Presented by

the

Government of Canada

Offert

par le

Gouvernement du Canada

DICTIONARY OF CANADIAN BIOGRAPHY

DICTIONARY OF CANADIAN BIOGRAPHY

DICTIONNAIRE BIOGRAPHIQUE DU CANADA

GENERAL EDITOR
GEORGE W. BROWN

DIRECTEUR ADJOINT
MARCEL TRUDEL

SECRÉTAIRE GÉNÉRAL
ANDRÉ VACHON

UNIVERSITY OF TORONTO PRESS

LES PRESSES DE L'UNIVERSITÉ LAVAL

DICTIONARY OF CANADIAN BIOGRAPHY

VOLUME I

1000 TO 1700

UNIVERSITY OF TORONTO PRESS

ENGLISH TRANSLATION OF FRENCH BIOGRAPHIES

D. M. Hayne, *Chairman* / J. F. Flinn / J. S. Wood

FRENCH TRANSLATION OF ENGLISH BIOGRAPHIES

Léopold Lamontagne, *Chairman* / Jean Darbelnet

BIBLIOGRAPHIC AND RESEARCH DEPARTMENT,
UNIVERSITY OF TORONTO PRESS

Francess G. Halpenny / Elizabeth W. Loosley / Constance P. McFarland

BUREAU DE RECHERCHE ET DE DOCUMENTATION DU *DBC*
AUX PRESSES DE L'UNIVERSITÉ LAVAL

Raynald Desmeules / Céline Dupré / Olga Jurgens

© University of Toronto Press and
Les Presses de l'université Laval, 1966
Printed in Canada
Reprinted 1966

CONTENTS

GENERAL INTRODUCTION	vii
INTRODUCTION TO VOLUME I	xiv
ACKNOWLEDGEMENTS	xxi
EDITORIAL NOTES	2
INTRODUCTORY ESSAYS	
The Indians of Northeastern North America Jacques Rousseau and George W. Brown	5
Glossary of Indian Tribal Names	12
The Northern Approaches to Canada T. J. Oleson and W. L. Morton	16
The Atlantic Region George MacBeath	21
New France, 1524–1713 Marcel Trudel	26
BIOGRAPHIES	39
APPENDIX	675
LIST OF ABBREVIATIONS	684
GENERAL BIBLIOGRAPHY	685
CONTRIBUTORS	711
INDEX	717

GENERAL INTRODUCTION*

THE *Dictionary of Canadian Biography/Dictionnaire biographique du Canada* was made possible by an imaginative and public-spirited bequest of the late James Nicholson, a Toronto business man, who left the residue and bulk of his estate to the University of Toronto for the purpose of creating a biographical reference work for Canada of truly national importance. The preparation of such a work had long been an obvious need and a cherished hope of Canadian scholars; but, although over the years a great deal of biographical material had been published, including many individual volumes and useful smaller reference works, there seemed no way of meeting the enormous expense of compiling, editing, and publishing a multi-volume dictionary of high quality until Mr. Nicholson's bequest translated the dream into a possibility.

JAMES NICHOLSON (22 AUGUST 1861 – 29 JUNE 1952)

MR. NICHOLSON'S BEQUEST, probably the most remarkable made thus far in Canada for a literary or historical purpose, arose out of his interest in Canadian and English history, which was maintained through a long life of varied activities. Born in Liverpool, he was the eldest of the three sons of John Nicholson of Forton, North Lancashire, England. His parents died when he was eight years of age, and he was educated in a private boarding school, Farndon Hall Academy in Cheshire. Later he was apprenticed for five years to W. H. Weightman & Son, the oldest architectural firm in Liverpool, and as a young man became a partner in the firm. From those early years the University of Toronto Press is fortunate to have some revealing fragments in the form of copy books, one of them done at the age of ten, and line drawings of old English buildings. In the copperplate schoolboy's hand advising us to "cultivate promising abilities" and to heed other bits of Victorian wisdom, and in the young architect's beautifully executed pen-and-ink sketches, we see clearly the love of symmetry and of careful workmanship so marked in later years.

In 1891, on the threshold of what must have appeared a promising professional career, Mr. Nicholson came to Canada. Just why we do not know, but it was characteristic of him that he should wish to strike out for himself. Characteristically, too, he made a very practical approach to his new environment by going to work on a farm near Lindsay, Ontario. The period was one of economic depression and there was

---

*This Introduction was written, just before his sudden death in October, 1963, by Dr. George W. Brown, who was appointed first General Editor of the Dictionary in 1959. At the time of his death, all major planning and most of the writing of Volume I had actually been completed. The work was thereafter brought forward to final publication along the lines established by the first General Editor, who devoted his last five years to the great task of launching the Dictionary. —THE PUBLISHERS.

little inducement to attempt a career in architecture. Farming, however, was not to his taste, and after a year he went to the city of London, Ontario, and entered the office of "Bart Cottam & Co., Importer and Manufacturer of Grocer's Sundries." First among the numerous items in the firm's advertisements was "bird seed," and doubtless it was in Bart Cottam's employ that Mr. Nicholson decided to concentrate upon the product which was in the next half-century to reward his business acumen and make it possible for him to found and endow the Dictionary.

Four years of practical business experience gave Mr. Nicholson the basis for another move, and in 1895 he settled in Toronto, establishing with J. W. Brock the firm of Nicholson and Brock with which he was identified during the remainder of his active business life. The time was favourable for new ventures. The economic tide was turning, and by the beginning of the century the new immigration and the settlement of the west were opening the gates for a country-wide expansion for many enterprises. In 1907 Mr. Brock retired from the firm and from that time Mr. Nicholson was the sole proprietor of a business ranging from Newfoundland to the Pacific Coast. The firm's best-known product, Brock's Bird Seed, soon gained a national reputation, and *Brock's Book on Birds*, written by Mr. Nicholson, published in both English and French editions, and circulated throughout the country, was to be found in every public library.

Mr. Nicholson's business interests kept him in touch for many years with all parts of Canada, and this was undoubtedly one of the influences which led him to think of a dictionary of Canadian biography. He learned French at a time when this was certainly an uncommon accomplishment for a Toronto businessman, and he himself prepared the French edition of his little book on birds. His activities outside his business were very numerous, and always they displayed the same combination of qualities and interests—a keen intellectual curiosity, a practical business sense, and a high idealism which gave direction and purpose to his thoughts and actions as a citizen.

In 1923 Mr. Nicholson married Janie Elliot Dalton, member of a prominent Toronto family and also related to the well-known Blake family of Toronto. For its intimate impressions, this biographical sketch owes much to Mrs. Nicholson, whose invaluable co-operation also made possible, as noted below, the beginning of work on the *Dictionary* in 1959.

First and foremost among Mr. Nicholson's broad community interests was his devotion to his church. For over 50 years he was a leading Anglican layman, not only in St. Paul's congregation in Toronto but also in the wider activities of the church throughout the country. First elected to the Toronto Diocesan Synod in 1899, he was a member for 52 years and Honorary Lay Secretary for 30. His membership in the Synod of the Ecclesiastical Province of Ontario extended from 1912 to 1946, and in it too he was Honorary Lay Secretary for a number of years. In the General Synod of the Church of England in Canada he was a member from 1918 to 1945, Assistant Honorary Lay Secretary 1921 and 1924, and Honorary Lay Secretary 1927 to 1934. He was "General Treasurer, Honorary" of the Anglican Sunday School Commission, later the General Board of Religious Education, from its beginning in 1909 until he retired in 1946. For many years he was a Sunday School teacher, and his interest in children and young people is commemorated by a carved screen enclosing the baptistry of St. Paul's Church in Toronto. Two memorials established by friends in his name, one in each of the Anglican colleges in Toronto, Trinity and Wycliffe, further attest his interest in religious education. He was also a member of the Council of Wycliffe College from 1916 to 1952, becoming vice-chairman in 1942, and serving as chairman, 1945 to 1952.

Along with his church activities his relations with the St. George's Society of Toronto held a special place in his affections. A member from 1903, he was elected a life member in 1916, an honorary life member in 1927, President of the Society twice, and in 1930 Marshal. His unflagging interest in, and extensive knowledge of, British history and institutions made him long remembered after his death. He was, said a member at the unveiling of his portrait in 1962, "the incarnation of the true spirit of the St. George's Society."

Mr. Nicholson's other social and business associations in Toronto were numerous. He was a member of the Royal Canadian Yacht Club, the Ontario Club, the Albany Club, the Canadian Manufacturers Association, and the Masonic Order. An active curler for many years, he was curling chairman of the Granite Club and Honorary Secretary of the curling section of the Empire Club.

Among Mrs. Nicholson's most vivid impressions of her husband is his love of reading. Books, she said, were his life; he was always "poring over them"; and often, he told her, in his early Liverpool days he had gone without a meal so that he could buy a book. Jokingly he recounted how in his first year in Canada he discovered that reading and ploughing were incompatible, a reason perhaps for his decision that farming was not "his line." Nor had he any aptitude for gardening, as Mrs. Nicholson discovered soon after their marriage when she asked him to plant a rosebush, which he did—upside down! This, she said, was his last venture into domestic horticulture. British history and literature were favourite studies, with the histories of France and Canada not far behind. Heraldry and English place and family names were a hobby, and he often lectured on these subjects and on famous persons and events in English history. Biography occupied a prominent section of his library. Literary form and style held immense interest for him. In fact, precision in words and facts was a constant preoccupation, and, Mrs. Nicholson reports, "he never read a book without jumping up to check this or that word or fact in his reference works," chief among which were the *Dictionary of National Biography* and the large *Oxford Dictionary*, both shelved within reach of his library chair. For music he had no ear, but consoled himself for this defect by reflecting that the learned Dr. Johnson suffered through the same deficiency.

Though studious by inclination, he was anything but a recluse. Always a welcome figure among his many and varied associates, he was, wrote one of them, gentle by nature and endowed with a winning personality. He had natural gifts for friendship and leadership, and to these were added a fine and tolerant judgement, a wide knowledge, and a practical wisdom which won him the respect and affection of all who knew him.

With all this in mind it is not difficult to imagine why Mr. Nicholson cherished the dream of a dictionary of Canadian biography. The idea appears to have come directly from his pleasure in and admiration for the *Dictionary of National Biography*. Among hundreds of pencilled marginal dates in his own copy of the *DNB*, showing on what date he read particular articles, two are of special interest in this connection: "15/6/24" in the Supplement, Vol. I, p. xi, opposite the "Memoir of George Smith," the founder of the *DNB*; and "3rd time 14/6/25" in Vol. LXIII, p. v, marking the beginning of the article "A Statistical Account." These two articles give a concise account not only of the life of George Smith and the origin, aims and content of the *DNB*, but of the tribulations of the editors, and of the enthusiastic and immediate recognition of the permanent value of this monumental work of scholarship. Apparently Mr. Nicholson pondered over these articles, and it may be that the idea of a Canadian dictionary came to him at this time. Not until after his death almost 30 years later, however, did his intention become known; to the best of her knowledge, said Mrs. Nicholson, the only person with whom he discussed the matter, and this was after his mind was made up, was his intimate friend of many years, the Rev. Dr. H. J. Cody, rector of St. Paul's Anglican Church and later President of the University of Toronto, 1932 to 1945.

The story of the origin and aims of the *DNB* made a deep impression on Mr. Nicholson. Paragraphs and sentences were marked in the margins of the two articles mentioned above; and later in his will he drew from these articles basic ideas and key phrases. George Smith's career must have interested Mr. Nicholson greatly, exhibiting as it did in high degree qualities and motives which were characteristic of the best in the business life of Victorian England and which he greatly admired. Smith was a magnanimous and public-spirited, but shrewd and successful, business man of an original turn of mind, who among his many enterprises was attracted most strongly to publishing. His founding in 1860 of the *Cornhill Magazine*, which achieved success under the editorship of Thackeray, was only one of his many contributions to the literary and cultural life of Britain. By the 1880's he was seeking for some final and significant project; and so it was that, after considering other possibilities, he decided to establish the *Dictionary of National Biography*. His desire was to produce a work which "should be of permanent value to his countrymen" by supplying "full, accurate and concise biographies of all noteworthy inhabitants of the British Isles and the Colonies (exclusive of living persons) from the earliest historical period to the present time." Fifty volumes were first envisaged, and Mr. Smith as an experienced publisher was well aware of the tremendous obligation he had undertaken. "The design," as the Preface said later with notable restraint, "satisfied none of the conditions of a merely commercial venture."

As already remarked, Mr. Nicholson was greatly influenced in making his will by the history of the *DNB*. The will itself is in its own way a remarkable document obviously drawn up with great care. In addition to the provisions for Mrs. Nicholson during her lifetime it contained directions for a generous number of personal and charitable bequests, two of them unusual but characteristic:

First to pay to the National Debt Redemption Fund established for the purpose of eventually redeeming the National Debt of Great Britain . . . the sum of ten thousand pounds Sterling. I do this in token of my admiration for His Majesty's Navy and of my faith in that great first line of defence, not only of Great Britain but of the whole Empire, and also in token of my admiration of the race of British Seamen.

Sixth: To pay to the City of Toronto, Ten thousand dollars, the same to be expended . . . in the purchase of seats and benches for the benefit of the public. Such seats to be placed in open spaces whether public parks, street car intersections or otherwise as shall best serve the public in Toronto.

Finally there was the provision for the endowment of a Dictionary of Canadian Biography:

Eleventh: As to any portion of the residue of my estate not required for payment of the gifts aforesaid, I desire that after the death of my wife the same shall be paid, or if in the form of Trustee securities shall be delivered to the proper authorities of the University of Toronto, and I desire that the capital shall remain in their hands and from the income from time to time available or as it may be accumulated or added to by other funds from other sources for the same purpose, such income shall be employed for the purpose of undertaking, and so far as possible carrying on from time to time as occasion may require, a work similar in principle and scope to the Dictionary of National Biography published in England, but devoted to the biographies of persons who were either born in Canada or subsequently resided therein. Without desiring to limit too rigidly the discretion of those who may be responsible for the publication of this work I suggest the following as certain main principles which express my desire, and which I would wish them to have in mind:

(a) The production of a complete Dictionary of National Biography which should supply full, accurate and concise biographies of all noteworthy inhabitants of the Dominion of Canada (exclusive of living persons), from the earliest historical period to the time of publication.

(b) That contributors shall seek information from first class authorities, including unpublished papers and records, and that they should append to each article a full list of the sources from whence their information was derived.

(c) That the biographies to be included shall be those whose lives are noteworthy from all points of view, and that the term "National" shall not be held to exclude the earlier settlers in British North America, or those born in Canada who may have gained distinction in foreign lands, nor shall it exclude persons of foreign birth who have achieved eminence in Canada.

(d) That the object shall be not only to supply an acknowledged want in Canadian literature, but that it should compete with or even surpass works of a similar character produced elsewhere.

(e) I leave it to the discretion of the authorities of the University of Toronto to appoint such Committee or such Trustees as in the opinion of the governing body of the University from time to time shall be best fitted to supervise and carry on a publication of this character.

Notable in these provisions is the combination of a clear general definition of aims with an absence of fettering particular directions. The debt to George Smith is obvious, but Mr. Nicholson was well aware that Canada would always have to make its own adaptations. One especially important departure from the example of the *DNB* was the provision that the income only from the bequest should be used, the result being that, although the need for additional funds will be felt for a number of years while the printed volumes are being completed up to date—a fact which Mr. Nicholson himself recognized—the permanence of the project is ensured. Moreover, all records and information collected in the course of the preparation of the printed volumes will be preserved.

It is difficult to praise too highly the conviction and clarity of judgement lying behind Mr. Nicholson's bequest. Without some such generous provision to launch it, a project on the scale which he envisaged would have been hopeless. The British and American dictionaries were made possible by business men with a high sense of public service, George Smith and Adolph S. Ochs of Smith, Elder & Co. and the *New York Times* respectively, and Mr. Nicholson doubtless had satisfaction in the thought that a business man would render the same service to Canada.

Unlike many other well-intentioned gifts, Mr. Nicholson's bequest fared well in both an altruistic and a material sense. Within a few years the increase in the principal and income of the estate reached the point where work could begin. Mrs. Nicholson, whose interest in the project equalled that of her husband, graciously consented to arrangements which made possible an early start, and her lively enthusiasm at each stage has given great encouragement to everyone associated with the *Dictionary*. In the spring of 1959 a General Editor was appointed, and the University of Toronto Press, which had been designated as the publisher, sent out an announcement to some 10,000 addresses scattered throughout the world. The association with the Press was a fortunate one since it made available to the *Dictionary* the full resources of a non-commercial press accustomed to handle annually in its editorial, manufacturing, and promotional departments a large volume of scholarly publications in the form of both books and journals. The interest in the announcement was attested by the receipt of over 2,000 return-cards requesting further information as issued. Work was started in July 1959, 1 July being designated as the formal date of the *Dictionary*'s establishment.

Mr. Nicholson's bequest came in many ways at an even more appropriate time than he could have realized. Since World War II a remarkable interest has been shown in dictionaries of national biography, which have been launched or projected in various parts of the world. The expense of such undertakings has made it necessary in almost all cases that they be in some sense official publications. This need not militate against their scholarly quality, but we are pleased to think that the Canadian like the British dictionary was made possible by the unselfish desire of a private donor to do something of "permanent value to his countrymen." From another point of view, also, the time of Mr. Nicholson's bequest was appropriate. The growth of Canadian scholarship in history and related fields has gained rapid momentum in recent years. Research has deepened and broadened, and the number of those engaged in it has greatly increased. A Canadian dictionary can now draw on resources which would have been unavailable a generation ago. It is indeed doubtful that a dictionary on the scale projected could have been successfully attempted at that time.

THE ESTABLISHMENT OF THE FRENCH EDITION, 9 MARCH 1961

OF SPECIAL INTEREST and importance is the fact that the Dictionary is published in two editions, English and French: the *Dictionary of Canadian Biography* by the University of Toronto Press; *Dictionnaire biographique du Canada* by Les Presses de l'Université Laval.

GENERAL INTRODUCTION

This arrangement breaks new ground since no comparable project of a similar kind in research and publication has previously been undertaken in Canada. At the time of the original announcement of the founding in 1959 it was stated that contributions would be accepted in either French or English and it was hoped that a French edition might also be arranged. It was clear, however, that such an edition must be suitably sponsored in French Canada, and in the preliminary consideration of this possibility a most important contribution was made by a French-Canadian Consultation Committee whose valuable assistance is recorded in the Acknowledgements below. It was on the recommendation of this committee that an approach was made to l'Université Laval, and there was sincere rejoicing at Toronto when the authorities at Laval enthusiastically undertook the responsibility. The formal announcement of the French edition was made at a *lancement* in Quebec on the evening of 10 March 1961, and on this occasion Mgr Vachon, Rector of l'Université Laval, said in part:

Ces deux éditions, l'une française et l'autre anglaise, qui seront publiées simultanément, nous apparaissent comme le symbole de la collaboration franche et entière qui doit exister dans notre pays entre les universitaires de langue française et ceux de langue anglaise.

Nous espérons que cette initiative servira d'exemple et de stimulant et qu'elle contribuera à consolider et à développer les mouvements d'échange et de bonne entente entre les deux grandes races qui constituent notre pays.

In these words Mgr Vachon expressed not only the sentiments of Laval, but equally those held at Toronto. Both greatly hoped that the *DCB/DBC* would prove to be not only a work of permanent historical value, but in a variety of ways a significant symbol of Canada's biculturalism. From the beginning it was planned that, apart from language, the French and English editions should be the same in content, and that the two editions of each volume would be issued simultaneously. The work was thus to be one not merely of translation, but of close collaboration at every stage of preparation.

Such close collaboration, requiring constant inter-communication and extending not only to the *DCB/DBC* offices but to researchers, authors, editors, and the two university presses, has proved, as had been expected, to be a complicated undertaking, but it has been a most rewarding one since it has brought together the resources of French- and English-Canadian scholarship in a spirit of co-operation which could not have been achieved in any other way. Without such co-operation it would in fact be impossible to create a work of this kind, which truly expresses Canada's duality.

GEORGE W. BROWN

INTRODUCTION TO VOLUME I

THE *Dictionary of Canadian Biography/Dictionnaire biographique du Canada* is in a venerable tradition, and among its many predecessors the *Dictionary of National Biography* and the *Dictionary of American Biography* have a leading place. For Canada itself, this project, which follows in the great tradition, and which will take many years and many volumes to complete, is of enormous import. It is fitting, however, that we acknowledge at the beginning the work of biographical record which has already been done for Canada, though on a much smaller scale, in a variety of publications and by a variety of people in both French and English.

The organization of material in a multi-volume dictionary of biography presents interesting and important problems. Various types of organization have been used in such works, each of them having particular advantages. No arrangement can, of course, be free from every possible objection. That adopted for the *DCB/DBC* avoids, however, some serious difficulties. The general organization of the English and American dictionaries was "alphabetical," running from A to Z through an entire set of volumes to a first terminal date: for the *Dictionary of National Biography* 63 volumes to 22 January 1901; for the *Dictionary of American Biography* 20 volumes to the end of 1935. One result of this arrangement was that no part of the series, and certainly no historical period, could be completed until the terminal date was reached and the volumes were all published. For the *DNB* this took fifteen and a half years; for the *DAB*, ten. Supplementary volumes were immediately added to both *DNB* and *DAB*, principally to include persons who had died while the work was in progress, but whose biographies had not been included because the volume in which they should have appeared had already been published. The original alphabetical arrangement was thus modified to some extent almost from the beginning. Following the first terminal dates, also, volumes have been added by a "period" arrangement, each volume covering a specific number of years. As a result there are at present three types of volumes in the two series.

The *DCB/DBC* is planned to have a consistent "period" arrangement throughout, volumes being arranged chronologically, each volume covering a specific number of years and being self-contained, with the contents arranged alphabetically from A to Z within the volume. The volume in which a biography is included is determined by the death date of the subject; or, if this is unknown, by the latest date of known activity, the "floreat" date. The periods will be arranged so as to produce volumes of approximately equal size, and will therefore be shortened as recent times are approached. Volume II is expected to cover the years 1701–40, and up to the mid-twentieth century there may be 18 to 20 volumes.

The most serious problem in the period arrangement is to provide means by which biographies may be readily located in the appropriate volume, since no reader can be expected to remember the thousands of death dates which will determine the locations of biographies in the various volumes. This difficulty, however, does not appear sufficient to outweigh other very important considerations, and will be taken care of by cumulative indexes and epitome volumes, which have, indeed, been found necessary in one form or another in any arrangement of material.

One of the most important advantages of the period arrangement for the compilers is the fact that in the various stages of selecting names, making writing assignments, and editing manuscripts, intensive work is possible on one or a few periods at a time, in contrast with the alphabetical arrangement which requires that the entire range of the national history be kept in mind in every volume. Biographies are also grouped logically, persons closely associated in their lives being brought more nearly together in their biographical articles than in an arrangement that scatters them through numerous volumes prepared at different times. This grouping makes possible a detailed comparison and cross-checking of articles at the editorial stage which is invaluable in the cases of many obscure figures. Moreover, a more even treatment of a period is possible since the same perspective may be applied in the writing of all biographies included in a single volume. The editors of the *DNB* were conscious of the fact that in the same volume there appeared individuals who had died centuries earlier and others who had died within recent months; this unevenness in perspective may not be too evident in the beginning but tends to appear more conspicuous with the lapse of time.

The reader of a volume prepared in the period arrangement shares also in the decided advantage of being able to purchase and to study self-contained volumes as they become available and to become acquainted with all the persons of various periods at one time. By making use of the cross-references, a reader will be able to pursue through many biographies the story of the explorations of the coast of North America and Hudson Bay, of Acadia and New France, the Huron missions and the Indians and thus build up his own picture of the history of the period. The self-contained character of the period-type volume also makes possible an index of the type which has been provided in Volume I.

In the long run, however, probably the most important of all considerations in favour of the period arrangement is the ease of revision, which, sooner or later, is a necessity for every reference work. With the period arrangement any volume may be revised independently at any time, and revision does not constitute the problem it does in an arrangement where an entire multi-volume series is involved. Since revision in these circumstances may require almost as much time and expense as the preparation of the original work, the temptation is to postpone it until it is long overdue.

The problem of the selection of names is a basic consideration in the preparation of a dictionary of biography, and a word should be said with regard to the general principles which the *DCB/DBC* is following. In his will Mr. James Nicholson, whose bequest made possible the founding of the *Dictionary*, stated that he wished it to "supply full, accurate, and concise biographies of all noteworthy inhabitants of the Dominion of Canada (exclusive of living persons)" and to include not only persons born and resident in Canada, but Canadians who had made reputations abroad, or persons from other countries who had made some contribution to Canadian life. Following the example of the *DNB*, the choice of persons was evidently to be a generous one, though each of those chosen should have some element of distinction or importance in his career to warrant inclusion.

What should be taken by the compilers of a biographical dictionary as constituting an element of distinction is by no means always clear. Where there is some definite accomplishment of significance in whatever field it may be, a decision is not difficult. High rank or office may, for example, be a guide in some cases, though this criterion will not carry us far. Choice is, of course, easy among those of first, second, or even third class importance; but as we get further down the scale the determining considerations become less clear. In what cases, for instance, should a share in a pioneering activity or participation in some notable event be taken as the criterion for inclusion?

The minor figures thus present the real difficulty, and an important influence on their selection is the over-all editorial policy as to lengths of articles. In the beginning it was planned to include in the *DCB/DBC* articles ranging from a minimum of 300 words to a maximum of 8,000–10,000. A very few articles, perhaps 1 per cent, would run to the maximum figure, the great majority coming within the range of 300–1,000 words. (It is interesting to note, by way of comparison, that the *Dictionary of American Biography*, had, in a total of almost 14,000 biographies, 70 articles which ran to about 10,000 words and 5 others which exceeded this limit.) A reconsideration of the *DCB/DBC* policy regarding lengths eventually led to the decision to include also notes of 200 words or even less, which meant that a good many more border-line cases among the minor figures would be brought in. Such an increase does not entirely eliminate problems of choice, but it greatly reduces them, and goes far to ensure that few if any of those for whom there is a clear-cut case for inclusion are omitted.

In determining lengths of biographies there are often, of course, other considerations than the importance of the individual to be taken into account. A lack of material may necessitate a shorter biography than the importance of the career would warrant; on the contrary, very ample materials may justify a longer biography than would otherwise be expected. In some cases also, the length may be increased by the necessity of indicating conflicting interpretations of a career, or of explaining the significance of events in which the person was involved. The period-type volume has made it possible also for special handling where several persons have been involved in the same events: the aim has been here to make the necessary background explanations in only one biography with suitable cross-references given in the others.

One general principle has been to omit the names of persons who have not set foot in what is now Canada, or at least approached its shores. This regrettably leaves out many persons who have had a great influence in Canadian history, while admitting others of lesser importance. To have done otherwise, however, would have opened the floodgate to a great number of persons, adequate treatment of whom would require a separate reference work. Many of these persons are referred to in one or more biographies, as are many lesser persons who do not merit a separate article, and a key to these references is provided by the index. In the cases of persons not born in Canada, the general principle has been to give the Canadian part of the career and its significance as full a treatment as possible within the allotted length, treating the career outside Canada very concisely but also providing bibliographical references for further reading.

In the preparation of the biographies themselves it has been the aim, as in other similar large-scale works, to provide not merely the essential factual material, but also an indication of the personality of the subject and the significance of the career. As a guide for the writing of the articles in Volume I, the following suggestions were included in the *Directives to Contributors/Instructions générales aux collaborateurs*:

The biography should be a fresh and scholarly treatment of the subject based upon reliable sources (where possible first-hand) precise and accurate in statements of fact, concise, but presented in attractive literary form. Though adequate factual material is of prime importance, biographies should not be mere catalogues of events. They should appraise circumstances which shaped careers, and should indicate the importance of such matters as ancestry, parentage, education, physical and social environment, and the other formative influences. So far as possible, they should leave the reader with a definite impression of the personality and achievements of the subject in relation to the period in which he lived and the events in which he participated. They should not be written to any one specification and should be interpretative in the best sense. They should be readable and make use of relevant anecdote and incident. In appraising the career of the subject, the article should aim at objectivity, fairness, and discrimination. It should indicate strengths and weaknesses, success and failure. Finally, while all these considerations must of necessity be controlled by limitations of space and materials available, the aim is to secure independent and original treatments and not mere compilations of preceding accounts.

These considerations obviously apply more fully to some biographies than to others, and perhaps in particular to biographies of several hundred words and more. In dealing with controversial figures or events contributors have been asked to indicate fairly the varying interpretations. This does not preclude the author leaving an impression of his own views, though the style of writing in a reference work of this kind should not be polemical. Extensive textual criticism of documents or of previous secondary sources is also out of place. Problems involving such criticism should, however, be pointed out, and we have requested that the bibliographies contain references which will enable a reader to follow up such problems if he wishes.

The creation of a Name File covering contributors to the whole of Canadian history was begun in 1959 when the *DCB* was established. It has been built through the work of the *DCB/DBC* staff and through information from outside sources. Some of this information, all of it welcome, has come unsolicited; much of it has come in response to inquiries or to Name Lists sent out for examination by scholars and institutions in Canada and elsewhere. The Name File continues to grow, and contributions to it will be received gratefully.

The Name File is maintained in duplicate in Toronto and in Quebec, and will be available for consultation by scholars and authors in search of information. These records, which will include eventually many more names than those appearing in the printed volumes, will constitute an invaluable source of information for historians, journalists, and inquirers in many other fields of interest.

CONTENTS AND PREPARATION OF VOLUME I

VOLUME I HAS PRESENTED a number of special problems because of the variety of groups included in the period covered and the specialized character of many of the sources which have had to be used. In these respects no subsequent volume appears likely to present equal difficulties though others will undoubtedly emerge since every volume will pose its own problems.

The names selected for inclusion in Volume I were drawn from a list which at one stage totalled over 1,300 entries. In making the final selection and determining the lengths of the biographies, helpful advice was received from more than 100 scholars in Canada and abroad. Although the various categories of biographies in this volume overlap somewhat, the total number of 594 articles may be classified approximately as follows: New France 318; Acadia 71; Hudson's Bay Company 34; Newfoundland 37; Maritime explorers beginning with the Norsemen 59; Indians 65; Appendix 10. The names selected are fewer than half of those in the Volume I file, and doubtless the choice might have been different in some instances. On the whole, the selection of names for Volume I has leaned to the generous side—a tendency specially justified, it was felt, for a period in which significant ideas and social and institutional patterns had their origin. The 16th and 17th centuries were such a period in Canadian history.

Volume I has a larger proportion of shorter articles on obscure persons than will probably be the case with later volumes. Since most of these obscure persons have hitherto had no place in reference works and general histories, it is perhaps by their inclusion more than in any other way that this volume breaks new ground. Reliance on source material, and not merely on secondary references, has been the aim throughout the volume, but nowhere more than in the preparation of the minor biographies. Work has been done or inquiries initiated not only in Canada, the United Kingdom, France, and the United States, but in the Scandinavian countries and elsewhere in Europe.

The research underlying the articles is indicated to some extent at least in the bibliographies, which are intended, however, to be useful rather than pretentious. Where there are controversial elements or conflicting interpretations which cannot be fully discussed in the text, and there are many such instances, references have frequently been included in the bibliography to give additional suggestions on the points in question.

Our effort has been to ensure a high standard of scholarship throughout the volume. The choice of competent authors was of course a basic consideration; in addition, a very thorough editorial examination of each article was made at Quebec and Toronto extending into source materials as well as secondary works; in a great many cases articles were sent to readers who were themselves authorities in the particular field involved; many special inquiries were also made in various places either by correspondence or by the *DCB/DBC* staff.

Following establishment of the text of articles by the authors and editors came translation at both Toronto and Quebec. Translations from French to English were made at Toronto, from English to French at Quebec. After translation, printer's copy was prepared for the French edition at Quebec, for the English edition at Toronto. It will thus be seen that neither edition is in the ordinary sense a translation of the other. They are together the product of a collaboration which has run through the entire process of preparation from the time the first *Preliminary list of names under consideration* ... was drawn up.

The self-contained nature of the volume has made possible the inclusion of the introductory essays, the aim of which is to provide for the biographies a framework of events and significant developments which will make many of them more understandable and meaningful. All the societies and countries of the American hemisphere were created by influences and patterns of thought and action brought from Europe and remoulded under the relentness pressures of geography and circumstance in the New World; and it was people who, as individuals, families and groups, brought these influences and patterns—by far the most important part of their baggage—and reacted to the challenge of the new environment. Canada, in this long and complex process of adjustment and creation, had its own distinctive share, beginning even with its "discovery" by the North Atlantic rather than the Columbia route. Into the northern half-continent which was in time to be Canada, the Gulf of St. Lawrence, the great River, and Hudson Bay were the gateways, and around them there centred areas of rivalry and conflict in trade, settlement, diplomacy, and strategy. It is against this epic background that the biographies, and especially the lesser ones, take on an added meaning; and in turn they may at many points add a touch of concrete significance to the impersonal recital of great historical events. Who then were the people caught up in these panoramic events and especially the leaders among them? Whence did they come? What did they bring with them of training and education, of traditions and loyalties? What mark did they leave? Such are the questions to which we should all like to have, even if imperfectly, the answers. Of the Indians we can know much less than of the Europeans; and yet for no group is an understanding of the individuals against their background more necessary. Their biographies, incomplete and based on fragmentary bits of evidence from the white man's sources, reveal, nevertheless, the shattering and revolutionary effects of European weapons, diseases, ideas, material objects, and conflicts transferred to the New World. On no group in this volume have contributors and editors worked with more interest than on the Indians.

Because of the inadequate or even equivocal nature of the evidence on which they are based, a number of other biographies have presented especially difficult problems. This is particularly true of the biographies of the maritime explorers from the days of the Norsemen on into the 17th century. In the field of maritime exploration, for example, very active research was proceeding at the time of preparation of this volume, and the *DCB/DBC* was fortunate in having obtained the help of a number of specialists in this controversial area. Owing to uncertainties and gaps in the available evidence, there are frequent conflicts in facts and in the legitimate interpretations which may be drawn from them. Moreover, new documents altering facts and interpretations may turn up at any time from collections not yet completely examined. There are many such possibilities in repositories public and private in western Europe. We have therefore not attempted, in the process of editing, to impose a framework of complete consistency with regard to disputable facts and interpretations. It would indeed have been improper to do so. We have, however, by means of cross-references and bibliographical interpolations, endeavoured to draw attention in interrelated biographies to variations which might otherwise puzzle the reader.

Finally, it may be remarked that ultimate usefulness to the reader has been high among the overriding principles in the preparation of this volume. It is hoped that he will find the aim realized in most respects at least.

GEORGE W. BROWN
MARCEL TRUDEL

ACKNOWLEDGEMENTS

THOSE entrusted with the preparation of the *DCB/DBC* are conscious of the great assistance given to them with unfailing generosity by many people and institutions. We should like to thank them all but for reasons of space are unable to include every name.

First among our acknowledgements should be that to Mrs. James Nicholson, not only for her generous co-operation which made possible the initiation of the work in 1959, but also for her continued interest and enthusiasm which have been a constant inspiration to the *DCB/DBC* staff at both Toronto and Quebec.

To the Canada Council goes a very special word of appreciation for its grant of $17,000 to provide for the translation costs of Volume I, an item which could not be carried within the regular budget. This grant, we believe, was a recognition of the significance of Canada's bicultural character, and of the value of the *Dictionary/Dictionnaire* as a product of Canadian scholarship in both French and English.

In connection with the establishment of the French edition, the valuable contribution made by the French-Canadian Consultation Committee has already been mentioned in the General Introduction. Its members were Dr. Pierre Dansereau, then Dean of the Faculty of Science, l'Université de Montréal, Professor M. Brunet, l'Université de Montréal, Professor Guy Frégault, then of the University of Ottawa, and Professor M. Trudel, then of l'Université Laval, the heads of the Departments or Institutes of History of their respective universities. Mgr Irénée Lussier, P.D., then Recteur de l'Université de Montréal, also gave very helpful advice at the time of the establishment of this committee. It is a matter of special regret that Professor Frégault's appointment as Deputy Minister of the newly created Department of Cultural Affairs of Quebec prevented him from writing the articles which he had undertaken to do. The *DCB/DBC* has, however, fortunately been able to benefit in various other ways from his advice and interest.

The contributors to Volume I are listed on page 711. With them the *DCB/DBC* has a special bond and a special reason for thanks since we have all come together through a period which was full of the experiences inevitable in the beginning of such a large project. We are proud of our list of contributors which includes authorities in a variety of fields from many scattered points, and which sets a high standard, we believe, for this and later volumes. Their patience in answering many queries has been greatly appreciated.

Among our contributors and consultants, though all were equally generous in co-operation, there were a number who at various times and in various ways gave special advice and assistance. In this connection, without any order of precedence or adequate explanation, but with a grateful sense of obligation, the following may be mentioned: Mgr Arthur Maheux, P.A., M. Gérard Morisset, and M. Antoine Roy at Quebec; M. Jean-Jacques Lefebvre of Montreal, whose suggestions especially in the early planning stage were very helpful; Dr. W. Kaye Lamb, whose great knowledge of archival and other source materials and of Canadian historical scholarship made his comments authoritative; Father René Baudry, C.S.C., of the Public Archives of Canada in Paris, whose advice at every stage of preparation was especially valuable; Dr. J.-Roger Comeau of the Public Archives in Ottawa, whose specialty is Acadian history; Father Clément Cormier, C.S.C., Recteur de l'Université de Moncton, whose library is a very important centre for Acadian studies; Dr. Gustave Lanctot, whose very broad knowledge of early Canadian history is based upon many years of research. For the Atlantic Provinces generous assistance was given by Dr. D. C. Harvey, Dr. A. G. Bailey, Dr. C. Bruce Fergusson, Mr. Allan M. Fraser, and Dr. George MacBeath. Others among our Canadian contributors to whom we are indebted for advice and help in various ways are the late Professor T. J. Oleson, Dr. C. P. Stacey, Professor W. J. Eccles, Mrs. Elsie McLeod Jury, Dr. Jean Lunn, Father Léon Pouliot, S.J., Dean Gordon Rothney, and Professor E. R. Seary.

In England, Professor David B. Quinn was most helpful and patient in connection with the tangled problems of early maritime exploration as was Mr. R. A. Skelton. Miss Alice M. Johnson's advice and help with regard to Hudson's Bay Company men were invaluable. Others in England who were of special help were Professor K. G. Davies, Mr. Taylor Milne, and Miss G. M. Townsend (now Mrs. Cell). Among the contributors in the United States, the following gave special advice and assistance: Mr. W. F. E. Morley (now at Queen's University), Dr. Ernest S. Dodge, Rev. Thomas Grassmann, O.F.M., CONV., and Dr. Paul A. W. Wallace. We should mention also the kind interest of the late Vilhjalmur Stefansson, who was responsible for the creation of the remarkable Stefansson Collection on the Arctic, and Mrs. Stefansson, the Collection's librarian.

A project such as the *DCB/DBC* could not exist without the interest and co-operation of members of the staff of archives, libraries, and museums. We have had the greatest possible assistance from such persons across Canada and beyond, and we owe them a tremendous debt of gratitude. We cannot list them all, though all deserve mention, but we may perhaps be forgiven if we make special reference here to the libraries and archives to whose collections we have referred constantly; in Toronto: the University of Toronto Library, the central branch of the Toronto Public Library, the Ontario Legislative Library, and the Public Archives of Ontario; and in Quebec: la Bibliothèque générale de l'Université Laval, les Archives du Séminaire de Québec, les Archives du Québec, and la Bibliothèque de la Législature.

To the above names should be added, if space permitted, the names of scores of persons who have received inquiries from us or who themselves inquired about the work. From many have come items of information which have enriched our files for all periods of Canadian history. We wish them to know that their interest has been a great encouragement.

In the broader aspects of policy there are a number of persons to whom the *DCB/*

ACKNOWLEDGEMENTS

DBC owes a great deal. In particular we may mention in this connection former Chancellor F. C. A. Jeanneret and President Claude Bissell of the University of Toronto and Mgr L.-A. Vachon, P.A., V.G., Recteur de l'Université Laval, Mgr A.-M. Parent, P.A., Vice-recteur de l'Université Laval, Abbé F. Gingras, Trésorier de l'Université Laval, and Abbé L. Roy, Directeur des Presses de l'Université Laval, who have always given understanding and encouragement to the *DCB/DBC*. It has benefited at every stage from the leadership, wise guidance in matters of policy, and publishing and editorial skill of Mr. M. Jeanneret, Director of the University of Toronto Press, and from the advice and encouragement of Miss Eleanor Harman, Assistant Director.

We have received help at various times from all the members of staff of the two university presses, and to them all we express our thanks. Over the course of preparation of volume I, the *DCB/DBC* offices have had a number of assistants who have contributed in special ways. Mrs. Laurier LaPierre (then Miss Paula Armstrong) was the first assistant to the General Editor. Mrs. J. Vassilev was over a long period associated with the large and responsible tasks of correspondence and record-keeping, as have been Mme Solanges Stewart, Mrs. H. L. McDougall, Mrs. E. M. Vida, and Miss L. Patrick for shorter periods. M. Marcel Hamelin, Mr. J. Buell, the late Miss Barbara Fraser, M. Michel Grenon, and Mr. W. G. Saywell assisted with the preparation of name lists. M. J.-G. Pelletier, Mlle P.-A. Rheault, and M. Laurier Renaud gave valuable help in bibliographical and other research and Mrs. B. Urquhart in checking proofs and preparing the Index for this edition. Miss Maud Hutcheson has given devoted service over almost the whole period of preparation in the area of bibliography and references, and in addition carried out a special assignment in research in England. With Jacques Monet, S.J., the *DCB/DBC* has had a happy association which goes back to its beginning and his help has lightened the task of our two offices.

DICTIONNAIRE BIOGRAPHIQUE DU CANADA   DICTIONARY OF CANADIAN BIOGRAPHY

The Centennial Commission has made available to the *DCB/DBC* a generous grant in the amount of $160,000, which has enabled the opening of an office in Ottawa for research. Its research is concerned with the Confederation period, that is with the years 1851–1900 in which the federation was established and developed. This indispensable biographical research into thousands of persons has the great advantage of being undertaken when the period is being intensively reviewed for the celebration of the Centennial. On it will be based the future volumes of the *DCB/DBC* for the Confederation period. The benefits of the gift of the Centennial Commission will thus be appreciated for years to come.

LES PRESSES DE L'UNIVERSITÉ LAVAL   UNIVERSITY OF TORONTO PRESS

DICTIONARY OF CANADIAN BIOGRAPHY

Editorial Notes

PROPER NAMES

The choice of a consistent form for name-entries was not easy in a chronological volume (*c.* 1000–1700) which includes Norse, Portuguese, Spanish, Italian, English, French, and Indian names, as well as the names of married women and members of religious orders. Persons have been entered under family name rather than title, pseudonym, popular name, nickname, or name in religion, an arrangement which has the advantage of bringing together prominent members of the same family [*see* LE MOYNE, AILLEBOUST, ALEXANDER, etc.]. Where possible, the form of the surname is based on the actual signature (although contemporary spelling of names was often erratic) and is given in the language of origin and in the spelling of the period: DENYS which later became "Denis," and so on.

FRENCH NAMES

In the case of French family names, "La," "Le," "Du," and "Des" (but not "de") are considered as part of the name and are capitalized. Compound French names and titles abound in this period: LE MOYNE de Longueuil et de Châteauguay, CHARLES; BIENCOURT de Poutrincourt et de Saint-Just, JEAN DE; etc. In such cases, cross-references are made in the text from the compounds to the main name-entry: from "Longueuil" and "Châteauguay" to "Le Moyne"; and from "Poutrincourt" and "Saint-Just" to "Biencourt." First names appear in the modern form: "Jean" rather than "Jehan"; "Noël" rather than "Noel."

NORSE, SPANISH, PORTUGUESE, AND ITALIAN NAMES

These names have been established by contributors in these areas and by three specialists, Professor J. H. Parker, Faculty of Arts and Science (Italian and Hispanic Studies), University of Toronto, W. F. E. Morley, formerly Bibliographer, John Carter Brown Library, Providence, R.I., and now at the Douglas Library, Queen's University, Kingston, Ontario, and Professor Humphrey Milnes, Department of German, University College, University of Toronto. Names are given in the language of origin with one exception: CABOT, where the English form has been selected in preference to the Italian form "Caboto." Norse name-entries are under the given name, as the patronymic changed from generation to generation.

INDIAN NAMES

Indian names, which are not properly speaking family names, have presented a particular problem, since an Indian might be known by his own name (spelled in a variety of ways by Europeans, French, English, or Dutch, unfamiliar with Indian languages), by a French, English or Dutch nickname, with the often present addition of a French first name, bestowed at baptism. Since there can now be no certainty as to the original spelling, the entry has been given under the form of the Indian name found in the indexes of sources such as *JR* (Thwaites); Champlain, *Works* (Biggar); Lescarbot, *History* (Grant); and so on. An effort has been made to include the major variants of the original name, as well as the nicknames, with relevant cross-references in the text. When the Indian name is not known, as is often the case with women, Indians are classified under their baptismal name.

NAMES OF MARRIED WOMEN AND NUNS

Married women and *religieuses* have been entered under their maiden names, with cross-references from their husbands' names or their names in religion, conforming to the general rule of entry under family name: BOULLONGNE, Marie-Barbe de; GUYART, Marie, dite de l'Incarnation.

NAMES OF RELIGIOUS

Jesuits, Recollets, and Sulpicians are entered under family name. Capuchins appear under their name in religion, followed by the province or house to which they belonged: IGNACE de Paris (an exception to the general rule, because family name, in most cases, is not known).

CROSS-REFERENCES AND POST-1700 NAMES

For each first mention, in an individual biography, of another person who also has a biography in Volume I, the family name is printed (in capitals and small capitals) in the form in which it appears alphabetically in the text: BUADE de Frontenac; Marie de l'Incarnation [*see* GUYART]. If there are two or more persons of the same family name, the first names also appear in capitals: CLAUDE PIJART; PIERRE PIJART. The names of most persons who died after 1700 are starred: John Nelson*, Saint-Vallier [La Croix*]. The majority of these persons will receive a biography in Volume II. Persons who died before 1700, mentioned incidentally in the text, as well as important persons who did not come to Canada, are included in the Index.

SPECIAL TERMS

Certain roles of varying importance in the 17th century have been explained in biographies: *autmoin* or *shaman* (medicine-man), p. 500; *dogique*, p. 632; *donné*, p. 414; *forain* (hawker); p. 661; *panis* (Indian slave), 452; *sachem*, p. 7; *sagamo*, p. 500; and *truchement* (go-between), pp. 131, 341.

PLACE-NAMES

The spelling most often encountered in the documents and maps of the period has been employed, in the original language. Complete consistency, however, has not been possible, nor has it been thought desirable. The English edition cites very well-known place-names in their present-day English form: St. Lawrence River; Quebec, Montreal; but uses Trois-Rivières rather than Three Rivers, for example. The modern form has also been used when no agreement exists among 17th-century writers: Kennebec for the river named by CHAMPLAIN "Quinibequi," by BIARD "Kinibequi," and by LESCARBOT, "Kinibeki," and by later English and French map-makers "Kennibek" and "Kennebeck."

Alternative and more familiar forms of place-names are included in parentheses after the original. The alternative is usually the modern name, based whenever possible on the *Gazetteers of Canada* issued by the Canadian Board on Geographical Names, Ottawa. Where biographies include both French and English protagonists, the alternative place-names in the English edition may be the French form; for example Moose Fort (Fort Saint-Louis or Monsipi), or Nashwaak (Naxouat).

In the present state of Canadian toponymy (only the gazetteers of New Brunswick and Nova Scotia, issued by the Canadian Board on Geographical Names were available for the place-names in volume I), no one work has been found entirely satisfactory. The following works have been useful as guides: for French names, Marcel Trudel, *Atlas historique du Canada français* (Québec, 1961); Champlain, *Œuvres* (Laverdière); *JR* (Thwaites); and P.-G. Roy, *Inv. concessions*; for Acadian names, Ganong, "Historic sites in New Brunswick"; for HBC names, HBRS, XXI and XXII (Rich); for Indian names, A. E. Jones, "'8endake Ehen' or Old Huronia," PAO *Annual Report*, V (1908); for Newfoundland names, E. R. Seary, *Toponymy of the Island of Newfoundland, check-list no. 1, Sources, maps* (1959); *check-list no. 2, Names, I, The Northern peninsula* (1960) (mimeographed; shortly to be published).

QUOTATIONS

Quotations have been translated when the language of the original passage is different from that of the text. All passages quoted from the *Jesuit Relations*, from Cartier's or Champlain's *Voyages*, as from some other relatively standard works, are given in the generally accepted English translations of those works, a fact which will account for some variant spellings between text and quotation and some irregularities. Direct quotations follow the originals, except in one particular. The "expanded method" has been used in the transcriptions of quotations from early documents and printed works: "i" is changed to "j" and "v" to "u" ("ivin" becomes "juin"); and some "u's" are changed to "v's" ("liue" becomes "live"). The original accents have been retained and contractions have been expanded.

DATES

The discrepancy between Old Style (Julian calendar, used in England until 1752) and New Style (Gregorian calendar, used in Italy, Spain, Portugal, and France from 1582) affects every biography in Volume I. Most biographies, of course, will present no problem: dates in those based entirely on English documents can be assumed to be Old Style; and in those based exclusively on French, Portuguese, etc. sources will surely be New Style. But where an article draws on both English and continental or Quebec sources, authors have been asked to make the dates in the article uniformly Old or New Style and to indicate after the dates used (O.S.) or (N.S.). It should be noted: (a) Old Style dates were 10 days behind New Style dates throughout the year in the 17th century; (b) the Old Style new year began 25 March and the New Style new year on 1 January (for Old Style dates between January and 25 March, the year is indicated as 1685/86; (c) in Scotland the new year commenced on 1 January, from 1600 on.

BIBLIOGRAPHIES

In order to avoid lengthy repetition, sources cited five or more times in individual bibliographies are listed there in shortened form and are cited in full in the General Bibliography (page 685). The individual bibliographies are arranged in three categories—each alphabetically—manuscript sources, printed sources, and secondary works. The General Bibliography contains descriptions of manuscript deposits, series of books, dictionaries, reference guides, and periodicals important for the study of Canadian history to 1700. In general the items in individual bibliographies are the sources as listed by the contributors, but this record has been supplemented by a considerable amount of bibliographical investigation in the *DCB/DBC* offices. Some instances of special bibliographical comment by contributors appear within square brackets.

A full description of the bibliographical style will be found in Constance McFarland, "The development of French and English styles for the *DCB/DBC*'s bibliographies," *Papers of the Bibliographical Society of Canada*, III (1964), 27–37.

TRANSLATION INTO ENGLISH (a note by the Committee for the English translation of French biographies)

In translating into English the biographies submitted originally in French to the *DCB/DBC*, the translators have tried to render the sense of the French text as faithfully as possible, while producing a clear and readable English version. At times the concision and brevity of the French necessitated a rather longer development in the English, but they have tried to avoid stylistic embellishments that would have misrepresented the French text.

Wherever possible, the translators have avoided using two distinct English words to translate the same French one in different passages or biographies, and also the use of a single English term to represent two or more French ones found in different contexts. Nevertheless the vagaries of the two languages have sometimes thwarted this desire for consistency; the French word "procureur" means both a legal representative and the financial officer of an ecclesiastical community, and it has been translated in some places as "attorney," and elsewhere as "bursar." On the other hand, English usage does not distinguish between "procureur" in the latter meaning and its synonym "économe"; thus the single English word "bursar" will be found doing duty for both. The greatest difficulty has of course been in trying to find suitable English equivalents for terms drawn from the political, religious, social, or economic background of 16th- and 17th-century life. The presence in the English version of occasional French words (e.g., *haute, moyenne, et basse justice*; *maître des comptes*; *donné*), which have no exact equivalent in English usage, will identify our least successful efforts in this direction. Occasional obscurity or ambiguity may have resulted from the difficulty of determining the precise meaning of certain words or expressions taken more or less directly from documents of the period, which are themselves not always free of obscurity or ambiguity. The value of certain words varied from one century to the other and they have had to be assessed in their context; thus "noble homme" becomes "nobleman" in a 16th-century text and simply "worthy man" in a 17th-century one. Indian terms are accompanied by an English equivalent or explanation. In accordance with editorial policy, full names of companies and institutions, such as "Compagnie de la Nouvelle-France" or "Conseil Souverain," have not been translated.

The Indians of Northeastern North America

JACQUES ROUSSEAU AND
GEORGE W. BROWN

THIS VOLUME of the Dictionary contains the biographies of 65 Indians. In many ways they are a group apart. For almost all of them the information is fragmentary. Like fireflies they glimmer for a moment before disappearing again into the dark forest of unrecorded history. More important, their stories must be extracted almost entirely from records which are not their own. The history of the Americas as we know it is the white man's history, written of necessity from his own records. The Indians' oral tradition has added a little, but not a great deal; archaeology in recent years has added much, but most significantly on the prewhite period. We can now begin, however, to understand more fully the tremendous drama of interracial and intercultural conflict, with all its tragic consequences, which followed the white man's "discovery" of the Americas. Here biography can help us, since the stories of individual Indians often give us clearer glimpses of these conflicts and tensions than we might otherwise have, for they are revealed to us in human terms and not as impersonal forces. For this reason the number of Indians included in this volume has on the whole leaned to the generous side.

Of the first natives met by Europeans in what is now Canada we have no individual records, though there are numerous references to such meetings in explorers' accounts. Amongst the Amerinds the Eskimos belong to a distinct linguistic and cultural family and were mainly encountered in the explorations of Hudson Bay, though they are mentioned also in the Norse sagas. Contacts with them were, however, brief and sporadic [*see* BAFFIN, BEST, HALL, KNIGHT, SNORRI Thorfinnsson, THORFINNR *karlsefni* Thordarson, WHITE].

At the beginning of the historical period the Eskimos had penetrated as far south as Havre-Saint-Pierre (formerly Pointe-aux-Esquimaux), on the north shore of the St. Lawrence. The first Indians of the Gulf region encountered by the early explorers [*see* HORE, PARMENIUS, WYET], were the Beothuks. Probably belonging to a distinct linguistic family, with a population of about 500 persons at the time of their discovery, they were entirely confined to Newfoundland. Their treatment by the whites in the early period was deplorable, members of the tribe being regarded as little better than animals by the Newfoundland fishermen who hunted them down. No missionaries were ever sent to the Beothuks and no colonist of the island ever learned their language. The tribe finally disappeared about the middle of the 19th century (*see* J. P. Howley, *The Beothuks or Red Indians, the aboriginal inhabitants of Newfoundland* (Cambridge, 1915); Jacques Rousseau, "Le dernier des Peaux-rouges," *Cahiers des Dix*, XXVII (1962), 47–76).

It is when we come to the Amerinds of the mainland that we find records of large numbers of identifiable persons from whom a representative selection for a volume such as this can be made. Northeastern North America was, however, a very large area stretching from Acadia westward through the entire region of the St. Lawrence and Great Lakes; and it is essential, as a background for the Indian biographies, that we recall that in the 17th century the Indians of this region present an often confusing mosaic of shifting tribes and bands at various levels of culture and with great differences in their ways of life. Beyond this also, if we are to have any true appreciation of the tension and tragedy in which both the Indian and the white man became involved, we must have some understanding of the basic rhythms and patterns of life which affected Indian thought and action.

In the northeastern region there were, broadly speaking, two linguistic groupings of Indian tribes: the Algonkian, migratory and primarily dependent on hunting and fishing; and the Iroquoian, semi-sedentary and semi-agricultural. Occupying the northern, and by far the larger, part of the region, were the many tribes of the Algonkian family. Farthest to the east were the Micmacs and the Malecites, inhabiting at the time of their discovery what is now the province of Nova Scotia, including Cape Breton Island, northern New Brunswick, and Prince Edward Island. The boundary between them was the height of land separating the waters that flow into the Saint John River from those that enter the Gulf of St. Lawrence; the Malecite territory extended to the shore of the St. Lawrence opposite present-day Tadoussac, and included also part of the state of Maine. The Malecites and several Algonkian tribes to the southward formed the Abenaki Confederacy (including, among others, the Passamaquoddy, Penobscot, and possibly the Sokoki Indians), which allied itself in the 17th century with the French against the Iroquois Confederacy and the English colonists of the Atlantic seaboard.

North of the St. Lawrence and east of the St. Maurice were the Montagnais; while further east along the north shore of the Gulf and stretching north into Labrador over a very great area were the roving bands of the closely related, and at times almost indistinguishable, Naskapis. West of the St. Maurice and occupying the Ottawa River basin were the Algonkians. Still further west were the Ottawas, on the route toward Georgian Bay; the Nipissings in the vicinity of Lake Nipissing; and the Chippewas or Ojibwas to the north around Lake Superior. North also of the Algonkians and Ojibwas, occupying the watershed of James Bay and stretching westward into present-day Saskatchewan, were the many roving bands of Crees.

The Algonkian peoples are usually described as migratory because so many individual tribes ranged more or less continually over wide expanses in search of game—moose, deer, caribou, smaller animals which were trapped—and fish. They also used wild plants to augment their diet and in certain places they gathered wild rice and made maple syrup in season. A few tribes also practised horticulture on a small scale, planting maize, beans, and squash [*see* TESSOUAT, fl. 1603–13]. Food was generally plentiful during the summer months but many of the tribes experienced severe food shortages in the winter.

Because the Algonkians were migratory, their material possessions were, of necessity, portable. Baskets and other containers were woven or made out of bark or wood. The single-family peaked or dome-shaped lodge or wigwam, as it is called, was the basic form of shelter used throughout the area. With its covering of birch-bark rolls, woven rush mats, or skins, this type of house was easy to assemble and dismantle. For winter travel, the Algonkians used the toboggan and snow-shoes and for summer expeditions, the graceful birch-bark canoe, one of the great Indian contributions to water transportation in North America.

The important socio-economic unit was the band, although there were tribal divisions which were known and recognized. Bands varied in size from a few families to several hundred individuals. In many ways, the Algonkian peoples inclined to individualism—so much so that they have been described by many authorities as "atomistic." The recognized leader of the band was usually an experienced hunter, noted for his astuteness and good judgement. In some instances, these positions were hereditary in a powerful family (descent among these people was through the male line). A particularly gifted man might become chief of the tribe when a number of bands joined in the conduct of war, in negotiations with other tribes, or with the white men's governments. At the local level, however, it was more often the shaman who exerted the greatest influence [*see* CARIGOUAN, PIGAROUICH].

With the rise of the fur trade, the Algonkians found their knowledge of the forest and the habits of the fur-bearing animals most valuable, as trapping became their major occupation. It was the European traders who introduced them to iron tools, guns, kettles, brandy, and other facets of white culture. In exchange, the traders received the pelts of lynx, otter, marten, fox, and, most important of all, beaver. In becoming trappers, the Algonkians had to relinquish much of their traditional woodland economy as they settled around the trading-posts. Thus they became dependent on the fur market, with all its vicissitudes, and were exposed to many evil aspects of European civilization, alcoholism in particular. Their participation in the fur trade as allies of the French involved them in conflicts with the Iroquois and, ultimately, dragged them into the struggle between England and France for North America itself.

In considerable contrast to the life of the Algonkians was that of the Iroquoian tribes, most prominent among whom in the early 17th century were the Hurons located south of Georgian Bay, and the Iroquois of the Five Nations Confederacy occupying the territory south of the St. Lawrence and Lake Ontario from the Richelieu River almost to Lake Erie. Situated in these well-watered and fertile regions of present-day southern Ontario and western New York, they had an hospitable environment for an extensive agricultural economy. Here they were able to grow maize, their principal crop, as well as beans, squash, pumpkins, tobacco, and other vegetable products, some in considerable quantity. The surrounding woodlands furnished them with a number of wild plants, game animals (deer in particular), and fish.

A rich, well-documented ethnohistorical literature describes the role of these peoples in the 17th century but their history before contact with the white man evokes considerable debate among archaeologists. It is now believed that the Hurons and the Iroquois shared a common origin in the south, having pushed into the region of the Great

Lakes from the southwest, following the line of the Ohio and splitting on lakes Erie and Ontario, some going to the north side of these lakes, some to the south. In 1534 CARTIER found Iroquois on the lower St. Lawrence; but, in the interval between then and the coming of CHAMPLAIN in 1608, they went back to the position south of the river which in the 17th century became a "buffer zone" between New France and the English colonies on the Atlantic seaboard.

Leagued in the Huron or Wyandot Confederacy were four tribes: Attignaouantan (Bear), Attingueenougnahak (Cord), Ahrendarrhonon (Rock), and Tahontaenrat (Deer). Adjoining the Hurons were other Iroquoian tribes: the Tobacco Nation or Petuns to the west, and the Neutrals to the south along the north shore of Lake Erie. The famous Iroquois Confederacy consisted in the 17th century of five tribes: the Mohawks farthest east toward the Richelieu River, and westward from them the Oneidas, Onondagas, Cayugas, and Senecas. South and west of the Senecas were the Eries, another Iroquoian tribe.

All these Iroquoian peoples lived in rather permanent villages which were abandoned after an occupancy of 10 to 15 years. These villages were usually situated on high ground near some source of water and were fairly large, attaining populations of several hundreds or more. Most were protected by a log palisade. The houses were multiple-family units, appropriately called "longhouses" because of their rectangular shape, and usually accommodated eight to ten families each, although some have been reported to house from 20 to 30 families.

The household was the basic unit of Iroquoian social organization, which may be described technically as a maternal lineage, with descent reckoned through the female line. The core of any household consisted of a number of females descended from a common ancestress. When a man married, he occupied his wife's house. Authority in these households was vested in an old woman. While not constituting a true matriarchate, these older women did exert a great deal of influence, particularly in the political sphere.

The clan, a larger kin group, consisted of a number of households and resembled somewhat a great family. Clansmen considered themselves siblings, intermarriage between them was prohibited, custom dictated that they aid one another in time of need, they held property as a corporate group, they redressed injuries to one another and avenged deaths. Most of the clans bore animal names, Bear, Wolf, and Turtle being almost universal.

The significant political unit was the tribe. It had a name, occupied a defined territory, and possessed a council of chiefs or sachems. Linguistic affinity and a common way of life did not, however, necessarily imply friendly intercourse. The Hurons, who became the irreconcilable enemies of the Iroquois, their linguistic and cultural kin, were on much better terms with the Algonkians, originally migratory hunters, speaking an alien dialect. Thus it was that by the time the white man arrived confederacies had been founded, the purpose of which was to maintain peace among the member tribes. The Five Nations referred to their confederacy as the "League of the Iroquois" or "the great peace." Its founders were the half-legendary DEKANAHWIDEH and Hiawatha. In this system those tribes which were not members of the League were theoretically considered at war with it.

The institutional structure of the League of the Iroquois was described in symbolic terms derived from the long-house, certain tribes being "keepers of the door," etc. [see FLEMISH Bastard]. The kinship bonds of the maternal line, representing the household, were extended across the member tribes, which were themselves divided into clans. Since certain clans extended across various tribes, it then followed that quarrelling between clan "brothers" would theoretically be unthinkable.

The decisions of the league were made by a federal council composed of 50 sachems, whose positions were hereditary in the female line. It was the old women who decided which eligible male relative would actually inherit. Indeed the older women, the heads of the households, made most of the decisions, while the men holding the titles of authority carried them out. The five tribes comprising the league did not, it might be noted, enjoy equal representation. The Senecas, for example, were represented by 8 sachems and the Onondagas by 14, with the three remaining tribes ranging in between. The requirement that decisions be unanimous offset this unequal representation, however. Sachems enjoyed high repute. Indeed, aside from warfare, the office of sachem was the only means whereby a man might gain prestige.

Eloquence was one of the prime qualifications for a great sachem [see KIOTSEAETON, OTREOUTI]. Oratory and the recitation from memory of the great legends surrounding the founding of the league were outstanding attractions at the annual meeting of the Federal Council held at Onondaga, New York. As an aid to memory, wampum belts were used, combinations of black and white beads (made from clam and other shells), signifying important ideas and events. At times wampum was also used as a form of currency.

Although members of the league did, on occasion, join one another to wage concerted war (the destruction of the Hurons is a case in point), the greater part of their military activities smacked of the vendetta. A few warriors would combine to conduct a raid, making the most of surprise attack. Scalps were taken and prisoners brought back to the village, where they were either killed or adopted. Each household which had lost a member had the right to select a captive to fill the vacancy. Death by torture was the fate of the remainder. To die without showing the slightest indication of pain was considered ideal behaviour and victims were supposed to exhibit contempt for their captors by presuming to enjoy the tortures they received. Whatever their warfare, small- or large-scale, during the historic period, the Iroquois suffered great losses, witness a passage in the Jesuit *Relations* to the effect that Huron and Algonkian captives made up two-thirds of the Oneida tribe in 1668 (*JR* (Thwaites), LI, 123).

Such in sketchiest outline are a few suggestions about the nature of Indian society at the time of the white man's arrival, but even these will help us to understand why the impact of 17th-century European culture on that of the Indian profoundly altered every aspect of Indian life and thought. That any remnants of Indian culture survived is a tribute to its strength and to the loyalty of the Indians to their traditions. The nature and devastating effects of this clash of cultures can be understood better now than by any observer at the time, though there are many penetrating recorded observations by both Indians and whites, especially by persons like Marie de l'Incarnation [*see* GUYART] and some of the Jesuits, for example, in their letters, relations, and journals.

For the Indians of northeastern North America there were three vital areas where they suffered the full impact of the culture clash: first, the ideological, in which their religious beliefs and tribal organization were shaken to their very roots and the authority and influence of chiefs and medicine-men were gravely weakened; second, the economic, in which the fur trade caused a revolution affecting every aspect of daily life, sowing discord among the tribes, and finally erupting into the fur-trade wars; and third, political, where the imperial rivalries of French and English relentlessly dragged the Indians into the white men's struggles for military supremacy. In each of these areas the results were inevitably far more profound and tragic for the Indians than for the whites. From the first limited contacts with the early explorers, subsequently multiplied a thousand-fold across the whole continent, the Indians found their ancient ways completely disrupted, and social and moral disintegration, aggravated by brandy and disease, began to haunt them. M. André Vachon in his "L'eau-de-vie dans la socété indienne," *CHA Report* (1960–61), 26–27, has vividly described this revolution:

"Indian society, which was extremely primitive, was in no way prepared for contact with Europeans. The Indian's first meeting with the white man was a brutal shock for him. Suddenly he discovered a world, the dimensions of which bore no relation to his own: the iron blades of the white men had more cutting power than the Indian's flint knives; their canoes were immense; their fire-arms killed from a distance with a noise like thunder. Surely the spirits on the side of the white men were infinitely more powerful than any others the Indian had ever encountered. Accustomed as he was to explaining natural phenomena in supernatural terms, the Indian recoiled from this first clash with western and Christian civilization, profoundly shaken in the very core of his existence—his religion.

"As these contacts with the white man became more frequent and prolonged, the Indian soul suffered a corresponding attrition. At first the French gave knives, axes, and kettles to the Indians in order to win their friendship. But this contact with European goods completely upset the Indian way of life. They could not resist the metal tools, so superior to their own in utility and convenience, which were, in their minds, imbued with power and strength, and they adopted them immediately. In consequence, they forsook their traditional crafts, they ceased to make their own weapons and utensils, they modified their methods of hunting to suit the new weapons. The French traded clothing, as well, in return for furs, also food and brandy. Each time the Indians accepted a European product, they abandoned a portion of their own culture. Little time elapsed before they became the slaves of the fur traders, for they were forced to bring more and more furs to the company stores in order to get all the new goods they needed. The Indian who, hitherto, had hunted only to satisfy his own limited needs, faced the brutal fact that he now lived in a competitive society which already had completely altered his life pattern . . . little by little, certain fundamental traditions were forgotten; and the demoralized Indian, conscious of his decline, gradually lost the will to live.

"Brandy, without question, played its part in this disintegration of the Indian culture. But we must guard against the temptation to isolate this element and to exaggerate its importance. Brandy was only one of the many factors which combined to bring about the physical and spiritual deterioration of the Indian."

The predominant influence in the ideological sphere was the impact made by the missions, initiated by the Recollets and later taken over by the Jesuits. The primitive Indians found it well-nigh impossible to reconcile the two dominant motives for the white man's penetration of their continent: the search for material wealth and the conversion of pagan souls. Neither motive seemed reasonable to men who provided merely for the material needs of the moment and who possessed an integrated system of belief peculiarly adapted to the natural environment in which it had evolved. Moreover, the Indians were further confused by a secular authority which revealed its will to them, sometimes through the black-robes, sometimes through Onontio (the governor), and sometimes through the traders. This multiple standard in the ideologies and behaviour of the white men was to make an indelible impression on the Indian. The ensuing clash of interests and cultural values was to beget a fatal violence at the very foot of the altar [*see* BRÉBEUF, GABRIEL LALEMANT] and does much to explain the obstacles encountered by both the missionaries and those whom they sincerely wished to aid in bridging the gulf separating the palaeolithic from the modern age. Many persons, both Indians and whites, whose lives are described in this volume found themselves struggling, often helplessly, with complex and almost insoluble problems created by this pioneer phase of Canadian history.

The Hurons and their fate, as allies of the French, provide perhaps the best and most tragic example of the results which followed the deep penetration of a primitive, indigenous culture by a European one, so far removed from it by centuries of civilization. Coming in a spirit of the utmost devotion and willing to suffer every hardship, even torture and death, the missionaries found themselves facing the baffling problem of bringing new concepts, religious and secular, to a people whose ways and language, in the beginning at least, they did not understand. And, an added difficulty, they soon found themselves, as important representatives of the small, educated minority in the colony, inextricably and often unwillingly involved in civil and commercial policy; in the disputes over the fur trade and the sale of brandy; and in the bitter Indian military conflicts which destroyed the Huron country and, for a time, threatened even the existence of New France itself.

Despite a high mortality rate, the native population had maintained its equilibrium before the arrival of the white men. Infectious diseases, hitherto unknown, were introduced by the Europeans, causing a catastrophic drop in population.

A too hasty judgement might attribute to warfare the numerical decline of the Indians. The majority succumbed first of all to these new diseases carried by the whites. When the Huron nation first allied itself with the French, its population numbered 30,000 in contrast with the Iroquois total of 15,000. Measles raged among the Hurons in 1634, which was soon followed by smallpox and some other unnamed epidemic. In 1640 the Hurons numbered no more than 12,000, while the Iroquois population remained substantially the same. This epidemiological disparity has its own explanation. The Huron and Algonkian allies, with their families, paid regular visits to the trading-posts of New France, camping there for weeks at a time, in contact with the colonists and thus exposed to fresh contagion. The French missionaries and traders, on their part, freely frequented the Indian villages, whereas the Dutch and English more rarely penetrated to the Iroquois country. The Mohawks lived in the forest heart and many a long portage was necessary before their emissaries arrived to complete their brief transactions at Fort Orange (Albany, N.Y.). Solitary and on foot, in a hurry to return home, they were better able to avoid contagion than were entire households, travelling in canoes and prepared to stay for an extended period. The Iroquois family was not welcome at Fort Orange, a fact which saved it. The Dutch supplied firearms to the Iroquois after 1643 but the French, fearing revolt, refused to arm their non-Christian Indian allies. In 1649, when the Five Nations gave the final blow to the Hurons, disease had already conquered them. History often overwhelms its victims. The Hurons and the Iroquois had been equal, both belonging to the same race, speaking the same language, with the same characteristics and social structure (*see* Jacques Rousseau, "Les premiers Canadiens," *Cahiers des Dix*, XXV (1960), 9–64).

The geographical location of the Iroquois in the western part of what is now the state of New York gave them an important military advantage, enabling them to attack from the south, with relative impunity, the routes along the St. Lawrence and Lake Ontario, both vital links in the French communications with the *pays d'en haut* (the up-country), their major fur supply, to which the Iroquois also sought access. Thus the Iroquois had a motive for aggression and the base from which to launch it, whereas the Hurons had no interest in attacking their neighbours to the south.

Unlike the Hurons, the Iroquois were in a strategic position for diplomatic bargaining with more than one European government. Although the Iroquois were caught, against their will, in the conflicts and rivalries between the French on the St. Lawrence and the Dutch (after 1664 the English) of the Hudson River valley and New York, their strong military position (though it proved vulnerable in the long run) allowed them through most of the 17th century to play off the Dutch or the English against the French and thus to gamble for high stakes in the fur trade, with all the diplomatic and oratorical arts in which their leaders excelled.

"Are there practical persons who believe that Champlain would have done better to form an alliance with the Iroquois? Others maintain that his idealism led him to take the side of the Hurons and Algonkins, exposed as they were to the foul deeds of the cruel Iroquois. Neither of these views is well founded. Champlain wanted to explore west from New France, to discover the route to China, and to create an agriculturally self-sufficient colony; but in the beginning he favoured the fur trade, the economic base for the young nation and the justification for the existence of the Compagnie des Cent-Associés, at that time masters of Canada. The north country harboured the finest furs—and the water routes leading into it were controlled by the Algonkins and the Hurons. The latter were, therefore, much more useful to the colony than were the Iroquois. The Hurons, moreover, profited from the same social structure as the Iroquois and they exceeded them by 10,000 to 15,000 men. The facts of the situation dictated Champlain's choice. But these tribes also had their problems. To participate in the fur trade they needed military aid against the Iroquois, with whom they had been at war for a half-century. Their enemies wanted to force them to join the Confederacy of the Five Nations. Independence is a prize for which a high price must be paid" (Rousseau, "Les premiers Canadiens," *ibid.*, 50).

For the fur trade the geographical location of the Iroquois during the 17th century was less favourable than that of the Hurons. They could not fall back on the rich resources to the west when their own fur supply became exhausted, and occupying the coveted Indian position of middleman between the hunting tribes or bands and the European purchasers, French, Dutch, or English, was thus beyond their reach. From the 1620's on, the European demand for furs was insatiable and the Hurons controlled access to the northern and western fur supply. They carefully prevented even the French from contacts at first hand with the Tobacco and Neutral nations which were their trading partners and with the Nipissings to the north who provided them with furs. For a brief period, the Allumette Island tribe (Algonkian), which inhabited an island in the Ottawa River, athwart the Huron-French trade route, cherished commercial ambitions, in spite of its numerical inferiority, but it was never successful in supplanting the Hurons, although its members were sufficiently powerful to exact tribute from the river traffic [*see* TESSOUAT; d. 1636]. Indian manoeuvres to control the fur trade are well illustrated by the career of the infamous OUMASASIKWEIE.

In the 1630's and 1640's, however, it was the Hurons who demonstrated, collectively and most strikingly, the powerful position of the middleman. Located just south of the Precambrian Shield they were able to build up a trading empire among the Algonkian tribes stretching from the Great Lakes to the St. Maurice River, and even beyond it to the Saguenay, and northward to Hudson Bay. Their trading canoes loaded with their own and European goods, they threaded their way through the lakes and rivers of this great area, bartering for furs which would then be carried down to Montreal and Quebec, the Ottawa being the principal convoy route. From their neighbours, the Neutral and Tobacco nations, who were jealously guarded against contact with the French, the Hurons obtained native products such as corn and tobacco to supplement their own articles of barter with the Algonkian tribes.

It was this Huron trading empire, already weakened by disease, which, along with the Jesuit missions, the Iroquois destroyed in 1649–50, so completely indeed that the Hurons ceased to exist as a people, their remnants being dispersed among the tribes north and west with some seeking refuge on the Île d'Orléans, later moving into Quebec itself and then, after ten years, to Notre-Dame-de-Foy, three or four miles west of Quebec.

"Of the 50,000 Hurons, Neutrals, and Eries who were in existence at the time the colony was founded, there remained only a remnant; in Oklahoma the Wyandots, their descendants, numbered scarcely 378 in 1905 and at Lorette, in the neighbourhood of Quebec, there were 835 Hurons in 1953. The majority of the fugitives merged with the Iroquois; Father [SIMON] LE MOYNE encountered 1,000 among the Onondagas in 1653. Three years later, the Iroquois presented an ultimatum to the vanquished in the vicinity of Quebec: assimilation or war to the death? The majority of Hurons bowed before this threat" (Rousseau, "Les premiers Canadiens," *ibid.*, 51). So completely did they lose their identity that the Iroquois fighting against DOLLARD at the Long Sault in 1660 could include adopted Hurons in their ranks. The dialogue between Dollard's Hurons and those of the enemy, as reported by Louis TAONDECHOREN, an Indian who escaped from the massacre, would tend to confirm this.

After 1650 the Iroquois never fully reaped the reward of replacing the Hurons in the fur trade, for the Ottawas fell heir to much of the Huron trade. The fierce forays of the Iroquois continued, however, far to the north and east, with ambuscades which at times closed the Ottawa to the fur convoys and with attacks on the settlements along the St. Lawrence which threatened the very existence of New France. Not until the arrival and campaign (1665–66) of the Carignan-Salières regiment under the Marquis de Tracy [*see* PROUVILLE] did the colony gain even a partial security in the military sense. Even then the long record of negotiations, treaty-making, and alternate intervals of war and peace did not end. It spanned, in fact, the entire 17th century, and spilled over into the 18th, for the Iroquois were then no less deeply involved in the Anglo-French wars and in the campaigns of the American Revolution. Thus the Iroquois provide the most striking example of the impact made on the Indians of northeastern North America by the white man's imperial rivalries, which dominated the new continent as well as the old.

What part geographical location and the fur trade played in the 17th century Iroquois history is impossible to determine exactly. That both had a very great influence there is no question, even if one cannot accept the too rigidly deterministic explanation put forward, for example, by George T. Hunt in *The wars of the Iroquois* (Madison, 1940). Between Hurons and Iroquois, even though they were linguistically and culturally closely related, there were important contrasts in ideologies and institutions. The Iroquois, for example, never responded as deeply to Christianity as did the Hurons. Missionary projects were not attempted by the Dutch and English, while French efforts, religious as well as secular, were centred north of the St. Lawrence and from this base expanded into the Mississippi regions. The devoted but tragic and unsuccessful attempt of Father JOGUES to found a mission in the Mohawk country was too slight and temporary an episode to affect the course of Iroquois cultural development. Whatever the explanation, the Iroquois were successful in defending themselves to some extent against catastrophic cultural changes, so that even today their descendants form a distinct cultural entity. Doubtless geographical location, leadership, the internal strength of Iroquois tradition and institutions, and other less tangible factors all played a part in their survival as a people. Of particular institutional significance was the famous Confederacy of the Five Nations. Although it was a voluntary association and its members acted with great freedom both in war and in peace, it undoubtedly had a cohesive influence, especially, it would appear, after 1660.

The clash of cultures, while affecting the Indian more drastically, also had its impact on the European, a stranger at first in the unfamiliar environment of the New World. Indeed, he owed to the Indian his own survival in these harsh surroundings. Cartier's description of his voyage of 1534 is our first authentic account of Indian-European contacts in northeastern North America. In it he described the Iroquoians whom he met in Gaspé Bay, explained their customs, and mentioned maize, a plant under cultivation there. The two young Indians, Domagaya and Taignoagny, taken to France with the reluctant permission of their father, DONNACONA, became in the next year the first Canadian interpreters at Stadacona. Through their good offices Cartier was able to learn something of the Great River of Canada, notably that it was *not* a strait leading into the Sea of Cathay. The cartographers of the Old World, drawing the first maps of Canada, were greatly indebted to the invaluable information collected from the Indians. From the Indians also, Cartier learned the spectacular cure for scurvy which beset his men in the winter of 1535–36 (Jacques Rousseau, "L'annedda et l'arbre de vie," *RHAF*, VIII (1954), 171–212).

The first and probably the most important contribution of the Indian to the white man was in exploration. It was the Indian, his canoe, his snow-shoes, and his interpreters (many of them children of the first unions between the French and Indian women) that enabled Champlain, JOLLIET, La Vérendrye [Gaultier*], and many others to thread their way towards *les pays d'en haut*, sometimes by streams which were little more than a trickle, and thus to discover a continent. It was also through the lore of the Indian and his knowledge of the fur-bearing animals that the *coureurs-de-bois* were able to make themselves at home in the forest and ultimately to build a commercial venture of world-wide importance, the development of which forms a dominant theme in early Canadian history.

The Indians' knowledge of native plants became of great importance to the European. Tobacco, maize, all types of squash or pumpkin, and beans, were unknown in Europe before Columbus. The Hurons made oil from the sunflower which they used to grease their hair. Champlain discovered the Jerusalem artichoke in eastern Canada but it was the historian, Marc LESCARBOT, who introduced it into Europe. The Canadian Indians were familiar with maple syrup though maple sugar, the *sucre du pays* was unknown to them. Some Indian foods have been incorporated into the European-American cuisine, such as corn cooked on the cob and in other ways, for example, as succotash (a mixture of Indian corn and boiled beans, a favourite dish in New England); game cooked with wild rice; and, finally, certain methods of making bread stuffs which have been perfected in the northern forests, much to the benefit of the modern explorers. The native peoples of Central and South America alone have given more than 100 plants to world agriculture and thus transformed the commerce and cuisine of the Old World. The potato, called *patate* in French-Canada and in several provinces of France, comes from Peru. Carib Indians contributed the manioc and the sweet potato. The pimento provided the principal condiment in Mexico and was highly esteemed there as a vegetable. Some species of cotton were cultivated in New Mexico. And among other species which came from the recently discovered continent, were the tomato, cocoa, peanuts, the pineapple, the avocado, and arrow root.

The French and English languages have also borrowed from the Indian dialects; in English, for example, *pow-wow*, *canoe*, *tepee*, *chipmunk*, *moose*, *hominy*, *squash*, *tamarack*, etc. In French no less than 100 words have been adopted, among them *canot*, *tobagane*, *wigwam*, and more than 25 names of plants and animals in the province of Quebec alone.

Thus the 65 Indian biographies in this volume are only a slight reminder of the part played by the Indians in Canada's early development, a token tribute to a host of other unnamed Indians. Unknown contributors to today's culture, obscure heroes who fell in many battles, interpreters and canoe-men, they helped literally to haul half a continent into the modern age. It is to this anonymous multitude that Canadian history owes some of its most striking pages.

GLOSSARY OF INDIAN TRIBAL NAMES

THE FOLLOWING LIST includes the tribal names which appear most frequently in the Indian biographies of this volume. It has been compiled by the staff of the Dictionary to assist the reader in identifying and locating geographically those tribes encountered by Europeans in the early exploration and development of Canada, but makes no claims to be a detailed and complete summary.

For background material, the following, among other reference works, have been used extensively; *Handbook of American Indians north of Mexico*, ed. F. W. Hodge; Jenness, *Indians of Canada*; Desrosiers, *Iroquoisie*; Hunt, *The wars of the Iroquois*; Jacques Rousseau, "Le Canada aborigène dans le contexte historique," *RHAF*, XVIII (1964), 39–63. The most important contemporary sources of information are listed in the General Bibliography, e.g. *JR* (Thwaites); Champlain, *Works*; Marie Guyart de l'Incarnation, *Lettres*; *NYCD* (O'Callaghan and Fernow), etc.

The American Indians, in their cultural context, had not evolved a system of writing and their various languages were in a state of constant evolution. These circumstances explain the difficulties encountered by the first European authors who wished to transcribe Indian names, also the large number of variants encountered in the texts of the period. Moreover, in the 17th century, French and English spelling were themselves still fluid. The reader will find in the glossary below some of the variants, between parentheses, following the main name-entry.

Abenakis (Abnakis, or Wabanaki Confederacy); in French Abénakis (Conféderation abénaquise). A loose alliance of tribes in what are now Maine and New Brunswick, which included, among others, the Malecites, Micmacs, Passamaquoddys, Penobscots, Norridgewocks, and possibly the Sokokis. The Abenakis were allies of the French in the struggle with the English colonists of New England and the League of the Iroquois. (Algonkian family)

Ahrendarrhonon (Rock nation of Hurons); in French, Nation de la Pierre. One of the four tribes making up the confederacy of the Hurons. *See also* HURONS.

Algonkians; in French Algiques (Algonkiennes). Members of the Algonkian linguistic family, which included several tribes.

Algonkins; in French Algonquins. The numerous bands, which inhabited the territory adjacent to the Montagnais on the east and the Chippewas or Ojibwas on the west, and south of the present city of Ottawa, were called Algonkins by CHAMPLAIN and other 17th-century writers. They and the Montagnais were allies of the French in their conflicts with the Iroquois. (Algonkian) N.B.: The spelling of the terms "Algonkian" and "Algonkin," a much-discussed matter, in the English edition of the DCB/DBC follows that employed by Jenness in his *Indians of Canada*.

Algonkins of the Island. *See* Allumette Island tribe.

Allumette Island tribe (Allumettes, Algonkins of the Island, Kichesipirini, called by the Hurons Ehonkehronons); in French Algonquins de l'île. These Indians inhabited Allumette Island in the Ottawa River (the present-day Morrison Island, near Pembroke, Ontario). Thus they were in a strategic position to control the river traffic, as it was necessary to portage around the rapids surrounding their island. They exacted stiff tolls from all other nations, which made them a wealthy and powerful tribe in spite of their small numbers. Like other tribes, they coveted the position of middlemen in the fur trade and attempted to prevent trade between the Hurons and the French and it was they who tried to keep CHAMPLAIN from visiting the Nipissings in 1613. Although they did not succeed in supplanting the Hurons, they traded far to the south and east, at Tadoussac and with the Abenakis in what is now Maine. Their allies were the small lower Ottawa River tribes, the Iroquets and the Petite Nation, which were relatively unimportant (the Petite Nation later joined the Allumette Island tribe). The Allumette Islanders were not actually defeated by the Iroquois but their power declined after 1650 and the Allumettes thenceforth existed as "hangers-on" around the French settlements. (Algonkian)

Almouchiquois. See ARMOUCHIQUOIS.

Amikoues (Beaver People, sometimes called Nez Percés). A separate and subsidiary Ottawa band. (Algonkian)

Andastes, Andastoguehronnons, Andastogues. See SUSQUEHANNAHS.

Anniehronnons. See MOHAWKS.

Armouchiquois (Almouchiquois). General term designating the various small tribes along the New England coast, particularly those belonging to the Abenaki Confederacy [q.v.]. (Algonkian)

Atichawata; in French Atichaouata. A tribe of the Algonkins [q.v.].

Attignaouantan (Bear Nation of Hurons, Charioquois, Outchetaguin); in French Nation de l'Ours. One of the four tribes making up the Confederacy of the Hurons. See also HURONS.

Attingueenongnahak (Cord Nation of Hurons); in French Nation de la Corde. One of the four tribes making up the Confederacy of the Hurons. See also HURONS.

Attikamegues (Whitefish Nation); in French Attikamègues (Poissons-Blancs). A hunting tribe, which inhabited the upper St. Maurice valley. The Hurons traded regularly with the Attikamegues and their circuitous northern trading route to the Attikamegue country was an alternative to the more direct Ottawa River route (open to Iroquois attack) which connected the Huron country with the French settlements. The Attikamegues were ravaged by smallpox, overwhelmed by Iroquois attacks, and disappeared as an entity around 1670, remnants of the tribe taking refuge with the Montagnais of Tadoussac. (Algonkian)

Attiwandaronk. See NEUTRALS.

Beothuk ("Red Indians"); in French Béothuk (Peaux-Rouges). The first aborigines encountered by early European visitors to Newfoundland, they probably belonged to a distinct linguistic family confined to Newfoundland and were exterminated by European fishermen and the Micmacs. The last known survivor died in captivity in 1829.

Canibas. See NORRIDGEWOCKS.

Cat Nation. See ERIES.

Cayugas; in French Goyogouins. One of the member tribes of the Five Nations Confederacy. See also IROQUOIS.

Charioquois. See ATTIGNAOUANTAN.

Cheveux Relevés. See OTTAWAS.

Chippewas (Ojibwas); in French Sauteux, Saulteux, "dwellers by the Sault." The Chippewas occupied the northern shores of Lake Huron and Lake Superior from Georgian Bay in the east to the prairies in the west and northwards to the territory of the Crees, to whom they were closely related (the boundary was the watershed where the rivers flow north into Hudson Bay). The Chippewas were divided into four groups or tribes: the Ojibwas of the Lake Superior region; the Missisaugas of Manitoulin Island and of the mainland around the Mississagi river; the Ottawas of the Georgian Bay area, and the Potawatomis on the west side of Lake Huron in what is now Michigan. The Lake Superior Chippewas, the Ottawas, and the Potawatomis formed a loose confederacy called in the 18th century the Council of the Three Fires. The first Chippewas known to the French prior to 1660 were those around the present Sault Ste. Marie, hence the name "Sauteurs." (Algonkian)

Conestogas. See SUSQUEHANNAHS.

Council of the Three Fires. See CHIPPEWAS, OTTAWAS, POTAWATOMIS.

Crees (contraction of Kristineaux, the French form of a name that a portion of the tribe applied to itself); in French Cris. It should be noted that the English and French terms are not synonymous. The French "Cris" include both the prairie and the woodland tribes, situated to the west of James Bay. The English "Crees" take in, as well as the prairie and woodland tribes, the Muskegons, the Algonkian band inhabiting the swampy land around James Bay, and also the Naskapis, the Montagnais-Naskapis, and the Montagnais [q.v.] of the Quebec peninsula [J. Rousseau]. (Algonkian)

Ehonkehronons. See ALLUMETTE ISLAND TRIBE.

Eries (Cat Nation); in French Ériés (Nation du Chat). A tribe living south and west of the Senecas and east of Lake Erie. After sheltering Huron fugitives following the destruction of Huronia in 1649, they were themselves defeated by the Iroquois 1654–57. (Iroquoian)

Etchemins. See MALECITES.

Five Nations Confederacy; in French Cinq-Nations. The Iroquois League or Confederacy of the Five Nations consisted of the Mohawks, Oneidas, Onondagas, Cayugas, and Senecas. After 1722, it became the "Six Nations" when the Tuscaroras moved north from Carolina and joined it. See also IROQUOIS.

Fire Nation; in French Nation du Feu. A term which referred roughly, at times, to the Chippewas [q.v.],

Mascoutens [*q.v.*] and probably to various other Michigan tribes.

Flint (Canienga) Nation. *See* MOHAWKS.

Foxes; in French Renards. *See* KICKAPOOS.

Gaspesians; in French Gaspésiens. *See* MICMACS.

Gens de Mer. *See* NIPISSINGS.

Gens du Puant. *See* NIPISSINGS.

Hurons (from the Old French *hure*, a "bristly head"). They were divided into four separate tribes: the Bear (Attignaouantan); the Cord (Attingueenongnahak); the Rock (Ahrendarrhonon); and the Deer (Tahontaenrat). A few smaller Iroquoian communities, and at least one Algonkian, united with them from time to time for protection against the Iroquois. The real name of the confederacy was *Wendat* ("Islanders" or "Dwellers on a Peninsula"). Hence the name Wyandot, adopted by the descendants of the Hurons in Oklahoma, Michigan, and Kansas. The Hurons built up a powerful trading enterprise, in which they acted as middlemen between the northern tribes and the French, and which was destroyed by the Iroquois in 1650. (Iroquoian)

Illinois; derived from the Algonkian word "Ilnout," meaning "the men," "the people." The great Illinois-Miami grouping of distinct and closely related Algonkian tribes occupied, at the time of its first contacts with Europeans, the valley of the Mississippi and its eastern tributaries in what is now the state of Illinois. The French referred to all Indian nations that came up from the south to trade at Point Saint-Esprit and Chequamegon Bay, as "Illinois." Trade with the latter became increasingly important as dwindling supplies of beaver pushed the fur trade westward. (Algonkian)

Iroquets. An Algonkin tribe of the lower Ottawa River, which once inhabited Montreal Island, they were allies of the powerful Allumette Island tribe [*q.v.*]. (Algonkian)

Iroquoians; in French Huronnes-iroquoises; members of the linguistic family comprising the Hurons, Iroquois, and several other tribes.

Iroquois; derived from an Algonkian word meaning "serpent." The five member tribes of the League of the Iroquois of the Five Nations Confederacy (Kayanerenh-kowa, "the great peace," also known as Kanonsionni, the "long-house") inhabited, in the 17th century, the territory south of the St. Lawrence River and Lake Ontario, from roughly the Richelieu River and Lake Champlain to Rochester, N.Y., in what is now the State of New York. From east to west, they were: the Mohawks, Oneidas, Onondagas, Cayugas, and Senecas. Their struggle with the Hurons for control of the fur trade largely dominated the military history of New France from the 1630's until the arrival of the Carignan-Salières regiment in the summer of 1665. (Iroquoian)

Island Savages. *See* ALLUMETTE ISLAND TRIBE.

Kaskaskias. Tribe of the Illinois confederacy. *See also* ILLINOIS.

Kanonsionni, "the long-house." *See* FIVE NATIONS CONFEDERACY, IROQUOIS.

Kayanerenh-Kowa, "the great peace." *See* FIVE NATIONS CONFEDERACY, IROQUOIS.

Kichegoueiaks. *See* KISKAKONS.

Kichesipirini. *See* ALLUMETTE ISLAND TRIBE.

Kickapoos; in French Kicapous. A tribe of the central Algonkin group, along with the Sauks and Foxes, to whom they were closely related, ethnically and linguistically. They were first encountered by Father ALLOUEZ between the Fox and Wisconsin Rivers, 1667–70. (Algonkian)

Kiskakons (Kichegoueiaks, Short-tailed Bear Clan of Ottawas). *See also* OTTAWAS.

Kristineaux. *See* CREES.

Mahicans (Mohicans); in French Loups. A powerful tribe to the east of the Five Nations Confederacy, which inhabited the Hudson valley and extended into Massachusetts. They were settled first at Schodac, on an island in the vicinity of Albany, N.Y., in 40 villages. After attacks by the Mohawks, they moved in 1664 to what is now Stockbridge, Mass. (Algonkian)

Malecites (Etchemins); in French Malécites (Etchemins). A tribe closely resembling the Micmacs (early writers confused the two tribes), which lived along the Saint John River in New Brunswick. Their territory stretched north beyond the drainage basin of the Saint John River and also, in the south, included a part of what is now the State of Maine. *See* ABENAKIS. (Algonkian)

Mascoutens (Mush-ko-dain-sug, the "people of the little prairie"). Close relatives of the Potawatomis, they were pushed into southern Michigan by the Ottawas and driven westward by the Neutrals about 1625, settling finally on the Fox River in Wisconsin. (Algonkian)

Miamis. A northern branch of the Illinois-Miami group (*see* ILLINOIS), inhabiting in the 17th century what is now northeastern Iowa or southeastern Minnesota. In the late 1660's and early 1670's they appeared in the Fox River–Green Bay region to trade. (Algonkian)

Micmacs (etymologically "the allies," Souriquois, Gaspesians [in French Gaspésiens], Miscouien). A member tribe of the Abenaki Confederacy, which, at the time of its discovery, occupied Nova Scotia, Cape Breton Island, the northern portion of New Brunswick, and Prince Edward Island. They are the Souriquois of the *Jesuit Relations* and the Gaspesians of LE CLERCQ. The tribe adopted agriculture, accepted the Christian teachings of the missionaries, intermarried freely with the French colonists, and, like their neighbours the Malecites, remained allies of the French throughout the wars of the 17th and 18th centuries. (Algonkian)

Minquas. *See* SUSQUEHANNAHS.

Miscouien. *See* MICMACS.

Mission Indians. Those Christianized Indians who lived in the various missions around the French posts, e.g., missions of Saint-Joseph, Sillery, etc.

Missisaugas. *See* CHIPPEWAS.

Mohawks (Anniehronnons); in French Agniers. A member tribe of the Five Nations Confederacy [*q.v.*]. *See also* IROQUOIS.

Mohicans. *See* MAHICANS.

Montagnais and Naskapis. These two tribes (practically indistinguishable) were the first to come into prolonged contact with Europeans. The Montagnais inhabited the huge territory bounded on the south by the north shore of the Gulf of St. Lawrence between the St. Maurice River and Sept-Îles and on the north by the watershed separating the rivers flowing into the St. Lawrence from those flowing into James Bay. The Naskapis occupied the Labrador Peninsula east of the imaginary line between Sept-Îles and Lake Nichikun and a second between Lake Nichikun and Ungava Bay, except for a narrow strip of coast from Ungava Bay to the Strait of Belle Isle, which belonged to the Eskimos. The Montagnais and the Naskapi were nomadic peoples who lived by hunting and fishing. Certain intermediary groupings, where it is difficult to determine whether the tribes are Naskapi or Montagnais, are called Montagnais-Naskapi. (Algonkian)

Mountaineers. *See* TOBACCO NATION.

Muskegons. *See* CREES.

Naskapis. *See* CREES, MONTAGNAIS AND NASKAPIS.

"Nasquapee Indians" (of Labrador). *See* MONTAGNAIS AND NASKAPI.

Nassauakuetouns. *See* OTTAWAS.

Nebicerini. *See* NIPISSINGS.

Neutrals (called Attiwandaronk by the Hurons); in French Neutres. At the end of the 16th century the Iroquoian tribes were grouped into three confederacies: the Hurons around Lake Simcoe; the Neutrals around Lake Erie; and the League of the Iroquois south of the St. Lawrence. In the 17th century, the first two confederacies were crushed by the third but all three appear to have had a similar organization. The Neutral Nation (it remained neutral in the Huron-Iroquois conflict) occupied the territory in southwestern Ontario between the Niagara River on the east, Lake Erie on the south, Lake St. Clair on the west, and an indeterminate northern boundary, roughly 75 miles from Huronia. They had moved in from the south in the wake of the Iroquois migration and retained their close relationship with their kinsmen, the Eries, with whom they were sometimes confused. They were trading-partners of the Hurons. (Iroquoian)

Nez-Percés. *See* AMIKOUES.

Nipissings (Gens de Mer, Gens du Puant, Nebicerini, Ounipigons, Sorcerers); in French Nebicerini (Sorciers, Puants). Their territory included the shore and islands of Lake Nipissing, which provided fish in abundance. They were not an agricultural people but their trade was extensive with the north and west. Their chief rival was the Allumette Island tribe with which they were on unfriendly terms. But they traded regularly with the Hurons, dried fish and furs in exchange for corn. (Algonkian)

Norridgewocks; in French Canibas. A tribe of the Abenaki Confederacy. *See also* ABENAKIS. (Algonkian)

Ojibwas. *See* CHIPPEWAS.

Oneidas; in French Onneiouts. One of the member tribes of the Five Nations Confederacy [*q.v.*]. *See also* IROQUOIS.

Onnontaehronnons. *See* ONONDAGAS.

Onondagas (Onnontaehronnons); in French Onontagués. One of the member tribes of the Five Nations Confederacy [*q.v.*]. *See also* IROQUOIS.

Ottawas; in French Outaouais (derived from an Algonkian word meaning "to trade") (Cheveux-Relevés). There were four tribes: Kiskakons; Ottawas du Sable; Sinangos; Nassauakuetouns. The Ottawas appear to have migrated westward from the Atlantic seaboard, until they reached the Strait and Peninsula of Upper Michigan and the eastern end of Lake Superior, where they divided into Chippewas, who moved westward along both shores of Lake Superior; Potawatomis, who pushed south into Michigan and inhabited the islands of northern Lake Huron; and the remaining Ottawas, who stayed behind in northern Michigan. Manitoulin Island was the home of the parent tribe and they traded as far west as Green Bay. In 1633 the Ottawas came down to New France, the first peoples of the "pays d'en haut" to visit the French, who henceforth referred to the whole of the Upper Lakes territory as the "Ottawa" country, a vague term which did not differentiate between the various tribes inhabiting the area. The Chippewas, the Potawatomis, and the Ottawas were associated in a loose confederacy, called in the 18th century the Council of the Three Fires. (Algonkian)

Ottawas du Sable. *See* OTTAWAS.

Oumamiouek Nation. A small Algonkian tribe, located near Sept-Îles, 300 miles from Tadoussac.

Ounipigons. *See* NIPISSINGS.

Outaouais. *See* OTTAWAS.

Outchetaguin. *See* ATTIGNAOUANTAN.

Papinachois. The early missionaries locate these Indians in the highlands between the Mistassini region and Labrador; ancestors of present Montagnais-Naskapi. (Algonkian)

Passamaquoddys; in French Pesmocodys. A small tribe which belonged to the Abenaki Confederacy but which spoke a dialect similar to the Malecites. The Passamaquoddys occupied all the regions around Passamaquoddy Bay, the St. Croix River and Schoodic Lake, on the boundary between Maine and New Brunswick. (Algonkian)

Penobscots; in French Pentagouets. A tribe of the Abenaki Confederacy which occupied the territory on both sides of Penobscot Bay and River and which laid claim to the whole Penobscot River basin. (Algonkian)

Peorias. One of the five Indian tribes in the Illinois confederacy found on the west side of the Mississippi by JOLLIET and MARQUETTE in 1673. *See also* ILLINOIS. (Algonkian)

Petite Nation. *See* WESKARINI.

Petuns. *See* TOBACCO NATION.

Porcupine Nation; in French Nation du Porc-Épic. Located at the mouth of the Métabetchouan River, the meeting-place of the tribes from the interior of the Saguenay. (Algonkian)

Potawatomis; in French Potéouatamis. *See* CHIPPEWAS, OTTAWAS.

Puants. Name given to different groupings, especially

to the Natchez in the south and to the Winnebagos of the Sioux family. (Siouan)

Quapaws. A tribe inhabiting the right bank of the Mississippi, a little beyond the present boundary of Arkansas and Louisiana, where the voyage of JOLLIET and MARQUETTE terminated, 17 July 1673. (Siouan)

Quieuenontatironone ("Mountaineers"). *See* TOBACCO NATION.

"Red Indians." *See* BEOTHUK.

Sauk. *See* KICKAPOOS.

Sauteux. *See* CHIPPEWAS.

Senecas; in French Tsonnontouans. One of the member tribes of the Five Nations Confederacy [*q.v.*]. *See also* IROQUOIS.

Sinangos. *See* OTTAWAS.

Sioux. They are not, strictly speaking, a Canadian tribe as they did not often cross into what is now Canada before 1876. In the 17th century, CHOUART Des Groseilliers and Radisson* encountered them in the neighbourhood of Lake Superior.

Sokokis; in French Socoquis. A tribe closely connected with the Abenakis and probably a part of the confederacy, which inhabited the banks of the Saco River in Maine, close to the mouth of the river.

Sorcerers. *See* NIPISSINGS.

Souriquois. *See* MICMACS.

Susquehannahs (known to the Hurons as Andastoguehronnons, which the French shortened to Andastes or Andastogues; to the Dutch as Minquas or White Minquas; and to the English as Conestogas and Susquehannahs). They inhabited the country around the headwaters of Chesapeake Bay and the Susquehannah River valley. Ancient enemies of the Iroquois, they once were induced by Étienne BRÛLÉ to raise a force in aid of the Hurons with Champlain. They maintained a close alliance with the Hurons, entered into complicated negotiations with them prior to the destruction of Huronia, but did not actually give them military aid against the Iroquois. Later in the 17th century, the Susquehannahs were themselves embroiled in a war with the Iroquois, who emerged as the victors. (Iroquoian)

Tahontaenrat (Deer Nation); in French Nation du Cerf, commonly known as Chevreuil in French Canada. One of the member tribes of the Huron confederacy. *See also* HURONS.

Tionon. *See* TOBACCO NATION.

Tobacco Nation (Petuns, Tobacco Hurons, Quieuenontatironons or "Mountaineers," Tionon); in French Gens du Pétun, Pétuneux, Tabacs. The Tobacco Nation occupied the territory to the west of Huronia in Bruce Peninsula, to the east of the Blue Mountains. They cultivated tobacco extensively, hence the name Petuns. Besides tobacco, they grew hemp, maize, beans and sunflowers. They lived in nine or ten villages with a total population of around 15,000. Economically, they were completely subservient to the Hurons, marketing their products through them. (Iroquoian)

Tuscaroras. *See* FIVE NATIONS CONFEDERACY.

Wabanaki Confederacy. *See* ABENAKIS.

Wendat (Wyandot) Confederacy. *See* HURONS.

Weskarini; in French Petite Nation (Petits Algonquins). Small Algonkian grouping on the Ottawa River, which occupied the site of the present Montebello. The remnant of these people, destroyed before 1664, merged with the Allumette Island tribe [*q.v.*]. (Algonkian)

White Minquas. *See* SUSQUEHANNAHS.

Whitefish Nation. *See* ATTIKAMEGUES.

Wyandot Confederacy. *See* HURONS.

The Northern Approaches to Canada

T. J. OLESON AND

W. L. MORTON

THE NATURE of the economy of the European northlands in the early mediaeval period, and the means by which man lived in the climate and on the land and water resources of the north, underlay the expansion of Norwegian Viking society from island to island across the North Atlantic. This expansion led to the pre-Columbian discovery of lands which were to become Canadian, and gave rise to a northern and maritime frontier which occupied and exploited the northlands from Norway to Greenland, and beyond Greenland to the eastern Canadian Arctic, Labrador, and possibly Newfoundland.

From the expansion of this northern economy came not only the discovery of Canada, but also —as the English, Portuguese, and French began to take over the old Norwegian maritime frontier —the extension in the 16th century of the frontier and the northern economy to Canada. As a result, the development of Canada had origins separate from those of the remainder of the Americas, and the economy and history of Canada from the beginning thus had a distinctive character which is still pronounced.

The characteristics of the northern economy were the extent of its spread and its dependence on metropolitan markets. Where agriculture was possible, the farmstead was the economic base; where not, the fishing village or the hunter's camp. From these bases, flocks and herds grazed over the hills; the hunter and trapper ranged still farther; the fishermen sought the distant banks and currents where the fish fed. Traders voyaged after timber, or the rare goods of the south, offering in exchange the northern staples of fish and fur, or such arctic exotics as ivory and oil. Northland society, if it were not to decline to the nomadic self-sufficiency of the Eskimo or the Lapp, required imports from the south to maintain the technology, the arts, and the religion derived, wholly or in part, from those more favoured regions.

The bringing of the north Atlantic and its islands into the orbit of Europe was the work of the Norwegians between A.D. 800 and 1000, in the period when they were greatly expanding their own maritime frontier. Not that they were the first to penetrate those northern seas—this had been done as early as the fourth century B.C. by Pytheas of Massilia and in the seventh and eighth centuries by the Irish. Pytheas may have visited Iceland and certainly Irish hermits were to be found there in the eighth and ninth centuries. But such ventures were without significant result and Europe was largely ignorant of the north Atlantic region until the Scandinavians —particularly the Norwegians—prompted possibly by over-population, launched on the stormy northern waters the seaworthy ships which they had developed over the centuries.

This expansive movement was only in part connected with the piratical and warlike descent of the Danes and Norwegians on the more culturally advanced British Isles and western Europe. Peacefully—because the lands were virtually uninhabited—the Norwegians worked their way north, establishing settlements as they progressed through the island clusters north of Scotland, the Orkneys, the Shetlands, the Faroes, to Iceland. Of these the most important was Iceland, which the Norwegians discovered between 850 and 870 and settled in the 60 years ending in 930. Here intermingled with the Irish settlers and slaves brought along with them, they were to form the Icelandic people and to create a brilliant culture. Beyond Iceland, too, at no great distance, lay the northern lands of the Western Hemisphere.

Just as the Norwegians brought the north Atlantic into the European orbit, the Icelanders introduced Greenland, the eastern Canadian Arctic, and the east coast of America (as far south as *c.* 35°N), thus opening the way to the discovery of North America. Although there had been earlier contacts with Greenland, the first enduring one was that of EIRIKR THORVALDSSON (Eric the Red). Exiled for three years from Iceland for manslaughter in 982 he spent those years exploring the west coast of Greenland, and then, on his return to Iceland, organized a party to settle the country to which he had given such an attractive name. Two colonies were established on the west coast. They were known as the Eastern (in the vicinity of present day Julianehaab) and the Western (in the region of the present day Godthaab Fjords) Settlements. The latter lasted until about 1342 and the former until the 16th century. Christianity was accepted about 1000 and a bishopric established in 1124. There were at least 12 churches in the Eastern Settlement and 4 in the Western, and Christianity was practised in the latter until the 16th century.

With the colonization of Greenland the discovery of continental America became inevitable. Its shores were first sighted by the Icelanders as early as 986 and then first explored by LEIFR *heppni* Eiriksson (Leif Ericsson or Leif the Lucky), the son of Eric the Red, about 1000. An attempt was made to found a colony in one of the three regions principally visited in the early years of the 11th century. This colony known as Vinland was, however, abandoned after two or three years, chiefly it seems because of the hostility of the aborigines of the region, and no further attempts at colonization south of the St. Lawrence were made. Contact, however, was maintained for centuries between the other two regions, Helluland (Baffin Island) and Markland (Labrador). The former supplied Europe through Greenland with the most prized bird for hawking, the white falcon, and the latter provided the Greenlanders with the wood which they needed to supplement the driftwood brought by the arctic current.

The location of Vinland has caused much heated discussion. Though claims have been made for a location as far south as New England, the name may have referred to a large tract of territory south of Labrador, including Newfoundland where remains of Norse buildings were reported to have been discovered in 1961. Further excavations of the buildings in 1962 revealed that they could be Norse but not necessarily so. A smithy and quantities of iron and slag indicated that iron may have been worked here in the same manner as in mediaeval Iceland and Greenland, but definitive tests have not been completed. Few artifacts were found except some nails. Carbon-14 datings of organic material from the site (L'Anse aux Meadows) have given a date about the year 1000. Archaeological evidence may thus throw further light on this thorny problem.

Much more important than the contacts with continental America were those with the islands of the Canadian Arctic. Here the attraction was principally economic—marine and land animals, fish, and birds. Whales and seals were important for the home economy and walrus, narwhal, and polar bears for export. Walrus ivory and ropes made from the hide of the walrus found a ready market in Europe and the best walrus-hunting was at the northern end of Baffin Bay. The long horn of the narwhal was prized in Europe for its supposed medicinal qualities. Polar bears were valued possessions of mediaeval kings, and the bear traps erected by the Greenlanders are to be found in northern Greenland, the islands of the arctic archipelago, and as far west as the Melville peninsula. Eider-duck nesting grounds, which provided an article of trade, testify to the presence of the Icelanders on Norman Lokyer Island (79° N.). Shelters or stone nests in which the ducks could lay their eggs were built in the nesting grounds, as has been customary in Iceland for centuries, and evidence of them still exists. Thus *via* Greenland these products, as well as skins and furs, reached Europe from the Canadian Arctic throughout the later Middle Ages.

Through 500 years the Icelanders in Greenland maintained themselves on an economy of husbandry and hunting, but eventually their settlements lost contact with Iceland and Europe. Farming seems to have been more important in the early centuries but to have been increasingly superseded by hunting towards the end of this period. Almost certainly this process was hastened after 1266 when the Skrælings (as the Icelanders called the aborigines whom they met in the northern hunting regions—Disko Island and farther north) began to make their way into first the Western and then the Eastern Settlement. There is no evidence to show that relations between the Icelanders and the Skrælings were anything but friendly, and the disappearance of the European-Christian culture, in the Western Settlement about 1342, and some two hundred years later in the Eastern, can only be explained by increasing intermarriage between the two peoples and the adoption of what may be called an Eskimo way of life on the part of the Greenlanders. We know from literary sources that from the time of the colonization of Greenland, numerous Icelanders left the districts in which husbandry was practised and took to hunting and fishing in the so-called "wastes" (*óbygðir*) of Greenland and America. There are good grounds for believing that these men are the Tunnits of the Eskimo legends—a tribe of gigantic size found especially on Baffin Island and Labrador and said to have come from Greenland. In any case it is known that racial intermixture occurred early, but it is more difficult to say who the Skrælings were and what people resulted from the racial intermixture. However, the view may be advanced provisionally that the Skrælings are the bearers of the so-called Dorset culture and the mixed race are the bearers of the so-called Thule culture.

It is often stated that contact with Greenland was lost after 1410. This was not so. The play did not end; there was rather a change of characters. Whereas up to the 15th century the Scandinavians are the most important agents in relations between Europe, Greenland, and the Canadian Arctic, their place is now taken by southern Europeans, principally the English, the Portuguese, and the French. There were various reasons for the decline of the Scandinavians, among them the debilitating effect of the Black Death on Norway after 1349, the increasing control of Norwegian commerce by the Hanseatic League in the 14th century, and the inroads of the Bristol merchants in the 15th. In the 15th century the geographical knowledge of North America, possessed by the Scandinavians through their centuries-long contact with the northern land of Canada, begins to penetrate into southern Europe, although distorted by the mediaeval view (shared by both northern and southern Europe) that there were only the three continents—Asia, Africa, and Europe. This assumption had led to the belief that Greenland was a peninsula of Asia, a concept which must have meant that it extended southeastward from the northwest corner of Asia. Its geographical features are fairly correctly represented on 15th-century maps, for example, those of Claudius Clavus. The arctic archipelago is referred to under various names, for example, the Falcon Islands; and the whole territory in America known to the Icelanders appears as Albania *magna* or *superior*. Relations between the courts of Denmark and Portugal (*see*, for example, S. K. Larsen, *The discovery of North America twenty years before Columbus* (London, 1925), and Carl V. Sølver, *Imago mundi: skitser fra de store opdagelsers tid* (København, 1951)) and even visits to Greenland by Portuguese envoys in the 1470's and 1490's, spread knowledge of the

Canadian Arctic. Brisk trade between Iceland and England (Bristol in particular), may have played its part, although there is no direct evidence for a knowledge of Greenland as distinct from Iceland. The result was that, when, at the beginning of the 16th century, the Scandinavian link with the Canadian Arctic was finally snapped, the English and Portuguese were in a position to forge another through the Bristol-Portuguese voyages, 1480–1509.

What connection there may have been between the English interest in the Iceland fishery and the beginning of English maritime exploration for the islands in the north Atlantic is uncertain. There were connections with the Azores and with the Portuguese, who were interested in the northern route overseas. What is certain is that an unsuccessful voyage of exploration into the Atlantic was made by John Lloyd of Bristol in 1480 [see Thomas CROFT and John JAY]. Other voyages from Bristol followed in 1481 and possibly in the two following years; there were perhaps others unrecorded. Still later voyages took place from 1491 to 1494. There is evidence, though not certain proof, that one of these voyages resulted in the discovery of North America by the English before 1492.

Again, what is certain is that these attempts of the Bristol men attracted the Italian navigator, JOHN CABOT, who, after an unsuccessful voyage perhaps in 1496, traced the outer coastline possibly from a landfall in Maine or southern Nova Scotia to Cape Race [see JOHN CABOT]. The next year Cabot apparently perished on a more ambitious voyage.

Other Bristol voyages were made down to 1505, perhaps in search of a northwest passage, but with no recorded result. A partner in these voyages was the Azorean, João FERNANDES, known as the Labrador, who had perhaps explored the west coast of Greenland and sailed with Cabot, somehow leaving his name to the continental coast. One of the captains of Terceira in the Azores, GASPAR CORTE-REAL, explored in the Greenland and Labrador region in 1500 and 1501. Gaspar perished on the latter voyage and his brother MIGUEL CORTE-REAL vanished searching for him in 1502.

Some time after the last Bristol voyage of 1505 and before 1509 SEBASTIAN CABOT, though some ascribe these details to the first voyage of his father John, sailed into the northwest up to, he claimed, latitude 67°30′N. He saw the opening of Hudson Strait and perhaps the bay beyond it. He believed it to be the open sea-way to Asia which he sought, but his men insisted on returning and Cabot was never to resume his voyage to the northwest. But the search for the northwest passage continued in the years up to 1585.

These voyages were probings for a sea route to Asia, but their immediate result was the establishment of the cod fishery of Newfoundland. Both the explorers and the fishermen used the brief spring period of comparatively favourable winds when the prevailing westerlies gave way to intermittent easterlies as the Iceland low shifted northwestward from its winter location south of Iceland. It was this phenomenon which explained the early and the continued use of the northern route to America.

After Sebastian Cabot's voyage of 1508–9, it became apparent that a sea route to Asia could lie only around the land mass which was North America. While explorers under French auspices, VERRAZZANO and CARTIER, continued to search for an isthmus or a river system which would afford a way to the Pacific, the idea of a sea-way to Asia continued to live on in England. The obscure voyages of the Englishmen John RUT and Richard HORE in 1527 and 1536 may, though it seems unlikely, have been intended to probe the northwest passage.

But nothing was done until 1553, when the search for the northeast, not the northwest, passage was taken up in London. It absorbed all English energy, although the year 1565 saw Humphrey GILBERT begin to petition for royal authority to undertake the quest for the route by the northwest. Gilbert did not obtain the terms he sought. Captain Martin FROBISHER took up his concept and in 1575 with his supporters received permission to undertake the search. In 1576 Frobisher reached Resolution Island and entered Hudson Strait. Subsequent voyages in 1577 and 1578 had as their object not only the further exploration of Hudson Strait, but also the mining of some ore thought to be gold bearing on Baffin Island, which Frobisher had discovered in 1576. This attempt to combine the exploitation of northland resources with exploration failed when the ore proved worthless.

Meanwhile, Gilbert at last procured in 1578 letters patent which authorized him to found a colony overseas. It seems that he intended to found a colony "in the North parts of America about the river of Canada" to serve as a base from which to pursue the possibilities of a river passage to the Pacific as suggested by Verrazzano and Cartier. When Gilbert himself perished after a reconnaissance of Newfoundland in 1583, the English turned back to the search for a northwest passage by sea. The development of the northern economy on the St. Lawrence and the search for a passage westward by that river was to be attempted by the English between 1593 and 1597 but was then left to be effectively carried on by the French.

In 1585, then, Captain John DAVIS, one of the ablest of the Elizabethan navigators, explored northward from the strait Frobisher had entered. He discovered the strait which bears his own name, and reached 66°41′N. In a second voyage of 1586 Davis made no discovery, but in 1587 sailed to 72°12′N up the Greenland coast and returned convinced that there was a passage to the westward.

For 15 years no one had time or interest to follow up Davis's work. Then in 1602 George WAYMOUTH in the service of the East India Company repeated the expedition of Frobisher and Davis in search of a northwest passage, as did James HALL and John KNIGHT in 1605 and 1606, in the service first of Denmark and then of the East India Company.

Their ineffectual voyages were a prelude to HENRY HUDSON's expedition to Frobisher's strait in 1610, which had an effect in spite of Hudson's tragic death. Since it seemed that he had discovered a passage to Asia, Hudson's backers organized themselves as the "Governor and Company of the Merchants of London, Discoverers of the North-West Passage," and dispatched Captain Thomas BUTTON with his ships to sail to Asia in 1612. Button encountered the west shore of Hudson Bay, wintered there and returned home, but still with the hope of a passage to the northwest. His discoveries and hardships were heroically and vainly repeated by the Danish navigator, Jens MUNK, in 1619, most of whose men perished in Churchill harbour.

The Discoverers in 1614 sent a third expedition under William GIBBONS, a cousin of Thomas Button, and which also included Robert BYLOT. They were unable to enter Hudson Strait and later were icebound on the Labrador coast. In 1615 Robert Bylot, with William BAFFIN as mate, sailed to investigate Button's report of a tide from the northwest in Foxe Channel. They concluded that this was not the way to the passage.

Bylot and Baffin, still backed by the Discoverers, therefore sought in 1616 the passage through Davis Strait. Working north to Smith Sound in latitude 78°N, they discerned and named both Jones and Lancaster Sounds. But Baffin, greatest of the arctic navigators, concluded that there was no passage westward free of ice, and the Discoverers accepted his conclusion.

The search for a passage from Hudson Bay was not resumed until 1629 when Luke FOX was convinced that Button's opening might yet be found. Captain Thomas JAMES planned a similar expedition. Both sailed in 1631 to complete the examination of the west shore of Hudson Bay. Fox worked down as far as Cape Henrietta Maria, and then pushed north into the channel and basin which bear his name, as far as 66°47′N, but found no opening to the west before returning to England. James examined the same coastline as Fox, but wintered in the bay to which his name is attached. In the following spring he sought a passage to the northwest, but was greatly hampered by ice and returned to England. The joint failure discouraged any further search for the passage for over a century. No way to the east was opened, no minerals, no fisheries were found.

The prolonged English search for the northwest passage had, however, revealed the great inlet of Hudson Bay and the shoreline of the arctic archipelago on Davis Strait and Baffin Bay. But it did not reveal a passage to Asia or lead to any occupation or exploitation of the Canadian northlands above the St. Lawrence. What was to tie the search for the passage to the occupation of the Canadian north was the westward movement of the Canadian fur trade, itself the development by the French of one aspect of the northern economy in Canada.

By 1660 two French fur traders, Médard CHOUART Des Groseilliers, and Pierre-Esprit Radisson*, had come to the daring conclusion that the region from which the best furs came could be reached more easily by Hudson Bay than by the St. Lawrence, hence their remarkable journeying to the Court of St. James's, the voyage of the *Nonsuch*, and the granting in 1670 of the charter to the "Governor and Company of Adventurers of England tradeing into Hudson's Bay."

The charter of the Company gave it lordship of the soil and exclusive trade in all the lands draining into Hudson Bay, on condition of a yearly payment to the Crown of two elks and two black beaver whenever the monarch should visit those territories, and referred to the voyage which had been undertaken by the *Nonsuch* and *Eaglet* "for the discovery of a new Passage into the South Sea." Thus the search for the passage was associated with the occupation and exploitation of the Canadian northlands, an association which continued until John Franklin's* first voyage in 1818. The great resource proved, of course, to be the fur trade.

The trade was conducted by ships bringing supplies to posts at the river mouths where the furs were exchanged by the Indians who came down the rivers. The first posts were in James Bay; not until 1682–84 was a post, York Factory, established on the rivers coming down from the basin of Lake Winnipeg.

The creation of the Hudson's Bay Company

provoked the founding of the French "Compagnie du Nord" in 1682, under the direction of Charles Aubert* de La Chesnaye. From that date until the Peace of Utrecht in 1713 the two countries and their respective companies contested the control of Hudson Bay. Finally, by the treaty of 1713, the French relinquished their claims, but for a time in the years of warfare at the end of the century they established a definite superiority. From 1697, the year of the Treaty of Ryswick, until 1713, they held all the posts in the Bay except Fort Albany. Thus the 17th century ended with the fur trade of the Canadian northlands at issue between French and English, but still exploited by the northern route which had long connected Europe and the Canadian Arctic and might still lead to Asia.

The Atlantic Region

GEORGE MacBEATH

BY REASON OF their geographic position it was inevitable that the Atlantic Provinces should be the first part of Canada to be known to Europeans. Just who the first European explorers of the region were, however, may never be determined. It is now accepted that North America was "discovered" by Europeans many centuries before the time of Columbus; yet conclusive evidence for pre-Norse voyages is so far lacking; and following the Norse voyages the evidence again fades out so that until the late 15th century we are left with only a few more legendary accounts of European visits to America.

With the last quarter of the 15th century we come to a very different period. Expanding trade, advances in the science of navigation, and international rivalries all pointed, as we can now see, to the imminence of a "break through" in western Europe's problem of penetrating the Atlantic and finding a short route to the Far East. In such a "break through" the region of the Gulf of St. Lawrence and the Atlantic Provinces was bound to become a critical area—a focus of international rivalries and of the earliest activities in trade and settlement. Even before the voyages of Columbus the rich fisheries of the West Atlantic were apparently known to fishermen from western Europe; and to quote J. A. Williamson's *The Cabot voyages and Bristol discovery under Henry VII* (London, 1962), "there is no doubt that from 1480, if not earlier, the merchants of Bristol were making voyages for the discovery of unknown lands to the westward of the British Isles" [*see* John JAY and Thomas CROFT]. That they succeeded before JOHN CABOT's voyage of 1497 is stated in the recently discovered John Day letter: "It is considered certain that the cape of the said land was found and discovered in the past by the men from Bristol who found 'Brasil' as your lordship well knows" (L.-A. Vigneras, "The Cape Breton landfall: 1494 or 1497; note on a letter from John Day," *CHR*, XXXVIII (1957), 228). The Bristol men concerned may have been Robert THORNE and Hugh ELIOT. In any event, John Cabot's voyages and his discovery or rediscovery of 1497 were widely reported in his own day, although from that time until the present opinions on his exact course, on the location of the "country of the Grand Khan" or the "Island of the Seven Cities," and on the role of his son SEBASTIAN have varied. It is now generally conceded that Sebastian struck farther north on his voyage of 1508 and from his account, if it is accepted, it may be deduced that he passed through Hudson Strait to the mouth of Hudson Bay. He believed he had discovered the opening of the northwest passage to Cathay.

While John Cabot was possibly the first to explore Canada's eastern coast, he was soon followed in the early years of the 16th century by other daring adventurers eager to probe the North Atlantic and to profit from western discoveries; among them João FERNANDES, the CORTE-REALS—GASPAR and MIGUEL—and a few years later João Alvares FAGUNDES, all from Portugal; from France sailed Giovanni da VERRAZZANO in 1524; and from Spain (1524–25), Estevão GOMES. Especially notable for Canadian history were the voyages of CARTIER in the mid 1530's, not only because of their importance in the

21

continuing quest for a sea route to the Orient, but because they gave Europeans their first clear report on eastern Canada. To Cartier goes the honour of discovering Île Saint-Jean (Prince Edward Island), northern New Brunswick, the Gaspé peninsula, and the majestic St. Lawrence which he systematically explored and mapped. The narrative of his explorations is of the greatest value, containing as it does a careful description of the area he saw and the Indians he encountered. "It does not seem too much to say," wrote W. F. Ganong, "that Cartier's voyages . . . are the key to the cartography of the Gulf for the remainder of the century" ("Cartography of the Gulf of St. Lawrence, Cartier to Champlain," *RSCT*, 2nd ser., VII (1889) sect.II, 51).

Thus by 1535 these maritime explorers had probed the coast from Greenland to Maine and unveiled the expanse of Canada's eastern regions to Europeans. Their voyages, however, brought no more immediate permanent result in the way of settlement than did the discoveries of Cabot. The problems of the northern environment were forbidding, such obvious sources of wealth as gold and precious stones, tobacco, and spices, were lacking, and many more years were to pass before a successful interest in colonization could be aroused.

Cabot's voyage had turned the attention of men of other nations to the fisheries beyond Iceland which Bristol men had been seeking since the 1480's. Cabot and his companions, said Raimondo de Soncino in a letter to the Duke of Milan dated 18 Dec. 1497, affirmed that "the sea there is swarming with fish, which can be taken not only with the net, but in baskets let down with a stone so that it sinks in the water. . . . These same English . . . say that they could bring so many fish that this kingdom would have no further need of Iceland . . ." (Williamson, *Cabot voyages* (1962), 210). Although the Iceland fishery remained of primary interest to English fishermen in the first half of the 16th century, word of the new discovery soon spread and the annual voyages of Breton, French, and Portuguese vessels to Newfoundland began, for fish was in constant and heavy demand in Europe as an article of diet.

The Bretons came as early as 1504 and the Portuguese in 1506. The Normans JEAN DENYS and Thomas AUBERT introduced to their compatriots the fishing grounds off the Avalon Peninsula and Bonavista. Portuguese fishermen also established themselves on the east shore after 1506. In 1512 a Basque captain of Capbreton was given permission to go the new lands and many Basques were undoubtedly fishing here by the first quarter of the century (La Morandière, *Historie de la pêche française de la morue*, I, 227–28). When Cartier sailed through in 1534, Bretons were frequenting the Straits of Belle Isle. H. A. Innis (*The cod fisheries*, 25) deduces from the date of departure of the vessels that the Banks fishery developed after the shore fishery, towards the middle of the 16th century.

It should be noted that the methods developed in carrying on the fishery had profound effects on the history of the region. The French and Portuguese, who possessed abundant salt supplies, used the "wet" or "green" method of curing in which the cod were dumped fresh into the ships' holds, layers of salt serving as a preservative. The French were able by this method to exploit the Banks fishery while the English, who lacked salt and had to buy supplies from the Portuguese, were limited to the fishery off Newfoundland's east coast. During the third quarter of the 16th century the English developed a "dry" method of preserving fish: cod was cleaned, lightly salted, and dried in the sun. As the Portuguese and Spanish fisheries declined towards the end of the century the English found an increasing market for their dried cod in the Mediterranean countries. French Basque fishermen and their financial backers in La Rochelle gradually adopted the dry method to supply the Spanish market. A large and increasingly widespread home market encouraged Bretons, Normans, and Biscains to exploit other fisheries off the south, west, and north shores of Newfoundland, off Gaspé, Cape Breton, Nova Scotia, and in the Gulf, where larger and superior cod were to be found in abundance.

At shore bases in these regions the fishermen came in contact with the Indians who wanted European goods, and trade soon sprang up as a highly profitable sideline. In Newfoundland itself the white men had few dealings with the Beothuk Indians who moved to out-of-the-way places in the island, probably because of persecution. On the mainland, contact was made chiefly with the Micmacs and Malecites who inhabited the eastern seaboard and with whom the French were to have a more successful relationship, making these tribes in fact their staunch allies. Of all the furs obtained by the fishermen, beaver pelts came after mid-century to have the greatest value owing to the discovery by hatters of their usefulness for making felt. Soon there was a great demand for furs and some of the French fishermen decided as early as 1569 to make the trip to Canada for furs alone. Toward the end of the century the fisheries and the fur trade reached such large proportions that groups of merchants began to seek charters of monopoly for such trade, the first being granted by France to Jacques NOËL in 1588. However, monopolies were impossible to enforce effectively, because of the number of men striving for quick profits from furs, and keen competition convinced the merchants that trading posts should be established to enable them to be close to the supply, and in a better position to compete. The fur trade, therefore, created the monopoly system which provided the financial base for subsequent exploration and settlement.

In Newfoundland, however, in contrast with the mainland, the fishery remained dominant and it was out of the fishery that the beginning of settlement emerged. Since the dry fishery required more permanent footholds than did the green fishery on the Banks, men from the fishing vessels began to stay behind for the winter, to cut timber for buildings and other shore equipment and to protect property. As we have seen, the English interests were largely concentrated along the east coast of the Avalon peninsula including St. John's, and England came to assume a kind of overlordship of this region and of the fishery carried on there. By the end of the 16th century a nationalistic element was added to the purely commercial one as Sir Humphrey GILBERT's ceremonial claim of possession for Queen Elizabeth in 1583 and Sir BERNARD DRAKE's damaging attack on the Spanish Newfoundland fleet in 1585 indicate.

Meanwhile France had been able to pay little attention to Canada. For 60 years following Cartier's voyages religious strife engaged her to the exclusion of officially sponsored overseas enterprises. The merchants and seamen of Brittany and Normandy were thus left largely to their own devices. With the end of the century, however, there were stirrings of new interest. TROILUS DE LA ROCHE de Mesgouez's ill-starred attempt in 1598 to establish a settlement on Sable Island (Île de Bourbon) was a dismal failure; but the triumph of Henri IV in uniting France had already set the stage for a new period of French exploration and settlement in the Gulf and St. Lawrence region. Since the crown was too poor to bear the costs involved, the obvious solution seemed to be the granting of a charter requiring the encouragement of settlement in return for the exclusive right to trade in furs. Such a charter was granted in 1603 to Pierre DU GUA de Monts, and in 1604 a fort was established at Île Sainte-Croix in Acadia, which in the next year was abandoned in favour of a new site, Port-Royal (Annapolis Royal). Though the founding of Quebec in 1608 meant the transfer of the major French effort to the St. Lawrence, the establishment of Port-Royal is a milestone, since it proved that Europeans could live the year round in Canada. Not only did it thus mark the beginning of French settlement in what is now Canada, it was the beginning also of French Acadia which has remained a permanent element in Canadian culture to the present day. It should be said that Acadia in the 17th century was an ill-defined region; roughly it may be stated to have comprised all of the present New Brunswick, Nova Scotia, Cape Breton, Prince Edward Island, most of northern Maine, and a part of Quebec south of the St. Lawrence.

In selecting Acadia as the site of his venture de Monts, who had already been to Tadoussac on the lower St. Lawrence, reasoned that, lying farther south than the St. Lawrence, it would be free of the bitter winter cold, that this area might reveal a passage through to Asia, and that it was close to the fishery. As in the St. Lawrence valley, the establishment of early Acadia owed much to religious motives and the support of missionary efforts by wealthy patrons in France. Thus religion entered into the tangled skein of rivalries which beset Acadia in the 17th century, setting Frenchmen not only against Englishmen but against one another as we shall see.

England also shared the increased interest in New World settlement which developed in the early years of the 17th century, an interest shown both in Newfoundland and in Virginia but with very different results. In 1610 the London and Bristol company was chartered by James I with the object of carrying on trade and founding a colony in Newfoundland. In the same year John GUY of Bristol established a settlement at Cuper's Cove (Cupids) on Conception Bay under the terms of this charter. Guy's colony lasted about 18 years but it was not a great success, and this was also the fate of two other attempts made in the next few years, notably that by Sir George CALVERT (Lord Baltimore) who established his little colony at Ferryland but soon found the climate and prospects too discouraging.

These difficulties were not the only obstacles to colonization, however. Fishing settlements were already scattered along the coast, and these fitted into the plans of the London and Bristol "sack-ship" owners who were interested in promoting their carrying trade in white wine and bullion, and in buying fish in Newfoundland for export particularly to Spain. But such plans flew directly in the face of the interests of the West Country fishermen from the ports of Dorset, Devon, Somerset, and Cornwall, who, as G. O. Rothney says, "wished to have as many foreigners as possible competing with the Londoners in purchasing their product and did not want to have inhabitants competing . . . in selling it"

(*Newfoundland from international fishery to Canadian province* (CHA Booklets, X, Ottawa, 1959), 6). The West Country men had established their fishery by annual voyages and by early in the 17th century they were sending as many as 300 ships and 3,000 fishermen across the Atlantic each summer, while 20,000 men were employed in England. Their dry-fishing operations required extensive shore space in all the good coves and harbours and over the years they had come to view Newfoundland as almost their own property. "Official settlement meant civil administration, which meant in turn, regular immigration, the growth of settlement, and the loss of the fishing monopoly to the inhabitants as had been the case in New England" (G. S. Graham, "Britain's defence of Newfoundland: a survey from the discovery to the present day," *CHR*, XXIII (1942), 260–79).

Included in the 17th-century nationalistic outlook was a belief, generally accepted by the European countries concerned, that the fisheries were a nursery for seamen. Throughout the century the West Country merchants with their immense stake in the fisheries would use this argument persuasively through Parliament to curb settlement in Newfoundland. The bitter conflict of interests prevented the establishment of civil government in Newfoundland not only in this period but indeed until early in the 19th century.

Through this long period of governmental anarchy the balance of power swayed back and forth, with the settlers as the principal victims, even though they were also participants in the violence and bloodshed which erupted at intervals in a most vicious fashion. To all the other troubles were added from time to time pirate raids by such famous buccaneers as Peter EASTON and Sir Henry MAINWARING. Newfoundland thus unhappily became, to use the apt phrase of one writer, "the sport of historic misfortune" (PRO, *Acts of P.C., col. ser., 1613–80*, xxix).

On 24 Jan. 1633/34 the West Countrymen appeared to win a decisive victory by obtaining, in letters patent known as the Western Charter, regulations of unspecified duration which subordinated the settlers and the shoreline to their control. Among the traditional practices now given the force of law was that of recognizing as admiral of a harbour the captain of the first ship to arrive in the spring. The fishing admirals had the authority to enforce the Western Charter in their respective harbours in Newfoundland. Appeal was theoretically possible to the mayor of any of the eight West Country ports, but the mayors always backed up the West Country admirals.

In 1637 the extremely unsettled state of affairs was complicated by a proprietary grant of the whole island to Sir DAVID KIRKE and his associates, backed by the London sack-ship owners, though it was specified that the regulations of the Western Charter must be respected. For a short time, Kirke, seated at Ferryland, gave the troubled shoreline a period of peace; but in the Civil War crisis he was marked as a supporter of the crown, and with the triumph of the Parliamentary cause he was brought down. Arrested in 1651 and taken a prisoner to England he died in 1654. Commissioners were sent out by the Commonwealth government [see John TREWORGIE], but neither in the 1650's nor in the Restoration period was a permanent solution for Newfoundland's conflict of interests worked out, and the settlers remained the principal victims of the uncertainty. In fact, the pressure for their entire removal, mooted at several points, actually increased until in 1671 an order-in-council declared that the regulation in effect since the 1630's but hitherto disregarded which forbade any planter from living within six miles of the shore would be enforced. In 1675 the commodore of the annual convoy of fishing vessels, Sir John BERRY, was instructed to warn Newfoundlanders that in the following year they would be removed either to England or to the West Indies. On his return to England, however, Berry so vigorously defended the settlers, supported by determined Newfoundlanders such as JOHN DOWNING and Thomas Oxford, that the plan of expulsion was never carried out, and provisions in an act of Parliament of 1699 actually made the situation of the settlers a little easier.

In the last year of the century, because of the failure to enforce England's mercantilistic customs regulations, Newfoundland became the centre of a remarkable unrestricted re-export and smuggling trade linking both sides of the Atlantic. "Newfoundland was a great hole in the wall of national self-sufficiency that the mercantilists sought to erect around the mother country and her colonies" (Lounsbury, *British fishery at Nfld.*, 202). The decade of the 1690's was, however, as we shall see, overshadowed by the Anglo-French war which broke out in 1689.

Meanwhile the situation in Acadia had been scarcely less stormy as a result not only of conflict among the French themselves but also of international rivalries, especially that between England and France. Both nations claimed the region, England on the basis of prior discovery, France by right of prior settlement. The Anglo-French struggle for Acadia was to last into the 18th century. It began in 1613 when the English captain Samuel ARGALL destroyed Port-Royal.

This had no permanent result since Port-Royal was repaired and reoccupied by the French under CHARLES DE BIENCOURT de Saint-Just, and outposts were established at Cap de Sable, La Hève, and Pentagouet on the Penobscot.

However, in 1621 a new element came into the situation when James I granted Acadia to Sir WILLIAM ALEXANDER, Earl of Stirling, under the name of New Scotland. In 1624 he was authorized to create, for a fee, baronets of Nova Scotia; and in 1629 under his son, Sir WILLIAM ALEXANDER the younger, a settlement was attempted. Its short and confusing history, in which the Alexanders, Sir David Kirke, the SAINT-ÉTIENNE de La Tours, Sir James STEWART (Lord Ochiltree), CHARLES DANIEL, and others were involved, illustrates the bewildering complexity of rivalries, personal and international, in the Acadia of this early period. In 1627 hostilities broke out between England and France; and the English gained control of Acadia as they did also of Quebec. This transfer of Acadia to England, the first of three changes of ownership during the century, was short-lived. In 1632 Acadia, like Quebec, was returned to France, and the Alexanders' attempt at colonization came to an end.

France now decided that peasants should be sent as colonists to the New World and the first of these arrived in Acadia with Governor Isaac de RAZILLY in 1632. They settled at La Hève and later moved to Port-Royal. These farmers were the first of the Acadians, a sturdy and vigorous people who showed a great love of the land and were unusually prolific. As their numbers grew, they spread through Acadia in a most successful experiment in colonization. Yet it must be said that this was achieved in the face of the neglect of the mother country and the hostility of the English who were establishing strong colonies to the south. It was the gentlemen-adventurers, the trading companies, and this little band of pioneers who struggled to maintain French interests in Acadia.

However, for a number of years the situation was a nearly chaotic one. By 1640 Acadia was governed by three men—MENOU d'Aulnay, NICOLAS DENYS, and Charles de Saint-Étienne de La Tour—each with his own territory to administer and in which he had exclusive right to trade. Fighting between the three for supreme control broke out and greatly hampered colonization. With d'Aulnay's death in 1650, peace was restored and more settlers were placed on the land. In 1654 a British force under Robert SEDGWICK captured all of Acadia except for the extreme northern portion, but during the next 13 years the English proprietors, TEMPLE and CROWNE, made no effective attempt to colonize Acadia, and in 1667 by the Treaty of Breda it was returned to France.

In the Newfoundland area the beginning of the 1660's was marked by a significant development in the rivalry of England and France. The great Colbert may be credited with the encouragement of the natural tendency of the French towards expansion in the north Atlantic, but with the aim of naval as well as commercial supremacy in accordance with the mercantilist plan. French fishermen had controlled the south coast of Newfoundland for many years but there were few permanent settlers. Plaisance (Placentia) was fortified in 1662, under DU PERRON, to serve as a secure base for the widespread fishery, as a port of call for convoys going to and from Quebec, and as a guardian of French possessions in North America. Plaisance, attached for governmental purposes to New France, became a bastion of French power and influence until finally lost by the Treaty of Utrecht in 1713.

With the reoccupation of Acadia in 1670 the French government was coming to be more concerned with the effectiveness of her Acadian settlements. It was noted that although great profits had been realized through the fur trade and fishing, insufficient progress had been made in the colonization of the new land, largely owing to the trading companies' lack of interest in settling the country. So it was that the seigneurial system was introduced, the first seigneuries being granted in 1672 to Martin d'APRENDESTIGUY de Martignon, to JOYBERT de Soulanges, and Jacques Potier* de Saint-Denys. While almost all the most advantageous places in Acadia were given as seigneurial tracts of land, this system proved a failure both for land cultivation and for settlement because the majority of the grantees did little or nothing to develop their holdings. A further hindrance to settlement was the repeatedly changing ownership of the country.

Both Acadia and Newfoundland suffered from raids by the Dutch during the second and third Anglo-Dutch Wars. In 1665 the Dutch, under De Ruyter, pillaged vessels and shore equipment in the outposts; they attacked St. John's in the next year and Ferryland in 1673. In 1676 the Dutch also raided Plaisance and destroyed the French fishing fleet in the area. Then, too, a Dutch ship under Jurriaen AERNOUTSZ had captured the French forts at Port-Royal, Penobscot, and Jemseg in 1674, and declared Acadia to be Dutch territory. By 1678, however, the Dutch had retired from the scene. There then followed ten years of relative peace, although unauthorized attacks on rival ships and establishments continued.

With the outbreak of general war between France and England in 1689 the conflict in the Gulf region entered a new phase which was to last with interruptions until the Treaty of Utrecht in 1713. In Boston, plans were quickly made for a new attack on Acadia, and in 1690 Sir William PHIPS set out with an expedition which captured Port-Royal, the Gut of Canso, and La Hève, though it failed at Quebec. At the same time, the French were busily engaged repairing and strengthening their fortifications at Plaisance. The garrison of regular soldiers was augmented and a series of privateer raids launched from that base on the island's English settlements. In retaliation, an English force raided Plaisance in 1690, tortured the governor, Antoine PARAT and removed the guns, but the town was returned to French control. Two years later it withstood a cannonade by units of the British navy and, over the next few years, Plaisance served as the base of operations for a series of hit-and-run attacks, in which Pierre Le Moyne* d'Iberville figured largely, which destroyed all the English settlements in Newfoundland with the exception of Bonavista and Carbonear. Thus the colonists paid for England's failure to resolve the problem of Newfoundland settlement; defence of the ports rested with the navy since none had been fortified.

Both Acadia and Newfoundland were thus embroiled in the clash between the two great powers. France had not been content to see the English win partial control in Acadia in 1690.

JOSEPH ROBINAU de Villebon was appointed governor in 1691 and he succeeded in reconquering the whole of Acadia. What is more, from his post at Naxouat (Nashwaak) he directed a spirited counter-offensive against Massachusetts, the marauding bands of French and Indians which he organized carrying out a series of bloody raids on New England settlements. In 1696, a New England expedition under Col. Benjamin Church* destroyed an Acadian settlement at Beaubassin (Chignictou) and led by Col. John Hathorne* attacked Villebon's fort at Nashwaak where it met stout opposition and was forced to retire. Late in the next year, the Treaty of Ryswick brought the fighting to a temporary end. Just prior to the signing of the treaty, England had sent two regiments and a naval squadron to recapture Newfoundland and when they arrived at St. John's they found not a single building left standing, stark evidence of the destruction that had taken place during the war years.

The peace treaty settled a few issues and in 1701 war was renewed. The Spanish, Portuguese, and Dutch were gone, but the grim struggle for economic and military control of the whole of North America from Newfoundland to the Antilles would go on; and in that struggle Canada's Atlantic region would continue to figure prominently as a focus of tensions and rivalries because of its great strategic importance as the eastern flank of the continent.

New France, 1524-1713

MARCEL TRUDEL

WHAT ASTONISHES most a student of the first two centuries of New France is that this colony, which was so slow in deciding on its location and becoming settled, should have all at once expanded until it covered nearly three-quarters of the North American continent.

Of all the countries facing on the Atlantic, France, at the end of the 15th century, was the richest and most powerful; under normal conditions, she should have taken the initiative in the discovery and occupation of the New World. Instead, it was small countries, Spain and Portugal, which experienced a colonial expansion of such scope that they soon shared, from the North Pole to the South, the territories not yet occupied by Europeans. France, centred on the Mediterranean and much more interested in Italy than in the New World, took part only in 1524 in the Atlantic race, and even then it was merely to seek what Spain had already been seeking for a quarter of a century: a sea route that would lead straight to Asia. The "happy shores of Cathay" remained inaccessible to VERRAZZANO, but in 1524 he discovered the coastline joining Florida and Cape Breton, thus placing at the disposal of François I an American empire as vast as that of Charles V. New France was entering history.

François I wanted primarily to discover a way through the continental barrier that Verrazzano had run up against: beyond America, it was Asia that fascinated him. In 1534, behind Newfoundland, CARTIER found a sea the shores of which he was the first to chart, and he established relations with natives from the interior. The following year, he discovered (and therein lies his finest claim to glory) one of the great rivers of the world, the *Rivière de Canada* (called 100 years later the River St. Lawrence), which was to become the indispensable axis of the French empire in America. Under the leadership of JEAN-FRANÇOIS DE LA ROCQUE de Roberval and of Cartier, centred on the great waterway that was expected to open on to a fabulous Saguenay, the proposed colony seemed to offer hopes of a glittering destiny; North America promised to be as rich as Peru. The enterprise floundered in 1543: Roberval, whose first concern was with his European possessions, had no experience of America; Cartier, a good navigator but not necessarily a good colonizer, and convinced that he had found gold and diamonds, parted company with his superior. In addition, the rigorous climate of the St. Lawrence region was the sort of obstacle that is overcome only after a generation or so. France withdrew from the St. Lawrence for half a century.

But she did not withdraw from America, and did not abandon her colonizing policy; for some years this policy was to remain linked with the Protestant problem. The most thoroughgoing and persistent effort at French colonization in 16th century America was carried out in terms of Protestantism. A New France had become necessary chiefly so that the Huguenots, persecuted at home, might set up a society there, in keeping with their religious reforms. This formula, which to a large extent was responsible for the astonishing success of England in the 17th century, did not work with the France of the 16th century. Assuredly, the failure of a New France in Brazil and Florida was due to some immediate causes (an obvious encroachment upon the Portuguese and Spanish empires, a treasure hunt rather than cultivation and consolidation), but above all there was the failure of Protestantism in France: according as Coligny's star rose or sank, Protestant colonial activity flourished or declined. The Massacre of St. Bartholomew brought an end to the Protestant leader's career, and at the same time to the vast plans for French colonization in the 16th century.

After Coligny's fall, colonization ceased for a long time to be the immediate concern of the state, which moreover was breaking up. Colonial activity had now perforce to be left to individuals. For the latter, however, this development took place at a propitious moment: American furs, which the cod-fishermen of Newfoundland had hitherto brought back only as extras, became, because of their abundance and quality, the prime reason for the Atlantic journeys. The state had no longer to stimulate the exploitation of America: the merchants had an interest in taking the initiative. A new formula for colonization therefore appeared; it consisted of guaranteeing an exclusive monopoly to a commercial enterprise, which in return would assume responsibility for settlement. Out of these merchants it would be the endeavour to make colonizers. But from 1588 on, obstacles arose which were to defer until the 17th century the establishment of a New France: on the one hand, those holding a monopoly were hardly likely to take kindly to colonization, always an extremely costly affair; on the other hand, those merchants who were denied this privilege would intervene, in the name of freedom of trade, in order to have the monopoly cancelled, or at least restricted in such a way that the slender margin of profits would render any colonization impossible.

There was no lack of serious efforts, but the means were not available. It was thought that the problem could be solved by choosing fresh sites: in 1597, TROILUS DE LA ROCHE de Mesgouez decided in favour of the Île de Sable, from which he hoped to be able to keep watch on the entrance to the Gulf of St. Lawrence; he supplied food to his settlement each year, except in 1602, but in 1603, when he again sent help, disaster was found. In 1600, PIERRE CHAUVIN DE TONNETUIT established himself at Tadoussac, the arrival point for the Laurentian furs. The first winter season (calamitous like all first experiences of wintering in North America), discouraged hopes, and Tadoussac remained a summer factory; as for the Sieur Aymar de Chaste's company, one gets the impression in reading the account of CHAMPLAIN that in 1603 it would prefer Acadia to the shores of the St. Lawrence. But by changing location, the founders merely modified their problem without solving it. England, also, thought she could make things easier for herself by moving her colonies. Newfoundland, Plymouth Bay, Rhode Island Bay, Chesapeake Bay, Cape Hatteras: in all these places, in very different latitudes, she tried vainly for a quarter of a century to get a foothold.

By the end of 1603, there was not yet in America a New England or a New France. The aims (evangelization and civilization) proclaimed by France were still not being realized. The natives' style of life had not been transformed into that of the French, and up to then the spiritual influence of France seemed to be non-existent. Despite the splendid religious declarations of 1540, France had not yet baptized a single native on North American soil, nor had any missionary laboured there.

The work of these 80 years does not represent a total loss: France had learned to know the continent; here and there she had scattered place-names, which was a minor form of taking possession; the four winter seasons in the Laurentians were a valuable experience; she had established firm relations with the natives, and had introduced her products into the very heart of the continent. It seemed more and more apparent that northeastern America was going to become France's territory. After all these attempts, one problem had remained: was it France's final intention to set up a colony or merely a fur-trading warehouse? Following a new survey made by FRANÇOIS GRAVÉ DU PONT and Samuel de Champlain in 1603, a new question presented itself: was France's choice to be the St. Lawrence or Acadia?

She preferred Acadia. It was here that a site was sought which would combine the ideal conditions for colonization: nearness to the sea, the proximity of peaceable natives, an abundance of mines, a fertile soil, a mild climate, and possible access to the Western Sea. As a concomitant of his trade monopoly, the Protestant DU GUA de Monts obtained the viceroyalty of a country that stretched to the 40th degree of latitude; in 1604, he chose the Île Sainte-Croix as a temporary base, then Port-Royal (Annapolis Royal, N.S.), until he could find the exact spot offering all the ideal conditions. The search went on for three years, and was still going on in 1607, when news arrived that the monopoly was revoked. In the autumn of 1607 the French settlers in Acadia returned to France, leaving ruins at Sainte-Croix and abandoned buildings at Port-Royal, whilst close by, at the mouth of the Kinibeki (now Kennebec), an English settlement was entering upon its first winter season, and, in those southern regions where Pierre Du Gua de Monts and JEAN DE BIENCOURT de Poutrincourt would have liked to find the ideal place for colonization, the English colony of Virginia was beginning, at Jamestown, a history that was to continue without interruption.

The French sojourn in Acadia, from 1604 to 1607, made possible tremendous progress in our geographical knowledge of this part of America: a long strip of coastline, from Cape Breton to Cape Cod (Cap Blanc), was added to the maps, and subsequently received only trifling corrections; and this same coastline was copiously supplied with French place-names. In addition, close relations had been established with the natives, and would not be allowed to slacken. Thenceforth the three great families that occupied the country, from Acadia to the Cap Anne, were known: the Micmacs or Souriquois, whose habitat embraced Acadia, Cape Breton, and the Gaspé Peninsula; the Etchemins, also called Malecites or Penobscots, who stretched from the Saint John River to the Rivière Penobscot; and the Armouchiquois, who were to be found between the Rivière Penobscot and the Rivière Chouacouët (Saco). Finally, the French had at their disposal a territory rich in mines and furs. LESCARBOT was to suggest enthusiastically that the surplus population of France should be deposited there. The Acadian experiment remained a valuable one, and was to contribute to the development of a New France; but for the moment, in the autumn of the year 1607, another set-back had to be recorded.

De Monts weathered the storm that swept away his Acadian settlement; on the advice of Champlain, the man who had publicized Acadia so much, he did, however, turn towards another region, the St. Lawrence River. Since no locality combined all the ideal conditions for colonization (at any rate those sought by De Monts), one might as well choose a river that offered hope of access to the Asian Sea, a place where lands appeared fertile, and where the natives were friendly in their behaviour; where above all it would perhaps be easier to protect his trade. Champlain therefore went back up the St. Lawrence in 1608, and, at a narrows called Quebec, established a depot. France was returning to where she had begun in 1535; this time, the establishment was to be permanent.

It is true that Quebec, for several years, continued to be only a storehouse for furs, around which gravitated the employees of the fur trade and the natives, a storehouse 140 miles distant from its maritime base of Tadoussac. Until 1615, Quebec consisted in reality only of a "habitation" and a warehouse; trade was the settlement's sole reason for existence. Then, thanks to Champlain, some Recollets came along, the first proper missionaries of the St. Lawrence valley; they built a chapel and a convent, and undertook to preach the gospel to the natives. The strictly commercial appearance of Quebec was changed. When LOUIS

HÉBERT established himself permanently, the first immigrant to settle on the St. Lawrence, and when the Jesuits came in 1625 to give a new impetus to religious life, the French colony began to assume the pattern of a civilized country.

Yet how frail was its existence! It could still support itself only by means of a commercial company, and that company required an exclusive monopoly. Yet the merchants of France were doggedly opposed to the formation of a monopoly, and when that monopoly was constituted the company remained powerless to protect its interests. In the "early spring" began the race to make contact with the native fur-traders, who were quickly put off by the same odious practices that certain Frenchmen had employed in Acadia. For the majority of merchants, the St. Lawrence valley was merely the source of a supply of furs; in their mind there was no question of building for permanence.

But gradually Champlain became a colonizer. His explorations in 1609 and 1613, his winter season in the Huron country in 1615–16, and the evidence of the other European settlements, convinced him of the rich potentiality of a vast empire; instead of a storehouse to be emptied in the spring with no further concern for the country, Champlain would have liked to make Quebec the centre of a French New World. One after the other, the companies that employed him bridled; they refused to establish settlers, because they well knew that those settlers would become a threat to the fur trade; they even attempted to jettison Champlain. But the latter acquired protection in high places, and gradually rose in dignity: the representative of a fur trading company soon became the representative of viceregal, then of royal, authority. As he rose, he maintained his colonizing programme against all comers.

Champlain gave a detailed explanation of this programme in 1618, in his reports to the king and to the Chamber of Commerce: it was to set up a completely organized colony, of which not only the furs but also all the abundant and varied resources would be exploited; to the profits that it would yield would be added the customs duties, since (as there was then every reason to expect) Quebec would become the unavoidable port on the route to Asia. It was a programme on a vast scale, which was to be matched only under TALON.

Fortunately, Champlain's persistence in maintaining the Quebec post in order to make of it a commercial settlement instead of a mere factory finally received approval from France: Richelieu wanted to raise up an empire in America, following the English and Dutch examples. It would really be starting from the ground up: in Acadia, the French, dispersed by the Virginians in 1613, had reappeared only in insignificant numbers; the Quebec settlement, after 20 years of existence, still consisted of about 70 persons only; a single family was permanently set up there, and the ground was as yet unturned by the plough.

To reverse this state of affairs, a ridiculous one by comparison with what the English and the Dutch were accomplishing in America, Richelieu founded in 1627 a large-scale company, which he put on a financial footing that was deemed very sound at the time. Bringing together important people (among them Richelieu himself and Champlain) and *bourgeois* who were each required to contribute 3,000 *livres*, the Compagnie des Cent-Associés, constructed on the model of the great English and Dutch companies, seemed to possess the guarantees necessary for success in its three fundamental aims: to populate the country with native-born Frenchmen, develop the American trade, and lead the Indians to the Christian religion and a civilized way of life. To this end, precise measures were decided upon: in 15 years the company was to establish 4,000 settlers (between 200 and 300 not later than 1628), all of them Catholics; in order to encourage the recruitment of workmen, they were promised, after merely six years of residence, the mastership that it was so hard to acquire in France; nobles and ecclesiastics would have the right to engage in trade, without loss of status; as for the natives, in order to make it easy for them to take their places in civil life, they had only to receive baptism to enjoy the same privileges as native-born Frenchmen. The company had very extensive responsibilities to bear, but it received an immense seigneury—the whole of North America, from Florida to the North Pole; it was guaranteed a monopoly of the fur trade in perpetuity, and a monopoly of all trade for 15 years; moreover, it would have no taxes to pay on any merchandise that it might manufacture in the colony if this were imported into France. Never up to then had such a powerful commercial company taken over the destiny of New France; there could be no further doubt about the success of the undertaking, and in 1628, at a cost of 400,000 *livres*, the company embarked a contingent of 400 immigrants.

Between France and England a state of war had been in existence for a year. The KIRKE brothers, serving with an English company that claimed Acadia and the St. Lawrence, captured the first shipment sent by the Cent-Associés, then prevented any help from getting through to Quebec. In 1629 Champlain capitulated, and returned to Europe with all the missionaries and his own people, except for the COUILLARD family and a few interpreters. The capitulation actually occurred at a time when international peace had been restored, but three long years of negotiation were necessary before the country again became a French possession.

The enthusiasm that had spurred forward the Compagnie des Cent-Associés had been blunted by these events: the company had lost its first convoy in 1628; the furs from the St. Lawrence poured wealth into English coffers until 1632; then, the company had to leave fur-trading to the de CAËN family until 1632, at the same time sustaining an endless lawsuit against them. After these first reverses, from which it was never to recover, it can be said that the company began its work only in 1633. It did send settlers, but recruiting in this period was much more the work of religious communities or of certain enterprising seigneurs, like ROBERT GIFFARD. In fact, the role of the Compagnie des Cent-Associés came to an end in 1645: after spending more than 1,000,000 *livres*, and at a moment when it was about to realize great profits, it was forced to hand over the exploitation of the Laurentian region to a junior company, the Communauté des Habitants.

With this company a new development occurred: for the first time, Frenchmen already settled in Canada were going to try to direct the exploitation of the St. Lawrence for their own benefit. These businessmen, the stock from which came the French régime's great landowners and the *bourgeois* who were to be its great fur-trading figures, were, from 1645 on, to infuse life into trade in New France and to play a leading role in the government of the colony. Yet the Communauté des Habitants, whose beginnings were auspicious, was destined to decline rapidly, because war paralysed the fur market. In the end, it ceased to pay what it owed to the Cent-Associés; it neglected its obligations with respect to population and defence; dissensions, favouritism, and intrigues were soon to disrupt the country. Nevertheless, in the period extending from 1633 to 1663 the Communauté des Habitants was the only secular foundation of any importance.

For the great undertakings of that age were those of the Church. From it came those remarkable foundations that were to guide New France's destiny. This was the period that has rightly been called a mystical one: it was because of these foundations that New France was then labelled a mission colony, for it was a colony that seemed, because of the predominating influence of the Church, to exist far more for religious ends than for secular ones.

The first in the series of these foundations was a Jesuit college, established in 1635 at Quebec "to educate the children of the ever growing families." Until the conquest it was to be the only college in New France. The education of the young and preparation for professional tasks were thenceforth ensured, within a religious framework. There were also the natives to be considered; in order to give them a better grounding in religion, it was thought desirable to civilize them according to the European conception, that is, to settle them permanently and accustom them to live after the French fashion. This problem was from the outset one of the missionaries' preoccupations. Hence came the French dream of setting up the natives on pieces of land that they would gradually be persuaded to cultivate. This was the object of the Sillery reserve in 1637, where at great expense ground was cleared and houses built, so that the natives would find everything prepared on their arrival. For the first time in North America, an attempt was made to acculturate natives, by transforming them first from nomads into settled people, and then into European farmers. Half a century later the Sillery venture was to be written off as a complete failure. All that could be done in future was to regroup the Hurons at Lorette, where, without becoming agriculturists, they would live a sedentary life on the edge of the great forest.

The Jesuits had undertaken the education of the boys at the same time as they tried to acculturate the natives; likewise, the Ursuline nuns who came in 1639 took charge of the education of the girls, and also attempted to acculturate the Indian girls by exposing them to the same programme. The second part of this programme was to prove less felicitous than the first, for according to Marie de l'Incarnation (*see* GUYART), a Frenchman more readily became a savage than a savage a Frenchman . . . Together with the Ursulines, Religious Hospitallers had landed, intending to devote themselves to the creation of an Hôtel-Dieu. Thus at the same moment, thanks to the Church, education and hospital care were set up: the essential needs of the community were fully met.

At the very period when the Ursulines and Hospitallers were starting upon a venture that was to assume a permanent form, another religious foundation was appearing that was to have an amazing future: Ville-Marie (Montreal). Since at least 1611, an establishment had been planned at the Sault-Saint-Louis (Lachine Rapids), not only to serve as a stage in the opening up of the continent, but also (since the rapids necessarily impeded navigation) to constitute a permanent meeting-place for French and native fur-traders.

The settlement's meagre resources, the Iroquois forays that were always so easy at a point so far inland, the opposition of the inhabitants of Quebec, who foresaw correctly that an establishment at the rapids would eventually corner the entire fur trade—all these rendered the project unattainable. It was an official from La Flèche, the tax-collector Jérôme Le Royer de La Dauversière, who in 1631 conceived the notion of establishing at Montreal a sort of mystical city. This project, unrealistic at first sight both because of its nature and because of the obstacles to be overcome, was characterized at each step by religious manifestations, and it came to fruition. The Société de Notre-Dame de Montréal founded Ville-Marie in 1642, in order to "labour there solely to bring about the glory of God and the salvation of the Indians." In 1657, the Sulpicians came to assume the spiritual direction, and in 1668 the teaching, of the "little schools"; the following year, 1658, Marguerite BOURGEOYS organized a congregation of women, who applied themselves to the education of girls. In 1659 Jeanne MANCE, who since 1642 had been providing hospital service there, brought in some Hospitallers to open the Hôtel-Dieu. Thus, as at Quebec, the essential needs of the Montreal community, education and hospital care, were provided for by the good works of the Church. But above all, thanks to the action of a group of mystics, a post was being created, the most remote post of the Laurentian colony, and it was rapidly to become as important as the capital itself.

The consummation of the religious organization of this colony was finally achieved in 1659, with the arrival of a vicar apostolic, François de Laval*. Until then, from the religious point of view, New France had been under the immediate direction of the superior of the Jesuit missionaries, it had been truly a mission country; the fact of being administered from Europe had raised awkward jurisdictional problems which would now be settled by the coming of a vicar apostolic. The life of the Church received a new impetus, and not only its material life, but especially its spiritual life, for this was the height of a period of mysticism. It was the age when, by a combination of circumstances, a number of ascetics were grouped in the colony, whose society bore the imprint of their mysticism: at Quebec were Bishop Laval, Marie de l'Incarnation, Catherine de Saint-Augustin (*see* SIMON); at Montreal, Jeanne Mance, Marguerite Bourgeoys; in the Huron country, the place of their labours and eventual martyrdom, were the Jesuit GABRIEL LALEMANT and his companion Jean de BRÉBEUF, an exceptional figure because of his moral stature and his works.

The outstanding achievements of this period, we must repeat, were those of the Church; its great figures were not soldiers or colonizers, but mystics; they marked the zenith of an incomparable religious life, and as they vanished so waned this epoch of mysticism.

But, while the colony was experiencing its loftiest manifestation of mysticism, it was also living through the most painful hours of its history. Garneau has reproached New France for devoting itself to the construction of religious houses, at a time when New England was building ships to trade with every nation. But the Church should not be held responsible for the material weakness of the State in comparison with its flourishing religious life. The Church at that time was dynamic, it had resources at its disposal, and it played its part fully; it was not because of the Church that the State did not achieve its ends, one of which was to protect the population against the Iroquois.

Since 1609, the colony had been subjected to more or less continuous warfare. In 1645 it was thought that a lasting peace had been concluded with the Iroquois, but war broke out again immediately, with more violence than before. All the efforts of the Iroquois were directed first against the Huron country. Established just north of the Iroquois, the Hurons had become the principal suppliers of furs, to the advantage of the French; by their control of the hunting-grounds in the north, they constituted a fundamental obstacle for the Iroquois, who supplied the Dutch: with the Huron country destroyed, the Iroquois tribes would be in a position to control the great hunting regions and obtain the most advantageous terms from the French or the Dutch. First the Hurons must be liquidated. These Indians, already decimated by diseases contracted from the whites, rotted by spirits, and accustomed to rely on French military assistance, were no more than a decadent ethnic group. The Iroquois speedily annihilated them. In 1648 they destroyed the village of Saint-Joseph (Teanaostaiaë), killing 700 persons there; in the spring of 1649, the village of Saint-Ignace (Taenhatentaron) likewise disappeared, with the loss of 400 persons; in the following autumn, the Iroquois attacked the village of Saint-Jean-Baptiste (Cahiagué), and massacred some 500 families there. The Hurons who survived tried to regroup on the Île Saint-Joseph (Christian Island), but illness and hunger finally struck them down. Those who remained came seeking refuge as far as the Île d'Orléans, east of Quebec. Under the governor's very nose, the Iroquois ferreted them out even in this distant sanctuary. The last survivors of the Huron nation were finally to put themselves under the immediate protection of Fort Saint-Louis, in a fortified place in the Upper Town of Quebec.

The Huron country no longer existed: a couple of years had sufficed for its disappearance. The Iroquois were able thenceforth to control the supply of furs, and, as necessity arose, to concentrate all their attacks against the French colony. The settlers were then harassed by continuous warfare, carried on by surprises and ambushes; those who left the stockades risked their lives; each of the three establishments (Quebec, Trois-Rivières, and Ville-Marie) lived withdrawn into itself, in a state of perpetual alarm. In 1660 DOLLARD Des Ormeaux, by the battle he fought at the Long Sault, saved the country from a general invasion (which he had not, however, foreseen), but the Iroquois forays were resumed in 1661, with a relentlessness hitherto unsurpassed.

The losses in manpower, which it has never been possible to estimate, were high: an allied nation, which had played an essential part in the fur trade, had vanished, and with it great missionaries who had acquired a thorough knowledge of the natives' mentality and territory; numerous Canadians, heads of families, had been killed. Deprived of effective protection, colonization was limited to the immediate confines of fortified places; rural cultivation had not begun. The civil administration was paralysed by internal quarrels. The fur trade, so prosperous in 1645 when the Communauté des Habitants had taken it over, was non-existent; around 1660, the merchants spoke of abandoning the country, and this, according to Marie de l'Incarnation, would have resulted in the general departure of the 2,000 or so inhabitants.

In Acadia, the colonial venture had become worthless. RAZILLY had undertaken, in 1632, to revive the Acadian settlement, and had given it La Hève (near Bridgewater, N.S.) as its capital. When he died in 1635, La Hève was abandoned for Port-Royal, and civil war soon broke out between Charles de MENOU d'Aulnay and CHARLES DE SAINT-ÉTIENNE de La Tour, to be continued between the latter and EMMANUEL LE BORGNE; it was still going on when, in 1654, the English began rapidly to occupy Acadia. Of the French settlement nothing remained except NICOLAS DENYS's establishment at Cape Breton; the Acadian peninsula had become an English possession.

The only alternatives were either to abandon everything or to found New France a second time. Governor PIERRE DUBOIS Davaugour requested the king to intervene personally in the colony's affairs; Bishop Laval and Pierre Boucher* went to France to plead the cause of the country and propose ways of re-establishing it. After receiving the report of a royal commissioner, Louis XIV adopted, from 1663 on, a series of measures that were tantamount to the founding of a new French colony in America.

Louis XIV first required the Compagnie des Cent-Associés to give up its American seigneury, and at the same time the Communauté des Habitants disappeared. The mother country was putting some order into the seigneurial régime: the large landowners who had not concerned themselves with populating their fiefs lost their titles in favour of seigneurs who were better disposed; the Island of Montreal, which from the administrative point of view had previously had an almost autonomous existence, was linked up with the government of the colony, a development which was to bring about the departure of Paul de CHOMEDEY de Maisonneuve.

Upon this unified colony, the king imposed a new form of administration that was to endure until the conquest. As in the French provinces where opposite the military governor was an intendant responsible for civil affairs, New France received in 1663 a government having two heads: the governor, upon whom devolved control of the army and external relations; the intendant, for the maintenance of justice, order, and sound finance, on whom the internal administration depended; both, by their respective jurisdictions, counterbalanced each other, and thus lessened the absoluteness of authority; both were better prepared for their own functions, and it was expected that a military governor would concern himself less and less with civil functions. Of course these new institutions were slow to adapt themselves. It had been thought that the replacement of a Dubois Davagour by a Mézy (*see* SAFFRAY) chosen by Bishop Laval would end the conflicts between church and state. But the first intendant, Robert, appointed in 1663, did not come, and Talon arrived only in 1665; prolonged rivalries, especially under Governor BUADE de Frontenac, were to hamper the smooth functioning of the new system. It had been forgotten that any form of administration is only as good as the men in it. Beginning with the 18th century, everything would finally be settled: the governor and the intendant would learn to confine themselves to their respective tasks.

In addition to dividing up control of the colony between two functionaries, the king suppressed the seneschal's court (a seigneurial court of justice established by the Cent-Associés), and introduced a new organization, the Conseil Souverain. This body was, in its first quarter-century, to have the role of an executive and legislative council and also of a supreme court, later rapidly becoming restricted to the role of a court of justice to which the lay and ecclesiastical tribunals of New France were answerable. The establishment of this Conseil Souverain brought in, in 1664, the use and custom of Paris, to the exclusion of the other provincial customs: the colony's laws and weights and measures were therefore to be those of Paris. In view of the wide variety of laws, weights and measures which had to be taken into account in France, from one province to another, it was decided not to transplant into New France the complications of Old France; a timely simplification was preferred.

Modifications were also made in the economic structure. Since the Cent-Associés were no longer involved, the king, in 1664, again granted the country, as a fief and seigneury, to the Compagnie des Indes occidentales, but this time the situation was not at all the same as in 1627: the company was not required to concern itself with civil or military administration. Although it was the seigneur of the country, and in this capacity was responsible for settlers, it was the state that would intervene, and build up the population by a dynamic policy. Indeed, from 1674 on, New France was never again to be the seigneury of a commercial company, and now came under the authority of the king and of the minister of marine, Colbert.

The country's defence had to be reorganized as well: the ludicrous weakness of this defence during the years of woe had placed the country in its most critical position. Hitherto the colony had relied upon the goodwill of the settlers and a few paltry troops maintained by the companies. In 1663, at Montreal, a militia was created; and this organization was to be extended six years later to the whole colony. Above all, the king decided to dispatch a whole regiment, the Carignan-Salières, the only regiment to come in full strength to New France. Under the command of PROUVILLE de Tracy, who had just been appointed lieutenant-general of America (with residence in the West Indies), and of a new governor, Daniel de RÉMY de Courcelle, this regiment arrived in 1665, and promptly in the following year marched into the Iroquois country: the effect of this expedition, less decisive than punitive, was at least to demonstrate the colony's new strength. The Iroquois thenceforth had to reckon with organized resistance, and the colony was about to experience some hours of peace. In addition, numerous members of the Carignan-Salières regiment were to settle down permanently: they founded those families of soldiers who were to save the country when great conflicts came.

The Canadian church played a part in this vast reorganization. It was already firmly installed, but as things turned out it was now to reach the peak of its political power. The vicar apostolic, Bishop Laval, had just succeeded in having the former governor recalled, and had had a governor of his own choosing appointed; the bishop shared, on the same footing as the new governor, in the appointment of members of the Conseil Souverain; on the political level, the church became as influential as the state. What the Canadian Church particularly lacked was cadres: Bishop Laval endeavoured to provide them. It was therefore planned to convert the office of vicar apostolic into a bishopric, but this project did not bear fruit until 1674. In order to form his clergy, Bishop Laval founded the Séminaire de Québec in 1663, which led in 1668 to the establishment of a *petit séminaire*, a house for training candidates for the priesthood. The upkeep of the priests had to be assured: in 1663 the tithe system was instituted. The colony was rapidly to cease being administered as a mission country. The Jesuit missionaries who were everywhere acting as parish priests gradually withdrew: at Montreal, they gave way to the Sulpicians in 1657, then, shortly afterwards, they handed over Quebec to the secular clergy, in anticipation of doing the same at Trois-Rivières, which they passed over to the Recollets in 1670. In 1664 the first properly organized parish was set up: Notre-Dame de Québec. Finally, for the spiritual training of the faithful, the Confrérie de la Sainte-Famille was established.

However, an important part of New France did not benefit from this reorganization: Acadia. Always sparsely populated, torn by fratricidal strife, then having become an English possession, it had been restored to France in 1667. The actual reoccupation, delayed for three years because of animosities, was only a resumption of the former civil war. The mother country did not seem concerned with giving cadres to Acadia, but merely ensured its territorial integrity; Acadia was to develop very slowly, with private enterprise as its only spur, and without a clearly defined policy. Its abandonment dates from well before 1713. It was the Laurentian colony that remained Louis XIV's main preoccupation.

Thus, for this colony, 1663 and the years immediately following meant a total reorganization in all domains: ecclesiastical, economic, civil, and military. It is in truth a new founding that we witness, a founding that thenceforth was to justify the most splendid hopes: it was the starting point of a surprising economic development, and of a territorial expansion that was to reach its height at the end of the century. This twofold progress was due to the impetus given by a minister like Colbert, whose responsibility the colonies were, and by a top-ranking intendant like Talon; unfortunately the latter was to stay in the country only five years. The gist of Talon's programme can be expressed thus: to obtain a total yield from the colony, and to extend its frontiers to the limits of America.

To carry out this programme, there had first to be a rapid increase in population. An intensive policy of developing man-power was therefore put into operation, by bringing in *filles de roi* ("king's daughters," orphans raised at the expense of the state), and by forcing bachelors to get married; dowries were given to needy girls, wedding presents were distributed to those who married very young, and large families were assisted by gratuities. This policy of increasing the birthrate did not apply to the European immigrants alone: marriages between French and Indians were also to be encouraged; it was Colbert's desire that French and Indians should thenceforth be of one blood. The population was studied closely by means of annual name-counts: the minister scrutinized the returns, and manifested his satisfaction or disappointment, accordingly as the figures showed an advance or a stagnation.

As the population increased, the seigneurial domains were extended by attracting more seigneurs. In the eyes of the state, they were only settlement agents, for the fiefs were at first allotted only on a strictly enforced condition: that the holders should establish settlers on them. Many seigneuries had been neglected, and large empty spaces on the banks of the St. Lawrence, particularly in the Richelieu River area, constituted a breach that facilitated the Iroquois invasions. Talon recalled the neglectful seigneurs to their duties: he closed the Richelieu gap by settling former officers of the Carignan-Salières regiment there. In 1672 alone, the authorities granted 46 seigneuries, the highest annual total ever attained in the whole history of the seigneurial régime.

The immigrants settled on the land had to be given the necessary equipment. Talon fetched pure-bred livestock (horses, cows, sheep) from France, and they were acclimatized to the country; he tested seed grain, and carefully sought the kind that would be best suited to the conditions along the St. Lawrence. At no time during the French régime was such a rational agricultural policy to be implemented as under Talon's intendancy.

But agriculture was only one of the intendant's concerns, for he dreamed of the total exploitation of the country. Working under the orders of a minister concerned with manufactures, and encouraged by the presence of the skilled workers who constituted the bulk of the immigrants, Talon found himself in the most favourable circumstances for the development of industry. He ordered research to be done on the most varied resources, had an oak timber survey carried out and had borings made in various places to find metals; he oversaw the yield of the fisheries, and spared no effort in order to set people to work upon products and by-products. He encouraged commerce, being anxious to bring about regular trade between Acadia and Canada; he even attempted to trade with the far distant West Indies. He would have liked New France not only to be self-sufficient, but also to supply the mother country with raw materials and, better still, finished products.

This policy of total yield was, alas, to be only a beautiful dream. Talon's stay was too short for him to make of New France an industrial colony. As for his successors, even if they had wished to carry on his work, they were held in check by the mother country: the factories that it was desired to set up were forbidden, because they might become a threat to those in France. In 1704, the minister was to put an end to all hope: a colony, he asserted, must exist only for the needs of the mother country that had established it. The colony had to return to the economic system obtaining before Talon's time, to the one that had been the despair of Champlain: an economy based on the fur trade.

And it is here that the fundamental explanation of a rapid drop in immigration is to be found. It has been claimed that the Frenchman did not emigrate; he did, but to places where there was a future; he did not come into the St. Lawrence valley. To attract immigrants, a country must offer an agriculture that yields more than immediate subsistence, or else an economic life vitalized by prosperous industry. France herself was self-sufficient in agricultural products; the colony was forbidden to trade with non-French colonies; and the Laurentian population, which was in any case settled for the most part on the land, was not sufficiently large to make the internal exchange of agricultural products worthwhile. As for industry, apart from that of the small craftsman, it was forbidden in the 18th century. One heavy industry, that at the Forges Saint-Maurice, was indeed allowed, but it was an industry for defence, and moreover, for want of small related industries, it always showed a deficit, even when the state assumed responsibility for it. An attempt was also made to start shipbuilding, but once more, because of the lack of secondary industries, a ship built at Quebec of Canadian wood cost more than a ship built in France from the same wood; like heavy industry, shipbuilding continued to show a loss, and was abandoned. What was left as exportable material? Unprocessed fur. If, at the least, it had required skilled labour, like tobacco-growing in Virginia, immigrants would have flocked in, but fur was the object of a mere transport trade: natives brought it to Montreal, and it had only to be loaded on to the ships. Local manpower sufficed. Under these conditions, New France did not attract immigrants, hence it is not surprising that in the whole history of the French régime not more than 10,000 persons came to Canada. On this point Talon's policy, in all respects similar to Champlain's, ended in failure.

The second point in Talon's programme was to extend New France to the frontiers of America, both in regions already occupied by the English or Dutch, and elsewhere. To the south of New France was New Holland, watered by a great river and enjoying the advantage of an ocean port open 12 months a year, whereas New France could use the St. Lawrence for only six months, being cut off from Europe for the rest of the year. Many times, the policy of expansion included the acquisition of New Holland, either by purchase or by conquest; and in 1689 Louis XIV instructed Frontenac to take possession of this colony, even if it meant then deporting the population, together or separately, to make room for a French colonizing venture.

It was obviously easier to expand into unoccupied regions, and it was here that the results were the most surprising. The rapid extension of New France was the most spectacular feature of this 17th century. In a single 25-year thrust, New France opened out as far as Hudson Bay, the Great Lakes, and the Gulf of Mexico. True enough, before Talon, long voyages had not been infrequent: in 1634, Jean NICOLLET reached Lake Michigan; from 1658 to 1662, Radisson* discovered the Upper Mississippi, explored Lake Superior, and, via the Albany River, got to Hudson Bay; but these were always individual adventures, which did not necessarily result in the official occupation of the places or a cartographical survey. With Talon began the explorations organized or followed very closely by the state: it was no longer a question of their merely covering ground, but of taking possession of the places, of binding the natives to the French cause, of returning with a methodical description of the regions visited.

The explorations of that period began with the exact study of a new route, that of the St. Lawrence. To get to the hinterland, the only known way was still the Rivière des Outaouais (Ottawa River), studied by Champlain in 1613, and again in 1615. In 1669-70, the Sulpicians BRÉHANT de Galinée and Dollier* de Casson established beyond dispute that Lakes Ontario, Erie, and Huron were connected; they made an accurate chart of this new route. Too many rapids were scattered along this waterway for it ever, under the French régime, to supersede the Ottawa River as a commercial route, but it was to be utilized as a military route of prime importance; by its posts and forts, it was to serve as a defensive bulwark against the English colonists of the Atlantic coast.

An important advance towards the west was carried out by DAUMONT de Saint-Lusson in 1671: he went to Lake Superior, established friendly relations there with natives who came from a great distance, and took possession, in the name of France, of the whole area as far as the Southern Sea. Shortly afterwards, in 1672, Denys* de Saint-Simon and the Jesuit ALBANEL (who had just explored the Lac Saint-Jean) undertook a long trip via the Lac des Mistassins (Mistassini) and the Rupert River; they reached Hudson Bay, took possession of the places they had passed through, and linked the natives politically with the French; even if they could do nothing against the English, who were beginning their rich fur trade, they extended the domain of New France; and the latter, in due course, would be able to derive profit from the fine and plentiful furs of that huge area draining into Hudson Bay.

Although it was decided on by Talon and connected with the search for a passage towards the Pacific, the voyage of exploration undertaken by Louis JOLLIET and the Jesuit MARQUETTE began only after the intendant's departure. In 1673, following a route already traced out by discoverers, Jolliet and Marquette reached the Upper Mississippi; they then went down it sufficiently far (to the 33rd degree of latitude) to ascertain that it could only flow into the Gulf of Mexico. It was to fall to CAVELIER de La Salle, ten years later, to reach the mouth of the Mississippi, and, in the name of France, to take possession of the gigantic basin of that river. La Salle committed a major error, which, however, was harmful only to himself. Convinced that the Mississippi which he had descended was not the Rio de Spiritu Santo (whose mouth the Spaniards had known since the 16th century), and bent on depreciating Jolliet's efforts, he wanted to prove that the credit for the discovery of the Mississippi's mouth was entirely his, and that this outlet had nothing to do with the Spiritu Santo. He consequently located his discovery in the north-west corner of the Gulf of Mexico. When he returned to the Gulf by sea in 1684, it was therefore on this shore that he disembarked, only to realize shortly that the river where he had stopped was not the Mississippi. Trying to locate it again by land, he met his death by assassination.

In 1684, therefore, New France, in the form that France claimed to possess it, stretched from the Gulf of St. Lawrence to beyond Lake Superior, and from Hudson Bay to the Gulf of Mexico. Yet it still numbered no more than about 12,000 inhabitants, almost all of whom clung timidly to the banks of the St. Lawrence between Quebec and Montreal. The expansion was not finished, all the same. New France needed all Hudson Bay, where the English, entrenched in forts, were exploiting the vast supply of furs; it needed Newfoundland in order to keep the fisheries, and at the same time to control the St. Lawrence more effectively. When the age of great explorations was over, New France endeavoured to expand by force of arms. A crisis had just come to a head in Europe, pitting the two blocks of Protestant and Catholic nations against each other: in America, the English and French worlds were about to clash in war.

When the conflict broke out the disparity between the forces was a frightening one. On the English side, there was a population of about 250,000 inhabitants, colonies made strong by flourishing external trade, all of them facing towards an ocean accessible to them the year round, all of them plentifully supplied with the most varied products because of the range of climates. On the other side, was a colony that, it is true, enjoyed an unlimited expanse of territory and was protected by natural defences, but that scarcely mustered 12,000 inhabitants (barely the population of the tiny Rhode Island of that time), a colony isolated from France six months of the year by its climate, possessing neither industry nor a navy, and still having as its economic foundation the beaver alone.

And yet this destitute colony had a military dynamism that was astounding. It was this colony that took the offensive, and that won. On land and then on sea, in a few years, it conquered the English forts in Hudson Bay; its limited troops seized Newfoundland, resisted in a poorly organized Acadia, and launched raids against New England and New Holland, where they spread terror. The English colonies decided to retort with crushing forces: a double invasion, that of 1690, which was designed to break through via the St. Lawrence and Lake Champlain, turned into a lamentable failure; and the Iroquois country, seeing the success of New France, toned down its policy of aggression and prepared itself for a permanent peace.

The Treaty of Ryswick, in 1697, confirmed the French power in America: if Newfoundland became once more an English colony, the treaty left Hudson Bay and Acadia to New France. But this triumph was only a truce; the forces remained poised, and war was resumed on all fronts in 1702. Again for New France it was an almost incredible series of successful engagements. With the assistance of imposing forces, New England attempted three invasions of New France: all three were failures. The island of Newfoundland was again conquered by the Canadians, and the latter still held firm in Hudson Bay; the powerful fleet of Sir Hovenden Walker*, who in 1711, by joining up with an army from Lake Champlain, was expected finally to eliminate New France, was lost on the reefs of the Gulf of St. Lawrence.

In 1712, New France had reached its zenith. Well established in Hudson Bay (militarily and commercially), it occupied Newfoundland, continued its colonization of Acadia, dominated the Iroquois country, which had made its peace, remained the serene mistress of the immense Great Lakes basin, and held absolute control over the Mississippi valley as far as the Gulf of Mexico, where it had just founded New Orleans. Arrayed against the English colonies, which were confined between the Alleghenys and the Atlantic, the French empire was built; the dreams of Champlain and of Talon had been fulfilled.

But dreams are fragile. A disastrous treaty, signed by France at Utrecht in 1713, began the demolition of this empire. France, conquered in Europe, sacrificed America. She handed Hudson Bay back to England, with all the rivers that flowed into it; she restored Newfoundland to England; she gave up Acadia; she agreed to allow the Iroquois country to be subject thenceforth to England.

What then became of New France? Although its whole economy was based on beaver, it no longer had access to the rich fur supply of Hudson Bay; the loss of Newfoundland deprived it not only of the old settlement of Plaisance (Placentia, Newfoundland), but of the control of the Gulf and its fisheries; by losing Acadia, populated with French settlers; it was cut off from the Atlantic coast; and, since the Iroquois country became in principle a territory belonging to England, the possession of the Great Lakes basin was going to be a matter of controversy. Finally, the French defeat in Europe brought about an immediate economic disaster in the colony: of all the paper money circulating in New France, the mother country refused to recognize more than one quarter.

In a word, the French empire was reduced to a long corridor. Its northern entry, in the Gulf of St. Lawrence, was under English control; its right flank was threatened from every direction: from Lake Champlain, where the natural frontier was less and less effective, from Lake Ontario, on whose shores the English had just established themselves, from the Alleghenies, which were no longer the impassable barrier of the 17th century. From the military point of view, New France had become a frail creature, who could be supported only by extremely costly measures, yet whose economic life was being stifled, because the north was closed to her. There only remained the region of the west, whose stocks of furs Gaultier* de La Vérendrye wanted to channel, from fantastic distances, towards Montreal.

And what were 20,000 inhabitants compared to the 400,000 that populated the English colonies from Newfoundland to South Carolina? Poorly equipped, deprived of Hudson Bay, pushed out of Newfoundland, Acadia, and the Iroquois country, the New France of the 18th century, despite its air of grandeur, was taking on more and more the appearance of a floundering colony. Nevertheless, in spite of its unfavourable position from this time on, New France, under the leadership of brilliant intendants, would attempt the consolidation in depth that had been desired for her in the previous century.

BIOGRAPHIES

ABRAHAM, JOHN, governor of Port Nelson; fl. 1672–89.

He joined the HBC about 1672 and served in James Bay 1672–75 and 1676–78 under Governor Charles BAYLY, against whom he brought charges of mismanagement. In 1679 Abraham was appointed second to John NIXON, Bayly's successor, and although he absconded with an advance of salary at sailing time, he was engaged in 1681 as mate of the *Diligence* (Capt. NEHEMIAH WALKER) and wintered in James Bay.

Despite Nixon's criticisms of him, Abraham was promoted captain of the *George* in 1683, his destination being Port Nelson, where Governor John BRIDGAR had gone in 1682 to establish a fort. En route Abraham assisted Nehemiah Walker to capture the interloper *Expectation* and, on arrival, finding that the Company's post had been destroyed and that Bridgar, with Benjamin Gillam* the New England interloper, had been captured and taken to Quebec by Radisson* and CHOUART Des Groseilliers, he assumed command. After a winter spent harassing and competing with Jean-Baptiste Chouart, Des Groseilliers's son, Abraham was homeward-bound when he received a commission as governor of Port Nelson. He returned, and during his first weeks of office York Fort was built under George GEYER's supervision and an attack, made by the newly arrived M. de Bermen* de La Martinière of the Compagine du Nord, was repulsed. After a winter of friction the French withdrew in 1685.

On learning that Abraham had left Port Nelson in 1684 before the arrival of the ships from England the Committee cancelled his commission and instead appointed him deputy to Governor Thomas PHIPPS. He served as such during 1685–86 and was then recalled because, for one reason, the Committee considered that his opposition to the French in 1684–85 had been "timerous & imprudent" when he was in the stronger position. One of his last duties in 1686 was to explore Churchill River, and it was his enthusiastic report of its possibilities which, not without reason, aroused the Committee's suspicions of his future intentions.

Abraham next undertook an interloping expedition to Hudson Bay in the *Mary*, but moves by the HBC to protect its monopoly prevented him from sailing until 1688, and by that time he had been joined by the dissatisfied John OUTLAW. The *Mary* was wrecked by ice in Hudson Strait, but her complement was taken aboard the Company's ships to Albany River where, under John MARSH, an attempt was made to settle peaceably near the French and re-establish the prestige and trade lost to Pierre de TROYES in 1686. Although both Crowns were at peace the rival parties clashed. Abraham, sent to the French as a hostage, changed his allegiance and apparently spent the rest of his life preying on English shipping in the St. Lawrence. References to his wife, Mary, are to be found in the company's records between 1677 and 1686.

ALICE M. JOHNSON

HBRS, VIII, IX (Rich); XI, XX (Rich and Johnson); XXI (Rich).

ADHASATAH. *See* TOGOUIROUI

AËOPTAHON. *See* ATIRONTA, d. 1650

AERNOUTSZ (Arentson, Aernoutson), JURRIAEN, Dutch sea-captain who conquered Acadia in 1674.

Little is known of Aernoutsz's career except for his brief involvement with Acadia. During the third Anglo-Dutch war he was commander of the frigate *Flying Horse*, based at Curaçao, in the West Indies. After the Dutch had regained New York, the *Flying Horse* was dispatched by the Governor of Curaçao to conduct hostilities against France and England in the North Atlantic. However, when Aernoutsz reached New York he learned that England and Holland had made peace by the Treaty of Westminster, 9 Feb. 1673–74 (o.s.) and his commission remained good only against the French. Aernoutsz's decision to attack Acadia resulted from his meeting with John RHOADES, a New Englander who described the country to him and agreed to serve as pilot for the expedition.

Aernoutsz conquered Acadia as quickly as SEDGWICK had done 20 years before. On 10 Aug.

Agariata

1674 (N.S.) the *Flying Horse* reached Pentagouet on the Penobscot, held by the Governor of Acadia, Jacques de Chambly, with approximately 30 men. Aernoutsz, with 50 men (BUADE de Frontenac says "110 corsaires hollandais"), took the fort by storm in two hours. Chambly, wounded in the encounter, was taken prisoner. Aernoutsz destroyed Pentagouet and proceeded eastward, pillaging all the French posts along the west shore of the Bay of Fundy (Baie Française) and capturing Chambly's lieutenant, Pierre de JOYBERT de Soulanges et de Marson, commander of Fort Jemseg on the Saint John River. In all, Aernoutsz spent a month in Acadia, a short time to justify his taking formal possession of the region, which he called "New Holland." He then sailed to Boston where he disposed of his plunder, even selling the cannon from Fort Pentagouet to the Massachusetts government. Some time in October 1674 he sailed for Curaçao, but left his prisoners and a number of his company in Boston, including John Rhoades.

Aernoutsz's efforts were soon negated by the action of Massachusetts. John Rhoades and the other men Aernoutsz had left in Boston, acting under Aernoutsz's orders to return to Acadia and maintain possession, began seizing New England vessels coming to trade with the Indians. Massachusetts apprehended Rhoades and his cohorts and tried them as pirates. Ultimately they were all released or banished from the colony, but in the meantime the French re-occupied Acadia unmolested. The Dutch government, hard pressed by Louis XIV, could only protest to Whitehall.

WILLIAM I. ROBERTS, 3rd

[For the outcome of the Dutch conquest of Acadia, *see* RHOADES.]

Documents pertaining to the Dutch conquest of Acadia are widely scattered among European and American depositories, but the principal ones have been printed in *Documentary history of Maine*, IV–VIII, and in Charles W. Tuttle, *Captain Francis Champernowne, the Dutch conquest of Acadia and other historical papers*, ed. A. H. Hoyt (Boston, 1889), which also contains the best secondary account of the episode. Some additional details are furnished by L.-A. Vigneras, "Letters of an Acadian trader 1674–1676," *N. Eng. Q.*, XIII (1940), 98–110, and *Mémoires des commissaires*, I, 51; *Memorials of the English and French commissaries*, I, 122. For the French account of the conquest see Correspondance de Frontenac (1672–82), in APQ *Rapport*, 1926–27, 73.

AGARIATA (Agoriata), Mohawk chief; fl. 1666.

Agariata's career can only be reconstructed, without too much certainty, from fragmentary and conflicting accounts (Le Roy* de Bacqueville de La Poterie alone gives him a name). He steps into history during the period 1663–66, when the Iroquois were prepared to make peace with the French after a series of disasters: defeat by their Indian enemies, disease, and, finally, the stand made against them by DOLLARD at the Long Sault in 1660. The French, moreover, were in a stronger military position after the arrival of the Carignan-Salières regiment in the summer of 1665. The presence in Quebec of PROUVILLE de Tracy, lieutenant-general of all the French possessions in North America, and of a new governor, Daniel de RÉMY de Courcelle, was also evidence of Louis XIV's serious interest in New France. The first move of the new régime was an attack against the Iroquois. In January 1666 Courcelle commanded an abortive raid against the Mohawks and in September of the same year Tracy led a successful invasion of the Mohawk country.

In July 1666 some Mohawk warriors, one of whom was Agariata, according to La Poterie, met a party of seven French officers from the Carignan-Salières regiment hunting on the borders of the Mohawk country in the vicinity of Fort Sainte-Anne, at the outlet of Lake Champlain. Among them were Louis de Canchy de Lerole and M. de Chazy, cousin and nephew of Tracy. A skirmish ensued in which Agariata (again according to La Poterie) killed Chazy. A Capt. de Traversy also lost his life and Lerole and the other Frenchmen were taken prisoner.

Lerole was one of the French captives brought to Quebec in late August 1666 by the FLEMISH BASTARD, a Mohawk chief who was seeking peace. In Perrot's* version, he was joined by another Mohawk chief, presumably Agariata, who had also delivered French prisoners to Montreal. Both chiefs were received hospitably by the Marquis de Tracy, who entertained them at his table. On the last occasion of their presence there, the Flemish Bastard's companion (it can only be assumed that he was Agariata) boasted that it was he who had killed M. de Chazy. Tracy, greatly incensed, ordered him strangled at once in the sight of the Flemish Bastard.

La Poterie's version of Agariata's fate is that Courcelle, to avenge the death of Chazy, ordered the Mohawks to surrender the culprit under threat of war. The Mohawks answered by sending 40 warriors to deliver Agariata, who was hanged by the French.

Doubt exists as to the date of the execution, if indeed it did occur. From the accounts of Perrot and La Poterie, it might be inferred that the execution took place between 28 August, the date of the report received in Quebec that the

Flemish Bastard was arriving with the French captives, and 14 September, the date of Tracy's departure for the Mohawk country. However, Marie de l'Incarnation [*see* GUYART], a contemporary witness, mentions in a letter 2 Nov. 1666 that the Flemish Bastard was present at Tracy's table and again 12 November that one of the Iroquois captives at Quebec (the name Agariata is not given) was hung for infringing the peace by Tracy after the army's return from the Mohawk country. The Jesuit Journal (*JR* (Thwaites), L, 203–5) states that Tracy returned to Quebec 5 Nov. 1666 and that the Flemish Bastard was sent home 8 November. It is possible, therefore, that it was Agariata who was hung on 6, 7, or perhaps 8 Nov. 1666.

THOMAS GRASSMANN

Charlevoix, *History* (Shea), III, 87–88, 93. Marie Guyart de l'Incarnation, *Lettres* (Richaudeau), II, 327–36. *JR* (Thwaites), L, 197, 201. La Pot(h)erie, *Histoire*, II, IV, tr. from the French, repr. in *Indian tribes* (Blair), I, 307. Perrot, "Memoir," repr. in *Indian tribes* (Blair), I, 201–2, 307. P.-G. Roy, *La ville de Québec*, I, 349–50.

AGRAMONTE, JUAN DE, Catalan sailor, a native of Lérida, thought to be an explorer of Newfoundland (1511).

Following the voyages of JOHN CABOT, Spain became concerned at the English intrusion into her territories in the New World, and planned to explore the north Atlantic coast in order to take possession of it. Consequently, in 1500, she placed Juan de Dornelos (or Dorvelos) in command of an expedition, which apparently did not put to sea.

It was with the same end in view that another sailor, Agramonte, signed a contract with Ferdinand of Aragon, whereby he undertook to lead an expedition of discovery and exploration to the "Tierra Nueva" or "Terranova." This contract was renewed on 29 Oct. 1511 by Juana, Ferdinand's daughter. Agramonte was made a captain at this juncture, and he was to hire two Breton pilots on the way to act as guides. The voyage was to be carried out at his expense, with the right to establish himself in the country and to trade in its products, provided that he made over one-sixth of the yield to the royal treasury, as well as one-tenth of any gold that he might discover. The expedition, which was to comprise two ships, had orders not to land on soil under the jurisdiction of the kingdom of Portugal. Up to now documentary history has failed to determine whether the voyage took place; it appears very doubtful. What constitutes the interest of the project is the recognition, by its promoters, that the banks of Newfoundland had previously been visited by the Bretons and that a part of the Newfoundland territory had been discovered by Portugal.

GUSTAVE LANCTOT

Anthiaume, *Cartes marines*, I, 44; II, 22–23. Martín Fernandez de Navarrete, *Colección de los viages y descubrimientos que hicieron por mar los Españoles desde fines del siglo XV...* (5v., Madrid, 1825–37), III, 77–78, 122–27. Hoffman, *Cabot to Cartier*, 32. *Precursors* (Biggar), xxii, 102–11, 115.

AHATSISTARI, EUSTACHE, a great Huron warrior, member of the Attingueenongnahak tribe (Cord people) and resident at the mission of Saint-Joseph II (Teanaostaiaë), near the present Hillsdale, Ontario; baptized Eustache, Holy Saturday 1642, at the age of 40; killed during August of the same year.

In the opinion of Father Charles GARNIER, Ahatsistari was a man of noble and generous nature as well as a great warrior, whose courage and yearly military exploits against the Iroquois merited for him the reputation of chief warrior in the Huron country.

In 1634 a peace had been agreed upon by the Senecas and the Hurons (*JR* (Thwaites), VIII, 115–17), which lasted, with some interruptions, until 1639, when the Hurons resumed the war against the Senecas (*JR* (Thwaites), XVII, 105). In 1641, as the chief of a band of 50 Hurons, Ahatsistari put to rout 300 Iroquois and even captured some of them. On another occasion, during the summer of the same year, while Ahatsistari and his companions were "crossing a great lake [Lake Ontario] which separates the Hurons from their Enemies," a number of large canoes filled with Iroquois endeavoured to attack them. Instead of seeking safety in flight, Ahatsistari urged his warriors forward. Jumping into an Iroquois canoe, he split the head of the first enemy he met, threw two others overboard, upset the canoe by plunging into the water, and, while swimming with one hand, killed with the other all who came near him. This sudden onslaught so disconcerted the Iroquois that they fled. Ahatsistari regained his canoe and captured the Iroquois who remained alive in the water.

In June 1642, Ahatsistari, with other Indians, convoyed Father JOGUES from the Huron country to Quebec, where they arrived safely after a journey of more than 35 days. Having completed the business which brought them to Quebec, Ahatsistari and his companions set out from Trois-Rivières 1 August, on their return journey to the Huron country. Forty persons, distributed among a number of canoes, made up the party.

Ahinsistan

In addition to Ahatsistari, Father Jogues, René GOUPIL, and Guillaume Couture*, the travellers included other renowned warriors and Huron Christians, Étienne TOTIRI, Charles Tsondatsaa, Joseph Teondechoren, and Thérèse OIONHATON, returning from the Ursuline Convent at Quebec.

On 2 August, those in the advance canoe noticed fresh footprints in the sand and clay on the shore of the river. A halt was made to discuss the situation. Some Hurons stated that the footprints belonged to enemies, while others identified them as the marks of Algonkins. Ahatsistari judged the tracks to represent a party which would not outnumber his own and encouraged everyone to continue without fear.

The journey was resumed but not long after the above episode, the occupants of the canoes were again startled by arquebus shots and the shouts of Mohawks, who rose from the grass and brushwood along the shore of the St. Lawrence. All was confusion. Some Hurons abandoned their canoes, weapons, and supplies and fled into the woods, while others resisted the attacking Mohawks. Eventually another band of Mohawks joined in the battle and overpowered the resisting Hurons and Frenchmen. Twenty-two in all fell into the hands of the Mohawks, including Ahatsistari, Father Jogues, René Goupil, and Guillaume Couture.

They were taken to the Mohawk country as captives and during the journey some received cruel treatment. Ahatsistari, for example, was deprived of both thumbs and a pointed stick was forced into the open wound up to his elbow. Once arrived at the Mohawk villages, the prisoners experienced further hardships. After seven days, the Mohawk chiefs decided to spare the lives of all the Huron captives except three, who were condemned to die by fire. One of these three was Ahatsistari. He suffered at the village of Tionontoguen (Teonontogen). Instead of uttering the usual cry of other dying captives, "Arise, someone from our bones as avenger" (*JR* (Thwaites), XXXIX, 199), Ahatsistari begged those of his Huron countrymen who were present not to allow the remembrance of his fate to influence in any way the conclusion of a peace with the Iroquois.

THOMAS GRASSMANN

Philip Alegambe and John Nadasi, *Mortes illustres et gesta eorum Societate Jesu* (Rome, 1657), 624. *JR* (Thwaites), XXI, 287; XXIII, 25–27, 117, 241; XXXI, 21–29, 35.

AHINSISTAN. *See* PASTEDECHOUAN

AIGRON *dit* **Lamothe, PIERRE**; b. at Saint-Étienne d'Estée, diocese of La Rochelle, son of Pierre Aigron and of Marie Daquin; d. some time after 1685 at Quebec.

Aigron came to Quebec as a seaman in 1660, and engaged in the sale of intoxicating liquors to the Indians, at the time when Bishop François de Laval* was leading an active campaign against this traffic. On 6 May 1660 the bishop had decreed excommunication *ipso facto* against whomever undertook such a trade. Eager for easy profits, Aigron continued to traffic. Laval decided to make a public example of him, and on 18 April 1661 excommunicated him by name, forbidding him to enter any church on pain of being "driven or thrown out." Faced with religious condemnation and general disapproval, Aigron submitted to public penitence on the following Sunday.

Aigron became a ship's master, and on 18 Jan. 1663, at Quebec, he married Marie-Madeleine Doucet, from the parish of Saint-Sauveur in La Rochelle. In 1680 he went to settle on the coast of Gaspé.

In 1682 he was employed by the Compagnie du Nord, in Hudson Bay. He was brought to London by Radisson* in 1684, and joined the HBC for a four-year term in 1685, at which time he returned to Canada.

GUSTAVE LANCTOT

Jug. et délib., *passim*. *Mandements des évêques de Québec* (Têtu et Gagnon), I, *passim*.
BRH, XVIII (1912), 113. Godbout, "Nos ancêtres," *APQ Rapport, 1951–53*, 467. Gosselin, *Vie de Mgr de Laval*, *passim*.

AILLEBOUST, MARIE-BARBE D'. *See* BOULLONGNE

AILLEBOUST DE COULONGE ET D'ARGENTENAY, LOUIS D', "engineer skilled in the profession of arms," governor and lieutenant-general of New France; b. *c.* 1612 at Ancy-le-Franc, in the province of Champagne, son of Antoine d'Ailleboust, counsellor-in-ordinary to the Prince de Condé, and of his second wife Suzanne Hotman, widow of Jean de Manthet d'Argentenay; d. May 1660 at Montreal.

His grandfather, Jean d'Ailleboust, was one of the principal doctors of Henri IV, who made him a nobleman. Louis was the nephew of Charles d'Ailleboust, Bishop of Autun (and not of Auxerre). His maternal grandfather was the famous François Hotman, a jurisconsult, a writer, and an ardent Calvinist (1524–90). Aegidius Fauteux informs us, quoting the *Journal de voyage* of Montaigne, that the latter, following "the example of all other scholars and men of letters,

Ailleboust de Coulonge

... stopped at Bâle [in Switzerland, where François Hotman had taken refuge] in 1580, to pay him a visit."

Louis d'Ailleboust had a half-brother, Nicolas, the issue of his father's first marriage, and a sister, Catherine, who was perhaps Suzanne Hotman's daughter. It was Nicolas who continued the line, and his son who was the first d'Ailleboust to found a family in Canada. Catherine became a nun at the abbey of Saint-Pierre de Reims.

In 1638 Louis d'Ailleboust, whose childhood and youth are equally unknown to us, was living in Paris, in the rue de Bièvre, within the parish of Saint-Étienne-du-Mont. He had the reputation of being a clever military engineer. He was 26 years old. On 6 September of the same year he signed his marriage contract in his parish, before Maître Philippe Perrier, at the hostelry "Aux deux Anges." His fiancée, Marie-Barbe de BOULLONGNE, was staying there at the time along with her mother, *née* Eustache Quéan (Quen), widow of Florentin de Boullongne, from Ravières in Champagne. As this town was quite near Ancy-le-Franc, the birthplace of Louis d'Ailleboust, the biographer Ernest Gagnon concluded that the betrothed were probably childhood friends.

The young couple went to Paris to live, in the rue des Morfondus, in the old quarter of Saint-Étienne-du-Mont. Three years later, Barbe d'Ailleboust listened as her husband unfolded to her surprising plans for the future. He was consumed with a desire to go to New France and work for the conversion of the unbelievers. He had been told of an impending expedition, the object of which was to found a missionary outpost on the island of Montreal. A society of gentlemen and elderly priests had acquired ownership of the island, and was attending to the embarkation and the various needs of a contingent led by a brave and devout gentleman, Paul de CHOMEDEY de Maisonneuve. The young wife's health was very delicate, and she was suffering from an illness deemed incurable by the doctors. She certainly could not think of following her husband to a country so distant, and so fraught with perils.

But in the face of her husband's insistence, she bethought herself of praying to God to restore her to health. In return she promised to accompany her husband to New France and to share his work of evangelization there. She consulted her director, who gave her his complete approval. This Jesuit was in no way surprised by the young woman's soul-searching and later by her decision, for he was also the confessor and confidant of Louis d'Ailleboust. The cure was brought about, according to a passage in the *Véritables motifs*.

Louis d'Ailleboust pushed on with the preparations for the journey. He learned that Philippine-Gertrude de Boullongne, his wife's eldest sister, had hastened to Paris at the news of Barbe's cure and extraordinary vow, and that she too was making up her mind to set out for Canada.

Following his director's advice, Louis d'Ailleboust paid a visit, with his wife and sister-in-law, to the Jesuit CHARLES LALEMANT, the procurator of the Canadian mission. Having been a missionary in that country since 1625, the priest could give them information about the kind of life they would experience as settlers and ambassadors of the faith. But above all the father advised these recruits to enter the Société Notre-Dame de Montréal, which they did at the first opportunity.

Louis d'Ailleboust and his female companions went to La Rochelle in the spring of 1643. They embarked towards the end of May on one of the three vessels leaving for New France. A contingent of 40 men was going there in order to give active assistance to the terribly exposed little post of Montreal. The crossing was long and stormy. Two of the ships arrived at Quebec only on 15 August. Ville-Marie was reached in September.

In that remote spot, people lived in anxious expectancy. Governor HUAULT de Montmagny, when he visited M. de Maisonneuve and his settlers in July, had announced good news concerning the annual shipments from France. Much could be hoped for in this direction, for even the king was taking an interest in the Montrealers. M. de Montmagny himself had received a communication from the king expressly recommending them to him. Moreover the king was offering them for their overseas settlement a ship of 350 tons, the *Notre-Dame*.

The arrival of the contingent brought confidence and joy back into the hearts of those at Ville-Marie. For the safety of all concerned, M. de Maisonneuve had great need of the help of a lieutenant such as d'Ailleboust, a man acquainted with the customs of military life. Better still, this lieutenant would soon be the skilful engineer that the governor was hoping for; he could undertake the construction of fortifications which were urgently required. Since the end of spring, when they had discovered the little post, the Iroquois had harassed it continually. Recently, in the month of July, four people had been killed and a number wounded at Ville-Marie. For her part Jeanne MANCE would now have the company of two women who were congenial, charitable, and able to look after the sick. Their presence would compensate for the imminent departure of Mme de CHAUVIGNY de La Peltrie, recalled to Quebec, and of Charlotte Barré, her lady companion.

Aillebout de Coulonge

At Ville-Marie Louis d'Ailleboust first had four bastions built, and the stockade of 1642 replaced by a solid surrounding wall. In addition he strongly advised the inhabitants of Ville-Marie to sow good French grain, for "the meager harvest of peas and Indian corn" that he had observed when he arrived at Montreal was really no longer sufficient for the needs of the settlers, whose number had increased.

In 1645 M. de Maisonneuve had to leave for France, and he entrusted the command of the post to M. d'Ailleboust, who replaced him from 1645 till the summer of 1647. When M. de Maisonneuve returned from France, he delivered to d'Ailleboust an important and unexpected message: the Compagnie des Cent-Associés, as well as the Société Notre-Dame de Montréal, was recalling d'Ailleboust to France forthwith. The reason was that a decision had been made to replace M. de Montmagny, after 11 years of faithful service as governor. The Conseil du Roi had at first chosen M. de Maisonneuve as his successor, but he had declined the offer in favour of Louis d'Ailleboust. Thus, the following year, d'Ailleboust was to return to Canada armed with his commission. We can imagine the satisfaction of the Montrealers. One of the distinguished settlers of Montreal was about to become, in the autumn of 1648, the ruler of the country.

Important changes would, moreover, accompany this appointment. Indeed, on the recommendation of the Compagnie des Cent-Associés, Mazarin, who had appointed M. d'Ailleboust as M. de Montmagny's successor on 2 March 1648, limited his term of office to three years. This decision would apply to all future governors. In conformity with the edict of 5 March 1648, the governor would inaugurate the new colonial administration as soon as he assumed office. Henceforth he would preside over a council of five members, whose function would include discussing and voting upon local laws, business affairs, questions of peace and war, legal judgements in civil and criminal matters, police regulations, and finances. The edict likewise set up a flying column composed of 40 soldiers who would bring immediate help to places threatened by the Iroquois. The new governor proposed to give the command of this flying column to his nephew, CHARLES-JOSEPH D'AILLEBOUST Des Muceaux, a young officer whom he had just brought out from France.

As soon as he was installed in the Château Saint-Louis, at Quebec, construction of which had been started the year before, an endless round of activity faced Louis d'Ailleboust. Mme d'Ailleboust and her sister Philippine also came here after an uninterrupted stay of five years at Ville-Marie.

M. d'Ailleboust eagerly set about fighting the Iroquois. He had had painful experience with this kind of war at Ville-Marie. The years 1648 and 1649 saw the almost total destruction of the Hurons; it was also the era of the great Jesuit martyrs. In 1650 Montreal was severely and ceaselessly besieged; the "book of the dead" was added to each day. The Montrealers were forced to take refuge in the fort, and to live there "more closely shut up than in the smallest monasteries of France." However, this far-sighted governor had increased, and was continually extending, his efforts to assist them. The most urgent as well as the most important of his first administrative acts had been the organization of the flying column. This group of bold fighters had taken to the field in the spring of 1649. They were considered so effective that the governor decided two years later to raise their strength to 70 men.

At the end of May 1649 M. d'Ailleboust went to Ville-Marie. He was accompanied by 12 soldiers, a number which was subsequently to become the normal escort. M. de Maisonneuve went out to meet him in a bark, and came up with him at the Sainte-Marie rapids. The governor announced to M. de Maisonneuve that the Compagnie des Cent-Associés was adding six soldiers to his personal garrison. His salary was consequently raised from 3,000 to 4,000 *livres*. These concessions had certainly been asked for by M. d'Ailleboust, for they were not in accordance with the decree of 5 March 1648. During his stay, the governor made a point of officially transferring to the Jesuits the possession of their Prairie-de-la-Magdelaine seigneury.

In 1650 thought was being given in all quarters to the problem of aiding the Huron nation, whose last survivors, pursued and hunted down by the Iroquois, seemed doomed to annihilation. The very small numbers of Indians who were able to escape took refuge in Ville-Marie, a post that was too exposed to the fury of the Iroquois. During the summer more than 300 Hurons reached Quebec under the leadership of Father RAGUENEAU. Through the entire winter 1650–51 they were helped and fed by the governor, the Jesuits, the Hospitallers, the Ursulines, and a few other persons. Of the three Huron tribes which thus came down to Quebec one only, the Cord tribe, did not want to leave Quebec in the spring, imploring M. d'Ailleboust's protection and asking permission to establish its members not far from Fort Saint-Louis. The descendants of this tribe can be found today at Lorette, near Quebec.

Towards the end of the year 1650 the governor had new fortifications erected at Trois-Rivières.

Ailleboust de Coulonge

M. Gagnon has published the document containing the very precise instructions given on that occasion by M. d'Ailleboust to Pierre Boucher*, the commandant of the post. These fortifications, the result of the extreme vigilance of the governor in regard to anything which might check the sanguinary progress of the Iroquois, "did indeed save the small town from complete destruction when it was beleaguered in 1653 by 500 Mohawks."

It is evident that in M. d'Ailleboust the soldier, the engineer, and the architect were on a level with the administrator and the statesman. Indeed, it was the statesman who attempted to resume the negotiations begun in 1647 by his predecessor, M. de Montmagny, in the hope of concluding with the colonies of New England a treaty of offensive and defensive alliance, in addition to the commercial union desired by the merchants of Boston, Plymouth, Connecticut, and New Haven. But as M. d'Ailleboust considered that the commercial treaty should not be signed unless the military treaty were signed also, the New England authorities hesitated, then finally refused any kind of alliance because of this last condition of the governor. This was a setback, but M. d'Ailleboust's prudence remains praiseworthy. He was only too justified in suspecting the intentions of a neighbour whose commercial designs were not exempt from egoism.

The governor likewise tackled the question of the traffic in spirits with the Indians. He issued severe orders for the cessation of this practice at the Tadoussac post.

For three years Louis d'Ailleboust de Coulonge, second titular governor of New France, faced with rare firmness and clearheadedness all difficulties and perils. The machinations of the Iroquois never caught him unprepared. Even when these enemies spoke of peace, he remained sceptical, and showed still greater vigilance. He often managed to see through their ruses, and would fight them then with a bravery that commanded their respect. This dauntlessness, the mark of a leader, nevertheless concealed many anxieties, for help from France was more clearly inadequate each year. Father Charlevoix* therefore remarked, rightly, that in handing over the reins of government, on 13 October 1651, to the new and weak governor JEAN DE LAUSON, "M. d'Ailleboust gave up without regret an office where he could only be witness to the desolation of the colony that he had not been given enough help to support with dignity."

D'Ailleboust and his wife retired in 1651 to their property at Coulonge, a league away from Quebec, and to which there was access by what was already called the Grande Allée. The governor had bought the Coulonge tract from Nicolas Gaudry dit Bourbonnière, 17 Oct. 1649. He built a house there, and spent the next years enlarging and beautifying his estate. "The name Coulonge," wrote Gagnon, "was for him both an estate name and a family name. Louis d'Ailleboust is called 'sieur de Coulonge' in a document executed in 1643, immediately before he first left France to go to Canada. This document is preserved in the archives of the Hôtel-Dieu de Québec."

M. d'Ailleboust's return to private life did not mean the abandonment of his public life. In July 1652 Governor de Lauson, in the name of the Compagnie des Cent-Associés, granted him the Argentenay fief and the Saint-Vilmé arriere-fief. Argentenay was another family name for d'Ailleboust. His half-sister, the daughter by his mother's first marriage, was named Dorothée de Manthet d'Argentenay, and had married Nicolas d'Ailleboust, Louis' elder brother. A little village in Champagne also had the name Argentenay, and another small town, not far away, bore the name Saint-Vilmé.

In 1653 M. d'Ailleboust was elected a syndic and a churchwarden of the parish of Quebec. In addition, by agreement with JEAN-PAUL GODEFROY and JEAN BOURDON, "he set up a fishing post at Percé, and sent a ship there with instructions to take to Saint-Christophe in the West Indies the catch made on the trip."

We must be careful not to think that this "Associate of Montreal" ever lost interest in the Ville-Marie venture. He often stayed there and lodged in his house, built inside the surrounding wall of the fort. M. de Maisonneuve still remained the best friend he had in New France.

It was also under M. de Lauson's administration that Louis d'Ailleboust was appointed director general of the trade in pelts in New France, "an office made particularly difficult by the opposing interests of the Grande compagnie and of the Compagnie des Habitants," which was created in 1645.

In 1655 M. d'Ailleboust and his nephew Charles-Joseph accompanied M. de Maisonneuve to France. The purpose was to ensure, with the help of the Société Notre-Dame, the continued existence of the Ville-Marie settlement, and "the implementation of M. Olier's plans concerning the spiritual side as well as the temporal side of the undertaking." The founder of the Compagnie de Saint-Sulpice, who was then very ill, nevertheless received with joy the visit of his fellow-Associates of Montreal. He promised to concern himself at once with the choice of four members of his company "to minister permanently to the île de Montréal."

Ailleboust de Coulonge

M. d'Ailleboust had to extend to nearly two years his stay in France, as did M. de Maisonneuve. A few weeks before d'Ailleboust embarked, the Compagnie des Cent-Associés handed letters patent to him, raising his Coulogne estate to a fief and castellany in recognition of his many services.

On 17 May 1657, at Saint-Nazaire, MM. de Maisonneuve and d'Ailleboust, as well as three Sulpicians under the leadership of Abbé Queylus [see THUBIÈRES], the first superior of Saint-Sulpice at Montreal, boarded the ship bound for Canada. The travellers, after a stormy crossing, landed on the Île d'Orléans, 29 July. In the middle of August the four Sulpicians, whom the Jesuits had kept as their guests for a few days in their residence, settled down at Ville-Marie.

Louis d'Ailleboust, who had followed his travelling companions to Montreal, returned to Quebec 12 September (*JJ*, 220), where he had been recalled by CHARLES DE LAUSON de Charny, then acting governor of New France. The latter, in a document signed 26 Aug. 1657 (*RSCT*, 3d ser., XXVI (1932), sect.I, 91), had handed over his powers to him pending the arrival in the country of the new governor, Pierre de Voyer* d'Argenson. Charles de Lauson, who had recently lost his wife, wished to become a priest and live in absolute reclusion. This meant asking of M. d'Ailleboust a very painful "act of devotion and abnegation," for none knew better than that gentleman the terrible difficulties which he was once more going to face, without being able to produce the slightest remedy for them. M. d'Ailleboust resumed the onerous task of government. There was indeed a continual succession of official parleys, meetings of notables, Hurons, and Algonkins, all called into consultation. Then suddenly all diplomatic efforts ceased. News got through to Quebec of massacres going on far away, in the Iroquois villages, and even at Ville-Marie, while peace was being hypocritically discussed at Fort Saint-Louis. Fortunately it was possible to arrest and imprison the 50 Iroquois delegates then visiting Quebec; they were precious hostages against future acts of treachery.

On 13 March 1658 M. d'Ailleboust, in his capacity as governor, and accompanied by Abbé VIGNAL, laid the corner-stone of the "church of the Petit Cap" (today Sainte-Anne de Beaupré). Taking advantage of the occasion, M. d'Ailleboust decided to oversee himself the building of the redoubts that were going up by his orders on the Beaupré shore. For the Iroquois were talking more and more about massacring not only the Hurons and Algonkins—a sinister work already accomplished—but also all the settlers in New France.

Shortly before the ceremonies at the Petit Cap, M. d'Ailleboust had to reassure the Hurons of the Cord tribe, who continually feared that the governor, yielding to Iroquois pressure, would order them to go and live among the Iroquois; the latter solemnly promised to treat them like brothers. The governor therefore caused a small fort to be put up where Hurons and Algonkins could take refuge, under the protection of the guns of the Château Saint-Louis. This construction, "quadrangular in form, each side having a length of 150 feet," was called "the little fort of the Hurons."

On 11 July 1658 M. d'Ailleboust handed over the keys of the fort to d'Argenson, the new governor. A few weeks later, having been unable to get on with this high official, he left for Ville-Marie with his wife, Abbé Queylus, and some 60 settlers.

As soon as he arrived, M. de Maisonneuve urged him to fortify the "highest point" of the Saint-Louis height and to lay the foundations of the future citadel of Montreal.

He was obliged however to return to Quebec the following year. He wanted to be among the first to do homage to the first bishop of New France, François de Laval*, who landed at Quebec 16 June 1659. In September, M. d'Ailleboust was still staying in the capital, for we find him interceding in a private capacity, at the request of the bishop and of the governor, in order to settle a point of contention that was arising between them. The issue was the location of the seats in which these eminent personages sat at church. M. d'Ailleboust handled the affair very well, to the satisfaction of both parties.

Louis d'Ailleboust died at Ville-Marie 31 May 1660, at the age of 48. He left no children. He was buried at Ville-Marie 1 June 1660, in the cemetery of the hospital that stood on the site of today's Place d'Armes.

We know of no authentic portrait of Louis d'Ailleboust de Coulonge. His family's coat of arms was "gules, chevron or between three estoiles of the second, two in chief, one in point."

MARIE-CLAIRE DAVELUY

Official documents of the third governor of New France are distributed among AJM, AJQ, APQ, Archives du Séminaire de Saint-Sulpice de Montréal, and PAC. AHDQ possesses the Papiers d'Ailleboust, in addition to other rare documents. ASQ and AHDM also have valuable holdings.

Charlevoix, *Histoire* (Shea). Dollier de Casson, *Histoire du Montréal*. *JR* (Thwaites). *JJ* (Laverdière et Casgrain). Morin, *Annales* (Fauteux et al.). [Jean-Jacques Olier?], *Les véritables motifs de messieurs et dames de la Société de Notre-Dame de Montréal pour la conversion des sauvages de la Nouvelle-France*, éd.

H.-A. Verreau (SHM *Mémoires*, IX (1880)). *Ord. comm.* (P.-G. Roy), I, 10–12.

E. R. Adair, "France and the beginnings of New France," *CHR*, XXV (1944), 246–78. Aegidius Fauteux, *La famille d'Ailleboust* (Montréal, 1917). Ernest Gagnon, *Feuilles volantes et pages d'histoire* (Québec, 1910). Amédée-E. Gosselin, "Notes et documents concernant les gouverneurs d'Ailleboust, de Lauzon et de Lauzon-Charny," *RSCT*, 3d ser., XXVI (1932), sect.I, 83–96.

AILLEBOUST DES MUCEAUX, CHARLES-JOSEPH D', soldier, acting governor of Montreal, civil and criminal judge of Montreal, business man, member of the Communauté des Habitants as well as of the Société Notre-Dame de Montréal; b. between 1623 and 1626 in France, son of Nicolas d'Ailleboust of Coulonges-la-Madeleine and Dorothée de Manthet; buried 20 Nov. 1700 at Montreal.

D'Ailleboust des Muceaux came to Canada with his uncle LOUIS D'AILLEBOUST, the recently appointed governor of New France. He arrived at Quebec on board the *Cardinal* 20 Aug. 1648, and immediately set out for Montreal, where he took command of a flying column, a troop of 40 men who were kept in constant readiness to repel the Iroquois. A year later he went back to France, probably to seek reinforcements, for he was listed among those who landed 8 Sept. 1650 at Quebec, and a few months later the strength of his column stood at 70 soldiers. CHOMEDEY de Maisonneuve, before sailing for France in 1651, entrusted to him the governorship of Montreal.

On 16 Sept. 1652 at Quebec, where he took up residence, he married Catherine, daughter of PIERRE LEGARDEUR de Repentigny; she was to give him 14 children. Then, having sold his properties at Quebec to Jean MADRY on 8 Aug. 1659, he went back to Montreal to live; since 1661 he had owned two sites there, in Notre-Dame street, and his residence was the most important one in the town.

In 1663 he was the lieutenant of the Montreal garrison; he was already dispensing seigneurial justice there, a function which he seems to have exercised from his arrival in 1659, but to which he was not officially appointed until 27 Sept. 1666, when TALON settled in favour of the Sulpicians, who were the seigneurs of Montreal, and of their candidate Charles-Joseph d'Ailleboust, a conflict of jurisdiction between the royal seneschal's court (created in 1663 by Governor de SAFFRAY de Mézy, with Louis-Arthus de SAILLY as the judge), and the seigneurial court set up by the members of Saint-Sulpice. Des Muceaux remained the civil and criminal judge of Montreal until 26 Aug. 1677, at which date he was replaced by MIGEON de Branssat.

In 1666 M. d'Ailleboust set off with PROUVILLE de Tracy's expedition against the Mohawks, but he was obliged to return to Montreal when he was bitten by a bear. From 1670 on he turned more and more towards business, but with indifferent success. In 1668 he had come to an understanding with his aunt, Mme Louis d'Ailleboust [*see* BOULLONGNE], in respect of the deceased governor's estate, and in 1673 he sold to the Hôtel-Dieu of Quebec his share of the Villemay, d'Argentenay, and Coulonges seigneuries. With his capital thus increased, he entered into partnership with the merchant François Le Noir* Rolland (18 March 1675). But in 1681 he was so poor that Governor BUADE de Frontenac had to obtain for him a pension of 150 *livres* from the king.

Since Governor Louis d'Ailleboust died childless, Charles-Joseph is the ancestor of all the d'Aillebousts in Canada.

J. MONET

Dollier de Casson, *Histoire du Montréal*, passim. *JR* (Thwaites). *JJ* (Laverdière et Casgrain). *Jug. et délib.* P.-G. Roy, *Inv. concessions.*

Claude de Bonnault, "Le Canada militaire, état provisoire des officiers de milice, de 1641 à 1760," *APQ Rapport, 1949–51*, 292. *BRH*, XV (1909), 53. Daveluy, "Bibliographie," *RHAF*, VI (1952–53), 147. Faillon, *Histoire de la colonie française*, II, 95f., 134f., 498; III, 75, 341. Aegidius Fauteux, *La famille d'Ailleboust* (Montréal, 1917). Godbout, "Nos ancêtres," *APQ Rapport, 1951–53*, 468. É.-Z. Massicotte, "Migeon de Branssat," *BRH*, XXI (1915), 232; "Les tribunaux et les officiers de justice à Montréal sous le régime français, 1648–1760," *RSCT*, 3d ser., X (1916), sect.I, 273–339. P.-G. Roy, "Le premier juge de Montréal," dans *Les petites choses de notre histoire* (3e sér., Lévis, 1922), 102–9. Régis Roy, *La famille d'Ailleboust* (Montréal, s.d.). Benjamin Sulte, "Le camp volant de 1649," *RC*, XVII (1881), 159–69.

AILLON, JOSEPH LA ROCHE D'. *See* LA ROCHE DAILLON

ALBANEL, CHARLES, priest, Jesuit, missionary, and explorer; b. 1616 (or 1613) in Auvergne; d. 11 Jan. 1696 at Sault Ste. Marie.

It has been claimed that he was born of English parents residing in France, but this opinion has no other basis than an incorrect reading of a text by Thomas GORST, storekeeper and secretary to the governor of Hudson Bay, Charles BAYLY. Of Albanel's youth nothing is known, except that he had finished two years of philosophical studies when he entered the Jesuit novitiate of the province of Toulouse 16 Sept. 1633. From 1635 on he taught, in succession, grammar, the humanities,

Albanel

and rhetoric at the colleges of Quercy (in Cahors), Carcassonne, Mauriac, and Aurillac. In 1636–37 he taught the second form of secondary school at Montpellier, and the following year he did a third year of philosophy at Billom. After his four years of theology at Tournon, he had to wait until 1648–49 to finish his religious training with the third year. It was in March of 1649 that he sailed for Quebec, where his arrival on 23 August was noted in the *Journal des Jésuites*. A month after landing at Quebec he left for Ville-Marie (Montreal), where his name appeared the following year in the little baptismal register.

During the next ten years he went to Tadoussac nearly every winter, returning to Quebec in the spring or summer. Dates allow us to chart his movements. On 22 Oct. 1650 he set out for Tadoussac with the intention of spending the winter among the Montagnais or Lower Algonkins, and returned on 22 April of the following year. On 2 May 1651 he sailed aboard a bark for Tadoussac and Gaspé. After a difficult winter with the nomadic Montagnais, he was back at Quebec in time to leave again on 4 May 1652 on a frigate with Father de QUEN. He returned 10 April 1653 with LOUIS COUILLARD de Lespinay. On 13 Nov. 1653 the *Journal des Jésuites* mentions that the Quebec fathers received letters from him brought by M. de Lespinay. On 24 Feb. 1654 we learn that he was spending his fourth winter among the Indians. Two years later, according to the *Journal*, M. de Lespinay brought news of him from Tadoussac on 31 October, and on 17 November the Indian Kahikohan passed on news of him from Le Bic. On 3 Feb. 1657 he left this place, and returned by foot along the south shore in company with Couillard and four Frenchmen; after a difficult trip they reached Quebec on 8 March. Between the time he left Quebec, 13 May 1658, and his return on 8 August, he worked at the Sainte-Croix mission near Tadoussac, where he had gone at the same time as Father DU PERON, Brother Nicolas Charton, and two Frenchmen. In 1659 he went again to Tadoussac. He left on 10 May and returned 31 August on Lespinay's vessel, which was coming back from hunting seals. The following winter he was again at Tadoussac. He had left Quebec 21 Nov. 1659 with four Frenchmen and he returned in April 1660.

On 8 July 1660 he went to Trois-Rivières with Governor Voyer* d'Argenson, and their boat was attacked by the Iroquois during their return trip. On 14 September of the same year he sailed as far as Montreal on his way to spend the winter among the *Bœuf* Nation. For a few years the *Journal des Jésuites* says nothing about Father Albanel, but we know that he had settled down at Cap-de-la-Madeleine, where he was the parish priest and superior. Father FRÉMIN replaced him in these charges on 17 Aug. 1665, but Albanel retained the main responsibility for the Montagnais or Algonkin missions, which at that time were being ravaged by the scourge of alcohol. The *Journal des Jésuites* mentions his departure from Trois-Rivières on 16 Nov. 1665 to go to serve as priest for a brief period at Fort Saint-Louis (Chambly) in place of Father Du Peron, who had died six days earlier. By 2 December he was at Trois-Rivières again, while waiting to go farther inland, probably to the upper Saint-Maurice River. In February 1666, shortly after being appointed parish priest at Fort Saint-Louis, he was accused by the governor, RÉMY de Courcelle, of having dissuaded the Indians from taking part in his war party that winter. Intendant TALON succeeded in persuading Courcelle to drop an accusation that was as surprising as it was unjustified. On 14 October of the same year Father Albanel accompanied the Carignan-Salières regiment as chaplain, along with Father Raffeix*, in a campaign against the Iroquois. PROUVILLE de Tracy and his soldiers were very pleased with him. In 1668–69 he spent a year at the Sillery mission; that same winter we find him again among the wandering tribes at the Sainte-Croix mission. He has left us two letters in which he has described his work during this period. In the course of his travels he visited the Papinachois Indians. On 15 June 1670 he left Tadoussac on a mission to evangelize the Oumamiois (Bersiamites), after obtaining two French companions from NICOLAS JUCHEREAU de Saint-Denis.

In 1671 Intendant Talon decided to send "two resolute men" to Hudson Bay. "Accordingly," Father DABLON tells us, "we fixed our choice on Father Charles Albanel, former missionary to Tadoussac, since he has had much intercourse with the Savages who possess a knowledge of that sea, who alone are able to act as guides over those hitherto unknown ways." The purpose of Albanel's voyage (1671–72) was to discover whether the Northern Sea was indeed Hudson Bay and to verify the presence there of Europeans who were said to be French. The persons concerned were in fact CHOUART Des Groseilliers and Radisson*, who had gone over to the service of the English.

Father Albanel was induced to make his trips to the Northern Sea because New France had long felt the fascination of a region that was generally considered as a natural frontier yet to be explored, as well as a rich territory where the Indians were for the missionaries persons to be converted and for the traders valuable allies in the trade in pelts. It was already known that Hudson Bay served as a passage-way for the English explorers in their search for the Western Sea. The French too had some hypotheses to verify concerning this passage. Thus, JEAN BOURDON had made a first attempt by sea in 1657 but had to turn back at the 55th parallel. In the same year possession was taken of the basin of the Northern Sea in the name of the king of France. In 1661 these attempts were complemented by the land expedition carried out on Governor Argenson's order. The group, to which belonged the Jesuits Dablon and DRUILLETTES, had reached a point a little beyond the watershed. This was only a postponement, for it was realized in New France that the country that held this region would at the same time be in possession of the entrance to the Western Sea and the inexhaustible wealth of beaver skins.

Father Albanel left Quebec 6 Aug. 1671 for Tadoussac, where he arranged to meet his two companions, Paul Denys* de Saint-Simon and a certain Sébastien Provencher. Upon his arrival on 8 August he secured the services of Montagnais guides. The group was at Chicoutimi on 26 August and left there on 29 August, reaching the far end of the lake on 7 September. Ten days later Albanel met five canoes bearing Attikamegue and Mistassini Indians and learned of the presence in the Bay of two English ships that were trading there. He then decided it would be well to have passports, which he sent messengers to obtain from the governor, the intendant, and the bishop in Quebec. The messengers did not return until 10 October, too late for the party to undertake the rest of the trip immediately. It was decided to spend the winter where they were, and Father Albanel took advantage of this to evangelize the Mistassinis and to baptize their children. The season was on the whole a hard one, according to Father Albanel, who thought that it was the most severe "of the ten winters [that he had spent] in the woods with the Indians." At that time he was only 55, even though Thomas Gorst considered him to be "a little old man." His guides abandoned him, and it was only his diplomacy that enabled him to find others.

On 1 June 1672 there was a new attempt, with 3 canoes bearing 3 Frenchmen and 16 Indians. On 9 June they were at the divide, that is to say, about the point reached by Father Dablon in 1661. The Mistassinis wanted to prevent them from going any farther. But Father Albanel succeeded with gifts and fair words in convincing them that the French would protect them against their enemies the Iroquois. On 18 June the expedition reached Lake Mistassini, and then Lake Nemiskau on 25 June, whence they went down the Rupert River, reaching its mouth on 28 June. There they found an English ship and two deserted houses: before leaving for England, everyone had gone hunting. Father Albanel took advantage of the absence of the English party to make the acquaintance of the Indians, to teach them and baptize some of them. After a few days sailing and exploring in James Bay, Albanel entrusted a letter for Radisson to the Indians and set out on the return trip on 6 July, without meeting any Englishmen or French deserters. Three days later the group raised the arms of the king of France at Lake Nemiskau. On 23 July the travellers were at Lake St. John, then on 1 August at Chicoutimi, where they were being awaited by the captain who was to take them to Tadoussac and thence to Quebec.

In the account of his trip Albanel reported that he had baptized 200 people, 100 adults and as many children. He had identified Hudson Bay, seen an English ship, and established firm ties with the Indians. But he had met no whites. The journey, he related, entailed many difficulties: an 880-league trip, 200 portages, falls, and dangerous passages, distrust on the part of the Indians, and so on. Finally he credited himself with the idea of such an undertaking. "Up till that time it had been felt that such a voyage was beyond the possibilities of the French, who, having already attempted it three times and having been unable to overcome the obstacles attendant upon it, despairing of success, had been obliged to give it up. What seems impossible becomes easy when it is pleasing to God. The leadership of this expedition was rightfully mine, after 18 years of attempts that I had made, and I had quite tangible proofs that God was reserving for me its successful completion."

"Fine beginnings," he concluded, in a way that forecast a new attempt before long. In fact, in a letter to Colbert (13 Nov. 1673), Frontenac [see BUADE], tells us: "I have utilized the zeal shown by Father Albanel, a Jesuit, for undertaking a mission to those regions in order to try to dissuade the Indians, among whom he is highly trusted, from following this route for trade with the English. . . . The aforementioned Father Albanel is to sound out Des Groseilliers, if he meets him, and to try to find out whether he can bring him back to our side."

Bearing a letter, dated 8 Oct. 1673, from Frontenac to Governor Bayly, Albanel left for Tadoussac, and by 13 Jan. 1674 he set off for the Northern Sea. On the way a burden fell on his back, immobilized him, and forced him to spend the winter in the region of Lake St. John. There he was visited by Father Crespieul*, in the month of January, then on 2 February and again on 3 March. The rest of the voyage is known to us only through English sources. Oldmixon, who summarizes Gorst, tells us that Albanel reached the Rupert River 30 Aug. 1674, along with a young Indian and a Frenchman born of English parents, probably Des Groseilliers's nephew. Albanel was carrying a letter for Des Groseilliers. Gorst claims that Albanel sought refuge with him in order to escape bad treatment from the Indians and in order not to have to make the return trip, which was so difficult. Despite Frontenac's letter, which was on the whole friendly, the English in Hudson Bay rather treated Albanel as a traitor, an enemy who had come to lure the Indians away from their alliance with them, in order to win them over to friendship and trade with the French. Albanel and his companion were detained by Bayly and then sent to England, after receiving hospitality, clothes, and money. In London Albanel is supposed to have obtained a letter exonerating him which he could deliver to his superiors, who he was afraid would accuse him of deserting the missions. Returning to France, the Jesuit embarked again for Canada and landed at Quebec 22 July 1676. He refused to talk about his voyage while on the ship, and later his companion promised to answer no questions until after the priest's death. Thus posterity was for ever deprived of important and valuable detailed information about this expedition.

Three days after his return to Quebec, a combination of circumstances led to his being appointed to the missions in the hinterland. He became superior at Sault Ste. Marie, even though he was "old and worn out," the author of the 1679 *Relation* informs us. His extraordinary talent for languages was responsible at that time for his beginning again a new missionary experience. He spent the rest of his life in these regions. Appointed superior of the Saint-François-Xavier missions (Baie des Puants, now De Pere, Wisconsin) on 25 July 1676, he was succeeded in this post by Father Henri Nouvel* in 1679. In the year of his appointment "he replaced the original chapel by an attractive church," Gérard Malchelosse informs us. In 1683, wrote Father Beschefer*, Father Albanel, though aged and trembling, had for some years been sharing with Father Louis André* the whole responsibility for the Sault Ste. Marie mission. On 11 Jan. 1696 he died there at 80 years of age.

GEORGES-ÉMILE GIGUÈRE

ACSM, f. 802. *Découvertes et établissements des Français* (Margry), I, 92–96. *JR* (Thwaites), LIII, 58–92; LVI, 148–217.
BRH, IX (1903), 216f.; XVIII (1912), 160, 192; XXII (1916), 226; XXV (1919), 111. N. M. Crouse, *Contributions of the Canadian Jesuits to the geographical knowledge of New France* (Ithaca, N.Y., 1924). HBRS, XXI (Rich). Séraphin Marion, *Relations des voyageurs français en Nouvelle-France au XVIIe siècle* (Paris, 1923), 168–78. Jacques Rousseau, "Les voyages du père Albanel au lac Mistassini et à la Baie James," *RHAF*, III (1949–50), 556–86. *See also* the bibliography for Thomas GORST.

ALEXANDER, SIR WILLIAM, Earl of Stirling, remembered in the land of his birth as a scholar, poet, courtier, and the favourite of James I and Charles I of England in their dealings with Scotland; and on this side of the Atlantic as the putative founder of a new Scotland under the aegis of both monarchs; b. *c.* 1577; d. 1640. Though his colonizing interest is the chief concern of cisatlantic readers, it cannot be understood without reference to his poetical works, which brought him first to royal notice and subsequently to royal favour and collaboration.

William Alexander was born in the village of Menstrie. He received a thorough classical education in the grammar school of Stirling, under Dr. Thomas Buchanan, nephew of George Buchanan, tutor of James VI of Scotland; and probably attended the University of Glasgow. He made "the grand tour" (France, Spain, Italy, and Holland) at the end of the century, as the companion of his kinsman, the seventh Earl of Argyle, who later introduced him to court.

Before going to court in London he had made some reputation as a poet, with his *Tragedie of Darius*, published at Edinburgh in 1603 and dedicated to James VI. This was reprinted in London in 1604, together with another tragedy, *Croesus*. Both reflect his classical education and foreshadow the main character of his poetical works. (*Aurora*, a sonnet sequence, published in the same year was obviously an earlier work; and *A Paraenesis to the Prince* was obviously a bid for royal favour.) These were followed in 1605 by *The Alexandrean Tragedy*; and in 1607 by a collected edition of his tragedies, including *Julius Caesar*, written in the interval. In this edition the author is described as a gentleman of the Prince's Privy Chamber.

In this year, 1607, he was granted the rights to the mines and minerals in the barony of Menstrie; and he shared equally with his father-in-law an annuity of £200. (He had married in 1601 Janet, daughter of Sir William Erskine a relative of the Earl of Mar, who in due course bore him ten children, seven sons and three daughters; and while he was climbing the ladder of fame Providence concealed from him the fact that a grandchild eight years of age was to enjoy for a few

Alexander

months only the heritage of an empty title by primogeniture.) In 1608, he and a relative were made agents for collecting debts due the Crown in Scotland from 1547 to 1588, on a 50 per cent basis; he was knighted in 1609.

In 1612 he wrote *An Elegie on the Death of Prince Henrie* and was appointed gentleman usher in the household of Prince Charles. Two years later, he published *Doomes-Day, or, The Great day of the Lords Judgement*, his last poetical work of importance. He had already won on his previous works and, from this date, would continue to win the warm praise of contemporary writers, above all that of Drummond of Hawthornden. Moreover, he had been chosen by King James as collaborator in translating *The Psalms of King David*.

It was, therefore, as a well-known literary figure, having close associations with both England and Scotland, that he was appointed in 1614 master of requests for Scotland—whose chief duty was to ward off needy Scots from the English court—and, in 1615, a member of the Scottish Privy Council, the highest advisory authority on Scottish affairs. It was in these two positions that he was most intimately associated with King James and, having won his complete confidence, was enabled to obtain his ardent support for his colonial adventures.

During his residence at court, though as a poet Sir William still maintained the futility of human ambition, nonetheless he mingled with those who were promoting the expansion of England overseas, became aware of Scotland's lack of any part in it, and, as a patriotic Scot, began to dream of making a name for himself by diverting the constant stream of Scottish manhood from the continental wars into a colony that should bear the name of Scotland.

He first approached Capt. John Mason, governor of Newfoundland, 1615–21, and author of *A briefe discourse of the New-found-land* for aid in getting room for a plantation there. Through Mason's influence he obtained a grant of the northwestern part of that island, from the Bay of Placentia to the Gulf of St. Lawrence, but, although he named it Alexandria, he made no use of it, because of a grander vision that emerged from the suggestion of Governor Mason that he consult Ferdinando Gorges, treasurer of the recently formed Council of New England. (In 1620 the London and Plymouth companies, which in 1606 were granted the territory between latitudes 34° and 45°N. under the name of Virginia, were reorganized and the northern part, extended to 48°, was granted to the Council of New England.)

Acting on Mason's advice, Alexander persuaded King James that the only way to get Scots to emigrate was to give them a new Scotland comparable to New France and New England; and the king conveyed the royal wish to the Council of New England and obtained from the latter the surrender of all their territory north of the Sainte-Croix. Thereupon the king immediately instructed the Scottish Privy Council to prepare a grant of this territory for Sir William Alexander. The grant was signed on 10 Sept. 1621 (o.s.), making Sir William, on paper at least, lord proprietor of what are now known as the three Atlantic Provinces and the Gaspé peninsula—to be called for all time New Scotland or Nova Scotia.

Unfortunately, this grant included the territory that had been claimed and nominally occupied by the French as Acadia. The much neglected CHARLES DE BIENCOURT and a little band of Frenchmen and their Indian allies were the unofficial representatives of French claims in the entire area; this same band under CHARLES DE SAINT-ÉTIENNE de La Tour was to play an important role in the later revival of French claims and in the final failure of Sir William's colonizing projects. Meanwhile in the six years during which his title was practically unchallenged, notwithstanding the continued favour of King James and his son Charles, Alexander was unable to plant permanently a single colonist in his far-flung domain.

This is perhaps not a matter of surprise when one considers his previous lack of experience with practical affairs, the difficulty of combining the roles of a dreamer and a man of action, and the magnitude of the task which he had undertaken single-handed; for he alone had to remould the Scottish national outlook and create a favourable public opinion, whereas the promoters of Virginia, New England, and Newfoundland were numerous and had the English nation behind them.

Though Sir William lacked experience he did not lack either courage or tenacity. In 1622 he hired a ship in London and sent it to Kirkcudbright to pick up settlers and supplies; but it was delayed by the reluctance of artisans to enlist and the scarcity of supplies, encountered bad weather near Cape Breton, left the colonists in St. John's, Newfoundland, and returned to London for more supplies. In 1623 he sent out another ship to pick up the colonists, but this party found that some of them had died, that others were out fishing, and that too few remained to found a colony. However, ten of these decided to go along with the ship to locate a fit site for a future settlement. They explored as far as Cap Nègre, landed at Port-Joli and Port-au-Mouton, formed a favourable opinion of the natural beauty and resources of the country, but returned to Newfoundland, whence they took passage to England with some of the West Country fishermen, leaving the ship to get its own load of fish. The remainder of the original party apparently became absorbed in the population of Newfoundland.

The net gain of Sir William's first venture, at an alleged cost of £6,000, was a rather vague but flowery description of New Scotland, which he embodied in his pamphlet *An encouragement to colonies*, published in 1624 and accompanied by a map on which he sprinkled a number of Scottish names. Thus the Sainte-Croix becomes the Tweed; the Saint John, the Clyde; and the whole is divided into two provinces Alexandria and Caledonia.

In this pamphlet he traces colonization from Abraham through the Greeks and Romans to the Spanish, French, and British, recounts the experience of his first venture, paints a glowing picture of its advantages to gentry and commoner, merchant and missionary, and concludes with an appeal to the king to further the project by making it appear a work of his own and thereby encouraging public "helps, such as hath beene had in other parts, for the like cause"—an obvious reference to the help given by the king to the plantation of Ulster, by the creation of knight-baronets, which brought £225,000 to the royal exchequer.

In response to this appeal, King James informed the Privy Council of Scotland that he had decided to confer the dignity of knight-baronet upon any worthy Scot who would undertake to furnish a number of settlers in return for a portion of New Scotland and instructed the council to prepare a proclamation to that effect. This they did on 30 Nov. 1624, offering a barony and the title of knight-baronet in return for setting forth six men fully armed, clothed, and provisioned for two years, within a year and a day after accepting the honour, at the cost of 2,000 merks and 1,000 merks to Sir William for resigning his interest in the barony. As there was no response to this offer, on 23 March 1624/25 the king wrote the council offering the baronies for a cash payment of 3,000 merks to Sir William, who would use the 2,000 merks for furnishing the settlers. Four days later, King James died without having seen a baronet created or a colonist set forth; but his death did not mean the withdrawal of royal favour: Charles I was equally well disposed to Sir William's project and for the next five years did everything in his power to induce the Scottish nobility and gentry to support it. By the end of May 1625 he had created eight baronets on the cash basis, with land three miles wide and six long, and on 12 July he renewed the charter of 1621 with additional provisions for a total of 150 baronets and for the incorporation of Nova Scotia into the kingdom of Scotland, in order that Sir William and the baronets could take seisin of their distant lands in the castle of Edinburgh without the necessity of going to Nova Scotia.

Despite the promising beginning, the response to the new charter was very disappointing. There was opposition on the part of the lesser barons to the special privileges offered to the knight-baronets. To meet this Charles demoted the secretary of state for Scotland, who had approved the protest of the lesser barons, and appointed Sir William in his stead. But by 25 July 1626 only 28 baronets had been created and, even if Sir William had received the full sum of 3,000 merks for each, he would have had only £4,666 13s. 4d. to finance his projected colony, considerably less than the £6,000 that he had already expended on the first attempt, for which he had a warrant from King James, still unpaid.

Accordingly, on 25 July 1626 King Charles authorized a committee of the council to meet frequently at stated times to see that the petitioners for the dignity of knight-baronet had satisfied Alexander and that he was prepared to surrender the lands specified, and to award the dignity forthwith. In the same commission the king awarded armorial bearings to the province. (It is from this commission that Nova Scotia derives its flag and present coat of arms.)

As only one baronet had responded by 3 March 1626/27, Charles wrote the council again to speed up matters and stated that unless the full number of baronets were created Sir William would be utterly undone, as he had already spent more on the two ships he was preparing than he had received.

The story of later creations may be summarized thus. Despite repeated urgings only 14 came forward in 1627, 21 in 1628, 7 in 1629, and even after the special badge was offered (27 Nov. 1629), 11 in 1630, and 4 in 1631. That is, 85 baronies only had been disposed of from 1625 to 1631 when Sir William was ordered to give up his colony at Port-Royal to the French and the creation of knight-baronets had degenerated into a scheme of raising money by the sale of titles. In fact 25 baronets were created between 1633 and 1637 after Port-Royal had been surrendered.

Until 1627, Sir William had to contend only with the problems of finance and the reluctance of the Scots to emigrate. But in the spring of that year he had to meet the competition of the powerful Compagnie des Cent-Associés, which Cardinal Richelieu had organized in Paris to control the destinies of New France and to challenge Sir William's claims to Nova Scotia. The outbreak of war between France and England also brought new adventurers into the field, notably the KIRKE brothers, whose brilliant achievements now threatened to supplant Alexander for the time being in the public eye. In 1628, after threatening Quebec, the Kirkes captured the supply ships of the Compagnie de la Nouvelle-France near Gaspé, brought CLAUDE DE SAINT-ÉTIENNE de La Tour, who was returning to Acadia after seeking help for the French against the British, a prisoner to England, and applied to the king for a grant of the monopoly of trade in Canada, under the Crown of England.

Meantime in February 1627/28 Sir William, whose eldest son, WILLIAM, was already in command of an expedition towards New Scotland, had induced the king to direct that all prize money collected in Scotland should be turned over to him and to grant him the lordship of Canada—an area of 50 leagues on each side of the St. Lawrence from its mouth to the mythical South Sea. He opposed the application of the Kirke brothers and, supported by the Privy Council of Scotland, obtained a compromise whereby the rival interests were united and agreed to operate under the crowns of England and Scotland. Accordingly, on 4 Feb. 1628/29 a commission was issued to Sir William Alexander the younger and others for a monopoly of the trade of the St. Lawrence, with power to confiscate the goods and ships of any interlopers, to make prizes of all French or Spanish ships, and to displant the French (*Royal letters*, 47).

It was under this commission that the Kirkes took the fort and trading post of Quebec and brought CHAMPLAIN and other Frenchmen prisoners to England. It was under the same commission that Sir William the younger helped Sir James STEWART, Lord Ochiltree, to plant a short-lived colony at Baleine in Cape Breton—it was uprooted two months later by CHARLES DANIEL—and that under the guidance of Claude de La Tour he planted a colony at Port-Royal (now Annapolis Royal, N.S.), which had a precarious existence until 1632.

The younger Sir William decided to remain in Port-Royal over the winter of 1629–30 and to send home his ships for supplies and reinforcement and Claude de La Tour with a draft agreement for his father to sign, whereby Claude and his son Charles were to receive a large barony (from Yarmouth to Lunenberg) in exchange for their allegiance and assistance. He also sent home the Indian chief SEGIPT and his wife and son to do homage to King Charles.

During the winter of 1629–30 Sir William managed to get together supplies and reinforcements for his colony, confirmed the agreement with Claude de La Tour, who married a Scottish lady, made him a knight-baronet, and sent him back in May with a patent for his son Charles. However, his own son, returning in the autumn of 1630, had to report that 30 of the 70 colonists had died during the winter, that Charles de La Tour had refused to accept the title of knight-baronet, and that Claude de la Tour had therefore lost face with both those whom he brought and the original settlers at Port-Royal. He in turn found his father deep in a struggle to resist the surrender of Nova Scotia to France in accordance with the Treaty of Susa, 23 April 1629, by which the British and French had agreed on mutual restoration of all territory and shipping taken subsequent to that date. Negotiations dragged on for two years. The British admitted that Quebec had been taken since that treaty but maintained that Port-Royal had been settled in unoccupied territory to which they had good title by discovery, strengthened by the charter of Virginia, the conquest of ARGALL, the charters of 1621 and 1625, and the homage of the Indian chief. The French insisted that both Quebec and Port-Royal be restored to their original condition or the possessor would have an unfair advantage in negotiation. Finally, King Charles, in dire financial straits, at outs with his Parliament, and lured by the prospect of receiving the half of his wife's dowry still unpaid by the French, agreed to instruct Sir William to withdraw his colonists with their effects and to destroy the fort and other habitations.

Though these instructions were drafted in 1631, they were not given to the French for submission to the colonists at Port-Royal until a year later, owing to the king's insistence that the marriage portion must first be paid to his banker. They sounded the death knell of Sir William's colonizing efforts (notwithstanding his later association with the Council of New England) and his hope of solvency, for by the end of 1632 the colony had been withdrawn and the king's warrant for £10,000 in compensation for his losses had been dishonoured. The monopoly of minting copper coins in Scotland, given at the time, failed to restore his finances. He died so heavily in debt that his creditors surrounded his death-bed in London, and denied him a peaceful burial in the church of Stirling.

He had enjoyed royal favour to the end so far

as the bestowal of titles was concerned (Viscount Stirling, Lord Alexander of Tullibody, 1630; Earl of Stirling, 1633; and Earl of Dovan [Devon], 1639), but this favour did not extend to saving his colony when put in the balance with the queen's marriage portion. On the other hand his close association with Charles in his attempt to foist episcopacy upon Scotland cost him the affection of many Scots who were neither his debtors nor his creditors.

As to his chief colonial venture, although two centuries were to elapse before unassisted Scottish emigration made New Scotland a reality, it cannot be regarded as a complete failure so long as the name Nova Scotia survives, and its citizens treasure their armorial achievement and their flag.

D. C. HARVEY

Champlain, *Works* (Biggar), VI, 50, 210. [Sir William Alexander], *The Earl of Stirling's register of royal letters, relative to the affairs of Scotland and Nova Scotia from 1615 to 1635*, ed. C. Rogers (2v., Edinburgh, 1885). *Mémoires des commissaires*, II, 193–276 *et passim*, and *Memorials of the English and French commissaries*, I, 38–43, 114, 141–44, 552–68 *et passim*. PAC *Report*, *1884*, Note D, lx–lxii; *1912*, 21–53. PRO, CSP, *Col.*, *1574–1660*. *Royal letters, charters, and tracts* (Laing).

DNB. G. P. Insh, *Scottish colonial schemes, 1620–1686* (Glasgow, 1922). Henry Kirke, *The first English conquest of Canada* (2d ed.; London, 1908). McGrail, *Alexander* (argues that the settlement of Port-Royal occurred in 1628, rather than 1629).

ALEXANDER, SIR WILLIAM, the younger, eldest son of Sir WILLIAM ALEXANDER, Earl of Stirling, founder of a Scottish colony at Port-Royal (Annapolis Royal, N.S.); b. *c.* 1602; d. 18 May 1638.

The younger Alexander was educated at Glasgow University, where Regent Blair remembered him as "my best beloved scholar." After his graduation in 1623 he entered the public service and was knighted 22 March 1627. Two months later he went on a privateering expedition with the larger of two ships which his father was preparing for New Scotland. In June he returned to Dumbarton with a prize, the *St. Lawrence of Lubec*, loaded with salt. The two ships lay at Dumbarton from June 1627 to 26 March 1628, while Alexander recruited colonists and secured supplies, after which they set out for Newfoundland, the River of Canada (St. Lawrence), and New Scotland. Alexander's route thereafter is uncertain and can be deduced only indirectly from his father's correspondence, in which it appears that he left a colony of "70 men and twa weemen" near Canada. It is probable that he joined forces with the KIRKES after they had captured the supply ships of the Compagnie de la Nouvelle-France in the summer of 1628, some of which supplies they left with Alexander's colonists at Gaspé or Tadoussac (Insh, *Scottish colonial schemes*, 225). (The assumption is that Alexander picked up these colonists before going to Port de la Baleine.)

On 4 Feb. 1628/29 Alexander, the Kirkes, and others obtained a monopoly of the trade to Canada. While the Kirkes went off to capture Quebec, Alexander joined forces with Sir James STEWART, Lord Ochiltree, helped him build a fort at Port de la Baleine (now Baleine) in Cape Breton, and then, under the guidance of CLAUDE DE SAINT-ÉTIENNE de La Tour, proceeded to Port-Royal. Here, in the summer of 1629, Alexander built a new fort in which he decided to pass the winter, sending back his ship for additional supplies and colonists. He also dispatched Claude de la Tour with an agreement for his father, Sir William, to sign, the terms of which conferred the title of knight-baronet and a large grant of land on Claude and his son CHARLES DE SAINT-ÉTIENNE de La Tour, in return for their assistance and allegiance. This agreement, slightly modified, was duly signed by Alexander's father 30 April 1630.

However, when Sir William returned to London that autumn, leaving Sir George Home in charge at Port-Royal, he reported that half the colonists had died during the previous winter. Claude de La Tour, moreover, having been unable to win over his son to the British cause, had lost the support of the Scots at Port-Royal, and had been induced by his son to return to his former French allegiance. Finding that Charles I was about to surrender the colony, Sir William did not return to Port-Royal. After the Treaty of Saint-Germain-en-Laye in 1632, the Scottish colony came to an end and the colonists were transported to England in the *Saint-Jean*, one of the ships which had brought Isaac de RAZILLY and French colonists to repossess Port-Royal.

Alexander continued for the rest of his life to be the loyal support of his father. In 1635 he was admitted as one of the extraordinary lords of the session, following his father's resignation, and in the same year he was appointed a member of the council of the New England company. In 1637 he was made deputy secretary of state for Scotland, with a salary of £300 per annum. Unlike his father, however, he was solvent at the time of his death, which occurred suddenly in London, 18 May 1638. He left only one son, a child of six, who, two years later, enjoyed for a few brief months the title and estates of his grandfather, the Earl of Stirling.

D. C. HARVEY

In addition to the references under Sir William Alexander, Earl of Stirling, see Couillard Després, Saint-Étienne de La Tour.

ALFONSE, JEAN. See FONTENEAU

ALLART, GERMAIN (baptized **Théodore**), Recollet priest, bishop; b. 1618 at Sézanne; d. 1685 at Vence.

He joined the Recollets of the province of Paris, where he made his profession on 22 Feb. 1637. He subsequently became reader in theology. Later he was, in succession, guardian at Corbeil in 1648 and 1649, at Rouen in 1650, definitor of his province from 1654 to 1657, and guardian of the monastery at Saint-Denys from 1657 to 1659. On three occasions, on 10 Aug. 1680, on 18 Nov. 1668, and on 4 May 1678, he was elected provincial of the province of Paris; he did not complete the last triennium, and resigned on 28 June 1679. Meanwhile he had governed the province of Saint-Antoine d'Arras from 1674 to 1677.

It was Allart who re-established the Recollets in New France after they were obliged in 1629 to leave the colony. In 1669 Louis XIV had asked him to send three religious there. A shipwreck off the coast of Portugal forced the missionaries to postpone their departure until the following year. This time the king ordered Father Allart to go himself, taking four religious with him. The provincial left La Rochelle at the end of May 1670, along with Intendant TALON, Fathers Gabriel de LA RIBOURDE, Simple Landon* and Hilarion Guénin*, Brothers Luc FRANÇOIS, who was a deacon, and Anselme (or Ignace) Bardou*, a lay-brother. When they arrived at Quebec on 18 August of that year, the population had a warm and appreciative welcome in store for them. Bishop Laval* turned over to Father Allart the house belonging to the Recollet order, but the provincial, after careful consideration, decided to build a new residence on the site of the old one. He then named Father de La Ribourde commissioner and first superior of the monastery. Governor RÉMY de Courcelle graciously consented to accept the office of first apostolic syndic of the Recollets. By December 1670, Father Allart was back in Paris.

Marie de l'Incarnation [see GUYART], who knew him at Quebec, was able to say of him and of the Recollets, "They are very zealous religious, whom the provincial [Father Allart], himself an outstanding man among them and possessing eminent qualities, has come in person to establish here." Intendant Talon for his part wrote to the king, "Father Germain Allart, the provincial, has conducted himself so judiciously and prudently during his stay that he has earned the esteem of even those persons who seemed as if they would only with difficulty be able to tolerate his presence. The establishment he has founded is taking good shape but he needs the King's generosity to maintain it."

In actual fact, Father Allart always enjoyed the king's favour; the great docility he displayed in carrying out the monarch's orders may perhaps be the explanation of this. On 13 April 1662, Louis XIV ordered him to join 11 Recollet monasteries in the Netherlands, which had recently been conquered by France, to the province of Saint-Denys. The proposal lacked any legal basis, but it was the king's wish and the army was ready to enforce the command. In 1666 the sovereign asked Father Allart, then guardian of the Paris monastery, to give spiritual assistance to the inhabitants of Dunkirk, who had been decimated by the plague. Without even waiting for his provincial's permission, the superior sent several religious to the town. In 1671, again at the king's request, he founded the monastery at Versailles.

On 10 Feb. 1675, Father Allart was elected commissioner-general of the three new custodies located in Flanders: Saint-Hubert, Saint-Pierre d'Alcantara, and Sainte-Famille. On 26 Sept. 1676, he was named commissioner of all the provinces of Recollets, Observants, and Cordeliers situated in France.

In recognition of his remarkable qualities and as a reward for his services, the king named Father Allart to the bishopric of Vence in June 1681. He was consecrated in the Recollet church in Paris on 12 July. In 1685 he took part in the Assembly of the Clergy, and died at Vence on 4 December of that year.

G.-M. DUMAS

Correspondance de Talon, *APQ Rapport, 1930–31*, 126f. Marie Guyart de l'Incarnation, *Lettres* (Richaudeau), II, 442. Le Clercq, *First establishment of the faith* (Shea), I, 12–13; II, 18, 68, 70–71, 99. Sixte Le Tac, *Histoire chronologique de la Nouvelle-France, ou Canada depuis sa découverte (mil cinq cents quatre) jusques en l'an mil six cents trente deux*, éd. Eugène Réveillaud (Paris, 1888), 123, 200.

Gosselin, *Vie de Mgr de Laval*, 183. M. Prévost, "Germain Allart," *DBF*, II (1936), 134–35. Antoine de Sérent, "Germain Allart," *Dictionnaire d'histoire et de géographie ecclésiastiques*, éd. Alfred Baudrillart et al. (14v., en cours de publication, Paris, 1912–60), II.

Allemand

ALLEMAND (Lalemand), PIERRE, pilot, cartographer, explorer, fur-trader; b. *c.* 1662 at Saint-Sauveur-de-Nuaillé (Charente-Maritime), son of Claude Allemand and Marie Mandet; d. 1691 at Quebec.

It seems that Allemand had the opportunity of crossing the Atlantic at least a number of times before settling finally in New France. We have little information, however, about his youth and his first voyages. In the 1681 census he is mentioned as living at Quebec and being 18 years old.

In 1682–83, Pierre Allemand took part as a pilot in an expedition to Hudson Bay directed jointly by Radisson* and CHOUART Des Groseilliers. This expedition had the financial backing of Charles Aubert* de La Chesnaye. The two ships, which had left Percé 11 July 1682, did not return to Quebec until the end of October of the following year, bearing English prisoners and a substantial quantity of furs. Among the prisoners was John BRIDGAR, the governor of Port Nelson.

In 1684 Allemand again served as a pilot, on a second expedition to Hudson Bay, led by Claude de Bermen* de La Martinière. The log of this expedition was kept by the chaplain, Father Antoine Silvy*, a Jesuit. Allemand was busy fur-trading during the whole winter, was sent as an envoy to treat with the English commander Bridgar, who was at the mouth of the Hayes (Sainte-Thérèse) River, and obtained from the Indians the most varied information, which was to enable him to draw up a map of the region. It was on his return from the voyage, 13 Nov. 1685, that he married, at Quebec, Louise Douaire de Bondy, granddaughter of Éléonore de GRANDMAISON and François de Chavigny. In November 1686, Governor Brisay* de Denonville, in a letter to the minister for the Marine, praised Allemand and called him a "very fine fellow," stressing the necessity of having in New France a greater number of pilots of his calibre. Allemand, having been unwell since his return from this second voyage to Hudson Bay, had not been able to complete the map that Denonville promised to send to France "at the first opportunity."

At the time Denonville wrote this letter to the minister, Pierre Allemand had already come back from another voyage to Hudson Bay, undertaken in 1686 with an expedition made up of some 100 men under the command of the Chevalier Pierre de TROYES. According to the log of the expedition, Allemand acted as "quartermaster," and was "a person of great usefulness, whose inventiveness and activity were of great help in this undertaking, where he served as a good canoeist, a soldier, a pilot and a geographer." This expedition followed the route of the Rivière des Outaouais (Ottawa), and it was anticipated that Allemand would be able to take command of an English ship if the French succeeded in capturing one, which occurred at Fort Charles (Rupert) early in July. Allemand was back at Montreal at the end of October.

Allemand then began the composition of a *Mémoire*, in which he proposed to continue the hydrographic map of the St. Lawrence Gulf and River that had already been started by Jean Deshayes*. To carry out surveys, he requested a corvette of 30–40 tons. He likewise volunteered to teach navigation to the young men of the colony, in order to ensure its defence and develop its fishing and its fur trade. This *Mémoire* was forwarded to the minister for the Marine on 6 Nov. 1687 by Governor Denonville and Intendant Bochart* Champigny.

In the spring of 1688, Pierre Allemand himself went to France, and, using as references the names of the governor, the intendant, and Bishop Saint-Vallier [La Croix*], he presented to Seignelay a second *Mémoire* composed in roughly the same terms, but it was no more successful than the previous attempts. That same year, Allemand was associated with a certain Landron in the operation of a brick-works. During the summer of 1689, he escorted Bishop Saint-Vallier on his rounds in Acadia and Newfoundland. Finally, still in 1689, a grant of land was made to him, as well as to Charles Aubert de La Chesnaye, François VIENNAY-Pachot, François-Mathieu Martin* de Lino, and a few others, in order that they could fish in the Gulf of St. Lawrence and off Newfoundland.

It can be seen, therefore, that Allemand had a quite varied career, in which illegal undertakings, and specifically smuggling, were not perhaps unknown.

On 27 May 1691, Pierre Allemand died at Quebec, when he was only about 29 years old. He had had five children. His widow married again, in 1693, her second husband being Nicolas Pinault*.

F. GRENIER

Chevalier de Troyes, *Journal* (Caron). *Documents relating to Hudson Bay* (Tyrrell). HBRS, XXI (Rich). *Ord. comm.* (P.-G. Roy), II, 49–53, 56. *Relation par lettres de l'Amérique septentrionale, années 1709 et 1710,* éd. Camille de Rochemonteix (Paris, 1904). P.-G. Roy, *Inv. concessions*, IV; "Le pilote canadien Pierre Allemand," dans *Les petites choses de notre histoire* (3e série, Lévis, 1922), 145–54) (includes extracts from Allemand's *Mémoires*); "Pierre Allemand," *BRH,* XXI (1915), 129–33.

ALLET, ANTOINE D', Sulpician priest and secretary of the Abbé Queylus [*see* THUBIÈRES];

b. *c.* 1634 in Paris, in the parish of Saint-Sulpice; d. some time after 1693 in France.

Allet, having come to the attention of M. Olier, at that time his parish priest, entered the Compagnie de Saint-Sulpice. While still a deacon, he came to Canada in 1657, as secretary of Abbé Queylus. If, as several authors claim, Allet was ordained on 15 Aug. 1659—which we strongly doubt, for he was at Quebec on 11 September of the same year—he must have gone to France in the autumn of 1658. It is tolerably certain that he was not ordained at Quebec: the chronicles of the period would not have passed over in silence what would have been the first ordination in this country. In any event, during the winter 1659–60 Allet stayed at the Hôtel-Dieu in Quebec. It was only on 27 April 1660 that his health allowed him to sail for Montreal. But the very next year he returned to France, probably with Abbé Queylus, who set out on 22 Oct. 1661. Allet landed again in Canada in 1668, together with Abbé Queylus. He continued to serve as the Abbé's secretary until 1671, when they both left Montreal and Canada for good. Back in France, Allet spent some years at Mont-Valérien, near Paris, until he was appointed, around 1683, confessor to the Filles de la Croix at Ruel. He was still living in 1693. He is the author of two memoirs on the Jesuits in Canada, which are reproduced in the works of Antoine Arnauld.

ANDRÉ VACHON

[Antoine Arnauld], *Œuvres de messire Antoine Arnauld* . . . (50 v., Paris et Lausanne, 1775–83), XXXIV. *JJ* (Laverdière et Casgrain), *passim*. Henri Gauthier, *La Compagnie de Saint-Sulpice au Canada* (Montréal, 1912), 23.

ALLOUEZ, CLAUDE, priest, Jesuit, missionary and explorer; b. 6 June 1622 at Saint-Didier-en-Forez; d. in the night of 27/28 Aug. 1689 in Miami territory, near Niles, Michigan.

Claude Allouez was 17 when, on 22 Sept. 1639, he entered the noviciate at Toulouse. He studied rhetoric (1641–42) and philosophy (1642–45) at the Collège in Billom, where he then became a teacher (1645–51); he studied theology at Toulouse (1651–55) and took his third probationary year at Rodez (1655–56); finally he was a preacher at Rodez until his departure for Canada.

The *Journal des Jésuites* notes his arrival at Quebec on 11 July 1658. At first he devoted himself to the study of the Huron and Algonkin languages. On 19 Sept. 1660, he left Quebec to take up an appointment as superior of the residence at Trois-Rivières. In 1663, he was named by Bishop François de Laval* vicar general of that part of the diocese of Quebec that today constitutes the central region of the United States. As a result of a misunderstanding he failed to set out in 1664, but was more successful the following year. This first trip, which is recalled for us by the *Relation* for 1667, was the most arduous of all, and it enables us to gauge the spiritual stature of Father Allouez. Scorned by the Ottawas, who did not want him among them, and abandoned on the shore of a lake as if he were a cumbersome dead weight, he took refuge in prayer: "In this abandoned state I withdrew into the woods, and, after thanking God for making me so acutely sensible of my slight worth, confessed before his divine Majesty that I was only a useless burden on this earth. My prayer ended, I returned to the water's edge, where I found the disposition of that Savage who had repulsed me with such contempt entirely changed; for, unsolicited, he invited me to enter his Canoe, which I did with much alacrity, fearing he would change his mind." The remainder of the voyage still held numerous hardships and humiliations in store for him; he was an awkward paddler, and was obliged to carry unaided over the 36 portages all his personal effects: some books, a portable altar, and a two-year supply of wine for masses.

On 1 October he arrived at Pointe du Saint Esprit, and made it the base for his apostolate. The humble birch-bark chapel that he erected there was the only one in existence west of Georgian Bay, and even west of Montreal. He gathered together the Christian Hurons who had not seen a Black Robe since the disaster of 1649. He taught the pagans of some ten nations who lived in those parts. In 1667, he went to Lake Nipigon to comfort the Christian Nipissings. He has the honour of having celebrated the first mass within the boundaries of the present diocese of Fort William. That same year, and again two years later, in 1669, he went down to Quebec in search of apostolic workers. But he did not linger there, and a few days after his arrival, he was already on the way back.

When, in 1671, DAUMONT de Saint-Lusson took possession of the expanses of the west in the name of the king of France, it was Father Allouez who delivered the address for the occasion. No one was better qualified to do so, both because of the prestige he enjoyed among the Indian nations and because of the fluency with which he spoke their languages and the way in which his kind of eloquence delighted his hearers. Some idea of Father Allouez's achievements can be had if one considers that he scoured in every direction the region around the Great Lakes: Huron, Superior, Erie, and Michigan; 3,000 miles of wild

Amantacha

country throughout which was scattered his nomadic flock: 23 nations of differing races, languages, and customs, according to the testimony of his superior, Father Claude DABLON. It is estimated that in the course of his 24 years of missionary apostolate, he personally baptized some 10,000 neophytes.

Father Allouez's written work is extensive and important. The *Relations* for the years 1667 to 1676 have preserved for us considerable extracts from his diary. One document however has been attributed to him which is not entirely from his hand. In his *Établissements et découvertes des Français*, Pierre Margry, on the authority of Father Dablon, published a document entitled "Sentiments du P. Claude Allouez." These notes, in Father Allouez's handwriting, were found in his papers after his death and sent to the superior at Quebec. The latter attributed them to Father Allouez and this attribution has persisted until the present. A careful study, however, allows us to question the attribution to Father Allouez of this work in its entirety. Almost all these notes are found, at times word for word, in the "Divers sentiments et avis" that conclude the *Relation* for 1635. Father Allouez had copied this document in his own hand, as it was important for its spiritual and apostolic value; and he thus had as his model to the very end of his life the portrait of the ideal missionary. Father Dablon can be forgiven for not having had a clear memory in 1690 of these texts from the *Relation* for 1635. But his mistake of attribution is the finest tribute he could pay to Father Allouez: that of having been the living confirmation of the essential characteristics of the perfect missionary.

A contemporary of and co-worker with those apostolic giants Jacques MARQUETTE and Claude Dablon, Claude Allouez is not their inferior in any respect. It has even been asserted, and this is our view, that he was the greatest missionary of the generation following that of the holy martyrs. "In Wisconsin," writes Father Gilbert Garraghan, "the earliest missionary endeavors on behalf of the Indian gather around the name of Claude Allouez. On Chequamegon Bay near the modern Ashland, at De Pere, and at various points in the interior of the state, he set up mission-posts that became so many starting-points for the civilizing influences that he sought to bring to bear upon the children of the forest. His appointment to the post of vicar general by saintly Bishop Laval, July 21, 1663, marked in a way the first organization of the Church in mid-America. From his pen came the earliest published account of the Illinois Indians, who were to give their name to the future state. No other figure at the dawn of Wisconsin history rises to a more commanding height. If the name of Jacques Marquette stands apart in the fervor of its appeal to sentiment and the historical imagination, the name of Claude Allouez deserves to be remembered as that of the first organizer of Catholicism in what is now the heart of the United States."

In the United States, and especially in Wisconsin, Father Allouez's memory has always been venerated. In 1899 the Wisconsin Historical Society erected a monument to him at De Pere. It is of interest to note that the then secretary of the Society was Reuben Gold Thwaites, the peerless editor of the collection of *Jesuit Relations and allied documents*.

LÉON POULIOT

Découvertes et établissements des Français (Margry), I, 58–72. *JR* (Thwaites), *passim*. *JJ* (Laverdière et Casgrain).
Campbell, *Pioneer priests*, I, 119, 121, 147–64. Delanglez, *Jolliet*. G. J. Garraghan, *The Jesuits of the middle United States* (3v., New York, 1938), I, 3–4. Francis Nelligan, "The visit of Father Allouez to Lake Nipigon in 1667," CCHA *Report*, *1956*, 41–52. Léon Pouliot, "La part du P. Claude Allouez dans les 'sentiments' qui lui sont attribués," *RHAF*, XV (1961–62), 379–95. Rochemonteix, *Les Jésuites et la Nouvelle-France au XVIIe siècle*, II, 353f.

AMANTACHA, baptized as **Louis de Sainte-Foi**, a Huron educated in France, later a friend and aide of the Jesuit missionaries; b. 1610? in the Huron country; d. probably 1636 in the Iroquois country.

Amantacha's father, Soranhes, lived in Teanaostaiaë (Mission of Saint-Joseph II) and was an early and active participant in the fur trade. When Father Nicolas VIEL was in the Huron country, Soranhes promised him that he would let his son live with the French and be educated by them. In this, as in his other dealings with the missionaries, he appears to have been motivated largely by the desire to gain favour with the French authorities at Quebec. In 1626 he took Amantacha, then aged 16, to Quebec where he entrusted him to the care of Father Joseph LE CARON. Several ships were willing to take the boy to France and a dispute as to his guardianship broke out between the Recollets, Jesuits, and ÉMERY DE CAËN. Finally Father Joseph gave over the Recollets' claim to the Jesuits.

Amantacha was taken to France by de Caën and once there was secured for the Jesuits by M. de Ventadour. He was baptized in the cathedral of Rouen, his godparents being the Duc de Longueville and Mme de Villars. A rumour that he was the son of the king of Canada attracted a large crowd to the baptism. He remained for two years in France where he was educated by the Jesuits and learned to read and write. On his return to Canada in 1628 his ship—one of the fleet of the Compagnie des Cent-Associés under the command of the admiral ROQUEMONT de Brison—was seized by the British. Hearing that he was the son of a native king and thinking that he might be useful in the future, the English kept Amantacha when they released the other passengers. He was taken to Quebec in 1629, but freed when the KIRKES discovered his real status. He then returned to the Huron country with Étienne BRÛLÉ.

Following their return, he sought to assist CHAMPLAIN and the Jesuits in their dealings with his people. He visited Quebec in the summers of 1632 and 1633, exhorting his people to trade once more with the French and showing some interest in religion, although the Jesuits had mixed feelings about his conduct. Amantacha, anxious to gain prestige among his people as a warrior, participated in their raids on the Iroquois. In 1634 he and his father were in a party of warriors ambushed by the enemy. His father escaped to the Neutral nation, but Amantacha was captured and managed to get away only after the Iroquois had cut off a finger. Back in the Huron country he did much to help the Jesuits, while his father, again hoping to win French favour in trade, attributed his escape to God and expressed the wish that his whole family be converted. The Jesuits went to his village and spent some time instructing them, but little came of this.

During holy week 1636 Amantacha visited the Jesuits. Then he left with his uncle on a raid into the Iroquois country from which he did not return. He was apparently captured, and while some members of his family believed that he continued to live with a Mohawk family, most were of the opinion that he had been killed. His father, Soranhes, died unbaptized on 24 Aug. 1637. He is said to have committed suicide through grief over the loss of his son.

BRUCE G. TRIGGER

JR (Thwaites), *passim* (gives details of Amantacha's later life). Le Clercq, *First establishment of the faith* (Shea). Sagard, *Histoire du Canada* (Tross), IV (the best primary source on Amantacha's early life). Desrosiers, *Iroquoisie*, 135.

AMBAULT, JACQUES DUCHESNEAU DE LA DOUSSINIÈRE ET D'. *See* DUCHESNEAU

AMIOT (Amyot), CHARLES, fur-trader and merchant; b. 26 Aug. 1636 at Quebec, son of Philippe Amiot and Anne Convent, buried there on 10 Dec. 1669.

He was educated at the Jesuit college and when he was barely 14 years old he accompanied Father BRESSANI as a servant on a trip to the Huron country. On 2 May 1660 Amiot married Geneviève de Chavigny, by whom he had three children. He opened a store at Quebec, at the foot of the Cap aux Diamants, on a site which his father-in-law had given him. He was then a merchant interested in eel fishing and in the fur trade. It was his travels among the Papinachois that gave him something of a reputation during his lifetime. On those occasions he accompanied Father Henri Nouvel*, a Jesuit who was born in 1621 or 1624 at Pézenas, in the department of Hérault, and who landed at Quebec in the summer of 1662.

A number of historians have confused the dates and routes of Father Nouvel's and Charles Amiot's journeys. According to the *Relations* they made their first voyage from April to June 1663, and a second from November 1663 to April 1664. They left Quebec in November 1663, and presumably went to the Île Verte and the Île aux Basques, then to the Île Saint-Barnabé, finally spending the winter with a band of Algonkins in the neighbourhood of Lake Matapédia or Lake Mitis. Amiot returned to the Île aux Basques in March 1664 and went down to Quebec, where he arrived on 5 April, whilst Father Nouvel remained on the island with his flock.

On 21 April 1664 Father Nouvel crossed to the north shore. He waited near Tadoussac for Father DRUILLETTES, who arrived only on 3 May. The latter decided to go and serve the Indians of the Saguenay. For their part, Father Nouvel and Charles Amiot, the the sole Frenchmen to accompany Druillettes, left Tadoussac the same day (3 May) and penetrated overland, with a band of Papinachois, as far as the river Peritibistokou (des Outardes), which they reached on 14 May. The travellers camped there until 2 June, went upstream for a whole day, and made a portage that brought them to the river Manikouaganistikou (Manicouagan). They got to Lake Sainte-Barnabé (Manicouagan) on 9 June. A band of Papinachois who had never met a white man was waiting for them there. The missionary preached the gospel and the traders bartered furs. Father Nouvel named the spot the Saint-Barnabé mission. The expedition returned to Quebec on 30 June 1664.

In November Father Nouvel again left Quebec for Tadoussac. This time Amiot apparently stayed at Quebec. Father Nouvel spent the winter of 1664–65 in the Lake St. John region, and returned in the spring. At the end of May 1665 he went back to the Saint-Barnabé mission together

Amiot

with two Frenchmen whom the *Relation* identifies as Amiot and Couture*. Father Godbout specifies that "for this last voyage among the nations of the north, he [Amiot] had taken Guillaume Couture, Noël Jérémie, and Sébastien Prouvereau, on 28 May 1665." They had arranged to meet the Papinachois at the mouth of the Manicouagan. But they had to go up the river without a guide, for the Indians did not appear at the rendezvous. They returned to Quebec on 26 July.

Father Nouvel returned to the north shore regularly until 1670, but the *Relations* make no further mention of Amiot's being with him. Perhaps the latter preferred to stay at Quebec with his family and attend to his general store. Amiot died on 10 Dec. 1669. "In consideration of the services rendered by the late Amiot in this country," TALON, on 3 Nov. 1672, made over to his widow the Vincelotte fief, in what is now the parish of Cap-Saint-Ignace. His son Charles-Joseph* inherited the fief and adopted its name. Charles Amiot was the brother of JEAN and MATHIEU AMIOT.

Father Nouvel had a much longer career. In the succeeding years he exercised his ministry between Michilimackinac and Sault Ste. Marie.

JEAN HAMELIN

JR (Thwaites) is the sole source of information on the expeditions of Nouvel and Amiot. For an exhaustive biography of Amiot see Godbout, "Nos ancêtres," APQ *Rapport, 1951–53*, 492. See also P.-G. Roy, "Les Amyot sous le régime français," *BRH*, XXIII (1917), 161–68.

AMIOT (Amyot), JEAN, interpreter and indentured employee of the Jesuits among the Hurons; son of Philippe Amiot and of Anne Convent, who came from the neighbourhood of Soissons around 1635, and brother of MATHIEU and CHARLES AMIOT, who were also associated with the Jesuit missionaries; b. probably in France about 1625; d. 1648.

Jean Amiot spent several years in the Huron country, and seems to have lived at Trois-Rivières from 1645 on. The Indians called him "Antaïok." In 1647 he outran and captured an Iroquois who had taken part in the martyrdom of Father Jean de BRÉBEUF. He was a remarkable athlete; in a tournament at Quebec he beat all the young Indians who tried to race against him, either on foot or on snowshoes. On 23 May 1648, when he was about to get married, Jean Amiot was drowned off Trois-Rivières with a companion, François MARGUERIE. His body was carried down by the current and recovered on 10 June opposite the Saint-Joseph de Sillery mission, where the burial took place. His possessions at Trois-Rivières were sold to JACQUES LENEUF de La Poterie on 18 Oct. 1649.

The 1648 *Relation* states that Amiot and Marguerie "were much regretted in that region, both for their virtue and for their knowledge of the languages. . . . They were both of them brave and skilful, and, what is more estimable still, they lived a most blameless life, according to everybody's opinion."

HONORIUS PROVOST

AJQ, Greffe de Guillaume Audouart, 18 oct. 1649. *JR* (Thwaites). *JJ* (Laverdière et Casgrain).
BRH, XI (1905), 217; XXIII (1917), 161. Godbout, "Nos ancêtres," APQ *Rapport, 1951–53*, 488.

AMIOT (Amyot), *dit* **Villeneuve, MATHIEU,** *donné*, interpreter, seigneur; b. between 1627 and 1629 probably near Chartres (Orléanais), son of Philippe Amiot and Anne Convent; d. 18 Nov. 1688 at Quebec.

His father, who came originally from the neighbourhood of Soissons, was at Quebec from the summer of 1635 on. Mathieu, like his brother JEAN, was for some years an interpreter for the Jesuits; he worked in their house at Trois-Rivières and perhaps also in the Huron country. Then he became a settler, and during the remainder of his life he managed to accumulate a fairly sizable number of properties. Thus, in 1649, Governor LOUIS D'AILLEBOUST made him a grant of land at Trois-Rivières; in addition, on the occasion of his marriage on 22 Oct. 1650, Marie Miville brought him as her dowry a property in the town of Quebec; in 1661 the Jesuits granted him a portion of land at Sillery, where he built a house for himself, whilst keeping his town residence; on 6 Sept. 1665 JEAN JUCHEREAU DE MAUR gave him an estate on Pointe Villeneuve, near Saint-Augustin de Portneuf, which he enlarged in 1677 and 1685; and on 3 Nov. 1672 TALON granted him another domain, as a fief and seigneury, at Pointe aux Bouleaux.

As his possessions increased, Mathieu became a more and more important person in the colony. A notable at Quebec, he had taken part in the election of a syndic in 1664, and three years later the king acceded to Talon's request to grant him letters of nobility. However, when these letters arrived in 1668 the intendant did not know whether he should have them registered in the Conseil Souverain of Quebec or in the Parlement of Paris. While awaiting the reply from Versailles he learned that Louis XIV had abolished all titles not yet registered (1669). Three other settlers had received letters of nobility at the same time as

Amiot. They or their descendants had them recognized despite the 1669 ruling. But as Amiot apparently made no claim in respect of his, they were finally annulled.

Villeneuve left his heirs more debts and worries than assets. In 1703 the debts encumbering the estate still amounted to 700 *livres*, and Marie Miville, who had sold the lands for 1,500 *livres*, had died (September 1702), a victim of the distress caused her by a lawsuit which her son Charles*, the eldest of her 15 children, had brought against her.

J. MONET

ASQ, Documents Faribault, 22, 104; Registre A, pp. 588–94. *Jug. et délib.*, *passim*. *Papier terrier de la Cie des I.O.* (P.-G. Roy), 42–44. P.-G. Roy, *Inv. concessions*, I, 276–78; II, 68: III, 4–6.
Lionel Audet-Lapointe, "Famille Amiot-Villeneuve," *BRH*, LX (1954), 121–35. Godbout, "Nos ancêtres," APQ *Rapport, 1951–53*, 488. P.-G. Roy, "Les Amyot sous le régime français," *BRH*, XXIII (1917), 164f.; "Mathieu Amiot Villeneuve," *BRH*, XXV (1919), 321–31.

AMISCOUECAN. *See* CHOMINA

AMOURS . *See* DAMOURS

AMYOT. *See* AMIOT

ANADABIJOU, Montagnais chief; fl. 1611.

It was probably Anadabijou's reputation as a "grand Sagamo" that led CHAMPLAIN and FRANÇOIS GRAVÉ Du Pont to seek out his cabin "à la pointce de Sainct Matthieu" three days after their arrival at Tadoussac 24 May 1603. With some 80 or 100 of his people, Anadabijou was celebrating a recent victory by an army of 1,000 Montagnais, Algonkins, and Etchemins warriors over the Iroquois at the mouth of the Iroquois (Richelieu) River. This was an important event, for these tribes were now moving towards the defensive in their relations with their ancient enemies, the Iroquois, who were returning to the St. Lawrence valley after their expulsion *c.* 1570–1603.

Expressions of friendship were voiced by both French and Indian. One of the two Indians whom Gravé had previously taken to France spoke of his experiences there and of the good reception granted him by the king of France, giving assurance that the king wished to people their country and would help in vanquishing their enemies. Anadabijou shared the ceremonial pipe with Champlain and Gravé, and expressed his appreciation of these sentiments. He pointed out "the advantage and profit they [the Indians] might receive from His said Majesty." This is the first recorded meeting where an alliance is suggested between the French and the Algonkins, the Montagnais, and the Etchemins against their common enemy the Iroquois, a policy which was pursued by the French, resulting in a century of French-Iroquois conflict.

The victory feast continued with eight or ten kettles filled with moose, bear, seal, beaver, and quantities of wild fowl. On the following day Anadabijou moved his people by canoe to Tadoussac where, about two weeks later, the feast was resumed with their allies, the Algonkins and Etchemins.

Champlain, on one occasion held discourse with Anadabijou on the subject of religion, discussing the nature of God, the origin of man, and prayer.

Later the same summer, on Anadabijou's recommendation, Gravé was given the son of BEGOURAT to take to France, with admonitions from Anadabijou to use him well and to let him see what the two above-mentioned Indians had seen.

On 12 July 1611, a party of Algonkins arriving at the Lachine Rapids offered to a son of Anadabijou a present to comfort him for the recent death of his father. In later years Anadabijou's son, MIRISTOU, stated that his father had "maintained peace among the other nations and the French."

ELSIE MCLEOD JURY

Champlain, *Works* (Biggar), *passim*. Desrosiers, *Iroquoisie*, 23–24.

ANDERSON, THOMAS, clergyman in the HBC's service; d. 1696.

Engaged in 1693, he was sent to York Fort and after only a year there was taken prisoner when the French under Pierre Le Moyne* d'Iberville captured the fort. Anderson, being learned in Latin, was called upon to write the terms of capitulation. The interpreter on the opposing side was the Jesuit, Father Gabriel Marest*. Evidently Anderson died while still a prisoner near Dinant, France, in 1696. Whether he was the Thomas Anderson who graduated B.A. from Cambridge in 1684 and M.A. in 1688 has not been established.

MAUD M. HUTCHESON

HBRS, XX (Rich and Johnson).

ANDIGNÉ DE GRANDFONTAINE, HECTOR D', officer in the Carignan-Salières regiment (1665–68), governor of Acadia (1670–3); baptized

Andigné de Grandfontaine

17 May 1627 at Ruillé-Froid-Fonds in Mayenne, son of Hector and Anne d'Andigné de Grandfontaine; d. 6 July 1696 at Brest.

Grandfontaine belonged to a very old noble family from Anjou. Some time before 1565 his paternal grandfather, Gaston d'Andigné, had acquired the property of Grandfontaine of which his descendants took over the name also. The youngest of four sons in a family which included many soldiers, Hector naturally entered upon a military career and became a knight of Malta.

On 17 Aug. 1665 he arrived at Quebec as a captain commanding a company of the Carignan-Salières regiment. The following October he supervised the building of a road along the Richelieu between Fort Saint-Louis (Chambly) and Fort Sainte-Thérèse. After a winter at Quebec, he took part in the campaign led by Prouville de Tracy and Rémy de Courcelle against the Mohawks and on 17 October signed the report of the taking-over of their territory (*BRH*, XIII (1907), 350–51). Talon recommended him among "the officers who deserve to be singled out for recognition," and probably took him back to France with him in the autumn of 1668.

The following year, when consideration was being given to forming companies of troops for the defence of Canada, Grandfontaine, along with four former officers of the Carignan regiment offered his services to raise a company, with the intention of acquiring a land grant and settling down in Canada. His offer was accepted, but instead of returning to the St. Lawrence, Grandfontaine was destined to go to Acadia, whose restitution to France, which had been decided by the Treaty of Breda (1667), had been held up until then by Sir Thomas Temple's opposition. He was commissioned by the king on 22 July 1669 to receive this restitution, but he was unable to leave immediately. The following spring (20 February), he was appointed governor for three years and embarked upon the *Saint-Sébastien* at La Rochelle with his company. He was the first French governor of Acadia after the English occupation of 1654–70.

As the English governor, Temple, resided at Boston, Grandfontaine went there and was courteously received. He presented the letters from Charles II and Louis XIV with which he had been supplied, and on 7 July 1670 he signed with Temple an agreement settling the conditions of the restitution. He then went to accept the return of Pentagouet by Richard Walker (17 July) and sent his lieutenant, Pierre de Joybert de Soulanges et de Marson, to take over the forts at Jemseg (27 August) and those at Port-Royal (Annapolis Royal, N.S.) and Port-La Tour (2 September).

While leaving him free to set up his principal post wherever he judged appropriate, his early instructions, drawn up by the intendant of Rochefort, Colbert de Terron, showed clearly a preference for Pentagouet, in order to hinder the encroachments of the English. Grandfontaine accordingly established his capital there. The choice of this site, lying in disputed territory and separated by the Bay of Fundy from the main settlement at Port-Royal, would create serious difficulties; but Grandfontaine was only obeying the instructions that he had received.

As soon as he had settled in, he dispatched a report to the king and the minister, sending them several maps and memoranda. In his reply of 11 Mar. 1671 Colbert laid down a very precise programme, reminding him that he was to act only upon the orders of the governor and the intendant of Canada. This subordination to multiple authorities, in France and in Canada, made action on his part difficult, and it was not easy to please all these superiors. Intendant Talon was fortunately interested in Acadia, and there was consequently a serious and concerted effort on both sides to take this colony in hand again and to develop it.

The most urgent task was to restore order and to meet the needs of the settlers. For twenty years the disputes among the heirs of Charles de Menou d'Aulnay, Emmanuel Le Borgne, and Charles de Saint-Étienne de La Tour, and the absence of a governor had given rise to a sort of anarchy. The population of Port-Royal, abandoned to its own resources, was managing to live off its crops and its herds, but lacked clothes and tools. Isolation had also developed the spirit of independence. Grandfontaine first revoked the authority of the seigneur Alexandre Le Borgne de Belle-Isle, whose misdemeanours had caused complaints, and enjoined the settlers to live in peace until a representative of the king could arrive to settle their disputes and lay down statutes for them. The supplies that he had brought from France and those that he obtained from Quebec or Boston provided for immediate needs. He also concerned himself with having boats built, while Talon asked for looms for the settlers.

The main effort was directed to populating the country. In addition to the soldiers and indentured employees who had arrived with the governor, the *Oranger* brought 60 passengers the following year, among them one woman and four girls, and the court paid 100 *livres* each for their passage and their setting-up. The soldiers seemed to like the country, for in the following years some 15 thought of settling there. It is impossible to

Andigné de Grandfontaine

determine exactly how many new settlers took up residence in Acadia at that time, but it was certainly the greatest number to arrive since the time of RAZILLY and d'Aulnay. Being in too exposed a position and provided with too little arable land, the settlement at Pentagouet did not last long, but several of its members were to be found later settled at Port-Royal and Beaubassin (Chignecto).

In order to provide better for the mutual defence of Acadia and Canada, Talon had conceived the plan of establishing a direct link between the Bay of Fundy and the St. Lawrence by opening an inland route and establishing a series of habitations as stopping-places. Two routes were available: the Kennebec or the Saint John River. To reconnoitre them Talon sent from Quebec his secretary PATOULET and two teams commanded by DAUMONT de Saint-Lusson and Louis de Niort* de La Noraye. For his part Grandfontaine sent two Frenchmen and two Indians in the direction of Quebec and established a first group of settlers at the portage at Kidiscuit. The route by the Kennebec to the Chaudière proved to be too difficult and not very dependable. Preference was given to the Saint John River route, which was already much used, and as early as 1672 the government of New France granted seigneuries along it to the Joybert brothers and to Jacques Potier* de Saint-Denis, while Martin d'APRENDESTIGUY, Sieur de Martignon, who had settled at the mouth of the river, was confirmed in his rights.

The minister, Colbert, had asked for an annual census of the population. Grandfontaine entrusted this survey to Father Laurent Molin, a Cordelier, parish priest of Port-Royal. This is the earliest extant list of Acadian settlers. It shows about 400 people living at Port-Royal, Cap de Sable, and on the east coast, but does not mention the new settlers at Pentagouet and on the Saint John River, so that in 1671 the total population of Acadia, including the garrisons, must have amounted to about 500 persons. This figure shows clearly the smallness of the colony.

The Treaty of Breda had decided only the question of the restitution of the forts, without fixing the boundaries of Acadia. Grandfontaine set these boundaries at the St. George River and flattered himself that by his honest dealings he could win for France the allegiance of the English settlers who were established on his side of the river. He sought to maintain the good relations with Boston which were necessary for him to obtain supplies. He bought a ketch from Temple, brought carpenters from New England, and granted fishing permits to ships from Boston. He endeavoured however to prevent English merchants from coming to barter for furs in French territory, had the fort at Pentagouet put back into shape, and maintained a garrison of about 30 men there, under the command of Jean-Vincent d'Abbadie* de Saint-Castin. Small detachments of about ten soldiers guarded the forts at Jemseg and Port-Royal. The only incident between the French and English was the capture of a French vessel coming from Jamaica, about which Grandfontaine sent his lieutenant to lodge complaints at Boston. The minister had also recommended that permanent fishing stations be set up, but Grandfontaine, busy establishing his settlers and reorganizing the colony, had no time to attend to the matter.

On the whole, Grandfontaine's brief governorship of Acadia was constructive. But his activity was hindered by serious disagreements with his lieutenant, Pierre Joybert de Marson, who complained about him. Moreover, Colbert de Terron accused him of being self-seeking. Yet Grandfontaine received only a small salary: 1,200 *livres* in 1670 and 2,400 the following year. It is possible that he engaged in commerce to add to his income and to meet the responsibilities of his office. We know for example that in 1672 famine raged at Pentagouet and that the governor had to send some men to spend the winter at Port-Royal.

Having been recalled 5 May 1673 and replaced by CHAMBLY, Grandfontaine returned to France the following December. Shortly afterwards he presented the intendant of Rochefort with a claim for 13,000 *livres* for expenses incurred during his service in Acadia. Terron, while he admitted that Grandfontaine had received funds from Rochefort for two years only and had kept the colony going for 36 months, refused to reimburse him, but suggested to the king that he be granted a post in the navy by way of consolation.

The ex-governor thus obtained employment at Rochefort, became a lieutenant-commander, then a ship's captain. He served on board the *Intrépide* in 1675 and took part in the expedition to Cayenne on board the *Glorieux* in 1676. He conducted himself bravely, was the first man to enter the town and was wounded in the arm. The following year he participated in the Tobago expedition against the Dutch and broke an arm, which he lost the use of for the rest of his life. Subsequently he lived at Brest and received an annual pension of 800 *livres*. He was included in the first list of Chevaliers de Saint-Louis in 1693, and died at Brest 6 July 1696 leaving no heirs.

RENÉ BAUDRY

Angibault

AE, Mém. et doc. Amérique, 5, f.277. Archives de la Mayenne (Laval), B. 2278–3291, *passim*. AN, Col., B, 2, f.571; 3, ff.19, 41, 55; C^{11D}, 1, ff.12, 139; 2, f.7; Marine, B², 10, f.38. BN, MS, Clairambault 866, ff.326, 363; 1306, f.153; Mélanges Colbert 167, ff.92, 186; 175, f.392; 176, ff.85, 103; MS Fr. 26541, 31233, 31567. Correspondance de Talon, APQ, *Rapport, 1930–31*. *Mémoires des commissaires*, I, xxj; II, 316–23, 325–26; IV, 288–89, 291, 303–5; and *Memorials of the English and French commissaries*, I, 24, 604–10 et passim. *BRH*, XXIII (1917), 57–58. Murdoch, *History of Nova-Scotia*, 145–53. Régis Roy et Malchelosse, *Le régiment de Carignan*.

ANGIBAULT *dit* **Champdoré, PIERRE,** ship's captain, member of the settlement in Acadia from 1604 to 1607 and in 1608.

In his poem Marc LESCARBOT called him a "naval captain" ("capitaine de marine") which seems like an exaggeration; in his *Histoire* he introduced him as the chief of navigation ("conducteur ès navigations"), entrusted with the command of the voyages ("la conduite des voyages"). In reality Champdoré's role would seem to have been limited to that of a simple ship's captain: Samuel de CHAMPLAIN for his part placed him on the same footing as Cramolet, "ship's master" ("maistre de barque"). Champlain, who lived in the same dwelling as Champdoré on the Île Sainte-Croix, blamed him on three occasions for being guilty of bad seamanship which imperilled the explorers' lives; a good carpenter for building ships, wrote Champlain, but in no way fitted for sailing them, he was obstinate and "little versed in the art of navigation." After an accident in April 1606 FRANÇOIS GRAVÉ Du Pont had Champdoré put in manacles until he could have him tried in France. However, as another boat had to be built, Champdoré was released for a time; as soon as the job was finished, he was put in manacles again. Another accident occurred; Champdoré saved the situation, and at his comrades' entreaties Gravé pardoned him. Lescarbot, who held him in high esteem, praised him in a sonnet and insisted upon his skill as a captain:

> Quand ta dextérité empêche d'abîmer
> La nef qui va sous toi du Ponant à l'Aurore...
> [When your skill saves from shipwreck the vessel which under your command sails from the west to the east . . .]

Champdoré took part in all the voyages of exploration: in 1604 in St. Mary's Bay (Nova Scotia) where he found the priest Nicolas AUBRY who had been lost, and in Champlain's voyage to the Kennebec River; in 1605 and 1606 down the New England coast; 1607 in the Bay of Fundy. Champdoré sailed back to France along with the whole settlement 30 July 1607. He returned to Acadia 1608: he sailed up the Saint John River for a distance of 50 leagues, went to Chouacouët (Saco Bay, Maine), reconciled the Armouchiquois and the Micmacs who had been at war the previous summer and had them formally conclude peace. He returned to France in the autumn and reported upon "the wondrous beauty of the wheat" that JEAN DE BIENCOURT de Poutrincourt had sown the previous year.

MARCEL TRUDEL

Champlain, *Works* (Biggar), I, 363 et n., 378–87, 458, *et passim*. Lescarbot, *Histoire* (Tross), II, 434 f., *et passim*; III, 57; *History* (Grant), II, 283, 361–62, 367–68, *et passim*.

ANNAOTAHA (Annahotaha, Anotaha), ÉTIENNE, Huron chief; d. 1660 at the Long Sault.

Annaotaha was mentioned by the Jesuits as early as 1649 as "This man whose life is but one series of combats and adventures," and furthermore, as "the most esteemed in the country for his courage and his exploits over the enemy." On 16 March 1649, he was present at Saint-Louis when the fatal Iroquois attack took place and was heard to upbraid stoutly those Hurons who would abandon the Jesuits Jean de BRÉBEUF and GABRIEL LALEMANT and flee from the battle.

He was one of the group of 300 Huron families who, when the Iroquois ravaged their country, took refuge on Ahouêndoë, or Île Saint-Joseph (now Christian Island), where the Jesuits and their party of Frenchmen under Father RAGUENEAU joined them. The winter of 1649–50 proved disastrous for the refugees. Famine and disease brought death to hundreds of the Hurons. Others lost their lives to ambushing Iroquois who were scouring the country. At one time, a band of 30 Iroquois landed on the island and erected a fortress from which they attacked the Huron settlement, murdering the bravest warriors.

In the late autumn (1649) another Iroquois band erected a fort on the mainland opposite the island. Annaotaha was one of the Hurons who fell into their hands. He pretended to believe the Iroquois claim that they brought peace and rich presents to the hungry Hurons, and led three Iroquois as ambassadors to the Huron village. He called together the inhabitants and told them that the Iroquois' "hearts have altered" and that "their thoughts are no longer of blood or of fires, except to change them into bonfires." The three ambassadors were treated to "everything that was most delicious in the village."

In the meantime Annaotaha conferred with the wisest of the Hurons, who were thoroughly suspicious of Iroquois designs. Annaotaha conceived and carried out a ruse whereby the women collected all their provisions and pounded corn as though for a three-day journey to the Iroquois country, "a land of promise." To remove all suspicion from the minds of the Iroquois Annaotaha went himself to their village. Embassies continued on both sides "as if there never had been war between them," until the Huron attracted over 30 of "the choicest and bravest of their [Iroquois] band" within their walls. These they seized and murdered with the exception of three who were allowed to escape for having spared the life of Annaotaha at Saint-Louis.

Annaotaha presumably accompanied, or followed, the Jesuits and the Huron remnant to Quebec in the spring of 1650. On 2 July 1652 he was at Trois-Rivières when a party of French, Hurons, and Algonkins were fired on by a band of Iroquois. In the parleys that followed, Annaotaha was one of three who met with three Iroquois representatives in mid-river. Undeceived by Iroquois talk of peace, Annaotaha, feigning to offer a loaf of bread, seized the leader, Aontarisati. The following day, Aontarisati and another Iroquois were baptized by Father MÉNARD and "were burned the next day."

In April 1660 Annaotaha set out with a band of 40, "the flower of all those of importance" in the Huron settlement at Quebec, to ambush Iroquois hunting parties. At Trois-Rivières he was joined by a few Algonkins, under Metiwemig. These Indians fought with DOLLARD Des Ormeaux and his party of 16 Frenchmen in the battle of the Long Sault. It was on the advice of Annaotaha that the party remained at the foot of the rapids, although Iroquois scouts had discovered their position. After seven days of seige, the arrival of 500 fresh Iroquois caused Annaotaha to suggest sending two Hurons and an adopted Oneida, with rich presents, to treat with the enemy, instructing them in what to say. They were enthusiastically received especially by the Hurons already in the Iroquois camp. This influenced 24 more Hurons to defect. The impetus thus added to the Iroquois attack led the French to fire into the negotiating party whereupon Annaotaha is reported to have said, "Ah Comrades, you have spoilt everything. You ought to have awaited the result of the council our enemies were holding."

In describing the battle, Marie de l'Incarnation [see GUYART] has said, "This captain did not reason wrongly." The Iroquois were enraged by the unexpected attack and launched their final and most savage assault on the few French and Indians who remained in the battered fort. Annaotaha died at the Long Sault. It is said that as he lay wounded by enemy arrows, he begged that they place his head in the fire, so that he might avoid the fate of being scalped by his long-time enemies.

ELSIE MCLEOD JURY

Marie Guyart de l'Incarnation, *Lettres* (Richaudeau), I, 154–61. *JR* (Thwaites), *passim*.

E. R. Adair, "Dollard Des Ormeaux and the fight at the Long Sault: a re-interpretation of Dollard's exploit," *CHR*, XIII (1932), 121–38. Gustave Lanctot, "Dollard Des Ormeaux and the fight at the Long Sault: Was Dollard the saviour of New France?" *CHR*, XIII (1932), 138–46. *See also* the bibliography for DOLLARD Des Ormeaux.

ANNENRAES, famous Onondaga chief; d. 1654.

Annenraes emerges from the troubled years immediately preceding the destruction of Huronia. After the peace neogtiations and treaty, 1645–46 (subsequently broken, *see* KIOTSEAETON), there was only a brief respite in the Huron–Iroquois struggle. During the early part of 1647, a body of Onondagas attempted an onslaught against Huron territory but met disaster. Two Susquehannah deputies also arrived in Huronia with the offer of help for their Huron allies if it were needed. A Huron embassy, headed by the chief ONDAAIONDIONT, was sent in April 1647 to the Susquehannah country.

Huron warriors had pursued the invading Onondagas, killed the chief, taken some prisoners, and dispersed the others. As usual, the prisoners were burned to death, with the exception of one named Annenraes, considered the most important of the captives. With the coming of spring, Annenraes learned that some of the Hurons resented the fact that he was still alive. He thereupon confided to a friend that he intended to escape and to return to his own people. His plan was communicated to some principal chiefs of the Huron council, who realized that they might gain a possible advantage with the Onondagas by assisting Annenraes to escape, as he was reputed to wield authority in his own country. Accordingly, Annenraes was provided with necessities for the journey, given presents, disguised, and permitted to start off by night.

Having passed Lake Ontario, Annenraes came upon 300 Onondagas, who were making canoes in which to cross the lake, their object being to attack the Hurons and thus to avenge his supposed death. These Onondagas were to join additional bands of Senecas and Cayugas, the total force to consist of 800 warriors, all intent upon war against Huronia. The unexpected

Anotaha

arrival of Annenraes upset the plans of the warparty, the members of which regarded him as one returned from the dead. Instead of continuing their military preparations, the warriors now considered the possibility of peace and returned to Onondaga, where they held a council.

Their deliberations resulted in the sending of an Onondaga embassy to the Hurons, bearing suitable gifts to pave the way for preliminary discussions on a peace treaty. This embassy arrived at the village of Saint-Ignace II (near Sturgeon Bay, Ontario), in the Huron country 9 July 1648. At its head was an Indian named Soines, born a Huron but naturalized as an Onondaga. Although negotiations were conducted back and forth between the Hurons and the Onondagas, peace did not ensue. The Onondagas seemed to favour peace, the Cayugas appeared to be of the same mind, the Oneidas were reported as not opposed, but the Senecas would not hear of peace and the Mohawks, it is stated, were against the proposal because they were jealous that the Onondagas had taken the initiative. The Huron embassy, headed by Ondaaiondiont, had also involved the Susquehannahs in the Huron–Iroquois negotiations.

These developments profoundly disturbed the Mohawks and the Senecas, who felt themselves, in consequence, increasingly isolated. After a series of inconclusive skirmishes in 1648, the desperate Mohawks and Senecas completely destroyed Huronia in 1649 and dispersed the Tobacco nation and the Neutrals in the years that followed.

Throughout the peace negotiations of 1648 between the Hurons and the Onondagas, the name of Annenraes is not mentioned. Six years later, in 1654, the French at Montreal were informed by some Onondagas that a new war was in progress. The Erie nation had attacked the Senecas as well as an army of Onondagas. These Onondaga warriors were returning to their own country after a victory won in the direction of Lake Huron, when the rearguard, composed of 80 picked men, was assaulted by Eries and completely cut to pieces. Annenraes, one of the greatest captains of the Onondagas, was captured by a group of Erie skirmishers almost at the gates of the Onondaga village. The exact month of the capture and subsequent death of Annenraes is not recorded. However, at Onondaga on 10 Aug. 1654, Father SIMON LE MOYNE addressed a general council of Iroquois (the Mohawks were absent) and offered 19 words or presents, the last of which is recorded as follows, "Finally, with the nineteenth present, I wiped away the tears of all the young warriors, caused by the death of their great Captain Anneneraes, who had been taken Captive by the cat (Erie) Nation not long before."

THOMAS GRASSMANN

JR (Thwaites), XXXIII, 117–25; XLI, 81, 109–13.

ANOTAHA. *See* ANNAOTAHA.

APOSTOLOS VALERIANOS. *See* FUCA [Appendix]

APRENDESTIGUY (Daprandesteguy, Arpentigny), MARTIN D', Sieur de Martignon, fur-trader and Acadian seigneur; b. *c.* 1616 at Ascain, in the Basque country of France, probably the son of Joanis d'Aprendestiguy; d. probably *c.* 1686–89. The Basque form of the name, "Aprendestiguy," often appears in official French documents as "Arpentigny."

In the 1650's in partnership with merchants of Saint-Jean-de-Luz, Aprendestiguy equipped a vessel which annually traded and fished on the Acadian coast, with the permission of Guillaume Lebel, the guardian of the late governor MENOU d'Aulnay's children. On such a trip in August 1656 Aprendestiguy's ship, the *Saint-Jean-Baptiste*, was captured and he and the crew taken prisoner by order of NICOLAS DENYS, who had purchased the fishing rights to the coast in 1653 and was subsequently appointed lieutenant-general of the region. Aprendestiguy was taken to Denys's headquarters at Saint-Pierre, Cape Breton, and then to France, where he was involved in legal proceedings. Two members of his crew escaped to Saint-Jean-de-Luz on a Basque fishing vessel and Aprendestiguy's associates then successfully took legal action to regain their ship and its cargo of furs and cod, on the grounds that notice of Denys's monopoly had not been posted in their port.

Aprendestiguy's relations with CHARLES DE SAINT-ÉTIENNE de La Tour were close, for he married Jeanne, La Tour's daughter by his first wife, and Aprendestiguy lent his father-in-law considerable sums of money. We may conclude, then, that Arpendestiguy probably settled in Acadia near La Tour—either at Cap de Sable or on the Saint John—in about 1660–62. In 1672 he was granted a seigneury at the mouth of the Saint John River and the title "Sieur de Martignon." The grant was extensive, but it yielded only a modest living by the fur trade. In fact, PERROT, in his Relation of 1686 said that there were only three people in the Saint John region, who lived miserably by the fur trade. Martignon repaired Menou d'Aulnay's fort at the mouth of the Saint John; it was then called Fort Martignon.

In 1686 Martignon's daughter, Marianne, aged 24, married Guillaume Bourgeois, a Port-Royal merchant who was the son of Jacques (or Jacob) Bourgeois*. It is probable that Martignon died between 1686 and 1689, for he was 70 years old at the time of the 1686 census and was not mentioned in that of 1689.

U. J. BOURGEOIS

AN, Col., C^{11D}, 2, f.20; E, 298^A, ff.440–41. Recensements (Acadie). *Pièces et documents relatifs à la tenure seigneuriale, demandés par une adresse de l'assemblée législative, 1851* (2v., Québec, 1852), II, 254.

René Baudry, "Quelques documents nouveaux sur Nicolas Denys," *RHAF*, IX (1955–56), 14–30. Ganong, "Historic sites in New Brunswick," 277–78, 309, 352. Placide Gaudet, "Acadian genealogy and notes/Généalogies des familles acadiennes accompagnées de documents," *PAC Report, 1905*, II, App. A, pt.III. Rameau de Saint-Père, *Une colonie féodale*, II, 403. Webster, *Acadia*, 210.

ARENTSON. *See* AERNOUTSZ

ARGALL (Argoll), SIR SAMUEL, leader of the first English expedtion to contest French settlement in Acadia; b. *c.* 1572, in Bristol, England, fifth son of Richard Argall, a military man of note of East Sutton, Kent, and his second wife, Mary, daughter of Sir Reginald Scott of Scott's Hall, Kent; d. before 1641, perhaps as early as 1626.

James I in 1606 established by charter two Virginia companies, one of London and the other of Plymouth. The first company was to establish a permanent colony in eastern North America between latitudes 36° and 41°N and the second between 38° and 45°. The Virginia Company of London established its settlement, Jamestown, and in 1609 received its confirming grant— sea to sea and 400 miles along the coast. The second company failed to found a settlement but its grant of 1606 was confirmed in the New England council grant of 1620. In the beginning all of this territory was called Virginia.

The records of the Guild of Merchant Tailors show that Capt. Samuel Argall was in the employ of the Virginia Company of London in 1609 and was commissioned to discover a shorter route to Virginia and to fish for sturgeon, valued for the caviar. He sailed west from the Azores to Bermuda and thence to the James River instead of going south to the tropics and west with the trade winds. His voyage took only nine weeks including two weeks becalmed. This new route enabled the English to avoid the Spaniards and to save provisions.

On his arrival at Jamestown, Argall found the new colony in dire straits. He supplied the colonists with all the food he could spare and returned to England at the end of the summer with a large catch of sturgeon. This help came to the colony at one of the most critical moments in its history.

Argall was back in Virginia in 1610 accompanied by Lord De La Warr and was appointed to the council by the governor. He was later driven off his course on a voyage to Bermuda, sailed and fished along the coast of New England to the mouth of the Penobscot on the coast of Maine. Charts of this coast which he made on this voyage were used later by Capt. John Smith and other voyagers.

In 1611 the *Grâce de Dieu* with CHARLES DE BIENCOURT and fathers BIARD and MASSÉ on board en route for Port-Royal (now Annapolis Royal, N.S.) was driven into Newport, Isle of Wight, by severe weather. Although LESCARBOT's work on New France had been translated into English and was available in London in 1610, this new evidence that French colonization was continuing near or in the territory granted to the Virginia Company and that the Jesuits were taking part alarmed the company. As a result the Trinity term of the Virginia court, acting under the authority granted them by James I, named Capt. Argall admiral of Virginia and he was commissioned by the governor under authority of the Great Seal of England to expel the French from all the territory claimed by England. Argall left for Virginia on 23 July 1612, in the *Treasurer*, a vessel of 130 tons mounting 14 guns and carrying 60 men. This vessel was owned jointly by Sir Robert Rich, later Earl of Warwick, and himself. In the spring of 1613 Argall sailed up the Potomac and abducting Pocahontas, the Indian chieftain's daughter, who had befriended the colony, took her a prisoner to Jamestown to secure the release of seven Englishmen held prisoners by her father Powhatan. Early in June he sailed north to investigate the reported French settlement.

In the meantime there was much discord in Port-Royal between the Jesuit fathers Biard and Massé, and JEAN DE BIENCOURT de Poutrincourt and his son Charles. Word of this strife reaching France, the Marquise de Guercheville, one of the chief ladies at the French court, equipped and sent out a relief expedition consisting of two vessels, *Jonas* of 100 tons and a pinnace of 12 tons under RENÉ LE COQ de La Saussaye, to

Argall

remove fathers Biard and Massé from the Port-Royal colony. Le Coq had a commission to settle on the coast to the south, which had been granted to Mme de Guercheville by the King of France. He reached Port-Royal in May 1613, took Biard and Massé on board, then sailed south to the Penobscot, and began to build a settlement named Saint-Sauveur.

Here Argall discovered them in July before they had fortifications erected. Their vessels were easily captured, as most of the French were ashore working on the settlement, and when Argall landed a small force some of them surrendered and the others fled into the woods. Several were killed including Gilbert DU THET, a Jesuit lay-brother. According to Biard, Argall searched Le Coq's chests, found his commission, concealed it, and treated the French thereafter as pirates. According to evidence given at an inquiry in England in 1614 Argall made the French three offers. He would (1) give them the small pinnace and enough food to take them to France, (2) give them passage to the fishing banks where they might meet French shipping, or (3) give Le Coq a shallop to make his own way with as many men as he would choose and to carry the rest to Virginia (BM, Cotton MS Otho E. VIII, 84, ff.252f.). The third course was followed. Father Massé went with Le Coq and they met a French fishing vessel and returned to France. Fathers Pierre Biard and JACQUES QUENTIN, Capt. Fleury of the *Jonas*, and La Motte-le-Vilin were among the 14 carried prisoners to Jamestown.

The council in Virginia decreed that Capt. Argall should sail immediately with his small fleet, the *Treasurer* and the two French vessels which he had captured, taking several of the French prisoners including Father Biard with him, and should destroy all the other French settlements to the north—to 46°, according to Champlain (*Works* (Biggar), IV, 20) or $46\frac{1}{2}°$, according to Biard (*JR* (Thwaites), IV, 35). Landing first at Saint-Sauveur, he destroyed the remnants of La Saussaye's settlement, cut down the cross planted by the Jesuits, and replaced it with one bearing the name of the king of England. He then proceeded to Sainte-Croix where he destroyed the remains of the old settlement and took a supply of salt stored there by French fishermen. Biard stated that he refused to guide Argall to Sainte-Croix but that he managed to find it anyway. He then steered across the bay to Port-Royal. Biard wrote that an Indian, the local sagamo, was captured by the English and guided them but Poutrincourt placed all the blame on Father Biard. No one suggests the obvious that there must have been enough charts and written directions in Le Coq's baggage and on the *Jonas* to guide Argall to both Sainte-Croix and Port-Royal. At any rate the surprise was complete. Biencourt had gone off with the Indians foraging for food and left neither sentinels nor anyone to man the fort. Argall looted the settlement of everything he wanted, butchered some of the livestock, and carried other animals off alive, then burned the settlement to the ground except for the mill and a few isolated barns. He also destroyed the crops in the fields.

Biencourt returned as the English were about to set sail and met privately with Argall on the shore. Argall blamed the Jesuits for causing the governor of Virginia to order the attack and Biencourt demanded the surrender of Biard to be hanged. An anonymous English authority (in Purchas, *Pilgrimes*, XIX (1906)) claimed that Biencourt offered to go over to the English if permitted to remain at Port-Royal under English protection and that Argall refused the offer. There seems to be no confirmation of this statement among other authors.

Argall's fleet left Port-Royal 13 November and almost immediately ran into a terrific storm. Argall in the *Treasurer* made his way back to Virginia stopping on the way, according to some authorities, to compel the small Dutch colony at the mouth of the Hudson to acknowledge English rule. The smallest vessel was never heard from again. *Jonas* with Lieut. Turner in command and with fathers Biard and Quentin on board was driven to the east and after stopping at the Azores for water and supplies made Pembroke in Wales. At the intervention of the French ambassador the Jesuits were permitted to return to France.

When Argall returned to England in 1614 there was an inquiry into his attacks on the French and it was agreed that the whole action was legal and proper to protect the rights granted to the Virginia Company by the Crown. The vessel *Jonas* was returned to Mme de Guercheville but her claim for 100,000 *livres* damages was disallowed.

Capt. Argall continued in the service of the Virginia Company and was elected deputy governor in 1616 and ruled the colony in the absence of the governor until 1619. The laws of the colony were severe as it was necessary to restrain the kind of settlers brought out at that time and Argall, finding the colony in disorder, enforced them harshly. Mostly for this reason many complaints went to London about him charging among other things extortion, waste of company revenues, and oppression of individuals.

While Argall was in Virginia the Earl of Warwick sent the *Treasurer* under another captain on a roving mission to the West Indies and as a result of this Argall was also charged with piracy but even in the eyes of the Spaniards he was exonerated.

The many references to Argall which show him up as a tyrant and a villain are based on these charges as written in the minutes of the Virginia colony by his bitter enemy Sir Edwin Sandys; they neglect all the evidence which refuted the accusations, especially a long inquiry after Argall's return to England in 1619 which exonerated him. On the other hand Father Biard who had the greatest reason to be bitter against him spoke very highly of him and obviously admired him.

While this inquiry was in progress he went on to further honours and greater responsibilities. In 1620 he was captain of a 24-gun merchant vessel and took part in an expedition against Algiers. On his return from the Mediterranean he was made a member of the Council of New England. He was very regular in his attendance at meetings of the council and actively interested in the colonization of this area. Later he was named admiral for New England. On 26 June 1622, he was knighted by King James. In 1624 he was nominated but not elected governor of Virginia and in the same year the king made him a member of his war council. In midsummer of 1625 he was the admiral of a fleet of 28 vessels which took many prizes off the coast of France and in October commanded the flagship in an unsuccessful attack on Cadiz.

A rather ambiguous letter was accepted by Brown as evidence that he died on board his ship 25 Jan. 1626, but other evidence indicates that he retired from the sea and was still alive as late as 1633.

W. AUSTIN SQUIRES

The often conflicting versions of Argall's activities in America may be found in: BM, Cotton MS Otho E. VIII, 84, ff.252–53. PRO, *CSP, Col., 1574–1660*. Champlain, *Works* (Biggar). India Office (London), Court Minute Book, IV, 392. *JR* (Thwaites). Purchas, *Pilgrimes* (1905–7), XIX, 213–16.

The genesis of the United States, ed. Alexander Brown (2v., Boston and New York, 1897). *DAB*. *DNB*. Huguet, *Poutrincourt*. R. A. Preston, *Gorges of Plymouth Fort* (Toronto, 1953). W. O. Sawtelle, "Sir Samuel Argall, the first Englishman at Mount Desert," *Sprague's J. of Maine Hist*., XII, no. 4 (1924), 201ff.

ARGENTENAY, LOUIS D'AILLEBOUST DE COULONGE ET D'. *See* AILLEBOUST

ARPENTIGNY, MARTIN D', SIEUR DE MARTIGNON. *See* APRENDESTIGUY

ASTICOU, sagamo of the Armouchiquois (Penobscots) on the frontiers of Acadia; fl. 1608–16.

According to LESCARBOT he was the successor of Bessabes, who succeeded Onemechin (Olmechin) on the latter's death in MEMBERTOU's war of revenge (1607). The cause of this war against the Armouchiquois was their slaying of PANOUNIAS in revenge for previous slayings of Armouchiquois by Touaniscou, a Micmac. Bessabes in turn had been slain by the English because of the treachery of his followers in dealing with their abortive colony of Norumbega or Sagdahoc, planted by Sir John Popham and others in 1607 but withdrawn the following year. In Bessabes' place the Indians "brought down from the back-country a chief named Asticou, a man grave, valorous and feared, who in the twinkling of an eye will gather together a thousand Indians." He, in a statesmanlike manner, demanded that ANGIBAULT *dit* Champdoré, who had been sent by DU GUA de Monts in 1608 to pick up any furs gathered in the winter and to report on his colony, send him a representative of the Etchemins (Malecites) to treat with him. As a result OUAGIMOU was chosen and peace concluded with due ceremony between the Etchemins and the Armouchiquois at Chouacouët (Saco) in 1608.

During the next five years the fate of Acadia lay in the hands of the BIENCOURTS and the Jesuits. BIARD had visited the site of the English colony with Charles de Biencourt in 1611 and thought that the French could forestall any future English attempt at settlement. When he and his fellow Jesuits, backed up the Marquise de Guercheville, set out in 1613 to found a colony on the English site, it was only by chance that they emerged from a fog at Île des Monts-Déserts, opposite the headquarters of Asticou.

Asticou now appears in a different role, as an ally of the French, hoping to induce the Jesuit colony to stay at Saint-Sauveur. His followers enticed Father Biard to visit him on the grounds that he was sick unto death and feared to die without baptism. Although Biard found that Asticou was suffering only from a cold, the ruse gave him an opportunity to examine Asticou's headquarters—apparently Pemaquid—with which he was so much impressed that, after consultation with his colleagues and Captain RENÉ LE COQ de La Saussaye, he decided to go no farther. But the plans of both Biard and Asticou were suddenly frustrated by Capt. Samuel ARGALL of Virginia, who attacked the settlement in July 1613 and carried off all the Frenchmen.

D. C. HARVEY

Champlain, *Works* (Biggar), I, 458 n. *et passim*. *JR*

Atarhea

(Thwaites), III, 71, 297. Lescarbot, *History* (Grant), II, 325, 368–69, 557; III, 497ff.

ATARHEA. See TAREHA

ATETKOUANON. See PASTEDECHOUAN

ATHASATA. See TOGOUIROUI

ATIC. See CHOMINA

ATIRONTA (Darontal, Durantal), one of the principal chiefs of the Ahrendarrhonon (Rock) nation of the Hurons; fl. 1615. Three distinguished Huron Indians bore the name "Atironta" in the 17th century, following the Indian custom of resuscitating and perpetuating the name of one who had died.

Atironta (fl. 1615) resided at Cahiagué (near Hawkestone, Ontario), the capital town of the Ahrendarrhonons, which according to CHAMPLAIN consisted of 200 long-houses.

According to Father PAUL LE JEUNE's description of the resuscitation of his name by a later chief in 1642, Atironta had been the first to make contact with the French at Quebec. He may have been one of the party of Attignaouantans (Bears) and Iroquets who met Champlain on the St. Lawrence in 1609, 1610, and 1611, and established the historic alliance for war and trade between the Hurons and Algonkins and the French.

Atironta was one of a war-party of Hurons and Algonkins led by Champlain in 1615 from the Huron country (near Georgian Bay) in an attack on an Iroquois village situated south of Lake Ontario. On the return journey, during a 38-day side-expedition for hunting, Atironta shared with Champlain his "cabin, provisions and furniture." Before this time, Champlain points out, he was "already on terms of some intimacy" with Atironta. After the return of the war-party to Cahiagué, the people of that village quarrelled with the Algonkins under IROQUET who were wintering near them. Councils were held at which Champlain mediated, and in which Atironta as a chief must have been involved, although no mention of his participation is made by Champlain.

In the summer of 1616 Champlain brought Atironta to Quebec, and there entertained him, referring to him as "my host." Atironta admired the French way of life and expressed a desire that, to ensure a safe passage on the river, settlement should be made at the Lachine rapids, a place where French and Indians might live as brothers. This Champlain promised to do.

According to SAGARD, a "great chief" Atironta ruled the Ahrendarrhonons in 1623–24.

ELSIE MCLEOD JURY

Champlain, *Works* (Biggar), *passim*. JR (Thwaites), *passim*. Sagard, *Long journey* (Wrong and Langton). Desrosiers, *Iroquoisie*, 63–67.

ATIRONTA (Aëoptahon), JEAN-BAPTISTE, a captain in the Huron Indian village of Cahiagué (near Hawkestone, Ontario), the largest in the Ahrendarrhonon (Rock) nation; d. 1650.

Atironta's original name was Aëoptahon, and it was on his selection as chief in 1642 that he took the name of a former chief ATIRONTA (fl. 1615). The leading men of the country had been called together and, as a mark of friendship for the French and because the earlier Atironta had been the first of the Hurons to meet the French in Quebec, the French who were then in the Huron country were also invited to attend and, furthermore, to name a successor. They declined, and the relatives of the dead Atironta chose Aëoptahon. The new chief, in accepting the name, took on the responsibilities of the dead chief, thus "resuscitating" the former Atironta, or bringing him back to life. This custom of renaming, or passing on the name of a dead person, was practised generally by the Hurons and, when a chieftainship was involved, was celebrated with great pomp and splendour.

When the mission of Saint-Jean-Baptiste had been founded at Cahiagué, in 1639–40, Atironta had shared his lodging with Fathers ANTOINE DANIEL and SIMON LE MOYNE. When feelings rose high against the missionaries, he sheltered them and assembled a council of elders before whom the fathers could declare publicly their innocence of the calumnies directed against them.

In 1642 Atironta and his brother were chiefs in a war-party against the Iroquois. His brother was captured, but Atironta escaped. He believed that his faith in God had saved him, because, before setting out, he had defied a demon who came in a dream to threaten him for his Christian leanings. On his return he was baptized and given the name Jean-Baptiste. He was the first adult Christian in good health at that mission. To demonstrate his joy, a splendid feast was held, with speeches.

Atironta took part in the peace council of 1645 which was attended by Iroquois, Hurons, Algonkins, and French at Trois-Rivières. This meeting was one of great moment in Indian history, being the last serious attempt to form an alliance that would ensure peace by allowing the Iroquois a share in the lucrative fur trade that had then developed between the Hurons and Algonkins and the French. At the conclusion Atironta spoke loudly and resolutely, rejoicing in the unity of the nations and admonishing the Iroquois to "betray no one. As for us, know that we have sound hearts."

During the winter of 1645–46, he and his family resided at the Hôtel-Dieu at Sillery. Ceremonies of baptism were completed for Catherine, his wife, and Mathieu, his small son, in the chapel at Quebec on 23 Dec. 1645. They sat in the governor's pew. Catherine received her first communion at midnight when the Christmas choral mass was accompanied by a violin and a German flute which proved to be out of tune. A cannon was shot at midnight as mass began. Candles lit the chapel which was heated by two great kettles; a few hours later the floor under one kettle caught fire.

In January 1646 Atironta was sought out by a Huron, Tandihetsi, to represent his tribe at Trois-Rivières in a council called as a result of the uneasiness of the Algonkins on hearing the rumour, afterwards proven to be true, that they had been left out of the 1645 peace-treaty by the Iroquois and the French [see KIOTSEAETON, PIESKARET]. Atironta left on 12 January and returned on the 27th, the council having "ended in nothing."

Visiting at Montreal in 1646, Atironta was impressed with the fine crop of corn and planned to settle his family there. The Jesuits hoped that Atironta's prestige among his people would influence other Hurons to do likewise. The Jesuits believed that if the Indians, particularly the Hurons, could be taught to live as Europeans, they would be more readily converted to Christianity, and also would be more valuable allies of the French, particularly at this time when attack from the Iroquois was imminent and the colony at Montreal especially vulnerable.

In 1647 Atironta again represented his people in an attempt to avert war with the Iroquois. While the Huron chief ONDAAIONDIONT was engaged in making an alliance with the Susquehannahs, Atironta with four other Hurons visited the Onondagas seeking a separate peace. In this way the Hurons hoped to divide and weaken the Iroquois forces. The journey required 20 days, followed by a month of treating, and a return journey of 30 days, for although the distance was not great, the danger from enemy attack along the route necessitated long detours. The Huron mission bore furs as presents and received in return wampum belts of 3,000 and 4,000 beads each. They had hoped for the freedom of some 100 Huron captives who were held by the Onondagas but only 15 were allowed to return with the peace mission.

In June 1650, Atironta, after wintering at Quebec, was returning to his own country with a party of Hurons and Frenchmen which included Father BRESSANI, when he and seven others were killed by a band of Iroquois. A few days later the party met the French and Hurons who, after the destruction of the Huron missions by the Iroquois, were escaping from the Huron country under Father RAGUENEAU.

ELSIE MCLEOD JURY

JR (Thwaites), *passim*.

ATIRONTA, PIERRE, Huron captain; d. 1672.

Atironta was a resident of the Huron village situated near Quebec from 1666 until his death. The inhabitants of this village were survivors of the Huron nation who, after a winter of starvation and death on Île Saint-Joseph (now Christian Island), escaped with the French party of priests, lay-brothers, workmen, and soldiers under Father RAGUENEAU, and arrived at Quebec 28 July 1650.

They first camped near the Hôtel-Dieu, moving to the Île d'Orléans the following March. In 1651, this nucleus was joined by the Hurons of the Sillery settlement and by those who had fled to Ekaentouton (Manitoulin Island). In 1654, still another group of Hurons who had been living at Trois-Rivières joined them. On 20 May 1656 they were stealthily attacked by Iroquois when several of their number were killed or made captive. For safety, they returned to Quebec where they remained until 1668; then, after a short sojourn at Beauport they settled at Côte Saint-Michel, Notre-Dame-de-Foy, in 1669. At this time they numbered about 210. They settled at Ancienne-Lorette in 1673. They were then increasing in population, partly from the addition of Iroquois converts. Basically the remnant of the mission to the Hurons, the Indians of this village were Christians under the care of the Jesuits.

During the six years that Pierre Atironta resided among the Huron exiles, he was deeply devoted to Christian beliefs and practices, and, although of advanced age, he learned by heart all the Huron prayers. He became *dogique* of his cabin, leading others in prayer night and morning. He held no resentment against the Iroquois by whom he was cruelly treated. He introduced, in the village, the practice of visiting and praying for the sick. Contrary to Indian custom, he reproved his children when necessary and also others whose behaviour offended him. While health permitted, he worked continually in the fields and in his house, and although he in the end endured great suffering, he gave no sign of pain.

ELSIE MCLEOD JURY

JR (Thwaites) *passim*.

AUBER, CLAUDE, royal notary, clerk of court then judge of the provost court of the seigneury of Beaupré; b. 1616 or 1617 at Sainte-Croix de Troarn (diocese of Bayeaux), son of Jacques Auber and of Marie Le Boucher; d. 1694 at Quebec.

His arrival in Canada is thought to date from 1645, and that of his wife Jacqueline Lucas and of his son Félix from 1648. Olivier LETARDIF made him a grant of land at Château-Richer on 22 May 1650. Shortly afterwards he began to practise as notary of the seigneury of Beaupré; his first act was dated 28 Oct. 1650. On 23 Jan. 1664 he even received from the Conseil Souverain a commission as royal notary in New France. According to the 1667 census he had fairly extensive holdings of farm land at Beaupré. Having long acted as notary and clerk of the seigneurial jurisdiction, he became its provost court judge on 19 Oct. 1671, by a nomination bearing the signature of Bishop François de Laval*, seigneur of Beaupré. He sold his land to his son Félix on 20 Feb. 1675 and resigned as a judge in 1676, but he remained at Château-Richer at least until the census of 1681. However he went to Quebec later on, was deputy judge of the Conseil Souverain there in 1684, and was buried in Quebec on 20 March 1694. His descendants now write their name "Aubert."

HONORIUS PROVOST

AJQ, Greffe de Paul Vachon, 20 févr. 1675. Recensements de 1667, 1681. *BRH*, XXIV (1918), 347. Godbout, "Nos ancêtres," APQ *Rapport, 1951–53*, 516–17. J.-E. Roy, *Histoire du notariat*, I, 54–55.

AUBERT, THOMAS, sailor from Dieppe, one of the first French navigators to visit American shores after the Breton fishermen, who arrived there as early as 1504.

Aubert must have come to America shortly after 1504, since in 1508 Jean Ango, senior, the great Dieppe shipowner, gave him the command of *La Pensée* for a fishing and reconnoitring voyage in the New World. From that trip Capt. Aubert brought back the first American Indians ever to come to France, and they caused a great stir at Rouen with their costumes, arms, and canoes. It is he who pointed out to the Normandy fishermen the fishing banks of Bonavista. According to some historians, VERRAZZANO may have taken part in the voyage of 1508.

GUSTAVE LANCTOT

Eusebii Caesariensis episcopi chronicon, éd. Henry Estienne (Paris, 1512). *JR* (Thwaites), III, 21–283. Ramusio, *Terzo volume delle navigationi et viaggi* (1st ed., Venetia, 1556), tr. in Hakluyt, *Divers voyages* (1850).
Bréard, *Documents relatifs à la marine normande*. É.-H. Gosselin, *Nouvelles glanes historiques normandes*. Harrisse, *Jean et Sébastien Cabot*. Hoffman, *Cabot to Cartier*.

AUBIGNY, CLAUDE DE BOUTROUE D'. *See* BOUTROUE

AUBRY, NICOLAS, priest, accompanied Pierre DU GUA de Monts to Acadia in 1604; b. in Paris; d. some time after 1611.

According to LESCARBOT, Aubry was a young man from a good family, who had sailed for New France against the latter's wishes. With him was another priest, sometimes called the priest of the parish of Port-Royal; the latter, whose name is unknown, was carried off by scurvy during the winter of 1605–6. A Protestant minister was also a member of the expedition. CHAMPLAIN reports a violent quarrel on the subject of religion between the minister and "nostre curé," which was fought with fists. This "curé" was probably Nicolas Aubry.

Nicolas Aubry drew attention to himself because of an adventure which befell him at Baie Sainte-Marie (N.S.), around 16 June 1604. During a walk through the woods with a number of others he lost his sword. He left the group to go and look for it, but lost his way, and despite the efforts of the French and of the Indians it was impossible to find him. Sixteen days later ANGIBAULT *dit* Champdoré, who had come from Sainte-Croix to fish near Île Longue, noticed him on the shore of the Baie Française (Bay of Fundy), waving his hat and his handkerchief at the end of a pole. The young ecclesiastic had kept himself alive on sorrel and on berries found in the woods. It took him some while to recover from these privations, and he returned to France either in 1604 or in 1605. Nicolas Aubry was still living in 1611, and maintained a keen interest in Canadian affairs.

LUCIEN CAMPEAU

Champlain, *Œuvres* (Laverdière), I, 164–65 [Aubry may be the curé referred to on 706 and 709]. *JR* (Thwaites), II, 184. Lescarbot, *History* (Grant), *passim*.

AUDOUART *dit* **Saint-Germain, GUILLAUME,** secretary of the first council of New France and notary; fl. 1648–63.

Audouart began his career at Trois-Rivières in 1648, as clerk in the court registry and tabellion ("*commis au greffe et tabellionnage*"). In the autumn of 1649 he settled at Quebec, where until 1663 he was secretary of the first council of New France, an office whose holder was entitled to practice as a notary public. Audouart was in fact the first official notary of New France, his predecessors (secretaries of governors, clerks of court, seigneurs, settlers) having practised the profession of notary only on sufferance. Audouart set about collecting their scattered documents and making them a part of his own registry, which comprises 1067 minutes. He also sat as seneschal judge of the seigneury of Beauport, as well as acting in the capacity of deputy to the seigneurial attorney at Quebec. On 22 Oct. 1663 he signed his last notarial act, and a few days later sold his registry to Pierre Duquet. It is not known whether Audouart ever married, but it was at this period that his house passed into the hands of his creditors. He seems to have returned to France in the autumn of 1663.

André Vachon

AJQ, Greffe de Guillaume Audouart, 1634–63. *Jug. et délib.*, I, *passim. Papier terrier de la Cie des I.O.* (P.-G. Roy), *passim*. J.-E. Roy, "Guillaume Andouart Saint-Germain (1648–1663)," *RC*, XXVII (1891), 213–17. André Vachon, *Histoire du notariat canadien, 1621–1960* (Québec, 1962).

AUGER, FRANÇOIS D'. *See* Dangé

AULNAY, CHARLES MENOU D'. *See* Menou

AUOINDAON, chief of the Attignaouantan (Bear) nation, the largest of the Huron groups, resident at Quieunonascaran (near the present-day Penetanguishene, Ontario), where the Recollet mission of Saint-Joseph was situated; fl. 1623.

It was necessary to have Auoidaon's permission to travel to Quebec. Similarly, his brother Onorotandi was, within the limits of the Huron country, master of roads and rivers that led to the upper Saguenay.

Auoindaon had a great affection for the French priests and served them "as a sort of Father Syndic in the country." He once offered to spend the night with Sagard, who was alone, because the chief feared that the priest might be harmed by the Iroquois who had invaded the Huron country and also by the evil spirits. Sagard spoke of him as "this good old man, full of kindness and goodwill."

In October 1623, Sagard accompanied Auoindaon on the annual fishing expedition into Georgian Bay, which continued for longer than a month. They lived in wigwam-type lodges on islands. Nets were set at night and brought in at daybreak. Hemp cord with wood and bone barbs were also used. Some fish were gutted and dried on racks; some were smoked on poles, before being packed in casks; and some of the largest were boiled for oil. When fishing was good there was a perpetual round of merry feasts.

The various rituals of fishing were observed. The bones of fish were not thrown on the fire lest the spirits warn the other fish against being caught; and the nets also, they believed, could see, hear, eat, and impart information to the fish. While everyone in the lodge lay flat on his back, a fish-preacher eloquently addressed the fish in order to attract them to the nets, and tobacco was thrown on the fire, with incantations, to ensure success.

In 1634, on his return to the Hurons, Brébeuf, with two other priests and one layman, lodged with one Aouandoie, possibly a descendant or a namesake of Auoindaon. He was one of the richest of the Hurons, formerly of Toanché; then at Ihonatiria—two villages near Quieunonascaran in the Penetanguishene peninsula. Toanché had twice been burned but Aouandoie's cabin alone escaped. Some residents, in jealousy, attempted to set fire to his cabin but Aouandoie, a generous man, prepared a feast and offered to the less fortunate one of his two bins of corn, each of which held 120 bushels.

Elsie McLeod Jury

JR (Thwaites), *passim*. Sagard, *Long journey* (Wrong and Langton), *passim*.

AUTEUIL, DENIS-JOSEPH RUETTE D'. *See* Ruette

AUTRAY, JACQUES BOURDON D'. *See* Bourdon

AVAUGOUR, PIERRE DUBOIS D'. *See* Dubois

AVÈNE DE DESMELOIZES, FRANÇOIS-MARIE RENAUD D'. *See* Renaud

B

BABIE (in later generations spelled "Bâby," and in Michigan historical collections "Baubee"), **JACQUES**, soldier, farmer, and fur-trader, founder of the distinguished Canadian family of this name, son of Jean "Bavis" and Isabeau Robin of the parish of Monteton, diocese of Agen; b. France *c.* 1633 (1639 according to the census of 1681); d. 28 July 1688 at Champlain.

Jacques Babie came to Canada in 1665 as a sergeant in the Carignan-Salières regiment, sent by Louis XIV and Colbert to fight the Iroquois. After peace had been signed at the end of 1666 between the Iroquois and Alexandre de PROUVILLE, Marquis de Tracy, commander-in-chief of Louis XIV's forces in North America, Babie obtained his discharge from the army and settled in Champlain on the St. Lawrence near Trois-Rivières, in a fertile region known as the "cradle of explorers and fur-traders."

He was attracted to fur-trading and farming and engaged in both. As early as 1668, and for many years thereafter, he traded with the Indians of the upper Saint-Maurice and upper Ottawa rivers, and was among the government-accredited merchants who participated in the great fur mart held annually at Montreal. In 1669, he bought two tracts of land in Champlain and farmed them. By the year 1681 he had acquired two more tracts of land in the same locality as well as another at Gentilly across the St. Lawrence. In 1670, he married Jeanne Dandonneau, daughter of Pierre Dandonneau* *dit* Lajeunesse, Sieur du Sablé, one of the substantial citizens of Trois-Rivières, who had settled in Champlain about 1660. Jacques Babie died in 1688, at the age of about 55, in Champlain, leaving a comfortable fortune. Very avid for profits, and a hard-headed businessman, he had numerous differences which frequently brought him before the Conseil Souverain.

The youngest of his 11 children, Raymond Babie*, who followed in his father's footsteps as a fur-trader, was the father of Jacques Duperron Bâby* and François Bâby*. Both distinguished themselves in the early years of British rule.

MARINE LELAND

AJTR, Greffe de Guillaume de La Rue, 1 juin 1670. APQ, Documents divers, I, Lettres de Jacques Babie et de son épouse, Jeanne Dandonneau, à Antoine Adhémar. Additional MS material in Detroit Public Library, Burton Hist. Coll.; Ontario Hist. Soc.; Public Archives of Ontario; University of Michigan, William L. Clements Library; Université de Montréal, Coll. Bâby. Recensement de 1681. *Jug. et délib.*, II, III, V, VI, *passim*. P.-B. Casgrain, "Jacques Babie," *BRH*, X (1904), 329–32; *Mémorial des familles Casgrain, Bâby et Perrault* (Québec, 1898).

BÂBY. *See* BABIE

BAFFIN, WILLIAM, arctic explorer; b. 1584?; d. 1622.

As with many of the early explorers and navigators, little is known of the life of William Baffin until the voyages upon which his reputation rests. The 11th edition of the *Encyclopaedia Britannica* gives 1584 as the year of his birth but does not supply the source of that important date. He was probably a native of London or vicinity and a self-educated man of humble origin but great talent, for Purchas speaks of him as "that learned-unlearned Mariner and Mathematician who, wanting art of words, so really employed himself to those industries, whereof here you see so evident fruits."

In 1612 Baffin was chief pilot with Capt. James HALL's ship *Patience* on the expedition when that unfortunate mariner was slain by revengeful Eskimos on the coast of Greenland. The *Patience* accompanied by the *Heart's Ease* sailed from the Humber on 22 April and returned to Hull, 11 September under the command of Andrew Barker. Baffin kept a journal, printed in part in Purchas, beginning 8 July to the end of the voyage. In this account we get the first of his many and important astronomical observations. He also describes the Greenland Eskimos and their country, and tells of Hall's tragic end.

When Baffin returned from this voyage he took service with the Muscovy Company which was trading with Russia and sending whalers to the Spitzbergen region. In 1613 the Company sent a fleet of seven vessels to the whaling grounds, and again the chief pilot was William Baffin, sailing on the *Tiger* under Capt. Benjamin Joseph. He sailed again with Capt. Joseph on a similar Spitzbergen voyage in 1614 on the *Thomasine* with a fleet of 11 ships and 2 pinnaces. Ice conditions extended well south making it a difficult season for northern navigation, but nevertheless Baffin explored a considerable section of the Spitzbergen coast returning to London 4 Oct. 1614.

Baffin's fourth adventure was in the service of the Northwest Company to search for the northwest passage. This voyage was a continuation of three previous expeditions, under HENRY HUDSON (1610–11), who was abandoned by his men after wintering in Hudson Bay; Thomas BUTTON, who wintered near Churchill (1612–13); and William GIBBONS, who holed up on the Labrador coast (1614). The stout ship *Discovery*, used by all three of the previous expeditions, was fitted out under the command of Robert BYLOT and Baffin again sailed as pilot on 15 March 1614/15. On

26 April, Baffin by observing an occultation of a star by the moon obtained the first longitude ever figured at sea while under way. Hudson Strait and the western end of Southampton Island were carefully examined, with particular attention given to the tides. The great 19th-century explorer, W. E. Parry*, checked Baffin's observations over two hundred years later and found them very nearly correct. Baffin kept a full journal of this expedition which is accompanied by the only surviving example of one of his maps. The expedition abandoned its search for the northwest passage because of ice conditions at a place where land showed to the northeast; Parry later named the land Baffin Island "out of respect to the memory of that able and enterprising navigator." The expedition returned in the fall of 1615. On his return from this voyage, Baffin concluded, quite correctly, that no navigable passage to the west existed out of Hudson Bay.

Baffin's fifth and most important voyage was also undertaken in the *Discovery* with Bylot as captain. Leaving Gravesend, 26 March 1616, they passed John DAVIS's farthest north at Hope Sanderson on the Greenland coast and continued for another 300 miles to 77°45′ which remained the farthest north reached for 236 years. They then sailed around and mapped the entire shore of "Baffin's Bay," including the entrances of "Sir Thomas Smith's," "Alderman Jones," and "Sir James Lancaster's" sounds. Lancaster Sound was not recognized, however, as the entrance to the sought-after northwest passage. It is an ironic historical fact that Baffin's greatest discovery, at first accepted, gradually became suspect and was reduced and finally eliminated from maps until rediscovered and confirmed by Sir John Ross* on his first expedition in 1818. Baffin's papers and map relating to Baffin Bay were given to Purchas, who suppressed them with exasperating casualness.

Baffin is certainly the most proficient navigator and observer of all the arctic explorers of his period. Following his return from the discovery of Baffin Bay, but without finding the northwest passage, he decided to seek that elusive waterway from the western end if he could find employment that would take him to the Pacific. The opportunity came in 1617 and he sailed 4 February as master's mate on the *Anne Royal* in the fleet of Capt. Martin Pring for the East India Company. The fleet arrived at Saldanha Bay 21 June and at Surat in September. The *Anne Royal* was detached and sent to Mocha and visited other ports in the Red Sea and the Persian Gulf area, where Baffin worked steadily, surveying and charting.

In September 1619 the *Anne Royal* was back in the Thames. Baffin had not been anywhere near the northwestern coast of North America but he was commended for his charts of Persia and the Red Sea.

The following year Baffin sailed again for the East Indies in the *London*, flagship of the fleet under Capt. Andrew Shilling who had been captain of the *Anne Royal*. Leaving the Downs 25 March the fleet arrived at Swally Roads 9 November, and, hearing of a fleet of Portuguese and Dutch ships awaiting them, they went in search of the enemy. In the engagement which took place 28 December in the Gulf of Oman, Capt. Shilling received wounds from which he died on 6 Jan. 1620/21. A year later 20 Jan. 1621/22 the English fleet arrived off Ormuz to lay seige to the Portuguese. William Baffin was sent on shore 23 January to make observations on the height and distance of the castle wall to find the range, "But as he was about the same, he received a shot from the Castle into his belly, wherewith he gave three leaps, and died immediately." And Purchas records: "In the Indies he dyed, in the late Ormus businesse, slaine in fight with a shot, as hee was trying his mathematicall projects and conclusions."

Mrs Baffin, a "troublesome, impatient woman," made claim against the East India Company for his wage and a large settlement. After three years of negotiations her claims were finally settled for £500.

Thus the only part of Baffin's life of which we are certain is the final decade, 1612 to 1622. The vast majority of his observations, records, surveys, and maps has disappeared but enough has survived to show us that during this time he became the best astronomical observer among all the navigators of his day.

ERNEST S. DODGE

Purchas, *Pilgrimes* (1905–7), XIV 365–411. *The voyages of William Baffin, 1612–1622*, ed. C. R. Markham (Hakluyt Soc., 1st ser., LXIII, 1881). *DNB*. Dodge, *Northwest by sea*. Encyclopaedia Britannica (11th ed., 29v., incl. Index, Cambridge, 1910–11). Oleson, *Early voyages*, 167–68. W. E. Parry, *Journal of a second voyage for the discovery of a north-west passage from the Atlantic to the Pacific; performed in the years 1821–22–23 in His Majesty's ships* Fury *and* Hecla (London, 1824). J. Ross, *A voyage of discovery, made under the orders of the Admiralty, in His Majesty's ships* Isabella *and* Alexander *for the purpose of exploring Baffin's Bay, and inquiring into the probability of a north-west passage* (London, 1819).

BAILLIF, CLAUDE, best-known and most prolific builder of 17th-century New France; b. *c.*

Baillif

1635; drowned at sea while returning to France on a ship that left in 1698.

Little is definitely known of Baillif's personal life. A conjecture is that he was born and trained in Lower Normandy (where "Baillif" is a common name), that he may have met Laval* on the bishop's 1671 visit to Paris, and been recruited there to teach in the seminary branch of the school of the arts and crafts founded in 1668 to provide instruction in "carpentry, sculpture, painting, gilding for church decoration, masonry, and woodworking." At any rate, the "Livre de Comptes" of the seminary of Quebec, recording his arrival in Quebec on 22 Sept. 1675, calls him "a stone mason" and notes that he is "engaged [at the school] for three years." His name appears inconsequentially in Quebec records in connection with several lawsuits; Tanguay cites the Registre de Beauport, 9 Oct. 1688 as recording his marriage to Catherine Sainctar; and there is a notice of his having drowned at sea. Otherwise, we know him only through contracts and other documents relating to his work on five specific buildings. These are as follows:

(1) In 1683 Baillif signed a contract to build a house for Louis JOLLIET in the Lower Town. Inasmuch as he was the best, if not the only, qualified master-builder in Quebec at the time, we may suppose that Jolliet's house was not Baillif's only venture in domestic architecture. No known works by him in this category survive, however.

(2) In 1684 Baillif was in charge of a programme of enlarging the cathedral of Quebec, instituted by Bishop Laval with the assistance of special grants from Louis XIV totalling over 10,000 *livres*. This was the building which had been designed in 1645 and completed in 1647, largely with Jesuit resources and inspiration, to serve as the parish church of Quebec under the title Notre-Dame de Québec, replacing in this capacity successively the first parish church built by the Recollets in 1615 and destroyed by DAVID KIRKE in 1629; CHAMPLAIN's votive church of Notre-Dame-de-la-Recouvrance, built in 1633 and burned 1640; and a temporary chapel in the house of the Cent-Associés used between 1640 and 1647. The parish church had become Laval's cathedral in 1674. The programme called for lengthening the stone walls of the nave by 50 ft., with (probably) a new façade in front of it, and stone towers at either side which would serve as entrances to new side-aisles. Of this, only the south tower, carrying a wooden *clocher* sheathed in tin, was completed under Baillif's direction; it still stands. Probably Laval's deteriorating health and consequent resignation as bishop had something to do with such desultory progress; in any event, no sooner had his successor, Mgr de Saint-Vallier [La Croix*] been consecrated in January 1688 than he wrote to Quebec officials (22 Feb.) that he was sending out to them "a skilled and clever building contractor called Larivière, along with six masons and three carpenters, to work on Our cathedral and succursal church. . . . Put them to work quickly." Hilaire Bernard* *dit* Larivière and his men evidently completed the enlargement of the nave, but the final result was none too happy: "The cathedral," wrote Charlevoix* in his 1720 *Journal*, "would make but an indifferent parish church in one of the smallest towns in France. . . . The most tolerable feature is a rather high tower, strongly built, which is fairly presentable from a distance." Charlevoix's impression is confirmed by the well-known drawing in the cathedral archives bearing the signature of Chaussegros* de Léry, which represents the front elevation as it was when he began his embellishment of it in 1744 (this we can tell by comparing the drawing with Short's* engraving of the cathedral in 1759, which shows it as Léry left it); the 1684 programme did indeed leave the cathedral "exactly like the architecture of a country church"—stark and simple, with only the tower and *clocher* having any hint of elegance. For this, circumstances and not Baillif were to blame, apparently. It would not be the last time a famous Québecois builder had his plans for this façade frustrated by delays, compromises, and economies; a century and a half later the design for it which was to have been Thomas Baillargé's* masterpiece ended in a similar fiasco, as the present façade bears witness.

(3) The "succursal church" referred to in Mgr Saint-Vallier's letter of February 1688 was evidently begun, with Bailiff in charge, in the spring of that year, to serve the inhabitants of the Lower Town. Originally dedicated to "L'Enfant-Jésus," it was renamed Notre-Dame-de-la-Victoire while under construction, in honour of what was considered the Virgin's miraculous help in repulsing the attack of PHIPS on Quebec. In 1711, when another attack by Sir Hovenden Walker* met disaster, the church received its present name of Notre-Dame-des-Victoires. Of Baillif's work here we can say for certain only that very little, probably nothing at all, remains today. Wolfe's* artillery wrecked the original church thoroughly (as Short's* drawing made in 1759 shows very well), and despite signs proclaiming it to tourists as "the oldest church" in Quebec, Notre-Dame-des-Victoires today represents a rebuilding of 1765, heavily if not entirely altered on several occasions between 1830 and 1860, probably by

André Pâquet* *dit* Lavallée. Evidences are that Baillif may have intended his church to have side-aisles like the cathedral's, and a small *clocher* over the crossing.

(4) In January 1693 Baillif signed a contract with Mgr Saint-Vallier to take charge of building his episcopal palace, preliminary work on which had already begun. Among other specifications, a façade was called for to be $24\frac{1}{2}$ ft. high, crowned by a "cornice, frieze, and architrave in the Tuscan order." Baillif set to work, and when the bishop returned from a trip to France in 1697, his palace was substantially complete. It was probably the most elaborate building of 17th-century New France. La Poterie [Le Roy*] in his *Histoire* described it with enthusiasm as "a large building of cut stone; the main body of it, with the chapel making up the central section, faces the channel [i.e., the St. Lawrence]. It has a wing 72 ft. long, with a pavilion at the end [in other words the plan—although irregular because of site—was that of a typical 17th-century French palace, a main body enclosing a *cour d'honneur*, with a wall and ornamental entrance on the fourth side]. The chapel is 60 ft. long; its façade is of the composite order, built of fine cut stone, which is a sort of rough marble. Its interior is magnificent, by reason of its altar retable, the ornaments of which are an abridgement of that in the Val-de-Grâce. There would be few episcopal palaces in France that could rival it, were it finished" (this last referring to the never-completed second wing). In La Poterie's accompanying plate the body of the chapel is shown set into the palace building at right angles, the façade projecting. Better known is the plate in Short's series; it depicts the façade as a "Jesuit" type of the 17th century, in two stories joined by reversed scrolls, and articulated by pilasters and cornice. The palace was repaired after the cession, and used through the 1830's (it appears in a good many early 19th-century views of Quebec); material from its walls was used in the present palace, designed by Thomas Baillargé and opened in 1844.

(5) The Livre de Comptes of the church of Sainte-Anne de Beaupré states that Claude Baillif was in charge of rebuilding during the years 1689–95; it specifically mentions a *clocher* built in 1696 "according to the designs of Claude Baillif" by the carpenters R. Leclaire and Jean Marchand. This was a complete renovation of the church built on the site *c.* 1676; when it was demolished in 1878 to make room for the fourth church (which stood until 1922, the present church dating from 1923), its materials were used in the construction of a commemorative chapel, on which this *clocher* is still to be seen. The importance of this reference is both to suggest something of Baillif's role in building operations, and to connect his name with the type of parish church established by Bishop Laval.

Baillif's precise function as a builder is uncertain. Apparently he was more than an artisan—not only do records indicate his working on three buildings at once, but there is also mention of his "plans." But it is evident, too, that Laval and Saint-Vallier took much more than a passive patron's interest in the design of churches and official buildings in their diocese; all such plans had, in fact, to be approved by both bishop and intendant before building operations could begin. The logical inference is that Baillif's "plans" were on the order of working drawings for designs devised jointly by himself and the bishop. Laval and Saint-Vallier were gentlemen, familiar with the advanced architectural ideas of Louis XIV's court. Baillif and the other workmen charged with executing their ideas were, however, trained in traditional modes and means of craftsmanship; in them mediaeval traditions were unusually strong, the more since rigid religious orthodoxy was a prime requirement for immigration to New France. The result of such collaboration was a fusion of mediaeval and Baroque traditions which created the first distinctly Canadian architectural expression. It was seen first and best in the six stone churches erected between 1669 and 1680 in parishes founded by Laval—Sainte-Anne du Petit Cap (Sainte-Anne de Beaupré), 1676; Sainte-Famille, 1669; Notre-Dame de Beauport, 1672; Saint-Joseph de la Pointe-Lévy, Lauzon, 1675; Ange-Gardien, 1675; Notre-Dame de Château-Richer, *c.* 1680—and in those immediately following them, such as the 1688–89 reconstruction of Sainte-Anne de Beaupré and the 1695 church of Saint-Laurent, Île d'Orléans, as a distinctive combination of classically inspired elements (round-headed arches in *clocher* arcades, quoins, interior forms) with the rugged fieldstone walls and steeply vertical proportions of a mediaeval tradition. It is in his contribution to the latter that Baillif takes his place as one of the main founders of the Québecois architectural tradition.

ALAN GOWANS

ASQ, MSS, C, II (1674–86) [Livres de comptes, II], p. 225. Archives de la Basilique de Sainte-Anne, Recettes et comptes, I (1659–1729). P.-F.-X. de Charlevoix, *Journal of a voyage to North America*, ed. L. P. Kellogg (2v., Chicago, 1923), I, 107. La Pot(h)erie, *Histoire* (1722), I, 233–34. Richard Short, *A view of the cathedral, Jesuits college, and Recollect friars church, taken from the gate of the governor's house*

Bailloquet

(London. 1761); one of a series of engravings executed by an English officer in Quebec, 1759–60.

Alan Gowans. *Church architecture in New France* (Toronto, 1955). 46ff., 61, 90, 120, 122–23, 126, 129. Gérard Morisset, *L'architecture en Nouvelle-France* (Québec, 1949), 127–28. P.-G. Roy, *La ville de Québec*, II, 179–80; *Les vieilles églises de la province de Québec 1647–1800* (Québec, 1925), 1f. Tanguay, *Dictionnaire*, I, 22.

BAILLOQUET, PIERRE, priest, Jesuit; b. 14 Oct. 1613 at Saintes, in France; d. 7 June 1692 at the Saint-François-Xavier mission among the Ottawa Indians.

Pierre Bailloquet entered the Society of Jesus on 17 Nov. 1633 at Bordeaux. He taught at Bordeaux and Poitiers before going to Quebec, where he arrived in June 1647. For 45 years he served faithfully the French settlers and native tribes in the missions that extended from Port-Royal in Acadia to the Sioux in Illinois.

J. MONET

ACSM, f.4015. *JR* (Thwaites), *passim*. *JJ* (Laverdière et Casgrain), *passim*.

BAILLY, GUILLAUME, priest, Sulpician, missionary and architect; date and place of birth unknown; d. 1696 in the diocese of Chartres.

He arrived in Canada 7 Sept. 1666. During all the time he spent in the country Bailly was associated with the Congrégation de Notre-Dame as its superior or as a confessor.

In 1668 the Sulpicians had founded a fixed mission at Kenté (Quinte), at the entrance to Lake Ontario, and another at Gentilly (near Dorval) in 1672. Neither had succeeded to the missionaries' liking. A third was established around 1676 on the slopes of Mount Royal. M. Bailly was sent to direct it and to teach: "He had a talent for languages, was not lacking in experience, and his devotion knew no bounds." But upon contact with the Indians, who had a taste for dreams, superstitions, and ghosts, he fell a prey to their failings and had to be recalled to the seminary.

Then came the period of the Lachine massacre (1689). The whole population of Montreal was profoundly disturbed by it, and in particular the religious communities: one worthy nun claimed that she was having visions and was receiving messages from the other world. She was backed up by a triumvirate that was remarkable for its virtue and devotion: M. Joseph de La Colombière*, M. Étienne Guyotte*, and M. Guillaume Bailly. The affair reached such a point that the superior of the Société de Saint-Sulpice in Paris had to recall to France the three *confrères* who were in part responsible for this spiritual unrest.

In addition to his incontestable qualities as a missionary priest, Bailly had a talent as an architect to which Sister Marie Morin*, the annalist of the Hôtel-Dieu of Montreal, bore testimony. He it was who drew up the plans for this hospital, which was rebuilt in stone in 1688.

After his return to France in 1691, Bailly was unable to adapt himself to the life of the Sulpicians. He left the society and went to the diocese of Chartres, where he died in 1696.

OLIVIER MAURAULT

Faillon, *Histoire de la colonie française*, III, *passim*. Henri Gauthier, *Sulpitiana* (Montréal, 1926). Albert Jamet, *Marguerite Bourgeoys, 1620–1700* (2v., Montréal, 1942), II, 416 *et passim*. Lefebvre, *Marie Morin*. Morin, *Annales* (Fauteux *et al.*).

BAILLY dit **Lafleur, FRANÇOIS**, master-mason; b. in France *c*. 1627 (1630 according to the census of 1681); d. 1690.

Bailly was hired by the Abbé Queylus [*see* THUBIÈRES] at La Rochelle 8 June 1659. With his wife, Marie, and his father-in-law, Jérémie Fonteneau, he arrived in Montreal the same year. Jeanne MANCE soon engaged him to build a barn for the Hôtel-Dieu, inside Fort Ville-Marie, and on 4 April 1660, he entered into partnership with mason Urbain Brossard*. Later he worked in partnership with the other leading Montreal mason of the period, Michel Bouvier*; the contract they jointly signed to build a bakery in 1683 calls them "architect-masons." Bailly was in the militia of Sainte-Famille in 1663 and he was also a civic official, serving as sergeant-royal (*huissier*) from 1667 and prison warden (*geôlier et concierge des prisons*) from 2 July 1676 until his death. Bailly's chief work, however, was on the parish church of Notre-Dame begun under the leadership of Dollier de Casson* in 1672, and completed in 1683. Constructed entirely of stone, 129 ft. long and 38 ft. wide, it was considerably larger and more impressive than Laval's* cathedral in Quebec. Bailly was buried 25 July 1690 and his wife on 29 Oct. 1692.

ALAN GOWANS

AJM, Greffe de Bénigne Basset, 15, 26 févr. 1660; 23 déc. 1662; 24 juin 1663; 22 févr. 1666; 19 août 1667; 7 oct. 1668; 31 juillet 1670; 8 févr. 1672; 6 oct. 1676; 10 févr. 1686; 23 sept. 1689. Recensement de 1681. Faillon, *Histoire de la colonie française*, III, 17. Alan Gowans, *Church architecture in New France* (Toronto, 1955), 64, 112, 115. É.-Z. Massicotte, "Maçons, entrepreneurs, architectes," *BRH*, XXXV (1929), 137–38; "Une recrue de colons pour Montréal en 1659," *Can. Antiquarian and Numismatic J.*, 3d ser., X (1913), 63–96.

BAILY, Baley. *See* BAYLY

BALTIMORE, CHARLES CALVERT, THIRD LORD. *See* CALVERT

BARTHÉLEMY, a Parisian youth who accompanied Robert CAVELIER de La Salle on his last and fatal expedition and who afterwards defamed him; fl. 1687.

After the murder of La Salle on a branch of the Trinity River in what is now the state of Texas, Barthélemy was one of the group under the leadership of Joutel*, La Salle's faithful companion, which started on the return trip to New France via Henri de Tonty's* post at the mouth of the Arkansas River. Although Joutel mentions that Barthélemy was left behind somewhere on the Arkansas, the boy must have made his way to the fort, because a "Relation" based on the report of Jean Couture*, the commander of the post, contains Barthélemy's statements.

The boy apparently said that his chief, La Salle, "was so enraged at his failures that he did not approach the sacraments for two years; that he nearly starved his brother Cavelier*, allowing him only a handful of meal a day; that he killed with his own hand 'quantité de personnes' who did not work to his liking; and that he killed the sick in their beds without mercy, under the pretence that they were counterfeiting sickness in order to escape work." Parkman terms this a "ridiculous defamation."

HENRY B. M. BEST

AN, Col., C^{13C}, 3, f.118, "Relation de la Mort du S^r. de la Salle, suivant le rapport d'un nommé Couture à qui M. Cavelier l'apprit en passant au pays des Akansa, avec toutes les circonstances que le dit Couture a apprises d'un François que M. avoit laissé au dit pays des Akansa, crainte qu'il ne gardât pas le secret" (translation in PAC *Report, 1899*, Supp., 21–23). *Découvertes et établissements des Français* (Margry), III, 91–534. V. W. Crane, *The southern frontier, 1670–1732* (Durham, N.C., 1928, and Philadelphia, 1929), 42–43. Parkman, *La Salle and the discovery of the great west* (12th ed.), 408–9, 430.

BASSET DES LAURIERS, BÉNIGNE, notary, clerk of court and surveyor at Montreal, son of Jean Basset, lute-player for the pages of the king's chamber, and of Catherine Gaudreau; b. c. 1639 in Paris; d. 4 Aug. 1699 at Montreal.

Bénigne Basset seems to have arrived at Montreal in 1657, together with the first Sulpicians, who made him their representative in the bailiff's court. In 1657 also, following the assassination of Jean de SAINT-PÈRE, they appointed him seigneurial notary and clerk of the tribunal. He further became the secretary of the charitable organization and council of the parish of Notre-Dame. The Sieur GAUDAIS-DUPONT appointed him royal notary, and his appointment was ratified by the Conseil Souverain on 18 Oct. 1663. When royal justice was abolished at Montreal (1666), Basset once more became a seigneurial notary. He was also a surveyor: we owe to him the plan of the first streets of Montreal in 1672. As a notary Basset, who made a proud show of his fine handwriting, long had the best clientele in the town. He signed some 2,525 acts, which have come down to us in a perfect state of preservation.

He did however have difficulties of a professional nature. In 1677 he lost his position as a clerk of court and was forbidden by Judge MIGEON de Branssat, who often complained of his negligence, to exercise the profession of notary. His name was cleared shortly afterwards, and he was able once more to draw up documents as a notary. Moreover, from 1686 to 1690 he was clerk of court for the intendant's subdelegate. He passed away in 1699 at Montreal.

In November 1659, at Ville-Marie, he had married Jeanne de Vauvilliers, a native of Paris like himself, who had arrived in the country the preceding summer and had received a dowry from LOUIS D'AILLEBOUST, the former governor of New France. She died in the summer of 1699, a few days before her husband.

In 1662 Basset had received a grant of land at the foot of the hill called Mont Royal, to the west of what is today the avenue du Parc. A small street in that locality still recalls his name. He also had two other properties, in the rue Saint-Paul.

JEAN-JACQUES LEFEBVRE

AJM, Greffe de Bénigne Basset, 1657–99. *Jug. et délib.*, I, 33.
BRH, XXXVII (1931), 122, 126, 312; XLII (1936), 73–76; XLIII (1937), 106; XLIX (1943), 165. William McLennan, "Anciens montréalais, I: Bénigne Basset, notaire royal, 1639–1699," *Le Canada Français*, 2e série, III (1919–20), 469–77. É.-Z. Massicotte, "Les colons de Montréal de 1642 à 1667," in *RSCT*, 3d ser., VII (1913), sect.I, 25, and in *BRH*, XXXIII (1927), 238. J.-E. Roy, *Histoire du notariat*, I, 68. Tanguay, *Dictionnaire*, I, 28.

BASSET DU TARTRE, VINCENT, surgeon major of the Carignan-Salières regiment, with which he landed at Quebec in the summer of 1665.

As the troops of the regiment comprised 24 companies, Basset had under his orders a similar number of surgeons or *fraters*. Some of these

Bâtard Flamand

practitioners remained in the colony when the regiment was disbanded. On 9 Jan. 1666 Basset appears to have accompanied RÉMY de Courcelle on his expedition against the Five Nations. The militiamen of the country who helped the regular troops had their own surgeon, Jean MADRY, who was subordinate to the surgeon-major. After his return to Montreal, Basset set out again for France, and there is no trace of him after 1668.

Massicotte has wondered whether he was related to the notary BÉNIGNE BASSET. Perhaps he belonged to the family of Bonaventure Basset, a Lyons doctor who is mentioned in Guy Patin's letters in 1657.

GABRIEL NADEAU

É.-Z. Massicotte, "Les chirurgiens de Montréal au XVIIe siècle," *BRH*, XX (1914), 254; "Les colons de Montréal de 1642 à 1667," *RSCT*, 3d ser., VII (1913), sect.I,53 and *BRH*, XXXIII (1927), 542; "Les chirurgiens, médecins, etc., de Montréal sous le régime français," APQ *Rapport, 1922–23*, 134. Régis Roy et Malchelosse, *Le régiment de Carignan*, 69. Sulte, *Mélanges historiques* (Malchelosse), VIII, 85, 131.

BÂTARD FLAMAND. See FLEMISH BASTARD

BATISCAN (Batisquan), Algonkin chief of the Trois-Rivières country; fl. 1610–29.

When CHAMPLAIN arrived in Quebec in April 1610, he was met by the interim commander, Capt. PIERRE CHAUVIN DE LA PIERRE, and the native chief Batiscan and his companions, who had been awaiting him. The Indians rejoiced with song and dance, and Champlain held a feast for them. In return, he was invited, with seven others, to a feast, "which is no small favour amongst them." Again, on his arrival in Quebec in 1611, Champlain was met by Batiscan and a group of Algonkin Indians. They refused to give aid in exploring the region of Trois-Rivières and the St. Maurice River but provided accurate information on the tribes that lived there and their origin.

Batiscan was one of a council of five chiefs, with CHOMINA as head, which was proposed by Champlain in June 1629 to strengthen his position with the native tribes. Shortly before the fall of Quebec to the English, the recommendation was accepted at a general council of the Indians of the district.

ELSIE MCLEOD JURY

Champlain, *Works* (Biggar), *passim*. Desrosiers, *Iroquoisie*, 45.

BAUBEE. See BABIE

BAUDOIN, JEAN, priest, Sulpician, missionary at Beaubassin (Chignecto) in Acadia; b. c. 1662 at Nantes; d. towards the end of the summer of 1698 at Beaubassin.

Abbé Baudoin studied at the Collège in Nantes, at first taking up a military career and becoming a musketeer in the king's guards. He soon embraced the ecclesiastical life and after beginning at Nantes theological studies that he concluded at Paris under the direction of Abbé Tronson, he became a priest in 1685. Since he aspired to be a missionary and was preparing himself for that at the Séminaire des Missions étrangères in Paris, he met there, in 1687, Bishop Laval* who had just resigned as bishop of Quebec, and Bishop Saint-Vallier [La Croix*], his successor. Abbé Baudoin's choice then fell upon Acadia, where he arrived in 1688. From Port-Royal he soon moved to Beaubassin, where, together with the Sulpician Claude Trouvé*, he carried on his priestly duties in the farthermost reaches of the Baie Française (Bay of Fundy). He occasionally took part in Indian expeditions against New England.

During his stay in Acadia, Baudoin was accused of exerting undue influence in civil matters, and he had clashes with Governor JOSEPH ROBINAU de Villebon in this connection. A stern letter from Versailles required him to go to France with Bishop Saint-Vallier in the fall of 1694 in order to exonerate himself. He returned in the spring of 1696 with Pierre Le Moyne* d'Iberville, who was entrusted with an expedition against the English. Abbé Baudoin accompanied him both as chaplain and as an expert on Acadian problems. He thus took part in the capture of Pemaquid and in the conquest of Newfoundland, leaving a detailed diary of the whole expedition. He returned, exhausted, to his mission at Beaubassin, and died there towards the end of the summer of 1698.

HONORIUS PROVOST

AN, Col., B, 17; C[11D], 3, ff.27–40. *Coll. de manuscrits relatifs à la Nouv.-France*, II, 148–55, 215. H.-R. Casgrain, *Les Sulpiciens et les prêtres des Missions-Étrangères en Acadie (1676–1762)* (Québec, 1897). Auguste Gosselin, *Journal de M. Beaudoin* (Les Normands au Canada; Évreux, 1900). Webster, *Acadia*.

BAUDOUIN, GERVAIS, surgeon; b. c. 1645 at Saint-Brice (diocese of Chartres), son of Gervais Baudouin and Jeanne Desrues; d. 1700 at Quebec.

Baudouin came to Canada about 1677. On 6 Oct. 1683 he married Anne Auber, daughter of the notary Claude AUBER, at Quebec. Baudouin was doctor to the Ursulines and to the seminary of Quebec, for which he received 100 *livres* in 1690 and 140 *livres* in 1691. He is not known to have had any apprentices.

He was assistant to the chief surgeon, Félix de Tassy, who was practising in France, and it was in this capacity that in September 1694 he denounced the surgeon René Gaschet as incompetent. In 1695 he was surgeon-major of Quebec. On 28 Sept. 1697 he bought two pieces of land at Montreal, and that is why it has been supposed, although incorrectly, that he had practised his art in that town.

On 4 Dec. 1700 he succumbed to an epidemic and was buried in the church of Notre-Dame de Québec the next day. Eight of his children survived him, one of whom, Gervais, was a surgeon, and another, Michel*, was a Jesuit missionary in Louisiana. Two of his daughters joined the Ursulines and another was a nun in the Hôpital Général. His wife died in June 1728.

GABRIEL NADEAU

AJQ, Greffe de Gilles Rageot, 4 nov. 1683. ASQ, MSS, C, II (1674–86) [Livres de comptes, II], 274f. Ahern, *Notes pour l'histoire de la médecine*. BRH, IV (1898), 339. Godbout, "Nos ancêtres," APQ *Rapport, 1953–55*, 506f. Albertus Martin, "La famille Beaudoin," BRH, XL (1934), 693–700.

BAYLY (Baily, Baley), CHARLES, first overseas governor of the HBC; fl. c. 1630–80.

This remarkable man, whose life was strangely affected and strongly influenced by the religious struggles of his time, was born in London of French Roman-Catholic parents and, to use his own words, "tenderly brought up about the Court of England." The nationality of his parents and his upbringing as a Roman Catholic at a Protestant court in an age when the older church was unpopular with the majority of Englishmen imply that Bayly senior was probably a member of Queen Henrietta Maria's household. The quarrels of Charles I with Parliament and the impending Civil War brought changes to court life which, in turn, led Bayly's parents to send their son to France. He was then about 12 or 13 years of age. Some time later he returned without permission and when at Gravesend en route to London he was enticed on board a ship about to sail for America.

In "Maryland in Virginia," as he usually described his American abode, he was forced to endure 14 years of misery and hardship as a bond-servant. Punishment meted out to him (according to his own account) and the length of his servitude may possibly indicate that Bayly tried unsuccessfully to escape from the situation into which he had been trapped. On gaining his freedom Bayly chose to remain in America and to labour with his hands rather than to return to Europe to find his relations. It was during this period of his life, in 1656 or 1657, that he came under the influence of Elizabeth Harris, the Quaker missionary, and it was on 14 Jan. 1657/58 (or the 14th day of the 11th month 1657, according to Quaker dating) that he was reported to her by a resident of Ann Arundel County, Maryland, as "abiding convinced."

Bayly left for England about the spring or summer of 1660. The journey was apparently inspired by religious zeal rather than a desire to find his relatives, and after brief stays in London and Dover, which must have occurred about the time of the Restoration, he joined forces with another Friend, Jane Stokes, to go to Rome for the purpose of helping the fanatical John Perrot, who was imprisoned there, it is said, for having tried to take the Quaker message to the pope. Their efforts led to their being examined and imprisoned by the Inquisition and Bayly, in "the Prison or Hospital of mad men," endured a self-imposed fast of 20 days "as a witness against that bloody Generation." By the end of May all three were released and began the journey back to England.

In the summer of 1661 Bayly was imprisoned for two months near Dieppe for proselytizing. After his release he continued his missionary activities in northern France, but when he reached Dunkirk his efforts were frustrated by the English governor's putting him aboard a royal frigate for England. Bayly was in Dover but 24 hours before he was arrested at a meeting of Friends and on refusing to take the oath of allegiance he was committed to prison on 13 Oct. 1661. It was during his seven months' confinement with other Quakers in Dover Castle that notice was first taken of his "mad actions," and that he began to fall out of repute with Friends. Influenced by John Perrot, whose sufferings in Rome had left him with a spiritual pride which brought him into conflict with Quaker leaders in England, Bayly shared with him the responsibility for the ensuing schism which resulted from their practice of carrying to extremes the Quaker revolt against traditional ways of worship. The heretics, who had a considerable following, made no distinction between "hat honour" to men and reverence due to God, and among other things committed the further extravagancy of growing long beards. It was about 1666 or 1667 before "this strange Fire," as the Quaker historian Sewel called it, "was altogether extinguished," and by then George Fox had accounted Bayly as having come to naught.

On being released from Dover prison early in May 1662 Bayly went to London where he was

Bayly

soon caught up in the storm of persecution which resulted after the passing of the first act of Parliament against Quakers. Between 27 June 1662 and about March or April 1663 he was imprisoned four times for refusing to take the oath of allegiance, and on one occasion was brought before and released by the lord mayor, Sir John Robinson, who was to be deputy governor of the future Hudson's Bay Company. By 1 May 1663 Bayly was imprisoned in Newgate, Bristol, for speaking to two priests in the street, and it was from this gaol that he wrote to Charles II in the following September, threatening him with "a share in the whirlwind of the Lord," advising him to "avoid rioting and excess, chambering and wantonness," and referring to the time when they had last spoken together. This reference becomes a matter for speculation. If king and Quaker had indeed spoken together the occasion could have been as recent as within the preceding three years, or as long ago as their childhood.

Bayly was next in the custody of the mayor of St. Albans, but in January 1664 he was transferred to that of Sir John Robinson, lieutenant of the Tower of London. The charge against Bayly was one of seditious practices, but he appears never to have been examined. As the Tower was reserved for prisoners of rank and importance Bayly's transfer there is puzzling, but a possible explanation is that the king, who was himself tolerant of Nonconformists and Roman Catholics, was responsible. By their concerted activities and bold refusal to accept what they considered wrong in the existing order, Friends were understandably and rightly regarded as enemies by its guardians. The charge against Bayly of seditious practices was doubtless due to his constant refusal to take the oath of allegiance, and to his being at cross-purposes with Fox and other Quaker leaders. There seems to be no confirmation of the statement made by the Venetian ambassador in France to the doge and senate that Bayly either aspired to being, or was recognized as, "the principal and most famous in the sect of Quecquers," or that he was concerned in a "conspiracy" of Friends at Colchester in the latter part of 1663.

In 1667 Bayly addressed "a few words of good counsel and advice" to the king, and in the summer of 1669 he obtained a conditional release to go to France for some, as yet, unknown purpose. In late August he was seen in Paris by the disgraced courtier, Henry Savile, caring for the children of the recently deceased Lady Lexington, and was described by him as an "old quaker with a long beard." Bayly, back in the Tower, petitioned the king in December 1669 for his liberty. This was granted on condition he betook himself "to the Navigation of Hudsons Bay, and the Places lately Discovered and to be Discovered in those parts," and he was assured of "conditions and allowances . . . agreeable to reason and the nature of his employment."

By this time the founder members of the HBC (including Sir John Robinson) had the satisfaction of knowing that the first voyage to Hudson Bay— that of CHOUART Des Groseilliers and Zachariah GILLAM in 1668–69—had been a success, and that a royal charter to protect their privileges was to be granted to them. This charter, dated 2 May 1670, gave the "Governor and Company of Adventurers of England trading into Hudsons Bay" the authority to appoint governors to serve overseas and Bayly was the first one to hold that rank. The true reason for such an apparently unsuitable choice has yet to be discovered. The king, interested but not financially involved in the Hudson Bay venture, may have seized the chance not only of ridding himself of an obstinate prisoner but also of helping an old acquaintance by making the conditions of release those of exile with dignity and remuneration. Sir John Robinson, knowing Bayly to be a travelled, fearless, and honest man, as well as a stubborn one, may have made the recommendation. The conditions of release were, no doubt, quite acceptable to Bayly who, after so many years of frustration, must have been spiritually discouraged and materially bankrupt.

Before sailing to Hudson Bay Bayly became a stockholder in the HBC to the extent of £300. This holding must have been surety for good behaviour, and as he had been on the king's allowance when in the Tower, it is probable that Sir John Robinson, or even the Lexington children's grandfather, Sir Anthony St. Ledger, was his guarantor. The stock remained in Bayly's name until some time between 1673 and 1675.

Early in June 1670 Bayly sailed from the Thames for Port Nelson in the *Wivenhoe* (Capt. Robert Newland). He had Pierre-Esprit Radisson* as a fellow-passenger and aboard the *Prince Rupert* (Capt. Zachariah Gillam), which sailed in company, was Des Groseilliers. The ships parted company on 18 August at the western end of Hudson Strait. The *Prince Rupert* arrived safely at Charles Fort on Rupert River, but it was only with difficulty that the *Wivenhoe* reached Port Nelson. Fogs and contrary winds made the river entrance hard to find, but in September Bayly went ashore and, nailing His Majesty's arms "in Brasse" on a tree, formally laid claim to the territory. By this time the Indians had left for inland and Bayly's men were so discouraged that it was decided to sail for Rupert River. By the middle of October, when the *Wivenhoe* was safely docked there, her captain and chief mate were both dead, presumably from scurvy, and the command had devolved upon Bayly.

The governor "repeated and confirmed" the agreements with the Indians which Capt. Gillam had made at Rupert River in 1668 and his relations with them were friendly. In the spring of 1671 Bayly and Radisson went to Moose River where they traded all the beaver skins taken to London that year in the *Wivenhoe*. Whilst preparations were in hand for the homeward voyage Bayly, accompanied by Thomas GORST and others, energetically explored the coast and islands of James Bay in shallops. They found signs of past human, but not of Indian, habitation, and assumed the place to be where HENRY HUDSON had ended his days. They also landed on Charlton Island, where they found traces of Capt. Thomas JAMES's expedition. As he was unable to get volunteers to stay in the country and was unwilling to make demands, Bayly had no option but to return to England, where he arrived in command of the *Wivenhoe* in October 1671.

From that time until he returned in the summer of 1672 to Charles Fort, Bayly was busily engaged in London helping to dispose of the 1671 homeward cargo and preparing the new outfit. It is extremely probable that it was during the winter of 1671–72 that he married, for it was after he had left for the bay a second time that his wife's name (Hannah) first appeared in his account in the Company's grand ledger.

On his return to Charles Fort in 1672 Bayly was ordered to settle a post at Moose River. A small house was accordingly built on Hayes Island in 1673, but it does not appear to have been occupied during the whole season. Also, in 1673, Bayly sent Des Groseilliers to trade at Port Nelson, but the trip was unsuccessful as the Indians were inland. The winter of 1673–74 was severe and the consequent shortage of fresh food inevitably resulted in scurvy. Difficulties were further increased by the enmity of the "Nodway" Indians who threatened to destroy Charles Fort, and at one time the back-sliding Quaker himself led a party in pursuit but "could not come near enough to do any Execution." Bayly's friendship with the "Cuscudidahs" may have been the cause of a small part of the "Nodways'" enmity, but most of it was almost certainly due to their dissatisfaction at the rates of exchange for their furs. This dissatisfaction no doubt resulted from Father Charles ALBANEL's activities at Rupert River in 1672, just prior to Bayly's return. Albanel had successfully demonstrated that James Bay could be reached overland from Canada and had laid claim to the territory in the French king's name.

By the summer of 1674 Bayly felt the effects on his business of the French traders strategically placed on the rivers flowing to James Bay and, as a result, he was the first Company governor to advocate sending men inland to meet the challenge.

During the summer of 1674 Bayly went to Moose River where he made a successful trade by, it is suspected, manipulating the rigid standard of trade laid down by the Company in London. He then sailed on 16 July "to discover Shechittawam [Albany] River" where "no Englishman had been before." He entered into a treaty with the Indians but as his visit was unexpected he did but little trade. He promised to return in the following year and on 21 July sailed northwards towards Cape Henrietta Maria. Passing the island now known as Akimiski, he named it after a Company committee-member, Sir Robert Vyner. Bayly saw many signs of starvation among the Indians at Ekwan River and at New Severn and, hearing that there was no beaver to be had and that the sea beyond Cape Henrietta Maria was full of ice, decided to return. A forced landing on Charlton Island delayed his arrival at Rupert River until 30 August.

Soon after, Father Albanel arrived at Charles Fort overland from Quebec. On this second visit to James Bay he brought Bayly a friendly letter from BUADE de Frontenac, but if the seduction of the English governor's allegiance was any part of the French plan, it was unsuccessful even during the particularly difficult conditions which prevailed in James Bay during the winter of 1674–75.

The delay in the arrival of the supply ships in 1674 made Bayly so uneasy that he formed tentative plans to evacuate the fort and return to England in the barque *Imploy*. But on 17 Sept. 1674, when he was on the point of sailing, two ships arrived and he learned that he had been recalled to London and that his successor, William LYDALL, had arrived. However, it was now too late in the season for the ships to return, so Bayly had not only to surrender his command, but also to submit to the humiliation of serving under the newcomer during the 1674–75 season. With so many extra mouths to feed the James Bay veterans advised immediate rationing, but Lydall would not agree and so, later in the season, the men at Charles Fort were "forc'd to pinch harder than they needed have done." The experienced Bayly managed better at Moose River. Lydall, disgruntled and disgusted, returned to England in 1675 and Bayly resumed the command which he was to hold until his second recall in 1679. He continued to explore James Bay so far as sea transport would allow and, before he left for London, he established and placed John BRIDGAR

Bazire

in charge of the first English post to be settled in Albany River.

During his last summer in James Bay Bayly was visited by Louis JOLLIET who had come overland from Quebec under instructions from Frontenac to report on the English posts and to persuade the Indians to trade with the French. Bayly received the French party in friendship but, at the same time, by a recital of English achievements in the bay since 1674, he indicated that he had nothing to fear from them.

Bayly arrived in London towards the end of 1679 to face certain charges which had been brought against him. The Company's surviving records of the period give but few clues as to the nature of the accusations, but there is no doubt that, besides being concerned with the forbidden practice of private trade, they were also connected with the mismanagement of company property due to lack of attention to detail and to slipshod, but not dishonest, methods. These charges were being prepared when Bayly died on 6 Jan. 1680/81 at the Strand home of William Walker of the HBC, the father of Capt. NEHEMIAH WALKER. Two days later, by torchlight and attended by the officers of the ship *John and Alexander* in which he had returned to London, Bayly was buried at the Company's expense in the church of St. Paul's, Covent Garden. Later in the year his successor, John NIXON, received an "escutcheon" from the governor and committee with instructions to have it "set up for the observation of the Indians, that they may be made to understand he [Bayly] is dead, and that the Company used him kindly." Bayly was survived by his wife, Hannah, who entered into a lengthy argument with the Company about his salary (£50 per annum until 1678 and £200 per annum afterwards); final agreement was not reached until 1683.

When Bayly first went to Rupert River he had already "come to naught" as far as Friends were concerned, and if he had not already shed all his Quaker beliefs the remaining ones could have suffered further in his close companionship with a limited number of highly individual characters under the harsh living conditions of James Bay. The attempt to punish the "Nodways" was one sign of changing views, and since George Fox considered music to be almost as dangerous as gunpowder the purchase of a "violl & shells & strings" was another. But it is not known if his failure to make public use of the prayer books, Bibles, and books of homilies sent to James Bay by the governor and committee was the result of a growing indifference to religion, or to a remaining objection to, and rejection of, an "established" order of worship.

Although Bayly was recalled to face charges of mismanagement, his career in the HBC was still an honourable one. Clearly he was a man of action who could not be bothered with book-keeping detail, but his loyalty, enthusiasm, and energy in James Bay were of great value to the Company during the first decade of its existence.

ALICE M. JOHNSON

The most informative of Bayly's own writings are: *A true and faithful warning unto the people and inhabitants of Bristol . . . with a brief account of some tryalls and sufferings . . .* (London, 1663); "The third of the Sixth Month, 1661 [i.e., 3 Aug. 1661] From the Common Goal [*sic*] in Burkdou in France, about thirty leagues from Dover, where I am a sufferer for speaking the word of the Lord to two Priests" in *A narrative of some of the sufferings of J.P. in the city of Rome* (London, 1661), 11–16; and *A seasonable warning and word of advice to all Papists, but most especially to those in the Kingdome of France* (London, 1663).

For references to Bayly and guidance to published and MS source material *see*: *Documents relating to Hudson Bay* (Tyrrell), 383–97; HBRS, V, VIII (Rich); XI (Rich and Johnson); XXI (Rich); PRO, *CSP, Venice, 1661–64*; W. C. Braithwaite, *The beginnings of Quakerism*, ed. H. J. Cadbury (2d rev. ed., Cambridge, 1961); *The second period of Quakerism* (London, 1919); Nute, *Caesars of the wilderness*, 131ff.

BAZIRE, CHARLES, receiver general of duties and of the king's domain, seigneur, merchant, agent of the Compagnie des Indes occidentales; b. 1624, son of Jean Bazire, a native of Saint-Vincent de Rouen, and of Jeanne Le Borgne; d. 1677.

He seems to have had only one sister, Marie, who married PHILIPPE GAULTIER de Comporté. On 11 Jan. 1666, at Quebec, he married Geneviève Macard, the daughter of Nicolas Macard and Marguerite Couillard; Charles, their only child, was born 21 Sept. 1666 and died two weeks later.

Charles Bazire came to New France about 1660 as receiver general of duties and of the king's domain. He immediately became active in business, and went into partnership with Charles Aubert* de La Chesnaye. In the 1667 census, 14 persons are listed as sharing his house at Quebec; in addition to his wife, his employees lived with him. The notarial documents of the period show Bazire involved in a large number of transactions dealing with real estate and various exchanges. Until 1674 he was the agent of the Compagnie des Indes occidentales, which held the fur-trading monopoly in New France. On 3 September of the same year, the governor-general, BUADE de Frontenac, in order to "make up the number of judges required to judge the charges of impugnment brought by" François-Marie PERROT, governor of

Montreal, against certain members of the Conseil Souverain, appointed him a member of this body, along with a number of others.

On 20 July 1672 Intendant TALON granted to him, and simultaneously to Pierre Denys* de La Ronde and Charles Aubert de La Chesnaye, a seigneury one league square on the mainland, opposite the Île Percée. Factories for fishing were set up on the Petite Rivière (at the mouth of the brook Barachois, at Saint-Pierre de La Malbaie), and at Percé. Pierre Denys seems to have been the one chiefly responsible for the smooth functioning of this establishment, which specialized in cod-fishing.

With Charles Aubert de La Chesnaye, Bazire likewise obtained a land grant for the purpose of cutting timber on the Rivière-du-Loup and Madawaska seigneuries. Several other land grants were also made to him. In this way he received from Bishop Laval* on 21 July 1677, jointly with Charles Aubert de La Chesnaye, the arriere-fief of Charlesville, near Montmorency Falls. We also know that he owned, again jointly with Charles Aubert de La Chesnaye, the fief and seigneury of Lachenaie (arriere-fief of the Beaupré heights).

Charles Bazire thus stands out as one of the first business men in New France. At his death, he left a tidy little fortune and various assets. In his will, drawn up before the notary Romain BECQUET on 14 Dec. 1677, the day preceding his death, he did indeed bequeath 50,000 *livres*, to be divided between the parochial council of Notre-Dame de Québec, where he had been a churchwarden in 1671 and 1673, the Jesuits, the Ursulines, the Hôtel-Dieu, his father, and the Recollets. His wife, with whom he had a joint estate, received half of his possessions. She was married twice more, first to François Provost*, major of the Château Saint-Louis and then governor of Trois-Rivières, and subsequently to Charles-Henri d'Aloigny*, Marquis de La Groye.

FERNAND GRENIER

ASQ, MSS, C, II (1674–86) [Livres de comptes, II], pp. 95–112, 280–3; Paroisse de Québec, 145; Seigneuries, III, 27; Séminaire, VI, 16, XXXIII, 11, XXXV, 34–37. BN, MS Clairambault, 1016, f.297. *Jug. et délib.*, I, II, III, V. *Ord comm.* (P.-G. Roy), I, 120-6, P.-G. Roy, *Inv. concessions*, I, 66, 264; II, 127; "La famille Bazire," *BRH*, XLII (1936), 66–72.

BEARE, JAMES, English mariner with the FROBISHER expeditions, 1577–78; fl. 1577–85.

James Beare, to whom are attributed "the first maps to show with reasonable accuracy the eastern approaches to the Canadian Arctic," was master of the 30-ton *Michaell* (Gilbert Yorke, captain) on the second (1577) Frobisher voyage and master of the *Anne Francis* (George BEST, captain) on Frobisher's third voyage in 1578.

During July 1577, the *Michaell* broke her "Stéerage" and the topmasts were blown overboard in a great storm. On 28 July, nevertheless, the *Michaell* entered an inlet which was named "Beares Sound," near the most westerly point reached that year in Frobisher Bay (mistaken for the northwest passage).

Beare also took part in the 1578 expedition as master of the *Anne Francis*. Frobisher's fleet left Harwich 31 May 1578, landed and took possession of Greenland for England, and sailed on to "Meta Incognita." Thick fog shrouded the coast and fierce tides swept them south across the entrance of the "mistaken straites" (Hudson Strait). Frobisher consulted with his men, sending "his Pinnesse aboorde to heare each mans opinion, and specially of James Beare, mayster of the Anne Francis, who was knowen to be a sufficient and skilful Mariner, and having bin there the yeare before, had well observed the place, and drawne out Cardes of the coast."

The *Anne Francis* ran on a sunken rock 10 August and lay there until the flood-tide lifted her. Two thousand strokes of the pump were needed to clear the water; and the crew built a pinnace as a precaution against shipwreck. There was a smith on board but no tools to make nails and knees. A gun-chamber was pressed into service as an anvil and a pickaxe as a sledge-hammer. The ship was laid aground on 30 August while eight gaping leaks, caused by rocks and ice, were stopped. The same day the crew attended a communion service conducted on shore by Master Wolfall, chaplain of the fleet.

Beare was with Best 11 August, when a stone cross was erected on Hatton's Headland "in token of Christian possession" of this place. Here they found "plentie of blacke Ore and divers preatie stones." Best had already found, on the island named Bestes Blessing, 9 August, masses of black ore of which he wrote, "if the goodnesse myghte aunswere the greate plentye thereof, it was to be thoughte that it might reasonably suffice all the golde gluttons of the worlde." The fleet brought back more than 1,000 tons of this ore; but it proved to be "fool's gold."

Later, James Beare (probably the same man) was master of the *Judith* of London, which was taken by Barbary pirates. In a letter to John Tipton, English consul at Algiers, dated 30 March 1585, William Harborne, ambassador at Constantinople, refers to Beare as a captive in Algiers (Hakluyt, *Principal navigations* (1903–5), *V*, 281).

Two maps in George Best's *A true discourse* are attributed to Beare: an engraved oval world map and a map of Meta Incognita. That Beare drew the latter map is reasonably certain from the reference in *A true discourse* to his "Cardes of the coast" and the fact that Best and Beare sailed together in 1578. Beare may well have drawn the world map also. Although neither map indicates that he was a talented cartographer, since both are roughly drawn, still the maps combine the discoveries of Frobisher with the previous theories of a passage; they are properly proportioned and correctly orientated; and they do constitute the first maps in a new phase of English cartography of America.

It is not certain that Beare was principal surveyor on the Frobisher expeditions, as stated in *Sixteenth-century maps relating to Canada*, since he did not sail with the 1576 expedition and he was not on board Frobisher's flag ship on the later voyages. However, he seems to have been treated as the chief cartographer of the voyages after returning in 1578.

THOMAS DUNBABIN

Best, *A true discourse* (repr. in *Three Voyages of Frobisher* (Stefansson), I, 4ff. and in Hakluyt, *Principal navigations* (1903–5), VII. *Sixteenth-century maps relating to Canada: a check-list and bibliography*, ed. T. E. Layng (PAC pub., 1956), 167–68.

BEAUDOIN. *See* BAUDOIN

BÉCANCOUR, RENÉ ROBINAU DE. *See* ROBINAU

BECHOURAT. *See* BEGOURAT

BECQUET, ROMAIN, notary, court officer, clerk of the diocesan officiality (*l'officialité diocésaine*), seigneurial judge and seigneur; b. 1640 or shortly before at Le Bec (or Becq), near Rouen; d. 20 April 1682 at Quebec.

Becquet, the son of a surgeon, Julien Becquet, and of Anne Vasse, married at Quebec (1) Romaine Boudet, 5 June 1666, and (2) Marie Pellerin, 2 May 1677; only two daughters survived him. But the name of the family has been preserved through the seigneury of Saint-Pierre-les-Becquets, which was granted to it in 1672. The presence of Romain Becquet at Quebec can be traced back to 31 July 1661.

He exercised the profession of notary from 1665 on, even styling himself "notaire royal," although he seems never to have had a commission of this kind. On 20 March 1668 the intendant TALON granted him a commission as court officer and sergeant. On 23 Oct. 1678, at the request of Bishop François de Laval*, seigneur of Beaupré, Becquet became judge or "baillif haut-justicier" of the county of Saint-Laurens (Île d'Orléans) and of the shore of Beaupré. It was in this capacity that he drew up the first registry of the land belonging to the seigneury. The bishop had also made him clerk of his officiality on 18 April 1675. Becquet's registry, preserved in the judical Archives of Quebec, is one of the most important for the study of 17th-century Quebec.

HONORIUS PROVOST

AJQ, Greffe de Romain Becquet, 1637–82. ASQ, Documents Faribault, 117b, 121, 123b, 129a, 226; Paroisse de Québec, 28, nos 4 et 5; 92, no 19, p. 7; 120; 147; 151–53. *Ord. comm.* (P.-G. Roy). J.-E. Roy, *Histoire du notariat.* P.-G. Roy, *Inv. ins. prév. Québec.*

BEGOURAT (Bechourat), a chief of the Montagnais Indians; fl. 1603.

Begourat led a successful war-party against the Iroquois in the summer of 1603. CHAMPLAIN described the events that transpired before the departure of this party in June. The Indians assembled in a "public square" at Tadoussac, dressed in the richest of fur garments, beads, and coloured cord, bearing bows and arrows, clubs, and round shields, with Begourat, their war-chief, at their head. They first marched single-file, sporting and play-acting, and then danced. After they had finished, the women disrobed and commenced to dance, finally taking to their canoes for a playful mock battle. When the women returned to their lodges, the warriors set off.

At the end of June, Champlain passed the party encamped in oak-bark lodges behind timber palisades thrown up at the mouth of the River of the Iroquois (Richelieu). Their canoes lay side by side on the bank ready for flight in the event of a surprise attack by the enemy.

In early August, Champlain met the same party on their return to Tadoussac after a successful encounter of 10 of their number with three canoes of Iroquois on Lake Champlain. They bore with them the heads of the defeated Iroquois. Only one Montagnais was wounded.

When the French departed from Tadoussac on 16 August, Begourat gave his son to FRANÇOIS GRAVÉ Du Pont to take to France on the recommendation of ANADABIJOU who had heard the satisfactory reports of the two Indians who had previously accompanied Gravé to France. An Iroquois woman captive whom they had intended to eat was also taken to France on this voyage.

ELSIE MCLEOD JURY

Champlain, *Works* (Biggar), *passim.*

BELESTRE, PIERRE PICOTÉ DE. *See* Picoté

BELLEBORNE, JEAN NICOLLET DE. *See* Nicollet de Belleborne

BELLE-ISLE, ALEXANDRE LE BORGNE DE. *See* Le Borgne

BELLENGER, ÉTIENNE (Stephen Bellinger in Hakluyt), merchant of Rouen and explorer of what are now the Atlantic Provinces; fl. 1580–84.

Bellenger was probably a general merchant who dealt indifferently in fish and furs. Before 1582 he had been on two voyages to the Maritimes, possibly as cape merchant (purser) on Norman vessels which visited Cape Breton to trade with the Indians, and had penetrated some way along the coast of Nova Scotia. It was probably on his initiative that the aged Cardinal Bourbon, archbishop of Rouen, took up, in association with the Duc de Joyeuse, admiral of France, a project for exploring and trading along the coast south and west of Cape Breton and establishing there a small outpost, which it was hoped would later become the nucleus of a colony.

In the summer of 1582 Bellenger was borrowing money in Rouen, perhaps with a view to financing the trading part of the venture although he had recently received payment for his part in financing Strozzi's ill-fated expedition to the Azores. Later, in November, the bark *Chardon* of 50 tons, belonging to Jacques de Chardon de Tressonville, gentleman in ordinary to the cardinal, was prepared for Bellenger's voyage. Michel Costé, an experienced Rouen pilot, was engaged for the voyage, and was permitted to purchase a third share in the ship. Costé was to be captain and pilot and was to supply a crew of 10 men; Bellenger was to have command of 20 men who were to be taken across the Atlantic and left there with provisions. The destination was to be kept secret and revealed by Bellenger only after the ship had left the English Channel. The vessel was to return to France when it had completed its mission.

The *Chardon* left Havre-de-Grâce (Le Havre) on 19 Jan. 1583 (N.S.), carrying a small pinnace. She must have been favoured with easterly winds as she reached Cape Breton in 20 days, that is about 7 February. How much Bellenger knew of the coast and where he had first intended to settle we do not know. The *Chardon*, under his direction, proceeded to make a thorough survey of the coast, west-southwestwards from the cape, charting bays and harbours, rocks and islands, and sounding shallows and deeps. Some 50 to 60 leagues down the coast he noted the appearance of a large island, which he identified as the island of St. John (Isle St. Jehan). Whatever it meant to other cartographers, it is clear that to him it was what we know as the westerly part of Nova Scotia, divided from the "mainland" probably at Halifax harbour. He coasted down one side of what he eventually sketched as a triangular island, lying about 50 leagues east and west, that is to Cap de Sable, and then turned to enter "the great bay of that island," namely the Bay of Fundy (Baie Française). As he noted that "the entrance is so narrow that a culverin shot can reach from one side to the other" it would appear that he passed (if the coast has not changed in the meantime) between Long Island and Digby Neck into the bay. He explored some 30 leagues up the southern shore of the bay, which would bring him almost to the entrance of Minas Basin, which he does not seem to have entered, though he evidently regarded it as the northern part of the channel between the Isle St. Jehan and Cape Breton. He planted marks of possession at the head of the bay by attaching the arms of Cardinal Bourbon to a tall tree (perhaps to be found there by Champlain in 1607 as a very old cross, all covered with moss).

Bellenger described the Bay of Fundy as being 20 leagues wide though it is less than half that except at its mouth. He gave names to many places as he continued to explore the bay and some of those which he gave to the northern shore survived his voyage. We are told that some 20 leagues to the west of the Isle St. Jehan, the outlines of which he had now established, he found a great river, up which he penetrated for seven leagues in his pinnace. He expressed the opinion that it was navigable for 60 or 80 leagues. It would appear that he emerged from the Bay of Fundy between Grand Menane (now Grand Manan) Island and the mainland and that he ran along the Maine coast to the opening of the Penobscot and entered that river. It would seem that he did not proceed westwards beyond the river. The range of his exploration is given as 200 leagues from Cape Breton and in the latitudes of 42° to 44°. Since Cape Breton is in 46°, we may probably modify these figures to between approximately 44° and 46°, which would include the mouth of the Penobscot. From the drafts he brought home Bellenger soon completed a general map, which he presented to the cardinal.

The *Chardon* or her pinnace put Bellenger on land frequently, ten to a dozen times. He made a close examination of the resources of the land, its timber, its possibilities for making salt, and its presumed mineral wealth, bringing home an ore believed to contain lead and silver. He also made frequent contacts with the Indians. Those who

Bellenger

lived from 60 to 80 leagues westward from Cape Breton he found cunning, cruel, and treacherous; he lost two of his men and his pinnace to them as he made his way back along the Nova Scotia shore. The Indians farther to the west were gentle and tractable. He visited an Indian village of 80 houses on a river 100 leagues from Cape Breton, not far, that is, from Cap de Sable. He had a quantity of small merchandise for trade, and acquired from the Indians in return for it dressed "buff" (probably elk), deer, and seal skins, together with marten, beaver, otter, and lynx pelts, samples of castor, porcupine quills, dye-stuffs, and some dried deer-flesh.

Having found so much, Bellenger abandoned his plan to remain in America. He was probably ready to leave early in May and he may have arrived home before the end of the month after an absence of about four months in all. He presented many mementos to the cardinal and sold, at a high profit, the skins bought on his own adventure.

In 1583 Jacques de Vaulx, a celebrated pilot of Le Havre, was working on two copies of a remarkable illustrated work on cosmography, "Les Premiéres Euvres de Jacques de Vaulx pillote en la marine." In his first version (BN, MS Fr. 9175), presented in 1584 to M. de Riberpré, he drew a map of the Americas using a stereotyped coastline from Cape Breton westward to the "R. de Gamas" (MS Fr. 9175, f.25), but in his second (BN, MS Fr. 150) he included evidence from Bellenger's voyage in the form of a triangular "Isle St. Jehan," for Nova Scotia, and other changes (f.26). He went on to compile a map of the North Atlantic using similar material (ff.29–30) and then returned to his first version to include a comparable "improved" map (MS Fr. 9175, ff.29–30), with somewhat more Bellenger material than in the others. De Vaulx intended his major version (MS Fr. 150) for the Duc de Joyeuse, who probably commissioned it, and he dedicated it to him before the end of 1583.

The close association of both de Vaulx and Bellenger with Joyeuse demonstrates how Bellenger's material became available so rapidly to the former. In 1584 de Vaulx compiled a more detailed map of the Americas which survives only in an incomplete form (BN, Cartes, Réserve, Géographie, C.4052). This preserves a much fuller version of the results of Bellenger's voyage, taken, with little doubt, from his own map. It shows a greatly modified coastline from Cape Breton to the "R. de Gamas," the western limit of the new information, which is therefore equated with Bellenger's "great river" (Penobscot). The new nomenclature comprises 15 names, all deriving, almost certainly, from Bellenger. The Bay of Fundy becomes "Pasaige de St. Jehan," and the coastline westwards from Passamaquoddy Bay, at "C. de Mont," to the "R. de Gamas" is greatly elongated.

We owe most of our knowledge of this voyage to the Rev. Richard Hakluyt, who had arrived at the English embassy in Paris as chaplain in October 1583, but who mainly concerned himself with collecting information on America. From André THEVET, the royal cosmographer, and Valeron Perosse, a Paris skinner who was already dealing in North American furs, he learned at the end of 1583 that "Duke Joyeuse, Admiral of France, and the Cardinal of Burbon and their frendes, have had a meaning to send out a certayne ships to inhabite some place for [i.e., in] the north part of America, and to carry thither many friers and other religiouse persons" (letter of 7 Jan. 1584).

With our knowledge of Bellenger's voyage earlier in 1583 we can probably envisage the objectives of the cardinal and the admiral. Bellenger had gone out to lay foundations for a colony by setting up a trading post, which was intended as a prelude to a larger settlement, which, in turn, was thought of as a centre for missionary efforts amongst the Indians. Unlike the projects of TROILUS DE LA ROCHE de Mesgouez this was directed towards the Maritimes and not the St. Lawrence valley. Bellenger's return may have underlined the dangers from the Indians such a venture might well experience even though he had had favourable geographic and economic reports to make, since Hakluyt adds (in the letter already cited) that "I thinke they be not in haste to do yt."

Hakluyt, however, using the English intelligence network, made contact with Bellenger's relative, André Mayer, a compass-maker in Rouen (and perhaps himself an agent) and through him with Bellenger. Hakluyt hurried to Rouen in late January or February and saw Bellenger in his house in the rue des Augustines, next to the sign of the Golden Tile (*Huille deor*, i.e., *Tuile d'Or*). Bellenger proved very forthcoming, giving a detailed account of his expedition, showing Hakluyt various skins and other goods brought back, and giving him specimens of ore and other things, besides letting him see the draft of his map of his discoveries, the fair copy of which he had already presented to the cardinal. Moreover, he proved willing to repeat some of his information to various members of the English community in Rouen (who were at once enlisted by Hakluyt to support English projects for American voyages which were then in preparation). Hakluyt reported that Bellenger was preparing another bark and pinnace at Honfleur to set out on a further voyage —solely a trading one it would appear—by 1 March 1584. We learn nothing further of Bellenger, who may not have returned from this voyage. He had made a valuable contribution to the knowledge of the coastline between Cape Breton and Maine even though it was not fully assimilated by his contemporaries. Cardinal Bourbon's and the admiral's plans for the Maritimes were soon subordinated to a more ambitious expedition which was in preparation during 1584, sponsored by the Duc de Joyeuse, and which was to be under the command of Guillaume Le Héricy, with Jacques de Vaulx as chief pilot, ostensibly to coast the whole of eastern America from Brazil to Labrador. It left in 1585 and eventually returned in 1587 but its North American relevance, if any, is not known.

Richard Hakluyt referred to Bellenger's voyage in his "Discourse of western planting" which he wrote in England during the summer and early autumn of 1584, but his fuller account of the voyage, "The relation of master Stephen Bellanger dwelling in Roan . . . of his late voiadge of discoverie of two hundreth leagues of coast from Cape Brittone . . . west-south-west at the charges of the Cardinall of Borbon this last yere 1583" (BM, Add. MS 14027, ff.289–90v), which he wrote for Dr Julius Caesar, judge of the Admiralty, has remained unknown. Studies by La Roncière, Anthiaume, and Ganong brought the de Vaulx materials to light and it is now possible to combine them with the Bellenger documents into a coherent story.

DAVID B. QUINN

BM, Add. MS 14027, ff.289–90v. BN, MS Fr. 150 et 9175; Cartes, Réserve, géographie, C.4052 (maps, etc., by Jacques de Vaulx). Hakluyt, *Original writings* (Taylor), I, 205–7; II, 211–326 ("Discourse of western planting.").
Anthiaume, *Cartes marines*. Philippe Barrey, "Le Havre transatlantique de 1571 à 1610, "*Mémoires et documents pour servir à l'histoire du commerce et de l'industrie en France*, éd. Julien Hayem (12 parties, Paris, 1911–29), 5e partie (1917), 45–210. Bréard, *Documents relatifs à la marine normande*, 267. W. F. Ganong, "A monograph of the cartography of the Province of New Brunswick," *RSCT*, 2d ser., III (1897), sect.II, 313–427; "Crucial maps, IX." La Roncière, *Histoire de la marine française*, IV (1923); "Une carte française encore inconnue du Nouveau Monde (1584)," *Bibliothèque de l'école des Chartes*, LXXI (1910), 588–601. T. N. Marsh, "An unpublished Hakluyt manuscript?" *New Eng. Q.*, XXXV (1962), 247–52. D. B. Quinn, "The voyage of Etienne Bellenger to the Maritimes in 1583: a new document," *CHR*, XLIII (1962), 328–43.

BELLOT *dit* **Lafontaine,** governor of Plaisance (Placentia) 1664–67.

After the brief governorship of DU PERRON, who died by an assassin's hand during the winter of 1662–63, only a few months after his arrival, the king sent a new governor, Bellot *dit* Lafontaine, to Plaisance. French fishermen had frequented the shores of Newfoundland for a long time, but the resident population of Plaisance did not yet exceed 200. To help them subsist, the king had to send them food and munitions every year; a fort and a small garrison assured their defence.

Far from working towards strengthening the colony, the new governor contributed rather to weakening it through his negligence, his exactions, and his misuse of his power. The only official document concerning him that has been preserved notes that he "has discharged his duty badly." He was recalled in 1667 and replaced by La Palme (or de Palme).

RENÉ BAUDRY

AN, Col., C^{11C}, 1, f.24 (copy in BN, MS, NAF 9282 (Margry), f.230). BN, Mélanges Colbert, 144, f.523. La Morandière, *Hist. de la pêche française de la morue*, I, 417–18.

BERGIER (or possibly **Clerbaud-Bergier**), initiator of a project for a shore fishery in Acadia and one of the leading members of the Compagnie des Pêches sédentaires de l'Acadie formed in 1682; lieutenant for the king in Acadia in 1684; fl. *c.* 1680–5.

Bergier, a Huguenot merchant of La Rochelle, desired to establish a company to promote fishing and trading in Acadia, and in 1680 obtained permission from NICOLAS DENYS to visit Acadia. Bergier and his associates being Huguenots, the grand vicar of Quebec, M. DUDOUYT, protested that their project would be contrary to the interests of the state and religion and to the intentions of the king in founding the colony. To meet this objection, Bergier associated himself with Gabriel Gautier, Boucher, and de Mantes, of Paris. Organized into a company by the Marquis de Chevry [*see* DURET], Bergier and his associates received from the king of France on 28 Feb. 1682 a grant on the coast of Acadia and the Saint John River as a suitable area for fishery and trade. Bergier then proceeded to Acadia to select a base of operations.

Favourably impressed by its climate, its soil, its timber, and its advantages for fishing, he chose Chedabouctou (now Guysborough), left men to clear land and erect buildings, and went back to Paris to report. Returning to Acadia in 1683, he sowed wheat, oats, and barley, and planted vines and fruit trees at Chedabouctou and

Bermen

urged the inhabitants of Port-Royal to engage in fishing. Chedabouctou had previously been the site of one of the fishing establishments of Nicolas Denys; his son RICHARD and son-in-law Michel Leneuf* de La Vallière still occasionally hunted and fished there.

The trading monopoly of the fishing company was disputed by the heirs of CHARLES DE SAINT-ÉTIENNE de La Tour, MENOU d'Aulnay, and EMMANUEL LE BORGNE. Attempts to enforce it drew protests from various quarters and led to conflict with New Englanders, for La Vallière, seigneur of Beaubassin (Chignecto), who had been placed in charge of Acadia in 1678, had been selling licences to New Englanders to fish along the coast and use its harbours. Early in 1684 the Conseil d'État authorized the Company of Acadia to seize foreign vessels trading or fishing along the coast, and La Vallière was dismissed from his post and forbidden to issue licences to the New Englanders, although the intendant, Jacques Demeulle*, had ordered La Vallière in 1683 to prevent Bergier from establishing his fishery without express permission. By a decree of 14 April 1684, Bergier was appointed lieutenant for the king in Acadia for three years. About this time he and his son—and agent—Bergier Deshormeaux (or Des Ormeaux) came into conflict with La Vallière, his son Alexandre Leneuf* de Beaubassin, and Richard Denys (Deshormeaux's procès-verbal, 12 mai 1685, AN, Col., C^{11D}, I, f.192). Bergier himself was accused of trying to engage in the fur trade and in trafficking with the English.

Bergier seems to have played a less important role in Acadia after this year, for Charles DURET de Chevry de La Boulaye replaced him as lieutenant for the king and another merchant, Antoine Héron, acted as director of the fishing company in La Rochelle. In 1686, after repeated requests, Gabriel Gautier, a member of the company, received a grant of fishing rights at Cape Breton, Île Saint-Jean (Prince Edward Island), and the Îles de la Madeleine for a period of 20 years. The company extended its operations to Port-Royal in 1687. In that year there were 150 persons at Chedabouctou, 80 of whom were fishermen. Bergier's protests at the French court against Denys and La Vallière were rewarded in April 1687 with the Cape Breton concession, which had been Nicolas Denys's. (In compensation, Denys was given a large seigneury at Miramichi.)

The Company of Acadia suffered heavy losses in 1688, when Chedabouctou was pillaged by New Englanders, and in 1690, when Fort Saint-Louis was demolished by Capt. Cyprian Southack* following PHIPS's capture of Port-Royal. After the Treaty of Ryswick in 1697 it endeavoured to revive its operations in Acadia. In 1698 it established a fishing station at Chibouctou (the future Halifax), but its employees soon absconded to Boston or to Port Razoir (later Port Roseway and now Shelburne). Thereafter, for a few years, it had to content itself with a dwindling trade at Port-Royal, until all its effects were returned to France in a king's ship in 1703.

C. BRUCE FERGUSSON

Among the many sources on the company and Bergier are: AN, Col., B, 13, f.186; C^{11A}, 1, f.211 (the Bergier here referred to, a bourgeois of La Rochelle who attempted to establish sedentary fishing in Acadia from 1645, may be Bergier's father); C^{11A}, 6; C^{11D}, 1, f.192; 2, f.165; Col., E, 277; E^1, 536^B, ff.493–94; Marine, liasse 21; B^2, 50, 52, 56, 57; B^3, 62, 64, 69. BN, MS, NAF 9283 (Margry), f.35; NAF 21395 (Arnoul), f.21. Public Archives of Nova Scotia, MS docs. II, 18–20, 27–28, 40, 45; III, 14, 24. Recensement de 1686 (Acadie).

Coll. de manuscrits relatifs à la Nouv.-France, I; II, 361–62, 368, 378. Denys, *Description and natural history* (Ganong), 13, 16, 40. Le sieur de Dièreville, *Relation of a voyage to Port Royal in Acadia or New France*, ed. J. C. Webster (Champlain Soc., XX, 1933). La Morandière, *Hist. de la pêche française de la morue*, I, 356–62. *Mémoires des commissaires*, II, 327; and *Memorials of the English and French commissaries*, I, 614. PRO, *CSP, Col., 1681–85*, p. 688; *1685–88*, nos. 545, 925.

Antoine Bernard, *Le drame acadien* (Montréal, 1936), 120–21, 124, 140–44, 185–86. "Chedabouctou, d'après l'Intendant de Meulles (1686)," *BRH*, XXXV (1929), 304. Roger Comeau, "Nicolas Denys, pionnier Acadien," *RHAF*, IX (1955–56), 31–54. Robert Le Blant, *Le baron de St-Castin* (Dax, s.d.), 44. Bruce T. McCully, "The New England–Acadia fishery dispute and the Nicholson mission of August, 1687," Essex Institute *Hist. Coll.*, XCVI (1960), 277–90. "Richard Denys, sieur de Fronsac, and his settlements in northern New Brunswick," Historical-geographical documents relating to New Brunswick, ed. W. F. Ganong, 4, N. B. Hist. Soc. *Coll.*, [III], no. 7 (1907), 15–16. Robert Rumilly, *Histoire des Acadiens* (2v., Montréal, 1935), I, 119. Webster, *Acadia*, 124, 206–8.

BERMEN, LAURENT, notary at Quebec from 1647 to 1649.

Since the time of Nicolas (first clerk to have signed an act in New France, 1621), it had been customary to allow clerks of court to receive acts and agreements. But Laurent Bermen was the first, in the acts which he drew up, to style himself royal notary. He had no reason to assume this title, since from 1627 to 1663 the Compagnie des Cent-Associés held the right of *haute, moyenne et basse justice* in New France, and alone could appoint officials and officers of justice. Bermen could have been only a sort of seigneurial notary in the service of the Company, which itself held seigneury over New France, for only the king, or one of his representatives specifically designated, could appoint royal notaries. Claude Lecoustre (1647–1648), Guillaume AUDOUART (1649–1663), Jean Durand (1653–1654) and Louis ROUER de Villeray (1653–1654) had no more right than Bermen to the title of royal notary, and for the same reasons. From 11 Aug. 1647 to 27 Oct. 1649, Bermen received 39 notarial acts. Nothing more is known about him.

ANDRÉ VACHON

AJQ, Greffe de Laurent Bermen, 1647–49. "Les notaires au Canada," APQ *Rapport 1921–22*, 11f. André Vachon, *Histoire du notariat canadien, 1621–1960* (Québec, 1962); "Inventaire critique des notaires royaux des gouvernements de Québec, Montréal et Trois-Rivières (1663–1764)," *RHAF*, X (1956–57), 97f.

BERNIÈRES, HENRI DE, first parish priest of Quebec, vicar general of the diocese, first superior of the seminary of Quebec and dean of the chapter; b. *c.* 1635 at Caen (Normandy), son of Pierre de Bernières, Baron d'Acqueville, and of Madeleine Le Breton; d. 1700.

He was nine years old when his father died, a victim of his devotion to sick prisoners. The young boy's upbringing was undertaken by his uncle, Jean de Bernières de Louvigny. This personage was the founder, about 1644, of the Hermitage at Caen, which played a remarkable part in the religious history of France. After the dissensions and religious wars that followed the Lutheran Reformation, the need for a revival made itself apparent everywhere, and aroused powerful tendencies towards austerity and mysticism within the Catholic nations. The Council of Trent was the main inspiration of the Roman Catholic renaissance. The dissemination of the council's decisions throughout the various classes of society owed a great deal to the efforts of eminent men such as St. Charles Borromeo, St. François de Sales, and St. Vincent de Paul. Distinguished women also played their part, as did a number of laymen, grouped in various associations. The Compagnie du Saint-Sacrement, and the Hermitage at Caen which was linked with it, were among these. Laymen and ecclesiastics met there to discuss religion, spiritual matters, mysticism, apostleship, and evangelization; at these sessions there was a great deal of prayer. Jean de Bernières was the initiator of the Hermitage, and its guiding spirit until his death in 1659. Abbé Montigny, that is to say François de Laval,* the future bishop of Quebec, frequented the Hermitage; the young Henri de Bernières was brought up and educated there. The Hermitage adjoined a monastery of Ursuline nuns founded by Jourdaine de Bernières, Jean's sister. This convent brought the same influence to bear on girls and women as the Hermitage did on men.

The colony of New France had come to life again after the Treaty of Saint-Germain-en-Laye in 1632. The Jesuits, who had followed the Recollets in 1625, opened a classical college at Quebec in 1635, and made it the centre of their evangelizing activity among the Indians and Europeans. The Sulpicians established themselves at Ville-Marie (Montreal) in 1657. Trois-Rivières and the Beaupré shore already had primitive parishes. The colony, around 1650, was still a great dream rather than a great reality. However, the French court took pride in this dream, and was formulating plans: the colony might be transformed into a real province of France. The Church also had lofty designs: Quebec might become a bishopric, at the least an apostolic vicariate. The colony did in fact become a province, and a vicar apostolic was appointed. According to Gallican custom, the bishops—and vicars apostolic—were chosen by the king and presented to the pope. François de Laval was first recommended for the apostolic vicariate of Tonkin, but shortly afterwards was designated for New France. He was consecrated in Paris and was to leave for Quebec in the spring of 1659. He would take some priests with him; his choice fell on Abbés Jean Torcapel, Philippe Pelerin, CHARLES DE LAUSON de Charny, and Henri de Bernières. The latter, aged 24, and a mere tonsured cleric (he had been tonsured when 9 years old), seems to have been the youngest of the four. He had been proposed to Bishop Laval by M. Jean de Bernières himself. The little group sailed from La Rochelle on 13 April 1659 and reached Quebec two months later, on 16 June. Father JÉRÔME LALEMANT made the crossing with them. No residence had been provided at Quebec for the bishop and his group, but they found temporary quarters.

The most pressing matter was to allocate the various tasks: Charles de Lauson became the official, in charge of legal and canonical affairs; Torcapel was entrusted with the responsibility of ministering to the future parish of Quebec. Young Henri de Bernières was the bishop's chaplain; he would continue his theological studies and tackle the Iroquois language. He was ordained priest on 13 March 1660. M. Torcapel left again for France in the autumn of 1660. The bishop appointed M. de Bernières in his place to look after the religious needs of the district of Quebec, which was not to be constituted a parish until 1664. The young priest supervised the building of a presbytery, which would also be the bishop's palace; two years sufficed for this. Bishop Laval departed for France in 1662; he entrusted the administration to MM. de Lauson and de Bernières, whom he appointed vicars general. The bishop's return in the summer of 1663 brought about a very important change: Bishop Laval had been authorized to construct a seminary; he had a royal charter signed by Louis XIV, a document which set up a corporation possessing wide powers to carry on teaching and to obtain all the help required for that purpose. It was at first a grand seminary, that is, a theological college. The Jesuit Fathers had been operating a classical college since 1635. Theoretically, the Jesuits' college could have had graduates by 1640, and it could be hoped that certain of them would elect to become priests. Other young men might come from France. By 1665, the seminary appeared to be progressing sufficiently well for it to be given a superior, and Bishop Laval selected M. de Bernières for this post. He held it on four occasions: 1665–72, 1673–83, 1685–88, and 1693–98, a total of 25 years.

M. de Bernières' work, both as parish priest of Quebec and as superior of the seminary, is most important. The parish of Quebec was the first in New France, and its organization would serve as a model for the establishment of other parishes. The seminary developed by stages: first a grand seminary (1663), then a classical college (1668), then seigneurial properties (1668, etc.), then a single vast corporation, capable of ensuring the maintenance of all priests entrusted with missions. M. de Bernières was a witness of and an agent in all these stages with his associates, of whom the chief ones were Abbés Louis Ango* Des Maizerets and Jean Dudouyt, and all were in perfect harmony with their father and master, Bishop Laval. In a new country, temporal backing was a necessity. The priests engaged in the ministry looked to the seminary for support; the latter relied on the Séminaire des Missions étrangères in Paris, by virtue of an agreement concluded in 1665 and renewed in 1676. When M. de Bernières died in 1700, the seminary had behind it 37 years of active existence; it had formed a number of priests. Its founder, Bishop Laval, was still alive, but he had resigned as bishop: his successor, Bishop Saint-Vallier [La Croix*], thought fit to introduce changes, the most typical of which was to make the parish priests independent of the seminary. As for seigneuries, the seminary owned the one at Beaupré and the one at the Île-Jésus, as well as the Sault-au-Matelot and the Saint-Michel fiefs, located at Quebec itself. Other resources came from France, by arrangements with various priories and abbeys. Wealthy families gave generously; the French Crown sometimes made a contribution. The ardent desire for missions among the Indian tribes had already forced the seminary to extend towards the banks of the great Mississippi River, particularly among the Tamaroas Indians, and towards Acadia. Henri de Bernières took part in all this progress. He had given to the seminary his substance, and, to the colony, a third of a century of labour, privation, and prayer.

ARTHUR MAHEUX

ASQ, Chapitre; Documents Faribault; Lettres; Paroisse de Québec; Paroisses diverses; Polygraphie; Séminaire; *passim*. Auguste Gosselin, *Henri de Bernières, premier curé de Québec* (Les Normands au Canada, Québec, 1902); *Vie de Mgr de Laval*.

BERRY, SIR JOHN, rear-admiral and captain of the Newfoundland convoy; b. 1635 in North Devon; d. 14 Feb. 1689/90 at Portsmouth; buried in Stepney Church.

John Berry was the second son of the vicar of Knoweston, near Ilfracombe, of a family long established and influential in the area. The Civil War, however, saw the family fortune committed to the Royalist cause and on his father's death in 1652 John and his elder brother went to sea. In 1663 Berry joined the Royal Navy as a boatswain but outstanding service in action gained him his first command on 17 Sept. 1665. After further commands, in the Mediterranean and the Caribbean particularly, he came to the notice of the Duke of York while in action with the *Resolution* in the Battle of Southwold Bay (1672). He was knighted immediately afterwards and the favour he found with the Duke of York was a prominent factor in his personal advancement in later years. In 1682 Berry commanded the *Gloucester*, carrying the duke to Scotland, and survived the court-martial which followed when the ship ran aground in the Humber. In 1683 he reached flag-rank and was second-in-command to Lord Dartmouth in the raid on Tangier. From 1684 he served as one of the navy commissioners and in 1688, after the defection of Lord Dartmouth, he commanded the naval forces deployed against William of Orange when he moved against James II.

In 1675 this prominent sailor was captain of the annual Newfoundland convoy. At this time it seemed certain that the long dispute between the Bristol Society of Merchant Venturers and opposing interests among the London merchants and the settlers in Newfoundland had been finally resolved in favour of the West Country men. The decision of the Committee for Trade and Plantations not only re-affirmed that of March 1670 but gave way to the strongest claims of the western adventurers and ordered that the permanent settlers should remove themselves to other colonies in America or be forcibly removed to England. As captain of the annual convoy, Berry was the representative of royal authority in the island and it was his duty to inform the settlers of the council's decision.

Berry was soon convinced that most of the charges made against the colonists were unjust. His reports of July and September 1675 (PRO, *CSP, Col., 1675–76*, 275–77), provided the first organized inquiry and subsequent annual reports followed the lines which he had laid down. He did his best to present the planters' case in the most favourable possible light and his views found immediate confirmation in a separate report from a Mr Page. Early in 1676 John DOWNING came to England to protest against the actions of the fishermen in that year and another independent report in favour of the planters came from the commander of the 1676 convoy, Capt. Russell. In 1677 a survey made by Capt. Poole estimated that there were 523 colonists scattered about 28 tiny settlements, mainly on the east coast.

The combined weight of these appeals brought the temporary suspension of the charter regulations of 27 Jan. 1675/76 and a commission was formed to investigate the situation yet again. No change was made in the government—or lack of government—pending the final judgement of this commission, although the English government continued to send out annually convoy captains with lists of heads of inquiry on which they reported after their return. But after 1680 the commission hardly functioned and no such judgement was ever achieved. Petitions for the governorship continued to be presented by such people as Capt. Robinson*, William HINTON, and Mr Coney but the final outcome of all the disputes since 1670 was inconclusive.

Among those who were responsible for the preservation of a permanent settlement in Newfoundland at this time Berry is perhaps the most important. Unlike the leaders of the planters' cause with which he identified himself, he had no direct interest in the colony and had no aspirations to the governorship. He entered the dispute at a crucial time and, while he achieved this by no means single-handed, he was instrumental in ending the West Country monopoly in Newfoundland and in the eventual reversal of British policy. Berry was appointed a commissioner for Virginia in 1677, presumably in recognition of his Newfoundland achievements (PRO, *CSP, Col., 1677–80*).

C. M. ROWE

[*See also* HINTON and DOWNING.]

PRO, *Acts of P.C., col. ser., 1613–80, 1680–1720, Unbound papers; CSP, Col., 1669–74, 1675–76, 1677–80, 1681–85; CSP, Dom., 1665–66, 1672–73, 1673, 1680, 1683, 1684–85*.

Several secondary works dealing with Berry's part in the determination of the dispute include: *DNB*. Innis, *Cod fisheries*. C. B. Judah, *The North American fisheries and British policy to 1713* (University of Illinois Studies in the Social Sciences, XVIII, nos. 3–4, 1933). Lounsbury, *British fishery at Nfld*. Prowse, *History of Nfld*. Rogers, *Newfoundland*.

BESOUAT. *See* TESSOUAT (fl. 1603–13)

BEST (Beste), GEORGE, chronicler of the three FROBISHER voyages "for the discoverie of the passage to Cataya and the East India, by the Northwest"; d. *c.* March 1583/84.

Best was a member of the second expedition (1577) as lieutenant to Frobisher and of the third (1578) as captain of a ship, the *Anne Francis*, and ship's complement assigned to establish a settlement in Frobisher's Meta Incognita "for further discovery of the Inland & secreats of those countries." Nothing is known of his career before the Frobisher voyages but that he called himself "a souldiour and one professing armes" who owed his duty "moste" to Sir Christopher Hatton, favourite of Queen Elizabeth, vice-chamberlain to Her Majesty, and investor in the Frobisher voyages. Best's dedication to Hatton of his account of the Frobisher voyages suggests that Best undertook to join Frobisher's second voyage at Hatton's behest, "to make a true reporte of al Occurrents."

Best's claim to enduring fame rests on the uncultivated but none the less sound scholarship his narratives evidence; on the range and precision of his observations; on the judicious niceness of the conclusions he drew from his studies and observations. Other contemporaries of Frobisher and participants in the voyages set down accounts of the voyages and the lands visited; only Best seems to have observed with more than a casual eye and to have fitted together his observations of the new land into geographical, meteorological, and sociological conclusions that time has proven correct. From the studies of "the science of Cosmographie & the secrets of Navigation" by which he prepared himself for his first voyage with Frobisher, he insisted that those going into

Biard

the Arctic must accept as a basic datum that the Arctic was far from being the frigid antithesis of a torrid Tropics (a belief commonly held in the 16th century); a proper reading of the shape of the earth and its relation to the sun, for instance, says that long warming days and the briefest of cooling nights must bring tropical heat to the Arctic during its summers. He was the first to suggest (from observation of the Baffin Island Eskimos' possession and use of iron objects) the view that late 19th-century anthropologists confirmed: that the Baffin Island Eskimos, marvellous and strange as they were to the Frobisher party, had probably trafficked with Europeans before the arrival of Frobisher.

Best's concluding chapter of his Frobisher *Voyages*, "A general and briefe Description of the Countrey, And condition of the people, which are Found in *Meta Incognita*," is humanely perceptive of the qualities of the native people (no small triumph of observation in the 16th century) and precisely descriptive of their appearance, dress, tools, manners among themselves and among strangers, and their prowess as hunters and fishers. His hazards on the geography and climatology of the land are many of them today's facts; his descriptions of the abundant and varied beasts and fowls are of an age of plenty now gone by, but time has not changed "a kinde of small flye or gnat that stingeth and offendeth sorelye," the only approach to "a hurtefull thing" that Best found in Elizabethan Meta Incognita.

Best was killed six years after his return to England in a duel with Oliver St. John, later Viscount Grandison. He had apparently gone from the Frobisher voyages back to "soldierly" service with Sir Christopher Hatton: Hatton refers to him a few months after his death as "a man of mine." In 1863, Charles Francis Hall*, using Frobisher's own words, recalled Best's name to history when he presented to the British people relics he had found on Kodlunarn (Frobisher's Countess of Warrick) Island of " 'a wall of good height . . . called Best's Bulwark, after the lieutenant's name, who first devised the same' " (*Frobisher* (Collinson), 374).

ALAN COOKE

Best, *A true discourse*, repr. in *Three voyages of Frobisher* (Stefansson), I; in Hakluyt, *Principal navigations* (1903–5), VII; and in *The three voyages of Martin Frobisher, in search of a passage to Cathaia and India by the North-West, A.D. 1576–8, reprinted from the first edition of Hakluyt's Voyages, with selections from manuscript documents in the British Museum and State Paper Office*, ed. Richard Collinson (Hakluyt Soc., 1st ser., XXXVIII, 1867). Harris Nicolas, *The life and times of Sir Christopher Hatton, K.G.* (London, 1847).

BIARD, PIERRE, Jesuit priest, missionary in Acadia; b. 1567 or 1568 at Grenoble, presumed to be the son of Jean Biard, royal notary and chatelain of Gières near Grenoble, and of Jeanne de Cluzel; admitted 3 June 1583 into the noviciate of the Society of Jesus, at the Collège in Tournon; d. at the noviciate of Avignon, 17 Nov. 1622.

After his noviciate and his literary studies he taught at Billom, studied philosophy and theology at Avignon, and was ordained a priest in 1599. In the years following he taught theology at Tournon, then at the Collège in Lyon, which he left in August or September 1608 in order to go to Bordeaux, and there await an opportunity of getting to Canada. He had to bide his time until September 1610, when the provincial of the Jesuits of Paris summoned him to the capital in order to send him and Father Énemond MASSÉ to Port-Royal (Annapolis Royal, N.S.) on the ship belonging to CHARLES DE BIENCOURT, son of JEAN DE BIENCOURT de Poutrincourt. When they reached Dieppe towards the end of October 1610, the two missionaries encountered opposition from two Calvinist merchants who were rigging the ship. [*See* CHARLES DE BIENCOURT.] But Antoinette de Pons, Marquise de Guercheville generously solved the difficulty by buying up the merchants' shares in the cargo, at a cost of 4,000 *livres tournois*. The noble lady stipulated that the missionaries should be partners of Poutrincourt, and should have half of the revenues of the expedition as their share. The contract was signed 20 Jan. 1611. The aim of the Marquise was to establish what was called a foundation for the maintenance of the missionaries. The capital which would be recovered on the ship's return by the sale of the merchandise was to be reinvested in the following expedition, whereas the half of the profits accruing to the Jesuits would serve to pay for their maintenance. But this half was from the beginning hypothetical since the missionaries shared in all the expenses, whatever they were, not only those of the commercial expedition, which brought profits both to them and to Poutrincourt, but also those involved in the maintenance of the Port-Royal settlement, which was advantageous only to Poutrincourt.

Father Biard left Dieppe 26 Jan. 1611, and after a long and hard crossing of four months' duration, reached Port-Royal 22 May. That same year he made three journeys along the coasts of New Brunswick and Maine, going as far as the Kennebec River, in an attempt to appease the quarrels among the French and to inculcate in the Indians the rudiments of Christianity. He incurred Biencourt's rancour when he decided to baptize the Indians only after he had been able to give them some instruction, since he saw that those who were already Christians had retained all their pagan customs. As it happened, Biencourt was counting on the number of baptisms conferred by Abbé FLÉCHÉ for propaganda purposes in Europe and for raising funds. [*See* JEAN DE BIENCOURT.] Moreover Father Biard, who could not learn Indian languages at Port-Royal, conceived the idea of going and asking the help of young ROBERT GRAVÉ Du Pont, Biencourt's rival. Biencourt was vexed at this, and refused to let the missionary leave. Thus immobilized, the Jesuit faced with the others the winter of 1611–12 and all its hardships, which were further accentuated by the shortage of supplies.

Meanwhile, Poutrincourt, who had returned to France, had sold off the cargo from the previous voyage. As a result of his administration, neither he nor the missionaries were left with a single *denier* for investment in a new expedition. The Marquise de Guercheville's suspicions were aroused, but she agreed to meet the entire cost of a new cargo, 3,000 *livres*, and she entered into a partnership with the master of Port-Royal in her own name, and no longer in that of the Jesuits. At the same time she got Sieur Pierre Du GUA de Monts to make over to her all the American Atlantic coast, excepting only Port-Royal. This news reached Biencourt at the end of January 1612, at the same time as the ship with the new supplies, and aggravated still further his aversion for Father Biard, whom Biencourt considered responsible for the usurpation of his rights over New France.

Poutrincourt's agent, Simon Imbert, arrived on this ship with the Jesuit brother Gilbert DU THET. Imbert accused the latter of regicidal utterances. [*See* DU THET.] The falseness of this charge was soon established, but Biencourt refused to dispense the justice demanded by Father Biard, and prevented the friar from returning to France to defend himself. Father Biard boarded a ship in secret; he was fully entitled to depart anyway. Biencourt used force to keep him at Port-Royal, and in this way incurred the sanctions laid down in canonical law. Father Biard, a prisoner of Biencourt, considered the settlement as excommunicated. A reconciliation did take place after three months, but the missionaries, spurned by the French and discredited among the Indians, could no longer pursue their work of evangelization. The winter of 1612–13 was to be spent seeking means of survival and waiting for relief to arrive. [*See* CHARLES DE BIENCOURT.]

The first voyage undertaken by the Guercheville-Poutrincourt partnership does not seem to have been a financial success. The agent of the Marquise at Dieppe had the vessel seized upon arrival, and the liquidation was carried out under legal supervision. Poutrincourt once again found himself without funds. The Marquise was disturbed about the fate of the missionaries, who had not been able to send any letters to France; she accordingly got her agent René LE COQ de La Saussaye to offer Poutrincourt the renewal of the partnership. She placed 750 *livres* at Poutrincourt's disposal, but required that he should put up the same amount. The agreement between Poutrincourt and La Saussaye was concluded on 17 Aug. 1612. The loading of the cargo was completed towards the beginning of October, but at that time Brother Du Thet arrived in France, and told of the bad treatment to which the Jesuits had been subjected. The noble lady then decided to break with Poutrincourt and to prepare an expedition to go to another part of New France, under the command of La Saussaye. The latter picked up Fathers Biard and Massé at Port-Royal in May 1613, and went to found Saint-Sauveur. [*See* CHARLES DE BIENCOURT.]

Construction work was held up there by dissension among the French. On 2 July 1613 Samuel ARGALL, a Virginian captain, seized the French ship and the fort which had been begun. Father Biard was taken to Jamestown with Father Jacques QUENTIN, a newcomer from France, and narrowly missed the gallows. He also escaped Biencourt's hatred when he was taken back to Acadia; then, while returning to Virginia with the prospect of being hanged, he was driven across the ocean by a storm and finally reached France in April 1614. [*See* ARGALL and CHARLES DE BIENCOURT.]

He returned to his ecclesiastical province, that of Lyon, and until his death was variously employed on popular missions, in disputations with the Calvinists, and as a military chaplain. Around 1620 he wrote an "Apologie" to defend himself against the insinuations made by LESCARBOT in his re-edition of the *Histoire de la Nouvelle-France* in 1618. This "Apologie," never published, has been lost. In the works cited below will be found Father Biard's writings, which are of great interest for Canadian history and for Indian ethnology.

LUCIEN CAMPEAU

BM, Cotton. MS Otho E. VIII, 84, ff.252–53. *Factum* (1614). *JR* (Thwaites), I–IV, including Biard's Relation of 1616 (III, 21–283; IV, 7–117). Lescarbot, *History* (Grant), III, 46–72. Purchas, *Pilgrimes* (1905–7), XIX, 213–16. Sources for this biography will appear in an early volume of *Monumenta Novae Franciae*, now

Biencourt de Poutrincourt

in preparation, part of the collection *Monumenta historica Societatis Iesu*, published in Rome.

Biggar, *Early trading companies*, 261–70. *Encyclopedia of Canada*, ed. W. S. Wallace (6v., Toronto, 1935–37), I, 222. Huguet, *Poutrincourt*, *passim*. Le Jeune, *Dictionnaire*, I, 166–69. Rochemonteix, *Les Jésuites et la Nouvelle-France au XVIIe siècle*, I, 22–84. Pierre de Saint-Olive, "Les Dauphinois au Canada," repr. from the *Bulletin de l'Académie delphinale (1935)*, 16–17; *Les Dauphinois au Canada: essai, de catalogue des Dauphinois qui ont pris part à l'établissement du régime français au Canada, suivi d'une étude sur un Dauphinois canadien: Antoine Pécody de Contrecœur* (Paris, 1936).

BIENCOURT DE POUTRINCOURT ET DE SAINT-JUST, JEAN DE, baron, governor of Méry-sur-Seine, lieutenant-governor of Acadia, commander of the first permanent settlement established in Acadia; b. 1557; d. 1615.

Poutrincourt was the fourth son of Florimond de Biencourt and Jeanne de Salazar. There were nine children recorded of this marriage. The eldest son, Louis, a page of the King's Bedchamber, disappeared in the battle of Dreux, 1562, fighting under the Guises. The second son, Charles, died while fighting in the Catholic advance at Moncontour in 1569. The third, Jacques, a page to Charles IX, inherited the title. A sister, Jeanne, was maid of honour to Mary Stuart. Jean was given the seigneury of Marsilly-sur-Seine in 1565 and was destined to inherit the seigneuries in Champagne, including the barony of Saint-Just, through his mother, who was a Salazar.

On 14 Aug. 1590, a marriage contract was drawn up between Jean de Poutrincourt and Claude Pajot, the daughter of Isaac Pajot. Two sons were born to the couple, CHARLES and Jacques. Six daughters are also recorded.

At an early age Jean de Poutrincourt entered the army in the service of the Duc d'Aumale and served with distinction in the siege of Paris against Henri IV. In 1593 Poutrincourt embraced the cause of the king after Henri's conversion and reconciliation with the members of the Catholic League. Henri IV appointed him his "Gentleman of the Chamber" and LESCARBOT tells us that the king once referred to him as one of the finest and most valorous men in his kingdom. Poutrincourt was appointed chevalier of the king's order and governor of Méry-sur-Seine. Devoted to the monarchy and to the king himself, he amassed more honour than fortune, despite his many titles and his high position at court, having lost much of his wealth in the religious wars of France.

In the year 1603, Jean de Poutrincourt learned that his friend DU GUA de Monts had received a grant in New France and was planning an expedition there. The challenge of such an expedition appealed to Poutrincourt's great love of adventure for he dreamed of founding a great agricultural colony in the New World. He was granted permission by Henri IV to accompany de Monts who was delighted to have Poutrincourt's support which greatly eased the problem of obtaining volunteers for the expedition. It was Poutrincourt who obtained the necessary arms and soldiers for the defence of the settlement de Monts planned to establish in America.

The expedition to Acadia, consisting of two ships, set sail on 7 March 1604, from Havre-de-Grâce (Le Havre). The voyage was long and filled with peril. Many times the captains of the two ships advised a return to France but both de Monts and Poutrincourt were determined to complete the journey. The coast of North America was finally reached and after months of hazardous explorations, de Monts decided to seek somewhere to winter the expedition. It was during this search that the vessels passed the place that was later to be named Port-Royal. This beautiful section of the country gave so much pleasure to Jean de Poutrincourt that he asked for and was given it as a grant by the Sieur de Monts on his promise to colonize the land. This grant, which included fur-trading privileges and fishing rights, was confirmed by the king on 25 Feb. 1606.

De Monts and most members of the expedition decided to spend the winter on an island they named Île Sainte-Croix. Poutrincourt did not remain in North America, having been sent to France by de Monts that autumn with a rich cargo of furs.

In the spring of 1606 Poutrincourt returned to Port-Royal (Annapolis Royal, N.S.) as lieutenant-governor of Acadia to take command of the settlement at Port-Royal and to continue exploration of the coast to the south of it with a view to establishing a new settlement. Poutrincourt brought with him a number of workmen, as well as LOUIS HÉBERT, Marc Lescarbot, and his own son Charles. Soon afterward Poutrincourt and CHAMPLAIN explored the coast to Cape Cod and established friendly relations with MESSAMOUET and SECOUDON, but the idea of a second settlement was abandoned after a battle with some unfriendly Indians during this trip.

Poutrincourt devoted all his energy to strengthening the settlement at Port-Royal. He erected a number of buildings, among them the first water-driven grist-mill in North America. Under his direction fields were prepared and crops planted; the early dream of an agricultural empire

Biencourt de Poutrincourt

was always foremost in his thoughts. He organized the fur trade and his men made regular visits across the bay to the mouth of the Saint John River, the richest source of trading in Acadia. Jean de Poutrincourt made friends with the Indians who trusted him implicitly. His treatment of the natives was always fair and just; he counselled treating them without the barbarity and cruelty practised by the Spanish in the Indies. By their conduct in Acadia the French under Poutrincourt set a pattern of behaviour which was greatly to their credit.

In the autumn of 1607, the ship *Jonas* returned to Acadia, with dispatches stating that the ten-year trading monopoly given de Monts's company had been revoked by the king. The inhabitants of Port-Royal were forced to return to France. They took with them a cargo of cod and samples of wheat, corn, minerals, and Canada geese to prove the value of the settlement.

Many things contributed to the failure of the colony at this time. The profits of the fish and fur trade had been less than expected owing to the large number of vessels poaching in the territory assigned to de Monts. Dutch vessels had also found their way to the St. Lawrence and carried off rich harvests of furs. The merchants who were financing de Monts found their profits on furs and fish being seriously cut by these intruders and were loath to put up more funds. Other Norman and Breton merchants and fishermen, exasperated at being excluded from trade in Canada, were complaining bitterly. The character of the recruits for the settlement had also contributed to some extent to the failure, many of the settlers having proven unfit for pioneer life. Another handicap in this period was the lack of interest in France in colonizing *per se*; some of the ladies at the French court were indeed interested in colonization, but rather as a means of evangelizing the Indians. The desirability of a permanent agricultural colony was thus obscured by the greater interest in trade or religion.

Despite the setback, Jean de Poutrincourt still planned to settle Acadia. Lescarbot attributes the extension of de Monts's monopoly for one year to Poutrincourt's presentation of the "fruits of the earth" of Acadia to the king. It seems that Poutrincourt himself received, in about 1608, a commission from the king, the terms of which are unknown, although the grant of Port-Royal seems to have been confirmed. To draw the support of the court he emphasized the conversion of the Indians to the Roman Catholic faith.

Poutrincourt was a good Catholic; he had tried in vain to induce priests to accompany the 1606 voyage and failing this in 1608 he wrote Pope Paul describing how on his previous trip to Port-Royal he had set Lescarbot to instructing the Indians. Lescarbot, to whom we owe much of our knowledge of the early years in Acadia, wrote, "at the request of our chief, M. de Poutrincourt, I devoted some hours each Sunday to the religious instruction of our men, both in order to improve their minds and to offer an example to the Indians of our manner of living." Poutrincourt received the pope's blessing for his projected third voyage to New France, and through the papal nuncio, Ubaldini, arranged that Father FLÉCHÉ should accompany him.

However, the Jesuits, who had influence with the king through his confessor, Father Coton, and with many of the ladies at court, were also interested in christianizing New France. The king therefore decided that Poutrincourt should take Jesuits with him on his return to Port-Royal. Father Coton chose fathers BIARD and MASSÉ for the mission and Father Biard repaired to Bordeaux where for a year he waited to sail.

Poutrincourt did not return to Acadia until 1610. The delay was due in part to the death of his mother, the need to settle her estate, and trouble with financial backers, and in part to his disinclination to take the Jesuits with him. Biencourt shared the prejudice current in some circles at this time against Jesuit missionaries, whom rumour accused of being too interested in commercial profit.

Poutrincourt finally sailed on 25 Feb. 1610 from Dieppe with Father Fléché, CLAUDE and CHARLES DE SAINT-ÉTIENNE de La Tour, his own two sons, and Thomas Robin, Vicomte de Coulogne, who had invested heavily in the expedition.

The two-month voyage to Acadia was broken by a mutiny of the crew, but Port-Royal was finally reached in May and found to be in good repair. The furniture was untouched and the buildings sound except for a partial falling-in of the roofs. Poutrincourt worked hard tilling the soil and with the aid of Father Fléché set about converting the Indians with a new zeal, wishing to prove to the French court that he did not need the Jesuits. The old chief MEMBERTOU was baptized along with all his family. Twenty other natives followed Membertou's example. Poutrincourt was so pleased with his success in this religious endeavour that he prepared an extract from the baptismal register to be carried to France in a ship returning with a cargo of furs under the charge of his son Charles. Young Biencourt sailed in July 1610 and while he was passing the Grand Banks a fisherman gave him the news that Henri IV had been assassinated.

Biencourt de Poutrincourt

When Biencourt reached France he obtained an audience with the queen regent, Marie de Medici, and presented her with the list of baptisms. The queen expressed her pleasure in the success of the missionary effort but any hopes the Biencourts had that the Crown could be dissuaded from sending Jesuits were soon dashed. The Jesuits had a powerful ally at court in the person of Antoinette de Pons, Marquise de Guercheville, the wife of Charles du Plessis, Duc de Liancourt and governor of Paris, who was herself the first lady-in-waiting to the queen. This deeply religious noblewoman fully supported the Jesuit desire to found American missions and she raised money at court so that fathers Biard and Massé could become partners with the Biencourts in the expedition after other backers withdrew [see CHARLES DE BIENCOURT].

Young Biencourt set sail in the *Grâce de Dieu* on 26 Jan. 1611 with a group of colonists—including possibly Mme de Pourtincourt (Biard's letter of 31 Jan. 1612)—the two fathers, and supplies for Port-Royal. The crossing took four months during which part of the provisions for the colony were consumed. On 22 May they were met at Port-Royal by a group of half-starved settlers.

Poutrincourt immediately determined to sail across the Bay of Fundy (Baie Française) to visit his Etchemin friends and trade for food and furs. On his arrival the Indians entreated him to punish a French captain, trading illegally in the area, who had robbed them and killed a woman; they also advised him of the presence of three other French vessels, trading without the viceroy's permission. On board one ship was ROBERT GRAVÉ Du PONT who had escaped detention after committing an outrage on an Indian woman. This offence, if unpunished, could have endangered the trust and friendship Poutrincourt had worked carefully to foster. Father Biard's intervention on young Gravé's behalf occasioned the first clash between Biard and Poutrincourt. The viceroy pardoned the young man, but the interference of the priest in civil affairs annoyed him. Soon afterwards Poutrincourt sailed for France to exchange the furs collected for trade goods, leaving Port-Royal under the charge of his son, who had received the post of vice-admiral in the seas of New France.

Poutrincourt arrived in France in August 1611. He talked to Mme de Guercheville who was still interested in the colony. Unable to raise money for his people elsewhere, desperate with worry over his son and companions at Port-Royal, and at the end of his financial resources, Poutrincourt was again forced to accept the help of Mme de Guercheville (Huguet, *Poutrincourt*, 364–65). He was able to outfit one small boat with provisions for Port-Royal; this arrived 23 Jan. 1612 carrying Poutrincourt's agent, Simon Imbert-Sandrier, and Mme de Guercheville's agent, the Jesuit Gilbert DU THET.

The arrival of Imbert and Du Thet only exacerbated the unhappy situation at Port-Royal and mutual accusations of disloyalty and incompetence were soon received in Paris from Biencourt and Biard. However the struggle between the Biencourts and the Jesuits and their allies was unequal, as Huguet comments; Poutrincourt was soon discredited at court.

While still desperately trying to raise money, Poutrincourt was approached by the courtier RENÉ LE COQ de La Saussaye in August 1612 with a financial proposition which would eliminate his problem. Believing La Saussaye to be acting for the Jesuits, Poutrincourt accepted the proposal and as a consequence entered into an agreement whereby he borrowed money to pay his share toward outfitting a ship and sending La Saussaye to Port-Royal with supplies. In a letter written later to Lescarbot, Poutrincourt explained that La Saussaye had withdrawn at the last moment and claimed the arrangement made with La Saussaye was a trick to ruin and discredit him. Unable to settle his debts he was thrown into prison. On his release, ill and discouraged, he arranged a legal separation from his wife to make it possible for her to keep any money and property she still owned. In the meantime, Mme de Guercheville had bought Du Gua de Monts's lands in New France: the title of viceroy of Canada was bestowed on Henri de Bourbon, Prince de Condé.

In 1613 the dauntless Poutrincourt was able to form a partnership with several ship outfitters of La Rochelle, including Georges and Macain, by promising them a share of the fur trade in the Port-Royal region, which he still controlled, and on 31 Dec. 1613 he again set sail for Port-Royal. He arrived 27 March 1614 to find the fort in ruins and the inhabitants starving, after Capt. ARGALL's raid the previous November. Records show that one mill and some barns had escaped destruction as had most of the planted fields but these were insufficient for the continuance of the colony at that time. Poutrincourt had no choice but to return to France with most of the colonists. He was also able to take back enough furs to more than cover the cost of the trip. Poutrincourt deeded to his son the title of all his lands in the New World and Biencourt remained in Acadia.

It is ironic that Poutrincourt who loved peace and wished to devote his life to agricultural development should die a violent death, having been summoned at the moment of fresh troubles in France and ordered by his queen to recapture Méry-sur-Seine in Champagne. Pierced by many bullets, he died in December 1615 at the age of 58. Various historians have given different versions of his death but the most accepted is that Poutrincourt died in an effort to forestall his commander-in-chief from receiving the surrender of Méry-sur-Seine, of which Poutrincourt was governor. Poutrincourt felt that he alone should capture it. He met his death at the hands of his own party. With him was his son Jacques who was taken prisoner.

Jean de Poutrincourt has been described by contemporary historians as a man of great energy and enterprise. During his sojourn in Acadia he endeavoured, with his musical ability, scholarship, and sensitive taste, to foster in the little colony for which he was responsible a love of the finer things in life. Poutrincourt gave ten years of his life in a struggle to build for France a new agricultural empire. His efforts to make this dream come true impoverished his family and brought the disgrace of a prison term on his honoured name. If the affairs of France had progressed differently it would seem that Poutrincourt might have achieved for Acadia what Champlain was later able to do for Quebec.

Poutrincourt was buried at Champagne where a large monument was erected to his memory.

IN COLLABORATION WITH
HUIA RYDER

AN, H, no. 1964. Champlain, *Works* (Biggar). *Factum* (1614). *JR* (Thwaites); Biard's Relation of 1616 is in III and IV. Lescarbot, *History* (Grant). *Mémoires des commissaires*, I, 140, 145; and *Memorials of the English and French commissaries*, I, 197, 201. Purchas, *Pilgrimes* (1905–7), XIX, 213–16.

Biggar, *Early trading companies*, esp. 261–70 and 292–94, containing an assessment of the relative objectivity of the primary sources. Lucien Campeau, "Autour de la Relation du P. Pierre Biard," *RHAF*, VI (1952–53), 517–35. Charlevoix, *History* (Shea), I, III. Huguet, *Poutrincourt*, a thoroughly documented biography. Parkman, *Pioneers of France* (25th ed.). B. Sulte, "Poutrincourt en Acadie—1604–1623," *RSCT*, II (1884), sect.I, 31–50, one of the first studies of Biencourt, containing, however, a number of errors.

BIENCOURT DE SAINT-JUST, CHARLES DE, baron, vice-admiral of Acadia and successor to his father as commander of the settlement at Port-Royal (Annapolis Royal, N.S.); b. 1591 or 1592 in Champagne; d. 1623 or 1624 at Port-Royal.

Biencourt de Saint-Just

Charles de Biencourt was the elder son of JEAN DE BIENCOURT de Poutrincourt and Claude Pajot. Of the early life and education of Charles de Biencourt we have no record, although he has been described by contemporary writers as a youth far beyond his years in character and capability.

Biencourt sailed with his father in the *Jonas* from La Rochelle 13 May 1606, on Poutrincourt's second voyage to New France. We are told he rapidly learned the Indian dialects and was of great assistance in the construction of buildings and in the preparations for farming.

In 1607 word came to Poutrincourt that DU GUA de Monts's monopoly was rescinded and it was learned that the establishment at Port-Royal could no longer be supported, the majority of labourers at the fort being in the pay of de Monts's company. With a heavy heart Poutrincourt, his son, and the other colonists returned to France. Early in October 1607, they anchored in the harbour of Saint-Malo.

It was not until the spring of 1610 that Poutrincourt, with young Biencourt, was able to return to Acadia. Accompanying them was Father FLÉCHÉ, a priest whom the Sieur de Poutrincourt hoped would prove to the court that two Jesuit fathers he had left behind in France were not necessary to the spiritual welfare of the colony. Charles de Biencourt's knowledge of the Indian language proved of great assistance to Father Fléché in his efforts to catechize the Indians.

Soon afterwards, Biencourt was placed by his father in charge of a vessel loaded with furs for France and instructed to present a petition to the king for certain trading privileges. An extract from the baptismal register was also to be presented in an effort to show that missionary work, which was of special concern to the queen and her ladies, was being emphasized. Before his arrival in France, Biencourt learned from fishermen on the Grand Banks that Henri IV had been assassinated.

When Biencourt reached Paris he presented his petition, the list of baptisms, and an article by LESCARBOT on the conversions to Marie de' Medici who had been appointed regent, and who both expressed satisfaction with the missionary endeavours and assured him that the late king had had the interest of the Port-Royal colony at heart. According to Lescarbot, he was informed at the same time by the Jesuits that Henri IV had granted them 2,000 *livres* a year for the establishment of their society in Acadia.

During this visit to France of 1611, Charles de Biencourt received the post of vice-admiral in the seas of New France. He also received letters of

Biencourt de Saint-Just

encouragement from the young King Louis XIII, Queen Marie, and the Marquise de Guercheville. They wished him and his father to continue the missionary work among the Indians of Acadia and in this regard they insisted he take with him on his return to Acadia the Jesuit fathers Pierre BIARD and Énemond MASSÉ.

Biencourt made arrangements with two Huguenot merchants of Dieppe, Du Jardin and Du Quesne (Duchesne according to CHAMPLAIN), who agreed to equip a vessel and furnish supplies for Acadia in return for a share of future profits in the fish and fur trade. These merchants upon learning of the additional passengers refused to have any part in an undertaking in which Jesuits were involved. The murder of King Henri IV had stirred both Huguenots and Catholics alike, and some believed the death had been plotted by Jesuits. Despite orders from the queen the merchants were adamant. Father Biard informed Father Coton, the friend and advisor of Mme de Guercheville, of the merchants' decision and through her efforts a subscription of more than 3,800 *livres* was collected to buy out the merchants' interest in the Port-Royal venture. Under the agreement drawn up, the Jesuits became partners with Jean de Poutrincourt and Thomas Robin de Coulogne in the profits of the trade. This business agreement strengthened later accusations that the members of the society were as much interested in trade as in missionary work (*see* Huguet, *Poutrincourt*, 350–1).

Biencourt, with Fathers Biard and Massé, finally set sail from Dieppe with 36 colonists on 26 Jan. 1611, on the *Grâce-de-Dieu*. The journey took four months during which the supplies intended for the relief of Port-Royal were almost exhausted. The colony of half-starving settlers had hoped for relief with the coming of the ship and were bitterly disappointed. The situation worsened when friction developed between the Jesuits and Poutrincourt over their respective spheres of authority.

At the end of June Jean de Poutrincourt decided to return to France to obtain further aid. He took with him a cargo of furs, planning to use the proceeds from their sale to purchase supplies. Before leaving he placed the colony of Port-Royal under the charge of his son.

This young man had to face many responsibilities and difficulties as the acting governor of the colony in enforcing his authority over the fishermen and traders visiting the coast and over the missionaries, who naturally were ignorant of the customs and language of the Indians and who lacked the older settlers' experience in dealing with them.

The illness of the Indian chief MEMBERTOU that fall caused the first real disagreement between Biencourt and the priests. Membertou, the colony's first convert, was important to the French because of his power and prestige over the Indians. Knowing he was about to die, the old chief asked for and received the last rites of the church. He then made Biencourt promise to bury him with his own people. Father Biard, however, refused to allow such a burial because the Indian burial place was not hallowed ground. Biencourt suggested the place could be blessed but, as this would mean heathens would also be buried in consecrated ground, Biard again refused. The affair caused much unpleasantness and at last Membertou relented upon being told the priests would not say prayers over his grave. Charlevoix* writes that "the obsequies paid to [Membertou] were such as would have been rendered to the commandant himself."

Biencourt concentrated on his trading. During the year 1609, the fur trade had once again been thrown open to the merchant marine of France as it had been prior to the granting of monopolies but it seems that the King's grant to Poutrincourt gave him the right to levy a *quint* or fifth on the French vessels visiting the Port-Royal area. Biencourt, as vice-admiral of the seas of New France, had a vaguely defined power to "command all manner of persons and visit their vessels." This Biencourt attempted to do. He did not, however, have enough soldiers to enforce his authority and so was able to control relatively little of the trading and fishing. He also made voyages along the coast. On one of these journeys he discovered an English fort which had been abandoned by the Virginia Company in 1609. To counteract the English claim, Biencourt set up the arms of France on the most conspicuous height of the fort and then returned to Port-Royal.

Biencourt's troubles were added to when in January 1612 Capt. L'Abbé's vessel, carrying the small amount of supplies Jean de Poutrincourt had been able to gather, anchored at Port-Royal. On board was the Jesuit Gilbert DU THET, who had come to Acadia as the representative and administrator of Mme de Guercheville. Poutrincourt's agent, Imbert-Sandrier, was also on board. The ensuing quarrels pervaded the whole colony and were a disturbing influence on the Indians who did not know which faction they could trust.

Biencourt refused to allow the Jesuits to leave Port-Royal to pursue their missionary endeavours in other parts of Acadia because of his fear that they would engineer some mischief against him. Biard then defied Biencourt's authority by secretly sending Massé to the other side of the Bay of

Fundy (Baie Française) to evangelize the Etchemins (Malecites). After his return, the three Jesuits again tried to leave for France, but Biencourt stopped them, saying that since he had been ordered by the queen, against his will, to bring them to Port-Royal, he would need a new order from the court to allow them to return. Finally, the Jesuits secretly boarded the ship, but on discovering this, Biencourt arrested the captain and ordered that the missionaries be put ashore, whereupon Biard said he would excommunicate anyone who touched them. When an attempt was made to remove them, Father Biard excommunicated Biencourt and the ship's captain, L'Abbé. The fathers finally disembarked but refused to conduct any further services in the colony. Letters from Biencourt to his father and from Biard to the superiors of his order and Mme de Guercheville were carried back to France; these varying accounts naturally put the actions of the protagonists in the best light.

It seems clear from these events that, as an anonymous contemporary account in Purchas says, Biencourt was a "youth at that time of more courage than circumspectnesse." In recording his impressions of Biencourt before this, Biard had described him as "an imitator of the virtues and good qualities of his father, both zealous in the service of God." Huguet's judgement seems reasonable, in view of the fact that Biencourt was only 20 or 21 years of age: "with all his precocious experience, Biencourt did not know how to maintain—when he had to act on his own initiative—the tact and balance that distinguished the viceroy. He lacked, in these difficult situations, the prestige of age, the authority of a long, honourable career of service to his country."

Du Thet managed to escape from the colony shortly afterwards on a fishing boat. Back in France, he complained to Mme de Guercheville of the misconduct, lack of proper organization, and ill-treatment of the Jesuits by Biencourt; she began making plans to remove them from Port-Royal and to found a new colony that would eclipse Port-Royal in importance. On 12 March 1613, a small craft of 100 tons, under the command of RENÉ LE COQ de La Saussaye, sailed from Honfleur with priests, colonists, horses, goats, and all the necessities of a new settlement.

After exploring the coast, La Saussaye anchored at Port-Royal and, finding Biencourt absent, showed LOUIS HÉBERT the queen's order to allow Biard and Massé to depart, took on board the two Jesuit priests, and sailed to the south, anchoring in a harbour on the east side of Île des Monts-Déserts (now Mount Desert Island) where the Indian ASTICOU lived. The company went ashore, raised a cross, and named their new home Saint-Sauveur. It was here that they were later found and taken prisoner by Capt. Samuel Argall.

In November Argall also attacked the defenceless Port-Royal settlement in Biencourt's absence. After confiscating everything he could carry away he set fire to the buildings and most of the crops and left the place in ruins. Accounts differ as to Argall's reasons for attacking Port-Royal. Biencourt himself laid the blame for the attack on Father Biard who had been captured by Argall at Saint-Sauveur and was on board the ship when it attacked Port-Royal. However, according to the testimony at his trial in London in 1614, Capt. Argall had been given instructions to prevent the French from obtaining a foothold in North America and he had spent the previous fall and winter at Jamestown making preparations for the expedition against French settlements to the north. In defending himself Father Biard declared that he had refused to help Argall locate Port-Royal and that it was an Indian, taken aboard by Argall, who showed the way.

Biencourt returned to Port-Royal before Capt. Argall sailed and, according to the unconfirmed account in Purchas, offered to serve the English and asked to be given Father Biard "with a purpose to hang him." Champlain attributes to an unnamed Frenchman at Port-Royal a speech advising that Biard be killed.

On 27 March 1614, Poutrincourt finally returned to Port-Royal and found most of it in ashes. One water-mill had escaped ruin as well as a few cattle, pigs, weapons, and some grain. Biencourt and his men had spent a winter of dreadful hardship, existing on roots and lichen. Poutrincourt transported most of the colonists to France. A few decided to remain behind with Biencourt. Poutrincourt deeded over his holdings in Acadia to his son.

During the next few years Charles de Biencourt built up what appears to have been a profitable fishing and fur-trading business in partnership with the La Rochelle shipowners, Jean Macain and Samuel Georges. During this period, David LOMERON acted as his commercial agent in France. Despite the growing activity of French and English as well as Dutch traders in the region the trade was profitable and some of the rival vessels were captured by Biencourt. Between 1614 and 1617, the trade along the coast became so good that vessels from La Rochelle visited Biencourt each spring. Biggar writes that according to Capt. John Smith's estimate, the French collected 25,000 furs in 1616. During the same period Biencourt launched several court actions over illegal trading in the area under his control.

Bienville

In September of 1618, Biencourt appealed unsuccessfully to the mayor and aldermen of Paris to establish a fortified post at Port-Royal and elsewhere on the coasts, urging the importance of protecting the fishing and fur-trading, from which Paris derived so much benefit, against the English. He added that the French would soon be altogether dependent upon the English and claimed that if France could help the colonists for two years they would become self-supporting. Time and again he was to complain of the neglect of Port-Royal by France, particularly in view of the growth of New England. Considering the fact that his pleas went unheeded, Charles de Biencourt did a remarkable job of holding the settlement together and thrusting off English encroachment in the area.

Fur-trading activity in Acadia slackened between 1618 and 1623. Port-Royal was gradually crumbling through neglect and the fact that the only new recruits the settlement received were the occasional sailors who left their ships. We are told that in his last years Biencourt lived more and more with the Indians.

Charles de Biencourt died in 1623 or 1624. A letter from CHARLES DE SAINT-ÉTIENNE de La Tour to King Louis XIII, dated 25 July 1627, says of Biencourt "he has been dead four years," but a passage in Champlain's *Voyages* has led some historians to give the year of his death as 1624. However, Charles de La Tour was with him at the time of his death. Lauvrière, among others, repeats the charge that Biencourt was poisoned by La Tour, but a descendant, the Marquis de Biencourt, in a letter written in 1847 declares, "no document exists which corroborates this version." Couillard Després says Biencourt "left his goods to one of his most faithful friends, to his relative Charles de La Tour."

Charles de Biencourt shared with his father a genuine desire to establish a self-supporting settlement based on agriculture. Without the ruinous rivalry of the Jesuits, the destruction caused by the Argall raid, and with even a slight amount of support from the Crown to establish the colony, the accomplishments of the Poutrincourts—father and son—might have been of a far higher order. As it was they did prove that Europeans could live in Acadia on the resources of the land and their experiences in this regard were to have value in later colonizing schemes.

IN COLLABORATION WITH
HUIA RYDER

See bibliography for Jean de Biencourt. *See also*: Couillard Després, *Saint-Étienne de La Tour*. Émile Lauvrière, *La tragédie d'un peuple: histoire du peuple acadien de ses origines à nos jours* (2v., Paris, 1922; éd. rev., 1924). Mass. Hist. Soc. *Coll.*, 4th ser., IX (1871), 45, 46. *Mémoires des commissaires*, I, 140, 143; and *Memorials of the English and French commissaries*, I, 197, 199. W. O. Sawtelle, "Sir Samuel Argall, the first Englishman at Mount Desert," *Sprague's J. of Maine Hist.*, XII, no. 4 (1924), 201ff.

BIENVILLE, FRANÇOIS LE MOYNE DE. *See* LE MOYNE

"BIG MOUTH." *See* OTREOUTI

BISSOT. *See* BYSSOT

BIZARD, JACQUES, town-major of Montreal 1677–92, one-time aide-de-camp to BUADE de Frontenac, gave his name to the large island in the Lac des Deux-Montagnes on the northwest side of the island of Montreal; b. Neuchâtel, Switzerland, in 1642, son of David Bizard, a Calvinist minister, and Guillemette Robert; d. 5 Dec. 1692.

He served in Crete as an officer in the Meuron regiment which was fighting with the Venetian forces against the Turks. While there, in 1669, he came to the notice of the Comte de Frontenac who was also serving with the Venetian forces, as a lieutenant-general. Frontenac acquired Bizard as one of his aides-de-camp. This was an unfortunate move for Bizard as shortly afterwards Frontenac was summarily dismissed from the Venetian service, with his aides-de-camp, and obliged to return to the mainland in September 1669. Frontenac later claimed that during the three months that Bizard served with him he succeeded in converting him from the Calvinist to the Roman Catholic faith.

Subsequently, Bizard obtained a commission as ensign with the Swiss mercenary troops serving with the French army but resigned his commission to accompany Frontenac to Canada in 1672 as a lieutenant in the governor's corps of guards. The following year Frontenac sent Bizard to Montreal to arrest certain *coureurs de bois* and in carrying out these orders Bizard deliberately provoked the governor of Montreal, François-Marie PERROT, into arresting him. This incident provided Frontenac with an excuse to arrest Perrot and remove him from office, causing considerable furore in the colony.

In 1676, when Zacharie DUPUY the town-major of Montreal died, Frontenac obtained the vacant appointment for Bizard who took office on 1 May 1677. His salary was a modest 400 *livres* a year. On 25 Oct. 1678 Frontenac granted him the seigneury of Île Bonaventure, later named Île Bizard, but he made no attempt to fulfil his obligation to develop the seigneury. On 16 Aug. 1678

Bizard married Jeanne-Cécile Closse, only daughter of Lambert Closse, a former town-major of Montreal who was killed by the Iroquois in 1662. By her, he was to have six children, five of whom survived infancy. The following year Frontenac succeeded in obtaining a 300 *livres* supplement to Bizard's salary. This caused the intendant, Jacques Duchesneau, some annoyance and he complained to the minister that far from carrying out his duties and arresting those who broke the king's edicts, Bizard contravened them himself by sending *coureurs de bois* to trade illicitly in the Indian villages. It was, in fact, only Frontenac's continued protection that prevented Bizard being dismissed from office for he had by this time earned a reputation as a drunkard and a bully who practised petty extortion on the tradesmen of Montreal. He also refused to obey orders of the governor of Montreal which required physical effort. The reason for this last was made plain by governor Le Febvre de La Barre, who succeeded Frontenac in 1682 and who informed the minister that Bizard was "a Swiss sunk in wine and drunkenness, useless for all duties because of the sluggishness of his body." He requested that Bizard be replaced in office by Charles Le Moyne de Longueuil. This request the minister ignored and in 1686 Bizard, perhaps through the continuing influence of Frontenac, was commissioned deputy governor of Montreal during the absence of Louis-Hector de Callières* on the campaign against the Senecas; but Brisay* de Denonville, recently appointed governor of the colony, declined to promulgate the commission on the grounds that Bizard was unfit for the post. The following year Bizard's request that he be accorded French naturalization papers was granted by the king.

In 1691 Frontenac, after his reappointment to the governor's post, obtained a new commission for Bizard as deputy governor of Montreal. The intendant, Bochart* Champigny, however, immediately wrote to the minister to remind him that Denonville had returned a similar commission on a previous occasion because Bizard had been deemed unworthy of the office. "There is more reason than ever now," wrote Champigny, "to deny him. There is not an officer who has not had trouble with him and in fact, even if he did not drink too much he still would lack the qualities needed for the post." When the minister queried Frontenac on this point, the governor defended Bizard stoutly, declaring that despite the weakness "his nation was sometimes subject to," he had more merit than anyone Frontenac knew and he would personally guarantee his fitness to perform his duties.

The question of Bizard's competence was never definitely settled for three months after Frontenac wrote to defend him, on 5 Dec. 1692, Bizard died, leaving his family penniless. Frontenac now pleaded with the minister that he concur in a settlement he had made in favour of Bizard's widow lest she be forced to beg in the street. Were this favour not to be granted, Frontenac declared, he would lose face in the colony since everyone knew how much he had always had Bizard's interests at heart. But Mme Bizard was not unable to care for herself; less than two years after her husband's death, on 8 Nov. 1694, she was married to Raymond Blaise* Des Bergères de Rigauville.

W. J. Eccles

There are references to Bizard scattered through the official correspondence of the governors and intendants, contained in AN, Col., C[11A]. Correspondance de Frontenac (1672–82), APQ *Rapport, 1926–27*; (1689–99), APQ *Rapport, 1927–28*. See also P.-G. Roy, "Jacques Bizard, major de Montréal," *BRH*, XXII (1916), 293–303.

BJARNI, HERJÓLFSSON, first European to sight the east coast of North America, son of Herjólfr Bárdarson, one of the early settlers of Iceland, and his wife, Thorgerdr; fl. *c.* 986.

Bjarni was a part of the remarkable migration which in the tenth century established Norse settlements in Iceland and Greenland, and almost inevitably therefore reached the shores of mainland North America. The Saga of the Greenlanders relates that Herjólfr, Bjarni's father, sailed to Greenland with Eirikr Thorvaldsson (Eric the Red) in 986 when the latter led a group of settlers to the island and founded an Icelandic settlement there. At this time Bjarni was a merchant who spent each summer abroad trading in Scandinavia, returning to Iceland in the autumn to spend the Yuletide with his father. When he reached Iceland in the late summer of 986 he was greeted with the news that his father had emigrated to Greenland. Immediately he set sail thither, but met with stormy and cloudy weather and was driven off course for several days. When the weather cleared he sighted a land which he described as wooded and having low hills. Bjarni said this could not be Greenland and sailed north for two days, when a second land—level and wooded—came into view. Bjarni did not stop there, but continued on a northward course for three days when he sighted a mountainous land covered with glaciers. Because Bjarni did not believe this to be Greenland, he sailed away from it. After four days he sighted a country which he declared answered the description given him of

Greenland and by a stroke of fortune he landed at his father's estate.

Scholars have disagreed as to what parts of the coast of America Bjarni saw and indeed as to whether there is any factual basis to the narrative. In recent years, however, the historicity of the *Saga* has been increasingly admitted. There are strong arguments for the view that the three lands seen by Bjarni were Newfoundland, Labrador, and Baffin Island.

Bjarni made no attempt to visit or explore the lands he sighted but LEIFR *heppni* Eiriksson, the son of Eric the Red, later bought Bjarni's ship and undertook this task, discovering Vinland, which has been variously located in Newfoundland, the Atlantic Provinces, Massachusetts, and elsewhere. For discussion of the location of Vinland see LEIFR.

T. J. OLESON

Johann S. Hannesson, *The sagas of Icelanders* (Islandica, XXXVIII, 1957). Hennig, *Terrae incognitae* II, 295ff., 311, 324, 342ff.; III, IV, *passim*. Halldór Hermannsson, *The northmen in America* (Islandica, II, 1909). Oleson, *Early voyages*, 19–22; "The Vikings in America: a critical bibliography," *CHR*, XXXVI (1955), 166–73.

BOCHART, CHARLES DU PLESSIS-. *See* DU PLESSIS–BOCHART

BOISBRIAND, MICHEL-SIDRAC DUGUÉ DE. *See* DUGUÉ

BOISDON, JACQUES, sometimes wrongly called Jean, first innkeeper and taverner at Quebec in 1648.

Of Boisdon's career nothing is known except that on 19 Sept. 1648 the council of New France permitted him "to the exclusion of all others . . . to keep a pastry shop and hostelry for all comers." At the same time the council drew up what is the oldest legislation dealing with the management of inns and taverns in New France. Boisdon was required to reside on the public square, not far from the church; to prevent any unseemliness, drunkenness, blasphemy, or games of chance in his house; to close his establishment during religious services on Sundays and feast days; in short, he was generally subject to the ordinances and regulations applicable to business. These few basic rules reappear in all subsequent legislation concerning inns and liquor shops. On the other hand, the council guaranteed Boisdon the shipment of "eight barrels gratis" from France to Quebec, and the use of the brewery of the Communauté des Habitants for three years. This monopoly was granted to him for a period of six years altogether; how long the innkeeper did ply his trade in Quebec cannot however be stated.

ANDRÉ VACHON

ASQ, Documents Faribault, 79. Philéas Gagnon, "Le premier cabaret tenu à Québec," *BRH*, IV (1898), 116f.

BOISSEAU, JOSIAS, agent general of the gentlemen with interests in the tax-farm; b. *c.* 1641; d. at a date unknown.

Boisseau probably arrived in the colony in 1678, accompanied by his wife, Marie Colombier. It was he and Charles Aubert* de La Chesnaye, one of the tax-farmers, who, in the spring of 1679, sent Louis JOLLIET to explore Hudson Bay. The agent general's relations with Aubert de La Chesnaye and Jolliet were excellent at that moment. But a disagreement which turned them against each other during the winter of 1679–80 rapidly grew more bitter.

During this period the country was rent by party quarrels: Frontenac [*see* BUADE] and DUCHESNEAU were in open opposition. All the powers, great and small, claimed the backing of either the governor or the intendant; neutrality was a difficult position to maintain, for the most innocent words and gestures were distorted and misconstrued. To repeat Louis XIV's own expression in a letter to Duchesneau, the conduct of individuals invariably received approval or disapproval, to the extent that they were friends or enemies of the adversary.

Boisseau was protected by Frontenac, with whom, according to Duchesneau, he was in league for the smuggling of furs. The vindictive governor took up the agent general's quarrel. La Chesnaye, his brother-in-law Lalande*, and his niece's husband Jolliet obtained the support of the intendant. What started the conflict is in fact not known, but it was extremely violent. On 10 April 1680, Boisseau put on record a protest against Duchesneau, whose ordinances had, he asserted, always been prejudicial to the company of the tax-farmers, and denounced the "abuses, wrong doings, extortions and malpractices" perpetrated by La Chesnaye and his supporters: the "assassination" (?) of one of his servants, defamatory libels posted on the doors of churches, threats, lawsuits, and so on.

Relentlessly, during the whole of the year 1680, Boisseau pursued his enemies, particularly Aubert de La Chesnaye, whom he attacked through Lalande and Jolliet. In March, he accused the latter two of illegal trafficking with the English in Hudson Bay, calling for a fine of 2,000 *livres* against them, the confiscation of their boat, and the seizure of their goods. Duchesneau endeavoured to parry the blow; finally he had to take action, but he reduced the penalty demanded by the agent general. Incredible as it may seem, the crime had been invented in every detail, as Delanglez has proved. To gratify his desire for vengeance, Boisseau therefore did not shrink from calumny. Twenty times, from 22 March to 15 October, alone or surrounded by witnesses, he appeared before one or other of the notaries of Quebec to sign declarations aimed at the destruction of his adversaries: La Chesnaye, Lalande, Jolliet, and probably Duchesneau, not overlooking PHILIPPE GAULTIER de Comporté, Jacques Le Ber*, and CHARLES LE MOYNE.

In 1681, the agent general exploded with rage. On 9 January, swearing and cursing "several times," he tore up, stamped on, and threw into the fire two ordinances of Duchesneau handed to him by a court officer, declaring that he would do the same thing to the intendant if he got his hands on him. In March, accompanied by one of the governor's guards, he passed Duchesneau's son, aged 16 or 17, and Vaultier his servant, in the street. Insults flared up on both sides. Frontenac, informed of this, demanded redress; the intendant sent his son and Vaultier to him. Far from offering his excuses, the young Duchesneau provoked Boisseau. Frontenac, in a fury, rushed at the youth, struck him a number of times with his cane, and tore his clothes. Duchesneau finally escaped, and managed to get to the law courts; his father, lest the governor should carry off the young man by force, barricaded the building and armed his servants. If the intendant is to be believed, the young seigneur none the less spent a month in the prisons of the fort, together with Vaultier. Finally, in August, "behaving in an unheard of way, swearing horribly against God and like a lion," Boisseau manhandled "extraordinarily" René Favre, whom he punched and kicked, seizing him by the thoat and threatening to strangle him.

Meanwhile, the agent general had not been afraid to attack the Conseil Souverain and the legal officers of the colony. Judge MIGEON de Branssat, for example, was singled out for abuse by Boisseau for having dared to arrest certain *coureurs de bois* who were confederates of François-Marie PERROT, the governor of Montreal and an accomplice of the agent general. Libellous writings, violence, and calumny were Boisseau's favourite weapons. The council would have willingly brought an action against him; but the majority of the councillors, who were proceeding against the agent general on their own account, would have had to disclaim competence, in order to avoid being both judges and litigants. What the councillors finally did, "in view of the protection given by the Governor to the said Boisseau," was to refer the matter, on 10 Nov. 1681, to the king's justice.

At that date, Boisseau was on the point of sailing for France. His unrestrained behaviour in 1680 had been the subject of numerous reports to the authorities in the homeland; Duchesneau, for one, had written many of them. The king ordered the company to dismiss Boisseau, but reproached the intendant for his partiality towards Aubert de La Chesnaye and the animosity that he had displayed in this matter. The announcement of Boisseau's recall must have reached Quebec shortly before 15 July (1681), the date on which he was styled "former" agent general.

Boisseau departed, but he announced his early return; moreover, he left at Quebec his wife and his two children, who had been born in Canada; they did not return to France until the autumn of 1682. In Paris, Boisseau felt more reluctant to go back to the colony when he learned that his protector Frontenac and Duchesneau would perhaps not be continued in their offices: it was even said, according to DUDOUYT, "that he [did] all he [could] in order not to return." And in fact Duchesneau and Frontenac were recalled. Boisseau endeavoured from then on to attach himself to the new governor, M. LE FEBVRE de La Barre, in the capacity of secretary; but, stated Dudouyt, the matter was not to be arranged, for La Barre "knew the Sieur Boisseau." The former agent general's Canadian adventure was at an end.

This headstrong man, apt at times to act foolishly, had the misfortune to reside in New France during years when the disagreements over authority, and the aggravated state of passions, allowed him to give free rein to his tendency to excess. Closely protected on the one hand by a Frontenac too like himself and just as grasping as he, Boisseau was assured of an almost complete impunity, which, following his master's example, he made use of blithely; on the other hand, the partiality and unrelenting hostility of the opposing party, and of Duchesneau in particular, helped to exasperate him, at the same time as they gave him an apparent justification for his violent actions. In other times and in a more benign climate, Josias Boisseau might perhaps have been a completely different man, whose energy, dynamism, and determination would have caused the uncouth and impetuous element of his character to be overlooked.

ANDRÉ VACHON

AJQ, Greffe de Romain Becquet, 10 avril 1680, etc.; Greffe de Pierre Duquet, 1663–84, *passim*; Greffe de

Boivin

Gilles Rageot, 1666–1702, *passim*; Greffe de François Genaple, 1682–1702, *passim*. ANDQ, Registre des baptêmes, mariages et sépultures de la paroisse Notre-Dame de Québec, 20 avril et 14 août 1680, 23 juin 1681. APQ, Ordres du roi, VIII, *passim*. ASQ, Lettres, N, 52, 57, 61, 62; Polygraphie, III, 51. Recensement de 1681.

Correspondance de Frontenac (1672–1682), APQ, *Rapport, 1926–27,* 120–6, 132. "Lettre de l'intendant Duchesneau au Marquis de Seignelay, fils de Colbert (13 nov. 1681)," *BRH*, XXVI (1920), 275–86. *Jug. et délib.*, II; *passim*. *NYCD* (O'Callaghan and Fernow), IX, 141, 157, 159f. *Ord. comm.* (P.-G. Roy), I; 287–90. Delanglez, *Jolliet*, 274, 285–97. Eccles, *Frontenac*, 146, 149, 151. Tanguay, *Dictionnaire*, I, 63.

BOIVIN, FRANÇOIS, master-carpenter, the earliest church-builder to whom there is specific reference in New France; b. 1612 or 1616 at Saint-Laurent, diocese of Rouen; d. *c.* 1675–76.

François Boivin came to Canada prior to 1639 with two of his brothers, Charles and Guillaume, also carpenters, who were Jesuit *donnés*. (Charles was brought to Sainte-Marie, the Huron mission, as architect in 1640.) François received a grant of land at Cap de la Madeleine from Father BUTEUX, 1 June 1649.

In 1649, François Boivin appeared at Trois-Rivières as chief signatory on a contract, dated 24 June, to roof a parish church there. This contract made between "Francois Boivin, *Maître-charpentier*" and the "*honorable homme* JEAN BOURDON, *procureur et commis général de la Communauté de la Nouvelle france,*" is the most important piece of evidence extant for building practices in the first half of the 17th century in Quebec. The dimensions of the church to be roofed (a rather remarkable 90 ft. long by 27 ft. wide, with a round apse and flanking chapels forming a transept) are specified, as are the sizes of the various rafters, beams, joists, and so forth that Boivin is to use. The carpenter is obligated to provide the wood himself, and bring it to the site. Presumably, then, he followed the old practice of master-builders, which survived in barn-raisings even into the 20th century, of cutting and shaping the various parts on the ground where the felled trees lay, then assembling them all in one "bee" with pegs and notches. As an artisan well trained in traditional methods, he needs no plan or drawings, for none are mentioned—but it is stated that his work will be inspected to make sure it conforms "to the art of carpentry" by "people knowing about such things." For all this he will receive remuneration of 1620 *livres*, "in addition, Bourdon promises to supply six barrels of flour while the work is going on." Finally—and this is a frontier touch, indeed, "it has been promised by *Monsieur le Gouverneur* that the said Boivin and one of his men will be exempt from guard duty during the said work." About the church we know no more; it was not until 1664 that the first parish church of Trois-Rivières was finally built—a much smaller structure than that called for in 1647, and all of wood.

According to the 1666 census and that of 1667, François Boivin lived on the Beaupré shore with his nephew Pierre, whom Boivin, a widower, had made his heir, and his wife, Thiennette Fafard, aged 14 years. The household does not seem to have been a happy one, as François Boivin, before the Quebec notary, Romain BECQUET, made a will 27 Jan. 1675, disinheriting his nephew and leaving his estate to the Hôtel-Dieu. After Boivin's death, which occurred between 27 Jan. 1675 and 15 Oct. 1676, his nephew contested the will and won a settlement.

ALAN GOWANS

AJQ, Greffe de Pierre Duquet, 15 oct. 1676; Greffe de Romain Becquet, 27 janv. 1675. AJTR, Greffe de Séverin Ameau, 1er juillet 1664. ASQ, Séminaire, VI, 23. P.-G. et A. Roy, *Inv. greffes not.*, II, 171; III, 128; XI, 75.

Archange Godbout, "Origine des familles canadiennes-françaises," extrait de *l'État civil français*, 1ère série (Lille, 1925), 27. Alan Gowans, *Church architecture in New France* (Toronto, 1955), 19–21. A. E. Jones, "'8endake Ehen' or Old Huronia," PAO *Annual Report*, V (1908). Wilfrid and Elsie McLeod Jury, *Sainte-Marie among the Hurons* (Toronto, 1954), 50. "Les frères Boivin," *BRH*, XLVII (1941), 309.

BONAMOUR, JEAN DE, king's doctor, one of the first medical doctors to practise in New France in the 17th century.

He arrived in the country in the summer of 1669, bearing letters naming him a king's doctor. His stipend was 600 *livres*, and he had received an equal amount "to outfit himself." His office required him to treat the poor of the town and of the Hôtel-Dieu of Quebec. He had authority over the surgeons and midwives. He was also doctor to the Ursulines in 1671.

On 9 June 1672 he was called to take a seat in the Conseil Souverain "in order to make up the number of judges." On 23 October of that year his presence is recorded at the signing of PHILIPPE GAULTIER de Comporté's marriage contract, and on this occasion he was called "the worthy man Jean de Bonamour." This was his last public act. Shortly afterwards he sailed for France on the pretext of family affairs. In November 1672 Governor BUADE de Frontenac vainly asked the minister to send Bonamour back to Canada.

Until Sarrazin's* return in 1697 there was no other medical doctor, or king's doctor, in Canada.

GABRIEL NADEAU

Correspondance de Frontenac (1672–82), APQ *Rapport, 1926–27*, 23. *Jug. et délib.*, I, 669, 685. P.-G. Roy, *Inv. contrats de mariage*, VI, 197. Ahern, *Notes pour l'histoire de la médecine*.

BOND, WILLIAM, HBC captain from the Thameside parish of Rotherhithe; fl. *c.* 1655–94.

He joined the Company in 1672 as gunner of the *Imploy* and sailed to Charles Fort, where he wintered before going on the first trading expedition to Port Nelson in the summer of 1673. Bond's knowledge of the country made him a useful employee, and when he returned to England in 1679 his services would have been retained but for the high value he set upon them after the death of Governor Charles BAYLY early in 1680.

By December 1681 Bond's terms were more reasonable, and in 1682 he was given command of the *Craven* pink which had been built for service in James Bay. But just before sailing he refused to take the oath of loyalty and to make a promise not to engage in private trade. However, when faced with dismissal, "this young blade" submitted, but his "stubborne Sullen disposition" had aroused the suspicions of the London Committee and he was recalled in 1683. After taking the *Albemarle* from Charlton Island to Port Nelson during the summer he accordingly returned to England in command of the *George*.

Bond, restored to favour, commanded the *Happy Return* in both 1684 and 1685 on successful voyages to and from Port Nelson. He was reprimanded, however, for not keeping company with the *Perpetuana Merchant* on the outward voyage in 1685. Had he done so he might have prevented her being taken at the western end of Hudson Strait by two French ships under the direction of Claude Bermen* de La Martinière.

On 10 July of the following year, when bound for Charlton Island, the *Happy Return* was lost in the ice in Hudson Strait, but Bond and his crew reached York Fort (Bourbon), presumably in the *Abraham and Robert* (Capt. Robert Porten). Bond returned to England in the same year as a passenger in that ship, and in 1687 commanded the *Dering* on a successful voyage to and from York Fort.

An effort was made in 1688 to recover part of the advantage lost to the French in 1686 when, at a time of peace, Pierre de TROYES had captured the Company's three forts in James Bay. A new governor, Capt. John MARSH, sailed with Bond in the *Churchill*, and a new deputy, Capt. Andrew HAMILTON, sailed with John Simpson in the *Yonge* for Albany River where, on account of the treaty of neutrality concluded between the English and French kings in November 1686, they were to live at peace with their French neighbours. Bond, the man of most experience, was to be senior to the deputy governor when in council, and at sea he was to be "Admirall." In Hudson Strait the ships met the interloper *Mary* in distress and took her company aboard, including captains John ABRAHAM and John OUTLAW, before continuing to Albany River, where they arrived about 10 September. From the beginning the French harassed the English party and in December 1688, when Bond and his mate were hunting partridges, they themselves were "caught like woodcocks." Later that season the French gained complete victory in Albany River.

Bond was sent overland to Canada where he was held until he was sent to France in 1691. This transfer was no doubt made because of the war which had broken out in 1689, and with the object of depriving the Company of the services of its most experienced captain. Because he had not returned to England by June 1692 the Governor and Committee were suspicious that he was concerned in a French plot against York Fort. If, however, Bond was identical with the "Wm. Bond" who commanded the Greenland Company's ship *George* in November 1694, these suspicions could have been unfounded. References to Bond's wife, Susan, are to be found in the Company's archives, but nothing further is known about his family.

ALICE M. JOHNSON

HBRS, V (Rich), 75; VIII, IX (Rich); XI, XX (Rich and Johnson).

BONNEMERE, FLORENT, lay brother, Jesuit, apothecary, surgeon; b. 1600 at Bordeaux (France); d. 16 Aug. 1683 at Quebec.

Bonnemere, who arrived at Quebec 14 Aug. 1647, had joined the Jesuits in Paris 23 July 1619. He appears to have been chiefly an apothecary; however, he is known to have taken an interest also in medicine and surgery.

The practice of the apothecary's art, regulated in France from the time of Charles VII, was in the 17th century controlled by a guild just as medicine was. The apothecaries had their own college, and after an apprenticeship of seven years they had to submit a master's thesis and a pharmaceutical "masterpiece." Their principal function was that of preparing medicines as prescribed by doctors; they were obliged to deliver them to the patients at home and to observe their effect. Apothecaries made use of a considerable quantity of medicines compounded from chemical products and medicinal plants and played an important role in the care of the sick. For Louis XIV's needs alone, there were nine apothecaries in ordinary.

Apothecaries were comparatively numerous in New France. The first one was LOUIS HÉBERT, the son of an apothecary of Paris. Several of them were religious, particularly Jesuits, which is perhaps attributable to the fact that the apothecary's art was not subject to the same restrictions as medicine and surgery with respect to its practice by members of the clergy. The Sulpician Gabriel SOUART, the first parish priest of Montreal, having studied medicine before entering holy orders, had to obtain papal authorization to practise his art after his arrival in the colony.

The Recollet brother, Pacifique DUPLESSIS, was an apothecary. The Jesuits, who were in charge of a sizable store of medicines, included a fair number of apothecaries: Brothers Noël Juchereau [see JEAN JUCHEREAU DE LA FERTÉ], Gaspard Gouault, Florent Bonnemere, Jean Vitry, Jean Boussat*, Jean-François Parisel, Charles and Jean Jard Boispineau. It is likely that Bonnemere also practised medicine and surgery. He treated the Ursuline Marie de Saint-Joseph [see SAVONNIÈRES] for dropsy. According to Bonnemere, this nun appeared to him on two occasions after her death (1652), once in order to warn him of mortal danger when he was crossing the St. Lawrence on the ice.

In a notebook entitled "Miracles arrivez en leglise de Ste-Anne du petit Cap Coste de Beaupré en Canadas," assembled in 1687 by the parish priest Thomas MOREL, there is reproduced a document that Bonnemere had signed, adding after his name: "practising medicine at Quebec."

The *Journal des Jésuites* (September 1659) contains the following two notes: "de F. Bonnemere; moderanda actio chirurgi circa foemineum sexum" (re Brother Bonnemere: he is to desist from surgical activity for the female sex). And, in the margin: "Chirurgus non curet foeminas" (As a surgeon he is not to attend women). From these two notes one has reason to think that Bonnemere was in regular surgical practice.

ANTONIO DROLET

ASQ, Paroisses diverses, 84, p. 11, and Polygraphie, XIII, 2, p. 18 (Thomas Morel, "Miracles arrivez en leglise de Ste Anne du petit Cap Coste de Beaupré en Canadas," 1687). Marie Guyart de l'Incarnation, *Lettres* (Richaudeau), I, 529–31. *JR* (Thwaites), XXXVIII, 163–65; XXXIX, 267; XLV, 115; LXXI, 147 *et passim*. *JJ* (Laverdière et Casgrain).

Maude E. Abbott, *History of medicine in the Province of Quebec* (Montreal, 1931). Ahern, *Notes pour l'histoire de la médecine*, 65. Boissonnault, *Histoire de la faculté de Médecine de Laval*, 45. Paul Delaunay, *La médecine et l'Église: contribution à l'histoire de la pratique médicale par les clercs* (Paris, 1948). *Dictionnaire encyclopédique des sciences médicales* (1ère série, 26v., Paris, 1864–82), V. J. J. Heagerty, *Four centuries of medical history in Canada, and a sketch of the medical history of Newfoundland* (2v., Toronto, 1928). Gabriel Nadeau, "Le dernier chirurgien du roi à Québec: Antoine Briault (1742–1760)," *L'Union médicale du Canada*, LXXX (1951), 705–26, 855–61, 981–98, 1106–15. *Les Ursulines de Québec*, I, 193f.

BOQUET, CHARLES, a *donné* of the Society of Jesus; b. *c.* 1630; d. some time after 1681.

We have no information concerning Charles Boquet's life until 1657; after this date he appears fairly frequently in the *Journal des Jésuites* and the *Relations*. Indeed, up to 1667 he appears to have been one of the best of the guides and interpreters on the expeditions to the Iroquois country; in any event he accompanied all important missions that went there. In 1657 he was a member of the mission of Father Louis Mercier* to Sainte-Marie-de-Ganentaa, and the following year he took an active part in the secret flight of the French. He returned three times to the Iroquois country in 1666: once in February and March as an interpreter to Father Pierre Raffeix* and to Governor RÉMY de Courcelle's troops; then in July with Father Thierry Beschefer* and the embassy proceeding to Fort Orange (Albany); lastly from September to November, with Father Charles ALBANEL and PROUVILLE de Tracy's expedition.

He took part with Fathers Jacques FRÉMIN and Jean PIERRON in the reopening of the Iroquois mission in 1667. Between 1658 and 1666 his chief employment seems to have been that of supervising the transporting of supplies between the Jesuit residences at Quebec and Trois-Rivières. In 1669 Mother Marie de l'Incarnation [see GUYART], described him in very warm terms of praise as a courier doing his rounds between the places where the fathers were. "He knows all the routes perfectly," she said, "[and] he is known by all the Indians, who esteem and fear him." The 1681 census—in most cases an unreliable source— states that he was about 51 years old, and was one of the *donnés* residing at the Jesuit college at Quebec.

J. MONET

Recensement de 1681. Marie Guyart de l'Incarnation, *Lettres* (Richaudeau), II, 415. *JR* (Thwaites), *passim*. *JJ* (Laverdière et Casgrain).

BOUCHARD, ÉTIENNE, surgeon; b. *c.* 1622 in the parish of Saint-Paul, Paris; d. 1676 in Montreal.

On 10 May 1653 Bouchard, who ordinarily lived in the town and duchy of Épernon, entered into an agreement with Paul de CHOMEDEY de Maisonneuve and Jérôme Le Royer de La Dauversière to act as a surgeon for the settlement of Montreal for a period of five years. He arrived in Canada 22 Sept. 1653, at the same time as two other surgeons, LOUIS CHARTIER and Pierre Piron. Having received authorization to break his 1653 contract, Bouchard made an agreement with a group of settlers of Ville-Marie on 3 March 1655, whereby he undertook to give free treatment to them and to their families in exchange for 100 *sous* paid annually in two instalments by each settler.

His practice must have been extensive. He first had in his service Jean Auger *dit* Le Baron, who left him 16 Aug. 1656. On 2 Feb. 1660 he engaged François Caron as surgeon's aid, and, on 15 November of the same year, Nicolas Colson as journeyman-surgeon. Colson left him at a date unknown, but certainly not after 26 July 1664, when he was in the employ of Jean MADRY. On 5 August of the following year Bouchard replaced him by Gilles Devennes. Bouchard's last professional act was performed with Jean Martinet* de Fonblanche, as an officer of the surgeons' guild.

Bouchard had married Marguerite Boissel at Quebec, 6 Oct. 1657; they had seven children of whom at least three survived their father. When he died at his colleague Martinet's home, 19 July 1676, he was a sick man, abandoned by his wife and separated from his children. He had been a doctor at the Hôtel-Dieu.

GABRIEL NADEAU

AJM, Greffe de Bénigne Basset, 5 août 1665 *et passim*; Greffe de Lambert Closse, 3 mars 1665; Greffe de Jean de Saint-Père, 16 août 1656. AJQ, Greffe de Guillaume Audouart, 23 juillet 1657. Lionel Audet-Lapointe, "Étienne Bouchard, chirurgien à Ville-Marie en 1653," SGCF *Mémoires*, XIII (1962), 241–43. Godbout, "Nos ancêtres," APQ *Rapport, 1959–60*, 292f. É.-Z. Massicotte, "Les chirurgiens, médecins, etc., de Montréal sous le régime français," APQ *Rapport, 1922–23*, 132f., 146f. Maria Mondoux, "Les 'Hommes' de Montréal," RHAF, II (1948–49), 71.

BOUCHER DE GRANDPRÉ, LAMBERT, officer and town major of Trois-Rivières, where he had been baptized on 12 Aug. 1656 and where he was buried in 1699.

The son of Pierre Boucher* and Jeanne Crevier, Boucher de Grandpré took up a military career. In 1689 he was an ensign in Guillaume de Lorimier's* company; the following year he took part in the defence of Quebec and for his conduct received, on 16 March 1691, royal confirmation of his ensign's rank. First Brisay* de Denonville and then Frontenac [*see* BUADE] praised him, and the latter granted him (1691) the rank of lieutenant on half pay, which the king confirmed on 1 March 1693. The previous year, on 7 April 1692, Louis XIV had appointed him major of the town of Trois-Rivières. Owner since 1681 of part of the Île Saint-Joseph, Lambert Boucher acquired part of the Grosbois fief from his father, on 2 July 1692, although he had no time to undertake its settlement. Indeed he died prematurely and was buried at Trois-Rivières on 3 April 1699. He was survived by his wife, Marguerite Vauvril de Blason, whom he had married at Quebec on 13 Aug. 1693, and two children.

ANDRÉ VACHON

Correspondance de Frontenac (1672–82, 1689–99), APQ *Rapport, 1927–28*, 26, 84, 108; *1928–29*, 282, 345, 363, 365. Godbout, "Nos ancêtres," APQ *Rapport, 1959–60*, 303. L.-A. Leymarie, "Le fief Grosbois," *NF*, I (1925–26), 259. P.-G. Roy, "Les officiers d'État Major," *RC*, XXI (1918), 378–79.

BOULLÉ (Boulay, Boullay, Boullet, Boulé), EUSTACHE, brother-in-law and lieutenant of CHAMPLAIN, became a Minim priest; b. *c.* 1600 in France, son of Nicolas Boullé, a secretary in the king's privy chamber, and of Marguerite Alix; d. sometime after 1638.

Eustache Boullé accompanied Champlain to New France in 1618. During the absence of the founder of Quebec (1618–20), he held out against the rebellious clerks. When he returned, Champlain had little Fort Saint-Louis built on the extremity of Cap-aux-Diamants and he entrusted its defence to Boullé, making himself responsible for that of the Habitation. On 26 Aug. 1621, they both were witnesses at the marriage of GUILLAUME COUILLARD and GUILLEMETTE HÉBERT. On 24 October of that year, Boullé was godfather to Eustache Martin.

In 1624 Boullé returned to France with Champlain and his wife HÉLÈNE, Boullé's sister. Two years later, Champlain, about to return to Quebec, wrote from Dieppe that his brother-in-law was at that time "doing honourable service as lieutenant at the fort." During his stay in New France, Boullé had found himself entrusted with important missions by Champlain, who placed complete faith in him. Thus, in 1627, Champlain sent him to Trois-Rivières as an ambassador for peace. Boullé was successful in delaying the Iroquois war "until all the ships had arrived and the Indians of the other nations had assembled." On 26 June 1629, when the English were threatening Quebec, Champlain gave his brother-in-law a new task:

to go to France to make known the critical situation of the colony and ask for help. Unfortunately Boullé was captured by the KIRKE brothers, who repatriated him. After the surrender of Quebec, which took place 19 July of that year, Boullé was never again to come back to America.

He chose to cross into Italy, where he joined the Minims. Mme de Champlain, who had had a major part in his conversion from Calvinism to Roman Catholicism, paid him a handsome pension during the ten years he spent in that country.

We do not know the place and date of Father Eustache Boullé's death. Some writers have confused this personage with a captain in JEAN DE BIENCOURT de Poutrincourt's regiment, a Sieur Boulay (Boullet) whose presence in Acadia was recorded in 1604 and in 1609–10.

ALBERT TESSIER

ANDQ, Registre des baptêmes, mariages et sépultures de la paroisse Notre-Dame de Québec. PRO, C.O. 1/5, 91, 92. Champlain, *Œuvres* (Laverdière). Dionne, *Champlain*. Lanctot, *Histoire du Canada*, I, 179. Robert Le Blant, "La famille Boullé 1586–1639," *RHAF*, XVII (1963–64), 55–69.

BOULLÉ, HÉLÈNE, wife of Samuel de CHAMPLAIN and founder of the Ursulines of Meaux (France); b. 1598 in Paris, daughter of Nicolas Boullé, a secretary in the king's household, and of Marguerite Alix, both of whom were Calvinists; d. and buried 20 Dec. 1654 at Meaux.

Of the four Boullé children Hélène was the most interesting. In 1610 she was given in marriage to Samuel de Champlain, 31 years her senior. As she had not yet reached the age of consent, the marrage contract required a lapse of two years before cohabitation of the couple. At first persistent in her beliefs, the young woman studied her husband's religion and adopted the Catholic faith at the age of 14. In 1620 she decided to accompany M. de Champlain to Canada. At Tadoussac the traveller met her brother EUSTACHE, who had been in America since 1618. As Champlain was almost continuously occupied with his duties as a commander, his wife found herself isolated and out of her element in an environment so different from Paris. Her habits did not lead her to frequent Mme Hébert [*see* ROLLET] and her daughter, and she sought occasional diversions among the Indians, who admired her face, her clothes, and especially the mirror hanging at her belt. After four years of exile Mme de Champlain returned to France for ever. From a distance she continued to watch over her husband's interests; in his name she instituted proceedings against GUILLAUME DE CAËN (1627), and ordered him to pay emoluments to Champlain. While her husband was still alive Hélène formed the intention of becoming an Ursuline nun. Champlain's death, which occurred suddenly on 25 Dec. 1635, left her free to carry out her plans, but various affairs delayed for 10 years her retirement from the world. Amongst other troubles were those occasioned by Champlain's will, which designated Notre-Dame-de-la-Recouvrance as the heir to all his property. Mme de Champlain, who had no liking for legal squabbles, gave up the rights conferred upon her by her marriage contract, and a first cousin, who had had the will set aside, won the day.

In November 1645 Hélène de Champlain entered the monastery of the Ursulines of Paris. It was there that she took the white veil under the name of Sister Hélène de Saint-Augustin. Because of her age, and of the independence to which she was accustomed, she apparently found the yoke heavy. While still a novice—which supports our conjectures—she left the convent of the Faubourg Saint-Jacques to go and found a monastery in the town of Meaux. The *Chroniques de l'ordre*, somewhat inclined though they are to fulsome praise, do however say that Mother Hélène de Saint-Augustin had to endure heavy trials which her lively temperament made doubly painful to her. She died in odour of sanctity on 20 Dec. 1654, after a week's illness.

MARIE-EMMANUEL CHABOT, O.S.U.

Les Chroniques de l'Ordre des Ursulines (Paris, 1673). *JR* (Thwaites). Morris Bishop, *Champlain: the life of fortitude* (New York, 1948). Bourde de la Rogerie's article in Société archéologique d'Ille-et-Vilaine *Bulletin*, LXIII (1932), published separately as *Hélène Boullé, femme de Samuel Champlain* (1938). Faillon, *Histoire de la colonie française*, I. Robert Le Blant, "La famille Boullé, 1586–1639," *RHAF*, XVII (1963–64), 55–69; "Le testament de Samuel Champlain, 17 novembre 1635." *ibid.*, 269–86.

BOULLET, EUSTACHE. *See* BOULLÉ

BOULLONGNE (Boulogne, Boulonge, Boullogne, Boulongue), MARIE-BARBE DE, wife of Governor LOUIS D'AILLEBOUST, co-founder of the Confrérie de la Sainte-Famille at Montreal, benefactress of the Hôtel-Dieu at Québec; b. *c.* 1618 at Ravières (Champagne), daughter of Florentin de Boullongne and Eustache Quéan; d. 1685 at Quebec.

Nothing is known about Barbe de Boullongne's youth. On 6 Sept. 1638, in Paris, she married Louis d'Ailleboust, the future governor of New France. They had no children; according to a tradition, they had taken the vow of continency.

At the beginning of her marriage she was a

timid, sickly young woman; she would have been unable to bring herself to follow her husband, who was determined to go to New France, had it not been for a cure considered to be miraculous, which put matters right and gave a new direction to the guidance being offered by their spiritual counsellors, in particular CHARLES LALEMANT and Jean-Jacques Olier. From then on Barbe de Boullongne's history is associated with that of her husband.

Once already, after her marriage, and with her husband's consent, she had had a taste of religious life among the Ursulines of Quebec, where her sister Philippine-Gertrude *dite* Mother Saint-Dominique lived. But this experiment, tried in January 1653, had lasted only a month. Her thoughts turned again in this direction, this time more seriously, after her husband's death in 1660. The management of her property prevented her from taking any action until 1663. But having by then settled all her affairs at Montreal, she re-entered the Ursuline noviciate, at 45 years of age. According to *Les Ursulines de Québec* she could not get used to the rules; she realized this and withdrew of her own accord after eight or nine months, in order "to resume in the world her life of good works and edification." Subsequently she turned down a number of splendid offers of marriage. Jeanne-Francoise Juchereau* *dite* de Saint-Ignace states that she was sought in marriage by Governor RÉMY de Courcelle, and especially by Intendant TALON, who lavished attention upon her. But she was detached from the world and thenceforth given up entirely to charity and piety.

The principal work associated with her name, as with Father CHAUMONOT's, is the establishment of the Confrérie de la Sainte-Famille. It was founded at Montreal during the years 1662–63, and afterwards established at Quebec, where it received the approval of Bishop Laval* in a pastoral letter of 4 March 1665, after being honoured, in the month of January, by a special bull, and endowed with indulgences by Pope Alexander VII.

Mme d'Ailleboust, who was dedicated to the sick in the Hôtel-Dieu of Quebec, gave herself to this institution by notarial contract on 5 July 1670, together with her remaining possessions; she spent the rest of her days in a small house adjoining the hospital, in the company of a shrewish old servant whom she had kept with her purely out of a spirit of self-mortification. She died as a predestinate on 7 June 1685, and was buried in the original nun's chancel. The Hôtel-Dieu still preserves her family papers, as well as certain other mementoes, and still calls her "our benefactress."

According to the 1647 *Relation* Mme d'Ailleboust took an interest in the natives, had studied their languages, and is supposed to have received from the Algonkins the name *Chaouerindamaguetch*, meaning "She who takes pity on us in our wretchedness."

HONORIUS PROVOST

AHDQ, Papiers d'Ailleboust. AJQ, Greffe de Gilles Rageot, 5 juillet 1670. ASQ, Documents Faribault, 83b; Polygraphie, II, 10; III, 41; XXII, 61b, 61d; Séminaire, VI, 22, 51, 52c. [P.-J.-M. Chaumonot], *Un missionaire des Hurons: autobiographie du père Chaumonot de la Compagnie de Jésus et son complément*, éd. Félix Martin (Paris, 1885). *JR* (Thwaites), *passim*. *JJ* (Laverdière et Casgrain). Juchereau, *Annales* (Jamet) *La solide dévotion à la Très-Saint Famille, de Jésus, Marie, et Joseph, avec un catéchisme qui enseigne à pratiquer leurs vertus* (Paris, 1675).

Marie-Claire Daveluy, "Bibliographie," *RHAF*, XV (1961), 146–54, 466–72, 611, 612. Aegidius Fauteux, *La famille d'Ailleboust* (Montréal, 1917). Ernest Gagnon, *Feuilles volantes et pages d'histoire* (Québec, 1910). Honorius Provost, "La réserve de M. d'Ailleboust à Québec," *BRH*, LIII (1947), 178–87. Régis Roy, *La famille d'Ailleboust* (Montréal, s.d.). *Les Ursulines de Québec*, I, 259–61.

BOURDON, JEAN (sometimes called M. de Saint-Jean or Sieur de Saint-François), seigneur, engineer, surveyor, cartographer, business man, procurator-syndic of the village of Quebec, head clerk of the Communauté des Habitants, explorer, attorney-general in the Conseil Souverain; b. *c.* 1601 at Saint-André-le-Vieil in Rouen; d. 1668 at Quebec.

He arrived in the colony on 8 Aug. 1634, together with his friend Abbé JEAN LE SUEUR; he was a bachelor and had the title of engineer to the governor. As soon as he arrived he settled on the outskirts of Quebec, on the Sainte-Geneviève hill. On 5 April 1639 Governor HUAULT de Montmagny made him a commoner's grant of the 50 acres of land that he had been occupying from the beginning, and that he had named "terre Saint-Jean." He built a mill, and a chapel where his friend Jean Le Sueur was to officiate. Later, on 19 March 1661, the Compagnie de la Nouvelle-France was to transform this first land-concession into a noble fief.

Jean Bourdon received several other seigneuries in return for his services. On 30 July 1636 he obtained the Rivière au Griffon seigneury, which was one league by three in area. On 1 Dec. 1637 he was granted the seigneury of Autray, measuring half a league by two, which he was to give to his son JACQUES on 20 Dec. 1653. On 10 March 1646 Montmagny granted him commoner's rights to the Saint-François domain, on condition that he

Bourdon

would build a wooden fort there to protect Quebec from the Iroquois. At first Bourdon owned only a part of this land, but Abbé Le Sueur subsequently gave him his portion. Governor JEAN DE LAUSON, on 25 April 1655, made this property into a noble fief. On 15 Dec. 1653 Bourdon received the seigneury of Dombourg (anagram of Bourdon), which was situated at the spot now called Pointe-aux-Trembles, and which he intended for his son JEAN-FRANÇOIS. A few days later, on 21 December, the governor granted him the seigneury of La Malbaie, which was four leagues in depth. On 30 March 1655 he acquired the arriere-fief of Saint-Anne, in the Lauson seigneury, which he was to give to the Ursulines to pay his daughter Anne's dowry.

Jean Bourdon does not seem to have devoted too much time to exploiting his seigneuries. He lived on the Saint-Jean fief, which he had put under cultivation and on which he had constructed "a large main building, and a smaller block of buildings including a chapel, two barns, and three granaries." He carried on his profession as an engineer and surveyor. He instituted a survey of the town of Quebec, directed building operations, and settled disputes relating to land. During his stay in France in 1641–42 he even drew up a detailed map of the region between Quebec and Cap Tourmente, including the Île d'Orléans. In 1653 he went into partnership with JEAN-PAUL GODEFROY and LOUIS D'AILLEBOUST, in order to establish three-way trade between Canada, the West Indies, and France.

Jean Bourdon became a prominent figure in the colony. In 1645 he was appointed acting governor of Trois-Rivières. The following year he went with Father JOGUES to the Iroquois country, to consolidate the peace treaty concluded the previous summer at Trois-Rivières between Montmagny and the Indian chiefs, who had been represented particularly by the orator KIOTSEAETON. He set off on 16 May and arrived in the Iroquois country on 7 June. On the tenth the meeting with the chieftains took place. The peace treaty was renewed, but with some reservations. An epidemic of smallpox among the Iroquois coincided with the departure of Jogues and Bourdon from the Iroquois country; some warlike chieftains accused Jogues of witchcraft and the peace was broken. Jogues and Bourdon were back at Trois-Rivières on the twenty-ninth.

The creation of the Communauté des Habitants raised Bourdon to the highest level of Quebec society. In 1647 he was elected procurator-syndic of the town of Quebec, then the governor appointed him head clerk of the Communauté. This last appointment required him to travel all over the colony in the following years, for he had to supervise the fur trade. In 1650 he went to France with Godefroy, who according to Burke-Gaffney proposed to negotiate the setting up of the Compagnie de Tadoussac. Apparently at Lauson's request, the Compagnie de La Nouvelle-France appointed Bourdon its fiscal attorney, with the responsibility of supervising the activities of the Compagnie de Tadoussac.

He was working for the Communauté when he undertook his famous journey to Hudson Bay. La Poterie [Le Roy*], Charlevoix*, and Garneau* give the date of this journey as 1656. Their error possibly stems from a forged document composed much later on under the administration of Governor Brisay* de Denonville, with the object of substantiating France's claim to Hudson Bay. The *Relations* and the documents of the period agree on the year 1657. Bourdon left Quebec on 2 May with 16 Frenchmen and 2 Hurons, and apparently went to Kibokok, at the mouth of the Ashouanipi River, latitude 55° north. The assassination of his Huron guides prevented him from continuing his journey. He returned to Quebec on 11 Aug. 1657. At the time of the diplomatic negotiations between France and England for the possession of Hudson Bay, the French tried to base their right of ownership on this voyage by Bourdon. It was of no avail, for Bourdon had not gone to Hudson Bay and had not officially taken possession of it.

On 18 Oct. 1660 he went to France. It is presumed that he was instructed to place before the minister the military situation in the colony, and to ask for troops to be dispatched. He may have drawn a map of Quebec for that purpose.

In 1662 Bourdon was called upon to reply to charges laid against him by JEAN PERONNE Dumesnil, who was making investigations for the Compagnie de la Nouvelle-France. Dumesnil accused Bourdon of having failed to keep an exact account of the furs traded by the Communauté des Habitants. ROUER de Villeray was also implicated in the affair, about which we have very conflicting evidence. Poor bookkeeping, resulting from the incompetence of the Communauté's administrators, may have given rise to Dumesnil's charges. It is undeniable that some people did deliberately create confusion; but Bourdon could not have been involved.

Despite the charges weighing upon Bourdon, Bishop Laval*, when an administrative reorganization was undertaken in 1663, called upon the latter's experience: he recommended him to the governor and had a hand in his appointment as attorney-general. Except for two periods when he was replaced by LOUIS-THÉANDRE CHARTIER de

Lotbinière, Bourdon occupied this office until 1668. The Council's records show that he was a regular attendant at the meetings, where he often sided with the bishop. This aroused the anger of Governor SAFFRAY de Mézy, who twice attempted to remove him from his post. In September 1664 he appointed new councillors to ensure that his point of view would prevail in the quarrel between himself and Bishop Laval, but Bourdon refused to leave his post, banking on the text of the decree that set up the Conseil Souverain; this text made no provision for any procedure whereby the attorney could be dismissed. Mézy was furious, ordered Bourdon to be expelled, and gave him 24 hours to leave for France. On 23 September Bourdon sailed with his son Jean-François. He spent his spare time in Paris drawing up a map of the surroundings of Quebec. An investigation by PROUVILLE de Tracy, who arrived in Canada in 1665, led to the reinstatement of the former councillors in 1666, and Bourdon, who had returned to Quebec on 16 July 1665, became attorney-general again on 6 Dec. 1666.

Once again he was not to occupy his seat for long. Since 1663 he had been a prey to gout. On 12 Jan. 1668 he died at Quebec. He was buried the next day in the Chapelle du Scapulaire, in the church of Notre-Dame de Québec.

Jean Bourdon had married twice. On 9 Sept. 1635, in the church of Notre-Dame-de-la-Recouvrance at Quebec, he had married Jacqueline Potel, who died on 11 Sept. 1654 after bearing him eight children. His four daughters became nuns. Geneviève, under the name of Mother Marie-de-Saint-Joseph, was the first Ursuline born in Canada; Anne*, called Mother Sainte-Agnès, became a superior of the Ursulines; Marguerite*, *dite* Mother Saint-Jean-Baptiste, entered the Augustines and was one of the three founders and the first superior of the Hôpital Général of Quebec, where Marie, who chose the name of Mother Marie-Thérèse-de-Jésus, took the veil.

On 21 Aug. 1655 Jean Bourdon married his second wife, Anne Gasnier, the widow of Jean de Clément Du Vault de Monceaux. She was born in 1611, and died on 27 June 1698. She was a friend of Barbe de BOULLONGNE d'Ailleboust, and had emigrated to Canada with the intention of devoting her life to the destitute. Marie de l'Incarnation [*see* GUYART] calls her "the mother of the unfortunate and the example for all kinds of good works." She took pity upon Jean Bourdon, who had been left a widower with seven young children. She agreed to marry him, but on condition that they live as brother and sister. He consented. Marie de l'Incarnation writes that Bourdon "experienced continually the sense of God's presence and of union with his divine Majesty."

After her husband's death, Anne Gasnier continued to concern herself with good works. She devoted herself especially to the welfare of immigrant girls. She made several trips to France to recruit respectable girls desirous of making a home in Canada. When they reached Quebec, she would give them lodging and food in a house that had been left to her in the Lower Town by her husband.

JEAN HAMELIN

Charlevoix, *Histoire*, I; 476. *JR* (Thwaites). *JJ* (Laverdière et Casgrain). La Pot(h)erie, *Histoire* (éd. 1722), I, 141. *NYCD* (O'Callaghan and Fernow), IX, 286 (Jacques René Brisay de Denonville, "Memoir on the state of Canada, Nov. 12, 1685), *et passim*. PAC *Report, 1883*, Note C, 173–201 ("Transactions betweene England and France relateing to Hudsons Bay, 1687"). P.-G. Roy, *Inv. concessions*.

Burke-Gaffney, "Canada's first engineer: Jean Bourdon 1601–1668," CCHA *Report, 1956–57*, 87–104. Delanglez, *Jolliet*, 245–62. "Éloge de la famille Bourdon (Lettre de la Mère Marie de l'Incarnation à son fils, 1668)," *BRH*, XXXIV (1928), 52f. Garneau, *Histoire du Canada*, I, 446. Godbout, *Les pionniers de la région trifluvienne*, 28. Auguste Gosselin, *Jean Bourdon, 1634–1668* (Les Normands au Canada; Évreux, 1892); *Jean Bourdon et son ami l'abbé de Saint-Sauveur: épisodes des temps héroïques de notre histoire* (Les Normands au Canada; Québec, 1904). "Jean Peronne Du Mesnil et ses mémoires," *BRH*, XXI (1915), 172, 193f, 198. Parkman, *The old régime* (25th ed.), 131–44. J.-E. Roy, "Jean Bourdon et la Baie d'Hudson," *BRH*, II (1896), 2–9, 21–23; "Les seigneuries de Jean Bourdon," *BRH*, XLII (1936), 336–38.

BOURDON D'AUTRAY, JACQUES, officer in the colonial regular troops, explorer, seigneur; b. 30 Sept. 1652 at Quebec, son of JEAN BOURDON and Jacqueline Potel; d. 1688.

He studied at the Jesuit College. From his father his received the fief of Autray (Lanoraie), but gave scant concern to its cultivation. By temperament he was an adventurer; he entered CAVELIER de La Salle's service in 1675 and served him loyally until his death. He was even one of La Salle's trusted associates. He was with La Salle during the latter's stay at Fort Cataracoui, took part in the building of the Conti and Crèvecœur forts in 1678 and 1680, and in 1682 was a member of the expedition that went down the Mississippi. On 9 April he signed the document recording the taking over of the Mississippi basin. He was then a lieutenant in the first company of troops maintained by the naval ministry. In return for his loyalty and his services, La Salle

Bourdon de Dombourg

granted him a fief of 126 *arpents* in length by 42 in depth at Fort Saint-Louis-des-Illinois. This was on 26 April 1682, and was La Salle's first grant of land in this region. In addition to the rights of *basse justice*, fishing, and hunting, d'Autray also enjoyed the privilege of being able to trade with the Indians. However, La Salle reserved to himself the monopoly of the bison skins, and stipulated that all trade must be conducted at Fort Saint-Louis.

In that same year, 1683, d'Autray associated himself with Henri de Tonty*, La Salle's lieutenant in charge of Fort Saint-Louis, to defend La Salle's interests against the scheming of LE FEBVRE de La Barre. In 1684 he helped Tonty to defend the fort when it was attacked by 200 Iroquois. In 1687, together with the French from the Illinois region, he went to the help of Governor Brisay* de Denonville, who was fighting the Senecas, and he took advantage of this trip to go down to Quebec. He spent the winter of 1687–88 at Montreal. In the spring he escorted the convoy that was on its way to take supplies to Fort Cataracoui. On the return journey he fell into an Iroquois ambush and was slaughtered. He was 36 years old, and a bachelor.

JEAN HAMELIN

Découvertes et établissements des Français (Margry), I, 502, 514, 518, 594, 604, 605; II, 108, 109, 118, 127, 131, 137, 139, 185, 193. *Jug. et délib.*, III, 249–50, 1071; IV, *passim*.

The French foundations, 1680–1693, ed. T. C. Pease and R. C. Werner (Illinois State Hist. Library Coll., XXIII, French ser., I, 1934), 19–27, texte de la concession de la seigneurie de d'Autray par La Salle. Auguste Gosselin, *Jean Bourdon, 1634–1668* (Les Normands au Canada, Évreux, 1892); "Les sieurs de Dombourg et d'Autray," *BRH*, VII (1901), 122–24. Parkman, *La Salle and the discovery of the great west* (12th ed.), 185, n. 1. Benjamin Sulte, "Le Fort de Frontenac, 1668–1678," *RSCT*, 2d ser., VII (1901), sect.I, 47–96; "La mort de Cavelier de La Salle," *RSCT*, 2d ser., IV (1898), sect.I, 3–31; "Les Tonty," *RSCT*, 2d ser., XI (1893), sect.I, 3–31.

BOURDON DE DOMBOURG, JEAN-FRANÇOIS, seigneur and ship's captain; b. 2 Feb. 1647 in Quebec, son of JEAN BOURDON, a seigneur and engineer-surveyor, and Jacquelin Potel; d. 1690 at La Rochelle.

Upon finishing his studies at the Jesuit college, he chose to be a sailor and became a captain in the merchant marine. His career led him to give up his rights to his father's property, which he could not work. On 28 Aug. 1677 he let the Sieur BAZIRE, a Quebec *bourgeois* and merchant, have for 3,000 *livres* the share that he had inherited of the fiefs of Saint-Jean and Saint-François. On 12 Nov. 1680 he sold his seigneury of Dombourg to Nicolas Dupont*, Sieur de Neuville. It was probably at this time that he decided to go to live in France.

He settled at La Rochelle and married Jeanne Jannière. Every year he sailed between Canada and La Rochelle, which was in control of trade with New France at that time. From there sailed the king's ship and those of the merchants, which supplied the colony with cloth, finished articles, and wines. Upon the death of his older brother, JACQUES BOURDON d'Autray, he spent some time in Canada in 1688 settling the estate. He died in 1690 at La Rochelle. In a letter to the king in 1686, Bochart* Champigny described him as "a very honest and experienced man."

After her husband's death, Jean-François Bourdon's widow came to Canada to obtain from the Conseil Souverain a statement attesting officially that her father-in-law had indeed died in the exercise of his duties as attorney general, as well as to settle her husband's estate. In 1693 she took as her second husband Simon-Pierre Denys*, Sieur de Bonaventure, a naval commander and the king's lieutenant in the government of Acadia.

JEAN HAMELIN

Coll. de manuscrits relatifs à la Nouv.-France, I, 372; II, 117. Ivanhoë Caron, "Les censitaires du côteau Sainte-Geneviève (banlieue de Québec) de 1636 à 1800," *BRH*, XXVII (1921), 132f. Auguste Gosselin, "Les sieurs de Dombourg et d'Autray," *BRH*, VII (1901), 122–24.

BOURDON DE ROMAINVILLE, JEAN, lieutenant; b. 1627 in Paris, son of Nicolas Bourdon, bourgeois, and Geneviève Amaugère; the date of his death is unknown.

He came to Acadia about 1650, and on 13 July 1653, at Port-Royal, he married Madeleine Daguerre, who had been born in the colony and brought up by Mme Menou d'Aulnay [*see* MOTIN]. From the latter Mlle Deguerre received a dowry consisting of half a league of land at Port-Royal.

In 1654 Romainville was a lieutenant at the habitation of NICOLAS DENYS at Nipisiguit (Bathurst, N.B.), and was forced, because of the forays made by the English, to return to France. He took up residence in the parish of Saint-Nicolas-des-Champs in Paris.

It is known that he had a daughter, Catherine, who was baptized 19 Aug. 1654; she does not seem to have lived. Her godfather was Pierre Lebon, from Le Havre, the captain of the *Grand Cerf*, who at that time was fishing at Percé.

We do not know whether Jean Bourdon de

Romainville returned to Canada. A court officer of the same name, a bachelor aged 37 appears, in the Quebec census of 1666; this officer prepared legal documents for the Conseil Souverain during the years 1663–68. It has not been possible to determine whether the two persons are in reality the same.

J.-ROGER COMEAU

AN, Y, 192, f.13–14v., ratification par Jean Bourdon, sieur de Romainville, et Madeleine Daguerre de leur contrat de mariage, passé à Port-Royal, le 13 juillet 1653. Acte passé devant Levasseur et Moufle, notaires au Chatelet, le 30 décembre 1654. Recensement de Québec, 1666. *Jug. et délib.* P.-G. Roy, "Jean Bourdon de Romainville," *BRH*, XXII (1916), 307.

BOURGCHEMIN ET DE L'HERMITIÈRE, JACQUES-FRANÇOIS HAMELIN DE. *See* HAMELIN

BOURGEOYS, MARGUERITE, *dite* du Saint-Sacrement, founder of the Congrégation de Notre-Dame de Montréal; b. 17 April 1620 at Troyes in Champagne (France); d. and buried 12 Jan. 1700 at Montreal; beatified 12 Nov. 1950.

Marguerite Bourgeoys was born in France in the century of the Thirty Years' War and the Fronde, during the period of the mighty triumphs of organization achieved by Richelieu and Colbert, during the period of the great mystics of the French school: Jean-Jacques Olier, Pierre de Bérulle, Charles de Condren. She was marked by her environment and by her time, and was destined to be both a great realist and a profound mystic, and also to assume the figure of a forerunner.

By her father, a master candle-maker and a coiner in the mint at Troyes, as well as by her mother Guillemette Garnier, Marguerite belonged to the 17th-century French bourgeoisie. The detailed inventory of Mme Bourgeoys's estates and jewellery, and an examination of the Garnier family, give proof of the high quality of the social relations maintained by the parents and of the comfortable circumstances in which they lived.

Up to 1950 the biographers of Marguerite Bourgeoys continued to assert that she became an orphan at the age of 12, and that from that time on she was responsible for keeping house and for the education of her brothers and sisters. Recently discovered documents prove, on the contrary, that Marguerite, the sixth of the 12 Bourgeoys children, was 19 at her mother's death, and that an elder sister, Anne, was still at home in 1639. It was in 1640—when Marguerite was 20—that she passed the first milestone in the astonishing odyssey that was to bring her to New France.

The Congrégation de Notre-Dame, founded in 1598 by Alix Leclerc at the instigation of Abbé Pierre Fourier, had a convent at Troyes. These cloistered nuns, who could not go outside the monastery to exercise their calling, had recourse to a compromise: a so-called external congregation, that is, a group of girls who met in the monastery for religious instruction and lessons in pedagogy.

"Notwithstanding all the entreaties which had been made to her," Marguerite Bourgeoys had always refused to enter the external congregation, lest she be "thought a bigot." But in 1640, during the procession of the Rosary, a sudden unforeseen incident changed her destiny. She wrote: "We passed again in front of the portal of [the abbey of] Notre-Dame, where there was a stone image [of the Virgin] above the door. When I looked up and saw it I thought it was very beautiful, and at the same time I found myself so touched and so changed that I no longer knew myself, and on my return to the house everybody noticed the change, for I had been very light-hearted and well-liked by the other girls."

Marguerite Bourgeoys's first step was to enter the external congregation. The director of the congreganists was then Mother Louise de Chomedey de Sainte-Marie, sister of Paul de CHOMEDEY de Maisonneuve, the governor of Ville-Marie (Montreal). Through her, Marguerite heard about Canada, and then was introduced to Maisonneuve, who was passing through Troyes in 1652. Sister Louise de Chomedey and a few associates begged Maisonneuve to take them to Montreal. But he refused, saying that under the conditions prevailing at the time a religious community would be unable to exist at Ville-Marie. Marguerite Bourgeoys, who was then 33, offered to go there, and Maisonneuve accepted her.

Having been inexplicably refused admission to the Carmelites and to some other orders, she was free to go to Ville-Marie. In February 1653 she left Troyes, and finally landed at Quebec, after many difficulties, on 22 September.

When she reached Ville-Marie, Marguerite Bourgeoys found there were no children of school age, because of the infant mortality: "For about eight years we were unable to find any children to raise." Meanwhile, she acted like an older sister to the settlers. Already, on the boat, her presence had been a moral lesson for them, had in fact almost converted them, for on their arrival "they were changed like clothes that are put in

Bourgeoys

the wash." In 1657 she seems with her winning ways to have persuaded them to make up a work-party for the construction of the chapel of Notre-Dame-de-Bon-Secours (the first stone church built on the island of Montreal), which, despite many transformations, still stands today in the same spot. The testimony of her contemporaries affirms that people had recourse on every occasion to Marguerite, a real social worker before the invention of the term.

But the mission towards which her inclinations and her natural disposition urged her was teaching. On 30 April 1658 Marguerite Bourgeoys was finally able to receive her first pupils in a stable that had been given her by Maisonneuve for want of something better. The deed of grant stated that it was "a stone building 36 feet long by 18 wide, situated at Ville-Marie, near the Hôpital Saint-Joseph."

Marguerite, however, had greater ambitions, for she returned to France that same year, 1658, "with the intention of bringing back some girls to help me to give lessons to the children." She did bring back three worthy bourgeois girls, Edmée Châtel, Marie RAISIN, Anne Hiou, as well as a "sturdy wench" for the heavy jobs. Thanks to her companions' help, Marguerite Bourgeoys was soon to be in a position to receive the *filles du roi*, the young orphan girls sent by Louis XIV to New France "to start families." She went "to meet them at the shore," and prepared them for their future role. It was to her house that the settlers of Ville-Marie came to seek a wife, and they had to undergo a rigorous examination. They seem moreover to have appreciated this unusual matrimonial agency, as well as the teaching given to the children at Marguerite Bourgeoys's school, for in 1667, at a "settlers' meeting," they resolved to ask the king to grant letters patent to the "filles de la Congrégation," the name by which "Sister Bourgeoys" and her companions were already known at Ville-Marie.

For his part, Bishop François de Laval*, the apostolic vicar of New France, at the time of his 1669 visit, gave his approval in the form of an ordinance authorizing the teachers of Ville-Marie to instruct on the Île de Montréal and in all other places in Canada that should ask for their services.

Marguerite Bourgeoys therefore decided, in 1670, to go and "ask the King for letters patent" in order to guarantee the existence of her community. This was perhaps the most astonishing of all her journeys. She set off, the only woman, with ten *sols* in her pocket. Reaching Paris, "without money, clothes or friends," she made her way into the king's presence. Jean TALON, in his report dated 10 Nov. 1670, had pointed out to Colbert the services rendered to Canada by this "kind of congregation formed to teach children not only reading and writing, but simple handiwork." And Colbert had written in the margin: "This institution must be actively encouraged." The ground was thus well prepared, and in May 1671 Marguerite Bourgeoys obtained from the king the desired letters patent. "Not only," wrote the king, "has she performed the office of schoolmistress by giving free instruction to the young girls in all the occupations that make them capable of earning their livelihood, but, far from being a liability to the country, she has built permanent buildings, cleared land-concessions, set up a farm. . . ."

Marguerite Bourgeoys brought back from France three of her nieces: Marguerite, Catherine, and Louise Sommillard. Marguerite and Catherine were later to become sisters of the Congrégation, and Louise the wife of a settler named Fortin.

This period (1672) was for Marguerite Bourgeoys the beginning of the golden age of her work in New France, a decade of great expansion.

At the request of the noble and bourgeois families who had previously sent their daughters to Quebec, Marguerite Bourgeoys opened a boarding-school at Ville-Marie, in 1676.

But Marguerite Bourgeoys's preferences went to young girls less favoured by fortune. For them she set up the first domestic training school in the country, the needle-work school (Ouvoir de la Providence), at Saint-Charles point. In addition she sent her assistants to all those who could not come to the boarding-school. Thus small schools were founded at Lachine, Pointe-aux-Trembles (Montreal), Batiscan, and Champlain. The little Indian girls were always special favourites of hers. From the time she came to Ville-Marie, Marguerite Bourgeoys had always attracted and welcomed a few to her school. Around 1678 she established a mission in the Indian village of Montagne. The sisters taught in cabins made of bark. It was only at the turn of the century that they were housed in the towers of the fort built by M. Vachon* de Belmont; these towers can still be seen today on the ground occupied by the Grand Séminaire of Montreal.

As she saw her work developing to an extent that had been unforeseeable at the beginning, Marguerite Bourgeoys became concerned about the future. Before sending them on a mission, she had indeed given her companions training in pedagogy, and especially in a rule of life that was suited to a secular community and that she had elaborated in imitation of Our Lady's earthly existence. Already, it is true, Bishop Laval and Louis XIV had agreed that this type of life should be tried, and the settlers had long called them "sisters." But Marguerite Bourgeoys and her companions could make only promises valid in civil law, since the official hierarchy of the Church had not approved a formal status for them.

For this reason Marguerite Bourgeoys undertook a third voyage to France in 1680, this time with Mme Perrot, the wife of François-Marie PERROT, the governor of Montreal. Bishop Laval, who was in Paris, overburdened with cares, received her coldly and even forbade her to attempt any recruiting.

This journey, however, was not useless. Marguerite Bourgeoys met Mme de Miramion, but lately a celebrity at the court, who was living in retirement and directing a group of young girls doing charitable works—a "mother of the church," as Mme de Sévigné put it. Marguerite returned to Canada having acquired valuable experience of religious life in France and better prepared to face the difficulties which would soon beset her young community.

In December 1683 Sister Bourgeoys intended to resign and to proceed to the election of a new superior. But it so happened that during the night of 6 to 7 December a fire destroyed the mother house and caused the death of the two candidates for election, Marguerite Sommillard and Geneviève Durosoy.

So Sister Bourgeoys courageously resumed office. The succeeding years recall those of the great foundations; it was the beginning of the Quebec era. In 1685 Bishop Saint-Vallier [La Croix*], who succeeded Bishop Laval, brought the sisters of the Congrégation to the parish of Sainte-Famille on the Île d'Orléans. Sister Mayrand and Sister Marie Barbier* *dite* Marie de l'Assomption, were to be the heroines of this difficult foundation. A few months later the bishop, delighted with Sister Bourgeoys's work at the Ouvoir de la Providence, decided to set up a similar charity school at Quebec. To this end he bought "a house near the great square of Notre-Dame, opposite the close of the reverend Jesuit Fathers," then he fetched from the Île d'Orléans Sister Barbier, who was soon joined by a companion from Montreal, Sister Marie-Catherine Charly.* It was in this same house of Providence that Bishop Saint-Vallier was to open his Hôpital Général in 1689, appointing two sisters of the Congrégation as nurses to take care of the aged.

In 1692 the whole organization of the Congrégation at Quebec was modified. At the request of the parish priest of Quebec and to Sister Bourgeoys's delight, the sisters of the Congrégation opened a school for little girls from the poor families of the Lower Town.

As for the activities of the Hôpital Général, Bishop Saint-Vallier housed them in the former convent of the Recollets on the Saint-Charles River, and entrusted them thenceforth to the Hospitallers.

The resignation of Sister Bourgeoys was finally accepted at Montreal in 1693; Sister Barbier was elected superior general. Yet Marguerite Bourgeoys, at 73 years of age, was not yet to withdraw to the infirmary, there to enjoy the peace that comes from the completion of one's labours. Bishop Saint-Vallier reopened the question of the essence and of the very existence of the Congrégation by trying to merge the sisters with the Ursulines, or to impose upon them the cloister and a rule of his own making. But finally, with the help of M. Tronson, the superior of the Sulpicians in Paris, and sustained by the lucid will of the founder, Sister Barbier succeeded in having this rule modified to fit the requirements "of secular nuns." On 1 July 1698, the day preceding the Visitation, in the presence of Bishop Saint-Vallier, Marguerite and her companions took simple vows in the Congrégation de Notre-Dame, which was canonically constituted a community. Marguerite Bourgeoys was henceforth to be called "Sœur du Saint-Sacrement," a name that sums up the last two years of her life, two years of solitude and prayer. From 1695 the mother house of the Congrégation finally had a chapel, thanks to the gifts made by Jeanne Le Ber,* who had asked in return to live there as a recluse for the rest of her life.

Marguerite Bourgeoys's death, following the model of her life, was marked by realism and mysticism. Sister Catherine Charly was dying; to save this young nun's life, Marguerite Bourgeoys offered her own: "Oh God," she prayed, "why do you not take me instead, I who am useless and good for nought!" The evening of that very day, according to Glandelet, who cites letters from witnesses of the occurrence, Sister Charly was saved, and Sister Bourgeoys, who was well up to that time, was taken with a heavy fever. She died a few days later, on 12 Jan. 1700.

For forming an idea of Marguerite Bourgeoys's stature in the eyes of her contemporaries there is no more revealing source than their tributes of esteem and veneration at the time of her death. Popular admiration had already canonized her 250 years before her beatification; the objects which had been placed in contact with her hands, during the afternoon when the public was admitted to see the body lying in the chapel of the

Congrégation, were considered relics. The unanimity of the praises addressed to her cannot be misleading. A further testimony of esteem was the discussion about the possession of her remains, which had moreover to be settled by a compromise; the parish of Ville-Marie kept her body and the Congrégation de Notre-Dame her heart.

Marguerite Bourgeoys's pedagogy comprised the great principles of teaching used in 17th-century France, and more particularly those of the excellent educator Pierre Fourier; she had been trained in his methods by the external congregation at Troyes. But she adapted what she had acquired to the setting of New France. In a century when people in France were still wondering whether education was necessary for daughters of the lower orders, she insisted that schooling should be free: "To be able to give free instruction, the sisters content themselves with a minimum, do without everything and live sparsely everywhere."

The competence of the teacher seems to be a quite modern requirement of our century. Yet Marguerite Bourgeoys called for it, with an astonishing perspicacity: "The sisters must take the trouble to acquire knowledge and skill for all kinds of tasks. The members of the Congrégation sacrifice their health, their satisfaction and their rest for the sake of the girls they teach."

In an age when the birch-rod was still widely employed, Mother Bourgeoys recommended the use of chastisement only "very rarely, always with prudence and extreme moderation, it being remembered that one is in the presence of God."

Thanks to this goodness, which was so to speak the hallmark of her pedagogy, Marguerite Bourgeoys managed to win over the little Indian girls and to form the first two nuns to come from the native races of America: an Algonkin, Marie-Thérèse Gannensagouas, and an Iroquois, Marie-Barbe Atontinon*.

It is above all in the founding of her community, the Congrégation de Notre-Dame, that Marguerite Bourgeoys appears modern to us; through her wonderful adaptations and her magnificent achievements she stands in the forefront of our history. In New France, in the 17th century, she founded a community of non-cloistered sisters, an extraordinary innovation at that time, for the cloistered life was the only one known for women. She did not succeed without difficulties. On two occasions she had even to resist respectfully her bishop's desire to link up the Congrégation with the Ursulines of Quebec, in order to avoid increasing the number of religious orders in a poor colony and exposing himself to the risks of a bold new venture.

Marguerite Bourgeoys hit upon a formula which was wonderfully suited to the new country. Her nuns, although they took vows, were "secular," that is to say they "were not cloistered," any more than Our Lady herself: "The Holy Virgin was not cloistered, but she everywhere preserved an internal solitude, and she never refused to be where charity or necessity required help." For this reason the first nuns went on horseback, on foot, or by canoe, to teach the catechism in the dwellings scattered along the shores of the St. Lawrence. And "in order not to be a burden to anyone," they had to see to their own subsistence.

The uniform costume given by Marguerite Bourgeoys to her nuns did not seem very well suited, one would say, to such a laborious life. But however complicated and cumbersome it might appear today, one must admit that at that period it was fairly well "in fashion," similar to what women then wore: long dress, fichu and headdress of "Rouen cloth."

Marguerite Bourgeoys's nuns were of a profoundly religious cast of mind; she imparted to her community a strong spiritual quality. Following the example of Mary, the sisters of the Congrégation were intended to be "wanderers and not cloistered."

In this entirely original fashion Marguerite Bourgeoys built an edifice of which the survival is certainly the most convincing proof that its mysticism is based upon realism. She promised her nuns nothing but "bread and soup," a prospect that scarcely invited entry into her community. Yet at her death in 1700 there were 40 sisters to continue her work. By 1961 the community numbered 6,644 nuns. In that year, in 262 establishments in Canada, the United States, and Japan, the Congrégation de Notre-Dame reached nearly 100,000 pupils through its teaching, a diffusion of the gospel which prolongs in time and space the presence of Marguerite Bourgeoys.

At the age of 78 Marguerite Bourgeoys wrote her memoirs. Disturbed by the way in which the early austerity was being relaxed, the clear-sighted founder put down in writing her warnings, her ideas on the spirit of the community, and some personal memories which explain the founding of the Congrégation de Notre-Dame. This point of view and this mood account for the style and tone of the memoirs and the choice of the memories. Several of Marguerite Bourgeoys's manuscripts were lost in the fire that destroyed the mother house in 1768. Those that escaped destruction were copied at that time of the informative enquiry for the cause of beatification in 1867, and the copies were preserved in the archdiocesan archives at Montreal. The original, kept at the Congrégation de Notre-Dame, was almost entirely consumed in the fire of 1893. That same year some sisters went to the archdiocesan archives to copy the transcription of the documents written in 1867 for the cause of beatification. In the archives of the mother house, at Montreal, are to be found today, in addition to the 1893 copy, the microfilm of the first copy belonging to the archdiocesan archives, and of the copy sent to the Vatican in 1868, and the bound photostats of these two copies.

HÉLÈNE BERNIER

ACND, MS, M¹, V¹, V², Écrits autographes de sœur Marguerite Bourgeois. [Marguerite Bourgeoys], *Marguerite Bourgeois*, éd. Hélène Bernier (Classiques canadiens, III, Montréal et Paris, 1958).
A great deal has been written on Marguerite Bourgeoys. Only the principal biographies are listed below, in chronological order: Charles Glandelet, Le vray esprit de Marguerite Bourgeoys et de l'Institut des sœurs séculières de la Congrégation de Notre-Dame établie à Ville-Marie en l'Isle de Montréal en Canada, 1701; unpublished MS, copies in ACND, particularly valuable because the author, Marguerite Bourgeoys's spiritual director, wrote it only a few months after the death of the foundress and used the accounts and recollections of her contemporaries. [Étienne Montgolfier], *La vie de la Vénérable Marguerite Bourgeoys dite du Saint-Sacrement* (Ville-Marie [Montréal], 1818), known as the *Vie de 1818*, and the first biography printed in Canada. [É.-M. Faillon], *Vie de la Sœur Bourgeoys, fondatrice de la Congrégation de Notre-Dame de Villemarie en Canada, suivie de l'histoire de cet institut jusqu'à ce jour* (2 v., Ville-marie [Montréal], 1853). Sister Saint Ignatius Doyle, *Marguerite Bourgeoys and her Congregation* (Gardenvale, P.Q., 1940). Albert Jamet, *Marguerite Bourgeoys, 1620–1700* (2 v., Montréal, 1942). Yvon Charron, *Mère Bourgeoys (1620–1700)* ([Montréal], 1950). L.-P. Desrosiers, *Les dialogues de Marthe et de Marie* (Montréal et Paris, [1957]).

BOUTET DE SAINT-MARTIN, MARTIN, (referred to, indiscriminately, as Boutet and Saint-Martin), first lay-teacher at Quebec, fosterer of church music, and eminent teacher of navigation; b. 1612? in France; d. 1683? at Quebec.

Boutet came to Quebec a short time before 1645, with his wife Catherine Soulage and two daughters, to tutor sons of Frenchmen. Mentally a mathematician, Saint-Martin was, emotionally, a musician. As a singer and violinist, he was an active member of the parish choir from December 1645 onwards. In September 1651, he signed a contract with the council and wardens of the parish church to direct a choir school. Shortly afterwards he accepted, from the Jesuit college, board and lodging in lieu of the salary promised him by the parish. In the following years he was referred to at one time as principal chanter and at another, as clerk of the parish. Meanwhile, he earned pocket-money by surveying.

His interest in money waned after his younger daughter, Marie (b. 1642 at Saintes, France) made her profession as an Ursuline nun in 1659. Wishing to give up all for God, he presented himself to the Jesuits, to serve and assist them in such ways as they should deem to contribute most to the glory of God. They adjudged that he could best use his talents by teaching mathematics, or what was called mathematics in those days. For about five years he had been teaching mathematics, with special emphasis on applications to surveying and navigation, when, in 1666, Jean TALON urged him to teach the principles of navigation, not only to the students of the college, but also to all young men who aspired to be pilots. The Jesuits approved of, and co-operated in this project, which led to Boutet's making his name as "the mathematician" of Quebec. His approval became a requirement to obtain a licence to survey. A questionnaire from France on the meteorology and tidology of Quebec was turned over to Boutet to answer.

In 1671, Talon related to Louis XIV the good work being done by Sieur Saint-Martin and expressed the hope that Quebec would become a nursery of navigation. Talon's hopes were well founded. Fifteen years later, Brisay* de Denonville reported to Seignelay that Boutet had been dead for some time, and that in the past three years the country had suffered much for want of a teacher of the principles of navigation, for Boutet "formed all whom we have of those who are skilled in navigation." In response to Denonville's representations, J.-B.-L. Franquelin* was appointed hydrographer royal at Quebec to do the work which Boutet had done, without title or remuneration, for 17 years.

M. W. BURKE-GAFFNEY

AN, Col., C¹¹ᴬ, 8, pp. 20–22 (marquis de Denonville à marquis de Seignelay, 8 mai 1686). ANDQ, Arpentage, 5 juillet 1655. ASQ, Documents Faribault, 89a, "Marché et accommodation faits par les sieurs et marguilliers de Québec avec Martin Boutet," 2 sept. 1651. BN, MS, Clairambault 1016, f.168. Correspondance de Talon, APQ *Rapport, 1930–31*, 157–58. *JR* (Thwaites), LX, 104–47; "Lettre de P. Jean Enjalran," 13 oct. 1676; XLII, 268–89, "Catalogue des bienfaiteurs de N. Dame de Recouvrance de Kebec." *Jug. et délib.*, I, *passim. Les Ursulines de Québec*, II, 53–54.

BOUTROUE D'AUBIGNY, CLAUDE DE, chevalier, intendant of New France 1668–70; b. 1620, in Paris; d. 1680.

His family were members of the *noblesse de robe* who had served the Crown for some few generations. In 1654 he held the post of councillor in the *cour des monnaies*, a special court located in Paris to deal with offences committed by employees of the thirty royal mints. In 1666 he published an important study of ancient French coins, *Recherches curieuses des monnayes de France depuis le commencement de la monarchie* (Paris, 1666). He married Marie Lescot (or Lescault); they had one daughter.

Early in 1668 he was chosen by Colbert to replace Jean TALON, who had asked to be allowed to return to France on grounds of ill health. He arrived at Quebec in September, accompanied by his daughter. He was described by a nursing sister at the Hôtel-Dieu, Quebec, as being a tall, handsome man, very knowledgeable and courteous, "who knew how to make himself both feared and liked." He was fortunate in that Talon's secretary and deputy, Jean-Baptiste PATOULET, had remained in the colony and was of great assistance, advising him on Canadian affairs and drafting the annual dispatches to the minister. Boutroue was, however, reputed to be assiduous in his duties and was instrumental in having an edict passed by the Conseil Souverain to curb the sale of brandy to the Indians, who committed the most heinous crimes when inebriated. Unfortunately, he did not get on well with RÉMY de Courcelle, the governor-general of the colony—few men did—and Courcelle complained to Colbert that Boutroue was too much under the influence of Bishop Laval*. Colbert defended Boutroue, informing Courcelle that the intendant was held in high regard in France and had always fulfilled his duties in a proper manner.

In 1670 Jean Talon, who had been reappointed intendant, reached Quebec and Boutroue returned to France that autumn. Talon, in a letter to Colbert, declared, rather condescendingly, that although Boutroue lacked some of the qualities needed for the post of intendant in New France, he had done his best and had earned the esteem of the leading citizens in the colony. In France, Boutroue took up residence in Paris and was occasionally consulted by Colbert on Canadian affairs before his death in 1680.

W. J. ECCLES

The letters and dispatches of Boutroue have not survived. The *édits* and *ordonnances* enacted by the Conseil Souverain during his term of office may be found in *Jug. et délib.*, I. AN, Col., C^{11G}, 12; repr. in PAC *Rapport*, *1899*, Supp. 237f., 240f. Caron, "Inventaire de documents," APQ *Rapport*, *1939–40*, 207ff., Résumé des instructions du roi au sieur Boutroue s'en allant au Canada comme intendant, 5 avril 1668.

Ord. comm. (P.-G. Roy), I, 85–95. "Armes de Bouteroue," *BRH*, VIII (1902), 343. "Commission de l'intendant Bouteroue pour la récepte du 10% (20 juillet 1670)," *BRH*, XXXIII (1927), 125f. "Inventaire des ordonnances, 1669," *BRH*, VIII (1902), 341–43.

BRADLEY, THOMAS, probably accompanied JOHN CABOT on his North American voyage in 1498; fl. 1484–1505.

Bradley appears to have been in the service of Richard III, who presented him (1484–85) with a Breton prize, the *Michael* of Crozon, then lying at Bristol. Bradley subsequently entered the service of Henry VII. After John Cabot had returned from his 1497 voyage to North America Henry VII manned and victualled a ship at Bristol, on which Cabot sailed as "chief patron." It was probably for this ship that payments were made by the king between 22 March and 6 April 1498, amounting in all to £113 8*s*., sufficient to outfit a moderate-sized vessel. The ship belonged to Lancelot THIRKILL of London and Bradley is named with Thirkill in a payment made 1–3 April and is described as "going to the new Isle." He is also named with Thirkill in the record of the payment of the final instalment. It appears likely that he was intended to look after the king's interest on the voyage. If he sailed, as he most probably did, he survived the voyage, since it was almost certainly he who accompanied an English mission to the queen of Naples at Valencia in 1505 as intrepreter.

DAVID B. QUINN

BM, Harley MS 433, f.82. PRO, E. 101/414, 16 (payments between 22 March and 6 April 1498). *The great chronicle of London*, ed. Isobel Thornley (London, 1939), 287. PRO, *Memorials of King Henry the Seventh* (Gairdner), 223–24. Williamson, *Cabot voyages* (1962); *Voyages of the Cabots* (1929), 33, 181.

BRANSSAT, JEAN-BAPTISTE MIGEON DE. *See* MIGEON

BRAS-DE-FER DE CHATEAUFORT, MARC-ANTOINE, Knight of Malta, acting commandant of New France from December 1635 to June 1636, commandant of Trois-Rivières from 1636 to 1638.

Chateaufort, who had arrived at Quebec in 1634 or 1635, had been appointed by the Compagnie des Cent-Associés to assume command in the event of Samuel de CHAMPLAIN's death. The letters confirming his appointment had been entrusted to the Jesuit PAUL LE JEUNE, who was commissioned "to produce them in proper time and place," and this he did immediately after

Champlain's funeral: the letters "were opened and read that very hour before the population assembled in the church." Champlain had acted as governor, without however bearing the title: in 1628, in a letter that he had written him, the king called him "commandant in New France" in the absence of Cardinal Richelieu; that is why Chateaufort was called "lieutenant-general for his Eminence the Cardinal, Duc de Richelieu, over the St. Lawrence River in all its length in New France."

On 11 June 1636 HUAULT de Montmagny landed at Quebec. The Compagnie des Cent-Associés had appointed him in January 1636 (before Champlain's death was known in France) to govern New France. Chateaufort handed over to him the keys of Fort Saint-Louis and shortly afterwards went to Trois-Rivières to act as commandant (the title of governor not yet being officially employed). The records of this town first make mention of this 28 Aug. 1636, but the Relation for 1637 entitles us to believe that Chateaufort had already been there for some time. It is not known whether he succeeded LAVIOLETTE, who was at Trois-Rivières until 17 April 1636 at least, or the Chevalier Antoine-Louis de BRÉHAUT Delisle.

Little is known of Chateaufort's administration at Trois-Rivières. In July 1637 he detained the Abenakis, whom he charged with trading at Trois-Rivières although it had been forbidden by Montmagny; he had their baggage searched, without finding any beaver pelts in it, and confiscated three arquebuses; he helped the Jesuits to enrol young Hurons for their seminary; he acted as godfather to young Indians; on 5 September Father Le Jeune, who was making a short stay at Trois-Rivières, found him very ill and gave him the sacrament. The records of Trois-Rivières last mention Chateaufort 6 Feb. 1638, but, contrary to what has been written, Chateaufort remained some months more at Trois-Rivières, since on 31 August of the same year he was present with Montmagny at the taking possession by Jean GODEFROY of the seigneury of Lintot. We do not know what became of Chateaufort after that date.

MARCEL TRUDEL

JR (Thwaites), VIII, 218, 308; IX, 208; XI, 82, 126–28, 130, 241; XII, 40–42, 110, 188, 236. P.-G. Roy, *Inv. concessions*, I, 31f., 152. BRH, IX (1903), 186f. P.-G. Roy, *La ville de Québec*, I, 135f., including a facsimile of Chateaufort's signature.Benjamin Sulte, *Mélanges historiques* (Malchelosse), XIV, 63f.

BRÉANAINN. *See* BRENDAN, ST. [Appendix]

BRÉBEUF, JEAN DE (called Échon by the Hurons), priest, Jesuit, founder of the Huron mission; b. 25 March 1593 at Condé-sur-Vire in Lower Normandy; martyred 16 March 1649 at the village of Saint-Ignace in the Huron country (in the region of Midland, Ontario), canonized 29 June 1930 by Pius XI and proclaimed by Pius XII on 16 Oct. 1940 patron saint of Canada along with his seven martyred companions.

Among Jean de Brébeuf's ancestors are said to have been companions-in-arms of William the Conqueror and of St. Louis, king of France, and his family, it is said, may be related to the English earls of Arundel. We know nothing of his immediate family. History has however preserved the names of two of his nephews: Georges de Brébeuf (1617–61), a minor poet of the 17th century, and Nicolas de Brébeuf (1631–91), prior of Saint-Gerbold, on the outskirts of Caen.

When he was 24 Brébeuf entered the Jesuit noviciate in Rouen. After two years (1617–19) under Father Lancelot Marin's direction he was appointed teacher of the first form in the secondary school (1619–20), then of the second form (1620–21) at the Collège in Rouen. During his second year of teaching he was incapacitated by illness, but he had enough strength left to prepare for the priesthood, which he received in 1622 at Pontoise. From 1622 to 1625 he stayed at the Collège of Rouen, where he held the office of steward. Then he was chosen for the missions in New France by the provincial of France, Father Pierre Coton. He sailed from Dieppe in April 1625 and landed at Quebec in June, along with Fathers CHARLES LALEMANT and Énemond MASSÉ and two lay brothers, François Charton and Gilbert Burel.

Five months of a roving existence in the cold and the snow (20 Oct. 1625–27 March 1626) with a group of Montagnais Indians who lived near Quebec constituted his apprenticeship for the missionary life. Scarcely had he been initiated in the language and custom of the Algonkins when in the same year 1626 his superior designated him, with Father Anne de NOUË, for the Huron country. In July for the first time Brébeuf travelled by canoe the 800 miles that separated Quebec from the Huron territory. The pages that he wrote later about conditions on this trip make of him, along with CHAMPLAIN, SAGARD, CHAUMONOT, and ALLOUEZ, one of the principal chroniclers of this great route to the West which missionaries, traders, and explorers long followed. This route led the travellers via the St. Lawrence, the Ottawa, the Mattawa, the Rivière à la Vase, Lake Nipissing, and the French River to Georgian Bay and the Great Lakes. This was

Brébeuf

a 20- to 30-day trip which the numerous portages, the tramping through the forests, the plague of mosquitoes, supply difficulties, lack of hygiene among the Indians, etc., often made exhausting.

Ties which were already very old, dating from Champlain's first explorations, linked the Hurons and the French. In a colony the existence and growth of which depended principally upon the fur trade, the Hurons were precious allies. Champlain had realized this. Indeed, the Hurons formed a compact, sedentary, agricultural group gifted with a real genius for trade. Their economy, which was relatively balanced and which was based upon the cultivation of the soil, supplemented in season by picking of fruit in summer, by fishing and hunting in the autumn, conferred upon them an undeniable superiority over the neighbouring tribes. From the time of their earliest contacts with the French, the Hurons realized that they were primarily interested in obtaining furs. Immediately they increased their trade. Taking advantage of their situation, which was economically and geographically privileged, they played the role of middlemen between populations with different kinds of economies. They accumulated in their villages huge quantities of furs that they bought from the nomadic hunters of the regions of Lake Nipissing, Lake Timiskaming, the Ottawa and St. Maurice rivers, and even the Hudson Bay territories. In return they offered these hunters corn, flour, tobacco, pumpkins, nets, which they obtained from their own district or from the tribes to the south and the west—the Neutrals, the Tobacco nation, the Eries, the Nipissings and the Ottawas. The Hurons thus became the great traders of the period. As soon as seeding was ended, they would load their canoes and go off to trade with the French, from whom they received European goods in exchange: metal arrow-heads, pots, hatchets, needles, fish-hooks, knives, blankets, and above all, porcelain, a material more precious than gold in the Indians' eyes.

The alliance with the Hurons presented other advantages: it facilitated exploration of the interior of the country and permitted the establishment of settlement outposts in the St. Lawrence basin, and above all it furthered the evangelizing of the Indians. For the missionaries, the evangelization of fixed and friendly populations was incontestably more promising than that of the nomadic Algonkins. There was however another side to this alliance, which with the years was to prove to be formidable: in allying themselves with the Hurons the French were committing themselves to lend them military support against the Iroquois, their hereditary enemies. For years the fur trade, the development of the colony, and the evangelizing of the Indians would be dependent upon the assistance that France would give the Laurentian coalition (Algonkins, Montagnais, and Hurons) against the Iroquois. Initially this alliance brought about a great increase in the trade in furs and facilitated the missionary enterprise.

Upon his arrival among the Hurons, Brébeuf took up residence at Toanché I, among the Bear tribe, the most important of the four great families in the Huron confederacy (the Bear, the Cord, the Rock, and the Deer tribes). The greatest benefit that Brébeuf derived from this first stay in the Huron country (1626–29) was no doubt, along with his apprenticeship in the language, a better knowledge of the Huron *milieu*. His efforts at evangelization met apparently with no success. In 1629 Brébeuf was recalled in haste to Quebec. He was present when the post was captured by the KIRKES in July and subsequently had to return to France with the other missionaries in the colony. He was appointed to Rouen and was assigned to serve the Church as a preacher and confessor. It was at this time (January 1630) that he took his final vows as a Jesuit. From 1631 to 1633 we find him at the Collège in Eu, acting as steward, minister, and confessor all at the same time. Brébeuf returned to New France in 1633, and the following year he went into the Huron country again, accompanied by Fathers ANTOINE DANIEL and Ambroise DAVOST.

This time he was entrusted by his superior, Father PAUL LE JEUNE, with the task of founding and organizing a real mission. From the outset the Jesuits of New France pinned their greatest hopes on this mission. In Le Jeune's eyes it represented a privileged testing-ground for the evangelizing of the Indians and was to constitute a sort of prototype which he intended to use as a model for the other missions. Brébeuf's first act as superior was to choose a centre from which the work of the mission would radiate. After careful consideration, on 19 Sept. 1634 he settled at Ihonatiria (Saint-Joseph I), a village near Toanché, where he had stayed from 1626 to 1629. Until 9 June 1637 the Huron mission was confined to this one residence. After a relatively satisfying phase the work of evangelization soon met obstinate and increasing resistance among the Hurons. Brébeuf attributed this resistance to three factors: the immorality of the Hurons, their attachment to the custom of the country, that is, to everything that until then had made up their world of beliefs and pleasures, and finally the epidemics that ravaged the country.

This last factor in particular greatly delayed the flow of conversions. The epidemics of 1634 (smallpox combined with dysentery), 1636 (malignant influenza), and 1639 (smallpox), reduced to 12,000 a population that Sagard, Brébeuf, and Champlain estimated at 30,000 souls. Contact with the Europeans was disastrous for the American Indians, taken by surprise by the viruses that had been brought from Europe. In this respect the Iroquois were better protected than the Hurons, since the Dutch and English settlers mixed little with the Indians and were content to wait for them in the shelter of their factories. In the Huron country these repeated scourges made the missionaries' presence odious. The epidemic of 1636–37 roused the whole nation against Brébeuf and his companions. For months on end, under the direction of the witch doctors, a clever campaign was carried on, made up of hypocritical insinuations, then of open and violent threats, which were accompanied by attempts at murder. In the autumn of 1637 the whole mission almost collapsed. In this emergency Brébeuf sent to Father Le Jeune a sort of letter-testament in which he announced the possibility that all the missionaries might be massacred.

At the end of August 1638, after founding a third post at Teanaostaiaë (Saint-Joseph II), Brébeuf handed direction of the mission over to Father JÉRÔME LALEMANT, who had recently arrived from France. He himself became the superior of the residence that he had just founded. It was in this ministry that Brébeuf had to suffer the harshest persecution of his career. After a smallpox epidemic the dramatic events of 1637 were repeated, but staged even more riotously: crosses were torn down, stones were thrown at the chapel, there were beatings and threats with hatchets and flaming embers. During this storm Brébeuf even saw part of his flock desert the faith that they had just embraced. In April 1640 an uprising broke out, in the course of which Pierre Boucher* was wounded in the arm, while Brébeuf and Chaumonot were beaten. In the month of May the Indians' tumult led Lalemant to give up the residence.

In the autumn of 1640, after taking counsel together the missionaries decided to start two new missions: one among the Algonkins, the other among the Neutrals. Brébeuf and Chaumonot were appointed to the latter. Preceded by secret Huron agents who depicted the missionaries as the most maleficent of witch doctors, the two of them travelled throughout a violently hostile region, rejected, abused, reviled everywhere. These were five months of fruitless labour (November 1640–March 1641). As a crowning misfortune, on the way back from this mission Brébeuf fell on the ice while crossing a frozen lake and broke his left clavicle. Father Lalemant felt that it was his duty to send Brébeuf back to Quebec and entrust him to a doctor's care; at the same time he could fill there the post of mission procurator which Father RAGUENEAU held. In the spring of 1642 Brébeuf reached Quebec, after seven consecutive years with the Hurons.

The task of procurator of the Huron mission consisted of supplying the missionaries with everything that they might need (books, paper, religious objects, etc.) and of organizing supply convoys for them. This was a painful trial for Brébeuf; twice, in 1642 and 1643, the convoys he prepared were seized by the Iroquois and were a complete loss. In addition to this function, during his stay at Quebec Brébeuf had to attend to the teaching of six young Hurons who had been entrusted to his care (September 1642–June 1643). He also served as confessor, spiritual director, and adviser to the Ursulines and Religious Hospitallers. And finally, on Sundays and feast days he preached and heard the confessions of the French inhabitants of Quebec.

On 7 Sept. 1644 Brébeuf was back in the Huron country, this time for good. He took up his post again at the very moment when the death-struggle of the Huron country was beginning. In fact, the conflict that had been going on for a long time between the Iroquois and the Hurons was on the point of coming to an end. In 1628 the victory of the Mohawks over the Mahicans made the Iroquois the suppliers of pelts to the Dutch at Fort Orange. From then on the Iroquois began to enjoy the advantage of trading with the Europeans. Their cupidity was aroused. They prevented the other tribes from crossing their territory to exchange their furs with Fort Orange. They aspired to play vis-à-vis the Dutch the same role that the Hurons did with the French. But then furs began to be scarce in their territory. Consequently, the Iroquois thought of capturing the Hurons' rich convoys. From the year 1637 on, the Mohawks became the pirates of the fur trade. To help them in their struggle they asked the Dutch traders for fire-arms, and succeeded in obtaining them. In 1641 they had at their disposal 39 muskets; in 1643, 300. Aggressive by nature, they were spurred on further by the weakness of their adversaries, whose numbers had from 1634 to 1640 been reduced by two-thirds as a result of epidemics. The Iroquois dreamt therefore of exterminating the Hurons. This policy was supported by New Holland, aware that the ruin of the Huron meant that of the French trade and by the same token of New France. "We

Brébeuf

have had letters from France," wrote Father VIMONT, "that the design of the Dutch is to have the French harassed by the Iroquois, to such an extent that they may constrain them to give up and abandon everything—even the conversion of the Savages."

In 1641 the insecurity in New France and on the route to the Huron country became so great that Father Vimont, at the request of Governor HUAULT de Montmagny and of the settlers, sent Father Le Jeune to France to set forth the situation to the king and to Richelieu. In 1642 began the disasters which were to go on increasing each year. The Mohawks and Senecas launched a vast offensive which extended from New France to the Huron territory. Divided into small bands, they systematically blockaded the routes along the Richelieu, the Ottawa, and the St. Lawrence. The French colony was weak; it had only 400 inhabitants and had available only 100 soldiers. The *Relations*, which previously had been crammed with details concerning conversions and epidemics, no longer spoke of anything but massacres and pillage. The year 1642, which saw the founding of Ville-Marie, was marked also by the capture of Isaac JOGUES, René GOUPIL, and Guillaume Couture*. In two years (1642–43) the mission convoys were captured three times, on the way either up or down. In 1644 Father BRESSANI was captured and tortured. The treaty of 1645 constituted only a short-lived truce in this nightmare, since Jogues was murdered in October 1646. During the summer of 1647 fear of the Iroquois was so great that the Hurons did not go down to Quebec.

The years 1647–48 marked the beginning of the annihilation of the Huron nation. Until then the Iroquois had restricted themselves to surprising the traders' convoys on the St. Lawrence and Ottawa routes. Now they were in the heart of the Huron country. In 1647 they massacred the population of a Neutral village. On 4 July 1648, taking advantage of the fact that the Hurons had gone trading, a band of Indians threw themselves upon the villages of Saint-Joseph and Saint-Michel and took 700 prisoners. Father Antoine Daniel fell, riddled with arrows. The village of Saint-Joseph II (Teanaostaiaë) formed with Ossossanë (La Conception) and Sainte-Marie the triangular base of Huron resistance. On 16 March of the following year (1649) more than 1,000 Iroquois attacked Saint-Ignace (Taenhatentaron), then Saint-Louis, where Brébeuf and GABRIEL LALEMANT were carrying on their work. They were taken prisoner and carried off to Saint-Ignace, where they suffered one of the most atrocious martyrdoms in the annals of Christianity. Brébeuf's torture has been told us with moving simplicity by the *donné* Christophe Regnault, who saw his remains: "Father de Brébeuf had his legs, thighs, and arms stripped of flesh to the very bone; I saw and touched a large number of great blisters, which he had on several places on his body, from the boiling water which these barbarians had poured over him in mockery of Holy Baptism. I saw and touched the wound from a belt of bark, full of pitch and resin, which roasted his whole body. I saw and touched the marks of burns from the Collar of hatchets placed on his shoulders and stomach. I saw and touched his two lips, which they had cut off because he constantly spoke of God while they made him suffer.

"I saw and touched all parts of his body, which had received more than two hundred blows from a stick. I saw and touched the top of his scalped head; I saw and touched the opening which these barbarians had made to tear out his heart.

"In fine, I saw and touched all the wounds of his body, as the savages had told and declared to us...."

In the face of the Iroquois attack, instead of recovering themselves the Hurons were seized with panic. Almost the entire Bear tribe took refuge with the Tobacco nation. Others sought asylum with the Neutrals, the Eries, the Algonkins, or fled to the nearby islands. The Huron confederacy fell completely to pieces. As the residence at Sainte-Marie-des-Hurons had at its disposal only 8 soldiers, 22 *donnés*, and 7 servants, the Jesuits decided to abandon it. On 14 June 1649 they set fire to the building and betook themselves with a few hundred Hurons to the Île Saint-Joseph (Christian Island), located a few miles from there in Lake Huron. The new establishment had scarcely been finished when a new misfortune was added to the previous ones; in December the village of Saint-Jean, in the territory of the Tobacco nation, was attacked and pillaged. On the Île Saint-Joseph the situation soon became desperate. Famine, contagious maladies, new attacks by the Iroquois, forced the missionaries and the Indians to leave. On 10 June 1650 300 Hurons, accompanied by the Jesuits and their servants, set out in canoes for Quebec. In the spring of 1651 these fragments of the Huron nation settled down on the Île d'Orléans; soon there were 600 of them, under Father Chaumonot's direction.

Brébeuf's apostolate in the Huron country lasted 15 years. The Huron mission died with him who had begun it. But by a striking contrast, at the same time as the nation was being crushed, its spiritual regeneration was taking place. The *Relations*, which for a long time could count the conversions only one by one, speak of hundreds and even of thousands of baptisms in the latter years. For the year 1649–50 alone, Father Ragueneau gave the figure of 3,000 baptisms. The consequence of the dispersion of the Huron nation was to spread the Christian faith among the nations of the Great Lakes basin and on the shores of the Rivière des Hollandais (Mohawk River). These converts were to form the elements of the Christian communities which the Jesuits were to go to found among the Iroquois and the nations of the west.

What we know of Brébeuf comes to us from the *Relations des Jésuites* and especially from his own writings. These writings, very varied in nature, cover a period of 18 years, that is from 1630 to 1648. Among them are two *Relations* (those for 1635 and 1636), a spiritual diary composed of 44 fragments, 15 letters addressed to the superior general of the Society of Jesus or to local superiors, instructions or catechisms, a dictionary, a grammar, and even two Huron texts. Several of these writings have been lost. Those that remain, about 20, amounting to some 300 pages, enable us to recognize in Brébeuf the founder of missions, the ethnographer, the mystic, and the writer.

The necessity for Brébeuf to understand thoroughly the *milieu* in which he was trying to evangelize resulted in a precious contribution to the ethnography of the Amerinds; 15 years of living with the Hurons allowed him to become better acquainted with their manners and customs than anyone else. Along with Champlain and Sagard, Brébeuf remains the most important witness of this period of first contacts. He lays stress for his part on the social, political, and religious life of the Hurons; in this respect he completes Champlain and enlarges upon Sagard. On these three points the 1636 *Relation* remains a unique document that is mentioned in first place in all the monographs concerning the Hurons. Brébeuf's testimony is all the more valuable from the ethnological point of view in that it establishes the picture of the Hurons at the time when they were still themselves, before successive epidemics, war, and massacres had reduced them to the state of human wrecks; his testimony has all the interest and the intensity of a snapshot, so to speak.

As the founder of the Huron mission Brébeuf was called upon to give it its earliest orientation. His administration was devoted to different tasks. First of all, there was the setting up of the first residences. During his superiorship he founded Saint-Joseph I at Ihonatiria (19 or 20 Sept. 1634), then the residence of L'Immaculée-Conception (9 June 1637) at Ossossanë, and finally that of Saint-Joseph II at Teanaostaiaë (25 June 1638). These posts, which were situated in the midst of the two main tribes (the Bear and the Cord), enabled him to become deeply assimilated into the Huron environment. Secondly, he applied himself to mastering the language. Brébeuf had been chosen the first time, in 1626, by Father Charles Lalemant to be the apostle to the Huron country because of his talent for languages. After his first three-year stay Brébeuf knew enough Huron to be able to translate the catechism of the Jesuit Ledesma. When he returned to New France in 1633, Brébeuf became Father Daniel's and Father Davost's teacher. As soon as they had arrived in the Huron country in 1634, their initiation continued, the team being completed by Fathers François LE MERCIER, PIERRE PIJART, Pierre CHASTELLAIN, Charles GARNIER, and Isaac Jogues, all of them working under Brébeuf's direction on the compilation of a dictionary and the preparation of a grammar. In 1639 mastery of the language had been achieved. This study, representing eight or nine years of austere and assiduous toil, was above all Brébeuf's work. As a third task, when he had been initiated into the Huron *milieu* and was master of the language, Brébeuf undertook the major work of evangelization. After first working with the children, he soon realized that all depended upon the adults, in particular the chieftains and elders, who were the real sources of influence. The work of conversion advanced very slowly at first. The first conversion of an adult in good health took place in 1637. Four years later, in 1641, there were still only 60 Christians.

Brébeuf's correspondence and still more his spiritual diary reveal to us a soul that had manifestly entered upon the paths of higher prayer and that had long been familiar with divine communications. Three important commitments mark Brébeuf's spiritual ascension: in 1631, the promise to serve Christ even to the sacrifice of his life; in 1637–39, the vow never to refuse the grace of martyrdom; in 1645, the vow of perfection. Several passages from the spiritual diary reveal that Brébeuf, like Jogues, had been favoured with a special vocation for the cross. From 1636 to 1641 insulted, beaten, stoned, jeered at, subjected to physical injury, Brébeuf was in the Huron country, like St. Paul, the "sweeping" of the world. Engaged in apostolic action, he was purified in that action and by that action. If in 1645, four years before his martyrdom, he was able to take the vow of perfection, it was because his soul had by that time long been completely submissive to God's will. The consummation of this saintliness came to Brébeuf through martyrdom. Among the influences which contributed to the shaping of Brébeuf's soul one must mention especially St. Ignatius Loyola's *Spiritual Exercises*, the *Imitation of Jesus Christ*, St. Paul's letters, and then the probable influence of Father Louis Lallemant, a great 17th-century French master of the spiritual life.

Finally, Brébeuf shows himself a writer without any pretentions, but a very gifted one. The two *Relations* in particular, in which Brébeuf recorded his observations as a traveller, ethnographer, and missionary, are written in very firm language of astonishing vigour, with a wealth of words and images, which had not yet been affected by the refining but impoverishing influence of the French *salons*. This language recalls the zest and the smile of Montaigne. Nowhere will one find more delightful observation or richer colour than in the chapters in which Brébeuf describes the conditions of life in the Huron country, the manners of the Hurons, the great Feast of the Dead. Nothing is more nobly lyrical than the *Avertissement d'importance* addressed to the young religious of France. Brébeuf's language has not grown old. Humbler, but how precious are the few notes that remain to us from his private diary; these fragments represent the earliest pages of mystical literature in Canada.

Among the missionaries of the period Brébeuf's personality stands out as one of the most colourful. However, if Brébeuf stood out, it was not primarily because of his qualities of intelligence, although they were remarkable. All those who came into contact with him recognized indeed that his judgement was excellent. His correspondence in particular and his two *Relations* reveal a very discriminating observer, who readily indulged in a certain type of humour. His letters to the superiors of the Society of Jesus remain models of clarity, composition, and practical good sense. One does not however find in him the bold conceptions typical of Lalemant or the constantly renewed initiatives of Le Jeune. Brébeuf is characterized rather by very robust good sense, by a kind of supernatural empiricism; in his undertakings he always combined human prudence and wisdom from above. His magnificent gifts always remained those of the heart and the will. There was no pettiness in this man, no meanness. One would look in vain in his writings for any sign of rancour, of bitterness in judgement, of secret jealousy. His mildness was proof against all scorn. The audacity which marked some of his actions was less a trait of his character than a form of his apostolic zeal. Two extremes were blended in him: on one hand, the realistic man, a friend of tradition, who appeared in the college steward, the mission organizer, the humble religious, and on the other hand the ardent, energetic apostle, courting all occasions for martrydom and all the irrationality of the cross. Such was he who has been called "the giant of the Huron missions," and more recently "the apostle whose heart was devoured."

RENÉ LATOURELLE

ACSM, "Mémoires touchant la mort et les vertus des pères Isaac Jogues . . ." (Ragueneau), repr. APQ *Rapport*, 1924–25, 3–70 passim. JR (Thwaites), VIII, X. *Positio causae*.

Desrosiers, *Iroquoisie*. *Jésuites de la N.-F.* (Roustang). A. E. Jones, " '8endake Ehen' or Old Huronia," PAO *Annual Report*, V (1908). R. Latourelle, *Étude sur les écrits de saint Jean de Brébeuf*, (2 v., Montréal, 1952, 1953). Félix Martin, *Hurons et Iroquois. Le P. Jean de Brébeuf, sa vie, ses travaux, son martyre* (Paris, 1877). Pouliot, *Étude sur les Relations des Jésuites*. J. Robinne, *L'Apôtre au cœur mangé, Jean de Brébeuf: étude sur l'époque et sur l'homme* (Paris, 1949). Rochemonteix, *Les Jésuites et la Nouvelle-France au XVIIe siècle*. F.-X. Talbot, *Saint among the Hurons: the life of Jean de Brébeuf* (New York, 1949). André Vachon, "L'eau-de-vie dans la société indienne," CHA *Report*, 1960, 22–32; "Mgr de Laval et la menace iroquoise," *BRH*, LXVII (1961), 36–46.

BRÉHANT DE GALINÉE, RENÉ DE, priest, Sulpician, prior of Saint-Maur de Nazar (Saint-Brieuc); b. c. 1645 in the diocese of Rennes; d. 1678 in Europe.

The Bréhant family, "descended in direct line from the ancient chivalric nobility," had as its motto: *Foi de Bréhant vaut mieux qu'argent* ("The pledged word of a Bréhant is better than silver"). It had followed St. Louis on his crusades and was descended from a crusader who bore the name of *Galilée*, which later became *Galinée*. Under François I, the seigneur Mathurin de Bréhant married the only daughter of the seigneur de Galinée. From this stock was born René de Bréhant de Galinée, who came to New France in 1668.

He was a licentiate in theology from the Sorbonne and had studied mathematics and astronomy. As soon as he arrived in the country, he set about learning Algonkin.

In those days the Sulpicians dreamt of going to evangelize the Potawatomis, a tribe living in the region of the Mississippi. In 1669 M. de THUBIÈRES de Levy de Queylus, the superior of the seminary of Montreal, had chosen for this mission François Dollier* de Casson and Michel Barthélemy*. They were about to set out with Robert CAVELIER de La Salle, when M. de Queylus, being suspicious of the famous explorer's loyalty, replaced M.

Barthélemy by M. de Galinée, whose knowledge of mathematics and astronomy might be valuable in case of desertion. In actual fact La Salle, who had fallen ill, separated himself from the missionaries at the tip of Lake Ontario.

The missionaries had followed the south shore of Lake Ontario, then had crossed the Niagara River and continued on to the region of the present city of Hamilton. Leaving La Salle and his men there, they continued their journey to the north shore of Lake Erie, where they spent the winter. As a wave had carried off during the night the canoe that contained what was necessary for religious ceremonies, the missionaries decided to return to Ville-Marie [Montreal]. However, so that their voyage would not be useless, they came back by a different route, going by way of the Detroit River, Lake Huron, the mission at Michilimackinac, Georgian Bay, Lake Nipissing, and the Ottawa River.

Back in Ville-Marie, M. de Galinée fell ill. He took advantage of his illness to write an account of his voyage and to draw up a map of the places he had seen. This map, one of the first to be published, came into the hands of the minister, Colbert, by 1670, thanks to SALIGNAC de La Mothe-Fénelon. A replica, corrected and perfected, was delivered to Intendant TALON.

His account, which is extremely interesting, was published under the title *Voyage de MM. Dollier et Galinée*, the first time in 1875 by the Société historique de Montréal, by Margry in *Decouvertes et établissements des Français . . .*, and then by James H. Coyne, under the auspices of the Ontario Historical Society. In it one can read that the Sulpician missionaries used to take possession of the territories that they reached by setting up a cross bearing the arms of France. Subsequently Talon enjoined DAUMONT de Saint-Lusson to do likewise at Sault Ste. Marie.

M. de Galinée returned to France in 1671, with M. de Queylus. He died on 16 Aug. 1678, while on his way to Rome.

OLIVIER MAURAULT

René de Bréhant de Galinée, ". . . Exploration of the Great Lakes, 1669–1670 . . . ," ed. J. H. Coyne, Ont. Hist. Soc. *Papers and Records*, IV (1903). "Voyage de Cavelier de La Salle avec les sulpiciens Dollier de Casson et Bréhan de Galinée," dans *Découvertes et établissements des Français* (Margry), I, 101–66. ". . . Voyage de MM. Dollier et Galinée," (SHM, Mémoires, VI, 1875). Dollier de Casson, *Histoire du Montréal*.

W. H. Atherton, *Montreal, 1535–1914* (3v., Montreal, Vancouver, Chicago, 1914). Faillon, *Histoire de la colonie française*, III, *passim*. Olivier Maurault, "Sur les pas des missionnaires-explorateurs," *Revue de l'Université d'Ottawa*, I (1931), 316–41.

BRÉHAUT DELISLE, ACHILLE (Antoine-Louis?), DE, Knight of Malta, lieutenant of Governor HUAULT de Montmagny, commandant of Trois-Rivières on two occasions, judge at Quebec in 1638.

He arrived at Quebec 11 June 1636 at the same time as Governor de Montmagny to whom he acted as lieutenant. "He is a very worthy gentleman," wrote the author of the *Relation* of 1636. He was a professional soldier, and, like the governor, was a Knight of Malta. Upon his arrival, Montmagny sent him to Trois-Rivières to reassure the settlers who had been without a leader since the departure of LAVIOLETTE on 17 April previous. He was in command there, without however having any official title, until 28 August, at which time the post was entrusted to Marc-Antoine BRAS-DE-FER de Chateaufort, who had acted as governor at Quebec during the interregnum between the death of CHAMPLAIN and the arrival of Montmagny. Bréhaut Delisle went back to Trois-Rivières in 1637 to organize a defence against the crafty attacks of the Iroquois. He showed himself to be a skilful diplomat in the negotiations, particularly when the Hurons sought to abandon the French, whom they accused of being the cause of the epidemics that were decimating the tribe. Like the governor, Bréhaut Delisle enjoyed splendour and always appeared at the Indian councils in full battle attire. He was very much esteemed by the Jesuits, who often referred in the *Relations* to his piety, his uprightness, and his presence at religious ceremonies. In 1638 he held an appointment as judge at Quebec, and the 1642 *Relation* mentions him as being still in that town. Then we lose sight of him.

We are not certain of the real first name of this personage. Was he called Achille or Antoine-Louis? Benjamin Sulte stated, without giving the sources of his information, that Bréhaut Delisle was of Breton stock, that he had been made a Knight of Malta in 1631, and that his name was Antoine-Louis. On the other hand, in at least two documents preserved at the seminary of Quebec, he himself used the names "Achilles de Lisle" and "Achilles Delisle," Knight of the Order of St. John of Jerusalem. Moreover, the *Relations des Jésuites* mention that he was godfather to an Indian and that he named him Achille. The available documents provide us with no further enlightenment on this subject.

RAYMOND DOUVILLE

ASQ, Documents Faribault, 5, 8, 9, 13, 17, 19, 27; Paroisse de Québec, 27. *JR* (Thwaites), XX, 204; XXIV, 52, *et passim*. Desrosiers, *Iroquoisie*. Godbout, *Les pionniers de la région trifluvienne*, 23. P.-G. Roy,

Brésoles

La ville de Québec, I, 143, 146. Sulte, *Mélanges historiques* (Malchelosse), XIV, 63f.

BRÉSOLES, JUDITH MOREAU DE. *See* MOREAU

BRESSANI, FRANÇOIS-JOSEPH (Francesco-Giuseppe), priest, Jesuit, missionary; b. 6 May 1612 in Rome; d. 9 Sept. 1672 in Florence.

Bressani entered the Society of Jesus 15 Aug. 1626, at the age of 14. He held in succession the chairs of literature, philosophy, and mathematics. Like so many others he was attracted by the foreign missions, and sought the privilege of being sent to New France. His superiors granted his wish in 1642. He first spent some time at Quebec in order to adapt himself; from there he went to Trois-Rivières (1643), a post much frequented by the Indians during the summer months. The missionary aspired to more arduous tasks; he obtained permission to penetrate 900 miles into the interior of the country, where the Hurons lived.

On 27 April 1644, as soon as the snows melted, he set out, together with one Frenchman and six Christian Hurons. He did not know that some ten bands of Iroquois were in ambush at strategic points on the route followed by the convoys of the French or those of their allies. Seven or eight miles from Fort Richelieu, when they were on their third day of travel, Father Bressani and his companions were attacked by a band of 27 Iroquois. The assailants took them prisoner, and dragged them by short stages towards their tribal territory, which they reached on 30 May. Father Bressani, weakened and mutilated, was only at the beginning of his sufferings. He bore stoically the most savage tortures; on 19 June, when he was awaiting death, his torturers handed him over to an old Iroquois woman, to replace her grandfather who had earlier been murdered by the Hurons. This unexpected outcome gave him a little respite and enabled him to write a long letter to the general of the Jesuits. This document, taken from the *Breve Relatione*, is dated 15 July 1644, and recounts in detail the sufferings he underwent. It opens with these lines: "I know not whether Your Paternity will recognize the letter of a poor cripple, who formerly, in perfect health, was well known to you. The letter is badly written and quite soiled, because, in addition to other inconveniences, he who writes it has only one whole finger on his right hand; and it is difficult to avoid staining the paper with the blood which flows from his wounds, not yet healed; he uses arquebus powder for ink, and the earth for a table."

The captive could not be the slightest use to the old woman, who got rid of him by turning him over to the Dutch for a trifling ransom. The religious was well treated, and was able to return to France: he reached the port of La Rochelle 15 Nov. 1644. He asked to go back to New France. In July 1645 he was once again at Trois-Rivières, where he took part in the peace palavers of an Iroquois delegation, fraternizing with his former torturers. In the autumn of the same year, he started out again for the Huron country.

The Huron missions, continually harassed by the Iroquois, lived in terror. The situation was such that in 1648 the decision was made to appeal to Governor HUAULT de Montmagny. Father Bressani, at the head of 250 Hurons, was to go and ask help. The assemblage arrived at Quebec at the end of July 1648. All that the governor could do was to grant an escort of 12 soldiers; the Jesuits sent a few religious as reinforcements. The fleet of 60 canoes, bringing back the 250 Hurons and 26 Frenchmen, reached the Huron country without mishap. Father Bressani was dumbfounded to hear that during his absence the Iroquois had wiped out the village of Saint-Joseph (Teanaostaiaë), murdered Father ANTOINE DANIEL, and killed more than 700 Hurons. This was only a beginning. On 6 March 1649, when the winter was scarcely over, the Iroquois reappeared, and ruthlessly massacred both Hurons and missionaries. The powerful Huron nation was reduced to a few hundred fugitives, whom the missionaries took to the Île Saint-Joseph (Christian Island), in order to give them temporary asylum. Help had once again to be sought from Quebec. Once more Father Bressani was instructed to go and plead the cause of the Huron missions, before the new governor LOUIS D'AILLEBOUST. He was received with kindliness, but obtained no formal promises. The governor could not withdraw his troops from the posts on the St. Lawrence. The missionary wanted to return to his flock immediately, and he left Quebec with a few Hurons on 28 Sept. 1649. His journey was a wildly imprudent venture, and the Hurons forced the father to turn back at the Rivière des Prairies, in the vicinity of Montreal. He returned reluctantly to Quebec, but was to leave again for the Huron country in June 1650 with a flotilla of some 23 canoes, carrying about 30 Frenchmen and 30 Indians, including J.-B. ATIRONTA. Meanwhile, after painful deliberation, the missionaries in the Huron country had decided that it was impossible to maintain their position in that region, and that it was better to bring back to the St. Lawrence the few hundred Hurons who had escaped the massacre. Father Paul RAGUENEAU was leading a group of 300 survivors towards

Quebec in the summer of 1651 when he met the rescue column led by Father Bressani. They had to go back to the capital (28 July 1650).

All the missionaries from the Huron country were available for new duties. The superior decided to send some of them back to France, to await better times. Father Bressani was among them. He sailed 2 Nov. 1650. He returned to Italy and devoted himself to preaching and to his apostolate.

During his eight years of evangelizing in Canada, Father Bressani had acquired valuable experience of the country and its inhabitants. He recorded his discoveries and observations in a work devoted principally to the Huron country and its martyrs. The *Relation abrégée* of Bressani, written in Italian, has been translated into French by Father F. Martin, a Jesuit.

ALBERT TESSIER

[F.-J. Bressani], *Relation abrégée de quelques missions des pères de la Compagnie de Jésus dans la Nouvelle-France par le R. P. Bressany de la même compagnie*, ed. Félix Martin (Montréal, 1852). *JR* (Thwaites). *JJ* (Laverdière et Casgrain). "Une lettre inédite du R. P. Bressani," *BRH*, XXXVIII (1932), 546–47. Rochemonteix, *Les Jésuites et la Nouvelle-France au XVIIᵉ siècle*, II, 36–37. Yvon Thériault, *L'apostolat missionnaire en Mauricie* (Trois-Rivières, 1951), 37–44.

BRICE, MADAME DE, teacher at Port-Royal (Annapolis Royal, N.S.); she arrived in Acadia in 1644 and returned to France probably in 1652.

In 1640 Cardinal Richelieu had made over to the Capuchins his share in the Compagnie de Razilly, in order to establish a "seminary" (school) in Acadia for the Indians. Two houses were built with this object: one adjoining the Capuchin monastery, for the boys, and the other for the girls. Father Pacifique de Provins, the prefect of missions, secured a gift of 1,500 *livres* from Anne of Austria in 1644, and persuaded a widow from Auxerre, Mme de Brice, to go to Acadia and devote herself to the education of the young Indian girls. She arrived at Port-Royal in the summer of 1644 and took charge of the girls' school. She managed to bring together some 30 pupils, and at the same time occupied the position of tutor to Governor MENOU d'Aulnay's children. All her contemporaries acknowledged her worth, and the governor, in his will, paid tribute to her devotion. Two of her sons who were Capuchins, fathers Léonard and Pascal d'Auxerre, had come to join her. After the governor's death in 1650, she was much harassed by EMMANUEL LE BORGNE, one of d'Aulnay's creditors. The schools were closed and Mme de Brice was imprisoned for five months. She probably succeeded in returning to France, and another of her sons, Brice de Sainte-Croix, the intendant of Mme d'Aulnay [*see* MOTIN], negotiated a partnership with the Duc de Vendôme in Mme d'Aulnay's name. One article of this agreement provided for the reinstatement of Mme de Brice as the directress of her school. But Le Borgne's irksome interference prevented her return, and this promising endeavour came to nothing.

RENÉ BAUDRY

Candide de Nant, *Pages glorieuses*, reproduces most of the original documents.

BRIDGAR, JOHN, an early governor of HBC forts on Hudson and James bays; fl. 1678–87.

He was engaged by the HBC on 19 April 1678 at a salary of £40 a year and arrived in James Bay on 22 August to serve under Governor Charles BAYLY. When Bayly returned to England the following year he left Bridgar in charge of the newly founded Albany post. Two years later Bridgar went back to London and on 15 May 1682 was commissioned governor of Port Nelson and of the west mainland of the Bay north from Cape Henrietta Maria, at £100 a year for three years. At the same time he was instructed "to Penetrate into the Countrey to make what discoveries you can, and to gett an Acquaintance and Comerce with the Indians thereabts."

He sailed on the Company's ship *Prince Rupert* (Zachariah GILLAM captain) accompanied by the *Albemarle* (Esbon SANFORD captain), and in September entered the mouth of the Nelson. But Pierre Esprit Radisson* was there ahead of him as agent for the French—who planned to drive the HBC from the Bay—and challenged his right to be there. Radisson and his brother-in-law Médard CHOUART Des Groseilliers had built a fort on the right bank of the Hayes River to the south. Bridgar chose a spot on the north shore of the Nelson, and there built the first HBC establishment in that area.

Twelve years previously Radisson, then in the employ of the English company, had landed at the mouth of the Nelson and had astutely perceived that it would be the gateway to the fur trade of the great Northwest. But the ship on which he and Governor Bayly had arrived was driven out to sea by a storm and no fort had been erected there.

Misfortune also dogged Bridgar's venture. His deputy, Sanford, died on 6 October; and on 21 October the *Prince Rupert* was blown out into the bay during a gale and sunk with all on board, including Zachariah Gillam, who had learned from Radisson that his son Benjamin Gillam* from New England was trading farther upstream

Brigeac

at his post on Gillam Island in defiance of the Company's charter—a fact still unknown to Bridgar.

Early next year Radisson captured young Gillam's fort and ship with their inhabitants and in the summer took possession of the Company's fort, making Bridgar and his men prisoner. In the New Englander's ship he took Bridgar to Quebec, where the Englishman was released by Governor Le FEBVRE de La Barre to return home by way of New England. In 1685 he sailed again for James Bay, apparently aboard the *Success* (John OUTLAW captain), to become deputy governor of that district under Henry SERGEANT—whom he was supposed to succeed as governor of "the Bottom of the Bay"—and took over the command of Moose Fort.

On 10 June (20 June N.S.) 1686 he set sail with his officers for Charles Fort; the very next night a French force from Montreal under Pierre de TROYES and three of the LE MOYNE brothers stormed Moose Fort and captured it from the remaining 17 leaderless traders. But Bridgar was not to escape so easily. In their birchbark canoes the Montrealers followed his ship to Charles Fort, boarded and captured it, and took the fort; so once more the luckless Bridgar found himself a prisoner of the French.

However, he was again released and wintered either at New Severn or at Port Nelson, returning to England in 1687. There shortly afterwards he appears to have left the Company's service, thus ending his short but stormy career on Hudson Bay.

CLIFFORD P. WILSON

HBRS, VIII (Rich), 213, 235; IX (Rich), 141 nn. 2, 3; XI (Rich and Johnson), 377; XXI (Rich), 134, 137–8, 178, 214, 216. Nute, *Caesars of the wilderness*, 188–96.

BRIGEAC (Brisac, Brigeart, Brijat), CLAUDE DE, soldier, secretary to Governor Paul de CHOMEDEY de Maisonneuve; b. at Ligny-en-Barois (Lorraine) *c.* 1631; killed by the Iroquois in 1661.

Brigeac, who arrived at Montreal in 1659, was referred to as a gentleman and a grenadier. He was attached to the garrison as a soldier, and became Governor Maisonneuve's secretary. On 25 Oct. 1661 he was ordered to accompany and protect a team of some 12 men who were going under the direction of the Sulpician Abbé VIGNAL to look for stones on the Île à la Pierre, adjoining the Île Sainte-Hélène. Brigeac was one of the last to arrive, and did not have time to arrange for the party's safety before 35 Iroquois made a surprise attack upon the scattered workers, who fled in confusion towards their canoes. Fearlessly, Brigeac faced the enemy single-handed, but a volley of shot shattered his right arm and mortally wounded Abbé Vignal. The Iroquois captured them, as well as two companions, René Cuillerier* and Dufresne, and made camp at La Pierre-de-la-Madeleine. Dufresne was then given to the Mohawks, the Oneidas keeping the two other captives for themselves. Subsequently Cuillerier was adopted by the tribe, whereas Brigeac, who managed to get a note to Father SIMON LE MOYNE informing him of his capture, was subjected to the cruellest tortures for two days and finished off at last with a knife. His body was put in the pot and provided a meal for his enemies.

GUSTAVE LANCTOT

ACND, MS M¹, Écrits autographes de Sœur Marguerite Bourgeoys. Dollier de Casson, *Histoire du Montréal*, 163–65, 241, 250, 252. *JR* (Thwaites), XLVII, 176–78, contains a letter from Brigeac, written when he was an Iroquois prisoner. *JJ* (Laverdière et Casgrain), *passim. Premier registre de l'église Notre-Dame de Montréal* (Montréal, 1961). Faillon, *Histoire de la colonie française*, II, 361, 505–12. É.-Z. Massicotte, "Brigeac, Brigeart ou Brijat," *BRH*, XXXV (1929), 639–40.

BRISON, CLAUDE ROQUEMONT DE. *See* ROQUEMONT

BRUCY, ANTOINE DE LA FRENAYE DE. *See* LA FRENAYE

BRÛLÉ, ÉTIENNE, interpreter of the Huron language, probably the first white man to make his way into the Huron country and Pennsylvania, and to see lakes Huron, Ontario, Superior, and Erie; b. *c.* 1592 probably at Champigny-sur-Marne (near Paris); murdered by the Hurons *c.* June 1633.

Étienne Brûlé has unfortunately left no personal description of his life among the Indians, or of his discoveries. The thread of his existence must be sought in the works of CHAMPLAIN, SAGARD, and BRÉBEUF, and even there it can be picked up only in haphazard fashion. In them the explorer's image, eluding any systematic pursuit, as in a forest studded with clearings, appears and disappears in turn, enigmatic and fascinating.

We know almost nothing of his origins. The year of his arrival in Canada was for long the subject of conjecture, because Champlain identifies Étienne Brûlé clearly only in 1618. At that date Champlain referred to him by his name, specifying that Brûlé had been living for eight years among the Indians. In 1610, a "youth who had already spent two winters at Quebec" asked Champlain's permission to go and live with the

Indians in order to learn their language. This youth was the first European, and the only one that year, to attempt such a venture. Cross-checking leads us to suppose that the "youth" of whom Champlain speaks was indeed Étienne Brûlé, and that he had been at Quebec since 1608.

Had Brûlé taken part in Champlain's first two clashes with the Iroquois? There is no indication of it. It is possible, however, that he was involved at least in the encounter that took place in the summer of 1610, since it was on the day immediately following this battle that he voiced to Champlain his desire to go and live among the Indians. Champlain, who had already conceived the plan of training interpreters, accepted readily, and entrusted Brûlé to the Algonkin chief IROQUET, receiving in exchange a young Huron called SAVIGNON, who was to accompany him to France.

No documentary trace remains of this first experience of a Frenchman living among the Canadian Indians, or of the journey that Brûlé may have made with the Algonkins, and more specifically with the tribe of the Iroquets. The forest swallowed up the young adventurer, and we lose sight of him. He must have wintered with Iroquet, but where? The Algonkin chief may just as well have spent that winter in the Huron country as in his village, somewhere in the valley of the Ottawa (Outaouais) River. All that Champlain tells us about the young man's exploit is that he was the first white man to shoot the Sault-Saint-Louis (the Lachine rapids, near Montreal) in a canoe. When later on Champlain, in his turn, ventured down these rapids with the Indians' help, he admitted that he had never yet done it unaided, "nor had any other Christian, except my young man of whom I have already spoken [Étienne Brûlé]."

Brûlé and the Indians returned as arranged one year after their departure, about 13 June 1611. It was a memorable event, which Champlain describes with a certain emotion: "I also saw my French boy who came dressed like an Indian. He was well pleased with the treatment received from the Indians, according to the customs of their country, and explained to me all that he had seen during the winter, and what he had learned from the Indians. . . . My lad . . . had learned their language very well." A new figure had come into being: the interpreter (*truchement*), destined to play an important role in the early days of the colony. Living among the Indians, in their fashion, he was accepted by them as one of their own people. He constituted a liaison officer between the colonizers and the natives, and was an indispensable cog in the mechanism of the fur trade.

During the four years following his return, Brûlé again vanished. From certain facts it can be presumed that he stayed in the Huron country —where subsequently he was to take up residence —for at least a part of this period. It is therefore probable that he was the first European to see that region and to make the long trip there via the Ottawa and Mattawa rivers, Lake Nipissing, the French River, and Georgian Bay. His discovery of the Huron country—assuming it took place— was the first of the numerous peregrinations of the interpreter between the years 1615 and 1626.

In 1615, Brûlé started out on an expedition that was to make him famous. Champlain and the Hurons, undertaking their third campaign against the Iroquois, were on their way that year towards the village of the Onondagas (situated not far from the present city of Syracuse, N.Y.), when they decided to send a delegation to the Susquehannahs, allies of the Hurons, to request their support for the projected battle. The Susquehannahs lived to the south of the Five Nations of the Iroquois (in the present county of Tioga, N.Y., probably between Elmira and Binghamton). To get there quickly, the delegation had to cross enemy territory; 12 of the best Huron braves were selected. Brûlé asked Champlain for permission to follow them, "to which I readily agreed," wrote Champlain, "since he was drawn thereto of his own inclination, and by this means would see their country and could observe the tribes that inhabit it." The delegation left Champlain at Lake Simcoe, the Huron army pushing on northwards, Brûlé and the 12 braves heading towards the south. As always when Brûlé was involved, no precise report has been made of the route taken on this journey. However, historians are generally agreed that the party must have followed the Humber River to its mouth (where the city of Toronto is now situated), gone around the western end of Lake Ontario, then landed somewhere on the south shore, perhaps between the Niagara and Genesee rivers, pushing on after that towards Carantouan, the Susquehannah capital. The mission of the Hurons and Brûlé did not prove successful. Although they succeeded in raising an army of Susquehannahs, it reached the meeting-place agreed upon with Champlain two days late, at a time when the Huron army, already defeated by the Iroquois, had abandoned the spot. After this reverse, Brûlé returned with the Susquehannahs to Carantouan to continue his exploration.

In the account that Brûlé later gave Champlain of his adventures in the country of the Susquehannahs, he stated that he had spent the autumn and winter investigating the neighbouring nations

Brûlé

and regions, and "making his way along a river which discharges on the coast of Florida," and that he had continued "his route along the said river to the sea, past islands and the coasts near them." As he probably did not possess the necessary knowledge to draw a map or to determine co-ordinates, Brûlé gave only a vague description of the region visited. In view of the geographical position of Carantouan, it seems likely that the river was the Susquehanna, which Brûlé may have gone down by starting at one of its branches rising in the county of Otsego, N.Y., that he reached Chesapeake Bay, which is indeed filled with islands, and that he went as far as the ocean. The bay itself had already been discovered in 1608 by Capt. John Smith. The latter had not been able, however, to go up the river, because of the obstacles. Étienne Brûlé, the first European to see Lake Ontario, would then also be the first to tread the soil of what is now Pennsylvania. But, according to Brûlé's account, the trip was not yet finished. On the way back he apparently lost his way, and fell into the hands of the Senecas. The Iroquois seemingly had time to subject him to the opening stages of the physical torment reserved for prisoners, adding to his exploits the sorry privilege of being the first white man to have experienced their tortures. However he managed to persuade the Indians to release him, through a ruse—by interpreting the sudden appearance of a storm as an intervention by heaven in his favour. Having set him free, the Indians accepted him as a member of the tribe and even included him in their feasts. Zeller questions the truth of the part of Brûlé's account relating to the miracle. The Senecas, anxious to conclude peace and to trade with the white men, may have released Brûlé on his promise "to make them friends with the French and their enemies, and to make them swear friendship for one another." Realizing that the conclusion of a Franco-Iroquois peace would compromise the interests of his friends the Hurons, Brûlé may have invented the rescue by heaven in order to explain to Champlain the hospitality of the enemy.

The expedition that Brûlé next undertook, in fulfilment of an earlier promise to Champlain, led him to discover Lake Superior. Butterfield, who has studied all his movements, places this voyage in 1621–23. Despite the lack of written sources, he reconstructs the route with a fair degree of probability. Accompanied by a certain Grenolle, Brûlé seems to have set out from Toanché, a Huron village of the Bear tribe where he had established his residence. The two adventurers may have gone northwards in a canoe, making their way along the shore of Georgian Bay as far as the copper mines worked by the Indians, on the north shore of what is known today as the North Channel. In fact Sagard recounts that "at about 80 or 100 leagues from the Hurons, there is a copper mine, from which the Interpreter Brûlé showed me an ingot when he returned from a voyage that he made to the neighbouring Nation with a certain Grenolle," the "neighbouring nation" being, according to what can be deduced from the description given by Grenolle elsewhere, a tribe then inhabiting that region. The two companions may then have gone via the St. Marys River as far as Lake Superior. Butterfield supposes that Brûlé and Grenolle continued their journey by following the north shore of Lake Superior to the spot on the St. Louis River where the cities of Duluth and Superior now stand. Yet there is no proof that Brûlé did actually cross the lake, although Sagard seems to state it by implication: "The Interpreter Bruslé and a number of Indians have assured us that beyond the *mer douce* [Lake Huron] there is another very large lake, which empties into the former by a waterfall, nearly two leagues across, which has been called the Gaston falls [Sault Ste. Marie]; this lake, with the freshwater sea, represents about a 30-day trip by canoe according to the Indians' statement, and according to the interpreter is 400 leagues long." The fact that Brûlé had a different opinion from that of the Indians might indicate that he had made the trip and was giving a personal estimation of it. The obscure Brûlé would in that case have preceded Daniel Greysolon* de Dulhut and Nicolas Perrot*.

To the regions traversed by Brûlé it is probably necessary to add the country of the Neutrals. According to Butterfield, he was there about 1625. This hypothesis, very probable though it is, rests on no documentary proof. We can only refer to a sentence in which Father JOSEPH DE LA ROCHE Daillon, in 1626, expressed the desire to go to the Neutral country, about which, he said, the interpreter Brûlé reported wondrous things. The Huron and Neutral nations moreover maintained frequent and friendly relations, a circumstance which makes Brûlé's voyage still more plausible, considering the number of years that he had spent in the Huron country. If Brûlé went to the Neutral country, he must have seen Lake Erie. Thus he would be the discoverer of four of the Great Lakes.

Some authors attribute to Brûlé the additional merit of having shared in the writing of Brother Sagard's dictionary of the Huron language. This is merely a supposition; it is certain only that in the beginning Brûlé helped Sagard to learn the language. It has also been maintained that Brûlé rendered the same service to Brébeuf, who lived three years (1626–29) in the same place as he, at Toanché. It is unlikely that he did so, for relations between Brûlé and Brébeuf were never good. Besides, Sagard complained that the interpreters banded together subsequently to refuse to teach the missionaries the native dialects.

With remarkable exploits to his credit, Brûlé was unfortunately guilty of reprehensible actions that have sullied his memory. In espousing the customs of the Indians, he had also adopted their morals. ". . . this man was recognized as being very vicious in character, and much addicted to women," wrote Champlain. In the eyes of Champlain and the missionaries, this degradation of a European to an inferior state of civilization stemmed from the desire to live in debauchery, and constituted a sin that they found difficult to pardon. In Brûlé's defence it should be remembered that he was very young when he set out in 1610 to live among the Indians. Furthermore, he is said to have had only a very sketchy religious upbringing. One day, recounts Sagard, when Brûlé was in danger of death, the only prayer he was able to recite was the *Benedicite*. In these circumstances it is understandable that he should have been beguiled by the free, primitive customs of the Indians. But Champlain also harboured resentment against him for another reason: that he was working—like his associate Nicolas MARSOLET, an interpreter of the Montagnais and Algonkian languages—for the benefit of the merchants rather than for that of colonization. Brûlé indeed received from the business men an annual salary of 100 *pistoles* to encourage the Indians to come and trade. None the less, all these faults would probably have been forgotten by posterity if in the year 1629, when Quebec was captured, Brûlé had not agreed, with three other companions, to abandon Champlain and enter the service of the KIRKE brothers. Champlain accused him of treason, and Brûlé went back to the Huron country. This episode represents the blackest page in his story. When Champlain returned to New France in 1633, Brûlé was dead.

The circumstances surrounding his death are shrouded in mystery. For some reason unknown, the Hurons, among whom he had lived as a brother for 20 years, killed him and ate him. The crime weighed upon the whole Huron nation. When Brébeuf returned to Toanché he found the place deserted. The Bear tribe had abandoned the village and split up. The Bears did not manage to "purge themselves" of this murder, and admitted that "no satisfaction had been obtained" from the interpreter's death. Pursued by epidemics, haunted by the memory of Brûlé "whose wounds are still bleeding," they attributed the cause of their misfortunes to the avenging spirit of the dead man's sister or brother, which, they said, breathed a curse on them. For a long time, suspicion centered around the tribe's chief, Aenon, but the latter denied that he was guilty. For want of proof, the enigma of Brûlé's murder remains unsolved.

Thus, Étienne Brûlé ended by paying very dearly for his mistakes. Endowed with a great spirit of independence, with initiative and indisputable courage, he had, despite all his failings, a remarkable and colourful personality. He is a striking example of the fascination that the free life of the Indians held for young Frenchmen in the first century of the colony's history.

OLGA JURGENS

Champlain, *Œuvres* (Laverdière), 368–70, 397–404, 408, 507, 523, 590, 621–29, 1043, 1045, 1064–65, 1228–29, 1249–51. *JR* (Thwaites). Sagard, *Histoire du Canada* (Tross), 306, 328, 338, 430–32, 456–57, 589, 716–17, 752–53; *Long journey* (Wrong and Langton). Morris Bishop, *Champlain: the life of fortitude* (New York, 1948). C. W. Butterfield, *History of Brûlé's discoveries and explorations, 1610–1626* (Cleveland, 1898). Benjamin Sulte, "Étienne Brûlé," *RSCT*, 3d ser., I (1907), sect. I, 97–126. J. Tremblay, "La sépulture d'Étienne Brulé," *RSCT*, 3d ser., IX (1915), sect. I, 145–64. A. G. Zeller, *The Champlain-Iroquois battle of 1615* (Oneida, N.Y., [1962?]), 19, 22.

BUADE DE FRONTENAC ET DE PALLUAU, LOUIS DE, soldier, Comte, governor-general of New France; one of the more turbulent and influential figures in the history of Canada, chiefly noted as the architect of French expansion in North America and defender of New France against attacks by the Iroquois confederacy and the English colonies; b. posthumously 22 May 1622, at Saint-Germain; d. 28 Nov. 1698 at Quebec, buried in the church of the Recollets at Quebec. He was the only son of Henri de Buade, Comte de Frontenac and Baron—later Comte—de Palluau, and Anne Phélypeaux de Pontchartrain who was the daughter of one secretary of state and niece of another. He was baptized 30 July 1623, with Louis XIII as his godfather. He had two sisters. All that is known of one is that she was a nun at Dourdan; the other was married to the Marquis de Saint-Luc, son of Maréchal de Saint-Luc, chevalier of the order of Saint-Esprit and lieutenant-general of Guyenne.

The Buades were an old family of the *noblesse d'épée*, known in Périgord since the end of the 13th century. The fief from which they derived the title "Frontenac" was situated in Guyenne,

Buade de Frontenac

between Agen and Castillones. Antoine de Buade, Frontenac's grandfather, a chevalier of the order of Saint-Esprit, served as Henri IV's personal equerry for several years before being appointed governor of Saint-Germain-en-Laye and *premier maître d'hôtel du Roi*. His son, Henri de Buade, was colonel of the regiment of Navarre and a member of Louis XIII's entourage.

Where Frontenac was educated is not known. It is known, however, that he attended for several years the same college as the Abbé Tronson, the superior of the Messieurs de Saint-Sulpice; very likely they were educated at a Jesuit college, then the best in Europe. Certainly Frontenac's correspondence indicates that he had received a very good education. While still in his teens he entered the French army, served in several campaigns in the Thirty Years' War and in February 1643 was commissioned colonel (*maître de camp*) of the Normandie regiment. While in command of this regiment at the siege of Orbitello in 1646, his right arm was permanently crippled. As recompense, he was given the rank of *maréchal-de-camp*, equivalent to the rank of brigadier in the present-day Canadian army. Unless he were left-handed, however, and his hand writing does not suggest that he was, his injury could not have been too serious since there is no discernible difference in his handwriting before and after the event. Unfortunately, no portrait of him is known to exist and none of his contemporaries who mentioned him in their writings gave any hints as to his physical appearance. If he resembled his grandfather, whose portrait is in the Bibliothèque Nationale, he was a small, wiry man with a wide forehead, long thin nose, hollow cheeks and narrow pointed chin; altogether rather unprepossessing.

When not on active service Frontenac resided at the royal court. Like so many of his class he lived extravagantly and became encumbered with debts. In October 1648 he secretly married Anne de La Grange, daughter of the seigneur de Trianon et de Neufville, a wealthy *maître des requêtes*. She was noted for her rare physical beauty—her portrait hangs in the palace of Versailles—a very imperious temperament, and a quick, biting wit. In addition, apart from her father's estate, reputed to be worth some 200,000 *écus*—over 1,000,000 dollars in present-day funds—she stood to inherit a considerable fortune left in trust for her by her mother until she came of age. Frontenac's father-in-law had placed every obstacle in the way of the marriage, even incarcerating his daughter in a convent to prevent it. When he learned that the marriage had nevertheless taken place clandestinely, he disinherited his daughter and eventually, by means of legal chicanery, prevented her from obtaining the inheritance due to her from her mother's estate. In May 1651 the Frontenac's only child, François-Louis, was born, and after the custom of the age and his class the child was reared by servants. Frontenac, at about this time, became a member of the entourage of Gaston d'Orléans, the uncle of Louis XIV, who had the well-earned reputation of being the most treacherous man in France. The Comtesse de Frontenac joined the entourage of Gaston's daughter, Mlle de Montpensier, shared the turbulent "Grande Mademoiselle's" adventures during the Fronde, and accompanied her to the provinces as a lady-in-waiting when she was exiled from the court. Mademoiselle eventually came to suspect that Frontenac and his wife were intriguing against her and the Comtesse de Frontenac was dismissed from her household.

Frontenac and his Comtesse then took up residence in Paris where their time was spent at the court, living well beyond their means. His extravagance, even in the extravagant court circles, was the subject of comment. In her memoirs Mlle de Montpensier remarks on his expensive tastes and his colossal vanity. In the summer of 1653 she spent a few days at his château at l'Île Savary, which she described as being "fine enough for a man such as he." When he showed her the plans he had made for the embellishment of his château she tartly commented: "One would have to be minister of finance to execute them." On another occasion she depicted him as affecting to hold a court at Saint-Fargeau, one of the royal châteaux where she resided, and of his expecting to be treated as a *grand seigneur* by all who came to dine with him. This she regarded as ridiculous and remarked: "Frontenac praised everything that he owned; he never came to dinner or supper without talking of some dish or new preserve that he had been served, crediting it to the excellence of his staff. Even meat, according to him, had a different taste at his table to what it had elsewhere.... Everyone who came to Saint-Fargeau he took to see his stable and in order to please him one had to praise his very indifferent horses; in short, he is like that in all things."

In 1653 Frontenac had to sell or relinquish the colonelcy of his regiment and by 1664 his debts were far in excess of 350,000 *livres*. In that year he legally bound himself to repay that much of his debts within four years, but he made no attempt to honour the commitment. He succeeded in evading his creditors by accepting an appointment as lieutenant-general with the Venetian forces in Crete which were defending the island

Buade de Frontenac

against the Turks. In June 1669 he sailed for Crete to take up this appointment, accompanied by his son who served as one of his aides-de-camp. He was not long with the Venetian army, however, before he began quarrelling with the other senior officers and he quickly came to be regarded with dislike and distrust by Francesco Morosini, captain-general of the Venetian forces and one of the foremost soldiers in Europe. Eventually, in September, he was dismissed from the Venetian service and ordered off the island by Morosini.

Some three years later, in the spring of 1672, Frontenac obtained the appointment as governor-general of New France. Although the salary and perquisites of the post were meagre indeed to one of Frontenac's habits, being only 24,000 *livres* a year, the appointment effectively blocked his creditors' attempts to seize his properties, for along with his commission as governor-general he obtained an order from the Conseil d'État lifting the seizure placed on his properties and deferring his legal obligation to repay his debts. This was by no means an unusual procedure in the circumstances and no stigma was attached to Frontenac's bankrupt condition.

On 28 June 1672, Frontenac sailed from La Rochelle for New France. His wife did not accompany him but Frontenac had his salary as governor-general paid directly to her, and throughout his career in Canada she used her not inconsiderable influence at the court on his behalf. She appears, in fact, to have been of greater assistance to him in this way than she could have been as his *châtelaine* at Quebec. It has been claimed that his relations with his wife were far from amicable but this claim is based largely on the memoirs of the Duc de Saint-Simon, who wrote some 35 years after the incidents he mentioned and was obviously recalling rather ancient court gossip. Mlle de Montpensier, in her memoirs, states that on one occasion Mme de Frontenac had displayed a marked aversion for her husband, refusing to share his bed, but she also makes it plain that on other occasions no such aversion existed. Thus, there would appear to be little foundation to the statements that they could not abide each other; in fact, considering that in the age and society in which they lived marital fidelity was something to be sneered at, their relations appear to have been surprisingly good.

RÉMY de Courcelle, the retiring governor of the colony, had already left when Frontenac arrived at Quebec in the early autumn and Jean TALON, the intendant, sailed for France in November. Perhaps because he had spent most of his adult life in the army where as colonel of a regiment his word had been virtually law, Frontenac failed to realize that even though he was the governor-general of the colony and the representative of Louis XIV, there were distinct limits to his authority. The administrative system of the colony, established by Louis XIV and Colbert, the minister in charge of colonies, was very similar to that existing in the provinces of France. There were some significant differences owing to the colony's remoteness from the seat of government in France and the conditions peculiar to North America, but there was a separation of powers of the senior officials. Frontenac, as governor, had complete control over military matters, he also had a veto power over the decisions of the other officials, but this last he could use only in extreme circumstances. He was instructed by the minister not to usurp the functions of the intendant, the Conseil Souverain, or the officers of justice in the lower courts.

Normally, the intendant was responsible for all matters concerning justice, finance, and general administration; it was this official who had authority in all civil matters. But with the intendant absent from the colony, and in view of Colbert's failure to appoint a deputy or to issue instructions concerning the derogation of the intendant's powers, Frontenac, not without reason, assumed that these powers devolved upon him. The manner in which he used these powers, however, soon brought him into conflict with the Conseil Souverain, the governor of Montreal, and several of the leading families in the colony.

Some of the more serious of these disputes centred about the fur trade. A few years prior to Frontenac's arrival peace had been made with the powerful Iroquois Confederacy. This had made it possible for the Canadian fur-traders to voyage into the west to obtain furs from the Indian tribes of the Great Lakes area. Jean Talon had espoused an expansionist policy; he had sent parties to the west to explore, to claim the western lands for France, and to establish trade relations with the Hurons, Ottawas, and other tribes. He had wanted to establish fortified posts in the west and to create a vast fur-trading empire extending far into the interior of North America. Colbert, however, had opposed this policy. This far-seeing minister desired to establish the colony in the valley of the St. Lawrence on a firm basis before undertaking any such expansion. Frontenac was quick to see the latent possibilities in the western fur trade. Before he had been in the colony a year, and without informing the minister of his intentions, not to mention obtaining authorization, he established a fur-trading post on Lake Ontario, at the mouth of the Cataracoui River—

Buade de Frontenac

where the city of Kingston stands today. The merchant fur-traders and habitants of Montreal were incensed by this, the former because they feared that this advanced trading post, called Fort Frontenac (or sometimes Cataracoui), would forestall them and deprive them of some part of the western fur trade; the ordinary habitants because Frontenac had called them out on *corvée* and obliged many of them to spend a good part of the summer in constructing the fort and transporting supplies to it. Consequently, during the autumn and winter of 1673 the people of Montreal were in an ugly mood. The governor of the town, François-Marie PERROT, himself an active participant in the fur trade, did all he could to foster this mood in an effort to hinder Frontenac's attempts to gain control of a large part of the western fur trade. To stifle this opposition and to maintain his authority Frontenac had Perrot arrested, under rather dubious circumstances, and charged with defying the authority of the governor-general. When the case was brought before the Conseil Souverain Perrot defended himself very ably. Meanwhile, in Montreal, a member of the clergy, the Abbé Fénelon [*see* SALIGNAC], spoke out from the pulpit in criticism of Frontenac's actions and he too was arrested. Despite the great pressure that Frontenac brought to bear on the members of the Conseil Souverain they finally concluded that the issues involved were beyond their jurisdiction; they ordered that the cases should be referred to the king and that Perrot and the Abbé Fénelon should be sent to France to answer the charges laid against them. Louis XIV and Colbert, after studying the evidence, concluded that all concerned had been at fault, especially Frontenac, and he was severely censured for his actions.

Colbert now took steps to check Frontenac in these abuses of his authority. He appointed an intendant for the colony, Jacques DUCHESNEAU, who was empowered to act as president of the Conseil Souverain and to perform all the other functions of a provincial intendant. This meant that Frontenac's authority was restricted to military matters and to supervising, but not interfering with, the other officials. At the same time the governor-general's power to appoint members of the Conseil Souverain conjointly with the bishop was removed. They were now granted royal commissions and all future appointments were made by the king. This made the Conseil Souverain virtually an independent body, able to defy the governor on occasion. In a negative sense Frontenac can be given the credit for this important development.

Frontenac, however, was bitterly resentful because his authority had been curbed and it was not long before he became embroiled in bitter disputes with the intendant and the Conseil Souverain. On one occasion he arbitrarily imprisoned the clerk of the court; on another he had a Montreal judge who had annoyed him incarcerated for two months and fined 200 *livres*. Then, during the winter of 1678–79, he attempted to reduce the intendant and the Conseil Souverain to subservience. The dispute began when Frontenac claimed the powers that were specifically denied him by the king's *Déclaration* of 1675, to preside over the meetings of the council. When, in July 1679, the Conseil Souverain refused to accede to this demand, he exiled from Quebec the attorney general, RUETTE d'Auteuil, and two councillors. They were ordered to remain at designated seigneuries outside Quebec until the ships sailed in November, then to cross to France to account to the king for their refusal to submit to their governor's direct command. During this time the work of the Conseil Souverain was completely disrupted. Only one of the three officials was finally obliged to go to France but his account of events convinced Louis XIV and Colbert that Frontenac had been in the wrong. It took all the influence that Frontenac's friends at court could bring to bear, and their assurances that he would not be guilty of such excesses in future, to prevent his recall.

The Conseil Souverain had scored a decisive victory over Frontenac; its members had resisted vigorously his attempts to reduce them to subservience and they had been upheld by Louis XIV and Colbert. Thus emboldened, they now began prosecuting some of Frontenac's associates for infringements of the royal edicts governing the fur trade. After establishing the post on Lake Ontario, Frontenac had become closely associated with CAVELIER de La Salle, to whom he gave every assistance in the establishment of a monopoly of the fur trade in the vast area south of the Great Lakes. In expanding French control into the west in this fashion, Frontenac's associates came into conflict with the Iroquois who were determined to seize the Ohio valley area for themselves. Until 1675 the Iroquois had been unable to oppose the establishment of French posts on lands they either regarded as their own or coveted, owing to their war with two powerful tribes to the east and south of them, the Mahicans and the Andastes. By 1675, however, they had forced these tribes to come to terms and were now able to resist French encroachment. From this date on they became increasingly more hostile. They began attacking Indian tribes allied to the French and under French protection. When

Buade de Frontenac

these tribes appealed to Frontenac for aid he offered none; instead he tried to appease the Iroquois, which merely emboldened them to begin pillaging French canoes and attacking French posts in the west. At the same time another threat to New France was developing in the north. The recently established Hudson's Bay Company was inducing Indian tribes that usually traded with the French to take their furs to the Company's posts on the Bay. Some in the colony advocated strong measures to remove this threat, but Frontenac refused to allow any action that might cause strife with the English.

It was at this juncture of events, in 1682, that Frontenac was recalled to France. It was not, however, his failure to cope with these military and economic threats that caused the king and the minister to dismiss him, for they were unaware of the seriousness of this situation; it was his continued wrangling with the intendant, the Conseil Souverain, and the clergy. In the case of the latter group, the underlying causes of the trouble were the fur trade and the anti-clerical attitude of the court in general and Colbert in particular. The Jesuits were Colbert's *bête noire*; he was convinced that in both France and New France they wielded far too much influence and were attempting to establish a theocracy in Canada. Thus, when a dispute arose over the unrestricted sale of brandy to the Indians, Frontenac was easily able to convince Colbert that this was merely another example of the clergy's continual attempts to encroach on the royal authority. The clergy, and particularly the Jesuits since they were mainly concerned with missionary activities among the Indians, were adamant in their opposition to the use of brandy in the fur trade, claiming, with good cause, that the Indians were cheated out of their furs by unscrupulous traders who first got them drunk; that they became utterly debauched and committed the most heinous crimes when brandy was brought into their villages. Bishop Laval* had declared the trading of brandy to the Indians to be a mortal sin and those known to have engaged in the practice were denied the sacraments of the church. Frontenac, along with many but by no means all of those engaged in the fur trade, regarded brandy as necessary for the trade and he accused the bishop of interfering in civil affairs and the Jesuits of desiring to gain control of the fur trade for themselves. Louis XIV eventually tried to settle the dispute with a compromise decision which was easily evaded, consequently the clergy continued to complain of Frontenac's attitude and he, in turn, did his best to discredit them.

Although in his disputes with the clergy Frontenac had the support of Colbert, in his violent quarrels with the intendant and the Conseil Souverain he did not. In 1680 the minister informed him that all the public bodies and many individuals were complaining of his tyranny. New France, Louis XIV wrote on 29 April 1680, "runs the risk of being completely destroyed unless you alter both your conduct and your principles." The following year he was warned that unless he changed his ways, it would be necessary to recall him. But Frontenac proved incapable of heeding warnings or orders. In violent displays of temper he imprisoned, first the teen-age son of Intendant Duchesneau, then MATHIEU DAMOURS DE CHAUFFOURS, an elderly member of the Conseil Souverain, for what he claimed were failures to show due respect for his person. Thus, it came as no surprise to anyone that he was dismissed from his post and ordered to return to France.

When he left the colony the civil administration was in a turmoil as a result of his wrangling. The fur trade had been divided between two rival and warring factions, that of Frontenac and his associates and that of the Montreal fur-trading merchants. Some of the latter group were also Frontenac's enemies in the Conseil Souverain. To some extent Frontenac was sinned against as well as sinning. His opponents had found it very easy to annoy and incite him to the excesses that resulted in his recall, but in the final analysis his lack of self-control was his downfall. His most serious fault, however, was his failure to take effective action in the face of the Iroquois threat. The danger had become very real that, as a result of his inaction, the French would be driven out of the west, that their hold on the fur trade, which was the economic life blood of the colony, would be lost, and that the Iroquois would, before long, launch attacks on the colony proper. Frontenac had failed to take any precautions in the face of this threat; the colony was virtually without defences. The settlements were very scattered; there were no fortified places where the settlers could find security in the event of attack; and the militia was untrained and without arms.

This was the situation that confronted Frontenac's successor, LE FEBVRE de La Barre, and it proved too much for him. Unable to cow the Iroquois with the forces available, he was obliged to make peace on their terms and in consequence he was recalled by Louis XIV. He had, however, at least succeeded in making the king and the minister of Marine realize the seriousness and urgency of the situation in Canada. M. de Brisay* de Denonville was now sent out as governor, with a considerable body of troops, and he succeeded

Buade de Frontenac

in bringing the Iroquois to accept his terms for peace. Before this treaty could be ratified, however, the war of the League of Augsburg broke out in Europe and the Iroquois learned from the New York authorities that France and England were at war before the news was received in Canada. Thus, a surprise attack by the Iroquois on the settlements at Lachine on 4 Aug. 1689 caught the Canadians unawares. Heavy casualties were inflicted and many farms destroyed.

Meanwhile, in France, Frontenac had for some time been striving to convince Louis XIV and his ministers that he merited another appointment. In this endeavour he was ably assisted by his influential friends and relatives at the court. He must have been living in very straitened circumstances for his creditors appear to have succeeded, at last, in seizing most of his properties. In 1685 he had received a gratuity of 3,500 *livres* which could have been but small financial comfort to a person accustomed to consuming well over ten times that amount in a year. Then, in 1688, Denonville sent his second in command, Louis-Hector de Callières*, the governor of Montreal, to Versailles to report on the state of affairs in the colony and to submit plans for a combined land and sea attack on New York; this last being regarded as the most effective way to bring the Iroquois to heel by denying them the supplies they needed to attack the French. As soon as England declared war on France Louis XIV had accepted this proposal and Frontenac was appointed to command the expedition. He was, at the same time, appointed to replace Denonville as governor of New France. He had received this appointment in April 1689 some four months before the Iroquois launched their sudden attack in August on the settlements at Lachine. Thus it would not be correct to claim that Frontenac was reappointed governor of New France to save the colony from disaster. He was reappointed because Denonville was worn out by his exertions and had asked to be replaced. Frontenac's own influence and that of his friends at the court was sufficient to obtain the appointment for him. Moreover, with France at war against a coalition of European powers, the better military commanders could not be spared for service in Canada, even had they been willing to accept the appointment.

The expedition against New York, with Frontenac in command, was delayed six weeks at La Rochelle owing to lack of crews for the ships. When it finally sailed on 23 July it encountered strong head winds and did not reach Quebec until 12 October. It was, by this time, too late in the season to undertake the overland assault on Albany and Manhattan and the enterprise was abandoned. When Frontenac now took stock of the situation with which he was faced, it was anything but reassuring. He had to defend the colony against the Iroquois who were continuing their devastating attacks on the settlements; face the possibility of attacks by the English colonies; and at the same time afford military aid to the Indian allies in the west. He had under his command a sizable force of regular troops, some 1,400 in all, as well as the Canadian militia, and in addition he had three very capable men to assist him: the intendant Jean Bochart* Champigny, Louis-Hector de Callières, the governor of Montreal, and Philippe de Rigaud* de Vaudreuil, commander of the regular troops. They were men of exceptionally strong character, not lacking in influence at the court—Callières's brother, for example, was one of Louis XIV's private secretaries—thus Frontenac had to defer to their judgement in many things. At the same time, he was in a much stronger position than he had been during his first term as governor, for within a year of his appointment, the Marquis de Seignelay, Colbert's son and successor, died and was succeeded by Frontenac's kinsman, Louis Phélypeaux de Pontchartrain. When Frontenac learned that his relative had been appointed minister of Finance and minister of Marine, his personal ambitions and expectations rose considerably. The position of governor-general of New France, so eagerly sought after a short time earlier, now seemed inadequate. Immediately upon hearing of Pontchartrain's appointment he wrote to request that he be given a more important and less arduous post. He stated that he was confident the minister would not wish to see a member of his own family fall into decrepitude and end his days without adequate means, without befitting dignity, and without the distinction his long services merited. This plea met with no response from the minister, although it was repeated year after year.

The Iroquois Confederacy responded in a similar fashion when Frontenac attempted to arrange a peace settlement with its member tribes. He greatly over-estimated his influence over them and their only reply was to torture to death some of his emissaries, whereupon they renewed their attacks on the Canadian settlements. The Canadians found it extremely difficult at first to parry these surprise assaults but their other foe, the English colonies, which were supplying the Iroquois with arms and urging them on in these attacks, could be dealt with. Before Frontenac's return to the colony the Canadians had been eager to attack Albany, the main supply base for the Iroquois, and had this town been destroyed the Iroquois would have been rendered impotent

Buade de Frontenac

for a time. Frontenac was quick to see that a military victory against the English would raise morale in the colony and his own prestige as governor. In January 1690 he mustered three war-parties to ravage the English border settlements, but instead of concentrating the assault against Albany, as many in the colony urged, he had his forces attack three small settlements at widely scattered points: Schenectady in New York, Salmon Falls on the Maine Coast, and Fort Loyal on Casco Bay. At all three places the farms and homes were destroyed, many of the English settlers killed, and some prisoners taken. These raids succeeded admirably in raising morale in New France and spreading terror along the English colonial frontier, but they also spurred the English colonies to unite their forces for a combined land and sea assault on Canada. Their plans called for a large force of militia from New York, New England, and Maryland to unite with the Iroquois for an attack on Montreal while a maritime expedition sailed from Boston under the command of Sir William Phips, to attack Quebec by way of the St. Lawrence. Owing to poor organization and an epidemic of smallpox in the ranks of the militia, the large-scale assault on Montreal had to be abandoned, consequently when word reached Frontenac at Montreal that a Boston fleet was approaching Quebec he was able to concentrate all the military forces in the colony on the defence of the town. On 17 October an officer from the Boston fleet came ashore and was taken before Frontenac and his senior officers and officials. This emissary delivered an ultimatum from Phips demanding the surrender of the colony within the hour, failing which Quebec would be taken by force of arms. To this Frontenac replied with the ringing phrase: "I have no reply to make to your general other than from the mouths of my cannon and muskets" (AN, Col., F³, 7, f.40).

This brave defiance heartened the defenders of Quebec and dismayed the New England forces. When the latter learned that the entire military forces of the colony awaited their assault, their military ardour faded appreciably. They put over a thousand men ashore on the Beauport flats, facing Quebec across the St. Charles River, but failed to launch an attack and after three days of marching and repelling forays by small bands of Canadian militia, with the weather growing bitterly cold, they finally returned to their ships and sailed away. Frontenac had thus successfully defended Quebec and the colony with the minimum of casualties by merely sitting tight. No battle had been fought and the enemy's withdrawal took Frontenac by surprise, but it was a decisive victory none the less. The English colonies launched no more full-scale assaults on Canada; for the ensuing seven years of war they relied on the Iroquois to do their fighting for them. Nor were Canada's military forces sufficient to invade the English colonies in strength. Frontenac therefore pursued a policy of guerilla warfare and the Canadians quickly became as adept as the Iroquois in this forest war of ambush and stealthy attack, where to be taken prisoner meant subjection to the worst forms of torture that could be devised by savage minds.

Frontenac played little part in this aspect of the war. The actual war-zone comprised the French settlements from Montreal to Trois-Rivières and the fighting was done by war-parties sent out from Montreal to attack the Iroquois on their own territory. The men responsible for the tactical direction of this *petite guerre* were Callières and Vaudreuil. Both were competent men and Frontenac did not interfere with them. To some extent this is a tribute to the strength of their characters; it is also a tribute to Frontenac's judgement, and for this he deserves credit.

For most of the year Frontenac resided at the Château Saint-Louis in Quebec, making only the occasional trip to Montreal when the Indian allies came from the west to confer with him—always an occasion for feasting and long speeches, which Frontenac appeared to enjoy. At Quebec he maintained a large establishment: a corps of guards, two or three secretaries, a chaplain, a physician, and a large number of servants. Although it would be ridiculous to assume that the Château Saint-Louis was a small-scale Versailles, Frontenac did entertain lavishly and in consequence he was popular with the ladies of Quebec. He held frequent banquets and receptions; when the ships from France arrived with the year's supplies, and perhaps word of fresh victories won by the armies of Louis XIV on the battlefields of Flanders or the Rhineland, then Frontenac would have a Te Deum sung, order all the houses in the town to be illuminated, salutes to be fired from the ships in the river below, and a display of fireworks. During the winter amateur theatricals were held at the château and some of the parts were taken by the ladies, to the horror of the clergy. On one occasion, when the bishop learned that Molière's *Tartuffe*—a biting satire on religious bigotry—was to be enacted, he raised a great outcry, excommunicated Jacques de Mareuil who was to take the leading role, and had the whole colony in an uproar. Louis XIV had to intervene before calm was finally restored.

During these years Frontenac made the expansion of the fur trade his main concern and the war

Buade de Frontenac

greatly facilitated this expansion. Under the guise of military activities he sent large forces to the western posts each year, paid for by the Crown. It soon became apparent that far from serving any military purpose, these expeditions merely afforded an opportunity for Frontenac's friends and associates to gain wealth by trading furs. The western Indians were kept fully occupied hunting beaver and had no time to carry the war to the Iroquois. New fur-trading posts were established in the west and the Canadian traders began to push beyond the forest belt to the great plains west of the Mississippi and around Lake Winnipeg. The Ottawa Indians, traditional commercial partners of the French, became very disgruntled by this expansion; they had been the middlemen, collecting furs from the tribes in the west to trade to the Canadians. Now the Canadian *coureurs de bois* were obtaining the furs directly, eliminating the Ottawas as middlemen. Worse still, the Canadians began trading with the Sioux, traditional enemies of the Ottawas, and supplying them with firearms. Thus, when the Iroquois approached the Ottawas to make peace and form an alliance against the French, their overtures were welcomed. The French commercial empire in the west was now in jeopardy. French officers and missionaries at the western posts and the senior officials at Montreal and Quebec began appealing to Frontenac to take swift action to counter this grave danger. They demanded that he organize a full-scale assault on the Iroquois villages, claiming that this was the only effective way to prevent disaster. Frontenac, however, was extremely reluctant to undertake the campaign. The Iroquois, while negotiating with the Ottawas, had kept the French inactive by entering into peace negotiations with Frontenac who believed them to be sincere, despite the efforts of Callières and the intendant to convince him that he was being duped. It was only after the Iroquois had brought the Ottawas to terms, then renewed their attacks on the French settlements, and after Frontenac had received direct orders from the minister of Marine, that he undertook a campaign against the Iroquois villages.

In July 1696 the army, composed of regular troops, militia, and Indian allies from the missions in the colony, numbering in all some 2,150 men, left Montreal with Frontenac nominally in command but with Callières and Vaudreuil in charge of operations. In the final march on the Onondaga village Frontenac, now in his seventy-fourth year, but determined not to be excluded from an active part in events, was carried through the forest in an arm-chair. When the Onondaga village was reached, only ashes remained. The enemy had fled into the forest after burning everything to the ground. The army set to work destroying the corn in the fields and all the food supplies they could find cached in and about the village. Vaudreuil, with over six hundred men, went on to the Oneida village, burned it to the ground and destroyed the crops. This work done the army returned to Montreal. Its total casualties had been three men drowned and one soldier killed by a lurking Iroquois while on the homeward route. Only one Iroquois was killed, an old Onondaga chief, captured because he was too old and feeble to flee. Frontenac permitted the Mission Indians to burn him slowly to death, a fate that he endured without a whimper.

Despite the failure to come to grips with the enemy, this campaign broke the resistance of the Iroquois. During the preceding few years the tide of the *petite guerre* had turned against them. At the beginning of the war they had been able to attack the French settlements with impunity, but the Canadians had rapidly become skilled in forest warfare tactics. More and more frequently Iroquois war- and hunting-parties were being ambushed on their own territories by Canadian war-parties; more and more frequently Iroquois warriors failed to return to the long-houses. With their villages and food supplies destroyed, the Onondagas and Oneidas now had to depend on the aid afforded by the three other Iroquois nations and the English colonies. When they appealed to the officials at Albany they received little help, for New York, the frontiers of which had been constantly harassed by Canadian war parties, had little to spare. In addition, the Ottawas, upon seeing the state to which the Iroquois were now reduced, abrogated their treaty and began attacking them anew. Nine years of war and the ravages of disease had already reduced their fighting strength by half, from an estimated 2,800 in 1689 to 1,320 in 1698, while the strength of the French, despite heavy losses from war and disease, had increased from a population of 10,523 in 1688 to 12,768 in 1695. Under these circumstances, and fearing that the French would destroy their remaining villages in further compaigns, they had no alternative but to sue for peace. This time, however, Frontenac was by no means convinced that they were sincere and for another three years the fighting continued intermittently in the forest. In Europe, meanwhile, the War of the League of Augsburg had ended. In February 1698 delegates from Albany arrived to inform the French that the Peace of Ryswick had been signed.

When Frontenac had arrived in New France in 1689 to take up the post of governor-general for the second time, the colony had been reeling under the constant assaults of the Iroquois. Although, with the exception of the defence of Quebec in 1690, he had played little real part in the tactical direction of the war, the responsibility had still been his. Had the colony been conquered he would have been held accountable; since it was successfully defended he deserves credit.

Any assessment of his attitude towards the fur trade is faced with a paradox. The policy of the government in France was to curb the fur trade to prevent its undermining the establishment of the colony on sound economic and social principles. The government wished the Canadians to be concentrated in the central colony, engaged in agriculture, fishing, and such other industries as shipbuilding, lumbering, and the manufacture of some consumer goods. In short, they wanted the colony to be self-sufficient in the essential commodities. They did not want a large segment of the Canadian population to be scattered about at posts in the interior of the continent. Frontenac, however, flouted this policy and under his governorship the fur trade expanded more than ever before; new trading-posts were established in the west, the commands given to his associates and military funds employed to further their trading activities. Clearly, Frontenac's motives were dominated by the financial interest of himself and his associates. Yet the fact remains that shortly after his death the government at Versailles, for political and dynastic reasons, abandoned the policy of restraining western expansion and adopted instead an imperialist policy of occupying all of North America west of the Alleghenies, between the Great Lakes and the Gulf of Mexico. The western posts established by Frontenac were vital to this new policy; had he not had them built and manned, the government would have had to begin creating them. It would be easy to assume prescience here on the part of Frontenac, but much more difficult to find evidence of it.

Again, in civil affairs, it is by no means easy to form a judgement of Frontenac. Certainly during his second term the administration was not completely disrupted as it had been during his first term as governor. With the exception of one violent dispute with Bishop Saint-Vallier [La Croix*] over the intended performance of Molière's *Tartuffe*—and it was the bishop rather than Frontenac who created the furore—his relations with the clergy were relatively peaceful. Nor did he create serious difficulties in the Conseil Souverain; but his relations with the intendant left a good deal to be desired. When Champigny tried to implement the royal edicts designed to curb abuses in the fur trade Frontenac overrode him and was supported by the officials in the ministry of Marine. By 1695, however, the ministry was brought face to face with the fact that the market for beaver in France was completely glutted. The amount of beaver pelts shipped from Canada had risen astronomically during the preceding ten years and the lease on the beaver monopoly expired in 1697. This lease brought 500,000 *livres* a year into the royal exchequer and there was a serious danger, with the market glutted, that no one would be willing to purchase the monopoly when the existing lease expired. The minister, when he investigated this situation, became convinced that Frontenac's persistent disregard for the edicts governing the fur trade was the main cause of the trouble. Frontenac's critics, who for some time had maintained that the huge military expenses incurred by the governor had served, not military purposes, but the extension of Frontenac's interests in the fur trade, were now believed. In 1692 the colony's military budget was 75,000 *livres*; by 1694 it had increased to 200,000 *livres*. The minister complained that over the preceding few years the excess of expenditures over allotted funds totalled 550,000 *livres*, and that little appeared to have been accomplished.

In 1697, when Frontenac became involved in a dispute with the intendant over the disposition of a ship prize and annulled his ruling, the minister revoked Frontenac's annulment, censured him severely, and warned him that he could not continue to protect him by excusing his conduct to the king. The patience of both Louis XIV and the minister was now exhausted. Instead of heeding this warning, however, the following year Frontenac became involved in a fresh dispute with the intendant when he attempted to prevent one of his western post commanders, Lamothe de Cadillac [Laumet*], being brought to trial for flagrant abuses of his authority while at Michilimackinac. During the course of this controversy it became plain that, far from striving to enforce the king's edicts governing the fur trade, Frontenac had actively encouraged the members of his following, men whom he had commissioned in the colonial regular troops and placed in command at the western posts, to disregard the edicts intended to limit their trading activities. At a time when the minister was striving to reduce the amount of beaver fur produced to the amount that the market could absorb, Frontenac continued to send large parties, loaded with trade goods, to the western posts in defiance of the king's explicit orders. In the light of these revelations, and the fact that his credit at the court was at a very low ebb, he stood in danger of being once again dismissed from his post. The minister, however, was spared the necessity for making this decision.

"Budai Parmenius Istvan"

For some weeks in the autumn of 1698 Frontenac had been in poor health, suffering from asthma. He had to sleep propped up in an armchair and his strength now began slowly to ebb away. By mid-November he realized that his end was near and he calmly prepared for it. He made his peace with his old antagonists, the intendant and the bishop, and on 28 November the bishop administered extreme unction. Shortly afterwards death came for the old governor and he was buried in the church of the Recollets of Quebec.

He was survived, until 20 Jan. 1707, by the Comtesse de Frontenac whose declining years were made difficult at times by straitened circumstances. They had no heir; their son, François-Louis, had died in 1672 or 1673 in Germany while serving as colonel in the forces of the Bishop of Münster.

One final point remains: the Frontenac legend. Until recently, only two studies of Frontenac and his régime, based on the original documents, had been made. The one by the American historian, Francis Parkman, entitled *Count Frontenac and New France under Louis XIV*, was first published in 1877; the other, by the French historian, Henri Lorin, entitled *Le comte de Frontenac*—and more a panegyric than a critical historical study—appeared in 1895. Their characterizations of Frontenac, and more particularly that of Francis Parkman, were accepted almost without question by all but a very few later historians and writers. Unfortunately, neither Parkman nor Lorin examined the evidence very critically. Frontenac was a prolific and gifted writer; he sent very lengthy accounts of all that happened in New France to his wife for circulation in court circles. These annual journals, running to 90 pages, were skilfully contrived to make everything redound to the greater glory of Frontenac; every success, no matter how ephemeral, was extolled, and every setback was plausibly explained away or at least minimized. But to accept his account of events uncritically ensured a colourful narrative particularly pleasing to the romantic historians—and reading public—who subscribed to the "great man" concept of history. When, however, Frontenac's accounts are closely checked against all the available evidence from other sources, the discrepancies, the subtle half-truths, the calculated omissions and the distortions are very apparent.

Unfortunately, most authors of the more recent biographies of Frontenac and general studies of the period, have preferred to paraphrase Parkman rather than to examine critically the evidence contained in the masses of original documents. Thus, they have perpetuated, and enhanced, the Frontenac legend by repeating old errors and, too often, creating new ones.

W. J. Eccles

[Original source material dealing with Frontenac's pre-Canadian career is rather scanty. There are some items in the Manuscript Division, BN, Paris, and a few documents in the Departmental Archives, Châteauroux. Mlle de Montpensier, in her memoirs, has not a little to say about the Comte and Comtesse de Frontenac, not much of it to their credit (*see* Anne Marie Louise de Montpensier d'Orléans, *Mémoires*, éd. A. Chéruel (4v., Paris, 1858–59), II, 279; III 16–17. Frontenac's dispatches to the court and those from Louis XIV and the minister to him are printed in APQ, *Rapport, 1926–27*, 1–144; *1927–28*, 3–211; *1928–29*, 247–384. To obtain a balanced view of Frontenac and his activities in Canada, however, the correspondence of other officials and notables in the colony must be consulted. The bulk of this material is to be found in AN and BN, Paris; transcripts and microfilm of these documents are available in PAC, Ottawa. Other pertinent documents are to be found in ASQ, AJM, and the state archives at Albany and Boston. A selection of Frontenac's correspondence, annotated and with a brief introduction, is printed in Guy et Lilliane Frégault, *Frontenac* (Classiques canadiens, 2, Montréal et Paris, 1956).

There have been several biographies of Frontenac, the first significant one being Francis Parkman, *Count Frontenac and New France under Louis XIV*, which has run through various editions but which was first published in Boston, 1877. Like most scholars of his generation, Parkman unfortunately judged New France by the values of his own day rather than those of Frontenac's age. Henri Lorin's *Le comte de Frontenac* (Paris, 1895) is little more than a panegyric wherein liberties are taken with historical evidence. Jean Delanglez's *Frontenac and the Jesuits* (Chicago, 1939) is an antidote to the anti-clericalism of both Parkman and Lorin. It deals only with the one aspect of Frontenac's career, however, but is nevertheless quite a sound piece of scholarship. The most recent, and critical, biography of Frontenac is by Eccles, *Frontenac: the courtier governor*. The biographies by W. Lesueur, *Count Frontenac* (Toronto, 1906), and Colby, *The fighting governor*, are based mainly on Parkman's earlier study and are of little real value. W.J.E.]

"BUDAI PARMENIUS ISTVAN." *See* PARMENIUS

BUTEUX, JACQUES, priest, Jesuit, missionary, explorer; b. 10 April 1599, son of Jean Buteux, a tanner of Abbeville in Picardy; killed 10 May 1652 on the upper St. Maurice River.

At the age of 21 he entered the noviciate of the Jesuits at Rouen; from 1622 to 1625 he studied philosophy at the Collège in La Flèche, where Father Massé, the pioneer of the Acadian missions in America, maintained a sacred fervour for the missions of the New World; from 1625 to 1629 Jacques Buteux taught grammar at Caen, then went back to La Flèche, where he attended the theology courses for four years; he was ordained priest in 1633. In the following year he was at Quebec, where he spent only a few months, because his superior, Father PAUL LE JEUNE, entrusted to his care the new habitation that CHAMPLAIN was having built at Trois-Rivières. The construction work, started 4 July under LAVIOLETTE's direction, was not yet completed when Father Buteux took over his new post, 8 Sept. 1634. He was to minister to Trois-Rivières until his death in 1652.

Trois-Rivières was at that period a gathering-place used by the Montagnais, Algonkin, and Huron Indians. In his Relation of 1636, Father Le Jeune pointed out that "As the Savages like the three Rivers better than Kébec they stop there oftener, and in greater numbers. That is why the Fathers who have been living this year in our Residence of the Conception have baptized more people than did those who remained at Kébec, where these Barbarians do not stay so long."

Father Buteux was appointed superior of the Trois-Rivières mission in 1639, and displayed great zeal. He endeavoured to give stability to a number of Indians by settling them at the Cap de Trois-Rivières, on the left bank of the St. Maurice River. In a letter dated 1640 he rejoiced to see Indians taking an interest in the cultivation of the land. When this attempt to form an Indian village failed, the religious recruited some French settlers; in 1649, 14 land-grants were made; this is the origin of the present town of Cap-de-la-Madeleine.

The annihilation of the Huron missions in 1649 induced the missionary to reply to the pressing invitations extended by the Attikamegues who were established in the upper St. Maurice basin. "In all these regions," wrote Buteux, "there are many other Tribes,—more than we can baptize, even if we had still forty years to live; and those people have no intercourse with us. It is from them that the Hurons, before their own country was desolated, obtained nearly all their Beavers,—the supply of which, being no longer diverted elsewhere, will now come to our French settlements, if the Iroquois do not disturb our repose."

On 27 March 1651 Father Buteux, accompanied by two Frenchmen and some 40 Attikamegues, undertook the journey northward. The expedition lasted three months. The travellers reached regions inhabited by tribes who had had no contact with white men. Wishing to go as far as Hudson Bay the following year, Father Buteux had presents sent "to the Captains of some Tribes further to the North." On 18 June 1651 he was back at Trois-Rivières. During July he set out on a mission in the direction of Tadoussac and Gaspé.

At the end of the account of his journey to the source of the St. Maurice, the missionary had expressed his desire to push on further with his evangelizing explorations: "I hope next Spring to make the same journey, and to push still further toward the North Sea, to find there new tribes and entire new Nations wherein the light of the faith has never yet penetrated. Since that journey, the Iroquois have entered that country which seemed almost inaccessible" (Lake Kisagami). In a letter to Father RAGUENEAU he added: "I would never have thought that they could have found or reached that lake with their canoes. On the journey that I made to these regions, we walked about twenty days on the snow, before coming to it."

Despite the menace of the Iroquois, Father Buteux set off northwards once more on 4 April 1652, with an escort of some 60 Attikamegues. His dream of reaching Hudson Bay was not realized. After five weeks of forced marches, when they should have reached, if not passed, the watershed, Buteux and his companions, the soldier Pierre Fontarabie and the converted Huron Thomas Tsondoutannen, were attacked by the Iroquois: "The Huron, who was walking in front, was seized so suddenly that he had no time to take a single step backward. The two others, a little farther away, were brought to the ground by the discharge of the enemy's muskets at them. The Father fell, wounded by two balls in his breast and another in his right arm, which was broken. . . . They were stripped entirely naked, and their bodies thrown into the river."

Thus ended tragically, 10 May 1652, a daring apostolic venture. Word of the drama was brought back to Trois-Rivières on 8 June by the Huron Tsondoutannen, who had managed to escape.

Father Buteux has left letters, an account of his 1651 journey, and numerous documents in the parish registers of Trois-Rivières.

ALBERT TESSIER

Archives de la paroisse de l'Immaculée-Conception, Trois-Rivières, Registres. ACSM, Mémoires et lettres du P. Jacques Buteux, dans "Mémoires touchant la mort et les vertus des pères Isaac Jogues . . ." (Ragueneau), repr. APQ *Rapport, 1924–25*, 3, 25, 26, 28, 45, 49. *JR* (Thwaites). *JJ* (Laverdière et Casgrain).

Ernest Gagnon, "Le Père Buteux et le drame du St-Maurice (1652)," *La Nouvelle-France*, XIV (1915), 85–89. Albert Tessier, *Jacques Buteux, le premier évangélisateur de la région du St-Maurice (1634–1652)* (Pages Trifluviennes, série B, no. 6, Trois-Rivières, 1934); "Le Père Jacques Buteux," *Cahiers des Dix*, I (1936), 157–70. Yvon Thériault, *L'apostolat missionaire en Mauricie* (Trois-Rivières, 1951), ch.III et IV.

Button

BUTTON, SIR THOMAS, naval captain and explorer, fourth son of Miles Button, of Worleton in the parish of St. Lythans, Glamorganshire, and Margaret, daughter of Edward Lewis of Van, Caerphilly, Glamorganshire; d. April 1634, probably at Worleton.

Thomas Button married Mary, daughter of Sir Walter Rice of Dynevor, Carmarthenshire, and the eldest of his three sons, Miles, married Barbara, daughter of Rhys Merrick, from whom she inherited the family estate of Cottrell in Glamorganshire: the Buttons were thus connected by marriage with some of the more influential landowning families in South Wales.

Little is known of Button's early career, but his letters in his old age suggest that he first saw service in the navy in the critical years 1588–89. In 1601, at the time of the Spanish invasion of Ireland, he was commended for gallantry as captain of the Queen's pinnace, *Moon*, at Kinsale, and was awarded a pension of 6*s*. 8*d*. *per diem* for life. In 1602 he sailed in command of the *Wylloby* on privateering raids in the West Indies. The *Wylloby* was owned by his fellow Welshmen, Sir Robert Mansel, who became treasurer of the navy in 1604, and Sir John Trevor, surveyor of the navy; owing to their influence, and his close friendship with Phineas Pett, the naval shipwright, he gained more important commands in the navy. It was with their backing that Button was selected in 1612 to command the expedition to find out what had become of HENRY HUDSON, set adrift by a mutinous crew in the previous spring, and to complete "ye full and perfect discovery of the North-west Passage."

Button's instructions were drawn up by Edward Wright, mathematician and tutor to Prince Henry, eldest son of James I, and indicate clearly that Button was expected to observe carefully the elevation, declination, and variation of the compass, "the beginning and ending of the Eclipse that will happen on the 20th of Maye next"; he was not to waste time entering "Bais, inlets or sands," but rather to observe the set of the tides, "remembering that your end is West, we would have you stand over . . . in the latitude of some 58 degrees, where, riding at some headland, observe well the flood; if it come in SOUTH WEST, then you maie be sure the passage is that waie: yf from the NORTH Or NORTHWEST, your course must be to stand upp into it." No mention is made in these instructions of Henry Hudson.

In April 1612 Button sailed in command of the *Resolution* (which had been specially selected by Pett and Button) and the *Discovery*. The "Company of the Merchants Discoverers of the North-West Passage" (known as The Northwest Company) was granted its charter on 26 July 1612. Among its members are cited Button and several who sailed with him, including Robert BYLOT who had sailed with Hudson and was later to make further expeditions to the northwest in company with BAFFIN, William GIBBONS, a relative of Button, and William HAWKERIDGE who respectively led the fruitless expeditions of 1614 and 1625.

Button's own journal of his voyage has been lost, but according to the fragments of it published in Capt. Luke Fox's *North-west Fox* in 1635, (taken largely from the accounts of Button's companions, Abacuk Pricket and William Hawkeridge, and abstracts from Button's journal by Sir Thomas Roe) Button penetrated Hudson Strait, naming the island at its entrance after his own ship, and eventually sailed southwestwards across what is now called Hudson Bay, and made landfall at a point which he called "Hopes Checkt." He then sailed southwards and wintered at the mouth of a river which he named after Robert Nelson, master of the *Resolution*, who died there. The winter was extremely hard, and Button lost many men, but in the spring he sailed northwards from this area which he had called New Wales. Creeping uncertainly forward in fog and storms, Button probably reached his most northerly point towards the end of July in the channel afterwards named "Sir Thomas Roe's Welcome," and then turned southwards, mistakenly believing that he was embayed. In August he reached the island he named after his friend and kinsman, Mansel, and reluctantly decided to return home.

Button's skilled seamanship in the combined operations against rebels in the west of Scotland in 1615 earned him high praise and in 1616 he was knighted. One of the few to emerge with credit from the unsatisfactory expedition against the pirates of Algiers in 1620–21 when he served as rear admiral, Button served for many years as "Admiral upon the Irish Coast," and became involved in endless quarrels with the Commissioners of the Navy over victualling for his undermanned ships, and the non-payment of monies due to him. In 1631 Button was delighted to be consulted when the voyages of Luke Fox and Thomas JAMES to the northwest were being planned, for he was still confident that the northwest passage existed, "W'ch I doe as confidently beleave to be a passage as I doe there is on[e] either between Calis and Dover or between Holy Head and Ireland." A courageous seaman and an able navigator, Button had the misfortune to serve during a period of considerable corruption in the Stuart navy, and this is inevitably reflected in his obstinate and intractable behaviour in his old age, and the scores of contentious letters which he wrote to the naval authorities in London.

ALED EAMES

Many letters from and to Button as admiral on the Irish station are in PRO, *CSP, Dom.*, and *CSP, Ireland* (particularly for the 1625–32 period). Also scattered references in the Rawlinson MSS in the Bodleian Library, Oxford, e.g., Rawlinson MSS, A455. The charter granted to the Company of Merchants Discoverers of the North-West Passage, 26 July 1612, and the fragments relating to Button's voyage have been printed in *Voyages of Foxe and James* (Christy). For Button's naval career see *Naval tracts of Sir William Monson*, ed. M. Oppenheim (5v., Navy Records Soc., XXII, XXIII, XLIII, XLV, XLVII, 1902–14), *passim*; and *The autobiography of Phineas Pett*, ed. W. G. Perrin (Navy Records Soc., LI, 1918).

G. T. Clark, *Some account of Sir Robert Mansel, and Admiral Sir Thomas Button* (Dowlais, 1883). *DNB*. Dodge, *Northwest by sea*, 129–34. Oleson, *Early voyages*, 166–67. D. W. Waters, *The art of navigation in Elizabethan and Stuart times* (London, 1958), 251–88.

BYLOT, ROBERT (the accepted spelling of a name which has several variants), seaman on HENRY HUDSON's last voyage and later with Sir Thomas BUTTON, William BAFFIN, and William GIBBONS; fl. 1610–16.

Bylot was promoted mate on the Hudson voyage but was degraded from that rank just prior to the marooning of Hudson and part of the crew in James Bay (June 1611). Despite his professed innocence in that transaction, Bylot became second-in-command of the mutineers under Henry Greene, and on the latter's death took complete charge. It was no doubt his feat in bringing the ship home with a depleted crew of starving disobedient wretches, thus saving that classic voyage from oblivion, which procured his pardon.

He sailed again to Hudson Bay with Sir Thomas Button (1612–13), and in 1615 commanded the *Discovery* (with William Baffin as pilot) on a voyage past the north shore of Southampton Island which did much to prove the non-existence of a western outlet from Hudson Bay. In 1616 Bylot and Baffin, again in the *Discovery*, made their great voyage around Baffin Bay, locating the historic sounds of Smith, Jones, and Lancaster. Baffin, to whom chief credit is given for the scientific results of these two voyages, testifies to Bylot's skill as an ice-pilot and to his attentiveness, where health and morale were concerned. Otherwise he remains an incorrigibly elusive personality to whom neither Pricket nor Baffin, though gifted narrators, can give a spark of vitality.

L. H. NEATBY

For sources *see* bibliographies of Henry Hudson and William Baffin. Bylot is known only through his association with these two navigators.

BYSSOT (Bissot) DE LA RIVIÈRE, FRANÇOIS, a native of Pont-Audemer, in the Department of the Eure (Normandy); b. 1612 or 1613, son of Jean Byssot Du Hommée, bourgeois, and of Marie Assour; d. 1673 at Quebec.

His presence in the colony is noted for the first time when the Jesuits took possession of the Île aux Ruaux, 2 July 1639.

Having subsequently settled at Pointe-Lévy, on the Lauson shore, Byssot went into partnership with Guillaume Couture*, whose neighbour he became. In 1647 Couture cleared a piece of land and constructed a main building, while Byssot supplied the money and materials. This property was 40 *arpents* deep by 5 wide, and bordered on the St. Lawrence. On 15 Oct. 1648 JEAN DE LAUSON (senior), in Paris, gave a formal title-deed, over his signature, to his first two copyholders (*censitaires*), Byssot and Couture. At Quebec, ten days later, Byssot, at the age of 34, married Marie Couillard, the fifth child of GUILLAUME COUILLARD and Guillemette HÉBERT.

On 9 Aug. 1653 he was named a deputy member of the body of syndics of Quebec, to represent the Lauson shore. In 1655 he had a mill constructed for the settlers at Pointe-Lévy. Taking part in the organization of seigneurial justice, he became seigneurial attorney for the Lauson estate and seigneury on 19 April 1650, and succeeded Charles SEVESTRE as provost judge after the latter's death in 1657. As a member of the Communauté des Habitants, Byssot also concerned himself with fishing and fur-trading. In 1650 he went into partnership with several persons, including CHARLES LEGARDEUR de Tilly and JEAN-PAUL GODEFROY, with a view to seal-fishing in the Tadoussac region.

On 25 Feb. 1661, for the purpose of hunting and fishing, Byssot received from the Compagnie des Cent-Associés title to the first piece of land granted on the north shore of the St. Lawrence: "L'Isle aux Oeufs as far as the Sept Isles and into the Grande Anse, towards the Esquimaux country where the Spaniards usually fish." It was as a result of this grant of land that Byssot set up a post at Mingan, in Labrador. Did he ever make use of this grant? Despite J.-E. Roy's assertions, it is questionable, for there is no documentary confirmation. On 4 March 1663, Byssot and 17 members of the Communauté obtained from

Cabot

PIERRE DUBOIS Davaugour the "Tadoussac trading concession" for two years, but on 4 October the new governor, SAFFRAY de Mézy, cancelled the agreement entered into by his predecessor.

On 8 March 1664, according to J.-E. Roy, Lauson made Byssot a new grant of land for services rendered; this estate had an area of 400 acres. When CHARLES DE LAUSON left, Byssot, together with Eustache LAMBERT, rented the seigneury. In 1668 he built at Point-Lévy the colony's first tannery, on the ground that he had received in 1648. A sluice-gate was built in the stream separating his estate from Couture's; a wooden conduit channelled the water into the tannin vats. Intendant TALON advanced 3,268 *livres* for the undertaking, while the Compagnie des Indes occidentales allocated 1,500 *livres* for it. The tannery specialized in the tanning of the skins of cows, calves, and porpoise, which were used for the making of shoes, ankle-boots, muffs, and covers for chests and trunks. It is noteworthy that in the inventory of Byssot's possessions, drawn up after his death, not a single sealskin is mentioned.

In 1671 Byssot applied to Talon, and received, in conjunction with NICOLAS JUCHEREAU de Saint-Denis, "concessions for the fishing of cod and seal, and for the oil therefrom," but his success in the realm of fishing remains unknown.

On 3 Nov. 1672 he was granted the Vincennes seigneury, a piece of land 70 *arpents* by one league, which he registered in the name of his sons Charles-François* and Jean-Baptiste*. The son of the latter, François-Marie*, was the founder of the post of Vincennes, in Indiana. Byssot had 12 children; one of his daughters, Claire-Françoise, married Louis JOLLIET. Byssot died 26 July 1673 at Quebec.

His widow, Marie Couillard, married again in 1675; her second husband was Jacques de Lalande* de Gayon. In October 1690 she was taken prisoner by the English and kept on the flag-ship of PHIPS. The latter sent her back to Quebec on the eve of his departure, in order to suggest an exchange of prisoners between the two camps.

RÉGIS DE ROQUEFEUIL

ASQ, Documents Faribault, 21, 78, 80; Polygraphie, XVI, 26. *Coll. de manuscrits relatifs à la Nouv.-France*, I, 213–14. Great Britain, Privy Council, Judicial Committee, *In the matter of the boundary between the Dominion of Canada and the Colony of Newfoundland in the Labrador Peninsula, between the Dominion of Canada of the one part and the Colony of Newfoundland of the other part* (12v., London, 1927), VII, 3511–27. *JR* (Thwaites). *Jug. et délib.*, I; II; III; V; VI, 10–12. *Papier terrier de la Cie des I.O.* (P.-G. Roy), 41–44, 202, 262–64. P.-G.Roy, *Inventaire de pièces sur la côte de Labrador conservées aux Archives de la Province de Québec* (2v., Québec, 1940–42), I, 3; *Inv. concessions*, I, III.

Godbout, "Nos ancêtres," APQ *Rapport, 1957–59*, 383–84. J.-E. Roy, "François Bissot, sieur de la Rivière," *RSCT*, 1st ser., X (1892), sect. I, 29–40; *Histoire de la seigneurie de Lauzon*, I, *passim*. Émile Vaillancourt, *La conquête du Canada par les Normands* (Montréal, 1933), 46.

C

CABOT (Caboto), JOHN (Giovanni), Italian explorer, leader of voyages of discovery from Bristol to North America in 1497 and 1498; d. 1498?

Neither the place nor the date of birth of Giovanni (or Zuan) Caboto, commonly called John Cabot, is known. The earliest historical document which refers to him records his naturalization as a Venetian citizen in 1476, under a procedure by which this privilege was granted to aliens who had resided continuously in Venice for 15 years or more. The resolution of the Venetian Senate, dated 28 March 1476, reads (in translation): "That a privilege of citizenship, both internal and external [*quae intus et extra*], be made out for *Ioani Caboto*, on account of fifteen years' residence, as usual." This decision, possibly confirming an earlier grant made between November 1471 and July 1473, implies that Cabot had been in Venice at least since March 1461, perhaps longer. When in London in 1497–98, Cabot was variously spoken of as a Venetian and as "another Genoese like Columbus," and some 60 years later he was believed by English writers, probably on the authority of his son SEBASTIAN, to be of Genoese origin. The surname Caboto, while absent from 15th-century records of Genoa, is found from the 12th century in those of Gaeta, where a Giovanni Caboto is named as late as 1431; and the family may have left Gaeta for Venice following Aragonese proscriptions after 1443, or an earthquake of 1456. The suggestions made by some modern writers that John Cabot was of Venetian, English, or Catalan origin are without foundation.

Documents in the Venetian archives, of dates between 27 Sept. 1482 and 13 Jan. 1485 (printed in R. Gallo, 1945) disclose that Giovanni Caboto (John Cabot), a merchant, was the son of Giulio Caboto deceased and had a brother Piero; that his wife Mattea was Venetian; and that by December 1484 he had two or more sons. These documents relate to property transactions in Chioggia and three other parishes; and as late as 1551 Sebastian Cabot was in communication with the Council of Ten about his patrimony in Venice. In the royal patent granted to John Cabot in England in 1496, his three sons are named, doubtless in order of seniority, as Lewis (i.e., Ludovico), Sebastian, and Sancio; and if they are the "sons" cited but not named in the Venetian record, the first two at least must have been born before 11 Dec. 1484.

From 1461, or earlier, until 13 Jan. 1485 John Cabot's residence in Venice is attested. On his employment during the next 11 years, in which he must have formulated his project for a westward voyage to the Indies, the evidence is indirect and equivocal. Italians who spoke with him in London in 1497 learnt that he had been engaged in the spice trade of the Levant, claiming even to have reached Mecca; they noted that he was "a most expert mariner" and a maker of maps and globes; and their reports of his conversation reveal that he was familiar with Marco Polo's account of the Far East and with the new discoveries made for the crowns of Portugal and Spain. Documents in the Valencia archives (Epist. vol. 496) show that a Venetian named John Cabot Montecalunya ("*johan caboto montecalunya venesia*") was resident in Valencia from the middle of 1490 until, probably, February 1493, and that he prepared plans for harbour improvements which he expounded to King Ferdinand in two interviews. Although the epithet "montecalunya" has defied interpretation, the identification of this man with John Cabot the explorer is very probable, while not positively established. Acceptance of it may carry the implication that he was present in Valencia when, in April 1493, Christopher Columbus passed through the city on his way to Barcelona, there to report to the Spanish sovereigns the triumphant issue of his western voyage. According to Pedro de Ayala, the associate Spanish envoy in London, writing on 25 July 1498, Cabot had, before coming to England, sought support for his own project in Lisbon and Seville (Archivo General en Simancas, Estado, Tratados con Inglaterra, leg.2, f.196; an English summary is in PRO, *CSP, Spanish, 1485-1509*, no. 210). We do not know whether these applications were made before or after Columbus' voyage; their want of success may be explained by the Portuguese rejection and the Spanish approval of Columbus' proposals and claims. But if John Cabot in fact witnessed the return of Columbus in the spring of 1493, his reading of Marco Polo may well have led him to discredit Columbus' belief that he had reached Cathay, and to suppose that the western sea route to Asia remained to be discovered.

At some date before the end of 1495 John Cabot arrived in England with a plan for reaching Cathay by a westward voyage in higher latitudes, and so by a shorter route, than those of the trade-wind zone in which Columbus had made his crossing. To Cabot's objectives and the means by which he proposed to reach them, and to the experience and reasoning by which he formulated his project, we have only indirect testimony, since no writing from his hand or of his composition survives on these matters. Converging evidence of various kinds points to hypothetical conclusions which are logically related to one another and to the various projects for Atlantic exploration in the last two decades of the 15th century. These conclusions, although subject to the reservation that they may be modified by new evidence, enable us to reconstruct Cabot's motives and to account for his movements.

The discovery of land by any of the Portuguese expeditions which, during the 15th century, sought islands in the western Atlantic is unauthenticated. From 1480 or earlier, by a more northerly route, English venturers from Bristol [for example, CROFT and JAY] set forth regular voyages in search of the "Island of Brasil," shown on contemporary charts to the west of Ireland; and at some date before 1494 their search was crowned by the discovery of a mainland, with which Cabot's crew were to identify the North American landfall made on his first voyage in 1497. The Bristol men were interested in fishing grounds, not in a trade route to East Asia; but, if Cabot had, at some time before the end of 1495, received news in Spain or Portugal about the Bristol discovery, perhaps by a "leakage" through trade channels, his move to England in expectation of official support and a base for his voyage can be explained. Bristol, the westernmost port of England, could provide seamen who had mastered the winds and navigation for a westward passage in these latitudes. The land which they had found might turn out to be at worst an island which would serve as a station on the voyage to Cathay, at best the northeast point of Asia which could be coasted in a southwesterly direction to the lands of the Great Khan in tropical latitudes, far to the west of Columbus' discovery. Thus the pattern of land and water which probably ruled Cabot's thought when he went to England in or before 1495, and certainly did so after his return from his voyage of 1497, having "discovered . . . the country of the Grand Khan" and coasted it for 300 leagues from west to east, must have corresponded to that illustrated in the later world

Cabot

maps of Contarini-Rosselli (1506) and Ruysch (1508).

On 21 Jan. 1496 Gonsalez de Puebla, the Spanish ambassador in London, wrote a report (not now extant) to his sovereigns, who replied on 28 March, referring to what he had said "of the arrival there of one like Columbus for the purpose of inducing the King of England to enter upon another undertaking like that of the Indies" (A.G.S., Estado, Tratados con Inglaterra, leg.2, f.16). On 5 March 1496, Cabot received letters patent from King Henry VII for a voyage of discovery from Bristol; and the lengthy process by which agreement on the terms of the patent was reached must have been set on foot some time earlier, although its initiation cannot much have antedated Puebla's letter. The argument that Cabot had conducted or inspired earlier voyages from Bristol, perhaps going back to 1491, rests on three documents. In his letter of July 1498 Pedro de Ayala recorded that "for the last seven years" the men of Bristol had sent ships to seek the island of Brazil and the Seven Cities "according to the fancy [or reckoning] of this Genoese" ("*con la fantasia desto Genoves*"); if John Cabot were in Valencia in 1490–93, Ayala's phrase must be taken to indicate merely Cabot's later interpretation of the objectives of the Bristol voyages, and not his direct association in or with them. Sebastian Cabot's world map of 1544 (now in BN, Paris) is accompanied by printed legends, the eighth of which ascribes the landfall made by John and Sebastian Cabot in the Cape Breton area to the year 1494; although the map and its legends doubtless incorporate information from Sebastian, his father, while in London in 1497–98, referred to his landfall of 1497 as a new discovery and made no allusion to any earlier successful voyage by him. The date in the legend of the 1544 map is in all probability a misprint for "1497," the last four digits, written in Roman numerals, having been misread by the printer (IIII for VII). Finally, John Dee in 1580 attached the date "Circa An. 1494" to his note on the discovery of "the New Found Lands" by Robert THORNE and Hugh ELIOT, merchants of Bristol (BM, Cotton MS Augustus I. i.1). As a record of a successful Bristol voyage before Cabot's, this may be authentic, for Dee took his information from the papers of Thorne's son; but the extant copies of these papers do not ascribe to the discovery any year-date, which must be taken to be a gloss by Dee, perhaps derived from Sebastian Cabot's map, and without earlier authority. The balance of evidence suggests that John Cabot made no westward voyage before the grant of his patent in March 1496. Moreover, this patent makes no mention of any earlier discovery by Cabot, although his later patent, granted in 1498, cites the successful voyage of 1497 which had preceded it.

The petition for letters patent was presented to King Henry VII on 5 March 1496 by "John Cabotto, Citezen of Venice" and his three sons (PRO, P.S.O. 2, 146). The letters patent, under the same date, authorized Cabot, his sons, their heirs, and their deputies to sail with five ships "to all parts, countries and seas of the East, of the West, and of the North," thus excluding them from the region of the Spanish discoveries in the Caribbean. They were however empowered to "discover and find whatsoever isles, countries, regions or provinces of heathens and infidels, in whatsoever part of the world they be, which before this time were unknown to all Christians"; if Cabot found new land in the zone to which he was restricted by the preceding clause, he was therefore permitted to follow its coast into the latitudes of discoveries by other nations. The patentees were to hold newly found lands under the king and received other privileges; no other subjects of the king might frequent lands discovered by the patentees without their licence.

In 1496, under the authority of his letters patent, John Cabot made an abortive voyage from Bristol with one ship, turning back because of disagreement with his crew, shortage of food, and bad weather. The evidence for this is an undated letter written late in 1497 or early in 1498 by the English merchant John Day and addressed to a correspondent in Spain whom he styles "Almirante Mayor" and whom there are good grounds for identifying with Christopher Columbus. Day's letter is also the only document which establishes the earlier discovery of "Brasil" by the Bristol men; and it gives a detailed narrative of Cabot's voyage of 1497. The other evidence for the course of this voyage comprises three contemporary letters written by foreigners in London (23 Aug. 1497, Lorenzo Pasqualigo to his brothers in Venice; 24 Aug. 1497, an anonymous Milanese correspondent to the Duke of Milan; 18 Dec. 1497, Raimondo de Soncino to the Duke of Milan), a passage in a Bristol chronicle written by Maurice Toby (in or after 1565), and the world maps of Juan de la Cosa (1500) and Sebastian Cabot (1544). From their data, in spite of a few discrepancies, it is possible to construct a coherent narrative of the voyage.

John Cabot sailed from Bristol on 2 May (Toby's date; "towards the end of May," Day; about the middle of May, Pasqualigo) in a small ship named the *Matthew* (Toby), with a ship's company of 20 (Day; 18, Soncino), including a crew of Bristol seamen, two or more Bristol merchants (Toby, who ascribes the discovery to them and does not name Cabot), a Burgundian and a Genoese barber, both companions of Cabot. Sailing past southern Ireland he made a passage of 700 leagues (Pasqualigo; 400 leagues, anonymous Milanese), in 35 days with ENE winds before sighting land (Day); two or three days earlier he had run into a storm and noted a compass declination of two points ($22\frac{1}{2}°$) west. The landfall was made on 24 June, St. John the Baptist's Day (Toby and the 1544 map); a reckoning of 35 days back would give 20 May as the date of departure. In the wooded country near his landfall Cabot went ashore, seeing no people but signs of habitation, and made a ceremonial act of possession. This was his only landing; after a coasting voyage of 300 leagues (Pasqualigo) from west to east, lasting one month, he made his departure from the "cape of the mainland nearest to Ireland" and 1,800 miles west of Dursey Head (Day). A return voyage of 15 days brought him with a fair wind to Brittany (Day) and so to Bristol on 6 August (Toby). He reported to Henry VII in London before 10 or 11 August, when the king's daybooks record a payment of £10 "to hym that founde the new Isle." By 23 August, when Pasqualigo wrote, Cabot was back "with his Venetian wife and his sons at Bristol," where he rented a house in St. Nicholas Street on St. James's Back.

The claims made by Cabot for his discovery and the impression which they made at the English court are attested by the contemporary reports. The mainland found was "the country of the Grand Khan" (Pasqualigo), "far beyond the land of the Tanais" (Soncino); it is also identified with the Island of the Seven Cities (anonymous Milanese; Day); it produced brazil-wood and silk, and the sea swarmed with cod-fish (Soncino; Day). Cabot "is called the Great Admiral, and vast honour is paid to him, and he goes dressed in silk, and these English run after him like mad" (Pasqualigo). He had made a world map and a globe showing where he had been (Soncino); by the beginning of 1498 John Day had a transcript of the map in his possession and had sent to the "Almirante Mayor," in Spain, "a copy of the land which has been found" (presumably a chart of the coasts discovered), naming "the capes of the mainland and the islands"; and another version of Cabot's world map was by July 1498 in the hands of Ayala, who supposed the Spanish government to have received a copy.

The identification of the point at which the landfall was made on 24 June 1497 and of the coasts traversed by Cabot in the ensuing 30 days has been much debated. La Cosa's world map undoubtedly incorporates, in its representation of North America, information from Cabot's first voyage in 1497 and possibly also (with much less certainty) from his second voyage, in 1498. The channels by which this material could have come into La Cosa's hands are illustrated in the letters of Day and Ayala. By the middle of 1498 a copy or copies of Cabot's world map had reached Spain, together with "the copy of the land" sent by Day, perhaps a sketch-chart with a list of places and distances. All these originals are now lost, and some caution is necessary in trying to reconstruct Cabot's geography from the map of La Cosa. The map is constructed in two distinct sections; the New World is drawn, on a larger scale than the Old World, from recent disjunct discoveries, completed by conjectural or theoretical interpolation. Since the scale is not uniform, it is impossible to correlate latitudes on the two sides of the Atlantic or the distances on the map with those reported to have been logged by Cabot. La Cosa's outlines, like the originals from which they were compiled, are drawn by compass bearings; and, to bring this part of the map into true orientation, it must be rotated anti-clockwise through some 22 degrees. The surviving example of the map appears to be a copy, with resultant generalization of outlines and considerable corruption of the place-names, some of which in the course of time have become wholly or partly illegible. The map is in one hand throughout; and, in spite of attempts to assign it to a later date, its content is consistent with a compilation date of 1500 or a little earlier.

It is generally agreed that, in this map, the section of North American coast trending E-W and marked by five English flags reflects John Cabot's coasting voyage in June-July 1497, although it may also include information from that of 1498. Of the 22 named features, the easternmost cape is styled *Cauo de ynglaterra*, one further west *C° de lisarte* (Lizard?), and a gulf to the west of the named features *mar descubierto por inglese*. Widely divergent identifications of the coast so delineated have been made (most of them before John Day's detailed report of the voyage came to light in 1956). It has been variously held to represent the north shore of the Gulf of St. Lawrence; the south coast of Newfoundland; the east coasts of Newfoundland and Labrador; Nova Scotia and Newfoundland; or even the west coast of Greenland.

The basic statement made by La Cosa's map is that Cabot traversed a coastline facing generally SSE across open sea; this seems to exclude the closed waters of Belle Isle strait or the Gulf of St. Lawrence. Day confirms that the coasting was from west to east, and his "cape nearest to

Cabot

Ireland" may be identified with La Cosa's *Cauo de ynglaterra*. The length of the coastal traverse—900 miles (Pasqualigo) in a month (Day)—is therefore to be measured back from the point of departure, at *Cauo de ynglaterra*, to Cabot's first sight of the land called by Day (also by the anonymous Milanese) the Island of the Seven Cities and located by him about latitude $45\frac{1}{2}°$N. Pasqualigo and the anonymous Milanese refer to two islands seen by Cabot on the way back to England; and Day identifies the cape of departure as the "Brasil" discovered by the Bristol men, referring to the wealth of fish, and places it about latitude $51\frac{1}{2}°$N, i.e., that of Cape Bauld. This latitude is irreconcilable with the duration of the coastal voyage from a landfall in $45\frac{1}{2}°$N and with La Cosa's delineation.

These details indicate either Cape Race or Cape Breton as Cabot's point of departure for home. Cape Race is more easily reconcilable with the Bristol discovery and with La Cosa's delineation (in spite of the *y: verde* which he draws, perhaps after a cartographic tradition, in the ocean east of *Cauo de ynglaterra*). Cape Breton would admit the two islands sighted on the homeward voyage; but this cape is marked as the point of landfall (*Prima tierra vista*) on the world map of 1544, the authority of which may be suspect. Even if the 900 miles of coasting be substantially reduced, in view of Cabot's need to keep in sight of land, a long shore voyage which ended at Cape Race must have begun on the Coast of Maine, and one which ended at Cape Breton still farther to the southwest. If the testimony of La Cosa's map be taken in conjunction with the documentary evidence, there are fewest difficulties in supposing the coasting voyage to have extended from a landfall in Maine or southern Nova Scotia to Cape Race. This hypothesis must be qualified by uncertainty about the reliability and precision of the several sources. It is nevertheless consistent with the geographical ideas which nourished both the plan for John Cabot's first voyage of reconnaissance and his proposals for further exploration of the route to Cathay, founded on his interpretation of his discovery as "a part of Asia."

In December 1497 Cabot expounded these proposals to the king in London. Soncino records the enthusiasm of the Bristol seamen about the rich fishing-grounds revealed; but Cabot, he adds, "has his mind set upon even greater things, because he proposes to keep along the coast from the place at which he touched, more and more towards the east [i.e., westward towards East Asia], until he reaches an island which he calls Cipango, situated in the equinoctial region, where he believes all the spices of the world to have their origin, as well as the jewels." This terminology plainly echoes Marco Polo's description of Cipangu and the eastern archipelago; and the association of ideas is strengthened by the wording of Day's letter, written about the same time, with which he sent to his correspondent "the other book of Marco Polo and the copy of the land which has been found." Similarly Ayala, after inspecting the records of the voyage of 1497, reported to his sovereigns that "what they have discovered or are in search of [i.e., on the voyage of 1498] is possessed by Your Highnesses because it is at the cape which fell to Your Highnesses by the convention with Portugal"—an allusion doubtless to Cuba, taken by Columbus to be a cape or peninsula of Cathay.

Cabot's purpose therefore was to follow the coast in a southwesterly direction from his first landfall until he came to the realm of the Great Khan. The preparations for his new expedition also suggest the intention to establish a "colony" or trading-post, either on the coast of Cathay or at an intermediate station on the route; this was to be manned by "malefactors" or prisoners supplied by the king, and some Italian friars were also to go with the expedition. On 3 Feb. 1498 royal letters patent authorized "John Kaboto, Venician," to impress six English ships of 200 tons or smaller burden, to conduct them "to the londe and Iles of late founde by the seid John," and to take with him out of the realm any of the king's subjects who would go on the voyage. The composition of the fleet is disclosed by a London chronicle of which variant versions, derived from a lost original composed in 1509 or later, survive from the 16th century. There were five ships; one was equipped by the king and perhaps hired from the London merchants Lancelot THIRKILL and Thomas BRADLEY, who seem to have sailed in her, while the other four ships were from Bristol and were fitted out by merchants of Bristol and London, whose names are unknown. Of Cabot's other companions only three names are recorded: John Cair "going to the newe Ile" (a payment in the Household books, 8–11 April 1498), Messer Giovanni Antonio de CARBONARIIS, a Milanese cleric (letter of Agostino de Spinula to the Duke of Milan, 20 June), and "another Friar Buil" (Ayala's letter, 25 July). The ships were provisioned for one year and carried cargoes of merchandise. Cabot's favour with the king is attested by the grant of an annual pension of £20, to be paid from the Bristol customs and subsidies (13 Dec. 1497), and by a "reward" of 66*s.* 8*d.* (8–12 Jan. 1498); the warrant for the first payment of the pension was issued on 22 Feb. 1498.

No narrative record of Cabot's second voyage is

extant, and the train of events can only be inferred from scattered allusions. The ships sailed from Bristol at the beginning of May, according to the London chronicler; by 25 July Ayala had heard that one ship, damaged in a storm, had put into an Irish port. That this ship may have been Cabot's and have subsequently resumed the voyage is suggested by a passage of Polydore Vergil (written 1512–13): "John [Cabot] set out in this same year and sailed first to Ireland. Then he set sail towards the west. In the event he is believed to have found the new lands nowhere but on the very bottom of the ocean, to which he is thought to have descended together with his boat . . . since after that voyage he was never seen again anywhere" (*The Anglica Historia of Polydore Vergil, A.D. 1485–1537*, trans. D. Hay (Royal Hist. Soc., Camden ser., LXXIV, 1950), 116–17). Although Cabot's pension was paid, not necessarily to him in person, in each of the two years 1497–98 and 1498–99 (Michaelmas to Michaelmas), it may be taken that he never returned to England, where his fate remained unknown.

By mid-September 1498 no more news of the expedition had reached London; but it is very probable that, if Cabot was lost, one or more of its other ships survived the voyage and that reports of it came back to England and Spain. The evidence for this, positive and negative, is slight but cumulatively significant. In the summer of 1501 the Portuguese crew of one of GASPAR CORTE-REAL's ships obtained from natives, probably on the Newfoundland coast, "a piece of broken gilt sword" of Italian workmanship and two silver Venetian earrings; of the previous expeditions recorded to have visited these coasts, namely those of the Bristol men, before 1494, of Cabot in 1497 (when he encountered no inhabitants), and of Cabot in 1498, the last-named seems the most probable source for the objects. Some news of the course of Cabot's ships evidently reached the Spanish government before 8 June 1501. On that date the sovereigns issued letters patent to Alonso de Ojeda for a voyage of exploration along the mainland coasts of the Caribbean, from south to north, commencing at Cabo de la Vela, in Colombia, which Ojeda, in company with La Cosa and Vespucci, had reached on a westerly traverse from Trinidad in 1499. He was now instructed to "follow that coast which you have discovered, which runs east and west, as it appears, because it goes towards the region where it has been learned that the English were making discoveries; and that you go setting up marks with the arms of their Majesties . . . so that you may stop the exploration of the English in that direction." In July 1498 Ayala, "having seen the course they are steering and the length of the voyage," had warned his government of Cabot's intention to follow the coast in a southwesterly direction into the tropics; and Ojeda's patent suggests that one or more of the English ships advanced either into the Caribbean or far enough to the south, along the North American coast, to alarm the Spaniards. How far this penetration extended cannot be positively affirmed. If any cartographic evidence of it exists, it is to be sought only in the coastline drawn by La Cosa from the *mar descubierto por inglese*, at the western limit of his "English coast," in a general WSW direction down to the latitude of Cuba. The conventional appearance of the drawing may be due to generalization by the copyist, and the absence of place names does not exclude the possibility that the design is a record of experience. Many students have in fact associated this delineation with the voyage of 1498, identifying certain details of it with real geographical features (Cape Cod, the Hudson River, the Delaware, Florida). The most that can be said is that, if La Cosa here records the results of an expedition of discovery, that expedition is more likely to be Cabot's of 1498 than any other.

During the 16th century John Cabot's reputation was eclipsed by that of his son Sebastian, to whom the discovery of North America made by his father came to be generally attributed. This misapprehension, which Sebastian did nothing to remove before his death in 1557, arose in part from confusion between John Cabot's expedition of 1498 and the later westward voyage made by Sebastian under the English flag, in part from ambiguity in some of the early records (including those derived from Sebastian) relating to the Cabot voyages, and in part from ignorance of other records. Thus the passage in the London chronicle describing the expedition of 1498 referred to its leader simply as "a Venetian," whom John Stow, in *The chronicles of England from Brute unto this present yeare of Christ, 1580* (London, 1580) and Richard Hakluyt, in *Divers voyages touching the discoverie of America* (London, 1582), identified as Sebastian Cabot, although Hakluyt printed, also in his *Divers voyages*, the letters patent issued to John Cabot and his sons in March 1496. Until the second quarter of the 19th century historians could still credit Sebastian with the conduct of his father's two expeditions, identifying that of 1498 with the voyage into high arctic latitudes made by Sebastian and described by him to Peter Martyr between 1512 and 1515 and to Ramusio in 1551. The Spanish, Venetian, Milanese, and English documents which came to light during the 19th century enabled Henry Harrisse (1882 and 1896) to restore to John Cabot

Cabot

the credit for the ventures of 1497 and 1498, and G. P. Winship (1900) to review the chronology and to isolate the aims and course of Sebastian's independent voyage, which he assigned to the years 1508–9.

Although some 20th-century historians associate Sebastian's statements about his own voyage with that of 1498, Winship's views, as adopted and developed by J. A. Williamson and R. Almagià, have commanded fairly general consent. They establish indeed a coherent and progressive relationship between the geographical concepts and objectives of the three voyages. As the scanty records place beyond doubt, John Cabot sailed in 1498 with the intention of running southwest from his discovery of 1497 along the coast which he supposed to be that of East Asia. If, as seems probable, either he or his companions executed this design, they found neither Cathay nor any westward sea passage. That this "intellectual discovery of America" may have resulted directly from the 1498 voyage is suggested by the fact that (as Williamson has pointed out) the records of subsequent English voyages to the west contain "no more talk of Asia as lying on the other side of the ocean." By 1508 Sebastian Cabot was seeking a northern passage round the continent which lay across the seaway to Cathay.

No contemporary portrait of John Cabot is known to exist; an ideal representation of him and his three sons was painted by Giustino Menescardi in 1762 on the wall of the Sala dello Scudo in the Palazzo Ducale, Venice. The memorials erected in England and Canada to celebrate the quatercentenary of his discovery, in 1897, include the Cabot Memorial Tower at Bristol.

R. A. Skelton

The primary or manuscript sources are extremely numerous, but they are gathered together in the various works cited below, in chronological order. The best general collections of documents on both the Cabots are those of Biggar (1911) and Williamson and on Sebastian Cabot, that of Toribio Medina. Significant new documents, or groups of documents, are those published by Ballesteros-Gaibrois, Gallo, Vigneras, and Pulido Rubio.

R. Biddle, *A memoir of Sebastian Cabot* (Philadelphia and London, 1831; London, 1832). Henry Harrisse, *Jean et Sébastien Cabot* (1882). Francesco Tarducci, *Di Giovanni e Sebastiano Caboto: memorie raccolte e documentate* (Venezia, 1892); Eng. trans., H. F. Brownson (Detroit, 1893). S. E. Dawson, "The voyages of the Cabots in 1497 and 1498," *RSCT*, 1st ser., XII (1894), sect.II, 51–112; 2d ser., II (1896), sect.II, 3–30; III (1897), sect.II, 139–268. Henry Harrisse, *John Cabot, the discoverer of North America, and Sebastian Cabot his son* (London, 1896). G. E. Weare, *Cabot's discovery of North America* (London, 1897). C. R. Beazley, *John and Sebastian Cabot* (London, 1898). G. P. Winship, *Cabot bibliography, with an introductory essay on the careers of the Cabots based on an independent examination of the sources of information* (London, 1900). H. P. Biggar, *The voyages of the Cabots and of the Corte-Reals to North America and Greenland, 1497–1503* (Paris, 1903); *Precursors* (1911). Williamson, *Voyages of the Cabots* (1929). Ganong, "Crucial maps, I." G. E. Nunn, *The mappemonde of Juan de La Cosa: a critical investigation of its date* (Jenkintown, 1934). Roberto Almagià, *Gli italiani, primi esploratori dell' America* (Roma, 1937). Manuel Ballesteros-Gaibrois, "Juan Caboto en España: nueva luz sobre un problema viejo," *Rev. de Indias*, IV (1943), 607–27. R. Gallo, "Intorno a Giovanni Caboto," Atti Accad. Lincei, Scienze Morali, *Rendiconti*, ser. VIII, III (1948), 209–20. Roberto Almagià, "Alcune considerazioni sui viaggi di Giovanni Caboto," Atti Accad. Lincei, Scienze Morali, *Rendiconti*, ser. VIII, III (1948), 291–303. *Mapas españoles de América*, ed. J. F. Guillén y Tato et al. (Madrid, 1951). Manuel Ballesteros-Gaibrois, "La clave de los descubrimientos de Juan Caboto," *Studi Colombiani*, II (1952). Luigi Cardi, *Gaeta patria di Giovanni Caboto* (Roma, 1956). Arthur Davies, "The 'English' coasts on the map of Juan de la Cosa," *Imago Mundi*, XIII (1956), 26–29. L.-A. Vigneras, "New light on the 1497 Cabot voyage to America," *Hisp. Amer. Hist. Rev.*, XXXVI (1956), 503–6; "The Cape Breton landfall: 1494 or 1497? Note on a letter by John Day," *CHR*, XXXVIII (1957), 219–28. Roberto Almagià, "Sulle navigazioni di Giovanni Caboto," *Riv. geogr. ital.*, LXVII (1960), 1–12. Arthur Davies, "The last voyage of John Cabot," *Nature*, CLXXVI (1955), 996–99. D. B. Quinn, "The argument for the English discovery of America between 1480 and 1494," *Geog. J.*, CXXVII (1961), 277–85. Williamson, *Cabot voyages* (1962).

CABOT, SEBASTIAN, Italian explorer and cosmographer; son of John Cabot; leader of an expedition for discovery of a northwest passage, 1508–9; fl. c. 1484–1557.

Sebastian Cabot was born in or before 1484 at Venice, where his father had some years earlier acquired rights of citizenship. This is attested by a Venetian document of 11 Dec. 1484, showing that at this date John Cabot already had sons, and by the English letters patent granted to him in March 1496, in which Sebastian is named second in order of his three sons. Sebastian made four legal declarations of his age in Spain in the years 1536, 1538, and 1543, implying birth-dates respectively before 1486, about 1479, about 1488 and about 1483. If the extreme dates be set aside, this evidence suggests that he was born not much earlier than 1484; and, as he informed Pietro Martire d'Anghiera (Peter Martyr) between 1512 and

1515, he was still "almost a child" (*pene infans*) when, before the end of 1495, he accompanied his father to England. The inference that John Cabot's three sons, mentioned in his patent of 1496, must then have been of full age is almost certainly unfounded; the absence of their names from the second patent, which in 1498 authorized the impressment of shipping by their father, suggests in fact that at this date they were still minors.

Sebastian Cabot was accordingly Venetian by birth, and he was so described both in an English record of 1505 and in declarations which he himself made in Spain to Peter Martyr, before 1515, and to the Venetian ambassador, in 1522. Only after his return to England in 1548 did he claim English nationality, doubtless to protect himself against extradition and return to Spain. The false account of his early years which he then put into circulation was reported by Richard Eden (*The decades of the newe worlde or west India*, 1555): "Sebastian Cabote tould me that he was borne in Brystowe, and that at iiij. yeare ould he was carried with his father to Venice, and so returned agayne into England after certayne years, whereby he was thought to have been born in Venice."

To Sebastian's participation in his father's voyage of discovery in 1497, the only testimony is the eighth printed legend accompanying his world map of 1544 (now in the BN): "This land was discovered by John Cabot the Venetian and Sebastian Cabot his son. . . ." Nor does any evidence exist that Sebastian took part in his father's second expedition in 1498, with which Sebastian's statements about his own later voyage came to be associated. This gave rise to the erroneous belief, prevalent from the 16th to the 19th century, that Sebastian, and not John, Cabot conducted the two expeditions of 1497 and 1498; hence also the reaction which led Henry Harrisse (1896), with no better justification, to condemn Sebastian's "disregard of truth" on the supposition that he had claimed credit for his father's discoveries.

Sebastian Cabot's name does not appear in any of the documents, from 1501 to 1506, connected with the operations of the Anglo-Portuguese syndicate known as the Company Adventurers into the New Found Lands [*see* FERNANDES and GONSALES]. The royal letters patent issued to the company in 1501 and 1502 did not overlap with or supersede the privileges granted to John Cabot and his heirs in 1496; for these privileges were "heritable in perpetuity," and Sebastian Cabot was in 1550 to obtain a certified copy of the original document. On 3 April 1505 King Henry VII awarded to "Sebastian Caboot Venycian" an annuity of £20 "in consideracion of the diligent service and attendaunce" rendered by him in and about "our Town and poort of Bristowe." (PRO, E. 159, 20 Hen. VII). The terms of this grant, which may have been prompted by information or assumption of John Cabot's death and the consequent lapse of his pension, do not suggest that Sebastian had been involved in the activities of the Company Adventurers, or indeed in any other oceanic enterprise of interest to the Crown. It is nonetheless possible, if not probable, that in this period he acquired the nautical experience which qualified him to command an expedition in 1508–9 and that the company's voyages to lands which remain unidentified had some bearing on his own project.

On Sebastian Cabot's voyage no official documents or contemporary narratives have survived. Its date is recorded by three writers of the 16th century, one of whom had known and spoken with him. These were Peter Martyr, who in his *De orbe novo*, Decade VII, composed in 1524, referred to the discovery of the "Bachalaos" by Sebastian Cabot in the 16th year back (*anno ab hinc sexto decimo*), i.e., in 1508 or 1509; Marcantonio Contarini, who reported to the Venetian Senate in 1536 (Wien, Oesterreichische Nationalbibliothek, codex 6122) that Sebastian Cabot had sailed in the reign of Henry VII and returned after the king's death; and George BEST, whose account of Frobisher's voyages (*A true discourse*, 1578) ascribed Cabot's expedition to the year 1508. The validity of these concurring testimonies outweighs the contradictory evidence of other 16th-century writers who, generally confusing Sebastian's voyage with those of his father, variously dated it in 1496, 1497, or 1498. It commenced either in the spring of 1508, or (with less likelihood) in the spring of 1509, and it ended at some date after 21 April 1509.

The objective and course of the voyage were in later years described by Sebastian Cabot to several persons, who recorded them with slight variants. In his Decade III, composed in 1515 and printed in 1516, Peter Martyr wrote down what he had been told by Cabot, who had been a guest in his house in Seville; further details were added by the editor (probably Giovanni Battista Ramusio) of the *Summario de la generale historia de l'Indie occidentali* (1534) compiled from Peter Martyr and other sources. In 1520–1 Cabot spoke of his "discovery" to a Venetian agent in England, and in 1522 to Gasparo Contarini, Venetian ambassador in Spain, in terms reported by Contarini in a dispatch dated from Valladolid 31 Dec. 1522. In 1550 Ramusio printed, in his *Navigationi et viaggi*, a garbled account of the voyage supplied by an unnamed "Mantuan gentleman," who

Cabot

claimed to have had it from Cabot's mouth some years earlier. In 1551 Cabot, then in England, was in correspondence with Ramusio, who printed in the *Terzo volume della navigationi et viaggi* (1556), a summary of a letter in which Cabot had described the voyage to him. Finally, during Cabot's later life in England from 1548 and after his death in 1557, various Englishmen, notably Richard Eden (1555), Sir Humphrey GILBERT in *A discourse of a discoverie for a new passage to Cataia* (London, 1576; written in 1566), and Richard Willes in *The history of travayle in the West and East Indies* . . . (London, 1577), made statements about his voyage and discovery of 1508–9 derived from his maps and papers. Other early writers to give details of the voyage, of unknown provenance, are the Spanish chronicler López de Gómara (1552), the Portuguese António Galvão (1563), and the Swiss Urbain Chauveton (1579).

Common to all these sources is the indication that Sebastian Cabot's expedition was directed, in the first instance, to high arctic latitudes, far north of the coasts traversed by his father in 1497. It is an inescapable inference, drawn by Winship in *Cabot bibliography* (1900) and Williamson in *Voyages of the Cabots* (1929), that at some date after 1498 the "intellectual discovery of America" had been made, that Sebastian in 1508 sought a sea passage by the north of the continent, and that he believed himself to have discovered such a passage. Gómara, who may have known Cabot in Spain, makes the positive statement that he intended "to go by the north to Cathay, and to bring thence spices in a shorter time than the Portuguese did by the south," besides ascertaining "what sort of land the Indies were to inhabit," i.e., for settlement.

The two most explicit accounts of the voyage, both of which cite Cabot as their authors' informant, are those of Peter Martyr (1516) and Ramusio (1556); variant details in the other reports must be considered of inferior authority. Peter Martyr: "He equipped two ships at his own cost in Britain, and with three hundred men steered first for the north, until even in the month of July he found great icebergs floating in the sea and almost continuous daylight, yet with the land free by the melting of the ice. Wherefore he was obliged, as he says, to turn and make for the west. And he extended his course furthermore to the southward owing to the curve of the coastline, so that his latitude was almost that of the Straits of Gibraltar and he penetrated so far to the west that he had the island of Cuba on his left hand almost in the same longitude with himself. . . . Those coasts . . . he called the Bacallaos."

Ramusio: "He told me how, having gone on for a long time towards the west and a quarter north along the islands situated by the side of the said land, at the latitude of $67\frac{1}{2}$ degrees under our pole, on the 11th of June, and finding the sea open and without any obstacle, he firmly believed that by that way he could pass towards Eastern Cathay, and he would have done it if the ill-will of the master and sailors, who were mutinous, had not compelled him to turn back." These reports, supplemented by further details given by Gómara, indicate that Sebastian sailed, with two ships (probably equipped at the joint expense of himself, the king, and the merchants) and 300 men (an improbably high figure), from an English port (unnamed), by way of Iceland and southern Greenland to a landfall on the Labrador coast, which he followed north and west to $67\frac{1}{2}°N$ (Gómara, "58 degrees, although he himself says much more"; Galvão, "60 degrees"). Here he found open sea before him, but his crew refused to go on. He then traversed the North American coast south and west to the latitude of Gibraltar (Gómara: "to 38 degrees") before returning to England.

If Sebastian Cabot's account be admitted, he must be held to have passed through Hudson Strait to the mouth of Hudson Bay. He believed himself to have discovered the opening of the northwest passage to Cathay, and the maps drawn by him in later life and described by English writers, notably Willes (1577), showed a broad lead running west from a point between 61° and 64°N for about ten degrees before broadening out, with a southerly trend, into the Pacific. These maps are now lost; but the representation of the passage in the surviving globe of Gemma Frisius, 1537 which according to Willes depicted it in the same way, enables us to visualize Sebastian's concept of the passage, the discovery of which he claimed. The search for a seaway to Cathay was to dominate his subsequent career in Spanish and English service and to furnish motives for some obscure and tortuous transactions in it.

On 1 May 1512 Cabot was paid for making a map of Gascony and Guyenne and in the same month he accompanied the English army sent to Spain for the invasion of France. Whether he hoped to obtain Spanish support for further exploration is a matter for conjecture. It is however significant that in 1511 the Spanish government had projected an expedition "to ascertain the secret of the new land" called "Terra nova" and that soon after his arrival in June 1512 Cabot went to the Spanish court at Burgos and had an interview with colonial officials. On 13 September King Ferdinand instructed the English commander to send Cabot to him; and on 20 October Cabot was appointed a naval captain in the Spanish service. He was given leave to return to England and bring back his family, and he settled at Seville. In 1515 he received the further appointment of "Pilot to his Majesty." Although he had been consulted by the king on matters of discovery in March 1514, and in the following year Peter Martyr wrote of a projected expedition, which was to sail in 1516, "for him to discover this hidden secret of nature," i.e., the western passage, no voyage by him under the Spanish flag at this time is recorded. Ferdinand's death in January 1516 may have stopped the project, and his successor Charles V appointed Cabot on 5 Feb. 1518 to the office of pilot-major in the Casa de la Contratación, in succession to Juan Díaz de Solís.

The abandonment of the Spanish plans for a voyage in 1516 perhaps explains why Cabot kept other strings to his bow and maintained communication with the governments of England and Venice. He may have visited London briefly in 1516, and an abortive English voyage "unto the new found land" in 1517 was said by Richard Eden, in 1553, to have been projected "under the governaunce" of Cabot and Thomas Spert. Better attested is Cabot's association, in the years 1520–21, with the plans formulated by Henry VIII and Cardinal Wolsey for a voyage "towards the Newefound Iland." Cabot (as he told Gasparo Contarini at the end of 1522) was offered by Wolsey "high terms if I would sail with an armada of his on a voyage of discovery." Although, in conversation with Contarini, he professed to have made his acceptance of the offer conditional on the permission of the king of Spain, the English merchant companies invited to invest in the venture were given to understand that he would be the commander. The reluctance of the London companies to subscribe was partly based on this proposal. The Drapers, considering the matter in March 1521 after consultation with the Mercers, suggested the employment of native-born English "maisters & mariners . . . having experience, and excercised in and about the forsaid Iland"; and they thought it too risky to hazard ships and goods "uppon the singuler trust of one man, callyd as we understond, Sebastyan, whiche Sebastyan, as we here say, was never in that land hym self, all if he makes reporte of many things as he hath hard his ffather and other men speke in tymes past." Against the scepticism of the merchants about Cabot's claims as an explorer must be weighed the evident acceptance of these claims by Wolsey, who must have been aware of the voyage of 1508–9 and its results. For reasons not relevant to this issue the project of 1520–21 was abandoned.

To Contarini in 1522 Cabot asserted that he withdrew from the venture, in remorse at forgetting the interests of his "native land" (Venice), after conversation with a Venetian friar in London, to whom he said that he "had the means of rendering Venice a partner in this navigation and of showing her a passage whereby she would obtain great profit; which is the truth for I have discovered it." After returning to Seville Cabot continued this intrigue through a Ragusan intermediary with the Council of Ten in Venice, who instructed Contarini to interview Cabot and, if he thought fit, to invite him to Venice "to explain his project." When Cabot visited Contarini in December 1522, at the latter's request, he was alarmed to discover that his private negotiations were known to the Venetian ambassador, whom he begged "to keep the thing secret, as it would cost me my life"; he declined to reveal his plan to any but the Ten, but offered to go to Venice, with the emperor's permission, "on the plea of recovering his mother's dowry." Correspondence on the arrangements for this proposed visit continued until the end of July 1523. That it was then broken off is probably to be ascribed to the difficulty which Cabot, as pilot-major, would have had in obtaining leave of absence at a time when negotiations between Spain and Portugal on the Moluccas were imminent.

The duties of the pilot-major, as laid down for the first incumbent, Amerigo Vespucci, in 1508, embraced instruction in navigation and in instrument-making, the examination and licensing of pilots, the scrutiny and correction of the official charts, and the compilation of hydrographic information from pilots' journals. The pilot-major was accordingly the principal geographical consultant of the Spanish government in matters concerning overseas navigation. Following the return of the *Vitoria*, the only surviving ship of Magellan's squadron, in 1522, diplomatic exchanges were set on foot regarding the location of the Spice Islands in relation to the eastern extension of the *raya*, or demarcation line agreed in the Treaty of Tordesillas (1494) between Spain and Portugal. On 15 April 1524 Cabot, with two other experts, signed a "Report on the longitude of the Molucca Islands," and on 25 April, with 12 others, a letter to the emperor informing him of the breakdown of the discussions between the Spanish and Portuguese members of the commission or *junta* of pilots.

In 1524 a company of Seville merchants was formed to promote a commercial voyage to the Pacific by way of South America. In September

Cabot

Cabot, who had been appointed to the command, secured the consent of the Council of the Indies and the Crown's support of the expedition by contributions to its cost and equipment. Charles V's interest in the venture appears to have differed from that of its original sponsors and to have been directed to exploration of the South American coasts before "going to the Indies." In the course of 1525, the preparations for the voyage were completed, not without much intrigue reflecting the divergent objectives of its promoters. The fleet comprised 4 ships and about 200 men. Cabot, who retained his office of pilot-major, to be served in his absence by two deputies, and had secured reversion of its supplementary emoluments to his wife, was appointed captain-general, with Martín Méndez as lieutenant-general and Miguel de Rodas as pilot in the *capitana*; the other ships were commanded by Gregorio Caro, Francisco de Rojas, and Miguel Rifos; their companies included the cosmographer Alonso de Santa Cruz and two Englishmen, Roger Barlow and Henry Patiner.

The expedition "for the discovery of Tharsis, Ophir and Eastern Cathay" sailed from Sanlucar de Barrameda on 3 April 1526 south to the Canaries and to the Cape Verde Islands. The SSW course then adopted by Cabot against the advice of the pilots took them into a zone of calms, with adverse winds; they spent over a month crossing to a landfall north of Pernambuco, three months coasting south to Cabo Frio, and another month to Santa Catarina island in 27°S, where the *capitana* ran aground and was lost on 28 October. By now Cabot, from the information of Portuguese settlers and Spanish survivors of earlier expeditions, had decided to explore the Plata region in search of the precious metals in which it was believed to be rich. Méndez, Rojas, Rodas, and other officers who, mindful of the commercial objectives of the expedition, opposed this decision were marooned at Santa Catarina. In February 1527 Cabot's squadron entered the Rio de la Plata and five months were spent exploring the estuary. In August a fort named San Salvador was constructed at the junction of the Rio Uruguay and the Rio San Salvador, and the two larger ships were left there. With the brigantine and a galley built at Santa Catarina, Cabot took an exploring party in search of gold up the Rio Paraná, building the small fort of Sancti Spiritus on the Rio Carcarañá, and then up the Rio Paraguay. After losing 18 men in an ambush he returned to San Salvador, meeting on the way Diego García, leader of a new Spanish expedition to the Plata. Cabot sent one ship back to Spain, to convey his reports and his accusations against the mutineers and to request fresh supplies, and spent the winter of 1528–29 at San Salvador. In the spring he went back upstream to Sancti Spiritus, where, during his temporary absence in the autumn of 1529, the fort was captured and sacked by Indians; Cabot recovered the heavy guns and withdrew to San Salvador where, at a council on 6 Oct. 1529, it was decided to return to Spain. In company with García, Cabot sailed to São Vicente, where Rojas joined García; thence, after purchasing 50 Indian slaves and coasting Brazil, Cabot arrived at Seville on 22 July 1530 with one ship and 24 men.

Between this date and the end of the year he was arraigned on criminal charges brought by the Crown, by Rojas, and by relatives of Méndez and Rodas, both of whom had died. On charges of disobeying instructions, committing arbitrary acts, and causing the death of officers under his command, he was tried by the Council of the Indies and condemned, in May–July 1531, to two years' banishment to Africa and payment of heavy damages; on appeal, the sentence of banishment was, on 1 Feb. 1532, increased to four years. During these proceedings, the emperor was absent in Germany; on his return in the spring of 1532 Cabot presented to him a description of the Plata region, with a proposal for another voyage to "Tharsis, Ophir, Eastern Cathay and Cipangu." While his salary and arrears of pay were attached to pay the damages and costs arising from the lawsuits, Cabot never went into exile; and, although no pardon has been traced, he evidently resumed his duties as pilot-major during 1532. There could hardly be a clearer indication that Charles V was satisfied with the geographical results of the expedition to the Plata (even if it be too much to identify, with J. A. Williamson, the emperor as "the real wrecker of the Spice Islands voyage") and that he expected further useful service from Cabot.

The voyage nonetheless exposed Cabot's weaknesses as a man of action: he had abandoned the grounded *capitana* prematurely; he was guilty of hasty and vindictive, yet ineffectual, reaction to discontent among his subordinates. The charges against his reputation as a navigator are unconvincing and must be held unproven.

On 24 June 1533 Cabot wrote to the secretary of the Council of the Indies about three maps which he had made for the emperor and about a method of determining longitude from magnetic variation. In 1534 the Casa de la Contratación conducted an inquiry into his examination of pilots; that he was vindicated is attested by a royal *cédula* of 11 December instructing him to examine pilots for the Indies. In the following year Cabot gave evidence on the *pleitos* brought against the Crown by the heirs of Columbus; in the course of it he affirmed ignorance whether the lands to the north of the Gulf of Mexico were "a continent or not." On 11 March 1541, in Seville, he signed a contract with two German printers "Lazaro Noremberguer" (Lazaro Aleman or Cromberger) and "Gabriel Miçel" (Gabriel Witzel?) to produce a world map, showing the latest discoveries, which they were to print; this contract seems to have been renewed in 1545, when the map had already been engraved, although no imperial privilege had yet been obtained. The map can almost certainly be identified with the large world map accompanied by 22 printed legends in Spanish and Latin, the 17th of which ascribes it to Sebastian Cabot and to the year 1544; this map, the unique copy of which is in the Bibliothèque nationale, Paris, is the only surviving example of Cabot's cartographic work. That it is copied from the Spanish *padrón real*, or official master-chart, is improbable, and its derivation, in the main, from a world map of the Dieppe school is patent; but references, in the map itself and in the 7th, 8th, and 17th legends, to the voyages of the Cabots may well stem from Sebastian, as do no doubt the instructions for navigation in the 17th legend.

In these years Sebastian Cabot, as pilot-major, was concerned with the revision of the *padrón real* and with problems of chart-construction, on which opinion among the Spanish cosmographers and pilots was divided. This work brought Cabot not infrequently into conflict with other pilots and cosmographers of the Casa de la Contratación and perhaps diminished the emperor's confidence in him. The most controversial issue in which he was involved was the proposal made in 1544 by the cosmographer Diego Gutiérrez to correct the *padrón real* by the introduction of a double graduation for latitude. Cabot supported Gutiérrez and produced reports on the numerous errors of the *padrón*; but the opinion of other cosmographers prevailed, and Cabot was in 1545 forced to acquiesce in the official condemnation of Gutiérrez' proposed reform and to require him to make his charts accord with the *padrón*.

Cabot's views on magnetic variation and its relation to longitude are quoted by several contemporaries. As early as 1522 he described to Contarini a method of "ascertaining by the compass the distance between two places from east to west"; he more than once emphasized the significance of marking in maps the line of no variation as a meridian; and he is reported to have expounded his views to King Edward VI, in England, between 1549 and 1553. A second method proposed by Cabot for finding the longitude, and described by Alonso de Santa Cruz, made use of the declination of the sun, observed with the quadrant.

Cabot seems to have become increasingly dissatisfied with Spanish service, and as early as 1538 he was soliciting employment in England; a memorandum from Sir Thomas Wyatt, ambassador in Spain, quotes him as "desirous, if he might not serve the King [of England], at least to see him, as his old master." What reply came from England is unknown; that Cabot was the "pilot from Seville," recorded in a dispatch from London as being retained there in 1541 by the king, is very doubtful. Six years later, after Henry VIII's death, the English government evidently invited Cabot into its service; on 9 Oct. 1547 the Privy Council issued a warrant for £100 "for the transporting of one Shabot, a pilot, to come out of Hispain." Cabot now made guarded arrangements for his departure: on 6 March 1548 he delegated his duties as pilot-major to Hernando Blas and Diego Gutiérrez, on 11 May he made his will, and on 9 July he was granted five months' leave of absence "to go to Germany." Payments of his salary were authorized by royal *cédulas* of 19 Oct. and 8 Nov. 1548; but by this time Cabot was probably no longer in Spain. On 6 Jan. 1549 King Edward VI granted him an annuity of £166 13*s*. 4*d*., payable from Michaelmas 1548 (perhaps the date of his arrival in England), "in consideration of . . . services done and to be done unto us" by him; and on 11 Sept. 1549 Henry Ostryge took up the £100 warrant "for conducting of Sebastian Sabott."

The Emperor, Charles V, in a dispatch forwarded from Brussels to the Privy Council on 25 Nov. 1549, demanded the return of Cabot, "a verie necessary man for the Emperor whose servant he is [and] hath a pension of him." To this the council replied on 21 April 1550 that "Cabot . . . of himself refused to go either into Spain or to the Emperor, and that he being of that mind and the King's subject, no reason nor equity would that he should be forced to go against his will"; an interview between Cabot and the Spanish ambassador in London was equally unfruitful; and a final request, addressed by the Emperor to Queen Mary on 9 Sept. 1553, to give Cabot leave to come to Spain for consultation was answered by Cabot on 15 Nov. 1554, excusing himself on grounds of ill-health, although (he added) before dying "I want to disclose to Your Majesty the secret which I possess." This was not the only door kept open by Cabot, for in 1551 he had been in correspondence with Venice, offering professional advice and enquiring once more about his patrimony.

Cabot

Hakluyt's statement that Cabot was appointed "Grand Pilot of England" by Edward VI is of doubtful validity. Cabot was certainly consulted in or before 1553 about a plan for an Anglo-French descent on Peru (the "secret" of which he wrote to Charles V); but his principal task was to be that of expert adviser on the English ventures for discovery of a northeast passage. He became governor of the company subsequently known as the Muscovy Company, which was constituted in the spring of 1553; and in this capacity he drew up the instructions, dated 9 May 1553, for the company's first voyage, under Sir Hugh Willoughby and Richard Chancellor. Cabot remained governor after the grant of a new charter to the company in 1555, and he assisted in the preparation of the expedition sent out by the company in 1556 under Stephen Borough. Borough's narrative, printed by Hakluyt, relates that Cabot himself (now aged about 74) came down to Gravesend, went aboard the pinnace, and then, entertaining the ship's company at the inn, "for very joy . . . entred into the dance himselfe amongst the rest of the young and lusty company."

In February 1557 his successor as governor of the company was in office. In March Cabot drew his quarterly pension in person; in May the pension was re-granted to him and to William Worthington jointly, and to the survivor of them; in June and September the pension was drawn on behalf of Cabot; and by December, when payment was made to Worthington alone, "de annuitate sua," Sebastian Cabot must have been dead. No will of his later than that made in Seville on 11 May 1548 has survived.

In 1582 Hakluyt referred to Cabot's "owne Mappes and discourses drawne and written by himself, which are in the custodie of . . . Master William Worthington," and to a proposal (by Hakluyt himself?) to publish them. Unhappily nothing came of this; and the only surviving literary remains of Sebastian Cabot are the Spanish documents printed by Harrisse (1882 and 1896), by Toribio Medina (1908), and by Pulido Rubio (1950), the English documents printed by Hakluyt (1589), and indirect quotations from his conversation and letters preserved by 16th-century writers. Of his maps, only the printed world map of 1544, with its legends, survives in a single copy, although a second copy of the Latin legends, in pamphlet form, also exists. Of the version of this map "sett out" or "cutt" (engraved?) by Clement Adams, apparently in 1549, with variant readings of the legends, copies were seen in various libraries during the 16th and 17th centuries, and described in terms which show that its revision in England, doubtless at Cabot's direction, illustrated his concept of the northwest passage of which he supposed himself to be the discoverer. Copies of his map were still in the royal collection about 1660 and probably perished in the burning of the Palace of Whitehall in 1691 and 1697.

An oil painting of Sebastian Cabot in old age, perhaps identical with one seen by Purchas in the royal collection at Whitehall before 1625, was in the 18th and 19th centuries in the possession, successively, of Lord Errol, of C. J. Harford of Bristol, and of Richard Biddle of Pittsburg, Pa. It was destroyed by fire in 1845; copies made by J. G. Chapman are owned by the Massachusetts and New York historical societies and by the Mayor and Corporation of Bristol. The portrait appears to be an ideal one, executed after Cabot's death.

On Cabot's family only scattered notices survive. That he was married and had offspring in England before 1512, when he entered Spanish service, is attested by his journey to London at the end of that year to bring his wife and family (*su mujer y casa*) to Seville; by a reference in a Spanish document of 14 Sept. 1514, indicating that by this date his wife Juana (Joanna?), of the parish of St. Giles in London, was dead; and by the English record of a legacy to his daughter Elizabeth, on 7 May 1516, from her godfather William Mychell of London. Cabot evidently remarried in Spain; and various official documents, from 25 Aug. 1525, name his wife as Catalina de Medrano. Witnesses in the lawsuits following Cabot's return to Spain in 1530 testified that his wife was a domineering woman who interfered in his affairs; she died on 2 Sept. 1547. A daughter died in 1533; she is unnamed, and it is not known whether she was born in England or Spain. The reference to "sons" of Catalina de Medrano, found in one document only, of 1525, may be merely an official formalism. An English document of 1586 refers to Henry Ostryge, who conveyed Cabot to England in 1548, as his "son-in-law." No descent from Sebastian Cabot can be proved.

R. A. SKELTON

The titles of works here given by author and date only are found under JOHN CABOT. The list is chronological. R. Biddle (1831). H. Harrisse (1882). F. Tarducci (1892). H. Harrisse (1896). C. R. Beazley (1898). G. P. Winship (1900). H. P. Biggar (1903 and 1911). J. Toribio Medina, *El veneciano Sebastián Caboto al servicio de España* (Santiago de Chile, 1908). J. A. Williamson (1929). R. Almagià (1937). José Pulido Rubio, *El piloto mayor de la Casa de la Contratación de Sevilla* (Sevilla, 1950). R. Almagià, *Commemorazione di Sebastiano Caboto nel IV centenario della morte* (Venezia, 1958). J. A. Williamson (1962).

CAËN, ÉMERY DE, captain in the service of the Compagnie de Caën, commandant of Quebec 1624–26 and in 1632–33; son of Ézéchiel de Caën and Marie Sores (Sors or Soré); baptized at Rouen 21 April 1603.

Merchant, *bourgeois*, and shipowner, Ézéchiel de Caën was engaged from the beginning of the 17th century in the American and East Indies trade; in 1613 he was associated with the Compagnie des Marchands de Rouen et de Saint-Malo in the trade with Canada; he took part in an expedition to the Sunda Isles in 1616 and in an expedition to the East Indies in 1619. He was a partner in the commercial enterprise carried on by his nephew GUILLAUME DE CAËN and his son Émery in New France.

In company with his cousin Guillaume de Caën, who had just received the monopoly of the fur trade in New France, Émery de Caën arrived at Quebec in 1621, to succour the colony and at the same time to begin the fur trade. After that he returned each year with the Company's ships. From 1624 to 1626 he was in command at Quebec, in Samuel de CHAMPLAIN's absence. When he came to Canada in 1629 to bring supplies to Quebec and to load on board the furs which Guillaume de Caën had left there, he encountered the KIRKES and was defeated. He reappeared in New France in 1631 to direct the fur trade which belonged that year to Guillaume de Caën, but the English refused him any liberty to carry on trade; on 22 August, on board the *Don-de-Dieu* before Quebec, he drew up a formal protestation and returned to France.

When in 1632 Guillaume de Caën was entrusted by Richelieu with organizing the handing-back of Quebec, Émery de Caën was named commandant of Quebec on 4 March and sent to New France. Accompanied by his lieutenant, DU PLESSIS-BOCHART and the Jesuit PAUL LE JEUNE, he arrived at Quebec and on 29 June he called upon the English to withdraw. They continued their trading, however, to the detriment of the Company; on 6 July Émery de Caën presented his credentials: the English put him off for a week. Finally on 13 July they handed over the fort and left. Émery de Caën then governed the colony from the summer of 1632 till the spring of 1633. On 22 May he handed the keys of the fort over to Du Plessis-Bochart who the next day restored them to Champlain. Émery de Caën then left the country, never again to return.

During his two periods of office as commandant of Quebec, and especially during the second one, Émery de Caën did not deserve the severe condemnation or the scornful judgement which he incurred in certain quarters. The documents reveal a leader who was perfectly in sympathy with the missionaries and the Indians; in 1632 he visited the Jesuits readily. For a long time people wondered whether he was Catholic or Protestant. The investigations carried out by the genealogist Archange Godbout have established that Émery, son of the Catholic Ézéchiel de Caën, was born a Catholic and was a Catholic during his lifetime. It is understandable why Richelieu sent him to New France, whereas the Protestant Guillaume de Caën was set aside.

MARCEL TRUDEL

For the bibliography concerning Émery de Caën, *see* that for GUILLAUME DE CAËN.

CAËN, GUILLAUME DE, nephew of Ézéchiel de Caën [*see* ÉMÉRY DE CAËN], general of the fleet of the Compagnie de Montmorency and of the Compagnie de Ventadour; authorized to trade in furs in New France from 1621 to 1627, and again in 1631 and 1632; Baron of Cap Tourmente in 1624, Baron of the Bahamas in 1640.

Guillaume de Caën the elder was a native of Dieppe who had settled at Rouen. He was an important shipowner, who had been sending ships to Holland and Newfoundland since 1583. On 20 July 1598 he had married Marie Langlois, a business woman whose name is frequently mentioned in the legal proceedings involving the de Caëns, and who still owned three ships in 1628. From this marriage Guillaume was born; he was a Protestant like his parents.

From 1619 on Guillaume de Caën the son was a naval captain; in 1624 he became Baron of Cap-Tourmente, a fief which comprised the cape, the Île d'Orléans, and a few other islands; as early as 1626 he bore the title of Seigneur de La Motte; in 1640 he added to his name the title of Baron of the Bahamas; in 1642 he was Seigneur de La Motte Saint-Lys, and he was styled "major-general and battle-sergeant of the naval forces of His Majesty." In documents he is always called "worthy man," a status attributed to those who did not belong to the nobility. Régis Roy, convinced that de Caën was a noble, and having no proof whatsoever to offer, even supposes that the appellation "de Caën" is a surname: there is nothing to substantiate this argument. In any case, he signed thus.

Since the system had been inaugurated in 1541 on behalf of Jean-François de LA ROCQUE de Roberval, the support and populating of New France had been entrusted to private companies which received in return the monopoly of trade. The preceding company having failed to fulfil its undertakings, Admiral Henri II, Duc de Montmorency, recently appointed viceroy of New

Caën

France, made an agreement on 8 Nov. 1620 with another society, directed by Guillaume de Caën and by his uncle Ézéchiel; on 12 Jan. 1621 the king approved the transfer and on 23 January Montmorency named Guillaume de Caën general of the fleet of the new company. In return for an 11-year monopoly, later extended by four years, the de Caëns undertook to pay the stipends of Montmorency and his lieutenant Samuel de CHAMPLAIN, to put ten men each summer at the latter's disposal, to provide for the upkeep of six Recollets and to settle six families, each numbering at least three persons.

Champlain was ordered to seize the preceding company's merchandise. Feeling most uncomfortable because of the regard which he had for FRANÇOIS GRAVÉ Du Pont, who represented the company at Quebec, Champlain allowed them to continue fur-trading. A fresh decision from France relieved the situation for everybody; for that year, 1621, both companies were authorized to trade concurrently, provided that they contributed equally to the upkeep of the settlement. On 20 March 1622 Louis XIII amalgamated the two companies into one, which from 1 April was called the Compagnie de Montmorency. At its head were the de Caëns: Ézéchiel, Guillaume (still general of the fleet), and Émery. This monopoly, valid in theory until 1636, was based on the same conditions as that of 1621.

This company, called also the Compagnie de Caën, was composed of Roman Catholics and Huguenots; of the three heads, one was Protestant (Guillaume), the two others, Ézéchiel and Émery, were Roman Catholics. It sometimes happened that the crews, formed mostly of Huguenots, clashed over religious matters. As early as 1621, in a petition taken to France by the Recollet LE BAILLIF, the notables of Quebec had asked that the Huguenots be excluded from New France, but Louis XIII had preferred to respect the relative liberty which the Edict of Nantes guaranteed to the Protestants.

Whatever may have been written on the subject, Guillaume de Caën was not personally responsible for these disputes: SAGARD described him as a "polite, liberal and understanding man"; it was through him that the Jesuit CHARLES LALEMANT was enabled in 1626 to study languages with an interpreter who had refused for ten years to impart anything at all to the Recollets; and, speaking of the Jesuits who were with him on the 1626 crossing, the *Relation* states that he treated them courteously. According to Dolu, intendant of the Compagnie de Montmorency, "there were hopes that de Caën might become a Catholic." It is true that the Jesuits were not received in 1625 in the way that they had expected, but nothing had been planned for them and Guillaume de Caën had assumed responsibility only for the Recollets. Moreover, the Jesuit Lalemant's letter is not bitter: "Monsieur the General, after having told us that it was impossible to give us lodging either in the settlement or in the fort, and that we must either return to France, or withdraw to the Recollet Fathers', obliged us to accept the latter offer"; thus the Jesuits became indirectly de Caën's responsibility, since it was he who provided for the needs of the Recollets. There is also the dispute between de Caën and the Jesuit NOYROT at Honfleur in 1627, but religion was not the cause of it. Various accusations have been laid against Guillaume de Caën: he defended himself to the satisfaction of the authorities, and a close examination of the documentary evidence reveals that his conduct was in no sense that of a fanatical Huguenot; Recollets and Jesuits are united in their praise of him. Being intimately associated with Roman Catholics (his uncle Ézéchiel and his cousin Émery), Guillaume de Caën could hardly attack the Catholics as such.

The Huguenots were moreover gradually being ousted: Richelieu entered the Conseil d'État in 1624; in January 1626 the Compagnie de Caën was required to nominate two Catholic captains for its fleet, of whom one would be appointed to navigate the ships; Guillaume de Caën, who still held the monopoly, had no longer the right to proceed in person to New France. The following October Richelieu became grand master and superintendent of navigation; in January 1627 he suppressed the office of admiral, and three months later he revoked the Edict of Nantes as applied to New France and founded the Compagnie des Cent-Associés, which he started upon a programme of intensive colonization, exclusively Catholic in character. It meant the end of the Compagnie de Caën.

This company now had to be liquidated. Champlain was ordered to draw up the inventory of possessions; in 1628 the de Caëns were forbidden, "under pain of death," to send ships and merchandise to New France, but their clerks were permitted that year to trade certain goods which they still had in the St. Lawrence valley. In 1629, on pretext of coming to the colony's assistance, but in reality to go and get 50,000 *écus* worth of pelts which he had at Quebec, Guillaume de Caën vainly sought permission to proceed to New France. While involved in lawsuits against the Cent-Associés and against the former Compagnie des Marchands de Rouen et de Saint-Malo, Guillaume de Caën learned in the autumn of 1629 that the KIRKES had carried off to England

Caën

some furs which he had had at Quebec; he went to London at the beginning of 1630 with Jacques Couillard de Lespinay, and on 9 April the Privy Council granted his request for the return of his furs. But despite the notices served upon the Kirkes, first the keys of the warehouse could not be found, then it was ascertained that a considerable proportion of the furs had disappeared. De Caën now claimed 266,000 *livres*; the English courts declared partially in his favour, but eight years later the judgement had still not been enforced, and de Caën was still proceeding against the Kirkes.

In 1631 Guillaume de Caën once more obtained the monopoly of fur-trading in the St. Lawrence, but the English cornered all the furs, despite Émery de Caën's protests. In 1632 Richelieu instructed Guillaume de Caën to arrange for the reoccupation of Quebec: de Caën was given a ship, 10,000 *livres* and the monopoly of the fur trade for that year, on condition that he did not go there himself and that those who wintered at Quebec were Roman Catholics; his cousin Émery was named commandant. Émery made his appearance in the St. Lawrence, but the English played for time, so as to make sure of the spring fur trade; in addition Émery found the Habitation burned down, with the loss of the 9,000 beaver skins that belonged to de Caën. The latter complained to Richelieu, who replied: "With time you will find ways to make good your losses, which for myself I earnestly desire to see."

De Caën worked hard to have himself reimbursed. He sued the Compagnie des Cent-Associés, from which he received at last, in 1643, a compensation of 350,000 *livres*, a sum equal to a capital amount of 150,000 *livres*, plus interest. Furthermore, because he had prematurely lost his monopoly and his barony of Cap Tourmente, Richelieu granted him in January 1633 the ownership of five small islands in the Antilles not previously occupied by Europeans. This gift was confirmed in 1640, when de Caën took the title of Baron of the Bahamas. In 1642, we find him once more very busy making claims: he served a writ on the Kirkes for the 137,000 *livres* which were owing to him; he had a Turkish ship sold by auction to compensate himself for 22,000 *écus* which he had lost to Algerian privateers; he obtained judgement against a certain Le Faucheur for a sum of 30,000 *livres*. From this point we lose sight of him. He had married Suzanne Petit about 1625, and had had at least two children by her, Hélène and Marie.

Canadian history has recorded that Guillaume de Caën, authorized to trade in furs in New France and responsible for the business of that country, did not concern himself with colonization. Champlain, the viceroy's lieutenant, dreamed of a true new France, with regular institutions and a stable population, and the full exploitation of the country's resources. But the population of the colony diminished instead of increasing. The commandant of Quebec found it hard to muster the ten men promised by the company for completing the Habitation and for working on the fort. In 1627 HÉLÈNE BOULLÉ was even reduced to taking legal action against de Caën to make him pay Champlain his emoluments. "Provided that the fur trade is carried on, that is all they want," wrote Champlain.

Guillaume de Caën saw in New France nothing more than a base for the fur trade; and the fur trade could produce a handsome yield: in 1628 it showed a profit of 100,000 *livres*. But the risk was high; they had to struggle unremittingly against smuggling, particularly smuggling by the men from La Rochelle, who rushed across the ice in early spring to carry off the furs. Besides this, the requirements of France, ridiculously slight from the point of view of colonization, show clearly that before 1627 French officialdom gave no serious thought to it: it is not by settling six families that one populates a country! These factors have to be taken into account before Guillaume de Caën is condemned. There are achievements to his credit: it was at the expense of his company that the Habitation was completed, that the fort was constructed (even if de Caën was at first opposed to it) and supplied with arms; he provided for the needs of the Recollets; he brought cattle and had a farm built at Cap Tourmente; while he was in charge three important fiefs were granted (Sault-au-Matelot, Lespinay, and Notre-Dame-des-Anges); he erected a small fort on the Île Miscou. The record is meagre, but that of the Compagnie des Cent-Associés, for all its extensive resources, did not prove to be very much more impressive. In any case, it is with de Caën that the history of the small commercial companies responsible for colonization comes to an end, and de Caën is also the last Protestant to hold the monopoly of the fur trade in New France.

MARCEL TRUDEL

The relevant sources are numerous but scattered. A large number of documents are in the following collections: AE, Mém. et doc., Amérique, 4, ff.119f. AN, Col., C^{11A}, 2; F^3, 3; E, 63, 86, 87a–b, 88a, 95a–b, 111, 117, 126, 167c; G^7, carton 1312, no. 194; V^6, cartons 59, 60, 62; Série Z^{1d} (for the de Caën lawsuit of 1626 to 1651, liasse 105 in particular). Two sources in BN are worthy of note; MS Fr. 8028 and 16738, ff.132, 143, 148; MS, NAF 9269 (Margry). Documents relating

Calvert

to the activities of de Caën in London 1630–33 have been published in Champlain, *Œuvres* (Laverdière), 990–1015. Documents for 1630 and 1631 have been published by Joseph Le Ber, in his "Documents inédits," *RHAF*, III (1949–50), 587–94. The documents of 1630–31, reproduced in this article, are accompanied by a study by Le Ber, and, particularly important, by a long note, p. 592, in which the genealogist, A. Godbout, proves, on the basis of the Rouen archives, that Émery de Caën was a Roman Catholic by birth and that he was the son of Ézéchiel. PRO, *Acts of the P.C., col. ser., 1613–80* [pp. xxxi–iv, 139–56, *et passim*] contains negotiations regarding the disposal of furs captured by the English; *CSP, Col., 1574–1660* [*see* Decaen].

Champlain, *Works* (Biggar). Ducreux, *History* (Robinson and Conacher) (the author states, I, 134, that Guillaume de Caën was named commandant of Quebec in 1632, when actually it was Émery, and the editors have failed to correct this error in a note). *JR* (Thwaites), IV, 170, 204–6, 210, 256–58, 267; V, 41–43, 59–70, 159, 202, 209, 275, 283; VI, 73; VIII, 288 (the editor, in both his notes and his index, confuses Émery with Guillaume). Lescarbot, *History* (Grant) (the editors, in II, 26, n.1, repeat the error of an English writer, Josselyn, who in 1672 explained that the name "Canada" was derived from that of De Caën, pronounced "Cane"). P.-G. Roy, *Inv. concessions*. Sagard, *Histoire du Canada* (Tross), I, 95.

The following studies have been selected from those published to date: E. R. Adair, "France and the beginnings of New France," *CHR*, XXV (1944), 246–78. Biggar, *Early trading companies*, 115–32, 147, 150, 152, 154ff., 158, 160, 163, 165. Bréard, *Documents relatifs à la marine normande*, 125, 131–34, 216–26. Dionne, *Champlain*, II, 75, n.1, 73–87, 261–70. É.-H. Gosselin, *Nouvelles glanes historiques normandes*, 47–50. La Roncière, *Histoire de la marine française*, IV, 296–306, 334–37, 658f. Régis Roy, "Guillaume de Caën," *BRH*, XXXII (1926), 531f.

CALVERT, SIR GEORGE, 1st Baron Baltimore, colonizer in Newfoundland; b. at Kipling, Yorkshire, *c*. 1580 the son of Leonard Calvert and his wife Alice, daughter of John Crosland of Crosland; d. 15 April 1632 in England.

George Calvert was educated at Trinity College, Oxford, and, in 1606, was appointed private secretary to Sir Robert Cecil. Advancing rapidly in the public service, he became clerk of the Privy Council in 1608 and was elected M.P. for Bossiney in 1609. Knighted in 1617, two years later he was made secretary of state and a member of the Privy Council. One of the leaders of the court party, he proved an effective exponent of the royal policy in Parliament until his conversion to Roman Catholicism in 1625 led to his resignation as secretary of state. On his retirement from politics he was created Baron Baltimore of county Longford, Ireland, as a reward for his loyalty to the king.

He now had leisure to devote to the colony in Newfoundland which he had acquired from William VAUGHAN. Four years earlier, in 1621, he had despatched Capt. Edward WYNNE with 12 men to establish a small settlement there at Ferryland, about 50 miles south of St. John's. This struggling colony was strengthened in the following year by the arrival of a second group of settlers, 22 in number, under the command of another of Calvert's agents, Capt. Daniel Powell. Encouraged by glowing reports from Wynne and Powell exaggerating the progress of the settlement, Calvert on 7 April 1623 procured a royal charter for his plantation, officially styled "the province of Avalon," a name, according to Lloyd in his *State Worthies*, adopted "in imitation of old Avalon in Somersetshire, where Glastonbury stands, the first-fruits of christianity in Britain, as the other was in that part of America."

Two years later, Calvert made plans to visit Avalon but was prevented from doing so because the ship *Jonathan* on which he intended to sail was requisitioned for the king's service. By 1627, however, Baltimore had come to realize that inefficient management by his two local agents was ruining his plantation and that only his personal presence and direction could save it from failure. He arrived in Avalon in July and, although his stay was short, it was long enough, apparently, to convince him of the urgent need to give close attention to his Newfoundland interests. He returned there in 1628, evidently prepared to settle permanently as he brought with him his wife and all his children except his eldest son. (This was his second wife, Jane, whom he had married after the death in 1622 of his first wife Anne, daughter of George Mynne of Hurlingfordbury, Herts., who had borne him six sons and five daughters.) He lived in considerable style, taking up residence in a substantial stone mansion, of which, in later years, Sir DAVID KIRKE was to be another distinguished occupant.

England and France were at war in 1628—the year of Buckingham's ill-fated expedition to the Isle of Rhé—and much of Baltimore's energies, during his stay at Ferryland from the spring of 1628 to the fall of 1629, was occupied in repulsing the French privateers that were preying upon English fishing vessels in the harbours of Avalon. Shortly after Baltimore's arrival at Ferryland, "de la Rade, of Dieppe" (probably Raymond de La RALDE), with three French ships, attacked the nearby harbour of Cape Broyle, capturing two English fishing craft in the port. Baltimore immediately ordered two men-of-war to the scene, rescued the two English vessels, and forced La Rade to flee northward leaving behind 67 members of his crew as prisoners. Baltimore's ships set off in hot pursuit but, being outdistanced by the French, had to abandon the chase. In retaliation, Baltimore descended on six French fishing craft which had put in at Trepassey, some 50 miles south of Ferryland, captured them all and sent them to England as prizes together with their cargoes of codfish and cod oil. The prizes, incidentally were the cause of a dispute between himself and the English merchants whose ships had assisted in the seizure, a dispute in which Baltimore with characteristic shrewdness sought to strengthen his case by having his letters of marque antedated. Profiting from his experience of French raids, Baltimore requested Charles I to despatch two warships to guard the coast of Avalon; only one ship, however, the *St. Claude*, was sent out, under the command of Leonard Calvert (1606–47), Baltimore's second son, who later acted as the first governor of Maryland for his brother Cecil Calvert, the first proprietor.

Baltimore was plagued also by the opposition of some of the colonists to his policy of religious toleration. They resented the presence of the Roman Catholic priests whom he had brought out from England. The leader of the malcontents, Erasmus STOURTON, a puritan clergyman, was banished by Baltimore for attempting to prevent the illegal celebration of mass in the colony. On his return to England, Stourton promptly denounced Baltimore to the authorities, but, apparently, without effect.

French raids, sectarian bickerings, and, above all, the severity of the winter climate decided Baltimore to abandon his infant colony. On 19 Aug. 1629, he wrote to the king from Ferryland, complaining that the winter lasted from October to May, that half his company of 100 were sick and that 10 of them were dead. He went on to petition Charles for a grant of land in Virginia, to which he could transfer some 40 of his settlers from Avalon. Without waiting for a reply to this appeal, he left for Virginia, whither his wife had preceded him in the fall of 1628. At Jamestown he was confronted with a requirement that he take the oaths of allegiance and supremacy as a condition of establishing himself there and so he returned to England. In 1632, he was given the territory north of the Potomac River which became the province of Maryland, but he died before receiving the charter for Maryland which was granted to his son, Cecil.

The Calvert family continued its interest in Newfoundland for several years. Cecil Calvert appointed William HILL as his deputy governor of Ferryland in 1634 and strongly protested the grant of Ferryland to Sir David Kirke in 1637. Following the Restoration he succeeded in securing recognition of the validity of his father's Avalon charter of 1623.

Genuinely interested in colonization, Baltimore lacked the determination needed to triumph over the privations of the pioneer. Too easily discouraged by adversity, he had no lasting influence on the history of Newfoundland.

ALLAN M. FRASER

For the land purchased from Vaughan see John Mason's map in William Vaughan, *Cabrensium Caroleia* (London, 1625; another issue, 1630); the enlargement by royal charter in 1623 is in PRO, C.O. 1/2, 23. Baltimore's will is in Somerset House, P.C.C. 39 Audley. Other contemporary sources are: PRO, C.O.1/4, 1/5; *CSP, Col., 1574–1660*. William Vaughan [Orpheus Junior, *pseud.*], *The golden fleece* (London, 1626); *The Newlanders cure* (London, 1630). Richard Whitbourne, *A discourse containing a loving invitation . . .* (London, 1622). Edward Winne [Wynne], *A letter to Sir George Calvert* ([London?], 1621).

DAB. DNB. J. P. Kennedy, *Discourse on the life and character of Sir G. Calvert* (Baltimore, 1845). Prowse, *History of Nfld.* L. D. Scisco, "Calvert's proceedings against Kirke," *CHR*, VIII (1927), 132–36.

CAPITANAL (Kepitanal, Kepitenat), Montagnais chief, orator, friend of the French; fl. 1615–34.

Capitanal's father, a friend of CHAMPLAIN, was killed in the battle (1615) against the Iroquois in which Champlain himself was wounded. Capitanal was only a child when his father died; but with the passing of the years he heard the old men of his nation narrate how Champlain first came to their country and how the Montagnais endeavoured to persuade him to live with them.

Capitanal and a number of Montagnais from the direction of Trois-Rivières arrived at Quebec on 24 May 1633 in 18 canoes, only a few days after Champlain's return following the English occupation of New France [*see* KIRKE]. He had been absent for almost four years. Champlain, on his voyage up-river, had seen three English vessels at Tadoussac, which had received permission to trade in the St. Lawrence. Fearing that the Montagnais would continue down the St. Lawrence to barter with the English, Champlain addressed the Indians through Olivier LETARDIF, the interpreter, recalling the former friendship that had existed between the Montagnais and the French; how the father of Capitanal fought and was killed at Champlain's side; how he, Champlain, had returned to see them again; and further, how the Montagnais, despite their earlier good relations with the French, now intended to trade

Carbonariis

with the English at Tadoussac instead of remaining at Quebec to deal with their friends and allies. When Champlain ended his address, Capitanal replied with modesty and dignity, and "with a keenness and delicacy of rhetoric that might have come out of the Schools of Aristotle or Cicero," assuring Champlain that he and the other Indians had heard the old men speak in favour of the French, that he would instruct the members of his group not to approach the English at Tadoussac, and that the French missionaries would be welcome among his people.

During the autumn of the next year (1634) Capitanal died. He was survived by his wife and three children, a boy of about 17 and two little girls. Before dying, Capitanal charged the principal men of his nation to preserve the good understanding with the French which he had established. As a proof of his love for the French, he had himself carried to the new settlement of Trois-Rivières to be buried near his friends. He also requested that he be borne to his grave by Frenchmen for whom he designated a present. Capitanal's wishes were granted, as Champlain caused an enclosure to be placed around the grave. The Jesuit, Father PAUL LE JEUNE, considered Capitanal to be a man of good sense and a firm friend of the French.

THOMAS GRASSMANN

Du Creux, *History* (Conacher), I, 145–47. *JR* (Thwaites), V, 203–5, 207, 209–11, VIII, 55, 253.

CARBONARIIS, GIOVANNI ANTONIO DE, Italian priest, probably sailed with JOHN CABOT's expedition, 1498; fl. 1489–98.

Carbonariis appears to have been involved in the complex diplomatic relationships between the Italian states, the papacy, France, Spain, and England—the background against which the Cabot voyages took place. Apparently a man of note, Carbonariis spent some time in England, as an envoy or agent of the dukes of Milan. In 1489, Henry VII of England sent him as a royal messenger to Gian Galeazza Sforza, and in 1497, Ludovico Sforza's envoy in England, Raimondo de Soncino, speaks of Carbonariis as "the Reverend Master" whose advice he would take while in England.

Prior to the sailing of Cabot's 1498 expedition, the duke sent a letter to Carbonariis in England, which Agostino de Spinula—in a letter from London, dated 20 June 1498—said he would keep until Carbonariis's return: he had "left recently with five ships, which his Majesty sent to discover new islands." Carbonariis may have sailed on the London ship victualled at the king's expense by Lancelot THIRKILL and Thomas BRADLEY, and not on one of the two Bristol ships immediately under John Cabot's command. Nothing further is known about Carbonariis, although he may well have returned to England.

THOMAS DUNBABIN

PRO, *CSP, Milan* [1385–1618], 250–1, 321, 344, 348. Williamson, *Voyages of the Cabots* (1929), 38–39, 181; *Cabot's voyages* (1962).

CARIGOUAN (Carigonan), renowned Montagnais medicine-man, hostile to the French; d. 1634.

Carigouan was one of the band with whom the Jesuit, PAUL LE JEUNE, spent the winter of 1633–34, sharing their nomadic life in the mountains and valleys that lie to the south of the lower St. Lawrence. Carigouan's brother Mestigoït, a brave hunter of good disposition, was his host. Carigouan had two other brothers over whom he had great influence, PASTEDECHOUAN and Sasousmat.

Carigouan, then the most famous of Montagnais medicine-men, was held in awe by his people who obeyed him implicitly in performing the rites and ceremonies demanded by him, even in the night hours or cold weather.

Father Le Jeune witnessed and described their feasts, dances, prayers, and death-rites, including feasts of the Bear and of the "Leg of the Manitou," when a crooked leather sack filled with beaver hair was hung where Carigouan was seated. Le Jeune observed tent-shaking rituals, and he saw Carigouan "kill," by rite, a sorcerer in Gaspé over 100 leagues distant. At times Carigouan withdrew alone to a cabin a short distance from the settlement, for eight or ten days, crying, shouting, and beating his drum.

Le Jeune related conversations with Carigouan and his followers concerning the creation; the nature of the universe and all that inhabits it, which they believed was restored by Messou after a general destruction by flood; the nature of the "genii" who were acquainted with events in the future, and who were called upon in the tent-shaking ritual; the souls of men and animals (the souls being shadows with physical attributes, therefore they must eat, sleep, drink, and hunt); and the village of departed souls. He describes dreams, songs, dances, drums, sweat-baths, and the curing of sickness.

Carigouan remained hostile to the priest who described him as "vile to the last degree." He made heavy demands for presents, especially of tobacco, and he bitterly resented Le Jeune's attempts to discredit him. "This was like tearing his soul out of his body," Le Jeune wrote. Carigouan had a natural aversion to the French. He retarded Le

Jeune's study of the language, he blasphemed in his presence, and he continually led his followers in sneers and derision against the father, often threatening him with death. Only at Christmas, in a period of great want, did he join in prayers.

The following winter, 1634–35, Carigouan was burned alive when his cabin was set on fire by one of his own people to relieve himself of the burden of the then sick medicine-man. At his death, his son was brought to Le Jeune and baptized in 1636.

ELSIE MCLEOD JURY

JR (Thwaites) *passim.*

CARTIER, JACQUES, navigator of Saint-Malo, first explorer of the Gulf of St. Lawrence in 1534, discoverer of the St. Lawrence River in 1535, commander of the settlement of Charlesbourg-Royal in 1541–42; b. probably some time between 7 June and 23 Dec. 1491 at Saint-Malo (Brittany), where he died in 1557.

Cartier had no doubt been going to sea since his youth, but nothing is known of his career before 1532. According to Lanctot, Cartier may have taken part in VERRAZZANO's expeditions in 1524 and 1528. Cartier's absences from France which coincide with the voyages of the celebrated Florentine, the objective assigned to Cartier in 1534, his point of arrival in Newfoundland which corresponds to the final point reached on the 1524 voyage, a Danish map of 1605, and a statement of the Jesuit Pierre BIARD in his Relation for the year 1614—from all these Lanctot concludes that Cartier sailed along the North American coast in 1524. He further states that Cartier, after Verrazzano's death, took command of the ship to return to France.

Several objections militate against this theory: if Cartier was absent from Saint-Malo during Verrazzano's voyages, he could easily have been elsewhere than on the *Dauphine*; moreover the expedition set out from Normandy, and one can hardly imagine a Breton joining forces, at that time, with the shipowners of Dieppe. Why does Cartier, in the accounts of his travels, never allude to Verrazzano or to the coast visited in 1524? When he compares the natives or the produce of Canada with those of Brazil, why does he never mention those of the North American seaboard? If Cartier had an important post on board the *Dauphine*, why does his name not appear in the Verrazzanian toponymy which recalls so many of the people associated with the Florentine? Finally, why do the French maps which rely upon Cartier for the valley of the St. Lawrence reject the Verrazzanian toponymy and utilize systematically the Spanish one? Lanctot's thesis is interesting, although it remains unproven and adds nothing certain to our knowledge of Cartier.

When in 1532 Jean Le Veneur, bishop of Saint-Malo and abbot of Mont-Saint-Michel, suggested to François I that an expedition be sent to the New World, he asserted that Cartier had already been to Brazil and to "Newfoundland." In fact Cartier's accounts do include several allusions to Brazil which are not merely recollections of things read; as for Newfoundland, Cartier knew the surrounding regions: a month before his departure he was aware that he was expected to reach the "Baie des Châteaux" (Strait of Belle-Isle), and he went directly there as if it were a familiar stopping-place.

The commission granted to Cartier in 1534 has not been located, but an order from the king, in March of the same year, enlightens us as to the objective of the voyage: "to discover certain islands and lands where it is said that a great quantity of gold, and other precious things, are to be found." The 1534 account suggests a second objective: the route to Asia. To those who credit Cartier, on this first voyage, with a concern for missionary work, Lionel Groulx's answer is: "Gold, the gateway to Cathay! If there is a *mystique* in all this, to use a word which is so debased today, it is a *mystique* of merchants, behind which looms a political rivalry." The 1534 account mentions no priest engaged in evangelization among the natives; it would moreover have been useless, because of the linguistic barrier. Although the ship's muster-roll has not been found, one may surmise that at least one priest was on board; when Bishop Le Veneur had proposed Cartier he had undertaken to supply the chaplains, and the account of the voyage alludes to the singing of mass.

Cartier set off from Saint-Malo on 20 April 1534, with 2 ships and 61 men. Favoured by "good weather," he crossed the Atlantic in 20 days. He visited places already known and named, from the cape of "Bonne Viste" to the Baie des Châteaux; then he entered the bay which had been set as the first stage in his journey. Ten leagues away, in the interior, was the port of Brest, a depot for supplying the codfishermen with water and wood. One hundred miles to the west of Belle-Isle, Cartier encountered a ship from La Rochelle; he directed it back on to its course. Cartier was not yet in a totally unknown world, but he freely assigned names to the geographical features of the north coast: Île Sainte-Catherine; Toutes-Isles; Havre Saint-Antoine; Havre Saint-Servan where he set up his first cross; Rivière Saint-Jacques; Havre Jacques-Cartier. For the land which he saw he had the utmost contempt:

Cartier

"along the whole of the north shore, I did not see one cart-load of earth," it was "the land God gave to Cain." On 15 June he steered "towards the south" and entered unexplored regions. He went along the west coast of Newfoundland, distributing French names, and reached what is today Cabot Strait, but he did not perceive that it was a navigable channel and turned westward.

He came across islands which appeared fertile to him by comparison with Newfoundland, among them Île Brion where he perhaps set up another cross, and on 26 June he reached the Îles de la Madeleine, which he assumed to be the beginning of the mainland. On the evening of 29 June he sighted another land, "the best-tempered region one can possibly see, and the heat is considerable"; he had discovered Prince Edward Island, without however being able to determine that it was an island.

Next, he explored bays that were disappointing, openings that held continual promise of being the passage to Asia, but which grew narrower as he advanced. To the southern tip of the "baye de Chaleurs" he gave the name of Cap d'Espérance, "for the hope we had of finding here a strait." From 4 to 9 July he made a systematic investigation, only to conclude that no passage existed, "whereat we were grieved and displeased." On 14 July he entered the Baie de Gaspé (which remained unnamed in 1534). He stayed there for a considerable time, until 25 July, which permitted him to establish some very important contacts with the Indians.

They were not the first natives whom he had encountered. On 12 or 13 June he had seen Indians in the "land of Cain"; they had come from inland to hunt the seal, and they have been identified by some as Beothuks, who are now extinct. At the beginning of July he had seen others on the Prince Edward Island coast, and on 7 July, in the Baie des Chaleurs, he had traded in furs with natives, probably Micmacs. Those whom he met at Gaspé were Laurentian Iroquois, who had come down in great numbers for their annual fishing. This nation was master of the St. Lawrence and was to assume historical importance. The Iroquois gleefully accepted small gifts, and an alliance was concluded, with dancing and jubilation. On 24 July Cartier erected a cross 30 ft. high, bearing the arms of France, at Penouille Point. If the crosses at Saint-Servan and on Île Brion were rather in the nature of landmarks or beacons, this one was much more: it is clear from the importance of the ceremony that the cross was intended to indicate that the territory was being taken possession of in the name of François I. Chief DONNACONA protested; he approached Cartier's boat with his brother and three of his sons to harangue the strangers. A pretence was made of offering him an axe. As he was about to take it, the French held on to his craft and forced the Iroquois to come on board the ship. Cartier reassured them and obtained permission to take away with him two of Donnacona's sons, Domagaya and Taignoagny, promising to bring them back. There was feasting, followed by a most cordial leave-taking. Cartier left the Baie de Gaspé on 25 July with these two Indians, who would be able one day to act as interpreters.

He could have turned westward, but he turned eastward, thinking that the strait 40 miles wide between the Gaspé Peninsula and Anticosti was nothing more than "the coast [which] ran back forming a bay, in the shape of a semi-circle." Cartier therefore missed discovering a river which would have taken him a long way into the interior of the continent. Until 29 July he sailed along the coast of Anticosti Island, and then around it; he took it for a peninsula. From 1 to 5 August he tried to find out whether he was in a bay or a waterway, and he finally realized that "the coast began to turn off towards the south-west." Once again he had all but discovered the river, but bad weather intervened, and Cartier decided to withdraw. After meeting some Montagnais at Natashquan point, he set his course straight for Newfoundland, and on 15 August started on the trip home.

Cartier had been the first to go right round the gulf. Perhaps JOHN CABOT, the CORTE-REALS, and João Alvares FAGUNDES had seen it before him, but no document offers any proof. Cartier discovered the gulf, he drew a map of it, and he had caught a glimpse of the hinterland. True, his geographical knowledge was limited; he did not notice the passage between Newfoundland and Cape Breton, he thought the Îles de la Madeleine were the mainland, he did not discover the entry to the river. For Cartier, this sea possessed only one certain outlet, the Strait of Belle-Isle, and another possible one, to the north of Anticosti, which he did not have time to investigate.

The discovery of an inland sea, the exploration of a new country, an alliance with natives from the west, the immediate possibility of penetrating deeper, the assistance of two Indians who were learning to express themselves in French, all this made a second expedition worth while, even if Cartier had so far found neither gold nor metals. He was back in Saint-Malo on 5 Sept. 1534, and as early as 30 October he received a new commission to complete his discovery, François I paying 3,000 *livres* towards the undertaking.

In 1534 Cartier had had only 2 ships and 61

men; in 1535 he had 3 ships and a crew of some 110 men. On board the *Grande Hermine*, Cartier had the shipmaster Thomas Fromont as his assistant; he took with him Claude de Pontbriand (son of a Seigneur de Montréal, in Languedoc), Charles de La Pommeraye, Jehan Poullet, thought to be the author of the account of the second voyage, and a few gentlemen. Guillaume Le Marié sailed the *Petite Hermine* under the command of Macé JALOBERT; the captain of the *Émérillon* was Guillaume Le Breton Bastille and the navigator Jacques Maingart. The undertaking had brought together numerous relatives of Cartier and of his wife Catherine Des Granches: Étienne Noël, a nephew; Macé Jalobert, a brother-in-law; Antoine Des Granches, Jacques Maingart, and three other Maingarts; Michel Audiepvre; Michel Philipot; Guillaume et Antoine Aliecte and Jacques Du Bog. Were there any chaplains? The ship's muster-roll mentions dom Guillaume Le Breton, and dom Anthoine immediately following. The word "dom" was at that time applied only to secular priests, unless it is here the abbreviation for "Dominique." Religious ceremonies were indeed performed on this voyage, but when Donnacona and his people asked for baptism (at a moment which it is difficult to specify), Cartier replied that he expected to bring priests with him on another voyage. Perhaps dom Le Breton and dom Anthoine were already dead? It is quite natural that chaplains should have accompanied such a large expedition, but no real proof of their presence can be found anywhere. Domagaya and Taignoagny were on the voyage also. During their eight and a half months' stay in France they had learned French, but had not yet been baptized.

Cartier left Saint-Malo 19 May 1535 and reached the gulf once more after a long, 50-day crossing. He immediately resumed his quest, sailing along the north coast. To mark his route he set up a cross in a harbour to the west of Natashquan. He stopped in a bay which he called Saint-Laurent (now Sainte-Geneviève); the name was soon to be extended to the gulf, and then to the river. Finally, on 13 August, following the instructions of his two native guides, he passed the crucial point. There before him was the whole geography of the region: the Indians showed him "the way to the mouth of the great river of Hochelaga and the route towards Canada," which narrowed continually as one went on; its waters, first salt then fresh, came from so great a distance that there was no record of any man ever having seen their source. Here at last, concluded Cartier, was the passage he was seeking.

He went up the river, examining the two shores as he advanced. He perceived on his right a "very deep and rapid" river which his guides told him was the route to the Saguenay, a kingdom where there was copper, and about which Donnacona was to tell wonderful tales. On 7 September Cartier reached the archipelago of Orléans, which was "where the province and territory of Canada begins," the name Canada being applied then only to what is now Quebec. After feasting with Donnacona, Cartier decided to lay up his ships in the river Sainte-Croix (Saint-Charles), at the mouth of the stream called Lairet. Opposite rose the cape of Stadacona, where there was a village which was probably unfortified, after the Montagnais fashion, although it was inhabited by Iroquois.

Cartier was eager to get to Hochelaga, but the two native interpreters had already begun to scheme against the French. There was also some anxiety at Stadacona about this trip. Donnacona wanted to secure for himself the monopoly of the trade which would develop, since he hoped to escape from the domination exercised by Hochelaga over the Iroquois of the valley. He tried to detain Cartier by gifts, then by a display of witchcraft. Cartier, however, set out on 19 September on the *Émérillon*, but without interpreters, which greatly lessened the usefulness of his trip. He stopped at Achelacy (in the region of Portneuf), and formed an alliance with the local chieftain. He reached the lake which he called "Angoulême" (Saint-Pierre), left his ship at anchor, and went on in long-boats with some 30 men. On 2 October he arrived at Hochelaga, a town enclosed and fortified after the Iroquois style, near a mountain which he named Mont-Royal. He was given a joyous reception which even took on the air of a religious ceremony; to the Iroquois, who presented their sick to be cured, Cartier read the gospel according to St. John and the Passion of Christ. Without delaying further, he visited the rapids which blocked navigation to the west. The Indians explained to him by signs that other rapids obstructed the river and that a watercourse, by which one could reach the gold, silver, and copper of the Saguenay, flowed into the river from the north. But Cartier did not pursue his investigation; he left Hochelaga the next day, 3 October. On 7 October he stopped at the mouth of the "rivière de Fouez" (Saint-Maurice), and set up a cross there.

When Cartier returned to Stadacona, he found his men building a fort. The natives feigned joy on seeing him again, but their friendliness had vanished; new intrigues by the interpreters soon brought about a complete rupture. Relations were resumed only in November, in an atmosphere of mutual distrust.

Cartier

Then came winter, the Laurentian winter which the Europeans were experiencing for the first time, and which furthermore was a severe one. From mid-November to mid-April the ships were ice-bound. The snow reached a height of four feet and more. The river froze as far as Hochelaga. Still more terrible than the winter was scurvy, which appeared among the natives of Stadacona in December; despite an attempt to set up a sanitary barrier against it, it attacked the French. By mid-February not more than 10 of Cartier's 110 men were still well; 8 were dead, including the young Philippe Rougemont, on whom an autopsy was made. And the evil continued its ravages; 25 persons, all told, eventually died. Cartier and his men went in a procession to pray before an image of the Virgin, and Cartier promised to make a pilgrimage to Roc-Amadour. At last, by skilfully questioning Domagaya, who had had scurvy, Cartier learned the secret of the remedy: an infusion made from *annedda* (white cedar). The crew was quickly cured.

Cartier was eager to use his contacts with the natives to increase his knowledge. He is the first person to give us information on the religion and customs of the St. Lawrence valley Indians. The network of waterways was moreover beginning to take shape in his mind: the Richelieu, still unnamed, which came from "Florida"; the St. Lawrence, which was open to navigation for three months; to the north of Hochelaga, a river (the Ottawa) which led to great lakes and to a "freshwater sea"; great waterways which proved that the continental barrier was much broader than had been believed. All the wonderful stories that he heard about the fabulous kingdom of Saguenay, the legend of which was perhaps a relic of Norse traditions (unless the Mississippi basin was meant), were recorded by Cartier. This continent was already extremely rich in surprises!

When spring came they prepared to return to France. As his crew was not large enough, Cartier abandoned the *Petite Hermine*. Her remains were thought to have been found in 1842 and one portion was deposited with the Quebec Literary and Historical Society, the other being sent to Saint-Malo. But, as N.-E. Dionne has written, it has never been proved that this wreckage was that of the *Petite Hermine*.

Before leaving, Cartier wanted to strengthen the position of the French; the ethnic, linguistic, and political unity of the Laurentian valley already gave them an advantage, which was however endangered by the conduct of Donnacona and of his two sons. Cartier learned that a rival, Agona, was aspiring to power. A plan for a revolution became clear: to eliminate the ruling party on behalf of Agona. Cartier cunningly took advantage of a religious ceremony—the erection of a cross on the festival on 3 May—to capture Donnacona, the interpreters, and a few other natives. He appeased the crowd by promising to bring back Donnacona in 10 or 12 months, with lavish presents from the king.

On 6 May he left Sainte-Croix with his two ships and about ten Iroquois, including four children who had been given to him the previous autumn. In his cargo were a dozen pieces of gold and some furs. This time, as he sailed between Anticosti Island and the Gaspé Peninsula, he ascertained that the Îles de la Madeleine, then called the Araines, were in fact islands, and discovered between Newfoundland and Cape Breton the passage which he had not noticed in 1534. On 16 July 1536 he arrived back in Saint-Malo, after an absence of 14 months.

This second voyage had been much more profitable than the first: Cartier had discovered a river by means of which one could penetrate deeply into the continent; he had opened up a new access route to the gulf; he had seen the natural resources of the St. Lawrence and had got to know its inhabitants; he had returned with an old chieftain who boasted of having visited the fabulously wealthy country of the Saguenay; and he had gold.

Immediately on his return Cartier presented a report to François I; he spoke of a river 800 leagues long which might lead to Asia, and he got Donnacona to add his testimony. The king enthusiastically gave him the *Grande Hermine*.

However, the Saint-Malo navigator could not resume his explorations immediately. War broke out between François I and Charles V; Savoy effaced the thought of America. What became of Cartier? Lanctot ascribes to him a memoir of 1538, which outlines a colonization plan, but there is no documentary proof to lend support to this argument. Similarly Lanctot has attempted to forge a dramatic link between Cartier and the escape of the Irish rebel Gerald Fitzgerald, who styled himself a king. A first report from a spy states that Cartier went to Ireland to get Fitzgerald, a version which Lanctot hastily accepts; but in a second report drawn up by the same spy after a more extensive enquiry, Cartier's role is limited to that of welcoming the refugee to Saint-Malo.

It was not until 17 Oct. 1540 that the king gave Cartier a commission for a third voyage. The discoverer was named captain-general of the new expedition, and he was to proceed to "Canada and Hochelaga, and as far as the land of Saguenay," with individuals of "all kinds, arts and industries," including some 50 men whom he was authorized to take from the prisons; exploration was to be carried out, and they were to live with the natives "if need be." Cartier made ready: he arranged to have the 50 prisoners delivered to him, he asked certain spiritual favours from Rome, and he persuaded the king to intervene to hasten the recruitment of his crew.

On 15 Jan. 1541 a royal decision changed everything; the Protestant Jean-François de LA ROCQUE de Roberval received a commission which placed him instead of Cartier at the head of a great colonizing undertaking. Lanctot has argued that Cartier remained on an equal footing with Roberval, the one concerned with colonization, the other with navigation. Yet the text of the commission is clear: Roberval was named the king's "lieutenant general," the "chief, leader, captain" of the undertaking, with authority over all those who would be part of "the said undertaking, expedition and army," and all were to take "oath of fealty" to obey him; moreover, in this commission the king annulled the one granted in October. Cartier became in truth Roberval's subaltern.

Cartier was ready in May 1541, but Roberval had not yet received his artillery. As the king was anxious that Cartier should set sail at once, Roberval gave him "full authority to leave" and instructed him to represent him. Cartier made his will on 19 May and on 23 May put to sea with five ships, including the *Grande Hermine* and the *Émérillon*. A Spanish spy put the crew at 1,500 men. Among Cartier's companions might be mentioned two brothers-in-law: Guyon Des Granches, Vicomte de Beaupré, and the pilot Macé Jalobert; a nephew, Étienne Noël; and the shipmaster Thomas Fromont *dit* La Bouille, who was to die during this voyage. None of the Iroquois whom he had brought to France in 1536 returned to Canada; they had all died, except for a little girl.

On 23 Aug. 1541 Cartier reappeared before Stadacona. The Indians received him with numerous demonstrations of joy. Cartier announced Donnacona's death, but stated that the other Iroquois were living in France like lords and did not want to return, which must have delighted Agona. The friendly relations nonetheless did not last. The abandonment of the Sainte-Croix site can no doubt be explained by this mutual distrust. Cartier went up the river and established himself at the western extremity of the cape, at the mouth of the Rivière du Cap-Rouge. The settlement was first called "Charlesbourg-Royal." This site appeared much more favourable than the first one; moreover white cedar was found there, and especially stones which were thought to be diamonds (hence the name Cap aux Diamants), and "certain leaves of fine gold."

On 2 September Cartier despatched Jalobert and Noël, with two ships, to France, to make a report; then he began two forts, one at the base of the cape, the other at the top. On the seventh he left the settlement under the command of the Vicomte de Beaupré and sailed for Hochelaga, greeting his friend the chieftain of Achelacy on the way and entrusting to him two boys so that they could be taught the language. They were the first two Europeans to become pupils of the natives. Cartier's intention was to examine the Hochelaga rapids in order to be able to clear them the following spring. The Indians proved to be affable, as they were in 1535, but Cartier had no interpreters. He made no progress in his knowledge of the hinterland, but persisted in his hypothesis of 1535.

When he returned, Cartier noticed that the Iroquois' distrust was increasing. Even the chieftain of Achelacy abandoned him. The French made ready to defend themselves. As the account of this voyage breaks off suddenly, we do not know exactly what happened during the winter season. We may infer from one sentence in this account that there was some scurvy, readily overcome thanks the the infusion of white cedar; according to some testimonies, the natives kept the settlement in a state of siege and boasted of having killed more than 35 Frenchmen. Cartier struck camp in June 1542.

At the port of St. John's (Newfoundland) he met Roberval, who had finally put in an appearance with his settlers and who ordered him to turn back. Believing that he was carrying gold and diamonds with him, or not wanting to face the natives again, Cartier headed for France under cover of darkness, thus depriving Roberval of manpower and of precious experience.

Cartier's fleet was the fleet of illusions: the gold ore was nothing but iron pyrites, and the diamonds were quartz, hence the proverb "as false as Canadian diamonds." It is not known whether Cartier was reprimanded for his insubordination; in any case he was not given the mission of repatriating Roberval in 1543, and he was not entrusted again with any long-range expedition.

Later Cartier had to sort out his accounts from Roberval's, and he appeared before a special tribunal in the spring of 1544. He proved that he had been a faithful trustee of the king's money and of Roberval's and was repaid about 9,000 *livres*, although certain merchants claimed in 1588 that the people of Saint-Malo had not yet received what Cartier declared that he had paid them.

Cartier

In 1545 appeared the *Brief récit*, an account of the second voyage, published anonymously, and mentioning once only in the text the name of Cartier. The navigator is said to have written in this period a "book in the nature of a sea-chart," but it has not been discovered. He received the Franciscan André THEVET, to whom he gave extensive information about Canada. An hypothesis has been advanced according to which a meeting between Rabelais and the explorer furnished some material for *Pantagruel*. This hypothesis has received less and less credence, and the last critic to mention it, Bernard G. Hoffman, does not accept it at all.

From this time on, Cartier apparently concentrated upon business and upon the exploitation of his estate of Limoilou. He acted as godfather, or served as a witness at court on various occasions. Cartier was no doubt a man who liked to do himself well; a note in a registry of births, marriages, and deaths associates him with the "hearty tipplers." The documents of this period usually designate him as a "noble homme," which places him in the well-established *bourgeoisie*. He died 1 Sept. 1557, at the age of 66 years.

In April or May 1520 he had married Catherine Des Granches, daughter of Jacques Des Granches, *chevalier du roi* and constable of Saint-Malo; she died in April 1575. They seem to have had no children. It was a nephew, Jacques NOËL, who was to try to carry on Cartier's work.

No authentic portrait of Cartier is known. According to Lanctot, who has made a special study of Cartier's iconography, eight pictures merit attention: a sketch about two inches high on the so-called Harleian Mappemonde (the latter is attributed to Pierre Descelliers and was made after 1542); a drawing on the Vallard map of 1547; a sketch one inch high in an edition of Ramusio in 1556; a portrait published in 1836 and made by Léopold Massart after the Descelliers sketch; a portrait by François Riso in 1839, reproduced by Théophile Hamel; a portrait published by Michelant, taken from a drawing which is said to have belonged to the BN and to have disappeared subsequently; a wooden medallion, 20 in. in diameter, dated 1704 and found in 1908 by Clarke in an old house in Gaspé; finally the copy of a portrait belonging to one of the Marquis de Villefranche. Lanctot is inclined to think that the only authentic one of all these portraits is "the sketch on the Descelliers map," the others being more or less accurate copies or even fanciful representations.

The accounts of Cartier's voyages raise a still more awkward problem. The account of the first voyage was published initially in Italian by Ramusio in 1565, then in English by Florio in 1580, finally in French by Raphaël du Petit-Val in 1598; it is this last text which was used by Marc LESCARBOT. A manuscript preserved in the BN (no.841 of the Moreau collection) was edited by the Quebec Literary and Historical Society in 1843, by Michelant and Ramé in 1867, by H. P. Biggar in 1924, by J. Pouliot in 1934, and finally by Th. Beauchesne in 1946. But this manuscript is only a copy of an original which has today disappeared.

The account of the second voyage was published in French as early as 1545, but anonymously. The original manuscript which served for this edition has not been discovered either. Three manuscripts of the account of the second voyage have been preserved in the BN: no.5589, the best one, that published by Lescarbot, and thought by Biggar to be the original; no.5644, which is faulty; no.5653, published at Quebec in 1843 and considered by Avezac to be the original. Robert Le Blant maintains in a recent study that none of the three is the original, and that all three are copies of a lost prototype.

Finally, for the account of the third voyage we possess only an incomplete English version compiled by Hakluyt in 1600, from a document which he had found in Paris around 1583 and which is now lost.

The authorship of the accounts is another problem which it has not been possible to resolve. The account of the third voyage, of which we have only the English version, gives us no indication. As for the account of the second voyage, Jehan Poullet has been suggested as the author. He was probably a native of Dol, in Brittany; he was first mentioned 31 March 1535, when he appeared before a meeting in Saint-Malo to submit the roll of the members of the next expedition. His name does not appear on this roll, but it occurs four times in the *Brief récit* published in 1545. It was in 1888 that Joüon Des Longrais submitted that Poullet, in view of "the obviously exaggerated importance given to him in the *Brief Récit*," must have had a hand in the writing of it, and he added: "Perhaps he is the author." In 1901 Biggar revived the same argument. Furthermore, perceiving a certain similarity of style between the accounts of the first two voyages, Biggar assumes that Poullet is also the writer of the account of the first voyage. In 1949 another hypothesis was advanced: Marius Barbeau maintained that Rabelais rewrote Cartier's accounts to present them to the king. Bernard G. Hoffman replied that they in no way recall the style of Rabelais, that the second account must of necessity have been sent to the king not later than 1536, that Rabelais did not know of Cartier's voyages before 1538, in short that the hypothesis was unfounded.

The problem would be simpler if the original documents could be found, and above all if one knew Cartier better. In Biggar's view it is obvious that the accounts, such as we know them, were taken from a ship's log kept by Cartier, and shaped into a literary story. But, argues Biggar, if Cartier could keep a ship's log, he was incapable of producing a literary story. That Cartier did not have the necessary literary talents has, however, never been demonstrated; to prove that he had not would be as difficult as to prove that he had. For the time being the author of the accounts remains unknown and the problem persists in its entirety.

Cartier has long been hailed by French-speaking historians as the discoverer of Canada. But did Cartier discover Canada? If we understand by that term the Canada of the 16th century, that is to say the region extending from approximately the Île d'Orléans to Portneuf, it is certainly Cartier who discovered it, but in 1535. Canada however has varied in its geographical dimensions: under the French régime it was identical with the settlement of the St. Lawrence, from Gaspé to the Vaudreuil-Soulanges region; the discoverer of this Canada was still Cartier. The same area, transformed in 1763 into the province of Quebec, became the Lower Canada of 1791, and in 1840 was merged with Ontario to form United Canada; up to Confederation the region called Canada still began only at the Gaspé Peninsula. Consequently one can affirm until 1867 that Cartier was the discoverer of Canada; the French-speaking historians were still perfectly correct. But Canada had not finished its development. By the Confederation of 1867 New Brunswick and Nova Scotia were added to it. If Nova Scotia was not reached by John Cabot, it certainly was by the Corte-Reals and by Fagundes; it appears on maps long before Cartier crossed the Atlantic. Finally, since 1949, the year that Newfoundland joined Confederation, the discovery of Canada in its present form must be attributed to the Italian Cabot, who had transferred his allegiance to England.

But even if Cartier's explorations are not on the same scale as the exploits of Hernando de Soto or of certain South American explorers, he does have a place among the great names of the 16th century. He was the first to make a survey of the coasts of the Gulf of St. Lawrence, to describe the life of the Indians of northeastern North America, and, what is most to his credit, in 1535 he discovered the St. Lawrence River, which was to become the axis of the French empire in America, the vital route which would carry eager explorers towards Hudson Bay, towards the mysterious horizon of the western sea, and towards the Mississippi. Cartier discovered one of the greatest rivers in the world, and he marks the starting-point of France's occupation of three-quarters of a continent.

MARCEL TRUDEL

The following publications reproduce the various documents relating to Cartier, known to date: Biggar, *Documents relating to Cartier and Roberval*. Hakluyt, *Principal navigations* (1903–5), VIII, 183–272 (Cartier's three voyages). *Jacques Cartier, Documents nouveaux*, éd. F. Joüon Des Longrais (Paris, 1888). *Precursors* (Biggar). André Thevet, *Les singularitez de la France antarctique, autrement nomée Amérique: & de plusieurs terres & isles découvertes de nostre temps* (Paris, 1558; autre éd., Anvers, 1558; éd. Paul Gaffarel, Paris, 1878), an account which belongs among these documents.

The principal editions of Cartier's voyages are as follows: Jacques Cartier, *Bref récit*; *Brief récit & succincte narration . . .* (Paris, 1545), reproduced by photostat in *Jacques Cartier et la "grosse maladie"* (XIXᵉ Congrès international de Physiologie Pub., Montréal, 1953); *Voyage de 1534*; [—— et al.], *Voyages de découverte au Canada, entre les années 1534 et 1542, par Jacques Quartier, le sieur de Roberval, Jean Alphonse de Xanctoigne, etc. suivis de la description de Québec et de ses environs en 1608, et de divers extraits relativement au lieu de l'hivernement de Jacques Quartier en 1535–36* (Société littéraire et historique de Québec, 1843). J.-C. Pouliot, *La grande aventure de Jacques Cartier: épave bi-centenaire découverte au Cap des Rosiers en 1908* (Québec, 1934). "Voyages de Jacques Cartier au Canada," éd. Th. Beauchesne, dans *Les Français en Amérique* (Julien), 77–197. *Voyages of Cartier* (Biggar). See also J.-E. Roy, *Rapport sur les Archives de France relatives à l'histoire du Canada* (PAC pub., VI, Ottawa, 1911), 669–72, which summarizes the history of the various MSS of Cartier's voyages and lists the various theories in regard to them.

Of the numerous published studies of Cartier only the most important are given here; certain of them include detailed bibliographies. These studies are listed in chronological order. N.-E. Dionne, *Vie et voyages de Jacques Cartier* (3ᵉ éd., Québec, 1934) (first published in 1889); *Étude archéologique: le fort Jacques Càrtier et la Petite Hermine* (Montréal, 1891). Biggar, *Early trading companies*. A.-J.-M. Lefranc, *Les navigations de Pantagruel* (Paris, 1905). [C.-J.-F. Hénault], "Extrait de la généalogie de la maison Le Veneur . . . ," *NF*, VI (1931), 340–43. Marius Barbeau, "Cartier inspired Rabelais," *Can. Geog. J.*, IX (1934), 113–25. Lionel Groulx, *La découverte du Canada, Jacques Cartier* (Montréal, 1934). Gustave Lanctot, *Jacques Cartier devant l'histoire* (Montréal, 1947); book reviewed by Lionel Groulx, *RHAF*, I (1947), 291–98. *Les voyages de découverte et les premiers établissements*

Caumont

(*XVe, XVIe siècles*), éd. Ch.-A. Julien, (Colonies et empires, 3e série, Paris, 1948). Hoffman, *Cabot to Cartier*, in particular 131–67. Robert Le Blant, "Les écrits attribués à Jacques Cartier," *RHAF*, XV (1961–62), 90–103.

For the cartography of Cartier, *see* Marcel Trudel, *Atlas historique du Canada français des origines à 1867* (Québec, 1961), cartes 14–23.

CAUMONT, PIERRE DE, priest, missionary, canon; b. *c.* 1641 in France; d. 1694 at Quebec.

The Abbé Caumont arrived from France 16 May 1669. Nothing is known about his previous history. His first mission that we know of was at Boucherville, where we find him in 1670; in that same year he built a chapel there. From there he carried his ministry to Longueuil, Varennes, and other localities. In 1683 Boucherville had 200 inhabitants; the missionary lived in the home of the seigneur Pierre Boucher*. From 1678 to 1680 M. de Caumont stayed at the seminary of Quebec because of an eye complaint which did not however prevent him from carrying on his ministry at the Côte de Beaupré and at Cap-Saint-Ignace. In 1684, upon the foundation of the chapter, he became one of the first canons of Quebec, and shortly afterwards, in 1685, he retired and took up residence in the seminary. According to a list for the year 1692 he was a member of the community of the seminary. He died 16 Feb. 1694 and was buried in the seminary chapel.

HONORIUS PROVOST

ASQ, Lettres, S, 66, M, 15; MSS, C, II (1674–86) [Livres de comptes, II]; Séminaire, II, 41.

CAVELIER DE LA SALLE, RENÉ-ROBERT, explorer, founder of Lachine, seigneur of Cataracoui, discoverer of the mouths of the Mississippi; b. 21 Nov. 1643 at Rouen (Normandy), son of Jean Cavelier, a wholesale haberdasher, and of Catherine Geest; assassinated 19 March 1687 in Texas.

René-Robert was baptized in the parish of Saint-Herbland, and brought up in the same district as Pierre Corneille, scarcely five minutes' walk from the great playwright's dwelling. He belonged to a rich family of the upper *bourgeoisie* of provincial France, and the name La Salle, which he was later to make famous, was that of an estate owned by his parents in the vicinity of Rouen.

He studied at the Jesuit college in his native town until 1658, the year when he entered upon his noviciate in the Society of Jesus in Paris. He was to spend nine years in that order. He made his vows in 1660, and for two years took up logic and physics at La Flèche, studies which he later completed by one year of mathematics after he had been a teacher in the second form of secondary school at Alençon. Then he taught once more, at Tours and Blois, from 1664 to 1666.

Apparently this young scholastic felt a perpetual need to change his occupation and environment. "Inquietus" was the word used to describe his lack of steadiness. He would grow bored and lose interest in his work, yet despite everything he displayed real gifts, particularly in mathematics. On the other hand, his superiors held his judgement in rather low esteem, and had a scarcely higher opinion of his discretion. They found him, moreover, by temperament emotional and imaginative, and at the same time unsociable, autocratic, and fiery, ill suited for conformity to rigid rule. The robust and impulsive Brother Cavelier, despite his efforts and his scrupulous conscience, was an elemental force that defied all attempts to master it. He himself, at the age of 22, tried to sublimate his indomitable energy, mobility of character, and spirit of independence, by asking on two occasions to be sent to a mission. But the authorities did not consider him sufficiently ready: his theological training was not completed, his religious preparation was still inadequate. So in October 1666 he resumed his studies at La Flèche, only to request soon afterwards permission to continue them in Portugal, with a view to preparing himself for his eventual missionary apostolate. He met with another refusal. Unable any longer to stand the strain, he had himself released from his vows, because of what he called his "moral frailties." On 28 March 1667, the convent doors closed behind him for ever.

Cavelier had at his disposal only meagre financial resources with which to make his way in the world. Legally he was excluded by his vow of poverty from sharing in any paternal legacy (his father had died shortly before the young man left the Jesuit order), and he possessed only a modest income. Furthermore, he had no profession. His restless urge to see ever new horizons had not left him, however. Then he had an uncle in the Compagnie des Cent-Associés and a brother who was a Sulpician at Montreal; he had, in addition, grown up in a city oriented towards Canada and situated in an archdiocese to which the Church in New France belonged as a dependency. Such a background could not fail to prompt him to go to America. He lost no time, and arrived in the colony between June and the beginning of November 1667. There the

Cavelier de La Salle

Sulpicians granted him a seigneury on Montreal Island.

On 9 Jan. 1669, after giving it relatively little attention, La Salle sold the major portion of the fief on the Côte Saint-Sulpice to its first owners, who had given it to him for nothing. The money realized from this transaction would later help him to gratify the demon of adventure lodged within him, the yearning for glory that consumed him. He dreamed of discovering the Ohio River, "in order not to leave to another the honour of finding the way to the Southern Sea, and thereby the route to China." Since La Salle's plans might fit in with the missionary programme of the Sulpician Dollier* de Casson, the governor requested the two men to join forces. However, the superior of the Sulpicians feared that La Salle's disposition, "known to be somewhat changeable," might cause him to abandon the expedition "at the first whim." Therefore he allowed the deacon BRÉHANT de Galinée, who had "some smattering of mathematics, and enough to put a map together after a fashion," to join the enterprise.

La Salle disposed of his Montreal properties, keeping only his house as a fur-trading factory. He left Ville-Marie (Montreal) at the beginning of July 1669 with a flotilla of nine canoes. From the start the voyage proved difficult, for La Salle was ill prepared, and his companions were not much better off. They were all more or less novices in the art of surviving in the woods, they had no guide, and if Galinée, by his own admission, was a mediocre cartographer, La Salle himself was no more competent as an astronomer. Finally, they would not be able to communicate with the Iroquois, among whom they were going, except by using as an interpreter a Dutchman who had little mastery of French. "M. de La Salle," wrote Galinée, "who said that he understood the Iroquois perfectly, and had learned all these things from them as a result of the perfect knowledge that he had of their language, did not know it at all, and was undertaking this voyage almost blindly, without knowing where he was going."

With much trial and tribulation, they reached Lake Ontario 2 August, and the approaches to the Seneca country six days later. About 10 August, some Indians came in a delegation to meet the French at a river called Karongouat. La Salle, Galinée, and a few men agreed to follow them to their village (on the site of what is today Boughton Hill, N.Y.), in the hope of obtaining a guide for the Ohio River country. The Senecas held a great council—in which La Salle admitted his ignorance of their language—and, while not openly refusing to lend their aid to the French, the natives advanced pretexts for deferring it. It seemed that they did not look favourably upon the idea of these Frenchmen going among their enemies. They even endeavoured secretly to discourage the Dutch interpreter. In the end their intrigues were so successful that the explorers were held up there for a month, disturbed at finding themselves in the neighbourhood of the relatives of a Seneca chieftain murdered in June by soldiers from the Montreal garrison. But the arrival of a traveller on his way to the north shore of Lake Ontario got them out of their difficulty. It was an Iroquois who was returning to Ganastogué, his village, and he offered to lead the white men to it. He assured them that they would easily find a guide there to take them to the Ohio via Lake Erie, a more convenient route, according to him, than the one through the Seneca country. At the far end of Burlington Bay, La Salle was struck down by fever: "Some said," remarked Galinée naïvely, or slyly, "that it was at the sight of three large rattlesnakes which he found in his path as he climbed up a rock." Then, on 24 September, he and his companions proceeded to Tinaouataoua (a few miles north of Hamilton), where they were to make a decisive encounter. Adrien, the brother of Louis JOLLIET, had been there since the previous day, having returned from a mission to the Great Lakes. He described to the two Sulpicians the route he had just traversed from the country of the Ottawas, where he had left his men searching for a large tribe not yet evangelized, the Potawotomis. The missionaries at once saw in this tribe a field for their apostolate that would enable them to reach the Belle Rivière (Ohio) region via the Great Lakes, a route that seemed to them all the easier because Dollier and Galinée spoke the Ottawa tongue.

However, La Salle had by this time lost his enthusiasm. He made his poor state of health a pretext for leaving Dollier and Galinée on 1 October, and for returning, so he said, to Montreal.

The true motive for this decision still gives rise to queries. Officially, the explorer was ill, and by reason of his inexperience and that of his party, was afraid to spend the winter in the woods. However, although several of his men did return to Ville-Marie, La Salle himself continued to travel.

In what regions? That particular question has caused much ink to flow, and is one of the more confused issues in Canadian history. It has been claimed that in 1669–70 La Salle explored the Ohio. More than that, certain admirers thinking that they were bestowing upon the city of Rouen

Cavelier de La Salle

the honour of being the birthplace of a conquistador after the fashion of Cortez—Margry, Chesnel, Gravier, and other historians of the same school—have gone so far as to maintain that La Salle discovered the Mississippi before Jolliet and Father MARQUETTE, that is before 15 June 1673. The archivist Pierre Margry's lack of care in editing the documents concerning his hero may have contributed to the growth and persistence of this double myth.

Very little is known for certain about La Salle's movements during the period under review. Nicolas Perrot* says that he met him early in the summer of 1670, hunting on the Outaouais (Ottawa River) below the Rapide des Chats, that is to say more than 700 miles, as the crow flies, from the Louisville Rapids, the point La Salle is supposed by some to have reached in exploring the Ohio. However, this testimony proves little, for Perrot is usually at variance with accepted chronology.

In any case, it is beyond doubt that La Salle came to Quebec, having discovered neither the Ohio nor the Mississippi, between 18 Aug. 1670, the date of TALON's return to the colony, and the following 10 November, the date of a letter in which Talon stated that he had sent La Salle southward, to find "the passage to Mexico." Furthermore, on 6 Aug. 1671 and 18 Dec. 1672, he was at Montreal again, in search of money, as is attested by documents deposited in the registry at Ville-Marie.

Then, at the beginning of 1673, we find him among the Iroquois, busy preparing for the expedition that Frontenac [see BUADE] was planning to Lake Ontario: the *Relations des Jésuites* and a letter from the governor are our sources of information here.

Consequently only two intervals remain during which La Salle could possibly have made the discovery of the Ohio or the Mississippi. Those periods fall respectively within the 10 months or so from the autumn of 1670 to 6 Aug. 1671, the date on which the explorer was at Montreal, and the 16 months separating the latter date from 18 Dec. 1672, the day on which he was again at Ville-Marie. No document belonging to these periods, at least in the present state of our knowledge, gives the slightest indication that La Salle could have discovered at that time either of the waterways in question.

Certainly nobody in the colony appears to have known anything about a discovery, not even Dollier de Casson, who, in the summer or autumn of 1671, when recounting Governor RÉMY de Courcelle's expedition to Lake Ontario, refers to the discovery of the Ohio as a goal still to be attained. More than that, Talon and Frontenac gave Louis Jolliet, who set out in the autumn of 1672, the task of looking for the Mississippi.

La Salle seems to have kept completely silent about his explorations at this time; it was even without Talon's knowledge that he turned up in August 1671 at Montreal, since on 2 November of that year the intendant declared that the explorer had not returned from his trip. Yet, if La Salle had had some important discovery to his credit, it was in his own interest to publish it widely; it was even his duty to report it to Talon, since the latter had entrusted him with an official mission. The only plausible explanation of La Salle's attitude is that he had found neither the Ohio nor the Mississippi.

The supporters of Cavelier de La Salle as the discoverer of the two great waterways rest their case on two later documents: the "Récit d'un ami de l'abbé de Gallinée," and the "Mémoire sur le projet du sieur de la Salle pour la descouverte de la partie occidentale de l'Amérique septentrionale entre la Nouvelle-France, la Floride et le Mexique." These texts were composed by the two *éminences grises* of La Salle who, in Europe, were busy behind the scenes of French colonial policy. The "Récit" is attributed to Abbé Eusèbe Renaudot, a grandson of the founder of the *Gazette de France*, of which he in his turn became the editor. An outstanding orientalist, a polyglot and a member of the French Academy, this personage, famed for his erudition, was very valuable to Louis XIV in that monarch's relations with Rome, England, and Spain. His passion for the sciences, among them geography, his religious zeal, tinged with Jansenism and hostile to the Jesuits, made him just the person to become the protector of La Salle, an explorer in perpetual conflict with the sons of Loyola.

The "Récit," which is not, it should be noted, an original document, but a copy the author and date of which are unknown, is an account of conversations alleged to have taken place in 1678, in Paris, between La Salle and Renaudot in the presence of friends. Despite the guarantees of veracity with which the learned ecclesiastic tries to shore it up, his text is none the less suspect. First, its objectivity is very doubtful, for it comes from a collection of anti-Jesuit manuscripts and is itself, in large part, a pamphlet directed against the Jesuits in Canada. Then too, it is difficult to take seriously a text based on the most unlikely geographical descriptions.

Abbé Claude Bernou, to whom we owe the "Mémoire" (presented at the court in 1677), does not produce any more solid testimony, since his

Cavelier de La Salle

is based on a lax chronology and inaccurate geographical details. Besides, he merely states vaguely: "In 1667 and the following years, he [La Salle] made various voyages involving much expense, in the course of which he was the first to discover many countries to the south of the Great Lakes, and also the great River Ohio."

The abbé had good reasons for wishing to attribute such a discovery to La Salle. In addition to being a member of Renaudot's circle, which brought together many influential persons who expressed the most lively curiosity concerning explorations in the New World and who supported the Recollets in their opposition to the Society of Jesus, Bernou (who himself carried out, on occasion, diplomatic missions), had definite personal ambitions that La Salle's success might advance. The priest, indeed, on his own admission, wished to become the explorer's paid agent, and even dreamed of an episcopate in the territories with which La Salle might be expected to enrich the kingdom of France.

However, Bernou was obliged to retract in 1685. During a controversy with Bishop Saint-Vallier [La Croix*], who was claiming for the diocese of Quebec the region around the Gulf of Mexico, where La Salle had gone to found a post, Bernou wrote quite explicitly: "It is true that Father Marquette discovered the Mississippi River, but he merely skirted it."

Among the other arguments used by La Salle's supporters in this controversy, one of the weightiest would seem to be the cartographic evidence. Two maps attributed to Louis Jolliet indicate the course of the Ohio, and, under the outline of the river, include respectively the following inscriptions: "Route of the sieur de La Salle for going into Mexico," and "River down which the sieur de La Salle went on leaving Lake Erie, to go into Mexico." These references have been construed as a tacit admission by Jolliet himself of the discovery of the Ohio by La Salle. But according to careful scientific research, particularly that of Father Jean Delanglez, both these inscriptions are interpolations having nothing to do with Jolliet, the first being of unknown origin, the second in the hand of Bernou himself.

Finally, a letter written by La Salle, dated 29 Sept. 1680, should suffice to settle the argument. The letter shows fairly clearly that the explorer was at that time still almost entirely ignorant of the Colbert River (Mississippi), in view of the elementary questions he admits having asked the Illinois about it.

In the autumn of 1673, La Salle returned to Montreal. The colony was then the scene of a tragi-comedy in which the rival protagonists were Perrot the governor of Montreal, Abbé Fénelon [see SALIGNAC], and Frontenac. There, siding with the governor of New France, whose vehement supporter he became, La Salle played a part akin to that of the valet in comedy. The two individuals had seemingly every reason to get on well together: their personalities were equally strong, but complementary, their respective interests could be of mutual advantage, and they shared an antipathy towards the Jesuits.

It was not long before La Salle benefited from his alliance with Frontenac. Thanks to his powerful protector, the discoverer managed, during a voyage to France in 1674–75, to secure for himself the grant of Fort Cataracoui (now Kingston), which he renamed Frontenac, and he even acquired letters of nobility for himself and his descendants. La Salle, who had ambitions of empire, knew well how he could profit from a post on Lake Ontario, which according to Talon, might be "the first opening towards an overland route to Florida."

Yet Fort Frontenac was not enough for him. In 1677, he returned to the court to seek authorization to construct, at his own expense, "two establishments . . . one at the entrance to Lake Erie, the other at the exit from the Lac des Illinois [Michigan]; [to become] seigneur of the lands that he might discover and populate . . . ; to receive ownership of all the cleared lands that the Indians might abandon of their own accord, as they do sometimes, and the office of governor in the said territories." Despite his detractors, in whose eyes his inordinate ambitions put him on the level of a fool "fit and ready for the madhouse," the explorer, thanks to his powers of persuasion and to the good offices of Bernou and Renaudot, obtained permission from the king, 12 May 1678, to reconnoitre the western part of North America between New France, Florida, and Mexico.

On 15 September following, La Salle arrived at Quebec with some 30 craftsmen, seamen, and gentlemen, among them Dominique LA MOTTE de Lucière and the Chevalier Henri de Tonty*, who was to be the explorer's confidential agent and his tireless lieutenant in his undertakings. Anxious to get started, La Salle, together with Tonty and a few men, joined La Motte at the Niagara River, around Christmas; La Motte had been sent on ahead as a scout, with Father Hennepin* and a small band of Frenchmen, to prepare for the building of a bark above the falls.

By January the boat was on the stocks, and construction began on the fort, which was to be called Conti. Because of unfortunate mishaps, La Salle found himself forced to go back

Cavelier de La Salle

immediately, on foot and under the worst conditions, to Fort Frontenac, and he did not return until the end of July.

During his absence, in spite of the most unfavourable circumstances, it proved possible to finish a boat of about 45 tons, armed with 7 cannon. The *Griffon*—so called in honour of Frontenac's coat of arms—was launched on 7 Aug. 1679. La Salle had on board, in addition to a pilot and some 30 men, Fathers Hennepin, MEMBRÉ, and LA RIBOURDE. After 20 days of extremely dangerous sailing, he reached the strait between lakes Huron and Michigan and went ashore at the Saint-Ignace de Michilimackinac mission. On 12 September he headed for the Baie des Puants (Green Bay). From there, notwithstanding the king's express order to him not to engage in "any trade with the Indians called Outaouacs and others who bring their beavers and other pelts to Montreal," he sent the *Griffon* back to Niagara loaded with a substantial cargo of furs, as well as merchandise intended to be stored at Michilimackinac until his return. With the coming of winter, he had to continue his journey by canoe.

On 19 Sept. 1679 La Salle set out with 14 men and 4 canoes. Amid wind and storm he went towards the south of Lake Michigan, stopping on 1 November at the mouth of the Rivière des Miamis (Saint-Joseph), where he had a rendezvous with Tonty. As the site had advantages, he caused a fort 40 feet by 30 to be built there, and decided to bring the *Griffon* from Michilimackinac. Nobody there, however, had seen the bark, according to Tonty, who turned up at the Rivière Saint-Joseph on the twentieth. Consequently La Salle set out again anxiously on 3 December, having doubled his forces and leaving instructions for the *Griffon* in case it should appear. He first went up the river, then crossed to the Téatiki (Kankakee), which led him to the Illinois.

On 5 Jan. 1680, the expedition reached the Illinois village of Pimitoui, in the vicinity of the present city of Peoria. La Salle outlined to the Indians his plan for building a fort and a bark in the neighbourhood, assuring them at the same time of his good intentions. His listeners willingly agreed. But the visit of a Mascouten chief soon caused them to change their attitude. They allowed themselves to be convinced of the insincerity of the explorer, who, they thought, was a dangerous ally of their mortal enemies, the Iroquois. They therefore did their utmost to dissuade him from his plan of exploring the Mississippi, trying to frighten the French with the description of imaginary dangers awaiting them on the river. Six valuable workmen, impressed by this talk, abandoned the party and slipped away. But despite everything, on 15 January, at a prudent distance from the Indian village, La Salle set about the building of the fort that was to be called Crèvecœur, an allusion to the manifold disappointments of the explorer. He was, however, only at the beginning of his troubles.

On 29 February La Salle sent Father Hennepin and two companions as an advance guard towards the upper Mississippi. He himself, lacking the tackle necessary to equip a new bark because of the disappearance of his first one, decided to set out in search of the *Griffon*. The unsettled spring weather, with its alternating periods of freezing and thawing, increased tenfold the difficulties of such an adventure. After 18 March, La Salle and the five men travelling with him had to abandon their canoe in order to continue their journey on foot. Six days later, weighed down under the burden of their equipment, they reached the end of a journey of 275 miles in all: the fort at the Rivière Saint-Joseph. Obtaining no information there about the fate of the *Griffon*, La Salle went on towards Lake Erie, "through woods so thickly intertwined with briars and thorns that in two and a half days he and his men had their clothes torn to shreds, and their faces so covered with blood and slashed that they were not recognizable." During the journey, some of his companions fell sick. To transport them, makeshift boats were assembled, and, sometimes on snow-shoes sometimes riverborne, the party reached Niagara on 21 April 1680. As a reward for his superhuman efforts, La Salle found the fort there burned down, and learned of the loss, in the Gulf of St. Lawrence, of a vessel bringing him more than 20,000 francs worth of goods. But, nothing daunted, the explorer mustered enough courage to go to Fort Frontenac, where on 6 May he completed "a voyage of nearly 500 leagues, and the most arduous that any Frenchman has ever undertaken in America."

He then hastened on to Montreal to settle some money matters, and quickly returned to Cataracoui, more in debt than ever. On 22 July two messengers sent by the Chevalier de Tonty, who had remained at Crèvecœur with Fathers Membré and La Ribourde, brought the news that the fort had been sacked and abandoned by the party that had been left there. This veritable catastrophe was a serious threat to the success of La Salle's explorations in the Illinois country. But he did not waste his time in useless lamentation. When he heard that several of the men were on their way to kill their master, after pillaging all the posts they came across where his goods were to be found, La Salle embarked on Lake Ontario, to hunt down the deserters. He lay in ambush in the Baie de Cataracoui, and captured them at the beginning of August.

Then, on the tenth of the same month, with 25 men, he undertook a second expedition to the territory of the Illinois. On the way he was to lose the last shred of hope of seeing the *Griffon* again: according to certain Potawatomis, a storm had beyond all doubt sunk the bark, sending to the bottom of Lake Michigan the equivalent of 10,000 *écus*.

The flotilla crossed Lake Ontario, and, by making use of the Humber River, Lake Simcoe, the Severn River, and Georgian Bay, reached the Sault Ste. Marie on 16 September. The next day La Salle left the mission, bound for Michilimackinac, where he believed he would be able to find out what had happened to Tonty, left helpless in a territory that the Iroquois had set out to attack. But his trip was fruitless: there was no news of his lieutenant. La Salle, consumed with apprehension, then hastened to Fort Saint-Joseph, and afterwards to Pimitoui.

On 1 December he arrived at an Illinois village that had been destroyed by the Iroquois, who had also massacred its inhabitants. La Salle searched in vain for traces of the worthy Tonty among the debris and the horribly mutilated corpses. Some 30 leagues farther on, the sight of the ruins of Fort Crèvecœur and of the unfinished bark was scarcely more heartening. More and more uneasy, La Salle went on down the Illinois River to the Mississippi, coming across other signs of slaughter on the way, but still finding no trace of Tonty.

He then retraced his steps as far as Fort Saint-Joseph, which he reached at the end of January 1681. From information he gleaned there, he concluded that a canoe which had been seen passing Michilimackinac was Tonty's. He immediately sent two men there, bearing a letter for his friend.

Meanwhile he himself endeavoured, by various negotiations, to encourage the Miamis and Illinois to unite against the Iroquois, in order to ensure the safety of the French establishment that he still planned to set up in the area.

At the beginning of March, some Outagamis (Foxes) revealed that Tonty had wintered among the Potawatomis. La Salle sent messengers to him, to arrange a rendezvous at Michilimackinac in May. Until that time, with unflagging energy, he was to go back and forth between the tribes he wanted to conciliate. Then, at the end of May, he finally met up with his confidential agent again, and heard the story of his distressing adventures, including the murder of Father La Ribourde by the Indians.

La Salle now made all speed to Montreal, whither Frontenac had summoned him. He took advantage of the occasion to draw up, on 11 Aug. 1681, a will in favour of his principal creditor—a whole pack of these were on his tracks—his cousin François Plet. And once more he set out, firmly resolved, this time, to get as far as the mouths of the Mississippi.

In the meantime, at Quebec, Intendant Jacques Duchesneau, who a year before to the day had denounced to the minister La Salle's illegal trading with the Outaouais (Ottawas), now made an accusation against the explorer: in a letter dated 13 Nov. 1681, he stated that La Salle's provocative attitude towards the Iroquois had incited them to war against the Illinois.

On 19 December, La Salle was back at the Rivière Saint-Joseph, where Tonty was waiting for him. About a month later, the expedition, comprising 23 Frenchmen and 18 Indians, was at Fort Crèvecœur. On 6 Feb. 1682 it reached the Mississippi itself, and a week later the breaking up of the ice made it finally possible to launch the canoes upon its waters. Six leagues farther on, they camped in shelters on the right bank, near the mouth of the Missouri. Then they set off again, paddling, hunting, and marvelling at the luxuriant country. About the fifth day, as evening drew on, they discovered on their left the turbulent waters of the mouth of the Ohio, that celebrated "Belle Rivière" which had so occupied La Salle's thoughts. Another stop was made in the neighbourhood of the present city of Memphis. There they had to wait some ten days for a member of the expedition who had become lost when hunting. While they were looking for him, La Salle had a fort built and this he called Prud'homme, from the surname of the luckless gunsmith (son of Louis Prud'homme) who was found starving and drifting downstream on a piece of wood.

La Salle and his party broke camp on 5 March. On the twelfth, the alarm was given: war whoops resounded on the right bank of the Mississippi, accompanied by a menacing roll of drums. They came from Arkansas Indians startled at the sight of the French canoes. The French quickly reassured them, and smoked the pipe of peace with them. The redskins welcomed the Pale Faces joyously, and supplied them sumptuously. La Salle, with all the customary ceremonies, took possession of the territory in the name of the king of France.

Tearing themselves away from the effusive and affectionate natives, who kept stroking their bodies by way of caressing them, the Frenchmen

Cavelier de La Salle

re-embarked, taking with them two guides. About 15 leagues farther on, they reached the mouth of the Arkansas River, where the voyage of Jolliet and Marquette had ended in 1673. The otter country was giving way to the crocodile country. On 22 March they camped among the Taensas, in whom could be recognized, wrote Tonty, "some of the qualities possessed by civilized people." These natives, of remarkable beauty, received their visitors with spectacular protocol, and in addition loaded them with presents.

Next they came to the Koroas, neighbours of the Natchez, who received them in their village and revealed to them that they were now only 10 days from the ocean. The expedition left at Easter, to come finally within sight of the sea on 6 April.

The next day La Salle, Tonty, and JACQUES BOURDON d'Autray began the exploration of the Mississippi delta. And on 9 April 1682, probably near the place now called Venice, the French took solemn possession of Louisiana. La Salle, clad in scarlet trimmed with gold—where did the splendour of the Great Century not manage to intrude itself!—to the sound of triumphant hymns and salvoes of musketry, erected a cross and a column bearing the arms of His Most Christian Majesty, and buried a copper plate engraved with inscriptions. In ringing tones he delivered the record of the territories that thus passed under the rule of the French crown. Finally the document was countersigned by twelve of the persons present.

But a man does not live by glory and fanfares alone, even if he is a Cavelier de La Salle. The French suffered from a shortage of food, having nothing to make a meal out of except potatoes and crocodile. Despite the inhospitable disposition of the Acolapissas, whose arrows they had had a taste of as they approached the mouths of the Mississippi, they had to resign themselves to seeking supplies from these barbarians. The journey upriver, on the way back to Canada, began on 10 April. Five days later, La Salle obtained a small quantity of maize, but at the price of a skirmish with the unco-operative Acolapissas. Suspecting the presence of some of them among the Koroas, whose country the French reached on the twenty-ninth, La Salle was prompted to hasten on to the territory of the Taensas. There his party again refreshed themselves copiously, acquired ample supplies, and re-embarked with much ceremony on 3 May.

In a greater hurry all the time, La Salle went ahead into the territory of the Arkansas, leaving Tonty behind him with part of the group. At the end of May, the faithful lieutenant joined his chief, who had fallen seriously ill, at Fort Prud'homme, among the Chickasaws. The explorer sent him to Fort Saint-Joseph, with instructions to write to the governor to recount the discovery to him; La Salle recovered just enough strength to start out again around 15 June. A month later he was at Crèvecœur, and from there, still convalescent, he went to Lake Michigan by land. Then he sailed towards Fort Saint-Joseph, and from there undertook a 120-league trek as far as Michilimackinac, where Tonty welcomed him in September 1682. Not being sufficiently recovered to travel to France and give an account of his discovery, La Salle went no farther, and confined himself to drawing up dispatches for which Father Membré was to be responsible. He wrote, in particular, to the governor of New France to ask him for help, at the very moment when Frontenac's successor, Joseph-Antoine LE FEBVRE de La Barre, landed in the colony.

On 30 December, he went back to the Illinois River, upstream from the present town of La Salle. This place had been chosen by the discoverer for the building of a fort, on an almost inaccessible rock. Fort Saint-Louis, which was to group under its protection the Miamis, Illinois, and Shawnees, was finished in May 1683.

As it happened, it was on the tenth of that month that the king sent to Intendant Demeulle* instructions in which he expressed his opposition to the undertaking of further explorations, agreeing only to allow La Salle's to be completed.

For his part, the latter, faced with an imminent Iroquois attack, appealed once more to La Barre for help. He was unaware of the hostility of this governor, whom he had not yet even met. From the beginning of his career, the discoverer, with a persistence bordering on paranoiac obsession, had never ceased to believe himself the victim of dark plots contrived against his undertakings and even against his life, by enemies—whether business men or Jesuits—who were inconvenienced by his explorations and establishments; now, when a plot against him was developing in Canada, he did not suspect it. La Barre, for mercenary reasons, had rallied the merchants, who saw La Salle as a dangerous rival in the fur trade. Consequently, using as a pretext the so-called abandonment of Fort Frontenac by La Salle the previous autumn, he relieved François Dauphin* de La Forest of the command which the explorer had entrusted to him, and made of the fort a business centre under the control of Jacques Le Ber* and Charles Aubert* de La Chesnaye. And when La Salle, in August 1683, left Fort Saint-Louis with the intention of going to the court to give an account of his discovery, he had not covered 15 leagues before he found himself face to face with the Chevalier Henri de Baugy*. This officer, on La

Cavelier de La Salle

Barre's orders, was on his way to take over the fort and send La Salle back to the authorities of the colony. La Barre justified himself this time by reviving a former complaint by Duchesneau: La Salle, by his imprudent relations with the enemies of the Five Nations, was compromising the peace negotiations between the French and the Iroquois. Furthermore, La Barre was not afraid to write to the minister, about the Sieur de La Salle "that his arrogance has turned his head; that he has been brazen enough to advise [him] of a false discovery." But the explorer, who was never behindhand when accusations were involved, was to assert, before he went back to the mother country, that La Barre, at the time of his meeting with the Iroquois at Montreal on 14 Aug. 1683, and in answer to their recriminations against La Salle, had given them permission to "kill him and the people who were assembled near his fort, without any consequence attaching to the matter." Obviously La Barre would defend himself vigorously!

It was with a perceptible decline in favour that La Salle, of his own accord but also on the governor's orders, boarded the *Saint-Honoré*, which carried him to La Rochelle shortly before Christmas.

The discoverer had barely set foot on French soil when he attempted to form a company of merchants, with a view to founding a colony among the Taensas. In the face of efforts that were patently useless, he decided to change his tactics.

He well knew that he could scarcely count on help from the king, who on the preceding 5 August had written to La Barre "that the Sieur de La Salle's discovery is completely useless [and that] such undertakings must in future be prevented." The explorer therefore let himself be persuaded to adapt to his own ends a plan presented to the court on 18 Jan. 1682 by Bernou. Because of his personal ambitions, the scheming priest had always had his heart set on his country's colonial expansion. He had therefore proposed to the minister an establishment on the Gulf of Mexico at the mouth of the Rio Bravo (Rio Grande), which would have the advantage of allowing the conquest of New Spain and its mines by Comte Diego de Peñalossa; the count, a former governor of New Mexico, had fled from the Inquisition and placed his sword at the service of France. Apparently Bernou, even before La Salle's arrival in the mother country, was thinking of using him for the implementation of his plan. Indeed, the account of the 1682 expedition, prepared by Father Membré, and the *Relation officielle* of the discovery of the Mississippi delta forwarded to the court in 1683 (which some ascribe to the same author), had been reworked, as Delanglez has shown, by Bernou or some other member of his circle, so as to make the description of the Mississippi valley coincide more or less with that of the Rio Bravo, the manifold advantages of which the priest had boasted to the king.

It was consequently La Salle's job to make his plan for an establishment in Louisiana attractive in the king's eyes, by presenting the settlement that he wanted to found as the ideal base for the invasion of New Biscay. To do this he agreed to falsify the geography of the Mississippi. He had maps made on which the River Colbert, as he called the Mississippi, deviated 250 leagues westward from its real course, and emptied into the gulf in the vicinity of New Mexico. One cannot, in defence of the explorer, plead involuntary error: even if he had lost his compass among the Illinois, he was too good an observer—he had already proved it—to deceive himself to that extent about the general course of the Mississippi. Pierre Le Moyne* d'Iberville was to note later: "M. de La Salle, although a man who passed for being clever, has marked the lower part of the Mississippi, on the map he has made, with 273 degrees . . . I believe that this comes from the strong desire he had to see himself near the mines of New Mexico, and thereby to induce the court to set up in that country establishments which could not but be very profitable thereafter." (*Découvertes et établissements des Français* (Margry).)

In addition, this time unbeknown to Bernou, four memoirs penned by La Salle, or by Renaudot, or by one of their followers, were addressed to the court at the beginning of 1684. They showed how the La Salle project and the Bernou-Peñalossa plan could be harmonized, for the greatest advantage of France. This thesis was supported by downright lies and wild exaggerations. Amongst them, to titillate the minister, the memoirs did not hesitate to say—although the explorer, better than anyone, was familiar with the petrified tree trunks that blocked the Colbert delta—that "the river he has discovered is an excellent port, which large vessels can ascend to a distance of more than 100 leagues inland, and small boats more than 500." They further declared that, to attack the Spaniards, La Salle could easily recruit an army of 15,000 Indians, having already 4,000 at his disposal around Fort Saint-Louis-des-Illinois. Finally they pinpointed the spot where the discoverer claimed to be able to found an establishment: the confluence of the Rivière Rouge and the Mississippi, that is to say in an area covered with marshes.

Not very alert, it seems, to the chimerical nature of the plan submitted to him, Seignelay allowed himself to be won over. And on 10 April 1684,

Cavelier de La Salle

while M. Tronson, speaking of La Salle, was writing to Dollier de Casson: "The king has listened to him, received him well and given him satisfaction," Louis XIV ordered La Barre to restore Fort Frontenac to La Salle through the intermediary La Forest. Four days later, the king granted La Salle a commission to command in all the territory lying between Fort Saint-Louis-des-Illinois and New Biscay. Louis XIV also gave him, among other things, 100 soldiers maintained at royal expense and commanded by 8 officers and non-commissioned officers, a warship carrying 36 cannon and a crew of approximately 70, called the *Joly*, in addition to the *Belle*, a bark of 60 tons armed with 4 small cannon. The convoy was to be completed by the *Aimable*, a flute of 180 tons fitted out by a La Rochelle merchant, and the *Saint-François*, a small ketch partly equipped by the intendant of Rochefort.

From the time of the first preparations for this expedition, which was doomed to be the most lamentable failure, difficulties arose. Not the least was the misunderstanding between La Salle and Taneguy Le Gallois* de Beaujeu, selected by the king to command the *Joly*. The two men were certain to offend each other: a gentleman of the old stock and a commoner recently ennobled were scarcely likely to fraternize. More than that, friction was inevitable between a military man accustomed to command—a hard-headed sailor trained in navigation on the high seas—and an inexperienced, domineering, and quixotic civilian. Finally, to add to La Salle's distrust of his colleague, Mme de Beaujeu had a Jesuit confessor!

La Salle and Beaujeu therefore came into conflict over each point in the organization of the undertaking: the estimated duration of the voyage, the choice and quantity of provisions, the stowage, the number of passengers, and above all the respective authority and prerogatives of the two leaders of the expedition. La Salle, as may well be imagined, had secured supreme control over the whole affair. But when the explorer claimed to be entitled to the obedience of the king's soldiers not only on land, but also on sea, the captain protested. The latter saw his role reduced to no more than directing the handling of the ship. La Salle's demands, according to Beaujeu, created "a great commotion at Rochefort among the officers, each one saying that a passenger had never been known to lay claim to being in command on a ship." Furthermore, he did not scruple to add, "There are very few who do not believe he is crazy. I have spoken of it to people who have known him for 20 years. Everyone says that he has always been something of a visionary."

La Salle's stubborn refusal to reveal to Beaujeu the destination of the voyage could also serve only to aggravate the situation. As well as being hurt in his pride, the captain was furious because he did not know what pilots to choose. Meanwhile, those responsible for recruiting the soldiers and the indentured workers were enrolling any kind of tatterdemalion or young blade who was ready to embark. Preparations dragged on, and La Salle became hesitant, irresolute, and irritable. Anxiety was probably taking hold of him, as he saw more and more clearly the enormous scale of the utopia that Versailles, at his own request, was sending him to create. On 2 Aug. 1684, Beaujeu summed up the situation thus: "I am going into an unknown country to seek something almost as difficult to find as the philosopher's stone, late in the season, laden above the water-line, and with an irritable man."

At the time when the captain was expressing himself in such a disillusioned manner, the expedition was already nine days out to sea. The convoy was transporting at least 320 persons, amongst whom, besides the 100 soldiers commanded by 5 officers and the 40 or so indentured workers and servants, were 6 missionaries, including the Sulpicians d'Esmanville and Jean Cavelier*, La Salle's brother, and the Recollets Membré and Anastase Douay. Also on the voyage were the engineer Minet, 9 volunteers (including Henri Joutel*, a *bourgeois* from Rouen, the author of the principal account of the expedition, and La Salle's right-hand man), about 8 merchants, and even some women and children. By La Salle's error, the *Joly*, which was planned for a crew of 125, had 240 persons on board, not to mention the goods between-decks, which "occupied the quarters of the soldiers and sailors," forcing them "to spend the whole voyage on the upper deck, in the sun by day and the rain by night."

As the ship's bowsprit had snapped on the second day out, they had had to head back to the Île d'Aix, putting out to sea again only on 1 August. A week later, the flotilla rounded Cape Finisterre (in northwestern Spain). Then, on the twentieth, it arrived off Madeira, where Beaujeu proposed to stop and take on water. La Salle refused, which brought about a further deterioration in his relations with the commander. On 6 September they crossed the Tropic of Cancer. La Salle, who by all accounts took himself very seriously, was opposed to the traditional burlesque ceremony of ducking on crossing the line. "Assuredly," admitted Joutel, "the sailors would gladly have killed us all . . . ."

Meanwhile, the unusual congestion on board the *Joly*, the heat, the slow speed, and the lack of drinking water were not long in having their

Cavelier de La Salle

effect. Some 50 persons, including La Salle, fell ill. It was therefore decided, on the eighteenth, to make for Santo Domingo as quickly as possible. However, instead of stopping at Port-de-Paix, as agreed, Beaujeu, perhaps thinking he could take advantage of a favourable wind, headed for the Petit-Goave (now in Haiti) which he reached, alas, only ten days later. Shortly after landing, the discoverer was stricken with a violent attack of fever, and was delirious for seven days. "M. de La Salle," noted Minet in his diary, "believed that all those he saw were coming to call him to account, saying that he had deceived M. de Seignelay." As soon as he had recovered, he went in quest of money—his pockets were always empty—and of supplies, and conferred with the government officials of the West Indies who came to meet him. On 2 October the *Aimable* and the *Belle*, which continually lagged behind, finally arrived. The *Saint-François*, however, a still slower ship, failed to appear. On 20 October fears were confirmed: the ketch, which carried the major part of the expedition's provisions and supplies, had been captured by the Spaniards. This was a heavy loss, responsibility for which La Salle imputed to Beaujeu. However, the governor of the Île de la Tortue having offered help to the explorer, the latter was able to speed up his preparations for departure. He was eager to weigh anchor, for desertions were increasing among his men. Determined to protect at least his own possessions, La Salle this time went on board the flute *Aimable*.

They got under way in the night of 25 November. By hugging the south coast of Cuba, the flotilla reached the entrance to the Gulf of Mexico around the middle of December. On the 27 and 28 of that month, they noticed the white colour of the sea, and the soundings revealed a sea bed of "fine, greyish and muddy sand": these are characteristics of the Mississippi delta, still visible today up to about 12 miles out from the coast of the gulf, which nowhere else has these particular features. For once it seemed that a good star had indeed guided La Salle straight to the objective. But it was not so. The explorer did not realize where he was: it was fairly easy, at that period, to calculate latitude correctly, but not to calculate longitude. Furthermore, the sea-charts of the region were all more or less inaccurate, and La Salle had made a mistake of two degrees when taking the latitude of the mouth of the Mississippi in 1682. The explorer therefore once more made a mistake in his reckonings, and, thinking he had got into the currents of the Gulf Stream of the force of which "several learned persons of Paris" had given him an exaggerated idea, he concluded that he had drifted 300 miles eastward, as far as Apalachee Bay. Nevertheless, La Salle, on 1 January, when he was less than 15 leagues from the Mississippi, wondered momentarily if he had not arrived in the vicinity of Cap Escondito, *by which the mouths of the Mississippi were marked on 17th century maps*. Unfortunately rather than following his intuition, he preferred to trust some log-books of Spanish navigators which confirmed him in his error about a drift to the east.

So they turned their prows westward, in search of the hypothetical Baie du Saint-Esprit, to the west of which the discoverer hoped to find his river again. In the night of 3–4 Jan. 1685, despite the fog, La Salle gave the signal for departure. Beaujeu, who was anchored further out to sea, apparently did not understand, or did not want to understand, and the other ships lost sight of the *Joly*. La Salle apparently did not give Beaujeu too much of an opportunity to catch up with him. In fact he sailed for 19 consecutive hours in the fog, then cast anchor in places where the *Joly* could not venture. On 6 January the *Aimable* and the *Belle* reached "a kind of bay" (probably that of Atchafalaya), which because of its reefs and sandbanks could not, according to La Salle, be the Baie du Saint-Esprit. They sailed on, going along the coasts of Texas. But about the eighteenth, the bend of the coast towards the south led La Salle to believe that they had in truth gone well beyond the Mississippi delta. They turned, and the next morning the *Joly* finally caught up with the other two ships, which were at anchor at the southwest tip of the island of Matagorda. Beaujeu and La Salle did not lose such an admirable opportunity for a quarrel, with mutual accusations of desertion. Then they spent several days hunting and exploring the seaboard, without managing to acquire any certainty as to the exact place where they had landed. La Salle was nonplussed, but nevertheless tried to convince himself that he had got to the mouth of one of the "outlets" of the Mississippi.

The stubborn explorer resumed his unflagging search. This time he changed his tactics: the soldiers were to move off by land, still towards the east, and the flotilla was to follow them offshore, at a reduced speed in order to help them if necessary. On 14 Feb. 1685, they all met off Matagorda Bay, to which La Salle was later to give the name Saint-Louis. An islet and reefs between the island and peninsula of Matagorda made access to the bay particularly difficult. However, the next day, reports Joutel, "M. de La Salle, who came ashore ... examined the entrance to the said river or bay. He found it a very fine one, and after he had considered everything, he decided to bring the *Belle* and the *Aimable* in that way, hoping as he did that this might be an arm of his

Cavelier de La Salle

river." A channel was therefore sounded and marked with buoys, and the *Belle* negotiated it successfully. But the *Aimable*, either because of La Salle's rashness or because of a mistake on the pilot's part, ran disastrously aground, spilling into the sea its cargo of foodstuffs, munitions, materials, and goods, only a small portion of which was recovered. Local Indians tried to take advantage of the shipwreck. In return, some of the French stole a number of their canoes. Fighting broke out: two people were killed and two wounded, among them La Salle's nephew, Crevel de Moranget. The situation was deteriorating. But this was only a beginning.

In the middle of March, Beaujeu, whose task was completed, returned to France, taking with him some members of the expedition who were abandoning the cause. For protection against the Indians, those who remained began to construct a fort out of the wreckage of the *Aimable*. On the twenty-fourth, La Salle set off with some 50 persons to reconnoitre the surrounding district, but succeeded in finding no trace of his river. Since sickness and death were taking their toll at the first camp because of the unhealthy locality, La Salle set up another one slightly to the northwest of Matagorda Bay; this site was just as badly chosen from the sanitary point of view. The building of Fort Saint-Louis, started in May 1685 on the right bank of the Rivière aux Bœufs (Lavaca), was to cost several men their lives. As Joutel says, "This excessive toil; the scant food of the workers, which was very frequently docked because they had not discharged their duty; M. de La Salle's vexation at not managing to accomplish things as he had imagined, which led him to treat his people harshly, often at the wrong time: all this saddened many, whose spirits visibly declined."

On Hallowe'en, La Salle set off in a canoe to go down the river as far as Matagorda Bay, where he wanted to examine the coves with minute care, still with the wild hope of finding an arm of the Mississippi. In mid-January 1686, Joutel, who was in command at Fort Saint-Louis, saw a lone figure returning: it was one of the men whom the explorer had taken with him. Pierre Duhaut, forced to stop in order to repair his makeshift footwear, had lost his way and had almost perished because of Moranget, who, ordered that day to bring up the rear, had refused to wait for him. La Salle's nephew was to pay dearly, later on, for his callousness.

As for the explorer himself, he came back to the fort at the end of March empty-handed, without his six best men, who had been killed by the Indians. The bark was missing. La Salle very much feared that the *Belle* had disappeared for good, somewhere in the bay, where it had been following from offshore his movements along the coast. This new misfortune seriously lessened La Salle's freedom of action, and the chances of the little colony's survival. The last resort was to try to discover the Mississippi by land, in order to go and seek help from Fort Saint-Louis-des-Illinois. La Salle started out at the end of April with some 20 companions, among them his brother and Father Douay. Three days later, Joutel took in at the fort of the Rivière aux Bœufs the five survivors from the shipwreck of the *Belle*, which its pilot had run aground when he was drunk. The rescued men brought with them La Salle's clothes and papers which they had saved.

Meanwhile the explorer was heading towards the northeast, crossing numerous rivers that he named as he went: the Princesse, the Mignonne, the Sablonnière, the Maligne, and the Rivière des Malheurs. Dominique Duhaut, as well as three or four other comrades, soon had to give up, and were sent back to the fort. On the way they became lost. The elder of the two Duhaut brothers was never to forgive La Salle for his younger brother's death.

The remainder of the party arrived among the Cenis Indians. There they obtained five horses. Then, judging the number in his troop—now eight people—too reduced to continue, La Salle retraced his steps. Back in Fort Saint-Louis once more, he was laid up in October by a painful hernia.

When he had recovered, La Salle began anew to prepare for departure. This time Joutel was to follow his chief. On 12 Jan. 1687 they set out on foot, 17 of them, to find their way towards the Illinois country; with the 25 people—7 of them of the female sex—left at the habitation, this was all that remained of the approximately 180 unfortunates who had been established in Texas two years earlier. It was certainly not a pleasure trip they were undertaking. Torrential rains flooded the countryside, rendering paths unusable and camping in shelters particularly arduous. The swollen watercourses were very difficult to ford, not to mention that the men, already overburdened, had to relieve the horses of the personal baggage of the Cavelier brothers, who had monopolized the animals. The priest alone made them carry, among other things, "several church ornaments, even a dozen habits . . . which could well have been dispensed with," as Joutel remarks. But, he added in exasperation, La Salle and the Sulpician "did not have the inconvenience of this, and it meant nothing to them." In addition, dense forests all around them proved to be uncommonly inhospitable. They advanced none the less, passing through numerous Indian villages which La Salle now approached tactfully, all too well aware how heavy had been the price, in dead men and futile wanderings, of his bad relations with the Texan tribes. The Indians, won over, showed themselves well disposed, and provided useful information about the country and its inhabitants. In the middle of March, the troop was in the neighbourhood of the Cenis Indians. On the fourteenth, they crossed the Trinity River, called by La Salle the Rivière aux Canots.

The next day, when they were camping two leagues from the left bank, La Salle sent his servant and his faithful Nika, a Shawnee hunter, together with Pierre Duhaut, the latter's surgeon, and three or four others, to dig up provisions that the explorer had buried a little farther on, during his last voyage. On the seventeenth, Moranget and two companions went to meet them with horses, to bring back the meat of the bison slaughtered by Nika. As soon as he arrived, La Salle's nephew flew into a rage against the men and claimed the flesh of the bison, which they had smoked and from which they had set aside the marrowbones for themselves. This really passed all bounds. Duhaut and his surgeon had long harboured a persistent resentment against Moranget, who had previously abandoned the former in the middle of the forest, and had requited the second with brutality for the careful attention he had lavished on his wounds at the time when the Indian canoes were stolen. A plot was therefore contrived, and during the night the surgeon, assisted by four accomplices, used an axe to kill Moranget, Nika, and La Salle's servant, who were sleeping side by side.

On the morning of 19 March 1687, La Salle, warned by sombre forebodings, hastened to the scene of the crime with Father Douay. The murderers had just as strong a grudge against their chief. Duhaut in particular, who as well as being his creditor held against him the disappearance of his brother Dominique, had no desire to let La Salle denounce the triple assassination. While the explorer was approaching, the merchant lay in wait, crouching in the tall grass with his musket. La Salle inquired about the fate of his nephew. Duhaut's servant replied impudently that the victim was adrift somewhere on a nearby stream. With a sudden angry gesture, La Salle turned towards the saucy fellow. A shot rang out. The discoverer slumped down, dead, with a bullet in his head. The "madmen" insulted the corpse, and, styling it a "grand bacha," they stripped it and left it naked in a thicket, to be devoured by wild animals. Then they seized La Salle's possessions, including his famous scarlet cloak, which had survived every shipwreck. Some time later, feeling the threat of impending justice, the conspirators, all but two, finished by killing one another off.

As for the rest of the troop, they reached Fort Saint-Louis-des-Illinois the following 14 September, and Montreal on 13 July 1688. During all that time, La Salle's tragic end was kept a secret at the request of Abbé Cavelier, who, being anxious to collect the furs owing to his brother, revealed his death only some weeks after having returned to France, 9 Oct. 1688. The covetous Sulpician, still through self-interest, subsequently composed an account of his voyage to the Gulf of Mexico, stuffed with lies which were to mislead several generations of historians.

Thus ended, paradoxically in blood, mud, and silence, a life given over to the frenzied pursuit of fame. However, history was again to invoke this man, René-Robert Cavelier de La Salle, to present him now as a hero worthy of inspiring a national holiday, now as a mere case for psychoanalysis. "Such is the fate of those men," remarked Charlevoix* very rightly, "whom a mixture of great defects and great virtues lifts above the common sphere. Their passions cause them to make mistakes; and although they do what others could not do, their undertakings are not to everybody's liking; their successes arouse the jealousy of those who remain in obscurity; they do good to some, and ill to others; the latter avenge themselves by discrediting them inordinately; the former exaggerate their worth. Hence the very different portraits that are made of them, no one of which is a likeness."

Few historical personages are more difficult to judge than La Salle. The merit of having discovered the last 700 miles of the lower course of the Mississippi certainly belongs to him, but it is sullied by the failure in Texas, for which he was to a large extent responsible. He had the lofty audacity to conceive vast plans for the extension of the kingdom of France, but his idealistic mind prevented him from seeing the exaggerated dimensions of his dreams, and led him to take his desires for realities.

Again, one must admit that during his explorations he displayed an almost superhuman strength, tenacity, and courage. Yet what energy he wasted, by his lack of organization, by his perpetual comings and goings in the Great Lakes and Illinois regions! One might easily assert, also, that he was afflicted with a persecution mania, but his frightful death shows that he was not after all completely misguided in his suspicions. Finally, if his austere and solitary nature made him choose the life of the woods, as he himself wrote, it did not prevent him, alas, and to his very great detriment, from dabbling in the intrigues of Versailles and in those created by the rivalry between Jesuits and Recollets.

It will be apparent that a definitive study of Cavelier de La Salle's life and work has yet to be made.

CÉLINE DUPRÉ

Among the numerous MSS and printed sources on La Salle the following are listed: AN, Col., B, 3–8, 10–13, C^{11A}, C^{13C}, 3; Marine, B^2, 50–2, 55, 58, 66, 104, B^4, 9, 10; Archives du Service hydrographique de la marine, carton 67^1, nos 15, 16; 115–19, no. 12. BN, MS, Clairambault 1016; MS, NAF 7497 (Renaudot), 21330, 21331 (Arnoul), 9288–94, 9300, 9301 (Margry).

[René de Bréhant de Galinée], *Voyage de MM. Dollier & Galinée* (SHM Mémoires, VI, Montréal, 1875); this incomplete edition is not worth consulting, except for the notes by Abbé H. A. Verreau; better is "Voyage de Cavelier de La Salle avec les Sulpiciens Dollier de Casson et Brehan de Gallinée" in *Découvertes et établissements des Français* (Margry), I, 101–66. *See also* the French-English edition of James H. Coyne, ". . . Exploration of the Great Lakes 1669–1670 . . ." in Ont. Hist. Soc. *Papers and Records*, IV (1903). Caron, "Inventaire de documents," APQ *Rapport, 1939–40*, 221–25. [Jean Cavelier], *The journal of Jean Cavelier: the account of a survivor of La Salle's Texas expedition, 1684–1688*, tr. and annotated by Jean Delanglez (Chicago, 1938); this work contains an extremely important critical analysis of the sources concerning La Salle, which clarify, in addition to La Salle's account, those of Douay and the pseudo-Tonty (*infra*). "Correspondance de Frontenac (1672–82)," APQ *Rapport, 1926–27*. "Correspondance de Talon," *ibid., 1930–31*. *Découvertes et établissements des Français* (Margry), I–III; the largest collection of printed sources, in which, however, the transcription is not always very faithful to the originals. Louis Hennepin, *Description de la Louisiane . . .* (Paris, 1683); *Nouvelle découverte d'un très grand pays dans l'Amérique entre le Nouveau Mexique, et la mer glaciale . . .* (Utrecht, 1697); *Nouveau voyage d'un païs plus grand que l'Europe, avec les réflections des entreprises du Sieur de La Salle . . .* (Utrecht, 1698); sources which are often quite untrustworthy. *JR* (Thwaites). [Henri Joutel], *Journal historique du dernier voyage que feu M. de la Sale fit dans le Golfe de Mexique . . . Où l'on voit l'histoire tragique de sa mort, & plusieurs choses curieuses du nouveau monde . . .*, éd. De Michel (Paris, 1713). *Jug. et délib.* Le Clercq, *First establishment of the faith* (Shea); *Premier établissement de la foy*, chap. XXI–XXV; chap. XII and XXIII contain the "Relation" of Membré and chap. XXV that of Douay. *NYCD* (O'Callaghan and Fernow), IX. Perrot, *Mémoire* (Tailhan). "Le procès de l'abbé de Fénelon devant le Conseil de la Nouvelle-France en 1674," APQ *Rapport, 1921–22*, 124–88. Raymond Thomassy, *Géologie pratique de la Louisiane* (Nouvelle-Orléans et Paris, 1860), 9–16, App. A et B; here are given, among other accounts, the official report (attributed to Membré) of La Salle's 1682 explorations. [Henri de Tonti], *Dernières découvertes dans l'Amérique Septentrionale de M. de la Sale . . .* (Paris, 1697); apocryphal account.

Charlevoix, *Histoire*. P. Chesnel, *Histoire de Cavelier de La Salle, exploration et conquête du bassin du Mississipi . . .* (Paris, 1901). Delanglez, *Jolliet*; *Some La Salle journeys* (Chicago, 1938); monographs of the greatest importance. Faillon, *Histoire de la colonie française*, III, 228f., 286–314, 353f., 472–77, 495–514. Désiré Girouard, *Les anciens forts de Lachine et Cavelier de La Salle* (Montréal, 1891). Gabriel Gravier, *Cavelier de La Salle de Rouen* (Paris, 1871), which provides a very useful bibliography; *Découvertes et établissements de Cavelier de La Salle, de Rouen, dans l'Amérique du Nord . . .* (Paris, 1870). Lionel Groulx, *Notre grande aventure: l'empire français en Amérique du Nord (1535–1760)* (Montréal et Paris (1958)), 111–37, 193–98. Marion Habig, *The Franciscan Père Marquette: a critical biography of Father Zénobe Membré . . ."* (Franciscan studies, XIII, New York, 1934). Gérard Malchelosse, "La Salle et le fort Saint-Joseph des Miamis," *Cahiers des Dix*, XXII (1957), 83–103. Nute, *Caesars of the wilderness*, 157–59, 201, *et passim*. Parkman, *La Salle and the discovery of the great west* (12th ed.). Rochemonteix, *Les Jésuites et la Nouvelle-France au XVIIe siècle*, III, 40–80, 162–64; best source for the years covering the religious life of La Salle. John G. Shea, *The bursting of Pierre Margry's La Salle bubble* (New York, 1879). Sulte, *Mélanges historiques* (Malchelosse), X, 66–89; "La mort de Cavelier de La Salle," *RSCT*, 2d ser., IV (1898), sect. I, 3–31. Roger Viau, *Cavelier de La Salle* (s.l., 1960). Marc de Villiers du Terrage, *La découverte du Missouri et l'histoire du Fort d'Orléans, 1673–1738* (Paris, 1925); *L'expédition de Cavelier de la Salle dans le golfe du Mexique, 1684–1687* (Paris, 1931): essential sources.

CENDRE CHAUDE. *See* OGENHERATARIHIENS

CHABANEL, NOËL, priest, Jesuit, missionary to the Hurons; canonized by Pope Pius XI on 29 June 1930; b. 2 Feb. 1613 at Saugues (Haute-Loire); killed out of hatred for the faith by a Huron apostate on 8 Dec. 1649.

Noël Chabanel entered the noviciate at Toulouse on 9 Feb. 1630. He taught in the college of that city (1632–39), studied theology there (1639–41), and did his third probationary year there (1641–42). After teaching rhetoric at the college of Rodez, he arrived at Quebec on 15 Aug. 1643, spent one year there and then went on to the Huron country.

Of the eight Canadian martyrs, he is the only one who had no flair for the study of languages. A brilliant teacher of rhetoric in France, he felt an inexpressible loathing for the ways and customs of the Indians. "Never, for all that," writes Father Paul RAGUENEAU, "would he break away from the

Cross on which God had placed him; never did he ask that he might come down from it. On the contrary, in order to bind himself to it more inviolably, he obliged himself, by a vow, to remain there till death, so that he might die upon the Cross." The *Relation* for 1650 has preserved for us the wording of this heroic vow.

At the beginning of December 1649, he was at the Saint-Jean mission among the Tobacco Indians, when he received orders to go to the main residence, Sainte-Marie II, on the Île Saint-Joseph. Having set out on 7 December he was the next day treacherously slain by a Huron apostate. The *Relation* for 1650 recounts Chabanel's death, but reveals no knowledge of the motives for the slaying. In the "Manuscrit de 1652," Father Ragueneau is better informed. He takes cognizance of the confession of the murderer, Louis Honarreennha, who stated that he had killed Chabanel because of his hatred for the faith.

LÉON POULIOT

ACSM, Notice manuscrite du P. Chabanel, rédigée par le père Félix Martin; "Mémoires touchant la mort et les vertus des pères Isaac Jogues . . . " (Ragueneau), repr. APQ *Rapport, 1924–25,* 3, 85–89. *Jésuites de la N.-F.* (Roustang), 315–22. *JR* (Thwaites). *Positio causae.* Rochemonteix, *Les Jésuites et la Nouvelle-France au XVIIe siècle,* II.

Father Chabanel, who aspired to be a martyr in obscurity and without bloodshed, has had two biographers in our own day: Alfred Raymond, *Saint Noël Chabanel, martyr du Canada (1613–1649)* (Montréal, 1946). Frédéric Saintonge, *Martyr dans l'ombre: Saint Noël Chabanel* (Montréal, 1958).

CHAMBLY, JACQUES DE, captain in the Carignan-Salières regiment, seigneur of Chambly and governor of Acadia, son of Philippe de Chambly and Louise de Laulne; d. 1687 in Martinique.

Descendant of an old and illustrious family which had been impoverished as a result of the wars, Chambly had served in Hungary and had commanded the regiment of the Maréchal d'Estrades. He arrived in Canada in June 1665 as captain of a company in the Carignan-Salières regiment; he directed the construction of Fort Saint-Louis on the Richelieu Rapids and took part in PROUVILLE de Tracy's expedition against the Iroquois cantons. The following year he received a gratuity of 400 *écus* from the king. When the regiment was disbanded, Chambly returned to France; but, having been recommended by TALON, he returned in 1670 as captain of a company of colonial regular troops. He began the establishment of a farming settlement around Fort Saint-Louis, where he lived, and received three of the horses that Talon had had sent out from France.

In 1672 he obtained the grant of a seigneury three leagues long and one deep on each side of the river, near the fort. This seigneury received his name. (It gave birth to the present-day village of Chambly.) Several of his soldiers settled near him. BUADE de Frontenac named him commandant of the south side of the river, from Rivière du Loup to Montreal. On 5 May 1673 he was appointed governor of Acadia, to replace ANDIGNÉ de Grandfontaine. In the autumn he went to Pentagouet from Quebec, on a small ship, the *Saint-Jean.*

He was not long in command there, for the very next summer he was attacked by a party of Dutch pirates commanded by AERNOUTSZ and RHOADES. His little garrison of 30 men was not able to withstand the assault and surrendered after a short combat. Chambly was taken prisoner and carried off to Boston with his ensign, Jean-Vincent d'Abbadie* de Saint-Castin, and Pierre JOYBERT de Soulanges, who had been captured at Jemseg. Saint-Castin succeeded in escaping and carried the news to Quebec. Frontenac paid the ransom, but Chambly could not be freed until the following year. Having returned to France, on 20 May 1676 he received command of Acadia once more. He had formed some ambitious projects which interested Colbert, who promised him 4,000 *livres* to pay for the passage of 30 soldiers and 100 settlers. Chambly does not however appear to have returned to Canada, since he had already been appointed military commander in the West Indies on 3 Sept. 1677. Having been named governor of Grenada 24 April 1679, he bequeathed his seigneury of Chambly to his fiancée Marie-Françoise de Thavenet, one of whose sisters, Marguerite*, had married Joseph-François Hertel* de la Fresnière. It was in this way that the seigneury of Chambly passed into the hands of the Hertel family. After being appointed governor of Martinique the following year, Chambly died there in 1687.

RENÉ BAUDRY

AN, Col., B, 1, 5, 7, 9; C^{11D}, 1. Correspondance de Frontenac (1672–82), APQ *Rapport, 1926–27.* Correspondance de Talon, APQ *Rapport, 1930–31.* P.-G. Roy, *Inv. concessions,* II, 196–97. *BRH,* XXII (1916), 374; XXIII (1917), 14–16. Robert La Roque de Roquebrune, "Les demoiselles de Thavenet," *NF,* V (1930), 86–91.

CHAMPDORÉ, PIERRE ANGIBAULT *dit.* *See* ANGIBAULT

Champflour

CHAMPFLOUR, FRANÇOIS DE, governor of Trois-Rivières, commandant at Fort Richelieu; b. into the Parisian branch of a family originally from Clermont-Ferrand, in Auvergne.

In 1636, a Bertrand de Champflour was a member of the Compagnie des Cent-Associés, and in 1639 M. HUAULT de Montmagny named François de Champflour governor of Trois-Rivières, with responsibility for reorganizing the defences of that fort and for negotiating with the enemy tribes. The commandant showed himself to be a firm and skilful diplomat. When in 1641 the Iroquois requested his presence to discuss a peace-treaty, Champflour sent François MARGUERIE to tell them, at the latter's suggestion it must be added, that the governor-general alone possessed this authority. Since the Indians insisted on his presence, he suspected a trap. He caused a reply to be made to them that he did not know their language, and delegated the excellent interpreters, Jean NICOLLET and Father Paul RAGUENEAU, to meet with them. This delay was necessary to allow M. de Montmagny to appear before the Iroquois in full official dress, and accompanied by a retinue capable of impressing them. The Iroquois withdrew farther towards the south, and the governor sent Champflour to Fort Richelieu as commandant in order to keep them there. He stayed there from August 1642 to December 1643, at which time he returned to Trois-Rivières with the title of governor. In July 1645 he received a visit from the Mohawk ambassadors, one of whom was KIOTSEAETON, who wished to open peace negotiations. He sent for Governor de Montmagny to come from Quebec. After long speeches on both sides, peace was concluded. In the fall of 1645 he went to Paris, apparently to settle his affairs with the intention of returning to the colony. In 1646, in Paris, he still bore the title of governor of Trois-Rivières. He did not return to New France, and in 1649 he sold the fief that the Compagnie des Cent-Associés had granted him at Trois-Rivières to JACQUES LENEUF de La Poterie.

RAYMOND DOUVILLE

Desrosiers, *Iroquoisie*, 303–8 *et passim*. E. Éverat, *Archives inédites de la famille de Champflour* (Clermont-Ferrand, 1928). P.-G. Roy, *Inv. concessions*, II, 71f. Benjamin Sulte, *Chronique trifluvienne* (Montréal, 1879); "Les gouverneurs des Trois-Rivières," *BRH*, II (1896), 67. *Mélanges historiques* (Malchelosse), XIV, 64, 71; XIX, 70–73.

CHAMPLAIN, ÉTIENNE PÉZARD DE LA TOUSCHE. See PÉZARD

CHAMPLAIN, HÉLÈNE DE. See BOULLÉ

CHAMPLAIN, SAMUEL DE, draftsman, geographer, explorer, founder of Quebec in 1608, lieutenant to Lieutenant-General Pierre DU GUA de Monts 1608–12, to Lieutenant-General Bourbon de Soissons in 1612, to Viceroy Bourbon de Condé 1612–20, to Viceroy de Montmorency 1620–25, to Viceroy de Ventadour 1625–27; commandant at Quebec in 1627 and 1628, between de Ventadour's resignation and the creation of the Compagnie des Cent-Associés; commander in New France "in the absence of my Lord the Cardinal de Richelieu" 1629–35; member of the Compagnie des Cent-Associés; b. *c.* 1570 at Brouage, in Saintonge (Charente-Maritime); d. 25 Dec. 1635 at Quebec.

As the parish registers of Brouage have been destroyed by fire, nothing is known of the date of Champlain's birth or of his baptism; he may have been born *c.* 1570, perhaps in 1567. Some have been inclined to see in Champlain the son of poor fisherfolk or of a naval captain, or even the bastard of a great family. Haunted by the mystery of Champlain's birth, Florian de La Horbe has endeavoured to solve it after the manner of an Alexandre Dumas; Champlain, he conjectures, was Guy Eder de La Fontanelle, a renowned ruffian who was sentenced to be broken on the wheel, and who is presumed to have escaped this punishment and to have turned up again as an honest man, under the name of Champlain. It is fruitless to seek in this hypothesis any serious proof which would lead one to doubt the traditional story; we are dealing here with nothing more than a very inferior detective novel.

We do not know whether Champlain was baptized a Roman Catholic or a Protestant; his biblical first name, which in Saintonge was seldom given except in Protestant families, and the fact that Brouage was then a Huguenot town, make it probable that Champlain was born a Protestant. His struggle against the Catholic League proves nothing, for opposition to the League was common among monarchists, Catholic or Protestant; his choice of a Protestant wife proves nothing either. If he was born a Protestant, Champlain very soon passed over to Catholicism, like the Jesuit PAUL LE JEUNE, who was born a Huguenot and later became a Catholic. In any case, when he began his Canadian career in 1603 Champlain was a Catholic; this is proved by the doctrine he expounded at that time to the Tadoussac Indians.

According to his marriage contract, Champlain was the son "of the late Anthoine de Complain, in his lifetime Captain in the Navy, and of Dame Margueritte Le Roy." We know nothing further about his parents, and the mystery of the "Provençal uncle" who played such an important role at the beginning of the explorer's career still remains to be cleared up. Was Champlain of noble birth? The little that we know of his family does not enlighten us any more than does the name he bears; his 1603 volume gives "Samuel Champlain" and the dedication to Admiral Montmorency is signed "S. Champlain," whereas in the *privilège*, in the same edition, there are the words "Sieur de Champlain," just as in the marriage contract of 1610 and in the 1613, 1619, and 1632 volumes. However, the particle proves nothing, for nobility was conferred only by direct noble descent or by letters of nobility. In the absence of the latter (whether they did not exist or have been lost), one must accept with considerable caution the titles that Champlain assumed or allowed himself to be given. In the 1610 marriage contract he was styled "noble homme," a title given to commoners of importance. In a notarial contract of 1615 Champlain was named an esquire; only nobles had a right to this title, although in practice quite a few bourgeois accepted it without demur. Further, in an agreement of 1617, he was called "noble homme," and likewise in a document of 1621; but in a notarial contract of 1625, and in 1626, at the time of the registration of this document, Champlain had once more his title of esquire; what is more, in the official list of the Cent-Associés in 1627, drawn up before the king bestowed upon the company letters of nobility for 12 associates who were commoners, Champlain was again styled an esquire. If it were possible to disregard the 1617 and 1621 documents, one might perhaps conclude that Champlain, a "noble homme" in 1610, acceded to the nobility before 1615; in that case his elevation would have occurred in 1612, when Champlain became lieutenant to a viceroy: it is difficult to imagine a Bourbon de Condé allowing himself to be represented in New France by a mere commoner, who was granted extensive powers that in theory only a noble could exercise. This is a hypothesis. The discovery of new documents will be necessary if it is to be supported more convincingly.

We have little reliable information about Champlain's pre-Canadian career. He may have practised an art necessary for a geographer, that of painter or draftsman. A factum drawn up by the merchants of Saint-Malo *c.* 1613 noted, concerning Champlain as he was in 1603: "He went [on this voyage] only as a passenger, his profession as a painter, as well as the money, inviting him to see the said country." In fact Champlain was an excellent draftsman. To him are attributed the very felicitous drawings of the *Brief discours* (they appear to be originals, whereas the text is only a copy). And the maps that he later drew of New France, particularly that of 1632, were magnificently executed.

He must have begun his sailing early, since he informed the queen in 1613 that the art of navigation had attracted him from his "tender youth." In 1632 he stated that he had served against the League in the army of Henri IV until 1598, with the title of sergeant; when the Spanish troops maintained in Brittany by Philippe II left Port-Blavet (Port-Louis, in Morbihan), Champlain embarked with them. From Spain, according to what he told the king in 1630 and 1632, he went as far as the West Indies, on a voyage that took him two years and a half. His presence at Cadiz was noted in July 1601, after which he returned to France.

Champlain wrote on two occasions that he had travelled in the West Indies; there is no good reason why one should reject this declaration by a man near the end of his career. What does complicate the problem is a work that Champlain never published but that is attributed to him, the *Brief discours des choses plus remarquables que Samuel Champlain de Brouage a reconnues aux Indes occidentales*. Claude de Bonnault and Jean Bruchési have been the first to cast doubt upon the authenticity of this document, and consequently upon the sincerity of Champlain. A recent study by L.-A. Vigneras re-examines the question, while retaining a few hypotheses: Vigneras notes that the *Brief discours* sometimes gives an itinerary incompatible with that of Coloma's *armada*, which Champlain is supposed to have accompanied; one must in addition, continues Vigneras, "entertain the most serious reservations about the alleged voyages to Mexico City, Porto-Bello and Carthagena." How are the gross errors of the *Brief discours* to be explained? According to Vigneras, Champlain did not make this trip (or all of it) with Coloma's fleet; again, he drew up the *Brief discours* from information collected in Spain, if not from the papers of the famous "Provençal uncle"; or else he recounted his journey only at a time when his memory was no longer reliable.

To be just towards Champlain, we must first remember that he did not publish this *Brief discours*; the work is not by him, or if it is he did not judge it worthy of publication. Another observation; what was published under Champlain's name, and that only after 1859, was not the original but a copy. To what extent is this copy accurate? The same fate has befallen the relation of VERRAZZANO, which was long known only through a truncated copy studded with errors. The Cèllere manuscript had to be

Champlain

discovered before historians could finally accord Verrazzano his proper merit. Until the original is found, we have no right to include the *Brief discours* among Champlain's works.

After his return from Spain, Champlain had the benefit of a pension at the court of Henri IV. It was then that Commander Aymar de Chaste, the holder of the trade monopoly in New France, invited Champlain to follow FRANÇOIS GRAVÉ DU Pont, whom he was sending on an expedition. On 15 March 1603, as a private passenger, Champlain went on board the *Bonne-Renommée* at Honfleur. He had no precise function; he was not yet a naval captain. When he published his account of the voyage, on his return, no title follows his name. Was he the king's geographer, as LESCARBOT was to hail him in a sonnet of 1607? Nowhere does Champlain bear this title, and no one but Lescarbot gives it to him; there is no confirmation that Champlain, while acting as a geographer, held the official post of king's geographer. He sailed in 1603 as a mere observer, and his presence on this voyage would have passed unnoticed had he not published his account; he is, moreover, the only one to give us an account of this voyage.

On 26 May, Gravé Du Pont's ships reached Tadoussac; there Champlain witnessed the "tabagies" (native feasts), during which the Algonkin women danced naked and the male Indians took part in races, for which presents were awarded. While the fur-trading was going on, from 26 May to 18 June, Champlain had time to study the natives' customs. He even gave them a course in religion. On 11 June, he went some 12 leagues up the Saguenay; he listened to descriptions of the whole Saguenay basin and its waterways, learned of the existence of a saltwater sea to the north, and without assuming, like all the travellers concerned, that this was the Asian Sea, he concluded with a confidence that surprises us: "It is some gulf of this our sea, which overflows in the north into the midst of the continent." In 1603, seven years before its discovery by the English, Champlain divined in some fashion the existence of Hudson Bay.

When the feasts and trading were over, Gravé, on 18 June, started to go up the St. Lawrence River, which Champlain was still calling, as in the time of CARTIER, the "rivière de Canada." Champlain went with him; he discovered nothing. What was new for him was not so for the French of his day; Levasseur, in 1601, had determined the configuration of the river as we know it, and his map mentions the place-names Tadoussac, Quebec, and Trois-Rivières. This 1603 journey did however furnish us with a more detailed and clearer description of the river than is to be found in Cartier's accounts. As he passed in front of Quebec, where his destiny was to be unfolded, Champlain showed little interest, merely remarking that if the lands were cultivated they would be as good as those of France. It was at Trois-Rivières that the future colonizer began to reveal himself; he saw there a place suitable for a "habitation," which at that time, however, he visualized only in its relationship to the safety of the fur-trading route. Did Champlain add to the list of place-names? It was probably he who christened Montmorency Falls. He gave a new name to "lac Angoulême," Saint-Pierre. He went up the Richelieu as far as the Saint-Ours Rapids, and got from the natives a good description of the upper reaches of the river. He was no more fortunate than Cartier, being blocked by the rapids at Hochelaga (Montreal). By questioning the natives, he made an amazing reconstruction of the network of the Great Lakes (including Niagara Falls), with measurements that often corresponded to actual fact, but he allowed himself to be persuaded that the Asian Sea was not far away.

He returned to Tadoussac on 11 July, and re-embarked with François Gravé Du Pont for Gaspé, where he stayed from 15 to 19 July—days of respite which permitted him to obtain a general notion of the region; he heard about Acadia, where he hoped to find the route to Asia, and the mines that SARCEL de Prévert was looking for in that area. These two Acadian possibilities, the route to Asia and the mines, fascinated Champlain in 1603 more than the St. Lawrence. When one reads him, one senses that Acadia would perhaps supersede the St. Lawrence, and that if the French returned, it would be principally in order to pursue the promises of that mysterious Acadia.

When Champlain went back to France, 20 September, he learned that de Chaste was dead. He presented a map of the St. Lawrence (which has not been found) to the king, delivered to him a "discourse" on what he had seen, and published his account, *Des sauvages*, the *privilège* of which is dated 15 November. The Protestant de Monts, who succeeded de Chaste, had seen nothing of the St. Lawrence except Tadoussac; he wanted to find a warmer country. Through his propaganda for Acadia in 1603, Champlain has his share of responsibility for the temporary abandonment of the St. Lawrence in favour of Acadia. Invited by de Monts and authorized by Henri IV, who apparently instructed him to make a report on his discovery, Champlain embarked once again in March 1604; he still had no official title, but the role he was to play and the completed tasks that he was to leave show that, without having the title, he did perform the duties of a geographer.

In early May 1604, the expedition stopped at Port-au-Mouton, on the east shore of Acadia. De Monts instructed Champlain to choose a temporary base for the settlement, until a site combining the most suitable conditions could be located. Champlain therefore set off on 19 May, sailed round the Cap de Sable, entered the Baie Sainte-Marie where he chose a harbour for the largest ship, noticed some mines, added to the toponymy, and came back to Port-au-Mouton after three weeks. De Monts took his ship into the safety of the Baie Sainte-Marie, and they went off in a bark to explore the Baie Française (the name given by de Monts to the Bay of Fundy). They first visited a bay that Champlain named Port-Royal (now Annapolis Royal, N.S.), went to the end of the Baie Française to look for Prévert's mines, and examined the mouth of the Saint John River, then, as they had to obtain temporary shelter, de Monts stopped at the Île Sainte-Croix (now Dochet Island, in the St. Croix River), which was Champlain's choice; the site and the summer season seemed to make it the best place. De Monts decided to have separate buildings constructed, and Champlain built himself a dwelling to be shared with MM. d'Orville and Pierre ANGIBAULT, *dit* Champdoré.

Before the winter, Champlain busied himself with exploration. After looking again for mines in the Baie Française, on 2 September he went back along the coast, in order to seek the ideal site for a permanent abode. He entered the Penobscot River and tried to reach the Kennebec, but he could not get beyond Pemaquid. On this month-long trip he covered some 150 miles, and penetrated as much as 50 miles into the lands adjoining the Penobscot River. Although not the first European to visit this region, he has given us the first precise description of it. He returned somewhat disappointed with what he had seen.

The winter seasons spent at Sainte-Croix, 1604–5, was disastrous because of scurvy and the exceptional severity of the cold. In the spring, de Monts, having received fresh supplies from Gravé Du Pont, set out again in search of a more favourable district, and with Champlain, on 17 June 1605, took the route southwards once more. On 1 July they entered the Kennebec River and continued towards the south, visiting various points on the coast: Baie des Sept-Îles (Casco Bay), Baie de Chouacouët (Saco Bay), Cap-aux-Îles (Cape Ann), Baie des Îles (Boston Bay), Port Saint-Louis (Plymouth Bay), and finally Cap Blanc (Cape Cod). De Monts rounded this and made a stop at Mallebarre (Nauset Harbour). After a journey of about 400 miles, he returned to Sainte-Croix without finding the ideal site for a settlement. Gosnold and WEYMOUTH had preceded him at some points on this coast, but the geographer Champlain has left us a set of such precise maps that he deserves the title of first cartographer of New England.

While waiting for something better to turn up, de Monts transported his colony to Port-Royal; experience led him to adopt this time the closed quadrilateral dwelling, and they settled in with a certain degree of comfort. For his part Champlain fitted himself up a work-room among the trees, and built a sluice in order to stock his own trout; he took "a particular pleasure" in gardening. At Port-Royal Champlain's role was still that of a mere observer. When de Monts returned to France it was not Champlain whom he named to command in his absence: it was first d'Orville, then Gravé Du Pont. Before the winter started Champlain set off again, unsuccessfully, to look for mines. The winter season of 1605–6, even though made miserable by scurvy, was less painful than the preceding one. During the summer of 1606, JEAN DE BIENCOURT de Poutrincourt turned up with a new contingent (among them the lawyer Marc Lescarbot and the pharmacist LOUIS HÉBERT) and replaced Gravé Du Pont, but Champlain remained a third winter. In September 1606 Poutrincourt, in his turn, searched southward for the site of a permanent settlement; Champlain went with him. Instead of making for Cap Blanc immediately, they lost time re-examining known places; it was only in October, therefore very late, that they got beyond the point they had reached at Mallebarre, but Port Fortuné, where they stopped, was the scene of a massacre of Frenchmen; they therefore returned without being able to get further than Martha's Vineyard. This voyage added little to the toponymy; Champlain gave his name to a small river, the Nashpee, east of Rhode Island.

The winter 1606–7 was a most merry one; pleasant temperature, food and wine in abundance. Champlain added to the high spirits by founding the Order of Good Cheer, a sort of carefree order of chivalry, whose members had to take their turn in providing game for the table and maintaining a joyful humour. In May 1607 it was learned that the trading privilege had been revoked; de Monts gave orders to his colony to return to France. Before leaving, however, Champlain went back to the Baie Française to look for a copper mine, but found only nuggets. When Champlain sailed, 11 August 1607, for Canseau (Canso), he took the opportunity to reconnoitre

Champlain

the coast in detail and to make a map of it. And it was thus that in 1607, thanks to him, all the Atlantic coastline, from Cape Breton to the south of Cap Blanc, was charted and decked out with French place-names. The English, who returned in 1607 to winter on the Kennebec, did nothing comparable in this domain.

The Acadian venture having been broken off, what was to become of Champlain? In 1603 he had influenced de Monts in the choice of Acadia rather than of the St. Lawrence; and he was the one, it seems, who was responsible for the return to the St. Lawrence in 1608. This time he received the first official function of his Canadian career; he became lieutenant to the Sieur de Monts. On 13 April 1608 he set out a third time for New France; he arrived on 3 June at Tadoussac, where he had not been for five years. It was in a bark, and not on board the *Don-de-Dieu*, that he went up the river to establish a habitation, on 3 July, at the "point of Quebec." "I at once employed a part of our workmen," he wrote, "in cutting them [the trees] down to make a site for our settlement, another part in sawing planks, another in digging the cellar and making ditches." He had built, along with a storehouse for provisions, three main buildings; the whole was surrounded by moats 15 feet wide and by stockades of stakes. Quebec was beginning its history.

A few days later, Champlain escaped a plot led by the locksmith Jean DUVAL, who had been with him in Acadia. To try out the soil, Champlain turned his attention to sowing wheat and rye; he planted vines, and made a vegetable garden. Like the first winter season in Acadia, the one at Quebec was marked by a severe onset of scurvy; of the 25 winterers, 16 died, including the surgeon Bonnerme [*see* DUVAL]. Champlain received fresh supplies from Gravé Du Pont in the spring of 1609, and set out on 28 June to discover the country of the Iroquois; he entered the Rivière des Iroquois (Richelieu) where he had already been in 1603; from the Chambly Rapids, taking with him only two Frenchmen, he pushed upriver with some Algonkin, Huron, and Montagnais Indians, and reached a great lake to which he was to give his name.

On the evening of 29 July, at Ticonderoga (Crown Point, N.Y.), his party encountered the Iroquois, and the next day the battle began; as the two sides clashed, the allies opened their ranks, Champlain advanced, fired with his arquebus, and killed two enemy chiefs; a shot fired into the woods by a companion produced panic among the Iroquois. Champlain was taking part for the first time in military operations in New France: although he was not responsible for the long Franco-Iroquois conflict, since the French had contracted an offensive alliance before 1603, he consolidated the prestige of the French; to honour Champlain, the allies reserved for him a brace of firearms and the head of one of the enemy. As a result of his voyage of exploration, Champlain enlarged the map of New France and opened up a route that was to be a strategic one for Europeans for two centuries; had he lingered on until September and gone a few miles farther south, he would have encountered the Englishman HENRY HUDSON, who was introducing Dutch supremacy into this region.

After his victory, Champlain left the command of Quebec to PIERRE CHAUVIN DE LA PIERRE, and returned to France with Gravé Du Pont; on 13 Oct. 1609 he was at Honfleur, whence he was to go and make a report to de Monts and the king. Although he did not manage to get his monopoly renewed, de Monts formed a society with some Rouen merchants: the latter would support the Quebec habitation, but on condition that it served as a warehouse for the fur trade; as a temporary compromise, Quebec would be exclusively a storage point for furs. After a false start and a month of illness, Champlain re-embarked with some artisans on 8 April 1610, and re-appeared at Quebec 28 April, after an unusually rapid voyage.

The Indians were awaiting Champlain, to start another expedition against the Iroquois: the allies had agreed upon a rendezvous at the mouth of the Richelieu; the Iroquois were already there, and well stockaded. Champlain led the attack, although wounded by an arrow which "split the tip of my ear and pierced my neck"; the assault was launched and the Iroquois fled. It was Champlain's last triumph over this enemy. Following this combat, Champlain entrusted to the chief IROQUET a young man, Étienne BRÛLÉ, who wanted to learn the Algonkin language; as a hostage he accepted the Huron SAVIGNON, who wanted to see France. Before he left for France, Champlain discovered that the fur trade that year was ruinous for those supporting him, and he learned that Henri IV had been assassinated. In that unfortunate combination of circumstances he set out from Quebec, 8 Aug. 1610, leaving 16 men under the orders of Jean de Godet Du Parc [*see* CLAUDE DE GODET]; he was at Honfleur by 27 September.

Without making any allusion to it in his writings, Champlain took an important step at the beginning of the winter; on 27 Dec. 1610, at about 40 years of age, he signed a marriage contract with a twelve-year-old girl, HÉLÈNE BOULLÉ. Because of the future bride's youthfulness, it was

Champlain

stipulated that the marriage would not be put into effect for two years. The betrothal took place two days later, and on 30 December the marriage was celebrated in the church of Saint-Germain-l'Auxerrois in Paris. Of the promised dowry (6,000 *livres*), Champlain received 4,500 *livres* the day before the ceremony, which was a valuable contribution to his undertaking.

He sailed again 1 March 1611, and arrived at Quebec 21 May. Forced by a mistake of the Indians to abandon his plan of exploring the St. Maurice River, he went to the Saint-Louis Rapids (Lachine); while waiting for the arrival of the native fur-traders he landed, and, 31 years before the founding of Montreal, he looked on that island for "the ground for building"; he finally chose what was to be Pointe Callières, a place where Indians had tilled the soil in Cartier's time. He ordered "the trees of the Place Royale to be cut down and cleared off, in order to level the ground and make it ready for building"; on an adjoining island, he had a wall constructed out of heavy earth, 10 fathoms long by 3 or 4 high, "to see how it would last during the winter." He noticed an island where it would be possible to "build a good strong town," and gave it the name of Sainte-Hélène in honour of his wife. Champlain's Montreal projects were never to go any further. At last, on 13 June, some Indians came down from the hinterland, and after parleys with them Champlain carried out a feat calculated to increase his prestige among the natives: with them, he shot the rapids in a canoe. Brûlé was the only white man to have done this before him. As soon as he returned to Quebec, he made repairs to the Habitation, planted rose-bushes, and put on board a cargo of "split oak" to be tried out in France. He arrived at La Rochelle 10 Sept. 1611.

Because they did not succeed in securing a monopoly, the Sieur de Monts's partners no longer wanted to support the Quebec venture; for their part the Saint-Malo merchants, finding their justification in Cartier's discoveries, demanded freedom of trade, which led Champlain to compare his work with that of the famous pilot of Saint-Malo; it was right, he asserted, "that we should enjoy the fruits of our labours." He drew up reports, published a map (the first that has come down to us), and begged the king to intervene. Finally, 8 Oct. 1612, Louis XIII named as his lieutenant-general in New France Charles de Bourbon, Comte de Soissons, who on the fifteenth of the month chose Champlain as his lieutenant to continue the Quebec undertaking. Champlain received power to exercise command in the lieutenant-general's name, to appoint "such captains and lieutenants as shall be expedient," to "commission officers for administration of justice and maintenance of police authority, regulations and ordinances," to make treaties with the natives or to wage war upon them, and to restrain merchants who did not belong to the society. It was also his duty to "find the easiest way to go through the said country to the Kingdom of China and the East Indies," to seek out the locations of mines of precious metals, and to exploit them. Shortly afterwards Bourbon de Soissons died. The king transferred the appointment to Henri de Bourbon, Prince de Condé, who on 22 November confirmed Champlain in his office. The supporters of the freedom of trade would try none the less to deprive Champlain of the support of a society of merchants; they would seek every expedient to prevent Champlain from publishing his commission. Champlain was to overcome this opposition only through the personal intervention of the king.

The autumn of 1612 had thus brought Champlain an important advancement. Since 1608, the year that marked his first access to an official position, he had been only the lieutenant to a lieutenant-general who possessed relatively little influence, the Sieur de Monts; in October 1612 he became the lieutenant of an important personage, the Comte de Soissons, who at that period, it is true, seems to have borne only the title of lieutenant-general; but the following November Champlain became lieutenant to a viceroy, the Prince de Condé. Moreover, he obtained the real powers of a governor, without however having either the title or the commission.

Shortly after, he added to his reputation by publishing his *Voyages* (an account that goes from 1604 to 1612), the *privilège* for which was dated 9 Jan. 1613.

On 6 March of the same year, on board François Gravé Du Pont's ship, he left Honfleur with his assistant, the Sieur L'Ange; on 29 March he arrived at Tadoussac, where he proclaimed his new commission; after a brief stop at Quebec, he reached the Saint-Louis rapids on 21 April. As in 1611, the fur trade yielded little profit. Disgusted by the tactics of the unauthorized merchants, the natives came only in small numbers. Champlain then decided to extend his exploration into the Huron country; with an Indian guide and four men (among them the Nicolas de Vignau who, in 1612 in Paris had boasted that he had seen Hudson Bay by going up the Ottawa River), Champlain set out on 27 May. He was the first European to give us a description of this "rivière des Outaouais" (Ottawa), which

191

Champlain

for two centuries was to be the main trade route to the Canadian west. Beyond the Chaudière Falls, to avoid rapids and a long meandering portion of the river, he went across country from one lake to the other (it was in one of these lakes, Green Lake, that in 1867 an astrolabe dated 1603 was found; it was attributed to Champlain, but without conclusive proof). He rejoined the river at the end of Allumette Island. In June he visited the home of TESSOUAT (fl. 1603–13), whom he had known at Tadoussac, and he invited the Algonkins to leave their land with its poor soil and settle at the Saint-Louis rapids. They accepted on condition that the French would build a fort there, an item which was already on Champlain's immediate programme. On the other hand, they tried to dissuade Champlain from going as far as the territory of the Nipissings. The Algonkins, for whom the tolls that they imposed upon the Indian tribes were a lucrative source of income, wanted to prevent the French from going farther up the river. During an interrogation to which they subjected Vignau, they induced him to declare that what he had said about the northern sea was false. This put an end to Champlain's voyage. Beside the Lac aux Allumettes, he erected a cross bearing the arms of France, and went back down the river with one of Tessouat's sons. The French route to the West had been opened up.

On the following 26 August Champlain was already back at Saint-Malo. Towards the end of that year, 1613, he published an account of the journey that he had just made, as well as a map of New France (it included only one addition to the preceding map: the upper part of the Ottawa River). In 1614, at Fontainebleau, where he went to make a report to the king, he formed a society with the merchants of Rouen and Saint-Malo for the support of the Canadian undertaking; this company, which bound the partners for 11 years, bore the name of Compagnie des Marchands de Rouen et de Saint-Malo, and also that of Compagnie de Champlain, because of the important role played by the lieutenant of the Prince de Condé. Despite an attempt by the merchants of La Rochelle to corner the Tadoussac fur trade, business was excellent in 1614. Champlain could indulge in the fondest hopes. He was also concerned with the furtherance of religious life; with the backing of Condé and of Louis Houel, a king's secretary, he secured four Recollets, among them Denis JAMET, their first superior in Canada, and the company undertook to feed them. With them Champlain set sail from Honfleur, 24 April 1615, and as soon as he arrived at Tadoussac, on 25 May, he set out for the Saint-Louis rapids to meet the natives. Bound by repeated promises to help them against the Iroquois, and wanting to push on with his "discoveries," Champlain, with two Frenchmen, one of whom was perhaps Étienne Brûlé, undertook his great voyage to the Huron country. This was on 9 July 1615. He went up the Ottawa River, continuing this time beyond Allumette Island, and reached the Rivière Mataouan; then, via the Lac des Népissingues (Nipissing) and the Rivière des Français (French River), he got to the great Lac Attigouautau (Huron), which he called a freshwater sea. On 1 August he at last arrived among the Hurons, in a country whose beauty and fertility amazed him.

The military rendezvous was at Cahiagué (on Lake Simcoe); he went there by easy stages, visiting the villages enclosed by their wooden stockades. After sending a delegation of 12 Huron braves—to whose number Brûlé was added—to warn their allies the Susquehannahs to the south of the Iroquois country, the expedition started out on 1 September. Passing through a country where the trees seemed to have been planted for the joy of it, they crossed Lake Ontario at its eastern tip; 14 leagues farther on they hid their canoes and struck into the interior. On 10 October, after following the Oneida River, they found themselves before an Iroquois fort (in a spot situated on the east side of Lake Onondaga, or, according to a reputable theory, at Nichols Pond, near Perryville, N.Y., to the south of Lake Oneida).

It was a fort protected by four stockades 30 feet high, and provided with galleries, in the form of a parapet, in which the Iroquois had fitted up troughs for putting out fires. Champlain was obliged by his allies' impatience to attack prematurely. He had to resort to the strategy used for besieging a fortress; a cavalier for shooting into the interior of the fort, mantlets to protect the besiegers, and wood to set fire to the stockade. The Hurons lacked discipline; their disorder caused the assault to fail, and Champlain himself was wounded twice in one leg by arrows, one of them striking his knee. After three hours it was necessary to withdraw. The allies waited in vain until 16 October for help from the Susquehannahs; seeing nothing arrive, they began their long retreat. Because of his knee, Champlain was carried for some days, trussed up in a basket on the back of a Huron, like "a little child in its swaddling clothes."

He wished to return to Quebec, but the Hurons were anxious for him to winter among them; he accepted, with much reluctance. Soon he set off with them on a great hunt during which, like the priest AUBRY in 1604, he got lost in the forest, stalking a strange bird from tree to tree;

without a compass, living on game and sleeping under a tree, he wandered for three days before finally meeting up with the band by chance. The hunt being over, they returned to Cahiagué on 23 December; he spent Christmas and New Year's Day there; on 5 Jan. 1616 he met the Recollet LE CARON again at Carhagouha. On the fifteenth, Champlain set off with the Recollet to visit the Tobacco Nation (to the south of Nottawasaga Bay), then the Cheveux-Relevés (Ottawas) (to the south of Georgian Bay), calling at the villages and inviting the natives to come to Quebec. He took advantage of this winter "to study their country, their manners, customs, modes of life": he has left us a detailed description of them which is an ethnographical compendium of the Huron country, He could however get only scant information about the mysterious west; because of the wars the Hurons had travelled little in that direction.

Finally, on 22 May 1616, Champlain left the Huron country; 40 days later, at the Saint-Louis rapids, he encountered Gravé Du Pont, who thought he was dead. Champlain again declared to the Hurons that he planned to build a habitation at the Saint-Louis rapids, and they pledged themselves to come and live there. On 11 July he was at Quebec; he enlarged the Habitation, and had the wheat cut to show it in France. He embarked 20 July and was at Honfleur 10 September.

There he learned that the Prince de Condé had just been arrested; which "made me infer," he wrote, "that our enviers would not be very slow in spewing out their venom." Indeed, Maréchal de Thémines had himself granted the office of viceroy; Champlain nevertheless remained a lieutenant, and the partners went so far as to show a sudden zeal for the colony. But everything "went up in smoke," and when Champlain decided to embark at Honfleur in 1617, the partner Daniel Boyer notified him that he was no longer the viceroy's lieutenant. Champlain left notwithstanding for New France, where he made only a brief stay (doubt has been cast on this 1617 voyage, but it remains possible, even if we find Champlain in Paris again on 22 July).

In February 1618, he attempted a major move by addressing two reports, one to the king and the other to the Chamber of Commerce, outlining his whole programme. He wrote to the king that by way of New France one could easily reach "the Kingdom of China and the East Indies, whence great riches could be drawn"; the customs duties that would be collected at Quebec on all goods coming from or proceeding to Asia "would surpass in value at least ten times all those levied in France"; the French would be masters of a country "nearly eighteen hundred leagues in length, watered by the fairest rivers in the world," and the Christian faith would be established among countless numbers of souls. To place New France on a solid footing, Champlain proposed that there be established at Quebec, in the valley of the St. Charles River, "a town almost as large as St. Denis, which town shall be called, if it please God and the king, *Ludovica*"; a fort would overlook this town; another would be built on the south bank of the river, a third at Tadoussac. To the country would be brought 15 Recollets, 300 families of 4 persons, and 300 soldiers; the king would send someone from his council to "establish and ordain fundamental laws of the State" and a free system of justice.

This programme of civilization was of a kind that would please the king. Champlain would interest the big speculators by enumerating the wealth that could be extracted from the country; this "great and permanent trade" would comprise the following items: fisheries of cod, salmon, sturgeon, eel, and herring; whale-oil and whale-wattles; timber "of marvellous height"; gum, ashes, tar; dye roots, hemp; mines of silver, iron, and lead; coarse cloths, pelts, gems, vines, livestock; finally, profits to be obtained from the "short route to China," via the St. Lawrence. In all, Champlain estimated the annual income at some 5,400,000 *livres*. In this estimate, the yield from agriculture had very little importance (for France could not be interested in Canadian agricultural products); furs amounted to only 400,000 *livres*. Like TALON subsequently, Champlain did not want all the economy of the country to be based on the one item of furs, and we notice that this evaluation by Champlain is fairly close to what they were to bring in on an average each year. Thus Champlain was dreaming of a country with a diversified economy. A wide-ranging programme! It is in the year 1618 that we find outlined for the first time a great colonizing policy.

The Chamber of Commerce was immediately convinced by it: on 9 Feb. 1618 it asked the king that Champlain be given the means to establish 300 families a year in New France, and that the partners be assured the monopoly of the trade in furs; on 12 March 1618 the king instructed the partners to assist Champlain "with things requisite and necessary" for the execution of the command that he had received, and to "carry on all work that he shall judge necessary for establishing the colonies that we wish to found in the said country." Armed with the king's support, Champlain embarked 24 May 1618, with his brother-in-law EUSTACHE BOULLÉ, who was 18

Champlain

years old; he reached Tadoussac on the 24 June following. At Quebec, three days later, he noticed that some progress had been made with cultivation, but he had to go to Trois-Rivières to pass judgement on the murder of two Frenchmen by two Montagnais in 1616, or more probably in 1617. Champlain preferred to "settle this affair amicably, and to pass things over quietly," in order to keep the friendship of the natives. When the fur-trading was finished, Champlain sailed again for Tadoussac on 26 July, hoping to return the following year "bringing a good number of families to people this country." He was at Honfleur by 28 August.

In France legal proceedings were now in full swing. From the king's Council the States of Brittany obtained freedom of trade; Champlain managed to have it revoked. The partners had been refusing up to that time to ensure the populating of the colony, fearing that they would then obtain furs only through the settlers, and that they would subsequently be ejected by those whom they had themselves established; but they realized that they would have to honour the population commitment. On 21 Dec. 1618 Champlain made them sign a statement whereby the partners undertook to convey to Quebec and maintain there 80 persons, with animals and seed; furthermore, on the twenty-fourth of the same month Champlain drew a pension of 600 *livres* provided for him by the king; and on the following 14 January he received the 1,500 *livres* owing to him from his wife's dowry. Everything seemed set fair for success. But now the partners, prompted by Boyer, sought to restrict Champlain to exploring and to entrust the command of Quebec to Gravé Du Pont. Champlain refused: "They thought . . . they were setting up a sort of republic there according to their own notions"; he claimed his right to command at Quebec and to devote his attention to the explorations that he deemed appropriate.

Sure of what he was doing, he set off for Rouen with his wife, in order to sail for Quebec. He showed the king's letter and the articles signed by the partners, and proved that he was the Prince de Condé's lieutenant. To no purpose: the partners refused point blank; the boat set sail; and Champlain returned to Paris to plead his case before the king's Council. "Now began our pettifoggery." A judgement confirmed him in his command ("which decree I make known to them in the open Exchange at Rouen"), but the 1619 trip nevertheless could not take place. During this enforced leisure, Champlain had written up the account of his *Voyages* from 1615 to 1618; the *privilège* is dated 18 May 1619.

The Prince de Condé was liberated in October 1619, and yielded his rights as viceroy to Henri II, Duc de Montmorency, admiral of France. The latter confirmed Champlain in his office, and appointed the Sieur Dolu, the Grand Usher of the kingdom, as an intendant to put the society "into a better condition of prosperity than it had been." On 7 May 1620, Louis XIII wrote to Champlain to enjoin him to maintain the country "in obedience to me, making the people who are there live as closely in conformity with the laws of my kingdom as you can." From that moment Champlain was to devote himself exclusively to the administration of the country; he was to undertake no further great voyages of discovery; his career as an explorer had ended.

In this spring of 1620 Champlain set out again for New France, this time with his wife (aged *c.* 22 years), whose first ocean journey it was; unfortunately it was a "rough passage." Arriving at Quebec in July, he had his commission read in public, and took possession of the country in the name of the viceroy de Montmorency. He undertook repairs: rain was coming into the Habitation and the storehouse was falling to pieces; despite the partners' aversion, he had a start made on Fort Saint-Louis, on the south cliff of the Cap aux Diamants. The construction lasted all autumn and all winter. In mid-May 1621, he learned that the fur trade had been handed over to the de Caën brothers, and that he was to take possession of the former society's goods. Champlain allowed the clerks, who were growing anxious, to continue trading meanwhile. Then, in June, Gravé Du Pont, who belonged to the earlier society, arrived at the same time as the de Caëns; a conflict was imminent, and Champlain braced himself. Parleys were held with both parties, but in the meantime it was ascertained that the king was allowing both companies to trade for that year. Guillaume de Caën planned, however, to seize Gravé's ship, and Champlain went down to Tadoussac to "render justice." De Caën seized the ship, then, changing his mind, pretended that the vessel was, after all, not fully armed and returned it to François Gravé. This conflict, and the rivalry of the two companies, were very indicative of the colony's unsettled state, and there were, moreover, other various complaints to be dealt with. On 18 Aug. 1621, with Champlain's permission, a general meeting of the settlers instructed the Recollet Le Baillif to go as their delegate and present the country's grievances in France. In the report that Le Baillif presented to the king, we find repeated the same arguments put forward

Champlain

by Champlain in 1618, including the reference to the route to Asia. The Recollet submitted the following requests: the exclusion of the Huguenots from the colony, the founding of a seminary for Indians, more power in the exercising of justice, a stronger military defence, and an increase in Champlain's pension. The king replied by merging the two companies, under the direction of the de Caëns. The latter committed themselves to support six Recollets and to settle six families; as for Champlain's pension, it was increased. Shortly after this general meeting, about which Champlain does not utter a word in his writings, the first ordinances were published at Quebec, 21 Sept. 1621. The texts of this first legislation in New France have not been found.

As a legislator, Champlain applied himself also to playing a political role among the natives. In order to "begin to assume a certain control over them," he succeeded in imposing on them a chief of his choice, MIRISTOU, and it was agreed that thenceforth only a chief acceptable to the French should be elected. The Indians, persuaded by Champlain to settle and till the land, began to clear ground near Quebec in the spring of 1622. In addition, in June, Champlain received a visit from some Iroquois who had come for peace parleys; he convinced his allies of the advantages of peace, and got them to send four of their men to the Iroquois country; he continued his efforts towards pacification when in July 1623, at the mouth of the Richelieu, he smoothed out a quarrel between some Hurons and Algonkins, and pardoned an Indian guilty of having killed some Frenchmen.

The material progress of the colony also concerned him. In August 1623 he went to visit the meadows at the Cap Tourmente, where he had 2,000 bales of hay put up, and from then on he thought of making of the spot "a good place for the pasturing of cattle." In November he opened up a road to give easier access to the Cap aux Diamants. During the winter of 1623–24, he drew up plans for a new Habitation, collected the materials, had the timber cut and hauled in. He laid the first stone on 6 May 1624. On 15 August, the construction being "in a forward state," Champlain left Quebec with his wife (who was not to return there again). On 1 October he landed at Dieppe, and from there went to Saint-Germain to make a report to the king.

The viceroyalty once more changed hands; Montmorency resigned in favour of Henri de Lévis, Duc de Ventadour. On 15 Feb. 1625 Champlain was confirmed by Ventadour in his office of viceroy's lieutenant, and received as his own lieutenant his brother-in-law Boullé. Ventadour instructed Champlain to "commission officers for the administration of justice, the maintenance of police, and the carrying out of regulations and ordinances," and encouraged him to look for the route to China. This last objective seems to have interested Champlain less and less, or else he no longer had the leisure to concern himself with it. After staying a year and a half in France, Champlain sailed again, 15 April 1626. He was at Quebec on 5 July, finding there the Jesuits who had arrived the previous year at the invitation of the Recollets. Champlain had the Habitation completed, and decided, despite the de Caëns and the partners, to raze the fort in order to build a larger one. For those attending to cattle-raising and hay-making, he personally supervised the construction of a habitation at the Cap Tourmente: two main buildings and a stable after the Normandy style. In the spring of 1627, faithful to his policy of peace, he prevented the allies from declaring war on the Iroquois by sending a French ambassador into the latter's country, a mission which was however to end in tragedy.

It was in 1627 also that Cardinal Richelieu, after suppressing the post of admiral and securing the resignation of the viceroy de Ventadour, took New France under his immediate supervision. He established the Compagnie des Cent-Associés, of which Champlain at once became a member. This new régime brought advancement to Champlain; since 1612 he had been lieutenant to a viceroy who, despite his rank, did not have the supreme control of the affairs of France. But on 21 March 1629 Champlain became the lieutenant and representative of Richelieu himself; the texts of this period refer to him as commander of New France "in the absence of my Lord the Cardinal de Richelieu." He had thus reached the height of his career. Yet though Champlain did exercise the functions of a governor, and though the *Relations* gave him this title, yet he never received a governor's commission.

The setting up of the Compagnie des Cent-Associés encouraged Champlain to hope for unqualified success, but meanwhile the colony continued to eke out its existence. At the beginning of 1628, Champlain noted an event of some importance. He tells us that on 27 April the land was "broken by the plough drawn by oxen," a labour which previously had had to be carried out by human strength. This advance took place a year after Louis Hébert's death. As the annual assistance was slow in coming, and a shortage of food was making itself felt, Champlain had a bark made ready to take some of the settlers to Gaspé. It was discovered early in July that the

Champlain

English had pillaged the Cap Tourmente habitation; then, on the tenth, some Basques brought Champlain a summons from the KIRKE brothers. Quebec was in a very bad way; each person was restricted to seven ounces of peas a day, and there remained only 50 pounds of gunpowder. Certain that help would shortly arrive, Champlain made a show of bravado, saying that one must "put on a bold countenance," and replied to the Kirkes that he was well provided for: "We are now waiting from hour to hour to receive you." The Kirkes did not press the point, but made arrangements to cut off all relief. On 8 July they had intercepted the first reinforcements sent by the Compagnie des Cent-Associés, a fleet of four ships carrying about 400 persons. Quebec found itself reduced to stark necessity. Frantic attempts were made to find means of subsistence; the inhabitants even went so far as to grind peas into pease-meal, and increase in this way the strength of the "soup".

As help still did not arrive in the spring of 1629, Champlain sent more people to Gaspé in order to have fewer mouths to feed, and those remaining turned to cultivation so as to have enough to exist on the following winter. Now, on 19 July, English ships appeared behind Pointe-Lévy, and a sloop came to present a summons from the Kirkes. This time Champlain could not put up a false front. He was forced to hand over Quebec, after obtaining the best terms of capitulation he could. On 24 July he left Quebec. On the way down to Tadoussac, Champlain, who was sailing with the Kirkes, met a ship commanded by ÉMERY DE CAËN: Champlain was ordered to go below decks, and the English and French joined battle. The English general later made Champlain come up and obliged him to serve as an intermediary; de Caën then announced that he was bringing help pending the coming of RAZILLY, and that peace must be made between French and English. The English refused to believe it. Champlain reached Tadoussac on 1 August, and he had to make a lengthy stay there. He had the opportunity to rebuke sharply Étienne Brûlé and Nicolas MARSOLET, who had gone over to the enemy, and he tried in vain to get permission to take to France the Indian girls CHARITÉ and Espérance, whom he had adopted.

Travelling on board an English ship, Champlain reached London on 29 October. He went immediately to the French ambassador and pointed out to him that the capture of Quebec had taken place two months after the signing of peace; he presented the original of the capitulation, some reports, and a map of Canada (this map has not been traced). At the beginning of December he was back in France, after an absence of three and a half years. He met the members of the company, Richelieu, and the king himself, and urged them to hasten the restitution of New France. In 1630, he submitted an appeal to the king which restated the arguments of 1618: the importance of a vast country; its usefulness "both for trade outside it and for the comforts of life inside it;" the "great and wonderful commerce" that would be carried on if the way to China were found; the "infinite number of savage peoples" to be converted. He enumerated the wide variety of resources in New France, and after his experience of the years 1628 and 1629 he added a new idea: to oblige the French "to cultivate the land, before all things, in order to have the basic foodstuffs on the spot, without being obliged to bring them from France." As early as April 1630, Louis XIII decided to demand the restitution of the country, but the negotiations were to drag on, in fact until the treaty of Saint-Germain-en-Laye in 1632. But, when everything was settled, it was Émery de Caën who, 4 March 1632, was provisionally appointed commandant of Quebec, and on 20 April following Isaac de Razilly was offered the lieutenancy of New France. He refused because he considered Champlain more competent, and finally, 1 March 1633, Champlain was again instructed to take over command of New France in Richelieu's absence.

What did he do during this three-year stay in France, besides make moves to hasten the restitution of the colony? He is known to have been at Brouage on 27 Sept. 1630, when he sold two houses there. On 13 Feb. 1632 Champlain and his wife made over their property to each other. During 1632 he published the *Voyages de la Nouvelle-France*, dedicated to Richelieu. This work contains an historical retrospect from 1504, his own voyages of 1603–29, and an account of what occurred in 1631. To this he attached a map of New France and his *Traitté de la marine et du devoir d'un bon marinier*.

Champlain reappeared at Quebec 22 May 1633, after an absence of nearly four years. Soon after his arrival, he had built at the expense of the Compagnie des Cent-Associés a chapel "in honour of our Lady." This was to be Notre-Dame-de-la-Recouvrance, near the fort, on the Cap aux Diamants (its foundations were unearthed in 1958, within the quadrilateral formed by the rues du Fort, Buade, du Trésor, and Sainte-Anne).

On 15 Aug. 1633, he wrote to Richelieu requesting him to terminate the English trading concession at Tadoussac and launch a great offensive against the Iroquois country. He wrote to him again, 18 Aug. 1634, to make a report: I have rebuilt the ruins of Quebec, enlarged the fortifications, constructed a habitation 15 leagues upstream from Quebec on an islet named Richelieu, whence one can command the river; I have had another one started at Trois-Rivières. He might have added that he had just sent Jean NICOLLET on a mission of peace and discovery amongst the tribes bordering on the Great Lakes. He wanted the Iroquois to be wiped out, or to be "brought to reason." This document, the last that we have from Champlain, is optimistic; the zeal of the company in fulfilling its obligations, and the arrival of those numerous families who came in 1634, gave Champlain "new courage."

In 1635 his health declined rapidly, which no doubt explains why, without any intimation of what had happened at Quebec at the beginning of the winter, Paris named a successor to Champlain in the person of Charles HUAULT de Montmagny, 15 Jan. 1636. In October 1635 Champlain had been stricken with paralysis. It was then that Champlain, in a gesture typical of that period, and forgetful of the agreements already entered into with his wife, appointed the Virgin Mary his heiress, thus leaving his furniture and his share in the company to the church of Notre-Dame-de-la-Recouvrance. This will, confirmed in Paris in 1637, was to be annulled two years later on the petition of a first cousin, Marie Camaret.

Attended until his last moments by the Jesuit CHARLES LALEMANT, Champlain died on 25 December 1635 or rather, according to Father Paul Le Jeune's colourful expression, "was reborn in Heaven." At the solemn funeral rites, Father Le Jeune pronounced the funeral oration: "I did not lack material," wrote the Jesuit; "although he died out of France, his name will not therefor be any less glorious to Posterity"; perhaps that was the theme of the address. Champlain was then buried temporarily in an unmarked grave, to be transferred later (probably in 1636, after Montmagny had enlarged the church) to a chapel built as an annex to the church, and called first the chapel of Monsieur le Gouverneur, and afterwards the chapel of Champlain. It was destroyed by a fire in 1640, at the same time as the church and residence of the Jesuits, and was immediately rebuilt, but nothing more was heard of it after 1664, and apparently in 1674 it no longer existed. The supposition is that the bodies interred beneath it were moved and placed beneath the new parish church (today Notre-Dame de Québec). As a consequence of the work done on the basement in 1877, any further possibility of tracing the remains of Champlain seems to have vanished.

Champlain wrote a great deal, but his works, which are extensive and abound in detail, reveal nothing of his private life. He kept silent about his background, his conversion (if he was born a Protestant), his marriage, and his wife. Once only does he speak to us, briefly, about an illness that he had undergone. On the other hand, his writings are almost the only source of information about the development of his career; from 1607 to 1625, the only facts we know about Champlain are those he has told us himself. When the *Relations des Jésuites* appeared, Champlain was a well-established man whom one respected and did not criticize, so that they merely add official details to the biography of the personage. Under these conditions it is difficult to construct an image of Champlain that conforms to reality.

From his written work we can deduce some dominant characteristics. First, a physical trait: a healthy, robust, resilient nature. He seems never to have suffered from scurvy, either in Acadia or at Quebec; the long sea voyages (from 1603 on, he crossed the Atlantic 21 times), the hazardous expeditions, the sojourns among the natives do not appear to have affected him at all; he was indomitable, and ran any kind of risk to win prestige for himself (for example, he shot the Lachine Rapids in a canoe). His health and energy were reflected in his moral qualities. Eager to see everything, to know everything, he was always out to make discoveries, whether it was a matter of examining a harbour, studying a type of soil or a tribe, looking for a mine. He was observant; it was while stalking a strange bird that he lost his way in the forests of the Huron country. He moved doggedly towards his goal; when de Monts withdrew, it was Champlain who, despite the most odious vexations, resisted those merchants who opposed every attempt at colonization. It was moreover in this conflict that the whole drama of Champlain's career lay. One would consequently expect to find in him an unbending man, hard towards others. On the contrary, he was jovial, a lover of good food and drink, the founder of the order of Good Cheer. He behaved towards the natives with the greatest amiability, making them laugh continually, forgiving their offences in circumstances which surprise us. He preferred winning them over to punishing them. This kindliness was not however to prevent him from letting fly a few shafts when necessary (as he did against Lescarbot), or from manoeuvring skilfully in order to apply a policy of domination. He prevailed upon the natives to adopt as their

Champlain

chief only a person who had been chosen by the French.

Champlain was a religious man. His zeal was revealed when in 1615, for example, the Recollets came to New France. It was also revealed in his writings, but here it is important to make distinctions. We must first set aside the dedications that cannot be by Champlain, because of their style (and it is in one of these dedications that the salvation of a soul is placed above the conquest of an empire). We must then distinguish between the early works and the last one. The writings of 1603–19 offer nothing distinctive from the religious point of view; besides, the Champlain of Acadia, concerned chiefly with discovering mines, had nothing of the apostle about him, and in the absence of a priest during the winter 1606–7, it was not he who was chosen to teach the catechism, but Lescarbot. It is not until the 1632 volume that Champlain's works disclose an obvious concern for spreading the gospel; this was the period when, according to the *Relations*, Champlain was leading the life of a devout man, having the lives of the saints read to him at supper, presiding over the self-examination and prayers that took place in common each evening. It would however be ridiculous to attempt to rank Champlain's writings alongside the letters of a Marie de l'Incarnation [see GUYART], or on a level with the work of Bishop Laval*. Champlain was no mystic.

Champlain did not have the humanist's preoccupation with describing man or his depth of meditation or refinement of style. He was a man of action, a geographer and ethnographer, who recounted what he had done and seen as one composes a work of information. Certainly one can regret that Champlain did not take care to describe for us society as it was in the early days of New France, its mentality and institutions, and this is the more regrettable because for the first 15 years of Quebec he is our only source of enlightenment. But he has left us, written with many technical details and sometimes in a picturesque style, a geographic inventory of Acadia, the St. Lawrence, and the Great Lakes, a compendium of Indian ethnography, and records as valuable as the *Relations des Jésuites*.

What was Champlain trying to do? By putting together phrases gathered at random, and insisting on his liking for gardening, some have sought to see in Champlain the founder of an agricultural colony. One could just as well, by the same unsound procedure, make of Champlain a man entirely dedicated to looking for mines! Champlain's programme is in the proposals of 1618: agriculture appears in it as a supporting element, for the colony had obviously to sustain itself as far as possible on what the country could produce; but Champlain, a realist, knew that France would have no use for an agricultural colony; he did not cease to assert that the greatness of France depended on the "great and permanent trade" of a colony of which all the natural wealth would be exploited. It is in this setting of large-scale commerce, and not in an agricultural setting, that Champlain is, before Talon, our first great colonizer.

Champlain was the man of ever-reviving plans: in Acadia, he hoped to discover several mines and the route to Asia; in the St. Lawrence, he wanted also to find the route to Asia, and to set up at Quebec a customs post between Europe and China; he had planned to build a habitation at Montreal; he wanted to move the Algonkins of Allumette Island and even the Hurons into the St. Lawrence valley; one item of his 1618 programme was the establishing of a great city, Ludovica, on the banks of the St. Charles River. He did not carry out these projects, but to him belongs the much greater merit of having established New France. If, despite the indifference of the authorities, he had not persisted in maintaining the presence of the French in the St. Lawrence region, one may suppose that foreigners would have filled the vacuum, so that there would not have been a New France. Furthermore, it was he who built up the great fur-trading organization, and who ensured the French hold on the Montagnais, Algonkin, and Huron tribes. Undoubtedly, when he died, the St. Lawrence colony was of little consequence (150 settlers, whereas Boston, five years old, already had 2,000), but thanks to Champlain the foundations were laid. At the starting-point of the uninterrupted history of Canada, we find Champlain. He is at its origin by his own choice, and because of the principles in which he believed. In him we must salute the founder of Canada.

We know of no authentic portrait of Champlain. A likeness has been circulated which is said to be a true one; but, as Biggar has shown, it represents an unscrupulous comptroller of finances, Particelli d'Émery. According to Lanctot, this "portrait of a stout, flabby man is a forgery which is an insult to the soldier and to the energetic and vigorous sailor" that Champlain was. The latter appears in an engraving illustrating the victory at Lake Champlain in 1609, but his facial features are much too vague, and it is not certain that the engraver intended to make a good likeness. By dint of ingenious deductions, the biographer Bishop conjectures that Champlain was thin and wiry, of a height below the average. The face is still to be recovered.

MARCEL TRUDEL

The works of Champlain, first edited in six volumes, Quebec, 1870 [*see* General Bibliography: Champlain, *Œuvres* (Laverdière)] were re-edited 1922–35 at Toronto by H. P. Biggar in the Champlain Society unnumbered series [*see* General Bibliography: Champlain, *Works* (Biggar)]. The latter edition, which includes the French text with an English translation, consists of six volumes, with a folder of maps, and is the edition chiefly used in the above article. It contains the *Brief discours*; the *Des sauvages* of 1603; the *Voyages* of 1613; the *Quatriesme voyage*; the *Voyages* of 1619; the *Voyages* of 1632 and the *Traité de la marine*. The editor also published, in an appendix, documents, which, until that date, had not been published, belonging to the years 1610–19 and 1629–34. Unpublished documents have also been given in *NF*, I (1925), 80–85; and in *RHAF*, III (1949–50), 594–97; IX (1955–56), 571–78.

Various manuscript sources have proved useful: AN, V^6, 62, no. 13; Col., C^{11A}, 1; Col., F^3, 3.

Among the contemporary printed sources which must be consulted, the following are cited: *JR* (Thwaites), IV, V, VI, IX, *et passim.*; Lescarbot, *Histoire* (Tross), II, III; Sagard, *Histoire du Canada* (Tross), III, IV; "La minute notariée du contrat de mariage de Champlain," éd. Emmanuel de Cathelineau, *NF*, V (1930), 142–55. The following studies include source material: [Samuel de Champlain], *Champlain*, éd. Marcel Trudel (Classiques canadiens, V, Montréal et Paris, 1956). [Samuel de Champlain], *Les voyages de Samuel Champlain, saintongeois, père du Canada*, éd. Hubert Deschamps (Colonies et Empires, 2e série, Paris, 1951), 1–45.

There are numerous studies on Champlain but only those of special interest are mentioned here. On the voyage to the Indies consult: Claude de Bonnault, "Encore le Brief discours: Champlain a-t-il été à Blavet en 1598?" *BRH*, LX (1954), 59–69; Jean Bruchési, "Champlain a-t-il menti?" *Cahiers des Dix*, XV (1950), 39–53; Marcel Delafosse, "L'oncle de Champlain," *RHAF*, XII (1958–59), 208–16; Jacques Rousseau, "Samuel de Champlain, botaniste mexicain et antillais," *Cahiers des Dix*, XVI (1951), 39–61; L.-A. Vigneras, "Le voyage de Samuel Champlain aux Indes occidentales," *RHAF*, XI (1957–58), 163–200; "Encore le capitaine provençal," *ibid.*, XIII (1959–60), 544–49.

For information on Champlain's astrolabe, *see* A. J. Russell, *On Champlain's astrolabe . . .* (Montréal, 1879); Charles Macnamara, "Champlain's astrolabe," *The Canadian Field Naturalist*, XXXIII (1918–19), 103–9.

Concerning the portraits of Champlain, *see* H. P. Biggar, "The portrait of Champlain," *CHR*, I (1920), 379f.; V. H. Paltsits, "A critical examination of Champlain's portraits," *BRH*, XXXVIII (1932), 755–59; Lanctot, *Histoire du Canada*, I, 207.

On the grave of Champlain, *see* Silvio Dumas, *La chapelle Champlain et Notre-Dame de la Recouvrance* (SHQ Cahiers d'histoire, X, 1958).

For Champlain's will, which was discovered in 1959, *see* Robert Le Blant, "Le testament de Samuel Champlain, 17 novembre 1635," *RHAF*, XVII (1963–1964), 269–86.

Recent short studies include Lucien Campeau, "Les Jésuites ont-ils retouchés les écrits de Champlain?" *RHAF*, V (1951–52), 340–61; Florian de La Horbe, *L'incroyable secret de Champlain* (Paris, 1959); A. Tessier, "France nouvelle ou simple colonie commerciale," *Cahiers des Dix*, XXII (1957), 43–51; A. Z. Zeller, *The Champlain-Iroquois battle of 1615* (Oneida, N.Y., 1962).

Finally, there are two important biographies: Dionne, *Champlain* [*see* General Bibliography] and Morris Bishop, *Champlain: the life of fortitude* (New York, 1948).

CHARITÉ, ESPÉRANCE, FOI (Charity, Hope, Faith), young Montagnais girls adopted by Samuel de CHAMPLAIN in 1628.

Champlain had for a long time wished to adopt some young Indians, in order to have them educated in France. But the obstacle was the very strong attachment of the Indians for their children: some parents, he writes, had turned down tempting offers. But on 2 Feb. 1628 the Montagnais came and offered him three girls aged 11, 12, and 15—one of them the daughter of Mécabou *dit* Martin. This move was an attempt to win back Champlain's friendship, which had been jeopardized the previous autumn by the murder of two Frenchmen. Champlain accepted the young Indian girls and named them Foi, Espérance, and Charité.

All three were apparently delighted at the idea of receiving a French education, but Foi soon went back to the woods. Espérance and Charité stayed at Fort Saint-Louis, where Champlain taught them "all that they were able to comprehend." He taught them "to use a needle, both for making clothes and for embroidering"; these tasks, Champlain notes enthusiastically, "they perform most neatly, and they are moreover highly civilized."

The war soon put an end to this family life and to the attempt at civilization. In July 1629, when Champlain was forced to surrender Quebec to the English, he asked LEWIS KIRKE for permission to take his two Indian girls to France. Kirke reluctantly agreed. Finally Espérance and Charité sailed for Tadoussac on 24 July, "animated by an intense desire to go to France," but Nicolas MARSOLET's interference was to spoil everything. Because he wanted to seduce Champlain's wards, he wrote to DAVID KIRKE that the Montagnais assembled at Trois-Rivières refused to let the two girls leave. Champlain argued that this was a mere lie, but Kirke, anxious to maintain his tactical position, was afraid of antagonizing the natives. Champlain insisted: he was ready to give them goods to the value of 1,000 *livres*. Kirke, at Marsolet's instigation, refused outright. Espérance and Charité were so upset that they refused to eat or drink.

One evening Kirke entertained the company at supper; his two brothers were there, with Champlain, the ships' captains, and Marsolet. Speaking to the latter, Espérance accused him of betraying the French, of importuning her with his indecent propositions, and of preventing herself and her companion from going to France "to learn to serve God there." And she added: "If you come near me in the future, I shall plunge a knife into your breast." Charité supported her: "If I had hold of your heart, I should eat it more readily and with greater spirit than I should eat any of the meats on that table." Marsolet "was shamefaced, and could give no reply other than that they were mad."

Nonetheless, Espérance and Charité stayed in the country. At the moment of parting, Champlain and his brother-in-law EUSTACHE BOULLÉ gave each girl a rosary. Champlain urged GUILLAUME COUILLARD, who was not emigrating, to "let them remain with his wife as long as they wanted to." Couillard sailed for Quebec on 14 Sept. 1629, with the two Montagnais girls. Champlain does not seem to have seen his adopted daughters again: he makes no mention of them on his return in 1633. The woods must have reclaimed them.

By instructing these native children Champlain was creating a precedent. CHOMEDEY de Maisonneuve, the Sisters of the Congrégation de Notre-Dame, and especially the Ursulines of Quebec were to continue this policy of acculturation. However, as far as we know the only Indian girl who did not return to the life of the woods is Marie-Madeleine Chrestienne, who married Pierre Boucher* about 1649.

MARCEL TRUDEL

Champlain, *Works* (Biggar), V, 248–53; VI, 60, 62, 70, 104–24, 144. Sagard, *Histoire du Canada* (Tross), IV, 829f., 908–11. Dionne, *Champlain*, II, 409–12. Marcel Trudel, *L'esclavage au Canada français: histoire et conditions de l'esclavage* (Québec, 1960), 8f.

CHARNY, CHARLES DE LAUSON DE. See LAUSON

CHARRON DE LA BARRE, CLAUDE, businessman, alderman of Quebec, police magistrate, churchwarden, syndic; b. some time between 1621 and 1627 in France; d. 1687 at Quebec. He appears to have signed himself "Charron" or "Charon," without distinction; one document only—the 1666 census—gives him the surname La Barre.

Arriving at Quebec in 1652 or shortly before, Charron and his wife Claude Camus (or Le Camus) settled first on the Île d'Orléans. Even at this time Charron had servants, which suggests that he had some financial resources. Two of his servants, perhaps planning to rob him, wounded him in the throat with a pistol on 29 April 1653.

On 20 May of that year, Governor JEAN DE LAUSON granted him a commoner's holding of ten acres on the Île d'Orléans. But Charron had little interest in clearing and cultivating land. Thus we soon find him back in Quebec, where he kept a shop. His business flourished to such an extent that on 7 March 1660 he sold his land on the Île d'Orléans, although he retained another property there to which he retired from time to time.

About 1660 Charron appears to have been one of the chief merchants of Quebec. On 5 November of that year he sailed for France, probably on a business trip, because in 1661 he imported goods to the value of "five or six thousand *livres*." In March 1663, he was one of the 17 merchants to whom Governor PIERRE DUBOIS Davaugour farmed out the Tadoussac trade. When this concession was annulled by the Conseil Souverain and the Tadoussac trade was put up for auction, Charron gave Aubert* de La Chesnaye—the wealthiest merchant of the day—a lively battle, bidding up to 46,000 *livres* and offering an advance payment of 15,000 *livres* for each year of the concession, before finally yielding to his powerful rival.

Being now one of the notables of Quebec, Charron could expect to receive appointments and honours. And in fact, on 7 Oct. 1663, the leading citizens of Quebec elected a mayor and two aldermen, of whom the Sieur Charron was one. But the mayor and his aldermen—and Charron in particular—"making little effort to fulfil the said functions," the council decided shortly thereafter to abolish these offices and "make do with a syndic." When the election of this officer took place on 3 Aug. 1664, the Sieur Charron was once again named by the few notables present. But the people opposed this choice, fearing that with Charron's support the merchants might acquire too much influence over the fixing of retail prices on goods sold in the colony. As a result the council suggested discreetly to Charron that he resign, and this he did in September 1664.

Although not a member of the Conseil Souverain, Charron was nevertheless often called upon to sit on the council in the absence of one of the regular judges. Furthermore he is mentioned in documents dated 8 Aug. 1669 and 7 Oct. 1671 as a churchwarden of the parish of Quebec. In 1673 and 1674 he was police magistrate of the town of Quebec, and in 1675 he was once again an alderman.

As a prominent businessman, having held public office and owning land at Quebec, on the Île d'Orléans, and at Montreal, Charron was one of 20 leading members of the colony selected by BUADE de Frontenac on 26 Oct. 1678, to give an opinion on trafficking in spirits. He expressed himself in favour of bartering with intoxicating liquors, as did the majority of the merchants present at this meeting.

As a result of his knowledge of the colony and his business experience, Charron had views of his own on New France's economic development. Although favouring the trade in spirits, he nevertheless deplored the fact that settlers were abandoning their lands in order to hunt beaver or live in the woods. In a brief addressed to the minister about 1680, Charron proposed the founding of a colony on the Detroit River in order to give stability to the settlers and create centres for the production of woollen material, cloth, and shoes. Lamothe de Cadillac [Laumet*] was to attempt just such a project a few years later.

Claude Camus died at Quebec on 12 April 1684. Charron was married a second time, on 21 August of that year, to Élisabeth, daughter of MATHIEU DAMOURS DE CHAUFFOURS and Marie Marsolet. On his death in 1687 he left behind him his second wife, four children—two of them by his second wife—and a sizable fortune.

ANDRÉ VACHON

ASQ, Paroisse de Québec, 124, 145. *JR* (Thwaites), *passim*. JJ (Laverdière et Casgrain). *Jug. et délib.*, I, II, III. P.-G. Roy, "Le sieur Charron de La Barre," *BRH*, XLII (1936), 484–87.

CHARTIER, LOUIS, surgeon; b. 1633 in France; drowned 1660 in the Ottawa River.

Louis Chartier crossed over to Canada with the great contingent of 1653 which was intended to strengthen the settlement of Ville-Marie (Montreal). Like his travelling companion Étienne BOUCHARD, he was one of the surgeons whom the Société Notre-Dame de Montréal had committed itself to placing at the settler's service free of charge. The general list of the contingent allocates to Chartier a guaranteed salary of 100 *livres* and a salary in advance of 120 *livres*. He acted as a witness for a will, several notarial acts, marriage contracts, bills of sale, drawn up during the years 1658, 1659, and 1660, and the title of "surgeon" or "master-surgeon of the island" is linked to his name. In one of these acts his name appears along with that of Adam DOLLARD Des Ormeaux. On 18 April 1660 he acted as a witness to the will of Jean Valets, who was getting ready to take part in Dollard's expedition. As a friend of the latter, Louis Chartier had lent him the sum of 30 *livres*. After Dollard's death he did not demand payment of this debt, being no doubt convinced that it could not be discharged.

Louis Chartier was 27 when he met his death by drowning in the waters of the Ottawa 20 July 1660, while taking part in the defence of Montreal Island against the Iroquois. His body was not recovered. The inventory of his belongings was made 19 Sept. 1660 by the notary BÉNIGNE BASSET. He died a bachelor. According to É.-Z. Massicotte, Chartier may have been the young surgeon mentioned in a relation of the period as being captured by the Iroquois at Ville-Marie in the spring of 1654 and brought back in the autumn.

In addition, mention is made of the presence of a certain Louis Chartier de La Broquerie at the marriage of Charles Philipeaux at Quebec 8 March 1654. It does not seem to be the same person, for in the acts drawn up at Montreal in which his name appears, he is always called merely Louis Chartier.

ANTONIO DROLET

AJQ, Greffe de Guillaume Audouart, 8 mars 1654. Maude E. Abbott, "Historic Montreal," *Annals of Internal Medicine*, VI (1933), 815–38; *History of medicine in the province of Quebec* (Toronto, 1931; McGill University pub., VIII, no. 63, 1932), 19. Ahern, *Notes pour l'histoire de la médecine*, 99. R.-J. Auger, *La grande recrue de 1653* (Montréal, 1955), 11, 15, 54–55, 120, 127, 135, 137, 141, 149, 150, 151. *BRH*, XV (1909), 30. J. J. Heagerty, *Four centuries of medical history in Canada, and a sketch of the medical history of Newfoundland* (2v., Toronto, 1928), I, 224, 232, 234, 241. É.-Z. Massicotte, "Les chirurgiens de Montréal au XVIIe siècle," *BRH*, XX (1914), 253; "Les chirurgiens, médecins, etc., de Montréal sous le régime français," APQ *Rapport, 1922–23*, 132; "Dollard des Ormeaux," *Can. Antiquarian and Numismatic J.*, 3d ser., IX (1912), 55. Tanguay, *Dictionnaire*, I, 120.

CHARTIER DE LOTBINIÈRE, LOUIS-THÉANDRE, seigneurial attorney and lieutenant general of the seneschal's court at Quebec, attorney general to the Conseil Souverain, lieutenant general of the provost's court at

Chartier de Lotbinière

Quebec; b. *c.* 1612 in Paris; d. some time after 1680 in France. He was the son of René-Pierre Chartier, a counsellor in the Parlement, physician in ordinary to the king, and royal professor, and of Françoise Bourcier.

The first known forbear, Philippe Chartier, the son of Joseph and Marguerite Amelotte, was born in 1345 at Dijon. The Chartier family received noble status at the beginning of the fifteenth century in the person of Alain (1382–1455), a receiver general of accounts and secretary of state under Charles VI. In the fourth generation, represented by Clément (b. 1456), the Chartiers adopted the surname of Lotbinière. They were allied to the Châteaubriands, the La Rochefoucaults, and the Polignacs, and of all the families who made their home in New France they were of the most ancient lineage.

Little is known of Louis-Théandre Chartier de Lotbinière's career before he came to Canada. He was prior of Saint-Étienne de Monays when a young man, but soon made over this living to his brother René. (The latter, who died in France on 19 Oct. 1655, had lived in Canada from 1643 to 1647 as chaplain to the Ursulines of Quebec.) In 1641, in Paris, Louis-Théandre married Élisabeth Damours, the sister of MATHIEU DAMOURS DE CHAUFFOURS and a relative of JEAN DE LAUSON, the future governor of New France. He had two children by her: René-Louis*—whom several historians have confused with his father—and Françoise.

It was perhaps at the request of M. de Lauson —with whom they made the journey, together with Mathieu Damours—that Chartier and his family went to New France. They landed at Quebec on 13 Oct. 1651.

It has been said of Chartier de Lotbinière that he is the "father of the Canadian magistrature." Like all such statements, this one is a little exaggerated, but it is not entirely false: M. de Lotbinière's legal career was in certain respects remarkable. When he arrived, the colony was still without any properly constituted court. It was customary for the governors to administer justice themselves, with the assistance of a few counsellors as occasion demanded. One of the first things accomplished by M. de Lauson was the establishment of a seneschal's court at Quebec, in the autumn of 1651. Chartier was appointed seigneurial attorney to the court, and in 1656 was promoted to be its lieutenant general for civil and criminal affairs. He kept this office until the autumn of 1663, when the seneschal's court was abolished following the setting up of the Conseil Souverain.

M. de Lotbinière was soon called upon to play a part in the new council. At the beginning of 1664, the attorney general JEAN BOURDON, together with the counsellors RUETTE d'Auteuil and ROUER de Villeray, had been arbitrarily removed from his office by M. de SAFFRAY de Mézy. On 10 March Saffray de Mézy appointed Chartier deputy attorney general; despite the opposition of Bishop Laval*, the council confirmed this appointment. But as Bourdon was reinstated shortly afterwards M. de Lotbinière resigned on 16 April. After a brief lull the governor's anger flared up again in September: on the nineteenth he dismissed d'Auteuil, Villeray, JEAN JUCHEREAU DE LA FERTÉ, and Bourdon; on the twenty-fourth, in the bishop's absence, he appointed Chartier de Lotbinière attorney general. Chartier held this position until 6 Dec. 1666, on which day M. PROUVILLE de Tracy restored to Bourdon his former office.

In the autumn of 1666 Chartier was also preparing himself for the presidency of another tribunal. The Compagnie des Indes occidentales, set up in 1664, had been authorized to "establish judges and officers wherever there will be need and wherever it will find it appropriate." The company made use of this privilege to create a provost's court at Quebec, and on 1 May 1666 named Chartier to it, with the function of lieutenant general for civil and criminal affairs. This court was to "deal in the first instance with cases of all kinds, whether civil, criminal, or concerning police, trade and navigation"; appeals were a matter for the Conseil Souverain. Chartier was installed in office on 10 Jan. 1667, and pronounced his judgements until he resigned in his son's favour on 25 Oct. 1677. The tribunal, officially abolished in 1674, was not resumed until 1677, yet it had not ceased to sit; on 13 May 1675, at a time when theoretically the provost's court did not exist, Louis XIV confirmed Chartier in his functions!

If a number of historians are to be believed, Chartier was a member of the Communauté des Habitants. We have found no documentary proof of this. It seems that a wrong interpretation has been given to his presence among the "17 individual settlers" who on 4 Oct. 1663 were deprived of the administration of the Tadoussac concession, which had previously been leased to them by PIERRE DUBOIS Davaugour. This association had nothing to do with the Communauté.

Shortly after his father's death in 1654 Chartier had brought a lawsuit against Marie Lenoir, René-Pierre Chartier's second wife. This matter of an inheritance, which had necessitated his taking a first trip to France in 1659, again required his presence in Paris in 1677. Then on 13 Nov. 1680

Intendant DUCHESNEAU wrote to the minister that Chartier's daughter, the widow of JOYBERT de Soulanges et de Marson, "has lost 1,000 *livres* which were granted to her last year, and a part of the 600 *livres* for the present year that her father the Sieur Chartier, to whom she had given powers of attorney, has consumed by his excesses, having continued to live in Paris."

This revelation of the behaviour of the "erstwhile" lieutenant general of the provost's court is one of the rare glimpses that we have of his character. As a relative of M. de Lauson, Chartier de Lotbinière occupied important offices from the time he arrived in New France. Yet he is rarely mentioned outside legal documents; moreover he does not seem to have enjoyed the Jesuits' esteem as much as did the other settlers of his social standing: the *Journal* rarely names him, and never in regard to the religious festivities in which the representatives of the best Quebec society took an active part. That M. de Lotbinière was not on the side of the Jesuits and—later—of Bishop Laval becomes evident when, in 1664, he sided with M. de Mézy and, against the bishop's opposition, accepted the post of attorney general in the Conseil Souverain. Nor do the clergy appear to have looked favourably upon the ball given by Chartier on 4 Feb. 1667—the "first ball in Canada," according to the *Journal des Jésuites*.

Did graver suspicions hang over Chartier in the Corruble affair? Ange Bouge, *dite* la Corruble, had been arrested by order of the council, and imprisoned because of scandalous conduct in the company of some young men. The next day, 18 July 1676, the jailer Genaple* released the prisoner, at Chartier's request. Asked to offer an explanation before the council, the lieutenant general refused to give his reasons, and furthermore his manner was peremptory and lacking in respect. He was summoned to appear again on 23 July, and he maintained that he alone had the right to decide upon imprisonments. He resorted to an attitude of arrogance, and refused to justify his action any further. On 3 August the council relieved him of his office, which he resumed however before the end of the month.

This officer of justice—whose career spanned almost 30 years, but whom TALON deemed "ill suited to this profession"—died in France some time after 1680. According to M. de Léry Macdonald he died in 1688.

ANDRÉ VACHON

APQ, Ins. cons. souv., I, 62. Correspondance de Talon, APQ *Rapport, 1930–31*, 103, 109, 110. *Édits ord.*, I, 46; III, 87. *JR* (Thwaites), *passim*. *JJ* (Laverdière et Casgrain), 233, 250, 267, 353. *Jug. et délib.*, I, II, *passim*. *Lettres de noblesse* (P.-G. Roy), II, 127–33. *Papier terrier de la Cie des I.O.* (P.-G. Roy). P.-G. Roy, *Inv. concessions*, I, 202f., 224, 271; II, 22; *Inv. ins. cons. souv.*, 9, 19, 29, 33, 39.

[François Daniel], *Histoire des grandes familles françaises du Canada ou aperçu sur le Chevalier Benoist et quelques familles contemporaines* (Montréal, 1867). J.-B. Garreau, "La Prévôté de Québec," *APQ Rapport, 1943–44*, 61–63. Le Jeune, *Dictionnaire*, II, 171f. A. De Léry Macdonald, "Louis-Théandre Chartier de Lotbinière, père de la magistrature canadienne," *BRH*, XXXIII (1927), 198–206. P.-G. Roy, *La ville de Québec*, I, *passim*.

CHARTRES, LÉONARD DE. *See* LÉONARD

CHASTELLAIN, PIERRE, called Arioo by the Indians, priest, Jesuit, missionary in the Huron country until 1650, author of religious writings; b. 25 June 1606 at Senlis (France); d. 15 Aug. 1684 at Quebec.

While still very young he stood out by virtue of his modesty and piety. Descended from an important family in Senlis, he had difficulty in obtaining his father's permission to become a Jesuit. He entered the noviciate in Paris 3 Sept. 1624.

After taking his first vows in September 1626 he was sent to the famous Collège de Clermont (Paris), where he was to spend ten years. At first a student in philosophy (1626–29), he remained there as a master and teacher (1629–32). At the same time he was a "dormitory scholastic," that is, a house-master in charge of the 300 boarders who were enrolled in this institution. He was still there for his theological studies, which he did with JOGUES and GARNIER, having the well-known Father Denis Pétau as his teacher. After a few months of the third year, he took the four vows of the professed of the Society of Jesus.

Before his departure from France in 1636, he was commissioned by Mme de Combalet, Richelieu's niece, the future Duchesse d'Aiguillon, to try to influence the Religious Hospitallers of Dieppe and Father PAUL LE JEUNE in favour of the founding of a hospital in New France. On 8 April 1636 he left Dieppe, in company with Father Garnier and Governor HUAULT de Montmagny. Landing at Quebec 11 June, he baptized his first Indian. By 1 July he was sailing to Trois-Rivières with Garnier in order "to wait for the canoes of the Hurons" there. Father Le Jeune went to join them on 21 July. On 12 August Chastellain reached Ihonatiria (Saint-Joseph I), where on 24 September he was stricken with purpura.

He spent two years (1636–38) at Ihonatiria with Isaac Jogues and PIERRE PIJART, then a few months at Ossossané (La Conception), before joining Jean de BRÉBEUF at Teanaostaiaë (Saint-Joseph

Chateaufort

II). From November 1639 on he was stationed permanently at the new central residence of Sainte-Marie-des-Hurons, with the task of "maintaining peace and good order." His knowledge of the Huron language, the pleasantness of his character, and his skill in directing consciences caused him to be designated to look after hospitality for passing Indians and the spiritual needs of all, including the missionaries. As an adviser, he approved the keeping on of the *donnés* (1643), the moving of the residence to the Île Saint-Joseph (Christian Island), and the departure of the Hurons for Quebec (1649 and 1650).

Throughout the period from 1650 to 1684 he was spiritual prefect and confessor of the Jesuits, admonisher, and adviser. His name appears in various notarial acts of the period and as a preacher on special occasions. For 32 years he was confessor and spiritual director of the Religious Hospitallers of Quebec and confessor extraordinary of the Ursulines, spiritual director to Catherine de Saint-Augustin [*see* SIMON], Mme d'Ailleboust [*see* BOULLONGNE], Governor RÉMY de Courcelle, and JEAN BOURDON, attorney-general, whose will he signed as a witness in 1657 and 1664.

After 60 years of religious life, he died 15 Aug. 1684. During his stay in the Huron country he had written in Latin a work entitled *Affectus amantis Jesum seu Exercitium amoris erga Dominum Jesum per tota hebdomada*, the first Canadian spiritual treatise.

GEORGES-ÉMILE GIGUÈRE

ACSM, MSS 124b, 310. ASQ, Carton Plante, 73, 86. Pierre Chastellain, *Affectus amantis Jesum seu Exercitium amoris erga Dominum Jesus per tota hebdomada* (Paris, 1648). *JR* (Thwaites), IX, 244–50; XIII, 126–28; XIX, 184–206. Juchereau, *Annales* (Jamet). *BRH*, II (1896), 21, 41, 43; IX (1903), 81. *Jésuites de la N.-F.* (Roustang). Rochemonteix, *Les Jésuites et la N.-F.-au XVIIe siècle*, II, 225, 292–93.

CHATEAUFORT, MARC-ANTOINE BRAS-DE-FER DE. *See* BRAS-DE-FER

CHÂTEAUGUAY, CHARLES LE MOYNE DE LONGUEUIL ET DE. *See* LE MOYNE

CHÂTEAUGUAY, LOUIS LE MOYNE DE. *See* LE MOYNE

CHAUDIÈRE NOIRE ("Black Cauldron"), one of the most formidable of the Onondaga chiefs, an enemy of the French; d. 1697.

In 1682, after 17 years of peace, the Iroquois were trying to pick a quarrel with the French. Some of these Indians, and particularly Chaudière Noire, bore them a great deal of ill will. In that year the great Onondaga warrior brought four Ottawa prisoners back to Montreal. In revenge for being badly received by the governor of the place, François-Marie PERROT, Chaudière Noire pillaged Fort Cataracoui (Frontenac), which he again attacked in August and September 1687.

In 1688 Chaudière Noire took part in the embassy that the Five Nations sent to Governor Brisay* de Denonville. In August 1691 the Onondaga chief and about 600 men, "like a river overflowing its banks," fell upon the most isolated villages. From Montreal the Chevalier de Callières* sent 300 Frenchmen and friendly Indians to war against the Iroquois. At a short day's march beyond Cataracoui the expedition terminated in a French victory.

In the spring of 1692 a group of Senecas, accompanied by Chaudière Noire and some of his men, were hunting at the Chaudière rapids. They were to spend the summer months there, ready to pounce upon the French who used to pass on their way to and from Michilimackinac. When they reached the Long Sault, the French were attacked and scattered by Chaudière Noire at the head of 140 men.

On 15 July 1692 at La Chesnaye Chaudière Noire carried off 3 Indian boys and 14 settlers who were busy drying their hay. Immediately Callières launched in pursuit a party of Frenchmen who were reinforced by 26 Indians from the Saint-Louis falls (Sault Saint-Louis) and the village of La Montagne (at Montreal). Two leagues above the Long Sault they caught up with Chaudière Noire, who succeeded in escaping by swimming across the Ottawa River. The expedition freed 9 Frenchmen and the 3 young Indians, killed a score of Chaudière Noire's warriors, and took about the same number of prisoners, among whom was the Iroquois chief's wife. Because she wished to escape, she was killed some months later. On their side the French lost 11 men, including 4 officers.

When Frontenac [*see* BUADE] was thinking of making peace with the Iroquois, Chaudière Noire came close to Cataracoui on the pretence of hunting and sent a message to the commanding officer, M. Dufrost* de La Jemmerais, saying that the elders of the upper cantons were going to Quebec to conclude peace. It was true. While these Iroquois were hunting game along the Bay of Quinte, 34 young Algonkins took them by surprise. Chaudière Noire was killed by a young Indian, Kiouet. His new wife and half the people in his expedition also perished.

HENRI BÉCHARD

Chaumonot

Charlevoix, *Histoire*, III. La Potherie, *Histoire*, III, IV. *NYCD* (O'Callaghan and Fernow), IX. Ferland, *Cours d'histoire du Canada*, II, 133. Gérard Malchelosse, "Ki8et et La Chaudière Noire," *La Revue Nationale*, IV (1922), 341–45. Vachon de Belmont, *Histoire du Canada*.

CHAUFFOURS, MATHIEU DAMOURS DE. *See* DAMOURS

CHAUMONOT (Calmonotius, Calvonotti, Chomonot), PIERRE-JOSEPH-MARIE, priest, Jesuit, missionary, called Échon (Héchon) by the Indians; specialist in the Huron language, co-founder of the Confrérie de la Sainte-Famille, founder of the Notre-Dame-de-Lorette mission near Quebec; b. 9 March 1611 at Châtillon-sur-Seine (Côte d'Or, Burgundy); d. 21 Feb. 1693 at Quebec.

In 1688, at Quebec, Father Claude DABLON asked Father Chaumonot to write the story of his life. This autobiography enables us to acquire a thorough knowledge of this missionary, who remains, as Gosselin says, "one of the finest figures in the Church in Canada and one of the purest glories of the Society of Jesus."

His father was "a poor vine-grower," and his mother "a poor daughter of a schoolmaster." After attending his grandfather's school, Pierre presented himself at the home of his uncle, a parish priest who wanted to make a cleric of him. But a comrade persuaded Pierre to accompany him to Beaune, where the Oratorian fathers taught. He took advantage of his uncle's absence at church to steal 100 *sols* from him and to take to flight. This petty theft was to lead him to the Jesuits' noviciate in Rome and then to the Huron mission in Canada.

Stranded without any funds, and being afraid of "being pointed at as a thief" if he returned home, he decided "to roam about the world as a vagabond." From Lyons he set off for Italy with another vagabond like himself. After many adventures, which are recounted in a picturesque manner in the autobiography, Pierre Chaumonot, who had been moved by a Jesuit father's sermon at Terni (Umbria), was presented to the provincial of the Jesuits and accepted by him, and entered St. Andrew's noviciate in Rome on 18 May 1632. He was 21 years old.

Six months later he was sent with three comrades to the new Jesuit noviciate at Florence where, a year and a half later, he took his vows. He travelled from Florence to Rome, then from Rome to Fermo, near Loreto. There he taught for two years and a half, while relearning his mother tongue which he had forgotten. Back in Rome to study philosophy in preparation for theology, he met Father PONCET de La Rivière, who showed him Brébeuf's *Relation* for 1636; on reading it he decided to apply for the missions in Canada. After repeated entreaties he obtained permission to drop his studies, to receive the priesthood as soon as possible, and to go to France (21 Sept. 1637).

Upon his ordination towards the end of 1637 or the beginning of 1638, Joseph-Marie said his first mass in a chapel erected under the name and invocation of the house of the Virgin in Loreto (it was at this time also that he obtained permission to use as his first name Joseph-Marie, because he held Mary in great veneration and because he had learned that Canada was under the protection of St. Joseph). Almost immediately after his ordination Father Chaumonot left Rome with Father Poncet and went to prepare for his mission at the noviciate in Rouen, at the same time doing his third probatory year. Finally the day of departure was set for 4 May 1639, from the quays of Dieppe. The flotilla consisted of three ships, including the flagship *Saint-Joseph*, which carried Father Barthélemy VIMONT, three Ursuline nuns, including Marie de l'Incarnation [*see* GUYART], four Religious Hospitallers, and Mme de CHAUVIGNY de La Peltrie. Father Claude Jager and Father Chaumonot embarked on the other two ships. Father Poncet also sailed on this voyage. The rough crossing, which has been described at length in the nuns' letters, did not end until the evening of 31 July; all the travellers, who were brought together on one boat at Tadoussac, landed on the western end of the Île d'Orléans. It was there that next morning the shallop belonging to M. HUAULT de Montmagny, the governor of New France, picked up the travellers to bring them to Quebec; they were received with open arms, for, according to Father PAUL LE JEUNE, the colony was receiving "a Jesuit college, a Hospitallers' house, & a Ursuline convent." The travellers went directly to the church; they sang the *Te Deum*, heard mass, and received Holy Communion; they dined at the governor's house. The people of Quebec took a holiday that day in honour of the new arrivals, who visited the town and its surroundings the very next day. Father Poncet and Father Chaumonot recorded their first baptisms of a few Indians.

On 3 Aug. 1639 Chaumonot was already on his way from Quebec to the Huron country with Father Poncet. Chaumonot himself has told us of this trip, which ended on 10 Sept. 1639 at Lake Isiaragui. Father Chaumonot, was assistant to Father François DU PERON and Father Paul RAGUENEAU at the former central residence at Ossossané, which had become the "Mission de la

Chaumonot

Conception." It had difficulties at the beginning, especially because of "a sort of smallpox" which scattered the population and for which the witch doctors blamed the fathers, as the French were not affected.

Between this first mission with Father Ragueneau and his departure for the Neutral Nation with Father Brébeuf, 2 Nov. 1640, Chaumonot stayed a short time with the Ahrendarrhonon (Rock) Nation at the Saint-Jean-Baptiste mission (Cahiagué), which at that time was under the direction of Father ANTOINE DANIEL. According to the autobiography and the 1640 *Relation*, this new position must have been entrusted to him early in the spring of 1640, probably in March, to permit him to learn the Huron language. "Father Daniel," he said, "gave me this advice. I had to go into a certain number of lodges every day to ask the Indians for the words of their language and to write them down when they were suggested to me." It was in dirty lodges, amid a thousand mockeries, that the missionaries were to learn the Huron language, "the most difficult of all those of North America," according to Chaumonot. He was to be rewarded for his work, for he himself declared: "It pleased God so to bless my work, that the Huron possesses no turn of phrase, no subtlety nor manner of expression, that I am not acquainted with and which I have not, as it were, discovered." After his death someone was to write: "All the Jesuits who will ever learn Huron will do so with the help of the examples, the roots, the speeches, and several fine works which he has left us in this language. The Indians themselves admitted that he spoke it better than they, who for the most part prided themselves on speaking well." Someone else was to write: "Father Chaumont [*sic*], who has lived for 50 years among the Hurons, has composed a grammar, which is very useful to those who come for the first time to this mission."

From that time on his life was to be nothing but a long series of moves in the midst of the greatest difficulties. After his stay with Father Daniel, Chaumonot was sent with Jean de Brébeuf to the Neutrals, with whom they stayed from 2 Nov. 1640 to 19 Mar. 1641. Then he returned with Father Daniel, staying sometimes at Saint-Jean-Baptiste, sometimes at Saint-Joseph II (Teanaostaiaë) or at Saint-Michel (Scanonaenrat). It was at Saint-Joseph II that Father Chaumonot was saved from death by Father Daniel, who very dexterously snatched a hatchet from the hand of an Indian who was about to fell the missionary.

From 1643 to 1645 Chaumonot worked at Saint-Michel with Father Du Peron. We lose sight of him during the years 1645–47, for the *Relations* make no mention whatsoever of him; it is not until the end of 1647 or the beginning of 1648 that we find him again, at the Saint-Ignace I mission (Taenhatentaron) with Father MÉNARD. After April 1648 and until 19 March 1649 he carried on his work at La Conception. We know that the Iroquois had sworn to destroy the Hurons. After harrying them for many years, they launched their final offensive in 1649. We also know that from 29 Sept. 1642 to 8 Dec. 1649 the Iroquois martyred eight persons. Having escaped the massacre, Chaumonot did not abandon the Hurons: he sought refuge with them among the Tobacco Nation from 19 March to 1 May 1649, and then on the Île Saint-Joseph (Christian Island) from 1 May to 10 June 1650, when they left for Quebec, which the "small remainder" reached on 28 July, to settle subsequently on the Île d'Orléans (29 March 1651).

On 12 Sept. 1655, in order to lure the Hurons to them, the Onondagas sent ambassadors to Quebec to request that priests be sent them. Following Father SIMON LE MOYNE's peace mission in 1654, Chaumonot left Quebec with Father Claude Dablon 19 Sept. 1655 and arrived at Onondaga 5 Nov. 1655. In July 1656 they established the Sainte-Marie-de-Ganentaa mission in Onondaga territory. It was there that Chaumonot delivered several addresses "in the style of the country," addresses that remained famous among the Indians as well as the French. As there was no end to the Iroquois' vexations, life rapidly became unbearable and all the French had to flee on 20 March 1658. They arrived back at Quebec on 23 April.

On 19 September Chaumonot was called to Montreal by Governor Voyer* d'Argenson to carry on negotiations with the Onondagas. As he was well acquainted with these Indians and with their habits and language, he was to be sent on embassy by the governor fairly often (13 May 1659, 2 July 1661).

On 2 June 1662 Chaumonot again set off for Montreal, this time "to succour the inhabitants . . . who were suffering from an extreme shortage of supplies." There, c. 1663, with M. SOUART's permission and the aid of Mme d'Ailleboust [*see* BOULLONGNE], he founded the Confrérie de la Sainte-Famille, which was to bear much fruit and which still exists. He was to establish the same congregation at Quebec in October 1664. Chaumonot was chaplain of five French companies from 23 July to 3 Oct. 1665. At the same time he continued to look after his Hurons. At the end of that year he was at the post between Quebec and Beauport—at Notre-Dame-des-Neiges—and he stayed there till April 1668. In the spring of 1669 he settled down at Côte-Saint-Michel, still serving the Hurons but sometimes preaching retreats to the nuns in Quebec and performing other ministries.

One of Father Chaumonot's finest claims to fame is that of having founded the celebrated Huron mission of Notre-Dame-de-Lorette, three leagues from Quebec. Since the time of his trip to Loreto in Italy he had dreamt of building in New France a chapel modelled on the one in Europe. At that time the missionaries were looking for tracts of land for the Hurons. After much searching and many prayers the Jesuits decided to bestow upon the Indians their seigneury of Saint-Michel which was three leagues from Quebec and to which they gave the name of Lorette. When the site for the chapel had been chosen, the plan for the village was drawn up, and in that same summer of 1673 the construction of a few lodges was quickly begun; on 28 December their first inhabitants moved into them. While waiting for the chapel to be built three Hurons generously lent their lodge, in which mass was said for ten months by the fathers, who themselves lived in a hastily erected lodge. On 16 July 1674 Father Claude Dablon, the superior general of the missions of the Society of Jesus in New France and rector of the college in Quebec, laid the first stone. He blessed the chapel 4 Nov. 1674; it had cost 5,000 *livres*. At the outset nearly 300 Indians (there would be only 146 at the time of the 1685 census) lived at the new mission, which was under the direction of Father Chaumonot. The *Relations* of the time contain a large number of accounts of the great virtues of the Hurons, who displayed much piety and much charity. The other missions had more inhabitants, but only those who openly professed Christianity and practised the highest virtues were chosen to live at Lorette. Father Chaumonot could see them praying in the chapel and hear them singing hymns in the fields.

Lorette rapidly became a place of pilgrimage for the French. Unfortunately, mingled with the pilgrims, were traffickers in spirits who took up with the Hurons. According to Father Chaumonot, drunkenness was the only vice they had to contend with; in 1687 he wrote that "with spirits moral perversion entered the village." Father Chaumonot resigned in 1691, after being the first religious to celebrate the golden jubilee of his sacerdotal career at Quebec.

In October 1692 he fell ill; he finally retired to Quebec, to the Jesuit college, and on 21 Feb. 1693 he died, after receiving the rites for the sick on 18 February. He was 82, and had spent 52 years working in New France.

ANDRÉ SURPRENANT

[P.-J.-M. Chaumonot], *Un missionnaire des Hurons: autobiographie du Père Chaumonot de la Compagnie de Jésus et son complément*, éd. Félix Martin (Paris, 1885); *Le Père Pierre Chaumonot de la Compagnie de Jésus: autobiographie et pièces inédites*, éd. Auguste Carayon (Poitiers, 1869); "Quelques remarques sur les vertus du P. de Brébeuf," dans ACSM, "Mémoires touchant la mort et les vertus des pères Isaac Jogues . . ." (Ragueneau), repr. APQ *Rapport, 1924–25*, 68–69; *La vie du R. P. Pierre-Joseph-Marie Chaumonot, de la Compagnie de Jésus, missionnaire dans la Nouvelle-France, écrite par lui-même par ordre de son supérieur, l'an 1688*, éd. J. G. Shea (2v., New York, 1858). Marie Guyart de l'Incarnation, *Écrits* (Jamet). *JR* (Thwaites). *Première mission des Jésuites au Canada: lettres et documents inédits*, éd. Auguste Carayon (Paris, 1864).

Campbell, *Pioneer priests*. Auguste Gosselin, *Vie de Mgr de Laval*. Jésuites de la N.-F. (Roustang). Parkman, *Jesuits in North America* (29th ed.); *The old régime* (25th ed.), 20–39. Rochemonteix, *Les Jésuites et la N.-F. au XVIIe siècle*, I, 399–408, *et passim*. André Surprenant, "Le Père Pierre-Joseph-Marie Chaumonot, missionnaire de la Huronie," *RHAF*, VII (1953–54), 64–87, 241–58, 392–412, 505–23.

CHAUVIGNY DE LA PELTRIE, MARIE-MADELEINE DE, secular foundress of the Ursulines of Quebec; b. 1603 at Alençon (France), a daughter of Guillaume de Chauvigny, Sieur d'Alençon et de Vaubougon, and of Lady Jeanne Du Bouchet; d. 16 Nov. 1671 at Quebec.

Since Guillaume de Chauvigny had no son to succeed him, he tried to arrange aristocratic matches for his daughters. Marie-Madeleine, the youngest, despite her inclination for the cloistered life, found herself obliged to marry the Chevalier de Gruel, Seigneur de La Peltrie. From this marriage, which lasted only five years, there was born one daughter who died in infancy. Widowed at the age of 22, Mme de La Peltrie devoted herself with singular zeal to the practice of virtue. She even went into solitary retirement in order to avoid her father's solicitous attempts to find her a second husband.

At this time the *Relation des Jésuites* for 1635 came to her attention, and Father PAUL LE JEUNE's appeal on behalf of the missions in New France seemed to be directed to her in particular: "Alas, my God!" he had written, "if the waste, if the superabundance of some of the Ladies of France were employed in this so holy work [the founding at Quebec of a convent of teaching nuns], what great blessings would it bring down upon their families!" From this moment forward, Mme de La Peltrie conceived the idea of devoting herself and her fortune to the conversion of the Indians.

But a serious illness interfered with her plans and brought her to death's door. While the doctors

Chauvin de La Pierre

thought her doomed and continued to visit her only as a formality, she made a vow to St. Joseph, promising, in return for her recovery, to go to Canada, to build a house there under his patronage, and to devote herself to the service of little Indian girls. The next day, contrary to everyone's expectations, she had no fever and was determined to carry out her promises. Her father, more intent than ever upon her remarriage, launched a new onslaught. Several persons urged her to yield to her father's desires, but she hit upon an ingenious device for allaying M. de Vaubougon's anxieties: a sham marriage with M. Jean de Bernières de Louvigny, a treasurer of France at Caen, who subsequently became procurator of the Ursulines at Quebec. This gentleman agreed to go through with the make-believe. In the meantime, M. de Vaubougon died and Mme de La Peltrie's affairs became complicated: her relations, thinking her unable to administer her fortune, sought to have her deprived of control over her estate. She appealed to the judicial court of Rouen, won her suit and, as a result, became mistress of her inheritance.

Eager to leave for New France, Mme de La Peltrie went to Paris and consulted M. Vincent [de Paul] and Father de Condren, the arbitrators of apostolic ventures. She was introduced to Father Joseph-Antoine PONCET de La Rivière, a Jesuit who told her about Marie de l'Incarnation [see GUYART], who likewise was filled with a longing to go to Canada. Mme de La Peltrie and M. de Bernières de Louvigny went to Tours and arrangements for the foundation were soon settled. In Mme de La Peltrie, Marie de l'Incarnation recognized the companion who had been revealed to her in a dream. In Paris the foundress signed the document that assured to the foundation the property called Haranvilliers, near Alençon, a bequest that represented an annual revenue of about 900 *livres*. When she was unable to find space for her baggage on the ships leaving for America, Mme de La Peltrie chartered a vessel at her own expense and loaded it with provisions and furnishings at a cost of 8,000 *livres*. To her party of three Ursulines she added a girl of 19, Charlotte Barré, who was to become the first professed nun in the Quebec convent, taking the name of Mother Saint-Ignace.

Upon her arrival at Quebec, 1 Aug. 1639, Mme de La Peltrie began to show her zeal for the conversion of the Indians. She was everywhere, exerting herself to multiply works of mercy, both on the physical and on the spiritual plane. As a result, the little Indian girls followed her with greater affection than children follow their own mother. Although she was of a frail constitution, she undertook the most menial duties in her desire to have a part in every charitable work. This yearning for absolute perfection explains her sudden departure for Montreal with Jeanne MANCE and Paul CHOMEDEY de Maisonneuve in the spring of 1642. Deprived of the financial resources, the furnishings, and especially of the presence of their foundress, the Ursulines were hard pressed to hold out. After an 18-month absence that might well have destroyed the Ursuline mission, Mme de La Peltrie returned to her nuns. When the noviciate was opened (1646), she sought the privilege of being admitted to the Compagnie de Sainte-Ursule, but the experiment did not last long. She resumed her secular dress, although continuing to live in the cloister and to observe all the rules of convent life.

On several occasions Marie de l'Incarnation paid tribute to Mme de La Peltrie, whom she called "a saint." On 12 Nov. 1671, the foundress contracted pleurisy, which caused her death six days later. The day after her death, her body was placed in a lead casket and buried in the Ursuline Chapel. In accordance with her last wishes, her heart was deposited with the Jesuits as a token of the respect and affection she had always felt for their Society.

MARIE-EMMANUEL CHABOT, O.S.U.

For a full biography and details of Mme de La Peltrie's romantic and apostolic adventures, consult: Marie Guyart de l'Incarnation, *Écrits* (Jamet). *JR* (Thwaites), LXI, *passim*. *Les Ursulines de Québec*, I.

CHAUVIN DE LA PIERRE, PIERRE, also called Chavin, Huguenot merchant and sea captain, temporary commandant at Quebec in 1609–10.

CHAMPLAIN normally calls him "Capt. Pierre," and only once names him "Pierre Chavin." But the latter's frequent dealings with PIERRE CHAUVIN DE TONNETUIT and his sister about an inheritance lead us to suppose that his family name was indeed Chauvin, a very common name in Normandy, and that he was a relative of his namesake, the Sieur de Tonnetuit, with whom he must not be confused.

He was a bourgeois of Dieppe and subsequently lived at Honfleur. The notarial register of that town contains several documents relating to him. In 1603 he sailed for Canada on the *Bonne Renommée*, with FRANÇOIS GRAVÉ Du Pont and Champlain. In 1607, as "king's captain in the navy" and in association with another captain named Tuvache, he bought a small vessel, the *Levrette*, on which he came again to Canada the following year. When Champlain went back to France in the autumn of 1609, he left the "worthy man . . . Pierre Chavin" in command of Quebec

Chauvin de Tonnetuit

during his absence, and subsequently mentioned him several times in the first edition of his *Voyages* (1613).

Chauvin returned to France in the autumn of 1610, and came back to Canada in 1611 on Isaac Martel's ship, to trade in furs. The following winter, at the same time as François de RAZILLY, he undertook a journey to Brazil on the ship *Perle*, after which time we lose trace of him.

RENÉ BAUDRY

Champlain, *Œuvres* (Laverdière). Bréard, *Documents relatifs à la marine normande*. Biographical note in Dionne, *Champlain*, I, 378–81.

CHAUVIN DE TONNETUIT, PIERRE DE, French naval and military captain, lieutenant of New France, called the founder of Tadoussac; b. Dieppe, Normandy; d. early in February 1603 in France (probably at Honfleur). He should not be confused with Capt. PIERRE CHAUVIN DE LA PIERRE, or Chavin, of Dieppe, whom CHAMPLAIN placed in command at Quebec during his absence in 1609–10.

He was of a wealthy merchant family, and married first Jeanne de Mallemouche, by whom he had one son, François, and second, Marie de Brinon. In 1583 he was serving under admiral Aymar de Chaste in the Azores, and in 1589 he was captain of the important Huguenot garrison at Honfleur, occupied by DU GUA de Monts the previous year. By 1596, as several notarized documents attest (reproduced in Bréard, *Documents*, 73ff.), Chauvin had developed an interest in commercial and maritime enterprises. He now owned four vessels, the *Don-de-Dieu*, the *Espérance*, the *Bon-Espoir*, and the *Saint-Jean*, and he was regularly engaged in the fur trade and cod-fishery of Canada and Newfoundland.

A Calvinist, he had given illustrious service in the wars against the League, and was soon rewarded with a position of influence in the new king's court. At the solicitation of FRANÇOIS GRAVÉ Du Pont, who also had made many trading expeditions to the St. Lawrence, Chauvin sought and gained from Henri IV, in 1599, a ten-year monopoly of the fur trade in New France. However, following the protest of LA ROCHE DE MESGOUEZ, who held a similar concession, Henri IV gave Chauvin a new commission on 15 Jan. 1600 which acknowledged only his "being one of the lieutenants" of La Roche.

Chauvin embarked from Honfleur in the early spring of 1600, with his four ships and the intended colonists, and Gravé as his partner and lieutenant. De Monts sailed with them as a passenger. Against the advice of Gravé and de Monts, Chauvin chose Tadoussac as his destination—inevitably, perhaps, for his trading post, but fatally for the colony. Strategically situated at the junction of the Saguenay and St. Lawrence rivers, the Indian trading routes to the interior, with a harbour adjacent, Tadoussac had long been a Montagnais summering place for barter, and for half a century a fur-trading and fishing resort for Europeans. But with the arms they received the Montagnais had ousted the Iroquois from the region; they were soon to be visited by a revenge of equal horror, and driven far into the interior. Tadoussac was to suffer; and as allies of the Montagnais, and soon of the Algonkins and Hurons too, all enemies of the Iroquois, the French and their fur trade were distressed for many years. Furthermore, the area was ill fitted for settlement because of the rugged terrain and poor soil, and because in winter "the cold is so great" Champlain says in his *Voyages* "that if there is an ounce of cold forty leagues up the river, there will be a pound of it here."

A house was built at Tadoussac, which Champlain saw and described as being "twenty-five feet long by eighteen wide and eight feet high, covered with boards with a fireplace in the middle," encompassed by a wattle palisade and a ditch. Champlain's map of Tadoussac in 1608, which appears in the *Works* (II, 19) depicts this structure on the east bank of a stream which enters the harbour; underneath are the words "abitation du Capp[n] chauvain de lan 1600" (habitation of Capt. Chauvin of the year 1600). After the colonists were settled, the monopolists devoted their energies to the traffic in peltry until the autumn, when they sailed for France with a cargo of beaver and other furs. At Tadoussac they left 16 men to face the unknown northern winter; only 5 survived, and these owed their lives to Indian hospitality.

According to contemporary documents Chauvin sent only one vessel, the *Espérance*, to the Saguenay the following spring (cf. Bréard, *Documents*, 69–70, 88), but did not sail himself. Doubtless the remnant of his colony returned with this ship in the autumn, and no others were set ashore to repeat the suffering. In April 1602, Chauvin commanded another expedition from Honfleur to New France, this time with only two ships, the *Don-de-Dieu* and the *Espérance*, and almost certainly no colonists. After a summer of trading in the Tadoussac region he returned, from this the third voyage of his monopoly, in October 1602. If the number of vessels employed is an indication, Chauvin had won no great success from his privilege.

209

Chefdostel

During half a century the Canadian fur trade had assumed considerable proportions, involving the capital of a great many investors. As with previous French grants of monopoly trading in Canada, Chauvin's patent was vigorously opposed by the excluded merchants of the French seaports. Henri IV had stood resolute in the larger cause; but after three summers, Chauvin had failed to establish a colony, and his rivals were as clamorous as ever. In 1602, therefore, the monopoly was extended to include certain other traders in Rouen and Saint-Malo, providing they undertook a share of the obligations. When this also failed to silence the outcry for free trade the king summoned a commission of inquiry, on 28 Dec. 1602, to meet in Rouen in a month's time. Here the commissioners (one of whom was the governor of Dieppe, Aymar de Chaste) received delegates from the Rouen and Saint-Malo merchants, and Chauvin himself, to discuss and arbitrate the monopoly and its colonization terms. An agreement to continue both was apparently reached and published (Biggar, *Early trading companies*, 45–46), but before the vessels could leave on another voyage, Chauvin died. The monopoly passed to de Chaste who, that same spring, dispatched three ships to New France. One, the *Bonne Renommée* belonging to de Chaste, was commanded by Gravé, whose task was to survey the resources of the region and find a more auspicious place for settlement; in this he was aided by Champlain, on his first visit to New France.

On 20 Jan. 1603, Chauvin was still living, for he gave a power of attorney to his sister Madeleine; in the absence of any known record we may accept the estimate of Bréard (*Documents*, 71), based on the evidence, that he died during the first days of February. The same writer shows that Chauvin had probably made a fortune during his lifetime, for he owned four ships and several smaller boats, more than one house, valuable personal property, and he had bought the land of Tonnetuit. Yet, at his death, his estate was so encumbered that both his wife and his son renounced it. Some historians have observed that Chauvin was more concerned with profit than with his colonists; but evidently his last years had only reduced his fortune, and he did send a ship to Tadoussac early in 1601, probably rescuing the surviving colonists, and in all likelihood he never replaced them. History, however, will remember him as the builder at Tadoussac, eight years before Quebec, of the first trading post, the first house, in Canada. A replica, serving as a museum, has been built on what is thought to be the original site.

WILLIAM F. E. MORLEY

Champlain, *Works* (Biggar), II, 19; III, 305–11. Biggar, *Early trading companies*, 42–46. Bréard, *Documents relatifs à la marine normande*, 65–92. Gustave Lanctot, *Réalisations françaises de Cartier à Montcalm* (Montréal, 1951), 45 f. La Roncière, *Histoire de la marine française*, IV (1923), 318–19. Joseph Le Ber, "Un document inédit sur l'Île de Sable et le Marquis de la Roche," *RHAF*, II (1948–49), 203 ff. Trudel, *Histoire de la Nouvelle-France*, I, 236.

CHEFDOSTEL, THOMAS, French sailor from Watteville, in Normandy; fl. 1597–1603.

Chefdostel, who was captain of the ship *Catherine*, entered into a contract with the Marquis TROILUS DE LA ROCHE de Mesgouez, viceroy of Canada, on 4 March 1597, whereby he undertook to lead to the Île de Sable an exploring and fishing expedition of which they were to share the profits. This expedition must have yielded satisfactory results, for the following year Chefdostel took La Roche himself there, and the latter set up on the island an exploration post manned by some 50 vagabonds and beggars recruited at Rouen. Each year, by La Roche's order, Chefdostel came to bring them supplies, except in 1602. The following year the viceroy instructed him to take stores to his men and to bring back the commander, Querbonyer, and a few associates. On his arrival he found that as the result of a mutiny the commander and other leaders had been slaughtered. He then brought back to France the 11 survivors left on the island, and claimed the right to keep as compensation all the skins which they had loaded on to his ship. But the Parlement of Rouen ordered them to be shared out, one-third going to Chefdostel and the remainder to the rescued men.

GUSTAVE LANCTOT

ASM, B (Parlement de Rouen), archives secrètes. Bibliothèque de l'Institut de France, Coll. Godefroy, 291 [escrit envoyé par le marquis Troille du Mesgouez de La Roche (1604)]. Anthiaume, *Cartes marines*, II, 95. Bréard, *Documents relatifs à la marine normande*, 59, 61, 63, 76, 79. É.-H. Gosselin, *Nouvelles glanes historiques normandes*. Gustave Lanctot, "L'établissement du marquis de La Roche à l'Île de Sable," CHA *Report 1933*, 33–42. Joseph Le Ber, "Un document inédit sur l'Île de Sable et le marquis de La Roche," *RHAF*, II (1948–49), 199–213.

CHEROUOUNY (called at various times **"The Murderer," "The Reconciled"**), Montagnais chief, one of the Indians implicated in the murder of two Frenchmen near Cap Tourmente in 1616; killed, on a peace mission to the Mohawks, 1627.

Though there is some uncertainty about this, Cherououny appears to be the man who instigated the 1616 murders. He frequented the French post at Quebec and that summer he had been insulted and beaten by the locksmith there. Soon after, when the locksmith and Charles Pillet, a sailor, went hunting in the vicinity of Cap Tourmente, Cherououny and a companion followed, slew them, and sank their bodies in the St. Lawrence. In 1618 the bodies were found and the French learned something about the slaying from an Indian hostile to the murderers [see CHOMINA]. Fearing French reprisals, the Indians of the area withdrew to Trois-Rivières, where SAGARD says they plotted to attack the French. Meanwhile, they sent EROUACHY, another Montagnais chief, to bargain with the French and to offer them the gifts they traditionally used to settle murders. Later, one of the murderers (LE CLERCQ suggests that it was Cherououny's accomplice) was persuaded to go with some of the principal chiefs to meet with the French at Quebec. The latter, fearing the Indians and not wishing to injure trade, decided not to insist that the murderers be put to death, although they delayed a final decision until the ships returned from France. CHAMPLAIN, when he arrived, agreed that it was best to avoid taking strong action. Hereafter, however, he did not allow Cherououny to return to Quebec and made a point of publicly humiliating him whenever they met.

After this, Cherououny's people, who already regarded the French with some ambivalence, looked on him as an important man. Early in July 1623, Erouachy revealed a plan which Cherououny had fomented for attacking the French simultaneously at Tadoussac and at Quebec. He may have been incited to do this by the independent Basque traders who are accused of inciting the Indians along the lower St. Lawrence against the French at Quebec. When French defensive measures defeated any hope of success, Cherououny denied knowledge of the plot. In the hope of avoiding more trouble, ÉMERY DE CAËN and others persuaded Champlain to grant him a royal pardon. This was done with considerable pomp on 31 July 1623. Champlain felt later that the Indians had interpreted this pardon as a sign of weakness.

In 1627 Cherououny was one of a number of chiefs to receive presents from the Dutch and their Indian allies, who urged them to break the peace of 1624 and attack the Mohawks. Though actively supporting this plan at first, Cherououny reversed his stand when he heard Champlain disapproved and he publicly denounced the project at Trois-Rivières. Despite the warnings of Cherououny and the French, some young warriors left for the Iroquois country and returned with two prisoners taken under the guise of friendship. Cherououny kept them alive until Champlain's arrival in mid-July. Champlain persuaded the Indians to return one of the captives and to treat for peace with the Iroquois.

On 24 July 1627, Cherououny set out for the Mohawk country, accompanied by two Indians and Pierre MAGNAN, a Frenchman. In August the French learned that Cherououny and his men had been slain by the Iroquois. There are two versions of this incident. An Algonkin who had escaped from the village where it happened said that the party was well received by the Mohawks; but that some Onondagas who had come to the village slew them, since they regarded them as allies of the Algonkins whom they had been fighting. (The murderers have also been identified as Senecas, *see: Handbook of American Indians north of Mexico*, ed. F. W. Hodge (2v., Washington, 1910), II, 507, 1112.) Later Erouachy reported that an Iroquois, held by the Mahicans, said that an Algonkin from Allumette Island, who had relatives among the Iroquois and who disliked Cherououny, had informed the Iroquois that the peace mission was merely a pretext for spying on the country. The Iroquois pretended to welcome the embassy, but then seized Cherououny and Magnan and cruelly tortured them to death, killed the third man while he was trying to escape, and adopted the last member of the party, who was of Iroquois stock and had been taken captive when he was very young.

Despite his vacillations Cherououny revealed himself as a vigorous individual who possessed notable powers of leadership. His initial injury, revenge, and reconciliation with the French at Quebec form the dominant themes of his life as we know it. Despite his co-operation with the French after 1623, it is doubtful whether he or Champlain ever regarded each other with any real friendship.

BRUCE G. TRIGGER

Champlain, *Works* (Biggar), *passim*. Sagard, *Histoire du Canada* (Tross). Desrosiers, *Iroquoisie*, 96–102.

CHEVALIER. *See* LA TOURASSE

CHEVRY DE LA BOULAYE, CHARLES DURET DE. *See* DURET

CHIHWATENHA (Chihouatenhoua, Chiohoarehra), baptized **JOSEPH**, model convert and friend of the Jesuit missionaries; b. 1602? in Huronia; slain 2 Aug. 1640, near Ossossané.

Joseph, whose uncle was an important chief, lived in Ossossané, where he participated in the fur trade and though not wealthy, had a voice in local councils. Throughout his lifetime Chihwatenha's people were being drawn into ever closer contact with the French. European goods were eagerly sought after by the Indians, but epidemics and increasing warfare among the leading tribes over control of the fur trade added to the already numerous problems which resulted from their contact with European culture, the technological superiority of which they clearly recognized. Particularly disturbing to the Indians were the teachings and admonitions of the missionaries who came to live among them, and whose theology and concepts of moral behaviour were in many ways different from their own.

Chihwatenha was a man of sober habits, and even before conversion the Jesuits regarded his behaviour as exemplary. From the time of their arrival in Ossossané Joseph showed great interest in their teaching, but the Jesuits wished to instruct him thoroughly before baptism. However, he was taken seriously ill and consequently was baptized soon afterwards on 16 Aug. 1637, while his wife, Marie Aonetta, and some other members of his family received baptism a little later. For about ten months his was the only Christian family in Ossossané.

Joseph gave every assistance to the Jesuits in their mission work, not only in his own village but throughout Huronia. He made a public profession of his faith, refused to attend pagan rites, defended the Jesuits in hostile councils, and exhorted the Hurons to become Christians. This was done at considerable personal risk, since the Jesuits were already accused of being sorcerers and were held responsible for the epidemics which were to halve the Huron population by 1640. Joseph's faith did not waver when many of his family died or were taken ill, or even when his sister-in-law sickened and died within 48 hours of her baptism. In the winter of 1637–38 the Jesuits taught him to read and write, apparently with considerable success. In 1639 he travelled to Quebec with Father LE MERCIER, where, probably as on previous visits, he was impressed by the charity and religious zeal of the French, and particularly by the convent and hospital. At the cost of considerable personal difficulty he managed to carry a number of holy relics back to the Huron country. There he argued with his countrymen that the French religion and culture were no less desirable than their trade goods.

In January 1640 he spent eight days performing spiritual exercises at the new mission centre at Fort Sainte-Marie, after which he attempted unsuccessfully to convert his brother. He accompanied the Jesuits on a number of missions that winter, including one to the Tobacco (Petun) tribe, where he had relatives or trading partners. On 2 August, while he was alone cutting wood near his village, he was slain, just one day before his annual departure for Quebec. Sensing danger, he had sent his nieces (one of them quite probably the young Thérèse OIONHATON), back to the village. The Huron chiefs investigated his death and attributed it to Iroquois raiders, an explanation which the Jesuits accepted. But Joseph may just as well have been murdered by Hurons who distrusted him for associating with the French priests and who especially resented his accompanying white men to the Tobacco country for fear they might attempt to promote the fur trade there. It was a Huron practice to murder undesirables in a way that would make the crime seem the work of enemy raiders.

The Jesuits were impressed with Joseph's ability and piety. His devotion and the continued devotion of his family under trying circumstances constituted a happy rebuttal to the Huron claim that it was impossible for an Indian to achieve the standard of morality required of a convert. Joseph was one of the first Hurons who managed to embrace whole-heartedly many of the spiritual as well as the material aspects of European civilization. This choice ran counter to the feeling of most of his people and tended to alienate him from them. His friendship for the French may eventually have brought about his death. Soon after, however, increasing numbers of Hurons came to feel that a more thorough-going acceptance of European ways was desirable. Joseph's brother, Joseph Teondechoren, a cult-healer, became a distinguished convert.

BRUCE G. TRIGGER

JR (Thwaites), *passim*. Léon Pouliot, *Le premier retraitant du Canada* (Montréal, 1958). B. G. Trigger, "The destruction of Huronia: a study in economic and cultural change, 1609–1650," Royal Can. Institute *Trans.*, XXXIII (1960), pt.I, 14–45; "Order and freedom in Huron society," *Anthropologica*, V (1963), 151–69.

CHIOHOAREHRA. *See* CHIHWATENHA

CHKOUDUN. *See* SECOUDON

CHOMEDEY DE MAISONNEUVE, PAUL DE, gentleman, officer, member of the Société Notre-Dame de Montréal, founder of Ville-Marie, first governor of the island of Montréal; b. Neuville-sur-Vanne in the province of Champagne and baptized there 15 Feb. 1612; d. 1676 in Paris.

Paul de Chomedey was the son of Louis de Chomedey, seigneur of Chavane, Germenoy-en-

Chomedey de Maisonneuve

Brie, and other places, and of his second wife Marie de Thomelin; the latter was the daughter of the worthy Jean de Thomelin, a king's counsellor and a treasurer of France in the generality of Champagne, and of Ambroise d'Aulquoy. He had as godfathers Paul Janson, a lieutenant in the bailiff's court at Villemort, and Gabriel de Campan; his godmother was Jeanne de Chabert.

The arms of Paul de Chomedey's grandfather, Hierosme, were "or, three flames gules." They were handed down by direct line to Paul de Chomedey, the eldest son of Louis, himself the son of Hierosme.

Paul de Chomedey grew up in the manor-house at Neuville-sur-Vanne, not far from the Maisonneuve fief, which his father acquired in 1614. He had two sisters and one brother. Louise, the eldest of the family, whose certificate of baptism has not been located, was later to become Mother Louise de Sainte-Marie, of the Congrégation Notre-Dame at Troyes. The date of her death is not known; we do know however that she survived her brother Paul, as is attested by the legacy which he made to her in his will dated 8 Sept. 1676. Odard, Paul's younger brother, was born in 1614. He died at the age of 33. Jacqueline, the youngest of the family, was born in 1618. In 1638 she married François Bouvot (not Bonnot) de Chevilly (not Chuly), by whom she had two daughters. One of them was later to assert her rights as the sole heiress of her uncle Paul. Jacqueline de Chomedey de Chevilly, who gave such effective protection to Marguerite BOURGEOYS before the latter's departure for Canada in 1653, met a sad end a short time afterwards. She died in 1655, assassinated by a sworn enemy of the family. Four years earlier her husband had suffered the same fate, by the same hand.

Paul de Chomedey's military career began early, as was customary in that period. Concerning the enlistment of the eldest of the Chomedeys, and also the incidents in his life as a young soldier winning his laurels, there is however a regrettable dearth of authentic documents. Leymarie admits that from 2 June 1624 to the year 1640 he was not able to find any document relating to him. Our only resort must therefore be to works in which the assertions are not at first-hand.

Dollier* de Casson, in his *Histoire du Montréal*, briefly recalled Paul de Chomedey's youth: Providence, which "had caused him to take up the profession of war in Holland at the age of 13, in order to give him more experience, had taken care to preserve his heart in purity in the midst of these heretical countries and among the free-thinkers to be found there." He added that "in order not to be obliged to go and seek distraction in the company of evil men, he learned to pluck the lute."

M. Dollier is almost the only historian to give details on M. de Maisonneuve's disposition, tastes, and unique character. In addition he offers us an insight into the circumstances that determined Maisonneuve's future plans. But we must give due weight, in all this, to an important statement by the Sulpician narrator. He warned his readers in the first lines of his *Histoire* "that they must not expect . . . that it will not contain a few slight errors in dates and times, or that . . . I shall not omit a very great number of such . . . , because the religion of these pious people . . . has never been able to tolerate anything unusual being published by booksellers concerning what has been done here, so much so that I am constrained today, when I have no authentic evidence of the same, to leave . . . shrouded in darkness what might deservedly be exposed to the brightest daylight." He also said, speaking of his sources, that they were all oral, and that he would restrict himself to recounting the gist of the history of Montreal.

M. Dollier, as a member of the Compagnie de Saint-Sulpice, which was so intimately linked through its founder Jean-Jacques Olier to the history of the early days of Montreal, could not help being deeply interested in the vocation of the first governor of Ville-Marie. He wrote: "The time having arrived when Providence wanted to employ him upon its work, it so increased in him the fear of divine retribution that to avoid this perverted world which he knew, he desired to go and serve his God, through his profession, in a number of very remote countries. One day, turning over these thoughts in his mind, he providentially came upon . . . a Relation from this country [New France] in which mention was made of Father CHARLES LALEMANT, who had returned from Canada some time before . . . ; he resolved to go and see the Father . . . to whom he revealed his inmost intention; the Father, judging that this gentleman was exactly the person that the Sulpicians of Montreal needed, recommended him to M. de la Doversière."

Jérôme Le Royer de La Dauversière, who was to impart a new direction to Paul de Chomedey's life, was a humble tax-collector in the little town of La Flèche, in the province of Anjou. In reality, he was one of the great servants of God in that period, an inspired soul, an architect of vast projects of a charitable, missionary, civilizing, or devotional nature. He was moreover merely one representative of the wave of mysticism that originated in Spain in the 16th century and invaded France in the 17th, numbering among its

Chomedey de Maisonneuve

great accomplishments the founding of the Compagnie du Saint-Sacrement, which played such an important role in France even after the interdiction of 1660.

Born 18 March 1597 at La Flèche (now in the department of the Sarthe), he was the younger son of Jérôme Le Royer, first seigneur of La Dauversière, and of Renée (or Marie) Oudin. His family originated in Brittany.

Jérôme was one of the first pupils of the Collège at La Flèche, founded in 1604 by Henri IV and operated by the Jesuits. There he met Father Charles Lalemant, who had entered the Society of Jesus in 1607 and was ten years his senior, and also Father PAUL LE JEUNE, who had entered in 1613. In addition to the philosopher René Descartes, he had as fellow-students several of the great missionaries of New France, such as François Ragueneau [see Paul RAGUENEAU], CLAUDE QUENTIN, Charles Du Marché, and Jacques BUTEUX. With them, he heard Father Énemond MASSÉ, in 1614, speak of the Acadian missions, recently abandoned as a result of the English conquest.

On his father's death, during the summer of 1618, Jérôme inherited the name and fief of La Dauversière, as well as the office of receiver of the *taille* at La Flèche. In 1620 he married Jeanne de Baugé, by whom he had six children. Possessed of firm piety and a wonderful zeal for good works, he soon became, with his elder brother Joseph, the promoter and organizer of the charitable undertakings in his small town. It is said that it was a supernatural vision that led him to found an institute of Hospitallers dedicated to St. Joseph. This vision would have occurred in 1632 or the beginning of 1633.

The second supernatural revelation that M. de La Dauversière is stated to have had can be set in the year 1635 or 1636. According to the text found in the *Véritables motifs* of the Société Notre-Dame de Montréal, printed in 1643, the "establishment of Montreal was conceived by a man of virtue whom it pleased divine goodness to inspire, seven or eight years previously with the desire of working for the Indians of New France, of whom he had no special knowledge before, and despite any repugnance that he might have felt for the task, as being beyond his strength, contrary to his status, and harmful to his family. Finally, several times urged on and enlightened by inner visions, which showed him in their reality the places, things and persons that he was to utilize ... encouraged inwardly to undertake it as a conspicuous service that God was asking of him, he responded like Samuel to his master's summons."

In 1639, on the advice of Father François Chauveau, a Jesuit at the Collège of La Flèche, he went to Paris with Pierre Chevrier, Baron de Fancamp, who had long been won over to the Montreal cause, in order to form a society capable of carrying through an undertaking of such magnitude: the founding of a missionary city in distant Canada. And then, at the end of February, occurred the meeting with Abbé Jean-Jacques Olier, a young priest of 31 who since 1636 had wanted to work for the conversion of unbelievers. He did not yet know, however, in what country. On this point we have his own testimony.

M. de La Dauversière and M. Olier met in the gallery painted by Simon Vouet, at the entrance to Chancellor Pierre Séguier's sumptuous dwelling in Paris. In this connection mention is made, erroneously, of an interview at the Château de Meudon, the abandoned residence of Charles de Lorraine, Duc de Guise, who had been living in Italy since 1631. For two hours they talked. Agreement was reached on the main features of the plan: the acquisition of the island of Montreal, the property of JEAN DE LAUSON, an intendant in Dauphiné and the future governor of New France, and also the founding of a society of gentlemen and ladies whose rapid recruitment certainly did not seem impossible. M. Olier was already prepared to answer for the consent of the Baron Gaston de Renty, one of the great philanthropists of the 17th century, and the superior of the famous Compagnie du Saint-Sacrement of which MM. de La Dauversière and Olier were members. M. Olier would likewise invite two more of his friends to enter the Société de Montréal.

Thought had soon to be given to finding a young leader, endowed with all the qualities necessary for directing this undertaking, which partook of both colonization and evangelization. One day Father Charles Lalemant, whom M. de La Dauversière consulted continually about the numerous requirements of his venture, said to him, after hearing once more his lamentations on the subject of this yet-to-be-discovered leader for the first Montreal contingent: "I know a worthy gentleman of Champagne named M. de Maison-neufve, who has such and such qualities; he might well meet your needs." M. de La Dauversière lost no time in having a conversation with Paul de Chomedey, to whom he entrusted with absolute confidence the direction of his overseas foundation. M. de Maisonneuve would be granted powers in Canada corresponding to the similar rights and duties, in France, of the directors of the Société Notre-Dame de Montréal. The latter would recruit, finance, and

Chomedey de Maisonneuve

assist in every way the little colony being formed. M. de Maisonneuve thus became one of the principal "Associates" of Montreal, to the great joy of MM. Olier and de Fancamp. A "gentleman of virtue and courage," as the anonymous authors of the *Véritables motifs* called him, he soon went to La Rochelle, the place of embarkation for the contingent.

On 9 May 1641 two ships left the port of La Rochelle, carrying out to sea, on their way to New France, the main portion of the Montreal settlers. In one of the vessels were M. de Maisonneuve with 25 men and a secular priest intended for the Ursulines; in the other were Jeanne MANCE, the nurse and bursar of the contingent, the Jesuit Father Jacques de La Place, and 12 men. The rest of the contingent (ten men) had left the port of Dieppe some weeks before. Three other women were on board: two of the workmen had refused to embark without their wives; one young local girl had "violently" pushed her way into the ship, resolved to go and serve God in the person of the poor Indians.

The ship bearing Jeanne Mance and Father de La Place reached Quebec without mishap, after a crossing of about three months. Dollier de Casson speaks of 8 August, a very likely arrival date. The ship bringing M. de Maisonneuve was less fortunate; it "met with such furious storms that it was obliged to put into port three times" in France. In these circumstances M. de Maisonneuve lost three or four men and his surgeon.

At what date did M. de Maisonneuve arrive at Tadoussac? Obviously very late; "so late," said the 1641 *Relation*, that the contingent would be quite unable to establish itself at Montreal before the following spring. Dollier de Casson favoured 20 August, an unlikely date, for only 12 days would have passed since Jeanne Mance's arrival. Jeanne Mance was full of concern, even of anxiety, since she heard it said on all sides that the arrival of fresh ships from France was becoming impossible at that season of the year. The only document known to us today that refers to Maisonneuve's presence in Canada in 1641 is a certificate of baptism dated 20 Sept. 1641, inserted in the register of baptisms at Sillery, without any indication of place (but in the margin of the document is the word Tadoussac). M. de Maisonneuve appears in it as the godfather and Jeanne Mance as the godmother of a little Indian girl baptized by Father Paul Le Jeune, very shortly before the latter's departure for France by the last ship. Can one conclude from this that the baptism took place at Tadoussac and not at Sillery, and that the date 20 Sept. 1641 might be the exact date of M. de Maisonneuve's arrival on Canadian soil? As far as Jeanne Mance is concerned, we can understand that she may have hastened to Tadoussac, to inform the leader of the contingent of the opposition manifested at Quebec against the plan to set up a small colony on the island of Montreal. "Foolhardy undertaking!" was the general outcry.

Paul de Chomedey was not upset by the hostility evidenced by the inhabitants of Quebec. Duly warned of the situation, he confronted his opponents. He was a wise man, possessed of unusual prudence, but also a resolute soldier. From the time of his first interview with Governor HUAULT de Montmagny he adhered to his decision to go up to Montreal the following spring, since the season was getting too advanced. A new move was attempted shortly afterwards by the governor and all the notables of Quebec. M. de Maisonneuve was offered the Île d'Orléans in exchange for the island of Montreal, in order that he might be more within reach of help in case of attack. And it was then that Paul de Chomedey uttered the proud words that Dollier de Casson has preserved for us: "Sir, what you are saying to me would be good if I had been sent to deliberate and choose a post; but having been instructed to go to Montreal by the Company that sends me, my honour is at stake, and you will agree that I must go up there to start a colony, even if all the trees on that island were to change into so many Iroquois." In the face of this inflexibility displayed with such dignity, all were obliged to yield. For his part M. de Montmagny, just as did Father Barthélemy VIMONT, the superior of the Jesuits, undertook to go personally to the island of Montreal in October, with several "persons, well versed in knowledge of the country," in order to choose the most favourable spot for the creation of this new post. It was impossible for M. de Maisonneuve to accompany them, for he was busy supervising the unloading of the ships and setting his men to work. Hence his name does not appear in the paragraph of the *Relations* recounting the little trip made on 15 Oct. 1641.

In addition to the tasks we have just mentioned, M. de Maisonneuve was acutely concerned with the question of housing for the contingent. It was late in the season. He could see no lodging suitable for the 56 (perhaps 58) persons who made up the little colony of Montreal. All the immediate difficulties, however, were settled following a visit to the seigneury of Sainte-Foy, in the neighbourhood of Quebec, where a rich septuagenarian, Pierre de PUISEAUX de Montrénault, expressed an earnest desire to receive M. de Maisonneuve. As soon as M. de Puiseaux had

Chomedey de Maisonneuve

made M. de Maisonneuve's acquaintance, and heard about the apostolic and civilizing mission being undertaken at Montreal, he asked to enter the Société Notre-Dame, in order to follow the founder of the post. As proof of the sincerity of his intentions, he offered, as an outright gift, his two seigneuries of Sainte-Foy and Saint-Michel (at Sillery). M. de Maisonneuve accepted the kindly old man's offer, and both then decided on the best use to be made of these rich seigneuries. The Sainte-Foy house, surrounded by fine oaks, could serve as a building-yard and as a shelter for the majority of the Montreal men; the Saint-Michel house would be assigned to MM. de Maisonneuve and de Puiseaux, to Jeanne Mance, to Mme de CHAUVIGNY de La Peltrie, who had hitherto been its tenant, and to some other persons. A few men of the contingent would also be housed there to do joinery work.

An unfortunate incident occurred in January 1642, bringing the governor-general and the local governor into conflict with each other. One of those thorny questions as to the extent or limitations of the power of each side arose for the first time in Canada, where they were to become very frequent. On 24 January, the eve of the conversion of St. Paul, M. de Maisonneuve's patron saint, the Montreal men had received some gunpowder from Jeanne Mance, the contingent's bursar, so that a salvo of artillery could be fired at dawn on the twenty-fifth, to mark M. de Maisonneuve's anniversary. The noise of the detonations was heard as far as Quebec. M. de Montmagny was offended because his consent to the firing of cannon in this way had not been sought. The gunner for the occasion was arrested and interned; he was Jean Gorry, a Breton from Pont-Aven, who was employed at Quebec by M. de Maisonneuve as a ship's master. Legal action followed. M. de Montmagny had finally to set Jean Gorry free, having really exceeded his authority. M. de Maisonneuve was able to show a letter from Louis XIV which authorized the Montreal contingent to possess artillery and to fire cannon. During these difficult days M. de Maisonneuve displayed moderation and endurance. He let the storm pass. But he took his revenge by helping the victim of the incident. He even went so far as to increase his wages.

M. de Montmagny endeavoured subsequently to atone for the extravagance of his behaviour. "On the seventeenth of May of the present year, 1642, Monsieur the Governor placed the sieur de Maison-neufve in possession of the Island, in the name of the Gentlemen of Mont-real, in order to commence the first buildings thereon. Reverend Father Vimont had the *Veni Creator* chanted, said Holy Mass, and exposed the Blessed Sacrament, to obtain from Heaven a happy beginning for the undertaking. Immediately afterwards, the men were set to work, and a redout was made of strong palisades for protection against enemies." Father Vimont, the superior of the Jesuit missions in Canada, to whom must be attributed the substance of this text, taken from the *Relation* of 1642, was an eye witness of, and took part in, these ceremonies.

Among the incidents pertaining to the founding of Montreal, one action of M. de Maisonneuve remains to be noted. The governor of Montreal, as we have seen, had set his men to work as soon as the civil and religious ceremonies were completed. Several trees had to be felled before erecting the stronghold of thick stakes. Sister Morin* tells us that the governor wished to fell the first tree himself.

Father Vimont, who celebrated the first high mass sung at Montreal, Sunday 18 May 1642, delivered an address in which he foretold, in a way, the future greatness of the town that had just been born.

The first baptism took place in the month of July. "On the twenty-eighth of July, a small party of Algonquins, who were passing that way, stopped there for several days. The Captain brought his son, aged about four years, to be Baptized. Father Joseph PONCET made him a Christian, and the sieur de Maison-neufve and Mademoiselle Mance named him Joseph on behalf of the Gentlemen and Ladies of Nostre Dame de Mont-real. This is the first fruit that this Island has borne for Paradise; it will not be the last. *Crescat in mille millia.*"

In the month of August the arrival of the French ships caused excitement among the Montrealers. They wondered what news they were going to receive from France. PIERRE LEGARDEUR de Repentigny landed one morning on the shores of Montreal. He brought with him the 12 settlers of the second contingent, a great quantity of provisions, sacred ornaments, munitions, and much good news. He informed M. de Maisonneuve and Mlle Mance that the *Dessein de Montréal*, written by M. de La Dauversière at Mlle Mance's suggestion and distributed in devout and influential circles, had noticeably increased the number of Associates in France. "About thirty-five persons of condition have joined together . . . in the Church of Notre Dame at Paris," and "consecrated the Island of Mont-real to the Holy Family . . . , under the special protection of the Blessed Virgin." The Montrealers gave free rein to their joy a few days later. The feast of the Assumption, 15 August, was celebrated with pomp. At this first great festival of Notre-Dame de Montréal, "The thunder of the cannons caused the whole Island to reëcho."

The year 1642, however, came to a dramatic close. The safety of the settlers was seriously threatened. The St. Lawrence river overflowed, and a flood became imminent. M. de Maisonneuve distinguished himself by his self-possession and especially by his lively faith. After consultation with the chaplains, Fathers Poncet and DU PERON, he promised, if the waters that were already surging against the gates of the fort subsided without causing any serious damage, to walk with a cross on his shoulders to the top of Mount Royal, and there to set it up. He put his promise in writing, had it read publicly, then he went and placed a cross, at whose foot was the written statement, on the bank of the roaring river: "the waters, having stopped a little while at the threshold of the gate, without swelling further, subsided by degrees, put the inhabitants out of danger, and set the Captain [M. de Maisonneuve] to the fulfillment of his promise."

The Iroquois, not knowing of the establishment of a post at Montreal, did not appear until the summer of 1643. But from then on they continually harried the Montrealers, using the tactics at which they were past masters: war by ambush. On the one day of 9 June 1643 they secured six victims, only one of whom was to escape, having cruelly suffered during his captivity.

A difficult life, full of unceasing, exhausting struggles, had now begun. It was to continue for a quarter of a century. The victims fell in great numbers, but prepared each morning for the supreme sacrifice by receiving the Eucharist. In the Montreal that, in 1643, was compared to the early church, they paid the ransom for all. And always M. de Maisonneuve stood out as the incomparable leader of a handful of heroes, both men and women. He also showed himself a skilful organiser. The *Véritables motifs*, written during the summer of 1643, offer us a picture of the little post, shortly after its founding: "The building consists of a fort for defence, a hospital for the sick, and a lodging already capable of housing 70 persons who live there . . . with two Jesuit Fathers who are like pastors to them; there is a chapel there that serves as a parish, under the title of Notre Dame to whom, with the island and the town which is designated by the name of Ville Marie, it is dedicated. The inhabitants live for the most part communally, as in a sort of inn; others live on their private means, but all live in Jesus Christ, with one heart and soul."

In July, on the day after the arrival of the first ships from France, M. de Montmagny went up to Ville-Marie. He had just received a personal letter from Louis XIII, enjoining him to give his most special protection to the little settlement at Montreal. He announced furthermore that the king was presenting the Associates of Montreal with a ship of 350 tons, called the *Notre-Dame*, which would cross the ocean each year. The Montrealers could also expect to receive effects of all kinds, and even, it was said, sums of money intended by an "unknown benefactress" for the construction of the hospital and for Mlle Mance. Patience was necessary, however, for the third Montreal contingent would arrive only in September. It would be led by a gentleman from Champagne, LOUIS D'AILLEBOUST de Coulonge et d'Argentenay, a talented military engineer; he was coming to settle at Montreal with his wife, Barbe de BOULLONGNE, who would be accompanied by her sister, Philippe or Philippine-Gertrude de Boullongne. All three, on Father Charles Lalemant's advice, had become members of the Société Notre-Dame. Two months later, the rejoicing inhabitants of Ville-Marie thronged around the new settlers. Everyone perceived also that the Associates in France were truly lavishing gifts upon their remote little outpost.

But that same autumn there were some departures as well. M. de Puiseaux, paralysed, "his brain weakened by his old age," asked for the return of his assets, in order to go to France for treatment. M. de Maisonneuve, generous and understanding as was his wont, agreed to this withdrawal. He also promised to recommend the worthy old man to the Associates of Montreal. Mme de La Peltrie and her companion, Charlotte Barré, likewise left. Mme de La Peltrie was recalled to Quebec by the Jesuits and by her charitable works, which could not survive without her help. She set off without too much anxiety, knowing that Mlle Mance would be sustained by the distinguished ladies, Mme d'Ailleboust and her sister, who had just arrived.

"Frenchmen," wrote Dollier de Casson, "were tired of seeing themselves insulted every day by the Iroquois." Anger had been building up in their hearts since the massacre of their fellow-workers the preceding year. They continually begged M. de Maisonneuve to allow them to match themselves against these assassins, who watched them unremittingly from the deep concealment of the forest. M. de Maisonneuve refused; he knew that they were unfamiliar with skirmishing, and considered them not sufficiently numerous to face 100 or perhaps 200 Iroquois. They obeyed, but "our fiery Frenchmen" eventually concluded that "M. de Maison-neufve was

Chomedey de Maisonneuve

afraid to expose himself." On 30 March 1644 the watch-dogs, which had been brought from France and which already possessed an extraordinary knack for tracking down the Iroquois, started, under the leadership of a bitch named Pilote, "to cry out and howl with all their might, looking towards the direction where they sensed the enemy." The settlers ran to find M. de Maisonneuve: "Sir, the enemies are in the wood in such and such a direction, shall we never go and find them?" To which the governor replied sharply, contrary to his habit: "Yes, you shall see them. Get ready right away to march, but see that you are as brave as you make out to be; I shall be leading you." Once in the wood the settlers, who numbered 30, perceived 200 Iroquois, well placed in various ambushes. The struggle promised to be uneven: seven against one! The French did the best they could so long as their bullets lasted. But when their powder ran out they had to beat a retreat. M. de Maisonneuve directed the expedition successfully. He withdrew only when he saw that the wounded were already at a distance and well guarded. But the settlers were no sooner out of the wood than they were stricken with panic, and bolted towards the fort, leaving M. de Maisonneuve alone and far in their rear. One of the Iroquois chiefs quickly overtook him; M. de Maisonneuve fired at him immediately. Then promptly, while the Iroquois was clawing at his throat, he discharged his second pistol and stretched the Indian dead at his feet. The enemy, thunderstruck, hesitated a moment, then rushed towards their chief; one of them loaded him on his shoulders, and they all plunged hastily into the wood. When M. de Maisonneuve entered the fort, the settlers flocked about him, showed their joy at his victory, praised his unusual bravery, and swore that in future they would take good care not to expose his life in such a way.

M. de Maisonneuve left for France in the autumn of 1645, having received news of his father's death. On leaving Ville-Marie he had entrusted his powers to Louis d'Ailleboust. On 9 Jan. 1646 we find him taking an "oath of fealty" and doing homage for the Maisonneuve fief, of which he had become the owner. He returned to Quebec after a year's stay in France, but on landing he found an urgent letter from M. de La Dauversière, requesting him to return to Europe with the least possible delay. Events concerning him personally, and others related to the affairs of Montreal, required his presence in France. M. de Maisonneuve was therefore unable to visit the Montrealers before sailing again, for in October he had to attend the meetings of the Communauté des Habitants, founded in 1645. At this time great changes had taken place with respect to the fur trade. The Compagnie des Cent-Associés had ceded "to the communauté des habitants in Canada . . . the right to trade in pelts, with the exception of the trade at Miscou, at Cap-Breton and in Acadia, while reserving to itself, in addition, the feudal and seigneurial dues collected in the country. In return the communauté undertook to meet the costs of the colony's administration, religious worship and defence, to send 20 settlers to Canada each year, and to pay the compagnie de la Nouvelle-France 1,000 beavers annually."

At the meetings of the council of the Communauté des Habitants the proceedings were often stormy. The *Journal des Jésuites* reported that "all those of the Council make strenuous efforts to augment their own pay and to requite their own services; which resulted in such confusion as was disgraceful. But, as Monsieur de Maisonneuve had not consented thereto, none of these gratuities were subscribed to." On 31 Oct. 1646, together with ROBERT GIFFARD, M. de Maisonneuve again sailed for France.

Although the governor of Montreal, when he reached his destination, had to concern himself with his personal interests, he certainly did not fail to attend equally to the proper conduct of the affairs of Montreal. There was much discussion, with M. de La Dauversière and on occasion with the other Associates, about the fur trade and the most recent incidents that had occurred before he left Canada. M. de La Dauversière endorsed M. de Maisonneuve's leadership.

The appointment of a successor to M. de Montmagny, who was to be recalled to France, was discussed with M. de Maisonneuve. The Associates offered him this high office. He refused, and proposed instead Louis d'Ailleboust. He took care not to mention his refusal, when on his return to Montreal in the summer of 1647 he warned M. d'Ailleboust that the latter had to go to France, that he would be appointed governor of New France there, and that he would return the following year with his commission.

M. de Maisonneuve had brought back some orders from the Société de Montréal concerning the distribution of the lands under his administration. This measure was now necessary. The first grantee, Pierre GADOYS, signed his deed of grant 4 Jan. 1648. At the bottom of the document, which was written entirely in M. de Maisonneuve's own hand, one reads: "Acceptance of the said grant made before the notary Jean de SAINT-PÈRE." As Benjamin Sulte stated: "It was from 1654 that grants of land were given in sufficient number to encourage the hope that the

Chomedey de Maisonneuve

island of Montreal would finally be settled permanently." "So long as M. de Maisonneuve was the governor, none but he made land grants, and the number of deeds issued by him was 123. It is evident, however, that we lack some of them, which will be found either complete, or mentioned in other documents." Is it not appropriate to stress in this regard the profound unselfishness of the Associates of Montreal, who had promised, from the first days of the town, to take, in this immense expanse of 250,000 acres, only the land necessary for their living? "The island of Montreal was therefore reserved entirely for real and genuine colonization," remarked Camille Bertrand. And he added that "M. de Maisonneuve never possessed a foot of ground, although he was resident governor for 23 years. Neither did Jeanne Mance ever own any land. It was as directress of the hospital that she received some pieces of land for the support of the poor in the Hôtel-Dieu." M. d'Ailleboust was the sole, although quite legitimate exception, since he was settling at Montreal in 1643.

As we have just seen, on 2 March 1648 M. d'Ailleboust had been appointed governor of New France for three years. He landed at Quebec 20 Aug. 1648, bringing with him his nephew, CHARLES-JOSEPH D'AILLEBOUST Des Muceaux, a brave career officer. The new governor moved soon after into the Château Saint-Louis with his wife. His sister-in-law, around the same date, joined the Ursulines.

Heart-rending news from Paris reached Mlle Mance in 1649. First, Father Rapine de Boisvert, a Recollet who had served as intermediary between the "unknown benefactress" and Mlle Mance, had died in December 1648; then the Société Notre-Dame de Montréal, which the death of the Baron de Renty and the withdrawal of a number of others had unsettled and weakened, was no longer showing any sign of life; and above all the mortal illness that afflicted M. de La Dauversière, the creator of the evangelizing undertaking at Ville-Marie and its guiding spirit, might put an end to the entire Montreal venture. These "three bludgeon strokes," wrote Dollier de Casson, forced Mlle Mance to sail at once for France. In truth peril reigned everywhere, in old France as in the new. Shortly after Mlle Mance's departure, news arrived of the martyrdom of Fathers Jean de BRÉBEUF and GABRIEL LALEMANT. Next came the almost total annihilation of the Hurons, of whom little bands arrived at Ville-Marie each day to take refuge there. Everyone could foresee then the mortal danger that would soon threaten Ville-Marie, for once the Hurons were conquered the Iroquois would turn their fury against the Montrealers. They were already swearing to destroy everything in that tiny, almost defenceless post; "ceaselessly," recorded M. Dollier, "we had them pressing upon us, there is not a month in this summer when our book of the dead has not been stained in red letters by the hands of the Iroquois." Mlle Mance's return, in the autumn of 1650, brought a little solace to the beleaguered. The directress of the hospital had successfully completed her mission. The Société Notre-Dame de Montréal would be restored to life, thanks to the complete support of M. Olier, who had agreed to direct it thenceforth. The Montrealers' distress had moved him. Moreover M. de La Dauversière, who had recovered, was also actively promoting the undertaking. And the "unknown benefactress" whom Jeanne had often visited remained the bounteous friend of the Hospitallers and of Jeanne Mance.

But in the spring of 1651 the Iroquois attacks became so frequent and so violent that Ville-Marie thought its end had come. M. de Maisonneuve made all the Montrealers take refuge in the fort. Mlle Mance, with her sick, her wounded, and her poor, came in also, reoccupying the rooms she had had when Ville-Marie was founded. Soon, exclaimed M. Dollier, no man ventured "to go four steps from his house without carrying his gun, his sword and his pistol. Finally, as we were getting fewer every day . . . , our enemies took heart from their greater number." M. de Maisonneuve saw fall, one by one, his beloved settlers whom he considered it his duty to protect. Gradually, he made up his mind to put an end to this slaughter. But now Jeanne Mance suddenly intervened: she placed at Maisonneuve's disposal 22,000 *livres* from the unknown benefactress, for the raising of a contingent of soldier-workmen.

In the autumn of 1651, the Montrealers saw M. de Maisonneuve leave for France. All things considered, the governor could not reject the offer made by the hospital's wise directress. As he handed over to d'Ailleboust Des Muceaux the direction of Ville-Marie, he uttered these few words: "I shall try to bring back 200 men . . . to defend this site; if I do not have at least 100, I shall not return, and everything will have to be abandoned, for indeed the place would be untenable."

M. de Maisonneuye's stay in Europe lasted two years. While, at Montreal, Major CLOSSE, his soldiers, and all able-bodied settlers were heroically resisting their attackers, M. de Maisonneuve was employing all possible means in France, with the assistance of M. de La Dauversière and the financial backing of the Associates of Montreal, to recruit numerous defenders for his post. But

Chomedey de Maisonneuve

first of all, with a diplomatic subtlety that we are able to glimpse through M. Dollier's account, M. de Maisonneuve decided to plead the cause of Montreal with the benefactress whose name Mlle Mance had disclosed to him. Without arousing the slightest suspicion in Mme Claude de Bullion—this was her name—that he knew the relations existing between her and Jeanne Mance, he had dwelt at length upon Ville-Marie's distress. The wealthy noblewoman was certainly impressed by it, for a short time later M. de Maisonneuve received from the hands of President Guillaume de Lamoignon, a cousin of the Bullions, and perhaps one of the Associates of Montreal, a sum of 20,000 *livres*, offered by a "person of quality" to M. de Maisonneuve to stimulate the recruitment of the settler-soldiers for Ville-Marie.

In the spring of 1653, the muster-roll could finally be drawn up. Out of the 154 men under contract, 120 honoured their signatures and embarked on the *Saint-Nicolas*, 20 June 1653, at Saint-Nazaire. On 22 September, after a miserable crossing during which several of the new settlers were stricken by a contagious disease, the ship entered the roadstead of Quebec.

The welcome in the capital was enthusiastic. A *Te Deum* was sung in the church. Not until several weeks later did the contingent go to Ville-Marie, for a fair number of the settlers, having barely recovered from the fevers of the disease, had to spend a period in hospital. It was with great relief that the Montrealers received these soldiers, who had come from the various provinces of France, chiefly Maine and Anjou. These 100 men were going to save not only Montreal, but the whole of New France, for the fall of Ville-Marie would inevitably have brought about the successive destruction of the other posts.

With the 1653 contingent there arrived at Ville-Marie a fine young woman, the future teacher of the little Montrealers and the young Indian girls: Marguerite Bourgeoys. The coming of this girl who had "a good mind," and "whose virtue is a treasure," was due to the sagacity of M. de Maisonneuve and of his sister, Mother Louise de Sainte-Marie, of the convent at Troyes. "This worthy girl whom I am bringing," M. de Maisonneuve had declared to Mlle Mance, ". . . will be a tremendous help at Montreal; moreover, this girl is yet another product of our province of Champagne, which seems to want to give to this place more than all the others put together."

Everything changed at Ville-Marie, and finally became settled. Thanks to the powerful reinforcements, the settlers gradually left the fort and went back to live in their little houses. Work in the fields kept many labourers busy. The governor of Montreal took advantage of the temporary peace, signed by the Iroquois in 1655, to return a fourth time to France. He had to induce M. Olier to consent, with the assistance of his ecclesiastics, to furnish the first parochial clergy of Montreal. The Jesuits found it difficult to carry on the ministry at Ville-Marie, for the number of their religious was barely adequate to staff their missions.

M. Olier acceded to M. de Maisonneuve's request. He designated for parochial worship MM. de Queylus [*see* THUBIÈRES], SOUART, Galinier, and D'ALLET. A few hours before their departure from Nantes, 17 May 1657, the Sulpicians learned of the death (2 April 1657) of their founder and superior M. Olier.

Jeanne Mance, who was getting old and whom an accident had deprived of the use of one arm, had brought back from France, in 1659, the first Hospitallers of St. Joseph, Mothers MOREAU de Brésoles, MACÉ, and MAILLET. She thus fulfilled one of the vows most dear to M. de La Dauversière, who, it should be added, helped her to the best of his ability.

A year later, on the arrival of the ships from France, the Montrealers received the news of the death of Jérôme Le Royer de La Dauversière, the founder of Montreal and of the Société Notre-Dame, who had passed away 6 Nov. 1659. The disappearance of the procurator of the Associates of Montreal, who died ruined, even bankrupt, following a reverse of fortune not long before, brought about some changes. The Société Notre-Dame, the number of whose associates had gradually been diminishing, saw itself obliged to abandon the Montreal seigneury. On 9 March 1663 the surviving members, in the presence of Mlle Mance who was then in Paris, and who brought them M. de Maisonneuve's consent, signed a deed of gift to the Séminaire de Saint-Sulpice.

As the Iroquois had resumed their bloody ambushes at Ville-Marie, M. de Maisonneuve created, on 27 Jan. 1663, the militia of the Sainte-Famille in order to meet the danger. It was composed of 139 settlers divided into 20 squads. Each squad had as its leader a corporal elected by a majority.

Finally, still in this same year, the Compagnie des Cent-Associés ceased to exist. On 24 February, the last meeting, attended by only a handful of partners, handed over New France to the Crown. The letters patent joining it to the royal domain were published the following month. Thenceforth Louis XIV was to guide the destinies of Canada. The following year the Communauté des Habitants (1645–64), completely ruined, disappeared in its turn.

Chomedey de Maisonneuve

The Marquis de Tracy [see PROUVILLE], newly appointed lieutenant-general of New France, landed at Quebec 30 June 1665 with four companies of soldiers, who came like himself from the West Indies. Already, the preceding 13 and 19 June, four other companies had arrived from France, a prelude to the dispatch of the famous Carignan-Salières regiment made up of 20 companies and comprising altogether some 1,000 fighting men. The king had decided to put an end to the Iroquois forays.

The salvation of Canada was thus assured sooner or later, and the settlers, so sorely tried for years by the Iroquois war, could not do other than rejoice over the fact. But at Ville-Marie, in September 1665, a grievous piece of news depressed the spirits of the Montrealers and went straight to their hearts. M. de Maisonneuve, their good governor, this honest judge of all their differences, had just received from Tracy the order to return to France on indefinite leave. Was he surprised to receive such an order, when he had to his credit 24 years of heroic service? Certainly not as much as one might think. For some years he had not enjoyed the favour of the governors-general. M. de SAFFRAY de Mézy, in particular, had displayed a truly regrettable intolerance and arrogance. To be persuaded of this one should read the accounts of Sister Morin, who can barely conceal her indignation. M. de Maisonneuve, a superior soul, bore everything with admirable dignity.

He left in the autumn of 1665, taking with him the regrets of his faithful little colony. He went to live in Paris, in seclusion, humble, ever discreet. The memory of the work accomplished at Ville-Marie kept his spirit serene and trusting until the end. He passed away 11 years later; at his bedside were his young friend Philippe de Turmenys, and his devoted servant Louis Fin (not Frin). His funeral took place at the church of the Fathers of the Christian Doctrine, situated not far from the abbey of Saint-Étienne-du-Mont, and there also he was buried.

Had it not been for the constant activity of Jérôme de La Dauversière in France and of Paul de Chomedey de Maisonneuve in Canada, the Société Notre-Dame de Montréal would have succumbed under the weight of countless trials and difficulties. Such tenacious leaders, such souls whose saintliness was readily discernible, were necessary to keep alive for a quarter of a century the little post of Montreal, isolated from the rest of the colony.

A monument was erected in 1895 on the Place d'Armes in Montreal, to the memory of M. de Maisonneuve. It is the work of the Canadian sculptor Louis-Philippe Hébert*. An imaginary model was used to represent Paul de Chomedey de Maisonneuve, for no authentic portrait of the first governor of Montreal exists.

MARIE-CLAIRE DAVELUY

[The definitive work on the character and achievements of the first governor of Montreal is still to be written. The biographies published to date are popular treatments, some of which present an overly romantic view. Critical appraisal is lacking. Although in this context an exhaustive bibliography is not appropriate, attention is drawn to the following works.]

Archives de l'Aube, Registre de catholicité de Neuville-sur-Vanne, acte de baptême, 1612. AHDM, Marie Morin, "Histoire simple et véritable de l'établissement des Religieuses Hospitalières de Saint-Joseph en l'Île de Montréal, dite à présent Ville-Marie, en Canada, de l'année 1659 . . ." AN, Col., C^{11A}, 1, f.233, "Articles accordez entre les directeurs associez en la Compagnie de la Nouvelle-France et les habitants du dit pays, 6 mars 1645" (see Gustave Lanctot, *Réalisations françaises de Cartier à Montcalm* (Montréal, 1951), 57). ANDQ, Registres des baptêmes de Sillery. Dollier de Casson, *Histoire du Montréal. JR* (Thwaites). "Inédits sur le fondateur de Villemarie: maintenue de noblesse, 1600," éd. L.-A. Leymarie, *NF*, I (1925–26), 20–33. É.-Z. Massicotte, *Répertoire des arrêts, édits, mandements, ordonnances conservés dans les Archives du Palais de Justice de Montréal, 1640–1760* (Montréal, 1919). Morin, *Annales* (Fauteux et al.). [Jean-Jacques Olier?], *Les véritables motifs de messieurs et dames de la Société de Notre-Dame de Montréal pour la conversion des sauvages de la Nouvelle-France*, éd. H.-A. Verreau (SHM *Mémoires*, IX (1880)). "Ordonnances de Mr. Paul de Chomedey, sieur de Maisonneuve, premier gouverneur de Montréal," in *Mémoires et documents relatifs à l'histoire du Canada* (SHM *Mémoires*, III, 1860), 123–44.

E. R. Adair, "France and the beginnings of New France," *CHR*, XXV (1944), 246–78. W. H. Atherton, *Montréal, 1535–1914* (3v., Montréal, Vancouver, Chicago, 1914). Camille Bertrand, *Monsieur de La Dauversière, fondateur de Montréal et des religieuses hospitalières de Saint-Joseph 1597–1659* (Montréal, 1947), 64. Daveluy, "Bibliographie," *RHAF*, VII (1953), 457–61, 586–92, *et passim*; *Jeanne Mance, 1606–1673, suivie d'un essai généalogique sur les Mance et les de Mance par M. Jacques Laurent* (Montréal, 1934), 284–88. Faillon, *Histoire de la colonie française*. Robert Le Blant, "Documents inédits: les derniers jours de Maisonneuve et Philippe de Turmenyes, 14 avril 1666–9 septembre 1676–3 août 1699," *RHAF*, XIII (1959–60), 262–80. L.-A. Leymarie, "Le fondateur de Montréal, Paul de Chomedey, sieur de Neufville, de Bourg-de Partie, de Saint-Chéron et de Maisonneuve (1672–1676)," *NF*, II (1926–27), 207–11; "Louise de Chomedey et les débuts de la congrégation de Notre-Dame à Ville-Marie," *NF*, II (1926–27), 28–32. É.-Z. Massicotte, "Memento historique de Montréal, 1636–1760," *RSCT*, 3d ser., XXVII (1933), sect.I, 111–31; "Notes et documents nouveaux sur le fondateur de Montréal," *BRH*, XXII

Chomina

(1916), 139–50; "Pierre Gadois, premier concessionnaire de terre à Montréal," *ibid.*, XXIX (1923), 36f.; "Les premières concessions de terre à Montréal, sous M. de Maisonneuve, 1648–1665," *RSCT*, 3d ser., VIII (1914), sect.I, 215–29. Mondoux, *L'Hôtel-Dieu de Montréal*. Émile Salone, *La colonisation de la Nouvelle-France: étude sur les origines de la nation canadienne-française* (Paris, 1906).

CHOMINA (Choumin), Montagnais chief of the Tadoussac district; fl. 1618–29. Chomina was known by several other names: Atic; Crapaut; Petitchouan; "La Mer Monte"; Amiscouecan; "Vieille Robe de Castor." The French called him "Le Cadet," because of his extreme neatness in dress and fine French manners, and also "Le Raisin" (The Grape), a translation of his Montagnais name, although LE CLERCQ says it was because he liked liquor.

Chomina was identified with the French for several years (1618–29). CHAMPLAIN wrote of him that "we had not known one who was a more faithful and serviceable friend." He wrote further that Chomina was a man whose word carried weight, who was intelligent, of good judgement and with a good perception of events, not ungrateful, and of great courage. Although closely attached to the French priests, Chomina never accepted Christianity.

He "adopted" as a brother Father Joseph LE CARON, who spent the winter of 1618–19 with his people. He gave the priest every assistance and Chrestien Le Clercq has written that he laboured ardently to build a house for Le Caron, encouraging others of his tribe to help in the project. In the same winter, Chomina's wife bore a son whom he was determined to call Père Joseph to show his affection for Father Le Caron.

At this time, Chomina requested that Father Le Caron take another son, Naneogauchit, then nine or ten years old, to teach him to live like the Recollets themselves. SAGARD describes at some length the steps taken and the difficulties that arose before the boy was baptized 23 March 1627. Chomina, subsequently influenced by non-religious French, did all in his power to entice the boy from the Recollets. Naneogauchit was given the name Louis by Champlain and Mme Hébert [*see* ROLLET] his godmother. The baptism was not public as had been planned because of Champlain's fear of sudden attack by the Indians during the ceremony. The boy was baptized in the chapel of Notre-Dame-des-Anges with Father Le Caron officiating. Nearly all the French and all the Indians were present although his father, Chomina, did not attend. The Te Deum was sung, followed by a salute of two cannon and several musket shots.

The principal relatives, the captains, the clergy, and the leading French were afterwards entertained at the Habitation by Champlain. A feast for Indians was held in the home of Mme Hébert, at which 56 wild geese, 30 ducks, 20 teals, and quantities of other game were consumed. Most of the French brought contributions: the "Messieurs de la Traicte," 2 barrels of biscuits, 15 or 20 pounds of prunes, 6 baskets of corn, 2 cranes, and more. All went into Mme Hébert's great cauldron. Soon after, however, Louis reverted from Christianity to his native beliefs.

In 1629, Chomina was regarded with some suspicion by his people for having accused another Indian of murdering two Frenchmen at Cap Tourmente the previous year. Champlain released the suspected murderer to Chomina. This was for the French a prudent gesture because of the scarcity of food at their disposal and also because of their dependence on the Indians during this critical time, when the English menaced New France. It also served to exonerate Chomina in the eyes of the Indians, a matter of concern to Champlain who required, as a condition of the prisoner's release, that a council, headed by Chomina, should be accepted by the Indians. Its purpose was to discuss and decide upon matters of mutual concern to all the Indians and the French. Other members of the council were EROUACHY, BATISCAN, TESSOUAT (d. 1636), and one other. The plan was accepted by the Indians, although Champlain doubted the sincerity of their spokesman, Erouachy. Ceremonies to establish the council were to be held on the arrival of the vainly awaited French ships. With the fall of Quebec to the English, the council passed into oblivion.

This distinction for Chomina caused jealousy among the Indians who were already critical because he had brought food to Quebec for the French when the Indians themselves were in need. However, hope of similar honours led other Indians to give food to the French.

As well as assisting in this fashion, Chomina kept Champlain informed on numerous Indian plots. He and his brothers remained near Quebec through that winter and in the spring, with the consent of the Jesuits, he worked a little plot of their land. His brother Ouagabemat or Neogabinat (whom Biggar identifies as NEGABAMAT) took Father Le Caron fishing.

In May 1629, Chomina's son Louis and two Frenchmen were sent by Champlain to Tadoussac to beg provisions and passage home for some of the French at Quebec. When supplies were perilously low at Quebec, Chomina went to Trois-Rivières seeking corn-meal from the Hurons who were then arriving for the annual trade. He was allowed a few knives to trade and loaned a pikeman's weapon, "we had such confidence in him." His brother set off for the Etchemins, with a Frenchman who lived near that country, in search of powder. Low waters, however, forced their return.

Chomina and his brother were the only natives who offered to take up arms with the French against the English. According to Le Clercq, Chomina urged that two or three missionaries should retire to the woods and thence make their way to the Tadoussac region rather than abandon the country altogether. Father Le Caron concurred in the plan but it was forbidden by those in authority during the capitulation of Quebec.

ELSIE MCLEOD JURY

Champlain, *Works* (Biggar), *passim*. Le Clercq, *First establishment of the faith* (Shea), I, 30–33, 132–33. Sagard, *Histoire du Canada* (Tross), I, 63–64, II, 284–85, 307, 498–517; IV, 884–85, 888, 892.

CHOMONOT, PIERRE-JOSEPH-MARIE. *See* CHAUMONOT

CHOUART DES GROSEILLIERS, MÉDARD, explorer and one of the originators of the HBC; baptized 31 July 1618, in the parish church at Charly-sur-Marne in the old French province of Brie, not far from Château-Thierry; d. 1696?

He was the son of Médard Chouart and Marie Poirier, whose farm, Les Groseilliers (the Gooseberry Bushes), may still be visited across the Marne from Charly. Little is known of Chouart's family or early life, except that in 1647 his parents were living at Saint-Cyr and that he reached Canada at a youthful age, perhaps in 1641, having lived at some earlier time in the home of "one of our mothers of Tours," according to Marie de l'Incarnation [*see* GUYART], the first mother superior of the Ursuline nuns in Quebec.

By 1646 the young man had become a part of the Jesuit mission of Huronia in modern Simcoe County, Ontario, perhaps as a *donné*, or lay helper, or, more likely, as a soldier. The Jesuit Relation of 1646 lists Des Groseilliers among the men "who returned this year from the Hurons." He may well have been Mother Marie's informant about recent geographical discoveries beyond the Hurons, which she recounts in a letter to her son, 10 Sept. 1646, mentioning "a great sea that is beyond that of the Hurons," obviously a reference to either Lake Michigan or Lake Superior.

Shortly after his return, Des Groseilliers (he is usually so mentioned in contemporary accounts) married a young widow. The parish records of Notre-Dame de Québec state, under date of 3 Sept. 1647, that he married Hélène, daughter of ABRAHAM MARTIN (for whom the Plains of Abraham appear to have been named), and widow of Claude Étienne. Étienne was probably connected in some way with CHARLES DE SAINT-ÉTIENNE de La Tour, who is known to have made plans at one time to explore Hudson Bay with the financial aid of Major-General Edward Gibbons of Boston. In 1653 Des Groseilliers visited La Tour in Acadia and later sought financial aid in Boston for a projected trip to Hudson Bay. It is conjectured, therefore, that La Tour may have been the source of Des Groseilliers' interest in and knowledge of Hudson Bay, which resulted in his trips to that region and the formation of the Hudson's Bay Company.

A son, Médard, was born in 1651(?) and lived to maturity. Another child had died in 1648. Sometime in the early 1650's Hélène also died. His second wife was also a widow, Marguerite Hayet, former wife of Jean Véron de Grandmesnil, and mother of two sons, Guillaume and Étienne, and possibly of a daughter. She was the daughter of Sebastien Hayet and Madeleine Hénaut and came from the parish of Saint-Paul in Paris. At the time of the wedding she was living in Trois-Rivières in the home of JEAN GODEFROY de Lintot, an interpreter famous in the annals of American exploration. Her half-brother was Pierre-Esprit Radisson*, the explorer and first known author of a descriptive account of the upper Great Lakes region, as well as Des Groseilliers' companion on many exploratory expeditions.

To Médard and Marguerite were born: Jean-Baptiste (bap. 5 July 1654), Marie-Anne (bap. 7 Aug. 1657), Marguerite (bap. 15 April 1659), and Marie-Antoinette (bap. 8 June 1661).

These and the several preceding years were a harrowing period in New France. Iroquois incursions destroyed Huronia. Many French residents of hamlets along the St. Lawrence—including Jean Véron—were massacred, others were captured and often tortured to death. The result of these raids was the almost complete cessation of the traffic in furs, heretofore brought annually from the region between the Hurons and the far western tribes, who now were also driven from their homes in what the *habitants* of New France called the "pays d'en haut," or the "country of the Ottawa Indians." Since New France's only export of consequence was furs, it looked for a time as though the country must be abandoned. At this juncture Des Groseilliers and an unknown companion came to the rescue.

Huron and Ottawa Indians reached Trois-Rivières in a roundabout way in the spring of 1653 and explained their predicament. They said that they were now hiding from the Iroquois in a region beyond Huronia and had a big accumulation of furs and that they hoped to come down the

Chouart Des Groseilliers

following year in sufficient numbers to defy the Iroquois.

In 1654 a peace was arranged between the French and the Iroquois and the western Indians did arrive late in the summer, bringing furs and news of "a great river" above their country "which empties into a great sea." This was enticement enough for Des Groseilliers. When the tribesmen returned to their homes, he and another man were with them to ferret out the hiding-places of the displaced natives, formerly the mainstay of New France's commerce.

It has been assumed by most historians that Radisson was Des Groseilliers' companion, but the facts disprove this assumption. Though the young brother-in-law claimed in his narrative of 1669—which is our only available source of detailed information—that he accompanied Des Groseilliers, he was both too young to go on such an expedition and, in addition, is known to have been in Quebec during the period of the trip, for on 7 Nov. 1655 he signed a deed of sale in that city (Greffe d'Audouart).

Just where Des Groseilliers and his companion journeyed cannot be stated in detail, for the Radisson narrative in the French language has been lost and only a contemporary translation has survived—a translation by an unknown person who was unacquainted with conditions among the natives of North America and who surely did not improve an already confused and difficult manuscript. However, it is possible to follow the explorers along the route that soon became the usual one for fur-traders, for Radisson's descriptions of numerous places enable us to follow him up the Ottawa River to Lake Nipissing, down the French River to Georgian Bay and into Lake Huron, even though there were as yet almost no geographic names in the whole western country. We can also follow them south of the traders' route in Lake Huron, past deserted Huronia, and probably through Lake St. Clair to the site of Detroit. After the "detroit" between Lake Huron and Lake Erie it is more difficult to find their track. Seemingly they crossed over the lower Michigan peninsula into Lake Michigan and followed its west shore up to the Straits of Michilimackinac. The return trip to Quebec again is plain, for Radisson could always describe clearly any region with which he was well acquanted.

For Des Groseilliers the trip's significance lay in the fact that he learned about the region west and south of Hudson Bay. Radisson writes: "We had not a full and whole discovery, w[ch] was that we have not ben in the bay of the north, not knowing anything but by report of ye wild Christinos [Crees]." The Jesuits in New France were much impressed by the new geographical facts afforded by the report of the two men upon their return, and they devote considerable space to it in their Relation of 1655–56. An outstanding merchant of New France, Charles Aubert* de La Chesnaye, also recalled many years later "the two individuals who returned in 1656, each one with from 14 to 15 thousand livres, and brought with them a flotilla of Indians with 100,000 écus worth of treasures."

The years from 1656 to 1659 are well documented for Des Groseilliers' career. We know when his children were born and by whom they were baptized, that his home was in Trois-Rivières, and that he and his wife were becoming well-to-do. The village records have been preserved and contain many documents relating to Des Groseilliers and his wife. They were a litigious pair and were often in court—to the satisfaction of historian and biographer, if not to neighbours of this typically frontier family.

Court records cease abruptly for Des Groseilliers, however, in the summer of 1659. The reason, of course, was that he had gone once more into the Upper Country. Radisson by this time was back from two sojourns in the Iroquois country—one while a captive and the other as a member of a Jesuit missionary venture at Onondaga—and he was now old enough to accompany his brother-in-law. The two men set out in August 1659 and returned the following summer.

Again we must rely principally upon Radisson's narrative of 1669 for details, but this time it is clear and consecutive. The governor, Pierre de Voyer* d'Argenson, was opposed to the expedition unless one of his men accompanied the explorers. Des Groseilliers in his blunt fashion announced that it was a case of "discoverers before governors" and slipped away undetected, largely because he was captian of the borough of Trois-Rivières and had "the keys of the Brough," according to Radisson.

They met returning tribesmen farther up the St. Lawrence, who helped repel an Iroquois attack on the Ottawa River; followed the traders' route to Lake Huron; passed along its northern coast to Sault Ste. Marie; portaged around the falls there; idled along the picturesque south shore of Lake Superior, whose sand dunes and portalled cliffs delighted the young Radisson; and came to the large inlet known today as Chequamegon Bay but given no name by Radisson in his account. Here, beyond the sand spit (La Pointe) guarding the bay from northeasters and close to the Apostle Islands, the displaced Ottawas, Hurons, and Chippewas turned inland to their temporary homes, probably on Lac Courte-

Chouart Des Groseilliers

Oreille, or Ottawa Lake. After caching their trade goods and building a rude shelter, the Frenchmen also went on to that lake.

The following winter was a severe one. Heavy snow-falls made it impossible to kill game for food and starvation faced even the white guests more than once. Toward spring the Sioux, the permanent residents of much of the region south and west of Lake Superior, sent representatives and gifts, inviting the strangers to visit them. Before doing so the Frenchmen witnessed a great Feast of the Dead, faithfully described in Radisson's narrative, our earliest account of the culture of the "eighteen severall nations" that he says participated in the festivities.

Six weeks, according to Radisson, were then spent among the Sioux, who were practically unknown to white men before this time. Spring having now begun, the two white men returned with some Chippewas to their cache near La Pointe, and then crossed Lake Superior to its north shore.

Here today is a Gooseberry River, which began to appear on French maps soon after Des Groseilliers' visit as Rivière des Groseilliers and may well have been named for him, although it was moved up and down that shore at the whim of the cartographer. As late as 1775 the Pigeon River, now the boundary line between Canada and the United States just west of Lake Superior, was called the River "des Groseilliers" by Alexander Henry* in the entries for 8 and 9 July in his *Travels & adventures in Canada . . . between the years 1760 and 1776*, ed. James Bain (Toronto, 1901), 236, 237.

Though Radisson injects at this point in his narrative a very brief account of a trip from Lake Superior to Hudson Bay, it is certain that this was wholly imaginary and only inserted in 1669 to further his plans of the moment, namely, a trip to Hudson Bay financed by Londoners. Such a journey could not have been made in the remaining time in 1660 before the return trip to Quebec. While on the north shore the explorers visited the Cree Indians and probably learned of the Grand-Portage—an important spot in North American history as the subject of international dispute over ownership (1783–1842) and because it was the beginning of practically the only good canoe route to the far west (via Pigeon River and the lakes and rivers of the present international boundary line).

The summer months of 1660 were spent in returning to the lower St. Lawrence. Accompanying the two Frenchmen were many Indians and a rich harvest of furs. At the Long Sault on the Ottawa River Radisson describes the remains of the DOLLARD massacre, which had occurred a few weeks earlier, and mentions that it was here on an earlier trip that Des Groseilliers was shipwrecked and lost his diaries. A document of 22 Aug. 1660 (Greffe de Bénigne Basset) shows that the brothers-in-law stopped briefly in Montreal to make a business agreement with one of the hamlet's outstanding merchants, CHARLES LE MOYNE de Longueuil (quoted in *BRH*, XX (1914), 188, but wrongly dated).

The Jesuits were eager for news of the countries to the west and duly reported in the year's Relation their interviews with Des Groseilliers upon his return. Three of their company, including the first missionary to Lake Superior Indians, Father René MÉNARD, and six other Frenchmen, five of them traders, immediately started back with the returning tribesmen, and from that moment there was never a time when French fur-traders were absent from the *pays d'en haut* as long as it was claimed as a part of the French empire. Those who went into the Ottawa country in 1660 to trade have been identified by Louise Phelps Kellogg as: Jean-François Pouteret de Bellecourt *dit* Colombier, Adrien Jolliet (elder brother of Louis JOLLIET), Claude DAVID, the Quebec mechanic from Paris, Pierre-Noël Levasseur* *dit* L'Espérance, and a man named Laflèche, probably related to the Nipissing interpreter Jean Richer.

There is good evidence that the western trip of the two brothers-in-law saved the colony from economic ruin—probably preserved its very existence—but Governor d'Argenson seized the explorers' furs, fined them, and, according to Radisson, threw Des Groseilliers into jail, presumably for departing without his sanction. This treatment infuriated both men and they resolved to seek assistance for their trading and exploration plans from New France's enemies and rivals, the English in New England or the Dutch in New Holland.

It was a crucial moment. A decision in ownership of much of the continent and possession of the lucrative beaver trade was in the making. Some persons at the time believed that the defection of these two men decided the issue. Two perspicacious individuals, Marie de l'Incarnation and Father Paul RAGUENEAU, long at the head of Jesuit missions in New France and formerly the tutor of the Great Condé, were quite explicit in their letters to France (Marie Guyart de l'Incarnation, *Lettres* (Richaudeau), II, 293; BN, Mélanges de Colbert, 125, Ragueneau to Colbert 7 Nov. 1664), linking the English conquest of New Holland in 1664 with the two renegades. A train of events, therefore, was started by them which

Chouart Des Groseilliers

would come to an end only with the British conquest of Canada in 1763.

The details of Des Groseilliers' preparations for his next venture—to the Ottawa country by way of Hudson Bay—are rather involved. With his brother-in-law he eventually departed down the St. Lawrence in a bark canoe with ten voyageurs in late April or early May 1662, having returned the previous year from a trip to France. There an agreement had been made with a La Rochelle merchant, Arnaud Peré (brother of the explorer-trader, Jean PERÉ for whom the Albany River was long named by the French) to supply a vessel to take him to Hudson Bay from Île Percée. Something—perhaps Jesuit opposition—fouled his plans at Île Percée and turned him instead to Boston.

In Massachusetts he found men willing to venture with him, and several journeys to Hudson Bay were begun. Because of inclement weather, lack of proper provisions for an arctic undertaking, and other impediments, nothing practical was accomplished, however, though New Englanders were then probably better versed than anyone else in knowledge of the Hudson Bay area. Something worthwhile was achieved, nevertheless, for commissioners, including Sir George Cartwright, from the newly restored king of England, sent to win truculent New Englanders' support for the new régime in England, met the Frenchmen, learned of their plans, and persuaded them to go to Charles II's court. After capture on the high seas by a Dutch caper (privateer) and a landfall in Spain, the two explorers went thence to London, Oxford, and Windsor, arriving in time to witness the ravages of the plague in 1665 and the Great Fire of 1666.

The next three years saw the fruition of Des Groseilliers' plans, though many mistakes and false starts were made, and though Dutch and French adventurers tried to anticipate him in his first sea voyage into Hudson Bay. Finally in 1668 two small vessels carrying the brothers-in-law departed from England for the Bay. Des Groseilliers' vessel, captained by a New England mariner, Zachariah GILLAM, found the difficult way into the "Sea of the North" and anchored at the mouth of a river, which the Englishmen named the Rupert and where they established Charles Fort and spent the winter. Radisson's voyage in a naval vessel lent by the king was unsuccessful, and he returned to London to spend the winter completing the writing of his narrative, which had been commanded at an interview with the king. For its translation five pounds sterling was paid in June 1669 to an unknown translator, perhaps Nicholas Hayward, later the Hudson's Bay Company's French interpreter. The original French manuscript has been lost, but the translation has been preserved in the papers of Samuel Pepys in the Bodleian Library in Oxford, England.

Meantime the English financial backers of the two Canadians formed a corporation, which received its charter on 2 May 1670 (O.S.) and has been known since as the Hudson's Bay Company. Like several of its predecessors in the settlement of English colonies in North America it was a joint stock company with governing powers and territorial rights in much of the northern part of the continent. It proceeded at once to establish settlements and to elect a colonial governor, Charles BAYLY. Gillam and others captained its vessels, which henceforth were to maintain almost yearly communication between the Bay and the mother country.

From 1670 to 1675 the two Frenchmen were employed by the new corporation, making trips to the Bay, founding fur-trading posts, supervising trade with the Indians, and making trips of exploration. Their activity was watched with increasing apprehension by French and Canadian officials, especially TALON and BUADE de Frontenac, as well as by Marie de l'Incarnation and the Jesuits, all of whom wrote letters to Colbert, to members of the French court, and even to other individuals, mentioning the English aggression and deploring the lack of effective French countermeasures. Talon attempted retaliation by sending CAVELIER de La Salle, Jean Peré, and Simon-François DAUMONT de Saint-Lusson to the west in 1670 and 1671, and Father Charles ALBANEL and Paul Denys* de Saint-Simon to Hudson Bay in 1671. Frontenac was even more determined to outdo the English and his response came in the form of Louis Jolliet's journey down the Mississippi in 1673 and La Salle's and Father Hennepin's* trips on the same stream in ensuing years.

An attempt was made by the new English company to have Radisson found a colony on the west coast of Hudson Bay at the mouth of the Nelson River, but it was unsuccessful, as the diary of Thomas GORST, a sort of supercargo on Des Groseilliers' vessel of that year (1670–71) reveals. Nevertheless, the attempt was to prove of value some years later, when an earnest effort was made in the late 1680's to resolve the conflicting territorial claims of France and Great Britain in the Hudson Bay area. Then each side to the dispute tried to provide conclusive evidence that its explorers or traders had been first in various parts of that region. A year's neutrality was decreed by the treaty of 16 Nov. 1686 to enable both sides to find the necessary evidence for specially appointed commissioners to adjudicate

Chouart Des Groseilliers

the issue ("Transactions betweene England and France relateing to Hudsons Bay, 1687," *PAC Report, 1883*, Note C, 173–201). The names and journeys, or reputed journeys, of many persons were brought to the attention of the commissioners, and the North American adventures of Radisson, Des Groseilliers, Father Albanel, Saint-Simon, JEAN BOURDON, Guillaume Couture*, the two brothers Jolliet, Le Moyne* d'Iberville, and others were taken up in their relation to the right of France to lay claim to parts of the Hudson Bay region. The Hudson's Bay Company, on its part, supplied records of the two Frenchmen, of its ships' captains, and of still earlier explorers operating under the British flag in the first half of the century. The year of neutrality had not ended when the "Glorious Revolution" took place in England, resulting in war between the two countries instead of the almost-achieved line of demarcation (the 49th parallel was the suggestion) between New France and British possessions to the north.

In 1676 Des Groseilliers and Radisson returned to Canada, after spending a year in France. They had gone to that country after Father Albanel had seduced them back to a French allegiance while the priest was held in England by the Hudson's Bay Company, following his 1674 journey to Hudson Bay, where he had been captured by the English. By the early 1680's the two Frenchmen were having another adventure in Hudson Bay, this time in the employ of a Canadian company, the Compagnie du Nord, under the direction of Aubert de La Chesnaye.

This man was a Canadian who combined knowledge, wealth, influence, and determination to an unusual degree. His conviction was that the salvation of Canadian trade lay in a maritime approach and increases in the quantities of coat beaver, obtainable chiefly from the west coast of Hudson Bay and beyond. In Paris in 1681 he got in touch with Radisson and laid plans for future action by means of a Canadian fur-trading company. Colbert was interested and *sub rosa* granted a charter in 1682 under the name of "La Compagnie de la Baie d'Hudson" (Compagnie du Nord). However, there was no official sanction of the scheme and that fact produced confusion and misunderstandings in Canada, where Frontenac refused a permit to Aubert de La Chesnaye, when he and Radisson returned to that country in 1682. Finally a permit to fish on the coast of Anticosti was secured from the governor. He was soon recalled to France and LE FEBVRE de La Barre served in his place.

La Chesnaye's plan actually was to get into the coat beaver country at the spot at the mouths of the Nelson and Hayes rivers where Radisson had attempted to found a colony in 1670. Unfortunately for the Canadians, the Hudson's Bay Company in that same year, 1682, reverted to its original plan; and Benjamin Gillam*, of Boston, the son of Captain Zachariah Gillam, planned an interloping venture to the same spot. Therefore, in September 1682 three separate groups appeared there and it became a question of which one arrived first or could outwit the others. Later each group claimed prior occupancy and it is now impossible to judge from the many accounts of practically guerrilla warfare in the Bay which claim is correct. The experience and knowledge of wilderness ways possessed by the two Canadians soon determined the issue in their favour and they came out apparent victors, taking most of the others captive, including John BRIDGAR, the newly appointed governor of the new English colony, securing its furs, and burning its forts. However, the Canadian company, in endeavouring to evade payment of the *quart* on the furs to the farmer-general in Quebec, brought about a governmental decree, which sent most of the Canadian participants, including Des Groseilliers and Radisson, to France for adjudication of the case.

In Paris they found that Colbert was dead and they were met with a complaint from the English company, whose governor was James, Duke of York, brother of the king and a person not to be trifled with by the French (he was their one hope of reconverting England to the Roman Catholic faith). The upshot of the ensuing intrigue between a special envoy sent from the English court, his spy, ministers of Louis XIV, and others, was that Des Groseilliers returned to his home in Canada and Radisson went back to the Bay in 1684 in the employ of the company whose post and furs he had just purloined.

There he tricked his nephew, Jean-Baptiste Chouart, into yielding up the post and the furs that the young man had been protecting during the absence of his father and uncle, transported him and his companions to England in the same year, enlisted them in the employ of the company, and took them back to the Bay with him on his next trip in 1685. Des Groseilliers' son has been regarded by some as the first white man to explore far into the hinterland back of Port Nelson, even anticipating Henry Kelsey* in this respect. Whether he did so at all is uncertain; and if he did go into the interior, it is uncertain whether he acted in the interest of the company or in an endeavour to carry out a scheme hatched by Daniel Greysolon* de Dulhut and other Canadians, who were trying to get him back to New

Choumin

France by way of Dulhut's post on Lake Nipigon. At all events, he stayed in the Bay until 1689, then returned to London, where his later career is unknown.

Likewise unknown is the elder Chouart's fate. He rejected a Company offer to re-enter its service, and sometime between April and November 1684 returned to New France. Where and when he ended his adventurous career is uncertain. In the 1690's Radisson, still serving the Company in London, stated that his brother-in-law had "died in the Bay." However, the date he gave—about 1683—is an impossible one, for we know that Des Groseilliers was alive beyond that time. Some other faint evidence points to Sorel, about 1696, as the place and time of his death. There is no proof of either conjecture. A Marguerite Des Groseilliers was interred in Trois-Rivières in 1711. Whether she was his wife or his daughter is uncertain.

Des Groseilliers' career was not merely adventurous and romantic. His daring led him to explorations that were crucial for French and English territorial claims in North America; and his intelligence enabled him to see quickly and clearly that the easiest and quickest route to the richest fur region of the continent was not by the difficult, dangerous, and time-consuming canoe highway through the Great Lakes and along the Grand-Portage–Lake of the Woods waterway, but across Hudson Bay in ships carrying large cargoes quickly and easily to the very heart of the continent. In addition he had the address sufficient on the one hand to assuage Indian fears of white men and on the other to persuade European officialdom and businessmen to carry out his ideas. The Hudson's Bay Company continues to this day to prove the correctness of his judgement.

GRACE LEE NUTE

For MS sources see Nute, *Caesars of the wilderness*, 359–63. *Coll. de manuscrits relatifs à la Nouv.-France*, I, 245–61. Marie Guyart de l'Incarnation, *Lettres* (Richaudeau), I, 292; II, 67, 447, 448. HBRS, V, VIII, IX (Rich.); XI, XX (Rich and Johnson); XXI, XXII (Rich). *JR* (Thwaites), XXVIII, 229; XL, 219–21, 235–37, 296 n.11; XLIII, 155–57. [Pierre-Esprit Radisson], *Voyages of Peter Esprit Radisson, being an account of his travels and experiences among the North American Indians, from 1652 to 1684, transcribed from original manuscripts in the Bodleian Library and the British Museum*, ed. G. D. Scull (Prince Soc., XVI, Boston, 1885; New York, 1943), 123–34, 172, 174, 175, 209–17.

J. B. Brebner, *The explorers of North America 1492–1806* (New York, 1955). L. P. Kellogg, *The French régime in Wisconsin and the Northwest* (Madison, 1925), 114, 115. Nute, *Caesars of the wilderness*.

The explorations of Pierre Esprit Radisson from the original manuscript in the Bodleian Library and the British Museum, ed. A. T. Adams (Minneapolis, 1961), a recent edition of the *Voyages*, offers another theory to explain the discrepancies in the sources.

CHOUMIN. See CHOMINA

CLARKE (Clark), RICHARD, of Weymouth, Dorset, English navigator and privateer who made voyages to Newfoundland; b. Buckhurst, Essex; fl. c. 1541–96.

Clarke went to sea and rose to be master of the *Mary Fortune*, trading to Bordeaux, in 1572. By 1582 when he appears in American waters he is a veteran sailing master and a skilled navigator. It is likely that he had already made fishing voyages to Newfoundland. In July 1582 he crossed the Atlantic to Newfoundland in command of the *Susan Fortune*, 200 tons, which was in consort with Sir John Perrot's ship, the *Popinjay*, 60 tons, Henry Tayler master. The *Susan Fortune* belonged to the Southampton merchant and shipowner Henry Oughtred, who had a grievance against the Spaniards because of losses caused to him in Spain for which he could get no redress. He had commissioned Richard Clarke as captain and master to take his ship to Newfoundland, armed as a privateer, to seize Spanish and Portuguese fishing vessels in satisfaction of his losses. Sir John Perrot, at that time prominent in the administration of Wales, was apparently his partner, and he may have had some unofficial encouragement from anti-Spanish officials at court. William Hawkins had tried such a raid in 1571, while Sir Humphrey GILBERT had advocated in 1577 a clean sweep of the Spanish Newfoundland fishing fleet.

At the end of July Clarke had both his ships at Fermeuse, but the fishing vessels were in Renewse harbour, which the *Susan Fortune* could not enter. Therefore Clarke took a boarding party into harbour on the *Popinjay* and made to take over the three Portuguese vessels there, alleging to the French port admiral and to the masters of the English ships—including one of John Hawkins's, which he found there—that he had a royal commission to take up Spanish shipping, though he later admitted to the English fishermen that his commission was from Don Antonio, the Portuguese royal claimant only (and even that was false). The ships were taken without resistance to Fermeuse where two of them were rifled and the third, the *Sao João*, 100 tons, laden with all the fish and gear she could carry, was brought away by a prize crew.

The master and part-owner Francisco Fernandes, went back to Portugal with the other two ships, carrying a testimonial signed by the English shipmasters as evidence of what took place. Clarke and Tayler got back to England with the prize after rifling other Portuguese ships at Newfoundland, and some 200,000 fish, a little train oil, and the ship were disposed of to Oughtred's benefit. Fernandes brought suit against Clarke in the High Court of Admiralty but, so far as is known, he received no satisfaction, although Oughtred's commission, when he produced it, was from the Duc d'Alençon and was dated after the ships had sailed. The raid disturbed the fishermen but yielded private revenge to Oughtred. It was not pressed home into a general attack on Iberian shipping in North American waters.

It was probably a vague report of Clarke's voyage, together with some confusion about Sir Humphrey Gilbert's in the following year, which led Anspach, in his *History of the island of Newfoundland* (1819), to invent a voyage by Sir Thomas Hampshire, who was said to have gone to Newfoundland in 1582 with five ships and, under a commission from Queen Elizabeth, to have regulated the drying stages used by the fishermen. No such man existed and no such expedition took place, even though the story finds a place in many Newfoundland histories.

When Sir Humphrey Gilbert set out for the North American mainland by way of Newfoundland in June 1583 he took Richard Clarke as his chief navigator. As master of the flagship, the *Delight*, Clarke had William Winter as captain on the way out, but exchanged him for Maurice Browne at Newfoundland. Clarke brought his ship into St. John's harbour on 3 August, had a stout boat or pinnace built there which later saved his life, and took the *Delight* out again on 20 August, on course for Sable Island. On the 29th the vessel went aground in bad weather and was wrecked. Clarke was later accused of bad navigation, but defended himself vigorously, claiming that on the 28th Gilbert, who was sailing in the *Squirrel*, had, against his better judgement, instructed him to change his course. Clarke thought that on the new course he might strike Sable Island and he may well have done so, although some modern commentators insist that he had reached Cape Breton Island and that the *Delight* came to grief at the entrance to Gabarus Bay.

Clarke made a dramatic escape. The ship's boat was on tow and Clarke, with 15 others, managed to get into her. Clarke took charge and with a single oar steered the overladen boat to safety in southern Newfoundland a week later, despite great hardships. Finding enough food to keep alive, he took his men westwards until they found a French Basque whale fisherman who brought them safely across the Atlantic. At Pasaje they were in danger from Spanish officials, but were concealed by the Frenchman and they slipped over the frontier into France, reaching England late in the year. The loss of the *Delight* was fatal to Gilbert's plans; he turned back and was himself lost on this voyage. How great was his, or Clarke's, responsibility for the wreck remains uncertain, but Clarke's skill and resourcefulness were well illustrated by his conduct thereafter.

Clarke disappears from view for a number of years, though he may have returned more than once to Newfoundland to fish. He reappears as master of the *Pilgrim*, 100 tons, belonging to Richard James of Newport, Isle of Wight, in 1596. Fishing on the Banks, he was still, late in September, short of his full lading and of salt. He hoped to find some of the latter on land at St. John's. Three French Basque vessels were in the harbour on 24 September. Next day he breakfasted with the admiral, Michel de Sancé of Saint-Jean-de-Luz, who offered help in catching fish to make up his lading. On the 26th Sancé, pretending illness, got Clarke to come aboard his ship and enticed a number of his men to follow him. Suddenly the French set on them, "crying out *rendez vous, rendez vous.*" On surrendering, Clarke and his men were imprisoned in the hold, while the Frenchmen went on to overpower and pillage the *Pilgrim*. After nine days the crew were released and given back their ship, which had been stripped down to a few sails and a little food. Thus Clarke was paid back for his actions in 1582. On his return to England Clarke and Richard James laid charges of piracy against Sancé and the rest without effect. We do not hear anything further about him.

Richard Clarke was clearly a skilful navigator who became well accustomed to transatlantic voyages and who might, but for misfortune in 1583, have played an important part in English American enterprises. With Richard WHITBOURNE he was one of the few English seamen to be found making voyages to Newfoundland over an extended period. His adventures in 1582 and 1596 illustrate the unsettled state of the fishery during this period.

DAVID B. QUINN

Hakluyt, *Principal navigations* (1903–5), VIII. L. A. Anspach, *A history of the island of Newfoundland* (London, 1819). *Voyages of Gilbert* (Quinn). W. G. Gosling, *The life of Sir Humphrey Gilbert* (London, 1911). G. Patterson, "Termination of Sir Humphrey Gilbert's expedition," *RSCT*, 2d ser., III (1897), sect.II, 113–27. For the 1582 episode add to the authorities in *Voyages of Gilbert* (Quinn), I, 55–56: PRO, *CSP,*

Clerbaud-Bergier

For., May–Dec. 1582, Jan.–June 1583; *CSP, Spain., 1580–86*; for that of 1596 see PRO, *CSP, Col., 1574–1660*, and PRO, H.C.A. 24/66, no. 51.

CLERBAUD-BERGIER. See BERGIER

CLOSSE, RAPHAËL-LAMBERT, merchant, seigneurial notary, sergeant-major of the Ville-Marie garrison, acting governor of Montreal; b. *c.* 1618 at Saint-Denis de Mogues, in the Ardennes, son of Jean Closse and Cécile Delafosse; killed 6 Feb. 1662 at Montreal.

We have no information concerning Lambert Closse's youth, and no details about his family. He certainly received a good education; in the light of the affection that the missionaries in Canada had for him, it was perhaps from the Jesuits. On occasion they wrote to him quite confidentially. We can also assume that his military career began fairly early. He acquired a sound knowledge and much experience in his profession. The authority that M. de CHOMEDEY de Maisonneuve gave him over the soldiers of the garrison in the fort, and his title of sergeant-major, which he held until his death, help to explain why Dollier* de Casson constantly praised his valour.

It is difficult to determine exactly the date of Closse's arrival in the settlement. M. Massicotte, making his deduction from a notarial document that Closse signed 2 May in the office of Jean de SAINT-PÈRE, refers to his presence at Ville-Marie in 1648. He must have arrived a year earlier with the contingent that M. de Maisonneuve had brought from France. Besides, M. Massicotte mentions no new settler in that year, 1648. A passage written by Sister Marie Morin* cannot but leave the historian puzzled: "Monsieur de Chomedey, who sought only to glorify God and to work for his own sanctification and that of the persons whom God had associated with him in his task, applied himself to establishing several little practices of virtue and devotion, of a simple and humble nature, to which he referred everything; he set up a fraternity of five brothers and five sisters; he was the first of the brothers, followed by Monsieur Lambert Closse, Monsieur Lucau, Monsieur Minime Barbier, Monsieur Prudhomme; the sisters were Madame d'Alleboust, Madame de La Peltrie, Mademoiselle MANCE, Mademoiselle de Boulogne, Mademoiselle [Charlotte Barré] who was as I said Madame de La Peltrie's lady companion; they called each other only brothers and sisters, made a point of deferring to each other in everything, of serving all people when they were in need, of consoling them, of serving the sick, &c.; they made many novenas and pilgrimages to the mountain, on foot, and at the risk of their lives because of the Iroquois."

The presence at Ville-Marie of certain of the settlers mentioned above gives us the date of these pious journeyings. Mme d'Ailleboust [*see* BOULLONGNE] and her sister arrived at Ville-Marie only in September 1643; Mme de CHAUVIGNY de La Peltrie and her attendant, Charlotte Barré, had already returned to Quebec in the summer of 1644. Therefore, from September 1643 to May 1644, out of the 10 people indicated by Sister Morin, eight were living at Ville-Marie beyond all question. There remain Lambert Closse and Louis PRUD'HOMME, whose presence at Montreal in 1643 must be proved. All that one can say is that they might have formed part of the contingent of 40 settlers brought to Canada that year by LOUIS d'AILLEBOUST.

M. Massicotte lists the titles and functions of Lambert Closse as follows: sergeant-major, merchant, notary. If this professional soldier carried on business, what was its nature? A solitary document throws a little light on the question: the inventory of Lambert Closse's personal possessions and real estate, drawn up in 1662 by the notary BÉNIGNE BASSET, indicates that the sergeant-major of Ville-Marie traded in furs with the Indians, like all his contemporaries. P.-G. Roy offers the following explanation in this connection: "Some who are unfamiliar with the habits and customs of the age when Closse lived have been almost scandalized on reading this document. How, said these scrupulous people, could a hero like Lambert Closse take part in the fur trade? Well, yes, Closse did trade in furs like all his contemporaries. Officials and even religious communities did so in that period. It must be admitted that this fraudulent system was allowed and encouraged by the king. He paid starvation wages to his officers, to his judges, to all those whom he employed, and in order not to die of hunger they were forced to do fur-trading. Some did it discreetly and honestly, others used every means to swell their nest-egg. . . . Closse's inventory . . . gives us an almost complete list of all the objects used for the fur trade."

Jean de Saint-Père and Lambert Closse, the first two scriveners [*tabellions*] of Montreal, must have been the same age according to M. Massicotte. In any case, they practised their profession alternately. The first document from the office of Jean de Saint-Père was dated 4 Jan. 1648, and that from the registry of Lambert Closse 6 July 1651. Closse's file is composed of 30 documents, from 1651 to 1656; 16 are in the hand of M. de Maisonneuve, 6 are written by an unknown copyist, and the rest by M. Closse. M. Massicotte points out: "M. Closse's script fairly closely resembles that of M. de Saint-Père; it differs from it by some spelling mistakes peculiar to our soldier, and by the handwriting which is lighter and more tapering."

Nobody can deny to Lambert Closse the title of saviour of Montreal during the years when the Iroquois terror paralysed all progress and decimated the population. In 1651, "only about fifty French remain there," said the *Relations*. In such tragic circumstances, Lambert Closse showed himself a leader of heroic calibre, with unfaltering will-power, a man whose qualities were exalted by the greatest perils instead of being weakened, and who knew how to keep his soldiers screwed to a pitch of valour that made the slightest action effective.

The writings of the time are unanimous in their praise, gratitude, and admiration. Long and circumstantial accounts prove the truth of this; in them stirs an enthusiasm that we still sense today. The Jesuits, Dollier de Casson, Marie de l'Incarnation [*see* GUYART], Marguerite BOURGEOYS, Sister Morin, Mother Juchereau* de Saint-Ignace, all have immortalized in their narratives the exploits and the name of Lambert Closse.

Dramatic circumstances surrounded the marriage of Lambert Closse, who was 39, and Élisabeth Moyen, who was 16. In 1655, when Élisabeth was living with her parents on Île aux Oies, below Quebec, a party of Iroquois suddenly appeared. Her father and mother, Jean-Baptiste Moyen Des Granges and Élisabeth Le Bret, were slaughtered on the spot; Élisabeth and her sister Marie were taken as captives to an Onondaga village. This story soon became known at Ville-Marie. The Montrealers, who were battling unceasingly with the Iroquois bands, then kept a close watch on their enemies. They hoped to discover some day the murderers of the Moyen family; this did happen in fact when CHARLES LE MOYNE returned from Quebec, for he recognized some of them. Dollier de Casson has told of the vicissitudes of the struggle that immediately began, and in which the artfulness and guile of Charles Le Moyne, the foresight of Maisonneuve, and the bravery of Lambert Closse and his soldiers brought about victory. This was followed by the exchange of several Iroquois chieftains being held in the fort for all the French prisoners in the hands of the Onondagas. Thus the young Moyen girls, half dead with fear and grief, reached Ville-Marie. Jeanne Mance received them at her Hôtel-Dieu, and under her care they gradually recovered.

In the autumn of that same year 1655, MM. de Maisonneuve and Louis d'Ailleboust left Ville-Marie for France. In M. de Maisonneuve's absence it was Lambert Closse who was in command at Ville-Marie. It is to be supposed that the acting governor paid many visits to the Hôtel-Dieu, for Jeanne Mance, with her judgement and her peculiar power of foreseeing difficulties and often of solving them, was a counsellor esteemed by all. Lambert Closse then had the opportunity of seeing Élisabeth Moyen and of chatting with her. The latter's feelings of gratitude towards one of her deliverers were gradually transformed into affection. On 12 Aug. 1657 the marriage of Lambert Closse and Élisabeth Moyen was celebrated by the Jesuit Father CLAUDE PIJART.

M. de Maisonneuve returned to Canada 29 July 1657, together with Louis d'Ailleboust and four Sulpicians. The governor's return gave Lambert Closse a little more freedom. He hastened to instal his young wife as comfortably as possible. He owned a property of 30 acres, which he had acquired 10 March 1652. The deed of sale was signed before Nicolas Gastineau-Duplessis. Six months after his marriage, that is 2 Feb. 1658, Lambert Closse was granted by M. de Maisonneuve, as a fief, "100 *arpents*, beginning 10 rods from the big river, by 40 rods wide." This fief began at the rue Saint-Laurent, and it is in honour of Lambert Closse that the côte Saint-Lambert bears that name.

Two children were born to the Closse family. The elder, Élisabeth, born early in October 1658, died the same day; the younger, Jeanne-Cécile, born 1660, had Jeanne Mance as her godmother. In 1678 she married Jacques BIZARD, the town-major of Montreal and the seigneur of Île Major (Bizard), who died in 1692. Jeanne-Cécile remarried in 1694; her second husband was Raymond Blaise* Des Bergères de Rigauville.

Lambert Closse disappeared in 1662, "killed by a band of Iroquois when he was going to aid some Frenchmen in danger." This "brave Mons. Closse," wrote Dollier de Casson, . . . "died like a brave soldier of Jesus Christ and of our Monarch, after having a thousand times exposed his life most courageously, without fearing to lose it on such occasions, which he clearly stated to some who said to him shortly before his death, 'that he would get himself killed because of the readiness with which he exposed himself everywhere in the service of the country,'—to this he replied— 'Gentlemen, I came here only in order to die for the sake of God while serving him in the profession of arms; if I did not think to die here I would leave the country to go and serve against the Turks and not be deprived of that glory.' "

The *Relation* of 1662, for the edification of posterity, also published the hero's funeral eulogy:

Cloutier

"He was a man whose piety was no whit inferior to his valour, and who possessed extraordinary presence of mind in the heat of battle . . . and justly won the credit of saving Montreal, both by his might and by his reputation. Hence it was deemed advisable to keep his death concealed from the enemy, for fear that they might take advantage of it. This Eulogy we owed his Memory, since Montreal owes him its life."

We know of no authentic picture of the town-major of Ville-Marie. An imaginary representation of Lambert Closse has been made by the sculptor Louis-Philippe Hébert, and forms part of Maisonneuve's monument in Montreal.

MARIE-CLAIRE DAVELUY

AJM, Greffe de Bénigne Basset, 22 nov. 1659, 8, 20 févr. 1662, 1er, 27 févr. 1667; Greffe de Lambert Closse, 1651–56; Greffe de Jean de Saint-Père, 1648–51, 1655–57, passim. AJTR, Greffe de Nicolas Gastineau, 10 mars 1652. Dollier de Casson, Histoire du Montréal. JR (Thwaites). JJ (Laverdière et Casgrain). Morin, Annales (Fauteux et al.). Premier registre de l'église Notre-Dame de Montréal (Montréal, 1961).

Aristide Beaugrand-Champagne, "Les origines de Montréal," Cahiers des Dix, XIII (1948), 57. Faillon, Histoire de la colonie française. É.-Z. Massicotte, "Les actes des trois premiers tabellions de Montréal, 1648–1657," RSCT, 3d ser., IX (1915), sect.I, 189–204; "Les colons de Montréal de 1642 à 1667," ibid., 3d ser., VII (1913), sect.I, 3–65, and BRH, XXXIII (1927), 238ff.; "L'inventaire des biens de Lambert Closse," BRH, XXV (1919), 16–31; "Memento historique de Montréal, 1636–1760," RSCT, 3d ser., XXVII (1933), sect.I, 111–31; "Les premières concessions de terre à Montréal, sous M. de Maisonneuve, 1648–1665," ibid., 3d ser., VIII (1914), sect.I, 215–29. P.-G. Roy, Toutes petites choses du régime français (2v., Québec, 1944), I, 69–73. Félicité Angers [Laure Conan], L'oublié (Montréal, 1900). [This historical novel, which the author has considered as fictional biography because of its fidelity to the facts and its truthful depiction of personality, is of classical stature. The clearly delineated characters are in striking relief, so that the work resembles a fresco in which the figures possess an intense life. M.-C. D.]

CLOUTIER, ZACHARIE, master carpenter, pioneer at Beauport, originally from Saint-Jean-Baptiste de Mortagne in Perche; b. c. 1590; d. 17 Sept. 1677 at Château-Richer.

Having married Xainte Dupont on 18 July 1616, Cloutier entered into an undertaking at Mortagne with ROBERT GIFFARD, the seigneur of Beauport, on 14 March 1634; by the terms of this agreement he was to come to Canada that same year with his fellow-countryman JEAN GUYON DU BUISSON, senior, and he received at the same time the grant of an arriere-fief at Beauport. The two settlers took formal possession of their lands on 3 Feb. 1637. The previous year, if not before, their families had joined them in Canada, for the two households figure in the marriage contract of Robert DROUIN and Anne Cloutier on 27 July 1636.

Cloutier's holding, the fief of La Clouterie (or La Cloutièrerie) brought him into conflict with his neighbour Guyon and with Giffard, his seigneur. He sold it to Nicolas Dupont* de Neuville on 20 Dec. 1670 in order to go and settle at Château-Richer, where he had already received a grant of land from Governor JEAN DE LAUSON on 15 July 1652. Zacharie Cloutier brought up five children; he appears to be the ancestor of all the Cloutiers in Canada. He signed himself with a mark shaped like an axe.

HONORIUS PROVOST

AJQ, Greffe de Jean de Lespinasse, 3 févr. 1637; Greffe de Gilles Rageot, 20 oct. 1670, 20 déc. 1670. ASQ, Documents Faribault, 2, 48. JR (Thwaites), passim. JJ (Laverdière et Casgrain). F.-L. Desaulniers, Recherches généalogiques . . . (Montréal, 1902). [T.-E. Giroux], Robert Giffard, seigneur colonisateur au tribunal de l'histoire, ou la raison de fêter le troisième centenaire de Beauport, 1634–1934 (Québec, 1934).

COBBIE, WALSALL, carpenter with the HBC; fl. 1676–82.

In the Company's service by 1676, Cobbie sailed the following year as mate of the Shaftesbury (Capt. Joseph THOMPSON). He was on the same ship when it was wrecked off the Scilly Isles on the homeward journey in 1678.

Another voyage as mate of the John and Alexander was followed by promotion to captain of the yacht Colleton in 1680. Before he took it to the Bay that year, he was instructed to keep "a perfect account" of his voyage and send home a copy by the Prudent Mary. That unfortunate vessel was wrecked off Tetherley's Island in James Bay and Governor NIXON assigned to Cobbie the salvaging of her boards, etc., for the storehouse he was building.

The winter of 1681–82, spent on Charlton Island, was a difficult one, for Capt. NEHEMIAH WALKER drank heavily and created general disturbance. Antagonism between him and Cobbie brought them to blows. Cobbie, who had been well recommended for his ability and integrity, gave strong support to Nixon, who entrusted him with a duplicate of the Hudson's Bay packet (letters) to take home in 1682. Cobbie still had a year to serve, but his wife had died and he wanted to look after his "childerine and his goods."

During Cobbie's absence his family was provided for with payments of wages made to his sister, Diana Hall, and his mother, Mrs. Eliza Cobbie, who acted as his attorney. Evidently he was not employed after 1682, although Nixon rated him "most fit for the Company's service."

MAUD M. HUTCHESON

HBRS, VIII, IX (Rich); XI (Rich and Johnson).

COCREAUMONT ET DE SAINT-MAURICE, JEAN-BAPTISTE DUBOIS DE. *See* DUBOIS

COLIN, MICHEL, a Frenchman buried at Quebec, in 1616.

In his *Histoire du Canada* Brother SAGARD records the death of Michel Colin, whom Father Jean DOLBEAU "had entombed" at Quebec on 24 March 1616 "with the ceremonies customary in the Holy Roman Church," and who was "the first person in the country to receive that grace."

The Recollet adds a few lines later that on 15 July following Father Dolbeau "for the first time gave extreme unction to a woman named Marguerite Vienne, who had arrived that same year in Canada with her husband, thinking that she would get used to it, but who fell ill soon after she landed, who died during the night of the nineteenth and was buried towards the next evening with the ceremonies of the Holy Church."

It has often been stated, following the example of N.-E. Dionne and of P.-G. Roy, that Marguerite Vienne was Michel Colin's wife. However, nothing in the two texts of Sagard warrants such a correlation. Quite the contrary. "A Frenchman named Michel Colin" was buried at Quebec on 24 March 1616. Now by that date the gulf and the river were not yet open to shipping. Colin had therefore been in the colony at least since 1615. As for Marguerite Vienne, who died on 19 July 1616, she "had arrived the same year . . . with her husband." Consequently she could not have been the wife of Colin, who had wintered in Canada.

Colin was probably a bachelor or had been married in France, and must have been a clerk employed in the fur trade. For their part, Marguerite Vienne and her unnamed husband are the first French couple mentioned at Quebec. Admittedly, it has been claimed that the families of ABRAHAM MARTIN, Pierre Desportes, and Nicolas Pivert had preceded them to the colony. This assertion, however, while not totally improbable, rests on no documentary proof.

ANDRÉ VACHON

Sagard, *Histoire du Canada* (Tross), I, 44. Dionne, *Champlain*, II, 47, 423, 436, 471. Roy, *La ville de Québec*, I, 57f.

Colston

COLSTON, WILLIAM, colonizer, deputy governor of the first English colony in Newfoundland; fl.1610–12.

William Colston was almost certainly of Bristol origin, but the many Colstons dwelling in the city at the time make his parentage difficult to establish. It is likely, however, that he was the son of William Colston, who served as sheriff of Bristol from 1599 to 1600, and of his wife Elizabeth Gittens. If this is so, he was still a minor in 1582 when his grandfather, William Gittens, bequeathed £25 each to him and his brother when they came of age. Colston was probably a merchant like his father, and may have been the William Colston who joined the Bristol Spanish company in 1605.

In 1610 Bristol became involved in the scheme for the plantation of Newfoundland and a number of her prominent citizens subscribed to the company which undertook the venture. Colston was not among these but he did go to the island that year as one of the first settlers. The colony at Cuper's (Cupids) Cove was governed by John GUY of Bristol and it has been said that Colston was Guy's brother-in-law (Prowse, 94, who has been followed by many historians), but there appears to be no documentary proof of this. Neither Guy nor any other contemporary mentions the relationship; when writing of Colston, Guy refers to him as "one Master Colton, a discreete yong man" and, immediately afterwards, to "my brother Philip Guy" (Purchas, XIX, 416).

When Guy returned to England in the autumn of 1611, he left Colston and Philip Guy in charge of all affairs in the island; there is no evidence as to how the infant settlement fared under their governorship. Colston kept the official journal of weather and events that winter, as instructed by the company in 1610. Guy returned to his post in 1612 and Colston left for England in June. His report to the company's treasurer, John Slany, was evidently encouraging and enthusiastic for Slany wrote: "The good news of our newffoundland business doth much Reioyse the Company . . . and the helth of the Cuntry Far passeth England as aperes by master Colson thatt hath bin there this 2 yere without an ower of sicknes."

There are no further references to Colston's presence in Newfoundland; it was not he who kept the colony's journal during the winter of 1612–13 (Prowse, 128) but Henry CROUT (Middleton MSS, Mi X 1/66), and the statement that he served as deputy governor again from 1613 to 1614 (Prowse, 102) appears to be without foundation. After his return to England, he does

Côme de Mantes

not seem to have played any part in the civic life of Bristol.

GILLIAN T. CELL

For Colston's activity in Newfoundland see: Nottingham University, Middleton MSS, Mi X 1/1-66. Purchas, *Pilgrimes* (1905–7). Prowse, *History of Nfld.* Other sources: A. B. Beaven, *Bristol lists* (Bristol, 1889). *Bristol wills*, ed. T. P. Wadley (Bristol and Gloucestershire Arch. Soc., 1886). T. Garrard and S. G. Tovey, *Edward Colston* (Bristol, 1852). *Records relating to the Society of Merchant Venturers of the city of Bristol in the seventeenth century*, ed. P. McGrath (Bristol Record Soc., XVII, 1952).

CÔME DE MANTES, priest, Capuchin, superior of the mission at Pentagouet in Acadia, guardian of convents in France; b. at Mantes (France); d. some time after 1658 and perhaps as long as 15 years after that date, probably in France.

He joined the Capuchins of Paris and in 1632 was one of the seven Capuchins who accompanied Governor RAZILLY to Acadia. After the latter's death in 1635, he went back to France because of the disagreements between Charles de MENOU d'Aulnay and CHARLES DE SAINT-ÉTIENNE de La Tour.

He returned to Acadia in 1642, and we find him again at Port-Royal, where, on 20 Oct. 1643, he and seven other Capuchins signed a document attesting an armed raid made on that place by La Tour and some Englishmen. Father Côme then carried his missionary efforts into the Saint John River district, where on 10 May 1648 he baptized two Indian children, and afterwards delivered a baptismal certificate to the parents. A copy of this document is preserved in the parish register of Sillery. Does this imply that Father Côme made a trip to Quebec, as stated by Abbé Tanguay? Not at all; it was the child's parents who, passing through Sillery, had the baptismal certificate registered at the mission. Furthermore the blank spaces in the register and the incorrect spelling of the names cannot be explained if Father Côme were present.

In 1648 when he was named superior of the mission at Pentagouet (now Castine, Maine), he wrote to the Jesuits at Quebec to beseech them to come and carry on their ministry among the Abenakis in his territory. After d'Aulnay's death in 1650 there appeared in Acadia one of the chief creditors of the deceased, the La Rochelle merchant EMMANUEL LE BORGNE. The Capuchins were to suffer as a result of the unpleasantness that ensued upon his arrival. In 1652 the merchant's soldiers went as far as to imprison Côme de Mantes, whom they held captive on one of Le Borgne's ships for five months until he returned to France for good.

In his homeland Father Côme de Mantes was named guardian of the convent of Dreux in 1658 and then of those of Poissy, Béthune, Melun, and Laon in succession. The exact date of his death is not known. In view of the likely number of years he must have spent at each of his posts, one can presume that he lived for about another 15 years after 1658.

G.-M. DUMAS

Coll. de manuscrits relatifs à la Nouv.-France, I, 118. Candide de Nant, *Pages glorieuses*. Ivanhoë Caron, "Les pères capucins en Acadie," *BRH*, XLVII (1941), 128–31. Tanguay, *Répertoire du clergé*, 41.

COMPORTÉ, PHILIPPE GAULTIER DE. *See* GAULTIER

CONTRECŒUR, ANTOINE PÉCAUDY DE. *See* PÉCAUDY

CORTE-REAL, GASPAR, Portuguese explorer; b. *c.* 1450–55.

The third son of João Vaz Corte-Real, governor of the southern half of Terceira Island and of St. George Island in the Azores, Gaspar is mentioned in several documents as acting governor during the absence of his father in 1488 and of his elder brother in 1497.

In 1498, King Manoel of Portugal (1495–1521) manifested an interest in western exploration, for the probable reason that the land discovered in the previous year by JOHN CABOT was thought to fall within the territory assigned to Portugal by the treaty of Tordesillas [signed 7 June 1494 between Spain and Portugal to settle conflicts arising from Columbus's first voyage]. During the next four years, Pedro de Barcelos, João FERNANDES "Labrador," the brothers Gaspar and MIGUEL CORTE-REAL, and João Martins (all prominent residents of Terceira Island) took part in the search for land across the North Atlantic. Martins, indeed, had been a *criado* (employee) of João Vaz Corte-Real, Gaspar's father.

The first Portuguese discovery occurred in 1500, when Gaspar sighted "Ponta d'Asia" (Greenland), in the probable vicinity of Cape Farewell. He was, however, prevented from landing, either by the ice floes or by the weather. According to Biggar (*Voyages*, 88–91), the Portuguese rounded the southern tip of Greenland and entered Davis Strait, exploring the west coast as far as Sukkertoppen in 65°20′. Positive evidence that the Portuguese penetrated that far north is, however, lacking. Biggar relies on some very doubtful statements published by Damian de

Goes in 1566, more than 60 years after the voyage was made, in which he mentions that the explorers saw white bears and natives who looked like Laplanders. Damian de Goes, it would seem, has confused the 1500 voyage with that of 1501.

A different view of the 1500 voyage is given by Henry Harrisse (*Discovery*, 50, 61–62). After sighting Greenland, he thinks, the Portuguese crossed Davis Strait, landing somewhere on the east coast of Newfoundland, possibly in the vicinity of Notre-Dame Bay. Gago Coutinho, the Portuguese admiral, has put forward a very bold theory in a recent study (*Ainda Gaspar Corte-Real*, 29–30), namely that Gaspar Corte-Real, after coming within sight of Greenland, was unable to land there but reached Newfoundland. He sailed around the island and penetrated into the Gulf of St. Lawrence by the northern route (Belle Isle strait), coming out through Cabot Strait. The latter theory, ingenious though it is, is not backed by documentary evidence. Our only positive information about the Portuguese voyage of 1500 is derived from a legend on the Cantino map, which states that the Portuguese sighted Greenland—mistakenly taking it to be East Asia—but were unable to land there. Any other theory is pure conjecture.

In 1501 Gaspar made another voyage with three caravels. There is a fair amount of information about this new undertaking in three letters written from Lisbon by Pietro Pasqualigo and Alberto Cantino in October 1501. These letters reveal that the expedition first tried to reach the land sighted the previous year. Finding the sea frozen, the Portuguese were forced to change course and, after apparently crossing the entrance to Davis Strait, they found a coast where many large rivers flowed into the sea. They sailed up one of these estuaries for about one league and disembarked in a country where pine trees and wild berries grew. They also captured a number of natives.

In the view of H. P. Biggar, the Portuguese had entered Hamilton Inlet, "which they explored as far as the Narrows, 35 miles up, where the breadth is only one third of a mile" and he identifies the aborigines brought back to Portugal as "Nasquapee Indians who still inhabit Labrador" (Biggar, *Voyages*, 96–97, 100). Harrisse, on the other hand, believes that the land of large rivers, tall pines, and wild berries described by Cantino must be the east coast of Newfoundland, where there are huge forests and streams of considerable size, like the Gander and the Exploits (Harrisse, *Discovery*, 69).

Gago Coutinho noted that the natives brought back to Portugal seemed to belong to two varying climatic regions, since some were dressed in skins, while others were naked. He concludes that Gaspar had explored two different sections of the American coast, one in Newfoundland and the other much farther to the south (Coutinho), *Corte-Real*, 30–32). Coutinho's deductions may contain some elements of truth but he is wrong in his assumption that Gaspar reached America by the southern route and that he explored the coast all the way from Florida to Newfoundland, for he could not then have found the sea frozen on his way to America. It is much more logical to suppose that Gaspar, if he discovered a temperate land, must have done so by sailing south from Newfoundland.

Two of Gaspar's three ships returned to Lisbon in October 1501 but the third, with the leader of the expedition, was lost, never to be heard from again. (*See* MIGUEL CORTE-REAL for his attempt in 1502 to find his lost brother, Gaspar.)

The land discovered by Gaspar appears for the first time on the Cantino map (1502) as the "Terra del Rey de Portugall." Other maps picturing it are those known as Kunstmann II and III ("Terra de Corte Real"). What is the exact location of the territory and how far north did it extend?

It is generally believed that it included the eastern shore of Newfoundland. On the Pedro Reinel map known as Kunstmann I, the new land is given an extension of 10° in latitude, from 49°N to 57°N. This has led Heinrich Winter and Ellen Taylor to believe that "Corte-Real Land," which also became known as "Codfish Land," extended far beyond the Strait of Belle Isle, as far as Cape Chidley.

It is true that the configuration of the coast on Reinel's map, as well as on other maps, seems to comprise present-day Labrador, in addition to eastern Newfoundland, but this is probably the result of later exploration. This author, however, doubts that the Corte-Reals sailed as far north as Cape Chidley, since Antonio Galvão states that Gaspar struck land at a latitude of 50°N and since the coast discovered by the Portuguese extended only from Cape Race to Bonavista, according to Pierre Crignon (*see* Ramusio, *Terzo volume delle navigationi et viaggi*, 417, 423–24).

It is possible, of course, that Reinel may have embodied in his map other data than those derived from the Corte-Real voyages. As soon as Newfoundland became known, vessels from England, France, Spain, and Portugal quickly established new fishing grounds. As early as 1506, for example, a tithe on Newfoundland fish was levied in Portuguese ports by order of the king. Reinel may have obtained considerable information from pilots of fishing vessels which may have ventured up Davis Strait. His map is undated but may have been drawn as late as 1510.

L.-A. VIGNERAS

Alguns documentos do Archivo National da Torre do Tombo (Lisboa, 1892), 123–27, 131–32, 150–52. Antonio Galvão, *Tratado dos descobrimentos* (Porto, 1944), 149. Damiano de Goes, *Chronica do felicissimo rei dom Manuel* (Lisboa, 1566), ff.65–66. *Raccolta Colombiana* (Roma, 1892), pt.III, v.I, 87–90, 151–52. G. B. Ramusio, *Terzo volume delle navigationi et viaggi nel quale si contengono Le Navigationi al Mondo Nuovo* (1st ed., Venetia, 1556), 417, 423–24.

H. P. Biggar, *The voyages of the Cabots and of the Corte-Reals to North America and Greenland, 1497–1503* (Paris, 1903). Gago Coutinho, *Ainda Gaspar Corte-Real* (Lisboa, 1950). Henry Harrisse, *The discovery of North America: a critical, documentary, and historic investigation, with an essay on the cartography of the new world* . . . (London, 1892), 59–76; *Les Corte-Real*. Hoffman, *Cabot to Cartier*, 26–29. S. E. Morison, *Portuguese voyages to America in the fifteenth century* (Cambridge, Mass., 1940), 68–72. Oleson, *Early voyages*, 143–44. *Precursors* (Biggar), 32–40, 59–70, 92–98. E. G. R. Taylor, "Hudson's Strait and the oblique meridian," *Imago mundi*, III (1939), 48–52. Heinrich Winter, "The pseudo-Labrador and the oblique meridian," *Imago mundi*, II (1937), 61–74.

MAPS: Friedrich Kunstmann, *Atlas zur Entdeckungsgeschichte Amerikas* (München, 1859), charts I–IV. *Portugaliae monumenta cartographica*, comp. A. Cortesão et A. Teixeira da Mota (5v., Lisboa, 1960–62), I, plates 4, 5, 6, 8.

CORTE-REAL, MIGUEL, Portuguese explorer, second son of João Vaz Corte-Real, m. Isabel de Castro, two daughters; b. *c*. 1450; probably d. 1502.

Miguel invested large sums in fitting out the 1500 and 1501 expeditions [*see* GASPAR CORTE-REAL] and in return Gaspar promised to share with him the lands he might discover. Miguel, however, did not accompany his brother but commanded one of the vessels sent by King Manoel to help the Venetians against the Turks in the summer of 1501.

During the winter of 1501–2, after his brother had failed to return from Newfoundland, Miguel organized a relief expedition. In confirmation of his previous agreement with Gaspar, King Manoel granted Miguel the captaincy of any fresh lands he might discover on his present voyage. Miguel sailed from Lisbon May 1502 with three ships in search of his brother. He apparently reached the shores explored by Gaspar the year before. There the three ships separated to widen the search but agreed on a rendezvous for 20 August at a spot identified by Biggar as St. John's Harbour on the south coast of Newfoundland. While two of the caravels came to the rendezvous at the appointed time, the other, with Miguel Corte-Real on board, failed to appear and was never heard of again.

In the following year, Vasco Añes Corte-Real planned an expedition to look for his missing brothers but the king would not let him sail, fearing that he might share their fate. Two ships were sent, however, which returned in the fall. Although their search had been in vain, Vasco Añes did not give up his claims to Newfoundland and had them confirmed by the king at various times.

Some 40 years ago Prof. Delabarre put forward the controversial hypothesis that an inscription on the Dighton Rock (in southern New England on the banks of the Taunton River) gives evidence of Miguel's fate. Delabarre deciphered the inscription as follows: MIGUEL CORTEREAL V DEI HIC DUX IND A D 1511. He saw in it a "proof" that Miguel had become chief of an Indian tribe and that he was still living in 1511. It must be remembered that in the 18th and 19th centuries some historians fancied that they had seen runic characters on the same stone, a "proof" that the Norsemen had been there. The Dighton rock is covered with scratches, drawings, and inscriptions, and it is hard to tell whether they are authentic or the work of pranksters. The inscription relating to Miguel Corte-Real is subject to other interpretations.

L.-A. VIGNERAS

See works cited for GASPAR CORTE-REAL.

E. B. Delabarre, *Dighton rock* (New York, 1928). F. F. Lopes, *The brothers Corte Real*, tr. F. de Andrade (Lisboa, 1957). G. S. Marques, *Pedra de Dighton* (New York, 1930).

COSINEAU DE MAREUIL, JACQUES-THÉODORE. *See* MAREUIL

COUILLARD DE LESPINAY, GUILLAUME, carpenter, seaman, and caulker, son of Guillaume Couillard and Élisabeth de Vesins, son-in-law of LOUIS HÉBERT; and native of Saint-Malo or of the parish of Saint-Landry in Paris; b. *c*. 1591; d. 1663 at Quebec.

Couillard married GUILLEMETTE, daughter of Louis Hébert, at Quebec, about 26 Aug. 1621. By her he had 10 children, and because of the numerous descendants of these children Couillard appears in the genealogy of almost all the old French-Canadian families.

He had come to Canada about 1613 according to CHAMPLAIN, who spoke highly of him in 1628. Couillard was one of the first to settle permanently in the colony. Louis Hébert, the first farmer, arrived at Quebec only in 1617. After his death in 1627, Couillard took over from him the farming of his lands, having inherited, through his wife, half of Hébert's estate. Moreover, in the same year (1627) Champlain also granted to Couillard, for personal reasons, "a hundred acres of land to clear and seed," which bordered on the St. Charles River. By 1632 Couillard had nearly 20 acres under cultivation, and in 1639 he owned a flour mill. On 8 July of the same year HUAULT de Montmagny appointed him a "clerk responsible for inspecting the sown lands and the food of the settlers of Quebec." He had been the first person to make use of a plough, in the spring of 1628. In 1643 he was making lime for the Compagnie des Cent-Associés.

At the end of June 1628 Champlain, alarmed by the approach of the English and the threat of famine at Quebec, decided to send someone to Tadoussac to repair and bring back a boat, for the purpose of moving unessential people out towards the Gaspé. Couillard, the only man capable of carrying out this operation, stubbornly refused to do it, despite his normal readiness to be of help. In dread of being slaughtered by the Indians, "he feared for his skin, and did not want to leave his wife, for fear of losing her."

When Quebec was captured in 1629, Guillaume Couillard's family was the only complete family that agreed to live under the occupation, and Champlain entrusted to it two young Indian girls, CHARITÉ and ESPÉRANCE, whom he had adopted. After the French returned in 1632 Couillard continued to work unsparingly for the colony and to be held in high regard generally: he took part in the defence against the Iroquois, frequently piloted boats between Quebec and Tadoussac, and became churchwarden of the parish, after having given a part of his land for the reconstruction of the church. Since he could not write, he used as his mark a most original little design, which appears on several historical documents that have been preserved.

In December 1654, under Governor JEAN DE LAUSON's administration, he was ennobled by the king, "on account of services rendered to the country of Canada." According to family papers, Couillard's coat of arms was "azure, a dove with wings outspread or, holding in its beak an olive branch proper," with the device: "*Dieu aide au premier colon.*"

Guillaume Couillard died in his house on 4 March 1663, and was buried in the chapel of the Hôtel-Dieu in recognition of the gifts made by him to that institution. Three years later his widow sold his house and a good portion of his land to Bishop Laval*, for the establishment of the seminary of Quebec. The site of the house is marked today by a cairn in an inside courtyard of the seminary, and Guillaume Couillard has his statue, the work of the sculptor Alfred Laliberté, near Louis Hébert's monument beside the city hall of Quebec.

HONORIUS PROVOST

ASQ, Documents Faribault, 20. Champlain, *Œuvres* (Laverdière), *passim*. *JJ* (Laverdière et Casgrain), *passim*. *JR* (Thwaites), *passim*. Couillard Després, *La première famille française au Canada*.

COUILLARD DE LESPINAY, LOUIS, fisherman, hunter and seigneur; b. 1629, third child and eldest son of GUILLAUME COUILLARD and GUILLEMETTE HÉBERT, baptized 18 May 1629 at Quebec just two months before its capture by the KIRKES; d. 1678.

He received some education from the Jesuits but early showed a liking for movement and adventure. At 17, with four gay companions of about his own age—all rascals ("tous fripons") comments the *Journal des Jésuites*—he made a voyage to Old France. Never daunted by danger, he had many narrow escapes and repeatedly turned up safe and sound after rumours of his capture or death. At the age of 21 he formed an association with seven other young men, for hunting seals, an occupation which entailed months of extreme hardships on the shores of the gulf.

On 29 April 1653, he married Geneviève Després. The following year he bought half the seigneury of the Rivière-du-Sud about 30 miles below Quebec on the south shore of the St. Lawrence. A year later, with the acquisition of the other half, he became the third seigneur of a domain originally granted to Governor HUAULT de Montmagny (1646).

He did not settle down on it, however, but continued his voyages. Going to and fro between Quebec and Tadoussac or the gulf, his boat transported a variety of passengers: frequently a Jesuit father, sometimes a government official, and once a fugitive from justice who was hanged the day after Lespinay landed him at Quebec.

In October 1656, he broke the Canadian record for cod-fishing by catching 1,000 in one day at Malbaie. In 1659 he caught 220 seals on a flat rocky island opposite Tadoussac. Later this rock (Île Rouge) was ceded to him exclusively. In 1664 Lespinay's discovery of a mine earned him a grant of 1,000 *livres* from the Conseil Souverain.

The Intendant TALON was well pleased with his enterprising spirit. His activities produced results which were tangible proof of the colony's potential wealth. Seal-hunting, for instance, furnished oil in such abundance that it could be exported to the Antilles. In 1665, in three weeks' hunting, Lespinay cleared a profit of 800 *livres*.

Coulonge et d'Argentenay

Guillaume Couillard was granted letters of nobility in 1654 and his son Louis, on the recommendation of Talon, received them in 1668. These letters, although not yet registered by 1669 when Louis XIV abolished such unregistered titles, were none the less valuable to Couillard and his descendants for no one questioned the title. On 30 June 1692 the Conseil Souverain even ordered that the patent be inscribed in the council's registers. Couillard still took pride in what he earned by work, however, as is evident in the motto he chose: *Prix des travaux n'a rien de vil.*

At the age of 45 he transferred his energies from the water to the land. He had his seigneury surveyed by his brother-in-law JEAN GUYON DU BUISSON (1619–94) and grants made to prospective settlers, most of them connections of the Hébert family. He himself, says his descendant, Couillard Després, supervised the clearing of the land and shared the toil with his tenants.

A manor house of stone, 40 ft. by 24 ft., surrounded with a palisade for protection against the Iroquois, was erected on a slight promontory overlooking the junction of the Rivière du Sud with the St. Lawrence. Nearby was a waterfall which could turn a mill-wheel. Lespinay engaged a skilful builder to construct a flour mill and equip it with everything necessary for the production of good flour. It cost 900 *livres*.

The expenses of clearing and building exhausted his capital. As well as selling hereditary land at Quebec he borrowed money from the Jesuit fathers and from Charles BAZIRE.

To his seigneury he gave the name La Couillardière but the old name, Rivière-du-Sud, later prevailed. The parish was called Saint-Thomas de Montmagny.

He died in the summer of 1678 at the age of 49. His creditors seized his seigneury (his debts by this time had passed through several hands) and his wife and six children were left with nothing. His wife, however, was legally entitled to claim her dowry; she did so and with it bought back the land. It remained in the possession of the family, says Couillard Després, for another century and a half.

ETHEL M. G. BENNETT

JR (Thwaites) frequently note Lespinay's activities. Couillard Després gives complete information about the seigneury in his *Histoire des seigneurs de la Rivière-du-Sud et leurs alliés canadiens et acadiens* (Saint-Hyacinthe, 1912); lists the genealogy in "Dictionnaire généalogique et historique de la famille Couillard et de ses diverses branches, 1613–1918," *BRH*, XXIV (1918), 91–94; cites letters patent in "Anoblissement des Couillard," *ibid.*, XX (1914), 221–24; and inventories Couillard's possessions at the time of his death in "En marge de l'histoire de la Rivière-du-Sud," *ibid.*, XXI (1915), 116–22. See also *Jug. et délib.*, III, 641.

COULONGE ET D'ARGENTENAY, LOUIS D'AILLEBOUST DE. *See* AILLEBOUST

COURCELLE (Courcelles), DANIEL RÉMY DE. *See* RÉMY

COURSERON, GILBERT, provost's lieutenant at Quebec in 1621.

CHAMPLAIN had held all legislative, executive, and judicial powers in the colony since 1612. He had acted first as the representative of the company operating the trading-post at Quebec, then, from 1612 on, as lieutenant to the viceroy. When the king ordered him to administer justice to all his subjects in the colony (1620), Champlain appointed in 1621 the country's first law-officers: LOUIS HÉBERT became king's attorney, Gilbert Courseron provost's lieutenant, and one named Nicolas clerk of court of the jurisdiction of Quebec. Where did Courseron come from, and how long did he remain at Quebec? It is impossible to answer either of these questions.

ANDRÉ VACHON

Champlain, *Œuvres* (Laverdière), V, 328; VI, 5f., 22. Le Clercq, *First establishment of the faith* (Shea), I, 167; *Premier établissement de la foy*, I, 186. André Vachon, *Histoire du notariat canadien, 1621–1960* (Québec, 1962), 10, 26.

CRAPAUT. *See* CHOMINA

CREVIER DE SAINT-FRANÇOIS, JEAN, fur-trader, a prominent person in the colony; b. 3 April 1642 at Trois-Rivières, son of Christophe Crevier *dit* La Meslée and Jeanne Énard; d. shortly after August 1693.

On 26 Nov. 1663, at Trois-Rivières, he married Marguerite, daughter of Jacques HERTEL and Marie Marguerie. He fell foul of the law with respect to his fur-trading with the Indians who frequented Cap-de-la-Madeleine. He bought the Saint-François-du-Lac seigneury from his brother-in-law Pierre Boucher* in 1673. He obtained ordinances from the intendants DUCHESNEAU and Demeulle*, forbidding anyone to hunt or fish throughout the area of his seigneury. He was one of the 20 principal settlers summoned to Quebec by Governor BUADE de Frontenac on 26 Oct. 1678 to express their opinion on trading in spirits, and he voted in favour of it, attributing the crimes committed by the Indians to their savage disposition rather than to the use of liquor. He was carried off by the Iroquois during a raid on Saint-François in August 1693, and just as they were getting ready to burn him alive he was ransomed for 50 *livres* by Major Peter Schuyler*, the commandant of the Albany garrison; but he died shortly afterwards, as a result of his wounds. His son Louis had been killed 27 March 1690, during the expedition of François Hertel* against Salmon Falls. His widow and his son Joseph*, on 23 Aug. 1700, gave part of their seigneury to the Abenakis and the Sokokis, for whom the Jesuits opened a mission which still exists today.

THOMAS CHARLAND

ASQ, Polygraphie, XIII, 47. *Coll. de manuscrits relatifs à la Nouv.-France*, I, 589f. *Découvertes et établissements des Français* (Margry), I, 405–20. *NYCD* (O'Callaghan and Fernow), IV, 66; IX, 554f. T.-M. Charland, "Enlèvement et mort du seigneur Crevier," *BRH*, XLIII (1937), 346–48; *Histoire de Saint-François-du-Lac* (Ottawa, 1942). J.-A. Maurault, *Histoire des Abénakis* (Sorel, 1866), 278–80.

CRISAFY (Crisasy, Crisaci, and **Crisacy), THOMAS,** officer, Knight of Malta, originally from Messina in Sicily; d. 29 Feb. 1696 at Montreal.

A first cousin of the Prince de Monaco, Crisafy belonged to the house of Grimaldi, one of the most powerful families in Italy. He took part in the Sicilian uprising against the prince who ruled the island in the name of the king of Spain. With his elder brother, the Marquis Antoine de Crisafy*, he declared himself on the side of the king of France. As soon as the revolt was suppressed and peace restored, their possessions were confiscated, and they asked help and protection from France. They were both reduced to accepting command of a company of colonial regular troops bound for Canada, where they arrived probably in 1684.

Thomas Crisafy conducted himself gallantly. He served under Philippe de Rigaud* de Vaudreuil. In 1690 it was he who came to the help of the mother of Madeleine de Verchères [JARRET*] when the former was attacked by a band of Iroquois. The following year he drove off a detachment of Oneidas at Repentigny. He was also the right-hand man of Governor BUADE de Frontenac, who in 1695 instructed him to go and relieve Fort Cataracoui (Frontenac). Governors Frontenac and Brisay* de Denonville, as well as Intendant Bochart* Champigny, commended him highly to the minister, but in vain: they did not succeed in obtaining for him the pension that he sought.

"One could not determine," said Charlevoix* of him, "what one should most admire; his skill in war, his shrewdness in counsel, his conduct in the undertakings that were entrusted to him, his fearlessness, or his presence of mind in action...."

LÉOPOLD LAMONTAGNE

Charlevoix, *Histoire*, II, III. *NYCD* (O'Callaghan and Fernow), IX. *Royal Fort Frontenac* (Preston and Lamontagne). *BRH*, VI (1900), 320, 346f.; XXIII (1917), 53; XXIX (1923), 315f.; XXXII (1926), 524–28; XL (1934), 341f. Tanguay, *Dictionnaire*.

CROFT, THOMAS, English official who financed an early voyage of discovery; third son of William Croft of Croft, Herefordshire; b. 1442; d. 1488.

Brought up with Edward of York, Croft went to court on Edward's accession as Edward IV. He was given various grants and minor offices by the king, being described as "the king's servitor." A lawyer of Lincoln's Inn, he was also M.P. for Leominster, 1478. Among his offices were those of joint collector of customs at Bristol, water-bailiff of Bristol (1478), and joint deputy butler of Bristol and other ports (1483). He remained faithful to Richard III until late in 1484 but deserted to Henry Tudor. Though he lost his Bristol appointments at the opening of the new reign he was rewarded with others by Henry VII for service in "our last victorious field" (the battle of Bosworth) and otherwise. He died in 1488, and his will, made in 1485, has survived.

Although as a collector of customs at Bristol he was not supposed to engage in trade, he received, on 18 June 1480, with three Bristol merchants, William Spencer, Robert Straunge, and William de la Fount, royal licence to trade for three years in any goods except staple goods (wool and cloth), with two or three ships of 60 tons each or less. (It may be inferred that Croft, a customs officer, received his permission in order to engage in exploration.) On 15 July following, the first recorded English expedition to seek lands in the Atlantic left Bristol under the command of a certain Lloyd (*see* John JAY) in search of the Isle of Brasil. It is not clear that this expedition was one with which Croft and his associates were concerned, or whether theirs was a rival project, since it would appear that their grant was to cover voyages of exploration. The 1480 venture did not succeed.

However, on or about 6 July 1481, two vessels left Bristol on a further attempt to find the Isle of Brasil. Both are described as ships or balingers, the latter name being used for a ship of not more than 60 tons, and normally between 20 and 50.

Crout

They were the *George*, probably the same as that described in a list of Bristol shipping of this time as of 52 tons, and the *Trinity*. Of each of these ships Thomas Croft owned one-eighth part. We may assume that his partners, Spencer, Straunge, and de la Fount, owned the bulk of the remainder, though John Jay, who had a share in the ship which sailed in 1480, may also have been a part-owner. Thomas Croft also played a part in equipping the ships for their voyage by contributing 40 bushels of salt, worth 20s., to their lading. This substantial amount of salt would suggest that one purpose of the voyage was to find and exploit fishing grounds. No record has yet been found of the result of the voyage, nor do we know whether or not Thomas Croft sailed on either of the vessels although he could have done so.

We know, however, that he was in Bristol on 24 Sept. 1481, when an inquiry was held into his participation in the setting out of the ships in spite of the regulation which forbade him, as a customs officer, to engage in trade. The terms of the inquiry also imply, though they do not state, that the ships had returned by that date. The result of the inquiry brought to light the names of the ships, Croft's shares in them, and his investment in their lading. It declared that the latter was for the renewal, strengthening, and maintenance of the said ships or balingers and not by cause of merchandise "but to the intent to search and find a certain isle called the Isle of Brasile" (*pro reparacione artillacione et sustentacione predictarum Navium sive Balinger et non causa mercandisandi set causa scrutandi et inveniendi quandam insulam vocatam le Ile of Brasile*). On 20 Jan. 1483 a pardon was issued to Thomas Croft in the same terms for his part in the expedition.

In view of the statement by John Day in 1498 (*see* JOHN CABOT) that "in times past" the English had discovered the Isle of Brasil before Cabot's voyages, it may reasonably be suggested that the expedition of 1481 could have discovered land across the Atlantic adjacent to a fishing ground, such as the Newfoundland Banks. This makes Thomas Croft of more potential significance in American discovery than has hitherto been thought, but until further evidence appears the full achievement (if any) of the 1481 expedition cannot be authoritatively assessed.

DAVID B. QUINN

Biography in J. C. Wedgwood and A. E. Holt, *History of Parliament: biographies of the members of the Commons house, 1439–1509* (3v., London, 1936), 239–40 (omits Croft's activities at Bristol). *The overseas trade of Bristol in the later Middle Ages*, ed. E. M. Carus-Wilson (Bristol Record Soc., VII, 1937), 157–58, 161–65, for the documents of 1480–81 with commentary.

See also W. E. C. Harrison, "An early voyage of discovery," *Mariner's Mirror*, XVI (1930), 198–99. Oleson, *Early voyages*, 124. D. B. Quinn, "The argument for the English discovery of America between 1480 and 1494," *Geog. J.*, CXXVII (1961), 277–85; "Edward IV and exploration," *Mariner's Mirror*, XXI (1935), 277–84. Carl V. Sølver, *Imago mundi: skitser fra de store opdagelsers tid* (København, 1951). L-.A. Vigneras, "The Cape Breton landfall: 1494 or 1497? Note on a letter by John Day," *CHR*, XXXVIII (1957), 219–28. Williamson, *Cabot voyages* (1962).

CROUT, HENRY, settler in the first English colony in Newfoundland; fl. 1612–17.

Nothing is known of Crout's life beyond the Newfoundland venture; his name suggests a Devonshire origin, but in 1612 he was living in Lambeth. In February 1612 Crout purchased, for £20, a half-share in the London and Bristol company for the settlement of Newfoundland, which had established a colony two years previously under JOHN GUY. He was apparently drawn into the venture by Sir Percival Willoughby, a subscriber to the company in 1610. Crout went to Newfoundland to represent Willoughby's interests there and to act as guardian to Thomas WILLOUGHBY, Sir Percival's son.

In May 1612 Crout reached Renewse, and in August he took up residence at Cuper's (Cupids) Cove whence he wrote a series of letters to Willoughby, recording his generally favourable impressions. He considered Newfoundland suitable for settlement—potentially fertile and promising mineral wealth, drugs (such as sarsaparilla), and a fur trade with the Indians such as that established by the French in Canada. Any criticisms which he made were of the company rather than of the country: he particularly questioned the practice of sending out apprentices rather than skilled men. Crout said surprisingly little of the colonists' day-to-day activities but did describe the raids of Peter EASTON, the pirate, on the fishermen. Two journeys which Crout made to Ferryland to negotiate with Easton led to his being accused by Willoughby of too great a familiarity with the pirates.

Crout's main duty was to explore the land which Willoughby hoped to receive from the company, namely the peninsula dividing Conception and Trinity bays, north of a line drawn from Carbonear to Heart's Content. At first, hindered by lack of a boat, he relayed to Willoughby the reports of fishermen who told of tracts of good, open land, woods frequented by deer and beaver, and harbours teeming with fish. Having failed to reach Trinity Bay overland, in October Crout went on the coasting expedition, led by Guy, which made contact with the Beothuk Indians there.

The winter of 1612–13 was spent at the settlement where he was evidently a person of some importance, for he was appointed to keep the colony's official journal (Middleton MSS, Mi X 1/66). This was primarily a record of the weather; each day wind direction, periods of sunshine, rain, or snowfall, and the severity of frost were noted. The terms used are subjective but the trends of the weather are apparent. The journal is an invaluable document, unique for this date. Furthermore, it provides a wealth of detail on the colony's life during that hard winter. By the early months of 1613, Willoughby was already critical of Crout for not having undertaken more extensive exploration. That spring he did return to Trinity Bay but the Beothuks proved elusive. Crout was prepared to winter again in Newfoundland but, by August, it had been decided that he should go to England to report more fully to Willoughby.

Apparently he remained in England until 1616, but by May of that year he was again in Cuper's Cove. Willoughby's desire that Crout establish a separate settlement on his land at Carbonear was frustrated by lack of men. Crout spent that winter in the island but Willoughby was increasingly dissatisfied with Crout's management of his affairs, and especially with this new delay. It seems probable that Willoughby recalled him, for nothing more is heard of Crout in Newfoundland and by 1619, Willoughby had a new agent there, Thomas ROWLEY.

GILLIAN T. CELL

Crout's letters, his journal, and other papers relating to him form part of a collection of documents on the first English colony at Nottingham University, Middleton MSS, Mi X 1/1–66. For accounts of the colony see: Purchas, *Pilgrimes* (1905–7), XIX. Prowse, *History of Nfld.* Rogers, *Newfoundland.*

CROWNE (Crown), WILLIAM, colonizer, independent minister in the Parliament of Cromwell, colonel in the British militia, Rouge-Dragon; b. 1617 (nothing is known of his place of birth or of his education); d. 1682 in Boston, North America.

William Crowne married, between the years 1635–40, Agnes (Mackworth) Watts, widow of Richard Watts and daughter-in-law of John Watts, an alderman and lord mayor of London, 1606. Mrs. Crowne was the sister of Humphrey Mackworth of Breton Grange, county of Shrewsbury. Three children were born to Agnes and William Crowne; the eldest, John, became a well-known English dramatist.

In 1636, William Crowne, in his nineteenth year, accompanied as a member of his suite the Earl of Arundel on a mission to the emperor Ferdinand II. He subsequently wrote an account of this journey. On 24 Sept. 1638, at the Red Tavern Inn, Richmond, the Earl of Arundel created Crowne Rouge-Dragon, entitling him to armorial bearings. William Crowne held this office after he went to America. He returned to London and officiated as Rouge-Dragon at the coronation of Charles II on 23 April 1661. Crowne resigned 25 May 1661.

Nothing is known of Crowne immediately following his marriage but at the outbreak of the Civil War he allied himself with the Parliamentary cause. In 1641 he was serving Basil Feilding, 2d Earl of Denbigh, as secretary. In July 1644, Crowne was in London requesting more strength and money for Denbigh. Four letters are known to have been sent out over his signature. In December 1649, he was acting as Humphrey Mackworth's secretary. On 2 April 1650 he was granted a commission as captain of foot and on 19 April he became a lieutenant-colonel of foot for Shropshire, under Humphrey Mackworth. He was an M.P. in 1654.

In the year 1656, Crowne tied up his fortune in a venture in the New World. He became joint proprietor, with Col. Thomas TEMPLE, of Nova Scotia, by buying CHARLES DE SAINT-ÉTIENNE de La Tour's patent as baronet of Nova Scotia. By this purchase, Crowne and Temple agreed to pay La Tour's debt of £3,379 to the widow of Maj.-Gen. Edward Gibbons of Boston and Temple assumed the cost of the English troops which had earlier captured the fort on the Saint John River [*see* SEDGWICK]. According to his statement of losses in about 1668, Crowne supplied the money and security for the purchase.

Col. Temple, Col. Crowne, his son John Crowne, and a group of settlers came to America in 1657. Crowne's name first appears in the records of Suffolk County, Mass., in September 1657 on an agreement between Temple and Crowne to divide Acadia, Temple taking the eastern part and Crowne the western, including the fort of Pentagouet (now Castine, Maine). The articles of agreement were not signed until 15 Feb. 1657/58 when Governor Endicot and John Crowne witnessed them. Each party gave a bond of £20,000.

Crowne took possession of his part of Acadia and built a trading post on the Penobscot River at a place called "Negu," or "Negu alias Cadascat." His son attended Harvard for the next three years. On 1 Nov. 1658 Crowne leased the whole territory to Capt. George Corwin and Ensign Joshua Scottee, and in 1659 to Col. Temple for four years. In each case the consideration was £110 per year. At this time Col. Crowne was living in Boston. He was made a freeman of Boston 30 May 1660.

The claim of Temple and Crowne to the grant of Nova Scotia by Cromwell was threatened at the Restoration by both French and English claims. Thomas Elliott, one of the grooms of the bedchamber to Charles, petitioned his master for a grant of the province. Sir LEWIS KIRKE and associates and the heirs of Sir WILLIAM ALEXANDER also petitioned for it. In 1661 the French ambassador claimed it for France. That same year Crowne, accompanied by his son, went to England with a petition, signed by the three original grantees (himself, Temple, and La Tour) which he submitted on 1 March. On 22 June 1661 he submitted a statement on the manner in which he and Temple became proprietors. While in England, Col. William Crowne also pleaded the cause of the colonists before the council and lord chamberlain on 4 Dec. 1661. Temple arrived in England in February 1662 and prepared a statement in answer to the French ambassador's claim, which gained him and his heirs a grant of Acadia and Nova Scotia and the governorship for life.

Crowne returned to America on 8 Oct. 1662. As a reward for his services while in London the General Court of the Massachusetts Bay colony granted him five hundred acres of land. This was laid out for him near Sudbury, Mass., in 1665. During the preceding five years Crowne had been involved in a lawsuit to recover lands and damages. The case was finally ended when the General Court of Massachusetts declared the entire matter beyond its jurisdiction. He moved to Mendon in 1667 and was chosen as the town's first clerk and selectman on 7 June 1667, offices he held for many years. Crowne lost the residue of his fortune in 1667 when by the Treaty of Breda Charles II ceded Acadia to France. His life in Mendon was marked by endless disputes with his neighbours over rents and other financial matters. On 27 May 1669, in answer to a special petition of the townspeople, the General Court appointed him a magistrate to solemnize marriages. He moved from Mendon by 1674 and lived then at Prudence Island, near Newbury, Mass. In 1679, he was living in Boston.

Agnes Crowne did not accompany her husband to America. That she was alive in 1674 is known because at that date Crowne was ordered to return to her in England. John Crowne also stayed in England and was forced by the loss of his patrimony to earn his living as a playwright.

Up until the time of William Crowne's death on 24 Dec. 1682, both he and his son endeavoured to collect promised restitution from the Crown for his property in Nova Scotia. Crowne's will was probated in Suffolk County 26 Feb. 1682/83. He died a poor man, as is evidenced also by records dated July 1682 containing his petition for financial assistance to the General Court of Massachusetts on the grounds of illness and need. He received two grants, one for £5 and one for £15. John Crowne continued for the rest of his life his father's struggle to obtain restitution for the Acadian losses. But although he won Charles II's favour through his plays, John Crowne also failed to regain financial security and died in poverty in 1712.

IN COLLABORATION WITH
HUIA G. RYDER

BM, Lansdowne MS 849, f.51, Crowne's memorial concerning the English title to Penobscot and adjacent lands, 4 Jan. 1697/98. "Mass. Archives," II, 506. *Annals of the town of Mendon from 1659 to 1880*, comp. J. G. Metcalf (Providence, R.I., 1880). *Documentary history of Maine*, IV, 175–76, 197; VII, 280; X, 25 and *passim*. Maine Hist. Soc., *Province and court records of Maine*, I, II. *Mémoires de commissaires*, I, 49, 56, 61, 96, 106; II, 278–79, 280–81, 289–90, 511; IV, 126, 307, 329; and *Memorials of the English and French commissaries*, I, 120, 126, 138–39, 167–68, 176, 579, 727. PRO, *Acts of P.C., col. ser., 1613–80*; *CSP, Col., 1574–1660, 1661–68, 1698–99*, no. 151. *Records of the Massachusetts Bay* (Shurtleff), IV, pts. 1 and 2, V.

William H. Davis, "Colonel William Crowne and his family," *N. Eng. Hist. and Geneal. Register*, LVII (1903), 406–10. *DAB* (John Crowne; William Crowne). *DNB* (John Crowne). Samuel Jennison, "William and John Crowne," *N. Eng. Hist. and Geneal. Register*, VI (1852), 46. J. L. Sibley, *Biographical sketches of graduates of Harvard University* (3v., Cambridge, Mass., 1873–85), I, 577. A. F. White, *John Crowne: his life and dramatic works* (Cleveland, 1922).

CRUSE, THOMAS, independent settler in Newfoundland; b. *c.* 1599, fl. 1677.

The little that is known of Cruse's life comes from a deposition which he made in 1677, as part of the evidence collected at Totnes in the Privy Council's inquiry into the dispute between the fishing industry and the colonists. Its object was to establish whether a governor should be sent to the island and fortifications erected in case the French, then settled in Placentia (Plaisance) Bay, should attack the English fishery. At this time Cruse described himself as a merchant of Ashprington, Devon.

Cruse had first visited Newfoundland more

than 50 years previously when, he said, there were but two or three inhabitants there and no governor; in fact the colony at Cuper's (Cupids) Cove must have been already established and governed by JOHN GUY or John MASON. About four years before the arrival of Sir DAVID KIRKE in 1638, Cruse returned to Newfoundland and settled in Bay Bulls, a harbour south of St. John's, much frequented by English fishermen. There he remained 18 years, doubtless living mainly by the fishery but dependent, with his fellow settlers, on visiting fishing ships for supplies since the barren land yielded insufficient food to support them.

Before 1638, according to Cruse, settlers and fishermen alike pursued the trade without hindrance, paying neither tax nor imposition. After Kirke's arrival all inhabitants were compelled to pay rent for their homes and fishing places. Kirke brought about 30 servants with him to enforce his demands. In 1640 Cruse agreed to pay a yearly rent of £3 6s. 8d. with a hog or a further 20s., for his house and land. Kirke also forced the settlers to hold licences for the keeping of taverns, although the sale of alcohol in Newfoundland was forbidden by the Western Charter of 1634 which had introduced regulations for the conduct of the fishery. Cruse himself held such a licence for which he paid Kirke £15 annually. About 1653 Cruse returned to England and of his life there we know nothing, save that he was a merchant.

Cruse's deposition shows an intimate knowledge of Newfoundland with its sparse settlements, not far apart but isolated by difficult terrain or frozen harbours, making a governor and a fort worthless because inaccessible. Above all, his evidence, like that of his fellow witnesses, reveals the bitterness felt by West Country fishermen against Kirke particularly and organized settlement generally. In 1677 when the London and Bristol merchants demanded government protection of the industry through the appointment of a governor, the men of the West Country ports opposed any interference in the trade that was their livelihood. To Cruse and many others, settlement and government were identified with the decline and eventual destruction of the industry.

GILLIAN T. CELL

There are copies of Cruse's deposition in the PRO, S.P. 29/223, no. 126 and in the Plymouth Central Library, MS 360/76. For the background to the inquiry see: PRO, *Acts of P.C., col. ser., 1613–80. CSP, Col., 1675–76, 1677–80.* C. B. Judah, *The North American fisheries and British policy to 1713* (University of Illinois Studies in the Social Sciences, XVIII, nos. 3–4, Urbana, Ill., 1933). Lounsbury, *British fishery at Nfld.*

Cunningham

CRYN. *See* TOGOUIROUI

CUNNINGHAM, JOHN, Scottish explorer in the employ of Denmark; b. 1575; d. 1651.

Contact between Denmark and the New World had been virtually non-existent from about 1500 until the 17th century, when Christian IV of Denmark dispatched three expeditions (1605, 1606, 1607) to recover the lost Scandinavian colonies in Greenland. Since England (now united with Scotland under James I) was the only country which had re-established communications with Greenland [*see* FROBISHER and DAVIS], the Danes were naturally eager to secure the services of English and Scottish seamen who might be familiar with the route to Greenland. Dynastic ties were also close between the royal families of both countries (James I of England was the brother-in-law of Christian IV of Denmark) and Andrew Sinclair, a Scot, was one of the most trusted servants of the Danish king.

Cunningham entered the service of Christian IV in 1603 as a captain in the navy. In 1605 the king sent out an expedition under Cunningham's command to recover Greenland, consisting of three ships, *Trost* (*Consolation*), *Löven* (*Lion*), and *Marekatten* or *Katten* (*Cat*), John KNIGHT, captain. Cunningham's ship was the *Trost* and on it he had as his first mate and "pilot" of the expedition another Englishman, James HALL.

From Hall's valuable report to the king of Denmark we learn that after reaching Greenland *Löven* left the other two ships and soon returned home, but Cunningham and Hall sailed to Davis Strait and made a landfall in Greenland about 67°N at a spot named by Hall "Denmarkes Haven" on the south side of "Cunninghams Mount" (now Qaqatsiaq). After exploring parts of the country the expedition returned to Denmark with valuable cartographical data.

In 1606 King Christian sent out five ships, this time under the leadership of Godske Lindenow. Cunningham now commanded *Löven* and Hall was again pilot of the expedition and wrote an account of it. On this voyage they approached the shore of Labrador, then sailed almost to the mouth of Cumberland Sound and east to Greenland. This was Cunningham's last voyage to Canadian waters. He remained in the Danish navy until 1619 when he became governor (*lehnsman*) of Vardöhuus in northern Norway, a post which he held until 1651, shortly before he died.

T. J. OLESON

Purchas, *Pilgrimes* (1905–7), XIV, 318–38. *A collection of voyages and travels* [comp. Awnsham and John Churchill] (2d ed., 6v., London, 1732), VI. *Danish arctic expeditions* (Gosch), I.

D

DABLON, CLAUDE, priest, Jesuit, missionary, superior-general of the Jesuit missions in New France, geographer; b. 21 June 1619 (*al.* February 1618) at Dieppe (Normandy); d. 1697 at Quebec.

Father Dablon lived in New France from 1655 until his death. As his apostolate took him from Lake Nekouba (Nikabau) to Lake Ontario and Lake Superior, his zeal for the conversion of the Indians was heightened by a special interest in the geography of America, the interior regions of which were still unknown to European scholars. But Father Dablon's importance lies above all in the fact that he was the superior-general of the Jesuit missions in New France.

When Father Dablon reached Quebec, late in the summer of 1655, Father François LE MERCIER, the superior, sent him immediately with Father CHAUMONOT to the south of Lake Ontario, to work among the Onondaga nation of the Iroquois; the Onondagas had been requesting missionaries for two years, and had been promised them by Father SIMON LE MOYNE. Father Dablon's account of his journey contains a fairly precise description of the St. Lawrence River, from Montreal to Lake Ontario. A second trip in 1656, the object of which was to found Sainte-Marie-de-Ganentaa, allowed him to add certain details about the natural resources of the country and the customs of the inhabitants. After the failure of this mission, Father Dablon returned to Quebec, where for ten years he was to hold various offices: minister, bursar, class prefect, director of the Grande Congrégation, teacher of humanities and rhetoric.

In 1661, with Father Gabriel DRUILLETTES and five Frenchmen, he proceeded up the Saguenay as far as Chicoutimi, went to Lac Saint-Jean, and undertook an exploratory expedition with the object of determining whether the northern sea was linked in some manner to the western sea and the southern one. Having got to Nekouba the group had reached the level of the watershed, and dread of the Iroquois struck terror into the Montagnais who were acting as guides for the French.

In 1669 Father Dablon was named superior of the western missions; their centre was Sault Ste. Marie. A journey around Lake Superior with Father ALLOUEZ supplied information for a map which for the period was admirable in its exactness, and which American geographers have called *Carte des Jésuites*. It depicts Lake Superior and the beginning of lakes Huron and Michigan.

His appointment as superior of the Jesuit missions in New France brought Father Dablon back to Quebec in 1671. He served in this capacity for two terms: 1671–80 and 1686–93. Being interested in the exploration of the country, he recorded in the *Relations* the accounts of the journeys of Fathers MARQUETTE and ALBANEL to the Mississippi and to Lac Saint-Jean.

Father Dablon was obliged to take a stand on certain contentious matters: the trade in spirits and the acculturation of the Indians. He managed to do so tactfully according to all contemporary testimony, including that of M. Louis Tronson, the superior-general of the Sulpicians in Paris.

From 1655 to 1672 Father Dablon wrote several chapters of the *Relations*; the account of the journey to the northern sea (Hudson Bay) was published in 1662. The *Relation* of 1672, the last to be published in the 17th century, and the annual reports from 1673 to 1679, which remained unpublished for nearly two centuries, are also his work.

MARIE-JEAN-D'ARS CHARETTE, C.S.C.

ACSM, MSS 402, Notice biographique du P. Claude Dablon (1868), par Félix Martin. ASQ, MSS, 43, "Étude sur les Relations des Jésuites," par Félix Martin. *JR* (Thwaites). *JJ* (Laverdière et Casgrain). Delanglez, *Jolliet*. Marie de Saint-Jean-d'Ars, "A la recherche de la mer du Nord, 1661," *RHAF*, VIII (1954–55), 220–35. Rochemonteix, *Les Jésuites et la Nouvelle-France au XVIIe siècle*, II, 143–49, 361–75, *et passim*; III, 4, *et passim*.

DAILLEBOUST. *See* AILLEBOUST

DAILLON, JOSEPH DE LA ROCHE. *See* LA ROCHE

DALMAS, ANTOINE, Jesuit priest, missionary; b. 4 Aug. 1636 at Tours, France; assassinated 4 May 1693 at Fort Sainte-Anne (Albany), Hudson Bay.

Antoine Dalmas entered the Society of Jesus in Paris on 8 Oct. 1652, and studied at La Flèche, Bourges, and Paris. After taking his vows as a spiritual coadjutor on 2 Feb. 1670, he set out for Canada, where for nine years he carried on his ministry among the French at Laprairie, Cap-de-la-Madeleine, Sillery, and Quebec. During the ten years following this period he was employed at the Tadoussac mission, except for one year (1683) when he taught the lower grades at the Collège at Quebec. Finally, in 1693, he started out for Hudson Bay, where he joined Father Antoine Silvy*. There he was struck down with an axe by a Frenchman, who had just confessed another murder to him.

J. MONET

ACSM, MS 378, copy of a letter from Reverend Father Claude Dablon to the provincial of France on the subject of the murder. *JR* (Thwaites), LVIII, 295. Rochemonteix, *Les Jésuites et la Nouvelle-France au XVIIe siècle*, III, 274. See also HBRS, XXI (Rich), 303.

DAMOURS (d'Amours) DE CHAUFFOURS, MATHIEU, town-major of Quebec, ship-owner, member of the Conseil Souverain, Seigneur de Matane; b. 1618, son of Louis Damours, counsellor at the Châtelet in Paris, and of Élisabeth Tessier; buried 9 Oct. 1695 at Quebec.

Mathieu Damour's ancestors belonged to the French nobility and had possessed seigneuries in Anjou. The seigneury of Chauffours, situated near Angers, had been acquired in 1586 by Jean Damours, counsellor in the Parlement of Brittany. Mathieu Damours arrived at Quebec in 1651, along with his sister Élisabeth and his brother-in-law LOUIS-THÉANDRE CHARTIER de Lotbinière, on 13 October, probably on the same ship which brought Governor JEAN DE LAUSON. On 16 March 1652 Mathieu Damours signed before ROLLAND GODET a marriage contract with Marie Marsolet, daughter of Nicolas MARSOLET, the famous interpreter for the French in their dealings with the Algonkins. The *Jugements et délibérations du Conseil Souverain* inform us about the earliest activities at Quebec of Mathieu Damours, who "shortly after his arrival . . . was chosen to be Major of this town, and subsequently to be in command of a flying column."

When the Conseil Souverain was set up in 1663, Governor SAFFRAY de Mézy and Bishop Laval* appointed Mathieu Damours to be a councillor. He was present at the first meeting, 18 Sept. 1663, thus commencing a long career, for he was a member of the Conseil Souverain until his death. Damours was involved in some incidents which arose among the members of the council. Thus, from the spring of 1664 on, in the conflict which set the governor against the bishop, Damours was on the side of the governor, who maintained him in his functions. When the council was reorganized in December 1666, PROUVILLE de Tracy reappointed Damours as a councillor.

Subsequently the councillor's career was fairly peaceful, at least until 1681. In April of that year Damours obtained a fur-trading licence and spent part of the summer on his seigneury at Matane, whence he returned with a well-filled boat. As soon as he arrived at Quebec he was summoned to appear before Governor BUADE de Frontenac, who reproached him with having broken the terms of his contract by bringing back more merchandise than had been authorized. In spite of the councillor's protestations, the governor had Mathieu Damours imprisoned 12 Aug. 1681 in one of the rooms of the Château Saint-Louis. Despite the intervention of the members of his family and his friends, Damours was not released until more than two months later, on 20 October. It was perhaps an act of vengeance on Frontenac's part against a councillor who had not been too much in sympathy with him the previous year in the council.

On 8 Nov. 1672 Damours had acquired the seigneury of Matane, upon which he made absolutely no effort to develop agriculture and made no grants of land. It seems to have been solely the supplies of fish in the Rivière Matane that interested the seigneur, who had besides received a grant of land on the Saint John River that was reputed to be prosperous. He also received a land grant on the Rivière Métis from Intendant DUCHESNEAU, on 26 June 1677, with fishing rights on the St. Lawrence River.

Mathieu Damours died 9 Oct. 1659 at Quebec, and his wife, who had borne him 15 children, died 24 Nov. 1711 at Montreal. Several of their children settled in Acadia, where the Damours family was able in this way to take root. His sons, including MATHIEU DAMOURS DE FRENEUSE, carried on the line.

F. GRENIER

AJQ, Greffe de Rolland Godet, 16 mars 1652. *Jug. et délib.*, I, II, III. *Lettres de noblesse* (P.-G. Roy), II, 3–14. Claude de Bonnault, "Le Canada militaire, état provisoire des officiers de milice, de 1641 à 1760," APQ *Rapport*, 1949–51, 293. *BRH*, IV (1898), 110; XX (1914), 147. *DBF*, II, 707–11. P. de Montagu, "Les familles d'Amours de Serain et d'Amours de Chauffour," *BRH*, XXXIII (1927), 328–31. P.-G. Roy, "Mathieu Damours de Chauffours," *BRH*, XXXII (1926), 385–92.

DAMOURS (d'Amours) DE FRENEUSE, MATHIEU, seigneur in Acadia and member of the Conseil Souverain of New France in succession to his father; b. 14 March 1657 at Quebec, the son of MATHIEU DAMOURS DE CHAUFFOURS and Marie Marsolet; d. 1696.

Mathieu Damours studied for the priesthood and was in orders from 1677 to 1680 at the Quebec seminary but withdrew. Thanks to his father's influence, he and three of his brothers—Louis, Sieur de Chauffours*; René, Sieur de Clignancour*; Bernard, Sieur de Plaines*—received large seigneurial grants in Acadia. That of Mathieu Damours, dated 1684, included the land between Jemseg and "Nacchouac" (Nashwaak) on the River Saint John. Here he developed the best cultivated seigneury on the river and with the help of his brother Louis built a lumber mill. He brought in settlers, erected a residence and barns, built up a herd of livestock and was soon raising crops. In addition, he appears to have engaged in trade with the Indians. In 1689 he was appointed to the Conseil Souverain but only in the absence or on the death of his father; he appeared before that body for the oath-taking ceremony in 1690. He and his brothers were disliked by Governor JOSEPH ROBINAU de Villebon who complained to the home authorities that they were licentious and disobedient, making little effort to improve their properties—charges which were unreasonable in the case of Mathieu Damours.

In 1696, a New England expedition under Col. John Hathorne* attacked Fort Saint-Joseph (Nashwaak), headquarters of Governor Villebon. Mathieu Damours figured prominently in its successful defence. When Hathorne and his men withdrew, they burned Damours's home and killed his cattle. Damours himself fell ill from exposure suffered during the attack and died soon afterwards.

His widow—Louise Guyon*, the widow of Charles Thibault, whom he had married in 1686—moved to Port-Royal (Annapolis Royal, N.S.) when Governor Jacques-François de Brouillan* established his headquarters there. There seems little doubt that during the years she was at Port-Royal she was on intimate terms both with the governor and the Sieur Denys* de Bonaventure, a prominent naval captain. This caused her to be one of the most talked about persons in New France. In 1708 she was sent to Quebec and there received in high social circles. Three years later she reappeared at Port-Royal, now in English control, having crossed the Bay of Fundy in a birch-bark canoe in mid-winter with only an Indian and her youngest son to help. She was given permission to settle there. Soon afterwards a force of English soldiers was ambushed and that same evening Mme Damours was taken to safety by a French force, adding weight to the suspicion that she had only returned to Port-Royal to serve the French cause.

GEORGE MACBEATH

AN, Col., B, 16, 17, 19 (see PAC Report, 1899, Supp., 296, 307, 309 f., 314). Jug. et délib., III, IV. Lettres de noblesse (P.-G. Roy). P.-G. Roy, Inv. concessions, IV, 2; Inv. contrats de mariage, II, 119.

W. O. Raymond, The River St. John, its physical features, legends and history from 1604 to 1784, ed. J. C. Webster (Sackville, 1943). P.-G. Roy, "Mathieu Damours de Chauffours," BRH, XXXII (1926), 385–94; "Mathieu Damours de Freneuse," ibid., 577–82. Webster, Acadia, 16, 17, 86–87, 170–74.

DANGÉ, FRANÇOIS, a musician accepted as a boarder by the Jesuits of Quebec in 1662. Father JÉRÔME LALEMANT in the *Journal des Jésuites* spells the surname "dangé" and "d'Anger"; J.-E. Roy gives it as "d'Augé" or "d'Auger."

The Jesuits began to accept college students as boarders in 1659; their policy was to finance "each only for the period of a year, so that they might be able to extend the charity to several." (Gosselin, in *Canada and Its Provinces*, XVI, 362, speaks of the "seminary" but as that was not founded until 1663 he must mean "college.") The Jesuit college had "about a score" of boarders in 1663. Lalemant wrote with reference to November 1662: "About this time, we received as boarders francois dangé, a musician, and la Marque, out of charity; for they knew not what would become of them." At Christmas of that year, the singers had been treated to a liberal share of beer and wine. "This made Amador so hoarse that he could not sing any more on the feasts; the same happened to other musicians, françois d'Anger and others." Lalemant's last reference to Dangé mentions that "On the 15th or 16th [December 1663] françois, the musician returned. We undertook to feed him out of charity, and Monseigneur the Bishop or the parish to supply him with *vestitum* [clothes]." The Jesuits' treatment of this young musician testifies to the importance they attached to musical talent.

HELMUT KALLMANN

JR (Thwaites), XLVII, 293, 295, 311. *BRH*, II (1896), 157–58. A.-E. Gosselin, "Education in Canada under the French régime," in *Canada and its provinces* (Shortt and Doughty), XVI, 361–73.

DANIEL, ANTOINE, priest, Jesuit, missionary to the Hurons; canonized by Pope Pius XI on 29 June 1930; b. 27 May 1601 at Dieppe; killed 4 July 1648 in Huronia.

Antoine Daniel had already begun his legal studies when he entered the noviciate of the Society of Jesus at Rouen on 1 Oct. 1621. He was a teacher of junior classes at the Collège in Rouen (1623–27), studied theology at the Collège in Clermont (1627–30), taught humanities (1630–1631), and was minister at the Collège in Eu (1631–32). On 1 Aug. 1626 Father CHARLES LALEMANT wrote from Quebec to his brother JÉRÔME: "A little Huron is going to see you; he longs to see France. He is very fond of us and manifests a strong desire to be instructed; nevertheless, his father and the Captain of the nation wishes to see him next year, assuring us that, if he is satisfied, he will give him to us for some years. It is of importance that he should be thoroughly satisfied, for if this child is once instructed, it will open the way to many tribes where he will be very useful." AMANTACHA *dit* Louis de Sainte-Foi, was baptized at Rouen during the time that Father Daniel was a teacher at the college. Certain historians have asserted that Father Daniel had prepared Amantacha for baptism; this affirmation has not been completely proved. But the presence of the young Huron at Rouen did not escape Daniel's notice, and it may be that it played some part in his missionary vocation.

In 1632 Father Daniel arrived at Cape Breton, where the habitation was under the command of his brother, Capt. CHARLES DANIEL. The following year, on 24 June 1633, he was at Quebec and was assigned, with Jean de BRÉBEUF, to the Huron mission, but their departure did not take place until 1634. No missionary experienced the hardships and perils offered at that period by the trip into Huronia as much as Father Daniel did; in 1634, and again in 1638, he was abandoned on the way by his guides; he soon found himself not only alone but ill, and he attributed to special divine protection the fact that he was able to reach his destination at all. The return trip he made in 1636 was equally arduous, and when he arrived at Trois-Rivières he was literally exhausted.

He made rapid progress in learning the language, and he had soon taught the children to sing the Pater and the Credo in Huron. His kindness, his gentleness, and his gifts as a teacher caused him to be assigned to a new apostolate that the missionaries, in their lack of experience of the actual circumstances, thought both feasible and full of promise for the propagation of the faith: the founding at Quebec of a seminary to which young Hurons would come to be trained in Christian knowledge and virtues. So great were the hopes aroused by this foundation that Huronia sacrificed for it one of its best missionaries, and the Jesuits at Quebec deprived themselves of the services of five very useful servants. Two years' experience was to show that the children of Huronia were not suited to, and not suitable for, this European type of education. The splendid dream came to naught, and brought about Father Daniel's return to active missionary life. He devoted himself to it indefatigably and effectively for ten years. On 4 July 1648 the Iroquois overran the Saint-Joseph II mission (Teanaostaiaë, near Hillsdale, Simcoe County, Ontario) just as Father Daniel was finishing his mass. He encouraged the neophytes and spoke so movingly of the truths of the faith that the pagans in large numbers asked him to baptize them. After wreaking havoc in the village, the Iroquois attacked the chapel: "Flee," said the missionary to his congregation, "and keep the faith to your dying breath." As for himself, his life belonged to the souls in his charge. He left the chapel and strode towards the enemy, who were astonished by such courage. When the first moment of stupefaction had passed, his body was riddled with arrows. A bullet struck him in the chest, passing through his body, and he fell uttering the name of Jesus. After desecrating his body, the Iroquois threw it into the fire that was consuming the chapel. As the first martyr of Huronia, Father Daniel, even after his death, inspired in his brother missionaries a wealth of tenderness and encouragement. The Relation for 1649 has preserved two instances of this for us.

The Hurons had given Father Daniel the name of An8ennen.

LÉON POULIOT

ACSM, "Mémoires touchant la mort et les vertus des pères Isaac Jogues . . ." (Ragueneau), repr. APQ *Rapport, 1924–25*, 3, 51. *JR* (Thwaites), in particular the Relation of 1649 (XXXIV, 86–96) *et passim*. *Positio causae.*

Campbell, *Pioneer priests*, II, 197–244. Lucien Campeau, in *Lettres du Bas-Canada*, II (1948), gives a critical study of the three accounts of the death of Father Daniel that have come down to us. Much the best study is by Fernand Potvin, "Saint Antoine Daniel, martyr canadien," *RHAF*, VIII (1954–55), 395–414, 556–64; IX (1955–56), 74–92, 236–49, 392–409, 562–70; X (1956–57), 77–92, 252–56. Rochemonteix, *Les Jésuites et la Nouvelle-France au XVIIe siècle*, II, 74.

DANIEL, CHARLES, sea captain, member of the Compagnie des Cent-Associés, founder of Fort Sainte-Anne on Cape Breton, second son of Antoine Daniel, a Dieppe merchant, and Marguerite Martin; d. 1661.

He was a brother of the Jesuit, ANTOINE DANIEL. His older brother André, a doctor, and one of his younger brothers, François, were also sea captains. In 1626 Charles Daniel, who already had experience in sailing to New France, was in partnership with GUILLAUME DE CAËN in the Compagnie de Ventadour and was engaged in fishing off Cape Breton. He had several skirmishes with the Basques, which resulted in some loss of life.

At the time that the Compagnie des Cent-Associés was being set up, he and his brother André became members of it. In 1629 he hired out two of his ships to the company and was to join at La Rochelle RAZILLY's fleet, which had the mission of coming to Champlain's aid at Quebec. However, as peace had been restored, Razilly was picked to go to Morocco, André Daniel was sent to London to demand the return of Quebec and

Daprendesteguy

Acadia, while Charles Daniel received command of the flotilla of four ships and a bark which were sent to Canada.

A gale scattered these ships off the Newfoundland Banks and Daniel reached Cape Breton alone. There he learned of the capture of Quebec and of the settlement which a Scottish lord, James STEWART, Lord Ochiltree, had established at Port de la Baleine, from which he was holding fishing boats to ransom. Daniel went there, besieged and captured Fort Rosemar, demolished it, then returned to Cibou (Bras d'Or Bay), where he built Fort Sainte-Anne, with a dwelling, a chapel, and a magazine. There he left two missionaries, one of whom was Father VIMONT, and a garrison of 40 men, and took back to France James Stewart and 17 prisoners after leaving the others, including Capt. FERRAR, in England. For four years, using Fort Sainte-Anne as his base of operations, he traded in the Gulf, as far as Miscou and Tadoussac, sharing expenses and receipts equally with the Compagnie de la Nouvelle-France.

In the autumn of 1632 the Cent-Associés, who had regained possession of Canada but who were half-ruined, organized a private company to continue their operations in the St. Lawrence and sold Cape Breton Island to Pierre Desportes de Lignères. Daniel then dropped his interest in the parent company, which still owed him money for the construction of Fort Sainte-Anne, and sold his share to a merchant from Paris, Nicolas Libert. Shortly afterwards, however, he joined a private company, along with Desportes and Libert, for the development of Cape Breton. At that time he returned to Canada and entered into relations with CHARLES DE SAINT-ÉTIENNE de La Tour and David LOMERON for the purchase of furs. He ceased to have an interest in this company when it passed into Jean Tuffet's hands in 1636, but until 1639 he kept up business relations with Libert and La Tour.

About this time Richelieu called Capt. Daniel to take command of a warship. Under the Comte d'Harcourt's orders Daniel took part in a naval expedition against Spain, raided Sardinia and the islands, and was wounded in the neck by a shot from an arquebus. From that time on he was almost constantly on official service. In 1638 he commanded eight ships which had the responsibility of assuring freedom of trade for the French in the English Channel. In 1641 he was captain in command of the port of La Rochelle and inspector of the fleet. He had acquired the noble properties of Mesnil-Gaillard and Du Verger, and in 1648 he received letters of nobility. In 1659 he was the senior captain on the pay-roll. He died at the beginning of 1661, after frequenting Canadian waters for about 10 years and serving for nearly 40 years in the navy. His posterity was assured through his grand-daughter.

RENÉ BAUDRY

[For the French and English versions of the capture of the Scottish fort, see also MALAPART and STEWART.]

Voyage à la Nouvelle-France du Capitaine Charles Daniel de Dieppe, 1629, éd. J. Félix (Rouen, 1881): the chief source. Champlain's voyages in Champlain, *Œuvres* (Laverdière). *JR* (Thwaites). PRO, *CSP, Col., 1574–1660,* 104, 105, 106, 112.

Biggar, *Early trading companies,* 271–73. Robert Le Blant, "Les compagnies du Cap-Breton, 1629–1647," *RHAF,* XVI (1962–63), 81–94.

DAPRANDESTEGUY, MARTIN. See APRENDESTIGUY

DARONTAL. See ATIRONTA (fl. 1615)

DAULAC (Daulat), ADAM. See DOLLARD

DAUMONT DE SAINT-LUSSON, SIMON-FRANÇOIS, regimental officer, explorer; d. some time after the spring of 1677.

He arrived at Quebec probably in 1663, together with the investigating commissioner GAUDAIS-DUPONT. In January 1664 he obtained a tract of the HÉBERT fief, near Beauport, which was to cause him legal complications from 1668 to 1671.

On 3 Sept. 1670 Intendant TALON appointed him a deputy commissioner "to seek out the copper mine in the country of the Ottawas, the Nez-Percés [Amikoues], and the Illinois, and of other nations discovered or to be discovered in North America in the region of Lake Superior or Freshwater Sea." What was being undertaken was a systematic study of the country, following the accounts brought back by the first travellers and the details supplied by the first explorers CAVELIER de La Salle, BRÉHANT de Galinée, Dollier* de Casson, Adrien Jolliet, and MARQUETTE. Indeed Daumont de Saint-Lusson, as well as making soundings at the Lake Superior copper mine, was to attempt to discover the northwest passage in a northerly direction, whereas La Salle was instructed to proceed towards the "southern sea." It was Talon's reply to the English expansion into Hudson Bay.

Saint-Lusson, accompanied by the interpreter Nicolas Perrot*, left Montreal in October 1670 via the Ottawa River, Lake Nipissing, the Rivière des Français (French River), and the Great Lakes; he went ashore at the village of Sault Ste. Marie, where the Jesuits maintained a fairly prosperous

Daumont de Saint-Lusson

mission. On 4 June 1671 he called together all the Indian nations that could be reached; there were 14 of them.

In the presence of this important gathering of nations and a few prominent Frenchmen a ceremony took place which had important diplomatic consequences. The interpreter Perrot, in the name of the king of France, began to read in the Indian language from the document that confirmed the appropriation by France of this immense territory, discovered and yet to be discovered, which stretched from the seas of the north and west to that of the south. Then they erected a cross, "to bring forth there the fruits of Christianity," and immediately beside it a cedar post bearing the arms of France. As the crowd, made up of both French and Indians, uttered repeated cheers of "Long live the king," a "sod of earth" was lifted in the air three times, in a symbolic gesture. Henceforth this part of a continent belonged to the king of France, and these 14 nations were dependent on His Majesty and subject to his laws and customs. In return they could count on his protection. The French intoned the *Vexilla Regis*, to the great wonderment of the Indians. Then Father ALLOUEZ delivered a harangue to the Indians in which he extolled the power of Louis XIV, "the Captain of the greatest Captains." Daumont de Saint-Lusson then spoke, and expressed himself "in martial and eloquent language." In the evening a splendid bonfire was lighted, presents were exchanged, and a *Te Deum* was sung to thank God, in the Indians' name, for having made of them "the subjects of so great and powerful a Monarch."

Some Hurons and Ottawas, who arrived late for the ceremony, likewise swore allegiance to Louis XIV. Saint-Lusson's official journey, which cost the king of France nothing and which added a segment—somewhat symbolically it is true—to his empire, in fact marks the beginning of the planned explorations that were to lead to James Bay, the Gulf of Mexico, and the Rocky Mountains.

As soon as Saint-Lusson returned to Quebec late in the summer of 1671, he was again sent on a mission, with instructions to proceed with the establishment of a means of communication between Quebec, Pentagouet (Castine, Maine), and Port-Royal (Annapolis Royal, N.S.), and to examine a copper deposit in Acadia. He returned the following 11 November, half-dead: "the sieur de Saint-Lusson returns from Pentagouet," Talon reported to the minister, "but so broken down by the fatigue of his journey, and so enfeebled by the hunger he suffered, that I doubt his ability to go to France, whither I should be very glad he would repair to have the honor to inform you, in person, what he saw at the Rivers Pemcuit and Kiniliki." Consequently the intendant, after extolling the explorer's courage and devotion, seized this opportunity to solicit for him a post at Quebec or in Acadia.

However, Saint-Lusson made a rapid recovery, since he embarked soon afterwards on the *Saint-Jean-Baptiste*, bound for Dieppe. He reached there in January 1672, bringing exotic mementoes: "A live moose about six months old, a fox and 12 large wild geese, which he hastened to go and present to the king." On 3 November of the same year he was granted the Île aux Lièvres seigneury, in the lower St. Lawrence region. On the following 31 December he was already back in New France, since he was present at the signing of the marriage contract between Jean DEMOSNY and Catherine Fol at Quebec.

What became of him subsequently? All we know is that at an undetermined date he returned to the mother country, whence he was preparing to get back to the colony in the spring of 1677; this is revealed by the correspondence of Abbé DUDOUYT with Bishop Laval*. Indeed on the 12 May M. Dudouyt wrote from Paris: "Saint-Lusson is making ready to go back to Canada without knowing what he will do there. I am likewise afraid that he will be what he was before." In another letter he noted: "Monsieur de Saint-Lusson is returning to Canada with no clear notion of what he should do. I see no change in his conduct; he says he wants to live differently from before." These comments, less flattering than the intendant's, appear to lend veracity to an enigmatic remark by Bacqueville de La Poterie [Le Roy*] on the subject of Saint-Lusson's expedition to Sault Ste. Marie: "his behaviour on that undertaking was so disorderly, to say nothing stronger," wrote La Poterie, "that I will content myself with reporting that he was dispatched to Acadia to be sent back to France."

About Saint-Lusson's family we possess nothing but confused and fragmentary information. According to Talon's letter of 11 Nov. 1671 to the minister, Saint-Lusson had at that period a wife and daughter in France, as well as another daughter in the colony. The latter is probably the "Magdeleine daumont St Lusson" whose signature appears on Demosny's marriage contract, and who is mentioned in the *Armorial de France* of d'Hozier as being the daughter of Simon-François Daumont de Saint-Lusson and Marguerite La Verge. On the other hand Tanguay's dictionary gives Marguerite Bérin as the name of Saint-Lusson's wife. Did the explorer marry twice? That is a matter for conjecture. Be that as

Dauphin de Montorgueuil

it may, this Marguerite Bérin must not be confused, as has often been done, with her namesake Marguerite Berrin, who married Julien Bouin on 2 July 1675; at that date Saint-Lusson was still alive, and moreover Marguerite Berrin was never the widow of Julien Bouin, who survived her and married again in July 1684. Finally, Saint-Lusson is said to have had a son, christened Jean-Baptiste, in June 1673.

LÉOPOLD LAMONTAGNE

ASQ, Lettres, N, 48²ᵉ, p.10; S, 93, p.5. *Coll. de manuscrits relatifs à la Nouv.-France*, I, 213, 217–18. Correspondance de Talon, APQ *Rapport, 1930–31*, 159, 165, *et passim*. *Découvertes et établissements des Français* (Margry), I, 87f., 92–99. *JR* (Thwaites), LV, 104–14. *Jug. et délib.*, I, III. La Pot(h)erie, *Histoire*, II, 124–30. *NYCD* (O'Callaghan and Fernow), IX, 74, 803f., *et passim*. Perrot, *Mémoire* (Tailhan), 126–28, 290–95. P.-G. Roy, *Inv. concessions*, II, 274f.; III, 116. *BRH*, XLVI (1940), 159f. Delanglez, *Jolliet*. Faillon, *Histoire de la colonie française*, III, 307–9. Ernest Gagnon, *Louis Jolliet, découvreur du Mississipi et du pays des Illinois, premier seigneur de l'île d'Anticosti* (Montréal, 1946), 48–59. Godbout, "Nos ancêtres," APQ *Rapport, 1959–60*, 325. Lionel Groulx, *Notre grande aventure: l'empire français en Amérique du Nord (1535–1760)* (Montréal et Paris [1958]). L. P. d'Hozier et A.-M. d'Hozier de Sérigny, *L'armorial général, ou registres de la noblesse de France* (6 registres en 10v., Paris, 1738–68). P.-G. Roy, "Jean Peré et Pierre Moreau dit la Taupine," *BRH*, X (1904), 219. Benjamin Sulte, "Les Français dans l'Ouest en 1671," *RSCT*, 3d ser., XII (1918), sect.I, 1–31. Tanguay, *Dictionnaire*, I, 159.

DAUPHIN DE MONTORGUEUIL, naval officer, JOSEPH ROBINAU de Villebon's lieutenant, son of the governor of Châtellerault (France); d. probably 1694.

On 1 June 1689 the king had appointed him Villebon's lieutenant at Port-Royal (Annapolis Royal, N.S.). The following spring Sir William PHIPS seized this post. A few days after the departure of Phips's soldiers, 14 June, Villebon returned from France. Fearing that the occupation troops from Boston would arrive very soon, he decided to set up the seat of French government at Fort Jemseg, on the Saint John River. A messenger was dispatched to Fort Saint-Louis de Chedabouctou (Guysborough, N.S.), carrying orders to Lieut. Montorgueuil, who was in command there with about 12 men, to come and rejoin Villebon. But Chedabouctou had already been captured by Phips's soldiers, under the leadership of Capt. Cyprian Southack*. The two chief participants in the event, Southack and Montorgueil, have each left an account of the battle. The former says that it took place on 5 June 1690 (O.S.), whereas the latter places it on 14 June (N.S.). The heroic defence put up by Montorgueuil on that occasion earned him the praise of BUADE DE Frontenac in a dispatch addressed to the minister in November of the same year.

Montorgueuil was a prisoner of the English in August 1690 at Bilbao; in 1691 he was again taken prisoner, this time by a privateer from Middleburg, and was released some while later. At that time he was appointed a naval ensign. On 7 May 1692 he was listed among the naval officers selected by the king to serve on the ships that his majesty was having fitted out at Rochefort for Canada.

It is very likely that Dauphin de Montorgueuil is the person of the same name, a "lieutenant serving on a frigate or a flute from the port of Rochefort," who died 26 July 1694 on board the *Solide*, off the Santo Domingo coast.

J.-ROGER COMEAU

AN, Col., B, 15, f.83; C¹¹ᴬ, 11, p.190 (PAC copy); Marine, B³, 62, ff.278–82; 64, ff.330–31v. PAC, FM 8, Cor. off., A 1, 7. PRO, C.O. 5/1081. *Coll. de manuscrits relatifs à la Nouv.-France*, I, 505–6. Aegidius Fauteux, "Dauphin de Montorgueuil," *BRH*, XXVIII (1922), 159. J.-F.-L. d'Hozier, *L'Impôt du sang, ou la noblesse de France sur les champs de bataille*, éd. Louis Paris (3v., Paris, 1874–81); *NYCD* (O'Callaghan and Fernow), IX, 921. Webster, *Acadia*, 8, 9, 207–8.

DAVAUGOUR, PIERRE DUBOIS. *See* DUBOIS

DAVID, CLAUDE, *voyageur*, settler; b. 1621 in France; d. 1687 at Cap-de-la-Madeleine.

Although one author has coupled the title of doctor with his name, there is no evidence that he practised medicine in Canada. On 2 June 1647 Governor Charles HUAULT de Montmagny granted him permission to clear the Île aux Cochons (Île du Milieu, today Île Maillet) situated at the junction of the St. Maurice River and the St. Lawrence. In 1649, at Trois-Rivières, he married Suzanne de Noyon, born in 1633, daughter of Édouard de Noyon and Catherine Chevalier. Claude David had seven children, all of whom were baptized at Trois-Rivières. An act granting land and dated 20 Oct. 1654 speaks of "Île de Claude David," next to the fief of Île Saint-Christophe. In an act of 7 April 1660 he figures as the owner of a grant at Trois-Rivières, adjoining that of MATHIEU and CHARLES AMIOT.

Claude David took part in a trading expedition, led by CHOUART Des Groseilliers, which left Montreal in 1660 for Lake Superior; the voyage, which was to take a year, lasted three. In a letter dated 2 June 1661 and sent from the mission of Notre-Dame-du-Bon-Secours, which he calls "Chassahamigan" (Baie Sainte-Catherine or Keweenaw Bay, Michigan), the Jesuit René MÉNARD mentions his companion Claude David, "who repairs the fire-arms."

On the occasion of a dispute with the Jesuits of Trois-Rivières, which was brought before the Conseil Souverain 30 Jan. 1664, Claude David and two of his fellow-settlers represented the inhabitants of the locality.

On 20 Jan. 1679 he granted a loan to Michel Pelletier de La Prade, seigneur of Gentilly. David died at Cap-de-la-Madeleine, near Trois-Rivières, and was buried there 2 Dec. 1687.

ANTONIO DROLET

ASQ, Documents Faribault, 161; Fonds Verreau, VIII, liasse 1, f.3, p.4; f.7. *JR* (Thwaites), XLVI, 142, 301f.; LXXI, 86. *Jug. et délib.*, I, 112. P.-G. Roy, *Inv. concessions*, I, 247; II, 29, 71. L. P. Kellogg, *The French régime in Wisconsin and the Northwest* (Madison, Wis., 1925), 115. P.-G. Roy, "Mathieu Amyot Villeneuve," *BRH*, XXV (1919), 323; *Noms géographiques de la province de Québec* (Lévis, 1906).

DAVIS (Davys), JOHN, navigator and explorer, discoverer of Davis Strait and the Falkland Islands, compiler of first *Sailing Directions* for the East Indies; b. 1550? on a small freehold at Sandridge near Dartmouth, Devon; married 29 Sept. 1582, to Faith Fulford, daughter of Sir John Fulford, by whom he had a daughter and four sons, three of whom survived him; d. 27 Dec. 1605 off Bintang Island, East Indies.

His childhood neighbours and lifelong friends were Humphrey and Adrian GILBERT and their younger half-brother, Walter Raleigh. Nothing is known of his early life, but his writings and his later friendships with the outstanding English mathematicians and cartographers of his day suggest he had at least a grammer school education, and certainly, by 1579 he was already highly regarded as a seaman and navigator.

Like many of his contemporaries, he was convinced of the existence of a northwest passage; his great ambition was to discover it and thus provide English commerce with a direct route to the Indies free from Spanish or Portuguese interference. By 1585 his friends had succeeded in persuading the queen's secretary, Sir Francis Walsingham, to lend his patronage to such a voyage of discovery; ships and money had been provided by wealthy merchants of London and Devon, and Davis was placed in command. He sailed from Dartmouth 7 June, 1585, with the *Sunneshine* of London (50 tons) and the *Mooneshine* of Dartmouth (35 tons)—which Davis persistently called the *Moonelight*—and returned 30 September. He had reached Greenland, whose existence had been forgotten by most Europeans since contact with its Norse colonies had been lost in the 13th century, and, after crossing what was subsequently named Davis Strait, he had made landfall on the east Baffin coast in Exeter Sound at about 66°40′N. He had not found the passage, but was now confident it lay either west up Cumberland Gulf (now Sound) or farther north up Davis Strait.

On 7 May 1586, Davis set out on his second arctic voyage. In addition to the two original ships he had also the *Mermayde* (120 tons) and a pinnace, the *North Starre* (10 tons). The *Sunneshine* and the *North Starre*, detached to search for a "Northward" passage between Greenland and Iceland, were turned back by ice, and the *North Starre* was lost in a storm. The *Mermayde* and the *Mooneshine* continued on to Davis Strait where conditions were less favourable than in the previous year. The *Mermayde* proved unwieldy in the ice and was finally sent home. Crossing to the west side of the strait, the *Mooneshine* continued alone until stopped by ice at roughly 67°N. Standing well off shore because of the wind, Davis sailed south to about 54°30′N (Hamilton Inlet) where he replenished his food supplies with abundant catches of cod. He returned home 14th October.

Davis sailed again 19 May 1587. This time the *Sunneshine* and the bark, *Elizabeth* of Dartmouth, were to engage in cod-fishing while Davis, in the 20-ton pinnace, *Ellen (Helene)* of London, continued his explorations. Conditions along the west Greenland coast were exceptionally favourable and he reached 72°12′N through ice-free waters before stiff winds forced him to alter course. Here, at his farthest north, he named a high cliff "Sanderson, his Hope" (now Hope Sanderson) in honour of his chief backer, William Sanderson, wealthy merchant of London. He then sailed west until further progress was blocked by the ice-stream of the Canadian current. He turned south down the Baffin coast, explored again Cumberland "Gulf," and noted the entrances to Lord Lumley's Inlet (now Frobisher Bay) and Hudson Strait which he described as a "furious overfall." He named Cape Chudleigh (now Chidley), its southeastern limit, entered the Labrador fiord which still bears his name (Davis Inlet) and finally reached the vicinity of Hamilton Inlet. He returned home 15 September, having successfully navigated his tiny vessel through more than 20° of arctic waters. He had charted long stretches of the Greenland, Baffin, and Labrador coasts, had

Davost

made careful observations of ice conditions, terrain, rock formations, weather, vegetation, and animal life. His description of the Eskimos is one of the earliest, and certainly one of the most accurate and sympathetic accounts of their habits of life. His "Traverse book" of this third voyage became the model on which ships' logs have since been patterned. Davis's original charts of these voyages have been lost, but the records of his discoveries were recorded on the maps of the period published after his return, especially the great map of the world (1598–1600) by his friend, the mathematician, Edward Wright, and the famous Molyneux globe (1592). It is, in fact, believed that it was probably Davis who introduced Molyneux to Sanderson, their mutual patron.

Never again was he to explore the Arctic. English energies were now absorbed in the struggle with Spain and, with the death of Walsingham in 1590, "the voyage was friendless." Davis, however, convinced that the discovery of this northwest passage would contribute to the growth of England's trade and thus to her national greatness, endeavoured to continue the search. In 1591 he joined the expedition of Thomas Cavendish who was attempting his second circumnavigation of the globe. It was agreed that once the Straits of Magellan were cleared, Davis and his ship would be released to continue exploration up the "backe side of America" in search of the western entrance of the passage. The expedition was a disastrous failure, its only achievement being Davis's discovery of the Falkland Islands. In 1595 he published his treatise, *The worldes hydrographical discription*, but this effort to gain support for the search so dear to his heart proved fruitless.

From 1598 to 1600 he served with distinction as pilot to the second Dutch expedition to the Indies, and on his return to London was appointed chief pilot to the highly successful first expedition of the East India Company. He returned home September 1603.

In December 1604, as pilot to Sir Edward Michelborne, he sailed aboard the *Tiger* (240 tons) on his third Indies voyage during which he charted the west coast of Sumatra and compiled the first known "Sailing directions" of the area. Off the east coast of Malaya the *Tiger* took a Japanese pirate ship in custody and, on 27 Dec. 1605, during a search of this ship, the pirates broke loose, killing Davis as their first victim.

Davis's life as a sailor and explorer was dedicated to the service of his country and the science of navigation in the best tradition of Elizabethan seamanship. Although during the wars with Spain he served in the naval campaigns, he was essentially a man of peaceful pursuits and quiet humour, highly regarded by his colleagues and crews for his fine character and outstanding competence, his patient, sympathetic understanding, his measured judgments, and his ability to command. He was scholarly in his approach to the problems of navigation and seamanship and his *Seaman's secrets* (1599), which for many years remained the mariner's handbook of practical navigation, was published in order to share with fellow mariners the knowledge he had acquired in a lifetime of intelligent observation and experience at sea. He invented the backstaff, or Davis quadrant, which remained the approved instrument for determining latitude until the introduction of the reflecting quadrant in 1731. His treatise *The worldes hydrographical discription* (1595) provided a masterly summary of the geographical knowledge of his time, particularly in relation to the northwest passage. It has been rightly said of him that, in his arctic discoveries, he lighted HENRY HUDSON into his strait and BAFFIN into his bay and indicated to Hans Egede the scene of his Greenland labours.

MARGARET MONTGOMERY LARNDER

Most of the original accounts of Davis's voyages, as well as *The worldes hydrographical discription* (London, 1595) are published in vols. III and IV of *Hakluyt's collection of the early voyages, travels and discoveries of the English nation* [ed. R. H. Evans] (5v., London, 1809–12), and in *A selection of curious, rare and early voyages and histories of interesting discoveries, chiefly published by Hakluyt, or at his suggestion, but not included in his . . . compilation, to which, to Purchas, and other general collections, this is intended as a supplement* [ed. R. H. Evans] (London, 1812). See also: Hakluyt, *Principal navigations* (1903–5), VII. The account of his last voyage and his death, written it is thought by Michelborne himself, is found in Purchas, *Pilgrimes* (1905–7), II, 347–66. There are also two excellent biographies: *The voyages and works of John Davis, the navigator* by A. H. Markham (Hakluyt Soc., 1st ser., LIX, 1880), which also contains a reprint of *Seaman's secrets* ("Newly corrected by the Author," London, 1599) and C. R. Markham, *A life of John Davis, the navigator, 1550–1605, discoverer of Davis Straits* (London, 1889). See also Oleson, *Early voyages*, 77, 88, 156–60.

DAVOST, AMBROISE, priest, Jesuit, missionary; b. 13 Nov. 1586 at Laval (Maine, France); d. 27 Sept. 1643 at sea.

Ambroise Davost became a Jesuit on 14 Oct. 1611 at Rouen, and studied principally at Bourges. In 1632 he went with Father ANTOINE DANIEL to Cape Breton Island. He remained at the Sainte-Anne post, which was in charge of Father Daniel's brother, Capt. CHARLES, until May 1663, when CHAMPLAIN took him to Quebec. In 1634 he set out for the Huron country, on the same expedition as Fathers BRÉBEUF and Daniel; he returned from it two years later, with the young Hurons [see TEOUATIRON] who were to help found Father Daniel's "seminary" near Quebec, where Davost stayed for two years as a tutor to the French children. During those years he was ill almost the whole time, particularly from scurvy; in 1643, stricken with a heavy fever, he left to seek treatment in France. He died before arriving and was buried at sea.

J. MONET

ACSM, Notes biographiques. *JR* (Thwaites), V, 290; XXXVI, 249. René Latourelle, "Saint Jean de Brébeuf, routier de la Huronie," *RHAF*, IV (1950–51), 325–26. Fernand Potvin, "Saint Antoine Daniel, martyr canadien," *RHAF*, VIII (1954–55), 558–63; IX (1955–56), 74–84, 92, 236.

DAVYS. *See* DAVIS

DEKANAHWIDEH (Deganawidah, the Heavenly Messenger), reputed founder of the Five Nations Confederacy, and the culture hero of the Iroquois.

The legend that grew up about him long served as a guide to Iroquois conduct, at home and abroad. In its various recorded versions it now appears a strange medley of religion, mythology, constitutional law, wisdom literature, animal lore, and folk custom. But the core of the narrative, which describes the practical steps taken by Dekanahwideh, the "Heavenly Messenger," to establish a firm League of Nations under the Tree of Peace, has a grandeur of conception unsurpassed in popular tradition anywhere in the world.

According to the legend, Dekanahwideh was born among the Huron Indians near the Bay of Quinte, on what is now the Thayendanaga or Deseronto Reservation. His virgin mother had been informed in a dream by a messenger from the Creator that she was to bear a son destined to plant the Tree of Peace at Onondaga (Syracuse, New York).

When the child was born, he was named Dekanahwideh. On reaching manhood, he explained to his mother the mission on which the Great Spirit had sent him, which was to bring "the good news of peace and power" to men: to show them how to make their desire for peace and justice effective by union under civil authority backed by military potential. When the time came to say farewell, he took his mother to a tree on a hill near the water and instructed her to come there once a year after his departure and strike the tree with a hatchet. If blood flowed from the cut, she would know that he had failed; if sap, that he was alive and successful. The hill is still held in reverence by the Iroquois people. Chiefs from the Six Nations Reserve near Brantford, Ontario, visit it at least once a year to burn sacred tobacco and offer prayer to the Great Spirit.

Crossing Lake Ontario in a canoe made of white stone (his first miracle), Dekanahwideh came to the country of the Onondagas. There he sought out a notorious murderer and cannibal, resolved to make this encounter the first test of his power. Finding the man's cabin empty, Dekanahwideh climbed to the bark roof and, lying prone, peered down through the smoke hole. Below him he saw a kettle of water on the fire. When the Onondaga warrior returned to his cabin and looked into the kettle, he saw a reflection of Dekanahwideh's face. Since no one else was in the cabin, the warrior thought it was a reflection of his own face; and he was struck by the contrast between the brutal life he was leading and the strong, gentle nobility of the face looking up at him out of the water. In revulsion, he emptied the kettle of its human contents and sat brooding by the fire over his failure to live up to what he now recognized to be his own true nature. When Dekanahwideh entered the cabin and delivered his message of peace and power, the warrior eagerly "took hold," offering himself as a disciple. Together the two laid plans for a campaign to bring neighbouring nations into a peaceful confederacy, with the intent that, as a 17th-century Iroquois was to say, "The land shall be beautiful, the river shall have no more waves, one may go everywhere without fear." The great obstacle to such a union was Atotarho, head chief of the Onondagas, a hideous tyrant whose body had seven crooks in it and whose hair was a tangle of live snakes. "You shall be called Hiawatha [He Who Combs]," said Dekanahwideh to his disciple, "for you shall comb the snakes out of Atotarho's hair."

Hiawatha (from whom Longfellow took little but the name) served as Dekanahwideh's spokesman. Some such arrangement appears to have been necessary, for, if the late William Dewaserage Loft of Ohsweken was correct, the name "Dekanahwideh" means "double row of teeth."

The two men separated for a time, Dekanahwideh going alone to the Canienga or Flint Nation (Mohawk). There the message of peace and power won many adherents, but sceptics demanded a sign. To satisfy them, Dekanahwideh climbed a tall tree on the edge of a cliff overlooking the Mohawk River. He instructed them to cut the tree down so that it would fall with him

Dekanahwideh

into the rapids. If he survived, they would know that his words were true. Having cut down the tree as directed, the Mohawks waited long on the bank, hoping to see cause to believe in him; but, as time passed and he did not reappear, they returned sadly to their village. Early next morning, a curl of smoke was seen on the bank where Dekanahwideh had fallen, and the Heavenly Messenger was observed sitting quietly beside his fire eating breakfast. The Mohawks reassembled, took hold of his message, and have forever since ranked as founders of the Iroquois Confederacy.

Hiawatha joined him here and the two were adopted into the Mohawk nation. Heading a band of Mohawk warriors and singing the peace hymn—"To the Great Peace bring we greeting . . . ," which ranks as the Iroquois national anthem—they proceeded west to the country of the Oneidas. These good friends of the Mohawks quickly took hold and joined the marching train. By-passing the Onondagas, who were terrorized by Atotarho, they went on to the Cayugas, who joined them, and all entered the Seneca country.

Here they found division, one party among the Senecas accepting but another rejecting the "good news." Dekanahwideh was constrained to perform another miracle. At his command, according to one version of the legend, "the sun went out and it was complete darkness." That sign was sufficient, and the dissident Senecas took hold.

Then the warriors of the four nations advanced on Atotarho in his "bulrush swale" near the shore of Onondaga Lake. Modern Indians locate the site on what is now the campus of Syracuse University. The threat of visible power, sweetened by the offer of the head-chiefship of the united nations if he would come in, brought Atotarho to reason, and Hiawatha combed the snakes out of his hair.

Thereupon Dekanahwideh "planted the Tree of Peace": a great white pine with "white [healthy] roots" extending to the four quarters of the earth in order to guide men everywhere who desired to trace peace to its source. Above the tree, he placed the "eagle that sees afar, symbol of military preparedness, to spy out danger. Under it he opened a cavern into which he threw the weapons of war. He put antlers on the heads of 50 chiefs representing the Five Nations (their names to become titles for the chiefs who succeeded them), and delivered to them the words of the "great law"—the constitution of the Five Nations.

His work accomplished, Dekanahwideh took leave of his people, instructing them to bring in other nations to sit with them under the Tree of Peace. He admonished the chiefs to exercise patience: "Your skins must be seven thumbs thick to withstand the darts of your enemies." He encouraged them to stand fast should evil days come upon them. If a high wind (war) should uproot the Tree of Peace, they were to look about for a great swamp elm and re-form the confederacy under its shelter. (After the Revolutionary War they found such an elm on the banks of the Grand River in Ontario.) If they ever found the league in extreme danger, he said, "Call on my name in the bushes and I will return." Today this last promise is much in Iroquois minds. Several times in the present century the chiefs have seriously debated whether the time had come to call on his name in the bushes.

At Deseronto, Ontario, the Mohawks have erected a stone monument on which are inscribed the traditional words of the founder: "I am Deganawidah, and with the Five Nations' Confederate lords I plant the Tree of the Great Peace . . ."

But the best monument to Dekanahwideh is the Six Nations Reserve by the Grand River. There the ancient forms of the league are still preserved. There the matrons nominate the chiefs, who are installed with the solemn rites instituted, it is traditionally believed, by Dekanahwideh. On such occasions, old nostalgic chants are heard: "Hail, my grandsires! Now hearken while your grandchildren cry mournfully to you —because the Great League which you established has grown old. . . . You have it as a pillow under your heads in the ground where you are lying . . . although you said that far away in the future the Great League would endure."

The confederacy is officially known as Kayanerenh-kowa (the Great Peace), a term which describes its function. It is also known as Kanonsionni (the Long-house), a term that describes both its geographical extent and its constitutional form. The long-house, typical Iroquois dwelling built of saplings and bark, was in shape not unlike a modern Pullman car but 80 to 100 or more feet in length. Several families of the same lineage occupied it, each within its own bark-partitioned apartment and with its own hearth fire, but all under the superintendence of an elder matron of the lineage.

So the Five Nations—Mohawks, Oneidas, Onondagas, Cayugas, and Senecas—stretched west along a war-path or ambassadors' road that extended through the Mohawk Valley and the Finger Lakes region; and so also each nation retained its sovereignty while at the same time joining its neighbours in giving a measure of authority to the Great Council at Onondaga, where chiefs of the Five Nations met to discuss their problems round "the fire that never dies." The sense of unity among these fiercely independent peoples was fostered by many ingenious devices, not least of which was the legend of Dekanahwideh and the sense of mission it evoked.

Women were highly honoured in Iroquois life, their status being in no way inferior to that of men. Not only was descent reckoned in the female line, but matrons of those lineages holding chiefly titles had power both to appoint the civil chiefs and, if these failed in their duty, to recall them—always, however, after consultation with the incumbent chiefs as well as with the "warriors and women," that is, the general public.

Although these and many other details of the social and political organization of the Five Nations are traditionally attributed to Dekanahwideh, it is probable that his function was not so much to create new laws as to codify existing customs among the several nations and provide a final stimulus for union.

Some scholars, while not denying historical foundation of a kind for the legend, question the historicity of Dekanahwideh himself. It has been suggested (see Anthony F. C. Wallace, "The Dekanawideh myth analyzed . . . ," *Ethnohistory*, V (1958), 118–30) that Dekanahwideh may have been the projection of an Indian prophet's vision. Undoubtedly popular imagination has contributed much to the growth of the legend over centures of oral transmission. Nevertheless the substantiality of the league itself, a phenomenon that the legend seeks to explain, is sufficiently attested by events in North American history.

That the league is very old can hardly be disputed. Benjamin Franklin in 1750 wrote that "it has subsisted ages and appears indissoluble." In 1654 the Jesuit missionary LE MERCIER noted in his Relation (*JR* (Thwaites), XLI, 87) that it had been in existence *de tout temps*, "from the earliest times." But the date of the founding is a subject of debate. There is evidence that the final union was the culmination of a long process of consolidation marked by a series of local confederacies—of Mohawk with Oneida and Seneca with Cayuga. Horatio Hale, a Canadian scholar who was at home among the Iroquois on the Six Nations Reserve as well as at Onondaga and who published *The Iroquois book of rites* in 1883, came to the conclusion that the union was completed "about the middle of the fifteenth century." The fact that, according to astronomical calculation (see Theodor von Oppolzer's *Canon der Finsternisse* (Vienna, 1887)), a total eclipse of the sun was visible in the Seneca country in 1451 (cf. Dekanahwideh's blotting out of the sun) is a curious coincidence if it is nothing more.

PAUL A. W. WALLACE

For information about Dekanahwideh and the founding of the Five Nations, the best sources are surviving versions of the legend: Seth Newhouse's MS, prepared on the Six Nations Reserve (with an English translation) in 1885, a photocopy of which is in the Amer. Philos. Soc. Library, Philadelphia; Newhouse's revision, published by Arthur C. Parker as "The constitution of the Five Nations, or the Iroquois book of the great law," *N.Y. State Bull.*, 184 (Albany, 1916); a version prepared by chiefs on the Six Nations Reserve in 1900 and published by D. C. Scott as the "Traditional history of the Confederacy of the Six Nations," *RSCT*, 3d ser., V (1911), sect.II, 195–246; a fuller and more philosophical version dictated by Chief John Arthur Gibson of the Six Nations Reserve to J. N. B. Hewitt of the Smithsonian Institution, 1899, and translated by William N. Fenton, still in MS at the Smithsonian; a still longer version by Chief Gibson dictated to Alexander A. Goldenweiser of Ottawa in 1912, now reposing, untranslated, in the Smithsonian. See also Paul A. W. Wallace, *The white roots of peace* (Philadelphia, 1946), a synthesis of the foregoing versions. Horatio Hale, *The Iroquois book of rites* (Philadelphia 1883; reprinted Toronto, 1963).

DELISLE, ACHILLE (ANTOINE-LOUIS?) BRÉHAUT DE. See BRÉHAUT

DEMESNU, JEAN-BAPTISTE PEUVRET. See PEUVRET

DEMOSNY, JEAN (or **Jean-Baptiste**) (the elder) deputy to the chief barber and surgeon to the king; b. 1643, son of Paul Demosny and Marie Filleul, from Grande in Normandy; d. 1687.

His duties made him reponsible for supervising the surgeon-barbers of New France, for examining their qualifications, and for checking on their knowledge and their medical competence. He was also the surgeon appointed to the Hôtel-Dieu at Quebec, succeeding Jean MADRY. On 9 Jan. 1673 he married Catherine Fol, who gave him two sons and five daughters, two of whom became Hospitallers of the Hôtel-Dieu in Quebec. In 1684–85 he was a churchwarden holding office in the parish of Notre-Dame de Québec. He died in 1687, leaving his widow in a precarious financial position; she remarried in 1691, becoming the wife of Claude Chasle. During his lifetime, Demosny had had to prosecute a good many patients who refused to pay for his treatments and for the remedies he had supplied to them. Some litigious cases were settled only several years after his death. He signed a good many

Denis de la Trinité

apprenticeship contracts such as that concluded between him and the parents of Ignace Pelerin, son of Pierre Pelerin de Saint-Amant and Louise de Mousseaux. By the terms of this notarial document, Demosny undertook to teach the young Pelerin "the art and craft of a surgeon and everything connected therewith," and to "furnish and supply him with subsistence, food and drink in his house, fire, bed and lodgings, and to treat him kindly and humanely as is proper."

One of his sons, also named Jean Demosny, was, like his father, surgeon at the Hôtel-Dieu of Quebec. He attempted to have his father's creditors pay their bills, and trafficked in liquor, which was probably more lucrative than surgery and the sale of remedies that the patients, once they were cured, neglected to pay for. Born 12 June 1674 at Quebec, he married on 18 Jan. 1701 Julienne Bisson, who bore him two children, the first of whom lived only a few weeks. He took as his second wife (1704) Marie-Louise Albert, daughter of Guillaume Albert. Seven children were born of this marriage. The younger Demosny died 11 June 1715.

CHARLES-MARIE BOISSONNAULT

Maude E. Abbott, *History of medicine in the Province of Quebec* (Toronto, 1931; McGill University pub., VIII, no. 63, 1932). Ahern, *Notes pour l'histoire de la médecine*. Boissonnault, *Histoire de la faculté de Médecine de Laval*.

DENIS DE LA TRINITÉ. *See* DENYS

DENYS, JEAN, a captain from Honfleur in Normandy; made a fishing trip to the coasts of America in 1506 with the pilot Gamard.

Denys is the first French sailor whose name is known to us after the expeditions to the New World made by unnamed Bretons as early as 1504. It is likely that he subsequently stopped over on occasion in Newfoundland, one of the ports of which bore the name "Le Hâvre de Jean Denys" (Jean Denys's Harbour); called Rognoust by the Basques, its name has now become Renews. It has been claimed that he made maps of the American coasts; indeed, a map entitled "Mouth of the St. Lawrence" is attributed to him. It can confidently be stated that this is a wrong attribution; the outline includes 17th-century names. Furthermore, French cartography had not yet come into existence in Denys's time.

GUSTAVE LANCTOT

JR (Thwaites), III, 21–283, IV, 7–117, Father Biard's Relation of 1616. *Memorials of the English and French commissaries*, I, 104. G. B. Ramusio, *Terzo volume delle navigationi et viaggi*... (1st ed., Venetia, 1556).

Anthiaume, *Cartes marines*. Henry Harrisse, *Découverte et évolution cartographique de Terre-Neuve et des pays circonvoisins, 1497, 1501, 1769* (Paris, 1900). Louis Legendre, *Vie du cardinal d'Amboise* (Rouen, 1724). *Sixteenth-century maps relating to Canada: a check-list and bibliography*, ed. T. E. Layng (PAC pub., 1956).

DENYS, NICOLAS, one of the leading figures in Acadia for over half of the 17th century; b. 1598 in Tours; d. 1688.

Probably a descendant of JEAN DENYS, the famous explorer who is said to have made a map of Canada in 1506, he was the son of Jacques Denys de La Thibaudière and Marie Cosnier. He himself stated that he belonged to "a family of engineers." While little is known of his early years, we can say he received little formal education but became proficient in navigation, the fishing business, lumbering, and administration. In 1632 we find him a merchant at La Rochelle and charged as agent and representative of the Compagnie de la Nouvelle-France with the responsibility of recruiting volunteers and fitting out the expedition being sent to Acadia under the command of Isaac de RAZILLY to take possession of the country under the terms of the Treaty of Saint-Germain-en-Laye and to establish a colony there.

The Razilly party, numbering some 300 men in three vessels, arrived at La Hève (near the modern Bridgewater, N.S.) on 8 Sept. 1632. Shortly afterwards, Denys started a sedentary fishing operation at Port Rossignol (now Liverpool). In 1634 Denys received from the commander a grant to a large, heavily wooded area at La Hève and the next year he began cutting white oak in the form of planks and beams for export to France in vessels owned by Razilly, his partner in this first Canadian lumbering venture. Razilly's death late in 1635 resulted in a severe set-back for the colony generally and Denys in particular. Charles de MENOU d'Aulnay, one of Razilly's lieutenants and his cousin, now assumed full authority and refused Denys permission to export his timber. This and the seizure without compensation of a ship and cargo of cod in a Portuguese port a few months earlier were the first misfortunes in this dauntless man's life. Indeed misfortune was to plague him continuously and limit sharply any lasting effect he was to have in the development of Acadia.

In the face of d'Aulnay's enmity and the confusion and strife that prevailed, Denys returned to La Rochelle where he again acted as the representative of the Compagnie de la Nouvelle-France. In addition, he arranged his own fishing and trading voyages to the coasts of Newfoundland and the Gulf of St. Lawrence, probably for the most part to the latter. About 1645 he obtained a concession from the company and built a fortified fishing and trading post on the south shore of Miscou Harbour. In addition he had land cleared and crops planted by the colonists he established. However, d'Aulnay by this time held the king's commission as governor of Acadia and refused to recognize the company's right to grant this privilege without his concurrence. In 1647 he seized the Miscou post and expelled Denys. Although he agreed to pay for the trade goods and other property seized, this was never done. There is a possibility that following this set-back Denys built a trading post on the Miramichi.

We do know, in any case, that on the receipt of the news of d'Aulnay's death in 1650, Denys went to Cape Breton with his brother, SIMON, for the purpose of fishing and trading. In the fall of 1651, soldiers sent by Mme d'Aulnay [see MOTIN] captured two posts occupied by the Denys, Saint-Pierre and Sainte-Anne, and took the two Denys as prisoners to Quebec. This seizure cannot have been recognized as legal by authorities there because Denys soon obtained his release and returned to Saint-Pierre. While remaining active there, in 1652 he built another branch at Nipisiguit (Bathurst). But he was not to enjoy this success for long. D'Aulnay had died heavily indebted to EMMANUEL LE BORGNE, a La Rochelle merchant who now claimed d'Aulnay's rights in Acadia until his claim against the estate was satisfied. In 1653 he ambushed and captured Denys at Saint-Pierre, seized all his goods found there and at Nipisiguit, and took him a prisoner to Port-Royal where Denys was chained and placed in a dungeon. Although he could not save himself, Denys had managed to warn CHARLES DE SAINT-ÉTIENNE de La Tour, who was able to withstand Le Borgne's subsequent attack on his fort. On Denys's release he hastened to France where he lodged a protest, for he claimed his post had been built under a commission from the company. Again, as in his dispute with d'Aulnay over the capture of his property at Miscou, the king ruled in Denys's favour. No compensation for loss was received, however, although the posts themselves were restored.

During this visit to France, Denys late in 1653 purchased from the Compagnie de La Nouvelle-France for 15,000 *livres* the rights to the coast and islands of the Gulf of St. Lawrence from Cap Canso to Cap des Rosiers on the Gaspé. This vast territory included Cape Breton as well as the Îles de la Madeleine, Île Saint-Jean (Prince Edward Island), and all other islands in the gulf. Shortly afterwards he was appointed governor and lieutenant-general of this territory. Denys now turned to organizing a fishing and trading company to operate within the limits of his grant. Partners with him in the venture were Christophe Fouquet de Chalain and the brothers Jacob and Abraham Duquesne. The new company made annual voyages between 1654 and 1664. Their vessel would leave France at the beginning of May and return in October with cod and furs. On the average, 15 sailors, 10 soldiers, and 16 tradesmen made up the party. The cost of each of these trips varied from 12,000 to 15,000 *livres*, exclusive of salaries.

Once this latest business venture was launched, Denys returned to Saint-Pierre and was successful in re-establishing his fishing station and his trade with the Indians, both there and at Nipisiguit, where JEAN BOURDON DE ROMAINVILLE was his lieutenant. Saint-Pierre remained his headquarters, and there he fished, traded, did some farming, built several small vessels, and cut timber. About 1659 he built another fishing establishment at Chedabouctou (Guysborough). In addition, he brought in cattle and settlers to fish and work the land. He began growing wheat, and made plans for a flour mill and the making of beer, which he hoped would replace imported wine as a beverage. The following year he dispensed with the services of all soldiers in his employ and moved with his family to Chedabouctou. The fact of the matter is that his fishing and trading company had not been a success. By 1658, his debts in this venture amounted to 51,520 *livres*. In 1664, he wrote Fouquet, president of the company, that he would not be able to pay off debts that his partners estimated were now close to 100,000 *livres*. Because of this, avenues of possible financial assistance were closed to him in the future.

Meanwhile, things were not going at all well at Chedabouctou. A M. de Canger and his lieutenant, La Giraudière, had been located there since 1658. By trickery and misrepresentation they succeeded in having the Compagnie de la Nouvelle-France extend their concession to include Denys's Chedabouctou post. An armed clash resulted and the conflict persisted for some years until Denys went to France and quickly secured a reaffirmation of his rights in Acadia by a grant issued on 9 Nov. 1667.

During the dispute with Canger, Denys had apparently moved his family back to Saint-Pierre. It was here his checkered career reached one of its lowest points during the winter of

Denys

1668–69 when his home and business at Saint-Pierre were completely destroyed by fire. This catastrophe brought him to financial ruin. Already, because of fire, plunder, and war, his business losses had amounted to well over 100,000 *livres*, a sizable sum for those days. Now, already a man of 70, he was forced to move his family to the post he had built at Nipisiguit (now Bathurst, N.B.). It consisted of an 18-foot-high stockade with four bastions enclosing his red sandstone house. Here it was that he turned to yet a new career: that of author.

It should be understood that Denys's most lasting contribution was neither as fisherman-trader, nor as promoter of settlement, but rather as the author of *Description géographique et historique des costes de l'Amérique septentrionale: avec l'histoire du païs*. This work was written at Nipisiguit and is one of the most valuable accounts of Acadia produced in the 17th century. On its completion, Denys prepared to leave for France to see to its publication because he obviously felt it would focus favourable attention on the country and stimulate settlement here. Before leaving, he appointed his son, RICHARD DENYS de Fronsac, as lieutenant, to be assisted by his mother, Marguerite Lafite. She had married Denys in 1642, accompanied him to Acadia, and bore: Richard; Marie, who married Michel Leneuf* de La Vallière; and possibly Marguerite, who married Capt. James Forsayth.

In France, Denys succeeded in having his study published in 1672. It comprised two volumes. The first is devoted to a description of the coastal area of Acadia from the Penobscot to Gaspé and to some of his experiences in this region. The second volume deals with fish and fishing, the natural resources generally of the region, and the Micmac Indians among whom he had lived for 40 years. It carries the title *Histoire naturelle des peuples, des animaux, des arbres et plantes de l'Amérique Septentrionale, & de ses divers climats. Avec une description exacte de la pesche des moluës, tant sur le Grand-Banc qu'à la Coste; & de tout ce qui s'y pratique de plus particulier*.

Poorly written, indicating both the author's lack of literary skill and his poor education, still this book is entertaining and of great value. Denys himself states in its pages: "You will excuse a fisherman. If I had given as much time to study as I have to instructing myself, and to investigating means, for following the Cod, ... I should have given you more satisfaction in all this account than I have done." In writing, Denys appears to have made few notes, relying mainly on his recollections at the cost of a number of errors. Yet he provides an invaluable picture of the country and its people, as well as of his own activities and those of such contemporaries as Razilly, d'Aulnay, La Tour, and Le Borgne. His description of the cod-fishery, for instance, has been termed the most complete and authoritative available. Those sections that deal with the other natural resources are, for the most part, remarkably enthusiastic and reflect his unquenchable optimism for the country. When we come to the Indians, he supplies the most satisfactory description that had yet appeared. In all, the book is clearly the product of the man of action, one who has a thorough knowledge of his subject but who lacks the fluency of style necessary to capture the attention of a large body of the reading public.

In Denys's eyes, the book must have seemed largely a failure because it neither cured his financial plight nor aided his efforts to settle Acadia. Yet, with his unbounded confidence in the future of this land, he continued to interest himself in his vast domain, although he apparently remained in France.

Of the several families of colonists which Denys had succeeded in bringing to Acadia, few remained. In 1662, for instance, he had only seven families of permanent settlers. Yet, by the terms of his 1653 grant, he had agreed to establish 80 such families. As a result of this failure to settle his lands as called for in his grant, the company from 1663 started issuing grants to part of Denys's territory, making concessions at Îles de la Madeleine, Chedabouctou, and Percé to others, such as Gautier [*see* BERGIER]. This breaking up of his seigneury was to trouble him deeply during these last years of his life. Even Denys's natural optimism must have been severely strained by this whittling away of his Acadian domain and by the fact that he was now absolutely without financial resources. We read, for instance, that early in 1685 he was living in beggary in Paris. It was probably in that same year he returned to Acadia to spend his last years at Nipisiguit. Because of his advanced age, it is unlikely that he took much part in business, being content to leave the management to his son. In 1687 the original grant to Nicolas Denys was revoked and on 17 April of that year the right to a large seigneury, "later to be chosen" was issued.

Nicolas Denys died in 1688 at the age of 89, in all probability at Nipisiguit. From his own writings and those of contemporary chroniclers we are able to piece together an impression of the man himself. He was blessed with a vigorous constitution, so much so that we gain the impression that he thrived on hardship. Little is known of his physical appearance except that he had a full, white beard which caused many of the Micmacs to refer to him as "*La Grande Barbe*." Among these Indians he exerted a strong influence. Tracing his activities, we become aware of an individual endowed with courage and determination, ability to command, business skill, and confidence in himself. Above all, he had no interest in war and conflict, having "no other aim than to devote myself in my district to my establishment and my business without mixing in the affairs of others." That he was unusually generous is borne out by the fact that twice he befriended the children of men who had done him ill. Possibly his prime quality was his honesty, a trait of character that is accepted by almost all historians. As a result, we are able to place unusual confidence in his statements concerning Acadia at a time when its development had been brought to a standstill by domestic squabbles and war.

A visionary, always striving to transform his dreams into reality, Denys sought to develop a great seigneury on New Brunswick's north shore. A forceful merchant, fisherman, and pioneer in the work of settlement, this man of astonishing activity clearly dreamed of his lands under cultivation, his ships loading cod and other fish for the European market, and great logs being rafted down the rivers to the sea for shipment to France. Unquestionably, much of this good would have been realized had his plans not been blocked and his financial ruin brought about by war, fire, heavy costs, and ruinous rivalries. What is more, his failure was no worse than that of a half dozen of his contemporaries, among them Le Borgne and d'Aulnay. Had he lived in another era, he might well have succeeded. As it was, none of his posts at Miscou, Nipisiguit, Saint-Pierre, and Chedabouctou became permanent. Yet the very fact that he had established these posts and through his writing made the country better known later encouraged others to come to these places and continue the work of pioneering. He himself observes in his study, "I believe that I have not altogether lost my time, even though it has been thwarted by a thousand misfortunes." Above all else, he was intimately connected with the material development of the country, a maker of history in Acadia for over half a century. His is the distinction of being the first Acadian author and lumberman, an arresting figure whose remarkable ability and force made him one of the principals in this new land during its infancy.

GEORGE MACBEATH

Denys, *Description and natural history* (Ganong). *JR* (Thwaites). *Mémoires des commissaires*, I, 48, 83, 135–37, 147, 154–55; II, 503; IV, 77, 79, 80, 83, 88–100, 118, 135, 147–48, 151, 166–68, 170, 174, 183, 201–2, 206–7, 209–10, 211, 219, 274, 392, 447, 451, 499, 518, 523–33; and *Memorials of the English and French commissaries*, I, 120, 157, 192–94, 202, 209, 295, 297, 299, 301, 321, 525, 719.

René Baudry, "Quelques documents nouveaux sur Nicolas Denys," *RHAF*, IX (1955–56), 14–30. Roger Comeau, "Nicolas Denys, pionnier Acadien," *RHAF*, IX (1955–56), 31–54. La Morandière, *Histoire de la pêche française de la morue*, I, 353–54. Robert Le Blant, "Les études historiques sur la colonie française d'Acadie, 1603–1713," *Revue d'Histoire des Colonies*, XXXV (1948), 94–102 (mentions all the known texts on Nicolas Denys); "Les compagnies du Cap-Breton, 1629–1647," *RHAF*, XVI (1962–63), 81–94. W. I. Morse, *Gravestones of Acadie: and other essays on local history, genealogy and parish records of Annapolis County, N.S.* (London, 1929).

DENYS DE FRONSAC, RICHARD, administrator, colonizer, trader, and fisherman; b. *c.* 1654, son of NICOLAS DENYS and Marguerite Lafite; d. 1691.

Richard Denys was born at Saint-Pierre, Cape Breton, where his father had just re-established himself after purchasing from the Compagnie de la Nouvelle-France the rights to the north coast of Acadia from Canso to Cap des Rosiers in Gaspé and being granted the title of governor and lieutenant of the king. Richard spent an eventful youth at Saint-Pierre, although it is noteworthy that the Denys family was not affected by SEDGWICK's capture of Port-Royal in 1654. The Denyses continued to reside at Saint-Pierre until the winter of 1668–69 when their buildings and business were destroyed by fire, whereupon they moved to Nipisiguit (now Bathurst, N.B.). Here Nicolas Denys had constructed a post around 1652. Because of his losses and the financial obligations incurred in trying to establish himself in difficult circumstances, the elder Denys determined to return to France, publish a book on the country, and seek a larger measure of support for his Acadian undertakings. This he did in 1671, leaving his wife and his seventeen-year-old son Richard in charge of his affairs. The early misfortunes of the elder Denys retarded the enterprises which the son was to administer and eventually to inherit.

Richard managed to wrest a living from forest, farm, and sea. He grew peas and wheat, and even pears and apples. He maintained the posts at Nipisiguit and Miscou. His participation in the defence, in 1676, of his father's Cape Breton coal beds against three English ketches shows that he attempted to exploit all available resources, but the fur trade and fishery were mainstays. Richard's

Denys de Fronsac

salary of 800 *livres* a year was never paid and by 1682, when it had accumulated to the amount of 9,600 *livres*, a new settlement gave Richard first claim on his father's estate for payment in arrears.

Most references to Richard Denys, in this period, relate to his exercise of authority on behalf of his father. The elder Denys's rights and jurisdictions were not invariably respected, or in any case, upheld, by the government at Quebec. There was much confusion as to titles and boundaries: on one occasion, for example, without reference to possibly existing commitments, the Intendant TALON conferred on Pierre Denys* de La Ronde, a relative of Nicolas, the rights to Île Percée. The settlers at that place petitioned Richard Denys for redress from La Ronde, who had withheld their deeds, since Richard was regarded as having paramount authority there.

A more serious jurisdictional dispute was that between Richard Denys and BERGIER's Compagnie de la Pesche sédentaire de l'Acadie. After Nicolas Denys's rights in the Chedabouctou (now Guysborough, N.S.) area had been reaffirmed in 1667, Richard and his brother-in-law Michel Leneuf* de La Vallière continued to hunt and fish periodically in the region, where he came in conflict with Bergier's company, active there in the 1680's. Bergier's complaints at the French court led to the concession of Cape Breton to Bergier in April 1687, on the grounds of the Denys's non-fulfilment of terms. A large seigneury, to be chosen later, was promised Nicolas in compensation.

Nicolas died the following year, and as no effective authority could be imposed from the distant Port-Royal, Richard Denys petitioned to have his late father's rights as governor—which in fact he himself had exercised for 18 years—conferred upon him. The government seems to have complied with his request, since his jurisdiction extended over the whole area until his death in 1691, except for a brief period in 1690 when he was a prisoner of the English after PHIPS had captured Port-Royal. At the same time, in place of the princely grant hitherto enjoyed, he inherited a seigneury at Miramichi—the one promised his father in 1687—and here he established himself, on the north bank of that river, about opposite the "tickle" that ran between what is now known as Wilson's Point and Beaubears (now Boishébert) Island. The seigneury was 15 leagues square; one-third had to be cleared within three years, and the remainder in the three years following. His house was of free stone, set in a wooden fort with four bastions, and defended by ten cannon, four of brass and six of iron. Already he had begun to cultivate grain, vegetables, fruits, and grass, all by hand. In 1689 he stated that he hoped soon to work the land with oxen, to have a water-mill, and a sedentary fishery.

In 1689, while residing at Fort Sainte-Croix on the Miramichi, he also maintained a settlement at Ristigouche (now Restigouche), and exercised his rights at Nipisiguit, in the midst of litigation lasting to 1691. (The latter involved one of his settlers, Philippe Énault*, whose obligation consisted of the payment of one pistole and one otter skin in the form of a bag, with tail, paws, and teeth, as rent and homage, every two years.) So energetically did Richard promote settlement that by 1689 he had 103 French settlers within his domain, a large number when compared with the small total of population in Acadia at that time. Of these 31 were in his immediate employ, 23 at his seigneury of Sainte-Croix, and 8 on the Baie des Chaleurs. Besides these he had "seated two villages of Indians" near his establishments, one on the Baie des Chaleurs of 60 families or 400 Indians, and the other at Miramichi of 500 in 80 wigwams.

In the interest of both the French and the Indians, Richard Denys encouraged the establishment of missions in his territories, mostly by the Jesuits and Recollets, but on one occasion by the seminary of Quebec. The grant to the Recollet order on 13 Aug. 1685 of three leagues square at Ristigouche, Miramichi, and in Cape Breton was revoked on 6 May 1690. The seminary's efforts in 1685 proved abortive, and a renewed Recollet attempt at Miramichi, under an agreement of 16 Oct. 1686, failed also. In 1688 Richard Denys reported that he had maintained at his own expense both Jesuits and Recollets for a period of years and for two years a priest from Quebec, but the ecclesiastical authorities, to the injury of both French and Indians, had removed them. Nevertheless he continued to the end of his life to serve the interests of France and the church with intelligence, vigour, and a degree of high-mindedness that gives him a claim to be regarded as the most distinguished of the native-born colonists of Acadia in the 17th century.

Richard Denys de Fronsac was first married, probably in 1680, to Anne Parabego (Partarabego), an Indian girl, and by her he had a daughter Marie-Anne, baptized on 25 May 1681 at Jemseg on the Saint John River and married in 1709 to Jean Merçan*, of Quebec. Also by this marriage he had a son Nicolas, born in 1682, who like his father married an Indian woman, and perished with his three children in 1732. On 15 Oct. 1689, Richard Denys was again married, this time at Quebec to Françoise Cailleteau, who bore him a son, Louis, on 31 Oct. 1690. In the autumn of 1691, at the age of 37, Richard Denys lost his life at sea. The vessel, the *Saint-François-Xavier*, in which he set out from Quebec, was never heard of again. Three years later, on 17 July 1694, his estate was settled in favour of his widow, and his son Louis presumably having died at an early age, it was inherited by the children of his widow's subsequent marriage to Pierre Rey Gaillard.

Contrary to what some historians have written, the title of "Sieur de Fronsac" was never held by Nicolas Denys, but was assumed by his son Richard in about 1677. Two members of the Denys family had been ennobled in the reign of Henri III, but the event which appears to have given Richard warrant for the assumption of his title was the ennoblement of his uncle, SIMON DENYS, in 1668. Fronsac was the name of a place in the neighbourhood of Bordeaux, France, but had, in honour of Cardinal Richelieu who was Duc de Fronsac, been given to a locality on the Strait of Canso near which Richard Denys was born.

ALFRED G. BAILEY

AN, Col., C^{11D}, 1, f.192, Bergier des Ormeaux's complaints, 12 May [1687?] against Leneuf de La Vallière, Leneuf de Beaubassin, and Richard Denys; Col., E, 277 (dossier La Vallière). BN, MS, Clairambault 1016, f.331. Denys, *Description and natural history* (Ganong). *Jug. et délib.*, III, IV, V. P.-G. Roy, *Inv. concessions*, IV. Ganong, "Historic sites in New Brunswick," 233, 292–94, 298–99, 300, 317–18, 319–20. "Richard Denys, sieur de Fronsac, and his settlements in northern New Brunswick," Historical-geographical documents relating to New Brunswick, ed. W. F. Ganong, 4, N.B. Hist. Soc. *Coll.*, [III], no. 7 (1907) 7–54.

DENYS (Denis) DE LA TRINITÉ, SIMON, member of the Conseil Souverain, second son of Jacques Denys de La Thibaudière and Marie Cosnier, younger brother of NICOLAS DENYS; ennobled by Louis XIV; b. 1599 at Tours, d. in Canada between 1678 and 1680.

Simon Denys came of a family of some distinction, with a record of service to the state in both military and civil affairs. During the greater part of his life Simon was established at Tours. He was at some time "conseiller du roi et lieutenant civil au grenier à sel de Tours," presumably in charge of the collection of the salt tax, or *gabelle*. He was twice married in France, first to Jeanne Dubreuil, also of Tours (d. 1639), secondly to Françoise Du Tartre (1621–70), and founded a large and notable family.

In 1632 Simon accompanied his brother, Nicolas, to Acadia. Nicolas established a fishery at Port Rossignol (near the present-day Liverpool, N.S.) and put Simon in command of a vessel purchased for the trade. When the ship was unloading its first cargo of cod at Oporto, hostilities broke out between France and Spain, of which Portugal was then a part, with the result that the ship was lost and Simon was imprisoned in Madrid. On his release he returned to France, bearing confidential messages from the French ambassador to Cardinal Richelieu. As compensation for his sufferings, the cardinal gave Simon command of one of the king's ships.

Subsequently Simon rejoined his brother in the New World, but precisely when is not clear. Evidently he was there in 1650 or 1651. In 1645 Nicolas had set up a post at Miscou, holding a concession possibly from the Compagnie des Cent-Associés. In 1647 MENOU d'Aulnay was appointed governor of Acadia and, asserting his authority over the whole domain, seized the post. At some later date, perhaps after the governor's death in May 1650, Nicolas attempted to establish himself in Cape Breton, setting up a habitation at Saint-Pierre, while Simon rebuilt Capt. CHARLES DANIEL's post at Sainte-Anne. In 1650 or 1651 Mme d'Aulnay [*see* MOTIN], widow of the governor, sent forces to seize these posts. The brothers were taken prisoner and, in October 1651, were sent to Quebec. Thus Simon, too, was drawn into the complicated rivalry between Menou d'Aulnay and the company.

Nicolas returned to Acadia but Simon remained in Canada. In August 1652 the Jesuits, seigneurs of Notre-Dame-des-Anges, granted him a concession, called the "ferme de la Trinité." He subsequently received several additional grants, established himself and his family, and put his land under cultivation. In addition he is mentioned in 1660 as being seigneurial attorney and receiver general ("*procurer fiscal et receveur général*") for the Compagnie des Cent-Associés. In September 1664 he was appointed to the Conseil Souverain, serving until 6 Dec. 1666.

Simon Denys apparently amassed no great fortune but he won the esteem of the authorities for, on the recommendation of the intendant, TALON, he was ennobled by the king in 1668. Although the patent of nobility was not registered by the Conseil Souverain until 1680, after Simon's death, no one contested the right of Simon or his descendants to bear arms. Louis XIV's abolition of unregistered titles in 1669 had, in practice, no application in New France.

JEAN LUNN

Denys, *Description and natural history* (Ganong). Hugolin Lemay, *Le père Joseph Denis, premier récollet canadien (1657–1736)* (2v., Québec, 1926). *JR*

Dermer

(Thwaites), *passim*. Thomas Guérin, *From the Crusades to Quebec: "The Knights of Malta in the New World"* (Montreal, 1949), 202. Le Jeune, *Dictionnaire*, I, 493–94. "Lettres d'annoblissement de Simon Denys," *BRH*, XII (1906), 345–46. *Lettres de noblesse, généalogies, érections de comtés et baronnies insinuées par le Conseil souverain de la Nouvelle-France*, éd. P.-G. Roy (2v., Beauceville, 1920). Benjamin Sulte, *Histoire des Can. fr.*, III. P.-G. Roy, "Les conseillers au Conseil souverain de la Nouvelle-France," *RSCT*, 3d ser., IX (1915), sect.I, 175.

DERMER, THOMAS, of Plymouth, England, navigator, pioneer, and explorer; d. 1621 in Virginia.

Dermer went first to New England with Capt. John Smith, who was sent out in 1614 by London merchants to lay the foundations of a new plantation and to trade with the Indians there. Dermer was to have accompanied Smith on his 1615 voyage to New England but the ship, after encountering pirates and the French, finally made its way back to Plymouth with great difficulty.

Dermer spent some time in Newfoundland, 1616–18, with his friend and associate, Governor John MASON, at Cuper's Cove (now Cupids), where he was possibly engaged in the fishing business but more likely involved in explorations of the island's natural resources. He wrote a letter, dated September 1616, from Cuper's Cove, in which he describes in flattering terms the fertility of the soil, abundance of wild life, and mineral potentialities, an evidence of his interest in the commercial possibilities of the area.

It was during this stay in Newfoundland that Dermer met TISQUANTUM (or Squanto), the New England Indian, who, with others, had been seized by Capt. Thomas Hunt in 1614 to be sold into slavery in Spain. Tisquantum eventually escaped and reached Cuper's Cove. Finding him very intelligent and with the ability to speak English and knowing that there was need for an interpreter between the New England colonizers and the Indians, Dermer had no difficulty in persuading Tisquantum to assume this role. Accompanied by Tisquantum, Dermer returned to England to confer with Sir Ferdinando Gorges, who was at that time attempting to colonize New England. Gorges, who favoured co-operation with the Indians as a matter of policy, was delighted with Dermer's plan to make Tisquantum an interpreter, in order to promote better understanding between the settlers and the Indians. He commissioned Dermer as commander of his 1619 expedition to New England. Tisquantum was a member of the expedition, was restored to his own people, and his work among them as interpreter amply fulfilled the expectations of Gorges and Dermer.

Dermer did not return to Newfoundland but remained in New England as Gorges's employee. Here he made extensive explorations along the coast from Cape Cod to Virginia, which he reached in November 1619; he then returned to New England where he spent the next year. He established that Long Island was an island (hitherto it was thought to be a part of the mainland). He prospected for gold and other minerals in the vicinity of Cape Cod, sending back samples of the earth to England. In 1621 he went again to Virginia, where he died of wounds inflicted by the Indians.

Dermer emerges from the records as a man of exemplary character, "this worthy gentleman . . . giving us good content in all hee undertook." In particular, his dealings with the Indians appear to have won their confidence and esteem. Standing high in their good graces, he was warmly welcomed all along the coast. In no small measure, therefore, he paved the way for the Pilgrim Fathers who landed in New England 11 Dec. 1620.

E. HUNT

Purchas, *Pilgrimes* (1905–7), XIX. *Bradford's history of the Plymouth settlement 1608–1650*, ed. Valerian Paget (New York, 1909). John Smith, *Travels and works*, ed. Edward Arber (2v., Birmingham, 1884), I, 217–18, 220–27; II, 747. H. F. Howe, *Salt rivers of the Massachusetts shore* (Rivers of America, New York, 1951). R. A. Preston, *Gorges of Plymouth Fort* (Toronto, 1953). Prowse, *History of Nfld*. Rogers, *Newfoundland*. A. L. Rowse, *The Elizabethans and America* (London, 1959).

DERRÉ DE GAND, FRANÇOIS (also called **de Ré** and **Sieur Gand** or **de Gand**), commissary general of the Compagnie des Cent-Associés, benefactor of the missionaries and the Indians; d. 20 May 1641 at Quebec.

Sent to New France as commissary general of the Compagnie des Cent-Associés, Derré probably accompanied CHAMPLAIN on the latter's return to Quebec in 1633. He was a sort of holy layman, or mystic, as noteworthy for his humility as for his charity to the Indians, for whom he frequently acted as godfather and whose wounds he himself dressed. It appears that little is known of his official activity as commissary general. An attentive study of his work, however, leads to the realization that, along with the kindliness and understanding shown to the Indians, whom he persuaded to trust the French, he was also an effective servant of the Compagnie des Cent-Associés.

Adaptable, diplomatic, and a student of human

nature, François Derré could also be firm. In 1636 in particular, he showed himself to be consummately clever when he realized that a group of Algonkins were seeking to come to an understanding with the Dutch in order to dispose of their furs. In the presence of the Algonkin chiefs gathered at Trois-Rivières, he declared that it was eminently just that the French should abandon them to their fate, if they preferred to have the Dutch take up their cause and defend them. Now the Algonkins were well aware that the Dutch were interested only in their furs and that they were not anxious to antagonize the Iroquois, especially the Mohawks, sworn foes of the Algonkins.

After Champlain's death in 1635, François Derré became a real protector and father to the little French settlement at Quebec. His charitableness was unlimited if anyone had recourse to him for advice. The *Jesuit Relations* praise him endlessly. In 1636, at his own expense, he sent a particularly brilliant young Indian to study in France. The supply warehouse of the company was always open to needy Indians. He himself went several times to carry provisions to the lodges of Indians too weak to make their way to the warehouse. Every time that troops of young redskins, pursued by the enemy, came to take refuge in the fort, the Jesuits sheltered the young men and M. de Gand accepted responsibility for the girls.

The exemplary life led by this charitable man did not preclude his being an excellent business man or prevent him from carrying out in every respect the duties of his office. From the moment of his arrival in New France he had realized that the resources of this new country gave promise of a brilliant future, and he applied himself to constructing sound spiritual and physical foundations for it. We have seen what a conciliatory policy he adopted towards the Indians in order to conserve their friendship and their furs. As soon as the Ursulines arrived at Quebec he assisted them in every possible way. The Jesuits found him a constant pillar of strength. He it was who, in 1638, took possession of the seigneury of the Île d'Orléans on behalf of a group of members of the Compagnie des Cent-Associés. Beginning in 1639 he took a special interest in the establishment at Sillery, where the Jesuits, urged on by M. Noël Brulart de Sillery, were proposing to found a village for Roman Catholic Indians. This territory had been granted to François Derré in 1637. He made a gift of his property rights to the Jesuits in 1639, and even sent workmen to give assistance to the missionaries, in addition to supplying them continually with provisions.

Generous to excess, François Derré, who had never married, lived very frugally himself. During the last years of his life, he made do with one little room located beneath the sacristy of the simple chapel erected in the building of the Cent-Associés after the fire at Notre-Dame-de-la-Recouvrance. It was there that he died 20 May 1641. He was buried beside M. de Champlain the next day. "He died in a sublime practice of patience; in a word, he died as he had lived—that is to say, as a man who seeks God in truth."

RAYMOND DOUVILLE

JR (Thwaites), XXI, 108, *et passim*. Desrosiers, *Iroquoisie*. Dionne, *Champlain*, II, 461–65; "François de Ré dit M. Gand," *BRH*, IX (1903), 23–27. "François de Ré, sieur de Gand," *BRH*, VII (1901), 23. P.-G. Roy, *La ville de Québec*, I, 153f. H.-A. Scott, *Une paroisse historique de la Nouvelle-France: Notre-Dame de Sainte-Foy: histoire civile et religieuse d'après les sources* (Québec, 1902).

D'ESCHAMBAULT. *See* FLEURY

DES CHATELETS, NOËL JUCHEREAU. *See* JUCHEREAU

DESDAMES, THIERRY, deputy representative of the Compagnie de Montmorency and captain of Miscou; fl. 1622–46.

Desdames arrived in New France in 1622 and the following year brought Father Nicolas VIEL and Brother Gabriel SAGARD from Tadoussac to Quebec. He was still in the colony in 1624, since in January he acted as godfather to Marguerite, ABRAHAM MARTIN's daughter. In 1628 it was he who brought to Quebec the news of the arrival of Claude ROQUEMONT de Brison at Gaspé; he feared a disaster, however, as he had heard the sound of cannon shortly after leaving Gaspé. In this state of suspense, CHAMPLAIN entrusted him with finding out what had happened to Roquemont and with obtaining provisions for the starving settlement. After a perilous journey that lasted more than a month, Desdames returned to Quebec and brought confirmation of the defeat of the French flotilla. He was instrumental in obtaining from Juan Chou, the Indian chief of Gaspé, an offer to shelter some of the French for the winter. Twenty settlers accepted this offer, but they were captured by the English, except for Desdames who succeeded in returning to France on Captain Joubert's ship.

Desdames returned to New France. In appreciation of his qualities as a sailor and confidential agent, he was appointed captain of Miscou and held this office from 1639 to 1646 at least.

MARCEL HAMELIN

Des Groseilliers

Champlain, *Œuvres* (Laverdière). *JR* (Thwaites), XII, 212–75; XXIV, 152; XXVIII, 200; XXX, 136. Dionne, *Champlain*, 405–7, *et passim*; "Miscou, hommes de mer et hommes de Dieu," *CF*, II (1889), 445–47.

DES GROSEILLIERS, MÉDARD CHOUART. See CHOUART

DES LAURIERS, BÉNIGNE BASSET. See BASSET

DESMARAIS (Desmarets, Des Maretz), CLAUDE GODET DE. See GODET

DESMELOIZES, FRANÇOIS-MARIE RENAUD D'AVÈNE DE. See RENAUD

DES MUCEAUX, CHARLES-JOSEPH D'AILLEBOUST. See AILLEBOUST

DES ORMEAUX, ADAM DOLLARD. See DOLLARD DES ORMEAUX

DESPORTES, HÉLÈNE, said to be the first white child born in New France, daughter of Pierre Desportes and Françoise Langlois; m. Guillaume Hébert 1634; d. 1675.

The date of Hélène's birth has not been definitely fixed. Dionne says that she came to Quebec with her parents in 1613, Sulte that she was born in Quebec about 1622. Statistics from other sources indicate that she was 14 years old in 1634, 38 in 1659, 46 in 1666, and 48 in 1667. Anne Hébert, according to CHAMPLAIN, had died in childbirth previous to 1620; but since there is no further mention of her child, it was presumably still-born. Eustache Martin was born in October 1621. If, however, we assume Hélène's birthdate to be 1620, which seems most probable, her claim is established as being the first white child born alive in the St. Lawrence region. (Sulte, to be sure, claims for GUILLEMETTE HÉBERT the honour of being the first-born *Canadienne*, on the assumption that LOUIS HÉBERT had his wife with him in Acadia in 1606, but LESCARBOT's evidence refutes this (*History* (Grant).)

Pierre Desportes probably came to Quebec in 1614 with ABRAHAM MARTIN: their wives were sisters. Desportes' occupation is not known, but he must have had some standing in the community and sufficient education to be able to write, for he signed on behalf of the inhabitants the document of 1621 appealing to the king. No other facts are known about him. (He is not to be confused with Pierre Desportes de Liguère, to whom the Compagnie de la Nouvelle-France ceded Île Royale (Cape Breton) in 1636.) Neither of Hélène's parents witnessed her marriage contract, drawn up in Quebec in October 1634.

Her husband was Guillaume Hébert. About this only son of Canada's first settler little is recorded except an occasional instance of his helping the priests in their relations with the savages. Since he had inherited half his father's land, which included some acres on the St. Charles as well as the original site above the cliff, it is to be assumed that his chief occupation during his short life was the cultivation of his fields. He was but a little boy when he came to Quebec with his parents in 1617, therefore probably still in his twenties when he died in 1639. Three children were born of this marriage, one of whom died in infancy. The other two were a son JOSEPH and a daughter Françoise (b. 1638) who married Guillaume Fournier, 1651.

Hélène's second husband was Noel Morin (1616–80), a wheelwright, who became one of the early pioneers of Montmagny. Their son Germain* became one of the first pupils of the seminary of Quebec and was consecrated to the priesthood by Mgr Laval* in September 1655, the first Canadian-born priest. Another son, Jean-Baptiste (1645–94) was a member of the Conseil Souverain. Hélène died 24 June 1675.

ETHEL M. G. BENNETT

For information about the Desportes family in Quebec see Léon Roy, "Pierre Desportes et sa descendance," SGCF *Mémoires*, II (1946–47), 165–68. See also Azarie Couillard Després, *Louis Hébert: premier colon canadien et sa famille* (Lille, Paris, Bruges, 1913; Montréal, 1918); *La première famille française au Canada*. Dionne *Champlain*, II, *passim*. Sulte, *Hist. des Can.-fr.*, II, 37, 78.

DETHUNES, EXUPÈRE, Recollet priest, missionary; b. c. 1644 in France; d. in 1692 at the convent of Sainte-Marguerite, near Gisors.

Exupère Dethunes joined the Recollets of the province of Saint-Denis in 1665. On 28 May 1668, at Rouen, he became a subdeacon, and the following 26 May a deacon; we do not know the date of his ordination. In 1671 he joined the Canadian mission and sailed with Fathers Claude Moireau*, Léonard Duchesne, Étienne Saulnier, and Brother Innocent Desmarais. Father Exupère Dethunes was assigned to the Recollets' house at Quebec, and divided his time between prayer, the study of Indian languages, and the exercise of his ministry among the settlers scattered along the north shore of the river. His presence at Dombourg, Cap-Rouge and Rivière-aux-Roches, as well as at Bourg-Royal, is in fact revealed by the local registers.

To comply with the invitation of the provincial commissioner, Father Gabriel de La Ribourde, he agreed, in May 1673, to provide religious services at Percé, where about 500 people came to fish during the summer. In the autumn he returned to Quebec to exercise his ministry there, as is testified by the parish registers of Notre-Dame de Québec (1673), L'Ange-Gardien (1675), and Cap-Santé (1679).

In 1680 he accompanied Father Chrétien Le Clercq, who had been commissioned to go to France to obtain authorization from the king whereby the Recollets might establish a hospice at Quebec and Ville-Marie (Montreal). This mission was successfully completed. In 1683 he was appointed vicar of the convent at Quebec and novice-master, and the following year he succeeded Father Henri Leroy* as superior of the same convent. It is in this capacity that on 7 Oct. 1684 he signed a brief presented to the intendant Jacques Demeulle* relating to the litigation which had arisen between the Recollets and Bishop François de Laval* about the building of the belfry for their hospice in the Upper Town. He returned to France during the summer of 1685, and died at the Sainte-Marguerite convent near Gisors, 26 Aug. 1692.

Frédéric Gingras

ASM, G. BN, MS Fr. 13875, Nécrologe des Frères-Mineurs Récollets de la province de Saint-Denys en France. Le Clercq, *First establishment of the faith* (Shea), I, 9, 27; II, 76, 80; *New relation of Gaspesia with the customs and religion of the Gaspesian Indians*, tr. and ed. W. F. Ganong (Champlain Soc., V, 1910); Hugolin Lemay, *L'établissement des Récollets à l'Île Percée (1673–1690)* (Québec, 1912).

DIDACE, FRÈRE. *See* Pelletier

DIESCARET. *See* Pieskaret

DOLBEAU, JEAN, Recollet priest, missionary in New France; b. 2 March 1586 in the Duchy of Anjou; d. 1652 at Orléans (France).

In 1605 he joined the Recollets of Balmette, near Angers. After his philosophical and theological studies, he sought permission from his superiors to go and preach the faith in the East or West Indies. Named to the Canadian mission, he sailed from Honfleur on 24 April 1615. On 25 May of that year his ship dropped anchor off Tadoussac and on 2 June he was at Quebec. As soon as he arrived he busied himself with building little rooms for the missionaries and a chapel, which he dedicated to St. Charles. On 25 June he celebrated the first mass said at Quebec.

In December of the same year, he was given charge of the Montagnais mission at Tadoussac. But the threat of failing eyesight soon obliged him to return to Quebec where he officiated at the burial of Michel Colin on 24 March 1616. After a short visit to Trois-Rivières at the end of June, he accompanied Samuel de Champlain and Father Joseph Le Caron back to Quebec on 11 July. While Champlain and Father Denis Jamet and Le Caron went to France to interest the Compagnie des Marchands de Rouen et de Saint-Malo and all men of goodwill in the Canadian missionary undertaking, Father Dolbeau remained at Quebec to minister to the French, to evangelize the Indians who came there, and to bolster the courage of the settlers who had, in the words of Gabriel Sagard, "many crosses and little bread."

After making a trip to France in the summer of 1617 to try in his turn to overcome the greed and covetousness of the merchant partners, Father Dolbeau arrived back in Quebec on 27 June 1618. He returned with the title of provincial commissioner and brought from France a jubilee —the first ever gained in Canada—which he proclaimed on 29 July in the chapel at Quebec "to the great satisfaction and solace of every one." On 3 June 1620 he blessed the corner-stone of the "first convent and first seminary" in the country, in the building of which both French and Indians worked under the leadership of François Gravé Du Pont. In the autumn of that same year, Father Dolbeau returned to France, taking with him an Indian boy named Pierre-Antoine Pastedechouan, in order to have him educated.

In France, Father Dolbeau served successively as master of novices and definitor; in May 1633 at Toledo he attended the chapter of his order in his capacity as custodian of the province of Sainte-Madeleine.

In demand as a spiritual director, he passed away at the convent of Orleans on 9 June 1652. At his death he left a manuscript in which he had recorded the marvellous workings of grace in the soul of Anne de Pichery, whom he had directed. This manuscript, which is supplemented by an abridged life of Father Dolbeau, was slightly revised for publication by the Benedictine monk Dom Gilles Jamin, but it was never printed. The manuscript is preserved in the Municipal Library of Orleans in five versions, each differing slightly from the others.

Frédéric Gingras

Bibliothèque municipal d'Orléans, MS 509, manuscrit du XVIIe siècle. Le Clercq, *First establishment of*

Dolebeau

the faith (Shea), I, 82, 85, 87, 89, *et passim.* Sagard, *Histoire du Canada* (Tross). *The Catholic encyclopedia, an international work of reference . . . of the Catholic Church,* ed. C. G. Herbermann *et al.* (17v., New York, 1907–22). Jouve, *Les Franciscains et le Canada (1615–1629).* Conrad Morin et Archange Godbout, "Le Père Jean Dolbeau, récollet, missionnaire en Nouvelle-France, 1615–1620: I, Vie; II, Lettres spirituelles," *Chronique franciscaine du Canada,* déc. 1941, 169–236.

DOLEBEAU (**Dolbeau** is sometimes found), **JEAN**, priest, Jesuit, missionary at Miscou, in the Baie des Chaleurs; b. 4 Jan. 1608 at Langres (France); died at sea during the summer of 1643.

Father Jean Dolebeau (not to be confused with Father Jean DOLBEAU) had entered the noviciate of the Society of Jesus on 16 Oct. 1628 in Paris. He had then taught at the Collège in Vannes (1630–32) and in Caen (1632–34). He had done his theology at the Collège in La Flèche (1634–38) and had been ordained priest. After teaching classics at the Collège in Moulins (1638–39), he completed at Rouen the final year of spiritual training required of Jesuits, then sailed to Canada in 1640. Together with Father André Richard he was made responsible for ministering to the parish of Miscou, a small French fur-trading and fishing post on an island in the Baie des Chaleurs. Nothing is known of his missionary labours in this place, except that he was obliged to concern himself principally with the traders and fishermen, since the local Micmacs had only just begun to make contact with the missionaries. At Christmas 1642 he was struck down by a painful illness, which in April 1643 left him paralysed in his arms and hands. Thierry DESDAMES, a former assistant clerk in the service of the de CAËN family and commandant of the post since 1639, helped Father Dolebeau most devotedly during his illness and arranged for his return to France in the summer of 1643. During the crossing the ship was attacked by three frigates, whose nationality is nowhere mentioned. While the captive vessel was being pillaged, the powder-magazine caught fire, and the explosion threw Father Dolebeau into the sea. He was drowned; the exact date of his death is unknown.

LUCIEN CAMPEAU

JR (Thwaites), XXIV, 152; XXV, 28. Rochemonteix, *Les Jésuites et la Nouvelle-France au XVIIe siècle,* I, 198, n.2. "Les Pères d'Olbeau," *BRH,* VI (1900), 278–80.

DOLLARD DES ORMEAUX (called **Daulat** in his death certificate and **Daulac** by some historians), **ADAM**, soldier, "garrison commander of the fort of Ville-Marie [Montreal]"; b. 1635, killed by the Iroquois at the Long Sault in May 1660.

Nothing is known of Dollard's activities prior to his arrival in Canada except that "he had held some commands in the armies of France." Having come to Montreal as a volunteer, very probably in 1658, he continued his military career there. In 1659 and 1660 he was described as an "officer" or "garrison commander of the fort of Ville-Marie," a title that he shared with Pierre PICOTÉ de Belestre. We do not however know what his particular responsibility was. Dollard was perhaps contemplating becoming a settler. At the end of 1659 CHOMEDY de Maisonneuve gave him a piece of land comprising 30 *arpents.* In 1661 the sum that Dollard had devoted "to having work done on the aforementioned grant" was calculated at 79 *livres,* 10 *sols,* "for 53 days' labour."

Dollard had an excellent reputation at Montreal. First-hand evidence, it is true, is rare: the *Relation* calls him "a man of accomplishments and generalship," and Dollier* de Casson calls him "a youth of courage and of good family." But Dollard had earned the governor's confidence and the esteem of his fellow-townsmen. For anyone who is acquainted with the social and religious climate of Ville-Marie in 1660, is any better recommendation needed? It would have been unthinkable for example for Maisonneuve to promote to garrison commander an officer whose conduct had not been irreproachable. Would Lambert CLOSSE have chosen him to be godfather to his daughter Élisabeth (3 Oct. 1658)? Would his presence have been sought, a score of times, to witness the signature before BÉNIGNE BASSET of contracts of all sorts, if Dollard had not been a thoroughly honourable man? Finally, would Maisonneuve have let him leave for the Long Sault in April 1660 if he had not had complete confidence in him?

To be sure, much ill has been spoken of Dollard, accused of stealing furs and of being headstrong. These accusations, however, are not based upon any documentary proof and in addition are contradicted by the facts. But the temptation to criticize was great. Dollier de Casson states that Dollard "may have been very glad of an opportunity to distinguish himself, to be of use to him on account of something which was said to have happened to him in France." What was this "something," and how serious had it been? We know nothing of it. It would be unreasonable to construct hypotheses upon a piece of information so fragile and which seems to be pure hearsay. Let it suffice to record that Dollard led an orderly life at Montreal and that he was well thought of by his superiors and his fellow-townsmen.

Dollard Des Ormeaux

This then was the man who, in the spring of 1660, assumed the leadership of an expedition to the Ottawa. Like him, his 16 companions all came from Montreal and all were unmarried. Eight of them had landed at Ville-Marie in 1653: Jacques Brassier, aged 25; François Crusson *dit* Pilote, 24; René Doussin, 30, a miller and soldier; Nicolas Josselin, 25, originally from Solesmes in Normandy; Jean Lecompte, 26, a digger and woodcutter from the parish of Chamiré-en-Charnie in Le Maine; Étienne Robin *dit* Des Forges, 27; Jean Tavernier *dit* La Lochetière, Sieur de La Forest, 28, an armourer, originally from Roëzé in Le Maine; and Jean Valets, 27, a ploughman from the parish of Thorie (or Teillé) in Le Maine. The remaining eight had arrived in 1658 or shortly before; Christophe Augier *dit* Desjardins, 26; Jacques Boisseau *dit* Cognac, 23; Alonié Delestre, the oldest of the Seventeen, 31, a lime-burner; Simon Grenet, 25; Roland Hébert *dit* Larivière, 27; Robert Jurie, 24; Louis Martin, the youngest of the group, 21, a cowherd; and Nicolas Tiblemont, 25, a locksmith.

Of the military exploit of 1660 there is a traditional, though relatively recent, version. In the 17th century Dollard and the defence of the Long Sault had quickly been forgotten. Except for the Jesuit Charlevoix* and François-Xavier Garneau, who both devoted a short paragraph to it, historians and chroniclers for nearly two centuries made no mention of this episode in the Iroquois wars. It was only in the 19th century, after the discovery of Dollier de Casson's manuscript of the *Histoire du Montréal*, that Abbé Jean-Baptiste Ferland and Abbé Étienne-Michel Faillon gave detailed accounts of the combat of 1660 which were not lacking in emotion and grandiloquence, particularly Faillon's. Dollard and his companions, "whom one was tempted to venerate as martyrs of the faith" (Ferland), went knowingly to their deaths to save their religion and their country. Forthwith the Seventeen acquired the stature of national heroes. "These brave men carried out . . . the finest feat of arms recorded in modern history"; more than that, "in the history of the Greeks and Romans, nothing is comparable to the action of these heroes" who "sacrificed their lives for the pure motives of the Faith" (Faillon).

It was in this patriotic and religious light that Ferland and Faillon presented the event of 1660. The Iroquois "having sent forth a great army and being resolved to destroy every last French person in Canada," Dollard "conceived . . . the noble project of going . . . to meet this army" in order to "spread terror among the Iroquois by such a daring resolution and so heroic a death." "In order not to be deterred by any consideration from going to face death nobly, [Dollard and his companions] all made their wills, came forward devoutly to receive the sacraments of Penitence and Holy Communion, and before the holy altars pledged themselves by a solemn oath neither to ask for nor to accept any quarter, and to fight until their last breath." Dollard and his men went up the Ottawa as far as the foot of the Long Sault, where a party of 40 Hurons and 4 Algonkins joined them. Scarcely had they time to put an old, abandoned fort into shape, when 300 Iroquois burst forth along the river. They were the advance-guard of an army corps which was on its way to the Richelieu islands where 500 warriors were awaiting them in order to attack the colony in force. Driven back several times with severe losses, the enemy decided to call to their aid the army of the Richelieu, which arrived on the fifth day. Despite the treachery of the Hurons who, with the exception of their chief ANNAOTAHA, all went over to the side of the Iroquois, Dollard and his men defended themselves valiantly for three days more against 800 besiegers. Having exhausted their ammunition and their strength, they finally gave in under the weight of numbers. On the French side the only survivors were a few Hurons who had deserted to the enemy. A third of the Iroquois army is said to have perished in the battle: "It is at least certain that the number of dead was very great, and even so excessive that, appalled by the fact that the defence put up by 17 Frenchmen had been so murderous for them, the Iroquois abandoned their undertaking. . . . Their reasoning, in which they all concurred, was as follows: 'If 17 Frenchmen, whose only defence was a wretched reduit that they happened upon, have killed so many of our warriors, what reception should we then have at their hands if we went to attack them in stone houses laid out for defence and in which would be gathered men of like courage?' " They withdrew therefore to their own territory. "Thus the heroic self-sacrifice of gallant Dollard . . . and his companions saved all of Canada in this emergency." Such is, in brief, Faillon's account, scarcely different from Ferland's, which is a little more restrained.

For a long time the historians—Abbé Rousseau, Parkman, Sulte, Mgr Tanguay—supported the thesis advanced by Ferland and Faillon. Only one discordant voice arose, which people pretended not to hear: that of the historian William Kingsford, who endeavoured to reduce the "exploit" to more realistic proportions.

In 1912 and 1913 in the *Canadian Antiquarian and Numismatic Journal* É.-Z. Massicotte made available numerous unpublished documents

Dollard Des Ormeaux

concerning Dollard and his companions: notarial papers, wills, death certificates for the Seventeen, inventories of their possessions, etc. It was the most important contribution to the historiography of the Dollard affair in 50 years. Unfortunately Massicotte did not himself make use of this wealth of material; although he corrected certain of Ferland's and Faillon's affirmations, he did not depart from their interpretation of the facts. In 1920 the Comité pour le Monument de Dollard des Ormeaux republished Massicotte's articles in the form of a brochure with a preface by Aegidius Fauteaux. The same year, and for the first time since Kingsford, a historian dared to attack the traditional thesis on Dollard. In his review of Massicotte's brochure Gustave Lanctot based his argument on the documents presented there—which had not been available to Kingsford to prove his point—and showed that Dollard and his companions did not believe that they were going to certain death, that they did not know of the imminence of an Iroquois invasion, and consequently that they were not volunteers who had sacrificed themselves, as people had wanted to believe. Despite the novelty and the boldness of these affirmations, Lanctot's article did not have any immediate repercussions. But in certain circles Dollard, whom publicity campaigns had made fashionable, was already a subject of discussion.

Suddenly in 1932 a historian set off the explosion. Professor E. R. Adair of McGill University maintained in a lecture that Dollard had not saved New France, that he was an ambitious young man who was eager to "regain a lost reputation" and who succeeded only in aggravating the warlike ardour of the Iroquois; not to mention, added the historian, that Dollard was unaware of the plan for invading the colony and that he was very badly prepared to encounter the enemy; in short, Dollard did more harm than good. The newspapers of 21 March 1932 gave a summary of this lecture. A lively controversy ensued. The historian William H. Atherton (26 March) and Émile Vaillancourt (29 March) came to the defence of the traditional thesis; on 2 April Adair refuted the arguments put forward by Vaillancourt, who replied five days later; on 8 April Adair answered Vaillancourt briefly and refused to continue the debate, announcing that the text of his lecture was shortly to appear in the *Canadian Historical Review*. On 7 and 11 May Abbé Lionel Groulx put his signature to a long study in *Le Devoir*, "Le Dossier de Dollard," which became in a way the Bible of the partisans of the traditional interpretation. In June the *Canadian Historical Review* published, in addition to Adair's article, a reply by Gustave Lanctot. Started in the newspapers, continued in the specialized magazines and later on radio and television, the controversy still rages 30 years later. There are few historians who have not at one time or another added fuel to the flames; but, a noteworthy phenomenon, the public, and especially the younger generation, has entered the debate, which has long since ceased to be the historians' preserve.

Since the debate has become a public issue and Dollard has been delivered into the hands of an impassioned public, the historians, in addition to having to refute their colleagues' opinions, are called upon to lend an ear to rumours and to reply to accusations which are often fanciful; ideological considerations having intruded into the controversy, a further result is that some people embark upon the slippery path of "committed" history. These factors create around the Dollard affair a climate of tension and distrust which is unfavourable to an attentive examination of the sources, to which we must return in order to see the battle of the Long Sault in its correct dimensions.

We must, then, re-examine, point by point, the traditional account and, through a patient and objective analysis of the sources, try to cast light upon this episode of the Iroquois wars, without entering into the virulent polemics and bitter debates which it has provoked up till now.

The purpose of the Long Sault expedition constitutes the most troublesome and most discussed aspect of the Dollard affair. Did the Seventeen know that an Iroquois army was preparing to invade the colony? Did they set off to meet the enemy with the intention of voluntarily sacrificing themselves? And if, perchance, they were unaware of the Iroquois' plans, what was their objective?

Not one of the sources of the Dollard affair says, even implicitly, that the Seventeen knew of the imminent arrival of the enemy army. The preceding year, it is true, there had been disquieting rumours, which Marie de l'Incarnation [*see* GUYART] echoed: "It has been learned from a Huron who has left them [that the Iroquois] are preparing a powerful army to come to carry off our new Christians and, so I believe, as many of the French as they can." Father JÉRÔME LALEMANT specified that the enemies were making ready "to burst upon [New France] with an army—next Spring, at the latest." These invasion rumours were not new in the colony. They were to be heard every year. Consequently people attached more or less credence to them: "People are indeed saying," wrote Marie de l'Incarnation in 1659, "that an

Dollard Des Ormeaux

army of our enemies is preparing to come here; ... if the situation were risky, I should be the first to advise you of it ..., but thanks be to God, we do not see nor believe that that will happen." When the first moments of fright had passed, these troubling prospects were quickly forgotten; in the spring of 1660, the Ursuline testifies again, "no one was on his guard, nor even suspected that the enemy was to come." This is proven by the commotion at Quebec which followed the announcement, shortly after 15 May, of the impending arrival of the Iroquois army. "You can imagine how this news surprised us," Marie de l'Incarnation was to write on 25 June. On 15 May, then, no one yet suspected the danger that threatened the colony; by this date Dollard and his companions, who had left Montreal a month earlier, were probably already dead.

According to Dollier de Casson, the Seventeen, before leaving, "all made their wills," made their confession, received Holy Communion, and "agreed under no circumstances to ask for mercy, taking oath to that effect." Quite wrongly, many people have seen in these preliminary arrangements an additional proof that Dollard and his companions were going knowingly to certain death. First, not all of them made their wills. Only Tavernier and Valets showed this foresight. Moreover, the fact that one dictates his last wishes does not necessarily imply that one *knows* that his death is imminent. Furthermore, Tavernier specified that his will would be valid if he died during the 1660 expedition but that it would "be annulled and of no value" if he came back; likewise Valets made his will "in case an accident should happen to him in the aforementioned voyage or in others that he might make afterwards." Both were setting out upon a dangerous adventure. They were right—and it was a custom that numerous *coureurs de bois* were later to adopt—to set their affairs in order before leaping into their canoes. Let us not forget that it was a time when scarcely anyone in France undertook a trip outside his own province without first signing his will. Similarly it was normal, in the religious climate of the colony, to fulfil one's religious obligations before going off for several weeks far from the centres of population. In recounting another feat of arms the annalist of the Hôtel-Dieu of Quebec wrote: "They went off after making a thorough confession, for at that time one did not go off to battle without taking this precaution...."

The act of "taking an oath of fidelity" would seem however to have been less common. But it must be noted that several historians, beginning with Faillon, have exaggerated the importance of this pact: "Before the holy altars they pledged themselves by a solemn oath neither to ask for nor to accept any quarter, and to fight until their last breath" (Faillon). However, Dollier de Casson had confined himself to writing: "They agreed under no circumstances to ask for mercy, taking an oath to that effect." Considered by itself, without amplification, this gesture is not as extraordinary as it has at times been thought to be. Nothing would seem more natural than that a group of young men who were on the verge of launching out into a long and dangerous undertaking should exchange their word of honour to respect the aims of the undertaking and to aid one another. It was in a way a verbal contract of partnership among the Seventeen, examples of which moreover are preserved, in written form and notarized, in the archives of the French régime.

Up to this point there is no basis for believing that Dollard and his men were aware of the threat presented by an invasion army which they had resolved to stop. If there remain any doubts, there is one argument that should remove them at once. The documents—all of which were written after Dollard's departure—establish that the Iroquois were grouping their warriors near the Richelieu. The enemy, wrote Marie de l'Incarnation, "had their rendezvous at Roche-Percée near Montreal, where 400 others were to come to join them so that ... they would then all sweep down together on Quebec.... It has been learned since that they were at the Richelieu, waiting for the right moment and the opportunity to destroy us all...." CHAUMONOT, the *Relation*, and Casson confirm this piece of information: the Iroquois were at "the Richelieu islands," where they were, according to d'Argenson [Voyer*], "accustomed to do their hunting and to assemble their army." In the spring of 1660 the Iroquois were therefore concentrating their forces on the Richelieu islands; why, if he knew of the enemy's presence and if he were burning to go to encounter them, did Dollard go off towards the Ottawa River—in exactly the opposite direction?

As for the objective of the expedition, the sources agree in the evidence they offer. Father Chaumonot, whose account was reproduced verbatim by Marie de l'Incarnation in a letter to her son dated 25 June 1660, writes: "In the month of April 1660, 17 gallant French volunteers from Montreal formed the project of risking their lives to go to prepare an ambush for the Iroquois...." The 1659–60 *Relation* bears out this statement: "Forty of our Hurons ... toward the close of last winter set out from Quebec to wage petty warfare (*petite guerre*), and lay ambuscades for the

Dollard Des Ormeaux

Iroquois when returning from the chase.... Then arriving at Montreal, they found that seventeen Frenchmen... had already formed a league for the same purpose as their own...." Radisson* also gives a quite similar version: "You must know that 17 ffrench made a plot wth foure Algonquins to make a league wth three score hurrons for to goe and wait for the Iroquoits in the passage att their retourne wth their castors on their ground, hoping to beat and destroy them wth ease, being destitut of necessary things. If one hath his gun he wants his powder, and so the rest." Finally, Dollier de Casson does not say anything else: "Towards the end of April M. Dollard ... was anxious to perform here some bold stroke befitting his bravery. He therefore tried to entice away fifteen or sixteen Frenchmen in order to take them as a detachment above this island, which had not yet been attempted." Even if the persons who related the battle of the Long Sault had omitted to inform us of Dollard's project, we should have the testimony of one of the Seventeen; in his will Jean Valets declared that he was eager "to accompany the Sieur Dollard, to attack the small bands of Iroquois and our enemies...." Can one wish for more complete unanimity?

The documents establish without any possibility of doubt the military nature of the Long Sault expedition; but it was a military undertaking in the style of the Indians. The "*petite guerre*" consisted of a "detachment"—a few dozen men at the most—"attacking the small bands" of the enemy and "laying ambuscades" for them, with the aim of "destroying" them or taking them prisoner. Essentially this was a war of surprise, in which patience and endurance must go with courage and ruse; a war that has its own requirements and its own laws. Once the enemy has been detected, you lie in wait until the moment arrives to attack him by surprise, if you are the stronger party; if the adversary is superior in numbers, it is customary to avoid the combat. A real hunt for human game, perfectly adapted to the forests of New France. Dollard was going off to a "*petite guerre*"; but he had not left the choice of his itinerary to chance. He directed his canoes towards the Long Sault, by which the Iroquois would inevitably pass "on their return from hunting."

The Iroquois wars, of which the battle of the Long Sault was only one painful episode, were above all economic in nature. The Iroquois needed furs and could no longer find any in their own territories. Consequently they were forced to hunt in the northern regions of the Ottawa and in the area around the Great Lakes. Generally they spent the winters there, returning via the Ottawa in the spring. In 1671 the Sulpician SALIGNAC de La Mothe-Fénelon described these annual migrations: "The Iroquois hunt in small, widely separated bands, dispersed over a distance of nearly 150 leagues. They return from the hunt in small groups, heavily laden with their booty of furs and meat. This would make it very easy for the French to wait for them on their route with canoes from which everything has been removed and which carry only men and arms." Does not this cast light, 11 years afterwards, upon Dollard's project? By 1660 the Iroquois had already been carrying on in this way for 20 years, and no one in New France was unaware of it. "In the spring," wrote d'Argenson, "the [Iroquois] hunters have not yet all come together and are probably not well supplied with ammunition to wage war, since they have used it all in their winter hunting...." One would think that one was reading Radisson: "If one hath his gun he wants his powder, and so the rest." It was partly to take advantage of this dispersion of the Iroquois hunters and of their low state of ammunition that Dollard fixed his choice upon the Ottawa River and stopped at the foot of the Long Sault, where the great difficulty in handling their canoes because of the currents would put the enemy at his mercy.

Without denying completely the military objective of the expedition, certain historians subordinate it to another purpose; the "capture" from the Iroquois by force of arms of the "valuable stocks of furs." In proof of this they advance as an argument the promissory note that Dollard signed at Montreal 15 April 1660: "I the undersigned recognize that I owe Mr. Jean Haubichon the sum of 45 *livres* plus 3 *livres* that I promise to pay him on my return...." Dollard promised to pay off this debt upon his return, it is argued, because he was sure that he would bring back furs. The note does indeed permit such a supposition; strictly speaking, it does not furnish proof of it. Certainly it was not possible for Dollard to be ignorant of the fact that the Iroquois canoes would be heavily laden with pelts; it was normal and quite fair that he should dream of rich spoils. Nevertheless, the virtual certainty that this was so does not authorize a historian to claim that capturing the Iroquois furs was the chief aim of the expedition. That would be contrary to all the testimonies of the time.

Besides, Dollard was not expecting to encounter hunters only. The presence of warriors on the Ottawa at this period of the year was too well known for him to have any illusions. In their search for furs the Iroquois had long before conceived the idea of intercepting the convoys on

Dollard Des Ormeaux

their way to the trading factories on the St. Lawrence. Hidden along the "passages," they would lie in wait for the canoes, massacre their crews, and carry off their cargoes. More than once the blockade of the Ottawa brought New France to the brink of ruin. Is it possible that, for the first time in the history of the colony, Dollard took upon himself the mission of assuring freedom of navigation for the allied flotillas by clearing the shores of the Ottawa? Radisson, who was particularly interested in this operation, asserted it explicitly: "Att ye other side [the Iroquois] wthout doubt had notice that ye travelers (we who had gone up to the Great Lakes) weare abroad, and would not faile to come downe wth a company, and to make a valiant deede and heroick action was to destroy them all, and consequently make the ffrench tremble as well as the wildmen, ffor the one could not live wthout the other; the one for his commodities, the other ffor his castors; so that ye Iroquoits pretending to wait for us at ye passage came thither fflocking. The ffrench [the Seventeen] and wild company [the 40 Hurons and 4 Algonkins], to putt the Iroquoits in some feare, and hinder his coming there so often wth such confidence, weare resolved to lay a snare agst him."

On top of that, there is no doubt that Dollard's expedition was seeking, among other purposes, to protect the descent of the Ottawas—or *Nez-Percés*—led by Radisson and CHOUART Des Groseilliers. The Jesuit Chaumonot was the only one to mention it, but his declaration is straightforward: "An Onondaga chieftain advanced without arms to within speaking distance to ask who were in the fort and why they had come there. He received the reply that they were Frenchmen, Hurons and Algonkins . . . who were coming to meet the *Nez-Percés*." Viewed in the context of what has preceded, this declaration casts a glaring light upon what may well have been the ultimate objective of the Seventeen.

When his project had received "the approbation and agreement of those in command," Dollard presumably spent part of the winter making his preparations, recruiting volunteers and laying in supplies "for ye whole summer." Lambert Closse, CHARLES LE MOYNE and Pierre Picoté de Belestre would have liked to join him if Dollard had agreed to "defer the enterprise until after the seeding"; but Dollard refused, since he would have had to give up "the honour of being in command." The departure was set for 19 April.

Hardly had the canoes left shore on the appointed day when cries were heard coming from the Île Saint-Paul, opposite Montreal. Hastening there, Dollard's troop forced a party of Iroquois to scatter into the woods, but they were too late to save the three Frenchmen who were the victims of this attack: Nicolas Duval had been killed and his companions, Blaise Juillet and Mathurin Soulard, had been drowned while trying to escape from the enemy. Dollard seized the Iroquois canoe, took Duval's body back to Ville-Marie, and probably attended his funeral the next day. On setting out the second time the expedition included a seventeenth volunteer who, after failing to keep his word the previous day, had now changed his mind.

Was Dollard accompanied from the beginning of his voyage by the 40 Hurons and 4 Algonkins who were to fight at his side? Chaumonot's and Radisson's accounts give this impression, and the *Relation* expressly states it. Dollier de Casson, however, relates that the Indians did not join the Frenchmen until the Long Sault. All things considered, this latter hypothesis seems the more probable. It would explain on the one hand the fact that neither Chaumonot nor the author of the *Relation*, whose informants were some Huron survivors, mentioned the incident at Île Saint-Paul, in which the Indians would not have taken part; and on the other hand it would explain why the Seventeen, who were "unskilled in managing canoes," were "held up for eight days by a little rapid at the end of this island [Montreal]." Although he left Montreal on 20 April, Dollard did not reach the Long Sault until 1 May (Chaumonot). Despite the presence of drift-ice on the river and the fact that "they journeyed by night to avoid discovery," it is certain that with the help of skilful Indian canoeists the French would have reached their destination much sooner. But all this is only a hypothesis, as the documents give contradictory versions concerning the moment at which the Indians joined Dollard's party.

On reaching the foot of the Long Sault (1 May), Dollard installed his troop in a makeshift way in an abandoned fort that the Algonkins had built the preceding autumn on a little rise. The next day, a Sunday, scouts spotted some Iroquois who were reconnoitring and who immediately fled. News of this encounter caused some anxiety among the Hurons, one of whom even insisted that they return to Montreal at once; it was finally agreed that "next day they would make a counter-palisade to protect the one that they had found there." But the enemy, who had been alerted by their scouts, did not give them time to do so; with "a hatchet in the belt" and "a musket at the Canoe's prow and a paddle in the hand," 200 (or 300) Onondagas soon came into sight on the river. "Surprised by so prompt and orderly an

Dollard Des Ormeaux

advance," Dollard and his men abandoned the meal that they were preparing and hastily shut themselves up in the fort. Firing broke out on both sides before they even had time to recognize each other.

After a few salvoes an Onondaga chieftain advanced unarmed to enquire "who were in the fort, and what they had come there for." "Frenchmen, Hurons and Algonkins, a hundred in all, who are here to meet the *Nez-Percés*," was the reply. The Iroquois then proposed a truce, to enable them to take counsel; anxious to reinforce their shelter, the French accepted, on condition that the enemy retire to the other side of the river. But far from going to the other side, the Iroquois began to raise stockades, while the allies were busy fortifying themselves as strongly as possible.

Dollard and his men had certainly not foreseen such an encounter. They had hoped to find the usual small, scattered bands of hunters. Now, in an unusual move, in 1660 the Iroquois had assembled on the Ottawa on their way back from the hunt because they had a rendezvous in the Richelieu islands with 500 warriors who were awaiting them in order to attack the French colony. Dollard had thus come up against a corps of the invasion army. This was not to be the last of his surprises.

Before the allies had finished fortifying their shelter, the Iroquois were already attacking. Heavy fire speedily compelled them to retire in disorder, leaving behind them dead and wounded. Some Hurons sprang beyond the palisade, cut off the head of an Onondaga chieftain, and "stuck it on a pike above the palisade as a trophy." Furious, the Iroquois made a second attempt, attacking the allies from the rear, it seems, in order to achieve greater surprise. This time too they were repulsed so vigorously that by the Onondagas' own admission, if the allies "had chased them, they would have destroyed them all." In not ordering a sortie, Dollard perhaps committed the error that cost him the victory.

After this second failure the Onondagas dispatched a canoe to the Richelieu islands to seek the aid of the 500 Mohawks and Oneidas who were waiting for them there. These reinforcements did not arrive until the fifth or seventh day following. In the meantime, well hidden behind their stockades, the Iroquois kept constant watch on the allies' fort, firing each time any one tried to leave it. Trapped in their confined reduit, almost without water because they were on a hill, the French and their allies soon found themselves in an extremely difficult situation: "The cold, the stench, the lack of sleep, hunger and thirst, wearied them more than the enemy. The scarcity of water was so great that they could no longer swallow the thick flour that soldiers are accustomed to live on in these extremities. They found a little water in a hole in the palisade, but when it was divided they scarcely had enough to moisten their mouths. The younger members made sorties from time to time over the stakes, for there were no gates, to fetch water from the river under cover of a heavy fusillade which drove back the enemy; but as they had lost their large receptacles [which had been left behind at the river's edge upon the enemy's arrival], they carried only small ones, which could not meet the needs of 60 persons both for drinking-water and for *sagamité*." In addition, as the Hurons and Algonkins prided themselves on replying to every shot fired by the enemy, ammunition began to run low.

Such was the precarious situation of Dollard's party when the 500 warriors arrived from the Richelieu. From then on it was no longer possible to cherish any illusions about the outcome of the battle. Therefore Annaotaha, the chief of the Hurons, proposed that they try to obtain "some satisfactory settlement" through the intermediary of a member of his group, an Oneida who had been adopted by the Hurons. When this suggestion was accepted, the Oneida and two "of the more important" Hurons were laden with presents and told what they were to say. While these bearers of a flag of truce were on their way to the enemy camp, their comrades in arms were offering prayers "to commend to God the outcome of this embassy." On the other hand, some Hurons who had been adopted by the Iroquois and who belonged to the Iroquois army took advantage of the truce to beg their compatriots in the French party to give up an unequal combat while there was still time, giving them assurances as to the welcome that the Iroquois had in store for them. Several Hurons—24 or 30—crossed the barricade and went over to the other side. Hoping that the whole troop would lay down their arms, some Iroquois came up to the small fort "with the intention of getting hold of those who wanted to flee." Disturbed by this move and having little confidence in the outcome of the embassy, the French opened fire, shooting down those who had ventured closest. Annaotaha upbraided his companions sharply for their haste: "Ah! comrades, you have spoiled everything. . . . Now that you have embittered them, they will charge upon us in such a rage, that we are without doubt lost." The Huron chief was right; in breaking the truce before the parley had failed, the French had just committed their second error.

As Annaotaha had foreseen, the Iroquois were incensed and rushed to attack the little fort. They

Dollard Des Ormeaux

were met with a hail of lead, but were not long in coming back, carrying for protection "mantlets of three pieces of wood lashed side to side, which covered them from the crown of the head to the middle of the thigh." Sheltering behind these makeshift shields, several of them were able to come up to the palisade and to slip "under the loop-holes," where they set to work to breach the walls. Aware of this new danger, the French "[took apart] two pistols and packed the barrels with powder," and setting fire to a fuse, they used them as grenades, but without much result. Then they had the idea of using in the same manner a keg of powder which hit something (the top of the palisade or a branch of a tree) and exploded on falling back inside the fort. Taking advantage of this mishap, the Iroquois took control of the loop-holes and fired from the outside on everything that moved inside the French reduit. One of the Frenchmen, "seeing that all was lost, and that several of his companions who had been mortally wounded were still alive, . . . despatched them with sturdy blows of his hatchet, to deliver them, by this inhuman act of mercy, from the fires of the Iroquois." When the enemy penetrated into the fort, they found only five Frenchmen and four Hurons alive.

According to Chaumonot, the battle of the Long Sault was begun on 2 May; according to Radisson and Chaumonot it probably lasted seven days, eight according to Dollier de Casson and ten according to the *Relation*. If we except the five survivors who fell into the enemy's hands, Dollard and his companions must have perished between 9 and 12 May 1660. One of the French prisoners was tortured to death on the scene of the combat; the remaining four were distributed among the Mohawks, Oneidas and Onondagas and suffered the same fate a little later. In Montreal Bénigne Basset compiled the inventory of the belongings of Jacques Boisseau on 25 May, of René Doussin and Jean Valets the following day. On 3 June Abbé SOUART drew up the death certificates of the Seventeen. The news of the disaster reached Quebec on 8 June, "towards midnight."

It was not until 6 Nov. 1660 that Basset proceeded to compile Dollard's post-obit inventory. His belongings, which were not numerous, were valued at 38 *livres*, 10 *sols*; his debts came to 32 *livres*, 10 *sols*; however, various notes signed by Dollard and not mentioned in the inventory bring the liabilities up to 119 *livres*, 10 *sols*. To the deceased's assets should be added the sum of 79 *livres*, 10 *sols* that he had devoted to developing his grant of land. On 2 May 1661 this property was assigned by Maisonneuve to Pierre Picoté de Belestre on condition that he pay back to Dollard's estate the 79 *livres*, 10 *sols* previously mentioned. Dollard's belongings were put up for auction 13 Nov. 1661. The sale of 9 of the 14 articles offered brought in 40 *livres*, 12 *sols*.

Did Dollard and his companions save New France by their resistance and death at the Long Sault? Opinions are divided, because agreement has not been reached upon the meaning of the expression "to save New France." If it is used in its absolute sense, and if it is affirmed that Dollard saved the colony from certain destruction and that he subdued the Iroquois for good, then it is obvious that the Seventeen did not save New France. But if a relative meaning is given to this expression, and if it is affirmed that in these particular circumstances Dollard momentarily averted from the colony a grave menace, then there is no doubt that the Seventeen saved New France. It should nevertheless be added that they did it involuntarily and by chance, since they had not foreseen meeting on the Ottawa a corps of the invasion army, of whose existence they were unaware.

But in addition, if Dollard saved New France, even involuntarily, the real reason must be given. Dollier de Casson reports that the French "had killed so many of the enemy that these used their bodies to climb over the palisades of the fort." Therefore, seized with fright, the Iroquois are supposed to have said: "If seventeen Frenchmen dealt with us in that fashion when they were in such a wretched hole, how shall we be treated when we have to attack a strong building in which are collected numbers of such people? We must not be so mad as to go any farther, to do so would mean death to us all. Let us go home." Thus, according to the Sulpician, the Iroquois probably gave up their invasion plan because of the terror which the vigorous defence by the Seventeen and the very considerable number of their own dead are believed to have caused them.

Were the Iroquois losses as great as was claimed by Dollier de Casson and Vachon* de Belmont, who wrote that "the enemy lost a third of their force"? Certainly not. On one hand, Indians did not expose their warriors to useless slaughter, fleeing unhesitantly and unashamedly from too costly a fight, even trying to obtain "some satisfactory settlement." The Iroquois probably did not act otherwise at the Long Sault. Moreover, they made only three or four assaults against the little fort. The rest of the time, well protected behind their stockades, they waited for the warriors from the Richelieu to arrive, being content to keep watch on the allies' fort to prevent

Dollard Des Ormeaux

them from coming out of it. For these reasons it seems impossible that the number of their dead was very high.

It is true that Radisson said that he believed "for certain that ye Iroquoits lost many men"; but that is merely an opinion, which we must interpret, asking ourselves what was meant at that time by losing "many men." Two documents connected with the Dollard affair allow us to establish a scale of reference; the 1660 *Relation* and a Dutch report written at Fort Orange and dated 15 June 1660. After the combat, recounts the *Relation*, the Iroquois "divided their captives. Two Frenchmen were apportioned to the Agnieronnons, two to the Onnontagueronnons, and the fifth to the Onneioutheronnons, to give them all a taste of French flesh, and . . . to invite them to a bloody war for avenging the deaths of a score of their men killed on this occasion." The author of the *Relation* had obtained this piece of information from some Hurons who had survived the Long Sault. In the Dutch document can be read the version by the Iroquois themselves: "Nothing new concerning the savages has happened here, except that the *Maquas* and *Sinnekus*, six hundred strong, have attacked a fort, defended by seventeen Frenchmen and one hundred savages; . . . they have lost fourteen killed; nineteen were wounded." A score of deaths is a much more probable figure than the great slaughter of which Dollier de Casson and Vachon de Belmont speak.

A poor judge of the Indians, Dollier de Casson was wrong when he ascribed the abandonment of the invasion project to the fact that the Iroquois were afraid. The latter were acting normally in returning immediately to their cantons, just as Marie de l'Incarnation wrote: "It is the characteristic of these Indians, even if they have taken or killed only a score of men, to go back to display them in their country." The *Relation* does not offer a different explanation of the Iroquois' decision: "After this distribution [of the prisoners] they departed, abandoning their intention to come and overwhelm our settlements, in order the sooner to conduct to their several countries those wretched victims, destined to appease the rage and cruelty of the most barbarous of all Nations."

Like all the original inhabitants of North America, the Iroquois were blindly obeying time-honoured laws. In the autumn of 1660, for example, having raised an army of 600 men, they advanced on New France. On the way some warriors raced off in pursuit of a stag. A shot meant for the animal killed the leader of the expedition. Taking this accident as a bad omen, the army broke off its project and dispersed. This new failure did not discourage the stubborn Iroquois; in 1661 they sowed terror in the colony, where they killed more than 100 of the French.

Thanks to a conjunction of circumstances, then, Dollard and his companions diverted the Iroquois army temporarily from its objective in 1660, thereby allowing the settlers to harvest their crop and escape famine and allowing Radisson to reach Montreal safe and sound with a load of furs valued at 200,000 *livres*. The Seventeen did not die in vain. And their merit was great. They were the first to take the offensive against the Iroquois when they left populated regions to destroy the enemy bands before they could strike at the colony. This tactic was ahead of its time since, except for the expedition by the Carignan-Salières regiment, it was not taken up until much later.

We must nevertheless take care not to exaggerate the importance of this episode in the Iroquois wars. During the heroic years of New France confrontations were frequent and the defenders of the colony valorous. Although little known, many feats of arms were no less splendid than that of the Seventeen. It is only the aura in which the battle of the Long Sault has been enveloped and the polemics to which it has given rise that explain the important place it occupies in Canadian historiography, as well as the nature and length of this present study, without however justifying them. In the picture of the first war between the French and Iroquois we must not relegate to the background, in favour of Dollard, people like Claude de BRIGEAC, JACQUES GODEFROY de Vieux-Pont, JEAN DE LAUSON (the younger), and especially someone like Lambert Closse, who were not inferior to him in courage and determination. It is fitting to recognize the merit of each, without trying to add to his glory.

ANDRÉ VACHON

APQ, Manuscrits concernant la Nouvelle-France, I, 321–26, 353–55. Dollier de Casson, *History of Montreal* (Flenley), 252–64. Marie Guyart de l'Incarnation, *Lettres* (Richaudeau), II, 148–75 (*see* the letters of 25 June, 17 and 23 September, and 2 November 1660 which, at least in part, bear on the affair of the Long-Sault; 154–62, Mémoire de Joseph-Marie Chaumonot. *JR* (Thwaites), XLV, 244–60; XLVII, 48–50. *JJ* (Laverdière et Casgrain), année 1660. *NYCD* (O'Callaghan and Fernow), XIII, 175. [Pierre-Esprit Radisson], *Voyages of Pierre Esprit Radisson, being an account of his travels and experiences among the North American Indians, from 1652 to 1684, transcribed from original manuscripts in the Bodleian Library and the British Museum*, ed. G. D. Scull (Prince Soc., XVI, Boston, 1885; New York, 1943), 234–36. Vachon de Belmont, *Histoire du Canada*, 10–11.

To enable the reader to follow the historiography of

Dollard, the studies listed below are given in chronological order. Charlevoix, *Histoire*, I, 347. Garneau, *Histoire du Canada*, I, 278–79. Ferland, *Cours d'histoire du Canada*, I, 455–62. Faillon, *Histoire de la colonie françias*, II, 395–420. Parkman, *The old régime* (1st ed.). P. Rousseau, *Histoire de la vie de M. Paul de Chomedey, sieur de Maisonneuve, fondateur et premier gouverneur de Ville-Marie* (Montréal, [1886]), 149–59. William Kingsford, *The history of Canada* (10v., Toronto and London, 1887–98), I, 261–62. Benjamin Sulte, "Le siège du Long-Sault," *Pages d'histoire du Canada* (Montréal, 1891), 273–82. Cyprien Tanguay, "Dollard et ses compagnons," *BHR*, VI (1900), 26–27. É.-Z. Massicotte, "Dollard Des Ormeaux," *Can. Antiquarian and Numismatic J.*, 3d ser., IX (1912), 45–73; "Les compagnons de Dollard Des Ormeaux," *Can. Antiquarian and Numismatic J.*, 4th ser., X (1913), 1–44. W. H. Atherton, *Montreal, 1535–1914* (3v., Montreal, Vancouver, Chicago, 1914), I, 163–72. É.-Z. Massicotte, *Dollard Des Ormeaux et ses compagnons: notes et documents* (Montréal, 1920); review by Gustave Lanctot in *CHR*, I (1920), 394–95. E. R. Adair, "Dollard Des Ormeaux and the fight at the Long Sault: a reinterpretation of Dollard's exploit," *CHR*, XIII (1932), 121–38. Gustave Lanctot, "Dollard Des Ormeaux and the fight at the Long Sault: Was Dollard the saviour of New France?" *CHR*, XIII (1932), 138–46. Lionel Groulx, "Le dossier de Dollard: la valeur des sources, la grandeur du dessein, la grandeur du résultat," *Le Devoir* (Montréal), 7, 11 mai 1932; publié en plaquette (Montréal, 1932); "Le dossier de Dollard," in *Notre maître le passé* (3v., Montréal, 1924–43), II, 25–53. L.-P. Desrosiers, "Dollard Des Ormeaux dans les textes," *Cahiers des Dix*, X (1945), 41–85. Lanctot, *Histoire du Canada*, I, 303–9. Lionel Groulx, *Dollard est-il un mythe?* (Montréal et Paris, 1960). Adrien Pouliot et Silvio Dumas, *L'exploit du Long-Sault: les témoignages des contemporains* (SHQ Cahiers d'Histoire, XII, 1960). Gustave Lanctot, "Gloire et respect à Dollard," *RUL*, XV (1960–1), 315–20. Adrien Pouliot, Series of articles on Dollard in *RUL*, XV (1960–1), 321–27, 430–40, 619–31, 814–31, 879–93; "L'exploit du Long-Sault: ses motifs, ses résultats," *RHAF*, XIV (1960–1), 3–15, 157–70. Silvio Dumas, "Le billet de Dollard," *RUL*, XV (1960–1), 709–15. Jacques Rousseau, " 'L'affaire Dollard,' de Fort Orange au Long-Sault," *RHAF*, XIV (1960–1), 370–7. André Vachon, "L'affaire du Long-Sault: valeur de la source huronne," *RUL*, XVIII (1963–64), 495–515.

DOMBOURG, JEAN-FRANÇOIS BOURDON DE. See BOURDON

DONNACONA, chief of Stadacona until May 1536, taken into exile by Jacques CARTIER along with two sons (Domagaya and Taignoagny); d. in France probably in 1539.

In July 1534, in Gaspé Bay ("la baie d'Honguedo"), Jacques Cartier entered into relations with Indians who had come from Stadacona (Quebec) to fish. When Cartier erected a cross there 24 July 1534, their chief, Donnacona, felt that he had been wronged; he harangued the French; his canoe was seized and he was forced to go aboard the ship along with those who were accompanying him. Cartier feasted him and persuaded him to let his two sons, Domagaya and Taignoagny, sail away with him, promising to bring them back. The French needed to train interpreters. Donnacona accepted and his two sons left for France. They spent eight months there and sailed again with Cartier 19 May 1535, without, however, having been baptized. They had learned French, they were able to give valuable information about their country; thanks to them, Cartier discovered in 1535 the great river which he had missed the previous year. Under the guidance of his two interpreters Cartier sailed up the river and took "the route to Canada"; on 7 September the interpreters finally arrived home, in "the province of Canada."

At this point Cartier, who was attracted by the hypothesis of a route to Asia, wanted to go on, to reach Hochelaga; from then on the interpreters began to intrigue against the French; Taignoagny in particular, we are told, "was intent on nothing but treason and malice." To dissuade Cartier from making this voyage they put on for him a scene of sorcery, which had no effect; Donnacona vainly offered gifts. Cartier left for Hochelaga without his interpreters. On his return, he found that his allies were no longer to be relied upon; he built fortifications. The chief of Achelacy (in the neighbourhood of Portneuf) put him on his guard against Donnacona and his sons: having become familiar with business practice in France, Domagaya and Taignoagny took their kinsmen to task for accepting trifling articles of no value in return for their goods, and Stadacona became more demanding. Relations were even broken off for a time; they were renewed 5 November, with the greatest benefit to the French. Indeed, Cartier obtained from Donnacona, who claimed to have travelled a great deal, much information about the country and also about the fabulous kingdom of the Saguenay which could be reached by the river which bears that name today and where "there are immense quantities of gold, rubies and other rich things, and . . . the men there are white as in France and go clothed in woolens," along with many other "marvels too long to relate." In addition, during the winter, when scurvy was ravaging the little French colony, it was Domagaya who unwittingly saved the day; Cartier learned from

Donnacona

him by ruse the secret of the infusion of *annedda* (white cedar).

The mutual distrust flared up again in the spring of 1536: Donnacona absented himself mysteriously and returned with people who had never been seen before; Cartier sent him an embassy, but Donnacona refused to receive it. It was finally learned that a quarrel had broken out at Stadacona between Chief Donnacona and his rival Agona. The interpreter Taignoagny asked for Cartier's help to eliminate Agona; for the French it involved carrying Agona off into exile. Cartier saw how he could turn the situation to good account and was "determined to outwit them." Since there was a crisis at Stadacona, it was better to get rid of Donnacona and his sons who were hindering the policy of the French; and, another advantage in carrying Donnacona off to France, the chief could recount personally all he knew to François I. Cartier pretended therefore to join in the plot against Agona; the interpreters promised to come back the following day for the feast of the Holy Cross (3 May). Donnacona and his people arrived for the religious ceremony, albeit very distrustfully; upon an order from Cartier, Chief Donnacona, his two sons, and two other headmen were seized. The inhabitants of Stadacona were upset; Cartier assured them ("and spoke thus to set their minds at rest") that Donnacona would come back in 12 moons, laden with gifts, after describing to the king the marvels of the Saguenay. On 6 May 1536 he left Stadacona with ten Iroquois on board: old Donnacona, his sons Domagaya and Taignoagny, a little girl of ten or 12 years of age, and two little boys whom Cartier had received as gifts the preceding autumn, a little girl of eight or nine years of age whom the chief of Achelacy had given him, and three other Indians. The way was clear for Agona.

It was not until 23 Aug. 1541 that Cartier arrived again at Stadacona; he returned without the Indians whom he had captured five years earlier. He announced to Agona, who was still chief of Stadacona, that Donnacona had died in France, that the others were living there as great lords, and that they were married and had not wished to come back: all of which naturally did not cause Chief Agona any grief.

In reality, of the ten Iroquois nine were dead; there remained only one little girl whose fate is unknown. Upon their arrival at Saint-Malo 16 July 1536, Chief Donnacona and his companions proceeded to live at the king's expense. Donnacona accepted questioning, even before a notary, about what he had seen on his voyages; the monk and historian André THEVET, who specialized in interrogating travellers, claimed that he had had a long conversation with Donnacona. The old chief was presented to François I: he talked to him about mines which were very rich in gold and silver, of an abundance of cloves, nutmeg, and pepper (the spices of which Europe dreamed); he enumerated many marvels, such as men with wings on their arms like bats, who flew from the trees to the ground. François I was very enthusiastic; someone said to him that the Indian chief was perhaps relating all this simply in order to obtain the opportunity of returning home; but the king in reply insisted upon Donnacona's veracity. On 25 March 1539 three of the Indians whom Cartier had brought back were baptized; the register does not identify them, we know only that they were males. Perhaps they were baptisms *in articulo mortis*? It was in any event towards this time that Donnacona, according to Thevet, died a Christian; and except for the little girl of ten years of age, his companions died about the same time.

When Cartier returned in 1541, Agona was then the only chief remaining at Stadacona. Franco-Iroquois relations were not improved thereby: Cartier's second voyage to Hochelaga (again without interpreters) undoubtedly had some bearing upon this, as did Agona's fear of suffering Donnacona's fate; even the chief of Achelacy, long faithful to Cartier, turned against the French. A veritable war finally broke out between the Indians of Stadacona and the colonists at Charlesbourg-Royal (at Cap-Rouge, near Quebec); the Indians were to boast of killing more than 35 of Cartier's men.

Agona was avenging Donnacona. We must go back to this wintering-over of 1541–42 to date the beginning of the wars between the French and the Iroquois. They were the result of Cartier's policy.

MARCEL TRUDEL

Biggar, *Documents relating to Cartier and Roberval*, 69–70, 75–82, 128, 456–57, 463. Hakluyt, *Principal navigations* (1903–5), VIII, 283–90 (English version of Cartier's third voyage). André Thevet, *Les singularitez de la France antarctique, autrement nommée Amérique: & de plusieurs terres & isles découvertes de nostre temps*, éd. Paul Gaffarel (Paris, 1878), 407. *Voyages de Jacques Cartier au Canada*, éd. Th. Beauchesne in *Les Français en Amérique* (Julien), 77–197. *Voyages of Cartier* (Biggar).

A. G. Bailey, "The significance of the identity and disappearance of the Laurentian Iroquois," *RSCT*, 3d ser., XXVII (1933), sect.II, 97–108. Hoffman, *Cabot to Cartier*, 131–60, 197–215. W. D. Lighthall, "Hochelagans and Mohawks; a link in Iroquois history," *RSCT*, 2d ser., V (1899), sect.II, 199–211. Jacques Rousseau, "L'annedda et l'arbre de vie," *RHAF*, VIII (1954), 171–201; "Ces gens qu'on dit sauvages," *Cahiers des Dix*, XXIII (1958), 71; "Le mystère de l'annedda," in *Jacques Cartier et "la grosse maladie"* (XIXe Congrès international de Physiologie Pub., Montréal, 1953), 105–16.

DOUBLET, FRANÇOIS, apothecary, shipowner; b. 1619 or 1620 at Honfleur (Normandy), son of François Doublet, a merchant, and of Marguerite Auber; d. before 1678.

François Doublet concerned himself with seaborne trade, and about 1659 he was in partnership with a Dieppe shipowner, Pierre Gellée; they traded in goods imported from Canada, especially cod, whale-oil, bearskins, and beaver pelts. In 1662 he decided to become a shipowner himself, and to turn his attention towards Canada. The Compagnie de la Nouvelle-France granted him, 19 Jan. 1663, the Îles de la Madeleine, de Saint-Jean (today Prince Edward Island), des Oiseaux, and de Brion, so that he could develop colonization and fisheries there. But, 10 years earlier, these islands had been made over to NICOLAS DENYS, and furthermore, a group of Basques had just finished settling in the Îles de la Madeleine.

After obtaining in Holland a ship of 300 tons, which was given the name *Saint-Michel*, François Doublet acquired two other small vessels. Before setting out, he formed a partnership with Philippe Gaignard on 23 April 1663, in order to exploit the Îles de la Madeleine. The ships put to sea towards the end of April 1663, carrying, in addition to the crews, 25 men who were to become the first settlers on the islands. The crossing was rather long, and marked by a number of incidents; for instance, as soon as they were on the high seas they discovered on board one of the ships a seven-year-old boy, Jean-François, François Doublet's son, who was later to become a privateer of some repute. The majority of the details that we have concerning this first voyage come from the account written by his son.

Towards mid-May, the expedition reached the Île de Brion, where some 20 Basques were found, living in a wooden house. During the rest of the summer, some dwellings and a store were built, and the men went hunting and fishing. Doublet returned to France in the autumn, leaving some 20 of his men to spend the winter on the islands. The following spring, he found the island completely abandoned by his associates, and the buildings started the previous summer already in ruins. Doublet was therefore obliged to go back to France, dissolve the partnership formed the winter before, and sell his ships.

That same year, having planned his return to New France, he boarded a ship at Le Havre which sailed for Quebec, where he landed 2 Oct. 1664. This time he came as a commissioner instructed "to sink a shaft into a lead mine which had recently been discovered on the shores of Gaspé." This new adventure was not much more successful, since by the end of the summer of 1665 the total quantity of lead ore extracted did not exceed four or five tons. Doublet then came back to Quebec, where his son Jean-François was studying under the Jesuits. On 21 July of the same year, in his capacity as head clerk of the Compagnie des Indes occidentales at Gaspé, he obtained from the Marquis de Tracy [*see* PROUVILLE] an authorization "to trade in pelts for and on behalf of the gentlemen of the said company along the coasts of Canada, Acadia, Newfoundland and elsewhere." He apparently spent two further years in New France, and his presence is noted at Fort Richelieu in 1665 and 1666.

In 1668 Doublet was back at Honfleur, and he seems to have spent the rest of his career in the service of a society of merchants who were carrying on trade along the coasts of Africa. He appears to have died before 1678.

On 1 Feb. 1643 François Doublet had married Madeleine Fontaine, Jacques Fontaine's daughter, by whom he had 16 children; the best known of them, Jean-François, "a privateer and lieutenant on a frigate . . . occupies a distinguished place in the naval history of Normandy."

Some have asserted that the Îles de la Madeleine owe their name to François Doublet, who is thought to have called them after his wife. It is more probable, however, that the name of these islands comes from the appellation "La Magdelene," given by CHAMPLAIN to Amherst Island on his map of 1632.

F. GRENIER

BM, Add. MS 14034, f.66 (concession of the Magdalen Islands in 1663). Correspondance de Talon, *APQ Rapport, 1930–31*, 22. [Jean Doublet], *Journal du corsaire Jean Doublet de Honfleur, lieutenant de frégate sous Louis XIV*, éd. Charles Bréard (Paris, 1884), 5–7, 27, 281–83. *Mémoires des commissaires*, I, 154; II, 521, 524–27; and *Memorials of the English and French commissaries*, I, 208–9, 736, 739. *Ord. comm.* (P.-G. Roy), I, 24–25. P.-G. Roy, *Inv. concessions*, II, 94. Charles Bréard, *Le vieux Honfleur et ses marins: biographies et récits maritimes* (Rouen, 1897), 86–92. "Les disparus: Jean-François Doublet," *BRH*, XXXIII (1927), 206. La Morandière, *Hist. de la pêche française de la morue*, I, 373.

DOWNING, JOHN, fl. 1647–82, and **WILLIAM,** d. 1681; settlers in Newfoundland.

Drake

Their father John Downing senior, a London merchant, was appointed deputy governor of Newfoundland in 1640 during Sir DAVID KIRKE's absence; he settled and died there. The younger John Downing became prominent in the island's affairs when, in 1676, he came to London to represent the planters' interests in the struggle for the survival of settlement on the island. The long conflict between planters and the western fishing merchants had culminated that year in an order that the inhabitants leave. The enforcement of the order was delayed first by Sir John BERRY's support of the settlers and then by John Downing's powerful representation of their case.

Downing's purpose was to have a governor appointed with authority over both inhabitants and visiting fishermen. He employed two main arguments: that it was the fishermen who committed abuses and the planters who brought order to the island, and that the French threat from Plaisance (Placentia Bay) was so great that, if the planters left, Newfoundland and its fishery would be lost to the Crown. Downing also held that the settlers had a legal right to live there because of the earlier proprietary patents. As a result of his pleading the Privy Council ordered an investigation to be made by the convoy commodore. (Such investigations soon became an established practice.) The hearing of evidence from both sides dragged on and early in 1677 Downing asked permission to return to Newfoundland where his family needed him. He seems to have gone to the island later that year and was still living in St. John's in 1682.

By 1679 his brother William had become the planters' agent and put forward arguments very similar to those used by John. With a fellow settler, Thomas Oxford, he proposed the fortification of certain key harbours. By now the inhabitants' plight had grown so desperate because of the fishermen's violence that they considered returning to England or seeking French protection. Early in 1680 William reported that the settlers were prepared to withdraw to four harbours and restrict the settlement to its present size. He renewed his plea for the appointment of a governor whom the planters offered to support; the suggestion was accepted on condition that the money could be raised voluntarily.

Such was the position when William Downing left for Newfoundland early in 1681 but in June he was reported to have died at sea. The steady opposition of experienced planters like the Downings to the pressure to end settlement in Newfoundland was a major factor in the defeat of the charter regulations of 27 Jan. 1675/76. The situation remained fluid, the government undecided, until the passing of the Newfoundland Act in 1699 when the position of the inhabitants was confirmed.

GILLIAN T. CELL

[*See also* BERRY and HINTON.]

For the official petitions and representations made by the Downings see PRO, C.O. 1/38, nos. 33, 70, 73, 74; 1/39, nos. 12, 45, 49, 50, 53, 56, 57; 1/43, nos. 16, 41, 51, 83; 1/44, nos. 18, 23, 27, 34; 1/47, nos. 15, 52; 391/1 nos. 305–7; 391/2, nos 22–26, 31–38, 323–35; 391/3, nos. 3, 4, 159, 160. BM, Egerton MS 2395, ff.560–66v. *See also:* PRO, *Acts of P.C., col. ser., 1613–80*; CSP, *Col., 1675–76, 1677–80, 1681–85*. William Downing's will is at Somerset House, P.C.C., 40 North. Lounsbury, *British fishery at Nfld.* Prowse, *History of Nfld.*

DRAKE, SIR BERNARD, commander of an English expedition to Newfoundland; b. *c.* 1537, d. 10 April 1586.

He succeeded his father in 1558 as head of the Drake family of Ashe, Musbury, Devon, and occupied himself in building up his estates and in local government. He was a first cousin of Sir Richard Grenville and may have been distantly related to Sir FRANCIS DRAKE. He married Gertrude Fortescue and had several children.

Bernard was first attracted to American ventures by Sir Humphrey GILBERT in 1582 and he undertook to lead a party of adventurers to settle whatever part of North America Gilbert had sold him on paper. However, he did not go or participate in any overseas ventures, so far as is known, until 1585, when he agreed to take part under Sir Walter Raleigh in the venture for planting Virginia. He was to lead a second squadron through the West Indies, with its chance of Spanish prizes, to Roanoke Island (modern North Carolina) where a colony was to be settled by Sir Richard Grenville, who had left Plymouth in April. Drake's ship, in which Amyas Preston—a gentleman of Cricket, Somerset, who was afterwards to be a prominent privateer and naval commander—had a share, was the 110-ton *Golden Riall* of Topsham, where Bernard Drake had a house. With her was associated Sir Walter Raleigh's *Job*, 70 tons, Capt. Andrew Fulford, and apparently a vessel commanded by Hugh Drake, perhaps the pinnace *Good Companion*. There were others too among the "divers good Ships under his command" which Richard WHITBOURNE saw at Newfoundland, possibly one large and two smaller, of which we have no details.

On 26 May the Spaniards clapped an embargo on English shipping in Bilbao harbour, as they were doing all over Spain; the ship *Primrose* fought her way clear and brought the news to

London. There it was decided to release a large number of privateers in reprisal and to take precautions against other merchant ships' being caught in Spain. On 10 June Raleigh was authorized to impress ships for a voyage to be made to Newfoundland so as to warn English fishing vessels there not to take fish direct to Spain or Portugal (the triangular trade being already well established), and to seize any vessels belonging to subjects of the king of Spain they could find. Commissions to lead such expeditions were issued to Carew Raleigh and to Bernard Drake on 20 June, and the latter was ordered about 27 June to abandon his Virginia voyage and take himself off to Newfoundland; Carew Raleigh apparently remained at home.

Drake probably set out early in July and reached Newfoundland by the end of the month, though we have no precise dates for the voyage. On the way over, the *Golden Riall*, perhaps with her pinnace, sailed far enough south to capture a rich, sugar-laden Brazilman. This valuable Portuguese prize was put in charge of Amyas Preston and was sent home, duly arriving at Exmouth, while Bernard Drake went on his way. In the absence of a narrative of the voyage we cannot say precisely how Drake made contact with his other ships, but he probably encountered them only at a rendezvous at St. John's, the obvious first port of call for the performance of his dual mission. It would have been here that Whitbourne saw him. After warning the English fishing captains and impounding enemy shipping there, he is likely to have dispersed his squadron, in convenient groups, to the other harbours which the English fishermen frequented.

Though the episode is usually characterized as the seizure of the Spanish fishing fleet, Drake did not, and was unlikely to, meet with more than an occasional fishing vessel, as the Spanish fishery was based on the southwest and west shores of Newfoundland, while the Portuguese shared harbours with the English in the southeast and east, and had already in 1582 suffered from English anti-Spanish reprisals following on the Spanish conquest of Portugal in 1580 [*see* CLARKE]. Bernard Drake himself took the *Golden Riall* south to Bay Bulls where he encountered George Raymond in command of the *Red Lion* of Chichester, 100 tons. Raymond was from Chichester, Sussex, and had sailed with Grenville to Virginia in April and landed his quota of colonists at Croatoan on the Carolina Outer Banks in June, before coming on to Newfoundland, where, it is not unlikely, he was already looking for Portuguese prizes. Drake joined forces with him and together they made more captures.

Leaving their consorts and prizes to make their own way home the two commanders sailed to the Azores where they were highly successful in prize-taking, overpowering a straggler from the homeward-bound Spanish West Indies fleet, which had some wine and ivory on board (though we do not know what its main cargo was), and no less than three Portuguese Brazilmen all laden with sugar. Another prize was a ship of La Rochelle from Guinea with a little gold. (Though brought to England she was later restored to her owners as she may have been under charter to English merchants.) We have no precise inventory of the Portuguese fishing vessels taken, but they totalled 16 or 17 in all. Some did not reach England. Their captors met with very bad weather and anything from two to seven of them may have been lost at sea, while the *Lion* of Viana, 180 tons, with Thomas Raynsforde as captain of her prize crew, along with Raleigh's *Job*, were forced into Breton ports and held captive there. Raymond brought a Brazilman to Chichester and some fishing vessels to the same port and to Portsmouth; the other two Brazilmen and the Spaniard followed Preston's prize into Exmouth, while by mid-October 600 Portuguese fishermen were scattered with their vessels amongst other southwestern ports.

The total haul of 21 or 22 vessels represented an appreciable victory for the English. The Brazilmen and the Westindiaman were worth at least £10,000 and the fishing vessels perhaps as much again, though values up to £60,000 were mentioned, and it is likely that much spoil went clandestinely to the seamen. Profits were high, as the initial cost of the expedition was about £3,500. The government, not to be robbed of customs duties and the lord high admiral's share, appointed commissioners in Devon, Somerset, and Dorset to appraise the prizes and distribute the proceeds, allowing the captives 3*d*. a day maintenance until repatriated. Raleigh and Sir John Gilbert appear to have had a major say in the final division, though particulars of it have not survived, except that four of the five most valuable prizes went to Bernard Drake and his son, though they withheld Amyas Preston's share in the one he brought home. This, Sir John Gilbert was finally ordered by the Privy Council to repay in 1589, as he had handed the vessel to the Drakes.

Bernard Drake had the crew of one of the Portuguese vessels brought to Dartmouth imprisoned in Exeter: the charge must have been a criminal one (mutiny perhaps). He made them no allowance and they starved through the winter except for some charity shown them by the citizens. He himself went to London where, at Greenwich on 9 Jan. 1585/86, Queen Elizabeth knighted him in recognition of his success. The Exeter assizes opened on 14 March. The chief justice of common pleas, Sir Edmund Anderson, who was on circuit, when he learnt of the plight of the 38 prisoners—all now seriously ill—reprimanded those responsible for their malnutrition and Drake in particular. The trial judge was Baron Flowerday and he had with him on the bench a group of local justices of the peace, including Sir Bernard Drake. There was a great stench when the prisoners were brought to the bar and it is not known that any sentence was passed on them, but within a little more than three weeks the judge, 8 J.P.s and 11 of 12 jurors, with some of the court officials, were all dead of an infection caught from the Portuguese. Sir Bernard Drake, when he fell ill, struggled as far as Crediton on his way home but died there on 10 April and was buried two days later. An epidemic of what was apparently typhus raged in Devonshire for more than a year. If it was entirely the consequence of the Newfoundland raid, which is not established, the cost of the latter in loss of life was very great. John, Drake's eldest son, succeeded to the estate of Ashe and to the family's new and old wealth.

DAVID B. QUINN

BM, Lansdowne MS 148, ff.127–28. PRO, H.C.A. 14/23, nos. 164(a-b)–165; C.142/211/175; S.O.3, Ind. 6800; S.P.12/144, no.59; 12/179, nos.1–2; 12/183, no.13; 12/185, no.60; 12/186, no.8; *Acts of P.C., 1588–89*, 383–84; *CSP, Spain, 1580–86*, 535. R. Holinshed, *Chronicles*, ed. H. Ellis (3d ed., 6v., London, 1807–8), IV, 868–69.
C. Creighton, *History of epidemics in Britain* (2v., Cambridge, 1891). *DNB* [see articles on Sir Bernard Drake, Edward Flowerdew, Sir Amyas de Preston]. *English privateering voyages to the West Indies 1588–95*, ed. K. R. Andrews (Hakluyt Soc., 2d ser., CXI, 1959) [for George Raymond and Amyas Preston]. *Roanoke voyages* (Quinn), I, 171–73, 234–42. A. L. Rowse, *The England of Elizabeth* (London, 1950). *The visitations of the County of Devon, comprising the herald's visitations of 1531, 1564 and 1620*, ed. J. L. Vivian (Exeter, [1895]). *Voyages of Gilbert* (Quinn), I, 61, 95; II, 333.

DRAKE, SIR FRANCIS, English navigator, probably the first European to sight the west coast of Canada; b. near Tavistock, Devonshire, c. 1540; d. 28 Jan. 1595/96 on board his ship off Portobelo, Panama.

One of the great seamen of the Elizabethan age, Drake made several voyages to the West Indies in 1565–73 and commanded a final expedition in 1595, but his fame rests chiefly upon his voyage around the world in 1577–80, for which he was knighted in 1581, and on the defeat of the Spanish Armada in 1588.

On his world voyage, Drake left Plymouth in December 1577. He spent some time in the South Atlantic; then, in September 1578, he passed through the Strait of Magellan and entered the Pacific. After harrying Spanish ships and settlements on the South and Central American coasts, he seized Huatulco in Mexico. Here, in the spring of 1579, he planned his homeward voyage. Geographical ideas at the time were much influenced by Abraham Ortelius, whose famous map of the world showed the northern coast of North America as being south of 60°, with a polar sea beyond which communicated with the Atlantic by a northwest passage and with the Pacific by the Strait of Anian. Drake decided to attempt to return to England by this polar route. He set out from Huatulco on 16 April, but some six weeks later bad weather made him change his mind, and eventually he sailed across the Pacific and Indian oceans and returned to Europe by rounding Africa.

The supposition that he sighted Canada is based upon the nature of the winds and currents that normally prevail in the North Pacific in the spring months. These revolve clockwise in a vast circle—a phenomenon noted by Claret* de Fleurieu, a French naval officer, and as a consequence known as "Fleurieu's whirlpool." Sailing ships must take it into careful account; otherwise they may spend many days battling with head winds.

After leaving Huatulco, Drake first sailed a considerable distance to the west, and then turned north. On 5 June he was still far from the North American coast, somewhere between latitude 42° and 48°; on 17 June he dropped anchor in a bay near San Francisco. The only way in which he could possibly have travelled between these two points in only 12 days was by following the edge of the whirlpool, and being swept along by its winds and currents. These probably carried him within sight of the coast of Vancouver Island and the State of Washington, and the earliest accounts of the voyage seem to bear this out.

W. KAYE LAMB

P. R. Bishop, "Drake's course in the north Pacific," *B.C. Hist. Q.*, III (1939), 151–82 (for the theory that Fleurieu's whirlpool carried Drake within sight of the coast of Vancouver Island and the State of Washington). E. G. R. Taylor, *Tudor geography, 1485–1583* (London, 1930), *passim*. H. R. Wagner, *Sir Francis Drake's voyage around the world* (San Francisco, 1926). J. A. Williamson, *The age of Drake* (London, 1938), *passim; Sir Francis Drake* (London, 1952), *passim*.

DRAPER, THOMAS, HBC captain; fl. 1670–81.
Although probably with the Company as early

as 1670, Draper's service was intermittent. Despite extensive preparations in 1674 he did not sail that year. In 1676 as chief mate on the *Shaftesbury* (Capt. Joseph THOMPSON) he made the trip out and back in the same season.

Four years later he commanded the *Albemarle*, bearing a commission from His Highness Prince Rupert to serve on Governor NIXON's council. Although it was "of great moment" that a factory be established at New Severn Draper did not carry out this instruction just then.

Of intriguing interest is an amount of £10 credited to his account in August 1680 "for secret service." Details are not available but speculation could link it with the irritating interloping trade. He brought the *Albemarle* home in 1681.

Draper later received a reprimand occasioned by the wreck, off Tetherley's Island in 1680, of the *Prudent Mary*, a vessel accompanying Draper's *Albemarle*. Failure to save her beaver cargo was laid primarily on Governor Nixon but Draper shared the blame as an "evil counsellor." In fact, the Company now considered him "so ill a man that we shall never think worth our imployment any more."

MAUD M. HUTCHESON

HBRS, V, VIII, IX (Rich); XI (Rich and Johnson).

DREUILLETTES (Drouillet, Drouillettes, Droulletes, Druilletes), GABRIEL. *See* DRUILLETTES

DROUIN, ROBERT, pioneer on the Beaupré shore; b. 6 Aug. 1607 at Saint-Barthélemi du Pin-la-Garenne, Perche, son of Robert Drouin and Marie Dubois; buried 1 June 1685 at Château-Richer.

The date of Drouin's arrival in Canada is not known, but it is certain that he was here by 1636. In 1641 he already had a farm near the Rivière aux Chiens on the Beaupré shore, although he did not receive the concession for it until 17 April 1646. By his marriage with Anne Cloutier, which was celebrated 12 July 1637, he had three daughters; by his second marriage, with Marie Chapelier on 29 Nov. 1649, he had eight more children.

It is almost impossible to trace any French-Canadian genealogy without encountering Robert Drouin among the earliest ancestors. That would seem to us to be his greatest claim to fame. It is also to be noted that his marriage contract with Anne Cloutier (which preceded by nearly a year the religious ceremony), concluded 27 July 1636 in ROBERT GIFFARD's house and drawn up in the absence of a notary by JEAN GUYON DU BUISSON, senior, is the oldest marriage contract preserved in the original in Canada.

HONORIUS PROVOST

ASQ, Documents Faribault, 2; Seigneuries. *JR* (Thwaites). *Jug. et délib.*

DRUILLETTES (the following forms are also found: **Dreuillettes, Drouillettes, Drouillet, Droulletes, Drueillettes, Druilletes**), **GABRIEL,** priest, Jesuit, missionary, and explorer; b. 29 Sept. 1610 at Garat (diocese of Limoges, France); d. 8 April 1681 at Quebec.

Gabriel Druillettes entered the noviciate of the Society of Jesus 28 July 1629 at Toulouse. He studied philosophy at Le Puy, taught at Mauriac, Béziers, and Puy, followed the course in theology at Toulouse, was ordained priest in 1641 or 1642, and sailed to Canada on 15 Aug. 1643, immediately after completing his training as a Jesuit. This missionary, whose name survives especially because of his explorations, has also other claims to be remembered by history. Among the Jesuits of New France, none perhaps made such a deep and rapid impression upon the Indians. No man, in any case, presented such an alliance of burning zeal with the gifts of the miracle-worker and the conquering power of gentleness.

The sources reveal Father Druillettes as specializing in wintering with Indian hunters. His career was decided by an early reverse. In September 1643 he was to accompany BRÉBEUF to the Huron country, but he was detained at Quebec by the Iroquois blockade. Consequently he was sent to Sillery to learn Montagnais. In the autumn of 1643 the Christian Montagnais asked him to go hunting with them. Druillettes set off in November or December, carrying his baggage on his shoulders as they did, together with his sacred vessels; like them he ranged the woods on snowshoes after moose, slept in filth amongst the dogs, shared the *sagamité* or the smoked meat of the natives, and their fasts of several days' duration as well. The worst ordeal was the smoke of the lodges. Druillette's eyes gradually grew weaker; he became completely blind, and his companions had to assign him a child to lead him. An old woman offered to give him treatment, and she scraped the cornea with a rusty knife. The remedy was worse than the disease. Finally the missionary called his flock around him and asked them to pray for him. He began a mass of the Virgin Mary, from memory. Suddenly, in the middle of the service, the light of day appeared to him again, shining and splendid. The mass was concluded with thanksgiving, and Druillettes never again suffered from his eyes. [*JR* (Thwaites), XXVII, 215–19.]

Duboct

This was the starting point of his extraordinary power of intercession on behalf of the Indians, who were to consider him everywhere as a miraculous being. Druillettes spent other winter seasons in a similar way in 1647–48, 1649–50, and 1664–65; for these periods we have evidence, but there are probably others. He travelled through the woods of Nouveau-Québec to the north of Tadoussac, those of the south shore in the region of Matane and the Notre-Dame mountains, and perhaps went to Sept-Îles and to Lac Saint-Jean. Apart from these winter journeys, he accompanied the Montagnais in war and regularly conducted the Tadoussac mission during the summer. The natives flocked from the most distant forests to hear his words, took them back with them, and themselves made converts.

Father Druillettes is known as the missionary to the Abenakis. In 1646, influenced by NEGABAMAT, these Indians of the Kennebec River basin asked for a missionary. Father Druillettes set off from Sillery on 29 August to go to them. He learned their language in three months, visited the Abenaki villages and the English settlements, and even went by sea to the Penobscot River, meeting the Capuchins who were missionaries in these parts. His preaching, further reinforced by amazing cures, conquered the Indians. Druillettes went hunting with the Abenakis in the region of Lake Moosehead (Maine), encountering the usual difficulties but gaining his companions' confidence more and more. From that time on the Abenakis, without being baptized, were won over to the faith. The Capuchins declared to the superior of Quebec that they feared a conflict of authority, and consequently Father Druillettes was not sent back to Maine in 1647 or 1648, despite the Indians' entreaties. But the Capuchin superior then changed his mind, and Father Druillettes returned there 1 Sept. 1650, with the *donné* Jean Guérin. This time Druillettes was the governor of Quebec's ambassador for the preparation of an alliance with New England against the Iroquois. He also carried on missionary work in Maine, acquired valuable friendships among the English, through almost all of whose country he travelled, and returned to Quebec in the spring of 1651, with hopes which were however not to come to fruition. He set off again on 22 June of the same year, to exercise his apostolate among the Abenakis and to continue his embassy. It was a fearful journey, by an enormous detour, since he had to go far up the Saint John River in order to reach the headwaters of the Kennebec. The amazing effects of the missionary's prayers delighted the Indians on several occasions; they adopted him as one of their own people and the English urged him to remain in the country. But he had to go back in 1652, eating on the way the boiled leather from his shoes and his moose-skin jerkin, and the thongs of his snow-shoes.

Less well known among Father Druillettes' merits is the fact that he was the true initiator of the grandiose project for establishing the western missions. Following up the reports of Radisson* and CHOUART Des Groseilliers, and also of Indians encountered at Tadoussac, he located and took censuses of the various tribes of these regions. This was in 1655. In 1656 he set off for the west with Léonard GARREAU, having already joined up with a party of Algonkins. Before reaching Montreal Garreau was mortally wounded by the Iroquois, and Druillettes, abandoned by the Algonkins, was obliged to turn back. In 1661 he conceived the fantastic plan of resuming this journey by way of Tadoussac, the Saguenay, and Hudson Bay. With Claude DABLON he succeeded in reaching the watershed, at Lac Nikabau. But fear of the Iroquois, even in those distant regions, caused the defection of his Indian guides, who went back to Tadoussac. Druillettes, with his body worn out by so many hardships but his courage still indomitable, had to wait until 1670 in order to realize his dream, when, as a stiff-jointed old man of 60, he went up to take charge at Sault Ste. Marie. There the great deeds of his maturity were repeated, and each year the report from the Sault, in the *Relations*, gave longer lists of the extraordinary favours that lent lustre to his apostolate. Around 1680 this old campaigner for Christ was brought back to Quebec, where he died in his seventy-first year. The few writings of Father Druillettes that will be found in the works quoted below have no literary interest; his real works were the men whom he formed and inspired: Pierre BAILLOQUET, Charles ALBANEL, Jacques MARQUETTE, Claude Dablon, Henri Nouvel*.

LUCIEN CAMPEAU

Charlevoix, *Histoire*, I, 279–81, 310–11, 326–27. *JR* (Thwaites). François Elesban de Guilhermy, *Ménologe de la Compagnie de Jésus . . . Assistance de France, comprenant les missions de l'Archipel, de l'Arménie, de la Syrie, . . . du Canada, de la Louisiane . . .*, éd. Jacques Terrien (2pts., Paris, 1892), I, 471–74. Le Jeune, *Dictionnaire*, I, 535. Rochemonteix, *Les Jésuites et la Nouvelle-France au XVIIe siècle*, I, 267–73; II, 131–35, 151, 368–69.

DUBOCT. *See* DUBOK

DUBOIS DAVAUGOUR, PIERRE, baron, governor of New France 1661–63 (the last to serve under the jurisdiction of the Compagnie des Cent-Associés); d. fighting againt the Turks at Serinvans-Zrin, on the borders of Croatia, 24 July 1664.

Davaugour, whose family could trace descent from a cadet branch of the counts of Brittany, had spent some 40 years in the army prior to his Canadian appointment. This would indicate that he was in his late fifties when he came to Canada. During the Thirty Years' War in Germany he served with distinction as a colonel in the French cavalry and during the closing stages of the war he was attached to the Swedish forces allied to France. In 1646 he acted as liaison officer for the great French general Turenne with the commander of the Swedish armies in Germany, to co-ordinate joint plans for the ensuing campaigns in the Rhineland against the armies of the Hapsburg Holy Roman Emperor. He subsequently served as Louis XIII's *résident*, or agent, in Germany and then was posted to the French armies in Flanders to supervise the implementation of the terms of the Treaty of Westphalia which ended the war between France and her allies on the one side and the emperor on the other. In 1658 he was sent on a diplomatic mission to Sweden, then, in 1661, on the recommendation of the queen he was appointed governor of New France for a three-year term, to succeed Voyer* d'Argenson.

In character he was very forthright, not given to compromise, rather hasty in his judgements at times, and quick to resent the slightest disagreement with his expressed views. He made his decisions very swiftly, sometimes without sufficient reflection, and was very loath to rescind an order, once given, even though the consequences were manifestly undesirable. Colbert, in 1661, commented on "his bizarre and rather untractable character." These were, however, almost the distinguishing marks of the French soldier and aristocrat of the period.

Yet Davaugour had one outstanding gift: imagination. From the moment of his arrival in New France on 31 Aug. 1661, he grasped the great potentiality of the country and he later wrote: "I believed, as did everyone else, that Canada was a country as savage as it was forsaken . . . and to tell the truth nothing in the world has appeared to me so beautiful as the river St. Lawrence, so pleasing to the eye, so fruitful for commerce, and so advantageous for the establishing of the fleurs de lis. . . ." But before any such vision of future greatness could begin to be realized, the colony had to be relieved of the constant harrying attacks of the Iroquois. Since the days of CHAMPLAIN the savage warriors of the five Iroquois nations had waged an intermittent war of ambush and surprise attack against the French settlers in an attempt to destroy their hold on the western fur trade. Not only did these attacks inflict heavy casualties on the French, but they prevented the development of the colony's resources; fields were left idle and cattle could not put out to pasture. Davaugour, with the contempt of the European soldier for irregular warfare, was of the opinion that a few hundred regular troops would quickly quell the Iroquois but he made it plain that the colony could not support the expense of maintaining such a force. In fact, the 100 soldiers he had brought with him from France were too great a burden for the colony to bear and in a letter to the Prince de Condé, dated 13 Oct. 1661, he bluntly stated: "If with the knowledge of this the king do not interpose, and do not send me my bread and that of the hundred soldiers whom I have brought with me, I shall have the honour of saying something more on this subject to your Highness next year, with God's help. And, in my opinion, I would rather rob the altar than impose upon them a burden they cannot yet bear." To clarify his views on what should be done he sent Pierre Boucher*, a long-time resident of the colony and governor of Trois-Rivières, to France. The choice of Boucher for this task proved to be an excellent one; he returned the following year with 200 settlers, 100 soldiers, and the assurance of much greater aid in the very near future.

Meanwhile, in addition to informing the members of Louis XIV's Conseil d'État of what could, and should, be done for the development of Canada, Davaugour was busy with more immediate problems. After visiting all the outlying settlements of the colony he returned to Quebec and appointed to its Conseil the superior of the Jesuits, on the ground that it was they who had done the most for the country. At the same time, he conspicuously failed to invite Bishop Laval* to take a seat at the council table. He did, however, support Bishop Laval, and the Jesuits, in their determined efforts to ban the sale of liquor to the Indians. Their opposition to this commerce stemmed from the fact that the Indians drank only to become intoxicated. They believed that liquor transported them into the strange world of their primitive gods and they themselves became akin to the gods when drunk. But, lacking the inhibitions of Europeans, too many of them lost every vestige of self-control, committed horrible crimes while inebriated, and afterwards disclaimed all responsibility for their actions. So eager were many of them to obtain liquor that they would trade all their furs for a jug or two of brandy. For the more unscrupulous of the French traders this

Dubois Davaugour

offered an excellent opportunity to make large profits. The clergy, however, were appalled by the effects liquor had on the Indians and in 1660 Bishop Laval had declared that anyone selling liquor to the Indians would be excommunicated *ipso facto*. The following year, in September, Davaugour strengthened the clerical injunction by issuing an edict forbidding all trade in liquor to the Indians on pain of the severest penalties and to show that he meant it, the following month, two men, convicted of contravening the edict, were shot [*see* VUIL] and a third flogged in the public square at Quebec. These harsh penalties had a very salutary effect.

Then, in January 1662, a woman of Quebec was caught contravening the edict and sent to prison by order of the governor. Her family and friends pleaded with Father JÉRÔME LALEMANT to intercede on her behalf. This he did, and he apparently irked Davaugour in doing so. The governor, accustomed to the stern discipline of the army, could not abide exceptions being made to his orders. He feared that this would result in a general flouting of the edict and a consequent loss of respect for law and authority in the colony. He brusquely informed Father Lalemant that if it were not a crime for this particular woman to trade brandy to the Indians, then it would not in future be considered a crime for anyone. He accused the Jesuit of inconsistency in wanting to save the woman, while opposed in principle to the brandy trade. Having once said this, he refused to reconsider his decision and immediately issued a new edict which removed the restrictions on the brandy trade.

When tales of the violent excesses once again being committed by the Indians reached the bishop, he renewed his mandamus of excommunication. This meant that the clergy were forbidding what the secular authority had specifically allowed. Relations between Bishop Laval and the Jesuits on the one hand and Davaugour on the other now became very strained indeed. Any who supported the clergy's stand became aware of the governor's displeasure. Bishop Laval therefore decided to go to France to plead at the court that some means be found to end the disorders caused by the brandy traffic.

Meanwhile the governor of Montreal, CHOMEDEY de Maisonneuve, issued an edict of his own forbidding the sale of brandy to the Indians, after a citizen of the town had been brutally killed on his own doorstep by a drunken Indian. This action on the part of Maisonneuve annoyed Davaugour and he attempted to undermine Maisonneuve's authority. He also attempted to impose a 10 per cent duty on goods imported by the seigneurs of Montreal and to impose restrictions on the town's merchants. When Maisonneuve came to Quebec with Jacques Le Ber*, one of the leading merchants of Montreal, intending to cross to France, Davaugour refused to allow Maisonneuve to leave the colony, had Le Ber arrested and ordered his goods seized on a charge of having fomented sedition in Montreal.

These extravagant and authoritarian actions provided Davaugour's enemies with ample ammunition to use against him. Letters of complaint from all quarters in the colony crossed on the ships that carried Bishop Laval to France. On 6 Nov. 1662 the Comte d'Estrades, French ambassador to the Court of St James's wrote to Colbert from London: "I learn with great regret, by a letter from the Bishop of Petraea that M. d'Avaugour is behaving very badly at Quebec and that all the people are extremely dissatisfied with his conduct. The quickest remedy that one can apply to this disorder is to send out a new governor." (BN, MS, Mélange Colbert, 112 bis, f.573.) The following year Louis XIV took possession of New France from the Compagnie des Cent-Associés, placing it directly under the Crown to be governed and administered by royal officials. At the same time, despite the strenuous objections of Davaugour's friends at the court, the decision was made by Colbert and Louis XIV to recall him to France.

It was not, however, until 5 July 1663, that word of this—and that the colony had been taken over by the Crown—reached Quebec. In the meantime Davaugour was drafting a lengthy memorial to the minister on what he thought the Crown should do for its colonies in America. The settlements in Newfoundland, Cape Breton, and on the Gaspé coast were not, he thought, worth bothering much about, but no expense or effort should be spared to establish a strong colony in the St. Lawrence valley. The defences at Quebec, he declared, could be made impregnable by building forts on both sides of the river; 3,000 soldiers would be required for three years to quell the Iroquois, and that done they could remain in the colony as settlers. The establishment of a fort on the Hudson River, with other connecting forts down the Richelieu and Lake Champlain, to open up year-round communications by sea would be an easy matter. These things done, Quebec would become the keystone of ten great provinces stretching into the interior, and these ten would guarantee the security of a hundred others. "When I reflect," he wrote, "on the object of the wars of Europe for fifty years, and the progress to be made here in ten, my duty not only obliges, but impels, me to speak boldly." The cost of implementing his great plans he estimated at 400,000 francs a year, for ten years, plus the cost of 3,000 infantry for three years. "I am much mistaken," he wrote, "if that does not suffice to establish a vast design, and to doubt it I must have forgotten all the idle expenditure that I have seen at divers points."

At the same time as he was projecting the future expenditure of millions of *livres* on the colony, Davaugour was having a hard time raising enough revenue to meet the day-to-day expense of his administration. In March 1663, on his own authority he leased the collection of the 25 per cent tax on furs exported from Quebec to a group of 17 residents of the colony for a lump sum of 50,000 *livres* a year. In addition these tax farmers also received the sole right to trade with the Indians at Tadoussac. Six months later, after Davaugour's departure, at one of the first meetings of the newly established Conseil Souverain, this contract was declared null and void because it had been executed without any consultation with the old council, duly established to deal with such matters.

Then, on 7 July, the ships arrived from France and Davaugour learned that he was being recalled. This came as a rude shock to him and in his impulsive fashion he made ready to leave the colony immediately, without waiting for his successor to arrive. He appointed his lieutenant, Jacques de Cailhault* de La Tesserie, acting governor and sailed from Quebec on 23 July.

On 4 August, he added a few bitter sentences to his memorial on Canada, declaring that he had never expected the charges of his critics would be taken seriously. "When I permitted them to repair to the court," he wrote, "I in no wise doubted but they would have composed verses in my praise, but the interest of the King's service, and forty years' experience under the bravest men that ever commanded, appeared to me a strong protection against such base spirits. To terminate this bickering, I shall content myself, through the respect I owe their cloth, by assuring you, my Lord, that I have served, by God's grace, not only well and faithfully, but right honestly, according to my means, and that my acts, when better understood, will never excite the King's wrath, nor that of the Queen Mother."

In France, Davaugour did not tarry long at the court. He took service with armies of the elector of Mayence, then helping to stem the advance of the Turks into Hungary. On 24 July 1664 he was killed, fighting valiantly, at Serinvans-Zrin on the borders of Croatia.

It could not be said that he had been a very successful governor of New France. He was too much the rough, blunt soldier to perform successfully the functions of civil administrator. Nor had he had available adequate military forces to end the constant assaults of the Iroquois on the colony. His projected plans for the future development of Canada were visionary, quite outside the realm of practicality. In his conflicts with the clergy and the authorities at Montreal, his combative nature had made a difficult situation worse. Although he was to some extent sinned against as well as sinning, the decision to recall him was the only practicable one the king and his ministers could have taken. Yet his recall did not of itself solve, or remove, these problems. His immediate successors were to encounter as much difficulty as he had in their relations with the clergy, perhaps because they were men of the same mould as Davaugour; masters of everything but themselves and more suited for army life than colonial administrative posts. It was, in fact, to be a few years yet before a group of well-trained colonial administrators were to emerge under Colbert's tutelage. Meanwhile, France had to make use of men such as Davaugour, and all things considered, the country could have been worse served.

W. J. ECCLES

[*JR* (Thwaites), XLVI, 149–53 and *NYCD* (O'Callaghan and Fernow), IX, 13–17, 20–1 contain items of Davaugour's correspondence and his memorial to Colbert. Faillon, *Histoire de la colonie française* III, 25, 30–66 gives a detailed account of events in Canada during Davaugour's administration. Lanctot, *Histoire du Canada*, I, 317–36. Francis Parkman, in *The old régime* (25th ed.), 120–30, briefly discusses some of the events of Davaugour's régime, but with his habitual, very anti-clerical bias. W.J.E.]

On the dispute between the civil authorities and the clergy over the brandy trade, see: André Vachon, "L'eau-de-vie dans la société indienne," CHA *Report 1960*, 22–32.

DUBOIS DE COCREAUMONT ET DE SAINT-MAURICE, JEAN-BAPTISTE, esquire, artillery commander and staff officer in the Carignan-Salières regiment; fl. 1665–67?

Having landed at Quebec only a short time before, Dubois arrived on 21 Oct. 1665 at Fort Sainte-Thérèse, where he spent the winter. In the autumn of 1666 he took part in the expedition against the Iroquois with instructions to take possession in the name of the king of France of the "Mohawk forts," which he duly did on 17 Oct. 1666. Nothing more is known of this soldier who probably returned to France in 1667 or 1668.

This officer should not be confused with his namesake Jean-Baptiste Dubois d'Esgriseilles (not "Des Prinzèles"), chaplain of the Carignan-Salières regiment, who landed at Quebec on 19

Dubok

Aug. 1665 with Henri de Chastelard*, Marquis de Salières. We have scarcely any more information about this person. He was at Montreal on Christmas Day 1665, then at Quebec on 19 Aug. 1666, when he conducted the opening religious exercises for the Jesuits. In the autumn he took part in the expedition against the Mohawks. Not much is known about what happened to him afterwards. In May 1671 he is mentioned as being at Trois-Rivières. Did he sail for France that same year, as Caron maintains? Was he actually at Montreal in 1674, as Sulte claims? In any event, if he remained in the colony after 1671, he did not attract much attention. Once, on 11 April 1676, he is named in an act of the Conseil Souverain, although we do not know if he was then in Canada; the act mentions his procurator, Sieur Jean Le Chasseur* (secretary of BUADE de Frontenac), which is not, of course, necessarily an indication that the abbé was then in France. Tanguay, Allaire, and Sulte, after Noiseux—whose information is very frequently incorrect—state that he left Canada in 1680. We ourselves believe that he had returned to France some years before that date.

ANDRÉ VACHON

On Dubois de Cocreaumont see "Mémoire de M. de Salières," Régis Roy et Malchelosse, Le régiment de Carignan, 51, and "Procès verbal de la prise de possession des forts d'Agnié (17 oct. 1666)," Sulte, Mélanges historiques (Malchelosse), VIII, 57f. On Abbé Dubois see: JR (Thwaites), L, passim. JJ (Laverdière et Casgrain), 333, 348. Jug. et délib., II, 18.

J.-B.-A. Allaire, Dictionnaire biographique du clergé canadien-français (6v., Montreal, 1910–34), I, 181f. Lucien Brault, "Les instruments de musique dans les églises de la Nouvelle-France," CCHA, Rapport, 1956–57, 95. Ivanhoë Caron, "Prêtres séculiers et religieux qui ont exercé le saint ministère dans la Nouvelle-France (1659–1669)," BRH, XLVII (1941), 196f. François Noiseux, Liste chronologique des évêques et des prêtes tant seculiers que reguliers, employes au service de l'église du Canada depuis l'établissement de ce pays . . . (Québec, 1834). Régis Roy et Malchelosse, Le régiment de Carignan, 113. Sulte, Mélanges historiques (Malchelosse), VIII, passim. Tanguay, Répertoire du clergé, 47. Les Ursulines de Trois Rivières, I, 431.

DUBOK (Duboct), "soldat empyrique" (charlatan); fl. 1645–46.

At the end of 1645 Dubok was asked to attend the sick at the mission post at Sillery. He lived there "from 20 November or thereabouts to 22 January." He had little success, and when his real profession was found out, he was in all likelihood dismissed. The Jesuit Journal observes that he was detested by both Indians and French.

Attempts have been made to identify him with the Laurent Dubocq who married the Huron girl Marie-Félix at Quebec in 1662 and who was probably born in 1634, according to the census of 1667, or in 1636 according to Tanguay. If we accept either of these two dates, we must be dealing with two different people, for in 1645 the charlatan Dubok would then have been merely some ten years old.

ANDRÉ VACHON

Recensement de 1667. JR (Thwaites), XXVII, 101. JJ (Laverdière et Casgrain), 14–15, 312. Tanguay, Dictionnaire, I, 202.

DU BOS, NICOLAS, priest; b. c. 1653 at Abbeville (Picardy), son of Nicolas Dubos and Antoinette Caron: d. 1699 at Quebec.

He came from France when he had finished his theological studies, arriving at Quebec in 1684. Bishop Laval*, who had to leave for Europe in search of a successor and who did not anticipate coming back for some time, quickly conferred holy orders upon him in November 1684. Du Bos was given charge of the parish of Charlesbourg, north of Quebec; he carried out this ministry for six years (1684–90), without living in the parish. Later, under compulsion from Bishop Saint-Vallier [La Croix*], Abbé Du Bos tried to live at Charlesbourg, but his health, which was already poor, was permanently affected as a result. At this place, according to a text of the period, "there is a little wooden chapel without a presbytery, which, being completely rotten, is falling into ruin . . . it carries an extra stipend of 250 livres." In addition to serving as parish priest at Charlesbourg, Du Bos was given on 9 Nov. 1684 the appointments as chaplain of the altar of Sainte-Anne and vicar of the chapter of Quebec.

From 1686 to 1692 he was a curate of the parish of Quebec. On 14 Aug. 1698 he was named penitentiary. In 1698 the bishop appointed him confessor and chaplain to the Ursulines. Previously, 1 May 1697, he had been appointed an officer of the seminary of Quebec, and he assumed his functions 1 Jan. 1698. He died 2 May 1699.

ARTHUR MAHEUX

ASQ, Chapitre, 10, 21, 31; A.-E. Gosselin, "Notes pour servir à la biographie des prêtes du séminaire de Québec, avec références en marge," 165–68; Lettres, M, 25, N, 95, O, 26, S, 101; MSS, 17, p.478 (Documents relatifs à Mgr de Laval); Paroisses diverses, 42, 46; Polygraphie, IX, 21; XXII, 22; Séminaire, I, 11, 31b; II, 41; V, 10; XCII, 19. BRH, III (1897), 57; XVI (1910), 138; XXII (1916), 207.

DU BOURG. See RÉMY

DU BOURG, MORILLON. *See* Morillon

DU BREUIL, NICOLAS LE CREUX. *See* Le Creux

DU BUISSON. *See* Guyon

DU CHESNE, ADRIEN, surgeon, interpreter, from Dieppe (Normandy); brother of Judith Du Chesne, the mother of Charles Le Moyne; known to have been in Canada during the period 1631–48; d. some time after 1656.

It is not known whether he was married, or at what exact date he arrived in New France. Benjamin Sulte, and following him Maude E. Abbott (the latter and John J. Heagerty call Du Chesne a Huguenot), are of the opinion that he came to Quebec as early as 1618. Basing himself on Faillon, Heagerty writes that he arrived with the Kirke brothers in 1629. Be that as it may, there is no evidence of his presence at Quebec until 9 Feb. 1631, when his name appeared on the certificate of baptism of a daughter of Guillaume Couillard. In the colony he acted as a surgeon, and as an interpreter in the service of the Jesuits. In the 1634 *Relation* he is given the title of "Chirurgien de l'habitation." The same *Relation* and that of 1636 recount that he accompanied the Jesuits on their visits to the Indians' lodges, and that with Fathers Paul Le Jeune and Jacques Buteux he had occasion to serve as godfather to several Indian children and a number of adults, who were being baptized after it had been noted that they were in danger of death.

On 9 July 1637 Du Chesne acquired a grant of land on the outskirts of Quebec; on 5 April 1639 this grant was to be confirmed by a title-deed issued by the Compagnie des Cent-Associés. In 1641 he was at Dieppe. He reappeared in Canada in August 1645 with Pierre Legardeur de Repentigny's fleet. In the same year he turned over to Abraham Martin the land that had been given to him at Quebec, on what are now the Plains of Abraham. In the autumn of that year, the *Journal des Jésuites* reported that Du Chesne "was sent to 3 rivers as soldier and Interpreter." We have news of him again in 1648, at Quebec.

There is one last document that does seem to refer to Adrien Du Chesne. This is a notary's deed from Dieppe, dated 17 Jan. 1656. In it mention is made of "Maistre Adrien Du Chesne, a surgeon at present living on the island of Guadeloupe." Might it be on this island that he ended his career?

Antonio Drolet

AJQ, Greffe de Jean Guitet, 17 oct. 1637. ASM, Tabellionage dieppois, 17 janv. 1656. ASQ, Documents Faribault, 14, 19, 157; Séminaire, LVII, 16. *JR* (Thwaites), VI, 126–28, 132; VIII, 258, 312; XXVII, 90. *JJ* (Laverdière et Casgrain). P.-G. Roy, *Inv. concessions*, I, 36.
Maude E. Abbott, *History of medicine in the Province of Quebec* (Toronto, 1931; McGill University pub., VIII, no. 63, 1932), 16. Ahern, *Notes pour l'histoire de la médecine*, 186–89. "Biographies canadiennes: Adrien Duchesne," *BRH*, XXVII (1921), 279. Boissonnault, *Histoire de la faculté de médecine de Laval*, 30–2. Archange Godbout, "Les origines de la famille Lemoyne, *RHAF*, I (1947–48), 533–40. J. J. Heagerty, *Four centuries of medical history in Canada, and a sketch of the medical history of Newfoundland* (2v., Toronto, 1928), I, 223–24. Joseph Le Ber, "Adrien Duchesne," SGCF *Mémoires*, IV (1950), 62; "Les origines de la famille LeMoine," *RHAF*, I (1947–48), 101–7, 257–70. Sulte, *Hist. des Can. fr.*, II, 37. Tanguay, *Dictionnaire* I, 207, 379.

DUCHESNEAU DE LA DOUSSINIÈRE ET D'AMBAULT, JACQUES, intendant of New France (1675–82), chevalier, counsellor to His Majesty, a treasurer of France, commissary for the generality of Tours *c.* 1664 and general of the king's finances in Touraine, son of Guillaume Chesneau, chevalier, seigneur, cup-bearer to the king, and of Anne de Lalande; d. 1696 at Ambrant, near Issoudun (Berry).

His titles of squire and chevalier are said to go back to the year 1511, to his great-great-grandfather. His ancestors were seigneurs of Breux, Montargis, and La Doussinière, and his paternal grandfather was chamberlain to Charles VII. Jacques Duchesneau belonged to a junior branch of the family and was the only one of his name. He had powerful protectors at court; he was even held in high esteem there by Colbert and the king, who, in appointing him to the office of intendant, stressed the wise conduct that his devoted subject had displayed in his office as a treasurer of France at Tours and in the various commissions that had been given him. His Majesty had also noticed the zeal and the loyalty that he had displayed in his service.

Duchesneau arrived at Quebec in the month of August 1675, bearing the edict of the preceding 5 June which reorganized the Conseil Souverain. He was provided with a salary of 12,000 *livres* a year and 3,000 *livres* for travelling expenses. The colony had been without an intendant since Jean Talon's departure in 1672. In the three-year interval Buade de Frontenac had fulfilled the double function of governor and administrator. It was perhaps as a result of Frontenac's quarrel with Fénelon [*see* Salignac], the Sulpician, and Perrot, governor of Montreal, that the king had

Duchesneau de La Doussinière

decided to fill the vacancy in the office of intendant. Be that as it may, Frontenac must not have been pleased with the arrival of this high official with whom he was going to have to share authority. On 23 September a session of the Conseil Souverain was held. In conformity with the instructions that he had received, the intendant presided over the meeting. Frontenac considered that his prerogatives had been encroached upon and ordered Duchesneau to call him by his title of "head and chairman of the Council." The intendant refused. This marked the beginning of seven years of quarrels which were disastrous for the progress of New France. A voluminous correspondence exchanged between the mother country and the colony gives us ample information on this subject. The minister's instructions were as clear as Versailles' policy. Generally speaking, the governor represented the king in the colony. He was head, and in a way honorary chairman of the council. On the other hand, the intendant, who in order of precedence occupied the third place in it, after the governor and the bishop, was its actual chairman; according to the declaration of 5 June 1675 the intendant "asks for opinions, takes the vote, and announces decrees."

Would the governor, who had a very lofty view of his position as viceroy, who held the foremost place in the council, and who for three years had directed all the affairs of the colony as he had pleased, be content to express an opinion and to vote like everyone else? According to Thomas Chapais, Duchesneau was "a man who clung to his rights and prerogatives, and he was endowed with great energy and rare tenacity of character . . . fussy, stubborn, meticulous, and aggressive despite a correct and apparently moderate manner. Frontenac was arrogant, irascible, imperious, and vindictive. Obviously one of these two men at Quebec would have to go." From that time on each strove fervently to ruin the other at court: Frontenac through his charming wife, Duchesneau thanks to his family's connections with the Voyer d'Argenson family and with Robert de La Lande, Louis XIV's deputy governor. This quarrel over titles was to become increasingly acrimonious until it reached its culmination early in the year 1679. In the face of the resistance put up against his claims, Frontenac lost his temper to the point of confining to their residences the attorney-general, Denis-Joseph de RUETTE d'Auteuil, and two other members of the council who were favourable to Duchesneau: Louis ROUER de Villeray and CHARLES LEGARDEUR de Tilly. The council's activity was thus paralysed, and the dispute was submitted to the king for decision. In the meantime a compromise was suggested to the governor: it was proposed that the deliberations of the council should be resumed without any specific title being given the contending parties. Frontenac first rejected this idea, but sensing clearly that he would not receive the sovereign's support in this affair, finally accepted it. And indeed the king, in his reply, decided in the intendant's favour: His Majesty chided Frontenac for his conduct and ordered him to be content with his title of governor and lieutenant-general of the colony.

Peace was however far from being restored, for there were other subjects of dissension. For example, the visit that Duchesneau made to La Prairie-de-la-Magdelaine, as soon as he arrived, in the month of June 1675, and which the *Relation* for that year records. Accompanied by his son, by Perrot, governor of Montreal, and by more than 50 important persons of the colony, including the parish priest of Ville-Marie (Montreal), the intendant proceeded with great pomp to this mission. He granted a league and a half of land to the Indians and held a general council of the Five Nations of the Iroquois, who were joined by some representatives of the Hurons and the Mahicans. On this occasion he offered a great feast and distributed gifts to the Indians. This display of magnificence on the part of the new intendant was not calculated to reassure the king's representative, who was so jealous of his prerogatives.

Conflicts of personalities apart, the court fully intended to divide powers in order better to rule over the colony. Jurisdictions, which were fairly clearly defined in theory, overlapped and were often in conflict in practice. Telling the governor that he represented the king's person, granting him a special guard of honour, was tantamount to inviting him to direct the state as he wished. It would subsequently be difficult to restrict his attributions. For they were not unlimited. It is true that he had absolute and sovereign authority in the conduct of military matters and in relations with the Indian tribes. But even in this domain he had to turn to the intendant for questions of clothing, food, transport, and pay. In matters of justice and finance it was the intendant who had the upper hand; however, in certain cases the governor had independent jurisdiction. As far as religion and public order were concerned, the two senior officials shared rights and often had to take decisions together. On many points the intendant had broader authority than the governor, who became a sort of comic-opera king, possessing only the right of veto. In case of divergences of opinion, they had to submit the matter to Versailles. But there again the intendant was often the stronger, since normally he had had long experience with administration and had protectors at court. This tangle of powers and this sharing as it were of functions presupposed a good measure of self-denial and a great spirit of conciliation in the two men. These were certainly not the predominant qualities of Frontenac, or of Duchesneau.

With these two stubborn men, discussions ended in quarrels that were often dramatic. According to Chapais, "M. Duchesneau's administration was nothing but one long conflict between him and the governor." There was the squabble over titles; there were many others. The quarrel over the trade in spirits was very serious. Dismayed by the ravages that alcohol caused among the Indians, Bishop Laval* used all his authority to have trade in it forbidden. The intendant, who was known for his piety, concurred in his opinion. Yet in the clergy's eyes Duchesneau remained too hesitant still. "He did considerable harm to himself and to all matters because of the excessive respect that he had for M. de Frontenac and several others." Frontenac was thinking of business and saw clearly that if the French traders did not have brandy to offer to conclude their transactions successfully, the Indians would go to deal with the English, who had no scruples about supplying them with rum. After violent discussions, it was decided to propose a compromise, which the king accepted. Henceforth it would be forbidden to sell spirits to the Indians except in French establishments. This decision satisfied neither party, and the *coureurs de bois* continued their traffic. These traders, moreover, were already a source of discord between the governor and the intendant. Duchesneau accused Frontenac of favouring these adventurers and of profiting himself from their clandestine trade. In a letter to Seignelay dated 13 Nov. 1681 he complained that "the King's orders are not carried out . . . and the guilty remain unpunished." He cited the example, among others, of the bad conduct of CAVELIER de La Salle and Greysolon* de Dulhut; pelts were still being taken to the English, who paid more for them than did the French and who sold merchandise of better quality and more cheaply. But Frontenac knew his adversary's tactics: "M. Duchesneau always begins as a general rule by accusing others of what he is doing or intends to do." He did indeed protect Charles Aubert* de La Chesnaye, Jacques Le Ber*, CHARLES LE MOYNE, LOUIS JOLLIET, and Jacques de Lalande*, who trafficked in pelts publicly and with impunity. The governor asked the minister to institute an inquiry to clear up this question. If he were found guilty, he agreed to suffer just punishment for his faults. Meanwhile, he would send Dulhut to the court to exculpate himself. For his part, the minister tried to keep the disagreement from becoming worse. On 15 May 1678 he wrote to Duchesneau that he was going beyond his duties, that he was seeking a quarrel with Frontenac in all his acts, that he must behave differently, under pain of being recalled the following year. On 2 June 1680 there was a new admonition from the minister warning the intendant that he would be confined to Tours, in France, if he did not strictly respect the king's orders. Again, on 2 May 1681, the minister, acting in the king's name, called upon him to change his ways, on pain of being recalled. On 30 April 1681 the king sent word to Frontenac that everything he wrote "against the said intendant concerning his participation in trade and the interest he takes in the *coureurs de bois* appears to be put forward in a spirit of recrimination rather than with any real foundation."

Nevertheless they both continued to misuse their powers. In turn each of them had the *coureurs de bois* who were connected with the other side arrested and those in his own camp freed. There is even the case of a member of the Conseil Souverain, MATHIEU DAMOURS DE CHAUFFOURS, who had obtained through the intendant a trading licence that was valid for the region of Matane. Frontenac had him arrested and brought before the council. Duchesneau defended the accused and once again stirred up the governor's anger. Two other events contributed to the deterioration of the situation. The attorney-general of the council, Ruette d'Auteuil, had to retire because of age, but he would have liked to be replaced by his son, François-Madeleine-Fortuné de Ruette* d'Auteuil de Monceaux. The father had been on the intendant's side at the time of the famous quarrel over the governor's rights, and Frontenac had too good a memory to have forgotten the father's insulting attitude. Moreover, the son was not of the required age for sitting on the council. Duchesneau sowed the wind in nevertheless proposing François d'Auteuil's appointment to the position of attorney-general. He reaped the whirlwind, which, once more, died down at the foot of the throne in Versailles, where the bold young man had to go to plead his case and have the age requirement waived.

Another event savours of melodrama. In the spring of 1681 some of Frontenac's people, while walking in the streets of Quebec, saw in the distance the intendant's son, who was 16 or 17 years old; accompanied by his servant, he was sitting "on the palisade which overlooks the path that leads from Lower to Upper Town, . . . singing for his own amusement an air without words." The two groups quarrelled. From foul words they went on to insults. Frontenac, to whom the altercation was reported, considered that he had been insulted and ordered young Duchesneau and his servant to be arrested. The intendant anticipated this, barricaded his house, and prepared to defend himself. The order for the arrest was not carried out. But discussions were begun between Duchesneau and Frontenac through Bishop Laval. The bishop went to and fro between the intendant's house and the governor's *château*. Frontenac demanded that those who had insulted him come to offer their apologies to him. Duchesneau, who feared his enemy's vindictiveness, asked for guarantees. And so the bishop went to seek assurances from one, and to calm the apprehensions of the other. Duchesneau finally took the risk and sent his son and his servant to see the governor. As usual, Frontenac flew into a rage. The servant received some blows from his cane and went, along with his young master, to expiate in prison his lack of respect towards the king's representative. The lesson lasted a month.

Duchesneau was far from being pleased. For his part, Frontenac, giving vent to his dissatisfaction, wrote to the minister, 2 Sept. 1681, that everyone was entitled to complain of the wrongs that he might have suffered, but that to do so juridically in the proceedings of the Conseil Souverain "amounts to informing publicly against a governor and to wanting to submit him to the jurisdiction [of the members of the Council]." He attributed to Duchesneau the disorder that reigned in the council's affairs, criticized the "poor order in which he wants the records to be kept" and the "changes that he often makes in the decrees after they have been passed." As proof he had copies of five or six reports of proceedings submitted to the minister. But above all the governor complained that the intendant resisted his orders and tried to foment a rebellion against him. For his part Duchesneau informed Seignelay of his grievances on 13 November of the same year. The minister would have ample opportunity to improve his knowledge in reading these six long memoirs from the intendant. He would learn from them, what he doubtless knew already, that things were not going very well in the colony, "that the King's orders are not carried out, that justice is oppressed, that its officers are persecuted, and that the guilty go unpunished." In addition, the *coureurs de bois* caused all sorts of disorders and destroyed French trade by going to take their furs to the English. Trade in Acadia, which could be lucrative, was dwindling. Another memoir was devoted particularly to the bad conduct of La Salle and Dulhut, friends of the governor; a third dealt with the activities of Josias BOISSEAU, a protégé of Frontenac. And all this ended with a general picture of the state—past, present, and future—of the king's tax farm.

That was enough. Tired of these grievances, seeing clearly that his remonstrances were of no effect, Louis XIV decreed the recall of his excessively hot-headed servants, who returned to France in the autumn of 1682.

From Duchesneau's seven years of administration some 30 ordinances are extant. It is regrettable that his time, his talents, and his experience were wasted in large measure in long and futile quarrels.

On his return to France Duchesneau withdrew to Ambrant, in Berry, where, retired from the world, he prepared for death, which came to him in 1696.

LÉOPOLD LAMONTAGNE

AN, Col., B; C^{11A}. ASQ, Évêques, 224; Lettres P, 46; M, 23, p.27; S, 93, p.5; Polygraphie, IV, 58; XXII, 35, *et passim*. Caron, "Inventaire de documents," APQ *Rapport, 1939–40*, 231–46. "Correspondance de Frontenac (1689–99)," APQ *Rapport, 1927–28*, 16. "Documents inédits sur l'histoire du Canada," éd. H.-A. Verreau, *RC*, X (1873), 623–34, 683–99. *Édits ord.*, I, 83f.; III, 42f. HBRS, VIII (Rich), xliii. *JR* (Thwaites), LIX, 284–90, 316, *et passim. Jug. et délib.* "Lettre de l'intendant Duchesneau au marquis de Seignelay, fils de Colbert (13 nov. 1681)," *BRH*, XXVI (1920), 275–86. *Mémoires des commissaires*, I, 151; II, 569, 573, 578; and *Memorials of the English and French commissaires,* I, 206, 746, 751, 755. *NYCD* (O'Callaghan and Fernow), IX. *Ord. comm.* (P.-G. Roy), I, 176–323. PAC *Rapport, 1885*, xxxvi–xli; *Rapport, 1899*, Supp., 38–39, 64–73, 248–56. P.-G. Roy, "Les ordonnances des six premiers intendants de la Nouvelle-France," *BRH*, XXV (1919), 170–74. *Royal Fort Frontenac* (Preston and Lamontagne).

Thomas Chapais [Ignotus], "Notes et souvenirs," *La Presse* (Montréal), 13 juillet 1901, 23. Delalande, *Le Conseil souverain*, 174–92. Eccles, *Frontenac*. Auguste Gosselin, *Vie de Mgr de Laval*, II, 274–78, 307, *et passim*. HBRS, XXI (Rich), 126. Gustave Lanctot, *L'administration de la Nouvelle-France* (Paris, 1929). Henri Lorin, *Le comte de Frontenac: étude sur le Canada français à la fin du XVIIe siècle* (Paris, 1895). Régis Roy, "Les intendants de la Nouvelle-France," *RSCT*, 2d ser., IX (1903), sect.I, 76f.; "Jacques Duchesneau," *BRH*, IX (1903), 182–84.

DUDOUYT, JEAN, priest, official, canon, vicar general, first procurator of the seminary of Quebec; b. *c.* 1628; d. 1688 in Paris.

Dudouyt was probably ordained to the priesthood in 1658. He appears to have come originally from Normandy, for he had inherited land at Périers, a few leagues from Coutances. Moreover, it was in Normandy that he made his first appearance in history, at the hermitage in Caen directed by Jean de Bernières de Louvigny. He quite evidently became acquainted there with his future companions in Canada, Bishop Laval* and abbés Henri de BERNIÈRES and Louis Ango* Des Maizerets.

The devout horror with which Jansenism was regarded at the Caen hermitage is well known. Bertrand* de Latour recounts that in 1660 Dudouyt, although dangerously ill, refused to receive the last rites from the parish priest because the latter was suspected of Jansenism. As a result of the scandal caused by this episode, the hermits of Caen moved to Paris; from there Abbé Dudouyt, having barely recovered from his illness, went to Canada at the very time that Bishop Laval was sailing back to France (1662).

On his return to Quebec, the bishop appointed Dudouyt promoter of the officialty on 20 Oct. 1663; but above all he made him the mainspring of the seminary he had just founded, by naming him its procurator as well as administrator of his own possessions. In this double capacity, the entire material care of the bishopric, the seminary, and the parishes was henceforth his responsibility. In addition he became vicar general in 1671 and, the following year, ecclesiastical superior of the Hôtel-Dieu.

In the autumn of 1676 he left for France as Bishop Laval's delegate to the court in the matter of the liquor trade, which the bishop consistently opposed, and which BUADE de Frontenac openly favoured.

The absolute necessity of having a representative in France to serve the interests of the seminary and the church in Canada kept Dudouyt there from that time forward, and he was moreover fully occupied, as some thirty letters of his attest. He lived at the Séminaire des Missions étrangères in Paris. Bishop Laval, for his part, did not forget his faithful representative. When he organized his chapter in 1684, he had Dudouyt appointed precentor, although he was absent.

After being a close witness of the first clashes between Bishop Saint-Vallier [La Croix*] and the Seminary of Quebec, Dudouyt died in Paris on 15 Jan. 1688, leaving to the seminary a small annuity amounting to some 1,000 *livres*, which had been purchased by his family. Bishop Laval, who was in France at the time, carried back to Quebec a few months later the heart of this priest who had spent 14 years in Canada. The bishop's thoughtfulness was appreciated by the whole population. The heart, encased in lead, was given solemn burial in the cathedral.

HONORIUS PROVOST

ASQ, Lettres; Séminaire. "M. Dudouyt à Mgr de Laval, 1677, 1681 et 1687," PAC *Rapport, 1885*, xcvii–cxxx. Bertrand de Latour, *Mémoires sur la vie de Laval, premier évêque de Québec* (Cologne, 1761). Maximilien Bibaud, *Le panthéon canadien*, éd. Adèle et Victoria Bibaud (Montréal, 1891), 83. Auguste Gosselin, *Henri de Bernières, premier curé de Québec* (Les Normands au Canada, Québec, 1902), *passim*.

DU GUA DE MONTS, PIERRE, explorer, trader, governor of Acadia, and founder of the first permanent settlement in Canada; b. 1558? in Saintonge, France, probably at Le Gua; d. 1628 in France, probably in the Ardennes.

The son of Guy Du Gua and Claire Goumard, he married Judith Chesnel by whom he had no children. A Calvinist, de Monts distinguished himself fighting in the cause of Henri IV during the religious wars in France. The king later awarded him an annual pension of 1,200 crowns and the governorship of the town of Pons in Saintonge in recognition of his outstanding service.

De Monts seems to have made several voyages to Canada during the closing years of the 16th century, one as a member of PIERRE CHAUVIN DE TONNETUIT's expedition to Tadoussac in 1600. France at the time was showing a growing interest in Canada as an area for both colonization and exploitation. Because of the depleted state of the country's treasury, this work was being left to individuals under an arrangement whereby they would establish settlements in New France in exchange for the exclusive right to trade with the Indians. Few such settlements had been attempted before de Monts and all of them had failed. In 1603, de Monts was granted the privilege of trade and responsibility of settlement by the king. Under the terms of his commissions, he was given a trading monopoly and appointed lieutenant-general "of the coasts, lands and confines of Acadia, Canada and other places in New France," there to establish 60 colonists a year and to win the Indians to the Christian faith.

De Monts turned at once to organizing a trading company. Merchants in Rouen, Saint-Malo, La Rochelle, and Saint-Jean-de-Luz who were willing to purchase shares were invited to join. With the promise of handsome profits, many of the merchants became partners, and a powerful company with capital of 90,000 *livres* was formed on 8 Feb. 1604. The principal collaborator was the Dutchman Cornelis (Corneille) de Bellois who was a merchant in Rouen, but de Monts withdrew his trust when Bellois's nephew, Daniel Boyer,

Du Gua de Monts

was caught trading illegally in 1606. With the means to equip an expedition to explore and colonize, de Monts had ships fitted out, the necessary supplies purchased, and he recruited both Protestant and Roman Catholic participants. These were men of varying skills such as artisans, architects, and carpenters, masons and stone cutters, soldiers and vagabonds, several noblemen whose motives in joining the daring venture ranged from a quest for riches to a desire—as in the case of JEAN DE BIENCOURT de Poutrincourt—to win new lands for France, as well as two priests, including Nicolas AUBRY, and a minister. De Monts invited Samuel de Champlain to accompany him and he acted as a geographer and cartographer. [*See* CHAMPLAIN.]

Early in the spring of 1604, de Monts sent three vessels to trade for furs on the St. Lawrence. Meanwhile, the work of fitting out the two ships he and his party would use to explore and colonize was rushed to completion. The first of these left Havre-de-Grâce (Le Havre) on 7 March, according to LESCARBOT, with FRANCOIS GRAVÉ Du Pont as senior officer and Capt. Timothée as sailing master. De Monts followed in Capt. Morel's vessel on 10 March 1604. He arrived on 8 May at Cap La Hève (La Have) on the Nova Scotia coast where he waited for François Gravé Du Pont who assessed the extent of de Monts's monopoly before joining his leader. A few days after his arrival, de Monts discovered and captured the *Levrette* of Jean Rossignol, for illegal trading in the area. As Rossignol and several Rouen merchants had equipped the vessel and obtained a permit to fish off the coasts of "Florida," they took legal action against de Monts and in 1608 de Monts agreed to repay Rossignol's expenses in recovering his ship as well as 900 *livres* compensation for the seized pelts. The place of the capture de Monts named Port Rossignol. The next day, while they were exploring another bay nearby, one of the sheep fell overboard and was drowned, which prompted de Monts to call the place Port-au-Mouton. De Monts decided to remain here while Jean Ralluau his secretary, and Champlain explored the coast south to the Baie Française (Bay of Fundy) in the ship's boat. When these two men returned, the vessel was taken to Baie Sainte-Marie at the entrance to the Bay of Fundy where it was left once more while de Monts and Champlain explored these unknown waters in the ship's long boat. Delighting in the country as they explored the coast, de Monts and Champlain were especially pleased with the beautiful region now called the Annapolis Basin. Poutrincourt was later to express the wish to have the place and to one day settle there with his family. De Monts forthwith gave him the basin area, a gift later approved by the king. The explorers continued up the bay, seeking both a site for their settlement and a valuable metal deposit Jean SARCEL de Prévert had reported the previous year to be in the area. So it was that they reached Chignictou (Chignecto) and then turned westward to coast the New Brunswick shore. On 24 June they entered the mouth of a great river and they named it the Saint John, the saint whose day it was. In this search for a place to settle, fear of the Indians made them look for a spot that would be easy to defend. So they continued west along the coast crossing Passamaquoddy Bay where they entered a river, coming probably on 26 June to an island that de Monts and his companions all seem to have felt suitable for their first settlement.

Île Sainte-Croix (Dochet Island) as it came to be called was chosen for its central position, its good anchorage, its ease of defence against attack, and because little time remained to prepare for the winter season. ANGIBAULT *dit* Champdoré, the expedition's pilot, was sent with orders for the two vessels and the rest of the men to move up to Sainte-Croix from the Baie Sainte-Marie. Work began almost at once and the rate of progress indicates both the careful preparations de Monts had made in France as well as the vigour of his leadership. Following a plan drawn by Champlain, some dozen houses were built around a court, being connected in some places by a palisaded wall so that the whole settlement resembled a fort. It is of interest that some of these houses were partially built of lumber brought from France. In addition there were service buildings such as a storehouse, kitchen, and common living-dining hall. Also included was a Catholic chapel. While construction was pressed forward, gardens were planted both on the island and the mainland opposite, where the first wheat to be grown in New France was sown.

Yet the season was already late and crops must have been small that first year. This was to be a very serious matter because the winter proved an abnormally severe one. The first snow fell on 6 Oct. 1604 and we are told it still lay three to four feet deep at the end of April. Even worse, ice floes in the river were so thick that it became dangerous—and sometimes impossible—to cross the river. The island was proving to be a prison. With supplies of fresh food exhausted, they were reduced to salt meat; fresh water was scarce and melted snow had to be used as a substitute. With the poor food and enforced idleness, scurvy developed and almost half of the men died of it.

Spring brought an end to the wretchedness of

Du Gua de Monts

the brave band. By March 1605, Etchemin (Passamaquoddy) Indians had started to call there to trade fresh meat and soon after the strongest men in the expedition were able to hunt game themselves. The arrival of warm weather also brought the supply ships from France with a relief party of 40 men under Ralluau and Gravé Du Pont. De Monts now decided to move his place of settlement. Champlain was sent on an exploratory trip down the New England coast with PANOUNIAS and his wife as interpreters and guides, but his report on settlement possibilities there was unfavourable. Orders were then given to dismantle the houses and carry them by ship to the Annapolis Basin, for building there not far from the present Annapolis the Port-Royal habitation. Once work was well under way, de Monts arranged to leave for France since recent news from home indicated his trading company was in financial difficulties and his monopoly in a critical condition. He left François Gravé in charge of the settlement because the Sieur d'Orville, a gentleman of some social standing who had joined the expedition and was to have assumed this responsibility, was ill from the effects of scurvy. Champlain was to direct further exploration.

De Monts set out for France in September 1605, taking with him all but three of the survivors of the winter on Sainte-Croix—Fougeray, Champdoré, and Samuel de Champlain. When he arrived after a crossing of 31 days, he learned that many of the fur-trading merchants who were not members of the company were making a serious effort to have his trading privileges revoked. He quickly came to the decision to remain in France to better protect his company's interests.

On 13 May 1606, having secured backing from the famous La Rochelle merchants Macain (or Macquin) and Georges, he sent out a ship to Acadia with supplies and a new party of men, including Jean Ralluau, Marc Lescarbot, and the young CHARLES DE BIENCOURT, under the command of Jean de Poutrincourt. His orders were to take charge of the Port-Royal colony and to continue the search for a better situation for the colony to the south. The party arrived late (the end of July), to find that the bulk of the good furs had already been taken by Basque interlopers.

At Port-Royal, François Gravé was able to report success in the growing of grain and other food, although he himself had concentrated on exploration, but 12 more men had died of scurvy during the winter of 1605–6. While Guillaume Des Champs, the surgeon, had performed autopsies he had failed to discover the cause of the dread disease. The next year, to keep the men active and interested, the Order of Good Cheer was formed; because of it and the mildness of the winter, scurvy claimed but seven victims, but bad news was to arrive with the spring.

De Monts reported in a letter sent out with Jean Ralluau in 1607 that the opposition of the merchants of Saint-Malo not included in the monopoly and of the Duc de Sully, and the intrigues of the Paris hatters' corporation had caused the king to revoke his privileges. Champlain, Poutrincourt, and the others were to return to France. That fall, the affairs of de Monts's company were wound up. The final accounting showed that during its three years of activity revenues had been high but costs even higher. De Monts's loss alone was said to be 10,000 *livres*. The chief reason for the failure was the volume of the illicit trade in furs. In 1604 alone, for example, at least eight vessels had been seized for trading with the Indians without licence, and many times that number had not been apprehended. It must be remembered that those who traded illegally did not bear the burden imposed on the de Monts company to supply colonists and their necessities.

Happily, de Monts succeeded in having the monopoly extended for one more year, 1607–8, on his pledge that he would establish a post on the St. Lawrence and renew his efforts to colonize the new land. Money was raised for a new expedition, organized by Lucas Legendre, of three vessels. One was to go to Port Royal (under Angibault *dit* Champdoré), a second to the lower St. Lawrence, and the third to found a post at Quebec under the direction of Champlain. A modest profit was realized from the trading venture and, more important, the station actually built at Quebec was both a post for trade and a base for exploring the country to the west. However, the monopoly was not renewed at the end of 1608, partly because of the lack of success there had been in colonizing under this system, in force since 1600. The fur trade was now thrown open to all. With the establishment of a system of free trade, de Monts was granted a compensation of 6,000 *livres*, but this money was never actually paid. Nevertheless, he and his partners, Collier and Legendre, decided to continue their operations. These were roughly divided into two phases with Champlain to continue to explore and have charge of the Quebec post while Gravé Du Pont took charge of the fur trade. It was during the 1611 season that de Monts arranged for a shipload of oak—the first timber to be exported from Canada—to be sent to France. Until the fall of 1611, de Monts regularly sent out ships with supplies for the colonists and goods for the trade in furs. The post at Quebec was maintained,

Du Gua de Monts

contact made with new Indian nations, and the exploration of the country pressed forward. Yet all other traders could share in the trade with none of this expense. Operating as they were at a loss, de Monts's two partners determined they could no longer afford to maintain the post at Quebec. With his unbounded faith in the country and his conviction of the importance of the work of exploration being undertaken by Champlain, de Monts determined that Quebec would not be abandoned. He therefore bought the shares of the others.

In 1612 Champlain and de Monts succeeded in having the title of viceroy given to the Comte de Soissons and then to the Prince de Condé. Under their protection, de Monts organized a company with certain privileges. By now, any rights he had in Acadia had been given to the Marquise de Guercheville [see BIARD and JEAN DE BIENCOURT] so that efforts were to be restricted to Canada where the new partners had won the monopoly. He continued to participate actively in the Canadian trade and to encourage the exploration and settlement of the country until 1617. After that he withdrew to his *château* in the Ardennes, although he continued to be a shareholder in succeeding trading companies as late as 1622 when he and Cornelis de Bellois became members of that of Montmorency.

Despite the tremendous contribution made by this far-seeing and broadminded individual to the development of Canada, he has seldom been accorded his rightful place in accounts of its history. Here is the man who made possible so much of what Champlain accomplished. He it was who, inspired with the noble impulse of making a new France in America, founded the first permanent colony here. With his interest in trade simply as a necessary source of funds for colonization and discovery, he sacrificed personal gain for the greater goal, one in which Champlain was his staunch ally. From the day he and his valiant band planted their settlement on Île Sainte-Croix, the continent was never to be without a European settlement. It was de Monts who proved that people from Europe could live here permanently and that agriculture could be carried on successfully.

What is more, he was instrumental in making Canada far better known in Europe. He assembled a collection of animals and birds, portraits of Indians, artifacts, and other curiosities. Part of this material was taken to France by Poutrincourt in 1604 and the rest by de Monts himself in 1605. These objects were examined by the distinguished humanist Nicolas de Peirese and his descriptions are among the earliest we have concerning certain of the birds and animals of North America. The energetic direction, support, and encouragement de Monts gave to exploration which was subsequently reported in the writings of such men as Champlain and Lescarbot represents a contribution of inestimable value. Speaking of the task undertaken by de Monts to promote settlement, to explore the land, and to expand commerce, Lescarbot says this in the dedication of his *Adieu à la France* (1606):

> *De Monts, tu és celui de qui le haut courage*
> *A tracé le chemin à un si grand ouvrage:*
> *Et pource de ton nom malgré l'effort des ans*
> *La feuille verdoyra d'un éternel printemps.*

> [De Monts, it is you whose high courage has traced the way for such a great undertaking, and for this reason, in spite of the attack of time, the leaf of your fame will grow green in an eternal spring.]

Had his monopoly been enforced and maintained by the French government, the undertakings of de Monts in Acadia and Canada might well have succeeded in full measure instead of falling short of the goals he had set. In many ways the monopoly arrangement for the fur trade was a good one at the time for developing the country, in that it gave reasonable assurance of profits large enough to pay the cost of founding settlements and to allow shareholders in the company a fair return on their investment, while imposing desirable obligations respecting colonization. Yet those who ruled France did little effectively to support the trading companies. Spanish, Dutch, and especially French vessels in sizable numbers defied the trading monopoly with little risk and the result was a drastic cut in fur-trading profits. What is more, jealousy prevailed, intrigue was rampant, and de Monts saw his exclusive trading privilege, granted for a ten-year period, revoked without just cause at the end of three. The monopoly system, even at best, could probably only have produced modest profits because of the high cost of placing colonists on the land, the quantity of supplies that had to be imported, the expense of building and maintaining posts both for trade and protection, in addition to the regular overhead of a company such as that of de Monts. References make it abundantly clear, however, that de Monts was a man interested in commercial profit only as a means to develop a new domain for France in this great, strange land across the Atlantic. To de Monts must be accorded an important part of the credit for the fact that this goal was ultimately reached.

GEORGE MACBEATH

AN, Minutier, XXIV, 229, 232. Champlain, *Works* (Biggar). Lescarbot, *History* (Grant). *Mémoires des commissaires*, I, IV, *passim*, and *Memorials of the English and French commissaries*, I, *passim*.

Biggar, *Early trading companies*. Ganong, "Historic sites in New Brunswick," 262–66. É.-H. Gosselin, *Documents authentiques et inédits pour servir à l'histoire de la marine normande et du commerce rouennais pendant les XVIe et XVIIe siècles* (Rouen, 1876), 18–19; *Précis analytique des travaux de l'Académie de Rouen* (Rouen, 1871–72), 331. Francis W. Gravit, "Un document inédit sur le Canada: raretés rapportées du Nouveau-Monde par M. de Monts," *RUL*, I (1946–47), 282–88. *Pierre Du Gua, sieur de Monts; records: colonial and "Saintongeois,"* ed. W. I. Morse (London, 1939), reproduces excellent documentary material on the subject.

DUGUÉ DE BOISBRIAND, MICHEL-SIDRAC, one of the first seigneurs in the Montreal area; b. *c.* 1638 at Persevil, diocese of Nantes, France, son of Pierre Dugué de La Boulardière and of Perrine de Chambellé; d. 1688.

Entering the army as a lieutenant in the Montagu regiment, he later transferred as a captain to the Chambellé regiment, commanded by his uncle. When Louis XIV determined to dispatch an élite corps to New France Dugué's company was incorporated in the Carignan-Salières regiment, in which Dugué retained the rank of captain. He arrived at Quebec in September 1665. In June 1666 Dugué was doing garrison duty in Montreal, where he became military commander, in the absence of a governor, from the spring of 1670 until August of that year when M. Perrot assumed his duties.

For his labours in the district the Gentlemen of Saint-Sulpice granted Dugué in January 1672 the land later known as the seigneury of Senneville at the western end of Montreal Island, but in 1679 he sold it to Charles Le Moyne and his brother-in-law Jacques Le Ber*. In October 1672 he obtained seigneurial title to Île Sainte-Thérèse near Repentigny at the east end of Montreal Island. Although he had received the right to cultivate this property earlier, he apparently showed more interest in the fur trade. He also obtained in 1683 the seigneury of Mille-Îles extending from Terrebonne to Rivière du Chêne, $11\frac{1}{2}$ x $7\frac{1}{2}$ miles in extent. Under the Edict of Marly, 1711, this property because of non-settlement was forfeited to the crown, but regranted immediately to his two sons-in-law Jean Petit* and Charles-Gaspard Piot* de Langloiserie.

In 1673 Dugué as a captain took part in Buade de Frontenac's expedition to Lake Ontario and in later years he frequently participated in others. In 1683 his name was considered for governor of Montreal, but he did not receive the appointment owing to the opposition of M. Le Febvre de La Barre. In 1684 and in 1687 he was a member of Brisay* de Denonville's rather ineffectual expeditions against the Indians.

His real interest, however, continued to be in the fur trade and to promote his interests therein, as one of the delegates called in 1678 to discuss the advisability of selling spirits to the Indians, he favoured completely "free trade." Yet despite his participation in the fur trade, he apparently lived much of the latter part of his life in poverty.

In 1667 he married Marie Moyen, daughter of Jean-Baptiste and Élisabeth Le Ber (Le Bret, according to Tanguay), who died 24 Oct. 1687 at Île Sainte-Thérèse. Dugué died in Montreal 18 Dec. 1688. He was survived by seven of his nine children.

From his life and activities one may deduce that Dugué was a typical frontier settler. More interested in fur-trading and fighting than in peaceful pursuits, he took little part in the development of the colony, but did play a considerable role in the defence and geographical extension of its territory.

W. Stanford Reid

AJM, Greffe de Bénigne Basset, 1 nov. 1667. AN, Col., C11A and other collections. Recensement de 1681. Lefebvre, *Marie Morin*. Le Jeune, *Dictionnaire*. *Royal Fort Frontenac* (Preston and Lamontagne), 45. Benjamin Sulte, "Michel-Sidrac Dugué, sieur de Boisbriand," *BRH*, X (1904), 221–23. Tanguay, *Dictionnaire*, I, 209–10; III, 512; VI, 375.

DU HÉRISSON, MICHEL LENEUF. *See* Leneuf

DUMESNIL, JEAN PERONNE. *See* Peronne

DUMONS, SIEUR. *See* Monts, Sieur de

DU PERON, FRANÇOIS, priest, Jesuit, missionary, called Anonchiara by the Indians; b. 26 Jan. 1610 at Lyon, France; d. 10 Nov. 1665 at Chambly.

Father Du Peron joined the Jesuits at Avignon 23 Feb. 1627 and studied at Dôle, Vesoul and Lyon. On 1 May 1638 he left for Canada. He was sent to minister to the Hurons; on the way he came across Father Simon Le Moyne and helped him. On 27 April 1639 he wrote to his brother, Joseph-Imbert, also a Jesuit, a letter that describes in detail his labours in the Huron country. Leaving this mission in 1649, he sailed back to France on 23 Aug. 1650 and remained there for five years. In 1657 he seems to have accompanied Father RAGUENEAU to the Onondaga country, to have returned to spend a period at Quebec, and to have left again for France. In 1664 he was at Carpentras, in France, requesting the general of the Society by letter to send him back to Canada. He reached Quebec on 30 June 1665. He was appointed chaplain to Fort Saint-Louis, at Chambly, and died shortly afterwards in his new office. He was buried at Quebec 16 Nov. 1665.

In the course of the demolition of the Jesuit college in 1875, his bones were found and were transferred in state to the Ursuline chapel in 1891.

His brother, Joseph-Imbert Du Peron, carried on his ministry in Canada from 1640 to 1658, working principally in the regions of the Richelieu and Trois-Rivières and at Sillery.

J. MONET

ACSM, ff.237, 240. *JR* (Thwaites), XIV, 288. Rochemonteix, *Les Jésuites et la Nouvelle-France au XVIIe siècle*, I, 226.

DU PERRON, THALOUR, governor of Plaisance (Placentia) (1662–63), native of Nantes, in France; assassinated 1663 in Newfoundland.

Du Perron was still very young when he was appointed governor of Plaisance and sent to take possession of this colony in the king's name, after Fouquet's disgrace and Feuquières' resignation.

He set off for Newfoundland in July 1662, on board the *Aigle d'Or*, with Nicolas GARGOT. His brother accompanied him, and a small party recruited in a most casual fashion; they had a supply of food and munitions. They did not arrive until October. Gargot went on to Quebec. A few months later, during the winter, as Du Perron and his brother were returning from hunting, they were attacked by a party of their men and shot down. The assassins then rushed to the storehouses, got drunk, and set to killing one another, to such effect that 12 or 15 corpses remained. The chaplain accompanying them had fled to the woods, but cold and hunger forced him to return to the fort, where his head was split open with an axe. The following spring the murderers tried to cross to the mainland with the most valuable part of their booty, but they were shipwrecked.

When Capt. Guillon, Gargot's second-in-command and the captain of the *Jardin de Hollande*, reached Plaisance with fresh supplies in 1663, he learned this news and managed to capture 15 of the criminals, whom he brought back to Quebec and handed over to Gargot. The trial gave rise to a conflict of authority; the Conseil Souverain demanded the prisoners, but Gargot claimed jurisdiction in the affair. He set up a court martial with the officers of his two ships, and one of the scoundrels, convicted of the murder of the chaplain, had his hand cut off, and was then hanged and burned on a raft, in full view of Quebec.

RENÉ BAUDRY

AN, Col., C^{11A}, 2, f.38. [Pierre Groyer], *Mémoires de la vie et des aventures de Nicolas Gargot, capitaine de marine* [Paris, 1668]; *Les aventures du rochelais Nicolas Gargot dit "Jambe-de-Bois,"* éd. Charles Millon (La Rochelle, 1928). *Jug. et délib.*, I, 6. La Morandière, *Hist. de la pêche française de la morue*, I, 414–16. P.-G. Roy, *La ville de Québec*, I, 301–2.

DUPLESSIS, PACIFIQUE, Recollet friar, missionary; b. at Vendôme; d. 1619 at Quebec.

After being a practising apothecary, he joined the Recollets of the province of Paris, and made his profession in that city in 1598.

He was one of four Recollets who, in 1615, established the Canadian mission, of which Father Denis JAMET was the first superior. At Quebec he was in charge of the building of a chapel dedicated to the Immaculate Conception. In the spring of 1617 he was sent to Trois-Rivières, where he devoted himself to preaching the gospel to the Indians, to teaching children, and to caring for the sick. He is thought to have been the first schoolmaster in the colony. By his zeal and gentleness he won the confidence of the Indians and helped to dissuade them from a plot they had hatched against the whites in the spring of 1618.

In July 1618, Brother Duplessis went back to France with Father HUET to plead the cause of the missions before the Compagnie des Marchands. He returned to Canada the following year. Shortly after his arrival, he fell ill and died at Quebec on 23 (or 26) Aug. 1619. He was the first missionary to die in the colony and on Champlain's orders "his funeral was marked by all the solemnity that the state of the colony . . . would permit" (Le Clercq). He was buried in the chapel at Quebec.

G.-M. DUMAS

ASQ, MSS, 200, Mortuologe des Recolets. Champlain, *Œuvres* (Laverdière). Le Clercq, *First establishment of the faith* (Shea), I, 83, 113, 120f., 129f., 147, 281; *Premier établissement de la foy*, I, 53f., 56f., 101, 111, 115, 124, 155. Sagard, *Histoire du Canada* (Tross), I, passim. Jouve, *Les Franciscains et le Canada: aux Trois-Rivières*, 1–5; *Les Franciscains et le Canada (1615–1629)*.

DU PLESSIS-BOCHART, CHARLES, naval officer, lieutenant of ÉMERY DE CAËN, head clerk of the Compagnie des Cent-Associés; known in Canada between 1633 and 1636.

It has been hinted, although no real proof has been advanced, that Du Plessis-Bochart was related to Cardinal Richelieu and the Duchesse d'Aiguillon; that is not impossible. However that may be, the protection given by these two personages is apparent in Du Plessis-Bochart's work in New France. He proved worthy of it, for he displayed unflagging activity in the service of the Cent-Associés.

The treaty of Saint-Germain-en-Laye having restored Canada to France on 29 March 1632, Émery de Caën was deputed to go and retake possession of it with his lieutenant, the Sieur Du Plessis-Bochart. The fort of Quebec was officially handed over to them on 13 July. On 22 May 1633, as CHAMPLAIN was back at Quebec, Émery de Caën entrusted the keys of the fort to Du Plessis-Bochart, who handed them over to Champlain the next day, "according to the cardinal's decree." In the autumn of the same year Du Plessis-Bochart received the order to take the fur-trading vessels back to France. He returned the following spring in command of four ships, one of which brought ROBERT GIFFARD, his family, and his party of emigrants.

Bochart served as a constant link between France and her colony, and carried out his mission zealously and intelligently. He made efforts to familiarize himself with the Indian mentality and its propensities, he convoked various tribes, and tried to make them settle. He founded a fur-trading post at Tadoussac and actively assisted Champlain, who wanted to strengthen the strategic fort of Trois-Rivières. His numerous voyages had, however, undermined his health, and he went back to France on 23 Aug. 1636, his name disappearing finally from our history at the period when changes were being made in the governing body of the Cent-Associés. In the command of the fleet he was replaced by M. de Courpont and in the office of head clerk by François DERRÉ de Gand.

In the index of the *Jesuit Relations* (Thwaites) Charles Du Plessis-Bochart has been confused with Guillaume GUILLEMOT, also called Du Plessis-Kerbodot.

RAYMOND DOUVILLE

JR (Thwaites). *JJ* (Laverdière et Casgrain). Desrosiers, *Iroquoisie*. Godbout, *Les pionniers de la région triflu-vienne*, 11. Sulte, *Mélanges historiques* (Malchelosse), V, 9–28.

DU PLESSIS-KERBODOT. See GUILLEMOT

DUPONT, FRANÇOIS GRAVÉ. See GRAVÉ

DUPONT, LOUIS GAUDAIS-. See GAUDAIS

DU PONT, ROBERT GRAVÉ. See GRAVÉ

(DU) PRÉVERT, JEAN SARCEL DE. See SARCEL

DUPUY, ZACHARIE, sometimes called "sieur de Verdun," from the name of his fief on the St. Lawrence; commandant of the forts of Quebec and of Onondaga (Onnontagué); town-major, commandant, and acting governor of Montreal; b. 1608 or 1610 at Saverdun in Gascony; d. 1676 at Montreal.

We do not know the exact date of Dupuy's arrival in New France, and more particularly at Quebec, where as early as 1656 he was in command of the fort. That same year the Jesuits, impressed by his qualities as an honest and excellent officer, accepted his offer to join the expedition which had been organized to found a mission among the Onondagas. On his return in 1658 he settled in Montreal, with the title of assistant town-major. He succeeded Major Lambert CLOSSE in 1662 and served as acting governor of Montreal in 1665, replacing M. de CHOMEDEY de Maisonneuve.

In 1671 the seigneurs of Montreal granted to Dupuy 320 acres, at the Saint-Louis rapids, as a noble fief without rights of justice; this was the Verdun fief. In the following year he received a new grant, this time from TALON, consisting of the Île aux Hérons and other islands, opposite the Verdun fief. In 1673 Dupuy and his wife, "desirous of withdrawing from the cares of the world and of devoting themselves to God," made over all their property to the Congrégation de Notre-Dame. The sisters of the Congrégation undertook to pay Dupuy and his wife a pension for life.

On 15 May 1674 the old town-major—he stated his age as 66—attended Easter mass in Notre-Dame church; he heard the Abbé SALIGNAC de Fénelon's sermon in which he attacked BUADE de Frontenac. When the witnesses were interrogated afterwards, Dupuy shrewdly deemed it more prudent to claim that he was "deficient in hearing and in memory," and he was not called to give testimony in the sensational case that followed.

Dupuy was buried at Montreal 1 July 1676. His widow appears to have returned to France shortly afterwards. His first wife, Jeanne Fauvenel, probably died before he came to New France; his second wife was Jeanne Groisard, whom he

Du Quesnoy

married on 25 Oct. 1668 at Quebec. Dupuy left no descendants.

ROLAND-J. AUGER

AJM, Documents judiciaires, 10 oct. 1662; 27 janv. 1667; 14 janv. 1669: Greffe de Bénigne Basset, 12 nov. 1673. AJQ, Greffe de Pierre Duquet, 22 oct. 1668. AN, F, 178, pp. 308–41 (PAC copy). Recensement de 1667.

JR (Thwaites), *passim.* "Le procès de l'abbé de Fénelon devant le Conseil Souverain de la Nouvelle-France en 1674," APQ *Rapport, 1921–22,* 138.

BRH, XXI (1915), 309–10; XXXIII (1927), 237. *Cahiers des Dix,* VII (1942), 84–87; VIII (1943), 239; X (1945), 228. Faillon, *Histoire de la colonie française,* II, 517, 524–27. Parkman, *The old régime* (25th ed.), 20–39. J.-E. Roy, *Histoire de la seigneurie de Lauzon,* I, 159.

DU QUESNOY, JEAN TALON. See TALON

DUQUET DE LA CHESNAYE, PIERRE, explorer, royal notary, attorney-general, seigneurial judge, seigneur; b. 14 Jan. 1643 in Quebec; d. 13 Oct. 1687 in Quebec.

Son of Denis Duquet and Catherine Gauthier, Pierre was one of the first pupils of the Jesuit college of Quebec. The *Journal des Jésuites* stresses on different occasions the role that he played in the musical portion of the religious ceremonies.

Shortly after leaving the college, Duquet, at the age of 20, bought the registry of the notary Guillaume AUDOUART, whom he succeeded as royal notary. His commission, dated 31 Oct. 1663, made him the first Canadian-born notary.

At this time Duquet had only just returned from an expedition, directed by Guillaume Couture*, which had taken him during the summer a little beyond Lake Nemiskau, about a hundred miles from Rupert River. This was the second attempt by the French to reach Hudson Bay by land.

Like most of the notaries of his period, Duquet had a well-filled career: he was often given power of attorney by litigants, and in addition he was commissioned to carry out several inquiries into irregularities in the liquor traffic. In the autumn of 1666 he went with the Carignan-Salières regiment into Iroquois territory and signed on 17 October the *Procès verbal de la prise de possession des forts d'Agnié.* Deputy attorney-general (1675–1681), attorney-general (1681–1686), seigneurial judge of Notre-Dame-des-Anges, of the Île d'Orléans and of Orsainville, he was moreover the owner of several properties at Quebec and Lévis and of two seigneuries granted to him in 1672 and 1675. His multifarious occupations prevented him however from giving the desired attention to his notarial acts, in which are to be found many errors and omissions. His registry, which is nevertheless very interesting, is preserved in the Judicial Archives of Quebec.

On 25 August 1666 Duquet had married at Quebec Anne Lamarre, who came originally from the parish of Saint-Sulpice in Paris.

ANDRÉ VACHON

AJQ, Greffe de Pierre Duquet, 1663–84; Ins. Prév. Québec, I, 303. AN, Col., C^{11A}, 10, ff.96s. APQ, Ins. Cons. souv., I, 6. *JR* (Thwaites), *passim. JJ* (Laverdière et Casgrain), *passim. Jug. et délib., passim. Ord. comm.* (P.-G. Roy), I, 21. Ordre de M. d'Avaugour au Sr. Couture pour aller au Nord, *BRH,* VII (1901), 41. *Papier terrier de la Cie des I.O.* (P.-G. Roy), 250–52. "Procès verbal de la prise de possession des forts d'Agnié (17 oct. 1666)," dans Sulte, *Mélanges historiques* (Malchelosse), VIII, 57f. Delanglez, *Jolliet,* 248, 255, 260. P.-G. Roy, *Inv. concessions, passim.*

"Les notaires au Canada," APQ *Rapport, 1921–22,* 22. J.-E. Roy, *Histoire du notariat,* I: 76f., 89–91. P.-G. Roy, *Fils de Québec* (4v., Lévis, 1933), I, 10–12. André Vachon, *Histoire du notariat canadien, 1621–1960* (Québec, 1962), *passim.*

DURANTAL. See ATIRONTA (fl. 1615)

DURET DE CHEVRY DE LA BOULAYE, CHARLES, lieutenant for the king in Acadia, 1685–90; b. *c.* 1645; d. 1691?

He was a first cousin of Charles-François Duret de Chevry, marquis de Villeneuve, called the marquis de Chevry (d. 16 Nov. 1712), under whose sponsorship La Compagnie des Pêches sédentaires de l'Acadie was organized [*see* BERGIER]. La Boulaye distinguished himself as an officer in Flanders in 1677 and by 1685 he was lieutenant for the king in Acadia, replacing Bergier. He was at Chedabouctou, which was the base of operations of the fishing company, about 7 or 8 leagues from Canseau, when Jacques Demeulle*, the intendant of New France, arrived there on 5 June 1686. At Canso, while on the way to Chedabouctou, Demeulle found the fishing company's ship *Saint-Louis* which had arrived 8 or 10 days earlier to fish for cod. The establishment of the company at Chedabouctou then consisted of Fort Saint Louis and several roughly built huts. La Boulaye had 15 or 20 hired men with him there and 3 leagues from the fort three or four inhabitants had cleared and manured 3 acres of land. La Boulaye accompanied Demeulle on his visit to Cape Breton in 1686. So as not to fall into the hands of buccaneers, La Boulaye escaped to Quebec in 1688. In 1689, not having received his pay, he applied for a grant of mines and for a leave of absence to return to France.

Although it is said that when Capt. Cyprian Southack* captured Chedabouctou in 1690, La Boulaye was taken prisoner and sent to Boston, where he died, DAUPHIN de Montorgueil, who was at that time commandant at Fort Saint-Louis, and Bochart* Champigny reported in 1690 that La Boulaye had returned to France.

C. Bruce FERGUSSON

There is much material on the marquis's company and on Duret in French archives, among which *see*: AN, Col., B, 13, f.186; C^{11A}, 1, f.211; C^{11D}, 1, ff.3, 150–70, 195–98; C^{11D}, 2, ff. 57–58, 63 (descriptions of Chedabouctou), 165, 176, 185; Col., E, 81 (petitions of the marquis's heirs, including a memoir giving the history of the company); F, 6, ff.176–77; F, 8, ff.30, 226. BN, MS, NAF 9283 (Margry), f.35; NAF 21395 (Arnoul), f.21. Recensement de 1686 (Acadie). *Coll. de manuscrits relatifs à la Nouv.-France*, I, II (*see* Laboulaye).
Acadiensia Nova (Morse), I, II. A. C. Jost, *Guysborough sketches and essays* (Guysborough, N.S., 1950). La Morandière, *Hist. de la pêche française de la morue*, I, 356–62. Murdoch, *History of Nova-Scotia*. Webster, *Acadia*, 205, 208.

DU TARTRE, VINCENT BASSET. See BASSET

DUTCH BASTARD. See FLEMISH BASTARD

DU THET, GILBERT, Jesuit brother; b. *c.* 1575 at Chantelle (Allier), made his noviciate at the Collège at Verdun from 1594 to 1596; d. 3 July 1613 at Saint-Sauveur (near Ellsworth, Maine).

He lived several years in the noviciate house, made a trip to Italy, and from 1609 was in Paris, living in the professed house.

Around November 1611 Antoinette de Pons, Marquise de Guercheville, supplanted Fathers Pierre BIARD and Énemond MASSÉ in the partnership which they had formed with Jean DE BIENCOURT de Poutrincourt, seigneur of Port-Royal (now Annapolis Royal, N.S.). She entrusted her outlay of 3,000 *livres tournois* to Brother Du Thet, who was gullible enough to let Poutrincourt appropriate 1,200 *livres* of it. Du Thet sailed in December 1611 and reached Port-Royal 26 Jan. 1612. He noticed some irregularities in the administration of Simon Imbert, Poutrincourt's agent, and suggested to CHARLES DE BIENCOURT, the son of Poutrincourt and chief of the colony, that the intendant be asked to give an account of himself. Imbert avenged himself on the friar by attributing to him remarks which approved the regicide of Henri IV, 14 May 1610. Charles de Biencourt made an investigation, ascertained that there was no case, but refused to issue the necessary affidavits and to allow the friar to go to France to defend himself. It was following this incident that Father Biard was the victim of violence, the result of which was the canonical interdict laid upon Port-Royal.

After the reconciliation of the Jesuits with Biencourt, 25 June 1612, Brother Du Thet was allowed to go back to France. He must have done so on a fishing or trading vessel and have arrived only late in the autumn. He could not do otherwise than tell the Marquise de Guercheville of the treatment received by the missionaries. The noble lady then broke off the partnership which she had renewed with Poutrincourt on 17 Aug. 1612. She had a new ship rigged, the *Jonas*, commanded by Capt. Charles Fleury, to go and withdraw Biard and Massé from Port-Royal and found a new settlement on the American coast. Brother Du Thet, with Father JACQUES QUENTIN, went on the expedition, but they were to return to France if they found their associates safe and sound. Brother Du Thet, however, wanted to end his days in Canada.

A site was chosen at Saint-Sauveur, but delays occurred in building through the fault of RENÉ LE COQ de La Saussaye, the commander of the settlement, and despite the protests of Charles Fleury, who wanted to return to France. On 3 July 1613 Samuel ARGALL's surprise attack was launched; the *Jonas*, and then the fort which had just been started, were quickly overcome. Seeing the English coming, Du Thet had gone with Fleury on to the ship, to help with the defence. The Jesuit took the place of the gunner who was absent, but to little purpose. He was hit in the chest by a bullet and struck down among the wounded. The victorious English took him ashore and he died the next day, attended by Father Biard. He was thus the first French Jesuit to die in America.

LUCIEN CAMPEAU

Archivum Romanum Societatis Iesu, codex Gal. 94 I, f.171, lettre du frère Du Thet au père Ignace Armand, Nancy, 10 mai 1603; codex Franc. 22, catalogue des maisons et des personnes de la province de France. Bréard, *Documents relatifs à la marine normande*, 121–23. *Factum* (1614), *passim*. JR (Thwaites), III, 21–283; IV, 7–117, Relation du père Biard. Lescarbot, *History* (Grant), III, 58–64. É.-H. Gosselin, *Nouvelles glanes historiques normandes*, 41–43. Huguet, *Poutrincourt*. [See also bibliography for JEAN DE BIENCOURT.]

DUVAL, JEAN, locksmith; hanged at Quebec 1608.

Duval had been a member of the colony at Port-Royal (Annapolis Royal, N.S.) in 1606–7. He had participated with JEAN DE BIENCOURT de

Easton

Poutrincourt and Samuel de CHAMPLAIN in the voyage southwards in the hope of finding a better location for the settlement. At Port Fortuné (Stage Harbour, Cape Cod) in October 1606, along with some sailors who refused to return to the ship for the night, he was attacked by Indians. He was one of the rare survivors and returned wounded by an arrow: "It would have been better if he had died there," wrote Marc Lescarbot.

The Habitation was being started at Quebec in July 1608 when Duval formed the scheme of killing Champlain in order to hand Quebec over to the Basques or the Spaniards, and to make his fortune in doing so. Duval found four accomplices, one of whom was the locksmith Antoine Natel, and they undertook to suborn all their comrades, including Champlain's lackey. Shortly before the time set for the crime, Natel was seized by remorse and went to warn Captain Testu who was on his way from Tadoussac; he revealed all the details of the scheme and obtained pardon through Testu's intervention.

The same evening Champlain had the four accomplices lured on board a boat under the pretext of offering them something to drink, and took them prisoner. Others who had been implicated in the affair informed against their leaders. Champlain formed a council composed of FRANÇOIS GRAVÉ DU PONT, Testu, the surgeon Bonnerme who at one moment had been under suspicion, and the officers in charge of navigation. The accomplices were tried and condemned to be hanged. Duval was executed immediately as an example, and his head was stuck on a pike at the highest point of the fort; the other three were sent to Pierre DU GUA de Monts in France, "in order that more ample justice should be done to them." Natel did not long survive the man he had informed against; he died of dysentery the following November. Bonnerme's death, probably from scurvy, followed in the spring of 1609.

MARCEL TRUDEL

Champlain, *Works* (Biggar), I, 376, 449; II, 25–34, 53, 59. Lescarbot, *Histoire* (Tross), II, 520, 546; III, 596f. Biggar, *Documents relating to Cartier and Roberval*, 55. Bréard, *Documents relatifs à la marine normande*, 86.

E

EASTON, PETER, once a loyal English seaman, later turned pirate, whose well-equipped fleet of warlike ships and intensive raids on both English and foreign ships earned him the appellation "arch-pirate"; fl. 1610–20.

Easton arrived in Newfoundland 1612 "with ten sayle of good ships well furnished and very rich" and proceeded with impunity to raid coastal harbours from Trinity Bay to Ferryland at his own good pleasure. He made Harbour Grace his headquarters, where he repaired his ships, built a fort, and added men to his crews by persuasion, and, if necessary, by force. In addition to his depredations in the waters adjacent to Harbour Grace, where he took two ships, 100 men, and provisions from every ship, Easton plundered 30 English vessels in the harbour of St. John's and raided French and Portuguese ships at Ferryland. The total damage inflicted by Easton on the fishing fleets was estimated at £20,400.

Easton's peripatetic exploits brought him into personal contact with RICHARD WHITBOURNE (afterwards Sir Richard), a long-time, legitimate trader, and JOHN GUY, governor of the colony at Cuper's (now Cupids) Cove. It must be said in Easton's favour that he did no actual harm to the settlement. Indeed, on one occasion, the settlers gave him two pigs. There was only one clash with the colonists, in which one of them was wounded by error. Easton did, however, capture Whitbourne, whom he kept on board his ship for 11 weeks, attempting all the while to convert him to piracy. He only released Whitbourne on condition that the latter should go to England and seek a royal pardon for him.

When Whitbourne arrived in England, he found that a pardon had already been granted to the pirate, February 1612, but that it had never reached him. It was re-granted 26 November. Capt. Roger Middleton was commissioned to deliver the pardon to Easton in Barbary, as the pirate had left Newfoundland to sail to the Mediterranean in search of Spanish treasure-ships. According to Whitbourne, Easton, consumed "with a longing desire and full expectation to be called home, lost that hope by too much delaying of time by him who carried the pardon."

Easton's pardon had still not reached him in March 1613, whereupon he sailed into Villefranche, Savoy, free port of the pirates. Because of his reputed wealth—two million pounds of "gold"—he was warmly welcomed by the Duke of Savoy, whose finances were then at a low ebb. At Villefranche Easton bought a palace, set up a warehouse for his booty, lived in luxury, and acquired the title "Marquis of Savoy." Being at that time a handsome man around 40, according to contemporary descriptions, he crowned his career by marrying a very wealthy lady. He remained in the service of the Duke of Savoy until 1620, when he is lost to history.

Easton was the leading corsair of his day and one of the most famous in the whole annals of piracy. He possessed all the requisite skills for his infamous trade but he was neither a blood-thirsty monster nor a swashbuckling cut-throat. On the contrary, he proved himself an outstanding navigator, an able, brave, and bold seaman, an expert tactician, and highly competent in gun-laying. He controlled such seapower that no sovereign or state could afford to ignore him and he was never overtaken or captured by any fleet commissioned to hunt him down.

E. HUNT

Nottingham University, Middleton MSS, Mi X 1/1–66. PRO, H.C.A. 1/47, 14/42 give details of his raids on English and French vessels returning from Newfoundland in 1610 and on the French in Newfoundland in 1612 (on the latter *see also* PRO, P.C.2/27 and *CSP, Ireland, 1611–14*, 383); H.C.A. 13/42 concerns his raids on the Dutch, 1612; H.C.A. 24/76, no.160; C.O.1/1, no.179; *CSP, Dom., 1611–18*, 119, 158; *CSP, Venice, 1610–13; 1613–15; 1619–21*.

The life and works of Sir Henry Mainwaring, ed. G. E. Manwaring (2v., Navy Records Soc., LIV, 1920, LVI, 1922), I. Purchas, *Pilgrimes* (1905–7), XIX, 417. *Westward hoe for Avalon in the New-found-land as described by Captain Richard Whitbourne, of Exmouth, Devon, 1622*, ed. T. Whitburn (London, 1870). Richard Whitbourne, *A discourse and discovery of New-found-land* (London, 1620).

ECHEVETE, MATIAS DE, reputed to be the first Spaniard to reach Newfoundland; b. *c.* 1525; d. 1599, aged 74.

According to the testimony of his son early in the 17th century, Matias was in Newfoundland when he was 15 years old, serving as carpenter on a French ship from Saint-Jean-de-Luz. The date given in the testimony is 1545; but it must be an error, since Echevete was then 20 years old and not 15. We know moreover that in 1541–42 several Spanish vessels went to Newfoundland, since some of the crew members, upon their return, gave information to the Spanish authorities on the whereabouts of CARTIER and JEAN-FRANÇOIS LA ROCQUE de Roberval. It also seems unlikely that Matias de Echevete was the first Spaniard to reach Newfoundland, for as early as 1527 Spanish fishing vessels were found in Newfoundland waters by the John RUT expedition. According to his son's testimony, Matias de Echevete made 28 voyages to Newfoundland as carpenter and as pilot.

L.-A. VIGNERAS

Museo Naval (Madrid), MSS in Collection Vargas Ponce. C. Fernández Duro, "La pesca de los Vascongados y el descubrimiento de Terra Nova," in *Arca de Noé* (Madrid, 1881), 313–14.

EDGCOMBE (Edgecombe), LEONARD, captain with the HBC; d. June 1696.

Master of the ship *John and Thomas*, chartered by the HBC, he sailed in 1684 to Charlton Island, the Company's *entrepôt* in James Bay.

For the next few seasons Edgcombe's services were otherwise engaged, but he served the HBC again in 1687, commanding the *John and Thomas*, with instructions to assist Governor George GEYER at Port Nelson and serve on his council. Edgcombe was cautioned to use extreme care in approaching Port Nelson lest it be in enemy hands, for the Company's three posts on James Bay had been taken by de TROYES the previous year. Back in England by October 1687, Edgcombe was able to report that the posts at Port Nelson and New Severn were in good condition. He sailed to York Fort in 1688 but by the time the next voyage was due England and France were at war.

He was now taken into the Company's regular service and by virtue of his faithful record and his "skillfullnesse" in navigation he was chosen in 1689 to command the *Royal Hudson's Bay* frigate which set out with the *Northwest Fox* (Capt. John Ford). The ships got no farther than the Scillies when they were attacked by three French privateers. After an eight- or nine-hour engagement Edgcombe brought his vessel limping back to Plymouth but the *Northwest Fox* fell prey to the enemy. It was too late that year for ships to reach the Bay so there was no communication with Rupert's Land for 12 months.

Edgcombe was again in command of the *Royal Hudson's Bay* on the 1690 voyage, carrying letters of marque, and on the voyage of 1691 he was designated chief or admiral of the voyage because of his "wonted courage and conduct." With similar rank he sailed the *Dering* [III] in 1692, accompanied by three other ships, and also in 1693, when he was warned to destroy the company's "pacquet" of letters if in danger of seizure by the enemy.

In February 1694 Edgcombe bought the ship *Supply* from the HBC for £2,200. Two years later, when commanding the East India Company's *Mocha* (*Mocca*) frigate, he met death at the hands of pirates. Their ringleader, James Kelly, alias Gillam, alias Sampson Marshall, was executed in London in 1700 for piracy and was generally considered to be responsible for Edgcombe's murder.

MAUD M. HUTCHESON

Eirikson

PRO, H.C.A. 1/14, pt.3, no.213; H.C.A. 1/53. *CSP, Col., 1699. CTP, 1697–1701/02.* HBRS, IX (Rich); XI, XX (Rich and Johnson); XXI (Rich).

EIRIKSON, LEIFR *heppni.* See LEIFR

ELIOT (Elyot, Eliott, Ellyot), HUGH, merchant of Bristol who is claimed to be, with Robert THORNE the elder, the English discoverer of America; fl. 1480–1510.

Little is known of Eliot's life. Involved in a Chancery action in 1485, he is found trading to France, Spain, and elsewhere from 1492 onwards. He was sheriff of Bristol in 1500–1 and was a party in various lawsuits there until 1510. Robert Thorne, the younger, in 1527 claimed that his father, and Hugh Eliot had been "the discoverers of the Newfound Landes." John Dee saw this statement when studying the English title to North America, 1577–80, and endorsed Thorne's claim, adding, with unknown authority (or none) the date "Circa An. 1494."

No evidence, except the disputed "1494" legend on the 1544 Cabot map [*see* SEBASTIAN CABOT], has come to light on a voyage of this year. Eliot and Thorne are often considered to have accompanied JOHN CABOT in 1497 and, by having the first sight of land, to have made the discovery then. The statement by John Day, in 1497–98, that the English discovered the Isle of Brasil "in other times," might seem to put them back as independent discoverers in an earlier period. Eliot may, for instance, have been associated with the voyages of 1480 and 1481 [*see* John JAY and Thomas CROFT].

In 1502 Eliot, Robert Thorne, and William Thorne his brother, bought a ship, the *Gabriel,* at Dieppe, perhaps for an American enterprise. On 9 Dec. 1502, Hugh Eliot's name appeared in the charter granted by Henry VII to him, Thomas Asshehurst, João GONSALES, and Francisco Fernandes to continue the voyages to North America begun in 1501 by the Anglo-Portuguese "Company Adventurers into the New Found Lands." He continued to be active in the company while it lasted, investing money and shipping, though we do not know that he crossed the Atlantic himself, but the Company broke up in 1505 and he was subsequently involved in proceedings for debt against Francisco Fernandes. The link he provides between the late 15th- and early 16th-century American enterprises is an important one.

DAVID B. QUINN

The great red book of Bristol, ed. E. W. W. Veale (5v., Bristol Record Soc.), pt.III (XVI, 1951). *The staple court books of Bristol,* ed. E. E. Rich (Bristol Record Soc., V, 1934). *Precursors* (Biggar). D. B. Quinn "The argument for the English discovery of America between 1480 and 1494," *Geog. J.,* CXXVII (1961), 277–85. Williamson, *Cabot voyages* (1962); *Voyages of the Cabots* (1929).

ENTREMONT, PHILIPPE MIUS (Muis) D'. *See* MIUS

ERIC, BISHOP. *See* EIRIKR *upsi* GNUPSSON, [Appendix]

ERIC THE RED. *See* EIRIKR THORVALDSSON [Appendix]

EROUACHY (Eroachi, Esrouachit), known to the French as "La Ferrière," "La Forière," "La Fourière," "La Foyrière"; chief of the Montagnais Indians around Tadoussac; frequently acted as self-appointed negotiator between his people and the French; fl. 1618–36?

Erouachy professed friendship for the French and sought favours from them. In 1618 he was sent to Quebec to negotiate with the French concerning the murder of two Europeans by Montagnais Indians near Cap Tourmente two years before. In July 1623, he warned the French of an impending attack on Tadoussac and Quebec, which CHEROUOUNY, another Montagnais leader, was fomenting, perhaps at the instigation of the independent fur-traders.

In 1627 the Montagnais were still annoyed by French restrictions on trade, claiming that the trading company charged more for goods than did the independent traders. When two more Frenchmen, Dumoulin and Henri, the servant of Mme Hébert [*see* ROLLET], were murdered near Quebec in October of that year, the French exacted three young men as hostages until those responsible were delivered to them. Erouachy again undertook to negotiate with the French. In May 1628, he came to Quebec with a man whom CHOMINA, a Montagnais Indian friendly to the French, had accused of the murders. Erouachy tried to justify his companion by blaming the killings on some Algonkins. When CHAMPLAIN refused to believe his story and arrested the suspect, he urged him to treat him well and to await further evidence. Erouachy spent the winter among the Abenakis, and in April 1629 he returned to Quebec to propose an alliance between that tribe and the French. The proposal greatly pleased Champlain, since the Abenakis were said to grow corn and he thought some Frenchmen might winter among them if the ships from France, captured the previous summer by DAVID

Kirke and again threatened by the English, did not succeed in reaching Quebec.

Erouachy also affirmed his friendship for the French and warned them to beware of the Indians at Tadoussac, whom they already knew had given aid to Kirke, who had captured that post in the previous year. Erouachy also offered to send one of his own men along in order to protect any Frenchmen who were hunting or fishing away from the settlement. He also repeated a story he had heard among the Mahicans, blaming the machinations of an Allumette Island Indian for the death of Pierre Magnan and Cherououny, while on a peace mission to the Iroquois country. At this time Erouachy again pleaded for the prisoner, and Champlain promised he would do nothing until the return of the ships and the annual gathering of the Indians.

In June, when the French at Quebec had run out of food, Erouachy insisted that the prisoner, now ill from unaccustomed confinement, be released. Fearing the Indians and in precarious circumstances, Champlain ultimately agreed to this, but only if a new hostage were given and if Chomina, to whom went the final credit for the prisoner's release, were elected as the chief representative of the tribes who traded with the French. This action seems to have been prompted partly by French distrust of Erouachy, to whom Chomina was also hostile.

Champlain's brief accounts throw little light on the character of Erouachy or on the broader aspects of his life. Like his enemy and possible rival Cherououny, he seems to have felt far from well disposed toward the French at Quebec. There is no evidence that he commanded any positive respect among his own people. Perhaps a weak man by nature he sought to gain the favour of the French but never succeeded in winning their confidence.

In 1636 the Jesuits mention that Erouachy's wife offered his daughter for baptism. It is not clear whether Erouachy was alive or dead at this time.

BRUCE G. TRIGGER

Champlain, *Works* (Biggar), *passim*. *JR* (Thwaites), IX, 32. Sagard, *Histoire du Canada* (Tross), *passim*. Desrosiers, *Iroquoisie*, 111. P.-G. Roy, *La ville de Québec*, I, 65–66.

ESCHAMBAULT, JACQUES FLEURY D'. *See* Fleury

ESPÉRANCE. *See* Charité, Espérance, and Foi

ESROUACHIT. *See* Erouachy

F

FAGUNDES, JOÃO ALVARES, Portuguese explorer; fl. 1521.

Fagundes, a native of Viana, Portugal, seems to have been a member of a company organized by residents of that city who wished to found a colony in Newfoundland. Fagundes received letters patent from King Manoel of Portugal (1495–1521) granting him the captaincy of any lands he might discover between "Cortereal Land" (the eastern shore of Newfoundland) and the territories assigned to Spain by the treaty of Tordesillas [signed 7 June 1494 between Spain and Portugal to settle conflicts arising from Columbus's first voyage]. On 13 March 1521, he had a Lisbon notary duly record his discoveries, made during a recent voyage, probably the year before. Among them he mentioned the three islands in Watering-Place Bay (Baya d'Auguoada), other islands which he called "Fagundas," the archipelago of Saint-Pantaléon, the archipelago of the 11,000 Virgins, and the island of Santa Cruz.

The archipelago of the 11,000 Virgins appears for the first time on the Reinel-Miller "Carta Atlantica" (BN, Paris). It is generally taken for granted that this archipelago is the Saint-Pierre-Miquelon-Langlade group with the small islands around it. H. P. Biggar and W. F. Ganong have identified Watering-Place Bay with Chedabucto Bay, between Cape Breton Island and Nova Scotia, where there are three relatively large islands (Madame, Janvrin, and Petite-de-Grat); but since the line of demarcation between the lands assigned to Spain and those assigned to Portugal was generally thought to cut through Cabot Strait, it is unlikely that Fagundes would have laid claim to Cape Breton Island, which was included in the Spanish zone. Harrisse has identified Watering-Place Bay with the Gulf of St. Lawrence, and Hoffman (*Cabot to Cartier*, 35) has suggested that "after 1521 Fagundes transferred his operations to Nova Scotian waters." There is no doubt that Fagundes discovered the southern coast of Newfoundland, between Cape Race and Cape Ray; but whether he also explored Cape Breton Island and penetrated into the Gulf of St. Lawrence remains a matter of speculation.

Farrar

An island called "Fagunda" appears on later Portuguese maps (by Lopo Homem, Vaz Dourado, etc.). It is placed to the southeast of Cape Breton, fairly near the present location of Sable Island. This island may be the one Fagundes named Santa Cruz, and which he located "at the foot of the bank."

Nothing more is known of Fagundes's venture. He spent large sums of money, but we do not know if he actually founded a colony. It does seem however that Portuguese fishing establishments were set up along the shore of Newfoundland, probably by men from Viana or from the Azores.

L.-A. VIGNERAS

"1516–1521. Descobertas de Joao Alvares Fagundes," *Archivo dos Açores*, IV (1882), 466–67. E. A. de Bettencourt, *Descobrimentos, guerras e conquistas* . . . (Lisboa, 1881) 132–35. Armando Cortesão, *Cartografia e cartógrafos portugueses dos séculos XV e XVI* (2v., Lisboa, 1935), I, 287–88. W. F. Ganong, "Crucial maps, II." Henry Harrisse, *The discovery of North America: a critical, documentary, and historic investigation, with an essay on the cartography of the new world* . . . (London, 1892), 182–88. Hoffman, *Cabot to Cartier*, 35, 100–1. *Precursors* (Biggar), xxii–xxiv.

FARRAR, CONSTANCE. *See* FERRAR

FÉNELON, FRANÇOIS DE SALIGNAC DE LA MOTHE-. *See* SALIGNAC

FERNANDES, JOÃO, significant early Portuguese explorer, said to have been the source of the name "Labrador"; fl. 1486–1505.

Bristol customs records for 1486 show "ffornandus and Gunsalus" as Portuguese traders in that port and for 1493 show "Johannes ffornandus." In 1501 Henry VII granted a charter to the Anglo-Portuguese syndicate, which included João Fernandes, Francisco Fernandes, and João GONSALES. It is probable that João Fernandes had traded with Bristol from 1486 on and so became linked with the English voyages to America as well as with Portuguese voyages. The Hamy King map of 1503 shows Greenland as "Terra de Labrador" and the Labrador-Newfoundland region as "Terra de Corte Real," implying that Greenland had been discovered by the labrador, João Fernandes before GASPAR CORTE-REAL coasted it in 1500.

In October 1499 King Manoel granted a charter to João Fernandes of the island of Terceira in the Azores, a landholder or labrador under the captaincy of the Corte-Real family. From a comparison of Fernandes's charter with that of Corte-Real in 1500, it does not seem that he had taken part in any Portuguese voyages of discovery previous to 1499. Yet his charter promised him governorship of any islands "which he might discover and find anew" (Biggar, *Precursors*, 31). JOHN CABOT discovered Cape Breton Island and south Newfoundland in 1497. His second voyage in 1498 reached East Greenland, crossed to Baffin Island and coasted as far as Chesapeake Bay (Harrisse, Dawson, Biggar, and others; but Winship, Williamson, Almagià, and Skelton do not accept this reconstruction). The Weimar map of 1530 has a legend near Greenland: "This land was discovered by the English of the town of Bristol but in it there is nothing of value. And as the one who first gave notice of it was a Labrador of the Azores, they gave it the name." The Italian maps of Maiollo from 1504 on carry similar legends. Santa Cruz in his manuscript of 1541 described the Land of the Labrador: "it is said that two Portuguese brothers, named the Corte Reals, . . . asserted that the great main land of the West Indies [North America], of which they occupied the extreme end, was separated from that island of the Labrador [Greenland] by a very large and wide sea channel, of which the pilot Antonio Gaboto . . . also had information. It was called the land of the Labrador because a labrador of the islands of the Azores gave notice and information about it to the King of England when he [*sic* had] sent in search of it Antonio Gaboto, the English pilot and father of Sebastian Gaboto, who is now Your Majesty's pilot-major. Adjoining the coast of . . . Bacallaos [Newfoundland] where the Corte Reales, the two Portuguese brothers, went to colonize, and which was first discovered by the pilot Antonio Gaboto, the Englishman, . . . there are many islands. . . . "

It is now known that John Cabot went down with his ship on the 1498 voyage. The most reasonable interpretation of the evidence is that Fernandes went with Cabot in 1498 as a pilot and charted the coasts from Greenland to Newfoundland and Chesapeake. On his return to England he showed his charts of these discoveries to the king. His special knowledge of these new lands gained him a charter from King Manoel the following autumn to "discover and find anew." It placed him also as the chief Portuguese member of the Anglo-Portuguese syndicate which got a charter from Henry VII in March 1501. It is possible that the name Labrador was given to the continuous mainland from Greenland to east Newfoundland, found during the 1498 Cabot voyage. Thirty-one maps, from that of Pedro Reinel of 1504, show such a continuous mainland and the map of Juan de la Cosa of 1500 also shows a continuous mainland. Newfoundland was soon established as an island. Corte-Real by 1501 found that Greenland was quite separate from the mainland of North America and confined the Labrador to Greenland as shown on the Hamy King and 11 other maps. The English seem to have retained "Labrador" for the present region after the Norse name, "Greenland," was re-adopted for that island, by 1560 or so.

On 9 Dec. 1502 a second charter to the Anglo-Portuguese syndicate specifically excluded João Fernandes from visiting the lands discovered by the English. It would appear that he was engaged on a rival scheme for King Manoel; perhaps he took part in the Corte-Real voyages. In 1506 Barcellos petitioned the Portuguese monarch: "I received a command from the King, our master, to go on a voyage of discovery, I and a Johã Fernandes, landholder, on which discovery we were absent (from Terceira) for three good years and when I returned to the said island, I found my people driven from the said lands . . ." (Biggar, *Precursors*, 98). His request was favourably received and the above statement confirmed by the monarch.

A. DAVIES

René Baudry, "D'où viennent les noms 'Bras d'Or' et 'Labrador'?" *RHAF*, VI (1952–53), 20–30. *Precursors* (Biggar). Arthur Davies, "João Fernandes and the Cabot voyages," Congresso internacional de historia dos descobrimentos, *Actas*, II (1961). Denys Hay, "The manuscript of Polydore Vergil's 'Anglica Historia,'" *EHR*, LIV (1939), 240–51. Hoffman, *Cabot to Cartier*. "The last voyage of John Cabot," *Nature*, CLXXVI (1955), 996–99. Fridtjof Nansen, *In northern mists: arctic exploration in early times* (2v., London, 1911), II. Williamson, *Voyages of the Cabots* (1929). Heinrich Winter, "The pseudo-Labrador and the oblique meridian," *Imago mundi*, II (1937), 61–74.

FERRAR (Farrar), CONSTANCE, army captain, who served in the Low Countries, the Palatinate, the Île de Ré, and La Rochelle, and who commanded the fort at the colony of Sir James STEWART (Lord Ochiltree) at Port de la Baleine, near English Harbour (later Louisbourg); fl 1629.

Ferrar, with his wife and family, crossed the Atlantic with Lord Ochiltree and his other colonists. At the suggestion of Capt. Ogilvie, they built a fort named "Rosemar." Within a few weeks, however, an end was put to this nascent settlement, when Capt. CHARLES DANIEL of Dieppe, one of the Compagnie des Cent-Associés, captured and razed it and took the settlers to Cibou (now St. Ann's, Cape Breton), where they remained for about five weeks before being taken back across the Atlantic. Daniel's men with the help of 20 of the captives built Fort Sainte-Anne at Cibou. Some of the prisoners, including Ferrar, were landed at the Lizard, Cornwall, but Ochiltree and 17 others were taken to France as prisoners. After his return to England Ferrar petitioned the king to take steps for the release of Lord Ochiltree and his associates.

C. BRUCE FERGUSSON

PRO, C.O.1/5, 41 (summary in *CSP, Col., 1574–1660*, 104), Ferrar's petition to Charles I. Champlain, *Works* (Biggar), VI, 153–61, Capt. Daniel's account.

FILLION, MICHEL, court sergeant, surveyor, secretary to Governor PIERRE DUBOIS Davaugour, clerk of the seneschal's court and of the Conseil Souverain, deputy to the attorney-general, seigneurial attorney, seneschal judge and royal notary; b. *c.* 1633 at Saint-Germain l'Auxerrois in Burgundy; d. 7 June 1689 at Beauport. He is not to be confused with a contemporary named Michel Feuillon, who had settled at Champlain.

Fillion, the son of André Fillion and of Gabrielle Senler (Senlet or Sanlerg), arrived in Canada before 10 April 1654, at which date we find him a court sergeant at Quebec. He acted in various capacities: among others, as clerk of the seneschal's court in 1662, as a royal notary by commission of the Conseil Souverain dated 23 Sept. 1663, and shortly afterwards as clerk of this same council. Except for an interval of three years (1671–74) during which he had "been out of his mind," he practised as a notary until his sudden death at Beauport on 7 June 1689.

On 26 Sept. 1661 he had married Marguerite Auber, widow of Martin Grouvel. She was still living on 22 April 1693. Tanguay is therefore wrong when he attributes to him a second marriage in 1667. More probably the marriage in question was that of his brother Antoine, who was himself living at Quebec according to the 1667 census, and who later died prematurely. Michel Fillion, who had had no children, adopted two of his brother's orphan children, Jean and Antoinette. Thus the mystery of his so-called descendants is cleared up.

The *Journal des Jésuites*, in February 1661, mentions a person named Fillon, who had "provided music" with Pierre DUQUET de La Chesnaye. Can we take this musician to be our Michel Fillion? Fillon's companion, Duquet, it is true, was also a notary; but how can we be sure that at that time there was not another individual at Quebec named Fillon, more skilled in music than Michel Fillion? The latter always signed himself, very legibly, in this way.

HONORIUS PROVOST

Fisher

AJQ, Greffe de Michel Fillion, 1660–88; Greffe de François Genaple, 22 avril 1693. AJTR, Greffe de Séverin Ameau, 17 mars 1665; Greffe de Jacques de La Touche, 15 oct. 1668. ASQ, Documents Faribault, 94. *JR* (Thwaites). *JJ* (Laverdière et Casgrain). *Jug. et délib. Papier terrier de la Cie des I.O.* (P.-G. Roy), 108. *BRH*, XLIX (1943), 372f. "Les notaires au Canada," APQ *Rapport, 1921–22*, 20, 22. J.-E. Roy, *Histoire du notariat*, I, 92–94, *et passim*. Tanguay, *Dictionnaire*.

FISHER, RICHARD, narrator of an English voyage to the Magdalen Is. and Cape Breton; fl. 1593.

Nothing is known of him except that he was the servant of a Thames-side shipowner, Master Hill of Rotherhithe, and that he kept the journal (being purser or cape merchant) on the ship owned by Hill, the *Marigold*, 70 tons (Richard Strong of Topsham, master), in 1593, when she set out, with ten hunters, butchers, and coopers on board, to take walrus from a base on the Magdalen Is. in the Gulf of St. Lawrence. A clue to Richard Fisher's family may be the fact that a Robert Fisher of Rotherhithe, whose sister became the second wife of Peter Hill between 1595 and 1602, may well have been a relative, possibly his father or uncle (*see* Will, 28 March 1602, Somerset House, London, P.C.C. Montague 25, printed in *Surrey Arch. Coll.*, X, 306).

In 1591 intelligence had reached Lord Burghley that the St. Lawrence contained valuable walrus, whale, and fur resources. A Breton vessel, the *Bonaventure*, belonging to LA COURT de Pré-Ravillon, was brought into Bristol with her share of the tusks and hides from 1,500 walrus and 80 tuns of oil taken by her and her consort. William James of Bristol obtained information about harbours in Ramea (the Magdalen Is.) where the walrus were taken, from an anonymous member of the crew (probably the master) of the *Bonaventure* and reported on 19 September to Lord Burghley. Only a month later, on 9 October, Edward Palmer wrote to Lord Burghley from Saint-Jean-de-Luz that a Basque ship from Canada, carrying fine furs and oil, had been taken into Weymouth and that he should investigate her cargo and sources of supply (PRO, S.P. 94/4, ff.64–66).

It may have been Burghley who induced Hill to send the *Marigold* to the southwest to take part in an English walrus-hunting venture. In the same year, a Basque pilot Stevan de Bocall, who knew the gulf came to Bristol and gave his services to a ship which went to the St. Lawrence [*see* WYET]. It is possible that he undertook to pilot George Drake of Topsham, who was to be ready to join with the *Marigold* in April.

The two ships did not leave Falmouth until 1 June. Fisher tells us that the ships parted company at sea. Drake, he learnt, got to Newfoundland first and succeeded in reaching the Magdalens (suggesting that he had a pilot). He found both harbours—Basque Harbour and either House Harbour or Grand Entry—occupied by Basques and Bretons, but in one was a single Breton ship (conceivably one belonging to La Court de Pré-Ravillon), almost ready to sail. Taking fright, as she was from a Catholic League port and feared an English attack, she slipped away at night, leaving George Drake to capture three of her boats, which were out hunting with 23 men on them, and, apparently, some walrus carcases. He stayed only a short time to hunt further and did not wait for the *Marigold*, but returned to England.

Fisher tells us the *Marigold*, after passing through Cabot Strait, missed the Magdalens and, as she afterwards found, overshot them. She landed men at Cape Breton, and finally worked her way, some 50 or 60 leagues westwards and southwestwards, along the shores of Cape Breton and Nova Scotia, possibly as far as the present-day Halifax Harbour. She then proceeded to beat up and down the coast of Arambec (the Micmac name for Nova Scotia) until late September, doing a little fishing. Fisher gives no explanation of the lack of decisive action. He had recorded the trees and fruits he saw and something about the Cape Breton Indians when he went ashore there several times, and was the first Englishman to do so, but he said nothing about similar visits on the Nova Scotia coast, though he did note the sighting of seals, porpoises, and whales at sea. Presumably, the *Marigold* was waiting for Drake's ship to pick her up.

Finally, the master persuaded the crew to make for the Azores in the hope of taking an enemy prize, but the only Portuguese ship they met was too strong for them. The *Marigold* got to the Downs on 22 December and was unable to make the Thames by Christmas, so that the voyage was, for her, a complete failure, and was not, apparently, repeated.

Fisher's narrative is sensible, but in no way outstanding. However, the novelty of his accounts of the Micmacs, limited though they are, makes his narrative of some significance.

DAVID B. QUINN

[For the continuation of the Magdalen Is. (Ramea) enterprises *see* Charles LEIGH.]

Hakluyt, *Principal navigations* (1903–5), VIII, 150–62. Biggar, *Early trading companies*. S. E. Dawson, *The St. Lawrence Basin* (London, 1905). R. Douglas,

"Place-names on Magdalen Islands, Que.," Geog. Bd. Can., 17th Report (1922), 66–74; "La nomenclature géographique des Isles Madeleine, Province de Québec," Bulletin de la Société de Géographie de Québec, XIX (1925), 228–40, 301–5.

FLÉCHÉ, JESSÉ, also Jossé Flesche (Biard), Josué Fleche (Champlain), Fleuchy and Fleuche; priest, missionary in Acadia; b. at Lantages, in the diocese of Langres (France); d. 1611 (?) in France.

In 1607 Henri IV had allowed JEAN DE BIENCOURT de Poutrincourt to continue his colonizing endeavours in Acadia, but on condition that he take some Jesuits there to preach the gospel to the Indians. Not desiring the presence of Jesuits, Poutrincourt, when he finally sailed from Dieppe on 25 Feb. 1610, took with him only one priest, Abbé Fléché. The latter, according to LESCARBOT, may have received his powers from the Nuncio Roberto Ubaldini. Rochemonteix, however, questions this statement, "for the Nuncio," he said, "was not unaware that the king had appointed two Jesuits for the Canadian mission," Fathers BIARD and MASSÉ.

Fléché landed at Port-Royal at the end of May or the beginning of June 1610. On 24 June, less than a month after his arrival, he administered baptism to the Micmac chief MEMBERTOU and 20 members of his family. One may justifiably be surprised at such haste, even if Lescarbot does warn us that during Poutrincourt's first stay in Acadia, in 1606 and 1607, these Indians had received some instruction. Since Fléché did not know the Indian language, it was CHARLES DE BIENCOURT, Pourtrincourt's son, who at his father's request undertook to teach the catechism to the Indians.

In precipitating events Fléché had apparently yielded to the pressure of Poutrincourt, who through the zeal that he showed for evangelization hoped to retain royal favour, to obtain the financial support of pious and wealthy individuals, and to prove to the court at one and the same time that the Jesuit ministry was not really necessary in Acadia. CHAMPLAIN perhaps provides the explanation for this haste when he writes that shortly after the ceremony the governor sent his son Biencourt to France, "to carry the good news of the baptism of the Indians." It appears certain that Poutrincourt, although genuinely desirous of winning over Indians to the faith, had good reasons—perhaps of a financial nature—for displaying such fervent apostolic zeal.

Lescarbot tells us that more than a hundred Indians were thus baptized in 1610 and 1611. When the Jesuits Biard and Massé finally arrived (1611), they were astounded to discover that the baptized Indians were ignorant of even the rudiments of the faith. A fresh start had to be made to teach the gospel. The learned theologians of the Sorbonne moreover disapproved of this speedy fashion of conferring baptism. The Jesuits put this experience to good use: from then on they baptized adults in good health only after a long probation.

Jessé Fléché, who had been nicknamed the "Patriarch" by the Indians, sailed for France in June 1611. According to certain historians, he died in France that same year.

ANDRÉ VACHON

Champlain, Œuvres (Laverdière). JR (Thwaites). Lescarbot, Histoire (Tross). Huguet, Poutrincourt. Rochemonteix, Les Jésuites et la Nouvelle-France au XVIIe siècle.

Flemish Bastard

FLEMISH BASTARD (Bâtard Flamand, Dutch Bastard, Smits Jan, Smiths John [Indian name unknown]**),** Mohawk chief, son of a Mohawk mother and a Dutch father, intermediary between the French, the Dutch, and the English; fl. 1650–87.

In July 1650 the Flemish Bastard led a band of 25 to 30 Mohawks in an attack on Trois-Rivières. Early in 1654 he brought letters to Quebec from Fort Orange (now Albany, N.Y.). Later, in July 1654, again at Quebec, he delivered two French hostages and complained because the Jesuit, Father SIMON LE MOYNE, was sent on an embassy to the Onondagas instead of to the Mohawks. The Mohawk chief asked, "Ought not one . . . to enter a house by the door, and not by the chimney or roof of the cabin, unless he be a thief, and wish to take the inmates by surprise? We, the five Iroquois Nations, compose but one cabin; we maintain but one fire; and we have, from time immemorial, dwelt under one and the same roof . . . will you not enter the cabin by the door, which is at the ground floor of the house? It is with us Anniehronnons, that you should begin; whereas you, by beginning with the Onnontaehronnons, try to enter by the roof and through the chimney. Have you no fear that the smoke may blind you, our fire not being extinguished, and that you may fall from the top to the bottom, having nothing solid on which to plant your feet?" (JR (Thwaites), XLI, 87–89.)

The Flemish Bastard again appears, 30 Aug. 1656, when he led an attack on a group of Ottawas and Hurons at the Lac des Deux-Montagnes. In the battle, the Jesuit, Father Léonard GARREAU, was shot with a musket, which broke his spine. The Mohawks carried the priest to Montreal, where he died 2 Sept. 1656. According to Nicolas Perrot*, who gives a different version of the affair, the Flemish Bastard delivered the body of Father Garreau, stating that he had been murdered by a French deserter.

The Flemish Bastard was reported at Pointe Sainte-Croix (now Point Platon, N.Y.), with a party of 40 Mohawks, intent upon war. Perrot claims that he was at Corlaer (now Schenectady, N.Y.), when Rémy de Courcelle arrived there in February 1666, on his punitive expedition against the Mohawks. The governor, however, returned to Quebec on 17 March, without having accomplished his mission.

On 24 July 1666, M. de SAUREL, a captain in the Carignan-Salières regiment, led a force of 300 men, which he had organized in May of that year, against the Mohawks to avenge the deaths of two officers of the regiment, Capt. de Traversy and M. de Chazy [see AGARIATA] and the capture of other Frenchmen, including M. Canchy de Lerole, all of whom had been stationed at Fort Sainte-Anne on Lake Champlain. But before Saurel reached the Mohawk villages, he met a peace embassy, headed by the Flemish Bastard, who was bringing back Lerole and the other French captives. M. Saurel, therefore, abandoned his march and all returned to Quebec.

On 14 Sept. 1666, PROUVILLE de Tracy and M. de Courcelle set out for the third and actual invasion of the Mohawk country, from which they and their troops returned to Quebec 5 Nov. 1666. It was not until 8 July 1667 that a general peace was concluded with the Five Nations. On this date the Mohawks finally ratified the peace between their nation and the French, which had earlier been interrupted, perhaps by Agariata's execution (although the facts are not certain). The Flemish Bastard, however, was sent back to his country 8 Nov. 1666 with an elder of the Mohawks and was instructed by the French to return within four moons with Huron and Algonkin captives.

In 1667 he was the bearer of letters from Col. Richard Nicolls, the first English governor of New York (1664–68). Nicolls insisted that only "Smits Jan," should transmit certain communications which he, the commissaries at Albany, and Arent van Curler had addressed to the governor of New France. Tracy, in his turn, acknowledged receipt of the letters through the Flemish Bastard.

A final reference to this Mohawk chief (as "Smiths John") mentions him as being among the Christian Indians during the expedition of Brisay* de Denonville against the Senecas in 1687 ("Examination of Adandidaghko, an Indian prisoner," dated at New York, 1 Sept. 1687 (o.s.), *NYCD* (O'Callaghan and Fernow), III, 435).

THOMAS GRASSMANN

JR (Thwaites), XXXV, 211–13; XLI, 85–89; XLII, 225–39; XLV, 97; L, 197, 201–3, 205. *NYCD* (O'Callaghan and Fernow), III, 146, 147, 148, 151–52, 435. Perrot, "Memoir," in *Indian tribes* (Blair), I, 157–58, 199, 201–3.

FLETCHER, JOHN, British naval captain; d. 1697.

Fletcher, who was twice taken by the enemy during the war of the League of Augsburg (1688–97), became captain of the fireship *Terrible* (238 tons) in 1694, and in January 1695 sailed with the fleet to the West Indies. He became commander of H.M. frigate *Hampshire* (479 tons) in May 1695 and remained on duty at Jamaica after the fleet returned to England in the following August. He was recalled the next year and reached the Thames in January 1697.

In accordance with Admiralty orders Fletcher, in the summer of 1697, undertook the task of convoying the HBC's ships *Royal Hudson's Bay* (Capt. NICHOLAS SMITHSEND) and *Dering* (Capt. Michael Grimington*) to York Fort which, in the previous year, the last-named captains had helped to recapture from the French. The fireship *Owner's Love* (Capt. Lloyd) which also joined the expedition was crushed by ice, but Fletcher and the Company's captains, after unsuccessfully attacking the French ship *Le Profond*, commanded by Pierre Dugué* de Boisbriand, in Hudson Strait, continued their voyage. When off Port Nelson on 26 August (o.s.) they encountered and attacked Pierre Le Moyne* d'Iberville in his flagship *Le Pélican*. In an engagement lasting several hours both it and the *Hampshire* were damaged. Iberville claimed that a broadside from *Le Pélican* was responsible for the sudden sinking of the *Hampshire* and the loss of Fletcher and his crew, but it is doubtful if guns of that period could have instantaneously sunk so large a ship. An English account of the action mentions a French tribute to Fletcher's bravery and expresses doubt as to whether battle damage or "a fflaw of Wind" caused the *Hampshire* to sink. This account supported Mary Fletcher's successful petition to the king for a pension as compensation for the death of her husband.

The loss of the *Royal Hudson's Bay* and the surrender of York Fort [called Bourbon by the French] by Governor Henry Bayley* swiftly followed Fletcher's disaster and so began the French occupation of the Hayes River area which was to continue until ended by the Treaty of Utrecht (1713).

ALICE M. JOHNSON

Information on Fletcher will be found in PRO, Adm. 51/4367, 4212; Adm. 6/4, f.64; Adm. 8/3; *CSP, Col., 1693–96*. PAC *Report, 1934*, 6–9. [Nicolas Jérémie], *Twenty years of York Factory 1694–1714: Jérémie's account of Hudson Strait and Bay*, tr. from the French ed. of 1720 with notes and intro. by R. Douglas and J. N. Wallace (Ottawa, 1926), 28–30. N. M. Crouse, *Lemoyne d'Iberville: soldier of New France* (Ithaca, 1954), 139–54 (it should be noted that the Captain Smithsend referred to is Nicholas rather than Richard).

For another account of the sinking of the *Hampshire* see Guy Frégault, *Iberville le conquérant* (Montréal, 1944).

FLEUCHE (Fleuchy). *See* FLÉCHÉ

FLEURY D'ESCHAMBAULT, JACQUES, Canadian priest, missionary in Acadia; b. 15 Aug. 1672 at Quebec, son of Jacques-Alexis Fleury, Sieur d'Eschambault, and of Marguerite de Chavigny; d. 29 Aug. 1698 at Mines (Minas Basin).

He was the eldest son of one of the most eminent families in the country. His father, a lawyer in the Parlement of Paris, had emigrated to Canada in 1671; he had married the same year, had become king's attorney at Montreal, and had distinguished himself in the great expedition led by BUADE de Frontenac against the Iroquois.

Fleury d'Eschambault received his classical education and began his theology at Quebec. He was still only a sub-deacon when he left for Acadia with Abbé THURY in 1693. From there he went to France, where he was ordained priest for the seminary of Quebec. He returned to Canada in 1694, spent a year at Quebec, and went back to Pentagouet (Castine, Maine) as assistant to M. Thury.

In 1697 the French court organized an expedition against the English colonies in America. Indians and troops from Canada were to wait for the squadron at Pentagouet. But the Duc de Nesmond, the commander of the fleet, having lost two months' time at sea, did not venture to attack Newfoundland and because the season was far advanced he returned to France with nothing accomplished. The Indians, however, after waiting all summer, decided to organize a foray before dispersing. A group of 120 braves was to go down the Penobscot and join up with an equal number of Abenakis from the Kennebec River. When they reached the Îles de Pemaquid, the Indians encountered three English vessels, which gave chase to them. A fight ensued which lasted several hours and caused some loss of life on both sides. Abbé d'Eschambault, who accompanied the expedition, has left us an account of it. He died on 29 Aug. 1698 at Mines. He was only 26 years old.

RENÉ BAUDRY

AN, Col., C^{11A}, 3, f.66, f.179 (publié dans la Correspondance de Talon, APQ *Rapport, 1930–31*, 154). ASQ, Amédée-E. Gosselin, "Notes pour servir à la bibliographie des prêtres du Séminaire de Québec, avec références en marge." Maximilien Bibaud, *Le panthéon canadien*, éd. Adèle et Victoria Bibaud (Montréal, 1891), 93–97. *BRH*, XXII (1916), 206–8. H.-R. Casgrain, *Les Sulpiciens et les prêtres des Missions-Étrangères en Acadie (1676–1762)* (Québec, 1897).

FOI. *See* CHARITÉ, ESPÉRANCE, and FOI

FONTENEAU, JEAN, better known by the name of **Jean Alfonse,** French navigator; b. 1484 in a village in Saintonge; d. 1544 at La Rochelle.

At the age of 12 he joined the merchant service at La Rochelle, which was to become his home port and his place of residence. He sailed on coastal vessels to ports in Spain and Portugal. While still young he married a Portuguese girl, Valentine Alfonse. Following the custom of nicknames, he was given his wife's name, which finally replaced his own. It is this surname, together with his knowledge of Portuguese, which has given rise to the belief that he was a native of Portugal. The voyages which he undertook for commercial reasons seem to have taken him to the Baltic in the north and to the Mediterranean in the south; in the east, he sailed the coasts of Africa, visited the Red Sea, and even got as far as Japan. In addition he familiarized himself with the coasts of America, from Nova Scotia to the Antilles.

We almost certainly owe to him the invention of the "jeannette," a small sail placed at the top of the main mast to facilitate the manoeuvring of ships. He was a sailor, and an outfitter of ships when the opportunity occurred; he quickly acquired the title of master navigator with the reputation of never having lost a vessel. It was because of this reputation that he was chosen as "captain and pilot of King François I," to lead to Canada LA ROCQUE de Roberval's expedition, which left La Rochelle 16 April 1542. It was probably on the return trip, at the end of the summer, that he ventured on a cruise in search of the northwest passage to China. He passed through the Strait of Belle-Isle, and seems to have got as far as Davis Strait, being the first Frenchman to reach what was later to be called Baffin Bay. He was back in La Rochelle in May

Forestier

1543. War having broken out with Spain, he armed as a raider and captured some enemy ships. The following year, not knowing that peace had been signed in September, he took a few more prizes; but he was attacked off Cape Saint-Vincent in Portugal by Menendez and his squadron, who chased him as far as La Rochelle; there, in the ensuing battle, he fell mortally wounded.

GUSTAVE LANCTOT

Jean Fonteneau (Jean Alfonse) has left the following writings: *La cosmographie avec l'espère et régime du soleil du nord par Jean Fonteneau dit Alfonse de Saintonge, capitaine-pilote de François 1er . . .* , 2e éd., P. L. G. Musset (Recueil de voyages, XX, Paris, 1904). "Routier de Jean Alphonse," in Hakluyt, *Principal navigations* (1903–5), VIII, 275–83. *Les voyages avantureux du Capitaine Ian Alfonce* (Poitiers, 1559).

Champlain, *Œuvres* (Laverdière). Anthiaume, *Cartes marines*, I, *passim* (*see* Alfonse). Biggar, *Early trading companies*. Harrisse, *Jean et Sébastien Cabot*. Hoffman, *Cabot to Cartier*. La Roncière, *Histoire de la marine française*, III (1908). *Sixteenth-century maps relating to Canada: a check-list and bibliography*, ed. T. E. Layng (PAC pub., 1956). *Voyages of Cartier* (Biggar), which reproduces Jean Alfonse's description of his voyage to Canada.

FORESTIER, MARIE, *dite* **de Saint-Bonaventure-de-Jésus,** one of the three original Religious Hospitallers of Quebec, second superior of the Hôtel-Dieu; b. *c.* 1615 at Dieppe; d. 1698 at Quebec.

We know nothing of her childhood or of her parents. Her family must have been well off, since it made considerable gifts to the nun. She entered the mother house of the Hospitallers at Dieppe when she was only eight, and made her religious profession in 1632. She volunteered for the Canadian mission and arrived at Quebec 1 Aug. 1639 with Anne Le Cointre, *dite* de Saint-Bernard, and Marie GUENET, *dite* de Saint-Ignace, to establish a hospital.

For more than 50 years Marie Forestier was the soul and the support of the house that had been founded and built through her efforts. She was appointed superior 9 May 1645 and was re-elected six times at varying intervals up till 1683. In the intervals the principal positions of responsibility in the community were all entrusted to her.

In 1655 she was involved in a controversy with Jeanne MANCE. The Hospitallers of Quebec wanted to extend their work to Montreal, but Mademoiselle Mance and CHOMEDEY de Maisonneuve were opposed to this. Here is what Father PAUL LE JEUNE conveyed to Mother de Saint-Bonaventure in 1656: "I have spoken to monsieur de maisonneuve. There is nothing to do for you at Montreal." Nevertheless the Abbé Queylus [*see* THUBIÈRES] succeeded in the autumn of 1658 in bringing two Hospitallers to Montreal, but in the face of Jeanne Mance's opposition they had to return to Quebec.

On 21 Jan. 1664 Marie Forestier obtained from Bishop Laval* "the separation and distinction between the funds for the poor and those of the community, so that, being guided in the future by what one would have to spend for the Nuns and for the hospital, one might limit" expenses.

Marie Forestier played a major role in the writing of the *Annales* of the Hôtel-Dieu. Mother Jeanne-Françoise Juchereau*, *dite* de Saint-Ignace, tells us that she kept "lovingly the little notebooks in which Mother Marie de Saint Bonaventure de Jésus wrote down what took place in her time. Her style is simple and naïve. I have tried to imitate it by continuing as she had begun. . . . Some years before she fell into her second childhood, we urged her to write down what she had often told us about the beginnings of this house. She gave in to our requests, and it is partly from what she left us that I have drawn what I shall say about that here." According to the *Annales* again, Marie Forestier saw in a vision the "entry into heaven" of Mother Catherine de Saint-Augustin [*see* SIMON]. She also received in a dream a warning of the imminent death of JEAN LE SUEUR, the nuns' former chaplain.

Marie Forestier died 25 May 1698. During her last years "her great age had impaired her mind . . . , but the saintly habit of the virtue of obedience which she had acquired made her so submissive, that when she asked for something that it was felt should not be granted her, she who took care of her had only to tell her that our Mother was not willing; that was sufficient for her not to show any more desire for what she wanted previously and for her to remain quiet." To express their admiration for the nun the Indians "had always called her the lovely, the good, and the kindly one."

JEAN-GUY PELLETIER

AHDQ, T. 21, C. 500, Notices biographiques des premières Mères. Recensement de 1681. "Acte de loi réception et approbation pour L'establissement de L'hopital de Québec par Monsieur le Gouverneur," PAC *Rapport, 1939*, 41–42. *JR* (Thwaites). Juchereau, *Annales* (Jamet). *Jug. et délib.*, I. H.-R. Casgrain, *Histoire de l'Hôtel-Dieu de Québec* (Québec, 1878). P.-G. Roy, *A travers l'histoire de l'Hôtel-Dieu de Québec* (Lévis, 1939).

FORRESTER (occasionally **Sorester), ANDREW,** military officer in Acadia; fl. 1632.

He participated in the great colonization attempt launched by Sir WILLIAM ALEXANDER the elder during the 1620's. As ALEXANDER the younger's lieutenant, he probably accompanied the Scottish settlers who occupied Port-Royal in 1628 or 1629. Here the expedition built Charles Fort, and Forrester assumed command of the garrison. Thirty of the party of 70 died of scurvy and hardship during the winter of 1629–30. Alexander the younger left for England in the fall of 1630, giving command of the colony to Sir George Home.

After the return of Home to Scotland, Forrester took charge of the colony. In 1632, following the signing of the Treaty of Saint-Germain-en-Laye, which transferred the country to France, Alexander sent directions to Forrester to prepare to abandon the settlement. However, on 18 September, and despite the fact that France and England were now at peace, Forrester assembled a force of 25 men and sailed to the Saint John River in 2 vessels with the purpose of capturing the French fort there. He entered the harbour that evening and no opposition to his landing was offered by Jean-Daniel Chaline who had been left in command of the fort by CHARLES DE SAINT-ÉTIENNE de La Tour. According to the sworn testimony made by Chaline and his men, and substantiated in good part during a hearing in Boston later, Chaline welcomed Forrester and his men and offered no objection to their entering the fort. Forrester and 15 of his party did so, but once inside they made the garrison prisoners and tortured Jean Beaujot of the Compagnie de la Nouvelle-France to learn the whereabouts of the fort's stock of furs, merchandise, and food. The prisoners were then taken to the vessels, as were the 1,550 pelts, the food, small arms, and powder seized. After knocking down the large wooden cross standing in the fort and the arms of France, Forrester sailed to Port-Royal where he landed the captured goods, and then took the prisoners to Pentagouet where they were turned over to the English.

In December, Isaac de RAZILLY appeared at Charles Fort and presented the order from the two crowns to take possession. Forrester complied, and soon after he and the 41 Scottish pioneers who chose to return home were given passage in the French vessel *Saint-Jean*. They landed in England early in February 1633.

GEORGE MACBEATH

ACM, B. 5654. PAC *Report, 1912*, App.B. Couillard Després, *Saint-Étienne de La Tour*. Insh, *Scottish colonial schemes*. Lanctot, *Histoire du Canada*. McGrail, *Alexander*. Beamish Murdoch, *History of Nova-Scotia*. Edmund Slafter, *Sir William Alexander and American colonization* (Boston, 1873). *Winthrop's journal* (Hosmer) in *Original narratives* (Jameson).

FOUCHER, manager on the farm of CHAMPLAIN at Cap Tourmente from 1626 to 1628.

His first name is unknown. He appears in Canadian history in 1626. He was employed by the company of the sieurs de CAËN, and from July 1626 to July 1628 was in charge of the farm set up by Champlain at Cap Tourmente in order to feed the livestock of the Habitation, without having to transport the hay from the natural meadows located in that area. Foucher passed all the seasons of the year there, with a staff of eight people under him. Around 9 July 1628 a band sent from Tadoussac by the KIRKE brothers and made up partly of French renegades invaded the farm, and took prisoner Foucher, Nicolas Pivert, the latter's wife and niece, and two other servants. The buildings were systematically pillaged; of the animals—about 50—some were killed, and the remainder burned with the stable and the two main buildings. Foucher, although badly manhandled by the English, managed to escape with the Indians' help, but in his flight the enemy "singed his moustaches" with their arquebuses. He spent the following winter at Quebec, and on 26 June 1629, on board the bark belonging to EUSTACHE BOULLÉ, he sailed for Gaspé, hoping to find there a means of returning to France.

LUCIEN CAMPEAU

Champlain, *Œuvres* (Lavredière), 1110, 1155–56, 1214, 1244. Sagard, *Histoire du Canada* (Tross), I, 155; IV, 830–35, 837–38, 840–41, 892–95; *Long journey* (Wrong and Langton), 48, 299.

FOX (Foxe), LUKE, English navigator and arctic explorer, son of Richard Fox, master mariner of Hull; b. 20 Oct. 1586 in Kingston-upon-Hull, Yorkshire; married Anne Barnard, of Whitby, 1613 (there is no record of any children); d. *c.* 15 July 1635.

Fox's formal education was limited but he became well read in navigation and arctic history. As a youth he sailed in European waters and acquired ability, as he says, in "the use of the globes and other mathematicke instruments." By the age of 20 he was fascinated by the possibility of discovering a northwest passage to the Orient. Gaining the patronage of Henry Briggs, the mathematician, and Sir John Brooke, late in 1629 he petitioned King Charles for assistance in a voyage. He was successful, and the stimulus of a rival plan of Capt. Thomas JAMES at Bristol won

François

Fox the further support of a group of London adventurers, including Sir Thomas Roe.

Preparations advanced with Fox's usual thoroughness, and H.M.S. *Charles*, a pinnace of 70 or 80 tons, with 20 men, 2 or 3 boys, and 18 months' provisions, left London 28 April 1631 (MS journal), quitting Deptford 5 May (published journal), 2 days after James left Bristol. Fox was captain and pilot. By way of the Orkneys, Fox reached Hudson Strait 22 June, skirted the western shore of Hudson Bay "never without sight of land," but discovered no likely opening (he apparently missed Chesterfield Inlet). At Port Nelson he found relics of Sir Thomas BUTTON's 1612–13 wintering. He met James by chance, 29–31 August, near Cape Henrietta Maria, turned north, and was the first to sail beyond Foxe Channel (named by Parry* nearly 200 years later) into Foxe Basin. He followed the coast of what is now Foxe Peninsula, making soundings and tidal observations all the way, to the point he named Cape Dorchester, the land about being whimsically dubbed (22 September) "Fox his farthest" and by his reckoning just beyond the Arctic Circle (66°47′N) but more likely about 1° south of it. Turning homeward, he reached the English Channel 31 October, "Having beene forth neere 6 monethsh."

Fox did not discover a northwest passage, though he considered what is now Roes Welcome Sound promising. He cancelled the last hope for Hudson Bay, and found the tide through Foxe Channel to be from the southeast (not from the west, as HENRY HUDSON and Button had encouragingly reported); these were negative discoveries, but they abated the zeal for arctic exploration for almost 200 years. Moreover, he writes that he had gone farther than any predecessor "in lesse time and at less charge." His return in the same year undoubtedly saved lives (his genuine concern) and money, but it gave rise to adverse criticism, and Fox found it necessary to append a defence to his book.

This work, fancifully named *North-West Fox* ... (London, 1635), is now rare, excessively so with Fox's circumpolar map, described by C. H. Coote (*DNB*) as "one of the most interesting and important documents in the history of Arctic exploration." The British Museum has a copy of an MS version of Fox's narrative. The book begins with a review of arctic explorations, perhaps the first ever attempted, including the only contemporary account of Button's great voyage to Hudson Bay. The journal of Fox's own voyage illustrates the span of his curiosity, embracing observations on tides, soundings, ice formations, aurora, and arctic flora and fauna. He describes a native burial ground on an island he named Sir Thomas Roe's Welcome (now applied to the encompassing strait). In the same vicinity he honoured other patrons in naming islands Brooke Cobham (now Marble Island) and Brigges His Mathematickes (now disused). His geographical designations are numerous; Christy (p. cix) lists 27 of them, 8 surviving in usage. *North-West Fox*, which Markham aptly calls "the quaintest and most amusing narrative in the whole range of Polar literature," Fox himself recognized as being "rough hewn." Self-made, he was somewhat vain and pedantic, but a diligent researcher and an able navigator, being one of the first to use logarithms (learned from Briggs) in his navigation and to write of the use of log and line in measuring a ship's run.

Though he was frugal and temperate, the years after his voyage were spent in poverty, "having received neither sallery, wages, or reward." Perhaps if he had lived on after the publication of his book he might eventually have benefited; but he died in unmerited neglect a few months after it appeared.

WILLIAM F. E. MORLEY

North-West Fox ... has been reproduced in *Voyages of Foxe and James* (Christy). Dodge, *Northwest by sea*, 156–64. *DNB*. C. R. Markham, *The lands of silence* (Cambridge, Eng., 1921), 151–56. *Narratives of voyages towards the North West in search of a passage to Cathay and India 1496 to 1631*, ..., ed. Thomas Rundall (Hakluyt Soc., 1st ser., V, 1849), 152–86. Oleson, *Early voyages*, 169–70.

FRANÇOIS, CLAUDE, *dit* **Frère Luc,** Recollet friar, painter and architect, son of Mathieu François, "maître-saîteur" or cloth manufacturer, and of Perrette Prieur; b. at the beginning of May 1614 in the city of Amiens in Picardy; d. 1685 in Paris.

It was not by chance that, when they returned to New France in 1670, the Recollets included in their number an artist who was also an architect and a painter. In this order of Friars Minor as well as in the other orders, it was traditional that each monastery should be self-sufficient in artistic as well as material matters. This tradition was maintained among the Recollets of New France until the disappearance of the order in the year 1813. Let us mention in passing Father Augustin Quintal*, a painter and architect, Father Juconde Drué*, an able builder, Brother Anselme (or Ignace) Bardou*, a resourceful overseer, Father François [Brekenmacher*], a painter of portraits and religious pictures. The best-known of these Recollet artists is undoubtedly Brother Luc.

Little is known of the early years of Claude

François, except the account of an accident which probably was a determining influence in his life. One day—25 April 1630 according to one chronicle—"this young man who, in accordance with his disposition and the humour of his age, delighted in riding, was proudly taking a horse to water near the Moucreux bridge [at Amiens, on the Somme], where, through a mistake on the rider's part, the animal got out of its depth and was carried away with its rider; thus, seeing himself in such obvious and manifest danger and having already gone under the surface several times without leaving his mount, he remembered to call upon *Notre-Dame-de-Foy*, begging her to save his life . . .; then, letting the horse go, without his knowing at what moment or by what means, he slipped underneath the grating and between the posts and the barrier which block the aforesaid bridge, through which one cannot imagine how a man could pass, much less a horse; then coming to the surface of the water on the other side of the bridge and being out of danger, with the horse swimming after him, he realized that he was outside the city in the direction of the suburb. . . ." "For such a signal favour," adds the chronicler, Claude hastened with his mother to give thanks to Notre-Dame-de-Foy in the church of the Augustinians. Later, when he had become a member of the Recollet order, he was to recall this accident in one of his most charming pictures (in the church of Neuville-lès-Loeuilly, near Amiens).

At the time of the accident at the Moucreux bridge, Claude François had for some years been studying drawing and painting. He probably took some lessons from one of the itinerant artists who, in the reign of Louis XIII, used to stay for longer or shorter periods in the different cities of the kingdom. Not satisfied with this, he tried his luck in Paris. In 1632 he joined the studio of Simon Vouet, who had returned from Rome five years before. There he acquired, as did Le Brun, professional skill, some magical tricks of the trade, and a taste for Italian painting.

In 1635 Claude François was in Rome. He worked hard there for three or four years, made copies of the finest works that he could find, and compelled recognition from the critics for his character as much as for his activity and his talent. We know who his idols were: Raphael, Francesco da Ponte, Guido Reni, Guercino, Honthorst, Caravaggio. He was never to forget them.

Claude returned to Paris probably in 1639. There he saw again his master Vouet, who presented him to Sublet de Noyers, superintendent of the king's buildings. The superintendent's great project was the decoration of the Galerie du Bord de l'Eau in the palace of the Louvre, and that of his château at Dangu. To direct this great enterprise he brought Nicolas Poussin back from Italy; then he enrolled young painters, giving preference to those who had studied in Rome. Thus Claude François joined the team working in the Louvre; as a result of his two years of work (1640–42) he obtained the title of "king's painter."

Upon the death of his mother (1644) he joined the Recollets of Paris; he made his profession there on 8 October of the following year and took the name of Brother Luc (Luke), undoubtedly in remembrance of the patron of artists. If Brother Luc had taken leave of the world, he had not given up painting. On the contrary, he pursued a double career as a painter of church pictures and as a teacher.

He decorated with great Franciscan compositions most of the Recollet chapels of the province of Saint-Denis: Paris of course, Melun, Sézanne, Chalons-sur-Marne, Saint-Germain-en-Laye, Rouen, Versailles. He also painted some portraits and some small pictures of an edifying nature which he entrusted to the most skilful engravers of his time.

We know the names of some of his pupils: Louis de Nameur (1627–93), Roger de Piles, an art historian (1639–1705), Jacques Galliot (1640–?), Claude de Saint-Paul (1666–1716), Desmarets. These unfamiliar names of painters and engravers do not constitute any great glory for Brother Luc. Probably he had little free time for giving lessons to daubers of mediocre talent—except for Roger de Piles, whose writings do not lack precision.

In the spring of 1670 Brother Luc left Paris for New France. He was one of a group of six Recollets who, under the direction of Father Germain ALLART, the future bishop of Vence, were going to raise from its ruins their monastery at Quebec. At the end of May they sailed from La Rochelle on the ship which bore the Intendant TALON. They landed at Quebec on 18 August.

The task which they were undertaking was greater than they had thought, for they found their monastery, which had been abandoned in 1629 after the capture of Quebec by the KIRKES, in such a dilapidated state that they had to rebuild it completely. They set to work resolutely, with the certitude of being able to count upon public generosity as well as upon the king's gifts. On 22 June 1671 Jean Talon laid the foundation-stone of the chapel; in October Bishop Laval* celebrated mass in the church which already had its roof.

This chapel, the oldest in Canada, still stands; it is the chapel of the Hôpital-Général. Brother

François

Luc made the plans for it and sketched out the retable as it is today; he even painted the "Assumption" which adorns this Recollet retable, the first one belonging to the Canadian School. Brother Luc showed his skill in the general composition and in the fitting-together of the component parts.

Moreover, it is not the only work of architecture which he has left. The wing of the procurator's office, in the seminary of Quebec, was erected in 1677–78 following his design. The retables of the chapels of the Recollets in Paris, Sézanne, and Châlons-sur-Marne are also among his most beautiful architectural works.

Of the retable in the Recollet chapel of Quebec it can be said that it enjoyed considerable popularity in New France. There are still a few others (in the Ursuline convent and in the Hôtel-Dieu in Quebec, at Verchères, at Sault-au-Récollet, at Ange-Gardien, etc.) which are masterpieces of composition and of wood-carving.

The Recollet artist produced a great deal during his 15-month stay at Quebec. After his departure in October 1671 he continued to paint pictures for the churches of New France, and even portraits; and a long time after his death, in 1817 to be precise, certain of his works, which had been removed from churches in Paris at the beginning of the Revolution, belonged to Abbé Philippe-Jean-Louis Desjardins* and were sold at Quebec as part of his collection of pictures.

Let us mention first of all the works which he did during his stay in New France. I have already referred to the "Assumption" in the Recollet chapel. Other pictures by Brother Luc were to be seen there: for example, an expressive head of Saint Francis of Assisi, which is today in Montreal. The other pictures were taken in 1693 to the Recollet chapel in the Upper Town; they were destroyed in the fire on 6 Sept. 1796. The "Holy Family" which he painted in 1671 for the cathedral of Quebec was destroyed in 1759, along with a "Descent from the Cross."

Fortunately however all was not destroyed. The "Guardian Angel" in the church of the same name (Ange Gardien) is one of the artist's most harmonious compositions; the serenity of the expressions in this picture and its delightful colouring make of it a masterpiece. The two expressive heads in the church of Saint-Joachim—"Jesus as a Young Man" and the "Virgin of Sorrow"—are works of edification, as are other works of the same sort that we are acquainted with through prints. But the "Holy Family" in the church of the same name (Sainte-Famille, Île d'Orléans) recalls the nostalgic pictures which the "Poverello" suggested to the Recollet painter. I could say the same of the "Holy Family à la Huronne" (Ursuline convent in Quebec), of a "Nun Hospitaller nursing Christ in the figure of a Patient" and two "Ecce Homo" (Hôtel-Dieu in Quebec), and of "France bringing the Faith to the Indians of Canada" (Ursuline convent in Quebec). These works do not necessarily possess great originality, but they are touching, naïvely expressive, bursting with tenderness. Other pictures preserved in the Ursuline convent, particularly "Tobias and the Angel," do not display the same skilful touch.

I do however discover the nostalgic expression of the subjects again in the two compositions that Brother Luc painted in 1677 for the church of Sainte-Anne de Beaupré—"Saint Joachim and the Virgin" and the "Madonna and Child." In these pictures all is restrained affection and grief: Saint Joachim and the Virgin, one might say, have a presentiment of the future and seem to see in the distance the cross of Golgotha. The artist often stressed this sentimental note. In the museum in Amiens, for example, an ex-voto represents the Madonna holding her child, to whom an angel descending from heaven is offering a cross. The picture bears the phrase: "Croix aimable à Jésus quoiqu'ignominieuse"—the Alexandrine line formed by the French title plays upon the name of the donor, François Quignon.

In the church of Saint-Philippe at Trois-Rivières is to be seen an immense ex-voto with rather gorgeous colours. It represents the Immaculate Conception. On the left a cherub holds a lance and shield, upon which can be read: IPSA CONTERET CAPUT NUNC; on the right are the kneeling donors. The face of the donor's wife recalls strangely that of Mother Catherine de Saint-Augustin [see SIMON]. The Recollet painter had already chosen this emaciated face to use in the "Nun Hospitaller nursing Christ in the figure of a Patient." In still another picture, "The Last Communion of Saint Catherine of Siena," we find again the features and the expression of the portrait of Mother Catherine de Saint-Augustin, which Father Hugues POMMIER painted in 1668. We are obliged to believe that Brother Luc had fallen under the spell of the sorrowful expression of the nun on her deathbed. This "Last Communion of Saint Catherine of Siena" is one of the two paintings which came to us from Paris with the Desjardins collection in 1817. The other is "Christ dictating to Saint Francis the Statutes of his Order"; it dates from 1679 and was painted for the Recollet chapel in Paris; a replica exists in the former chapel of the Recollets in Sézanne.

In the Recollet's works are included some painted portraits. Two of them are at Quebec:

"Jean Talon," in the Hôtel-Dieu, and "Bishop Laval" in the seminary. They date from the years 1671–72. Bishop Laval has a serious, slightly frowning expression. Talon on the other hand is smiling; in any event he does not have the stiff and somewhat pretentious expression which characterizes the copies that have been made of this lifelike portrait.

Our artist returned to France in the autumn of 1671 and the following year he received his teaching certificate for the monastery at Sézanne in Champagne. There he painted some ten pictures for the chapel and one portrait, that of the lawyer Charles Poullet. Returning to Paris in 1675, he continued to occupy himself with painting. But he conceived the idea of interesting himself in the Canadian missions. He constituted himself their advocate and agent in Paris, writes the editor of the *Mortuologe*. He had interviews with Colbert; he transmitted to the bishop of Quebec the minister's intentions concerning the role of the Recollets in New France; finally, he undertook to find recruits for the needs of the Church in Canada.

In 1684 the monk left his studio, never to see it again. Nor do the documents mention him again, except to announce his death: he died peacefully on 17 May 1685.

GÉRARD MORISSET

ASQ, MSS, 200, Mortuologe des Recolets. BN, Estampes, Da. 40. Boitel, *Annuaire du département de la Marne pour 1850–1851* (Châlons-sur-Marne, 1851). Charles-Philippe Chennevières-Pointel, *Recherches sur la vie et les ouvrages de quelques peintres provinciaux de l'ancienne France* (4v., Paris, 1847–62), III, 305–6. Florent Lecomte, *Cabinet des singularitez d'architecture, peinture, sculpture et gravure* (2ᵉ éd., 3v., Bruxelles, 1702). Hugolin Lemay, "Un peintre de renom à Québec en 1670: le diacre Luc François, récollet," *RSCT*, 3d ser., XXVI (1932), sect.I, 65–82. Gérard Morisset, *La vie et l'œuvre du Frère Luc* (Québec, 1944). Roger de Piles, *Abrégé de la vie des peintres, avec des réflexions sur leurs ouvrages* (Paris, 1715).

FRÉMIN, JACQUES, priest, Jesuit, missionary; b. 12 March 1628 at Reims; d. 20 July 1691 at Quebec.

Father Frémin became a Jesuit in Paris on 21 Nov. 1646, and taught for five years at Alençon before being ordained in 1655 at Moulins. He came to Canada the same year, and in 1656 took part in the expedition to the Onondagas which resulted from SIMON LE MOYNE's embassy. Until 1667, except for wintering near Rechibouctou (Richibucto, N.B.) in 1658–59 and a trip to France in 1659–60, he remained among the Montagnais near Trois-Rivières. Then, in the capacity of superior, he left for the Iroquois mission, in the reopening of which Jean PIERRON and Charles BOQUET took part in 1667. He exercised his ministry there until 1679, working especially among the Onondagas, the Cayugas, and the Mohawks. After 1671 he directed his mission from the Caughnawaga centre near Montreal, and endeavoured to familiarize the Indians with French customs. He also took an active part in the quarrels over the trade in spirits. In 1679–81 he was back in France to see to the interests of his mission; but on his return he was forced because of his numerous infirmities to retire to Quebec. There he acted as a confessor to the nuns of the Hôtel-Dieu until his death.

Father Frémin's intelligence was not great, and his manners lacked refinement, but his courage and good sense were particularly outstanding. It is estimated that during his apostolate he baptized some 10,000 natives.

J. MONET

ACSM, ff.375, 40004, 40006. Campbell, *Pioneer priests*, I, 172–89. E. J. Devine, *Historic Caughnawaga . . .* (Montreal, 1922), 20–66. Rochemonteix, *Les Jésuites et la Nouvelle-France au XVIIᵉ siècle*, II, 406; III, 365.

FRENCH, JOHN, M.A., first clergyman to serve with the HBC in the Bay; d. 1687.

He was sent to Albany in 1683 equipped with Bibles, prayer books, and homilies. Items like parsnips, rice, and French barley were provided for his personal use. The voyage outward with Governor SERGEANT's party was made eventful by the capture of an interloping ship—one trespassing on the company's monopoly—the *Expectation*, commanded by Richard LUCAS, a renegade HBC employee.

"Extravagant demands" and poor trade returns accounted largely for Governor Sergeant's recall in 1686. Instructions to bring his family "and Mr. French, the Minister, too" had not arrived when Albany was captured by Pierre de TROYES. Articles of surrender were drawn up with much ceremony, clergyman John French acting as intermediary. He was despatched with a group of prisoners on the yacht *Colleton* to Port Nelson. While account books show him as being still alive on 7 Feb. 1686/87 he presumably died before returning to England. In January 1687/88 the balance of his salary was "accounted with Lawrence French, his executor," an HBC stockholder.

MAUD M. HUTCHESON

HBRS, IX, (Rich); XI (Rich and Johnson).

FRENEUSE, MATHIEU DAMOURS DE. *See* DAMOURS

Frobisher

FROBISHER, SIR MARTIN, mariner, privateer, explorer, the first Englishman after the CABOTS to seek a northwest passage; b. 1539?; d. 1594.

He was one of five children of Bernard Frobisher and his wife, the daughter of a knightly family named York. When Martin was of an age to be schooled, his widowed mother put him in the care of her brother, Sir John York, then master of the Mint and resident in London. The extant personal papers of Frobisher suggest that he leaned little towards scholarly pursuits, as lad or man; but as Lok says in his account of the first voyage, his uncle perceived him "to be of great spirit and bould courage, and naturall hardnes of body." In 1553, Sir John sent Martin to Guinea with the Wyndham expedition, in which Sir John had invested; Martin was among the quarter of the expedition who survived. In 1554, he joined another trading expedition to Guinea; on this venture he was detained some months by an African chief as a hostage.

From the close of his second Guinea voyage until 1573, Frobisher's rise in prestige and worldly influence followed the pattern of Elizabethan England's myriad daredevil, swashbuckling, fortune-seeking marine careerists. In 1571 and for a year or two after, he was employed by the queen herself in her campaign to subjugate Ireland. Meanwhile, he had engaged in legitimate merchant trade and also privateering, sometimes with a licence, sometimes not. Although never brought to trial, he was at least three times taken into custody on charges of piracy, the charges probably dismissed when balanced against the booty his forays added to the queen's treasury. The spirit and boldness his uncle observed in him did not diminish; to them the years added brilliant seamanship. In 1569, he caused the merchants of Rye to petition the Privy Council for special protection against his harrying of French vessels carrying Rye merchandise: "no six of their ships were fit to cope with Frobisher." In 1564, according to Admiralty Court records, "his name was as well known to Philip of Spain and as well hated as that of Hawkins himself."

No contemporary document dates the year in which Frobisher's seaman-venturer's imagination began to work on opening a route west across the northern seas between Elizabeth's England, feverish for gold, and Cathay, treasure house of the known world. At his uncle's house, even before being sent to sea, young Frobisher would have heard constant talk of the wealth of the Orient and of routes to it. Likely enough, coming from such a household, his ears and fancy were pricked by the tales of a captain on the Wyndham expedition, one Pinteado, who declared that such a passage not only existed but that Pinteado himself had earlier passed "this streicte." By 1561 Frobisher had laid before his friends a map by which he proved a northwest passage voyage "easie to bée performed" (G. BEST, "The fyrst booke of the first voyage of Martin Frobisher..."). For 15 years thereafter he offered his services for such a voyage to likely entrepreneurs of the time. Unable to promise them "sure, certayne, and present gaynes," he despaired of opening their purses and took his plan to the queen's court.

Ambrose Dudley, Earl of Warwick, brought Frobisher to the favourable attention of members of the Privy Council who, in December 1574, recommended to the Muscovy Company that it grant him a licence for a northwest exploration. When the Muscovy Company, itself under licence from the Privy Council to search out a northwest passage, refused to support Frobisher, the Council ordered the company either to attempt the exploration by an expedition of their own or to grant a licence to someone who would attempt it. Michael Lok, the director of the Muscovy Company, had meantime become enthusiastic about Frobisher's proposal; he persuaded the company to grant Frobisher a licence for north-west passage exploration without further opposition.

From 18 of many persons solicited, Lok and Frobisher were able to raise £875. Lok agreed to assume the remaining cost, more than £700. They built a ship of about 20 tons, the *Gabriell*, and bought the *Michaell*, a ship of about 25 tons, and a pinnace of about 10 tons. Dr John Dee, Elizabethan England's most famed astrologer, mathematician, and sometime magician passed the spring of 1576 on board Frobisher's ships, instructing the men in the new art of cosmological and mathematical navigation.

On 7 June 1576, the fleet, with Frobisher its admiral and pilot, sailed from Ratcliffe. Christopher Hall was captain of the *Gabriell*, Owen Griffyn of the *Michaell*; the crews numbered in all, 35. The queen herself waved them farewell as they passed Greenwich. On 26 June, having been delayed by wind, they reached the Shetland Islands, then sailed westward.

On 1 July, Frobisher sighted the east coast of Greenland; this he took to be Friesland, an island then charted on most maps of the North Atlantic Ocean, but now known not to exist. [*See* Appendix for a discussion of the ZENO brothers' map.] Ice and fog along the coast prevented a landing. While they were near Greenland, a great storm arose in which the pinnace and its crew of four were lost, the *Gabriell* nearly swamped, and the *Michaell* separated from the *Gabriell*. Capt.

Griffyn of the *Michaell* was so frightened by the ice encountered that he decided to turn back. When he arrived in London, he reported the rest of the expedition lost.

Undaunted by the loss of his sister ship and pinnace, Frobisher continued westward "knowing that the Sea at length must néedes have an endyng, and that some lande shoulde have a beginning that way." On 28 July he sighted a coast (probably Resolution Island) that he named Queen Elizabeth's Foreland. Directly north of it he discovered a "greate gutte, bay or passage," dividing, or so he thought, Asia on the north from America on the south. He sailed some 60 leagues into the passage which, following the precedent of Magellan, he named for himself—Frobisher's Strait. The "strait" is in fact the deep bay in Baffin Island that still bears Frobisher's name.

In late August, natives came to the ship to trade meat and furs for trinkets and clothing. One native agreed, by signs, to pilot the ship into the "West Sea." Frobisher sent the native, accompanied by seamen, back to shore to prepare himself for the journey. Contrary to Frobisher's orders, the five men who rowed the native ashore landed out of sight of the ship. Two of the five rowed into sight again, but then headed back to shore, and none of the five was ever seen again. Frobisher, hoping they would return, stood by for three days; he then proceeded along the coast with the plan of capturing other natives whom he might ransom for his own men. He found no other natives and when he returned to the place where his men had disappeared he found the natives who had been there gone. In despair, he decided he must return home. Just before leaving Frobisher's "strait," he captured a native who had come to the ship in his kayak to trade and took him to England.

The *Gabriell*'s arrival in London, on 9 October, was greeted with joy and admiration, not only because the ship had been supposed lost, but also, as Lok said, because of the "strange man and his bote, which was such a wonder onto the whole city and to the rest of the realm that heard of yt as seemed never to have happened the like great matter to any man's knowledge." Frobisher was "highly commended . . . for the great hope he brought of the passage to Cataya" (Best) but his prisoner, who had taken a cold at sea, soon died.

Frobisher gave to Michael Lok, according to a promise he had made, "the fyrst thing that he founde in the new land," a piece of mineral. Lok took the mineral to three assayers, each of whom identified it as marcasite. A fourth assayer, an Italian named Agnello, returned to Lok three tiny amounts of gold for the three pieces of marcasite he had tested. When Lok asked Agnello how he had succeeded where others failed, the Italian replied: "It is necessary to know how to flatter nature."

The rumour of gold made the supporters of the first voyage eager to join in financing a second. In March 1577 they formed the Cathay Company, under royal charter; Lok was appointed governor and Frobisher styled "high admiral." Queen Elizabeth subscribed £1,000 to the new company and lent a ship of 200 tons, the *Ayde*.

Frobisher's commission for his second voyage, according to Best, "directed hym . . . only for the searching of the Gold Ore, and to deferre the further discoverie of the passage untill another tyme." On 31 May 1577, Frobisher set out from Harwich with 3 ships and about 120 men. He, his lieutenant, George Best, with Charles Jackman as mate, sailed in the *Ayde*; Edward Fenton captained the *Gabrielle*, and Gilbert Yorke the *Michaell*. They were off Greenland on 4 July, but ice prevented a landing. On 17 July they reached the island from which the marcasite had been taken but, finding the ore body meagre, Frobisher moved to another island in his "strait" for mining. While the five miners and other members of the expedition loaded the *Ayde* with about 200 tons of ore, Frobisher searched for his lost men. No trace of them was found. Before they left the mine, on 23 August, Frobisher took prisoner a native man and a woman with a child, all of whom died about a month after they reached England.

During the winter of 1577-78, disagreements, both among the investors of the Cathay Company and among the refiners, arose over the smelting of the ore. The disagreements terminated when the refiners declared the ore poor and the Company decided upon a third, more ambitious voyage. On 31 May 1578, Frobisher, in the *Ayde*, led a fleet of 15 vessels from Harwich with the double object of establishing a settlement in Frobisher's "straits" and of bringing back to England 2,000 tons of ore.

On 20 June, Frobisher took possession of Greenland (he still thought it Friesland) in the name of Queen Elizabeth and renamed it West England. On 2 July the expedition sighted the new land—Meta Incognita, Queen Elizabeth had named it—but ice and unfavourable winds prevented their landing immediately. Driven south, they sailed some 60 leagues into a "mistaken straytes." Frobisher consulted with his subordinates, especially with James BEARE, a master in the fleet who had made a chart of the coast in 1577, and Christopher Hall, his chief pilot. At

Frobisher

first Frobisher insisted, against Hall's opinion, that it was "Frobisher's strait." He explained later that he had hoped, by maintaining the newly discovered strait was his own, to follow it to China. A quarter of a century elapsed before George WAYMOUTH, in 1602, and HENRY HUDSON, in 1610, demonstrated that the "mistaken straytes" led not into the South or West Sea, as Frobisher believed, but into the inland sea now called Hudson Bay.

Ice, currents, and contrary winds held the fleet from its destination during most of July. One ship sank, crushed by the ice, but its crew was saved; another ship, with its full complement of men, deserted to return to England. At the end of July the fleet gathered in the sound within Frobisher's "strait" which the admiral had named for the Countess of Warwick. Here Frobisher led a search for ore, and in the short season remaining the sailors mended the damaged ships; the miners and gold refiners dug out and tested the ore, assisted by the "Gentlemen [who] for example sake laboured hartily, and honestlye encouraged the inferiour sorte to worke" (Best). Because most of the building timber had been lost with the sunken ship, the establishment of a wintering colony, one of the objects of the expedition, was given up. Frobisher caused to be built near the mines a house of lime and stones so that the effect of an arctic winter on them might be observed in the future. (Charles Francis Hall* in 1861–62 found the site of Frobisher's mines; Hall divided between the Smithsonian Institution and the Royal Geographical Society the relics he found at the mines, but both sets of relics have since been lost.)

At the end of August, the 13 vessels left the Countess of Warwick's Sound with their cargo of ore. In England, attempts to refine gold from the ore continued at least until 1583; finally both refiners and investors admitted failure. Many of the documents relating to the organization and the financing of Frobisher's three arctic voyages have been preserved in the records of the litigations following on the failure of the Cathay Company. Had the voyages turned out more favourably to the investors, the company's earlier records would probably by now have been lost or destroyed.

Frobisher continued in naval service after the failure of the Cathay Company. In the autumn of 1578 he participated in a campaign to put down a rebellion in Ireland. In 1582 he planned—but never made—an expedition to Cathay by way of the Cape of Good Hope. In 1585 Sir FRANCIS DRAKE, with Frobisher as vice-admiral, led a privateering expedition of 25 vessels to the West Indies; the fleet returned to England in July 1586, having done great damage to the Spanish settlements and taken a booty of £60,000. In 1588 Frobisher held one of the chief commands in the naval defence of England against the Spanish Armada; for this service he was knighted. In the spring of 1589, Sir Martin assisted Drake in harassing Spanish shipping, an activity he continued, in positions of command, until 1594. In that year the Spanish king sent a force to Brest to assist a faction warring against the king of France. Elizabeth sent a force to support the French. In the course of storming a fort held by the Spanish at Crozon, Sir Martin was shot in the side. He died of his wound a few days later, on 22 Nov. 1594, at Plymouth.

Little is known of Frobisher's personal life. His first wife, Isabel, evidently died some time after his third arctic voyage; by 1591, he had married Dorothy, the widow of Sir William Widmerpole. He had no children, but named as heir his nephew Peter Frobisher.

Stefansson has given a useful assessment of Frobisher's character, in view of the derogatory comments of some of his contemporaries:

"Though he is frequently described as a hasty, choleric, or passionate man, this estimate appears to be based mainly on the abuse heaped upon him by his old friend Lok when schemes went wrong. That the brave admiral was not unloved by those under him appears from the narrative of the sailor Thomas Ellis, and the various poems written by him and others in praise of Frobisher, as well as from the references to his heroism, his feats of strength, his desire to treat the natives kindly, in the various accounts of his voyages by other participants."

ALAN COOKE

George Best, *A true discourse of the late voyages of discoverie, for the finding of a passage to Cathaya, by the northwest, under the conduct of Martin Frobisher generall . . .* (London, 1578); reprinted in Stefansson ed. (*infra*), I, in Hakluyt, *Principal navigations*, VII (1903–5), and in Collinson ed. (*infra*). Thomas Ellis, *A true report of the third and last voyage into Meta incognita: atchieved by the worthie capteine, M. Martine Frobisher, esquire, Anno. 1578* (London, 1578), reprinted in Stefansson ed., II, and in Collinson ed. Dionyse Settle, *A true reporte of the laste voyage into the west and northwest regions, &c. 1577. worthily atchieved by Capteine Frobisher of the sayde voyage the first finder and generall* (London, 1577); reprinted in Stefansson ed., II.

The three voyages of Martin Frobisher in search of a passage to Cathaia and India by the north-west, A.D. 1576–8, ed. R. Collinson (Hakluyt Soc., 1st ser., XXXVIII, 1867). *The three voyages of Martin Frobisher in search of a passage to Cathay and India by the north-west, A.D. 1576–8: from the original 1578 text of George Best,* ed. Vilhjalmur Stefansson (2v., London, 1938); all quotations in the text above are from this edition. *DNB.* William McFee, *The life of Sir Martin Frobisher* (New York and London, 1928). Oleson, *Early voyages,* 148–54. Sharat K. Roy, *The history and petrography of Frobisher's "Gold Ore,"* Field Museum of Nat. Hist. Pub., 384, Geol. ser., VII (1937), 21–38. E. G. R. Taylor, *Tudor geography, 1485–1583* (London, 1930).

FRONSAC, RICHARD DENYS DE. See Denys

FRONTENAC, ET DE PALLUAU, LOUIS DE BUADE DE. See Buade

G

GADOYS, PIERRE, first farmer at Montreal, churchwarden at Ville-Marie (Montreal); b. *c.* 1594 at Saint-Martin d'Igé (near Mortagne in Perche); d. in October 1667 at Montreal.

Pierre Gadoys may have been bought to the colony by Robert Giffard with his Beauport settlers, most of whom came from Perche. We find him at Quebec as early as 1636, at which time a son, of whose fate we know nothing, was born to him. From 1643 to 1645 he was apparently in the employ of the Société Notre-Dame de Montréal at Sainte-Foy. In October 1645, Hurons and Algonkins broke into Gadoys's house on several occasions to steal food from him and beat him.

He must have moved to Montreal about 1646 or 1647. He had the honour, in January 1648, of being the first person to whom the governor, Paul de Chomedey de Maisonneuve, made a grant of land; 40 acres in area, it extended from Saint-Paul street in a northwesterly direction to the west of Saint-Pierre and Bleury streets. Hence Dollier* de Casson gave him the title of first farmer of Ville-Marie. In 1666 he received another grant of 60 acres to extend the first one. In 1660 Pierre Gadoys became the fourth churchwarden of Notre-Dame church. In March 1661, when he was well on in his sixties, he fought bravely in defence of Charles Le Moyne and some colonists who had been attacked by the Iroquois. In 1672, when the street map was drawn, Saint-Pierre street, which bounded his property, was so named in his honour.

In France, about 1620, he had married Louise Mauger (1598–1690). Three of their children are known to us: Roberte (1621–1716) who in 1650 married the pioneer Louis Prud'homme: Pierre (1632–1714), born in France, died at Montreal; and Jean-Baptiste (1641–1728) born at Quebec, died at Montreal; both the sons were gunsmiths. Their descendants have survived to the present day. An older sister of Pierre Gadoys, Françoise, the wife of Nicolas Godé, had come to Montreal in May 1642.

Jean-Jacques Lefebvre

Dollier de Casson, *Histoire du Montréal. JR* (Thwaites), XXVII, 91. É.-Z. Massicotte, "Les colons de Montréal de 1642 à 1667," *BRH,* XXXIII (1922), 170–92; *RSCT* 3d ser., VII (1913), sect.i, 3–65; "Pierre Gadois, premier concessionnaire de terre à Montréal," *BRH,* XXIX (1923), 36–37. Tanguay, *Dictionnaire.*

GAGNON, (Gaingnon, Gangnon, and **Gaignon), MATHURIN,** farmer, business man, member of the Communauté des Habitants; b. 1606 at Saint-Aubin de Tourouvre (Perche), son of Pierre Gagnon (Gaignon) and Madeleine-Renée Roger; d. 1690 at Château-Richer.

The propaganda of Robert Giffard and of Noël Juchereau, who were recruiting settlers in Perche, probably had an influence on Mathurin Gagnon, and he decided to establish himself in Canada with his brothers Pierre and Jean. They arrived at Quebec before 1640. They went in for business, and worked in partnership. A number of notarial documents of the period bear as a signature "Sieurs Mathurin, Jehan, and Pierre Gangnon, brothers." Mathurin was the best educated of the three: he alone knew how to write. Consequently he acted as head of the firm. It was he who went to France in 1642, to settle their family and business affairs. Around 1651 the Gagnon brothers built a store on the square in the Lower Town, near the store belonging to the Communauté des Habitants.

However, the Gagnons loved the land. In 1640 they had taken up tracts of land on the Beaupré shore, at Château-Richer. Between 1635 and 1660 several natives of Perche settled in this area, where they introduced the ritual of the devotion to Sainte-Anne, which was observed at that time at the famous "Carrefour de Sainte-Anne" in Perche. Mathurin applied himself to clearing his land. He was a member of the Communauté des Habitants; he worked on his farm in the summer and concerned himself with business at Quebec in the winter. He did not settle finally at Château-Richer until 1650, in which year he received a grant of land six *arpents* wide and one and a half leagues in depth.

Gaillard

Mathurin was married on 30 Sept. 1647. His wife, Françoise Goudeau, was only 13; she gave him 16 children. He was appointed churchwarden in 1662, and was an important figure in the parish. According to the various census-takings, he was one of the most energetic of the farmers; in 1681 he owned 20 horned beasts and 45 acres of land under cultivation. He died on 20 April 1690, aged 84 years. He was buried the next day in the parish cemetery. From Mathurin is descended one of the largest families in French Canada.

JEAN HAMELIN

Recensement de 1681. Philéas Gagnon, "Une vieille famille canadienne," *BRH*, XVII (1911), 268–86, 298–311, 324–31. Lucien Serre, "L'ancêtre Mathurin Gagnon," *BRH*, XXXIV (1928), 177–83.

GAILLARD, MATHIEU, commissary in ordinary to the navy and subdelegate for the intendant at Montreal; fl. 1683–94.

Gaillard arrived at Quebec 9 Oct. 1686, preceded, according to Governor Jacques-René Brisay* de Denonville, by a good reputation. He was commissioned to take charge of "His Majesty's affairs in the region of Montreal." Denonville, Bochart* Champigny, and BUADE de Frontenac unanimously praised his integrity, exactness, and loyalty. In 1687 he took part in Denonville's expedition which went to crush the Iroquois in their own territory. He was one of those who signed the act when Niagara was taken over on 31 July 1687.

On 7 June 1689 the king sent instructions to Frontenac about a plan for attacking New York; he enjoined him to take along the commissary Gaillard to draw up an inventory of the enemies' possessions. For reasons of health, Gaillard could not remain in the colony. On 10 July 1690 the king appointed him commissary in ordinary to the navy at the port and arsenal of Rochefort. Frontenac regretted losing this official since, according to him, it was difficult to find a man "who was as zealous in the King's service." Gaillard did not leave until the spring of 1691 and he was still at his post in Rochefort in February 1694.

MARCEL HAMELIN

AN, Col., B, 12, ff.20, 39, 40½; 15, f. 6½; C^IIA, 8, pp. 192, 220, 320 (copies in PAC); 10, pp. 147, 291, 371, 411 (copies in PAC); 11, pp. 205, 391 (copies in PAC). *Coll. de manuscrits relatifs à la Nouv.-France*. P.-G. Roy, "Mathieu Gaillard," *BRH*, XXI (1915); 87–89.

GAINGNON. See GAGNON

GALINÉE, RENÉ DE BRÉHANT DE. See BRÉHANT

GALLERAN, GUILLAUME, Recollet priest, visitor of the Canadian missions in 1622; b. Franconville; d. 1636 at Metz.

He made his profession with the Recollets of the province of Saint-Denis in 1599 and received the tonsure in Paris on 27 May 1600. Guardian of the monastery of La Charité-sur-Loire from 1613 to 1615, he became in 1618 the first superior of the monastery at Montereau. Then from 1619 to 1621 he was in charge of the community at Melun.

On his appointment as visitor to the missions in New France he sailed from Dieppe on 15 May 1622 with the title of provincial commissioner. During the crossing he baptized a young Indian whom the Recollet LE BAILLIF had taken to France the year before and who, having been seriously ill for several days, died at sea shortly afterwards. Father Galleran had orders to carry on the work of the seminary at Notre-Dame-des-Anges and to establish a noviciate at Quebec "with special power to receive into our holy habit not only Frenchmen but also the Indians of our seminary if in due course one could make them sufficiently Christian to warrant the hope of bringing them to a state of evangelical perfection." In September he gave the Recollet habit to Pierre LANGOISSIEUX, who had for three years been teaching the Indians at Trois-Rivières. Ever since his arrival at Quebec the provincial commissioner had been carrying out his inquiry into the condition of the missions. In the fall of 1622 he sent to Father Le Baillif, the general agent for Canadian affairs at the court, a memorandum entitled "Advice on the present state and needs of the Canadian mission."

After spending a year in Canada, Father Galleran was in 1623 again named superior of the monastery at Montereau, and in 1626 became superior at Clamecy. His strong sense of charity had often led him to assist victims of the plague; he was himself stricken and died at Metz on 17 June 1636.

G.-M. DUMAS

ASQ, MSS, 200, Mortuologe des Recolets. Le Clercq, *First establishment of the faith* (Shea), I, 175, 330, 343. Sagard, *Histoire du Canada* (Tross), I, *passim*. Jouve, *Les Franciscains et le Canada (1615–1629)*. Hugolin Lemay, "L'œuvre manuscrite ou imprimée des Récollets de la mission du Canada, (Province de Saint-Denis), 1615–1629," *RSCT*, 3d ser., XXX (1936), sect.I, 115–26.

GAMELAIN DE LA FONTAINE, MICHEL, surgeon, colonizer, business man; b. in 1640 at Blois (France) if one is to believe the census of 1667; son of Michel Gamelain, a wine merchant, and Françoise Bellanger; d. *c.* 1676.

The first mention made of him goes back to 1661, the year of his marriage to Marguerite Crevier, the sister of Jean CREVIER de Saint-François. Gamelain lived at Trois-Rivières and later at Cap-de-la-Madeleine, where he received a grant of land in 1662. He must have practised his profession there, since we find him involved in a court case with Louis PINARD, another surgeon practising in those parts, who feared competition from Gamelain. Thus, when Louis Pinard complained of the slenderness of his earnings as surgeon to the garrison at Trois-Rivières, the Conseil Souverain replied to him that, if he was not satisfied, he would be replaced by Michel Gamelain. The latter preferred to devote himself to the fur trade. In order to do so, he made use of his pharmaceutical knowledge, manufactured beer from wheat, and exchanged it for furs. His lodges, one on the Île Saint-Ignace, the other at the mouth of the Rivière Sainte-Anne, were frequently the setting for most disgraceful scenes in which Indians and squaws indulged too freely in beer, while Gamelain wheedled their furs out of them, all the more easily because he spoke the language of the natives of the region fluently. Although he was found guilty by the Conseil Souverain on 20 June 1667 of being a "trafficker in liquor," he nevertheless carried on this trade until the end of his days. Even after having sold his seigneury to two officers of the Carignan-Salières regiment, Thomas de LANOUGUÈRE and Edmond de Suève, in 1670, Michel Gamelain continued to trade in furs, sending his former copy-holders who liked life in the woods to carry on the trade in the hinterland, and buying their surplus produce from those who preferred to devote themselves to farming, which was a terrible encroachment on the rights of the new seigneurs. From 1670 to 1674 he occasionally provided surgical services for the Hôtel-Dieu de Montréal.

The Gamelain household seems to have included four children, one of whom, Françoise, married Claude Pinard, son of the surgeon. Gamelain died about 1676; his widow remarried, becoming the wife of François Renou *dit* La Chapelle.

CHARLES-MARIE BOISSONNAULT

Ahern, *Notes pour l'histoire de la médecine.* Boissonnault, *Histoire de la faculté de médecine de Laval.* Raymond Douville, "Chirurgiens, barbiers-chirurgiens et charlatans de la région trifluvienne sous le régime français," in *Cahiers des Dix*, XV (1950), 81–128 and in *Visages du vieux Trois-Rivières* (Trois-Rivières, 1955), 33–91; "L'Épopée des petits traiteurs," *Cahiers des Dix*, XIV (1949), 41–63; *Premiers seigneurs et colons de Sainte-Anne de la Pérade (1667–1681)* (Trois-Rivières, 1946).

GAND, FRANÇOIS DERRÉ DE. *See* DERRÉ

GANDEACTEUA (Gandeacteüa, Gandeaktena, Gandeaktewa, Gandiaktua, Ganneaktena), CATHERINE, an Erie belonging to the Cat nation, responsible for the founding of the Saint-François-Xavier mission at Prairie-de-la-Magdelaine (moved in 1717 to Caughnawaga); d. 1673 at the mission.

In the autumn of 1654 the Mohawks completely razed Gentaienton, a Cat village, and before the end of the year they had annihilated this people of Iroquois stock which had been established on the south shore of Lake Erie. Gandeacteua and her mother were carried off as slaves to the Oneida village of Ganouaroharé. The story is told that she soon won everyone's heart. Towards 1656 she was married to a Christian Huron, François-Xavier TONSAHOTEN, who had been adopted by the Iroquois.

In 1667 she met Father Jacques Bruyas*, a Jesuit who had come to carry on his work in her village. She taught him Iroquois and in return he taught her the truths of the faith. Gandeacteua helped him to convert a dying woman. Shortly afterwards her husband took her on a trip to Montreal. She suggested to him that they should continue as far as Quebec. There, at the end of the summer of 1668, Bishop Laval* baptized her, as well as a small group of Oneidas and Mohawks. When the neophytes were back in Montreal, Father Pierre Raffeix*, a Jesuit, received them and invited them to spend the winter with him at Prairie-de-la-Magdelaine. Thus the "newly-baptized people returned in autumn and landed at la prairie, where in the course of time they and many others have built a fine village.... At the beginning of the winter, they set out to go hunting."

In the spring of 1669 Catherine and the other Indian women sowed some corn. The crop was excellent. Three other Iroquois lodges were built that year. Catherine Gandeacteua's charity and zeal attracted more and more pagans. In 1671, to her great satisfaction, more than 20 Iroquois families belonged to the Saint-François-Xavier mission. The neophytes decided to stay there permanently. In this same year the Jesuit Philippe Pierson, a Belgian, introduced the new converts to the Confrérie de la Sainte-Famille. Catherine had a preponderant influence in it, and even today the Confrérie still exists among the Indians of the mission.

Gangnon

Before the end of 1673 the Great Mohawk [see TOGOUIROUI] brought some 40 of his people to Prairie-de-la-Magdelaine. By this time there were more than 200 Indians there, representing at least 22 nations. Catherine Gandeacteua had practically finished her work. This woman, whose charity, humility, tenacity, and tact were extraordinary, died after a short illness on 6 Nov. 1673. Everyone, French as well as Indians, had such esteem for her that when the cemetery was being moved in 1689, 16 years after her death, they quarrelled as to where her remains would be kept. It was finally decided that they would be kept at the mission. In the opinion of her contemporaries Gandeacteua, the foundress of Caughnawaga, was a true saint.

HENRI BÉCHARD

Charlevoix, *Histoire*. *JR* (Thwaites), LXIII, 154–82; LXI, 194–208. *JJ* (Laverdière et Casgrain). *The Positio on Katharine Tekakwitha. Positio super virtutibus servae Dei, Catharinae Tekakwitha* (Rome, 1940). E. J. Devine, *Historic Caughnawaga* . . . (Montréal, 1922). Hunt, *Wars of the Iroquois*, 101–2. Félix Martin, *Relation des années 1673–1674 pour faire suite aux anciennes relations avec deux cartes géographiques* (Paris, 1861). Rochemonteix, *Les Jésuites et la Nouvelle-France au XVIIe siècle*.

GANGNON. See GAGNON

GANNEAKTENA. See GANDEACTEUA

GARAKONTIÉ (Garakonké, Harakontie), baptized as **DANIEL**, almost certainly the "sagochiendagehte" referred to in the Jesuit Relation, 1654, Onondaga chief and a leading negotiator with the French from that date until his death in the winter of 1677–78.

Although he was apparently not a hereditary chief, Garakontié was highly respected and influential among the Five Nations Iroquois. He was a skilful orator and deeply imbued with Iroquois traditions. He consistently sought to serve the best interests of the Five Nations through a pro-French policy, often in the face of opposition among his own people.

The first references to Garakontié reveal him struggling to preserve the general peace of 1653, and Father Jean de Lamberville* later credits him with giving the Jesuit settlement at Onondaga, founded in 1656, warning of the attack which the Mohawks and his tribesmen were planning in March 1658. He played a leading role in bringing about a new truce between the western Iroquois and the French in 1661. In the summer of that year Father SIMON LE MOYNE visited Onondaga where he was very enthusiastically received. He stayed there while Garakontié led an embassy to Montreal to negotiate with the French. Nine French prisoners were taken along to be released. While en route Garakontié's party learned of OTREOUTI's raid against Montreal. Garakontié persuaded those with him to go on, pointing out that Father Le Moyne's presence at Onondaga was enough assurance for their safety. He also bought off an Oneida war party which was planning to stir up trouble with the French. In December 1665 he led another Onondaga, Cayuga, and Seneca mission to Quebec to confirm a new peace, bringing back CHARLES LE MOYNE, who had been a prisoner of the Iroquois. He asked for time to persuade the Mohawks and Oneidas to join in this peace before the French expeditions led by PROUVILLE de Tracy and RÉMY de Courcelle were sent against these tribes in 1666.

Following the general French-Iroquois peace of 1667, Garakontié did much to promote the work of the Jesuit missions. In 1668 he persuaded Father Julien Garnier* to stay at Onondaga, and brought Father Étienne de Carheil* and Father Pierre Millet* from Quebec. Nevertheless Garakontié remained undecided about being baptized. Perhaps over the years an interest in Christianity that at first was mainly political developed into genuine belief. In any case, in 1669 he finally expressed a desire to be baptized. The next year while at Quebec, helping to settle a dispute which threatened to result in the outbreak of war between the Iroquois and the Algonkins, he expressed his enthusiasm for Christianity in such strong terms that he overcame any fears the Jesuits may have had concerning the premature baptism of a man of his importance. Garakontié was baptized in the cathedral of Quebec by Bishop Laval*. Daniel de Rémy de Courcelle, the governor, whose name Garakontié was given, was his godfather, and Mlle de Boutroue (daughter of the intendant BOUTROUE d'Aubigny), his godmother. To emphasize how important the French regarded Garakontié's conversion the governor provided a feast for the assembled tribes. Garakontié led an exemplary Christian life and continued to do much to aid the Jesuits in their work among the Iroquois. The Jesuits, in turn, began to teach him to read and write. While visiting New Netherland he sharply rebuked the Protestants there who ridiculed his faith.

This zeal led some of his tribesmen to try to undermine his authority by questioning his sanity and his loyalty to the Onondagas. Nevertheless, he continued to enjoy wide respect and influence in village affairs and in dealings with the Europeans. When the Indian allies assembled to greet

Buade de Frontenac at Cataracoui in the summer of 1673, Garakontié was the first to speak for them. He died of an illness in the winter of 1677–78, at an advanced age and was buried in European fashion, as he had wished, by Father de Lamberville.

According to the Jesuits, Garakontié was distinguished by his integrity and patience, and by skill in oratory and politics. The policy which he followed unswervingly in his public life was a rare blend of honest dealing and shrewd bargaining, through which he sought to protect the interests of the Five Nations in a time of ever increasing problems in their dealings with the Europeans. He is credited with saving more than 26 Frenchmen from death by torture. He ransomed these men at various times and kept them until he could persuade his people to release them, often in exchange for Iroquois held by the French. At no time, however, did he become merely a tool of French policy. He seems to have been convinced that the best course for his people was to ally themselves with the French and to learn from them. Like any Iroquois leader, he did not enjoy the unswerving support of his people. In particular, his influence with the French sometimes aroused the jealousy of other chiefs, who sought to hinder him. Nevertheless he was able to play a leading role whenever they became convinced that good relations with the French were desirable.

BRUCE G. TRIGGER

Charlevoix, *History* (Shea), *passim*. *JR* (Thwaites), *passim*. *NYCD* (O'Callaghan and Fernow), *passim*. The reader should note that O'Callaghan does not distinguish between this Garakontié and his brother, who resuscitated the latter's memory and who is sometimes designated as Garakontié II. Lanctot, *Histoire du Canada*, I, 312, 313, 320; II, 27, 66, 67.

Gargot de La Rochette

GARGOT DE LA ROCHETTE, NICOLAS, nicknamed Peg-leg (*Jambe de Bois*), lieutenant, naval captain, and Chevalier de Saint-Michel, governor of Plaisance; b. 20 Feb. 1619 at La Rochelle (France), son of Hilaire Gargot and Anne Lardeau; d. and buried 16 Dec. 1664 in that same city.

Gargot was a grandson of the La Rochelle sailor, Jacques Lardeau, who had saved young Henri IV's life. His father, an eminently respectable man, was a Huguenot merchant but did not belong to the upper middle class. Nicolas was converted to catholicism. His elder brother, Jean, traded along the coasts of Africa and became a salaried captain in the navy.

Nicolas became a soldier at the age of 13; he took part in a battle against the Spaniards in the Mediterranean in 1636, and in the attack of the Îles Sainte-Marguerite in 1637. In 1638 we find him in Acadia, serving as a commissary and storekeeper. He also fulfilled the functions of lieutenant to CHARLES DE SAINT-ÉTIENNE de La Tour, and contributed to improving the fort on the Saint John River. On his return from Acadia in 1639, Gargot was captured by the Spaniards. When he regained his liberty he was assigned to guard the coasts of Brittany. He joined forces with La Tour against MENOU d'Aulnay and went to Boston and to France in order to solicit assistance against their mutual enemy, whose fort, situated at Port-Royal, was actually attacked in 1643. Having been made an artillery commissioner in 1645, Gargot served at the siege of La Mothe in Lorraine, where he lost a leg. In 1648 he was promoted to ship's captain, and had a part in the victory at Castellammare.

In the summer of 1650 he set his course for Newfoundland, where he had differences with some Spanish fishermen. The following year he was taken prisoner by his mutinous crew and turned over to the Spanish authorities. On being set free, he went back to France and applied himself to the service of his country. In 1658 he was admitted to the Ordre de Saint-Michel.

At about that same time the king granted him the port of Plaisance (Placentia) as a hereditary fief, including with it a grant of land 26 leagues in depth on the south shore of Newfoundland. In 1660, a royal commission did indeed name Gargot Comte de Plaisance and governor of the island. The minister of finance, Nicolas Fouquet, who had private interests in this region, was not without a hand in this appointment. When the English trespassed on his fief, Gargot set out at the head of a naval expedition and seized the settlements at Grand-Plaisance, Petit-Plaisance, and Petit-Paradis. The following year the king acceded to a request made by the inhabitants of the region and duchy of Brittany, and forbad Gargot to molest them when they were fishing off Newfoundland. Gargot set sail for that island in the *Aigle d'or* and the *Flûte royale* in July 1662. On the voyage, which lasted four months, scurvy claimed several victims. The following year, Gargot undertook the same trip in the *Aigle d'or* and the *Jardin-de-Hollande*. Only the latter ship, commanded by Cap. Jean Guillon, landed at Newfoundland; the *Aigle d'or* continued on to Quebec carrying the first bishop of Canada, Bishop Laval*, Governor SAFFRAY de Mézy, the commissioner GAUDAIS-DUPONT, and a certain number of troops. At Plaisance, Guillon learned that the previous winter the soldiers of the garrison had assassinated Governor DU PERRON, his brother,

Garland

and the chaplain of the fort, and had then begun killing one other. He managed to capture some of the culprits and brought them back to Quebec where Gargot tried them and had one of them hanged on a raft off shore.

After returning to France, Gargot made a trip to Sweden in his country's service and returned seriously ill. He died three months later, leaving his wife but no children. Thus ended a life dogged by trials and misfortunes; among others he had suffered from the ruinous partnership to which Maréchal Louis Foucault de Saint-Germain-Beaupré, Comte de Dognon, had subjected him in 1649. The latter, a vice-admiral and subsequently governor of Brouage and La Rochelle, was not satisfied, in return for his modest share in the expenses, with a third of the prizes, and had extorted 242,000 *livres* from Nicolas Gargot. Had it not been for a pension of 2,000 *livres* he obtained from Anne of Austria, Gargot would have starved to death. His career, as brilliant as it was active, was characterized by courage, zeal, and loyalty to his country.

J.-ROGER COMEAU

ACM, B.218. AE, Mém. et doc., Amérique, 5, ff.40–41v. AN, E¹, 347ᴀ, f.334. BN, MS, Baluze 149, ff.5, 10, 11–12v, 93; MS Fr. 22643, f.82, MS, Mélanges Colbert, 109 bis, f.847; NAF 9281 (Margry), f.153–153v, 9282 (Margry), f.224; *Acadiensia Nova* (Morse), I, xxii, 40; II, 49–54, 67–68, 74, 98–101. [Pierre Groyer], *Mémoires de la vie et des aventures de Nicolas Gargot, capitaine de marine* [Paris, 1668]; *Les aventures du rochelais Nicolas Gargot dit "Jambe-de-Bois,"* éd. Charles Millon (La Rochelle, 1928). *Jug. et délib.*, I, 6.

William Hubbard, *A general history of New England from the discovery to MDCLXXX* (Mass. Hist. Soc. Coll., 2d ser., V, VI (1815); reprinted 1848), II, 478–79. A. Jal, *Dictionnaire critique de biographie et d'histoire* (2e éd., Paris, 1872), 474. La Morandière, *Hist. de la pêche française de la morue*, I, 18, 220, 409–16. L. Maschinet de Richemond, *Les marins rochelais* (2e éd., Niort et La Rochelle, 1906), 29–41. P.-G. Roy, "Une exécution capitale dans le porte de Québec en 1663," *BRH*, XXIX (1923), 137–40; "Les familles de nos gouverneurs français," *BRH*, XXVI (1920), 261–62. Régis Roy, "Nicolas Gargot," *BRH*, XXIX (1923), 178.

GARLAND, THOMAS, a seaman with the HBC; fl. *c.* 1678–87.

He sailed in the *Prince Rupert* (Capt. Richard POWER) to James Bay in 1678 and returned to England next year. In 1680 he was appointed chief trader at New Severn where Capt. Thomas DRAPER was commissioned to establish and command a factory, a plan not completed at that time.

During the winter of 1681–82, which Garland spent at Charlton Island under Governor John NIXON, friction developed. Garland allied himself with Capt. NEHEMIAH WALKER'S "discontented party" against Nixon, who sent home a lengthy and damaging account of the situation. In spite of this adverse report, when Garland returned to England he was made master of the yacht *Colleton* in 1683. He spent the three following seasons in James Bay and was among those taken prisoner when de TROYES captured the Company's three factories there in 1686. He managed to secure release and wintered either at New Severn or Port Nelson on Hudson Bay and evidently severed his connection with the Company after he had returned to England in 1687.

His wife Katherine is mentioned in HBC records, requesting on occasion that he be allowed to return home.

MAUD M. HUTCHESON

HBRS, VIII, IX (Rich); XI (Rich and Johnson).

GARNIER, CHARLES (called **Ouracha** by the Indians), priest, Jesuit, missionary, martyr; b. 1606 (or 1605) in Paris; d. 1649 in the Huron country.

He was baptized 25 (or 26) May in the parish of Saint-Gervais, and was the second son of Jean Garnier, an under-secretary in Henri III's private household and later *maître des comptes* in Normandy, and of Anne de Garault, who came from a noble family of Orléans. After attending the Collège de Clermont in Paris, which was under the direction of the Jesuits, he entered the noviciate of the Society of Jesus in 1624. He was ordained priest in 1635, was nominated for the missions in New France, and landed at Quebec 11 June 1636, at the same time as Governor HUAULT de Montmagny. In July, together with Father Pierre CHASTELLAIN, he reached the territory of the Hurons. In 1639 and 1640 he wintered in the land of the Tobacco nation, which he vainly tried to convert. From 1641 to 1646 Garnier was employed at the Saint-Joseph (Teanaostaiaë) mission, among the Cord clan. Finally, in the autumn of 1646, he was again sent to the Tobacco Nation, on the shores of Georgian Bay, and there he established a mission that this time flourished; he also met his death there, being slaughtered by the Iroquois on 7 Dec. 1649 when they attacked the village of Saint-Jean, at the time of the destruction of the Huron missions. His body, lacerated by two bullet wounds and two blows from a hatchet, was found a few steps from the ruins of his chapel. He was canonized by Pope Pius XI on 29 June 1930.

FLORIAN LARIVIÈRE

"De la prise et désolation de la mission de Saint-Jean, par les Iroquois, et de la mort du P. Charles Garnier, qui y était en mission," and "Abrégé de la vie du Père Charles Garnier," in ACSM "Mémoires touchant la mort et les vertus des pères Isaac Jogues . . ." (Ragueneau), repr. APQ *Rapport, 1924–25*, 76–85. APQ *Rapport, 1929–30*, 1–43, "Lettres de Saint Charles Garnier." *JR* (Thwaites), XXXV, 118–44; *et passim. Positio causae.* Florian Larivière, *La vie ardente de Saint Charles Garnier* (Montréal, 1957). Rochemonteix, *Les Jésuites et la Nouvelle-France au XVIIe siècle*, I, 97–100, 409–18.

GAROHIAÉ (Garonhiaqué). See OGENHERATARIHIENS

GARREAU, LÉONARD, priest, Jesuit, missionary; b. 11 Oct. 1609 (or in September 1610) at Aridieux (Saint-Yrieix) near Limoges; d. 2 Sept. 1656 at Montreal.

Léonard Garreau came from a noble family. He distinguished himself in his classical studies at Limoges and Bordeaux, before becoming a Jesuit at Bordeaux on 27 Sept. 1629. While training for the priesthood he taught at Poitiers, Pau, Agen, Bordeaux, and Rome, where he made repeated requests to the general of the Jesuits to be allowed to go to Canada.

He reached Quebec on 15 Aug 1643. After a year at Sillery he set out for the Huron country, where he exercised his ministry, especially among the Tobacco Nation, until 1649. From 1650 to 1654 he was responsible for the Huron mission on the Île d'Orléans, then he was sent to Trois-Rivières to serve as an interpreter and a missionary among the Algonkins. He was also a parish priest there for some time in 1656. That same year he set out with a large expedition of Ottawa braves to establish a mission in their territory. The group was attacked by the Mohawks near Montreal on 30 August, and Father Garreau was mortally wounded, perhaps by the FLEMISH BASTARD. The latter, when accused of the assassination, vehemently denied his guilt. It is not impossible that Garreau was killed by an Indian or a French deserter.

J. MONET

ACSM, ff.133, 229. *JR* (Thwaites), XXIII, 328. Perrot, *Mémoire* (Tailhan), 84ff. "Les ordonnances du Gouverneur de Lauzon," APQ *Rapport, 1924–25*, 391. Campbell, *Pioneer priests*, II, 377. Rochemonteix, *Les Jésuites et la Nouvelle-France au XVIIe siècle*, II, 151.

GAUDAIS-DUPONT, LOUIS, royal commissioner in New France (1663), whom several authors have confused with Nicolas Dupont*, Sieur de Neuville.

In 1661 and 1662 Louis XIV had made himself acquainted with several reports on New France; he had granted hearings to prominent people of the colony; he had even sent a royal investigator, the Sieur de MONTS, to America. A distinct change of policy was quite obviously necessary. At the beginning of 1663 the monarch accepted the resignation of the Compagnie des Cent-Associés. New France again became the property of the king.

Louis XIV resolved to supervise personally the progress of Canada, and decided to send a commissioner there to take possession of the country in his name and to set up the new administrative and judicial institutions that had been granted to the colony. On 7 May 1663 he appointed the Sieur Gaudais, to whom he assigned the responsibility of going "to examine Canada," and he gave him precise instructions: to describe the colony in detail, study its trade, analyze the financial and legal administration of the previous few years, take a census of the population, investigate the extent of land clearance, agriculture, and natural resources, suggest means whereby the revenues from the fur trade could be turned to the profit of the Crown and the seigneurial rights of the king established over Canada; in short, to transmit any piece of information which would help in the organization and development of New France. Gaudais' commission and instructions were accompanied by a secret document ordering him to make discreet enquiries into the conduct and views of the previous governor and the newly appointed one, of Bishop Laval*, and of the Jesuits. The king wanted to discover the reason for the quarrels that had taken place between PIERRE DUBOIS Davaugour and the clergy.

Gaudais had a heavy task to perform and little time at his disposal, since the king required him to return by the same ship that would take him to New France. He landed at Quebec on 15 September with Bishop Laval and Augustin de SAFFRAY de Mézy, and on 18 September attended the first session of the Conseil Souverain, of which the king had made him a member. A few days later, perhaps on the twenty-second, he set out for Trois-Rivières and Montreal, a journey which took him "16 or 17 days." Gaudais' activities in New France are recounted in a letter of Marie de l'Incarnation [*see* GUYART]: "He has settled all the affairs of the country. He has appointed officers to dispense justice according to the prescription of the law. He has also established an administration to take care of trade and maintain civil society. All the inhabitants of the country have without exception rendered faith

Gaultier de Comporté

and homage to him, declaring themselves dependent on the king because of his castle at Quebec."

As early as 20 September the conflict between the directors of the Communauté des Habitants and the talkative JEAN PERONNE Dumesnil, the intendant of the Compagnie des Cent-Associés, had been referred to Gaudais. The Conseil Souverain had instructed the royal commissioner to examine Dumesnil's claims. But Gaudais, for want of time, had to sail for France before being able to announce his conclusions. In a report to Colbert the following year Dumesnil did not spare Gaudais, whom he accused of partiality and of collusion with the Jesuits and the former directors of the Communauté des Habitants. Colbert, ever suspicious, appears at least momentarily to have held the Sieur Gaudais responsible for the affronts suffered by Dumesnil. In his turn Gaudais addressed a report to the minister, giving a different version of the facts and clearing himself of the accusations levelled by the intendant, whom he considered lacked judgement and moderation.

Gaudais had sailed for France on 26 Oct. 1663, four days after marrying his niece, Michèle-Thérèse Nau, to Joseph Giffard*, the son of the seigneur of Beauport. In the colony he had left his own son, Nicolas Gaudais, Sieur Du Chartran, who is mentioned as being at Quebec on 2 Dec. 1663 and who sailed for France on 30 Aug. 1664.

No trace has been found of the report that Gaudais made to the king on his "examination" of New France.

ANDRÉ VACHON

AN, Col., C11A, 125, 217. APQ, Ins. cons. souv., I, 2v. *Édits ord.*, III, 22–27. Marie Guyart de l'Incarnation, *Lettres* (Richaudeau), II, 266f., "Marie de l'Incarnation à son fils, 1663." *JJ* (Laverdière et Casgrain), 321, 328. *Jug. et délib.*, I, 1–2, 3–6, 33–34. "Mémoire du sieur Gaudais-Dupont à Mgr Colbert," éd. P.-G. Roy, *BRH*, XXI (1915), 227–31. Caron, "Inventaire des documents," APQ *Rapport, 1939–40*, 197–98. "Jean Peronne Dumesnil et ses mémoires," *BRH*, XXI (1915), 169–71. Régis Roy, "Nicolas Gaudais, sieur de Chartran," *BRH*, XL (1934), 320.

GAULTIER DE COMPORTÉ, PHILIPPE, soldier, seigneur, commissary of the king's warehouses, provost of the marshalsea, naval commissary; b. 1641 at Comporté, near Poitiers, son of Philippe Gaultier, Sieur du Rinault, and of Gillette de Vernon; d. 22 Nov. 1687 at Quebec.

Philippe Gaultier, of a noble family, enlisted in the Carignan-Salières regiment, and accompanied it to Canada. He reached Quebec on 18 June 1665, but on 10 May a court of law in Poitou had condemned him in his absence to capital punishment for the death of two persons (prominent in the district), who had died following a brawl in which he had taken part in order to avenge an insult to the regiment. It was not until 15 years later that the sentence imposed upon him became known in the colony. Because of his honourable life, and thanks to the intercession of the civil and religious authorities, the king granted him letters of remission in June 1680. After leaving the army, Gaultier de Comporté played an important part in the administration of the colony. On 20 July 1670 he was appointed by Intendant BOUTROUE as the receiver of the 10 per cent tax levied on merchandise arriving in the country. He subsequently became a commissary of the king's warehouses (1672–78), the first provost of the marshalsea (1677), and, at least on a temporary basis from 1685, a naval commissary. In all these posts he seems to have won general confidence. TALON twice made him his personal procurator, and the nuns of the Hôtel-Dieu de Québec chose him in 1675 to represent them on a commission set up by Bishop Laval* to appraise all their possessions. He was also elected a churchwarden of the parish of Quebec—a great honour in the 1670's—and as such he was involved in the quarrel over precedence, in which BUADE de Frontenac and the Conseil Souverain took sides against the vicars general and the seminary, in February-March 1675.

He was successful in business. Two seigneuries (Comporté and La Malbaie) were granted to him; he did not clear them, but sold them at a reasonably good price; later on (1683), he was one of the founding members of the Compagnie du Nord. He went to France as a delegate to obtain the protection of the court, and returned after successfully completing this mission.

On 22 Nov. 1672 he had married Marie Bazire, the sister of Charles BAZIRE, one of the most important merchants of Quebec. Gaultier de Comporté and Marie Bazire had 11 children; two of the daughters entered the monastery of the Ursulines; another, Angélique, married Denis Riverin*, a member of the Conseil Souverain, and lieutenant-general of the provost's court of Quebec; and another, Marie-Anne, had as her first husband Alexandre Peuvret* de Gaudarville, the clerk of the Conseil Souverain.

J. MONET

Jug. et délib. P.-G. Roy, *Inv. concessions*. Nute, *Caesars of the Wilderness*. P.-G. Roy, "La famille Gaultier de Comporté," *BRH*, XL (1934), 321–52.

GAULTIER DE VARENNES, RENÉ, officer in the Carignan-Salières regiment, seigneur, governor of Trois-Rivières; b. *c.* 1635 at Bécon (Anjou),

Gaultier de Varennes

son of Adam-Pierre Gaultier de La Vérenderie and Bertrande Gourdeau; d. 4 June 1689.

As a lieutenant he belonged to Arnoult de Broisle de Loubias' company, which was stationed at Trois-Rivières in the autumn of 1666. On 26 Sept. 1667 he married Marie, the 12-year-old daughter of Pierre Boucher*, governor of Trois-Rivières. The marriage contract, drawn up before the notary Séverin Ameau* on 22 September, stipulated that Boucher should board his daughter and her future husband for a period of six months, and that M. RÉMY de Courcelle, the governor of New France, should be respectfully requested to obtain for Varennes the office and the privileges of his father-in-law.

Pierre Boucher had in fact decided to leave Trois-Rivières to settle on his seigneury at Boucherville, which he did in 1667. René Gaultier probably took over the office of governor as soon as Boucher left, but he appears as such, in the extant records, only on 10 June 1668. His official appointment was to come in 1672.

In 1671 Gaultier de Varennes took part in de Courcelle's expedition to Lake Ontario, and acquitted himself well. In October of the following year TALON granted him the Varennes and Du Tremblay seigneuries, "in consideration of the good, useful and commendable services that he has rendered to His Majesty in various places, both in Old and New France. . . ." In addition, in 1673 Governor BUADE de Frontenac granted him as a noble fief the La Vérenderie seigneury, also known as La Gabelle.

In 1681 the governor wrote to Colbert that "the Sieur de Varennes and the Sieur de Boucher, his father-in-law, have each five canoes and ten fur-traders in the woods." This additional source of income did not prevent the governor of Trois-Rivières from living in poverty, so modest were his emoluments. As a governor he received initially 1,200 *livres* a year, then, from 1685, 3,000 *livres*. Against this he had to maintain at his own expense the officer and seven soldiers of the Trois-Rivières garrison. Moreover his three seigneuries yielded very little, since their total population 1681 was 101 settlers. Du Tremblay then numbered 30 persons, it had only 67 acres under cultivation, and its livestock consisted of only 3 horned beasts. At Varennes there were only 71 settlers, 218 acres under cultivation, and 57 horned beasts. As for the La Gabelle fief, it was uninhabited.

Gaultier sometimes went there to make contact with the Indians, and carried on with them a clandestine fur trade which, incidentally, brought upon him the remonstrances of the court. Intendant Demeulle* in particular complained sharply about it in a letter dated 28 Sept. 1685. "M. de Varennes, the governor of Trois-Rivières," he wrote, "uses his authority to trade privately with Indians in a place named La Gabelle, four leagues from Trois-Rivières; this is forbidden by His Majesty's ordinances, which permit it only at Trois-Rivières. I have not failed to express my feeling about it several times to the said Sieur de Varennes, who has not appeared to be very pleased as a result. . . ." So displeased was he that Demeulle, if we are to believe his word, was forced to suffer the thunderous ire of Gaultier's cousin, M. de Montortier, and of Governor Brisay* de Denonville. The latter is even supposed to have pointed out to the intendant that in France "intendants come after the governor," which provoked the retort "that governors here [such as the one at Trois-Rivières] should properly be considered as majors or mere commandants. . . ." Moreover, had not M. de Varennes married "the daughter of a man who was an indentured employee of the Jesuits for 36 months, and who served them in the capacity of a cook, [and] this same man had had as his first wife an Indian woman. . . ."

In March of the following year the king informed the governor of Trois-Rivières that he had been apprised of the trade which he was carrying on, and that he hoped this would not recur. Be that as it may, M. de Denonville was to recommend the renewal of Gaultier de Varennes' commission, stressing that "he is a very worthy gentleman whose only vice is poverty." The latter therefore found his commission renewed every three years until his death.

His young widow survived him by 44 years. She first spent some years in her father's house at Boucherville, then settled at Varennes, and in 1712 went to Montreal for good. She belonged to one of the most illustrious families in Canada, the Bouchers, to whose fame she made a substantial contribution, for the majority of her nine children played a prominent part in the life of New France.

ALBERT TESSIER

"Documents et renseignements inédits sur la Vérendrye et sa famille," ed. Antonio Champagne, *BRH*, LXII (1956), 60–75, 171–93. "Documents inédits, Les Gaultier de la Vérenderie en France et au Canada et leurs relations par delà l'Océan," éd. Antonio Champagne, *RHAF*, XII (1958–59), 262–77, 411–27; XIII (1959–60), 97–122. "Documents sur Pierre Gaultier de la Vérendrye," éd. Jean-Jacques Lefebvre, APQ *Rapport*, 1949–51, 33–67. *NYCD* (O'Callaghan and Fernow), IX. Ivanhoë Caron, "René Gaultier de Varennes, gouverneur des Trois-Rivières," *BRH*, XXIII (1917), 117–24. Aegidius Fauteux, "Les Gaultier de Varennes et de la Vérendrye," *BRH*,

XXIII (1917), 244–49. Benjamin Sulte, "Les Gaultier de Varennes," *RC*, X (1873), 781–89, 849–56, 935–50; "Les gouverneurs des Trois-Rivières," *BRH*, II (1896), 69, 72; "Officiers de Carignan," *BRH*, XVII (1911), 193–97; "La Vérenderie avant ses voyages au Nord-Ouest," *BRH*, XXI (1915), 111.

GENDRON, FRANÇOIS, surgeon, *donné* of the Jesuits, later priest, king's counsellor and almoner; b. 18 April 1618 at Voves (diocese of Chartres), son of Éloi Gendron, a farmer, and Gillette Doussineau; d. 1688 in France.

After studying surgery at Orléans for at least five years, François Gendron went to New France in 1643. He was the first doctor known to have lived in Ontario and among the North American Indians. It was in 1644–45, from Sainte-Marie-des-Hurons, that he wrote his letters, which were published in 1660 by Jean-Baptiste de Rocoles. In the Huron country, according to the testimony of Father RAGUENEAU, Gendron "helped the French and the Indians with great charity ... always lived in a very edifying manner ... without any pay, without any profit ... for the love of God." He spent seven years in the Huron territory as a Jesuit *donné* and left for France again 23 Aug. 1650, after the destruction of the Huron country; he travelled in company with Louis PINARD and Father Pierre PIJART, and took with him an ointment for fistulas, stubborn ulcers, and cancers. Its base was a powder that came from stones which he had discovered on the shores of Lake Erie and which he called "Erie Stones" ("*Pierres Ériennes*"). This ointment was to make his fortune in France and in 1664 was to bring him the honour of treating the queen, Anne of Austria, who was suffering from cancer of the breast.

Gendron was ordained 25 May 1652, became curate of his native parish, and a doctor of the poor. His popularity increased to such an extent that he soon had to devote himself exclusively to caring for the ill, among whom were to be found persons of distinction. His treatment of the queen created jealousies among members of the profession, in which he was much decried. His cassock especially made him suspect of charlatanism in the eyes of the envious. Nevertheless, despite his great humility and his timidity, he became famous at the court and in the whole country, in which he had travelled a great deal in order to pursue his studies and his experiments in the treatment of cancer.

When he left the court he returned to Voves, provided with tangible evidence of the royal family's gratitude, even though he had only been able to alleviate the queen's malady. Thus on 27 Aug. 1665 he was appointed by the king commendatory abbot of Maisières in Burgundy. He used the gains which royal favour brought him for the benefit of indigent patients. Each year he sent 200 *livres* to Father Ragueneau in Canada.

In 1671 he took up residence in Orléans, in the house of a nephew whose son, Claude Deshaies-Gendron, was to become in the 18th century the doctor of the regent, Philippe II d'Orléans. François Gendron practised until his death, which occurred 2 April 1688. A great number of his writings have been preserved, among them a long "Memoir ... concerning his conduct with regard to the treatment of the cancer of the late Queen Queen Mother."

GABRIEL NADEAU

[François Gendron], *Quelques particularitez du pays des Hurons en la Nouvelle France, remarquées par le Sieur Gendron, docteur en médecine, qui a demeuré dans ce pays-là fort long-temps*, éd. J.-B. de Rocoles (Troyes et Paris, 1660; réimprimé à Albany, 1868). *JJ* (Laverdière et Casgrain), 143. Philippe Champault, "Les Gendron 'médecins des rois et des pauvres,'" *RSCT*, 2d ser., VI (1912), sect.I, 35–120. A. Dureau, *Notice sur la famille Gendron* (Chartres, 1868). J.-Frédéric Gendron, *Nicolas Gendron et ses descendants* (Montréal, s.d.). Léon Gérin, "Le Sieur Gendron," *BRH*, XXXI (1925), 124. Benjamin Sulte, "Le Sieur Gendron," *BRH*, XIII (1907), 182f.

GENEVIÈVE-AGNÈS *dite* de Tous-les-Saints. *See* SKANUDHAROUA

GEYER (Guyar, Guyer), GEORGE, governor of York Fort, Hudson Bay; fl. *c.* 1672–97.

Outside his career in the HBC, which began in 1672 when he became associated with Governor Charles BAYLY "in a constant Discovery ... yea, in very dangerous Places" (*Parl. Rept.*, 1749, p.273), nothing is known of George Geyer. He was to have returned to England from James Bay in 1680, but the wreck of the *Prudent Mary* that year delayed his arrival in London until 1681.

Geyer, under contract for three years and with instructions to obtain isinglass at Slude (now Eastmain) River, sailed to James Bay in 1682 but, after wintering as chief at Rupert River, he again went to London in 1683. His early return may have been caused by Governor John NIXON's inability, or lack of enthusiasm, to undertake the isinglass project. But Geyer's services were retained for, after spending the winter of 1683-84 looking after an Indian who had been brought to London at the Company's expense, he sailed for Port Nelson in 1684.

Geyer had been appointed a member of Governor John ABRAHAM's council as well as chief of the fort to be established at New Severn, but this new settlement could not be formed immediately as help was needed at Port Nelson against the French who had not altogether lost the advantages they had gained there in 1682. Geyer therefore remained at Port Nelson, taking part in repulsing the attack made by Claude de Bermen* de La Martinière in September 1684, and supervising the building of the first York Fort on the north bank of Hayes River. After the French withdrawal in 1685 he was able to establish New Severn.

In 1686 Geyer became governor of York Fort. This was the year in which resources there were severely strained by the addition to the normal personnel not only of the men from the wrecked supply ship *Happy Return*, but also of Governor Henry SERGEANT and the other released prisoners from the Company's forts in James Bay which had been captured by the Chevalier de TROYES.

In 1688 Geyer's dignity as governor was confirmed by a commission from James II, and in 1689, the year which saw the start of war between England and France, this was replaced by one from William and Mary. In 1690 Geyer successfully repulsed a French attack on York Fort, and in 1693, when he could not be induced to stay any longer in Hudson Bay, Walsh* succeeded him as governor and he finally returned to England. It was during Geyer's period as governor that the first attempt was made to settle at Churchill River (in 1689) and that Henry Kelsey* went "up into the Country of the Assinae Poets" (in 1690). Geyer applied for re-entry into the Company in 1697 but there was no suitable opening for him at that time, and no further references to him have been found in the Company's archives.

ALICE M. JOHNSON

For detailed information on Geyer's career *see* HBRS, VIII, IX (Rich); XI, XX (Rich and Johnson).

GIBBONS, WILLIAM, arctic explorer, cousin of Sir Thomas BUTTON; fl. 1612–14.

Nothing is known of the life and career of Capt. William Gibbons beyond what appears in Purchas and Fox, and a few odd bits of information gleaned by Miller Christy for the notes and introduction to the Hakluyt edition of the Fox and JAMES voyages.

Capt. William Gibbons was a cousin of Sir Thomas Button and served with him as a volunteer on Button's expedition to Hudson Bay in 1612. He was apparently a seaman of considerable experience in whom Button had great confidence.

The return of the Button expedition in 1613 raised the hopes of those who felt that the northwest passage would ultimately be found through Hudson Bay. Consequently Capt. Gibbons, now an arctic veteran, commanded the next expedition for the Company of the Merchants Discoverers of the North-West Passage, and he is listed as one of the Adventurers in that company. Some support for the voyage was also contributed by the East India Company.

Gibbons sailed in March 1614 in HENRY HUDSON's old ship *Discovery* accompanied by Robert BYLOT a veteran of both the Hudson and the Button voyages. Very little is known of this voyage. It was a year of unusually heavy ice which forced the ship from the entrance of Hudson Strait down the Labrador coast where for ten weeks Gibbons remained ice bound in a bay about $58\frac{1}{2}°$ latitude, which was called Gibbons' Hole, now believed to be Saglek Bay. At last, free of the ice with the season far gone Gibbons sailed back to England, accomplishing nothing.

The fruitless results of this voyage by no means prove that Gibbons was incompetent; he was, more likely, simply unfortunate in his season as many other good arctic explorers have been.

ERNEST S. DODGE

Purchas, *Pilgrimes* (1905–7), XIV, 379. *Voyages of Foxe and James* (Christy), I, vi, 164n., *et passim*; II, 284, 646.

GIFFARD, MARIE-FRANÇOISE, *dite* **Marie de Saint-Ignace,** Hospitaller of the Hôtel-Dieu of Quebec, first nun of Canadian birth; b. 1634, daughter of ROBERT GIFFARD and Marie Regnouard; d. 1657.

In 1634 Giffard, having been granted a seigneury, returned to New France with his wife and his two children. On 11 June, a week after their arrival at Quebec, Françoise was born; she was baptized by Father CHARLES LALEMANT. In the autumn of 1646 she took her vows at the Hôtel-Dieu of Quebec. She received the name of the mother superior and foundress, who had died 5 November.

Marie-Françoise Giffard's niece, Mother Juchereau* de Saint-Ignace, has traced a portrait of her that seems authentic: "She was very intelligent, endowed with great gentleness and a prudence beyond her age. Her innocence and purity were angelic; she had a sincere and deep humility, an ardent charity and an unfailing readiness to endure all in God's name." Mother Giffard de Saint-Ignace died 15 March 1657 at Quebec, after terrible suffering. She was buried

Giffard de Moncel

under the chancel in the Hôtel-Dieu chapel. Her contemporaries admired her saintly qualities.

MARIE-JEAN-D'ARS CHARETTE, C.S.C.

JR (Thwaites). Juchereau, *Annales* (Jamet). *BRH*, VII (1901), 86–89.

GIFFARD DE MONCEL, ROBERT, master surgeon, colonizing seigneur, member of the Communauté des Habitants, first doctor of the Hôtel-Dieu of Quebec and doctor in ordinary to the king; b. 1587, the son of Marc Giffard and Jeanne Poignant, in the parish of Saint-Jean-Baptiste in Mortagne (Perche); d. 14 April 1668 at Beauport.

His marriage contract with Marie Regnouard was drawn up on 12 Feb. 1628 at Mortagne. Established at Beauport, less than two leagues from Quebec, Giffard was the first colonizing seigneur in New France. This vocation was superimposed upon that of "naval surgeon," a title that he bore in 1627, when mention of his coming to Canada was first made. In 1640 he became the first doctor of the Hôtel-Dieu of Quebec, apothecary and even "doctor in ordinary" to the king, a purely honorary title which crowned his career and his prestige.

At the time of his voyage in 1627, if not sooner, Giffard had built himself a "cabin" at La Canardière, in the region of Beauport, probably for hunting and fishing. Apparently he already intended to settle in the colony, since, when he came back in 1628 with ROQUEMONT's fleet, bringing with him a considerable amount of equipment, he was captured and despoiled by the KIRKES when half-way up the St. Lawrence. Later the Compagnie de la Nouvelle-France recognized his attempt at colonization and indemnified him for "the losses that he incurred in this context when he was captured with the fleet."

He returned to France, but in 1634 came back to Canada for good, with his wife and two children. The company, which was having difficulties in meeting its obligations with respect to immigration, had just granted him on 15 January one of the first seigneuries in Canada, "a league of ground to be taken up along the shore of the St. Lawrence River for a depth of a league and a half inland, at the place where the River called Notre Dame de Beauport flows into the said St. Lawrence River, the first-mentioned river being included within the area." The document stipulated that in return the colonists brought out by Giffard "will be credited to the said Company, to reduce the number that it is to send out," and this "without the said Giffard being allowed however to trade in furs and pelts at the said place or elsewhere in New France."

Robert Giffard was therefore launching what was solely a colonizing enterprise, and as early as 1634 he concluded a hiring agreement with JEAN GUYON DU BUISSON senior, and Zacharie CLOUTIER, to take them forthwith to Canada, each being accompanied by one of his children, to begin the operations of land-clearing and settling. This was the starting-point of what has been called the immigration from the Perche, which was continued by Noël LANGLOIS, JEAN JUCHEREAU DE MAUR, Gaspard and Marin Boucher, and others, all of whom were the forefathers of important families in the French-Canadian nation. In Giffard's house was drawn up, on 27 July 1636, the oldest marriage contract preserved in any Canadian archives (ASQ), that of Robert DROUIN and Anne Cloutier, the daughter of Zacharie. The seigneury of Beauport was enlarged on 21 March 1653 and extended to a depth of four leagues. At the 1666 census it comprised at least 29 households and 184 persons.

Robert Giffard rendered a number of services to the colony. In 1637, near Trois-Rivières, he risked his life to repulse the Iroquois. In 1645 he was a churchwarden in the parish of Quebec. On 6 March of the same year was founded the Communauté des Habitants, a society for trade with the Indians, all the members of which could also carry on trade on their own. Giffard immediately became a member and subsequently signed all of its official documents. He also had a small ship for the trade. Because of the abuses of PIERRE LEGARDEUR de Repentigny and the other directors of the Communauté des Habitants, who were related to each other, Giffard with CHOMEDEY de Maisonneuve undertook a trip to France during the winter of 1646–47. In 1648 he was named to the council of Quebec, which had been established by order of the king in 1647.

In return for his services Giffard first received two other seigneuries: that of Saint-Gabriel, to the northwest of Quebec, on 11 April 1647, and that of Mille-Vaches, below Tadoussac, on 15 Nov. 1653. He did not however take possession of these lands; he gave a quarter of the seigneury of Saint-Gabriel to the Nuns Hospitallers of Quebec (later the fief of Saint-Ignace) as a dowry for his daughter, MARIE-FRANÇOISE GIFFARD *dite* Marie de Saint-Ignace, who became the first Canadian nun. The rest he gave to the Jesuits as an extension to their seigneury of Sillery. With the support of Governor Voyer* d'Argenson, Giffard obtained for himself and his lineal descendants one of the first letters of nobility granted to a resident of Canada, signed by Louis XIV in

March 1658 and registered by the Conseil de Québec on 8 September.

Robert Giffard died on 14 April 1668 in his manor-house at Beauport. An excellent Christian, a friend and benefactor of the Jesuits, he was favoured with the attendance of Father Étienne de Carheil* throughout his illness. His funeral took place in the presence of Bishop Laval* and the clergy. The Giffard name died out in Canada with his son Joseph*, who left no issue. Besides his daughter who was a nun and another son who returned to France after only a short stay, Giffard had three other daughters: Marie, the wife of JEAN JUCHEREAU DE LA FERTÉ; Louise, married to CHARLES DE LAUSON de Charny, and Marie-Thérèse, the wife of NICOLAS JUCHEREAU de Saint-Denis. At Giffard, a municipality situated between Quebec and Beauport, a monument commemorates Robert Giffard.

HONORIUS PROVOST

ASQ, Documents Faribault, 2, Accord de mariage entre Robert Drouin et Anne Cloutier, chez Giffard de Mortagne, 27 juillet 1636. *JR* (Thwaites), *passim.* Juchereau, *Annales* (Jamet), *passim.* P.-G. Roy, *Inv. concessions, passim.*
Ahern, *Notes pour l'histoire de la médecine*, 258–75. Edward-C. Bailly, "Additional notes on the French-Canadian background of a Minnesota pioneer: Alexis Bailly," *BRH*, LX (1954), 161–64. Joseph Besnard, "Les diverses professions de Robert Giffard," *NF.*, IV (1929), 322–29. *BRH*, VIII (1902), 314f.; IX (1903), 267–70; XXI (1915), 159f.; XXII (1916), 31f., 188f. Alfred A. Cambray, *Robert Giffard, premier seigneur de Beauport et les origines de la Nouvelle-France* (Cap-de-la-Madeleine, 1932). T.-E. Giroux, *Robert Giffard, seigneur colonisateur au tribunal de l'histoire, ou la raison de fêter le troisième centenaire de Beauport, 1634–1934* (Québec, 1934). L. de La Sicotière, "L'émigration percheronne au Canada," Société historique et archéologique de l'Orne *Bulletin*, VI (1887).

GILBERT (Gylberte, Jilbert), SIR HUMPHREY, Elizabethan explorer who annexed Newfoundland to England, second son of Otho and Katherine Gilbert of Compton and Greenway, Devonshire, half-brother (through his mother) of Sir Walter Raleigh and Sir Carew Raleigh; b. *c.* 1537; d. 1583.

Gilbert is said to have been to Eton and to Oxford University and in 1558 was living in one of the Inns of Court (New Inn) in London. He had then been for some time in the service of Princess Elizabeth; after her accession to the throne she continued to remember him. In 1562–63 he served with an English force at Havre-de-Grâce (Le Havre) and is thought there to have met Frenchmen who had been across the Atlantic and who first interested him in America.

On his return he began to study academic geography in order to see whether or not there was a water passage by the northwest of America to Asia. He petitioned the queen late in 1565 to allow him and his brothers to try to find such a passage. With Anthony Jenkinson, he debated the rival claims of northwest and northeast passages before Queen Elizabeth and the men finally agreed to co-operate, although they never did so. By 30 June 1566 Gilbert had completed a treatise, the title of which, when later revised, was "A discourse of a discoverie for a new passage to Cataia," to prove the existence of a northwest passage. His geography, if learned and often ingenious, was mostly preposterous. However, he put forward proposals not only for trading with Asia, but also for utilizing North America on his way. He thought a colony and half-way station should be set up "about the Sierra Nevada," in northwest America, and he considered trade with North American Indians might be a good and profitable thing in itself.

Gilbert served as an officer in Ireland for three and a half years, being an M.P. in the Irish Parliament of 1569–70, and on 1 Jan. 1570 was knighted for his services by Sir Henry Sidney, the lord deputy. Gilbert was deeply involved with Sidney in planning a large-scale settlement of Ulster by Devonshire gentlemen and their dependents and in making colonizing proposals for Munster. Although Ulster and Munster were not in fact planted at this time, the idea of exploiting unlimited land remained with Gilbert and reappeared later in his American plans.

He returned to England in 1570 and married Anne Aucher, an heiress of a Kent county family, by whom he was to have no less than six sons and a daughter. He was elected M.P., with John Hawkins, for Plymouth in the Parliament of 1571. He received rewards from the Crown in the shape of leases and licences and associated himself from late in 1571 with an alchemical project, in which Sir Thomas Smith, the secretary of state, was deeply concerned, for transmuting iron into copper and antimony and lead into mercury. With more significance, he led the first English force, a thousand men, to the assistance of the Dutch sea-beggars in their attack on Spanish power in the Netherlands. Based on Flushing from July to November 1572, he occupied substantial Spanish forces without, himself, showing outstanding military qualities. For some years, he was given little to do by the queen and settled down to study and make plans for reforming the government of Ireland and for setting up, in England, a new "modern" type of institution of higher learning where modern languages, science, and applied

Gilbert

mathematics would be taught. He also took out and refurbished his "Discourse" on the northwest passage. Michael Lok and Martin FROBISHER consulted him about their plans from 1574 onwards to establish a company to exploit the supposed passage. Gilbert gave advice and his name as a subscriber, but nothing more, except that his "Discourse" was at last published in 1576, possibly without his consent.

From 1576 onwards Gilbert is regarded as an authority on America and he does his best to become one. He turned in 1577 to the making of extreme anti-Spanish plans—to seize a major island in the West Indies, to capture the foreign fishing vessels at Newfoundland (his first known association with the island), and to convert them into a privateering fleet—for which he failed to get support at court.

He then produced a more concrete scheme, which led the queen to grant him letters patent on 11 June 1578 to discover and occupy in the next six years a site for a colony not already in European hands. It is clear from the fact that he was authorized to expel any intruders who planted within 600 miles of him, that the coast of eastern North America was his objective. He himself could hold land there and convey it to others, but all would in turn be held from the Crown, while his colony was to be governed by laws agreeable to those of England.

Gilbert now prepared to take advantage of his newly granted rights by planning an ambitious expedition across the Atlantic. He received advice from the learned Dr. John Dee, who was mainly interested in finding routes to Asia, and from the elder Hakluyt, who made sensible suggestions for settling Englishmen in lands between 35° and 40°N. We know, too, that he was in close touch with Sir Francis Walsingham, the secretary of state. It is also probable that he heard about the possibilities of settlement in Newfoundland from Anthony PARKHURST. There is little doubt that Gilbert expected to rob and plunder any Spanish ships he encountered, and that he favoured working round by the Caribbean and up the North American coast, but we cannot say where he had finally decided to settle.

By mid-November Gilbert had assembled a fairly powerful squadron at Plymouth, consisting in all of ten vessels, heavily armed and manned (175 guns, 570 men). Many of the men were pirates and some had been reprieved from execution to go with Gilbert. Not surprisingly, some of them refused to obey Gilbert's orders: Henry Knollys took off three ships for a purely piratical cruise (one or more of the remaining ships joining him later). Gilbert's remaining seven vessels left Plymouth on 18 November, but soon had to put into Cork harbour, since the *Falcon* and perhaps Gilbert's own flagship, the *Anne Ager* (or *Anne Aucher*), were leaking, while another had to return to England for the same cause. Stores also were apparently quite inadequate. The result was that, although Gilbert set off into the Atlantic again about February 1579, he had to return to Dartmouth by the end of April. The *Falcon* alone, with Walter Raleigh in command and the Portuguese Simon Fernandez—a captured Caribbean pilot reprieved by Walsingham and given to Gilbert—as pilot, reached the Canary Islands and made out to sea for the West Indies and the eastern coast of North America under Fernandez' guidance. She failed, however, to get there and had to return to Plymouth in May. The failure of the expedition was complete. It revealed grave defects in its leader's organizing capacity and involved the loss of the greater part of Gilbert's personal fortune, and part of his family's.

Gilbert was now glad to take temporary service with the Crown and to serve with three ships off the Irish coast from July to October 1579, but he soon reverted to his American plans. The mishaps to his 1578 venture had the negative effect of turning him away from southeastern North America to New England and Newfoundland. He equipped his tiny 8-ton frigate, the *Squirrel*, for an American reconnaissance, and she sailed under the command of Simon Fernandez, with a crew of ten, to North America and back within three months—a fine achievement. We have no specific evidence where she made her landfall, but her reports of the country were clearly encouraging. By this time Dr. John Dee had convinced Gilbert that his most desirable objective would be the River of Norumbega, or "Refugio," of VERRAZZANO (Narrangansett Bay, R.I.), while he himself acquired Gilbert's rights to all land north of 50°, including northern Newfoundland, most of the St. Lawrence valley, Labrador, and the northwest passage as shown on his map of 1580. This would indicate that Gilbert's objective lay to the south. We know little of Gilbert's activities during the latter part of 1580 and early in 1581, except that he was an active M.P. (for Queenborough, Kent) between January and March 1581, and that his final preparations for an American venture began in the summer of that year.

Gilbert's main proposition to potential supporters was that there were vast quantities of land, fertile and in good climates, waiting to be occupied by Englishmen, and that he would, for a consideration, give them title to great estates there. This appealed especially to loyal English

Roman Catholic gentlemen, who were now subject to crippling fines as recusants as long as they refused to conform to the Church of England, but who did not want to go into exile amongst her enemies on the continent. Sir George Peckham of Denham, Bucks., and Sir Thomas Gerrard of Bryn, Lancs., emerged as the leaders of this group and did their best to assemble their co-religionists behind Gilbert. Between June 1582 and February 1583 Gilbert assigned no less than 8,500,000 acres of land in America to them, the area to be around the River of Norumbega and the bay of the five islands lying nearby, the Roman Catholics undertaking to make their own way to America. Gilbert himself concentrated on mobilizing the townsmen and gentry of the south and southwest of England—the town of Southampton was awarded a monopoly of trade from the colony—promising some of them land and others trading rights. The main settlements would be knit into a single proprietory polity under his personal government, while a commercial corporation was to be founded to control trade and provide the mechanism for continuing the flow of settlers after Gilbert had departed for America.

However, the Catholic group was badly weakened during 1582 by attempts of their clergy and by Spanish agents to dissuade settlers on the grounds of religious disloyalty or danger. Consequently, no expedition under Catholic auspices sailed early in 1583, as had been originally planned. Moreover, Christopher Carleill, stepson of Sir Francis Walsingham, on whose goodwill Gilbert relied for official tolerance of his project, was also in the field with a semi-independent project. Depending on the Bristol merchants, and trying to get support from the Muscovy Company as well, his plan, ostensibly, was to settle 100 men at 40°N or thereabouts, as a base for fishery, lumbering, and trade with the Indians. Carleill, however, proved willing to let Gilbert get away first.

In the meantime a great deal of news-gathering about North America had been done. The younger Richard Hakluyt was commissioned to put together all he could gather from printed or manuscript sources and brought out his *Divers voyages touching the discoverie of America* in May 1582 (republished Hakluyt Soc., 1st ser., VII, 1850), with documents ranging from JOHN CABOT's patent in 1496 to Verrazzano's account of his 1524 voyage and Ribault's narrative of the 1562 Florida colony, as well as lists of American commodities and advice on colonization. David INGRAM, Simon Fernandez, and a certain John Walker, who had made a voyage in 1580 to an inlet which was either the Penobscot or the Bay of Fundy, were interviewed in August and September by Walsingham, Peckham, and others. During 1583 Ingram's travels were published, as were Carleill's proposals and also a poem on Gilbert's voyage by Stephanus PARMENIUS. North America was therefore much in evidence.

Gilbert knew the elaborate map of North America which John Dee made for Queen Elizabeth in 1580 and which assembled all the knowledge at that time available to Englishmen, while he also acquired a circumpolar map which Dee made specially for him in 1582–83. Both had some influence on his geographical conceptions. Dee believed particularly in the existence of a passage through North America in temperate latitudes by way of the St. Lawrence or the River of Norumbega. (*See*: Ganong, "Crucial maps, IX." The Gilbert map is now in the Elkins Collection, Philadelphia Public Library.) He was also supplied with an elaborate set of instructions to enable mapping of the coast to be developed and a survey made of natural resources, including flora and fauna, and of Indian peoples (with pictures) to be in the charge of a man, Thomas Bavin, otherwise unknown. Professor E. G. R. Taylor (*Mariner's Mirror*, XXXVII, 48) considered that William Borough, clerk of the Navy Board, was partly responsible for their drafting, while the two Hakluyts, the lawyer and his younger clergyman cousin, are also likely to have been concerned (*see*: *Roanoke voyages* (Quinn), I, 49–54). The discovery of the instructions suggests that Gilbert's planning was on a more advanced scientific level than had hitherto been thought likely, though the scale of the projected survey was probably quite out of proportion to the resources at his disposal.

Gilbert had to choose from a number of alternatives in planning his voyage. His final decision was to follow the well-known track of the Newfoundland fishing fleet to the Banks and then, making for Cape Breton, to follow the mainland coast southwards until he found an attractive site for a colony or reached Dee's Verrazzanean harbour. He expected to get away early in the spring of 1583, but the queen urged him, as "a man noted of not good happ by sea," to stay behind. On 16 March she relented however and sent him a token of her goodwill ("an ancor guyded by a Lady"), but he was not ready until June. He had then five vessels at Plymouth—the *Delight*, 120 tons, owned by William Winter, her captain, and Gilbert's elder brother Sir John; the flagship, on which he was to sail as "General" of the expedition; the *Bark Raleigh*, 200 tons, owned and commanded by his rising young half-brother Walter Raleigh; the *Golden Hind*, 40 tons,

Gilbert

owned and commanded by Edward HAYES, whose account is the chief authority for the voyage; the *Swallow*, 40 tons, commanded by Maurice Browne (to which Gilbert had only a dubious title), on which the Hungarian Stephanus Parmenius sailed; and the *Squirrel*, 8 or 10 tons, now under William Andrewes, Gilbert's little frigate which had made the 1580 voyage.

They set out on 11 June. Bad luck again afflicted Gilbert, since the *Bark Raleigh* turned back shortly after sailing, but the remaining vessels kept company on a slow voyage until 23 July when the ships were not far from Newfoundland, though well to the north of the fishery. They then separated in fog and the *Golden Hind* had to work down from what Capt. Hayes reckoned was 51°N to Conception Bay, where she picked up the *Swallow*, and then to St. John's, where she found the *Squirrel* outside the harbour, and, on 3 August, the *Delight*. Although the port admiral was an Englishman, he had mobilized the crews of the 36 ships, Portuguese, Basque, and French as well as English, to deny passage to Gilbert. The reason for this was the piracy by the *Delight*'s master, Richard CLARKE, against Portuguese ships in the harbour in 1582, which the fishermen were determined to stop. Gilbert flourished his royal commission (evidently his patent) and the English fishermen gave way, so that his little squadron entered the same day.

Gilbert had already fully formed the plan of taking possession of Newfoundland for the English Crown. This was not precisely forecast in any earlier pronouncements, though it was envisaged as a possibility by Anthony Parkhurst in 1578. To make such sovereignty effective he would need an armed shore establishment, which could issue licences to fishermen and assign shore stations. What Gilbert did was to issue to each of the 36 vessels in the harbour a certificate authorizing it to continue fishing (a version of one of these has recently been found in Seville, Archivo de Indias, Patronato 265, ramo 40), while, in return, he levied a contribution in kind from the fisheries for the supply of his own ships, poorly provisioned to begin with and worse off for having been over seven weeks at sea instead of the normal three or four. On 5 August Sir Humphrey Gilbert formally took possession of Newfoundland and of the land 200 leagues to the north and south (i.e., from approximately 37°35″N to 57°35″N). The merchants and fishermen assembled before his tent, a rod and turf were cut and delivered to him in virtue of his personal title to the soil, and he proclaimed the land to be the queen's in perpetuity. He promulgated "laws" to be observed—no public exercise of religion apart from that of the Church of England, no opposition (on pain of punishment for high treason), no disrespect to the queen (without cutting of ears and seizing of ships and goods). To all these his audience assented, being unable to do otherwise, and, no doubt, glad to get off so lightly. A formal marker was set up at St John's— a wooden pillar with the royal arms in lead attached. Further, he assigned drying stages in perpetuity to certain fishermen (previously the first comers had obtained them). All this presupposed continuous occupation and was almost meaningless without it.

On 4 August Gilbert had gone ashore to look at a wild garden with roses and raspberries, which had some young English peas growing in it. After the 5th he went out with the parties which tried to enter the almost impassable forest and examined the shore and inland hills for signs of minerals. His Saxon mineral expert, Daniel, collected iron ore and what he said was silver. Gilbert made a great show of secrecy about the latter. Hayes and Parmenius made some observations of the land and of its potentialities. His men were in bad shape—some were determined to go no farther so the *Swallow* was sent back with the sick and recalcitrant (including the captains of the *Delight* and *Squirrel*). Hayes tells us that Gilbert was so attracted to Newfoundland and its minerals that he was determined to return there, but that his obligations to his friends— Peckham and those who hoped to settle farther south—bound him to continue his voyage down the mainland coast, so as to take formal possession of the land there before his patent expired in June 1584.

Leaving with his three remaining ships on 20 August, Gilbert worked down to Cape Race, off which they did some cod-fishing, and then sent shore parties to sample the soil on Trepassey and Placentia bays before sailing for Sable Island on 22 August. They had had a course worked out for them by a Portuguese fisherman at St. John's who recommended them to visit the island to obtain some wild cattle and pigs loose there (released he said by the Portuguese some 30 years before). The voyage was slow but uneventful until the 28th. Then Gilbert, sailing in the *Squirrel*, quarrelled with Richard Clarke about his course, and made him change from westsouthwest to northwest; William Cox, master of the *Golden Hind*, disapproved of the change. After a windy night, the ships found themselves in shoal water on the morning of the 29th, and the *Delight*'s crew, keeping a poor look-out, were unable to prevent her going aground and rapidly breaking up. Richard Clarke rescued 15 men in the ship's boat, but the rest—Parmenius, Saxon miner, ore, and all—were lost.

The *Golden Hind* and the *Squirrel* "cast about Eastsoutheast, bearing to the South, even for our lives into the windes eye," as Hayes tells us, and so escaped. Although George Patterson argued that the traverses given by Hayes would have brought them to Gabarus Bay, not Sable Island, this is not established as the courses are open to several interpretations. It appears probable, however, that if the men were correct in their calculations, they had in fact passed to the north of Sable Island and were caught on the shoal (the West Bar) which stretches out to the west behind the island.

The loss demoralized both the remaining crews: they were now quite sure that their poor equipment and stores would be insufficient. Consequently, and after much discussion with Hayes and Cox, Gilbert decided on 31 August to return. The wind was now in their favour and they sped back to Cape Race in two days and were soon clear of land. Gilbert had hurt his foot on the *Squirrel* and, on 2 September, came on board the *Golden Hind* to have it dressed and to concert means of keeping the two little ships in company with each other. He refused to leave the *Squirrel*, and the vessels set out on the Atlantic crossing. After a sharp storm, they had a spell of good weather and made fair progress: Gilbert came aboard the *Golden Hind* again, talked and made merry with Hayes, and insisted once more on returning to the frigate, even though Hayes maintained she was over-gunned and unsafe for sailing. Some 900 miles on from Cape Race they encountered very heavy seas, "breaking short and high Pyramid wise," said Hayes. On 9 September the *Squirrel* was nearly overwhelmed but recovered, and in a calmer spell Gilbert hailed the *Golden Hind*. He was sitting towards the stern with a book in his hand, repeatedly calling out "We are as neare to Heaven by sea as by land." It is thought that the book was More's *Utopia* and the passage which had struck his imagination in these desperate circumstances was: "He that hathe no grave is covered with the skye: and, the way to heaven out of all places is of like length and distaunce." It was to be Gilbert's last—and famous—recorded saying. At midnight the frigate's lights went out; the watch cried "the Generall was cast away," and at that moment, in Hayes' words, "the Frigat was devoured and swallowed up of the Sea." The *Golden Hind* continued on her course and reached Falmouth on the 22nd, sailing on to bring the tragic news to Sir John Gilbert at Dartmouth.

On board ship on the way home, Hayes had found Gilbert "wholly fixed on the New found land." He was determined to return there in 1584 while Hayes and Cox would take over the southward exploration of the mainland coast. He was also optimistic about his chances of getting two squadrons to sea, since he believed the queen would lend him £10,000. The basis for this belief seems to have been his confidence that he could assure her, in spite of the loss of the ore samples on the *Delight*, that there was silver to be mined in Newfoundland. Or else, perhaps, he was letting his obsessive fancy take hold of him.

Sir Humphrey Gilbert's personality is difficult to assess. He was an able soldier, but evidently more an ingenious tactician than an organizer or strategist. He had some appreciable intellectual ability. He was physically brave and had considerable determination. Clearly, he spoke with authority to his men on land or sea. But he was cruel—Thomas Churchyard tells us that when he received submissions of some Irish lords in his tent, a border leading to it was lined with the heads of their associates. He was liable to break out into violent rages when he would inflict physical violence on his dependents. He was intermittently homosexual (Sir Thomas Smith said that the only way to soothe his temper was to send a boy to him). He was vain and, one suspects, sometimes pompous. His American plans and dreams became something of an obsession. His vision of a transplanted English gentry exploiting vast new American lands in a feudal setting was not wholly unrealistic (it was to be realized later, to some extent, in Maryland) but his plans were far too wide-ranging for his resources and there was some lack of scruple in his easy disposal in bulk of lands which he had never seen. He did not realize the slow, painful, and expensive character of colonization in temperate climates. His impatience is also shown in his dealings with Newfoundland. Control of the fishery had superficial attractions, but it would need an expensive shore establishment (and settlers proved hard to keep on Newfoundland in the 17th century) and even then, since the French and other foreigners might well keep away from the English-dominated areas or even arm posts of their own, it would not necessarily pay its way. Gilbert seems to have been far too optimistic, on too little evidence, about the value of Newfoundland minerals. His ventures, however, focussed attention sharply on the possibilities of North American colonization and helped greatly to make it a continuing English objective.

Walter Raleigh had Sir Humphrey Gilbert's patent reissued him in his favour early in 1584, with Newfoundland excluded from its scope, and sent a series of colonies to Roanoke Island in North Carolina. Newfoundland, in theory, should have been governed according to elaborate arrangements made with Peckham and Sir John Gilbert, but though Sir John sent ships there in 1584 he evidently found any control of fishery and fishermen impracticable and did not renew the attempt (we lack any narrative of events there in 1584). Sir George Peckham was still in the field, even if most of his Roman Catholic supporters had deserted him. He made the best he could of the Newfoundland events and of the prospects of mainland estates in his *A true report* which he finished on 12 Nov. 1583, and which was published soon after. But, although he was trying to collect subscribers early in 1584, he was making so little headway that the authorities sent him back to prison as a recusant and he passes out of the colonizing story.

Christopher Carleill, undoubtedly influenced by Gilbert, continued the latter's preparatory work. His objective was land to the southwest of Cape Breton and perhaps the St. Lawrence. He had reports of French activity there and received further news in the spring of 1584 through the younger Richard Hakluyt, now attached to the Paris embassy. Carleill sailed as far as Ireland early in the summer, but, for a reason so far unknown (perhaps the discovery that his supplies were inadequate), he turned over his three ships for government service in Irish waters at the beginning of August and, himself, settled down in military employment in Ireland for some nine years (with an interval in 1585–86 when he served on Sir FRANCIS DRAKE's West Indian voyage and may well have entered Newfoundland waters on his way homeward). Later he returned to his plan made with Edward Hayes, which was a fresh scheme for settling in the region of the Atlantic Provinces and the Gulf of St. Lawrence in 1593–94 [*see* HAYES].

Dr John Dee had planned to follow up his grant of 1580 from Gilbert by getting a patent to prospect for northerly passages, but he was diverted by an invitation to go to Poland, which he accepted in September 1583. He relinquished his projects (and apparently his grant) to Adrian Gilbert, Sir Humphrey's younger brother, who was duly given a patent for the discovery of a northerly passage in February 1584. From this sprang the masterly explorations of John DAVIS, 1585–87.

From Gilbert, then, derived the attempts to settle the Roanoke Island colonies and also the most fruitful northwestern voyages of the 16th century. He also, by annexing Newfoundland, (though this remained a formality until 1610), gave Englishmen a continuing interest in what went on in the fishing industry and provoked subsequent plans by Hayes and others to control the fishery, leading in the end to the Jacobean colonies. He attracted attention to New England and the region of the Atlantic Provinces as possible sites for English settlements, and, by his elaboration of the concept of proprietorial colonization, influenced later events in Newfoundland, Nova Scotia, Maine, and Maryland.

DAVID B. QUINN

BM, Add. MS 38823, ff.1–8 (*see* E. G. R. Taylor, "Instructions to a colonial surveyor in 1582," *Mariner's Mirror*, XXXVII (1951), 48–63). BM, Lansdowne MS 144, f.384, Dr. Thomas Wilson to Captain Augustine Clarke, 10 April 1580. PRO, H.C.A. 13/23, 14 Nov. 1578, Thomas Gager, 20 May 1579, John Webster, 26 May 1579; S.P. 12/42, no. 23.

Sir Humphrey Gilbert, *A discourse of a discoverie for a new passage to Cataia* (London, 1576); repr. in *Voyages of Gilbert* (Quinn), I, 129ff. *Voyages of Gilbert* (Quinn) includes almost all the Gilbert documents and a biography. Edward Hayes, "A report of the voyage and successe thereof, attempted in the yeere of our Lord, 1583. by sir Humfrey Gilbert knight..." in Hakluyt, *Principall navigations* (London, 1589), 679–97; repr. in 2nd ed. Hakluyt, III (1600), 143–61; Hakluyt Soc. ed. (1903–5), VIII, 34–77. *Index to administrations in the Prerogative Court of Canterbury*, ed. C. H. Rudge (British Record Soc., LXXVI, 1954), 65, contains probate of will of Gilbert, Oct. 1584. Peckham, *A true report. Queen Elizabethes Achademy*, ed. F. J. Furnivall (Early English Text Soc., extra ser., VIII, 1869), 1–12. ["The erection of an Achademy in London for educacion of her Majestes Wardes, and others the youth of nobility and gentlemen [by Humphrey Gilbert?].] *Sir Humfrey Gylberte and his enterprize of colonization in America*, ed. Carlos Slafter (Prince Soc., XXIX, Boston, 1903).

Ganong, "Crucial maps, IX." W. G. Gosling, *The life of Sir Humphrey Gilbert* (London, 1911). G. B. Parks, "George Peele and his friends as 'ghost' poets," *J. English and Germanic Philology*, XLI (1942), 527–36. D. B. Quinn, "Simão Fernandes," Congresso internacional de historia dos descobrimentos *Actas*, III (1961), 449–65. *Roanoke voyages* (Quinn), I, 49–54. Joan Wake, *The Brudenells of Deene* (London, 1953). Portraits: painting by anonymous artist (perhaps painted after his death), in Compton Castle, Devonshire; engraving by Robert Boissard (from lost portrait) in *Bazilωlogia* (1618), re-engraved for Henry Holland, *Herωologia anglica* (1620) (*see*: Engraving in England in the sixteenth and seventeenth centuries: a descriptive catalogue, intro. by A. M. Hind (2v., Cambridge, 1952–55), I, xxiv, 187–92).

GILLAM, ZACHARIAH, HBC captain; b. in Boston, Mass., 30 July 1636 (o.s.); d. at Hudson Bay 21 Oct. 1682.

He was the second son of Benjamin Gillam, a shipwright who came to New England and was made a freeman of Massachusetts 6 May 1635, and of his wife Hannah. Benjamin prospered and his descendants married into prominent New England families. On 26 July 1659 Zachariah married Phoebe, daughter of Major William Phillips, a prominent citizen of Charlestown and Boston, and of his first wife, Mary. Major Phillips had been the Massachusetts commissioner for Maine in 1653, but not liking the Puritans, he had removed to Saco, Maine, with his third wife Bridget (the mother of ESBON SANFORD by a former marriage) and acquired a large tract of wilderness land back of Saco and Wells, formerly called Phillipstown, where the present town of Sanford now stands. Major Phillips deeded to Zachariah Gillam and his brother-in-law, Ephraim Turner, 500 acres on West Brook in Maine.

Like many young Bostonians of that day, Zachariah followed the sea. He engaged in the New England coastal trade, but he was interested in the scheme of CHOUART Des Groseilliers and Radisson* to open a new fur-trading route through Hudson Bay. Some Boston merchants in 1663 fitted out an expedition, led by the two explorers, which reached the mouth of Hudson Strait but then turned back. Although the attempt was abortive, Des Groseilliers and Radisson were fortunate in catching the attention of the British commissioner Col. George Cartwright in Boston in 1665, who convinced them to go to England to present information on the possibilities of their project to the group of courtiers, gentlemen, financiers, and some members of the infant Royal Society who were interested in exploring and establishing such a trading route. The Frenchmen sailed for England 1 Aug. 1665 in the *Charles*, commanded by Capt. Benjamin Gillam, the elder brother of Zachariah.

It seems likely that through Des Groseilliers and Radisson Zachariah became known to the "Adventurers"; in any case he was captain of the 43-ton ketch *Nonsuch*, which, with Charles II's ketch *Eaglet*, was fitted out by the adventurers for the historic voyage to Hudson Bay in 1668–69. Des Groseilliers sailed with Gillam in the *Nonsuch*, Radisson in the *Eaglet*. When the latter ship had to turn back to England in August 1668, the burden of the voyage fell on the *Nonsuch*.

Gillam carried out his instructions (printed in *Minnesota History*, XVI, 419–23) quite successfully. He and Des Groseilliers established friendly relations on the coasts of Hudson Bay with the Indians, who led them to the mouth of the Rupert River; they built a house, called Charles Fort, the forerunner of Rupert House, in which they wintered and from which they traded in the spring; Gillam kept a log (published as a "Breviate" about 1675 by John Seller in the *English Pilot*) giving information on navigation and trade; he made a "treaty" with the Indians by which he "purchased" the Rupert River and the surrounding land; and he and Des Groseilliers secured a cargo of fine beaver pelts which realized over £1,300. On his return to London in 1669, Gillam gave information to the Royal Society, several of whose members had helped finance the voyage and who, with the other "Adventurers," formed the HBC, which was formally incorporated on 2 May 1670.

In that same month Gillam was sent out again, in command of the frigate *Prince Rupert* ($75\frac{1}{2}$ tons) carrying Des Groseilliers and Thomas GORST, in company with the *Wivenhoe*, carrying Charles BAYLY and Radisson. The purpose of the expedition, aside from the immediate one of trade, was to establish a main fort on the Nelson River from which Bayly was to govern the region for the HBC. This was not accomplished, and Bayly and Radisson joined Gillam and Des Groseilliers at Charles Fort in the "Bottom of the Bay" where the latter party had built a new house [*see* Gorst's journal in Nute, *Caesars of the wilderness*]. In the winter Radisson made an exploratory expedition to Moose River and in the spring the Indians came to trade. Both ships returned to England in October 1671 with cargoes of skins and information on the coast of the bay. Gillam was captain of the *Prince Rupert* on the 1672–73 voyage and again in 1674–75, although he had been dismissed from the service of the HBC, when he had returned in 1673, for private trading. Some dispute also arose between Gillam and Radisson, who accused each other of misconduct and peculation. Thereafter Gillam returned to Boston and the coastal trade. He was in North Carolina from 1677 until 1680 and, suspected of taking part in the Culpeper rebellion, he was taken in custody to England.

In January 1682 he applied for re-employment in the HBC and he was hired, since he was an old servant and had done good service in the past. He was to have £100 a year "from the day he breakes ground" at Gravesend and 20s. a week until that time. In March he was given command of his old ship, the *Prince Rupert*, but in May he was charged with misconduct in being absent from his ship during its loading and he faced dismissal. However, Gillam sailed at the beginning of June 1682 with John BRIDGAR, the governor of Port Nelson. Five ships were sent out; three were to proceed to the Bottom of the Bay and two, the *Prince Rupert* and the *Albemarle*

Girard de La Place

(commanded by Esbon Sanford, the deputy governor of Port Nelson), were to proceed to the Nelson and Hayes rivers, there to establish Port Nelson.

But the HBC ships had been preceded by two separate parties: that of Zachariah's son Benjamin Gillam* and that of Radisson and Des Groseilliers. Benjamin, under a licence from the governor of Massachusetts and probably aware of the HBC's intentions from his father, arrived on an interloping voyage from Boston 18 Aug. 1682 in the *Bachelor's Delight* and established a camp up the Nelson River. The French party, financed by Aubert* de La Chesnaye and sanctioned by the governor of Quebec, Le Febvre de La Barre, intended to establish a French claim to trade in the Bay; it arrived a few days later and settled on the Hayes River. Returning from a visit to Gillam, intended to intimidate him, Radisson witnessed the arrival on 7 September of the *Prince Rupert* at the mouth of the Nelson, come to establish Port Nelson.

The HBC men decided to winter on the north shore of the Nelson River, despite the French threat. But they were beset with many mishaps: the *Albemarle* did not reach Port Nelson that fall; her captain, Sanford, had died 6 October; worst of all, on 21 Oct. 1682 the *Prince Rupert* dragged her anchor in a severe storm, drifted out to sea, and was lost with about nine crew members, many of the supplies, and her captain, Gillam. Thus Captain Zachariah ended his varied and stormy career. The next year Radisson captured both posts and sailed to Quebec with the captives, Gillam and Bridgar. There they were released and they made their way to New England.

When the first news of these events reached England, the HBC was naturally disturbed but it hesitated to proceed against Benjamin Gillam for some time as Radisson had claimed the region for France and left a group of his people there to hold it. The company would need to establish the prior arrival of Benjamin to make good its claim to the territory. In April 1683, while ignorant of the deaths of captains Gillam and Sanford, it revoked the latter's command of the *Albemarle*, ordered Zachariah to return to England in ballast, to transfer his cargo to other ships, and to bring Sanford with him. The HBC also secured an order-in-council directed to the governor of Massachusetts to permit the commissioner to arrest the Gillams and Sanford in case they should come to New England.

During his wanderings, Zachariah's home was in Boston where his wife and children remained. By Phoebe he had Martha (b. 1660), Zachariah (b. 1661), and Benjamin (b. 23 March 1662/63), the interloper. On 14 April 1676 the executors of Zachariah's father set off to him certain land at Fort Hill in Boston and by a deed in 1692 his sister Hannah Sharpe, widow, deeded to Benjamin all her interest in the land at Fort Hill. The family was continued by his descendants.

Zachariah Gillam was evidently a very able and skilful seaman, resolute and resourceful, but at times unscrupulous and not entirely to be trusted. Nevertheless, he appears to have been reasonably loyal to the HBC in his last days.

G. ANDREWS MORIARTY

"Mass. Archives," LXI, 9. Mass. Hist. Soc., Thwing MSS. Boston, Record Commissioners, *Ninth report: births, baptisms, marriages and deaths, 1630–1699*, ed. W. H. Whitmore and W. S. Appleton (Boston, 1883), *passim*.

C. T. Libby and Sybil Noyes, *Genealogical dictionary of Maine and New Hampshire* (Portland, Me., 1928–39), pt. III, 262; pt. IV, 548. HBRS, V, VIII, IX (Rich); XI, XX (Rich and Johnson), XXI (Rich). G. A. Moriarty, "Captains Gillam and Sanford of the Hudson's Bay Company," *Genealogists' Mag.*, X (1947–50), 568–71. Nute, *Caesars of the wilderness*. L. Parke, "The Savage family," *N. Eng. Hist. and Geneal. Register*, LXVII (1913), 200–1. C. H. Pope, *The pioneers of Massachusetts, a descriptive list . . . (from town, church and other records)* (Boston, 1900), 187. W. H. Whitmore, "Gleanings," *N. Eng. Hist. and Geneal. Register*, XIX (1865), 254.

GIRARD DE LA PLACE, SIMON, priest, Recollet, the first missionary to live among the Malecite Indians of the Saint John River (if we except Father Massé, who spent the summer of 1612 there); b. 1657 in Rouen; d. 1 Jan. 1699 in Acadia.

Simon Girard de La Place joined the Recollets of the province of Aquitaine in 1673. He was appointed a missionary to New France and landed at Quebec in the summer of 1683. He stayed there until the spring of 1685, when he was put in charge of the post on the Saint John River. He took up his abode at Medoctec (now Meductic), the principal Malecite village, and there he received on 18 May 1686 a visit from Bishop Saint-Vallier [La Croix*], who esteemed him very highly. For ten years he laboured to teach the Indians the truths of the faith with a zeal that earned him the praise of the bishop of Quebec as well as that of JOSEPH ROBINAU de Villebon, governor of Acadia. In the autumn of 1695 he went up to Quebec to present the intendant, Bochart* Champigny, with the census that he had taken of the Indians of the Saint John River.

Back in Acadia in the spring of 1696, Father

Simon accompanied as chaplain some 150 Indians who were taking part in Pierre Le Moyne* d'Iberville's expedition against Pemaquid. On 26 August he came back to Fort Naxouat (Nashwaak), the seat of the governor of Acadia, to announce the victory of the French and the capture of Pemaquid by the Malecites. During the winter of 1696–97, as Fort Naxouat was without a chaplain, he took it upon himself to provide religious services on Sundays and feast days. His strength soon gave way under the ardour of his zeal, and on 1 Jan. 1699 he died in odour of sanctity. His brother, Father Louis-Hyacinthe Girard* de La Place, likewise a Recollet, tells us in a letter to his mother that on the orders of the governor of Canada the body of Father Simon was taken to Quebec to be buried in the Recollet church there.

FRÉDÉRIC GINGRAS

AN, Col., C11D, 3, ff.118, 125, 132. *Coll. de manuscrits relatifs à la Nouv.-France*, II, 187, 190, 243. Webster, *Acadia*, 16–17, 91, 143, 198.

GLORIA, JEAN, clerk in charge of stores, procurator of the Communauté des Habitants, royal notary, and merchant; b. shortly before 1630 at Saint-Jacques de Dieppe, Normandy; d. 15 Oct. 1665 at Quebec.

Son of Pierre Gloria, "bourgeois and merchant of the town of Dieppe," and of Perrette Vaulthier, he was already at Quebec on 1 Jan. 1650 as a servant of the Jesuits. Despite his youth, Gloria rapidly became a prominent figure in Quebec, perhaps as a result of his marriage to Marie Bourdon on 9 Jan. 1652. At any rate, this alliance brought him substantial material advantages and the support of JEAN BOURDON, his uncle by marriage, of JEAN LE SUEUR, the Abbé Saint-Sauveur, and of LOUIS D'AILLEBOUST. From 27 March 1652 on, Gloria was "clerk in charge of stores in this colony," which title he was to bear until 1661 or later; in 1658 he was also referred to as "procurator" of the Communauté des Habitants. Although he was an employee of the Communauté, he nevertheless had his own business, and after his death his wife was to continue to operate his shop in the Lower Town of Quebec.

In the year 1663, two honours came to Gloria; he was made churchwarden of the parish of Quebec, and became, by commission of the Conseil Souverain dated 20 September, the first royal notary in New France. He carried on his notary's duties until 8 Sept. 1664. It appears likely that the illness which was to cause his death a year later obliged him to withdraw from active life after that date.

Gloria was buried on 16 Oct. 1665 in the church at Quebec.

ANDRÉ VACHON

AJQ, Greffe de Guillaume Audouart, 27 déc. 1651. APQ, Ins. cons. souv., I, 6v. ASQ, Documents Faribault, 97–101, 107; Registre A, p. 575. "Documents inédits: tabellion de Dieppe," *RHAF*, V (1951–52), 267f., 275f. *JR* (Thwaites), XXXV, 30–31; *JJ* (Laverdière et Casgrain), 132. *Jug. et délib.*, I, 5.

GNUPSSON, EIRIKR (Eric) *upsi*. See EIRIKR *upsi* GNUPSSON [Appendix]

GODEFROY, JEAN-PAUL, interpreter, trading clerk at Trois-Rivières, businessman, comptroller-general of the Communauté des Habitants, naval commander, and counsellor; b. *c.* 1602 in Paris, of a family from Normandy; d. in 1668 or shortly before, probably in France.

He was the son of Robert Godefroy, who was king's counsellor and treasurer-general for supplementary war expenses, and, in 1627, one of the Compagnie des Cent-Associés, and of Marie Marteau, of the parish of Saint-Nicolas-des-Champs in Paris.

Several historians have settled on 1626 as the date of Jean-Paul Godefroy's arrival in New France. It is nevertheless quite possible that he came as early as 1623. Indeed CHAMPLAIN, in his *Voyages*, speaks in that year of "a sailor named Jean Paul," whom Laverdière identifies, somewhat hastily perhaps, as Godefroy. In any event it is certain that, even before the KIRKE episode [see SIR DAVID KIRKE], Godefroy was one of Champlain's interpreters, and returned to Europe with him in 1629.

Did Godefroy come back to Quebec in 1633 as has been claimed? We do not know. But it is known that in 1636 he was at Trois-Rivières serving as a trading clerk. The *Jesuit Relations* allude to his apostolic zeal among the Indians, over whom he had great influence by virtue of his complete mastery of their language and his athletic prowess.

Champlain's erstwhile interpreter continued to interest himself in trade. In 1644 the Communauté des Habitants sent him, together with PIERRE LEGARDEUR de Repentigny, to France as its delegate to seek certain changes in the trading monopoly, and at the same time, if possible, to obtain the return to the colony of the Recollets. Although unsuccessful in the latter respect, the Godefroy-Legardeur mission did secure for the Habitants a very favourable agreement with the Compagnie des Cent-Associés (1645). We find Godefroy going to France again in 1650 to request, although with no more success than

Godefroy de Lintot

before, the return of the Recollets, to whom it was proposed to entrust all parish duties.

In addition to being one of the leading members of the Communauté des Habitants, of which he was comptroller-general in 1648, Godefroy maintained a personal interest in the fur trade, in sealing, and in the cod-fisheries. As the owner of at least one ship, he joined forces with LOUIS D'AILLEBOUST and JEAN BOURDON in 1653 to fish for cod. Their association aimed at creating a triangular trade between Canada, the West Indies, and France. The outcome of this bold plan is, however, unknown.

Being an enterprising individual and a colonial of far-ranging ideas, Godefroy was often called upon to exercise important functions: after serving as a delegate to France in 1644 and 1650, as comptroller-general of the Communauté and member of the colony's first council in 1648 and as admiral of the fleet in 1649, he was entrusted in 1651 with the delicate mission of meeting with the representatives of the New England colonies.

Since 1647 negotiations had in fact been taking place between the New England colonies and New France with the idea of establishing commercial relations. The council of New France, while favourable to the project, was nevertheless insisting that the commercial agreement be accompanied by a defensive and offensive alliance against the Iroquois and such other tribes as were hostile to the Christian Indians. On 20 June 1651 the council empowered Jean-Paul Godefroy and the Jesuit Gabriel DRUILLETTES to meet the representatives of New England in order to bring the discussions to a successful conclusion. On 30 Oct. 1651 Godefroy returned. The mission had been a failure; the English refused to fight the Iroquois.

In 1652 Godefroy was churchwarden of the parish of Quebec, but after that date he is mentioned only occasionally, once in 1653 and once in 1657. It appears likely that about this time he settled in France with his wife, Marie-Madeleine Legardeur de Repentigny, whom he had married at Quebec on 3 Oct. 1646, and with his daughter Barbe. As for his second daughter, Charlotte, she was probably entrusted to the Ursulines of Quebec, in whose community she later became a nun.

Jean-Paul Godefroy died sometime before 23 Oct. 1668, apparently in France.

ANDRÉ VACHON

APQ, Manuscrits concernant la Nouvelle-France, I. ASQ, Séminaire, VI, 6a. Champlain, *Œuvres* (Laverdière), VI, 58. *JR* (Thwaites), IX, 33, 57. *Papier terrier de la Cie des I.O.* (P.-G. Roy), 272f., 276. Lanctot, *Histoire du Canada*, I, 272. Le Jeune, *Dictionnaire*. P.-G. Roy, "Jean-Paul Godefroy," *BRH*, X (1904), 246–50. Benjamin Sulte, "Les interprètes du temps de Champlain," *RSCT*, 1st ser., I (1882–83), sect.I, 53.

GODEFROY DE LINTOT, JEAN (not "Jean-Baptiste" as he has usually been called by historians on the authority of the 1666 census; "Lintot," from the name of a small municipality in the district of Caux, and not "Linctot"), interpreter, seigneur, member of the Communauté des Habitants; b. 1607 or 1608, son of Pierre Godefroy, esquire, and of Perrette Cavelier of Lintot, district of Caux in Normandy; d. 1681 at Trois-Rivières.

Brother of THOMAS GODEFROY de Normanville, Jean Godefroy arrived in New France with him about 1626 and served under CHAMPLAIN in the capacity of interpreter. After the capture of Quebec by the KIRKES in 1629, Jean Godefroy stayed on in the colony, living in the woods with the Indians.

Soon after the return of the French, Godefroy settled at Trois-Rivières (1633?), where he was to spend the rest of his life. On two occasions in 1636, he is referred to as a "settler at Trois-Rivières," where he was furthermore granted a seigneury on 1 Dec. 1637.

Having become a seigneur-settler, the former interpreter turned to clearing the land, although continuing to trade in furs. From 1646 on, together with his relative JEAN-PAUL GODEFROY, he was a member of the Communauté des Habitants.

Head of the Godefroy de Tonnancour family, Jean Godefroy had married, probably towards the end of 1636 (the private marriage contract is dated 15 December), Marie Leneuf, daughter of Mathieu Leneuf, Sieur du Hérisson, and of Jeanne Le Marchant of Caen, Normandy, and sister of MICHEL LENEUF. Out of this marriage there were born between 1637 and 1658 11 children, of whom 8 were sons who almost all distinguished themselves in the service of New France.

Jean Godefroy's worth was recognized by Intendant TALON, who in 1668 obtained letters of nobility for the former interpreter and his family; unfortunately, because of an administrative error, these letters could not be registered within the required time and were, theoretically, cancelled. In practice, however, the intendants DUCHESNEAU and Demeulle*, in 1681 and 1685, as well as the king himself, officially recognized the Godefroy arms in 1718.

Participation in the fur trade and the cultivation of his seigneury had not brought wealth to Godefroy. In 1672 the governor, BUADE de Frontenac commended him to the king's generosity, as "one of the first to have come to this colony . . . , burdened with a very large family, having several daughters and six sons [two others having died, one sometime before 1655, the other in 1661], all of whom are courageous men who are the first to offer to go on any expedition ..., there being no better canoemen in the whole colony"; the Sieur Godefroy however "is not too comfortably off, [having] a daughter whom he cannot marry because he has nothing to give her as a dowry." The king turned a deaf ear to this request.

Godefroy lived on his lands until 1681, dying shortly after 8 July of that year. His wife died at Trois-Rivières on 27 Oct. 1688.

ANDRÉ VACHON

ASQ, Documents Faribault, *passim.* Correspondance de Frontenac (1672–82), APQ *Rapport, 1926–27,* 17. Correspondance de Talon, APQ *Rapport, 1930–31,* 88. *Lettres de noblesse* (P.-G. Roy), I, 197–213. *Ord. comm.* (P.-G. Roy), I, 293f. *Papier terrier de la Cie des I.O.* (P.-G. Roy), 286–89. P.-G. Roy, *La famille Godefroy de Tonnancour* (Lévis, 1904), 7–10. Benjamin Sulte, "Un mariage d'autrefois," *Revue de Montréal,* IV (1880), 357–62; *Mélanges historiques* (Malchelosse), XI. Roy and Sulte state that Jean Godefroy was a member of the Conseil de la Nouvelle-France. Both have confused Godefroy de Lintot with his relative JEAN-PAUL GODEFROY.

GODEFROY DE NORMANVILLE, THOMAS, interpreter, brother of JEAN GODEFROY de Lintot; b. *c.* 1610 at Lintot in the district of Caux, Normandy; d. 1652 in the Iroquois country.

Thomas Godefroy arrived in New France about 1626, together with his elder brother, Jean Godefroy. After serving CHAMPLAIN as an interpreter, he went to live among the Indians while Quebec was under English occupation from 1629 to 1632. When the French returned he settled in the Trois-Rivières region, as did his brother and his relative JEAN-PAUL GODEFROY. But, unlike these, he continued to act as an interpreter.

Normanville was one of those go-betweens or interpreters (*truchements*) of the early days of New France who were so well able to reconcile the interests of business and religion. One often finds him assisting and even replacing missionaries; he catechized Indians, led them in prayer, sometimes even baptized them. Speaking Algonkian, Iroquoian, and in all probability Huron, he rendered invaluable service to the colony.

His bravery was well known. On three occasions he fell into the hands of the Iroquois: in February 1641, when he was captured with his companion, François MARGUERIE; in the spring of 1648, and in August 1652. On the first two occasions he escaped without too much difficulty. In 1652, however, the Iroquois carried him away to their cantons and killed him.

In 1641–42, Normanville had accompanied Father PAUL LE JEUNE to France on a trip made for "the common and public weal of the colony," and in 1651, he, along with Father BUTEUX and three other Frenchmen, had been the first white men to travel up the St. Maurice River as far as the territory of the Attikamegues.

ANDRÉ VACHON

APQ, Coll. de pièces jud. et not., 2158. Dollier de Casson, *Histoire du Montréal,* 66f. *JR* (Thwaites), XXI, 23–45, XXIV, 197, XXVII, 263, XXXVIII, 59. *Papier terrier de la Cie des I.O.* (P.-G. Roy), 287. P.-G. Roy, *La famille Godefroy de Tonnancour* (Lévis, 1904), 118–23. Sulte, *Mélanges historiques* (Malchelosse), XI.

GODEFROY DE VIEUXPONT, JACQUES, fur-trader and interpreter, son of JEAN GODEFROY de Lintot; baptized on 6 March 1641 at Trois-Rivières; d. in 1661 to the north of that town.

In the spring of 1661, while "on a fur-trading expedition," he left Trois-Rivières with one Frenchman and some 30 Attikamegue Indians. On the way the group was attacked by a band of 80 Iroquois. The fight was bitter and lasted 48 hours. According to the *Relation,* had it not been for an unfortunate dissension between two chiefs, the courage of the Indians and of the two Frenchmen would have assured them of victory. Jacques Godefroy displayed admirable coolness and boldness; but finally, with several bullets in his body, he died in the arms of his companions. One lone Attikamegue survived to bring the news to Trois-Rivières. Twenty-four Iroquois had perished in the skirmish.

ANDRÉ VACHON

JR (Thwaites), XLVI, 208–10. P.-G. Roy, *La famille Godefroy de Tonnancour* (Lévis, 1904).

GODET, ROLLAND, soldier, notary and clerk of court 1651–53.

In 1651 Governor JEAN DE LAUSON had created at Quebec a seneschal's court of justice. Godet was its first notary, and in addition functioned as its clerk. Between 16 Jan. 1652 and 23 June 1653 he received 19 acts. This "soldat notaire," as he was styled by the Jesuit de QUEN, may also have been the secretary of the governor, but we have found no document confirming this assertion, made by the archivist of the province of Quebec. It is not known where Godet came from and what became of him after the month of June 1653.

ANDRÉ VACHON

Godet Des Maretz

AJQ, Greffe de Rolland Godet, 1652–53. APQ, Coll. de pièces jud. et not., 2160. "Les notaires au Canada," APQ *Rapport*, *1921–22*, 16, J.-E. Roy, *Histoire du notariat*, I, 45f.

GODET DES MARETZ (Desmarets, Desmarais), CLAUDE DE, infantry officer, trader, son-in-law of François Gravé Du Pont; d. 1627 or shortly before.

Descendant of a noble family, he was the eldest son of Cléophas de Godet Des Maretz, a lawyer. He first came to New France in 1609. On his return to Normandy in 1610 he encouraged the preparations being made by the ship-owners of Honfleur for cod-fishing and the fur trade; he lent money to assist in the chartering of ships. Godet Des Maretz crossed over again to Canada in 1610, 1620 and 1623, always with Gravé Du Pont. In 1621 he bore the title of Captain on the Coast of Touque (coastguard captain) in Europe.

By Jeanne Gravé Du Pont, whom he had married when he was an infantry officer, he had two children, Christine and François. The latter, born about 1616, following in his grandfather Gravé's footsteps, went to Canada in 1627 and stayed there until the capture of Quebec by the Kirkes. In 1645 he married Marie de La Marck, had one son, Paul, a future bishop of Chartres, and died 2 July 1652.

Claude de Godet was accompanied on his first voyage to New France by his supposed brother Jean Godet Du Parc. The latter was Champlain's lieutenant, and it was to him that Champlain, before leaving for France in 1610, had confided the command of the fort at Quebec and of the 16 men remaining in it. Du Parc also was in charge of the wintering-over in 1612–13 and was in command at Quebec in 1616. He died 16 Nov. 1652 in France, at Saint-Germain-de-Clairefeuille.

Marcel Hamelin

Champlain, *Œuvres* (Laverdière), 321, 326, 330, 354, 371, 1043. Bréard, *Documents relatifs à la marine normande*. Dionne, *Champlain*, 142, 203, 416, 431. Huguet, *Poutrincourt*.

GOMES, ESTEVÃO (in Spanish Esteban Gómez), Portuguese explorer; b. 1483–84, probably in Oporto; d. 1538 in South America.

In his youth Gomes served on Portuguese ships going to India. Then he left Portugal and entered the service of Spain, being appointed pilot of the Casa de la Contratación in Seville (10 Feb. 1518). He sailed with Magellan in August 1519 but deserted later and brought his ship back to Spain in May 1521.

In 1523, he convinced Charles V that he could find between Florida and Newfoundland a shorter and easier passage to the Isles of Spices than the one discovered by Magellan. For that purpose he built in Bilbao a 75-ton caravel named *La Anunciada*. A detailed account of the sums spent for the building of the caravel, the purchase of supplies, the maintenance of the crew and of the Indian captives, has been found recently in the Archivo de Indias in Seville (*see* Vigneras, 189–207). The caravel sailed from Coruña on 24 Sept. 1524, with 29 men on board, the two leaders of the expedition being Gomes (captain and pilot) and Pedro de Luna (controller).

After making port at Santiago de Cuba to load fresh supplies, the *Anunciada* sailed along the eastern seaboard all the way from Florida to Cape Race. It failed to find a western passage, and returned to Spain, reaching Coruña on 21 Aug. 1525. The voyage had lasted 10 months and 27 days.

The theory generally accepted by historians (Harrisse, Biggar, Ganong, Hoffman, etc.) that Gomes made his voyage north-south, is based on an erroneous statement by Antonio Herrera, and evidence is overwhelmingly against it. (For a discussion of this problem, *see* Vigneras, 196–97). It is most likely that the stop-over at Santiago de Cuba took place on the way to America and not on the return trip, and that Gomes made his voyage south-north, as Verrazzano had done a few months before.

Not wishing to return empty-handed, Gomes kidnapped on the coast of Maine or Nova Scotia a large number of Indians whom he planned to sell as slaves. We know that at least 58 reached Spain alive. These Indians were freed later by order of Charles V.

As a result of Gomes's failure to find a western passage, Spanish maps drawn after his return showed a continuous coastline from Florida to Newfoundland. They also pictured the "Land of Esteban Gómez" which included roughly New England and Nova Scotia. The first map to do so was the "Castiglione Map," drawn by Pedro Ribero in 1525 in Coruña, shortly after Gomes's return.

Alonso de Santa Cruz, in his "Islario general del mundo" (1542?), also gives information relating to Gomes's voyage, and pictures the Nova Scotia peninsula as the "Isla de San Juan." Apparently Gomes did not try to enter Cabot Strait, which looked to him just like another bay, but sailed past it.

In 1535, Gomes sailed to the Rio de la Plata as chief pilot of the armada of Pedro de Mendoza. In February 1537, he accompanied Juan de Ayolas on his famous trek across the Gran Chaco in search of silver and gold. After 14 months, Ayolas, Gomes, and their companions returned to the banks of the Paraguay, where they were all ambushed and killed by the Indians in the spring of 1538.

L.-A. VIGNERAS

Archivo de Indias (Sevilla), Patronato real 37, Contaduria 2, 425, 426, 427. Alonso de Santa Cruz, "Islario general de todas las islas del mundo," in *Precursors* (Biggar), 183–94 and Henry Harrisse, *The discovery of North America: a critical, documentary, and historic investigation, with an essay on the cartography of the new world* . . . (London, 1892), 243–48. Ganong, "Crucial maps," IV. J. Toribio Medina, *El Portugués Esteban Gómez al servicio de España* (Santiago de Chile, 1908). *Portugaliae monumenta cartographica*, comp. A. Cortesão et A. Teixeira de Mota (5v., Lisboa, 1960–62), I, 95–98, plate 37. *Precursors* (Biggar), xxv–xxix, 183–94. L.-A. Vigneras, "El viaje de Esteban Gómez a Norte América," *Revista de Indias*, LXVIII (1957), 189–207.

GONSALES (Gonsalves, Gonçalves) JOÃO, Portuguese explorer; fl. 1501–2.

It is known that Gonsales sailed for the shores of Newfoundland, that he was granted a pension of £10 a year for his good services, and that although born in the Azores, he was allowed to assume English nationality so long as he paid English taxes. Documentary mention of him occurs in letters-patent issued by Henry VII of England 19 March 1501 giving rights of exploration to three merchants of Bristol, Richard Warde, Thomas Asshehurst, and John Thomas, and to three Portuguese explorers, João FERNANDES, Francisco Fernandes, and "John Gunsalus, born Isle of Surrys" (Azores). The voyage was sufficiently successful to warrant a payment "to men of bristoll that found thisle" on 7 Jan. 1502 (BM, Add. MS 7099) and another payment on 26 Sept. 1502 to "ffraunceys ffernandus and John Guidisalvus" as well as the issue of a second charter dated 9 Dec. 1502 in favour of the syndicate of two Bristol merchants, Hugh ELIOT and Thomas Asshehurst, and two Portuguese, Gonsales and Francisco Fernandes. The expedition sailed from Bristol early in 1503 but nothing is known of the outcome.

SYLVIA SEELEY

Documents are printed in Henry Harrisse, *John Cabot, the discoverer of North America, and Sebastian Cabot his son* (London, 1896); *Precursors* (Biggar); and Williamson, *Voyages of the Cabots* (1929). See also Hoffman, *Cabot to Cartier*.

GORST, THOMAS, employee of the HBC and author of detailed accounts of life in James Bay during 1670–71 and 1672–75; fl. c. 1668–87.

Gorst was a passenger in the *Eaglet* which was forced by storm damage to abandon the precharter voyage of 1668, but he apparently sailed again in 1669, this time in the *Wivenhoe*, on Captain William Stannard's second abortive attempt to reach Hudson Bay (HBC Arch., A.14/1, f.35).

In 1670 Gorst sailed in the *Prince Rupert* to Charles Fort where he spent the trading season of 1670–71, and before returning to London he accompanied Governor Charles BAYLY on an exploration of the coast and islands of James Bay. In 1672 he again went to Rupert River where he was employed first as Bayly's secretary and later, during 1674–75, as Governor William LYDALL's storekeeper.

Gorst came home in 1675 and in 1676, as purser of the *Prince Rupert*, was associated with Capt. Thomas SHEPARD in the abortive search for the elusive Busse Island (*ibid.*, A.15/1, p. 4). After Gorst's return in the same year from this voyage his employment was terminated. He applied for work in 1680, but was not re-engaged as his demands were too high. He was presumably identical, however, with the Thomas Gorst who went to James Bay in 1685 and who was captured by the French in 1686. Nothing more is known of him after 1687, by which time he had been released and sent to Port Nelson, where he may have died.

ALICE M. JOHNSON

John Oldmixon used information from Gorst's journals for 1670–71 and 1672–75 in vol. I of *The British Empire in America* . . . (London, 1708). For a reprint of the relevant part see: *Documents relating to Hudson Bay* (Tyrrell), 383–97. A contemporary manuscript "Extract" from the 1670–71 journal is among the papers of the 17th-century experimental philosopher Robert Hooke, in the Guildhall Library, London. The "Extract" is printed in Nute, *Caesars of the wilderness*, 286–92. Information on Gorst will also be found in HBRS, V (Rich); VIII (Rich), 50, 52, 309, 310; XI (Rich and Johnson).

GOUPIL, RENÉ, surgeon, brother, Jesuit, missionary and martyr; canonized by Pope Pius XI on 29 June 1930; b. 13 May 1608 in the little town of Saint-Martin in the diocese of Angers; d. 29 Sept. 1642 in the Iroquois country.

We know for certain that René Goupil was already a surgeon at the time he entered the noviciate at Paris on 16 March 1639. His name does not appear in the official lists for the ensuing years. But a note preserved in the archives of the Jesuits of Chantilly, near Paris, informs us that he had to discontinue his noviciate because he was afflicted with deafness: "*Renatus Goupil a tirocinio Parisiensi exclusus erat, quia surdaster.*"

Grand Agnier

When he arrived in Canada in 1640 he seems to have sought to carry out his missionary vocation as a layman. And all the evidence inclines us to believe that he was bound to the Society by the promise of the *donnés* ("given men"). We find him at the Saint-Joseph de Sillery mission, near Quebec, from 1640 to 1642. He was in the service of the missionaries, who valued above all his gifts as a surgeon.

On 1 Aug. 1642, he left Trois-Rivières along with Isaac JOGUES, Guillaume Couture*, several Huron chiefs, among them Eustache AHATSISTARI and Joseph Teondechoren, and the latter's niece, daughter of the famous Joseph CHIWATENHA, Thérèse OIONHATON, who had been trained in the practice of the Christian virtues by the Ursulines. This flotilla, which comprised 12 canoes and included about 40 persons, set out for the Huron country where Goupil was henceforth to follow his surgeon's calling. A few days later the whole party fell into the hands of Iroquois who carried Goupil off into their own territory. There, at Ossernenon (Auriesville, N.Y.), he met his death by the hatchet of an Iroquois who had been provoked by seeing him make the sign of the cross over a child. This was on 29 Sept. 1642. A few days earlier, he had taken his religious vows before St. Isaac Jogues. He is venerated as the first Jesuit martyr in Canada.

The account of his death, contained in the *Relation* for 1643, prompted the coming to Canada of one of his comrades: " . . . another young surgeon, well versed in his art, and well known in the Hospital at Orléans, where he has given proofs of his virtue and of his competence, has chosen to take the place of his comrade; he has crossed into New France. . . ." This text, in conjunction with that in the Society's list, is sufficient to establish that Goupil had studied surgery and that he was not merely a barber-surgeon.

LÉON POULIOT

For the life, virtues, and death of René Goupil one may profitably consult the *Relations* for 1643 and 1647 (*JR* (Thwaites), XXIII, XXIV, XXXI) and ACSM, "Mémoires touchant la mort et les vertus des pères Isaac Jogues . . ." (Ragueneau), repr. APQ *Rapport, 1924–25*, 1, 3, 30, 34, 38, 89–93. But the most important document is undoubtedly the biographical note devoted to him by St. Isaac Jogues (*JR* (Thwaites), XXVIII, 116–34), which is reprinted in *Jésuites de la N.-F.* (Roustang), 254–61. Archivum Romanum Societatis Iesu, codex Franc. 22, f. 359v. *Positio causæ*.

GRAND AGNIER, LE. *See* TOGOUIROUI

"GRANDE GUEULE" ("Big Mouth"). *See* OTREOUTI

GRANDFONTAINE, HECTOR D'ANDIGNÉ DE. *See* ANDIGNÉ

GRANDMAISON, ÉLÉONORE DE, seigneuresse, in turn the wife of Antoine Boudier de Beauregard, François de Chavigny de Berchereau, Jacques Gourdeau de Beaulieu, and Jacques de Cailhault de La Tesserie; b. *c.* 1620 at Clamecy, in Nivernais; d. 1692 at Quebec.

She was still in her teens at the time of her first marriage, in France, to Antoine Boudier de Beauregard, of whom little is known.

She very soon became a widow, and married again, probably in 1640; her second husband was François de Chavigny de Berchereau, born about 1615. They went to New France in the spring or summer of the following year. As early as December 1640 they had received from the Compagnie de la Nouvelle-France grants of land in the town and outskirts of Quebec, as well as at Sillery, and a seigneury on the north shore of the St. Lawrence, 15 leagues from Quebec. This fief was later ceded to Chavigny's son-in-law, Jacques-Alexis Fleury* d'Eschambault, who gave it his name. In 1647 the company granted Chavigny a further extension of this fief. On 24 June of the same year Governor HUAULT de Montmagny granted him two acres fronting on the Cap-Rouge road. Finally in March 1649 Olivier LETARDIF, in the name of the seigneurs of the Île d'Orléans, made over to Chavigny and his wife a seigneury (later given the name of the Beaulieu fief) on the western extremity of the island.

Chavigny was present in May 1649 with JEAN BOURDON, the chief engineer of New France, at the signing of the report drawn up by Governor LOUIS D'AILLEBOUST to fix the boundaries of the fief granted to the Jesuits at La Prairie-de-la-Magdeleine (now Laprairie, near Montreal).

Éléonore de Grandmaison's second husband stood high in the favour of M. de Montmagny, who chose him as his replacement at the head of the colony during his absences. When the Conseil de Québec was created in 1648, Chavigny was summoned to sit on it with ROBERT GIFFARD and JEAN-PAUL GODEFROY. Like CHOMEDEY de Maisonneuve, Jeanne MANCE, and Marguerite BOURGEOYS, he came from Champagne, and was their friend and counsellor.

Chavigny and his wife resided first at Sillery, then, in 1645, on the Chavigny fief, which was an undeniable sign of courage; nobody at that time, because of the Iroquois menace, dared to live far from Quebec. In 1648 they moved to the Île d'Orléans, where no white woman was believed to have dwelt before.

In 1651 François de Chavigny decided to return

to France to have medical treatment. He died at sea. Éléonore de Grandmaison had had by Chavigny five daughters and one son, François,* who accompanied DAUMONT de Saint-Lusson when he took possession of the western territories at the Sainte-Marie falls (Sault Ste. Marie) in 1671.

On 13 Aug. 1652, in the chapel of the Île d'Orléans, Father CHAUMONOT celebrated the marriage of Éléonore de Grandmaison with Jacques Gourdeau de Beaulieu. Gourdeau, the son of a king's attorney at Niort, in Poitou, was born around 1614; as early as 1637 he was at Quebec, where he became a clerk of the seneschal's court and from 1662 a notary. Gourdeau de Beaulieu was assassinated on 29 May 1663 by one of his servants, who to hide his crime set fire to the house.

Four children were born of this marriage, of whom three reached adult age: Antoine, *contrôleur du castor* (beaver) at the *Bureau des Fermes;* Jacques*, seigneur of Beaulieu; and Jeanne-Renée, who married, in 1686, Charles Macart*, councillor in the Conseil Souverain.

Éléonore's fourth marriage was on 15 Oct. 1663, with Jacques de Cailhault de La Tesserie, who was born around 1620 and came from Saint-Herblain near Nantes. The Cailhaults were of the old nobility, and were seigneurs of La Chevrotière, in France. He was an important person in the colony, and was in turn a member of the council of the fur trade and, from 1664 to his death, a member of the Conseil Souverain. In 1666 Cailhault acted as an interpreter for Fathers Beschefer* and BAILLOQUET when a deputation was sent to Fort Orange (Albany). In the same year he discovered a mine at Baie Saint-Paul, where he had been sent by the intendant TALON. In 1668 he swore fealty for the La Grossardière fief, situated on the Île d'Orléans and adjacent to the Beaulieu fief. He died in 1673. His spouse was to survive him by nearly 20 years.

Éléonore appears to have been a woman with a head for business. In 1651 the remnants of the Huron nation took refuge on the Île d'Orléans, under the guidance of Father Chaumonot. Éléonore de Grandmaison rented lands to them, and they lived there until 1656. In October 1674 we find her taking proceedings against Louis JOLLIET and others, in respect of a society for trading in the Ottawa country of which she was a shareholder. She also appeared before the Conseil Souverain, as the agent of her last husband. Nevertheless, she does not seem to have become rich. In 1679 the intendant DUCHESNEAU interceded on her behalf with the minister, calling her a "poor widow." He added: "the lady de La Tesserie [. . .] has children and very little money; her eldest son, named La Chevrotière, who has been urged several times to go into the woods, has always resisted this suggestion despite his poverty."

Éléonore de Grandmaison died in February 1692 at Quebec. She was the ancestress, among others, of Charlotte Fleury* d'Eschambault, wife of the Marquis Pierre de Rigaud* de Vaudreuil de Cavagnial, the last governor of New France.

JEAN-JACQUES LEFEBVRE

JR (Thwaites), XI, 68, 278; XVIII, 255; XXVII, 311f.; XXXVII, 92. *Jug. et délib.*, I, 20, 118, 196, 863, *et passim.* P.-G. Roy, *Inv. concessions.* L.-E. Bois, *L'Île d'Orleans* (Québec, 1895). P.-G. Roy, *La famille de Chavigny de la Chevrotière* (Lévis, 1916); "François de Chavigny de Berchereau," *BRH,* XXI (1915), 311–17; *L'Île d'Orléans* (Québec, 1928). Sulte, *Hist. des Can. fr.*, II, 80, *et passim.* Tanguay, *Dictionnaire*, I, 163, 186, 279. L.-P. Turcotte, *Histoire de l'île d'Orléans* (Québec, 1867).

GRANDPRÉ, LA COURT DE PRÉ-RAVILLON ET DE. *See* LA COURT

GRANDPRÉ, LAMBERT BOUCHER DE. *See* BOUCHER

"GRANGULA" ("Grangular"). *See* OTREOUTI

"THE GRAPE." *See* CHOMINA

GRAVÉ DU PONT, (also called **Dupont-Gravé, Gravé Le Pont, Pont-Gravé**, or simply **Le Pont** or **Gravé**), **FRANÇOIS**, "noble homme," a captain in the navy, in command at Tadoussac in 1603, at Port-Royal in 1605–6 and at Quebec in 1619–20; b. *c.* 1554 at Saint-Malo; d. in France sometime after 1629.

Gravé Du Pont had borne arms before becoming a merchant. He came up the St. Lawrence to trade furs at a very early date, reaching Trois-Rivières before 1599. CHAMPLAIN credits him with playing a decisive role in obtaining the trading monopoly for PIERRE CHAUVIN DE TONNETUIT, which explains the fact that Troilus de LA ROCHE de Mesgouez, feeling that his rights had been encroached upon, accused François Gravé of betraying "all those traders from Saint-Malo who had been his partners." In 1600 Gravé Du Pont left Saint-Malo to take up residence at Honfleur. In the spring of this same year, he sailed for Tadoussac with Chauvin. He would have liked to go farther up the river, but his partner refused to do any exploring.

Gravé Du Pont

In 1603 we find Gravé Du Pont in the service of Aymar de Chaste, the new holder of the monopoly: the latter was in charge of the expedition, which Champlain had joined merely as an observer, and brought out with him two Indians whom he had taken to France on a previous voyage; with Champlain, François Gravé ascended the river as far as the falls later called Saint-Louis and made a new inventory of the St. Lawrence River.

After de Chaste's death, Gravé became the deputy of the Sieur DU GUA de Monts, the newest successful bidder for the trading rights. On his 1604 voyage, he concerned himself exclusively with trading. In 1605 he brought supplies to the Acadian colony, and along with Champlain, he chose Port-Royal as the site for a new settlement; in 1605 and 1606, de Monts entrusted him with the command of the colony.

François Gravé Du Pont does not turn up in New France again until 1608 when, attempting to drive off the Basques who were trading despite prohibitions, he was defeated and wounded; in the autumn he returned to France, taking with him DUVAL's accomplices in the plot against Champlain. From 1609 to 1618 inclusive, he came back into the St. Lawrence every year. In 1619 the merchants joined together to name him to replace Champlain at Quebec; the latter protested "that as far as the Sieur du Pont is concerned, I am his friend & his age will make me respect him like my father: but as for agreeing that he be given what by right & in all reason belongs to me, I shall not stand for it. . . . The Sieur du Pont & I having in the past lived on friendly terms, I want to continue to do so." Champlain was obliged to remain in France, and Gravé was in command of the colony at Quebec until the spring of 1620, when Champlain presented himself, bearing a commission naming him lieutenant to the viceroy.

Another conflict occurred the following year. The trading monopoly now belonged to the de CAËNS, but Gravé arrived in the St. Lawrence to traffic in the name of the former associates. Champlain attempted to negotiate, but GUILLAUME DE CAËN confiscated François Gravé's ship and then, disillusioned, returned it to him. When the de Caën company was merged by the king with that of the former associates, Gravé Du Pont entered Guillaume de Caën's service, working for him continuously until 1629. He passed the winter at Quebec in 1622–23, returned in 1624, then spent the winter there again in 1625–26. Next Gravé, more than 70 years old, and having had heart trouble in Acadia and suffering badly from gout (this ailment had been particularly violent in the previous few years) reappeared at Quebec in 1627, to the surprise of all. As a result of his long experience with the Indians, Gravé was an indispensable person; it was for this reason that de Caën had asked him to come back once more. He remained at Quebec until 1629, suffering both from the famine and from his gout. In the spring of 1629, Champlain wanted him to go down the river to Gaspé in a boat fitted with a bedroom and in the care of people who would look after him. Gravé at first accepted, then changed his mind. He was still at Quebec, ill in bed, when it capitulated. Finally he set sail with the Jesuits for Tadoussac and thence to England. We do not know what became of him subsequently.

His unwavering friendship for Champlain, his personal services to the Recollets, the assistance he sometimes gave in exploration when he was responsible only for trading, his popularity with the Indians, all make of Gravé a very likable character; according to SAGARD he was "jovial by nature," even if he did sometimes lose his temper, "drink his liquor straight" and then roar for "relief from the pain of his gout." Despite his old age and his recurrent periods of illness, he astonished his contemporaries by his indomitable energy, which in 1606 earned for him the praise of LESCARBOT in the latter's *Adieu aux François*.

Married to Christine Martin (who was still living in 1677), Gravé Du Pont had at least two children, ROBERT and Jeanne, who later married CLAUDE GODET Des Maretz.

MARCEL TRUDEL

Bréard, *Documents relatifs à la marine normande*, 65, 93–99, 100–34 (*passim*), 223–26 contains the inventory of all documents concerning Gravé Du Pont (no new ones have since come to light). Champlain, *Works* (Biggar), I, 125–65, 422n., 426, and n., *et passim*; II, 11–14, 32–35, 143–48, *et passim*; III, 24ff., 177ff., 228–230, *et passim*; *IV*, 361–66, *et passim*; V, 24–27, 39–48, *et passim*; VI, 29–38, *et passim*. Escrit of La Roche, quoted in Gustave Lanctot, "L'établissement du marquis de La Roche à l'ile de Sable," CHA *Report, 1933*, 40. *JR* (Thwaites), I, 66, 76–80, "La conversion des sauvages"; 168–70; II, 26, 230; IV, 26. Lescarbot, *Histoire* (Tross), II, 426 f., 479–83, 521, 544–46, *et passim*; III, 17, "Les Muses de la Nouvelle-France." Sagard, *Histoire du Canada* (Tross), I, 67, 243; IV, 859–61, 891.

GRAVÉ DU PONT (also called **Pont-Gravé** and **Du Pont-Gravé**), **ROBERT**, naval captain, furtrader, founder of the first European settlement in what is now New Brunswick and possibly the first white man to become completely familiar with the language and customs of the Etchemin (Malecite) Indians; b. *c*. 1585 at Saint-Malo, the son of

François Gravé Du Pont and Christine Martin; d. 9 Nov. 1621.

In the spring of 1606 he sailed for Acadia with Jean de Biencourt de Poutrincourt. That fall he accompanied Champlain and Poutrincourt on a voyage of exploration along the coast to Cape Cod and had part of his hand blown off when his musket exploded during an attack by some 400 Indians. He returned with the party to Port-Royal, and there became active in the fur trade.

By 1610 his trading activities had concentrated on the Saint John River and in that year he was arrested by Poutrincourt following complaints lodged by the Etchemins that Gravé had abducted one of their women. It was also felt that his loose morals and defiance of the law were creating a bad impression of the white man among the Indians. Gravé escaped and went to live among the Indians whom he endeavoured to turn against French authority and the efforts being made to convert them.

When Father Biard arrived in Acadia in the spring of 1611, he learned of this situation and a few weeks later, he persuaded the governor to pardon Gravé. This was only achieved after heated discussion during which Poutrincourt voiced his strong objection to Biard's interfering in civil matters. Gravé then gave himself up and swore to recognize Poutrincourt's authority. Later that same year, however, word reached Charles de Biencourt, who had been left in charge in Acadia, that Gravé was plotting to overthrow the Poutrincourts. Louis Hébert was sent with a force of men to capture him at Emenenic (Caton's Island) on the Saint John River. This trading station organized by young Gravé was the first attempt at settlement yet made in New Brunswick. Hébert captured the post but both Gravé and his aide, Capt. Merveille, were absent, although details of the plot were confessed by the man left in charge of the post. On 3 Oct. 1611, Biencourt organized a force of 16 men and, accompanied by Father Biard and two Indian guides, they set out for Gravé's post on the Saint John. Again, both Gravé and Capt. Merveille were absent, but Merveille was captured that evening, Gravé remaining at large. Father Biard admired Gravé's "great physical and mental strength" and was relying on him to serve as his interpreter with the local Indians. He therefore went to find him after receiving Biencourt's word that he would not be harmed. A few days later he returned with Gravé who was pardoned after promising to reform.

Gravé continued to live at his post on the Saint John until 1618, apparently making regular trips to France with furs obtained there. In 1619 he had command of the *Espérance* sent with a French expedition to the East Indies. His ship was burned there by the Dutch in 1621 and he died at sea soon afterwards.

George MacBeath

JR (Thwaites). Lescarbot, *History* (Grant). Bréard, *Documents relatifs à la Marine normande*, 94, 215–20, 226. Huguet, *Poutrincourt*.

THE GREAT MOHAWK. *See* Togouiroui

GROSEILLIERS, MÉDARD CHOUART DES. *See* Chouart

GUENET, MARIE, *dite* de Saint-Ignace, Hospitaller of the Augustine order; b. 28 Oct. 1610 at Rouen, daughter of Roger Guenet, counsellor in the Parlement, and of Anne Desloges; d. at the age of 36 at the Hôtel-Dieu in Québec.

It is told of Marie Guenet that even when she was very young she could not bear to see a poor person without being inconsolable if he were not helped. If her parents were willing she would "run and give everything she can lay hands on, however valuable it may be." Intending to devote her life to the service of God and of her fellow-man, she turned her thoughts before the age of 14 to the Hôtel-Dieu of Dieppe. After a long wait, she secured her father's consent and entered the noviciate at Dieppe in 1626. She was to make her solemn religious vows there, 19 March 1628.

In 1633 the plague broke out at Dieppe. The hospital was full. Turning a deaf ear to all remonstrances, Marie saw in the pestilence an urgent invitation to sacrifice herself. But the hardships of this era, combined with the demands of hospital service in these periods of epidemics, overcame the strength of the young nun. Struck down by a disease thought to be fatal, she recovered after making a vow to devote her life to the assistance and the conversion of the Indians of the New World, if her superiors gave their approval.

Already the secular foundress of the Hôtel-Dieu of Quebec, the Duchesse d'Aiguillon, had assured herself at Dieppe of the support of the Hospitallers. She obtained from the Cent-Associés the necessary site in the centre of Quebec, and a fief on the outskirts. The founding agreement was signed in Paris 16 Aug. 1637. The enterprise, endowed by the generosity of its benefactress, was launched at Quebec by three Hospitallers: Anne Le Cointre, *dite* de Saint-Bernard, Marie Forestier, *dite* de Saint-Bonaventure-de-Jésus, and Marie Guenet, *dite* de Saint-Ignace, selected by an elective mandate at the Dieppe monastery, 2 Feb. 1639. Their ages were 29, 28, and 22 respectively.

Guenet

Mother de Saint-Ignace was elected and proclaimed first superior of the Hôtel-Dieu of Quebec. The queen, Anne of Austria, at once honoured her by a mark of her extreme benevolence. She wrote to her, promising her protection and asking to be included in her prayers. At the same time the king granted letters patent for "the establishment of the Religious Hospitallers of Dieppe at the Hôtel-Dieu of Quebec." The Duchesse d'Aiguillon, in a letter to the new superior, praised God for the holy resolve she and her companions had taken.

The departing travellers, delayed for two weeks in the roadstead of Dieppe by frightful weather, set sail 4 May 1639 on the flagship *Saint-Joseph*, commanded by Captain Bontemps. They encouraged each other as they bade farewell to the shores of France. "Farewells are the more painful the more they are prolonged" Mother de Saint-Ignace was to say to her sister nuns, "but already our thoughts are winging their way towards those whom we are going to aid." The crossing, made in the company of the first Ursulines, was a most perilous one and lasted three months.

Early in the morning of 1 Aug. 1639, "several rounds fired from swivel-guns and muskets, and a ... fire in the woods" on the Île d'Orléans, alerted Quebec. A scout brought the news. The governor immediately dispatched a specially decorated sloop to meet the nuns. They were greeted by M. de Montmagny [*see* HUAULT], by Father PAUL LE JEUNE, and by an enthusiastic following; after kissing the ground of Quebec, they stopped at the church of Notre-Dame-de-la-Recouvrance to place their apostolate under the protection of the Blessed Virgin.

An epidemic broke out among the Indians. For six whole months the Hospitallers were attending so many smallpox victims that huge bark lodges were set up around the nuns' shelter to receive them.

This rigorous introduction was followed by expulsion from their quarters. In a few hours one night, the church, the governor's chapel, and the Jesuit house were consumed by flames. "This fiery wreck," sighed Father Le Jeune, "reduced us to the hospital." It was pointless to search elsewhere; there was nothing left.

The duchess thought well of a plan to erect the hospital at Sillery, the village favoured by the Indians. It had been the Jesuits' first wish to settle the nomadic tribes there; nothing more was needed in the present situation to persuade Marie de Saint-Ignace to decide upon an immediate transfer and the starting of a building at Sillery: a large stone house, two storeys high, which was still far from finished in December 1640 when the little community, supplemented by two recruits from France, moved in. The fact that the death of the latest arrival, Jeanne de Sainte-Marie (aged 28), occurred in less than eight months is sufficient to indicate the rigours of this initial period.

Furthermore, a wave of Iroquois raids sowed terror and threatened Sillery first of all. Fear was felt for the safety of the Hospitallers. The latter, according to the 1641 *Relation*, nevertheless opened a seminary for little Indian girls who were too far away from that of the Ursulines at Quebec. They were also to take in French girls as boarders, among them two little daughters of ROBERT GIFFARD. The elder of these, MARIE-FRANÇOISE, was to become, at the Hôtel-Dieu a few years later, the first Canadian nun.

The Iroquois peril forced the nuns to return to Quebec. "Remove to their house in Kebec," the *Relation* of 1644 points out, "not without great inconvenience, because the building had as yet but the four walls and the roof." While waiting for their new quarters, the Hospitallers contributed to the progress of construction, helping out as labourers until the ships arrived with additional workmen. An enclosure fenced with stakes allowed the Indians to set up their lodges there, where the sisters carried their meals to them; fear of the Iroquois kept them from going hunting.

After five years this appeared to be the only gain in return for such labour. The achievement may seem slight; it was at best an introduction, a prelude. Marie de Saint-Ignace was to see nothing of the results of the undertaking, but she clearly believed firmly in it.

The last great exertions were too much for the Hospitaller. "Fear that she would die threw us into a state of great affliction, which she readily detected. She herself consoled us in such tender fashion and with such submissiveness to the commandments of God that she charmed us. We asked her for her blessing, and we dissolved into tears as we received it ... after recommending several very practical things to us, she died saying: 'My God, Thy will be done; I am Thine'." This was on 5 Nov. 1646. One incident added to the emotions experienced by her daughters in religion: "The very day ... we were to move into our house ... She was the first to be carried in, for ... the burial service."

The *Relations* devoted a chapter each year to the hospital. Mother de Saint-Ignace's accounts furnished the information for it. Father VIMONT, in 1647, expressed his appreciation freely and reported, with respect to the last moments of this faithful soul, her "incredible satisfaction to die in Canada, in the service of these poor Barbarians" whom she loved. "She has been," he added, "equally regretted by the French and by the Savages, her charity having won all hearts."

Mother de Saint-Ignace furnished the bulk of the information offered to historians of New France by *Les Annales*. Her "notes or memoirs," compiled by the annalist, constituted their source.

SAINTE-JEANNE-DE-CHANTAL MARTIN, O.S.A.

Archives des Hospitalières de Dieppe, "Précis de ce qui s'est passé depuis l'an 800, jusqu'à l'an 1645, où il est parlé de quelle manière nous avons été établies dans cette ville de Dieppe au commencement de ce siècle. Tiré de nos Annales de la Maison de Dieppe, première de notre institut." AHDQ, Parchemin, T. 2, C. 50, "Lettre patente du roy Louis XIII pour la fondation de l'Hôtel-Dieu de Québec, 15 avril 1639," T.21, C.500, "Notices biographiques des premières Mères." *Constitutions de la congrégation des religieuses hospitalières de la miséricorde de Jésus de l'ordre de saint Augustin*, précédées de la bulle du pape Alexandre VII et d'une préface de 1666 (Québec, 1923). *JR* (Thwaites). Juchereau, *Annales* (Jamet). René Piacentini, *Origines et évolution de l'hospitalisation: les chanoinesses augustines de la miséricorde de Jésus* (Les grands ordres monastiques et instituts religieux, XLVIII, Paris, 1957).

GUER. See KIRKE

GUILLEMOT, GUILLAUME, (also called **Du Plessis-Kerbodot**), governor of Trois-Rivières 1651–52; killed by the Iroquois on 19 Aug. 1652.

We must accept the name that he signed and under which he is known in our history: Guillaume Guillemot, seigneur of the Kerbodot fief in Brittany. If he has been called Du Plessis, it is because the word *plessis*, in Norman, means village, fief, like the Breton word *ker*. In the index of the *Jesuit Relations* (Thwaites), this person has been confused with DU PLESSIS-BOCHART. The identity of each has subsequently been established beyond dispute.

Guillaume Guillemot certainly enjoyed great prestige in official circles, for on 2 Jan. 1651 his name was proposed to the king by the Compagnie des Cent-Associés, together with those of JEAN DE LAUSON (senior) and Pierre Robinau, as a replacement for LOUIS D'AILLEBOUST as governor of New France. M. de Lauson was named to this office, but Du Plessis-Kerbodot was appointed governor of Trois-Rivières. He arrived at Quebec on 13 October of the same year, and his presence was noted at Trois-Rivières on 1 December. This latter post was no sinecure, and the new governor wanted above all to protect the interests of the Compagnie des Cent-Associés there. He quickly realized that he had to force the Indians to make peace, for Trois-Rivières was at that period the outpost against Iroquois attacks. An emergency squad was formed, called the flying column. By virtue of his office, the governor undertook to lead it himself. This was the first mistake on his part, for he was not a soldier and was totally ignorant of Indian tactics.

Despite the warning of a man of experience, Pierre Boucher*, and of a number of other settlers, Kerbodot ordered his flying column blindly to seek out the enemy in the woods around the town. The hastily organized troop obeyed. It comprised some 60 men, including 12 Indians who were allies. On the morning of 19 August they embarked in two sloops and followed the banks of the St. Lawrence. As soon as the troop landed, it fell into the ambush set by the Iroquois, who, following their usual tactics, had been watching its approach. Twenty-two Frenchmen, including the governor himself, were killed outright or taken prisoner.

Du Plessis-Kerbodot had married Étiennette Després in 1647 in Paris, and she had followed him to New France with their two children, Anne and François.

RAYMOND DOUVILLE

JR (Thwaites). *JJ* (Laverdière et Casgrain). Sulte, *Mélanges historiques* (Malchelosse), V, 9–28. Albert Tessier, *Les Trois-Rivières: quatre siècles d'histoire 1535–1935* (Trois Rivières, 1934).

GUY, JOHN, colonizer, explorer, governor of the first English colony in Newfoundland; d. *c*. March 1629.

From the beginning of the 17th century John Guy was prominent in the civic and commercial life of Bristol. In 1603 he was elected to the Common Council on which he served until 1629; he was also a member of the Bristol Society of Merchant Venturers. In 1606, when sheriff of the city, he and the mayor, Thomas James (the father of Capt. Thomas JAMES), became the principal Bristol subscribers to the North Virginia Company. Four years later he was appointed governor of the colony to be established in Newfoundland by the London and Bristol company.

It is possible that Guy was the originator of this movement to colonize Newfoundland. In 1608 he had visited the island and the following year, according to Purchas, he wrote a tract—of which no copy is known—advocating the settlement of Newfoundland. Early in 1610 a petition for a grant of incorporation was submitted to the Privy Council by John Slany, treasurer of the company, and John Guy, as representatives of the two groups of subscribers from London and Bristol. By its charter, sealed in May 1610, the company was granted the whole island, with

Guy

particular emphasis on the area of the Avalon peninsula. Before leaving, Guy received detailed instructions as to the employment of his men and the requirements of a good site. Elaborate provision was also made for the government of the colony: Guy had supreme authority and was to govern without assistance; if he died without naming a successor, his brother Philip, who was also a subscriber to the company, was to be governor. In the event of Philip's death, William Chatchmaid was to succeed.

On 5 July 1610, John and Philip Guy and the other colonists, including COLSTON and probably ROWLEY, sailed from Bristol, reaching Newfoundland in August. The actual choice of site was entrusted to John and, on arrival, he decided on Cuper's Cove (now Cupids) rather than on Colliers Cove, also in Conception Bay. Much of our knowledge of the settlement's early history comes from Guy's letters home, which reveal his preoccupation with making the colony self-supporting. From the outset the planters' industry was remarkable and a tribute to Guy's leadership, which always seems to have been well accepted by his men. The first winter was mild: of the 39 settlers, only 4 died. Their time was occupied in building and fortifying their habitation, in exploring and farming.

Guy returned to England in the late summer of 1611; he was at this time treasurer of the Merchant Venturers. Before leaving, he issued orders for the regulation of the fishery, to reform the disorderly practices of the visiting fishermen and placed his brother, Philip, and William Colston in charge of the colony. Early in 1612 he returned to the island, bringing more colonists.

That summer was a difficult time for Guy because of the raids of the pirate, Peter EASTON. The fishermen ignored Guy's advice to attack the pirate and so suffered heavily. Guy himself was with Easton for 14 days and seems to have won immunity for the colony; there was only one incident when a colonist was shot in error. However, Easton's visit forced Guy to abandon the company's plan to establish a settlement at Renewse that year. He withdrew his men and concentrated on strengthening Cuper's Cove.

Also hindered was the journey of exploration to Trinity Bay which Guy had intended that summer. Not until October did he set out with 18 men, including PEARSON, and 2 boats. He explored Trinity Bay with some care, looking vainly for a passage to Placentia Bay, but his main purpose was to establish contact with the Beothuk Indians, which he did at Bull Arm. George Whittington, one of the colonists, was chosen to go ashore first to convince the Indians that they came in friendship. Guy's journal of the expedition gives a charming account of the encounter, the exchange of gifts, and the shared meal. Some furs were obtained and, after an eventful journey, Guy regained Cuper's Cove late in November. That winter was the most severe yet experienced; 22 of the 62 settlers suffered from scurvy, though only 8 died. In April 1613 Guy suddenly left for England and the expedition which he had intended to lead that summer was abandoned.

It was expected that Guy would return in the autumn of 1613, but in September he was still in Bristol. Probably he did go to Newfoundland early in 1614 but stayed only for the summer, since in December 1614 he was again in Bristol. At this time his relations with the company became strained and Guy complained bitterly of their treatment of himself and the other colonists: he had not received the land promised him nor had the men received their wages. A letter which he wrote in 1614 strongly suggests that his dispute with the company had gone to law (Middleton MSS, Mi X 1/28); however his land must have been allotted to him by 1626, when he bequeathed it to his sons. In 1616 John Slany accused Guy of having deceived the company over the island's mineral resources. About this time John MASON was appointed governor of the colony.

Probably Guy never returned to Newfoundland but he had left the colony firmly established with over 60 inhabitants, both men and women. Cargoes of fish and merchantable timber which would help towards the cost of the enterprise had been sent home; new areas of a little-known country had been explored; a fur trade with the Indians had been begun. By comparison with the careers of the first governors of other such ventures, Guy's had been most successful.

He took up life in Bristol with renewed vigour; in 1618 he served as mayor and, the following year, became an alderman. From December 1620 until 1622, he represented Bristol in the House of Commons and was particularly prominent in the long debates on the bill for the greater liberty of fishing voyages to North America. Guy consistently opposed the bill as jeopardizing the freedom of the Newfoundland planters in the fishery. In September 1621 he represented Bristol in the government inquiry into the decline of trade. He was master of the Merchant Venturers in 1622 and in 1624 he was returned to Parliament for a further year when he again supported the Newfoundland planters in the renewed debate on the fishery.

In February 1626 Guy made a will bequeathing extensive property to his seven children and his wife, Anne; his Seaforest estate in Newfoundland he divided among three of his sons. He attended his last meeting of the Common Council in June 1628, and in May 1629, probate was granted to his wife. A monument was later erected to his memory in St. Stephen's Church, Bristol.

GILLIAN T. CELL

There are letters from John and NICHOLAS GUY, and papers relating to them, at Nottingham University, Middleton MSS, Mi X 1/1-66. John Guy's journal is at Lambeth Palace, MS 250 (ff.406–12 are reproduced in *The New World: a catalogue of an exhibition of books, maps, manuscripts and documents held at Lambeth Palace library between 1 May and 1 December 1957* (London, 1957), 52–64). His will is at Somerset House, P.C.C., 48 Ridley.

Other sources are: PRO, C.O. 1/1. Trinity House, Trans., 1609–25. *Proceedings and debates of the British Parliaments respecting North America*, ed. L. F. Stock (5v., Washington, 1924–41), I. Purchas, *Pilgrimes* (1905–7), XIX. A. B. Beaven, *Bristol lists* (Bristol, 1889). John Latimer, *The history of the Society of Merchant Venturers of the city of Bristol* (Bristol, 1903). J. W. Damer Powell, "John Guy: founder of Newfoundland," *United Empire*, XXIV (1933), 323–27.

GUY, NICHOLAS, one of the first English colonists in Newfoundland; fl. 1612–31.

No relationship can be definitely established between Nicholas and JOHN GUY, though a relationship is very probable. Both Nicholas Guy and his wife were in Newfoundland by 1612 and, on 27 March 1613, a son was born to them—possibly the first English child born in Newfoundland. In 1631 Nicholas was still in Newfoundland and about to enter into partnership with Sir Percival Willoughby, one of the subscribers to the Merchant Venturers company in 1610. Guy was to manage Willoughby's land which consisted of the northern part of the peninsula between Conception and Trinity bays. By 1631 he had already left Cuper's (now Cupids) Cove to settle on Willoughby's land at Carbonear where he was farming profitably. How much longer Nicholas Guy continued to live in Newfoundland is unknown, but he is an identifiable example of a settler who persevered after official interest appears to have died.

GILLIAN T. CELL

[*See* bibliography for JOHN GUY.]

GUYAR (Guyer). *See* GEYER

GUYART, MARIE, *dite* **Marie de l'Incarnation,** Ursuline nun, foundress of the Ursuline order in New France; b. 28 Oct. 1599 at Tours (France); d. 30 April 1672 at Quebec.

A daughter of Florent Guyart, master baker, and of Jeanne Michelet, Marie was baptized in the former church of Saint-Saturnin. Her mother was descended from the Babou de La Bourdaisières, an old and noble family that had distinguished itself in the service of church and state. But Jeanne Michelet had married a simple and honest workingman who was well established and honoured in his guild. The Guyarts gave their seven children, three boys and four girls, a deeply Christian upbringing and a sound education. Marie went to school at an early age. Her earliest recollections are of trundling a hoop in a playground with a companion. One night she saw the Lord in a dream. Bending down to her, he asked her: "Do you want to be mine?" "Yes," she replied. A "yes" which was to make of her existence an uninterrupted series of generous impulses. Marie Guyart was a little girl who was drawn towards divine realities. While still quite young, she used to spend hours telling her "personal matters" to God. Standing on a chair, she would repeat the sermons she had heard in church, and she used to stare after the priests whom she met in the street. What she called "a slight sentiment of prudence" kept her from kissing their footsteps and running after them. Marie early revealed a rich yet balanced character, apt for both mystical experiences and practical deeds. She was indeed a daughter of the first half of the 17th century: a period of chivalry and of good sense, a period in which speculation and action meet in a harmonious synthesis.

At the age of 14, Marie Guyart showed an inclination towards the life of the cloister; but, finding her of a gay and agreeable disposition, her parents thought instead that she was suited for marriage. Even though she was devout, Marie read novels and presented a cheerful exterior to the world. Claude Martin, a master silk-worker, came forward as a suitor, and Marie allowed herself to be contracted in this marriage which did not bring her happiness. She always remained reticent about this period of her life, but her first biographer, Dom Claude Martin, speaks of trials of a rare and new sort. A mystery, which conceals domestic troubles caused by a jealous mother-in-law and financial difficulties which were to terminate in bankruptcy. It is possible that the precarious state of his business brought Claude Martin to his grave. He died in the last months of 1619, after two years of married life, leaving his 19-year-old widow with a son 6 months old. Little Claude, born 2 April, had been the only ray of sunshine in their marriage. As soon

Guyart

as she was free, Marie returned to her father's house and her longings for the life of the cloister became overwhelming. But the pitiful state of her affairs and her infant son kept her from withdrawing from the world. From all sides she was urged to remarry in order to re-establish her financial situation and provide for her son's education. After some hesitation, she decided to follow her inclination towards the secluded life. Retiring to an upper room, she began to read works of piety and to converse closely with God.

Suddenly the Lord burst into her life. She herself relates the mystical experience which brought about what she called her "conversion." One morning as she was going to her work, an irresistible force descended upon her and stopped her in the middle of the street. In a moment the eyes of her spirit were opened and all her faults and imperfections were revealed to her collectively and severally, with "a clearness more certain than any certitude." At the same moment she saw herself immersed in the blood of the Son of God. She confessed to the first priest that she saw in the Chapel of the Feuillants and returned so completely changed that she was no longer the same person. This occurred on 24 March 1620. Marie was only 20 years old. By her dress and her bearing she indicated that she no longer had ambitions for herself in the world. As she had a great deal of talent for business, her sister, who was married to Paul Buisson, the owner of a carrier business, induced her to come to live in her home. At first Marie took upon herself the most humble tasks in the house. In turn cook, maid, and nurse, she would sit down at table with some 30 drivers in order to keep them from uttering blasphemies, and when they were ill she took care of them like a mother. Being already bound to God by the vow of chastity, she also took the vows of poverty and obedience. We can imagine what she had to put up with from her sister and brother-in-law, who suspected nothing. In 1625 Paul Buisson entrusted her with the entire responsibility of his business. There she was, caught up in the worries of business, engaged in conversation with a numerous clientele, on the wharfs along the Loire, even in the Huguenots' shop. She had however the experience of "an inner paradise," and received ineffable revelations concerning the mystery of the Holy Trinity. She was 27, and her son Claude had just turned 8. He was a frail, timid little boy whom his mother prepared gently for the final separation.

Mme Martin knew that the moment for leaving the world was at hand. Aided by the advice of Dom Raymond de Saint-Bernard, a member of the Order of Feuillants, she waited for the ways of the Lord to be made clear. She would undoubtedly have been accepted by the Feuillantines, the nuns of the Order of the Visitation, the Carmelites, or the Benedictine nuns of Beaumont-lez-Tours, but she chose the Ursulines, because a secret voice told her that was what God wanted for her. On 25 January she left her aged father, entrusted her son Claude to the care of her sister, and, completely shattered with grief, entered the noviciate of the Ursulines of Tours. No human explanation can justify such an action. Like Abraham, Marie was obeying divine demands, which were approved by her spiritual adviser and by Bishop Bertrand d'Eschaux of Tours. Recalling this painful episode later, Marie was to admit that she "had suffered a living death." Nothing was more painful for her than her son's flight. Having a presentiment of something unusual, he had run away from home before his mother's departure. He was found again three days later, on the wharfs of Blois. Then the poor child stormed the convent with a band of school boys. In the midst of the uproar Marie could pick out the voice of her son, who was crying aloud: "Give me back my mother, give me back my mother."

Mme Martin became an Ursuline nun under the name Marie de l'Incarnation and took her vows in 1633. Claude continued his schooling with the Jesuits in Rennes. Soon Marie was assistant mistress of novices and instructor in Christian doctrine. She had, however, the secret conviction that the convent of Tours was only a stopping-point for her. Gradually her apostolic vocation became clear. In a dream God took her to a vast country full of mountains, valleys, and heavy fogs. Later the Lord said to her explicitly: "It was Canada that I showed you; you must go there to build a house for Jesus and Mary." The mystery was resolved, the difficulties vanished. The Jesuit *Relations* informed Marie about the missions in New France. Father PONCET de La Rivière enabled her to meet Mme de CHAUVIGNY de La Peltrie, who also was eager to devote her life to the evangelization of little Indian girls. In human terms the undertaking seemed sheer madness: how could one picture frail women on a sea infested with reefs and pirates? Manifold objections sprang up in the way of the project. Certain Jesuit priests wanted to substitute the Ursulines of the Faubourg Saint-Jacques for those of Tours. Mgr d'Eschaux at first turned a deaf ear; the Compagnies des Cent-Associés refused passage to Mme de La Peltrie, who applied too late. Finally Marie de l'Incarnation, Marie SAVONNIÈRES de La Troche *dite* Marie de Saint-Joseph, and Mme de La Peltrie went off to Paris.

They hoped to enlist there a third Ursuline; but the archbishop refused to expose Mother Saint-Jérôme to "the ravages of the sea and of the barbarians." Mother Cécile de Sainte-Croix, an Ursuline from Dieppe, filled out their number at the last minute. Three Hospitallers also sailed for Canada: Mother Marie GUENET *dite* Marie de Saint-Ignace; Anne Le Cointre *dite* Anne de Saint-Bernard; and Marie FORESTIER *dite* Marie de Saint-Bonaventure. On 4 May 1639 the *Saint-Joseph* sailed off to the New World. Marie de l'Incarnation has left a picturesque description of the crossing and of the enormous iceberg which almost smashed the ship. On 1 August 1639 the travellers arrived at Quebec.

Marie de l'Incarnation's apostolic life was thus intimately linked with the history of New France. Mother Marie proved first to be a business woman. She took up residence as best she could in a house in the Lower Town—makeshift accommodation that she subtly called her "Louvre." To ward off the cold the sisters had to sleep in chests lined with serge. In 1642 they moved to the top of the cape, into the handsome convent all in stone, with three floors, 92 ft. long and 28 wide, a marvel for the country. During the night of 31 December fire destroyed the dwelling, the fruit of immense sacrifices. Marie de l'Incarnation started rebuilding. She held out thanks to her energy, ingenuity, and alms. She knew how to draw up contracts and defend her rights against certain gentlemen who tried to take her privileges away from her.

On top of all that she had new and personal ideas about the country's economy. The discovery of mines and salt-pits interested her. She suggested that if she were in the merchants' place, she would export porpoise oil. She herself cultivated a garden, operated a farm, had wells dug. Her correspondence abounds in details of daily life. In our presence she counts her last *sous*, pays the workmen, kneads her barley bread. She even stops to look at her winded oxen. Governors, intendants, and notables of the colony consult her on temporal matters. She had great dreams for France, rejoiced in her compatriots' exploits, measured the progress achieved at Quebec. In 1639 she had arrived in a little village composed of not more than a few houses; in 1663 there was talk of electing a mayor and aldermen. The custom of collecting tithes for the upkeep of the seminary and the founding of parishes had been established, and there were even plans for building a law-court and a prison. "In short all that sounds promising, and is off to a good start . . . ," wrote Marie de l'Incarnation.

With the help of the Jesuits she drew up Constitutions which were suited to New France—a monument of practical and supernatural wisdom. Marie de l'Incarnation was indeed a mystic imbued with a sense of action. For 32 years the whole weight of the responsibility for the foundation rested on her shoulders. She defied Iroquois raids, bad weather, the ill will of men who are skilful in sowing tares in the field of the just.

Marie de l'Incarnation used her talents as a leader for serving souls. It was indeed for this evangelical work that God had supplied her with the gifts of nature and of divine grace. In Canada she emulated the priests of the Society of Jesus, whose confidante and support she was. She accompanied them in her thoughts right into the Huron country, she corresponded with them, even wished to share their martyrdom. The Jesuits were her spiritual advisers and her instructors in Indian languages.

At the grill of the convent parlour Mother Marie received the secrets of the Frenchmen who were entrusted with the administration of the colony. They talked about spiritual matters even more than about their temporal undertakings. MM. Louis D'AILLEBOUST, JEAN BOURDON, PIERRE LEGARDEUR de Repentigny, and Alexandre de PROUVILLE de Tracy regarded her as their best friend. But Marie de l'Incarnation had above all come to educate the little French and Indian girls. Immediately following their arrival at Quebec the Ursulines took in all the young French girls who could be found, to instruct them in godliness and morality. Because of the scarcity of money, the young ladies' board was paid in kind. Hence the quaintness of the records, such as this extract from the year 1646:

Received 13 January for Mlle C's board:
    $3\frac{1}{2}$ cords of firewood.
   "   6 March—4 cords of firewood.
   "   13 March—1 pot of butter
          weighing 12 lbs.
   "   13 November—1 fat pig,
          1 barrel of peas.
   "   . . . .—1 barrel of salted eel.

The Ursulines' boarding-school was first composed of 18 to 20 boarders who paid 120 *livres* per year for their board. As the years passed, the number kept increasing and the task became heavy and pressing. "If it were not for the Ursulines," wrote Mother Marie, "[the young girls] would be in danger for their salvation." The reason for this? Too much freedom was allowed the young girls. On the whole the Canadian girls had "an upright character," and became steadfast in the right when they were aware of it, but sometimes it was necessary to teach them "in one year to read, write, count ... and everything that a girl should know." Before her death Mother Marie had the solace of bestowing the religious habit upon several native-born Canadians who had come to carry on the work.

But Marie de l'Incarnation always kept the best of herself in reserve for the little Indian girls. She received them with open arms, cleaned them up, taxed her ingenuity to understand them, to catechize them, and to make them happy. Her letters brim over with picturesque stories describing the fervour, the struggles, and the pranks of the children of the woods. These documents reveal Mother Marie's deep understanding and her apostolic insight, as well as the mentality of the neophytes. She recommended to all the nuns, especially when dealing with the pupils of the seminary, to use "greetings and little expressions of affection." Often she called them the "delights" of her heart and "the brightest jewels" in her crown.

In 1668 the King's ministers took measures to encourage the Indians to adopt the French way of life. In the Jesuit establishments, in the seminary of Quebec and the Ursuline convent, the experiment proved to be disastrous. "It is however a very difficult thing, if not an impossible one, to adapt the Indians to French customs or to civilize them. We have had more experience with it than anyone else, and we have observed that of a hundred girls who have passed through our hands, we have scarcely civilized one."

The flowers of the woods did not, however, fail to blossom, to Mother Marie's delight. Among others, there was Marie-Madeleine Chrestienne, a former pupil of the Indian seminary of the Ursulines of Quebec, who became the wife of Pierre Boucher*, a future governor of Trois-Rivières.

Mother Marie's apostolate to the adult Indians was also intensive. She catechized them and regaled them with *sagamité* (a dish of corn-meal and meat). When more than 40 years of age, she started to study the Indian languages and mastered them to such a degree that she wrote French-Algonkin, Algonkin-French and Iroquois dictionaries and a catechism in Iroquois. Some of these works disappeared in the fire of 1686, the rest were given to Oblate missionaries who were leaving for the Canadian north.

After the fire in 1650 the Hurons were afraid of losing Marie de l'Incarnation and her companions. Chief Taiearonk addressed them in these moving terms: "Courage, saintly maidens, do not let yourselves be overwhelmed by love for your family, and prove today that your affection for the poor Indians is an act of heavenly charity that is stronger than the bonds of nature." After that, it is understandable that the Hurons of Lorette should have sent a postulatory letter to Pius IX in the autumn of 1875. In recognition of the services that Marie de l'Incarnation had lavished upon their fathers, they requested for her the honours of beatification.

Certainly Marie de l'Incarnation had much to suffer from the Iroquois, who devastated her farms and killed her servants and her best friends. In 1660 her convent was besieged. Each year she wondered in anguish whether they should not have to return to France. The spiritual mother of the Canadian church, she felt the repercussions of all the trials inflicted upon her adopted country.

For 33 years she took part in the unremitting struggles of the French to establish themselves in North America. Her letters recount this vibrant epic of efforts, defeats, victories, and bravado. At the beginning it is the story of the hesitant little colony under the direction of Charles HUAULT de Montmagny. Then came the sacrifice of the martyrs and the arrival of Bishop François de Laval* in 1659. His Excellency had first resided in Mme de La Peltrie's house, a humble dwelling located a few paces from the Ursuline convent. In mentioning this episcopal residence Bishop Laval wrote: "We consider it rich enough because it is sufficient unto our poverty. We have three priests with us, who are our table-companions, two servants, and that is all." Marie de l'Incarnation had lent him her garden, and her perspicacious eye had quickly discerned the Bishop of Petraea's tastes: "I do not say that he is a saint, that would be saying too much; but I will truthfully say that he lives like a saint and apostle." In April 1660 Bishop Laval had paid his first episcopal visit to the Ursulines and had declared that he intended to bring about important changes in the Constitutions of 1646, which had been drawn up with such care by Father JÉRÔME LALEMANT. Having resided in Canada since 1639, Marie de l'Incarnation understood better than the newly arrived Bishop Laval all the basic problems. Without taking "eight months or a year" for reflection, she felt that the proposed changes would ruin the Constitutions. Therefore she wrote, in a respectful but very firm tone: "... the matter has been thoroughly considered and our mind is fully made up: we will not accept it, unless we are pushed to the limits of obedience." Along with tenacity went prudence and the gift of depicting people in a lifelike way: "We are however saying nothing, in order not to embitter matters; for we are dealing with a

Prelate whose piety is so great that, once he is convinced that God's glory is at stake, he will never accept reconsidering the matter, and we shall have to give in, which would be very prejudicial to our observances." Bishop Laval kept the former Constitutions with the exception of five articles. In 1681, nine years after Marie's death, the act of affiliation between the Ursulines of Quebec and those of Paris was to be signed.

After Tracy's expeditions came years of peace and prosperity which were rendered illustrious by the measures initiated by the intendant TALON. Mother Marie had worked very hard. Prolonged penances, illnesses that she had treated casually, had worn her out. What she called her "hepatic flux" was sapping her strength unceasingly. Sometimes her letters contained a bulletin on her health that was far from reassuring; she could no longer remain on her knees, her sight was failing, everything she ate had the bitterness of wormwood. And yet she exulted in the thought that the end was approaching, that soon she could see God face to face. Before dying she went over her life and felt that the time for departing had arrived: the Lord had showered her with mystic favours, the work of the Ursulines was going very well, and her son Claude had become her glory and her delight. He had joined the Benedictines of Saint-Maur in 1641 and had been promoted to the office of superior in 1652. In 1668, as assistant to the superior-general, he had taken his place among the principal superiors of his order. Just before dying, Marie de l'Incarnation sent him an affectionate message: "Tell him that I am carrying him with me in my heart." She said farewell to her little Indian girls and passed away on 30 April 1672, at the age of 72 years and 6 months.

When the funeral ceremony was over, the body was lowered into the vault; but it was shortly brought up again for a portrait to be made, so that "the ray of majesty which God caused to shine forth from her face" should not be buried. Unfortunately the painter who was sent by the Governor, Daniel de RÉMY de Courcelle, was a second-rate artist; he fixed on the canvas only the features of a dead woman. There was no one to make a death mask. The painting of 1672 perished in the flames in 1686. In 1699 the Ursulines of Quebec received another portrait of their venerable Mother: a copy of the original, according to the traditions of the convent. However that may be, this awkwardly retouched replica portrays Marie de l'Incarnation as a woman in her seventies, worn out by age and infirmities. With her eyes shut and her hands swollen, she has lost the halo of transfiguration.

This painting is preserved in the Ursuline convent in Quebec. Neither the engraving by Jean Edelinck, done for the editions of Dom Claude Martin's work (1677 and 1681), nor the portrait by Poilly, made for the Charlevoix monograph (1724), do justice to Marie de l'Incarnation. More successful than his predecessors, the painter Botoni (1878) has given us a Marie de l'Incarnation in ecstasy; but this creation of the imagination does not correspond to the physiognomy which emerges from her letters. In order to get an idea of it, let us instead reread the portrait which Dom Martin left of his mother: "She was," he writes in the *Vie*, "of a good height for one of her sex, grave and majestic in her bearing, which had however nothing ostentatious about it, as it was tempered by a humble and modest gentleness. In her youth, and before her penances and her labours had affected it, her face had been rather beautiful, and even in her old age the regularity of her features showed clearly enough what she had formerly been like. There was however nothing languid about this beauty, but rather one could see in her face the marks of the great courage which she showed whenever an occasion arose for undertaking and suffering anything that she realized to be to God's glory and for the salvation of souls. Her courage was matched by her strength, as she was of a sound temperament and a strong and vigorous physical constitution, suited to bearing up under the great labours which God required of her in service. She was of an agreeable disposition, and although God's continual presence imparted to her a feeling of gravity and restraint which had about it a certain celestial quality, one could not however meet a more accommodating and affable person."

From 1672 on Marie de l'Incarnation was venerated as a saint. The objects that she had used were sought after as relics. Father Jérôme Lalemant, who during almost all her time in Canada had been her spiritual adviser, wrote: "If his Excellency the Bishop had been here, he would not have quit her during her illness, so great was his esteem for her; in his absence M. Henri de BERNIÈRES, his vicar general and superior of the monastery, did everything for her that one may expect from a pastor of souls, and our Society manifested all the proofs of respect and affection which were due to her merit. Furthermore, the memory of the deceased will for ever be blessed in these regions, and as for myself, I have much confidence in her prayers and I hope that she will be of greater help to me in dying in the faith than I was to her. I was for her in everything and everywhere a useless servant, contenting myself with being the observer of the works of the Holy Ghost in her, without interfering in anything, for fear of undoing everything, since I saw her in such good keeping."

One of the finest eulogies bestowed upon Marie de l'Incarnation is the letter that Bishop Laval wrote under date of 12 Nov. 1677 to Dom Claude Martin to be inserted at the beginning of his edition of that year. It deserves to be quoted here (in part):

"We consider as a special blessing the acquaintance which it pleased God to give us with her [Marie de l'Incarnation], putting her under our pastoral guidance, and the testimony that we can give of her is that she was eminently endowed with all the virtues, especially with the gift of such lofty prayer and with so perfect a union with God, that she preserved His presence amongst the various occupations in which her vocation involved her and in the midst of the worries caused by the most difficult and most distracting affairs. She was dead to herself to such a degree, and Jesus Christ possessed her so completely, that one may assuredly say of her, as of the Apostle, that it was not she who lived, but Jesus Christ in her, and that she lived and acted only through Jesus Christ. Having chosen her to inaugurate the founding of the Ursulines in Canada, God had given her the plenitude of the spirit of her Rule. She was a perfect superior, an excellent mistress of novices; she was capable of carrying out all the works of religion. Her life, ordinary on the outside but very regular and animated by a completely divine inner nature, was a living rule for her entire community. Her ardour for saving souls and especially for the conversion of the Indians was so great and so far-reaching, that it seemed as if she bore them all in her heart, and we do not doubt that she contributed greatly by her prayers to obtaining from God the blessings which He has showered on this new-born Church."

Towards the middle of the 18th century the worship accorded the memory of Marie de l'Incarnation was about to be brought officially to the knowledge of the Holy See. But the Treaty of Paris, which handed Canada over to England, held up the proceedings that had been prepared. In 1867 circumstances seemed favourable to the renewal of the project. At the request of his Excellency Charles-François Baillargeon*, Bishop of Quebec, the proceedings preparatory to the introduction of the cause of the servant of God were started. Here are the principal steps in these proceedings: introduction of the cause in the Court of Rome, 1877; process of absence of cultus, 1882; process concerning the reputation of sanctity, 1891; inquiry regarding the writings, 1895; validation of the processes conducted at Quebec, 1897; process of the practice of virtues in a heroic degree, 1907–1910; decree asserting the existence of evidence of the heroic virtues of Marie de l'Incarnation (19 July) 1911. Only two miracles, obtained through the intercession of Mother Marie, are lacking for the solemn proclamation of her beatification.

Marie de l'Incarnation wrote a great deal, but not all of her writings have come down to us. There remain: a *Relation autobiographique*, written in 1633 in Tours; some *Lettres de conscience*, dating from the years 1625–34; some spiritual notes, *Exclamations et élévations*, which go back to the years 1625–38; an *Exposition du Cantique des Cantiques*, written between 1631 and 1637; the *École Sainte: explication des mystères de la foi*, written between 1633 and 1635; a *Relation autobiographique*, written at Quebec in 1654; a *Mémoire complémentaire* to the preceding *Relation*, written in 1656; the *Correspondance*, made up of letters of a historical and spiritual nature. In 1677 Dom Claude Martin published a *Vie*, the story of his mother's life, which contains fragments of the two *Relations*. A *Recueil de Lettres* followed in 1681. Today Dom Claude's edition has become very rare. The more learned and more complete one by Dom Jamet comprises two volumes of religious writings and two volumes of letters (1639–60).

The *Relation* of 1633. Marie de l'Incarnation, who was at the time an Ursuline nun in the convent at Tours, wrote this memoir at the request of Father de La Haye, rector of the Collège at Orléans. This priest had several conversations with Mother Marie, and seeing the exceptional quality of his interlocutress, "he wanted her in addition to put down in writing all the favours that she had received from God since her childhood, with the use that she had made of them, so that he could make a more accurate judgement of [her] state."

Before his death (1652) Father de La Haye bequeathed this *Relation* to the Ursulines of Saint-Denis (France), with the injunction that they keep it secret until Marie's death. They respected this order so faithfully that Dom Claude spent 20 years searching for this document. After 1672 the Ursulines sent it to him "very obligingly upon learning that he was working on the *Vie* [of his venerable mother]."

Dom Claude cut up the *Relation*, taking 87 fragments from it which he spread through the 757 pages of the *Vie*, and then sent the precious document back to its owners. By means of comparisons and cross-checking Dom Jamet succeeded in making a rational reconstitution of the *Relation* of 1633. Thus it is possible to follow the various stages in the mystical itinerary of Marie de l'Incarnation.

Lettres de conscience. Under this title are grouped some letters from Marie to her spiritual adviser, Dom Raymond de Saint-Bernard; his absences from Tours motivated Marie's correspondence between 1622 and 1634. The samples which remain show that despite her noviciate, her vow of obedience to her spiritual father, and the reading of treatises on prayer, the Ursuline nun had kept her personal quality. One day she took the liberty of telling Dom Raymond that he must detach himself from everything, even from God's gifts.

Exclamations et élévations. Under these two headings may be grouped the *epithalamia* or lover's complaints which Marie wrote "to dissipate the fervour of the spirit." Most of them were burned, but the remnants which escaped the fire reveal the emotion of a woman who has encountered life in the utmost recesses of her being. Rejecting all metaphors, all analogies, Marie describes God exactly as she experiences Him: "No, my love, You are not fire, You are not water, You are not what we say. You are what You are in Your glorious eternity. You are: that is Your essence and Your name. You are divine life, living life, unifying life. You are all bliss. You are infinitely adorable, ineffable, incomprehensible unity. In a word You are Love and my Love."

Entretien spirituel sur l'épouse des Cantiques. As assistant mistress of novices Marie de l'Incarnation gave instruction to the young religious of the convent in Tours. These lectures dealt with the *Mysteries of the faith*, the *Psalms* and the *Song of Songs*. Only one of her lectures has come down to us. Marie had the gift of speech and according to the grace granted at that particular moment would break into improvisations that filled the listeners with wonder: "I could not keep silent," she wrote, "and I found it very easy to present my thoughts to my sisters who were all astonished to hear me speak in this way. One among them, having found in her French Bible a passage uttered by the Bride of the *Songs*, said to me: 'Preach to us a little, Sister Marie; tell us the meaning of *Let him kiss me with the kisses of his mouth.*' Our mistress was present, and to mortify me she had a chair brought for me. Without further ado I began with these words: *Let him kiss me with the kisses of his mouth:* this led me on to an address, so that, starting from this quotation, no longer being in control of myself, I spoke for a very long time, under the influence of the love which possessed me. Finally I lost my voice, as if the Spirit of my Jesus had wanted the rest for Himself. I could not restrain myself on this occasion, which subsequently caused me much confusion, something which has since happened to me unexpectedly on other occasions."

L'École Sainte. The *École Sainte*, or *Explication familière des mystères de la foy*, was, according to Father Charlevoix*, one of the best catechisms available in French. The venerable Mother based her teaching upon the Scriptures, which she explained in a simple and clear manner. Not satisfied with enlightening the mind, she stirred up the heart and urged it on to sanctify itself. Marie used to speak extempore, being surprised by her own facility: "I felt greatly illuminated on the subject, and I bore in my soul a grace of knowledge which sometimes made me say things that I should not have desired or dared to utter of my own accord."

The *Relations d'oraison*. Dom Claude Martin published these *Relations* under the title *Retraites de la Vénérable Mère Marie de l'Incarnation*. They are notes on prayer set down for her own use. These confidences, which were submitted to her spiritual adviser, explain all the ways in which the divine spirit acts upon a soul that is faithful to its inspirations. It was from this little book of *Méditations*, "more useful than 20 treatises on mystical theology," that Henri Bremond took the principal elements of his study on the spiritual psychology of Marie de l'Incarnation.

The *Relation* of 1654. This second autobiography is more extensive than the first, which it does not reproduce. Marie de l'Incarnation wrote it by fits and starts, at the long-repeated instances of her son and on the order of her adviser, Father Jérôme Lalemant. "In the midst of a period of great distraction caused by her everyday affairs," Marie related the story of her life. After enjoining that it be kept secret, she speaks freely of the favours that she has received, and of the heights that God has made her climb. Her shrewd psychology sorts out the interplay of the faculties and the ineffable touches of divine love. This *Relation* is sufficient in itself to class Marie among the most sublime mystics of the universal Church. Theologians, philosophers, and linguists have not finished making use of this journal, which is still of intense interest.

Marie de l'Incarnation sent this long letter to her son with this recommendation: "If you have difficulties with it, you can point them out to me by indicating the passages." The prior of the monastery of the *Blancs-Manteaux* sent a long list of questions to Quebec. In 1656 he received a *Supplément* of which only a few articles are known to us.

Guyart

The *Correspondance*. Marie de l'Incarnation was a born letter-writer. It is estimated that she must have written about 13,000 letters in her life. Five or six of the originals have escaped oblivion. Dom Claude Martin published 221 of them, a very limited number which was to be reduced further because certain items had been divided into two. Richaudeau and Dom Jamet were fortunate enough to find some of these letters. If most of Marie's letters have disappeared, the *Registre des bienfaiteurs des Ursulines de Québec* gives us the list of the principal recipients. The list is incomplete but huge enough to make us deplore the loss brought about by the destruction of a multitude of letters. If we are to judge them by some very extensive specimens, a number of them must have been veritable treatises on the spiritual life and chapters on the history of the colony.

Marie touched on every subject, wrote as her pen ran on, at night by candlelight. Her letters were only rough drafts which she sent off without having time to reread them. The ships were waiting and her hand would become so tired that she had difficulty guiding it. In such a conjuncture she could have limited herself to the essential, sending laconic notes, requests and thanks in telegraphic style. Not at all! She allowed herself the pleasure of recounting picturesque scenes drawn from life and full of exciting topical news. Straight away she shows us her entire self as well as her period and her contemporaries. It is above all in her letters that she opens her heart unrestrainedly, revealing all the facets of her inspired personality. One can feel the beatings of her heart, which is that of a mother, friend, nun, and patriot. She talked about everything even though she had not gone to specialized schools, she settled the most complex problems, all because she looked at the world in the light of eternity, with eyes that were detached from all unhealthy desires. And her style, flowing and cheerful, assumed all the inflexions of the human register. As soon as she left the parlour she put her impressions down on paper, upon which immediately appeared figures of unforgettable accuracy and life. Mother Marie's letters have all the qualities and all the defects of writings that have been spontaneously poured out; but some negligence of form is pardoned a person who knows how to use the magic wand of life. A daughter of the 17th century, Marie de l'Incarnation possessed a sense of order and harmony. The unity that she achieved in her own being appears in her writings, as limpid as her soul, which was detached from all trifles.

In 1645 Marie de l'Incarnation desired the union of all the congregations of French Ursulines. Her dream was realized in Canada in 1953. Her daughters were grouped under the direction of a superior-general and provinces were created at Quebec, Trois-Rivières, and Rimouski. Faithful to the missionary spirit of their foundress, the Canadian Ursulines have spread to Japan (1935) and South America (1961).

MARIE-EMMANUEL CHABOT, O.S.U.

Archives manuscrites des Ursulines de Québec. Archives manuscrites du Couvent des Ursulines du Faubourg Saint-Jacques, Paris. P. F.-X. de Charlevoix, *La vie de la Mère Marie de l'Incarnation, institutrice et première supérieure des Ursulines de la Nouvelle-France* (Paris, 1724). Eugène Griselle, *La vénérable Mère Marie de l'Incarnation, première supérieure des Ursulines de Québec: supplément à sa correspondance* (Paris, [1909?]). Marie Guyart de l'Incarnation, *L'école sainte ou explication familière des mystères de la foy pour toutes de personnes qui sont obligées d'enseigner la doctrine chrétienne* (Paris, 1684); *Écrits* (Jamet); *Lettres* (Martin); *Lettres* (Richaudeau); *Retraites de la Vénérable Mère Marie de l'Incarnation, religieuse ursuline, avec une exposition succincte du "Cantique des cantiques"* (Paris, 1682); *Le témoinage de Marie de l'Incarnation, Ursuline de Tours et de Québec*, éd. Albert Jamet (Paris, [1932]); *La vie de la Vénérable Mère Marie de l'Incarnation, première supérieure des Ursulines de la Nouvelle-France, tirée de ses lettres et de ses écrits*, éd. Claude Martin (Paris, 1677). *JR* (Thwaites), *passim. JJ* (Laverdière et Casgrain), *passim*.

J.-L. Beaumier, *Marie Guyart de l'Incarnation, fondatrice des Ursulines au Canada 1599-1672* (Trois-Rivières, 1959). Henri Bremond, *Histoire littéraire du sentiment religieux en France depuis les guerres de religion jusqu'à nos jours* (12v., Paris, 1916–36), VI (1926): *La conquête mystique: Marie de l'Incarnation*. H.-R. Casgrain, *Histoire de la Mère Marie de l'Incarnation, première supérieure des Ursulines de la Nouvelle-France, précédée d'une esquisse sur l'histoire religieuse des premiers temps de cette colonie* (Québec, 1864). Marie-Emmanuel Chabot, *Marie de l'Incarnation d'après ses lettres* (Québec et Ottawa, 1946). Henri Cuzin, *Du Christ à la Trinité, d'après l'expérience mystique de Marie de l'Incarnation* (Lyon, 1936). *Glimpses of the monastery: scenes from the history of the Ursulines of Quebec during two hundred years, 1639-1839, by a member of the community* (Québec, 1897). Georges Goyau, "La première française missionaire: la vocation canadienne de Mère Marie de l'Incarnation," *Études*, CCXXVII (1936), 145–68. Fernand Jetté, *La voie de la sainteté d'après Marie de l'Incarnation, fondatrice des Ursulines de Québec* (Ottawa, 1954). Joseph Klein, *L'itinéraire mystique de la Vénérable Mère Marie de l'Incarnation, Ursuline de Tours et de Québec, 1599-1672* (Issoudun et Paris, 1938). *Marie de l'Incarnation*, éd. Marie-Emmanuel Chabot (Classiques canadiens, XXV, Montréal et Paris, 1962). *Marie de l'Incarnation fondatrice du Monastère des Ursulines de Québec* (Québec, 1935). M. T.-L. Penido, *La conscience religieuse: autour de*

Guyon Du Buisson

Marie de l'Incarnation (Paris, 1935). A. Poisson, *La dévotion au Saint-Esprit illustrée par le témoignage de Marie de l'Incarnation de Tours et de Québec* (Paris, 1960). Paul Renaudin, *Une grande mystique française au XVIIe siècle, Marie de l'Incarnation, Ursuline de Tours et de Québec; essai de psychologie religieuse* (Paris, 1935). Agnes Repplier, *Mère Marie of the Ursulines: a study in adventure* (New York, 1931). *Les Ursulines de Québec*, I.

GUYON, JEAN, painter, canon of the chapter of Quebec; member of the Guyon family, originally from Perche; son of Simon Guyon, who was called "habittant" in the 1666 census, and of Louise Racine, b. at Quebec in 1641; b. 5 Oct. 1659 at Château-Richer; d. 1687 in Paris.

Entering the seminary about 1670, Jean Guyon studied the humanities there and, according to all indications, took up painting, urged along in this direction probably by the example of Brother Luc [*see* FRANÇOIS], Father POMMIER and, in 1675, M. de Cardenat. He entered the Grand Seminary on 8 Dec. 1677, the day that the building which still stands was officially opened, and he received minor orders four days later.

In the summer of 1678 Guyon went to France to continue his philosophical and theological studies. We learn this from a letter dated 9 March 1681 from Abbé DUDOUYT to Bishop Laval*: "Mr. Guyon will travel [to New France] with the first ships." Dudouyt added: "He [Guyon] is fairly well at present. He has benefited in his painting. He has not applied himself as much to his philosophy this year, because of his illness . . . I hope that he will do well and that he will give you cause for satisfaction."

Returning to Quebec in August 1682, Guyon completed his theology and was ordained priest on 21 Nov. 1683. He was appointed a canon of the chapter on 7 Nov. 1684 and almost immediately left Quebec as secretary to Bishop Laval and went to Paris. He died there on 10 Jan. 1687, "with feelings of great confidence." A letter from Abbé Dudouyt, dated 17 April 1687, gives few details about the young priest's works: "I am sending you some lacquer which Mr. Guion had bought, having got a bargain, some plaster statues, some prints and some small tools which he used for working on the statues. . . ."

There are solid grounds for thinking that Father Guyon's production was not great. Some of his works probably perished in the fires at the seminary in 1701 and 1705; others have perhaps been so badly damaged that it is impossible to identify them. At the present time there remain a portrait in oils, of astonishing grace and charm, and some water-colours which have kept their subtlety and freshness.

The portrait (at the Hôtel-Dieu in Quebec) represents Mother Jeanne-Françoise Juchereau* *dite* de Saint-Ignace. Born at Quebec in 1650, she was several times superior of her convent; she was also its annalist. Her expression—intelligent, amiable, smiling shrewdly, well-bred—makes us think of her style of writing. The artist has reproduced her face and dress with great simplicity and admirable skill, and with deep perceptiveness.

Abbé Guyon probably did his water-colour paintings to help in the teaching of botany. They represent items of the Laurentian flora. The drawing is accurate and lively, the colours fresh and transparent; the composition is arranged in an orderly but natural manner.

GÉRARD MORISSET

ASQ, Lettres, N, 52; O, 1; A.-E. Gosselin, "Notes pour servir à la biographie des prêtres du séminaire de Québec, avec références en marge." Caron, "Inventaire de documents," APQ *Rapport, 1939–40*, 234, 248f., 254, 258, 275, 279.

GUYON DU BUISSON, JEAN (senior), master mason, pioneer at Beauport; b. at Saint-Jean-Baptiste de Mortagne in Perche; d. 30 May 1663.

On 14 March 1634, at Mortagne, Guyon and his fellow-countryman CLOUTIER signed an undertaking with ROBERT GIFFARD. Guyon settled at Beauport that same year, and a year or two later brought out his wife, Mathurine Robin and his children, of whom he had at least eight. When he received from Giffard an arriere-fief near the Rivière du Buisson, he assumed that nobiliary surname. He died 30 May 1663. Several of his descendants now bear the name Dion.

HONORIUS PROVOST

ASQ, Document Faribault, *passim*.; Séminaire, LVII. *JR* (Thwaites), XXVII, 314. *JJ* (Laverdière et Casgrain), *passim*. *BRH*, XLIX (1943), 268–72. Louis Guyon, *Étude généalogique sur Jean Guyon et ses descendants* (Montréal, 1927). É.-Z. Massicotte, "Les arpenteurs de Montréal sous le régime français," *BRH*, XXIV (1918), 304.

GUYON DU BUISSON, JEAN (junior), royal surveyor; b. 1 Aug. 1619 at Mortagne (in Perche); d. 13 Jan. 1694.

Jean Guyon probably came to Canada with his father in 1634. On 27 Nov. 1645, at Quebec, he married Élisabeth Couillard, a daughter of GUILLAUME COUILLARD; she was to bear him 12 children. Trained perhaps by JEAN BOURDON or Martin BOUTET, both of whom were surveyors, Guyon became the first surveyor to learn his trade in Canada. He was already in practice on 12 April 1662, with the title of surveyor for the seigneury of Notre-Dame-des-Anges. Subsequently (1667) he came to style himself "king's surveyor in this colony." He was to finish his days at Château-Richer, where he had been given a grant of land in 1650.

HONORIUS PROVOST

ASQ, Documents Faribault, 117; Paroisse de Québec, 151. Séminaire, XXXVI, 1c. *BRH*, XLIX (1943), 268–72. Louis Guyon, *Étude généalogique sur Jean Guyon et ses descendants* (Montréal, 1927). É.-Z. Massicotte, "Les arpenteurs de Montréal sous le régime français," *BRH*, XXIV (1918), 304.

GYLBERTE. *See* GILBERT

H

HAIES. *See* HAYES

HALL, JAMES, arctic pilot and navigator, participated in three expeditions to Greenland in Danish service and led a fourth expedition in English service; d. 1612 and buried in Greenland.

The results of John DAVIS's explorations had excited the interest of Christian IV of Denmark, who determined to re-establish communication with the Scandinavian colonies known to have existed formerly in Greenland. In 1605 he sent out an expedition of three ships under John CUNNINGHAM. Hall—a native of Hull about whose personal history nothing is known—served as first mate and pilot. Hall probably had accompanied one of the Davis voyages. John KNIGHT, a captain in the fleet, may also have had experience in arctic navigation. The expedition made landings at King Christian's Fjord and at other parts of the west coast. They saw nothing of the lost colonists, but they took captive some Eskimos and collected some ore that they wrongly thought was silver-bearing. In 1606 the king sent out a five-ship expedition to Greenland in which Hall again served as pilot and first mate to the commander, to continue mineralogical exploration in the same area. Ice and currents in Davis Strait forced the ships westward until they had reached about 66°N when an opportunity came to sail eastward to the Greenland coast. While on the western side of Davis Strait they sighted Baffin Island but made no landing. They brought back more ore that proved worthless and more Eskimo captives. In 1607 Hall accompanied a third royal expedition of two vessels, which ended in failure, for the ships were prevented by ice from reaching Greenland.

In 1612, having returned to England, Hall persuaded four merchants of London to join him in financing an expedition to Greenland for the purposes of mineralogical exploration and trade. He sailed with the *Patience* and *Heart's Ease* to Cape Farewell and followed the west coast of Greenland north. On 22 July in Rammel's (Amerdlok) Fjord, Hall was evidently recognized by a group of Eskimos from whom he had earlier taken captives. One of them struck him in the side with a spear, and he died the next day. According to his last wish he was buried on a nearby island rather than at sea.

Hall's fourth expedition provided William BAFFIN, who probably sailed as pilot in the *Patience*, with his first arctic experience. Baffin's geological observations were the most important result of the expedition. Hall's report to the King of Denmark on the voyage of 1605 was accompanied by four maps, results of the earliest attempt to map the west coast of Greenland. This report and others published by Purchas formed a valuable source of knowledge about Greenland which England used to greater advantage than did Denmark.

ALAN COOKE

Danish arctic expeditions (Gosch), I, includes narratives of Hall and his contemporaries. *DNB*. Dodge, *Northwest by sea*. Vilhjalmur Stefansson, *Greenland* (London, 1943).

HAMELIN DE BOURGCHEMIN ET DE L'HERMITIÈRE, JACQUES-FRANÇOIS, ensign, then lieutenant, commandant first at Contrecœur and then at Fort Saint-François, seigneur; b. 6 Jan. 1664 at Louze, Maine (department of Sarthe), son of François de Bourgchemin, nobleman and seigneur, and of Madeleine Guitton; d. between the end of 1695 and the beginning of 1698, probably in France.

It is not known exactly when Bourgchemin arrived in New France. In any case, after becoming an ensign on 17 March 1687 he was in Canada on 13 November of that year, because he married Elisabeth Dizy, the 15-year-old daughter of Pierre Dizy, Sieur de Montplaisir, at Champlain on that date. On the marriage certificate he had himself styled "chevalier," a title without foundation even in the letters of nobility granted to his family, and which led the genealogist Cyprien

Tanguay to confuse him with a soldier living in Acadia at the time and called Chevalier [*see* LA TOURASSE].

In 1690 he was at Contrecœur to direct its defence against the Iroquois. There he received the rank of half-pay lieutenant in 1691, which rank was confirmed on 1 March 1693 and raised to that of lieutenant on 15 April 1694. On 24 January of the latter year, in a document in the parish registers of Batiscan, he described himself as commandant of Fort Saint-François. Between 1690 and 1694 we find him on various occasions at Champlain, at Batiscan, and at Sorel, where he behaved scandalously. For example, in February 1690, when Bourgchemin's wife had by her arrogance provoked a sharp retort from a Batiscan settler, the husband took his axe to the impertinent fellow to punish him. Moreover, early in 1694, this unruly officer was reported to BUADE de Frontenac by Bishop Saint-Vallier [LA CROIX*], although without justification apparently, for having refused, along with François Desjordy* de Cabanac, to attend mass on Sexagesima Sunday. This was at a time when, in addition, Bourgchemin was involved in the legal proceedings before the Conseil Souverain instituted by Desjordy and Marguerite Dizy-Debryeux* against the parish priests Claude Bouquin* and Nicolas Foucault*. Bourgchemin's friend and his sister-in-law had just been placed under interdict in announcements from the pulpit in the churches of Champlain and Batiscan as a result of a pastoral letter from the bishop censuring the behaviour of certain officers in these villages. The repercussions of the litigation and the bravado of the two officers aggravated the situation. The affair dragged on, until it was finally referred to the king's privy council in 1695 and lost sight of. That same year Bourgchemin's case was further complicated: he was accused of trying to poison his wife, and Frontenac, in his letter of 4 Nov. 1695 to the minister for colonies stated that he was obliged to send him back to France. There is no trace of him after this date, but we assume that he returned to the mother country and died there shortly afterwards, since his widow remarried on 26 Jan. 1698.

Frontenac, probably to annoy Bishop Saint-Vallier, had, on 1 March 1695, transferred to Bourgchemin a grant of land made to Pierre Dorfeuille in 1672; and on 20 June of the same year he gave him a seigneury on the Yamaska River—the Bourgchemin fief—a grant confirmed by the king on 19 May 1696. Bourgchemin had had three children by Elisabeth Dizy: Anne-Marie, baptized on 10 Nov. 1689, François, baptized on 27 Oct. 1691 and buried on 7 April 1703, and lastly Marguerite, of whom we know only that she died sometime before 1724.

IN COLLABORATION WITH
HONORIUS PROVOST

ASQ, MSS, 132, 133, Laffilard, Officiers français aux colonies, 1627–1780. *Coll. de manuscrits relatifs à la Nouv.-France*, I, 580. Correspondance de Frontenac (1689–99), APQ *Rapport, 1928–29*, 281. *Jug. et délib.* Lettre de M. de Lamothe Cadillac, 28 sept. 1694, APQ *Rapport, 1923–24*, 80–93. P.-G. Roy, *Inv. concessions.* F.-J. Audet, *Contrecœur, famille, seigneurie, paroisse, village* (Montréal, 1940). Raymond Douville, "Deux officiers 'indésirables' des troupes de la Marine," *Cahiers des Dix*, XIX (1954), 67–83. Ægidius Fauteux, "Le Sieur de Bourchemin," *BRH*, XXXIV (1930), 317–19. O.-H.-A. Lapalice, *Histoire de la seigneurie Massue et de la paroisse de Saint-Aimé* (s.l., 1930), 9–22, 416; "Le sieur de Bourgchemin," *BRH*, XXIV (1918), 273–74. É.-Z. Massicotte, "Le Sieur de Bourchemin, ses noms, son âge, sa noblesse," *BRH*, XXV (1919), 210–14.

HAMILTON, ANDREW, deputy governor for the HBC in James Bay; fl. 1688–89.

Under the treaty of neutrality concluded in November 1686, before the news of de TROYE's activities in James Bay had reached London, the French retained the Company's forts even though they had been captured during a time of peace. In 1688 Hamilton was associated with governor John MARSH, William BOND, and John Simpson in an attempt to re-establish trade for the Company in Albany River (called by the French the Quichicouane). From the time they arrived in September they were harassed by the French. Bond, who took precedence of Hamilton in council because of his experience in the country, was captured in December 1688 and when Marsh died in January following, the command fell to Hamilton. By March Hamilton had surrendered to Pierre Le Moyne* d'Iberville. The French sent him with about 30 other prisoners to sail for New England in the captured *Huband*, but once at sea the company "resolved for England." Contrary winds and shortage of food forced them into Limerick, where Hamilton sold the Company's ship and shared the proceeds with his companions. Nothing more is known of him.

ALICE M. JOHNSON

HBRS, XX (Rich and Johnson).

HARAKONTIE. See GARAKONTIÉ

HATEOUATI. See OTREOUTI

HAUTEVILLE, NICOLAS LE VIEUX DE. See LE VIEUX

Hawkeridge

HAWKERIDGE (Hawkridge), WILLIAM, English navigator, made voyage to Hudson Strait in 1625; fl. 1610–31.

Very little is known about William Hawkeridge, except that he came from Devon and was a cousin of Phineas Pett, master shipwright of the Deptford dockyard. In 1610 he sailed with Capt. Richard WHITBOURNE, as servant, in the Newfoundland trade, and it is recorded that they both encountered a creature they supposed to be a mermaid in the harbour of St. John's, which Whitbourne described as "a strange Creature . . . looking cheerfully as it had been a woman, by the Face, Eyes, Nose, Mouth, Chin, Eares, Necke and Forehead; . . . the same came shortly after unto a Boate, wherein one William Hawkridge, then my seruant, was, . . . and the same Creature did put both his hands upon the side of the Boate, and did strive to come in to him and others then in the said Boate: . . . Whether it were a Maremaid or no, I know not; I leave it for others to judge." (*A discourse and discovery of New-found-land* (London, 1620).)

Hawkeridge sailed with Sir Thomas BUTTON in 1612–13, as volunteer, to Hudson Bay. A few years later he was in command of a voyage to discover the northwest passage under the auspices of Sir John Wolstenholme and the East India Company. There is some question as to the date of this voyage. Rundall notes that, according to his own research, it was 1619. However, Christy states that the voyage probably took place in 1625. The expedition sailed in two pinnaces (whose names are not recorded according to Luke Fox, but one of which is listed as *Lions Whelp* by Dodge) from the west coast of England and reached the entrance to Hudson Strait on 29 June, after first having sailed, in error, into Frobisher Bay (called Lumley's Inlet). However, it was not until 22 July that Hawkeridge actually entered the strait. He sailed to the Western extremity of Hudson Strait, and then seems to have cruised aimlessly about, making no new discoveries, until 16 August when he turned around for home, passing Resolution Island on 7 September. The only extant record of Hawkeridge's voyage was made by Luke Fox, either from Hawkeridge's own log, or with the help of Hawkeridge himself. Though full of detail, the account is very confused and Hawkeridge's course is almost impossible to chart on a map. It is not known whether Hawkeridge was incompetent and lacking in ability, despite his many years' experience, or merely extremely unlucky. However, the results of his voyage were completely valueless to those who followed him. This voyage is considered the last of the "Golden Age of Arctic Research." The dismal failure of this well-equipped expedition dampened the enthusiasm for arctic exploration until 1631 when Fox and JAMES set sail.

Of Hawkeridge's later life there is no record other than that he was the owner of a cargo ship that was captured in 1631 off Algiers and that he himself was held in slavery for ransom.

NORA T. CORLEY

Accounts of Hawkeridge's voyage can be found in the three following books: *Danish arctic expeditions* (Gosch), II: *The expedition of Captain Jens Munk to Hudson's Bay in search of a north-west passage in 1619–20. Narratives of voyages towards the north-west, in search of a passage to Cathay and India* . . . , ed. Thomas Rundall (Hakluyt Soc., 1st ser., V, 1849). *Voyages of Foxe and James* (Christy), I, 248–59.

See also: Miller Christy, "Captain William Hawkeridge and his voyage in search of a north-west passage in 1625," *Mariner's Mirror*, XIII (1927), 51–78. Dodge, *Northwest by sea*.

HAYES (Haies), EDWARD, English explorer, writer, and colonial promoter; b. *c.* 1550 at West Derby near Liverpool, Lancs.; d. *c.* 1613.

Hayes's father was a small landowner and merchant who soon after his son's birth went to live in Liverpool. Hayes was at King's College, Cambridge, in 1565 and reappeared there in 1571, but did not obtain a degree. He entered the service of Elizabeth, Lady Hoby (Lady Russell from 1574), at Bisham Abbey, Berks., possibly as tutor to one of her sons, during which time he seems to have come to the notice of the lord treasurer, Lord Burghley, Lady Russell's brother-in-law. Thereafter he is often in touch with Burghley and is likely to have enjoyed some patronage at his hands from time to time.

For five years, 1578–83, he was very closely associated with the American voyages and colonizing schemes of Sir Humphrey GILBERT. In 1578, as "Mr Haies gent. of Leerpolle," he subscribed to the expedition which Sir Humphrey GILBERT was preparing to find a site for an English settlement and he may have sailed on the abortive voyage of that year, although we have no record that he did so.

He took to sea as a merchant captain about 1579. Late in 1581 or 1582 he bought the *Samuel* of Weymouth, renamed her the *Golden Hind* in honour of Sir Francis DRAKE's ship, and engaged in at least one privateering voyage in her. From 1580 onwards, however, he worked closely with Gilbert in preparing a second venture. Like Gilbert, he turned away from southeastern to northeastern America and may, indeed, have been influenced by the propaganda of Anthony PARKHURST in favour of English settlement in Newfoundland, though Gilbert's own interests centred on the mainland south from Cape Breton, and principally in what was later to be called New England. By 1582 he was already known to Richard Hakluyt and was involved in the planning of the voyage (and probably doing propaganda for it). He contributed his bark, the *Golden Hind* of 40 tons. Its master was the tough, experienced seaman, William Cox of Limehouse, formerly in command of a privateer in the West Indies, 1576–78, who was later to distinguish himself (and die) in the Armada campaign.

Hayes may have been appointed to write a journal of the voyage or have decided to do so for himself. In any event, his vivid and dramatic account, "A report of the voyage . . . ," published in the 1589 edition of Hakluyt's *The principall navigations*, is the chief authority for the voyage and we see it very much through his eyes. He writes well, especially when he is telling a straight story, and his narrative is deservedly famous. The *Golden Hind* left Plymouth with the expedition on 11 June and sighted land near the Straits of Belle Isle on 30 July. Sailing cautiously south from an estimated 51°N.Lat., Hayes first sighted Funk Island, then Baccalieu Island and Cape St. Francis, picking up the *Swallow* at Conception Bay. He was joined by Gilbert in the *Delight* (Richard CLARKE, master) at St. John's harbour. After Gilbert arrived on 3 August, Hayes went on shore, where, the following day, he saw a little of the land round the harbour but he suffered an injury (we are not told how) and was immobilized for some days. He was thus largely dependent on reports from the parties that Gilbert dispatched from his base, though they were not able to penetrate far into the interior [*see* Stephanus PARMENIUS]. He summarized the reports carefully and gave an intelligent account of the climate, estimated the fishing resources of the island, and concluded that all northern commodities, whether or not already present—timber products, hemp, flax, furs, and, he thought, wheat—could be grown and exploited; but the rigorous winters would have to be faced as they were in Scandinavia. He picked up something about trees, fruits, birds, and animals, and stressed the mineral potentialities of the island, in iron, copper, lead, and, he thought, silver.

Hayes tells effectively the story of the next leg of the voyage (24–29 August) and all he knew of the wreck of the *Delight*. Hayes, following, appears to have taken a southwesterly course to safety [*see* Sir Humphrey GILBERT]. But the expedition was reduced too far for it to proceed; the *Golden Hind* and the *Squirrel* were unable to face the blustery weather and the long autumn reconnaissance down the coast from Cape Breton which they had planned. Gilbert, from the *Squirrel*, came to confer with Hayes and Cox and they decided reluctantly, Hayes says, to abandon the voyage.

Gilbert, however, had not abandoned his plans. At a last conference he told Hayes and Cox that they should command the expeditions he would get to sea in 1584 towards the south (down the mainland coast), while he himself would command a northern (Newfoundland) voyage. But on Monday night, 9 September, the *Squirrel*'s lights went out and Hayes had to assume she had foundered. Next day there was no trace of her or her occupants. So the *Golden Hind* came home alone, reaching Falmouth on the 22nd, putting in at Dartmouth to tell Gilbert's brother the sad news and then sailing to Weymouth where the men were dispersed. His crew had remained healthy and united throughout the voyage and its many frustrations. Hayes, though he had lost much in the enterprise, remained optimistic. He had shown himself an able and resourceful voyager.

Hayes did his best on his return to see that Gilbert's enterprise was continued, contributing much to Sir George Peckham's tract, *A true report* (1583), by which he hoped to revive support for the venture. But its Catholic supporters had mostly abandoned the project and the investors with Gilbert had lost too much money already. Whether Hayes prepared and circulated his own report in manuscript we do not know. Christopher Carleill set out in May 1584 but got no farther than Ireland. Hayes, however, was convinced that Newfoundland offered great prospects if sufficient backing could be got to exploit it, so he did not associate himself with Walter Raleigh and Sir Francis Walsingham, his supporter, who were soon planning colonies just north of Spanish Florida.

Instead, he turned to win the support of Lord Burghley, his old patron, whose interests overseas were centred on the encouragement of fisheries, the fur trade, and the production of naval stores—timber products, flax, and hemp, especially. By 10 May 1585, when Hayes wrote to Burghley (BM, Lansdowne MS 37, ff.166–67), he had worked out several detailed documents on Newfoundland and handed over early in 1596 both "A discourse of Master Haies of the new lande discovered" (BM, Lansdowne MS 100, ff.83–87), in which the climate and commodities of Newfoundland are discussed against a background of English political rights and economic

Hayes

needs; and also another "Platt" (plot or plan) (*ibid.*, ff.88–94) for putting into effect his schemes for a colony which would control the fishery.

He showed some detailed knowledge of the fishery and expressed his belief that both Englishmen and foreigners would submit to control and taxation in the harbours in order to gain security against attack [*see* Richard CLARKE, Sir BERNARD DRAKE]. He proposed that a corporation be established, representing the fishing interests in all the principal ports and headed by some nobleman of rank, which would be open to other English participants in the fishery. This was not unlike the fur-trading consortium worked out for New France in 1603. It is possible that Hayes had backing from southern ports like Southampton and Weymouth but the southwestern ports were satisfied with the existing system and all the fishermen concerned were in any event strongly individualistic. Moreover, the prospects of being able to control and tax foreign fishing vessels were by no means assured. His own contribution was to offer to take out 200 convicts to do the hard work of galley-slaves and labourers. He implies too that he should be general of the expedition. Burghley may well have been sympathetic but he did nothing to implement the scheme. It is of some significance, however, in bringing consideration of Newfoundland as a possible colony under closer scrutiny.

The appearance of Hayes's report of the Gilbert voyage in the first edition (1589) of *The principall navigations* publicized his vivid and dramatic account and also gave his views on English colonization in general, along with "A brief relation of the New found lande," the earliest systematic description to be published. (This was reprinted in the second edition, III (1600), 143–61.) Hayes did not confine his activities to the promotion of colonization alone, for throughout his adult life, from 1579 to 1613, he frequently advocated projects to Burghley and his successors as lord treasurer and to Sir Robert Cecil, Burghley's son. Some were plans for domestic reforms, many of them for improving the coinage system in England or Ireland, or for reorganizing the militia; others, maybe, for improving the water-supply of London, or some other local purpose. Most of them contained proposals for his employment in implementing them. In addition, this active and resourceful man engaged in privateering from 1589 to 1591.

By about 1593 Hayes had revived his interest in North America but by this time he had decided that Newfoundland was too cold for permanent settlement. What was needed was the plantation of the mainland coast between 40° and 45°, where English colonists could settle in a climate more congenial to them, or else down the valley of the St. Lawrence where the French had reached 45°, and along which there was a substantial possibility of finding a passage to the South Seas. The colony should be built up economically on the profits of fur-trading with the Indians, the gradual establishment of small settlements, and the eventual attraction of the Newfoundland fishermen to the mainland coasts, where new fishing grounds and shore bases could be developed for them. Later, when settlement had developed, large numbers of intending settlers, 20,000 if need be, could be carried on the outward-bound fishing vessels and so a strong dominion established for the crown of England, while the discovery of a passage to the Pacific would make not only the settlers but also England rich.

The project owes much to the ideas of Christopher Carleill, who planned to settle the coasts north of 40° in 1583–84 [*see* Sir Humphrey GILBERT] but who had been diverted to various military employments in Ireland. Returning to England in 1593 he may well have joined forces with Hayes (and quite possibly Richard Hakluyt as well). The result was an elaborate and valuable proposal for the colonization of what are now Canada and northern New England, which has remained unpublished, "A discourse concerning a voyage intended for the plantation of Christian religion and people in the northwest regions of American in places most apt for the constitution of our bodies and the speedy advancement of a state" (Cambridge University Library, MS Dd. 3.85). The limiting dates for it are 1593 to 1595, but by the latter date Carleill was said to have sailed with Sir Francis Drake on his last voyage and in 1596 Hayes declared himself willing to follow Sir Walter Raleigh to Guiana. Who else was concerned in the proposals is not known but these proposals may well have been directed to Lord Burghley, who was at this time interested in plans for penetrating the St. Lawrence [*see* Richard FISHER, Sylvester WYET, Charles LEIGH].

When the "discourse" appears in print under Hayes's name, as an appendix to John Brereton's *A brief and true relation . . .* (1602), this document is much abbreviated: it is linked more closely with the attempts to explore and settle Maine and Massachusetts with which Bartholomew Gosnold's voyage in 1602 had been concerned. The St. Lawrence references are removed (the English have now left the valley finally to the French), but the title, "A treatise, containing important inducements for the planting in these parts, and finding a passage that way to the South Sea and China," still stresses the possibility of finding, if not by the St. Lawrence, then by other rivers, a westerly passage to the Pacific. But lists of commodities to be found on the Atlantic seaboard include a few new scraps of information from the Nova Scotia area, probably gathered by Hakluyt.

Hayes now ceases to concern himself in American ventures. From 1599 to 1603, he is employed in government service in and concerning Ireland. How he was employed otherwise we do not know; he preferred to live in London but he is found living at various times in Fittington, Essex, and in Hamsell, Sussex. He was, from 1601 to 1603, in charge of a coinage debasement scheme in Ireland, which he himself had proposed. He was associated with various inventions, or their application, mostly for coinage purposes. In his latter years, from 1603, he was a government pensioner. But he retained a lively interest in North America from 1578 until at least 1606, in which year he and his relative, Thomas Hayes, approached Lord Salisbury with a scheme for the public financing of the proposed Virginia Company.

To Hayes we owe the finest description of any 16th-century English voyage to what is now Canada but in addition he must be regarded as the most devoted propagandist for Elizabethan settlement within Newfoundland, the Atlantic Provinces, and the St. Lawrence. Of these areas only the first was planted by Englishmen in his lifetime, but it seems probable that at least he had kept English interest in that area alive, even if he is not known to have been associated with the Newfoundland Company of 1610.

DAVID B. QUINN

Hayes's account of the Gilbert voyage, "A report of the voyage and successe thereof, attempted in the yeere of our Lord, 1583. by Sir Humfrey Gilbert knight . . ." was printed in Hakluyt's *Principall navigations* (London, 1589), 679–97. (It contains "A brief relation of the New found lande.") Modern reprintings: *Principal navigations* (1903–5), VIII, 34–77; *Voyages of Gilbert* (Quinn), II, 385ff. Hayes's "A discourse of Master Haies of the new lande discovered" is in BM, Lansdowne MS 100, ff.83–87; and in the appendix to John Brereton's *A brief and true relation of the discovery of the north part of Virginia . . .* (London, 1602). W. G. Gosling, *The life of Sir Humphrey Gilbert* (London, 1911). Prowse, *History of Nfld*. D. B. Quinn, "Edward Hayes, Liverpool colonial pioneer," Lancashire and Cheshire Hist. Soc. *Trans.*, CXIII (1960), 25–45.

HAYMAN, ROBERT, poet, colonizer, governor of Bristol's colony in Newfoundland; b. 1575, first son of Nicholas Hayman and Amis Raleigh; d. Nov. 1629 in Guiana where he was buried.

Hayman spent his early life in Totnes, Devon, where his father, a merchant, was twice an M.P. In 1590 he matriculated from Exeter College, Oxford; in July 1596 he was admitted to the degree of B.A. and that October became a student in Lincoln's Inn. Between receiving his degree and July 1600 he studied at Poitiers, according to a letter which his father wrote to Sir Robert Cecil, asking him to find employment for Robert. Whether Cecil's help was forthcoming or not, Hayman later claimed to have known the court of Elizabeth well. At Oxford he enjoyed a reputation as a poet and was acquainted with other poets including William VAUGHAN, founder of the colony at Trepassey Bay, Newfoundland.

The origin of Hayman's connection with Bristol is not clear; however, one of his sisters married John Barker of Bristol and Hayman's poems show that his acquaintance there was large. Bristol had been involved in the plantation of Newfoundland since 1610 and the first governor of the Cuper's Cove colony had been a Bristolian, JOHN GUY. Perhaps Guy's quarrel with the company about five years later prompted members of the city's Society of Merchant Venturers, during Barker's years of office as master (1617–18), to apply for a separate grant of land. They received land around Harbour Grace on Conception Bay, which they called Bristol's Hope, a name that still survives.

Little is known of Hayman's career as governor of this colony although, according to contemporary reports, the settlement flourished. Even the date of his appointment is unknown but possibly he took office at the colony's foundation about 1618. He was certainly governor for some years: his first visit lasted 15 months and he spent several summers there until ceasing to be governor, which must have been by 1628. There were still settlers at Bristol's Hope in 1631 but it is not known whether a second governor was appointed. While in Newfoundland Hayman, having little to do but oversee the labour of others, as he himself put it, wrote verse and translated works by John Owen, Rabelais, and others, which he published in 1628. A group of his own poems he addressed to the promoters of the various Newfoundland plantations, praising those who, like George CALVERT, Lord Baltimore, persevered and chiding those who, like Lord Falkland, had become discouraged. About 1628, also, he tried to enlist royal support for a colony, through the mediation of the Duke of Buckingham. He argued that private resources had proved insufficient and attempted to show how the

Hébert

nation might profit by the full exploitation of the island's resources.

From Newfoundland Hayman turned to Guiana. In November 1628 he left for the Amazon with Robert Harcourt, reaching Wiapoko (now Oyapock) in the following February. In November 1629 he died of a fever while on an expedition up river.

GILLIAN T. CELL

Hayman's book is entitled *Quodlibets, lately come over from New Britaniola, Old Newfound-land* (London, 1628); his letter to Buckingham and address to Charles I are in the BM, Egerton MSS, 2541; his will, dated 28 Nov. 1628 and proved 23 Jan. 1633, is at Somerset House, P.C.C., 1 Russell. Other sources: Bristol Society of Merchant Venturers, Book of charters, I. *The book of examinations and depositions*, 1622–44, II, ed. R. C. Anderson (Southampton Record Soc., XXXI, 1931), 65–69. Hist. MSS Com., 9, *Salisbury (Cecil) MSS*, X. *Register of the University of Oxford* (1571–1622), ed. C. W. Boase and A. Clark (2v. [II in 4 pts.], Oxford Hist. Soc., 1884–89), II, pts. 2, 3.

DNB. G. C. Moore-Smith, "Robert Hayman and the Plantation in Newfoundland," *EHR*, XXXIII (1918), 21–36. J. A. Williamson, *The English colonies in Guiana and on the Amazon, 1604–1668* (Oxford, 1923). Anthony à Wood, *Athenae Oxonienses: an exact history of writers and bishops who have had their education in the University of Oxford* (3rd ed., 4v., London, 1813–20), II.

HÉBERT, GUILLEMETTE, daughter of LOUIS HÉBERT and Marie ROLLET, m. GUILLAUME COUILLARD 26 Aug. 1621; b. in Paris or Dieppe c. 1606; d. at Quebec 1684.

On Louis Hébert's death, his daughter Guillemette and her husband Guillaume Couillard inherited half the estate. Guillaume Couillard became the head of the family, as his wife's brother Guillaume was still a minor. Up to 1632, the Hébert house on the brow of the cliff was the only private dwelling in Quebec. Farther up along the edge was CHAMPLAIN's little wooden fort, and directly below it, on the shore, was the Habitation with the small Recollet chapel beside it. The only other buildings in the settlement were the convents of the Recollet and Jesuit orders on the St. Charles River, a mile away beyond dense woods. Guillemette and her mother were frequently alone on their property for Couillard was often on the river and the servant, Henri, whom the Héberts had brought from France, was murdered by the savages the same year that Louis Hébert died (1627).

Like her parents, Mme Couillard was interested in Indian children and was often godmother at their baptisms. After the English captured Quebec in 1629, she received into her home CHARITÉ and Espérance, two of the three Indian girls, protégées of Champlain, whom he had hoped to take to France with him. When DAVID KIRKE refused permission for the journey, the girls asked to be sent to Mme Couillard. They must have formed part of a cosmopolitan household, for it contained also OLIVIER LE JEUNE, a negro boy from Madagascar brought up the river by the English, sold to Olivier Le Baillif, and given by him to the Couillard family. Guillemette and her mother arranged for his religious instruction and he was baptized in 1633. By 1648 the Couillards had other servants and ten children, a lively—entries in the *Journal des Jésuites* would suggest even an unruly—ménage. At the marriage of the third daughter, Élisabeth, in November 1645, there were two violins in the chapel, a thing never before heard in Canada. The early 1660's, however, brought bereavement to Mme Couillard. Two sons, first Nicolas, aged 20, then Guillaume, aged 27, and her nephew JOSEPH HÉBERT fell victim to the Iroquois, 1661–62, and in March 1663 her husband died.

Being rich in land (the Héberts owned property other than their original homestead), Mme Couillard jointly with her husband had made various gifts for charitable and religious purposes: to the church in 1652, and to the Hôtel-Dieu in 1655 and 1659. As a widow, she sold to Bishop Laval* in 1666 the land for the "petit séminaire." Her disposal of this valuable property (the fief of Sault-au-Matelot), on which her father had first established himself, met with strong objections from the younger generation. The litigation begun by these prospective heirs was to continue generation after generation, even into the 20th century.

Saddened no doubt by the dissensions in her family, and somewhat infirm in body, she withdrew to the convent of the Hôtel-Dieu, where, as a boarder, she spent her last years. In 1678, when her father's bones were re-interred, she had herself carried to the Recollet chapel to witness the ceremony. She died October 1684, "aged 78 years or thereabouts" and was buried beside her husband in the chapel of the Hôtel-Dieu. At that time her descendants numbered over 250. The number at the present day could hardly be estimated.

ETHEL M. G. BENNETT

There are brief references to Mme Couillard in Sagard, *Histoire du Canada* (Tross); Champlain, *Works* (Biggar); and in the records of the Jesuits. Sons and servants are mentioned in the *Journal des Jésuites* (see: *JR* (Thwaites), *passim*). Chrestien LE CLERCQ, who was in Canada 1673–87 and who often talked with her, gives details of her later life (*see: First establishment of the faith* (Shea), *passim*). For more complete information consult Azarie Couillard Després, *Histoire des seigneurs de la Rivière-du-Sud et leurs alliés canadiens et acadiens* (Saint-Hyacinthe, 1912); *Louis Hébert: premier colon canadien et sa famille* (Lille, Paris, Bruges, 1913; Montréal, 1918); "Louis Hébert et ses descendants," *BRH*, XX (1914), 281–85; and *La première famille française au Canada*.

HÉBERT, JOSEPH, grandson of Canada's first settler, only son of Guillaume Hébert and Hélène DESPORTES; b. Quebec 3 Nov. 1636; d. 1661 or 1662.

Joseph Hébert's father, only son of LOUIS HÉBERT, died in 1639. On 12 Oct. 1660, Joseph married Marie-Charlotte de Poytiers. Not long afterwards he was captured by the Iroquois, perhaps by the same band who killed his cousin Nicolas Couillard and six other Frenchmen on the Île d'Orléans in June 1661. A letter written by a companion in captivity states that, wounded in the arm and shoulder, he was given to the Iroquois of Oneida. After the usual tortures, he was finally stabbed to death by drunken members of the tribe. His death was not definitely known in Quebec until the summer of 1662.

Meanwhile on 5 Oct. 1661 his wife had borne a son, Joseph. Since the records contain no further mention of this child, it is assumed that he died in infancy. In that case, Canada's first settler has no direct descendants bearing the Hébert name. There were, however, other Héberts in the colony at an early date, who may have been related; for example, one Jacques Hébert signed the inventory of Jean NICOLLET's possessions 7 Nov. 1642.

ETHEL M. G. BENNETT

The letter written by Joseph Hébert's companion in captivity is cited in *JR* (Thwaites) XLVII, 90. Other information is collected in Azarie Couillard Després, *La première famille française au Canada* and in Léon Roy, "Pierre Desportes et sa descendance," *SGCF Mémoires*, II (1946–47), 167–68.

HÉBERT, LOUIS, apothecary, first officer of justice in New France, first Canadian settler to support himself from the soil, m. Marie ROLLET; b. Paris 1575?; d. Quebec, January 1627.

According to his descendant, Couillard Després, he was the son of a Louis Hébert who was apothecary at the court of Catherine de' Medici. Documents more recently discovered in Paris indicate that his father was Nicolas Hébert, an apothecary, and that Louis was born in the *Mortier d'Or*, a house near the Louvre. The niece of Nicolas Hébert's wife married JEAN DE BIENCOURT de Poutrincourt, in 1590. This relationship would explain Louis Hébert's interest in the early settlements in Acadia and his presence in DU GUA de Monts's expedition.

LESCARBOT, in Port-Royal (Annapolis Royal, N.S.) in 1606, speaks with respect of his skill in healing and his pleasure in cultivating the soil, and, on his map of that region, indicates an island and a river named for Hébert. In the summer of 1606 Hébert sailed with CHAMPLAIN and Poutrincourt along the coast to the southwest, seeking other sites suitable for settlement. Poutrincourt and Hébert were so attracted by what is now Gloucester, Mass., that they planted a clearing there to test the soil's fertility. Both hoped to bring their families to settle in the New World. On this voyage Hébert showed that, though intent on peaceful pursuits, he could be counted on for quick and courageous action in an emergency. With Champlain, Poutrincourt, and several others, he leaped from the ship into a small boat, unclothed, in the middle of the night, in response to frantic cries from some foolhardy men who, having defied orders and remained on shore, were being attacked by Indians. The *Jonas*, arriving from France in June 1607, brought the unwelcome news that, because of the cancellation of de Monts's concessions, the company must return to France.

In 1610, Hébert was again in Port-Royal, with the group whom Poutrincourt hoped to establish there. As apothecary, he treated both French and Indian patients. Apparently meals as well as medicine received his consideration; he prepared and administered both to chief MEMBERTOU in his last illness. He was in charge of the settlement when, in 1613, RÉNE LE COQ de La Saussaye came with the Marquise de Guercheville's colonists, withdrew the two Jesuit fathers from Port-Royal, and sailed away to start a new settlement elsewhere. The capture of this expedition at Île des Monts Deserts by the English that same summer was followed by their destruction of Port-Royal (November 1613), and once more Hébert was forced to return to France.

In the winter of 1616–17 he renewed acquaintance with Champlain who was in Paris seeking support for his colony at Quebec. This post, having survived for nine years, probably seemed to Hébert a safe place for settlers, especially as Champlain obtained for him a favourable contract from the fur-trading company in control of the St. Lawrence region. Relying on these promises—200 crowns a year for his services as apothecary, and food and shelter for his family while getting land cleared—Hébert sold his house and garden in Paris and took his wife Marie

Hébert

Rollet and three children, Anne, GUILLEMETTE, and Guillaume, to Honfleur ready to embark. There he discovered that the company had no intention of honouring its agreement. The best he could obtain was a new contract, halving his salary and his land grant and stipulating that his family and his servant should be at the service of the company without pay. Having no alternative, he accepted and sailed with his family 11 March 1617.

In Quebec his apothecary's skill and his small store of grain were a godsend to the sick and starving winterers. In spite of the company's demands on his and his servant's time, he succeeded in clearing and planting some land. Champlain, on his brief visit of 1618, found cultivated land "filled with fine grain" and gardens in which flourished a variety of vegetables.

For many years Hébert was the only man besides Champlain himself who took any interest in cultivating land. The trading company did their utmost to discourage him. Both Champlain and SAGARD say that the unlawful restrictions they imposed upon him and upon the disposal of his products prevented him from enjoying the fruits of his labours.

When in 1620 Champlain returned from France with (nominally) full authority over the colony, he gave Hébert responsibility in the administration of justice by appointing him king's attorney. In this capacity he signed the colony's petition to the king in 1621. Hébert enjoyed the confidence also of the Indians, whom he, in contrast to many of his contemporaries, considered as intelligent human beings lacking only education. Many instances bear witness to their respect and affection for him. There is some question of trade relations with GUILLAUME DE CAËN, but in view of the fact that the surname Hébert is a very common one, this may be a case of mistaken identity.

In 1622 he petitioned the viceroy for a title to his land and on 4 Feb. 1623 received the grant guaranteeing him possession. Known later as the fief Sault-au-Matelot, the land included sites at present occupied by the Basilica, the seminary, and Hébert and Couillard streets. This title was ratified on 28 Feb. 1626 by the succeeding viceroy and some acres along the St. Charles—the fief Saint-Joseph, later known as fief de Lespinay—were added, both holdings to be enjoyed "en fief noble." Hébert had achieved his cherished ambition: he had brought under his control enough of the wild land of the New World to support himself and his family in independence. The meadows along the St. Charles afforded pasture for cattle; on the higher ground he had grain fields, vegetable gardens, and an orchard planted with apple trees brought from Normandy. All this had been achieved in spite of the company's opposition. Moreover, it had been accomplished with hand-tools only, not even a plough. (It was not until a year after the death of Hébert, that land was worked with plough and oxen and agriculture on a larger scale could begin.)

The winter of 1626 he had a fall on the ice which proved fatal. He died 25 Jan. 1627 and was buried in the Recollet cemetery. In 1678 his bones, still in their cedar coffin, were transferred to the vault of the newly erected Recollet chapel and with those of Brother Pacifique DUPLESSIS were the first to rest there.

ETHEL M. G. BENNETT

Hébert is mentioned in the following works of his contemporaries: Champlain, *Works* (Biggar), *passim*. *JR* (Thwaites), *passim*. Lescarbot, *History* (Grant), II, 209, 234, 328, 331; III, 246. Sagard, *Histoire du Canada* (Tross), I, 53, 83, 158–59. LE CLERCQ, while not strictly a contemporary, is near enough to the period to have gathered first-hand information and to have talked with Hébert's daughter. He gives information about the family in *First establishment of the faith* (Shea), I, 164–67, 281. Documents concerning company agreements, land grants, etc., are cited in Biggar, *Early trading companies* and in Azarie Couillard Després, *La première famille française au Canada* and *Louis Hébert: premier colon canadien et sa famille* (Lille, Paris, Bruges, 1913; Montréal, 1918). The two latter works give detailed and imaginative, but as far as possible documented, accounts of the family and its members. Madeleine Jurgens, "Recherches sur Louis Hébert et sa famille," SGCF *Mémoires*, VIII (1957), 106–12, 135–45; XI (1960), 24–31. This is the general title of a series of three articles: the second (VIII (1957), 135–45) deals mainly with Nicolas Hébert; the third (XI (1960), 24–31) with Louis.

HÉBERT, MARIE. *See* ROLLET

HERJÓLFSSON. *See* BJARNI

HEROVIN, MARIE, *dite* **de la Conception.** *See* IRWIN

HERTEL DE LA FRESNIÈRE, JACQUES, soldier, interpreter, and settler, father of the famous François Hertel*; b. at Fécamp (Normandy), son of Nicolas Hertel and Jeanne Miriot; d. 10 Aug. 1651 at Trois-Rivières.

It is probable, although there is no written proof of it, that he arrived in the country about 1626, as a soldier. He spent among the Algonkins the years during which Quebec was occupied by the KIRKE brothers. No doubt as a reward for the good relations that he had maintained with the Indians, the Compagnie des Cent-Associés granted him, by a title-deed dated 16 Dec. 1633 at Paris, a 200-acre tract of land at Trois-Rivières; with JEAN GODEFROY de Lintot he was the first settler there, before the official founding of that post. Hertel served as an interpreter for the Jesuits among the Indians, and was the settlers' syndic in 1647. He died 10 Aug. 1651 in the prime of life, it is believed accidentally. On 23 Aug. 1641 he had married Marie Marguerie, a sister of the interpreter, by whom he had had three children: François, nicknamed the "hero of Trois-Rivières," who was baptized by Father BRÉBEUF 3 July 1642, whose godfather was François MARGUERIE, and whose godmother was Marguerite Couillard, the wife of Jean NICOLLET; Madeleine, b. 2 Sept. 1645, who on 29 Aug. 1658 married Louis PINARD, the surgeon of the fort at Trois-Rivières; and Marguerite, b. 26 Aug. 1649, who became the wife of Jean CREVIER, the seigneur of Saint-François, in 1663. In 1652 Marie Marguerie remarried; her second husband was Quentin Moral de Saint-Quentin.

RAYMOND DOUVILLE

Archives de la paroisse de l'Immaculée-Conception, Trois-Rivières, Registres. *JR* (Thwaites). P.-G. Roy, *Inv. concessions*, II, 4–5. Godbout, *Les pionniers de la région trifluvienne*.

HILL, WILLIAM, sea captain, colonizer, governor of Lord Baltimore's [*see* CALVERT] colony at Ferryland; fl. 1634–38.

Nothing is known of Hill's career before about 1634 when he was appointed deputy governor of the colony in Newfoundland by Cecil Calvert, the second Lord Baltimore. The settlement appears to have been without a governor since 1629 when George Calvert had left the island and transferred his interest to the more hospitable shores of Maryland.

Hill took up residence in Baltimore's deserted mansion house at Ferryland. There are no accounts of his rule over the colonists and visiting fishermen. In 1629 the settlers had numbered 100 but probably only a small proportion of these now remained.

Hill was still at Ferryland in June 1638 when the *Pembroke* of London, commanded by Capt. Henry Tilliard, arrived to prepare for the coming of Sir DAVID KIRKE. Kirke and his associates, the Marquis of Hamilton and the earls of Pembroke and Holland, were the new proprietors of the island under a charter granted in November 1637, in disregard of Baltimore's charter of Avalon. A month later Kirke himself arrived and demanded that Hill quit the mansion house. Hill at first refused but found himself unable to hold out against Kirke's superior strength. He "withdrew himselfe into a little house adjoyning and not being able to doe otherwise yeelded up the possession of the said Chiefe Mansion house to the said Sir David Kirke." Later Hill moved to the north side of the harbour "where after some yeeres of dwelling hee . . . departed his life." (PRO, H.C.A.13/65, 12 & 29 March 1652, depositions of James Pratt and Robert Alward.)

GILLIAN T. CELL

For other references to Hill see: PRO, C.O. 1/14, no. 9. PRO, *CSP, Col., 1574–1660*. Lounsbury, *British fishery at Nfld*. L. D. Scisco, "Calvert's proceedings against Kirke," *CHR*, VIII (1927), 132–36.

HINTON, WILLIAM, courtier and Newfoundland planter who campaigned for civil government and aspired to governorship; b. *c*. 1624–26; d. *c*. 1688.

William Hinton was born into a well-connected, propertied family in the West Country. His grandfather, Sir Thomas Hinton, owned extensive lands in Devon, was J.P. for the County of Wiltshire, and was able to exert considerable influence at the courts of James I and Charles I. His father, also named William Hinton, was a Gentleman of the Privy Chamber from about 1620 onwards. The younger William, therefore, was led directly into close contact with the Stuart court and, after the establishment of republican government in 1649, he and his father followed Prince Charles into exile on the Continent, almost as a matter of course.

It is possible, though by no means certain, that Hinton already had some connections, either direct or otherwise, with Newfoundland for in later life he repeatedly claimed that he was specifically promised the governorship of Newfoundland many times after 1654. Early in his stay in Flanders he married the daughter of Jacobus Boeve, a merchant at Middleburg in Zeeland and one of the many men who supported the royal exile and his retinue during the Interregnum. Boeve was later to ask that his son-in-law be made governor of Newfoundland as reward for his own financial help to the future Charles II; Hinton himself maintained that his family suffered a loss of several thousand pounds in the Civil War and the years of exile.

In 1659 the younger Hinton was back in England where he raised a troop of horse for the abortive Royalist rising led by Sir George Booth in Cheshire and North Wales. The rising, intended to cover the whole country, was confined to the northwest. It ended in utter rout at Nantwich but may well have had some effect in hastening the Restoration.

Hirouin

After 1660 the elder Hinton became tenant of Bradninch Manor and added the title of "Provider of the Queens Robes" to that of "Gentleman of the Privy Chamber." He died eventually in 1669.

His son was involved in landowning disputes in Pembrokeshire in 1661 but was soon afterwards established as a planter in Newfoundland, apparently with the express purpose of furthering his claims to the promised governorship when a government should finally be established. By 1667 he had successfully achieved an unofficial position as spokesman for the inhabitants in the dispute over the Newfoundland trade and offshore fishery. In 1668 he went to England to press his case for civil government and his own plans to become the first governor. His forceful personality and boundless optimism were sufficiently impressive to cause a Mr Francis at Whitehall to write to Mr Saunders at Scarborough that "The ship with Mr Hinton, appointed Governor of Newfoundland, put into Weymouth Road" on 27 Aug. 1668. This is plainly impossible, as the first official governor was appointed in 1729, but it may well be an indication of Hinton's faith in the promises he had received some ten or more years before.

This faith shows itself consistently in the frequent petitions made by Hinton between 1668 and 1681. His participation, on behalf of the inhabitants and himself, in that period of the long dispute between London and West Country merchant interests concerning the regulation of the trade and fishery is roughly contemporary with that of Capt. Robert Robinson*. Whereas Robinson, however, was an enthusiastic theorist, there can be little doubt that Hinton was far more concerned with personal advancement than with strategic or economic considerations. His view, apparently, was that he could hardly become governor unless civil government were brought about beforehand.

In spite of his ambitious motives, Hinton did achieve considerable success in presenting the planters' case; and it seems that his vigorous campaigning, simultaneously with that of WILLIAM DOWNING, had great significance among the pressures brought to bear on the Privy Council. Hinton's petition played a large part in the investigation into the fishery made by the Committee of Trade and Plantations in 1675. Hinton was also prominent, together with John BERRY, Thomas Oxford, and the Downings, in re-opening the question immediately after the 1675 decision had gone against them.

Even the passage of so many years and a long illness in 1677–78 did not deter him from further efforts to secure the governorship. In March 1679 he presented a further petition, hoping that "in consideration of his pains and cost in endeavouring to settle Newfoundland he may have the benefit of his Majesty's promise." In 1680 he presented a vast series of "Observations" on the island, running to 21 clauses, and a last desperate petition, backed by the Bishop of London, came forward in February 1680/81. The whole question by now, however, was obviously further than ever from resolution and a disappointed Hinton turned at last to other fields before his death some short time after 1686.

C. M. ROWE

[See also BERRY and DOWNING]

PRO, Acts of P.C., col. ser., 1613–80; new ser., 1621–23; 1629–30; CSP, Col., 1669–74, 1675–76, 1677–80, 1681–85; CSP, Dom., 1654, 1660–61, 1663–64, 1667–68, 1675–76, 1679–80. Hinton's petitions are especially interesting for the light they throw upon his character.

C. B. Judah, *The North American fisheries and British policy to 1713* (University of Illinois Studies in the Social Sciences, XVIII, nos. 3–4, 1933). Lounsbury, *British fishery at Nfld*, has the best history of the fishery dispute. Prowse, *History of Nfld*.

HIROUIN, MARIE, *dite* **de la Conception.** See IRWIN

HONATTENIATE (known also as "Le Berger" [the lover or shepherd]), Mohawk Indian, friend of the French and protector of Father JOGUES; b. in the Mohawk Valley of present New York State; d. 1650 in Paris.

The story of Honatteniate illustrates the devotion which he and many nameless Indians felt for the French. His mother was the adopted "aunt" of Father Isaac Jogues during his first captivity, 1642–43, in the Mohawk country, a relationship honoured by her son at the risk of his own life.

Honatteniate played a role as hostage in the crucial peace negotiations of 1645 [see KIOTSEAETON]. He was one of two Mohawks captured during the spring of 1645 by a war-party of Algonkins under PIESKARET secreted on an island in Lake Champlain. Brought unharmed to Sillery by the Algonkins, the two Mohawks were delivered 18 May to Governor HUAULT de Montmagny, who ordered them transferred to Trois-Rivières with instructions to the commandant, Sieur de CHAMPFLOUR, to liberate Tokhrahenehiaron, a Mohawk captured previously by the French. The latter was told to inform his nation that Honatteniate would be set free after the Mohawks had advised the governor of their peaceful intentions.

Tokhrahenehiaron and two prominent Mohawk envoys were present 12 July 1645 during the important peace negotiations at Trois-Rivières, where Kiotseaeton, the famous Mohawk orator, presented 17 words (there were 17 divisions in his address) and each was confirmed by a belt of wampum. The seventeenth and last belt was one which had been worn by Honatteniate in his own country and which his mother had sent in gratitude that her son's life had been spared by the French. As a result of the peace treaty ratified in May 1646, Honatteniate and his companions returned home. Father Jogues, with JEAN BOURDON, was in the Mohawk country 16 May–29 June to confirm the peace.

Father Jogues started on his third and last journey to the Mohawk country, 24 Sept. 1646, to found a mission there. Unknown to the priest, the Mohawks had repudiated the recently established peace. On his arrival at the Mohawk village, he was seized and treated as a prisoner. But Honatteniate was with him when a Mohawk hatchet struck him down on the evening of 18 Oct. 1646. The Indian attempted to avert the blow but was disabled by a gash in the arm. A second, swift stroke, and the priest was dead.

Honatteniate delivered himself into the hands of the French at Trois-Rivières, 30 May 1648. He said that he had loved them from the time they spared his life. His trust was not reciprocated and his feet were shackled. Even this indignity did not turn him against the French. Later he proved his sincerity by acting on several occasions as intermediary between the French and other Mohawks, who frequented the vicinity of Trois-Rivières.

Honatteniate was now a man without a country and a target for Mohawk retaliation. Eventually it was decided that, as a safety precaution, he should be sent to France in the care of the Jesuit fathers. He left Quebec in the company of a priest, Oct. 1649. The two arrived at Havre-de-Grâce (Le Havre), 7 December and from there travelled to Dieppe. In Paris Honatteniate developed a serious fever around 20 Jan. 1650. He died 26 January, a short time after his baptism, aged about 35 years.

THOMAS GRASSMANN

JR (Thwaites), XXVII, 229–45, 247, 251–65, 267–73. XXVIII, 137, 189, 207, XXIX, 47–61, XXXI, 109, 111, 117, XXXII, 149–53, XXXVI, 21–23, 25–27, 29, 33–39, 41–45.

HORE (Hoore), RICHARD, merchant and navigator, who brought a group of English gentlemen to see Newfoundland in 1536; fl. 1507–40.

Citizen of London and leather-seller, Hore engaged in the Spanish trade with William Dolphyn, a London draper, and Sir Thomas Spert, a naval official and shipowner, between 1536 and 1540, signing a petition in Spain against the Spanish Inquisition in 1540. Hakluyt describes him as "a man of goodly stature and of great courage, and given to the studie of Cosmographie"; though some of his commercial transactions show him to have been unscrupulous.

Early in 1536 he chartered from Dolphyn the *William* of London, Richard Elyot master, for a voyage to Newfoundland. She had a Breton pilot, Alayne Moyne. Late in August, at the end of her voyage, she was at anchor at "the Isle of Spere" (Spear Island), completing her lading of fish and repairing, with timber sawn from trees felled near the harbour, three leaks caused "by reasons of labouring at the seas and long lying at Newfoundland." Despite a further leak on the return voyage she was back in the Thames by early October. Nothing is said, in the documents which tell this story, about discovery, or passengers. Hakluyt, citing Thomas Butts, says there were two ships, the *Trinity*, 140 tons, Capt. Hore, on which Butts sailed, and the *Minion* (for the *William*?). With the king's goodwill they carried 30 gentlemen, including John RASTELL, the younger, on "a voyage of discoverie upon the Northwest parts of America." Hore took his ships to Cape Breton and then coasted southern and eastern Newfoundland to Penguin (Funk) Island, where they killed great auk and bear.

Thus far the story is credible. Hakluyt then switches to a narrative by Oliver Dawbeny, who claimed to have sailed on the *Minion*. He recalled some contacts with the Beothuk Indians, and then told of starvation suffered in harbour (where, it is not stated), culminating in cannibalism by one of the seamen. He said disaster was prevented only by the arrival of a French ship which the English seized. They exchanged their ship for the French one and finally arrived, much emaciated, in Cornwall late in October. Dawbeny and Butts told their stories some 50 years later; part of Dawbeny's, if applied to the *William*, is demonstrably false. Nothing is certainly known of how the *Trinity* fared after she left Funk Island.

Though usually considered to have voyaged up the eastern shores of Labrador, Hore cannot be proved to have left Newfoundland waters. However, a possible explanation of the objective and course of the voyage is suggested by the employment of the Breton pilot, Alayne Moyne, namely the following of Jacques CARTIER's track of 1534 through the Straits of Belle Isle, along the southern shores of Labrador or northwest Newfoundland, into the Gulf of St. Lawrence. The taking of sea-birds for food at Funk Island might be thought to have copied Cartier's action two years before. The exhaustion of food supplies could

Horehouasse

then have been caused by delays brought about by the leaking of the ship and its repair. The barren coast could be southern Labrador. Finally, the appearance of a French ship, and her robbery if not permanent seizure, would parallel Cartier's discovery of a La Rochelle vessel fishing in these waters. An exaggeration of hardships encountered and of time taken would account for the rest of the story with its omission of the voyage to southern Newfoundland (through the Straits of Belle Isle rather than by Cabot Strait) to fish and refit. This theory of the voyage is proposed with little confidence as it is, at present, impossible to prove it. It may well be that any attempt to reconcile the two stories in Hakluyt is impossible if one of them is substantially false.

The combination of sightseeing, fishing, and perhaps some original exploration was novel. It gave a number of educated Englishmen, for the first time, an opportunity to see part of North America, and it may thus be a link with the revived interest of Elizabethan intellectuals in Newfoundland after about 1575. Richard Hore may therefore be a valuable link between the early and later English ventures in this area.

DAVID B. QUINN

PRO, H.C.A.13/2, ff.51–53, 61–65, 100–53v; 24/2, 13; 30/542, 56–58. Thomas Butts's and Oliver Dawbeny's accounts are found in Hakluyt, *Principal navigations* (1903–5), VIII, 3–7. E. G. R. Taylor, "Master Hore's voyage of 1536," *Geog. J.*, LXXVII (1933), 469–70. *Voyages of Cartier* (Biggar), 273–77. Williamson, *Voyages of the Cabots* (1929).

HOREHOUASSE. *See* OUREHOUARE

"HOT ASH" ("Hot Powder"). *See* OGENHERATARIHIENS

HOTEOUATE (Hotrehouati, Houtreouati). *See* OTREOUTI

HUAULT DE MONTMAGNY, CHARLES, called by the Indians "**Onontio,**" first governor and lieutenant-general of New France from 1636 to 1648; b. *c.* 1583 in France; d. apparently in 1653, on the Île Saint-Christophe in the West Indies.

The Huault family goes back at least as far as Henri II, to whom Jacques Huault was a counsellor and a secretary. The Huaults owned extensive estates. They were marquis of Vaires and of Bussy-Saint-Martin (Seine-et-Marne), and seigneurs of Bernay, Montmagny, and Richebourg (Seine-et-Oise).

Charles Huault was educated by the Jesuits, and entered the Order of Malta on 3 Aug. 1622. He was posted to the men-of-war of the order which maintained peace in the Mediterranean area, and he served his apprenticeship there as a naval officer, fighting against the Turks and the pirates from Algiers and Tripoli. In 1632 he was one of the directors of the Compagnie de la Nouvelle-France.

In 1635, while CHAMPLAIN was still alive, Montmagny was appointed governor of Canada. His family ties with JEAN DE LAUSON (senior), a director of the company, partly explain this appointment. Montmagny's gifts as an administrator, as well as his personal qualities, had, however, already shown that he was worthy to continue Champlain's work. His first commission as governor dates from 15 Jan. 1636. He was therefore the first titular governor of New France, since Champlain bore the title of "commandant in New France in the absence" of Richelieu. Montmagny was to receive subsequently three commissions: in 1639, 1642, and 1645.

He arrived in the colony on 11 June 1636, together with Lieut. BRÉHAUT Delisle, his secretary Martial Piraube, and three officers. He immediately went to the church, where the *Te Deum* was sung, and M. BRAS-DE-FER de Chateaufort handed over to him the keys of Fort Saint-Louis. Montmagny was then 53. He was an impressive personality; the Jesuit correspondent was frequently to extol "his piety, his industry, his prudence, and his wisdom."

Charles Huault spared neither strength nor courage in the king's service. In September 1636, in order to find out for himself what the state of the settlers was, he made a tour of the colony which took him from Cap Tourmente to the Île Montmagny (Jésus). He was struck by the population's insecurity, and as soon as he got back to Quebec he gave his attention to the reorganization of the military defences. He ordered the Château Saint-Louis to be transformed into a stone and brick fortress with a garrison. He instructed the engineer and surveyor JEAN BOURDON to draw up a plan for the future town, and himself chose the names of the first streets: Saint-Louis, Sainte-Anne, and Mont-Carmel. At Trois-Rivières he built a storehouse and a platform fitted with cannon.

The Iroquois were indeed threatening the country. During the occupation of Quebec by the English they had broken the peace concluded by Champlain, around 1622, and in 1634 had again begun their incursions into the colony. Everything might have been settled had it not been for the Dutch from Fort Orange (Albany, N.Y.), who in

Huault de Montmagny

1639 began to barter with the Iroquois, giving them arquebuses in exchange for beaver furs. In this way the Iroquois, who were rivals of the Hurons in the fur trade, had an undeniable military superiority, for Montmagny, continuing Champlain's policy, forbade the French to sell fire-arms to the Indians. Emboldened by the support of the Dutch, the Iroquois formally declared war on the French in 1641. Montmagny held a parley with them at Trois-Rivières in June, but to no avail. The negotiations degenerated into a brief combat, in which the governor was victorious.

The dark hours of the colony had just begun. What could 300 settlers (including women and children), scattered between Beaupré and Trois-Rivières, do against an enemy as cunning as the Iroquois? Montmagny hastily blockaded the Richelieu, the traditional Iroquois route. In August 1642 he constructed Fort Richelieu, on the site of the future Sorel, using for that purpose the 40 soldiers who had arrived from France. Montmagny was under no illusions as to the effectiveness of this fort. Consequently he sought peace. In 1645, at Trois-Rivières, he concluded a treaty with the Mohawks; the famous orator, KIOTSEAETON, took an active part in drawing it up. The Jesuit JOGUES and Jean Bourdon endeavoured to consolidate the peace by going to the Iroquois country in June 1646. Jogues was to return there in the autumn, but only to meet his death. The Iroquois had already planned the destruction of the Huron country; they were to carry out their scheme in 1648–49, at a time when Montmagny had returned to France.

Despite the Iroquois war, important achievements marked Montmagny's term of office. In 1639 the governor was delighted by the arrival of two religious communities who wished to devote themselves to the welfare of the population: the Ursulines, financed by Mme CHAUVIGNY de La Peltrie, proposed to concern themselves with the education of young girls; the Augustine Hospitallers, encouraged by the Duchesse d'Aiguillon, proposed to found a hospital. Then came the founding of Montreal. In the autumn of 1641 the first contingent of the Société Notre-Dame reached Quebec. The leader, CHOMEDEY de Maisonneuve wanted to establish himself on the Montreal Island. Montmagny considered that to choose an island so far up the river and so exposed to Iroquois attacks was a "foolhardy venture," and urged the Montrealers to establish themselves on the Île d'Orléans. But Maisonneuve stood firm, and Montmagny was obliged to hand over Montreal Island to the members of the society. Subsequently Montmagny always kept the Montrealers at a distance. Perhaps he deemed the project too rash, perhaps also he did not forgive the society for having the privilege of letters patent that granted it a wide administrative and religious autonomy. Whatever the reasons may be, Montmagny showed little inclination to assist the Montrealers when they were at grips with the Iroquois in 1647 and 1648; it was even rumoured that he attempted to keep at Quebec the few soldiers at his disposal.

After the founding of Montreal came the creation of the Communauté des Habitants; an important consequence of this was the limitation of the governor's powers. Practically speaking both the civil and the military authority were vested in Montmagny. He saw to the country's security, held smuggling in check, presided at councils with the natives, and settled disputes arising among individuals. A lieutenant, a clerk of court, and an attorney assisted him in his functions. However, the irregularities that took place in the administration of the Communauté led the Conseil du Roi, on 27 March 1647, to enact a law for "establishing order and surveillance in Canada." The decree created a council composed of the governor, the superior of the Jesuits, and the governor of Montreal. The council appointed the general and the captains of the fleet, the clerks and comptrollers of the fur trade, in addition to a secretary able to act as a notary public. In fact, the council had jurisdiction over everything that concerned the fur trade and the general interest of the country.

Montmagny was replaced in 1648, and it is not known whether this was because of his age, of his reserve towards the members of the Société de Montréal, of the indecision that had for some time marked his policy towards the Iroquois, or of the designs of the Order of Malta in America. The Conseil du Roi, which included the three members of the Société de Montréal, first thought of Maisonneuve as his successor. The latter stood down in favour of LOUIS D'AILLEBOUST, who was appointed on 2 March 1648. Montmagny betrayed no acrimony. He received the new governor with elaborate ceremony on 20 Aug. 1648 and sailed for France on 23 September. On his arrival he was appointed receiver of the priory of France by the grand master of Malta. The latter, in 1652, entrusted to him the government of Saint-Christophe, in the West Indies. Montmagny is thought to have died there in 1653.

He was remembered after his death as a conscientious administrator, concerned with the progress and well-being of the population, but over-assertive. He never let pass an opportunity to show his compassion for the poor and his friendship for the common people, whom he often invited to public celebrations. Thanks to him, the theatre made its appearance at Quebec: in 1640 his secretary Piraube played the principal role in a tragi-comedy, and on 31 Dec. 1646 the people of Quebec were able to witness a performance of *Le Cid*.

The Indians had named Montmagny "Onontio," meaning "great mountain." This name was subsequently passed on to all the governors of New France, in the same way that "Achiendassé," the name given to JÉRÔME LALEMANT, later designated the superiors of the Jesuits at Quebec.

JEAN HAMELIN

The documentation on Montmagny is scanty, as his correspondence has never been found. *JJ* (Laverdière et Casgrain) and *JR* (Thwaites), are the best documentary sources. ASQ possesses about 50 documents relative to the judgments, concessions, and orders signed by Montmagny. See also: *Édits ord.*, III, 15. *Ord. comm.* (P.-G. Roy), I, 1–9. *Inv. concessions* (P.-G. Roy), I, *passim. Mémoires des commissaires*, I, 156–57; II, 499; IV, 180; and *Memorials of the English and French commissaries*, I, 211, 365, 715.

Among the secondary sources, Gustave Lanctot, in his *Histoire du Canada*, I, provides useful and precise details and, especially, the historical background. J.-E. Roy has devoted several articles to Montmagny, as well as his *L'ordre de Malte en Amérique* (Québec, 1888), in which he advances the theory that Montmagny would have liked to make the Château Saint-Louis a fortress of the order.

For the reasons behind Montmagny's departure, the following works may be consulted: *BRH*, XVI (1910), 11–17; XLVII (1941), 32, and *Coll. de manuscrits relatifs à la Nouv.-France*, I, 249. See also E. R. Adair, "France and the beginnings of New France," *CHR*, XXV (1944), 246–78.

HUDSON, HENRY, English navigator and discoverer, and, in a sense, a founding father of both New York City and the Hudson's Bay Company; fl. 1607–11.

The antecedents and early life of Hudson are obscure. He first appears in 1607 already in middle life and of international reputation. In that year he was employed by the English Muscovy Company to seek a short route to China by way of the North Pole. He succeeded only in setting a "farthest north" record and in making observations which led to the founding of the Spitzbergen whale fishery. His search in 1608, on behalf of the same employers, for a northeast passage through the Russian Arctic was a complete failure.

It may be taken as an indication of Hudson's reputation for zeal and competence that his ill success convinced his countrymen that these enterprises were impracticable. Less easily discouraged, the directors of the Dutch East India Company hired him to re-attempt the northeast passage. He sailed in 1609 in the *Half Moon* with a mixed crew of Dutch and English (including a former shipmate, the cantankerous Robert Juet). On meeting the polar ice beyond the North Cape of Norway, the crew mutinied and refused to go farther. The captain therefore put about to seek a route to China by way of North America. He ascended the Hudson River (discovered in 1524 by the Italian VERRAZZANO) as far as Albany and proved the trading potentialities of that inland waterway. On the homeward voyage he put in at an English harbour and there received an order from the Privy Council forbidding him to return to the Netherlands, or to re-enter the service of a foreign power.

This prohibition mattered less to the discoverer as he found immediate employment with his own countrymen. His last voyage, though unsuccessful, had revived hopes of a genuine passage to China elsewhere. Sir Thomas Smith, incorporator and first governor of the East India and Northwest Passage companies and treasurer of the Virginia Company, Sir Dudley Digges, a wealthy young gentleman interested in explorations, and Mr (later Sir) John Wolstenholme, a famous Yorkshire promoter of expeditions, in association with a number of merchants, financed a fresh expedition and appointed Hudson to the command. He was to direct his search towards Davis Strait [*see* John DAVIS], a region which, with the nebulous Strait of Anian in mind, he regarded as affording the best promise of success.

The ship *Discovery* was manned with a larger and more miscellaneous crew than had sailed with Hudson on his previous English-based voyages. He carried Juet with him as mate. It is a sign of weakness on the explorer's part that he could not refuse this important post to one with whose unpleasant disposition he was fully acquainted. Possibly to lessen his dependence on the troublesome old man, he shipped, although with no higher rank than that of seaman, Robert BYLOT, a first-class navigator, and, as he was to prove, a man of stolid but invincible courage. Four landsmen were taken aboard, Edward Wilson, surgeon (not to be confused with William Wilson, later promoted boatswain, and a principal conspirator against his captain), Abacuk Pricket, a servingman of Sir Dudley Digges, Thomas Wydowse (or Woodhouse), a mathematician, who may also have owed his berth to Digges, and (without the knowledge of the owners) one Henry Greene. This last was a dissolute young man, disowned by his well-to-do Kentish family, whom Hudson had befriended, and whom he now, with characteristic good-nature and want of judgement, took on board, promising, despite Greene's unauthorized position, to procure him a seaman's wages when the voyage was over. Greene was a man of some education; and Hudson, who was plainly naïve in all but purely professional relationships, may have fancied that he had found in him the counterpart of John Janes, the friend of John Davis and picturesque chronicler of some of his voyages.

The *Discovery* sailed from London on 17 April 1610, and after a prosperous voyage as far as Iceland put into a bay to refresh her crew while they waited for the ice-fields to the west to disperse. There the first symptoms of discord appeared. Greene, who was arrogant and of great physical strength, quarrelled with Edward Wilson and beat him so severely that "wee had much adoe to get the surgeon aboard." Though the crew were much incensed at this, Hudson shielded his favourite and fixed the blame for the quarrel on Wilson. They were again at sea when the drunken Juet, who, like the surgeon, detested the pretensions of the young upstart, openly declared that Hudson had shipped Greene to act as a spy on officers and men. The captain, on hearing this, flew into a rage and was with difficulty dissuaded from putting back to Iceland and sending the old mate home with the fishing fleet. This was an undignified and disheartening prelude to a season of hardship which only the highest degree of subordination and harmony could make tolerable. Late in June they raised the Island of Good Fortune (later Resolution Island) which marked Davis Strait on the right hand and Hudson Strait to the left.

Hudson Strait does not owe its discovery to the man after whom it is called. On his third voyage to Meta Incognita (1578), FROBISHER had entered it by mistake and, so he asserted, sailed up it 60 leagues. Sir Martin, however, was an indifferent navigator—at least in the opinion of his sailing master, Christopher Hall—and was noted, even in that uninhibited age, for overstatement. Experienced pilots put more weight on the observations of Davis (in 1587) and on the voyage of Capt. WAYMOUTH who in 1602 attempted the passage of the strait until thwarted by his crew who put the ship about and sailed for home. In 1606 John KNIGHT had approached the strait entrance only to perish mysteriously on the Labrador coast.

There are vaguer claims of discovery far antedating that of Frobisher. G. M. Asher, the 19th-century historian, believed that Hudson Strait was known to SEBASTIAN CABOT; and on the strength of old maps, unsupported by any trustworthy record, credited Portuguese navigators with having passed through the strait clean into the bay. The claim on behalf of Sebastian Cabot has the modern endorsement of J. A. Williamson. The best informed of Hudson's contemporaries harboured no such beliefs. Luke Fox ignores all earlier claimants to assert that it was Davis and Waymouth who "did (I conceive) light Hudson into his Streights." In the absence of incontrovertible evidence it is a fair conclusion that while both Portuguese and English navigators had been aware of the strait and had groped hesitantly about its eastern entrance, Hudson first supplied the daring and resolution to grasp the clue and follow without faltering wherever it led.

An ambiguous remark of Pricket suggests that it was the captain's intention to go north up Davis Strait—in conformity with his belief in an ice-free sea at higher latitudes—when the ship was caught in the tide and swept south of Resolution Island into the ice-clogged waters of Hudson Strait. Once in, he dared not turn back, as his frightened and divided crew might have insisted on abandoning altogether so dangerous an enterprise. With the ship battered by ice and swept back and forth by the tide-race in uncharted and, as they feared, reef-strewn waters, men fell sick from fear; and Hudson himself, as he later confessed to Pricket, was almost daunted.

When near Akpatok Island the crew mutinied at the instigation of the unforgiving Juet and clamoured to have the ship put about, the carpenter, Philip Staffe; stood loyally by his captain, who with a mixture of objurgation and entreaty reduced his unruly followers to obedience. A careful pilot, Hudson missed no opportunity of fixing landmarks on both sides of the strait, and after a devious voyage of six weeks passed between Cape Wolstenholme on the Quebec mainland and Digges Island (names bestowed in honour of the voyage's patrons) into Hudson Bay itself.

In the "larger discourse" of Pricket, which furnishes graphic glimpses of the voyage rather than a connected survey, Hudson appears chiefly in moments of passionate contention. Yet he must have displayed great patience and resolution to carry his ship through the manifold dangers of the strait which two centuries later, despite their foreknowledge, were to impress Franklin* and Parry*. His progress was slow, on an average ten miles a day of distance gained, and in an atmosphere of "indescribable gloom" calculated to excite the superstitious fears of the best-disposed among his company. The conquest of the strait

Hudson

confers on Hudson a greatness which his subsequent folly and mismanagement cannot annul.

Hudson hove to near Digges Island and sent Pricket ashore in the boat, accompanied by Bylot and Greene. They came back reporting abundance of wildfowl and the finest grass they had seen since leaving England. Pricket urged the captain to remain for two days in order to refresh the crew and build up his depleted food supply; but Hudson, confident that he had duplicated the feat of Magellan and was now in the Pacific, rejected the advice in a tone of annoyance. There was some justification for Juet's vicious taunt that Hudson was an unpractical visionary who expected to be in the Spice Islands by Candlemas.

While steering away to the south Hudson took advantage of his increased prestige to revenge himself on the mutineers who had nearly wrecked the expedition at Akpatok Island. Juet was arraigned before the crew (a dangerous precedent), convicted of inciting to disobedience, and degraded from the office of mate. This appointment, with the pay attached to it, was transferred to Robert Bylot. The boatswain was, for the same reason, deposed from his post. William Wilson was appointed in his place and the pay of the rank divided between him and John King, a loyal but ignorant fellow whom his shipmates tended to despise. Hudson was weak enough to apologize to the men whom he had disgraced and to promise that if their future conduct were satisfactory he "would bee a meanes for their good, and that hee would forget injuries."

The popularity which emboldened the captain thus to assert himself was short-lived. In October the voyagers found themselves in the bay later named for Thomas JAMES, "a labyrinth without end." Lacking the resolution to confess failure in that quarter Hudson wasted some weeks in seeking a southerly outlet, and found himself compelled to winter in the southeast angle of the Bay—presumably at the mouth of Rupert River. His own natural irritation was shared by the men who saw themselves cheated of the rewards promised for the actual discovery of a passage and faced by a winter of certain but incalculable hardship.

This state of suppressed ill-temper was aggravated by Hudson's indiscretion. About this time John Williams, the gunner, died, and according to custom his effects were sold by auction before the mast. Included was a grey cloth gown, a garment coveted by all the men now that the sub-arctic winter was upon them. Hudson gave great offence by appropriating this and handing it over to his favourite Greene, who had neither cash nor assured wages to pledge in payment of the debt.

Hudson, who a week before had impatiently rejected Staffe's suggestion that a building be erected on land to house the crew, now ordered him to build one. Staffe exclaimed that it had grown too cold and that "hee neither could nor would goe in hand with such worke." Hudson, who had been indulgent towards coarse and hardened offenders, betrayed his weakness by unrestrained severity to one whose fidelity was incorruptible. "Hee ferreted him [Staffe] out of his cabbin to strike him, calling him by many foule names, and threatning to hang him." After a day or two, through the loyal temper of Staffe, and perhaps also through the remorse of the hasty but generous captain, the quarrel was settled and the house built. But in the meantime the insolent Greene showed his contempt for Hudson by treating Staffe with special civility. The incensed captain deprived him of his gown, which he handed over to Bylot, and, taunting Greene with the vices which he himself had condoned, threatened to retract his promise of wages.

The *Discovery* was very ill provided for the many months which must elapse before she reached a home port. Pricket, who was in a position to know, asserts that Hudson could have obtained a more generous provision, but with characteristic optimism rejected it, probably wishing to keep the ship light for the dangerous navigation which she was certain to encounter in the ice. Though short rations were supplemented by partridge and other wildfowl, many suffered from scurvy during the winter. About the time that the ice broke up the explorers were visited by an Indian who after a kind reception took his leave promising by signs to return "after so many sleepes." The travellers never saw him again. In desperation Hudson took the boat and went in search of the natives to obtain "flesh." He discovered their settlement, but the natives refused all intercourse and set the woods on fire to keep the unwelcome visitors at a distance. The returns from fishing were disappointing and the fears of the men were aggravated by uncertainty as to how much food they had in hand.

Greene, less placable than Staffe, was labouring to discredit Hudson with the crew. Pricket states that he and William Wilson, a coarse but resolute fellow, plotted to steal the shallop and "shift for themselves"—an incredible story unless those seasoned vagabonds planned not to return home but to join the Indians and lead the life of savages. As long as Bylot remained loyal Hudson was safe from direct mutiny, for as Juet was deemed incapable of carrying the ship home, those two alone could pilot the others out of the wilderness. But about this time, on what grounds it is not known, Hudson transferred the post of mate to the subservient and illiterate John King. Greene, Wilson, and Juet could safely plot the captain's destruction, now they were assured of the friendship or neutrality of Bylot.

The voyage home was begun 12 June 1611. Hudson divided what purported to be the remaining rations among his company, telling them that they must live off that until they reached Digges Island. The men were certain that he was withholding a reserve supply, but could only guess at its amount. Candour on that point might even then have saved him.

On the night of 23 June, the ship being then becalmed off the island later named Charlton by Thomas James who wintered there in 1631–32, Greene and William Wilson entered Pricket's cabin to inform him of their intention to mutiny and turn the captain and the feebler men (still suffering from the effects of scurvy) adrift and so secure for themselves an enlarged ration which might suffice for survival. After a timid protest the frightened serving-man prevailed upon the two ringleaders and their accomplices to take an oath to "doe nothing but to the glory of God and the good of the action in hand, and harme to no man" (he does not explain the construction that he put upon this) and withdrew his opposition. At daybreak Hudson, his son JOHN, Wydowse, and five others were seized and pushed overboard into the shallop. Scorning to save his life by conniving at such a crime, Staffe voluntarily followed his captain into the boat. The mutineers then cut the shallop adrift and ran some distance to the north before heaving-to to ransack the ship. They turned up a concealed food hoard of some size, but not an excessively large emergency supply for a company of 21. While they were thus engaged the shallop came into sight and the more pitiful urged that the castaways be readmitted to the ship. The resolute Wilson prevailed, and they hoisted sail and fled, "as from an enemy."

By force of character and the prestige of his gentle birth Greene asserted his authority over the diminished band. He snubbed the unfortunate Juet and restored Bylot to the post of mate. Pricket now learned that it had been Greene's intention to maroon him with the rest and that he owed his life to the more prudent conspirators who looked to him to procure their pardon through his master, Sir Dudley Digges. The luckless serving-man's hope of proving his innocence by his hypocritical device of an oath was shrewdly thwarted by Greene who fixed on him the character of a chief conspirator by installing him (much against his will) in Hudson's cabin and putting him in charge of rations.

Bylot carried the ship directly to Digges Island, no inconsiderable feat of navigation, as reckoning had been confused by their devious course in James Bay in the autumn before. There they met with Eskimos of whom, on the way in, they had seen only traces. Greene was confident of obtaining food from these people. With incredible rashness he landed and committed himself and an unarmed party to the frightened and suspicious natives. They were set upon: Greene fought courageously to protect the retreat of his comrades with the broken staff of a pike and was struck dead by an arrow as he was clambering into the boat; William Wilson and one other man were mortally wounded. The desperate survivors put in at another part of the island and secured enough wildfowl for a pittance on the voyage home. Juet died on the way and the rest were brought to the point of starvation. When all others were reduced to despairing indifference, the skill, patience, and wooden courage of Bylot barely prevailed to bring the ship to the south of Ireland where help was obtained to carry them on to London.

Nothing is known of the ultimate fate of the victims of their crime. Later visitors to James Bay—Thomas James, Radisson* and others—discovered traces which have been conjecturally associated with Hudson and his men. The plot which cost them their lives appears the more odious from its rarity. Polar travellers have often risked and, in one instance at least, have sacrificed their lives rather than abandon disabled comrades. Yet in view of the privations endured by the eight survivors it might be supposed that had the crew of the *Discovery* remained intact all must have perished from want. This inference is, however, by no means forced. Pricket mentions no excessive privation in the period between the marooning of Hudson and the second arrival of the ship at Cape Digges. We may assume that all 21 could have survived to that point; and 21 men under leadership more prudent than that of Henry Greene might well have eluded the treachery of the natives and secured provision for the voyage home. Such a feat of survival would have been no more remarkable than John Davis's return voyage from Patagonia 20 years before.

For the incidents of this celebrated voyage and the last episode in the life of its commander we are chiefly indebted to the "larger discourse" of Abacuk Pricket. His truthfulness has naturally been questioned. He had to save not only his own character but those of his living comrades who could repay in kind any testimony he brought

Hudson

against them. Under these circumstances the fact that he spared the living and laid the burden of guilt almost entirely on the dead has troubled the critics. Yet he is plausible and consistent throughout, and the critical parts of his narrative are not without corroboration. We know that Greene bore an evil character before the voyage began; and a fragment, luckily preserved, of the diary of Thomas Wydowse supports Pricket's portrayal of Juet as disloyal and a confirmed trouble-maker. There is a strength and realism about the villain Wilson which Pricket, who was no Shakespeare, could not have coined. The tragedy of Hudson is probably as accurately recorded as any historical transaction which depends chiefly on one primary source and that not wholly disinterested.

With the qualifications noted above Pricket's account of these transactions is graphic and convincing. Without much intelligence or aptitude for geography he had the gift of his fellow-Puritan Bunyan for exact observation and vivid expression and he furnishes the material for a just estimate of the discoverer with whom his fortunes were linked. Hudson was a man in whom courage, vision, and intensity of purpose were vitiated by lack of the more commonplace qualities of good leadership. He had not the rude force of Sir FRANCIS DRAKE, or the robust good nature of John Davis, which enabled those captains to bend men to their will in times of danger and uncertainty. He showed little discretion either in his choice of favourites or in the extent to which he countenanced them. Hence, like his more modern counterpart, William Bligh, his trouble was chiefly with his officers. There must have been honest sturdy men of the type of Philip Staffe among the crew or the voyage would have terminated with Juet's first mutinous gesture at Akpatok Island. Hudson also must have had his share of moral force and persuasiveness to survive that crisis and rally his panic-stricken company for a fresh effort.

Hudson's achievement gives him a very high rank in the band of navigators from the British Isles who have done so much to unfold the map of the Canadian sub-continent. Parry and Franklin alone can compare with him in the extent to which he outstripped his predecessors and in the sum total of his original discoveries; but Parry was supported by a large, well-trained staff and a disciplined crew, while Franklin owed more to the journeys of Hearne* and Mackenzie* than Hudson to the nebulous findings of Cabot and the Portuguese navigators. The records of the latter, however meritorious, were unfruitful and did little to smooth the path of those who followed them. Single-handed Hudson blazed the way through the 400 miles of his strait and opened up the vast tract of inland sea beyond. More than that, his colossal effort gave his countrymen such an impetus that, barely five years after his disappearance, the rough chart of his bay was nearly complete and BAFFIN could assert with reasonable confidence that it was a closed sea with no navigable outlet to the west. It was not Hudson's fault that the English then proved less enterprising than his previous Dutch employers allowing a half-century to elapse before they undertook the commercial exploitation of his last magnificent venture.

Ironically, the very importance of Hudson's achievement served to shield the *Discovery*'s eight survivors—who were at least guilty of conniving at his fate—from the vengeance of the law. Foremost among these was Robert Bylot whose plea that he had had no share in the mutiny would have been given less weight in a criminal court than the palpable fact that he had been assigned high rank by the mutineers as soon as their crime was accomplished. If he were granted the pardon to which he seemed entitled through his splendid service in retrieving the expedition and its records (as well as his value as a pilot on future voyages in search of a passage beyond the Bay), the others could hardly be treated with severity. Hence, though some or all of the eight men suffered a period of detention, and the High Court of Admiralty held enquiries over a number of years, there is no record of a prosecution until 1618 when Pricket (who in the meantime had taken part in BUTTON's expedition to Hudson Bay), Edward Wilson, and two of their former comrades were subjected to a form of trial before the Admiralty court. In view of the lapse of time and mitigating circumstances, the authorities evidently wished to close the case with an acquittal. The four were arraigned, not on the inescapable charge of mutiny, but of murder—and it was not murder to turn experienced seamen adrift near a shore that was neither totally barren nor uninhabited. All four were acquitted.

L. H. NEATBY

Abacuk Pricket's narrative and other contemporary documents relating to Hudson have been collected by G. M. Asher in *Henry Hudson, the navigator: the original documents in which his career is recorded, collected, partly translated, and annotated* (Hakluyt Soc., 1st. ser., XXVII, 1860). An excellent biography is Llewellyn Powys's *Henry Hudson* (London, 1927), which provides a comprehensive bibliography and reprints the documents relating to the trial of Pricket and three other mutineers, which were unknown in Asher's time.

DAB. DNB. Dodge, *Northwest by sea*, 114–29.

C. R. Markham, *A life of John Davis, the navigator, 1550–1605, discoverer of Davis Straits* (London, 1889). L. H. Neatby, *In quest of the North West Passage* (Toronto, 1958), 14–29. Oleson, *Early voyages*, 163–66. *Voyages of Foxe and James* (Christy). *The voyages of William Baffin, 1612–1622*, ed. C. R. Markham (Hakluyt Soc., 1st ser., LXIII, 1881).

HUDSON, JOHN, son of HENRY HUDSON and his father's companion on his voyage to the high Arctic (1607) and to Nova Zemlya (1608); 1592?–1611?

John Hudson did not obtain a berth on the Dutch-sponsored expedition to the Hudson River but joined the *Discovery* on his father's last voyage (1610–11). Although he was only 19 years old, he was put overboard by the mutineers, who doubtless dreaded the effect of his testimony if he were allowed to live. Asher considers the relationship between the two Hudsons unproved, despite the testimony of Purchas on that point.

L. H. NEATBY

See bibliography for HENRY HUDSON.

HUET, PAUL, Recollet priest, missionary; d. 1665 at Vitry.

He had made his profession with the Recollets of the province of Paris in 1604. On 11 April 1617, he sailed from Honfleur. On landing at Tadoussac, he built a chapel of branches and foliage there, and on 11 July 1617 celebrated in it what appears to have been the first mass ever said in that place. He was the first priest to live at Trois-Rivières, where he stayed from 29 June to 14 July 1618; he celebrated mass during the whole time he was there. In the interests of the mission, Father Huet sailed for France on 26 July 1618 in company with Father Pacifique DUPLESSIS. In Paris he consulted the theologians of the Sorbonne on the administration of baptism to the Indians, and employed himself in collecting alms with a view to building a monastery and a seminary at Quebec. On his return to the colony the following year, he undertook the construction of the monastery, which was completed in 1621. In 1622 Father Huet assumed the direction of the mission at Trois-Rivières, replacing Father POULAIN. On 4 Jan. 1624, he was again at Quebec, where he baptized Marguerite Martin, daughter of ABRAHAM MARTIN.

After leaving Canada, he worked energetically for the return of the Recollets to New France, but without any immediate success. He occupied various ecclesiastical posts in France: at Metz in 1637, at Rouen in 1650. At Montargis he was director of junior clergy, among whom was Louis Hennepin*, the future companion of CAVELIER de La Salle. Father Huet died suddenly at Vitry in Champagne on 16 Feb. 1655.

G.-M. DUMAS

ASQ, MSS, 200, Mortuologe des Recolets. Champlain, *Œuvres* (Laverdière). Le Clercq, *First establishment of the faith* (Shea), I, 116, 118–20, *et passim*; *Premier établissement de la foy*. Sagard, *Histoire du Canada* (Tross), I, *passim*. Jouve, *Les Franciscains et le Canada: aux Trois-Rivières*; *Les Franciscains et le Canada (1615–1629)*. P.-G. Roy, *La ville de Québec*, I.

I

IGNACE DE PARIS, priest, Capuchin, chronicler; d. 1662 in Paris.

It is unfortunately impossible to give precise details as to this person's birth and family. We do know however that he made his profession in the Order of Friars Minor Capuchin of Paris on 2 Feb. 1621. In 1641 he landed at Port-Royal (Annapolis Royal, N.S.), the principal religious centre of the region served by his community since 1632. He spent 11 years in the following Capuchin missions: Port-Royal, the Saint John River, Canseau, Saint-Pierre, Nipisiguit (Bathurst, N.B.), Kennebec, and Pentagouet (Castine, Maine). He was the superior at the latter place in 1646 and 1647. There he welcomed the Jesuit Gabriel DRUILLETTES, who in 1646 carried out a special mission among the Abenakis. In May 1650, after the accidental death of MENOU d'Aulnay, the syndic of the Capuchins, it was Ignace de Paris who received the body and buried it in the chapel at Port-Royal. Two years later the intrusion of the La Rochelle merchant EMMANUEL LE BORGNE into the government of Acadia forced him to return to France for good. He died 29 Jan. 1662 at the convent of Saint-Honoré in Paris, after having been a preacher in Tours.

Father Ignace de Paris has left, among others, two important writings: a letter dated 6 Aug. 1653 giving evidence in favour of d'Aulnay, and a "Brève relation de la mission d'Acadie," drawn up in 1656 at the request of the Sacred Congregation of Propaganda. According to Father Alexis the second work constitutes the best extant account of the Capuchin mission in Acadia at that period. It is an official document, remarkable for the precise and authentic nature of the facts presented in it. Father Ignace's object was first to advocate the return to the French of important places such as Pentagouet, the Saint John River, and Port-Royal, and the restoration of the Capuchin mission; he wanted next to demonstrate the flourishing state of the Acadian mission under the Capuchins and the illogicality of replacing them by new missionaries; he hoped in addition to develop his views as to the most suitable means of spreading the gospel in Acadia. The Capuchins had had to withdraw to France following the second conquest of the country by the English in the preceding year. Ignace de Paris's statement, intended to induce the Propaganda to encourage the return of his order to Acadia, had no success. Indeed it was not until the end of the 19th century that the Capuchins were to resume their missionary activity. In this same account Ignace de Paris holds Le Borgne responsible for the loss of three French posts and the departure of Mme de BRICE, the directress of the college for young Indian girls at Port-Royal, and the governess of d'Aulnay's daughters.

Father Ignace was full of admiration for the native tongues of Acadia. While conceding that they were particularly difficult, he saw in them great beauty and richness of expression. According to Father Albéric, Ignace de Paris is the first historian of the Acadian church. He was undeniably one of the most competent and zealous members of his order to exercise his apostolate in Acadia.

J.-ROGER COMEAU

Archivum Sacrae Congregationis de Propaganda, Rome, Lettere Antiche, 260, f.25, Ignace de Paris, "Brevis ac dilucida . . ." ("Brève relation de la mission d'Acadie . . . 1656") (photocopy with a translation in PAC, M.G. 17, I; *see* PAC *Report, 1904,* App. H, 333–41). BN, MS Fr. 25055, f.79. *Coll. de manuscrits relatifs à la Nouv.-France,* I, 136–39 (Father Ignace's letter of 1653).

Maurice Albéric, "Les capucins en Acadie, 1632–1654," *La Nouvelle-France,* XIV (1915), 337–45; 416–25, 565, 573; XV (1916), 27–34. Alexis, *Le Canada héroique et pittoresque* (Bruges et Paris, [1927]), 50–58. Candide de Nant, *Pages glorieuses,* 215, 233–34, 273.

INGRAM, DAVID, English mariner, who claimed to have walked from Mexico to Acadia, 1568–69; fl. 1523–83.

Ingram, a native of Barking, Essex, was one of 100 seamen who were set ashore, 8 Oct. 1568, on the Gulf of Mexico, near the mouth of the Tampico River, by John Hawkins, after his disastrous defeat by the Spaniards near Vera Cruz. The party divided, some going north, and a sub-group, according to Ingram, consisting of himself, Richard Browne, and Richard Twide (both conveniently dead before Ingram published his tale in 1583) walked northward, keeping within 20 or 30 miles of the coast, and covering, he estimated, 2,000 miles in 11 or 12 months before they were rescued by Capt. Champion (or Champaigne) of the ship *Gargarine* of Le Havre. Brought to the Lizard in 20 days, and then to Le Havre, Ingram reached England by the end of the year and was rewarded, he said, by Hawkins in January 1569/70.

David Ingram told his story to a group of men, headed by the secretary of state, Sir Francis Walsingham, and including Sir George Peckham, in August and September 1582, when they were collecting material on North America for Sir Humphrey GILBERT's projected settlement there. The story was evidently considered plausible since it was published in 1583 and Ingram, who accompanied Gilbert to Newfoundland that year, returned with his reputation untarnished. Richard Hakluyt, who reprinted Ingram in his *Principall navigations* (1589), left him out (as unreliable) in the second edition of 1598–1600.

The case for accepting Ingram's story that he walked to Cape Breton rests solely on his own statements. There are some discrepancies in his more general statements—11 or 12 months for the length of the journey; 50 leagues (150 miles) or 60 leagues (180 miles) for the distance he was from Cape Breton when rescued, but these, in themselves, are not serious. His claim that he had walked on the north side of America, and was told by the Indians about European-like ships with sails, is consistent with his encountering Micmac Indians on the Gulf of St. Lawrence. An accidental meeting with a Norman vessel in this region (west or south of Cape Breton) was possible and the 20-day voyage to the English Channel plausible.

The case against acceptance is much stronger. The full distance cannot have been less than 3,000 miles: this requires a rate of march which, averaging nearly 9 miles a day, with stops of some days and even weeks at certain places (even if we could admit that the travellers followed a direct route), seems incredible. Moreover, Ingram admitted under close examination that not more than three months were spent north of the "River of May" (St. Johns River, Florida), which telescopes his progress northwards still further and impugns his credit as he had elsewhere given seven months for this part of the journey. The name of this river and of a bay and river of St. Mary's are the only place-names found in other documents of the time. His discrepancies in naming places are serious, e.g., he was rescued on the "River of Banda," at the head of a river called "Garinda." Such instances clearly demonstrate the farcical nature of much of his information. No reputable Indian scholar has been able to correlate his information on Indian life and nomenclature with that of other travellers (though play has been made with a few of his names and incidents): some part of it appears to be derived from African and Caribbean observations, the rest, largely garbled or invented in the 13 years after his return.

It is, however, difficult to deny some basis for Ingram's tale. Hawkins was still alive in 1582–83 and could well have denounced Ingram as a liar (though it is not certain that he did not). The framework of the story has some degree of plausibility, even if the details have little coherence. Ingram could, less incredibly, have walked to some part of the coast north of the Spanish posts scattered from St. Augustine to Santa Elena on Port Royal Sound: in 1568 Dominique de Gourges had shattered the forts of the St. Johns River and between then and 1580 the French were trading and refitting their ships along the coast of what is now South Carolina. An accidental meeting with a French ship on this coast is credible, the distance less unlikely. More plausibly still he could have been picked up by a French privateer on the Gulf of Mexico and have gone with her to take water and fuel along the coast of the Carolinas, conceivable ending up with a call near Cape Breton before sailing for Europe.

Ingram lied in things greater or smaller, but his tales of North America in the 1560's may have just sufficient substance to repay some further research by scholars with time on their hands.

DAVID B. QUINN
THOMAS DUNBABIN

Ingram's narrative of his alleged travels, *A true discourse of the adventures and travailes of David Ingram*, was published in 1583, but no copy is known to survive (*see* W. A. Jackson, "Humphrey Dyson's library," Amer. Biblio. Soc. *Papers*, XLIX (1949), 285, and *Roanoke voyages* (Quinn), I, 3–4). It was reprinted by Richard Hakluyt in *Principall navigations* (1589), 557–62, only (and in *Voyages of Gilbert* (Quinn), II, 283–96). Another version is in BM, Sloane MS 1447, ff.1–11 (printed in P. C. G. Weston, *Documents connected with the history of South Carolina* (London, 1956), 7–19, and collated in Quinn, *supra*). A third version is in the Bodleian Library, Tanner MS 79, ff.172–80 (printed in *Mag. Amer. Hist.*, IX (1883), 200–8). "Certaine questions to be demanded of Davy Ingram," PRO, S.P. 12/175-95 (printed in *Voyages of Gilbert* (Quinn), II, 281–83), and his detailed replies, dating from the autumn of 1582, are in "Reportes of ye contrie Sir Humfrey Gilbert goes to discover," PRO C.O. 1/1, 2. There is another version in Calthorpe MS 162 (now BM, Add. MS 48151), ff.161–66, collated in *Voyages of Gilbert* (Quinn), II, 296–309. Ingram is also cited in Peckham, *A true report*.

For varying views of the credibility of Ingram's tale, *see*: B. F. DeCosta, "Ingram's journey through North America in 1567–69," *Mag. Amer. Hist.*, IX (1883), 168–76 (credulous but scholarly). *Voyages of Gilbert* (Quinn), I, 64–65 (highly sceptical). Rayner Unwin, *The defeat of Sir John Hawkins* (London, 1960) (half sceptical, half romantic). H. Wendt, *I sought Adam* (London, 1955) (somewhat credulous). J. A. Williamson, *Sir John Hawkins: the time and the man* (Oxford, 1927), 237–38 (scornful).

IROQUET (Yroquet), Algonkin chief; fl. 1609–15.

Iroquet was the first Algonkin chief to meet CHAMPLAIN in June 1609 near Quebec, where he had come with Outchetaguin, a Huron chief, to seek an alliance with the French in making war against the Iroquois. Champlain agreed to join them, and his first attack on the Iroquois on Lake Champlain took place a few days later.

Champlain then agreed to meet with Iroquet and Outchetaguin at the mouth of the River of the Iroquois (Richelieu) the following year, thus initiating the historic diplomatic and trading alliance between the Huron and Algonkin Indians and the French.

Iroquet and Outchetaguin arrived too late in 1610, however, to take part in Champlain's second attack on the Iroquois, but a three-day council was held by them with Champlain on Île de Saint-Ignace. Champlain requested that Iroquet take a young French lad [possibly Étienne BRÛLÉ] to winter at his home 80 leagues above the Rapids (Lachine) so that he might learn his people's language, observe the various tribes, and explore their water-ways and mines. Iroquet agreed, but his followers feared the consequences if harm came to the boy. Champlain, however, won their consent by accepting a young Huron lad, SAVIGNON, to return to France with him.

The following year, 1611, Iroquet and Outchetaguin, according to plan, were met by Champlain in the St. Lawrence with a salvo of arquebuses, muskets, and small pieces, also two salutes from 13 pinnaces that had arrived for the trade. All this badly frightened the Indians, most of whom had never seen a European. Champlain traded with them at length at the Rapids, at the same time learning of the geography of the country. Although uneasy about many of the other French traders, the Indians reiterated their trust in Champlain, promising to show him their country. Champlain in turn promised to request the king to send a small army to go to their country with him; he also promised to establish a settlement there.

Champlain was entirely satisfied with Iroquet's

treatment of the French boy, and this year a second boy, attached to the trader Boyer or Bouvier, was allowed to return with the Algonkins. Champlain specified that he must reside with Iroquet only.

In 1615 the promises of 1611 were fulfilled when Champlain travelled to the Huron country with a band of French soldiers. Iroquet was the war-chief of the Algonkins in the Huron-Algonkin war-party against the Iroquois, which Champlain led from the Huron country bordering Georgian Bay to the Iroquois country that lay south of Lake Ontario.

After returning from the raid, Iroquet and his Algonkins wintered near the Huron village of Cahiagué (near present-day Hawkestone, Ontario). Animosity developed between the two communities as a result of Iroquet's treatment of a captive whom the Hurons had handed over to him for the customary torture. Iroquet treated the captive, who was a good hunter and an intelligent man, with fatherly kindness. In resentment at this behaviour the Hurons appointed one of their men to kill the captive. In reprisal, the Algonkins killed the slayer; whereupon the Hurons, further insulted by the death of one of their own people, attacked the Algonkins, and Iroquet was wounded by two arrow shots.

In order to secure peace, the Algonkins were required to give to the Hurons "fifty wampum belts with one hundred fathoms of the same," also a great number of kettles and hatchets, and two women captives. But the situation remained hazardous for the Algonkins, and, in Champlain's opinion, these unsettled affairs among the natives were perilous for the French residents of the district and could bring ruin to the trade.

Two inhabitants of Cahiagué sought out Champlain, who was some distance away, to beg him to attempt a reconciliation. He agreed, but first visited a settlement of Nipissing Indians with whom he had planned to make a voyage of discovery to the north. To his profound regret he found that Iroquet had already been there, and with gifts of wampum had secured the promise of the Nipissings to postpone the voyage. Iroquet's action in this matter may have been a precautionary move against Champlain's making alliances for trade with other nations; or it may have been born of fear for the safety of his relatively small band who were faced with danger from the populous village of Cahiagué which at that time, Champlain states, consisted of some 200 long-houses.

In 1623–24 SAGARD records that an Indian named Iroquet, who was well known in those areas, had been to the Neutral country with 20 of his men, hunting for beaver, of which they had taken "fully five hundred." He could not be induced, however, to divulge to the French the route from the St. Lawrence to the Neutral country that bordered Lake Erie. Thus did the Algonkins and Hurons guard jealously the furs that were basic to the economy of New France at that period.

As was customary, the tribe of Iroquet was often known by the name of its chief. In 1644 the Iroquets were described by Father Barthélemy VIMONT as "extremely insolent, arrogant, full of superstitions and very profligate," whereas their chief at that time said that they were "a remnant of one of the most flourishing tribes that ever dwelt in this country."

ELSIE MCLEOD JURY

Champlain, *Works* (Biggar), *passim*. *JR* (Thwaites), *passim*. Sagard, *Histoire du Canada* (Tross), III, 803. Desrosiers, *Iroquoisie*, 61–64. Hunt, *Wars of the Iroquois*, 57, 63.

IRWIN (Kirwin, Herovin, Hirouin), MARIE, *dite de la Conception,* Hospitaller; b. 1626 in Scotland; d. 14 Nov. 1687 at Quebec.

The records of the Hôtel-Dieu of Quebec mention the arrival in Canada in 1642 of a young Scottish girl whose family was related to Mary Queen of Scots. She is described as the "daughter of a Scottish nobleman who had sought refuge in France with his whole family to keep his religion." She was sent by the nursing order of Dieppe, for she desired to take her religious vows in Quebec and she remained as a boarder at the Hôtel-Dieu from 1642 until about 1643. At this time she returned to Dieppe and entered the convent of the nursing sisters. In 1657 Marie Irwin returned to New France, this time as a nun. She entered the Hôtel-Dieu, in accordance with her own desire, where she was known as Mère Marie de la Conception.

Mère Marie de la Conception is described in the *Annales* as possessing "all the virtues, simple obedience, respectful deference for her superiors, unchanging sweetness, surprising patience and equilibrium, and to complete our praise in a few words, she possessed a deep humility, never judging herself capable of doing anything, nevertheless succeeding in everything. . . ." Mère Marie fell dangerously ill on 6 Nov. 1687 and died eight days later.

HENRY B. M. BEST

Juchereau, *Annales* (Jamet), 42, 76, 84, 95, 155, 231–32. P.-G. Roy, *A travers l'histoire de l'Hôtel-Dieu de Québec* (Lévis, 1939).

JACQUELIN, FRANÇOISE-MARIE, Acadian heroine, wife of CHARLES DE SAINT-ÉTIENNE de La Tour; b. 1602 in France; d. 1645 at Fort La Tour.

Nothing factual is known about her background. Although Charles de MENOU d'Aulnay states she was the daughter of a Le Mans barber and became an actress in Paris, proof is lacking and it seems more probable that she was the daughter of a member of the lesser nobility. In 1640 she accepted a proposal of marriage from Charles de La Tour delivered by his La Rochelle agent, Desjardins Du Val. She sailed for Port-Royal (Annapolis Royal, N.S.) where the ceremony was performed that same year. The couple settled at La Tour's fort situated at the mouth of the Saint John River. Here she made her home and gave birth to a son.

Almost immediately after her marriage she became her husband's courageous supporter in a struggle with d'Aulnay for power in Acadia. In 1642 she evaded d'Aulnay's blockade of the Saint John and made her way to France where she successfully appealed against the king's order that her husband be arrested and brought to France on charges of disloyalty. She was given permission to take back a warship with supplies for Fort La Tour at Saint John harbour. Two years later, she again sailed for France, this time to find La Tour completely discredited at court owing to charges brought by d'Aulnay. Despite the fact that she herself was forbidden to leave France, Mme de La Tour borrowed money from friends and escaped to England where she bought supplies and chartered a ship to carry her to the Saint John. The trip lasted six months, the ship's commander, Capt. Bailey, having stopped on the Grand Banks to fish. Off Cap de Sable, the vessel was stopped by d'Aulnay but Mme de La Tour hid in the hold and escaped detection. When the vessel landed in Boston, she sued the captain both for unnecessary delay and for not taking her to the Saint John as he had agreed. With the £2,000 she received in settlement, Mme de La Tour hired three ships to run the blockade d'Aulnay was maintaining at Saint John harbour and arrived home in the closing days of 1644.

Early in the new year, d'Aulnay launched an unsuccessful attack on Fort La Tour. Soon afterwards La Tour, cut off from supplies from France, elected to go to Boston and seek aid from the English. Word that he had left the fort and that it was now garrisoned by but 45 men was carried to d'Aulnay by deserters. He promptly decided to attack again and arrived at the Saint John on 13 April with a force of some 200 men. His emissary, carrying the summons to surrender, was promptly dismissed by Mme de La Tour who had assumed command of the fort and was determined to fight if she must. The ensuing battle raged for three days and has been termed by the late Dr. W. F. Ganong the most dramatic event in the history of New Brunswick.

Although casualties were relatively heavy, the action continued. By Easter Sunday—the fourth day of the siege—d'Aulnay's bombardment had knocked out a portion of the fort's parapet and he had been able to land a force of men with two cannon. It is said that a Swiss mercenary at the fort—Hans Vaner (or Vannier)—allowed this land-force to creep up to the walls of the fortification while its defenders were resting and holding Easter service. The noise of the storming of the palisade alerted the garrison and they rushed to defend their post. A hand-to-hand clash ensued within the confines of the fort itself, and losses on both sides were heavy. Finally, d'Aulnay called off his men and swore that he "would give quarter to all" if Mme de La Tour would capitulate. With her small garrison reduced by casualties, the fort heavily damaged, and both food and ammunition running low, Mme de La Tour concluded that her position was hopeless. She ordered her men to surrender.

The events that then transpired are shrouded in bias and personal animus, and made all the more confusing by scholastic prejudice. Consequently, we may never have a clear view of subsequent happenings. However, relatively unbiased accounts, such as that of NICOLAS DENYS, agree in substance. We are told that, once in possession of the fort, d'Aulnay went back on his word, disregarded the terms of capitulation, and ordered the arrest of the La Tour garrison. A gallows was erected at once and all of the soldiers captured at Fort La Tour hanged, except for one man—probably André Bernard—who agreed to be the executioner of his comrades. Madame de La Tour was forced to watch the hangings with a rope around her own neck. She herself died there three weeks later.

This gallant woman had spent but five years in Acadia, yet her position in the history of this country is assured. Hers was the distinction of being the first European woman to have lived, to have made a home, and to have raised a family in New Brunswick. Neither the perils of the sea, the dangers of war nor the horrors of a long siege could still her courage. Here, truly, was the most remarkable woman in Acadia's early history.

GEORGE MACBEATH

Jalobert

Aulnay's version of these events is found in AN, Col., C^{11D}, 1 (modern copies in BN, MS, NAF 9281, 9282 (Margry)). Less biased sources are Denys, *Description and natural history* (Ganong), 114–16 (and the sources listed therein) and *Winthrop's journal* (Hosmer) in *Original narratives* (Jameson). Charlevoix, *History* (Shea). *Suffolk deeds*, I, 9. Couillard Després, *Saint-Étienne de La Tour*.

JALOBERT, MACÉ, brother-in-law and companion of Jacques CARTIER on his voyages. Son of Bertrand Jalobert and Jehanne Maingard, he had married Alizon Des Granches, sister of Cartier's wife, about 1528.

As captain and pilot of the *Petite Hermine*, Jalobert was a member of the 1535–36 expedition, which included several of Cartier's relatives. The *Petite Hermine* set sail on 19 May 1535, along with the *Grande Hermine* and the *Emérillon*, but it was separated from the others by bad weather from 25 June on, and Jalobert succeeded in rejoining Cartier only at Blanc Sablon, on 26 July. In the autumn of 1535, Jalobert was among those who accompanied Cartier to Hochelaga. He returned to France in July 1536.

In May 1541, Jalobert joined the expedition consisting of five ships which Cartier was responsible for leading to Canada. The crossing from Brittany to Newfoundland took three months; then on 2 September of the same year, Jalobert and Étienne Noël [*see* Jacques NOËL] took to sea again, for Cartier sent them back to report to François I "what had been done and found." What then became of Macé Jalobert? We do not know whether he returned to Canada in 1542 with LA ROCQUE de Roberval's expedition. In 1555 he was still going to sea, because a document describes him as master of the *Marguerite Bonaventure* sailing out of Saint-Malo. This is the last mention of Jalobert.

MARCEL TRUDEL

Biggar, *Documents relating to Cartier and Roberval*, 37, 54, 394 n.1, 405, 408–10, 490, 534. *Jacques Cartier, documents nouveaux*, éd. F. Joüon Des Longrais (Paris, 1888), 130. *Les Français en Amérique* (Julien), 119, 143, 191. Hoffman, *Cabot to Cartier*, 186.

JAMAY. *See* JAMET

JAMES, THOMAS, English navigator and explorer who, in 1631–32, explored the west coast of Hudson Bay and James Bay in an attempt to find a northwest passage; b. 1593?; d. 1635?

Little is known of James's ancestry and early life. Available evidence indicates that he was a son of Thomas James, mayor of Bristol in 1605 and 1614, and that before he turned to the sea he was a Bristol barrister, probably wealthy.

James's opportunity to head a northwest passage expedition arose through the commercial rivalry between London and Bristol merchants. Capt. Luke Fox had persuaded a group of London merchants to support him in a search for a northwest passage. The Bristol Society of Merchant Venturers determined to send a similar expedition, for they feared the London merchants might secure a monopoly of whatever markets or trade Fox might discover. Capt. James represented the Bristol merchants at court and obtained for them from Charles I a promise of equal rights and privileges in whatever discoveries either expedition might make, in proportion to each city's investment in the dual venture.

On 3 May 1631, James sailed from Bristol in a 70-ton ship, named *Henrietta Maria* after England's queen, with a crew of 22 men. He took no one who had ever sailed on a northern voyage for fear that opinion based on previous experience might conflict with or diminish his own authority. On 5 June the ship entered the ice near Davis Strait and there James and his men began an almost uninterrupted series of harrowing adventures.

They took nearly a month to penetrate Hudson Strait, and ice prevented them from proceeding farther north than Nottingham Island. On 16 July James turned southwest into Hudson Bay and, on 11 August, after a miserable crossing, he sighted Hubbert's Hope, near present-day Churchill.

During the latter part of July, James and Fox separately explored the Hudson Bay coast south of Cape Churchill, a coast James named the New Principality of South Wales. On 26 July James lay in the estuary of a great river that he named the New Severn. On 29 and 30 July occurred the only meeting of James and Fox in Hudson Bay, a meeting that Fox records with scorn.

On 3 September James sighted and named Cape Henrietta Maria and on the 7th he began his only independent exploration, a reconnaissance of the west coast of the bay to which he gave his name. James planned to plumb this bay, to round "Cape Monmouth" (a non-existent projection of land that he imagined separated an "east" bay from the "west" bay which HENRY HUDSON had discovered and in which he had perished), and then to seek a route to the St. Lawrence River. In early October, greatly troubled by storms, shoals, and ice, James sought an anchorage and found one off Charlton Island, where he wintered—the first deliberate wintering of a European party in the Canadian north.

During October and November, the crew built cabins on the island. On 29 November James sank his ship in a desperate move to prevent its being swept away by storms. Fearing the ship could not be raised again, he attempted to build a pinnace of local wood during the winter. Because of inexperience and inadequate provisions and clothing, James and his men suffered from cold and malnutrition. By February, 1632, most of the crew showed symptoms of scurvy. Four men died. Throughout these tribulations, James carefully recorded scientific information, taking special note of low-temperature phenomena.

In April, the party discovered to their surprise that the sea had not frozen solid and that water drained from the ship's hold at low water. They repaired the damaged hull and pumped out the ship. During May they complained of the daily heat, although the nights continued freezing cold. In June they rehung the rudder with great difficulty and moved the ship into deeper water. They had restored their health by eating green plants found along the shores. Mosquitoes, they learned, were a more painful affliction than the cold of winter.

On 24 June 1632, James took possession of Charlton Island in the king's name. On 1 July, when the expedition took formal leave of its dead, James recited a poem he had written for the occasion, a poem that Robert Southey praised in his *Omniana* (1812). The next day, on Danby Island, James found two stakes that "had beene cut sharpe at the ends with a hatchet, or some other good Iron toole, and driven in, as it were with the head of it." These stakes were possibly relics of Henry Hudson and his men, who had been abandoned thereabouts some 20 years earlier.

Hindered by severe ice conditions, the ship took nearly three weeks attaining Cape Henrietta Maria and approached Cape Tatnam only on 14 August. James then sailed northeast across Hudson Bay and, on the 24th, sighted Nottingham Island. He attempted to penetrate what is now called Foxe Channel, not knowing that his rival had explored it on his homeward trip the previous year. James reached about 65°30′N before he turned back. The *Henrietta Maria* arrived at Bristol on 22 October in such a state that her crew thought it a daily miracle that she did not sink.

Of the two voyages, Fox's was the more productive in geographic discovery, and it was easily executed; Fox's rough common sense and professional seamanship are in strong contrast to James's academic qualities and his amateurish misadventures. But James's narrative, a literary success, had the greater popularity. Some critics think that Coleridge drew upon James's account of hardship and lamentation in writing *The rime of the ancient mariner*. Robert Boyle quoted many passages from it in *New experiments and observations touching cold* (London, 1665).

James rightly concluded that no northwest passage existed south of 66°N. This conclusion and the account of his sufferings in James Bay so discouraged promoters of expeditions seeking a northwest passage that the search, begun by FROBISHER in 1576, was interrupted until 1719 when James Knight* began a new chapter in northwest-passage exploration. There was no recorded voyage into Hudson Bay, after James, until 1668, when CHOUART Des Groseilliers and Zachariah GILLAM accomplished the fur-trading mission that resulted in the formation of the HBC.

Upon his return from Hudson Bay, the Admiralty appointed James to a command in the Bristol Channel squadron. The circumstances of his death are not known, and his place of burial is disputed. James's knowledge of mathematical navigation was unusual for the time. His account of his voyage, one of the classic narratives of exploration, demonstrates the author's fluent grace of expression, learning, and scientific curiosity.

ALAN COOKE

Records relating to the Society of Merchant Venturers of the city of Bristol in the seventeenth century, ed. P. McGrath (Bristol Record Soc., XVII, 1952). *Voyages of Fox and James* (Christy): *see* Introduction, I, cxxxi–ccix, and James's "The strange and dangerous voyage of Captaine Thomas James, in his intended discovery of the northwest passage into the South Sea wherein the miseries indured, both going, wintering, returning; & the rarities observed, both philosophicall and mathematicall, are related in this journall of it," II, 447–611.

DNB. Dodge, *Northwest by sea*. C. M. Macinnes, "The north-west passage," in *A gateway of empire* (Bristol, 1939), 107–23. J. F. Nicholls, *Capt. Thomas James and George Thomas, the philanthropist* (Bristol Biographies, II, 1870). Oleson, *Early voyages*, 169–70. J. W. Damer Powell, *Bristol privateers and ships of war* (Bristol, 1930).

JAMET (Jamay), DENIS, Recollet priest, first superior of the Canadian mission in 1615; d. 1625 at Montargis.

Father Jamet, having gained valuable experience by exercising the highest functions of government in the religious province of Saint-Denis, was chosen in 1615 to superintend the establishment of the church in Canada. He sailed from Honfleur on 24 April 1615 with three other Recollets, Fathers Joseph LE CARON, Jean DOLBEAU, and Pacifique DUPLESSIS, and landed at

Jay

Tadoussac on 25 May. On 8 June he reached Quebec, and set out the same day for the falls later called Saint-Louis. On 24 June Fathers Le Caron and Jamet celebrated at Rivière des Prairies the first mass ever said on Montreal Island. When Father Jamet returned to Quebec he entrusted to FRANÇOIS GRAVÉ Du Pont who was going to France, a relation dated 15 July and addressed to Cardinal François de Joyeuse; in this relation, following a few remarks on the topography, climate, inhabitants, customs, and religion of the country, he clearly indicated the conditions necessary for the progress of religion in New France.

On 20 July 1616, on behalf of the mission, Father Jamet left for France with CHAMPLAIN and Father Le Caron. During the four years of a protracted stay there, Father Jamet, at the same time as he was working actively in his position as procurator of the Canadian missions, served successively as superior of the convents of Saint-Denis in 1617, Châlons in 1618, and Sézanne, which he founded in 1619.

He was again appointed provincial commissioner to Canada, and sailed 5 April 1620 on the *Sallemande*, commanded by Deschênes; he took Brother Bonaventure and a few workmen with him. He reached Quebec on 11 July, and on the strength of the financial backing given by Charles de Boves, vicar general of Pontoise, by Henri de Bourbon, Prince de Condé, and by the Sieur Louis Houel, he undertook the building of the convent of Notre-Dame-des-Anges, which he blessed on 25 May 1621. On 18 August a memoir, bearing Jamet's signature next to Champlain's, was addressed to the king, bringing to his attention the measures required to preserve religion and suppress disorder in the infant colony. At Quebec he applied himself to his priestly functions, blessing GUILLEMETTE HÉBERT's marriage on 26 August and baptizing Eustache Martin on 24 October. In the spring of 1622 he returned to France; he died at the convent of Montargis on 26 Feb. 1625, after devoting his life to the conversion of the Indians and endowing the colony with its first religious institutions.

FRÉDÉRIC GINGRAS

BN, MS, Cinq-Cents de Colbert, 483, Relation du Père Jamet. Champlain, *Œuvres* (Laverdière), 495, 497, 499, 506–7, 593–94. Le Clercq, *First establishment of the faith* (Shea), I, 82, 85, *et passim*. Sagard, *Histoire du Canada* (Tross), I, 28, 36, 44, 68–79.
The Catholic encyclopedia, an international work of reference . . . of the Catholic church, ed. C. G. Herbermann *et al.* (17v., New York, 1907–22), VI, 301. Jouve, *Les Franciscains et le Canada: 1615–1629*.

JAY, JOHN, merchant of Bristol, participant in North American ventures, 1480–1505.

Jay's identity is puzzling; he was certainly the nephew of John Jay, tucker, of Bristol, thought to have died in 1480, and may have been the son of John Jay, merchant of Bristol (d. 1468). The latter left a ship called the *Trinity* to his son, while a John Jay and John Withipoll supplied in 1477 five ships for the king's use: if these references are to our John Jay he was already an important shipowner by 1480.

In that year he was named by William Worcester as part-owner of the first ship known to have left England on a voyage of discovery in the Atlantic. Worcester's account, translated, runs: "1480, on July 15, a ship . . . and of John Jay, the younger, of the burden of 80 tons, began a voyage from the Kingroad at Bristol to the Island of Brasylle in the western part of Ireland, to traverse the seas for . . . and Thloyde is the most expert shipmaster of all England; and news came to Bristol on Monday, September 18, that in the said ship they sailed the seas for about 9 months [*recte* weeks], but were driven back by storms to a port . . . in Ireland for the preservation of the ship and the sailors." (The gaps were left by the writer to be completed subsequently.)

"Thloyde" evidently was master of the vessel, and is probably "John Lloyd," the shipmaster and merchant who was trading from Bristol between 1461 and 1480. The Welsh surname "Lloyd" would sound like "Thloyde" in English, which could also be intended for "Th[omas] Loyde," although no man of this name has yet been found. The voyage was clearly unsuccessful. Other partners in the voyage may have included Thomas CROFT, a customs official, and his associates, who received a royal licence on 18 June 1480, apparently to make exploring voyages, and who sent out a further expedition of discovery in 1481 in which Jay could also have participated.

John Jay lived in a house in Broad Street, Bristol, and engaged in trade to Spain, Portugal, Norway, and other places. He was bailiff of the city, 1486–87, and sheriff, 1498–99. Though no evidence has yet been found to make it certain, he is likely to have been one of the Bristol merchants associated with JOHN CABOT's voyages in 1497–98 and with the Company Adventurers into the New Found Lands which sent out expeditions to America between 1501 and 1505, since he was in close commercial relations during the latter years with Hugh ELIOT, Thomas Asshehurst, and William Clerk who were concerned in the company. He survived to be mayor of Bristol in 1518 and died in 1528.

DAVID B. QUINN

Bristol and Gloucestershire Arch. Soc. *Trans.*, XLVII (1925), 123–29. *The great red book of Bristol*, ed. E. W. W. Veale (5v., Bristol Record Soc.), pts. III, IV (XVI, 1951, XVIII, 1953). *The overseas trade of Bristol in the later Middle Ages*, ed. E. M. Carus-Wilson (Bristol Record Soc., VII, 1937), 157–63, with Latin text of William Worcester. The English translation is given in Williamson, *Voyages of the Cabots* (1929), 18–19, and *Cabot voyages* (1962), 187–88.

JEAN ALFONSE. See FONTENEAU

JÉRÉMIE *dit* **Lamontagne, NOËL,** trader, clerk in the employ of the Tadoussac trading organization, son of Claude Jérémie and Hélène Macart; b. in 1629 (according to the census of 1666), in 1636 (census of 1667), or in 1638 (census of 1681), at Mareuil-sur-Oge in Champagne (France); d. some time between 1694 and 1697, in New France.

On 29 Jan. 1659, shortly after his arrival in Canada, Jérémie married Jeanne Pelletier at Quebec. He had already been interested in the fur trade, travelling with his brother-in-law François Pelletier among the northern tribes. On 28 May 1665 Jérémie entered into partnership with CHARLES AMIOT, Guillaume Couture*, and Sébastien Prouvereau* for the purpose of "travelling among the tribes called Papinachoises and the northern tribes." This traffic did not however enrich him in the slightest.

By a grant from PIERRE DUBOIS Davaugour (4 Sept. 1662), Jérémie became seigneur of the Île de la Patience, which he later gave to his relative Bécart* de Granville. In addition he owned a house in the Lower Town of Quebec which had been given him by Charles Aubert* de La Chesnaye, and a piece of land at Côte Saint-Ignace, where he took up residence at the end of 1666 or the beginning of 1667. But in 1671, after three years of litigation, his two pieces of property at Quebec and Côte Saint-Ignace were sold to satisfy his creditors. Shortly afterwards he moved his family to Batiscan, where they were still residing in 1681.

Jérémie turns up again in 1694. At that time he was "clerk in the employ of the Tadoussac trading organization," and his family was again living in the region of Quebec. He died some time between July 1694 and July 1697.

ANDRÉ VACHON

AJQ, Greffe de Guillaume Audouart, 3 févr. 1659; Greffe de Pierre Duquet, 28 mai 1665. ANDQ, Mariages, 1621–67, 169. APQ, Coll. de pièces jud. et not., 53, 78, 143, 1995; Seigneuries, île de la Patience. ASQ, Séminaire, VI, 20. Recensements de 1666, 1667, 1681. *Jug. et délib.*, I, III, IV. *Papier terrier de la Cie des I.O.* (P.-G. Roy), 115 f., 159. J.-E. Roy, *Histoire de la seigneurie de Lauzon*, I, 223; II, 31. P.-G. Roy, *Inv. concessions*, I, 217 f.

JILBERT. See GILBERT

JOGUES, ISAAC, Jesuit, missionary among the Hurons and later among the Iroquois, ambassador for peace to the Iroquois; b. 10 Jan. 1607 at Orléans (France); murdered by the Iroquois 18 Oct. 1646 at Ossernenon (Auriesville, N.Y.); canonized 29 June 1930 with seven of his fellow martyrs.

The fifth of nine children, Jogues was born in a prosperous family that included notaries, lawyers, apothecaries, and merchants. He began his studies in the family home under the direction of a private tutor and continued them at the Jesuit college which had just been founded at Orléans in September 1617. He completed his courses at the age of 17. He could have taken up the flourishing business left by his father, or else he might, like his uncles, have chosen law or officialdom. But he preferred to follow his teachers, the Jesuits, and in October 1624 he was the first Jesuit from Orléans to enter the noviciate at Rouen, where he became a disciple of Father Louis Lallemant, an author of spiritual writings and a novice-master of repute. He made his first vows two years later and entered upon his studies in philosophy at the Collège at La Flèche, where the intense missionary spirit implanted there in 1613 by Father Énemond MASSÉ still prevailed.

In 1634 Jogues began to study theology at Clermont (Paris), a celebrated institution that then numbered 2,000 students. He was at the same time the prefect responsible for discipline among the lay students. For reasons that are obscure, he was unwilling to continue the theological studies which his intellectual gifts would easily have allowed him to carry on. Indeed, he had always been studious; he had a thorough knowledge of Latin and Greek, and he expressed himself in a smooth flowery style that corresponded admirably to the courteous and refined manners of this renaissance gentleman. And yet he asked to be released from the rest of his studies. Was he perhaps impatient to set out for the American missions about which his reading of the *Jesuit Relations* had informed him?

Jogues's ordination to the priesthood, which was conferred upon him at the end of January 1636 in the chapel of Clermont, brought all the closer his departure for the missions. His first mass, said in the church at Orléans on the first Sunday in Lent, brought joy mingled with sadness to his family. His mother consoled herself

Jogues

by preparing some priestly vestments and a few accessories, the only gifts that the missionary accepted for his crossing to the New World. The young priest, concluding his training, felt himself ever more deeply committed to his religious and missionary vocation. He detached himself from every worldly preoccupation, even those connected with his family, but did so with great delicacy and affection. The letters he wrote to his mother at this period and in subsequent years reveal him to us in his true light.

The departure, after several postponements, took place 8 April 1636. In the convoy of eight ships, Jogues took his place with Father Georges d'Endemare on the vessel that was to call at the Île de Miscou near Baie des Chaleurs. After eight weeks of sailing, the missionary arrived at this trading post which numbered 25 Frenchmen and 2 Jesuits. A week later he resumed his sea voyage, spending two days at Tadoussac where he made contact with the Indians, and then continuing towards Quebec, which he left immediately again to go on to Trois-Rivières. The sight of his colleagues Ambroise DAVOST and ANTOINE DANIEL, emaciated and terribly aged after a few years of life as missionaries, made a deep impression on him. He witnessed the torture of an Iroquois prisoner at the hands of Huron warriors. Despite the famous "important admonition" of Father BRÉBEUF, he could not remain unmoved. Still, his letters do not contain any evidence of fright; they exude only zeal and strength of character. He landed at Ihonatiria (Saint-Joseph I) on 11 September after 16 days' travelling; he was given the name "Ondessonk" (bird of prey).

Jogues, who had been free of any illness during the crossing, was the first to be overcome by fever in September. The epidemics that raged among the Hurons at this period imperilled the lives of the missionaries, for the Indians believed them to be caused by the presence of the religious. In 1637 the situation became so acute that the Huron grand council decided upon the death of the priests. It was in that year that the missionaries met at Ossossané for a farewell feast in Huron style, at which Brébeuf drew up the celebrated testamentary letter that all the Jesuits present signed. The epidemic ended without the execution of the death sentence. Some time afterward, 16 Aug. 1637, the first baptism was administered to a Huron, Joseph CHIHWATENHA, a sublime spirit whose profoundly Christian temperament was to lend support to the missionary effort. His whole family followed his example on 19 March 1638.

The following August Father JÉRÔME LALEMANT succeeded Father Brébeuf as superior of the Huron mission. The new superior, proceeding to reorganize the mission, decided to set up a central residence for the missionaries. The building of Fort Sainte-Marie was entrusted to Father Jogues. Subsequently the latter was sent with Father GARNIER to the Tobacco nation. In September 1641, Jogues and Charles RAYMBAUT went into the territory of the Sauteurs (Chippewas). They pushed on a considerable distance to the west and came to the Sainte-Marie falls (Sault Ste. Marie). They were warmly welcomed, the meeting was a productive one, and the priests had to promise to come back to preach the gospel.

In June 1642 the Hurons were preparing a trading expedition to the French settlements, but the St. Lawrence River was under constant surveillance by the Iroquois between Ville-Marie (Montreal) and Trois-Rivières. Moreover the missionaries needed to replenish their supplies and to exchange news with Europe. Furthermore Father Raymbaut, gravely ill, required hospitalization. Jogues was designated by Lalemant to accompany the convoy, which set off for Quebec. When their business was done, the travellers embarked for the return trip. They reached Trois-Rivières in the last few days of July. In addition to Jogues, the group included Guillaume Couture*, the donné René GOUPIL, another Frenchman, and some Hurons, one of whom was AHATSISTARI; in all there were about 40 persons divided among 12 canoes. The party finally got under way 1 Aug. 1642. The day following their departure, the canoes were craftily attacked by some Iroquois in ambush. Historians are not entirely agreed on the location of the attack. Be that as it may, it must have occurred around Sorel, around Berthier, or, more likely around Lanoraie. After a brief exchange of gunfire, Jogues, Goupil, Couture, and a group of the Hurons were carried off as prisoners into Mohawk territory and put to the most appalling tortures: floggings, bites, mutilations, strippings, forced marches, and insults.

The moral anguish, even more acute than the physical torment, Jogues bore with extraordinary fortitude. He endured it all the more fondly because he had sought it out. For, as he himself assures us, he had cast himself into the hands of the Iroquois of his own free will. "I was watching this disaster," says the father, "from a place very favorable for concealing me from the sight of the enemy, being able to hide myself in thickets and among very tall and dense reeds; but this thought could never enter my mind. 'Could I, indeed,' I said to myself, 'abandon our French and leave those good Neophytes and those poor Catechumens, without giving them the help which the

Jogues

Church of my God has entrusted to me?' Flight seemed horrible to me; 'It must be,' I said in my heart, 'that my body suffer the fire of earth, in order to deliver those poor souls from the flames of Hell; it must die a transient death, in order to procure for them an eternal life.' My conclusion being reached without great opposition from my feelings, I called the one of the Hiroquois who had remained to guard the prisoners."

René Goupil was killed (22 Sept. 1642) by an Iroquois in front of Jogues, who was kept captive under constant threat of death until November 1643. An old Iroquois woman had adopted him and he acted as a servant. He had been so weakened by blows and hardships that the only work he could do was a task reserved for women: gathering wood to feed the fire in the lodge on the hunt.

With the complicity of the Dutch, Jogues embarked at the beginning of November 1643 on a ship that reached England at the end of December. He took another ship and the next day, Christmas Day, he disembarked on the coast of Brittany. Finally, 5 Jan. 1644, he reached the nearest Jesuit house, the Collège at Rennes. His superiors were unable to recognize him, so transformed was he by his sufferings and mutilations. He took some rest in order to recover from his fatigue and pain, attempting to hide from the admiration that people wanted to lavish on him. He was obliged, however, to yield to the entreaties of the queen regent, Anne of Austria, who insisted upon beholding this martyr. Before her and before Mazarin and the directors of the Compagnie des Cent-Associés, he bore witness to the wretchedness and the needs of New France.

While he was in France, steps were taken to seek from the pope an indult that would permit Jogues to celebrate mass despite his mutilated fingers. The sovereign pontiff readily granted him this favour, believing that it was not proper that a martyr for Christ should not be able to offer Christ's blood ("*Indignum esset Christi martyrem Christi non bibere sanguinem*").

In the colony nothing was yet known of Jogues's fate, and his escape was learned of only when he landed at Quebec early in July 1644. Despite the torment he had suffered, he eagerly sought from his superiors the privilege of devoting himself to the evangelizing of the Iroquois. But peace had not been restored among the Mohawks, and Father VIMONT preferred to assign Father Jogues to the post at Ville-Marie, founded two years earlier. This was to be a calmer period for Jogues, which would allow him to compose various important texts for posterity: the account of his captivity and that of the death of his companion Goupil, and what may be considered the earliest description of New York.

Peace, of which there was still no sign on the Iroquois side, finally came about following the freeing of Father BRESSANI in August 1644. Exchanges of prisoners, as proposed by Governor HUAULT de Montmagny, encouraged negotiations. Jogues became an important personnage when he appeared before the council meeting held by the governor at Trois-Rivières 12 July 1645, in the course of which the Mohawk orator KIOT-SEAETON played a prominent part. From 15 to 25 September, a new council brought confirmation of the peaceful intentions of the Mohawks, but the French persisted in having serious doubts about their good faith.

As soon as Father Jérôme Lalemant was appointed superior-general of the Jesuits in New France, Jogues again expressed his desire to go and work for the evangelizing of the Iroquois. But the guarantees of peace were not yet sufficiently firm, and were built up only gradually during the councils held on 22 Feb. and 13 May 1646. Jogues was then accepted by Father Lalemant and by the governor as an ambassador for peace to the Mohawks. The joy with which Jogues received the news of his appointment was tinged with very justifiable misgivings. To Father Jérôme Lalemant he made this reply: "Would you believe that, on opening the letters from your Reverence, my heart was, as it were, seized with dread at the beginning, apprehending lest what I desire, and what my spirit should most prize, might happen. Poor nature, which remembered the past, trembled; but our Lord, through his goodness, has calmed it and will calm it still further. Yes, my Father, I desire all that our Lord desires, at the peril of a thousand lives. Oh, what sorrow I would have, to fail at so excellent an opportunity! Could I endure that it should depend on me that some soul were not saved? I hope that his goodness, which has not forsaken me on [past] occasions, will assist me still; he and I are able to trample down all the difficulties which might oppose themselves." The missionary took thought for immediate preparations for his future apostolate by bringing together a box of warm clothes for the winter, the sacred vessels for masses, and gifts for the Indians.

After leaving Trois-Rivières 16 May 1646, the expedition ascended the Richelieu and crossed Lake Champlain. Jogues was the first white man to see Lake George, which he named Saint-Sacrement, as his companion JEAN BOURDON noted on his map. The Mohawks were intrigued by the mysterious box that Jogues wanted to leave with them. At the conclusion of the parleys, the diplomats set out on the return trip on 16 June, called at Fort Richelieu on 27 June, at Trois-Rivières on 29 June, and arrived at Quebec on 3 July. Jogues gave an account of his mission to the authorities, who once again refused to allow him to leave to spend the winter among the Iroquois. Having returned to Montreal, Jogues was recalled at the end of August to Trois-Rivières, where the peace council authorized him to take part in a new embassy being planned by the Hurons. This time Jogues had decided to stay the winter. He left on 24 September with Jean de La Lande and with the Hurons, abandoned them at Fort Richelieu. The two Frenchmen pushed on with a single Huron. They met a hostile reception; towards the middle of October, they were taken prisoner. The feeling of the Iroquois had completely changed because, mystified by the small box left at the Mohawk village by Jogues, they saw in it the confirmation of their suspicions about the cause of the epidemic, the drought, and the famine that had followed his summer embassy. On 18 October, at Ossernenon, Jogues was killed by a hatchet blow in the head. La Lande perished in the same way, probably the next day.

Parkman has asserted that Jogues might truthfully have aspired to literary fame. It has even been said that in him the humanist could die only with the saint, so completely did his intellectual qualities complement his spiritual ones and thus give him his maximum value as a writer. Like several of his fellow missionaries in New France, he was a mystic, but in one sense he surpassed them all because he knew how to express the experience that he, like them, had previously undergone. His spiritual writings, equally as limpid as those of Father Brébeuf, surpass the latter's by a lyricism which achieves great literary perfection. He controls his pen as readily as he disciplines his sensibility, his memory, and all his faculties. Even in the depths of grief, he never bursts out, but makes us feel that he is aware of living through an adventure that overpowers him, but does not crush him. The truth is that under a timid and frail exterior he concealed an astonishing fortitude and spiritual independence. He was a sensitive person, fired with love, whose interior joy never yielded to grief. Divine love had once and for all enveloped his whole being.

In collaboration with
Georges-Émile Giguère

ACSM, "Mémoires touchant la mort et les vertus des pères Isaac Jogues . . ." (Ragueneau), repr. APQ *Rapport, 1924–25*, 3–41, *passing*; various autograph writings and *apographes* by Jogues, including a note on René Goupil (May 1646) and several letters. *JR* (Thwaites); an important printed source, with bibliographical information. "Lettre du père Jogues, captif chez les Iroquois, au gouverneur de Montmagny," *BRH*, XXXVI (1930), 48–49. *Positio causae*.

John Joseph Birch, *The saint of the wilderness: St. Isaac Jogues* (New York, 1936). *BRH*, V (1899), 88–90; XVIII (1912), 91. Lucien Campeau, "Un site historique retrouvé," *RHAF*, VI (1952), 31–41. Charlevoix, *Histoire*, I, 232–77. N.-E. Dionne, "Le père Jogues et les Hollandais," *BRH*, X (1904), 60–4. *Jésuites de la N.-F.* (Roustang). Louis-Raoul de Lorimier, "Jogues (en marge de l'histoire, 1607–1646)," *RC*, XIX (1917), 336–51. Lucien Lusignan, "Essai sur les écrits de deux martyrs canadiens," *BRH*, L (1944), 174–92. Félix Martin, *Le R.P. Isaac Jogues de la Compagnie de Jésus, premier apôtre des Iroquois* (Paris, 1873). Henri Petiot [Daniel-Rops], *Les aventuriers de Dieu* (Paris, 1951), 121–42. Rochemonteix, *Les Jésuites et la Nouvelle-France au XVIIe siècle*, I, II, 429–43. Francis Talbot, *Saint among savages* (New York and London, 1935); *Un saint parmi les sauvages* (Paris, 1937). W. H. Withrow, "The adventures of Isaac Jogues, s.j.," *RSCT*, 1st ser., III (1885), sect.ii, 45–53.

JOHNSON, GEORGE, English separatist, who, with three companions, searched Canada for a site for a Pilgrim settlement in 1597 and wrote of his experiences; b. 1564; d. 1605.

From 1590 Puritan separatists, known as Brownists, were harshly persecuted in England. Four of them were destined to come into contact with Canada: Francis Johnson (1562–1618), formerly a Fellow of Christ's College, Cambridge, and an Anglican clergyman, had become a follower of the separatist Henry Barrow (executed in 1593), and pastor of a London congregation of Barrow's followers, that was arrested *en bloc* in 1592; Daniel Studley, an elder in Barrow's own congregation, of whose background little is known, but who was sentenced to death and reprieved, 1593; John Clarke (or Clerke) a husbandman of Wallsoken, Norfolk, and a prisoner since 1590; and George Johnson who had been to Christ's College, Cambridge, and was a schoolmaster when arrested in 1593. An act of Parliament in 1593 required sentences of death or banishment for all separatists unreconciled to the Church of England, and, from then on, separatists were released and went into exile in Amsterdam where they formed a congregation, the leaders still remaining in prison. Francis Johnson, as early as 1593, had petitioned for the separatists to have leave to withdraw to some part of the queen's dominions where they might exercise their religion freely. In 1597 the opportunity arose. Captain Charles LEIGH and his friends, who may have been backed by the aged Lord Burghley, offered them the possibility of an English settlement on Ramea (the Magdalen Is.) in the Gulf of St. Lawrence. A petition by the imprisoned Brownists to go there was accepted by the Privy Council on 25 March 1597. Four of them were to set out at once, and were "to take with them such household stuff and other implements as may serve them for their necessary use," since they, with one of the ships, were to winter on the islands and be reinforced by the remaining exiles in 1598.

The ships *Hopewell* and *Chancewell* made their way from the Thames to Falmouth in April 1597, Francis Johnson, as the leader of the congregation, and Studley, as an elder, accompanying Capt. Leigh on the *Hopewell*—their story is now Capt. Leigh's—while George Johnson with John Clarke, chosen no doubt for his knowledge of practical agriculture, were on the *Chancewell*. There was some trouble at Falmouth. George Johnson had circulated among the crew the Brownists' *credo*, *A true confession of the faith* ([Amsterdam], 1596), with its preface by Henry Ainsworth, poignantly characterizing the separatists—"wee are but strangers and pilgrims warring against many and mightie adversaries"—which was clearly seditious. Capt. Stephen van Harwick of the *Chancewell* wished to take severe action against George but Francis Johnson intervened and enabled the expedition to set out. (There were further attempts by George to convert the sailors at Newfoundland, and more dissensions, once again assuaged by Francis.) The ships crossed the Atlantic together, reaching Newfoundland waters on 18 May. After losing contact briefly they made a rendezvous at Conception Bay on the 20th and then worked their way down the Newfoundland coast, finally losing touch with each other in a fog on 5 June off Placentia Bay.

The *Chancewell* had evidently no pilot for the Magdalens and made no attempt to reach them, but sailed for Cape Breton. Her captain may have intended to fish, or look for prizes along the coast, although he may have also had some intention of allowing his Puritan passengers the chance to prospect for alternative settlement sites. However, in a great bay, some 18 leagues (about 54 miles) from Cape Breton (to the west, and perhaps St. Ann's Bay) the *Chancewell* was wrecked, "the ship," says George Johnson, "being thorow the headines of the Master in a faire sunne shine day run upon the Rocks." They got the *Chancewell* off the rocks and beached her, but they had taken no precautions to safeguard her before she was over-run by French Basque fishermen from Ciboure, a flotilla of whose boats was fishing nearby. They stripped the ship and the men, leaving them little but their boats. Johnson and Clarke lost all their settlers' gear, and were on bad terms at least with Capt. van Harwick. He was now in a dangerous position and thought his best course was to attempt a counter-attack on the French, but the consciences of his Puritan passengers, unwilling to countenance robbery, stood in his way. He offered, tauntingly, to leave them to live among the Indians (and perish), to be taken by the French (and compelled to hear mass), or to join with him in attacking a fishing vessel. Neither John Clarke nor Johnson would choose: they would accept "what he would lay on them," and would undergo it with God's help, but the captain was reluctant to make their decision for them and deferred it. In the meantime van Harwick equipped his men and rigged his shallops as best he could. Three or four days later he and George were walking on the shore "conferring of these things," when "suddenly (being quick sighted) he saw a ship far off in the sea, and said I see a shipp." George Johnson replied, "it may be the Lord wil send us help thereby," and urged van Harwick to send out a shallop to make contact. This was done. On shore the newcomer was soon identified as an English ship; hope grew that she was the *Hopewell*, and so she proved to be. On 27 June there was a joyful reunion between the four exiles, "yea I cannot now write without teares, remembering such a wondrous providence of God even in a strange land," George wrote in 1603. Francis shared his goods and food with his brother and the *Hopewell*, with her expanded complement, began her course of reprisals against the French which was to occupy Capt. Leigh until 5 August following. There was no attempt to discuss further plans of settlement; we may assume that Francis Johnson and Studley were disillusioned by their experiences on the Magdalens, or at least could see no prospect of building a stable settlement.

On shipboard the Puritans were preoccupied with their own affairs. George Johnson alleged that Daniel Studley stood aloof from the reunited brothers and that he had incited him, George, to "exhort and admonish" Capt. Leigh about certain, unnamed, shortcomings. The captain naturally resented such interference even though he was in sympathy with his passengers' beliefs, and the result was a quarrel with George—"who before had long bene deare frends." Then too it was Studley, George tells us, who revived the theological criticism of Francis Johnson's wife's manner of dress which had already divided the congregation in prison. We have a vivid picture of George and Studley, lying in their cabins and putting out their heads to hurl scriptural arguments against one another on this abstruse matter. All this time the ship was searching for the *Chancewell*'s goods on the Cape Breton coast and then working along southwest Newfoundland, taking a Breton prize and trans-shipping to her before setting out for home on 5 August. In mid-Atlantic the arguments had become so fierce that George was ostracized by the rest and Francis Johnson urged, so George claimed, that Capt. Leigh should keep him on shipboard in case he disrupted the congregation at home. Reaching the Isle of Wight on 5 September, the frustrated pilgrims made their way to London from Southampton, trying to force George to keep quiet and not draw attention to them. Of the discussions with the rest of the congregation in London, now on parole, we have no record. They decided against emigration to America (although Leigh was still in favour of settlement on the Magdalens), and they left London to reassemble their congregation, with the earlier emigrants, in Amsterdam.

George Johnson was an unbalanced man: he continued to divide the church by his controversies with his brother and Daniel Studley, was expelled, and wrote his *Discourse of some troubles* (1603, extant only in copies in Trinity College, Cambridge, and Sion College, London), recounting, amongst other things, his experiences in Canada. He then returned to England and to prison where he died at Durham in 1605. Studley maintained a career of controversy until 1612. George Johnson tells us he "kept things in writing against me which fel out in our banishment when we were at sea and at New found land, never dealing with me for them but tolde them in open congregation." Unfortunately, we lack his American journal. Of John Clarke no more is heard. Francis Johnson bravely led the "Ancient Church," as it was later known, through various vicissitudes in Holland and at Emden, until his death in 1618. He is not known, personally, to have revived the plan of moving to America. But William Bradford, the founding father of Plymouth colony, regarded the pilgrims of 1597 as the precursors of the pilgrims of 1620. In his "Dialogue" (written about 1648, and given in A. Young, *Chronicles of the pilgrim fathers* (2d ed., Boston, 1844), 440–1), he says of the Brownists—"the truth is, their condition for the most part was for some time very low and hard. It was with them, as, if it should be related, would hardly be believed. And no marvel. For many of them had lain long in prisons, and then were banished into Newfoundland, where they were abused, and at last came into the Low Countries, and wanting money, trades, friends or acquaintances, and languages to help themselves, how could it be otherwise." The Ramea venture was a false step on the road to Plymouth.

DAVID B. QUINN

For further details of the expedition and a bibliography *see* LEIGH.

JOIBERT. *See* JOYBERT

JOLLIET, LOUIS, explorer, discoverer of the Mississippi, cartographer, king's hydrographer, teacher at the Jesuit college at Quebec, organist, business man, and seigneur; baptized 21 Sept. 1645 at Quebec, son of Jean Jollyet, a wheelwright in the service of the Compagnie des Cent-Associés, and of Marie d'Abancourt; d. 1700 in New France.

Can the historian fail to deplore the ill luck that seems to have dogged the personal papers of Louis Jolliet and the documents concerning him? Various mishaps and regrettable omissions have as it were wantonly contrived to set up zones of silence and obscurity in the career of this great Canadian. The trouble begins even with his birth, of which we know neither the place nor the date. Was he born at Quebec, on the Beaupré shore or in one of the adjoining seigneuries, territories which in 1645 all came within the boundaries of the parish church of Quebec where he was baptized? The certificate of baptism dated 21 Sept. 1645 gives no precise details on the place, any more than on the date of birth of this child "*recens natum.*"

Louis Jolliet was only five and a half when he lost his father, 23 April 1651. His mother married again on 19 October; her second husband was Gefroy Guillot, who was drowned in the St. Lawrence in the summer of 1655. On 8 Nov. 1665 Marie d'Abancourt was married a third time, to Martin PRÉVOST.

Around the age of 11, Jolliet entered the college of the Jesuits at Quebec, where he did his classical studies. Intending to enter the priesthood, he took the minor orders, 19 Aug. 1662. At that time Jolliet was already becoming interested in music, and he shared with Germain Morin* the title of music officer in the college. As first organist of the cathedral of Quebec, he apparently played the organ from 1664; a document of 1700 states that he "played on the organ" there for "many years."

In 1666, Jolliet—whom the census of that year styles a "cleric"—was finishing his philosophical

Jolliet

studies. On 2 July, together with Pierre Francheville, he defended a "thesis in philosophy." Bishop Laval*, MM. Prouville de Tracy, Rémy de Courcelle, and Talon were present. "Monsieur the Intendant, among others, made a strong argument," noted the *Journal des Jésuites*; "Monsieur Joliet and Pierre Francheville replied very well, upon the whole subject of logic." This "disputation," as was the custom, must have been conducted in Latin, a language that Jolliet knew well; he would have recourse to it in 1679 in Hudson Bay.

No longer feeling drawn towards a priestly vocation, Jolliet left the seminary around the month of July 1667. In October, thanks to a sum of 587 *livres* lent by Bishop Laval, he embarked for France. We do not know the object of this voyage, during which he stayed in Paris and at La Rochelle, dividing his time about equally between the two cities. He must have devoted some thought, however, to the direction that he would henceforth give to his life. When he returned to Quebec his mind was made up: on 9 Oct. 1668 he bought from Charles Aubert* de La Chesnaye a considerable stock of goods for fur-trading. Jolliet would be a fur-trader! But in this vast country of New France, with its inviting rivers and ready mirages, one temptation awaited fur-traders and travellers: exploration. Would the erstwhile "cleric" succumb to it?

Although having a rich supply of merchandise, Jolliet apparently did not leave for the West in the autumn of 1668. He was certainly at Quebec on 14 October, and perhaps at Cap-de-la-Madeleine on 9 November, which were very late dates for undertaking such a journey; his presence is further vouched for at Quebec, 13 April 1669, too early for him to be already back from the Great Lakes, unless one assumes that he returned before the melting of the snows and the break-up of the ice. But it is difficult to concede that an inexperienced traveller like Jolliet would have plunged into an adventure dreaded by the most hardened and by the most courageous *coureurs de bois*. It is more likely that he spent the winter at Quebec. How then did he dispose of his fur-trading goods? Did he keep them for a journey that he may have made in 1669–70? It is not impossible, although we possess no indication of it. In 1669, it is true, a "sieur Jolliet" set off with Jean Peré, in search of a copper mine on Lake Superior, but it has been possible to demonstrate that this is a reference to Adrien, Louis's brother. In short, it must be admitted that with the exception of his presence at Quebec 13 April 1669, nothing is known of Louis Jolliet from the autumn of 1668 to the summer of 1670.

On 4 June 1671, at the Sainte-Marie falls (Sault Ste. Marie), some Frenchmen "who were fur-trading in the locality" signed the document whereby Daumont de Saint-Lusson took possession of the territories of the West. Louis Jolliet was one of the number. He had probably left Quebec in the autumn of 1670; on 12 Sept. 1671 he was back. We do not know how he was engaged during the year that preceded his departure for the Mississippi, but it is certain that he did not go back to the West.

The Mississippi! The mysterious river that for nearly 15 years haunted the imagination of missionaries and explorers. In 1660 and 1662, on the assurance of the Indians, the Relation reported the existence towards the west of a "beautiful River, large, wide, deep, and worthy of comparison . . . with our great river St. Lawrence." This river, which was thought to flow into the Gulf of Mexico, or, in the direction of California, into the "mer Vermeille" (Gulf of California), was not perhaps the Mississippi, the name of which will moreover appear (in the form "Messipi") only in 1667; but at least, the missionaries' investigations concerning this waterway did lead them to a knowledge of the Mississippi. In 1670, with only the information supplied by the Indians, the Jesuit Dablon managed to give a good description of it. The following year the Sulpicians Dollier* de Casson and Bréhant de Galinée became in their turn interested in the river that they named Ohio or Mississippi ("*Ohio*," in the Iroquois language, and "*Mississippi*," in the Ottawa language, both mean "beautiful river," *belle rivière*). Thus, before any white man in New France had seen it, and although inevitably some confused ideas existed about it, the Mississippi was in 1672 relatively well known by the missionaries, who had acquired certain fairly precise notions regarding it from their contacts with the native populations of the Great Lakes. Its mouth still remained, however, a disquieting and undiscovered secret: might this river be at last the coveted waterway to the China Sea, the insubstantial stuff of the eternally disappointed dreams and quests of so many explorers?

Talon himself had not escaped the general obsession. In 1670, for example, he had instructed Daumont de Saint-Lusson to "seek out carefully . . . some communication" with the Southern Sea. The intendant had certainly heard of the Mississippi by then; but the additional information supplied during 1671 by Saint-Lusson and by the Relation of 1669–70 kindled a new hope in him. He resolved to send someone "to discover the Southern Sea, by way of the country of the Mashoutins [Mascoutens], and to go to the great

Jolliet

river that they call Michissipi and that is thought to empty into the Sea of California." For this ambitious scheme, Talon chose Louis Jolliet; shortly before sailing for France, in 1672, he suggested his candidate to Frontenac [see BUADE], who accepted him. The mission entrusted to Jolliet was not so much to discover the Mississippi as to ascertain into what sea, the Gulf of Mexico or the "mer Vermeille," this "beautiful river" flowed. Here was the riddle to be solved.

For the moment, the explorer was facing other problems. Talon had warned him that the state would not subsidize his expedition, any more than it had done for Saint-Lusson in 1670. To acquire funds, Jolliet formed a commercial society, the revenues of which would serve especially to meet the cost of his voyage of discovery. On 1 Oct. 1672 François de Chavigny* de La Chevrotière, Zacharie Jolliet, Jean Plattier, Pierre Moreau, Jacques Largilier*, Jean Thiberge (Téberge), and Louis Jolliet agreed, before Gilles RAGEOT, to "make together the journey to the Ottawa Indians, [and to] trade in furs with the Indians as advantageously [as possible]." On 3 October the partners attended to the last details of their preparations and settled certain matters with the notary Rageot. They probably left Quebec the next day, two days after the appointed date.

On 6 Dec. 1672 Jolliet arrived at Michilimackinac. There he delivered to Father Jacques MARQUETTE a letter from Claude Dablon, the superior of the Jesuits in New France, ordering the missionary to join the expedition to the Southern Sea. In 1670 Marquette had been about to proceed via the Mississippi to the country of the Illinois, but the sudden worsening of relations between the Hurons, Ottawas, and Sioux had obliged him to cancel his plan. It was with enthusiasm and gratitude that he agreed to accompany Jolliet and to "seek . . . new nations that are unknown to us, to teach them to know our great God." If Jolliet, the official envoy of the state, represented the economic and political aims of New France, Marquette represented its religious aspirations. Thus can be seen, felicitously combined in the 1673 expedition, the two great forces that launched the astonishing territorial expansion of the colony: the dictates of trade and the zeal for evangelism.

Did Jolliet spend the winter of 1672–73 at the Sainte-Marie falls, busy with his fur-trading, as it has been claimed? More probably he stayed at the Saint-Ignace mission at Michilimackinac, together with Marquette. On the one hand, he had to interrogate the Indians closely about the Mississippi and the peoples along its banks:

Michilimackinac was the rallying-point of several nations, and Marquette was an expert in Indian languages. On the other hand Michilimackinac, the starting-point of the voyage of discovery, was the best place in which to complete the preparations for the expedition. An extract from the "Voyages du P. Jacques Marquette" (composed by Dablon) suggests this interpretation: "we obtained all the Information that we could from the savages who had frequented those regions; and we even traced out from their reports a Map of the whole of that New country; on it we indicated the rivers which we were to navigate, the names of the peoples and of the places through which we were to pass, the Course of the great River [Mississippi], and the direction we were to follow when we reached it." It is not impossible that Jolliet also stayed for some time at the Sainte-Marie falls; his presence would not be absolutely necessary since his partners and, particularly, his brother Zacharie were looking after his interests there, thus assuring to him the calm and the leisure necessary for the perfecting of his great plan.

Towards the middle of May 1673 the expedition set forth. It comprised seven men, in two canoes. In addition to Jolliet and Marquette, the group no doubt included some of Jolliet's partners. Chavigny, however, who was at Fort Frontenac in July 1673, was not with them; we must also exclude Zacharie Jolliet, who seems to have remained at the Sainte-Marie falls to watch over his brother's interests. The other partners (Largilier, Moreau, Thiberge, and Plattier) probably accompanied Louis Jolliet; the seventh person remains unidentified. In short, among the discoverers of the Mississippi, two only—Jolliet, the leader of the expedition, and Marquette—are known with certainty; for the others, one can, it is true, juggle with probabilities, but they will never yield more than hypotheses and conjectures.

The discoverers' route, and more so the question of chronology, remain obscured by doubt, owing to the absence of a log-book. It seems almost certain, however, that from Michilimackinac the explorers headed westward, going along the north shore of Lake Michigan, then along the west shore of the Baie des Puants (Green Bay), as far as the Saint-François-Xavier mission (near De Pere, Wisconsin); from there they followed the Rivière aux Renards (Fox River) as far as the village of the Mascouten Indians (near Berlin, Wisconsin). After some 20 days of navigation, the expedition had just reached the limit of known territory. From the Mascoutens, the French learned of the existence—only three leagues away—of a tributary of the Mississippi;

guided by two Indians, they made a "portage of half a league," going from the Rivière aux Renards to the Rivière Meskousing (Wisconsin). On 15 June, after a journey of more than 500 miles, 118 of them along the Wisconsin, the canoes finally entered the Mississippi. An intense feeling of joy and triumph surged through the little band; but Jolliet was careful not to forget that the discovery of the Mississippi, however thrilling it might be, was only a stage in his glorious mission, and that he had promised Frontenac he would see the mouth of this river.

Pushing on with their advance along the Mississippi, the French gazed in wonderment at the new scenery, so different from anything they had known before; soon strange birds appeared, exotic plants, and formidable bison, in herds some of which numbered more than 400 animals. Of Indians, however, there was no sign. For eight or ten days the banks remained obstinately deserted, as far as the mouth of the Iowa, where at last the discoverers perceived their first village of Illinois Indians, the Peorias. They were received there with numerous gestures of friendship and welcome. Jolliet and his men took to their paddles once more, and pursued their journey, which was marked by two other important stages: they encountered first the Missouri and then the Ouabouskigou (Ohio), two stately rivers that flow into the Mississippi. The Indians were numerous in this region, and were as hospitable as the Peorias. When they got to the mouth of the Ohio the French had covered some 1,200 miles from Michilimackinac. Once again, as they got farther away from the Ohio, the landscape and climate changed rapidly; the Indians also became more distrustful, if not hostile; Marquette, although he spoke six native tongues, no longer managed to make himself understood. The little band finally stopped at the village of the Quapaws (Kappas), some 450 miles from the Ohio.

The Quapaws lived on the right bank of the Mississippi, a little this side of the present boundary of Arkansas and Louisiana, at lat. 34°40′N. There Jolliet's voyage was to end. The growing hostility of the Indians, the danger of falling soon into the hands of the Spaniards to whom the Arkansas nation were known, the certainty, acquired from the natives, that they were only 50 leagues from the sea—in reality they were more than 700 miles from it—and the fear of compromising the results of the expedition: all these factors induced Jolliet and his companions to turn back. In the second fortnight of July the canoes were launched against the current in the Mississippi; the return journey was carried out via the Illinois River, the Chicago portage, and Lake Michigan to the Baie des Esturgeons (Sturgeon Bay); thanks to a further portage, the canoeists passed into the Baie des Puants and went down to the Saint-François-Xavier mission, which they reached towards the middle of October.

Louis Jolliet had completed his mission. He had not seen the mouth of the Mississippi, but he had advanced sufficiently far south to acquire the certainty that the river emptied into the Gulf of Mexico. This news was a profound disappointment to all those who already believed that they possessed the passage to the China Sea; so much so that Jolliet's very important contribution to what was then known of the geography of North America and to the territorial expansion of New France was not always appreciated at its true worth. But the obsession with the West was so firmly rooted and hopes were so keen that people immediately began once more to dream of another waterway, this time along one of the tributaries of the Mississippi.

Jolliet spent the winter of 1673–74 at the Sainte-Marie falls, engaged in making copies of his log-book and of the map that he had drawn during the course of his expedition. Towards the end of May 1674, leaving replicas of these precious documents in the care of the Jesuits, he set out for Quebec. When he reached the Saint-Louis rapids, towards the end of June, his canoe was capsized: two Frenchmen and a little Illinois slave given to him when he went down the Mississippi were drowned; Jolliet, the sole survivor, was saved in the nick of time "after being four hours in the water"; the box that contained his log, his map, and his personal papers disappeared beneath the surface. The discoverer did not get off with this disaster: the copies of his log and map left at the Sainte-Marie falls were destroyed in a fire; and to complete the circle of misfortune Marquette's diary has not come down to us. On the discovery of the Mississippi the historian therefore possesses only the information supplied from memory by Jolliet and documents based on second-hand knowledge, particularly Dablon's account. Hence there are numerous gaps: who is to say, for instance, whether Jolliet officially took possession, in the name of France, of the territories discovered in 1673?

Back from the Mississippi, Jolliet began to think of settling down. On 1 Oct. 1675 he signed a marriage contract with Claire-Françoise Byssot, aged 19, the daughter of François Byssot de La Rivière and Marie Couillard; the latter had just married a second time (7 Sept. 1675), her new husband being Jacques de Lalande* de Gayon.

Jolliet

The religious ceremony was celebrated in the cathedral at Quebec, 7 October. In the following year Jolliet asked Colbert for permission to settle, with 20 men, in the land of the Illinois which he had discovered. The reply, dated 23 April 1677, was negative. The minister wrote: "we must increase the number of settlers before thinking of other lands."

This refusal did not catch Jolliet unawares. From the time of his return from the Mississippi, he had resumed his commercial activity; but following upon his marriage with Claire Byssot—whose father had traded in the region of Sept-Îles where the family still had interests—Jolliet abandoned the hinterland for the north shore of the St. Lawrence River. On 23 April 1676 he joined the society consisting of Jacques de Lalande, his father-in-law, Marie Laurence, the widow of Eustache LAMBERT, and Denis Guyon; on 2 May the partners hired Guyon's bark to meet the needs of the fur trade at Sept-Îles. Jolliet and Lalande, however, were not long in obtaining their own boat: on 2 Nov. 1676 they bought from Michel Leneuf* de La Vallière a ketch in which they made the trip to Sept-Îles the following spring.

Jolliet rapidly acquired a place among the merchants of consequence. On 20 Oct. 1676, for example, he was among the settlers assembled by DUCHESNEAU to fix the price of beaver. Two years later, 26 Oct. 1678, he was one of the notables of the colony consulted by Frontenac about the traffic in intoxicating drink. Jolliet's qualified opinion was the one adopted by Louis XIV in the ordinance of 24 May 1679, permitting traffic in spirits within the colony but forbidding it in the woods.

With Frontenac's consent, in the spring of 1679, Josias BOISSEAU, the agent for the syndicate holding the Tadoussac trading concession, and Charles Aubert de La Chesnaye instructed Jolliet to "visit the nations and the territories of the king's domain in this country." By virtue of his commission the explorer was to go as far as Hudson Bay. It is difficult to state the exact object of this trip, but one may suppose that Jolliet assumed himself to have a double objective: to estimate the extent of English influence on the tribes in the Hudson basin, and perhaps to lay the foundations for a trade alliance with the Indians in the north. According to Father Crespieul*, who was working in the Lac Saint-Jean region in 1679, Jolliet's role was to "establish the fur trade and the St. François Xavier mission at Nemiskau." This testimony does not invalidate the two-fold hypothesis just formulated; it seems beyond question, indeed, that the task entrusted to Jolliet did not concern solely the fur-trading post—or the mission—at Nemiskau, which was only a stage in his expedition.

The 1679 voyage was not a voyage of discovery. After three fruitless attempts on the part of the French to reach Hudson Bay by sea (JEAN BOURDON in 1657), and by land (Michel Leneuf de La Vallière, Claude Dablon, and Gabriel DRUILLETTES in 1661; Guillaume Couture* in 1663), the Jesuit Charles ALBANEL, together with Paul Denys* de Saint-Simon and Sébastien Pennasca, had in fact reached the mouth of the Rivière Nemiskau in June 1672. The Jesuit repeated the journey in 1674. These precedents did not, it is true, lessen the terrible difficulties of the routes. In Albanel's words, "There are 200 saults, or water-falls, and consequently 200 portages. . . . There are 400 rapids."

On 13 April 1679 Jolliet embarked at Quebec with eight men, one of whom was his brother Zacharie. Two Indians, who acted as their guides, probably joined them on the way. The expedition apparently adopted the following itinerary: the Saguenay, Lac Saint-Jean, Rivière and Lac Mistassini, Rivière à la Marte (Marten) to Nemiskau, and Rivière Nemiskau, which flows into Rupert Bay, to the south of James Bay. The journey, in Jolliet's estimation, covered 343 leagues, "because of the detours." In the bay the explorer encountered some Englishmen, who welcomed him with a great show of politeness, and particularly Governor Charles BAYLY, who gave him ship's biscuits and flour for the return trip. Bayly had heard of Jolliet and of his discovery of the Mississippi; he congratulated the Canadian, assuring him that "the English have a high regard for discoverers." After collecting all his information, and turning down a tempting offer from the governor, who invited him to enter the service of the English, Jolliet took leave of his hosts. He returned along the Rivière Nemiskau and the Rivière à la Marte, crossed Lac Mistassini and Lac Albanel, and, via the Rivère Temiscamie, went into the Rivière Peribonca, Lac Saint-Jean, and the Saguenay. On 25 October he regained Quebec.

During his voyage Jolliet had become convinced that in Hudson Bay the English were doing "the finest trade in Canada." They "gathered in" beavers, "as many as they wanted," and even hoped to "make this enterprise more extensive in the future." The circle of their influence was growing larger all the time, and each spring the rivers of the Hudson basin brought down towards the English posts the heavily laden canoes of nations as numerous as they were distant. "There is no doubt that if the English are left in this bay [they] will make themselves masters of all the trade in Canada in less than six [ten?] years."

Jolliet

The Ottawas, indeed, who were the suppliers of the French, "do not hunt beaver, but go and seek them from the nations in the baie des Puants or from those in the neighbourhood of Lake Superior"; now it was to be feared that those nations would prefer to take their furs directly to the English, as certain of them had begun to do. And Jolliet discreetly requested His Majesty to "remove the English from this bay" or, at least, to "prevent them from establishing themselves any further, without driving them out or breaking with them."

Jolliet was aware of the disastrous results that a drive by the English in Hudson Bay would have on the Tadoussac trading concession, and he also knew how much his own trade on the north shore was threatened. His interest in this region, which adjoined the king's domain, was all the keener because on 10 March 1679 Intendant Duchesneau had granted him, in joint ownership with Jacques de Lalande, the Mingan islands and islets. Jolliet, however, lacked neither ambition nor optimism. In March 1680 he obtained Anticosti Island from Duchesneau. He proposed to set up, there and at Mingan, fishing-grounds for cod, seals, and whales, and "by this means to trade in this country and in the islands of America [West Indies]."

Because of this second grant of land, Jolliet incurred the fierce opposition of Josias Boisseau, the agent for the king's domain, who had just quarrelled with Aubert de La Chesnaye, Jolliet's uncle. The trade that Lalande and Jolliet were carrying on with the Indians of the Sept-Îles was thought to be doing harm to the tax-farmers of His Majesty's domain. Counting on Frontenac's support, Boisseau demanded in vain the cancellation of the Anticosti concession, as well as of certain fur-trading privileges granted by Duchesneau to Jolliet and his partners. The Crown's agent made a lot of fuss, launched unfounded accusations, and indulged in such excesses of language and conduct that in the summer of 1681 he was relieved of his duties and recalled to France.

Despite Boisseau's untimely complaints and extravagant behaviour, Jolliet continued his trading on the north shore. As early as 1680 or 1681 he had a dwelling on Anticosti, where he spent the summer months with his family and a few servants; in winter he lived at Quebec. Because of the scarcity of documents concerning him during the years 1680–93—in 1682 his papers were burned in a fire—little is known of Jolliet's activities between his voyages to Hudson Bay (1679) and to Labrador (1694). He exploited his fisheries at Mingan and Anticosti; but it is impossible to say whether he traded in the West Indies. During his frequent travels, Jolliet had completed a map of the St. Lawrence River and Gulf, which was sent to the minister in 1685. On that occasion Brisay* de Denonville requested for Jolliet the post of teacher of navigation. This reward was not accorded him. In 1690 the fleet commanded by Phips seized Jolliet's bark, confiscated goods worth 10,000–12,000 *livres*, and took the discoverer's wife and mother-in-law prisoners; two years later, two English ships sacked and burned his outposts at Mingan and Anticosti. Jolliet was ruined.

Jolliet had perhaps made a journey to Labrador in 1689, if we can believe a document dated 1693. He dreamed of going back there, but needed a subsidy, which the court seemed little inclined to grant him. Fortunately a Quebec merchant, François Viennay-Pachot, came to the rescue and agreed to cover the costs of the undertaking. Several explorers—Davis, Waymouth, Knight, Jean Bourdon, Chouart Des Groseilliers, and Radisson*—had already sailed along the coasts of Labrador, but none had produced a tolerably exact account of them, or even a map. Jolliet was to be the first to reveal the secret of this region that extended from the Saint John River (15 miles west of Mingan) to the present Zoar, situated at lat. 56°8′N.

On 28 April 1694, at Quebec, Jolliet boarded a vessel armed with 6 swivel-guns and 14 cannon, belonging to Pachot; the crew comprised 18 persons, one of whom was a Recollet. They dropped anchor first at Mingan, where Jolliet stayed for more than a month to traffic in furs and to reconstruct the buildings burned down by the English. On 9 June they set sail for Labrador. Jolliet sailed along the coast, which he described and mapped out systematically, doing a little trading when the opportunity presented itself. Shortly after 9 July the ship passed the Pointe du Détour (Cap Charles), and entered unknown waters. Continuing his slow advance, Jolliet charted the coastline and described the Eskimos with whom he made contact. When he drew level with Zoar, the explorer decided to turn back. The season was well advanced, and the ship, fitted with poor rigging, would not have withstood the heavy weather of autumn; besides, trade with the few Eskimos along the coast could not "pay what the vessel cost every day"; finally, the ship was carrying salt "which had to be used for cod." On 15 August Jolliet started on the way home. He reached Quebec around the middle of October, after having fished, and after having probably stopped at Mingan to take on board his wife and children, who had spent the summer there.

Joybert de Soulanges

Jolliet hastened to give a final form to his travel log. This relatively extensive document contains, in addition to a description of the Labrador coasts and their inhabitants, 16 cartographic sketches. It is the first account of the shoreline between Cap Charles and Zoar, hence its historical importance; moreover, it was in 1694 the most complete and precise portrayal of the Eskimos so far made. As for the territories visited, Jolliet found the soil barren and the inhabitants few in number; he noted the rapid disappearance of cod as soon as one proceeded northward; the only trade possible with the Eskimos was in whale oil and seal oil, but even then it would be necessary to count on cod "to cover part of the costs." Jolliet was not put off because of that: he applied for the privilege—which he was not to receive—of trafficking alone, for 20 years, with the Eskimos of Labrador.

In the autumn of 1695, when the season was well advanced and navigation in the river and gulf dangerous, he was selected by the governor and the intendant to pilot the *Charente*: he was "perhaps the only man in this country, according to Frontenac, capable of performing this work properly." For this task Jolliet received 600 *livres*. He spent the winter in France, and returned to Quebec before 13 June 1696 with the promise of his appointment—confirmed 30 April 1697—to the office of hydrographer. In a document of 1692 he had already been given the title of hydrography master: was this a *lapsus*, or was Jolliet teaching hydrography at the Jesuit college, without holding the post officially? Be that as it may, Jolliet and the maps that he was able to make to render navigation in the river and gulf safe were often mentioned during these years. One of the maps, dated 1698, has come down to us.

On 30 April 1697 Jolliet had received from Frontenac and Bochart* Champigny a small fief on the Rivière des Etchemins, which he did not have time to develop. In winter he taught at the Jesuit college; in summer he probably lived on Anticosti Island or at Mingan. Unfortunately the last three years of his life are shrouded in uncertainty. Was it on his lands on the north shore that he died in the summer of 1700, in circumstances that have not been revealed? Nothing is known of this, and despite active research his burial-place has not yet been discovered.

Thus ended, between 4 May and 15 Sept. 1700, the remarkable career of this explorer; his broad education, his culture, the diversity of his talents as much as his courage and ambition, made of him one of the greatest and most illustrious sons of his country. Born in New France, formed in its institutions, Jolliet attained international fame during his lifetime: in France, Spain, Italy, Holland, Germany, England, works extolled his name and the discovery of the Mississippi. Beyond all doubt, the Canadian Louis Jolliet is one of the most genuine and most impressive examples of the heroes produced by New France.

ANDRÉ VACHON

Acte de baptême de Louis Jolliet (21 sept. 1645), APQ *Rapport, 1924–25*, 198. Acte de mariage de Louis Jolliet et de Claire-Françoise Bissot (Québec, 7 oct. 1675), APQ *Rapport, 1924–25*, 224. AJQ, Greffe de Romain Becquet, 7 mai 1666; 1er oct. 1675; 9 mai 1679; 16 avril 1680; Greffe de Pierre Duquet, 2 nov. 1676; 9 févr. 1679; Greffe de François Genaple, 14 mars 1680; Greffe de Gilles Rageot, 21 avril 1669; 1er oct. 1672; 3 oct. 1672; 23 avril 1676; 2 mai 1676; 4 déc. 1676; 17 avril 1680. APQ, *Ins. cons. souv.*, II, 3. Contrat de mariage de Louis Jolliet et de Claire Bissot (1er octobre 1675), *APQ Rapport, 1924–25*, 240. Correspondance de Frontenac, *APQ Rapport, 1926–27, 1927–28* et *1928–29, passim*. Correspondance de Talon, APQ *Rapport, 1930–31, passim*. [Claude Dablon], "Voyages du P. Jacques Marquette, 1673–75," in *JR* (Thwaites), LIX, 85–211; *ibid., passim*. *JJ* (Laverdière et Casgrain), 330, 345. [Louis Jolliet], "Journal de Louis Jolliet allant à la descouverte de Labrador, 1694," éd. Jean Delanglez, in APQ *Rapport, 1943–44*, 147–206. *Jug. et délib., passim. Ord. comm.* (P.-G. Roy), I, 322f. P.-G. Roy, *Inventaire de pièces sur la côte de Labrador conservées aux Archives de la Province de Québec* (2v., Québec, 1940–2), I, 3–9. Recensement de 1666.

Delanglez, *Jolliet*. Ernest Gagnon, *Louis Jolliet, découvreur du Mississipi et du pays des Illinois, premier seigneur de l'île d'Anticosti* (Montréal, 1946); "Où est mort Louis Jolliet?" *BRH*, VIII (1902), 277–79. Godbout, "Nos ancêtres," APQ *Rapport, 1951–53*, 459. Amédée-E. Gosselin, "Jean Jolliet et ses enfants," *RSCT*, 3rd ser., XIV (1920), sect.I, 65–81. Lionel Groulx, *Notre grande aventure: l'empire français en Amérique du Nord (1535–1760)* (Montréal et Paris [1958]), 139–74. Pierre Margry, "Louis Jolliet," *RC*, VIII (1871), 930–42; IX (1872), 61–72, 121–38, 205–19. Adrien Pouliot et T.-Edmond Giroux, "Où est né Louis Jolliet?" *BRH*, LI (1945), 344–46, 359–63, 374.

JOYBERT (Joibert) DE SOULANGES ET DE MARSON, PIERRE DE, soldier, seigneur, and administrator of Acadia; b. 1641 or 1642 in Saint-Hilaire de Soulanges in Champagne; baptized in 1644; d. 1678.

At an early age he apparently joined the Briquemault regiment and served in Portugal. In 1665, he arrived at Quebec as a lieutenant in Hector d'ANDIGNÉ de Grandfontaine's company of the Carignan-Salières regiment, and took part in PROUVILLE de Tracy's expedition against the Iroquois the next year. He returned with his commander to France in 1667 because of the war

Joybert de Soulanges

over the Spanish Netherlands. When, late in 1669, Grandfontaine was selected to take possession of Acadia under the terms of the Treaty of Breda, Joybert was one of the men chosen to accompany this officer. Their vessel was wrecked on the coast of Portugal near Lisbon in January 1670, but Joybert and the others were saved, and as soon as possible the expedition was reorganized and dispatched to Boston in the *Saint-Sébastien*. Joybert was present at the handing over to French authority of Fort Pentagouet, and on 14 August he was ordered to accompany RICHARD WALKER, who had been Col. Thomas TEMPLE's deputy governor of Acadia, in the *Saint-Sébastien*, to take possession of various other posts in Acadia. On 27 August he accepted the surrender of Jemseg, the fortified trading-post that had been built in 1659 by Temple on the Saint John River 50 miles from its mouth, and on 2 September at Port-Royal, he took possession of that place and also accepted the surrender of Fort La Tour at Cap de Sable.

That fall Joybert was ordered to Boston by TALON to deliver some letters and to secure information about the French merchant vessel *La Fontaine* that had been seized by the English, together with her valuable cargo. His conduct on this mission was criticized by Grandfontaine who sent him to Quebec to explain his conduct to Talon. Talon reported the dispute to the king but was unable, or unwilling, to deal with the serious disagreement, the details of which are not known. It was at Quebec, in 1672, that Joybert married Marie-Françoise, daughter of the attorney-general of New France, LOUIS-THÉANDRE CHARTIER de Lotbinière.

On 20 Oct. 1672, in recognition of his "good and praise-worthy service to the King, both in Old and New France" he received a seigneurial grant on the east bank of the Saint John, measuring 1 league in depth and extending 4 leagues up the river from its mouth. This large area included a part of the site of the present city of Saint John. At the same time, he was promoted to "Major des troupes" in Acadia and assigned command of Fort Jemseg (called Gemisick by the French) and the river Saint John by BUADE de Frontenac. It is doubtful if there was a single white resident at the time on the Saint John and his appointment appears to have been part of a plan to settle soldiers and families on that river as an aid in establishing an inland route of communication between Quebec and Acadia. On the very same day, his brother Jacques was issued a seigneurial grant adjoining that of Joybert at the mouth of the Saint John.

Joybert turned his attention to repairing and strengthening the post at Jemseg. But, with his garrison of nine men, he was in no condition to resist when a Dutch force under Jurriaen AERNOUTSZ pillaged the post and took Joybert a prisoner to Boston on 7 Aug. 1674. A ransom of 1,000 beaver pelts, or the equivalent, was placed on Joybert. Word of the capture reached Frontenac at the end of September and he immediately sent men with canoes to find out what was happening in Acadia, and to bring Mme de Soulanges with her infant daughter via the Saint John–Rivière du Loup route to Quebec. Joybert appears to have remained a captive at Boston until ransom had been arranged by Frontenac, probably late in 1675. He then went to Quebec, reporting to Frontenac for duty and being sent back to command the Saint John River area. On 12 Oct. 1676 he received a grant at "Nachouach" (Nashwaak) measuring 2 leagues wide by 2 leagues deep on both sides of the river, and including the site of the present Fredericton. This concession was made by Frontenac in consideration of Joybert's service in Acadia and "desiring to engage him to continue them." Just four days later, Joybert's petition to the king for another grant was heard. In this, he spoke of using his own funds to repair Jemseg both before and after the Dutch raid, and of the fact that he had lost everything as a result of that raid. His request was complied with, and the grant issued included Fort Jemseg itself, together with land measuring 1 league on either side of it and 2 leagues in depth. In all, the three seigneuries comprised more than 100 square miles.

In 1677 Joybert was named administrator of Acadia, succeeding Jacques de CHAMBLY, and Jemseg became the seat of French power and the capital of the country. He died about 1 July the following year and was succeeded by Michel Leneuf* de La Vallière. Joybert was survived by his widow and two children. The elder, Louise-Élisabeth, afterwards became the wife of Philippe de Rigaud* de Vaudreuil, governor-general of Canada, and the mother of ten children, including Pierre de Rigaud* de Vaudreuil de Cavagnial, who was the first native-born governor of Canada. Joybert's second child, Pierre-Jacques, became a soldier and died of smallpox at Quebec in 1703. A third child died in infancy.

In the years following her husband's death Mme Joybert appears to have divided her time between Quebec and the Saint John River, where she continued Joybert's fur-trading activity. However, her circumstances were such that Intendant DUCHENEAU felt obliged to give her 300 *livres* following Joybert's death, and an annual pension in the same amount was eventually granted. On 31 March 1691 the widow received a new seigneurial concession on the Saint John opposite

Juchereau de La Ferté

Jemseg including much of the present Camp Gagetown. Title to this grant, and to the three that had been granted Joybert, was to lapse due to non-fulfilment of conditions. Mme Joybert herself died in Paris in 1732.

GEORGE MACBEATH

AN, Col., C¹¹A, 3. *Collection de manuscrits relatifs à la Nouv.-France*, I. Correspondance de Frontenac (1672–82), APQ *Rapport, 1926–27*, 17, 73, 74, 88, 90, 96, 111. Correspondance de Talon, APQ *Rapport, 1930–31*, 156, 157, 176, 179. *Jug. et délib. Mémoires des commissaires*, I, 151; II, 323–26, 566–70, 573–75; IV, 37, 288–89; and *Memorials of the English and French commissaries*, I, 25, 206, 413, 611–13, 744, 746, 748. P.-G. Roy, *Inv. concessions*, II, III, IV.

Claude de Bonnault, "Branche canadienne des Joybert," *BRH*, XLII (1936), 110–16. Ganong, "Historic sites in New Brunswick," 274–75, 277, 309–12, 314. Beamish Murdoch, *History of Nova-Scotia*. Rameau de Saint-Père, *Une colonie féodale*. W. O. Raymond, *The River St. John, its physical features, legends and history from 1604 to 1784*, ed. J. C. Webster (Sackville, 1943). P.-G. Roy, *La ville de Québec*, I, 362. Régis Roy, "La famille de Joybert," *BRH*, XV (1909), 223; ——— et Malchelosse, *Le régiment de Carignan*. Sulte, *Mélanges historiques* (Malchelosse), VIII.

JUCHEREAU DE LA FERTÉ, JEAN, merchant, member of the Conseil Souverain; b. *c.* 1620 at La Ferté-Vidame (Eure-et-Loir, France), son of JEAN JUCHEREAU DE MAUR and of Marie Langlois; d. 16 Nov. 1685 at Quebec.

Juchereau de La Ferté was the eldest son of the family; he arrived in Canada with his parents in 1634 and married Marie Giffard on 21 Nov. 1645 at Quebec. He played a distinguished part in the trade, magistrature, and society of the new-born colony. On 7 Sept. 1661 he received a grant of land on the Île d'Orléans from CHARLES DE LAUSON. On 18 Sept. 1663 he was appointed a member of the newly instituted Conseil Souverain. The following year, with the majority of the members of the council, he opposed the appointment of a syndic for the settlers. Consequently on 19 Sept. 1664 Governor SAFFRAY de Mézy relieved him of his duties, together with three other members of that body. PROUVILLE de Tracy, on 31 May 1666, annulled this action as *ultra vires*, and Juchereau was once again to be found witnessing, as "former" councillor, the registration of the letters patent of RÉMY de Courcelle, TALON, and Le Barroys. Tracy, having taken the time to inquire into the 1664 quarrel, did not deem it expedient to reinstate La Ferté, who was replaced in the council by de Gorribon.

In 1672 Jean Juchereau inherited the de Maur seigneury, at Saint-Augustin near Quebec. He died at the Hôtel-Dieu in Quebec and was buried in the paupers' cemetery. His wife, Marie Giffard, born about 1628 in France, had died on 11 Aug. 1665, also at Quebec, and had been buried the next day. The Juchereaus belonged to the bourgeoisie, and at that time had not yet been ennobled.

Jean Juchereau and Marie Giffard had seven children: three sons and four daughters. None of the sons was to leave any descendants. The eldest, Noël, born 3 July 1647 at Quebec, was the first Jesuit and the first religious born in Canada. He entered the noviciate at Nancy as a lay brother on 30 Jan. 1665, and was sent to Lyon to study pharmacy for two years, from 1667 to 1669. In this latter year he returned to Quebec, where he was drowned on 3 Nov. 1672 while on his way to minister to the sick. The second son, Paul-Augustin Juchereau *dit* de Saint-Denis, was born 3 June 1658; he inherited his father's seigneury and devoted himself to trade. He went as a delegate to France in 1700, with the sieur Pascaud*, to ask for freedom of trade on behalf of the Canadians; there he negotiated the formation of the Compagnie de la Colonie, for which he acted as receiver of moneys until his sudden death in 1714 in a shipwreck near the Île de Sable. The youngest, Denis-Joseph Juchereau de La Ferté, born 20 June 1661, chose the army as his career. He was with Greysolon* de Dulhut at the Sainte-Marie falls (Sault Ste. Marie) in 1684, with Le Moyne* d'Iberville at Hudson Bay in 1689, and with JOLLIET in Labrador in 1694, and it was he whom the king sent to warn Frontenac [*see* BUADE] of an imminent English attack in 1697. He died 9 Aug. 1709 at Quebec.

Of the four daughters only one, Marie-Louise, born 9 Sept. 1652, got married; she became the wife of Charles Aubert* de La Chesnaye at Beauport, on 10 Jan. 1668. She had six children, the only posterity of Jean Juchereau de La Ferté, and died on 7 March 1678 at La Rochelle. The other three girls became nuns. Jeanne-Françoise joined the Hospitallers of Quebec and became the celebrated Mother Juchereau* de Saint-Ignace. Charlotte became an Hospitaller at La Rochelle, where she was superior. Marie became as it were the eldest Hospitaller at Quebec, where she took her vows on 25 Jan. 1678. She was called Marie Juchereau de Saint-Thérèse, was of ailing health, and died in piety on 25 March 1697.

LUCIEN CAMPEAU

Alphonse Gauthier, "Noël Juchereau de La Ferté: premier jésuite et religieux canadien," *Lettres du Bas-Canada*, XIII (1959), 211–19. P.-G. Roy, *La famille Juchereau Duchesnay* (Lévis, 1903), 18–56.

Juchereau de Saint-Denis

JUCHEREAU DE MAUR, JEAN, seigneur, member of the fur-trading council and churchwarden, brother of NOËL JUCHEREAU Des Chatelets; b. *c.* 1584 at La Ferté-Vidame (Eure-et-Loir, France); d. 7 Feb. 1672 at Beauport.

It was in 1634 that Jean Juchereau, his wife, and four children came to New France. Juchereau was a friend and collaborator of ROBERT GIFFARD, with whom he probably made the crossing, and he was of considerable help in establishing immigrants from Le Perche in the colony.

Furthermore, as early as 15 Jan. 1635 the Cent-Associés granted him the stretch of land lying between the Cap aux Diamants and the valley of Cap-Rouge. A little later, however, since HUAULT de Montmagny considered it preferable to leave around Quebec a strip of land forming part of the region for which dues would be payable to the company, Juchereau's fief was exchanged for an area of equal size situated beyond Cap-Rouge. JEAN DE LAUSON, senior, the intendant of the Cent-Associés, took the trouble to write to Juchereau on 19 March 1636, to explain to him the company's new policy.

In 1647 Juchereau's land holdings were extended: on 21 March, in the presence of Teuleron, a notary at La Rochelle, Noël Juchereau Des Chatelets purchased in his brother's name the fief of Saint-Michel, owned by M. de PUISEAUX, and on 18 September the governor granted to Jean and Noël Juchereau the seigneury of Maur, or Saint-Augustin. This concession was ratified by the company on 29 March 1649, and Jean Juchereau, having inherited from his brother who had recently died, was given possession of his seigneury on 9 April 1650.

Juchereau took a great interest in clearing land and in colonization, but he was none the less active in the affairs of the Communauté des Habitants. A document of 1667 mentions him as "formerly assessor to the Sovereign Court of this country [Conseil Souverain], and member of the council established by the King for the direction of the commerce and of the fur trade of the said country...."

By the time he took over the seigneury of Maur, Juchereau had obviously become an important person in the colony; in 1647, 1650, and 1651 he carried the canopy in the Corpus-Christi processions; on New Year's Day 1651 he was one of the small group of prominent people who received gifts from the Jesuits; and in 1656 and 1657 he was a warden of the parish church of Quebec. Juchereau was a prominent citizen of Quebec and one of the leading men in the Communauté des Habitants; he was also among the many accused of malpractices by JEAN PERONNE Dumesnil, who was a hot-tempered, unreasonable individual.

From 1663 Juchereau, who was growing old and no longer held any actual office, was chosen on occasions by the Conseil Souverain or by the parties concerned as an arbitrator or as the trustee of an estate. In 1668 PROUVILLE de Tracy suggested to the king that Juchereau, together with some of the principal settlers, should be ennobled—a suggestion which the king failed to adopt.

Finally on 4 January, aware that his end was near, Juchereau signed an act with his inheritors whereby he bequeathed his seigneury of Maur to his eldest son, JEAN JUCHEREAU DE LA FERTÉ.

His wife, Marie Langlois, had been buried at Quebec on 15 Jan. 1661. Jean Juchereau de Maur himself died at Beauport "in the dwelling of M. de Saint-Denys, his son [*see* NICOLAS JUCHEREAU], on 7 Feb. 1672.

ANDRÉ VACHON

AJQ, Greffe de Guillaume Audouart, 15 mars, 1 oct. 1651; Greffe de Gilles Rageot, 4 janv. 1672. ANQ, Registre des sépultures, 15 janv. 1661. APQ, Coll. de pièces jud. et not., 26; Fois et hommages, Régime français, I, 199. ASQ, Documents Faribault, 78, 97–100; Polygraphie, XII, 22; XXII, 47.

"Contrat de Teuleron, 21 mars 1647," *RHAF*, V (1951–52), 123–25. *JR* (Thwaites), *passim*. *JJ* (Laverdière et Casgrain). *Jug. et délib.*, I, *passim*. *Papier terrier de la Cie des I.O.* (P.-G. Roy), 25, 124, 261. "Précis des actes de foy et hommage, I," PAC *Rapport, 1885*, 31. P.-G. Roy, *Inv. concessions*, I, 270–2.

Phileas Gagnon, "La seigneurie de Maur," *BRH*, VII (1901), 52f. "Jean Peronne Dumesnil et ses mémoires," *BRH*, XXI (1915), 194. Jean Langevin, *Notes sur les archives de Notre-Dame de Beauport* (Québec, 1860), 10, 132. P.-G. Roy, *La famille Juchereau Duchesnay* (Lévis, 1903), 15–18.

JUCHEREAU DE SAINT-DENIS, NICOLAS, seigneur, colonizer, business man, member of the council of the colony for the fur trade, director of the Tadoussac trade, soldier; b. *c.* 1627 at La Ferté-Vidame, near Chartres (France), son of JEAN JUCHEREAU DE MAUR and Marie Langlois; d. 4 Oct. 1692 at Quebec.

Nicolas Juchereau came to Canada in 1634 with his father, who was a person of some means. His uncle, NOËL JUCHEREAU Des Chatelets, had come to Canada probably two years earlier, to attend to the interests of the Compagnie des Cent-Associés, and later became the head clerk of the Communauté des Habitants.

Nicolas Juchereau possessed vast domains. He obtained by grant, gift, or purchase, properties at Quebec, Beauport, and the Île d'Orléans. In 1656 he obtained as a grant the seigneury of

Juchereau Des Chatelets

Grande Anse (Saint-Roch-des-Aulnaies), comprising islands and shore-lines, where there was little or no farming. In 1673 the GIFFARDS granted him the fief of Duchesnay, comprising a frontage of nine *arpents* and extending to the whole depth of the seigneury of Beauport: Juchereau saw to its being peopled and worked.

For his son Joseph, who was six, he obtained from Governor BUADE de Frontenac the seigneury of Saint-Denis in 1679. Although he is sometimes called seigneur of Beauport, Nicolas Juchereau never possessed this seigneury. It was his son, Ignace Juchereau* Duchesnay, who received it as a gift 17 Feb. 1683 and took possession of it in 1696.

Nicolas Juchereau was also active in the trade in pelts. Like his father, he was for a time a member of the council of the colony for the fur trade. From 1649 on we find him going off with the Indians for the great hunt. From 1660 to 1665 he made several excursions in the region of Tadoussac, often in company with Father DRUILLETTES. In 1663 he was a member of the group of 17 Canadians to whom Governor PIERRE DUBOIS Davaugour farmed out the collection of the 25 per cent levy on beaver pelts and of the duties on wine and spirits, as well as the Tadoussac trade. When the lease was annulled by the Conseil Souverain some months later, his brother JEAN JUCHEREAU DE LA FERTÉ was appointed to collect the revenues. For several years Nicolas Juchereau was to have an interest in the Tadoussac lease, and he was to be for some time the director of trade at this locality. It was there that Father ALBANEL met him in 1670 and obtained from him two Frenchmen as travelling companions. In 1672 the same missionary obtained passage from Chicoutimi to Tadoussac on a boat belonging to Nicolas Juchereau, whom he called at that time "captain of Tadoussac."

In 1679 Juchereau took into his home his brother-in-law, CHARLES LEGARDEUR de Tilly, a member of the Conseil Souverain who had been exiled from Quebec by Frontenac. In 1684 he was among the 18 notables whom the intendant consulted about the country's finances. In the same year Denis Riverin*, agent of the tax farmers for the fur trade, challenged his right to fish, hunt, and trade on his fief of Saint-Denis; these "privileges," which had been "overlooked" in 1679 when the fief had been granted, were to be granted officially to Juchereau's wife in 1697.

He also distinguished himself as a soldier. In 1666, at the head of a militia company, he took part in the expeditions led by Governor RÉMY de Courcelle and by the Marquis PROUVILLE de Tracy against the Iroquois. Subsequently he was to remain in command of this company. When PHIPS attacked Quebec in 1690, Nicolas Juchereau was stationed with his 80 or so militiamen at the place where the English troops landed, with the mission of harassing them and of blocking their path. He had an arm broken by a shot while he was trying to repel the invaders. As the militia troops of Beauport and Beaupré had captured six enemy cannon, he received one as a trophy. In February 1692 he was ennobled as a reward for his services as a colonizer and soldier.

He died 4 Oct. 1692 at Quebec and was buried in the cemetery of Beauport. On 22 Sept. 1649 he had married Marie-Thérèse Giffard, who bore him 12 children. His wife died in 1714.

BERNARD WEILBRENNER

AN, Col., C^{11A}, 6, ff.437–38, Déclaration de Nicolas Juchereau sur la traite de Tadoussac, 18 oct. 1684. *Coll. de manuscrits relatifs à la Nouv.-France*, I, 523; II, 53. *JR* (Thwaites). *Jug. et délib., passim. Papier terrier de la Cie des I.O.* (P.-G. Roy). P.-G. Roy, *Inv. concessions*, I, II, III.

JUCHEREAU DES CHATELETS, NOËL, Bachelor of Laws, member of the Compagnie des Cent-Associés and head clerk of the Communauté des Habitants; brother of JEAN JUCHEREAU DE MAUR; b. at La Ferté-Vidame (Eure-et-Loir, France) towards the end of the 16th century; d. 1648 at Orléans (France).

Noël Juchereau received an excellent education: he completed a course in the humanities, followed by a course in law which earned him a Bachelor's degree.

A member of the Cent-Associés, he came to New France in 1634 (or 1632), probably as representative of the syndicate of eight members set up to administer the company after the disaster which befell ROQUEMONT's fleet in 1628.

Juchereau was a prominent figure at Quebec: he received grants of land and took an active part in the life of the colony. The governor sought his assistance frequently when certain delicate legal matters had to be decided.

It was he, who, together with PIERRE LEGARDEUR de Repentigny, conceived in 1644 the idea of the Communauté des Habitants, of which he was appointed head clerk in 1645. Henceforth Juchereau was very much to the fore in the colony; as a churchwarden in 1645–46, he had a part in all religious ceremonies, which were the essence of Quebec's social life at this period. The *Journal des Jésuites* refers to his carrying the canopy, distributing consecrated bread, or washing the feet of Indians on Maundy Thursday.

But in January 1646 the officers of the Communauté des Habitants were taken to task by the "ordinary members" who seemed "to be about to rise up against those who held the appointments and offices." Juchereau, among others, was reproached with "living too well." It appears that the settlers had some grounds for rebellion, but the governor quickly repressed this would-be mutiny by punishing the more vocal objectors. In October 1646, Des Chatelets was nevertheless promoted to "clerk in charge of naval purchases."

All, however, was not well at Quebec and in the Communauté. A reorganization of the colonial administration was needed. As a result several memoranda were addressed to the king in 1647, requesting the elimination of various abuses. Des Chatelets himself sailed for France in October, in order to lay the colony's problems before the king.

These efforts were subsequently to lead to the royal regulations of 1648. But Juchereau did not live to see them implemented, for he died on this trip, in the city of Orléans, shortly before 31 July 1648.

Noël Juchereau Des Chatelets never married.

ANDRÉ VACHON

ASQ, Documents Faribault, 6, 30, 45, 60. *JR* (Thwaites), *passim*. *JJ* (Laverdière et Casgrain). Thomas Chapais [Ignotus], "Noel Juchereau, sieur des Chatelets," *BRH*, VIII (1902), 86–89. "Jean Peronne DuMesnil et ses mémoires," *BRH*, XXI (1915), 171. Lanctot, *Histoire du Canada*, I.

K

KÉLUS. *See* THUBIÈRES

KEPITANAL. *See* CAPITANAL

KERBODOT, DU PLESSIS-. *See* GUILLEMOT

KERTK. *See* KIRKE

KIOTSEAETON (Kioutsaeton) *dit* "**Le Crochet**" (**The Hook**), Mohawk chief, orator, and envoy to the French during the peace negotiations, 1645–46, between the French, their Indian allies, and the Mohawks; fl. 1645–46.

Kiotseaeton was a famous Mohawk orator, first of all a professional speaker for the council chiefs, appointed to speak for them, not for himself, and only secondly a man who handled words dramatically. Eloquence, however, was regarded by the Indians as second only to courage in hunting and in war. Their oratory was slow and deliberate, but fluent; logical, repetitious, rhetorical, frequently sarcastic, rich in simile and metaphor, and invariably dignified (Jenness, *Indians of Canada*, 200–1). Woven belts of wampum were used as gift exchanges by the orator to confirm his statements.

In 1645 both the French and the Mohawks were eager for peace. The negotiations of that year represent a serious attempt by the Mohawks to end the long strife with the French and their Indian allies, in which the fur trade was deeply involved. In 1642 Iroquois hostilities had broken out against the Hurons, middlemen in the northern fur trade with the French, as the Mohawks had less furs to trade. They began a series of raids on the Huron fur convoys, which used the Ottawa River as their trading route. French settlements were menaced, colonization came to a standstill, and no military aid was available from France itself.

In the spring of 1644, the famous Algonkin chief, PIESKARET, with six members of his tribe, was on a hunting trip to Lake Champlain, where they fell in, by chance, with a party of 13 Mohawks, 11 of whom they killed. Tokhrahenehiaron, one of the two survivors, with two other released captives, was sent back to the Mohawk country by the French with a proposal from HUAULT de Montmagny, the governor, "to bring about universal peace among all the Nations." The Mohawks responded by dispatching Kiotseaeton to discuss terms for peace. He arrived at Trois-Rivières 5 July 1645, accompanied by two other Mohawks and Guillaume Couture*, who had remained as a prisoner in the Mohawk country, after his capture with Father Isaac JOGUES three years previously. Tokhrahenehiaron, also, was one of the party. Kiotseaeton, profusely adorned with wampum, declared the purpose of his people "to enter into the designs of the French, of the Hurons, and of the Algonquins." CHAMPFLOUR, the commandant at Trois-Rivières, welcomed the embassy. News of its arrival was sent to the governor at Quebec, who came to Trois-Rivières and appointed 12 July as the date for a conference.

Father Jogues, who had come from Montreal, was also present at the great peace council, attended with ceremonial pomp and pageantry on the part of both the Indians and the French. In addition to the French and Mohawk delegations, Huron, Algonkin, Montagnais, and Attikamegue deputies were also represented but their most important spokesmen were absent. Seventeen wampum belts were presented by Kiotseaeton,

Kirke

with an equivalent number of "words" or addresses. The seventeenth or last present was the collar worn at home by HONATTENIATE, one of the two Mohawks most recently captured by the French. The governor made his reply to the embassy, 14 July, presenting 14 gifts with as many messages to the visiting Mohawks.

There is some uncertainty surrounding the discussions. Two recent secondary sources (Hunt, *Wars of the Iroquois*, 77–78, 82, 86 and Desrosiers, *Iroquoisie*, 303–8, 321–24, 328–36) infer that the Mohawks demanded a share of the northern fur trade, in which the Hurons acted as middlemen for the French. The settlement, as recorded in *JR* (Thwaites), XXVII, states merely that "Thus was peace concluded with them [the Mohawks]," subject to the following conditions, "that they should commit no act of hostility against the Hurons, or against the other Nations who are our [French] allies, until the chiefs of those Nations who were not present had treated with them." It is clear, however, that two private conversations took place between the governor, "Le Crochet" (by inference, Kiotseaeton), and Couture. At the first of these meetings, Kiotseaeton proposed that the Algonkins be excluded from the terms then under discussion. Montmagny, however, refused to abandon his allies, whereupon Kiotseaeton showed himself "chagrined at this repulse." Nevertheless, in the second conference, the governor made the proposal to include the Christian Algonkins only in the protective terms of the treaty. (*JR* (Thwaites) XXVIII, 149, 151, 315.)

It is evident that the Jesuits at Quebec and Sillery had no knowledge of this secret condition (*JR* (Thwaites), XXVIII, 147–51) until news was brought from Trois-Rivières 8 Jan. 1646 by Tandihetsi, a Huron, that all the Algonkins were planning to hold a council there. Its purpose was to inform the Algonkins that some Mohawks had "spoke in confidence to Tandihetsi, who was accompanying them, and told him the secret of their country,—to wit, that no peace was desired with the Atichawata [Algonkins], but it was desired with the Hurons and the French; that the French had consented thereto, and that consequently nothing but the opportunity was now awaited for exterminating the Atichawata, and that 300 Annieronons [Mohawks] could certainly come by the middle of February [1646] for the execution of this plan" (*JR* (Thwaites), XXVIII, 149).

Fathers JÉRÔME LALEMANT and Jean de QUEN, who were surprised that their confrères at Trois-Rivières had not informed them of the proposed council and its objectives, reported Tandihetsi's message to the governor, who then told them what had transpired earlier in the two private discussions with Kiotseaeton. In the interval between the deliberations, Montmagny, fearing that peace would be endangered by refusing Kiotseaeton's demands, had consulted Fathers Barthélemy VIMONT and PAUL LE JEUNE, who "thought that the difficulty might be smoothed over." (There is no evidence in the *Relations* that Vimont and Le Jeune had actually been present at the two meetings with Kiotseaeton.) On 23 Jan. 1646, Pierre Boucher*, Toupin, his brother-in-law, and a Mohawk, arrived in Quebec from Trois-Rivières, bearing letters which stated that everything which "the Huron Tandihetsi had said was false,—at least, in the main" (*JR* (Thwaites), XXVIII, 155).

A second parley was held between the French, Mohawks, Hurons, Algonkins, and Iroquets, 18–20 Sept. 1646 and the peace terms were subsequently ratified in the Mohawk villages. Two Algonkins, two Hurons, and two Frenchmen were included in the embassy, headed by Couture, which was sent to the Mohawk country on behalf of the French, while three Mohawks remained in New France. The French embassy, accompanied by seven Mohawk ambassadors, did not return to New France until February 1646.

Kiotseaeton was again present at Trois-Rivières 7 May 1646, as head of a third Mohawk peace embassy. Following this meeting, Father Jogues and JEAN BOURDON set out 16 May for the Mohawk country to confirm the peace. After his return, 7 June, Father Jogues received permission to go back to the Mohawk country as a missionary and left Montreal on 24 September. His devoted efforts, however, soon ended in tragedy. Despite the treaty, hostilities were renewed, and the murder of Father Jogues in the Mohawk country 18 Oct. 1646 was an ominous prelude to the bloody war which culminated in the destruction of the Huron trading "empire" in 1649.

THOMAS GRASSMANN

Du Creux, *History* (Conacher), II, 408–13, 436–37. *JR* (Thwaites), XXVII, 247–73, 275–303; XXVIII, 147–51, 291–303, 315; XXIX, 47–49.

KIRKE (in French sources called **Kertk, Quer(que)**, or **Guer), SIR DAVID**, adventurer, trader, colonizer, leader of the expedition that captured Quebec in 1629, and later governor of Newfoundland; b. *c.* 1597 in Dieppe; d. 1654 near London.

David was the eldest of five sons of Gervase (Jarvis) Kirke of Derbyshire, merchant of London and Dieppe, and Elizabeth Gowding (Goudon), who may have been the daughter of an English merchant settled in Dieppe (BM, Add. MS 5533, 215). As an importer from Dieppe, Gervase undoubtedly had good information on French operations in North America. In 1627 some London merchants, including Gervase, formed a company whose object was trade and plantation on the St. Lawrence. When war broke out that year between France and England, the company financed an expedition, under David Kirke, which was commissioned by Charles I to displace the French from "Canida." Accompanied by his brothers LEWIS, THOMAS, John, and James (sometimes called Jarvis), David Kirke set off with three ships probably in company with a fleet bringing settlers to Sir WILLIAM ALEXANDER's projected colony at Port-Royal. Kirke may have stopped at Ferryland, the colony of Lord Baltimore [see CALVERT] in Newfoundland before ascending the St. Lawrence and capturing Tadoussac. He seized one supply ship going to Quebec and then sent Basque fishermen to CHAMPLAIN demanding the surrender of the post. Champlain rejected the demand because he was expecting relief from France, and Kirke decided against an attack on the fortified settlement. The English ships turned back to England, but off Gaspé encountered the French supply fleet of four vessels under Admiral ROQUEMONT de Brison and captured them without loss in a short engagement. When news of these events reached Paris the Kirke brothers were burned in effigy because, having been born in Dieppe, they were considered French citizens and their actions were therefore treason against King Louis.

Impressed with the achievement of the Kirkes, their backers applied for a patent giving them the sole right to trade and settle in Canada. Sir William Alexander complained that such a patent would infringe upon the land granted to him under the Great Seal of Scotland in February 1627/28. The two groups compromised by joining in the Company of Adventurers to Canada to establish an Anglo-Scottish colony at Tadoussac with Alexander holding all the land within 10 leagues of Tadoussac on both sides of the river and with the united company having the right to free trade and use of the harbours.

The second fleet, of six ships and three pinnaces, left Gravesend in March 1629 under the Kirke brothers, with Jacques Michel, a deserter from Champlain, again acting as pilot on the river. From Quebec, where the small garrison were now on the point of starvation, Champlain sent a party to meet the expected relief fleet which, under ÉMERY DE CAËN, was bringing word that peace had been declared in April by the Treaty of Susa. Although the party did meet de Caën in the Gulf, they were captured by the English on their way back to Quebec. David Kirke, now aware of the desperate conditions at Quebec, sent Lewis and Thomas on to that post from Tadoussac, and Champlain, having no alternative, surrendered on 19 July 1629.

Despite the Treaty of Susa, Charles I refused to restore the captured lands in North America until his wife's dowry was paid by his brother-in-law, Louis XIII of France. Protracted negotiations over the dowry and ownership of the furs seized at Quebec by the Kirkes were ended in 1632 by the Treaty of Saint-Germain-en-Laye and the adventurers were ordered to restore Quebec and Port-Royal to the French. During the intervening years the English had retained control of Quebec while the Company of Adventurers to Canada prosecuted the fur trade, contended with attempts at trade by both French and English interlopers, maintained 200 men in Canada, and explored "400 leagues" into the interior. In recognition of their services, David Kirke was knighted in 1633 and Lewis (who was knighted in 1643) received a patent of dubious validity to trade in the St. Lawrence.

In 1635 Sir David wrote a description of Newfoundland based on a visit of uncertain date, and on 13 Nov. 1637 he was made co-proprietor of that island with the Marquis (later Duke) of Hamilton and the earls of Pembroke and Holland, the prior right of Lord Baltimore in Avalon being set aside because he was accused of deserting his settlement at Ferryland [but see HILL]. The patent issued to the Company of Adventurers to Newfoundland forbade any settlement within six miles of the shore and any interference with visiting fishermen. Complete freedom of the fisheries was guaranteed but Kirke was authorized to collect an impost of 5 per cent of all fish and oil taken by foreign fishermen. The coat of arms granted to these Adventurers is that of the Province of Newfoundland today. In 1639 Sir David, as the first governor of Newfoundland, took possession of Baltimore's "Mansion House" and the other property at Ferryland. In the same year the four eldest Kirke brothers were naturalized as English citizens.

As governor of Newfoundland Sir David soon came into conflict with the fishing merchants of western England, the so-called "Western Adventurers," who were intent on preserving their control of the Grand Banks fisheries by excluding settlement from the island. Sir David had brought out about 100 colonists, erected forts at Ferryland, St. John's, and Bay de Verde, and collected tolls from all fishing vessels. The charges of the Western Adventurers were that he had rented

Kirke

preferred fisheries to foreigners, destroyed curing buildings, and disrupted the industry by establishing taverns along the coast. Kirke replied showing the bias of his accusers and the faults of these summer visitors.

Because of family connections and dependence on royal favour Sir David supported the cause of Charles I in the English Civil War. After Prince Rupert induced part of the navy to join Charles's forces in 1648, the Puritan government feared that Newfoundland under Kirke might be used as a royalist base for counter-revolutionary naval operations. Sir David, sometime correspondent of Archbishop Laud, hired 400 sailors in 1649 ostensibly as fishermen. The island was therefore kept under naval surveillance and strict controls were placed on access to the island, as in the case of Sir Lewis Kirke.

In 1651 Sir David was called to England to answer charges that he had withheld taxes collected in the name of the government. His property was put in charge of commissioners, including TREWORGIE, who were also directed to collect the impost on foreign fishermen. The following year other commissioners were appointed to manage "the affairs and interest of the Commonwealth in Newfoundland" which included guarding the island against Prince Rupert. Treworgie appears to have remained in control *in situ* until 1659.

Kirke's estate was temporarily sequestered and in England he was called before the Council of State several times. As sole survivor of the original patentees Sir David transferred five-sixths of the patent rights to Cromwell's son-in-law, perhaps for political reasons. The charges against Sir David were never substantiated and his wife was allowed to return to Newfoundland to superintend his business. Sir David, however, was imprisoned on a suit by Lord Baltimore's heir for the seizure of Ferryland in 1639, and while in prison, probably in the Clink in Southwark, he died about the end of January 1654. The commissioners sent to Newfoundland in 1651 were in turn arrested on the suit of James Kirke for £1,100 owing to Sir David's estate.

Apparently Lady Kirke and her sons, George, David, and Philip, continued to reside in Newfoundland, but after the Restoration Cecil Calvert, second Lord Baltimore, successfully reclaimed his father's patent for Avalon though he never exercised his rights. On behalf of his eldest nephew, George, Sir Lewis demanded compensation for improvements made at Ferryland by the Kirkes. Lady Kirke petitioned Charles II that George be made governor of Newfoundland, an arrangement suggested by the Newfoundlanders themselves, but no resident governor was appointed. Lady Kirke and her children were still in Ferryland in 1673 when a Dutch fleet sacked and burned the settlement. A decade later, in 1683, Sir John Kirke, whose daughter had married Radisson* and who was himself a member of Prince Rupert's Hudson's Bay Company, asked the king for compensation to himself and the families of Sir David and Sir Lewis for the losses incurred in the conquest of Canada in 1629, a claim that the French had never paid. The last reference to George Kirke appears to be in 1680 when he was proposed as a collector of the toll levied on all boats fishing in Newfoundland waters.

David Kirke's character remains obscure and controversial, heroic to some English writers, piratical to some French. His actions at Quebec have been denounced as those of a violent and grasping religious bigot, yet his relations with Champlain seem to have been gentlemanly and even cordial. In an age of violence Kirke behaved in Newfoundland like a self-appointed king of the fishery island, ousting Lord Calvert's agent and imposing his own order on the transient fishing fleet. Yet the investigations of the Puritan parliamentarians into the activities of this known Royalist failed to produce any evidence of malfeasance on his part.

JOHN S. MOIR

The MS sources for Kirke's life are relatively few and scattered, but the majority are to be found in PRO, C.O. 1/5, 6, 10, 12, 14–17, 21, 22, 24, 25, 34, 44, and 66, and in S.P. 25/16, 18, 25. The diplomatic correspondence concerning the restoration of Quebec and the disposal of the captured furs is in S.P. 78/85–91, and related material can be found in *Acts of P.C., col. ser., 1613–80*. Documentary evidence concerning the time and place of Sir David Kirke's death is found in Somerset House, Surrey and Sussex wills, Alchin, f.379.

Contemporary material in print includes Champlain, *Works* (Biggar), VI and Sagard, *Histoire du Canada* (Tross), especially IV. Lescarbot, *History* (Grant), III, gives a brief account of the capture of Quebec. Du Creux, *History* (Conacher), picks up the story of the English conquest only in 1632. Eighteenth-century accounts appear in *Mémoires des commissaires*, I, 42–43, 71, 160; II, 275–77, 484–88; IV, 279–80, 301 and *Memorials of the English and French commissaries*, I, 115, 145, 214, 401, 421, 569, 571.

Léon Pouliot, "Que penser des frères Kirke?" *BRH*, XLIV (1938), 321–35, discusses the problem of the nationality of the Kirke brothers. L. D. Scisco has published "Kirke's memorial on Newfoundland" in *CHR*, VII (1926), 46–51. The only monograph on the Kirkes is Henry Kirke's *The first English conquest of Canada* of which the second edition (London, 1908) corrects many inaccuracies from the first edition (1871), but omits all documentary references. The best account of the relationship of the Kirkes to events in Canada and Acadia is given by Biggar, *Early trading companies*. A contemporary ballad celebrating Kirke's victory has been published recently: Martin Parker, *England's honour revived by the valiant exploytes of Captaine Kirke: News from Canada, 1628*, ed. J. Stevens Cox (Beaminster, Dorset, 1964).

KIRKE, SIR LEWIS, adventurer and trader, brother of Sir DAVID and THOMAS KIRKE; b. *c.* 1599 at Dieppe; d. ante 1683.

Lewis accompanied his brothers David, Thomas, John, and James as second-in-command of the expeditions to capture Quebec in 1628 and 1629. In the latter year he carried David's letter, demanding surrender of the post, to CHAMPLAIN. He was distinguished by the French for his gentlemanly behaviour and generous treatment of the Roman Catholic clergy captured at Quebec. He was in Quebec in 1631 and again in 1632 when the post was restored to the French and may have been there throughout the occupation.

In 1633 he received a patent from Charles I to trade and colonize in the St. Lawrence valley and Nova Scotia. He was sent out in the *Mary Fortune* by David Kirke and a number of other adventurers with a £12,000 cargo which was seized by the French and for which no compensation was received. His patent was also challenged by Sir WILLIAM ALEXANDER the elder, who had a prior patent in the area. In 1634 he commanded a fleet of three vessels dispatched to Canada by David Kirke and his associates but it was forced to put back into Plymouth because of a storm. The next year Lewis was made captain of the naval ship *Leopard* and was engaged in battles with Dunkirk ships and in a search for Turkish pirates near Guernsey. He was in command of the *Repulse* in 1636 but the following year was transferred to the *Margaret* when he refused to serve under Admiral Rainsborough in the fleet off the Netherlands. He was next found in Newfoundland collecting the 5 per cent levy of the fish and oil taken by foreign fishermen, which the patent of 1637 had authorized [*see* Sir DAVID KIRKE]. His actions brought him into conflict with the Basque fishermen in Trinity Harbour. In 1640 he was lieutenant-colonel in charge of levies in the eastern division of Northampton County. He was charged jointly with Lord Morley in 1641 with the murder of a Capt. Peter Clarke and was convicted, although it was generally believed that the acquitted Lord Morley was the principal agent in the murder.

Lewis Kirke must have subsequently been pardoned for he served in the royalist army during the Civil War and was knighted in 1643. He was governor of the stronghold of Bridgnorth in 1643 and 1644, and was later accused of torturing supposed parliamentary informers in that town. He surrendered to the revolutionary forces and compounded under the Oxford Articles of 1646, but was arrested in 1647 on the suit of a man whose estate he had seized during the war. Sir Lewis pleaded benefit of the Oxford Articles which was denied because he had not paid the fine imposed on compounders. In 1650 he gave two sureties of £1,000 each for his good behaviour towards the revolutionary government before being allowed to visit his brother Sir David in Newfoundland.

He appears to have been reconciled with the government for in 1654 with his brothers John and James he petitioned Cromwell's Council of State for the claim of £48,000 unpaid from the 1632 settlement with the French regarding Quebec. Provision for a final settlement was contained in the French treaty of 1655, but as late as 1667 the terms had not been fulfilled and Sir Lewis was asking Charles II not to return Nova Scotia to the French until they complied. After the Restoration he and John also petitioned the king to force Thomas TEMPLE to return lands and property in Nova Scotia which they claimed belonged to them under the patent of 1633. Sir Lewis was appointed captain and paymaster of the corps of Gentlemen-at-Arms by Charles II, perhaps as compensation for the loss of his claims in North America. His heirs are mentioned in a petition of Sir David Kirke's widow in 1683.

JOHN S. MOIR

See sources for Sir DAVID KIRKE.

KIRKE, THOMAS, adventurer, younger brother of Sir DAVID KIRKE; b. *c.* 1603 in Dieppe; d. post-1641.

Thomas Kirke accompanied his brothers David LEWIS, John, and James in the expeditions to capture Quebec in 1628 and 1629. Upon the surrender of CHAMPLAIN at Quebec in 1629 Thomas took him as a prisoner to the English headquarters at Tadoussac. En route he encountered a French relief ship under Émery de Caën, which had slipped past David Kirke, and captured it after a pitched battle. Following this, Thomas was left in charge of the fur-trading post at Quebec where he acted as governor for the English and Scottish merchants who had financed the expedition. He had to contend with English and French interlopers in the St. Lawrence. In 1631, having returned to England, he brought out the English supply ship and apparently wintered at Quebec, then returned to England in 1632 with

Kirwin

his brother Lewis when the colony was restored to the French.

He entered the navy, probably in that same year, with the rank of captain and "Vice Admiral of the English Fleet." In March 1635 he was appointed captain of the *Sampson* but was transferred to the *Swallow* in the following year after being accused by his lieutenant of exceeding his powers. He may have been the Thomas Kirke connected with the collection of ship money in Cambridgeshire in 1637. During the Civil War in England he served in the royalist forces as a lieutenant-colonel, and it was probably Thomas, rather than Lewis, also a lieutenant-colonel, who was wounded while capturing Knock Castle near Trim, Ireland, in 1642.

He does not seem to have left any family as he is not mentioned in a petition of 1683 requesting compensation to heirs of the Kirke brothers for losses incurred in the conquest of Quebec. Thomas Kirke may have died during the Civil War, or he may be the person of that name engaged in 1661 to hunt down supporters of the Cromwellian régime in Connecticut and Massachusetts. He is not to be confused with a namesake and probable relative who was appointed English consul at Genoa in 1689.

JOHN S. MOIR

See sources for Sir DAVID KIRKE.

KIRWIN, MARIE, dite de la Conception. *See* IRWIN

KNIGHT, JOHN, English navigator, explorer; d. June 1606 in Labrador.

Knight is first heard of in 1605 when he captained the pinnace *Marekatten* or *Katten* (*Cat*) in a Danish expedition to Greenland led by John CUNNINGHAM, with James HALL as chief pilot. By 1606 he had quit Danish service and was employed by the East India and Russia companies to search for a northwest passage. In April he received a safe-conduct from the companies and, later that month, sailed from Gravesend in the *Hopewell* of 40 tons. On 19 June he sighted the coast of Labrador and followed it southwards, intending to explore as much as possible during the summer and to winter ashore. His plans went astray when the ship was badly damaged in a storm, probably in the vicinity of Nain. On 26 June, Knight and three companions, including his brother Gabriel, went ashore; they never returned. His crew denied that they had borne any grudge against the commander whom they deserted, claiming that ice and hostile Eskimos prevented their searching for him.

GILLIAN T. CELL

There are three sources for the voyage: PRO, H.C.A. 13/38 (narratives by several members of the crew); Knight's own journal, continued after his disappearance by Oliver Brownel or Browne (Olivier Brunel), and printed in *The voyages of Sir James Lancaster, Kt., to the East Indies . . . and the voyage of Captain John Knight (1606) to seek the North-West Passage*, ed. C. R. Markham (Hakluyt Soc., 1st ser., LVI, 1877); and an abridged version of the journal in Purchas, *Pilgrimes*, XIV (1905–7), 353–65.

DNB. Dodge, *Northwest by sea. The first letter book of the East India Company*, ed. G. Birdwood and W. Foster (London, 1893). W. Foster *England's quest of eastern trade* (London, 1933).

KOLNO. *See* SCOLVUS [Appendix]

KRYN. *See* TOGOUIROUI

L

LA BARRE, CLAUDE CHARRON DE. *See* CHARRON

LA BARRE, JOSEPH-ANTOINE LE FEBVRE DE. *See* LE FEBVRE

LA BOULAYE, CHARLES DURET DE CHEVRY DE. *See* DURET

"LABRADOR, THE." *See* FERNANDES

LA CHESNAYE, PIERRE DUQUET DE. *See* DUQUET

LA COMBE-POCATIÈRE, FRANÇOIS POLLET DE. *See* POLLET

LA COURT DE PRÉ-RAVILLON ET DE GRANPRÉ, French *armateur*, who by himself, or by means of his seamen, discovered for the Bretons the walrus-fishery in the Magdalen Islands (Îles de la Madeleine), under the name of Ramea (Ramée); fl. 1591.

Knowledge of the 1591 voyage comes chiefly from an account written in English by an anonymous member, perhaps the master, of the *Bonaventure* set out with a consort by "Monsieur de La court Pre Ravillon and Grand Pre" of Saint-Malo (Hakluyt, *Principal navigations* (1903–5), VIII, 150–54) and from a letter by Thomas JAMES (*ibid.*, VIII, 155, *see also* 156–57). James speaks of *two* small ships which came and went to Ramea, in connection with the capture, near the Scilly Isles, of the *Bonaventure* by the Bristol privateer *Pleasure*, which brought the prize back to Bristol with her cargo. The capture is referred to in BM, Lansdowne MS 67, ff.146, 190, and Harleian MS 598, f.15v., the last describing her as "on Leaguer prize Laden with trayne oyell, feshydes and teeth," her forty tons of oil, with walrus hides and tusks being officially worth £793 10s. (not more than half their real value). The sister ship of the *Bonaventure* seems to have reached Saint-Malo safely. The anonymous account makes it clear that La Court's two ships set out with "the fleet that went to Canada," i.e. to the St. Lawrence, probably to Tadoussac. The *Soudil* and the *Charles* with which the *Bonaventure* kept company were also ships in that fleet. La Court may have been in the *Bonaventure*'s consort as the author of the narrative refers to "my Masters" as being on board her (Hakluyt, VIII, 152).

The *Bonaventure* was at Cape Ray ("Cape de Rey") 6 May 1591, Bird Rocks (Isles of Aponas) 7 May; circled the Magdalens (the writer's "Ramea," used for the group as we today use "Magdalens"), keeping between Duoron (likely Entry Island) and Amherst Island, and entering Pleasant Bay and Basque Harbour (Harbour of the Isle Ramea) between Amherst Island and Grindstone Island (Hupp) where the walrus were taken.

La Court himself remains a mystery. He is not identified by his names in the Saint-Malo parish registers, yet Lord Burghley notes that the *Bonaventure* belonged to "Frenchmen of St Mallows" (BM, Lansdowne MS 67, f.146). He may have been a sea-captain, a merchant, or merely a financier. La Roncière, however, states that he was empowered to set out his ships by Jacques NoËL, one of the heirs of Jacques CARTIER's Canadian rights. Pierre Bergeron, in his *Traicté de la navigation*, though he uses mainly the documents printed by Hakluyt, adds that La Court touched at Saint-Pierre on his way out (he may be developing a phrase in Hakluyt rather than using an independent source).

The *Bonaventure* was sold in Bristol, but it is possible that her owners recovered her and that she, with her consort, may have come to the Magdalens again. There was at least one Breton ship there in 1593 and more than two in 1597 [*see* Richard FISHER and Charles LEIGH], so that La Court's penetration of the Basque monopoly of the Gulf of St. Lawrence fisheries established a profitable trade for Breton seamen and merchants.

DAVID B. QUINN

BN, MS Fr. 15452, 15454. BM, Harley MS 598; Lansdowne MS 67. P. Bergeron, *Traicté de la navigation* (Paris, 1630), 122. Hakluyt, *Principal navigations* (1903–5), VIII, 150–57. La Roncière, *Histoire de la marine française*, IV, 314.

LA DOUSSINIÈRE ET D'AMBAULT, JACQUES DUCHESNEAU DE. *See* DUCHESNEAU

"LA FERRIÈRE." *See* EROUACHY

LA FERTÉ, JEAN JUCHEREAU DE. *See* JUCHEREAU

LAFLEUR, FRANÇOIS *dit. See* BAILLY

LA FLEUR, GUILLAUME RICHARD *dit. See* RICHARD

LAFONTAINE, BELLOT *dit. See* BELLOT

LA FONTAINE, MAURICE POULIN DE. *See* POULIN

LA FONTAINE, MICHEL GAMELAIN DE. *See* GAMELAIN

LA FOREST, GABRIEL TESTARD DE. *See* TESTARD

"LA FORIÈRE" ("La Fourière," "La Foyrière"). *See* EROUACHY

LA FRENAYE DE BRUCY (Lafrenaye, Lafresnaye, Lafresnay, La Frenay, Lafraynaye), ANTOINE DE, lieutenant in the Auvergne regiment, ensign of the first company ("la Colonelle") in the Carignan-Salières regiment, lieutenant of François-Marie PERROT (governor of Montreal); b. *c.* 1650 at Carlepont in the diocese of Noyon (Department of the Oise), son of Martin de La Frenaye and Geneviève Lepage; d. 1684 in Canada.

As a lieutenant in the Auvergne regiment, he came from the West Indies to Canada, arriving with PROUVILLE de Tracy in 1665. By a notarial contract drawn up 26 Aug. 1667 at Quebec, he purchased from Dominique Lefebvre Du Guesclin, for the sum of 500 *livres*, a commission as ensign of a company which was part of the Carignan regiment, and decided to settle in Canada. In 1670 he became the lieutenant of the governor of Montreal, François-Marie Perrot. As the governor could not personally concern himself with the trading in furs for which he possessed the rights in the island bearing his name, he appointed Brucy in his place. As

La Fresnaye

Perrot's partner Brucy acted as an intermediary between him and certain *coureurs de bois*, and furthered the governor's ambition by trafficking in furs with the Indians who came down the Ottawa river to Ville-Marie (Montreal). In 1673 Frontenac [*see* BUADE] learned that the corrupt practices of the *coureurs de bois* were attributable to Perrot and Brucy. Summoned to amend their ways, the two traders complied; indeed, shortly afterwards, when Frontenac arrived at Montreal on his way to Cataracoui (Kingston), Perrot received him with respect and Brucy was entrusted with a command in the expedition led by Frontenac himself. But the following year the conflict began again more fiercely than ever, and the infractions of the ordinances on the part of the two accomplices were one of the causes of the notorious legal disputes in 1674–75, involving the Abbé Fénelon [*see* SALIGNAC], Perrot, and Brucy. The Conseil Souverain referred the whole matter to Colbert in Paris. Various sentences were handed down; Brucy, as Perrot's principal agent, was condemned to a term of imprisonment and a fine of 200 *livres*.

Antoine de Brucy obtained several fiefs by notarial contract, among others the one granted by Perrot, on his island, 1 Jan. 1676: 10 *arpents* in length by 30 in depth, opposite Sainte-Anne-de-Bellevue. On 5 Feb. 1684 Dollier* de Casson, the superior of the Montreal seminary, conveyed to him a tract of land 2 *arpents* wide by 20 deep, attached to the fief of Jacques Le Ber* near Senneville.

Brucy, a very skilful and moderately scrupulous businessman, succeeded in acquiring a fortune. He owned a house and a store at Montreal, at the northwest corner of Saint-Paul and Saint-Pierre streets. The inventory of his possessions reveals a remarkable wealth for a gentleman of the period. On 10 Oct. 1682 Brucy had attended an assembly of notables called specifically to discuss the Iroquois question.

In 1676, at Lachine, he had married Hélène, daughter of Pierre PICOTÉ de Belestre, a Montreal merchant; she bore him five children. When she became a widow, Hélène Picoté de Belestre married again, in 1686. Her second husband was Jean-Baptiste Céloron* de Blainville.

MARIE BABOYANT

P.-G. Roy, *Inv. concessions*, I, II, V. Valérien Carrière, *Histoire de l'île Perrot, de 1662 à nos jours* (Valleyfield, 1949). Faillon, *Histoire de la colonie française*, III; 449–51. Henri Lorin, *Le comte de Frontenac: étude sur le Canada français à la fin du XVIIe siècle* (Paris, 1895). Gérard Malchelosse, "Perrot, neveu de Talon," *Cahiers des Dix*, VII (1942), 129–60. É.-Z. Massicotte, "Le sieur La Fresnaye de Brucy," *BRH*, XXXVI (1930), 644–67. Régis Roy et Malchelosse, *Le régiment de Carignan*. Tanguay, *Dictionnaire*.

LA FRESNAYE. *See* RÉMY

LA FRESNIÈRE, JACQUES HERTEL DE. *See* HERTEL

"LA GRANDE GUEULE" ("Big Mouth"). *See* OTREOUTI

"LA GRENOUILLE." *See* OUMASASIKWEIE

LA HAYE, FRANÇOIS MARGUERIE DE. *See* MARGUERIE

LA LANDE, JEAN DE, a *donné* of the Society of Jesus, native of Dieppe, canonized by Pope Pius XI, 29 June 1930; killed by the Iroquois in October 1646.

La Lande was a *donné*, and by that we mean that he was not bound to the Society of Jesus by religious vows, but by a contract under the terms of which he placed himself completely at the disposal of the missionaries, who in return guaranteed him lodging, food, and help in case of illness. The first indication of his presence in the colony was on 14 Dec. 1642, when the effects of the late Jean NICOLLET were up for auction and he came forward as purchaser of two books of piety which had belonged to the famous interpreter of the Algonkins. From 1642 to 1646 he seems to have been attached regularly to the Trois-Rivières residence. Father Anne de NOUË was then in charge of the residents of the house; this missionary was later buried at Trois-Rivières after an heroic death which was a noble inspiration to Jean de La Lande.

On 21 Aug. 1646 Father JÉRÔME LALEMANT, the superior of the Jesuits of Quebec, decided to send Father Isaac JOGUES to the Iroquois country in order to maintain peaceful relations with the Indians. For an associate he was given Jean de La Lande, who was not unaware of the danger to which he was exposing himself. Jogues, La Lande and a few Hurons left Quebec on 24 Sept. of that year. The little band had scarcely got beyond Trois-Rivières when all the Hurons save one turned back, so impressed were they with the dangers of such a journey. With Jean de La Lande the sense of duty prevailed over everything else; he had promised to follow Jogues, and he was going to keep his word. When they reached their destination, the ambassadors of peace were treated as enemies. Victims for their faith, they were both killed: Jogues on 18 October, La Lande on 18 or 19 Oct. 1646.

The news did not reach Quebec until June 1647. The *Relation* gives a long account of Jogues's martyrdom. Of his associate it says: "One must not forget the young Frenchmen who was slain with the Father. That good youth, called Jean de la Lande,—a native of the City of Dieppe, as has been said,—seeing the dangers in which he was involving himself in so perilous a journey, protested at his departure that the desire of serving God was leading him into a country where he surely expected to meet death. This frame of mind has enabled him to pass into a life which no longer fears either the rage of those Barbarians, or the fury of the Demons, or the pangs of death."

LÉON POULIOT

JR (Thwaites), XXXI, 122 (the one passage in the *Relations* concerning Jean de La Lande). Additional information may be found in *Positio causae* and in Archange Godbout, *Les pionniers de la région trifluvienne*, 67.

LALEMAND, PIERRE. See ALLEMAND

LALEMANT, CHARLES, first superior of the Jesuits of Quebec (1625–29), missionary at Quebec (1634–38), procurator of the mission of New France, in Paris (1638–50), son of a criminal-court lieutenant of Paris; brother of JÉRÔME LALEMANT; b. 17 Nov. 1587; d. 18 Nov. 1674 in Paris.

Charles Lalemant entered the noviciate at Rouen on 29 July 1607. He studied philosophy at the Collège in La Flèche (1609–12), taught the lower classes at the Collège in Nevers (1612–15), studied his theology at La Flèche (1615–19), and did his third probationary year in Paris under the direction of the celebrated Father Antoine Le Gaudier (1619–20). He was then a teacher of logic and physics at the Collège of Bourges (1620–22), and from October 1622 to March 1625 was principal of the boarding-school at the Collège de Clermont.

He was made responsible for setting up a mission of the Society of Jesus in Canada, and in April 1625 he left Dieppe with Fathers Énemond Massé, Jean de Brébeuf and two lay brothers. He arrived at Quebec in June. Neither the directors of the Compagnie de Montmorency nor the settlers amongst whom the pamphlet *Anti-Coton* was then circulating had any liking for the Jesuits. But the Recollets received them with great kindliness and gave them hospitality until they could have their own house. Father Lalemant was quick to realize that the progress of the colony was being impeded by the very people who ought to have promoted it, the de CAËNS, who were interested exclusively in the fur trade. A change was imperative. Therefore, as soon as Father Philibert NOYROT arrived in 1626 he was ordered, because of the good standing that he enjoyed at the court, to take ship again for France, with the object of advancing the welfare of the colony. One result of this move was the revocation of the Edict of Nantes where New France was concerned. Father Noyrot had arranged for supplies to be sent to his Quebec colleagues, but they never reached their destination. According to Father Chrestien LE CLERCQ, they were seized at Honfleur by Raymond de LA RALDE and GUILLAUME DE CAËN. Hence Father Lalemant returned to France in the autumn of 1627. The ship that was bringing him back to Canada in 1628, and that was commanded by Claude ROQUEMONT de Brison, fell into the hands of the KIRKE brothers. The latter made Lalemant their prisoner and dispatched him to Belgium, whence he got back to France. A fresh start, made in 1629, was interrupted by a shipwreck in the Strait of Canseau. Lalemant had to return to France on a Basque fishing vessel which was itself wrecked near San Sebastián in Spain [*JR* (Thwaites), IV, 229–44]. These were personal misfortunes, to be superseded in the apostolic soul of Father Lalemant by a greater one: Quebec was in the hands of the English, and what the missionaries had accomplished was already overthrown.

But Lalemant lost no time in setting to work to restore the ruins. He launched crusades of prayer in the Paris monasteries; as rector of the Collège in Eu, then of the Collège in Rouen, he followed closely the negotiations which were to culminate in the Treaty of Saint-Germain-en-Laye (1632). By December 1631 he was convinced that Canada would be given back to France, and he asked to return to the colony. His wish was not to be granted until 1634, and he was to return to France for good in 1638. It was he who helped CHAMPLAIN during his last illness and who celebrated the funeral mass. A letter that he addressed to his brother Jérôme Lalemant, on 1 Aug. 1626, reveals the soul of the man. He was under no illusions as to the difficulties of the missionary apostolate: "The conversion of the Savages takes time. The first six or seven years will appear sterile to some; and, if I should say ten or twelve, I would possibly not be far from the truth. But is that any reason why all should be abandoned? Are not beginnings necessary everywhere? Are not preparations needed for the attainment of every object? For my part, I confess that, if God shows me mercy, although I expect no fruits as long as it will please him to preserve my life, provided that our labours are acceptable to him, and that he may be pleased to make use of them as a preparation for those who will come after us, I shall hold myself only too happy to employ my life and my strength, and to spare nothing in my power, not even my blood, for such a purpose." These words reveal a clear grasp of the difficulties, linked with the spiritual strength to overcome them: precious qualities in the founder of a mission. He did not labour in vain. The residence that he had built at Quebec was to receive Father PAUL LE JEUNE in 1632, and he was to live there himself from 1634 to 1638. Indeed, Father Lalemant's zeal was particularly manifest in his efforts on behalf of the French population of Quebec. He had left such pleasant memories there that 12 years after his departure the Communauté des Habitants was to recommend him to the queen as the first bishop of Quebec.

In 1626 when Father Lalemant reported to the general of the Society Father Noyrot's return to France, he said that the object of his voyage was to inform certain benefactors and even his colleagues in Paris about the needs of the Jesuit mission in New France. Lalemant added that, after the return of Father Noyrot in the spring, it would be necessary to replace him with a person who would look after the interests of the Canadian mission in France. What Father Lalemant was suggesting was a procurator for the mission, a post that he was to be the first to hold and that would allow him to play a very important part in the founding of Montreal. It was through his personal intervention with M. JEAN DE LAUSON, the future governor of New France, that the island was ceded to the Société de Montréal. It was he who introduced Paul de CHOMEDEY de Maisonneuve to Jérôme Le Royer de La Dauversière. He likewise had a decisive influence in bringing Jeanne MANCE, LOUIS D'AILLEBOUST de Coulonge, and his wife Marie-Barbe de BOULLONGNE to Montreal.

Father Lalemant's ministry, like that of his successors in Paris, Fathers Le Jeune and Paul RAGUENEAU, was devoted to preaching and spiritual leadership. In 1660 he published *La vie cachée de Jésus-Christ en l'eucharistie*, which was reprinted in 1835, 1857, and 1888. Father Lalemant died in Paris 18 Nov. 1674, at the age of 84. His contribution to Canadian history, if less spectacular than that of men such as Le Jeune and Ragueneau, is very important. In particular, he occupies a distinguished place in the gallery of people who never saw Montreal, but among whom one must seek the explanation of its heroic origins.

It is known that Father Charles Lalemant had been the superior of the professed house in Paris, and for a time vice-provincial. It was in this capacity that he authorized Cramoisy, on 3 February 1652, to publish the 1651 *Relation*.

Father Lalemant was an unflagging correspondent. His letter of 1 Aug. 1626 to Father Jérôme was the 68th of that year, and it was not the last. What has become of them? We do not know.

LÉON POULIOT

Le Clercq, *First establishment of the faith* (Shea); *Premier établissement de la foy*. E. R. Adair, "France and the beginnings of New France," *CHR*, XXV (1944), 246–78. Campbell, *Pioneer priests*, II, 247–76. Robert Le Blant, "Le testament de Samuel de Champlain, 17 novembre 1635," *RHAF*, XVII (1963–64), 273–77. In *Ville, ô ma ville* (Montréal, 1941), 63–71, the author has described the part played by Father Charles Lalement in the founding of Montreal. Rochemonteix, *Les Jésuites et la Nouvelle-France au XVIIe siècle*, I, 137f.

LALEMANT, GABRIEL, priest, Jesuit, missionary and martyr; canonized by Pope Pius XI, 29 June 1930; b. 3 Oct. 1610 in Paris; killed by the Iroquois 17 March 1649.

Gabriel Lalemant was the son of a lawyer in the judicial court (Parlement) of Paris. The 1649 *Relation* implies that he belonged to the nobility: "Although, in leaving the world, he had left the share which his birth gave him in honorable offices. . . ." He was 20 when he entered the noviciate in Paris on 24 March 1630. Two years later he was granted permission by his superiors to add to the three usual religious vows that of devoting himself to foreign missions; 14 years were to elapse between the taking of this vow and Gabriel's arrival in Canada. In the interval he was a teacher at the Collège in Moulins (1632–35), studied theology at Bourges (1635–39), was minister to the boarding-school pupils at the Collège in La Flèche (1639–41), was philosophy teacher at the Collège in Moulins (1641–44), and prefect of the Collège in Bourges (1644–46). The *Journal des Jésuites* records his arrival under the date 20 Sept. 1646. We know little about his stay in Quebec (1646–48). Early in September 1648 he arrived at Sainte-Marie-des-Hurons and he was diligent in the study of the language. His success was so prompt that in February 1649 he replaced at the Saint-Louis mission Father Noël CHABANEL, who had been called away.

On 16 March 1649, a war-party of 1,000 Iroquois overran the little town of Saint-Ignace and captured it before sunrise, almost without striking a blow. From there they went on to the Saint-Louis mission, about a league away. Here the Hurons defended themselves stoutly, and drove back two separate attacks. But by weight of numbers the Iroquois were victorious here as well.

Jean de BRÉBEUF and Gabriel Lalemant were at that time at the Saint-Louis mission. They were urged to flee; they refused, "and, during the heat of the combat, their hearts were only fire for the salvation of souls." As soon as they were captured they were stripped of their clothes, their nails were torn out, and they were taken to the little town of Saint-Ignace (half-way between Coldwater and Vasey, in the county of Simcoe, Ontario).

Brébeuf died 16 March, at four in the afternoon. Was Lalemant aware of his fellow missionary's suffering? We do not know. As for him, his martyrdom began 16 March at six in the evening and lasted until the following morning. Here is the account of it given in the *Relation:* "At the height of these torments, Father Gabriel Lallemant lifted his eyes to Heaven, clasping his hands from time to time and uttering sighs to God, whom he invoked to his aid." He "had received a hatchet blow on the left ear, which they had driven into his brain, which appeared exposed: we saw no part of his body, from the feet even to the head, which had not been broiled, and in which he had not been burned alive,— even the eyes, into which those impious ones had thrust burning coals."

His body, buried with Brébeuf's beneath the chapel of the Sainte-Marie residence, was taken up and moved to Quebec in the spring of 1650.

LÉON POULIOT

Almost all that we know about Gabriel Lalemant we owe to the *Relation* of 1649 (*JR* (Thwaites), XXXIV, 24–36). *JJ* (Laverdière et Casgrain), *passim.* See also ACSM, "Mémoires touchant la mort et les vertus des pères Isaac Jogues . . ." (Ragueneau), repr. APQ *Rapport, 1924–25*, 3–93, *passim. Positio causae.* Christophe Regnaut, "Récit veritable du martyre et de la bien heureuse mort, du Père Jean de Breboeuf et du Père Gabriel l'Alemant en la Nouvelle france, dans le pays des hurons par les Iroquois, ennemis de la foy," 1678, in PAC *Report, 1884,* Note E. lxiii.

Léon Pouliot, "Notice sur Gabriel Lalemant," dans *Les saints martyrs canadiens* (Montréal, 1949), 25–28; 115–21. Rochemonteix, *Les Jésuites et la Nouvelle-France au XVIIe siècle,* II.

LALEMANT, JÉRÔME (called **Achiendassé** by the Hurons), Jesuit priest, superior of the Huron mission (1638–45), superior of the Jesuits in Canada (1645–50 and 1659–65); b. 27 April 1593 in Paris; d. 26 January 1673 at Quebec; brother of CHARLES and uncle of GABRIEL LALEMANT.

Jérôme Lalemant entered the Jesuit noviciate in Paris 20 Oct. 1610; he studied philosophy at Pont-à-Mousson (1612–15) and theology at the Collège de Clermont (1619–23). In the interval he had been prefect of the boarding-school at Verdun (1615–16) and teacher at the Collège in Amiens (1616–19); after finishing his theology he taught philosophy and the sciences at the Collège de Clermont (1623–26), and did his third probationary year at Rouen (1626–27); then he became minister of the Collège de Clermont (1627–29) and principal of the boarding-school of this same college (1629–32), rector of the Collège in Blois (1632–36); from 1636 to 1638 he was again at the Collège de Clermont, this time as spiritual adviser. Few Jesuits had had as wide experience as Father Jérôme Lalemant before coming to Canada, an evidence of the high esteem in which he was held by his superiors.

It is not astonishing, in view of this, that he was named superior of the Huron Mission in 1638, the very year of his arrival in the country. He succeeded Jean de BRÉBEUF. His first act was to make a count of the population living within the Huron country: 12,000 people divided among 32 towns or villages.

His name remains associated with the central residence of the missionaries in the field: Sainte-Marie-des-Hurons. Begun in 1639, this first important establishment west of Quebec developed at the same pace as the mission. It comprised in 1649 a chapel, the fathers' residence, that of the lay personnel, carpentry and ironworking shops, a hospital, a retreat house for the neophytes, guest quarters for the non-Christians who were passing through, a cemetery, a farm with a poultry-yard and farm animals. A base for apostolic operations, Sainte-Marie-des-Hurons was, from 1639 to 1649, and in every sense of the word, the stronghold of the mission.

This prominent place in Canadian religious history deserved a better fate than the oblivion which was its lot for two centuries. By collaborating to restore it to life in the 1960's, the Jesuits of the district of Upper Canada and the archaeologists Kidd and Jury are enabling us to have a better understanding of the greatness of soul of those Frenchmen of the 17th century and of the gigantic tasks which they took upon themselves in order to implant Christian civilization in the very midst of barbarousness and to carry it ever forward.

The material realization of Sainte-Marie-des-Hurons would have been impossible without an

Lalemant

institution introduced into Canada by Father Jérôme Lalemant: the *donnés* ("given men"). The lay brothers, who were responsible for the domestic tasks, were too few to be able to keep up with the constant development of the mission. Moreover, their status as religious forbade them to carry arms; yet it was not prudent for the missionaries to remain defenceless in the Huron country. The *donnés*, who dedicated their lives to the mission but without taking vows of religion, assisted the lay brothers and could in case of need take up arms. It would be difficult to exaggerate their importance in the development of the mission. Thus, to take just one example, in 1649 there were in the Huron country 16 fathers, 4 lay brothers, and 22 *donnés*.

In 1644 Father Jérôme Lalemant was appointed superior of the Jesuits in Canada with his residence at Quebec. As the mail bringing him this news had been intercepted by the Iroquois, he did not take up his post until September 1645. This first period of office (1645–50) had very great trials in store for him. It was during this time that the martyrdom occurred of Isaac JOGUES, ANTOINE DANIEL, Jean de Brébeuf, GABRIEL LALEMANT, Charles GARNIER, Noël CHABANEL, and Jean de LA LANDE. We must add also the devastation of the Huron mission, which he had organized and administered so well. He was deeply affected by these events, but he was too submissive to God's will to be depressed by them. It was a great consolation for him to be able, in the summer of 1650, to venerate the remains of Brébeuf and of his own nephew Gabriel, which had just been brought to Quebec. In the autumn of that year he sailed for France, in order to plead there the cause of the Canadian missions. When he returned in 1651 he obeyed his successor, Father Paul RAGUENEAU, as simply as a novice. In 1656 he was recalled to France, and two years later he was named rector of the Collège royal de La Flèche.

At the pressing request of Bishop François de Laval*, who had shortly before been appointed apostolic vicar of New France, Father Lalemant returned to Quebec as superior of the Jesuits in 1659. He was received enthusiastically by his fellow religious; and this was the starting-point of a second glorious period for the Society's missions in Canada. A man of infinite discretion, he was able in the difficulties which were at that time disturbing Canada to retain the esteem of Bishop Laval and the confidence of the governors of the colony. He was the spiritual adviser of Marie de l'Incarnation [*see* GUYART], who frequently praises him in her letters. She wrote to her son on 30 Oct. 1650: "He is the father of the poor, French as well as Indians: he is the ardent servant of the Church who seems to have been brought up in all the ceremonies, which is not usual for a Jesuit. Lastly, he is the most saintly man I have known since I was born." It was he who in 1646 had drawn up the Constitutions of the Ursulines of Quebec. It was under Father Jérôme Lalemant's administration that Huron families were settled on the Jesuit lands at Beauport.

We are indebted to Father Jérôme Lalemant for the *Relations* concerning the Hurons for the years 1639 to 1644. To him are also attributed those which were published during his two periods of office at Quebec. A manuscript by Father Félix Martin, which is preserved in the archives of the seminary of Quebec, informs us that Father Lalemant "is said to have put the finishing touches to a Huron catechism in which he had brought together the principal truths of religion." Research workers are grateful to him for his immense contribution to what has survived of the *Journal des Jésuites*. These entries, made from day to day concerning the events, great or small, connected with the history of the colony, are the necessary complement to the *Relations;* they take us more deeply into the social, political, and religious life of Canada at that time.

The Hurons had named Father Lalemant "Achiendassé." He has himself recounted for us the origins of this custom: "The reason for these surnames arises from the fact that the Savages, not being ordinarily able to pronounce either our names or our surnames—as they do not have in their language several consonants that are found therein—get as near to them as they can; but if they cannot succeed, they seek instead words used in their own country, which they can readily pronounce, and which have some connection either with our names or with their meaning. But inasmuch as it sometimes happens that they make rather unsuitable guesses, the confirmation or change of names that they have given during the voyage is made when they reach home." According to Father SIMON LE MOYNE, the name "Achiendassé" subsequently designated the superiors of the Jesuits of Quebec, just as that of "Onontio," first given to Charles HUAULT de Montmagny, designated the governors of the colony.

LÉON POULIOT

ASQ, MSS, 43, "Étude sur les Relations des Jésuites," par Félix Martin. Marie Guyart de l'Incarnation, *Écrits* (Jamet), IV, 307; *Lettres de la vénérable Mère Marie de l'Incarnation, première supérieure des Ursulines de la Nouvelle-France: divisées en deux parties*, éd. Claude Martin (Paris, 1681). *JR* (Thwaites), passim. *JJ* (Laverdière et Casgrain), *passim*; reprinted in *JR* (Thwaites), XXVIIf.

J.-O. Bégin, "Le Père Jérôme Lalement, supérieur de la mission huronne: étude critique sur la valeur historique des Relations des Hurons (1639–1644)," thèse de maîtrise présenté à l'Institut d'Histoire de l'Université de Montréal, 1952. Campbell, *Pioneer priests*, II, 279–324.

For more detailed information on Sainte-Marie-des-Hurons, consult the following: Jean Côté, "Domestique séculier d'habit, mais religieux de cœur," *RHAF*, X (1956–57), 183–90, 448–53 (bibliography); "L'institution des donnés," *RHAF*, XV (1961–62), 344–78. Wilfrid Jury and Elsie McLeod Jury, *Sainte-Marie among the Hurons* (Toronto, 1954). Kenneth E. Kidd, *The excavation of Ste Marie I* (Toronto, 1949). Rochemonteix, *Les Jésuites et la Nouvelle-France au XVIIe siècle*, I, II.

LAMBERT, EUSTACHE, *donné*, interpreter, settler, fur-trader; b. *c.* 1618, probably near Boulogne in France; d. 1673 at Quebec.

The *donné* Eustache Lambert, who came to New France probably in the early 1640's, appears for the first time in Canadian history in August 1646, on the occasion of a return journey to Sainte-Marie-des-Hurons. This was his second or third trip to the mission, and he seems to have remained in the service of the Jesuits at least until 1651, when we find him accompanying Father CHAUMONOT to the Île d'Orléans and to Tadoussac.

In 1653 Eustache Lambert acquired a tract of land at Pointe-Lévy, in the seigneury of the LAUSON family. It was there that he built the house which he named Sainte-Marie in honour of his youth spent in the Huron country, and which became a favourite meeting-place for the Huron and Algonkin fur-traders passing through Quebec. Lambert hunted and fished there fairly successfully, it seems, for in 1671 he managed to free himself from his seigneurial dues by paying a sum of 300 *livres*, half in money, half in beaver. He was also said to be the owner of a merchants' bank, a house in the Lower Town of Quebec, in Sault-au-Matelot street, and a dwelling at Saint-Joseph de Beauport. In 1653, at Quebec, he was the commander of a flying column of 50 men, and on 8 Aug. 1669 became a churchwarden of the parish of Notre-Dame. Eustache Lambert married Marie Laurence in 1656. They had a large number of descendants.

Lambert was buried 6 July 1673 at Quebec.

J. MONET

ASQ, Paroisse de Québec, 124; Polygraphie, XVI, 26. *JR* (Thwaites), *passim*. *JJ* (Laverdière et Casgrain), *passim*. Claude de Bonnault, "Le Canada militaire, état provisoire des officiers de milice, de 1641 à 1760," APQ *Rapport*, *1949–51*, 294. A. De Léry Macdonald, "La famille Lambert Du Mont," *RC*, XIX (1883), 633. J.-E. Roy, "Eustache Lambert, frère donné et interprète," *La Kermesse*, X (25 nov. 1892), 136–40; *Histoire de la seigneurie de Lauzon*, I, 254.

LAMONTAGNE, NOËL JÉRÉMIE *dit*. See JÉRÉMIE

LAMOTHE, PIERRE AIGRON *dit*. See AIGRON

LA MOTHE-FÉNELON, FRANÇOIS DE SALIGNAC DE. See SALIGNAC

LA MOTTE DE LUCIÈRE, DOMINIQUE, companion of CAVELIER de La Salle in his explorations, commandant of Fort Conti at Niagara, substitute captain of the guards of the king's farms, of noble birth; b. 1636 at Vernix (Normandy), son of Jean de La Motte and Clémence de Badon; d. 18 Sept. 1700 at Montreal.

In 1678 he agreed to accompany La Salle to New France and lent him 1,374 *livres*. He sailed with him from La Rochelle 21 July and reached Quebec 15 September. La Salle charged him with taking his men and his belongings to Ville-Marie (Montreal), then to Cataracoui (Kingston). From there La Motte set out again on 18 November to go to choose the site of Fort Conti on the Niagara River. After enduring a multitude of dangers, he entered the river on 6 December. The next day he visited the great falls, "the greatest in the world," wrote Hennepin*, who accompanied him. The two travellers were charged with the mission of persuading the Senecas to agree to the construction of a fort on the river and also the building of the large bark which La Salle had ordered. The Iroquois would give no definite answer. However, a little later, as La Salle had succeeded in convincing the Indians, the shipwrights set to work building the *Griffon*.

La Motte was not able to stay long at the building site. Being in danger of losing his sight, he returned to Montreal. There he married on 24 Dec. 1680 Alixe de La Feuillée, the widow of Louis Des Granges de Mauprée. He lived in Notre-Dame street. La Motte did not long enjoy La Salle's esteem, as the suspicious explorer classed him in 1682 among his innumerable persecutors, real or imaginary, accusing him of having done his utmost at the time of the Niagara River expedition to steal his workmen away from him.

On 26 July 1683 La Motte asked for and obtained the abandoned seigneury of Lussaudière. The following year he bought a piece of ground in

Lamotte de Saint-Paul

the Saint-Jacques street next to his dwelling. He enlarged his house in 1691 in order to rent part of it to Alphonse de Tonty*, and later to Mme. Lamothe-Cadillac.

He lived, however, in poverty, and in 1697 he acknowledged that he owed the Sulpicians the sum of 1,092 livres. On 9 July 1699 he did fealty and homage for his fief of Lussière (Lucière), and in October he was appointed substitute captain-commandant of the guards of the king's farms for the government of Montreal, with a salary of 400 livres a year. He died 18 Sept. 1700, two months before his wife.

He has been mistaken for several persons of the same name, among others Pierre LAMOTTE de Saint-Paul and Louis de La Rue, Chevalier de La Motte.

LÉOPOLD LAMONTAGNE

Découvertes et établissements des Français (Margry), I, passim.; II, 7–10, 229f. Louis Hennepin, *Voyage ou nouvelle découverte d'un très grand pays . . .* (Amsterdam, 1704), 72–91. *Royal Fort Frontenac* (Preston and Lamontagne), 34, 476. Philéas Gagnon, "Noms propres du Canada-Français . . . ," *BRH*, XV (1909), 51. "Les La Mothe du régime français," *BRH*, XL (1934), 49–54. Charles de La Roncière, *Le père de la Louisiane, Cavelier de La Salle* (Tours, 1936), 26–29. Léon Lemonnier, *Cavelier de La Salle et l'exploration du Mississipi* (Paris, 1942), 74–79. É.-Z Massicotte, "Les actes de foi et hommage conservés à Montréal," *BRH*, XXVI (1920), 94; "Dominique de La Motte, sieur de Lucière," *BRH*, XXVII (1921), 189–91; "Le travail des enfants, à Montréal, au XVIIe siècle," *BRH*, XXII (1916), 57. Parkman, *La Salle and the discovery of the great west* (12th ed.) 116f., 123–29. Sulte, *Mélanges historiques* (Malchelosse), VIII, 98f. Roger Viau, *Cavelier de La Salle* (s.l., 1960), 46–49.

LAMOTTE DE SAINT-PAUL, PIERRE, captain commanding a company in the Carignan-Salières regiment, regimental officer (1665–70).

Lamotte landed at Quebec in August 1665 and was given the task in the autumn of the same year of opening up a road from Fort Sainte-Thérèse to Fort Saint-Louis (Chambly).

In the spring of 1666 he was commissioned to build Fort Sainte-Anne on the island that bears his name (Lamotte), at the entrance to Lake Champlain. It was from there that the troops under PROUVILLE de Tracy and RÉMY de Courcelle set out in the autumn of 1666 on an expedition into the Mohawk country, in the region around Orange (Albany, N.Y.). The following winter Lamotte, whose position of command at Fort Sainte-Anne, the most exposed in the colony, required great bravery, had in addition to cope with an epidemic and famine which ravaged his garrison. Dollier* de Casson, who had come in haste from Ville-Marie (Montreal) at the risk of his life to help the victims, has left an account of those tragic days.

Towards the end of 1668 or in 1669 Lamotte de Saint-Paul became commandant of Montreal, succeeding Zacharie DUPUY. In an act drawn up at Montreal and dated 11 Aug. 1669 (at the baptism of his godson Pierre Le Ber*, the son of Jacques*, coseigneur of Senneville), Lamotte is described as commanding officer of the regiments in New France. He still bore this title in Abraham Bouat's marriage contract in March 1670. This is the last mention of his stay in Canada. Benjamin Sulte declares that he left for France at the beginning of the summer of 1670. He did not come back.

In praising the officers of the Carignan-Salières regiment on 27 Oct. 1667, TALON wrote: "One above all, M. de la Motte, senior captain and commandant of the most advanced fort against the Iroquois, obliges me to single him out from the others and to ask you for a gratuity for him because of his wise and prudent conduct, which is accompanied by all the zeal that one can desire of a very good officer. . . ."

If it has been claimed that Lamotte de Saint-Paul was commandant of Fort Niagara in 1679, it was because he was confused with Dominique LA MOTTE de Lucière. It was also believed that he died at Saint-François-du-Lac in 1690; he had been incorrectly identified with Louis de La Rue, Chevalier de La Motte, a lieutenant who was killed fighting the Indians.

JEAN-JACQUES LEFEBVRE

Correspondance de Talon, APQ *Rapport, 1930–31*, 45, 78, 92, 171. Dollier de Casson, *Histoire du Montréal*, 183–93. Perrot, *Mémoire* (Tailhan), 122–25. "Les La Mothe du régime français," *BRH*, XL (1934), 49–54. [Joseph M.], *Le fort et la chapelle de Ste-Anne à l'Ile La Motte, sur le lac Champlain* (Burlington, Vt., 1890). P.-G. Roy, "Les gouverneurs de Montréal," *BRH*, XI (1905), 161–74. Sulte, *Mélanges historiques* (Malchelosse), VIII, 98f., 108, 136.

"LA NASSE." *See* MANITOUGATCHE

LANE, DANIEL, mariner, of the parish of St. Mary Aldermary, London; b. c. 1654.

He was in the service of the HBC by 1680, when he refused Governor John NIXON's offer to command a sloop between Charlton Island and other Hudson Bay posts as being too hazardous. Besides, he wanted to go home. Since the only vessel returning that season, the *Prudent Mary*, was wrecked while still in James Bay, his return to England was delayed until 1681.

He signed for a further three-year term in 1682

but within a month accepted a much more tempting offer from a group of interlopers (trespassers on the Company's monopoly). The interloping vessel, the *Expectation* (Capt. LUCAS) was captured in 1683 by the HBC ship *Diligence* (Capt. NEHEMIAH WALKER) and Lane was brought to England and imprisoned. His promise "to ingeniously confess all matters" brought release and he testified in the Company's favour when it brought suit against the interlopers in the High Court of Admiralty.

Received back into service, Lane voyaged again in 1684 and 1685 to Hudson Bay. Further adventures awaited him, for he was taken prisoner when de TROYES captured Moose Fort in 1686, a time of peace. He must have succumbed to the rigours of that winter, since he was not among the released prisoners sent to Port Nelson or among those reaching France in the autumn of 1687. His wages were "accounted for" with Thomas Dowse, his administrator, in April 1688.

MAUD M. HUTCHESON

HBRS, VIII, IX (Rich); XI (Rich and Johnson).

LANGLOIS, NOËL, pilot of the St. Lawrence River, early settler on the seigneury of Beauport; b. *c.* 1603 at Saint-Léonard in Normandy, son of Guillaume Langlois and Jeanne Millet; d. 15 July 1684.

Following the relinquishment of New France by the British in 1632, ROBERT GIFFARD, the seigneur of Beauport, persuaded Langlois to become a settler in the new land. It is probable that ABRAHAM MARTIN *dit* L'Écossais, the king's pilot at Quebec, and possibly related to him by marriage, greatly influenced his decision. Langlois and his future wife, Françoise Grenier (Garnier), left France with Giffard's prospective settlers in the spring of 1634 and arrived at Quebec on 24 June. Following his marriage at Quebec in July, Langlois settled at Beauport. Three years later he received from Giffard a grant of land in perpetuity. His wife, the mother of 10 of his 11 children, died in November 1665. In July 1666 Langlois married Marie Crevet, the widow of Robert Caron. Langlois himself died at Beauport in July 1684, survived by his widow and 8 of his 11 children.

H. C. BURLEIGH

AJQ, Greffe de Claude Auber, 7 juillet 1666. Université de Montréal, Coll. Bâby (land grants (concessions), 1626–1718). *JR* (Thwaites), *passim*. Dionne, *Champlain*, II, 338, 457. Léon Roy, "La terre de Noël Langlois à Beauport," *BRH*, LIV (1948), 240–54. P.-G. Roy, "Noël Langlois senior et Noël Langlois Junior," *BRH*, XXII (1916), 86, 245–46. Tanguay, *Dictionnaire*, I, 345. Émile Vaillancourt, *La conquête du Canada par les Normands* (Montréal, 1933), 148.

LANGOISSIEUX, CHARLES (baptismal name **Pierre**), Recollet brother, the first Frenchman to become a religious in New France; originally from the city of Rouen; d. 1645 at Gisors.

He probably arrived in Canada in 1619 and he had been devoting himself to teaching the Indians in the region of Trois-Rivières for three years when he expressed his desire to join the Recollets. Father Guillaume GALLERAN "received him therefore into the noviciate; the ceremony of the taking of the habit took place in the month of September 1622 in our church of Notre-Dame-des-Anges, in the presence of his excellency the governor, of all the French inhabitants, and of a multitude of Indians. He was called Brother Charles, after our first syndic, Father Charles de Boves."

During his noviciate Brother Charles almost lost his life in circumstances that Gabriel SAGARD has described in his *Histoire du Canada*. When his noviciate was ended he made his profession and in 1624 returned to the post at Trois-Rivières to continue teaching the Indians. The surrender of Quebec put an end to his apostolate on Canadian soil. On 9 Sept. 1629, along with the other Recollets, he left Quebec for France, where he landed on 29 October.

After carrying out the humblest tasks reserved for the lay brothers in different convents of his province, he passed away at Gisors 23 Oct. 1645.

FRÉDÉRIC GINGRAS

ASQ, MSS, 200, Mortuologe des Recolets. Le Clercq, *First establishment of the faith* (Shea), I, 190. Sagard, *Histoire du Canada* (Tross), I, 104–7. Jouve, *Les Franciscains et le Canada: aux Trois-Rivières*; *Les Franciscains et le Canada (1615–1629)*.

LANOUGUÈRE, THOMAS DE, ensign in the Carignan-Salières regiment, seigneur of Sainte-Anne, acting governor of Montreal in 1674, lieutenant and later captain of Governor Frontenac's [*see* BUADE] guards; b. 1644 at Mirande (Guyenne), son of Jean de Lanouguère, king's counsellor in a state fiscal subdivision, and of Jeanne de Samalins; d. 1678 in Canada.

He signed himself Lanouguère, a name which became Lanaudière, Tarieu de Lanaudière, and Tarieu de la Pérade in the case of his descendants. He himself did not have the surname Tarieu. Coming from a noble French family of long standing, Thomas de Lanouguère arrived in

La Peltrie

Canada in September 1665 as ensign in the company of Pierre de Saint-Ours* d'Eschaillons (Carignan-Salières regiment). Shortly after its arrival, his company received orders to go and second Capt. Pierre de SAUREL in the construction of a fort at the mouth of the Richelieu River. Like the majority of the officers and soldiers of the Carignan-Salières regiment, Lanouguère took part in the expedition led by the Marquis de Tracy [see PROUVILLE] against the Iroquois tribes in 1666.

His father and mother both being dead, he decided at the time of the disbanding of the troops to remain in Canada. On 29 Sept. 1670, acting conjointly with Edmond de Suève, the lieutenant of his company, an unmarried man who considered him as his son, Lanouguère purchased a tract of land along the Rivière Sainte-Anne; the tract had previously been granted to Michel GAMELAIN de La Fontaine and a few settlers had begun to clear it. These lands, located in what is now the parish of Sainte-Anne de la Pérade, were officially granted to them by Intendant TALON 29 Oct. 1672. A soldier by preference and by career, M. de Lanouguère was only slightly interested in his seigneury. At first he left this responsibility to M. de Suève. Then he entrusted the task to his wife, Marguerite-Renée Denys, whom he had married at Quebec 16 Oct. 1672 and who was the daughter of Pierre Denys* de La Ronde and of Catherine Leneuf de La Poterie.

In that same year, 1672, the Comte de Frontenac was appointed governor of New France. Lanouguère pleased him as an officer, and he kept him close to himself. He appointed him lieutenant of his guards after their return from the Cataracoui expedition, where in the governor's opinion Lanouguère had conducted himself like a gallant soldier. In the spring of 1673, Lanouguère wanted to try his hand at the fur trade. But the commandant at Montreal, François-Marie PERROT, having been imprisoned, Frontenac wanted to replace him by a man he could trust, and he delegated his *protégé*, who was officially appointed 10 Feb. 1674. Frontenac, by an ordinance of 20 Oct. 1674, caused him to be given half of the withheld salary of Governor Perrot, and in his reports to the minister, Colbert, he never tired of praising this officer "who is very energetic and very zealous in the service." Anticipating that Perrot would return, Frontenac requested for Lanouguère the post of town-major of Montreal, and in the meantime appointed him captain of his guards at Quebec.

This appointment as captain of the guards did not, however, prevent Lanouguère from spending brief periods on his seigneury, which was barely 20 leagues from Quebec. Able to count on the governor's protection, he could look forward to a prosperous future. However, he died suddenly at Quebec in May 1678 and was buried in the little chapel of his seigneury.

His twenty-one-year-old widow settled down on his seigneury and lived there for 30 years among her copy-holders (censitaires), whom she assisted by her advice and her example. On 9 July 1708 she married Jacques-Alexis Fleury* d'Eschambault, the widower of Marguerite de Chavigny, daughter of Éléonore de GRANDMAISON; he was the lieutenant-general of the royal jurisdiction of Montreal. Marguerite-Renée Denys died 3 Feb. 1722 at Montreal.

Three children had been born of the Lanouguère-Denys marriage. One of them, Pierre-Thomas, inherited the seigneury of Sainte-Anne and in 1706 married the celebrated Madeleine de Verchères [Jarret*].

RAYMOND DOUVILLE

[François Daniel], *Histoire des grandes familles françaises du Canada ou aperçu sur le Chevalier Benoist et quelques contemporaines* (Montréal, 1867). Raymond Douville, *Premiers seigneurs et colons de Sainte-Anne de la Pérade (1667–1681)* (Trois-Rivières, 1946). Faillon, *Histoire de la colonie française*, III, 482–500, *et passim*. P.-G. Roy, *La famille Tarieu de Lanaudière* (Lévis, 1922). Sulte, *Mélanges historiques* (Malchelosse), VIII.

LA PELTRIE, MARIE-MADELEINE DE CHAUVIGNY DE. *See* CHAUVIGNY

LA PIERRE, PIERRE CHAUVIN DE. *See* CHAUVIN

LA PLACE, SIMON GIRARD DE. *See* GIRARD

LA POIPPE, governor of Plaisance (Placentia, Newfoundland), naval lieutenant, native of Lyons; d. 1684.

La Poippe was appointed commandant at Plaisance 20 Feb. 1670, to replace La Palme. The intendant of Rochefort, Colbert de Terron, and the minister, Colbert, gave him instructions to protect the fishermen and strengthen the settlement. As soon as he arrived, La Poippe took a census. The settled population numbered as yet only 73 persons. To provide for their subsistence and meet the needs of government, the mother country granted 10,000 *livres*. As the commandants received only a meagre stipend, some of them had taken to speculating on the king's provisions and supplies by demanding from the fishermen a third of their haul. La Poippe had been clearly warned to put an end to this abuse, and does not appear to have indulged in it himself. Two years later, Colbert de Terron described him as "a very good fellow and an upright gentleman."

The settlement experienced a difficult period at the time of the war with the Dutch, because of enemy privateers. The king, in 1675, forbade the ships to leave port. But the following year he reinstituted fishing, and sent two escort vessels to protect the Newfoundlanders' return. Commissioner Benne, who accompanied the expedition, has left a long memoir in which he describes the Plaisance habitation as a collection of wretched shacks, covered with bark and protected only by a palisade of stakes. The port, however, was magnificent, surrounded by fine gravel beaches, and serving as a meeting-place for the Saint-Malo, Basque, and Breton fishermen, who came there to get supplies and sell their fish. This port, during the fishing season, thus became a very active centre of trade, and the commandant had a good deal of trouble in maintaining peace among this motley and transient population, as well as in defending the rights of his subjects against the fishermen of other nationalities established in the neighbouring ports.

It seems likely that La Poippe traded on his own account, like all the other commandants, but he managed to avoid clashes, to refrain from corrupt practices, and to give satisfaction, for he was appointed to Plaisance for 3 years and remained there for 15. It was during his administration that the naval ordinance of 1681 was passed, regulating French fishing off Newfoundland. He died in 1684, probably at Plaisance, and was replaced by PARAT.

RENÉ BAUDRY

AN, Col., B, 2, f.64; 3, f.44; Col., C11C, 1, f.36; Col., F1A, 1, ff.107–10, 114; Col., G1, 467; Marine, B2, 11, f.196v.; Marine, C1, 161, f.460, BN, MS, NAF 22253, f.11bis; MS, Mélanges Colbert, 163, f.251; 176, f.127v. La Morandière, *Hist. de la pêche française de la morue*, I, 421–28; II, 1009–10, reproduces several original documents.

LA POTERIE, JACQUES LENEUF DE. *See* LENEUF

LA RALDE (La Rade), RAYMOND DE, lieutenant of GUILLAUME and ÉMERY DE CAËN, founder of the post at Miscou; known in Canada between 1621 and 1632.

The de Caën family held the monopoly of the fur trade *c.* 1620–7; from 1628 to 1632 this monopoly was shared with the Compagnie des Cent-Associés, and in 1632 was again granted for the year to the de Caëns. Raymond de La Ralde's principal task seems to have been to keep a watch on the Basque, Flemish, Spanish, and French ships that were trading in furs clandestinely in the Gulf of St. Lawrence, thus infringing the monopoly granted by the king to the Compagnie de Caën. As lieutenant of the de Caëns, La Ralde possessed extensive powers in that region; furthermore, the exercise of these powers kept him very busy, which explains why he was to be found at one time at Gaspé or at Percé, at another in the Baie des Chaleurs, and especially on the Île de Miscou, where he had decided to build a habitation (or storehouse), and where he maintained a store for the company's benefit. La Ralde appears to have come to New France regularly each year.

In 1626 a ruling of the king's Conseil d'État called upon the Compagnie de Caën to give command of its fleet to a Catholic, at the same time forbidding the Protestant Guillaume to show himself in the colony. In conformity with this order, Guillaume de Caën entrusted the fleet that was proceeding to Canada to Raymond de La Ralde, a Catholic and an associate of the de Caëns, since he had married a sister or a daughter of Guillaume de Caën senior. La Ralde, who had gone back to France in the autumn, must have returned to Canada the following spring. Sagard in fact records his presence at Quebec at the end of August 1627. He gives him at that time the title of "vice-admiral of the fleet sent by sieur Guillaume de Caën, for the trade in pelts." In two letters dated 25 Aug. 1628 and addressed to Charles I of England and to the Duke of Buckingham, George CALVERT, Lord Baltimore, complained of a certain "Mons. De la Rade" of Dieppe, in connection with the vexatious interference by the French in the English fisheries off Newfoundland. Very probably the reference was to Raymond de La Ralde. The last mention of La Ralde is made in the *Relations* in August 1632, when it seems that he was at Quebec.

According to Sagard, Raymond de La Ralde was not on good terms with the Jesuits, who accused him of "discourtesy," and attributed to him a "determination to bring about the downfall of the Church," but the same author adds that he later heard that La Ralde "had returned to the bosom of the Church."

MARCEL HAMELIN

Champlain, *Œuvres* (Laverdière). "Documents inédits," éd. Joseph Le Ber, *RHAF*, III (1949–50), 592. *JR* (Thwaites). PRO, *CSP, Col., 1574–1660*, nos. 56, 57. Sagard, *Histoire du Canada* (Tross), 812f. Dionne, *Champlain*; "Miscou, hommes de mer et hommes de Dieu," *CF*, II (1889), 445–47.

La Ribourde

LA RIBOURDE, GABRIEL DE, Recollet priest, missionary, chaplain and companion of CAVELIER de La Salle; b. *c.* 1620 in the Champagne section of Brie; killed in the territory of the Illinois in 1680.

Scion of a noble Burgundian family, of which he was the sole heir, he gave up his entire inheritance and took his vows on 1 Nov. 1638. After a period of preaching, he was named superior and director of novices of the monastery at Béthune in Artois.

In May 1670, he came to Canada with Father ALLART, the provincial of the province of Paris, with Fathers Landon* and Guénin*, and with Brothers Luc FRANÇOIS and Anselme (or Ignace) Bardou*. In the autumn of that year, after being named provincial commissioner and superior, he strove to recover the former Recollet seigneury and to restore the monastery and church of Notre-Dame-des-Anges. In the autumn of 1673 he went to the newly built Fort Cataracoui (Frontenac), where he acted as chaplain for nearly three years. He then returned to the monastery at Quebec, of which he was to be the superior until September 1677.

After spending four months at the Trois-Rivières mission, he returned to Fort Frontenac; three other Recollets, Fathers Louis Hennepin*, Zénobe MEMBRÉ, and Mélithon Watteau*, joined him there on 2 Nov. 1678. La Salle arrived on 16 December to prepare for his expedition to the Gulf of Mexico. Father de La Ribourde was named spiritual leader of the expeditionary party, which arrived at Fort Niagara on 30 July 1679, went on board the *Griffon* on 7 August, crossed lakes Orléans (Huron) and Conty (Erie), landed at Baie des Puants (Green Bay), crossed Lake Michigan in birch-bark canoes, then descended the Miami and Illinois rivers. It was in this area that the party passed the winter and the following summer. Then, reduced by desertions, absences and sickness to six persons, the party embarked on 18 Sept. 1680 in a dilapidated birch-bark canoe to go back up the Illinois River and try to return to Canada. The following day, 19 September, they went ashore to repair the canoe. Father La Ribourde decided to pass the time saying his breviary in the coolness of the woods. His return was awaited in vain; he did not come back. He had been killed, scalped and stripped, probably by Kickapoo warriors. Thus perished this saintly missionary whose piety, virtue, courage and tact were praised by all who knew him.

LÉOPOLD LAMONTAGNE

ASQ, MSS, 200, Mortuologe des Recolets. *Découvertes et établissements des Français* (Margry) I, *passim.* Louis Hennepin, *Description de la Louisiane . . .* (Paris, 1683), 19f.; *Nouvelle découverte d'un très grand pays, situé dans l'Amérique entre le Nouveau Mexique, et la mer glaciale . . .* (Utrecht, 1697), 108, 239, *et passim.* Le Clercq, *First establishment of the faith* (Shea), I, 15; II, 71, 73, 145–49, *et passim*; *Premier établissement de la foy,* II, 93f. BRH, XVIII (1912), 26; XX (1914), 59; XXVI (1920), 14. O.-M. Jouve, *Le Père Gabriel de la Ribourde, récollet* (Québec, 1912).

LA RIVIÈRE, FRANÇOIS BYSSOT DE. *See* BYSSOT

LA RIVIÈRE, JOSEPH-ANTOINE PONCET DE. *See* PONCET

LA ROCHE DAILLON, JOSEPH DE, Recollet priest, first missionary to the Neutrals, son of Jacques de La Roche, seigneur of Daillon in Anjou, and of Jeanne Froyer of La Baronnière; d. 1656 in Paris.

After leaving Dieppe 24 April 1625, Father Joseph de La Roche Daillon landed at Quebec on 19 June of that year. His superiors having requested him to go and lend his assistance to Father Nicolas VIEL, a missionary to the Hurons, he had already gone as far as Trois-Rivières in the company of Father Jean de BRÉBEUF, when he learned of Father Viel's death, which had occurred on 25 June. Both Hurons and French then persuaded them to turn back.

On 14 July 1626 he set out again, and after a successful trip made in Huron canoes, he at last arrived at the village of Toanché. After staying a short time with the Hurons, he departed on 18 Oct. 1626 for the territory of the Neutrals, where he spent some months studying their language and catechizing them, as he tells us in his account dated 18 July 1627. This text which, according to the *Relation* for 1641, was judged worthy of publication, constitutes, despite its brevity, the first study of the customs of the Neutrals and one of the earliest descriptions of the Huron peninsula. After narrowly escaping death at the hands of the Neutrals, Father Daillon returned to the Huron country.

Back in Quebec in the autumn of 1628, he carried on his ministry, as is attested by the first page of the parish register of Notre-Dame de Québec, where, on 18 May 1629, he administered the rite of baptism to LOUIS COUILLARD de Lespinay.

After serving as Latin interpreter on the occasion of the capitulation of Quebec, Father Daillon, together with his fellow religious, took ship for Tadoussac on 9 Sept. 1629; this was the first leg of a journey that took him to Dover on 29 October and thence to the convent in Paris.

Thus concluded the missionary career of this priest "who had renounced worldly honours in favour of the humility and poverty of the religious life." He passed away in France on 16 July 1656.

FRÉDÉRIC GINGRAS

Champlain, *Œuvres* (Laverdière), 1077, 1112, 1184. *JR* (Thwaites), *passim*. Le Clercq, *First establishment of the faith* (Shea), I, 234, 236, 241, 246, 261, 263–72. Sagard, *Histoire du Canada* (Tross), II, III, IV, *passim*. *The Catholic encyclopedia, an international work of reference . . . of the Catholic church* ed. C. G. Herbermann *et al* (17v., New York, 1907–22). D. Harris, *The Catholic Church in the Niagara peninsula* (Toronto, 1895). Jouve, *Les Franciscains et le Canada (1615–1629)*.

LA ROCHE DE MESGOUEZ, TROILUS DE, Marquis de La Roche-Mesgouez, in Brittany, viceroy of New France, founder of the outpost on Sable Island in 1598; b. probably in 1540 at La Roche-Coatarmoal (Brittany); d. 1606 in France.

At 13 La Roche was a page at the court of Henri II. Subsequently, having won the favour of Catherine de' Medici, he was in turn made a *chevalier*, a captain, and a counsellor of state. In 1565 he became governor of Morlaix (Brittany). This position opened his eyes to the profits brought to Saint-Malo by the fisheries and the fur trade on the American coasts, and suggested to him that he should undertake the "exploitation" of the "Terres-Neuves." In March 1577 he obtained from Henri IV a commission allowing him to appropriate to himself the territories "of which he could make himself master." On 3 January of the following year a second commission made him the first holder of the title of viceroy in New France, and granted him the right to govern the country. With the assistance of Honorat de Bueil, the vice-admiral of Brittany, and the co-operation of a few shipowners, he fitted out a ship and a pinnace for his undertaking. But, recalling that in 1575 he had had dealings with James Fitzgerald, an Irish rebel who according to certain authors was a pretender to the Irish throne, England suspected him of wanting to assist the Irish insurgents. Four British vessels captured his ship, probably in June (1578), while the pinnace escaped.

In 1583 a trading voyage under Étienne BELLENGER, of which the expenses were met by Cardinal Charles de Bourbon and Anne de Joyeuse, Admiral of France, was a financial success. Encouraged by this example, La Roche, with their support, organized a second expedition, in association with some shipowners of Saint-Malo and of Saint-Jean-de-Luz. He set sail from the latter port at the beginning of 1584 with a flotilla carrying 300 men, but his principal ship sank off the coast of Saintonge, and this put an end to the expedition.

During the civil war between Roman Catholics and Huguenots, which deferred any resumption of his plans, La Roche rallied to the side of Henri III and Henri IV against the League. In 1589 he exchanged his governorship of Morlaix for that of Fougères, north of Rennes. While on his way to defend the town, he fell into the hands of the Leaguers at Sablé; their leader, the Duc de Mercœur, kept him a prisoner for seven years in the castle at Nantes. He was finally freed in 1596, on payment of a ransom, and "seeing himself without a command" he went back to his plan for developing trade across the Atlantic. On 16 Feb. 1597 Henri IV granted him "authority" to undertake a new expedition. La Roche, on 4 March, signed an agreement with Thomas CHEFDOSTEL, captain of the ship *Catherine*, under the terms of which the latter piloted to America an exploratory mission commanded by Capt. Kerdement. The marquis, satisfied with the information thus obtained, received new letters patent from the king, dated 12 Jan. 1598, appointing him lieutenant-general of the territories of Canada, Newfoundland, Labrador, and Norumbega. These letters granted him title to the area and the monopoly of the fur trade, and forbade all others to trade in furs without his consent, on pain "of losing all their ships and merchandise." They further authorized him to recruit hardened criminals for his undertaking.

From the prisoners delivered to him La Roche chose those who possessed "considerable means," and offered them the opportunity of purchasing their freedom for a large sum, which he sometimes set at 500 *écus*. The courts, when informed of how justice was being cheated, refused all further requests for prisoners. La Roche then got the Parlement of Rouen, on 16 March 1598, to hand over to him 250 "vagabonds and beggars." Among those who agreed to make the voyage he selected some 40 of the most vigorous, to whom he attached about 10 soldiers. He embarked them on two ships, Chefdostel's *Catherine* and Capt. Jehan Girot's *Françoise*, which took them to the Île de Sable (Sable Island); La Roche rebaptized it the Île de Bourbon in honour of François de Bourbon, Duc de Montpensier, governor of Normandy. The viceroy settled his party on the north coast, on a small waterway forming a narrows which he named the Boncœur River. There he built living quarters, and a storehouse in which were placed provisions, clothes, tools,

La Rochette

arms, and furniture. Leaving the post under the orders of a commandant, Querbonyer, La Roche accompanied the ships to the Newfoundland fisheries. According to an agreement previously concluded, the profits from the fishing were to go to the ships' captains, whereas the furs exchanged on the spot were to be divided, two-thirds being given to the captains and the remainder to the viceroy. On their return trip at the beginning of September a violent storm prevented the ships from calling at the island post, and drove them straight to the French coast.

Following the report that the marquis made of his voyage to Henri IV, the king promised, as a subsidy, to "grant him one *écu* for each barrel of merchandise coming to and being loaded in the ports of Normandy." Thanks to this subsidy, which over the years was to bring him in 12,000 *écus*, La Roche maintained his settlement. Each spring he had it supplied by Chefdostel with "wine, coats and clothing": the deportees got their food from the fish and game available locally, as well as from the cattle that had been landed on the island probably by the Portuguese FAGUNDES around 1520. At the same time they cultivated "French gardens," which supplied them with vegetables.

Meanwhile, on 22 Nov. 1599, the Huguenot shipowner PIERRE CHAUVIN DE TONNETUIT, of Honfleur, managed to obtain a commission similar to La Roche's. In the face of the latter's protests Henri IV issued new letters patent on 5 Jan. 1600, by which Chauvin was only "one of the lieutenants" of the viceroy, with fishing rights from the Gulf of St. Lawrence to Tadoussac, where he soon set up a post with FRANCOIS GRAVÉ DU PONT.

In 1602, for an unknown reason, La Roche did not dispatch the annual supply of wine and clothes. It seems likely that complaints on this score, as well as about the administration of Commandant Querbonyer and Capt. Storekeeper Coussez, reached the court in the autumn. To counter them, the viceroy instructed Chefdostel, on 21 Feb. 1603, to go and take supplies to the post and to bring back Querbonyer, Coussez, and three other persons. In addition, Chefdostel was to take a commissioner there, whose task was to inquire into the island's resources in order to give the king information relevant to a plan for making it into a reliable and suitable colony.

But on the island itself, during the winter (1602–3), and probably as a result of the lack of food supplies, the deportees, exasperated by their long detention in a wilderness, had revolted, and butchered the two leaders Querbonyer and Coussez; this seditious act had soon been followed by further murders among the deportees. After a stay on the island—about which nothing is known—Chefdostel took on board the 11 principal rebels, together with the remaining stock of furs. When they got back to France these deportees, making great display of their animal skins, were presented to Henri IV, who had each of them given the sum of 50 *écus*. This treatment staggered La Roche, who was indignant that "instead of their being hanged for their misdeeds, they have been given money, although they have themselves admitted to the murders."

During subsequent years, the viceroy appears to have kept and utilized his establishment in America: after the foundation of Port-Royal (Annapolis Royal, N.S.), he wrote in 1604 that DU GUA de Monts was not "in full view of everyone as I am on the Île de Bourbon." That same year, in a *mémoire* to the king, he requested payment of the grants and dues to which he was entitled, and at the same time offered to fortify all the harbours from Labrador to Port-Royal. Henri IV remained deaf to this appeal. Without apparently obtaining any satisfaction, La Roche died during the year 1606.

GUSTAVE LANCTOT

ASM, B, Parlement de Normandie, archives secrètes. Bibliothèque de l'Institut de France, Coll. Godefroy, 291, Escrit envoyé par le marquis Troille de Mesgouez de La Roche (1604), Bréard, *Documents relatifs à la marine normande*. Cartier, *Voyage de 1534*. Champlain, *Œuvres* (Laverdière). Hakluyt, "Discourse on western planting." Lescarbot, *Histoire* (Tross).

Biggar, *Early trading companies*. N.-E. Dionne, *La Nouvelle-France de Cartier à Champlain* (Québec, 1891). *Édits ord*., III. É.-H. Gosselin, *Nouvelles glanes historiques normandes*. Gustave Lanctot, "L'établissement du Marquis de La Roche à l'île de Sable," CHA *Report, 1933*, 33–42. La Roncière, *Histoire de la marine française*, IV. Joseph Le Ber, "Un document inédit sur l'île de Sable et le Marquis de la Roche," *RHAF*, II (1948–49), 199–213. D. B. Quinn, "The voyage of Étienne Bellenger to the Maritimes in 1583: a new document," *CHR*, XLIII (1962), 328–43.

LA ROCHETTE, NICOLAS GARGOT DE. *See* GARGOT

LA ROCQUE DE ROBERVAL, JEAN-FRANÇOIS DE, lieutenant-general in Canada; b. c. 1500, probably at Carcassonne, of which his father was the governor; d. 1560 in Paris.

He was the son of Bernard de La Roque *dit* Couillaud, the seigneur of Châtelrein, and of Isabeau de Poitiers. His maternal grandmother was Alix de Popincourt, the dame de Roberval in Picardy. The La Roques belonged to a very old noble family in the south of France. Bernard de

La Rocque de Roberval

La Roque was a gentleman of the king's household, an ambassador, and an officer of the Comte d'Armagnac; he was involved in the trial of the Maréchal de Gié. La Rocque de Roberval lived at the court in the circle of Prince François d'Angoulême who, on becoming king of France, continued to be his protector. This fact saved him in 1535. As a Protestant convert, he was outlawed, along with other Protestants, including Clément Marot. He soon returned to France and again lived at the court. A portrait of La Rocque de Roberval by Clouet is among the 310 portraits of members of the French court in the collection at the Château de Chantilly.

Roberval had, however, jeopardized his fortune. He borrowed from his cousins: the La Roque de Blaizins in Languedoc, the La Roques in Armagnac, and the Popincourts in Picardy. It was then that he seems to have conceived the idea of recouping his fortune in Canada. In 1540 he had completely recovered the favour of François I. Had he by then returned to the Catholic faith? François I appointed him as his "lieutenant-general in the country of Canada," where he was charged with "spreading the holy Catholic faith." The terms of his commission were clear-cut: his mission was to found a colony where he was to construct churches and fortified towns. He received a subsidy of 45,000 *livres*, and he fitted out three ships, the *Valentine*, the *Anne*, and the *Lèchefraye*. Some gentlemen were to accompany him, and the king gave him authority to take criminals from the prisons in order to begin his colony. "On 15 January 1541," says the historian Gustave Lanctot, "François Ier signed the commission that marked the beginning of French colonization." Jacques CARTIER was to serve as Roberval's guide. But Cartier left in May 1541 with his ships, while Roberval did not leave until the following year. They met at St. John's (Newfoundland) and Cartier returned to France despite Roberval's orders.

Roberval had had difficulties in organizing his expedition; he had been obliged to sell some properties and to borrow money. At this time he was associated with Bidoux de Lartigue and was sailing the seas as a pirate. The English ambassador complained to François I about the seizure by Roberval of English ships; the king pretended to be angry with La Rocque. The latter's preparations for the voyage had made the Spaniards uneasy and one of Charles V's spies informed him that the destination of the voyage was Canada. The three ships, piloted by Jean FONTENEAU, sailed from La Rochelle. The crossing lasted from 16 April to 8 June, on which date Roberval met Cartier at Newfoundland.

The expedition navigated the Gulf of St. Lawrence and the river without incident except for the romantic adventure of Roberval's "relative," the young lady Marguerite de LA ROQUE, who was left on an island with her lover. Roberval established his colony at Charlesbourg-Royal on Cap Rouge, where Cartier had already built a fort. Like the courtier he was, La Rocque de Roberval gave his Canadian colony the name France-Roy and called the river France-Prime in honour of François I. A fort was erected, and André THEVET wrote in his *Cosmographie* that they built "a fortified house," and that another "was begun on the bank of a river called in the language of the barbarians the land of Sinagua." The "land of Sinagua" was probably the Saguenay.

Roberval undertook some exploring; he went up the St. Lawrence and tried to get through the Lachine rapids. He attempted to explore the Saguenay, where he thought he would find precious stones and gold. His boats, manned by 70 men and under the command of Lespinay, La Brosse, Longueval, and Frotté, returned without having found either the kingdom of Saguenay or the precious stones. One of the craft had gone down with Noirefontaine and Le Vasseur aboard. But the severest test was the winter spent in the forts. The little colony was sorely tried by cold, famine, and sickness. The situation became tragic. Apparently Roberval had to suppress uprisings. A passage in Thevet shows him behaving with thoroughly Calvinistic harshness: "Capt. Roberval was very cruel in dealing with his men, forcing them to work; otherwise they were deprived of food and drink. If anyone failed in his duty, Roberval had him punished. One day he had six of them hanged and some he ordered to be banished to an island, in leg-irons, because they had been caught in petty thefts involving not more than five *sous*. Others, both men and women, were flogged for the same offence." If Roberval displayed such terrible severity, it was because his colony was composed principally of habitual criminals. He did, however, exercise his right of pardon in favour of a man named Aussillon de Sauveterre, who, it is true, had accompanied Roberval of his own volition. When he killed a refractory sailor, Sauveterre received a letter of remission. This document, dated in Canada on 9 Sept. 1542 and bearing the handwritten signature "J. F. de La Rocque," is the first and oldest official Canadian document.

Roberval appears at an early date to have had doubts about the success of his enterprise, and he sent a ship to France bearing Sauveterre and Guignecourt to seek the king's help. He then embarked with his whole company on the vessels

La Rocque Roberval

sent by François I. His colony had lasted only a few months. Certain historians have said that Jacques Cartier was in charge of this rescue expedition, but this fourth voyage to Canada by Cartier is extremely doubtful. In the king's order of 26 Jan. 1543 to Aussillon de Sauveterre, who was sent to Roberval's assistance, there is no mention of Cartier. Charlevoix* claimed that Roberval made a second voyage to America with "his brother Pierre de La Roque" and that they perished in a shipwreck in 1549. But Roberval certainly did not perish in 1549, because in 1554 he carried on a lawsuit against Jean de Boutillac. And his brother, whose name was not Pierre but Jean de La Roque, did not sail the seas, for he was a monk and prior of his order in Normandy.

Roberval's attempt at settlement was disastrous for himself, for Canada, and even for Jacques Cartier. The "precious stones" gathered on Canadian soil and the "gold" were neither precious stones nor gold. "When the chemists tested them," says Gustave Lanctot, "the gold was found to be iron pyrites, the diamonds were mica. With the evidence of the crucible, the hopes of the kingdom had crumbled in cataclysmic fashion. A dream that disappoints us is never forgiven. Of Cartier's great achievement, of his three expeditions there remained in France only the proverb, 'as false as Canadian diamonds.' Cartier ceased to be the experienced captain, the great explorer on whom were fixed the eyes of a whole nation." And Canada no longer interested anyone in France for 50 years, until the coming of CHAMPLAIN.

There were several reasons for this failure. First among these was the character and position of Roberval. Not at all a sailor, but a professional soldier, he was above all a courtier, as proven by his presence among the troops of the Maréchal de La Marck and the inclusion of his portrait among the likenesses of the members of the French court. What was he seeking in America? Probably, like the *conquistadores*, he wanted to make his fortune. But his crotchety temper and his roughness of manner had alienated his companions in adventure. Furthermore, this group was very unevenly constituted: gentlemen, courtiers like himself, even society women, and above all a pack of criminals taken from the prisons. He was commissioned to found a Roman Catholic colony and he was himself a Protestant. He is thought to have been an engineer because he later had himself entrusted with the operation of the mines of France, but he had no need to be an engineer for that. Lastly, his voyage had been badly prepared. His faulty administration of his own assets shows moreover that he possessed none of the qualities essential for a great colonizer.

Ruined by his Canadian colony, he struggled with great difficulties. In 1544 he appeared before the commission established to examine his accounts and those of Jacques Cartier and the latter won his case. In 1555 Roberval's holdings were mortgaged and his *château* threatened with seizure. The letters patent that king Henri II had given him for the operation of the mines of France do not seem to have made him rich.

By his loyalty to his Protestant faith, Jean-François La Rocque de Roberval became one of the first victims of the Wars of Religion. Coming out of a Calvinist meeting one night in 1560, he was attacked, along with his fellow Protestants, and was killed at the corner of the Cimetière des Innocents in Paris. The remnants of his fortune passed into the hands of his creditors; his *château* at Roberval was bought back by his nephew Louis de Madaillan, the son of Charlotte de La Roque. In the 18th century this *château* belonged to the Prince de Soubise, and in 1817 became the property of M. Davène de Fontaine. Completely transformed, the *château* no longer resembles in any way what it was in the time of Jean-François de La Rocque. His personal papers are, however, preserved there. Published by H. P. Biggar, these documents have revealed part of the life of this man who, in the 16th century, tried to colonize Canada.

What is curious in the case of Roberval is that his personality and his adventures in Canada have left their traces in 16th-century French literature. Rabelais speaks of him, calling him Robert Valbringue; the Queen of Navarre recounts the romantic story of his relative Marguerite de La Roque; André Thevet gives us valuable information about him and about his colony; the court poets Clément Marot and Michel d'Amboise dedicated works to him. Lastly, a Protestant-inspired Latin poem, *Robervalensis Epitaphium* is included in an anonymous collection of poetry in the Bibliothèque Nationale in Paris. This work recalls Roberval's voyage to Canada and his assassination in 1560.

It has been possible to identify some of Roberval's companions, among whom, however, one must distinguish between those who went to Canada as volunteers and the criminals taken from the prisons and forced to set sail.

Among the gentlemen who made the voyage, one can identify with certainty Paul d'Aussillon de Sauveterre, thanks to a document in which his first name, his family name, and the name of his land are inscribed: the letter of remission of 9 Sept. 1542. Aussillon de Sauveterre was a mariner and was in command of the *Anne*, one of Roberval's three vessels. It was he whom his chief would later send with Guignecourt to seek the king's aid. He belonged to the Aussillon family, who were seigneurs of Sauveterre and La Cabarède, in Languedoc in the bishopric of Castres.

Longueval likewise can be identified: Robert de Longueval, the seigneur of Thenelle, was related to Roberval, for he had married the daughter of Catherine de La Roque and Robert de Hangard. He was a gentleman of the king's bedchamber. Longueval took part in the Saguenay expedition in which Noirefontaine and Le Vasseur were drowned.

The other companions of Roberval cannot be positively identified. Nevertheless one can well believe that Nicolas de Lespinay is the same person as the Nicolas de Lespinay who was a son of Hutin de Lespinay, seigneur of La Neuville; Nicolas did homage for this seigneury to the Duc d'Orléans, Comte de Clermont in Beauvaisis, on 28 April 1545. Nicolas de Lespinay married Marie de Caulincourt in 1550. Noirefontaine might be one of the Noirefontaines who were seigneurs of Le Buisson in Champagne. Guignecourt (Guignicourt) perhaps belongs to the family of Guignicourt, seigneur of La Motte, near Laon. Beauvaisis, Champagne, and the town of Laon are all near the Château de Roberval. As for Jean de La Salle, could he be Jean de Lartigue, seigneur of La Salle, who was a gentleman of Queen Marguerite of Navarre? The Lartiques were a family from Gascony, a region where Jean-François de La Rocque had lands and family connections.

H. P. Biggar identified some 15 of the criminals taken from prisons by Roberval under the authority of the royal letters of 1541. M. Robert Marichal has added seven names to the list. These individuals of deplorable reputation all died in Canada or returned to France. Among them the only one who deserves mention is Pierre Ronsard, because of the role that he was able to play during the expedition. For, if Blarye *dit* Titailt, a murderer; Jacques Le Gall, a thief; Louis de Villaine, an assassin; Le Page *dit* Chaudron, a cook in the service of the Duchesse de Nevers and an assassin, had no influence on the fate of Roberval's colony, Pierre Ronsard seems to have had a job on the expedition which was, to say the least, unusual.

This Pierre Ronsard, born about 1480, was approximately 60 years old when Roberval obtained his release from prison. The master of the mint at Bourges, he had been condemned for falsification and for "altering coins." But he was a technician, and Roberval needed him, in view of the fact, says the royal letter of 31 March 1541 "that the said Ronsard might render great service to the said La Roque on the voyage to be made by him to the territories across the seas." This indicates that Roberval's objective in going to Canada was above all to discover precious metals. It may have been Ronsard who "assayed" the stones gathered in the Saguenay district and who declared them to be gold. And thus, writes R. Marichal, Ronsard might be the person really responsible for the tremendous disillusionment which was to put a halt to colonization in Canada for half a century.

R. La Roque de Roquebrune

AN, E, 191, 193; N.X. 2 A91; Z^{1b}, 32. Archives du Vatican, 57. Archivo de Indias (Sevilla), 2. Archivo General en Simancas, Estado, 53. BN, MS Fr. 15452–53 ("Le grand insulaire et pilotage d'André Thevet, Angoumoisin, cosmographe du Roy, dans lequel sont contenus plusieurs plants d'isles habitées et deshabitées et description d'icelles"); 20291; 29007 (P.O. 2523); 30612 (Carré d'Hozier 383); 31096 (Cabinet d'Hozier 215).

Biggar, *Documents relating to Cartier and Roberval*. Charlevoix, *Histoire*. Hakluyt, *Principal navigations* (1903–5), VIII, 283–89 (the only English account of Roberval's 1542 voyage, first published in 1600). Marguerite de Navarre, *L'Heptameron des nouvelles* (Paris, 1559). *Mémoires des commissaires*, I, 149; and *Memorials of the English and French commissaries*, I, 205.

Emmanuel Cathelineau, "D'une épitaphe sur Roberval," *NF*, VI (1931), 302–12. Hoffman, *Cabot to Cartier*. Lanctot, *Histoire du Canada*, I, 98, 99, 101–7, 116, 413; *Jacques Cartier devant l'histoire* (Montréal, 1947). A.-J.-M. Lefranc, *Les navigations de Pantagruel* (Paris, 1905). R. Marichal, "Les compagnons de Roberval," *Humanisme et Renaissance*, I (1934), 51–122. Robert La Roque de Roquebrune, "Roberval, sa généalogie, son pére et le procès du maréchal de Gié, le portrait de Chantilly," *RHAF*, IX (1955–56), 157–75.

LA ROQUE, MARGUERITE DE, related to Jean-François de La Rocque de Roberval; deported to an island in the St. Lawrence River. The date and place of her birth and death have never been ascertained.

She was co-seigneuress of Pontpoint, of which Roberval owned a part. Her principal lands, however, for which she had pledged fealty and homage in 1536, were in Périgord and Languedoc. Her family relationship to Roberval was very close, according to Thevet.

Among Roberval's companions on his voyage to Canada were Marguerite and a young man, her lover, but the latter is not named either by the Queen of Navarre or by Thevet, both of whom recount this romantic adventure. Shocked by Marguerite's conduct, Roberval set her down on an island called Île des Démons, in the St.

La Salle

Lawrence near the mouth of the Rivière Saint-Paul. According to Thevet, the young man joined her there. In the Queen of Navarre's account, it was the young man who was put off the ship and Marguerite who went to share his fate. The servant-girl Damienne, "a native of Normandy," accompanied them. Marguerite gave birth to a child, who died; the young man succumbed too, as did the servant-girl. Marguerite stayed on alone on the island, using her firearms against the wild animals; she managed to survive and was one day picked up by fishermen who took her away to France.

There are considerable differences between the accounts given by the Queen of Navarre and by Thevet, but Thevet is much more precise. He indicates the family relationship between Roberval and Marguerite de La Roque, and provides certain details that are historically accurate, such as the separation of Jacques CARTIER's ships and those of Roberval, the presence on the ships of men and women intended for the colony, and the location of the Île des Démons. All this gives Thevet's narrative an authenticity which both confirms and supplements the skilfully contrived little romance of the Queen of Navarre.

Thevet states that he was told of this episode by the heroine herself, whom he met at Montron in Périgord. The Queen of Navarre says that it was "Captain Roberval" who told her this story, from which she derived one of the tales of her *Heptameron*. Historians have conceded that the accounts of these two contemporaries of Roberval and Marguerite de la Roque are based on an actual happening.

R. LA ROQUE DE ROQUEBRUNE

AN, Anciens hommages et aveux, 1536, pièce 820, Languedoc, 556, Foi et hommage de Demoiselle Marguerite de La Roque pour ses terres. BN, MS Fr. 15452–53 ("Le grand insulaire et pilotage d'André Thevet, Angoumoisin, cosmographe du Roy, dans lequel sont contenus plusieurs plants d'isles habitées et deshabitées et description d'icelles"); 15454, ("Relation de deux voyages faits par André Thevet aux Indes australes et occidentales)." Marguerite de Navarre, *L'Heptameron des nouvelles* (Paris, 1559). Thevet, *Cosmographie universelle*.

Henry Harrisse, *Notes pour servir à l'histoire, à la bibliographie et à la cartographie de la Nouvelle-France et des pays adjacents, 1545–1700* (Paris, 1872). Pierre Jourda, "Marguerite, reine de Navarre," thèse pour le doctorat ès lettres, Université de Paris, 1930. Lanctot, *Histoire du Canada*, I, 104–5. Henri Malo, "L'Île des Démons, la reine de Navarre et Alcofribas," *Mercure de France*, LXXXVI (1910), 639–45. Robert La Roque de Roquebrune, "Marguerite de La Roque et l'île de la Demoiselle au Canada," *NF*, VI (1931), 131–42.

LA SALLE, RENÉ-ROBERT CAVELIER DE. *See* CAVELIER

LA SAUSSAYE, RENÉ LE COQ DE. *See* LE COQ

LA TOUR, CHARLES and **CLAUDE SAINT-ÉTIENNE DE.** *See* SAINT-ÉTIENNE

LA TOURASSE, CHARLES (known as **Chevalier**), sergeant in the French garrison at Port-Royal in Acadia, temporary English commandant there, 1690–3; ensign in the company of Sébastien de Villieu*, in Acadia; d. 1696.

In the spring of 1690 Sir William PHIPS captured Port-Royal (Annapolis Royal, N.S.) and the French governor of Acadia, Louis-Alexandre Des Friches* de Menneval. Phips himself remained at Port-Royal only for 10 or 12 days after its capitulation. Before he left it, however, he assembled as many of the inhabitants as he could and had them take the oath of allegiance to William and Mary. Then for the preservation of peace at Port-Royal, pending the arrival of a governor from Boston, Phips constituted a council, of which La Tourasse was appointed president, and the remaining members were six other leading inhabitants, one of whom was ALEXANDRE LE BORGNE de Belle-Isle. La Tourasse continued as English commandant at Port-Royal for some time, with the approval of JOSEPH ROBINAU de Villebon, a military officer who returned from France to Acadia in June 1690. The English did not establish a garrison at Port-Royal. Villebon attributed their failure to do so to the fact that the inhabitants at Port-Royal refused, as he had told them to do, to sign a guarantee for the actions of the Indians in the event that an English garrison should be sent to Port-Royal.

In the autumn of 1691 the vessel in which Villebon, now the governor of Acadia, was returning from France via Quebec to Acadia, captured a New England vessel carrying Col. Edward TYNG, who had been named governor of Nova Scotia by the New England authorities, who claimed Acadia by right of conquest. Upon his arrival at Port-Royal on 26 Nov. 1691, Villebon found the English flag flying, but still no Englishmen to defend it. The next day he assembled the inhabitants and in their presence took formal possession of Port-Royal and of all Acadia, in the name of the French monarch. Villebon did not even find it necessary to disturb the provisional government set up there by Phips. All he had to do was to instruct La Tourasse to favour the French cause whenever he could do so without embarrassing his relations with the English; then he continued in the direction of Fort Jemseg, where he established his government. Subsequently Villebon directed La Tourasse to take no steps save those which he prescribed for him. When Abraham Boudrot offered to go to Boston, under the pretext of trading, in order to see what designs were afoot there, La Tourasse suggested that his own wife, née Catherine Bugaret, in whom the English had confidence, might accompany Boudrot in order to give Villebon proof that she was a loyal Frenchwoman. Villebon gave his consent to this proposal, but La Tourasse's wife died on the voyage to Boston in 1693, and after her death, La Tourasse abandoned the post given to him by the English.

On 15 Feb. 1694 La Tourasse received a commission as an ensign, and on the 13 March following, in a "memorandum intended for the instruction of the sieur de Villebon," who was then established at Fort Naxouat (Nashwaak), the minister wrote: "His Majesty has had the vessel *La Bretonne* fitted out to bring help.... This vessel carries 10 soldiers to replace those who may be missing from among the 40 that His Majesty wishes to maintain at the said fort with the sieur Chevallier [La Tourasse], whom His Majesty has made an ensign in the Sieur de Villieu's company, in recognition of his faithfulness and of the devotion that he has displayed in His Majesty's service since the coming of the English to Acadia."

When Benjamin Church* decided to seize the Bay of Fundy and lay siege to Fort Naxouat, La Tourasse acted as a scout under Villebon's orders; he was killed in an ambush on or about 9 Oct. 1696.

IN COLLABORATION WITH
C. BRUCE FERGUSSON

Recensement de 1693 (Acadie). *Coll. de manuscrits relatifs à la Nouv.-France*, II, 4–5 ("de la Tourasse"), 146, 241–47 ("Chevalier"). PAC *Report, 1912*, App. E, 54–66; App. F, 67–73 ("Latourasie" and "Lattoras"). Murdoch, *History of Nova-Scotia*, I. Parkman, *Count Frontenac and New France* (24th ed.). Webster, *Acadia*.

LA TOUSCHE CHAMPLAIN, PÉZARD DE. See PÉZARD

LA TRINITÉ, SIMON DENYS DE. See DENYS

LA TROCHE, MARIE SAVONNIÈRES DE. See SAVONNIÈRES

LAUSON, GILLES, Montreal settler, forefather of all the Lauzons of Canada and the United States; b. in the parish of Saint-Julien in the town of Caen (France) in 1631, the son of Pierre Lauson and Anne Boivin; d. at Montreal in 1687.

Lauson exercised the copper-smith's trade, having qualified as a master craftsman before he landed in Canada in 1653 with the great contingent brought from France by CHOMEDEY de Maisonneuve. Having decided to settle at Ville-Marie (Montreal), Lauson bought 50 rods of land and a house from Urbain Tessier *dit* Lavigne, in March 1655. On 20 August of the same year there were added to this property, as grants from Maisonneuve, 30 acres "below the Coteau Saint-Louis" and one acre "within the town." Being henceforth in a position to support a wife and family, Lauson married Marie Archambault, aged 12, daughter of Jacques Archambault and Françoise Toureault, on 27 Nov. 1656, at Ville-Marie. As a good citizen Lauson enlisted in the militia of the Sainte-Famille and held the position of churchwarden of the parish of Montreal from 5 Jan. 1670 to 11 Jan. 1672.

Marie Archambault died on 8 Aug. 1685, leaving 13 children; on 21 Sept. 1687 Lauson himself died.

ANDRÉ VACHON

R.-J. Auger, *La grande recrue de 1653* (Montréal, 1955), 79f. L. Lauzon, *Un pionnier de Ville-Marie, Gilles Lauzon et sa postérité* (Québec, 1926).

LAUSON, JEAN DE, senior, governor of New France; b. *c.* 1584; d. 16 Feb. 1666 in Paris.

Jean de Lauson came from an old legal family of Breton origin that had been established in Poitou since the 16th century; he was the eldest son of François de Lauson, seigneur of Lirec, counsellor in the Parlement, and of Isabelle Lottin, daughter of the seigneur of Charny. While still young he began to follow the path traced by his ancestors. On 3 Feb. 1613 he was appointed a counsellor in the Parlement, and on 23 May 1622 *maître des requêtes*. In this latter capacity he was required, in 1632, to examine the case against Henri II, Duc de Montmorency, and two years later that against the Duc d'Épernon. Subsequently he was in turn president of the Grand Conseil, intendant of Provence, then of Guyenne, and, about 1640, intendant of Dauphiné. But already, in about 1627, he had become involved in the affairs of New France in a way which was to yield him key posts in its administration for 30 years to come. When Richelieu decided to form the Compagnie des Cent-Associés, Jean de Lauson was accepted as one of its first members, on the very day of its founding, 29 April 1627. He played the major part in its organization, and a few months later, at the request of the first

Lauson

associates, he was appointed by Richelieu its intendant or director. This was an office much sought after, for it was in the intendant's own residence that the discussions were to be held and the accounts presented; in fact M. de Lauson replaced Richelieu in his absence, and became the pivot of the company.

As intendant, Lauson was required to make arrangements for restoring Canada to France after the capture of Quebec by the KIRKE brothers. In 1929, CHAMPLAIN had written to him from Dover to inform him of what had taken place, and in 1631 the founder of Quebec paid Lauson the tribute of saying that it was thanks to the latter's influence that the restitution of the colony was negotiated. At the same time Lauson supported the Jesuits in their campaign to have themselves granted exclusive missionary rights in Canada. The Recollets claimed priority, and the Capuchins could call upon the influence of Father Joseph, Richelieu's adviser. Lauson suggested that the Capuchins should accept instead the Acadian mission, previously manned by the Recollets; however he himself refused the latter free passage to Canada and their yearly allotments of 600 *livres*. In 1634 and 1635 he again opposed their departure. Then in January 1651, in the face of their reiterated complaints to the directors of the company, he managed to have their request referred to the Conseil de Québec. By that time he had already been appointed governor, and the decision, which could only be negative, thus came before himself.

In his capacity as intendant of the company, Lauson also took advantage of his influence to have vast estates made over to his family: to his eldest son François he granted a piece of land stretching from the Rivière des Iroquois (the Richelieu) to the present-day Châteauguay. Then, by making use of straw men, he obtained for himself Montreal Island, an eighth part of the Beaupré seigneury and of the Île d'Orléans, and the whole expanse of the seigneury that thenceforth (1636) bore his name. By 1640 the Lausons, father and sons, had become the biggest landowners in the colony.

Around 1640 Jean de Lauson was appointed intendant of Dauphiné, with residence at Vienne. It was there that in August 1640 he received a visit from Father CHARLES LALEMANT, who was negotiating the purchase, on behalf of the Société Notre-Dame de Montréal, of the island where it was planned to found Ville-Marie. (According to some authors, Lauson sold it at the exorbitant figure of 150,000 *livres*, the Cent-Associés annulled the sale, and regranted the island in December 1640.)

Meanwhile, the situation in New France was becoming more and more precarious because of the Iroquois wars. Both the Compagnie des Cent-Associés and the young Communauté des Habitants found their business adversely affected. Lauson may have offered his services at that time for the solution of the difficulties. In any case, on the recommendation of the Cent-Associés and with Father JÉRÔME LALEMANT's backing, he was appointed governor of New France on 17 Jan. 1651, his commission to take effect on his arrival in the colony. M. de Lauson landed at Quebec on 13 Oct. 1651, and stayed there as governor until September 1656. He brought a letter from the king, dated 8 May 1651, conferring on him the right to promulgate "with sovereign authority and as a last court of appeal . . . such statutes and regulations as you shall deem reasonable, whether for the armies, for justice, for sound administration, . . . or for the beaver trade." And he indeed lost no time in making use of his vast powers.

In the very first months of his administration, Lauson saw to the setting up of his sons JEAN and Louis, who had landed with him. He appointed the former grand seneschal of New France, and made him several grants of land in the Lauson seigneury and in the area around Cap-Rouge. To Louis, Sieur de La Citière, he granted a new seigneury called Gaudarville in honour of Marie Gaudar, Mme de Lauson, who had apparently died in France. To his youngest son CHARLES, who had arrived at Quebec 1 July 1652, he gave the title of grand master of the waters and forests, in addition to several fiefs, including those of Charny and Lirec. Having endowed them with estates of this kind, the governor also saw that his sons married into the founding families of the colony. Jean, the grand seneschal, married Anne Després, sister-in-law of Guillaume GUILLEMOT; Charles married Marie-Louise, daughter of ROBERT GIFFARD; Louis took as his wife Catherine Nau, sister-in-law of Joseph Giffard* of Beauport and niece of GAUDAIS-DUPONT. Did Lauson, by thus establishing his sons, who might have held enviable posts in France—François, the eldest, was already a counsellor in the Parlement of Bordeaux—seek to inspire confidence in the settlers, who were discouraged by poverty and by Indian attacks? In any case, of all the French governors, he was the only one to encourage the cultivation of the land by setting up his sons in Canada.

M. de Lauson also endeavoured to solve the Indian problem. Since 1649, the Iroquois had been masters of the fur-trading routes, and the colony was barely eking out an existence. In 1653, when the settlers were thinking of going back to France, he succeeded in concluding a treaty with the Mohawks, who sent their chief, Andioura, to Quebec to negotiate. But three years later the same Mohawks, jealous because of the promise of the French to set up a post among the Onondagas, decided to attack the Hurons on the Île d'Orléans. On 20 May 1656, 300 of them landed on the island and reduced the Huron village to ashes, murdering or capturing their enemies. On their way back they passed by the walls of Quebec, chanting insults at the French; the latter did not dare to give chase or snatch the prisoners from them. The inhabitants of Quebec wanted to intervene, but Lauson, who had had the Jesuits' residence fortified in case of emergency, vetoed this categorically, no doubt having in mind the meagreness of the resources at his disposal. He nevertheless continued to encourage the expedition into the territory of the Onondagas led by Father SIMON LE MOYNE, which he had himself approved.

In the meantime, he also encountered great difficulties over the question of the fur trade. Since 1648, the prosperity of the colony and of its governor had been declining steadily, despite the harsh measures adopted by Lauson in 1652 in order to control trade and increase his own income. After he signed the peace treaty with the Iroquois in 1653, their attacks momentarily ceased, but there was no perceptible improvement in trade. Hence, in 1654, having obtained a renewal of his mandate, Lauson arrogated to himself the monopoly of the fur trade, by forbidding anyone to set out without his written permission, and by sending into the interior two of his own supporters (one of them being CHOUART Des Groseilliers, apparently). In view of these abuses, the settlers deputed a syndic to go to Paris; the latter lodged a complaint with the Cent-Associés, and, through their intermediary, with the king. Louis XIV consequently decreed (15 March 1656) that the seigneurial attorney of the Cent-Associés should thenceforth sit on the council, to which the fur-trading accounts would be presented. At Quebec, the council hastened to comply with the decree by granting all the settlers the right to engage in the fur trade throughout the whole country. M. de Lauson, feeling himself the particular target of the king's decree, decided to return to France to build up influential support. He left the administration of the colony to his son Charles, Sieur de Charny, and set out from Quebec in September 1656. Before leaving, he seized a substantial share of the furs, valued at 300,000 *livres*, that Des Groseilliers had unloaded at Quebec during the summer; then he had Charles SEVESTRE, the company's receiving clerk, pay him 3,000 *livres* for the cost of the journey which he made on one of the company's ships, presumably without dipping into his own purse. It seems difficult not to censure the old governor's ambition and greed, even if the sons he had given to the colony and left there were to do honour to New France by their talents and their sacrifices. The directors of the Cent-Associés, however, exonerated him, while regretting (in a decree dated 7 March 1657) the cornering of the fur trade "by the most powerful . . . who draw the profit to themselves alone." Later on, Lauson was appointed to the post of subdean of the Conseil Royal.

The correspondence of missionaries and other contemporaries alludes to Lauson as being a virtuous and cultured man. He apparently possessed one of the richest libraries in France, and used it. But he was also said to be ambitious and cowardly, inexperienced, poorly advised, and lacking in decisiveness. One thing is certain: whether or not he had the requisite attributes for a governor, he had to face a decade of reverses which made this period one of the most difficult in the history of New France.

J. MONET

APQ *Rapport, 1924–25*, 377–91, "Les ordonnances du gouverneur de Lauzon." "De la famille des Lauson," éd. Louis-Hippolyte Lafontaine, dans *Mémoires et documents relatifs à l'histoire du Canada* (SHM Mémoires, II, 1859), 65–96. *Édits, ord.*, III, 16. *JR* (Thwaites). *Mémoires des commissaires*, I, 157; II, 501; IV, 180, 219; and *Memorials of the English and French commissaries*, I, 117, 211, 365, 717. P.-G. Roy, *Inv. concessions*.

T.-P. Bédard, "Le gouverneur Jean de Lauson et ses trois fils, étude historique (1651)," *Nouvelles Soirées canadiennes*, I (1882), 55–61, 84–90, 115–22. *BRH*, XXI (1915), 140; XXII (1916), 33; XXVI (1920), 343. Couillard Després, *La première famille française au Canada*, 266–73. Garneau, *Histoire du Canada*, I. Amédée-E. Gosselin, "Notes et documents concernant les gouverneurs d'Ailleboust, de Lauzon et de Lauzon-Charny," *RSCT*, 3d ser., XXVI (1932), sect.I, 83–96. Lionel Laberge, *Histoire du fief de Lotinville, 1652–1690* (L'Ange-Gardien, 1963). Lanctot, *Histoire du Canada*, I. L. Lauzon, *Un pionnier de la Ville-Marie, Gilles Lauzon et sa postérité* (Québec, 1926). J.-E. Roy, *Histoire de la seigneurie de Lauzon*, I. P.-G. Roy, *La ville de Québec*, I.

LAUSON, JEAN DE, junior, grand seneschal of New France; b. presumably between 1620 and 1635 in France, son of JEAN DE LAUSON, future governor of New France, and of Marie Gaudar; killed 22 June 1661 during an Iroquois raid on the Île d'Orléans.

It is difficult to give the exact date of the birth

of Jean de Lauson junior. Several authors, without indicating their sources, say he was 17 when he became grand seneschal in 1651. Pierre-Georges Roy makes him 22 at the same period, and J.-Edmond Roy suggests that it was to him that Marie de l'Incarnation [*see* GUYART] was alluding in a letter of 2 Aug. 1644, when she wrote: "Among this year's arrivals, there is a young man of very noble birth, 22 years old, whom God has inspired to serve Him in this country, for the salvation of the Indians. . . . This young man . . . has held a command in the French armies." A document of 1660, in the registry of the notary AUDOUART, describes him as "now in his majority, 25 years old." What is certain is that he was in Quebec, at least briefly, at the end of August 1644, when he acted as godfather for little Anne*, the daughter of JEAN BOURDON and Jacqueline Potel. And finally, he came to Quebec again with his father on 13 Oct. 1651, having resigned in France from the Navarre and Picardy regiments. As soon as he arrived, Jean received from his father several grants of land in the Lauson seigneury and in the area around Cap-Rouge; on 23 Oct. 1651, at Quebec, he married Anne Després, who had made the crossing with him. Father Barthélemy VIMONT solemnized the marriage, and the wedding festivities lasted three days.

Governor Lauson, a former counsellor of state, and consequently well acquainted with the organization and routine of tribunals, resolved to put the administration of justice in New France in order. Until then, civil and criminal justice had been administered very irregularly at the Château Saint-Louis, and almost arbitrarily. Lauson therefore created a seneschal's court modelled on those in the French provinces. For Quebec and Trois-Rivières, he set up courts presided over by a lieutenant-general with the assistance of a clerk and an attorney, and of a special civil and criminal lieutenant for the lower courts (Montreal retained its seigneurial court under CHOMEDEY de Maisonneuve). To preside over this entire organization, he appointed his son Jean, giving him the title of grand seneschal of New France, and the right to sit on all courts. The title and rights of the grand seneschal were to be chiefly honorary. For although it was stated, in several documents relating to the grants of seigneuries, that the judgements of the seigneurial courts "will be under the jurisdiction of the grand seneschal of New France," justice was usually administered by subordinate officers (the general and special lieutenants and the seigneurial attorney), and appeals were brought before the governor.

During the administration of his father, an old man of about 70 years, who was incapable of waging war, Jean de Lauson's chief concern was to give the colony the benefit of his army experience. In February 1652, he made a military inspection visit to Trois-Rivières, and among other feats of arms, at the end of the following August, he took an active part in the defence of the same town, at the time of the Iroquois attack during which Governor GUILLEMOT met his death. After his father's departure in 1656, he retired to his estate of Beaumarchais, near Beauport. He never resided in his Lauson seigneury.

The guerilla warfare being waged by the Iroquois was then at its worst. A band of Iroquois, returning from a murderous descent upon Tadoussac, stopped at the Île d'Orléans to slaughter some 15 Frenchmen. Quebec was living in terror, and in the grand seneschal's circle anxiety was felt particularly about his brother-in-law, LOUIS COUILLARD de Lespinay, who was overdue from a hunting expedition. Lauson set out on 22 June 1661 with six companions to seek him, but himself fell into the hands of a troop of some 80 Iroquois. After a valiant and long struggle (during which the man for whom they had ventured out, having heard the sound of muskets, hurried vainly to Quebec to seek help), the seven Frenchmen were massacred. The next day the grand seneschal's body was found, covered with wounds and decapitated. His head had been carried off to the Iroquois country as a trophy. With his six companions, he was buried on St. John the Baptist's day in the church at Quebec.

By his marriage with Anne Després, Jean de Lauson had six children, of whom only two daughters (later to become Ursulines) lived to adulthood. His widow remarried 7 July 1664, her second husband being Claude de Bermen* de La Martinière, and died in 1689.

The annalist of the Hôtel-Dieu and Father JÉRÔME LALEMANT pointed out how serious for Quebec was the loss of the third seigneur of Lauson. He was loved for his cheerfulness and his easy friendliness; he was respected for his authority. He was very courageous; he always seemed ready to pursue the enemy, and the young men followed him. After his death, confusion ensued on all sides, and discouragement left almost everyone at the mercy of the Iroquois.

J. MONET

"De la famille des Lauson," éd. Louis-Hippolyte Lafontaine, dans *Mémoires et documents relatifs à l'histoire du Canada* (SHM Mémoires, II, 1859), 65–96. *JR* (Thwaites). P.-G. Roy, *Inv. concessions*.

T.-P. Bédard, "Le gouverneur Jean de Lauson et ses trois fils, étude historique (1651)," *Nouvelles soirées canadiennes*, I (1882), 55–61, 84–90, 115–22. Couillard Després, *La première famille française au Canada*, 266–73. Lanctot, *Histoire du Canada*, I. E. Lareau, *Histoire du droit canadien* (2v., Montréal, 1888–89), I. J.-E. Roy, *Histoire de la seigneurie de Lauzon*, I. P.-G. Roy, *La ville de Québec*, I.

LAUSON DE CHARNY, CHARLES DE, acting governor of New France, then priest, official, vicar general, ecclesiastical superior of the Hôtel-Dieu of Quebec; b. *c.* 1629 probably in Paris, son of JEAN DE LAUSON, governor of New France, and of Marie Gaudar; d. some time after 1689 in France.

The Lauson family, whose ancestors were from Poitou, had established themselves in Paris. The surname given to Charles came to him from a great-grandfather, the seigneur of Charny, in the Department of the Yonne. Jean de Lauson had acquired immense estates in New France; but it was done for the advantage of the three sons whom he summoned to come and join him, and who did in fact marry and settle in the country, with the intention of remaining there. Charles came last, on 1 July 1652, on a ship that ran aground on the Île aux Coudres. When he arrived his father gave him the title of grand master of the waters and forests, a title more high-sounding than meaningful in a colony still in its infancy. Shortly afterwards he ceded to him his share (one-eighth) of the Beaupré seigneury and of the Charny and Lirec fiefs on the Île d'Orléans.

On 12 Aug. 1652, barely six weeks after his arrival, Charles de Lauson married Louise Giffard, aged 13 years, daughter of ROBERT GIFFARD, the seigneur of Beauport. Father JÉRÔME LALEMANT pronounced the nuptial blessing, in the presence of M. GUILLEMOT *dit* Du Plessis-Kerbodot, governor of Trois-Rivières, and of M. LE VIEUX de Hauteville, lieutenant-general of the seneschal's court.

In June 1656 Jean de Lauson, wearied of administration, returned to France, leaving as acting governor his son Charles. The latter bore the title of administrator or "commandant of New France" until 20 August of the following year, when he received a commission as governor from the king, pending the arrival of M. Voyer* d'Argenson who was designated for this post. Subsequently he styled himself "Charles de Lauson, *chevalier*, seigneur of Charny, governor and lieutenant-general for the king in New France," with the "powers, authorities, and rights with which it has pleased the king to honour us." But he himself, on 26 Aug. 1657 (*RSCT*, 3d ser., XXVI (1932), sect.I, 9), delegated the office of temporary administrator to the former governor LOUIS D'AILLEBOUST, and sailed for France.

His young wife had died at the Hôtel-Dieu on 30 Oct. 1656, two weeks after giving him a daughter. Out of respect for the Lauson family and for that of Giffard, which had just given the Hôtel-Dieu its first Canadian nun, the deceased had been buried in the vault of the monastery as she had requested. For the repose of his wife's soul, M. de Lauson de Charny asked that each year the office for the dead and a high mass be celebrated at the Hôtel-Dieu, in return for a grant of land on the Lauzon shore [of the St. Lawrence] which at that time had "an annual revenue of 200 *livres*, because of the eel fishing which was very plentiful."

Having put out his daughter to nurse, the acting governor left Quebec on 18 Sept. 1657 bound for France, where he entered orders. His appointment on 24 Feb. 1657 as first prefect of the congregation that the Jesuits had just founded at Quebec had already been an acknowledgement of his piety. M. de Lauson de Charny became a priest on 12 April 1659, and his first action was to come straight back to Canada. He made the crossing with the new vicar apostolic, Bishop Laval*, who reached Quebec on 16 June 1659. On 27 September the new priest was appointed *official* (ecclesiastical judge). The next year he became vicar general and accompanied the bishop on his pastoral visit to Trois-Rivières and Montreal. He lived at the Jesuit college from his arrival until the spring of 1664, when he went to live at the seminary with the bishop and the other secular priests. Officially, however, he was never a member of the Quebec seminary. On 15 July 1664 he became the ecclesiastical superior of the Hôtel-Dieu of Quebec, where he exercised his ministry with great zeal.

While serving the diocese, he continued to manage his fiefs and even those of his family. After the death of his brother, the grand seneschal JEAN DE LAUSON, who was killed by the Iroquois on 22 June 1661, he had to assume the guardianship of the latter's children who were under age and concern himself with the seigneury of Lauson, which was a part of the estate. M. de Lauson senior died on 16 Feb. 1666 in Paris, and the abbé had to sail on 17 October to go and settle the affairs of his family, which possessed extensive property. In addition Bishop Laval, by an enactment dated 21 October, made him responsible, in France, for watching over the interests of the Hôtel-Dieu of Montreal. M. de Lauson de Charny was back again by 1668.

Before leaving to become a priest he had already sold his share in the Beaupré and Île d'Orléans seigneuries to Julien Fortin *dit* Bellefontaine. With the sale of his arriere-fief to Bishop Laval he divested himself of his last piece of land in New France. In the autumn of 1671 he returned to France for good. We know the two main reasons for his leaving. The first resulted from his position as vicar general, which involved him in the friction between Bishop Laval and the civil authorities; the second concerned the future of his daughter, born in 1656, who wanted to become a nun. The sisters of the Hôtel-Dieu had had her as a boarder since the age of six and appreciated her fine qualities; but despite the assurance that she would receive 12,000 *livres* as a dowry, they refused to accept the condition laid down by her father: that she should be given a special menu because of her delicate constitution. In view of this, M. de Lauson de Charny took her off to France, with one of her cousins, and both girls became nuns of the Hôtel-Dieu of La Rochelle. The abbé lived at the Jesuit college in that town until his death, which occurred sometime after 1689.

HONORIUS PROVOST

AJQ, Greffe de Romain Becquet, 2 sept. 1666. ASQ, Album Gaspé, p.121; Carton Plante, 60; Fonds Verreau, Saberdache rouge, L, p.196ff.; MSS, 17, Documents relatifs à Mgr de Laval, p.125; Polygraphie, III, 14; XIX, 12. Juchereau, *Annales* (Jamet), *passim*. Amédée-E. Gosselin, "Notes et documents concernant les gouverneurs d'Ailleboust, de Lauzon et de Lauzon-Charny," *RSCT*, 3d ser., XXVI (1932), sect.I, 83–96. J.-E. Roy, *Histoire de la seigneurie de Lauzon*, I.

LAVIGNE, JEAN LEVASSEUR *dit*. *See* LEVASSEUR

LAVIOLETTE, first commandant of Trois-Rivières; fl. 1634–36.

The site of Trois-Rivières very early entered history. Jacques CARTIER, returning from Hochelaga, had stopped there on 7 Oct. 1535 to explore the mouth of the Saint-Maurice. Shortly before 1600 FRANÇOIS GRAVÉ Du Pont, perhaps wanting to find a more suitable trading-post than the one at Tadoussac, or else with the intention of outstripping his competitors, had gone there to meet the Indians. And as early as 1601 Trois-Rivières appeared for the first time on a geographical map (Levasseur's).

Gravé Du Pont returned there in 1603, together with CHAMPLAIN. At that period the Indians of the Laurentian coalition (Algonkins, Montagnais, Hurons) were at war with the Iroquois. The latter, making use of the Richelieu River route, were trying to intercept the fur convoys on the St. Lawrence, on their way to Tadoussac. Champlain immediately realized the strategic importance of Trois-Rivières, an advanced post from which one would be able to keep the Iroquois in check and assure unmolested passage along the river for the fur-traders.

However, it was only in 1618 that, for the first time since the founding of Quebec, exchange of furs took place at Trois-Rivières. The same thing occurred in 1620, 1621, and 1622; from 1623 to 1629 the spring fair was held at Cap-de-la-Victoire, near the Richelieu, except in 1624 when it took place at Quebec. In 1632 Trois-Rivières was finally decided upon for the annual meeting between the Indians and the fur-traders.

Champlain had not forgotten his plan of 1603. In 1634 he decided to establish a habitation at Trois-Rivières, prompted by the economic and strategic advantages of the site. He named an employee of the fur trade, called Laviolette, to command the post. Laviolette set out with some artisans and a handful of soldiers, and had a stockade built, within which were erected a few buildings to serve as dwellings and stores. In the same year the Jesuits PAUL LE JEUNE and Jacques BUTEUX set up a permanent mission there.

Laviolette commanded at Trois-Rivières from 4 July 1634 to 17 April 1636. That is all we know of him. He probably returned to France at the end of the summer of 1636.

Who is entitled to be called the founder of Trois-Rivières? The majority of historians say that Champlain was the real founder of the post, and Laviolette a subordinate. Was it not Champlain who recognized the economic and strategic importance of the site of Trois-Rivières and who chose the right moment to set it up?

So long as it remained the annual meeting-place of traders and Indians, the "town" of Trois-Rivières prospered. But around 1660 it was supplanted by Montreal and began to mark time. In 1666 it had almost as many inhabitants as Montreal and Quebec; at the end of the French régime its population was scarcely greater than in 1666, whereas that of the other two towns had increased tenfold. The Forges Saint-Maurice, which were attempted there in the 18th century, were not enough to fill the gap left by the loss of the fur trade.

ANDRÉ VACHON

Recensement de 1666. Champlain, *Œuvres* (Laverdière), *JR* (Thwaites), IV, 261. L.-P. Desrosiers, "Les Trois-Rivières," *Cahiers des Dix*, X (1946), 63–95. Sulte, *Hist. des Can. fr.*, II, 48–54.

LE BAILLIF, GEORGES, Recollet, priest, missionary in Canada; fl. 1620–21.

Having been appointed to the Canadian missions, Le Baillif, member of a noble French family, left Honfleur around 8 May 1620 with Samuel de CHAMPLAIN, and reached Quebec in mid-July.

Father Le Baillif was the friend and counsellor of Champlain, who had been asked by Henri II, Duc de Montmorency and viceroy of New France, and by the Sieurs Villemenon and Dolu, "to undertake nothing without the participation of this worthy Father." They assured Champlain "that they would always approve of what he would do in association with Father Le Baillif," who, continued Chrestien Le Clercq, "was a man of great uprightness, sound doctrine and prudence." Father Le Baillif had many opportunities to display his talents.

On 17 July 1621 Champlain sent him to Tadoussac, with full authority to settle on his behalf the differences between FRANÇOIS GRAVÉ Du Pont and GUILLAUME DE CAËN. A provisional agreement was reached, and the dispute was referred back to France.

At the assembly of notables, held at Quebec on 18 August of that year, Father Le Baillif was selected to go and place before the king the complaints of the colony. The esteem already shown to him by Louis XIII made him the natural choice for this responsible appointment. He left Quebec 7 Sept. 1621.

He was received on two occasions by the king, and submitted to him the needs of New France: the protection of the colony in case of attack by a foreign power; the building of a fort on Cap aux Diamants; the banning of an arms supply to the Indians by the Huguenot business men of La Rochelle; the cessation of the quarrels dividing the two companies of merchants; the maintenance and expansion of the Roman Catholic religion; the forbidding of any observance of the Protestant cult in the colony; the founding of a seminary at Quebec for 50 Indian children; the establishment of a stronger system of justice against wrong-doers; an increase in Champlain's salary and authority.

The Recollet was successful in respect of the main issues: the conflict between the rival companies came to an end; Protestant worship was forbidden in the colony; the building of a seminary was decided upon and letters patent were promulgated accordingly. Thus, by his influence, Le Baillif made an important contribution to the restoration of peace in the colony.

At the Duc de Montmorency's request, Father Le Baillif remained in France, as chief representative of the Recollets stationed in Canada. It was in this capacity that he appointed Brother SAGARD, who was their first historian, to the Canadian missions; obtained gifts of land for the Trois-Rivières and Tadoussac missions; pleaded in favour of sending Jesuits to New France, and in 1625 presented to Louis XIII the dictionary of the Huron, Algonkin and Montagnais languages compiled by the Recollet Joseph LE CARON.

By his calm, prudent, and effective action, Father Le Baillif was an agent of peace and progress for the colony in its early days.

G.-M. DUMAS

BN, Imprimés, LK[12], 774, [Georges Le Baillif], Plainte de la Nouvelle France dicte Canada, à la France, sa Germaine. Pour servir de Factum en vue d'une cause pendante au Conseil (fin 1621 ou début 1622). Champlain, Œuvres (Laverdière), 995f., 1001f., 1008–12, 1018. Le Clercq, *First establishment of the faith* (Shea), I, 152, 162–66, *et passim*. Sagard, *Histoire du Canada* (Tross), I, *passim*.

Ferland, *Cours d'histoires du Canada*, I, 192. Jouve, *Les Franciscains et le Canada (1615–1629)*. Hugolin Lemay, "L'œuvre manuscrite ou imprimée des Récollets de la mission du Canada (Province de Saint-Denis), 1615–1629," *RSCT*, 3d ser., XXX (1936), sect.I, 115–26. Trudel, *Histoire de la Nouvelle-France*, II.

"LE BERGER." *See* HONATTENIATE

LE BORGNE, EMMANUEL, merchant, backer of and claimant to estate of Charles de MENOU d'Aulnay, consular magistrate of La Rochelle, governor of Acadia 1657–67; b. 1610 at Calais; d. 5 Aug. 1675 at La Rochelle.

Le Borgne, a prosperous and influential merchant of La Rochelle, had made large advances to d'Aulnay for his Acadian enterprise. Upon receiving word of the latter's death by drowning at Port-Royal (Annapolis Royal, N.S.), Le Borgne obtained on 9 Nov. 1650 a formal recognition from René de Menou de Charnisay, the aged father of d'Aulnay, that 260,000 *livres* were due him. To satisfy his claim upon the d'Aulnay estate, Le Borgne sent an expedition to Acadia the following spring, hoping to take over the whole trade, in which CHARLES DE SAINT-ÉTIENNE de La Tour at Saint John and NICOLAS DENYS at Cape Breton were also active. His agent Saint-Mas took possession of Port-Royal and the goods there belonging to his debtor's widow, Jeanne MOTIN. His second son ALEXANDRE LE BORGNE de Belle-Isle visited Boston on 10 June 1651 to seek good relations with the New Englanders, presenting letters from d'Aulnay's father, widow, and Saint-Mas, and asserting his

Le Borgne

father's claim (Mass. Hist. Soc. *Coll.*, 3d ser., VII (1838), 114–18). Le Borgne's men appear to have raided Denys's establishments at Saint-Pierre and Sainte-Anne in Mme d'Aulnay's name, for Denys and his brother were taken prisoner and sent to Quebec in October. The Capuchins at Port-Royal persuaded the widow to send her steward, Brice de Sainte-Croix, the son of Mme de BRICE, to France to seek protection. He was provided with a power of attorney for her goods in France, dated 11 July 1651. Exceeding his authority, Brice made a contract with the king's uncle, the Duc de Vendôme, on 18 Feb. 1652, under which the duke took over from the widow the seigneuries of Saint John and Île Saint-Pierre in exchange for his protection. Presumably in retaliation, Le Borgne's men seized and imprisoned Fathers CÔME de Mantes and Gabriel de Joinville and Mme de Brice at Port-Royal in 1652, and then took them to France, while the other Capuchins withdrew from Port-Royal.

In 1653 Le Borgne himself came to Port-Royal, and on 30 August made the widow, who in July had married her husband's rival in the hope of safeguarding her interests, sign an account showing that 206,286 *livres* were still due him. He used this document as authority to seize property belonging to the d'Aulnay heirs both in Acadia and in the French ports. Continuing his effort to monopolize the Acadian trade, he captured the posts at Pentagouet (Castine, Maine), La Hève, Saint-Pierre, and Nipisiguit (Bathurst, N.B.); Nicolas Denys was once more taken prisoner, though later allowed to return to France, where he sought damages of 50,000 *livres*. On 3 Dec. 1653 Denys obtained a large grant from the Compagnie de la Nouvelle-France which ran from Gaspé to Cap Canseau (Canso), and on 30 Jan. 1654 a royal commission as governor of the whole Gulf of St. Lawrence region, with a monopoly of shore-based fisheries as far south as "Virginia." With his title to the northern Acadian trade thus reinforced, Denys returned to Saint-Pierre in the spring of 1654 in time to warn La Tour at Saint John of Le Borgne's impending attack upon him.

Le Borgne had reached an agreement with the Duc de Vendôme, and under his patronage returned to Port-Royal in 1654 in the ship *Châteaufort*, laden with 75,000 *livres* of merchandise, provisions, and munitions, to enforce the duke's claim to Saint John and Saint-Pierre under the 1652 transaction. But Le Borgne failed to capture the Saint John fort and La Tour before his operations were interrupted by SEDGWICK's 1654 expedition to capture Acadia. Le Borgne was accused of favouring the New Englanders, since he refused to supply La Tour with needed provisions and munitions, and of having maintained a treasonable correspondence with them. In the capitulation of Port-Royal (16 August), which he signed along with Father LÉONARD de Chartres, he requested that his ship and his merchandise be returned to him. In the light of the charges made against him, it is significant that he was permitted to return to France in the *Châteaufort* late in 1654, leaving his eldest son, Emmanuel Le Borgne Du Coudray, as a hostage at Port-Royal, and Alexandre Le Borgne de Belle-Isle in charge of La Hève and other posts which the English let him have.

Once back in France Le Borgne seized all the furs and merchandise belonging to the d'Aulnay heirs, and continued to enjoy the revenues of the estate under the transactions of 1650 and 1653. Nicolas Denys obtained an *arrêt* of the Conseil Privé du Roi on 15 Oct. 1655, ordering Le Borgne to return furs belonging to Denys, which the former had seized from the Sieur de La Meilleraye. This same decree ordered Le Borgne and other claimants to the d'Aulnay estate not to take any action against the posts granted Denys by the Compagnie de la Nouvelle-France. Le Borgne then proceeded to obtain from the company on 20 Nov. 1657 a grant running from the Rivière Verte (Sainte-Marie; now St. Mary's) to New England, except for those lands conceded to La Tour. On 10 December he received a royal commission as governor of Acadia, in place of La Tour who had sold his interests to the English, with the right to command for nine years in the region from Canseau to New England. Thus there remained no legitimate source of conflict between Le Borgne and Denys except in the matter of shore-based fisheries, and the latter had no such establishment below Canseau. On 25 July 1658 the Parlement of Paris confirmed the 1650 agreement, despite the protests of the d'Aulnay heirs, and Le Borgne remained in possession of their lands, though the key posts were occupied by the English.

Le Borgne seems to have gone to England early in 1658 to press for the restitution of Saint John, Port-Royal, and Penobscot, while in May Belle-Isle captured La Hève and the furs and provisions there belonging to Col. Thomas TEMPLE, who with William CROWNE of Boston had purchased La Tour's interests in Acadia in 1656 and had become Cromwell's lieutenant-general of Nova Scotia. Temple promptly retaliated, taking Belle-Isle prisoner, and drawing up a complaint against the elder Le Borgne the following November. By 6 Sept. 1659 (o.s.), how-

Le Borgne de Belle-Isle

ever, Temple was writing Lord Keeper Fiennes of his willingness to give up La Hève to Le Borgne, reputed to be a very honest man who had nearly ruined himself in the Acadian trade, and who wanted to establish his son in the fishery there.

At the time of the formation of the Compagnie des Indes occidentales in 1664, Le Borgne vainly tried to get a concession of the La Tour and d'Aulnay lands. He also urged the company to support his son [Emmanuel?] Le Borgne Du Coudray at Canseau on 27 Dec. 1664. But the company renewed his own grant in 1667, with an added concession. Belle-Isle received a royal commission as governor and lieutenant-general in Acadia. Although the Treaty of Breda of that year provided for the return of Acadia to France, and Belle-Isle went to Acadia to take possession on 9 Oct. 1668, he was advised to return home by MORILLON Du Bourg, who on a visit to Boston had found that Temple was not ready to surrender the posts. When the transfer finally took place in 1670, Belle-Isle returned to Acadia with the new governor, ANDIGNÉ de Grandfontaine, to protect the Le Borgne interests, despite the fact that that Andigné told the people to regard him as a simple *habitant* (AN, Col. C^{11D}, I, f.139v).

Emmanuel Le Borgne died at La Rochelle in 1675, reputedly ruined by his Acadian enterprises, although a *mémoire* of 1667 in the La Tour interest alleges that he had received much more than the amount due him while he had enjoyed the revenues of the d'Aulnay estate. Belle-Isle continued to press his father's and his own claims, which were finally settled by an *arrêt* of March 1702. After the English withdrawal in 1670, Emmanuel Le Borgne and his sons enjoyed the monopoly of the Acadian trade for which he had struggled for twenty years.

MASON WADE

ACM, B.194. AN, Col., B, 15, ff.44–44v; 23, f.133v; C^{11D}, 10, *passim;* E, 277 (dossier La Vallière); F^3, 1, ff.253–54; 3, ff.249–50; 6, ff.34–35v. Archivum Sacrae Congregationis de Propaganda, Rome, Lettere Antiche, 260, f.25, Ignace de Paris, "Brevis ac dilucida . . ." ("Brève relation de la mission d'Acadie . . . 1656") (photocopy of the original with a translation in PAC, MG 17, 1; *see* PAC *Report, 1904,* App.H, 333–41). BN, MS, Clairambault 867, f.890. BM, Egerton MS 2395, ff.313v–319.

Coll. de manuscrits, relatifs à la Nouv.-France, I, 132, 137, 141–49, 151–55, 197–98, 441; II, 351–80 *passim.* Denys, *Description and natural history* (Ganong), 6–7, 26–27, 38, 57–70, 98–101, 116. *JR* (Thwaites), XXXVI, 143. Mass. Hist. Soc. *Coll.,* 3d ser., VII (1838) [XXVII of the *Coll.*], 114–18. PRO, *CSP., Col., 1574–1660,* 469–70.

J. B. Brebner, *New England's outpost: Acadia before the conquest of Canada* (New York, 1927), 30–6. Couillard Després, *Saint-Étienne de La Tour,* chaps. XXIV–XXVI, *passim.* Candide de Nant, *Pages glorieuses,* 271–74, 305–11. W. O. Raymond, "The Acadians and early history, 1604–1713," in *Canada and its provinces* (Shortt and Doughty), XIII, 48, 50.

LE BORGNE DE BELLE-ISLE, ALEXANDRE, temporary governor of Acadia, seigneur of Port-Royal; b. 1640 or 1643 at La Rochelle, son of EMMANUEL LE BORGNE and Jeanne François; d. *c.* 1693 at Port-Royal.

Emmanuel Le Borgne had advanced considerable sums of money to MENOU d'Aulnay, the former governor of Acadia, to further the latter's plans for colonization. On d'Aulnay's death in 1650, Le Borgne sought to recover his outlay. His claims and the steps that he took in consequence were to involve him in sharp quarrels which were a blot upon the history of the colony at that period. Young Alexandre thus grew up in an atmosphere of litigation between people whose roles are still appraised in varying ways by historians.

In the autumn of 1656, two years after the capitulation of Port-Royal (Annapolis Royal, N.S.) to SEDGWICK, Acadia was ceded by CHARLES DE SAINT-ÉTIENNE de La Tour to two English colonels, Thomas TEMPLE and William CROWNE. The following year Emmanuel Le Borgne was appointed governor of Acadia by the king of France, but being unable to leave Europe he sent his son Alexandre to the colony with some 50 men, to take possession of his holdings. The little force seized the fort of La Hève in May 1658 and appropriated for itself the food and pelts that Temple had stored there. Carrying on its campaign, it then unsuccessfully attacked Temple's fort, constructed at Port-La Tour. Thomas Temple, anxious to avenge the insult, hastened up from Boston and attacked Alexandre Le Borgne's improvised fort. Le Borgne was wounded during this engagement then taken to London, where he was held captive for some years. When the Treaty of Breda restored Acadia to France in 1667, Emmanuel Le Borgne recovered his former possessions. The following year he entrusted the government of the colony to his son Alexandre, who from then on took the name of Le Borgne de Belle-Isle.

On 9 Oct. 1668 Alexandre Le Borgne sailed along the Acadian shore, accompanying MORILLON Du Bourg, who was the French king's delegate for the execution of the Treaty of Breda and the representative of the Compagnie des Indes occidentales. Before continuing his journey

Le Borgne de L'Île

towards New England, the delegate officially installed Belle-Isle in command of the colony. As soon as he got to Boston, Morillon Du Bourg learned that Temple had received a further letter from Charles II, giving him strict instructions not to hand over the Acadian posts before certain islands in the West Indies had been restored by France to England in accordance with the treaty; Temple complained also about the capture of Port-Rossignol which had meanwhile been carried out by Belle-Isle. Morillon, accepting Temple's arguments, wrote Alexandre Le Borgne to warn him to return to France until the litigation concerning the islands was settled. Belle-Isle followed Du Bourg's advice, but considered that the supplying of his men had represented for him a loss of 20,000 *livres*. He came back to Acadia in 1670, with Governor ANDIGNÉ de Grandfontaine, to defend his family's Acadian interests.

Very little is known about Belle-Isle's activities in connection with Acadia between 1670 and 1693. Mention is made of him in a deed recording a grant of land in 1679. In 1690 he and Pierre MELANSON acted as interpreters in the negotiations concerning the surrender of Port-Royal to William PHIPS; the latter appointed Belle-Isle a member of the council set up on the spot to govern the conquered territory.

A number of reports from governors of Acadia allow us to infer a good deal about Belle-Isle's conduct and character. Grandfontaine had tried to limit his powers. According to PERROT, Belle-Isle was addicted to wine. When drunk he was capable of granting the same piece of land to several settlers at once, which could not but cause the farmers considerable vexation. Des Friches* de Meneval had gone so far as to put him in prison for a few days in November 1689, because of irregularities of this nature. JOSEPH ROBINAU de Villebon wrote in 1699 that former settlers had told him that Belle-Isle had withdrawn from the records all documents which might incriminate him. Finally Villebon was also convinced that Belle-Isle had not fulfilled his seigneurial duty, which was to see to the development of his lands.

Although he seems to have enjoyed until about 1686 the privileges attaching to the grant of land made to his father, Alexandre Le Borgne was threatened by the legal proceedings instituted in France in 1671 by Dame Marie de Menou d'Aulnay, the canoness of Poussay, who was endeavouring to regain possession of the lands that had been granted to her father. On the other hand, a letter from the minister to Des Friches de Meneval in 1688 reveals that the Le Borgnes were at that moment contesting their eviction from some of their properties in Acadia. When Dame Marie d'Aulnay died in 1691 the action was continued by her half-brothers and half-sisters, the children of Charles de Saint-Étienne de La Tour and Jeanne MOTIN. One of their sons in particular, Charles*, carried on the litigation energetically in France against Belle-Isle's brother, André Le Borgne Du Coudray, against the Duc de Vendôme, and against the Marquis de Chevry, who was a member of the Compagnie des Pêches sédentaires in Acadia.

Alexandre Le Borgne died about 1693 at Port-Royal. He had married Marie de Saint-Étienne de La Tour (d. 1739). They had had seven children. The descendants of this family were sorely tried at the time of the expulsion; people named Le Borgne and Belisle are to be found today in Canada and the United States.

CLÉMENT CORMIER

AN, Col., C¹¹ᴰ, 1, ff.55–60v, 126; 2–4; Col., E, 277 (dossier La Vallière). *Coll. de manuscrits relatifs à la Nouv.-France*, I, 153–54, 197, 324, 365, 386, 425–26, 439–41; II, 292–93, 351–80 *passim*. *Mémoires des commissaires*, I, 286–88; II, 305–8, 310–12 and *Memorials of the English and French commissaries*, I, 20–4 *passim*, 121, 591–96, 599–600. PAC *Report, 1912*, App. E, F. PRO, *CSP, Col., 1574–1660*, 15 [Laborne]; *1661–68*, nos. 1868, 1877, 1898.

Azarie Couillard Després, *En marge de La tragédie d'un peuple de M. Émile Lauvrière ou erreurs sur l'histoire d'Acadie* (Bruges, 1925); *Saint-Étienne de La Tour*, 446–47. John Knox, *An historical journal of the campaigns in North America for the years 1757, 1758, 1759 and 1760*, ed. A. G. Doughty (3v., Champlain Soc., VIII–X, 1914–16), I, notes by Placide Gaudet accompanying a map of Annapolis. Émile Lauvrière, *La tragédie d'un peuple: histoire du peuple acadien de ses origines à nos jours* (2v., Paris, 1922; éd. rev. 1924), I. Le Jeune, *Dictionnaire*, II, 124. Geneviève Massignon, "La seigneurie de Charles de Menou d'Aulnay, gouverneur de l'Acadie, 1635–1650," *RHAF*, XVI (1963), 474. Murdoch, *History of Nova-Scotia*, I. Rameau de Saint-Père, *Une colonie féodale*, I. Webster, *Acadia*, 123–24 (translation of a report of Robinau de Villebon to Pontchartrain, 1699).

LE BORGNE DE L'ÎLE. *See* TESSOUAT (d. 1636); TESSOUAT (d. 1654)

"LE CADET." *See* CHOMINA

LE CARON, JOSEPH, priest, Recollet, first missionary among the Hurons; b. *c.* 1586 somewhere near Paris; d. in 1632 near Gisors.

Father Le Caron entered the priesthood and was chosen as chaplain and tutor to the Duc d'Orléans. When the latter died, Le Caron joined the Recollets and made his profession in the order in 1611. Four years later CHAMPLAIN brought four Recollets to New France; Father Le Caron was among them, as well as Father JAMET, who became their first superior. Father Caron left Honfleur 24 April 1615, landed at Tadoussac on 25 May, and a few days later was on his way with the traders in pelts towards the Saint-Louis rapids, in order to meet the Hurons there and to try to follow them into their own country. Sure of carrying out his plan, he went down to Quebec again to equip himself with the objects necessary for worship, and around 23 June he was once more at the Rivière des Prairies. The next day mass "was sung most devoutly by Fathers Denis and Joseph on the bank of the said river." He then exposed to Champlain his plan of going to live among the Attignaouantans (Bear nation of the Hurons) "to learn their language . . . and to proclaim God's name to these natives." After a trip that has been described for us by LE CLERCQ, Father Le Caron took up residence at Carhagouha. On 12 August, in the presence of Champlain and of the Frenchmen who were with him, he celebrated the first mass in the Huron country. In January 1616 Champlain, having returned from his military expedition, joined Father Le Caron again and visited with him the nation of the Petuns, as well as seven other villages allied to them; the natives received them with the most cordial hospitality, and the French struck up a friendship with them. Leaving this region on 20 May, Father Le Caron reached Quebec on 11 July after stopping at the Saint-Louis rapids and at Trois-Rivières. The mission in the Huron country was established.

On 20 July 1616 Champlain, together with Fathers Jamet and Le Caron, started back for France. They were going to lodge a complaint with the heads of the Compagnie des Marchands de Rouen et de Saint-Malo about the behaviour of its agents, who were hindering the spread of the gospel. This task completed, Father Le Caron sailed again on 11 April 1617; he was returning to Quebec with the title of provincial commissioner. He stayed there for one year, replacing the Recollet Jean DOLBEAU who went to France, and during that time he blessed the marriage of LOUIS HÉBERT's eldest daughter Anne to Étienne Jonquet. On Father Dolbeau's return the following year, Father Le Caron went to the Montagnais at Tadoussac; he stayed with them until 1619, acting in the double capacity of missionary and schoolmaster, as he stated himself: "I have taught the alphabet to some who are beginning to read and write fairly well. . . . In this way I have been busy running a free school in our house at Tadoussac." In 1624 he would be able to write, referring to the seminary that the Recollets had opened at Quebec in 1620: "Our seminary would be of great assistance if we had the means to provide for everything, but given the poverty of the country, we can support only a small number of Indians."

He returned to Quebec, where on 18 Aug. 1621 he signed a petition addressed to King Louis XIII, pleading the cause of New France, then went back to the Montagnais at Tadoussac; the following May he returned to Quebec again to take part in the spiritual exercises of the retreat at the convent of Notre-Dame-des-Anges. In 1623, after a second stay among the Montagnais, he welcomed some new recruits at Quebec and planned to go to the Huron country with Father Nicolas VIEL and Brother Gabriel SAGARD. He and his companions took up their abode in the village of Carhagouha. His stay was marked by an incident which would have cost him his life had it not been for a powerful Huron chief who defended him. Back in Quebec in June 1624, Father Le Caron passed on to Brother Sagard, who was preparing to go to France, a relation written in his own hand, large extracts of which have been preserved for us by Le Clercq. This relation is a detailed study of the Indians of New France, of their customs and of the obstacles in the way of their conversion. The introduction reveals the existence of a second memoir, the manuscript of which is now lost.

Having gone back to France at the end of August 1625, Father Le Caron was appointed by the missionaries to make a supreme effort against the Compagnie de Montmorency, which was paralysing the development of the Church. To this end he drew up and had printed two documents intended to enlighten the king's council; the first, 15 pages long, was entitled: *Plainte de la Nouvelle France dicte Canada, à la France, sa Germaine*; the second, with the title *Avis au Roi sur la Nouvelle-France*, comprised 23 pages. These two manuscripts, preserved in the Bibliothèque nationale in Paris, constitute a violent indictment of the Compagnie des Marchands and its director. On this same trip Le Caron had brought his dictionary of the Huron language and two others, of the Algonkin and Montagnais languages, which were presented to the king by LE BAILLIF. None are extant today.

Having completed his assignment, Father Le Caron once more returned to Quebec, where he again concerned himself with spreading the gospel. The capitulation of 1629, by making New France an English possession, also put an end to his missionary activity in this country; on 9 September Father Le Caron and his fellow-Recollets returned to France, where they landed on 29 October.

Le Clercq

Father Le Caron was named superior of the convent of Sainte-Marguerite, near Gisors, and died there of the plague on 29 March 1632, aged 46; that very day was signed the Treaty of Saint-Germain-en-Laye restoring Canada to France.

Of the Recollets who came to New France, Father Le Caron was one of the most outstanding, both because of his culture and of his apostolic zeal. He had contributed effectively to the establishment of the Church in Canada and had founded the first mission in the Huron country.

FRÉDÉRIC GINGRAS

ASQ, MSS, 200, Mortuologe des Recolets. BN, Imprimés, LK[12], 733, [Joseph Le Caron], Au Roi sur la Nouvelle-France (1626). This is the only memoir which could have been written by Caron (see Trudel, *Histoire de la Nouvelle-France*, II). The "Plainte de la Nouvelle France dicte Canada, à la France, sa Germaine . . ." may have been written by Father Le Baillif at the end of 1621 or at the beginning of 1622 [see bibliography of Georges LE BAILLIF]. Champlain, *Œuvres* (Laverdière), 495, 497f., 501f., 504, 506f., 517, 1040f., 1050. Le Clercq, *First establishment of the faith* (Shea), I, 31, et passim; II, 45. Sixte Le Tac, *Histoire chronologique de la Nouvelle-France ou Canada depuis sa découverte (mil cinq cents quatre) jusques en l'an mil six cents trente deux*, éd Eugène Réveillaud (Paris, 1888). "Mémoire faict en 1637 pour l'affaire des Pères Recollectz . . . ," *Découvertes et établissements des Français* (Margry), I, 3–18. Sagard, *Le grand voyage* (Tross), passim; *Histoire du Canada* (Tross), I–IV, passim. *The Catholic encyclopedia, an international work of reference . . . of the Catholic church*, ed. C. G. Herbermann et al. (17v., New York, 1907–22), VI, 301. Jouve, *Les Franciscains et le Canada (1615–1629)*.

LE CLERCQ, CHRESTIEN, priest, Recollet, missionary to the Micmacs of the Gaspé Peninsula, historiographer; b. 1641, probably at Bapaume (Pas-de-Calais, France); was still living, in France, 1700 (Hennepin*).

In 1668 he joined the Recollets of Saint-Antoine-de-Padoue, in Artois, and was the first novice and first professed of the order in that province, as he tells us himself. He received the name Chrestien upon taking the habit. Two members of his family belonged to the same order and followed him to New France: Father Zénobe MEMBRÉ, his cousin, and Father Maxime Le Clercq, who was either his brother or his cousin. Both of them, missionaries and companions of CAVELIER de La Salle in the Mississippi country, were massacred in 1689 at Fort Saint-Louis-des-Illinois by the Indians of that region.

At Béthune Father Le Clercq had as novice master Father Gabriel de LA RIBOURDE, who in the spring of 1670 sailed for Quebec to establish the Recollets again in New France. This order had been the first community of permanent missionaries in this country, where they had carried on their work from 1615 to 1629. It was a reformed branch of the order of St. Francis which had developed in Spain, and then in France from 1592 on. The religious wore a grey habit with a white cord.

We possess absolutely no details about Father Le Clercq's activities in the years 1670–5; perhaps during this time he was pursuing his studies in preparation for the priesthood, which he must have received shortly before his departure for Canada.

On 15 March 1675 Father Le Clercq was appointed to the missions in Canada. Before sailing he made a brief visit to his village, Bapaume, where he won a recruit for the Recollet noviciate, Emmanuel Jumeau*, who seven years later became his companion in the missionary work in the Gaspé Peninsula. Father Le Clercq sailed from La Rochelle in the month of June in company with Fathers Louis Hennepin, Luc Buisset, and Zénobe Membré; on the same ship had also embarked Bishop Laval*, the newly appointed titular bishop of Quebec, Robert Cavelier de La Salle, and Intendant DUCHESNEAU. The group landed at Quebec two months later. In the middle of October Father Le Clercq left for the missions in Gaspé; he reached Percé on 27 October, after meeting with a violent gale in the Gulf of St. Lawrence. The post at Percé, which served as a shelter for French fishermen, had been ministered to since 1672 by Fathers Hilarion Guénin* and Exupère DETHUNES. Le Clercq seems to have been the first missionary of this group to be assigned specifically to the missions to the Micmacs, whom he called *Gaspésiens*. Indeed, if the two previous Recollets had carried on a ministry among these Indians, they would have recommended to him "the study of the prayers in the language of Gaspé" instead of writings in the Algonkin language which the Indians scarcely understood.

Le Clercq quickly learned the dialect of the inhabitants of Gaspé and was able to teach them religion thanks to a system of figurative letters that he invented. This hieroglyphic writing subsequently remained in use and served as the basis for the present-day writing. The Recollet also composed a dictionary for the future apostles to these peoples.

In the spring of 1676 he visited the Gaspé Indians; he spent the summer with the Micmacs of Restigouche, and in September he went to

Nipisiguit (Bathurst, N.B.). In January 1677 he visited Miramichi (near present-day Chatham); travelling with a Frenchman and two Indians, he became lost and was almost dead of cold and hunger when an Indian, who happened to be passing, helped him. The Micmacs of this area brought great and pleasant consolation to the missionary because of their habit of carrying the cross "next to the skin and on their clothes." This custom, which was rather paradoxical in a tribe that had not yet been deeply affected by Christianity, furnished the Recollet with the theme of a long treatise on the origin, the extent, and the import of this practice among these Indians; in token of this, he gave them the name of *Porte-Croix* (Cross-Bearers).

During the summer of 1678 Father Le Clercq went to Quebec in order to renew his spiritual strength and to visit his superior. During the following winter he was beset by discouragement brought on by the paltry results of his zeal among the Indians. He thought of giving up his post; in the months of April and May 1679 he wrote to his superior, Father Valentin Leroux, to reveal to him his difficulties. Leroux sent him a long letter in which he requested him not to give up his work; and in fact the missionary remained a further eight years with the Micmacs. He did however take advantage of the permission that his superior accorded him to come to spend the winter at Quebec. On 30 Oct. 1679, on the Beaupré shore, he solemnized the marriage of Catherine Pelletier, sister of Brother Didace PELLETIER, a Recollet; then on 2 Feb. 1680 he officiated at a baptism at the Côte Saint-Ange (Cap-Rouge), where he drew up the certificate that remains the only autograph of his that we possess.

Before returning to Percé, Le Clercq was sent to France with Father Dethunes to obtain the authorizations necessary for the founding of a hospice at Quebec and a house at Montreal. Immediately upon his arrival he sent the documents concerning his request to Father ALLART, the provincial of Paris, and went to visit his relatives at Bapaume. After a rest he sailed from La Rochelle in the summer of 1681 with Father François Masson and reached Quebec 30 days later. Then he accompanied Governor BUADE de Frontenac to Montreal as his chaplain. There he received from M. Dollier* de Casson, superior of the Sulpicians, a grant of four acres of land near the river, as the contract signed on 26 Oct. 1681 proves. On his return to Quebec, Le Clercq does not seem to have continued on to the missions at Percé immediately. He would even seem to have spent the winter in Quebec, since he officiated at a baptism on 23 Jan. 1682 on the Île d'Orléans, as is indicated by the parish records of Saint-Laurent.

After this date Father Le Clercq's comings and goings are almost completely unknown to us; he tells us that he returned to his Indians of Gaspé, where he was received "with all the warm welcome that they were capable of." We find him back at Quebec on 7 Oct. and 5 Nov. 1684.

He must have remained at Percé during the summer of 1685. On 2 December of that year he was at Sorel, where he spent the winter as a replacement for the parish priest. The consecration of the church at Percé, which he presided over himself, must have taken place during the summer of 1686. Then he said good-bye to the Micmacs and returned to France. In February 1687 he called upon Bishop Saint-Vallier [La Croix*], who was making a short stay in Paris. In 1690 he was superior of the convent at Lens (Pas-de-Calais). At the request of the mayor and the aldermen he preached the Advent sermons in 1697 at Saint-Pol. According to Father Hennepin, he was definitor of the province of Artois in 1698, and then we last hear of him as superior of the Recollets in Saint-Omer in 1700.

Father Le Clercq owes his place in history principally to the two precious volumes he published to recount his apostolate and that of the Recollets in Canada.

The *Nouvelle Relation de la Gaspésie* was published in Paris in 1691 and in Lyon the following year, this time without the author's name. The Recollets had from 1615 on acquired the habit of sending relations or yearly letters to their superior, and their relatives and friends; the *Relations des Jésuites* came later.

The *Nouvelle Relation* is devoted entirely to the Micmacs, among whom the author carried on his apostolate for 12 years. The book begins with a description of the Gaspé Peninsula (Father Le Clercq was the first to use the name "Gaspésie"). The following chapters study in logical order everything concerning the inhabitants of Gaspé— their origins, birth, dress and ornaments, dwellings, food, language, religion, beliefs and superstitions, government, laws, marriage, war, hunting, feasts and dances, maladies and death. The author mentions in passing his apostolic labours and those of the Recollets who lived in this region. Although it is of local interest, this information is very important. Le Clercq recounts facts as he observed them, and since he knew the language and was held in great esteem by the Indians, his report takes on the value of authentic evidence. He informs us himself in his book that in his story he intended simply to write of things as he knew them. Some inaccuracies however

Le Clercq

found their way into it, and his personal chronology, particularly from 1679 on, is rather confused; as for the worship offered to the cross by the Indians of the Miramichi region, modern historians, without denying the fact, have tended to recognize in this cross the stylized figure of the tribal totem, which was originally a bird with outspread wings.

Certain authors have minimized the value or the usefulness of this document. Father Charlevoix*, a Jesuit, declared loftily that "there is not enough of interest in it to fill a volume of 600 pages." Séraphin Marion is more caustic: he said that the chapter concerning child-birth among the Indians of Gaspé is filled "with mediocre details about the life and the everyday customs of the tribe." On the other hand Ganong, who translated and analysed Father Le Clercq's work, maintains that the *Nouvelle Relation* constitutes one of the finest pages on the native population of Canada, and in speaking of Chapter v he made this pertinent remark: "Nowhere does our literature offer a finer picture of the family life of the Indians."

Father Le Clercq's other work, entitled *Premier établissement de la foy dans la Nouvelle-France*, which was published in 1691, was reprinted the same year under the title *Établissement de la Foy*. In 1692 a second edition, entitled *Histoire des colonies francaises*, was published in Lyon.

The author divided his work into three parts: the first runs from 1615 to 1629 and tells of the first planting of the faith in New France by the Recollets; the second, for the period from 1632 to 1663, mentions the efforts by these religious to return to their former missions; the third, extending from 1663 to 1691, speaks of the Recollets' return to this country, La Salle's discoveries, and Frontenac's victories over the Indians and the English.

In this book, unlike the *Nouvelle Relation*, the author plays the part of a historian rather than a witness; he was not a witness of the events except for a brief episode in the third part of the work. He had necessarily to accumulate material and to have recourse to written and oral sources. His testimony will be worth what the documents he consulted are worth. But Father Le Clercq warns us that he has founded his account only upon the truth: "As truth is the soul and the very essence of history, this account does not need to seek support and authority elsewhere." No one has seriously doubted Le Clercq's good faith; impartial critics are of Ganong's opinion: "Without doubt this author always intended, to my way of thinking, to tell the exact truth." Nevertheless, with the aid of present-day documents, one cannot help pointing out here and there some more or less important errors: Le Clercq gives 1635 as the year of the founding of Trois-Rivières, and 1636 for that of Montreal; he changes Father Nicolas VIEL's French companion at Rivière des Prairies into a Huron; he is in error about Father Leroux's successor and the end of his term at Quebec. But on the whole these are not serious. The major error with which Father Le Clercq has been charged is that he criticized the *Relations des Jésuites* and suspected these fathers of having thwarted the Recollets' return to New France after 1632. To what extent was he right? The question is not easily settled. What is certain is that Le Clercq took too literally certain affirmations in the *Relations*, and he hastened to put things in their true light with statements such as the following: "Would to God that all these churches described in the *Relations* were as real as the country knows them to be imaginary." We know today that the *Relations*, which had been composed largely for propaganda, betray here and there pious exaggerations.

Is the *Premier établissement* indeed Father Le Clercq's work? Certain persons have denied his authorship. Father Hennepin, a contemporary of the author, attributed this book to Fathers Valentin Leroux and Zénobe Membré. Shea maintains that several persons had a hand in the work. Ganong admits that certain parts of the volume are not by Le Clercq. Guy Frégault, in *Iberville, le conquérant*, speaks of a "pseudo-Leclercq." None of these affirmations is based upon any decisive proof. On the contrary, it is obvious on reading the text that the *Premier établissement* is certainly the work of a Recollet; and for anyone who has read the book attentively, this Recollet can be no other than Father Le Clercq. On the title-page he presents himself as the sole author, and throughout the account brief but precise personal references oblige us to attribute this work to him.

The *Nouvelle relation* and the *Premier établissement* remain valuable sources of information about the history of Canada. Father Le Clercq's writings emerge as a work of great value from the literary, social, religious, and historical point of view. The language is lively, harmonious, and correct, in keeping with the canons of the 17th century, and the ideas are clear and well organized. For studying the Micmacs of the Gaspé Peninsula the *Nouvelle Relation* provides valuable and original documentation; for the history of the Recollets and of Catholicism in North America, the *Premier établissement* continues to be a reliable and sincere guide. Consequently Father Chrestien Le Clercq ranks among the great historiographers of New France, and as such he merits our profound admiration.

G.-M. Dumas

Recensement de 1681. [Jean Cavelier], *The Journal of Jean Cavelier. The account of a survivor of La Salle's Texas expedition, 1684–1688*, translated and annotated by Jean Delanglez (Chicago, 1938), 9. Charlevoix, *Histoire*. Le Clercq, *First Establishment of the faith* (Shea); *New relation of Gaspesia with the customs and religion of the Gaspesian Indians*, tr. and ed. W. F. Ganong (Champlain Soc., V, 1910); *Premier établissement de la Foy*. Frégault, *Iberville*. Archange Godbout, "Leclercq," dans *Centenaire de l'histoire du Canada de F.-X. Garneau* (Montréal, 1945), 269–90. Séraphin Marion, *Relations des voyageurs français en Nouvelle-France au XVIIᵉ siècle* (Paris, 1923), 53–57. H. A. Scott, *Nos anciens historiographes et autres études d'histoire canadienne* (Lévis, 1930). Marc de Villiers du Terrage, *L'expédition de Cavelier de la Salle dans le golfe du Mexique, 1684–1687* (Paris, 1931), 196f.

LE COQ (Le Cocq), ROBERT, supervisor of buildings at Sainte-Marie-des-Hurons; d. 20 Aug. 1650 near Trois-Rivières.

We do not know from what part of France he originated. His biographer Father Paul Desjardins has identified him, not unconvincingly, with the carpenter Le Coq, an employee of Émery de Caën at the time when the latter had come to grief while reconnoitring near Quebec in July 1629. Robert Le Coq accompanied the missionaries as soon as they returned among the Hurons in 1634, in the capacity of a *donné*, bound by vows and contract to serve them. Being responsible for supplying the mission with food, he travelled annually to Quebec, from 1635 to 1640. In 1639 a terrible illness nearly cost him his life. During the time that he was entrusted with the supervision of the buildings and equipment at the residence of Sainte-Marie-des-Hurons he made his last trip to Quebec, in 1649, to relieve the mission, which was in desperate straits. He was able to start back only in 1650, but he did not complete the journey, for at the beginning of July he met the Hurons and their missionaries who were coming down to Quebec. A month and a half later he took part in an expedition against the Iroquois, in which he met his death.

Lucien Campeau

ACSM, Paul Desjardins, "Auxiliaires laïques des missions de la Nouvelle-France: le donné Robert Le Coq." Champlain, *Œuvres* (Laverdière), 1246–47. *JR* (Thwaites).

LE COQ DE LA SAUSSAYE, RENÉ, agent and lieutenant of Antoinette de Pons, Marquise de Guercheville, in Acadia; normally resided at Gaillon-sur-Seine (Eure); d. some time after 1613.

René Le Coq appears in history as the agent of the Marquise de Guercheville, who was associated with Jean de Biencourt de Poutrincourt for the purpose of trading in New France. Poutrincourt's *Factum* systematically ascribes to the Jesuits all the misfortunes which befell this gentleman, since Poutrincourt himself did not dare to attack the noble lady. We have no space here to discuss the errors of the *Factum*; we shall merely outline what happened. On 17 Aug. 1612 La Saussaye undertook, by a notarial contract, to charter and rig a vessel at Havre-de-Grâce (Le Havre) to assist Port-Royal (Annapolis Royal, N.S.), Poutrincourt paying 750 *livres* in silver and Mme de Guercheville being required to provide the same amount. The seigneur of Port-Royal had borrowed this money from a Rouen merchant against a bond due in two months. On the arrival of Brother Du Thet in France at the beginning of October 1612, the marquise broke off her association with Poutrincourt, who attempted to take proceedings against La Saussaye in order to recover the money or the goods purchased. But as Poutrincourt himself had to pay his bond on 17 October, he was prosecuted in his turn by the Rouen merchant, cast into prison, then sentenced to discharge his debt before receiving the goods, which he does seem to have obtained eventually.

The Marquise de Guercheville appointed La Saussaye as her lieutenant for the founding of a new colony in Acadia. He left Honfleur on 12 March 1613 and landed on 16 May at La Hève, where he took possession of all the American coast, except Port-Royal, in the name of the marquise. He then withdrew Fathers Biard and Massé from Port-Royal and followed the coastline to Frenchmans Bay, in Maine. The obstinacy of the crew obliged him to stop at this spot, which they named Saint-Sauveur. Instead of pushing on with building La Saussaye started to till the soil, despite the protests of the more important people, and particularly of his lieutenant Nicolas de La Mothe, whom we shall meet again at Quebec in 1618–19.

On 29 June 1613 they received warning that an English vessel, in fighting order, was fishing off the mouth of the Penobscot, but La Saussaye was not disturbed by the news. On 2 July the English appeared in the bay; the French ship, loaded, was still at anchor in the roads. Capt. Fleury, with Brother Du Thet and a handful of men, clambered aboard to defend it. But La Saussaye had kept the majority of the defenders on shore; Argall, the English commander, seized the French ship and then landed, while La Saussaye

"L'Écossais"

took refuge in the woods with his party. The English looted the camp and pilfered from a chest the commander's official papers. When La Saussaye reappeared he could offer no good reason for his presence there, and Argall pretended to consider him a pirate. He did, however, agree to let the 30 Frenchmen have a longboat, so that they could make for the Acadian peninsula and seek a fishing vessel. La Saussaye accepted, but Father Biard intervened, and pointed out that such an arrangement was tantamount to exposing them to certain shipwreck. So the French divided up into two groups and La Saussaye set out in the longboat with Father Massé and 13 others. He reached France during the month of October 1613, and there is no further trace of him. But it is evident enough from this account that La Saussaye did not belong to the race that founds colonies.

LUCIEN CAMPEAU

[For other accounts of the events of 1612 and 1613 see JEAN DE BIENCOURT and Samuel ARGALL.]

AN, Minutier, VI, 413, contrat entre Jean de Biencourt et René Le Coq, 17 août 1612. BN, MS, NAF 9283 (Margry), 4–5, copie du rapport de Charles Fleury, Rouen, 27 août 1614. PRO, *CSP, Col.*, 1574–1660, 15. *Factum* (1614), 38–42. *JR* (Thwaites), I–IV. Lescarbot, *History* (Grant), III, *passim*. *Mémoires des commissaires*, I, 37, 141; and *Memorials of the English and French commissaries*, I, 111, 197. Purchas, *Pilgrimes* (1905–7), XIX. Huguet, *Poutrincourt*.

"L'ÉCOSSAIS." See MARTIN, ABRAHAM

LE CREUX DU BREUIL, NICOLAS, lieutenant at Canseau and Port-Royal (Annapolis Royal, N.S.), collaborator of RAZILLY and MENOU d'Aulnay, a native of Belle-Isle-en-Mer (France); d. some time after 1652.

He had married Anne Motin, daughter of Louis Motin, a member of the Compagnie Razilly-Condonnier; consequently he probably arrived in Acadia with Commander Isaac de Razilly as early as 1632. Le Creux was in command of Fort Saint-François at Canseau and was working at fortifying it when, on 31 July 1635, he had to repulse Indians who had been stirred up by Jean THOMAS, the captain of a fishing boat. Le Creux, who had received two sword wounds, had a report drawn up and immediately informed Commander Razilly. The latter sent Capt. MAROT to seize Thomas's ship. An inquiry was held before the provost of La Hève, and Thomas, who was accused of smuggling and sedition, was arraigned by Le Creux himself before the Admiralty at La Rochelle. The following year, on board the *Saint-Jean*, he brought to Acadia a contingent of 12 settlers (6 of them farm-labourers) who had been recruited at Dijon. At the same time he brought his wife and part of his family, including Jeanne MOTIN, his sister-in-law, who was to become the wife of Governor Charles de Menou, Sieur d'Aulnay. Le Creux made several more voyages to France to carry shipments of pelts and to bring back supplies for the colony. In 1642 he went halves with d'Aulnay to buy a ship of 180 tons, the *Georges*. Despite his links with Acadia, he seems to have left it for good some years before 1650. He was still living in 1652 and resided at Saint-Eusèbe-sur-Bois in Burgundy.

RENÉ BAUDRY

ACM, B.5654–55. Couillard Després, *Saint-Étienne de La Tour*. Archange Godbout, "Le rôle du Saint-Jehan et les origines acadiennes," SGCF *Mémoires*, I (1944), 19–30.

"LE CROCHET." See KIOTSEAETON

LE FEBVRE DE LA BARRE, JOSEPH-ANTOINE, governor-general of New France (1682–85), counsellor in the Parlement of Paris in 1645, *maître des requêtes c.* 1650, intendant of Paris during the Fronde, then intendant of Bourbonnais, Auvergne, and Dauphiné, ship's captain, governor and lieutenant-general of Guiana *c.* 1666; b. 1622 in France, son of Antoine Le Febvre de La Barre, a counsellor in the Parlement of Paris and *prévôt des marchands*, and of Madeleine Belin; d. 1688 in Paris.

In 1659, when La Barre was serving in Dauphiné, Colbert complained of his administration and wrote to Cardinal Mazarin that M. de La Barre was hated by the people, to which the minister replied that "M. de La Barre should be taken at his word if it is true that he has asked to be relieved."

This was done, for he left the service of the government. From 1661 on, we find this civilian in the royal navy, where he was a ship's captain, which suggests that he had powerful protectors. However, he proved himself to be a good sailor and an excellent administrator. In 1664 he was sent to Guiana at the head of a squadron—together with PROUVILLE de Tracy, who had just been appointed lieutenant-general of the whole of French America in November 1663—and recaptured Cayenne from the Dutch; the latter capitulated and handed over Fort Nassau to La Barre in May 1664. La Barre, appointed governor of Guiana, made of it a colony which promised to become flourishing, experimented with different types of cultivation, and drew up plans for the fortifications of Cayenne.

Le Febvre de La Barre

When all the islands possessed by France in America had been ceded to the Compagnie des Indes occidentales, Colbert de Terron, one of the directors, wrote to the minister, Colbert: "M. de La Barre did not seem to me very suitable as a commander," and La Barre was recalled, although this last letter was apparently not the reason for it.

Despite the enmity of the Colberts, La Barre was made lieutenant-general in 1666 and sent to the West Indies. In November 1666 he suggested the conquest of Nevis (Niévès) to the war council, which did not agree to it. In April 1667, while commanding the ship *Armes d'Angleterre*, he did battle with the English ship *Colchester*, off the tip of Nevis Island. La Barre emerged victorious from a terrible struggle during which he was wounded, and he returned to Martinique, where he was handed an indent for supplies from the govenor of Île Saint-Christophe (St. Kitts) which was being blockaded by the English. As France was then an ally of Holland, La Barre and Clodoré, the governor of Martinique, supported by Admiral Abraham Crynssen's fleet, joined battle with William Willoughby, governor of Barbados and the Caribbean Islands, on 20 May. After a savage combat La Barre disengaged and sailed towards Saint-Christophe. He was accused by Clodoré of having changed the battle order and shown lack of courage, and by Crynssen, in his report, of having taken to flight. M. de La Barre, said the same document, "made many excuses . . . to the effect that his vessel did not sail well" (May 1667). Back in Martinique, La Barre and Clodoré wasted time arguing, until the English admiral Sir John Harman reconciled them by attacking them. The English ships bombarded the French ships in the roadstead of Saint-Pierre. La Barre, who seems to have lost his head, gave orders for his ships to be scuttled. The Treaty of Breda, July 1667, rendered Sir John Harman's victory pointless by stipulating the return of colonies on both sides.

In 1671, in Paris, Le Febvre de La Barre published a *Relation de ce qui s'est passé dans les îles de l'Amérique en 1666–1667*. It was, in the words of Father Labat, "rather a Factum against M. de Closdoré, the governor of Martinique, than an exact and sincere account of what occurred there."

When a dispute broke out between two captains concerning a manoeuvre, a jury was assembled to consider the "Point of honour." The proceedings were signed by eight officers, including Le Febvre de La Barre: his name was among those of the best sailors in the royal navy.

In 1673 La Barre was commanding one of the ships in the squadron of Admiral d'Estrées: as France and England had united against Holland by the Treaty of Dover in 1670, the English and French vessels fought side by side against de Ruyter's fleet. Le Febvre de La Barre served with distinction, particularly at the battle of Schooneveldt, where he was in command of the *Sage*. The allies defeated the Dutch there, 7 June 1673, and La Barre was cited, by the French ambassador in London, among the officers who had conducted themselves very well during this combat. The defeat of the Dutch at Schooneveldt forced them to withdraw. In 1674, he commanded the *Maure* in the Chevalier de Valbelle's fleet in the Mediterranean.

On 1 May 1682, King Louis XIV appointed Le Febvre de La Barre governor-general of New France. He was then 60 years old and had had a long career in the navy. In Canada he succeeded a man of fine character, who was difficult to replace: the Comte de Frontenac [*see* BUADE]. The period was a tragic one, for the Iroquois, who had conquered the other tribes, were becoming a menace for the French. There was also the English threat in Hudson Bay. And when the new governor and Intendant Demeulle* landed at Quebec, at the end of September 1682, they found half the town destroyed by the great fire of August 1682. Despite these unpropitious circumstances, M. de La Barre wrote highly confident letters to the king and the minister, assuring them that he would be able to overcome the Iroquois, who must, he said, be familar with his victories over the English in the West Indies. He also declared to the minister, Colbert de Seignelay, that he would not follow the example of his predecessors, who had made their fortunes in Canada through trade.

La Barre's first official act, 10 Oct. 1682, was to convene an assembly of the religious and lay notables of the colony, to discuss the best policy to adopt in the face of the Iroquois peril. Both missionaries and soldiers were of the opinion that the Iroquois wanted to destroy the Indians allied with the French, and then to fall upon the Canadian settlers. Father Jean de Lamberville* had written to Frontenac a month earlier: "the Iroquois . . . have no fear of them [the French], and are ready to attack Canada, as soon as they are given any reason for doing so."

As a result of repeated pressure by Intendant Demeulle and La Barre, Louis XIV finally sent 200 soldiers and 20,000 *livres* the following year. But the king advised La Barre to settle the conflict with the Indians by diplomatic means, and to make the decision to attack them only if he were morally certain that he could conquer them quickly.

443

Le Febvre de La Barre

The governor concerned himself with internal administration, and had a list of land grants prepared which he sent to the minister by the courier of 1682. He supported the clergy in its attempts to remain independent of the civil authority, and in 1684 increased the salaries of the parish priests. This last measure was censured in a letter from the minister. In the same year, La Barre set up the Compagnie du Nord, which entered into competition with the English posts in Hudson Bay.

Notwithstanding his apparent determination to wage war on the Iroquois, the governor's main activity was to organize his own trade with them. He pretended to believe in the trustworthiness of the Iroquois, who had promised, at CHARLES LE MOYNE de Longueuil's request, to send delegates to Montreal. But in the month of May 1683 the Iroquois began attacking the allies of the French. La Barre tried naively to negotiate an understanding with the governor of New York, Col. Thomas Dongan, who was trading with the Indians and selling them goods cheaper than those of the French. The king of England had instructed Dongan to come to an agreement with La Barre, but the New York governor continued to support the Iroquois and arouse them against the French. Le Moyne managed, however, to take 13 Senecas to La Barre in Montreal on 20 July 1683. This embassy was a prelude to the one on 14 Aug. 1683 composed of 43 Iroquois chiefs, who according to La Barre demanded the expulsion of CAVELIER de La Salle from the Fort Saint-Louis, and promised to forward the governor's requests to their nations. The governor wanted, in particular, to see the Iroquois make peace with the Hurons, Algonkins, and Ottawas. The delegates left Montreal satisfied, promising to send their braves the following spring to ratify the agreement. However, though the Senecas replied frankly enough to the proposals that were made to them, the rest of the Indians, according to La Barre, desired only to play for time. He knew, he said, that they had increased their fighting strength by 150 men, and that they were continually weakening the Miami and Illinois Indians. His conclusion was that the Senecas did not want to embark on a war lightly, but that they were quite resolved to fight.

In the spring of 1683, Governor La Barre instructed two officers, Olivier Morel* de La Durantaye and Henri de Baugy*, to go to the region around the Great Lakes and to the Illinois country, in order to check the abusive practices of the *coureurs de bois*; the latter were trafficking in furs without licences. In the course of their inquiries into La Salle's activities in these parts, the officers were also to invite the Indians to come and trade their furs at Montreal and meet the new governor. Fort Frontenac (Cataracoui), which belonged to La Salle, was detrimental to the business of the Montreal merchants, for it intercepted the fur trade with the Indians. La Barre made an economic alliance with the merchants Aubert* de La Chesnaye and Le Ber*, an agreement directed mainly against La Salle. In his letters to the minister, Intendant Demeulle accused the governor of selling a great number of fur-trading licences and even of having commercial dealings with the English and the Dutch. La Barre wrote in his own defence: "I should be a very wretched man, if I were capable of doing things such as I am accused of."

Frontenac's successor wanted above all to get rid of La Salle, and he devoted all his efforts to making the latter's position untenable and driving him out of all the posts that he had founded. The governor undertook a veritable smear campaign against the discoverer, writing to the minister that his explorations were mere fabrications. La Salle seems to have been still unaware, in the spring of 1683, of the governor's machinations, for he wrote two letters to him, on 2 April and 4 June, to ask for his protection. Nevertheless, at this period, La Barre sent Aubert and Le Ber to take possession of Fort Frontenac and all La Salle's merchandise. The pretext for this seizure was that La Salle had not complied with the conditions in return for which he had received the ownership of the fort.

At the end of the summer, the Chevalier de Baugy, on La Barre's orders, took possession of the Fort Saint-Louis on the Illinois River, where Henri de Tonty* was in command in the name of La Salle, who had constructed this fur-trading post. On 21 March 1684, the Iroquois attacked Fort Saint-Louis, where they were repulsed by Tonty and Baugy.

The Iroquois' assault against Fort Saint-Louis was perhaps, as certain historians have asserted, what induced M. de La Barre to go and attack them in their own territory. But the governor's real motive, according to his contemporaries, was rather to save the trade in beaver pelts carried on by five or six merchants, as Intendant Demeulle wrote to the minister on 8 July 1684. For Demeulle stated openly that the war against the Iroquois in 1684 had been decided upon by Governor La Barre and six of the most important businessmen in the colony, with the hope that they would oblige the Indians to trade with them and no longer with the English. The intendant claimed that the fur-trader Aubert de La Chesnaye was the closest adviser of the governor, who had not

Le Febvre de La Barre

even consulted the military. Everyone said that this expedition was only a business affair, and that La Barre would conclude peace after having frightened the Iroquois, in order to trade with them: such was the tenor of the intendant's letters to Versailles.

The department of the Marine, under whose jurisdiction Canada came, first approved M. de La Barre's action against the Iroquois, for on 30 July 1684 the king wrote to the governor that he endorsed "his decision to attack the Iroquois because of their action against the Fort Saint-Louis"—which did not prevent the king from blaming La Barre a year later. The latter had moreover a very personal grievance against these Indians. Out of hatred for La Salle, whom he wanted to ruin completely, and with the aim of sparing La Chesnaye any commercial competition, the governor had been unwise enough to authorize the Iroquois to attack and pillage any canoe the owner of which could not show a fur-trading licence signed by him. Now the Iroquois, fortified by this official permission, set about attacking all canoes indiscriminately, even those carrying goods belonging to M. de La Barre. This, according to Abbé Vachon* de Belmont, sent him into a towering rage.

The Jesuits recommended a policy of prudence. The Fathers, who had missions in the region around the Great Lakes, knew from experience how to deal with Indians. Fathers DABLON and FRÉMIN had already given advice to Intendant DUCHESNEAU. Father Thierry Beschefer* had drafted a lengthy report on the subject. The Jesuits, and especially Father Jean de Lamberville, who maintained a regular correspondence with La Barre from July to October 1684, said that it was essential not to provoke the Iroquois, or to meddle in their war with the Illinois. Their advice was to call the chiefs together in a conference, but not to scare them by too great a display of military strength, which would offer a pretext for war. For their part, according to Rochemonteix, the notables and ecclesiastics of Quebec who had been present at the assembly of 10 Oct. 1682 "were not opposed to the war, but they did not want to undertake it before having secured fresh troops from France and exhausted all the resources of diplomacy in the effort to maintain peace."

M. de La Barre disregarded these opinions. He had only militiamen and a few companies of regular troops at his disposal. Brimming over with presumptuousness, he thought he was certain to succeed. In a letter to the minister, the governor declared: "I shall go into the Iroquois country with 1,200 settlers and spend the winter there, in order to entice all the Indians to come and attack us in the spring of 1684, when they will be destroyed. They number 2,600 braves, but our young men are hardened and accustomed to the woods, beside the fact that we shall make war better than they, and that a few cannon will give us a great advantage." This confidence was to be belied by the events. The governor set out from Montreal on 30 July 1684, with a small army of 700 Canadians, 150 regulars, and 400 Indian allies, and went as far as Fort Frontenac. He began parleys with the Iroquois, and made contact with them on 29 August northeast of Oswego, on Lake Ontario, in a place that bore the ill-starred name of Anse de la Famine (Famine cove). La Barre had established himself in a very bad spot, marshy and difficult to defend. Fever ravaged his troops; provisions ran out. The Onondagas, Oneidas, and Cayugas, under the leadership of OTREOUTI (Grande Gueule) and GARAKONTIÉ, had agreed to enter into negotiations, with Le Moyne de Longueuil acting as intermediary, but the Mohawks and the Senecas, through fear of Dongan, refrained from sending an ambassador, and they were represented only by Téganissorens*, a prisoner of La Barre. At a conference on 5 Sept. 1684, the Onondaga chiefs maintained a tone of lofty pride. They gave the governor to understand that it was for them, not for him, to dictate the peace. While contending, among other things, that the pillage of which the Senecas were guilty did not constitute a sufficient reason for war, the Indians none the less promised that the French should receive compensation. They also asked La Barre, in particular, to return to Quebec with his army, and to agree to the substitution of the Anse de la Famine for Montreal or Cataracoui as the place for subsequent deliberations. The Five Nations were willing to make peace and not to attack the Miamis again, but they refused to cease hostilities against the Illinois. La Barre was forced to bow to the will of the Iroquois, and, what was very serious, he left the Illinois, the allies of France, in their hands. He returned in sorry state to Montreal, with his troops decimated by illness.

His expedition had in no way intimidated the Indians. Intendant Demeulle wrote treacherously to the minister on 10 October: "The general [the governor] goes at the head of a small army corps to make war on the Iroquois, and far from doing that, he grants them all they ask." This treaty highly displeased not only the court, but also the whole colony. The Indian tribes of the West who were allies of the French accused La Barre of treason, and the French reproached the governor, among other things, for dragging them from their

Legardeur de Repentigny

homes to no purpose, and for calling them to arms only in order to be subjected to a bitter humiliation. "Thus," wrote Garneau, "through the pusillanimity of the general, an expedition failed which, had it been well led, would have had quite different results. The Five Nations had the glory . . . of signing with the Canadian governor a treaty that put the French to shame."

La Barre's return to Quebec almost coincided with the arrival there of 300 soldiers sent by the king. Had this help been sent earlier, it might have changed the complexion of things. But M. de La Barre was dogged by misfortune everywhere. His enemy La Salle, who had gone to France, had completely reinstated himself in the good graces of the king and the minister, Seignelay. Forts Frontenac and Saint-Louis were restored to him. Harsh letters reached the governor. On 10 March 1685, Louis XIV wrote to Intendant Demeulle, expressing his dissatisfaction with "the shameful peace that he [La Barre] has just concluded with the Iroquois." The same letter added that La Barre was going to be recalled and replaced by Brisay* de Denonville.

Le Febvre de La Barre left Quebec in August 1685. His administration had been disastrous. He left to his successor Denonville a difficult situation. The Iroquois made no pretence of observing the terms of the treaty. They continued to attack the French, to wage war on the Indian allies, and to maintain commercial relations with the English. The tragic years that followed M. de La Barre's government were due in part to his unsound policy regarding the Indians, his egotistic and overweening character, and his unco-ordinated strategy.

He retired to France, where he lived thenceforth without holding any office. But he possessed a large fortune, which was squandered by his son. In 1645 Governor La Barre had married Marie Mandat, the daughter of Galiot Mandat, a *maître des comptes*. M. de La Barre died 4 May 1688 in Paris, and was buried in the church of Saint-Gervais. His grandson, the Chevalier de La Barre, achieved celebrity as a result of his trial and punishment in 1766. He was accused of impiety and of having mutilated a crucifix, and was condemned to death by judgement of the Parlement of Paris. Voltaire defended him, but could not save him from the scaffold.

R. LA ROQUE DE ROQUEBRUNE

AN, Col., B, 10, 11, C11A, 6, F3, 6; Marine, B4, campagnes, 1673. ASQ, Lettres, N, 61, p.26, 62, pp.1–2, 79, p.4; P, 51, p.6. BN, MS, Mélanges Colbert, 164. [Henri] de Baugy, *Journal d'une expédition contre les Iroquois en 1687: lettres et pièces relatives au fort Saint-Louis des Illinois*, éd. Ernest Serrigny (Paris, 1883). Caron, "Inventaire de documents," APQ *Rapport, 1939–40*, 155, 246, 250. *Coll. de manuscrits relatifs à la Nouv.-France*, I. *Découvertes et établissements des Français* (Margry), I, 613–14; II, 307–51, 370–73; III, 28–36. *Édits ord.*, III, 44–45. I.C.S.D.V., *Relation*. *JR* (Thwaites), XLIX, LXII, LXIII *et passim*. *Jug. et délib.*, II, III. Jean-Baptiste Labat, *Nouveau Voyage aux Isles de l'Amérique. Contenant l'histoire naturelle de ces pays*, . . . (La Haye, 1724), ij. L.-A. Lahontan, *Nouveaux voyages . . . dans l'Amérique Septentrionale . . .* (2v., La Haye, 1703). J.-A. Le Febvre de La Barre, *Description de la France Equinoctiale, cy-devant appelée Guyanne, et par les Espagnols, El Dorado . . .* (Paris, 1666); *Journal du dernier Voyage du Sr de la Barre en la Terre-Ferme, & Isle de Cayenne, accompagné d'une exacte description du Pays, moeurs & naturel des Habitans*, in I.C.S.D.V., *Relation*. *Mémoires des commissaires*, I, 152; II, 583, 587; and *Memorials of the French and English commissaries*, I, 207, 761, 765. *NYCD* (O'Callaghan and Fernow), III, IX. *Ord. comm.* (P.-G. Roy), I, 323–28; II, 7–93. PRO, *CSP*, *Col.*, *1669–74*. PAC *Rapport, 1885*, xl–xliv; *1899*, Supp., 40, 73–78. Vachon de Belmont, *Histoire du Canada*.

L.-P. Desrosiers, "L'expédition de M. de la Barre," *Cahiers des Dix*, XXII (1957), 105–35. Eccles, *Frontenac*, 157–72. Garneau, *Histoire du Canada*. HBRS, VIII, XXI (Rich); XI (Rich and Johnson). A. Jal, *Abraham Duquesne et la marine de son temps* (2v., Paris, 1873). Lanctot, *Histoire du Canada*, II, 113–21. La Roncière, *Histoire de la marine française*, V. Henri Lorin, *Le comte de Frontenac; étude sur le Canada français à la fin du XVIIe siècle* (Paris, 1895). Rochemonteix, *Les Jésuites et la N.-F. au XVIIe siècle*, III, 154–84. J.-E. Roy, "La famille Lefebvre de la Barre," *BRH*, II (1896), 82–87. Régis Roy, "Joseph-Antoine Lefebvre, sieur de la Barre, gouverneur de la Nouvelle-France en 1682," *BRH*, XX (1914), 46–51.

LEGARDEUR DE REPENTIGNY, PIERRE, Governor HUAULT de Montmagny's lieutenant, director of the Communauté des Habitants, admiral of the fleet; b. probably in the first decade of the 17th century at Thury-Harcourt (Haute-Normandie), son of René Legardeur de Tilly and Catherine de Cordé; d. 1648 at sea.

Pierre Legardeur reached Quebec on 11 June 1636 with his mother, his sister Marguerite, wife of JACQUES LENEUF de La Poterie, and his brother CHARLES LEGARDEUR de Tilly. He therefore formed part of the group of Normans and representatives of the lesser nobility that arrived with Montmagny. The name Repentigny came to him from a neighbourhood in Calvados.

Marie de l'Incarnation [*see* GUYART] states that he was Governor Montmagny's lieutenant. Probably he succeeded BRÉHAUT Delisle in this office; of the latter there is no trace after 1642. Pierre Legardeur came into prominence in 1644,

Legardeur de Tilly

when he and NOËL JUCHEREAU Des Châtelets won over the important persons of the settlement to the idea of an association of settlers, which would take over the monopoly of the fur trade. With the Jesuits' backing, Legardeur went to Paris with JEAN-PAUL GODEFROY in the autumn, to negotiate with the directors of the Compagnie des Cent-Associés the transfer of the fur-trading monopoly; this was effected on 14 Jan. 1645 and ratified by the king on 6 March following. The new company adopted the name of Communauté des Habitants. The success of the negotiations was chiefly due to the Jesuits, in particular to Father CHARLES LALEMANT, who had contacts at court.

The lack of working capital, however, prevented the start of commercial activity. Legardeur obtained funds from Hilaire Leclerc, a treasurer of France at Poitiers. He was then able to load five ships, which put to sea late in the spring of 1645. The zeal that he displayed earned him the title of admiral, that is to say commander of the fleet. He reached Quebec on 5 Aug. 1645.

Unfortunately it was not long before the Communauté des Habitants, under Legardeur's leadership, began to take on the appearance of a family business. All the directors were related by marriage. The ordinary people were suspicious, and protested; they were supported by CHOMEDEY de Maisonneuve, who went to France with ROBERT GIFFARD in 1646 to denounce the directors' actions. The Conseil du Roi recorded the protests of Maisonneuve and Giffard, and on 27 March 1647 passed a "statute to establish order and sound administration in Canada." This ruling created an administrative and supervisory council.

Meanwhile Legardeur (director of transport to New France in 1645 and 1646) was plying between the colony and the mother country. He would leave Quebec in the autumn with the furs collected during the winter and reappear in the spring with the supplies required for the fur trade. Before he left in 1647 he was made to open his accounts to the administrative council. It was apparent that his methods of book-keeping were inadequate and that he was not niggardly about expenses. He was admonished, but retained in his position. In the spring of 1648 Pierre Legardeur gave vent to his dissatisfaction with regard to the appointment of LOUIS D'AILLEBOUST to the post of governor. The king took firm action by appointing d'Aillebout general of the fleet for the return voyage to Canada.

According to the royal orders, Legardeur was to resume his office only in the autumn of that year. He did not, however, have the opportunity to do so. He had barely left La Rochelle, in May 1648, before an epidemic broke out on the ship that was carrying him. He became seriously ill and succumbed rapidly, "his body half covered with blackish purple spots as large as two-denier pieces."

His wife, Marie Favery, lived until 29 Sept. 1675. She had had four children, two of whom, Marie-Madeleine and Catherine, married Jean-Paul Godefroy and CHARLES-JOSEPH D'AILLEBOUST Des Muceaux respectively. Marie Favery inherited the Repentigny and Bécancour seigneuries, which her husband had obtained in 1647. In 1657 she founded the Confrérie du Saint-Rosaire.

JEAN HAMELIN

ASQ, Documents Faribault, 34, 74. Marie Guyart de l'Incarnation, *Lettres* (Sulte), 36f. *JR* (Thwaites). *JJ* (Laverdière et Casgrain). Le Clercq, *Premier établissement de la foy*, I, 494, 497; II, 12. P.-G. Roy, *Inv. concessions*, I, 244, 251, 257.

Gabriel Debien, "Engagés pour le Canada au XVIIe siècle vus de La Rochelle," *RHAF*, VI (1952), 187. Faillon, *Histoire de la colonie française*, II, 94f., *et passim*. Lanctot, *Histoire du Canada*, I. "La mort de Pierre Le Gardeur de Repentigny," *BRH*, XXXII (1926), 45–46. P.-G. Roy, "La famille Le Gardeur de Repentigny," *BRH*, LIII (1947), 165–76, 195–98; "Jean-Paul Godefroy," *BRH*, X (1904), 246–50.

LEGARDEUR DE TILLY, CHARLES, navigator, governor of Trois-Rivières, member of the Communauté des Habitants, business man, fur-trader, councillor of the Conseil Souverain of New France; b. probably 1614 at Thury-Harcourt (Haute-Normandie), son of René Legardeur de Tilly and Catherine de Cordé; d. 10 Nov. 1695 at Quebec.

Charles Legardeur was 22 when he landed at Quebec in 1636, with his brother PIERRE LEGARDEUR de Repentigny. He was said at that time to be "proficient in the art of navigation," which is quite probable, since in 1645 we find him in command of a ship that was plying between Quebec and the mother country.

Like his brother Pierre, he played an active part in the organization and administration of the Communauté des Habitants. He held the office of governor of Trois-Rivières from 1648 to 1650. When he returned to Quebec, he concerned himself with business. He entered into a partnership with François BYSSOT and JEAN-PAUL GODEFROY in order to hunt seal at Tadoussac and to trade in beaver. In the autumn of 1650 he went to France to obtain from the Compagnie des Cent-Associés the fishing monopoly at Tadoussac.

Le Grand Agnier

Charles Legardeur rapidly became a person of importance and influence. In 1652, with other associates, he received the Cap-des-Rosiers seigneury. In 1653 he represented the Côte Saint-Michel in the election of the syndic of Quebec. His name appears in the list of the first councillors of the Conseil Souverain. He was one of the clique grouped around Governor SAFFRAY de Mézy which was promoting the sale of spirits. His commercial activities determined his opinion. At the time of Mézy's coup d'état, in September 1664, he was not dismissed from office. The governor even bequeathed him 500 *livres* in his will. Legardeur continued his career as a councillor under the governorship of BUADE de Frontenac, who at first took a liking to him; when Frontenac travelled to Lake Ontario in 1673, he entrusted Legardeur with the military command of Quebec. In April 1675 the latter was appointed a life member of the Conseil Souverain.

Shortly afterwards his relations with Frontenac were to deteriorate. Indeed, when the council was reorganized in 1675 the king had decided that the intendant should act as a chairman to call for expressions of opinion and count votes. Frontenac took offence at the conferring of these powers upon Jacques DUCHESNEAU. During the winter of 1678–79, he proclaimed his right to preside over the council in the absence of the intendant. The latter in turn took exception, with the support of the majority of the council members. Tension increased. On 4 July 1679 Frontenac ordered ROUER de Villeray and Legardeur de Tilly to withdraw from Quebec. Tilly went into exile at Beauport, in the home of his brother-in-law NICOLAS JUCHEREAU de Saint-Denis. However, Frontenac and Tilly both climbed down a little: the first because he had received remonstrances from the king; the second because he needed employment in order to meet the needs of his family. Tilly broke with his associates, made his submission to Frontenac, and regained the latter's friendship. He remained in office until 1688, when he made way for his son, Pierre-Noël Legardeur* de Tilly.

On 1 Oct. 1648, at Quebec, Charles Legardeur had married Geneviève, the daughter of JEAN JUCHEREAU DE MAUR; she was to give him 15 children. As a dowry she brought him what she had inherited from her uncle NOËL JUCHEREAU Des Châtelets, namely the land at Saint-Michel cove, which the Compagnie des Cent-Associés made into a fief on 7 April 1660, and which Tilly sold to the seminary of Quebec on 26 April 1678.

Tilly lived in great poverty, in a state of penury that sometimes bordered on destitution. Frontenac wrote that he was ruined by the Iroquois, who pillaged him during the wars. In 1688 he was recommended to Seignelay as "being very poor and very old." He died 10 Nov. 1695.

JEAN HAMELIN

ASQ, Documents Faribault, 112, 113, 126a, 158; Polygraphie, IV, 55; I, 68; Registre A, pp. 144, 599–602. *JR* (Thwaites). *Jug. et délib.*, I, 278–80; *passim*. P.-G. Roy, *Inv. concessions*, I, 105, 272; II, 14, 65f., 68. Delalande, *Le Conseil souverain, passim*. Eccles, *Frontenac*. P.-G. Roy, "Charles Legardeur de Tilly, conseiller au Conseil souverain," *BRH*, XXVIII (1922), 65–73; "La famille Le Gardeur de Tilly," *BRH*, LIII (1947), 99–123, 133–46. E. Villaret, "Le premier congréganiste canadien-français (Charles Le Gardeur de Tilly)," *BRH*, XLV (1939), 33–42.

LE GRAND AGNIER. *See* TOGOUIROUI

LEIFR *heppni* **EIRIKSSON (Leif Ericsson or Leif the Lucky),** first European to set foot on the mainland of North America; d. *c.* 1020.

Leifr's father was the famous EIRIKR Thorvaldsson (Eric the Red), who established the Greenland settlements. The circumstances of the landing of Leifr on the east coast of America are obscure. According to one of the two main sources on the Vinland voyages (*Saga of Eric the Red*), he spent some time at the court of King Olaf Tryggvason of Norway in the year 1000, was baptized, and returned to Greenland with a priest to undertake the conversion of its inhabitants to Christianity. On his way thither he was driven off course and after many days sighted a hitherto unknown land. On going ashore he found self-sown wheat, wild grapes, and trees called *mösurr* (possibly maples). Leifr loaded his ship with these products, made his way to Greenland, and en route rescued some shipwrecked sailors, earning by this deed the nickname "Lucky" (*heppni*). He then settled down in Greenland, but his brother Thorsteinn in the next year made an abortive attempt to visit the land Leifr had found. Some time later THORFINNR *karlsefni* Thordarson made an attempt to settle Leifr's land.

According to the other main source (*Saga of the Greenlanders*) BJARNI Herjólfsson sighted America as early as 985 but did not land. Leifr is thus not the first discoverer of America, and his interest in it stems from Bjarni. He was, indeed, at the court of King Olaf in 1000, returned to Greenland with a priest, but did not discover any new lands on this voyage, although he earned his nickname by rescuing sailors. He then bought Bjarni's ship and retraced the latter's course, coming first to a land covered with glaciers and, between them and the shore, what appeared to be a high, flat expanse of rock. To this land Leifr gave the name of Helluland (Flagstoneland). Sailing on, he next reached a level wooded land with many beaches of white sand and gave to it the name of Markland (Woodland). Leifr then sailed in a southwesterly direction for two days until he reached land again. He landed on an island off it where the dew tasted sweet and then proceeded to the mainland where he built houses and wintered. There was good salmon fishing and no frost in the winter so his cattle were able to forage for themselves. "Day and night were of more equal duration there than in Iceland; about the time of the winter solstice the sun was in *eyktarstafr* [the place on the horizon over which the sun is at about 3 or 3:30 P.M.] and in *dagmalastafr* [the place over which the sun is at 9 A.M.]."

One day, Tyrkir, a native of southern Europe who had long been in the service of Leifr and his father, discovered wild grapes and vines. Leifr then set his men to picking grapes and felling vines and trees. He loaded his ship with this cargo and, after giving the land the name of Vinland (Wineland), sailed in the spring for Greenland, again rescuing en route shipwrecked sailors.

Leifr himself undertook no further voyages to Vinland, but his brother Thorvaldr made an expedition on which he perished and then another brother, Thorsteinn, failed in an attempt to bring back Thorvaldr's body. This was followed by the expedition of Thorfinnr *karlsefni* and finally by another led by Leifr's sister Freydis, that proved a most bloody affair.

As is evident from the above there is a very considerable discrepancy between the two main sources on the Vinland voyages and scholars have long argued about which is the older and more reliable. For many years the *Saga of Eric the Red* has been preferred but fresh research in recent years has to a considerable extent re-established the view that the *Saga of the Greenlanders* is the older, written probably about A.D. 1200 i.e., 50 to 75 years before that of Eric.

Again, scholars have spent endless time in attempting to identify the geographical positions of Helluland, Markland, and Vinland. The first two do not present many difficulties. Helluland may confidently be identified with Baffin Island and Markland with Labrador. Vinland is a much more difficult case. It must be said that both sagas are too vague, too confused, and too brief in their accounts of the course followed by the Icelanders to Vinland, of the geographical and topographical features, of the flora and fauna, and so on, to enable positive identification. Even the passage in the *Saga of the Greenlanders* on the length of day in Vinland, which at first sight would seem very helpful, has proved a broken reed. Its interpretation involves highly technical definitions and astronomical calculations, leading to such great diversity of opinion that, on the basis of the passage, Vinland has been located as far north as 58°26′N and as far south as 31°N, or even Florida. Each scholar has had to juggle the narratives, assume copyists' errors, supply missing details, and so on, in order to make his favourite locality fit the meagre details the sagas provide. By such means Vinland has been located as far south as Florida, as far north as Hudson Bay (where the climate is assumed without evidence to have been much warmer in the year 1000 than at present) and as far inland as the Great Lakes. Helge Ingstad has even suggested that there existed a North and South Vinland, the latter on the New England coast and the former in Newfoundland.

It remains a fact, however, that no relics of the Norsemen have been found in America which might help one to locate Vinland, unless indeed, the houses which Ingstad excavated in 1961 in northern Newfoundland prove to be the work of Icelandic explorers of the 11th century, as he believes. These ruins, however, need not in any case be from Vinland or from any of the recorded voyages, for there is no doubt that many more unrecorded trips were made to America throughout the five centuries the Greenland colony existed. Finally it may be said that, as far as there is any agreement, the most likely location of Vinland is in the region of Cape Cod, but certainty will never be obtained unless archaeology furnishes new and compelling evidence.

T. J. OLESON

Íslenzk fornrit, ed. Sigurður Nordal (Reykjavík, 1933–54+), IV, *Eyrbyggja saga . . . Eiríks saga rauða*, ed. E. O. Sveinsson og Matthías Þórdarson (1935), 118–36. Jón Jóhannesson, "Aldur Grænlendingas sögu," in *Nordæla* (Reykjavík, 1956), 149–58. H. Hermannsson, *The problem of Wineland* (Islandica, XXV, 1936); *The Vinland sagas* (Islandica, XXX, 1944). Helge Ingstad, *Landet under Leidarstjernen* (Oslo, 1959), 253–72. Rolf Müller, "Altnordische Eyktmarken und die Entdeckung Amerikas," *Greinar*, II, no.3 (1949), 33–82. Oleson, *Early voyages*, 22–23, 32. A. M. Reeves, *The finding of Wineland the Good* (London, 1890). J. R. Swanton, *The Wineland voyages* (Smithsonian Misc. Coll., CVII, no.12, 1947).

LEIGH, CHARLES, merchant and voyager, first Englishman to attempt to establish a colony on the St. Lawrence; third son of John Leigh and

Leigh

Joan Oliph of Addington, Surrey; *b.* Addington, 12 March 1572; *d.* 1605.

Nothing is known of Leigh's early life though it is probable that he spent some years at sea and in trading abroad before he appears as a colonial *entrepreneur* in 1597. He had by then come under the influence of the Brownist separatists against whom church and state had turned hostile (George JOHNSON spoke of "master Leigh . . . a brother in the faith unto us"). He was also associated with two Dutch merchants, Abraham and Stephen van Harwick, settled in London, the former of whom may possibly have had sympathies with the Brownists, but who had metal-working interests at Rotherhithe, Surrey, as well. There Abraham van Harwick could have encountered the Master Peter Hill who had invested in 1593 in an unsuccessful walrus-fishing expedition to Ramea (the Magdalen Is. in the St. Lawrence), it would seem at the instance of Lord Burghley [*see* LA COURT de Pré-Ravillon, FISHER, and WYET].

Since Ralph Hill, a London goldsmith and perhaps a relative of Peter Hill, was concerned in the expedition of 1597, it is logical to see it as the continuation and elaboration of the project for a walrus fishery in the St. Lawrence, first aroused by the capture of a Breton ship in 1591. The difference between this and earlier attempts was that a permanent settlement was envisaged, to hold the islands against both Bretons and Basques and to begin the fishery early in the year before ships could penetrate into the gulf. The personnel of the colony was to be supplied from an imprisoned group of Protestant separatists led by their pastor Francis Johnson who wished to gain their freedom, and yet live under the queen's allegiance. How Leigh came to be entrusted with the delicate task of taking these "Brownists" to America is not known. (It is not at all unlikely to have been the work of the aged and ailing Lord Burghley.) In any case the four leading Brownists [*see* George JOHNSON] were to go out with Leigh, and were to stay over the winter on the Magdalens with one ship (and presumably some walrus-hunters), where they would be joined by the rest of the congregation in the spring of 1598. They were obliged to promise to obey Leigh and not to return without his permission.

The 120-ton *Hopewell* of London, with Leigh as captain, William Craston as master, and Francis Johnson, Daniel Studley, and Ralph Hill as passengers, and the 70-ton *Chancewell*, Stephen van Harwick captain and Stephen Bennet master, with the other two Brownists on board, left the Thames 8 April and Falmouth 28 April or just after. The ships made a good Atlantic crossing, arriving together on the Grand Banks on 18 May. They lost each other briefly in fog but made a rendezvous at Conception Bay, on 20 May. Leigh worked down the coast trying to buy boats—shallops for fishing and hunting—from English fishermen at Farillon (Ferryland) and Renewse, but getting only one damaged pinnace. After repairing it, they turned Cape Race and in foggy weather the ships lost each other 5 June at the entrance to Placentia Bay. The *Hopewell*, which is likely to have had a pilot who had previously been to Ramea, continued alone, sighting Cape Breton on 11 June, and working into the gulf. Leigh was the first Englishman to remark on the great bird colonies on Bird Rocks; his party also saw many walrus on the rocks; off Île Brion they caught good cod. It was not until the 18th that they rounded the southwestern end of the Magdalens and finally penetrated into the inner harbour, Basque Harbour, which they called by its Basque name, Halabolina (between Amherst Is. and Grindstone Is.), showing clearly that some of the men had been here before. The *Hopewell* did not find the Magdalens unoccupied. In Halabolina were two Breton ships (perhaps representing La Court de Pré-Ravillon's 1591 syndicate) and two Basque vessels from Ciboure, on the French side of the border. There were other Basque and Breton ships in the other harbour (now Grand Entry Harbour). Moreover, there were cod-fishing stages on Île Blanche so that more than walrus-hunting was in progress. Nor were there only Europeans on the islands: large summer fishing parties of 300 Indians (evidently Micmac from what is now Prince Edward Island and the mainland) were trading with the French as well as fishing.

Leigh was the intruder in the harbour, but he offered hospitality to the other captains. The Bretons responded; one of the Basques appeared and satisfied Leigh that his ship was French, from Ciboure, the other remaining under suspicion of being a Spanish Basque and therefore a lawful prize. Leigh demanded that the Basques should hand over their powder and ammunition as proof of good faith and when this was refused sent a boarding party into one vessel. Leigh stopped their pillaging and returned all except the munitions. But the men, apparently led by William Craston, an old privateering seaman, were planning to seize the Basque vessel when a force of Bretons and Basques appeared on shore, on 20 June. There were some 200 men, gathered from the ships in both harbours, who mounted 3 guns on land and brought out some 300 Indians as well The "battle" could have been only intermittent firing between ship and shore. Finally Leigh sent Ralph Hill and the bosun's mate on land to parley. Capt. Charles, from a Breton ship, came to demand their small pinnace, got at Farillon, and tried to manoeuvre his own ship so as to board the *Hopewell*, though this move was thwarted. Leigh handed over the pinnace but did not get back the two hostages. Not till he cut his cables did the French let Hill and his companion go. By that time the *Hopewell* had drifted on to a rock and Leigh was too busy to seek revenge. (It is noteworthy that the French were satisfied with his withdrawal and did not attack further.) The *Hopewell* was got clear on the 21st and moved up the coast to Île Blanche to try to get back her boat and her anchor but was warned off by a shot from a cannon mounted on shore. The French had won and were seen to be too well entrenched for any colony to be possible. Leigh now tried to set course for Grande Coste (probably the gulf coast, northwest of Anticosti) to prospect for an alternative site for a settlement, but the master, William Craston, was now in control of the ship and refused to take her further, so it was decided to work back to Cape Breton. They reached Menego (St. Paul Is.) on 25 June, worked along the coast towards the cape, and, on the 27th had the extraordinary luck to encounter the *Chancewell*'s shallop, sent out, as George Johnson recounted, to attract the attention of their heaven-sent rescuers. Since the *Chancewell* had been wrecked and looted by Basque fishermen, her men had little but their shallops left. All were now taken on board the *Hopewell*. The four pilgrim Brownists were reunited and it was probably here, at or near St. Ann's Bay, that Leigh formally released them of their promise to stay in Canada and so brought the colonizing project to an end.

Leigh now began a long and arduous campaign to get back from the Basque ships some of the gear stolen from the *Chancewell*. Some he recovered from a Ciboure ship in the bay; later he got more from the Spanish Basque vessel, *Santa Maria de San Vicente*, at English Port (Mira Bay?) though, when it looked as if he might try to make a prize of her, Basques and Bretons again combined to chase him away. Meantime he did some cod-fishing and made contact with the Indians, taking a birch-bark canoe and giving it back with presents when the Indians returned to request it. This in turn brought down the local chief and his wife and followers to the shore. Leigh learnt that his name was Itarey and the harbour called Cibo (from Ciboure?), so that it seems likely that the Indian spoke some French. Presents were again given and Leigh clearly tried to establish good relations, perhaps with the idea of returning subsequently to Cape Breton.

Craston and the men on the *Hopewell* were determined to take a prize by some means or other, so they now turned to the Basque shore on southern Newfoundland which Wyet had visited in friendship in 1594. On 18 July in St. Lawrence's Bay (apparently Great St. Lawrence) Craston surprised the 120-ton Spanish-Basque *Catalina*, of Orio, laden with fish and oil. Next day Craston was trying to restore contact with the *Hopewell*, when he was captured by the crew of a Rocheller, who held him and his men as hostages for the return of the *Catalina*. This was arranged after some complex bargaining and the *Hopewell* finally left for St. Mary's Bay where her last attempt at prize-taking, on 25 July, was successful. After a fierce but not very bloody fight in which Capt. Leigh narrowly escaped injury, a 200-ton ship of Belle-Isle, a Catholic League port in Brittany, and probably a lawful prize, was captured, Leigh himself taking over the prize. He then insisted on making for home, not raiding northern Newfoundland as Craston wished. On 5 August the *Hopewell* sailed by way of the Azores to seek further prizes, Leigh and the Pilgrims reaching the Isle of Wight on 5 September, where Francis Johnson and the rest of the Pilgrims went on shore, while Leigh took the prize to London to be appraised and the spoil divided.

The Brownists made no attempt to follow up the venture and went into exile in Holland. Leigh, however, was anxious to continue what he had so unsuccessfully begun. He wrote a good account of the voyage, together with a description of the Magdalens—the first we have—in which he made clear his belief that they were suitable for settlement. Moreover, on 4 October, he set down, in his "Briefe platform," his plan to go out in 1598 with three ships and plant a settlement which would permanently deprive the French of the islands. By getting to the Magdalens a month ahead of the French and by fortifying the small island at the mouth of Basque Harbour called Duoron (now Île d'Entrée) and a similar commanding site at the other harbour, they would keep the French away. The king of Spain would thus be deprived of fish sent him by the French, while settlers would find the islands habitable, though colder than England. The Privy Council, to which the document was addressed, offered no support and the plan was dropped, but hints and suggestions for a settlement on the St. Lawrence continued until 1602 when, it seems, the English abandoned the field finally to the French.

We do not know whether Leigh made further

Le Jeune

prospecting voyages in 1598 or 1599, but after 1599 he deserted North America. He had married young and had two children, the elder, Olyph, being born early in 1597. He was trading at Algiers in 1600–1 and, in 1601–2, led an expedition against English pirates and Spanish merchantmen in the Mediterranean. On his return from Barbary he went prospecting in Guiana in 1602 and selected the river Wiapoco (now Oyapock) as a site for a small trading settlement. This he established in 1604, maintaining himself there until relief came in 1605, but, weakened by disease, he died on shipboard, in March 1605. The colony maintained a tenuous existence until the following year.

Leigh was a man of some enterprise and vision. He was aware that small settlements must have a specific economic function if they were to have the chance of succeeding. The Magdalens provided a possible site for such an experiment, though the seasonal nature of the fishing and hunting made a colony scarcely essential, but he was unable to overcome the advantage in force and familiarity which the Bretons and Basques had built up and the close co-operation which they were prepared to display against the English intruder. His attempt to enlist the idealism of the Pilgrims was also far-sighted but it was not appropriate to the setting in which he proposed to exploit it. [For further details of the expedition see George JOHNSON].

DAVID B. QUINN

BM, Add. MS 12505, ff.474–78. Hist. MSS Com., 9, *Salisbury (Cecil) MSS*, XI. PRO, H.C.A. 13/32, Deposition of Francisco de Cazanova, 7 Nov. 1597; *Acts of P.C., new ser., 1596–97, 1597, 1597–98*. Hakluyt, *Principal navigations* (1903–5), VIII, 166–82. George Johnson, *A discourse of some troubles* ([Amsterdam], 1603). Purchas, *Pilgrimes* (1903–5), XVI.

R. Douglas, "Place-names on Magdalen Islands, Que.," Geog. Bd. Can., *17th Report* (1922), 66–74. G. Leveson-Gower, "Notices of the family of Leigh of Addington," *Surrey Arch. Coll.*, VII (1880), 77–123, for the best account of the Leigh family. Rogers, *Newfoundland. The Victoria history of the counties of England: Surrey*, ed. W. Page (5v., 1902–14), II–IV. J. A. Williamson, *The English colonies in Guiana and on the Amazon, 1604–1668* (Oxford, 1923).

For the Brownists, see Champlin Burrage, *The early English dissenters* (2v., Cambridge, Eng., 1962). H. M. Dexter, *The Congregationalism of the last 300 years* (London, 1880); —— and Morton Dexter, *The England and Holland of the Pilgrims* (London and Boston, 1906). F. J. Powicke, *Henry Barrow* (London, 1900).

LE JEUNE, OLIVIER, a negro belonging to GUILLAUME COUILLARD; baptized 14 May 1633 in Quebec, where he was buried on 10 May 1654.

He came from Madagascar or Guinea, and was brought to Quebec when still very young by one of the KIRKE brothers, who sold him for 50 *écus* to Le Baillif, a French clerk who had entered the service of the English. In July 1632 Le Baillif gave him to Guillaume Couillard. At his baptism this negro had received the Christian name Olivier in honour of Olivier LETARDIF, the head clerk; at his burial we find him bearing the family name of the Jesuit PAUL LE JEUNE, who had catechized him. In 1638 he was "chained up for 24 hours" for slandering Nicolas MARSOLET; he signed his confession with an X. We do not know whether Couillard treated him as a slave or set him free, for in the burial register the negro Olivier is listed as a servant. No text certifies that he was a slave. His situation may very well have been the same as that of the Indian girls CHARITÉ and Espérance, whom CHAMPLAIN was unable to obtain permission to take to France and whom Couillard adopted.

Slavery was not to be legalized in New France until 13 April 1709, by an ordinance of Intendant Raudot*; it nevertheless existed in the 17th century: the word "*esclave*" (slave) is used in the records of Lachine, on 28 Oct. 1694, to describe René Chartier's "*panis*." Certainly the slave trade had started before 1694: the trader Pierre Ducharme bought a little *panis* prior to 1691, and Laurent Tessier's widow sold an Indian sometime around 1689. The custom on the part of the French of accepting Indian slaves had begun even earlier: in 1674 Louis JOLLIET brought from the Mississippi region a little slave who had been given him there; in 1671 the Iroquois gave Governor RÉMY de Courcelle two Potawatomi slaves to appease his wrath. Slavery did therefore exist in fact in the 17th century and the ordinance of 1709 merely sanctioned an established practice. One must in addition keep in mind the international principle in force at the time: a negro was a slave wherever he might be, unless he had been emancipated.

If Olivier Le Jeune was the first negro to appear in the St. Lawrence Valley, he had been preceded in New France by the anonymous negro who died of scurvy at Port-Royal during the winter of 1606–7, and by Mathieu de Coste (de Costa), the negro of the Sieur DU GUA de Monts, who is supposed to have served in Acadia around 1608.

MARCEL TRUDEL

ASQ, Documents Faribault, 17. *JR* (Thwaites), V, 62, 64, 196–98. Lescarbot, *Histoire* (Tross), II, 455. Marcel Trudel, *L'esclavage au Canada français: histoire et conditions de l'esclavage* (Québec, 1960), 3–17.

Le Jeune

LE JEUNE, PAUL, superior of the Jesuits of Quebec from 1632 to 1639, first editor of the *Relations des Jésuites de la Nouvelle-France*, missionary at Quebec, Sillery, Tadoussac, Trois-Rivières, and Montreal from 1639 to 1649, procurator of the Canadian mission (1649–62); b. 1591 at Vitry-le-François in the diocese of Châlons-sur-Marne; d. 7 Aug. 1664 in Paris.

Paul Le Jeune was born of Calvinist parents in the province of Champagne which gave so many exceptional souls to New France: Paul de Chomedey de Maisonneuve, Jeanne Mance, Louis d'Ailleboust, the blessed Marguerite Bourgeoys, Jacques Marquette, and so on. According to Fressencourt he was 16 when he embraced Catholicism. In 1613 he entered the noviciate of the Jesuits of Paris. Two years later he studied philosophy at the Collège Henri IV at La Flèche. This was at the time when Father Énemond Massé, who had returned from Acadia, was minister of the boarding-school pupils and was communicating to the young a missionary fervour, of which Canada was before long to receive the fruits. Among Father Massé's young disciples at La Flèche from 1614 to 1625 were Charles Lalemant, Barthélemy Vimont, Anne de Noüe, Charles Du Marché, François Ragueneau, Jacques Buteux, Alexander Vieuxpont, all of them future missionaries to Canada. After finishing his philosophical studies Father Le Jeune was a teacher at the colleges in Rennes (1618–19) and Bourges (1619–22); he studied theology for four years at the Collège de Clermont in Paris, taught rhetoric at Nevers from 1626 to 1628, did his third year of the noviciate at Rouen under the direction of the famous Father Louis Lallemant. In 1629–30 he was once more professor of rhetoric, but this time at Caen.

The following year he was preaching at Dieppe, and he was in charge of the Jesuit residence in this town when he was appointed superior-general of the mission in Canada. Although he had lived in an intense missionary atmosphere at La Flèche and at the Collège de Clermont, he had not asked for an apostolate in a distant land. And yet the provincial's letter which assigned him to Canada was one of the happiest events in his life. He wrote: "Having been notified by you on the last day of March that I should embark as early as possible at Havre de grace [Le Havre], to sail directly for New France, the joy and happiness that I felt in my soul was so great that I believe I have experienced nothing like it for twenty years, nor has any letter been so welcome to me. I left Dieppe the next day. . . ." In these words is revealed Father Le Jeune's whole soul: an extraordinary and serene optimism which freed itself easily from the past to devote itself entirely to the task assigned to it. He was later to write: "I thought nothing of coming to Canada when I was sent here; I felt no particular affection for the Savages, but the duty of obedience was binding, even if I had been sent a thousand times further away; but I may say that even if I had had an aversion to this country, seeing what I have already seen, I should be touched, had I a heart of bronze." This assiduity in his duty was to make Father Le Jeune responsive to the lessons of experience and was to make of him one of our great missionaries.

A man of this stamp was needed to rekindle the apostolate of the Jesuits in New France, for after three years of English occupation everything had to be begun again. Confronted with the lamentable condition in which he found the Jesuit residence he did not give himself up to vain recriminations: "When a person is in dire distress, he must deliver himself as best he can. It is a great deal that such a guest [the Kirkes] has left our house and the entire country." There was a still more serious problem: his ignorance of the language, manners, and customs of these peoples whom he was coming to evangelize. With neither a grammar nor a dictionary, he had to resort to the direct method, to conversation with the Indians. After a few fruitless attempts at Quebec, he decided to accompany the Indians on their winter hunt (1634–35), a heroic undertaking for a refined 17th-century intellectual, but at the same time an experience of which he bore the burden without complaining and which had the most satisfactory consequences. Not only did he acquire mastery of the language and earn the goodwill of the Indians, but he also conceived means of carrying out the apostolate which were to prove to be effective: the necessity of making the nomadic Indians sedentary in order better to teach them the truths of the faith, the necessity of a hospital to care for the aged and the ill, of schools for educating the young; the need of a carefully selected European population which would be capable of completing the apostolic work of the missionaries by its devotion and its own example. When he came to be replaced as superior by Father Barthélemy Vimont in 1639, this ambitious programme was to be well on its way to being realized. Father Le Jeune is justly regarded as the founder of the Jesuit missions in Canada. Such toil did not prevent him from collaborating in the founding and maintaining of the post at Trois-Rivières and in the starting-up again of the Huron mission.

As superior of the Jesuits of Quebec from 1632 to 1639, Father Le Jeune was held in very high

Le Jeune

esteem by the civil authorities. He took pleasure in recognizing in the *Relations* the profoundly Christian spirit of the first two governors, CHAMPLAIN and HUAULT de Montmagny. In 1635 he pronounced the former's funeral oration, for which he wrote: "I did not lack material. Those whom he left behind have reason to be well satisfied with him, for though he died out of France, his name will not therefor be any less glorious to Posterity." It was he who presided over the ceremony by which BRAS-DE-FER de Chateaufort succeeded Champlain temporarily. In the 1636 *Relation* he greeted Montmagny's arrival with an enthusiasm that was never to flag. Through the *Relations* he openly carried on his role as a missionary and colonizer; what he wanted was quality, not quantity: "I beg those who shall come, to come with a desire to do good. New France will some day be a terrestrial Paradise if our Lord continues to bestow upon it his blessings, both material and spiritual. But, meanwhile, its first inhabitants must do to it what Adam was commanded to do in that one which he lost by his own fault. God had placed him there to fertilize it by his own work and to preserve it by his vigilance, and not to stay there and do nothing. I have more desire to see this country cleared, than people. Useless mouths would be a burden here, during these first years." But if there was always perfect harmony between the superior of the Jesuits and the governors, there is no indication that Father Le Jeune intervened in the administration of the colony.

Having become once again a simple missionary in 1639, Father Le Jeune exerted himself unsparingly, with his customary simplicity and optimism, at Quebec, Sillery, Tadoussac, Trois-Rivières, and Montreal. In 1641 and 1643 he was delegated to go to France to obtain help against the Iroquois peril. The immediate result of his first voyage was the building of Fort Richelieu (1642), on the site of the present-day Sorel. That was not all; for several years previously he had been hoping that a missionary post would be founded at Montreal. He was in the French capital when the dedication of Montreal Island to the Holy Family took place in February 1642. The personal relations he established at that time with Jérôme Le Royer de La Dauversière and the other members of the Société Notre-Dame de Montréal were of the greatest importance. In M. de La Dauversière's project, which was called a "mad enterprise" by so many others, he saw the finger of God. He wrote in the 1642 *Relation*: "Such an enterprise would have seemed as rash as it was holy and daring, had it not been based upon the power of him who never fails those who undertake nothing except under the impulse of his will. And everyone who learns what is being done to carry out this great design successfully will at once see that Our Lord is certainly the author thereof." He joined in the project enthusiastically, published the text of the first plan of the Messieurs de Montréal, placed at the service of the cause his vast personal prestige and the excellent publicity medium constituted by the annual *Relation*. At the formal request of M. de La Dauversière he was to spend the winter of 1645–46 at Montreal, along with Father Isaac JOGUES.

In 1649 Father Le Jeune returned to France and was assigned the office of procurator of the mission. Did his superiors think that the destruction of the Huron mission was likely to discourage the benefactors and dampen the zeal of the aspiring missionaries, and did they think that Father Le Jeune's presence was consequently more useful in France than in Canada? Everything leads us to that view. It is certain that, as mission procurator, he had the responsibility of publishing the annual *Relation* and that he did not fail in the task. When the manuscripts left Quebec but did not reach Paris, he made up for them, thanks to the epistolary exchange that he kept up with Canada; this is the case for the *Relations* of 1653, 1655, 1657, and 1658. Thus can be seen the importance that he attached to the publications of this annual report; and he was well placed to measure its effect.

The office of mission procurator was not enough to occupy completely a man as active and an apostle as untiring as Father Le Jeune. In Paris he was a director of souls and a much-sought after and very reliable preacher, as is proven by his *Épistres spirituelles*, published in Paris by his friends soon after his death, in 1665. But though the *Épistres* enlighten us about Father Le Jeune's religious doctrine, they add little to our historical knowledge. The names of the recipients, most of whom were still alive, were discreetly omitted; the names of persons—except that of Jogues which appears once—and the dates were likewise omitted. Out of a total of 288 extracts, only 11 seem to us to have been written in Canada; four bear the exact date, five do not but they announce Jogues's death, which was known in Canada in the spring of 1647. During his years in Paris Father Le Jeune was first and foremost procurator of the mission in Canada; he was not only known as such, but he was also identified with the mission by his numerous correspondents. The role of spiritual adviser did not prejudice that of procurator; rather it was very useful to him in that it kept an important and influential public attached to the interests of New France.

Did Father Le Jeune make a final voyage to Canada in 1660? Abbé Auguste Gosselin asserted that he did; Father Rochemonteix denied it. The argument of silence which the latter presented has not met with general acceptance. The testimony of Marie de l'Incarnation [see GUYART], combined with certain allusions in the *Épistres spirituelles*, makes us inclined to believe that Father Le Jeune did come to Canada in 1660. An attentive study of the *Relation* for that year lends support to this view; in it can be recognized his style, his spirit, his manner, and a warmth of tone which is hard to explain if the author was not giving the evidence of his own eyes and ears. In 1662 he was replaced as mission procurator by Father Paul Ragueneau. He died 7 Aug. 1664 in Paris. He was 73 years old.

Of all Father Le Jeune's merits the greatest was undoubtedly that of being the first, the most prolific, and the most efficient of the editors of the *Relations des Jésuites*. It is consequently not irrelevant to describe here this collection which before becoming a written source of Canadian history was a marvellous instrument of missionary propaganda.

Just as Father Le Jeune had never requested to be sent on foreign missions, so he had never thought of making a collection of historical documents. The letter which he sent to the provincial of Paris on 28 Aug. 1632, "from the midst of a forest more than 800 leagues in extent, at Kebec," was quite simply a report of his voyage and his arrival in New France. He had kept his diary, for from 1 April till 5 July the main events are dated with unusual precision. But the letter that he wrote was not a dry, cold catalogue of facts. In it can be felt the soul of a great missionary, which was moved by the sad condition of the unbelievers whom he observed attentively and whom he already loved. This account, made up of things which were so astonishing for a Frenchman of the 17th century and which were so beautifully told, pleased Father Barthélemy Jacquinot, the provincial of Paris, who immediately ordered it to be published. The 1633 *Relation* was also, in Father Le Jeune's mind, a private document, destined for the provincial of Paris alone: 216 pages of solid text, without chapter divisions and without marginal notes. The wealth of its contents justified its publication also.

Since the *Relation* was henceforth in the public domain, Father Le Jeune made its presentation more attractive. He wrote in 1634: "I shall divide the Relation of this year into chapters, at the end of which I shall add a journal of things which have no other connection than the order of time in which they happened." And henceforth, with few exceptions, when the manuscript left Quebec it was ready for publication. "Annual reports sent by the Superior of Quebec to the Provincial of Paris, printed in the 17th century, disseminated among the general public, the aim of which is to attract sympathy and temporal and spiritual benefactors for the Jesuit missions in New France," such would appear to be an accurate description of the *Relations*. Thus, although the missionary documents prior to 1632 or later than 1673 retain all their historical value, they are not, properly speaking, *Relations*. We must also observe that the *Relations* are not a complete and sequential history of New France. The superiors of the Jesuits of Quebec were neither by vocation nor by official designation the historiographers of the colony. Father Le Jeune wrote in 1635: "In regard to our French people, they are occupied in fortifying, in building, in clearing and cultivating the land. However, I do not pretend to describe all that takes place in this country, but only that which concerns the welfare of the faith and of Religion."

On the *Relations des Jésuites* there is a rather vast literature. We are obliged to make a choice. Here is what Charlevoix said of them: "As these fathers were scattered among all the nations with whom the French had any intercourse, and their missions obliged them to enter into all the affairs of the colony, we may say that their memoirs contain a very detailed history. There is indeed no other source to which we can resort to learn the progress of religion among the Indians, and to know those nations, all whose languages they spoke. The style of these relations is extremely simple, but this very simplicity has contributed to give them a great vogue, not less than the curious and edifying matter with which they are filled."

There are three editions of the *Relations des Jésuites de la Nouvelle-France*. The original edition is composed of 41 small duodecimal volumes, the first of which appeared in 1632 and the last in 1673. The 1637 *Relation* was printed at Rouen, by Jean Le Boullenger; all the others were printed in Paris, by Cramoisy. As the *Relations* had a purely practical aim, and appeared at a time when love of books was not as widespread as it is today, complete collections of the original edition are rare. If we limit ourselves to North America, Laval University in Quebec and Brown University in Providence, R.I., own complete sets of this edition.

In 1858, thanks to a subsidy from the Canadian government, there appeared at Quebec the

Le Jeune

Relations des Jésuites contenant ce qui s'est passé de plus remarquable dans les missions des Pères de la Compagnie de Jésus dans la Nouvelle-France. These three fat volumes contain the exact text of all the *Relations* published in France from 1632 to 1673. They also contain the *Relation de la Nouvelle-France* by Father Pierre BIARD, which was published at Lyon in 1616, as well as the letter sent from Quebec on 1 Aug. 1626 by Father Charles Lalemant to his brother, Father JÉRÔME LALEMANT. The editors of the Quebec edition wanted to save a very important source of Canadian history from destruction and make it accessible to a wide public, and this aim was attained in large measure. The hour of the learned edition had not yet arrived; but the third volume ended with an analytical table and an alphabetical index which made this edition easier to consult.

The great merit of the Quebec edition is, in our opinion, that it prepared the way for the edition which bears the name of its director, Reuben Gold Thwaites. This edition, which is entitled *The Jesuit Relations and allied documents*, consists of 73 octavo volumes and was printed in Cleveland from 1896 to 1901 by Burrows Brothers. It is not our role to talk about the allied documents here. As for the Relations, the original French text is accompanied by an English translation. Bibliographical information and learned notes are included at the end of each volume. The collection ends with many and various tables and indexes which make it a wonderful tool. In 1960 Pageant Books Inc. of New York brought out a photographic edition of Thwaites's work in 34 volumes, proof of the growing importance of the *Relations*. It is unfortunate that the notes have not been brought up to date, for in the past 60 years history has made far from negligible strides.

The *Relations* have had their detractors, but no serious historian casts doubt nowadays upon their historical value. Parkman has accorded them this praise: "With regard to the condition and character of the primitive inhabitants of North America, it is impossible to exaggerate their value as an authority. I should add, that the closest examination has left me no doubt that these missionaries wrote in perfect good faith, and that the *Relations* hold a high place as authentic and trustworthy historical documents." They did not tell everything: that was not their aim; but what they did affirm is worthy of credence. If really extraordinary facts, the truth of which the reader might question, are concerned, the authors merely recount and indicate their sources; or else they state formally what they themselves—and they were remarkably well-balanced—had seen and heard. If in the beginning they happened to utter hasty judgements, subsequently they added the necessary corrections. Never has their honesty been found wanting. As men of the 17th century they knew how to observe, discriminate, and express themselves clearly. Let us add that their language was in no way inferior to that of better-known authors who wrote in France at the same period; numerous are the pages of the *Relations* which would figure honourably in an anthology of French prose-writers of the 17th century.

To instruct and edify the European reader and hence to bring about his collaboration in the essential aim which the missionaries were pursuing: such were the reasons for the existence of the *Relations*. But the events which they related took place in time and space. That is why there is much information about the means of communication between Europe and Canada, between the various regions of the country itself, about its fauna and flora, about its climate. In them we become better acquainted with the peoples who inhabited Canada at that time, with the multifarious problems and the achievements of the missionary apostolate. Finally, we are indebted to the *Relations* for almost everything that we know about the great Indian chiefs of the period, about their eloquence and their military strategy; these volumes give us information non-existent elsewhere on the personalities of the missionaries, their souls, their labours, their sufferings, and the heroic deaths of the Canadian martyr-saints. What Edmund Bailey O'Callaghan wrote in 1847 is still true: "No historian can do thorough research on the circumstances surrounding the early settlements in this country without knowing them, and those who claim to be able to do so, without studying them beforehand, only give proof of their unfitness for this type of work."

Before becoming a written source for Canadian history, the *Relations* were an indispensable source of life, as much for the apostolate to the unbelievers as for the French colony. Like all missions, those in New France entailed very heavy expenses. The apostles and their servants had to be lodged, clothed, and fed; innumerable needy had to be helped in a country where famine and epidemics appeared more frequently than not; as the faith progressed, chapels and residences had to be built and supplied with all the appurtenances. The Jesuits of France could not meet so many expenses by themselves. The alms inspired by the reading of the *Relations* seem to have been the most important material contribution.

Émile Salone, Georges Goyau, and more recently Father Gilles Chaussé have brought out the vital role of the *Relations* in the peopling of the country by settlers from France. The reading of the *Relations* aroused in the monasteries and religious institutions of France a vast movement of sympathy, prayers, and devotion in favour of the missions in Canada. It was the starting-point for the missionary apostolate of women in the Roman Catholic Church. When the Ursulines and Hospitallers, answering the appeal of the *Relations*, arrived at Quebec in 1639, it marked the first time that cloistered nuns had crossed the seas to carry out an apostolic mission. "This participation of women in evangelization is a creation of Catholic and French origin, and it is what gives the colonization of Canada its true originality," wrote Dom Jamet (Juchereau, *Annales* (Jamet), III). Though the project for Montreal, in M. de La Dauversière's mind, was earlier than the *Relations*, the reading of the latter had a singular impact upon its development. M. de La Dauversière's particular vocation was to assure the founding of Montreal without leaving his little town of La Flèche and without giving up his office as tax-collector. He therefore needed a deputy on the spot, but it had to be a man with his stamp of mind, disinterested, and capable of understanding the sublime beauty of the project for Montreal. This indispensable man did indeed exist: his name was Paul de Chomedey de Maisonneuve, and it was the 1649 *Relation* that led him to M. de La Dauversière. The *Relation* for 1639 inspired the missionary vocation of Jeanne Mance, the laywoman from Champagne who founded the first hospital in Montreal and whose cause for beatification is registered in the court of Rome. Mother Marie de l'Incarnation and Mme de CHAUVIGNY de La Peltrie owed their vocation in Canada to the reading of the *Relations*. The 1647 *Relation*, which recounted the martyrdom of Saint Isaac Jogues, decided the coming to Canada of the great mystic of the Hôtel-Dieu of Quebec, Marie-Catherine de Saint-Augustin [*see* SIMON].

This simple enumeration is already imposing; it is not complete. It does suffice, we believe, to establish the unrivalled influence of the *Relations des Jésuites* on the history of Canada at its origins. And it is fitting to point out Father Le Jeune's immense merit: he created the marvellous instrument of propaganda embodied in the *Relations*; he assured their success by the beauty and the communicative warmth of his style, and by the loftiness of his thoughts; he imposed New France upon the attention of the mother country. The first 11 *Relations* are his work, and that was the golden age of the missions. From that period date institutions and works which, after serving the particular aim which had been their inspiration, have endured to our own days: the Ursulines and Hospitallers of Quebec, the founding of Montreal, and so on. Of the 41 volumes which make up the original edition, 15 are entirely Le Jeune's; and he contributed to all the others until 1662.

LÉON POULIOT

[At the beginning of his edition of the *Epistres spirituelles* (*Lettres spirituelles*, Paris, 1875), Father Fressencourt has provided an interesting article on Father Le Jeune. After being forgotten for nearly three centuries this is now enjoying a deserved popularity. In November 1957 there appeared in the collection *Classiques canadiens*, No. 7 (Fides), *Paul Le Jeune, S.J. (1591–1664)*, a choice of texts drawn from the first 11 *Relations*. In December of the same year Father Gilles Chaussé, S.J., presented to the University of Montreal a Master's thesis: "Le P. Paul Le Jeune, missionnaire-colonisateur." At the beginning of 1958 Father Jean Bouchard, S.J., defended before the Faculty of Missiology of the Gregorian University a doctoral thesis: "Les méthodes missionnaires du P. Paul Le Jeune." In a paper which he presented to the Royal Society of Canada in 1942, "Aux sources de l'histoire de Montréal" (*RSCT*, 3d ser., III (1942), sect. I, 83–94), Victor Morin maintained on the basis of internal criticism that the 1642 *Relations*, hitherto attributed to Father Barthélemy Vimont, belonged to Father Le Jeune. This author accepts his opinion, without however accepting the consequences that he tried to draw from it. In *L'Exploit du Long-Sault: les témoignages des contemporains* (SHQ Cahiers d'Histoire, XII, 1960), 58–61, Father Adrien Pouliot, S.J., and Sylvio Dumas attributed the 1660 *Relation* to Father Le Jeune. Their arguments seem to us to merit the most serious attention. On the Gosselin–de Rochemonteix controversy one should read the former's study, "Quelques observations à propos du voyage du P. Le Jeune au Canada en 1660 et du prétendu voyage de M. de Queylus en 1644," in *RSCT*, 2d ser., II (1896), sect. I, 35–58, and Father de Rochemonteix's reply in *Les Jésuites et la Nouvelle-France au XVIIe siècle*, I, 430–46. Émile Salone, *La colonisation de la Nouvelle-France: étude sur les origines de la nation canadienne-française* (Paris, 1906) and Georges Goyau, *Une épopée mystique: les origines religieuses du Canada* (Paris, 1924) stress Father Le Jeune's influence on the peopling of the colony. For a better knowledge of Father Le Jeune as a missionary, nothing equals reading the first 11 *Relations*, which are all by him. We have also, by Father Le Jeune, works of spiritual advice, among which are the *Lettres spirituelles*, of which we have already spoken, and his *Solitude de dix jours sur les plus solides véritez et sur les plus saintes maximes de l'Évangile*, which has appeared in several editions. The credit for restoring the *Relations* to a place of honour in the 19th century belongs to Edmund Bailey O'Callaghan, *Jesuit Relations*, New York, 1847. This opuscule was translated into French by Father Félix Martin *Relations des Jésuites . . . en Canada . . . (1611–1672) . . .*; tr. de

Le Maistre

l'anglais avec quelques notes, corrections et additions (Montréal, 1850). Francis Parkman made excellent use of the *Relations* in *The Jesuits in North America* (1st ed., 1867). The same must be said of Garneau, Ferland, Father de Rochemonteix and all the historians who have studied the history of New France. We shall be excused if we mention at this point our *Étude sur les Relations des Jésuites*. Those who are interested in the bibliography of the *Relations* as well as in the various editions and variants of the 17th century will profitably consult James McCoy, *Jesuit Relations of Canada: a bibliography*, with introduction by Lawrence P. Wroth (Paris, 1937). This is a conscientious work which does honour to its author and which is a tribute of unusual quality to this important source for Canadian history.   LÉON POULIOT]

LE MAISTRE, JACQUES, priest, Sulpician, bursar of the seminary of Saint-Sulpice at Montreal; b. *c.* 1621 in Normandy; killed by the Iroquois 29 Aug. 1661.

We have little precise information about Jacques Le Maistre. Together with the Sulpician Guillaume VIGNAL he sailed from La Rochelle, 29 June 1659, on the *Saint-André*, as chaplain to the Hospitallers Catherine MACÉ, Judith MOREAU de Brésoles, and Marie MAILLET. He reached Quebec on 7 September, and proceeded to Ville-Marie (Montreal), where he was appointed bursar of the seminary of Saint-Sulpice, a function that he performed until his death, which occurred on 29 Aug. 1661. On that day he was in a field belonging to the Saint-Gabriel farm, west of Ville-Marie; he had drawn aside from a group of workmen in order to recite his breviary, and was surprised by some Iroquois under OTREOUTI. Le Maistre seized a cutlass and tried to place himself between the Indians and the workmen, but he was killed by a shot from an arquebus. After cutting off his head, the Iroquois stripped him of his cassock, and Otreouti put it on.

According to a legend, the Indians wrapped Le Maistre's head in a white handkerchief taken from his pocket. "This piece of cloth received such a strong imprint of his face that a perfect image was left stamped upon it," and when one saw the cloth one could recognize "Aaouandio" (the Iroquois name for Le Maistre). On hearing this story, SIMON LE MOYNE tried to acquire the handkerchief, but his efforts were of no avail.

OLGA JURGENS

Morin, *Annales* (Fauteux et al.), 146–48. Dollier de Casson, *Histoire du Montréal*, 157–60, 240. Marie Guyart de l'Incarnation, *Lettres* (Richaudeau), II, 206–7. *JR* (Thwaites), XLV, 110, 112; XLVI, 188, 216–18; XLVII, 94, 102–4. *JJ* (Laverdière et Casgrain), 263, 265, 303.

LE MERCIER, FRANÇOIS-JOSEPH, priest, Jesuit, missionary in the Huron country and superior-general of the missions in New France; b. 3 Oct. 1604 in Paris, son of Paul Le Mercier, goldsmith and valet to the king, and of Marie Du Jardin; d. 12 June 1690 in Martinique.

He was admitted into the noviciate of the Society of Jesus on 22 Oct. 1622 in Paris. All the early part of his religious career was spent in Paris, where after his noviciate he followed the philosophy and theology courses at the Collège de Clermont; he also taught for four years in the same college. He was ordained priest in 1633, sailed to New France as soon as his training as a Jesuit was completed, and reached Quebec 20 July 1635. Three days later he set off by canoe for the Huron country, which he reached on 13 August.

At that period the missionaries usually lived at Ihonatiria (Saint-Joseph I), under the authority of Jean de BRÉBEUF. Under this pioneer missionary Father Le Mercier obtained a working knowledge of the language and had his first experience of the apostolate. He was named "Chaüosé" by the Hurons, and was immediately and conspicuously successful in the study of their language. The missionaries lived in bark lodges built after the manner of the country. The chapel itself was in a similar style. Eating, reading, or conferring together squatting on the ground, without furniture, without blankets, sleeping fully dressed on mats, the Jesuits lived in every respect after the Indian fashion. From Ihonatiria they spread out into the neighbouring villages; frequently they were unwelcome guests of the natives, lodging in their tents, distressed by the promiscuity, filth, and smoke, and annoyed by the dogs. Their food was that of the Indians, *sagamité*, a liquid paste made of water and crushed maize, and sometimes flavoured with overripe or dried fish. Pumpkins, declared excellent by the Jesuits, were an important part of the menu. Maize and pumpkins were the principal foods grown by the Hurons, in fields which they maintained adjoining their villages and abandoned every ten years or so when they shifted their dwellings. Meat and fresh fish were rare, hunting and fishing being only spasmodic and very seldom productive. On the missionary journeys the Hurons themselves provided the priests with food, not without receiving in payment small objects, knives, awls, and so on, which the fathers always had with them. At the central residence the servants tilled the soil in Indian fashion and went hunting or fishing for the Jesuits.

The French missionaries adapted themselves well to the Indian style of habitation and food, but they also were liable to be struck down by the epidemics which afflicted the Hurons at that time. Father Le Mercier was designated as a male nurse, which gave him a good deal of work in 1636. The following year, because of these same illnesses, the hostility of the Hurons became so intense that in their councils they decided upon a general massacre of the missionaries. At the same time Brébeuf was attending to the establishment of a new post, Ossossané, which in 1637 became the second main base of operations for the apostles. Le Mercier was put in charge of it. It was at Ossossané that Brébeuf presided at the farewell banquet that was to precede the Jesuits' death. He drafted the admirable letter of 28 Oct. 1637, which all the fathers signed and in which he proclaimed the firmness and resignation of all in face of death. The threat was not put into effect at that time, but the maltreatment continued until 1640, and Father Le Mercier himself was personally attacked and narrowly escaped being burned. His courage and eloquence saved him on that occasion.

With the arrival of Father JÉRÔME LALEMANT as superior of the mission, on 28 Aug. 1638, the missionary technique was to change. Until then the missionaries had lived among the Hurons, at Ossossané, where Father Lalemant resided for a while, and at Teanaostaiaé (Saint-Joseph II), which Brébeuf had chosen in the spring of 1638 instead of Ihonatiria. Father Lalemant had a census made of the Huron villages, whose population amounted to about 12,000 souls. Then he decided to concentrate the missionaries in an isolated residence, Fort Sainte-Marie, which was built in 1639 on the land where Midland, Ontario, now stands. The Jesuits were to radiate from this centre in their journeys through the Huron villages. As minister and procurator, Father Le Mercier certainly had a great part in the building of this post, but he did not neglect the apostolate on that account. His great facility in the Huron language frequently took him away from Sainte-Marie in the early years, the domestic tasks being left to Fathers Isaac JOGUES and PIERRE PIJART. However, as the missionaries' residence became a regular rallying point for the Christian Hurons, Father Le Mercier was able to exercise his ministry among them without moving from the spot. It was he who not only watched over the administration of the house but also was responsible for the neophytes who were passing through. As early as 1642 Father Lalemant realized that he would have to divide up the apostles further, and disperse them among the villages in small, firmly knit groups. Sainte-Marie-des-Hurons remained a centre for retreats and rest, where the fathers came for meditation and the recovery of their strength, and where the Indians came to complete their instruction and receive baptism in more solemn ceremonies than elsewhere. Father Le Mercier presided over all this. He also supervised the *donnés* and the servants, who were busy with household tasks, with tilling the fields, hunting, and fishing, as well as being concerned with the defence of the establishment if necessary. Under his general direction "the soil was cleared and planted, livestock and poultry were brought up from Quebec, by dint of unbelievable efforts. The new establishment became an important farm. Harvests, hunting, fishing and trading were sufficient after a few years to support the community, the donnés and the servants" (Rochemonteix, I, 396). Father Le Mercier thus lived at the central residence under the two superiorships of Fathers Jérôme Lalemant and Paul RAGUENEAU.

It is known that the Iroquois, in 1648–49, embarked upon the systematic destruction of the Huron nation. After the martyrdom of Fathers Jean de Brébeuf and GABRIEL LALEMANT in the spring of 1649, the surviving Hurons begged the priests to emigrate with them to the Île Saint-Joseph (Christian Island). Fathers Ragueneau and Le Mercier agreed, and burned their residence at Sainte-Marie on 14 June 1649. They built a similar one on the island, with the same name. Despite Father Le Mercier's administrative foresight, the following winter ended in a deprivation beyond belief; this, combined with the latest Iroquois forays on the mainland, forced the missionaries and a fair proportion of the Hurons to go down and take refuge near Quebec in 1650.

Father Le Mercier, back from the Huron country, resided during the subsequent years in Quebec. In 1652 he was engaged in obtaining help for the Trois-Rivières settlement, which was threatened by the Iroquois. Despite the opinions of the settlers themselves, he had fortifications put up which made it possible, in 1653, to hold off 500 Iroquois who had sworn to destroy the post. On 6 Aug. 1653 news came of his appointment as rector of the Collège at Quebec and superior-general of the missions in New France. It was in this capacity that he was to take part in the peace negotiations with the Iroquois. He did not hesitate to share himself the dangers to which he exposed his subordinates by sending them among the Indians. On 11 May 1656 he designated Father Jérôme Lalemant vice-superior of the mission, until such time as the general of the Jesuits named his successor; Father Jean de QUEN was to replace him during the summer. As for Lemercier himself, in May he joined the missionary expedition to the Iroquois country, organized following the embassies of Father SIMON LE MOYNE to the Onondaga country. The Iroquois named Father Le Mercier "Teharonhiagannra." His absence lasted a year. On 1 June 1657 he was back in Quebec, which he left again on the 27th of the same month, possibly intending to return once more among the Iroquois. However, Father Ragueneau, who had left Quebec a few days before him and whom it was desired at that time to keep at a distance from the place of government, was the only one to accompany the expedition beyond Montreal; Father Le Mercier returned to Quebec and concerned himself with various missionary labours.

On 6 Aug. 1665 Father Le Mercier was once again appointed rector and superior-general of the missions. This second mandate was to be attended by the revival of the Jesuit missions both among the Iroquois and among the Ottawas of the region around the Sainte-Marie falls (Sault Ste. Marie). At the same period Father MARQUETTE was preparing the expedition that was destined to make him famous. The Laprairie area near Montreal was opened up for colonization by the superior. After six years Father Le Mercier was relieved of his burden and became *primarius*, that is to say prefect of the Collège at Quebec. But he held this post for only a year, being recalled to France by the provincial of Paris in the summer of 1672.

Father Paul Oliva, the general of the Society of Jesus, had in fact been considering the already veteran missionary, with a view to entrusting to him the reorganization of the French Jesuit missions in the West Indies, which were at the height of an internal crisis. In 1673 the superior of these missions was recalled to France and Father Le Mercier was sent to replace him, with the responsibility of visiting all the missionaries in the general's name. The visitor assumed his duties on 17 Dec. 1673, had a look at all the missions, smoothed out the difficulties, and was finally appointed superior-general on 12 Oct. 1674. This new superiorship ended only on 26 March 1681, the date on which Father Le Mercier was replaced by Father Martin Poincet. The former superior was spiritual director and confessor in Martinique for a year, and was also given the responsibility for directing the Jesuits of that island; he held this from 1682 until his death in his eighty-sixth year.

Father Le Mercier has left a good deal of written material, mostly incorporated into the *Relations des Jésuites* series. They consist of letters or extracts of letters, but also of several relations or parts of relations drawn up in his hand. In 1637 and 1638 Jean de Brébeuf was already entrusting to him the task of writing the relation of the Huron mission. He likewise drafted the annual reports sent to France during his years as superior. His style is clear, precise, lively, reflecting the man of action and the zealous missionary that he was.

LUCIEN CAMPEAU

Archivum Romanum Societatis Iesu, Codex Franc. 22, 23, Catlogues annuels des maisons et des personnes de la province de France; Codex Gal. 109, I, 134–35, 144, 159–60, 164, 204–5, 237–38, 261–62, 264–65, 266–67, 280–1, 286–87, 315, Lettres originales. *JR* (Thwaites). François Elesban de Guilhermy, *Ménologe de la Compagnie de Jésus . . . Assistance de France, comprenant les missions de l'Archipel, de l'Arménie, de la Syrie, . . . du Canada, de la Louisiane . . .*, éd. Jacques Terrien (2 pts., Paris, 1892), I, 727–28. Rochemonteix, *Les Jésuites et la Nouvelle-France au XVIIe siècle*, I, II, passim.

LEMIRE, JEAN, master-carpenter; b. 1626 in France; in Quebec by 1653, when his marriage to Louise Marsolet is recorded; d. 1685 at Quebec.

In civic records Lemire is named as preparing an estimate for the building of the presbytery in Quebec in November 1664; as preparing a report, along with Paul Chalifour—both are called "carpenters" (*charpentiers*)—on a house at Coulonge on 5 April 1664; and, on 21 June 1664, as delivering it. The most important notice of him, however, is as a carpenter working on the enlargement programme for the cathedral of Quebec undertaken in 1684. A contract for the work was signed by him 4 Jan. 1684, and he is credited with constructing "out of oak from Batiscan" a *clocher* on the south tower of the cathedral, under the direction of Claude BAILLIF. Since he died soon after beginning work on the cathedral, it is to be presumed that Lemire constructed the *clocher* on the ground for later installation; perhaps it was finished, after his death, by one of his many sons.

ALAN GOWANS

AJQ, Greffe de Guillaume Audouart, 14 juillet 1653. ASQ, Paroisse de Québec, 46, 51, 131; Polygraphie, XXII, 61, 61A; Séminaire, V, 10. Recensements de 1660, 1667, et 1681. *Jug. et délib.*, I, II, IV. *Papier terrier de la Cie des I.O.* (P.-G. Roy), 128, 130. P.-G. Roy, *Inv. concessions*, I, 147; II, 8; *Inv. ins. cons. souv.*, 63f.; *La ville de Québec*, I, 273, 341, 353, 430. Alan Gowans, *Church architecture in New France* (Toronto, 1955).

LE MOYNE, SIMON, Jesuit priest, missionary to the Hurons, ambassador of peace to the Iroquois; b. 22 Oct. 1604 at Beauvais; d. 24 Nov. 1665 at Cap-de-la-Madeleine.

Le Moyne

Simon Le Moyne entered the Jesuit noviciate at Rouen on 10 Dec. 1622. He studied philosophy at the Collège de Clermont in Paris (1624–27), taught at the Collège in Rouen (1627–32), and took theology courses at La Flèche (1632–36); he again became a teacher at the Collège in Rouen (1636–37), where he also did his third probationary year. On 30 June 1638 he arrived at Quebec and by the end of September he was in the Huron country.

A letter from his confrère, Father François Du Peron, informs us that Father Le Moyne was deserted on the way by his Huron guides. For 15 days, abandoned in the immense forest, he had to live on the results of his young French companion's hunting. Thanks to the fact that Father Du Peron came by unexpectedly, Father Le Moyne was able finally to reach his destination. He devoted his efforts to the Huron country until 1649, and was of the same intellectual and apostolic calibre as his companions Jean de Brébeuf, Isaac Jogues, Jérôme Lalemant, Paul Ragueneau, Antoine Daniel, Charles Garnier, and others. After the destruction of the Huron nation, he returned to Quebec in 1650, and shared in the labours of his confrères at Sillery, on the Île d'Orléans and at Trois-Rivières. No one except Father Chaumonot spoke better Huron and Algonkian than he did. The Hurons had given him the name "Ouane." During his Iroquois period he was known as "Ondessonk," a name that had been given to Jogues.

It is above all as an ambassador of peace to the Iroquois that Father Simon Le Moyne has a place in history. In 1653 a short-lived truce had been signed between the Iroquois and the French. Following this flimsy and frequently violated treaty, Father Le Moyne on six occasions from 1654 to 1662 made trips into Iroquois country, each time as an ambassador of peace and each time risking his life. This official envoy of Onontio (the governor) was himself held prisoner, took his place on the enemy's scaffold, was threatened more than once by the hatchet of a drunken Iroquois or of one who believed it necessary to strike him down to fulfil a dream. And yet after all this, he considered the finest day of his life to be that on which he undertook, in 1661, his last trip into the Iroquois country.

Nothing is more effective in showing us the superior and attractive spirit of Father Le Moyne than the diary of his first trip to Iroquois territory. He left Quebec on 2 July 1654, taking with him as a companion a young Frenchman from Montreal, and he was back at Quebec on 11 September. The trip, exhausting in itself, was made still more arduous by heavy rains. Father Le Moyne describes the features and the beauties of the landscape, the warm sympathy shown him by the Iroquois, the ineffable comfort he derived from seeing again Huron prisoners who had remained steadfast in their faith and eager to hear the Black Robe tell them about God. But that did not prevent the practical man in him from noting the existence, near Syracuse (N.Y.), of a salt water spring. On 16 August he wrote: "We arrive at the entrance to a little lake in a great basin that is half dried up, and taste the water from a spring of which these people [the Iroquois] dare not drink, as they say there is an evil spirit in it that renders it foul. Upon tasting of it, I find it to be a spring of salt water; and indeed we made some salt from it, as natural as that which comes from the sea, and are carrying a sample of it to Quebec."

Father Le Moyne's peace embassy proved to be a success. In the name of the superior of the Jesuites at Quebec he had promised that missionaries would come and dwell among the Onondagas in 1655. This explains why, on 19 September of that year, Fathers Chaumonot and Dablon set out for the tribal territory of the Onondagas. On 30 March 1656 Father Dablon returned to Montreal, the bearer of good tidings. It was a time for optimism and heroism, and Quebec witnessed, on 17 May 1656, a large-scale missionary departure. Father François Le Mercier, the superior of the Jesuits at Quebec, Fathers René Ménard, Claude Dablon, Jacques Frémin and Brothers Ambroise Brouet and Joseph Boursier were going to join Father Chaumonot. They were accompanied by about 50 French workmen. Their task was to erect in record time a central residence, Sainte-Marie de Ganentaa, which would be to the Iroquois what the residence of Sainte-Marie had formerly been to the Hurons. The work of construction began 17 July and was carried on, not without some difficulties. The missionaries, however, became aware that they had been lured into a trap and that the ultimate design was nothing less than the massacre of all the Frenchmen and their allies. For this reason, it was decided to abandon Ganentaa. On 20 March 1658 fathers and workmen left secretly and arrived at Montreal on 23 April. Father Le Moyne's embassy and its sequel, that is to say the founding of Sainte-Marie de Ganentaa, were doomed from the beginning. Both of them had been undertaken without the knowledge of, and without any assistance from, the Mohawks, and they were for the benefit of the Onondagas. The Mohawks, who considered themselves the leading nation of the Iroquois, took umbrage at this; moreover, they feared lest this alliance between French and Onondagas harm their trade with the Dutch.

Le Moyne

They became more arrogant and more threatening than ever; and, feigning peaceful intentions, they sought Black Robes for themselves. If their wishes were not acceded to, the truce would be more imperilled than ever.

For the general good of the colony, Father Le Moyne was to travel into Mohawk territory as an ambassador of peace four times: from 17 Aug. to early November 1655; from the beginning of September to 5 Nov. 1656; from 27 Aug. 1657 to 21 May 1658; and from 7 May to 3 July 1659. These recurring negotiations make it clear that no one of them was entirely successful; but they prove also the esteem in which Father Le Moyne was held by both French and Iroquois. During these tragic years he personified the hopes of the civil and religious authorities in the face of the Iroquois menace.

During his 1657–58 stay, at which time he was considered a captive and was free only under surveillance, Father Le Moyne made the journey from Ossernenon (Auriesville, N.Y.) to New Amsterdam (New York). He wanted to thank Pastor Jan Megapolensis for the kindness the latter had earlier shown to Father Isaac Jogues. He was received with the greatest cordiality. He told his host about the salt spring at Lake Onondaga. They also discussed religion, for the Dutch minister writes that the missionary, on his return to Ossernenon, sent him three documents: one on the papal succession, a second on Church councils, and a third on heresies. Father Le Moyne, while making his way to Ossernenon over difficult roads, had set down in his own hand these theology lessons for Pastor Megapolensis. The *Journal des Jésuites* notes Father Le Moyne's arrival at Quebec on 21 May 1658.

On 21 July 1661, Father Le Moyne started out again for the Iroquois territory, in order to work for the release of the French captives. When he returned to Montreal on 31 Aug. 1662, he brought back 19 of them. Lastly, the *Journal des Jésuites* informs us that on 31 July 1663 he went to Montreal in order to be able to seize the first opportunity of going back among the Iroquois, but he does not appear to have gone any farther than Montreal.

His efforts to promote peace had not been in vain. A renowned Onondaga chieftain, GARAKONTIÉ, who was soon to occupy a prominent position, had at an early stage been won over to Father Le Moyne and to his mission of peace. In 1658 he returned two French captives to Montreal. In 1661 he shared his lodging with Father Le Moyne, built a chapel for him, protected him and encouraged his religious apostolate, although he was himself still a pagan.

When Father Le Moyne passed away at Cap-de-la-Madeleine on 24 Nov. 1665, four of the five Iroquois tribes were seeking peace with the French. Garakontié, spokesman of the Onondagas, was present at the council that was then taking place at Quebec. When he learned of the death of his old friend, he spoke these words: "Ondessonk, hearest thou me from the country of the dead, whither thou hast so quickly passed? Thou it was who didst so many times expose thy life on the scaffolds of the Agniehronnons; who didst go bravely into their very fires, to snatch so many Frenchmen from the flames; who didst carry peace and tranquillity whithersoever thou didst go, and who madest converts wherever thou didst dwell. We have seen thee on our council-mats deciding questions of peace and war; our cabins were found to be too small when thou didst enter them, and our villages themselves were too cramped when thou wast present, —so great was the crowd of people attracted thither by thy words. But I disturb thy rest with this importunate address. So often didst thou teach us that this life of afflictions is followed by one of eternal happiness; since, then, thou dost now possess that life, what reason have we to mourn thee? But we weep for thee because, in losing thee, we have lost our Father and Protector. Nevertheless we will console ourselves with the thought that thou still holdest that relation to us in Heaven, and that thou hast found in that abode the infinite joy whereof thou has so often told us."

In the Onondaga of old, now Syracuse, the centre of the missionary's apostolate of peace, Le Moyne College, under the direction of the American Jesuits, recalls to mind this great French Jesuit and honours his memory.

LÉON POULIOT

JR (Thwaites), *passim*. An English translation of a letter from Megapolensis to his religious superiors in Amsterdam, 28 Sept. 1658, is given in *Narratives of New Netherlands* (Jameson), 403–5, in *Original narratives* (Jameson). The letters from Megapolensis to Father Lemoyne, mentioned in the *Journal des Jésuites*, 15 Aug. 1658 (*JJ* (Laverdière et Casgrain), 239; *JR* (Thwaites), XLIV, 105), appear to have been lost.

Campbell, *Pioneer priests*, I, 75–100. Rochemonteix, *Les Jésuites et la Nouvelle-France au XVIIe siècle*, I. The most complete study devoted to Father Le Moyne is perhaps that of Alexander M. Stewart, "Le Moyne, the peacemaker," in *Annual Diocesan Review (1938)*, Supplement of the *Catholic Courier*, newspaper of the Rochester diocese, X (1939), 4, 6–8, 10–14, 19. Its author corrects certain errors which have slipped into the otherwise outstanding work of the Rev. Charles Hawley, *Early chapters of Seneca history* (Auburn, New York, 1884).

Le Moyne de Longueuil

LE MOYNE DE BIENVILLE, FRANCOIS, soldier; b. 10 March 1666 at Montreal, son of Charles Le Moyne and Catherine Thierry; d. 7 June 1691 at Repentigny.

He was the fifth son of Charles Le Moyne de Longueuil. As a cadet, then an ensign, in the colonial regular troops, he may have taken part with his older brother, Jacques Le Moyne de Sainte-Hélène, in Governor Brisay* de Denonville's campaign against the Iroquois in 1687. In February 1690 he accompanied his brothers Sainte-Hélène and Pierre Le Moyne* d'Iberville in the expedition against Corlaer (Schenectady, N.Y.). In the spring of 1691 he went in pursuit of the Iroquois who had been ravaging the region about Montreal since the beginning of May. With Philippe de Rigaud* de Vaudreuil and about a hundred volunteers, who had been recruited with difficulty, he set off at the beginning of June 1691 in pursuit of a band of Oneidas who were prowling about east of Montreal. Having located them in a deserted house in Repentigny, the Frenchmen decided to attack them during the night of 6–7 June. The Indians were resting unconcernedly, and about 15 of them were lying outside, near the door. These were massacred, but the slaughter alarmed those who were inside the house and they defended themselves vigorously after unsuccessfully proposing peace. During this engagement François de Bienville met his death, along with seven or eight comrades. Having come too close to a window, he was killed by a gunshot. But the enemy did not meet a better fate. Vaudreuil had the cabin set on fire. Eight warriors were killed when they tried to get out. Three were forced back into the fierce fire. This was one of the rare occasions during this war that the French were able to overcome a group of Iroquois on Canadian territory.

François de Bienville was buried at Montreal. His title went to his brother, Jean-Baptiste Le Moyne* de Bienville, the twelfth child of Charles Le Moyne and the founder of Louisiana.

Jean Blain

AN, Col., C11^A, 11, ff. 299–300. Ferland, *Cours d'histoire du Canada*, II, 233f. Frégault, *Iberville*, 128–40. A. Jodoin et J.-L. Vincent, *Histoire de Longueuil et de la famille de Longueuil* (Montréal, 1889), 149. Charles de La Roncière, *Une épopée canadienne* (Paris, 1930).

LE MOYNE DE CHÂTEAUGUAY, LOUIS, soldier and sailor; b. 4 Jan. 1676 at Montreal, son of Charles Le Moyne and Catherine Thierry; d. 1694.

He was the tenth child of Charles Le Moyne de Longueuil. When still very young he took part in the expedition to Hudson Bay with his brother, Pierre Le Moyne* d'Iberville, who in 1693 requested a midshipman's commission for him, alleging that Châteauguay was "able to manage a ship by himself as far as piloting and commanding are concerned." During the siege of Port Nelson (York Fort), when he was responsible for preventing the besieged from breaking out, Châteauguay was killed by a musket shot 4 Oct. 1694. He was serving as sub-lieutenant under his brother, Joseph Le Moyne* de Sérigny.

Jean Blain

JR (Thwaites). Frégault, *Iberville*. A. Jodoin et J.-L. Vincent, *Histoire de Longueuil et de la famille de Longueuil* (Montréal, 1889), 155–56, 180, *et passim*. Charles de La Roncière, *Une épopée canadienne* (Paris, 1930), 79–81.

LE MOYNE DE LONGUEUIL ET DE CHÂTEAUGUAY, CHARLES, soldier, interpreter, trader, seigneur, son of Pierre Le Moyne, innkeeper, and of Judith Du Chesne; b. 2 Aug. 1626 at Dieppe (Normandy); d. February 1685 at Montreal.

The fact that his maternal uncle, the surgeon Adrien Du Chesne, was in the colony, encouraged Charles Le Moyne to come to New France. He was 15 years old when he arrived in 1641. At first he was an indentured employee of the Jesuits in the Huron country, and over a period of four years he familiarized himself with the Indian languages.

In 1645 he was serving in the Trois-Rivières garrison as an interpreter, a clerk, and a soldier. The following year he settled at Ville-Marie (Montreal), where he was to remain throughout his whole career. His life there took the form of continual skirmishes with the Indians, who plagued the fort unceasingly with their attacks. In 1646, and again in 1648, he took a number of Iroquois prisoner. In the spring of 1651, with the pioneer Jacques Archambault, he barely escaped a massacre in which several settlers perished; there was only one other survivor, Jean Chicot, and he had been scalped. On 18 June of the same year he repelled another attack, and for his bravery he was named storekeeper of the fort.

In another ambush, in 1655, he and Lambert Closse took half a dozen Indians prisoner, among them a chief. During a trip he made to Quebec in 1657 he instituted an exchange of French and Iroquois prisoners. He very nearly set out with Dollard Des Ormeaux on the 1660 expedition; he did not go, however, because he wanted it to be postponed until after seed-time.

Le Moyne de Longueuil

During an attack by 160 Indians in February 1661, only Le Moyne had a weapon with which to defend himself. Just as he was about to be captured he was saved by Mme Celles Duclos, who brought him an armful of weapons. In the summer of 1665 he was taken prisoner by an Iroquois party, but set free thanks to GARAKONTIÉ, a friend of the French and a chief of the Onondagas.

In January 1666 Le Moyne was in command of the settlers of Ville-Marie who served as the advance guard for Governor RÉMY de Courcelle's fruitless expedition to the Iroquois country. In the autumn he was to be found at the head of the Montreal settlers in the campaign against the Mohawks, which was personally conducted by the lieutenant general, PROUVILLE de Tracy. On his return he escorted the army chaplain to Fort Sainte-Anne on Lake Champlain. In addition, in the summer of 1671, he took part, as an interpreter, in a new expedition to Lake Ontario organized by Courcelle. In 1673 he resumed his role as an interpreter for the chiefs of the Iroquois tribes, when Governor BUADE de Frontenac went to Lake Ontario to lay the foundations for the settlement of Cataracoui.

In the autumn of 1682 he took part in the assembly of the notables of the country, called by Governor LE FEBVRE de La Barre to decide whether New France should take the offensive against the Iroquois territory. In the spring of 1683, he was again delegated by La Barre, this time to go with four Indian chiefs from Laprairie, near Montreal, to the south shore of Lake Ontario; they were to take gifts to the Five Nations, who were once more defying the authorities of New France and neglecting to send their deputies, according to agreement, to negotiate the terms of the fur trade and of the alliances.

In the year of his marriage (1654), Charles Le Moyne had received from CHOMEDEY de Maisonneuve a gift of money and a grant of 90 acres of land, since called Pointe-Saint-Charles, and a site in Saint-Paul Street, where for 30 years he had his home and his headquarters.

The Lauson family, in 1657, granted him a fief of 5,000 acres, in accordance with the uses and customs of Le Vexin in France; this was on the south shore at Montreal, cut directly out of the huge seigneury of La Citière. To this fief was added in 1665 grants of land on the Île Sainte-Hélène and the Île Ronde. In 1669 he had an establishment at the Saint-Louis rapids.

In 1672 Governor Frontenac and Intendant JEAN TALON confirmed him in his title to the seigneury of Longueuil by augmenting it with the unallotted lands between Varennes and Laprairie, and by extending it to one and a half leagues in depth. The following year, "because of the zeal that he has always shown in the service of the king," Frontenac granted him a seigneury at Châteauguay two leagues across by three in depth, and the Île Saint-Bernard, now called the Île Châteauguay, at the mouth of the Rivière du Loup. In 1676 the intendant DUCHESNEAU, in compliance with his request, still further extended the depth of his seigneury of Longueuil, and Le Moyne collected all his fiefs under the name of Longueuil.

With his brother-in-law and business associate Jacques Le Ber* he acquired in 1679 the Boisbriant fief, which subsequent documents situate "at the upper end of the Île de Montréal," which took the name of Senneville, and of which Le Ber became the sole holder. Under M. de La Barre's administration he obtained with Le Ber the right to trade in furs at Fort Cataracoui and to ship supplies there, in compensation for funds advanced to CAVELIER de La Salle, a bad debtor.

In 1682 he had been one of the shareholders of the Compagnie du Nord, whose agents, Radisson* and CHOUART Des Groseilliers, went over to the English in the Hudson's Bay Company.

He made application, in 1684, for the purchase of the fief of the Île Perrot, which had belonged to François-Marie PERROT, the governor of Montreal.

In addition to his residence in Saint-Paul Street —the finest at Ville-Marie—Le Moyne, from 1674, owned a house and buildings on his fief of Longueuil. In 1675 he had there some 20 copyholders (*censitaires*). In 1684, in favour of his eldest son Charles*, he relinquished his Longueuil fief, which was to be elevated to a barony in 1700.

With Pierre GADOYS, Le Moyne was elected a warden of the parish church of Ville-Marie in 1660, and when the royal government was set up at Montreal in 1663 he was given the office of attorney-general, which he filled for a year of two.

In 1668 Le Moyne received letters patent of nobility. These letters, which were not registered within the prescribed time-limit and which were therefore theoretically cancelled, were nevertheless recognized by the authorities of the colony and by the king himself. Nobody, moreover, seems to have challenged the right of Le Moyne or of his descendants to their titles between 1668 and 1717, at which time the situation was regularized by the registration of the letters patent in the Parlement of Paris and the Cour des Aides.

Governor Le Febvre de La Barre, asserting that Le Moyne had done more than any other person in the war against the Iroquois, recommended him in 1683 for the post of governor of Montreal.

Shortly afterwards, Le Moyne was to perform

Le Moyne de Sainte-Hélène

his final service for his country. It was he who in the summer of 1684, with the help of Father Jean de Lamberville*, saved from disaster La Barre's unfortunate expedition against the Iroquois, by inducing the latter to negotiate for peace at Anse de la Famine (Famine Cove).

Worn out before his time, Charles Le Moyne was not yet 60 when he dictated his last will and testament on 30 Jan. 1685. He passed away a few days later and was buried in the crypt of the church of Notre-Dame at Montreal.

At Ville-Marie, in 1654, he had married Catherine Thierry (1640–90), the adopted daughter of Antoine Primot and of Martine Messier. His wife survived him by only five years. He had by her two daughters and 12 sons, almost all of them famous: of the latter several died in battle of their wounds; others were commandants of different localities; and one, Pierre Le Moyne* d'Iberville, was the most renowned soldier of New France.

The inventory of Charles Le Moyne's possessions, which was drawn up shortly after his death by the notary Bénigne Basset, enumerated, in addition to the titles of landed property quoted earlier, personal possessions to the value of more than 125,000 *livres*; this makes Le Moyne the richest Montreal citizen of his day.

Jean-Jacques Lefebvre

AJM, Greffe de Bénigne Basset, 1657–99, *passim*. Dollier de Casson, *Histoire du Montréal*. *NYCD* (O'Callaghan and Fernow), III, IX. *Royal Fort Frontenac* (Preston and Lamontagne).

Crouse, *Lemoyne d'Iberville*. Faillon, *Histoire de la colonie française*, II, III. E. Falardeau, *Les pionniers de Longueuil, 1666–1681* (Montréal, 1937). Frégault, *Iberville*, 9–64. A. Jodoin et J.-L. Vincent, *Histoire de Longueuil et de la famille de Longueuil* (Montréal, 1889). Sulte, *Mélanges historiques* (Malchelosse), VIII. Tanguay, *Dictionnaire*.

LE MOYNE DE SAINTE-HÉLÈNE, JACQUES, soldier; b. 16 April 1659 at Montreal, son of Charles Le Moyne and Catherine Thierry; d. 1690 at Quebec.

In 1684 Sainte-Hélène, one of the famous Le Moyne brothers, fought a duel with François-Marie Perrot, the governor of Montreal who had been dismissed from his office. In that year Jacques Le Moyne accompanied his father on the expedition which Governor Le Febvre de La Barre commanded and which had unfortunate consequences.

It was however from 1686 on that he won fame. He associated himself as first lieutenant with the Chevalier de Troyes, who had been given the task of driving the English out of Hudson Bay. In addition to contributing to the glory of giving back to France territories that she claimed as hers, Sainte-Hélène, with his brothers Pierre Le Moyne* d'Iberville and Paul Le Moyne* de Maricourt, represented in this expedition the interests of the Compagnie du Nord, with which his father, Charles Le Moyne, was closely associated. After an 85-day trip via the Ottawa River, Lake Timiskaming, and the Abitibi and Moosonee Rivers, the little force arrived in sight of Fort Monsipi (Moose or Saint-Louis) on James Bay. The Chevalier de Troyes entrusted Sainte-Hélène and 18 men with the task of attacking the left flank of the fort, which seemed to be strongly built. Once over the stockades, Sainte-Hélène forced his way into the place, sword in hand. Resistance crumbled. Negotiations had begun, when one of the English thought better of it and decided to aim a cannon at the invaders. Immediately a bullet struck him right in the forehead. As Sainte-Hélène had the reputation of being a good marksman, the shot was attributed to him. After Monsipi the next objective was Charles Fort (Rupert House) and an English ship that was calling there. Having been sent to make a reconnaissance, Sainte-Hélène reported that neither the fort nor the ship was capable of putting up a good defence. While d'Iberville was to seize the ship, Sainte-Hélène was given the task of taking the fort by storm, which he succeeded in doing with very great ease.

Their efforts were then directed against the third fort, Quichicouanne (Albany). Saint-Hélène was again chosen to reconnoitre the area. Quichicouanne was better guarded than the other posts. The Chevalier de Troyes decided to lay siege to it. Saint-Hélène and Iberville acted as gunners. The English capitulated. The French renamed the fort Sainte-Anne. The Chevalier de Troyes's expedition was a complete success, but the credit for it was due above all to Iberville and Sainte-Hélène.

Jacques Le Moyne's short career knew little respite. In the summer of 1687 we find him at the head of 300 Indians in the vanguard of the expeditionary corps led by Governor Brisay* de Denonville against the Senecas. In the same year Iberville requested the command of a company for him. Denonville made him lieutenant to M. de Merville. In the summer of 1689 the Compagnie du Nord wanted to supply Iberville on Hudson Bay with fresh provisions and to request him to return to Quebec with a load of pelts. At the same time it wanted to try out a new route which was supposed to take one to the Bay in 28 days. The company entrusted the task to Sainte-Hélène, who was accompanied by a detachment of 38 men, including several sailors, and who was commissioned to sail to Quebec the

Le Moyne de Sainte-Hélène

English ships that had been seized in Hudson Bay. Leaving on 5 July, Sainte-Hélène met his brother 15 August at Fort Sainte-Anne (Quichicouanne). After discharging his mission, he returned to Quebec in November 1689, just in time to take part in the winter campaign of 1690 against the English establishments in New England.

In 1690 Governor BUADE de Frontenac decided to reply to the attacks directed against New France by the Iroquois and encouraged by the English. He raised three expeditionary corps, one of which was recruited at Montreal, another at Trois-Rivières, and the third at Quebec, and which had the task of paying the English back in their own coin, as well as of restoring French prestige among their Indian allies.

The Montreal detachment was composed of 210 men, 114 of whom were French. It was under the command of Le Moyne de Sainte-Hélène and Nicolas d'Ailleboust* de Manthet. Leaving Montreal at the beginning of February, the little corps hesitated between two possible objectives, Albany (N.Y.) and Corlaer (Schenectady), then decided upon the second place, as it presented fewer risks and was better suited to the sort of surprise attack that was being contemplated. On 18 February, at nightfall, they were in sight of the post, which was inhabited mainly by Dutch people. As at Lachine the preceding year, the inhabitants were asleep, with no suspicion of what was in store for them. Sainte-Hélène and Manthet stationed their men around the village and at the strategic points. Then the signal for the attack was given.

The inhabitants of Corlaer suffered hours of terrible anguish until dawn. Some 60 persons were massacred. Others succeeded in fleeing in the direction of Albany under pitiful conditions. The assailants took 25 prisoners and spared about 50 people, most of whom had put up no resistance. The houses, about 80 of them, were left to the Indian allies, who set fire to all but five or six. The next day Sainte-Hélène set off again for Montreal with his men, leaving behind him a scene of utter desolation. These raids as authorized by Frontenac in 1690 have been severely censured by a number of historians, particularly those of American origin, because of the savagery and cruelty which they occasioned. The blame also falls upon the commanders of these expeditions, in particular upon Sainte-Hélène. French-Canadian historians have not failed to point out that in the 17th century the rules of war, particularly on the American continent, were not as rigid as they can be today, and that, moreover, we are concerned with punitive expeditions that were intended to check the barbarous attacks by the Iroquois against New France. By inflicting upon a few New England posts the fate that had been reserved for the post at Lachine, it was hoped that the English would be made to think twice before hurling the Iroquois against the French establishments. In any event, the expedition against Corlaer throws light upon the personalities of Sainte-Hélène and his companions. By this time they were already displaying the characteristics that distinguished the Canadian soldier of the 17th and 18th centuries as opposed to the French regular soldier. Like his brothers, Sainte-Hélène had learned the art of fighting in the immense savagery of the North American continent. He derived from the Indian his technique, his courage, and also his cruelty.

In October 1690 we find Sainte-Hélène back at Quebec. He had come to aid his people who were defending the capital of New France againt PHIPS's attacks. He was posted to the artillery. On 18 October some of Phips's ships, including the flagship, neared Quebec to bombard it. The retort was fierce. Sainte-Hélène's firing was accurate. Next day two of the ships had to retreat and two others tried vainly to take shelter in the Anse des Mères. The flagship was leaking and its mainmast was nearly shot away. Many of its crew were dead or wounded.

Meanwhile, Major Walley* had landed downstream from Quebec and was trying vainly to advance towards the town. He was prevented from doing so by gunners at Beauport and Beaupré and by a detachment of men from Montreal led by Sainte-Hélène. On 20 October an engagement was fought between the advance guard of the English army and the corps from Montreal. The English soldiers had to withdraw. Sainte-Hélène was wounded in the leg, and after a few days the wound, which had been thought to be insignificant, became worse. Sainte-Hélène was taken to the Hôtel-Dieu at Quebec, and there he died at the beginning of December, 1690. According to Charlevoix* the colony had just lost "one of the bravest Men that it had ever had."

On 7 Feb. 1684 Jacques Le Moyne de Sainte-Hélène had married Jeanne Dufresnoy Carion in Montreal. As she was only 12, a dispensation was necessary, which Bishop Laval* gladly granted because of "the fidelity . . . with which he has always refused to misuse the liquor trade with the Indians, but rather to be guided by the fear of God in his dealings with it." Sainte-Hélène had three children, one of whom, Jacques*, carved out a career for himself in Louisiana.

JEAN BLAIN

ASQ, MSS, 17, p. 433.
"Acte de sépulture de Lemoyne de Ste-Hélène,"

BRH, XXXV (1929), 707. Charlevoix, *Histoire*, I. *Coll. de manuscrits relatifs à la Nouv.-France*, I, 482–531, 551–59. *JR* (Thwaites), LXIV, 60, 275. La Pot(h)erie, *Histoire*, I. Chevalier de Troyes, *Journal* (Caron). Frégault, *Iberville*. HBRS, XXI (Rich). A. Jodoin et J.-L. Vincent, *Histoire de Longueuil et de la famille de Longueil* (Montréal, 1889), 138–43 *et passim*. Robert Le Blant, *Histoire de la Nouvelle-France: les sources narratives du début du XVIIIe siècle et le Recueil de Gédéon de Catalogne* (1 v. paru, Dax, s.d.), 169–272. É.-Z. Massicotte, "Le Moyne de Sainte-Marie et Le Moyne de Martigny," *BRH*, XXIII (1917), 125–27. P.-G. Roy, "Le duel sous le régime français," *BRH*, XIII (1907), 131f. *1690, Sir William Phips devant Québec: histoire d'un siège*, éd. Ernest Myrand (Québec, 1893).

LENEUF DE LA POTERIE, JACQUES, seigneur of Portneuf, governor of Trois-Rivières, acting governor of New France, brother of MICHEL LENEUF Du Hérisson; b. 1606 at Caen (Normandy); d. some time after 1685.

Jacques Leneuf de La Poterie arrived at Quebec in 1636. In January of the same year he had managed to acquire the seigneury of Portneuf, a concession which was to be confirmed 16 April 1647. He likewise obtained, on 29 March 1649, the marquisate of Sablé—which despite its name was land held by a commoner—the fief of the Île aux Cochons (29 March 1649), the fief of La Poterie or Niverville (7 April 1660), which were lands situated in the region of Trois-Rivières, and also the seigneury of the Cap-des-Rosiers, in Gaspesia, which he shared with CHARLES LEGARDEUR de Tilly and a few others.

He lived at Trois-Rivières from 1640 on. On several occasions he was to act as deputy governor of this small town: from 17 Nov. 1645 to 2 Sept. 1648, then in 1650, 1652–53, 1658–62. On 13 May 1665 the Conseil Souverain ordered a commission to be registered by virtue of which the governor SAFFRAY de Mézy had nominated him "to be his Lieutenant after his demise." The governor had died on 5 May. The Council, on 27 May, refused to allow him the majority of the prerogatives of this office, conceding him only the command of the militia.

On 18 Oct. 1666 Jacques Leneuf sailed on the *Moulin d'Or*, on his way first to Acadia then to France. His titles of nobility were confirmed by Louis XIV in 1667 and registered in the Conseil Souverain of New France in 1675. He was possibly back in Canada by 1667; in any case he was at Quebec 22 May 1668. Mention of his name is found in public documents up to 1685.

While in France Jacques Leneuf had married Marguerite Legardeur, sister of PIERRE LEGARDEUR de Repentigny and of Charles Legardeur de Tilly, members of one of the most illustrious Canadian families. His son Michel Leneuf* de La Vallière, born in October 1640, was to play an important role in Acadia.

Leneuf de La Poterie had always been interested in the fur trade—as well as in the trafficking of spirits. He was one of the members of the Communauté des Habitants. He was a wily business man who often had brushes with the law.

LÉOPOLD LAMONTAGNE

Édits ord., II, 25f. *JR* (Thwaites), VIII, 220; IX, 142; XVIII, 90; LXXIII, 79. *JJ* (Laverdière et Casgrain). *Jug. et délib.*, I, 344, 347, 350, 436, 996, 1001; II, 1045. *Lettres de noblesse* (P.-G. Roy). *Papier terrier de la Cie des I.O.* (P.-G. Roy). P.-G. Roy, *Inv. concessions*. *BRH*, II (1896), 67–69; VI (1900), 29; IX (1903), 160, 311–14; XXI (1915), 46. Raymond Douville, "La dictature de la famille Le Neuf," *Cahiers des Dix*, XX (1955), 61–89. Hugolin Lemay, *Le père Joseph Denis, premier récollet canadien (1657–1736)* (2v., Québec, 1926), I, 40f. Sulte, *Mélanges historiques* (Malchelosse), XVIII, 6f., 9, 19; "Premiers seigneurs du Canada, 1634–1664," *RSCT*, 1st ser., I (1882–83), sect. I, 131–37. Tanguay, *Dictionnaire*, I, 381. E. Vaillancourt, *La conquête du Canada par les Normands* (Montréal, 1933).

LENEUF DU HÉRISSON, MICHEL, seigneur, member of the Communauté des Habitants, syndic, acting governor of Trois-Rivières, royal judge; b. c. 1601 at Caen (Normandy), son of Mathieu Leneuf and Jeanne Le Marchant; d. probably in 1672.

Michel Leneuf landed at Quebec 11 June 1636 along with other members of his numerous family: his adopted or illegitimate daughter Anne; his mother, Jeanne Le Marchant, widow of Mathieu Leneuf; his sister, Marie Leneuf (who was to marry the Trois-Rivières pioneer, JEAN GODEFROY de Lintot); his brother, JACQUES LENEUF de La Poterie, who was bringing from France his daughter Marie-Anne and his wife, Marguerite Legardeur de Repentigny; PIERRE LEGARDEUR de Repentigny and CHARLES LEGARDEUR de Tilly. They made up a veritable family clan, as was said later, which for several years sought to acquire a monopoly of the fur trade and which took the initiative in the founding of the Communauté des Habitants.

The Leneuf family went to settle at Trois-Rivières the same year it arrived. Michel secured title to substantial grants of land: among others the Dutort (later Bécancour) fief, 1 Dec. 1637; 50 acres fronting on the St. Lawrence River at Trois-Rivières, 16 July 1638; the fief of Vieux-Pont, 29 March 1649; part of the seigneury of

467

Léonard de Chartres

Cap-des-Rosiers (the rest of which belonged to his brother, to the Le Gardeurs, and others), 9 March 1652. With the backing of his younger brother, Jacques, in whose house he lived, he managed to acquire, jointly with Jacques, effective control of the town of Trois-Rivières. The 1667 census credits him with 100 acres of land under development at Trois-Rivières. He also owned a flour mill. He had his farms cultivated by tenant farmers with whom, as a result of his violent temperament, he was in constant difficulty and litigation, especially with Sébastien Dodier and Guillaume Isabel. He was also continually at odds with the Jesuits in connection with the boundaries of their adjacent grants of land.

His public life was similarly very active. He capitalized on the prestige of his brother Jacques, who was governor of Trois-Rivières almost without interruption from 1645 to 1662. Michel Leneuf was chosen syndic of the settlers in 1648 and in 1649. In 1661, while his brother was still governor and when his brother-in-law, Charles Legardeur de Tilly, was a member of the Conseil de la Nouvelle-France, Michel had no difficulty in obtaining the post of general civil and criminal lieutenant in the seneschal's court of Trois-Rivières; then, from 1664 on, he replaced Pierre Boucher* as royal judge after the latter's resignation. When the Leneuf brothers had the control of the key offices which they had sought for a long time, their abuses involved them in numerous difficulties. In 1665–66 an inquiry into the liquor trade with the Indians proved that the governor's wife herself, Marguerite Legardeur, was one of the leading figures in this flourishing business. The Conseil Souverain suspended Michel Leneuf from his post as a judge by a decree dated 29 May 1665 and replaced him temporarily by Councillor Louis Peronne de Mazé, who was appointed "special commissioner" for the time being.

Shortly afterwards Michel Leneuf was reinstated in office. In the records of a hearing held on 19 May 1666 he is listed as civil and criminal lieutenant, and the following year, on 8 June, a petition addressed to him by Michel Gamelain dit Lafontaine refers to him as "Royal Judge."

The archives of the courthouse of Trois-Rivières have preserved for us some of the judgements handed down by Michel Leneuf. In general they are marked by fairness and common sense. These archives also contain an absorbing account of the numerous lawsuits that took place between the fiery seigneur and his tenant farmers. He was a typical Norman country squire, intelligent and wily, but fond of legal quibbles.

The documents provide us with very little information about his private life. When he arrived in New France he was single or a widower, for he brought out with him a little girl of four who still bore the name Anne Du Hérisson and not Anne Leneuf Du Hérisson. It is possible, as has been claimed, that she was his illegitimate daughter. No precise information is given in this young woman's marriage contract with Antoine Desrosiers dated 24 Nov. 1647.

Michel Leneuf's burial certificate is not recorded in the Roman Catholic registers of Trois-Rivières, which are preserved intact from 1634. We may, however, assume that he died in 1672, for he was replaced in his post as judge by Gilles de Boyvinet on 26 October of that year.

Michel had acted as governor of Trois-Rivières in 1668, as a temporary replacement in this office for René Gaultier de Varennes.

Raymond Douville

AJTR, MSS, Registres des audiences de la cour de juridiction civile et criminelle. APQ, Documents de la prévôté de Trois-Rivières. Recensement de 1667. Papier terrier de la Cie des I.O. (P.-G. Roy). P.-G. Roy, Inv. concessions, I, II, V. Raymond Douville, "La dictature de la famille Le Neuf," Cahiers des Dix, XX (1955), 61–89; Visages du vieux Trois-Rivières (Trois-Rivières, 1955). Godbout, Les pionniers de la région trifluvienne. Sulte, Mélanges historiques (Malchelosse), XI, 7–38; XIV, 65–67; XIX.

LÉONARD DE CHARTRES, priest, Capuchin, missionary and vice-prefect of the religious of his order in Acadia; b. at Chartres (France); assassinated 1654 at Port-Royal (now Annapolis Royal, N.S.).

He joined the Capuchins in Paris in 1616. He was sent to Port-Royal in 1649 as a custodian to replace Father Pascal de Troyes, who was drowned at Blois that same year on his return from Acadia. As soon as he arrived Father Léonard visited the various posts ministered to by the Capuchins and baptized several persons. During a baptism on 14 July 1649 an Indian let fly an arrow at him, which nearly brought about his death. But he recovered, and resumed his missionary travels.

After Governor Menou d'Aulnay's death in 1650, Emmanuel Le Borgne, a merchant of La Rochelle who had advanced considerable sums of money to the governor, sought to recover his outlay by securing the Acadian trade and taking possession of the posts. For the Capuchins these circumstances were to create difficulties. Some of them were even imprisoned by Le Borgne's soldiers, others returned to France, or else took to the woods, where they lived with the Indians. Father Léonard remained at Port-Royal. The following year he blessed a new monastery and a new church. In July 1653 Father Léonard officiated at the marriage of d'Aulnay's widow [*see* MOTIN] to CHARLES DE SAINTE-ÉTIENNE de La Tour and signed the marriage contract.

The following year he was present at the capture of Port-Royal by SEDGWICK and with Le Borgne he countersigned the articles of capitulation (16 August). This document stipulated freedom for the Capuchins, but they were expelled just the same; only the superior, Father Léonard de Chartres, remained at Port-Royal, where he died the same year, a victim of the new rulers. He is considered to be the first Capuchin to have shed his blood for the Catholic faith in North America.

G.-M. DUMAS

Archivum Sacrae Congregationis de Propaganda, Lettere Antiche, 260, f.25, Ignace de Paris, "Brevis ac dilucida . . ." ("Brève relation de la mission d'Acadie . . . 1656") (photocopy of the original with a translation in PAC, MG 17, 1; *see* PAC, *Report, 1904*, App. H, 333–41). *Coll. de manuscrits relatifs à la Nouv.-France*, I, 145–49 (capitulation of Port-Royal). Candide de Nant, *Pages glorieuses*; "Silhouettes de missionnaires, I: le Père Léonard de Chartres," *La Nouvelle-France*, X (1911), 316–23. Ivanhoë Caron, "Les pères capucins en Acadie," *BRH*, XLVII (1941), 128–31. Couillard Després, *Saint-Étienne de La Tour*, 408 (marriage contract of d'Aulnay's widow and Charles de La Tour).

LE PIAT, IRÉNÉE. *See* PIAT

LE PICARD, MARC-ANTOINE *dit. See* OLIVIER

LE PONT, FRANÇOIS GRAVÉ. *See* GRAVÉ DU PONT

"LE RAISIN." *See* CHOMINA

LESCARBOT, MARC, lawyer, traveller, and writer; b. *c.* 1570 at Vervins in Thiérache, a frontier region between France and the Spanish Netherlands; d. 1642.

His family probably came from Guise, but he himself tells us that his ancestors originated in Saint-Pol-de-Léon, Brittany. He first studied at the Collège in Vervins, then at Laon. Thanks to the protection of Mgr Duglas, the bishop of this latter town, he was able to go and complete his studies in Paris, with a bursary from the Collège of Laon. He received in Paris a very thorough classical education, learned Latin, Greek, and Hebrew, and acquired a wide knowledge of ancient and modern literatures. He then studied canonical and civil law.

He graduated as a bachelor of laws in 1598, and took a minor part in the negotiations for the Treaty of Vervins, between Spain and France. At a moment when the discussions seemed doomed to failure, Lescarbot delivered a Latin *Discours* in defence of peace. After the conclusion of the treaty, he composed a *Harangue d'action de grâces*, wrote a commemorative inscription, and published *Poèmes de la Paix*. He was called to the Parlement of Paris as a lawyer in 1599, and translated into French three Latin works: the *Discours de l'origine des Russiens* and the *Discours véritable de la réunion des églises* by Cardinal Baronius, and the *Guide des curés* by St. Charles Borromeo, which he dedicated to the new bishop of Laon, Godefroy de Billy, but published only after that dignitary's death (1613).

He normally lived in Paris, where he associated with men of letters, such as the scholars Frédéric and Claude Morel, his first printers, and the poet Guillaume Colletet, who wrote a biography of him that has unfortunately been lost. He was likewise interested in medicine, and translated into French a pamphlet by Dr. Citois, *Histoire merveilleuse de l'abstinence triennale d'une fille de Confolens* (1602). But he also travelled and maintained contact with his native region, where he had relatives and friends, such as the Laroque brothers, his rivals in poetry, and where he recruited a number of clients. The loss of a case because of the venality of a judge gave him a temporary distaste for the bar. Consequently, when one of his clients, JEAN DE BIENCOURT de Poutrincourt, who was associated with the Canadian entreprises of the Sieur DU GUA de Monts, proposed that he accompany them on a voyage to Acadia, Lescarbot lost no time in accepting. He composed an *Adieu à la France* in verse, and embarked at La Rochelle on 13 May 1606. He reached Port-Royal (Annapolis Royal, N.S.) in July, spent the remainder of the year there, and the following spring made a trip to the Saint John River and the Île Sainte-Croix. But in the summer of 1607 the revocation of de Monts's licence obliged the whole colony to go back to France.

On his return there, Lescarbot published an epic poem on *La défaite des sauvages armouchiquois* (1607), then undertook to compose a vast history of the French establishments in America, the *Histoire de la Nouvelle-France*. The first edition of this work appeared in Paris in 1609, published by the bookseller Jean Millot. The author recounted first the voyages of Laudonnière, Ribaut, and Gourgues to Florida, and those of Durand de Villegaignon and Jean de Léry to Brazil, then those of VERRAZZANO, CARTIER, and Roberval [*see* JEAN-FRANÇOIS LA ROCQUE] to Canada. This last part, the least original of his work, is little more than a second-hand compilation.

He next undertook to recount de Monts's

Lescarbot

ventures in Acadia, and this part of his book is clearly original. He had spent a year at the Port-Royal habitation and met the survivors of the short-lived settlement at Sainte-Croix; he had talked with the promoters and members of the earlier voyages, FRANÇOIS GRAVÉ Du Pont, de Monts, and CHAMPLAIN; he had visited old fishing captains, who knew Newfoundland and the Acadian coasts; he therefore reported what he had himself seen or learned from those who had taken part in the events or witnessed them at first hand.

In the successive editions of his *Histoire*, in 1611–12 and 1617–18, and in his complementary pamphlets, *La conversion des sauvages* (1610) and the *Relation dernière* (1612) he reshaped and completed his account. He described the re-establishment of the colony by Poutrincourt, the disputes of the latter and of his son CHARLES DE BIENCOURT with their competitors and the Jesuits BIARD, MASSÉ and DU THET, and then the ruin of the colony by ARGALL. He had not seen these incidents, and narrated them only according to Poutrincourt, Biencourt, Imbert, or other witnesses. These testimonies might appear to show some bias, or to be designed for publicity purposes; but Lescarbot, by retaining them, has brought to our knowledge incidents and texts that we would not have known were it not for him.

Lescarbot devoted the whole of the last part of his *Histoire* to a description of the natives. He was keenly interested in the Indians, and frequently visited the Souriquois (Micmac) chiefs and braves; he observed their customs, made a collection of their remarks, noted down their chants. In many respects he judged them more civilized and virtuous than Europeans, but, like a good Frenchman, he pitied them for their ignorance of the pleasures of wine and love!

Throughout his work, Lescarbot did not confine himself to narration, but expressed many personal ideas. He had very precise opinions about the colonies, which he saw as a field of action for men of courage, an outlet for trade, a social benefit, and a means for the mother country to extend her influence. He favoured a commercial monopoly as a way of meeting the expenses of colonization; for him, freedom of trade led only to anarchy, and produced nothing stable. In Poutrincourt's dispute with the Jesuits, he obviously sided with his protector; but he could not possibly have composed the *Factum* of 1614 [*see* General Bibliography] that some authors attribute to him; he was staying in Switzerland when this lampoon appeared.

All the editions of the *Histoire* include, as an appendix, a short collection of poems called *Les muses de la Nouvelle-France*, also published separately. In his dedication to Brulart de Sillery, Lescarbot begs him to forgive these "unkempt and rustically garbed" muses, sprung from the forest. Indeed, if the author did possess real poetic gifts, poetry for him, as for his contemporary Malherbe, was never more than an occasional diversion and a means of pleasing the great. He possessed a feeling for nature and a keen sensibility, and sometimes lighted upon agreeable rhythms and images; but his verse, clumsy and hastily wrought, was dictated by the bad taste of the period and added nothing to his glory.

His *Théâtre de Neptune*, which is part of the *Muses*, does however offer some interest. It is a kind of nautical spectacle, organized to celebrate Poutrincourt's return to Port-Royal. The god Neptune comes in a bark to bid the traveller welcome; he is surrounded by a court of Tritons and Indians, who recite in turn, in French, Gascon, and Souriquois verse, the praises of the leaders of the colony, and then sing in chorus the glory of the king, while trumpets sound and cannon are fired. This performance, a mixture of barbarism and mythology, in the impressive setting of the Port-Royal basin, was the first theatrical presentation, and no ordinary one, in North America.

Shortly after the second edition of his *Histoire*, dedicated to President Jeannin, Lescarbot accompanied Jeannin's son-in-law, Pierre de Castille, to Switzerland; he went as the secretary of the latter, who had been appointed ambassador to the Thirteen Cantons. Lescarbot must have valued this post, which allowed him to travel, to visit part of Germany, and to frequent the watering-places. He took advantage of the opportunity to compose a *Tableau de la Suisse*, in poetry and in prose, a half-descriptive half-historical production thanks to which, perhaps, he obtained the office of naval commissary, and which earned for him when it was published (1618) a gratuity of 300 *livres* from the king. This excursion of the poet into diplomacy and administration nevertheless represented only a brief and brilliant episode in his life.

Although he was appreciative of female society, Lescarbot remained for long a bachelor. An idyll with a young lady named de Mouroy, in 1609, had indeed brought him before a notary; they had even drawn up their marriage contract when, for reasons unknown, their splendid plans evaporated and their vows were annulled. Lescarbot was obliged to resort to the law in order to recover an engagement ring that the faithless beauty refused to give back. This misadventure made him cautious. He was nearly 50 when on 3 Sept. 1619, at Saint-Germain-l'Auxerrois, he married a young widow of noble birth, Françoise de Valpergue, who had been entirely ruined by swindlers; by way of a dowry, she brought him only a fine lawsuit to defend. Her family's house and estates, burdened with undischarged obligations, had been seized by creditors who had been occupying them for 30 years. Lescarbot, a gallant man and a brilliant lawyer, used all his resources to restore his wife's heritage. He succeeded in obtaining possession once more of the Valpergues' house, in the village of Presles, and of an agricultural estate, the farm of Saint-Audebert. But he had to defend these properties tirelessly, in an endless series of court actions, which swallowed up all the slender revenues from these unprofitable lands and embittered the remainder of his life.

In 1629, he endeavoured to attract Richelieu's attention by two accounts in verse of the siege of La Rochelle: *La chasse aux Anglais* and *La victoire du roy*. He kept up his interest in New France and maintained his relations with Charles de Biencourt and CHARLES DE SAINT-ÉTIENNE de La Tour. The embarkation list of a ship taking supplies to La Tour in 1633 mentions a Marc Lescarbot among the passengers, but it was probably a nephew of the lawyer, with the same first name. We know, however, that he corresponded with Isaac de RAZILLY. The governor's reply to one of his letters has been preserved; it is dated 16 Aug. 1634. Razilly gave him interesting details about the founding of La Hève, and invited him to come and settle in Acadia with his wife. But Lescarbot was to spend the last years of his life at Presles. He died childless in 1642, leaving his assets to his brother Claude and to his nephew. His wife survived him.

Lescarbot, a very picturesque figure, has a special place among the annalists of New France. Between Champlain, the somewhat unpolished man of action, and the missionaries concerned with evangelization, this lawyer-poet appears as a scholar and a humanist, a disciple of Ronsard and Montaigne. He possessed the intellectual curiosity, the taste for learning, and the Graeco-Latin culture of the Renaissance. Although a Roman Catholic, he maintained friendships with Protestants, and preserved in religious matters an attitude of independent judgement and of free inquiry that caused him to be considered unorthodox. By all these traits of character, he was a faithful reflection of his period, and showed himself a worthy subject of King Henri IV, whom he venerated.

His abundant and varied literary production is evidence of his intelligence and of the range of his talents. Apart from the works already mentioned, we know that he wrote some manuscript notes and some miscellaneous poems. In addition, he probably composed several pamphlets, published anonymously or left in manuscript, including a *Traité de la polygamie*, of which he himself spoke. He was also a musician, a calligrapher, and a draughtsman, and Canadian folklorists can claim him as their precursor, since he was the first to record the notation of Indian songs.

But his magnum opus, by its physical size and influence, is surely his *Histoire de la Nouvelle-France*. This large work went through three editions, adorned with maps. It was written in a pleasant style, was widely disseminated in France and abroad, and received the honour of a German translation and two English ones, by Erondelle and by Purchas. It appears certain, from the numerous quotations from this work, that it exercised a considerable influence, and contributed, among other factors, to the colonial movement that took place in Europe at the beginning of the 17th century. Charlevoix cited him with praise; H. P. Biggar has called him the "French Hakluyt," and G. Atkinson proclaims him "the best of the historians of New France." Despite the reservations which judgements so favourable might call for, it remains evident that Lescarbot is the author of one of the first great books in the history of Canada.

RENÉ BAUDRY

The second edition of the *Histoire de la Nouvelle-France* (Paris, 1611 et 1612) was reproduced by Edwin Tross (3v., Paris, 1866). The third edition (Paris, 1617 et 1618) has been reprinted, with an English translation which in part follows that of Erondelle, by W. L. Grant with Introduction by H. P. Biggar (3v., Champlain Soc., I (1907), VII (1911), XI (1914)). *Le Théâtre de Neptune en la Nouvelle-France* has been re-published separately and translated as *The Theatre of Neptune in New France*, by H. T. Richardson (Boston, 1927).

ACM, B.5654, no. 33. AN, H, 2803[7]; T, 201[143]; X[1b], 1135; Y, 160, f.323; Minutier central des notaires, une quinzaine d'actes. Bibliothèque de Laon, MS 166bis, tome 1, p. 123. BN, Imprimés, Rés. Thoisy 414, f.336; Rés. Z. Payen 1064, p. 69; MS, Fr. 4519, f.153v; 13423, f.349; MS, Lat. 9956, f.3; MS, NAF 9281 (Margry), f.9.

G. Atkinson, *Les nouveaux horizons de la Renaissance française* (Paris, 1935), *passim*; *Les relations de voyages français du XVIIe siècle et l'évolution des idées* (Paris, 1927). V. Beuzart, "La religion de Marc Lescarbot," Société de l'histoire du protestantisme français *Bulletin*, LXXXVII (1938), 237–60. H. P. Biggar, "The French Hakluyt: Marc Lescarbot of Vervins," *AHR*, VI (1901), 671–92. G. Chinard, *L'Amérique et le rêve exotique dans la littérature française au XVIIe siècle et au XVIIIe siècle* (Paris,

1913), 100–15. A. Demarsy, *Note sur Marc Lescarbot, avocat vervinois* (Vervins, 1868). A. Jal, *Dictionnaire critique de biographie et d'histoire* (2e éd., Paris, 1872). *La Thiérache: Bulletin de la Société archéologique de Vervins* (Aisne, 1873–1949) contains several articles on Lescarbot by M. Noël, M. G. Lecocq, E. Dedrus, E. Creveaux, and others.

L'ESPÉRANCE, PIERRE LEVASSEUR *dit*. *See* Levasseur

LESPINAY, GUILLAUME and **LOUIS COUILLARD DE**. *See* Couillard

LE SUEUR, JEAN, also called **Abbé Saint-Sauveur**, priest, chaplain of the Hôtel-Dieu of Quebec; b. *c*. 1598 in Normandy; d. 29 Nov. 1668 at Quebec.

He was the first secular priest to come to the St. Lawrence colony. He arrived in 1634 and carried on his ministry in the region around Quebec, under the jurisdiction of the Jesuits, who at that time had spiritual charge of the colony. He had been ordained a priest around 1623 and had first been a parish priest in Normandy, in the parish of Saint-Sauveur in Thury-Harcourt (diocese of Bayeux, department of Calvados).

The history of Abbé Le Sueur is interesting because it is connected with that of Jean Bourdon, who had arrived on the same ship. This fact provoked some queries on the part of Abbé Auguste Gosselin: "Had these two men known each other previously? Had they collaborated in their plans to emigrate to New France? Or had they simply met by chance? What is certain is that from that moment they contracted an unbreakable friendship, a friendship such that their fates were henceforth linked together and their lives inseparable."

Jean Bourdon had settled in the suburbs of Quebec, on a fief that he named Saint-Jean, and there Abbé Le Sueur joined him in 1650, when a chapel was being built near the house. Hence the modern appelations: rue Saint-Jean and faubourg Saint-Jean-Baptiste. The chapel of Saint-Jean served from that time on as the parish church for the inhabitants on the Sainte-Geneviève hill, under the direction of Abbé Le Sueur, who was also the tutor of Jean Bourdon's children. Bishop Laval* mentioned the chapel in his 1660 report to the Holy See, in which he enumerated the eight churches or chapels in the government of Quebec. Jean Bourdon finally left this chapel to his friend in a codicil dated 20 Sept. 1664.

Bourdon received another grant from Governor Huault de Montmagny on 10 Mar. 1646, and on 31 October of the same year Abbé Le Sueur obtained for himself the grant of an adjoining piece of land situated on the Sainte-Geneviève hill. These two grants made up the fief of Saint-François, of which the holders obtained, 30 Dec. 1653, an extension as far as the St. Charles River. Finally Abbé Le Sueur made over his holdings of land to his companion by donations dated 3 May 1654 and 26 Feb. 1655.

Abbé Le Sueur was closely connected with the founding of the Hôtel-Dieu of Quebec. In the year before the arrival of the nuns, the foundress had obtained for them lands near Sillery, which were subsequently called "the Virgin Mary's lands" ("*terres de Sainte-Marie*"), and he was entrusted with overseeing the workmen who were sent to clear the land and build the dwelling. When the nuns did arrive in 1639, he made for them a mattress of branches with his own hands. At the request of the superior of the Jesuits he served as chaplain to the nuns; in their name he took official possession of their lands on 26 Jan. 1640 and of another grant on 9 May 1650. Over a period of 10 or 11 years he rendered them a thousand temporal and spiritual services; he was the confessor of Mother Catherine de Saint-Augustin [*see* Simon].

Meanwhile he remained at the Jesuits' disposal for the parish of Quebec and for the mission at the Beaupré shore, which he went to visit periodically at the request and the expense of the Compagnie de Beaupré. Several details of his ministry are recorded in the *Relations* and especially in the *Journal des Jésuites*. He took pleasure in acting as godfather to the Indians, and he was very well versed in church singing, even directing it on great occasions. Abbé Le Sueur died at the Hôtel-Dieu, after lingering for several months. A Quebec parish, partly situated on the lands that he had owned, bears the name Saint-Sauveur.

Honorius Provost

AJQ, Greffe de Louis Rouer de Villeray, 26 févr. 1655. ASQ, Documents Faribault, 28. *JR* (Thwaites). *JJ* (Laverdière et Casgrain). Juchereau, *Annales* (Jamet). P.-G. Roy, *Inv. concessions*.
Ivanhoë Caron, "Les censitaires du coteau Saint-Geneviève (banlieue de Québec), de 1636 à 1800," *BRH*, XXVII (1921), 105–6, 132–33. Auguste Gosselin, *Jean Bourdon, 1634–1668* (Les Normands au Canada, Évreux, 1892); *M. Jean Le Sueur, ancien curé de Saint-Sauveur-de-Thury, premier prêtre séculier du Canada, 1634–1668* (Les Normands au Canada, Évreux, 1894). P.-G. Roy, *La ville de Québec*, 203–4.

LE SUISSE, PIERRE MIVILLE *dit*. *See* Miville

LETARDIF, OLIVIER, interpreter, head clerk of the Compagnie des Cent-Associés, judge of the court of the seigneury of Beaupré; b. *c.* 1604 in Brittany, in the diocese of Saint-Brieuc; d. 1665 at Château-Richer.

Letardif was at Quebec from at least 1621 on, since he signed the report of the meeting of leading citizens in that year; his presence is then noted from time to time until 1629. By that date he was an assistant clerk for the de CAËNS; "experienced" in the Montagnais, Algonkian, and Huron languages, he served also as an interpreter. In July 1629, acting on behalf of FRANÇOIS GRAVÉ Du Pont, who was ill, he handed over the keys of the Habitation to LEWIS KIRKE. We find him in Quebec again in 1633, promoted to be head clerk of the Cent-Associés, and fulfilling the functions of interpreter or witness as required. It was at this period that Letardif collaborated in the missionary effort: he supported the Jesuits and acted as godfather to Indians; he even administered baptism and, following CHAMPLAIN's example, adopted three young Indians. In May 1637 he received, jointly with Jean NICOLLET (who shortly thereafter became his brother-in-law), the tract called Belleborne on the outskirts of Quebec (a commoner's grant of 160 acres). In April 1646 he acquired one-eighth of the seigneury of Beaupré. On becoming a member of the Compagnie de Beaupré, with the title "general and special procurator," he made a score of grants in the years 1650 and 1651.

Then in 1653 Letardif gave up his Belleborne property, which was to become the castellany of Coulonge, and obtained land at Château-Richer, where he settled. From this time onward, until 1659, it would appear that he exercised the functions of seigneurial judge of Beaupré; his "premature senility" apparently caused him to neglect his duties. On 13 April 1662 he sold his fief in the seigneury of Beaupré. This former colleague of the de Caëns, of Gravé Du Pont, of Champlain, and of the Jesuit PAUL LE JEUNE died at Château-Richer in January 1665, and was buried there on the 28th of that month.

Letardif's first wife, whom he married on 3 Nov. 1637, was 13-year-old Louise Couillard, daughter of GUILLAUME COUILLARD. Left a widower in November 1641, he married Barbe Esmart, widow of Gilles Michel and sister-in-law of Zacharie CLOUTIER, at La Rochelle on 16 May 1648. Only one child is known to have been born of the first marriage; three more followed from the second. Olivier Le Tardif is the forefather of the Letardifs or Tardifs of North America.

MARCEL TRUDEL

ASQ, Documents Faribault, *passim*; Registre A, *passim.*; Seigneuries, III, 10; Séminaire VI, *passim*; XXXV, 25A, 27–27L; XXXVI, 1, 11; XXXVII, 3, 4. Champlain, *Works* (Biggar), V, 95, 209; VI, 62–63. Du Creux, *History* (Conacher), I, 176, 319, 359. *JR* (Thwaites). *Jug. et délib.* P.-G. Roy, *Inv. concessions*, I, *passim*. Sagard, *Histoire du Canada* (Tross), I, 83.

A.-Émile Ducharme, "Olivier Le Tardif," SGCF *Mémoires*, XII (1961), 4–20. Archange Godbout, "Origine d'Olivier Le Tardif," SGCF *Mémoires*, IX (1958), 151. Amédée-E. Gosselin, "Olivier Letardif, juge-prévôt de Beaupré," *RSCT*, 3d ser., XVII (1923), sect.I, 1–16. Léon Roy, "La famille Michel-dit-Taillon," *BRH*, LII (1946), 373–79.

LEVASSEUR, *dit* **Lavigne, JEAN,** "master joiner of Paris," first court officer of the Conseil Souverain; b. 1622, son of Noël Levasseur and Geneviève Grange; buried 31 Aug. 1686 at Quebec. He was the grandfather of the wood-carver Noël Levasseur* and one of the founders of the Confrérie de Sainte-Anne, at the parish church of Quebec.

In 1648, in Paris, he married Marguerite Richard, daughter of a master lapidary and of Jeanne Bonnet. He probably arrived at Quebec in 1651, with Governor JEAN DE LAUSON. On 13 Aug. 1654, Father JÉRÔME LALEMANT and the churchwardens of Notre-Dame entrusted to Jean Levasseur the upkeep of the parish church, particularly of the casement windows of the edifice, "providing him with the paper and the oil," and paying him a daily wage of 30 *sols*.

In 1655, LOUIS D'AILLEBOUST made him two grants of land: one in the *censive* of Quebec, the other in the seigneury of Coulonge. Three years later, d'Ailleboust granted him more land, this time on the north slope of the Île d'Orléans.

Marguerite Richard had left assets in Paris, specifically a house located on Guérin-Boisseau Street, in the quarter of Saint-Nicolas-des-Champs, "where hangs a sign bearing the likenesses of Ste Barbara, Ste Anne and Saint Francis." On two occasions, 13 Aug. 1658 and 18 Oct. 1660, she authorized her husband to go and sell this property. It seems that Jean Levasseur's journey to France took place in the autumn of 1660, since on 31 October of that year, in Quebec, Levasseur undertook to pay, on behalf of Raymond Pajet *dit* Carcy, the sum of 150 *livres* to "Nicolas Marsollet, in the town of Rouen, in his lodging which is at the bottom of the rue de la Vicomté, in the dwelling of the Sieur de la Marre, master locksmith." This obligation was cancelled, but it is nevertheless certain that Levasseur made the voyage to France with his son Louis, then 10 years old; on 18 Sept.

Levasseur, dit L'Espérance

1662, Louis Levasseur was boarding with Gilles de Beddé, at Montreuil-sous-Bois.

The position of court officer of the Conseil Souverain, which Jean Levasseur assumed, left him little opportunity for the diligent practice of his trade. He became as it were an intermediary between the joiners and the government of New France, and indulged in speculation in real estate —as can be ascertained from some of the contracts of the notaries DUQUET and RAGEOT.

When the marriage contract was drawn up between his daughter Anne-Félicité and Jean Hamel, 23 April 1685, Jean Levasseur was stated to be absent by reason of an indisposition.

GÉRARD MORISSET

AJQ, Greffe de Guillaume Audouart, 13 août 1654, 20 oct. 1655; Greffe de Pierre Duquet, 1663–84, *passim;* Greffe de Gilles Rageot, 1666–1702, *passim.* ASQ, Documents Faribault; Séminaire, *passim.* Musée du Québec, Inventaire des œuvres d'art . . . , Dossiers Levasseur. *JR* (Thwaites). P.-G. Roy, *Inv. concessions.*

Marius Barbeau, "Les Le Vasseur, maîtres menuisiers, sculpteurs et statuaires (Québec, *circa* 1648–1818)," *Les Archives de Folklore,* III (1948), 35–49. D. Levack, *La Confrérie de Sainte-Anne à Québec* (Sainte-Anne-de-Beaupré, 1956). Tanquay, *Dictionnaire.*

LEVASSEUR, *dit* **L'Espérance, PIERRE,** joiner; b. 1629, son of Noël Levasseur and Geneviève Grange; d. some time after 1681. Brother of JEAN LEVASSEUR and grandfather of the woodcarver Pierre-Noël Levasseur*.

On 23 Oct. 1655, at Quebec, he married Jeanne de Chaverlange, daughter of Antoine de Chaverlange and Marthe Guérin, from Saint-Oursin (near Bourges). The couple had eight children.

Levasseur was one of the founders of the Confrérie de Sainte-Anne, at the parish church of Quebec.

On 4 March 1657 he purchased a piece of land situated in the *censive* of the Messieurs de la Nouvelle-France.

Around 1661, even before securing title to the property, he built a house and outbuildings on a piece of land belonging to the Argentenay seigneury, on the Île d'Orléans; but as "he has not had an opportunity to accustom himself to the said place, by reason of inconveniences which exist there both for himself and his family," he waived his rights in favour of Vincent Chrétien, for the sum of 140 *livres.*

In 1674, Pierre Levasseur worked in the joiner's shop attached to the church at Beauport. We know this from an account of a quarrel between the joiner and Robert Mossion, a Quebec tailor. Because of a debt of 35 *livres* 5 *sols* for goods supplied, Levasseur had to submit to the seizure of payments owed him by the parochial council at Beauport.

GÉRARD MORISSET

AJQ, Greffe de Guillaume Audouart, 4 mars 1657, 26 août 1663; Greffe de J.-B. Peuvret de Mesnu, 1er et 25 nov. 1658. P.-G. Roy, *Inventaire d'une collection de pièces judiciaires, notariales, etc., etc., conservées aux Archives judiciaires de Québec* (2v., Beauceville, 1917), I, II. Marius Barbeau, "Les Le Vasseur, maîtres menuisiers, sculpteurs et statuaires (Québec, *circa* 1648–1818)," *Les Archives de Folklore,* III (1948), 35–49. D. Levack, *La Confrérie de Sainte-Anne à Québec* (Sainte-Anne-de-Beaupré, 1956). Tanguay, *Dictionnaire.*

LEVERETT, JOHN, official commander of the forts in Acadia, 1654–57; governor of Massachusetts 1673–79; b. 1616, in Boston, England; s. of Thomas Leverett and Anne Fisher; d. 16 March 1678/79 (o.s.).

Leverett migrated to Massachusetts, with his parents, in 1633. He engaged in foreign trade and had a distinguished military and public career on both sides of the Atlantic. He joined the Ancient and Honourable Artillery Company in 1639 and continued as a member of it for 32 years. He became a freeman of Boston in 1640. Four years later he went to England, where he received a command in the Parliamentary army and gained distinction in the war. He returned to Boston, Mass., by 1648. In 1651 he was elected to the General Court and became one of the selectmen of the town of Boston. By 1653–54 the apprehensions felt in Massachusetts respecting Dutch, Indian, and French neighbours had resulted in plans for an expedition against the Dutch in Manhattan. Cromwell sent out three or four ships, and the General Court of Massachusetts took steps to enlist 500 volunteers, to be commanded by Major Robert SEDGWICK and his son-in-law Capt. John Leverett. Before the expedition was ready, peace was signed with the Dutch, and it was decided to turn it against the French in Acadia.

Sedgwick captured the forts at Saint John, Port-Royal (now Annapolis Royal, N.S.), and Penobscot, the last capitulating on 2 Sept. 1654; and designated Leverett as commander of these forts. Leverett was not with Sedgwick's expedition, as we know from his letter dated at Boston on 8 Sept. 1654 (Rawlinson MSS A18, f.58).

Although the documentary evidence is inconclusive, it is to be presumed that Leverett went to Acadia, for he was addressed by Cromwell in a letter of 3 April 1655 as "Commander of the Forts lately taken from the French" and was urged to use "your utmost care and circumspection, as well to defend and keep the forts above said." He continued to be regarded as commander until the forts were delivered up to Col. Thomas TEMPLE on 1 May 1657, although Leverett had been appointed colonial agent in England on 13 Nov. 1655. Several of Leverett's petitions for compensation for his expenses as commander in Acadia were among the many facing the Council of State during these troubled years and after the Restoration Leverett was still petitioning for his losses.

On his return to Massachusetts, Leverett was again elected to the General Court for 1663–65. He was major-general of all Massachusetts forces from 1663 to 1673. From 1665 to 1670 he was a member of the council and from 1671 to 1673 he was deputy governor of Massachusetts. He was elected governor of that colony in 1673 and was re-elected annually until his death in 1678/79. He married Hannah Hudson and after her death in 1646, Sarah Sedgwick, the daughter of Robert Sedgwick, in 1647.

C. BRUCE FERGUSSON

Bodleian Library, Rawlinson MSS, A16, f.52; A18, f.58. Documents in Essex Institute, Salem, Mass., "Mass. Archives"; Mass. Hist. Soc., Saltonstall Coll. Maine Hist. Soc. *Coll.*, 1st ser., I, V, VI, IX; 2d ser., III, V, VI; *Documentary history of Maine*, IV, V, VI, VIII, IX, XI, XIII; *Province and court records of Maine*, I, II, III. Mass. Hist. Soc. *Coll.*, 3d ser., VII (1838) [XXVII of the *Coll.*], 122; *Proc.*, 2d ser., XIII (1900), 407. *Mémoires des commissaires*, I, xv, xl, 97; II, 290–91; IV, 283, 307; and *Memorials of the English and French commissaries*, I, 19, 45, 167, 403, 580. *NYCD* (O'Callaghan and Fernow), III, IX. PRO, *CSP, Col., 1574–1660*, passim. *Records of the colony of New Plymouth in New England (1620–1692)*, ed. N. B. Shurtleff *et al.* (12v., Boston, 1855–61), V, 75–80. *Records of the Massachusetts Bay* (Shurtleff), IV, pt. 1.

DAB. DNB, supp.III. James Hannay, *The history of Acadia from its first discovery to its surrender to England by the Treaty of Paris* (Saint John, N.B., 1879), 195–98. C. E. Leverett, *Memoir of Sir John Leverett, knight, governor of Massachusetts* (Boston, 1856). Murdoch, *History of Nova-Scotia*, I, 126–27, 139.

LE VIEUX DE HAUTEVILLE, NICOLAS,

lieutenant-general for civil and criminal affairs in the seneschal's court at Quebec, son of Nicolas Le Vieux de Hauteville, secretary of the council of finance of His Royal Highness, Seigneur de La Mothe, d'Esgry et de Hauteville, and of Marguerite Lyonne.

During the five years he spent in New France, from 1651 to 1656, Hauteville was lieutenant-general for civil and criminal affairs in the seneschal's court established at Quebec by Governor JEAN DE LAUSON, with whom he had arrived at Quebec on 13 Oct. 1651. It fell to him to preside at two investitures of grants of land; one to the Indians at Sillery, 6 Feb. 1652, and the other for the benefit of the parochial council of Quebec, 26 July. When, on 10 Sept. 1654, he married Marie Renardin de La Blanchetière, the daughter of Vincent de La Blanchetière, an attorney at the presidial seat of Nantes, and of Françoise Ouary, Hauteville was granted by Governor Lauson a site on the Quebec quay, and on 20 September he purchased from Christophe Crevier a piece of land popularly called "La Cabane aux Taupiers" ("Molecatchers' Cabin"), to which he gave the name "Hauteville fief." When he returned to France along with Lauson, probably in June 1656, he was the father of one daughter. Two years later, he sold off his properties at Quebec.

HONORIUS PROVOST

ASQ, Documents Faribault, 92; Lettres, 0, 152; Polygraphie, XIII, 22. *JR* (Thwaites), *passim*. *JJ* (Laverdière et Casgrain), 163. *BRH*, XXII (1916), 33–35.

LEVY DE QUEYLUS, GABRIEL THUBIÈRES DE. *See* THUBIÈRES

L'HERMITIÈRE, JACQUES-FRANÇOIS HAMELIN DE BOURGCHEMIN ET DE. *See* HAMELIN

LIDDALL. *See* LYDALL

LIÉGEOIS, JEAN,

Jesuit friar; b. in 1600 (or 1599) in the diocese of Verdun (France); became a member of the Jesuits of the Province of France at Paris in 1623; killed by the Iroquois at Sillery, near Quebec, on 29 May 1655.

Skilled in the building trades and equipped with a sound education, Brother Liégeois landed at Quebec on 2 June 1634. He was first assigned to the residence of Notre-Dame-des-Anges, but he soon went to Trois-Rivières (about 1640), "where he built a commodious house with a chapel for our missionaries and their Indians." Subsequently he was to be found on all the Jesuits' construction sites: at the mill at La Vacherie (1646), at the college in Quebec (1648) as superintendent of construction, and at Sillery (1655).

Because of his intelligence and initiative, this indefatigable builder won the confidence of his superiors. In 1644–45, it would seem, then in 1648–49, 1649–50 and 1650–52, he spent periods in France "in the service of the mission and for matters concerning our different buildings." He was moreover—in 1645 and 1646 at least—bursar of his community. Brother Liégeois likewise enjoyed the esteem of the public; we find him on occasion settling quarrels about precedence within the carpenters' brotherhood or, during his trips to France, concluding certain pieces of business on behalf of settlers in the colony.

This friar, "who was esteemed by the Governors of his time," an old chronicle affirms, was murdered by seven or eight Mohawks at Sillery on 29 May 1655, when he was directing the building of a fort for the Indian converts. Scalped and decapitated, he was buried on 31 May in the chapel of the college in Quebec.

ANDRÉ VACHON

APQ, Coll. des pièces jud. et not., 9. Du Creux, *History* (Conacher), I, 178; II, 689f. *JR* (Thwaites), *passim*. JJ (Laverdière et Casgrain), *passim*. Gabriel Debien, "Liste des engagés pour le Canada au XVIIe siècle (1634–1715)," *RHAF*, VI (1952–53), 189, 379. [Melançon], *Liste des missionnaires jésuites: Nouvelle-France et Louisiane, 1611–1800* (Montréal, 1929).

LINTOT, JEAN GODEFROY DE. See GODEFROY

LIONNE, MARTIN DE. See LYONNE

LOMERON, DAVID, merchant of La Rochelle, Huguenot; b. October 1591 at Chinon (France) or in the vicinity, son of Daniel Lomeron de La Martinière and Suzanne Georges.

David Lomeron was the nephew of the famous La Rochelle merchants Samuel Georges and Jean Macain, who were partners of the BIENCOURT family, and who sent him to Canada in 1613. He took part in the disputes that set the Biencourts against the Compagnie de la Nouvelle-France. When Lomeron had returned to Port-Royal in 1615, Charles de Biencourt made him his *chargé d'affaires*. The following year they together seized the *Ange-Saint-Michel*, a ship belonging to the Compagnie du Canada. In 1617, Lomeron, while continuing to act for Biencourt, founded a society comprising Pierre Georges, a regular traveller to Canada, and Pierre Garat, who went there in 1620. Lomeron continued in his double capacity until Charles de Biencourt's death in about 1623.

After that date it is not too clear what became of him. In 1627 there was in existence near the Cap Fourchu (Yarmouth, N.S.), a post called Port-Lomeron, and NICOLAS DENYS stated that Lomeron for several years owned an establishment there, which was destroyed by the English about 1628. It is known that he worked for CHARLES DE SAINT-ÉTIENNE de La Tour between 1633 and 1636, but we do not know at what date he had entered his service.

Lomeron seems to have left La Rochelle for good; he had married Jeanne Duquerny there, 12 May 1622.

IN COLLABORATION

ACM, B, Amirauté de La Rochelle; E, Notaires. Denys, *Description and natural history* (Ganong). Robert Le Blant, "L'avitaillement du Port-Royal d'Acadie . . . ," *Revue d'Histoire des Colonies*, XLIV (1957), 138–64. Étienne Trocmé et Marcel Delafosse, *Le commerce rochelais de la fin du XVe siècle au début du XVIIe*, avant-propos de Fernand Braudel (École pratique des Haute-études, VIe section, Centre de Recherches historiques, Ports–Routes–Trafics, V, Paris, 1952).

LONGPRÉ, MARIE-CATHERINE DE SIMON DE. See SIMON

LONGUEUIL ET DE CHÂTEAUGUAY, CHARLES LE MOYNE DE. See LE MOYNE

LOTBINIÈRE, LOUIS-THÉANDRE CHARTIER DE. See CHARTIER

LOUIS DE SAINTE-FOI. See AMANTACHA

LUC, FRÈRE. See FRANÇOIS, CLAUDE

LUCAS, RICHARD, of Rotherhithe (London), HBC captain; b. c. 1656.

Lucas may have been in the company's service by 1673 although he is first mentioned in its records in 1678 as second mate and gunner on the *Prince Rupert* (Capt. Richard POWER). He returned to England on the *John and Alexander* in 1679 and sailed next year on the *Prudent Mary* (Capt. Richard Greenway).

High adventure seemed to be his lot, for the *Prudent Mary* was wrecked off Tetherley's Island in James Bay just after setting out homeward.

With much larger reward in view, Lucas accepted command of an interloping ship (i.e., one trespassing on the HBC's monopoly) in 1682, thus heightening suspicion that he had hidden some of the *Prudent Mary*'s most valuable beaver for his own use. It was 1683 when the interloping vessel the *Expectation* sailed with Lucas in command, only to be captured by Capt.

NEHEMIAH WALKER, who "clapt" Lucas and crew on board and brought them to England. When this series of events led to suit in the High Court of Admiralty Lucas turned witness on behalf of the Company which promptly re-engaged him.

Commanding the *Owner's Goodwill* in 1685 he met two French vessels with their capture, the *Perpetuana Merchant*, refused to strike or come on board, and escaped, reaching the Bay with damaged rigging. Deciding that he could profit himself better than in the Company's service, he asked for release in 1686 and was given a certificate for "true and faithful service."

MAUD M. HUTCHESON

HBRS, VIII, IX (Rich); XI (Rich and Johnson); XXI (Rich).

LUCIÈRE, DOMINIQUE LA MOTTE DE. *See* LA MOTTE

LYDALL (Lyddall, Liddall), WILLIAM, second governor for the HBC in Hudson Bay; b. *c.* 1625.

A son of Sir Richard Lydall, he was appointed in 1674 to replace Charles BAYLY, who had filled the post since 1670. He was recommended by Sir John Griffith, a member of the London Committee, as having "made many voyages to and from Russia and lived many years therein that country." He had in addition served from 1665 to 1673 as a lieutenant in the Royal Navy.

Before sailing, Lydall received special instructions to suppress private trading by the Company's servants, a practice that was assuming serious proportions. Arriving late in 1674 the ships (*Prince Rupert* and *Shaftesbury*) remained in James Bay, Lydall wintering at Charles Fort (Rupert River) and Bayly at Moose. Provisions at Charles Fort ran so low that Thomas GORST, the storekeeper, proposed rationing, but Lydall refused. "If we starve we'll starve together," he ruled. Since he took passage home next year on the ship that had brought him out, his brief term in the Bay was not a successful one. In fact, when John NIXON became governor in 1679 he tried to mark out a path for his successor, "leest he break his shins as Lydall did."

Lydall evidently re-entered the navy in 1678 and petitioned for a pension in 1692. Although lacking two years of the stipulated superannuation period he was in ill health and burdened by debt. Records show that his petition was still ungranted in 1695.

MAUD M. HUTCHESON

PRO, *CSP, Dom., 1695*; *CTP, 1556–1696*. HBRS, V, VIII, XXI (Rich). *A descriptive catalogue of the naval manuscripts in the Pepysian Library*, ed. J. R. Tanner (4v., Navy Records Soc., XXVI–VII, XXXVI, LVII, 1903–22), I, 379.

LYONNE (Lionne, Lyonnes), MARTIN DE, Jesuit priest and missionary; b. 13 May 1614 in Paris; met his death by accident on 16 Jan. 1661 in the Baie de Chedabouctou (Guysborough, N.S.).

He was admitted into the Society of Jesus on 8 Dec. 1629 at Nancy. After three years of philosophy at the university of Pont-à-Mousson (1631–34), Martin de Lyonne taught at Sens and Charleville (1634–38), then was sent to study theology in Rome (1638–42). He was ordained priest at 1641, returned to France to complete his spiritual training at Rouen (1642–43), and sailed for Canada, reaching Miscou on 15 Aug. 1643. Father de Lyonne was intended for the Huron mission, but he agreed to replace Father Jean DOLEBEAU, the priest for Miscou, who was obliged to return to France. This fur-trading and fishing post was set up on an island in the Baie des Chaleurs. The settlement had suffered considerably from scurvy, and in 1637 only 9 of the original 23 settlers were left, the others having died meanwhile. The Jesuits who had succeeded one other there had not been more fortunate: one had died and three others had had to leave the spot. Father Lyonne was ill himself from May to September 1644, so much so that there was talk of sending him back to France, but he refused to go. In fact he recovered, and the epidemic came to an end.

The evangelization of the Indians, for which Father Lyonne shared the responsibility with Fathers Jacques de La Marche and André Richard, began to have some success in this region in 1645. The chief obstacle was alcohol, which the French exchanged with the Indians for furs. Nevertheless the missionaries did baptize a good number of adults, especially in 1647, both at Miscou itself and in a reduction founded in 1644 at Nipisiguit (Bathurst, N.B.), to the south of the bay. This success prompted the three fathers to go to Quebec in the summer of the same year, probably to confer with Father JÉRÔME LALEMANT on missionary strategy. Father Lyonne was kept at Quebec by his superior, who perhaps wished to prepare him for his solemn profession. He set off for France on 23 Sept. 1648 and took his vows on 2 Feb. 1649, sailing back afterwards to Miscou. Yet in September 1649 he was again at Quebec. From 1650 to 1659 he was to go to France almost every year, leaving in the autumn and returning in the spring, in order to obtain the essentials required by the missionaries.

Macé

These journeys involved considerable fatigue and danger; one might cite, for example, that of 1651, which was undertaken at the approach of winter, and in which one of the two vessels was lost, and the other, after narrowly escaping shipwreck, was pillaged when it arrived in port.

Father Lyonne did not however forget his missions in the Gulf of St. Lawrence, and wished to go back to them. He intended to do so in 1657, but he had to prolong still further his career as a traveller. It was not until 1659 that he was back in Miscou, taking part in the work of bringing religion to this region. In 1660 he looked after the Indians of Chedabouctou. When illness broke out among his flock he gave of himself unstintingly, until he was himself stricken. And even then, when an Indian requested his services in the depth of winter, he hastened to him, falling into an icy stream on the way. When he got back he was ridden with fever, which brought him to his grave at the age of 46.

LUCIEN CAMPEAU

Charlevoix, *Histoire*, I, 222. *JR* (Thwaites). Rochemonteix, *Les Jésuites et la Nouvelle-France au XVIIe siècle*, I, 198–99.

M

MACÉ, CATHERINE, nun, Religious Hospitaller of Saint-Joseph, co-foundress of the Hôtel-Dieu, Laval (France), second superior of the Hôtel-Dieu, Montreal; b. 1616 at Nantes, daughter of Guillé Macé, a rich ship-owner, and Philippe Martineau; d. 1698.

She was received into the order of the Hospitallers at La Flèche in September 1643. In 1650 she shared with Mother Judith MOREAU de Brésoles and Mother Marie MAILLET the honour of being a foundress of the Hôtel-Dieu in Laval. In 1659 she was its assistant superior.

Very early her qualities had been recognized by the clear-sighted founders of Ville-Marie. Mother Marie de La Ferre "founded great hopes on her virtue," and Jérôme Le Royer de La Dauversière realized that God wanted her "to help in establishing Montreal." She was therefore appointed assistant to Mother Moreau de Brésoles. On 7 Sept. 1659 she arrived at Quebec with her, and with Mother Maillet and Jeanne MANCE.

Mother Macé was superior of the Hôtel-Dieu of Montreal from 1663 to 1681. She also served as bursar and as mistress of novices. Sister Marie Morin*, who shared her missionary life for 36 years, had ample time to observe her great qualities, which to her seemed excessive, reaching "a degree that was suited only to her."

Her brother, René Macé, a Sulpician, exercised in Paris the functions of procurator of the nuns of Saint-Joseph. He obtained from the court relatively large sums which were sent to the hospital in Montreal. As a result Sister Morin bestowed upon her "very dear and highly respected Mother Macé" the title of "distinguished benefactress," for the establishment existed only thanks to her brother's gifts.

Mother Macé died 25 Sept. 1698, at 81 years of age.

ESTHER LEFEBVRE, R.H.S.J.

AHDM, Registre des entrées et professions (contient l'acte de profession de Mère Macé); Contrat de fondation des Filles Hospitalières de Sainte-Joseph de Montréal (9 juin 1659); Acte fait par les trois premières Mères durant leur séjour à La Rochelle, le 12 juin 1659, par lequel elles s'engagent à ne jamais sortir de la maison "sans permission de Monseigneur l'Evêque"; "Obédience" de Monseigneur de Laval confiant le mandat aux trois premières Mères (20 oct. 1659); Requête présentée à Monseigneur l'Evêque de Pétrée pour la solennité des vœux (7 oct. 1671); Marie Morin, "Histoire simple et véritable de l'établissement des Religieuses Hospitalières de Saint-Joseph en l'Île de Montréal, dite à présent Ville-Marie, en Canada, de l'année 1659 . . ."; and other documents. Morin, *Annales* (Fauteux *et al.*). Lefebvre, *Marie Morin*. Mondoux, *L'Hôtel-Dieu de Montréal*.

MADOG AB OWAIN GWYNEDD. *See* MADOC [Appendix]

MADRY, JEAN, garrison surgeon at Trois-Rivières, lieutenant and clerk to the chief barber and surgeon of the king; b. *c.* 1625; d. 1669.

He came to Canada around 1651, and from 1653 to 1655 he was garrison corporal and surgeon at the Trois-Rivières fort. In 1657 he was settled in Quebec, and in the autumn of that year he sailed for France. On 2 April 1658 François de Barnoin, chief barber to the king, conferred upon him the master's status and authorized him to confer it upon others. The letters were however not ratified until November 1663. On the tenth of that month Madry became lieutenant and clerk to Barnoin and thereby obtained powers of surveillance over the surgeons in the colony.

Madry was a churchwarden of Notre-Dame of Quebec in 1663. On 7 October Claude CHARRON and he became the first two aldermen for the town; they were to lose their function shortly afterwards, to be replaced by a syndic. Madry had also been made one of the directors of the Tadoussac trading organization by a lease dated 4 March, which was annulled on the following 4 October.

On 13 Oct. 1668 he rendered fealty and homage to Bishop Laval* in the name of the nuns of the Hôtel-Dieu for their arriere-fief of Saint-Laurent on the Île d'Orléans.

Madry died of drowning 26 July 1669 during a trip to Trois-Rivières and was buried in the paupers' cemetery of the Hôtel-Dieu at Quebec, according to a wish that he had expressed.

Madry was a good surgeon. He seems however to have been of a rather stubborn, violent, and over-bearing character, if we are to judge by his obstinacy in refusing to accept the guardianship of the under-age children of Guillaume Gauthier, whose cousin he was through his wife, and by the obstacle that he tried to put in the way of Pierre Rouffray's marriage on the pretext that Rouffray was "his domestic servant, having been assigned to him by order of the Council." Like several of his colleagues at that time, Madry often appeared before the Conseil Souverain to claim fees that he considered were due him. On several occasions he reappeared as a plaintiff for other reasons, but most of the time in money matters.

On 19 Jan. 1660 at Quebec he had married Françoise Duquet, who was 15 years of age and a sister of the notary Pierre DUQUET; he had no children. After the surgeon's death his wife remarried in 1670; her second husband was Olivier Morel* de La Durantaye, a king's counsellor on the Conseil Souverain. Madry owned the fief of Grand-Pré at La Canardière, which the Jesuits had granted him in 1659. Later he was to build on it a house which was called the Château Bigot.

GABRIEL NADEAU

Jug. et délib., I. Ahern, Notes pour l'histoire de la médecine. Boissonnault, Histoire de la faculté de médecine de Laval, 55f. Raymond Douville, "Chirurgiens, barbiers-chirurgiens et charlatans de la région trifluvienne sous le régime français," Cahiers des Dix, XV (1950), 110f. J.-E. Roy, "Jean Madry," BRH, XX (1914), 156f. P.-G. Roy, L'Île d'Orléans (Québec, 1928); La ville de Québec.

MAGNAN, PIERRE, first Frenchman known to have been tortured to death by the Iroquois; b. Tougne, in the vicinity of Lisieux, Normandy; d. 1627.

Little is known about the early life of Pierre Magnan, except that he had clubbed a man to death in France, whereupon he fled to New France. Here he became involved in the tortuous web of French-Indian diplomacy.

In 1627 Mahigan Aticq [MIRISTOU], a Montagnais chief, informed CHAMPLAIN of proposals made by the Dutch and the Mohicans at Fort Orange (Albany, New York) to Montagnais and other Indian nations that they attack the Mohawks. Champlain, who did not wish to jeopardize the peace of 1624, achieved at such cost to himself, warned the Montagnais to refuse the proposals. The Indians held a council at Trois-Rivières, which ÉMERY DE CAËN attended in an endeavour to discourage the projected war. But a group of young warriors, who would not listen to the Frenchman's advice, travelled to Lake Champlain, captured two Mohawks by feigning friendship, and brought their captives back to Trois-Rivières, where they maltreated them.

A council was held, at which Champlain again warned the Montagnais of the possible consequences of this treacherous act. The council then decided to send a peace embassy to the Mohawks, which would include one of the prisoners and also a Frenchman. Pierre Magnan agreed to join the embassy, thus undertaking a mission of great importance under the most urgent circumstances. He and the prisoner, a Montagnais chief CHEROUOUNY, known as "The Reconciled," and two other Indians left Trois-Rivières for the Mohawk country, 24 July 1627. On 25 August, news was received at Quebec that the entire embassy had been slain upon arrival among the Mohawks.

Not until 16 April 1629 were there explanations of the fate of the embassy. EROUACHY, a Montagnais chief, reported that an Algonkin of Allumette Island, who hated Cherououny, had advised the Mohawks beforehand that the ambassadors who were coming to treat for peace were actually spies. The Mohawks accepted this accusation without further inquiry and had cruelly murdered the deputies, including Pierre Magnan, the first Frenchman known to have been slain in a Mohawk village.

THOMAS GRASSMANN

[For an alternative account of the embassy's end see CHEROUOUNY.]

Champlain, Works (Biggar), V, 214–26, 229–32, 308–13. Le Clercq, First establishment of the faith (Shea), I, 284. Sagard, Histoire du Canada (Tross), II, 445–46.

MAHEUT, LOUIS, probably the first surgeon born in Canada, son of René Maheut, a bourgeois of Paris, and Marguerite Corrivault; baptized 12 Dec. 1650 at Quebec; d. there in 1683. The name Maheut is the Breton form of Mathieu, which has also produced Maheu, Maheux, and Mayo.

Louis Maheut received the same first name as his elder brother, likewise a surgeon who lived at various times in Canada. He had as godfather and

Mahigan Aticq Ouche

godmother Governor LOUIS D'AILLEBOUST and Jacqueline Potel, the wife of JEAN BOURDON.

In October 1668, after some sort of apprenticeship as a surgeon-barber, Louis Maheut sailed on the *Sainte-Anne*, proposing to go and continue his surgical studies in France. For this purpose he had borrowed the sum of 146 *livres*, 13 *sols* from his stepfather Jean Maheut, his mother's third husband. He could not have stayed more than five years in France, since on 12 June 1673, at Quebec, he married his cousin Geneviève Byssot, daughter of François BYSSOT. The day before, he had obtained from the bishop dispensation from the fourth degree of relationship, thought to be the first of this kind granted in New France. The marriage contract had been signed on 29 May 1673. By this union Louis Maheut became the brother-in-law of the discoverer of the Mississippi, Louis JOLLIET, himself the godson of Louis Maheut the elder. Louis Maheut owned a property at Rivière-des-Roches on the St. Lawrence, opposite the Île d'Orléans. He died 24 Nov. 1683 in the Lower Town of Quebec, in the house that he had received from his father. The inventory of his possessions listed as many nautical instruments as surgical ones, and of the ten books that he possessed only one dealt with medicine. Maheut had no descendants: a posthumous child lived for less than a year.

ANTONIO DROLET

AJQ, Greffe de Pierre Duquet, Contrat de mariage de Louis Maheust et Geneviève Bissot, 29 mai 1673. ASQ, Séminaire, XCII, 19, p.6. *Jug. et délib.*, *passim*. *Papier terrier de la Cie des I.O.* (P.-G. Roy), 101. P.-G. Roy, *Inv. contrats de mariage*, IV, 118.
Ahern, *Notes pour l'histoire de la médecine*. Boissonnault, *Histoire de la faculté de Médecine de Laval*, 40–44. Phileas Gagnon, "Noms propres au Canada français," *BRH*, XV (1909), 143. Archange Godbout, "Origines des Cormiers," SGCF *Mémoires*, IV (1950), 179–83. "Origine de quelques noms canadiens," *BRH*, XI (1905), 269. SGCF *Mémoires*, I (1944), 219.

MAHIGAN ATICQ OUCHE. *See* MIRISTOU

MAILLET, MARIE, nun, Hospitaller of Saint-Joseph, first bursar of the Hôtel-Dieu, Montreal; b. 1610 at Saumur (Anjou), daughter of Jean Maillet, a merchant, and Marie Rivard (or Pinard); d. 1677.

Until she was 35 she lived at Saumur "on her income, very comfortably, devoted to God and in the sincere desire to honour and serve Him." She decided to devote herself to the service of the poor and entered the Hôtel-Dieu of La Flèche 5 April 1646.

Appointed depositary at La Flèche and then at Laval (France), she kept this office when she was designated for Ville-Marie. She owed this designation which she had desired so much to Jérôme Le Royer de La Dauversière himself, "who was her director and who asked for her to be the third person in his establishment at Ville-Marie." She arrived at Quebec 7 Sept. 1659 with Jean MANCE and Mothers MOREAU de Brésoles and MACÉ. She carried out her functions as bursar "in a very virtuous manner," we are told by Marie Morin*, the annalist of the Hôtel-Dieu.

The capable depositary was at the same time a nun who had entered upon the ways of mysticism, as had a great number of fervent souls of her time. Here is Sister Morin's testimony on this subject: "Sister Maillet was a nun of very superior gifts of prayer.... The late M. Olier had appeared to her several times, bathed in glory, to strengthen and console her in her inward sufferings.... She also saw M. de La Dauversière after his death on the same subject. These great servants of God assured her in His name that this work [the Hôtel-Dieu] was His and that it would subsist despite the opposition of those men who in that respect were acting blindly, not knowing His designs; but that He would be well able to create out of these difficulties His glory and the advantage of this house, which was founded and sustained by the Cross."

Although a nun above all else, Mother Maillet was also an excellent Hospitaller: "she surpassed herself by the lengths to which she went to relieve the sufferings" of her patients. Consequently they loved her greatly, and the Indians themselves never called her anything else but "their dear mother."

Mother Maillet died "towards the end of the month of November 1677, which year was the 18th of her stay at Ville-Marie."

ESTHER LEFEBVRE, R.H.S.J.

AHDM, Registre des entrées et professions (contient l'acte de profession de Mère Maillet); Contrat de fondation des Filles Hospitalières de Saint-Joseph de Montréal (9 juin 1659); Acte fait par les trois premières Mères durant leur séjour à La Rochelle, le 12 juin 1659, par lequel elles s'engagent à ne jamais sortir de la maison "sans permission"; "Obédience" de Monseigneur de Laval confiant le mandat aux trois premières Mères (20 oct. 1659); Requête présentée à Monseigneur l'Evêque de Pétrée pour la solennité des vœux (7 oct. 1671); Marie Morin, "Histoire simple et véritable de l'établissement des Religieuses Hospitalières de Saint-Joseph en l'Ile de Montréal, dite à présent Ville-Marie, en Canada, de l'année 1659..."; and other documents. Morin, *Annales* (Fauteux *et al.*). Lefebvre, *Marie Morin*. Mondoux, *L'Hôtel-Dieu de Montréal*.

MAINWARING (Manwaring, Maynwaringe), SIR HENRY, famous Jacobean pirate; b. 1587 near Ightfield, Shropshire; d. 1653.

He was the second of four sons and two daughters of Sir George Mainwaring and his wife, of the branch of the Mainwarings of Peover in Cheshire, educated at Brasenose College, Oxford, where he obtained his B.A. degree at the age of 15.

As a skilful seaman, he was commissioned in 1610 by the lord high admiral to try to capture the pirate Peter EASTON, but failed. He was then given command of a privateer under letters of marque to plunder Spanish shipping in the West Indies, and sailed in the *Resistance* of 160 tons, well armed and manned. However, he changed his mind on the high seas and turned pirate.

Based at Mamora on the Barbary coast, he soon had a large fleet of captured vessels at his command for international pillage and plunder. To recruit men and obtain supplies of fish he made the Atlantic crossing in 1614 and arrived in Newfoundland waters 4 June 1614 with eight war-like ships. He raided the harbours, taking with him, when he left in mid-September, carpenters, ammunition, 10,000 fish from a French vessel at Harbour Grace, and 400 men (at the rate of one out of every six sailors on the fishing vessels).

In 1615 he was sued in the High Court of Admiralty for his attack on the *Hound* of Flushing at Newfoundland (PRO, H.C.A.14/41, 9). Offered a free pardon by King James I if he would give up piracy, he accepted and was pardoned in 1616 under the Great Seal, on the grounds that "he had committed no great Wrong." In gratitude for his pardon, Mainwaring wrote a discourse entitled "Of the beginnings, practices, and suppression of pirates," which he dedicated to James I. He sailed for Dover and later rescued a Newfoundland trading fleet captured by pirates near Gibraltar.

He was knighted in 1618, appointed deputy warden of the Cinque Ports and lieutenant of Dover in 1620, elected M.P. for Dover in 1621, and ended his naval career as a vice-admiral in 1639. Because of his royalist sympathies, he was removed from his position as master of Trinity House, but his *Seaman's dictionary* was printed in 1644, despite his political views, by order of Parliament. In 1646 he accompanied Prince Charles into exile in Jersey, where he lived in poverty. He compounded an estate of £8—consisting of a horse and wearing apparel—with the Commonwealth in 1651. Eighteen months later he died. No tombstone marks his grave in St. Giles's Church, Camberwell.

He was a linguist and scholar of no mean ability, and one of the greatest seamen of the age. His skill in naval attack and his mode of boarding and resisting the enemy were said to be without equal in England. He was one of the greatest of the Jacobean pirates and was regarded as a "patriotic pirate" by those who maintained that he never molested English vessels.

E. HUNT

There are many references to Mainwaring in the PRO, H.C.A.14/41. *The life and works of Sir Henry Mainwaring*, ed. G. E. Manwaring (2v., Navy Records Soc., LIV (1920), LVI (1922)); I contains a biography of Mainwaring; II, "Of the beginnings, practices and suppression of pirates" (also known as "Discours of pirats," printed from BN, Royal MS 17 A XLVII) and "The seaman's dictionary, or an exposition . . . of all parts and things belonging to a ship." Richard Whitbourne, *A discourse and discovery of New-foundland* (London, 1620). Philip Gosse, *The history of piracy* (New York, 1934), 116–28. Prowse, *History of Nfld*.

MAISONNEUVE, PAUL DE CHOMEDEY DE. *See* CHOMEDEY

MAKHEABICHTICHIOU (Makhatewebichtichi), sometimes identified as a Montagnais chief; probably b. in the vicinity of Trois-Rivières; d. 1640 or 1641.

Father PAUL LE JEUNE mentions Makheabichtichiou in 1637. A daughter, Agatha Khisipikiwam, was baptized at the mission of Saint-Joseph (Sillery) according to a register of baptisms for the year 1638–40 and the death of his oldest son is mentioned by Father Le Jeune in the *Relation* of 1640–1.

Makheabichtichiou is said to have been strong and hardy, a good warrior with a ready tongue. Although he was not the captain or chief of his tribe, he was, nevertheless, usually recognized as the chief of his band. Consequently he often fulfilled the duties of captain or chief and thereby unofficially acquired his title. During the year 1637, having erected a camp near Quebec, Makheabichtichiou sought to gain the goodwill of the governor, HUAULT de Montmagny by stressing his acquaintance with the Jesuit missionaries. In fact, before leaving Trois-Rivières, Makheabichtichiou asked Father Jacques BUTEUX for a letter to Father Le Jeune requesting access for him to the residence of the Jesuits at Quebec.

Makheabichtichiou achieved his desire. The governor extended a hearty welcome but made it evident that a close friendship was reserved for those Indians who were instructed in the Christian faith. Makheabichtichiou thereafter manifested a

Malapart

more than ordinary interest in Christian doctrine. He frequented the residence of the Jesuits even at night in order, as he declared, to avoid intruding upon the time of the many French who came daily to consult the missionaries. During the year 1637, Makheabichtichiou often conversed with Father Le Jeune about Christianity. He sometimes preached to his fellow Indians but also, on occasion, he exhibited anger towards Father Le Jeune. Father Le Jeune's *Relation* for 1637 and 1638 implies that Makheabichtichiou repeatedly protested his belief in Christianity but could not bring himself to give up polygamy. The Christian Indians at Sillery disapproved of Makheabichtichiou, which caused him to remove with his two wives to the land of the Abenakis where, during the winter of 1640–1, he met a violent death, supposedly at the hands of an intoxicated member of that tribe who lived "near the sea."

THOMAS GRASSMANN

JR (Thwaites), XI, 149–65, 167–83, 225; XIV, 133, 265; XX, 209–11, 309 n.10; XXI, 10, 67, 69.

MALAPART, ANDRÉ, Parisian soldier who served under Capt. CHARLES DANIEL of Dieppe in Acadia and published with his own additions Daniel's report of the capture in 1629 of James STEWART, Lord Ochiltree, and the garrison of the Scottish fort at Port de la Baleine.

In May 1629 Daniel had orders from Richelieu to sail with Isaac de RAZILLY from La Rochelle to revictual CHAMPLAIN at Quebec. Razilly was ordered elsewhere, and so the fleet of the Compagnie de la Nouvelle-France set forth without him. Daniel lost touch with his companion vessels in fog and storms on the Atlantic, and on 28 August entered what is now St. Ann's Bay, Cape Breton, alone. The French fishermen there had no news of Quebec, but told him that Lord Ochiltree, after occupying Port-Royal (now Annapolis Royal, N.S.), had established himself on the west coast of Cape Breton in June and was exacting one-tenth of their catch from all French fishing vessels in the Gulf.

According to Daniel's account, he at once attacked the Scottish fort, which stood on a rock surrounded on two sides by water. Despite the fact that Ochiltree had armed the fort with cannon and had a garrison of 60 men, the French force of 53 sailors hastily trained in the use of arms captured the place by frontal assault under cover of bombardment from their boats. Malapart lost an eye and part of his hand in the fray. After razing the Scottish fort and using its material to build a new fort, Sainte-Anne, to guard the passage, Daniel abandoned the idea of relieving Quebec, probably because of the lateness of the season, and returned to France. On his way home he landed 42 of his prisoners at Falmouth, while the remainder, including Stewart, were imprisoned at Dieppe for a month.

Daniel drew up his report of the expedition for Cardinal Richelieu at Paris 12 Dec. 1629, and it was published by Malapart the following year at Rouen under the title, *La prise d'un seigneur écossais et de ses gens qui pilloient les navires pescheurs de France, par Monsieur Daniel, dedié à M. de Lauzon par le sieur Malapart, parisien, soldat dudit sieur Daniel*.

Malapart's additions to Daniel's straightforward report, which take up 13 pages to Daniel's 6, are not notable. His intention was to supplement the omissions due to Daniel's modesty and to the nature of a summary report. He notes that the French fishermen sent a petition to Daniel, urging him to attack the Scots. His most important observation is that some 200 French vessels now yearly visited this coast in search of cod, salmon, and whale oil, and that the whole industry gave employment to at least 100,000 men at home and abroad. He praised the company's work, which had produced "this heroic action," and closed with some complimentary verses addressed to Daniel.

Little is known of Malapart's later life. Various acts attest his presence at Quebec in September 1634 and at Trois-Rivières in 1635, 1639, and 1649. Malapart was commander of the fort of Trois-Rivières for some time. He is not to be confused with the Malepart who arrived in June 1636 with HUAULT de Montmagny.

MASON WADE

Daniel's report was reprinted in Champlain's *Voyages* of 1632 (*see* Champlain, *Works* (Biggar), VI, 157, and *Œuvres* (Laverdière), 1283–88), and as *Voyage à la Nouvelle-France du Capitaine Charles Daniel de Dieppe, 1629*, éd. J. Félix (Rouen, 1881). The English version of events in 1629 is given in PRO, *CSP, Col., 1574–1660*, 104–6.

ASQ, Séminaire, VI, 2, 40. Biggar, *Early trading companies*. Philéas Gagnon, "Noms propres au Canada-Français: transformations de noms propres, établies par les signatures autographes ou par les écrits de contemporains où ils sont mentionnés," *BRH*, XV (1909), 143. La Roncière, *Histoire de la marine française*, IV (1923), 636. P.-G. Roy, "Les familles de nos gouverneurs français," *BRH*, XXVI (1920), 258; *La ville de Québec*, I, 143. Benjamin Sulte, "Les gouverneurs des Trois-Rivières," *BRH*, II (1896), 67. Tanguay, *Dictionnaire*.

MALDONADO, LORENZO FERRER. *See* FERRER [Appendix]

MALHERBE, FRANÇOIS, Jesuit lay brother; b. 1 March 1627 in Saintonge (France); d. 19 April 1696 near Chicoutimi.

François Malherbe arrived in Canada around 1645 as a *donné*, and set out for the Huron country, where he stayed until this mission was abandoned in 1650. In March 1649 he helped to bring from Saint-Ignace to Sainte-Marie the remains of the martyrs Jean de BRÉBEUF and GABRIEL LALEMANT, and to prepare them for burial. After remaining some four years among the Huron refugees near Quebec, he went back to France, to become a Jesuit lay brother in Paris on 30 Dec. 1654. He took his final vows as a temporal coadjutor on 15 Aug. 1655. In 1658 he was already back in Canada, where he was to work for 16 years as an interpreter among the Montagnais and the Algonkins of Trois-Rivières. In 1676 he was sent to Sillery, and in 1682 to the Tadoussac mission. There he gave unstintingly of himself until his death, particularly as a joiner and as a farmer at Saint-Charles, the central post set up near Chicoutimi by Father de Crespieul* to serve as a residence and a supply point for the missionaries and Christian natives of the region. According to what his superiors have written, Brother Malherbe was a very prudent religious, gentle by nature, endowed with a rare patience, and especially fitted for manual tasks.

J. MONET

ACSM, f.400. *JR* (Thwaites), XLVI, 303. "Lettre du père Crespieul sur le père Malherbe," *BRH*, XLVII (1941), 56f. F.-X.-E. Frenette, "Les pères Cocquart et de La Brosse et le frère Malherbe," *BRH*, XLI (1935), 416–32. "Ici ont passé: le monument du coteau du Portage," Soc. Hist. du Saguenay *Pub*, II (Chicoutimi, 1937), 25–27. A. E. Jones, "'Ŝendake Ehen' or Old Huronia," PAO *Annual Report*, V (1908).

MANCE, JEANNE, founder of the Hôtel-Dieu of Montreal; b. at Langres in Champagne (France), baptized 12 Nov. 1606, daughter of Catherine Émonnot and Charles Mance, attorney in the *bailliage* of Langres; d. 18 June 1673 at Montreal.

The Mance family hailed from Nogent-le-Roi (today Nogent-en-Bassigny, Haute-Marne), and the Émonnot family from Langres, where Jeanne Mance's parents went to make a home. The two families belonged to the administrative middle class; Charles Mance and Catherine Émonnot had married in 1602. They had six boys and six girls. Jeanne, their second child, was probably among the first pupils entrusted to the Ursulines, who had come to establish themselves at Langres in 1613. She was a little over 20 when she lost her mother. Very devout, and with the ability to be unmindful of herself, she became together with her sister the support of her father, and looked after the education of her young brothers and sisters. She experienced the hardships of the Thirty Years' War, which spared scarcely any of the frontier towns of France. Hospitals were founded at Langres. The bishop, Sébastien Zamet, concentrated his efforts and poured out his gold for the construction of a charity-hospital in his town. Better still, he established a society of pious ladies directed towards charitable activities of an external and social nature. It was probably in this type of work that Jeanne Mance first served as a nurse. By it she no doubt learned to give emergency care to the wounded and the sick. How else can we explain her deftness at Ville-Marie, at the bedside of the horribly mutilated victims of the Iroquois? As her brothers and sisters grew up, she had more and more time to attend to charitable works, and her father was no longer there to require her care. He had died about 1635.

Around the middle of April 1640, Jeanne learned of the presence at Langres, where he was staying with her uncle Simon Dolebeau, of Nicolas, the eldest son of the Dolebeau family; he was the chaplain of the Saint-Chapelle in Paris and tutor to the Duc de Richelieu, the nephew of the Duchesse d'Aiguillon. Jeanne had a high regard for this cousin. She willingly followed his advice, although he was about her own age (he was born 18 Aug. 1605 at Nogent-le-Roi). Jeanne eagerly went to visit him. The young man spoke to her of New France. He could barely contain his emotion, for his younger brother Jean [*see* DOLEBEAU], a religious of the Society of Jesus, had just set sail for the missions in the colony. Nicolas also informed Jeanne that not only were courageous men of God hastening to those regions, but that since the summer of 1639 society women and nuns were landing there too, testifying to the same surge of faith and the same dauntlessness as their missionary companions. He described the astounding vocation of Mme de CHAUVIGNY de La Peltrie and of the Ursulines whom she brought out to New France, and also that of the Hospitallers of Saint-Augustin sent there by the Duchesse d'Aiguillon. Dollier* de Casson, to whom we owe the account of these events, assures us that it was at that moment that Jeanne Mance felt for the first time the desire to go to New France.

A few days passed. Jeanne meditated and prayed. She decided to consult her director about her intention to sail for America. Whitsuntide was approaching. Her director, who is still unknown, urged her to submit all her aspirations to the scrutiny of the Holy Spirit. Finally the priest

Mance

allowed her to sail for Canada. It was agreed that she should leave for Paris on "the Wednesday after Whitsun; that there she should go and see Father C[HARLES] LALEMANT who looked after Canadian affairs, that as her director she should take the rector of the Jesuit house nearest to the place where she would be living." She then spoke to her relatives and friends of her plans.

It was on the last day of May that Jeanne Mance left Langres. In Paris she went to the house of her cousin, Mme de Bellevue (née Antoinette Dolebeau, Nicolas's only sister). Mme de Bellevue lived in the Faubourg Saint-Germain, not far from another of her brothers, Father Charles Dolebeau, a discalced Carmelite. Encouraged by the warmth of feeling shown to her, Jeanne abandoned her reserve. She spoke of her great missionary aspirations. She also zealously and punctiliously carried out the programme outlined for her by her director at Langres. She first presented herself at the Jesuit convent in Pot-de-Fer street (now Bonaparte). She saw Father Charles Lalemant, the procurator of the Canadian missions, who immediately took an interest in her plans. At the convent Jeanne also saw Father Jean-Baptiste Saint-Jure, whom the Society of Jesus, even at that time, considered one of its greatest masters. Unfortunately, for several months, it was impossible for Father Saint-Jure to receive her. In the meantime Jeanne immersed herself in the active life of charity led by her cousin. She made numerous acquaintances. Among others she was introduced to a great Parisian lady, Mme de Villesavin (née Isabelle or Isabeau Blondeau; wife of Jean Phélypeaux, seigneur of Villesavin). Jeanne did not suspect that in a few months this gracious lady would do her a remarkable service. For it was Mme de Villesavin who, one day, protested when she heard Jeanne regret not having had Father Saint-Jure's advice as to her missionary aptitude. She promised Jeanne that she would plead her case before the religious, and she was successful; Jeanne was requested to go to the parlour as often as she thought fit. Other important women wished to make Jeanne's acquaintance, notably Charlotte-Marguerite de Montmorency, Princesse de Condé, the wife of Chancellor Pierre Séguier, the Duchesse d'Aiguillon, the Marquise de Liancourt, Louise de Marillac, and Marie Rousseau, the celebrated Paris clairvoyante. Finally the queen herself, the devout Anne of Austria, expressed the desire to see her.

Dollier de Casson informs us that "a provincial of the Recollets, a man of great merit named Father Rapin, came to Paris; as she [Jeanne] knew him already she visited him and told him how things stood." Father Rapine was glad to see Jeanne again. He was touched by her trust in Providence. Consequently, having approved her decision to go to Canada and work for the conversion of the Indians there, he added "that that was good, that she must forget herself in this way, but that it was well that others should take the necessary care of her." A few days later, Father Rapine wrote to ask her to be good enough to go the the Hôtel de Bullion, in Platrière street. There Jeanne met Father Rapine again; he introduced her to a distinguished and very wealthy lady, the discreet but bountiful protectress of the majority of French charitable works. This person was Angélique Faure, the widow of Claude de Bullion, the French superintendant of finance and a cousin of Father Rapine. Angélique Faure was the daughter of Guichard Faure de Berlise, a king's secretary and master in ordinary to His Majesty, and of Madeleine Brulart de Sillery; the latter was the sister of Noël Brulart de Sillery, the founder of the Sillery mission in Canada, and of Nicolas, chancellor of France. From her union with Claude de Bullion, Angélique had had five children.

As these two great Christian women had made an excellent first impression on each other, Jeanne's visits to the Hôtel de Bullion became more frequent. On the fourth occasion, Mme de Bullion asked Jeanne Mance "whether she would not consent to take charge of a hospital in the country to which she was going, because she proposed to found one there with what would be necessary for its maintenance, and on that account she would have been very glad to know what endowment was given to the hospital at Kebecq by Mad. Deguillon." Jeanne raised some objections, but without rejecting the project absolutely. Mme de Bullion then requested her to be good enough to inquire about the approximate cost of the Hôtel-Dieu at Quebec, for she was prepared to give as much money for her hospital, if not more. Jeanne accepted. The Duchesse d'Aiguillon, she was informed, had allotted to the Hôtel-Dieu at Quebec a sum of 22,000 *livres*, which she raised a little later to a total of 40,500. Cardinal Richelieu, of course, had assumed responsibility for a part of these gifts. Meanwhile Jeanne went to the Jesuits and consulted Father Saint-Jure, to find out whether she should accept the offers made to her by Mme de Bullion.

After praying and meditating, Father Saint-Jure replied that she must go to Canada, "that it was infallibly Our Lord who wanted this association" with the wealthy lady. Mme de Bullion was delighted with Jeanne's decision. She asked Jeanne to be sure, in the future, to maintain the most complete secrecy about all that concerned her, about her name, her person, and the gifts that she expected to make. Jeanne, deeply moved by such unselfishness, undertook to keep silent. On the last visit she made to the Hôtel de Bullion, she received a purse and other expensive gifts.

In April 1641 Jeanne took leave of her relatives and friends, and set off for La Rochelle. On her arrival she met the Jesuit Jacques de La Place, who informed her of the wonders that would attend the journey to New France. The next day Jeanne, on entering the church of the Jesuits, passed a gentleman. They exchanged a look charged with an extraordinary clairvoyance, for, in the words of the *Véritables motifs*, "no sooner had they greeted each other, without ever having seen or heard of each other before, than in an instant God implanted in their minds a knowledge of their inner selves and of their design that was so clear, that upon this mutual recognition they could not but thank God for His favours."

This devout personage, in his forties, was Jérôme Le Royer de La Dauversière, a receiver of the *taille* at La Flèche, in Anjou, whom God had inspired with the project for Montreal in the cathedral of Notre-Dame in Paris in 1635. Since that date he had developed his plan and obtained the approval of the Jesuits, his former masters at the Collège of La Flèche. In 1639, his efforts led to the founding of the Société Notre-Dame de Montréal, whose "Associates" acquired the island of Montreal. Paul de CHOMEDEY de Maisonneuve was chosen to take charge of the new post.

M. de La Dauversière made urgent appeals to Jeanne. The Associates of Montreal needed a person of precisely her type, wise, devout, intelligent, and resolute, as bursar and later as nurse for the Montreal contingent. M. de La Dauversière obtained her consent as soon as she had consulted by letter first Father Saint-Jure, then Mme de Bullion. Jeanne then became a member of the Société Notre-Dame de Montréal.

On 9 May 1641 the contingent embarked on two ships. M. de Maisonneuve boarded one with a part of the contingent; the Jesuit father La Place, Jeanne Mance, and 12 men went aboard the second. But before the sails could be unfurled, M. de La Dauversière conversed for the last time with Jeanne. It was then that she suggested to him an extension of the Société de Montréal, which would, in her view, provide the support indispensable to their colonizing endeavours. She proposed that M. de La Dauversière should set down in writing an outline of the "Montreal project," and deliver several copies to her. She would then address invitations to membership in the Société de Montréal to the distinguished and generous ladies and to the devout women with whom she had associated in Paris, and would attach to each invitation a copy of M. de La Dauversière's draft. M. de La Dauversière promised to distribute the missives as soon as he reached Paris.

Jeanne Mance landed at Quebec at the beginning of August, the eighth, we are told by Dollier de Casson, who adds that "the ship carrying Mademoiselle Mance experienced little other than calm weather, M. de Maison-neufve's encountered such violent storms that it had to put back to port three times." The leader of the contingent apparently arrived at Tadoussac only on 20 September, when hope of his appearing that year was being abandoned.

The opposition manifested at Quebec against the founding of a post at Montreal, which was styled a "foolhardy undertaking," dismayed Jeanne Mance. But M. de Maisonneuve, once he had got to his destination and been duly warned of this situation, decided to disregard it, although he did so with his usual courtesy. The founding was none the less postponed until the following spring because of the lateness of the season. Jeanne spent the winter at Sillery together with M. de Maisonneuve, Mme de La Peltrie, who displayed a keen affection for her, and M. Pierre de PUISEAUX de Montrénault. The winter was marked by a few conflicts with the governor, HUAULT de Montmagny, who at the beginning was not in favour of the project of founding Montreal. In the face of M. de Maisonneuve's firmness, he finally yielded. According to the *Relations*, the founding of Montreal took place 17 May 1642. On that date "Monsieur the Governor placed the sieur de Maison-neufve in possession of the Island, in the name of the Gentlemen of Mont-real, in order to commence the first buildings thereon."

The founding of the Hôtel-Dieu at Montreal took place in the autumn of the same year. Here again it is a text of the *Relations* that fixes the date: "Of all the Savages, there remained with us [in the spring of 1643] but one, Pachirini, . . . he had always wished to live with us, together with two other patients, in the little Hospital which we had erected there [in the fort] for the wounded." The construction of the hospital proper, however, took place only in 1645.

In 1649, Jeanne was at Quebec when some letters reached her from France. When she read them, she received, said Dollier de Casson, "three bludgeon strokes." She learned from them first the death of Father Rapine, "who used to obtain for her, from his lady, all that was needed," the

Mance

lady being Mme de Bullion. She was likewise informed that M. de La Dauversière was seriously ill and was on the brink of ruin. Finally she was told that the Associates of Montreal had all dispersed. Jeanne decided to leave as soon as possible for France. She wrote to M. de Maisonneuve, acquainted him with the predicament of the Montreal post, and notified him of her immediate embarkation.

When she returned a year later, all the difficulties had been smoothed out. M. de La Dauversière had completely recovered and was concerning himself zealously with the interests of Montreal. The Société de Montréal had revived under the guidance of Jean-Jacques Olier, one of its founders. Finally Mme de Bullion, admirably well-disposed as ever towards Montreal and its hospital, had agreed with Jeanne upon a new method of communication which would allow her not to divulge her name.

But from the spring of 1651 on, the struggle against the Iroquois became more and more bloody and recurrent. "The Iroquois," wrote Dollier de Casson, "having no more atrocities to commit . . . because there were no more Hurons to destroy, . . . turned their attention towards the île de Montreal . . . ; there is not a month in this summer when our book of the dead has not been stained in red letters by the hands of the Iroquois." Jeanne Mance had to close the hospital and take refuge in the fort. All the settlers did the same. On the abandoned sites it was necessary to put garrisons; "we were getting fewer every day," added Dollier de Casson.

At the end of the summer of 1651 M. de Maisonneuve, discouraged, and even profoundly distressed at the sight of settlers whom he loved and had undertaken to protect falling continually around him, resolved to bring an end to this slaughter at whatever cost. It was clear that they would all meet the same fate sooner or later. He would go to France, and try to obtain assistance in order to bring a good number of soldiers back to Ville-Marie. Or else, if he failed to gain the support of the Associates of Montreal, he would abandon the undertaking and order the settlers to return to France.

It was then that Jeanne intervened. Her trust in Providence had suddenly revealed to her the way to come to the assistance of all of them. She went to M. de Maisonneuve's house and said to him that "she advised him to go to France, that the foundress had given her for the hospital 22,000 *livres*, which were in a certain place that she pointed out to him,—and that she would give him the money so that he could get help." M. de Maisonneuve accepted the proposal in principle. Before making a final decision he wanted to pray, meditate, and consult the chaplains. He was also thinking about the way to compensate Mme de Bullion for the loss of the capital that she was putting at his disposal. He sailed for France a few weeks later, not without some hope. By her advice to the governor, Jeanne Mance had just saved Montreal, for M. de Maisonneuve came back with help.

A few years later, 28 Jan. 1657, as she was returning from mass, Jeanne Mance fell on the ice, fractured her right arm, and dislocated her wrist. This fall had serious consequences. The doctors managed to set the fracture, but they failed to notice the condition of the wrist; although cured, Jeanne was unable to use her arm. Because of this infirmity she was obliged to consider having herself replaced as the head of the hospital. She waited, however, for the return of M. de Maisonneuve, who had set out for France again in 1655. He was to return only at the end of July 1657, together with the first parish clergy for Ville-Marie, which would consist of three Sulpicians under the leadership of Abbé Queylus [*see* THUBIÈRES]. But as ill luck would have it M. Olier, who had himself chosen these four missionaries, passed away just a few days before the priests went on board. Jeanne, who had lost no time in consulting M. de Maisonneuve on his arrival, had to postpone her journey to France until the following year. Her state of health left much to be desired. She set out in the autumn of 1658, together with Marguerite BOURGEOYS, who had become her faithful friend. M. de Queylus had taken advantage of Jeanne Mance's impending departure to send for two Hospitallers from Quebec. This was in accordance with a promise which he had made to the Hospitallers of Quebec, to entrust to them the management of the hospital at Montreal. The Quebec nuns were however obliged to go back to their convent when Jeanne Mance returned with the Hospitallers from La Flèche.

In France, Jeanne had to make the trip from La Rochelle to La Flèche on a stretcher. Her arm was giving her terrible pain. With M. de La Dauversière she made all the necessary arrangements, so that she could shortly take back to New France the three Hospitallers of Saint-Joseph whom he would himself choose. She confessed to him her hope of getting some funds from Mme de Bullion to help in establishing these nuns at Montreal. Her success was everywhere complete, and to it was even added an incident which has been considered as miraculous. In the Sulpicians' chapel she had placed the relic of M. Olier's heart on her injured arm, and had recovered the use of it. She re-embarked for New France with Mothers Judith MOREAU de Brésoles, Catherine MACÉ, and Marie MAILLET, and arrived in the colony 7 Sept. 1659. Marguerite Bourgeoys, with a few female companions, was on the same ship. M. de La Dauversière, who had gone to La Rochelle, gave to all the women a final benediction. One of his most cherished wishes was being realized.

In 1662 Jeanne made her last journey to France. On this occasion an event of great importance had to be superintended: the replacement of the Société Notre-Dame de Montréal, which had withdrawn, by the Compagnie des Prêtres de Saint-Sulpice, which was becoming the seigneur and owner of the island of Montreal. The Société de Montréal was in the process of breaking up, and moreover M. La Dauversière, the tireless founder and providential benefactor of Ville-Marie, was no longer there to stir the Associates to action. He had died 6 Nov. 1659. Jeanne returned to Montreal in 1664.

From 1663 on, great changes had been taking place in the government of New France. Louis XIV had insisted on personally guiding the destinies of his overseas settlement. In the first place he had concerned himself with putting down the Iroquois. But since 1665 Ville-Marie had been plunged into the deepest affliction. M. de Maisonneuve had been requested to return to France on indefinite leave. No account had been taken of his 24 years of incomparable service. He had accepted this decision heroically, and he left New France in the autumn of 1665. Soon Jeanne Mance, too, encountered the inability of authorities whom she revered to understand her deeds of deliverance in earlier days. Ever courageous and resigned, she carried out her task to the end. Her last administrative act dates from January 1673. She died 18 June 1673 "in odour of sanctity," affirmed Mother Juchereau* de Saint-Ignace in her *Annales* of the Hôtel-Dieu of Quebec.

A small picture signed L. Dugardin, preserved at the Hôtel-Dieu of Montreal, seems to represent the true face of Jeanne Mance. In any case one can read on the back of the work: "Authentic copy of the portrait of Mademoiselle Mance." This inscription has been identified as probably being in the hand of Sister Joséphine Paquet*, the archivist of the Hôtel-Dieu from 1870 to 1889.

MARIE-CLAIRE DAVELUY

Archives de l'hôtel de ville de Langres (Haute-Marne), Registres des baptêmes ... de la paroisse Saint-Pierre et Saint-Paul. Dollier de Casson, *Histoire du Montréal*. *JR* (Thwaites). Juchereau, *Annales* (Jamet). Morin, *Annales* (Fauteux *et al.*). [Jean-Jacques Olier?], *Les véritables motifs de messieurs et dames de la Société de Notre-Dame de Montréal pour la conversion des sauvages de la Nouvelle-France*, éd. H.-A. Verreau (SHM *Mémoires*, IX (1880)). Daveluy, "Bibliographie," *RHAF*, VIII (1954–55), 292–306, 449–55, 591–606; IX (1955–56), 141–49; *Jeanne Mance, 1606–1673, suivie d'un essai généalogique sur les Mance et les De Mance par M. Jacques Laurent*. (1ère éd., Montréal, 1934; 2e éd., Montréal et Paris, [1962]). [Étienne-Michel Faillon], *Vie de Mademoiselle Mance et histoire de l'Hôtel de Villemarie en Canada* (2v., Paris, 1854). Robert Le Blant, "Notes sur Madame de Bullion, bienfaitrice de l'Hôtel-Dieu de Montréal, après 1587–26 juin 1664," *RHAF*, XII (1958–59), 112–25. Lefebvre, *Marie Morin*. Léo-A. Leymarie, "Les commencements de Montréal," *Cahiers Catholiques*, 132 (1925), 3706–10. Mondoux, *L'Hôtel-Dieu de Montréal*. Louis-N. Prunel, *Sébastien Zamet, évêque-duc de Langres, 1588–1655* (Paris, 1912). René Roussel, *Le lieu de naissance et la famille de Jeanne Mance* (Langres, 1932), extract from Société historique et archéologique de Langres *Bulletin*, X.

MANITOUGATCHE (Manitoucharche, Manitouchatche, known as "La Nasse"), JOSEPH, Montagnais Indian and friend of the French, one of the first Indians to adopt, in part, the French way of life; fl. 1629–34.

On the morning of 19 July 1629 Manitougatche brought news to Quebec that three English ships were approaching the Île d'Orléans destined for Quebec. This message was confirmed the same day when English vessels arrived at Quebec and an officer came ashore with a letter from LEWIS and THOMAS KIRKE calling upon CHAMPLAIN to surrender the fort and settlement to the English. After negotiations, the surrender was effected on Friday, 20 July 1629.

Prior to the surrender by the French, Manitougatche and his family lived near Quebec in a cabin on cleared land given to him by the Jesuits. Following the expulsion of the Recollets and the Jesuits by the English in 1629, Manitougatche, molested by the new régime, removed "to the Islands" (identity unknown) and continued to farm the land. When Quebec was restored to the French in 1632 the Jesuits returned the same year and Manitougatche visited the missionaries, promising to again construct his cabin near them and to commit his son to their care. The Jesuits agreed to educate the boy.

On 13 Oct. 1633, Manitougatche and other Indians placed their goods and belongings in care of the Jesuits for safekeeping, probably because they were absent on a bear hunt from which they returned on 24 October. On this occasion Manitougatche, in the words of Father PAUL LE JEUNE, "carried with him a great shield, very long and

Mantes

very wide. . . . They raise it up and cover themselves with it. It is made of one single piece of very light cedar . . . a little bent or curved, the better to cover the body; and, in order that if an arrow or blow should split it, it might still hold together, it was sewed at the top and bottom with a leather string." Shortly thereafter, on 8 Nov. 1633, Manitougatche and his entire family, consisting of two or three households, arrived and camped near the house of the Jesuits. The reported presence of a considerable number of Iroquois near Quebec, 13 Nov. 1633, caused Manitougatche to lead his entire group to cabins near the settlement where protection was provided; but he himself returned to the house of the Jesuits stating that if he was destined for death it was his wish to die near the missionaries. Evidently Manitougatche adopted some French customs because on 30 Nov. 1633, he started building a cabin of wood, fashioning boards with a hatchet, and using nails obtained by burning a derelict boat.

The known life of Manitougatche does not include great deeds as a warrior. It can probably best be described as that of an Indian adopting, in part, new customs and acquiring convictions unknown to his ancestors. Little is recorded of his family other than that he had a son and sons-in-law. Among the latter, Pierre PASTEDECHOUAN is mentioned. When residing near the Jesuits, Manitougatche participated in Christian religious services. His baptism was delayed by the missionaries who always required adult Indians to undergo a lengthy period of probation to test their sincerity. Toward the end of 1633, suffering from an unnamed disease, Manitougatche was cared for at the Jesuit dwelling where he was baptized on 3 April 1634 and named Joseph. He died on Holy Saturday 1634 and was buried according to the ritual of the Roman Catholic Church. Champlain released his people from work and sent them to attend the funeral of Manitougatche.

THOMAS GRASSMANN

Champlain, *Works* (Biggar), VI, 49–66. Du Creux, *History* (Conacher), I, 49–52, 137, 141 (the "Nassa" referred to, 137, 141, is "La Nasse"). *JR* (Thwaites), V, 57, 93–97, 103–5, 107, 111, 121, 163; VI, 119–25. Le Clercq, *First establishment of the faith* (Shea), I, 289. Sagard, *Histoire du Canada* (Tross), IV, 895–97, 904.

MANTES, CÔME DE. See CÔME DE MANTES

MANWARING. See MAINWARING

MARCH. See MARSH

MAREUIL, JACQUES DE, half-pay lieutenant of a detachment of colonial regular troops, amateur actor; he arrived in Canada in the spring of 1693 and left again in the autumn of 1694.

This officer, to whom Abbé Auguste Gosselin gives the name of Jacques-Théodore Cosineau de Mareuil, is principally famous for the scandal he caused during his brief stay at Quebec, and he might be considered the first free-thinker in Canada. He lived at the Château Saint-Louis.

The carnival season at Quebec has always been the occasion for social merry-making. The first governors took advantage of the winter season to have plays staged at the Château Saint-Louis. These performances brought together the military and civil *élite* of the colony. The bishop of Quebec, just as did Bossuet and Massillon, frowned most severely on the theatre. At his request, Governors La Barre [see LE FEBVRE] and Denonville* had desisted from giving any such dramatic presentations. Frontenac [see BUADE], at the beginning of his second term of office, imitated their discretion. The year 1693 had, however, been a particularly good one, and it was proposed to celebrate the carnival with more than the usual lustre by preparing entertainments. The theatre was taken up again, probably because Lieut. Mareuil, Frontenac's protégé, had a liking for the stage and was himself an enthusiastic actor. Corneille's *Nicomède* and Racine's *Mithridate* were staged; preparations were even being made to put on *Tartuffe*, when the bishop, dismayed by the harm that this play might do to his flock, decided to interpose his authority and that of the Church. It was the principal actor and perhaps even the unofficial director of the little *château* troupe that he was attacking when, on 10 January, he asked the parish priests of Quebec to condemn the theatre in general and Lieut. Mareuil in particular. Then on 16 Jan. 1694 the prelate published two pastoral letters in quick succession, one "on impious speech," directed against the free-thinker Mareuil by name, the other "about plays," aimed at Mareuil, who had the title role in *Tartuffe*. However, Mareuil was not the sort of man to take things lying down.

On 19 January he presented a petition to the intendant, Bochart* Champigny, demanding that M. Dupré*, a priest of the parish of Quebec, supply him with a copy of the sermon delivered at high mass in the parish church. The priest refused. The matter was brought before the Conseil Souverain. There the bishop testified that he had "several times charitably warned him [Mareuil], and had had him warned by persons of authority who were most trustworthy, so that he would repudiate the blasphemous and shockingly lewd remarks that he had made during the year that he had been in the country, both against God and against the Blessed Virgin and the saints. . . ." The council postponed action, through fear of displeasing the governor. On 15 March Mareuil called upon the council to give a ruling, and to declare invalid and improper the pastoral letter that had been read against him in the cathedral. The council finally ordered Mareuil's arrest and asked the bishop to produce the letters in question. It was Frontenac's guards who carried out the arrest, on 14 October. The prisoner was forbidden to communicate with any other person. On 15 November the bishop, foreseeing that he would not get complete satisfaction from the council, declared that he was referring the whole matter to France. At last, on 29 November, Frontenac argued before the council that the case had been badly handled, that a great number of "one-sided views, intrigues and private passions" had become mixed up in it, that no proof had yet been adduced against the accused; that consequently he was obliged to release the prisoner, "a man whose person is perhaps hated more than the crime that he is alleged to have committed." Jacques de Mareuil was set at large the same day, and Frontenac had him embarked secretly on the last ship bound for France.

LÉOPOLD LAMONTAGNE

AN, Col., B, 17, ff.99, 115; C¹¹ᴬ, 13, ff.95, 129, 178; F³, 5, ff.186–270 *passim* (*see* PAC *Report, 1885*, lxi; *1899*, Supp., 92, 310–11). APQ *Rapport, 1922–23*, 8–10. Caron, "Inventaire des documents," APQ *Rapport, 1939–40*, 315, 317, 320–2, 324, 327–28. *Jug. et délib.*, III. *Mandements des évêques de Québec* (Tetû et Gagnon), I, 301–8.

Jean Béraud, *350 ans de théâtre au Canada français* (Encyclopédie du Canada français, I, [Ottawa, 1958]), 11–14. Cahall, *The Sovereign Council of New France*, 85–93. Delalande, *Le Conseil souverain*, 198–202. Eccles, *Frontenac*, 297ff, 302–5. Auguste Gosselin, "Un episode de l'histoire du théâtre au Canada (1694)," *RSCT*, 2d ser., IV (1898), sect.I, 53–72. "Ordonnance de M. Bochart Champigny . . . (19 janv. 1694)," *BRH*, XXXIX (1933), 125–27. Alfred Rambaud, "La vie orageuse et douloureuse de Mgr de Saint-Vallier, deuxième évêque de Québec (1653–1727)," *RUL*, IX (1954–55), 90–108.

MARGUERIE DE LA HAYE, FRANÇOIS, interpreter; b. Rouen (Normandy) where he was baptized 12 Oct. 1612, son of François Marguerie, *bourgeois* and oar-maker, and of Marthe Romain; drowned 23 May 1648 at Trois-Rivières and buried at Quebec.

One of the most daring figures of the early days of the colony, François Marguerie was called "the double man" by the Indians, because he had earned for himself the reputation among them of being the paleface who had adapted himself most completely to their customs and to their tongues. Although the *Relations des Jésuites* do not record his presence in the colony until 1636, it is possible, as some historians claim, that he was in Canada before 1629 and that he went to seek refuge among the Algonkins during the KIRKES' occupation of the colony, thus becoming familiar with the way of life and language of this tribe.

Marguerie spent the winter of 1635–36 at Allumette Island and on 28 March he arrived in the Huron country in the company of four Algonkins, one of whom was TESSOUAT (d. 1636), bringing the missionaries news of the civilized world. The spontaneous sympathy that the Indians manifested towards him was very useful to the Jesuits, for whom he acted as guide and interpreter on their trips and in their missionary endeavours. During the years 1637–40, however, he scarcely left Trois-Rivières and we know that he was the chief interpreter at that place from 1642 to 1648.

In the month of February 1641 he went hunting in the surrounding woods with another specialist in Indian languages, THOMAS GODEFROY; they were taken prisoner by a party of Iroquois and carried off to their village. The two interpreters remained there for several weeks, and took advantage of the opportunity to become familiar with the Iroquois language.

During the period of their captivity, the two prisoners became aware that the Iroquois were preparing to descend upon Trois-Rivières early in the summer, and that they would be using the two Frenchmen as guides and as a lure. The two of them for their part devised a plan to thwart the Indian scheme. When the party reached a point directly across the St. Lawrence River from Trois-Rivières, Marguerie volunteered to go in person to negotiate with the authorities of the town. Thomas Godefroy was to be kept as a hostage, and Marguerie gave his word of honour that he would return and be a prisoner again if he achieved no results. On 5 June he appeared at the fort, and without giving a thought to his personal safety, he dissuaded the governor, M. de CHAMPFLOUR, from accepting the Iroquois proposals, as they concealed a trap. Then he went back to turn himself over to the Indians. In the meantime the authorities of Trois-Rivières deliberated and decided to send Jean NICOLLET and Father RAGUENEAU to attempt negotiations with the Iroquois. At last an agreement was reached, and the two captives were freed. Their boldness and their courage had helped to save the settlement at Trois-Rivières.

Marie-Catherine de Saint-Augustin

Both were shortly to meet tragic deaths. François Marguerie was drowned, along with a companion, JEAN AMIOT, 23 May 1648; his canoe had capsized in the St. Lawrence off Trois-Rivières. Godefroy was tortured to death four years later. The death of these two young men was an irreparable loss to the colony, as the *Relation* of 1648 notes: ". . . two young Frenchmen, who have been greatly regretted in this country on account of both their virtue and their knowledge of languages."

François Marguerie had married at Quebec, 26 Oct. 1645, Louise Cloutier, daughter of Zacherie CLOUTIER, one of the Beauport pioneers. They had no children. His widow married Jean Mignot *dit* Chatillon and later Jean-Pierre Mataut.

RAYMOND DOUVILLE

JR (Thwaites), X, 320f; XXI, 20–58; XXXII, 136. *Papier terrier de la cie des I.O.* (P.-G. Roy), 301. Desrosiers, *Iroquoisie*. Godbout, *Les pionniers de la région trifluvienne*. Sulte, *Chronique trifluvienne* (Montréal, 1879). Albert Tessier, *Les Trois-Rivières: quatre siècles d'histoire 1535–1935* (Trois-Rivières, 1934).

MARIE-CATHERINE DE SAINT-AUGUSTIN. *See* SIMON

MARIE DE LA CONCEPTION. *See* IRWIN

MARIE DE L'INCARNATION. *See* GUYART

MARIE DE SAINT-BERNARD. *See* SAVONNIÈRES

MARIE DE SAINT-BONAVENTURE-DE-JÉSUS. *See* FORESTIER

MARIE DE SAINT-IGNACE (Hospitaller of the Augustine order). *See* GUENET

MARIE DE SAINT-IGNACE (Hospitaller of the Hôtel-Dieu, Quebec). *See* GIFFARD

MARIE DE SAINT-JOSEPH. *See* SAVONNIÈRES

MAROT, BERNARD, surgeon and ship's captain; b. apparently in the Basque country of France; fl. 1610–50.

Marot came to Port-Royal (Annapolis Royal, N.S.) as a qualified surgeon in 1610 or 1611. It was he who in 1630 was sent from Bordeaux by Jean Tuffet, director of the Compagnie de la Nouvelle-France, with two ships carrying letters and supplies for CHARLES DE SAINT-ÉTIENNE de La Tour and his men at Cap de Sable. While there, he traded for furs to help pay for the voyage. The favourable report he carried back to the company helped win for La Tour the title of lieutenant-general in Acadia. However, he was reprimanded by Tuffet for having sent his second vessel back to France empty. Soon afterwards Marot was caught carrying on unauthorized fishing and fur-trading in Acadia and sent a prisoner to France by order of La Tour, who later withdrew the charges. On his release, Marot joined Isaac de RAZILLY in Acadia and was given the rank of captain. In 1635 he led the party of soldiers sent by Razilly to capture Jean THOMAS who instigated the first rebellion in Acadia.

After Razilly's death, Marot served under his successor, Charles de MENOU d'Aulnay. In 1640 he was sent by d'Aulnay to reinforce the garrison at Fort Pentagouet on the Penobscot. He took part in the successful attack on Fort La Tour at Saint John in 1645 and was one of the signers of a statement concerning that action [*see* JACQUELIN and MENOU]. That same year he was sent to the Rechibouctou area to seize a bark and her crew trading there for furs for the Miscou company. From then until 1650 he appears to have been employed mainly in capturing vessels and trading and fishing in Acadia without the consent of d'Aulnay. Nothing definite is known of his subsequent career, although he may have been the Capt. Marot who commanded a merchantman voyaging to Quebec in 1657.

GEORGE MACBEATH

ACM, B.187, 5655, 5656. Champlain, *Works* (Biggar). *Factum* (1614). Couillard Després, *Saint-Étienne de La Tour*. Huguet, *Poutrincourt*. Candide de Nant, *Pages glorieuses de l'épopée canadienne: une mission capucine en Acadie* (Montréal, 1927).

MARQUETTE, JACQUES, Jesuit, missionary; b. at Laon, France, on 10 June 1637; d. in the territory of the Illinois Indians, near the present-day Luddington, Michigan, 18 May 1675.

The son of Nicolas Marquette, seigneur of Tombelles and councillor of Laon, and of his second wife, Rose de La Salle, Jacques Marquette descended from two distinguished families of warriors and officials, his father's being one of the most ancient and prominent in the Laon district. At the age of 17, in October 1654, he entered the Jesuit noviciate at Nancy, and, after studies and teaching assignments at Auxerre, Rheims, Charleville, Langres, and Pont-à-Mousson, he began his theological studies at Pont-à-Mousson in the autumn of 1665. Since 1658, however, he had been repeatedly expressing both to his immediate superiors and to the general of the Jesuits in Rome, his strong desire to become a missionary.

Marquette

In March 1665, he had written a second letter to the general, urging "that your Paternity order me to set out for foreign nations of which I have been thinking from my earliest boyhood," and begging that he be allowed to go without the usual course in theology. "A reason for my not tarrying so long," he insisted, "is that I feel a repugnance to getting up the speculative sciences and by nature and disposition am not so well suited for them." He had, nevertheless, been obliged to begin theology; but his course was, by exception, abbreviated to one academic year.

Accordingly, at the beginning of June 1666, Marquette left La Rochelle, arriving in Quebec on 20 September. Three weeks later, on 10 October, he left for Trois-Rivières where he spent a year with Father Gabriel DRUILLETTES in the study of Montagnais and other Indian languages —among which, by 1673, he was fluent in six. On 20 May 1668, he left Quebec for the Ottawa mission, joining Father Claude DABLON in the establishment at Sault Ste. Marie, a mission post that served some 2,000 Algonkins. A year later, in September 1669, he transferred to the western extremity of Lake Superior, founding, at La Pointe du Saint-Esprit in Chequamegon Bay, a mission which ministered to refugee Ottawa and Huron tribesmen from the shores of Lake Huron and Georgian Bay. It was here that he first made contact with the Illinois Indians, whose gentle and courteous manners contrasted with those of the fierce Hurons. The latter, having become involved in a quarrel with the Sioux, and finding themselves outnumbered, hurriedly abandoned La Pointe and fled to Lake Michigan. Marquette followed, and in the summer of 1671, founded the mission of Saint-Ignace on the north shore of the straits of Michilimackinac. There he remained until 1673, except for a sojourn at Sault Ste. Marie where he took his final vows as a Jesuit on 2 July 1671. There also, on 8 Dec. 1672, he welcomed Louis JOLLIET, who came with a commission to lead an expedition of discovery to the Mississippi.

After a winter of plans and preparations, Marquette and Jolliet left in mid-May 1673 for the great voyage. A month later they entered the Mississippi, and, at a spot somewhere on the Iowa shore, were greeted at a Peoria village by an aged man who exclaimed: "Never is the sun so bright, O Frenchman, as when thou comst to visit us"—a sentence which was inscribed in 1937 on the pedestal of the Marquette monument in Laon. Jolliet and Marquette sailed on to a point near the modern boundary of Arkansas and Louisiana, turning their canoes in mid-July, and heading up-stream, back through the Chicago River to Lake Michigan, which they reached in September. Marquette, his health sadly impaired, remained at the mission of Saint-François-Xavier, near the present-day De Pere, Wisconsin, while Jolliet returned to Montreal.

By the following summer, 1674, Marquette had recovered sufficiently to renew his missionary activity. He set out to fulfil his promise to the Kaskaskia Indians that he would return to them. Accordingly in October 1674, he left Green Bay (Baie des Puants) with two *voyageurs*, Jacques Le Castor and Pierre Porteret, for the Illinois territory; but he suffered much from the stormy weather and frost; his dysentery returned; and the three travellers were forced to stop on 14 December and to spend the winter at a spot which is now in the suburbs of Chicago. They were frequently visited by parties of Illinois Indians; on 30 March 1675, Marquette decided to continue on to their village on the Illinois River which he reached with his companions on 8 April. It was Holy Week, and on Holy Thursday he preached in the open air to a magnificent circle of 500 chiefs and old men squatting around him, while 1,500 young braves stood behind. However he was already a dying man. Shortly after Easter, he left for Saint-Ignace hoping to reach the mission before the end. He did not. Carried ashore by his two companions, he expired in the wilderness on a spot at the mouth of the river since named after him. Two years later, a convoy of some 30 canoes of Kiskakon Indians disinterred his body, and solemnly transported it to Saint-Ignace.

Perhaps because he is the most renowned of all Jesuit missionary-explorers in the early story of North America, Marquette has been the centre of a great deal of controversy. In the last 30 years or so this has tended to concentrate on three main points: the authorship of the *Récit* of the 1673 expedition; Marquette's ordination to the priesthood; and the personality and relative importance of the man as a missionary and explorer. Until 1927, Marquette was generally taken to be the author of the *Récit* which was, in fact, written in the first person. In that year, however, Francis B. Steck published *The Jolliet-Marquette expedition of 1673* in which he challenged this traditional belief, claiming that the *Récit* was not Marquette's but rather Jolliet's journal recast by Father Claude Dablon with the aid of other sources. Steck's conclusions were thoroughly reviewed in "The Jolliet-Marquette expedition of 1673," *Thought*, IV (1929), 32–71, by Father J. G. Carraghan who questioned Steck's critical methods and concluded in turn that although there was some mystery about the *Récit*, it must continue to be considered as substantially Marquette's own journal of the voyage. To this Steck replied with

Marquette

a pamphlet, *Father Garraghan and "The Jolliet-Marquette Expedition of 1673,"* in which he reiterated his original stand and, in turn, criticized Garraghan's methods. In 1945, Jean Delanglez began a series of articles on the *Récit* and claimed, after examination of a bewildering record of manuscripts, publications, and maps, that the *Récit* had indeed been composed (in the first person as a literary device) by Father Claude Dablon with the aid of other documents but not Jolliet's journal, a conclusion which he incorporated, with a huge bibliography, in his *Life and voyages of Louis Jolliet*, and *Louis Jolliet: vie et voyages*.

The debate on the second controversial point, Marquette's ordination, is based especially on the argument from silence (there is no record of it), on the fact of Marquette's request of 1665 to be sent to the missions without the regular course in theology; and, finally, on different interpretations of the document of Marquette's final vows in the Jesuit order. In a review of Delanglez' *Jolliet* in the *Wisconsin Magazine of History*, XXXII (1948), 227–29, J. C. Short claims that Jacques Marquette was not a priest but a catechist, a claim he reiterated in "Jacques Marquette, cathechist," *RUL*, III (1948–49), 436f. In "Attempted mayhem on Père Marquette," *Mid-America*, XXXI (1949), 109–15, Jerome V. Jacobson refutes this, both by arguments taken from the Jesuit Constitutions, and by publishing a new document that records the ordination of a Jacques Marquette at Toul on 7 March 1666. He repeats these arguments and adds the testimony of the triennial catalogue of the Jesuit province of Champagne (to which Marquette belonged) in another article in the same periodical, "Marquette's ordination" (*Mid-America*, XXXII (1950), 46–54). These arguments for and against Marquette's priesthood are reviewed again in Claude Corrivault's "Le Père Jacques Marquette," *BRH*, LVI (1950), 46f.

The discussion about Marquette's personality and place in history is largely a by-product of the other two debates. Viewed from the *Récit*, the *Journal*, other letters, and the *Relations*, Marquette appears as a robust, optimistic, gentle, and truly zealous missionary who exercised an intense personal influence over the Indians, and whose reputation for great missionary initiative as well as personal holiness began with his own immediate contemporaries. As such he has appealed to posterity, and has deserved to be commemorated by monuments (a statue in the Capitol in Washington, among others) and the bestowal of his name on a university, a railroad, a river, a number of cities, districts, and countless avenues. By using other documents, however, by re-evaluating the *Récit* and from the ordination controversy, some have found Marquette to be a "synthetic hero," one whom his superiors in France, during his first years as a Jesuit, found in fact to be "mediocre" or at best "good," and temperamentally "bilious" and "melancholic." They underline that he only spent six and one-half years at the missions; that he founded none, except Saint-Ignace; that, except for the Mississippi expedition, he merely followed in the footsteps of others, especially Father Claude ALLOUEZ; and that on the Mississippi expedition itself, Jolliet was the leader and not Marquette, as Charlevoix* had claimed. In an unpublished mimeographed collection of ten essays on Marquette, Steck rehearses all his previous arguments about the exaggerated place in history given to Marquette, and adds additional ones. These he published in *Marquette Legends*. But these, again, were closely re-examined and criticized in a review by Lucien Campeau (*RHAF*, XIV (1960–61), 282–86).

Judging from the record of the past 30 years, the last word has not yet been written in this three-pronged debate, which, even in a short view of history, does not really matter. For it concerns a man who left behind him as many mysteries as any man will, and, being human, must have had the defects of all his qualities.

J. MONET

Charlevoix, *Histoire*. JR (Thwaites), LIX. *Narratives of the Northwest* (Kellogg) in *Original narratives* (Jameson). *Mission du Canada: Relations inédites de la Nouvelle-France (1672–1679) pour faire suite aux anciennes relations (1615–1672) avec deux cartes géographiques*, [éd. Félix Martin] (2v., Paris, 1861). J. G. Shea, *Discovery and exploration of the Mississippi valley with the original narratives of Marquette, Allouez, Membré, Hennepin, and Anastase Douay* (New York, 1852). Melchisédech Thévenot, *Recueil de voyages de Mr. Thévenot* (Paris, 1681).

Lucien Campeau, "Marquette legends," *RHAF*, XIV (1960–61), 282–86. C. Corrivault, "Le Père Jacques Marquette," *BRH*, LVI (1950), 46–48. Jean Delanglez, "The discovery of the Mississippi," *Mid-America*, XXVII (1945), 219–31; XXVIII (1946), 2–22; *Jolliet* ; "Marquette's autograph map of the Mississippi River," *Mid-America*, XXVII (1945), 30–53; "The 'Récit des voyages et des découvertes du Père Jacques Marquette,' " *Mid-America*, XXVIII (1946), 173–94, 211–58. G. J. Garraghan, "The Jolliet-Marquette expedition, 1673," *Thought*, IV (1929), 32–71; *Marquette—ardent missioner, daring explorer* (New York, 1937). "Some hitherto unpublished Marquettiana," *Mid-America*, XVIII (1936), 15–26; "Some newly discovered Marquette and La Salle letters," *Archivum historicum Societatis Iesu*, Anni IV, Fasc.II (Iul.-Dec., 1935), 268–90. Alfred Hamy, *Au Mississippi: la première exploration, 1673: le Père Jacques Marquette de Laon, prêtre de la Compagnie de Jésus*

(*1637–1675*), *et Louis Jolliet, d'après Ernest Gagnon* (Paris, 1903). Jerome V. Jacobson, "Attempted mayhem on Père Marquette," *Mid-America*, XXXI (1949), 109–15; "Documents: Marquette's ordination" *Mid-America*, XXXII (1950), 46–54.

L. P. Kellogg, *The French régime in Wisconsin and the Northwest* (Madison, Wis., 1925); "Jacques Marquette," *DAB*, XXII, 294–95; "Marquette's authentic map possibly identified," State Hist. Soc. of Wisconsin *Proc.*, 1906, 183–93. Agnes Repplier, *Père Marquette: priest, pioneer and adventurer* (New York, 1929). J. C. Short, "Jacques Marquette, catechist," *RUL*, III (1948–49), 436–41; review of Jean Delanglez, *Life and voyages of Louis Jolliet*, in *Wisconsin Mag. of Hist.*, XXXII (1948–49), 227–29. Jared Sparks, "Father Marquette," in *The Library of American biography*, ed. Jared Sparks (10v., Boston and London, 1834–36), X, 263–99. Francis Borgia Steck, *Essays relating to the Jolliet-Marquette expedition, 1673*, ed. August Reyling (2v., Quincy, Ill., 1953 [for private distribution]); *Father Garraghan and "The Jolliet-Marquette expedition, 1673"* (Quincy, Ill., 1929 [privately printed pamphlet]); *The Jolliet-Marquette expedition, 1673* (The Catholic University of America, Studies in American Church History, VI, 1927); *Marquette legends*, ed. August Reyling (New York, 1960).

MARSH (March), JOHN, HBC governor in Hudson Bay; d. 1688/89.

Recommended by Lord Churchill (later Duke of Marlborough), Marsh was appointed governor of James Bay in 1688 when the Company's three forts had been for two years in French hands. He was instructed to build a new settlement on Albany River to re-establish the HBC's trade but in doing so to avoid "annoyeing" the French, for a truce was in effect between the two nations.

For the new fort Marsh chose an island in James Bay and began building operations. The ships *Churchill* (Capt. William BOND) and *Yonge* (Capt. John Simpson) were to winter with him and assist him. He was to take strong measures against private trading and interloping (trespassing on the Company's monopoly). On the way out his party did meet an interloping ship, the *Mary*, which had become jammed in the Hudson Strait ice and they took its captain and 20 men on board before the ship sank next day.

The expedition was ill-fated. While out hunting, Bond and his colleagues became careless of their safety and were surprised and taken prisoner by the French. Marsh, who was ill at the time, died on 30 Jan. 1688/89 (HBC Arch. A.15/3, f.158). He was succeeded by Capt. Andrew HAMILTON, his deputy, who shortly afterwards surrendered to the French, under Pierre Le Moyne* d'Iberville. Marsh left a widow, Elizabeth, who received settlement of his account in May 1690.

MAUD M. HUTCHESON

[On the events of 1688/89 see also ABRAHAM, OUTLAW, and VERNER.]

HBRS, XI, XX (Rich and Johnson); XXI (Rich).

MARSOLET DE SAINT-AIGNAN, NICOLAS, interpreter, clerk in the fur trade, ship's master, trader, and seigneur, coming from the neighbourhood of Rouen—perhaps from Saint-Aignan-sur-Ry, as his name suggests; b. 1587, if the burial certificate is to be believed, or 1601, according to the 1666 census; d. 15 May 1677 at Quebec.

Historians do not agree as to the date of Marsolet's arrival in New France: some favour 1608, others 1613 or 1618. The only affirmation that is at all explicit comes from CHAMPLAIN; recounting the events of 1629, he wrote of Pierre Raye, Étienne BRULÉ, and Marsolet that he had taken them "upon our expeditions over fifteen or sixteen years before." Now we know that Champlain had in fact left France in 1613 for a sixth stay in Canada, during which time he went up the Ottawa River as far as Allumette Island in the Algonkin country. In our opinion it was in this year that Marsolet, a future interpreter of the Montagnais and Algonkin languages, landed in the colony, together with the founder of Quebec.

In Marsolet's long career two periods are distinguishable, during which he adopted in turn each of the two conceptions of colonization whose partisans were at variance in New France. On the one hand the merchants and their clerks, concerned solely with furs and wealth, were opposed to the establishment of a French population; on the other hand Champlain and his associates were struggling to populate the colony and preach the gospel to the Indians. Until about 1636 Marsolet seems to have supported the merchants; subsequently he went over to the other camp.

Little information prior to 1629 is available in respect to Marsolet. In 1623 and 1624 his presence at Tadoussac was noted; on 24 March 1627 he was in Paris; in the summer of 1627 he was back in Canada and took part in fur-trading at Cap-de-la-Victoire. Finally, the "interpreter" who spent the winter of 1626–27 with the Jesuits of Quebec while incapacitated by pleurisy and who agreed to impart his linguistic knowledge to Father CHARLES LALEMANT, was perhaps Marsolet.

From the moment he reached New France, Marsolet probably divided his activities between the posts at Tadoussac, Quebec, Trois-Rivières, and the Algonkin villages of the Ottawa River region, living with the Indians in the greatest licence and continually on the look-out for substantial profits. This at least is what Champlain hinted at in 1629, when he accused Marsolet and

Marsolet de Saint-Aignan

Brûlé of remaining "without religion, eating meat on Friday and Saturday," of indulging themselves "in unrestrained debauchery and libertinism," and especially of having "betrayed their King and sold their country" for love of money, by putting themselves at the disposal of the English when Quebec was taken by the KIRKE brothers.

Champlain had another reason to complain of Marsolet. The interpreter wrecked his plan to take back to France CHARITÉ and Espérance, two Indian girls whom the founder of Quebec had adopted. Perhaps with the intention of keeping the young girls near him, because, as Champlain wrote, he "wished to debauch" them, or in order to punish Espérance for having repulsed his advances, the "rascal" misled Kirke—who was very anxious to keep the Indians' goodwill—into thinking that they would look with disapproval upon the girls' departure. Despite Champlain's indignant denials and his offer to appease the Indians by a valuable gift, DAVID KIRKE did not authorize him to take his two protégées with him. Champlain and Espérance heaped bitter reproaches upon Marsolet for such double-dealing.

At the end of the summer of 1629 the majority of the French sailed for France. Marsolet remained behind. He continued to carry on his occupation as an interpreter, for the benefit of the English. In 1632 the French returned, and again Marsolet changed his allegiance, although not entirely his attitude. The Jesuit PAUL LE JEUNE wrote in 1633: " In all the years that we have been in this country no one has ever been able to learn anything from the interpreter named Marsolet, who, for excuse, said that he had sworn that he would never teach the Savage tongue to anyone whomsoever." Only "Father Charles Lallemant won him." Nicolas Marsolet was still harbouring the inveterate distrust felt by the majority of the fur-traders towards the missionaries and the settlers, for they dreaded their influence over the Indians who supplied the fur trade.

Nevertheless, the interpreter was soon to abandon his prejudices. By about 1636 there seemed to be no possibility that the movement towards populating and evangelizing the country would be checked, although it was still only at its beginning. Marsolet sided with the general opinion and resolved to settle down. In 1636 or 1637 (we know the first child was baptized on 22 Feb. 1638) he married Marie Le Barbier, and on 6 Oct. 1637 took possession of the seigneury of Bellechasse (Berthier). This seigneury, with a frontage of a quarter of a league and a depth of one and a half leagues, had been granted to him by the Cent-Associés on the preceding 28 March; three years later, on 20 Nov. 1640, he bought from René Maheu a tract of land on the Sainte-Geneviève hill. From then on Marsolet lived a steady life. In 1643, for example, the *Relation* spoke of him as a valued collaborator of the missionaries.

Thanks to his long experience of Indian questions and of the fur trade, Marsolet obtained a post as clerk to the Cent-Associés about 1642; but while he continued to act as an interpreter, an occupation which he never abandoned, he soon began to traffic on his own account. Marsolet was on bad terms with the directors of the Communauté des Habitants; he disapproved of their luxurious living; and after inciting a movement of protest against them in January 1646, which was swiftly suppressed by the governor, he had to rely on his own resources to carry through his commercial undertakings. By 1647 at the latest he was the owner of a boat which he utilized in his fur-trading trips to Tadoussac. Later, about 1660, he appears to have operated a shop at Quebec: in December 1664, for instance, he was accused of retailing wine at 25 *sols* a jug, despite the rulings of the council. In 1663 he was one of the 17 settlers to whom the governor PIERRE DUBOIS Davaugour, on March 4, had rented the Tadoussac trading concession for two years; this lease, however, was judged irregular and annulled shortly afterwards by the Conseil Souverain.

The "little king of Tadoussac," totally engrossed in the fur trade, took scant interest—perhaps for lack of capital—in exploiting the numerous grants of land that had been made to him. After the Bellechasse seigneury which he made over to M. Berthier* on 15 Nov. 1672, Marsolet had received the following: from Abbé La Ferté on 5 April 1644 the Marsolet meadows, an arriere-fief with a frontage of half a league and a depth of two leagues, in the Cap-de-la-Madeleine seigneury; from the Compagnie de la Nouvelle-France on 16 April 1647 an equal area of land, in part of the future Gentilly seigneury, which he sold to Michel Pelletier de La Prade on 23 Oct. 1671; and from Jean TALON on 3 Nov. 1672 the Marsolet fief, half a league long and one and a half leagues wide, in the future Lotbinière seigneury. None of these fiefs was lived on or cleared by Marsolet's efforts. In the *censive* (seigneurial area) of Quebec Marsolet owned two other estates: 71 acres on the Sainte-Geneviève hill, granted by the Compagnie de la Nouvelle-France on 29 March 1649, and 16 acres on the St. Charles River, made over by LOUIS D'AILLEBOUST on 10 Feb. 1651. Only the land on the Sainte-Geneviève hill was brought under cultivation—and 1668 Marsolet declared that the 71 acres were "now ploughed" and that on them he had "had built two buildings and a barn"; it seems, as is suggested by the farming lease made between Marsolet and Raymond Pajet *dit* Carcy in 1656, that this land was chiefly worked by farmers.

Shortly before 1660, and although he still acted as an interpreter if occasion arose, Nicolas Marsolet ceased to make excursions to Tadoussac in order to devote himself to his business at Quebec. It is here that he died on 15 May 1677. His widow, who had given him 10 children, married Denis Le Maistre on 8 May 1681. She was buried at Quebec on 21 Feb. 1688. As for Marsolet's children, some of them became connected by marriage with the best families in the colony.

In the person of the old interpreter there passed away, in 1677, one of the last witnesses of the earliest years of Quebec. They were heroic years, and Nicolas Marsolet had certainly lived them intensely. We take pleasure in recognizing in him one of those men venturesome in spirit, courageous, rugged in endeavour, who even although they were not always above reproach contributed to the building of New France.

ANDRÉ VACHON

AJQ, Greffe de Guillaume Audouart, 10 févr. 1651, 10 juillet 1656; Greffe de Henry Bancheron, 16 avril 1647; Greffe de Pierre Duquet, 15 nov. 1672; Greffe de Jean Guitet, 6 oct. 1637; Greffe de Martial Piraube, 20 nov. 1640; Greffe de Gilles Rageot, 23 oct. 1671. Recensement de 1666. Champlain, *Œuvres* (Laverdière), 1062, 1228, 1249–50, 1253–63. *JR* (Thwaites), IV, 206–14; V, 112; XXIV, 132; LXXI, 84. *JJ* (Laverdière et Casgrain), 30–1, 86, 94, 147–48, 154–55. *Jug. et délib.*, I, *passim*. *Ord. comm.* (P.-G. Roy), I, 3–4. *Papier terrier de la cie des I.O.* (P.-G. Roy), 37–39. P.-G. Roy, *Inv. concessions*, I, 243, 245–46; II, 7, 187–88; III, 76–77. Sagard, *Histoire du Canada* (Tross), II, 333–34, 522–23. "La famille Marsolet de Saint-Aignan," *BRH*, XL (1934), 385–409.

MARTIGNON. *See* APRENDESTIGUY

MARTIN, ABRAHAM (*dit* "l'Écossais" or "Maître Abraham"), pilot; b. 1589 in France; d. 8 Sept. 1664 at Quebec.

Martin arrived in New France with his wife, Marguerite Langlois, her sister Françoise and brother-in-law Pierre Desportes (the parents of Hélène DESPORTES) about 1620. Martin may have been of Scottish descent or he might have used the sobriquet if he had been enrolled in military service or had been a member of an illegal organization: such names were used to avoid detection by officials looking for deserted soldiers or in case the records of an illegal organization were seized. It is also possible that he acquired the name because he had made several voyages to Scotland as a young man. There is some question as to whether Martin was really an official pilot or not, although he was referred to as "king's pilot" in his own day. However, he did fish well down into the Gulf of St. Lawrence.

It is presumed that the Plains (or Heights) of Abraham are named after Martin. It is picturesquely said that the "Côte d'Abraham" was the path that Martin used to descend to the St. Charles River to water his animals. His property amounted to 32 acres in all, 12 received from the Compagnie de la Nouvelle-France in 1635 and 20 as a gift from Sieur Adrien DU CHESNE, ship's surgeon to PIERRE LEGARDEUR de Repentigny in 1645. This land was sold by the Martin family to the Ursulines in 1667. It is possible that this is the same Martin who was employed by JEAN DE BIENCOURT and DU GUA de Monts as navigator on the coast of Acadia, although he would have been very young at that time. When DAVID KIRKE captured Quebec in 1629 and left his brother LEWIS as governor until 1632, Martin and his family stayed on. In his later years Martin fell in the estimation of his fellow citizens when he was accused of improper conduct with regard to a young girl in Quebec. He was imprisoned for this on 15 Feb. 1649.

As far as can be found from the records, Abraham Martin and Marie Langlois had nine or ten children. Anne Martin, born in France and married 17 Nov. 1635 to Jean Côté, was probably not Abraham's daughter. Eustache, baptized 24 Oct. 1621 and the godson of EUSTACHE BOULLÉ, was the first child born in Canada. Marguerite, born 4 Jan. 1624 and married 22 May 1638 to Étienne Racine had many descendants, including the two bishops Racine*. Hélène, born 21 June 1627, was a god-daughter of Samuel de CHAMPLAIN. She married first Claude Étienne in 1640 and on 3 Sept. 1647 Médard CHOUART Des Groseilliers. Charles-Amador*, born 7 March 1648, the godson of CHARLES DE SAINT-ÉTIENNE de La Tour, was the second Canadian-born priest. It is possible that Brother Dominique Scot, spoken of in the Jesuit Relations as having gone to the Huron country as a young man, was also a son. It is also possible that a young man who is mentioned as having been in the Huron country at the same time (1634–35) was Eustache Martin.

HENRY B. M. BEST

Collection de manuscrits relatifs à la Nouv.-France, I, 61. *JR* (Thwaites). P.-B. Casgrain, "La fontaine d'Abraham Martin et le site de son habitation," *RSCT*, 2d ser., IX (1903), sect.I, 145–55. Dionne, *Champlain*. A. G. Doughty and G. W. Parmelee, *The siege of Quebec and the battle of the Plains of Abraham* (6v., Quebec, 1901), II, 289–309. John Knox, *An historical journal of the campaigns in North America for the years 1757, 1758, 1759 and 1760*, ed. A. G.

Martin

Doughty (3v., Champlain Soc., VIII–X, 1914–16), II, 97n. J. M. LeMoine, *The Scot in New France, an ethnological study* (Montreal, 1881). É.-Z. Massicotte, "Au sujet d'Anne Martin," *BRH*, XXVIII (1922), 116–17. Léon Roy, "Anne Martin, épouse de Jean Côté," *BRH*, XLIX (1943), 203–4. P.-G. Roy, *La ville de Québec*, I, II. Tanguay, *Dictionnaire*.

MARTIN, CHRISTOPHER, native of Cockington, Devon, master mariner and fisherman planter in Newfoundland for many seasons; fl.1661–78.

Martin, in his deposition before the Committee of Trade and Plantations 28 Jan. 1677/78 states that for 17 years he had commanded his own ship, mostly in fishing voyages to Newfoundland, and that he had traded with the inhabitants of St. John's, where, he said, "I have been often Admirall of the Fishing Shipps." During this period he distinguished himself by his heroic resistance to piratical marauders and enemy invaders. In June 1665, when the Dutch under de Ruyter attacked St. John's, Martin made a gallant attempt at defence, as he also did in 1667, when the Dutch again invaded and pillaged St. John's. In 1673, he beat off four pirate ships under the command of the notorious Cornelis Evertsen and successfully repelled his attack on St. John's by building, at his own expense, a crude battery near Chain Rock in the Narrows, on which he mounted 6 guns from his own ship, manned by 23 men.

Martin appears to have been a wise and sensible man. Unlike many of his contemporaries, the fishing admirals and "Western Adventurers" who opposed settlement and stable government in the island, and contrary to the home government which disallowed it, he strongly advocated immigration, a ruling governor, and organized government. Martin took the side of the planters against the fishing merchants because he believed that if the planters left, fewer fish would be taken, since the planters supplied timber and also kept the fishing stages and other construction in repair. He also thought that the planters' removal would enable the French to advance from Placentia Bay and to take control of the island. Martin's views did find support among some of his fellow fishermen—two of whom, Thomas Martin and Nehemiah Trout by name, testified in 1677 when Martin did—and from many of the convoy commodores. The government which in 1676 had ordered the planters to leave did not enforce the decree.

E. HUNT

PRO, C.O. 1/42, 20, 21, 22. L. E. F. English, *Historic Newfoundland* (St. John's, 1955). Prowse, *History of Nfld.*

MASON, JOHN, sailor, explorer, cartographer, colonizer, second governor of the first English colony in Newfoundland and founder of New Hampshire; b. 1586 at King's Lynn, Norfolk, son of John and Isabella Mason; d. in London, 1635.

Nothing is known of Mason's life before 1606 when he married Anne, daughter of Edward Greene of London, although there is a possibility that he may have been the John Mason of Hampshire who matriculated from Magdalen College, Oxford, in 1602 (Dean, pp. 34–35). His career becomes more certain from 1610 when he was commissioned by James I as commander of four vessels to assist Bishop Andrew Knox in reclaiming the Hebrides. This suggests that Mason, although not yet 30, had both considerable naval experience and private means, for he bore the expedition's costs of over £2,000 himself. In recompense, the Scottish Privy Council awarded him the assize of herring in the northern seas but the Dutch fishermen refused to pay, while the Scottish fishermen had him imprisoned. When next heard of, in 1615, Mason was regarded as a pirate by the Scots and imprisoned in Edinburgh. There is no evidence of a trial but in August he surrendered his ship to the deputy treasurer for Scotland.

About this time Mason became governor of the colony at Cuper's Cove (now Cupids), Newfoundland, in succession to JOHN GUY. There is no satisfactory explanation of his appointment; it has been thought that it was a reward for his service to the king in the Hebrides, but it seems unlikely that anyone but the council of the Newfoundland company would make the appointment. No doubt Mason's naval experience did influence the company, which was perturbed by the frequent attacks made on the island by pirates. By June 1616 Mason was at Cuper's Cove and had already begun those explorations which enabled him to produce the first known English map of Newfoundland, based on personal survey. In August 1617 he wrote to Sir John Scot that "as huswives have many lett[s] to good housewifry, Frontlett[s], bracelett[s] partlet[s] etc.;—so have Inlett[s], outlett[s], bayes Coves &c through their discovery, ben so many obstacles and hinderanc[s] to my duty" (National Library of Scotland, Advocates MS 17. 1. 19, ff.221, 222v) and so the map did not appear until 1625 when William VAUGHAN's *Cambrensium Caroleia* was printed; it was also included in Vaughan's *The golden fleece* (1626). Mason appears to have lived continuously in the colony until October 1619, when he left for England to persuade the company to have the scope of their patent enlarged so as to give the colonists greater authority over the visiting fishermen. During Mason's governorship the conflict between settlers and fishermen, that is, between London and West Country trading interests, had flared up and a series of charges and counter-charges had been presented to the Privy Council. His fellow-colonists did not know whether Mason would return, since his wife, who had probably been with her husband during most, if not all, of his residence there, had left in September.

While in England, Mason probably supervised the publishing of his *A briefe discourse of the New-found-land* which appeared in 1620. This rare and attractive little work described the geography and climate of Newfoundland, its flora, fauna, and natural resources realistically, for it was Mason's intention to correct previous exaggerations. His motive seems to have been to interest his Scottish acquaintances in the plantation of the island and much space was devoted to proving how profitable and relatively easy settlement would be. He was apparently successful for, in a petition which the Newfoundland company presented to the Privy Council in March 1620, asking that Mason be appointed king's lieutenant in the island to suppress piracy, "the Scottish vndertakers of the plantations" are mentioned; Sir William ALEXANDER, Earl of Stirling, promoter of the settlement of Nova Scotia, certainly held land in the south of the island.

In May Mason received a commission from the lord admiral to command a vessel against the pirates and he probably did return to Newfoundland that year for the last time. About 1621, for a reason now unknown, Mason relinquished his connection with Newfoundland in favour of New England. Unfortunately there is very little documentary evidence on which to base an assessment of Mason's career in Newfoundland. It does appear, however, that the colony was still reasonably successful: in 1620 the Privy Council had given the company permission to transport iron ore to Newfoundland for smelting there. This would suggest, as do letters written by a colonist, Thomas ROWLEY, that there were still a considerable number of settlers. It was after Mason's departure that effort seemed to flag.

In his New England ventures Mason acted in co-operation with Sir Ferdinando Gorges who was a commissioner for the regulation of the Newfoundland fisheries. In 1622 Mason received two grants of land in New England; one between the "Naumkeck" and "Merimack" rivers; the other, held jointly with Gorges. was the future province of Maine. He had not entirely abandoned his interest in Newfoundland for, in 1623, his agent there was trying to obtain certain fish due to him. The outbreak of war with Spain in 1624 and with France two years later distracted Mason from colonial affairs. In 1625 he was made commissary general, responsible for victualling the Cadiz expedition and, in 1626, became treasurer and paymaster of the English forces. Peace was made in 1629 and that year Mason was granted the area to be known as New Hampshire. Furthermore, in association with Gorges and others, he established the Laconia company to develop land on Lake Champlain. In 1630 a successful colony was set up on his land on the Pascataway (Piscataqua). He became a member of the Council of New England in 1632 and, later that year, vice-president. He received further grants of land in 1635 and, when the council surrendered its patent, Mason was created vice-admiral of New England.

Meanwhile, in England, he had organized a scheme to encourage the fisheries in home waters at the expense of the Dutch. In 1633 the king granted a charter for "An association for the three kingdoms for a general fishery"; Mason was treasurer. The following year he was made captain of Southsea castle and inspector of all forts and castles on the south coast. Mason was making preparations to visit New Hampshire when he died in December 1635, bequeathing his vast estates in New England to his wife and then to his four grandchildren. So ended an extraordinarily active career to which his achievements in New England were a fitting memorial, even if those in Newfoundland were transitory.

GILLIAN T. CELL

Most of the letters, papers, and grants in the PRO and elsewhere relating to Mason have been printed in *Capt. John Mason, the founder of New Hampshire, including his tract on Newfoundland*, ed. J. W. Dean (Prince Soc., XVII, Boston, 1887). Other manuscript sources: Bodleian Library, Malone MSS, 2, ff.1v–13v, 130–38v. National Library of Scotland, Advocates MS 17. 1. 19, ff.221, 222v. Nottingham University, Middleton MSS, Mi X 1/1–66. *See also*: PRO, *Register of the P.C. of Scotland, 1610–13, 1613–16*. Sir W. Alexander, *An encouragement to colonies* (London, 1624). PRO, *CSP, Col., 1574–1660*. *DNB*. Insh, *Scottish colonial schemes*. J. Mason, *A briefe discourse of the New-found-land* (Edinburgh, 1620). R. A. Preston, *Gorges of Plymouth Fort* (Toronto, 1953). Prowse, *History of Nfld*. Sir W. Vaughan, *Cambrensium Caroleia* (London, 1625; another issue, 1630); *The golden fleece* (London, 1626).

MASSÉ, ÉNEMOND, Jesuit priest and missionary; b. 3 Aug. 1575 at Lyon, eldest son of François Massé, independent baker, and of Philippe Bica; entered the Company of Jesus at the noviciate of Avignon, on 22 Aug. 1595; d. 12

May 1646 at Sillery. He had been baptized with the name of Nesmes, which he changed to Énemond when he became a religious.

After his noviciate he taught at the Collège of Tournon (1597–99), and was also assistant to the bursar; at the same time he began his theological studies, which he completed at the Collège of Dole in 1602. After his ordination to the priesthood, we find him again at Tournon, then at the Collège in Lyon, as minister or bursar, a function which he was to perform during a great part of his life. In 1609 he left the province of Lyon to become the associate of Father Pierre Coton, the confessor to Henri IV, at the court. Rochemonteix wrongly identifies him with Father Imbert de Masso, his predecessor in this office.

In September 1610 Father Massé was selected to accompany Father BIARD to New France, where he arrived on 22 May 1611. From that time on he displayed a practical common sense which was to make him indispensable wherever he went, and to earn him the surname of Father Useful (*Père Utile*). In the summer of 1612 Massé ventured on a hunting trip with a Micmac family, and very nearly lost his life as a result. He was driven out of Acadia by ARGALL, and was back in France in October 1613. He spent a year at the Collège de Clermont in Paris, and was then sent as minister to La Flèche, where he stayed until 1625. He subjected himself to harsh mortifications in order to be deemed worthy of returning to New France, and he was in fact among the first group of Jesuits who landed at Quebec in 1625. He made his home with the Recollets, and Father CHARLES LALEMANT entrusted him with the work of completing Notre-Dame-des-Anges, in which the missionaries began to live in 1626. After he and his companions had been reduced to starvation, he was again expelled by the English under DAVID KIRKE in 1629.

Following a second stay at La Flèche, Father Massé sailed again for Canada in 1633. He lived at Notre-Dame-des-Anges until 1642, gladly undertaking all the most menial daily tasks. From 1641 on, as age and fatigue began to weigh more heavily, he concerned himself more with giving his associates the benefit of his counsel and experience. In 1643, however, he was still to be found taking care of the Indians at Sillery, where he taught the Montagnais language to Father DRUILLETTES. By the end of 1645 the venerable pioneer of the Canadian mission was reduced to inactivity. His life came to a peaceful close at Sillery, when he was 70 years old. His memory is recalled today by a monument erected over his grave in 1870, on the site of the old chapel which was still unfinished at the time of his death.

Father Massé has left little written material; he obviously wielded a tool more readily than a pen. We know of three short letters of his. Father JÉRÔME LALEMANT quotes a portion of his spiritual notes, and we have found the copy, in his handwriting, of a letter of Father Biard's.

LUCIEN CAMPEAU

Champlain, *Works* (Biggar). *Factum* (1614). *JR* (Thwaites). Lescarbot, *History* (Grant), III. Campbell, *Pioneer priests*, II, 49–61. Charlevoix, *Histoire*, I, 121–40, 159, 178, 367. Huguet, *Poutrincourt*. *Jésuites de la N.-F.* (Roustang). Léon Pouliot, *Premiers ouvriers de la Nouvelle-France: les pères Énemond Massé et Anne de Nouë, missionaires jésuites* (Montréal, 1940). Rochemonteix, *Les Jésuites et la Nouvelle-France au XVIIe siècle*, I, 23–72, 140, 152, 158, 166, 174, 176, 189, 276–79.

MAUGUE, CLAUDE, notary, clerk of court, deputy to the attorney-general; b. c. 1646 in the parish of Saint-Amand, diocese of Clermont-Ferrand (Auvergne), son of Antoine Maugue, merchant, and of Françoise Rigaud; d. 1696 at Montreal.

The first mention of Maugue in Canada is in August 1673, when he appeared as a schoolmaster at Beauport. On the following 9 December Governor BUADE de Frontenac appointed him notary of the seigneury of Lauson. In this capacity Maugue drew up 19 acts, particularly grants of land.

He was summoned to Montreal in 1677, and succeeded BÉNIGNE BASSET in the office of court clerk of the jurisdiction; he held this post for seven years, while continuing to function as a notary. In 19 years he signed some 3,000 acts, which have come down to us in a perfect state of preservation.

While serving as deputy to the attorney-general of Montreal in 1692, Maugue died in his fifties after a brief illness, and was buried 9 Nov. 1696.

In October 1679, at Montreal, he had married Louise Jousset, who was married again in 1698, to Jean de La Sague.

JEAN-JACQUES LEFEBVRE

AJM, Greffe de Claude Maugue, 1677–96. AJQ, Greffe de Claude Maugue, 16 mai 1674–20 juin 1679. É.-Z. Massicotte, "Les tribunaux et les officiers de justice sous le régime français," *BRH*, XXXVII (1931), 127. J.-É. Roy, *Histoire du notariat*, I. Tanguay, *Dictionnaire*, I, 422.

MAUPASSANT, EUSTACHE, Recollet priest, provincial commissioner of his order in New France; b. c. 1627 in France; d. 29 June 1692 at Châlons.

He joined the Recollets of the province of Saint-Denis in 1647. After being superior of the convents of Vitry (1669), Sézanne (1670), and Rouen (1672), he was named, in 1673, to succeed Father Gabriel de LA RIBOURDE in the offices of provincial commissioner of the Recollets in Canada and guardian of the convent of Notre-Dame-des-Anges at Quebec. He went to Canada during the summer of that year, and remained there until 1676.

Being a gifted preacher, he was invited upon his arrival at Quebec to deliver the eulogy of St. Francis Borgia on the occasion of the dedication of the Jesuit church in Quebec in August 1673. He was chaplain of the Château Saint-Louis and was also the confessor of Louis de BUADE de Frontenac. These duties, together with the jealousy of the ecclesiastical authorities towards the Recollets, contributed in no small measure to paralysing his apostolic efforts. He complained bitterly of this to Colbert in a letter dated 12 Nov. 1674. Frontenac himself echoed his complaint: "when you [the Recollets] were sent to this country," he wrote, "it was not done to have you lead the contemplative life here, but to have your help in labouring in the Lord's vineyard, in which some would not desire to give you a large share." Father Eustache's conduct was even termed scandalous by those who thought he deferred too much to civil authority.

After a visit to the Percé mission in 1676, he went back to France. He was a preacher at Châlons (1677); he was superior at Montargis (1680), at Verdun (1681), and at Metz (1683) where he delivered the funeral oration of Queen Marie-Thérèse; he was provincial definitor in 1683, visitor-general of the custody of Saint-Nicolas in Lorraine in 1686, and guardian at Paris in 1687. He passed away at Châlons 29 June 1692.

FRÉDÉRIC GINGRAS

BN, MS Fr. 13875 (Nécrologe des Frères-Mineurs Récollets de la province Saint-Denys en France); MS, Mélanges Colbert, 171, f.54 (Lettre de Frontenac au provincial des Récollets, 10 nov. 1674); f.57 (Lettre du P. Eustache Maupassant à Colbert, 12 nov. 1674). Hyacinthe Lefebvre, *Histoire chronologique de la province des Récollets de Paris, sous le titre de Saint-Denys, en France, depuis 1612, qu'elle fut érigée jusqu'en l'année 1676* (Paris, 1677).

MAUR, JEAN JUCHEREAU DE. See JUCHEREAU

MAY, HENRY, English mariner and early visitor to Cape Breton Island; fl. 1591–94.

May was purser of the *Edward Bonaventure*, commanded by Sir James Lancaster, on the first English voyage to the East Indies, under George Raymond, general of the expedition, in the *Penelope*, and in company with Samuel Foxcroft in the *Merchant Royal*. The ships left Plymouth 10 April 1591.

The voyage was fraught with illness, mutiny, and disaster, but the *Edward Bonaventure*, after rounding the Cape of Good Hope 31 March 1593, reached the small West Indian island of Mona in June, where Lancaster was aided by a French vessel. May, who spoke French, set out for Europe from Laguna in Hispaniola, 30 November, in a French ship, the captain of which was named La Barbotière, and which was wrecked, 17 December, on the Bermudas. May helped the crew to build an 18-ton bark in which they sailed from the Bermudas, 11 May 1594, reaching land near Cape Breton on 20 May. Here, in the mouth of a river, they took in wood, water, and ballast, and encountered Indians, "clothed all in furs, with the furred side unto their skins," who "brought with them furres of sundry sorts to sell, besides great store of wild ducks." The French traded small beads for ducks and May wrote, "This should seeme to be a very good countrey."

On the Grand Banks they met various ships, not one of which would "take in a man of us," until a Falmouth bark agreed to accept the whole crew on board. "With her," says May, "we tooke a French ship wherein I left capitan de la Barbotier, my deere friend, and all his company." May reached Falmouth in August 1594.

THOMAS DUNBABIN

Hakluyt, *Principal navigations* (1903–5), X, 194–203 (especially 202–3). Purchas, *Pilgrimes* (1905–7), II, 288, states that May was purser of the *Edward Bonaventure*.

MAYNWARINGE. See MAINWARING

MAZÉ, LOUIS PERONNE DE. See PERONNE

MELANSON, CHARLES, ploughman, settler; b. 1643; d. some time before 1700.

Historians agree neither on his ethnic origin nor on the date of his arrival in Canada. Undeniably, he "came from Scotland"; but, as a notarial contract designated him "Sieur de La Ramée," and as his brother Pierre was nicknamed "La Verdure," Placide Gaudet concluded that the family might have been of French origin, and that, because it was Huguenot, it might have emigrated to Scotland, whence it went to Acadia. Some writers claim that the Melansons belonged to the settlement founded by Sir WILLIAM ALEXANDER, the younger. According to Placide Gaudet, the family arrived in the colony in 1657 with

Membertou

Governor TEMPLE; it settled at Port-Royal; later it is thought to have emigrated to Boston, leaving in Acadia Pierre and Charles, the only members of the family whose names have been preserved in history.

The elder, Pierre, *dit* La Verdure, a tailor, husband of Marie-Marguerite Mius d'Entremont, was one of the founders of Grand-Pré. Charles, a "*laboureur*" (ploughman), according to the 1671 census, worked the paternal estate and became prosperous; in 1664, after renouncing Protestantism, he married Marie Dugas, by whom he had several children. Their descendants have been numerous.

CLÉMENT CORMIER

Recensements de 1671, 1686. Placide Gaudet, notes, correspondence, genealogical studies in the PAC and Université de Moncton; study published in *Weymouth Free Press*, 6 Jan. 1899. Bona Arsenault, *L'Acadie des ancêtres: avec la généalogie des premières familles acadiennes* (Québec, 1955), 39–41, 143–44. James Hannay, "Our first families," *New Brunswick Magazine*, I (1898), 129, 177–86; II (1899), 92–96; III (1899), 17. Rameau de Saint-Père, *Une colonie féodale*. A. W. Savary, "The Acadian Melansons," *New Brunswick Magazine*, I (1898), 360; II (1899), 222. The "Laverdure" referred to in PAC *Report*, 1912, App. E, 56, 58, and App. F, 69, may be Pierre.

MEMBERTOU, HENRI, chief of a Micmac band, ally of the French; first native baptized in New France; d. 18 Sept. 1611 at Port-Royal (Annapolis Royal, N.S.).

According to Lescarbot, Membertou was already more than 100 years old in 1607. This is probably an exaggeration. The old man stated that at a period when he was himself already married and the father of a family he had known Jacques CARTIER. His eldest son Louis is supposed to have been 60 in 1610; and that also appears exaggerated, since all Louis's children were then very young. The exploits attributed to Henri Membertou during a fighting expedition in 1607 are ill suited to a centenarian. In the same way the pompous titles conferred on Membertou by the French should not be taken literally. He commanded a small following of Micmacs who hunted and fished in the basin of the river and harbour of Port-Royal, and on the shores of St. Mary's Bay in Nova Scotia. It would be unwise to give to this band a precise figure; that of 100 souls seems a generous estimate. Messire FLÉCHÉ, who baptized all the Indians passing through Port-Royal, scarcely reached the number of 140 in a year.

The chief of a band, or *sagamo*, assumed responsibility for directing and protecting a group of individuals and families moving about in a given area. No doubt there was nothing very stable about the composition of a band, since ambitious men frequently set themselves up as sagamos. For payment the chief received presents and a proportion of the yield from hunting and fishing. The young people were under his authority; the married men, partly emancipated, paid him tribute. The sagamo was hardly any richer in consequence, since his income was used up in supporting his attendants and meeting the cost of alliances with his neighbours. Honour, and little else, was his chief reward.

With his position as sagamo Membertou combined that of *autmoin* or *shaman* (medicine-man). In return for gifts he made prophecies on the outcome of hunting or war. When called to attend the sick, he would blow upon them to drive out the devil, dance, go into wild contortions, conduct still stranger ceremonies, and make pronouncements on the recovery or approaching death of the patient. The prestige of the autmoin reinforced that of the sagamo and gave him a special authority in the councils. Membertou, inhabiting a remote region of no interest to French fishermen, suddenly found himself in the limelight when DU GUA de Monts came to settle at Port-Royal in 1605. To be the host of the Europeans, within immediate range of their merchandise, was an advantage which all the sagamos envied highly. The jealousy of his fellow-sagamos earned for the old chief the "reputation of being the most evil and treacherous among all those of his nation," according to CHAMPLAIN. But this perhaps not impartial judgement is offset by the profound esteem of the French. Father Biard wrote: "This was the greatest, most renowned and most formidable savage within the memory of man; of splendid physique, taller and larger-limbed than is usual among them; bearded like a Frenchman, although scarcely any of the others have hair upon the chin; grave and reserved; feeling a proper sense of dignity for his position as commander." He showed an unswerving loyalty towards his European allies. The Port-Royal habitation, when it was left for three years entirely in his hands, did not suffer in any way. His touching friendship with JEAN DE BIENCOURT de Poutrincourt was clearly evident in his last address, but also in all his conduct towards this gentleman.

Only one example of his military bravery is known. In 1607 he led an expedition to the River Chouacouët (Saco) to avenge the murder of PANOUNIAS, who was both his follower and his son-in-law. After the usual palavers with his allies in a stockaded hut, erected near Port-Royal, the sagamo set out at the head of 400 men, according to Lescarbot, or more likely 30 or 40, as Champlain said. His passage through the Abenaki country, where he had some allies, occasioned a number of skirmishes; Membertou himself approached his enemies under the pretence of friendship and trade, and then treacherously fell upon them. He reported that he had killed 20 men and wounded 10 or 12 others, but he brought back no prisoners; none of his men lost his life. The story of this episode, written by Lescarbot, appears to belong as much to the realm of fancy as to that of history.

The fact that this Micmac sagamo was the first Indian to receive solemn baptism in New France remains his principal claim to distinction. Others before him had been baptized in France, only to return to their pagan customs as soon as they got back. In 1610 Poutrincourt, who was destitute but anxious to get settled in Acadia in order to satisfy Henri IV's impatience, conceived the plan of raising money in the form of gifts for the Indian neophytes. He landed at Port-Royal with a priest, Jessé Fléché, around 17 June, and tried to seek out the Micmacs, who were scattered for the fishing. He located only the Membertou family of 21 persons, who were baptized ceremoniously on 24 June. The sagamo received the name of the king, Henri; his wife was called Marie, like the queen; his eldest son was given the name of the dauphin, Louis, who by this date had already become Louis XIII. These baptisms, for which there had been no preparation, changed nothing in the behaviour of the neophytes, who preserved their pagan habits, to the scandal of the Jesuits.

Henri Membertou was as ignorant as the others; he did however show exceptional aptitude. He completely renounced the profession of shaman, and took on Christian responsibilities to the extent that he could understand them. When his son Actodin fell ill and all were preparing to subject him to the tribe's traditional rites, Membertou listened without impatience to Father Biard's reprimands and followed his instructions. He urged the missionaries to learn the Micmac tongue, for he earnestly desired to be catechized and thereafter admitted into their apostolate. His steadfast refusal to practise polygamy, a custom of the sagamos, was greatly admired. At the end of August 1611 Membertou, a victim of dysentery, came to Port-Royal, where Father MASSÉ received him into his hut during Father Biard's absence. The latter, when he returned on 8 September, shared with his companion the nursing of the ailing man. But when the old man's wife and daughter arrived, he had to be removed from the habitation, because CHARLES DE BIENCOURT refused to admit him into another part of it. On 16 September Membertou made his farewell speech, after having confessed his sins. He announced his wish to be buried with his pagan ancestors. Father Biard opposed this, whereas Biencourt, acting as an interpreter, agreed with the sick man. The Jesuit withdrew in order to make his disapproval clear, but returned to give extreme unction to the dying Indian. Two days later Membertou changed his mind and asked to be buried with the French. He died Sunday, 18 September, after vespers, and on the Monday he was given a solemn funeral.

LUCIEN CAMPEAU

All the sources concerning Membertou may be found in the following: Champlain, *Works* (Biggar); *Œuvres* (Laverdière), 234 *et passim*. *Factum* (1614), 15–17. *JR* (Thwaites), I–IV, *passim*. Lescarbot, *History* (Grant).

MEMBRÉ, ZÉNOBE, Recollet, missionary in New France and companion of Robert CAVELIER de La Salle on his expeditions in Louisiana; b. 1645 at Bapaume; d. 15 Jan. 1689.

He joined the Recollets of the province of Saint-Antoine in Artois around 1668. In June 1675 he took ship at La Rochelle for New France, with four of his fellow-religious. As soon as he reached Quebec, he began his priestly activities; this is confirmed by the parish registers of Sainte-Anne de Beaupré in April 1676 and by those of Trois-Rivières under the date of 17 Jan. 1678.

In October of the same year he was chosen to be one of the chaplains on La Salle's first expedition, and he went to Fort Cataracoui (Kingston, Ont.), where he was joyfully welcomed by Fathers Gabriel de LA RIBOURDE and Luc Buisset on 2 November. They left this post during July 1679, and arrived at Fort Crèvecœur on 11 March 1680. Father Membré stayed some months among the Illinois, whom he followed in their wanderings and whose language he learned.

On 18 September he started on the return journey with the expedition. The following day he lost his companion, Father Gabriel de La Ribourde, who was assassinated by the Kickapoos, and the shipwreck of his "wretched bark canoe" forced him "to complete the journey by land, walking barefoot in the snow and over the ice, with no other food but acorns."

The failure of this first expedition did not stop him from taking part in that of 1681–82 and reaching the Mississippi, which they went down as far as the mouth. On 6 April 1682 La Salle solemnly took possession of the whole of "Louisianne" in the French king's name, and planted a cross which was blessed by Father Membré. Proud of his success, La Salle requested the

Ménard

Recollet to go to France in order to give the king the first news of the discovery. Father Membré left Fort Miami on 8 October, reached Quebec on 15 November, the day before the ships were leaving, and embarked on the vessel of the governor, BUADE de Frontenac in order to make the crossing.

After staying nearly two years in France, during which time he held the office of superior of the convent at Bapaume, he left his country once more on 24 July 1684, with La Salle, and accompanied him on his third expedition. After numerous vicissitudes, the explorers reached the Gulf of Mexico and went up as far as Fort Saint-Louis. It was here that Cavelier de La Salle met his death, and that Father Membré was slaughtered on 15 Jan. 1689. Thus perished a man who was the faithful friend and the steadfast associate of La Salle, and whom historians have too readily left in obscurity.

Father Zénobe Membré has left three important documents concerning all these voyages. The first is a letter dated 3 June 1682 from the Mississippi River; a copy made at the time is in the Bibliothèque nationale in Paris, and constitutes the first account made by an eye-witness of the 1682 expedition. The second is a detailed relation of Membré's voyage in 1682 which the latter, on his way through Quebec, delivered to his superior. Finally, Father Habig has established by a critical study that Father Membré was indeed the author of the document known under the following title: "Relation de la découverte de l'embouchure de la rivière Mississippi dans le golfe de Mexique, faite par le Sieur De La Salle, l'année passée 1682."

FRÉDÉRIC GINGRAS

BN, MS, Clairambault 1016, ff.163–65. The official report of La Salle's 1682 expedition, "Relation de la découverte de l'embouchure de la rivière Mississippi dans le golfe de Mexique, faite par le Sieur De La Salle, l'année passée 1682," by Membré, was first published in Raymond Thomassy, *Géologie pratique de la Louisiane* (Nouvelle-Orléans et Paris, 1860), 9–16; App. A, 197–98. Le Clercq, *First establishment of the faith* (Shea), I, 15, 20, 28–31, 109, 112; II, 88 *et passim*; *Premier établissement de la foy*, II, 161–95, Father Membré's Relation of his voyage which he delivered to his superior on his way through Quebec in 1682. Jean Delanglez, *Some La Salle Journeys* (Chicago, 1938), 67f., n.10. Marion Habig, "The Franciscan Père Marquette: a critical biography of Father Zénobe Membré . . ." (Franciscan studies, XIII, New York, 1934). *Découvertes et établissements des Français* (Margry), I, 545–70; II, 206. J. G. Shea, *Discovery and exploration of the Mississippi valley with the original narratives of Marquette, Allouez, Membré, Hennepin and Anastase Douay* (New York, 1852).

MÉNARD, RENÉ, priest, Jesuit, missionary; b. 2 Mar. 1605 in Paris; disappeared into the forest in the Wisconsin district in August 1661.

Father Ménard joined the Jesuits 7 Sept. 1624 in Paris and studied at La Flèche, Bourges, and Orléans. After his solemn profession in the order, he was sent to Canada, where he arrived 8 July 1640. In 1641 he went off to Sainte-Marie-des-Hurons and later was a missionary to the Nipissings and Algonkins. From 1651 to 1656 he was the superior of the residence at Trois-Rivières. Then he took part in the move to the Onondaga country, which was a consequence of SIMON LE MOYNE's diplomatic mission, and went to spend two years among the Iroquois. In 1660 he accompanied an expedition of Ottawas who were returning to their home in the region of modern Michigan. The following year he started out from there to go to join some Hurons who were encamped near the mouths of the Black River, in the Wisconsin district, but he became lost in the woods. Several years later his breviary and his cassock were discovered in the possession of the Sioux, who had found them and placed them among their manitous on an altar upon which they offered up prayers to the Great Spirit. In confidential memoranda to Rome Father Ménard's colleagues praised highly his intelligence and judgement, adding that he had a special talent for winning the Indians' confidence.

J. MONET

ACSM, MS biography based on the catalogues of the Archivium Romanum Societatis Jesu in Rome, which corrects some of the data given in *JR* and Rochemonteix below. *JR* (Thwaites), XVIII, 256, 257; XLVI, 144. Perrot, "Memoir," in *Indian tribes* (Blair), I, 171f., M.136. *BRH*, XXXVI (1930), 23. H. C. Campbell, *Père René Ménard* (Parkman Club publications, XI, Milwaukee, 1897); *Pioneer priests*, I, 215. Rochemonteix, *Les Jésuites et la Nouvelle-France au XVIIe siècle*, I, 429.

MENOU D'AULNAY, CHARLES DE, sea captain, lieutenant to RAZILLY, and governor of Acadia; b. *c.* 1604 at the Château de Charnisay (France), son of René de Menou, councillor of state under Louis XIII, and of Nicole de Jousserand; d. 1650 at Port-Royal (Annapolis Royal, N.S.). D'Aulnay belonged to a very ancient noble family that originated in Perche. His second name came from the seigneury of Aulnay, near Loudun, bequeathed to him by his mother.

Charles de Menou served first in the navy, as his cousin Isaac de Razilly's lieutenant. When Razilly was appointed governor, Menou went to Acadia (4 July 1632), where he became one of his most active collaborators. Almost every year he went to France with pelts, fish, or masts, and brought back supplies. He borrowed funds, hired ships, and recruited men. Since Razilly's interests, at least at the beginning, were linked with those of the Compagnie de la Nouvelle-France, d'Aulnay acted both in Razilly's name and in that of the company. But this system gave rise to difficulties and in 1633 d'Aulnay found it very hard to get the company to pay his seamen. A private company, Razilly-Condonnier, was organized in 1634, and from then on d'Aulnay acted only for it.

In 1635 his commander, Razilly, entrusted him with a dangerous mission. The post at Pentagouet, founded by CLAUDE DE SAINT-ÉTIENNE de La Tour in about 1625, had been captured by the English, who still held it. Razilly instructed d'Aulnay to retake it with the help of CHARLES DE SAINT-ÉTIENNE de La Tour. The latter had agreed to co-operate with Razilly, but refused to work under d'Aulnay, who none the less managed to retake the post and to defend it against an English counter-attack. But in the following year the Compagnie de la Nouvelle-France, where the La Tours could number some friends, granted the Vieux-Logis at Pentagouet to Claude de La Tour. This conflict was to give rise to a long and costly rivalry between the two competitors.

Isaac de Razilly's death in 1635 was a severe blow for Acadia. But the majority of his collaborators remained at their posts, and the colony was not prevented by his death from receiving substantial reinforcements at the beginning of 1636. Claude de Launay-Rasilly, the dead governor's brother, had been granted Port-Royal, La Hève, and the Île de Sable in his own name, and inherited his brother's shares in the Compagnie de Razilly-Condonnier. His family responsibilities and his post in the navy prevented him from coming personally to Acadia. According to NICOLAS DENYS he made an arrangement with his cousin Charles de Menou, whereby the latter became his lieutenant in Acadia, while he himself looked after the company's affairs in France.

This temporary measure worked for several years, without d'Aulnay's having the title of governor. The right to nominate to this office belonged to the Compagnie de la Nouvelle-France; for various reasons it did not consider nominating d'Aulnay, who nevertheless exercised absolute authority at La Hève and Port-Royal, in perfect accord with Claude de Rasilly. He very soon decided, no doubt in agreement with his chief, to set up the colony's principal post at Port-Royal. This site offered a double advantage: it had fertile lands, which La Hève lacked, and it was hoped to establish salt-pans there, in order to be able to gather near at hand the salt needed for the fisheries. Claude de Rasilly sent saltmakers, and the construction of dikes was begun. The majority of the settlers at La Hève gradually came and established themselves at Port-Royal, where agricultural development advanced at a good pace.

Meanwhile the old bipartite administration continued to exist in Acadia, under the authority of the Compagnie de la Nouvelle-France. D'Aulnay, as Rasilly's lieutenant, was in command at Port-Royal and La Hève, whereas La Tour commanded at Cap de Sable and the Saint John River. Each of them received one-half of the revenue from the trading concession and had the right of inspection in the other's territory. This system could not but lead to clashes of interests and personalities. D'Aulnay, already on bad terms with Nicolas Denys, apparently wanted to assume some measure of authority over La Tour and to insinuate himself into his affairs. Their disagreement was submitted to the court; Boutilier, on 10 Feb. 1638, sent d'Aulnay a letter setting out rules of conduct, signed by the king.

This letter made a most clumsy attempt to divide up the Acadian territory between the two lieutenants. It granted d'Aulnay the title of lieutenant-general in Acadia, confirmed his authority over Port-Royal and La Hève, and assigned to him the direction of Pentagouet. If his status had been only a subordinate one up to then, this letter, in the absence of an explicit commission, recognized his powers and was evidence of the court's confidence in him. The same year d'Aulnay married Jeanne MOTIN, daughter of Louis Motin, an interested party in the Compagnie de Razilly, and sister-in-law of his colleague Nicolas LE CREUX Du Breuil. This marriage was a clear indication of his intention to settle in the country.

At about the same time La Tour, despairing of seeing his rival leave, was inveigled into acts of aggression. He is said first to have incited the Indians against him, then in 1639 to have intercepted a pinnace sent to Pentagouet and to have held the nine men of the crew prisoner. In 1640 d'Aulnay, himself returning from Pentagouet with two small ships, came under cannon-fire from La Tour, and one of his vessels lost its mast. This rash aggression turned to La Tour's disadvantage: Pierre Jamin, the captain of his ship, was killed; La Tour himself, as well as his lieutenant Desjardins Du Val, and the whole crew were taken prisoner. On the intervention of the Capuchins, an agreement was made whereby La Tour recovered his liberty, while the matter was reported to France. These incidents marked the start of a minor war between the king's two lieutenants in

Menou d'Aulnay

Acadia. The struggle caused the loss of several lives, engendered a goodly number of useless proceedings and negotiations, consumed their energies and their money for five years, and left them both half ruined.

While Jamin's widow, backed by Desjardins, was obtaining the seizure at La Rochelle of the *Saint-François*, the Compagnie de Razilly's ship, d'Aulnay was having reports prepared, and through the intermediary of his father he submitted his complaints to the Conseil du Roi. The skirmish of 1640 helped considerably to strengthen his position. In the following spring the ships brought to La Tour an order to go to France and give an account of himself, and d'Aulnay received instructions to administer La Tour's forts. In accordance with these orders La Tour handed over the fort of Cap de Sable, which it was difficult for him to defend, but refused to leave the country and took refuge at the Saint John River settlement.

The same year the Dutch made a number of forays on the Acadian coasts, so that d'Aulnay had at the same time to defend himself against La Tour, to assist Pentagouet which was constantly threatened, and to assure the defence of Acadia. To face these dangers he had asked the company for 30 or 40 men as reinforcements, but he received only six. Claude de Rasilly, hampered by the Jamin lawsuit, had managed to liberate his ships and pelts through the intervention of the Compagnie de la Nouvelle-France. But these vexations had blocked the fur trade and caused losses. By way of encouragement the partners granted d'Aulnay, on 15 Feb. 1641, a free share in the company, but they could not do more. D'Aulnay went to France to seek help.

During this trip he was extraordinarily active, and with his father's support he succeeded in obtaining considerable advantages. He first tried to clarify his standing with the Compagnie de Razilly. The principal person concerned was still Claude de Launay-Rasilly. But the latter had already poured vast sums into Acadia without getting anything in return. Moreover, the open war that had just been declared between his lieutenant d'Aulnay and La Tour offered the prospect of serious difficulties. Neither he nor his partners were inclined to sink more funds in this ruinous undertaking, but thought rather of withdrawing. As d'Aulnay, on the other hand, seemed full of hope and ready to commit himself to the full, the partners arranged to give him a chance and to ease the way for him to take effective control of the company.

Launay-Rasilly, by a notarial contract dated 16 Jan. 1642, made over to d'Aulnay his four shares, worth more than 60,000 *livres*, and his rights over La Hève and Port-Royal, for the paltry sum of 14,000 *livres*, payable in seven years at the rate of 2,000 *livres* a year. In addition he gave him (19 February) 4,000 *livres*, charged against his expected inheritance from his brother's estate, so that d'Aulnay could purchase the Rivière Sainte-Croix concession. Furthermore, thanks to the help of Father Pascal de Troyes, d'Aulnay became the administrator of the share that Cardinal Richelieu had given to the Capuchins. Thus, from being a mere lieutenant, d'Aulnay rose to be master of the greater portion of Acadia. To meet his new obligations and to finance the colony, he concluded agreements the following May with a Huguenot merchant of La Rochelle, EMMANUEL LE BORGNE, who became at the same time the man responsible for fitting out his ships, his banker, and his business agent. That same year Le Borgne made him an advance of 18,000 *livres* so that d'Aulnay, with the aid of some relatives also, was able to charter three ships and purchase a fourth. He thus returned to Port-Royal with imposing forces. As soon as he arrived he despatched three gentlemen and four seamen to notify La Tour of the court's new orders. But La Tour, on an angry impulse, crumpled up the documents and imprisoned the messengers. D'Aulnay then resolved to cut off his supplies, in order to starve him into submission. D'Aulnay's ship, the *Vierge*, remained five months at the mouth of the Saint John River and managed to stop La Tour's supply ship, the *Saint-Clément*, and an English ship from putting in there. A landing was attempted but it failed.

La Tour did however succeed in rejoining the *Saint-Clément* and in getting to Boston, where he chartered four merchant ships, with which he returned to the Saint John. Faced by these superior forces, d'Aulnay prudently withdrew to Port-Royal. La Tour followed him there, but his English allies refused to attack the fort, and, with 30 volunteers, he had to content himself with attacking a mill defended by some 20 soldiers. He was able to set fire to it, kill three men, and take a long-boat loaded with pelts.

This second attack showed d'Aulnay how vulnerable his position was. If the English, with their superior strength, had wanted to attack the siege would have been difficult to withstand. D'Aulnay immediately started building a new fort. This attack did however furnish him with fresh arguments against La Tour. He had reports prepared by the provost André Certain, by the Capuchins, and by former supporters of La Tour, drafted two long statements himself, and went in person to France to request further

Menou d'Aulnay

help. He obtained a new decree from the council, on 6 March 1644. Le Borgne disbursed 50,000 *livres* for the thorough fitting-out of a ship, and hired out to him a 200-ton frigate, the *Grand Cardinal*, armed with 16 cannon. Meanwhile a man in his trust, the sieur Marie, probably a Capuchin in civilian clothes, went to Boston to protest against the help given to La Tour.

D'Aulnay's ships, one of which was commanded by Bernard MAROT, took up their watch again off the Saint John settlement. In the spring, learning that La Tour had left his fort to go to Boston and discuss plans, d'Aulnay decided to attempt a siege. He put some cannon ashore, brought his ships up in front of the fort, and submitted it to a bombardment that destroyed part of the parapet. After promising to allow his soldiers to pillage, he gave orders for an attack on Easter Monday 1645. The fort fell, despite a desperate resistance. It seems certain that a number of the 45 defenders perished on the spot and that the others were hanged, except for a few who were pardoned. Mme de La Tour, *née* Françoise-Marie JACQUELIN, was taken prisoner and died soon afterwards. D'Aulnay had lost eight men and paid compensation to their families.

The victor then had the La Tour fort restored and considerably strengthened, and set up a profitable trading-post there. According to Denys, he traded as many as 3,000 moose skins a year at this post. The king and the queen mother wrote to him on 27 and 28 Sept. 1645 to congratulate him and to promise him a supply ship. But they neglected to send it, and d'Aulnay, the following year, reminded them in vain of their promise; he never received any material aid from the court. The trade in pelts constituted his sole source of revenue. To help in the support of the colony, he adopted the expedient of felling trees, organized seal-fishing, and developed agriculture.

The question of a peace treaty with the New England states, which had been debated since 1643, remained in abeyance. An initial agreement with Boston, signed in 1644, was ratified in September 1645. But d'Aulnay claimed an indemnity of 8,000 *louis* for the losses caused by the English merchants who had supported La Tour. His three delegates were received most courteously in Boston, and after three days of discussion signed a treaty with the New England states. As symbolic reparation, d'Aulnay was offered a sedan-chair taken by a pirate from the viceroy of Mexico.

In February 1647, thanks to Séguier's patronage, d'Aulnay received very generous letters patent from the court, in recognition of his services and to compensate him for his huge expenses. After a laudatory reference to his services, the letters confirmed him in his powers as governor of the whole of Acadia, from the St. Lawrence to the sea and as far as Virginia, and he obtained the sole privilege of the trade in pelts, to the exclusion of all competitors.

But these same letters, obtained without the recommendation of the Compagnie de la Nouvelle-France, aroused the latter's protests, the more because d'Aulnay had already anticipated their tenor and was applying them rigorously. He had, indeed, begun, in 1644 and 1645, to send his ships to patrol along the coasts in order to seize the fishing vessels engaged in trading in pelts and he had also seized some ten ships from the Basque country, Bordeaux, and Brittany. In 1646, in the Gulf of the St. Lawrence, he had even captured some long-boats belonging to the Compagnie de Miscou. In September 1647 he took possession of Fort Saint-Pierre at Cape Breton, which belonged to Gilles Guignard and of the fort of Nipisiguit (Bathurst, N.B.), which had been granted to Nicolas Denys. These harsh acts, which it was difficult to justify, resulted in numerous counter-seizures and proceedings before the Admiralty courts, and in appeals to the Conseil du Roi. But d'Aulnay's standing at court was very firm, and the company's protests were heard only in 1652, after the death of the governor and of his father.

Despite his efforts, d'Aulnay was never able to repay the annual expenditures required by the colony. The accumulated deficits already came to more than 200,000 *livres* in 1648. Le Borgne, refusing to contribute further, went to Port-Royal to demand payment of his arrears. A somewhat sharp altercation resulted and Le Borgne had to go back with an empty ship. He started legal proceedings and had the estate of d'Aulnay seized. The governor was not checked by these difficulties, and he found other suppliers at Nantes and Bayonne. He was engaged upon clearing further tracts of land when he died suddenly, on 24 May 1650. His canoe capsized in the Port-Royal basin, and he died of exhaustion after remaining an hour and a half in the icy water. He left eight children, all quite young, and a heavily encumbered estate. He had drawn up his will on the preceding 20 January. Burial was in the church at Port-Royal. His father, René de Menou, became the children's guardian, and his widow, Jeanne Motin, by an ironic twist of fate, became the wife of his former adversary La Tour.

What he achieved was appreciable. According to the testimony of the earliest settlers, he had had three forts built, equipped with 60 cannon, and he maintained garrisons there. He had fetched some 20 families from France, and in order to establish them he had brought grass-lands under cultivation, organized two farms at Port-Royal, and cleared stretches of land at Pentagouet and the Saint John River. To supply his settlers, he had three or four ships come each year from France; he had two mills constructed, and built two small ships of 70 tons, five pinnaces, and several sloops. He had also established two schools, and at his death he left a population of about 500 souls, divided among four posts and served by 12 Capuchins.

These results may seem rather slight, but they assume considerable proportions when one remembers that d'Aulnay obtained them by his own efforts, with no official help. Such achievements betoken a high degree of intelligence and energy. While his rivals were almost entirely concerned with trade, d'Aulnay's ambition was to establish a lasting colony, and he realized that this could be done only by settling families in the country and by giving them the means of subsisting on the spot and by themselves, through the cultivation of the land, through fishing, and through industry. The colony that he left in Acadia was well rooted and vigorous enough to resist the English occupation and the 20 years of neglect that followed. That is enough for d'Aulnay to deserve consideration as a great colonizer and as one of the first architects of the plan to give to the Atlantic provinces a European population.

RENÉ BAUDRY

Information on this period is found chiefly in the memoirs of d'Aulnay and La Tour and is often contradictory. The original sources are: AN, Col., C^{11D}, 1, ff.63–81; BN, MS Fr. 15621, ff.265–72, 18593, ff.365–415, and NAF 9281 (Margry), ff.69–129; "Mass. Archives"; and ACM. *See also* Archivum Sacrae Congregationis de Propaganda, Rome, Lettere Antiche, 260, f.25, Ignace de Paris, "Brevis ac dilucida . . ." ("Brève relation de la mission d'Acadie . . . 1656") (photocopy of the original with a translation in PAC, FM 17, 1; see PAC *Report, 1904*, App. H, 333–41); and Denys, *Description and natural history* (Ganong). Several documents are reproduced in *Coll. de manuscrits relatifs à la Nouv.-France*, I, 115–26, II, 351–80 *passim*, in *Mémoires des commissaires*, I, x, xlviii, 46–47, 71, 79–84; II, 281–86, 495–96; IV, 169–74 *passim*, 203–8, 219, 223–49 *passim*, 259, 260–68, 272–74, 280–81, 302–5, 393, 446–47, 451, 517, 531; in *Memorials of the English and French commissaries*, I, 15, 53, 118–19, 147, 155–56, 347, 349, 353, 367, 375–81, 385, 401, 403, 525, 571–76, 711–12; and in the works of Couillard Després and Candide de Nant [*infra*].

Several modern historians have sided violently with d'Aulnay or with La Tour, and their works contain more polemic than history. Célestin Moreau in his *Histoire de l'Acadie françoise (Amérique septentrionale) de 1598 à 1755* (Paris, 1873), Émile Lauvrière in *La tragédie d'un peuple: histoire du peuple acadien de ses origines à nos jours* (2v., Paris, 1922; éd. rev., 1924) and in *Deux traîtres d'Acadie et leur victime: les Latour père et fils et Charles d'Aulnay* (Paris et Montréal, 1932), and Candide de Nant in *Pages glorieuses* are partial to d'Aulnay. Azarie Couillard Després defends the memory of La Tour in his *Observations sur l'histoire de l'Acadie françoise de M. Moreau, Paris 1873. Réfutation et mise au point* (Montréal, 1919), in *En marge de La tragédie d'un peuple de M. Émile Lauvrière ou erreurs sur l'histoire d'Acadie* (Bruges, 1925), and above all in *Saint-Étienne de La Tour*.

Rameau de Saint-Père, *Une colonie féodale*, and Parkman, *The old régime*, are more objective. *See also* two articles in *RHAF*: XI (1957–58), 218–41, "Charles d'Aulnay et la Compagnie de la Nouvelle-France," by René Baudry, and XVI (1962–63), 469–501, "La seigneurie de Charles de Menou d'Aulnay, gouverneur de l'Acadie, 1635–1650," by Geneviève Massignon.

MERLAC, ANDRÉ-LOUIS DE, a young priest whom Bishop Saint-Vallier [La Croix*] brought from France in 1688 and made his vicar-general (*grand vicaire*); fl. 1667–98.

On 9 Feb. 1690 the bishop appointed Merlac canon and precentor or "chief cantor"—whose function, according to Langevin, was "the supervision of the chanting, ceremonies, and the external aspects of worship"—of the chapter of the Quebec cathedral. The chapter had been established by Laval in 1684 and the first precentor had been Jean DUDOUYT. Because of the initial opposition of the other canons he was not installed as canon until 29 Aug. 1692.

In 1690 Merlac replaced Louis Ango* Des Maizerets as chaplain or superior of the Hospitallers, the nuns of the Hôtel-Dieu. In this position he was unpopular and failed to justify the bishop's trust in him. In 1694, after his departure, the chronicler of *Les Annales* expressed relief and thanked God "for having spared us the misfortunes that might have arisen, had the depravity of this wretched priest been able to lead astray some of our nuns, who in their simpleness listened to what he had to tell in order to captivate their minds and ruin them. With this in mind, the nuns put down in writing some atrocious remarks that he had made to them, so that the Mother Superior found herself obliged to ask Monsignor the Bishop to remove this undignified minister from this community." The bishop agreed and Merlac left for France on 2 Oct. 1694. Joseph de La Colombière* was appointed superior of the Hospitallers de l'Hôtel-Dieu in the same year.

Merlac was accused by Glandelet*, syndic of the chapter of Quebec and an opponent of Mgr de Saint-Vallier, of distributing "certain suspect and dangerous books touching the new doctrine" (Jansenism). Examples were listed and Merlac was further accused of questioning certain points of Catholic doctrine. An editorial footnote in *Les Annales* connects Merlac with a reference in Laval's letter of 1696 to Saint-Vallier in which the latter is reproached for having taken away from the seminary priests their parochial duties and having entrusted these to priests whose very bad conduct Saint-Vallier could not have ignored.

In assessing this criticism it must be noted that Merlac's unpopularity also arose from the fact that he was a protégé of Mgr de Saint-Vallier and that he was caught in the various disputes between the bishop on the one hand and the chapter and the Seminary of Quebec on the other.

In 1698 Merlac was living in France. He did not return to Canada.

HELMUT KALLMANN

ASQ, Chapitre, 31, Mémoire de Glandelet, 1690, "Prétentions de Mgr de Québec sur le Séminaire de Québec...," 9, 57–59, *et passim*; Lettres, O 23, pp.13, 19, *et passim*. Juchereau, *Annales* (Jamet). *Jug. et délib.*, III, 747–49, 754, 756. Auguste Gosselin, *L'Église du Canada depuis Monseigneur de Laval jusqu'à la conquête* (3v., Québec, 1911–14), I, 51, 55, 124; *Henri de Bernières, premier curé de Québec* (Les Normands au Canada, Québec, 1902), 137–41. Edmond Langevin, *Notice biographique sur François de Laval de Montmorency, 1er évêque de Québec* (Montréal, 1874), 193, "Notes historiques sur le chapitre de la cathédrale de Québec, 1684–1794."

MESGOUEZ, TROILUS DE LA ROCHE DE.
See LA ROCHE

MESNU, JEAN-BAPTISTE PEUVRET DE.
See PEUVRET

MESSAMOUET, a Souriquois (Micmac) sagamo of the La Hève River; fl. 1604–7.

Messamouet was chosen, in 1604, to guide Samuel de CHAMPLAIN in quest of the copper mine that SARCEL de Prévert's men claimed to have discovered, with the guidance of Indians. Champlain and Messamouet set sail in a pinnace of five or six tons, manned by nine sailors. Between Île Sainte-Croix and the Saint John they located two mines, neither of pure copper.

In 1606 JEAN DE BIENCOURT de Poutrincourt and Champlain left Port-Royal (now Annapolis Royal, N.S.), for the Sainte-Croix River, where they met Messamouet and SECOUDON. The two Indians joined the Frenchmen, for they wanted to go to Chouacouët (Saco) to meet chiefs Onemechin and Marchin and form an alliance. Onemechin and Marchin gave Poutrincourt a Souriquois they were holding prisoner; Messamouet gave them presents of French articles and harangued them, saying that he knew what the friendship of the French could bring them, for he had stayed in France at the house of M. de Grandmont, the governor of Bayonne.

In return, Onemechin offered Messamouet Indian corn, squashes, and so on. But these gifts, or the lack of a similar harangue, displeased Messamouet, who immediately began to think of making war.

EILEEN C. CUSHING

Champlain, *Works* (Biggar), I, 278, 393. Lescarbot, *History* (Grant), II, 323.

MESSIER, MARTINE, wife of Antoine Primot; b. at Saint-Denis-le-Thiboult (or le Petit-Bourg), in the diocese of Rouen, in 1607; d. at Montreal some time after 1672.

Primot and his wife were married in France and are mentioned for the first time in 1650 as being at Montreal, although Abbé Faillon maintains that they had been there since 1642. The adoptive mother of Catherine Thierry, who in 1654 married CHARLES LE MOYNE, Martine Messier seems to have imparted to the famous LE MOYNE brothers, her grandsons, the courage and sang-froid which she exhibited on at least one occasion.

On 29 July 1652, at twice the distance of a gun shot from the fort of Montreal, Martine was attacked by three Iroquois. Although she was unarmed, she defended herself "like a lioness." Having suffered several hatchet wounds, she finally fainted; but just as one of the Iroquois grasped her by the head to scalp her, "our Amazon" recovered consciousness, "rose more furious than ever and seized the brute so violently in a place which modesty forbids mentioning, that he was barely able to escape." Her strength failed her and she fainted again, but her assailants fled at the approach of the defenders of the fort who had been aroused by the victim's cries.

Martine was not dead, as was quickly realized. In a gesture of compassion, one of the settlers who had come to her rescue took it into his head to embrace her. Recovering consciousness, Martine immediately "dealt him a lusty box on the ear." She explained to the astonished witnesses in her patois: "*Parmanda*, I thought he wanted to kiss me." This retort caused great laughter, and subsequently Martine was never called by anything but the nickname *la bonne femme Parmanda*.

Martine Messier was still living in 1672.

ANDRÉ VACHON

Martine Messier's exploit is recorded in: Dollier de Casson, *Histoire du Montréal*, 84f. Marie Guyart de

Mézy

l'Incarnation, *Lettres* (Richaudeau), I, 470. *JR* (Thwaites), XXXVIII, 50–52. *JJ* (Laverdière et Casgrain), 174. Vachon de Belmont, *Histoire du Canada*.

For information about Martine Messier, her husband, and adopted daughter, consult: AJM, Greffe de Bénigne Basset, 20 mai 1660. Recensements de 1666 et 1667. Faillon, *Histoire de la colonie française*, II, 145. Archange Godbout, "Les origines de la famille Le Moyne," *RHAF*, I (1947–48), 539. É.-Z. Massicotte, "Les colons de Montréal de 1642 à 1667, *RSCT*, 3d ser., VII (1913), sect.I, 12f.; *BRH*, XXXIII (1927), 184.

MÉZY (Mésy), AUGUSTIN DE SAFFRAY DE. *See* SAFFRAY

MIGEON DE BRANSSAT, JEAN-BAPTISTE, merchant, clerk in the Compagnie des Indes occidentales, seigneurial attorney, subdelegate of the intendant, judge and seigneur; b. 1636 at Moulins in Bourbonnais, son of Jean Migeon, merchant, and of Marie Desbordes; d. August 1693 at Montreal.

Migeon de Branssat seems to have come to New France in 1665, or not long before. In 1665 he was a merchant at Montreal. The following year he was a clerk in the Compagnie des Indes occidentales, and in 1667 became attorney of the seigneury of Montreal. He was to hold this office for ten years, with Sieur Jean Gervaise as his deputy.

In November 1665, at Montreal, he married Catherine Gauchet de Belleville, a native of Senlis. She was of a noble family, and was related to M. SOUART, superior of the seminary of Saint-Sulpice; she had come to Canada with the contingent that arrived in 1659. In May 1664 she had been granted an arriere fief, later known as Lagauchetière, to which a thoroughfare of the city still gives access today.

In December 1665 Migeon himself was granted an arriere fief, adjoining his wife's. At that time he was engaged in fur-trading, and made numerous real estate deals.

In the winter of 1672 Migeon, with Pierre PICOTÉ de Belestre, Jean-Vincent Philippe de Hautmesnyl, CHARLES LE MOYNE, and Jacques Le Ber*, formed part of a deputation that tried to make respectful representations to the governor of Montreal, François-Marie PERROT, about his repeated violation of the laws governing trade in pelts. For this so-called insolence Perrot had Migeon put in prison; the latter, replacing CHARLES-JOSEPH D'AILLEBOUST in his function as judge, had made himself the spokesman of the group.

At the time of a quarrel over precedence in the parish church of Notre-Dame, in 1675, Migeon de Branssat bore the titles of bachelor of laws and lawyer in the Parlement. On several other occasions this same status was attributed to him.

In August 1677 he succeeded d'Ailleboust, the civil and criminal judge in the bailiff's court of Montreal, despite the protests of d'Ailleboust's son, who laid claim to the office. His installation address is recorded in the register of the bailiff's court of Montreal.

Migeon de Branssat has been reproached with having frequently ignored the edicts concerning the fur trade and the *coureurs de bois*, although his very office required him to see that they were observed.

He became the subdelegate of the intendant Jacques Demeulle* in September 1685, and resigned from his post as seigneurial judge in 1690.

He was named royal judge of Montreal by the edict of 15 March 1693 that created this office, but he died in the following August, before the appointment had been conferred upon him. It was Charles Juchereau* de Saint-Denis who assumed this function.

After 13 years as a widow, his former wife became a nun of the Hôtel-Dieu at Montreal, where one of her daughters had preceded her. She died there in 1721, aged 77 years. It has been said that she had originally come to New France with the intention of becoming a nun.

Migeon de Branssat and Catherine Gauchet de Belleville had at least six children who reached adult age.

JEAN-JACQUES LEFEBVRE

Jug. et délib., I, 1014; II, 157, 183, 191, 547–49, 575, 617f., 675f.; III, 760f., 924f. *Ord. comm.* (P.-G. Roy), I, 252–58. Faillon, *Histoire de la colonie française*, II, 360f.; III, 82, 216, 452f. É.-Z. Massicotte, "Les juges de Montréal sous le régime français, 1648–1760," *BRH*, XXVII (1921), 177–83; "Migeon de Branssat," *BRH*, XXI (1915), 232–35, 303f.; "Les tribunaux et les officiers de justice de Montréal sous le régime français," *BRH*, XXXVII (1931), 302–13. Régis Roy, "Migeon de Bransat," *BRH*, XXVI (1920), 313–17.

MIRISTOU (Mahigan Aticq Ouche, meaning "Wolf," "Stag," "Canoe"), Montagnais chief; d. 1628.

Miristou, a son of ANADABIJOU with whom CHAMPLAIN had first allied himself in 1603, received his chieftainship in 1622 through the influence of Champlain. He had protested great friendship to the French, and Champlain, after some delay, had agreed to influence his tribe to this end if Miristou, with his 30 companions, would promise to settle and cultivate land near Quebec. Miristou fulfilled this obligation admirably and although there were other claimants,

Champlain effected his election. Thus Champlain planned to establish friendly groups of natives near Quebec who could be trusted to aid in exploration and the fur trade. Also he wished to set an example for other tribes who, by seeking aid from the French in the election of their chiefs, would gradually come under French control. At this time, Miristou changed his name to Mahigan Aticq or Mahigan Aticq Ouche, meaning "Stag" and "Wolf," indicating that he could be equally gentle or cruel.

To give special distinction to Mahigan Aticq's installation as chief, Champlain presented him with two swords, explaining that by accepting them a chief "entered into an obligation" to bear arms against those who might harm the French. Although Mahigan Aticq had assisted in driving off the Iroquois in an attack on the St. Charles River earlier that year, he was never called upon to show his loyalty. Rather, Mahigan Aticq's efforts were directed toward peace with the Iroquois. He was a leader of those natives who were "sick and tired" of the wars that had lasted over 50 years and who wished to ensure safe hunting in areas from which they had been prevented from travelling because of these wars. In June 1622 a peace council was held with Iroquois representatives in Mahigan's cabin. Negotiations with the enemy continued in 1623. During these parlays Mahigan sought and relied on the advice of Champlain. In 1624, a council representing more nations than had hitherto been assembled, including Iroquois, met at Trois-Rivières. Mahigan Aticq arrived with Champlain. The peace that resulted from this meeting was maintained for three years.

Early in 1627, however, it was threatened by a request of the Dutch, and the Indians of their region, to certain Montagnais to join in war against the Mahicans. Again Mahigan Aticq, wishing to avoid war, sought the advice of Champlain who consulted fully with him in the matter. He and Champlain's brother-in-law, EUSTACHE BOULLÉ, were dispatched by Champlain to dissuade the Indians from going to war. When on the action of "nine or ten young hot-heads," however, the peace was broken, Mahigan Aticq and Champlain again travelled together to attend a council where they continued to assert their influence for peace. On Champlain's advice envoys, including a Frenchman, Pierre MAGNAN, were sent to the Iroquois but these were murdered in an Iroquois village, thus terminating hope of peace. Throughout this period it would appear that Mahigan Aticq and Champlain were mutually interdependent for prestige and for influence among both friendly tribes and enemies.

According to SAGARD, Mahigan Aticq was the murderer of two Frenchmen, Dumoulin and Henri, Mme Hebert's [see ROLLET] servant, at Quebec in October 1627. Le CLERCQ repeats this version of the crime. Champlain, however, suspected another Montagnais whom he held under arrest. There is no indication that Champlain entertained any suspicions of Mahigan Aticq's guilt, although Sagard states that CHOMINA informed Champlain that Mahigan Aticq was guilty. Sagard may have been confused, for his version of Mahigan Aticq's subsequent fate is essentially the same as Champlain's account of his "suspected murderer." Champlain says that news of Mahigan Aticq's death was brought to him in late April 1628, and that the trial of the suspected murderer continued in May. It was only in the spring of 1629, faced with a serious food shortage in Quebec, that Champlain released the prisoner into the custody of Chomina and EROUACHY.

ELSIE MCLEOD JURY

Champlain, *Works* (Biggar), *passim*. Sagard, *Histoire du Canada* (Tross), II, 443, 515; III, 813–22, 855–56. Desrosiers, *Iroquoisie*, 76, 95–96, 98.

MISSENDEN, SAMUEL, employee of the HBC; fl. 1685–88.

"A gentleman for whom the Company had good future expectations," he entered upon a somewhat dramatic career in 1685. He was assigned to Port Nelson where he served as chief warehousekeeper, presumably until 1686. He was then advanced to the post of chief at New Severn and deputy governor at Port Nelson and commended for his study of the Indian language.

Suddenly he was back in England in 1687, claiming to have come over in the Company's service. Subsequently it turned out that Pierre Radisson* had urged him to witness to charges against Governor GEYER that proved to be "falce and malitious." Instead of returning as governor of the Bay, as Radisson had promised, Missenden was dismissed from the Company's employment.

A few days after returning to England in 1687 Missenden was required, with other Company employees, to present himself at Whitehall. "The concerne of this Compa. against the French," i.e., the capture by de TROYES of three Company posts on James Bay in time of peace (1686), was to be laid before the king.

He is next heard of on the Continent. He went to Hamburg to visit his father, who probably had mercantile interests in that important trading centre, and he wrote from Amsterdam, hinting at

Mius

interloping ships to the Bay. (Interlopers were trespassers on the Company's monopoly.) His offer to return to Company service in 1688 was declined as not being "to the conveniency of the Company."

MAUD M. HUTCHESON

HBRS, XI, XX (Rich and Johnson).

MIUS (Muis) D'ENTREMONT, PHILIPPE, esquire, first baron of Pobomcoup (Pubnico), near Cap de Sable, lieutenant-major, king's attorney, settler, the first of the d'Entremonts of Nova Scotia; b. *c.* 1601 (or 1609) in Normandy (probably at Cherbourg); d. *c.* 1700 (or 1701).

According to Placide Gaudet, the Norman Philippe Mius was related by marriage to the Bourbon family and was made Sieur d'Entremont by Louis XIV; but according to a descendant, H. Léandre d'Entremont, the titles of nobility are said to go back to the 11th century in Savoy, and a branch of the Savoy family is thought to have emigrated to Normandy during the 16th century. In 1649 the Sieur d'Entremont married Madeleine Hélie (or Élie) Du Tillet (b. 1626). He was then a captain in a regiment. It was in 1650 (*Coll. de manuscrits relatifs à la Nouv.-France*, II, 329) or 1651 (R. Le Blant) that he, with his wife and a daughter, was brought to Acadia by the new governor CHARLES DE SAINT-ÉTIENNE de La Tour, a childhood friend, as lieutenant-major and commander of the king's troops. To reward him for his services, La Tour offered d'Entremont in 1651 or 1653 the letters patent of the Pobomcoup fief, as a barony. The feudal rights conferred upon the baron a territory stretching from Cap Nègre to Cap Fourchu (Yarmouth). The feudal castle was built near the entry to the natural harbour of Pubnico, on the east side.

D'Entremont played an important part in the colony's history both because of what he did as an administrator and because he was one of the rare Acadian seigneurs to concern himself with cultivation and with clearing land; he attracted to his estate "several indentured workers and a few families from Port-Royal [now Annapolis Royal, N.S.] and this seigneury eventually formed a small centre of population."

Besides their daughter whom they had brought from France, the d'Entremonts had four children who were born on Acadian soil: two of their sons, Jacques*, b. 1659, and Abraham*, de Plemazais (or Plemarch), b. 1661 or 1662, married respectively Anne and Marguerite, the daughters of Governor Charles de La Tour and Jeanne MOTIN; the third son, Philippe*, whose life is more difficult to piece together, may have married a daughter of Jean-Vincent d'Abbadie* de Saint-Castin. As for the daughters, Marie-Marguerite, born in France, married Pierre Melanson *dit* La Verdure [*see* Charles MELANSON]; the other, Madeleine, seems to have remained a spinster.

Around 1670, at the time when the Treaty of Breda was being put into force, Governor ANDIGNÉ de Grandfontaine was establishing himself at Pentagouet on the Penobscot. D'Entremont was named king's attorney, an office which he held for 18 years despite his advanced age. We know of reports which were made by Mius d'Entremont and Jacques Bourgeois* on the subject of the Acadian frontiers, and sent to the minister, Pontchartrain, by JOSEPH ROBINAU de Villebon. Towards the end of his life d'Entremont left his seigneurial estate, bequeathing the title of baron to his eldest son Jacques, and went to settle at Port-Royal with his wife and two of his children. He died at the end of 1700 or the beginning of 1701, a venerable patriarch more than 90 years old. According to tradition it was at Port-Royal that he died, but Léandre d'Entremont indicates Grand-Pré, where d'Entremont may have gone to reside with his daughter Marie-Marguerite Melanson, as the more likely place of death. Philippe Mius d'Entremont has left a large number of descendants in Acadia; the barony of Pobomcoup remained in the family until the expulsion of the Acadians; and after more than three centuries some hundred families of the same name can still be counted at Pubnico.

CLÉMENT CORMIER

Coll. de manuscrits relatifs à la Nouv.-France, II, 134, 329. Recensement de 1686 (Acadie). Placide Gaudet, notes preserved in the PAC and at the Université de Moncton; études published in *Moniteur Acadien* (Shediac, N.B.), 17 Dec. 1886, 11 and 25 Jan. 1887. George S. Brown, *Yarmouth, Nova Scotia: a sequel to Campbell's history* (Boston, 1888), 151–52. A. Cameron, study published in the Halifax *Herald*, 1 Jan. 1886, of which the translation was published in the *Moniteur Acadien*, 21 Jan. 1886; *see also* issues of 7, 14 Jan. 1886, 17 Dec. 1886, 11 Jan. 1887. H. L. d'Entremont, *The Baronnie de Pombcoup and the Acadians, a history of the ancient "Department of Cape Sable," now known as Yarmouth and Shelburne counties, Nova Scotia* (Yarmouth, 1931); *The forts of Cape Sable of the seventeenth century* (n.p., 1938); study on the genealogy of the Acadian families of Yarmouth county, published in the Yarmouth *Herald* beginning 20 Feb. 1940. Robert Le Blant, "Les trois mariages d'une Acadienne, Anne d'Entremont (1694–1778)," *NF*, VII (1932), 211. Rameau de Saint-Père, *Une colonie féodale*, II, 320. P.-G. Roy, "Les marquisats, comptés, baronnies et châtellenies dans la Nouvelle-France," *BRH*, XXI (1915), 48. Webster, *Acadia*, 121.

MIVILLE *dit* **le Suisse, PIERRE,** master-joiner, pioneer and captain of the Lauson shore; d. 14 Oct. 1669.

Swiss by birth, Miville came to Canada via La Rochelle at a date that has not been established with certainty but that was previous to 28 Oct. 1649, on which date he, along with his son François, received from the governor, Louis d'Ailleboust, a grant of land in the seigneury of Lauson, which was later raised to the status of an arriere-fief. Miville apparently tried to entice some of his compatriots to Canada. In fact, on 16 July 1665, M. de Prouville de Tracy granted him, along with his sons and four other persons, a concession measuring 21 *arpents* by 40 at Grande Anse (La Pocatière), naming the locality "the Canton of the Fribourg Swiss." This undertaking was unsuccessful. Pierre Miville stayed at Lauson until his death, 14 Oct. 1669. In France he had married Charlotte Maugis, who bore him six children at least; one of them, Jacques, was the founder of the Miville-Deschênes families of North America.

Honorius Provost

"Le canton de Suisses Fribourgeois," *BRH*, XX (1914), 233f. J.-E. Roy, *Histoire de la seigneurie de Lauzon*, I, 69–71.

MOHIER (Moyer), GERVAIS, Recollet friar and missionary; b. 1599 at Chartres; d. 1662 at Châlons.

After making his profession with the Recollets of the province of Paris on 2 June 1625, he was sent to Canada the following year to replace Brother Sagard. He sailed from Dieppe on 24 April with Father Le Caron and Champlain, and reached Quebec on 4 July. He spent a year at the monastery at Notre-Dame-des-Anges, where he worked hard at instructing a young Montagnais who was baptized on Whitsunday 1627 and given the name of Louis.

In July 1627 he went to join the Indians who had gathered at Cap-de-la-Victoire for the fur trade. The Montagnais had brought with them two Iroquois prisoners, one of whom was slaughtered despite Brother Mohier's protests. A few days later, an Algonkin medicine man, Napagabiscou, fell ill; having been moved for some time by the preaching of Father Le Caron, he requested baptism, which was administered to him *in extremis* by Brother Mohier.

In 1628 the Algonkins entreated Brother Mohier and Father Le Caron to go and live in their territory in order to save the missions being threatened by the Kirke brothers. The Recollets set out, but soon returned when it was announced that the English had withdrawn. The following year, however, after the surrender of Quebec, Brother Mohier, along with all the other missionaries, was obliged to leave Canada permanently. He died at Châlons in Champagne on 10 May 1662.

G.-M. Dumas

ASQ, MSS, 200, Mortuologe des Recolets. Champlain, *Œuvres* (Laverdière). Le Clercq, *First establishment of the faith* (Shea), I, 260, 293, 335, 344, 366. Sagard, *Histoire du Canada* (Tross), II, IV, *passim*. Jouve, *Les Franciscains et le Canada (1615–1629)*.

MONCEL, ROBERT GIFFARD DE. See Giffard

MONCHY. See Mouchy

MONS, Sieur de. See Monts

MONTIGNY. See Rémy

MONTMAGNY, CHARLES HUAULT DE. See Huault

MONTORGUEUIL, DAUPHIN DE. See Dauphin

MONTS, Sieur de, thus called by Marie de l'Incarnation [*see* Guyart], but also designated under the names **Dumons** and **de Mons**; royal commissioner in New France; fl. 1662.

In 1662 Pierre Boucher* had met Louis XIV and had discussed with him the problems and needs of New France. The king had promised him substantial assistance for the following year; but meanwhile he sent some 100 soldiers to Canada, under the orders of a gentleman named de Monts.

The task of the Sieur de Monts was to study the situation and the needs of the colony and to make a report to the king. But numerous delays held up the departure of the ships until the end of June, which to some extent adversely affected the royal commissioner's assignment. The crossing was rough. It lasted four months, during which the Sieur de Monts, according to Marie de l'Incarnation, was "most sorely treated by the captain of the King's vessels, not to mention that he had provisions for only two months, and was four on the way."

On the journey de Monts called at Plaisance (Placentia), of which he officially took possession in the name of the king, leaving there 30 soldiers, a priest, and food for the winter.

Monts

The ships finally reached Tadoussac on 27 October. The soldiers and settlers—the latter numbering 200—made their way to Quebec in row-boats. De Monts himself, who had to return to France before the end of the sailing season, made haste to inspect the colony, noting "the lands, the mountains, the rivers, the shores and their approaches." He paid particular attention to the town of Quebec, then proceeded to Trois-Rivières, where in the name of the king he installed the new governor, Pierre Boucher. De Monts does not appear to have visited Montreal. Indeed he spent only seven days in the colony. He landed at Tadoussac on 27 October, and reached Quebec the same day; he probably spent the 28th there, leaving for Trois-Rivières only on the 29th. Marie de l'Incarnation affirms that he took two days to get to the latter town (say the evening of the 30th). But on 3 November de Monts sailed again for France. He therefore did not have time to go to Montreal. Even if he had looked over no more than a very small part of New France—and that very rapidly—the Sieur de Monts nevertheless departed "very pleased," promising to return "in eight months' time to further his Majesty's intentions," but already convinced "that a kingdom can be set up in this country larger and finer than that of France."

De Monts did not return to New France. In 1633 another royal commissioner, the Sieur GAUDAIS-DUPONT, was appointed in his place.

ANDRÉ VACHON

[Parkman, in *The old régime* (25th ed.) 131, attributes to "Dumont" the account of a voyage which was published anonymously in the *Relation* for the year 1663. De Monts was here only seven days, but the author of this account affirms that he was in the colony for a year: the attribution cannot be supported. Marie Guyart de l'Incarnation, *Lettres* (Richaudeau), II, 223–25, Marie de l'Incarnation à son fils, Québec, 6 nov. 1662. *JJ* (Laverdière et Casgrain), 313f. Lanctot, *Histoire du Canada*, I, 329.   A.V.]

MONTS, PIERRE DU GUA DE. *See* DU GUA

MOREAU DE BRÉSOLES, JUDITH, nun, Hospitaller of St. Joseph, co-foundress of the Hôtel-Dieu, Laval (France), foundress and first superior of the Hospitallers of the Hôtel-Dieu de Montréal; b. 25 March 1620 at Blois, daughter of François Moreau de Brésoles, commissary for the wars, and of Françoise Gailliard; d. 1 July 1687 at Montreal.

Judith Moreau de Brésoles' family held a place of importance in the city of Blois. From the time she was six, Judith used to accompany her mother on her charitable visits. When she was barely 15, she learned to do blood-letting and to compound remedies. She soon became an assiduous visitor to the sick in the hospital in Blois, and wanted to become a nursing nun. Her parents were resolutely opposed to this. Nevertheless they finally allowed her to enter the convent of the Visitation in her native city, but this trial was unsuccessful. Nothing but hospital service attracted the girl, and her spiritual directors permitted her to follow her vocation despite her family's opposition. On 5 Nov. 1645, accompanied by an old servant, she fled the paternal *château* to go to present herself to Mother Marie de La Ferre, the foundress of the Religious Hospitallers of St. Joseph, at La Flèche. Her nursing talents were soon put to use. She determined "to learn from a skilful chemist the secret of extracting spirits, essences, and other most difficult pharmaceutical products." She was consequently able to render valuable services to the Hôtel-Dieu at La Flèche as well as to that at Laval. With Mother Catherine MACÉ and Mother Marie MAILLET she shared the honour of being a foundress of the hospital at Laval. She was its novice mistress.

Mother Brésoles, "who was in truth a Judith in courage and fidelity," was likewise to distinguish herself by her great virtues. She had the honour of being chosen by the founder of Montreal, Jérôme Le Royer de La Dauversière, and the bishop of Angers, Henri Arnauld, to be the foundress of the convent of the Hospitallers of Montreal.

Arriving in Canada 7 Sept. 1659 with Jeanne MANCE, Mother Macé, and Mother Maillet, she organized her little community, keeping for herself the difficult and menial tasks. Her medical and pharmaceutical talents made of her a most competent Hospitaller. "Consequently," wrote Sister Morin*, "it was said that her medicines were miraculous." She served the sick, "French as well as Indian," for 20 years. Her reputation as a good nurse became so firmly established that her patients believed naïvely that it would be impossible for them to die if it was she who took care of them.

The first superior of the Hospitallers of the Hôtel-Dieu de Montréal died 1 July 1687. She was 67. All the population of Canada, says the chronicle, mourned the loss of this great Sister of Mercy and true servant of the poor.

ESTHER LEFEBVRE, R.H.S.J.

AHDM, Acte de baptême de Mère de Brésoles; Registre des entrées et professions; Rôle d'embarquement sur le Saint-André; Contrat de fondation des Filles Hospitalières de Saint-Joseph de Montréal

(9 juin 1659); "Obédience" de Monseigneur de Laval confiant le mandat aux trois premières Mères (20 oct. 1659); Acte de prise de possession de l'Hôtel-Dieu de Ville-Marie (20 nov. 1659); Acceptation d'administration du bien des pauvres de l'Hôpital de Montréal par les Dames religieuses du dit Hôpital (10 oct. 1676); Marie Morin, "Histoire simple et véritable de l'établissement des Religieuses Hospitalières de Saint-Joseph en l'Ile de Montréal, dite à présent Ville-Marie, en Canada, de l'année 1659 . . ."; and other documents. Morin, *Annales* (Fauteux, *et al.*). Lefebvre, *Marie Morin.* Mondoux, *L'Hôtel-Dieu de Montréal.*

MOREL, THOMAS, priest, pastor to several parishes in New France, canon; b. 1636 at Amalis (diocese of Rennes, in Brittany); d. 1687.

He was one of the first five priests attached to the seminary of Quebec, and the first of the parish priests who were considered as life-time members of this institution. He devoted his life to ministration among the French settlers. He arrived at Quebec on 22 Aug. 1661, and served as a priest first at the Beaupré shore (1661–68) and on the Île d'Orléans (1661–71), then, from 1671 to 1683, almost exclusively on the south shore, starting at Pointe-Lévy and going down the river as the missions were set up. After a period of rest at the seminary, he attempted to resume his ministry at Champlain, but he contracted a serious illness there and went to Quebec, where he died soon after, on 23 Nov. 1687.

Abbé Morel had had the church of Sainte-Anne de Beaupré rebuilt because it was too near to the tides. In addition to the parish registers, drawn up with extraordinary care, he has left us a handwritten account of the first miracles performed at the Sainte-Anne sanctuary. The parish of Saint-Thomas de Montmagny owes its name to Abbé Morel, who officiated there for several years. In 1675, at the time of a quarrel over precedence, Abbé Morel was indicted for contempt of authority. He refused to appear before the Conseil Souverain, whose jurisdiction in ecclesiastical matters he called in question, and demanded that his case be placed before the diocesan officiality. He was imprisoned on 25 June, but set free on 22 July. The proceedings were then abandoned.

HONORIUS PROVOST

ASQ, Thomas Morel, "Miracles arrivez en leglise de Ste. Anne du petit Cap Coste de Beaupré en Canadas" (1687), dans Paroisses diverses, 84, et Polygraphie, XIII, 2; Paroisses diverses, 72, 87; Séminaire, II, 57; V, 10; *et passim. Jug. et délib.*, I *passim.*; II, 813, 834. Thomas Morel, "Recit des merveilles arrivées en l'eglise de Sainte Anne du Petit Cap, coste de Beaupray en la Nouvelle France," *JR* (Thwaites), LI, 86–100. *BRH*, XXXIII (1927), 680. Gosselin, *Vie de Mgr de Laval.* J.-E. Roy, *Histoire de la seigneurie de Lauzon,* I, 280–3. P.-G. Roy, "L'emprisonnement de l'abbé Morel," *BRH*, XLVII (1941), 127.

MORILLON DU BOURG (his first name is unknown), commissioner appointed by the king of France to carry out the Treaty of Breda in Acadia; fl. *c.* 1667–68; d. 10 April 1670, perhaps in Guinea (Africa).

According to a letter that he wrote from Boston 9 Nov. 1668 (o.s.) to the Compagnie des Indes occidentales, Morillon du Bourg, in order to conform with the instructions of Charles II and carry out the mission that Louis XIV had entrusted to him, had sailed along the shores of Acadia with ALEXANDRE LE BORGNE de Belle-Isle; his purpose was to see the places mentioned in his commission. He had left Belle-Isle at Port-Royal, after making over his powers to him, and had sailed for Boston to arrive at an understanding with the English governor of Acadia, Sir Thomas TEMPLE, concerning the cession of the territory to France. During Du Bourg's stay at Boston, Temple received from Charles II, who had revised his decision, the order not to give up Acadia so long as the French, for their part, had not turned over St. Christopher's Island (now St. Kitts), as the treaty required. Temple, on his own initiative, lodged a complaint with Du Bourg against the attack made by Belle-Isle on Port Rossignol. Du Bourg hastened to write to Belle-Isle to advise him to leave Acadia until the principal clauses of the treaty were respected. He forwarded reports to the Compagnie des Indes occidentales and to the French ambassador in London, M. Colbert de Croissy, then headed for St. Christopher's. The Acadian posts were ceded to the French only in August and September 1670.

On 1 Nov. 1669 a frigate, the *Justice*, had left Le Havre-de-Grâce (Le Havre), bound for Africa. It was engaged upon an expedition organized by the Compagnie des Indes occidentales, with the object of establishing commercial relations (the slave trade) with Guinea, through the creation of a post there. The vessel had aboard a "sieur du Bourg, with the title of commandant for the habitation." The latter died in Africa a year later. This was perhaps Morillon Du Bourg, who, after completing his mission in Acadia, may have returned to France via the West Indies, and then left again for Guinea.

IN COLLABORATION

AN, Col., C[11D], 1, f.126. *Coll. de manuscrits relatifs à la Nouv.-France,* I, 188, 197. *Journal du voyage du Sr Delbée, aux isles de la coste de Guinée,* 348, 386, 389, 393, 394, 400, 403, 404, 409, 410, 412, 463, in I.C.S.D.V., *Relation. Mémoires des commissaires du roi,* I, xviii, 49; II, 298–99, 302–12; IV, 286–87, 311; and *Memorials*

Motin

of the English and French commissaries, I, 21, 121, 411, 588–89, 591–96, 599–600. PRO, *CSP, Col., 1661–68*, nos.1868, 1877, 1898. Couillard Després, *Saint-Étienne de La Tour*, 446 (note that the dating seems to be incorrect).

MOTIN (Mottin), JEANNE, Acadian pioneer and governor's wife; b. *c*. 1615 in France, daughter of Louis Motin de Co(u)rcelles, who was associated with the Razilly-Condonnier trading company; d. *c*. 1666 at Cap de Sable.

She came to Acadia in 1636 with her two sisters and her brother-in-law, Nicolas Le Creux Du Breuil. In the same year, probably at Port-Royal, she married Charles de Menou d'Aulnay, by whom she had four sons, who entered the army and died in battle, and four daughters, all of whom took religious vows.

Following the death of d'Aulnay in 1650 she continued to reside at Port-Royal. She found her husband's estate had debts totalling well over 300,000 *livres*, and there was little hope of her being able to raise this sum. Persistent attempts to collect payments were made by creditors and those of Emmanuel Le Borgne did not stop short of raiding and looting her property. At the same time she sent one of her officers to dislodge Nicolas and Simon Denys from their posts at Cape Breton, claiming that these were on lands controlled by the d'Aulnay estate. In July of 1651 she had her steward (*intendant*), Brice de Sainte-Croix—the son of Mme de Brice—go to France to act in her interests. The unauthorized arrangements he made with the Duc de Vendôme, under which Vendôme assumed half the debts in exchange for half the d'Aulnay property and an equal share in the fur trade, only complicated the situation.

In a marriage of convenience she was wed in July 1653 to Charles de Saint-Étienne de La Tour, who had been d'Aulnay's chief rival for power in Acadia. They lived at the mouth of the Saint John until about 1656 when they moved to Cap de Sable. By La Tour she had five children—Jacques (m. Anne Melanson), Charles*, Marie (m. Alexandre Le Borgne), Marguerite (m. Abraham Mius* de Plemazais), and Anne (m. Jacques Mius* de Pobomcoup). A petition by her daughter, Marie, dated 1667 shows that Jeanne Motin was dead by that date.

George MacBeath

[See bibliography for Charles de Menou d'Aulnay and Charles de Saint-Étienne.]

For the litigation carried on by her daughter, Dame Marie de Menou, canoness of Poussay, and subsequently by her son Charles de Saint-Étienne* de La Tour, *see* AN, Col., C^{11D}, 1, ff.55–60v., printed in *Coll. de manuscrits relatifs à la Nouv.-France*, II, 351–63. Other references: *ibid.*, I, 132, 145–46; II, 292–93, 363–80 *passim*.

MOUCHY, NICOLAS DE, often erroneously called Monchy, a native of Lyon (France), notary, clerk of court, deputy attorney-general and member of the Conseil Souverain (1663–72).

Arriving at Montreal in 1663, or shortly before, Mouchy was, on 26 May 1664, appointed by the Conseil Souverain royal notary and clerk of the royal seneschal's court of Montreal, which was subsequently abolished on 18 Sept. 1666; he nevertheless continued to carry on the same duties within the framework of the seigneurial jurisdiction. On 14 Jan. 1669 he was promoted to the post of deputy attorney-general. He took up residence in Quebec, bringing with him his minutes, only six of which have come down to us although he drafted at least 35 documents. A year later, on 13 Jan. 1670, Mouchy was appointed to the Conseil Souverain, and on two occasions, on 21 Jan. 1671 and 28 March 1672, he was reappointed to membership. On 31 Oct. 1672, he took his seat in the council for the last time. A few days later he sailed for France, apparently leaving in the colony his daughter, who, in 1675, married François Sabatier in Montreal.

André Vachon

AJM, Greffe de Bénigne Basset, 18 déc., 1675. *Jug. et délib.*, I. É.-Z. Massicotte, "Nicolas de Mouchy, notaire royal à Montréal," *BRH*, XXV (1919), 83–89.

MOYER. *See* Mohier

MUNK (Munck), JENS ERIKSEN, Danish sailor, wintered at the mouth of Churchill River in 1620; b. 3 June 1579 at Barbo, near the present Arendal, Norway; second son of Erik Nielsen Munk; married Katherine Adriansdatter; divorced 1623; several children; d. 3 or 24 June 1628 and buried 3 July in Copenhagen.

Munk's early years were spent at sea. During the war with Sweden, 1611–13, he was commissioned a captain in the Danish navy, where he distinguished himself. From 1613 onwards he fulfilled various official duties at the command of his sovereign, Christian IV. He became actively interested in the arctic whale fisheries, in view of the profits that could be made, and was the first to introduce whaling as an industry to Denmark.

In 1619 Munk was instructed by Christian IV to make a voyage in search of the northwest passage to India. Munk chose two navy vessels, the *Enhiörningen* (Unicorn or Narwhal), a small frigate, and the *Lamprenen* (Lamprey), a sloop, which were outfitted under his own supervision. He set out in May 1619, sailing north of the Shetlands, past the Faeroes, and west towards Greenland. He sighted Kap Farvel (Cape Farewell), 30 June, ten days after nearing Greenland. By 8 July he had sighted the western shore of Davis Strait, but was prevented from approaching land by ice and fog. When the weather cleared he sailed into Frobisher Bay thinking it was Hudson Strait. On discovering the error he sailed south until he was satisfied that the strait had been reached. Munk gave the name "Fretum Christian" to Hudson Strait. He perilously followed the north shore of the strait between the ice and the land. At a place called by Munk "Rinsund" he anchored and went ashore to talk to the natives, probably transient Eskimo, and to shoot reindeer. Munk took possession of this land in the name of Christian IV, setting up the king's arms and monogram brought for the purpose. After leaving Rinsund he was caught in the ice for six days. He explored a small cove, which he called "Haresund" 31 July, until the weather improved. There he found metalliferous rocks and talc. The position of Haresund is not precisely known.

Munk started out again 19 August to the WSW. His pilots thought they were in Hudson Bay, but Munk was not sure. Actually they were in Ungava Bay. After rectifying this mistake they made no more navigational errors. With adverse winds it took six days to regain the strait, and Hudson Bay was entered near Digges Island.

Munk called the whole of what is now known as Hudson Bay "Novum Mare Christian." At this time only the southern portion was known as "Hudson's Bay"; the western part was called Button's Bay. Munk's account of the bay is the first to treat the inland sea as a whole, and his map the first on which the whole of the bay is depicted.

On reaching Hudson Bay Munk sailed southwest to the western coast searching for a certain place—exactly what is not known, as there is no extant copy of his instructions. The crossing of the bay was without incident. Landfall was made at a spot later named Cape Churchill where Munk immediately sought shelter for his ships. The weather deteriorated shortly thereafter, it being early September, and Munk was forced to winter at Port Churchill in the estuary of the Churchill River, and planned to search for the passage the following spring. There is no mistaking the site as Munk's description is most explicit and, at a later date, relics of his stay were found. He called the estuary "Jens Muncke's Bay."

Munk was the first European to visit the area, though Button may have passed by in 1612 and 1613 without taking note of it. While wintering there Munk recorded various scientific observations and opinions such as the migrations of birds, an eclipse of the moon, parhelions, and his views on the origins of the icebergs he had seen in Davis and Hudson straits.

Munk encouraged his men to hunt and take exercise, but as the weather grew colder and the snow deeper they were confined to their ships. By January 1620 the men were beginning to succumb to scurvy. Though the ships had adequate stores of herbs, waters, and medicines, no one knew how to administer them. By March half the crew were dead, and by 4 June 61 had perished, leaving only Munk and two others, who were weakened by the disease. However, they recovered sufficiently to attempt a return to Europe in the sloop.

Munk's account of the homeward voyage is meagre. The course followed was much the same as that of the outward voyage. He reached Norway 21 Sept. and by 25 Dec. was again in Copenhagen. Munk was naturally disappointed in the failure of the expedition. He had not been prepared for the extreme cold—worse than he had experienced on his unsuccessful voyages to Novaya Zemlya (New Land). Also, he had planned to live off the land and so have fresh meat. He later made plans to return to the area with colonists to initiate the fur trade there. He made various preparations for this second voyage but it was postponed for several reasons.

The year 1623 saw him again sailing under King Christian's orders. In 1625 he was commissioned admiral and stationed on the Weser during the Thirty Years' War.

NORA T. CORLEY

Danish arctic expeditions (Gosch), II: *The expedition of Captain Jens Munk to Hudson's Bay in search of a north-west passage in 1619–20*, contains the most complete account of Jens Munk's life, together with a translation of his own account of his voyage, *Navigatio septentrionalis*, originally published in Copenhagen in 1624. The 2d ed., edited anonymously and published in 1723, includes a biography of Munk, which is believed to be extracted from his own journals. A 3d ed., consisting of an accurate reprint of the 1624 ed., was published in Copenhagen in 1883, with an Introduction and notes by P. Lauridsen, who included "some interesting additional information" found in the Danish State Archives. Munk's original, autographed MS, including most of the text, is the property of the University Library in Copenhagen. For a lively, modern account *see* Dodge, *Northwest by sea*, 144–53. Oleson, *Early voyages*, 171–72.

"THE MURDERER." *See* CHEROUOUNY

NEGABAMAT, NOËL, *dit* **Tekouerimat,** one of the principal Montagnais chiefs of Sillery; b. *c.* 1600; d. 19 March 1666.

Noël Negabamat's life is one of the best examples of the success of the policy of the French missionaries, who wanted both to convert the American Indians to Catholicism and to integrate them into the European way of living. When Father PAUL LE JEUNE founded a centre at Sillery where the nomadic tribes might settle down (1637), Negabamat, brother of the Montagnais chief CHOMINA and leader of a troop of Montagnais who had settled in the neighbourhood, asked permission to establish himself close to the Jesuits' residence. In the spring of the next year he and his followers settled permanently there with another chief, Negaskoumat. Around this nucleus of some 20 men the whole village was to develop. Negabamat, elegantly dressed in French fashion, was the first neophyte of importance in the colony; he presented himself for baptism at Quebec on 8 Dec. 1638. He adopted the name of Noël in honour of M. de Sillery. His wife decided to call herself Marie.

From that time on the friends and enemies of France were those of Negabamat. In 1645 he took an active part in the preliminary peace negotiations between the French, the Hurons, and the Algonkins on the one hand, and the Iroquois on the other. When the war began again three years later, he set out for Trois-Rivières with his men to bring help to his allies. In 1646 he exerted his powerful influence on the Abenakis to induce them to ask for a missionary. Father Gabriel DRUILLETTES was chosen, and Negabamat went with him as an ambassador. In 1650 he rendered the same service, and followed the Jesuit to Boston and Plymouth, in order to persuade the Sokokis, the Penacooks, and the Mahicans to join the French. Negabamat composed a very interesting account of this journey and sent it to France to his old friend, Father Paul Le Jeune, who sent him in return a magnificent robe woven with gold thread.

Meanwhile, in the winter of 1647–48, he set out once more with Father Druillettes to visit the small tribes of the lower St. Lawrence. There he negotiated a treaty with the Algonkin chief Étouat, and received as his share of the transaction the right to hunt in the richest game region near Tadoussac.

The French conferred several great honours upon Negabamat. He carried the canopy during the Corpus Christi procession at Quebec. In 1665, as "the oldest of the Christians," he also had a place of distinction at the great ceremonies that marked the arrival of M. de PROUVILLE de Tracy at Quebec.

The *Jesuit Relations* speak of Negabamat with nothing but praise. There one reads that he was handsome, well built, a powerful orator, intelligent, an exemplary Christian. Mother Marie de l'Incarnation [*see* GUYART] says that he was a true saint, and his own people wondered whether he did not want to become a Jesuit. In any case, he always exercised a great influence over his own kind, and was a constant friend to the French cause. "I am growing old, but the faith is not growing old in me," he declared in 1652, adding, apparently without nostalgia: "I am almost entirely French."

J. MONET

Marie Guyart de l'Incarnation, *Écrits* (Jamet), III, 376. *JR* (Thwaites), XXXVIII, 64; LII, 222; *et passim*. Léon Pouliot, *Étude sur les Relations des Jésuites*, 69, 173–76.

NICOLLET DE BELLEBORNE, JEAN, interpreter and clerk of the Compagnie des Cent-Associés, liaison officer between the French and the Indians, explorer; b. *c.* 1598, probably at Cherbourg (Normandy), son of Thomas Nicollet, king's postal courier between Cherbourg and Paris, and of Marie de Lamer; drowned 27 Oct. 1642 at Sillery.

Nicollet arrived in Canada in 1618, in the service of the Compagnie des Marchands de Rouen et de Saint-Malo. Like MARSOLET and BRÛLÉ, he was intended to live among the Indian allies in order to learn their language and customs and explore the regions they inhabited. Nothing is known of his education or temperament, except this remark of Father VIMONT in 1643: "his disposition and his excellent memory led one to expect worthwhile things of him."

CHAMPLAIN, at the time of his explorations, had established relations with the Algonkins in the upper reaches of the Ottawa (Outaouais) River. It is presumed that, in his desire to strengthen the alliance that was only just taking shape, it was Champlain who instructed Nicollet, the year he arrived, to go and spend the winter on Allumette Island. This place was the rallying-point of the great Algonkin family commanded by TESSOUAT (d. 1636). The island was located at a strategic spot on the Ottawa River, the fur-trade route. It was important, for the sake of trade, that the tribes living on the shores of the Ottawa should be friendly with the French. Nicollet stayed two years at Allumette Island, and carried out his mission very well. He learned the Huron and

Nicollet de Belleborne

Algonkin languages, lived the precarious existence of the natives, came to know their customs, and explored the region. They were not long in accepting him as one of their own. They made him a chief, allowed him to attend their councils, and even took him among the Iroquois to negotiate a peace treaty.

Nicollet returned to Quebec in 1620. He made a report on his mission and was given another: to make contact with the Nipissings who lived on the shores of the lake of the same name. These Indians were each year assuming a more important role in the fur trade, acting as intermediaries between the French and the Indian tribes of the west and of Hudson Bay. It was Nicollet's task to consolidate their alliance with the French, and to see that their furs did not find their way to Hudson Bay.

In the summer of 1620, Nicollet went to the country of the Nipissings. For nine years he was to live among them. He had his own lodge and a store. By day he traded with the Indians of the various tribes that were on their way to the shores of Lake Nipissing, and questioned them about their country; at night he noted down what he had gleaned. These "mémoires" of Nicollet, unfortunately lost today, have come to us indirectly through the *Relations*. Father PAUL LE JEUNE, who was able to consult them, drew upon them in order to describe the customs of the Indians in that region.

When Quebec was captured by the English in 1629, Nicollet, who was loyal to France, took refuge in the Huron country. He thwarted all the English plans to get the Indians to trade with them.

Nicollet appeared at Trois-Rivières and Quebec in 1633. He asked permission to set himself up at Trois-Rivières as a clerk of the Compagnie des Cent-Associés, and his wish was readily granted. Before taking up his new duties, however, he was requested, no doubt by Champlain, to undertake a voyage of exploration and pacification among the *Gens de Mer*, also called Puants, Ounipigons or Winnebagoes. These Indians lived at the far end of Green Bay (Baie des Puants), surrounded by Algonkin tribes with whom their relationship was somewhat cool, where the fur trade was concerned. An alliance between the *Gens de Mer* and the Dutch of the Hudson River region was to be feared. It was necessary to restore peace as soon as possible in this area. Nicollet was also supposed to use the trip to check the information that he had gathered concerning the China Sea, which according to the Indians was near to Green Bay. Nicollet therefore provided himself, before his departure, with a robe of Chinese damask, liberally strewn with flowers and multicoloured birds.

Nicollet set out in the summer of 1634, probably in mid-July. He followed the traditional Ottawa River route, branched off at Allumette Island in the direction of Lake Nipissing, then went down the French River (Rivière des Français) to get to Lake Huron. On the way he recruited an escort of seven Hurons. He headed for Michilimackinac, entered Lake Michigan, and reached Green Bay. Attired in his damask robe, he momentarily struck terror into the Winnebagoes, who took him for a god. He assembled 4,000 or 5,000 men, grouping together the different tribes of the region, and, while smoking their long-stemmed pipes, they concluded a peace.

Nicollet had attained the first objective of his journey. Unfortunately, he had not found the China Sea. In a fruitless attempt to do so, he went down the Fox River (Rivière aux Renards) as far as the village of Mascoutens, three days' distance from the Wisconsin River, a tributary of the Mississippi. A thrust southward, towards the Illinois River, was scarcely more rewarding. Probably disappointed by the incomplete success of his mission, he returned to Quebec in the autumn of 1635. It is none the less true that he was the first white man to explore the region now known as the American Northwest.

Nicollet settled finally at Trois-Rivières, as a clerk of the Compagnie des Cent-Associés. He received, "in common with Olivier LETARDIF, a grant of 160 acres of wooded land in the outskirts, 23 May 1637." It may have been at the same period that he obtained, in co-ownership with his brother-in-law Letardif, the Belleborne fief, which was probably on the Plains of Abraham, at Quebec. In October 1637 he married Marguerite, daughter of GUILLAUME COUILLARD and GUILLEMETTE HÉBERT, by whom he had a son and a daughter. The latter, whose first name was Marguerite, became the wife of Jean-Baptiste Legardeur* de Repentigny, a member of the Conseil Souverain. Until his death, Nicollet stood out as a leading figure in the little town of Trois-Rivières. The noteworthy services that he rendered to the colony, and his knowledge of Indian languages and customs, earned him the respect of everyone.

The *Jesuit Relations* often speak warmly of his exemplary conduct; unlike the majority of the *coureurs de bois* of his day, Nicollet appears always to have lived according to the principles of his religion. In 1628, however, he did have an illegitimate daughter, probably born of a Nipissing Indian woman. In 1633 he asked permission to stay at Trois-Rivières, "to assure his salvation," wrote Father Le Jeune, "by the use of the sacraments." His greatest joy, in the spare moments that his duties allowed him, was to act as an interpreter for the missionaries and to teach religion to the Indians.

Nicollet died prematurely in 1642 at Quebec. While he was temporarily replacing the head clerk of the company, his brother-in-law Letardif, he was asked to go with all speed to Trois-Rivières to save an Iroquois prisoner that the Hurons were preparing to torture. The shallop that was taking him to Trois-Rivières was overturned by a strong gust of wind, near Sillery. Being unable to swim, he was drowned.

JEAN HAMELIN

ASQ, Documents Faribault, 7; Registre A, 560f. (carries Nicollet's signature). Champlain, *Œuvres* (Laverdière), V, VI. *JR* (Thwaites), VIII, 247, 257, 267, 295f.; XXIII, 274–82; *et passim*.

C. W. Butterfield, *History of the discovery of the north-west by John Nicolet in 1634, with a sketch of his life* (Cincinnati, 1881). Godbout, *Les pionniers de la région trifluvienne*. Auguste Gosselin, *Jean Nicolet et le Canada de son temps* (Québec, 1905). Lionel Groulx, *Notre grande aventure: l'empire français en Amérique du Nord (1535–1760)* (Montréal et Paris, [1958]). Gérard Hébert, "Jean Nicolet, le premier blanc à résider au lac Nipissing" (La Société historique du Nouvel-Ontario, *Documents historiques*, XIII, Sudbury, 1947), 8–24. Henri Jouan, "Jean Nicolet (de Cherbourg), interprète-voyageur au Canada, 1618–1642," *RC*, XXII (1886), 67–83. Benjamin Sulte, "Jean Nicolet," *Journal de l'Instruction publique*, XVII (1873), 166f.: XVIII (1874), 28–32; "Jean Nicolet et la découverte du Wisconsin, 1634," *RC*, VI (1910), 148–55, 331–42, 409–20; "Le nom de Nicolet," *BRH*, VII (1901), 21–23; "Notes on Jean Nicolet" (Wisconsin Hist. Soc. *Coll.*, VIII, Madison, 1879), 188–94.

NIXON, JOHN, governor of HBC settlements 1679–83; b. *c.* 1623; d. in Carolina, 1692; nothing is known of his parentage.

Nixon was appointed governor in succession to Charles BAYLY and sailed from London in the *John and Alexander* (Capt. NEHEMIAH WALKER), on 23 May 1679. At the time of his arrival in Hudson Bay, the HBC occupied Moose Factory, Charles Fort in Rupert East River, and probably Albany, which Nixon later strengthened. His governorship was not marked by notable new settlements; though directed to occupy Port Nelson and New Severn, there is no proof that he did so. His main achievement (which proved short-lived) was the occupation of Charlton Island and the construction of buildings there. Nixon recommended a policy of expansion—the establishment of forts in the interior as well as the sending of men inland to induce the Indians to visit the Bayside—and he understood the necessity of pacifying warlike tribes if trade were to flourish. But he does not appear to have done anything himself to further these aims. Consolidation and attention to the details of business were the chief preoccupations of his governorship.

This assessment is suggested by Nixon's letter of 1682, the only governor's dispatch from Hudson Bay to survive from the 17th century and "the first detailed and substantial account of conditions by the Bay" (HBRS, XXI (Rich), 111). His concern was to check the spirit of lawlessness which he found amongst the Company's servants, fomented by crews of hired ships wintering in the Bay. The Company's policy at this time was to use Charlton Island as a magazine at which "great ships" from England could discharge cargoes and take on furs for the return voyage, the trading posts being supplied by sloops. Nixon argued cogently against this policy: Charlton Island, in his opinion, was remote from trade, difficult to defend, and ice-bound longer than the mainland. Nixon also criticized forthrightly the supply of trade goods and tradesmen. He wrote of "the heap of unventable goods which ly spoylling on oure hands . . . if wee had the prime coast of them and their fraught, layed out in ould sherie it would goe off better to oure comfort . . ."

Nixon's early years in the bay were undisturbed by active French competition. Plans to enter the maritime fur trade were being laid but did not mature until 1682. In that year the HBC sent John BRIDGAR, with a command independent of Nixon, to settle at Nelson River. At the same time Radisson* and CHOUART Des Groseilliers were leading a French expedition to Hayes River. These events and Bridgar's defeat and capture in 1683 seem to have taken place without Nixon's participation. His dispatch of 1682 does not dwell at length on the French menace, showing more awareness of the dangers of mutiny and Indian attack.

Nixon, it must be admitted, left few obvious marks on the Company's history in Hudson Bay. Some noise was made by his lowering of the standard of trade laid down by Governor Bayly: he not only reduced the number of beaver skins accepted for English trade goods but also lowered the equivalent of beaver in terms of other furs. His intentions in this do not appear. There is, however, no reason to question his honesty or loyalty in the Company's service. Returns in beaver during his governorship were 24,123 in 1681, 18,600 in 1682 and 20,355 in 1683, the proceeds of sales in London being well above the average in Governor Bayly's time. If it would be rash to give Nixon all the credit for this improvement, it is difficult to see who else (in the bay) was responsible. His own claim "I spend many hours (when others take their quiet rests,) to consider of what is most needfull to be doone" need not be doubted.

The decision to replace Nixon was taken on 31 Jan. 1683 and on 27 April following the Committee wrote recalling him "in regard of your great age and disability to travaile & endure the Hardship which the place you have for severall yeares held under us doe require." Nixon handed over to Henry SERGEANT on 27 Aug. 1683. Back in London, he had to wait some time for the settlement of his account. His commencing salary had been £100 a year, raised in 1680 to £200: a large part was still due on his return. At a number of meetings in June 1684 the Committee debated his case and whether a governor had power to alter the standard. Eventually, with the deputy governor dissenting, it was resolved to pay the balance of £305. After 1685 no reference to Nixon has been found in the HBC archives.

Modern historians have been hard on Nixon. E. E. Rich describes him as "a tetchy fellow," A. S. Morton calls him "a disappointment," while to Sir George Clark he was "sanctimonious" and to E. G. R. Taylor "a man of dour, puritanical habit." Certainly Nixon's letter contains some melancholy asides ("O Lord how hath the Northwest been corrupted"). It is also true that he condemned drunkenness. But he made no secret of his own partiality for liquor. "Water doeth not agree with me," he wrote, indenting for wine and brandy for his own use; and he refers more than once to the necessity of strong drink for the men. His remarks on "licentiousness" (which seem to have inspired Professor Taylor's verdict) refer not specifically to the common practice of keeping Indian women at the posts but to the general indiscipline of the company's servants.

Something of the man emerges from his long dispatch of 1682. He found difficulty in imposing himself on others by force of character, and so was unduly dependent on his status and commission as governor. In his clashes with Capt. Walker, both on the voyage out in 1679 and in the winter of 1681–82 on Charlton Island, Nixon on his own showing was the loser. The best he could do was to maintain a dignified silence and pretend to be superior to Walker's drunken antics and ridiculous behaviour. Apprehensive of mutiny, Nixon advised the Company to enlarge the governor's authority to enable him to inflict corporal punishment and he recommended the engagement of Scotsmen who would be not only hardier and cheaper but also more obedient. From his subordinates he expected the worst and he wrote feelingly of his own position "between two rocks": efforts to keep good order in accordance with his instructions led to complaints against him which might prejudice the Committee. Yet to buy the goodwill of his men, he thought "not worth three skips of a louse." Complaints there certainly were. In 1682 the Committee wrote to Nixon that most of the men who had returned to England the previous year reported that he carried himself with "tomuch inhumanity and cruelty towards the Natives." He was warned to take care that "the morossness of your temper turne not to the prejudice of our affaires."

Very little has been discovered of Nixon's life apart from his connection with the HBC. He himself stated that he had been in the East Indies but search in the records of the East India Company has been fruitless. There is, however, a strong case for identifying him with John Nixon of Carolina. In the first place, we know that Nixon came into the HBC at the instance of the Earl of Shaftesbury and Sir Peter Colleton, both Lords Proprietors of Carolina. In 1677 John Nixon was deputy to Colleton in Carolina. Secondly, and more conclusively, Nixon's will is extant in North Carolina: the upright, angular signature on this document is beyond doubt the same as the two signatures at the end of Nixon's dispatch of 1682.

Granted this identification, we still do not know a great deal about Nixon's life in America. He was presumably the "Mr Nixon" mentioned by John Locke in connection with Acts of Assembly of Albemarle County, Carolina, in 1669–70 (*CSP, Col., 1669–74*, no. 142); in 1673 he was a magistrate and in 1675 a member of the "Court of Albemarle" (Essex Institute, *Historical Collections*, II (1860), pp. 129–30). When the Culpeper rebellion broke out in Carolina in 1677 Nixon, with Thomas Miller, Shaftesbury's deputy, was imprisoned by the rebels (who included Capt. Zachariah GILLAM, later drowned in Hudson Bay during Nixon's residence there). In 1679 Miller was tried in Carolina for seditious words and blasphemy alleged to have been spoken in November 1675. Nixon's deposition in this case gives his age as 54. The deposition is undated, so that the year of Nixon's birth may have been any between 1621 and 1625. He must have been about 60 in 1683 when he was relieved of office on grounds of "great age." In his will, dated 4 Feb. 1687/88, he left three-quarters of his estate to his

Noël

wife Em, the remaining quarter to his daughter Ann at age 18 or on marriage. This is presumably the daughter for whose maintenance he appointed attorneys while in Hudson Bay: Em Nixon may, therefore, be a second or subsequent wife. Nixon's will was proved on 8 Aug. 1692.

K. G. DAVIES

A summary of Nixon's career in the HBC is in HBRS, IX (Rich), 331–33. This volume and vols. VIII and XI of the HBRS publications contain many references to him. His dispatch of 1682 is preserved at the Royal Soc., London (Boyle Papers, Misc., XL); there is a photostatic copy in the archives of the HBC, London, and the document is printed in HBRS, IX; Nixon's signatures are at pp. 49 and 52 of the MS. The Boyle Papers (Science, XXI) also contain Nixon's impressions of ice in Hudson Bay and an estimate of the magnetic variation of Charlton Island. HBRS, XXI (Rich), chap. IX, relates Nixon's governorship to the history of the company and the bay. Nixon's will is in North Carolina, State Department of Archives and History, North Carolina Wills, 1663–1789, XXII, 59; a photostatic copy has been placed in the HBC archives so that the signature may be compared with those of the Royal Soc. MS. References to Nixon's life in Carolina are in *The Colonial Records of North Carolina*, ed. W. L. Saunders (10v., Raleigh, N.C., 1886–90), I.

NOËL (Nouel), JACQUES, nephew of Jacques CARTIER and half-brother of Étienne Noël, explorer and trader.

Two nephews of Jacques Cartier took part in the exploration of the St. Lawrence: Étienne and Jacques Noël. Étienne, a son of Jean Noël and Jeanne Cartier (the discoverer's sister), is believed to have sailed on the voyage in 1535, if the provisional muster-roll of 31 March 1535 can be relied upon; in any event he took part in the 1541 voyage. He arrived 23 August and already by 2 September he was on his way back to France with Macé JALOBERT, both of them being described in the narration as excellent pilots.

Even though certain historians may call him a great-nephew of Cartier and give 1551 (which is much too late) as his year of birth, Jacques Noël was a nephew of the famous native of Saint-Malo, as is asserted by the 16th-century documents; he is believed to have been born of Jean Noël's second marriage, which would make him a half-brother of Étienne. Jacques Noël, who owned a chart by Cartier and had himself made a sketch, knew Canada well from having been there in 1585 at least; he had seen the ruins of his uncle's forts, had gone as far as the rapids of Hochelaga (Montreal), and had climbed Mount Royal to try to see what lay beyond the horizon. During the voyage he had brought back to France an Indian who subsequently returned to his own country.

In 1587 Jacques Noël's two sons, Jean and Michel, sailed into the St. Lawrence, where they lost four luggers in the course of a battle between rival traders.

As a result of this expedition Jacques Noël asked for the monopoly of the mines and the fur trade; he was at that time in partnership with Étienne Chaton de La Jannaye, a sea captain who had distinguished himself at La Rochelle and in Brittany, but who had never been to Canada. Alleging that Cartier had recommended to him "the continuation of his enterprise," Noël pointed to his past experience and undertook to build forts and settle the country if his request were favourably received. In conferring the monopoly 12 Jan. 1588 Henri III declared that the commission granted to Cartier 17 Oct. 1540 would have the same effect as if Noël and La Jannaye were named in it; he authorized the handing-over to them of 60 prisoners for Canada each year.

The following month the bourgeois of Saint-Malo, and after them the states of the province of Brittany, contested this privilege: to their mind La Jannaye could in no way make use of the name of Cartier; as for Noël, they said, he was exaggerating his previous role; he was Cartier's heir only "in very small part," and the country was "not at all fertile"; finally, the bourgeois preferred not to ask for the monopoly for themselves, as they would have to build and keep up forts. The inhabitants of Saint-Malo in 1588 wanted to profit from the St. Lawrence without the expenses of colonization. However, Henri III revoked his decision. By 9 July Noël and La Jannaye no longer held anything but the right to exploit the mines that they might discover. They waived their right, and thus ended the last activity by the Cartier family in the St. Lawrence. This dispute in 1588 was also the first episode in a long conflict which was to oppose the partisans of trade to the partisans of colonization. For the first time the historic dilemma arose: colonization sustained by an exclusive monopoly, or freedom of trade and no colony. In 1588 the partisans of trade had won out and the scheme for colonization advanced by Cartier's nephew was not followed up.

MARCEL TRUDEL

Biggar, *Documents relating to Cartier and Roberval*, 53–56. *Jacques Cartier, documents nouveaux*, éd. F. Joüon Des Longrais (Paris, 1888), 131, 145–48, 152–58, 160. Alfred Ramé, *Documents inédits sur le Canada* (Paris, 1865), 24–51. *Voyages of Jacques Cartier* (Biggar), 251–53, 313ff., App. VI. N.-E. Dionne, *La Nouvelle-France, de Cartier à Champlain, 1540–1603* (Québec, 1891), 124f.

NORMANVILLE, THOMAS GODEFROY DE. *See* GODEFROY

NOUË, ANNE DE, officer of the Privy Chamber, then priest, Jesuit, missionary; b. 7 Aug. 1587 near Rheims; frozen to death 1 or 2 Feb. 1646 on the St. Lawrence, near Sorel.

Descendant of a noble family, Anne de Noue spent several years at the court of Henri IV, where M. de La Vieuville had taken him into his service as a page. He was called "the handsome page." Later he was an officer of the Privy Chamber. In September 1612 he entered the noviciate house of the Jesuits of Paris; he studied at Paris, where he acted as prefect—or supervisor of studies—during his theological courses (1618–22), and then at La Flèche and Nevers. After two years as minister of the Collège in Bourges (1622–24), he came to Canada in 1626. He spent the winter in the Huron country with Father de BRÉBEUF, then went to stay with the Montagnais, but although he was a keenly intelligent man, he was unable either to learn the Indians' languages or to become accustomed to their kind of life. On the other hand he was a skilful fisherman, which enabled him to feed the community and its friends during the dire period of 1627–28 at Quebec.

Back in France 1629–32, he was minister of the colleges of Amiens and Orléans, and then returned to Canada to look after the numerous workmen at the residence in Quebec. He stayed there until 1642, in which year he left for Trois-Rivières. During the winter of 1646 he set out to administer the sacraments to the soldiers of the garrison at Sorel. He lost his way in a blizzard. Six miles up-stream from Sorel his body was found, in a kneeling position, bare-headed, his eyes turned towards heaven. He was buried at Trois-Rivières.

J. MONET

ACSM, ff.38, 4015; MS biography based on the old Jesuit catalogues, and "Mémoires touchant la mort et les vertus des pères Isaac Jogues . . ." (Ragueneau), repr. APQ *Rapport, 1924–25,* 41–51. *JR* (Thwaites), IV, 266. *Positio causae.* Campbell, *Pioneer priests,* II, 187–93. A. M. Pope, "The first martyr of the Canadian mission," *Canadian Register and Canadian Extension* (now *Canadian Register*), Toronto, 3 Mar. 1921. Rochemonteix, *Les Jésuites et la Nouvelle-France au XVIIe siècle,* I, 158.

NOUEL. *See* NOËL

NOYROT, PHILIBERT, Jesuit; b. October 1592 near Autun (France); drowned 24 Aug. 1629 in a shipwreck near the Strait of Canso.

Philibert Noyrot entered the Society of Jesus 16 Oct. 1617 in Paris, and upon finishing his theological studies in Bourges he was appointed treasurer of the college there. During his stay in Bourges he became renowned for his lessons in the catechism to the children and the poor; he was called "the children's Father." In 1624 he became confessor to Henri de Lévis, Duc de Ventadour, who on his advice purchased the viceroyalty of New France the following year and asked the Recollets of Canada to give the Jesuits a part in their missionary efforts.

In 1626 Father Noyrot himself left for Quebec, where he arrived in July with 20 workmen ready to begin building a residence for the Jesuits. But his superior, Father CHARLES LALEMANT, immediately sent him back to Paris to try to bring about the revocation of the monopoly which was held by the Huguenots of the Compagnie de Montmorency. Father Noyrot therefore had an audience with Richelieu and, thanks to the intervention of his former penitent, the Duc de Ventadour, he obtained from the cardinal, at the time of the founding of the Compagnie des Cent-Associés (1627), the revocation of the application to New France of the Edict of Nantes. It would appear that it was also at Father Noyrot's suggestion that Ventadour resigned his viceregal office and that Antoinette de Pons, Marquise de Guercheville, gave up her rights to Acadia.

In 1627 Father Noyrot took steps to have a shipload of provisions sent to Canada, but his attempt failed when the ship was seized at Honfleur by GUILLAUME DE CAËN and Raymond de LA RALDE. In 1628 Noyrot himself fitted out another ship with enough provisions to succour the missions for a year and left La Rochelle with ROQUEMONT's expedition. When the KIRKES stopped them in the Gulf of St. Lawrence, taking Roquemont prisoner, Father Noyrot succeeded in escaping and sailing his ship back to France. In 1629 he set out a third time in a convoy made up of four ships and a bark, under the command of Captain CHARLES DANIEL. But a violent gale near Cape Breton Island sent to the bottom the ship that he himself had chartered, and Father Noyrot was drowned, along with 14 members of the crew.

According to his contemporaries, Father Noyrot was indefatigable and a man of sound common sense, even though he expressed himself with difficulty.

J. MONET

ACSM, MS biography based on the old Jesuit catalogues: Étude sur les Relations des Jésuites, by Félix Martin (*see also* ASQ, MSS, 43, pp. 141–56); two unpublished articles: Lucien Campeau, "Les Récollets ont-ils appelé les Jésuites?" and Euclide Gervais, "Le Père Philibert Noyrot." Champlain,

Nutt

Œuvres (Laverdière), II, 1107–8, *et passim*. *JR* (Thwaites), IV, 267; LXXI, 138. Sagard, *Histoire du Canada* (Tross).

Jésuites de la N.-F. (Roustang). Lanctot, *Histoire du Canada*, I, 174. Sixte Le Tac, *Histoire chronologique de la Nouvelle France ou Canada, depuis sa découverte (mil cinq cents quatre) jusques en l'an mil six cents trente-deux*, éd. Eugène Réveillaud (Paris, 1888). Rochemonteix, *Les Jésuites et la Nouvelle-France au XVIIe siècle*, I, 145.

NUTT, JOHN, Newfoundland pirate; fl. 1620–32.

Nutt, a native of Lympstone, Devon, and a gunner on a Dartmouth vessel, went in 1620 to Newfoundland, where he and other seamen seized a French ship and turned pirates. They then took a large Plymouth ship and another "Fleming" vessel of 200 tons. After plundering the fishing fleet, Nutt sailed for England.

He seems to have been a humane man, for a pirate: he had a wife and children at Torbay; he gave his crew good wages and paid them regularly; and when royal orders came to Sir John Eliot, vice-admiral of Devon, to press seamen for the navy, Nutt warned the sailors, hundreds of whom fled to Newfoundland.

Nutt was "in his third year" of piracy when he wrote, in May 1623, from his "man-of-war" at Torbay to Eliot, who had been ordered to arrest him, offering £300 in return for a pardon. Nutt later agreed to pay £500; but when he landed, his period of grace had run out and he was arrested by Eliot, who was about to hang him. However, Sir George CALVERT, later Lord Baltimore, intervened. A letter, written in August, by Calvert, the secretary of state, reveals that he had granted Nutt one pardon and would be glad to secure him another, "wherein I have no other end but to be grateful to a poor man that hath been ready to do me & my associates courtesies in a plantation which we have begun in Newfoundland, by defending us from others which perhaps in the infancy of that work might have done us wrong." With the pardon, Nutt received £100 as compensation and Eliot was put in prison.

After receiving his pardon in 1623, John Nutt appears to have remained within the law. As master of various ships he received letters of marque against the French during the war with France. But some doubts as to the firmness of his conversion from piracy remained in 1632: when the king pardoned John's brother, Robert Nutt, in that year and commissioned captains Thomas Ketelby and John Nutt to deliver the pardon, the fear was expressed that John might take the opportunity to join his brother.

Thomas DUNBABIN

PRO, *CSP, Dom., 1619–23; 1623–25; 1628–29; 1629–31; 1631–33*. John Forster, *Sir John Eliot: a biography* (2d ed., 2v., London, 1872), I, 24–43.

O

OAGIMONT. *See* OUAGIMOU

OCHILTREE, SIR JAMES STEWART, fourth Lord. *See* STEWART

OGENHERATARIHIENS (also occurs as **Ogeratarihen** ("Cendre Chaude" meaning "Hot Ash" or "Poudre Chaude" meaning "Hot Powder" in Iroquois), **Garonhiagué** ("In-the-Sky" or "Celestial"), and **Garohiaé**), **LOUIS,** an Oneida chief according to La Poterie [Le Roy*], a Mohawk chieftain according to Father Charlevoix*; b. *c.* 1646 and killed 1687.

Charlevoix and La Poterie claimed that he had been one of Father BRÉBEUF's torturers. Cendre Chaude was born too late for this to have been possible.

In his village Ogenheratarihiens had married Marie Garhio (Garhi), an Indian girl. In 1676, with her and her entire family, Cendre Chaude received baptism at the Saint-François-Xavier mission at the Saint-Louis Rapids, which had been moved from Prairie-de-la-Magdelaine. He was soon chosen to be the fourth chief of the village, and not later than 1683 he became the first.

A great orator, Cendre Chaude fought effectively against lewdness and drunkenness in the mission. He won over a good number of Oneidas to his cause and extended his influence as far as the Five Nations. In 1677, for example, he joined Kateri TEKAKWITHA's brother-in-law and a Huron from Lorette for a missionary trip to the Mohawks. That same year he brought Kateri from Gandaouagué (Fonda, N.Y.) to the Saint-François-Xavier mission.

In 1683, in his role as chief, he declared his attachment to the French when the question of war with the pagan Iroquois came up. He even undertook a diplomatic mission to the enemy. Subsequently the Oneidas invited him to go to govern their canton, and to do so without giving up his faith. He preferred to stay at Saint-François-Xavier, in order to remain a good Christian.

In 1684, unlike the other Christian chiefs, Cendre Chaude refused to take part in Governor LE FEBVRE de La Barre's expedition to La Famine. When Governor Brisay* de Denonville assumed the reins of government, Cendre Chaude was among the first to recognize his authority. During his campaign against the Senecas, Cendre Chaude and two other Christian Iroquois were killed 14 July 1687. "Few missionaries," wrote Father Charlevoix, "won over to God as many unbelievers as he did."

HENRI BÉCHARD

Charlevoix, *Histoire*, I. *JR* (Thwaites), LXI, 56–60; LXIII, 196. La Pot(h)erie, *Histoire*, I, 347, 349f., 355. *The Positio on Katharine Tekakwitha. Positio super virtutibus servae Dei, Catherinae Tekakwitha.*

OGERATARIHEN. See OGENHERATARIHIENS

OIONHATON, THÉRÈSE, Huron girl better known by her Christian name, niece (Du Creux states daughter) of the celebrated convert, Joseph CHIWATENHA, seemingly a resident of Ossossané, educated by the Ursulines at Quebec; fl. 1628–55.

Oionhaton was the innocent victim of the interminable strife between the Iroquois and New France. The exact date of her birth is not known, but in 1642 she is mentioned as being 13 or 14 years old. In 1640 her uncle, Joseph Teondechoren, brother of Chiwatenha, placed her in the care of Marie de l'Incarnation [see GUYART] and the Ursuline nuns at Quebec, to carry out the wishes of Chiwatenha, who had been slain by the Iroquois during the same year.

Little Oionhaton endeavoured to conform with the religious practices of the nuns and even spoke to visiting Hurons about religion. After living at Quebec for two years, Oionhaton was provided with everything necessary for her marriage and in 1642 started on her return journey to the Huron country. The convoy in which she was to travel included some of the most courageous and renowned warriors of Huronia: AHATSISTARI, TOTIRI, Tsondatsaa, and two of her uncles, one of whom was Teondechoren. With it were three Frenchmen: Father Isaac JOGUES, René GOUPIL, and Guillaume Couture*. At Trois-Rivières, Oionhaton wrote in Huron a short and touching letter of thanks to the Mother Superior (her Indian relatives marvelled to see her read and write) and entrusted the letter to the care of Father Joseph Du Peron.

Within two days of their departure, the travellers were attacked by a war-party of Mohawks, while still on the St. Lawrence River. The survivors were taken as captives into the Mohawk country. Oionhaton "was taken prisoner by the Hiroquois with her parents," states the Jesuit *Relation* for 1642. Other references to the same episode mention only the uncles of Oionhaton. The captives received "almost as many blows as there were Iroquois" but two young children and Oionhaton were not injured.

The French made repeated efforts to secure the release of Oionhaton from the Mohawks during the critical peace negotiations of 1645 [see KIOTSEAETON]. Throughout her captivity she was steadfast in her faith and told her beads on her fingers. Father Jogues, who went with JEAN BOURDON to the Mohawk country 18 May 1646, as ambassadors for the French, encountered Oionhaton among some Iroquois fishermen, spoke with her, questioned her, and instructed her. "Jogues encouraged her to hope for deliverance, telling her that for the sake of the Ursulines at Quebec Montmagny [see HUAULT] was doing everything possible, and that the Algonquins were doing what they could to secure her freedom. He promised to speak to the Annierronons [Mohawks] himself at the first opportunity; meantime he told her to trust in God." Later the priest presented 5,000 wampum beads to the Mohawks for Oionhaton's freedom (she had been given in marriage by the Mohawks to an Onondaga). The Mohawks declared themselves willing to release her as soon as she should return to their country, offering 1,500 wampum beads as a pledge of good faith.

In 1654 Father SIMON LE MOYNE found Oionhaton living in a cabin apart from the Onondaga village, where she reared her family in peace. In the fall of 1655, she travelled with a baby in her arms three leagues from her home to await the arrival of the "Black Robes." This last reference to Oionhaton is given by fathers CHAUMONOT and DABLON on the occasion of their journey from Quebec to Onondaga.

The day after their meeting with Oionhaton, the missionaries also met her sister, a prisoner among the Onondagas. Her name is not recorded nor are the circumstances of her capture. There is a reference in the *Relation* of 1652–53 to a sister of Oionhaton, who, at that time, was living as a young widow in the house of the Ursuline nuns at Quebec. There is a possibility, however, that Cécile and Agathe may be the names of these two sisters, since Du Creux mentions them at one time as the nieces of Joseph Chiwatenha and at another states that Chiwatenha was the father of Oionhaton.

THOMAS GRASSMANN

Du Creux, *History* (Conacher), I, 252, 335; II, 436, 439, 668, 707–8. Marie Guyart de l'Incarnation,

Olivier

Écrits (Jamet), III, 289. *JR* (Thwaites), XV, 77, 89–91; XXI, 147, 149, 155; XXII, 189, 193, 195, 197; XXIII, 297; XXIV, 281; XXVI, 191; XXVII, 287; XXVIII, 297–99; XXIX, 53–55; XL, 225; XLI, 103; XLII, 81.

OLIVIER. *See* LE JEUNE, OLIVIER

OLIVIER *dit* le Picard, MARC-ANTOINE, gold- and silversmith and soldier; fl. 1688–96.

A native of the region of Beauvais, Marc-Antoine Olivier probably served his apprenticeship under a master goldsmith in Amiens. In 1688 he enlisted in the company of fusiliers which François de Gallifet* raised in Picardy for service in New France—whence his surname. Scarcely had they arrived in Canada when Gallifet and his 300 men went to Montreal, the crucial point for the defence of the territory against the Indians.

Marc-Antoine Olivier appears to have followed Gallifet in his moves. In 1689 he belonged first to the garrison of Trois-Rivières. At the time of the Lachine massacre (3 Aug. 1689), he was at Pointe-Saint-Charles. On 17 June 1690 he married at Pointe-aux-Trembles (near Montreal) a young girl of 13, Françoise Dardaine. In the marriage certificate he is called "a soldier in Galifé's company." One of his brothers-in-arms, Michel Senau *dit* La Viazère, was present at the ceremony and declared, as did Olivier himself, that he did not know how to sign his name. In a private contract, which has not been found, the parents-in-law gave their daughter Françoise a piece of land situated at Saint-Sulpice, near Montreal, for her dowry.

For the next three years we have no information about Olivier. Perhaps he went with Gallifet, who had been appointed town-major of Quebec in 1692. Upon the birth of his first child Marc-Antoine Olivier, described as a gold- and silversmith, was not present at the baptism which took place in Montreal on 3 Jan. 1695. That same year, on 10 October, he gave up his land at Saint-Sulpice, claiming that he was "incapable of farming it."

At the baptism of his second son Simon, born 29 Feb. 1696, the officiating priest added the remark: "The father did not sign, since he is in France for the time being." This is the last authentic reference to the Olivier family that we know of at present.

Several documents attest to Marc-Antoine's having been a gold- and silversmith by trade, but no work which can be attributed to him has yet been found.

GÉRARD MORISSET

AJM, Registre des baptêmes, mariages et sépultures, N.-D. de Montréal, 1690, 1694–96. É.-Z. Massicotte, "Orfèvres et bijoutiers du régime français," *BRH*, XXXVI (1930), 30–2.

ONDAAIONDIONT, CHARLES, Huron Indian, admirable Christian of long standing, head of an embassy to the Susquehannah Indians; fl. 1645–49.

What is known of Ondaaiondiont's life coincides with the fateful years immediately preceding the destruction of Huronia, which finally ended the Huron-Iroquois struggle. Early in 1647, two Susquehannah Indians, who had been sent as deputies by their chiefs, visited the Hurons in Canada. They stated that ambassadors should be sent to the Susquehannah chiefs if the Hurons found themselves too weak to oppose their enemies. In response to this invitation, on 13 April 1647, an embassy did leave Huronia for the Susquehannah country, with the Christian Ondaaiondiont at its head and including four additional Christian and four non-Christian Hurons. This was one of two embassies—the second was sent to the Onondagas [*see* ANNENRAES].

The Huron envoys under Ondaaiondiont reached the Susquehannah country at the beginning of June. Here Ondaaiondiont represented the Huron country as "The Land of Souls," a place where war and fear of enemies created havoc; where blood covered the country and the cabins contained only corpses. The Susquehannah chiefs lamented the misfortunes suffered by the Hurons, adding that these calamities must be averted. Councils were held and qualified messengers were sent to the Oneidas, Onondagas, Cayugas, and Senecas to seek peace between these nations and the Hurons. The Susquehannahs promised that if the Mohawks refused to participate in the proposed peace, they would renew the war which they had waged with them for some years past. Thus the Hurons were negotiating for peace with the Onondagas directly through Annenraes and indirectly through the Susquehannahs.

While still among the Susquehannahs, Ondaaiondiont extended his journey by three days to visit the settlements of the Dutch and Swedes, Europeans friendly to the Susquehannahs, who were respectively located on the east and west banks of the Delaware River, which demarcates the present states of New Jersey and Pennsylvania. It is not known, however, whether Ondaairondiont visited one or both of these colonies. The captain of the European settlement was surprised to hear Ondaaiondiont preach Christian doctine in an authoritative manner. During this visit, a vessel arrived with news that Father JOGUES had been killed by the Mohawks the previous year (1646). Two letters (one of which was lost en route) and a printed page torn out of a book were given to Ondaaiondiont to deliver to the Jesuits in Huronia.

Returning to the Susquehannah country, Ondaaiondiont learned that the deputies sent to the Iroquois had not yet returned. Anxious to report to his people the action taken by the Susquehannahs, he appointed one of his companions to stay in the Susquehannah country to witness what should transpire, and he himself set out with his entourage, 15 Aug. 1647, on the homeward journey. Suspecting a Seneca ambush, Ondaaiondiont made a detour which required 40 days travel instead of the usual 10 days needed to go from the Susquehannah country to the land of the Neutrals.

The Susquehannah proposals to the Oneidas, Onondagas, Cayugas, and Senecas ended in failure. The Hurons were attacked repeatedly by their enemies, in particular the Mohawks and Senecas, until, in 1649, their country was completely devastated. The exaggerated picture of Huron misery, given to the Susquehannahs by Ondaaiondiont in 1647, was now the reality. Ossossanë (La Conception, "The Believing Village") was destroyed during March 1649 and with it fell Charles Ondaaiondiont, killed by an arquebus shot.

THOMAS GRASSMANN

JR (Thwaites), XXX, 57–59; XXXIII, 129–33, 135; XXXIV, 217. "Report of Governor Johan Printz, 1647," in *Narratives of Pennsylvnaia* (Meyers), 120–29, in *Original narratives* (Jameson), and maps of New Belgium or New Netherland by Visscher, van der Donck, and others in *ibid.*, in *Narratives of New Netherland* (Jameson), and in other vols. of *Original narratives* (Jameson).

OREHAOUE. *See* OUREHOUARE

OTREOUTI (Hateouati, Hoteouate, Hotrehouati, Houtreouati, Oureouhat, Outreouhati, *dit* **"La Grande Gueule" ("Big Mouth"), "Grangular," or "Grangula"),** famous Onondaga chief and orator, often a deputy from his nation in peace negotiations between the Iroquois and the French; fl. 1659–88.

The renowned Onondaga orator and chief, Otreouti, appears during the complicated peace negotiations, 1653–67, between the French and the Iroquois in the critical years following the destruction of Huronia in 1649. Otreouti is first named in a French reply, 28 April 1659, to peace proposals made at Quebec by Oneida ambassadors, on behalf of their own tribe and of the Onondagas and Mohawks. "If Otrewati and his eight comrades had not fled," said the French spokesman, "I would have gone back with them to Onnontage [Onondaga]." This doubtless referred to Otreouti and the Onondaga prisoners who escaped 19 Oct. 1658, after breaking two iron bars in the windows of their Montreal jail.

In the summer of 1661, while Father SIMON LE MOYNE was at Onondaga negotiating for peace, Otreouti led 30 Onondagas against Montreal, in retaliation for the insult of having been imprisoned there. In the vicinity of Montreal, Otreouti and his followers surprised Father Jacques LE MAISTRE, a Sulpician, and other Frenchmen, who were working in a field of grain. They killed two, including Father Le Maistre, and took one captive. Father Le Maistre they decapitated and, putting on the priest's cassock, Otreouti strutted defiantly in full view of the inhabitants of Montreal.

In September 1661, on the way back to Onondaga, Otreouti, who still wore the murdered priest's black cassock, and his companions, who were carrying some French scalps, met a Seneca and Onondaga embassy led by GARAKONTIÉ, an Onondaga chief friendly to the French, on its way to Montreal to deliver nine French captives. The ambassadors were shocked at the sight. They halted, deliberating in council for some time as to whether they would be safe in going on to Montreal. Garakontié prevailed in the end and the embassy, with the nine captives, reached Montreal 5 Oct. 1661.

Four years later, Otreouti was one of six Onondaga ambassadors who attested articles of peace 13 Dec. 1665 at Quebec with the French in the name of their own nation, and of the Senecas, the Cayugas, and the Oneidas. The role of Otreouti in the negotiations of 1665 is not clear, witness an enigmatic entry in the Jesuit *Journal* of 8 Dec. 1665: "La grand gueule ('big mouth') then learned, I know not from whom, of the design of Monsieur the governor respecting Anniee [Mohawks]; and he informed Garakontie of it in our reception room."

Otreouti is not mentioned again in colonial records for almost 19 years, until the time of Governor LE FEBVRE de La Barre's invasion of the Mohawk country in 1684. On 18 July 1684, the Jesuit, Father Jean de Lamberville*, wrote from the Onondaga mission to La Barre (whose small force had proceeded only as far as Lake St. Francis) about a council of Onondagas, Senecas, Cayugas, and Oneidas, in which Otreouti played a part. "La Grande Gueule," the priest reported, "and his triumvirate have assuredly signalized themselves in this rencounter"; and again, 17 Aug. 1684, "I gave La Grande Gueule your belt underhand, and have remarked to him the things you wish him to effect. He calls himself your best friend and you have done well to

Ouagimou

have attached to you this hoc [sic] who has the strongest head and loudest voice among the Iroquois."

La Barre had informed Governor Dongan of New York that he was obliged to wage war against the Iroquois and asked that English support be withheld. When Dongan heard of the councils at Onondaga, however, he sent Aernout Cornelissen Viele there to warn the Iroquois not to enter into conversations with the French without his, Dongan's, permission. Father de Lamberville reported this to La Barre 28 Aug. 1684, noting that La Grande Gueule considered Dongan's message strange, and was "exhorting all the warriors and chiefs not to listen to the proposals of a man who seemed to be drunk, so opposed to all reason was what he uttered." Despite Dongan's intervention, a meeting between the Iroquois and La Barre took place 5 Sept. 1684 at La Famine, on the south shore of Lake Ontario, where the Onondagas mediated between the French and the Senecas. On that occasion, "Hateouati, who is Orator of that Nation [Onondagas], spoke by fifteen presents, not only on behalf of the Senecas, but of the four Iroquois Nations also."

La Barre in 1684 obtained only a doubtful truce. Otreouti promised to give 1,000 beaver skins in recompense for recent Iroquois raids on the French in the Illinois country and to refrain from attacks upon the Miami Indians; but he refused to make peace with the Illinois, nor would he agree to respect French voyageurs in the Illinois country and in the neighbourhood of Fort Saint-Louis.

M. Demeulle*, the intendant, gave a somewhat critical account of the meeting at La Famine in a letter to M. de Seignelay, dated Quebec 10 Oct. 1684, "There came altogether on this embassy only a certain sycophant who seeks merely a good dinner, and a real buffoon, called among the French la Grande Gueule, accompanied by eight or ten miserable fellows, who fooled the General in a most shameful manner, as you will perceive by the articles of peace I have the honor to send you, and which I doubt not he also will send you."

Three years later, Governor Brisay* de Denonville gave a much more favourable picture of Otreouti in his "Memoir of the expedition against the Senecas, October 1687." "Last day of June [1687]. We arrived within half a league of Cataracouy [Cataraqui]. . . . On arriving at that Fort, I thought proper to send to the village of the Onnontagues [Onondagas], the son and the brother of an Indian named Hotre-houati, one of the most distinguished and influential of the said village, from whom we had derived great assistance in checking the incursions which the Senecas and other Iroquois had made the past year under the instigation of Colonel Dongan, Governor of New-York, and whose influence, as well as that of his other friends, Father de Lamberville made use of to frustrate the Colonel's ill designs."

Otreouti is again mentioned when the Onondagas, Cayugas, and Oneidas, after Denonville's defeat of the Senecas in 1687, executed a declaration of neutrality in the presence of Denonville at Montreal 15 June 1688. His name appears among those of the Onondaga signatories. Below the signatures and totems appears the following statement, "The man called La grande gueule by the French, and Otreouaté by the Iroquois, who spoke here at Montreal in public on several occasions in June, and twice repeated what precedes in the speeches, did himself, assisted by two Iroquois, affix the subjoined Totems and delineate with his own hand the figures of these Animals; which he did in quality of Speaker and Deputy of the three Iroquois Nations, to wit, Of the Cayugas, Onontagues [Onondagas] and Oneidas."

The last reference to Otreouti, as La Grande Gueule, appears in the "Relation of the events of the war, and state of affairs in Canada," dated Quebec, 30 Oct. 1688.

THOMAS GRASSMANN

JR (Thwaites), XLIV, 119; XLV, 89; XLVI, 219; XLVII, 73, 77, 93–97; XLIX, 179–81. L.-A. Lahontan, Nouveaux voyages dans l'Amérique septentrionale (2v., La Haye, 1703); Otreouti is the model for "La Grangula." NYCD (O'Callaghan and Fernow), III, 121–25; IX, 236–39, 247, 255–58, 362, 384–86, 388–93. Eccles, Frontenac, 169–70, 189. Lanctot, Histoire du Canada, II, 118, 142.

OUAGIMOU (Oagimont), chief of the neighbouring Indians when DU GUA de Monts and CHAMPLAIN established their settlement on Île Sainte-Croix in 1604. He was described as an Etchemin chief but the Indians of that region are now called Passamaquoddies.

Ouagimou is mentioned in connection with the Indian warfare and diplomacy of early Acadia. He petitioned the Armouchiquois (Penobscots) for the body of PANOUNIAS, who had been slain in revenge for a Souriquois (Micmac) attack on some of their tribe, and brought it to Port-Royal for burial in 1607. He then joined MEMBERTOU and SECOUDON with his warriors to attack the Armouchiquois in New England and the next year returned, at the request of ASTICOU, the new chief of the Armouchiquois, and with the assurance of French protection, as the representative of the Etchemins to make peace with them.

LESCARBOT records that Ouagimou gave some sea-biscuits to JEAN DE BIENCOURT de Poutrincourt in 1610 when he put in to Sainte-Croix after being driven out to sea by a storm. Lescarbot also refers to a daughter of Ouagimou about 11 years of age whom Poutrincourt wished to take to France and present to the queen but her father refused to consent to this.

It is considered highly probable that the head carved in relief on a slab of red granite found near Lake Utopia in 1863 represents Ouagimou and was carved by one of de Monts's stone-cutters at Île Sainte-Croix in the winter of 1604–5. This slab, known as the Utopia Medallion, is in the New Brunswick Museum at Saint John.

W. AUSTIN SQUIRES

Champlain, *Works* (Biggar), I, 442–43. Lescarbot, *History* (Grant), II, 359–60, 367–69; III, 42. *JR* (Thwaites), II, 145.

OUMASASIKWEIE (known to the French as "**La Grenouille**" ("The Frog")), Algonkin Indian of the Allumette Island tribe, traitor and intriguer; fl. 1633–36.

Oumasasikweie played a discreditable role in the trade rivalries between the Indians of New France and the Mohawks, who wished to prevent them from trading with the Dutch at Fort Orange ("Memorial presented by Kiliaen van Rensselaer"). He belonged to the Indian group known as the Algonkins of the Island (Allumette Island, now Morrison Island in the Ottawa River, near Pembroke, Ontario) and also as the Island tribe. Members of the Algonkian family, they were named Kichesipirini but the Hurons called them Ehonkehronons.

This captain visited the Jesuits 1 April 1633 in Quebec, presented some elk meat, engaged in conversation with them, and stated that he would be pleased to have his son educated by the Jesuits but that his wife did not agree. The same year, on 10 July, a son of La Grenouille became seriously ill at Quebec. Father BRÉBEUF and Father de NOUË went to his cabin, where they found the child at the point of death. With the consent of his parents, the child was baptized as François. Next evening he died.

The Jesuit *Relation* of 1635 mentions La Grenouille in connection with a rumour current in New France during August of that year. "I have heard," states the writer, Father PAUL LE JEUNE, "a report, I do not know how true it is, that a certain Savage named the Frog [La Grenouille] who acts as a Captain here, has said that the Hiroquois, with whom he had made a treaty of peace, have incited them [Algonkins of the Island] to kill some of the Hurons, and to make war against them." The *Relation* continues, "Those best informed believe that this is a ruse of those who trade with these Tribes, and who are striving to divert through their agency, the Hurons from their commerce with our French; which would happen if our Montagnais made war against them; and then they [the traders] would attract them to their settlements and there would result a very considerable injury to the Associated Gentlemen of the Company of New France." While the part played by Oumasasikweie is not clear, he seems to have been the instigator of the 1634 peace treaty (favourable to the Dutch) between the Algonkins, the Montagnais, the Onondagas, and the Mohawks, which was soon broken by an Iroquois attack on the Algonkins 10 Aug. 1635.

There is no doubt, however, that La Grenouille was distrusted in New France. "This *wicked* man," says the *Relation* of 1636, "had more authority than the Captains, and his influence extended even among all those Tribes. His plans were laid to divert them entirely from commerce and friendship with the French. To this end he had negotiated peace with his enemies; but God, who knew the malice of his heart, crushed him, and permitted the most wicked of the Savages [the Iroquois] to be involved in his crimes. For in trying to open a way to the Foreigners through the lands of their enemies, whom he thought he had won over, they imbrued their hands in his blood, slaughtering him miserably, as well as those whose pride had caused us the most trouble."

As the *Relation* states, Oumasasikweie was betrayed in his turn by the Iroquois, who were, he thought, favourably disposed to his plans. He and a number of his accomplices were massacred in the Iroquois country, while they were trying to open a commercial route to Fort Orange (Albany, N.Y.).

The date of Oumasasikweie's death is not fully recorded, but must have occured before 18 July 1636, because on that day, M. DU PLESSIS-BOCHART, who met some hundreds of Indians at the Richelieu River in an attempt to promote peace with the Iroquois, exonerated MAKHEABICHTICHIOU, a Montagnais captain, from the charge that he had received presents from the Iroquois and that he had betrayed Oumasasikweie and his companions. Oumasasikweie's wife survived him. A baptismal record (1638–40) of the mission of Saint-Joseph at Sillery contains this entry, "Cecilia Natoukwabekwe, wife of the late La Grenouille."

THOMAS GRASSMANN

Du Creux, *History* (Conacher), I, 148 n.3, 152–54. *JR* (Thwaites), V, 179–81, 227–33, 239, 291 n.57;

Ourehouare

VIII, 25, 59–61; IX, 95–97, 245; XX, 309. *Van Rensselaer Bowier manuscripts*, ed. A. J. F. van Laer (Albany, N.Y., 1908), 235–50.

OUREHOUARE (Orehaoue, Horehouasse), Iroquois war-chief, galley-slave, confidant, and ambassador of BUADE de Frontenac; b. *c.* 1650; d. 1698.

Ourehouare was a chief of the Cayuga villages which had been established on the Bay of Quinte before the founding of Fort Frontenac (Cataracoui) in 1673. In 1687 the governor, Brisay* de Denonville, invaded the Iroquois homeland and won a partial victory which prevented the Iroquois, backed by the English, from wresting the western fur trade from French control.

Bochart* Champigny, the intendant, went in advance of the main force, 17 June 1687, to Fort Cataracoui, where he seized a group of Cayuga hunters encamped near the fort. Another group he lured into the fort, on pretext of a feast, but imprisoned them instead. En route to the country of the Senecas, Jean PERÉ, another member of the expedition, captured Ourehouare and several other Indians near Montreal and these prisoners were added to the others in the fort. The tribesmen, numbering 51 braves, were stripped, and tied to stakes in the compound of the fort, where they underwent torture at the hands of the French and their Indian allies. On the return of the invading French army, the captives were transported down the St. Lawrence River to Quebec, leaving behind them 150 helpless women and children. In accordance with the French king's request, Ourehouare and his fellow captives were subsequently shipped to France where they were forced to serve in the king's galleys.

This treacherous behaviour on the part of the French unleashed savage warfare throughout the length of the St. Lawrence River for more than a decade. Raiding parties of Iroquois carried tomahawk, scalping knife, and torch to isolated communities and threatened the destruction of the French colony.

Alarmed at the deterioration of affairs in New France, Louis XIV in 1689 decided to return the Indian captives, and to replace Governor de Denonville with Count Frontenac. When the latter sailed for Quebec, he was accompanied by Ourehouare and 13 Cayuga braves, all that had survived two years of slavery in the king's galleys during France's wars against the Mediterranean pirates. On the long voyage Frontenac exerted himself to the utmost to gain the confidence and friendship of Ourehouare, inviting the chief to dine with him and showering him with gifts. In Quebec, Ourehouare was given a suite in the Château Saint-Louis, and was admitted to the governor's inner circle. As a result, he became a firm friend of Frontenac. He acted as the governor's ambassador in several attempts at reconciliation with the Iroquois and participated in retaliatory attacks on enemy posts. Ourehouare never returned to his homeland. He died of pleurisy in Quebec in 1698, before peace could be attained, and was buried there with full military honours.

H. C. BURLEIGH

AN, Col., C11A, 9, ff.32–38, 61–77. BM, Add. MS 16913, ff.173–80v. *Coll. de manuscrits relatifs à la Nouv.-France*, I, 485–88, 559. *JR* (Thwaites), LXII, 102–4, 272, *et passim*. L.-A. Lahontan, *New voyages to North America*, ed. R. G. Thwaites (2v., Chicago, 1905), I, 233. *NYCD* (O'Callaghan and Fernow), IX, 360, 681–82. Vachon de Belmont, *Histoire du Canada*, 20.

Eccles, *Canada under Louis XIV* (Canadian centenary series III, Toronto, 1964), 267; *Frontenac*, 181–83, 186–87, 207–8; "Denonville et les galériens iroquois," *RHAF*, XIV (1960–1), 408–29. Lionel Groulx, "Denonville et les galériens iroquois," *Action universitaire*, VII (1941), 6, 8–9, 12. Lanctot, *Histoire du Canada*, II, 138–39, 151, 154. Jean Leclerc, "Denonville et ses captifs iroquois," *RHAF*, XIV (1960–1), 545–58; XV (1961–2), 41–58. A. M. Machar, *The story of old Kingston* (Toronto, 1908), 36–39. Parkman, *Count Frontenac and New France* (24th ed.), 194–201. Rochemonteix, *Les Jésuites et la Nouvelle-France au XVIIe siècle*, III, 613f. *Royal Fort Frontenac* (Preston and Lamontagne), 46–48. F. B. Tracy, *Tercentenary history of Canada from Champlain to Laurier 1608–1908* (3v., New York and Toronto, 1908), I, 270–1. G. M. Wrong, *The rise and fall of New France* (2v., Toronto, 1928), II, 503–10.

OUREOUHAT. *See* OTREOUTI

OUTLAW, JOHN (Outlan or **Outlas, Jean)**, "Marriner & Shipwright" of Limehouse, England; d. *c.* 1696–97.

He served as mate on the *Bachelor's Delight*, commanded by Benjamin Gillam* who sailed from New England on 21 June 1682 and founded a post 26 miles up the Nelson River. Subsequently Radisson* and CHOUART Des Groseilliers, and John BRIDGAR established posts for the French and HBC respectively. Radisson captured the two rival posts in 1683. Some of the English prisoners were put on the unseaworthy *Sainte-Anne*, and Outlaw navigated it to James Bay, whence he returned to England in the HBC ship, *Diligence* (Capt. NEHEMIAH WALKER).

Despite Outlaw's being an interloper who had infringed their patent, the HBC hired him for their 1684 voyage. He was given command of the *Lucy* and sailing with the *Happy Return* made a successful voyage to and from Port Nelson.

Radisson, his captor of the year before and now in English pay, was a passenger on the *Happy Return*, and Henry Kelsey*, on his first voyage to the Bay, was aboard the *Lucy*.

Outlaw commanded the *Success* in 1685 and on the voyage out encountered two French ships from Port Nelson under Claude de Bermen* de La Martinière with the captured English vessel *Perpetuana Merchant*. He was unable either to seize the French ships or to release their prize. Homeward bound from Charlton Island the *Success* was wrecked by ice; passengers and crew made their way to Charles Fort on Rupert River. Outlaw spent the winter at Moose. In the spring of 1686 Pierre de TROYES captured Moose (which the French called Saint-Louis) and at Rupert River captured both the post and the HBC ship, *Craven*. Outlaw piloted the *Craven* to Moose where de Troyes loaded it with cannon before proceeding to capture Albany (Sainte-Anne). Outlaw and many of the English prisoners were sent in the *Colleton* to winter at Port Nelson and Severn, subsequently returning to England in 1687.

Outlaw and his crew were refused their wages for alleged negligence in losing the *Success*. Therefore in 1688, the disgruntled Outlaw joined John ABRAHAM in an interloping expedition on the *Mary* but she was wrecked by ice in Hudson Strait. The crew were happily rescued by the HBC ship *Churchill* (Capt. William BOND) which, with the *Yonge*, was taking a new governor, MARSH, and men to Albany to establish a post near the former English fort captured by the French in 1686. The new post was established but Pierre Le Moyne* d'Iberville captured it during the winter and Outlaw was taken prisoner by the French for the third time. He accepted his destiny and deserted to the French either then or shortly afterwards. In 1690 the HBC warned its servants that Outlaw was a potential interloper.

At Quebec in 1692 Outlaw married Françoise Denis (his first wife was Mary Saille of London) and had three children by her. He commanded a royal frigate *La Boufonne*, which left Quebec on a privateering expedition on 9 June 1696 (N.S.). He may have been the "sieur Outlas" to whom some land in Acadia was granted in 1697 and the "Outelas" forbidden by Governor JOSEPH ROBINAU de Villebon in August 1697 to go off on a cruise without further instructions. Outlaw died before July 1698, when his wife was remarried.

G. E. THORMAN

HBRS, IX (Rich); XI, XX (Rich and Johnson); XXI (Rich). *Coll. de manuscrits relatifs à la Nouv.-France*, II, 222. P.-G. Roy, *Inv. concessions*, IV, 135. Chevalier de Troyes, *Journal* (Caron). Tanguay, *Dictionnaire*, I, 456. Webster, *Acadia*, 106.

OUTREOUHATI. *See* OTREOUTI

P

PACHOT, FRANÇOIS VIENNAY-. *See* VIENNAY

PAIZS (Paizsos), ISTVÁN. *See* PARMENIUS

PALLUAU, LOUIS DE BUADE DE FRONTENAC ET DE. *See* BUADE

PANOUNIAS (Panoniac), Micmac chief, whose death precipitated savage warfare between the Indians of Acadia and the Armouchiquois (Penobscots) of New England; d. 1607.

When DU GUA de Monts and CHAMPLAIN, together with other Frenchmen and 20 sailors, embarked 18 June 1605 from Île Sainte-Croix to explore the coastal region inhabited by the Armouchiquois (Almouchiquois) in what is now the state of Maine, Panounias and his wife, an Armouchiquois, were engaged as interpreters and guides. This expedition continued south along the New England coast to the vicinity of Nauset Harbour, just below Cape Cod. But by 9 July, when the party met Onemechin (Olemechin), an Armouchiquois chief, on the Saco (Chouacoët) River, Panounias' wife was no longer with them and her husband was unable to interpret many of Onemechin's remarks without her. The expedition left for Île Sainte-Croix 25 July, arriving there 3 August.

Two years later, the death of Panounias was the cause of the most serious recorded conflict between the Indians of Acadia and the Armouchiquois, who killed the Micmac chief near the Saco to avenge deaths of their own tribesmen and allies. MEMBERTOU rallied the Acadian tribes for a retaliatory raid against the Armouchiquois. Joining their allies the Etchemins (Malecites) at the Saint John River, the warriors, under the command of Membertou, travelled west to the Armouchiquois country, where they defeated their enemy. In the battle, Bessabes, the most renowned Armouchiquois sagamo, and many lesser chiefs, were slain.

OUAGIMOU, an Etchemin (Passamoquoddy) chief, brought the news of Panounias's death, to the French and to SECOUDON, the Etchemin chief

Paquine

who was with them at Port-Royal (Annapolis Royal, N.S.). There is some uncertainty as to the year of Panounias's death but the historical evidence points to 1607 [see Champlain, *Works* (Biggar)].

THOMAS GRASSMANN

Champlain, *Works* (Biggar), I, 311–66, 435–36, 442–445, 458. Lescarbot, *History* (Grant), II, 368–69; III, 81, 104, 273.

PAQUINE. *See* PASQUINE

PARAT, ANTOINE, fire-ship captain, governor of Plaisance (Placentia); d. 8 Mar. 1696.

On 13 Jan. 1685 the court appointed Antoine Parat governor of Plaisance, after the death of Governor LA POIPPE. Parat assumed office on 2 June of that year. Immediately he took a census of the French colony in Newfoundland, which numbered at that time 640 people, 474 of whom were indentured employees. Plaisance consisted of just 18 houses; the rest of the population was scattered among some dozen ports along the coast. These posts offered refuge to about 60 fishing boats which each year took in approximately 140,000 quintals of cod from the Banks. With the ridiculously inadequate means at his disposal, it was not easy for the governor to assure the safety and to satisfy the needs of a scattered and turbulent population. One of Parat's first concerns was to request a bigger garrison and the repairing of the fort. In 1687 a detachment of 25 soldiers arrived, under the command of Philippe de Pastour* de Costebelle, but the governor had to be satisfied with patching up the fort at his own expense.

He lived on good terms with the English governor of Renewse and concluded a treaty of neutrality with him. He also traded with Boston, in order to obtain the stores and supplies that were needed. There was however great rivalry between the French and English fishermen who frequented the vicinity of Newfoundland and each side endeavoured to seize prizes. Parat had an English ketch, which had been seized by some French merchants, released, but this did not prevent a party of 45 privateers from attacking and pillaging Plaisance. They maltreated the governor and kept the population captive for six weeks. Thinking that the colony was lost, Parat asked the court to build a strong fort, to group the inhabitants together, and to send a frigate to cruise off the coasts. He considered Newfoundland to be "the most wretched country in the world," and asked to be recalled.

Moreover he had stirred up complaints by engaging in fishing, running a tavern, and trafficking in food and munitions; he kept a concubine, from whom the bishop of Quebec had to separate him, and he quarrelled with Costebelle, with the inhabitants, and with the Basques. A ticklish affair with a Huguenot apostate by the name of David Basset* also did him harm at court. His recall had been decided upon in 1687, but Jacques-François Brouillan*, his successor, could not set out until 1690. Overwrought by the siege and the ill-treatment that he had received the previous winter, Parat left in September, 1690, without even waiting for Brouillan to arrive. The inhabitants' complaints brought on an enquiry, which he got out of without any great harm to himself. He died 8 March 1696.

RENÉ BAUDRY

AN, Col., B, 11, 13, 15; C^{11C}, 1. BN, MS, Clairambault 1016, ff.467–68. Sixte Le Tac, *Histoire chronologique de la Nouvelle France ou Canada depuis sa découverte (mil cinq cents quatre) jusques en l'an mil six cents trente deux*, éd. Eugène Réveillaud (Paris, 1888), 236f. La Morandière, *Hist. de la pêche française de la morue*, I 429–37, 440–44, 447, 449, and the sources cited therein. Robert Le Blant, *Philippe de Pastour de Costebelle, gouverneur de Terre-Neuve puis de l'Île Royale 1661–1717* (Paris et Dax, 1935), 54–71.

PARIS, IGNACE DE. *See* IGNACE

PARKHURST, ANTHONY, merchant, explorer, and advocate of English settlement in Newfoundland; fl. 1561–83.

Possibly a son of John Parkhurst of East Lenham, Kent, he was recommended by Sir Thomas Challoner, English ambassador in Spain (1561–64), with whom he was serving, to John Hawkins as an adventurer on his second slaving voyage (1564–65). This took Parkhurst to West Africa, the Caribbean, and Florida, sharpened his observation, and gave him a taste for exploration. He became acquainted with Richard Hakluyt the elder who encouraged his interest in exploration. After a quarrel in 1573 with his father, who disinherited him (the Privy Council intervening to try to settle the matter), he moved to Bristol and set up as a merchant.

In 1565 he had been impressed on his way homeward by the fishing off Newfoundland, so he now bought a ship (perhaps of 70 tons), and became an *entrepreneur* in the fishery. He had three good seasons, 1575–77, and a bad one in 1578, the latter failing, he said, because some Portuguese did not deliver salt to preserve his fish. He was an exceptional merchant for he accompanied his ship each year, and spent much time in Newfoundland with his mastiff and eel-spear searching "the harbors, creekes and havens and also the land," he tells us, "much more than ever any Englishman hath done." Moreover, he went to northeastern as well as southeastern Newfoundland and collected information from French and Portuguese fishermen.

On the basis of his knowledge he decided that the English should colonize Newfoundland. Salt could thus be made on the spot and men could be engaged for a much longer period in the fishery. Occupation of the Straits of Belle Isle (and the fortification of Belle Isle itself) and of St. John's would give the English dominance over Spanish, Portuguese, and French fishermen. His views were expressed in letters in 1577–78, one to an unknown courtier (possibly Edward Dyer), the other to Hakluyt. The letter to Hakluyt included much on the natural resources of the island: woods, minerals (iron and copper), fruit, flowers, animals, birds, and fish. His observation was acute, his views on climate sensible. He thought the climate not unfavourable to settlement, as he had experimented successfully with English fruit, grain, and vegetable seeds. Settlement would bring advantages to the English economy: the exploitation of a product (fish) which need not be paid for expensively in exports but which would provide cheap food at home; the acquisition of an independent source of naval stores; prospects of iron mining and smelting; the training of seamen; the occupation of surplus population. Conversion of the Indians would also be possible.

Parkhurst was also the first Englishman to call attention to the Gulf of St. Lawrence and the river beyond. He offered to explore there or on the mainland south from Cape Breton (for he considered salt could be panned at 43°). Though he may have influenced Sir Humphrey GILBERT's proposal in 1577 to seize the Spanish fishing fleet, Parkhurst did not take part in the latter's abortive colonizing expedition of 1578 although he did subscribe in 1583 (but probably did not sail) when Gilbert set out for Newfoundland and New England. Later, after Gilbert had been lost, he contributed complimentary verses to Sir George Peckham's *A true report* (1583), expressing the hope that in America "Some good and well disposed men, An other England there would plant." With this expression of his views on English settlement in northeastern North America, in which he was a pioneer, he disappears from our knowledge. An intelligent and well-informed commentator, he was, with Edward HAYES, Newfoundland's most important early publicist.

DAVID B. QUINN

PRO, *Acts of P.C., new ser., 1571–75*; *CSP, For.,* 1564–65. Hakluyt, *Original writings* (Taylor), I; *Principal navigations* (1903–5), VIII, X. *Voyages of Gilbert* (Quinn).

PARMENIUS, STEPHANUS (in Hungarian **István Paizs(os)** or **Budai Parmenius István**), scholar, traveller, probably the first Hungarian to visit North America; d. 1583.

He tells us he was born of Christian parents in Turkish captivity, i.e., in the pashalik of Buda after 1541, and that he was educated by learned men before being sent, about 1579, to complete his education by a tour of European universities. On reaching England about 1581 he formed a friendship with Henry Unton, an English gentleman, later ambassador to France, who may possibly have visited Hungary and who became his patron. At Oxford he lodged at Christ Church with Richard Hakluyt the younger (who refers to him in the "Discourse of western planting" as "my bedfelowe in Oxforde"), and became friendly with the Puritan president of Magdalen College, Dr. Laurence Humfrey.

Parmenius was a Calvinist and it is probable that he took introductions to London Calvinists with him in 1582; the Huguenot printer and publisher, Thomas Vautrollier, printed for him a short religious work in verse, *Paean . . . ad psalmum Davidis CIV* (1582), with a dedicatory poem to Henry Unton. He renewed a close acquaintance with Hakluyt, who was then busy preparing publicity for several American colonizing ventures, and was introduced by him to Sir Humphrey GILBERT. Parmenius became so enthusiastic about Gilbert's proposed voyage that he published a poetic tribute in Latin to the venture, *De navigatione illustris et magnanimi aurati Humfredi Gilberti, ad deducendam in novum orbem coloniam* (London, 1582). This provided encouragement, if little factual information, for participants in the project, but it demonstrated the author's command of classical parallels and also the careful teaching on English maritime achievements he had had from Hakluyt. Hakluyt reprinted it in 1600 (*Principal navigations*, III, 137–43, with the slightly confusing date 31 March 1583). Unton, already a friend of Gilbert's, may have subscribed to the expedition, but Parmenius decided to go himself and to record what he saw.

He left Plymouth on board the *Swallow*, to whose captain, Maurice Browne, he later paid tribute, and had, he said later, a fine voyage, all the men being in good health when they entered St. John's harbour, Newfoundland, on 3 Aug. 1583. Edward HAYES, however, tells us that the *Swallow*'s crew were largely pirates, and being short of food when they reached Newfoundland,

Parmentier

they attacked and stripped a French ship, losing two of their own men through carelessness, for which the crew and ship were sent home by Gilbert from St. John's. Parmenius made some slight attempt to explore the country around St. John's and to penetrate into the interior, but everywhere the forests were blocked with dead timber and were thus impenetrable, for Gilbert refused to use fire to clear a way.

What Parmenius could see was not promising—great pine woods, good grass, some land which might be cultivable; he did not know what to write—"What shall I say . . . when I see nothing but a very wildernesse?" he commented to Hakluyt to whom he wrote, amongst others—the remaining letters not being extant—on 6 August. Only the fish moved him to enthusiasm, and his critical attitude should be compared with the eulogy on Newfoundland by Hayes. He wished to comment on the native peoples but could see or hear of none (showing how completely the Beothuk Indians had deserted southeastern Newfoundland). On the climate, he commended the heat, which made it necessary, however, each day to turn the fish drying on stages, but said he had learnt of the extreme cold of winter and of the danger which the fishermen encountered from icebergs in early summer. On 5 August he saw Gilbert carry out the ceremony of annexation at St. John's before turning to levy supplies from foreign and English vessels alike. His letter, in Latin, reached Hakluyt in time and told of his desire to be off towards more southern parts from which more and better things were to be expected. (Hakluyt published the letter with translation, in *The principall navigations* (1589), 697–99, and in *Principal navigations*, III (1600), 161–63.)

Parmenius shipped in the *Delight* under Capt. Browne, who had exchanged with Capt. William Winter, when she sailed on 20 August for Sable Island and Cape Breton. On 29 August the ship was in difficulties in shallow waters and went aground in bad weather, breaking up rapidly. Parmenius was not one of those whom Richard CLARKE brought to safety in the ship's pinnace. He was drowned on Sable Island, or conceivably Cape Breton. Edward Hayes got home and explained that Parmenius had "adventured in this action, minding to record in the Latine tongue, the gests and things worthy of remembrance, happening in this discoverie, to the honour of our nation, the same being adorned with the eloquent stile of this Orator and rare Poet of our time." By his premature death was thus lost an embryo chronicle of the voyage and perhaps also the beginnings of an epic poem.

DAVID B. QUINN

BM, copies of Parmenius's two pamphlets. Hakluyt, "Discourse on western planting"; *Original writings* (Taylor); *Principal navigations* (1903–5), VIII. A[biel] H[olmes], "Memoir and poem of Stephen Parmenius of Buda," Mass. Hist. Soc. *Coll.*, 1st ser., IX (1804), 49–74. *Voyages of Gilbert* (Quinn). C. S. Emden, *Oriel papers* (Oxford, 1948). István Gál, *Magyarország Anglia és Amerika* (Budapest, [1945]). W. G. Gosling, *The Life of Sir Humphrey Gilbert* (London, 1911). L. L. Kropf, "Budai Parmenius István," *Századok*, XXIII (1889), 150–54. Correspondence between the author and Dr. György Pajkoss, National Széchényi Library, Budapest.

PARMENTIER, JEAN, navigator, cartographer, and poet; b. 1494 at Dieppe; d. 1529 at sea, off the coast of Sumatra.

It is extremely difficult to prove, from the evidence available, whether or not Jean Parmentier actually came to Canada. According to Lanctot (*Histoire du Canada*, I, 112), Jean and his brother Raoul in 1520 loaded their boats with furs in the Cape Breton region. E. Guénin, however, in his *Ango et ses pilotes* (Paris, 1901) says only that c. 1510–20 Parmentier apparently made voyages to Newfoundland, as to other places, for the renowned shipowner Jean Ango. The brothers, moreover, kept the details of their route to the New World secret from all but their master. Although Jean was well known as a cartographer in his lifetime, none of his maps has survived and it is unlikely that, in any event, he entrusted his American secrets to them.

Jean and Raoul both died in 1529 on a voyage to the East Indies. The poet and astrologer, Pierre Crignon, who accompanied them on this expedition, published Jean Parmentier's poem, "Traicté en forme d'exhortation contenant les merveilles de Dieu et de la dignité de l'homme" as well as his own "Déploration sur la mort desditz Parmentiers" in 1531 and his poem "Plainctes sur les trépas de Raoul et Jean Parmentier" ten years later.

THOMAS DUNBABIN

The first account of the Parmentiers' voyages appeared in *Description nouvelle des merveilles de ce monde et de la dignité de l'homme . . .* (Paris, 1531), which includes Crignon's "Déploration sur la mort desditz Parmentiers." Louis Estancelin, *Recherches sur les découvertes des navigateurs normands en Afrique, dans les Indes orientales et en Amérique, suivies d'Observations sur la marine, le commerce et les établissements coloniaux des Français* (Paris, 1832) contains Crignon's "Journal du voyage de Jean Parmentier de Dieppe, à l'île de Sumatra . . . 1529." The "Journal" is republished in *Le discours de la navigation de Jean et Raoul Parmentier de Dieppe: voyage à Sumatra en 1529; description de l'isle de Sainct-Domingo*, éd. Christian Schefer (Recueil de voyages, IV, Paris, 1883). For a discussion of whether Crignon wrote the "Discorso . . ." published by Ramusio, and of the validity of the evidence for a North American voyage by Parmentier, see Henri Harrisse, *Découverte et évolution cartographique de Terre-Neuve et des pays circonvoisins, 1497, 1501, 1769* (Paris, 1900); Hoffman, *Cabot to Cartier*, 149, 169; and *Les voyages de découverte et les premiers établissements, XVe, XVIe siècles*, éd. Ch.-A. Julien (Colonies et Empires, 3e série, Paris, 1948).

PASQUINE (Paquine), French engineer of the department of Marine, who prepared plans for the re-fortification of Port-Royal (Annapolis Royal, N.S.); fl. 1681–88.

Pasquine, experienced in the mapping of the Mediterranean coasts of France and Spain, was sent to Acadia in 1688 at the request of Des Friches* de Menneval. His instructions, dated 10 April 1688, stated he was "to have an examination made of the posts which it is particularly necessary to occupy and fortify for the defence and conservation of the colony in case of war with its neighbour. . . ."

Pasquine arrived in Acadia aboard *La Friponne*, commanded by Barthélemy de Beauregard*. He drew a detailed plan of the river and country surrounding Port-Royal and visited the other posts on the Bay of Fundy (Baie Française). He also prepared several plans for the rebuilding of the fort at Port-Royal, on the same site and scale as the old one, dated at Paris 26 Dec. 1688 and an estimate of the expense involved. The first estimate was 9,952 *livres*, but he made a second one of 7,761 *livres*. Although this project was approved the execution of the proposals was entrusted to SACCARDY rather than Pasquine.

Pasquine left maps of the mouths of the Saint John, Penobscot, and Kennebec rivers, where he recommended that forts be erected. These maps, which are of great historical interest, reveal a man of talent.

ÉMERY LeBLANC

AN, Col., B, 15; C^{11D}, 2. Seven maps by Pasquine are preserved in AN (Archives d'Outre-Mer), Dépôt des fortifications des colonies, carton no.2, and in the BN, Cartes et plans. *Acadiensia Nova* (Morse), I, 58–60; II [*see* Paquine]. *BRH*, I (1895), 36. *Coll. de manuscrits relatifs à la Nouv.-France.* Étienne Taillemite, *Inventaire analytique de la correspondance générale avec les colonies, départ, Série B (déposée aux Archives nationales), I–, Registres 1 à 37 (1654–1715)* (Paris, 1959).

PASTEDECHOUAN (Patetchoanen, Ahinsistan, Atetkouanon), PIERRE-ANTOINE, Montagnais Indian, early victim of French-Indian cultural conflict; fl. 1620–36.

The life of Pastedechouan provides a tragic example of one aspect of the European impact on Indian culture. In 1620 he was taken as a child to France by the Recollets, baptized, and given the name Pierre-Antoine, with the Prince de Guémenée acting as his godfather. The latter supervised his studies for the next five years and Pastedechouan became proficient in both Latin and French.

He was persuaded to return to Canada in 1626 with the Recollet Father JOSEPH DE LA ROCHE Daillon, who arrived in August of that year. Pastedechouan lived for a time with the Recollets at Quebec but did not mix with the Indians, probably because he had almost forgotten his own language. He was, therefore, advised to return to his own district near Tadoussac and to live with his three brothers, CARIGOUAN (a famous medicine-man who had great influence over him), Mestigoït, and Sasousmat, so that he might again become fluent in his native tongue.

Here he was found in 1629 by the English, who, under the command of the KIRKE brothers, had come to invade Canada. At first Pastedechouan pretended that he could not understand the English who questioned him in both French and Latin but a French deserter exposed this feigned ignorance. The English held Pastedechouan as an interpreter, supplied him with goods to trade with the Indians at Trois-Rivières, and permitted him to start off alone. He did not return.

During the English occupation of Quebec, Pastedechouan turned away from Christianity and reverted to his native customs and way of life. In 1632, after the French regained New France, Pastedechouan visited ÉMERY DE CAËN, who employed him as an interpreter but later dismissed him as unreliable. On 13 Nov. 1632, Pastedechouan, who was now incapable of maintaining himself by hunting, took up residence with the Jesuit fathers at Quebec, where he was to teach Father PAUL LE JEUNE the Montagnais language. He refused, however, to continue with his lessons after Easter 1633 and rejoined his brothers. Le Jeune, anxious to master the language and to commence his missionary work, joined them in a hunting expedition. Pastedechouan, crazed by drink and completely under the domination of Carigouan (who hated the priest), proved of no help to Le Jeune during this winter of near starvation in the forests. He did, however, accompany his brother Mestigoït, who paddled Le Jeune to safety at Quebec through the early spring break-up of the frozen St. Lawrence.

Pastedechouan married a daughter of MANITOUGATCHE, who left him, whereupon he took a wife from another nation. He is said to have had four or five wives in all. Before he died the

Patoulet

women ridiculed him. In 1636 he died of starvation, alone in the woods.

THOMAS GRASSMANN

Du Creux, *History* (Conacher), I, 140, 141, 156. *JR* (Thwaites), V, 107–11; VI, 87; VII, 69, 173; IX, 69–71. Le Clercq, *First establishment of the faith* (Shea), I, 235–37, 273–74, 295–96. Sagard, *Histoire du Canada* (Tross), III, 785–87.

PATOULET, JEAN-BAPTISTE, secretary to Jean TALON, intendant of New France 1665–72; d. 8 April 1695 at Dunkirk.

He came to the colony with Talon in 1665, at a salary of 1,200 *livres* a year, one-tenth as much as Talon received. In 1667 he was sent back to France on the king's service and returned to Quebec two years later, during the intendancy of Claude de BOUTROUE. His talents were much appreciated by Boutroue who gave him the important task of drafting the dispatches to the minister of Marine. In 1670 he was again in France and was appointed a naval commissary. The following year he was sent by Colbert to report on conditions in Acadia and from there he proceeded to Quebec. In 1671, Talon, when asking the minister to be allowed to return to France for reasons of health, stated that Patoulet was competent to take over the intendant's duties, "provided that he accepted and followed the advice that [Talon] would give to him." This recommendation was not acted on and Patoulet returned to France with Talon in 1672. He was then appointed comptroller at the Atlantic naval base at Rochefort where he received intensive training in all aspects of naval administration by the intendant of the base, Colbert de Terron. During these years his advice on Canadian affairs was, on occasion, solicited by the minister. His views were always judicious and sometimes ran counter to the minister's prejudices, as, for example, when he defended Bishop Laval* and the Jesuits against the charge levelled at them by the governor of the colony, BUADE de Frontenac, that they encroached on the civil authority. In 1679 he was appointed to the important post of intendant of the French West Indies, where he endeavoured to stimulate trade between the islands and Canada. In 1683 he was recalled to France to become intendant of Dunkirk. Phélypeaux de Pontchartrain, minister of Marine, wrote of him in 1694: "I have observed that he is a completely honest man, good tempered and agreeable. He understands the navy very well, does his duty conscientiously, is respected and liked by both officers and seamen and in general by all who are under his orders." He was, in fact, an excellent example of the type of men brought into the government service under Colbert, their exceptional talents being, in no small measure, responsible for the resurgence of France under Louis XIV. He died at Dunkirk on 8 April 1695.

W. J. ECCLES

Correspondance de Talon, APQ *Rapport, 1930–31,* 150, Talon au ministre, Québec, 31 octobre 1671. BN, MS, Clairambault, 868, f.385; Mélanges Colbert, 164, ff.72, 185; 165, f.188; 273, f.259; 287, f.179. Chapais, *Talon*.

PAUMART, JEAN, missionary, supposed author of a travel account; b. 22 Jan. 1583 at Beauvais (France); d. and buried 14 Oct. 1648 at Neuilly-sous-Clermont in the region of Beauvais.

Son of Guillaume Paumart, royal provost of Angy, and of Marie Le Roy, he came to Canada as a missionary at a date which is uncertain but which was not in any case earlier than 1620. In 1625 he was secretly the chaplain of Queen Henrietta Maria in England. Some time later, at the request of His Excellency Bishop Pothier of Beauvais, he returned to his diocese. He died in 1648 while bearing aid to victims of the plague during an epidemic which had struck Neuilly-sous-Clermont.

An account of a voyage in America by Jean Paumart is said to exist, apparently in the Borel de Bretizel private collections, which are preserved in the Château du Vieux-Rouen.

MARCEL HAMELIN

Collection privée Borel de Bretizel, Château du Vieux-Rouen, "Un récit de voyage en Amérique." "Documents relatifs à Jean Paumart, prêtre, et au Père Simon Lemoine, tous deux de Beauvais, missionnaires au Canada (copiés sur les manuscrits de la collection Borel de Bretizel, au château du Vieux-Rouen)," *NF*, V (1930), 303–39. Régis Roy, "Jean Paumart," *BRH*, XXVIII (1922), 92f.

PEARSON, BARTHOLOMEW, yeoman of Wollaton, Nottingham, settler in the first English colony in Newfoundland; fl. 1612–34.

Pearson was one of a group of settlers who went to Cuper's Cove (now Cupids) in 1612 at the instigation and expense of Sir Percival Willoughby, also of Wollaton, a prominent member of the Merchant Venturers company formed in 1610 for the plantation of Newfoundland. Pearson's function seems to have been to assess the agricultural possibilities of Newfoundland but, after only a few months there, he condemned both the land and the climate. However, his letters reveal a genuine interest in the island's animal life. In October 1612 he took part in JOHN GUY's expedition to Trinity Bay and was among those shipwrecked at Green Bay (Bay de Verde) on the way back. Nine days later, near starvation, they regained Cuper's Cove, having walked to Carbonear where they had found a boat.

With 60 others Pearson wintered in Newfoundland but in April 1613 he wrote asking Willoughby for permission to come home. His letter was critical not only of Newfoundland but also of the management of the undertaking. He probably left with others of Willoughby's men later that year; he was certainly in Nottingham early in 1617, when he married Elizabeth Baguleughe. The remainder of Pearson's life seems to have been spent, less adventurously, in Nottinghamshire where he maintained his connection with Willoughby, leasing land and coal-pits from him.

GILLIAN T. CELL

Pearson's letters from Newfoundland and other papers relating to the colony are at Nottingham University, Middleton MSS, Mi X 1/1–66. For his subsequent career see: Middleton MSS, 1/1/9, 1/38/26, 6/170/117. *Nottinghamshire marriage licences*, ed. T. M. Blagg, I (Br. Record Soc., 1930).

PÉCAUDY DE CONTRECŒUR, ANTOINE, officer in the Carignan-Salières regiment, first seigneur of Contrecœur; b. 1596 at Vignieu (Dauphiné), probably the son of Benoît de Pécody and Énarde Martin; d. 1 May 1688.

The original family name, fairly common in the north of Dauphiné, was Picoud or Pécoud. Contrecœur was a regimental nickname. Thus Pécaud *dit* Contrecœur eventually became Pécaudy de Contrecœur. Pécaudy was also frequently written Pécody.

Antoine Pécaudy de Contrecœur went to New France in 1665. All the details known to us about his career before that date come from the letters of nobility that Louis XIV is said to have granted him in January 1661. The historian Pierre Saint-Olive has cast doubt upon the authenticity of this document, in which he has pointed out several inaccuracies, particularly errors of concordance in the dates and places quoted. It was only in 1687, that is to say 26 years later, that Contrecœur apparently bethought himself, at Quebec, of invoking his nobility. It is therefore possible that the document registered in the Conseil Souverain at Quebec on 25 Feb. 1687 was based only on a nonagenarian's recollections.

Pécaudy, who is thought to have begun his military career at the age of 40, belonged first to the Montezon regiment, then to that of Carignan-Salières, in which he was a lieutenant and after that a captain. He was wounded on several occasions. One may suppose that he was a courageous soldier. On 11 Jan. 1652, at Saint-Chef, at the age of 56, he married Anne Dubois, who had been left a widow by Jacques Lemort a year earlier. The widow's second marriage, like her first, was childless.

Pécaudy seemed to be interested in his wife's assets, and tried by every conceivable means to obtain a transfer of ownership, an arrangement to which the Dubois brothers were opposed. He was absent when his wife died, at Saint-Chef, and he arrived home only on 10 July 1663, the evening of the funeral. The Dubois brothers and Pécaudy came into conflict over the settlement of the estate, and at first the Dubois family prevailed. But fresh disputes arose, and in 1720 proceedings were still under way, involving the descendants of the Dubois, and those of Charles Pécaudy, Contrecœur's nephew.

In 1665 Pécaudy de Contrecœur embarked at La Rochelle in command of one of the 24 companies of the Carignan-Salières regiment, bound for New France. He landed at Quebec 17 Aug. 1665. After his first winter, spent at Montreal, he led his troops in the various campaigns undertaken by the Carignan-Salières regiment.

On 17 Sept. 1667, at the age of 71, he married again; his wife was a young girl of 15, Barbe Denys, the daughter of SIMON DENYS de La Trinité, a member of the Conseil Souverain. In a letter dated 19 Dec. 1667, Intendant TALON wrote to the minister, Louvois, that he was delighted at this marriage, which was going to contribute to the establishment of the colony. Three children were born of this union, among them François-Antoine*, b. 1680, who married Jeanne de Saint-Ours in 1701 and continued the line.

When the Carignan-Salières regiment was disbanded, Contrecœur chose to remain in Canada. On 29 Oct. 1672, Talon had a seigneury granted to him; it was two square leagues, on the south shore of the St. Lawrence, a few miles east of Montreal. The seigneury, referred to by the name of Contrecœur, had 69 settlers and 80 acres of productive land at the time of the 1681 census.

In July 1673 the seigneur of Contrecœur was among the officers who accompanied Governor BUADE de Frontenac at the founding of Fort Cataracoui (Frontenac). Although the name of the seigneur of Contrecœur is fairly often mentioned in the documents of the Conseil Souverain and in various other sources, it nevertheless seems that as an individual he was not associated with any outstanding event in the years preceding his death, which occurred 1 May 1688.

Later on, in the Pécaudy de Contrecœur family, it became the accepted thing to repeat that their ancestor had died "in the king's service." This should perhaps be taken to mean that he was killed when the Iroquois sent an expedition to the Montreal region.

Among his descendants, one should mention Claude-Pierre Pécaudy* de Contrecœur, who played an important role during the military operations of the Seven Years' War and was a member of the Conseil Législatif of Quebec.

F. GRENIER

AJQ, Greffe de Gilles Rageot, 6 sept. 1667. Recensement de 1681. Correspondance de Talon, APQ Rapport, 1930–1, 90. *Jug. et délib.*, I, III. P.-G. Roy, *Inv. concessions*, II, 154f. F.-J. Audet, *Contrecœur, famille, seigneurie, paroisse, village* (Montréal, 1940). *BRH*, IV (1898), 193; VI (1900), 219; X (1904), 320; XV (1909), 151; XVII (1911), 194; XXIV (1918), 226f. Auguste Gosselin, *Une famille de héros, les Pécaudy de Contrecœur* (Évreux, 1904). Régis Roy et Malchelosse, *Le régiment de Carignan*. Pierre Saint-Olive, *Les Dauphinois au Canada: essai de catalogue des Dauphinois qui ont pris part à l'établissement du régime français au Canada, suivi d'une étude sur un Dauphinois canadien: Antoine Pécody de Contrecœur* (Paris, 1936). Sulte, *Mélanges historiques* (Malchelosse), VIII.

PELLETIER, DIDACE (baptized **Claude**), Recollet lay brother and master-carpenter, whose cause for beatification was introduced as early as 1713; b. 28 June 1657 at Sainte-Anne de Beaupré, son of Georges Pelletier (baptized 1624 at Dieppe), who had come to New France in 1652 and married Catherine Vannier in 1656; d. 1699.

Confirmed by Bishop Laval* in 1666, Claude Pelletier in 1668 entered the Saint-Joachim School of arts and crafts, which the bishop had established that same year, and was trained as a master carpenter. His first work was on the second church of Sainte-Anne de Beaupré, begun about 1676, and here no doubt his inclinations to the religious life received strong reinforcement, for it was already a famous shrine. In 1658 a small "Sailors' Chapel" had been built on this site, at which miracles were reported; of the first church proper, begun in 1660, Mère Marie de l'Incarnation [*see* GUYART] wrote in 1665 that "seven leagues from Quebec there is a place called le Petit Cap, where there is a church of Sainte-Anne in which Our Lord does great miracles on behalf of this holy mother of the Holy Virgin. Paralytics may be seen walking there, blind recovering their sight, and the sick of every sort recovering their health." The larger church which in turn replaced the 1660 building was of stone, its design traditionally ascribed to the curé, François Fillon, though in fact probably determined by Bishop Laval and Claude BAILLIF; Pelletier's work must have had to do with the roof, *clocher*, and other structural woodwork.

Two years later (1678), the carpenter applied for admission to the Recollet order, was accepted in 1679, and in 1680 took the name "Frère Didace." From 1682 on he accompanied Father Joseph Denis*, also Canadian-born but educated and ordained in France, to various far-flung Recollet mission stations—to Percé on Île Bonaventure, to Plaisance (Placentia) in Newfoundland, to Ville-Marie (Montreal) for six years, finally to Trois-Rivières where on 21 Feb. 1699 he died of a cold contracted while working on the Recollet church there. He is buried in the former conventual chapel of the Recollets (now the Protestant church) on Notre-Dame Street, Trois-Rivières.

Long acquaintance with his manner of life and death convinced Father Denis of his lay assistant's sanctity, and with the assistance of Bishop Saint-Vallier [La Croix*] beatification proceedings were begun. The Archives du Séminaire de Québec contains a copy, made between 1720 and 1744, of Father Denis's account of some 22 miracles taking place in connection with Brother Didace's relics, and other letters concerning him. Nothing, however, came of the action, and Brother Didace was completely forgotten until the discovery in the later 19th century of contemporary engravings of him—"Le vray portrait du très religieux Frère Didace, mort en odeur de S'teté . . . 21 fev 1699" —one in Quebec, another in the BN, Paris; since that time interest in him has been steadily maintained. Of his carpentry no evidence, tangible or documentary, has survived.

ALAN GOWANS

ASQ, Fonds Verreau, 073, Actes du Très devot frère Didace Recollet mort en odeur de sainteté en 1699. Odoric-Marie Jouve, "Étude historique et critique sur les actes du Frère Didace Pelletier, récollet," *BRH*, XVII (1911), 54ff.

PERÉ, JEAN, merchant from La Rochelle, explorer, prospector, *coureur de bois*, interpreter, guide; d. some time after November 1699.

The first mention of Jean Peré in the archives of New France seems to have been made in a very vague way by the Jesuit *Journal*, which notes the arrival from France, 17 June 1660, of "Peré and other small merchants."

In 1699 Intendant TALON gave 1,000 *livres* to Peré and 400 to Adrien Jolliet, and both set off "to go and reconnoitre to see whether the copper mine situated to the north of Lake Ontario . . . is rich and of easy extraction." Peré however was apparently interested chiefly in the furs which he collected from among the Ottawa Indians and at Sault Ste. Marie. Talon complained that he was slow in fulfilling his mission and presenting a report on it. Finally it was learned that the explorer had discovered mines in the region around Lake Superior.

In 1677 Peré was at Cataracoui. In November 1679 Intendant DUCHESNEAU accused him of being a *coureur de bois*: he informed the minister, Seignelay, that Peré, having been at Orange to sell his furs to the English, had been taken prisoner by the local governor and sent to Major Andros* at Manate (Manhattan, N.Y.). The latter, added Duchesneau, had treated Peré very well, since he wanted to make use of him with a view to establishing trade relations with the Ottawas.

In 1684 Peré pushed on as far as Hudson Bay, where he was captured by the English. Two years later, during the attack on Fort Quichicouanne (Albany), the Chevalier de TROYES demanded that Peré be handed over. But he was informed that the captive had been dispatched to France by way of England.

Peré, however, was not long in returning to Canada, where he won the favour of Governor de Brisay* de Denonville. He was a member of the latter's expedition against the Iroquois and brought back a number of prisoners to him, among them the famous Indian chief OUREHOUARE. In 1690 he was thought of as a useful man for the foray planned against Manate; but that year he was at La Rochelle, in France, where he and his brother Arnaud were engaged in selling furs.

We find Jean Peré back at Quebec in 1692 and 1693, pleading a case before the Conseil Souverain. He seems to have returned to France subsequently, since at the time of a lawsuit opened in 1698 before the same tribunal he had a court officer represent him and signed a power of attorney on 12 June 1699 at La Rochelle. These legal differences were debated at Quebec until March 1700. As Peré was still absent at this period, it is not known whether he was still alive.

He had given his name to a river that rises in Lake Nipigon and empties into the southwest end of James Bay. On a map Franquelin* noted: "R. du Perray which is the name of the first European to navigate this river as far as Hudson Bay."

LÉOPOLD LAMONTAGNE

Coll. de manuscrits relatifs à la Nouv.-France, I, 409, 553, 558, 560; II, 5. Correspondance de Talon, APQ *Rapport, 1930–1*, 136f. *Découvertes et établissements des Français* (Margry), I, 81, 88, 296; VI, 19; *passim*. *JR* (Thwaites), XLV, XLVII, LV, *passim*. JJ (Laverdière et Casgrain), *passim*. *Jug. et délib. NYCD* (O'Callaghan and Fernow), IX.

Chapais, *Talon*, 406f. J. H. Coyne, "The pathfinders of the Great Lakes," in *Canada and its provinces* (Shortt and Doughty), I, 83f. Delanglez, *Jolliet*. Nute, *Caesars of the wilderness*. P.-G. Roy, "Jean Peré et Pierre Moreau dit la Taupine," *BRH*, X (1904), 213–18.

PERONNE DE MAZÉ, LOUIS, secretary to Governor PIERRE DUBOIS Davaugour, captain in the Quebec garrison, gentleman in ordinary of the king's bedchamber, member of the Conseil Souverain, son of JEAN PERONNE Dumesnil; death date unknown.

Peronne arrived at Quebec on 31 Aug. 1661 with Governor Davaugour. That same day, his brother Michel Peronne Des Touches was buried there. On 7 November he, together with Jacques de Cailhault de la Tesserie [husband of Éléonore de GRANDMAISON], received 15 acres of land on the Île d'Orléans, granted to them by CHARLES DE LAUSON; this became the fief of La Grossardière, adjoining the Beaulieu fief. From the summer of 1662 until that of 1663, Peronne was absent on a trip to France. On 24 Sept. 1664, Governor SAFFRAY de Mézy, at loggerheads with the bishop of Quebec in the matter of appointments to the Conseil Souverain, named three new councillors, Louis Peronne de Mazé among them. The latter then sat regularly on the council until the meeting of 6 July 1665; he was obliged to leave for France shortly thereafter, and did not return. On the previous 14 May he had, before the notary Pierre DUQUET, handed over to his partner La Tesserie his interest in the La Grossardière fief, which they had begun to clear together.

HONORIUS PROVOST

Jug. et délib., passim. P.-G. Roy, *Inv. concessions*, I, 108. *BRH*, I (1895), 152; XXI (1915), 164–66.

PERONNE DUMESNIL, JEAN, a native of Anjou, lawyer in the Parlement of Paris; d. before 14 March 1667.

Dumesnil landed at Quebec 7 Sept. 1660. He stated that he was provided with a commission as "comptroller general, intendant and sovereign judge in the said country of Canada," granted by the Compagnie des Cent-Associés, the seigneur of the country. He immediately undertook the task of inspecting all fur-trading transactions carried out since 1645, the year in which this trade was ceded by the Cent-Associés to the Communauté des Habitants. Such a commission could not be considered valid, because the king, in the charter of the "great company," had reserved to himself the right of establishing sovereign judges in New France. Moreover, the control of trade did not belong to the Cent-Associés but to the king, who,

Peronne Dumesnil

in 1647, had appointed a council to administer it. The only claim the Cent-Associés could legitimately insist on was that of a thousand pounds of beaver pelts by weight each year. This commitment was not met after 1650, but Dumesnil made no mention of that in his report. It is, therefore, not surprising that the Conseil de Québec, set up by the king, did not recognize the authority of the great company's delegate.

The methods used by Dumesnil were somewhat odd for a jurist. During the first year of his stay, he appears to have tried to extort information about the commerce of the country. He made himself so odious that on 30 Aug. 1661 four settlers of the colony murdered his son, Michel Peronne Des Touches. Indomitable, the father, at an unknown date, broke into the house of the notary Guillaume AUDOUART, the secretary of the council, and seized the Communauté's papers. These were the documents that the Conseil Souverain ordered ROUER de Villeray and JEAN BOURDON to go and take from his house, 20 Sept. 1663. Dumesnil, called upon to explain his conduct, refused in practice to accept the authority of the whole council. GAUDAIS-DUPONT prevented his being arrested for his outrageous behaviour towards the tribunal. The lawyer, stripped of his powers, decided to sail back to France. He has left a dramatic account of his departure, 21 Oct. 1663, with the cannon of the port pointed at him.

Dumesnil accused the settlers of the country of having "taken and misappropriated 3,000,000 *livres* or thereabouts." Here are the items: "2,400,000 and some odd *livres* belonging to the public and being proceeds of the sale of beaver and other pelts since the year 1645," "830,175 *livres* borrowed from public funds," and "400,000 and some odd *livres* given in alms." First of all, these sums in no way concerned the Cent-Associés, who had not disbursed them and had no right to them, except for the thousand pounds by weight of beaver pelts each year. The alms were the concern of the donors, who did not demand statements, and it is odious to suppose that the beneficiaries misappropriated them outright. The loans were the lenders' affair, and a part of the money had been repaid. The 2,400,000 *livres* represented the gross receipts from the trade in beaver pelts over a period of 15 years. They had been used to meet the costs of this trade, to finance the administration, upkeep, and defence of the colony, to pay back the loans, to discharge interest, and to pay off the seigneurial rent to the Cent-Associés over a period of five years. They could not then have been misappropriated entirely, or even in their greater part. It should be noted that the budget of the colony showed a considerable deficit under the administration of the Communauté des Habitants.

Whereas Dumesnil scarcely concerned himself at all with the genuine rights of the Cent-Associés, he plunged up to his neck into commercial accounts over which he had no jurisdiction. He called in question the powers of Governors LOUIS D'AILLEBOUST, Pierre de Voyer* d'Argenson, and PIERRE DUBOIS Davaugour, and of the commissioner Gaudais-Dupont, who were all established by the king; he rejected the authority of the councils, which were also constituted by the king. He piled up charges and slanders against all officials, against the Jesuits and the bishop. And he had the presumption to suggest to the king an administrative structure of his own fabrication to replace the one that the monarch had set up a few months previously. The falsest allegations can be found in his report. He asserted that Gaudais-Dupont had not published his commission, when it had been registered in the council on 18 Sept. 1663. He attributed to the Jesuits the embezzlement of 6,000 *livres*, which they had declined to accept earlier for the construction of a presbytery. He demanded from the "Sieurs Rosé Guinet and Company, merchants of Rouen," the 100,000 *livres*—which he raised to 120,000—that they had paid for the privilege of collecting the 25 per cent tax on beaver pelts for a two-year period; they were short of the amount by 12,650 *livres* because of the insufficient volume of trade. Dumesnil further estimated at about 22,000 *livres* the revenue from the 10 per cent levy on merchandise in 1662, whereas this levy had been farmed out to Aubert* de La Chesnaye for only 10,000. And so on.

We would not need Dumesnil's report to arrive at the conclusion that the Communauté des Habitants had been badly run, although, used with discretion, the report is valuable in that it gives us a more exact idea of the situation. The incompetence of the directors can readily be believed, but their dishonesty is not proven. Bad bookkeeping, unjustified expenses, uncalculated risks, doubtful legality, all that, at varying times, marked the management of the Communauté. Gaudais himself was less than delighted with a council composed of these same people: "But after casting one's eyes on several persons from whom to make up the aforesaid council, there were none more capable to be found. It was necessary to use and employ those who are now on it."

MARIE BABOYANT

Coll. de manuscrits relatifs à la Nouv.-France, I. *JR* (Thwaites). *Jug. et délib.*, I. Ferland, *Cours d'histoire du Canada*, I. Lanctot, *Histoire du Canada*, I. Parkman,

The old régime (Toronto ed.), chap.x. P.-G. Roy, "Jean Péronne Dumesnil et ses mémoires," *BRH*, XXI (1915), 161–73, 193–200, 225–31; "Mémoire du sieur Gaudais Dupont à Mgr Colbert," *ibid.*, 277–31; *La ville de Québec*, I, 303f.

PÉROT, GILLES, priest, Sulpician, parish priest of Montreal; b. *c.* 1625 in the diocese of Chartres, d. 17 (or 16) July 1680 in Canada.

He entered the Society of Saint-Sulpice in 1651. Pérot came to Canada in 1665. The following year he succeeded M. Gabriel SOUART as parish priest and missionary at Ville-Marie (Montreal). In 1678 he became the pastor or first curate, as the superior of the seminary had, at the wish of Bishop Laval*, been appointed honorary pastor in perpetuity.

He officiated at the mass on 25 March 1674 in the chapel of the Hôtel-Dieu, which at that time was being used as a parish church, when SALIGNAC de La Mothe-Fénelon delivered the famous sermon to which Governor BUADE de Frontenac took such great exception. Legal proceedings ensued, which resulted in the preacher's returning to France. M. Pérot did not express his approval of his colleague, but admitted that he had himself said just as much in his sermons without being disturbed.

As the parish priest of Ville-Marie for 15 years, M. Pérot was responsible for the building of the parish church, of which the foundation stone was laid on 30 June 1672, in the presence of Governor RÉMY de Courcelle and Intendant TALON.

M. Pérot died suddenly in the seminary garden on 17 (or 16) July 1680, as he was getting ready to say mass.

OLIVIER MAURAULT

Faillon, *Histoire de la colonie française*, III, 495–523 *et passim*. H. Gauthier, *Sulpitiana* (Montréal, 1926), 247. Olivier Maurault, *L'œuvre et fabrique de Notre-Dame de Montréal* (Montréal, 1959), 29.

PERRAULT, JULIEN, priest, Jesuit, missionary at Cape Breton; b. probably in 1602 at Clisson, near Nantes (France); d. 24 Nov. 1647 at Orléans (France).

According to Father Melançon, Julien Perrault was born 20 June 1598; but a directory dated 1625, at the time of Perrault's noviciate, indicates his age at that time as 23, which would advance his birthdate to 1602. He seems to have studied theology before joining the Jesuits. Immediately after his noviciate he studied moral theology for a year at Amiens (1626–27), then for one year was assistant bursar at the Collège in Caen. He was ordained priest in 1628, was named to the office of bursar at the same college, and exercised it until 1633, when he went to complete his spiritual training at the noviciate of Rouen (1633–34). On 27 Jan. 1634 Julien Perrault received from Father Barthélemy Jacquinot, the provincial of Paris, his appointment to the Cape Breton mission, together with Father André Richard. He left Dieppe on 20 March and made a successful crossing to Fort Sainte-Anne or Cibou (on St. Ann's Bay, Cape Breton Island), reaching it on 30 April. Father Richard followed him on another ship seven days later. The two missionaries were first of all to be pastors for the French fishermen who lived at this post or stopped there. But they also gave their earnest attention to observing the customs of the natives and learning their language. In the two letters of Father Perrault that have come down to us, the Micmacs are described with an obvious liking, and the task of spreading the gospel seemed full of promise. Although Father Melançon dates Father Perrault's return to France as 1635, we believe it must be placed a year later. The directory of the province of France does not show him in his homeland in 1634 and 1635, and the relation sent by him in 1635 leads us to suppose that he did not return that year. Perhaps the sickness that ravaged the establishments around the gulf in the early years forced Father Perrault to go back to France. He resided at the Collège in Rennes in 1636–37, then was bursar of the Collège in Vannes from 1637 to 1641; afterwards he was bursar of the Collège in Quimper, and finally of the Collège in Orléans, where he died.

LUCIEN CAMPEAU

Archivum Romanum Societatis Iesu, codex Franc. 22, catalogues annuels des maisons et des personnes de la province de France de la Compagnie de Jésus; Lettres originales, codex Gal. 109 I, ff.54–55, lettre autographe du P. Julien Perrault au P. Mutius Vitelleschi, général, Sainte-Anne, 19 sept. 1634. *JR* (Thwaites). R. Latourelle, *Étude sur les écrits de saint Jean de Brébeuf* (2v., Montréal, 1952–53), II, [39]–40, lettre au père Julien Perrault, datée de Rouen le 31 mai 1631. [Melançon], *Liste des missionnaires jésuites, Nouvelle-France et Louisiane, 1611–1800* (Montréal, 1929), 61.

PERREAULT, HYACINTHE, Recollet, eighth provincial commissioner of his order in New France; b. 1654 in France; d. 1700 in Paris.

Hyacinthe Perrault joined the Recollets of the province of Saint-Denis in 1670. When his theological studies were finished, his superiors appointed him reader in theology, an office he filled until 1686. He was engaged in preaching retreats to the religious of his order when, in 1692, the council of definitors of his province appointed him provincial commissioner of the Canadian Recollets and superior of the convent of Notre-Dame-des-Anges at Quebec.

His term of office was noteworthy for the construction in the Upper Town of a new convent, of which he became the superior after the convent of Notre-Dame-des-Anges had been transferred to the bishop by a contract signed 13 Sept. 1693. Anxious to provide his religious with a suitable place for retreats, Father Hyacinthe secured, 14 Nov. 1693, the permission of the bishop and the intendant to build a hermitage, "l'hermitage St-Roch," on the banks of the St. Charles River.

On 10 May of the next year, Bishop Saint-Vallier [La Croix*] was invited to open the first Recollet convent and church at Montreal. The ceremony, attended by Louis-Hector de Callières*, was marred by the unpleasantness of the "prayer-stool incident," as a result of which the bishop laid first the church and later the religious themselves under interdict. Father Hyacinthe devoted himself to the settlement of this dispute, in which the Recollets were the innocent victims. The matter was not resolved until the spring of 1695. When his term expired in 1696, Father Hyacinthe went back to France and died in Paris 26 April 1700.

FRÉDÉRIC GINGRAS

APQ *Rapport, 1923–24*, 75–79, Première, deuxième et troisième monitions de Mgr de St-Vallier aux révérends Pères Récollets, 19 juillet, 9 août, et 15 sept. 1694. BN, MS Fr. 13875, Nécrologe des Frères-Mineurs Récollets de la province Saint-Denys en France. PAC, FM 3, no.8 (AN, K), 3, 1232, no.48, pp. 193–213; 6, 1374, nos.85, 87. Auguste Gosselin, *L'Église du Canada depuis Monseigneur de Laval jusqu'à la conquête* (3v., Québec, 1911–14), I.

PERROT, FRANÇOIS-MARIE, Seigneur de Sainte-Geneviève, governor of Montreal 1669–84 and of Acadia 1684–87; b. 1644 in Paris; d. 1691.

He was a captain in the Picardie regiment. In 1669 he married Madeleine Laguide Meynier, a niece of Jean TALON, and by her he had six children. Through Talon's influence he obtained the appointment as governor of Montreal from the seigneurs of the island, the Messieurs de Saint-Sulpice, succeeding Paul de CHOMEDEY de Maisonneuve.

Accompanied by his bride and her uncle, Talon, Perrot sailed from La Rochelle 5 July 1669 but, the ship being wrecked on the coast of Portugal, they were forced to return to France. On 20 April 1670 on the nomination of M. de Bretonvilliers, superior of the Sulpicians in Paris, he received a royal commission as governor of Montreal. In mid-May 1670 he sailed again from La Rochelle, accompanied by Talon but not by his wife, and arrived at Quebec on 18 August. When he reached Montreal, Dollier* de Casson, superior of the Sulpician seminary, commented: "As he is a very handsome gentleman, of good birth, his arrival gave us all reason to hope much from him." In this expectation, however, the Sulpicians were to be sadly disappointed, as also were Perrot's creditors. When they had recourse to the courts to seize his property he obtained, in July 1671, *lettres d'état* from the king which protected him against confiscation during his period of service in Canada, since he was now unable to defend his interests in person in the law courts in France. This action was, however, normal procedure for officers serving abroad.

In 1671 Perrot accompanied RÉMY de Courcelle, the governor-general of the colony, to Lake Ontario to order the Iroquois to cease their assaults on the Indian tribes allied to the French and to abandon their announced intention to attack the French settlements. Courcelle's audacious expedition achieved its aim and war was averted. The following year Perrot obtained a seigneurial grant of the large island located at the junction of the Ottawa and St. Lawrence rivers that today bears his name. He established a fur-trading post on the island, employed *coureurs de bois*, and forestalled the fur-traders of Montreal. Such ventures were forbidden by royal edicts governing the fur trade but when the inhabitants of Montreal protested against his actions, Perrot employed force to make them desist.

In 1673 BUADE de Frontenac established a fur-trading post on Lake Ontario which posed a much graver threat to the Montreal traders than did Perrot's illegal activities and which aroused much greater resentment. Both Perrot and the people of Montreal protested vigorously and for a time they were united in their opposition to Frontenac. To quell this resistance Frontenac had Perrot arrested, under rather dubious circumstances [*see* BIZARD and SALIGNAC], then ordered the Conseil Souverain to bring charges against him and to commit him for trial. Perrot, however, was no coward; he refused to be intimidated and from his prison cell he made a very effective defence, refusing to recognize the right of the Conseil Souverain to try him since he held his commission from the king and was accountable only to him. Perrot succeeded in instilling in the councillors the fear that their attempt to bring him to trial would be regarded as *ultra vires*. To the great annoyance of Frontenac they eventually referred the matter to the king. Perrot was then sent to France by Frontenac to account to the king for his alleged refusal to obey the orders of the governor-general of the colony.

Louis XIV and the minister of marine, Colbert, condemned the actions of both Frontenac and Perrot, but to uphold the authority of the king vested in a governor-general, Perrot was punished by being sent to the comfortable seclusion of the Bastille for three weeks. Upon his release he was reinstated as governor of Montreal and Frontenac was ordered to treat him with more respect in future. Upon his return to New France Perrot made his peace with Frontenac and they entered into an uneasy alliance to further their illicit activities in the fur trade. From this point on, when complaints were made against Perrot by the seigneurs and the people of Montreal, Frontenac quashed them. Thus protected, Perrot rode roughshod over the people of Montreal; any who protested against his attempts to garner the bulk of the fur trade for himself were beaten by his guards or thrown into gaol without trial and held there during Perrot's pleasure. In these acts of tyranny Perrot was aided by Frontenac's man, Josias BOISSEAU, an agent of the Compagnie de la Ferme du Roi. In 1678 Perrot arbitrarily imprisoned MIGEON de Branssat, a judge of the seigneurial court at Montreal, for having ordered the arrest of a *coureur de bois* in Perrot's employ. When the Conseil Souverain decided to intervene, Frontenac forbade them to take any action. The council then referred the matter to the king who promptly issued a royal edict forbidding local governors to imprison or fine anyone without specific orders from the governor-general or the Conseil Souverain. This edict was accompanied by direct orders to Frontenac that on no account was he to order the arrest of anyone except for the crimes of sedition and treason, which, Colbert pointed out, "hardly ever occur," but to leave the administration of justice entirely in the hands of the established courts. By this royal edict and the accompanying orders the people of New France were thereafter afforded protection against arbitrary arrest. Ensuing events made it plain that the king and the minister of marine were determined that the edict should be enforced. Oddly enough, in England in that same year, 1679, and under somewhat similar circumstances, Parliament passed an act to serve the same purpose, the Habeas Corpus Act.

Perrot, however, paid no heed to the edict. Relying on the protection afforded by Frontenac, he continued his harassment of any residents of Montreal who complained of his illegal fur-trading activities. When the Ottawas came to Montreal to trade their furs he stationed his guards to prevent all but his own and Frontenac's men from trading with them. On one occasion he was reported to have traded the clothes off his back to an Indian who then paraded around the town in the governor's garb, and Perrot boasted that he had made a profit of 30 *pistoles* on the exchange. It was estimated that in 1680 alone he had made some 40,000 *livres* illegal profit in the fur trade and two years later it was reliably reported that he had realized 100,000 *livres* on the sale of beaver pelts at Niort in Poitou.

When the Conseil Souverain, in 1680 and 1681, tried to bring Perrot to account for his illegal activities Frontenac put every obstacle in its path, but in 1682 Frontenac was dismissed from his post. Despite the intercession of his brother, Perrot de Fercourt, and his influential friends at the court, the complaints against Perrot from the citizens of Montreal, the seigneurs of the island, the intendant, and the Conseil Souverain were too numerous and well authenticated to be ignored. In May 1682 the king informed LE FEBVRE de La Barre, newly appointed governor-general of the colony, that he had decided to dismiss Perrot from his post and La Barre was instructed to recommend an officer in the colony to succeed him. La Barre, however, defended Perrot, made light of his illegal fur-trading, and declared that the complaints against him were occasioned by the jealousy of the Montreal merchants. Since La Barre himself was quickly to become very active in the fur trade, despite strict orders forbidding him to have any part in it, directly or indirectly, La Barre was really excusing his own as well as Perrot's conduct. The minister, however, was not impressed by La Barre's advocacy and in 1683 Perrot was interdicted, stripped of his powers as governor, and informed that unless he mended his ways and made his peace with the seigneurs of the island he would be recalled to France. The following year Louis-Hector de Callières* was appointed governor of Montreal and Perrot was given the post of governor of Acadia.

Not a great deal is known of Perrot's career from this point on. Acadia was sparsely populated and sadly neglected by the French government, hence there were few officials in the colony and little correspondence with the ministry of marine. Moreover, of the correspondence that there must have been, little has survived to provide information. It is known, however, that Perrot went from Montreal to France and did not take up his post at Port-Royal (Annapolis Royal, N.S.) until September 1685. Despite the stern warnings of the minister it appears that he behaved in Acadia exactly as he had done at Montreal. He lost no time in seeking to monopolize the fur trade of the colony, traded brandy over the counter in his own

Petitchouan

house, shipped contraband to Boston and, in complete disregard for the king's orders, allowed New England seamen to fish in Acadian coastal waters upon purchasing a permit, for which he charged £5 per ketch. Once again the minister received complaints about Perrot's conduct from individuals and from BERGIER, a Huguenot merchant of La Rochelle and director of the Compagnie des Pêches sédentaires de l'Acadie. In consequence, Perrot was dismissed from his post in April 1687. He did not, however, return to France but remained in Acadia and continued his malpractices, despite warnings from the minister to desist or learn what it meant to incur the king's serious displeasure.

Then, in 1690, English freebooters succeeded where Louis XIV and his ministers had failed. In mid-May 1690 Sir William PHIPS, commanding a Boston expedition, arrived off Port-Royal and obliged the governor, Louis-Alexandre Des Friches* de Meneval, to surrender the fort, taking him and the garrison into captivity. A month later JOSEPH ROBINAU de Villebon, an officer in the Port-Royal garrison, returned from France on the *Union*, belonging to the Acadia fishing company, and took over command in the province. Accompanied by Perrot, he removed to the Saint John River. A few days later two pirate ships from the English colonies entered the river, captured the French vessels, and Perrot with them. Believing that he had hidden large sums of money, they tortured him to make him divulge its whereabouts, with what success is not known. Subsequently he was rescued by a French privateer and landed at a French port. He then took up residence in Paris and sought, unsuccessfully, to obtain his reappointment as governor of Acadia. He died on 20 Oct. 1691, allegedly as a result of his sufferings at the hands of the English freebooters.

W. J. ECCLES

The main documentary sources for Perrot's career are: AN, Col., B, 8, f.18; C^{11A}, 3, 4, 5; C^{11D}, *passim*, F^3, 2, 3, 4. BN, MS Fr. 6653, f.280. Much material concerning Perrot's conflict with Frontenac is contained in *Jug. et délib.*, I. Perrot's career as governor of Montreal is discussed in *Coll. de manuscrits relatifs à la Nouv.-France*, I, II, *passim*; Eccles, *Frontenac*; *Canada under Louis XIV, 1663–1701* (Canadian Centenary ser., III, Toronto, 1964). On Perrot's career in Acadia *see*: B. T. McCully, "The New England–Acadia fishery dispute and the Nicholson mission of August, 1687," Essex Institute *Hist. Coll.*, XCVI (1960), 277–90. PAC *Report, 1912*, App. E, F. Webster, *Acadia*.

PETITCHOUAN. *See* CHOMINA

PEUVRET DEMESNU, JEAN-BAPTISTE, soldier, secretary to Governor JEAN DE LAUSON, notary and clerk of the seneschal's court, seigneurial attorney for the Compagnie des Indes occidentales, receiver for crown lands, chief clerk and secretary of the Conseil Souverain, seigneur; b. 1632 at Bellême (France); d. 1697 at Quebec.

Son of Marie La Garenne and Jacques Peuvret, king's counsellor and criminal lieutenant for the fiscal subdivision of Le Perche, Peuvret received a sound education which permitted him to play an important role in New France. He arrived as a soldier in Canada on 12 Oct. 1651, along with his brother François who was drowned on 24 June 1657.

In 1653 Peuvret was acting as secretary to Governor Jean de Lauson. Then, from the end of 1653 till the summer of 1657, we lose sight of him temporarily. Perhaps he took a trip to France. In any event, in July 1657 Peuvret became notary and clerk of the seneschal's court of Quebec, which offices he held until the summer of 1659.

Peuvret was certainly in high favour in Quebec, since he married there on 10 July 1659 Catherine Nau de Fossambault, the widow of "the late Messire Louis de Lauson, knight, seigneur of [La] Citière," son of the former governor. Catherine Nau came from a family that had been ennobled in 1605. Her father, Jacques Nau de La Boissière et de Fossambault, had first been treasurer of supplementary war expenses for the province of Languedoc, then king's counsellor and receiver-general of finances for the province of Berry. Having come to Quebec with the intention of becoming a nun hospitaller, she had married the son of Governor Lauson the same year she arrived (1655). Shortly after their marriage Peuvret and his wife returned to France, and came back to Canada in the autumn of 1661.

For Peuvret a new career was about to begin. On 18 September 1663 he was appointed chief clerk and secretary of the Conseil Souverain, an office which he held until his death, except for the period from 19 Sept. 1664 to 6 Dec. 1666, when he was removed from office by Governor SAFFRAY de Mézy for having supported the policy of Bishop Laval*. To these already important offices were added, on 1 May 1666, that of seigneurial attorney of the Compagnie des Indes occidentales, and, about 1670, that of receiver of crown lands.

To all these titles Peuvret added another, that of seigneur. From the Lausons he inherited the seigneury of Gaudarville; he was in addition the owner of an arriere-fief on the Île d'Orléans by virtue of a grant from the Compagnie de Beaupré dated 12 March 1661.

By his marriage with Catherine Nau, Jean-Baptiste Peuvret had five children, one of whom, Alexandre*, succeeded him as chief clerk of the Conseil Souverain and as seigneur of Gaudarville. Another, Marie-Catherine, a god-daughter of Governor Rémy de Courcelle, married Ignace Juchereau* Duchesnay, seigneur of Beauport, in 1683. Jean-Baptiste married his second wife, Marie-Rogère Lepage, on 16 Oct. 1681. Peuvret died at Quebec on 23 May 1697.

ANDRÉ VACHON

AJQ, Greffe de J.-B. Peuvret, 1653–59. APQ, Ins. Cons. souv. *Jug. et délib.*, *passim*. Berneval, "Les filles venues au Canada de 1654 à 1657," *BRH*, XLVI (1940), 344. Azarie Couillard Després, "Louis Couillard de Lespinay," *RSCT*, 3d ser., XVIII (1924), sect.I, 118 J.-E. Roy, *Histoire du notariat*, I. P.-G. Roy, "Les conseillers au Conseil souverain de la Nouvelle-France," *RSCT*, 3d ser., IX (1915), sect.I, 184.

PÉZARD DE LA TOUSCHE CHAMPLAIN, ÉTIENNE, soldier, named to the governorship of Montreal, seigneur of Champlain, colonizer; b. 1624 at Blois (Orléanais), son of Claude Pézard de La Tousche and Marie Masson; d. *c.* 1696.

His arrival in Canada is generally dated as 1661, the same year that he was appointed lieutenant at Trois-Rivières. He must have distinguished himself in some way, since shortly afterwards he was promoted captain of the garrison. During his stay at Trois-Rivières it is thought that he helped Pierre Boucher* in the writing of his *Histoire véritable et naturelle . . .* (Paris, 1664).

He left Trois-Rivières in June 1664 to take over the command of the Montreal garrison. On 20 June, in the parish church of Notre-Dame, he married Madeleine Mullois de La Borde, who gave him five children. On the day of his marriage he was nominated governor of Montreal by SAFFRAY de Mézy. Between the latter and CHOMEDEY de Maisonneuve, who protected the rights of the seigneurs of the island, there was a certain coolness, and the nomination led to nothing because of the opposition of the seigneurs of Montreal, upon whom such a nomination depended. Probably Mézy wanted to compensate Pézard de La Tousche by granting him, on 8 Aug. 1664, the Champlain seigneury, which was a league and a half in length by one in depth. La Tousche, as distinct from the majority of the seigneurs of his day, took his role of "colony builder" seriously. He immediately erected a manor-house on the rocky promontory at the mouth of the Champlain River, and to attract settlers he began the construction of a church in 1665. Settlers thronged to the spot. In 1665 alone he granted more than 22 *censives*. His colonizing zeal made him a prominent inhabitant of New France. In 1670, in order to emphasize his merit, the intendant had no hesitation in giving him a mare from the royal stables. Later, in 1678, his name appeared among the 20 prominent persons summoned to decide upon the question of the trade in spirits.

The date of his death is not noted in the records. It is presumed that he died in 1696, for although the documents make mention of him in 1695, a text dated November 1696 speaks of the widow Marie-Madeleine Mullois. His wife lived until 1704.

JEAN HAMELIN

[Pierre Boucher], *Histoire véritable et naturelle des mœurs et productions du pays de la Nouvelle-France, vulgairement dite le Canada* (Paris, 1664; Société historique de Boucherville, I, 1964). *Jug. et délib.*, *passim*. P.-G. Roy, *Inv. concessions*, II, 105–7. Prosper Cloutier, *Histoire de la paroisse de Champlain* (2v., Trois-Rivières, 1915). Faillon, *Histoire de la colonie française*, III, 94f. P.-G. Roy, "Les gouverneurs de Montréal," *BRH*, XI (1905), 165.

PHIPPS, THOMAS, junior, HBC employee; fl. 1679–86.

He was warehousekeeper at Moose Fort in 1679–80 and presumably for the following year. In 1681 he was with Governor John NIXON on Charlton Island, a rendezvous for men from the several factories and the ships from England. The *Diligence* (Capt. NEHEMIAH WALKER) was late that year and after supplies were distributed ice conditions made it too hazardous for Nixon and his staff to reach the mainland by the yacht *Colleton*.

Nixon's decision to winter at Charlton Island had to be made known at Moose Fort (headquarters) and Phipps voluntarily offered to attempt the crossing in a small boat with four companions. After great difficulty the party reached the mainland and travelled—on foot and without snowshoes—100 miles to Moose in eight days. Phipps carried a commission from Nixon investing him with full authority as deputy governor to deal with any "distractions" or disorders, and his "prudant care" was highly commended when Nixon visited Moose Fort next spring.

About that time Phipps came under suspicion in London in connection with an interloping expedition in which his cousin, Thomas Phipps senior, a shareholder in the HBC, was heavily interested. When intercepted letters exposed this

Phips

scheme and the possibility that Phipps junior might be implicated, he faced dismissal.

Such good reports of his character, however, were furnished by colleagues returning from Hudson Bay that the Company reversed its decision, and in 1685 promoted Phipps governor at Port Nelson. Success went to his head. He demanded a 100 per cent salary increase which was flatly refused. Coming home in 1686 he haggled over terms until a subcommittee declared him "not so candid as reported."

A further black mark against him was gambling. His winning of £14 in one night from a colleague, Surgeon John Kerr, in 1684 led the Company to refuse to transfer sums between its servants' accounts in settlement of gaming debts. To his credit it may be added that Phipps was "one whom the Indians loved."

MAUD M. HUTCHESON

HBRS, VIII, IX (Rich); XI (Rich and Johnson); XXI (Rich).

PHIPS, SIR WILLIAM, sailor, adventurer, and colonial governor; b. (according to Cotton Mather) 2 Feb., 1650/1, near the mouth of the Kennebec River in what is now the state of Maine, the son of humble parents, James and Mary Phips; d. 18 Feb., 1694/95 in London, England.

After working as a shepherd for his widowed mother, he was apprenticed to a ship carpenter and subsequently practised this trade in Boston, where he married a wealthy widow, Mary (Spencer) Hull. He is also said to have been a ship captain. Becoming interested in the recovery of sunken Spanish treasure, he apparently made a first voyage to the Bahamas without much success; later, however, he went to England and succeeded in obtaining the loan of a naval vessel for another attempt. This (1683–84) also yielded a very small return. In 1686, nevertheless, Phips gained the support of the second Duke of Albemarle, who organized a joint-stock company to finance a search for a sunken treasure-ship believed to lie off Haiti. This venture proved triumphantly successful; in June 1687 Phips returned to England with treasure valued officially at over £207,600. His own share was over £11,000 (R. H. George, "The treasure trove of William Phips," *N. Eng. Q.*, VI (1933), 294–318). The incident brought him his knighthood, and James II appointed him provost marshal general of the short-lived Dominion of New England. Returning to England to complain of his reception by the authorities of the Dominion, he came in contact with Increase Mather, and thereafter the two were close associates.

In 1690 Phips underwent what seems to have been a politic religious conversion, being received into the Second Church of Boston by Cotton Mather. Almost simultaneously he was sworn in as major-general to command an expedition organized by Massachusetts against French Acadia. He sailed with seven vessels carrying a militia "Foot Regiment" about 450 strong, and after preliminary operations against settlements at Penobscot and Passamaquoddy entered the harbour of Port-Royal (Annapolis Royal, N.S.) on 19 May (N.S.). Next day a flag of truce was sent to the fort, and on 21 May the governor, Louis-Alexandre Des Friches* de Meneval surrendered. He had only about 70 men, and no guns mounted, and resistance would have been useless. On 22 May the "journal" of Phips's proceedings says, "We cut down the cross, rifled the Church, pulled down the High-Altar, breaking their images"; and on 23 May, "kept gathering Plunder both by land and water, and also under ground in their Gardens" (PAC *Report, 1912*, 54 ff.). After forcing the inhabitants to swear allegiance to King William and Queen Mary, Phips sailed back to Boston with his booty, leaving LA TOURASSE as interim president of the local council, and taking Meneval, the soldiers, and Fathers Trouvé* and Petit* with him as prisoners. Meneval subsequently claimed that Phips had taken some of his personal property, which he seems to have had difficulty in recovering even after the Massachusetts council ordered Phips to restore it.

Phips's bloodless success against Port-Royal was presumably considered to justify his appointment to command a more important expedition which was being organized at the time of his return. The New England colonies and New York dispatched a force overland against Montreal, which accomplished virtually nothing; while Phips, with about 32 ships (only 4 of which were of any size) and somewhat more than 2,000 Massachusetts militiamen, moved against Quebec by way of the St. Lawrence. Phips's expedition was inadequately supplied with ammunition; and it was delayed until unduly late in the summer by awaiting supplies hoped for from England which never came. It sailed from Hull, near Boston, only on 19 or 20 Aug. 1690. Bad weather, contrary winds, and lack of a St. Lawrence pilot hampered progress, and Phips did not anchor in the Quebec basin until 16 October.

Quebec's defences had hitherto been very slight; but during the past few months the governor, BUADE de Frontenac, had strengthened them considerably, constructing an improvised *enceinte* covering the side of the town facing the open country (but not enclosing the high ground where the modern Citadel stands). Before Phips's arrival the batteries facing the river were improved. Frontenac himself reached Quebec from Montreal on 14 October, and when all the militia whom he had summoned arrived he had nearly 3,000 men to defend the place. Frontenac had reason for confidence, the more so as he possessed a force of colonial regulars organized in three battalions and certainly superior in efficiency to Phips's amateur soldiery. (As it turned out, however, virtually all the fighting on the French side was done by the Canadian militia.) When on 16 October Phips sent Frontenac, by Major Thomas Savage, a summons to surrender, the governor made the famous reply that he had no answer to give "save from the mouths of my cannon and from my musketry."

The New Englanders' plan, prepared by a council of war, was to land their main force on the Beauport shore east of the St. Charles River, and move it across that river with the aid of the fleet's boats, which would also land the field guns on the Quebec side of the St. Charles. When the landing force was on the heights west of Quebec, the fleet would attack the front of the town and land another force there. Frontenac on his side pursued a cautious policy. He proposed to fight only a skirmishing action east of the St. Charles, holding his regulars in reserve for a European-style battle on the open ground west of Quebec. This battle never took place, for the English landing force, commanded by Major John Walley*, Phips's second-in-command, never got across the St. Charles. It landed on 18 October, and immediately began to be harassed by Canadian militia under JACQUES LE MOYNE de Sainte-Hélène. The ships' boats failed to give the expected co-operation, but did land the guns—on the wrong side of the St. Charles. The same evening, Phips's four large ships, quite contrary to the plan, anchored before Quebec and began to bombard the town. (The statement, made by Charlevoix* and others, that this took place on the 16th, immediately after Frontenac rejected Phips's ultimatum, is certainly inaccurate.) The bombardment continued on the 19th, and was broken off when the English had shot away most of their ammunition, and their ships, particularly Phips's flagship the *Six Friends*, had suffered considerable damage by the fire of the town batteries.

Walley's force remained inactive during the bombardment. His men were suffering from cold and complaining of shortage of rum, and there was smallpox among them. There was a skirmish on 20 October, during which Sainte-Hélène was mortally wounded. The same day Phips agreed, apparently reluctantly, to the recommendation of a council of war held by the officers ashore that the landing force should re-embark. This evacuation, at first proposed for the morning of the 21st, was postponed until the following night. It was carried out successfully, the French apparently not realizing what was happening; but the New Englanders left five of their six cannon behind them. A more enterprising commander than Frontenac showed himself to be might well have destroyed Walley's discouraged force before it could get away; but the governor was content to stand on the defensive to the end. Although the English had talked of landing at another point, nothing more was attempted. On 23 and 24 October an exchange of prisoners was negotiated and effected, and Phips's ships then made sail for Boston. Although his own account of the expedition claims that his casualties did not exceed 30 men, the loss by sickness or marine accident ran into hundreds; James Lloyd of Boston wrote in the following January, "7 vessels yet wanting 3 more cast away & burnt." Cotton Mather tells how one brigantine was wrecked on Anticosti; her crew maintained themselves on the island through the winter and were apparently rescued the following summer by a ship from Boston. Phips's defeat was complete and disastrous, but the French would have been in serious difficulties if the siege had been prolonged, for food was lacking for the large force assembled to defend Quebec. Phips himself had displayed no natural military talents to offset his lack of experience. It can be argued however that the absence of trained soldiers and adequate supplies had doomed the enterprise from the start.

This reverse was far from ending Phips's career. When William III granted a new charter to Massachusetts in 1691, the appointment of the governor was reserved to the Crown. On Increase Mather's recommendation, Phips was made the first royal governor, taking up his duties in May 1692. The witchcraft mania was then active in Massachusetts. After a period of uncertainty, Phips put an end to the executions, reprieving all condemned persons pending instructions from London. In 1693 a letter from Queen Mary supported his attitude and, Phips said, averted the ruin of the province (PRO, *CSP, Col.*, 1693–96, items 112, 545). Phips did effective work in defending the eastern frontier against the French and Indians, but he became violently embroiled with the authorities of the neighbouring colonies and with the local officers of the Royal Navy. He is also accused of using his position for his own profit in various ways. In 1693 he was instructed to co-operate with

Phokus Valerianatos

Sir Francis Wheler in a seaborne expedition against Quebec which had been planned in England; but the orders reached him belatedly, and when Wheler consulted him in July, Phips—whose experience before Quebec in 1690 had obviously left a deep impression—said that he would need at least four months to collect forces from the other colonies, that at least 4,000 men would be needed (Wheler's effective force was only 650) and that the expedition should have sailed not later than 1 July. Wheler accordingly limited himself to an enterprise against Placentia, which was foiled by the weather, and a raid on Saint-Pierre. In 1694 Phips was summoned to England to answer charges against him, including those relating to his assault upon and persecution of Capt. Richard Short, R.N. Phips died of fever before the investigation was completed. He was buried in the church of St. Mary Woolnoth, London.

Phips was amply endowed with energy and courage, and seems to have had considerable native ability; but he also possessed less admirable qualities. Sir John Fortescue, the editor of the colonial *State Papers* of his period, came to the conclusion that he was "ignorant, brutal, covetous and violent," and there is much warrant for this opinion. He had few qualifications for the military commands he held against Port-Royal and Quebec. The part he took in ending the witchcraft persecution is the most creditable incident of his public life.

C. P. STACEY

[The earliest biography of Phips was Cotton Mather's *Pietas in Patriam: the life of His Excellency Sir William Phips, Knt.* (London, 1697; reprinted in Mather's *Magnalia Christi Americana*, London, 1702 and 2v., Hartford, Conn., 1820); written to justify the Mathers' sponsorship of Phips, it is correspondingly unreliable. The most extended modern study, Alice Lounsberry's *Sir William Phips, treasure fisherman and governor of the Massachusetts Bay Colony* (New York, 1941), is a curious mixture of research and imagination, largely uncritical. Viola F. Barnes's article in *DAB* has an excellent critical bibliography; see also two articles by the same author in *N. Eng. Q.*, I, (1928): "The Rise of William Phips" (271–94) and "Phippius Maximus" (532–53). Rev. Henry O. Thayer's *Sir William Phips, adventurer and statesman . . .* (Portland, Me., 1927) is generally reliable.

None of the recent American studies is of much value on Phips's Canadian ventures. The best general account covering them is still that in Francis Parkman, *Count Frontenac and New France* (1st ed., Boston, 1877). A detailed account of the Quebec enterprise is "Sir William Phips' Attack on Quebec, 1690," in *Introduction to the study of military history for Canadian students*, ed. C. P. Stacey (5th ed., 2d rev., Ottawa, 1960). The official French accounts of this episode are in AN, Col., C^{11A}, 11. These and other French documents, and some English accounts, are printed in *1690, Sir William Phips devant Québec: histoire d'un siege*, éd. Ernest Myrand (Québec, 1893); the documents are more useful than the commentary. The chief New England accounts, including Phips's own, are in W. K. Watkins, *Soldiers in the expedition to Canada in 1690 . . .* (Boston, 1898). Many important documents relating to Phips are abstracted in PRO, *CSP, Col., 1689–92* and *1693–96*. Several contemporary documents on the Port-Royal and Quebec enterprises, including James Lloyd's letter, are in PAC *Report, 1912*. C.P.S.]

PHOKUS VALERIANATOS. *See* FUCA [Appendix]

PIAT (sometimes called **Le Piat**), **IRÉNÉE**, Recollet, priest, missionary; b. 1594 at Giens; d. 1674 at Nevers.

He entered the Recollet order at Nevers and made his profession there on 21 June 1612. On 15 May 1622, Father Piat sailed from Dieppe for Canada and arrived at Tadoussac about mid-June. There he gave a solemn blessing to a large cross he had caused to be set up and after building a chapel of branches, he celebrated mass in it.

In July he went to Quebec with ÉMERY DE CAËN. On 25 August he returned to Tadoussac, which he left on 13 December to go and spend the winter among the Montagnais. On the way, having been unable to prevent the Indian guide, whom he had befriended, from committing a murder at the instigation of the medicine-man, he abandoned the trip by way of protest; Father LE CARON undertook to replace him among the Indians. The following spring Father Piat attempted to resume his evangelical work among the Montagnais, but as the latter were preparing a war-party he had no other choice than to return to Tadoussac.

In 1624 he was chosen to go to France to recruit new missionaries. He left Quebec on 15 August with Brother SAGARD. His mission produced the desired result: the Jesuits, acting upon the invitation of the Recollets, arrived at Quebec in 1625. Father Piat, however, did not return.

He was guardian of the monasteries at Montargis (1629–31) and Metz (1636), and definitor of his province in 1632 and again in 1671. "He was," says the Mortuologe, "a priest of great simplicity and good-heartedness, and very intelligent." He died at Nevers on 28 June 1674.

G.-M. DUMAS

ASQ, MSS, 200, Mortuologe des Recolets. Champlain, *Œuvres* (Laverdière). Placide Gallemant, *Provincia Sancti Dionysii in Gallia* (Catalauni, 1649). Le Clercq, *First establishment of the faith* (Shea), I, 175, *et passim*. Sagard, *Histoire du Canada* (Tross), I, passim. Jouve, *Les Franciscains et le Canada (1615–1629)*.

PICOTÉ DE BELESTRE, PIERRE, merchant, fur trader, officer of the garrison of Montreal; b. *c.* 1637 in France, son of François Picoté de Belestre, a doctor; d. January 1679.

He came to Canada in 1659 as a member of the contingent accompanying the Religious Hospitallers of La Flèche, who had been authorized to come to Ville-Marie (Montreal). His sister Perrinne, one of Jeanne MANCE's two lay companions on the crossing, was for some time a novice with the Hospitallers.

Dollier* de Casson, who recorded Pierre Picoté de Belestre's arrival at Ville-Marie, declared that "he indeed graces this place in time of war as well as when we are enjoying peace, because of the outstanding qualities which he possesses for both of these occasions." In fact, we know little about him, although he seems to have had a certain prestige among the members of the settlement at Montreal. A trader at the annual fair at Montreal, an honorary churchwarden in 1671, he received that same year a grant of land at Pointe-aux-Trembles.

His name is most frequently associated with warlike episodes. In 1660 he was one of those who asked DOLLARD Des Ormeaux to postpone his undertaking until after seeding, so that they could take part in it. Later, upon receipt of the news of the defeat at the Long Sault and the possibility of an attack in force against the post, CHOMEDEY de Maisonneuve appointed him to take charge of the defence of the house at Sainte-Marie which belonged to the Sulpicians and which was situated half a league from Ville-Marie. In May 1662 he repulsed at this same place an attack by 50 Iroquois, whom he succeeded in routing. Two years later he was again involved in an Iroquois ambush. Finally, in 1666 he took part in PROUVILLE de Tracy's expedition as a lieutenant commanding the troops that had been raised at Montreal.

Pierre Picoté de Belestre had married Marie Pars in France. He had at least five children, including Hélène, who married Antoine de LA FRENAYE de Brucy; Marie-Anne, who married Alphonse de Tonty*; and Jeanne-Geneviève*, who was seduced by Pierre Le Moyne* d'Iberville.

JEAN BLAIN

AJM, Greffe de Bénigne Basset, 12 déc. 1684, Inventaire des biens de Picoté de Belestre. Dollier de Casson, *Histoire du Montréal*, 141, 143, 168, 180f. *BRH*, XV (1909), 153. Faillon, *Histoire de la colonie française*, II, 361, 389, 398, 418, 419, 517–19; III, 94–141. "La foire des pelleteries à Montréal au XVIIe siècle," *BRH*, XXVIII (1922), 373–80.

PIERRON, JEAN, priest, Jesuit, missionary; b. 28 Sept. 1631 at Dun-sur-Meuse, France; d. probably 20 Feb. 1700 at Pont-à-Mousson, France.

Jean Pierron became a Jesuit at Nancy on 21 Nov. 1650, and after periods of studying and teaching at Pont-à-Mousson, Verdun, and Metz, he arrived at Quebec 27 June 1667. He made his solemn profession in the Society of Jesus 5 March 1668.

Along with FRÉMIN and BOQUET he took part in the re-opening of the mission in the Iroquois country, where he stayed from 1667 to 1674, with the Mohawks among others.

He made a great impression upon these Indians because of his talent for sketching and painting. He spent the winter of 1674 in Acadia. That same year he travelled in disguise through New England, Maryland, and Virginia. At Boston he had several discussions on religious matters with Protestant ministers, but despite his disguise he was suspected of being a Jesuit and was summoned to appear before the General Assembly of Massachusetts. He was not, however, otherwise interfered with. In Maryland he met three English Jesuits and suggested to his superiors, though in vain, that he be sent there to help them. After three more years among the Iroquois he returned to France in 1678.

J. MONET

ACSM, f.301, biographical notes based on the old Jesuit catalogues. *JR* (Thwaites), *passim*. *JJ* (Laverdière et Casgrain), *passim*. Campbell, *Pioneer priests*, I, 215–25. Rochemonteix, *Les Jésuites et la Nouvelle-France au XVIIe siècle*, II, 404. J. G. Shea, *History of the Catholic Church in the United States* (4v., New York, 1886–92), I: *The Catholic Church in colonial days . . . 1521–1763*.

PIESKARET (Piescaret, Piescars, Diescaret), SIMON, Algonkin chief of the tribe Tessouat or "Le Borgne"; d. 1647.

Pieskaret, according to Nicolas Perrot,* was known as "the terror of the Iroquois" for they knew his valour well. Many extraordinary deeds had rendered him "redoubtable" to the enemy. The Algonkins spoke of him as "a very brave man," and the Jesuits wrote that he was "a man somewhat noted among his people."

Pieskaret was mourned as dead in 1643, believed to have been captured by Iroquois, but in early April he appeared with his band, opposite Montreal, bearing the head of an enemy, having escaped the pursuing Iroquois because of the

Pigarouich

swift break-up of the river. This return was celebrated with dancing, and a council was held after which Pieskaret and TESSOUAT (d. 1654) reported to CHOMEDEY de Maisonneuve their intention to go to Trois-Rivières to formulate plans for the future and to determine if the French were to keep their promise of assistance against the enemy.

In the early spring of 1645, while it was still necessary to drag their canoes on ice on the St. Lawrence, Pieskaret led a war-party to the Richelieu River and Lake Champlain, where they made successful raids on a band of Iroquois, killing several and taking two as captives. On their return to the mission at Sillery, the captives could be seen dancing in the canoes according to custom, and enemy scalps were floating from long sticks "like vanes" in the wind. The captive Iroquois (one of whom was HONATTENIATE) were treated kindly by the residents of Sillery in deference to the French. Pieskaret handed over the captives to the governor, HUAULT de Montmagny, who shortly after sent word to the Iroquois by another Iroquois captured at an earlier date, that the captives would be freed if the Iroquois were disposed to treat for peace. This resulted in the arrival of KIOTSEAETON, as ambassador from the Iroquois, in July.

A peace council was then held with the Iroquois, the French, and the Hurons, Algonkins, and Montagnais, at the end of which Pieskaret presented furs to the Iroquois ambassador, symbolizing "a rock or tomb" placed on the grave of the victims of the above-mentioned battle, so that all might be forgiven and no revenge sought. The ensuing short-lived, but important, peace and trade negotiations of 1645–46 openly allotted to the Mohawks a share of the northern fur trade (a clause which was never implemented), while secretly excluding the pagan Algonkins from French protection.

By 1646–47 many tribes had taken up residence in the Trois-Rivières area because of the growing intensity of the Iroquois menace. Confusion and controversies developed. To solve the difficulties the Indians appointed Pieskaret to maintain the peace between the French and the Indians, and between the Hurons and the Algonkins, with power to punish delinquents, especially if the fault were a religious one. He is said to have discharged his duty faithfully.

Pieskaret had been baptized at Trois-Rivières in 1640 or 1641, and given the name of Simon by M. de CHAMPFLOUR, the governor. However, in 1646–47, being affected by the sudden death of Joseph Oumasasikweie, a Christian convert and a nephew of Tessouat (d. 1654), he made public confession and renewed his faith, which he had accepted formerly for diplomatic reasons only.

Indirectly, Pieskaret's open avowal of Christianity may have been the cause of his death. When returning from hunting on the north shore of the St. Lawrence in March 1647, laden with muzzles and tongues of elks, Pieskaret met a band of Iroquois (now allowed to hunt in this area by the terms of the 1645 treaty), who were singing the peace-song. Although rumours of the secret clause in the treaty had already reached Pieskaret and there was general fear of an Iroquois attack, he, doubtless counting on his Christian faith to protect him, smoked the pipe with the Iroquois and they addressed each other with words of respect. But when the journey was resumed, Pieskaret, who walked in the centre, was treacherously killed and scalped by one of the Iroquois who lagged behind.

Numerous anecdotes attest to the prowess of Pieskaret. Perrot, for example, recounts that on one occasion Pieskaret entered an Iroquois village, killed a whole family, and hid in one of their woodpiles on two succeeding nights. On the third he was detected. He fled, but being "naturally agile and nimble," he out-distanced his pursuers and took refuge in a tree trunk. Later, when the Iroquois set up camp near by, Pieskaret killed them all in their sleep and "came back laden with their scalps." Another time, at the mouth of the Sorel [probably Richelieu] River, he, with four others, sank five Iroquois canoes by firing on them, then killed all the enemy but saved the captives who were travelling with them.

ELSIE MCLEOD JURY

JR (Thwaites), *passim*. Perrot, "Memoir," in *Indian tribes* (Blair), I, 194–96. Desrosiers, *Iroquoisie*, 298–300, 308, 327; "La rupture de la paix de 1645," *Cahiers des Dix*, XVII (1952), 169–81.

PIGAROUICH, ÉTIENNE, Algonkin medicine-man and Christian apostate; fl. 1639–43.

Pigarouich maintained that he had achieved his power as a medicine-man by fasting five days and nights in an isolated cabin. He held eat-all feasts, sang loudly during feasts, and interpreted dreams; he sang and beat on drums and to cure sickness he consulted the "genii" of "those who make the light." He killed men with his sorceries. He took robes and other presents for healing and he ordered that presents be given to the sick. For success in hunting he sang the song he had learned in a dream. As were all the leading medicine-men, he was greatly feared among his people.

Although he had burned the utensils of his trade some two years previously, his conversion and baptism described by Father PAUL LE JEUNE took place in 1639. This followed a narrow escape from the Iroquois when on a war-party, a deliverance which he attributed to prayer. Soon afterwards he was married, for a second time, by Christian ceremony. (A wife and children had died in an earlier epidemic.)

Pigarouich, while still a medicine-man, carried on long discussions with the priests, at times revealing with great sincerity "all his knaveries." He greatly feared the undermining of his practices by the Europeans. He was an able disputant and caused much concern to the fathers, both before and after his baptism.

Pigarouich discussed the tent-shaking ritual with Father Le Jeune. A tent about seven feet high was built of poles held together with a wooden "hoop." It was covered with robes and blankets. The genii were invoked by the sorcerer's singing, and the tent, although strongly built, would shake violently, moved by the wind. Sometimes the tent bent almost to the ground and the arms and legs of the sorcerer would be visible. In fact, so forcibly did it shake at times that the sorcerer would believe the earth had opened under him and would run from the tent in terror, while it continued to shake.

At Sillery, in 1643, he brought many to prayers. He chastised the wicked and preached eloquently at the chapel, speaking "as well as Father de Bressany [see BRESSANI], who had just preached a fine sermon."

Pigarouich was of a bold, active, and passionate nature. Molested by his own people at Trois-Rivières, presumably for giving up his trade as a sorcerer, he went to Quebec and there fell into evil ways. Although at times deeply repentant, he had several relapses into non-Christian practices during the winter of 1643–44 and was for a time exiled by both French and Indians.

Having decided to join a war-party and fearing imminent death, however, Pigarouich went to Trois-Rivières to beg absolution for his sins from Father BRÉBEUF. He was refused. He then sought Father BUTEUX at Montreal who heard his confession and wrote, later, that he had "never heard any Savage speak better or more boldly than he did in the Church, for the space of a quarter of an hour," adding that "what he will do is known to God alone, as He alone knows whether he is truly contrite." It was agreed by the Jesuits, however, that Pigarouich could do much to aid or to injure the progress of Christianity among the Indians. After 1644 they make no further reference to him.

ELSIE MCLEOD JURY

JR (Thwaites), *passim*.

PIJART, CLAUDE, priest, Jesuit, missionary, parish priest, teacher, founder of the parish of Charlesbourg; b. 1 Sept. 1600 in Paris, son of Claude Pijart and Geneviève Charon, brother of PIERRE PIJART; d. 16 Nov. 1683 at Quebec.

Claude Pijart's father was the jewellery dealer of Queen Marguerite de Valois and the leading figures at court. Claude was first educated at the colleges at La Flèche and Clermont before becoming a Jesuit 7 Aug. 1621, thus preceding his brother Pierre by eight years. While still a student he is said to have been cured of an infection in the knee by the appearance of the Virgin Mary the very day before an operation, which would have amputated the leg, was to take place. After some ten years of studying and teaching at Orléans, Caen, and Paris, he was ordained priest on 16 April 1631 and left for Canada in 1637. He worked for three years at Quebec and Trois-Rivières in order to learn Algonkin. Then he went off with Father Charles RAYMBAUT on a mission to the Nipissings and the Algonkins, among whom he worked until September 1643. He spent 1644 with the Algonkins again, and subsequently lived either in the Huron country or at Montreal, where he appears to have taken charge of the mission from 1646 on. After escaping from the Huron country in 1649, he proceeded to Montreal in 1650 and became the parish priest there in 1653. Four years later he handed his parish over to the Sulpicians and returned to Quebec. There he was parish priest and teacher at the Jesuit college. He was also the founder, in 1660, of the parish of Charlesbourg, near Quebec, and in 1664 he was confessor to Governor SAFFRAY de Mézy. He continued to teach senior classes in rhetoric and philosophy until he was 80.

A handsome and very intelligent man, Father Pijart attracted people above all by his congenial personality. He had such a reputation for saintliness that after his death the population took relics from his remains.

J. MONET

ACSM, f.106, notes biographiques. Daveluy, "Bibliographie," *RHAF*, VIII (1954–55), 450. Paul Desjardins, *Les Jésuites à Montréal: le Père Claude Pijart* (Montréal, 1941). Hunt, *Wars of the Iroquois*, 46. Rochemonteix, *Les Jésuites et la Nouvelle-France au XVIIe siècle*, I, 419.

PIJART, PIERRE, priest, Jesuit, missionary; b. 17 May 1608 in Paris, son of Claude Pijart and Geneviève Charon; d. 26 May 1676 at Dieppe.

Pierre Pijart followed his elder brother, CLAUDE PIJART, into the Society of Jesus in Paris 16 Sept. 1629. He studied and taught at Paris, Caen, and

Pinard

La Flèche. Better endowed with practical commonsense than with a talent for study, he did only one year of theology (La Flèche, 1634–35) before setting out for Canada. He reached Quebec 10 July 1635 and immediately departed for the Huron country, which he did not leave for nine years except for a fruitless journey among the *Tionnontatés* (Tobacco nation) in 1640. In 1644 he was obliged for reasons of health to return and carry on his ministry among the French settlers at Trois-Rivières and Quebec. He was also procurator (treasurer) of the Huron mission until he left for France 23 Aug. 1650.

J. MONET

ACSM, f.99b. *JR* (Thwaites), VIII, 290; *passim*. Rochemonteix, *Les Jésuites et la Nouvelle-France au XVIIe siècle*, I, 409.

PINARD, LOUIS, master surgeon, *donné* of the Jesuits, surgeon-major at Trois-Rivières; b. *c.* 1633, son of Jean Pinard and Marguerite Gaignier of Notre-Dame de La Rochelle; d. 1695.

He came to Canada about 1648 as a surgeon and Jesuit *donné*, and left for France again 23 Aug. 1650 with the surgeon François GENDRON to complete his surgical studies. A master surgeon upon his return in 1656 and established at Trois-Rivières, he immediately began to exercise his art for the benefit of the garrison. In 1666 Jacques Dubois was employed by him as a surgeon's aid. Pinard is said to have taken part in the expedition to Hudson Bay in 1685 along with the surgeon Jacques Meneux *dit* Châteauneuf. Around 1690 he became surgeon-major of the town of Trois-Rivières. His son Claude was also to become a surgeon and undoubtedly began his studies under his father's direction; he did his apprenticeship, however, under Jean DEMOSNY at Quebec. In 1692 Pinard was the agent of Claude Deshaies-Gendron, and distributed in the region around Trois-Rivières "the remedies which M. Gendron sent to Canada for charity."

On 11 June 1657 Louis Pinard had signed before the notary Séverin Ameau* a contract of marriage with Marie-Madeleine Hertel, daughter of Jacques HERTEL and Marie Marguerie. On 30 Nov. 1680 at Champlain he took as his second wife Marie-Ursule Pépin. Each of his wives bore him six children.

Pinard does not seem to have had a very peaceful career: we find him engaged in legal disputes over money matters with a great number of citizens of Trois-Rivières and Cap-de-la-Madeleine. In particular he had quarrels with MICHEL LENEUF Du Hérisson. Moreover he was in rivalry with the surgeon Michel GAMELAIN, whose competition he feared and who later became father-in-law to his son, the surgeon Claude Pinard. Nevertheless Louis Pinard seems to have been held in esteem, since he was for a long time one of the settlers' syndics, a churchwarden, and procurator of the church.

In 1670 he settled down on his seigneury of L'Arbre-à-la-Croix at Champlain (seigneury of La Pinardière). There he engaged in agriculture and the fur trade. Later we find him at Batiscan, where he was buried 12 Jan. 1695.

GABRIEL NADEAU

AJTR, Greffe de Séverin Ameau, 11 juin 1657. *JJ* (Laverdière et Casgrain), 143. *Jug. et délib.* Ahern, *Notes pour l'histoire de la médecine*, 441–44. Raymond Douville, "Chirurgiens, barbiers-chirurgiens et charlatans de la région trifluvienne sous le régime français," *Cahiers des Dix*, XV (1950), 118–21.

POLLET DE LA COMBE–POCATIÈRE, FRANÇOIS, came to Canada in the summer of 1665 with the headquarters of the Carignan-Salières regiment, as a half-pay captain and cavalry sergeant; was a native of the small town of Chélieu, in the diocese of Grenoble, and the son of François Pollet de La Combe, who styled himself Sieur de La Pocatière, and of Catherine Rossin; d. 1672.

When the troops were disbanded in 1668, Pollet de La Combe–Pocatière remained in the colony. On 29 Nov. 1669, at Quebec, he married Marie-Anne Juchereau, born 14 Aug. 1653 at Quebec, the daughter of NICOLAS JUCHEREAU de Saint-Denis and of Marie-Thérèse Giffard. On 18 Sept. 1670, by a contract drawn up before the notary Gilles RAGEOT, Nicolas Juchereau de Saint-Denis, a councillor of the Conseil Souverain of New France, made over to his son-in-law "a piece of land half a league wide by two leagues in depth, within the territory forming part of the fief and domaine of Kamisitsit, so named by the Indians, and called Grande-Anse by the French."

François Pollet de La Combe-Pocatière was a captain on the active list from 1669 until the time of his death on 20 March 1672, four days before the birth of his second daughter. On the following 29 October, his widow received from Intendant Jean TALON the title to the La Pocatière seigneury, "a league and a half along the river by the same distance back," which she developed slowly, as her resources permitted. The deed of grant required that she should be in residence on her estate, and that, in her contracts with her tenants, she should oblige them to undertake to settle on their lands within a year of the concession. Adding her first name, Anne, to that of the fief, and suppressing her dead husband's surname, the widow gave to her seigneury the name Sainte-Anne de La Pocatière.

By her marriage with François Pollet de La Combe-Pocatière, Marie-Anne Juchereau had two daughters: the elder, Marie-Louise, born 1670, married Augustin Rouer* de Villeray et de La Cardonnière in 1706; the younger, Marie-Thérèse, born 24 March 1672 at Beauport and baptized 27 March at Quebec, married Pierre Le Moyne* d'Iberville at Quebec, 8 Oct. 1693.

Marie-Anne Juchereau married again at Quebec, 23 Feb. 1683; her second husband was François-Madeleine-Fortuné de Ruette* d'Auteuil, seigneur of Monceaux, and attorney-general in the Conseil Souverain of Quebec.

GÉRARD MALCHELOSSE

Jug. et délib., I, 776. P.-G. Roy, Inv. concessions, II, III, IV. Régis Roy et Malchelosse, Le régiment de Carignan. Sulte, Mélanges historiques (Malchelosse), VIII. Tanguay, Dictionnaire.

POMMIER, HUGUES, priest, missionary, painter, and portraitist; b. c. 1637 in the region of Vendôme, southwest of Paris; d. 1686 in France.

Little is known of his life before he left for New France, except that he had been ordained as a priest and that he intended to do missionary work in Canada. He sailed in 1663, stopped off at Plaisance (Placentia, Newfoundland), where he exercised his ministry for several months, and did not reach Quebec until the spring of 1664. During the 14 years that he spent in New France, he served the few parishes which were then in the making—Sainte-Famille (Île d'Orléans), Boucherville, Lauson, Contrecœur, Sorel, and Beauport. The last mention concerning him dates from 1678. He returned to France, where he died in December 1686.

"He prided himself on being a painter, producing many pictures; no one liked them," wrote Louis Bertrand* de Latour in his Mémoire sur la vie de M. de Laval. It is advisable to distrust formulas of this sort. However that may be, there are in existence at the present time three pictures which were painted between 1665 and 1672 and which are certainly Pommier's work. One is a good copy of a print by Grégoire Huret representing the martyrdom of the Jesuit fathers in 1648–49. The painting is old, and as Huret's print arrived at Quebec in 1665, Pommier was the only painter capable of doing it at that time. This picture is in the Hôtel-Dieu in Quebec.

The same institution possesses a hallucinatory portrait, that of Mother Catherine de Saint-Augustin [see SIMON], who died on 8 May 1668. At that date Pommier was still the only Quebec painter practising his art and available to paint the portrait of the deceased.

On 30 April 1672 Mother Marie de l'Incarnation [see GUYART] died at the convent of the Ursulines in Quebec. She was buried with great ceremony. But some hours later it was decided to take her body out of the vault in order to have her portrait done. At the beginning of May 1672 Pommier was the only person who could "make a perfect likeness of this gentle face which was stamped with the marks of beatitude." The original of this portrait was lost in the fire of 1686; there is still in existence however a replica or a faithful copy.

These are the only works of this artist that are known at the present time. Even if he had painted only the moving portrait of Mother Catherine, Father Pommier would have proved his talent as a painter and portraitist.

GÉRARD MORISSET

ASQ, MSS, 29, "Histoire du Séminaire de Québec," par J.-A. Taschereau. Jug. et délib., I, 283. Auguste Gosselin, Vie de Mgr de Laval, I, 446. Louis Bertrand de Latour, Mémoires sur la vie de M. de Laval, premier évéque de Québec (Cologne, 1761), 107. Gérard Morisset, Peintres et tableaux (2v., Québec, 1936–37), II, 23–36.

PONCET DE LA RIVIÈRE, JOSEPH-ANTOINE, priest, Jesuit, missionary among the Hurons and the Indians in the neighbourhood of Quebec, Trois-Rivières, and Montreal; b. 7 May 1610 in Paris, son of Jean Poncet de La Rivière et de Brétigny, a member of the Compagnie des Cent-Associés, and of Marguerite Thiersault; d. 18 June 1675 in Martinique (he must not be confused with Joseph-Antoine Poncet, another Jesuit, b. 1652, and d. 12 Aug. 1697 in Newfoundland on his way to Canada).

Joseph-Antoine Poncet de La Rivière was admitted into the noviciate of the Jesuits in Paris on 30 July 1629. He taught at the Collège in Orléans (1631–34), then began his theological studies at the Collège de Clermont (1634–35), and went to Rome to finish them (1635–38). Having completed his spiritual training in Paris (1638–39) he sailed for Quebec, where he arrived on 1 Aug. 1639. That same year Father Poncet went up among the Hurons, but remained there only a year and returned to Quebec. At the beginning of 1642 he was at Trois-Rivières with Father BUTEUX, and in July went to take charge of the parish of Montreal where he remained until the spring of 1643. The last years of his stay in Canada seem to have been taken up with various occupations at Quebec and on the St. Lawrence.

Pont-Gravé

Three points are noteworthy in his career in Canada. The first is the part he played in the missionary vocation of Marie de l'Incarnation [see GUYART], whose son Claude he had known at the Collège in Orléans, and whom he had put in touch with Mme CHAUVIGNY de La Peltrie in the autumn of 1638. The two women became friends and came to Canada in 1639 with Father Poncet himself. The second episode is his capture by the Iroquois on 20 Aug. 1653. These Indians took him into their country and subjected him to the usual tortures inflicted on prisoners. Father Poncet lost his left index finger and apparently acquired a certain aversion for the Iroquois; but he got off with his life, was adopted by an old woman, and finally freed in November 1653. The third incident was brought about by the arrival in 1657 of Abbé Queylus [see THUBIÈRES], with a vicar general's powers received from the archbishop of Rouen. Father Jean de QUEN, the superior of Quebec, a man of peace if ever there was one, and who possessed the same powers, found himself in a most delicate situation. Father Poncet, at that time priest of the parish of Quebec, had already shown signs of being an unreliable and capricious character; by his refusal to obey Father de Quen he caused a conflict of jurisdiction between the superior and the dictatorial abbé. Father de Quen's gentleness smoothed things over fairly well, but Father Poncet, named to go among the Iroquois, preferred to be repatriated, and his wish was granted that same year, 1657.

However, Father Poncet never gave up the idea of returning to Canada; in France he took one step after another to achieve this. Not being successful, chiefly because of opposition from the Canadian Jesuits, he asked to be transferred to Rome. He went there in 1665, but was no more successful, so that finally in 1671 he agreed to be sent to the West Indies. His last years were spent teaching the gospel to the Negroes of Martinique. He died on that island at the age of 65, attended by his former Canadian superior, Father François LE MERCIER. Father Poncet had an attractive personality, and did not lack talent, virtues, or zeal, although his suspicious and irritable character made him unhappy and difficult to handle. He has left an account of his captivity among the Iroquois, quoted by Father Le Mercier in his 1653 *Relation*.

LUCIEN CAMPEAU

Marie Guyart de l'Incarnation, *Écrits* (Jamet), III, 93, 109–56, *et passim*. *JR* (Thwaites). Faillon, *Histoire de la colonie française*, II, 276–83. Rochemonteix, *Les Jésuites et la Nouvelle-France au XVIIe siècle*, I, 301–6; II, 137–40, 210–32.

PONT-GRAVÉ, FRANÇOIS. See GRAVÉ DU PONT

PONT-GRAVÉ, ROBERT. See GRAVÉ DU PONT

"POUDRE CHAUDE." See OGENHERATARIHIENS

POULAIN, GUILLAUME, Recollet, priest, the first missionary to the Hurons in the Nipissing region; b. *c.* 1594 in France; d. 1623 at Châlons.

He entered the Recollet order in 1615 and made his profession in it on 13 April 1616. In the spring of 1619 he sailed for New France along with Father Paul HUET and Brother PACIFIQUE DUPLESSIS.

As soon as he reached Quebec, Father Poulain was assigned to Trois-Rivières, where he stayed until the spring of 1622. At that time, joining the French and Indians who were going westwards for the fur trade, he reached the Huron country. This long voyage was marked by an incident which almost cost him his life. The Iroquois attacked the flotilla and Father Poulain, "who was in a canoe by himself, having landed, was surprised by the Iroquois in the woods, along with a Frenchman. The good priest suffered with the greatest fortitude and patience the indignities and cruelties of the savages." The Iroquois had already begun to torture him when they agreed to exchange him for several of their men who had been captured by the French.

This incident did not however keep him from continuing his trip westwards, as LE CLERCQ tells it: "Since his [Guillaume Poulain's] escape from the Iroquois he had completely recovered and had been able to continue with the four French canoes into the territory of the Nipissings." He added: "that the Indians whom he had met on his way had seemed to him to be fairly docile and tractable, [and] that since his departure he had baptized more than 30 persons, children as well as various adults who were desperately ill."

In the autumn of this same year Father Poulain returned to Quebec in order to go back to France and recover his health. He was not to come back. On 12 March 1623 he died in the convent at Châlons, in Champagne.

FRÉDÉRIC GINGRAS

ASQ, MSS, 200, Mortuologe des Recolets. Le Clercq, *First establishment of the faith* (Shea), I, 146–47, 178, 187. Jouve, *Les Franciscains et le Canada (1615–1629)*.

POULIN DE LA FONTAINE, MAURICE, seigneurial attorney, judge, and king's attorney at Trois-Rivières; b. *c.* 1620 at Villebadin (Department of Orne, Normandy), son of Pierre Poulin and Jeanne Ploumelle; d. between 9 Oct. 1670 and 4 Aug. 1676.

On 13 Dec. 1649 Maurice Poulin was at Trois-Rivières, where he acted as godfather to a young Indian girl. On 9 Sept. 1654 he married Jeanne Jallot (or Jalleau), the widow of Marin Terrier, Sieur de Francheville et de Repentigny, who had been captured and burned by the Iroquois in 1652, in the battle on the outskirts of Trois-Rivières.

On 12 Sept. 1657 Poulin succeeded Jean Sauvaget as seigneurial attorney at Trois-Rivières. He sat as a judge the following year and on 17 Nov. 1663 became a king's attorney, by decision of the Conseil Souverain. On 6 Sept. 1664 the Council granted him a yearly payment of 150 *livres* "on account of his office as deputy to the king's attorney at Trois-Rivières." On 28 Jan. 1665 the same body ordered "the payment to Sieur Maurice Poulain [*sic*], king's attorney at Trois-Rivières, of the sum of 225 *livres* for eighteen months' stipend which will fall due next March. . . ."

In 1663 Poulin requested authorization for clearing operations to be carried out on a tract of land bordering on the St. Maurice River. This privilege was granted to him by Intendant TALON on 10 Jan. 1668. The ground was made ready, buildings were put up, and Poulin distributed land to several settlers. The seigneury, which was to be handed over officially to his widow on 4 Aug. 1676 by Intendant DUCHESNEAU, had a frontage of one league along the river of Trois-Rivières and a depth of two leagues, with fishing rights on the river. The seigneury was designated as a fief with rights of justice.

On 9 Oct. 1670 Maurice Poulin acted as godfather to Maurice Cardin. According to Benjamin Sulte this is the last trace of him that can be found in the archives. Hence it was between this date and 4 Aug. 1676, when Jeanne Jallot was said to be a widow, that he died.

Maurice Poulin left Michel Poulin, born 4 May 1655, who took the name of Sieur de Saint-Maurice; Jean-Baptiste, Sieur de Courval, born 15 Jan. 1657; Marguerite, who married François Lemaître* Lamorille; and Catherine, who became the wife of Joseph Godefroy* de Vieuxpont.

It was François Poulin* de Francheville, a grandson of Maurice Poulin, who was to set up a company in the following century for the establishment of a foundry in his Saint-Maurice seigneury.

This name, which was given to the Poulin fief in accordance with the Christian name of the head of the Poulin line, subsequently designated the river along whose shore the seigneury ran. Until then, it had been called the river of Trois-Rivières, or the Métabéroutine, or else the Fouez (Jacques CARTIER's designation). In their turn Les Forges took the name of Saint-Maurice, which was then extended to the county, and finally to the surrounding region.

H. BIRON

Archives de la paroisse de l'Immaculée-Conception, Trois-Rivières. *Jug. et délib.*, I, 275, 314. P.-G. Roy, *Inv. concessions*, II, 115. Benjamin Sulte, *Les forges Saint-Maurice* (Montréal, 1920). Albert Tessier, *Les forges du Saint-Maurice, 1729–1883* (Trois-Rivières, 1952).

POUTRINCOURT ET DE SAINT-JUST, JEAN DE BIENCOURT DE. *See* BIENCOURT

POWER (Powers), RICHARD, HBC employee; d. 1681.

In 1674 Power seemed likely to be arrested "at the suite of James Tatnam," because he, Power, had evidently impounded the beaver which Tatnam had traded independently. Not content with taking home beaver· skins himself, Tatnam had enticed a seaman into bringing more, but was obliged to pay up when the man confessed. Private trading was a practice that the Company was determined to stamp out and since they offered to go bail and handle any suit against Power, he had probably brought this particular incident to light.

Power was mate on the *Prince Rupert* in 1676, second mate on the *Shaftesbury* the following year, and sailed as master of the *Prince Rupert* in 1678. While he was favourably regarded at headquarters in London and he was appointed to Governor John NIXON's council in 1680, his conduct in Hudson Bay was severely censured by Governor Nixon. When Nixon assumed his post in 1679 Capt. Power and a companion, Dr. Rainer, came on board at Point Comfort, "both so drunke as beasts" and used abusive language to the retiring governor, Charles BAYLY.

Power came home in command of the *Prince Rupert* in 1681 and died very suddenly a few weeks later of smallpox.

MAUD M. HUTCHESON

HBRS, V, VIII, XI (Rich).

PRÉ-RAVILLON ET DE GRANPRÉ, LA COURT DE. *See* LA COURT

PRÉVERT. *See* SARCEL

PRÉVOST (Provost), MARTIN, one of the pioneers of Beauport near Quebec; b. *c.* 1611, son of Pierre Prévost and Charlotte Vien, of

Prouville de Tracy

Montreuil-sur-le-Bois-de-Vincennes (now Montreuil-sous-Bois), near Paris; d. 26 Jan. 1691 at Beauport.

Prévost's presence at Quebec is referred to in the documents of the notary Piraube as early as the year 1639. On 3 Nov. 1644, he married, at Quebec, Marie-Olivier-Sylvestre Manitouabeouich. This is the first marriage between a Frenchman and an Indian mentioned in Canadian historical records. The young bride had been given by her parents to the interpreter Olivier LETARDIF, who had been her godfather and had then had her brought up as a French girl in the home of Sieur Guillaume Hubou.

From the time of his marriage until his death, we find Martin Prévost settled at Beauport as an "*habitant*," or farmer, which did not prevent him from having a piece of land and a house at Quebec in 1667. He was married a second time in 1665, to Marie d'Abancourt, the widow of Jean Jollyet and of Gefroy Guillot. Prévost had had at least nine children by his first wife.

Towards the end of his life, Prévost signed his name "Provost." His descendants have adopted one or other of the two spellings.

HONORIUS PROVOST

JR (Thwaites), IX, 103; XI, 93. *Papier terrier de la Cie des I.O.* (P.-G. Roy). Jean Langevin, *Notes sur les Archives de Notre-Dame de Beauport* (Québec, 1860).

PROUVILLE DE TRACY, ALEXANDRE DE, Marquis (or Chevalier), seigneur of Tracy-le-Val and Tracy-le-Mont (Picardy), king's counsellor, commissary general of the French army in Germany, commander-in-chief of the troops, lieutenant-general of America, commandant of Dunkirk, then of the Château Trompette at Bordeaux; b. *c.* 1596 (or 1603), probably the son of Pierre de Prouville, bailiff of the citadel of Amiens, and Marie Bochart de Champigny; d. 1670 in Paris.

A professional soldier, he was a captain in the light horse in 1632. He served gloriously in Germany (1641–49), where he took part in several battles; he commanded a regiment there, then was appointed commissary general of the king's army in that country, assuring liaison between the court and the French generals. In 1647 he was in charge of the negotiations at Ulm between France, Sweden, and the Elector of Bavaria. In addition he fought for a time in the ranks of the Fronde, but soon returned to put his sword at his sovereign's service. He was created a lieutenant-general of the king's armies on 10 July 1652 and served in Guiana.

On 19 Nov. 1663 he received his commission as "lieutenant-general throughout the length and breadth of the continental countries under our authority situated in South and North America, and of the islands, rivers. . . ." He was not, however, viceroy of these territories, since this title belonged to the Comte d'Estrades, whose commission had not been revoked and who was at this time the king's ambassador to Holland. M. de Tracy had the complete confidence of his sovereign, who, in naming him to this important post, gave him this high praise: he "has all the qualities necessary for discharging this office fittingly, and after the proofs that he has given of his worth in the positions of command that he has held over our troops in Germany and elsewhere and of his prudence in the negotiations that have been entrusted to him, we thus have reason to believe that we could choose no one better to command in the said country."

Tracy had a double mission: to drive the Dutch out of the West Indies, and in Canada to carry the war home to the Iroquois in order to exterminate them completely. Antoine-Joseph LE FEBVRE de La Barre accompanied him in his campaign in the West Indies. The flotilla sailed from La Rochelle 26 Feb. 1664. It carried 650 settlers and 4 infantry companies: de Broglie, Chambellé, Poitou, and Orléans. The operation was energetically carried out. On 16 May the French troops captured Cayenne from the Dutch. Tracy installed governors in the principal islands: Martinique, Tortuga, Guadeloupe, Grenada, Marie Galante.

On 25 April 1665 the fleet left Guadeloupe, sailed through Caicos Passage, rounded the Bermudas, entered the Gulf of St. Lawrence and cast anchor at Percé Rock a month later. The stocks of water and wood were replenished, merchandise was transferred to smaller vessels. After a few delays in the St. Lawrence River, the expedition arrived before Quebec on 30 June; its commandant was "so weak and so reduced by fever, that only his courage could sustain him." Quebec was given over to rejoicing; the town prepared a magnificent reception, but as he was ill the lieutenant-general refused all the festivities. Preceded by his 24 guards, all dressed in His Majesty's colours, and by four pages, accompanied by his aide-de-camp, the Chevalier de Chaumont*, and followed by six lackeys and several officers in sumptuous dress, the king's representative proceeded from the port to the church amidst the acclamations of the crowd. The bells pealed forth. Escorted by his clergy, Bishop Laval* received the saviour of the colony at the entrance to the nave; he offered him holy water and led him to his prayer-stool, but the general preferred to kneel on the floor like everyone else. The ceremony ended with the *Te Deum*.

Then M. de Tracy went to the palace, which was located approximately on the site of the present-day law-courts and which the Conseil Souverain had had put into repair for him. Tasks and anxieties were not lacking. The town consisted of some 70 houses. Religious and civil quarrels were acute. But for the moment diplomatic and military problems monopolized all his energies.

Indeed, the king had decided to have done with the Iroquois, who hindered the evangelizing of the peaceful Indian nations, diverted the trade in furs towards the English, and massacred the French settlers. In a letter of 18 March 1664 Colbert expressed clearly to Bishop Laval His Majesty's intentions: it was necessary "to destroy utterly these barbarians, whose numbers are already much diminished, according to the latest accounts that we have had of them, both as a result of the losses that they have suffered in warring against their enemies and because of a sort of contagious malady which has carried off a good number of them." For this purpose the court was sending a complete infantry regiment, the Carignan-Salières, which was commanded by M. de Salières [Chastelard*] which had fought the Turks in Hungary. Four companies were already there, having arrived 18 and 19 June, before Tracy appeared with his four; on 19 and 20 August eight more companies landed, and as many more on 14 September. Never had the port of Quebec hummed with such activity. There had however been an unfortunate accident: the ship carrying M. de Tracy's valuable belongings had sunk. Subsequently the king was to grant his representative generous compensation.

The late arrival of the ships and sickness caused the expedition against the Iroquois to be put off till the following year. Indeed, many soldiers had arrived ill: the Hôtel-Dieu was full of them, the church was filled right up to the altar-railing, and there were even patients in the neighbouring houses. There were 20 deaths. Nevertheless military preparations were to be all the more thorough. Four companies left Quebec 23 July 1665 for Sorel. They began constructing forts on the Richelieu River to protect the forward movement of the troops: Fort Richelieu on 13 August; Fort Saint-Louis, 25 August; Fort Sainte-Thérèse in September; Forts Saint-Jean, Sainte-Anne, and Lamothe (this last one built on an island in Lake Champlain) were to complete the chain of defences the following year. Four more companies left Quebec for Trois-Rivières on 1 October in order to protect the centre of the country.

In December some Iroquois tribes, frightened by so much warlike ardour, sent GARAKONTIÉ and a delegation to return their prisoner, CHARLES LE MOYNE, and to renew peace with the French. However, since he was not much convinced of the Indians' sincerity and since he particularly feared the Mohawks, who continued to be hostile, Tracy empowered Governor RÉMY de Courcelle to attack the latter. He left Quebec 9 Jan. 1666 with 400 or 500 men, on snow-shoes, some 60 of whom he lost mainly because of the cold. Having lost its way, the army found itself before the Anglo-Dutch establishment at Corlaer (Schenectady, N.Y.), where it received help. The remnants of the detachment got back to Quebec on 17 March, without having inflicted any serious losses on the Iroquois. The latter realized however that the French troops had been able to reach their country for the first time, and in May and July they sent ambassadors to Quebec to sign peace treaties; the Five Nations were represented there, but the Mohawks and Oneidas continued to inspire some fear. Tracy sent a French delegation to the cantons to ascertain whether the Indians were favourably disposed before accepting the peace that they proposed. But the news reached Quebec of new outrages committed by the Mohawks: they had just murdered a nephew of Tracy and captured one of his cousins. Tracy immediately recalled his ambassadors and imprisoned 24 Iroquois delegates. He had more redoubts built around Montreal and allowed M. de SAUREL to lead a raid with 300 men into the Mohawk country on 24 July in order to free the French prisoners. On the way the detachment met the FLEMISH BASTARD (an Iroquois chief, the son of a Dutchman and a Mohawk squaw), who was going to Quebec to make peace, accompanied by the prisoners, and Saurel abandoned his attack.

But Tracy was exasperated with the peace negotiations which had perpetually to be started again with the Mohawks. The authorities of the colony deliberated as to whether the war should be carried into their territory. On 1 Sept. 1666 Intendant TALON sent to Tracy and Courcelle a long memoir in which, after weighing the pros and cons, he recommended a punitive expedition into the Mohawk country. On 6 September Tracy fell in with his opinion.

All the necessary preparations had been made. The route was well protected by numerous forts, which were filled with munitions and supplies; flat-bottomed boats, large and small, had been built. The soldiers' morale was excellent: "It seems to all this army," wrote Marie de l'Incarnation [*see* GUYART], "that it is going to besiege paradise and that it aspires to take it and enter

Prouville de Tracy

into it, because it is for the good of the faith and religion that it is going to fight." Elsewhere she speaks of "1,300 picked men who are all going off to combat as if to a triumph." The troops prepared themselves for this campaign by a general confession and by all sorts of pious exercises; a score of Huguenots were converted; public prayers were to go on until the return of the expedition.

The departure took place from Quebec 14 September. The army paraded through the streets in view of the Flemish Bastard and the other Iroquois hostages, who wept for the destruction of their nation. The force was to consist in all of 600 regular soldiers, as many militiamen (110 were to come from Ville-Marie (Montreal)), and 100 Hurons and Algonkins, plus 4 chaplains, one of whom was Dollier* de Casson. The rendezvous was set for 28 September at Fort Sainte-Anne. From there the expedition moved off on 3 October. Courcelle had already left with 400 men as the advance party; Tracy followed him with the main body of troops. MM. de CHAMBLY and Berthier* brought up the rear, four days later. Three hundred small boats transported rations, baggage, and arms, among which were two field guns. There were more than 60 leagues to cover beyond the forts; the march was tiring, the rain fell in abundance; food was running out, rationing was imposed. They were nearing the famine point, when suddenly they came upon a forest that was laden with chestnuts. Finally they reached the Mohawk villages. All four were deserted. The soldiers seized all the goods that were of any use and set fire to the lodges and crops. At Andaraqué they took official possession of all the Mohawk territory in the name of Louis XIV; they sang the *Te Deum*, they set up a cross and a post bearing the arms of the king of France, and the four chaplains said mass. As the season was already well advanced, the commandant gave up the idea of going to punish the Oneidas, a neighbouring nation that was no less rebellious. The return trip was carried out with even greater difficulty than the outward one. Rains had swollen the rivers; a gale was blowing on Lake Champlain; two canoes with eight men were lost. The army arrived back at Quebec 5 Nov. 1666. A solemn procession and another *Te Deum* marked the end of this crusade.

Tracy had an over-bold Iroquois prisoner, who is believed to have been AGARIATA, hanged, to frighten the others. He sent three or four others from each nation back to their people to carry the news of his victory and to ask them to make known their intentions.

Talon told Colbert in a letter of the outcome of the expedition: "although the number of the Christians' enemies is not diminished . . ., the afflictions of their families caused by the burning of their forts and the devastation of their fields will perhaps weaken them appreciably and cause them to lose heart." If the Indians had not fled, he said, "after sacrificing the majority of these barbarians to the shades of so many Christians who have been slaughtered and burned, we could have seen the remainder on Your Majesty's galleys." The intendant regretted that the valiant French soldiers had been cheated of this double satisfaction.

Tracy stayed in Canada until August 28, 1667. He left a deep imprint upon it. "He is a person of merit and piety," wrote Bishop Laval. Mother Marie de l'Incarnation went further, saying that he "won over everyone by his good works and by the great examples of virtue and religion which he has given the whole country." Indeed, his charity was admirable. He had a chapel built for the Ursulines at a cost of 2,500 *livres*; he gave 500 *livres* to the Jesuits for their chapel; he paid for the education of young Indians; he donated the picture over the high altar in the chapel at Sainte-Anne; he himself tended the sick in the hospital. His piety was no less exemplary: a nun saw him praying in a church for six hours; he went on several pilgrimages to Sainte-Anne de Beaupré; he took part in all solemn ceremonies. Faithful to God, he was also faithful to his king. Nothing that His Majesty suggested was too difficult for him. He was 62 years of age when, crippled with gout, he undertook his formidable expedition. He had to be carried for two days.

He attended just as conscientiously to the affairs of the state. He settled the thorny problem of the tithes, presided over the meetings of the Conseil Souverain, which had been reorganized after Governor SAFFRAY de Mézy's quarrels with it: "he has set the affairs of Canada in such good order that I shall have little to do there," remarked Talon. Marie de l'Incarnation was of the same opinion; less than a month after Tracy's arrival she wrote: "Monsieur de Tracy has already introduced very fine regulations: I believe that he is a man chosen by God for the solid founding of these regions, for the liberty of the Church, and for sound justice." It is not astonishing that His Majesty treated him as a good servant and had a magnificent vessel, the *Saint-Sébastien*, fitted out for him, to bring him back to France. The annalist of the Hôtel-Dieu in Quebec noted that "Monsieur de Tracy took ship to return to France, after charming all Canada by his manners, his solicitude, and his benefactions."

On his return to France he was not sparing in his advice to Colbert. On 12 Dec. 1667 he was appointed commandant at Dunkirk, and on 26

October governor of the Château Trompette, the citadel of Bordeaux. He came to Paris to die on 28 April 1670, in the parish of Saint-Eustache. "After CARTIER and CHAMPLAIN, there is perhaps no one whose stay in New France left a more radiant beam of light on our history," comments Aegidius Fauteux.

From his first marriage, which had taken place before 1630, Tracy had had a son, Charles-Henri, who was killed at the siege of Landrecies in 1655, and a daughter. On 15 April 1657 at Saint-Eustache in Paris, he had taken as his second wife Louise de Fouilleuse.

LÉOPOLD LAMONTAGNE

ASQ, Lettres, N, 12, 14, 19, 20, 21; Polygraphie, V, 6; XIII, 2, p.39; Séminaire, VI, 73j; XXXIII, 5. Caron, "Inventaire de documents," APQ *Rapport, 1939–40*, 157–353. "Correspondance de Talon," APQ, *Rapport, 1930–1, passim*. Dollier de Casson, *Histoire du Montréal*, 179–93. *Édits ord.*, III, 27f. Marie Guyart de l'Incarnation, *Lettres* (Richaudeau), II, 289–354. *JR* (Thwaites), XLIX, L, LI. *JJ* (Laverdière et Casgrain). Juchereau, *Annales* (Jamet). *Jug. et délib*. *NYCD* (O'Callaghan and Fernow), III, IX. *Ord. comm.* (P.-G. Roy), I, 22–74. PAC *Rapport, 1905*, I, 1vi.

Raphaël Bellemare, "M. de Tracy et la Nouvelle-France," *BRH*, III (1897), 77ff. Chapais, *Talon*. Faillon, *Histoire de la colonie française*, III, 119–67. Aegidius Fauteux, "La carrière pré-canadienne de Monsieur de Tracy," *Cahiers des Dix*, I (1936), 59–93. Garneau, *Histoire du Canada*, I, 379–90. P.-G. Roy, 'Le palais occupé par M. de Tracy à Québec en 1665–1666," *BRH*, XXVII (1921), 353–58. Régis Roy, "Alexandre de Prouville, sieur de Tracy," *BRH*, XIV 1908), 285–87; "M. de Tracy était-il marquis?" *ibid.*, X (1904), 252f., 342–45. Sulte, *Mélanges historiques* (Malchelosse), VIII.

PROVOST. *See* PRÉVOST

PRUD'HOMME, LOUIS, pioneer, churchwarden, brewer, corporal and militia captain of Montreal, son of Claude Prud'homme and Isabelle Aliomet; b. *c.* 1611 at Pomponne (Île-de-France); d. 1 July 1671 at Montreal.

After arriving in New France in 1641 at the latest and being one of the first to settle at Ville-Marie (Montreal), he received in October 1650 a grant of land close to the fort and adjoining that of Michel Chauvin, whose bigamy he disclosed to Governor CHOMEDEY de Maisonneuve. As it happened, Prud'homme had discovered, in the course of a trip to France that very year, that Chauvin had a wife there whom he had married before setting out for the colony. Hence this second marriage to Anne Archambault, celebrated at Quebec in 1647, was annulled in 1651 and Chauvin was banished from Ville-Marie. This judgement is the earliest one pronounced by the founder of Montreal that has come down to us. In 1654, 1662, and 1666, Prud'homme received further grants of land.

In November 1650 Louis Prud'homme married Roberte Gadoys (1621–1716), daughter of Pierre GADOYS, who was called the first farmer of Ville-Marie. In 1644 Roberte Gadoys had already entered into an earlier contract of marriage with César Léger at Quebec, the notary being Guillaume Tronquet. This union, it appears, had subsequently been annulled.

When the Sulpicians arrived in 1657, Prud'homme was elected as one of the first three churchwardens of the parish of Notre-Dame. In 1663 when the militia of the Holy Family was constituted, he was corporal of a section. The following year he was elected police magistrate, along with four of his fellow-citizens; but the authorities of New France considered the institution of the police court too democratic and refused to confirm the results of the election.

Louis Prud'homme died at Montreal in 1671. He had been the brewer of longest standing in the town. The inventory of his possessions, drawn up by BÉNIGNE BASSET in 1673, provides a description of the equipment of his brewery. When his son François married in 1684, the deceased Louis Prud'homme was described by the officiating priest as "the first militia captain of Montreal."

In 1673 his widow, Roberte Gadoys, took as her second husband Pierre Verrier. Like her mother, Louise Mauger Gadoys, she died in her nineties.

One of his sons, Pierre (1658–1703), received from CAVELIER de La Salle in 1683 a grant of land in fief at the Illinois fort, which thereafter bore his name. The son of this latter Prud'homme, Louis (1692–1769), with the same name as the pioneer, was born and died at Montreal; in 1751 he was lieutenant-colonel of the militia forces of Montreal and was their commander at Sainte-Foy in April 1760.

JEAN-JACQUES LEFEBVRE

AJM, Greffe de Bénigne Basset, 29 juillet 1658; 11, 12, 14 janv., 2 juillet 1673. "La famille Prud'homme," *BRH*, XXXIV (1928), 151–70. É.-Z. Massicotte, "Pierre Prud'homme: un montréalais compagnon de La Salle," *BRH*, XXVIII (1922), 28–30; "Pierre Prud'homme, compagnon de La Salle," *Can. Antiquarian and Numismatic J.*, XI (1914), 21–31; "Les tribunaux de police de Montréal," *BRH*, XXVI (1920), 180–3. Tanguay, *Dictionnaire*, I, 502.

PUISEAUX, PIERRE DE, seigneur of Montrénault in France, of Saint-Michel and of Sainte-Foy in New France; b. *c.* 1566; d. some time after 21 June 1647 at La Rochelle.

Quen

Pierre de Puiseaux arrived in Canada shortly after having received from the Compagnie des Cent-Associés, 15 Jan. 1637, the seigneuries of Saint-Michel, near Sillery, and of Sainte-Foy, not far from Quebec. (Faillon, Ferland, and Scott place the arrival of Puiseaux in Canada at the time of CHAMPLAIN. Their documentation, however, remains either non-existent or incomplete.)

Dollier* de Casson, who made use of the stories of eye-witnesses when he wrote in 1672, gives us some details on this settler's past. First he affirms that he was 75 years old in 1641. Then he informs us that he was "a worthy old man most zealous for this country in which he had spent very great sums of money." He was very generous towards the pioneers around him; in 1640 he lodged in his house at Saint-Michel, called "the jewel of the colony," the nuns of the Hôtel-Dieu of Quebec, whose convent at the Sillery mission was not completed. In the autumn of the following year he virtually became a providential benefactor for M. CHOMEDEY de Maisonneuve and the Montreal contingent. They all settled, until the spring of 1642, on the Saint-Michel and Sainte-Foy seigneuries, which Pierre de Puiseaux, by a contract signed 23 Nov. 1641 before the notary Guillaume Tronquet, at Quebec, had just given to the Société Notre-Dame de Montréal through the intermediary of M. de Maisonneuve. Having become a member of that society, M. de Puiseaux attended, 17 May 1642, the ceremonies of the founding of Montreal, and there became, 5 March 1643, the godfather of the wife of a famous Algonkin, PAUL TESSOUAT (d. 1654).

He returned to France, very ill, in 1644. On 21 June 1647 he dictated his will at La Rochelle, where he died shortly afterwards. Before leaving New France, he had asked Maisonneuve to restore his seigneuries to him so that he might obtain funds for medical treatment. They were returned to him with all goodwill.

MARIE-CLAIRE DAVELUY

Dollier de Casson, *Histoire du Montréal*. *JR* (Thwaites). Juchereau, *Annales* (Jamet), 29. *Premier registre de l'église Notre Dame de Montréal* (Montréal, 1961), 49.
État de la maison du roi Louis XIII . . . comprenant les années 1601 à 1665, éd. Eugène Griselle (Paris, 1912), 27, 367. Faillon, *Histoire de la colonie française*, I, II. Ferland, *Cours d'histoire du Canada*, I. H. A. Scott, *Une paroisse historique de la Nouvelle-France: Notre-Dame de Sainte-Foy: histoire civile et religieuse d'après les sources* (Québec, 1902).

No personal documents of M. Puiseaux are known to the author of the above article and it also appears that no biography of Puiseaux has ever been written.

Q

QUEN, JEAN DE, priest, Jesuit, missionary, discoverer of Lac Saint-Jean, founder of the Saguenay missions, superior of the missions of the Jesuits of New France, annalist; b. May 1603 (*al.* 1600, 1604) at Amiens (Picardy); d. 8 Oct. 1659 at Quebec.

Jean de Quen entered the Society of Jesus 13 Sept. 1620. After his noviciate, three years of philosophy in Paris, one year as a regent and three years of theology at Clermont, one year as a regent at Amiens, and his third probationary year in Belgium, he taught for three years at the Collège in Eu, and then left for Canada. He arrived at Quebec 17 Aug. 1635.

He was first employed as a teacher at the college in Quebec, which opened its doors in 1635; he soon went to the fixed mission at Sillery, and returned to Quebec, where he was responsible for ministering to the parish of Notre-Dame-de-la-Recouvrance. In 1640 he went back to Sillery, and concerned himself more particularly with the hospital. There he wore himself down to the danger point; he recovered fairly quickly, and was sent to the Trois-Rivières residence; he thereby had the opportunity to bring about many conversions. He returned the following year to Sillery, and was in charge of that important mission centre for eight years (1642–49). He fulfilled a very active ministry there, which brought him into contact with Indians from almost everywhere, more particularly the Montagnais, whose language he learned perfectly.

In the spring of 1642 Jean de Quen was entrusted with the Montagnais mission, with which he concerned himself for 11 years. This mission had been founded the preceding year at Tadoussac, where between spring and the end of August the fur trade brought Indians from all parts of the vast territory of the Saguenay, from the great Lac Mistassini in the interior to the Sept-Îles, on the shore of the St. Lawrence estuary. Some also came from the south shore and from the Gaspé peninsula. Father de Quen was well prepared for this diversity of types, and was highly esteemed by the Montagnais; with the aid of Fathers Jacques BUTEUX, Gabriel DRUILLETTES, Martin de LYONNE, and Charles ALBANEL, following one upon another, he created a form of summer mission suited to the existence of these nomadic peoples, and made a success of it. He formed a solid nucleus of Christians who helped him to reach the most distant groups. (It was at Tadoussac that the first stone church in Canada was constructed, in 1646.)

During the summer of 1647, having learned that some neophytes on their way to the mission had been halted at Lac Piékouagami (Saint-Jean) by illness, he got two young Montagnais to take him there, and covered in five days a distance of 120 miles, with ten portages to slow his progress. During this journey he discovered Lac Saint-Jean and the route leading into the interior of the Saguenay, which the Indians had kept a secret from the white men. He arrived at the lake via the Belle-Rivière on 16 July. "This lake is so large," wrote Father de Quen, "that one hardly sees its banks; it seems to be round in shape. It is deep and very full of fish; they fish here for pike, perch, salmon, trout, dories, white-fish, carp, and many other kinds. It is surrounded by a flat country, terminating in high mountains, distant 3, four or five leagues from its shores. It is fed by the waters of fifteen rivers, or thereabout, which serve as highways for the small nations which are back in the country, to come to fish in this lake, and to maintain the intercourse and friendship which they have among themselves."

Crossing a part of the lake, he went to visit the Indians of the Porcupine nation at the mouth of the Rivière Métabetchouan, the meeting-place of the tribes from the interior of the Saguenay.

Father de Quen returned there in 1650 and again in 1652, on the latter occasion for a twelve-day mission that was subsequently to be repeated regularly. In 1651 and 1652 he did the same for the Oumamiwek (Bersamite) nation, a small tribe on the coast in the direction of the Sept-Îles, more than 300 miles from Tadoussac. One may therefore consider Father de Quen as the founder of the Saguenay missions.

Apart from the few months that these missions required annually, Jean de Quen concerned himself actively with his ministry at Sillery and Quebec, and in the vicinity (Beaupré shore, Île d'Orléans, etc.). In 1656 he was appointed superior of the missions in New France, a post which he occupied until 8 Sept. 1659, a month before his death. It was during his term of office that, with the arrival of Abbé de Queylus [*see* THUBIÈRES] as vicar general, the crisis over ecclesiastical jurisdiction in New France came to a head.

Father de Quen is the author of the *Relations des Jésuites* for the year 1655–56, and of the *Journal des Jésuites* from 25 Oct. 1656 to 7 Sept. 1659 (except during a few brief absences). He collaborated in the "Catalogue des bienfaicteurs de N. Dame de Recouvrance (1632–57)." He is also said to have undertaken correspondence in order to refute the accusations levelled against the Jesuits on the subject of the fur trade. The *Relations* several times mention his letters and quote certain passages from them. Here is one that illustrates his style of writing: "I sent to the hospital that good old man, Adam, the most aged of the savages. I rescued him from the death which these Barbarians intended to cause him by a rope, in order to rid themselves of a burden that greatly oppressed them. I begged our Frenchmen who were going down there to take him in their bark: I do not doubt that the Mothers will receive him willingly; they have already fed and aided him, during the whole of last winter. This worthy man has no other malady than that which he began to contract more than a hundred years ago."

Father de Quen, who had always given particular attention to the care of the sick, was finally a victim of his own devotion. The *Journal des Jésuites* recounts the event in this way, in October 1659: "On the 1st, Jean de Quen took to his bed; and on the 8th. he died from those contagious fevers that had been brought by the last ship. . . . Father de Quen was buried on the morning of the 9th." He had given Canada 24 years of untiring and fruitful activity.

His remains were uncovered under the chapel of the Collège des Jésuites when it was demolished in 1878. They were placed temporarily in the Belmont cemetery, and were buried solemnly in a vault under the chapel of the Quebec Ursulines on 12 May 1891. The historical record of these facts, composed by C.-E. Rouleau, contains a brief biographical notice of Jean de Quen, the only one that has ever been published.

VICTOR TREMBLAY

ACSM, "Mémoires touchant la mort et les vertus des pères Isaac Jogues . . ." (Ragueneau), repr. APQ *Rapport, 1924–25*, 40f., 47–49, Lettres du P. Jean de Quen. ASQ, MSS, 43, "Étude sur les Relations des Jésuites," par Félix Martin; Polygraphie, XIII, 22. Marie Guyart de l'Incarnation, *Lettres* (Richaudeau), I, 137–40, 208, *JR* (Thwaites), XX, 238; XXXI, 248–54; XLII, 9–262, 268–88; LXXI, 123; *et passim*. JJ (Laverdière et Casgrain), 199–263, 266; *et passim*.

Lanctot, *Histoire du Canada*, I, 285–87. *L'histoire du Saguenay: depuis l'origine jusqu'à 1870* (Soc. hist. du Saguenay pub., III, Chicoutimi, 1938). "Le Père Jean de Quen," *BRH*, XIX (1913), 256. Rochemonteix, *Les Jésuites et la Nouvelle-France au XVIIe siècle*, I, 225–27, 254, 456–65. C. E. Rouleau, *Découverte ces restes de trois missionnaires de la Compagnie de Jésus* (Québec, 1893).

Quentin

QUENTIN, CLAUDE, priest, Jesuit, missionary; b. 18 Feb. 1597; d. 31 Oct. 1676 at La Flèche, in Anjou.

Father Quentin became a Jesuit at Rouen on 5 Nov. 1617, and received almost all his education in that same city. He arrived in Canada in July 1635, and established himself at the Trois-Rivières residence. As he seemed unable to learn the native languages, he was sent in 1638 to minister to the French settlers on the Île de Miscou, in the Baie des Chaleurs. But some time later he had to return to Quebec because of his health. In 1641 he became procurator (treasurer) of the mission, a post that caused him to make several trips to France—in 1645, in October 1646—before his final return there on 21 Oct. 1647.

He has sometimes been confused with Father JACQUES QUENTIN, who had come to Acadia in 1613.

J. MONET

ACSM, biographical data based on the old Jesuit catalogues. *JR* (Thwaites), VIII, 290, *et passim* (the index of the Quebec ed. of the *Relation des Jésuites* confuses Claude and Jacques Quentin). Rochemonteix, *Les Jésuites et la Nouvelle-France au XVIIe siècle*, I, 433.

QUENTIN, JACQUES, priest, Jesuit; b. 1572 at Abbeville; d. 18 March 1647 at Charleville. Fathers CLAUDE and Jacques Quentin have sometimes been confused. They did not however live in Canada at the same period.

Jacques Quentin was a Master of Arts of the Collège of Douai and a priest when he entered the noviciate of the Society at Nancy in 1604. After teaching in the colleges at Bourges (1606–8) and Rouen (1608–9), he was appointed minister of the college at Eu. There he received Fathers Pierre BIARD and Énemond MASSÉ who were on their way to Acadia (1610). It lay within his province to introduce them into the various communities of the little town; it was doubtless he who made known to them the presence in the monastery of the Augustinians of the relic of St. Lawrence O'Toole, Archbishop of Dublin, which they took with them [*see* the bibliography for a note on O'Toole]. At the beginning of 1613 he was appointed to take charge of the new mission (Saint-Sauveur) planned by Antoinette de Pons, Marquise de Guercheville, in the event that the two missionaries had died. If this had not happened, he was to return to France. He reached Acadia on 16 May. Early in July the English from Virginia, under the command of Samuel ARGALL, seized the French possessions. Brother Gilbert DU THET was mortally wounded and the other Jesuits were taken prisoner. Father Quentin shared Father Biard's fate: "We remained in captivity during nine months and a half," wrote the latter. "We were in the ship all the time, except when we landed at Pembroke, as related. There were three months during which we daily received only about two ounces of bread, and a small quantity of salt fish, with water that was nearly always fetid." Upon his return to France in 1614 Father Quentin was assigned to the preaching ministry, residing most of the time at Charleville. He died there 18 March 1647.

LÉON POULIOT

Archivum Romanum Societatis Iesu. *JR* (Thwaites), *passim* (the index of the Quebec edition of the *Relations des Jésuites* confuses Claude and Jacques Quentin). *Première mission des Jésuites au Canada: lettres et documents inédits*, éd. Auguste Carayon (Paris, 1864). Rochemonteix, *Les Jésuites et la Nouvelle-France au XVIIe siècle*, I, 83.

Marquis de Saint-Pierre, "Note historique sur saint Laurent O'Toole, archévêque de Dublin, patron du fleuve Saint-Laurent," *BRH*, LXII (1956), 33–36. [In this note there is much excellent material and also much that is poor. One may accept the data on St. Lawrence O'Toole; but the documents relating to the transfer and return of the relic have been copied from the originals. The great river, however, owes its name to Jacques Cartier (1535). The Archbishop of Dublin's relic has nothing to do with the matter. L.P.]

QUER(QUE). *See* KIRKE

QUEYLUS, GABRIEL THUBIÈRES DE LEVY DE. *See* THUBIÈRES

R

RAGEOT, GILLES, clerk of court, notary, seigneur; b. *c.* 1642 at Saint-Jean-de-l'Aigle, diocese of Évreux (Orne, France), son of Isaac Rageot and of Louise Duret; d. at Quebec 1692.

Rageot came to Quebec in 1663 or shortly before. He began his career as recorder by virtue of being clerk of the registry of the Conseil Souverain. In 1666, however, he acquired more important functions. The Compagnie des Indes occidentales granted him two commissions in rapid succession: that of clerk of the seigneurial jurisdiction of the town of Quebec (5 May 1666), and that of notary in the jurisdiction of Quebec. Having been appointed by the company, Rageot had not the right to take the title of royal notary; Intendant TALON, however, who disputed the company's right to appoint notaries, issued a warrant dated 7 Nov. 1666, whereby Rageot could henceforth practise as a royal notary. When the company finally withdrew from Canadian affairs (1674), Rageot decided to make sure of the validity of his notary's commission, and asked the king himself for permission to continue in his office. This was granted by a commission signed by Louis XIV on 17 May 1675. The same day the king also renewed his commission as clerk of court. Rageot thus became the first notary of New France to receive a royal commission. But in 1685 the intendant, on the pretext that Rageot was sick, relieved him of his office of clerk and conferred it on François Genaple*. Rageot appealed to the king, who reinstated him on 24 May 1686.

Through his wife, Rageot became the owner of the arriere-fief of Saint-Luc, in the seigneury of Rivière-du-Sud.

Rageot had married Marie-Madeleine Morin on 29 May 1673, and from this union were born eight children. Three, following in their father's footsteps, became clerks of court and notaries: Charles*, born in 1674, Nicolas*, in 1676, and François, in 1682. The Rageot family, therefore, occupies an important place in the history of the profession of notary in Canada. Two other sons of Gilles Rageot, Philippe*, born in 1678, and Jean-Baptiste*, born in 1680, entered the priesthood, the first in 1701 and the second in 1700. The last-born son (1689) of the family, christened Gilles like his father, made his fortune in business.

Gilles Rageot was buried at Quebec on 3 Jan. 1692.

ANDRÉ VACHON

AJQ, Greffe de Gilles Rageot, 1666–1702; Ins. prév. Québec. APQ, Ins. cons. souv. *Jug. et délib.* P.-G. Roy, "Les Rageot de Saint-Luc et de Beaurivage," *BRH*, XXII (1916), 323–26.

RAGUENEAU, PAUL, priest, Jesuit, missionary, superior of the Huron mission (1645–50), superior of the Jesuits in Canada (1650–3), procurator of the Canadian mission in Paris; b. 18 March 1608 in Paris; d. 3 Sept. 1680 in the same city.

Father Paul Ragueneau has at times been confused with his brother François, likewise a Jesuit but 11 years his elder, having been born at Blois on 14 June 1597. Father François had been named to accompany Father CHARLES LALEMANT who was returning to Canada in 1628. The two Jesuits and three Recollets left Dieppe 8 May 1628 in the ship commanded by Claude ROQUEMONT de Brison in the name of the Compagnie des Cent-Associés. Two months later, at the mouth of the St. Lawrence, Roquemont was obliged to surrender to the KIRKE brothers. The two Jesuits were taken prisoner, transported to England and sent from that country to Belgium. On his return to France, Father François Ragueneau taught in Jesuit colleges and was even rector at Bourges. To the very end of his life he continued to interest himself in the Canadian mission, although it is not possible to state positively that he ever visited it. But one may assume that he conveyed his great missionary ideal to his brother Paul.

Paul Ragueneau entered the Paris noviciate on 21 Aug. 1626. From 1628 to 1632 he was a teacher at the Collège in Bourges, where for a period of three years the "Grand Condé" was one of his pupils. He studied theology at La Flèche from 1632 to 1636. On 28 June of the latter year he was at Quebec, and in 1637 he went on to the Huron country. The epidemic was then at the height of its violence; the missionaries were held responsible, and their death had been decreed. The famous testamentary letter of Jean de BRÉBEUF is dated 28 Oct. 1637, and is countersigned by Paul Ragueneau.

After having been the subordinate of Jean de Brébeuf and JÉRÔME LALEMANT for eight years, Father Ragueneau became superior of the Huron mission in 1645. We owe to him the "Relations des Hurons" for 1646, 1647, 1648, that of 1649 which recounts the destruction of the mission and the martyrdom of Fathers Brébeuf and GABRIEL LALEMANT, and that of 1650 which describes the ardours of the winter spent at Île Saint-Joseph (Christian Island) and the emigration and resettlement of the Hurons under the protection of the fort at Quebec.

Being of superior mentality, Father Ragueneau was amenable to the lessons of experience. In 1648 he wrote: "Had I to give counsel to those who commence to labor for the conversion of the Savages, I would willingly say a word of advice to them, which experience will, I think, make them acknowledge to be more important than it seems at first sight, namely: that one must be very careful before condemning a thousand things among their customs, which greatly offend minds brought up and nourished in another world. It is easy to call irreligion what is merely stupidity, and to take for diabolical working something that is nothing more than human; and then, one thinks he is obliged to forbid as impious certain things that are done in all innocence, or, at most, are silly, but not criminal customs. These could be abolished more gently, and I may say more efficaciously, by inducing the Savages themselves gradually to find out their absurdity, to laugh at them, and to abandon them—not through motives of conscience, as if they were crimes, but through their own judgment and knowledge, as follies. It is difficult to see everything in one day, and time is the most faithful instructor that one can consult." He recognized that the uncompromising attitude of the early missionaries was perhaps necessary in their time, but was no longer appropriate in his.

In the destruction of the Huron mission, only a small minority of the Hurons escaped death or captivity. Father Ragueneau was not indifferent to so much suffering unleashed all at once on his neophytes, or to the destruction of this missionary effort with all its high hopes. But how great he was in this time of trial: "It is a blessing for us that a part of this truly heavy cross is our portion for ourselves; that we have seen some of our brethren there shedding their blood and enduring torments, the cause of which may indeed enable them to pass some day for martyrs; that there is not one of us who may not expect to follow them in the midst of the burning fires, wherein they have been consumed; and that now the state of affairs is such that we are happily compelled to suffer much, and to fear everything, in the service of the great Master whose grandeur we announce in these Barbarous countries. We adore his divine guidance, over both us and our flock; we bless him for the past; and we await with love—and, I may say, with joy in our hearts—that which our nature would especially dread; for it is thus alone that he deserves to be served."

As superior of the Huron mission, Father Ragueneau had some major decisions to make in 1649 and 1650. The 300 or so Hurons who had escaped death or captivity and who had not fled saw their only salvation in the presence among them of the missionaries. But where should they go, for the situation at Sainte-Marie was untenable, the Iroquois being still on the warpath? Acceding to the wishes of the chiefs, Father Ragueneau decided to take up residence, along with his fellow-missionaries and servants, on the newly chosen site of the Île Saint-Joseph or Sainte-Marie II, now called Christian Island, in Georgian Bay. But before they left, another decision had to be made, and what a heart-breaking one for Father Ragueneau: the destruction of the Sainte-Marie residence and fort. He wrote: "That spot must be forsaken, which I may call our second Fatherland, our home of innocent delights, since it had been the cradle of this Christian church; since it was the temple of God, and the home of the servants of Jesus Christ. Moreover, for fear that our enemies, only too wicked, should profane the sacred place, and derive from it an advantage, we ourselves set fire to it, and beheld burn before our eyes, in less than one hour, our work of nine or ten years." This was on 14 June 1649.

A year later famine and Iroquois forays made another move necessary. At the request of the tribal chiefs, Father Ragueneau supervised the exodus to Quebec of the remnants of the Huron nation. The mission in Huronia had had its day. It was to survive in the hearts of its children who were seeking the protection of the fort at Quebec; and the numerous Hurons captured by the Iroquois were to give further proof that Father Ragueneau and his confrères had not toiled in vain.

When he left for France on 2 Nov. 1650, Father Jérôme Lalemant named Father Ragueneau vice-superior; it was the latter who was to direct the mission until 6 Aug. 1653, on which date he was to be replaced by Father François LE MERCIER. The missionaries in the Huron country had had nothing but praise for Father Ragueneau. "He is possessed of uncommon gifts in virtue, intelligence, prudence and learning," Father Charles GARNIER wrote to the general of the Society. And here is the testimony of Jean de Brébeuf: "He is an outstanding man, and in short he is so accomplished in every respect that he has not his like here and I doubt that he ever will have." It is therefore not surprising that he was thought of in 1650 as a likely first bishop of New France; but fortunately this proposal was not followed up. Indeed, the superiorship of Quebec, which made him a member of the Conseil of New France, was a stumbling block for Father Ragueneau. "Once he had become rector of Quebec and superior of the Canadian missions," wrote Rochemonteix, "he displeased the missionaries as superior by mixing too much in the civil and administrative affairs of the colony, and as a member of the Council he by the same token offended a large number of settlers."

As superior of the Canadian Jesuits, Father Ragueneau gave the initial impulse to the cause of canonization of the holy Canadian martyrs. On 21 March 1649, he had presided at the funerals of Brébeuf and of Gabriel Lalemant and had laid their bodies to rest beneath the chapel of the Sainte-Marie residence. He had caused to be placed in Brébeuf's grave a lead plaque inscribed with the name of the missionary and the date of his death at the hands of the Iroquois; this plaque was unearthed in 1954. In the 1649 *Relation*, Father Ragueneau had implied, but without anticipating the judgement of the Church, that Brébeuf and Gabriel Lalemant were martyrs in the canonical sense of the term. In 1650, before the final abandonment of Huronia, he had had the bodies taken up, and in his *Récit véritable* Brother Christophe Regnault informs us that the flesh was burned and the bones transported to Quebec. In 1652 Father Ragueneau undertook the collection of documents for the glorification not only of his two confrères in Huronia but also of the other missionaries in New France whom public opinion considered to be martyrs. This is the "Manuscrit de 1652" of which the original is preserved in the archives of the Collège Sainte-Marie in Montreal. It is undoubtedly an official and canonical document. There is no other explanation of the fact that the witnesses gave their testimony under oath and that Father Ragueneau confirmed it all in his capacity as superior of the Canadian Jesuits. In this respect as in several others, Father Ragueneau was ahead of his time. Less thought was given then than now to the glorification of those who had shed their blood for the faith or who had provided an example of great saintliness. All Father Ragueneau's confrères gave the same worship as he did to the missionaries who had died because of their zeal or their charity. But he alone thought that they would one day be canonized, and the "Manuscrit de 1652" prepared the way for the inquiries preceding canonization.

In 1656, Father Ragueneau was assigned to the residence at Trois-Rivières. The *Journal des Jésuites* informs us also that on 22 June 1657 he left for Sainte-Marie-de-Ganentaa. He lived through the tragic times that brought about the departure of Fathers P.-J.-M. Chaumonot, Simon Le Moyne and other missionaries and marked the failure of this first attempt at an organized apostolate among the Iroquois. Our account of it comes from him.

Father Ragueneau does not appear to have enjoyed the confidence of Governor Pierre de Voyer* d'Argenson. But the latter's successor, Pierre Du Bois Davaugour, had barely arrived at Quebec when he appealed to Ragueneau's good offices. He made the Jesuit chairman of a council that deliberated "every day on public affairs." In a letter dated 12 Oct. 1661 Father Ragueneau requested the "Grand Condé," his former pupil at Bourges, to employ his influence to secure the sending of troops to Canada, the only method of putting an end to the Iroquois threat. On 12 Aug. 1662 he left for France, in order to plead in person the same cause. He was never to return to Canada.

In Paris he succeeded Father Paul Le Jeune as the representative of the Jesuit missions in New France. And like Father Le Jeune, he too was much in demand as a spiritual director. "Providence," wrote Father Pierre Champion, "directed innumerable good souls to him, especially those who were treading unusual paths, and he devoted himself with boundless charity to aiding them both by word and by correspondence. People wrote to him from every quarter, and his replies carried enlightenment and the unction of the Holy Spirit to the hearts of those who received them."

At the suggestion of Bishop François de Laval*, who held him in high esteem, Father Ragueneau composed, and published at Florentin Lambert's in Paris in 1671, a *Vie* of the great mystic of the Hôtel-Dieu at Quebec, Catherine Simon de Longpré *dite* de Saint-Augustin; this became a document of the utmost importance in the cause of beatification of that servant of God. Father Ragueneau passed away at Paris on 3 Sept. 1680, at 72 years of age.

In the gallery of the great Jesuits of France at that period, Father Paul Ragueneau occupies a special place. When he was a teacher at the Collège in Bourges, he had had Father Louis Lallemant as rector and he had been deeply influenced by that master of the spiritual life. In *La Doctrine spirituelle du père Louis Lallemant*, Father Champion speaks of Father Ragueneau as follows: "He was a faultless religious, of great breadth of mind, of unusually penetrating and solid judgment, of heroic courage and capable of the greatest undertakings, of saintly simplicity, having an admirable trust in God and consummate experience in spiritual matters; a man completely detached from all worldly interests, who breathed only the love of God and a zeal for souls. He was one of the first missionaries in New France, and I know from Father Joseph Poncet and from Father François Le Mercier, two saintly religious who had been his colleagues in his apostolic labours, that there was no one who had rendered greater service to the Church in Canada, or who more richly deserved the title of apostle."

Two centuries later, Father Camille de Rochemonteix was to write: "Father Ragueneau was one of the most intelligent Jesuits Canada ever had." When he was moved from Quebec in 1656 he "accepted the order of his superior with a simplicity and a readiness that bear witness to his loftiness of soul. Numerous letters of his are to be found in the archives of the Society; not a single word betrays the slightest dissatisfaction. In all of them there is the same calmness, the same dignity; in all of them one recognizes the man of worth and the true religious. No Jesuit in Canada has written as much as, or better than, he."

Léon Pouliot

ACSM, "Mémoires touchant la mort et les vertus des pères Isaac Jogues . . ." (Ragueneau), repr. APQ *Rapport, 1924–25,* 3–93. Archives du Séminaire de

Raisin

Nicolet, Fonds Bois, La vie du P. Paul Ragueneau, de la Compagnie de Jésus, missionnaire du Canada. Et le recueil des réponses qu'il a faites sur les plus difficiles matières de la vie spirituelle. [The "Vie" (46pp.) is not at all complete, retaining only the essential facts contributing to a better understanding of the spiritual director. The author, who has not yet been positively identified, lived in Canada. He was a friend and admirer of Father Ragueneau; he notes the great esteem in which this missionary was held by Mgr de Laval; he has read Father Louis Lallemant's *Doctrine spirituelle*, which was first published in 1694. The existence of this MS in the Fonds Bois leads one to believe that it was written in Canada by a missionary who had had in his possession letters addressed by Father Ragueneau to the religious of the country. L. P.] ASQ, MSS, 43, "Etude sur les Relations des Jésuites," par Félix Martin.

JR (Thwaites), *passim*. *JJ* (Laverdière et Casgrain). [Louis Lallemant], *La vie et la doctrine spirituelle du père Louis Lallemant* ..., éd. François Courel (Collection Christus, III, Paris, 1959). Paul Ragueneau, *La vie de Mère Catherine de Saint-Augustin* (Paris, 1671).

E. R. Adair, "France and the beginnings of New France," *CHR*, XXV (1944), 246–78. Campbell, *Pioneer priests*, I, 141–57. A. E. Jones, "'8endake Ehen' or Old Huronia," *PAO Annual Report*, V (1908). Rochemonteix, *Les Jésuites et la Nouvelle-France au XVIIe siècle*, I, II.

RAISIN, MARIE, one of the first nuns of the Congrégation de Notre-Dame (Montreal), bap. 29 April 1636 at Troyes (Champagne), daughter of Edmé Raisin, a master-tailor, and Anne Collet; d. 1691.

Her parents lived near the house belonging to the parents of Marguerite BOURGEOYS. In 1659 Marie Raisin met Sister Bourgeoys, who had come to Troyes to recruit teachers. With her and two other companions she went to Paris. While there she obtained her father's permission to go to Canada. The travellers left La Rochelle 2 July 1659, and after a rough crossing they arrived at Quebec on 8 September, then reached Ville-Marie (Montreal) on 29 September. Until 1666 Marie taught in the stable converted into a school. Her name is found on the census list of Trois-Rivières for that year; in it she is called "a school-mistress to the girls of Trois-Rivières." In this same year of 1666 she entered the Ursuline convent at Quebec and spent three months there as a postulant. She came back to Ville-Marie in November, with Sister Bourgeoys. From this time on she held important positions at Ville-Marie and in the surrounding missions. In 1670 she was assistant superior. She then taught at Champlain, but in 1678 and 1683 she was at Ville-Marie. Her brother Nicolas, a lawyer in the Parlement of Paris, died in 1687, leaving her all his fortune. She donated it to the Congrégation de Notre-Dame on 7 March 1688. She died 5 Oct. 1691.

SAINT MIRIAM OF THE TEMPLE, C.N.D.

ACND, MS M¹, Écrits autographes de sœur Marguerite Bourgeois; et autres documents. AHDM, Marie Morin, Histoire simple et véritable de l'établissement des Religieuses Hospitalières de Saint-Joseph en l'Île de Montréal, dite à présent Ville-Marie, en Canada, de l'année 1659. . . . AJM, Greffe de Bénigne Basset, 7 mars 1688. Recensement de 1666. Morin, *Annales* (Fauteux *et al.*). *Premier registre de l'église Notre-Dame de Montréal* (Montréal, 1961). Louis Morin, *Deux familles troyennes de musiciens et de comédiens, les Siret et les Raisin* (Troyes, 1927), 12f.

RALLUAU (Ralleau), JEAN, explorer and secretary to DU GUA de Monts; fl. 1604–15.

He joined the de Monts expedition of 1604 and served as secretary to the leader. Soon after the arrival of the expedition at Nova Scotia, when de Monts decided to wait at Port-au-Mouton for his second vessel to make rendezvous, Ralluau and CHAMPLAIN used the opportunity to make a short voyage of exploration to the south of that place. At the end of August Ralluau was sent back to France to report the successful founding of the colony on Île Sainte-Croix (Dochet Island) to de Monts's partners in the trading company and to arrange for fresh stores to be sent out as soon as possible the next spring. He returned to Acadia with the supply ship in 1605, then accompanied de Monts back to France later that season. He sailed from La Rochelle on 13 May 1606 aboard the *Jonas*, being sent with supplies and a party of men that included Marc LESCARBOT and JEAN DE BIENCOURT de Poutrincourt. At Canseau (Canso) he left the *Jonas* and succeeded in finding at Port-Royal (Annapolis Royal) the settlers who, despairing of receiving relief, were on their way to France.

The next year, it was Jean Ralluau whom de Monts entrusted to carry word to Port-Royal that the company's exclusive trading privileges had been cancelled and the colonists were to abandon the settlement, but he found the news had already been received from Chevalier. There is reference to Ralluau with ANGIBAULT *dit* Champdoré making a trip to Port-Royal again in 1608 to trade and to examine its condition since de Monts's monopoly had been extended one more year. During this same visit they made a trip up the Saint John River for a distance of some 50 leagues in a search for SECOUDON, chief of the Indians there. They were likely the first Europeans to explore the Saint John for any distance and they supplied a good description of the country and its vegetation.

In 1612 he was involved, with de Monts, in lawsuits over supplies for the fur trade in America. By 1615 Ralluau was managing at Paris the interests of the Compagnie du Canada as well as acting as Sillery's secretary. At that time he had power of attorney from Champlain authorizing him to act for Champlain in an involved dispute over the fur trade with Samuel Georges, Jean Macain, and others.

GEORGE MACBEATH

Champlain, *Works* (Biggar). Lescarbot, *History* (Grant), II, 240. Huguet, *Poutrincourt*, 203, 234. Robert Le Blant and Marcel Delafosse, "Les Rochelais dans la vallée du Saint-Laurent (1599–1618)," *RHAF*, X (1956–57), 346–47. *Pierre Du Gua, sieur de Monts, records: colonial and "Saintongeois,"* ed. W. I. Morse (London, 1939), 62–64, 73–74, 82.

RANDIN (often found, incorrectly, as **Raudin, Rendin,** or **Renden**), **HUGUES,** French engineer in Governor BUADE de Frontenac's service, soldier, cartographer, architect of Fort Cataracoui (Frontenac); b. (according to Lejeune) 1628, in France; d. *c.* 1680 in New France.

Nothing is known of Randin's parentage and early life, and there is no record that he ever married while in New France. He came to Canada as an ensign with the Carignan-Salières regiment in the summer of 1665, and stayed when the regiment was repatriated in 1668. In 1671, the intendant, TALON, sent him to the western boundary of Acadia to report on the condition of Fort Pentagouet. For his services to New France he was granted a seigneury on the St. Lawrence by Talon in 1672, but this he sold a year later to Alexandre Berthier*; it is now called Berthierville, but an island opposite the town preserves the name Randin.

Randin accompanied Frontenac on his 1673 mission of peace and trade to the Iroquois at the mouth of the Cataracoui (where Kingston, Ontario, now stands), when a French post was established to divert furs from the Dutch and English. Randin designed the fort and directed its construction. The work proceeded with such zeal that the journal of the expedition (*NYCD*, IX, 104; original in Paris) reports that the officers had difficulty in stopping the men for sleep. Arriving 12 July, they began clearing the next day and, to the amazement of the assembled Indians, Fort Cataracoui (or Frontenac) was completed by the 19th and palisaded on the 20th. Three years later the fort was dismantled and rebuilt of stone.

In 1676 Frontenac deputed Randin to Sault Ste. Marie with gifts as an ambassador of peace to facilitate fur-trade relations, this time with the Sioux. The mission was successful and Frontenac secured a grant to his engineer in 1679 of a seigneury in Acadia; its gift, by Randin's brother and heir, to the Hôtel-Dieu, Quebec, was witnessed there before notary François Genaple*, 5 June 1684.

A coloured MS map survives (in John Carter Brown Library, Providence, R.I.), generally attributed to Randin: *Carte de L'Amerique Septentrionale Depuis l'embouchûre de la Riviere St. Laurens jusques au Sein Mexique*, which depicts the full extent of the French empire in North America. It is a testimony to its author's skill in draftsmanship. Though undated (and unsigned) it was evidently made after the "Jolliet" map of 1674, but possibly not later than 1676 since it bears no details of Randin's Lake Superior journey.

A memoir dated 13 Nov. 1680, from Intendant DUCHESNEAU to Jean-Baptiste Colbert in Paris (*NYCD*, IX, 142) complains of a trading agreement between Randin and his associates, and Frontenac. If Randin were living in November, he must have died within two months, for a document (AN, Col. C^{11A}, 6, f.111) exists which refers twice to the *feu* (late) Randin; it is dated 10 Jan. 1681.

WILLIAM F. E. MORLEY

Private information from the John Carter Brown Library, Providence, R.I. *NYCD* (O'Callaghan and Fernow), IX, 104, for tr. of the "Paris" document. Le Jeune, *Dictionnaire*. II, 500–1. Sara J. Tucker, *Indian villages of the Illinois country* (Springfield, Ill., 1942), 3, and pl.VI.

RASILLY. *See* RAZILLY

RASTELL, JOHN, the younger, eldest son of John Rastell; English lawyer, visited Newfoundland with Richard HORE; fl. 1510–40.

John Rastell, the elder, married Elizabeth, sister of Sir Thomas More, in London, 1512, where he combined a legal practice with a printing business, and undertook various tasks for Henry VIII. As a member of Sir Thomas More's circle, he took part in discussions on America and its potentialities.

The elder Rastell determined to explore and settle North America, influenced, apparently, by advice from SEBASTIAN CABOT that a half-way house on a northwest passage to Asia would be very profitable. With two London merchants, John Howting and Richard Spicer, he got letters from the king on 5 March 1517, and a small loan. One or more royal ships were assigned to the expedition, the preparation of which was supervised by Sir Thomas Spert, a naval officer (though he and the lord admiral, the Earl of Surrey, were later accused of faint-heartedness and sabotage).

Starting late in the summer, the expedition, consisting of at least four vessels with supplies and equipment for settlement, delayed at Sandwich, Dartmouth, Plymouth, and Falmouth. Dissension broke out among the men and their leaders. One ship returned to England, another touched Ireland and then sailed for France, while two ships seem not to have gone beyond Falmouth. The seamen clearly were unwilling to settle in Newfoundland or Labrador and to search the northwest passage for a way to Asia from this base. Set ashore in Ireland, the elder Rastell wrote a moral play entitled *A new interlude and a mery of the nature of the iiij elementes*, which he published when he returned to England about 1519 and which embodied both his own ideals of colonization and his use of oral evidence from those who made American voyages before 1506. His vision of an overseas empire, which he made no further attempt to realize, is the only one of its kind before Queen Elizabeth's reign to survive.

The younger Rastell was born in Coventry and in 1511 was entered, when a child, as a member of the Corpus Christi Guild. (The elder Rastell, too, had been born in Coventry, c. 1475, where he later became coroner before his move to London.) The son reached manhood at a time of crisis for his family. His father broke with his uncle, Sir Thomas More, when Henry VIII came into conflict with the papacy. The elder Rastell was a reformer in the Reformation Parliament of 1529–1536 but he went too far for Thomas Cromwell in challenging the continuation of tithes, was imprisoned, and died in 1536. It was probably before his father's difficulties became acute that the younger John had committed himself to join the expedition to Newfoundland which was to be led by Richard Hore and on which he left London in April 1536 with a number of other gentlemen adventurers. We do not know whether he sailed on the *Trinity* or the *William*. It is possible that one or both ships penetrated the Strait of Belle Isle and got into trouble on the coast of Labrador before returning to fish off Newfoundland, but all got home safely in the end. Beyond some appearances in the courts, little is known of the younger Rastell's subsequent career but the continuity of his American expedition with his father's projects is of some significance.

DAVID B. QUINN

Williamson, *Voyages of the Cabots* (1929), contains a number of documents [see Richard HORE for others]. *DNB* (Rastell, John the elder, and William). For a discussion of *A new interlude*, see G. B. Parks, "The geography of the 'Interlude of the four elements'," *Philological Q.*, XVII (1938), 251–62, and J. Parr, "John Rastell's geographical knowledge of America," *Philological Q.*, XXVII (1948), 229–40. A. W. Read, *Early Tudor drama* (London, 1926), deals fully with the biography of John Rastell the elder, and has most of what is known on John Rastell the younger.

RAUDIN. *See* RANDIN

RAVILLON, LA COURT PRÉ-. *See* LA COURT

RAYMBAUT, CHARLES, priest, Jesuit, missionary among the Hurons and the Indians of Lake Nipissing; b. 6 April 1602 at Senlis (France); d. 22 Oct. 1642 at Quebec.

He was admitted into the noviciate of the Jesuits at Rouen on 24 Aug. 1621. He studied his philosophy at La Flèche (1623–26), taught at Rennes (1626–28), studied theology at Bourges (1628–30), and after his ordination he taught for a further year at Blois and another at Amiens. Having completed his spiritual training at Rouen (1632–33), he remained at the noviciate of that town as bursar, and was also responsible for the interests of the Canadian mission (1633–37). In the summer of 1637 he arrived at Quebec and was immediately sent to join Father BUTEUX at Trois-Rivières, in order to learn the Algonkin language and begin his apostolate. Father Raymbaut was a tall man with a vigorous physique. He was thought very well qualified to investigate the tribes of the west, who were reputed to speak the Algonkin tongue. He therefore set out in 1640, with Father CLAUDE PIJART, to begin his work at Lake Nipissing. As the Indians belonging to these regions were not there, the two Jesuits went to the Huron country, where the Nipissing Indians themselves arrived soon after to pass the winter season. Fathers Pijart and Raymbaut learned their language, began to instruct them, and accompanied them the following summer to Lake Nipissing, where they witnessed their feast of the dead at the beginning of September 1641. Raymbaut returned to the residence of Sainte-Marie-des-Hurons, and at the end of that month started on a journey to the country of the Sauteurs with Father JOGUES. Though the autumn was well advanced, Raymbaut decided again to winter at Lake Nipissing with Father René MÉNARD. The difficulties of the journey were such that they were obliged to turn back, and Raymbaut fell seriously ill. He grew weaker all through the winter, and was sent to Quebec in the spring to await death, which struck down this robust man at the age of 40. He was the first Jesuit to die at Quebec, and Governor HUAULT de Montmagny had him buried beside CHAMPLAIN.

LUCIEN CAMPEAU

JR (Thwaites). Rochemonteix, *Les Jésuites et la Nouvelle-France au XVIIe siècle*, I, 419–28.

RAYNER (Reyner), JOHN, sea captain, deputy governor of Newfoundland for George CALVERT, Lord Baltimore; fl. 1661–62.

When, in March 1661, Lord Baltimore's patent of Avalon was declared still valid, captains Pease and John Rayner were sent to Newfoundland by Baltimore as his deputies. They made their headquarters at Ferryland but their administration was neither successful, because of their constant disagreements, nor popular, because Rayner tried to collect arrears of rent owing to Baltimore. The only account of Rayner's governorship, however, was written by an agent of the KIRKES and must therefore be suspect; "Captaine Reyner," he wrote, "is a desperado and looks not fore right."

While in Newfoundland Rayner and Pease claimed for Baltimore a half-share in two French prizes taken by the convoy ships. Rayner also seized a ship, the *John* of Topsham, on the pretence of enforcing the Act of Navigation as the master could not prove that the Dutch-built vessel was English owned. In 1662 the owner sued Rayner in the Admiralty court for recovery of his ship.

In September 1661 it was reported that Rayner had left for England but he was in Newfoundland in 1662 when he and Pease sent John Matthews to St. Mary's Bay to seize a Mr. Russell and an Indian who were taking furs without permission. Matthews was captured by the French, who said that the southern part of the island belonged to France. How much longer Rayner stayed in Newfoundland we do not know; certainly Baltimore's authority over the island was not long maintained for, in 1666, certain of the planters asked Sir DAVID KIRKE's son, George, to assume the governorship.

GILLIAN T. CELL

BM, Egerton MS 2395, ff.308–8v., 447, 471. PRO, C.O. 1/16, no.113; Dom., Car.II, S.P. 29/42, no.10; H.C.A. 13/74, 6 Nov. 1662, depositions of John Chettle, Robert Swanley, and William Reyner; *Acts of P.C., col. ser., 1613–80*. Lounsbury, *British fishery at Nfld*. Prowse, *History of Nfld*.

RAZILLY (Rasilly), ISAAC DE, naval captain, colonizer, and governor in Acadia; b. 1587 at the Château d'Oiseaumelle in the Touraine country of France, the son of François de Razilly and Catherine de Valliers, and the brother of Claude, a ship's captain and commodore, of Gabriel, a member of the order of Saint John of Jerusalem, who was killed at Montpellier in 1622, and of François, who directed the Maragnan expedition; d. 1635 at La Hève.

At the age of 18, Isaac was appointed a knight of the order of Saint John of Jerusalem. He became a member of the French navy and over the years saw much distinguished service. In 1621 he was appointed commander of Isle-Bouchard in Touraine. That same year he commanded a squadron of 13 vessels during the siege of the Huguenot-held port of Saint-Martin, his force capturing some 30 enemy craft during the action. In the attack on the Huguenots at La Rochelle in 1625 he was seriously wounded and lost an eye when one of the vessels in his fleet blew up. His other service with the navy took him to many parts of the world and further demonstrated his unusual ability.

Cardinal Richelieu came to seek his counsel on maritime matters and in 1626 he asked Razilly to prepare a brief setting forth his ideas on the country's trade and commerce. The report that resulted stated frankly that the nation's trade was at a low ebb owing to the government's mistaken notion that trade was not vital to the country's welfare. Refuting this idea, Razilly went on to observe that mastery of the sea would also bring France great power on land. In the section dealing with New France, he proposed that a large trading company with capital of 300,000 *livres* be organized, that steps be taken to block any English encroachment north of the 36th parallel, and that three to four thousand colonists be placed on the land both as a means to developing resources and to further ensure a hold on the country.

This report from a man of renown and high reputation was received favourably by Richelieu who set about putting the various proposals into force. Possibly the most important outcome was the founding the next year of the Compagnie de La Nouvelle-France, or the Compagnie des Cent-Associés as it is often called. Participants included Richelieu himself, CHAMPLAIN, and Razilly, who was appointed naval commander for the company. The company's first act was to prepare four ships and load them with settlers, cattle, food, and other supplies for Champlain at Quebec and CHARLES DE SAINT-ÉTIENNE de La Tour at Cap de Sable. They set out in the spring of 1628 but were intercepted by an English squadron and few of the supplies got through. The next year it was decided to send three warships commanded by Razilly, including that of Capt. CHARLES DANIEL, to guard the supply ships on the Atlantic crossing but, with peace between France and England

Razilly

about to be signed, Richelieu ordered Razilly to sail instead against Moorish pirates attacking French shipping in the Mediterranean.

Early in 1632 Cardinal Richelieu invited Razilly to accept the post of lieutenant-general of New France, but he declined, requesting instead to serve as a ship's captain under Champlain "because he is more competent in colonial affairs." On 27 March Razilly and Richelieu signed an agreement by which Razilly was to take possession of Port-Royal (now Annapolis Royal, N.S.) for the company and France under the terms of the Treaty of Saint-Germain-en-Laye and to make Acadia a French colony. Necessary authority to undertake this action was given Razilly in a royal commission dated 10 May. While the company also wished Razilly to begin settling the country, the losses it had suffered in the recent war with England had left it short of funds. The solution arrived at was to accord a part of its trading privilege to private companies on condition that such groups participate financially. So it was that Razilly and some of his friends formed a private trading association that came to be known as the Razilly-Condonnier company. While the Compagnie de la Nouvelle-France provided an equipped vessel and the sum of 10,000 *livres* for the 1632 expedition to Acadia, it was Razilly's private trading group which advanced the greater part of the money required. On 19 May, the company named Razilly lieutenant-general for the king in New France and granted him a tract of land at Sainte-Croix measuring 12 leagues by 20 leagues.

Three vessels were fitted out and, in addition to sailors and soldiers, workmen and craftsmen as well as some 12 to 15 families of colonists were recruited. In all "300 hommes d'élite," including six Capuchins and a number of noblemen made up the expedition. They sailed from the port of Auray in Britanny on 23 July 1632, were joined by a ship from La Rochelle, and reached Acadia on 8 September. Razilly, a seaman by training, chose the port of La Hève (now La Have) on Nova Scotia's south shore to be his headquarters and the capital of Acadia, a decision probably made because of its good harbour and its navigational advantages. On the site of the present village of Riverport, Razilly built a habitation consisting of his own residence, a store, and Fort Sainte-Marie-de-Grâce. A chapel for the Capuchins and other buildings for the families and the unmarried workmen were erected nearby. It was here at La Hève, too, that the Capuchins opened the first boarding-school in New France, one that was for the use of the colonists and especially the Indians.

Once the work of founding the settlement was well under way, Razilly turned his attention to the retaking of Port-Royal. Towards mid-December this post was peacefully surrendered to him by the garrison commander, Capt. Andrew FORRESTER. While a few of the Port-Royal settlers probably joined Razilly's colonists, most accepted his offer of passage home to England where they arrived in February 1632/33.

Working towards the goal of establishing the colony on a solid base, Razilly set some of the men to farming. Land for this purpose was cleared at Petite-Rivière (Green Bay) and in the course of time some 40 people were settled there. At the same time, other projects of significance were developed. Since the La Hève area was a good one for fishing, Razilly in partnership with one of his lieutenants, NICOLAS DENYS, developed an inshore fishing business based at Port-Rossignol. He also encouraged Denys in his successful efforts to cut timber near La Hève for export to Europe. However, he realized it was the successful development of the trade in furs that would best assure necessary funds for the continued progress of the venture, and it was the colonizing of Acadia that he considered his chief purpose. In fact, as Denys says, "he had no other desire than to people this land, and every year he had brought here as many people as he possibly could for this purpose". In his letters to Richelieu, Razilly spoke in the most glowing terms of the land of Acadia and of the number of people then living and suffering in France who could dwell in comfort in this "blessed land." "The soil," he writes, "is rich both on the surface and below; the sea abounds in fish that we are exporting to southern France." In 1634 he wrote Marc LESCARBOT lamenting his lack of means to accelerate the colonizing enterprise and observing that if he had the money himself he would willingly use it to foster this project.

That same year Razilly proposed that Richelieu ask the king for money to hire five vessels for use in Acadia. Two would be employed in the fur trade and the remaining three in cod-fishing. They would take these cargoes to France and return with European goods. Profits would mean that the number of vessels could be increased year by year. This project, he felt, would benefit the country by accelerating its settlement, by stimulating trade, by easing financial demands on the state, and by providing greater security against pirates.

To increase his fur-trade outlets, Razilly built a fortified port at Canseau (Canso) called Fort Saint-François. Here he placed Nicolas LE CREUX Du Breuil, in charge. This place had the distinction of being the centre of the first attempt at revolt in Acadia when in 1635 Jean THOMAS incited his crew and a band of Micmacs in the area to attack and capture Fort Saint-François. In a display of his usual energetic leadership, Razilly put down the rebellion, had Thomas made a prisoner, and prosecuted.

During all this time, Razilly had a good working relationship with Charles de La Tour who shared with him, under terms of the commissions issued by the Compagnie de La Nouvelle-France, control of the land and the coasts of Acadia. The company regularly sent out ships to Razilly with colonists and provisions. By early 1635 he felt strong enough to attempt to retake Fort Pentagouet on the Penobscot which by treaty had reverted to France but had never actually been abandoned by the New Englanders. So it was that Razilly assigned a force of men to one of his lieutenants, Charles de MENOU d'Aulnay, and ordered him to capture the fort at Penobscot and to inform the English they were to vacate all lands north of Pemaquid. This post was taken in August and its occupants ejected.

Razilly now had the satisfaction of knowing that all French interests in Acadia had been restored. Peace reigned and the many development projects he had set in motion were flourishing. His sudden death at La Hève in December 1635 proved a disastrous blow which had a lasting effect on the country.

During these years in Acadia, Isaac de Razilly had had the whole-hearted support of his brother, Claude de Launay-Rasilly (who signed his name thus), a member not only of the Razilly-Condonnier company and the Compagnie de la Nouvelle-France, but also of two private companies active in the St. Lawrence region. When, in 1634, the Compagnie de la Nouvelle-France was unable to repay the Razillys the money they had loaned, the company conceded them in the name of Claude de Rasilly the forts at La Hève and Port-Royal as well as half the profits to be derived from the fur trade over the next ten years. Following the death of his brother, who was a bachelor, Claude de Rasilly became responsible for the Acadian colony. Since business affairs obliged him to remain in France, he authorized Menou d'Aulnay to act for him in Acadia. However, he remained actively interested in the affairs of the colony and in all probability it is he who was largely responsible for continuing his brother's successful experiment of establishing farmers in Acadia. While totals are extremely difficult to estimate, it seems reasonable to suggest that some 120 permanent inhabitants were brought to Acadia by the Razilly brothers. At the beginning of 1642, Claude de Rasilly sold his interests in the Razilly-Condonnier company to d'Aulnay and, with this act, participation of the Razillys in affairs here ceased.

While Isaac de Razilly lived little more than three years in Acadia, his contribution to its development had lasting importance. He was one of the first Europeans to be more interested in settling the country than exploiting its other resources. It was under his direction that a good number of the original Acadian people, whose descendants today comprise some 300,000 of the population of the Atlantic provinces, were established on the land. Realizing that commerce was also essential to the success of this experiment, he successfully promoted the fur trade, timber cutting, and inshore fishing projects. What is more, he ruled the territory under his direction with vigour, intelligence, and foresight. As Champlain records, he was "prudent, wise, laborious, and impelled by a holy desire to increase the glory of God, and carry his courage to the country of New France, there to unfurl the standard of Jesus Christ and cause the lilies [of France] to flourish."

GEORGE MACBEATH

BN, MS Fr. 13423, ff.349v–350, letter from Razilly to Lescarbot of 16 Aug. 1634. Champlain, *Works* (Biggar). *Coll. de manuscrits relatifs à la Nouv.-France*, I, II. Denys, *Description and natural history* (Ganong). *JR* (Thwaites). René Baudry, "Charles d'Aulnay et la Compagnie de la Nouvelle-France," *RHAF*, XI (1957–58), 218–41. Roger Comeau, "Origine des Acadiens," SGCF *Mémoires*, VI (1955), 243–56. Couillard Després, *Saint-Étienne de La Tour*. Léon Deschamps, *Un colonisateur au temps de Richelieu: Isaac de Razilly* (Paris, 1887) (taken in part from the *Revue de Géographie* (1877)). La Roncière, *Histoire de la marine française*, IV. Michel-Gustave de Rasilly, *Généalogie de la famille de Rasilly* (Laval, 1903). J.-E. Roy, "Le commandeur de Rasilly," *BRH*, XIX (1913), 345–49.

Two documents which may indicate that Claude de Launay-Rasilly was in Acadia are in AN (Archives d'Outre-Mer), Dépôt des fortifications des colonies, 134, f.28 (Mémoire de Lhermitte, 1716), and in ACM, B.203, 206 (29 avril 1662).

RÉ, FRANÇOIS DE. *See* DERRÉ DE GAND, FRANÇOIS

"THE RECONCILED." *See* CHEROUOUNY

RÉMUS. *See* ROMIEUX

RÉMY DE COURCELLE (Courcelles), DANIEL DE, Sieur de Montigny, de La Fresnaye et de Courcelle, seigneur de Rouvray et Du Bourg; b. 1626; d. unmarried, possibly at Toulon, France, 24 Oct. 1698.

Rémy de Courcelle

Courcelle succeeded SAFFRAY de Mézy as governor of New France in 1665 and, along with PROUVILLE de Tracy, was instrumental in subduing the Iroquois who had periodically ravaged the colony since the days of CHAMPLAIN. Prior to his appointment as governor-general of New France 23 March 1665, he was governor of Thionville in Lorraine. He arrived at Quebec with the intendant, Jean TALON, 12 September. Tracy, the lieutenant-general of all the French possessions in North America, had arrived the previous June along with the Carignan-Salières regiment, sent to crush the Iroquois. As soon as he landed, Courcelle, "breathing nothing but war," concerned himself with the construction and garrisoning of the forts that Tracy had ordered built along the Richelieu River, the invasion route used by the Mohawks in their attacks on the French settlements.

At this time the Iroquois Confederacy was being hard pressed by its Indian foes and its ranks had been reduced by an epidemic of smallpox. When the member tribes learned that the French had received heavy reinforcements of troops and settlers their chiefs were quick to sound out the French missionaries on the possibilities of a peace settlement. Tracy, Courcelle, and Talon were convinced, however, that only after the Iroquois had been soundly defeated in battle would there be any hope of an enduring peace. They therefore decided to invade the Mohawk country in mid-winter when the enemy would least expect it.

On 9 January 1666, Courcelle left Quebec at the head of 600 men. By the time they reached the forts on the Richelieu River several of the men had had their limbs and faces badly frozen. A party of Algonkins was expected to guide the army but it failed to appear and on 29 January Courcelle gave the order to march without the Indians. The men, carrying their arms and supplies on their backs and unaccustomed to marching on snow-shoes in deep snow, were quickly exhausted. The intense cold made their ordeal all the worse. Owing to the lack of guides they followed many false trails and frequently had to retrace their path. On 15 February, hardly knowing where they were headed, they found themselves close to the Dutch settlement of Schenectady, three days march from the Mohawk villages. The only Mohawks they had so far encountered had ambushed the detachment sent in their pursuit, killing an officer and ten men.

When the officials at Albany learned that a large French force was in the vicinity they sent a delegation to inquire why the French had marched an army into the territory of the king of England without first informing the governor of New York province. (It was perhaps as well for all concerned that neither Courcelle nor the authorities at Albany knew that England and France had been at war for the past fortnight.) Courcelle, in fact, was surprised to learn that the English had gained title to New Amsterdam (now New York) from the Dutch and he ruefully commented "that the King of England did graspe at all America." He assured the delegates from Albany that he had no intention of molesting His Britannic Majesty's subjects, nor would he invade his territory. He arranged to purchase food supplies from Schenectady but when he and his men were invited to avail themselves of the shelter of that village he declined the offer, fearing that if his men once got near a chimney corner it would be difficult to get them away again. Seven of his wounded were taken to Albany where they were well cared for by the Dutch settlers.

When a sudden thaw set in and it began to rain heavily Courcelle was forced to abandon the campaign. On 21 February they began the long march home, pursued by Mohawk war parties. Over 60 men, weakened by exposure and hunger, perished during the return journey.

This campaign had come dangerously close to being a total disaster. Courcelle tried to blame the Jesuits for its sorry outcome, claiming it to be their fault that the Algonkin guides had not joined the expedition. Deprived of their Indian guides, they had failed to reach the Mohawk villages. The Marquis de Salières [Chastelard*] colonel of the Carignan-Salières regiment, with whom Courcelle had quarrelled earlier, placed the blame squarely on Courcelle's shoulders, maintaining that the governor had failed to provide his men with adequate equipment and winter clothing for such an expedition. Wherever the blame might lie, the expedition had failed in its purpose. The Mohawks now saw little cause to fear the French and another campaign was essential to restore French prestige and to halt the Iroquois attacks on the colony.

In late September 1666 Tracy and Courcelle at the head of 1,400 men, accompanied by 100 Hurons and Algonkins, left Fort Sainte-Anne at the foot of Lake Champlain and invaded the Mohawk country. The Mohawks fled before this army, the largest ever seen in that part of the world, which advanced steadily with banners flying and drums beating. The four villages of the Mohawks were put to the torch and all the food supplies destroyed. A large cross and a post bearing the arms of France were planted on the site of the principal village. The lands of the Mohawks were then claimed for Louis XIV by

Rémy de Courcelle

right of conquest and the army returned home. The Iroquois now accepted the French terms for peace, and this time they abided by them. It was clear, however, that they could be kept at peace only as long as the French could keep them "in a state of fear." To maintain this peace was to be Courcelle's principal task during the ensuing six years.

Meanwhile, on 6 Dec. 1666, Courcelle, Talon, and Tracy reconstituted the Conseil Souverain. Prior to this the intendant Talon had dispensed justice by himself. With the rapid increase in population, the number of cases coming before the Conseil Souverain increased considerably. In August 1667, in an attempt to expedite matters, the council agreed that all litigation should be examined first by Talon and allocated, as he saw fit, to the Conseil Souverain, to the Cour de Prévôté, or be retained by himself for summary judgement. Courcelle refused to agree to this edict on the grounds that it ran counter to the authority vested in him as governor, and was not in the public interest. The following January he again refused to agree to this proposal. He was apparently of the opinion that it was he, as governor, and not the intendant, who should hold the reins of power in the colony. He was always on good terms with the lieutenant-general but Tracy left the colony in August 1667, and from that date Courcelle's relations with Talon and with BOUTROUE, who replaced Talon as intendant for two years, grew steadily worse. In 1669 Colbert curtly informed him that a man in his position had to be tolerant of the faults of others and to make the best use possible of their good qualities in order that the king's intentions for the colony might be carried out. In 1670, when Talon returned to New France, his relations with Courcelle became very strained. In November of that year Talon informed Colbert that the governor appeared very jealous of the influence he, Talon, had with the minister and became very annoyed whenever Talon failed to agree with him. The following year Talon complained that Courcelle treated him as his inferior, almost as a valet, and did much to hinder his plans for the colony. Unfortunately, Courcelle's correspondence has not survived and Talon's dispatches to the minister give, of course, only his side of the dispute.

In one field that was properly his own, relations with the Indian nations, Courcelle showed great ability and won the respect of French and Indians alike. When, in 1669, a Seneca chief was murdered by three soldiers of the Montreal garrison, Courcelle took swift action lest the Iroquois regard the incident as a *casus belli*. The three men were quickly apprehended, tried and executed, before a large group of Iroquois, come to Montreal to trade. The Iroquois were much impressed with the fact that the French had condemned to death three of their own men for the murder of one Iroquois and the peace was preserved. The following year, however, the Iroquois began warring again with the Algonkins, killing several and taking some prisoners. The Algonkins immediately struck back. It looked as though hostilities would spread to all the tribes allied to the French and eventually to the French themselves. Courcelle ordered both sides to cease fighting and to return their prisoners. When the Iroquois showed no inclination to accept this order Courcelle threatened to march an army into their country. The western Iroquois defied him in a haughty reply, confident that their villages were too remote to be reached by a French army: "The governor threatens to ruin our country? We shall see if his arm is long enough to lift our scalps."

The following year the governor had a large flat boat built at Montreal, capable of transporting heavier supplies than canoes could carry, mustered 56 volunteers and on 2 June set off up the turbulent rapids of the St. Lawrence to show the western Iroquois that their country was not beyond his reach. Ten days later his force reached Lake Ontario, to the great consternation of the Iroquois hunting parties encountered on the way. Courcelle informed them that if they wished to continue warring with the Algonkins and to extend the war to the French as some of them had threatened, they were completely at liberty to do so; but if they did, he added, he would bring an army to Lake Ontario in large boats and destroy them. The Iroquois were so impressed by Courcelle's audacious move that they ceased all talk of war and made their peace with the Algonkins.

While at Lake Ontario Courcelle explored the eastern end of the lake for a suitable site to build a fort and trading-post to obtain from the Iroquois the pelts they garnered on the north side of the lake and which they traded with the Dutch at Albany. He suggested establishing a fort near the mouth of Lake Ontario but Colbert rejected the suggestion. Talon also suggested establishing two trading-posts on Lake Ontario, one on the north shore and one on the south. Although Courcelle had wanted a military fort, his successor, BUADE de Frontenac, two years later, established a trading-post at the mouth of the Cataracoui River—where the city of Kingston stands today. When Louis XIV was eventually shown a map of the area he expressed amazement that anyone should locate a "fort" at the place chosen by Frontenac, since, from a military point of view the obvious site was a point commanding the St. Lawrence.

Renaud d'Avène de Desmeloizes

Courcelle was also very disturbed over attempts made by the Ottawa nation, the chief suppliers of furs to the French, to trade with the Dutch and English either directly at Albany or through the Iroquois acting as middlemen. He successfully sowed suspicion in the minds of both the Iroquois and the Ottawas, saying that each nation intended to use this trade as a means to lure the other into a trap and there to destroy it. In this way he safeguarded the western fur trade for the French.

The exploration of the west by CAVELIER de La Salle, DAUMONT de Saint-Lusson, Jean PERÉ, JOLLIET, Dollier* de Casson and BRÉHANT de Galinée was actively encouraged by Courcelle. Vast areas, previously unknown, were now claimed for France and trading relations established with the Indian nations of these regions. It was also under Courcelle, acting on the orders of Louis XIV, that militia units were formed in New France and the able-bodied men from 16 to 60 drilled in the use of arms. It was this militia that was to bear the brunt of the fighting in the colony's future wars.

By 1671 Courcelle was anxious to return to France and, pleading ill-health, he asked to be recalled. The following year his request was granted. One of his last acts in the colony was to make a bequest of 1,000 *livres* to Dollier de Casson, superior at the seminary in Montreal, in favour of a six-year-old Iroquois girl whom he had adopted and placed in the care of the Sœurs de la Congrégation. In late November 1672 he sailed for France where he was appointed commander of the citadel at Arras. He is reported to have been governor of Toulon at the time of his death 24 Oct. 1698.

As governor of New France Courcelle's relations with certain of his subordinates may have left something to be desired but had his correspondence survived, it might indicate that they were as much at fault as he. Certainly the administration of the colony was not disrupted by these disputes, as was the case under both his predecessor and his successor in office. As a military commander his winter expedition against the Mohawks added little to his reputation, but it was the first such campaign ever waged by the French and they learned much from it. His most notable achievement, and one that does him great credit, was his curbing of the attacks made by the Iroquois on the French Indian allies. He deterred them from attacking the French settlements, and he accomplished his aim without the shedding of blood. When he returned to France he left the colony at peace, with the prestige of the French, in the eyes of both their Indian allies and the Iroquois, considerably enhanced.

W. J. ECCLES

As mentioned in the above article, the correspondence of Courcelle has not survived. "Sur le voyage de Monsieur de Courcelles gouverneur et lieutenant general pour le Roy en la Nouvelle France en l'année 1666," a satirical poem regarding his first expedition to the Mohawk country, which went the rounds of New France, may be found in *BRH*, XXXIII (1927), 264–82. *NYCD* (O'Callaghan and Fernow), III, *passim*. PRO, *CSP, Col., 1661–68*, 349, 392–93, 404, 438–41, 462–63, 470–71. Chapais, *Talon*, Faillon, *Histoire de la colonie française*, III. Francis Parkman, *The old régime* (25th ed.), 176, 186–90.

RENAUD D'AVÈNE DE DESMELOIZES, FRANÇOIS-MARIE, ensign on the king's ships and captain of a company of colonial regular troops; b. in 1655 (*al.* 1657) at Lormes, Burgundy, son of Edmé (or Aimé) Renaud d'Avène, seigneur Des Méloizes et de Berges, and Adrienne de Montsaulnin; d. 22 April 1699 at Quebec.

He entered Condé's regiment in 1668, became a standard-bearer in the dragoons in 1672, and a standard-bearer in the cavalry the following year. On 5 March 1685 he acquired a company in the colonial regular troops, and arrived with them at Quebec on 1 August. In 1687 he went with Governor Brisay* de Denonville on his expedition against the Senecas, and on 19 July signed the document recording the taking over of their country. Frontenac [*see* BUADE] seems to have held him in high esteem, since he considered him "one of the best and wisest officers" in Canada.

On 13 May 1687, at Quebec, Renaud d'Avène had married Françoise-Thérèse, daughter of Nicolas Dupont*, seigneur de Neuville. At the time of his marriage his wife's grandfather gave him the arriere-fief of La Cloutièrerie, located in the Beauport seigneury. He sold this land 29 July 1693. He also owned some property in the Upper Town of Quebec, since in 1695 his neighbour Pierre Ménage* brought an action against him in the provost's court of Quebec, for having dug a culvert which emptied into his well and made its water "extraordinarily muddy." Desmeloizes died 22 April 1699 at Quebec and was buried in the vaults of the basilica. He had nine children, one of whom, Nicolas-Marie*, carried on the line.

JEAN-GUY PELLETIER

AJQ, Greffe de Gilles Rageot, 10 mai 1687; Greffe de Louis Chambalon, 29 juillet 1693. APQ, La prévôté de Québec, registre de 1695, 25 novembre, 128–130. Correspondance de Frontenac (1689–99), APQ *Rapport, 1928–29*, 271–82. *Jug. et délib.*, IV, V. P.-G. Roy, *Inv. concessions*, I, 40f.; *BRH*, IV (1898), 112; XV (1909), 178; XVIII (1912), 114; XX (1914), 106, 148. E. Cheminade, "Les provinces de France et la Nouvelle-France, émigrants au Canada venant du Nivernais," *NF*, I (1925–26), 75f. P.-G. Roy, "La famille Renaud d'Avène Des Méloises," *BRH*, XIII (1907), 161–81; *La famille Renaud d'Avène Des Méloises* (Lévis, 1907). Tanguay, *Dictionnaire*, I, 514; VI, 538.

RENDEN (Rendin). *See* RANDIN

REPENTIGNY, PIERRE LEGARDEUR DE. *See* LEGARDEUR

REYNER. *See* RAYNER

RHOADES (Rhode seems to be the Dutch spelling), **JOHN,** New England trader instrumental in the Dutch conquest of Acadia; fl. 1674–76.

A Massachusetts resident thoroughly familiar with the fur trade on the coasts of Maine and Acadia, Rhoades not only persuaded Capt. Jurriaen AERNOUTSZ to attack the French posts there but also took the Dutch oath of allegiance and served as pilot for the expedition.

Rhoades was also a member of the group Aernoutsz appointed to maintain the Dutch conquest of the country and he probably arranged for the vessels and trade goods they secured in Boston on credit. This group sailed back to Acadia, where they proceeded to seize several New England trading vessels and their cargoes. Governor LEVERETT thereupon sent armed vessels against Rhoades, whom the Massachusetts authorities regarded as the leader of the group. Defeated in a naval fight in the Bay of Fundy, Rhoades and his companions were taken prisoner to Boston and tried as pirates. All but two of them were convicted of either piracy or theft. The two Dutch leaders of the group were pardoned but Rhoades was condemned to death. His execution was postponed because of King Philip's war and he was released in October 1675 on condition that he leave Massachusetts forever.

In September 1676 the Dutch West India Company made a belated effort to capitalize on Aernoutsz's conquest by granting Rhoades a commission to reside and trade in Acadia and by appointing Cornelis van Steenwijck, a Dutch merchant in New York, governor of Acadia. Rhoades attempted to use his commission, but was arrested on the St. George River by a lieutenant of Governor Andros* for trespassing on the territory of the Duke of York. He was taken to New York but released after a brief imprisonment. In the Treaty of Nimwegen (1678), ending the war between France and Holland, the Dutch conquest of Acadia was not even mentioned.

WILLIAM I. ROBERTS, 3rd

[For information on Rhoades, consult the sources cited under Jurriaen AERNOUTSZ.]

Richard

RICHARD *dit* **Lafleur, GUILLAUME** (styled **Sieur de La Fleur),** soldier of the Carignan-Salières regiment, captain of the Canadian militia, and at one time churchwarden; b. 1641, son of Jean Richard, grain merchant, and his wife, Anne Meusnier, of Saint-Léger, bishopric of Saintes, France; d. 1690.

A strong family tradition states that Richard was the descendant of John Richards, a Welshman, who, as a member of the king's bodyguard, assisted the French king, Charles IX, to escape through the back gardens of the palace during the frightful massacre of St. Bartholomew, 14 Aug. 1572.

Richard entered the French army as a young man, joining the Carignan-Salières regiment at its formation in 1664. On the last day of May of the following year he embarked for New France with his regiment, as a soldier in the company of Roger de Bonneau de La Varenne, arriving at Quebec 19 August, after a long and tempestuous voyage. Two years later, when his regiment returned to France, Richard chose to remain in Canada. Shortly thereafter he was appointed sergeant in the Canadian forces, in which rank he accompanied governor Frontenac [*see* BUADE] to Cataracoui where Fort Frontenac was founded in 1673. He remained at the new post as its first commandant when the French returned to Quebec. Richard continued in that capacity until the return of CAVELIER de La Salle in 1675, and was still at the fort in September 1677, according to a census of its garrison. Shortly thereafter he was appointed sergeant of the garrison at Montreal. By 1684 he was lieutenant of the vanguard company of that post and later still was captain of militia in the parish of Pointe-aux-Trembles de Montréal, where he had maintained his residence since 1679. Guillaume Richard *dit* Lafleur met a soldier's death on 2 July 1690, near Bout-de-l'Île de Montréal, when his small party of 25 was overwhelmed by a band of Iroquois warriors. Six days later the bodies of the fallen were buried hurriedly where they fell. In 1694 their remains were exhumed and reinterred in the cemetery of Pointe-aux-Trembles.

Richard's son, Jean-Baptiste, an interpreter, married Marie-Anne, the daughter of Pierre You* de La Découverte—an associate of La Salle in his discoveries on the Mississippi River—and of Elisabeth, a Miami squaw. Jean-Baptiste's daughter, Suzanne, became the wife of Gilbert Parant*, merchant and interpreter at Detroit. Jean-Baptiste's son, Jean* (b. 1721), according to tradition, was wounded and captured by western Indians, from whom he escaped three years later, finally reaching civilization on the lower reaches of the

Mohawk River. He, in turn, served as interpreter in the Loyalist forces during the Revolutionary War and after peace was established he settled on the Bay of Quinte, where he died in 1807.

H. C. BURLEIGH

MS sources include AN, Col., C^{11A}, 6, État des soldats de l'avant-garde, 14 août 1684. United Empire Loyalist Assoc. Archives, Bay of Quinte Branch, narrative of John C. Richards, 1875. É.-Z. Massicotte, *Faits curieux de l'histoire de Montréal* (Montréal, 1922), 184–88, 195–96. Régis Roy et Malchelosse, *Le régiment de Carignan*, 67–68, 72, 100. *Royal Fort Frontenac* (Preston and Lamontagne), 108–14, 124, 348, 467. Tanguay, *Dictionnaire*, I, 516, 591; VI, 237, 555, 557; VII, 491.

ROBERTS, LEWIS, merchant and writer; b. Beaumaris, Anglesey, in 1596, the son of Gabriel and Ann Roberts; d. March 1641 in London where he was buried.

In his youth Roberts, diverted "by adverse fortune or crosse fate, from the study of Arts to the studie of Marts," became an apprentice or factor to a London merchant, Thomas Harvey. He was sent to Constantinople, whence, in 1617, he petitioned the East India Company for employment. Roberts served both that company and the Levant Company in Constantinople and, on his return to England, became a member of both organizations and a director of the former.

In 1638 Roberts published his most important work, *The merchants mappe of commerce*, in which he set out to provide an exhaustive guide to the world's trade for the benefit of the young merchant. He dealt in turn with each of the four known continents, putting the trade with America first as being "the least and worst knowne." In this most painstaking and comprehensive of manuals, Roberts described the geography of each continent, the location of the principal cities and centres of commerce and the peculiarities of the methods of trade in each. He also advised on the techniques of business and revealed an intimate knowledge of the intricacies of trade in the early 17th century.

Much of his material was gleaned from personal experience including the brief description of Newfoundland which Roberts claimed to have visited in his younger days, although exactly when is not apparent. He gave a short but accurate account of the English fishery on the coast of Newfoundland and the Bank, stating that they were frequented annually by 500 English ships—an estimate which seems too high. He mentioned the method of sale of fish by contract, the use of sack ships and the transportation of the catch to Mediterranean markets.

In the last years of his life Roberts published two less well-known works. He died in March 1641 and his will is registered at Somerset House, P.C.C. 45 Evelyn, and was proved 9 April 1641 by his widow Ann.

GILLIAN T. CELL

Roberts's published works are: *The merchants mappe of commerce* (London, 1638; other eds. 1671, 1677, and 1700) which contains a portrait; *Warre-fare epitomized* (London, 1640); *The treasure of traffike* (London, 1641). *Familiae minorum gentium*, ed. J. W. Clay (4v., Hakluyt Soc., 1st ser., XXXVII–XL, 1894–96), I. PRO, *CSP, Col., East Indies, 1617–21, 1630–34*. DNB. H. A. Innis, *The cod fisheries* (rev. ed., Toronto, 1954).

ROBERVAL, JEAN-FRANÇOIS LA ROCQUE DE. *See* LA ROCQUE

ROBERVAL, MARGUERITE LA ROQUE DE. *See* LA ROQUE

ROBINAU DE BÉCANCOUR, RENÉ (called Outsitsony by the Hurons), Baron de Portneuf, ensign in Turenne's regiment, *Chevalier* of the Ordre de Saint-Michel, member of the Compagnie des Cent-Associés, chief road officer of New France; b. *c.* 1625 in Paris, son of Pierre Robinau de Bécancour and Renée Marteau; d. 1699 at Quebec.

His father, Pierre Robinau, secretary in the king's privy chamber, provincial receiver in the generality of Paris, then receiver general of finances at Tours, paymaster of the light cavalry of France, member of the Cent-Associés, was presented to the king as a candidate for the post of governor of New France, with Guillaume GUILLEMOT and JEAN DE LAUSON (the elder). It was the latter who was chosen, in 1651.

René Robinau, after serving in two campaigns as an ensign in Turenne's regiment, arrived at Quebec in 1645. He was in Governor HUAULT de Montmagny's employ when, in January 1646, he took part with Nicolas MARSOLET in the rebellion of the "petty habitans" against those "who had the public duties and offices" in the Communauté des Habitants. He was next an officer in the Quebec flying column. It was in this capacity that, on 26 Feb. 1652, he accompanied the grand seneschal JEAN DE LAUSON (the younger) and 15 Frenchmen on an expedition to Trois-Rivières. Before that town, on 2 July, he took part in a fight against the Iroquois and gave refuge to a Huron captive.

He seems to have gone to France in the autumn of 1656. His stay was a profitable one: the king made him a *Chevalier* of the Ordre de Saint-Michel, and the Compagnie de la Nouvelle-

Robinau de Bécancour

France granted him the little Bécancour fief "on the road to the great Cap Rouge." The company also bestowed upon him, in 1657, the office of chief road officer for Canada. He became the first to occupy this post, which according to P.-G. Roy "was then something of a sinecure." Indeed, the Canadian peasants preferred the waterway to land routes, and loathed the corvées necessary for establishing roads. It was only in the 18th century that the position of chief road officer acquired importance and began to lay real responsibilities upon its holder.

René Robinau seems to have concerned himself above all with trade. In October 1659 he made a journey to France and during this stay he replaced his father, who was of advanced age, in the Compagnie des Cent-Associés. In this capacity he signed a commercial treaty with Toussaint Guenet and several Rouen merchants on 5 Feb. 1660, granting their company the monopoly of the trade in beaver pelts and of imports into the colony. He apparently returned to Canada in 1661, and he left it again in 1663. On 23 Feb. 1663 he was one of the signatories to the letter by which the Cent-Associés gave up Canada to the king.

After that, until 1667, the records are silent about René Robinau. Since the 1666 nominal roll of New France makes no mention of René Robinau and his family, P.-G. Roy suggests that the Robinaus could have been in France at that time. René Robinau turned up again in 1667, when on 29 March the new Compagnie des Indes occidentales granted him "once again . . . the said function of chief road officer."

On 10 Oct. 1678 he was called upon to give his opinion about the sale of spirits to the Indians. He stated "that this traffic is necessary . . . and that it is of extreme necessity, for the establishment of trade and of religion, to . . . supply drink" to the Indians. He was no doubt interested in trading with them, since in 1679 Intendant DUCHESNEAU accused him of protecting the coureurs de bois. On the other hand, Sulte tells us that Robinau "often lived at Trois-Rivières for his trade in pelts."

He does not seem, moreover, to have been in the intendant's good graces. The latter again denounced him to the minister, on 13 Nov. 1680: "There is another officer of whom I complain, and that is the sieur de Bécancour, chief road officer, who since I have been here has always neglected to discharge his duties, whatever warnings I gave him. Finally, on my last journey to Montreal, because of the protests of the people, I was obliged to issue my ordinance, stating that he must make his visits without receiving any payments until he had brought me his reports on them, but very far from complying with this, he came and insulted me, with one of his children named Villebon" (JOSEPH ROBINAU de Villebon).

Duchesneau's hostility did not, however, have much influence on the king, who in March 1681 raised the Portneuf seigneury to the status of a barony. René Robinau had obtained this fief from his father-in-law, JACQUES LENEUF de La Poterie, 7 July 1671. Governor BUADE de Frontenac, on 23 March 1677, also granted him the Îles Bouchard, "situated near to and adjoining the great island that bears the same name"; these islands had first been granted, on 29 Oct. 1672, to his brother François Robinau de Fortelle, who never came to Canada.

In the autumn of 1693, René Robinau seems to have gone to France again, for the purpose of receiving an inheritance; he came back in 1694. He was buried 12 Dec. 1699 in the church of the Recollets, according to the wish he had expressed in his will.

On 21 Oct. 1652, at Trois-Rivières, by a contract drawn up before the notary Ameau*, he had married Marie-Anne, the daughter of Jacques Leneuf de La Poterie and Marguerite Legardeur; they had 12 children, among them Pierre*, Baron de Portneuf, who on 24 May 1689 obtained letters confirming his appointment by reversion to the office of chief road officer, and Joseph Robinau de Villebon, governor of Acadia.

JEAN-GUY PELLETIER

AJM, Greffe de Bénigne Basset, 7 juillet 1671. AJQ, Greffe de François Genaple, 23 oct. 1693, 4 avril 1699. AJTR, Greffe de Séverin Ameau, 21 oct. 1652. ASQ, Documents Faribault, 57, 112, 122, 125; Polygraphie, III, 141; IV, 8; Séminaire, XXXI, 7. Recensement de 1681.

Coll. de manuscrits relatifs à la Nouv.-France, I, 82, 245. *Découvertes et établissements des Français* (Margry), I, 405, 409f. Dollier de Casson, *Histoire du Montréal*, 265. *JR* (Thwaites). *Jug. et délib.*, I, II, III. *Lettres de noblesse* (P.-G. Roy), I, 95–102. *Papier terrier de la Cie des I.O.* (P.-G. Roy). *Pièces et documents relatifs à la tenure seigneuriale, demandés par une adresse de l'assemblée législative, 1851* (2v., Québec, 1852), I, 92f. [René Robinau de Bécancour], "Aveu et dénombrement de Messire René Robinau, seigneur de Bécancour, grand voyer de la Nouvelle-France, pour le fief et seigneurie de Portneuf (3 sept. 1677)," *APQ Rapport, 1925–26*, 340–42. P.-G. Roy, *Inv. concessions*, I, II, III, V; *Inv. ins. cons. souv.*; *Inventaire des procès-verbaux des grands voyers conservés aux archives de la province de Québec* (6v., Beauceville, 1923–32), I, II.

E.-J. Auclair, *Les De Jordy de Cabanac, histoire d'une ancienne famille noble du Canada* (Montréal, 1930), 148f., 187–93. Claude de Bonnault, "Le Canada militaire, état provisoire des officiers de milice, de 1641 à 1760," *APQ Rapport, 1949–51*, 293f. *BRH*, I (1895),

Robinau de Villebon

89; II (1896), 140; V (1899), 126; XIV (1908), 160; XV (1909), 179; XXI (1915), 48, 168; XXVI (1920), 37f., 68f.; XXVII (1921), 304; XXVIII (1922), 376. Ivanhoë Caron, "Historique de la voirie dans la province de Québec," *BRH*, XXXIX (1933), 198–215. Thomas Chapais [Ignotus], "Notes et souvenirs," *La Presse* (Montréal), 12 nov. 1898, 9; 28 déc. 1901, 4. Archange Godbout, "Les Robinau de Bécancourt," SGCF *Mémoires*, IV (1951), 158–62. Lanctot, *Histoire du Canada*, I, 242, 295f., 319. Henri Lorin, *Le comte de Frontenac: étude sur le Canada français à la fin du XVIIe siècle* (Paris, 1895), 182. P.-G. Roy, "Le premier baron de Portneuf," *Cahiers des Dix*, XIV (1949), 223–41; "Le premier baron de Portneuf," dans *Les petites choses de notre histoire* (3e sér., Lévis, 1922), 121–37; "Les grands voyers de la Nouvelle-France et leurs successeurs," *Cahiers des Dix*, VIII (1943), 181–96. Benjamin Sulte, "La guerre des Iroquois," *RSCT*, 2d ser., III (1897), sect.I, 86; *Mélanges historiques* (Malchelosse), XVIII, 22f. *Les Ursulines de Québec*, II, 335–39.

ROBINAU DE VILLEBON, JOSEPH, officer, captain, governor of Acadia; b. 22 Aug. 1655 at Quebec, son of RENÉ ROBINAU de Bécancour and Marie-Anne Leneuf de La Poterie; d. 5 July 1700 at Fort Saint-Jean in Acadia.

Robinau de Villebon's personality dominated the Acadian scene for a period of about ten years (1690–1700), at the time of the War of the League of Augsburg. To carry out the policy of Versailles a soldier was needed in Acadia, a man who was capable of holding out with very little aid. The choice of Villebon seems to have been a good one: a native of the country, he knew Acadia; in addition he had gone to France in his youth to finish his education and to serve in the army. Indeed, after serving as an officer in a dragoon regiment, he had been promoted to the rank of captain. Around 1681 he had returned to New France. He seems to have lived with his parents at the manor-house of Portneuf until 1684, in which year he took part in LE FEBVRE de La Barre's expedition against the Iroquois. Robinau de Villebon must have gone to Acadia soon after this campaign, around 1685 or 1686. There he had first assisted Governors PERROT and Des Friches* de Meneval, and had returned to France during the winter of 1689. Therefore he was absent when PHIPS attacked Port-Royal (Annapolis Royal, N.S.) in the spring of 1690. Villebon had sailed from La Rochelle on the *Union*, along with the engineer Vincent SACCARDY. He did not reach Acadia until 14 June 1690, after the departure of Phips who had taken off to Boston some 50 prisoners, one of whom was Governor Meneval. Because of these circumstances Joseph Robinau had become the official representative of the king of France in Acadia. Fearing that Phips might return to Port-Royal, where the fort had been destroyed, Villebon had gone to entrench himself in Jemseg and had removed the seat of French government there provisionally. This transfer had not been made without some difficulties, for English privateers had discovered them and had imprisoned Saccardy and captured the ship. Villebon had been able to elude the English, but, having lost all his cargo, he had decided to go by land to Quebec to ask for reinforcements from Governor BUADE de Frontenac. After a stay at Quebec and Montreal, he had continued on to France.

This then constituted Joseph Robinau's experience when on 7 April 1691 the king appointed him "commandant in Acadia," an appointment that he held until his death. In entrusting this role to him the king had given precise instructions as to the policy to be followed in this region. In a memoir from Louis XIV to Frontenac these instructions are summed up as follows: Villebon was "to take advantage of the favourable dispositions of the Canibats [the Abenaki Indians, allies of the French] towards serving His Majesty, of their hatred of the English and the proximity of the New England centres, to use them in waging continual and violent war against the aforementioned English, creating at the same time a diversion to secure Canada from their ventures. . . ." During his stay in Paris Joseph Robinau had perhaps contributed to the decision by Versailles to maintain Acadia under French rule and to the elaboration of this strategy. In any event, equipped with the memoir addressed to Frontenac and with supplies and arms, he sailed again for Canada on the *Soleil d'Afrique*, commanded by Capt. Denys* de Bonaventure. After a stop at Quebec the sailing-ship went on its way towards Acadia. In the Baie Française (Bay of Fundy) it met a Boston ship carrying the merchants John Nelson* and John Alden*, the latter's son William, and Col. Edward TYNG. Bonaventure and Villebon succeeded in capturing the vessel. Subsequently they released John Alden to allow him to return to New England to negotiate an exchange of prisoners; they kept the other prisoners as hostages. At Port-Royal Joseph Robinau replaced the English flag by that of France. Not feeling strong enough however to defend the place against a new English attack, he made no changes in the administration that Phips had set up there. The latter had entrusted Sergeant Charles LA TOURASSE with the command of Port-Royal. Knowing that he would defend the interest of the French settlers, Villebon left him in office, then went to set himself up at Jemseg.

Until the end of the war Villebon tried to carry

out the royal policy by having New England harried incessantly by the Indians, among whom he enjoyed great prestige. He was aided in this task by Abbé Louis-Pierre THURY and at times by Jean-Vincent d'Abbadie* de Saint-Castin. To thwart the policy of the French, Phips rebuilt, about 1692, Fort William Henry at Pemaquid and tried to win over the Abenakis to the cause of the English, without success however. Considering that he was faced with too great a threat at Jemseg, Villebon for his part built, farther up the Saint John River, another fort which he called Fort Saint-Joseph; this name did not last, for the fort was known rather under the name derived from the Indian: Naxouat (Nashwaak). This was a period of various raids by both sides. The French pirate Pierre Maisonnat* *dit* Baptiste succeeded in capturing some enemy vessels; Benjamin Church* laid waste various regions, among them that of Beaubassin (Chignecto Bay), but his attempt to capture Villebon failed. The great event of this period was the capture in 1696 of Fort William Henry, with the help of Pierre Le Moyne* d'Iberville.

In 1697 the Treaty of Ryswick brought peace. Acadia remained French, but the treaty had not put an end to the strife about the boundaries. A special commission was to be appointed to settle it. The French, for example, claimed that the boundary should follow the course of the Kennebec River. One of the reasons put forward to justify this claim was that the Indian allies of the French inhabited the region lying between this river and the Penobscot. On the other hand the English were of the opinion that the boundary should be on the St. Croix River. There was also another problem, that of the fishing rights in French waters. Villebon tried to settle it by proposing the creation of a system of permits, the revenues from which would be applied to maintaining fortifications. It seems that this plan was not carried out, any more than was the plan to attack Manate (Manhattan) and Boston which Villebon had always supported vigorously. The king allowed Joseph Robinau to proceed with the rebuilding of Fort Saint-Jean. Villebon dedicated himself to this task and transferred his seat of government to Fort Saint-Jean about 1698. It was there that he died, 5 July 1700. The Sieur de Dièreville*, who had visited him the very day of his death, described Villebon as "a man of sound judgment, tall & very well set up."

Villebon's personality has given rise to much controversy, for he often committed actions which it is difficult to see in their right light. During his stay in Acadia many complaints were made about him. In his report entitled "Mon séjour de l'Acadie," M. de Gargas (the principal recorder in Acadia during the years 1685–88) charged him with having intimidated and insulted the settlers and with having extorted exorbitant sums from them for goods, among other things. Gargas called Villebon the terror of the country. In 1696 the intendant, Bochart* Champigny, sent on to the minister other complaints agaínst Joseph Villebon: the seigneurs and the *habitants* of the Saint John River in particular accused the governor of "threats and bad treatment" towards them and "charge him with having secured for himself all trade in his fort." Villebon's brothers, who were at the time serving under his orders, were accused of aiding him in this business and of leading scandalous lives. One of the most picturesque accusations was that by Mathieu Des Goutins*, judge for Acadia in 1698, who affirmed, among several other grievances, "that the Sieur de Villebon has caused to be used up 112 pounds of gunpowder in the bonfire to celebrate the peace, while drinking healths to his mistresses, and that he and the Sieur Martel, his son-in-law, became drunk while so doing." It seems however certain that Villebon never married. Jean Martel* had married at Port-Royal a certain Marie-Anne Robinau, who was considered to be the illegitimate daughter of the governor.

Villebon did not turn a deaf ear to these complaints. He explained in his defence that they often sprang from jealousy and that he was at times obliged to call to order seigneurs who, being far from France, had become too independent and had lost the notion of good conduct and of the respect due to the government. These interventions were particularly necessitated by the behaviour of the Damours brothers, seigneurs with whom the governor had disagreements. One of them, MATHIEU DAMOURS DE FRENEUSE, owned a fief on the Saint John River between Jemseg and Nashwaak, Robinau's centre of activity. Around 1699 Villebon reproached the settlers of Port-Royal with indolently confining themselves to making their land produce just what was necessary to keep them alive. It was the same with a few personal reproaches. Thus for example, rightly or wrongly he accused the parish priest JEAN BAUDOIN (another former soldier) of taking to the woods instead of attending to his parishioners and of having struck down an Indian.

This free exchange of complaints and particularly their subject reveal to us a glimpse of a colourful period which was faithfully reflected in the personality of the rugged and turbulent governor. Villebon had had a very stormy career, and even at the moment of departing this life he could not help provoking a slight incident: Abbé

Rollet

Abel Maudoux*, with whom he had fallen out a short time before his death, required that he be paid his honorarium before agreeing to officiate at his funeral. Sébastien de Villieu*, Villebon's lieutenant, finally yielded to the priest's demands and paid, so that the governor would have a Christian burial.

Whatever one may think of Villebon, one must take into account the circumstances in which he was called to act: the war, the little help that France offered him, and the lack of settlers (according to the census made by Intendant Demeulle*, in 1686 Acadia had 885 inhabitants; in 1693 the total was apparently 1,009). In our opinion, it was principally because of his military talents and his skill in dealing with the Indians that the French government kept him in office and that Meneval, and above all Frontenac, always supported and defended him.

IN COLLABORATION WITH
ÉMERY LEBLANC

AN, Col., B, 16, 17, 19, 20, 22; C¹¹A, 12–14; C¹¹D, 2–4. BM, Lansdowne MS 849, f.47. "Mass. Archives." *Acadiensia Nova* (Morse), contains, among other documents, "Mon séjour de l'Acadie" by Gargas (I, 165–99). *Coll. de manuscrits relatifs à la Nouv.-France*. Correspondance de Frontenac (1689–99), APQ *Rapport, 1927–28; 1928–29*. Dièreville, *Relation of a voyage to Port Royal in Acadia or New France*, ed. J. C. Webster (Champlain Soc., XX, 1933), 152. *Jug. et délib*. IV, 327. *Mémoires des commissaires*, II, 333–34 and *Memorials of the English and French commissaries*, I, 30–1, 123, 620–1. *NYCD* (O'Callaghan and Fernow), IX. PAC *Report, 1912*, App. F. Webster, *Acadia*.

Azarie Couillard Després, "Les gouverneurs de l'Acadie sous le régime français, 1600–1700," *RSCT*, 3d ser., XXXIII (1939), sect.I, 273–80. Ganong, "Historic sites in New Brunswick," 273. P.-G. Roy, "Les Robineau," *Cahiers des Dix*, XVII (1952), 209–13.

ROLLET, MARIE, wife of LOUIS HÉBERT, Canada's first settler; d. 1649 at Quebec.

In 1617, with her husband and three children she came from Paris to Quebec, where she found starvation, sickness, and threats of Indian attack. A year after their arrival, says SAGARD, the first marriage solemnized in Canada with the rites of the church took place, that of their daughter Anne and Étienne Jonquet. Anne died in childbirth the following year, but there is no record of the child.

Marie Rollet aided her husband in caring for the sick and shared his interest in the savages, concerning herself especially with the education of Indian children. In 1627, at the baptism of CHOMINA's son, Naneogauchit, which the priests were striving to make an impressive occasion, she feasted a crowd of visiting savages out of her big brewing kettle. Her name appears often as godmother at the baptism of converted savages.

Two years after the death of Louis Hébert, on 16 May 1629, she married Guillaume Hubou. After seeking CHAMPLAIN's advice, she and her family (i.e., her second husband, her 15-year-old son Guillaume, and her daughter and son-in-law GUILLAUME COUILLARD) remained in Quebec during the English occupation and kept alive among the neighbouring savages the memory of French friendship. After the return of the French in 1632, her house became the home of Indian girls given to the Jesuits for training. She died in 1649, leaving her husband, her one surviving child, GUILLEMETTE HÉBERT, and a number of grandchildren. She was buried at Quebec, 27 May 1649.

ETHEL M. G. BENNETT

[For bibliography, *see* LOUIS HEBERT.]

ROMAINVILLE, JEAN BOURDON DE. See BOURDON

ROMIEUX (Romulus, Rémus), PIERRE (or Peter), surgeon; b. *c*. 1636; fl. 1675.

A surgeon of Béziers in Languedoc, he signed a three-year contract with Médard CHOUART Des Groseilliers in France in 1659 to work for François Renou *dit* La Chapelle of Trois-Rivières and evidently spent three years there. He was to work for 200 *livres* per annum, La Chapelle providing the medicines.

For several years he served as surgeon to Radisson* and Des Groseilliers, accompanying them in their journeys, and he was one of the "originals" who went with these two adventurers on the *Nonsuch* to Hudson Bay in 1668. Presumably he returned to England the following year. In the Company's records he appears as Peter Romulus, "ye French chirurgion." He made another voyage to the Bay in 1672 and was to "stay in the countrey." His medicine chest had evidently been too generously furnished: Mr Pelling, the apothecary, had overrated supplies by at least one-third and was "to bee spoken to." While Romieux was to "stay in the countrey," a replacement was appointed for him—surgeon Walter Farr—in 1674. Since no ships returned from Hudson Bay that year it was November 1675 before Romieux severed association with the Company.

MAUD M. HUTCHESON

HBC Arch. A.14/1, ff.79d–80, 101; A.14/2, 12 and 27 Nov. 1675. HBRS, V (Rich). Gabriel Debien, "Liste des engagés pour le Canada au XVIIᵉ siècle (1634–

1715)," *RHAF*, VI (1952–53), 391. Raymond Douville, "Chirurgiens, barbiers-chirurgiens et charlatans de la région trifluvienne sous le régime français," *Cahiers des Dix*, XV (1950), 124–25.

ROMULUS. *See* ROMIEUX

ROQUEMONT DE BRISON, CLAUDE, admiral of the fleet of the Compagnie des Cent-Associés in 1628.

Roquemont, who lived in Paris, was one of the six people to whom Richelieu confided the task of setting up the Compagnie des Cent-Associés, and he signed the act creating it immediately after the cardinal, 29 April 1627. Shortly afterwards war broke out between France and England, but the king nevertheless forced the company to dispatch a group of settlers in 1628. The Cent-Associés fitted out four ships (*Estourneau*, *Magdeleine*, *Suzanne* and one other), and the over-all command was entrusted to Roquemont. About 400 persons embarked, including a large number of settlers, "the flower of the youth of Normandy." One of the ships, which was carrying supplies for Acadia, was commanded by CLAUDE DE SAINT-ÉTIENNE de La Tour.

The fleet sailed from Dieppe 28 April 1628, followed by a supply ship that the Jesuit Philibert NOYROT had chartered, and by fishing-boats which sailed under its protection. Escaping at the moment of departure from two ships from La Rochelle (this city was at the time at war against the king), the fleet reached the Grand Banks after five or six weeks, then Anticosti Island where a cross was set up. At Gaspé Roquemont learned of the presence of English ships in the St. Lawrence: he unloaded "a number of sacks of flour" in order to lighten his ships in the event of a battle, sent Thierry DESDAMES to inform CHAMPLAIN of his arrival and, instead of remaining in safety in some port, he tried to go up the river under cover of mist.

The English fleet, commanded by the KIRKE brothers, moved in to attack 18 July, somewhere near Tadoussac. The fight lasted about 15 hours, during which, it appears, "1200 gun salvoes" were fired; then, as he was running short of ammunition, Roquemont had to capitulate. The French had lost only two men and Roquemont had been wounded in the leg. The English seized the ships and their cargoes; the Kirkes kept as prisoners Roquemont, Raymond de LA RALDE, the captains, the Jesuit and Recollet missionaries and "the most important Frenchmen" in order to furnish proof in England of the capture of the fleet and also in the hope of obtaining ransom for them. The Recollets and some of the French who before being captured had been going to settle in Canada were released a short time afterwards. The rest of the passengers received permission to return to France on a ship which the Kirkes left them.

The Jesuit Noyrot's ship had managed to escape before the battle and return to France. The first expedition of the Compagnie des Cent-Associés was annihilated. Not only was Roquemont himself lost, wrote Champlain, "but he left the whole country in ruins, and nearly a hundred persons, men, women and children, to die of hunger, and who would be obliged to abandon the fort and the habitation to the first enemy, as experience has shown." According to Champlain, Roquemont should have resorted more to ruse in order first of all to assure the safety of the colony, and should have shown prudence rather than bravery; but "too much courage led him to risk battle." Roquemont was entrusted with no other command by the Compagnie des Cent-Associés, whose documents from that time on make no further mention of him.

MARCEL TRUDEL

AN, Col., C^{11A}, 1, ff.107–14; E, 95, doc. 5, f.95. BN, MS Fr. 16738, f.147r. Champlain, *Works* (Biggar), V, 287–96. Du Creux, *History* (Conacher), I, 34, 39, 41–43, 47. *Édits ord.*, I, 6, 11, 18–20. Sagard, *Histoire du Canada* (Tross), IV, 852. Dionne, *Champlain*, II, 187–93, 336.

ROUER DE VILLERAY, LOUIS, soldier, clerk of court, notary, secretary of Governor JEAN DE LAUSON then of CHARLES de Lauson de Charny, provost court judge of the Beaupré Heights, special lieutenant of the seneschal's court and warehouse clerk of the Compagnie de la Nouvelle-France, member of the colony's first Conseil, first councillor in the Conseil Souverain, agent of the tax farm; b. 1629 at Amboise, near Tours (France), son of Jacques Rouer de Villeray, a valet to the queen, and of Marie Perthuis; d. 6 Dec. 1700 at Quebec.

Louis Rouer de Villeray belonged to a noble family that came originally from Italy; he was intelligent and hard-working, but lacked money; he was only just over 20 when he landed in Canada in 1650 or 1651. On his arrival he became a soldier at Quebec, then at Trois-Rivières, where he was noticed by Pierre Boucher*, who made him his confidential agent by constituting him, through an act signed before Séverin Ameau* on 20 Oct. 1653, "his general and special procurator . . . to deal with the accounts for the goods that the said Sieur Boucher wished to have brought to the aforesaid Trois-Rivières."

The following year Rouer returned to Quebec,

Rouer de Villeray

where Governor Jean de Lauson made him his secretary. De Lauson's son Charles kept him on in this position. He was also a notary, 1654–57, and clerk of court in the jurisdiction of Quebec. He likewise held the office, not a particularly burdensome one at that period, of provost court judge of the Beaupré shore.

His marriage with Catherine Sevestre, 19 Feb. 1658, did much to improve his circumstances. His father-in-law, Charles SEVESTRE, having died two months earlier, he inherited title to a piece of land one *arpent* wide by 10 deep between the Grande Allée and the river, with fishing rights. Governor LOUIS D'AILLEBOUST allowed him also to succeed Charles Sevestre in the two functions of special lieutenant of the seneschal's court and clerk of the warehouse of the Compagnie de la Nouvelle-France at Quebec.

The somewhat muddled financial records left by his father-in-law created difficulties for Villeray. When he was elected to the council of the fur trade shortly afterwards, he was accused of occupying that office illegally, since he had not yet settled Charles Sevestre's accounts. The complaints against Villeray reached the court, and by a royal edict dated 13 May 1659 he was relieved of his duties and ordered to go to France in the autumn, with the object of clearing himself and presenting Charles Sevestre's accounts together with supporting vouchers. When he returned the following spring he was reinstated. But as the council of the fur trade persisted in holding him responsible for the sums spent by his father-in-law on the sole authority of the governor of the time, Villeray, who nevertheless had Governor Voyer* d'Argenson's backing, had to go back to France in 1660 and 1662 to defend his case.

His efforts were not wasted. On 19 Jan. 1663 the Compagnie de la Nouvelle-France confirmed the grant to him of the lands inherited from his father-in-law, granted him the three or four acres the title of which was in dispute, and gave to the whole the designation of Villeray fief. In the same year he received an important promotion. When, on 18 Sept. 1663, Governor SAFFRAY de Mézy and Bishop Laval* chose the five members who with themselves were to constitute the Conseil Souverain, Villeray was the first one nominated. From that time on, Rouer de Villeray had a leading part to play in the conduct of the colony's judicial and administrative affairs.

One of the first actions of the Conseil Souverain was directed againt the lawyer Jean PERONNE Dumesnil, a superior officer whom the Compagnie de la Nouvelle-France had sent to the colony in 1660, as a comptroller general, an intendant of the Cent-Associés, and a sovereign judge; his accusations and inquisitions had turned all the men in high places against him. Villeray and JEAN BOURDON were given authority to seize the documents that Dumesnil had appropriated and to evict him from his house, which belonged to the colony. They carried out their task with the help of some ten soldiers.

In the council, disagreements between the governor and the bishop were not long in breaking out. After the council had sided with the bishop on the question of tithes, Mézy, by his ordinance 13 Feb. 1664, suspended Rouer de Villeray, RUETTE d'Auteuil, and Attorney-General Bourdon; he accused them of usurping the governor's authority and of conspiring with the bishop to foment sedition. He reversed his decision two months later, but fresh dissensions were aroused on the occasion of the election of a settler's syndic. A meeting of townspeople had finally been called by the governor alone to make a choice, and at this the councillors protested. Enraged at their opposition, the governor, on 19 Sept. 1664, dismissed Bourdon, Villeray, d'Auteuil, and JEAN JUCHEREAU DE LA FERTÉ; Villeray was absent, having sailed for France on the preceding 30 August. On 24 September the governor appointed three new councillors, but without the required consent of the bishop. In a report presented to the king, Villeray accused Mézy of being jealous of the council's powers and of being annoyed that he had not obtained an increase in salary. Only Mézy's death prevented him from being dismissed.

In France, Villeray probably met TALON, the newly appointed intendant of New France. He persuaded Talon to intercede with the minister, so that Villeray and some other Canadians could load on a ship belonging to the Compagnie des Indes occidentales the supplies bought in the mother country. It was also probably with the intendant that he returned to Quebec in the summer of 1665. On 6 Dec. 1666 he once more received the office of first councillor, this time from PROUVILLE de Tracy.

Up to this time, Villeray had been considered completely devoted to the bishop and the Jesuits. But it seems that shortly afterwards his attachment to Talon proved the stronger. When on 10 Nov. 1668 the intendant proposed a decree allowing the sale of spirits to the Indians, Villeray voted in favour of the measure. This was an insult to the bishop: had not Villeray been earlier elected churchwarden of the parish of Quebec? His relations with the bishop, however, continued to be good. And Talon, who was his protector, granted him the post of receiver of the 10 per cent tax imposed on dry goods arriving in Canada.

Rouer de Villeray

Governor RÉMY de Courcelle kept Villeray on in his office of councillor in 1669, but the following year, on 13 June 1670, he removed him from it, accusing him of being too closely associated with the bishop. Several important settlers protested against this eviction, which moreover had not been approved by the bishop. The Sieur PATOULET, Talon's secretary, judged the governor's action to be of doubtful legality, and in a report dated 25 Jan. 1672 he suggested that a royal decree should confirm Courcelle's decision and the subsequent decrees of the council, but should reinstate Villeray, the only person capable, according to him, of exercising judicial functions.

Nevertheless, BUADE de Frontenac, the new governor, was already thinking of depriving Villeray of his office as receiver of taxes. While admitting that Villeray was intelligent and well-educated, he thought he was a blunderer and an intriguer, completely won over to the Jesuits. In addition, in a letter addressed to Colbert, Frontenac said that he had received complaints against Villeray both from the merchants of La Rochelle, "creditors of the communauté du Canada" (who were to receive the money derived from duties), and from the settlers of the colony, who could not obtain receipts for the taxes they had paid. Furthermore, he accused Villeray of also exacting a levy of 5 per cent that had been abolished two years before. In 1673 Frontenac took from him his office of councillor to give it to the Sieur Peiras, M. de Courcelle's former secretary.

But Villeray had protectors. In the spring of 1674 the minister ordered Frontenac to reinstate him in his office of tax collector and in his rank of first councillor, his return to the council being guaranteed through his appointment to this post by the Compagnie des Indes occidentales, which possessed the sole right to confer it.

Frontenac obeyed with bad grace. Alleging that the letters patent had not been received, he seated Villeray on the council, but did not grant him the rank of first councillor. He also lost no time in correcting the erroneous information that the minister had received about Villeray. The minister, in his dispatch of 17 May 1674, had said that Villeray was one of the most well-to-do settlers in the colony, an important business man, and a pioneer in trade with the West Indies. Frontenac vehemently refuted all this: far from being rich, Villeray could not have existed if during the previous few years he had not been the factor of a La Rochelle merchant; he himself boasted that, having studied law and jurisprudence for ten years, he had not been able to engage in commerce. Frontenac had expressed some scepticism with regard to the legal knowledge of Rouer de Villeray, who possessed no diploma. But his library was a testimony to his studies. When an inventory was made of it after his death, it contained 41 titles—books of law, religion, and history.

Villeray knew how to utilize his legal knowledge at the time of the PERROT affair, to the great discomfiture of Frontenac. Since the governor of Montreal, François-Marie Perrot, had defied Frontenac's authority, the latter had him arrested and imprisoned at Quebec on 28 Jan. 1674. Perrot, questioned during the spring and summer, challenged the competence of his judges, and presented several petitions couched in legal terminology and referring to royal edicts more than a century old. Rouer de Villeray's hand is to be seen in this. He was probably the only man possessing sufficient knowledge of jurisprudence to draw up such learned petitions. He had been kept away from the interrogations; he was therefore free to help the accused. He had good reason for so doing: to avenge himself for the unjust persecutions inflicted upon him by Frontenac, who himself admitted that he had no cause for complaint against him, and to pay his court to his protector Talon, whose nephew Perrot was. Thanks to these skilful manoeuvres, Frontenac was compelled to give way and to send Perrot to be judged by the king. Frontenac was severely reprimanded, and Perrot kept his post.

The Conseil Souverain was reorganized by an edict dated 5 June 1675. It was put on the same footing as the Parlements in France; its members were appointed for life, by royal commission. Villeray was again appointed first councillor, by a commission dated 26 April 1675. He therefore continued to enjoy a distinction which, in the words of Governor Louis-Hector de Callières*, made him "primus inter pares." The king gave him further evidence of his esteem by having 2,500 *livres* paid to him, as his salary for the five years during which he had been excluded from the council.

Despite a sufficiently precise definition of their respective powers, difficulties between Frontenac and DUCHESNEAU soon made themselves manifest. But the most serious quarrel broke out in 1679, over the presidency of the council; Duchesneau sent Villeray and Bermen* de La Martinière as delegates to the governor, suggesting that the question be referred to the king. The governor refused point-blank, and demanded that the effective control be granted to him. The deadlock lasted for months. Finally Frontenac issued an ultimatum. The council held firm. On 4 July Frontenac sent written orders to three councillors to leave Quebec: Ruette d'Auteuil, the attorney-general, Villeray, and CHARLES LEGARDEUR de

Rouer de Villeray

Tilly. The latter was forced to withdraw to the Île d'Orléans. The councillors met at the intendant's house on 4 and 5 July, but to no avail. A provisional agreement was not concluded until 16 October: Ruette d'Auteuil and Tilly were allowed to return home, but Villeray was to go and explain his conduct to the king. To Frontenac's great surprise, Villeray, far from being upset at having to justify himself before the king, seemed confident of obtaining royal approval. Villeray was right. He returned in October with an order for his reinstatement to the council, and a dispatch, dated 29 April 1680, in which the king expressed his dissatisfaction and his condemnation of Frontenac's claims.

The intendant asked the king for a gratuity to compensate for the losses and expenses that the governor had caused Villeray. His exile, which occurred during the harvest season, had greatly inconvenienced him, since he lived on the produce of his lands. By 1668, through inheritance or purchase, he had brought together 103 or 104 acres, all of them between the river and the Grande Allée, west of the Saint-Louis gate. He had subsequently rounded out his estate. In 1675 he had bought from RENÉ ROBINAU de Bécancour a fief one *arpent* by 10. Later on he rented the *comté* of Orsainville from Talon, in return for 250 *livres* a year.

The governor's enmity was long-lived. At a session of the council in March 1681, Frontenac admonished Villeray and forbad him to use the title of esquire, despite the production by Villeray of his supporting documents. But Frontenac was recalled shortly afterwards, and the relations between his successors and Villeray were excellent. On 27 April 1684, Villeray obtained the Île-Verte seigneury for his sons. In the same year he was among the 18 notables consulted about the fur trade.

Governor Brisay* de Denonville had the highest opinion of his unselfishness and intelligence. He said that he had kept him back when he wanted to go to France, because he had nobody more capable of apprising him of the affairs of the Conseil Souverain. The governor approved Villeray's request to the king, whereby the office of special lieutenant of Quebec would be re-established, and Villeray's son appointed to it so that he could study and fit himself to succeed his father. But this request was rejected.

In 1686 Villeray began a new phase in his career, as agent of the tax farm. Gilles de Boyvinet, the agent sent by the company, had been drowned at Quebec on 22 July; consequently Intendant Bochart* Champigny, after consulting the governor, gave Villeray the commission of comptroller of the Compagnie du Canada, because of the doubtful honesty of the Sieur de La Héronnière, who had been appointed temporarily by Intendant Duchesneau.

In the autumn of the same year Villeray went to France. He obtained a gratuity from the king and the title of director general of the tax farm for the Compagnie Pointeau. When he returned, he found his house in ashes. The governor and the intendant asked for his gratuity to be continued.

In 1688 he secured for his youngest son the seigneury of Rimouski, his eldest son taking possession of the whole Île-Verte seigneury.

After Frontenac's return in 1689, Villeray was delegated to approach the governor in order to request him to attend the sessions of the council. After much negotiation, it was agreed to receive Frontenac with all the ceremony that he wanted, and this improved subsequent relations with him.

According to Intendant Champigny, Villeray carried out his duties as general agent of the tax farm with scrupulous fidelity. On 10 Nov. 1692 he was appointed procurator of the Associés de Paris, former tax farmers of the Compagnie d'Oudiette, who held a third of the shares in the Compagnie du Nord.

If we are to take the word of the offended Lamothe de Cadillac [Laumet*] Villeray was, in 1693, maintaining a butcher's shop in his house, with his servant retailing meat and his wife acting as cashier.

In 1694, when Pierre Le Moyne* d'Iberville needed funds for his expedition to Hudson Bay, a meeting of the Compagnie du Nord was called. Villeray, as procurator of the Associés de Paris, while admitting that he had received no instructions on this score, offered to borrow at 12 per cent interest in order to have a share in the undertaking, but his offer was refused.

The following year, Frontenac complained to one of his protectors that Villeray had had the effrontery to tell him on several occasions that he considered him as merely an honorary member of the council.

In 1698, by order of the minister, the intendant examined the lands of the Sieur de Villeray on which the fortifications of Quebec had been constructed. He reported that in 1690, 3 acres of turf had been taken up, 7 acres had been dug down to the rock for the redoubts, 23 acres altogether had been taken over, and an ice-pit had been removed; that consequently Villeray was asking for a substantial indemnity or an increase in his annual gratuity. The minister granted him a life pension of 400 *livres*.

In 1698 also, a quarrel had broken out between the settlers and the agents of the tax farm over the date at which all the furs were to be delivered. To hasten the departure of the ships, the agents wanted to fix the date as 1 October, the settlers as 20 October. The intendant suggested 10 October as a compromise.

On 6 Dec. 1700, at the age of 71, Villeray died during an epidemic that was raging at Quebec. On 19 Feb. 1658 he had married Catherine, daughter of Charles Sevestre and Marie Pichon. He had had three children by her: Augustin Rouer* de La Cardonnière et de Villeray, Louis Rouer d'Artigny, and Charles Rouer de Villeray. Catherine Sevestre had died in 1670 at Quebec. Louis Rouer had married again on 26 Nov. 1675; his second wife was Marie-Anne, daughter of Jacques Du Saussay de Bémont and of Anne Carlier, who returned to France some time after her husband's death. From 1702 on, the widow received a pension of 200 *livres*, and d'Artigny a pension of 150 *livres*, to compensate for the lands utilized for the fortifications.

Callières, the governor, by way of a funeral oration, wrote to the minister that Louis Rouer de Villeray had been appointed first councillor because of his merit and knowledge, and that his memory was respected throughout the whole country.

In Villeray the colony lost one of its great officials. Intelligent and active as he was, he had quickly attracted the attention of the governors. He had retained the protection of almost all the administrators of the country by his zeal, honesty, and good judgement, in legal as well as in financial matters. As first councillor, he had tried to impose respect for the powers and prerogatives of the Conseil Souverain, but he had remained content to follow the party with which he felt himself most in harmony, that of the bishop, and secondly, that of the intendant. One cannot hold against him his tilts with Frontenac: only the protégés of the governor were safe from his mighty rages. He had spent 50 years in the country. In his office as first councillor, which he had occupied for more than 30 years, in his position as agent of the tax farm, which he had held for nearly 15, as well as in the management of his estates, he had shown himself a capable and conscientious man. His inexhaustible energy had enabled him to manage several demanding tasks at the same time, frequently interrupted though these were by his numerous trips to France. He had acquired a good knowledge of the laws, of commerce, of agriculture. Thanks to his sterling qualities, he had carved out for himself an honourable and fruitful career.

BERNARD WEILBRENNER

AN, Col., B; C[11A]. ASQ, Documents Faribault, 94, 95, 126a; Lettres N, 39; 0, 1, p.2; Polygraphie IV, 55; Séminaire, XXXV, 27b; Registre A, 294–96. *JR* (Thwaites). *Papier terrier de la Cie des I.O.* (P.-G. Roy). P.-G. Roy, *Inv. des concessions*. Charles-P. Beaubien, "Louis Rouer de Villeray," *BRH*, V (1899), 356-58. "La bibliothèques de Louis Rouer de Villeray, premier conseiller au Conseil Souverain de la Nouvelle-France," *BRH*, XXVIII (1922), 178–80. Eccles, *Frontenac*. P.-G. Roy, "À propos de Louis Rouer de Villeray," *BRH*, XXXI (1925), 419f.; "La famille Rouer de Villeray," *BRH*, XXVI (1920), 33–52; 65–77; 97–111.

ROUSSEL, TIMOTHÉE, surgeon; b. *c.* 1639, son of Étienne Roussel and Jeanne Bouette, from Notre-Dame de Montpellier (France); d. 1700 at Quebec.

In 1669 he entered the Hôtel-Dieu at Quebec, but he apparently became its salaried surgeon only in 1687, after the death of Jean DEMOSNY. He received 200 *livres* a year. He is not known to have had an apprentice, but he did have a journeyman-surgeon, René Gaschet. In 1688 he had a stone house built in Buade street, later called "Maison du Chien d'Or" ("House of the Golden Dog") because of an inscription that he caused to be placed on it. In 1877 William Kirby was to immortalize this house and its owner in his novel *The Golden Dog*. About 1688–89, Roussel was the surgeon of the Ursulines.

He was a sharp-tempered and grasping man. From 1672 on, he appeared almost yearly before the Conseil Souverain in the roles of petitioner, defendant, respondent, or appellant. He was churchwarden of the parish of Notre-Dame in Quebec in 1685 and 1686. He died during the epidemic of 1700.

On 22 Nov. 1667 he had married Madeleine Du Mortier, by whom he had one boy and six girls: in 1694 his daughter Geneviève became the second wife of Louis Chambalon*, and another daughter, Louise, joined the Hospitallers of the Hôtel-Dieu at Quebec in 1693. After becoming a widower, Roussel had married again on 16 Aug. 1688; by his second wife, Catherine Fournier, he had eight children. Catherine, one of the daughters of this second marriage, also joined the Hospitallers, in 1713.

GABRIEL NADEAU

ASQ, Documents Faribault, 127b. Recensement de 1681. *Jug. et délib.* Ahern, *Notes pour l'histoire de la médecine*, 465–72. Auguste Gosselin, *Henri de Bernières, premier curé de Québec* (Les Normands au Canada, Québec, 1902), 175, 183. P.-G. Roy, *A travers l'histoire de l'Hôtel-Dieu de Québec* (Lévis, 1939), 106f. Benjamin Sulte "Le chien d'or," *BRH*, XXI (1915), 270–3. *Les Ursulines de Québec*, I, 460.

Rouvray

ROUVRAY. *See* RÉMY

ROWLEY (Rowlie), THOMAS, settler in the first English colony in Newfoundland; fl. 1612–28.

He was the son of Roger Rowley of Rowley, Shropshire, gentleman, a member of the London Haberdashers' company, as were several subscribers to the Newfoundland company of 1610. He himself did not subscribe but, as he was said to have lived in the island since its first plantation, he may have been one of the original colonists who went with JOHN GUY in 1610. Rowley was certainly in Newfoundland by 1612, when he went on the expedition, led by Guy, which established friendly relations with the Indians.

Later he became associated with Sir Percival Willoughby, an important member of the company, probably through Thomas WILLOUGHBY, Sir Percival's son, who had been a colonist. In 1618 or early 1619, Willoughby drew up a deed making over half his land in the island to Rowley and William Hannam, the son of John Hannam of Huish, Somerset, gentleman. Willoughby's grant, received from the company in 1617, consisted of the peninsula between Conception and Trinity bays, north of a line from Carbonear to Heart's Content. It was intended that Rowley and Hannam should develop this land independently of the original settlement at Cuper's (now Cupids) Cove. They were to hold the land under the same terms as Willoughby, paying him a peppercorn rent. However the document bears no signatures and Rowley later expressed discontent at not having received his land.

Rowley was also to act as Willoughby's agent in Newfoundland; early in 1619 he was in Bristol making preparations to sail. By September he was in the island, but his intention to settle independently at Carbonear that summer and at Heart's Content the following year had been frustrated by disagreements with Hannam, whom he accused of keeping two of his men and also of cheating him over the provisions. Rowley then decided to winter at the company's settlement in Cuper's Cove, from which he might explore Trinity Bay and trade with the Indians. Because of this delay, Rowley and Willoughby agreed to abandon the plan to settle at Carbonear and to go immediately to Heart's Content in 1620. That winter Rowley made preparations and enlisted eight men, including five fishermen, to accompany him.

There is no definite evidence as to what followed but the settlement cannot have been established for, in 1631, Willoughby was still looking for someone to plant his land. In February 1620 Rowley complained of not having received his land or any commission to prove his authority; perhaps he refused to act further for Willoughby. Nevertheless he seems to have persevered in his interest in Newfoundland, for in a poem by Robert HAYMAN, governor of the Bristol plantation, which was published in 1628, his constancy was praised: "from the first plantation [he] hath lived in Newfoundland, little to his profit." Nothing more is known of him, although he may have been the Thomas Rowley, haberdasher, whose will was proved in June 1641.

GILLIAN T. CELL

Rowley's letters and other papers relating to him and Hannam are at Nottingham University, Middleton MSS, Mi X 1/1–66. For Rowley *see also:* Guildhall Library, London, Act Book 7.77 P. R. Hayman, *Quodlibets, lately come over from New Britaniola* (London, 1628). Lambeth Palace, MS 250. *Visitation of Shropshire taken in the year 1623*, ed. George Grazebrook and J. P. Rylands (2 parts Harleian Soc., 1889) pt. 2. For Hannam *see:* Somerset House, P.C.C., 75 Fenner, 65 Soame.

RUETTE D'AUTEUIL, DENIS-JOSEPH DE, attorney-general of the Conseil Souverain at Quebec 1674–79; b. 1617, ennobled 16 Jan. 1643 by Louis XIII, emigrated to New France in 1648 or 1649, obtained a seigneury at Sillery, and established residence in Quebec; d. 9 Dec. 1679 at the Hôtel-Dieu, Quebec.

D'Auteuil was one of the original members of the Conseil Souverain, being appointed 18 Sept. 1663. The following September, however, he, along with Louis ROUER de Villeray, JEAN JUCHEREAU DE LA FERTÉ, and JEAN BOURDON, was arbitrarily dismissed from office by the governor, SAFFRAY de Mézy, for allegedly conspiring to thwart the governor's plan to introduce reforms in the local government at Quebec. Subsequently, PROUVILLE de Tracy, lieutenant-general over all the French possessions in North America, strongly recommended that d'Auteuil be appointed attorney-general to succeed the late Jean Bourdon but the minister rejected this recommendation. On 10 Sept. 1674, d'Auteuil again had a seat at the council table, serving as a substitute judge during the trials of François-Marie PERROT and the Abbé de Fénelon [*see* SALIGNAC]. Three weeks later he received a commission from the king, dated 29 May 1674, appointing him attorney-general, which angered BUADE de Frontenac. The latter informed the minister that d'Auteuil was incompetent and under the influence of the Jesuits. Frontenac, however, had no recourse but to allow the registration of d'Auteuil's commission by the Conseil Souverain on 3 October.

In 1679 a violent conflict erupted between the

governor and the Conseil Souverain. Frontenac insisted that he, rather than the intendant, must preside over the meetings of the council and be termed chief and president. D'Auteuil gave it as his opinion that this action was contrary to the king's *Déclaration* of 1675 and the council concurred. When the council members adamantly refused to bow to his will, Frontenac banished d'Auteuil and two of the councillors from Quebec and ordered them to cross to France to account to the king for their insubordination. D'Auteuil, however, was a very sick man, suffering from a serious lung ailment and Frontenac was persuaded to rescind his order, so that d'Auteuil might be spared the sea journey. He died at Quebec on 9 December, 12 days after the ships had sailed for France.

D'Auteuil's marriage, 18 Nov. 1647, in Paris, to Claire-Françoise de Clément Du Vault (or Vuault), daughter of Jean, seigneur of Monceau*, was not a happy one. The young couple was accompanied to Quebec by Claire-Françoise' mother, Anne Gasnier. Twice widowed in France, she became the second wife of Jean Bourdon in 1655. D'Auteuil and his wife lived on their seigneury at Sillery and in a rented house in Quebec. Their first child, a girl, was born at Sillery, 2 June 1652; the next four died in infancy; and the fifth was François-Madeleine-Fortuné*. Mme d'Auteuil, however, deserted her husband on two occasions. In 1650 she eloped with Charles Cadieu during the absence of her husband and her mother in France. Cadieu was subsequently imprisoned for his part in this adventure and Mme d'Auteuil was confined, in the care of the seigneur of Beauport, ROBERT GIFFARD, by order of the colonial authorities, until her husband's return to Quebec in 1651. In 1657, she obtained a separation of property and crossed to France, where she remained until her death in 1674. François-Madeleine-Fortuné was born during the voyage and baptized 17 Jan. 1658 in Paris. Before her death, Mme d'Auteuil disinherited her young son.

In 1660 Ruette d'Auteuil crossed to France, again with his mother-in-law. He failed, however, to persuade his wife to return with him to New France but he brought his son back to Quebec. Here he brought up the boy to assume the duties of attorney-general after his, d'Auteuil's, death, an appointment which was made by the intendant, with the sanction of the Conseil Souverain, despite the strong opposition of Frontenac. The following year, after a careful study of all the facts in the earlier dispute, Louis XIV upheld the contentions of the late attorney-general, rebuked Frontenac severely, and confirmed d'Auteuil's son in office.

There can be no doubt that Ruette d'Auteuil, a dying man, had shown considerable courage in defying Frontenac as he did and his actions contributed to a strengthening of the council's authority by freeing it from the arbitrary domination of the governor.

W. J. ECCLES

JR (Thwaites), *passim*. *Jug. et délib.*, I, contains transcripts of the proceedings of the council. On d'Auteuil's career as a member of the Conseil Souverain *see*: Cahall, *The Sovereign Council of New France*. W. J. Eccles, *Canada under Louis XIV 1663–1701* (Canadian Centenary ser., III, Toronto, 1964); *Frontenac*. Faillon, *Histoire de la colonie française*, III. P.-G. Roy, *La Ville de Québec*, I, contains some references to d'Auteuil.

RUT, JOHN, commander of an English expedition to North America; fl. 1512–28.

As yeoman of the crown and master of the king's ship *Mary Guildford*, normally employed to bring wine for the king from Bordeaux, John Rut (described as of Ratcliffe, Essex) was chosen by Henry VIII to command an expedition to America in 1527. With the *Mary Guildford* and the *Samson*, he was to find a passage to Asia around or through North America and to engage in trade when he had done so. Leaving the Thames on 20 May and Plymouth on 10 June, the vessels parted company in a storm on 1 July. The *Mary Guildford* met icebergs on 3 July and soon afterwards turned back (reports that some men died of cold are not, at that season, at all unlikely). The sources are corrupt and give figures as varied as 53° (perhaps for 58°) and 64° for the most northerly latitude she reached. Rut, on his way south, explored the Labrador coast, entering one inlet, probably St. Lewis Inlet (52°20′N), and landing with his men. He fished at Cap de Bas (at 52°N as he reckoned and probably Cape Charles) between 21 and 30 July, then sailed south to St. John's, Newfoundland, where he found 14 French and Portuguese fishing vessels, as he wrote on 3 August to King Henry. Rut was on his way to Cape Race to fish, expecting to rendezvous at Cap Espar (Cape Spear) with the *Samson* by mid-August and to set out "toward parts to that Ilands that we are commanded," as Purchas, most obscurely, makes him say.

The historian E. G. R. Taylor has argued that if he did not find a northwest passage he had orders to look for a passage or isthmus about latitude 40°N as shown on a map by Giovanni da VERRAZZANO, apparently presented to the king in 1525 or 1526. It was almost certainly the *Mary Guildford* (we must assume the *Samson* had been lost) which coasted eastern North America from

Saccardy

Cape Breton to the Florida channel during the autumn, the first English vessel known to have done so. It is possible that at one landing the pilot was killed by Indians. Nothing further is known of them until an English ship appeared at the island of Mona in the West Indies on 19 November, supposedly having been on a search for "Noruega" (Spanish for "Norway" but perhaps meant for Verrazzano's "Norumbega"). The *Mary*, we are told by our Spanish authorities, was well-armed, had a pinnace and long-boat, and about 70 men (that is 40 more than her normal crew of 30). A pinnace put men ashore at the city of Santo Domingo on 25 November, where they offered to exchange woollen cloth, linen, and pewter for dye-wood and food. They were well received but, next day, as the ship was being brought into the harbour, a stone shot was fired from a warning gun. The captain thereupon took fright and brought his vessel out. Later, at Ocoa, when the Spaniards refused to trade, the English took food by force, threatening to return as enemies, though they later traded peacefully at San German, Puerto Rico, The ship must have reached England in the spring or summer of 1528 since, between September and December, the *Mary Guildford* was employed once more, under John Rut, to bring the king's wine from Bordeaux. The voyage gave Englishmen some first-hand knowledge of the whole eastern coast of North America, enabling them, in this respect, to catch up with France and Spain. Its lack of success in finding a northwest passage to Asia meant that it was not followed up since Henry VIII had little interest in North America for its own sake.

One member of Rut's expedition, Albertus de Prato, has attracted a certain amount of attention through the letter he wrote to King Henry, 10 Aug. 1527 (Purchas, *Pilgrimes* (1905–7), XIV, 303–5; Williamson, *Voyages of the Cabots* (1929), 105, 258). He was thought by Biggar (*Mélanges*, 467) to be the "Alberto de Porto" who borrowed £19 15s. on 19 April 1527 from one Raphael Maruffo (PRO, *CLP, Hen. VIII*, IV, Part II, 1526–28). This, however, does not help to identify Prato. It has been suggested that the "canon of St. Paul in London" who Hakluyt thought was on the voyage (*Principal navigations*, VIII (1904), 1–2), was Prato but the lists of dignitaries of St. Paul's Cathedral have been searched for him in vain. Hakluyt heard of him as "a great Mathematician, and a man indued with wealth [who] did much advance the action, and went therein himselfe in person."

DAVID B. QUINN

Hakluyt, *Principal navigations*, VIII (1904), 1–2. PRO, *CLP, Hen. VIII*, IV, Part II, 1526–28. Purchas, *Pilgrimes* (1905–7), XIV, 303–5. *Spanish documents concerning English voyages to the Caribbean, 1527–68*, ed. I. A. Wright (Hakluyt Soc., 2d ser., LXII, 1929), 29–56 (on p. 48 "Norumbega" should read "Noruega"). Williamson, *Voyages of the Cabots* (1929).

H. P. Biggar, "An English expedition to America in 1527," in *Mélanges offerts à M. Charles Bémont* (Paris, 1913), 459–72. F. A. Kirkpatrick, "The first recorded English voyage to the West Indies," *EHR*, XX (1905), 115–24. *Precursors* (Biggar). E. G. R. Taylor, *Tudor geography, 1485–1583* (London, 1930), 11–12.

Biggar's account (*Mélanges*, 459–72) is the basis for the assumption made above that Rut's ship was the king's wine ship *Mary Guildford* (and not the *Mary of Gilford*) and that it was this ship (and not the *Sampson*) that reached the West Indies. For alternative views *see* Williamson, *Voyages of the Cabots* (1929), 258–61 and Hoffman, *Cabot to Cartier*, 121.

S

SACCARDY (de Saccardy, Saccardie), VINCENT, engineer-general for the French king in Canada; buried May 1691, at Amboise, France.

On 1 June 1689 Saccardy was appointed specifically to execute PASQUINE's plans for rebuilding Port-Royal (now Annapolis Royal, N.S.). He arrived at Chedabouctou (Guysborough, N.S.) on 4 September and at Port-Royal on 6 October. Saccardy spent about a month there, during which he began to tear down the old fort and build a larger one of four bastions, following a different drawing from that of Pasquine. This fort was to enclose the church, the priest's residence, the mill, the garrison, and the governor's residence. He was ordered back to France in November. The Marquis de Seignelay scolded him for having left open the palisade he had begun and adopting a project even more elaborate than Pasquine's. Nevertheless, Seignelay sent Saccardy back the following spring, after reducing the plan by half.

On 14 June 1690, JOSEPH ROBINAU de Villebon and Saccardy arrived on the *Union* at Port-Royal to find that the settlement had been captured by PHIPS on 21 May. Villebon decided to make his headquarters on the Saint John River, to which they sailed three days later. On 30 June the *Union* was attacked by two privateers belonging to the Bostonian, Jacob Leisler, and Saccardy was taken prisoner. On his return journey to France, Saccardy died. He was buried 7 May 1691 at Amboise.

Saccardy left maps of Acadia and interesting memoirs in which he discussed many questions about the colony. Several of his maps were signed by his son, who worked with him, and who became *garde de marine* at Rochefort, then engineer and captain of a frigate.

ÉMERY LEBLANC

AN, Col., B, 15; C¹¹ᴰ, 2. There are four maps in AN (Archives d'Outre-Mer), Dépôt des Fortifications des Colonies, carton no. 2, and in BN, Cartes et Plans. PAC *Report, 1912*, App.F. *Acadiensia Nova* (Morse), I, 201–22. *BRH*, XXXVIII (1932), 720. Webster, *Acadia*, 192.

SAFFRAY DE MÉZY (or Mésy), AUGUSTIN DE, chevalier, governor of New France 1663–65 (the first to serve directly under Louis XIV, after the king took over the administration of the colony from the Compagnie des Cent-Associés in 1663); died at Quebec in the night of 5–6 May, 1665.

A member of the old Norman nobility, dating back to the mid-14th century, Mézy was reputed to have been very dissolute in his youth. He was major of the town and *château* at Caen where he came under the influence of M. Jean de Bernières, head of a group of religious devotees at the Hermitage. He then became noted for his great piety. This drew him to the attention of François de Laval*, future bishop of Quebec, who became favourably impressed by Mézy's character.

In 1663, when Louis XIV and Colbert decided to recall the governor of New France, Baron Davaugour [*see* DUBOIS], they delegated to Bishop Laval the task of finding a suitable replacement. The main reason for doing so was not that Bishop Laval wielded such great power but that the king and his ministers were fully occupied with the internal problems of the kingdom. Moreover, it was extremely difficult to find competent officers to serve as governors in the colonies. When Colbert asked the Comte d'Estrades to suggest a man for the Canadian post he refused point blank, declaring, "it is so easy to misjudge men that I must decline to suggest anyone to you for Canada" (BN, Mélanges Colbert, 112 bis, f.573). Bishop Laval was equally reluctant to make the choice but the king insisted and so Laval, remembering the piety and apparent disinterestedness of Mézy, suggested his name. Mézy, however, appeared anything but anxious to accept the appointment, stating that his many heavy debts prevented him from taking up such a post. There being no other candidate available, Louis XIV is reputed to have offered to pay Mézy's debts if he would accept the appointment for a three-year term and to this Mézy agreed.

On 15 Sept. 1663, Mézy and Laval disembarked at Quebec. With them came 159 indentured labourers and prospective settlers; 60 others had died at sea. Their arrival, and the assurance that much greater aid would be sent from France in the near future, raised the spirits of the 2,500 people in the colony. They could now hope for an early surcease from the constant Iroquois assaults that had bled the colony white. At this time the Five Nations of the Iroquois Confederacy were being hard pressed by their Indian foes, the Hurons, Algonkins, Mahicans and Andastes; in addition they had recently suffered heavy losses from smallpox. When they learned from some of their French captives that reinforcements had arrived in the colony and that more were expected, their attacks on the French settlements slackened and their chiefs began sounding out the Jesuit missionaries on the possibility of a peace settlement. The Jesuit *Relation* for 1663 reported: "Our enemies, being this year engaged elsewhere, have suffered us to till our fields in safety, and to enjoy a sort of foretaste of the quiet which our incomparable Monarch is about to secure for us. . . . Montreal alone has been stained with the blood of Frenchmen, Iroquois and Hurons."

The retiring governor, Baron Davaugour, had already left for France when Mézy and Laval arrived and on 18 September the Conseil Souverain was established by virtue of the royal edict of the previous April, which empowered the governor and bishop to select jointly five councillors, an attorney-general, and a recording clerk to serve for a one-year term, renewable if the governor and bishop saw fit. The bishop, or in his absence the senior ecclesiastic in the colony, also had a seat in the council.

In the three days that had elapsed between the arrival of Mézy and the establishment of the Conseil Souverain he certainly had not had sufficient time to assess the merits of those appointed to this body. It is, therefore, more than likely that Bishop Laval selected Louis ROUER de Villeray, JEAN JUCHEREAU DE LA FERTÉ, Denis-Joseph de RUETTE d'Auteuil, CHARLES LEGARDEUR de Tilly and MATHIEU DAMOURS DE CHAUFFOURS as councillors, along with JEAN BOURDON as attorney-general and Jean-Baptiste PEUVRET Demesnu as recording clerk and secretary. These were men who had played leading roles in the direction of the colony's affairs under the rule of the Compagnie des Cent-Associés. In fact, in the general administration of the colony and in the method of dispensing justice, the Conseil Souverain took over where the preceding council had left off, serving as a court of appeal and of first instance, and also as the colony's legislative body. One of the first edicts it issued, on 28 September, forbade anyone to trade liquor, directly or indirectly, with the Indians on pain of heavy fines or

Saffray de Mézy

banishment. Thus, one of the main causes of conflict between the clergy and previous governors was again removed. To provide funds for the colony's administration Mézy auctioned off the right to collect the 25 per cent export tax on furs along with a monopoly on the fur trade at Tadoussac; this brought in the sum of 46,500 *livres* a year for a three-year term.

There was, apparently, a difference of opinion between Mézy and the bishop over his salary and allowances. Some of the clergy later maintained that he had made excessive demands and upon being refused he had "declared war" on the bishop and the Conseil Souverain. There appears to be little truth in these statements. At the meeting of the Conseil Souverain on 28 Nov. 1663 Mézy stated that some "difficulty" had arisen over this matter but he was willing to allow the Conseil Souverain to grant him the same amount as any of the last three governors had received. A week later the council voted to grant him the salary and appointments that had previously been granted to Voyer* d'Argenson. This amounted to 23,303 *livres*, out of which Mézy had to pay the wages and upkeep of the Quebec garrison.

The following year Mézy had the council remove the 10 per cent tax on all goods entering the colony except on wines, spirits, and tobacco. To protect consumers from overcharging by the merchants, the prices at which all imported goods could be sold was fixed, allowing for a 65 per cent mark-up over the prices paid for similar goods in France. At the same time ocean freight rates were fixed at 80 *livres* the ton. That these regulations were not to be disregarded was made plain when some merchants were heavily fined for charging more than the tariff allowed.

To encourage the settlers to clear more land and to grow more grain in the face of a large wheat surplus, in 1664 the Conseil Souverain purchased 1,000 bushels, at the generous price of 5 *livres* the bushel, to be stored for the use of the regular troops expected from France the following year. The wages of indentured labourers were also fixed by law at 60 to 90 *livres* a year for a three-year term, after which they were free to obtain land of their own. Thus, during the first year of Mézy's government some worthwhile legislation was enacted. But before that year was out, trouble had arisen between the governor and the bishop.

Mézy, although he represented the king in the colony and had supreme authority, had, in fact, less real power than had the bishop. Mézy had been appointed for only a three-year term and could be recalled by the king at any time. The bishop, on the other hand, was permanently appointed and, in addition to his seat on the council, had the power and prestige of his clerical rank. The clergy had clearly expected Mézy to remain subservient to Bishop Laval, deferring to him in all things, but the governor soon showed he was not prepared to accept a subordinate position.

During the winter 1663–64 Mézy appears to have become convinced that the bishop, supported by some members of the council, was seeking to undermine his authority. According to the royal edict establishing the Conseil Souverain the governor represented the person of the king; Mézy therefore decided to take steps to assert his prerogatives. On 13 February 1664 he sent the major of his garrison to inform the bishop of his intention to exclude Villeray, d'Auteuil, and Bourdon from the council on the grounds that they had formed a cabal and behaved in a manner contrary to the interests of the king and the people. He also declared that replacements for those now excluded would be chosen by a public assembly. Laval, as was to be expected, refused to entertain this innovation, or to sanction the dismissal of the two council members and the attorney-general. Tilly, La Ferté, and Damours, however, supported Mézy and signed an ordinance suspending Laval's adherents.

Without an attorney-general justice could not be dispensed and the settlers of the district who had litigation before the court protested vigorously. Mézy therefore asked the bishop to agree to the appointment of a deputy attorney-general. Laval refused to give his sanction but he did declare that he would not openly oppose the governor in any action he took on his own authority. On 10 March the rump council duly appointed LOUIS-THÉANDRE CHARTIER de Lotbinière to the vacant attorney-general's post and the work of the council proceeded. Subsequently, a reconciliation of the disputing factions was effected; Lotbinière gracefully retired and Bourdon was reinstated.

In July, however, trouble again erupted, this time over the election of a syndic for Quebec. The previous November the offices of mayor and alderman had been abolished by the council and it was then decided that the old office of syndic should be reinstituted to represent the interests of the local people before the council. Not until the following August was an election held, when Claude CHARRON, a merchant of Quebec, was elected in absentia by 23 local residents.

Meanwhile, nearly a year having elapsed since the establishment of the Conseil Souverain, Mézy repeatedly requested Laval to agree to the re-

Saffray de Mézy

placement of some of its members and the confirmation in office of the others. The bishop, obviously knowing which members Mézy wished to exclude, refused to accede to this legitimate request. On 25 August Mézy sent Laval a courteously worded note asking that they should cooperate in good faith to appoint a new council as laid down in the royal edict of April 1663. He proposed that he should draw up a list of 12 men suitable to hold office and that the bishop should select any four; or, the bishop could name 12 candidates and allow the governor to choose four of them. Under the circumstances this was a fair proposal. Laval, however, in a terse note, informed Mézy that he had received word from the minister of marine that Seigneur de Tracy [see PROUVILLE], recently appointed lieutenant-general over all French possessions in America with the powers of a viceroy, would arrive at Quebec the following spring and they should await his arrival before making any changes in the membership of the council. This meant that Mézy would have to face further opposition in the council for the best part of a year. Unfortunately, the terms of the royal edict establishing the Conseil Souverain gave no guidance as to how to cope with an impasse such as this.

After some of the citizens had protested the election of Charron as syndic on the grounds that too few people had voted in the election and that he was more likely to favour the interests of the merchants than those of the consumers, Charron was persuaded to resign and a new election was called. This assembly of voters was also poorly attended and no election was held. Mézy was convinced, rightly or wrongly, that his old foes the clergy and their adherents in the council were responsible for this state of affairs. He therefore sent notes to a large number of townspeople to attend a meeting without stating its purpose. When they had assembled he and Damours held the election and Jean LEMIRE was duly elected syndic. At the next meeting of the Conseil Souverain, La Ferté, d'Auteuil and the bishop's deputy, CHARLES DE LAUSON de Charny, protested this election and refused to allow Lemire to be installed. By this time Mézy's patience was exhausted. He regarded this latest move by the bishop's adherents as chicanery and being, he declared, unaccustomed to such ways, he decided to deal with the situation in the only way he knew how, as would a cavalier defending the king's interests. On his own authority he dismissed from the council on 19 Sept. 1664 Villeray (who had sailed for France a short time before), d'Auteuil, La Ferté, and Bourdon. As their replacements he appointed SIMON DENYS de La Trinité, LOUIS PERONNE de Mazé, and Jacques de Cailhault* de La Tesserie, with Lotbinière once again to serve as attorney-general and Michel FILLION as clerk. Jean Bourdon, however, unlike the others, refused to accept this dismissal, declaring the governor's action to be illegal, which it of course was. A violent argument ensued and Mézy lost control of himself. He attacked Bourdon, striking him first with his cane then with the flat of his sword, pursued him out of the chamber and wounded him in the hand. Bishop Laval immediately protested Mézy's reconstitution of the council, declaring it to be contrary to the king's edict. The following Sunday he made his views known to the public in a statement read from the pulpit by one of his priests. Mézy, lacking a pulpit, retaliated by posting notices about the town defending his own actions and attacking the bishop, whereupon he was refused absolution by the clergy. The governor's response was a threat to refuse the authorization of the payment of the semi-annual grant of funds to the clergy.

What the people of the colony thought of this fracas is not known but it certainly could not have enhanced their respect for either the secular or religious authorities. But through it all Mézy's reconstituted Conseil Souverain continued to function, meting out justice, carrying on the normal processes of the administration, and showing a proper sense of its responsibilities. Then, early in March 1665, Mézy fell seriously ill. When he expressed a desire to be reconciled with the clergy all their earlier rancour was forgotten. Before Mézy expired, during the night of 5–6 May, the bishop said mass for him every day and in his will the governor made bequests to the poor, to charitable institutions, to the church and to five residents of Quebec, one of whom was Villeray.

Shortly before his death Mézy had commissioned JACQUES LENEUF de La Poterie to succeed him as his deputy but when the acting attorney-general presented the commission to the Conseil Souverain this body refused to register it, maintaining that the governor had no power to appoint his successor—only the king could do this. In France, meanwhile, numerous complaints against Mézy's conduct had reached the court; Bourdon and Villeray were able to give their version of events at first hand. The minister was thus convinced that Mézy's conduct could not be condoned. Unaware that the governor was dead, Colbert ordered that the charges against him be investigated and if substantiated he was to be placed under arrest and sent back to France to stand trial.

It is unfortunate that Mézy's own papers have

Sagard

not survived; were they available to counterbalance the charges levelled at him in the writings of the clergy which have been preserved, he might appear in a better light. At least it can be said that his had been no easy position, sharing power with Bishop Laval. He acted with violence on occasion, it is true; but he did so not without some provocation. Although the clash of personalities played no small part in the conflict, strongly held differences of opinion on what should be done for the better administration of the colony were also involved. In the final analysis the main reason for the eventual impasse was the ill-conceived phrasing of the edict establishing the Conseil Souverain. The governor and the bishop had to share authority and were expected to co-operate in all things. If, for one reason or another, this became impossible, then either the government of the colony was hamstrung or one of them had to over-rule the other and to exercise arbitrary power if the administration were to function. This power the bishop clearly could not wield; but the governor, who was essentially a soldier accustomed to giving orders and being obeyed, readily could and did exercise his authority. In any event, these conflicts should not be allowed to obscure the fact that during Mézy's brief term as governor, royal government was established in the colony, justice was dispensed equitably and some useful legislation was enacted.

W. J. ECCLES

Much of the documentary source material is printed in *Jug. et délib.*, I. The best account to date of Mézy's administration is that contained in Cahall, *The Sovereign Council of New France*, 22–36. Faillon, *Histoire de la colonie française*, III. Gosselin, *Vie de Mgr de Laval*, I. Lanctot, *Histoire du Canada*, II. Parkman, *The old régime* (25th ed.), 145–58.

SAGARD, GABRIEL (christened **Théodat**), Recollet friar, missionary in the Huron country in 1623 and 1624, first religious historian of Canada; fl. 1614–36.

From an allusion by Sagard to Father Daniel Saymond (d. 1604), superior of the monastery of Verdun, we may conclude that Sagard was already a Recollet by that year. At the end of 1614 he was living in Paris with Father Jacques Garnier Chapouin, the provincial of the Recollets of Saint-Denis, and serving as his private secretary. At that time Louis Houel, a king's secretary and comptroller of the salt-works at Brouage, suggested to Father Chapouin that missionaries be sent to New France. Father Chapouin, encouraged by the French clergy, who were assembled for the Estates General, immediately appointed four religious: Denis JAMET, Jean DOLBEAU, Joseph LE CARON, and Pacifique DUPLESSIS. They left in the spring of 1615: ". . . I should have dearly liked to be one of them," wrote Sagard. His wish was not to be fulfilled until 1623, at which time he obtained permission to sail to Canada with Father Nicolas VIEL. The two Recollets left the monastery in Paris on 18 March and landed at Quebec on 28 June, after a crossing made up of "three months six days of sailing."

As soon as they arrived, the missionaries made plans to get to the Huron country. On 16 July Fathers Viel and Le Caron and Brother Sagard left the convent of the Recollets; they joined the French boats leaving for the exchange of furs, which took place that year at Cap-de-la-Victoire, at the mouth of the Rivière des Iroquois (Richelieu). When the trading was finished (2 August) the Hurons returned to their territory together with the three missionaries, who were divided up among the different canoes. After a most arduous journey Sagard reached Lake Huron on 20 August. Two days later he was at Ossossanë, the village of his guide and protector Oonchiarey.

Sagard passed "a fairly long time" in this environment; he was respected and loved as a guest, and divided his time between prayer, the study of the language, and the visiting of families. One day Father Viel suddenly arrived. Together they rejoined Father Le Caron at Carhagouha, some five leagues from Ossossanë. With the Indians' help the three Recollets built near the village a cabin in the Indian style; it measured "about 20 feet long and 10 or 12 wide, being constructed in the form of a garden bower." It was in this little convent that the Recollets exercised their ministry, celebrating the holy mysteries, administering the sacraments to the French, and receiving numerous Indians all the time; of these, some came to obtain religious instruction, others, more "spiteful," came "to steal our modest furnishings under pretext of paying us a visit."

Around May 1624 Sagard, together with the Hurons who were going to exchange furs, set off for Quebec, in order to acquire certain items necessary for the mission. On the way, they met the convoy headed by Étienne BRÛLÉ, which was also travelling in the direction of the St. Lawrence valley. The boats of the missionaries reached Quebec on 16 July, after a number of vicissitudes. As he was about to return, Sagard received a letter from the provincial, Father Polycarpe Du Fay, instructing him to come back to Paris.

Some months after the publication of his *Histoire* (1636), Sagard left the Recollets. They made repeated attempts to get him to join them again, but to no purpose, since Sagard died, probably, while with the Franciscans.

Three works of Sagard, dealing with the early days of New France, have come down to us. *Le grand voyage au pays des Hurons* (1632) appeared in two volumes. Six chapters recount the ocean crossing, the journey from Quebec to the "lac des Hurons," and the author's return to France. The remainder of the work studies the Huron customs and way of life, and the flora and fauna of the country. It is a brilliant, astonishingly precise fresco.

Four years later Sagard published *L'histoire du Canada* in four parts. The first deals with the apostolic activity of the Recollets in Canada from 1615 up to the author's journey in 1623; the two following parts reproduce *Le grand voyage*, revised and enlarged; the last is concerned with the period marked by the arrival of the Jesuits, the capture of Quebec, and the temporary abandonment of the colony. In addition to describing missionary life, the author relates the principal political, commercial, and agricultural events in which the Recollets played a part. It is an important work which corroborates and adds further detail to the writings of Samuel de CHAMPLAIN, and which provides us with a number of unique and outstandingly valuable documents.

At first sight the book is disconcerting: the historian takes up and amplifies his study of 1632, giving us information on the missionary work of the Recollets in the Holy Land, India, Tartary, Slavonia, Bulgaria, China, and America. The object of this panoramic view is to establish the injustice of excluding the Recollets when Canada was returned to the French in 1632. Sagard wants to prove, on the one hand, that the success of the Recollets as apostles in other countries is an argument in favour of their return to Canada, and to show on the other hand that the apparent failure of the first missionaries was due to the ill will of the companies for trading and colonizing and the disgraceful conduct of certain French settlers. A plea *pro domo*, perhaps, but in no way an extravagant panegyric. On the contrary, the eulogy has an attractive tone to it: the thesis appears only as a finely interwoven thread, and the monk uses a sly wit with great finesse.

The "Dictionnaire de la langue huronne" is a collection of French expressions translated into the Huron language. One can hold against Sagard —and several have not failed to do so—the fact that this so-called dictionary is not a dictionary, and that it contains errors. Sagard never had any pretentions in this respect. He was thoroughly aware of undertaking an irksome task: he acknowledged that the language was very difficult, had few if any rules, and was constantly changing. If, however, he tackled this thankless job, it was because of his earnest desire to supply those who were labouring to implant faith among the Hurons with the rudiments of the language. Nothing is likely to cast serious doubt on the value of this short work. Sagard draws upon the experience of interpreters, and upon that of his missionary associates, among them Father Le Caron, the author of a Huron dictionary now lost. Despite its imperfections, Sagard's dictionary remains, in the opinion of one linguist, the most complete compilation dealing with the old Huron language.

The qualities of the historian inspire confidence: "keenness of observation, strict accuracy, sincerity, straightforward simplicity." His work is founded upon authentic sources: letters and relations by his associates, ecclesiastical and civil documents, reports by Jesuits. In addition he uses Champlain's writings, from which he reports several facts without naming Champlain, and those of Marc LESCARBOT, whom he mentions once under the name of "Lescot." Finally Sagard recounts and describes events which to a large extent he witnessed himself.

As an historian he has been reproved for a credulousness which some have called extreme. Somewhat unlikely cases of possession by demons and of diabolical apparitions, with which certain chapters are concerned, are an indication of an undeniable credulousness. Is he to be condemned because of that? We must not forget the period when Sagard was writing, a period when a fervour not firmly established lent too ready credence to spells and interventions by the devil. In any case, great writers of the same period have hardly displayed any more caution.

Sagard is first and foremost a painter, who applies himself to the detail of things, to the daily life of the Indians. He is helped by a faculty for keen observation. Whether he is studying the habits and customs of the Indians, or tracing the topography of places, or describing the flora and fauna of the region, Sagard is precise and exact. These qualities are enhanced by an attractive form of expression and by a direct, smoothly flowing style, although there are some blemishes. Other narrators have a more elegant, refined prose; very few possess his completely uninhibited, natural, simple manner.

Gabriel Sagard continues to be a little-known figure whom our annals are wont to pass over. Even in the restricted circle of scholars Sagard does not enjoy the esteem of all. For some, this worthy monk is only a naïve person, with a superficial and over-credulous mind; for others he is a first-rate historian, with a mind that is

Sailly

discerning and luminous. But the fact remains that Sagard's work, devoted to the early days of New France, commands respect: the author is a reliable, competent, and honest witness.

JEAN DE LA CROIX RIOUX

Sagard, *Le grand voyage* (Tross); *Histoire du Canada* (Tross), *see* particularly introductory note by H.-Émile Chevalier; *Long journey* (Wrong and Langton). J.-C. Cayer, "Gabriel Sagard, Théodat," in *Centenaire de l'histoire de François-Xavier Garneau* (Montréal, 1945), 171–200. Archange Godbout, "L'historien Sagard," in *Les Récollets et Montréal* (Montréal, 1955), 89–97. Jouve, *Les Franciscains et le Canada (1615–1629)*. Séraphin Marion, *Relations des voyageurs français en Nouvelle-France au XVIIe siècle* (Paris, 1923). H.-A. Scott, "Que penser de l'historien du Canada, le frère Gabriel Sagard, récollet?" *Almanach de Saint-François* (Montréal, 1924), 40–4.

SAILLY, LOUIS-ARTHUS DE, merchant, royal judge; b. *c.* 1625 in France; d. April 1668 at Montreal.

Very little is known about his life before his arrival at Montreal in 1657. At Amiens, in Picardy, he married Anne-Françoise, the daughter of Médéric Bourduceau, a merchant who was apparently fairly successful in the West Indies trade, in which he was associated particularly with the Sulpician Gabriel SOUART. M. de Sailly lived for some time in Martinique, where he represented his father-in-law.

After taking up residence at Montreal, he made several more or less profitable transactions with his wife's parents, assisted in this by M. Souart and the Sulpicians. From 1 Feb. 1663 he was a corporal in the 14th militia squadron of Montreal. That same year a conflict arose between the royal government and the Sulpicians over the right to administer justice, and Governor SAFFRAY de Mézy appointed M. de Sailly judge of the royal seneschal's court. The Sulpicians protested, and created a seigneurial court with CHARLES-JOSEPH D'AILLEBOUST Des Muceaux as judge. The two courts functioned concurrently until TALON abolished the royal court in 1666. Despite his dismissal, M. de Sailly retained his title of royal judge until his death, which occurred unexpectedly when he was 43. His wife and children must have gone back to France, for we do not come across their name in Canada again after 1668.

J. MONET

Jug. et délib., I, 33f., 423. A. C. de Léry Macdonald, "Un petit point d'histoire: le juge de Sailly," *RC*, XIX (1883), 760f. É.-Z. Massicotte, "Louis Artus de Sailly, premier juge royal de Montréal," *BRH*, XXI (1915), 206–9; "Les tribunaux et les officiers de justice à Montréal sous le régime français, 1648–1760," *RSCT*, 3d ser., X (1916), sect.I, 273. Sulte, *Hist. des Can. fr.*, IV, 10.

SAINT-AIGNAN, NICOLAS MARSOLET *dit*. *See* MARSOLET

SAINT-DENIS, NICOLAS JUCHEREAU DE. *See* JUCHEREAU

SAINTE-GENEVIÈVE, SEIGNEUR DE. *See* PERROT, FRANÇOIS-MARIE

SAINTE-HÉLÈNE, JACQUES LE MOYNE DE. *See* LE MOYNE

SAINT-ÉTIENNE DE LA TOUR, CHARLES DE [the family name may well have been **Turgis**], trader, colonizer, and governor of Acadia; b. 1593, probably in the old French province of Champagne, the son of CLAUDE DE SAINT-ÉTIENNE de La Tour; d. 1666.

On 25 Feb. 1610 Charles set sail from Dieppe for Acadia with his father and a party of men led by JEAN DE BIENCOURT de Poutrincourt to re-occupy the abandoned settlement at Port-Royal (now Annapolis Royal, N.S.). During the years that followed, affairs in Acadia were most often in charge of Poutrincourt's son, CHARLES DE BIENCOURT. He and young La Tour were close friends, with La Tour serving as his lieutenant.

Following the destruction of Port-Royal by Samuel ARGALL in 1613, Biencourt and his men were forced to live with the Indians for a time. With little in the way of supplies and reinforcements arriving from France, Biencourt and La Tour were able to rebuild the Port-Royal buildings only in part. They largely abandoned settlement and farming in favour of the lucrative but risky fur trade, a commerce which each year attracted several vessels to the Acadian coasts. When Biencourt died in 1623, he left Charles de La Tour as his heir. La Tour took charge of the colony and soon after he built up a strong post at Cap de Sable, called Fort Lomeron in honour of David LOMERON who was his agent in France. Here he carried on a sizeable trade in furs with the Indians and farmed the land.

When La Tour learned of the outbreak of war between France and England in 1627, he was concerned for the future. For the past 20 years the French government had largely ignored Acadia, leaving it without defence or economic aid. The last remaining post France had in the country was La Tour's Fort Lomeron. He fully realized something had to be done quickly to strengthen

Saint-Étienne de La Tour

defences if Acadia were to remain French, and he wrote letters both to King Louis and to Cardinal Richelieu pointing out the lack of support and the fact, that, exercising the authority of administrator in Acadia as the heir of Biencourt, he had maintained the hold France had on Acadia. He went on to report that he had trained a mixed force of Frenchmen and Indians which he had used to prevent English attempts to trade and to fish in Acadia. He ended with a request for supplies and reinforcements as well as for a proper commission authorizing him to defend the area. La Tour's father presented the letters and was able to give a full account of conditions in Acadia.

The request for supplies and men was turned over to the powerful new trading association—the Compagnie de la Nouvelle-France (called also the Compagnie des Cent-Associés)—formed that same year, 1627, and given the right to trade with the Indians and to grant seigneuries while encouraging the settlement of New France. The next spring the company sent out under ROQUEMONT de Brison four ships laden with supplies for Quebec and Cap de Sable. Three ships, commanded by Sir DAVID KIRKE, which were accompanying some vessels carrying WILLIAM ALEXANDER the younger and his settlers, captured the French ships (and Claude de La Tour). As a result, no help got through to Charles. With the taking of Quebec by the English in 1629, the sole French stronghold left in New France was La Tour's Fort Lomeron.

After his capture, Claude de La Tour espoused the English cause and promised to win over his son, in exchange for a large grant of land in "New Scotland." The elder La Tour set out immediately afterwards with two British warships carrying colonists and soldiers to the Anglo-Scottish settlement at Port-Royal. A stop was made at Cap de Sable and Claude hastened to inform his son of all that had taken place. He urged Charles to give up this last possession of France in Acadia and to accept the title and generous land-grant being offered him by the English. The emphatic reaction of the younger La Tour, as Champlain tells us, was that "he would rather have died than consent to such baseness as to betray his King."

Since his urging and pleading were in vain, Claude resorted to force. For over 24 hours troops presumably led by Claude de La Tour attacked Fort Lomeron, but without success. Charles, then, was victorious in the cause of France, while his uncomfortable father was obliged to retire with the English to Port-Royal.

Shortly afterwards, two vessels of the Compagnie de la Nouvelle-France, sent by Jean Tuffet, arrived at Fort Lomeron with supplies and a relief party including workmen, artisans, and three Recollet priests. Bernard MAROT, the leader of the expedition, brought with him letters from the company appointing La Tour one of its associates and explaining that the food, arms, and men had been sent to enable him to build a habitation where he felt it would be most useful. The workmen were soon set to the task of enlarging and strengthening the post at Cap de Sable, and apparently it was renamed Fort La Tour (although Champlain called it "Fort sainct Louys" in his *Works* (Biggar), VI, 199). At the same time, Charles consulted with Marot and the Recollets about the problem of his father and then decided to allow Claude to return to Cap de Sable.

Because of the new interest shown by France in Acadia, La Tour resolved to build a fortified trading post at the mouth of the Saint John River, the richest source of furs in all Acadia. He reasoned that this would forestall any designs the English might have on that part of the country. La Tour immediately sent to France an emissary, Krainguille, for the additional men and supplies required for the project. On 8 Feb. 1631 Louis XIII signed a royal commission naming Charles de La Tour governor and lieutenant-general of the king; it was delivered either by Laurent Ferchaud or Krainguille, who brought out the requested materials for La Tour's use at Saint John. When the post there was completed, it was named Fort Sainte-Marie and Jean-Daniel Chaline, one of La Tour's lieutenants, was placed in charge of this first permanent establishment on the Saint John. On 18 Sept. 1632, a force of Scots from Port-Royal under command of Capt. Andrew FORRESTER attacked the new fort, tore down a large cross, damaged the chapel, and plundered the supplies. Not too many months elapsed before La Tour captured the English fort at Machias and pillaged it as a warning that his posts could not be molested with impunity.

With the signing of the Treaty of Saint-Germain-en-Laye in 1632, France recovered Acadia and Canada. Isaac de RAZILLY was given a commission as governor in Acadia and ordered to take possession of it. He arrived at La Hève that fall and a few months later secured the return of Port-Royal from the Scots. With the country once more under French control, La Tour went to France where he had the limits of his authority and that of Razilly clarified by the company: under this arrangement, Razilly was given control of La Hève, Port-Royal, and the Sainte-Croix area. While in France La Tour also recruited colonists for his headquarters, which he moved to Fort Sainte-Marie in 1635. Everything indicates that La Tour got on well with Razilly and that

Saint-Étienne de La Tour

under their direction trade flourished and settlers were attracted to the land. Just as conditions in Acadia were undergoing such an encouraging change, Isaac de Razilly died suddenly in 1635 and a period of confusion and strife began.

Claude de Rasilly succeeded his brother. Since he found it necessary to stay in France, he delegated the task of looking after the Rasilly interests in Acadia to his cousin, Charles de MENOU d'Aulnay. It was not long before d'Aulnay and La Tour, both energetic and ambitious men with indefinite areas of command, came into conflict. The story of Acadia for the next decade is largely a record of their strife, which worsened to armed conflict and paralysed colonization. This deplorable clash between noblemen of the same race, religion, and allegiance had the result of obscuring the history of the period to a surprising degree. What is more, the smoke-screen of prejudice, both contemporary and modern, has made it difficult to determine the facts that should be the basis of unprejudiced judgement by the historian. Happily, enough documentation remains to allow us to trace with a fair degree of accuracy the remarkable feud between La Tour and d'Aulnay.

In 1636, the Compagnie de la Nouvelle-France gave a trading post at Pentagouet (on the Penobscot) to Claude de La Tour. Built possibly about 1625 by the elder La Tour, the post had been captured by the New Englanders in 1626, then retaken by d'Aulnay in 1635. The company's action seems to have roused d'Aulnay's hatred for both La Tour and the company. D'Aulnay addressed himself directly to the king who in 1638 gave Pentagouet to d'Aulnay and made an unsuccessful attempt to divide all of Acadia west of Canseau (Canso) between them. In their ignorance, Louis XIII's ministers gave d'Aulnay the land lying north of the Bay of Fundy but not Fort Sainte-Marie, and La Tour the peninsular part of Acadia but not Port-Royal. This simply made matters worse and the struggle continued.

Under an arrangement instituted by the company some years before, Razilly and La Tour shared the expenses and the profits of the fur trade. However, when La Tour went to Port-Royal in 1640 to check the furs and supplies there, he was refused permission and it appears that he and d'Aulnay came to blows. The latter complained to the king about what he termed this act of aggression and was directed to carry orders to La Tour asking the latter to return to France and explain his conduct. This La Tour bluntly refused to do, on the grounds that the order was obtained through misrepresentation. Using this to best advantage, d'Aulnay was able gradually to improve his position at court. Under instructions from the king to put Fort La Tour in the hands of "faithful personages," he captured and burned the post, keeping all the goods he found there for himself.

When he learned that La Tour, cut off from trade goods and other supplies from France, had sent his lieutenant GARGOT to Boston asking for the right to trade and to recruit mercenaries, d'Aulnay hastened to France, to claim that La Tour had committed treason, and that he had shown disrespect for the Crown by refusing to face the king. In August of 1642 he returned to Acadia with orders for La Tour to appear before the king to answer these serious charges.

La Tour and his wife, Françoise-Marie JACQUELIN, decided it was best that she go to France and that he stay in Acadia to protect his interests. Once in France, Mme de La Tour won from the vice-admiral authorization for the Compagnie de la Nouvelle-France to send a vessel with soldiers and supplies to La Tour. Sailing in April 1643, it entered the Baie Française (Bay of Fundy) to find that d'Aulnay had established a three-ship blockade of the Saint John post. Since the relief ship was not able to get through, La Tour managed to reach her under cover of darkness and to persuade the captain to take him to Boston. There La Tour showed his authorization from the vice-admiral of France to receive supplies that were now illegally denied him by d'Aulnay, and he received permission to obtain private assistance. By mortgaging his property to Major-General Edward Gibbons of Boston he was able to hire four ships and a number of soldiers.

On sighting this fleet in the Bay of Fundy, d'Aulnay fled to Port-Royal where he was pursued by La Tour. There La Tour wished to discuss the matter of compensation for his losses but d'Aulnay refused to negotiate. La Tour then attacked with a force of his own men—augmented by a group of 30 English volunteers—defeated d'Aulnay's force, and burned the mill. D'Aulnay was not slow in lodging a complaint with the Crown, charging La Tour with open rebellion and having turned traitor in allying himself with the English for the purpose of driving the French from Acadia. The result was that La Tour was totally discredited with the French government. Soon after, when Mme La Tour arrived in France once more to obtain the supplies her husband desperately needed, she was even refused permission to leave the country and had to flee in disguise to England.

Having won the complete favour of the king, d'Aulnay hired soldiers, purchased both a warship and ammunition, and arrived at Port-Royal in September 1644. At this time he signed a treaty of peace with the English of Boston. There is no doubt that he as well as La Tour had been carrying on trade with the New Englanders, who preferred to deal with La Tour but strove to be impartial because of their fear of d'Aulnay. D'Aulnay then sent a representative to Boston asking for aid in his struggle with La Tour. Aid was refused and the suggestion made that he seek instead to make peace with his rival. Such a proposal fell on deaf ears. Victorious at court, he was determined to be victor in the field as well.

During La Tour's absence from the Saint John early in February 1645, d'Aulnay attacked Fort Sainte-Marie but was beaten off with heavy loss. When in April he learned from deserters that La Tour was once more away at Boston in search of food and trade goods, d'Aulnay resolved to attack again. This time he was successful, but more through deception than force of arms. News of the capture of his fort and of his wife's death reached La Tour at Boston while he was still preparing his relief expedition.

The next year Charles moved to Quebec where he was warmly welcomed by Governor Huault de Montmagny who gave him lodging at the Château Saint-Louis. During the four years that followed he was busily occupied in trade, assisted the Jesuits in their missionary efforts, and on at least one occasion fought with the Hurons against the Iroquois. When news of d'Aulnay's death in 1650 reached Quebec, La Tour decided at last to go to France to plead his case. There, he begged that an inquiry be made into his conduct as well as into the faults both he and the Compagnie de la Nouvelle-France had found in d'Aulnay's conduct. The inquiry was granted. It resulted in La Tour's being re-established in the royal favour; responsibility for the bloody fighting between the two was charged to d'Aulnay.

With his property and his commission as governor restored, La Tour gathered several families of colonists, including that of his childhood friend Mius d'Entremont, and sailed in the summer of 1653 for Port-Royal. He presented Mme d'Aulnay [Jeanne Motin] with a royal order restoring to him the fort at Saint John. Mme d'Aulnay and La Tour were both heavily in debt and anxious to bring the disastrous rivalry of their two factions to an end, and so, in due course, she accepted La Tour's proposal of marriage. Later that same summer Emmanuel Le Borgne, to whom the d'Aulnay estate owed over 200,000 *livres*, arrived at Port-Royal to collect the debt. He discovered La Tour was absent at Fort Sainte-Marie and took the opportunity to make off with all the pelts he could find. The next year Le Borgne made an attempt to take the fort at Saint John, which was unsuccessful since La Tour had been forewarned by Nicolas Denys.

On 14 July 1654, an English expedition sent by Oliver Cromwell under the command of Major Robert Sedgwick entered the harbour at Saint John and called for La Tour's surrender. Having few cannon, almost no ammunition, and a garrison of but 70 men to oppose a force of 500, La Tour was obliged to comply. He was made a prisoner and taken to England. Only in 1656 was he allowed to see Cromwell. He asked for the return of his property on the grounds that England and France had been at peace when the capture took place. Cromwell refused the request, agreeing only to recognize La Tour's right as a baronet of Nova Scotia as his father's heir, provided he accepted English allegiance and paid both the amount he owed Boston merchants and the cost of the English garrison that Leverett had maintained at Saint John. Discouraged with the turn of events and undoubtedly dispirited at the thought of the French creditors awaiting him and his wife, Charles accepted these conditions. (It is of interest to note that in 1700 the king of France indicated an understanding of this action when he recognized the rights in Acadia of La Tour's children.) To raise the some £15,000 involved, La Tour entered into partnership with William Crowne and Thomas Temple.

Soon afterwards—in September, 1656—La Tour, possibly finding this enforced arrangement with the English distasteful, sold his rights to his two partners, retaining only a small percentage of the profit. Temple took command of the fort at Saint John and Crowne that at Pentagouet. La Tour appears to have retired with his wife to Cap de Sable and there he died in 1666. In all, he had been a resident of Acadia for 56 years and his is the name that predominates during most of that period.

Charles de La Tour was married three times. The first marriage, to an unnamed Micmac girl, was blessed in 1626. By this union he had three daughters, two of whom entered religious orders and the third, Jeanne, who later married Martin d'Aprendestiguy de Martignon. La Tour's second marriage, to the valiant Françoise-Marie Jacquelin, took place at Port-Royal in 1640. They had one son who apparently died during childhood. La Tour's third wife was d'Aulnay's widow, Jeanne Motin, whom he married at Port-Royal in 1653; they had five children.

There is little doubt that La Tour remained loyal to his country until 1656, all of his previous dealings with the English occurring in peace-time and being a recognized practice. Unquestionably, La Tour would have preferred to obtain the goods

Saint-Étienne de La Tour

he required in France, but the acts of his rival had the very effect of forcing him more and more to turn to Boston for supplies. In fact, we may say that in the face of an all too often uninterested and short-sighted government he went to unusual lengths to preserve French power, although he was only a trader and was not really interested in colonization.

So far as his ruinous struggle with d'Aulnay is concerned, it is usually thought that La Tour struck the first physical blow, but there is no proof of this. Had he been willing to conciliate his vindictive enemy, the fratricidal battle might not have reached such heights.

Charles de La Tour, who must remain something of a controversial figure, was ambitious, confident of his own judgement, and the possessor of great natural ability and determination. He was a born leader with the happy faculty of making friends and of inspiring faith in his integrity. His associations with the French court, Huault de Montmagny, Boston merchants, and d'Aulnay's widow—if not with d'Aulnay—testify to his diplomatic persuasiveness, unusual in a man brought up from boyhood days in a wilderness land. The pages of Acadia's history are much richer for his presence.

GEORGE MACBEATH

ACM, B.187, f.19. AE, Mém. et doc., Amérique, 8. AN, Minutier, XV, 31; XX, 156; LXVI, 28. BN, MS Fr. 18593, f.373; NAF 9281 (Margry), ff. 69–129. "Mass. Archives." Champlain, *Works* (Biggar). Charlevoix, *History* (Shea). *Coll. de manuscrits relatifs à la Nouv.-France*, II, 351–80 *passim*. Denys, *Description and natural history* (Ganong). *Factum* (1614). *Mémoires des commissaires*, I, xiii, xxvi, xxxvii, 46–48, 71, 80–82, 84, 97, 106, 151; II, 276, 279–80, 286–89, 493, 511; IV, 86, 126, 162–63, 180, 224ff., 232–39, 241, 263, 305, 333, 443, 451, 499; and *Memorials of the English and French commissaries*, I, 17, 41, 43, 118, 120, 145–47, 155–57, 168, 176, 206, 337, 361, 369, 488, 525, 570, 576–79, 709, 727. PRO, *CSP, Col., 1574–1660* [see "Delatour"]; 1661–68 [see "St. Stephen"]; *1669–74*; *1697–98* [see "Delatour"]. *Suffolk deeds*, I, 6–10, 75–76; III, 265, 268, 272, 276. *Winthrop's journal* (Hosmer) in *Original narratives* (Jameson).

René Baudry, "Charles d'Aulnay et la Compagnie de la Nouvelle-France," *RHAF*, XI (1957–58), 218–41. J. B. Brebner, *New England's outpost: Acadia before the conquest of Canada* (New York, 1927). Couillard Després, *Saint-Étienne de La Tour*. Huguet, *Poutrincourt*. Émile Lauvrière, *Deux traîtres d'Acadie et leur victime: les Latour père et fils et Charles d'Aulnay* (Paris et Montréal, 1932). Edmund Slafter, *Sir William Alexander and American colonization* (Boston, 1873).

SAINT-ÉTIENNE DE LA TOUR, CLAUDE DE [the family name may well have been **Turgis**], fur-trader and prominent colonist in Acadia, father of CHARLES DE SAINT-ÉTIENNE de La Tour; b. *c.* 1570 in the province of Champagne, France; d. after 1636.

Claude de La Tour saw service as a ship's captain in the religious wars during which he suffered heavy financial loss. In 1609 he accepted an invitation from JEAN DE BIENCOURT de Poutrincourt to come to Acadia to assist him in forming a permanent colony at Port-Royal (now Annapolis Royal, N.S.), that settlement having been abandoned two years before. He sailed from Dieppe with Poutrincourt on 25 Feb. 1610 and after a passage of several months the party arrived at Port-Royal. Here Claude assisted in superintending the construction of buildings and the tilling of the soil, and he learned the various phases of the fur trade. With the destruction of Port-Royal by Samuel ARGALL in 1613, he appears to have turned his attention to fur-trading activities in the Penobscot area and there in the course of time built Fort Pentagouet, a combined fortified trading post and fishing station. This post, termed the first permanent settlement in New England, proved to be a highly profitable outlet for the fur trade.

About 1626, Claude de La Tour was driven from Fort Pentagouet by the Plymouth colony. He then returned to France to sell some of his lands in Champagne, and he also presented a request on behalf of his son Charles, acting governor of Acadia, for a commission and supplies. He was then assigned by the Compagnie de la Nouvelle-France to a supply ship being sent, apparently under the command of Father Philibert NOYROT, to Charles's post at Cap de Sable in the spring of 1628. This vessel and others on their way to Quebec, under the charge of Claude ROQUEMONT, were captured by an English squadron led by Sir DAVID KIRKE. Claude de La Tour was made prisoner and taken to England.

He was presented at court and there met many relatives and friends. He was evidently an adaptable man and it would appear that he felt his prospects to be better in England. At that time the English controlled the whole of Acadia with the exception of Charles de La Tour's post at Cap de Sable, and he may well have felt the country was lost forever to his homeland. What is more, the French government had shown an almost complete lack of interest in Acadia for many years, and his son's position in that province was both irregular and uncertain. The English considered Claude to be a great prize, for he apparently exaggerated his importance in Acadia, and his extensive knowledge of the country could prove of value. Claude in his turn was both clever and ambitious, and apparently never one to fret about

Saint-Étienne de La Tour

seemingly lost causes, so that he was quickly won over by the English. He became friendly with one of the ladies-in-waiting to Queen Henrietta Maria and he married her. One historian recounts that this lady was a relative of Sir WILLIAM ALEXANDER the elder, who had been granted Acadia by King James. Whether this fact had any influence on Claude's choice of a wife is not known, but it did prove very helpful.

Alexander had already evolved an ambitious scheme for colonizing Acadia whereby large tracts of land and the title of "Baronet of Nova Scotia" would be offered to men willing to participate in the project. Claude de La Tour appears to have impressed Alexander with his knowledge of Acadia, and he evidently expressed a willingness to join in the colonization project.

Details concerning his life during this period are lacking, but it would appear that he volunteered to accompany Sir WILLIAM ALEXANDER the younger as his assistant on an expedition that left for Acadia in the spring of 1629. He is believed to have spent most of that summer familiarizing the Scots with the country and gathering a cargo of furs in the Bay of Fundy area. On 6 October he apparently signed the rough draft of an accord with the younger Alexander at Charles Fort. In any case, he returned to England and on 30 November was made a baronet of Nova Scotia in recognition of his valuable assistance in exploring the country. It would seem that he then even promised to put the Alexander interests in possession of the whole of Acadia by persuading his son to surrender his fort at Cap de Sable and to accept English allegiance. On 12 May 1630, and unknown to Charles de La Tour, he accepted a baronetcy for his son. The titles brought with them a huge grant of land in the southern part of Nova Scotia.

Claude de La Tour and his wife sailed for Acadia with a group of colonists and two English men-of-war in May 1630. When the vessels dropped anchor off Cap de Sable, Claude hastened to inform his son of all that had happened, and of the titles and honours awaiting him from the English king. Charles refused to make good his father's promises and announced his firm intention of maintaining his French allegiance. Claude, having vowed to win over his son, tried entreaties, then threats, but Charles resisted all such efforts. At last the father declared he would be obliged to treat his son as an enemy. He rounded up a mixed force of soldiers and sailors from the two warships and attacked the fort at Cap de Sable. The ensuing battle between father and son lasted two days and a night and has no parallel in the history of the New World. This strange fight ended with the withdrawal of the English force in the face of the stout resistance put up by Charles.

Having cast his lot, Claude could do no more than accompany the English to Port-Royal. Then, with an appealing nobility, he informed his wife that since his prospects now seemed so bleak, she was free to return to England. This she refused to do, choosing to remain and share her husband's lot. It is here that we might expect Claude, stripped of both his reputation and his resources, to fade from the pages of history, but such was not the case. He wrote his son asking to be allowed to return to Cap de Sable and to French allegiance. On the advice of representatives of the Compagnie de la Nouvelle-France who had arrived with supplies and a governor's commission for him, Charles finally agreed to the request. Now wise to the ways of Claude, however, Charles insisted he live with his wife in a house outside the fort and not enter the post itself.

When Claude arrived at Cap de Sable he brought news that the garrison at Port-Royal had been strengthened and that a force would be sent to take the post at Cap de Sable, bringing the whole of Acadia under English control. Such an attack did not materialize and may well have been simply a product of Claude's fertile mind.

That he was an able man and valued as a fur-trader is borne out by the fact that when the Compagnie de la Nouvelle-France decided the next year to build a new post at the Saint John, the richest area for furs in all Acadia, it was resolved that Claude would be given the command of the new post. However, he remained at Cap de Sable and Jean-Daniel Chaline received the appointment instead.

After Fort Pentagouet was recaptured from the English, it and a grant of land were given Claude de La Tour by the French Crown "in recognition of the recent service he has rendered the king." The exact nature of that service is not known. It is unlikely, however, that Claude moved to Fort Pentagouet, for he seems to have remained in quiet retirement at Cap de Sable after 1631. It was there that NICOLAS DENYS, another of the prominent figures in the Acadia of those days, found him living in 1635. He reports him to have been the picture of domestic bliss, a genial host who waxed enthusiastic about his extensive garden. He died sometime after 1636, a turn-coat, an opportunist, a rogue perhaps, but one who lends colour to the early history of Acadia.

GEORGE MACBEATH

According to the researches of M. Robert Le Blant ("Du nouveau sur les La Tour," SGCF

Saint-François

Mémoires, XI (1960), 21–23), Claude de La Tour usually signed his name "de Saint-Étienne" but two notarial acts call him "Turgis, dit Saint-Étienne, écuyer, sieur de La Tour" and "Claude Turgis, dit Saint-Étienne et de La Tour." It would seem therefore that the family name of the La Tours was "Turgis" and that the family was of the lesser nobility.

On the documentary sources see PAC *Report, 1883; 1894; 1912,* 18, 23–24. Champlain, *Works* (Biggar), V, VI. *Coll. de manuscrits relatifs à la Nouv.-France,* I, 439; II, 351–80. Denys, *Description and natural history* (Ganong). *Royal letters, charters, and tracts* (Laing). Couillard Després, *Saint-Étienne de La Tour.* Huguet, *Poutrincourt.* Insh, *Scottish colonial schemes.* McGrail, *Alexander.* G. A. Wheeler, "Fort Pentagoet and the French occupation of Castine," Maine Hist. Soc. *Coll. and Proc.,* 2d ser., IV (1893), 113–23. *See also* bibliography for CHARLES DE SAINT-ÉTIENNE de La Tour.

SAINT-FRANÇOIS, SIEUR. *See* BOURDON, JEAN

SAINT-FRANÇOIS, JEAN CREVIER DE. *See* CREVIER

SAINT-GERMAIN, GUILLAUME AUDOUART *dit. See* AUDOUART

SAINT-JUST. *See* BIENCOURT, CHARLES DE and JEAN DE

SAINT-LUSSON, SIMON-FRANÇOIS DAUMONT DE. *See* DAUMONT

SAINT-MARTIN, MARTIN BOUTET DE. *See* BOUTET

SAINT-MAURICE, JEAN-BAPTISTE DUBOIS DE. *See* DUBOIS

SAINT-PAUL, PIERRE LAMOTTE DE. *See* LAMOTTE

SAINT-PÈRE, JEAN DE, clerk of court, notary, and syndic; b. at Dormelles in Gâtinois (France) c. 1618; son of Étienne de Saint-Père and of Étiennette Julian, he belonged to a respected family whose arms were "azure, three fusils or, placed fessways in pale"; d. at Montreal in 1657.

Saint-Père came to Montreal, probably in 1643, in order, as he himself declared, "to contribute to the conversion of the Indians," and from January 1648 he was the first clerk of court and the first notary at Ville-Marie (Montreal). He exercised this dual function from January 1648 to July 1651 and from April 1655 until his death. In 1651 he was the syndic of the Communauté des Habitants of Ville-Marie, and on 29 June 1654 he was elected "receiver of alms for the construction of the proposed church at Montreal." These different responsibilities entrusted to him by his fellow-citizens show their esteem for Jean de Saint-Père. M. de Maisonneuve displayed no less confidence and esteem when, at the signing of Saint-Père's marriage contract on 18 Sept. 1651, he made him a generous grant of land "to reward him for his good and faithful services, rendered over a period of eight years."

This man "who had as solid a piety, as alert a mind, and in general . . . as excellent a judgment as have ever been known here [at Montreal]" met with a tragic end on 25 Oct. 1657. For a short time there had been peace between the French and the Iroquois. A group of Oneidas appeared on the land of Nicolas Godé, who, together with his son-in-law Jean de Saint-Père and their servant Jacques Noël, was busy building a house. The Frenchmen received the visitors most courteously, and even gave them a meal. The Iroquois, who had come under the guise of peace and friendship but with treacherous intent, waited until their hosts had climbed back again onto the roof and were within range of their arquebuses; they then "brought them down like sparrows." To complete their work, the Oneidas scalped Godé and Noël, but cut off Saint-Père's head and carried it off "in order to have his fine growth of hair."

A curious story, reported by Dollier* de Casson, Marguerite BOURGEOYS and Vachon* de Belmont, is connected with this episode. While the Iroquois were fleeing with their wretched trophy, Saint-Père's head began to speak—in very good Iroquois, although during his life Saint-Père had always been ignorant of that language—reproaching them for their faithlessness: "You kill us, you inflict endless cruelties on us, you want to annihilate the French, you will not succeed, they will one day be your masters and you will obey them. . . ." It was useless for the Iroquois to put the head some distance away, to cover it or to bury it, the avenging voice continued to make itself heard. They finally got rid of the skull, but since they retained the hair the Iroquois could not help but hear the voice of Saint-Père coming from the place where they kept the scalp.

These strange happenings, affirms Dollier de Casson, were recounted by the Iroquois themselves to reliable persons; Sister Bourgeoys asserts in addition that M. Cuillerier*, at that time a prisoner of the Iroquois, testified to the truth of this occurrence.

On 25 September 1651, at Montreal, Jean de Saint-Père had married Mathurine Godé, by whom he had two children. He was buried on 25 Oct. 1657, in the same grave as his two unfortunate companions.

ANDRÉ VACHON

AJM, Greffe de Lambert Closse, 1651–56; Greffe de Jean de Saint-Père, 1648–51, 1655–57. *Premier registre de l'église Notre-Dame De Montréal* (Montréal, 1961). É.-Z. Massicotte, "Jean de Saint-Père," *BRH*, XXI (1915), 112–115; "Les trois premiers tabellions de Montréal." *RSCT*, 3d ser., IX (1915), sect.I, 190f. J.-E. Roy, *Histoire du notariat*, I, 64–66.

The account of Saint-Père's death is found in the following sources: Dollier de Casson, *Histoire du Montréal*, 122f. "Écrits autographes de Soeur Bourgeoys," in Faillon, *Histoire de la colonie française*, II, 365, n. 2. *JJ* (Laverdière et Casgrain), 224. [François Vachon] de Belmont, "Histoire du Canada," Lit. and Hist. Soc. of Québec *Trans*., XVIII (1886), 29.

SAINT-SACREMENT, MARGUERITE BOURGEOYS *dite* **DU.** *See* BOURGEOYS

SAINT-SAUVEUR, ABBÉ DE. *See* LE SUEUR, JEAN

SAKUMOW SAGMA. *See* SEGIPT

SALIGNAC DE LA MOTHE-FÉNELON, FRANÇOIS DE, priest, Sulpician, missionary; b. 1641 at the Château de Fénelon in Périgord (France); d. 1679 in France.

He was a half-brother of the famous archbishop of Cambrai, who was ten years his junior. Nothing is known of his early years, of his education, or of his studies. We do know however that in 1666 he was so eager to devote himself to the missions in New France that he obtained permission to leave after spending only 15 months in the seminary in Paris. He set sail 30 Jan. 1667 and arrived at Quebec on 27 June. Bishop Laval* ordained him priest 11 June 1668.

At this period those Iroquois who had settled down in the Kenté (Quinte) peninsula on Lake Ontario, came to Montreal to ask the superior of the seminary for missionaries. M. de Fénelon and M. Trouvé* made known their desire to accept the invitation. The superior, M. de Queylus [*see* THUBIÈRES] agreed to this and sent them both to Quebec to acquire the necessary civil and religious authorizations. They obtained from Governor RÉMY de Courcelle a grant of land on which to establish their mission and from Bishop Laval they received a warm letter of recommendation. On 28 Oct. 1668 they reached the village of Kenté. They spent the winter there.

In the spring M. de Fénelon went down to Montreal and Quebec by canoe "to seek payment for the Indians who were feeding them." He brought back with him his cousin, M. Lascaris* d'Urfé. Instead of spending the winter of 1669 with his two companions, he went to teach the Indians of Gandaseteiagon in their village located on Lake Ontario near the present Port Hope.

It was not to be expected that these missionaries would themselves provide a detailed account of their heroic enterprise. In 1669, when Bishop Laval wanted to publish the story of their exploits in the *Jesuit Relations*, M. de Fénelon made him this reply: "The greatest favour that you can grant us is not to have us mentioned at all." Nevertheless, in 1672 M. Dollier* de Casson appended to his *Histoire du Montréal* a long letter written by M. Trouvé, which is a résumé of the history of the Kenté mission. One can glimpse in it the great daring and stamina which characterized these athletic young missionaries who propelled their birch-bark canoes through rapids and ice floes as they travelled from Lake Ontario to Montreal and Quebec, wintering in the woods where at times they got lost, eating *sagamité* and pumpkin, sharing the wretchedness of the Indians, and succeeding only in baptizing children or a few adults on the point of death.

Fortunately there was interest in the Kenté mission in Paris, and it was decided to begin building there and to send out some animals, which was done in the course of the following decade.

At Montreal there was concern about the education of Indian children. It was thought necessary to move them away from the town, and consideration was given, as a site for settling them, to three islands in Lac Saint-Louis (above Lachine) which were given the name Gentilly. M. de Fénelon was summoned there, as he already had experience of Indian life. He arranged to have these islands granted to him in due form. On that occasion Governor BUADE de Frontenac wrote, 9 Jan. 1673: "The great zeal that Sieur Abbé de Fénelon has exhibited for several years in the propagation of Christianity in this colony, and the devotion that he has displayed in His Majesty's service, constrain us to seek every kind of means of recognizing them and of pressing him to keep up the zeal he has shown up to the present; a zeal whose ardour has prompted him to abandon all the substantial establishments that his birth and merit might have entitled him to expect in France, in order to devote himself entirely to the conversion and education of the Indians." On the shores of the island adjacent to the lake the seminary of Montreal erected the necessary buildings, in the hope of attracting some new settlers to this part of the island. Soon M. d'Urfé came to rejoin his colleague there.

Salignac de La Mothe-Fénelon

In 1674 we find M. de Fénelon at Montreal again. By virtue of his personal qualities and his name he was in the good graces of the governors of Quebec and Montreal, Frontenac and PERROT. But this situation was soon to change.

François-Marie Perrot, who had married TALON's niece and whom M. de Bretonvilliers, superior of the seminary of Saint-Sulpice in Paris, had appointed governor of Montreal at the request of the intendant, was not the personage one might have hoped for. He had come to Canada only to make his fortune and had soon revealed himself in his true light: grasping, arrogant, having no respect for the seigneurs, and taking improper advantage of his office; he had opened, on the island that bears his name, a trading agency, whose management he entrusted to his clerk, Antoine de LA FRENAYE de Brucy, and, scorning the regulations, he authorized frequent leaves for the *coureurs de bois*. Frontenac for his part, no less eager for gain, had used *corvée* labour to construct Fort Cataracoui (Frontenac), in order to protect and group the Indians; he made use of the fort, however, to carry on trade in pelts through the intermediary of his liegeman, Robert CAVELIER de La Salle, to whom he had given the post. Now it happened that two outlawed *coureurs de bois* came to Montreal and sought seclusion in the home of M. de Carion, a confidant of Perrot's. The judge of Montreal, CHARLES D'AILLEBOUST, wanted to seize them. Perrot resisted this. The judge wrote to Frontenac, who dispatched BIZARD. The latter was coolly received by Perrot, although it must be said that Bizard had behaved in very provocative fashion and had done so on Frontenac's orders. The governor gave Perrot notice to appear before him at Quebec and wrote to M. de Fénelon, their mutual friend, asking him to act as his intermediary. Fénelon prevailed upon Perrot and they both went down to Quebec. Upon their arrival Frontenac imprisoned Perrot, and Fénelon, in attempting to intercede for him, annoyed the governor and lost his friendship. Fénelon had realized, moreover, that Frontenac had taken advantage of his friendship and had deceived him.

On his return to Montreal, the abbé thought it discreet, in view of probable future difficulties, to turn over to the seminary his property holdings on the Îles Gentilly, where the seminary had, after all, met all the expenses. Fénelon, who was responsible for delivering the sermon at Easter high mass, preached to all the citizens of Montreal. In the second part of his sermon, dealing with the duties of those who are set in authority, he alluded to certain abuses, especially to burdensome *corvées*, and so on. La Salle created an uproar at that point; he stood up and drew the attention of the hearers to what the preacher was saying. The general opinion was that in his criticisms the abbé had been alluding to Governor Frontenac.

After mass all M. de Fénelon's colleagues condemned his sermon. The superior went to make his apologies to the local commandant, M. de LANOUGUÈRE, and wrote to the governor himself to dissociate the Society from the blunder committed by one of its members. Frontenac took a very high and mighty attitude and requested the superior to expel M. de Fénelon from the Society. (It should be pointed out that Sulpicians do not take any vow of obedience.) M. de Fénelon went away, however, of his own accord and carried on his ministry at Lachine.

In addition to his sermon on 25 March 1674, the abbé had committed another indiscretion: that of having the citizens of Montreal sign a petition protesting against the arbitrary imprisonment of Perrot at Quebec. Hence Frontenac ordered him to appear before him. M. de Fénelon went to Quebec and challenged the right of the Conseil Souverain to judge him. These scions of ancient families, proud of their noble birth, did not fear to speak bluntly before their peers. Furthermore, the suit that was being brought against Abbé Fénelon was contrary to both the ecclesiastical and the civil laws of the kingdom. Despite the intervention of Lascaris d'Urfé, a relative of the abbé and a friend of Frontenac, matters became so unpleasant that the Conseil Souverain decided to refer the litigation to the king himself. M. d'Urfé, for his part, sent off a conclusive report to the minister, Colbert.

Perrot and Fénelon went to France in 1674. Perrot was shut up in the Bastille for some months and then sent back to his governor's duties at Montreal. Frontenac was very severely reprimanded by the king for his attitude towards M. de Fénelon. It was solely to safeguard the governor's authority that the king refrained from publicly rebuking him. As a result of this episode, the members of the Conseil Souverain were thenceforth appointed by the king.

As for M. de Fénelon, forbidden by the king to remain in Canada, denounced by the seminary of Paris just as he had been by that of Montreal, he withdrew from the Society of Saint-Sulpice.

On 7 May 1675 M. de Bretonvilliers said to the priests of Montreal: "I urge you all to profit from the example of M. de Fénelon. By dint of too much intriguing in society and interfering in what did not concern him, he has marred all his undertakings and damaged those of his friends while trying to serve them. In matters of this sort, which are concerned only with private differences, neutrality will always be the desirable course."

Where did M. de Fénelon spend his retirement? Historians have so far been unable to find out. Was it with his uncle, the bishop of Sarlat, or, more likely, on the estate of his family in Dordogne? We know only that he died in 1679 at the age of 38.

It is a matter of regret that the career of this fearless missionary was so soon broken off. Not even a trace remains of the mission he founded at Kenté. Only his name lingers on, at Fenelon Falls on the Trent River.

OLIVIER MAURAULT

Ivanhoë Caron, "Inventaire de documents," *APQ Rapport*, *1939–40*, 221–25. Correspondance de Frontenac (1672–82), *APQ Rapport*, *1926–27*, 67–73, 81. Dollier de Casson, *Histoire du Montréal*. *Jug. et délib*. "Le proces de l'abbé de Fénelon devant le Conseil souverain de la Nouvelle-France en 1674," *APQ Rapport*, *1921–22*, 124–88.

"Le différend entre M. de Frontenac et l'abbé de Fénelon," *BRH*, XLII (1936), 614–17. Eccles, *Frontenac*. Faillon, *Histoire de la colonie française*, III. Aegidius Fauteux, "Les surprises de la généalogie," *BRH*, LI (1945), 391–94. Lionel Groulx, "Frontenac vs l'abbé de Fénelon: une tragi-comédie judiciaire," *RHAF*, XII (1958–59), 358–71.

SANFORD, ESBON (Ezbon Sandford), HBC captain; b. 25 Jan. 1645/46 at Portsmouth R.I.; d. 6 Oct. 1682 of unknown causes in the Port Nelson area of Hudson Bay.

He was the son of President John Sanford of Rhode Island by a second marriage; his mother, Bridget Hutchinson—who was a daughter of Anne Hutchinson, the famous religious disturber in Massachusetts—later married William Phillips, whose own daughter by a previous marriage, Phoebe, became the wife of Capt. Zachariah GILLAM in 1659.

Esbon Sanford entered the service of the HBC in 1672, undoubtedly through his connection with Capt. Gillam. That year he sailed for James Bay as mate of the *Messenger* dogger (Capt. Robert Morris) and wintered there. In the summer of 1674, he returned to James Bay, this time as mate to his kinsman, Zachariah Gillam, captain of the *Prince Rupert*.

Sanford must have left the HBC some time afterwards, for he is not mentioned again until 1681. In January of that year, when the plans for the establishment of Port Nelson were being prepared, the HBC committee offered him employment. But it was only after his "extraordinary demands" had been cut down that he was engaged as captain of the *Albemarle* and deputy to Governor John BRIDGAR. Sanford sailed a few months later, in the summer of 1682, arriving in the Port Nelson area on 18 September. He died there on 6 October and accordingly took little or no part in the intrigues brought about by the presence of the interloper, Benjamin Gillam*, his step-sister's son. Because of his kinship with Gillam, however, he was suspected of having been concerned with the venture, and the committee, before they learned of his death, cancelled his instructions, recalled him to England, and sent orders to Boston for his arrest, if he should come there.

Sanford married before 1674. On 6 August of that year he made a will in favour of his wife Sarah, signing himself "of Ratcliffe, Stepney parish, mariner." In December 1683, the HBC ordered that his wages be paid to his widow, and added £3 10s. for charity as he had died in the Company's service. Sanford's mother, Bridget Hutchinson Phillips, in her will dated 20 Sept. 1696, left a legacy to his daughter "in England."

G. ANDREWS MORIARTY

For the genealogy of the Sanfords and Gillams see: James N. Arnold, *Vital records of Rhode Island, 1636–1850, first series: births, marriages, and deaths* (20v., Providence, 1891). J. O. Austin, *The genealogical dictionary of Rhode Island* (Albany, N.Y., 1887), 171–72. G. A. Moriarty, "Captains Gillam and Sanford of the Hudson's Bay Company," *Genealogists' Mag.*, X (1947–50), 568–71; "President John Sanford and his family," *N. Eng. Hist. and Geneal. Register*, CIII (1949), 212–13. Sybil Noyes et al., *Genealogical dictionary of Maine and New Hampshire* (Portland, Me., 1928–39), pt.III, 262; pt.V, 607. *Records of the town of Portsmouth, R.I.*, ed. Clarence. Brigham (Providence, R.I., 1901).

For his career with the HBC *see*: HBRS, VIII, IX (Rich); XI (Rich and Johnson); XXI (Rich).

SARCEL DE (Du) PRÉVERT, JEAN, merchant of Saint-Malo; d. 22 April 1622 at Saint-Malo.

He had sailed up and down the coasts of New France in the early years of the 17th century, if not before. Prévert was in partnership with some Saint-Malo merchants; their ship was trading at the Île d'Orléans when, in 1600, some of their goods were carried off by the men serving under PIERRE CHAUVIN DE TONNETUIT. By a decree of the Conseil Privé on 21 Nov. 1601, Chauvin was ordered to compensate the merchants, and he complied on 23 Feb. 1602.

Prévert was probably one of those who gave Henri IV information about the Acadian region before Pierre DU GUA de Monts obtained his first commission. He claimed that he possessed a trading licence that was still valid on 13 March 1603, the date on which a captain from Saint-Malo was authorized to join him and FRANÇOIS

Saurel

GRAVÉ Du Pont for the explorations that were contemplated. Prévert reconnoitred the Acadian coasts as far as the Saint John River, and brought back to CHAMPLAIN specimens taken from two mines. He seems to have played a part in the decision taken by Du Gua to establish settlements towards the south.

Prévert joined the first company of de Monts 19 Feb. 1604 and withdrew from it in 1607. On 17 January of this latter year, he had obtained a loan with the intention of fur-trading on his own account. The following year Sarcel de Prévert and his former partners fitted out two ships for Canseau (Canso) and Percé. But they were indicted by de Monts before the Admiralty of Rouen and came to terms with him on 20 December. The last thing we know of Prévert's activity is that on 2 March 1609 he sold 200 beaver skins in advance to a Paris merchant.

In 1591 he had married Françoise Richomme at Saint-Malo. He was buried 22 April 1622 in that same city.

IN COLLABORATION

AN, V^6, 5, pièce 237; Minutier, XV et XXXV (minutes de Cuvilier et Dournel). ASM, Tabellionage de Rouen. Champlain, *Œuvres* (Laverdière) and *Works* (Biggar). Biggar, *Early trading companies*. Paul Paris-Jalobert, *Anciens registres paroissiaux de Bretagne (baptêmes–mariages–sépultures)* (11v.), IX (Saint-Malo, 1898–1914), no 1, 375.

SAUREL, PIERRE DE, captain of the Carignan-Salières regiment, seigneur; b. 1628 at Notre-Dame de Grenoble, son of Mathieu de Saurel and Jeanne de Giraud; d. 1682 at Montreal.

We know nothing of his career before he came to Canada. But he seems to have entered the army quite young, since in 1665 he was a captain in the Carignan-Salières regiment. On 14 May of that year, at La Rochelle, TALON, attending a review of the troops before they left for Canada, declared himself very satisfied with the bearing of the soldiers and particularly those of M. de Saurel; he advised the king to give the latter 15 or 20 pistoles, because his company "appeared the best in everyone's opinion." After a stormy crossing, on the *Paix*, Saurel reached Quebec with four companies about 18 August, the day after the arrival of the colonel of the regiment, M. de Salières [Chastelard*], and four other companies on the *Aigle d'Or*.

On 25 August he was sent with his men by PROUVILLE de Tracy to build a fort on the ruins of the one set up by HUAULT de Montmagny in 1642, at the mouth of the River of the Iroquois (Richelieu), the site of what is now the city of Sorel.

On 10 Nov. 1665, Father François DU PERON died at the nearby fort at Chambly; Saurel received the body "at the water's edge with all his soldiers under arms," and they guarded the corpse "all the night, with lighted tapers around him."

Saurel spent the winter of 1665–66 in his fort. On 27 July 1666, at Quebec, he assumed command of an expedition of 200 Frenchmen and some 100 Indians against a village of Mohawks who had killed or taken prisoner 7 Frenchmen. When he was nearly there, he met Indian ambassadors, including the FLEMISH BASTARD, who were bringing back two of the prisoners and coming "to offer all possible satisfaction for the murder of those who had been slain, and fresh guarantees of peace."

On 20 August, Saurel, together with the Indian chief, was back at Quebec. On 14 September he took part in Tracy's expedition against the Mohawk villages, and led the rearguard with Capt. Berthier*.

He took advantage of the disbanding of the regiment in 1668 to marry Catherine, daughter of CHARLES LEGARDEUR de Tilly and Geneviève Juchereau de Maur, on 10 October at Quebec. He then settled on the Sorel estate, which was officially granted to him as a seigneury in 1672. Talon had a high opinion of him, although in about 1673 he was disturbed by his ambition: he had "great designs and great plans, which make me fear in him, a Piedmontese, too great an establishment in a country so far removed from the primary authority."

He was one of the settlers consulted by BUADE de Frontenac in 1678 about the sale of spirits to the Indians. He approved of this traffic, for according to him the Indians would turn to the Dutch if the French defaulted. He was moreover actively engaged in fur-trading. In 1681, according to Frontenac, he had "5 canoes and 10 men in the woods carrying on the fur trade." He was also accused the same year, before the Conseil Souverain, of having allowed "many things in [his] house [. . .] in mockery of the king's orders and in defiance of the law."

In the summer of 1682, he entered into partnership with Aubert* de La Chesnaye, Radisson*, CHOUART Des Groseilliers, and several others for an expedition to Hudson Bay. He seems to have gone with them. On his return, he attended an assembly at Quebec, on 10 October, to discuss the Iroquois question. He died at Montreal, where his business had taken him, on 26 Nov. 1682; he left no descendants. His wife encountered difficulties over his estate, and had to sell the seigneury by auction in 1713. It was bought by Claude de Ramezay*.

JEAN-GUY PELLETIER

AJQ, Greffe de Romain Becquet, 9 oct. 1668. APQ, Philippe Sainte-Marie, "Esquisse de l'histoire de Saurel sous la domination française et sous la domination anglaise" (manuscript). Correspondance de Frontenac (1672–82), APQ *Rapport, 1926–27*, 123. Correspondance de Talon, APQ *Rapport, 1930–31*, 24, 47, 132, 174. *Découvertes et établissements des Français* (Margry), I, 405. *Édits ord.*, II, 103. *JR* (Thwaites). *JJ* (Laverdière et Casgrain). *Jug. et délib.*, I; II; IV; VI. Perrot, *Memoir*, in *Indian tribes* (Blair), I, 201. Recensement de 1681. P.-G. Roy, *Inv. concessions*, II, 167–68.

BRH, I (1895), 89; VI (1900), 219; XII (1906), 375; XV (1909), 58; XVII (1911), 194; XXVII (1921), 28–29; XXX (1924), 249–52; XLVI (1940), 115, 240. Charlevoix, *Histoire*. Azarie Couillard Després, *Histoire de Sorel de ses origines à nos jours* (Montréal, 1926); "Les origines de la seigneurie de Saurel: M. Pierre de Saurel, seigneur de Saurel, et ses premiers censitaires," *RSCT*, 3d ser., XVII (1923), sect.I, 183–91. Faillon, *Histoire de la colonie française*, III, 222. Germain Lesage, "L'arrivée du régiment de Carignan," *Revue de l'Université d'Ottawa*, XXXV (1965), 11–34. É.-Z. Massicotte, "Le tribunal seigneurial de Sorel et autres," *BRH*, L (1944), 13–14. Olivier Maurault, "A propos d'une visite princière," *Cahiers des Dix*, IV (1939), 119–20. Nute, *Caesars of the wilderness*, 186. Roy et Malchelosse, *Le régiment de Carignan*. Pierre Saint Olive, *Les Dauphinois au Canada: Essai de catalogue des Dauphinois qui ont pris part à l'établissement du Régime français au Canada, suivi d'une étude sur un Dauphinois canadien: Antoine Pécody de Contrecœur* (Paris, 1936). Sulte, *Mélanges historiques* (Malchelosse), VIII.

SAVIGNON, Huron youth who accompanied CHAMPLAIN to France in 1610.

Returning from the Iroquois country in June 1610, Champlain met a party of Hurons under Outchetaguin and Algonkins under IROQUET at the mouth of the River of the Iroquois (Richelieu). At their request he agreed to take Savignon, a young Huron, to France in return for a young French lad [possibly Étienne BRÛLÉ] whom he had persuaded Iroquet and his people to take to winter in their country to learn the language, observe the geography and the minerals, and to acquaint himself with the various tribes. Savignon, in return, was to report to his people on his observations in France. In this way Champlain hoped to build up a body of interpreters who would act as agents for the French in Indian territory.

Savignon returned to the St. Lawrence with Champlain in 1611 and was sent ahead from the Rapids (Lachine) to hasten the arrival of the Hurons and Algonkins who were expected; but because of a faulty canoe he was forced to return after passing the Lac des Deux-Montagnes. On the return trip he narrowly escaped death off "l'isle aux herons," where his canoe became engulfed in the whirling waters. Two companions, Louis, a young Frenchman in the service of DU GUA de Monts, and Outetoucos, a Montagnais chief, were lost. It is said that this incident gave the St. Louis Rapids its name.

Shortly after, the Hurons arrived with Chief Outchetaguin and Iroquet, and Tregouaroti, Savignon's brother. They were welcomed with a salvo of arquebus and musket shots, and small cannon, which frightened many who had never seen a European. Savignon gave a good account of his treatment in France, and Champlain was equally pleased with the report of the French lad [Brûlé?] who had come down with Iroquet. Savignon then returned to his own country parting from Champlain with regret. Champlain, however, confessed his relief at being free of the responsibility for him.

ELSIE MCLEOD JURY

Champlain, *Works* (Biggar), *passim*.

SAVONNIÈRES DE LA TROCHE, MARIE DE, *dite* **Marie de Saint-Joseph,** Ursuline nun, first known as **Marie de Saint-Bernard**; b. 7 Sept. 1616 at the Château de Saint-Germain in Anjou; d. 4 April 1652 at Quebec.

Her father, Simon de Savonnières de La Troche, of Saint-Germain, Les Hayes, and elsewhere, and her mother, Jeanne Raoul, were both noted for their nobility and integrity. From her childhood, Marie de Savonnières was much attracted to the pious life. She joined the Ursulines of Tours at the age of 14 and made her profession under the name of Marie de Saint-Bernard. Towards 1636, she heard about Canada, and her interest in distant missions was aroused. Three years later, she volunteered to accompany Marie de l'Incarnation [*see* GUYART] to Canada. Her heart-broken parents did not conceal their opposition to her departure. The young Ursuline then appealed to St. Joseph to change her family's attitude. To show her gratitude and to discharge a vow she had made, Mother Marie de Saint-Bernard assumed the name Marie de Saint-Joseph. She sailed for New France in 1639. On her arrival in the colony, she devoted herself to the study of the Huron and Algonkin languages. Contemporaries who knew her describe her as being extremely good-humoured, keen of mind, and well informed. As a result, she soon won the confidence of the Indians, who addressed her as their mother.

The last four years of her life were a continuous martyrdom which she endured in heroic fashion. After the destruction of the convent by fire (1650), her parents urged her to return to Tours, but she refused, wanting to offer her suffering for the conversion of the Indians. The community had received shelter in the house of Madame CHAUVIGNY de La Peltrie, and there the sick nun was made very uncomfortable by the crowded quarters, the noise, the smoke, and the smell of eels. She was soon suffering not only from tuberculosis but also from dropsy and gangrene. Mother Marie de Saint-Joseph died 4 April 1652, regretted by all, and especially by the Hurons who were inconsolable at the loss of so saintly and lovable a person. She was buried the following day in the convent garden. According to contemporary reports, it was the most impressive funeral procession ever witnessed in the colony. The history of the convent records several miraculous occurrences attributed to Mother Marie de Saint-Joseph's collaboration. To honour her companion and favourite nun, Marie de l'Incarnation composed an obituary in the form of a booklet that is of great interest despite its somewhat conventual tone. This document, most of which was incorporated into the *Relation* for 1652, provides ample proof that Mother Marie de Saint-Joseph was an exceptional woman and one of the glories of the Church in Canada.

MARIE-EMMANUEL CHABOT, O.S.U.

Marie Guyart de l'Incarnation, *Écrits* (Jamet). *JR* (Thwaites), XXXVIII, 79–91, 143. *Les Ursulines de Québec*, I.

SECOUDON (Secondon, Chkoudun), sagamo or chieftain of all the Saint John River Indians when CHAMPLAIN and DU GUA de Monts discovered the river in 1604; d. before 1616.

He was referred to as an Etchemin chief but the modern designation for the Saint John River Indians is Malecite. His headquarters at that time was a village called Ouygoudy (or Menagoueche according to Ganong) on the west side of what is now Saint John harbour. LESCARBOT, describing this village, which he visited in 1607, said it was enclosed by a strong stockade with many lodges inside, one of which was as large as a market hall with numerous families dwelling in it.

In 1605 Secoudon guided Champlain to an outcropping of copper ore on La Baye des Mines (Minas Basin) and later assisted Champlain and his companions when their pinnace was wrecked. He also acted as a guide to the French on two voyages along the New England coast. In 1606 JEAN DE BIENCOURT de Poutrincourt found Secoudon and MESSAMOUET trading articles they had obtained from the French with the Indians of the Penobscot area.

At the time of Lescarbot's visit to Secoudon at Ouygoudy he had assembled a war-party including Indians from as far distant as Gaspé. They were preparing to join MEMBERTOU of Port-Royal renown in an attack on the Armouchiquois of New England.

Father BIARD was much impressed by Secoudon's apparent interest in French civilization and by the fact that in imitation of the French he had erected a cross in front of his lodge and wore a cross around his neck. He also attended religious worship making a great show of piety.

In 1616 Father Biard referred to Secoudon as already dead at that time.

W. AUSTIN SQUIRES

Champlain, *Works* (Biggar), I; Lescarbot, *History* (Grant), II; *JR* (Thwaites), I, III.

SEDGWICK, ROBERT, Puritan, merchant, soldier, and colonist; led the English conquest of Acadia in 1654; b. 1611 at Woburn, Bedfordshire, England, son of William Sedgwick and Elizabeth Howe; d. 24 May 1656.

Sedgwick's deep Puritan convictions led him to New England at the age of 24, after a brief mercantile career in London, where he was a member of one of the militia companies. He resided in Massachusetts from 1636 to 1653, held several political offices, helped build its militia, and became major-general of the colony in 1652. As a merchant he pioneered in the development of the New England fishery and invested in several local enterprises.

In 1653–54 Sedgwick visited England, then at war with the Dutch. Because New Haven had petitioned Cromwell to reduce her rival, New Netherland, Sedgwick was sent to New England to organize an expedition against the Dutch colony, but news of peace overtook him in Boston. Since his commission from Cromwell of 8 Feb. 1653/54, as general of the fleet and commander-in-chief of all the New England coast, authorized him to make reprisals against French commerce for attacks on English vessels by French privateers commissioned by princes Rupert and Charles, he resolved to use this power to secure the rich fur-trading and fishing resources of Acadia for New England and the Protectorate.

CHARLES DE SAINT-ÉTIENNE de La Tour controlled Acadia at this time, but his defences were weak. He had outlasted his rival, Charles de MENOU d'Aulnay, only to suffer attack by d'Aulnay's creditor, the La Rochelle merchant EMMANUEL LE BORGNE. Sedgwick left Boston on 4 July 1654 with 170 men in three ships and a ketch. In ten days he reached the Saint John River where he found La Tour in his fort. Three days later La Tour and 70 fighting men surrendered. On 31 July Sedgwick's expedition sailed to Port-Royal (now Annapolis Royal, N.S.). Sedgwick was ambushed but won and took the fort. He then sailed to Pentagouet on the Penobscot, which he took on 2 September. He plundered the forts of their goods to the value of about £10,000. Early in September he was back in Boston; the General Court of Massachusetts ordered a thanksgiving for 20 September. His son-in-law, Major John LEVERETT, was appointed military governor of Acadia and Sedwick left for England, taking La Tour with him.

Cromwell welcomed Sedgwick because possession of Acadia provided additional bargaining power in negotiating with France. The Protectorate agreed to recognize La Tour's title to Nova Scotia under his grant from Sir WILLIAM ALEXANDER, Earl of Stirling, if he would undertake to reimburse Sedgwick for the cost of the conquest, nearly £1,800. This led La Tour to sell his rights to Sir Thomas TEMPLE and Col. William CROWNE, who became proprietors of Nova Scotia for the next 14 years. Sedgwick was rewarded with command of an expedition to reinforce William Penn and Robert Venables against the Spanish in the West Indies. Ultimately Cromwell appointed him supreme military commander in Jamaica but Sedgwick died on 24 May 1656, shortly after receiving the commission.

WILLIAM I. ROBERTS, 3rd

For information on Sedgwick's conquest of Acadia see Bodleian Library, Rawlinson MSS, A16, f.52; A18, f.58. Mass. Hist. Soc., Gay Papers. Thomas Birch, *A collection of the state papers of John Thurloe, Esq., secretary to the Council of State and the two protectors Oliver and Richard Cromwell . . .* (7v., London, 1742). *Coll. de manuscrits relatifs à la Nouv.-France*, I, 145–49; II, 358–59. *Documentary history of Maine*, IV, VI, VII, X. Maine Hist. Soc. *Coll.*, 1st ser., V, 231. *Mémoires des commissaires*, I, 56; IV, 499; and *Memorials of the English and French commissaries*, I, 126, 525. PRO, *CSP, Col.*, 1574–1660.

For other aspects of Sedgwick's career, see: *Suffolk deeds*, I, 20, 45. Bernard Bailyn, *The New England merchants in the seventeenth century* (Cambridge, Mass., 1955). *DAB. DNB*, 1st Supp., III. Oliver A. Roberts, *History of the Military Company of the Massachusetts, now called the Ancient and Honorable Artillery Company of Massachusetts, 1637–1888* (4v., Boston, 1895–1901), I. Henry D. Sedgwick, "Robert Sedgwick," Col. Soc. Mass. *Pub.*, III (1895–97), 156–73.

SEGIPT (sometimes called **Sakumow Sagma**), sagamo or chief of the Micmacs near Port-Royal; fl. 1629–32.

In 1629 Segipt and his family were sent to England by Sir WILLIAM ALEXANDER the younger, on a ship returning to pick up supplies for the newly founded Scottish colony. Chosen by the Micmacs as "representative of the rest" to acknowledge the suzerainty of Charles I over New Scotland and to crave his protection against the French, he had no doubt been influenced by CLAUDE DE SAINT-ÉTIENNE de La Tour who had been persuaded to join the English and Scottish cause and who was returning at the same time to obtain the approval of Sir WILLIAM ALEXANDER, Earl of Stirling to an agreement whereby Claude would become a "baronet of Nova Scotia."

While Claude, who had spent the previous winter about the court, needed no special attention, Segipt with his wife and son, travelling as king, queen and prince of Canada, were treated with the utmost courtesy. In December 1629, Sir James Bragg, governor of Plymouth, was instructed by Charles I to give every assistance to the agent whom he had sent to conduct the "royal party" to court, where they arrived in February 1630.

From the correspondence of the period it appears that they evoked much curiosity. One correspondent accepted them as genuine representatives of the aborigines, come to do homage to King Charles. Another regarded their visit as a publicity stunt, staged by the Alexanders to help in the creation of Knight-Baronets. In any event little seems to have been gained by their visit. They returned quietly with the Anglo-Scottish expedition of 1630, which failed to obtain the transfer of CHARLES DE SAINT-ÉTIENNE de La Tour's allegiance and caused grave loss of face to his father Claude.

D. C. HARVEY

[Sir William Alexander], *The Earl of Stirling's register of royal letters, relative to the affairs of Scotland and Nova Scotia from 1615 to 1635*, ed. C. Rogers (2v., Edinburgh, 1885). *Royal letters, charters and tracts* (Layng). Insh, *Scottish colonial schemes*. McGrail, *Alexander*.

SERGEANT, HENRY, succeeded John NIXON in 1683 as governor of the James Bay posts of the HBC for three years; fl. 1683–89.

The appointment appears to have been made on the personal recommendation of James, Duke of York, governor of the HBC from January 1683 to February 1685. Sergeant sailed for Charlton Island in the *Diligence* (Capt. NEHEMIAH WALKER) accompanied by Mr John FRENCH, the first minister sent to the Bay by the HBC, and three women: his wife, her companion, Mrs. Maurice, and a maidservant, the first white women to winter in James Bay. The voyage out was eventful both for the capture of the interloping ship *Expectation* (Capt. Richard LUCAS) and "the ill and evill carridg" of Capt. Walker.

Despite orders to make Albany his headquarters, Sergeant spent the winter of 1683–84 at Moose. He seems to have been irascible and highhanded in dealing with both the Indians and his own men. The Company criticized him severely for his failure to raise the standard of trade, for his extravagant indents, and for a marked decrease in the trade. The London Committee in 1685 decided to appoint BRIDGAR to succeed Sergeant and so informed him that year. But the formal order never reached him because the *Happy Return* was sunk en route; even had the order arrived, it would have come too late, for on 9 July 1686 (o.s.) the chevalier de TROYES, after capturing the Moose and Rupert River posts, appeared at Albany and demanded that Sergeant surrender. He refused but proceeded to put up a lackadaisical defence permitting the French to erect a battery practically unopposed. The fort was bombarded on 15 and 16 July and was ceremoniously surrendered with all the military amenities on the 16th. Sergeant has been blamed for losing the posts to a surprise attack despite repeated warnings from England and a direct threat from Zacharie Jolliet of an impending French attack. However, Sergeant must have reasoned that an attack delivered overland was impossible—as it should have been had the Moose fort defenders been alert—and that therefore there was no danger until navigation opened.

Sergeant and many of the prisoners were sent in the overloaded *Colleton* to winter at Port Nelson; the remaining prisoners were sent overland to Quebec. In 1687 the company gave "positive order" to their Port Nelson governor, George GEYER, that "Mr. Sergeant with the whole parcell of women appertaining to him" should be sent home.

Back in England he defended his surrender of Albany (called by the French Sainte-Anne) by blaming it on the mutinous conduct and cowardice of his men; they in turn accused him of lethargy and disinterest. De Troyes, a less prejudiced observer, attributed French success to the general laxity of the English defence. The HBC sued Sergeant, whose attorney was Thomas Sergeant, for £20,000 in the Court of King's Bench, and tried to prove that he had "lost his Fort either by neglect or cowardice." The case dragged on through postponement and arbitration until 1689 when the suit was dropped and Sergeant was paid his salary.

G. E. THORMAN

HBRS, IX (Rich); XI, XX (Rich and Johnson); XXI (Rich). *Documents relating to Hudson Bay* (Tyrrell) (note that Oldmixon's account of the siege of Albany is a little garbled). Chevalier de Troyes, *Journal* (Caron).

SEVESTRE, CHARLES, clerk in the Quebec warehouse, procurator-syndic of the Communauté des Habitants, special lieutenant of the seneschal's court of Quebec; son of Charles Sevestre and Marguerite Petitpas; d. 1657 at Quebec.

The Sevestre family came from Paris, where, some time around 1627, Charles had married Marie Pichon, the widow of Philippe Gauthier de La Chenaye. We know of four of Charles's brothers: Louis, who was a bookseller; Étienne, Ignace, and Thomas, who probably arrived at Quebec with Charles not later than 1636. They brought with them their widowed mother. The Compagnie des Cent-Associés granted them lands at Quebec in the spring of 1639.

Charles Sevestre's first occupation is unknown to us; he is referred to in 1641 only as a "settler living at the aforesaid Quebec." But in 1645, when the Communauté des Habitants was founded, Sevestre makes his appearance as clerk of the warehouse. On 23 Aug. 1648, at a meeting of all the notables of the Quebec region, he was elected procurator-syndic of the Communauté. It was in this capacity that he was required, in 1649, to initiate the construction of the first church at Trois-Rivières. On 8 May 1651 he is mentioned as being provost judge of the Lauson seigneury, an office that he was the first to hold. During the years 1651 and 1652 he was one of the churchwardens of the parish of Quebec. Finally, from 1651 until his death, he was the first appointee to the important office of special civil and criminal lieutenant in the seneschal's court of Quebec, created by Governor JEAN DE LAUSON.

Charles Sevestre died at Quebec and was buried on 9 Dec. 1657 under his pew in the church; his wife was to follow him on 4 May 1661.

It seems evident, however, that Sevestre's bookkeeping, while he was a clerk in the warehouse, was not all it should have been towards the end of his term, for his son-in-law, Louis ROUER de Villeray (who succeeded him in the position through the favour of the interim governor, LOUIS d'AILLEBOUST) was held responsible for Sevestre's errors or poor administration. Indeed, Villeray was forced to go to France to exonerate his father-in-law. This did not prevent the advocate, JEAN PERONNE Dumesnil, who arrived in 1660 as an inspector on behalf of the Compagnie des Cent-Associés, then in its death throes, from heaping abuse on Rouer and his father-in-law, along with other highly respectable citizens of Canada, Bishop Laval* included.

Charles Sevestre was the only member of his family to leave descendants in Canada and he left only girls, as his male descendants died without issue.

HONORIUS PROVOST

ASQ, Documents Faribault, 78, 86, 89a, 94, 95, 158; Séminaire, VI, 5, 6a, 34. *JR* (Thwaites). *JJ* (Laverdière et Casgrain). *Jug. et délib.*

SHEPARD (Shepheard), THOMAS, mate and captain in the HBC; fl. *c.* 1668–81.

He was chief mate of the *Nonsuch* (Capt. Zachariah GILLAM) on the pre-charter voyage of 1668–69 to James Bay. He would, therefore, have been present when Gillam and CHOUART Des Groseilliers took formal possession of Rupert River and would have assisted in building Charles Fort, the first English habitation in present-day Quebec.

The *Nonsuch* arrived back in England in October 1669 and then, or shortly afterwards, Shepard sought employment elsewhere. Whilst master of the *Golden Lyon* of Dunkirk he claimed to have re-discovered Busse Island, one of the "lost" islands of the Atlantic. It was supposed to have been seen originally in 1578 from one of the ships attached to Sir Martin FROBISHER's third expedition in search of a northwest passage. The circumstances in which Shepard sighted the elusive island on 22 Aug. 1671 are not known, but whatever his story, it interested the governor and Committee when he approached them in December 1673. He was requested to estimate the cost of an expedition to Busse Island and a move was made to obtain a royal charter. This charter was at length obtained on 13 May 1675 when the king granted to the HBC "All that Island called the Busse Island lying betweene fifty seaven and fifty nyne Degrees of Northerne Latitude or thereabouts," together with similar privileges to those enjoyed under the charter of 2 May 1670.

Meanwhile, in 1674, Shepard had commanded the Company's *Shaftesbury* pink to James Bay. Unfavourable ice conditions delayed his return to England until the autumn of 1675, by which time plans for an expedition to Busse Island had been made. What subsequently happened is not altogether clear as there are gaps in the Company's minutes and correspondence, but the account books show that Shepard sailed in command of the *Prince Rupert* in 1676 (HBC Arch., A.14/2, f.50), and that on 16 October of the same year petty expenses were paid "for severall post Letters & other Letters upon the first news of Capt. Shepards arrivall from attempting the discovery of Buss Island" (*ibid.*, A.15/1, p. 4). The account books have no record of any cargo brought back by Shepard, although they give details of that obtained on the 1676 voyage of the *Shaftesbury* (Capt. Joseph THOMPSON). This omission, together with the item for petty expenses, suggests that, unlike Thompson, Shepard did not go to James Bay in 1676, but searched unsuccessfully for Busse Island.

Shepard's employment with the company ended in 1676; although he was re-engaged in February 1681 he was dismissed in the following May for "haveing behaved himself Ill."

ALICE M. JOHNSON

Shepard's career in the HBC can be followed in HBRS, V, VIII (Rich). For appraisals of Shepard's re-discovery of Busse Island *see*: Miller Christy, "On 'Busse Island,' " in *Danish arctic expeditions* (Gosch), I, 164–202, and A. M. Johnson, "The mythical land of Buss," *Beaver* (Dec., 1942), 43–47.

SIMON DE LONGPRÉ, MARIE-CATHERINE DE, *dite* **de Saint-Augustin,** nun of the Hôtel-Dieu of Quebec, daughter of Jacques Simon, Sieur de Longpré, and of Françoise Jourdan; b. 3 May 1632 at Saint-Sauveur-le-Vicomte (Lower Normandy); d. 8 May 1668 at Quebec.

A precocious child, Catherine grew up under the care of her grandmother and her maternal grandfather, M. de Launé-Jourdan, "a man of prayer and grand almoner, whose virtue has been appreciated by everyone." At the age of three she showed herself to be imbued with a desire for the heroic and the absolute, and asked how she might in all things do God's will. Her spiritual adviser, the Jesuit Father Malherbe, explained this to her in the presence of a pauper covered with sores. Catherine concluded from his illustration that it is easier to find God in humiliation and suffering than in prosperity. The tiny tot then began, "with unbelievable earnestness," to wish for "many maladies." An ear infection that degenerated into bone decay started to torment her. Catherine undertook to accept everything joyfully and she was cured, despite the treatments of the surgeons of the period, wretched quacks whom Molière rightly held up to ridicule. Without turning a hair, Father Paul RAGUENEAU describes one of these "operators" in the act of pouring red-hot ashes into the ears of Mlle de Longpré.

At the age of ten, "unaided by any visible person," Catherine composed a "Donation" to the Blessed Virgin, a text worthy of an adult. Like her contemporaries in the first part of the 17th century, the little girl affirmed her yearning for epic deeds. And so her impetuosity burst forth in

Simon de Longpré

uncompromising formulas: "Remove from my heart every impurity, let me die now rather than allow my heart and soul to be soiled by the slightest blemish."

Despite their predisposition to panegyrize, the hagiographers record a complete reversal of Catherine's attitude. Was this a normal adolescent crisis, or an awareness of her deep and engaging femininity? Catherine realized that she was pretty, intelligent, and attractive, and made use of her charms to conquer those about her. To some extent she imitated the precious ladies of the Hôtel de Rambouillet; she sang love songs, and read novels, perhaps *L'Astrée* and *Polexandre*. In summarizing this brief period of exuberance, Catherine wrote: "I took pleasure then in being loved and in seeking friendship without wanting to appear to be doing so; on the contrary, I gave the appearance of much severity, in order to be considered an independent thinker."

When she was twelve and a half, Catherine underwent a "bad shakeup": she felt that God was calling her to the cloister, but she balked, because the world attracted her. "I tried," she said, "to stifle it all by seeking diversions." But ever pursued by her obsession with pleasing God, she became a Hospitaller of Bayeux on 7 October 1644, joining her elder sister there. Thinking herself "too young and too small" to make a final decision, she jauntily notified the authorities of the hospital that she was not coming to the noviciate with the express intention of staying there, "but merely to try it out and to see something of how the nuns live." She was put to the test "twofold," for fear that her vocation might have sprung from a desire for human esteem. Catherine remained firm, however, and openly challenged the mistress of novices: "Do what you like to me, you will not make me give up the nun's habit and I will not leave here except to go to Canada."

These prophetic words were not long in being fulfilled. The Hospitallers of Quebec were at that moment requesting reinforcements from their Mothers in France. The two de Longpré sisters were among the first to offer themselves, especially Catherine who was not old enough to make her profession. Her family became alarmed. The older sister yielded to her parents' entreaties, but the younger one resisted all pressures. M. de Longpré became annoyed and "petitioned the court" to prevent his daughter's departure. The novice was adamant and vowed to live and die in Canada if God would let her go there. Her father softened and gave his consent. The nuns, for their part, were reluctant to lose a recruit who gave promise of rendering such great services to the Bayeux convent. At last Catherine took ship for Quebec. She was not yet 16, the minimum age for profession. She was allowed to take ordinary vows, which she did in the chapel of Notre-Dame-de-Toute-Joie at Nantes. At sea she almost died of the plague. After three months on the ocean, she reached New France on 19 Aug. 1648.

At this period Quebec was only a little town in the midst of barbarism. Catherine was lodged in an Hôtel-Dieu that seemed "more like a hut than a hospital." And what an atmosphere there was in the country! The Iroquois were massacring the Hurons, martyring the missionaries, burning the dwellings, and threatening to destroy the colony. In a letter dated 9 Nov. 1651, Mother Catherine wrote: "We are in no hurry to finish the rest of our buildings, because of our uncertainty whether we shall be staying here for long."

Mother Catherine soon established for herself a reputation as an exemplary nun: she was considered to be a treasure, she was loved and was thought to be perfect by nature. But her health was so fragile that the Hospitallers of Bayeux became concerned and invited her to return to France. The young nun declined these offers: "I am too much absorbed in Canada," she exclaimed, "to be able to tear myself away. Believe, me, my dear aunt, only death or a general upheaval in this country can break this bond."

We find her becoming in turn depositary (1659), senior Hospitaller (1663), and mistress of novices (1665). In 1668 the community contemplated electing her superior, but on 20 April of that year she began spitting blood. On 8 May, she died at the age of 36.

After 1668, Mother Catherine's secrets were brought to light. In Canada, even in Europe, there was talk of the extraordinary occurrences at the Hôtel-Dieu in Quebec. In 1671 Father Paul Ragueneau published *La vie de Mère Catherine de Saint-Augustin*. At once the public penetrated into the innermost existence of the young nun. Until then she had appeared to be at peace with this world and the next; but suddenly a host of disturbing things were learned about this Hospitaller who had seemed so serene and so intent upon passing unnoticed. What a price she had paid for her saintliness! God had allowed her to be possessed, that is, to be tormented in visible and external fashion by the devil. At times, says Ragueneau, so great a horde of demons assailed Mother Catherine that they seemed as numerous "as the specks one sees in the air in sunlight" (p.160). In the presence of these dark angels, she underwent a kind of psychological dissociation from herself: despite her refined nature she was cohabiting with depraved beings. This ontological torture was aggravated by a sort of moral dualism: on the one hand she felt an unspeakable loathing for the slightest impurity; on the other hand she felt as if sin were imprinted in her heart and she regretted that she was not utterly impious, not "fully and completely like the demons" (p.125). It is not surprising that she skirted the abyss of despair: "I experienced a violent desire to be damned without delay" (pp.206–7).

Instead of crying for help and begging for deliverance, Mother Catherine advanced to the limit of magnanimity and uttered this pathetic prayer: "My Saviour and my All! If the demons' sojourn in my body is pleasing in your sight, I am willing that they should stay there as long as you wish; provided that sin does not creep in with them, I fear nothing, and I hope that you will grant me grace to love you for all eternity, even though I were in the depths of hell." (P.50.)

Catherine de Saint-Augustin tells that God gave her as director the Jesuit Father Jean de BRÉBEUF, another native of Bayeux, who had died in 1649. This missionary had never during his lifetime met Mother Catherine de Saint-Augustin. The nun says that from 1662 on, she frequently received visits from this blessed Jesuit, who was entrusted with guiding, comforting, and at times restraining her in her mortifications. But on certain days even he seemed to elude her. To win him to her, Mother Catherine spoke to him with childlike simplicity: "How happy I am, Father, that you are deriving some small joy and satisfaction now from seeing me thus crucified: be vexed with me as much as you like; I shall always look upon you and love you as my kind and charitable Father." (P.207.)

On many occasions Mother Catherine stated that it was for Canada, which was in danger of undergoing grave punishments for the crimes being committed there, that she was enduring suffering. This role of assumed victim for the colony has placed Mother Catherine among the founders of the Canadian Church. While others overcame the forest, the rivers, the winter, and the Indians, Mother Catherine bore the sins of her adopted country and grappled in close quarters with the powers of darkness.

What are we to think of these unusual revelations? In the first place, Father Ragueneau recounts them in uninspired fashion, in the style of the ancient hagiographers who were more skilful in giving a distaste for virtue than in effectively presenting their personages. This first biographer of Mother Catherine advises us, however, that he composed the *Vie* from the Hospitaller's own "Journal." Since the latter document has disappeared, internal criticism is required to evaluate Father Ragueneau's work. Until this scientific study is made, there are left to us a number of pieces of testimony in Mother Catherine's favour: the opinions of contemporaries who concur in their praise of the heroic nun.

First of all, the *Annales de l'Hôtel-Dieu de Québec* published an obituary notice which should be mentioned. Let us note this paragraph: "This dear Mother died in odour of sanctity, 8 May 1668, aged 36 years and 5 days, universally mourned by the whole Community and the whole colony as a soul who brought great blessings upon this poor land. She spent 20 years in Canada, where she was a source of great edification to everyone and gave great glory to God by the heroic acts of virtue she accomplished there, although externally she led an ordinary life that carefully concealed the treasures of grace that God had bestowed upon her."

Further on, the annalist noted that the *Vie* had the merit of displeasing the members of Port-Royal "who contemplated submitting it to the Sorbonne" apparently in the hope of having it condemned.

Here is how Mother Marie FORESTIER de Saint-Bonaventure, superior of the Hôtel-Dieu in 1668, announced the death of her daughter in religion to the Hospitallers of Bayeux: "We cannot possibly convey to you our sentiments at such a loss, for we have lost what we shall never regain, the best and most lovable person one might ever hope to see: the best formed and most attractive disposition one can conceive of; a girl who was as quiet, charitable, and prudent as anyone could imagine: her virtue was as exceptional as God's behaviour with her was unusual. Our grief is so legitimate and so palpable that we can speak of it and think of it only with tears."

Bishop François de Laval* for his part wrote personally to the Superior of the Hospitallers of Bayeux: "My dear Mother, there is every reason to glorify God for the course of action he has followed with respect to our Sister Catherine de Saint-Augustin. She was a soul he had chosen in order to impart to her very great and very special blessings. Her saintliness will be better known in heaven than in this life, for assuredly she is exceptional. She has accomplished much and suffered much with inviolable faithfulness and with a courage that was above the ordinary: her love for her fellow man was able to take in anything, no matter how difficult. I have no need of the extraordinary things which took place within her in order to be convinced of her saintliness; her real virtues make it perfectly known to me."

His interest aroused by all the marvellous stories

Skanudharoua

which were circulating about Mother Catherine, Father Joseph-Antoine PONCET de La Rivière, a former missionary in New France, consulted Marie de l'Incarnation [see GUYART]. After the burning of her monastery (30 Dec. 1650), the latter had lived for three weeks at the Hôtel-Dieu in Quebec. This stay had allowed her to meet Mother Catherine and to develop an admiration for her. Mother Marie de l'Incarnation was nevertheless cautious in her reply to Father Poncet: "I am quite unable to tell you my feeling about such extraordinary matters, as you ask me to, and I beg you to excuse me from doing so, seeing that persons of learning and virtue are suspending judgment on the question and are continuing in doubt, not daring to give credence to unusual visions of this type. Reverend Father Ragueneau is a scholar in these matters and he considers her blessed, because she has always been faithful in her duty, and has never yielded to the demon, over whom she has always been victorious. I am of the opinion that this fidelity in her obligations and her struggles makes her great in heaven, and I rely on that more readily than on the visions that I hear about. And what has further astonished persons of virtue and experience is the fact that she never said a word about her behaviour to her superior, who is a very enlightened person of great experience and of exceptional virtue." Further on, Marie de l'Incarnation was more explicit: "It was not for lack of loyalty or submissiveness that she kept all that secret, but because of the order she had received from her directors in view of the nature of her case which might well have been upsetting."

By the overflowing activity of her life as well as by her discretion and her good humour, Mother Catherine proved that she was by no means a hysterical woman. Aware that he was writing a book likely to arouse controversy, Father Ragueneau began it by a foreword. In this preliminary vindication, Mother Catherine appeared as a well-balanced person, secure from all the snares of the imagination. The *Vie* began with a symbolic picture engraved at Bishop Laval's request. At the bottom were to be seen Satan and the souls in purgatory; in the centre, angels helped Mother Catherine to support a large cross; in the sky Father Brébeuf was holding a palm in his hand; at the very top were the Virgin and Our Lord. This picture is a sort of condensed biography, which makes no impression on the 20th century. Instead of this complicated iconography, we prefer the likeness of the delicate face of Mother Catherine de Longpré that adorns the little private chapel in the Hôtel-Dieu in Quebec. Lively and wide-awake, this delightful young Norman girl hurled herself into paradise at a heroic pace. She must be depicted above all as a missionary on foreign soil, as a nurse, as an enterprising woman who died with a "*Te Deum*" on her lips. In that way she will emerge gloriously from the shadows, reassuring both theologians and psychiatrists.

MARIE-EMMANUEL CHABOT, o.s.u.

Marie Guyart de l'Incarnation, *Lettres* (Martin); *Lettres* (Richaudeau). *JR* (Thwaites), XXXII. Juchereau, *Annales* (Jamet). Paul Ragueneau, *La vie de Mère Catherine de Saint-Augustin* (Paris, 1671). P.-G. Roy, *La Ville de Québec*, I, 207–8. *Les Ursulines de Québec*, I, 9.

SKANUDHAROUA (Skannud-Haroï), **GENEVIÈVE-AGNÈS** *dite* **de Tous-les-Saints,** Hospitaller, first Indian girl to enter the religious life; b. 1642; d. 3 Nov. 1657 at Quebec.

Skanudharoua was born at the Huron village of Ossossanë, or La Conception, a daughter of a leading Huron chief, Pierre Ondakion, whose family had been the first of that nation to embrace Christianity, and his wife Jeanne Asenregéhaon. Their marriage was the first Christian union in the Huron country. At first, Skanudharoua lived with the Ursuline nuns at Quebec. In 1650, when the Ursulines' house burned, she was thought for some time to have been lost.

In May 1650 she was taken to the Hôtel-Dieu in Quebec where she learned the French language perfectly in less than a year and quickly mastered the art of reading and writing, surpassing her French companions. She acted as interpreter for the sick Hurons at the Hôtel-Dieu. In order "that she might always be kept in a spirit of submission," she was engaged in kitchen work, yet never was heard to complain. She was firm in her desire to remain with the nuns in the face of her parents' frequent attempts to compel her to leave. When "tried" before the whole community, she preferred harsh discipline to returning to her people. She overcame the native's natural impulse for freedom and was much loved by all for her humility, sincerity, and sweetness. Her godmother in Paris, Mme Bodeau, paid for her upkeep.

Geneviève-Agnès had an ardent desire to become a nun and was admitted to the noviciate on 25 March 1657. She suffered a lingering disease of the lungs and was moved to the hospital infirmary on 15 August. She continued to discharge her religious duties as long as her strength would allow "with as much exactness as an old professed nun." On 1 November she was given the holy garb and, at her own request, the name "Tous-les-Saints." A few hours before her death on 3 Nov.

1657, she took the final vows, the first Indian girl to enter the religious life. She was buried at the Hôtel-Dieu in Quebec with other nuns.

Mother Saint-Bonaventure-de-Jésus [see FORESTIER], superior of the Hôtel-Dieu, wrote after her death, "She had a very fine form and an exceedingly pleasing countenance . . . an intelligence above the average, not only of the Savages, but also of the French."

ELSIE MCLEOD JURY

Juchereau, *Annales* (Jamet), 85–86, 95–96, 99, 104. Marie Guyart de l'Incarnation, *Lettres* (Richaudeau), *passim*. *JR* (Thwaites), esp. XLIV, 261–75. Lefebvre, *Marie Morin*. P.-G. Roy, *La Ville de Québec*, I, 227–28.

SMITHS JOHN. *See* FLEMISH BASTARD

SMITHSEND, NICHOLAS, servant of the HBC, brother to RICHARD SMITHSEND, of the parish of St. John, Wapping; fl. 1685–98 (O.S.).

Nicholas was a sailor on the *Perpetuana Merchant* which was captured by the French in Hudson Strait in July 1685 and taken to Quebec [*see* RICHARD SMITHSEND].

It is not known exactly when Nicholas was next employed by the HBC, but he made a trip in the *Royal Hudson's Bay* to York Fort (Port Nelson) and Albany River, returning to London in 1694. As no ships were sent to the Bay in 1695, he commanded the *Prosperous* on a voyage to Newcastle but she was wrecked on her return voyage. Like other HBC captains, Smithsend was granted a letter of marque in 1696 and he commanded the new frigate *Knight*, accompanied by two other HBC ships and two of the Royal Navy, on an expedition which recovered York Fort, which had been captured by Pierre Le Moyne* d'Iberville in 1694. He commanded the *Royal Hudson's Bay* on the return voyage. In 1697 he commanded the same ship on the outward voyage in company with HMS *Hampshire* (Capt. John FLETCHER), the HBC's *Dering*, and a fireship. The flotilla was intercepted off Port Nelson by d'Iberville in *Le Pélican* and after the *Hampshire* was sunk, Smithsend surrendered his ship without a fight on 5 Sept. 1697 (N.S.) according to La Poterie [Le Roy*]. (Smithsend's account no longer exists.) A prize crew was put on board, but a bad storm wrecked the ship in Hayes River (called by the French Sainte-Thérèse), enabling Smithsend and some of his crew to slip their captivity and make their way to York Fort where Smithsend encouraged the defenders to resist. The fort was subsequently surrendered by Governor Henry Bayley* on 3 Sept. 1697 (O.S.).

Smithsend was presumably released with Bayley, Kelsey*, and others; in any case he was in London by 8 Dec. 1697 and was paid his outstanding wages by the HBC on 20 Jan. 1698/99.

G. E. THORMAN

HBC Arch. A.15/4, f.115; A.15/5, f.35. HBRS, XX (Rich and Johnson). [Henry Kelsey], *The Kelsey papers*, ed. A. G. Doughty and Chester Martin (Ottawa, 1929), 99–100. La Pot(h)erie, *Histoire*.

For a description of the 1697 battle *see* Crouse, *Lemoyne d'Iberville*, 142–51 (it should be noted that the Capt. Smithsend referred to here is Nicholas, not Richard), and Frégault, *Iberville*. *See also* FLETCHER.

SMITHSEND, RICHARD, HBC employee, 1685–91, but for over half this period a French prisoner; b. *c.* 1653.

In 1685 he was mate of the *Perpetuana Merchant* (Capt. Edward Hume), on which his brother NICHOLAS SMITHSEND also sailed. Bound for York Fort the ship was captured in Hudson Strait in July 1685 by Bermen* de La Martinière, whose two ships were returning from the Bay to Quebec. The *Perpetuana Merchant* was taken to Quebec where, despite being imprisoned, Smithsend managed to write to Mr John Hampson about "the Designes of the French upon Port Nellson the next year." This letter was read at the HBC Committee meeting held in London on 3 Feb. 1685/86.

In August 1686, after 11 months at Quebec, Smithsend was sent to Martinique for further imprisonment, but the ship's captain landed at Guadeloupe by error and the prisoners were released. Returning to England via Barbadoes, Smithsend arrived in London where he made an affidavit dated 15 Feb. 1686/87 describing his captivity, reports of the success of the Chevalier de TROYES' expedition of 1686, and the arrival at Quebec of two English ships (the *Craven* was one) captured by de Troyes at Moose.

Smithsend was given command of the *Huband* which sailed for Port Nelson in 1687. The *Huband* had not arrived at Port Nelson by 22 September and is presumed to have arrived there later. However, Smithsend may have wintered her at Charlton Island (AN, Col., C^{11A}, X, 237–40). There are no further references to the *Huband*'s activities until it was captured by Pierre Le Moyne* d'Iberville at Rupert River in the early summer of 1689.

Smithsend was sent overland to Quebec along with the other ships' captains whom Iberville had captured at Albany. He was shipped to France and imprisoned at La Rochelle. His wife together with other HBC "grass widows" petitioned Queen Mary on 1 Oct. 1691 to help obtain the release of their husbands, but Smithsend escaped later in the month. He did not re-enter the HBC service and assigned his gratuity of £10 to his brother John.

G. E. THORMAN

AN, Col., C¹¹ᴬ, 10, ff.146–47. HBC Arch. A.1/14, f.10d; A.1/84, f.15d; A.9/4, f.16–16d. HBRS, XI (Rich and Johnson), 214–15; XX (Rich and Johnson).

SMITS JAN. *See* FLEMISH BASTARD

SNORRI THORFINNSSON, first white child born on the North American continent, son of THORFINNR *karlsefni* Thordarson and his wife Gudridr, daughter of Thorbjörn; b. *c.* 1005–13.

The *Saga of Eric the Red*, supplemented by the *Saga of the Greenlanders*, is the main source of the few facts known about Snorri. His father, Thorfinnr, went from Iceland to Greenland. There he became interested in the new lands in North America to which the sons of EIRIKR Thorvaldsson (Eric the Red)—LEIFR *heppni* Eiriksson, Thorvaldr, and Thorsteinn—had made expeditions in the years following A.D. 1000. He determined to lead a colonizing expedition thither and set sail with 60 men and 5 women (*Saga of the Greenlanders*), and accompanied by two other ships, some time during the years 1003–10 (*Saga of Eric the Red*). Where he established his colony is not known. Newfoundland, Nova Scotia, and Massachusetts are among the many regions that have been suggested, although the likeliest spot is probably the vicinity of Cape Cod. The colony lasted for three years, and during the summers exploratory voyages were undertaken both north and south. Many scholars believe that the explorers sailed a considerable distance up the St. Lawrence River, and, according to the *Saga of Eric the Red*, even reached the "land of the Unipeds" of which CARTIER was to be told centuries later. The peace of the colony, however, was disturbed by troubles with the aborigines of the region, although there is no agreement among historians on whether these were Indians or Eskimos. Bloody fighting broke out. Whether because of this or for some other reason, the settlement was abandoned after three years and the settlers returned to Greenland. During their stay in America, however, a son was born to Thorfinnr and Gudridr and given the name of Snorri. He was taken to Iceland by his parents two years after the colony came to an end. There he lived out his life, but the date of his death is unknown. However, it is known that a "great and goodly lineage" sprang from him, including several of the early bishops of Iceland.

T. J. OLESON

On the expedition *see* the works cited under BJARNI Herjólfsson. As to the relative age and historical authenticity of the *Saga of the Greenlanders* and the *Saga of Eric the Red*, *see*: Halldór Hermannsson, *The problem of Wineland* (Islandica, XXV, 1936) and Jón Jóhannesson, "Aldur Grænlendingas sögu," *Nordæla* (Reykjavík, 1956), 149–58.

SORESTER. *See* FORRESTER

SOUART, GABRIEL, priest, Sulpician, first parish priest of Montreal and superior of the Sulpician seminary, doctor, and schoolmaster; b. *c.* 1611 in the diocese of Paris; d. 8 March 1691 in France. He was the nephew of the Recollet Joseph LE CARON.

Souart's calling was a late one; he entered the Sulpician order only in 1646, becoming a priest in 1650. He had studied medicine, which he practised, with his superiors' permission, while on missions; he also held the title of bachelor of canon law.

M. Souart was one of the first four Sulpicians chosen by M. Olier in 1657 to go and found the Séminaire de Montréal. Together with MM. de Queylus [*see* THUBIÈRES], Galinier, and d'ALLET, he arrived at Ville-Marie in the summer of 1657. The Jesuits, who had ministered to Ville-Marie (Montreal) since 1642, made way for him, and without more ado he started to organize the parish on a regular basis. Having been appointed officially as parish priest by M. de Queylus, on 21 Nov. 1657, he got the people to elect the first group of churchwardens. He always showed great zeal for the decorum and beauty of divine worship and for the sanctification of his flock. With Mme de BOULLONGNE d'Ailleboust and Father CHAUMONOT, he instituted the pious Confrérie de la Sainte-Famille, which soon spread throughout the whole of New France.

He often replaced his superior, Abbé Queylus, during the latter's numerous absences and was himself superior of the seminary, 1661–68 and 1674–76. He was also chaplain of the Congrégation Notre-Dame, 1659–76, and of the Hôtel-Dieu, which he saved from ruin by his generosity, 1661–84. He became a schoolmaster from 1668 on, and was very proud of this title.

He was priest of the parish of Ville-Marie during the settlement's most terrible years (1657–66): the time of the exploit of DOLLARD Des Ormeaux in 1660, of the massacre of the Sulpicians LE MAISTE and VIGNAL in 1661, and of the earthquake in 1663.

On 26 Dec. 1665, in his capacity as seigneur of Montreal Island, he created the arriere-fief of Hautmesny, between the St. Lawrence River and the Rivière des Prairies, and sent M. Dollier* de Casson as army chaplain to Lake Champlain in 1666. Later, in 1674, he tried to exercise a calming influence in the conflict that sprang up between Governor BUADE de Frontenac and Abbé Fénelon [see SALIGNAC].

Abbé Souart was apparently very wealthy: he made generous donations to the various institutions as well as to individuals in the colony; the nuns of the Hôtel-Dieu numbered him among their benefactors.

M. Souart probably made his first journey to France in 1667. He left Canada for good shortly after 1686—perhaps in 1688—and died on 8 March 1691.

OLIVIER MAURAULT

AJM, Greffe de Bénigne Basset, 1657–86, *passim.* ASQ, Séminaire, I, 20 (acte d'union spirituelle entre les séminaires de Saint-Sulpice et de Québec, 28 févr. 1688). Dollier de Casson, *Histoire du Montréal. JJ* (Laverdière et Casgrain). P.-G. Roy, *Inv. concessions*, I, 191f. Faillon, *Histoire de la colonie française*, II; III; *passim.* "Marguilliers de la paroisse de Notre-Dame de Ville-Marie de 1657 à 1913," *BRH*, XIX (1913), 276–84. É.-Z. Massicotte, "Fondation d'une communauté de frères instituteurs à Montréal en 1686," *BRH*, XXVIII (1922), 37–42; "Louis Artus de Sailly, premier juge royal de Montréal," *BRH*, XXI (1915), 206; "M. Philippe de Hautmesny," *BRH*, XXII (1916), 40. "Le premier prêtre ordonné au Canada," *BRH*, XII (1906), 57.

SQUANTO (Squantum). *See* TISQUANTUM

STEWART ("Stuart" in French documents), **SIR JAMES,** of Killeith, fourth **Lord Ochiltree** (or Ochiltrie), founder of a short-lived colony at Port de la Baleine, on Cape Breton; b. 1582? in Scotland; d. 1659.

He was the elder son of Capt. James Stewart of Bothwellmuir, the usurping Earl of Arran, and his wife, Lady Elizabeth Stewart, eldest daughter of John, fourth Earl of Atholl. In 1615 he became fourth Lord Ochiltree as the result of a family arrangement among the members of the Ochiltree branch of the Stewarts. Perhaps lack of money turned his attention to colonial enterprise. In 1629, after Sir WILLIAM ALEXANDER the elder had joined with London merchant venturers in an Anglo-Scottish company, Charles I authorized £500 sterling to be borrowed for Ochiltree's use in connection with the latter's expedition to Cape Breton for planting a colony there. The fleet sent out by that company reached Port de la Baleine, not far from English Harbour, the site of the future Louisbourg, on 1 July. There Ochiltree, with about 60 Scots, including Capt. Constance FERRAR, began a settlement and built a small fort named "Rosemar," while Sir WILLIAM ALEXANDER the younger proceeded to Port-Royal with other colonists. Within a few weeks, however, Capt. CHARLES DANIEL of Dieppe, one of the Compagnie des Cent-Associés who had left France to relieve CHAMPLAIN at Quebec, hearing of this nascent colony, overpowered it, captured its people, and carried them first to Cibou (St. Ann's) on Cape Breton Island and then back across the Atlantic. A number of Ochiltree's colonists were landed near Falmouth, but Ochiltree and 17 others were taken to France as prisoners. Released by the Conseil de la Marine, he petitioned Charles I in 1630 for compensation for his losses and denounced French "pretensions" to Canada and Acadia.

Ochiltree applied for a grant in Nova Scotia under Sir William Alexander's scheme on 18 April 1630, and he and several other baronets made plans to plant a colony "near unto the river of Canada." But a more serious misfortune now befell him. Having accused James, Marquis of Hamilton (and later first Duke of Hamilton)—who was a partner of Sir DAVID KIRKE in 1638—of high treason, his charges were investigated and found to be baseless. He was thereupon condemned to perpetual imprisonment in Blackness Castle, and his patent for a barony in Nova Scotia was cancelled before being registered. He remained a prisoner for 20 years, until the English invaders set him at liberty in 1652 after the battle of Worcester.

Twice married, by his first wife, Margaret, daughter of Uchtred Macdowall of Garthland, he had a son, who predeceased him, but whose son, William, became in turn the fifth Lord Ochiltree, though he died in his 16th year; by his second wife, Mary Livingstone, the fourth Lord Ochiltree had a son and three daughters. He died in 1659.

C. BRUCE FERGUSSON

[For the contemporary French version of the capture of "Rosemar," see MALAPART.]

AE, Corr. pol., Angleterre, 43, 44, 45. AN, E¹, 101A, 103A. PRO, C.O. 1/5, nos. 41, 46, 47. [Sir William Alexander], *The Earl of Stirling's register of royal letters, relative to the affairs of Scotland and Nova Scotia from 1615 to 1635*, ed. C. Rogers (2v., Edinburgh, 1885). Champlain, *Works* (Biggar), VI, 153–61 contains the French version of the founding and destruction of Ochiltree's fort. *Mémoires des commissaires*, I, 43; and *Memorials of the English and French commissaries*, I, 116. PRO, *CSP, Col., 1574–1660*, 104–6. *Royal letters, charters, and tracts* (Laing), 78, 120–3.

William Anderson, *The Scottish nation* (3v., Edinburgh and London, 1880). Richard Brown, *A history* of the Island of Cape Breton (London, 1869), 74–83. Insh, Scottish colonial schemes. McGrail, Alexander. Although Insh and McGrail differ as to the date of Alexander's and Ochiltree's settlements, it seems clear from such records as BM, Egerton MS 2395, f.23, and Harley MS 1760; Nat. Library of Scotland, Hawthornden MS IX, ff.148–50; some of the documents in the Earl of Stirlings's register; and Captain Daniel's narrative of his voyage in 1629 that Insh's view that the year was 1629 is correct.

STIRLING, EARL OF. See ALEXANDER, SIR WILLIAM (c. 1577–1640)

STOURTON, ERASMUS, probably the second Anglican clergyman (the first whose name is known) to come to Newfoundland; b. 1603, eldest son of Edward Stourton of Narborough, Leicestershire, and his wife Mary; m. Elizabeth Gravenor, by whom he had six children; d. November 1658, at Walesby, Lincolnshire.

Although Stourton describes himself only as "late preacher to the Colony at Ferryland" in a petition dated 9 Oct. 1628 (PRO, C.O. 1/4, 59), he is undoubtedly the Erasmus Stourton who, in 1619, matriculated from St. John's College, Cambridge, at the age of 16. He graduated with a B.A. in 1622–23 and was ordained September 1625.

After he secured his M.A. in 1627, Stourton went to Newfoundland to serve the colonists at Ferryland as chaplain. Here he came into conflict with Sir George CALVERT (later Lord Baltimore), who had sent out Capt. Edward WYNNE to establish a colony at Ferryland in 1621, which Calvert himself visited for the first time in 1627. In 1628, Calvert, a Roman Catholic, brought out, in addition to his family and 40 others of the Catholic faith, two priests who celebrated mass and carried out "all the other ceremonies of the Church of Rome in the ample manner as it was used in Spain." This so aroused Stourton's militant protestantism that the ensuing religious squabbles between the two men resulted in Stourton's banishment from the colony in 1628 on Calvert's orders. Stourton returned to England in the same year and there continued for a while his ineffectual efforts to stir up the Privy Council and other authorities against the "Popish Colony" at Ferryland.

Stourton later became chaplain to Christopher Villiers, Earl of Anglesey, and rector of Walesby in Lincolnshire, 1631–58, where he died in November 1658.

It is difficult to present a picture of Stourton as a human being, since so little has been written about him. While Calvert calls him "an audacious man, a narrow-minded sectary, and a troublesome meddlesome busy-body" and M. F. Howley, an eminent historian, later refers to him as "an aggressive Protestant, unbearable, and most likely seditious," it could be that, under the existing circumstances, such epithets were greatly exaggerated, by reason of enmity or prejudice. What might be said on Stourton's behalf, with some degree of justification, is that he fulfilled his work as missionary to those early colonists and settlers with some distinction and to the satisfaction of the hierarchy of his church in England. He shows himself a man of courage, no reed shaken by the wind, in his conflict with the powerful and influential Calvert. The mere fact of his coming to Newfoundland, his willingness to forgo the amenities of his home land, is evidence of commendable devotion and sacrifice. It would indeed appear that he possessed some of the qualities required for the life and work of the true pioneer.

E. HUNT

PRO, C.O. 1/4, 59. For details of Stourton's early life see: Lincolnshire pedigrees, ed. A. R. Maddison (3v., Harleian Soc., L–LII, 1902–4), III. Alumni Cantabrigiensis, ed. John and J. A. Venn (2pts. (10v.), Cambridge, 1922–54), pt.I, v.IV. M. F. Howley, Ecclesiastical history of Newfoundland (Boston, 1888). Prowse, History of Nfld. (the account given by Prowse of Stourton's arrival in Newfoundland in 1612 as chaplain to John Guy's colony is not supported by recent scholarship). Rogers, Newfoundland. A. L. Rowse, The Elizabethans and America (London, 1959).

STUART. See STEWART

SZKOLNY. See SCOLVUS [Appendix]

T

TAGASKOUÏTA. See TEKAKWITHA

TALON, JEAN (called at one time **Talon Du Quesnoy**), intendant of New France 1665–68 and 1670–72; b. at Châlons-sur-Marne, in Champagne, where he was baptized 8 Jan. 1626, son of Philippe Talon and Anne de Bury (or Burry, but not Beuvy); d. November 1694 in France.

According to certain authors the Talons were said to be of Irish origin. The first ancestor to settle in France, in the middle of the 16th century, was supposed to have been Artus Talon. However that may be, by the end of that century the

Talon

Talon family was divided into two separate branches: the Parisian branch, made famous by several magistrates who were related to the Gueffiers and the Phélypeaux de Pontchartrain family, and the one in Champagne, to which Jean Talon belonged.

Talon studied in Paris, with the Jesuits at the Collège de Clermont. Towards the age of 28 he joined the military administrative services: he was commissary for the wars in Flanders and intendant of Turenne's army in 1653, commissary of Le Quesnoy in 1654. In 1655 he became intendant of the province of Hainault. During the years that he held this office he often merited Mazarin's praise for his zeal and competence.

Created by Richelieu, the intendants—ill-received at first because they caused the royal power to be too closely felt—had an essential role to play in the administrative machinery of France. According to Pierre Clément, "they were required 'to deal with acts of oppression that the king's subjects might suffer at the hands of the officers of the law through corruption, negligence, ignorance or otherwise,' to report upon examples of incorrect procedure and extortion by magistrates, to judge on the authority of the council and to pronounce judgements without appeal, including the death penalty, to anticipate and repress anything that might threaten order, to keep watch over provisions and supplies and the state of the prisons. Informed by the attorneys-general of all abuses committed in the province, following the armies if necessary, they reviewed the troops in order to make sure that they were well equipped, and judged soldiers without appeal. Roads, canals, mines, lay within their competence, and in addition everything that concerned taxes." These manifold and somewhat overwhelming duties had in 1655 fallen to the lot of a young man 30 years of age. It was proof that Jean Talon was held in great esteem in high places.

In 1665 Louis XIV and Colbert were looking for an intendant for Canada. Louis Robert de Fortel had been appointed to this office on 21 March 1663; but, for reasons that have remained unknown, he never went to New France. The post was a difficult one, and Colbert was demanding. Jean Talon, until then intendant of the province of Hainault, was nominated. On 23 March 1665 he was given his commission, and on 24 May he sailed for New France on board the *Saint-Sébastien*, along with Governor RÉMY de Courcelle. After putting into port at Gaspé, where he collected some minerals, Talon arrived before Quebec on 12 Sept. 1665.

At the moment when Talon landed at Quebec, France was finally enjoying peace and order following the treaties of Osnabrück, Münster, and of the Pyrenees, and Louis XIV's succession to the throne: the same did not hold true for New France. For more than 20 years, weakened and disorganized, the colony had been at grips with a cruel and elusive enemy who threatened its fragile existence a little more each day. Canada was being drained of its lifeblood in the struggle with the Iroquois, whose "warlike and bloodthirsty mood" increased in proportion to their success. The whole life of the colony was affected by it: the fur trade, the economic foundation of the country, had all but died out, as had the enthusiasm and zeal of the Cent-Associés, to such an extent that the debility of the colony seemed to jeopardize its future. It was for this reason that Louis XIV and Colbert decided to intervene before it was too late. The appointment of an intendant, in particular, fitted into the plan for a necessary reorganization of New France.

Indeed, since CHAMPLAIN the governors had held the widest powers. Although the royal statutes of 1647 and 1648 had set up a council with legislative, executive, and judicial powers, this council nevertheless remained under the control of the governor, whose opinion always prevailed. Being thus in possession of a sort of right of veto, the governor continued in effect to hold the authority which Champlain and his immediate successors had enjoyed.

This system was too primitive to last. The increase in the population soon showed up its weaknesses. Towards 1660 the settlers were clamouring for a change. Moreover, tired of the inertia of the Compagnie des Cent-Associés, which could no longer fulfil its obligations, they were asking for its dissolution. Louis XIV, who had assumed power in 1661, was immediately made aware of the problem of New France, then on the brink of ruin, according to contemporary testimony. The king acquainted himself with numerous reports on the colony; he granted audiences to prominent persons; he even sent a royal investigator to America [*see* MONTS]. Quite obviously a new tack was called for. At the beginning of 1663 Louis XIV accepted the withdrawal of the Compagnie des Cent-Associés. New France became a royal possession again.

Louis XIV then proceeded to carry out a vast administrative reorganization of the colony. The governor's powers were conspicuously reduced, many being transferred to the intendant and the Conseil Souverain. The governor, the first personage in the hierarchy of New France, directed military matters and external policy (Indians and the English colonies in America), in addition to exercising a certain supervision over the clergy,

Talon

the religious communities, and education. For his part, the intendant was responsible for all the civil administration.

The creation of the Conseil Souverain in April 1663 marked the establishment of royal justice in New France. The seigneurial courts were not suppressed as a result, although their jurisdiction was speedily limited to lower justice, middle and high justice being henceforth the prerogative of the royal courts. In fact, from 1666 on the towns of Quebec and Trois-Rivières—Montreal followed suit in 1693—were both provided with a court of first instance, the *prévôté* (provost court) or *juridiction*, which likewise heard appeals from the seigneurial courts within its competence. Decisions of these *juridictions* could be appealed to the Conseil Souverain, the highest court in the country. This council was composed of the governor, the bishop, the intendant, and five councillors. Although it was above all a court of justice, the council nevertheless fulfilled at the beginning some administrative functions, of which it was to be relieved completely at the end of the century.

Scarcely a year had gone by since the retrocession of the colony to the royal domain by the Cent-Associés when in May 1664 Louis XIV created the Compagnie des Indes occidentales, to which he granted all rights of ownership, justice, and seigneury. The king reserved for himself, however, the privilege of delivering their commissions to the governors, as well as to the officers of the Conseil Souverain—and later to the intendants—who in theory were chosen and appointed by the company.

Upon his arrival in the colony Talon bore the title of intendant of justice, police, and finances in Canada, Acadia, the island of Newfoundland, and other countries of North American France. His duties were as numerous as they were varied: to attend councils of war, to hear complaints from all persons and to render good and swift justice, to investigate all undertakings against the king's service, to take action, including the carrying-out of the judgement, against those guilty of all crimes, to appoint the number of judges and legally trained persons required by law, in general to take cognizance of all crimes, abuses, and malpractices, to preside over the Conseil Souverain in the absence of the lieutenant-general and the governor, and to judge alone and without appeal in civil cases. In addition, in the field of finances he was to keep a watch on the control, handling, and distribution of funds intended for the upkeep of the soldiers or for provisions, munitions, repairs, fortifications, loans, taxes, and other expenses; to verify and close the statements and warrants forwarded by the lieutenant-general-in-chief; and to have presented for his examination statements of musters and inspections, rolls, and registers. Generally speaking, he was to do and order, within the limits of his function, whatever he considered necessary for the good and the advantage of the administration.

In the same year that Talon arrived, there landed at Quebec the troops promised by the king for subduing the Iroquois, whom Louis XIV was resolved to "exterminate completely." By the summer of 1665, in anticipation of future action, the lieutenant-general PROUVILLE de Tracy had three forts built on the Richelieu which were intended both to defend the approaches to the colony and to serve as outposts and stepping-stones on the road to the Iroquois country; two others were to be built the following year. The intendant showed great energy in procuring for the 1,300 soldiers the shelter, supplies, clothes, tools, and arms that they needed for passing the winter. In addition most of the material preparations for the projected expedition depended upon him. In particular the army had to be equipped with barks and flat-bottomed boats, which Talon had built in the colony. Instead of a single expedition, there were two: Courcelle's during the winter of 1665–66, and another led by Tracy himself in the autumn of 1666. The following year the Iroquois surrendered. If, at the request of Tracy and Courcelle, the intendant did not accompany the troops into the Iroquois cantons, he none the less had a very large share in the success of the French arms through his constant and meticulous care in placing at the disposition of the army everything that was necessary for the war, despite the poverty of the colony, the lack of roads, and the distances.

While collaborating with the military leaders, Talon neglected in no way the more pacific aspects of his mission and applied himself to executing the instructions that the king had given him on 27 March 1665. Perusal of this document recalls immediately the statement by Louis XIV and Colbert in 1664, in the charter of the Compagnie des Indes occidentales, to the effect that colonies and ocean traffic are "the sole and true means of giving trade the lustre that it enjoys in foreign countries." Indeed, the king incited Talon to take the most appropriate steps for the "expansion" of the colony, so that it would shortly be able to provide for its own needs and supply certain products necessary for the growth of industry in the mother country; to that end it was necessary to settle the country, develop agriculture and trade, and set up industries in it.

In particular, his instructions urged Talon to

study the administration of justice, in order to apply to it the necessary correctives; also, in collaboration with the Conseil Souverain, he was to see to "the establishing of sound administration." In September 1665 Talon found the colony virtually devoid of courts of justice, except for a few seigneurial tribunals: the former seneschal's court had been abolished in 1663, the Conseil Souverain had not sat since 6 July—it had indeed met on 23 September (1665), but for the sole purpose of registering Courcelle's, Talon's, and Le Barroys's commissions—and the Compagnie des Indes occidentales had not yet appointed any judges. At Montreal, it is true, there had been in existence since 1663 a royal seneschal's court, which had been set up by the Conseil Souverain in place of the seigneurial justice. This seneschal's court had, however, been established in violation of the rights of the Sulpicians; Talon therefore abolished it on 18 Sept. 1666, restoring by this move seigneurial justice in Montreal.

In the absence of regular tribunals, the intendant acted as arbitrator between litigant parties: "I have thus far settled out of court all the matters and all the law-suits that have come before me." This situation however could only be temporary. In the summer of 1666 Talon prepared a draft of regulations which he submitted to Tracy and Courcelle: he proposed to them the restoration of the Conseil Souverain, whose members were in fact appointed on 6 December of that year. From January 1667 on, the council met, but rather irregularly. In the meantime, on 1 May 1666, the Compagnie des Indes occidentales had appointed LOUIS-THÉANDRE CHARTIER de Lotbinière lieutenant-general for civil and criminal cases at Quebec; the council received his oath and installed him in his functions 10 Jan. 1667. At about the same time Trois-Rivières also received its court of first instance. As a result, in his "Mémoire sur l'état présent du Canada" in 1667 Talon was able to describe the administration of justice in the colony as follows: it "is rendered in the first instance by the seigneurial judge, then by a civil and criminal lieutenant named by the Company in each of the jurisdictions of Quebec and Trois-Rivières, and over all there is a Conseil Souverain which judges in the last resort all cases that are appealed."

The intendant wanted to cut down the number of law-suits, which were far too frequent in the colony. He believed in the effectiveness of the out-of-court settlements which he had tried out at the beginning of his administration and to which, he wrote, "I resort with pleasure": "this more gentle way . . . saves valuable time for the parties that live in distant places which they can leave only by canoe." On 20 Aug. 1667 he obtained from the Conseil Souverain—probably at his request, and despite Courcelle's opposition —that all lower court cases should first be brought before him, in order that he might "assign them to the jurisdiction which should deal with them" if he did not find any way of arriving at a settlement out of court or that, if the matter required him to take cognizance of it, he might assert his competency to judge it himself. In 1671, as Courcelle had created difficulties for him, Talon consulted the minister, who did not approve of his procedure, which he considered to be "a little contrary to the ways of justice." Colbert, who had urged Talon to "carry out the duties of a good paterfamilias," did not look with favour upon a judicial system which, although paternalistic, was too summary.

Being responsible for policing just as much as he was for justice, the intendant did not delay in giving his attention to it. As early as the summer of 1666, in his draft of regulations which was registered in the Conseil Souverain on 24 Jan. 1667, Talon revealed his intention of establishing order in the life of the colony. However, as most of his ordinances have been lost, it is difficult to see his work in this field. Nevertheless the records of the Conseil Souverain allow us sometimes to detect and often to guess at the intendant's influence in the drawing-up of the colony's legislation, the whole body of which, for the period spanned by Talon's two administrations, is remarkable for its cohesion and its realism. The intendant followed a well-defined policy, which had indeed been conveyed to him by the great Colbert himself: "You must always keep in mind the plan which I am outlining to you in a few words and which corresponds to what is contained at greater length in your instructions and to the interviews that I have had with you here, and you must never depart from it."

The first point in this "plan" concerned peopling the country. In order to increase the population, various measures, which were sometimes very energetic, were adopted. First, immigration was encouraged. From 1665 to 1672 1,500 settlers landed in Canada, either as indentured employees or simply as immigrants. The indentured employees, who were from 16 to 40 years of age, were recruited and transported to Canada in return for their promise to work for a settler for three years; their passage was assured and they received a modest salary. At the end of their engagement they received a tract of land, some supplies and tools. This system offered a double advantage: it provided the colonists with precious man-power and gave the newcomers time to

Talon

adapt themselves to the special conditions of farm work in New France. The immigrants who came on their own were granted a piece of land, two acres of which had been cleared and seeded, as well as essential tools and supplies for a year or two; in return they promised to clear two acres and to put them in cultivation for a future arrival. Indentured employees and immigrants thus received, through the intendant, considerable help.

Talon desired massive immigration; but Colbert adhered to the principle that Old France should not be depopulated for the benefit of New France. Nevertheless the minister had given him orders to encourage the soldiers of the Carignan-Salières regiment to get used to the colony. The intendant bent his efforts to this with all the more conviction as he counted very much upon colonization by the military for the defence of the country. Despite opposition from certain quarters, Talon succeeded in persuading several officers to take up land alongside their men; he obtained gratuities (about 44,000 *livres* in all) for the most zealous among them, so that it is estimated that 800 soldiers settled down in the colony, drawn from the Carignan-Salières regiment and from companies that had landed in 1670.

Indentured employees, soldiers, and settlers were expected to found homes. For them Colbert, effectively seconded by Talon, sent to New France a considerable number of female immigrants. In seven years more than 1,000 "king's daughters" (*filles du roi*) found husbands shortly after landing from their ships. Among them, some "girls of high birth" who were intended for the former officers of the Carignan-Salières regiment, received a dowry from the intendant, who wanted in this way to encourage their marriage. To the others Talon delivered "some provisions" and 50 *livres* "in goods suitable for their household."

So unfaltering was the intendant's will to encourage marriage and child-bearing, that he resorted to measures that sometimes ran counter to normal individual liberty. Not satisfied with urging parents to marry off their children as soon as they were old enough to fend for themselves, he even made the fathers of unmarried boys and girls appear at the registry office to explain themselves. Likewise, on 20 Oct. 1671 he signed an ordinance obliging bachelors to marry the young girls who arrived from France, under penalty of being deprived of the privilege of fishing, hunting, and engaging in the fur trade: one might well say that he deprived the recalcitrants of any chance of making a living in the colony. Along with these measures, the severity of which astonishes us, he had others adopted (His Majesty's decree of 5 April 1669) which were more humane in character: he wanted honours conferred upon the heads of the largest families, who would be chosen for civil offices; to fathers of 10 children "born in lawful wedlock and who are not priests, religious, or nuns" he gave an annual grant of 300 *livres*, and 400 to fathers of 12 children; to young men who married when they were 20 years of age or less he gave 20 *livres*. Talon was not disappointed in his expectations: in 1671, he announced proudly to Colbert, there had been between 600 and 700 births in the colony.

At the time of Talon's second administration, however, a relatively new phenomenon endangered his policy for increasing the population: the men and young men were more and more taking to going into the woods, giving up their homes, living like the Indians and carrying on "the veritable profession of bandits." On 5 June 1672 Talon issued an ordinance forbidding anyone to take to the woods without a licence from the governor or the intendant. At the time when, on Colbert's orders, Talon was applying himself to the acculturation of the Indians, to inducing them to live among the whites and to become united with them by marriage, he was witnessing, by an ironic reversal of the situation, the defection of the French. If he had stayed longer in the colony, Talon would have verified the accuracy of the remark made by Marie de l'Incarnation [*see* GUYART], that a Frenchman becomes an Indian more readily than an Indian becomes a Frenchman. Thus, on these two points, taking to the woods and assimilating the Indians, the intendant met with complete failure.

Nevertheless the policy of populating the country carried on by Colbert and Talon did on the whole give the desired results. Convinced, like his master, that men are the basic wealth of a state, the intendant pursued his objective with a veritable passion, with the result that, from 1666 to 1673, if we go by the censuses (which are not always very reliable), the population of Canada appears to have more than doubled, increasing from 3,215 to 7,605 souls.

Populating the country could not proceed without settlement. As early as the autumn of 1665 Talon made a point of encouraging in a rational manner the implantation of a large land-owning population. For it was above all else necessary, according to Colbert's desire, that the colony should become self-sufficient as soon as possible, particularly as far as food was concerned; Talon likewise wanted to make agricultural products one of the bases of Canadian trade with France and especially with the West Indies. His effort was therefore not only a matter of assuring for New

France a subsistence economy, but of putting agriculture on a commercial footing.

During the winter of 1665–66 Talon selected a large area of ground near Quebec for establishing three farming villages. This ground belonged to the Jesuits, who objected; but the intendant advanced the argument of the common good, which he set against the private advantage of the religious; Colbert gave his approval, and the Jesuits reluctantly gave up part of the seigneury of Notre-Dame-des-Anges, which had been granted them in 1626. In creating the communities of Bourg-Royal, Bourg-la-Reine, and Bourg-Talon, the intendant was pursuing a double objective: to provide an example of dwellings built next to one another, and to prepare at the same time the 30 or 40 pieces of land that Colbert had requested each year for the new families, to whom Talon added the soldiers who would settle in the country. In order to realize the first objective, Talon adopted for his villages a plan that was completely new in Canada: "The pieces of land were triangular," wrote Chapais, "and the dwellings, which were built at the apex of the triangle, were all grouped about the square or the rectangle where the church or the chapel was to rise." Without reducing the area of the pieces of land, this arrangement had the advantage of bringing together the inhabitants, who could better help one another, and of bringing them near the priest, the surgeon, and the notary.

Until that time indeed, the seigneurial régime had developed a little haphazardly: at the court it was deplored that seigneuries that were still heavily wooded created gaps along the St. Lawrence which were detrimental to the defence of the country (the Iroquois war had proved that), as well as to the centralization of services. Consequently it was necessary to increase the number of judges, notaries, and surgeons, who as a result made a poor living, because, on the one hand, settlement had not been carried on in an orderly manner, and on the other, seigneurs who were negligent or too generously endowed left standing veritable walls of forest along the limits of their domains.

Not satisfied with setting an example by putting his rural villages into cultivation, Talon tackled all the problems at once. He endeavoured to fill in the spots that were still empty along the shores of the St. Lawrence by distributing some 60 fiefs. Moreover, in an ordinance dated 22 May 1667 he had enjoined the seigneurs to include in their contracts for land grants the following clauses: an obligation on the copyholder's part to take up residence within 12 months of receiving the grant, and to clear and cultivate two acres each year on pain of retrocession of the property thus granted; a prohibition against sale of his land by the copyholder before he had built a dwelling on it and had cleared two acres. These measures were well calculated to assure the actual taking possession of the soil and the continuous settlement of the shores of the St. Lawrence. There remained however the seigneuries that were too vast and that their owners were unlikely to clear entirely. Talon turned his attention to them: beginning in 1666 and 1667 he ordered that a register of landed property be prepared, to permit a general survey of the situation. He had moreover conceived with Colbert a plan for reducing the dimensions of these domains, a tenth or a fifteenth of which could be granted each year to a more zealous or more capable seigneur. On 27 Sept. 1672, in anticipation of the application of this measure, the intendant required all those who owned more than 400 acres of land "obtained previous to the last 10 years," to declare the extent and the quality of the lands they owned, cleared or uncleared, the number of tenants, and other details calculated to enlighten him about the true state of settlement in the St. Lawrence valley. After Talon's departure (November 1672), this project does not seem to have been followed up.

This attempt to ensure rational settlement was the reason for the appointment of two surveyors: Louis-Marin Boucher, *dit* Boisbuisson (1 May 1672), and Jean Lerouge* (5 Nov. 1672).

In every respect Talon had followed out the precise directions contained in his instructions: endeavour to remedy the scattering of the population by having land cleared "step by step"; make the settlers take up residence; expropriate in favour of new settlers the parts not yet cleared of domains that were too extensive; prepare each year 30 or 40 dwellings for new families "by having the woods cut down and the lands that are cleared seeded at His Majesty's expense." We lack exact figures for evaluating Talon's work in its entirety, but the following will suffice to show that there was progress: from 1667 to 1668 the number of acres under cultivation in the colony rose from 11,448 to 15,649; in 1668 the wheat crop amounted to 130,978 bushels.

Wheat! "Up till now," admitted Pierre Boucher* in 1664, "our one thought has been of wheat . . . as being the most necessary to us." While encouraging the growing of this essential cereal and of vegetables such as peas and beans, which constituted the basic food of the settlers, Talon, in accordance with the directives that he received from the mother country, endeavoured to introduce into the colony hemp, flax, and hops, which

Talon

would supply the factories of which he was already dreaming. Having a predilection for energetic measures, he requisitioned in 1666 all the thread stocked in the warehouses of the colony, in order to make the settlers sow hemp. He distributed seed to them, not sparing his encouragements to them and requiring them to give him back the same quantity the following year. In 1669 the production of thread and cloth had begun; Talon bought their hemp crops from two settlers to prove to the colonists that they would find a market for this product. The production of flax and hemp seemed to have a glowing future: "In three years from now," wrote Talon in 1671, "the settlers will receive from their crops and their own manufacture most and perhaps all the cloth that they need for themselves," even though, on an average, the value of the annual consumption of cloth amounted to "more than 60,000 *livres*"; in six years, he forecast, cloth could be exported to France. In addition the manufacture of rope and other small kinds of cordage had been begun. He also encouraged the growing of hops and barley, which he bought for his brewery. Once again he set the example: he had 6,000 poles of hops planted on his land at Les Islets. In short, he gave such an impetus to agriculture, that the colony soon had a surplus: in 1667 and 1668 peas, both green and dried, hops, and barley were exported to the West Indies; in 1672 Frontenac [*see* BUADE] spoke of the products, in particular wheat, of which the colony had too much.

Talon was no less energetic in increasing livestock in New France, which up till then had consisted almost entirely of cattle and, to a lesser degree, pigs. Horses and sheep arrived from France almost every year, but in limited quantities (41 horses and 80 sheep from 1665 to 1668). Talon was so successful in encouraging the settlers to increase the number of their animals and took such suitable measures that in a few years astonishing results were obtained: by 1670 horses were sufficiently numerous for trading in them to be carried on; in 1671 no more salt pork was imported from La Rochelle, which ordinarily supplied 800 barrels of it each year; at the same period the colony was producing sufficient leather to shoe the whole population. Wool, however, was scarce: sheep were few, and Colbert was not inclined to send more to the colony; despite Talon's protestations, the minister remained adamant.

In five years Talon did a great deal for Canadian agriculture: he diversified its production and temporarily put it on a commercial footing, as well as interesting the settlers in breeding stock. Nevertheless, after him the growing of crops for industrial use, with which the settlers had not had time to become familiar, almost completely disappeared for lack of encouragement and markets; the colony quickly returned to growing wheat and to subsistence farming. Talon's stay had been too brief.

The abandonment of the cultivation of fieldcrops for industrial use was a consequence of the disappearance or the slowing-down of the manufacturing industries created by the intendant to absorb the agricultural surpluses. The absence of Talon, who knew how to encourage and stimulate the settlers, and the stopping of royal subsidies brought an end to a work that was still precarious, that had been laboriously set up without sufficient aid from the mother country: "The means to establish manufacturing there lies in the industry of the settlers and their work, rather than in the help that the King can give," Colbert had written as early as 1666.

At the beginning of his administration Talon had introduced looms into the colony. Not only did he urge women and girls to learn to spin, but he also had looms distributed to private homes; to the seminarists he supplied in addition hemp and wool. In 1671 he announced to Colbert that he had had the wool made into drugget, barracan, coarse muslin, and serge; now the colony was ready to make cloth. Moreover, he added, "Nearly a third of the shoes are made from native leathers, and at the present time I have from what is produced in Canada all that I need to clothe myself from head to foot." He had, in fact, set up at Quebec a hat factory and had made possible in 1668 the establishment of a tannery at Pointe-Lévy. With his son-in-law and partner Étienne Charest, François BYSSOT worked the hides of cattle, elk, deer, and even of porpoises and seals. Besides bestowing 3,268 *livres* upon Byssot, Talon ordered from him large quantities of shoes for the troops. The undertaking prospered so well that in 1673 the intendant (who was back in France) estimated the production of shoes at 8,000 pairs a year. This was, moreover, one of the rare industries to survive Talon's departure; most of them, like hat-making, being entirely supported by the intendant, did not last.

Talon's most important achievement in his search for outlets for the agricultural products was the brewery that he had caused to be built at Quebec between 1668 and 1670. In 1667 he had received from the king two vats which he wanted to use for making beer, and from Colbert he received permission to set up a brewery. At this time New France was spending 100,000 *livres* each year on the purchase of wines and spirits. In order to keep this money in the colony and to put to use the surplus barley and wheat, the intendant had the Conseil Souverain issue an ordinance encouraging the setting up of breweries by limiting to 1,200 hogsheads the annual importation of alcoholic beverages. Constructed during the period between Talon's two terms of office, the brewery began production in 1670; on 2 Nov. 1671 Talon informed Colbert that it could supply 2,000 hogsheads of beer for the West Indies and a like amount for local consumption, which would bring about the processing of 12,000 bushels of grain per year. Unfortunately, after the intendant's departure, the regulations concerning the importation of wines and spirits were eased; in 1675 the brewery closed down. After remaining empty a long time, the building was sold to the king by Talon in 1685 and was fitted up to serve as a residence for the intendants of New France.

If he applied himself to developing that basic resource, agriculture, Talon nonetheless did not neglect New France's other great resource, the forest. Everything concurred, it is true, to favour the setting up of a lumber industry: on one hand Colbert wanted to equip France with a powerful navy and merchant marine; the West Indies, on the other hand, needed wood for making the barrels, casks, and chests necessary for their trade. Towards these two poles Talon oriented the lumbering industry: to the mother country he sent masts and lumber; to the West Indies, lighter woods, and particularly stave wood. This industry was not entirely new in the colony: as early as 1630 николаs denys had undertaken it in Acadia; in the St. Lawrence valley some settlers had at various times shipped wood to France. But it fell to Talon to give it a new impetus and to push it on to a point that had not been attained up till then.

During the winter of 1665–66 Talon had the forests inspected, in order to receive information about the quantity and quality of the trees suitable for ship-building. Of all the woods, oak was the most sought after. Unfortunately there was hardly any close to the St. Lawrence; the intendant hit upon the idea of using the tributary rivers for floating the logs. In 1667 he sent off his first shipments: to the West Indies planks, stave wood, and some small masts; to France small masts, spars, and other pieces for building ships; at Quebec itself wood had been in use for a year for the ship-building yard. Anxious not to squander this resource, Talon signed three ordinances in 1670 and 1671 forbidding the settlers to cut down or burn oak and other species of trees suitable for ship-building before the king's carpenters had examined them.

The lumbering industry did not however become as important as the intendant would have liked. In particular, the absence of sawmills—there was only one in existence, it seems, which began operating at Montreal in 1670—constituted a major obstacle. Talon tried to bring from the English colonies workmen who were specialists in building these mills, but his scheme was not successful. Once again the new-born industry disappeared with the intendant. The trade in masts was to start up again in the colony, but much later.

From the Canadian forest Talon wanted to extract other products: tar, potash, and soft soap. At his request, Colbert de Terron sent to Quebec in 1670 a tar-maker. The following year production had reached 8 barrels, 2 of which were shipped to France. Emboldened by his tar-maker's promises, the intendant hoped for an excellent output; but it was soon realized that for a long time only a very little tar would be obtained, and at very high cost. patoulet, the intendant's secretary, expressed the opinion that it was better to let the settlers make it and to buy their goods; the scheme was given up. Talon had no more success with the potash and soft soap, despite the fact that in 1670 he had brought from France a specialist—or self-styled one—the Sieur Nicolas Follin, and that the king had granted the latter important commercial privileges. At the time of Talon's departure Follin had not yet seriously set to work. These failures however are rather to be ascribed to the difficulties which such industries met in New France in the 17th century than to the intendant, who, as was his wont, did not stint his aid or his encouragements to the makers of tar and potash.

Talon's interest in the growing of hemp, in the lumber industry, and in the making of tar was directly linked to the ship-building industry which he was endeavouring to establish in the colony; besides, he was well aware that these materials would be welcomed by Colbert, who, despite his mercantilist convictions, was forced to buy them in Scandinavia. The idea of building ships in Canada was however not new: for a long period, it is true, only barks and pinnaces had been built, principally to cope with emergencies; but in 1664, at Colbert's command and on the king's behalf, a galliot, a brigantine, and some ships of lesser tonnage had been laid down. Upon his arrival Talon took this activity in hand and with his special genius tried to establish it on solid foundations; he sought to produce in the colony the cordage, the tar, and even the iron fittings that were required.

The intendant succeeded in some of his ventures. He opened a shipyard on the Saint-Charles River, brought from France shipwrights and a

Talon

foreman. Talon's aim was to supply ships for the king on the one hand (Colbert had promised to order some from him), and to private individuals on the other, for the fishing industry and for trading with France and the West Indies. As early as the autumn of 1665 he had assembled some settlers to undertake the construction of ships of 20 and 40 tons burden; he hoped that for them the king would approve of his bringing from France the ironwork, canvas, and cordage. He himself had a vessel of 120 tons burden built, which was completed in the spring of 1667. With the collaboration of some private individuals and thanks to a fund of 40,000 *livres* created in 1671, he was able to lay down a ship of 400 to 500 tons, and soon afterwards another of 800.

Numerous difficulties arose however. Skilled labour was scarce: Talon reinforced the few shipwrights with "house carpenters," who, for the sake of the trade that they were learning, pledged themselves to work for four years "for their board and clothing only"; he even enlisted the help of soldiers and settlers who received training in "handling the axe" and were "formed to the trade." Moreover the iron fittings, anchors, cordage, tars, compasses, etc., still had to be imported from France. The ships were very costly.

In 1672 Frontenac, who had neither Talon's patience nor his tenacity, wrote to the minister that he did not know "whether, in view of the cost and the scarcity of workers which exists in this country, you would not find it more profitable for us to send you all the wood considered suitable for ship-building . . . rather than play at having them built here." This was an opinion that Colbert was quite disposed to listen to. Consequently, after the intendant's departure all effective aid to the ship-building industry ceased, and the settlers were simply encouraged to build boats for their own needs. There was hardly any interest except in the barks and flat-bottomed boats required for the army; only a few individuals occasionally built ships of greater tonnage for their trade. The ship-building industry had lost its impetus.

In Talon's mind ship-building was not unrelated to the need for developing the richest and perhaps the most accessible of the colony's resources: fish. What it had been possible to call "a manna which surpasses all that one can imagine," had up till then had only a very limited attraction for the settlers, who were, it has been said, too preoccupied with obtaining wheat for themselves; consequently, in 1663 a traveller compared the French in Canada to "paralytics lying beside a great treasure." They were satisfied with using this manna merely for their sustenance; a few only, who had gathered about François Byssot in 1650, made a commercial activity of fishing. However—and Talon made the observation in 1673—all of Europe was eating dried cod; France for its part had to import more than 1,500,000 *livres* worth of fish annually, without mentioning the West Indies and the Levant colonies, which ate Acadian cod supplied by the Boston fishing boats!

Although the king had not discussed fisheries with him in his written instructions, Talon concerned himself with them as soon as he reached Quebec. On 4 Oct. 1665 he announced to the minister that he had assembled some men for "fishing work." The following year he reported on cod-fishing in the St. Lawrence and told how he had sent men to hunt seals. He endeavoured to have the settlers realize the advantages and profits that they could derive from fishing: he commissioned nine of them to fish for cod to supply the troops and the West Indies trade, "in order to impart the desire to anyone who does not have it." And in fact, in 1667 he shipped to the West Indies salted salmon and eels, salt and dried cod, and seal oil.

Talon's ambition was to induce the settlers to develop fishing with a view to exporting. In 1666 he had an idea that bore fruit: "fixed" fisheries, which would be more profitable still than "roving" ones. The intendant dreamed of seeing the settlers located on their fishing grounds, attending to fishing in season and turning to lumbering or to hunting moose in the winter. This felicitous combination could not fail to attract enterprising spirits. Nevertheless it was not until 1671 and 1672—perhaps because of Talon's absence from 1668 to 1670—that the first fishing centres were set up in the Gaspé peninsula and Acadia, and on the Labrador coast.

Shortly before leaving the colony, Talon was working at forming a company which would have brought into association the principal settlers who were interested in the fishing industry. He did not have time to carry out his plan, or else, did he meet some resistance among the colonists? They, according to Frontenac, were afraid "that wishing to be their own masters and directors of their businesses, they would lose their freedom to carry on in their own way." Did they have the impression, which was perhaps justified, that the intendant would have interfered a little too much in their activities? However that may be, if the company did not come into existence, the movement in favour of fixed fisheries was so well launched that they were not given up after Talon's departure; although they were few in number, they enjoyed relative prosperity.

The efforts which Talon exerted in the fields of

agriculture, lumbering, and fishing, as well as his policy for peopling and colonizing the country, had as their ultimate aim the creation of a great trade. It was this aim that gave his work its admirable unity. In all sectors of the colony's economy he wanted to succeed in producing for export; to transport merchandise, ships were needed: Talon had them built: whence the development, not only of the basic natural resources, but also of complementary industries, such as those for making tar and cordage. Canadian products would, naturally, be shipped to France, where there was a market for furs, fish, wood, hemp, tar, potash, as well as for iron, copper, and coal; but most of Canada's products would be directed towards the West Indies, since New France's economy complemented the mother country's too little for there to be any hope of ever balancing their trade. Talon considered that it was possible however to balance Canada's trade through "the southern part of America [the West Indies]," which was "naturally deprived of the products necessary for food and clothing because of its exposure to the sun and its excessively hot climates...."

The intendant conceived of a three-way trade, Canada-West Indies-France, which, as a matter of fact, had been tried as early as 1653 by JEAN-PAUL GODEFROY and his partners, although the results are not known.

This triangular trade was started again by Talon in 1667, when he sent wood, fish, peas, and seal oil to the West Indies. The first trial was made by a ship belonging to the Compagnie des Indes occidentales, which returned to France laden with sugar. Each year after that two or three ships, some of which belonged to settlers, sailed to the West Indies with their cargo of products from Canada.

In 1673, shortly before leaving Canada, Talon was optimistic: this trade, he wrote, "is made up of the surplus of peas, salmon, salted eels, salt and dried cod, planks and stave wood, and it will grow with the surplus of wheat, which will be converted into flour, and it is estimated that Canada will be able to dispose of 30,000 bushels a year"; "the quantity of peas may amount to 10,000 bushels"; "salt meat, beef and pork, will not be the least important part of this trade, and I consider that ... Canada will shortly be able to supply salt pork, which already she has stopped importing from France"; "beer too enters into this trade, and I affirm that 2,000 hogsheads a year can be supplied to the Islands, and more, if they consume more"; there were even grounds for hoping soon to ship clothes of Canadian manufacture.

These forecasts were not unreasonable. Unfortunately, Talon's departure was fatal to his work and to the dealings with the West Indies: although they were not given up completely, they were never to justify the hopes that he had placed in them.

The fact that navigation on the St. Lawrence was shut down for six months in winter and that ships could make only one trip a year did not help in developing trade. Combined with the enormous distances to be covered, this factor had an effect upon the profit-earning capacity of the exchanges. In 1669 Colbert had asked Talon to set up in Acadia "some storage place" where ships would have been able to unload and take on their merchandise and also make up enough time to complete two trips a year. Talon did not have time to create these warehouses; it can be assumed however that the opening-up of the land route from Lévis to Pentagouet, of which he dreamed, was linked up with this plan.

Talon wanted to set his great trade going with Acadia and Boston as well as with the West Indies. A stock-growing country, Acadia could supply salted meats. In 1671 for example the intendant had bought 60 quintals of beef there. In return Canada would send cereals and flour. In this way, and thanks to the line of communications which he hoped to open up between the two colonies, the intendant would have joined closely two regions of New France that had up till then been juxtaposed. Acadia had long been obtaining its supplies on the Boston market; while trying to direct Acadia's trade towards Quebec, the intendant did not nevertheless want to cut off economic relations with the English in America. With the king's approval he made advances to the authorities in Boston in order to set up a system of exchange. His departure, however, put a definite end to this bold plan.

If the fruit of his efforts was almost entirely lost after Talon had returned to France, this can be ascribed in good measure to the lack of interest on the part of the court and the colonial administrators. Talon's projects were workable; the only thing that was to be lacking was effective support from his successors and financial aid from the mother country.

On leaving France in 1665 Talon had received from the king a promise that he would have to stay only two years in Canada. Consequently in November 1666 he had reminded the monarch that the end of his term of office was approaching; from Colbert he had requested permission to leave, in view of his ill health. Nevertheless on 5 April 1667 Colbert had told him that he was to spend a third year in New France. The following

Talon

autumn Talon had been more insistent: his health and family matters compelled him to return to France. Yielding to his requests, Colbert had appointed to replace him the Sieur de BOUTROUE, who landed at Quebec in September 1668. Talon left shortly afterwards, on 10 November, regretted by all: "Since he has been here as intendant," wrote Marie de l'Incarnation, "the country has developed and business has progressed more than they had done since the French have been here."

There was satisfaction too in France. Colbert did not try to conceal it: he received Talon and accompanied him into the presence of the king, who talked for an hour with the former intendant. Delighted with the colony's progress, Louis XIV and the minister were afraid that Talon's absence might harm Canada: they persuaded him to return there in the spring of 1669.

Talon took advantage of his stay in Paris to have certain measures adopted: freedom of trade for Canada, the decree of 5 April 1669 giving assistance to marriages, another on 16 April for the control of import duties on Canadian cod and coal, and the return to New France of the Recollets. In addition, at his request Colbert allocated 200,000 *livres* to the colony, providing for the passage of 150 *filles du roi*, 6 companies of 50 soldiers each, and of more than 30 officers and gentlemen; he gave orders for the sending of 12 mares, 2 stallions, and 50 ewes; finally, he allowed him some shipwrights.

Talon's new commission was signed on 10 May 1669; on the 17th he received his instructions and on 15 July he sailed from La Rochelle after settling his family affairs. Caught in a gale, the ship spent three months struggling against the elements; it finally put into Lisbon, to be shipwrecked shortly afterwards three leagues out of this port. Talon escaped safe and sound, but his arrival in New France was delayed by a year. It was not until 18 Aug. 1670, after being at sea for three months and going aground off Tadoussac, that he landed at Quebec.

Immediately Talon took up his task again, pursuing aims that he had set himself during his first term as intendant. This time, however, he concerned himself greatly with the external affairs of the colony, even infringing on occasion upon the governor's province. His new concerns, which caused him to send "resolute persons" to the four corners of the country—discoverers and ambassadors—are the outstanding feature of his second term of administration: he tried, in Lionel Groulx's words, "to relate New France to its natural ties, geographic as well as economic, in short, to its American *milieu*." Hardly had he arrived than he was writing to Colbert on 10 Nov. 1670: "This country is laid out in such a way that by means of the St. Lawrence one can go everywhere inland, thanks to the lakes which lead to its source in the West and to the rivers that flow into it along its shores, opening the way to the North and the South." Talon was hearing the fascinating appeal of the unknown regions; along the inviting network of the river routes he was about to send forth his explorers.

He was not however yielding to simple curiosity. His aim was to give the colony its natural frontiers, to organize its trade, to reinforce its alliances, so that what had been created on the shores of the St. Lawrence could attain its full development.

In particular Talon felt the full weight of the presence of the English on the continent. He had in fact been disturbed about it from the time of his first administration. On 13 Nov. 1666, for example, he had suggested to Louis XIV and Colbert the conquest or the acquisition of New Holland in order, he said, to provide a second way of access to Canada and to prevent pelts from being diverted to Manhattan and Orange; moreover, he added, this would be the means of putting the Iroquois at the mercy of the French and of shutting the English up inside the boundaries of their territories. This idea, which was to be taken up again at the end of the century, was not accepted by the court. Nevertheless Talon gave proof of keen political vision, as he also did when he confided to Tracy and Courcelle his fear that in the event of war the English would attack Canada simultaneously from the upper and lower reaches of the St. Lawrence. This was foreseeing, 24 years ahead, almost exactly the tactics of the English when, in 1690, they sought to hem in the colony.

During his second mandate Talon was even more obsessed by these preoccupations. Thus, in the autumn of 1670 he told the minister about the "acts of piracy" by the Iroquois, who were seizing French furs to sell them to the English and the Dutch. To put an end to this practice, which each year was costing Canada's trade "1,200,000 *livres* of beaver pelts," he suggested two posts, one to the north and the other to the south of Lake Ontario, to protect the movement of the Ottawa Indians coming to trade, and the building of a galley to ensure freedom of navigation on the lake. In order to carry out this project he asked for a company of 100 soldiers and 15,000 *livres*. In reply Colbert told him to transmit this idea to M. de Courcelle, on whom the responsibility rested, so that he might carry it out if it were worthwhile.

Still with a view to increasing the profits of the fur trade, Talon made another suggestion, a very daring one: that an attempt be made to harness the Ottawa Rapids, "which interfere to such an extent with the Indians' travelling by water, that sometimes they are discouraged from coming down to us to bring us their pelts." The Indians, who would profit from this, would pay in return "some slight tax" on the furs that they would be transporting.

The desire to get ahead of the English by taking possession of territory, the need to extend the trade in furs, the obsession with the China Sea, together with the search for mines: these were the motives that incited Talon to set in motion a veritable exploration programme. In his usual way he wanted these undertakings to be carried out in an orderly manner: "In all places these adventurers [the explorers] are to keep diaries and answer on their return to the instructions that I have given them in writing. In all places they are to take possession, set up the King's arms, and draw up reports to serve as title claims."

At the moment that Talon was writing these lines, in the autumn of 1670, a year had already gone by since CAVELIER de La Salle had set out, supplied with letters patent from M. de Courcelle and accompanied by the Sulpicians Dollier* de Casson and BRÉHANT de Galinée, to look for the Ohio River and the Gulf of California. However, by 1 Oct. 1669 the impetuous La Salle had left the two religious, on the pretext of returning to Montreal. Whatever he did after this date, it is certain that he did not go as far as the Ohio; at least he never claimed that he did, and no document substantiates it. The Sulpicians for their part had reached the north shore of Lake Erie, of which they had taken possession before returning to Montreal on 18 June 1670.

Shortly after his return to the colony Talon certainly met La Salle, whom he sent in the autumn of 1670 "towards the south," in search of the "passage" to the China Sea. Once again nothing is known of the comings and goings of the temperamental explorer, except that he was at Montreal on 6 Aug. 1671. In the autumn however Talon maintained that he had no news of him; he left the colony in 1672, before La Salle had given any news of himself. Clearly the explorer had not carried out his mission.

To the regions that had been visited by Dollier and Galinée, Talon sent Simon-François DAUMONT de Saint-Lusson, to whom he gave the task of taking possession, in the name of the king of France, of the whole central region of America. In addition Saint-Lusson was to go as far as possible, as long as he had "what he needed to live on," in order to ascertain "with care whether there is, by means of lakes and rivers, any way of reaching the Southern Sea, which separates this continent from China." Having left in October 1670 with Nicolas Perrot*, Saint-Lusson spent the winter on Manitoulin Island, whence he forwarded to several nations an invitation to assemble in the spring at Sault Ste. Marie. There, on 4 June 1671, in the presence of the delegates of 14 Indian nations and "with all the pomp and circumstance that the country would allow," Saint-Lusson took possession "of the aforesaid place of Sainte-Marie du Sault, as also of Lakes Huron and Superior, the Île de Caienton, and of all the other countries, rivers, lakes, and nearby or contiguous streams, already or still to be discovered, which are confined on the one side by the Northern and Western Seas and on the other by the Southern Sea, as well as in all their length or breadth." At one fell swoop part of an empire came under France's jurisdiction.

Saint-Lusson, it seems, scarcely pushed on past Sault Ste. Marie, bringing back at the most some second-hand information about the "link" with the Southern Sea. He probably told the intendant about the Mississippi, which was much talked about in the Great Lakes region and which, it was believed, flowed into the Gulf of California. In the summer of 1672, perhaps losing hope of seeing La Salle come back, Talon entrusted Louis JOLLIET with going to the mouth of this river in order to verify that it did indeed flow into the China Sea. In 1674 Jolliet was to return with the certainty that the Mississippi flowed into the Gulf of Mexico; hope was however to be preserved of finding, through one of its tributaries, the Western Passage that was so much desired.

In any event, thanks to Talon's vision three-quarters of the American continent, to the west and the south, came under French sovereignty in a period of a few years.

Talon's attention was also directed towards the north, still little known, whence came, through the hands of the Ottawa Indians, the finest furs. In the summer of 1671 he chose the Jesuit Charles ALBANEL and Paul Denys* de Saint-Simon to make an expedition in this direction: the explorers were to go to Hudson Bay, make reports on everything that they discovered, establish trade in pelts with the Indians, and take possession of the territories; in addition they were to investigate whether it was advisable to establish on Hudson Bay a warehouse which could "replenish supplies for the ships which will subsequently be able to discover by this route the connecting passage between the Northern and Southern Seas." Albanel and his companion were the first Frenchmen—Radisson* and CHOUART Des Groseilliers excepted—to reach James Bay, which they took

Talon

possession of, although the English were already there.

Talon was seeking on every side the passage to the Western Sea. He was very much interested in the suggestion made to him at this time by a certain Capt. Poulet, who proposed searching for this passage and accomplishing the circumnavigation of America, either by the Northern Sea or the Straits of Magellan. With the intendant's departure, however, this project came to naught.

In his endeavour to link all parts of the colony with the vital centre in the St. Lawrence valley, Talon did not overlook the eastern territories, and chiefly Acadia. Probably attracted by the idea of setting up there a seaport that would be open in all seasons, and aware of the necessity of defending this province that was adjacent to the rival American colonies, Talon conceived the plan of a land route which would link Acadia to Quebec; he thought of it as having at regular intervals dwellings which would serve as relay stations. To reconnoitre the ground, he formed two teams which had the task of studying the regions of the Kennebec and Saint John rivers. He fixed his choice upon the latter region. In 1672 Talon gave a start to the execution of his project by granting fiefs on the route foreseen from Lévis to Pentagouet.

From 1670 to 1672, then, Talon pursued major aims which explain his whole work: to link the different parts of New France firmly to the nerve centre of the colony on the St. Lawrence; to build up a network of alliances which would funnel towards Quebec the furs from the north, west, and south; to guarantee the integrity and defence of French territory by taking possession of it, by making economic and military treaties, and by developing the frontier regions; finally, to find the China Sea and, perhaps, a second outlet for New France.

To these aims must be added that of discovering mines, with which Talon had been concerned even before leaving for New France; following information he had received at La Rochelle, he had put into port at Gaspé in 1665 to pick up some lead ore there. During his first administration, he collected information about coal, iron, lead, and copper mines; he sent ore regularly to France to be analysed. But despite his efforts he met with only very relative success.

In addition to the coal mine which the intendant had discovered in 1666 in the cliff at Quebec but which was impossible to work, there was another on Cape Breton Island which was rich in coal of excellent quality. In 1670 Talon sent Capt. Poulet to inspect this mine, from which it was thought the ore could easily be extracted, so that a 150-ton ship could take on a full load in a week. The assays confirmed the excellent quality of the product, which was nevertheless considered to be a little too small for use in large furnaces. Despite the existence of this mine and the diminution of import duties on Canadian coal, there was only a very limited trade in it under the French régime.

As for iron, traces of it were detected in many places; but the veins were insignificant or the assays by the specialists inconclusive. However, Talon did not give up hope of setting up in the colony forges that would supply the iron necessary for ship-building. In 1670 he had brought from France an ironmaster, the Sieur de La Potardière, who affirmed that the deposits in the region of Trois-Rivières were very promising. Talon immediately sent him back to France with 20 barrels of ore and sand from Trois-Rivières. While waiting for the result of the analyses and La Potardière's return, he had ore extracted in anticipation of future working. Unfortunately the ironmaster did not come back and Talon had to return to France. The mine at Trois-Rivières was not worked until the 18th century.

Talon had even less success with lead. Immediately upon arriving at Quebec in 1665 he had given the metal-founder of the Compagnie des Indes occidentales the task of examining the mine at Gaspé. It was judged to be of poor quality. The following year the intendant sent a new team to Gaspé. An explosion killed two workmen; the expedition returned to Quebec and the project was abandoned.

It was in August 1667, when the Jesuit ALLOUEZ brought him a piece of very pure copper ore from Lake Superior, that Talon began to become interested in this mineral. In the autumn of 1668 he chose Adrien Jolliet and Jean PERÉ "to go to find out whether the copper mine . . . is rich and the ore easily extracted and brought down here"; the explorers were in addition supposed to look for an "easier route than the usual one" to transport the copper from Lake Superior to Montreal. Jolliet (who died during the voyage) and Peré could not find the mine; however, they discovered a new route, via Lake Huron, Lake St. Clair and Lake Erie, which allowed traffic to avoid the rapids on the Ottawa River.

In 1670, still eager to find the exact site of the mine, the intendant entrusted Saint-Lusson with the search for it; this was, in Talon's words, "the principal object of his mission." Saint-Lusson, we know, went to Sault Ste. Marie, of which he took possession; it is more than probable however that he did not see Lake Superior, neglecting the primary aim of his trip. At all events, he did not bring back any more news than had Peré about the famous copper mine, of which no one ever succeeded in discovering the lode. Frontenac had new searches carried out at the beginning of his governorship, but without any success. He considered besides that the distances to be covered made this mine impracticable.

Frontenac was probably right. The absence of suitable means of prospecting for and working mines, the lack of skilled manpower, the enormous distances, the difficulty of transport, all these were obstacles that made any mining development in New France in the 17th century almost impossible, despite the goodwill of administrators like Talon.

Talon's boundless activity during his two stays in Canada did not fail to antagonize some people. On a few occasions he complained, in his correspondence to the minister, of the opposition that he was encountering in carrying out his plans; he was not, he said, "to everyone's liking." In particular he clashed with M. de Courcelle, the merchants, the Compagnie des Indes occidentales, and the Church.

From the time of his first administration, and especially after M. de Tracy's departure, Talon had had to put up with certain vexations from Courcelle, who seems to have been somewhat jealous of the intendant's very extensive powers and offended by the influence that he wielded in the colony, where nothing was done without his approval. Courcelle was the first to experience the dramatic plight of the governors, to whom, under the French régime, the greatest honours were rendered but whose real authority was very much less than that of the intendants and whose prerogatives were limited to the areas of war and diplomacy. When he asked to be relieved of his office, moreover, Talon stressed, among other things, that the governor's attitude did not permit him to stay any longer in Canada. The disagreement was even more serious during Talon's second term of office, especially since he took it into his head to enter into the sector of external relations, thus encroaching upon the prerogatives of the governor. Courcelle may have been less imaginative and above all less active than he, but he rightfully became very resentful of this conduct: when he was afraid of meeting some opposition from the governor, Talon acted without consulting him, in fields in which the governor had a say. In short, it was whispered about in the colony that "M. Talon wanted to combine the role of the governor with that of the intendant." Courcelle, who could not be unaware of this, was certainly hurt by it. The rumour was not without foundation: in January 1672 Patoulet wrote to the minister that Talon wanted to be recalled, unless he remained alone in the country. Talon and Courcelle each had, it seems, his share of the responsibility for this dissension, which became deeper each day.

The business men also heaped upon the intendant reproaches which were similar to Courcelle's: Talon was encroaching upon the whole of business, to the detriment of the established merchants and companies; taking advantage of his privileged position, he was bringing in from France, free of charge, merchandise with which he was flooding the colony's market. This practice, it is true, was not to the advantage of the local merchants or those from France; it was however to the advantage of the colony as a whole. Nor did this criticism take into account the fact that Talon invested in Canada the sums that he took in from these operations, in the ship-building industry, the brewery, the manufacturing industries. He simply plunged into business and competed with the merchants. From the very beginning however he had come to an understanding with Colbert, who had given him his approval. Later, on 10 Nov. 1670, he brought up the question again:

"On this matter I must draw to your attention that if all the money that the King authorizes for Canada were brought here, and if it were used in cash, not only would this not be to the country's advantage, but double the amount would be spent. This practice of converting the King's money into products which are suitable for food, or into clothing or tools, and which serve for the setting up of soldiers, girls who get married, and new families which come here, is not agreeable to the merchants, who would like everything, be it of good or bad quality, to be bought from them, and at such high prices that expenditures would have to be doubled if we were reduced to doing what they desire. These goods also are of use to exchange for wheat, and it is for this purpose that I have sent some of them to various parts, where they are to be distributed to the settlers who live at a distance from Quebec, so that, finding the things they need on the spot, they will not have to leave their families for 3 or 4 days in order to come to get them at Quebec itself, and also so that the quantities of wheat received in payment can be transported here by a single boat. I am dealing with this matter and discussing it because I have been informed that a merchant in La Rochelle has complained to M. de Terron that I was meddling too much in business and that I had stores set up in Canada; I add that if I had not had some, several of the enterprises that are begun or already completed would have failed utterly, and nothing would please some people better."

On 11 Feb. 1671 Colbert again expressed his approval of Talon's reasoning and said in conclusion that it was "very important to continue sending goods and always to keep the money in the kingdom."

In his struggle with the Compagnie des Indes occidentales, which had been set up by Colbert himself, Talon did not obtain the minister's support so easily. From the time of his first contact with New France he had perceived that His Majesty's interests in the development of the country and those of the company were "very often opposed," and that the company was in many respects an obstacle to the progress of the colony. By the very fact of its existence it interfered with the machinery of the governmental institutions that had recently been created. The king continued in fact to appoint the governors and the intendants, with whom he remained in constant touch and through whom he directed the whole colonial policy. For their part the governors and intendants strove to put into effect the king's policy and to enforce royal authority everywhere. The intendants were already endeavouring to bring about a considerable centralization of the administration of justice. Consequently the royal policy often ran counter to the rights and privileges of the company, which considered that it was being wronged. On the other hand, the exclusive right of trade and shipping which the company held by virtue of Article 15 of its charter acted as a check upon the development of New France: this clause discouraged any spirit of initiative among the colonists and made them extremely dependent upon the company. Talon's idea was that only freedom of trade and shipping could ensure the colony's progress, which could only result from the joint effort of the authorities and the settlers.

While still at La Rochelle in 1665 Talon had had to intervene with the company's agents, who were refusing the inhabitants of Canada the right to import certain articles of merchandise; when he had arrived in Quebec, he had realized that the trade monopoly worked to the detriment of the population. Therefore on 4 Oct. 1665 he had presented the following alternative to Colbert: if, in setting up the company, the king wanted to enrich it, "without having as his aim the extension of the habitations in this country and the increasing of its settlers," it was necessary to safeguard all the company's rights and privileges; if, on the contrary, the king desired the colony's progress, "I cannot convince myself that he will succeed in his intention by leaving in hands other than his own the seigniory, the ownership of the land, the appointment of priests, and, I add, even trade, which is the soul of the foundation that he has in mind." This was declaring strongly—and courageously—against the very existence of the company. Although far from agreeing with him, Colbert nevertheless told Talon in his reply of 5 Jan. 1666 that His Majesty, as an experiment, had "had the Company condescend to give up [in the settlers' favour] trade with the Indians," and that in addition the company had consented "for this year" to grant freedom of trade "to all persons without distinction." In 1668 the Conseil Souverain wrote to the minister to request of him again this free trade which the company had allowed only for 1666. According to the councillors the stores were so poorly supplied with goods that the settlers were in danger of lacking essentials; furthermore, the prices demanded by the company were excessive. This letter and Talon's efforts led the king to decide to grant freedom of trade to Canada in 1669 once and for all.

At the same time that he was fighting for freedom of trade, Talon fought to obtain for the colony an adequate budget. But, by virtue of its charter it was the Compagnie des Indes occidentales that was supposed to assume the ordinary expenses of the country, as the Compagnie des Cent-Associés and the Communauté des Habitants had done previously. In order to discharge its obligations, the Communauté des Habitants had decided to impose a levy on beaver pelts amounting to a quarter of their value and a tenth on moose hides; to this initial fund was added a little later the revenue from the Tadoussac trading organization. The sums that were collected thus, called the "revenue of the colony," were allocated to the "ordinary expenses." The Compagnie des Indes occidentales claimed that these revenues had been ceded to it for 40 years, along with the seigniory of New France. Talon, who meant to be as independent of the company as possible, contested its ownership of these rights; he wanted at the least to make it record its receipts, so that its earnings could be known. On 5 March 1666 however Colbert answered him, saying that the company actually did hold the rights that he was contesting, and he sent him a copy of a decree dated 8 April 1666 which ruled upon this question.

There was still to be determined the amount of the country's ordinary expenses. On 18 Aug. 1666 Le Barroys offered to pay "all pay and expenses of the officers" according to a scale adopted by the agents of the company. Talon protested: according to the decree of 8 April the expenses were to be met "on the same basis as they were by the former company and by the . . . Communauté." A memoir by GAUDAIS-DUPONT indicated that the Communauté des Habitants paid the sum of 48,950 *livres*; Le Barroys however was offering only 29,200 *livres*. Talon brought the matter to the attention of the minister, who fixed the company's contribution at 36,000 *livres*, which was considerably less than the revenues of the Tadoussac trading organization alone. Talon was convinced from that time on that the company cared very little for the colony, but was seeking above all to increase its profits. The intendant had judged correctly: the system of company ownership did not suit New France; by 1674, ruined and stripped of its prestige, the Compagnie des Indes occidentales ended its career prematurely.

If Talon undertook his struggles with the merchants and the Compagnie des Indes occidentales on his own initiative, it was at Colbert's request that he began to keep an eye on the activities of the ecclesiastics in New France, in conformity with the following article in his instructions: ". . . the aforementioned Sieur Talon will take note that those who have given the most faithful and the most disinterested accounts of the said country have always declared that the Jesuits (whose piety and zeal have greatly contributed to attracting to that country the people who are now there) have acquired an authority that goes beyond the limits of their true profession, which must be concerned only with consciences. In order to maintain their position there, they were very happy to nominate the bishop of Petraea [Laval*] to carry out the episcopal functions there, as he is entirely under their sway, and right up to the present either they have nominated governors to represent the king in that country or they have used all possible means to obtain the recall of those who had been chosen for this task without their participation, so that, as it is absolutely necessary to maintain a just balance between the temporal authority which resides in the person of the King and of those who represent him, and the spiritual authority which resides in the person of the said bishop and the Jesuits, but in such a way that the latter be subordinated to the former," Talon was to take care to watch closely "the state of these two authorities in the country at present and the state in which they should normally be kept." Such a paragraph—even though it was full of erroneous details, particularly concerning the appointment and recall of the governors—could not help but incite Talon to examine closely the conduct of the ecclesiastics; in addition it supplied him with a precise guide with respect to what should be the position of the spiritual authority in relation to the temporal.

Talon, who was going to prove to be strongly Gallican, and very suspicious in addition, had illustrious examples in his own family: the attorneys-general Omer and Denis Talon, who were very famous in Paris, were out and out Gallicans; of Omer Talon it was possible to write that, not satisfied with exaggerating the doctrines of Pithou and Richer, "he enriched the code of gallicanism with new articles and was the first to put them into practice." Moreover, by his own behaviour Colbert was going to encourage Talon in his suspicions regarding the Canadian Church.

However, Talon's first report, which was sent to Colbert 4 Oct. 1665, was not unfavourable: ". . . I say that if in the past the Jesuits matched temporal authority with spiritual, they have very much amended their conduct, and provided that they always keep it as it seems to me to be today, there will be no need to guard against it in the future." This impression however changed little by little into a kind of hostility, which caused the intendant to commit the error that he was blaming the Church for: he interfered on a few occasions in questions which rested entirely with the bishop and belonged to ecclesiastical discipline. This change of attitude came about between October 1665 and November 1666, when he wrote that if he were willing "to leave the Church on the level of authority on which I found it, I should have less trouble and should receive more approbation." Must this change of attitude be attributed to the affair of the seigneury of Notre-Dame-des-Anges, which has been mentioned and which brought him into conflict with the Jesuits, who were not disposed to let their lands be expropriated? Or rather, was it due to the bad opinion that he had had of the Jesuit Albanel, who had been unjustly accused by M. de Courcelle of having dissuaded the Indians from taking part in his war party in the winter of 1666? In any event, nothing else seems to have troubled the relations between church and state in 1666.

In March 1667 the intendant made a great deal of fuss about what has been called the affair of the Dames de la Sainte-Famille. This pious association, which had been canonically founded by Bishop Laval, forbade its members to take part in society gatherings and dances. Now, during the carnival of 1667 people had had a very good time at Quebec: Louis-Théandre Chartier de Lotbinière had given the first ball in Canada, and there had no doubt been numerous joyful gatherings. Several of the Dames de la Sainte-Famille, it seems, had forgotten the regulations of the association. In agreement with the directors of the

Talon

sisterhood, Bishop Laval decided to suspend its meetings. Thereupon Talon lost his temper, seeing in the bishop's gesture an intrusion by the Church upon social liberties. A fine affair, indeed! On 14 March 1667 the intendant laid the matter before the Conseil Souverain, which ruled, through two commissioners, that gatherings during the carnival could not be condemned. Talon did not perhaps dare go further, and the incident ended there. Obviously the intendant had taken offence, intervening without any reason in the internal administration of a religious association which people were free to belong to and which, besides, in no way depended upon the state.

A little later that same year there arose the question of the tithe, which had been instituted in 1663 and set at a thirteenth but had not yet been put into force, in consequence of the settlers' firm opposition; even an ordinance by M. de Tracy had not been able to impose it. On 23 Aug. 1667 Tracy, Courcelle, and Talon set the tithe at a twenty-sixth for a period of 20 years. This diminution was certainly not agreeable to the clergy, whose needs were great; Bishop Laval had nevertheless to accept it. At the beginning of the 18th century Bertrand* de Latour claimed that Talon was responsible for the change made in the rate of the tithe, but there is no proof of this. It would however not be astonishing if Talon, engrossed in the settlement of colonists, wanted to lighten their burden; it was probably he, besides, who was responsible for the clause which exempted new colonists from this tax for five years.

More painful to Bishop Laval was Talon's *volte-face* when, after co-operating with the Conseil Souverain in forbidding the bartering of alcoholic beverages to the Indians, he had the council adopt, 10 Nov. 1668, an ordinance permitting this commerce but forbidding the Indians to become drunk. Although he was present at this meeting, Bishop Laval did not sign the minutes. Henceforth, except for a few restrictions, trade in spirits was going to be legal in the colony until the end of the French régime. It was a hard blow for the bishop and the Jesuits, who, for moral reasons, had fought this trade unceasingly.

The expropriation of part of the seigneury of Notre-Dame-des-Anges, the affair concerning the Dames de la Saint-Famille, the question of the tithes, and the authorizing of trade in spirits, these were the only episodes during his first term of office that brought Talon into conflict with the Church; moreover, during his second stay in the colony, not once did he enter into conflict with the ecclesiastical authority. Is all this sufficient to conclude that Talon was Gallican in sentiment? Perhaps not: in two of these incidents at least he did not act from Gallican principles. It is in his correspondence, however, that he shows himself to be deeply imbued with Gallican doctrines, continually accusing the Canadian Church of interfering with the temporal power and of disturbing people's consciences by recourse to spiritual constraints. But it is noteworthy that Talon never cites names, never gives precise details; he always confines himself to vague accusations. Moreover, in studying his two administrations, one finds few cases in which he had to intervene with the ecclesiastical authorities. It seems that, being suspicious by nature, very firmly convinced in addition of the eminent priority of the state, Talon often exaggerated small incidents, as in the affair of the Dames de la Sainte-Famille, seeing intrusions upon the temporal authority where there was none and lending a too willing ear to rumours and hearsay. Perhaps too, without ever saying so, he was in profound disagreement with the clergy on the question of the trade in alcoholic beverages, which would explain his surprising change of attitude on 10 Nov. 1668.

Talon, convinced that the Jesuits and the secular clergy—with the exception of the Sulpicians, whom he favoured as much as he could—"tormented" consciences and kept the population in a state of moral subjection, conceived the idea of bringing to New France a religious order which might counterbalance the influence of the former and exercise the ministry while respecting liberty of conscience. He applied himself to this matter in France in 1669, with the result that in 1670 he arrived in the colony together with some Recollets. However, Talon did not seem to realize how dangerous it was to set one part of the clergy against the other, no more indeed than he was conscious of his interference in the ecclesiastical affairs of New France.

Leaving aside his uneasy Gallicanism and his tendency to ignore an authority that was too close to his own, one can hardly criticize Talon, whose two administrations—five and a half years in all—changed the face of New France. Of a colony centred solely upon subsistence agriculture and the fur trade, he began to make an industrial and commercial country; to a population that was too small, he brought numbers; to an embryonic and as yet ill-balanced society he ensured order and justice; to a New France whose frontiers were too restricted, he gave the dimensions of an empire; in a word, he laid in America the bases of that "great Kingdom," of that "very great State," of which he had dreamt from the very first day.

The starting-point of his work was certainly the programme laid out by Colbert. In large measure the intendant simply complied with this programme; he was never, however, the blind executant of a plan that had been drawn up in advance. He had first of all the merit of understanding Colbert's plan and aims; he adapted his projects, adding to them or cutting them down as necessary, even fighting them when they clashed with his own views. He created for himself a personal conception of New France and strove, especially during his second term of office, to impose it. His inventive genius led him to make of what was simply a programme of colonization a veritable policy, all of whose elements were tightly knit together and which foresaw the complete development of the colony.

Gifted with a remarkable mind for synthesis, rapid in conceiving ideas as in realizing them, he had all the qualities necessary for his office. He was both the architect and the builder of his work. A true theorist, he did not abhor invoking the great political principles upon which he based his activity; a formidable dialectician, he knew how to expound and defend his projects as well as to fight contrary opinions. A talent for speculation complemented admirably in him the practical, realistic, and efficient man of action. Powerful in conception, steadfast in decision, and swift in execution: these characteristics in Intendant Talon suffice to account for his career in Canada.

In addition, throughout his stay in Canada Talon exhibited a social sense of which his period has left us few examples. From the time of his first term of office he had established personal contact with the population, visiting each of the settlers at census time, entering their homes and discussing with them their needs and aspirations. His social preoccupations can be detected, for example, in the reasons he gave for setting up dwellings in communities, in the type of aid and encouragement that he gave the settlers, in his plan to ensure Canadian society of an *élite* by distributing some patents of nobility, in the preambles to his ordinances, in particular to that of 5 June 1672 forbidding men to take to the woods (which would deserve to be quoted), and in his constant concern for teaching. In the workyards and factories of the colony, indeed, craftsmen from France taught their art to the settlers and soldiers; likewise the agricultural developments were in effect schools where the old settlers revealed their secrets about agriculture in Canada to the indentured employees who had recently landed; at Quebec, at Talon's request, a teacher introduced young Canadians to mathematics; in short, wrote the intendant, "the young men of Canada are dedicated and rush to the schools of science, into the arts and crafts, and especially into seamanship." Talon must receive credit for realizing that it was not enough to develop the economy in order to make something great of the colony; he subordinated his whole work to the welfare of the few thousand human beings who were entrusted to his care.

The "incomparable intendant," as Mother Juchereau* de Saint-Ignace called him, left the colony for good in November 1672. At the time of his departure Canada had become one immense work-yard: in the summer of 1671 nearly 350 men had been counted in the workshops that had been created by Talon. The whole of New France was looking confidently to the future.

Unfortunately this effort was not kept up. From 1672 on the king stopped giving any effective aid to the young colony in the form of funds; besides, and this is perhaps the most important factor, three years went by before a successor to Talon was appointed, so that New France was left under the sole direction of Frontenac, whose experience and ability were above all military. In several sectors Talon's work was soon undone. Other intendants came to Canada, some of whom were not lacking in talent, but circumstances were no longer as favourable as they had been in the period when Louis XIV and Colbert held the destinies of the colony firmly in their hands. New France's only great period, from 1665 to 1672, was gone for ever.

Shortly after returning to France, Talon, who had already been captain and governor of the *château* of Mariemont since 1670, received the important and very honourable office of first valet of the King's Wardrobe and secretary in his privy chamber. In addition Talon's property of Les Islets, which had been created a barony on 14 Mar. 1671, was raised to a countship in May 1675, under the name of Orsainville. These royal favours show in what esteem the former intendant was held by Louis XIV.

Occasionally he used his influence on behalf of New France and of his nephew, François-Marie PERROT, governor of Montreal. In particular, being favourable to the trade in spirits with the Indians, he became Colbert's adviser on this matter, which earned for him the enmity of the Canadian clergy. Thus, in 1681, when he thought of going to Canada to set up a general hospital, the churchmen became alarmed, thinking, rightly or wrongly, that his real intention was to return as intendant or even as governor. But this project was soon given up.

An influential personage, often in contact with Louis XIV, a friend of James II of England who was in exile in Paris, protected by Mme de Maintenon, Talon lived in affluence in Paris, in

Tanfield

the rue du Bac, when his duties did not require his presence at Versailles. In 1692 he sold his offices as valet and secretary, the first for 110,000 *livres* and the second for 143,000. As he felt his end approaching, he drew up his will 29 April 1694. He died a bachelor on the following 24 November and was buried in the chapel of Sainte-Catherine in the church of Notre-Dame-en-Vaux, at Châlons-sur-Marne.

ANDRÉ VACHON

Recensements de 1666, 1667. "Acte de naissance de Jean Talon," *BRH*, LXVII (1961), 62. Pierre Boucher, *Histoire véritable et naturelle des moeurs et productions du pays de la Nouvelle-France, vulgairement dite de Canada* (Paris, 1664). "Correspondance de Frontenac (1672–82)," APQ *Rapport, 1926–27*, 3–144. "Correspondance de Talon," APQ *Rapport, 1930–31*, 3–182. *Édits ord.*, I, 30–35, 40–48; III, 33–40. Marie Guyart de l'Incarnation, *Lettres* (Richaudeau), II, *passim*. *JR* (Thwaites), *passim*. *JJ* (Laverdière et Casgrain), *passim*. Juchereau, *Annales* (Jamet), *passim*. *Jug. et délib.*, I, *passim*. *Lettres de noblesse* (P.-G. Roy), I, 37–46. "Ordonnances de Talon," dans P.-G. Roy, *Inv. ord. int.*, III, 218–77 et *Ord. comm.* (P.-G. Roy), I, 26–85, 96–129. *Papier terrier de la Cie des I.O.* (P.-G. Roy). P.-G. Roy, *Inv. concessions*, *passim*.

Chapais, *Talon*. Pierre Clément, *Histoire de Colbert* (3e éd., Paris, 1892). Joseph Cossette, "Jean Talon, champion au Canada du gallicanisme royal, 1665–1672," *RHAF*, XI (1957–58), 327–48. J.-N. Fauteux, *Essai sur l'industrie au Canada sous le Régime français* (2v., Québec, 1927). René Gobillot, "La tombe de Jean Talon," *NF*, VI (1931), 251. Lionel Groulx, *Histoire du Canada français depuis la découverte* (4v., Montréal, 1950–52), I, 69–145. Roland Lamontagne, *Succès d'intendance de Talon* (Montréal, 1964).

TANFIELD, SIR FRANCIS, governor of Lord Falkland's colony in Newfoundland; fl. 1623–25.

The most probable identification of Tanfield is that he was the son of Clement Tanfield and his wife, Anne, of Gayton, Northamptonshire; b. 1565. He was knighted in July 1603 and, in September, accompanied the new ambassador, Lord Spencer, to the court of the Duke of Württemberg.

Tanfield was second cousin to Elizabeth, daughter of Sir Lawrence Tanfield—a subscriber to the Newfoundland company of 1610—and wife of Henry Cary, Lord Falkland. About 1620 Cary purchased two pieces of land in Newfoundland: the first, a strip of land between Renewse and Aquaforte, he bought from William VAUGHAN; the second, a larger area on Trinity Bay, he bought from the Newfoundland company. The scheme was well worked out and, in 1623, an appeal for subscribers and planters was published, land being offered in return for investment of capital or service in the settlement. By this date Sir Francis Tanfield had been appointed governor and it was probably that same year that he and the colonists left to settle at Renewse. Tanfield, who does not appear to have had previous experience of this kind of enterprise, was troubled by conflict between the planters and the fishermen. He was helped and advised by Sir Richard WHITBOURNE who twice visited the colony. There is no indication of the scale on which the plantation was undertaken and it survived for only two years. Nothing further is heard of Tanfield until 1630 when he was in England and preparing to go to Ireland on the king's service.

GILLIAN T. CELL

For Tanfield's life *see*: PRO, C. 2 James I, T 11/58, and P.C. 2/39, p.722. G. Baker, *The history and antiquities of the county of Northamptonshire*, II (London, 1841). For his career in Newfoundland *see*: BM, Sloane MS 3827, ff.67–68v. Sir William Alexander, *An encouragement to colonies* (London, 1624). T. C., *A short discourse of the New-found-land* (Dublin, 1623). William Vaughan, *The Newlanders cure* (London, 1630). R. Whitbourne, *A discourse containing a loving invitation . . .* (London, 1622) where the spelling "Tanfill" is found.

TAONDECHOREN, LOUIS, Huron chieftain, *dogique* of the mission at Notre-Dame-de-Foy; b. *c.* 1600; d. some time after 1677.

Louis was baptized at Sainte-Marie-des-Hurons in 1640. The missionaries, who considered him at the time to be "one of the noble spirits of the country [Huronia]" and "one of the best qualified for our mysteries," were not disappointed. He was noted for his fervour: an "excellent Christian," wrote Marie de l'Incarnation [*see* GUYART], who had a long conversation with him and presented him in 1671 with "a very beautiful wax relief Image of the holy Infant Jesus in his cradle." The *Relation* adds: "It is incredible how zealous this man is in all manners of piety." In 1668 Louis was *dogique* of the little Huron colony at Quebec, that is to say, he was responsible for leading the Indians in their prayers and for keeping watch over their conduct in the missionary's absence. He filled this role until 1677 at least. In addition to his piety and his zeal the Jesuits spoke highly of his eloquence: "very Eloquent in his own language," he delivered addresses that were "sensible and sound" and which "have nothing of the Savage about them."

Moved by a true apostolic spirit, Louis had long dreamed of proclaiming "the truths of our Religion" in his native region and in the Iroquois cantons. The opportunity to do so was soon offered. In 1673 he accompanied Governor BUADE de Frontenac on his journey to Lake Ontario.

Although infirm and ill, he prolonged his stay, acting at Onondaga as "preacher, both in public before meetings of the council and in private visits to the lodges." Father Jean de Lamberville* expressed his satisfaction at "having found such a vicar."

In 1660 Louis had been one of DOLLARD's companions at the Long Sault. Captured by the Iroquois, he had escaped 8 or 10 days later. He had been "4 days and 4 nights on the run, without a stop," before reaching Montreal around 25 May. It was he who was the chief source of information for Father CHAUMONOT and the author of the 1659–60 *Relation*, both of whom drew up an account of the battle of the Long Sault.

From 1677 on the *Relations* make no further mention of Louis, who by that time was nearly 80 years of age.

ANDRÉ VACHON

Marie Guyart de l'Incarnation, *Lettres* (Richaudeau), II, 162f. *JR* (Thwaites), XIX, 148–50; L, 210–12; LII, 236; LV, 266–68, 276, 300; LVIII, 134, 148, 150, 196–98; LX, 78, 306. André Vachon, "L'affaire du Long-Sault: valeur de la source huronne," *RUL*, XVIII (1963–64), 495–515.

TARATOUAN (Taratwane), Huron chief; b. 1577?; d. 1637.

Taratouan proved himself a staunch friend of the Jesuit missionaries during the years when their presence was arousing bitter opposition in the Huron villages. Once, when their lives were threatened in council, Taratouan rose to their defence by presenting a string of wampum with the words, "There is something to close your mouths and stop your talking." By this pledge of support on the part of an influential chief, the ill-will against the priests was dissipated.

In the summer of 1636, Taratouan, with a flotilla of Huron and Nipissing canoes laden with pelts, was forbidden passage on the Ottawa River by the Allumette Island tribe of Algonkins, about 150 leagues above Trois-Rivières. Thirteen Huron canoes were turned back, but Taratouan held firm until the arrival of Father ANTOINE DANIEL who interceded with the island tribe and refused to continue without the Hurons. The flotilla arrived safely in the St. Lawrence on 19 August and although there were few canoes, they carried "a great amount of merchandise." It was the usual custom of the Allumettes to harass the Hurons and the French, for it was their ambition to prevent commerce between the French and the Hurons in order to gain control of the fur trade for themselves.

However, even if the Hurons were ten against one in relation to the Islanders they would not pass their island if a single inhabitant objected, "so strictly do they guard the laws of the Country." A boundary tribute was paid customarily, and in the summer of 1636 special offerings were expected "to dry the tears" for the death of the Islander captain, Le Borgne [*see* TESSOUAT, d. 1636] who had not yet been resuscitated or "cached" in a ceremony by which his name and power would be given to another.

Taratouan visited the Jesuit seminary at Quebec and gave encouragement to the three recently arrived Huron students, especially to his nephew, TEOUATIRON. Father PAUL LE JEUNE believed him to be then (in 1636) "fully sixty years old." Taratouan was never instructed in the Christian faith, other than by Teouatiron who had explained to him some of the teachings at the seminary. Le Jeune described him as "a brave Captain," and again "this brave man."

In 1637, on the journey down to Trois-Rivières, Taratouan, who was again in charge of a fur flotilla of ten Huron canoes, met Teouatiron travelling up to the Huron country. He persuaded him to return to the seminary. On entering Lake St. Peter, Taratouan was captured, together with nine canoes and their rich cargoes of fur. During his torture he was heard to sing "as loudly and as gayly as if he were among his friends."

Shortly after this event Father Le Jeune, when accompanying a French war-party to the mouth of the River of the Iroquois (Richelieu), reported seeing a cross-bar ripped from a cross erected the year before by M. DUPLESSIS-BOCHART, which was fastened to a branchless tree on the spot where the massacre had taken place. On it were painted the heads of the 30 Huron captives. Variation in length of the lines indicated the quality and age of each. Two larger ones depicted captains and smaller ones, youths and children. Stripes in the form of plumes were on the heads of the bravest. All were red signifying their ultimate fate by fire, except one black head for the single Huron murdered at the time.

ELSIE MCLEOD JURY

JR (Thwaites), *passim*. Desrosiers, *Iroquoisie*, 150–52, 177–79.

TAREHA (Atarhea, Tarrigha, Tarsha, Tharca), an Oneida chief; fl. 1691–95.

On 10 June 1693, according to Father Charlevoix*, Tareha reached Montreal, bringing with him Saint-Amours, who had been a captive of the Iroquois for four years. He wanted to exchange him for his nephew, who was a prisoner at the Saint-François-Xavier mission at the Saint-Louis (Lachine) rapids. Immediately the Chevalier de

Tarrigha

Callières* sent Tareha to Quebec, where Frontenac [see BUADE] consented to the exchange. As proof of his sincerity the Indian had presented to the governor a letter from the Jesuit Father Milet*. He warned Frontenac that the French should be on the look-out at harvest-time. The Indians wanted peace, he added, and if he succeeded in reconciling his canton with the French, he would come and spend the rest of his days at the Saint-François-Xavier mission. Through him the Comte de Frontenac asked each of the Five Nations to send him two ambassadors in September, among whom he wished to see Téganissorens*, the famous Onondaga orator.

Towards the end of September Tareha returned to Quebec, accompanied only by one woman from his lodge who had always shown kindness to the French prisoners. The count was affable. Tareha apologized for not being surrounded by the delegates from his canton and cast all the blame on the English. As Benjamin Fletcher, the governor of New York, had suggested, the Indian advised Frontenac to send a representative to Albany, where, it was said, the English wanted to negotiate with the French and the Indians. Frontenac was indignant; he dismissed Tareha, but not without giving him the customary presents.

Téganissorens and eight delegates finally appeared at Quebec in the month of May 1694. Tareha and the two Oneida ambassadors did not arrive until 1 November, after Milet's liberation; they were badly received by the irascible Frontenac, who however calmed down on receiving the Jesuit's testimony, to whom Tareha had "rendered good services during his captivity." Tareha's relative who had already made the trip to Quebec had arrived at the Saint-Louis Rapids with all her family at the same time as Father Milet. There she was baptized and received the name Suzanne.

According to the Oneidas, who recalled his memory in 1757, Tareha lived until the time of Philippe de Rigaud* de Vaudreuil and always proved himself to be the ally of the French.

HENRI BÉCHARD

Charlevoix, *Histoire*, II. Correspondance de Frontenac (1689–99), APQ *Rapport*, *1927–28*, 211. *NYCD* (O'Callaghan and Fernow), III. W. M. Beauchamp, *A history of the New York Iroquois, now commonly called the Six Nations* (New York State Museum Bull., 78, Albany, 1905). E. J. Devine, *Historic Caughnawaga* . . . (Montréal, 1922), 112–15.

TARRIGHA (Tarsha). *See* TAREHA

TASQUANTUM. *See* TISQUANTUM

TEGAKWITHA. *See* TEKAKWITHA

TEHORENHAEGNON, Huron medicine-man, considered one of the "two greatest sorcerers in the country"; fl. 1628–37.

Indian medicine-men had a profound knowledge of medicinal herbs, considerable skill in healing wounds and tumours, and also exercised tremendous influence by treating illness and diverting disaster by calling on supernatural forces, by practising frauds, and by enforcing ceremonial dances, songs, and games, for which they received handsome rewards.

In 1628 and again in 1635, Tehorenhaegnon, having failed to fulfil his promises of rain, proclaimed that the cross which stood before the Jesuit house at Toanché II and at Ihonatiria (in the Penetanguishene peninsula) was the cause of droughts, famine, and fires by which three villages had recently been destroyed. He held a feast to avert bad luck from an eclipse of the moon that occurred on 27 Aug. 1635.

In the epidemics of 1637, he boasted of a secret remedy learned from the demons after a 12- or 13-day fast in a cabin on the shore of the lake. The village of Ossossané (La Conception), accordingly, requested his services. Tehorenhaegnon sent one of his associates, Saossarinon, to whom he communicated his power, giving him his bow and arrows to represent him. Three days of feasting were ordered as protection against disease for all who attended. Saossarinon made the rounds of the cabins and visited the sick, while the men of the village assembled in the largest cabin and spent the night singing, dancing, and beating on pieces of bark. At daybreak Saossarinon entered amid a profound silence. He was preceded by a captain bearing Tehorenhaegnon's bow and a kettle of water with which to sprinkle the sick. Saossarinon gravely fanned those present with a turkey wing and passed around a liquid to drink. Having thus inspired the company with courage, he withdrew. A feast followed. Then the men left the place to the women who sang and danced in turn, but did not partake of the feast. The second day's feast was given by Saossarinon, but the third was not held "for lack of fish." Before departing, Saossarinon taught his secrets to two residents of Ossossané, giving them turkey wings as tokens of his power. The ceremonies proved only partially successful, however, and a messenger went again to Tehorenhaegnon. Saossarinon returned but this time refused to visit the sick, insisting that they be brought to him. The people of Ossossané lost faith and the turkey wings were discarded.

As the epidemics continued to ravage the

country, Tehorenhaegnon's reputation is said to have dwindled, when his sweat-baths, feasts, potions, and ordinances proved of no avail.

ELSIE MCLEOD JURY

JR (Thwaites), *passim*.

TEKAKWITHA (Tagaskouïta, Tegakwitha), KATERI (Catherine), the first Indian to be named venerable, daughter of a Christian Algonkin squaw and a pagan Mohawk; b. 1656 at Ossernenon (Auriesville, N.Y.); d. 1680 near Montreal.

Kateri Tekakwitha's mother, who had been brought up by French settlers at Trois-Rivières, had been captured about 1653. Shortly afterwards she had been chosen by a Mohawk to be his wife. In 1660 she was carried off by smallpox, along with her husband and her last-born child. Young Catherine, whose face was pock-marked and whose eyes were badly affected, almost died too. She was taken in by her uncle, the first chieftain of the village and a declared enemy of the Christian faith.

In the autumn of 1666 PROUVILLE de Tracy came down from Quebec at the head of a punitive expedition and burned the centres of population of the Mohawk canton with all their stores. Ossernenon was rebuilt under the name of Gandaouagué, on the other side of the Mohawk River (Rivière des Hollandais), a little to the west of the former site. After this defeat the Mohawks begged for peace and asked for missionaries. They were sent Fathers Jacques FRÉMIN, Jacques Bruyas*, Jean PIERRON, and the *donnés* Charles BOQUET and François Poisson, who arrived at Gandaouagué in September 1667. During the three days that they stayed there, Kateri Tekakwitha had to take care of the Jesuits, whose piety and courteous manners impressed her.

On several occasions her relatives tried to make her marry, but she always refused, to their great displeasure. There is nothing surprising in this refusal, since two-thirds of the population of Gandaouagué was composed of Christian Algonkins and Hurons who had undoubtedly spoken to Kateri about the Ursulines of Quebec and the religious life.

In 1675 Father Jacques de Lamberville*, a Jesuit, entered her lodge for the first time. She revealed to him her desire to receive baptism. The ceremony took place on Easter Day, 1676, and the young Indian girl received the name of Kateri.

Her conversion brought upon her a veritable persecution. She was even threatened with death. Amidst all these trials Father Lamberville advised her to pray unremittingly and to go to live at the Saint-Louis (Lachine) rapids. In the autumn of 1677, with the aid of three Indian neophytes, she succeeded in fleeing.

It was at the Saint-François-Xavier mission that Kateri Tekakwitha definitely prepared herself for the Christian life. Anastasie Tegonhatsiongo, who had formerly been her mother's friend at Ossernenon, acted as her spiritual guide. Because of her exceptional qualities she was allowed to take her first communion by Christmas of 1677, sooner than was usual for converts. In addition, in the spring of 1678 she was received into the Confrérie de la Sainte-Famille, despite her youth.

The strength of Kateri Tekakwitha's spirituality lay in an extraordinary purity of body and soul and an efficacious charity towards all. This laywoman lived in full the life of the Indians, in the village as on the great winter hunts. Not until 1678, less than two years before her death, did she cease to accompany her people in their search for game; at this time the Eucharist had taken such a powerful hold upon her, that, even at the risk of suffering hunger, she no longer wished to be away from the church for long months. Even in the fervent environment of the mission she had to endure great trials, in particular false accusations. Later her slanderers were the first to praise her.

Kateri Tekakwitha would have liked to found a community of Indian nuns, but Father Lamberville persuaded her to give up the idea. On 25 March 1679, on the feast of the Annunciation, she was permitted to take in private the vow of perpetual chastity. It is easy to understand why posterity named her the Lily of the Mohawks.

She used to submit herself to painful mortifications, which she moderated on her director's order. She concealed this penitential spirit to the best of her ability; she liked jokes and would laugh heartily.

Kateri, whose health had always been mediocre, became aware at the beginning of 1680 that she was seriously ill. On the Tuesday of Holy Week she received the last sacrament. The next day, 17 April, at barely 24 years of age, she passed away very easily while uttering the names of Jesus and Mary.

After her death Father Cholenec* observed that Kateri's features, which had been marked by smallpox, had become remarkably beautiful. In consequence of conspicuous favours obtained through her intercession, there soon sprang up a strong devotion to her. In 1688 Bishop Saint-Vallier [La Croix*], the second bishop of Quebec, called her "the Geneviève of Canada," a theme that Chateaubriand was to develop in *Les Natchez*. In 1744 Father Charlevoix* wrote that she was "universally regarded as the Protectress of

Tekouerimat

Canada." Devotion to the Venerable Kateri Tekakwitha has spread to Canada, the United States, and throughout the world. Each year sees more pilgrimages made to Auriesville and to the Saint-François-Xavier mission at Caughnawaga, where her relics are preserved.

Since her death about 50 biographies of the Venerable Kateri Tekakwitha have appeared in some 10 languages.

HENRI BÉCHARD

Charlevoix, *Histoire*, I. Claude Chauchetière, *La vie de la bienheureuse Catherine Tegakouita dite à présent la saincte sauvagesse* (Manate, 1887). Pierre Cholenec, "Catherine Tegahkouita, la sainte sauvagesse," *BRH*, XX (1914), 26–32, 61–64, 99–103, 134–36, 168; *Catherine Tegahkouita, la sainte sauvagesse* (Beauceville, 1914). *JR* (Thwaites). *The Positio on Katharine Tekakwitha. Positio super virtutibus servae Dei Catherinae Tekakwitha*.

Guy Boulizon, *La croix chez les Indiens* (Montréal, 1958). G.-C. Bouvier, *Kateri Tekakwitha: La plus belle fleur épanouie au bord du Saint-Laurent* (Montréal, 1939). E.-X. Evans, "The literature relative to Katheri Tekakwitha," *BRH*, XLVI (1940), 193–209, 241–55. Édouard Lecompte, *Une vierge iroquoise, Catherine Tekakwitha: Le lis des bords de la Mohawk et du Saint-Laurent, 1656–1680* (Montréal, 1930). Robert Rumilly, *Kateri Tekakwitha, le lys de la Mohawk, la fleur du Saint-Laurent* (Paris, 1934). J. C. Steurer, *The impact of Katharine Tekakwitha on American spiritual life* (Washington, D.C., 1957). E. H. Walworth, *Life and times of Kateri Tekakwitha* (Albany, N.Y., 1926).

TEKOUERIMAT. *See* NEGABAMAT

TEMPLE, SIR THOMAS, baronet, governor of Acadia; b. January 1613/14 at Stowe, Buckinghamshire, England; d. 27 March 1674 at Ealing, Middlesex. He was the second son of Sir John Temple of Stanton Bury and his first wife Dorothy, daughter of Edmund Lee, and a grandson of Sir Thomas Temple, of Stowe.

Nothing is recorded of Thomas Temple until the year 1656 when he entered into partnership with Col. William CROWNE to buy most of CHARLES DE SAINT-ÉTIENNE de La Tour's interest in Nova Scotia. Lord Fiennes, an uncle of Thomas Temple and a member of Cromwell's council, advised his nephew, who was suspected of Royalist leanings, to take this opportunity to leave England. On 29 May 1656, the Council of State approved the joint petition of La Tour, Temple, and Crowne, and ordered a patent to be granted; on 14 July, articles of agreement were drawn up and a month later on 9 or 10 August, the patent was granted. La Tour gave up his title to Temple and Crowne on 20 Sept. 1656, in return for which Temple undertook to pay the cost of the English troops which had earlier captured the fort on the Saint John River [*see* SEDGWICK]—£1,800 according to Temple's petition of 1660—and Crowne and Temple, La Tour's debt to Maj.-Gen. Edward Gibbons of Boston.

At the same time, Cromwell ordered the commander of Acadia, LEVERETT, to surrender the forts of Saint John and "Pentacoit" (Pentagouet) to Temple. This Leverett did 1 May 1657 after Temple arrived with a party of settlers.

On 12 Sept. 1657 an agreement was made between Temple and Crowne for a division of their property. Temple's share extended from what is now Lunenburg in Nova Scotia to the River St. George in Maine, including the whole coast of the Bay of Fundy (Baie Française) on both sides and a hundred leagues inland. Crowne and Temple had many disputes over their property in Nova Scotia. In 1659, Col. Crowne leased his share of the grant to Thomas Temple for four years. The rent from Temple was secured by a bond of £440. Another challenge to Temple's assertion of authority over Acadia was ALEXANDER LE BORGNE de Belle-Isle's seizure of La Hève (now La Have) in May 1658. Belle-Isle acted under his father's concession in Acadia from the Compagnie de la Nouvelle-France. He was captured by Temple, taken to Boston, and there held prisoner for several years.

In a letter to Lord Fiennes dated 6 Sept. 1659 pleading for a new patent to Nova Scotia "with his name only on it," Temple describes some of his work in this colony. He says he repaired the fort at Saint John as much as he was able, built a trading house 150 miles up the river (this refers to Jemseg although the distance is incorrect), and built another in the bottom of the bay [of Fundy]. After the restoration of Charles II in 1660 petitions for a grant of Acadia were placed before the king by Thomas Elliott, a groom of the bedchamber, Sir LEWIS KIRKE, the heirs of Sir WILLIAM ALEXANDER, the French ambassador on behalf of Le Borgne, and others. In 1662 Temple was created a baronet of Nova Scotia and given the governorship for which he paid Elliott £600 per year.

Temple's possession of Acadia was short-lived. By the Treaty of Breda in 1667, Charles II ceded Acadia to Louis XIV and ordered Temple on 31 Dec. 1667 to surrender the five Acadian forts to MORILLON Du Bourg. In October 1668, Temple, having been told in August to "forbear delivery" until further notice, showed Du Bourg the king's order and raised several objections to immediate surrender. Du Bourg accepted Temple's argument that the island of St. Christopher was to be surrendered to the English before Acadia was returned to the French and wrote Le Borgne de

Belle-Isle accordingly. Charles II renewed his command to Temple to surrender Acadia on 8 March 1668/69 and 6 Aug. 1669. The transfer was effected in the summer of 1670 by Temple's deputy-governor, Capt. RICHARD WALKER, after Temple and ANDIGNÉ de Grandfontaine had signed an agreement in Boston.

During the uncertain period from 1667 to 1670 Temple lived in Boston and continued to petition the king for recompense for his expenses and losses in Nova Scotia. He claimed that Acadia yielded only £900, of which (for seven years) he had to pay Elliott £600 and Boston merchants £180 to remit it to England, leaving him an annual income of £120, with which he had "supported our pigmy war with the French, and preserved the the King's country. . . ." It is unlikely that he received the £16,000 he requested to cover his losses and debts of £7,000.

Temple seems to have prospered after he settled in Boston. He had begun to acquire property there while still living in Nova Scotia and he was very active in commerce, particularly real estate. He was prominent among those who attempted to develop some of the islands in Boston Harbour.

Temple had moved to London shortly before his death on 27 March 1674. He was buried at Ealing, Middlesex. His will bequeathed the bulk of his estate to his nephew, John Nelson*, of Boston.

IN COLLABORATION WITH HUIA RYDER

AE, Corr. pol., Angleterre, 91, 93, 94, 96; Mém. et doc., Amérique, 5, ff.2, 6, 7, 277–79. AN, Col., C^{11D}, I, ff.126, 135–36, 139; Marine, B², 9, ff.233–42; 10, ff.38–39. BM, Egerton MS 2395. "Mass. Archives." Suffolk County Court House (Boston, Mass.), Registry of Probate, VI, 102; XII, 165, 166. *Coll. de manuscrits relatifs à la Nouv.-France*, I. Maine Hist. Soc. *Coll.*, I (1831), 301, IV, V, VI, VIII; *Documentary history of Maine*, IV, VI, VII, IX, X. *Mémoires des commissaires*, I, xiv–xv, xix, xxii, xxv, xliv, 49–51, 94–98, 106, 161, 179; II, 279–80, 286, 290–91, 298–99, 302–10, 313–18, 325–26, 332, 511, 527; IV, 31, 95, 126, 280–81, 288, 291, 304–5, 307, 310–11, 329, 350, 361, 362ff., 384ff., 392, 451, 520–21, 534; and *Memorials of the English and French commissaries*, I, 18–23, 25, 27, 31, 49, 120–22, 165–69, 176, 215, 230, 403, 411, 413, 417, 421, 449, 451, 571, 580, 588–97, 601, 606, 613, 618, 727, 743. *NYCD* (O'Callaghan and Fernow), IX. PRO, *CSP, Col., 1574–1660, 1661–68, 1669–74*. *Records of the Massachusetts Bay* (Shurtleff), IV, pts. 1 and 2.

J. B. Brebner, *New England's outpost: Acadia before the conquest of Canada* (New York, 1927), 32–36. *DNB*. Ganong, "Historic sites in New Brunswick," 274–75. Thomas Hutchinson, *The history of the colony and province of Massachusetts Bay*, ed. Lawrence S. Mayo (new ed., 3v., Cambridge, Mass., 1936), I. Murdoch, *History of Nova-Scotia*, I, 134, 141–48.

TEOUATIRON (Tewathiron, Thewathiron), JOSEPH, a native of the Huron village of Saint-Ignace (near Waubaushene, Ontario); d. 1640 or 1641.

Teouatiron was one of the original six students of the Jesuit seminary at Quebec in 1636. Although 12 Huron boys had been promised to the Jesuits, the mothers and especially the grandmothers, were loath to see them depart to such a distance, and only one of the 12, Satouta, made the journey with Father ANTOINE DANIEL in the summer of 1636. The other five boys were recruited, but only after pleadings, promises, and many gifts, from their fathers whom they had accompanied to the trade. One, rather "peevish," returned to his village the first year, and two died. The following summer Aiandacé, the youngest, returned, leaving only Teouatiron and Andehoua. The boys lived apart, under the direction of Father Daniel and were furnished with all necessities. Their day was regulated by prayers, instruction, and free hours which they spent hunting and fishing, making bows and arrows, or clearing land.

They were "petted" by the French, dressed in French clothing, and taught French manners. Teouatiron was described as of an affable, compliant nature, but a little "duller" than his fellow Andehoua. He prepared himself for baptism in the winter of 1637–38 "by an extraordinary fast," by "diminishing the pleasures of the chase, to which he is strongly inclined," and by long inward reflection. His godparents, François DERRÉ de Gand and "Mlle Repentigny" [Mme PIERRE LEGARDEUR de Repentigny] gave him the name of Joseph. Andehoua was baptized at the same time and given the name of Jean-Armand. The two boys were united by strong and affectionate bonds and while at the seminary were never known to have a disagreement.

At one time Teouatiron remained obstinate about a wilful act and was summoned before Father PAUL LE JEUNE. He had been angered by imagining that he was being forced by threats to believe in God and had acted to show that his heart would not be won by fear. However, he looked on Father Daniel as a father, he maintained, and had no desire to leave. When supplies were low in Quebec, he and Jean-Armand elected to remain rather than return to the temptations of living with their own people.

In the summer of 1637 Teouatiron was given permission to go to his country, in company with Father RAGUENEAU to visit his mother who was "quite old." On the homeward route he met his uncle TARATOUAN who convinced him that he should return to the seminary. On Lake St. Peter the party was ambushed by Iroquois.

Tessouat

Teouatiron and his two companions were pursued to the south shore, where they rushed into the woods, abandoning all their luggage, even clothes. After a day in hiding, Teouatiron made his way to safety at Trois-Rivières in an abandoned Iroquois canoe. His companions were saved after lighting a great beacon fire on the south shore. Teouatiron proceeded immediately to the seminary suffering from cuts and scratches after running through brush and nettles.

In the early spring of 1638, when fear grew as to the fate of the French in the Huron country, Teouatiron and Andehoua offered to go there to assess the situation. They embarked with Father Daniel, a courageous young Frenchman, and a party of Algonkins. From Hurons travelling to Quebec, some of whom were friends of Teouatiron, they learned that conditions in the Huron country had improved and Father Daniel sent Teouatiron back to Quebec.

The transition from the freedom of their earlier life to the restaints of the seminary caused many problems and often confusion for the boys and also the Jesuits. The latter hoped that by teaching a nucleus of young men the European way of life, a Christian village of Huron Indians might be founded near Quebec which would afford protection against attack and which would be of assistance in promoting the fur trade.

Andehoua's fine example as a preacher to his people in the summer of 1638 led the priests to request that Teouatiron also be sent up as a preacher for "his populous town." Teouatiron spent two years in the seminary but after his return to his own country he reverted to the customs of his people. The Jesuits laboured, at times successfully, to maintain his Christian beliefs, meanwhile sympathizing with the difficulties suffered by one so young in withstanding the impact of his native culture. In the winter of 1640–41 an accidental fire caused his death. The priests who were present ran to his assistance and had the consolation of bringing him, in the end, into the Christian fold.

ELSIE MCLEOD JURY

JR (Thwaites), *passim*.

TESSOUAT (Besouat), Algonkin chief of Allumette Island; fl. 1603–13.

Tessouat was probably the Besouat who, as leader of an Algonkin party, had joined the Montagnais under ANADABIJOU and the Etchemins to defeat a band of Iroquois at the mouth of the River of the Iroquois (Richelieu) in 1603. A few days after CHAMPLAIN's arrival on the St. Lawrence (29 May 1603) he and FRANÇOIS GRAVÉ DU PONT attended the victory celebrations of this battle. Tessouat (Besouat) was seated in front of the women and girls and between two poles on which hung the scalps of the enemy. From time to time he arose to address the assembly.

Tessouat was a chief of considerable influence because of the strategic location of his tribe on Allumette Island, now Morrison Island, between Upper and Lower Allumette lakes (near Pembroke, Ontario). Rapids necessitating a portage surrounded this island and blocked the route of the Huron and other northern tribes to the St. Lawrence by way of the Ottawa River. It was Indian custom to recognize the rights of other tribes in matters of travel and trade, and not even the much stronger Hurons would pass the island without the consent of the inhabitants or without paying the required customs. Thus it was in the power of Tessouat virtually to control the flow of trade on the Ottawa River.

In 1613 Champlain journeyed to Tessouat's island, where a Frenchman Nicolas de VIGNAU, had spent the previous winter and had reported having travelled from there to the shores of the "Northern Sea" (Hudson Bay). Champlain's aims were threefold: to establish friendly relations with Tessouat, to promise military support against the Iroquois, and to continue with the aid of Tessouat's people to the land of the Nebicerini (Nipissings), whom Vignau had told him lived on the Northern Sea.

A feast was held at Tessouat's home. Then a council of elders met and after having "smoked plentifully" in silence for half an hour they received Champlain's request to be taken to the Nebicerini. This they refused and, although several reasons were advanced, the "Island" Indians were hereby introducing the policy, from which they never faltered, of hindering French advances toward other tribes that might reduce their own influential role in the practice of the fur trade.

The goodwill of Tessouat's tribe, therefore, was essential to the French. They were invited by Champlain to come to Sault-Saint-Louis (Lachine rapids) to trade, where there were four ships loaded with merchandise. They were, in fact, urged to move their village to the rapids, where Champlain promised to found a French settlement, a plan that they approved, saying that they lived on poor land because they had been forced there by their enemy, the Iroquois. In making this suggestion, Champlain probably had in mind that a friendly band of proven enemies of the Iroquois would provide a protective barrier for a French settlement at this important trading site.

Champlain described the cemeteries on Allumette Island. Upright boards bore the face of the person buried, rudely carved. For a man, there was also a shield, a sword-handle, a club, or bows and arrows; for a chief, a bunch of feathers; for a child, a bow and arrow; for a woman or girl, a kettle, earthen vessel, wooden spoon, and paddle. They were painted red and yellow "with various decorations as fine as the carving." In the gardens he noted "pumpkins, beans and peas like ours, which they are beginning to grow."

Before his departure from the island, Champlain erected a cross of white cedar, bearing the arms of France, as he had done from place to place along his route. He promised to return the following year when Tessouat agreed to provide large numbers of men to join him on the war-path.

Tessouat and Champlain parted with mutual respect, for Champlain writes of him "as the kind old chief," and Tessouat permitted his own son to accompany Champlain to Quebec.

SAGARD mentions a "Le Borgne of the Island," an Algonkin chief, being present at Trois-Rivières in 1617. This may have been Tessouat, or Besouat, or a successor, as the name Le Borgne seems to have been given to chiefs of this island whose names were variants of Tessouat, i.e., Tesouehat, Tesswehas.

ELSIE McLEOD JURY

Champlain, *Works* (Biggar), *passim*. Sagard, *Histoire du Canada* (Tross), I, 60. Desrosiers, *Iroquoisie*, 54. Hunt, *Wars of the Iroquois*, 43–45.

TESSOUAT (Le Borgne de l'Île), chief of the Allumette Island tribe of Algonkins (Kichesipirini), probably a successor of the TESSOUAT whom CHAMPLAIN visited in 1613; d. 1636.

Tessouat was a sagacious and ambitious Algonkin chief whose tribe wielded a power disproportionate to their numbers because of their strategic location on the Ottawa River route of the fur trade. Not satisfied with controlling traffic on the river by tolls and customs, they continually sought a monopoly of the role of middlemen. The importance of the goodwill of this tribe was early recognized by the French. In 1620 Champlain had sent the young Jean NICOLLET to live with them. In 1629 he named Le Borgne, or Tessouat, to a council of five Indian chiefs under CHOMINA, describing him as "a man of intelligence." The council, however, was rendered ineffective shortly after its ratification by the Indians when the English captured Quebec.

When the French returned to the Huron country in 1634, Tessouat was engaged in deflecting the fur trade from the upper country and spread the rumour that Champlain sought revenge against the people of the village of Ihonatiria in the Attignaouantan (Bear) nation for their part in the death of Étienne BRÛLÉ. Playing on the feeling of guilt and fear of these people, he hoped to dislodge the Jesuits from their village and thus to destroy their relations with the French. Father BRÉBEUF, however, foreseeing this development, determined to remain at Ihonatiria to build up confidence in the French among the inhabitants.

In March 1636, Le Borgne travelled some 300 leagues over ice and snow to the Huron country with four of his tribe and a young Frenchman, François MARGUERIE, who was wintering with them, seeking allies among the Hurons, Algonkins, and Nipissings for an attack against the Iroquois who had recently killed 23 of his people. He presented 23 wampum belts on this occasion. Again, Tessouat's diplomacy was directed against the Bear nation which was traditionally most closely related to the French. Its citizens were offered no presents and Tessouat even attempted to keep the matter secret from them. His mission was unsuccessful, the Bear being the most influential of the Huron tribes, and the Nipissings refused him aid because of the extortion practised on them when they passed his island.

In his speeches, Tessouat boasted of his power, in the hearing of the Jesuits, pointing out that the preservation of his people and himself meant the continuance of the Indian trade with the French. His body "was hatchets" he explained, and its preservation "was the preservation of the hatchets, the kettles, and all the trade of the French." He claimed further that he was master of the French. Before leaving the Hurons, however, he had a long, friendly talk with the Jesuits, urging them to leave the Huron country, especially the Bear nation; he dwelt on its wickedness in murdering Brûlé, Father Nicolas VIEL, and his companion in 1616, and shortly before this, eight of his own Island Indians. The Jesuits laboured to retain Tessouat's friendship for the French, and on his departure, presented him with a canoe and other little presents.

Tessouat died shortly after this encounter, in the spring of 1636. In August, when the Huron chief TARATOUAN with a Huron flotilla reached Allumette Island, he was refused passage by Tessouat's people until Father ANTOINE DANIEL arrived to intercede, because their recently demised chief had not yet been "cached," that is, his name and responsibility had not yet been taken over by another. This enabled them to make greater demands in tolls than was usual.

ELSIE McLEOD JURY

JR (Thwaites), *passim*. Desrosiers, *Iroquoisie*, 122–24, 150–52. *See also* note to biography of TESSOUAT (d. 1654).

Tessouat

TESSOUAT (Tesswehas, Le Borgne de l'Île), PAUL, Algonkin chief of the Allumette Island tribe; d. 1654.

Tessouat had one eye only and was, therefore, called "Le Borgne." He was described by the Jesuits as haughty and proud, clever, subtle, and unusually arrogant and malicious. Of himself he said, "I am like a tree—men are the branches thereof, to which I give vigor."

Wintering on the St. Lawrence in 1640–41, his people quarrelled with the Christians at Sillery and threatened murder. Tessouat enticed the Christians to return to paganism. Some Sillery Christians joined him in a war-party, which met a sudden defeat after the non-Christians were in consultation with their demons.

At Trois-Rivières, when Father BUTEUX interfered in a pagan ceremony to cure the sick, Tessouat threw burning cinders at his eyes and threatened to kill him with a rope. He later denied this intention to CHAMPFLOUR, the governor. In 1642, one of the two leading chiefs then resident at Trois-Rivières, he was again fomenting trouble. He forbade his people to attend mass. In November he moved to Fort Richelieu to be with others of his tribe for hunting or war.

In March 1643, he arrived at the new settlement of Ville-Marie, on the island Montreal, where his nephew Joseph Oumasasikweie was then living. (Joseph and his wife, Mitigoukwe (later Jeanne) were the first Indians to be baptized and married with full church rites at Ville-Marie.) To the surprise of all, Tessouat requested baptism and a Christian marriage. His conversion was greatly prized because of his importance as chief and because of his former hostility. Great solemnity therefore was observed in the ceremonies on 9 March. CHOMEDEY de Maisonneuve and Mlle MANCE, who were his godparents, gave him the name of Paul. M de PUISEAUX and Mme CHAUVIGNY de La Peltrie were godparents to his wife, who was given the name of Magdelaine. Maisonneuve presented Tessouat with an arquebus and invited him and his wife to dine with the French. Tessouat later held a feast for the Indians, which the French attended. He expressed his gratitude to Maisonneuve, and also his desire to settle near him. Maisonneuve granted land to Tessouat and gave him two men to help cultivate it.

Although the haughtiest man in the world before his baptism, Tessouat became as gentle and humble as a little child, the Jesuits recorded. He showed zeal for the faith and preached often, inclining others of his tribe to follow his example.

In 1644, however, Tessouat was giving support to PIGAROUICH, a former medicine-man of his tribe, then in disrepute with the French. To reinstate himself, he afterwards made a submission which was "very galling to a man of his temper."

Tessouat wintered at Montreal in 1645–46 where he planted corn, but he withdrew to Trois-Rivières, urging others to do likewise, in the face of reports that Iroquois raids were imminent. This probably resulted from his learning that the French had abandoned non-Christian Algonkins in the 1645 treaty with the Iroquois.

Tessouat was described as one of the greatest orators of his time and in May 1646 he spoke eloquently for all the Algonkins at peace councils held with the Iroquois ambassadors. In his speech, however, there were overtones of suspicion and fear that the French might betray their allies, the Hurons and the Algonkins, and sign a separate peace with the Iroquois. In token of his goodwill he presented the Iroquois with 14 elk robes, handsomely painted and well trimmed. Four robes each were given to three Iroquois villages, entreating them to return with safety the children and adult Algonkins whom they held captive.

Returning to his country in August, his party was ambushed. On this occasion he lost one young man who returned to Montreal with an arquebus wound, and two women, one very aged.

In 1648, Tessouat was at Sillery, concerned over the prohibition of non-Christian Indians from that mission at a time when Iroquois war-parties were sweeping the country. He was there accosted by NEGABAMAT for refusing to accept Christianity and at the time gave some hope of reconversion.

Nicolas Perrot*, writing of Le Borgne or Tessouat, said that he "was regarded as the terror of all the peoples, even of the Iroquois." He relates the story that the French priest accompanying the Hurons in the escape from their country in 1650 gave orders to pass Le Borgne's island without payment of toll, saying that the French were masters of all the nations. Tessouat, who then had 400 warriors at his command, forced the party to be brought before him and ordered that the priest be "suspended from a tree by the armpits." (Perrot, however, confused the superior of the Huron mission, Father Paul RAGUENEAU, with Father JÉRÔME LALEMANT, who was not one of the party.) The next year, Perrot continues, Tessouat went down to the French colony. He was carried ashore in his canoe, and despite the fact that guards never left him, he was arrested and thrown into a dungeon for a few days in punishment for his treatment of the priest.

In 1654 the "famous one-eyed man," the greatest orator of his time, died a Christian at Trois-Rivières.

ELSIE MCLEOD JURY

JR (Thwaites), *passim*. Perrot, "Memoir," in *Indian tribes* (Blair), I, 176–78. Desrosiers, *Iroquoisie*, 330–31, 335; "La rupture de la paix de 1645," *Cahiers des Dix*, XVII (1952), 180. Hunt, *Wars of the Iroquois*, 106.

[Note: Since the name "Tessouat" (or a variation of it), and the title "Le Borgne [meaning one-eyed] de l'Île" were "resuscitated" among the chiefs of the Allumette Island tribe, it is extremely difficult to determine which chief is actually referred to in the early documents. The biography of TESSOUAT (d. 1654) may possibly combine the careers of two chiefs but it appears more likely that the events recorded concern one man, who, like many other Indians of his time, wavered in his allegiance to the Christian faith.]

TESSWEHAS. See TESSOUAT (d. 1654)

TESTARD DE LA FOREST, GABRIEL, officer, commandant of Fort Bourbon, Hudson Bay; b. 1661 at Montreal, son of Jacques Testard de La Forest and Marie Pournin; d. 1697 in London.

In 1694, under Pierre Le Moyne* d'Iberville, he took part in the capture of Fort Bourbon (York Factory). Iberville left the fort at the beginning of September 1695, leaving La Forest there in command of a garrison of about 70 men. The following year the fort was besieged by five English ships, two of which were warships. Two French boats, which were bringing help, too late, returned to France. After a three-day bombardment Testard de La Forest surrendered, 1 Sept. 1696. The commander of the English forces, Capt. William Allen, had granted very honourable terms: the honours of war, the right to keep the year's furs, and the transportation of the whole garrison to Plaisance (Placentia, Newfoundland). However, violating the terms of surrender, Allen confiscated the furs and carried off the French to England as prisoners.

La Forest, when he reached Plymouth in October, referred his complaint to the Lord Commissioners of the Board of Trade, and a report was made to the Privy Council. But the affair dragged on. Testard died 27 Aug. 1697 in London. His claims were communicated to the French plenipotentiaries negotiating the Treaty of Ryswick who obtained a favourable decision thanks to its article on North America.

BERNARD WEILBRENNER

AN, Col., C^{11A}, 14, ff.24–29 (mémoire touchant la capitulation du fort Bourbon en 1696); Marine, B^2, 124, ff.346^2–346^5 (rapport de M. de Belleville Lestendart et Blondel . . . 14 nov. 1696).
Documents relating to Hudson Bay (Tyrrell). HBRS, XX (Rich and Johnson); XXI (Rich), 330f., 337–41, *passim*. [Nicolas Jérémie], "Relation du Détroit et de la Baie d'Hudson par Monsieur Jérémie," Soc. historique de Saint-Boniface *Bulletin*, II (1912), 3–23; *Twenty years of York Factory, 1694–1714: Jérémie's account of Hudson Strait and Bay*, tr. from the French ed. of 1720 with notes and intro. by R. Douglas and J. N. Wallace (Ottawa, 1926).
BRH, IX (1903), 188. Faillon, *Histoire de la colonie française*, II, 360f. "M. de la Forest à la Baie d'Hudson," *BRH*, XII (1906), 220–3.

THARCA. See TAREHA

THÉODAT, GABRIEL SAGARD-. See SAGARD

THÉODORE (Recollet). See ALLART

THEWATHIRON. See TEOUATIRON

THIRKILL, LANCELOT, explorer and shipowner, who sailed with JOHN CABOT in 1498; fl. 1498–1501.

Most probably a London merchant, he is described as "of London," and as receiving payments for the victualling of his ship. King Henry VII, after Cabot's return from his 1497 voyage, decided to subsidize a further voyage in 1498. Accordingly, between 22 and 27 March 1498, £20 were advanced "to Lanslot Thirkill of London . . . for his Shipp going towardes the new Ilande," a further £20 on 31 March "to Launcelot Thirkill going towardes the new Ile"; a third payment of £30, between 1 and 3 April, was made to "Launce" Thirkill and Thomas BRADLEY described as "going to the new Isle," and a fourth, of £43 0s. 8d. between 4 and 6 April, to them jointly. These payments made up a total of £113 8s., a sum sufficient to victual a moderate-sized vessel. Other evidence indicates that John Cabot sailed as "chief patron" on the vessel which the king had had manned and victualled for him at Bristol. This is likely to have been Thirkill's ship. That the ship on which Thirkill sailed returned from the voyage may be presumed from a bond which he made on 6 June 1501, referred to in a royal document of 1505.

DAVID B. QUINN

BM, King's book of payments, Add. MS 21480, f.35v. PRO, E. 101/414, 16 (payments between 22 March and 6 April 1498). Williamson, *Cabot voyages* (1962); *Voyages of the Cabots* (1929).

Thomas

THOMAS, JEAN, illegal fur-trader and instigator of the first Indian revolt against the French in Acadia; b. probably in France; fl. 1635.

In 1635 Thomas obtained permission from Cardinal Richelieu to fish for cod on the Grand Banks, but was expressly forbidden to engage in any sort of trade with the Indians. He hired the 150-ton vessel *Saint-Pierre* at Brouage, loading her with both salt and wine as well as regular supplies for the trip. Despite the restrictions placed on his actions by Richelieu, Thomas went to the Canseau (Canso) area and began trading with the Micmacs for furs. According to a charge later laid by Nicolas LE CREUX Du Breuil, commander of Isaac de RAZILLY's Fort Saint-François at Canseau, Thomas incited the Indians through talk and plying them with wine to attack and pillage the fort on 31 July 1635. Once word of this affair reached Commander Razilly at La Hève, he instructed Capt. Bernard MAROT to capture Thomas and this was done. Two inquiries were held that same summer at La Hève, with testimony being given both by residents at Canseau and members of the Thomas crew. Soon afterwards Thomas was sent to France and placed in the prison at La Rochelle, being released on bail 27 Sept. 1635. Nothing further is known of Capt. Jean Thomas whose stay in Canada was short but turbulent.

GEORGE MACBEATH

ACM, B.187. Candide de Nant, *Pages glorieuses*. Couillard Després, *Saint-Étienne de La Tour*, 214–16.

THOMPSON, JOSEPH, HBC employee; fl. 1674–79.

Thompson entered the Company's service in 1674 as mate on the *Shaftesbury* (Capt. Thomas SHEPARD). In 1676 he was given "a medall and chayne" for sailing the same ship to Hudson Bay and back in six months and bringing home a cargo of beaver that realized £1,972. On the return voyage he committed the error of "wearing the King's Jack" (flying the king's flag) and the lords of Admiralty promptly called him to account. Pardon was immediately forthcoming when Prince Rupert answered on his behalf and it is of more than passing interest that Thompson's journal of the 1676 voyage went to Prince Rupert for his library.

When Thompson was en route home in 1678 fortune turned fickle. After leaving Kinsale, Ireland, the *Shaftesbury* was wrecked off the Scilly Isles and that year's cargo of furs was lost. Events following this mishap are obscure but Thompson assigned £50 of HBC stock in part satisfaction of his debt to the Company on a £1,000 bond, and his account shows a mystifying debit item in 1679 for "money pd. the Bayleys (bailiffs) for arresting you."

MAUD M. HUTCHESON

HBRS, V, VIII, IX, XXI (Rich).

THORDARSON, THORFINNR. *See* THORFINNR *karlsefni*

THORFINNR *karlsefni* **THORDARSON,** first European to attempt to found a settlement on the American mainland; fl. 1000–20.

Thorfinnr was a wealthy Icelandic merchant who had made many merchant voyages before going to Greenland shortly after the year 1000 A.D. There he married Gudridr, the widow of Thorsteinn, the son of EIRIKR Thorvaldsson (Eric the Red). Some time between the years 1003 and 1015 Thorfinnr led an expedition to colonize Vinland. The course he followed and the location of his settlement have given rise to much speculation, as is the case with the voyage of LEIFR *heppni* Eiriksson. The most detailed account of Thorfinnr's venture is found in the *Saga of Eric the Red*, but it is vague enough to have given rise to the most varied views. There is no agreement among scholars, but a tentative and not unconvincing case may be made for the following itinerary.

Thorfinnr and about 160 men and women left the Eastern Settlement of Greenland and sailed first to the Western Settlement. Then with a north wind at their back they reached Helluland (Baffin Island) in two days. Again a north wind carried them in two days to Markland (northern Labrador). The expedition coasted southward for a long time until they came to a ness (headland) to which they gave the name of Kjalarnes (Keelness, possibly Cape Whittle) from the keel of a vessel they found there. The land lay upon the starboard and they sailed along its long strands and sandy banks, which they named Furdustrandir (Wonder Strands, possibly the south coast of Labrador).

The land then became indented with bays. They sailed into one where the current was very strong; to it they gave the name of Straumfjord (Bay of Strong Currents, possibly Baie des Sept-Îles) and to an island at its mouth, literally covered with birds and their nests, the name of Straumey. Here they wintered and were hard pressed, for the weather proved severe and they had taken no steps to lay in provisions.

Part of the expedition now left to return to Greenland, while Thorfinnr and the rest proceeded southward to find Vinland. They came to a landlocked bay, which they called Hop. Here, according to different versions of the saga, they spent either about two months or (more likely) a year. They found self-sown wheat growing on low-lying ground and vines or grapes on higher ground. There was an abundance of fish and many animals of all kinds in the woods. The winter was mild with no snow and plenty of forage for the cattle. Hop is difficult to identify because of the discrepant accounts in the saga, but the description would fit Cape Cod.

At Hop the expedition first met the aborigines of the country whom they called Skrælingjar (small, withered). They are described as swarthy, ill-countenanced with large eyes, ugly hair, and broad cheeks. At first relations with them were friendly and the Icelanders bartered gaudy cloth for skins to their great profit, but a bull frightened the Skrælings and they fled. However, they returned in three weeks and battled with the Icelanders, who were saved by Freydis, the daughter of Eirikr Thorvaldsson (Eric the Red). It is impossible, though many attempts have been made, to determine with certainty whether the Skrælings were Indians or (more likely) some type of Eskimo.

Discouraged, it seems, by the hostility of the natives, Thorfinnr returned to Straumfjord. He then sailed northward along Furdustrandir, rounded Keelness and continued westward with very heavily wooded land on the larboard, until he reached a river flowing from east to west. Here Thorvaldr, the brother of Leifr Eiriksson, had been killed by a one-legged man (*einfatingr*; some regard this word as a scribal error for *innfadingr*, or native) on his expedition (*c.* 1003–4). Having explored the country to some extent and finding it unattractive and the natives unfriendly, Thorfinnr returned to Straumfjord and wintered there. In the spring the whole expedition, including the three-year-old son of Thorfinnr, SNORRI, who was born at Straumfjord, returned to Greenland, ending the first and what proved to be the only attempt of the Icelanders in Greenland to settle on the North American continent. Thorfinnr, with his wife and son, soon returned to Iceland and resumed residence there.

The *Saga of the Greenlanders* includes a very brief account of Thorfinnr's expedition. It gives no names to localities, but describes the region where Thorfinnr settled in the same terms as the *Saga of Eric* uses of Hop. It also describes rather differently some details of the encounters with the Skrælings. No archaeological evidence, which might throw light on the location of the above-mentioned places, has so far been discovered.

T. J. OLESON

See the works cited under BJARNI Herjólfsson and LEIFR *heppni* Eiriksson [Appendix]. Also Oleson, *Early Voyages*, 24–25, 33.

THORFINNSSON, SNORRI. *See* SNORRI

THORNE, ROBERT, the elder (d. 1519), and his son ROBERT THORNE the younger (1492–1532), Bristol merchants associated with early voyages to America.

The elder Thorne was trading actively from Bristol to Spain, Portugal, Iceland, and elsewhere for nearly 40 years from 1479 onwards. In 1501 he was associated with Hugh ELIOT in the purchase of a ship; in 1510 he was a member of an admiralty commission for Bristol and he was mayor in 1515. He died in London in 1518, was buried in the Temple Church, and left money for the endowment of a grammar school in Bristol. His son, Robert the younger, also a merchant, moved to London and thence, shortly after 1520, to Seville, where he lived as a factor and merchant. He invested in SEBASTIAN CABOT's expedition of 1526 and returned to England by 1531, but died in 1532, leaving a large fortune.

The younger Robert in 1527 stated of his father that he "with an other Marchaunt of Brystow named Hughe Elliot were the discoverers of the Newfound Landes." This statement appears to have been made in good faith, but its meaning is not certain. It could mean an independent discovery prior to the time of JOHN CABOT, which is now not unlikely in view of John Day's statement in 1498 that the English had made a transatlantic discovery "in other times," conceivably in 1481 [*see* CROFT]. Between 1577 and 1580 Dr John Dee dated the alleged Thorne-Eliot voyage as "Circa An. 1494," though it is doubtful if he had evidence for doing so [*see* discussion of Sebastian Cabot's map of 1544 in JOHN CABOT]. It has also been thought that Thorne and Eliot may have been leading participants in the Cabot voyage of 1497. The elder Thorne is indeed likely to have been associated in the Cabot voyages and, most probably, with those of 1501–5, in association with Hugh Eliot. The younger Thorne was especially interested in the prospect of finding an English route to the Far East. In 1527 he compiled a "Declaration of the Indies," with a map, and sent them with a letter to Edward Lee, the English ambassador, for transmission to Henry VIII, in which he put forward a comprehensive scheme for an approach to Asia northward from England (and including the statement about his father). At his return from Spain he had a ship almost prepared for an exploring voyage when he died.

DAVID B. QUINN

Roger Barlow, *A brief summe of geographie*, ed. E. G. R. Taylor (Hakluyt Soc., 2d ser., LXIX, 1932). G. Connell-Smith, *Forerunners of Drake* (London,

1954). G. C. Moore-Smith, "The Withypoll family," Walthamstow Antiq. Soc. *Pub.*, XXXIV (1936). Williamson, *Cabot voyages* (1962); *Voyages of the Cabots* (1929).

THORVALDSSON, EIRIKR. See EIRIKR [Appendix]

THUBIÈRES DE LEVY DE QUEYLUS, GABRIEL (the name is sometimes written **Kaylus, Kélus,** or **Quélus,** but he signed **Queylus**), priest, Sulpician, abbé of Loc-Dieu, doctor of theology, member of the Société Notre-Dame de Montréal, vicar general of the archbishop of Rouen in Canada, founder and first superior of the Séminaire de Saint-Sulpice at Montreal; b. 1612 at Privezac, diocese of Rodez; d. 20 May 1677 in Paris.

Gabriel de Queylus came from a wealthy seigneurial family; he became the abbé of Loc-Dieu in his native Rouergue at the age of 11 (1623) and studied at Vaugirard (Paris), where he may have had as an associate Jean-Jacques Olier, of whom he later became one of the most loyal fellow-workers. Abbé Queylus was ordained a priest on 15 April 1645, and shortly afterwards received the degree of doctor of theology. The year 1645 was for the 33-year-old priest one of crucial decisions, which set his career upon its permanent course: on 26 July he entered the Compagnie des Prêtres de Saint-Sulpice—founded in 1641 by Olier—and at about the same time joined the Société de Montréal. Saint-Sulpice and Montreal: two centres of Queylus's activity which by a remarkable conjunction of events were to coincide perfectly in his career from 1657 on.

As soon as he was admitted to Saint-Sulpice, he became one of Olier's most active assistants. During his lifetime the founder permitted seven Sulpician seminaries to be established; he entrusted M. de Queylus with the task of laying the foundations of five of them: those of Rodez (1647), Nantes (1649), Viviers (1650), Clermont (1656), and Montreal (1657). In 1648, moreover, Abbé Queylus was made superior (on a temporary basis) of the mother community of Saint-Sulpice, in Paris. In the midst of these wanderings, there came a pause: from 1650 to 1656 Queylus lived in Vivarais, holding the appointment of parish priest of Privas and working to convert the Protestants.

Suddenly, in 1656, Queylus was recalled to Paris. He went there, probably in complete ignorance of the turmoil into which he was to be plunged.

A double plan had taken shape within the Société de Montréal: the establishment of a seminary of Saint-Sulpice at Ville-Marie and the appointment of a Sulpician bishop for Canada. M. Olier, in conformity with the society's views, nominated to lay the foundations of the seminary at Ville-Marie the same person who had already brought into existence four Sulpician communities: M. de Queylus's experience, the fact that he belonged to the Société de Montréal, his personal fortune, and his generosity made it inevitable that his superior should select him. Certain associates, however, conceived of a higher dignity for M. de Queylus: after a discreet approach had been made to him, he allowed himself to be recommended for the bishopric of Quebec. On 9 Aug. 1656 Bishop Godeau of Vence announced to the general assembly of the French clergy "that he had an abbé who was willing to accept this post [the bishopric], and to go and make the sacrifice of his wealth and his person among the Indians," but "that he could not yet name him." The candidate's name was disclosed only at the session held on 10 Jan. 1657.

Abbé Queylus's candidature was not acceptable to the Jesuits; in their turn, they put forward a priest of their choice, François de Laval*, the abbé of Montigny, who enjoyed the favour of the French court. It was rightly considered that the future bishop would have to command the support of the Jesuits, who since 1632 had alone guided the destiny of the Church in Canada. The intervention of the Jesuits destroyed M. de Queylus's hopes, and this rankled with him, as was to become apparent during his subsequent stay at Quebec.

But for the time being the preparations towards his departure for Canada had to be hastened. For the seminary at Ville-Marie Olier had appointed, in addition to M. de Queylus, two priests, MM. Dominique Galinier and Gabriel SOUART, and a deacon, M. Antoine d'ALLET. All four embarked on 17 May 1657 at Nantes, in the roadstead of Saint-Nazaire, after receiving ecclesiastical powers, conveyed by letters dated 22 April, from the archbishop of Rouen; on the same day the archbishop had delivered letters patent to M. de Queylus, naming him his official and his vicar general for the whole of New France.

The title of vicar general conferred upon M. de Queylus was going to aggravate the delicate question of ecclesiastical jurisdiction in New France. For years the Recollets, and later the Jesuits, had received their powers directly from the pope. But the archbishop of Rouen had long claimed the right to accredit missionaries, many of whom came from his diocese, or at any rate embarked there for the crossing to Canada. In 1647 and 1648 the Jesuits had consulted various authorities on this question; they finally acknowledged their dependency upon the archbishop of Rouen, who on 30 April 1649 gave letters of appointment as vicar general to the superior at Quebec. The Jesuits, however, kept this acknowledgment secret until 15 April 1653, at which time they proclaimed it from the pulpit—not without taking certain precautions beforehand in case of a protest from Rome or from the court. The discretion with which the change of jurisdiction was surrounded, and the prudence displayed by the Jesuits before accepting the archbishop of Rouen's authority and "making it . . . evident and declaring it openly," clearly show how ticklish this question was.

Abbé Queylus's letters of appointment as vicar general were good for the whole of New France, without at the same time explicitly revoking those of the superior of the Jesuits. Clashes were to be expected.

The ship on which the Sulpicians had made the crossing anchored before Quebec on 29 July 1657. M. de Queylus and his associates had already left the ship at the Île d'Orléans, and gone to M. Maheu's house. As soon as he heard of the ecclesiastics' arrival Father de QUEN, the superior of the Jesuits, hastened to the Île d'Orléans, welcomed the Sulpicians, and brought them to Quebec. The Jesuits' reception was cordial, Abbé Queylus most polite.

In the course of a conversation a few days later, Abbé Queylus showed the superior of the Jesuits his letters of appointment. Father de Quen apparently did not venture to stress the validity of his own: for the time being he recognized M. de Queylus's authority and agreed with him that he, de Quen, should make no move in his capacity of vicar general so long as the archbishop of Rouen had not made his intentions clear as to the powers of the superior of the Jesuits. After confirming Father PONCET in his office as priest serving the parish of Quebec, M. de Queylus sailed for Montreal with his associates.

The Sulpicians had handed to Father Poncet, with instructions to proclaim it from the pulpit, the Bull of Indulgence granted by Alexander VII on the occasion of his elevation to the pontificate. Without notifying his superior, the priest of the parish of Quebec read the papal document to the congregation. Offended by what he took to be a show of independence, Father de Quen—as he was entitled to do by reason of his formal agreement with M. de Queylus—relieved Father Poncet of his functions and replaced him by Father CLAUDE PIJART. Father Poncet, on his way to the Iroquois country, stopped at Montreal at the beginning of September, and informed M. de Queylus of this incident. The vicar general, taking

Thubières de Levy de Queylus

umbrage in his turn, ordered the Jesuit to accompany him to Quebec, where they arrived on the evening of 12 September. Queylus immediately took the control of the parish away from Father Pijart and announced his decision to take it over himself. In this way, as a consequence of the susceptibility of Father de Quen and of M. de Queylus, an incident trivial in itself launched a small-scale war.

Each side kept watch on the other, seeking to catch the adversary off guard. Abbé Queylus made the mistake of attacking the Jesuits from the pulpit on a number of occasions: on 21 Oct. 1657, in particular, he favoured them with a "satirical discourse," accusing them of trying to "check up" on him and comparing them to pharisees. On their part the Jesuits were imprudent enough to write "barbed missives" against the abbé; the incriminating letters fell into the hands of M. de Queylus, who was "shocked" to learn that he was "violent," and "more troublesome in his war against the Jesuits than the Iroquois were."

But the new parish priest of Quebec had other concerns: for instance, to find a place to live. Either, the presbytery was being used legally by the Jesuits as a residence, or it was not. Convinced of the second of these hypotheses Abbé Queylus—prompted by the churchwardens, according to Voyer* d'Argenson—submitted a petition to the lieutenant-general of Quebec, asking that the "Jesuit Fathers be required to leave their house, so that the said Abbé might be lodged there as priest of the parish of Quebec, or to repay 6,000 *livres* given to them by the Communauté [des Habitants] for building a presbytery." A writ, served by the court officer Lavigne [*see* JEAN LEVASSEUR] on 22 Nov. 1657, summoned the Jesuits to a hearing on the following Tuesday to reply to this petition. Unfortunately M. de Queylus had been mistaken: the residence belonged to the Jesuits in their own right, and they had paid the Communauté des Habitants the sum of 6,000 *livres* to have it built. This was affirmed by a judgement of LOUIS D'AILLEBOUST handed down on 23 Mar. 1658. Although they were in the right, the Jesuits must nonetheless have considered this court summons extremely high-handed.

The relations between M. de Queylus and the Jesuits did not seem likely to improve. On 1 Jan. 1658 the Jesuits had attempted a rapprochement: "Father Pijart went to see the abbé"; but "the said abbé did not return the visit." On 31 March there were still signs of tension: in their *Journal* the Jesuits deemed a "homily" of Abbé Queylus "exaggerated," and saw a "contradiction" in his words. Then, from April on—under some benign influence or other—a reconciliation seems to have

Thubières de Levy de Queylus

come about gradually: the superior of the Jesuits visited the vicar general when he was ill; certain of them were invited to hold services in the church; so that when M. d'Argenson arrived at Quebec in the summer of 1658 he expressed his surprise at finding "the Church in close union."

The actual cause of the conflict was moreover soon to disappear. In the autumn of 1657 the ships had carried the first news of the dispute to France. In order to restore peace, the archbishop of Rouen signed an act on 30 March 1658, declaring M. de Queylus and Father de Quen his vicars general, the first throughout the island of Montreal, the second in the remainder of New France. The document reached Quebec on 11 July, and was served on M. de Queylus—an exchange of courtesies—on 8 August. The abbé played for time, alleging that there was an irregularity in the letters of appointment as vicar general addressed to the superior of the Jesuits; however, at Argenson's request, he finally agreed, not without bitterness, to embark for Montreal, on 21 August.

In New France the question of ecclesiastical jurisdiction seemed to be settled; in France, it was being raised with a new sharpness. As early as January 1657 Louis XIV had presented to the pope the Jesuit candidate for the bishopric of Quebec. The matter dragged on, so much so that the bull appointing Bishop Laval was signed only on 3 June 1658: he was appointed vicar apostolic in New France, with the "foreign" title of bishop of Petraea. As vicar apostolic, Laval was completely outside the archbishop of Rouen's authority. Rome moreover denied the validity of the latter's claims.

But barely had Bishop Laval's appointment become known when the archbishop and Parlement of Rouen opposed it outright, forbidding Laval to "take upon himself the functions of vicar apostolic in Canada." On 8 Dec. 1658, in the middle of this chorus of protests, François de Laval managed to have himself consecrated secretly in Paris, by the papal nuncio, in a chapel not subject to the archbishop's jurisdiction. In quick succession the Parlements of Paris and of Rouen, on 16 and 23 December, seeing in this consecration a "blow against the rights of the [French] episcopacy and the liberties of the Gallican Church," forbade all the king's subjects "to recognize François de Laval as vicar apostolic." Archbishop Harlay of Rouen showed such dogged persistence that Bishop Laval set off for New France armed with a royal document which recognized the archbishop of Rouen's jurisdiction over Canada as concurrent with that of the vicar apostolic. However the queen mother, who was well disposed towards the Jesuits and Laval, had sent a letter to Governor Argenson correcting the purport of this document: she called upon him to proclaim, to the exclusion of all other, the jurisdiction of the bishop of Petraea over all Canada.

The ship carrying Bishop Laval dropped anchor before Quebec on 16 June 1659. The bishop was received with great pomp, but it was not without some hesitation that the female communities and some settlers recognized his authority. Was not the archbishop of Rouen, represented in the colony by M. de Queylus, "above Bishop Laval, who was only vicar apostolic?" The question was debated, and soon everyone rallied to the crook of the new shepherd. Time was passing, however, and M. de Queylus had not yet given any sign of life. Finally, on 7 August, he made his appearance, greeted the bishop, and submitted himself to his authority, promising that thenceforth he would accept no further letter of appointment as vicar general from the archbishop of Rouen.

But at the beginning of September a ship brought two letters, one from Archbishop Harlay, the other from Louis XIV, authorizing M. de Queylus to exercise the functions of vicar general of the archbishop of Rouen. Forthwith the abbé forgot his protestations of the previous month: "taking off his mask," he sought to have his powers recognized. Unfortunately for him the king had changed his mind: in a letter to Argenson he cancelled the authorization that he had just granted to M. de Queylus. The abbé yielded, and on 22 Oct. 1659 sailed for France.

Bishop Laval, certain that M. de Queylus would not give up easily, wrote to the cardinals of the Propaganda (in Rome) on 3 Oct. 1660, to put them on guard against any attempt aimed at undermining his authority. Likewise he entreated Louis XIV to prevent the abbé from returning to Canada. Bishop Laval had reason to distrust the persistent Sulpician, who was preparing once again, at the beginning of 1660, to cross the Atlantic. On 27 February Louis XIV, forewarned, forbade him absolutely to leave the kingdom without his express permission. This did not prevent the scheming abbé, after a vain attempt to have the prohibition rescinded, from going secretly to Rome in the autumn of 1660; there, unknown to the Propaganda, he abused the good faith of the Datary, from which he obtained a bull authorizing the establishment at Ville-Marie of a parish independent of the vicar apostolic, and granting the right of presentation of the incumbent to the superior of Saint-Sulpice and the right of appointment to the archbishop of Rouen. Back in France, Queylus had himself appointed parish priest of Montreal by Arch-

Thubières de Levy de Queylus

bishop Harlay, and sailed clandestinely for Quebec, where he arrived incognito on 3 Aug. 1661.

The unheralded arrival of Abbé Queylus, who had travelled from Percé to Quebec in a small boat in order to get there before the ship, and the purport of the document that he was carrying, greatly astonished Bishop Laval, who refused, pending further investigation, to put the Sulpician in possession of the parish of Ville-Marie. He begged him, in vain, to refrain from going up to Montreal for the time being; on two occasions, 4 and 5 August, he forbade him to do so. Despite the threat of inhibition from his priestly functions and the customary three canonical monitions contained in Laval's second letter, the Sulpician did not give up his plan for departure: during the night of 5–6 August he slipped into a canoe and made off towards Montreal. On 6 August Laval ordered him to return to Quebec, declaring him "inhibited" if he disregarded this order. Despite the gravity of the sentence, the abbé did not turn back.

Meanwhile Louis XIV had learned of Abbé Queylus's departure for Canada. Straightway he ordered PIERRE DUBOIS Davaugour, who was going to occupy the post of governor in the colony, to send M. de Queylus back to France. On 22 Oct. 1661 the vessel bearing the former vicar general sailed for Europe; thus ended the struggle between Bishop Laval and Abbé Queylus over the matter of jurisdiction. As for the archbishop of Rouen, the firm attitude of Rome, Louis XIV, and Bishop Laval forced him gradually to give up his claims.

M. de Queylus's return to France was a bitter blow to the few members of the Société Notre-Dame de Montréal who were still active. By his fortune, which he used generously for the benefit of Ville-Marie, he was the main support of the undertaking. His forced absence from New France perhaps hastened the members' decision to cede Montreal Island to the Séminaire de Saint-Sulpice (9 March 1663). Once the cession was made, the Sulpicians hesitated in their turn: without M. de Queylus's presence at Montreal their efforts seemed doomed to failure. Consequently they entreated Bishop Laval—who was then in Paris—to authorize the abbé to come to Canada. But in vain. The vicar apostolic displayed the inflexibility which was a dominant feature of his character, according to Marie de l'Incarnation [see GUYART].

With the passage of time, the passions aroused by the question of ecclesiastical jurisdiction in New France abated. For his part Abbé Queylus kept quiet, to use the description of Bishop Laval. In consequence the king, in 1668, allowed him to return to Canada as the superior of the seminary of Ville-Marie. Laval received him graciously and kindly, even giving him letters of appointment as vicar general on Montreal Island.

The untroubled atmosphere of the colony was to give M. de Queylus the opportunity to reveal his spirit of enterprise and his talents as a builder, which had remained almost unnoticed during his first two stays in Canada. In that disturbed period, he had nonetheless authorized the building of the churches of Sainte-Anne at Petit-Cap (Beaupré) and of Notre-Dame-de-la-Visitation at Château-Richer in 1658; the preceding year he had reorganized the parish of Montreal, and appointed his colleague, M. Souart, to it; in 1659 he had given some attention to the settlement of Ville-Marie, fixing the site of the town and making ready for the coming of new settlers, who were to clear the fiefs of Saint-Marie and of Saint-Gabriel.

This time M. de Queylus's work was more in accord with the missionary concerns of New France. The Sulpicians, with the possible exception of M. Barthélemy*, had scarcely taken any part hitherto in the apostolic endeavour. As soon as he arrived in the autumn of 1668, M. de Queylus appointed MM. Trouvé* and Fénelon [see SALIGNAC] to found a mission among the Onondagas of the Bay of Quinte (Kenté). The following year he added M. Lascaris* d'Urfé to their number. In 1670 the Sulpicians held three posts on Lake Ontario: Kenté, Gandaseteiagon, and Ganeraské. But M. de Queylus already had his eyes on new apostolic fields: in 1669 he had sent M. Dollier* de Casson and M. René BRÉHANT de Galinée to reconnoitre among the "Ottawa nations" of the Mississippi region; this voyage had taken the two Sulpicians as far as Lake Erie, of which they had taken possession in the king's name.

Simultaneously with this missionary undertaking, Abbé Queylus, at Montreal, also championed the cultural assimilation of the natives. At that period the mother country indeed insisted that the Indians be civilized. Bishop Laval, the Jesuits, the Ursulines knew from experience that this was a fanciful ambition; M. de Queylus, not yet disillusioned, gave himself up to it with a zeal that brought him tributes of satisfaction from the king and the minister. He accepted Indian boys in his seminary, and entrusted the girls to the sisters of the Congregation. These children were taught French, mechanical arts, good manners. At first this sincere effort appeared likely to yield good results. But it soon became evident, at Ville-Marie as at Quebec, just how premature the attempt was.

Meanwhile another ambitious plan had taken shape in M. de Queylus's mind: the founding of

Thubières de Levy de Queylus

a hospice at Ville-Marie for aged and sick Indians. Absorbed in his dream of assimilation, he hoped that the Indians, following their relatives who had retired to the hospice, would come to Montreal, establish themselves there, and gradually acquire the French language and civilization from their contacts with the settlers. The abbé obtained Bishop Laval's permission for the direction of this institution to be entrusted to the Hospitallers of Quebec, to whom he promised a generous grant of land and a fund of 10,000 *livres* (1671).

In appealing to the Hospitallers of Quebec, M. de Queylus was seeking to honour an old promise made to this community. In 1658, edified by the piety and devotion of these nuns, he had offered them the direction of the hospital at Ville-Marie, which was administered by Jeanne MANCE pending the arrival of Hospitallers from La Flèche. This community had been founded by M. Le Royer de La Dauversière, having in mind an establishment at Ville-Marie. M. de Queylus, a member of the Société Notre-Dame de Montréal since 1645, was not unaware of this. However, he devised a scheme to induce the Hospitallers of Quebec to assume responsibility for the hospital. Shortly before Mlle Mance's departure for France in the autumn of 1658, and without divulging his intentions, the Sulpician brought to Montreal two nuns from the Hôtel-Dieu in Quebec; one of them, he asserted, needed a "change of air" for her health. Neither Mlle Mance nor CHOMEDEY de Maisonneuve was taken in by the abbé's fine words. Furthermore, when Mlle Mance reached Quebec she learned of M. de Queylus's plans from the lips of the Hospitallers themselves. But having found, in France, a benefactress for the hospital at Ville-Marie, Jeanne Mance brought three Hospitallers from La Flèche to Canada in 1659. This put an end to the Quebec nuns' stay at Montreal —although Bishop Laval, who had recently arrived, was in agreement with M. de Queylus that the number of religious orders in Canada should not be greatly increased. Hence it is not surprising that the abbé—the admirer and benefactor of the nuns of the Hôtel-Dieu in Quebec—wanted to entrust to them the direction of the proposed hospice, which, however, he did not have the time to found.

For all that, the enterprising superior had not neglected the material organization of the Montreal settlement. On his arrival he had appointed M. Souart as a schoolmaster for the young French children. He had in addition concerned himself with peopling the colony, bringing in indentured workers who subsequently received grants of land. Encouraged by the peace of 1666, he granted fiefs outside the limits of the town. The population increased appreciably: from 624 in 1666, it rose to nearly 1500 in 1671.

M. de Queylus's exuberant activity earned him the praises of Louis XIV, Colbert, and TALON. Much reliance was placed upon his intelligent zeal and his initiative for the expansion and welfare of the Montreal colony. Unfortunately the Sulpician had to return to France in 1671 to undertake the division of his property between himself and his brothers. He did not come back: stricken by illness, he retired to the seminary in Paris. He died there on 20 May 1677, at the age of 65.

Thus, in the calm of retirement, the eventful career of a priest endowed with an unusual personality drew to a close. Undeviating in his friendships and animosities, he made faithful friends and irreconcilable enemies. Yet with one accord his contemporaries lauded his piety, his zeal, his virtue. What kind of man, then, was this abbé?

Uncompromising, skilful in conceiving plans, swift in his decisions, having a sense of organization, M. de Queylus had the temperament of a builder. Individualistic, extremely active, unswerving in the pursuit of his objectives, he was irked by authority as soon as it appeared to restrict his initiative and hamper his action; he would attack it as if it were an obstacle in his path. Fervent and zealous, he threw himself completely into his activities, with which his whole identity would finally be merged.

An individual whose personality is fashioned in this way displays the full sweep of his talents when circumstances are favourable to him. Thus, under the friendly and understanding authority of M. Olier, who placed deep confidence in him, Abbé Queylus's achievements were considerable; it was the same in 1668–71, when as seigneur of Montreal and superior of the Sulpician seminary, he had the support and goodwill both of Bishop Laval and of the civil authorities. Such a personality, however, rebels when it encounters any kind of opposition. When faced with contradiction or hostility, M. de Queylus proved to be suspicious, touchy, rancorous; he was all too apt to be harsh to his adversaries, towards whom he was sparing neither of his scorn nor of his irony; he was so persistent in his plans that he would go so far as to adopt any means—dissimulation, cunning, intrigue—to achieve his ends; in short, at such times, he readily lost his sense of proportion.

Highly strung, active, devoted, and generous, Abbé Queylus was essentially a man who identified himself with a cause, becoming its champion and giving to it unstintingly of his person and of his wealth. He had the soul of a crusader. Once launched upon a course, this intrepid fighter harboured no doubts and knew no retreat. And woe betide the obstacles!

ANDRÉ VACHON

Correspondance de Talon, APQ *Rapport*, *1930–31*, 110, 127, 147, 155, 165, 170, 172. Dollier de Casson, *Histoire du Montréal*. Marie Guyart de l'Incarnation, *Lettres* (Richaudeau). *JR* (Thwaites). *JJ* (Laverdière et Casgrain). "Lettre du ministre Colbert à l'abbé de Queylus (15 mai 1669)," *BRH*, XXXII (1926): 148. "Lettres inédites du gouverneur d'Argenson," *BRH*, XXVII (1921), 298–309, 328–39.

Caron, "Inventaire de documents," APQ *Rapport*, *1939–40*, 157–353. Daveluy, "Bibliographie," *RHAF*, XVI (1962–63), 455–463; *Jeanne Mance, 1606–1673, suivie d'un essai généalogique sur les Mance et les De Mance par M. Jacques Laurent* (2e éd., Montréal et Paris [1962]). Faillon, *Histoire de la colonie française*, II, III. Auguste Gosselin, "Quelques observations à propos du voyage du P. Le Jeune au Canada en 1660, et du prétendu voyage de M. de Queylus en 1664," *RSCT*, 2d ser., II (1896), sect.I, 35–58; *Vie de Mgr de Laval*, I. Olivier Maurault, "Saint-Sulpice et le Canada: l'imbroglio Queylus-Laval," *SCHEC Rapport*, *1955–56*, 73–81. Mondoux, *L'Hôtel-Dieu de Montréal*. Rochemonteix, *Les Jésuites et la N.-F. au XVIIe siècle*, II; *Réponse à un mémoire intitulé: Observations à propos du P. Le Jeune et de M. de Queylus par M. l'abbé Gosselin . . .* (Versailles, 1897). *Les Ursulines de Québec*, I, 327.

THURY, LOUIS-PIERRE, priest, missionary in Acadia; b. *c.* 1644 at Notre-Dame-de-Breuil in Normandy; d. 3 June 1699 at Chibouctou (Halifax, N.S.). Abbé Thury had probably begun his theological studies in France. He arrived in Canada about 1675, where he finished his theological studies, and was ordained by Bishop Laval* 21 Dec. 1677. He first served some parishes on both shores of the St. Lawrence and became busar of the seminary of Quebec.

In 1684, as the institution was planning to found a mission in Acadia, Bishop Laval sent Abbé Thury on an observation tour from Percé to Port-Royal (Annapolis Royal, N.S.). The missionary sent the bishop a long account and chose to settle at Miramichi, where RICHARD DENYS offered a piece of ground for a mission. He remained there three years, receiving the visit of Bishop Saint-Vallier [La Croix*], and occasionally went to the Saint John River and Port-Royal.

On Abbé Petit's* advice, he then went to settle at Pentagouet (Castine, Maine), near Jean-Vincent d'Abbadie* de Saint-Castin, where he remained eight years. He acquired great influence over the Abenakis and took part in their expeditions. In 1689 he accompanied Saint-Castin on the raid which resulted in the destruction of Pemaquid; of this he left a detailed account. In 1692 he went along with a war party against York (Maine). Two years later he applied himself to thwarting the endeavours of PHIPS, who wanted to keep the Abenakis neutral; Thury played an important role in retaining them under French influence. He took part in the attack against Pescadouet (Oyster Bay), and was present with ROBINAU de Villebon and a party of Abenakis at the capture of Pemaquid by Pierre Le Moyne* d'Iberville in 1696.

The bishop of Quebec made him his vicar general in 1698 and appointed him to be the superior of the missions in Acadia. About the same time Abbé Thury founded a new mission at Pigiguit (on Minas Basin) and planned to group the Micmacs in one huge settlement between Shubenacadie and Chibouctou. The court looked with favour upon this plan and granted him a sum of 2,000 *livres*. His death prevented him from carrying out this undertaking.

He died 3 June 1699 at Chibouctou and was buried by the Indians under a stone monument. Dièreville* saw this monument and heard the hymns which the missionary had translated into Micmac.

Endowed with great qualities, Abbé Thury had a full career and was a great missionary. His political role is more open to discussion and has been variously judged. The French officers praised his activity and Charlevoix* represented him as a "true apostle," whereas Parkman considered him merely an "apostle of carnage."

RENÉ BAUDRY

AN, Col., B, 17, 19, 20, 22; C^{11D}, 2, 3. ASQ, Documents Faribault, Lettres; Polygraphie; Séminaire; *passim*; A.-E. Gosselin, "Notes pour servir à la biographie des prêtres du Séminaire de Québec," with marginal notes. Jean-Baptiste de La Croix de Chevrières de Saint-Vallier, *Estat présent de l'Église de la colonie française dans la Nouvelle-France . . .* (2e éd., Québec, 1856), 45–52, reproduces the report of Thury to Bishop Laval.

H.-R. Casgrain, *Les Sulpiciens et les Prêtres des Missions étrangères en Acadie (1676–1762)* (Québec, 1897), 31–48, 139–143 (extract from Thury's account of the destruction of Pemaquid, from Charlevoix). Parkman, *Count Frontenac and New France* (1st ed.), *passim*. Webster, *Acadia*, 198f.

TILLY, CHARLES LEGARDEUR DE. See LEGARDEUR

TING. *See* TYNG

TISQUANTUM (Squanto, Squantum, Tasquantum), English-speaking Indian of Pawtuxet (Plymouth, Mass.); d. 1622 at Manamoick (now Chatham, Mass.).

Togouiroui

Tisquantum has been identified as one of the Maine Indians taken to England by Capt. George WAYMOUTH in 1605 but the authority for this is far from certain. He was put ashore at Cape Cod by Capt. John Smith in 1614. After the departure of Capt. Smith, Capt. Thomas Hunt seized more than 20 Indians, including Tisquantum, to be sold in Spain as slaves. Tisquantum escaped to London and lived there at the home of John Slaney, treasurer of the Newfoundland company, who sent him to Newfoundland two years later. He landed at Cuper's (now Cupids) Cove where John MASON and Thomas DERMER had settled. Dermer took Tisquantum back to England in 1618 but returning to America the next year, he cruised along the coast of New England and put Tisquantum ashore. He was then the sole survivor of his tribe, all the others having died of smallpox while he was away.

Tisquantum is best known as the Indian who visited the Pilgrims at Plymouth Bay in March 1621 and who became their interpreter.

Tisquantum should not be confused with Squando (Squanto in *JR*), the Sokoki or Abenaki sagamo at Saco, Maine, who burned the English settlement there on 18 Sept. 1675, after the English had drowned his wife and baby.

W. AUSTIN SQUIRES

DAB (Squanto). L. N. Kinnicutt, "Plymouth settlement and Tisquantum," *Mass. Hist. Soc. Proc.*, XLVIII (1914–15), 103–18. R. A. Preston, *Gorges of Plymouth Fort* (Toronto, 1953). John Smith, *Travels and Works*, ed. E. Arber (2v., Birmingham, 1884–1910). H. M. Sylvester, *Indian Wars of New England* (3v., Boston, 1910), I, 36, 74, 75, 115, 116, 140.

TOGOUIROUI (Togoniron, Kryn, Cryn, Athasata, Adhasatah), JOSEPH (Sosé), called the **Great Mohawk,** chief of the French Mohawks; d. 1690.

He had already distinguished himself in 1669, when the Mohicans had besieged Gandaouagué (Fonda, N.Y.). In 1672, after a disagreement with his wife, he went away from his village and during the winter hunt met near Chambly a Christian Indian woman and her husband, who was a catechumen at the Saint-François-Xavier mission at Prairie-de-la-Magdelaine. Won over by their example and by his conversations with them, he arrived at the mission with them in the spring and asked permission to become a Christian. Father Jacques FRÉMIN, a Jesuit, first made him go back to Gandaouagué to get his wife. He returned towards the end of June 1673, accompanied by his wife and some 40 friends. Seven years later, thanks in good measure to the Great Mohawk, there were more of his compatriots at the mission than in their native canton. In 1676 he brought along about 30 more, and others the following year. As long as the peace which had been imposed by PROUVILLE de Tracy in 1666 lasted, Togouiroui used to return from his trips with new recruits.

In 1683 a gale blew down the church at Saint-François-Xavier. To replace it the Great Mohawk handed over the fine lodge that he had just built for himself. Before leaving on Governor LE FEBVRE de La Barre's ill-fated expedition to La Famine, he offered to the chapel in 1684 a bronze candlestick worth four beaver pelts.

As a chief he was admired not only by his own people but also by the French, and was respected by all. In 1674, in a skirmish near Fort Chambly, a pagan Iroquois killed a Mahican chief. A neophyte from Saint-François-Xavier was accused of the killing. Immediately the Great Mohawk held an investigation and proved that none of the mission Indians was guilty. In this way he rendered a great service to the colony: a violation of the peace of 1666 between the French and the Five Nations would have caused a disaster.

In 1687 Governor Brisay* de Denonville seized some pagan chiefs by treachery at Cataracoui (Fort Frontenac) and sent them to the galleys in France. In the month of July he attacked the Senecas and burned their villages. The Great Mohawk fought under his orders. At the end of August he went to Lake Champlain and met some 60 Mohawks who were on their way to attack the colony. The Great Mohawk persuaded them to go back home quietly. Once more he had saved the lives of French settlers.

After the massacre at Lachine by the pagan Iroquois in 1689, the Great Mohawk remained faithful to the French. When the aged Frontenac [*see* BUADE], who had again become governor, declared war on the English at the beginning of February 1690, a detachment of Frenchmen and friendly Indians marched on Corlaer (Schenectady, N.Y.). The Great Mohawk harangued his men, and the village was attacked by surprise. The English, who had encouraged the Five Nations to wage war against the French, suffered a loss of 400,000 *livres* as well as many dead.

In another expedition under the command of René Legardeur* de Beauvais and the Great Mohawk, a small band of Frenchmen and Indians were bivouacking on the night of 4 June 1690 on the Rivière-aux-Saumons (Salmon River). A party of Algonkins and Abenakis, their allies, took them for the enemy and charged them before daylight. The Great Mohawk was the first to fall. He "was hardly less mourned by the French than by his compatriots," wrote Father Charlevoix*, "& of all those who regretted his death, the missionaries were those who felt this loss the most cruelly."

HENRI BÉCHARD

Charlevoix, *Histoire. JR* (Thwaites). La Pot(h)erie, *Histoire*, I, 347–49. *NYCD* (O'Callaghan and Fernow). *The Positio on Katharine Tekakwitha. Positio super virtutibus servae Dei Catharinae Tekakwitha.* E. J. Devine, *Historic Caughnawaga* . . . (Montreal, 1922). Eccles, *Frontenac*, 4–5, 157–72, 186–87, 191–92, 197, 208, 224–27, 331–32 *et passim*. Lanctot, *Histoire du Canada*, II, 152–54.

TONNETUIT, PIERRE CHAUVIN DE. See CHAUVIN

TONSAHOTEN (Tonsanhoten, Tonsohoten), FRANÇOIS-XAVIER (Pierre), a Huron, the first Christian Indian at the Saint-François-Xavier mission at Prairie-de-la-Magdelaine.

Tonsahoten had been baptized by Father Léonard GARREAU, a companion of the Canadian martyrs. He was adopted by the Oneidas after the destruction of Huronia. A valiant warrior, he was of a rather difficult temperament.

Towards 1656 he married Catherine GANDEACTEUA at Oneida. In November 1667 Father Jacques Bruyas*, a Jesuit, visited their village. It was just the right moment, for François-Xavier and his wife were to set out for Montreal and Quebec, where they hoped to find some Black Robes. The Indian enjoined his wife to treat the missionary well and to have him teach her the Christians' prayers. A little later, at Catherine's suggestion, he decided to go to Montreal to have himself treated at the Hôtel-Dieu for a leg ailment. According to Father Claude Chauchetière*, a Jesuit, Tonsahoten was probably accompanying Charles BOQUET, Father Bruyas's interpreter, when he left Oneida with his wife, his mother-in-law, his father, and two or three acquaintances. As soon as he was cured, he left the Hôtel-Dieu to go to Quebec. There his wife and his friends were baptized and confirmed, and Bishop Laval* blessed the marriage of François-Xavier and Catherine.

Towards the end of 1668, upon their return to Quebec, Father Pierre Raffeix*, a Jesuit, invited Tonsahoten and his people to settle at Prairie-de-la-Magdelaine. The following spring François-Xavier built his lodge there. Shortly afterwards, with his wife, he took several Oneidas to Quebec. They were converted to Christianity and wanted to remain near him. Thus was started the Saint-François-Xavier mission.

In the summer of 1671 the neophytes elected two leaders: François-Xavier was the first chieftain. In agreement with the lay religious leader, who was called the *dogique*, he decided that, to be a member of the Christian village, one had to give up idolatry, polygamy, and drunkenness. He became a member of the Confrérie de la Sainte-Famille, along with his wife.

Shortly before his wife's death in 1673 it was reported that François-Xavier was dead. The news was false, and on his return he presented to the chapel in thanksgiving a big porcelain necklace with which he decked himself out when he went to war. When his wife passed away, he wanted nothing that was not Christian at her funeral. In addition he distributed all the deceased's possessions to the poor.

In 1678, when the village moved from Prairie-de-la-Magdelaine to the Saint-Louis rapids, François-Xavier Tonsahoten gave his field for the new chapel to be built upon. In token of his affection for the faith, he went to war when he was 60 years of age. He died like a good Christian at the Saint-Louis rapids during the winter of 1688: he was called "the father of the believers," because he had been the first Christian Indian at the Saint-François-Xavier mission.

HENRI BÉCHARD

Charlevoix, *Histoire. JR* (Thwaites), LXIII, 154–82. Félix Martin, *Relation des années 1673–1674 pour faire suite aux anciennes relations avec deux cartes géographiques* (Paris, 1861). *The Positio on Katharine Tekakwitha. Positio super virtutibus servae Dei, Catharinae Tekakwitha.* Rochemonteix, *Les Jésuites et la Nouvelle-France au XVIIe siècle*. J. G. Shea, *History of the Catholic missions among the Indian tribes of the United States, 1529–1854* (New York, 1855).

TOTIRI (Totihri), ÉTIENNE, Huron Indian, staunch Christian convert, resident of the village of Teanaostaiaë or Teanaustayé (near Hillsdale, Ontario); fl. 1642–46.

In 1642 Totiri, who was of an influential family, gave over to the Jesuits the end of his cabin, where corn and wood were usually stored. A little chapel, dedicated to Saint-Joseph, was built in "that cabin's end." To be convenient, the priests also lodged with Totiri. He showered with a thousand courtesies the two Frenchmen who came to work on the chapel.

Because of the support he gave the priests, Totiri suffered at the hands of non-Christian villagers who blamed the Jesuits for the disease, famine, and wars that were sweeping their country. With zeal and valour, he led the Christian converts in the face of ostracism, calumnies, and violence. He became custodian of the chapel and instructed male converts in the Christian beliefs; his wife, Madeleine, his equal in intelligence and

Tracy

virtue, instructed the women converts. "Estienne makes of his Cabin a School of devotion," Father GARNIER wrote in 1643.

When no priest could be spared, Totiri and his brother carried on the mission to the Neutral Indians in the winter of 1643–44. They stayed in one of the villages "nearer the frontier," while another Huron convert, Barnabé Otsinnonannhont of the Neutral village of Saint-Michel, "penetrated to the heart of the country" and remained longer, for he had great authority among them, and also many relatives. As a result, 100 Neutrals visited the Hurons to witness the Christian church in action.

In 1646 Totiri was described as *dogique* of the village, carrying on the work of the priests in their absence. Teanaostaiaë, however, was particularly attached to the ancient beliefs and customs. Fearing a departure from them and regarding the new faith as too rigorous, the captains of the village renewed their attacks against the Christians. When a cross, erected in the cemetery by the Jesuits, was attacked by children, Totiri mounted his roof-top and in an "astounding" loud voice, such as was used when the enemy approached, assembled the people and spoke so forcibly against such practices that parents henceforth repressed their children's insolence.

Apart from his religious activities, we know only that Totiri, on a return journey to Huronia, lost nearly all his property when ambushed by Iroquois near Trois-Rivières, probably in 1643, and that in the summer of 1644, "he was about to leave for the war."

As well as his wife, his daughter Catherine, and his brother Paul, Totiri's mother, Christine, Tarihia was a devout Christian after her baptism in 1639. She requested, at her death in the winter of 1643–44 to be buried in the Christian cemetery at Sainte-Marie, some six leagues distant from Teanaostaiaë, the second person to be buried there.

ELSIE MCLEOD JURY

JR (Thwaites), *passim*. Desrosiers, *Iroquoisie*, 244.

TRACY, ALEXANDRE DE PROUVILLE DE. *See* PROUVILLE

TREWORGIE (Treworgy, Trewerghey), JOHN, merchant, colonizer, governor of Newfoundland; b. *c.* 1618; fl. 1660.

He was the son of James Treworgie and his wife, Catherine, who was the daughter of Alexander Shapleigh, a Dartmouth merchant. Shapleigh had interests in Maine, New England, and John Treworgie went there as his agent about 1635. He stayed until about 1650, living at Sturgeon Creek, Kittery, and returning to England briefly in 1640. In January 1646 he married a Miss Spencer of Newberry, Mass., and a son, John, was born in 1649.

Treworgie had experience of the New England fishery and perhaps also of Newfoundland; the Shapleigh family had engaged in the Newfoundland fishery throughout the century, as the Dartmouth port books reveal. This would explain Treworgie's nomination as one of six commissioners for Newfoundland in 1651. The commissioners were instructed to arrest the governor, Sir DAVID KIRKE, and his goods, to inquire into his alleged misdemeanours, regulate the fishery, and collect the imposition payable on fish and oil taken by foreigners. For the first time Newfoundland came directly under government control and remained so throughout the Interregnum as part of the tendency towards increasing imperial centralization. In 1651 the investigation into Kirke's conduct began. In the following year Walter Sikes, Robert Street, William Pyle, and Nicholas Redwood were sent as commissioners to the island, their instructions being very similar to those issued in 1651.

Meanwhile Treworgie must have remained in Newfoundland, for in May 1653, when the Committee for Irish and Scottish Affairs debated whether to send a new commission to the island, it was decided to entrust affairs to Treworgie who was then living there. In June instructions were forwarded, giving him authority over both planters and fishermen and ordering him to collect impositions on aliens, to defend the island and devise means for its fortifications, to receive all complaints against Kirke, and to report to the council at the end of the fishing season. Treworgie was prevented from carrying out these duties when he, together with Sikes and Pyle, was arrested by James Kirke because of their seizure of Sir David Kirke's estates. In vain they showed their commissions and protested that they had already returned Kirke's property to his wife. They were found guilty but, in 1654, petitioned Cromwell for a new trial.

The outcome of the suit is not known although it may be presumed that they were pardoned. Treworgie appears to have continued as governor of the island until 1659 or 1660. In April 1660 he petitioned the Council of State for a new commission as governor and requested two or three frigates to help him collect impositions and surprise any Spanish fishermen. The reasons which he gave for his return to England were want of supplies and the fact that he was owed six years' salary. Treworgie's petition was referred to the secretary for foreign plantations but, with the

Restoration, the controversy between Lord Baltimore [*see* CALVERT] and the Kirkes over the proprietary right to the island was reopened and, for a time, direct governmental control lapsed.

Treworgie never received his commission and disappears from Newfoundland history. It is possible that he was the John Trewethy described in December 1663 as "his Majesties Servant . . . Assignee of Ralph, late Lord Hopton," involved in a petition to the council concerning land in Virginia.

Treworgie seems to have been a just and able administrator who accomplished with some success the difficult task of governing the unruly planters and fishermen. With the return to proprietary rule conflict between the two groups sprang up with a new violence and rancour which came close to ruining both industry and settlement.

GILLIAN T. CELL

The official papers concerning Treworgie's career in Newfoundland are in PRO, C.O. 1/12, nos. 20, 21, 1/33, no.73; 25/29, pp.11–18, 22–24; 25/65, pp.243–44, 25/69, pp.160, 197, 204–10, 25/75, p.2/8, 25/121, p.51 (summarized in PRO, *CSP, Col., 1574–1660, 1675–76*). See also: BM, Egerton MS 2395, f.262. PRO, *Acts of P.C., col. ser., 1613–80*. Lounsbury, *British fishery at Nfld.* Prowse, *History of Nfld.*

For his connection with Maine see: PRO, H.C.A. 13/64, deposition of John Trewerghey, 19 March 1650/1. Maine Hist. Soc., *Documentary history of Maine*, III, IV, VI; *Province and court records of Maine*, I. J. Savage, *A genealogical dictionary of the first settlers of New England* (4v., Boston, 1860–2), IV.

TROYES, PIERRE DE, *dit* **Chevalier de Troyes,** officer, son of Michel de Troyes, an attorney in the Parlement of Paris, and of Madeleine Alard; d. 1688.

While a captain in the Piémont regiment, he married Marie Petit de L'Estang on 5 Feb. 1681.

He arrived at Quebec 1 Aug. 1685 together with Governor Brisay* de Denonville and reinforcements consisting of about 350 soldiers belonging to the colonial regular troops. He was in command of a company; he had been brevetted a captain on 5 Mar. 1685. On 12 Feb. 1686 Denonville entrusted him with a difficult and perilous mission which was financed in large measure by the Compagnie du Nord: to go and oust the English from Hudson Bay and capture the interlopers (unauthorized traders), especially those in the employ of Radisson* and his group. He had under his orders a detachment of 30 soldiers and 70 militiamen. Among his officers there were three LE MOYNES: JACQUES, Sieur de Sainte-Hélène, the first lieutenant; Pierre*, Sieur d'Iberville, the second lieutenant; Paul*, Sieur de Maricourt,

Troyes

the adjutant; he had also the Jesuit Silvy*, as chaplain, and Pierre ALLEMAND, an experienced pilot (the latter two were making this trip for the third time). The troop, divided into three sections, left Montreal on 20 March, went up the Ottawa (Outaouais) River, and utilizing the lakes and rivers, reached Hudson Bay on 20 June. They seized Fort Monsipi (Moose Factory or Saint-Louis), Fort Rupert (Charles Fort), and Fort Quichicouanne (Fort Albany). The Chevalier de Troyes was back in Quebec at the beginning of October 1686, leaving Pierre Le Moyne d'Iberville in command of the captured forts.

During the winter Governor Denonville was preparing his too famous attack against the Senecas. The Chevalier de Troyes was in command of one of the four companies of the expedition, which set out on 17 June 1687. By force and ruse Denonville succeeded in capturing about 200 Iroquois. He released most of them, but kept some of them, whom he sent to serve in the king's galleys. He next went to devastate the Seneca villages on the south shore of Lake Ontario, then proceeded to Niagara to rebuild the fort that CAVELIER de La Salle had previously constructed. On 31 July, when the work was finished, he left a garrison of 100 men there under the orders of the Chevalier de Troyes. The winter of 1687 was particularly distressing for the garrison, which was subjected to the avenging forays of the Iroquois. In addition scurvy wrought havoc among the troops, who attempted to revolt. There remained only a handful of men capable of resistance. The Chevalier de Troyes was himself struck down by this malady, and he succumbed to it on 8 May 1688.

In the three years he spent in Canada the Chevalier de Troyes had been in command of an important expedition and had taken part in another. He had acquired the confidence of the governor, who had entrusted to him the defence of a strategic post. Denonville considered that he was "the most intelligent and the most capable of our commanders," and that he possessed excellent qualities as a leader, that he was "wise and sensible and full of good will." Death put an end too soon to a career that gave promise of being a brilliant one.

LÉOPOLD LAMONTAGNE

AN, Col., C^{11A}, 8, 9. Charlevoix, *Histoire*, I. Jean-Baptiste de La Croix de Chevrières de Saint-Vallier, *Estat présent de l'Église et de la colonie française dans la Nouvelle-France . . .*, réimprimé . . . d'après l'édition de Robert Pepie, Paris, 1688 (Québec, 1857), 43–45. La Pot(h)erie, *Histoire*, I, 147f. *NYCD* (O'Callaghan and Fernow), III, 396; IX, 307, 335, 339f., 351, 359, 396. Chevalier de Troyes, *Journal* (Caron).

L. J. Boucher, "Une Abitibi traîtresse au XVIIe siècle," *RHAF*, XIII (1959–60), 93–96. Crouse, *Lemoyne d'Iberville*. Frégault, *Iberville*, 89–106, *et passim*. HBRS, XXI (Rich). Robert Le Blant, *Histoire de la Nouvelle-France: les sources narratives du début du XVIIIe siècle et le Recueil de Gédéon de Catalogne* (1v. paru, Dax, s.d.), I, 176, n. 37, 196. P.-G. Roy, "Le chevalier de Troye," *BRH*, X (1904), 284–87; "Les commandants du Fort Niagara: Pierre, chevalier de Troye," *ibid.*, LIV (1948), 131–33.

TURGIS, CHARLES and **CLAUDE**. *See* SAINT-ÉTIENNE DE LA TOUR

TYNG (Ting, Tynge), EDWARD, a member of the Council of Maine from 1678, commandant of Fort Loyal, Maine, 1681–82 and 1686–87, appointed governor of Port-Royal (Annapolis Royal, N.S.), 1691; b. 1649? in New England, son of Edward Tyng, who emigrated from England to Massachusetts in 1636; d. 1691 or later.

Near Fort Loyal in Falmouth (Portland), on 23 July 1680, Capt. Edward Tyng was granted a lot of land. He was commander of Fort Loyal 1681–82, at a salary of £60 per annum for himself and servant. In 1684 he was appointed by the General Assembly of the province to a committee to take care of repairing Fort Loyal and settling a chief officer there. He was commissioned as a member of Joseph Dudley's Council of New England on 13 Oct. 1685 and he took the oath of office when that council convened for the first time at Boston on 25 May 1686. A year later Capt. Tyng was again appointed to command Fort Loyal. On 10 Jan. 1687 he was appointed to the council of Sir Edmund Andros*, governor of New England and New York, with whom he was a favourite. Capt. Tyng conducted negotiations with the Indians of Maine in 1688 and commanded a company of soldiers in the garrison at Pemaquid. He was appointed lieutenant-colonel in Sagadahoc the same year.

After the fall of Port-Royal in 1690, when Massachusetts claimed Acadia or Nova Scotia, Tyng was selected as its governor. He visited Port-Royal in 1691, in a vessel owned and commanded by John Nelson*, a Boston merchant and the chief heir of Sir Thomas TEMPLE. But finding that the inhabitants would give him no guarantee against Indian attacks, he declined to remain. On the way back to Boston, Nelson's vessel called at Saint John, where it was captured by a French frigate, *Soleil d'Afrique*, commanded by Simon-Pierre Denys* de Bonaventure. JOSEPH ROBINAU de Villebon, the new French governor of Acadia, was on board this ship. Tyng, Nelson, and young William Alden were held as hostages, while John Alden* took the ketch on parole to Boston with a letter to the governor requesting an exchange of prisoners. Satisfactory arrangements not being made, Tyng was subsequently sent to Quebec, to be transferred later to France, where he died in captivity at La Rochelle.

Tyng's wife was Elizabeth, daughter of Ensign Thaddeus and Elizabeth (Mitton) Clarke. He had two sons and two daughters. In consequence of his father's hardships and expenses, Tyng's son Edward, a distinguished Massachusetts naval officer, was granted a tract of land by the Province of Massachusetts-Bay in 1736.

C. BRUCE FERGUSSON

Among the material on the capture of Port-Royal and of Tyng is: AN (Archives d'Outre-Mer), Dépôts des fortifications des colonies, article no. 56; Marine, B², 89, 90, 91, 92, 97, 107, 109; B³, 75, 76, 77. BM, Lansdowne MS 849, 41–43, 44–46. *Journals of the Rev. Thomas Smith and the Rev. Samuel Deane . . .* , ed. William Willis (Portland, 1849). Maine Hist. Soc., *Documentary history of Maine*, V. *NYCD* (O'Callaghan and Fernow), V, 527; IX. PRO, *CSP, Col., 1689–92*. *Records of the Massachusetts Bay* (Shurtleff). Suffolk deeds, I, 16, 26, 57.

J. B. Brebner, *New England's outpost: Acadia before the conquest of Canada* (New York, 1927). Maine Hist. Soc. *Coll.*, 1st ser., I (1831 and 1865); VI (1859); VIII (1881). Mass. Hist. Soc. *Proc.* 2d ser., XIII (1900), *passim*. W. D. Williamson, *The history of the state of Maine* (2v., Hallowell, 1832).

V

VALERIAN(AT)OS. *See* FUCA [Appendix]

VARENNES, RENÉ GAULTIER DE. *See* GAULTIER

VAUGHAN, SIR WILLIAM, scholar, writer, poet, colonial promoter; b. 1575, second son of Walter Vaughan of Golden Grove, Carmarthenshire, and his wife Katherine; d. August 1641 at Llangyndeyrn, Carmarthen, where he was buried.

Vaughan matriculated at Jesus College, Oxford, in 1592; in 1595 he received the degree of B.A. and two years later that of M.A. He supplicated for B.C.L. in December 1600 but went abroad before taking his degree. He travelled widely in Europe, receiving the degree of doctor of law in Vienna. He had returned to England by the summer of 1603 and in July 1605 was incorporated D.C.L. at Oxford.

At this time Vaughan settled at Llangyndeyrn,

became a justice of the peace, and married Elizabeth, the daughter of David ap Robert of Llangyndeyrn, by whom he had a son Francis. The child seems to have died young and his wife also died in 1608. Vaughan probably devoted most of his time to writing; his first book had been published in 1597 and in 1600 his most famous work, *The golden grove*, appeared. The purpose of the book was to assist "all such as would know how to gouerne themselues, their houses and their country"; it dealt with the three phases of man's life according to the Aristotelian concept—the moral, the economic, and the political.

In *The golden grove*, Vaughan revealed his preoccupation with the economic plight of Wales and it seems to have been the idea of helping his fellow countrymen that first interested him in overseas colonization. A colony, Vaughan thought, would relieve the overpopulation, poverty, and apathy surrounding him. In Wales he saw men starve while land went uncultivated and maritime enterprise was ignored, although across the Severn, trade—and especially the Newfoundland fishery —brought prosperity to Devon. To Vaughan, as to many contemporaries, colonization was a remedy for the ills afflicting their society.

As a site Vaughan thought first of Soldana or St. Helena but these he rejected as too distant, having a bad climate, and being liable to Spanish attack. He turned next to America; neither Bermuda nor Virginia attracted him and finally he chose Newfoundland as being easy of access and providing a staple, saleable commodity, fish. "I saw," he wrote later in *The golden fleece*, "that God had reserved the *Newfoundland* for us Britaines."

In 1616 Vaughan purchased land from the Newfoundland company which had been established in 1610. It was the first of a number of alienations made by the company, probably for financial reasons. Vaughan received part of the Avalon peninsula lying south of a line from Caplin Bay to Placentia Bay, according to John MASON's map (1625), and including the much frequented harbours of Ferryland, Fermeuse, and Renewse. The name which he bestowed upon his land reflected his impractical idealism; he called it Cambriol for it was to be a second Wales founded in the New World. His over-optimistic enthusiasm is revealed in *The golden fleece*: "This is our *Colchos*, where the *Golden Fleece* flourisheth on the backes of *Neptunes sheepe*, continually to be shorne. This is *Great Britaines* Indies, never to be exhausted dry."

That Vaughan was not the man to transform these dreams into reality became apparent in the first year of settlement. In 1617 he despatched his first colonists to Renewse. We do not know how many he sent or what sort of people they were, but as pioneers in a hard land they proved totally inadequate. Furthermore, they appear to have had no experienced leader for it was not until 1618 that Richard WHITBOURNE took up his appointment as governor. On arrival he found that they had not even built themselves a habitation but had lived out the winter with only the fishermen's shacks for shelter.

Although Whitbourne succeeded in reorganizing the settlement, by 1619 the venture had collapsed and the colonists left. The following year Vaughan, "finding the Burthern too heavy for my weake Shoulders," assigned a part of his grant to Henry Cary, later Lord Falkland. Subsequently, at the instigation of his brother, the Earl of Carbery, Vaughan made over some of his land to Sir George CALVERT (later Lord Baltimore). There remained to Vaughan the land south of a line from Renewse to Placentia Bay. About 1621 or 1622 Vaughan re-established his colony at Trepassey Bay; in 1624 it was said to be prospering but of its later fortunes we know little.

Vaughan certainly retained his interest in Newfoundland. In 1625 he published John Mason's map of the island in his book *Cambrensium Caroleia*, written to celebrate the accession of Charles I, and in the following year *The golden fleece* appeared. *The golden fleece* is an extraordinary work, in vivid contrast to the more prosaic and practical propagandist tracts on Newfoundland which Whitbourne and Mason had written. Its purpose was simple enough: Vaughan was anxious to promote the island as a place for settlement. Success, he believed, would relieve overpopulation at home, treble England's present income from the fishery which he estimated to be £20,000, and generally increase trade.

In none of this does *The golden fleece* vary much from other promotion literature; it is rather Vaughan's method of presentation which is unique. He imagines Apollo holding court as arbiter in all matters—religious, political, economic, and moral. The first part of the book is largely an attack on Roman Catholicism; the second deals with the ills afflicting the state and their remedies, the third with ways to obtain wealth so as to restore the state. It is this third part which is most concerned with Newfoundland. Vaughan calls on those most intimately connected with the colonization of the island, among them JOHN GUY and John Mason, to give evidence on Newfoundland's resources and potentialities; to prove, in fact, that the golden fleece is to be found there. Much of what Vaughan has to say here is sound and practical, if not very original; however, such passages are so well concealed amongst pages of fantasy, classical, biblical, and historical allusions, and tirades against Catholicism that, as a propaganda document, the whole makes very little impact.

One passage in *The golden fleece* suggests that Vaughan has been forced to suspend his colonizing activities through lack of funds (sig. Blv). Two years later, in 1628, the erstwhile governor of the Bristol plantation, Robert HAYMAN, encouraged Vaughan to take up the enterprise again; he also says that Vaughan had intended to visit the plantation himself but had been prevented by ill health. It has been said that Vaughan went to Newfoundland himself before this, the usual date given being 1622, that he wrote *The golden fleece* there, and returned to England in 1625 or 1626 (Prowse, *History of Nfld.*, 111; *DNB*). The source of this statement is most probably the title page of *The golden fleece* for the work is described as being "Transported from Cambrioll Colchos, out of the Southermost Part of the Iland, commonly called the Newfoundland." As the book is written in such a high, fantastic style and under the pseudonym of Orpheus Junior, it seems most likely that this is merely a poetic formula not to be taken literally. Vaughan describes his Newfoundland activities and gives a good deal of autobiographical material in both *The golden fleece* and *The Newlanders cure* (1630); if he had been to the island, he would surely have mentioned it. Moreover he was involved in a suit before the Exchequer court in 1624 (PRO, E146/113/21 Jac. I). These two facts, together with Hayman's statement, suggest that Vaughan did not go to Newfoundland, at least before 1628.

In that year Vaughan was in Ireland where he was knighted. There is a slight possibility that he did visit Newfoundland after this date for, about this time, he had interested a new group of adventurers in the scheme. Chief among them was his brother-in-law, Sir Henry Salusbury of Llewenni. Salusbury had apparently received from Lord Falkland a narrow belt of land, stretching north from Fermeuse to the boundary of Lord Baltimore's estates. Salusbury was given advice on plantation by such experts as John Guy, first governor of the Cuper's (now Cupids) Cove colony, and NICHOLAS GUY, a settler of long experience. He had taken no action by 1630 when Vaughan published *The Newlanders cure*. This was a medical work designed to help emigrants and it contained remedies for such maladies as scurvy and seasickness; it was perhaps occasioned by the sufferings of Baltimore's colonists in 1628. It has been said that Vaughan spent the years 1628 to 1630 in Newfoundland (*DNB*; Thomas, "Iscenum...," 121), but the impression which he gives in *The Newlanders cure* is that he is still hoping to go.

It is most probable, however, that the rest of Vaughan's life was spent in Wales. He had married as his second wife Anne, the daughter of John Christmas of Colchester, by whom he had six children. In the last years of his life he published two works of a religious nature and he died in August 1641, his will being proved at Carmarthen on 27 August.

As a colonial promoter Vaughan failed to realize his ambitions. His settlements, first at Renewse then at Trepassey, had a precarious existence partly through lack of money, partly because, with the exception of Richard Whitbourne, they do not seem to have had a competent and experienced governor. Such a man was essential, for Vaughan himself was not practical nor does he seem to have possessed powers of organization and leadership. His books reveal that many of his plans were sound. He saw that the fishery should not be the sole support of a colony; he intended that industry, agriculture, and fishing should be so co-ordinated as to provide income and employment throughout the year. But he lacked the ability to put his schemes into operation.

In defence of Vaughan it may be said that he displayed great qualities of perseverance and that few of his contemporaries met with much success in their attempts to settle in Newfoundland. Vaughan also provided us with some of the earliest English literature on North America.

GILLIAN T. CELL

Vaughan's published works are: Ἐρωτοπαίγνιον pium (London, 1597); Ἐρωτοπαίγνιον pium: Pars secunda (London, 1598); *Poematum libellus* (London, 1598); *Speculum humane condicionis* (London, 1598); *The golden grove* (London, 1600; 2d ed. 1608); *Natural and artificiall directions for health* (London, 1600; 2d ed., 1602; 3d ed., 1607); *Approved directions for health* (4th ed., 1612); *Directions for health* (5th ed., 1617; 6th ed., 1626; 7th ed., 1633); *The spirit of detraction conjured and convicted in seven circles* (London, 1611; another issue, with the title *The arraignment of slander*, 1630); *Cambrensium Caroleia* (London, 1625; another issue, 1630); *The golden fleece* [Orpheus Junior, pseud.] (London, 1626); *The Newlanders cure* (London, 1630); *The church militant* (London, 1640); *The soules exercise* (London, 1641).

National Library of Wales, MSS 1595 E, 5390 D. Nottingham University, Middleton MSS, Mi X 1/51. PRO, E. 146/113, 21 James I. R. Eburne, *A plaine path-way to plantations* (London, 1624). R. Hayman, *Quodlibets, lately come over from New Britaniola* (London, 1628).

Carmarthenshire Antiq. Soc. *Trans.*, X (1914–15),

70. *DNB*. *Dictionary of Welsh Biography down to 1940*, ed. J. E. Lloyd and R. T. Jenkins (London, 1959). J. J. Jones, "The golden fleece," *Nat. Library Wales J.*, III (1943–44), 58–60. Northwestern University Graduate School, *Summaries of doctoral dissertations*, XVII (1949), 30–34, summary of W. F. Marquardt's "A critical edition of Sir William Vaughan's *The golden grove*." Prowse, *History of Nfld*. *Register of the University of Oxford* (1571–1622), ed. C. W. Boase and A. Clark (2v. [II in 4 pts.], Oxford Hist. Soc., 1884–89), II, pts. 1–3. W. A. Shaw, *The knights of England* (2v., London, 1906). D. Ll. Thomas, "Iscennen and Golden Grove," Honourable Soc. of Cymmrodorion *Trans.*, 1940, 115–29. E. R. Williams, "Cambriol, the story of a forgotten colony," *Welsh Outlook*, VIII (1921), 230–33.

VERDUN, SIEUR DE. *See* Dupuy

VERNER, HUGH, HBC employee; fl. 1678–97.

Verner, who was probably a Scotsman, or had Scottish connections, first went to James Bay in 1678 and apparently showed much ability, for on the renewal of his contract in 1681, he was made chief factor at the post originally known as Charles Fort on Rupert River. In response to the entreaties of his wife, Elinor, Verner returned home in 1682, but in March 1683 he applied for his former position and, on account of his ability, experience, and loyalty, was re-engaged. As a passenger to Charlton Island, en route to Rupert River, in the chartered ship *Diligence* (Capt. Nehemiah Walker) Verner would have been a spectator at the capture of the interloping ship *Expectation*.

In September 1685 Verner received a warning of intended French aggressions against the Company's posts from Zacharie Jolliet, his competitor and near-neighbour at Nemiskau Lake. Zacharie, like his brother Louis Jolliet, had enjoyed hospitality at Charles Fort in Governor Bayly's time and that had been when he had first met Verner, whom he now advised to retreat from Rupert River. The French threat, made at a time when the English and French kings were at peace, was apparently not taken seriously by Governor Sergeant at Albany but Verner, according to his own account, started to get his post into a state of defence in the spring of 1686. Nevertheless, during the early hours of 23 June (3 July n.s.) he was completely surprised by a force of French soldiers and Canadians under the command of the Chevalier de Troyes, and after a very brief resistance, during which his ship-wrecked guest, Mrs Maurice (late companion to Mrs Henry Sergeant) was wounded, he was forced to surrender. Verner was released later in the year and allowed to sail to York Fort (called by the French Fort Bourbon) in the *Colleton*. He returned to England in the summer of 1687.

Verner was re-engaged as a trader at the "Bottom of the Bay" in 1688 and thus became a member of the expedition under Governor John Marsh which went to Albany River (Quichicouani) with instructions to re-establish the Company's trade and, owing to the treaty of neutrality of November 1686 between the English and French kings, to live at peace with the neighbouring French. The expedition was a failure. By 11 March 1688/89 (o.s.) (HBC Arch., A.15/3, f.184) Marsh was dead and William Bond, Andrew Hamilton, and the rest of the English party had all been captured. Verner was one of those sent overland to Canada later in the year. He reached England via France early in January 1691. Later that year Verner went to York Fort where he was employed as an assistant to Governor Geyer until he was recalled home in 1693. He again offered his services to the HBC in 1697 but as there was no opening suitable for him no further references to him are to be found in the Company's archives.

ALICE M. JOHNSON

HBRS, VIII, IX (Rich); XI (Rich and Johnson). Chevalier de Troyes, *Journal* (Caron).

VERRAZZANO ("Janus Verrazanus," the one extant signature on a deed dated 11 May 1526, now in the archives at Rouen, is generally conceded to be a Latinized form of the original Italian spelling), **GIOVANNI DA,** explorer, navigator, merchant adventurer, the first European, according to authentic record, to sail the coast of America from Florida to Newfoundland; b. *c.* 1485 in or near Florence (possibly at Greve) of Piero Andrea da Verrazzano and Fiametta Capelli, both of Florence; d. *c.* 1528 in the West Indies at the hands of cannibals.

Verrazzano's distinguished lineage has been traced to the early Middle Ages and the last member of the family died in Florence in 1819. Verrazzano had a younger brother, Gerolamo, to whom he must have been close; another, named Bernardo, was a prominent banker in Rome; and two others found in a genealogical register are given as Nicolo and Piero. It is not known if Giovanni ever married. The position of his family as well-to-do merchants and bankers, and his mastery of the elements of navigation and the literary culture revealed in his famous Letter, are sufficient evidence of a superior education.

Florence was well able to provide it; she was the golden city, a centre of geographical and navigational science. Her prosperous merchants travelled everywhere in prosecution of trade. The

Verrazzano

twin pursuits of navigation and commerce quickly occupied Verrazzano's attention for, imbued with the Renaissance spirit, he developed as a man of enlightened thought and imaginative action. As a young man he lived in Cairo for several years as a commercial agent and doubtless he learned his seamanship in the eastern Mediterranean for he was familiar with these waters, where Columbus also had gained experience. One source, Bacchiani, pictures the young Verrazzano as giving ear to a patriot group "nearly all friends of France, because enemies of the Medici and believers in citizen's rights." It is not unreasonable to assume that he left Florence, as did so many Florentines in this period, to escape the repressive atmosphere.

There have been suggestions that Verrazzano sailed to America in his early twenties with Thomas AUBERT's famous voyage to Newfoundland in 1508. It is a possibility sufficiently in character, but the evidence is inconclusive. Murphy, Buckingham Smith, and others have identified the navigator with a corsair, named Jean Florin or Florentin (the Florentine), who operated against Spanish and Portuguese treasure-ships during these years but Prospero Peragallo has effectively shown this to be a confusion of personalities. Verrazzano was not idle however; indeed one contemporary, writing after the navigator's return from his 1524 voyage, refers to his travels in Egypt and Syria and "almost through all the known world, and thence by reason of his merit is esteemed another Amerigo Vespucci; another Ferdinand Magellan and even more" (Carli letter). Apart from these speculations, there are no known records to enlighten us further on Verrazzano's early life.

When Verrazzano entered the maritime service of France is uncertain; the earliest documentary evidence placing him in that country is a report of 1522 from Portuguese merchants in France to their king, where it is said that Verrazzano is quietly soliciting the support of François I for a voyage. It was the eager desire of the age for a sea route westwards to the riches of China and the East Indies, and particularly the French king's ambition to have a share in the Iberian glories and profits of the New World, that presented Verrazzano with his opportunity. Though a continent south of the latitude of Florida seemed to bar the way to the east, the region northwards to Cape Breton, so far as surviving narrative indicates, was unexplored; here there was still hope for both a passage and new lands. The account of Verrazzano's voyage to this area is told in versions of a letter or relation he wrote to François I, who commissioned the voyage—the first to America under official French auspices.

The Letter is dated on board his ship, 8 July 1524, immediately upon his return to Dieppe. Although the autographic original has disappeared (it may yet be found), four Italian versions are extant. One is printed in Ramusio, and another is a transcribed codex found in the Strozzi Library, Florence, together with the Carli letter; there is also a manuscript fragment of this text in the Academy at Cimento. It was on the basis of these texts that Smith and Murphy raised the controversy of the latter half of the 19th century, when it was plausibly argued that Verrazzano never reached America and that the Letter was not his work at all. Brevoort, Dexter (in Justin Winsor), and other learned authorities came forward in a strong defence of both the missive and the voyage, restoring confidence in the navigator. After the discovery of the next and most important version, in the Library of Count Giulio de Cèllere, Rome, in 1909 (now in the Pierpont Morgan Library), all suspicions were finally dispelled; this codex bears what are regarded as Verrazzano's own marginal comments. The last version, a manuscript in the Vatican Library, was reported only in 1925. Still further supporting documents have been discovered in this century, more in fact than during the preceding 350 years.

The Letter says at the outset that the writer was sent by the king "to discover new lands," and later that "my intention was... to reach Cathay"; but there is much evidence indicating that Verrazzano had a keen mercantile as well as exploring interest in his voyages. Two manuscripts dated in March 1523, found in the Rouen archives, record inferentially, in connection with a voyage being planned, an agreement concerning the division of investment and profit among members of a Lyons syndicate which includes Verrazzano; the members are revealingly described as "tous marchans florentins."

From the Letter we find that its author set out from Dieppe late in 1523 with four ships, but that a storm forced him to find a haven in Brittany with only the *Normanda* and the *Dauphine*. After repairs, he skirted the Spanish coast harassing commerce and then, apparently under new orders, resumed his voyage with the *Dauphine* alone. He set sail from a deserted islet at the westernmost point of the Madeiras (probably Porto Santo) on 17 Jan. 1524 (N.S.), with a Norman crew of 50, his tiny caravel armed and victualled for an eight-month voyage. Sailing west on a course about 150 miles north of that of Columbus, he weathered a violent tempest on 24 February, continued west but bearing "somewhat to the north," and in 25 more days found "a new land never before seen by anyone." The position of this landfall, given

Verrazzano

as in 34°, has been variously placed from Florida (for he reported palm trees) to North Carolina, but was probably close to Cape Fear, North Carolina. After a short exploration southward in vain search for a harbour, he turned about, fearing to meet Spaniards, and coasted north as far as Nova Scotia and "near the land which the Britanni (Britons) found," Cape Breton—without, apparently, observing the Bay of Fundy. He went ashore at several places along the coast, abducted an Indian boy to take back to France, visited New York harbour, and spent 15 days in Narragansett Bay. His Letter records the earliest geographical and topographical description of a continuous North Atlantic coast of America derived from a known exploration, and his observation on the Indians is the first ethnological account of America north of Mexico.

Reaching Newfoundland ("Bacalaia" in the Cèllere version gloss) and finding his provisions failing, he set course for France, making Dieppe early in July 1524 "having discovered six hundred leagues and more of new land." His six-month voyage is one of the most important in North American exploration. Though it failed to reveal a passage to China, it enabled Verrazzano to be the first to report that the "New World which above I have described is connected together, not adjoining Asia or Africa (which I know to be a certainty)." Here is reasoning based on experience, freed from the ancient teaching of the schools that the Atlantic bathed both European and Asian shores. Verrazzano had, in fact, joined Canada to the rest of America—to the New World. The Letter concludes with a cosmographical description of the voyage, including detailed nautical and astronomical data which demonstrate Verrazzano's mastery of the scientific methods of the day.

The voyage was represented cartographically in coastlines from Florida to Cape Breton: Hakluyt ("Discourse on western planting") mentions a "mightie large olde mappe" (the basis of the 1582 Lok map) and an "Olde excellent globe," both seemingly made by Verrazzano (now lost); the world map of Vesconte de Maggiolo, 1527 (destroyed during the bombing of Milan in World War II), and, more clearly, Gerolamo da Verrazzano's world map of 1529 (now in the Vatican); and there are many others which derive this coastline from Verrazzano (Ganong describes them fully). The Robertus de Bailly globe of 1530, and the copper globe of Euphrosynus Ulpius, dated 1542, are notably Verrazzanian in their North American contours. The latter bears the inscription across North America "Verrazana sive Nova Gallia a Verrazano Florentino comperta anno sal. M.D." ("Verrazana, or New Gaul [i.e., New France], discovered by Verrazano the Florentine, in the year of Salvation M.D.," date incomplete). Bailly has "Verrazana" written across the North American seaboard. Both globes depict the Sea of Verrazzano, a curiosity beginning with Verrazzano's own gloss in the Cèllere version of his Letter, where he mentions an isthmus "a mile in width and about 200 long, in which, from the ship, was seen the Mare Orientale between the west and the north. Which is the one, without doubt, which goes about the extremity of India, China and Cathay." (Hall's translation in Stokes.) This isthmus, described by Hakluyt from the old map and globe as "a little necke of lande in 40. degrees of latitude," with the sea on both sides, is the line of islands and sandbars off the coast of North Carolina and the Mare Orientale (Western Sea) extending to Asia is no more than the broad Pamlico and Albemarle sounds. Yet this misconception of a willing mind persisted even into the 17th century. (The cartographical history of the Sea of Verrazzano is traced in Winsor.)

Verrazzano's voyage also left its impression in the nomenclature of subsequent maps, though regrettably almost every one of his place-names has now disappeared. Maggiolo's 1527 map is the first to use the appellation "Francesca" (François I) for North America and the chart of the navigator's brother, Gerolamo, is the earliest to show the names New France ("Nova Gallia") and Norumbega (if this is his "Oranbega"), a name later applied variously within the area between New York and Cape Breton. Both maps therefore record a French influence in North American exploration, due to Verrazzano, several years before CARTIER's first voyage. "Arcadia," the name Giovanni gave to Maryland or Virginia "on account of the beauty of the trees," made its first cartographical appearance in the 1548 Gastaldo map and is the only name to survive in Canadian usage. It has a curious history. In the 17th century CHAMPLAIN fixed its present orthography, with the "r" omitted, and Ganong has shown its gradual progress northwards, in a succession of maps, to its resting place in the Atlantic provinces.

Verrazzano's Letter was dispatched from Dieppe to a banker in Rome, but en route at Lyons its contents were evidently available to the merchants with whom the navigator had contracted for the voyage, since a copy of it accompanied a letter from the Florentine merchant Bernardo Carli, resident in Lyons, to his father in Florence, dated 4 Aug. 1524. The Carli letter contains some interesting, though indirect, hints on Verrazzano's

Verrazzano

earlier career and offers the hope of his associates that the king will entrust the navigator "again, with half a dozen good vessels and that he will return to the voyage," that "he may discover some profitable traffic." Verrazzano shared this hope and late in 1524 he had another French expedition in readiness for the Indies. The military defeats of France that year, however, left her in no mood for transatlantic enterprises; Verrazzano's ships and crews were commandeered. The evidence for this proposed voyage includes a record that the king, François I, later compensated its promoters for the loss of their investment. Even so, Hakluyt ("Epistle Dedicatorie" to *Divers voyages*), in speaking of America, says that Verrazzano "had been thrise on that coast"—though this may have reference to the Aubert voyage of 1508. In the same place Hakluyt refers to a map of Verrazzano "which he gave to King Henrie the eight," perhaps implying a visit to England, and it has even been argued that Verrazzano sailed in King Henry's service after his first voyage. This possibility is not countenanced by Bacchiani, but his arguments are unconvincing. It appears probable, nevertheless, that the navigator made only two voyages to America.

The final voyage, also under royal auspices, was planned in 1526; it is attested in a contract of that year by Chabot, the admiral of France, with Verrazzano and other speculators to furnish three vessels (two of them the king's) to make a trading voyage to the Indies for spices. Our navigator, as chief pilot, was to receive one-sixth of the fruits of the venture after certain expenses had been deducted. Other documents corroborate the voyage; one, a deed dated 11 May 1526, signed "Janus Verrazanus" in the Latin form (an aspect of his Renaissance classicism), is his only known autograph. Preserved in the archives at Rouen, a facsimile appears in Winsor. The deed appoints his brother Gerolamo his heir and attorney during the proposed mission. Another object of the voyage, besides trade, was to search for the elusive passage to Asia south of the region explored in the first journey. All was apparently ready in 1526, yet the start was unaccountably delayed for nearly two years. The arguments for a 1526 expedition, mainly liturgical (the naming of geographical features for the feast days on which they were discovered) are not demonstrable. The cause of the delay is still a matter of conjecture.

With Darien as its likely first destination, the fleet at last set its course in the spring of 1528 for Florida, the Bahamas, and the Lesser Antilles. On an island in the latter group, probably near Guadeloupe, Verrazzano landed with a party and was taken by Caribs, killed, and eaten within sight of his crew. The event is recorded in Ramusio, in Paolo Giovio's *Elogia* (Florence, 1548; Basel, 1575, copy in Library of Congress), and in a manuscript poem (in the Museo Civico, Como) by Paolo's nephew Giulio Giovio. Many have inferred that Gerolamo was an eye-witness to his brother's shocking death.

Among a group of edicts passed by the Parlement of Normandy in 1532, concerning the financing, fitting out, and lading with trade goods of Verrazzano's fleet is one which reveals an interesting sequel to his last voyage. It records the unlading from *La Flamengue*, the navigator's vessel, at Fécamp in March 1530, of a cargo of brazil-wood. From the context we know, therefore, that Verrazzano's own ship returned in 1530, and that it definitely visited the Caribbean area—perhaps while Verrazzano was still alive.

WILLIAM F. E. MORLEY

The primary sources for the voyages are the Letter in its four versions: Cèllere codex (probably 1524), first printed by A. Bacchiani, with commentary, in Soc. geogr. ital. *Bollett.*, XLVI (1909), 1274–1323, facsimile in Stokes [*infra*], II, plates 60–81, and tr. by E. H. Hall, in Stokes, IV, 15–19. G. B. Ramusio, *Terzo volume delle navigationi et viaggi nel quale si contengono Le Navigationi al Mondo Nuovo* . . . (1st ed., Venetia, 1556), III, 420–22; tr. in Hakluyt, *Divers voyages* (1850), 55–71. Strozzi, or Florentine, codex (late 16th cent.), tr. by J. G. Cogswell in N.Y. Hist. Soc. *Coll.*, 2nd ser., I (1841), 37–67. Vatican codex (presumably 16th c.), unpublished, but photostatic copy in Pierpont Morgan Library, New York. The Carli letter and Chabot agreement are appended to Murphy [*infra*], with his tr. Reproductions of the Maggiolo, G. da Verrazzano, and Gastaldo maps are in Stevenson [*infra*]. PAC has a Gastaldo 1548 Ptolemy. Pierpont Morgan Library has the Bailly globe, and the N.Y. Hist. Soc. the Ulpius globe.

Some secondary sources are: Bacchiani, commentary [*supra*]; and "I fratelli da Verrazzano," Soc. geogr. ital. *Bollett*, LXII (1925), 373–400. J. C. Brevoort, *Verrazano the navigator* (Albany, 1874). Ganong, "Crucial maps, III." Hakluyt, "Discourse on western planting." *The iconography of Manhattan Island, 1498–1909*, comp. I. N. P. Stokes (6v., New York, 1915–28), IV, 15–19. H. C. Murphy, *The voyage of Verrazzano* (New York, 1875). P. Peragallo, "Intorno alla supposta identità di Giovanni Verrazzano," Soc. geogr. ital. *Memorie*, VII, Rome, 1897, 165–89. Buckingham Smith, *An inquiry into the authenticity of documents* . . . (New York, 1864). E. L. Stevenson, *Maps illustrating early discovery and exploration in America, 1502–1530* (New Brunswick, N.J., 1903). Justin Winsor, *Narrative and critical history of America* (8v., Boston, 1884–89), IV. Consulted: L. C. Wroth, study of Verrazzano and his voyages, in preparation.

VIEL, NICOLAS, Recollet priest, missionary in the territory of the Hurons; b. near Coutances in Normandy; d. in 1625.

He had made his profession in 1598, with the Recollets of the province of Paris. Having been appointed missionary to Canada in 1623, he left Paris on 18 March with Brother SAGARD and reached Quebec on 28 June. On 16 July 1623 he left Quebec, together with Father LE CARON and Brother Sagard, for the country of the Hurons. He spent two years there, studying the language and taking notes which enabled him to supplement Father Le Caron's dictionary. In 1624 his two companions returned to Quebec, leaving him behind with nine other Frenchmen.

At the end of May 1625 Father Viel decided to go to Quebec. He set off with the Indians who were going down for the fur trade. While he was at the last rapids in the Rivière des Prairies, in a canoe occupied by three Indians, he was slaughtered by them and thrown into the water; a young man called Ahuntsic, who was following in another canoe, witnessed the crime, and suffered the same fate. The deed was committed on 25 June 1625, at the place now called Sault-au-Récollet; the body of the religious was recovered from the water a few days later and buried at Quebec.

The story of this tragedy, based on the accounts of Sagard, BRÉBEUF, PAUL LE JEUNE and LE CLERCQ, leaves no doubt about Father Viel's assassination. Was it caused by hatred of the Gospels? The Catholic Church has never stated its position in this regard; however, contemporary writers have no hesitation in proclaiming Father Viel the first martyr of the faith in Canada.

G.-M. DUMAS

ASQ, MSS, 200, Mortuologe des Recolets. Le Clercq, *First establishment of the faith* (Shea), I, 203f., 236, *et passim.* Sagard, *Histoire du Canada* (Tross). C.-P. Beaubien, *Le Sault-au-Récollet: ses rapports avec les premiers temps de la colonie* (Montréal, 1898), 47–91. R. Desrochers, *Le Sault-au-Récollet, paroisse la Visitation* (Montréal, 1936). Archange Godbout, "Le néophyte Ahuntsic," *BRH*, XLVIII (1942), 129–37. Jouve, *Les Franciscains et le Canada (1615–1629).* Hugolin Lemay, "L'œuvre manuscrite ou imprimée des Récollets de la mission du Canada (Province de Saint-Denis) 1615–1629," *RSCT*, 3d ser., XXX (1936), sect.I, 115–26. *Le père Nicolas Viel* (Notes bibliographiques pour servir à l'histoire des Récollets du Canada, II, Québec, 1932).

VIENNAY-PACHOT, FRANÇOIS, seigneur, merchant, director of the Compagnie du Nord, militia captain; b. at Bourg-d'Oisans (Dauphiné); d. 2 Sept. 1698 at Quebec.

As soon as he arrived in New France, probably before 1679, he opened a store in the Lower Town of Quebec. At that time he must have had the status of a hawker—a hawker could not traffic with the Indians or open a store at Montreal or Trois-Rivières from 15 June to 15 August—since on 24 April 1681 he presented a petition to the Conseil Souverain, in which he claimed the enjoyment of the privileges possessed by the other merchants. The Council acceded to his request. On 27 March 1684 he acquired a site in the Lower Town from the Quebec seminary, and then a second one on 4 Jan. 1686.

On 7 Jan. 1689 he obtained the Rivière-Mitis seigneury, which had an area of one square league. He intended to carry on cod- and seal-fishing there. Fishing was Viennay-Pachot's major concern. On 14 April 1689 he obtained, with several partners, "permission to fish for cod, whale, seal, porpoise and others that there may be in the St. Lawrence Gulf and River." On 8 March 1696 he signed an agreement with Marie Couillard [*see* BYSSOT] with respect to fishing and hunting throughout the whole extent of the Mingan islands. Furthermore, his name appeared among those of the directors of the Compagnie du Nord, in 1690.

François Viennay-Pachot died 2 Sept. 1698 at Quebec. He was married twice: to Jeanne Avamy, who died before his arrival in Canada, and to Charlotte-Françoise Juchereau* de Saint-Denis, daughter of NICOLAS JUCHEREAU de Saint-Denis, whom he married 17 Dec. 1680 and who gave him 16 children. She later married François de La Forest, calling herself Comtesse de Saint-Laurent in honour of the comté de Saint-Laurent, which she had bought from François Berthelot* on 25 Feb. 1702. This transaction involved her in disputes with Berthelot which have become famous.

JEAN HAMELIN

ASQ, Polygraphie, III, 113, 138, 141, 143, 144, 148. *Jug. et délib.*, II, 542f.; *passim.* P.-G. Roy, *Inv. concessions*, I, 74–76; III, 191; "La famille Viennay-Pachot," *BRH*, XXI (1915), 336–42; *L'Île d'Orléans* (Québec, 1928), 73–75.

VIEUX-PONT, JACQUES GODEFROY DE. *See* GODEFROY

VIGNAL (Vignar, Vignart, Vignard), GUILLAUME, priest, Sulpician, chaplain to the Ursulines of Quebec, bursar of the seminary of Saint-Sulpice at Montreal; b. *c.* 1604 (L. Le Jeune) or 1615 in the diocese of Périgueux (O. Maurault); killed by the Iroquois 27 Oct. 1661.

Little is known of Vignal's life before 1648. According to Le Jeune, he may have been ordained

Vignar

a priest about 1628. According to O. Maurault, he may have come to Canada as a secular priest to serve missions in the Gulf of St. Lawrence. In any case, on 13 Sept. 1648, we find him at Quebec with the title of chaplain to the Ursulines, as replacement for the prior, René Chartier, who had returned to France the preceding year. In return for an annual payment from the Ursulines of 100 *francs*, he concerned himself with various tasks on the community's behalf, one of them being to clear land on their Saint-Joseph farm. In 1653 he received from LOUIS D'AILLEBOUST an acre of land which he donated to the Ursulines on 4 Oct. 1655, "being on the point of sailing for France," a voyage from which he returned in 1656. On the occasion of a visit by Louis d'Ailleboust, then acting governor, to the Beaupré shore, Vignal accompanied him and, on 13 March 1658, blessed "the site of the church of the Petit Cap" (the future church of Sainte-Anne de Beaupré), the governor laying the first stone. Following the advice of M. de Queylus [*see* THUBIÈRES], Abbé Vignal decided to enrol in the Compagnie des Prêtres de Saint-Sulpice, which necessitated his going back to France that same year.

He returned to Canada on 7 Sept. 1659 together with the Sulpician Jacques LE MAISTRE, to take up his abode at Ville-Marie (Montreal). After Le Maistre's assassination in August 1661, he replaced him as bursar of the seminary of Saint-Sulpice. Before two months had elapsed he suffered the same fate as his colleague, at the hands of the same enemies. Being anxious to complete the seminary which was under construction, he had gone with a group of workmen to the Île à la Pierre, on 25 Oct. 1661, to collect the necessary materials. They were surprised by a band of Iroquois, and in the ensuing struggle Vignal was seriously wounded, captured and carried off with three other prisoners: a certain Dufresne, the settler René Cuillerier*, and Claude de BRIGEAC. Judging Vignal to be too badly hurt to survive, the Iroquois finished him off two days later near the Cap-de-la-Madeleine. After scalping him, they are said to have roasted and eaten his flesh.

From the evidence of the documents of the period, one can surmise that Vignal had a brave, devoted, deeply humble character. He was too trusting, however, and seems at times to have lacked prudence and foresight. Carried away by his eagerness to complete the seminary, he had indeed neglected warnings of the presence of Iroquois on the island; these warnings would have enabled him to avoid being slaughtered. According to JÉRÔME LALEMANT "he bore in life a very good repute among all the French, through his exercise of humility, charity and penitence—virtues which were highly developed in him, and made him beloved by every one." The Ursulines had esteemed him highly and keenly regretted his departure.

OLGA JURGENS

ASQ, Polygraphie III, 38. Dollier de Casson, *Histoire du Montréal*, 138–40, 162–65, 241. *JR* (Thwaites), XLII, 156, *et passim*. *JJ* (Laverdière et Casgrain), 232f., *et passim*. Gabriel Debien, "Liste des engagés pour le Canada au XVIIe siècle (1634–1715)," *RHAF*, VI (1952–53), 387. Le Jeune, *Dictionnaire*. Olivier Maurault, *Marges d'histoire* (3v., Montréal, 1929–30), III, 189–96. P.-G. Roy, *La ville de Québec*, I, 236 (facsimile of Vignal's signature). *Les Ursulines de Québec*, I, 67, 227, 231, 238–40.

VIGNAR (Vignard, Vignart). *See* VIGNAL

VIGNAU, NICOLAS DE, came to New France with CHAMPLAIN some time before 1612.

In 1611–12, Vignau wintered with TESSOUAT (fl. 1603–13), an Algonkin chief, on Allumette Island. Back in Paris in 1612 with "an account of the country which he said he had drawn up," Vignau stated that he had gone with a relative of Tessouat to the "northern sea" (Hudson Bay), and that he had seen a shipwrecked English vessel. The story was a likely one: in 1612 the English had entered Hudson Bay and had lost two ships there. The king induced Champlain to undertake such a voyage.

After Vignau had reaffirmed his statement before two notaries, Champlain set off with him in March 1613 to try and reach Hudson Bay by way of the Ottawa River. To get there they had to pass through the territory of the Nipissings. But Tessouat's Algonkins, on their island, controlled the head of the rapids and the access to the portage. They took advantage of their position to impose upon the native traders a more or less heavy toll, and they were in danger of losing this lucrative source of income if the French were themselves going to trade with the hinterland. In order to explain why they were opposed to Champlain's voyage, they therefore claimed that the Nipissings were an enemy nation (which was a lie). To reassure them Champlain made reference to Vignau's experience. The Algonkins protested vociferously; Tessouat declared to Vignau: "If you visited those tribes, it was in your sleep." Subjected to an interrogation that was loaded with threats, Vignau admitted that he had invented everything in order to get back to Canada. The Indians' reply was: "Give him to us, and we promise you he will tell no more lies." Champlain preferred to pardon a person whom he styled "the most impudent liar that has been seen for a long time." At the Saint-Louis Rapids Vignau asked to be left in the locality, but no one among the Indians wanted that, and Champlain added: "We left him in God's keeping." This is the last information that we have about him.

But had Vignau really lied? He lived among the Algonkins of the Island from the summer of 1611 until the spring of 1612; now according to Sagard the Algonkins were famous for the "journeys into distant lands" which they undertook, like the good merchants that they were; it is also known that they maintained constant business relations with the nations in the north; moreover the details supplied by Vignau on the northern sea correspond to what other sources have given us; all this authorizes us to believe that Vignau had in fact gone to Hudson Bay. Champlain, who did not yet know these Indians sufficiently well (he was making his first journey along the Ottawa River), seems to have been taken in by them; as for Vignau, he might have been the victim not of a dream but of the rigorous policy of the Algonkins of the Island, a people that Sagard calls "the harshest, the proudest and the least courteous."

MARCEL TRUDEL

Champlain, *Works* (Biggar), II, 255–307; IV, 151, 153–204. *JR* (Thwaites), IX, 274. Sagard, *Histoire du Canada* (Tross), II, 367; III, 739f.

VILLAIN, JEAN-BAPTISTE, gold- and silversmith; fl. 1666–70.

The first census list of New France, drawn up in 1666, bears the name of Jean-Baptiste Villain, 19 years old, "gold- and silversmith working on the Île d'Orléans." He was probably working on the land, and not at his trade. This very young craftsman has been mistaken for Jean Villain, who qualified as a master craftsman in Paris in 1670, was suspended in 1676 for complicity in a matter of false countermarks, and was debarred from the mastership in 1694. There is no proof that he came to Canada.

We next meet Jean-Baptiste Villain at Montreal. On 18 Oct. 1670 he was present as cousin of the fiancée at the signing of the private marriage contract concluded between Mathurin Bernier, a native of Bessay (near Luçon), and Jeanne Villain, "daughter of Jean Villain and of the late Jeanne Barbé, her father and mother, of the parish of Saint-Jacques-la-Boucherie in Paris." Ten days later the parish priest of Notre-Dame in Montreal drew up the marriage certificate of the Berniers; in it Jeanne Villain is called "daughter of Jean Villain, master gold- and silversmith in Paris, and of Jeanne Barbé." Jean-Baptiste Villain was present at the wedding as a cousin of Jeanne; his friend, the gunsmith-silversmith René Fézeret*, signed as a friend of the married couple.

Jean-Baptiste Villain declared in these two documents that he did not know how to write his name; moreover, his profession is not given. We have therefore only his declaration to the census-taker in 1666 to support his claim to being a gold- and silversmith. That is not enough, for at his age when he arrived in New France he could scarcely claim to be anything other than an apprentice.

GÉRARD MORISSET

AJM, Actes sous seing privé, 1134; Régistre des baptêmes, mariages et sépultures, Notre-Dame de Montréal, 28 oct. 1670. Recensement de 1666. *Catalogue de l'orefèvrerie du XVIIe, du XVIIIe et du XIXe siècles* (Paris, 1958), 14.

VILLEBON, JOSEPH ROBINAU DE. *See* ROBINAU

VILLENEUVE, MATHIEU AMIOT *dit. See* AMIOT

VILLENEUVE, ROBERT DE, engineer, cartographer, draughtsman, probably a pupil of Vauban, who recommended him at the beginning of 1685 as a military engineer for New France; b. c. 1645, place unknown; d. in France some time after 1692.

Villeneuve reached Quebec at the beginning of May 1685 and applied himself immediately to the instructions received from the king. An analysis of the tasks which he carried out from June to November of that year makes it clear that he had been instructed by Versailles to make accurate surveys of the promontory of Quebec, with the object of fortifying the town.

His first completed piece of work was a plan of Quebec. On it can be seen the houses which then existed, shown to scale. Two lines are also visible, intersecting at right angles: one passes along the centre of Sous-le-Fort street; the other is parallel to the Château Saint-Louis. On the east-west line, the engineer has set up two sections, which show the rock of Quebec in relief and the outline of the houses in the Upper and Lower Town. In this way we have a precise idea of the Château Saint-Louis, built by HUAULT de Montmagny in 1647; it was a long building of attractive proportions, with a hipped roof.

Despite frequent indispositions, Villeneuve completed a considerable amount of work up to November. He carried out surveys at Trois-Rivières and at Montreal; he went to Cataracoui and made sketches of Fort Frontenac and its

Villeneuve

surroundings. Meanwhile the Intendant Demeulle* instructed him to draw up the plans for a powder-magazine which was to be constructed in one of the bastions of Fort Saint-Louis; the contract prepared by François Genaple* on 12 Aug. 1685 tells us the name of the builder, Jean Lerouge*. This powder-magazine, completed in 1686, was demolished in 1893.

Villeneuve spent the winter of 1685–86 drawing the map of the surroundings of Quebec, with the help of notes made since his arrival in the country. Then he drafted a memoir on the state of the Château Saint-Louis; another on the digging of a well in the Upper Town; a third on improvements to the appearance of the Lower Town; and finally a fourth on the state of the prison. It was probably because of these memoirs that the disagreement between Governor Brisay* de Denonville and the engineer erupted. On 8 May 1686 Denonville wrote to Versailles: "I propose to send to Niagara this year the sieur Dorvilliers [Rémy Guilloust* (Guillouet) d'Orvilliers] with the sieur de Villeneuve, the draughtsman you gave me, in order to make a plan of it. . . . I shall see whether I cannot make a trip there myself, so that I can give you a more reliable report; for when it comes to trusting the Sieur de Villeneuve alone, he is a very good, very accurate and very true draughtsman, but in other respects his mind is not well enough ordered, and is too limited for him to be able to offer any views as to the establishment of a post, and to run it on his own." Villeneuve was often sick, and was ill adjusted to the climate. He spent the summer and autumn of 1686 doing numerous sketches of the surroundings of Quebec, the Île d'Orléans, Montreal, Chambly and La Prairie-de-la-Madeleine. But, wrote Denonville, "he did not have the leisure to make fair copies of them."

The following year the quarrel worsened. Villeneuve's delays in carrying out the surveys, his dissension with Major François Provost*, his difficult relations with some of the king's officials, everything contributed to make his life miserable. Denonville was exasperated: "This engineer of ours," he wrote to the minister on 8 June 1687, "is a fool, a libertine, a débauché, whom we have to put up with because we have business with him. . . . He is a spendthrift. Yet he works amazingly well with his hands, and very quickly when he wants to. Monsieur de Vauban can readily describe to you his type of mind. Had he not been staying in my house and receiving board from me, I should never have been able to get anything out of him. . . . The intendant will acquaint you with the way in which he has covered our magazine [powder-magazine]; the stone roofing, being made of blocks, has not been tight enough to prevent water from coming in through the jointing, besides which the lime and the cement which have been used do not stand up at all to the frost in this country. . . ." On 6 Nov. 1687, another letter from the governor, countersigned by Bochart* Champigny: "He is a very good draughtsman, and has an astonishing ability for mapping the outlines of a terrain; which is a great help for M. de Vauban, who can send us a plan from France for fortifying the terrain which we shall have reported to him."

Villeneuve, discouraged, asked to go back to France. The next day he changed his mind. On 13 Nov. 1687 he left the governor's residence and went to live in the Lower Town, at Étienne Landron's house. On 8 March 1688 he received an order from Louis XIV to return to France; however, with Denonville's authorization, he remained at Quebec and continued his work as a cartographer. Finally Vauban administered to him a series of reprimands which, as Denonville and Champigny wrote on 6 Nov. 1688, "made him more tractable and more amenable to reason." Having been recalled again on 1 May 1689, he put the finishing touches to the map of the surroundings of Niagara, completed the plan of Fort Frontenac, and left the country in November 1689.

Villeneuve returned to Quebec in April 1691. He no longer had any effective authority. It was his temporary successor, Jean-Baptiste-Louis Franquelin*, who in June 1691 drew the plans of the Batterie royale which Claude Baillif undertook to build at the end of Sous-le-Fort street. The following year, Villeneuve wanted to go back to France to explain to Vauban the relief drawing of the rock of Quebec. He left the country for good in November 1692.

That Denonville and Champigny somewhat exaggerated Villeneuve's weaknesses of character is possible. But they were right to praise his talent as a draughtsman. He was more of an artist than an engineer. And to his taste for sensitive and precise drawing we owe charming pieces of work —for example the excellent surveys of 1685 and the plan of Quebec during the siege of 1690.

Gérard Morisset

AJQ, Greffe de François Genaple, 12 août 1685, 13 nov. 1687. APQ, Manuscrits concernant la Nouvelle-France, 2ᵉ série, 1614–1727, IV, 271, 370, 374, 380, 385; V, 209, 220, 234f., 237, 303f., 318, 408, 420f., 445, 448, 452f., 476, 617; VI, 111, 197f.; VII, 240; Ordres du roi, XII, 65; XIII, 51; XV, 36, 56, 104f.; XVIII, 4. Correspondance de Frontenac (1689–99), APQ *Rapport, 1927–28*, 140f., 144. P.-G. Roy, "Le sieur de Villeneuve, ingénieur du roi," *BRH*, X (1904), 280–2.

VILLERAY, LOUIS ROUER DE. *See* ROUER

VIMONT, BARTHÉLEMY, priest, Jesuit, missionary, third superior of the Canadian mission; b. 17 Jan. 1594 at Lisieux (Normandy); d. 13 July 1667 at Vannes in France.

He entered the Society of Jesus at Rouen on 16 Nov. 1613. After his noviciate he took his philosophy at the Collège at La Flèche (1615–18), then taught for one year at Rennes and three years at Eu. From 1622 to 1626 he studied theology at the Collège de Clermont, in Paris; finally he returned to Eu as bursar (1626–29). It was from there that he left for Canada, on 26 June 1629, on one of Capt. CHARLES DANIEL'S ships; this convoy was also carrying Fathers Philibert NOYROT and Alexandre de Vieuxpont. The captain, cast up by a storm on the coast of Cape Breton Island, towards the end of August, built a fort at the entrance to the Grand-Cibou (today called St. Ann's), where he left a garrison with Father Vimont as the chaplain. Vieuxpont, after surviving the shipwreck in which Father Noyrot had perished, joined Vimont. Together they started to preach the gospel to the Indians of the district. But they were recalled to France the following year, as the colony had fallen into the hands of the KIRKE brothers.

After serving for eight years in various capacities at the Collège in Vannes and for one year as superior at the residence in Dieppe, Father Vimont arrived at Quebec on 1 Aug. 1639, together with Fathers CHAUMONOT and PONCET, to succeed Father PAUL LE JEUNE as superior of the mission in Canada. He was on the same ship as the Ursulines—among whom was Marie de l'Incarnation [*see* GUYART]—the Hospitallers, and Mme CHAUVIGNY de La Peltrie, who had all been entrusted to his care; with them, he was given a formal reception, on the report of which his signature appears.

Vimont remained the superior for six years. At first he seems to have lived chiefly at Sillery, and to have been successful with the Indians of this reservation. From there he went to witness the founding of Montreal. He himself wrote the account of it (*Relation* of 1642), for the superior of Quebec was responsible for making a report every year to the provincial of the Society in France. For this reason Father Vimont prepared the four *Relations* of the years 1642–45; JÉRÔME LALEMANT succeeded him in this duty.

In 1643, under the Vimont administration, the Huron seminary that had been established at the Notre-Dame-des-Anges residence was closed. In the same year, with the support of the directors of the Compagnie des Cent-Associés, Vimont had the task of clearing the name of the Jesuits in Canada; they had been charged with taking part in the fur trade. In 1645, at the time of the peace negotiations with the Iroquois (among whom was the orator KIOTSEAETON), Father Vimont's advice was solicited by Governor HUAULT de Montmagny.

At the same period, the fathers were taking turns in ministering to the parish of Quebec. It thus happened that Vimont baptized Louis JOLLIET, on 21 Sept. 1645. On 21 October Vimont set out for France; he went as a delegate from the fathers, to obtain clarification of certain jurisdictional questions. He returned to Quebec on 19 Aug. 1648, and for another 11 years he continued actively to serve the religious communities and the parishioners of the neighbourhood of Quebec, in particular those of Beauport. He also acted as adviser to the superior. On 23 Oct. 1651 he blessed the marriage of the seneschal, JEAN DE LAUSON, the son of the governor of the same name. Finally, on 22 Oct. 1659, he left the country; he died on 13 July 1667 at Vannes.

HONORIUS PROVOST

ASQ, Documents Faribault, 23, 25. Champlain, *Œuvres* (Laverdière), II, 1283–87. *JR* (Thwaites), XXII, 9–296; XXIII, 255–318; XXV, 9–78, 88–280; XXVII, 123–304; *et passim. JJ* (Laverdière et Casgrain), 93, 163, 185f., *et passim.* Auguste Gosselin, *La mission du Canada avant Mgr de Laval (1615–1659)* (Évreux, 1909), 55, *et passim.*

VUIL, DANIEL, executed at Quebec on 7 Oct. 1661 for carrying on an illegal traffic in spirits with the Indians.

Trafficking in spirits had always been prohibited in New France. But after the arrival of Bishop Laval*, church and state had combined their efforts to put an end to this profitable enterprise. While the civil power, in the person of Governor Voyer* d'Argenson, was punishing the traffickers severely, Bishop Laval announced on 6 May 1660 the *ipso facto* excommunication of any person giving intoxicating liquor to the Indians. For a time, this measure put a stop to irregular practices, but gradually the traffic was resumed.

Was it for trafficking in spirits that Daniel Vuil was imprisoned at Quebec in February 1661? Perhaps. At any rate, the prisoner "a relapsed heretic, a blasphemer and profaner of the Sacraments" was the cause of a dispute between the civil and religious authorities on the occasion of a sentence pronounced upon him by Bishop Laval. Was Vuil released shortly after, or did he remain in prison until the day of his execution? We do

Walker

not know. But it was unquestionably "for trafficking in spirits with the Indians" that he was executed by arquebus on 7 Oct. 1661. This exemplary punishment was meted out on the eleventh of the same month to another trafficker named La Violette.

In all probability the state was obliged to have recourse to these extreme measures because of the incorrigibility of these adventurers; Pierre AIGRON *dit* Lamothe, excommunicated in person in April 1661 for the same crime but having subsequently reformed, does not appear to have incurred the wrath of the civil power.

ANDRÉ VACHON

JJ (Laverdière et Casgrain), 282–303. G. Lanctot, "Une accusation contre Mgr de Laval," SCHEC *Rapport, 1944–45*, 11–26.

W

WALKER, NEHEMIAH, sea captain for the HBC; fl. *c.* 1670–90.

He was a son of the London goldsmith, William Walker, who was a stockholder in the Company from the 1670's and a committee member from 1682 to 1685. Nehemiah himself, apparently as security to the Company for good conduct, appears to have been a stockholder in 1670 when he sailed in the *Wivenhoe* (Capt. Robert Newland) to Hudson Bay as assistant to Governor Charles BAYLY. Walker was present when Bayly took formal possession of Port Nelson in September 1670 and he wintered with the remainder of the *Wivenhoe*'s company at Charles Fort, Rupert River. On his return to London in 1671 he found other employment.

Immediately after the loss of the homeward-bound *Shaftsbury* (Capt. Joseph THOMPSON) in the autumn of 1678, the Committee persuaded Walker to rejoin the Company, and in the following year he commanded the *John and Alexander* to and from James Bay. On this voyage both the outward-bound Governor John NIXON and the retired Governor Bayly suffered from his arrogance and ill-temper. Furthermore, Walker's reckless behaviour was largely the reason the *Colleton* (Capt. James Tatnam) did not reach James Bay that year, so it is understandable that with the return of the *John and Alexander* to the Royal Navy early in 1680 and the chartering of the *Prudent Mary* (Capt. Richard Greenway) for the voyage of that year, Walker was left unemployed. But the *Prudent Mary* was wrecked and the other ships sent out in 1680 remained in James Bay so, in 1681, the Committee again approached Walker. After an unsuccessful demand for very high wages, Walker accepted the command of the chartered ship *Diligence*. According to instructions he wintered at Charlton Island and his quarrelsome and drunken behaviour there caused Governor Nixon to complain bitterly to the Committee.

Walker returned to London in 1682 and in 1683 he again commanded the *Diligence* to James Bay. Nixon's successor, Henry SERGEANT, was a passenger and, like his predecessors, had reason to complain of Walker's behaviour. In Hudson Strait the *Diligence* came upon the interloper *Expectation* (alias the *Charles*) which was commanded by an ex-Company employee, Richard LUCAS. Acting on instructions from the Committee who sought to safeguard their privileges under the charter of 2 May 1670, Walker seized the *Expectation* and placed his own crew aboard. The vessel was wrecked shortly afterwards and Lucas and his men were brought back to England in the *Diligence* later in 1683.

The seizure of the *Expectation* led to a series of legal actions by the owners against both the Company and Walker who, early in 1684, was dismissed by the Committee not only because of his mismanagement when taking the interloper, but on account of his conduct to Governor Sergeant.

Walker, whose brothers William and James were also employed by the Company for short periods, described himself in 1687 as of the Thameside parish of Rotherhithe, and it is likely, but unconfirmed, that he was identical with the Nehemiah Walker, mariner of London, whose wife, Anne, was sole beneficiary under a will dated 21 June 1688 and proved in the Prerogative Court of Canterbury on 12 July 1690.

ALICE M. JOHNSON

HBRS, V (Rich), 14, 20, 24, 68; VIII, IX (Rich); XI (Rich and Johnson); XXI (Rich).

WALKER, RICHARD, deputy governor of Nova Scotia or Acadia, under Sir Thomas TEMPLE, in 1670; fl. 1637–80.

He was an early New England settler, and was a member both of the Honourable Artillery Company of London and of the Ancient and Honourable Artillery Company of Boston. He held the rank of ensign when he was surveyor of arms for Saugus in 1637. By 1640 he was a deputy in the General Court of Massachusetts Bay. By

1648 he held the rank of lieutenant and represented Reading in the General Court. By 1652 he had been promoted to captain.

At Boston on 7 July 1670, Sir Thomas Temple wrote a letter to Capt. Richard Walker, then in Nova Scotia, directing him, in accordance with orders from His Majesty dated 8 March 1668/69 and 6 Aug. 1669, to deliver Acadia ("namely the forts and habitations of Pentagouet, St. John [Jemseg], Port Royal, La Have, and Cape Sable") to ANDIGNÉ de Grandfontaine. Pursuant to these instructions, Walker handed over Pentagouet on 17 July 1670 to Andigné, Jemseg on 27 August and Port-Royal and Fort La Tour on 2 Sept. 1670 to JOYBERT de Soulanges.

By 1677 Capt. Richard Walker was living in Lynn, Mass., with his wife Sarah, the widow of Obediah Walker. He represented Lynn in the General Court in 1679–80.

C. BRUCE FERGUSSON

On the surrender of the Acadian forts *see*: AE, Corr. pol., Angleterre, 91, 93, 94, 96; Mém. et doc., Amérique, 5, ff.2, 6, 7, 277–79. AN, Col., C11D, 1, ff. 135–36, 139, etc.; Marine, B2, 9, 10. "Mass. Archives."

Charlevoix, *History* (Shea), III, 138. *Collection de manuscrits relatifs à la Nouv.-France*, I, 201–2. *Mémoires des commissaires*, I xxj, 50–51; II, 316–23, 325–26; IV, 304; and *Memorials of the English and French commissaries*, I, 24–25, 122, 421, 604–13, *et passim*. PRO, *CSP, Col.*, 1669–74, nos. 32, 95, 384. *Records of the Massachusetts Bay* (Shurtleff), I; II; IV, pts. I and II; V. *Suffolk deeds*.

John Farmer, *A genealogical register of the first settlers of New-England* (Lancaster, Mass., 1829). F. C. Lowell, "Memoir of Francis A. Walker, LL.D.," Mass. Hist. Soc. *Proc.*, 2d ser., XIII (1900), 303.

WAYMOUTH or **WEYMOUTH** (Purchas uses both spellings), **GEORGE**, explorer and navigator; fl. 1601–12.

Waymouth, an English mariner, was involved in three projected expeditions (only two of which actually took place) to the New World. He is described by James Rosier—who sailed with him on his 1605 expedition to explore Virginia for the Earl of Southampton and Lord Thomas Arundell of Wardour—as a man who knew "most of the Coast of England and most of other Countries (having beene experienced by implyments in discoveries and travails from his childehood)."

Waymouth appears to have been a man of some education. Between his voyage to Hudson Strait and his expedition to Virginia, he addressed to King James I a manuscript entitled "The jewell of artes," which dealt with navigation, shipbuilding, and instruments of war. During 1605, he prepared a manuscript "Errors and defects in the usual building of ships," written, he asserted, from 20 years' study of mathematics and shipbuilding. (Neither manuscript was ever printed and both are now in the British Museum.)

In September 1601, after previous negotiations with the Muscovy and Turkey companies, Waymouth agreed to seek a northwest passage to India for the newly formed (1601) East India Company. With him on this expedition were the Rev. John Cartwright, who later published an account of his travels in the East entitled *The preachers' travels* (1611) and who acted as chaplain, and John Drew, master of the *Godspeed*, Waymouth's consort. Waymouth was granted £100 by the company to cover the purchase of instruments and other necessary supplies and was promised £500, to be paid only if he found the passage. Queen Elizabeth equipped Waymouth with an illuminated letter to the "Emperor of China," with translations in Latin, Spanish, and Italian, and a tin box to hold them. (These he brought home; they are preserved in the Lancashire County Record Office, Preston, England.)

On 2 May 1602, Waymouth sailed from Ratcliffe on the Thames aboard the 70-ton *Discovery* (William Cobreth, master), accompanied by Drew's 60-ton *Godspeed*. The two vessels carried 35 men. On 28 June he sighted America at an estimated latitude of 62°30′N, but was driven off the coast in foggy weather. Land was sighted again at 63°53′ on 8 July, but there was much dangerous ice and it was not possible to examine the shore. Waymouth, in his own account of the voyage, reports that on 19 July "all our men conspired secretly together to beare up the helme for England, while I was asleepe in my Cabin." The following day, the mutineers presented their written reasons for the mutiny; they said they would not winter in the north but they would explore between 57° and 60°N. On 21 July, the crew "bore up the helm" and steered S by W. Challenged by Waymouth, the men stated that this decision had been made by "one and all." A simple misreading of the narrative erroneously makes Cartwright the leader of the mutiny (*see*: *DNB*, *DAB*). On 22 July, Waymouth, in the presence of Cartwright and Cobreth, sent for the ring-leaders and "punished them severely"; but at the entreaties of the two men he remitted a portion of the sentence. The same day, boats from the *Discovery* and the *Godspeed* narrowly escaped being capsized by an iceberg, which cracked and began to overturn as the men were breaking off ice to replenish their supply of fresh water.

The ships continued to sail to the south. On 26 July, Waymouth reckoned he was at the entry to an inlet (Hudson Strait) in the latitude 61°40′N, into which he sailed westward for 100 leagues

Whitbourne

(300 miles). Although Waymouth had "great hope of this Inlet," he turned back on 26 July, as the year was far spent and many men were ill. Nevertheless, in the words of Luke Fox, Waymouth did indeed "light HUDSON into his Streights."

The ships cleared Hudson Strait on 5 August and on 9 August the mainland of Labrador was sighted in the latitude 55°30′N. That night the *Godspeed* struck an iceberg which the crew feared "had foundred the Shippe," but no damage ensued. On 14 August, the ships stood to the westward to look for an inlet in the latitude 56°N, as Waymouth "had good hope of a passage that way, by many great and probable reasons"; but nothing came of the search. The ships rode out a great storm on 18 August and with a fair wind, they then cleared the land and ice, making sail for England. Waymouth reached Dartmouth 5 Sept. 1602.

The court of the East India Company examined Waymouth on 24 Nov. 1602; a decision was made to send a second expedition, which was not, however, implemented.

In 1605 Waymouth explored the shores of Massachusetts and Maine. On 27 Oct. 1607, James I granted him a pension of 3*s*. 4*d*. a day until "he shall receive from His Majesty some other advancement." The last mention of him is the payment of his pension, Easter 1612.

THOMAS DUNBABIN

PRO, *CSP, Col., East Indies, 1601–2*. For a contemporary record of the 1605 voyage *see* James Rosier, *A true relation* . . . (London, 1605), in Purchas, *Pilgrimes* (1905–7), XVIII, 335–60 (with additions), in *Rosier's relation of Waymouth's voyage to the coast of Maine 1605*, ed. H. S. Burrage (Gorges Soc., III, 1887), and in H. S. Burrage, *Gorges and the grant of the Province of Maine, 1622: a tercentenary memorial* (Portland, Me., 1923). Waymouth's own account of the 1602 voyage is given in Purchas, *Pilgrimes* (1905–7), XIV, 306–18, and in Luke Fox, *North-West Fox* . . . (London, 1635) in *Voyages of Foxe and James* (Christy).

DAB. DNB. G. B. Manhart, "The English search for a north-west passage in the time of Queen Elizabeth," in *Studies in English commerce and exploration in the reign of Elizabeth* (Philadelphia, 1924). *Narratives of voyages towards the north west in search of a passage to Cathay and India 1496 to 1631*, . . . , ed. Thomas Rundall (Hakluyt Soc., 1st ser., V, 1849), 51–71. Oleson, *Early voyages*, 161–62. Henry Stevens, *The dawn of British trade to the East Indies as recorded in the court minutes of the East India Company 1599–1603 containing an account of . . . Waymouth's voyage in search of the North-West Passage* (London, 1886).

WHITBOURNE, SIR RICHARD, sailor, merchant, colonizer, writer, governor of Sir William VAUGHAN's colony in Newfoundland; b. at Exmouth, Devonshire; fl. 1579–1628.

From the age of 15 Whitbourne was a mariner, engaged in trading to most parts of western Europe. In 1579 he made his first voyage to Newfoundland, to catch whales and trade with the Indians. After this he visited the island frequently, being a witness both of Sir Humphrey GILBERT's annexation in 1583 and of Sir BERNARD DRAKE's raid on Portuguese shipping in 1585. He commanded his own ship and three others against the Armada in 1588, subsequently receiving letters of recommendation from the lord high admiral, Lord Howard. His voyages to Newfoundland continued and, in 1612, Whitbourne was taken prisoner by "that famous Arch-Pirate," Peter EASTON, while two years later he saw the damage inflicted on the fishermen by Henry MAINWARING.

Early in 1615 he was commissioned by the High Court of Admiralty to hold vice-admiralty courts in Newfoundland and inquire into abuses committed by the fishermen. It was to correct these same disorders that JOHN GUY, governor of the English plantation, had issued a series of laws in 1611. Whitbourne amassed evidence from 170 masters of English fishing vessels but, judging from later controversies between the colonists and the fishing merchants, his action was no more effective than Guy's; indeed, it is difficult to see what one man could have been expected to accomplish.

From this time Whitbourne's interest in Newfoundland widened; previously it had been mainly commercial. In 1612, 1614, and 1616 he had ships there which he intended should go directly to the Mediterranean with their fish. Now he became concerned with the island's settlement and an advocate of the planters against the fishermen—a most unusual attitude in a West Country man who had himself been a fisherman. About 1617 he was consulted by William Vaughan, the first independent speculator to purchase land in the island from the London and Bristol company. Vaughan sent his first colonists out to Renewse in that year and in 1618 Whitbourne sailed as their governor. He found that the settlers had been so ineffectual that they had not even built themselves an adequate shelter. Despite the hindrance caused to his plans by an attack on one of his ships "by an English erring Captaine" sailing with Sir Walter Raleigh, he succeeded in reorganizing the settlement.

The Vaughan enterprise continued for some years but never with much success and Whitbourne's association with it seems to have ended by 1620 when he published his first *Discourse and discovery of New-found-land*. He had first submitted both his book and a proposition for a colony to the Privy Council. A committee appointed to consider whether a plantation should be assisted made no recommendation on this, but did approve the printing of the book and requested that the archbishops of Canterbury and York have it distributed in every parish. In 1621 the Privy Council asked for contributions from each parish to recompense him for his services and losses in Newfoundland.

In 1622 a second edition of the *Discourse* appeared and he also published *A discourse containing a loving invitation . . . to all Adventurers . . . for the advancement of his Majesties most hopeful Plantation in the New-found-land*. This he dedicated to Lord Falkland, for he was now involved in the latter's plan to establish a colony at Renewse. In December 1622 he wrote to Falkland, advising him on the financial organization and practical necessities of such a scheme. He recommended that a modest beginning be made in 1623 with only 12 settlers, all of whom should be craftsmen or fishermen. Between 1622 and 1626 he twice visited the colony which was governed by Sir Francis TANFIELD. In 1625 Whitbourne was knighted by Falkland but, by November 1626, he was looking for fresh employment. In a petition to the Duke of Buckingham he set forth his past services in Newfoundland and his fitness for further occupation there or elsewhere; this was supported by a reference from several prominent West Country gentlemen. He is next heard of serving as lieutenant on the *Bonaventure* under Sir John Chudleigh in October 1627. The date of Whitbourne's death is unknown, but he was alive in 1628 when Robert HAYMAN published a poem in praise of his books.

Whitbourne's works are a unique contribution to the early literature on Newfoundland. Their purpose was always to stimulate interest in the island and, particularly, to promote its settlement as profitable both to the individual and to the nation. But their uniqueness lies not in their purpose but in their content; there were other propagandists but no other writer of the day could rival Whitbourne's experience and knowledge or his ability to transmit enthusiasm. "What can the world yeeld," he wrote, "to the sustentation of man, which is not in her [Newfoundland] to bee gotten. Desire you wholesome ayre? (the very food of life) It is there. Shall any Land powre in abundant heapes of nourishments and necessaries before you? There you have them. What Seas abounding with fish? What shores so replenished with fresh and sweet waters? The wants of other Kingdomes are not felt here." (*Discourse* (1622), 75.) For his contemporaries he provided a wealth of detail on the geography, climate, and resources of the island, besides practical advice on settlement and the fishery; he even included a precise inventory of the cost of setting out a fishing vessel of 100 tons and 40 planters. For the historian he is an invaluable and lively source, reflecting the state of geographical knowledge and supplying important information on the method and organization of the fishery and the extensive trade in fish and oil.

GILLIAN T. CELL

Whitbourne's books are: *A discourse and discovery of New-found-land* (London, 1620), of which there is a MS draft in Whitbourne's own hand in the BM, Add. MSS, 22564; *A discourse and discovery of New-found-land: as also an invitation . . .* (London, 1622), extracts from which appear in *Westward hoe for Avalon . . .* ed. T. Whitburn (London, 1870); (another ed., 1623); *A discourse containing a loving invitation . . .* (London, 1622), a small part of which is reprinted in M. Carroll, *The seal and herring fisheries of Newfoundland* (Montreal, 1873). There are two letters from Whitbourne to Lord Falkland: BM, Sloane MS 3827, ff.15–18, 67–68v. Other MS sources: BM, Add. MS 11033, ff.18–19v. PRO, S.P. 16/31, 81; C.O. 1/4; P.C. 2/29, 30, 31.

DNB. R. Hayman, *Quodlibets, lately come over from New Britaniola* (London, 1628). Prowse, *History of Nfld*. W. A. Shaw, *The knights of England* (2v., London, 1906).

WHITE, JOHN, English artist and the first to draw Eskimos in Canada; b. *c.* 1540–50; fl. 1593 in County Cork, Ireland.

White was perhaps of Cornish stock, though his family and early career have not been traced with any certainty. But he is most likely to be identified with the John White who was a member of the Painter-Stainers' Company of London in 1580. He was intimately connected with Sir Walter Raleigh's colonizing expeditions in North Carolina and Virginia between 1584 and 1590, first as artist, later (1587–90) as governor of the new colony. The results of his artistic activities in Raleigh's Virginia, which have survived, are confined to a set of skilful and convincing water-colour drawings, in the British Museum, of Indians and the fauna and flora of this coastal area.

Yet these almost certainly were not his first records of the New World. Though his name does not appear in the documents there is strong presumptive evidence that he sailed with FROBISHER to South Baffin Island on his second voyage in 1577. This is supplied by a pen and water-colour drawing of a fight between Eskimos and Englishmen contained in an album of early 17th-century copies of White's drawings, acquired by Sir Hans Sloane from White's descendant a century later. The scene depicted is so authentic in detail that it may be presumed that White himself was an

Willoughby

eye-witness. The theory is supported by the likely identification of this incident with one described by Dionise Settle and George BEST in their accounts of the voyage. The Englishmen in their pinnace being attacked by Eskimos with bows and arrows, and attacking them in turn with muskets, the Baffin Islanders in kayaks, their tents in the background above the bay: all are mentioned in the accounts of the fight and illustrated in the drawing. Original drawings by White of an Eskimo man, and of a woman and her baby (which are found in the set of his drawings together with his Indians of Virginia) almost certainly portray the prisoners known to have been taken by Frobisher in 1577. Their costume is without doubt that of Baffin Islanders.

White may well have provided the original drawings from which engravings were made (or intended) for a publication licensed by the Stationers' Company to John Allde on 30 Jan. 1578, as "A discription of the purtrayture and Shape of those strange kinde of people whiche the worthie master MARTIN FOURBOSIER, brought into England in Anno 1576 and 1577." No copy of this book, if published, is known, but French and German editions of Settle's account of Frobisher's second voyage, published in 1578 and 1580, each include woodcuts, close in detail to each other, which were probably taken from a print in the lost publication. Both certainly include details of a man and woman Eskimo with her baby and of a kayaker, which definitely connect them with the known portraits by White. At least one other drawing in the same album of copies, the back view of the Eskimo man, indicates that White drew more portraits than the two original Eskimo subjects which have survived. Judging from his later Virginia material, it is likely that he made a much wider record of Eskimo life which, published or unpublished, must have played its part in extending the knowledge of this remote part of Canada among those most concerned with the possibilities of English expansion overseas.

P. H. HULTON

Roanoke voyages (Quinn), I. Kaj Birket-Smith, "The earliest Eskimo portraits," *Folk*, I (1959), 5–14. E. Croft-Murray and P. H. Hulton, *Catalogue of British drawings* (London, British Museum, 1960–   ), I: *XVI & XVII centuries*, 26–30. P. H. Hulton, "John White's drawings of Eskimos," *Beaver*, outfit 292 (summer, 1961), 16–20. *John White's American drawings, 1577–1590*, ed. P. H. Hulton and D. B. Quinn (2v., London and Chapel Hill, N.C., 1963), plates 62, 63, 84, 85, 147.

WILLOUGHBY, THOMAS, member of the first English colony in Newfoundland; b. 1593, the third son of Sir Percival Willoughby and his wife, Bridget, of Wollaton, Nottinghamshire.

Thomas's father had been one of the foremost subscribers to the Newfoundland company on its foundation in 1610 and had been appointed to the council which managed the company's affairs. Sir Percival had inherited a large but impoverished estate and engaged in many financial schemes to restore his fortunes; it was probably the speculative aspect of the Newfoundland venture which attracted him.

Thomas was evidently the black sheep of the family and, by 1612, had so angered his parents that he was sent out to the recently established colony at Cuper's Cove (now Cupids) to reform. In May 1612 Willoughby and Henry CROUT who was his guardian and agent to his father, reached Newfoundland. With a group of new settlers they landed at Renewse where they remained for some time, Crout making Willoughby help in the company fishery to keep him out of mischief and bad company. By August they had both joined the main colony under JOHN GUY at Cuper's Cove. Willoughby evidently found life as a pioneer a sobering experience for he soon wrote a most dutiful letter home, repenting of his former indiscretions and promising so to "indever [my] selfe in all goodnesse, that I hope in time you may live to se[e] mee become a newe man."

With 60 fellow settlers he spent that winter in the island. Severe weather caused the death of eight men and the loss of much livestock; it also immobilized the colonists but, when the weather permitted, Willoughby participated in their main activities of exploring and hunting. Crout informed Sir Percival that he should find his son much improved and Thomas was allowed to return to England in the late summer of 1613. A letter which he wrote to his mother in 1614 expressed his joy at being restored to favour.

In 1615 Sir Percival decided to make over the land in Newfoundland, which he hoped to receive from the company, to Thomas and his second son, Edward. This land was part of the peninsula between Conception and Trinity bays, north of a line drawn from Carbonear to Heart's Content. The grant, however, was not confirmed until 1617 by which time Sir Percival had changed his mind.

It would appear that Thomas had again fallen from grace for, in the previous year, he had been sent back to Newfoundland. It was his father's wish that he and Crout should establish an independent settlement at Carbonear but the plan was frustrated by the desertion of most of his men before they left England. Thomas wrote from Cuper's Cove telling his father of this and advising him to set out his own fishing vessel, as he considered fishing the only way to make any profit from the island. Young Willoughby's advice certainly was sound, for at this time only by fishing could the costs of supporting men in the island be covered.

It is not clear how long Willoughby remained in Newfoundland; he certainly spent the winter of 1616–17 there. In March 1617 his father wrote to Crout in Newfoundland that "for m^r Thomas, it is not words nor writinge but deeds and better courses, can geive me satisfaction" (Middleton MS, Mi X 1/45). It is probable that he left with Henry Crout, who had quit Sir Percival's service by 1619.

Thomas Willoughby does not figure in the family papers after 1621 when he was again at Wollaton. His total omission from the family pedigree (*Visitation of Nottinghamshire, 1569 & 1614*, p. 185, which includes material collected in 1631) suggests that he might have been disowned by his family. His father, however, was one of the most persistent promoters of the Newfoundland enterprise and maintained his interest in the island as late as 1631.

GILLIAN T. CELL

There is a large collection of papers relating to the Willoughby family at Nottingham University in the Middleton MSS; those particularly relevant are: Middleton MSS, 1/38/26, Mi X 1/1–66, Mi LM 27.

Other sources on the family: Cassandra Brydges, *The continuation of the history of the Willoughby family*, ed. A. C. Wood (Nottingham, 1958). Hist. MSS Com., 69, *Middleton MSS*. *Visitations of the county of Nottingham in the years 1569 and 1614*, ed. G. W. Marshall (Harleian Soc., IV, 1871), 185. *See also*: Prowse, *History of Nfld*. Rogers, *Newfoundland*.

WINNE. *See* WYNNE

WYET (Wyeth or **Wyatt), SYLVESTER,** English sailing-master and fisherman who visited Anticosti; fl. 1594.

Nothing is known of Wyet except in connection with the voyage of the *Grace* of Bristol (35 tons), belonging to Rice Jones, of which he was master in a voyage to the Gulf of St. Lawrence in 1594. The English interest in St. Lawrence voyages goes back to 1591 [*see* FISHER and LA COURT de Pré-Ravillon], but this is the first known English voyage to the western coast of Newfoundland and to Anticosti.

The bark left Bristol on 4 April 1594, and after sighting "Cape d'Espere" (Cape Spear), Newfoundland, on 19 May worked her way south and then west to the Bay of Placentia where codfishing was in the hands of Basque (French and Spanish) fishermen. Wyet saw only two ships of "Sibiburo" (Ciboure) before he rounded Cape de Rey and located the wrecks of two Basque ships which, according to survivors who reached Saint-Jean-de-Luz, had gone ashore in 1593 with a valuable cargo. On the southern side of St. George's Bay he found the ships, much battered, but got from them 700 to 800 whale-fins (that is whalebone) and some other gear, but no whale oil. Going round to Cape St. George and "being informed" (i.e., having Basque information) that wounded whales were cast ashore on the island of Assumption or Natiscotec (Montagnais: *Natiskotek*, our Anticosti)—which was, he knew, "in the very mouth of the great river that runneth up to Canada"—he took the *Grace* across the Gulf of St. Lawrence to the eastern end of the island. He worked round to the northern shore of the island and then back to the southern, seeing a little of the vegetation but finding no stranded whales. That being so, Wyet retreated again to the southern shores of Newfoundland, this time sighting Cape Breton to starboard on his way, and entered the Bay of Placentia where there were no less than 60 Basque vessels, only eight of them Spanish, engaged in fishing. They proved most co-operative, giving the English two pinnaces so as to enable them to complete a lading. Retiring to "Pesmarck" (either the Horse Chops in Fortune Bay or "Pesmarq," in the vicinity of Oderin in Placentia Bay), they made good progress until the Beothuk Indians set their boats adrift. Though they recovered the boats, they thought it wiser to move, and worked round to "Farrillon" (Ferryland), where there were 20 English fishing vessels. They filled their ship with fish and set off for home on 24 August, and re-entered the Hungroad, near Bristol, on 24 September.

It is clear from the narrative that Wyet is keeping back his evidence of how the ship was able to find her way so easily and to deal so expertly with the Basques. The reason was that she almost certainly had on board an expert Basque pilot called Stevan de Bocall. In an unaddressed and unsigned letter of 6 March 1595, information is given, probably to Lord Burghley, that a Basque pilot, then in Saint-Jean-de-Luz, called Stevan de Bocall, is anxious to re-enter the English service. He has an expert knowledge of the fisheries and fur trade of Canada and has dealt with the Indians. He has, moreover, already spent two seasons at Bristol and has taken out expeditions but, as the letter says, "he could not have that as he would for the victualling, and when he came thither his men would do nothing, and in a bark of 35 tons." The bark is almost certainly to be identified with the *Grace*, so that he is clearly the source of the information about the Basque wrecks and about the whales stranded on Anticosti, and also the cause of Basque friendliness at Placentia Bay. What the men would not do is less clear: perhaps Wyet would not take the risk of hunting whale the Basque way. If the reference to a 1593 pilotage does not refer to the *Grace*, and we have no record of her being in the gulf earlier, then Bocall may have piloted George Drake in his voyage of that year to the Magdalens [*see* FISHER].

Wyet's journal, printed by Hakluyt in 1600, is a good one, valuable for its clear account of the ship's progress, for place-names, for brief descriptions of natural resources at the places visited, and, above all, for a detailed and perceptive description of a Beothuk settlement on St. George's Bay, deserted though it was when they found it. He is the first known Englishman to have described the western coast of Newfoundland and Anticosti Island.

DAVID B. QUINN

PRO, S.P. 94/5, ff.9–10v. Hakluyt, *Principal navigations* (1903–5) VIII, 162–65. W. P. Anderson, "Place names on Anticosti Island," Geog. Bd. Can. *17th Report*, pt. III (1922), 53–65; "Nomenclature géographique de l'Ile Anticosti," *BSGQ*, XVIII (1924), 297–300; XIX (1925), 47–50, 95–99, 174–78. Biggar, *Early trading companies*.

WYNNE (Winne), EDWARD, captain, colonizer, first governor of the Newfoundland colony of Sir George CALVERT (Lord Baltimore); fl. 1621–26.

Wynne was a Welshman and may possibly have been introduced to Calvert by Sir William VAUGHAN from whom Calvert received his first grant of land in 1620.

In August 1621 Wynne established a colony of 12 men at Ferryland and later that month sent Calvert an extremely favourable report of the country. During the first year the settlers, helped by mild weather, worked with great industry in building, fortifying their habitation, and clearing land. In 1622 a new group of colonists arrived led by Capt. Daniel Powell; 32 people spent that winter in Newfoundland including 7 women. Wynne and other settlers continued to send home glowing, and probably over-optimistic, reports of their achievements. Thus encouraged, Calvert had his grant confirmed and enlarged by royal charter which, in 1623, created the province of Avalon.

Wynne remained governor until 1625 in which year Calvert intended but failed to visit the colony. There appears to be no foundation for the charge that Wynne cheated his employer (Prowse, *History of Nfld.*, 119) but it is probable that, like many of the inexperienced governors who were sent out at this time, he proved incapable of coping with the difficult conditions. By 1626 Wynne had been replaced as governor by Sir Arthur Aston, Calvert having realized that Wynne's claims were exaggerated and that the colony was in danger of failure. Calvert later found it necessary to supervise the venture personally.

GILLIAN T. CELL

Wynne later wrote a tract, dedicated to Charles I, advocating the exploitation of Newfoundland, entitled "The British India," BM, Royal MS 17 A LVII. His letters to Calvert are published in Edward Winne, *A letter to Sir George Calvert* ([London?], 1621) and in Richard Whitbourne, *A discourse and discovery of New-found-land: as also an invitation . . .* (London, 1622, another ed., 1623). Hist. MSS Comm., 23, *Cowper* (*Coke MSS*), I. PRO, *CSP, Col.*, *1574–1660*. William Vaughan [Orpheus Junior], *The golden fleece* (London, 1626). Prowse, *History of Nfld.*

Y

YONG (Yonge), THOMAS. *See* YOUNG

YONGE, JAMES. *See* YOUNG

YOUNG (Yonge), JAMES, of Wapping (London), captain with the HBC; fl. 1688–93.

"A stout and coragious man," he entered the service of the Company at a critical period. In 1688 only two forts—York and New Severn—remained in its possession. Three others had been captured by Pierre de TROYES in 1686. As captain of the *Dering* [I] Young was instructed to leave eight or ten hands at Churchill River to establish a settlement and then to winter at York 150 miles to the south. It was the following year (1689) before a house was built at Churchill, only to be burned and abandoned within a few months. Young's complement of men included a harpooner, Edward Mills, so that the whale fishery could be profitably developed. Although Mills had been "bread in the Greeneland whalefishing trade," he met stiff competition from the inexperienced Capt. Young who took just as many whales.

Young arrived back in England in 1689 bringing the disheartening news of Capt. MARSH's failure to resettle Albany. He sailed the *Dering* [II] frigate out in 1690 under an Admiralty pass, for Anglo-French rivalry had erupted into open war by then. The seas were full of French privateers, and possibly the prospect of continued danger prompted Young to seek release when his contract expired in 1691. However, he took out the *Loyalty* that season and in 1693 filled in at the last moment for Capt. John Simpson who had proven unsatisfactory.

MAUD M. HUTCHESON

HBRS, XX (Rich and Johnson); XXI (Rich).

YOUNG (Yong, Yonge), THOMAS, captain, reputed to have journeyed up the Kennebec River to the St. Lawrence; fl. 1634–40?

Thomas Young was granted a pass in April 1634 by Charles I, stating that he was employed "upon special and weighty affairs concerning our private service" for discovery in America. He arrived in Virginia about July 1634 in two ships with a surgeon and cosmographer aboard and with his nephew, Robert Evelin, a cousin of the diarist, as his lieutenant. Young apparently spent 18 months searching for a navigable passage from the Atlantic Ocean to the "South Sea." Confident of success, he petitioned on 22 May 1636 on behalf of himself and his associates for control over "any inland countries and rivers" bordering the strait which they hoped to discover.

According to a manuscript written about 1660, Capt. Young and three men went up the "Kenebeth" River in 1636 and "came into Canada River very neare Kebeck Fort." Young was sent to France and his company returned safely to New England. This expedition has been identified with that reported in Father PAUL LE JEUNE's *Relation* of 1640, when an Englishman who had departed from the lake or river Quinibequi [*sic*] in Acadia was discovered near Quebec and eventually sent to England by way of France. According to Le Jeune, the Englishman related some wonderful things about New Mexico. "I have learned that one can sail to that country through seas that are North of it. For two years I have ranged the whole Southern coast, from Virginia to Quinebiqui, seeking to find some great river or great lake that might lead me to peoples who had some knowledge of this sea which is to the North of Mexico. Not having found any, I came to this country to enter the Saguené, and penetrate, if I could, with the savages of the country, to the North sea."

THOMAS DUNBABIN

BM, Egerton MS 2395, ff.397–411 (printed in Mass. Hist. Soc. *Proc.*, 2d ser., I, 231–32). *JR*, XVIII, 236–237. PRO, *CSP, Col., 1574–1660*; *CSP, Dom., 1635–36*. Nute, *Caesars of the wilderness*, 89–90, 284. On the family *see: The Genesis of the United States*, ed. Alexander Brown (2v., Boston and New York, 1897), II, 887.

YROQUET. *See* IROQUET

Appendix

Persons whose identity is uncertain or who may never have come to what is now Canada

BRENDAN (Bréanainn), SAINT, Irish abbot and missionary, traditionally connected with voyages westward towards North America and possibly even to present-day Canada; b. *c.* 484; d. *c.* 578.

It is believed that he was born near Tralee, County Kerry, Ireland, the son of Christian parents. He was ordained at the age of 26 and later founded the important monastery at Clonfert, County Galway, of which he was abbot. Mt. Brandon, on Dingle peninsula, is named after the saint, and to the west of it is the supposed location of "St. Brendan's Isle."

St. Brendan is reputed to have visited such places as the Faeroe Islands, Iceland, Jan Mayen Island, the Antilles, the Azores, the Canaries, and even Greenland and the mainland of America. Although the Irish had reached and even established a religious community in Iceland before A.D. 800, there is nothing to connect Brendan with this venture. Nor is there any reliable evidence to show that either Brendan or any of his countrymen had ever reached Greenland or America. Very early a *Vita Sancti Brendani* was written and then later a *Navigatio* which incorporated parts of the *Vita* and the date of which is disputed (Selmer dates the earliest manuscript at the turn of the 10th to the 11th century). This *Navigatio* relates the voyage or voyages of the saint in search of the *paradisum terrestre* (*tir tairgirne*) or Promised Land of the saints. It was circulated in numerous manuscripts and translated into many languages.

It is a much more reasonable argument that, where the *Navigatio Sancti Brendani* contains what might be construed as information about the seas or lands west of Iceland, this was derived from accounts of the voyages of the Norsemen in the north Atlantic (or, in cases where Iceland seems to be indicated, from the Irish monks who fled Iceland at the approach of the Norsemen in 870) transmitted by the numerous Scandinavians who visited or settled in Ireland in the years 800–1200.

A close scrutiny of the relevant Icelandic sagas (*Saga of Eric the Red*, (chap. 12); *Eyrbyggja saga* (chap. 64); and the *Landnámabok* (chap. 171)) can lead only to the conclusion that they are inapplicable to any "White Men's Land" in America, and indeed no land is to be found in six days' sailing west of Ireland. St. Brendan or others like him may have crossed the Atlantic but there is no real evidence for this view. If they did, they left not even transient memorials, such as one would expect to find described in the Icelandic sagas. Therefore we may assume that the Norsemen did not come into contact with a flourishing Irish colony on the east coast of Canada or of the United States of America.

T. J. OLESON

Navigatio Sancti Brendani abbatis, ed. Carl Selmer (Notre Dame, Ind., 1959) contains a full bibliography and account of the MSS material. Geoffrey Ashe, *Land to the west* (London, 1962). Eugène Beauvois, *La découverte du Nouveau Monde par les Irlandais, et les premières traces du christianisme en Amérique avant l'an 1000* (Congrès international des Américanistes, Nancy, 1875). R.-Y. Creston, *Journal de bord de Saint-Brendan* (Paris, 1957). Jón Dúason, *Landkönnun og Landnám Íslendinga i Vesturheimi* (Reykjavík, 1941–47), 292–97, 665–70. Hennig, *Terrae incognitae.* Lanctot, *Histoire du Canada,* I, 45–59, 62. G. A. Little, *St. Brendan the navigator* (Dublin, 1945). Fridtjof Nansen, *In northern mists: arctic exploration in early times* (2v., London, 1911), II, 42–56. Denis O'Donoghue, *Brendaniana: St. Brendan the voyager* (Dublin, 1893). Oleson, *Early voyages,* 100, 125. E. G. R. Waters, *The Anglo-Norman voyage of St. Brendan* (Oxford, 1928).

EIRIKR (Eric) *upsi* **GNUPSSON,** bishop; fl. 1121.

Almost nothing is known of this man. Icelandic annals *s.a.* 1113 record "Voyage of Bishop Eric" and *s.a.* 1121 "Bishop Eric from Greenland went to look for Vinland." Claus C. Lyschander (1558–1624), not a very trustworthy source, says that he went to Vinland and there planted both the faith and a colony which still exist. Beyond this nothing is known of Bishop Eric except his genealogy and Lyschander says that he was buried at Gardar in Greenland in 1146. This paucity of information has, however, not prevented much writing and speculation: that Eric was bishop of Greenland and Vinland; that knowledge of the location of Vinland had been lost and Eric went to find it; that Vinland was an old colony and Eric was making a visitation to part of his diocese; that he was seeking to convert pagans to Christianity or regain apostates for the faith; that

Eirikr Thorvaldsson

vestiges of the Christian faith supposedly found in the 16th century among the Indians of Quebec and the Atlantic Provinces stem from Eric's work. Yet all that is known is that Eric went in search of Vinland, wheresoever it may have been.

T. J. OLESON

Hennig, *Terrae incognitae*, III, *passim*. C. C. Lyschander, *Dend Grønlanske chronica* (København, 1726). Oleson, *Early voyages*, 100. P. de Roo, *History of America before Columbus according to documents and approved authors* (2v., London, 1900).

EIRIKR THORVALDSSON (Eric the Red), first European to explore and settle Greenland; fl. 985.

His father Thorvaldr Asvaldsson was exiled from Norway and settled in Iceland where Eric was born. In 982 Eric was sentenced to three years outlawry for manslaughter. He determined to go in search of a land in the west, sighted many years before by Gunnbjörn Ulfsson and known as the Skerries of Gunnbjörn (likely the mountains on the east coast of Greenland). He sailed to Greenland and spent his three years of outlawry exploring the west coast. In 985 he returned to Iceland, organized a colonization company and led that year or the next a flotilla of 25 ships (14 of which reached their goal) to Greenland. These people formed the nucleus of the two Icelandic colonies, the Western and Eastern Settlements on the west coast of Greenland. The Western Settlement was deserted by its inhabitants *c*. 1340 but the Eastern Settlement endured into the 16th century. From these settlements the Icelanders made voyages north to the Canadian islands of the Arctic and south to the east coasts of Canada and the United States of America. Our sources say that Eric himself intended to lead an expedition to the shores of America but was prevented by an accident as he was preparing to depart. His son was Leif the Lucky [*see* LEIFR *heppni* Eiriksson].

T. J. OLESON

[For bibliography *see* LEIFR *heppni* Eiriksson.]

FERRER MALDONADO, LORENZO, Spanish navigator and adventurer, whose circumstantial account of his participation in a successful northwest passage voyage in the winter of 1588 has found some believers; d. 1625.

Maldonado submitted his *Relacion* to Philip III in 1609, probably in an attempt to profit by Spain's growing concern with English efforts to find a northwest passage.

Maldonado describes entering the Strait of Labrador (Davis Strait) at 60°, following it northwest 280 leagues to emerge at 75°, then following a generally westward passage of 790 leagues to emerge through a strait, in about 60°, that he believed to divide Asia from America, the Strait of Anian. After exploring the coast of America to about 55°, the expedition returned through the Strait of Anian and the northwest passage to Spain. Maldonado urged in strong terms the necessity of Spain's fortifying the Strait of Anian before the English reached it, and he dwelt glowingly upon economic and other advantages to the nation of controlling this short trade route to the Far East.

Maldonado was evidently familiar with English voyages of the period, especially those of John DAVIS, and probably he knew of Michael Lok's support of Juan de FUCA, who claimed to have discovered the Strait of Anian in 1592. Despite the ingenuity and persuasiveness of his argument, he was unable to obtain official interest in his supposed discoveries or support of his plans. Because of a general resemblance of Bering Strait to Maldonado's Strait of Anian, his claim to belief has been revived occasionally.

An unknown number of manuscript copies of the *Relacion* circulated in Maldonado's day. The Duke de Almodóvar gave it first publication in 1788, but it drew no attention until 1790, when Philippe Buache de La Neuville read a paper (later published in Spanish) before the Paris Academy of Sciences. His endorsement of Maldonado's claims stirred the Spanish government in 1791 to dispatch Alejandro Malaspina from Mexico on a new but unsuccessful search of the northwest coast for a strait near 60°. In 1811, Carlo Amoretti published an Italian translation of the *Relacion* that he had found in the Ambrosian Library, Milan, of which he was librarian. In 1812, he republished the work in French and appended a *Discours* defending the authenticity of the work. In 1849 Fernandez Navarrete and in 1881 Novo y Colson published condemnatory statements, and numbered the *Relacion* with the apocryphal accounts of Juan de Fuca and Bartholomew de FONTE.

Little is known about Maldonado's life. About 1600 he evaded action in a litigation in which he was charged with preparing false documents; he probably visited Newfoundland before 1609; he claimed to have discovered a means of finding longitude at sea with a magnetized needle, a secret he offered to divulge for 5,000 ducats; he wrote a geographical work, published after his death, which makes no mention of his supposed journey through the northwest passage.

ALAN COOKE

Lorenzo Ferrer Maldonado, "Relación del descubrimiento del Estrecho de Anian . . . ," in [Almodóvar],

Madoc

Historia política de los establecimientos ultramarinos de las naciones europeas (5v., Madrid, 1784–90), IV; *Imagen del mundo, sobre la esfera, cosmografía, y geografía, teórica de planetas, y arte de nauegar* (Alcalá, 1626); *Voyage de la mer Atlantique à l'océan Pacifique* . . . , traduit d'un manuscrit espagnol et suivi d'un discours qui en démontre l'authenticité et la veracité, par Charles Amoretti . . . (Plaisance, 1812). Philippe Buache de La Neuville, "Memoria leída en la Academia de la Ciencias de París por Mr. Buache," in *Sobre los viajes apócrifos de Juan de Fuca y de Lorenzo Ferrer Maldonado* . . . , ed. Pedro de Novo y Colson (Madrid, 1881), 123–53. Dodge, *Northwest by sea*, 183–84. *Enciclopedia universal ilustrada Europeo-americana* (72v., Barcelona, 1907?–1930), XXXII. Martin Fernandez de Navarrete, *Examen histórico de los viajes y descubrimientos geográficos de Capitán Lorenzo Ferrer Maldonado, de Juan de Fuca y de Almirante Bartolomé Fonte* . . . (Madrid, 1849). H. R. Wagner, "Apocryphal voyages to the northwest coast of America," Amer. Antiquarian Soc. *Proc.*, new ser., XLI (1931), 179–234.

FONTE, BARTHOLOMEW DE, reputed to have made a voyage to the northwest coast of America in the course of which a passage from the Pacific to the Atlantic oceans was discovered; fl. 1640.

The account of this voyage, first published in the *Monthly Miscellany or Memoirs for the Curious*, April and June 1708, took the form of a letter by de Fonte in which he described himself as "then Admiral of New Spain and Peru, and now Prince of Chili." This apocryphal account is now attributed to the editor or owner of the London magazine, James Petiver. There is no reliable evidence to authenticate either the existence of de Fonte himself or of the voyage. The publication of this highly imaginative account led to a lively controversy in the mid-18th century in which Arthur Dobbs, the Irish challenger of the exclusive charter rights of the HBC and a proponent of the discovery of the northwest passage by de Fonte, was joined by Henry Ellis* and Thomas Swaine Drage* in arguing in favour of the authenticity of the account. Of even greater interest was the manner in which two prominent French geographers, Joseph-Nicolas Delisle and Phillipe Buache, attempted to interpret de Fonte's imaginary geography in maps, notably the "Carte générale des découvertes de l'Amiral de Fonte et autres navigateurs espagnols, anglois et russes, pour la recherche du Passage à la Mer du Sud" published in November 1752 (*see* J.-N. Delisle, *Nouvelles cartes des découvertes de l'Amiral de Fonte* (Paris, 1753)).

WILLARD E. IRELAND

Dodge, *Northwest by sea*, 182–84, 197. HBRS, XXI (Rich), 556–86. H. R. Wagner, "Apocryphal voyages to the northwest coast of America," Amer. Antiquarian Soc. *Proc.*, new ser., XLI (1931), 179–234. Glyndwr Williams, *The British search for the northwest passage in the eighteenth century* (Royal Commonwealth Soc. Imperial Studies, XXIV, 1962).

FUCA (sometimes called Apostolos Valerianos or Phokus Valerianatos), JUAN DE, Greek seaman and explorer; b. 1536 at Valeriano on the island of Cephalonia (Ionian Islands); d. there 1602.

Fuca, according to a statement made by him in 1596, had served the king of Spain for 40 years as a mariner and pilot in the Americas. It appears that he was in Mexico from 1588 to 1593 or 1594; and he later claimed that in 1592 he was sent by the viceroy of Mexico to sail north along the California coast in search of the "Strait of Anian" which was reputed to connect the South Seas with the northwest passage. His story was that between latitudes 47° and 48° he found a broad inlet up which he sailed as far as the "North Sea" (Arctic Ocean) before turning back. Though the strait between Vancouver Island and the mainland bears his name, his story is obviously open to serious question. It was circulated in the late 16th century by Michael Lok, an important English merchant promoter of exploration who had helped to finance FROBISHER's voyages. Lok tried unsuccessfully to get assistance from the English government to bring Fuca to England so that he could pursue his explorations under the English flag. Lok's account of his meeting with Fuca appears in Purchas, *Pilgrimes* (1905–7), XIV, and is reprinted in H. R. Wagner, "Apocryphal voyages to the Northwest coast of America," Amer. Antiquarian Soc. *Proc.* new ser., XLI (1931), 179–234.

THOMAS DUNBABIN

MADOC (Madog ab Owain Gwynedd), possibly a younger son of Owain the Great, king of Gwynedd in North Wales or perhaps a member of his bodyguard, credited in the 16th century with making the first voyage to America; fl. 1170.

Mediaeval Welsh poets told how he left his home in the midst of family dissensions and went to sea. Meredudd ap Rhys (fl. 1450–85) compared his own life with that of Madoc who "sought nor flocks nor herds save in the vasty deep," but no mediaeval claim that he found lands to the west has so far been discovered. Nonetheless, in the 16th century, discussions of the new discoveries led to popular tales that Madoc had preceded Columbus. Dr. John Dee (1527–1608) first gave this academic currency when in 1578 he claimed that about 1170 Madoc "led a Colonie and inhabited in Terra Florida" (Williamson, *Cabot voyages* (1962), 201). Sir George Peckham's tract (1583) on Sir Humphrey GILBERT (*Voyages of Gilbert* (Quinn), II, 159-60) claimed that Madoc had returned with news of his discoveries. The story of two voyages, the second establishing a colony, was fathered on Humphrey Llwyd (1527-68) by David Powel (1522?-96) whose *The Historie of Cambria* (London, 1584) became the classic source for the story. Modern scholarship attributes its elaboration to Powel's own invention, possibly aided by his association with the Rev. Richard Hakluyt, who adopted the story in the same year as Powel printed it ([Hakluyt], *Original writings* (Taylor), II, 290). Sir Thomas Herbert, in *A relation of some yeares travaile* (London, 1634), 217-24, included "A discourse and proofe that Madoc ap Owen-Gwynedd first found out that Continent now call'd America," giving details of the colony planted on "the Gulph of Mexico" to which he had brought ten shiploads of colonists and supplies on his second voyage. Welsh scholars have found no evidence that these stories are anything but inventions.

The story was of value to the Elizabethans as it gave them a polemical argument to use against Spanish claims to America, since Elizabeth I could be put forward as the heir to the Welsh princes. Alleged Christian practices in America before the Spaniards arrived, and the supposition that North-American Indians spoke Welsh, seemed to offer some support for it. The story appears in Hakluyt's *Principall navigations* (1589), *Principal navigations* (1598-1600), III, and in Purchas' *Pilgrimes* (1625); but as early as 1599, George Abbot, in *A briefe description of the whole worlde...* (London, 1599), could say, "we have no invincible certainty hereof." This book went through nine editions between 1599 and 1636. The legend, indeed, rapidly faded out of English history. It flourished in Wales where it was a badge of cultural nationalism, and got a new lease of life at the hands of Theophilus Evans, in his *Drych y Prif Oesoedd* (Shrewsbury, 1716). The investigation and demolition of the Madoc story was done by Thomas Stephens in 1858, but it was not until his *Madoc: an essay on the discovery of America by Madoc ap Owen Gwynedd in the twelfth century*, ed. Llywarch Reynolds (London and New York, 1893) appeared that almost all serious students dropped the belief that the Madoc story rested in credible mediaeval evidence.

DAVID B. QUINN

Besides the works mentioned in the text, *The dictionary of Welsh biography down to 1940*, ed. J. E. Lloyd and R. T. Jenkins (London, 1959) is useful. Zeila Armstrong, *Who discovered America? The amazing story of Madoc* (Chattanooga, Tenn., 1950) and B. F. Bowen, *America discovered by the Welsh in 1170* (Philadelphia, 1876) are examples of continued belief in the legend. Geoffrey Ashe, *Land to the west* (London, 1962), maintains an entertaining scepticism. David Williams, *Cymru ac America: Wales and America* (Cardiff, 1946), is hostile.

NICHOLAS OF LYNNE, Franciscan friar, mathematician, and astronomer at Oxford; fl. 1360.

He is believed by many to have written the *Inventio fortunata*—a description of the arctic regions—no longer extant. The earliest mention of this work is on the map of Johannes Ruysch in the Rome Ptolemy of 1508, where it is said to describe a high magnetic rock under the Arctic Pole (a mountain in the vicinity of Thule in Greenland well known to the mediaeval Icelanders, who had by the 14th century noticed the deviation of the compass). Mercator on his 1569 world map (Ganong, "Crucial maps," I, 104) says that in 1364 a certain priest at the court of Norway told James Cnoyen of Bois-le-Duc, whose dates are unknown and whose works are lost, that in the year 1360 a certain English friar, a Franciscan and a mathematician of Oxford, came into the northern island. He then left, and passing farther by his magical arts described all those places he saw and took the height of them with his astrolabe. Hakluyt says the friar wrote the *Inventio fortunata* after a voyage he made in 1360. Travelling in company with others to the most northern island of the world he there left his fellows and travelled alone. The record of his travels, the *Inventio* "qui liber incipit a gradu 54. usque ad polum," he presented to King Edward III of England. This same friar "for sundry purposes after that did five times pass from England thither, and home again." Similar accounts are found in the writings of John Dee (who, however, believed the friar to have been the minorite, Hugo of Ireland, a traveller who flourished and wrote c. 1360) and of Peter Heylyn. None of these writers identifies the friar as Nicholas of Lynne, but most subsequent historians have made this identification. It is only in recent years, however, that Nicholas of Lynne has acquired a considerable reputation as an early English explorer of the Arctic, in spite of the absurdity of the statements that he travelled alone to the Pole and later made five further arctic expeditions. Thomas Blundeville seems to have come nearer to the truth when he wrote in 1589 that he did not believe that the friar had made a voyage to the Arctic "unlesse he had some colde Devill out of the middle Region of the aire to be his guide."

The *Inventio fortunata* was, however, as far as can be judged a trustworthy description of Greenland and the Canadian archipelago, as far as this had been traversed by the mediaeval Icelanders of Greenland. Moreover, this book had a large circulation in Europe and may have been used by Columbus. Its author, whether Nicholas of Lynne or not, almost unquestionably received his information, not first hand by travelling through the Arctic, but from the priest Ivar Bárdarson, who from *c*. 1340 to *c*. 1360 was administrator of the see of Gardar in Greenland and as such travelled widely and acquired directly or indirectly much information about the eastern Canadian Arctic. He wrote a description of Greenland which attained a wide circulation: it was translated for the use of HENRY HUDSON who carried a copy with him on at least some of his voyages. Ivar Bardarson was back in Norway, possibly by 1361 and certainly by 1364, and there the Oxford friar may have met him personally and compiled the *Inventio fortunata*. In any case the excerpts from the *Inventio* found in later works point conclusively to an Icelandic-Greenlandic source.

T. J. OLESON

Thomas Blundeville, "A briefe description of universall mapes and cardes ...," *M. Blundeville his exercises* ... (London, 1622), 747–99. Hakluyt, *Principal navigations* (1903–5), I, 303; X, 301ff. Peter Heylyn, *Cosmographie* (London, 1657). Johannes Ruysch map, "Universalior cogniti orbis tabula ex recentibus confecta observationibus," in Claudius Ptolemy, *In hoc opere haec continentur Geographiae* ... (Rome, 1508). B. F. DeCosta, *Inventio fortunata: arctic exploration with an account of Nicholas of Lynn* ... (New York, 1881); *Sailing directions of Henry Hudson from the old Danish of Ivar Bardsen* (Albany, 1869). H. R. Holand, "An English scientist in America 130 years before Columbus," Wisconsin Academy of Science and Letters *Trans.*, XLVIII (1959). N. A. E. Nordenskiöld, *Facsimile atlas to the early history of cartography, with reproductions of the most important maps printed in the XV and XVI centuries* ... (Stockholm, 1889). Oleson, *Early voyages*, 105–8. E. G. R. Taylor, "A letter dated 1577 from Mercator to John Dee," *Imago Mundi*, XIII (1956), 56–58.

SCOLVUS, JOHN, navigator and pilot who may have visited Labrador in 1476; fl. *c*. 1470–80.

His Christian name is often spelled Jean or Johannes; his surname spelled Scolnus, Scoluus, Scolus, Szkolny, Kolno, Skolvsson. Other variations are known. His nationality is disputed, but probably he was Danish or Norwegian; the suggestion of his being Polish is perhaps based on a corruption of *pilatus* to *polonus*. Nothing is known of his personal life.

Scolvus's place in history depends chiefly upon an inscription that Gemma Frisius placed on his globe of about 1536 within the Arctic Circle, north of a strait dividing "Terra Corterealis" and "Baccalearum Regio" from a westward projection of "Groélãdia." The inscription says, "Quij, the people to whom John Scolvus, a Dane, penetrated about the year 1476 (Quij populi ad quos Ioés Scoluus danus peruenit circa annum 1476)," (Bjørnbo, "Cartographia Groenlandica," Tavle IV, 250 ff.). A document prepared about 1575 in connection with FROBISHER's first voyage includes a similar statement: "In the north side of this passage [Streicte of the three Bretheren], John Scolus, a pilot of Denmerke, was in anno 1476" (*Three voyages of Frobisher* (Collinson), 4). Other 16th-century references probably derive from Frisius's inscription.

No details of his voyage are known, but it seems likely that he accompanied one at least of the expeditions under Pining and Pothorst sent by Christian I of Denmark to Greenland and perhaps beyond. Frisius appears to have obtained his information about Labrador from Portuguese sources. The Danes and Portuguese were, in Christian's reign, co-operating in a search for a northwest passage.

An examination of 16th-century maps and toponymy and, in particular, of Frisius's globe, suggests the strong probability that the Labrador visited by Scolvus was, in fact, Greenland.

ALAN COOKE

"State papers previous to the first voyage," in *The three voyages of Martin Frobisher, in search of a passage to Cathaia and India by the North-West, A.D. 1576–8*, reprinted from the first edition of Hakluyt's *Voyages*, with selections from manuscript documents in the British Museum and State Paper Office ed. Richard Collinson (Hakluyt Soc., 1st ser., XXXVIII, 1867), 3–4. A. A. Bjørnbo, "Cartographia Groenlandica," *Meddelelser om Grønland, udgivne af Kimmissionen for Ledelsen af de Geologiske og Geografiske Undersøgelser i Grønland*, XLVIII (1912). L. M. Larson, "Did John Scolvus visit Labrador and Newfoundland in or about 1476?" *Scandinavian Studies and Notes*, VII (1921–23), 81–89. S. E. Morison, *Portuguese voyages to America in the fifteenth century* (Cambridge, Mass., 1940), 35–41. Fridtjof Nansen, *In northern mists: arctic explorations in early times* (2v., London, 1911), II. Oleson, *Early voyages*, 118. E. G. R. Taylor, *Tudor geography, 1485–1583* (London, 1930). Heinrich Winter, "The pseudo-Labrador and the oblique meridian," *Imago Mundi*, II (1937), 61–74.

THEVET, ANDRÉ, Franciscan friar, first French historian to describe America; b. 1502 in Angoulême; d. 1590 in Paris.

Thevet embarked for the east *c*. 1537, where he travelled for five or six years. He claimed to have

Zeno

come to America in 1550 with the pilot Guillaume Testu but this statement is now generally considered to be false. From 10 Nov. 1555 to 31 Jan. 1556 he was in Brazil as almoner to Villegaignon, vice-admiral of Brittany, who had gone there to establish a French colony. Elevated to the position of almoner to Catherine de' Medici, he later became historiographer and cosmographer to the king. A bogus scholar and a naïve compiler of facts, he recorded indiscriminately everything he read or heard, while at the same time creating the impression that he himself had actually visited the countries (including North America) which he described.

Two works of Thevet are of direct concern to Canada: his MS "Le grand insulaire et pilotage d'André Thevet . . ." (BN, MS Fr. 15452–53) and *Les singularitez de la France antarctique, autrement nommée Amérique . . .* (Paris, 1558). Although Thevet himself never came to Canada, he was able to use, to a large extent, CARTIER's *Brief récit & succincte narration . . .*, 1545. He also availed himself of the works of Jean FONTENEAU (Jean Alfonse). Nevertheless, information supplied by Thevet, often resting on no known written source, has been proved by present-day scholars to be exact. He was the first, for example, to publicize the place-names Tadoussac, Anticosti, Miramichi; and to give important details about the warfare between the Indian tribes of the St. Lawrence valley, the accuracy of which has been substantiated in CHAMPLAIN's writings. It is clear that Thevet talked with explorers; that he was host to Cartier in Saint-Malo; that he cited the latter as verbal source at various points in his writings; that he must also have questioned the Indians whom Cartier had brought back to France and perhaps fishermen who had returned from the Gulf of St. Lawrence. In the course of these investigations he accumulated data to be found in no other sources, even though these are studded with gross errors and contradictions. In a recent evaluation of Thevet's work, Bernard G. Hoffman concludes that Thevet is "an amazing source" and that "Le grand insulaire" and *Les singularitez de la France antarctique* remain of inestimable value for the ethnography of eastern Canada.

MARCEL TRUDEL

André Thevet, *Cosmographie universelle; Les singularitez de la France antarctique, autrement nommée Amérique: & de plusieurs terres & isles découvertes de nostre temps* (Paris, 1558; autre éd., Anvers, 1558; éd. Paul Gaffarel, Paris, 1878). The 1878 édition also contains a biographical note, v–xxxiii, repr. in part in *BRH*, XVIII (1912), 321–33. Biggar, *Early trading companies*, 231–42. Ganong, "Crucial maps, I", 109–29. Hoffman, *Cabot to Cartier*, 171–79.

ZENO, NICOLÒ and **ANTONIO**, two Venetian brothers, reputed to have sailed to the north Atlantic *c.* 1380, to have made voyages to several islands in the north Atlantic, and even to have reached Nova Scotia; Nicolò b. *c.* 1326, d. *c.* 1402; Antonio d. shortly after 1403.

Their supposed voyage is based on a book published by a member of the Zeno family in Venice 1558, entitled *Dello scoprimento dell' isole Frislanda, Eslanda, Engrouelanda, Estotilanda e Icaria fatto sotto il Polo artico da' due fratelli Zeni, M. Nicolò il K. e M. Antonio.* According to this account, Nicolò and Antonio sailed to the north Atlantic about 1380 and entered the service of a local potentate there named Zichmni. While in his service, and sometimes accompanied by him, they made voyages to several islands in the north Atlantic, and even reached Nova Scotia, according to various interpretations of the *Dello scoprimento.* The narrative, however, is a crude fabrication and there is no other evidence for the presence of the brothers at any time in the north Atlantic. On the contrary, historians have established the fact that Nicolò spent the greater part of his life in the public service of Venice, including the years when he is supposed to have been with Zichmni. Nor did he die while in his service, as the narrative states, for he made a will in Venice in 1400 and died about 1402. Antonio died shortly after 1403.

The importance of the Zeno fabrications lies, not in the narrative, but in the map of the north Atlantic appended to this. It was accepted as genuine for more than a hundred years after its publication in 1558 and its mythical islands and fantastic names found their way onto several maps, including Mercator's map of 1569 and that of Ortelius, 1570, and misled geographers and mariners for many decades, for example, FROBISHER who seems to have thought that the east coast of Greenland was the "Frisland" of the Zeno map. It has, however, been shown conclusively that the Zeno map was based on the 1537 map of the northern regions executed by the Swede Olaus Magnus and on the 15th-century map of the Dane, Claudius Clavus. The search for the northwest passage may have been at least in part prompted by study of the Zeno map.

The literature on the Zeni brothers is voluminous and the number of those who have accepted their story as genuine is astounding. Many have, accordingly, attempted to identify Zichmni with a historical character. The most widely accepted identification is that made by J. R. Forster in 1784 when he argued that Zichmni was actually Henry Sinclair, 1st earl of the Orkneys, who was born in 1350 and died in 1404. Even if one overlooks the absurd contents of the Zeno narrative, there is not a shred of evidence, as F. W. Lucas conclusively showed in 1898, to suggest that Henry Sinclair made any transatlantic voyages (not to mention the discovery of Nova Scotia) or that he had either Nicolò or Antonio at his court. Thus the Zeno affair remains one of the most preposterous and at the same time one of the most successful fabrications in the history of exploration.

T. J. OLESON

J. R. Forster, *History of the voyages and discoveries made in the north, translated from the German . . .* (London, 1786). F. W. Lucas, *The annals of the voyages of the brothers Nicolo and Antonio Zeno* (London, 1898). A. da Mosto, "I navigatori Nicolò e Antonio Zeno," *Ad Allesandro Luzio gli archivi di stato italiano: miscellanea di studi storici* (2v., Firenze, 1933). *Nordisk familjebok: konversationslexikon och realencyklopedi* (Stockholm, 1922). Oleson, *Early voyages*, 108–9. *The voyages of the Venetian brothers Nicolò & Antonio Zeno, to the northern seas, in the XIVth century, comprising the latest known accounts of the lost colony of Greenland and of the Northmen in America before Columbus*, tr. and ed. R. H. Major (Hakluyt Soc., 1st ser., L, 1873).

GENERAL BIBLIOGRAPHY AND
LIST OF ABBREVIATIONS

List of Abbreviations

AAM	Archives de la chancellerie de l'archevêché de Montréal
AAQ	Archives de l'archevêché de Québec
ACM	Archives de la Charente-Maritime
ACND	Archives de la congrégation de Notre-Dame, Montréal
ACSM	Archives du Collège Sainte-Marie, Montréal
AE	Archives du Ministère des Affaires étrangères, Paris
AHDM	Archives des Religieuses Hospitalières de Saint-Joseph de l'Hôtel-Dieu de Montréal
AHDQ	Archives de l'Hôtel-Dieu de Québec
AJM	Archives judiciaires de Montréal
AJQ	Archives judiciaires de Québec
AJTR	Archives judiciaires de Trois-Rivières
AN	Archives nationales, Paris
ANDQ	Archives paroissiales de Notre-Dame de Québec
APQ	Archives de la province de Québec
ASM	Archives de la Seine-Maritime, Rouen
ASQ	Archives du Séminaire de Québec
BM	British Museum
BN	Bibliothèque nationale, Paris
BRH	*Bulletin des Recherches historiques*
CCHA	Canadian Catholic Historical Association
CF	*Canada Français*
CHA	Canadian Historical Association
CHR	*Canadian Historical Review*
DAB	*Dictionary of American Biography*
DNB	*Dictionary of National Biography*
HBC	Hudson's Bay Company
HBRS	Hudson's Bay Record Society
Hist. MSS Com.	Royal Commission on Historical Manuscripts
JJ (Laverdière et Casgrain)	*Journal des Jésuites*
JR (Thwaites)	*Jesuit Relations and allied documents*
NF	*Nova Francia*
NYCD	*Documents relative to the colonial history of the State of New York*
PAC	Public Archives of Canada
PANS	Public Archives of Nova Scotia
PAO	Public Archives of Ontario
PRO	Public Record Office, London
RC	*Revue canadienne*
RHAF	*Revue d'histoire de l'Amérique française*
RSCT	*Royal Society of Canada Transactions*
RUL	*Revue de l'Université Laval*
SCHEC	Société canadienne de l'histoire de l'Église catholique
SGCF	Société généalogique canadienne-française
SGQ	Société de géographie de Québec
SHM	Société historique de Montréal
SHQ	Société historique de Québec

General Bibliography

This General Bibliography is based on the sources most frequently cited in individual bibliographies in Volume I. It should not be regarded as providing a complete list of background materials for the history of Canada up to 1700. Sections I and II however do give a reasonably full guide to the documentation for this period. Section II (primary printed sources) will be found to include also printed works of the 17th and 18th centuries which may be regarded as contemporary sources.

I: ARCHIVES AND MANUSCRIPT SOURCES

ARCHIVES DE LA CHANCELLERIE DE L'ARCHEVÊCHÉ DE MONTRÉAL. These archives contain photographs, maps, 634 registers divided into 17 series which include the correspondance of the bishops of Montreal, and some 500,000 separate items. The latter are particularly relevant to Volume I since they date from 1675. On the French régime there are documents concerning the diocese of Quebec; the parishes of Notre-Dame de Montréal, Saint-François-de-Sales and Saint-Vincent-de-Paul on Île Jésus, Saint-Joseph of Rivière-des-Prairies, of L'Assomption and of Repentigny; the priests of Saint-Sulpice; the religious of the congregation of Notre-Dame; the religious hospitallers of Saint-Joseph; and the Hurons.

ARCHIVES DE LA CHARENTE-MARITIME, La Rochelle. The classification system is the same as that for all departmental archives in France. Marcel Delafosse, *Guide des Archives de la Charente-Maritime* (La Rochelle, 1958) gives an introduction to the contents of the archives and finding aids.

For Volume I persons, the following series are most important:
B (Cours et juridictions avant 1790), Amirauté de La Rochelle (B 174–264, 5580–6094)
E (Titres de familles, Communautés, Notaires), Notaires.

ARCHIVES DE LA CONGRÉGATION DE NOTRE-DAME, Montréal. These archives are in the process of being catalogued.
The most important document cited in Volume I of the DCB/DBC is:
M^1: Ecrits autographes de sœur Marguerite Bourgeois. The original manuscript was destroyed in a fire, but the archives possess a microfilm and photostats of the copy prepared for the cause of beatification, M^1, considered an original version; a copy sent to the Archives of the Vatican, V^2; and another, slightly different copy, V^1, also in the Vatican.

ARCHIVES DE LA PROVINCE DE QUÉBEC. At the Conquest, articles 43, 44 and 45 of the capitulation of Montreal—contrary to the custom of international law at that time—permitted the administrators of New France to take back to France the documents relating to the government of the colony. Only archives having a legal value for individuals were to remain in the country and these were to suffer various misfortunes before the office of the Archives of the Province of Quebec was formed in 1920, with Pierre-Georges Roy as archivist. (See Fernand Ouellet, "L'histoire des archives du gouvernement en Nouvelle-France," *RUL*, XII (1958), 397–415.) The archives now comprise 3,300 feet of documents—official and private papers, originals and copies—the majority for the period 1663–1867.

The following series are cited in Volume I:
Collection de pièces judiciaires et notariales, 70 bundles in 122 cartons, each collection of documents numbered very irregularly from 1 to 4,324. The series covers the entire French régime and also includes many documents from the English period.
Documents divers, 2 vols. Judicial and notarial documents relating especially to the government of Trois-Rivières under the French régime.
Fois et hommages, Régime français, 1666–1764, 4 vols.
Manuscrits concernant la Nouvelle-France, 2e série, 1614–1727, 11 vols. Manuscript copies of documents in various French archives.
Ordres du roi, 1663–1745, 81 vols. Copies of

documents in AN, Col., B series. Also on microfilm.

La Prévôte dé Québec, 1666–1759, 115 vols. numbered 1 to 110.

La Prévôté de Trois-Rivières, 1646–1757, 14 vols.

Registres des Insinuations du Conseil souverain, 10 registers, dated 23 Sept. 1663 to 21 Aug. 1758.

ARCHIVES DE L'ARCHEVÊCHÉ DE QUÉBEC. Contains about 650 feet of documents, an analytical card file for all the documents prior to 1940, and a Répertoire général des Registres de l'archevêché de Québec in 6 vols., from 1659 to the present.

The principal series concerning the French régime:

Lettres des évêques de Québec

Registres d'insinuation de 1659 à 1870, 30 cahiers

Registre de l'ancien chapitre de Québec, 1684–1773

Correspondance des vicaires généraux

Copies de lettres des évêques de Québec (copies of documents in Paris and the Vatican concerning Canada and Louisiana 1659–1763), 3 cahiers

Église du Canada (copies made in Paris of the correspondence of the bishops of Quebec with the Vatican and Paris), 7 manuscript vols.

Some of the documents are inventoried in Caron, "Inventaire de documents," *APQ Rapport, 1939–40*, 157–353.

ARCHIVES DE LA SEINE-MARITIME, Rouen. The classification system is the same as that for all departmental archives in France. For lists of analytical inventories *see*: France, Direction des Archives, *État des inventaires des archives nationales, départementales, communales et hospitalières au 1er janvier 1937* (Paris, 1938), and *Supplément, 1937–54* [by Robert H. Bautier] (Paris, 1955).

Important series for Volume I persons:

A: Actes du pouvoir souverain

B: Cours et juridictions (parlements, bailliages, amirautés). Parlements de Normandie et Rouen

E: Féodalité, communes, bourgeoisie et familles

G: Clergé séculier

ARCHIVES DE L'HÔTEL-DIEU DE QUÉBEC. Not catalogued.

ARCHIVES DES RELIGIEUSES HOSPITALIÈRES DE SAINT-JOSEPH DE L'HÔTEL-DIEU DE MONTRÉAL. In the process of being catalogued.

The chief document cited in Volume I of the DCB/DBC is:

Morin, Marie, "Histoire simple et véritable de l'établissement des Religieuses hospitalières de Saint-Joseph en l'Ile de Montréal, dite à présent Ville-Marie, en Canada, de l'année 1659. . . ." The published version is entitled: *Annales de l'Hôtel-Dieu de Montréal* [*see* section II].

ARCHIVES DU COLLÈGE SAINTE-MARIE, Montréal. These archives were founded by Father Félix Martin in 1844, and in that year received a rich gift from the religious of the Hôtel-Dieu in Québec. They contain many documents on the missions in Canada of the Company of Jesus, among them 75 items (originals, facsimiles, or photostats) from the 17th century: several originals such as MS 90, Father Isaac Jogues's "Novum Belgium, ou Description de la ville de New-Netherland [New York]," (1646); MS 296, Father Jacques Marquette's journal (1674); and MS 343, Father Claude Chauchetière's "Vie de Catherine Tegakouita" (1695); attestations of miracles; concessions of land, and so on. ACSM also possess "Mémoires touchant la mort et les vertus des pères Isaac Jogues . . . ," by Father Paul Ragueneau [section II]; "Etude sur les Relations des Jésuites," by Father Félix Martin, of which there is another copy in ASQ; 28 notebooks of documentation (including ff. 4004, 4006, and 4015) used in the preparation of Rochemonteix's *Les Jésuites et la Nouvelle-France au XVIIe siècle* [*see* section IV] and *Les Jésuites et la Nouvelle-France au XVIIIe siècle* (2v., Paris, 1906); biographical sketches of Jesuit missionaries by Father Martin (ff.38, 133, 301, 402); and copies from archives in Rome, Paris, Saint-Malo, and Vannes.

ARCHIVES DU MINISTÈRE DES AFFAIRES ÉTRANGÈRES, Paris. On the holdings of the archives *see* France, Archives des Affaires étrangères, *Inventaire sommaire des archives du département des Affaires étrangères* (6v., Paris, 1883–1903). Three volumes are devoted to each of the two main divisions of the archives: Correspondance politique and Mémoires et documents. *See also*: France, Archives des Affaires étrangères, *État numérique des fonds de la correspondance politique de l'origine à 1871* (Paris, 1936); Archives publiques du Canada, Division des manuscrits, *Inventaire provisoire, Fonds de manuscrits, no 5* (Ottawa, 1955), 6–8, 27–30; and W. G. Leland *et al.*, *Guide to materials for American history in the libraries and archives of Paris, Volume II: Archives of the Ministry of Foreign Affairs* (Carnegie Institution of Washington publication 392, 1943).

Documents concerning persons and events in Volume I are found in:
Correspondance politique, Angleterre, vols. 1–211
Mémoires et documents, Amérique, 4–5, 21–24

ARCHIVES DU SÉMINAIRE DE QUÉBEC. One of the most important deposits of documents in North America. The archives date from the founding of the Séminaire in 1663, but Mgr Thomas-Étienne Hamel and Mgr Amédée Gosselin may be considered to have founded the ASQ at the end of the 19th and the beginning of the 20th century. ASQ contains 1,172 feet of documents (seminary and private papers, the oldest from 1636 and the majority from 1675 to 1950), 2,000 maps and 160 feet of engravings and photographs.

For Volume I the following have been used principally:

Album Gaspé. 1 vol.; containing 146 pages and 138 separate manuscripts (numbered 147 to 284), and Index. Manuscripts, signatures, engravings, photographs.

Carton Plante. 266 pieces. 1734–1869

Chapitre. 1 carton containing 340 pieces. 1666–1785

Documents Faribault. 1 carton containing 300 various pieces. 1626–1860

Évêques. 1 carton containing 227 pieces. 1657–1920

Fonds Verreau. Includes Fonds Viger, hence frequently called Viger-Verreau. The collections of the Abbé Hospice-Anthelme Verreau and of Jacques Viger, principally composed of about a hundred cartons, several large notebooks, and the series of Viger's manuscript volumes entitled "Ma Saberdache."

A.-E. Gosselin, "Notes pour servir à la biographie des prêtres du Séminaire de Québec," with marginal references

Lettres. Carton M, 171 pieces; N, 180 pieces; O, 157 pieces; P, 207 pieces; S, 188 pieces

Manuscrits. A series of volumes of which the following are relevant: 17, "Documents relatifs à Mgr de Laval"; 29, "Histoire du Séminaire de Québec," by J.-A. Taschereau; 43, "Étude sur les Relations des Jésuites," by Félix Martin (another copy is in ACSM); 132, 133, "Personnel militaire et civil, Alphabet Laffilard, officiers français aux colonies, 1627–1780" (typewritten copy of AN, Col., D²ᶜ, 222, "Liste alphabétique des militaires et fonctionnaires coloniaux," compiled by F.-M. Laffilard, archivist of the Marine 1740–54); 200, "Mortuologe des Freres Mineurs Recolets de la Province de St. Denys en France dans lequel le nom et les qualitez de tous ceux des trois Ordres de St. François qui sont enterrez dans leurs couvents sont écrits"; C, vol. II (1674–86) [Livres de comptes] (vol. I is no longer in existence).

Paroisse de Québec. 1 carton containing 156 pieces. 1652–1877

Paroisses diverses. 1 carton containing 101 pieces. 1672–1880

Polygraphie. 248 cartons

Registre A. Register of copies of all the title-deeds of the seminary. 1663–1754

Seigneuries. Cartons I–XI, Sault-au-Matelot; XXIV–XXVI, Beaupré; XLVI, Île-aux-Coudres; XLVII–XLVIII, Coulonge-Saint-Michel; XLIX–LXVI, Île-Jésus

Séminaire. 204 cartons.

ARCHIVES JUDICIAIRES DE MONTRÉAL.

The following *greffes* and register contain material on persons in Volume I:

Bénigne Basset Des Lauriers, 1657–99
Raphaël-Lambert Closse, 1651–56
Claude Maugue, 1677–96
Jean de Saint-Père, 1648–51
Registre des baptêmes, mariages et sépultures de la paroisse Notre-Dame de Montréal, 1690, 1694–96

ARCHIVES JUDICIAIRES DE QUÉBEC.

The following *greffes* are cited in Volume I:
Claude Auber, 1652–93
Guillaume Audouart, *dit* Saint-Germain, 1634–63
Henry Bancheron, 1646–47
Romain Becquet, 1637–82
Laurent Bermen, 1647–49
Louis Chambalon, 1692–1716
Pierre Duquet de La Chesnaye, 1663–84
Michel Fillion, 1660–88
François Genaple de Bellefonds, 1682–1702
Rolland Godet, 1652–53
Jean Guitet, 1637–38
Jean de Lespinasse, 1637
Claude Maugue, 1674–79
J.-B. Peuvret de Mesnu, 1653–59
Martial Piraube, 1639–45
Gilles Rageot, 1666–1702
Louis Rouer de Villeray, 1653–56
Paul Vachon, 1644–93

Insinuations de la prévôté de Québec. 12 registres. 1667–1759.

ARCHIVES JUDICIAIRES DE TROIS-RIVIÈRES. For an indication of the documents in these archives *see*

J.-B.-Meilleur Barthe, "Inventaire sommaire des archives conservées au palais de Justice des Trois-Rivières," APQ *Rapport, 1920–21*, 328–49.

For Volume I the following *greffes* are useful:
Séverin Ameau, 1651–90
Nicolas Gastineau, *dit* Duplessis, 1650–53
Guillaume de La Rue, 1664–76
Jacques de La Touche, 1664–68

ARCHIVES NATIONALES, Paris. The Archives nationales were founded in 1789 to accommodate the original papers of the Constituent Assembly and later of the pre-Revolutionary administrations. The basic inventories are: France, Direction des Archives, *Inventaire sommaire et tableau méthodique des fonds conservés aux Archives nationales, 1ère partie, Régime antérieur à 1789* (Paris, 1871), and *État sommaire par séries des documents conservés aux Archives nationales* (Paris, 1891). Recent guides to finding aids are: France, Direction des Archives, *État des inventaires des Archives nationales, départementales, communales et hospitalières au 1er janvier 1937* (Paris, 1938), and *Supplément, 1937–54*, [by Robert H. Bautier] (Paris, 1955). J.-E. Roy, *Rapport sur les Archives de France relatives à l'histoire du Canada* (PAC pub., 6, 1911) and H. P. Beers, *The French in North America: a bibliographical guide to French archives, reproductions, and research missions* (Baton Rouge, La., 1957) give sketches of the history and organization of the archives. For copies in the PAC of documents in the Archives nationales see Archives publiques du Canada, Division des manuscrits, *Inventaire provisoire, Fonds des manuscrits N° 3* (Ottawa, 1953).

Series of documents relevant to persons in Volume I:
E: Conseil d'État du Roi
 E1: Conseil des finances (vols. 1–1683)
F: Administration générale de la France
G: Administrations financières et spéciales
H: Administrations provinciale et locale
T: Documents placés sous séquestre lors de la Révolution ou antérieurement
V: Grande Chancellerie et conseils
 V6: Conseil privé. Décisions et arrêts
X: Parlement de Paris
 X1b: Minutes du Parlement civil
Y: Châtelet de Paris
Z: Juridictions spéciales et ordinaires
Minutier central des notaires de Paris et du Département de la Seine

AN, Archives des Colonies. These archives date from about 1669. Colbert established the distinction between papers relating to the Marine and those concerning the colonies and also laid down the major series in the Archives des Colonies. The complicated development of the archives and its close proximity to the Archives de la Marine under the department of the Marine, as well as later subdivisions of series, sometimes make it difficult to identify the documents in this depository in various 19th- and 20th-century calendars. For copies of manuscripts in the PAC in the latest classification system *see: Inventaire provisoire, Fonds des manuscrits N° 1* (Ottawa, 1952).

Series containing information on persons in Volume I:
B: Lettres envoyées. Dispatches of the king, the minister of the Marine, and the Conseil d'État to officials in New France. For the 17th century see the following calendars: Étienne Taillemite, *Inventaire analytique de la Correspondance générale avec les colonies, depart, Série B (déposée aux Archives nationales), I–, registres 1 à 37 (1654–1715)* (Paris, 1959) and PAC *Report, 1899*, Supp., 245ff.

C11A: Correspondance générale. Letters of officials in New France to the king and the minister of the Marine and some drafts of documents sent to the colony. A calendar of 17th-century documents is published in PAC *Report, 1885*, xxix ff. and in D. W. Parker, *A guide to the documents in the Manuscript Room at the Public Archives of Canada, Vol. I* (PAC pub., 10, 1914), 227ff.

C11C: Amérique du Nord. Papers concerning Newfoundland, Îles de la Madeleine, and Gaspé. Calendared in Parker, *Guide*, 246ff. PAC *Report, 1887*, cccxciv ff.

C11D: Correspondance générale, Acadie. Dispatches to the minister of the Marine from Acadia. See calendars in PAC *Report, 1887*, ccxxxix ff. and in Parker, *Guide*, 238–41.

C11G: Correspondance Raudot-Pontchartrain et correspondance générale du Domaine d'Occident et de l'Île Royale. See calendars in Parker, *Guide*, 246, and PAC *Report, 1899*, Supp., 201–44.

C13C: Louisiana

D2C: Troupes coloniales. Many volumes contain information on officers who served in Canada. Alphabet Laffilard (vol. 222) is particularly useful. For copies in the PAC see: *Inventaire provisoire, Fonds des manuscrits, N° 1* (1952), 14–15.

E: Dossiers personnels. Correspondance regarding pensions, employment, and so on.

F1A: Fonds des colonies

F3: Collection Moreau Saint-Méry. Eighteenth-

and 19th-century copies of documents in the C^11A and B series and of others that have since disappeared. Papers relating to Canada, Louisiana, Île-Royale, Saint-Pierre, and Miquelon have been copied and microfilmed by PAC. Calendared in PAC *Report, 1899*, Supp., 39–191; *Report, 1905*, I, 447–505; and Parker, *Guide*, 249–53. [Note that volumes have since been renumbered to agree with AN classification.]

G: *See* AN, Archives d'Outre-Mer

AN, Archives de la Marine. The papers relating to the Marine, now housed in the Archives nationales, have been collected in the Archives de la Marine since the formation of the Marine under Colbert. In 1882 the Archives des Colonies were separated from the Marine. For descriptions of the archives and documents *see*: Didier Neuville, *État sommaire des Archives de la Marine antérieures à la Révolution* (Paris, 1898); ——— *et al.*, *Inventaire des Archives de la Marine, série B: service général* (9v., Paris, 1885–1930); and J.-E. Roy, *Rapport sur les Archives de France*, 157 ff. For copies of manuscripts in the PAC *see*: *Inventaire provisoire, Fonds des manuscrits, N° 2* (1953).

Series pertinent for Volume I:

B²: Ordres et dépêches. The kings' and the ministers' orders to the department of the Marine, military commanders, and intendants of the Marine in French ports.

B³: Correspondance des ports du Lévant et du Ponant. Comprises 797 volumes of dispatches and letters from the officers of the Marine to the minister, from 1644 to 1789.

C: Personnel

C¹: "Revues Laffilard" and "Alphabets Laffilard," in vols. 105–7, 151, 153–55, 157, 160–61

AN, Archives d'Outre-Mer. Two series of documents only are housed in the Archives d'Outre-Mer, which survive from the Ministère de la France d'Outre-Mer (the old Ministère des Colonies), no longer in existence. This special repository is under the authority of the AN, but has a chief archivist.

Série G: Registres de l'état civil, recensements et divers documents

460–61, Recensements de Canada, 1666, 1667, 1668, 1681, 1683, 1685, and later

466, Recensements de l'Acadie, 1671, 1686, 1689, 1693, 1695, 1698, 1700, and later

467, Recensements de Plaisance et Terre-Neuve, from 1671 and 1687. See PAC, *Inventaire provisoire, Fonds de manuscrits, N° 1*, 17–18.

Dépôt des fortifications des colonies. This series contains technical reports, maps, reports on discoveries, fisheries, commerce, and military campaigns, as well as papers on the Compagnie des Indes. *See*: PAC *Report, 1905*, I, pt. III, 1–43; J.-E. Roy, *Rapport sur les archives de France*, 536 ff; and PAC, *Inventaire provisoire, Fonds de manuscrits, N° 1*, 19.

ARCHIVES PAROISSIALES DE NOTRE-DAME DE QUÉBEC.

Registre des mariages, 1621–1667 (1 registre)
Registre des baptêmes
Registre des sépultures
Registre des baptêmes de Sillery

ARCHIVO DE INDIAS, Seville. The "Council of the Indies" series contains material on early exploration.

ARCHIVO GENERAL, Simancas. There are occasional references in the "Estado" series to the early explorers.

ARCHIVUM ROMANUM SOCIETATIS IESU, Rome. Despite the destruction of a large part of these archives following the brief suppression of the order in 1773, a number of valuable documents on the history of the Company of Jesus in North America have survived. These include correspondence between the general of the order and missionaries, annual letters from America, catalogues and death notices which provide biographical information. Unfortunately the archives are not open to researchers. However the American Jesuits and the Congregation have published certain of their more important manuscripts. The Institutum Historicum Societatis Jesu in Rome, has published the series "Monumenta Historica Missionum Societatis Jesu."

BIBLIOTHÈQUE NATIONALE, Paris. The library collection of the kings of France, from the time of François I, form the basis of the BN. In the 17th century the manuscripts and printed works were separated. From 1926 the libraries of the Arsenal, Opéra, and Conservatoire national de musique have functioned in conjunction with the Bibliothèque nationale. The main divisions at the present time are Cartes et Plans, Estampes, Imprimés, Journaux et Périodiques, Manuscrits, Médailles, and Musique. Most important for Volume I are the manuscripts, which number over 160,000. Most of the documents have been integrated with the Fonds français (Fr., nos. 1–33264) or with Nouvelles acquisitions françaises (NAF, nos. 1-   ); documents most recently integrated have double numbering. Among the collections not integrated are Baluze, Cinq-Cents and Mélanges de Colbert, and Clairambault. J.-E. Roy, *Rapport sur les archives de France relatives à l'histoire du Canada* (PAC pub., 6, 1911), 663 ff. outlines the organization of the BN and lists the 18-volume catalogue to the Fr. and NAF (1–10,000) for which there is a *Table générale alphabétique* (6v., Paris, 1931–48). Another guide is W. G. Leland, *Guide to materials for American history in the libraries and archives of Paris, Volume I: Libraries* (Carnegie Institution of Washington publication 392, 1932). See also BN, Département des manuscrits, *Catalogue des manuscrits de la collection Clairambault*, par Philippe Lauer (3v., Paris, 1923–32); *Catalogue des manuscrits de la collection des Cinq Cents de Colbert*, par Charles de La Roncière (Paris, 1908); *Catalogue des manuscrits de la collection des Mélanges de Colbert*, par Charles de La Roncière et P.-M. Bondois (2v., Paris, 1920–22); *Nouvelles acquisitions du département des manuscrits pendant les années 1898–1899, inventaire sommaire* (Paris, 1900), 49–85 ("Amérique, Canada, Nouvelle-France, Acadie, et Louisiane" [catalogue sommaire de la collection Pierre Margry], par Charles de La Roncière); Robert Latouche, "Inventaire sommaire de la collection Arnoul conservée à la Bibliothèque nationale," *Revue des bibliothèques*, XVIII (1908), 244–63.

BODLEIAN LIBRARY, Oxford University. The Malone, Rawlinson, and Tanner manuscripts contain material on Volume I persons.

BRITISH MUSEUM, London. Founded in the 1750's to house the Sloane, and other collections. For a brief guide to catalogues of the Sloane, Cotton, Egerton, Harley, King's, Lansdowne, Royal, and additional manuscripts see T. C. Skeat, "The catalogues of the British Museum, 2. Manuscripts," *Journal of Documentation*, VII (1951), 18–60; revised as *British Museum: the catalogues of the manuscript collections* (London, 1962). For copies of documents in the PAC see Manuscript Division, *Preliminary inventory, Manuscript Group 21, transcripts from papers in the British Museum* (Ottawa, 1955).

FRANKLIN DELANO ROOSEVELT LIBRARY, Hyde Park, N.Y. Contains the originals of the Livingstone Indian records.

HUDSON'S BAY COMPANY ARCHIVES, London. The HBC archives comprise over thirty thousand volumes and files of records dating from the founding of the Company in 1670. The archives as presently constituted were established in 1932. The work of organization proceeded thereafter, a publishing programme was undertaken by the Hudson's Bay Record Society [*see* section II], and in 1949 the HBC and the PAC arranged jointly to microfilm the records. On the organization of the archives *see* R. H. Leveson Gower, "The Archives of the Hudson's Bay Company," *Beaver*, outfit 264, no. 3 (December, 1933), 40–42, 64, and for copies in North America of documents *see* H. P. Beers, *The French & British in the old Northwest: a bibliographical guide to archive and manuscript sources* (Detroit, 1964), 187–88.

Documents on persons and events in Volume I are found in:

Section A: London Office records
    A.1/: Minute books of the Governor and Committee
    A.6/: London outward correspondence books—HBC official
    A.9/: Memorial books
    A.14/: Grand ledgers (London)
    A.15/: Grand journals (London)
    A.37/: Charters, deeds, agreements and byelaws

MASSACHUSETTS HISTORICAL SOCIETY, Boston, Mass. Founded in 1791, it is the oldest historical society in the United States. About half the holdings of the Society are manuscripts and transcriptions. *See* Stephen T. Riley, *The Massachusetts Historical Society 1791–1959* (Boston, 1959) and "The manuscript collections of the Massachusetts Historical Society: a brief listing," M. H. S. *Miscellany*, no. 5 (December 1958).

Of interest for 17th century Canadian history are the Parkman transcripts from European archives (1565–1768), 100 volumes; the F. L. Gay transcripts from English archives (1630–1776), 124 volumes; and the Annie H. Thwing typescript, in 22 vols., *Suffolk deeds, 1630–1800, compiled by streets* (1916) and card index, from Boston records.

MASSACHUSETTS, SECRETARY OF THE COMMONWEALTH'S OFFICE, ARCHIVES, Boston, Mass. These archives contain primarily the records of the General Court of Massachusetts from the 17th century until the present day.

The following series of documents are of interest for 17th-century Canadian history:
"Massachusetts Archives." This is the title usually given to the 326 volumes of legislative records rearranged in the 19th century by J. B. Felt and his successor according to subject. Excellent name card-indexes have been prepared for about 55 volumes on such subjects as colonial affairs

(including letters received and sent to other North American and West Indian colonies), commerce, depositions, foreign affairs, judicial and pecuniary matters, and military records.

Executive records of the Council (called Council Records), about 150 volumes. For the 17th century, the records cover 1650–56, 1686–87, and 1692 on.

Legislative records of the Council (called Court Records), 73 vols. Those for 1630 to 1686 were printed under the title *Records of the governor and company of the Massachusetts Bay* [see section II].

J. B. Poore's transcripts from French archives, from the discovery of America to 1780, 10 vols. Copies of these copies were published 40 years later by the Quebec legislature as *Coll. de manuscrits relatifs à la Nouv.-France* [see section II; see also H. P. Beers, *The French in North America: a bibliographical guide to French archives, reproductions, and research missions* (Baton Rouge, La., 1957), 153–56].

For copies of documents in the PAC see: *Preliminary inventory, Manuscript Group 18, pre-Conquest papers* (Ottawa, 1964).

NEW ENGLAND HISTORIC GENEALOGICAL SOCIETY, Boston, Mass. The society specializes in family history and genealogy and its collections are on the national scale. It also has one of the largest collections on this continent of copies of English parish records.

NEW YORK STATE, ARCHIVES, Albany, N.Y. On the development and present organization of these various archives see E. F. Rowse, "The archives of New York," *American Archivist*, IV (1941), 267–74, and Historical Records Survey, *Guide to depositories of manuscript collections in the United States* (Columbus, 1938), 76–77. On *NYCD* see H. P. Beers, *The French in North America: a bibliographical guide to French archives, reproductions, and research missions* (Baton Rouge, 1957), 145–53.

NOTTINGHAM UNIVERSITY LIBRARY, Nottingham, England. The Middleton Manuscripts are important for the early history of Newfoundland.

PUBLIC ARCHIVES OF CANADA, Ottawa. In 1873 the government of Canada commissioned the Abbé H.-A. Verreau to investigate the holdings of English and French archives with a view to copying documents concerning the early history of Canada. The work of transcribing and microfilming such manuscripts has proceeded since that time. Many unpublished finding aids are available only in the archives, but the Manuscript Division has published the following *Preliminary Inventories* and *Inventories*: *Fonds des Manuscrits N° 1, Archives des Colonies* (1952); *Fonds des Manuscrits N° 2, Archives de la Marine, N° 3, Archives nationales, N° 4, Archives de la Guerre* (1953); *Fonds des Manuscrits N° 5, Ministère des Affaires étrangères* (1955); *Manuscript Group 8, Quebec provincial and local records; Manuscript Group 9, Provincial, local and territorial records* (1961); *Manuscript Group 11, Public Record Office, London, Colonial Office papers* (1961); *Manuscript Group 18, Pre-Conquest papers* (1964); *Manuscript Group 21, transcripts from papers in the British Museum* (1955). See also "Guides to calendars of series and collections in the Public Archives," *PAC Report, 1949*, 451–59; H. P. Beers, *The French & British in the old Northwest: a bibliographical guide to archive and manuscript sources* (Detroit, 1964) and *The French in North America: a bibliographical guide to French archives, reproductions, and research missions* (Baton Rouge, 1957).

PUBLIC ARCHIVES OF NOVA SCOTIA, Halifax. These archives contain bound volumes of transcripts of documents from European archives relating to the earliest history of Acadia or Nova Scotia. See: *Catalogue or list of manuscript documents, arranged, bound and catalogued under the direction of the commissioner of public records . . .* (Halifax, 1877; 2d ed., 1886) and J. P. Edwards, *The public records of Nova Scotia* (Halifax, 1920).

PUBLIC RECORD OFFICE, London. For an introduction to the contents and arrangement of these archives see: *Guide to the contents of the Public Record Office* (2v., London, 1963).

The documentary series cited in Volume I include:

Admiralty
    Adm. 6: Admiralty and secretariat, registers, returns and certificates, various (1673–1859).
    Adm. 8: *Ibid.*, list books (1673–1893).
    Adm. 51: Admiralty and secretariat, log books, etc., captains' logs (1669–1852).

Records of the Chancery
    C. 2: Chancery files or brevia regia, judicial proceedings (equity side), proceedings, Chancery proceedings, series I, Elizabeth I to Charles I.
    C. 142: Chancery files or brevia regia, inquisitions, inquisitions post mortem, series II, Henry VII to Charles II.

Colonial Office (*see* R. B. Pugh, *The records of the Colonial and Dominion offices* (PRO Handbooks, III, 1964))
  C.O. 1: General series (1574–1757). Includes papers relating to America and the West Indies, preponderantly before 1688, from which date most of these papers are in C.O. 5.
  C.O. 5: America and West Indies, original correspondence ([1606] to 1807). Comprises the original correspondence and entry books of the Board of Trade and the secretary of state and other papers.

Records of the Exchequer, the King's Remembrancer
  E. 101: Accounts, various, Henry II to George III.
  E. 146: Deeds, forest proceedings, Henry III to 1653.
  E. 159: Inquisitions post mortem, memoranda rolls, 2 Henry III to 1926.

Records of the High Court of Admiralty
  H.C.A. 1: Criminal, oyer and terminer records (1535–1834).
  H.C.A. 13: Instance and prize courts, court minute books (prize), examinations, etc. (1536–1826).
  H.C.A. 14: *Ibid.*, exemplifications (1531–1768).
  H.C.A. 24: *Ibid.*, instance papers, libels, etc. (1519–1814).

Privy Council Office
  P.C. 2: Registers (1540–1920).

Privy Seal Office
  P.S.O. 2: Warrants for the Privy Seal, series II, Henry VII to Charles II.
  P.S.O. 3: *Ibid.*, series III, 1766 to 1851.

State Paper Office, State papers domestic and foreign
  S.P. 12: Domestic, Elizabeth I (1558–1603).
  S.P. 16: Domestic, Charles I (1625–49).
  S.P. 25: Domestic, Interregnum, Council of State, etc. (1649–60).
  S.P. 29: Domestic, Charles II (1660–85).
  S.P. 63: Ireland, Elizabeth I to George III (1558–1782).
  S.P. 78: Foreign, France (1577–1780).
  S.P. 94: Foreign, Spain (1577–1780).

ROYAL COMMISSION ON HISTORICAL MANUSCRIPTS, London. The commission was instituted in the reign of Queen Victoria to inspect and report on collections of manuscripts and records belonging to private families or institutions, other than those of the central government, to publish reports, and to record particulars in the National Register of Archives. For details of publications *see*: *Publications of the Royal Commission on Historical manuscripts: sectional list no. 17* (London, 1962); annual *Lists of accessions*; and *Bulletins* of the National Register of Archives.

SOMERSET HOUSE, London. This is the repository for registers of births, marriages, burials, wills, etc., including church records transferred there after 1857. The Prerogative Court of Canterbury (P.C.C.), with York, had jurisdiction to grant probate or administration when the diocesan court could not entertain the case because the deceased died possessed of goods above the value of £5 in each of two or more dioceses. This jurisdiction was transferred in 1857 to the High Court of Justice, Probate, Divorce and Admiralty division.

SUFFOLK COUNTY COURT HOUSE, Boston, Mass. Two groups of records are of interest for Volume I, the registry of probate and the registry of deeds. Although the probate records are not in print, there is an index: *Index to the Probate records of the County of Suffolk, Massachusetts, 1636 to 1893* (3v., Boston, 1895). Records of deeds from 1629 to 1697 only were published as *Suffolk deeds* [*see* section II].

II. PRINTED PRIMARY SOURCES

Acadiensia Nova (1598–1779): new and unpublished documents and other data relating to Acadia. Edited by W. I. Morse. 2 vols. London, 1935.

[ALEXANDER, SIR WILLIAM.] *The Earl of Stirling's register of royal letters, relative to the affairs of Scotland and Nova Scotia from 1615 to 1635.* Edited by Charles Rogers. 2 vols. Edinburgh, 1885.

—— *An encouragement to colonies.* London, 1624.

ARCHIVES DE LA PROVINCE DE QUÉBEC PUBLICATIONS
  APQ Rapports. Documents from the APQ—as well as from other archives—have been published in the *Rapport de l'Archiviste de la Province de Québec*. Volumes correspond to the fiscal years for 1920–21 to 1948–49 and

1959–60; those for the years 1949–51 to 1957–59 include two years; no volumes were published for 1961 or 1962, but publication was resumed in 1963.
Bulletin des Recherches historiques [*see* sect. IV].
Lettres de noblesse (P.-G. Roy).
Ord. comm. (P.-G. Roy).
Papier terrier de la Cie des I.O. (P.-G. Roy).
P.-G. Roy. *Index des jugements et délibérations du Conseil souverain de 1663 à 1716.* Québec, 1940.
—— *Inv. coll. pièces jud. et not.*
—— *Inv. concessions.*
—— *Inv. contrats de mariage.*
—— *Inventaire de pièces sur la côte de Labrador.*
—— *Inventaire des procès-verbaux des grands voyers.*
—— *Inv. ins. cons. souv.*
—— *Inv. ins. prév. Québec.*
—— *Inv. jug. et délib.*
—— *Inv. ord. int.*
—— *Inv. testaments.*
—— *et al. Inv. greffes not.*
[For complete descriptions see individual titles and P.-G. Roy, *infra*.]
BACQUEVILLE DE LA POTHERIE. See LE ROY.
BAUGY, [HENRI DE]. *Journal d'une expédition contre les Iroquois en 1687: lettres et pièces relatives au fort Saint-Louis des Illinois.* Édité par Ernest Serrigny. Paris, 1883.
Beatificationis seu declarationis martyrii servorum Dei . . . Brébeuf . . . Lalemant . . . Daniel . . . Garnier . . . Chabanel . . . Jogues . . . Goupil . . . Lalande e Societate Jesu: positio super introductione causae. Edited by A. Vico. Romae, 1916.
BELMONT, [VACHON DE]. *See* LITERARY AND HISTORICAL SOCIETY OF QUEBEC.
BERTRAND DE LATOUR, LOUIS. *Mémoires sur la vie de M. de Laval, premier évêque de Québec.* Cologne, 1761.
BEST, GEORGE. *A true discourse of the late voyages of discoverie, for the finding of a passage to Cathaya, by the northwest, under the conduct of Martin Frobisher generall.* . . . London, 1578. Reprinted in *Three voyages of Martin Frobisher* (Stefansson), I, 4ff., and in Hakluyt, *Principal navigations* (1903–5), VII.
BIGGAR, H. P. *A collection of documents relating to Jacques Cartier and the sieur de Roberval.* (Public Archives of Canada publications, XIV.) Ottawa, 1930. Contains the original French texts.
[BOUCHER, PIERRE.] *Histoire véritable et naturelle des mœurs et productions du pays de la Nouvelle-France, vulgairement dite le Canada.* Paris, 1664. (Société historique de Boucherville, I, 1964.)
[BRESSANI, F.-J.] *Relation abrégée de quelques missions des Pères de la Compagnie de Jésus dans la Nouvelle-France par le R. P. Bressany de la même compagnie.* Édité par Félix Martin. Montréal, 1852.
BRISTOL RECORD SOCIETY. Founded in 1929 "to make available something of the wealth of historical material contained in the city archives, and in the collections of lay and ecclesiastical corporations." Publications pertinent for Volume I:
II, IV, VIII, XVI, XVIII: *The great red book of Bristol.* Edited by E. W. W. Veale. 5 vols. 1931, 1933, 1938, 1951, 1953.
V: *The staple court books of Bristol.* Edited by E. E. Rich. 1934.
VII: *The overseas trade of Bristol in the later Middle Ages.* Edited by E. M. Carus-Wilson. 1937.
XVII: *Records relating to the Society of Merchant Venturers of the city of Bristol in the seventeenth century.* Edited by Patrick McGrath. 1952.
XIX: *Merchants and merchandise in seventeenth-century Bristol.* Edited by Patrick McGrath. 1955.
CANADA (NEW FRANCE, –1763). STATUTES. *Édits, ordonnances royaux, déclarations et arrêts du Conseil d'état du roi concernant le Canada: revus et corrigés d'après les pièces originales déposées aux archives provinciales.* 3 vols. Québec, 1854–56.
II: *Arrêts et règlements du Conseil supérieur de Québec, et ordonnances et jugements des intendants du Canada,* 1855.
III: *Complément des ordonnances et jugements des gouverneurs et intendants du Canada, précédé des commissions des dits gouverneurs et intendants et des différents officiers civils et de justice.* . . .
CARON, IVANHOË. "Inventaire des documents concernant l'Église du Canada," APQ *Rapport, 1939–40,* 157–353.
CARTIER, JACQUES. *Bref récit et succincte narration de la navigation faite en MDXXXV et MDXXXVI par le capitaine Jacques Cartier aux isles de Canada, Hochelaga, Saguenay et autres.* Édité par M. d'Avezac. Paris, 1863.
[——] *Brief récit & succincte narration.* . . . Paris, 1545. Reproduced by photostat in *Jacques Cartier et la "grosse maladie."* (XIXᵉ Congrès international de Physiologie publication distribuée to members.) Montréal, 1953.
[——] *Relation originale du voyage de Jacques Cartier au Canada en 1534: documents inédits sur Jacques Cartier et le Canada (nouvelle série).* Édité par H. Michelant et A. Ramé. Paris, 1867.

[———] *Voyage de Jacques Cartier au Canada en 1534. Nouvelle édition publiée d'après Ramusio par M. H. Michelant, avec deux cartes, documents inédits sur Jacques Cartier et le Canada communiqués par M. Alfred Ramé.* Paris, 1865.

[———] *Voyages de découverte au Canada, entre les années 1534 et 1542, par Jacques Quartier, le sieur de Roberval, Jean Alphonse de Xanctoigne, etc., suivis de la description de Québec et de ses environs en 1608, et de divers extraits relativement au lieu de l'hivernement de Jacques Quartier en 1535–36.* (Société littéraire et historique de Québec/Literary and Historical Society of Quebec, Historical Documents, D.3, 1st series.) Québec, 1843.

[CAVELIER, JEAN.] *The journal of Jean Cavelier: the account of a survivor of La Salle's Texas expedition, 1684–1688.* Translated and annotated by Jean Delanglez. Chicago, 1938.

CENSUSES. See RECENSEMENTS

[CHAMPLAIN, SAMUEL DE.] *Œuvres de Champlain.* Publiées par C.-H. Laverdière. 2ᵉ édition. 6 vols. en 4. Québec, 1870. Text paged continuously throughout the set.

[———] *Les voyages de la Nouvelle France occidentale, dicte Canada, faits par le Sr de Champlain . . . & toutes les descouvertes qu'il a faites en ce pais depuis l'an 1603 jusques en l'an 1629.* Paris, 1632.

[———] *Les voyages de Samuel Champlain, saintongeois, père du Canada.* Édités par Hubert Deschamps. (Colonies et empires, 2ᵉ série.) Paris, 1951.

[———] *Works.* Reprinted, translated and annotated by six Canadian scholars under the general editorship of H. P. Biggar. 6 vols. (Champlain Society publications, New Series.) Toronto, 1922–36. I: *1599–1607* (1922). II: *1608–1613* (1925). III: *1615–1618* (1929). IV: *1608–1620* (1932). V: *1620–1629* (1933). VI: *1629–1632* (1936). Includes original French text.

CHAMPLAIN SOCIETY. "Founded in 1905, with headquarters in Toronto, for the purpose of publishing rare and inaccessible materials relating to the history of Canada. Its publications are issued only to elected members, limited in number. . . ." Volumes relative to this work include:

PUBLICATIONS

I: Lescarbot, *History* (Grant), I.
II: Denys, *Description and natural history* (Ganong).
V: Le Clercq, *New relation of Gaspesia* (Ganong).
VII, IX: Lescarbot, *History* (Grant). II, III.
VIII: *Documents relating to Hudson Bay* (Tyrrell).
XX: Dièreville, *Relation of a voyage to Port-Royal* (Webster).
XXV: Sagard, *Long journey* (Wrong and Langton).

NEW SERIES

Champlain, *Works* (Biggar).
[For complete citations see individual listings.]

CHARLEVOIX [FRANÇOIS-XAVIER] DE. *Histoire et description generale de la Nouvelle France avec le journal historique d'un voyage fait par ordre du roi dans l'Amérique septentrionale.* 3 vols.; another edition 6 vols. Paris, 1744.

——— *History and general description of New France.* Translated, with notes, by J. G. Shea. 6 vols. New York, 1866–72.

[CLODORÉ, JEAN DE?] I.C.S.D.V. *Relation de ce qui s'est passé dans les Isles & Terre-Ferme de l'Amérique, pendant la dernière guerre avec l'Angleterre, & depuis en execution du Traitté de Breda. Avec un journal du dernier voyage du Sr de la Barre en la Terre-Ferme, & Isle de Cayenne, accompagné d'une exacte description du pays, mœurs & naturel des habitans. . . . Où est joint le journal d'un nouveau voyage fait en Guynée. . . .* Paris, 1671.

Collection de manuscrits contenant lettres, mémoires, et autres documents historiques relatifs à la Nouvelle-France. 4 vols. Québec, 1883–85.
[*See* Massachusetts, Secretary of the Commonwealth's Office, Archives, section I.]

"Correspondance échangée entre la cour de France et le gouverneur de Frontenac, pendant sa première administration (1672–1682)," *APQ Rapport, 1926–27,* 1–144.

"Correspondance échangée entre la cour de France et le gouverneur de Frontenac, pendant sa seconde administration (1689–1699)," *APQ Rapport, 1927–28,* 3–211; *1928–29,* 247–384.

"Correspondance échangée entre la cour de France et l'intendant Talon pendant ses deux administrations dans la Nouvelle-France," *APQ Rapport, 1930–31,* 3–182.

Danish arctic expeditions, 1605 to 1620. Edited by C. C. A. Gosch. 2 vols. (Hakluyt Society publications, 1st series, XCVI, XCVII.) London, 1897.
Book I: *The Danish expeditions to Greenland in 1605, 1606, and 1607; to which is added Captain James Hall's voyage to Greenland in 1612.*
Book II: *The expedition of Captain Jens Munk to Hudson's Bay in search of a north-west passage in 1619–20.*

Découvertes et établissements des Français dans l'ouest et dans le sud de l'Amérique septentrionale, 1614–1754: mémoires et documents inédits. Édités par Pierre Margry. 6 vols. Paris, 1879–88. Documents reproduced here should be checked against the originals.

DENYS, NICOLAS. *The description and natural history of the coasts of North America (Acadia)*. Translated and edited, with a memoir of the author, collateral documents, and a reprint of the original, by W. F. Ganong. (Champlain Society publications, II.) Toronto, 1908.

——— *Description géographique et historique des costes de l'Amérique septentrionale: avec l'histoire naturelle du païs* (Tome I). *Histoire naturelle des peuples, des animaux, des arbres, & plantes de l'Amérique septentrionale, & de ses divers climats: avec une description exacte de la pêche des molues* (Tome II). 2 vols. Paris, 1672.

DIÈREVILLE, SIEUR DE. *Relation of a voyage to Port Royal in Acadia or New France*. Edited by J. C. Webster. (Champlain Society publications, XX.) Toronto, 1933. Includes original French text.

Le discours de la navigation de Jean et Raoul Parmentier de Dieppe: voyage à Sumatra en 1529: description de l'isle de Sainct-Domingo. Édité par Christian Schefer. (Recueil de voyages, IV.) Paris, 1883.

Documentary history of the State of Maine. Edited by William Willis *et al*. 24 vols. (Maine Historical Society Collections, 2d series.) Portland, 1869–1916. Not to be confused with Maine Historical Society, *Collections and Proceedings* [*q.v.*].

Documents relating to the early history of Hudson Bay. Edited by J. B. Tyrrell. (Champlain Society publications, XVIII.) Toronto, 1931.

Documents relative to the colonial history of the State of New York, procured in Holland, England, and France. . . . Edited by E. B. O'Callaghan and Berthold Fernow. 15 vols. Albany, N.Y., 1853–87.

[DOLLIER DE CASSON, FRANÇOIS.] *Histoire du Montréal 1640–1672*. Avec apostilles par Pierre Margry et notes et appendices par J. Viger. (Société historique de Montréal, Mémoires, IV.) Montréal, 1868.

[———] *Histoire du Montréal 1640–1672*. (Literary and Historical Society of Quebec, Historical Documents, D.6, 3d series.) Québec, 1871.

[———] *A history of Montreal 1640–1672 from the French of Dollier de Casson*. Edited and translated by Ralph Flenley. Toronto, 1928.

DU CREUX, FRANÇOIS. *The history of Canada or New France*. Translated with an introduction by P. J. Robinson; edited with notes by J. B. Conacher. 2 vols. (Champlain Society publications, XXX, XXXI.) Toronto, 1951, 1952. Includes original French text.

EBURNE, RICHARD. *A plaine path-way to plantations*. [London], 1624.

——— *A plain pathway to plantations (1624)*. Edited by L. B. Wright. Ithaca, N.Y., 1962.

EDEN, RICHARD. *The first three English books on America*. [1511?]–1555 A.D. Edited by Edward Arber. Birmingham, 1885.

Édits ord. See CANADA (New France, –1763). Statutes. *Édits, ordonnances*. . .

Eyrbyggja saga . . . Eiríks saga rauða; Grænlendinga saga. . . . Edited by E. O. Sveinsson and Mattías Þórdarson (*Íslenzk fornrit*, edited by Sigurður Nordal, IV.) Reykjavík, 1935.

Factum du procez entre Messire Jean de Biencourt chevalier sieur de Poutrincourt, Baron de S. Just, appelant d'une part, et de Pierre Biard, Enemond Masse & consorts, soy disans Prestres de la Société de Jesus, intimez. Sans lieu, 1614.

FONTENEAU, JEAN [JEAN ALFONSE]. *La cosmographie avec l'espère et régime du soleil du nord par Jean Fonteneau dit Alfonse de Saintonge, capitaine-pilote de François 1ᵉʳ*. . . . Éditée par P. L. G. Musset (Recueil de voyages, XX.) Paris, 1904.

——— "Routier de Jean Alphonse." See Richard Hakluyt, *Principal navigations* (1903–5).

Les Français en Amérique pendant la première moitié du XVIᵉ siècle: textes des voyages de Gonneville, Verrazano, J. Cartier et Roberval. Édité par Ch.-A. Julien *et al*. (Colonies et empires, 2ᵉ série, I.) Paris, 1946.

The French foundations, 1680–1693. Edited by T. C. Calvin and R. C. Werner. (Illinois State Historical Library Collections, XXIII, French series, I.) Springfield, Ill., 1934.

[GENDRON, FRANÇOIS.] *Quelques particularitez du pays des Hurons en la Nouvelle France, remarquées par le Sieur Gendron, docteur en médecine, qui a demeuré dans ce pays-là fort longtemps*. Rédigées par J.-B. de Rocoles. Troyes et Paris, 1660. [Réimprimées à Albany, 1868].

GRISELLE, EUGÈNE. *La Vénérable Mère Marie de l'Incarnation, première supérieure des Ursulines de Québec: supplément à sa correspondance*. Paris, [1909?].

[GROYER, PIERRE.] *Les aventures du Rochelais Nicolas Gargot dit "Jambe-de-Bois."* Éditées par Charles Millon. La Rochelle, 1928. New edition of Gargot's *Mémoires*.

——— *Mémoires de la vie et des aventures de Nicolas Gargot, capitaine de marine*. [Paris, 1668.]

GUYART DE L'INCARNATION, MARIE. *Lettres de la révérende Mère Marie de l'Incarnation (née Marie Guyard), première supérieure du Monastère des Ursulines de Québec*. Éditées par P.-F. Richaudeau. 2 vols. Paris, Leipzig, Tournai, 1876.

——— *Lettres de la Vénérable Mère Marie de*

l'Incarnation, première supérieure des Ursulines de la Nouvelle-France, divisées en deux parties. Éditées par Dom Claude Martin. Paris, 1681.

────── *Lettres historiques de la Vénérable Mère Marie de l'Incarnation sur le Canada.* Éditées par Benjamin Sulte. Québec, 1927.

────── *Marie de l'Incarnation, Ursuline de Tours, fondatrice des Ursulines de la Nouvelle-France: Écrits spirituels et historiques: publiées par Dom Claude Martin.* . . . Éditées par Dom Albert Jamet. 4 vols. Paris, 1929–39.

HAKLUYT, RICHARD. "A particuler discourse concerning the greate necessitie and manifolde comodyties that are like to growe to this Realme of Englande by the westerne discoveries lately attempted." 1584. First published as "A discourse concerning western planting," edited by Charles Deane, in *Documentary history of Maine*, II, 1–241; also published in Hakluyt, *Original writings* (Taylor), II, 211–326, with the title "A discourse of western planting."

────── *Divers voyages touching the discoverie of America and the Ilands adjacent unto the same, made first of all by our Englishmen and afterwards by the Frenchmen and Britons.* London, 1582. Reprinted in 1850 in Hakluyt Society publications (1st series, VII), and edited by J. W. Jones.

────── *The original writings & correspondence of the two Richard Hakluyts.* Edited by E. G. R. Taylor. 2 vols. (Hakluyt Society publications, 2d series, LXXVI, LXXVII.) London, 1935.

────── *The principall navigations voiages and discoveries of the English nation, made by sea or over land to the most remote and farthest distant quarters of the earth at any time within the compasse of these 1500 yeeres: devided into three severall parts.* . . . London, 1589. Reprinted in facsimile, edited by D. B. Quinn and R. A. Skelton. 2 vols. (Hakluyt Society publications, Extra Series, [XXXIX].) Cambridge, 1965.

────── *The principal navigations, voiages, traffiques and discoveries of the English nation made by sea or over-land.* . . . 3 vols. London, 1598, 1599, 1600. [Titles of vols II and III vary slightly.]

────── *Hakluyt's collection of the early voyages, travels, and discoveries of the English nation.* [Edited by R. H. Evans.] 5 vols. London, 1809–12. Part of Vol. IV and Vol. V were issued separately under the title: *A selection of curious, rare and early voyages and histories of interesting discoveries, chiefly published by Hakluyt, or at his suggestion, but not included in his . . . compilation, to which, to Purchas, and other general collections, this is intended as a supplement.* [Edited by R. H. Evans.] London, 1812.

────── *The principal navigations voyages traffiques & discoveries of the English nation made by sea or over-land to the remote and farthest distant quarters of the earth at any time within the compasse of these 1600 yeeres.* 12 vols. (Hakluyt Society publications, Extra Series, I–XII.) Glasgow, 1903–5. The text of this edition is an exact reprint of that of 1598–1600.

The *Principal navigations* includes accounts of the voyages of the following explorers whose biographies appear in Vol. I: Nicolas of Lynne (Vol. I of the Hakluyt Society edition); Robert Thorne (II); John and Sebastian Cabot, Sir Humphrey Gilbert, Martin Frobisher, James Beare, John Davis, and Nicolò and Antonio Zeno (VII); Richard Hore, Anthony Parkhurst, Edward Hayes, Stephanus Parmenius, Richard Clarke, La Court de Pré-Ravillon, Thomas James, George Drake [see Richard Fisher], Sylvester Wyet, Charles Leigh, Jacques Cartier, Jean Fonteneau *dit* Alfonse, Jean-François La Rocque de Roberval, and Giovanni da Verrazzano (VIII); Sir Francis Drake (IX); and Henry May (X).

HAKLUYT SOCIETY publications. The society was formed in 1846 with the aim of printing rare or unpublished voyages and travels. Of the 221 volumes published to date, the following are relevant for Vol. I:

FIRST SERIES (London, 1849–99)

V: *Narratives of voyages towards the North West in search of a passage to Cathay and India 1496 to 1631.* . . . Edited by Thomas Rundall. 1849.

VII: Hakluyt, *Divers voyages* (1850).

XXVII: *Henry Hudson the navigator: the original documents in which his career is recorded, collected, partly translated, and annotated.* Introduction by G. M. Asher. 1860.

XXXVIII: *Three voyages of Frobisher* (Collinson).

L: *The voyages of the Venetian brothers Nicolò & Antonio Zeno, to the northern seas, in the XIVth century, comprising the latest known accounts of the lost colony of Greenland: and of the Northmen in America before Columbus.* Translated and edited by R. H. Major. 1873.

LVI: *The voyages of Sir James Lancaster, Kt., to the East Indies . . . and the voyage of Captain John Knight (1606) to seek the North-West Passage.* Edited by C. R. Markham. 1877.

LIX: *The voyages and works of John Davis, the navigator.* Edited by A. H. Markham. 1880.

LXIII: *The voyages of William Baffin, 1612–1622.* Edited by C. R. Markham. 1881.

LXXXVI: *The journal of Christopher Columbus (during his first voyages, 1492–93) and docu-*

GENERAL BIBLIOGRAPHY

ments relating to the voyages of John Cabot and Gaspar Corte Real. Translated by C. R. Markham. 1893.
LXXXVIII, LXXXIX: *Voyages of Foxe and James* (Christy).
XCVI, XCVII: *Danish arctic expeditions* (Gosch).
    SECOND SERIES (London and Cambridge, 1899–)
LXIX: Roger Barlow. *A brief summe of geographie*. Edited by E. G. R. Taylor. 1932.
LXXVI, LXXVII: Hakluyt, *Original writings* (Taylor).
LXXXIII, LXXXIV: *Voyages of Gilbert* (Quinn).
CIV, CV: *Roanoke voyages* (Quinn).
CXI: *English privateering voyages to the West Indies 1588–1595*. Edited by K. R. Andrews. Cambridge, 1959.
CXX: Williamson, *Cabot voyages* (1962).
    EXTRA SERIES
Hakluyt, *Principal navigations* (1903–5).
Purchas, *Pilgrimes* (1905–7).
Hakluyt, *Principall navigations* (Quinn and Skelton).
[For full citations for short titles above, see individual entries.]
HARRISSE, HENRY. *Les Corte-Real et leurs voyages au Nouveau-Monde ... suivi du texte inédit d'un récit de la troisième expédition de Gaspar Corte-Real.* [III.] *Les Corte-Real: Post-Scriptum: Gaspar Corte-Real: la date exacte de sa dernière expédition au Nouveau-Monde.* [III bis.] (Recueil de voyages, III, III *bis*.) Paris, 1883. See documents, III, 177–257.
——— *Jean et Sébastien Cabot, leur origine et leurs voyages, étude d'histoire critique suivie d'une cartographie, d'une bibliographie et d'une chronologie des voyages au Nord-Ouest, de 1497 à 1550, d'après des documents inédits.* (Recueil de voyages, I.) Paris, 1882. See documents, 309–66.
——— *John Cabot, the discoverer of North America, and Sebastian Cabot his son.* London, 1896. See documents, 385–469.
HENNEPIN, LOUIS. *Description de la Louisiane....* Paris, 1683.
——— *Nouveau voyage d'un païs plus grand que l'Europe, avec les réflections des entreprises du sieur de La Salle....* Utrecht, 1698. A continuation of the author's *Nouvelle découverte, infra.*
——— *Nouvelle découverte d'un très grand pays situé dans l'Amerique entre le Nouveau Mexique, et la mer glaciale....* Utrecht, 1697.
——— *A new discovery of a vast country, by Father Louis Hennepin, reprinted from the second London issue of 1698*, Edited by R. G. Thwaites. 2 vols. Chicago, 1903.
——— *Voyage ou nouvelle découverte d'un très grand pays....* Amsterdam, 1704.
HENNIG, RICHARD. *Terrae incognitae: eine Zusammenstellung und kritische Bewertung der wichtigsten vorcolumbischen Entdeckungsreisen....* 2d edition. 4 vols. Leiden, 1944–56.
HUDSON'S BAY RECORD SOCIETY. Initiated in 1938 by the Company after classification of its London Archives, begun in 1932, had progressed to the point where publication was feasible. Membership in the Society is limited. Inquiries should be directed to: the Hon. Secretary, Beaver House, Great Trinity Lane, London, E.C.4, England.
    PUBLICATIONS
General editor for vols. I–XXII, E. E. Rich: for vols. XXIII– , K. G. Davies. XXIV vols. published to date. Vols. I–XII issue in association with the Champlain Society, Toronto; vols. XXI and XXII issued in Toronto by McClelland & Stewart Ltd.
V: *Minutes of the Hudson's Bay Company 1671–1674.* Edited by E. E. Rich. 1942.
VIII: *Minutes of the Hudson's Bay Company 1679–1684: first part, 1679–82.* Edited by E. E. Rich. 1945.
IX: *Minutes of the Hudson's Bay Company 1679–1684: second part, 1682–84.* Edited by E. E. Rich. 1946.
XI: *Copy-book of letters outward &c. begins 29th May, 1680, ends 5 July, 1687.* Edited by E. E. Rich and A. M. Johnson. 1948.
XX: *Hudson's Bay copy booke of letters commissions instructions outward 1688–1696.* Edited by E. E. Rich and A. M. Johnson. 1957.
XXI: Rich. *History of the HBC. I: 1670–1763.*
XXII: Rich. *History of the HBC. II: 1763–1870.*
HUTCHINSON, [THOMAS]. *The history of the colony of Massachuset's Bay, from the first settlement thereof in 1628, until its incorporation with the colony of Plimouth, Province of Main, &c. by the charter of King William and Queen Mary, in 1691.* 2d edition. London, 1765. The 1st edition was published in Boston in 1764 and a 3d edition in Boston in 1795.
——— *The history of the province of Massachusets-Bay, from the charter of King William and Queen Mary, in 1691, until the year 1750.* 2d edition. London, 1768. The 1st edition was published in Boston in 1767 and a 3d edition in Boston in 1795.
——— *The history of the colony and province of Massachusetts-Bay, edited from the author's own copies of volumes I and II and his manuscript of

volume III, with a memoir and additional notes. Edited by L. S. Mayo. 3 vols. Cambridge, Mass., 1936. Volumes I and II include Governor Hutchinson's corrections of the 2d editions.

I.C.S.D.V. See [CLODORÉ?]

The Indian tribes of the upper Mississippi Valley and region of the Great Lakes, as described by Nicolas Perrot; Bacqueville de la Potherie; Morrell Marston; and Thomas Forsyth. Edited and translated by E. H. Blair. 2 vols. Cleveland, 1911, 1912.

Jacques Cartier, documents nouveaux. Édité par F. Joüon Des Longrais. Paris, 1888.

[JÉRÉMIE, NICOLAS.] *Twenty years of York Factory 1694–1714: Jérémie's account of Hudson Strait and Bay.* Translated from the French edition of 1720 with notes and Introduction by R. Douglas and J. N. Wallace. Ottawa, 1926.

The Jesuit Relations and allied documents: travels and explorations of the Jesuit missionaries in New France 1610–1791: the original French, Latin and Italian texts, with English translations and notes. Edited by R. G. Thwaites. 73 vols., including 2 Index vols. Cleveland, 1896–1901. Facsimile reproduction, 73 vols. in 36, New York, 1959. [For a discussion of the *Relations*, see pp. 455–57.]

Jésuites de la Nouvelle-France. . . . Édité par François Roustang. (Collection Christus, VI.) [Bruges ou Bruxelles], 1961.

Le journal des Jésuites, publié d'après le manuscrit original conservé aux Archives du Séminaire de Québec. Édité par les Abbés Laverdière et Casgrain. 2ᵉ édition; Montréal, 1892.

JUCHEREAU DE LA FERTÉ DE SAINT-IGNACE, JEANNE-FRANÇOISE, et MARIE-ANDRÉE DUPLESSIS DE SAINTE-HÉLÈNE. *Les annales de l'Hôtel-Dieu de Québec, 1636–1716.* Éditées par Albert Jamet. Québec et Montréal, 1939.

Jugements et déliberations du Conseil souverain de la Nouvelle-France [1663–1716]. 6 vols. Québec, 1885–91. *Index.* By P.-G. Roy. Québec, 1940.

LA CROIX DE CHEVRIÈRES DE SAINT-VALLIER, JEAN-BAPTISTE DE. *Estat present de l'Église et de la colonie française dans la Nouvelle-France. . . .* Paris, 1688; Québec, 1856 ou 1857.

LAHONTAN, LOM D'ARCE DE. See LOM

LA POT(H)ERIE, LE ROY DE BACQUEVILLE DE. See LE ROY

LE BLANT, ROBERT. *Histoire de la Nouvelle-France: les sources narratives du début du XVIIIᵉ siècle et le Recueil de Gédéon de Catalogne.* 1 vol. paru. Dax, sans date.

LE CLERCQ, CHRESTIEN. *The first establishment of the faith in New France.* Translated by J. G. Shea. 2 vols. New York, 1881.

—— *New relation of Gaspesia with the customs and religion of the Gaspesian Indians.* Translated and edited by W. F. Ganong. (Champlain Society publications, V.) Toronto, 1910.

—— *Premier établissement de la foy dans la Nouvelle-France.* 2 vols. Paris, 1691.

LE ROY DE BACQUEVILLE DE LA POT(H)ERIE, CLAUDE-CHARLES. *Histoire de l'Amérique septentrionale.* 4 vols. Paris, 1722; autres éditions Rouen, 1722, Paris, 1753.

LESCARBOT, MARC. *Histoire de la Nouvelle-France . . . suivie des Muses de la Nouvelle-France.* Nouvelle édition publiée par Edwin Tross. 3 vols. Paris, 1866.

—— *The history of New France containing the voyages, discoveries, and settlements made by the French in the West Indies and New France . . . from one hundred years ago until now. . . .* Translation by W. L. Grant; Introduction by H. P. Biggar. 3 vols. (Champlain Society publications, I, VII, XI.) Toronto, 1907, 1911, 1914. [Based on the 3d edition, Paris, 1618.]

LE TAC, SIXTE. *Histoire chronologique de la Nouvelle France ou Canada depuis sa découverte (mil cinq cents quatre) jusques en l'an mil six cents trente deux . . . publiée pour la première fois d'après le manuscrit original de 1689 et accompagnée de notes et d'un appendice tout composé de documents originaux et inédites.* Par Eugène Réveillaud. Paris, 1888.

"Lettres inédites du gouverneur d'Argenson." See [VOYER D'ARGENSON.]

Lettres de noblesse, généalogies, érections de comtés et baronnies insinuées par le Conseil souverain de la Nouvelle-France. Éditées par P.-G. Roy. 2 vols. Beauceville, 1920.

LITERARY AND HISTORICAL SOCIETY OF QUEBEC/ SOCIÉTÉ LITTÉRAIRE ET HISTORIQUE DE QUÉBEC. The oldest historical society in Canada, founded 6 Jan. 1824 in Quebec. It has published (a) a lengthy series of *Transactions*: old series, I (1824/29)–V (1862); new series, I (1863)–XXX (1924); (b) another collection, Historical Documents, consisting of 12 vols. in 9 series (1838–1915), numbered consecutively D.1, D.2, etc., irrespective of the fact that the first series contains 4 vols., while the remaining eight series contain only one vol. each; (c) *Bulletin*, I (1900)–IV (1907); (d) *Index to the archival publications . . . 1824–1924.* Québec, 1923. Relative to this volume are:

[CARTIER et al.] *Voyages de découverte au Canada. . . .* (Historical Documents, D.3, 1st series.)

[DOLLIER DE CASSON.] *Histoire du Montréal 1640–1672.* (Historical Documents, D.6, 3d series.)

[FRANÇOIS VACHON] DE BELMONT. *Histoire du*

Canada . . . in *Collection de mémoires et de relations sur l'histoire ancienne du Canada, d'après des manuscrits récemment obtenus des archives et bureaux publics en France, no 4.* (Historical Documents, D.2, 1st series.) Québec, 1840. Reprinted with the title *Recueil de ce qui s'est passé au Canada au sujet de la guerre tant des Anglais que des Iroquois,* in 1871 (Historical Documents, D.6, 3d series) and in 1886 (*Transactions,* XVIII, 21–56).

The Livinsgtone Indian Records 1666–1723. Edited by L. H. Leder. Gettysburg, 1956.

LOM D'ARCE DE LAHONTAN, L.-A. *New voyages to North America.* Edited by R. G. Thwaites. 2 vols. Chicago, 1905.

—— *Nouveaux voyages . . . dans l'Amérique septentrionale. . . .* 2 vols. La Haye, 1703.

MAINE HISTORICAL SOCIETY publications, Portland, Maine.
Collections, 1st series. 10 vols. 1831–91.
Collections and proceedings, 2d series. 10 vols. 1890–99.
Collections, 3d series. 2 vols. 1904–6.
Documentary history of the State of Maine [*q.v.*].
Province and court records of Maine. Edited by G. T. Libby *et al.* 4 vols., in progress. 1928–58– .

Mandements, lettres pastorales et circulaires des évêques de Québec. Édités par H. Têtu et C.-O. Gagnon. 9 vols. Québec, 1887–98.

MARGRY, PIERRE, ed. See: *Découvertes et établissements . . .*

MARTIRE D'ANGHIERA, PIETRO (PETER MARTYR). *De orbe novo.* Decade III. Alcalá, 1616. Decade VII. Alcalá, 1530. Decade VIII. Edited by Richard Hakluyt. Paris, 1587. [For other editions, *see* Hoffman, *Cabot to Cartier,* 230–31.]

MASSACHUSETTS HISTORICAL SOCIETY PUBLICATIONS, Boston, Mass.
Collections. 7 series of 10 vols. each plus 9 volumes published to date. 1792– .
Proceedings. 2 series of 20 vols. each plus 36 vols. published to date. 1879– .
Shipton. *Sibley's Harvard graduates.*
As a guide to contents and indexes see: *Handbook of the publications and photostats 1792–1935* (1937).

MASSICOTTE, É.-Z. *Répertoire des arrêts, édits, mandements, ordonnances conservés dans les Archives du Palais de Justice de Montréal, 1640–1760.* Montréal, 1919.

Mémoires des commissaires du roi et de ceux de Sa Majesté britannique, sur les possessions & les droits respectifs des deux couronnes en Amérique: avec les actes publics & pièces justificatives. 1ère édition. 4 vols. Paris, 1755, 1757. 2e édition. 6 vols. Paris, 1756–57. Vols. I–III (1ère éd.) were published in 1755 and vol. IV in 1757. The latter volume is probably in answer to the English *Memorials . . . ,* 1755 *infra.* Vol. I contains *Mémoires sur l'Acadie et sur l'isle de Sainte-Lucie;* Vol. II, *Pièces justificatives . . . sur les limites de l'Acadie;* Vol. IV, *Les derniers mémoires sur l'Acadie.*

Memorials of the English and French commissaries concerning the limits of Nova Scotia or Acadia. 2 vols. London, 1755. Vol. I relates to Nova Scotia; Vol. II, to St. Lucia. *See also: Mémoires, supra.*

MORIN, MARIE. *Annales de l'Hôtel-Dieu de Montréal.* Éditées par A. Fauteux, É.-Z. Massicotte et C. Bertrand. (Société historique de Montréal, Mémoires, XII. Montréal, 1921. This is an incomplete and inexact published version of the manuscript in AHDM [*q.v.*] by Marie Morin.

Narratives of the discovery of America. Edited by A. W. Lawrence and Jean Young. London, New York, and Toronto, 1931. Contains translations of the principal documents of discovery.

NAVY RECORDS SOCIETY, London. Founded in 1893 "for the purpose of rendering accessible the sources of [Britain's] naval history."
XXII, XXIII, XLIII, XLV, XLVII: *The naval tracts of Sir William Monson.* Edited by M. Oppenheim. 5 vols. 1902–14.
XXVI, XXVII, XXXVI, LVII: *A descriptive catalogue of the naval manuscripts in the Pepysian Library.* Edited by J. R. Tanner. 4 vols. 1903–22.
LI: *The autobiography of Phineas Pett.* Edited by W. G. Perrin. 1918.

NYCD (O'Callaghan and Fernow). See: *Documents relative to the colonial history of the State of New York . . .*

Ordonnances, commissions, etc., etc., des gouverneurs et intendants de la Nouvelle-France, 1639–1706. Éditées par P.-G. Roy. 2 vols. Beauceville, 1924.

Original narratives of early American history. Edited by J. F. Jameson. 19 vols. New York. 1906–17.
Early English and French voyages, chiefly out of Hakluyt. Edited by H. S. Burrage. 1906.
Voyages of Samuel de Champlain, 1604–1618. Edited by W. L. Grant. 1907.
Winthrop's journal "History of New England" 1630–1649. Edited by J. K. Hosmer. 2 vols. 1908.
Narratives of New Netherland, 1609–1664. Edited by J. F. Jameson. 1909.
Narratives of early Pennsylvania, west New Jersey and Delaware, 1630–1707. Edited by A. C. Myers. 1912.

Early narratives of the Northwest, 1634–1699. Edited by L. P. Kellogg. 1917.
Papier terrier de la Compagnie des Indes occidentales, 1667–1668. Édité par P.-G. Roy. Beauceville, 1931.
PERROT, NICOLAS. "Memoir on the manners, customs and religion of the savages of North America." Translated from the French in *Indian tribes of the upper Mississippi Valley and region of the Great Lakes.* Edited by E. H. Blair. 2 vols. Cleveland, 1911.
—— *Mémoire sur les mœurs, coustumes et relligion des sauvages de l'Amérique septentrionale.* Édité par J. Tailhan. Leipzig et Paris, 1864.
Pièces et documents relatifs à la tenure seigneuriale, demandés par une adresse de l'assembée législative, 1851. 2 vols. Québec, 1852.
Positio causae. . . . See: Beatificationis seu declarationis . . .
The Positio of the Historical Section of the Sacred Congregation of Rites on the introduction of the cause for beatification and canonization and on the virtues of the servant of God Katharine Tekakwitha, the Lily of the Mohawks. New York, [1940].
The precursors of Jacques Cartier 1497–1534: a collection of documents relating to the early history of the Dominion of Canada. Edited by H. P. Biggar. (Public Archives of Canada publications, V.) Ottawa, 1911.
Premier registre de l'église Notre-Dame de Montréal. Montréal, 1961.
Première mission des Jésuites au Canada: lettres et documents inédits. Éditée par Auguste Carayon. Paris, 1864.
PRINCE SOCIETY PUBLICATIONS, Boston, 1865–1920
XVI: Radisson, *Voyages* (Scull).
XVII: *Capt. John Mason, the founder of New Hampshire, including his tract on Newfoundland.* Edited by J. W. Dean. 1887.
XXIX: *Sir Humfrey Gylberte and his enterprize of colonization in America.* Edited by Carlos Slafter. 1903.
Province and court records of Maine. See MAINE HISTORICAL SOCIETY PUBLICATIONS
PUBLIC ARCHIVES OF CANADA
  NUMBERED PUBLICATIONS
I: *Index to reports of Canadian archives from 1872 to 1908.* 1909.
V: *Precursors* (Biggar).
VI: J.-E. ROY. *Rapport sur les archives de France relatives à l'histoire du Canada.* 1911.
VIII: H. R. HOLMDEN. *Catalogue des cartes, plans et cartes marines conservés au dépôt des cartes des archives canadiennes.* 1912.
X: D. W. PARKER. *A guide to the documents in the Manuscript Room at the Public Archives of Canada Vol. I.* 1914.
XI: *Voyages of Cartier* (Biggar).
XIII: MAGDALEN CASEY. *Catalogue of pamphlets in the PAC 1493–1931 with Index.* 2 vols. 1931–32.
XIV: BIGGAR. *Documents relating to Cartier and Roberval.*
  OTHER PUBLICATIONS
Annual Reports. 1881–1952 (irregular thereafter).
Sixteenth-century maps relating to Canada: a check-list and bibliography. Edited with an Introduction by T. E. Layng. 1956.
PUBLIC RECORD OFFICE PUBLICATIONS. The following calendars contain information on events in or affecting Canada before the 18th century:
Acts of the Privy Council of England. New series [1541–1631]. Edited by J. R. Dasent *et al.* 45 vols., in progress. 1890–
VIII: *1571–1575.* 1894.
XVII: *1588–1589.* 1898.
XXVI: *1596–1597.* 1902.
XXVII: *1597.* 1903.
XXVIII: *1597–1598.* 1904.
XXXVIII: *1621–1623.* 1932.
XLV: *1629–1630.* 1961.
Acts of the Privy Council of England. Colonial series [1613–1783]. Edited by W. L. Grant and J. Munro. 6 vols. 1908–12.
I: *1613–1680.* 1908.
VI: *"The unbound papers," 1676–1783.* 1912.
Calendar of letters and papers, foreign and domestic, of the reign of Henry VIII. Edited by J. S. Brewer *et al.* 21 vols. in 35. 1864–1932.
IV, Part II: *1526–1528.* 1872.
Calendar of state papers, colonial series. [1574–1736.] Edited by W. N. Sainsbury *et al.* 41 vols., in progress. 1860–   .
I: [America and West Indies] *1574–1660.* 1860.
II: [East Indies, China and Japan], *1513–1616.* 1862.
III: [East Indies, China and Japan], *1617–1621.* 1870.
V: *America and West Indies, 1661–1668.* 1880.
VII: [*America and West Indies*], *1669–1674.* 1889.
VIII: *East Indies and Persia, 1630–1634.* 1892.
IX: *America and West Indies, 1675–1676, with Addenda 1574–1674.* 1894.
X: *America and West Indies, 1677–1680.* 1896
XI: *America and West Indies, 1681–1685.* 1898.
XIII: *America and West Indies, 1689–1692.* 1901.
XIV: *America and West Indies, 1693–1696.* 1903.

XV: *America and West Indies, May, 1696–Oct., 1697*. 1904.
XVI: *America and West Indies, Oct., 1697–Dec., 1698*. 1905.
XVII: *America and West Indies, 1699, with Addenda, 1621–1698*. 1908.

Calendar of state papers, domestic series, of the reigns of Edward VI, Mary, Elizabeth I and James I. [1547–1625.] Edited by R. Lemon and Mrs. Everett Green. 12 vols. 1856–72.
IX: *1611–1618*. 1858.
X: *1619–1623*. 1858.
XI: *1623–1625*. 1859.

Calendar of state papers, domestic series, of the reign of Charles I. [1625–49.] Edited by John Bruce *et al*. 23 vols. 1858–97.
III: *1628–1629*. 1859.
IV: *1629–1631*. 1860.
V: *1631–1633*. 1862.
IX: *1635–1636*. 1866.

Calendar of state papers, domestic series, the Commonwealth. [1649–60.] Edited by Mrs. Everett Green. 13 vols. 1875–86.
VII: *1654*. 1881.

Calendar of state papers, domestic series, of the reign of Charles II. [1660–85.] Edited by Mrs. Everett Green *et al*. 23 vols. 1860–1947.
I: *1660–1661*. 1860.
III: *1663–1664*. 1862.
V: *Oct. 1, 1665, to July 31, 1666*. 1864.
VII: *1667*. 1866.
VIII: *Nov. 1667–Sept. 8, 1668*. 1894.
XIV: *Oct. 1672–Feb. 1673*. 1901.
XV: *March–Oct. 1673*. 1902.
XXI: *1679–Aug. 1680*. 1915.
XXIV: *Jan. 1–June 30, 1683*. 1933.
XXV: *July–Sept. 30, 1683*. 1934.
XXVII: *May 1684–Feb. 5th, 1685*. 1938.

Calendar of state papers relating to Ireland, of the reign of James I. [1603–25.] Edited by C. W. Russell and J. P. Prendergast. 5 vols. 1872–80.
IV: *1611–1614*. 1876.

Calendar of state papers, foreign series, of the reign of Elizabeth. [1558–July 1589.] Edited by the Rev. J. Stevenson *et al*. 23 vols. in 26. 1863–1950.
VII: *1564–1565*. 1870.
XVI: *May–Dec., 1582*. 1909.
XVII: *Jan.–June, 1583, with Addenda 1553 (?)–1583*. 1913.

Calendar of state papers existing in the archives and collections of Milan. Edited by A. B. Hinds. 1 vol. [1383–1618.] 1912.

Calendar of letters and state papers relating to English affairs, preserved principally in the archives at Simancas. [1558–1603.] Edited by M. A. S. Hume. 4 vols. 1892–99.
III: *Elizabeth, 1580–1586*. 1896.

Calendar of state papers and manuscripts relating to English affairs, existing in the archives and collections of Venice, and in other libraries of northern Italy. [1202–1674.] Edited by Rawdon Brown *et al*. 38 vols. in 40. 1864–1947.
XII: *1610–1613*. 1905.
XIII: *1613–1615*. 1907.
XVI: *1619–1621*. 1911.
XXXIII: *1661–1664*. 1932.

Calendar of Treasury papers. [1556–1728.] Edited by J. Redington. 6 vols. 1868–89.
I: *1557–1696*. 1868.
II: *1697–1702*. 1871.

Memorials of Henry the Seventh, Bernardi Andreæ Tholosatis vita Regis Henrici Septimi; necnon alia quaedam ad eundem Regem Spectantia. Edited by J. Gairdner. 1858.

Register of the Privy Council of Scotland. [1545–1625.] Edited by J. H. Burton and David Masson. 14 vols. 1877–98.

[*See also* British Government publications, Record publications: sectional list No. 24 (London, 1962).]

PULIDO RUBIO, J. *El piloto mayor de la Casa de la Contratación de Sevilla*. Sevilla, 1950. Reproduces documents on Sebastian Cabot's voyages.

PURCHAS, SAMUEL. *Hakluytus posthumus or Purchas his pilgrimes, contayning a history of the world, in sea voyages and lande travells, by Englishmen and others*. . . . 20 vols. (Hakluyt Society publications, Extra Series.) Glasgow, 1905–7. Reproduces the 4-volume edition of 1625.

QUINN, D. B. "The voyage of Etienne Bellenger to the Maritimes in 1583: a new document," *CHR*, XLIII (1962), 328–43.

[RADISSON, PIERRE ESPRIT.] *The explorations of Pierre Esprit Radisson from the original manuscript in the Bodleian Library and the British Museum*. Edited by A. T. Adams. Minneapolis, 1961. A recent edition of the *Voyages* which offers a new theory to explain the discrepancies in the sources.

[———] *Voyages of Pierre Esprit Radisson, being an account of his travels and experiences among the North American Indians, from 1652 to 1684, transcribed from original manuscripts in the Bodleian Library and the British Museum*. Edited by G. D. Scull. (Prince Society publications, XVI.) Boston, 1885; New York, 1943.

[RAGUENEAU, PAUL.] "Mémoires touchant la mort et les vertus des pères Isaac Jogues, Anne de Noüe, Anthoine Daniel, Jean de Brébeuf,

Gabriel Lallement, Charles Garnier, Noël Chabanel et un séculier René Goupil," manuscript in ACSM known as the "Manuscrit de 1652," reproduced in APQ *Rapport, 1924–25*, 3–93.

RAMÉ, ALFRED. *Documents inédits sur le Canada.* Paris, 1865.

RAMUSIO, G. B. *Primo volume delle navigationi et viaggi nel qual si contiene la descrittione dell' Africa.* . . . Venetia, 1550.

────── *Terzo volume delle navigationi et viaggi nel quale si contengono Le Navigationi al Mondo Nuovo.* . . . Venetia, 1556.

[For various editions of Ramusio see Hoffman, *Cabot to Cartier*, 254–55.]

RECENSEMENTS

ACADIE

1671: "Familles establies à l'Acadie," in Sulte, *Hist. des Can. fr.*, IV, 150–54.

1686: "Un Recensement de l'Acadie en 1686. Recensement des peuples de la rivière de Miramichy, de Chedabouctou, de Nepesiguy et de l'Ile Percée," *BRH*, XXXVIII (1932), 677–96, 721–34. Sulte, *Hist. des Can. fr.*, VI, 6–9.

CANADA

1666: "Estat general des habitans du Canada en 1666," APQ *Rapport, 1935–36*, 3–154. Sulte, *Hist. des Can. fr.*, IV, 51–63. "Le premier recensement nominal de Québec," éd. P.-G. R[oy], *BRH*, XXXVII (1931), 321–31, 385–404.

1667: Sulte, *Hist. des Can. fr.*, IV, 64–78.

1681: Sulte, *Hist. des Can. fr.*, V, 53–92.

See also Canada, Bureau of Statistics, Demography Branch. *Chronological list of Canadian censuses.* Ottawa. 1942.

[Since the printed versions of the censuses are not always accurate copies, it is preferable to consult the originals. See Archives nationales, Archives d'Outre-Mer, série G, in section I.]

Records of the governor and company of the Massachusetts Bay in New England. Edited by N. B. Shurtleff. 6 vols. in 5. Boston, 1853–54.

Recueil de voyages et de documents pour servir à l'histoire de la géographie depuis le XIIIe jusqu'à la fin du XVIe siècle. Publié par Christian Schefer et Henri Cordier. 24 vols. Paris, 1882–1923.

I: HENRY HARRISSE. *Jean et Sébastien Cabot.*
III, III bis: ──────. *Les Corte-Real.*
IV: *Le discours de la navigation.*
XX: JEAN FONTENEAU [JEAN ALFONSE]. *La cosmographie.*

Relations des Jésuites contenant ce qui s'est passé de plus remarquable dans les missions des pères de la Compagnie de Jésus dans la Nouvelle-France. 3 vols. Québec, 1858. [For a discussion of the *Relations*, see pp. 455–57.]

Relation par lettres de l'Amérique septentrionale, années 1709 et 1710. Édité par Camille de Rochemonteix. Paris, 1904.

The Roanoke voyages, 1584–1590. Edited by D. B. Quinn. 2 vols. (Hakluyt Society publications, CIV, CV.) London, 1955.

ROY, P.-G. *Inventaire de pièces sur la côte de Labrador conservées aux Archives de la Province de Québec.* 2 vols. Québec, 1940–42.

────── *Inventaire des concessions en fief et seigneurie, fois et hommages et aveux et dénombrements conservés aux Archives de la Province de Québec.* 6 vols. Beauceville, 1927–29.

────── *Inventaire des contrats de mariage du Régime français conservés aux Archives judiciaires de Québec.* 6 vols. Québec, 1937–38.

────── *Inventaire des insinuations de la prévôté de Québec.* 3 vols. Beauceville, 1936.

────── *Inventaire des insinuations du Conseil souverain de la Nouvelle-France.* Beauceville, 1921.

────── *Inventaire des ordonnances des intendants de la Nouvelle-France conservées aux Archives provinciales de Québec.* 4 vols. Beauceville, 1919.

────── *Inventaire des procès-verbaux des grands voyers conservés aux Archives de la Province de Québec.* 6 vols. Beauceville, 1923–32.

────── *Inventaire des testaments, donations et inventaires du Régime français conservés aux Archives judiciaires de Québec.* 3 vols. Québec, 1941.

────── *Inventaire d'une collection de pièces judiciaires, notariales, etc., conservées aux Archives judiciaires de Québec.* 2 vols. Beauceville, 1917.

────── et ANTOINE ROY. *Inventaire des greffes des notaires du Régime français.* 21 vols. parus. Québec, 1943–65.

ROYAL COMMISSION ON HISTORICAL MANUSCRIPTS PUBLICATIONS

Series 9, *Salisbury (Cecil), MSS.*
Series 23, *Cowper (Coke MSS).*
Series 69, *Middleton MSS.*

Royal Fort Frontenac. Translated by R. A. Preston; edited by Léopold Lamontagne. (Champlain Society publications, Ontario series, II.) Toronto, 1958.

Royal letters, charters, and tracts, relating to the colonization of New Scotland and the institution of the Order of Knight Baronets of Nova Scotia 1621–1638. Edited by David Laing. Edinburgh, 1867, 1886.

SAGARD, GABRIEL. *Le grand voyage du pays des Hurons, situé en l'Amérique vers la Mer douce, ès derniers confins de la Nouvelle-France, dite Canada.* . . . *Avec un dictionnaire de la langue huronne, pour la commodité de ceux qui ont à voyager dans le pays, et n'ont l'intelligence d'icelle langue.* 2 vols. Paris, 1632. Réédité par Edwin Tross. 2 vols. Paris, 1865.

—— *Histoire du Canada et voyages que les Freres mineurs Recollets y ont faicts pour la conversion des infidelles divisez en quatre livres . . . depuis l'an 1615 jusques à la prise qui en a este faicte par les Anglois. . . .* 4 vols. Paris, 1636. Réédition, *Histoire du Canada et voyages que les Frères mineurs Recollects y ont faicts pour la conversion des infidèles depuis l'an 1615 . . . avec un dictionnaire de la langue huronne.* Édité par Edwin Tross. 4 vols. Paris, 1866.

—— *The long journey to the country of the Hurons.* Edited by G. M. Wrong; translated by H. H. Langton. (Champlain Society publications, XXV.) Toronto, 1939.

SAINT-VALLIER, LA CROIX DE CHEVRIÈRES DE. *See* LA CROIX

SHEA, J. G. *Discovery and exploration of the Mississippi valley with the original narratives of Marquette, Allouez, Membré, Hennepin and Anastase Douay.* New York, 1852.

1690, Sir William Phips devant Québec: histoire d'un siège. Édité par Ernest Myrand. Québec, 1893.

SOCIÉTÉ HISTORIQUE DE MONTRÉAL. The Society was founded in 1857 to collect, preserve, and publish documents relating to the history of Canada. Of the 12 volumes of Mémoires published between 1859 and 1921 the following are cited in this volume:
II–III: *Mémoires et documents relatifs à l'histoire du Canada.* 1859–60.
IV: [Dollier de Casson], *Histoire du Montréal.*
VI: [René de Bréhant de Galinée.] *Voyage de MM. Dollier et Galinée.* [Notes de l'abbé H.-A. Verreau.] 1875. [Incomplete; *see* p. 184.]
IX: *Les véritables motifs* (Verreau).
XII: Morin, *Annales* (Fauteux *et al.*).

Suffolk Deeds. 14 vols. Boston, 1880–1906. Includes records from 1629 to 1697 in the Registry of Deeds, Suffolk County Court House, Boston, Mass.

Summario de la generale historia de l'Indie occidentali. [Probably edited by G. B. Ramusio.] [Venetia], 1534.

THEVET, ANDRÉ. *Cosmographie universelle . . . illustrée de diverses figures des choses plus remarquables vues par l'auteur. . . .* 2 vols. Paris, 1575.

—— *Les singularitez de la France antarctique, autrement nomée Amérique: & de plusieurs terres & isles découvertes de nostre temps.* Paris, 1558; autre édition, Anvers, 1558. Réédition, *Les singularitez de la France antarctique.* Edité par Paul Gaffarel. Paris, 1878.

THOMASSY, RAYMOND. *Géologie pratique de la Louisiane.* Nouvelle-Orléans et Paris, 1860. First printed the official report of La Salle's 1682 explorations, "Relation de la découverte de l'embouchure de la rivière Mississipi dans le golfe de Mexique, faite par le sieur De La Salle, l'année passé 1682," 9–16 (attributed to Père Zénobe Membré). App. A: "Decouverte des manuscrits de La Salle." App. B: "Relation inédite de la Salle sur la nécessité de poursuivre la découverte du Mississipi adressée au Comte de Frontenac, en novembre 1680."

The three voyages of Martin Frobisher, in search of a passage to Cathaia and India by the North-West, A.D. 1576–8, reprinted from the first edition of Hakluyt's Voyages, with selections from manuscript documents in the British Museum and the State Paper Office. Edited by Richard Collinson. (Hakluyt Society publications, 1st series, XXXVIII.) London, 1867.

The three voyages of Martin Frobisher in search of a passage to Cathay and India by the North-West, A.D. 1576–8. From the original 1578 text of George Best. Edited by Vilhjalmur Stefansson. 2 vols. London, 1938.

[TONTI, HENRI DE?] *Dernières découvertes dans l'Amérique Septentrionale de M. de la Sale, mises au jour par M. le Chevalier Tonti, gouverneur du Fort Saint-Louis, aux Islinois.* Paris, 1697.

TORIBIO MEDINA, JOSÉ. *El portugués Esteban Gomez al servicio de España.* Santiago de Chile, 1908.

—— *El veneciano Sebastian Caboto al servicio de España.* Santiago de Chile, 1908.

[TROYES, PIERRE DE.] *Journal de l'expédition du Chevalier de Troyes à la Baie d'Hudson, en 1686.* Édité par Ivanhoë Caron. Beauceville, 1918.

TRUDEL, MARCEL. *Atlas historique du Canada Français: des origines à 1867.* Québec, 1961.

[VACHON] DE BELMONT, [FRANÇOIS]. *See* Literary and Historical Society of Quebec.

Les véritables motifs de messieurs et dames de la Société de Notre-Dame de Montréal pour la conversion des sauvages de la Nouvelle-France. Édités par H.-A. Verreau. (Société historique de Montréal, Mémoires, IX.) Montréal, 1880. Attributed to J.-J. Olier.

VIGNERAS, L.-A. "The Cape Breton landfall: 1494 or 1497? Note on a letter by John Day," *CHR*, XXXVIII (1957), 219–28. Includes a translation of the letter.

—— "New light on the 1497 Cabot voyages to America," *Hispanic American Historical Review*, XXXVI (1956), 503–9. The original Spanish letter is printed here.

The Vinland sagas: the Norse discovery of America.

Grænlendinga saga and Eirik's saga. Translated with an Introduction by Magnus Magnusson and Hermann Pálsson. [Harmondsworth, Middlesex, 1965.]

Voyage à la Nouvelle-France du Capitaine Charles Daniel de Dieppe, 1629. Édité par J. Félix. Rouen, 1881.

The voyages and colonising enterprises of Sir Humphrey Gilbert. Edited by D. B. Quinn. 2 vols. (Hakluyt Society publications, LXXXIII, LXXXIV.) London, 1940.

The voyages of Captain Luke Foxe of Hull, and Captain Thomas James of Bristol in search of a north-west passage, in 1631–32; with narratives of the earlier north-west voyages of Frobisher, Davis, Weymouth, Hall, Knight, Hudson, Button, Gibbons, Bylot, Baffin, Hawkeridge and others. Edited by Miller Christy. 2 vols. (Hakluyt Society publications, LXXXVIII, LXXXIX.) London, 1894.

The voyages of Jacques Cartier. Translated by H.P. Biggar. (Public Archives of Canada publications, XI.) Ottawa, 1924. Includes the original French text.

[VOYER D'ARGENSON, PIERRE DE.] "Lettres inédites du gouverneur d'Argenson," *BRH*, XXVII (1921), 298–309, 328–39.

WATKINS, W. K. "The Expedition to Canada in 1690 under Sir William Phips," in *Society of Colonial Wars in the Commonwealth of Massachusetts Yearbook*, IV (1898), 111ff.

WEBSTER, J. C. *Acadia at the end of the seventeenth century: letters, journals and memoirs of Joseph Robineau de Villebon, commandant in Acadia, 1690–1700, and other contemporary documents.* (New Brunswick Museum, Monographic series, I). Saint John, 1934.

WILLIAMSON, J. A. *The Cabot voyages and Bristol discovery under Henry VII.* (Hakluyt Society publications, 2d series, CXX.) London, 1962.

—— *The Voyages of the Cabots and the English discovery of North America under Henry VII and Henry VIII.* London, 1929.

WRAXALL, PETER. *An abridgment of the Indian affairs contained in four folio volumes, transacted in the colony of New York, from the year 1678 to the year 1751.* Edited with an Introduction by C. H. McIlwain. (Harvard Historical Studies, XXI.) Cambridge, Mass., 1915.

III. REFERENCE WORKS

ALLAIRE, J.-B.-A. *Dictionnaire biographique du clergé canadien-français.* 6 vols. Montréal, 1910–34.

A bibliography of Canadiana: being items in the Public Library of Toronto, Canada, relating to the early history and development of Canada. Edited by F. M. Staton and Marie Tremaine. Toronto, 1934.

A bibliography of Canadiana: a first supplement. . . . Edited by G. M. Boyle, assisted by Marjorie Colbeck. Toronto, 1959.

BONNAULT, CLAUDE DE. "Le Canada militaire, état provisoire des officiers de milice de 1641 à 1760," *APQ Rapport, 1949–51*, 261–527.

CARON, IVANHOË. "Liste des prêtres séculiers et religieux qui ont exercé le saint ministère en Canada," *BRH*, XLVII (1941), 1604–29, pp. 76–78; 1629–59, pp. 160–75; 1659–69, pp. 192–201; 1670–79, pp. 225–35; 1680–90, pp. 257–68; 1691–99, pp. 289–99. [Title varies.]

The Catholic encyclopedia, an international work of reference . . . of the Catholic church. Edited by C. G. Herbermann *et al.* 15 vols., Index, 1 Supplement. New York, 1907–22.

DAVELUY, MARIE-CLAIRE. "Bibliographie de la Société de Notre-Dame de Montréal (1639–1663) et de ses membres, accompagnée de notes historiques et critiques," *RHAF*, V (1951–52), 139–48, 296–307, 445–60, 603–16; VI (1952–53), 146–50, 297–305, 458–63, 595–605; VII (1953–54), 457–61, 586–92; VIII (1954–55), 292–306, 449–55, 591–606; IX (1955–56), 141–49, 306–9, 458–62, 594–602; X (1956–57), 295–302; XI (1957–58), 137–42, 298–304, 449–57, 608–14; XII (1958–59), 144–47, 294–302, 443–53; XIII (1959–60), 137–49, 298–305, 450–60, 594–602; XIV (1960–61), 142–49, 302–11, 626–35; XV (1961–62), 141–54, 466–72, 611–16; XVI (1962–63), 294–307, 455–63; XVII (1963–64), 141–52.

DESAULNIERS, F.-L. *Recherches généalogiques.* . . . Montréal, 1902. Included are 25 biographies of important French-canadian families.

Dictionary of American biography [to 1928]. Edited by Allen Johnson and Dumas Malone. 20 vols., Index. New York, 1928–37. 2 Supplements [to 31 Dec. 1940], New York, 1944, 1958. New edition, comprising 22 vols. in 11, New York, 1959. *Concise DAB*, New York, 1964. In progress.

Dictionary of national biography [to 1900]. Edited by Leslie Stephen and Sidney Lee. 63 vols.;

Supplement, 3 vols.; Index and epitome. London. 1885–1903. 5 Supplements for the 20th century. *Concise DNB*, 2 vols., 1952, 1961. In progress.

Dictionnaire de biographie française. Sous la direction de J. Balteau et al. 9 vols., en cours de publication. Paris, [1932]– . Volumes "A" to "Delbos" have been published.

DIONNE, N.-E. *Inventaire chronologique des livres, brochures, journaux et revues. . . .* 4 vols. Québec, 1905–9.

Encyclopedia Canadiana. J. E. Robbins, Editor-in-chief. 10 vols. Ottawa, 1957–58.

The Encyclopedia of Canada. Edited by W. S. Wallace. 6 vols. Toronto, 1935–37.

GAGNON, PHILÉAS. "Noms propres au Canada français: transformations de noms propres, établies par les signatures autographes ou par les écrits de contemporains où ils sont mentionnés," *BRH*, XV (1909), 17–30, 49–61, 80–94, 112–24, 143–57, 177–86.

GAUTHIER, HENRI. *Sulpitiana.* Montréal, 1926.

GODBOUT, ARCHANGE. "Nos ancêtres au XVIIe siècle," APQ *Rapport, 1951–53*, 449–544; *1953–55*, 445–536; *1955–57*, 379–489; *1957–59*, 383–440; *1959–60*, 277–354. "A" to "Bousquet" included.

—— *Origine des familles canadiennes-françaises, extrait de l'état civil français: 1ère série.* Lille 1925.

HAMELIN, JEAN et ANDRÉ BEAULIEU. *Guide de l'étudiant en histoire du Canada.* Sainte-Foy, 1964. Mimeographed.

Handbook of American Indians north of Mexico. Edited by F. W. Hodge. (Smithsonian Institution, Bureau of American Ethnology, Bulletin 30.) 2 vols. Washington, D.C., 1907, 1910.

HOZIER, L.-P. D' et A.-M. D'HOZIER DE SÉRIGNY. *L'armorial général, ou registres de la noblesse de France.* 6 registres en 10 vols. Paris, 1738–68.

LANCTOT, GUSTAVE. *L'œuvre de la France en Amérique du Nord: bibliographie sélective et critique.* Montréal, 1951.

LECESTRE, LÉON. *Liste alphabétique des officiers généraux jusqu'en 1762 dont les notices biographiques se trouvent dans la Chronologie militaire de Pinard. . . .* Paris, 1903.

LECLERC, CH.-H. *Bibliotheca Americana: histoire, géographie, voyages, archéologie et linguistique des deux Amériques et des îles phillippines.* Paris, 1878. Suppléments, nos 1, 2. Paris, 1881, 1887.

LE JEUNE, L.-M. *Dictionnaire général de biographie, histoire, littérature, agriculture, commerce, industrie et des arts, sciences, mœurs, coutumes,* *institutions politiques et religieuses du Canada.* 2 vols. Ottawa, 1931.

MASSICOTTE, É.-Z. "Les chirurgiens, médecins, . . . de Montréal sous le Régime français," APQ *Rapport, 1922–23*, 131–55.

—— "Les colons de Montréal de 1642 à 1667," *RSCT*, 3d ser., VII (1913), sect.I, 3–65 and *BRH*, XXXIII (1927), 170–92, 224–39, 379–84, 433–48, 467–82, 538–48, 613–25, 650–52.

—— "Les tribunaux et les officiers de justice de Montréal sous le régime français, 1648–1760," *RSCT*, 3d ser., X (1916), sect.I, 273–303 et *BRH*, XXXVII (1931), 122–28, 179–92, 252–56, 302–13.

[MELANÇON.] *Liste des missionnaires jésuites: Nouvelle-France et Louisiane, 1611–1800.* Montréal, 1929.

"Les notaires au Canada sous le Régime français," APQ *Rapport, 1921–22*, 1–58. Contains biographies of nearly 200 notaires.

PINARD. *Chronologie historique-militaire, contenant l'histoire de la création de toutes les charges, dignités et grades militaires supérieurs. . . .* 7 vols. Paris, 1760–64. See volume VI; see also Lecestre *supra*.

ROY, P.-G. *Les officiers d'état-major des gouvernements de Québec, Montréal et Trois-Rivières sous le Régime français*, Lévis, 1919, and *RC*, XX (1917), 375–84; XXI (1918), 75–79, 210–20, 276–95, 373–79.

TANGHE, RAYMOND. *Bibliography of Canadian bibliographies/Bibliographie des bibliographies canadiennes.* Toronto, 1960. Published under the auspices of the Bibliographical Society of Canada. Pages 168–81 concern history.

TANGUAY, CYPRIEN. *Dictionnaire généalogique des familles canadiennes depuis la fondation de la colonie jusqu'à nos jours.* 7 vols. [Montréal], 1871–90.

—— *Répertoire général du clergé canadien par ordre chronologique depuis la fondation de la colonie jusqu'à nos jours.* Québec, 1868.

VACHON, ANDRÉ, "Inventaire critique des notaires royaux des gouvernements de Québec, Montréal et Trois-Rivières (1663–1764)," *RHAF*, IX (1955–56), 423–38, 546–61; X (1956–57), 93–103, 257–62, 381–90; XI (1957–58), 93–106, 270–76, 400–6.

WALLACE, W. S. *The Macmillan dictionary of Canadian biography.* 3d edition, revised and enlarged. London, Toronto, and New York, 1963.

WINSHIP, G. P. *Cabot bibliography, with an introductory essay on the careers of the Cabots based on an independent examination of the sources of information.* London, 1900.

GENERAL BIBLIOGRAPHY

IV. STUDIES

ABBOTT, M. E. *History of medicine in the Province of Quebec.* Toronto, 1931; McGill University publications, VIII, no.63, 1932.

ADAIR, E. R. "The evolution of Montreal under the French régime," CHA *Report, 1942,* 20–41.

—— "France and the beginnings of New France," *CHR,* XXV (1944), 246–78.

AHERN, GEORGES et M.-J. *Notes pour servir à l'histoire de la médecine dans le Bas-Canada depuis la fondation de Québec jusqu'au commencement du XIXᵉ siècle.* Québec, 1923.

ALMAGIÀ, ROBERTO. "Alcune considerazioni sui viaggi di Giovanni Caboto," Atti Accademia nazionale dei Lincei, Scienze Morali, *Rendiconti,* ser. VIII, III (1948), 291–303.

—— *Commemorazione di Sebastiano Caboto nel IV centenario della morte.* Venezia, 1958.

—— *Gli italiani, primi esploratori dell' America.* Roma, 1937.

—— "Sulle navigazioni di Giovanni Caboto," *Rivista geografica italiana,* LXVII (1960), 1–12.

ANTHIAUME, A. *Cartes marines, constructions navales, voyages de découverte chez les Normands 1500–1650.* 2 vols. Paris, 1916.

ATHERTON, W. H. *Montreal, 1535–1914.* 3 vols. Montreal, Vancouver, Chicago, 1914.

AUGER, R.-J. *La grande recrue de 1653.* Montréal, 1955.

BAILEY, A. G. *The conflict of European and eastern Algonkian cultures, 1504–1700: a study in Canadian civilization.* (New Brunswick Museum publications, Monographic series, 2.) Saint John, 1937.

BAILYN, BERNARD. *The New England merchants in the seventeenth century.* (Studies in Entrepreneurial History.) Cambridge, Mass., 1955.

BIGGAR, H. P. *The early trading companies of New France.* (University of Toronto Studies in History, edited by G. M. Wrong.) Toronto, 1901.

—— *The voyages of the Cabots and of the Corte-Reals to North America and Greenland, 1497–1503.* Paris, 1903.

BISHOP, MORRIS. *Champlain: the life of fortitude.* New York, 1948.

—— *White men came to the St. Lawrence: the French and the land they found.* London and Montreal, 1961.

BOISSONNAULT, C.-M. *Histoire de la faculté de médecine de Laval.* Québec, 1953.

BRÉARD, CHARLES et PAUL. *Documents relatifs à la marine normande et à ses armements aux XVIᵉ et XVIIᵉ siècles pour le Canada, l'Afrique, les Antilles, le Brésil et les Indes.* Rouen, 1889.

BREBNER, J. B. *The explorers of North America, 1492–1806.* New York, 1955.

—— *New England's outpost: Acadia before the conquest of Canada.* New York, 1927.

Bulletin des Recherches historiques. Lévis, Québec. Monthly journal of archaeology, history, biography, bibliography, numismatology, and so on. I (1895)– . Index: I (1895)–XXXI (1925). 4 vols. Beauceville, 1925–26. For subsequent years see the manuscript index in APQ. Founded by P.-G. Roy, it became in March 1923 the journal of the APQ.

CAHALL, RAYMOND DU BOIS. *The Sovereign Council of New France: a study in Canadian constitutional history.* (Studies in History, Economics and Public Law, edited by the Faculty of Political Science of Columbia University, LXV, no.1: whole no.156.) New York, 1915.

Cahiers des Dix. Montréal. I (1936)– . Annual revue published by "Les Dix," a group of historians who formed a legal association in 1935.

CAMPBELL, T. J. *Pioneer priests of North America 1642–1710.* 2 vols. New York, 1908, 1910.

Canada and its provinces: a history of the Canadian people and their institutions by one hundred associates. Edited by Adam Shortt and A. G. Doughty. 23 vols. Toronto, 1914–17.

Le Canada Français. Québec. First series. Journal published under the direction of a committee of professors of the Université Laval. I (1888)–IV (1891). Concerned with religion, philosophy, history, fine arts, science, and letters. Many documents on Acadia. Second series. Incorporated *Parler Français* and *La Nouvelle France.* Publication of the Université Laval; journal of the Société du Parler français au Canada. I (1918–19)–XXXIII (1945–46). Renamed *Revue de l'Université Laval* [*q.v.*].

CANADIAN CATHOLIC HISTORICAL ASSOCIATION/ SOCIETE CANADIENNE D'HISTOIRE DE L'ÉGLISE CATHOLIQUE. *Report/Rapport.* Ottawa. The bilingual society, founded 3 June 1933, annually publishes French and English volumes with entirely different contents. I (1933–34)– . Separate index for 1933–59.

CANADIAN HISTORICAL ASSOCIATION, Ottawa. The aims of the Association are "to encourage historical research and public interest in history; to promote the preservation of historic sites and buildings, documents, relics, and other significant heirlooms of the past; to publish historical studies and documents as circumstances may permit." Publications include: annual reports, 1915– and historical booklets.

The Canadian Historical Review. Quarterly. Toronto. I (1920)– *General Index,* I (1920)–X

(1929); XI (1930)–XX (1939); XXI (1940)–XXX (1949). Each issue includes a current bibliography of publications in English and French. A continuation of the annual *Review of Historical Publications relating to Canada.* Edited by G. M. Wrong, H. H. Langton, and W. S. Wallace. I (for 1896)– XXII (for 1917 and 1918). Indexes I–X, XI–XX.

CANDIDE DE NANT. *Pages glorieuses de l'épopée canadienne: une mission capucine en Acadie.* Montréal, 1927.

CASGRAIN, H.-R. *Les Sulpiciens et les prêtres des Missions-Étrangères en Acadie (1676–1762).* Québec, 1897.

CHAPAIS, THOMAS [IGNOTUS]. *Jean Talon, intendant de la Nouvelle-France (1665–1672).* Québec, 1904.

[CLOUTIER, PROSPER.] *Histoire de la paroisse de Champlain.* 2 vols. Trois-Rivières, 1915.

COUILLARD DESPRÉS, AZARIE. *Charles de Saint-Étienne de La Tour, gouverneur, lieutenant-général en Acadie, et son temps, 1593–1666.* Arthabaska, 1930.

—— *Charles de Saint-Étienne de La Tour, gouverneur en Acadie, 1593–1666, au tribunal de l'histoire.* Saint-Hyacinthe, 1932.

—— *Histoire des seigneurs de la Rivière-du-Sud et leurs alliés canadiens et acadiens.* Saint-Hyacinthe, 1912.

—— *Louis Hébert: premier colon canadien et sa famille.* Lille, Paris, Bruges, 1913; Montréal, 1918.

—— *La première famille française au Canada, ses alliés et ses descendants.* Montréal, 1906.

CROUSE, N. M. *Contributions of the Canadian Jesuits to the geographical knowledge of New France.* [Ithaca, N.Y.], 1924.

—— *In quest of the western ocean.* New York, [1928].

—— *Lemoyne d'Iberville: soldier of New France.* Ithaca, N.Y., [1954].

[DANIEL, FRANÇOIS.] *Histoire des grandes familles françaises du Canada ou aperçu sur le Chevalier Benoist et quelques familles contemporaines.* Montréal, 1867.

DAVELUY, M.-C. *Jeanne Mance, 1606–1673, suivie d'un essai généalogique sur les Mance et les De Mance par M. Jacques Laurent.* 1ère édition, Montréal, 1934; 2e édition, Montréal et Paris, [1962].

DAVIES, ARTHUR. "The 'English' coasts on the map of Juan de la Cosa," *Imago Mundi*, XIII (1956), 26–29.

—— "João Fernandes and the Cabot voyages," Congresso internacional de historia dos descobrimentos, *Actas* (1961), II.

DAWSON, S. E. "The voyages of the Cabots in 1497 and 1498," *RSCT*, 1st series, XII (1894),
sect.II, 51–112; 2d series, II (1896), sect.II, 3–30; III (1897), sect.II, 139–268.

DELALANDE, J. *Le Conseil souverain de la Nouvelle-France.* Québec, 1927.

DELANGLEZ, JEAN. *Frontenac and the Jesuits.* Chicago, 1939.

—— *Life and voyages of Louis Jolliet.* (Institute of Jesuit History publications.) Chicago, 1948.

—— *Louis Jolliet, vie et voyages (1645–1700).* (Les études de l'Institut d'Histoire de l'Amérique française.) Montréal, 1950.

—— *Some La Salle journeys.* Chicago, 1938.

DESROSIERS, L.-P. *Iroquoisie.* 2 vols. projected; I (1534–1646) published. Montréal, 1947.

DIONNE, N.-E. *La Nouvelle-France de Cartier à Champlain 1540–1603.* Québec, 1891.

—— *Samuel Champlain.* 2 vols. Québec, 1891, 1906.

—— *Vie et voyages de Jacques Cartier.* 3e édition. Québec, 1934.

DODGE, E. S. *Northwest by sea.* New York, 1961.

DOUVILLE, RAYMOND. *Premiers seigneurs et colons de Sainte-Anne de la Pérade (1667–1681).* Trois-Rivières, 1946.

—— *Visages du vieux Trois-Rivières.* Trois-Rivières, 1955.

ECCLES, W. J. *Canada under Louis XIV, 1663–1701.* (Canadian Centenary Series, III.) Toronto 1964.

—— *Frontenac: the courtier governor.* Toronto, 1959.

—— *Frontenac.* Traduit de l'anglais par Françoise de Tilly. (Collection Figures canadiennes, VIII.) Montréal, 1963.

ESSEX INSTITUTE. *Historical Collections*, I (1859)– . Indexes, 1859–1930 and 1931–49.

[FAILLON, É.-M.] *Histoire de la colonie française en Canada.* 3 vols. Villemarie [Montréal], 1865–66.

—— *Vie de Mademoiselle Mance et histoire de l'Hôtel-Dieu de Villemarie en Canada.* 2 vols. Paris, 1854.

—— *Vie de la Sœur Bourgeoys fondatrice de la Congrégation de Notre-Dame de Villemarie en Canada suivie de l'histoire de cet institut jusqu'à ce jour.* 2 vols. Villemarie, 1853.

FERLAND, J.-B.-A. *Cours d'histoire du Canada (1534–1759).* 2 vols. Québec, 1861, 1865.

FRÉGAULT, GUY. *Iberville le conquérant.* Montréal, 1944.

GAGNON, ERNEST. *Louis Jolliet: découvreur du Mississipi et du pays des Illinois, premier seigneur de l'île d'Anticosti.* Montréal, 1946.

GANONG, W. F. "Crucial maps in the early cartography and place-nomenclature of the Atlantic coast of Canada," *RSCT*, 3d series, sect.II: Part I, XXIII (1929), 135–75; Part II, XXIV (1930),

135–87; Part III, XXV (1931), 169–203; Part IV, XXVI (1932), 125–79; Part V, XXVII (1933), 149–95; Part VI, XXVIII (1934), 149–294; Part VII, XXIX (1935), 101–29; Part VIII, XXX (1936), 109–29; Part IX, XXXI (1937), 101–30. Reprinted as: *Crucial maps in the early cartography and place-nomenclature of the Atlantic coast of Canada: with an introduction, commentary, and map notes by Theodore E. Layng* (Royal Society of Canada special publications, VII.) Toronto, 1964.

——— "A monograph of historic sites in the province of New Brunswick," *RSCT*, 2d series, V (1899), sect.II, 213–357.

GARNEAU, F.-X. *Histoire du Canada, depuis sa découverte jusqu'à nos jours.* 1ère édition. 4 vols. Québec, 1845–52.

GARRAGHAN, G. J. *The Jesuits of the middle United States.* 3 vols. New York, 1938.

GODBOUT, ARCHANGE. *Les pionniers de la région trifluvienne (1ère série, 1634 à 1647).* (Pages trifluviennes, série A, no 14.) Trois-Rivières, 1934.

GOSSELIN, AUGUSTE. *L'Église du Canada depuis Monseigneur de Laval jusqu'à la Conquête.* 3 vols. Québec, 1911–14.

——— *La mission du Canada avant Mgr de Laval (1615–1659).* Évreux, 1909.

——— *Vie de Mgr de Laval, premier évêque de Québec et apôtre du Canada, 1622–1708.* 2 vols. Québec, 1890.

——— See also "Les Normands au Canada."

GOSSELIN, É.-H. *Documents authentiques et inédits pour servir à l'histoire de la marine normande et du commerce rouennais pendant les XVIe et XVIIe siècles.* Rouen, 1876.

——— *Nouvelles glanes historiques normandes puisées exclusivement dans les documents inédits.* (Les Normands au Canada.) Rouen, 1873.

GOWANS, ALAN. *Church architecture in New France.* Toronto, 1955.

GRAVIER, GABRIEL. *Cavelier de La Salle de Rouen.* Paris, 1871. *See* the Bibliography.

GROULX, LIONEL. *La découverte du Canada, Jacques Cartier.* Montréal, 1934.

——— *Histoire du Canada français depuis la découverte.* 4 vols. Montréal, 1950–52.

——— *Notre grande aventure: l'empire français en Amérique du Nord (1535–1760).* Montréal et Paris, [1958].

HARRISSE, HENRY. *Découverte et évolution cartographique de Terre-Neuve et des pays circonvoisins, 1497–1501–1769.* Paris, 1900.

——— *The discovery of North America: a critical, documentary, and historic investigation, with an essay on the cartography of the new world....* London, 1892.

——— *Notes pour servir à l'histoire, à la bibliographie et à la cartographie de la Nouvelle-France et des pays adjacents, 1545–1700.* Paris, 1872.

HOFFMAN, B. G. *Cabot to Cartier: sources for a historical ethnography of northeastern North America 1497–1550.* Toronto, 1961.

HUGUET, ADRIEN. *Jean de Poutrincourt, fondateur de Port-Royal en Acadie, vice-roi du Canada, 1557–1615: campagnes, voyages et aventures d'un colonisateur sous Henri IV.* (Société des Antiquaires de Picardie, Mémoires, XLIV.) Paris, 1932.

HUNT, G. T. *The wars of the Iroquois: a study in intertribal trade relations.* Madison, Wis., 1960.

INNIS, H. A. *The cod fisheries: the history of an international economy.* Revised edition. Toronto, 1954.

INSH, G. P. *Scottish colonial schemes, 1620–1686.* Glasgow, 1922.

JODOIN, ALEXANDRE, et J.-L. VINCENT. *Histoire de Longueuil et de la famille de Longueuil.* Montréal, 1889.

JOUVE, O.-M. *Les Franciscains et le Canada: aux Trois-Rivières.* Paris, 1934.

——— *Les Franciscains et le Canada: l'établissement de la foi, 1615–1629.* Québec, 1915.

KELLOGG, L. P. *The French régime in Wisconsin and the Northwest.* Madison, Wis., 1925.

KINGSFORD, WILLIAM. *The history of Canada.* 10 vols. Toronto and London, 1887–98.

LA MORANDIÈRE, CHARLES DE. *Histoire de la pêche française de la morue dans l'Amérique septentrionale (des origines à 1789).* 2 vols. Paris, 1962.

LANCTOT, GUSTAVE. *L'administration de la Nouvelle-France.* Paris, 1929.

——— *Histoire du Canada.* 3 vols. Montréal, 1959–64.

I: *Des origines au régime royal.* 1959.

II: *Du régime royal au traité d'Utrecht, 1663–1713.* 1963.

III: *Du traité d'Utrecht, au traité de Paris, 1713–1763.* 1964.

LANGEVIN, JEAN. *Notes sur les Archives de Notre-Dame de Beauport.* Québec, 1860.

LA RONCIÈRE, CHARLES DE. *Histoire de la marine française.* 1ère édition. 6 vols. Paris, 1899–1932.

LAUVRIÈRE, ÉMILE. *La tragédie d'un peuple: histoire du peuple acadien de ses origines à nos jours.* 2 vols. Paris, 1922; nouvelle édition revisée, 1924.

LEFEBVRE, ESTHER. *Marie Morin, s.h.s.j., premier historien canadien de Ville-Marie.* Montréal et Paris, 1959.

LORIN, HENRI. *Le Comte de Frontenac: étude sur le Canada français à la fin du XVIIe siècle.* Paris, 1895.

LOUNSBURY, R. G. *The British fishery at New-*

foundland 1634–1763. New Haven and London, 1934.
McGrail, T. H. *Sir William Alexander, first Earl of Stirling: a biographical study.* Edinburgh and London, 1940.
Mélanges historiques. See Sulte
Mondoux, Maria. *L'Hôtel-Dieu, premier hôpital de Montréal . . . 1642–1763.* Montréal, 1942.
Moreau, Célestin. *Histoire de l'Acadie françoise (Amérique septentrionale) de 1598 à 1755.* Paris, 1873.
Morison, S. E. *Portuguese voyages to America in the fifteenth century.* Cambridge, Mass., 1940.
Morisset, Gérard. *L'architecture en Nouvelle-France.* Québec, 1949.
Murdoch, Beamish. *A history of Nova-Scotia, or Acadie.* 3 vols. Halifax, 1865–67.
Neatby, L. H. *In quest of the North West Passage.* Toronto, 1958.
New England Historic Genealogical Society publications
New England Historical and Genealogical Register. Boston, 1847– . Indexes for volumes I–L were published in 1906–7 (persons), 1908 (subjects), and 1911 (places); Index for volumes LI–CXII compiled by M. W. Parsons and published in 1959.
Les Normands au Canada
Auguste Gosselin. *Henri de Bernières, premier curé de Québec.* Évreux, 1896; Québec, 1902.
—— *Jean Bourdon, 1634–1668.* Évreux, 1892.
—— *Jean Bourdon et son ami l'abbé de Saint-Sauveur: épisodes des temps héroïques de notre histoire.* Québec, 1904.
—— *M. Jean Le Sueur, ancien curé de Saint-Sauveur-de-Thury, premier prêtre séculier du Canada, 1634–1668.* Évreux, 1894.
—— *Jean Nicolet et le Canada de son temps.* Évreux, 1893; Québec, 1905.
—— *Journal de M. Beaudoin.* Évreux, 1900.
É.-H. Gosselin. *Nouvelles glanes historiques.*
La Nouvelle France. Monthly. Québec. I (1902)–XVII (1918). This periodical and *Parler français* were incorporated in September 1918 and named *Le Canada français* (2d series).
Nova Francia. Paris. I (1925–26)–VII (1932). Organ of the Société d'histoire du Canada, founded in France in 1924. Reproduces many documents.
Nute, G. L. *Caesars of the wilderness: Médard Chouart, Sieur Des Groseilliers and Pierre Esprit Radisson, 1618–1710.* New York, 1943.
Oleson, T. J. *Early voyages and northern approaches 1000–1632.* (Canadian Centenary Series, I.) Toronto, 1963.
Palardy, Jean. *Les meubles anciens du Canada français.* Paris, 1963, 1965.

—— *The early furniture of French Canada.* Translated from the French by Eric McLean. Toronto, 1963, 1965. Some inaccuracies in birth and death dates have been noted.
Parkman, Francis. *France and England in North America.* 8 vols. Boston, 1851–92. Many editions of each of the volumes in the series have been published, of which the following are used in the *DCB/DBC*, Vol. I:
I: *Pioneers of France in the New World.* 1st edition, Boston, 1865; 25th, revised edition, 1891.
II: *The Jesuits in North America in the seventeenth century.* 1st edition, Boston, 1867; 29th edition, 1891.
III: *La Salle and the discovery of the great west.* 12th, revised edition, Boston, 1891 or 1893 (1st edition under the title *The discovery of the great west*, Boston, 1869).
IV: *The old régime in Canada.* 1st edition, Boston, 1874; 25th edition, 1891; 29th, revised edition, 1893; new edition, Toronto, 1900.
V: *Count Frontenac and New France under Louis XIV.* 1st edition, Boston, 1877; 24th edition, 1891; new edition, Toronto, 1899.
For a summary of the various editions of Parkman's works *see*: *The Parkman reader from the works of Francis Parkman,* selected and edited by Samuel Eliot Morison (Boston and Toronto, 1955), Bibliography.
Pouliot, Léon. *Étude sur les Relations des Jésuites de la Nouvelle-France (1632–1672).* (Studia Collegii Maximi Immaculatae conceptionis, V.) Paris et Montréal, 1940.
Prowse, D. W. *A history of Newfoundland.* London, 1895.
Quinn, D. B. "The argument for the English discovery of America between 1480 and 1494," *Geographical Journal,* CXXVII (1961), 277–85.
Rameau de Saint-Père, F.-E. *Une colonie féodale en Amérique: l'Acadie (1604–1881).* 2 vols. Paris et Montréal, 1889.
Revue canadienne. Monthly. Montréal. First series, I (1864)–XVI (1879). Second series, XVII (1881)—L–LI (1906), with numbering peculiar to the series, and intermittent. Third series, I–II (1908)–XXVII (1922). Indexes.
Revue d'histoire de l'Amérique française. Quarterly. Montréal. I (1947–48)– . Publication of the Institut d'histoire de l'Amérique française. Founded and directed by Canon Lionel Groulx.
Revue de l'Université Laval. Quarterly. Québec. I (1946–47)– . Publication of the University and organ of the Société du Parler français au Canada. Continuation of the review *Le Canada Français.*

Rich, E. E. *The history of the Hudson's Bay Company 1670–1870. Volume I: 1670–1763; Volume II: 1763–1870.* (Hudson's Bay Record Society publications, XXI, XXII.) London, 1958–59. Another edition, 3 vols. Toronto, 1960.

Rochemonteix, Camille de. *Les Jésuites et la Nouvelle-France au XVIIe siècle.* 3 vols. Paris, 1895–96.

Rogers, J. D. *Newfoundland.* (C. P. Lucas, *Historical geography of the British colonies (dominions)*, V, Part IV.) Oxford, 1911; 2d edition, 1931.

Rousseau, Jacques. "Le Canada aborigène dans le contexte historique," *RHAF*, XVIII (1964), 39–63.

Roy, J.-E. *Histoire de la seigneurie de Lauzon.* 5 vols. Lévis, 1897–1904.

——— *Histoire du notariat au Canada depuis la fondation de la colonie jusqu'à nos jours.* 4 vols. Lévis, 1899–1902.

Roy, P.-G. *Fils de Québec.* 4 vols. Lévis, 1933.

——— *L'Île d'Orléans.* Québec, 1928.

——— *Noms géographiques de la province de Québec.* Lévis, 1906.

——— *Les petites choses de notre histoire.* 7 vols. Lévis et Québec, 1919–44.

——— *La ville de Québec sous le régime français.* 2 vols. Québec, 1930.

Roy, Régis, et Gérard Malchelosse. *Le régiment de Carignan: son organisation et son expédition au Canada (1665–1668): officiers et soldats qui s'établirent en Canada.* Montréal, 1925.

Royal Society of Canada/Société royale du Canada. Under the patronage of The Marquess of Lorne, the society was formed in 1882 for the encouragement of literature and science in Canada. Originally the society was composed of five sections—two for literature and three for sciences. The annual *Mémoires* of Section I and the *Transactions* of Section II include historical articles. First series: I (1882–83)–XII (1894). Second series: I (1895)–X (1904). Third series: I (1907)–LVI (1962). Fourth series: I (1963)– . Indexes.

Salone, Émile. *La colonisation de la Nouvelle-France: étude sur les origines de la nation canadienne-française.* Paris, 1906.

Shipton, C. K. *Sibley's Harvard graduates.* (Massachusetts Historical Society publications.) 10 vols., in progress. Cambridge and Boston, 1933– . A continuation of Sibley, *infra.* Vols. IV–XIII include graduates of the years 1690 to 1755.

Sibley, J. L. *Biographical sketches of graduates of Harvard University, in Cambridge, Massachusetts.* 3 vols. Cambridge, 1873–85. Includes graduates of the years 1642 to 1689.

La Société généalogique canadienne-française, *Mémoires.* Organ of the society, which was founded on the initiative of P. Archange Godbout, 3 Sept. 1943. I (1945)– .

Société historique de Québec. Founded in 1937, the Society has, to date, published chiefly studies, in the series Cahiers d'histoire. 15 vols. published. Québec, 1947–63. Cited in this volume are:

X: Silvio Dumas. *La chapelle Champlain et Notre-Dame de Recouvrance.* 1958.

XII: Adrien Pouliot et Silvio Dumas. *L'exploit du Long-Sault: les témoignages des contemporains.* 1960.

Sulte, Benjamin. "Les Français dans l'Ouest en 1671," *RSCT*, 3d series, XII (1918), sect.i, 1–31.

——— *Histoire des Canadiens français, 1608–1880.* 8 vols. Montréal, 1882–84.

——— *Mélanges historiques: études éparses et inédites.* Edités par Gérard Malchelosse. 21 vols. Montréal. 1918–34. Cited in Vol I:

V (1919 [1920]): "Les deux Duplessis," 9–28.

VIII (1922): *Le régiment de Carignan.*

X (1922): "Lachine," 66–89.

XI (1923): "La famille Godefroy," 7–38; "Les Godefroy de Maubœuf," 39–70.

XIV (1928): "Les gouverneurs des Trois-Rivières," 62–71.

XVIII (1931): *Trois-Rivières d'autrefois*, 1ère série.

XIX (1932): *Trois-Rivières d'autrefois*, 2e série.

Taylor, E. G. R. *Tudor geography, 1485–1583.* London, 1930.

Tessier, Albert. *Les Trois-Rivières: quatre siècles d'histoire 1535–1935.* Trois-Rivières, 1934.

Traquair, Ramsay. *The old architecture of Quebec: a study of the buildings from the earliest explorers to the middle of the nineteenth century.* Toronto, 1947.

Trudel, Marcel. *Histoire de la Nouvelle-France.* 3 vols. parus. Montréal, 1963– .

I: *Les vaines tentatives 1524–1603.*

II: *Le comptoir, 1604–1627.*

III: *La seigneurie des Cent-Associés, 1627–1663.*

Les Ursulines de Québec, depuis leur établissement jusqu'à nos jours. 4 vols. Québec, 1863–66; 2e édition, 1866–78.

Les Ursulines des Trois-Rivières depuis leur établissement jusqu'à nos jours. 4 vols. Trois-Rivières 1888–1911.

Vachon, André. "L'eau-de-vie dans la société indienne," *CHA Report, 1960*, 22–32.

——— *Histoire du notariat canadien, 1621–1960.* Québec, 1962.

Les voyages de découverte et les premiers établissements, XVe, XVIe siècles. Edités par Ch.-A. Julien. (Colonies et Empires, 3e série.) Paris, 1948.

Contributors

ROLAND-J. AUGER. Généalogiste, Archives du Québec, Québec.
Zacharie Dupuy.

MARIE BABOYANT. Bibliothécaire et directrice du département des Canadiana, bibliothèque de la ville de Montréal, Québec.
Antoine de La Frenaye de Brucy. Jean Peronne Dumesnil.

ALFRED G. BAILEY. Vice-President (Academic); Professor and Head of the Department of History and Anthropology, University of New Brunswick, Fredericton, New Brunswick.
Richard Denys de Fronsac.

RENÉ BAUDRY, C.S.C. Représentant des Archives publiques du Canada en France.
Hector d'Andigné de Grandfontaine. Bellot, dit Lafontaine. Mme de Brice. Jacques de Chambly. Pierre Chauvin de La Pierre. Charles Daniel. Thalour Du Perron. Jacques Fleury d'Eschambault. La Poippe. Nicolas Le Creux Du Breuil. Marc Lescarbot. Charles de Menou d'Aulnay. Antoine Parat. Louis-Pierre Thury.

HENRI BÉCHARD, S.J. Vice-postulateur de la cause de béatification et de canonisation de la vénérable Kateri Tekakouitha, Montréal, Québec.
Chaudière Noire. Catherine Gandeacteua. Ogenheratarihiens. Tareha. Kateri Tekakouitha. Joseph Togouiroui. François-Xavier (Pierre) Tonsahoten.

ETHEL M. G. BENNETT. Historical novelist, Toronto, Ontario.
Louis Couillard de Lespinay. Hélène Desportes. Guillemette Hébert. Joseph Hébert. Louis Hébert. Marie Rollet.

HÉLÈNE BERNIER. Professeur de français au cours secondaire à la commission des Écoles catholiques de Montréal, Montréal, Québec.
Marguerite Bourgeoys.

HENRY B. M. BEST. Assistant to the President, York University, Toronto, Ontario.
Barthélemy. Marie Irwin, dite de la Conception. Abraham Martin.

HERVÉ BIRON. Éditeur adjoint, *Le Journal des Débats*, Assemblée législative, Québec, Québec.
Maurice Poulin de La Fontaine.

JEAN BLAIN. Professeur assistant, département d'histoire, université de Montréal, Montréal, Québec.
François Le Moyne de Bienville. Louis Le Moyne de Châteauguay. Jacques Le Moyne de Sainte-Hélène. Pierre Picoté de Belestre.

CHARLES-MARIE BOISSONNAULT. Publiciste, poète, historien, critique littéraire, Québec, Québec.
Jean Demosny. Michel Gamelain de La Fontaine.

U. J. BOURGEOIS. Médecin, Tracadie, Nouveau-Brunswick.
Martin d'Aprendestiguy.

† GEORGE W. BROWN. First General Editor, *Dictionary of Canadian Biography/Dictionnaire biographique du Canada*, University of Toronto Press, 1959–63; Professor Emeritus, Department of History, University of Toronto, Toronto, Ontario.

M. W. BURKE-GAFFNEY, S.J. Professor Emeritus, formerly Professor of Astronomy and Lecturer in History of Science, Saint Mary's University, Halifax, Nova Scotia.
Martin Boutet de Saint-Martin.

H. C. BURLEIGH. Medical doctor, Bath, Ontario.
Noël Langlois. Ourehouare. Guillaume Richard, dit La Fleur.

LUCIEN CAMPEAU, S.J. Professeur d'histoire ecclésiastique au scolasticat de l'Immaculée-Conception, Montréal, Québec.
Nicolas Aubry. Pierre Biard. Jean Dolebeau. Gabriel Druillettes. Gilbert Du Thet. Foucher. Jean Juchereau de La Ferté. Robert Le Coq. René Le Coq de La Saussaye. François-Joseph Le Mercier. Martin de Lyonne. Énemond Massé. Henri Membertou. Julien Perrault. Joseph-Antoine Poncet de La Rivière. Charles Raymbaut.

GILLIAN T. CELL. Instructor, Department of History, University of North Carolina, Durham, North Carolina, U.S.A.
William Colston. Henry Crout. Thomas Cruse. John and *William Downing. John Guy. Nicholas Guy. Robert Hayman. William Hill. John Knight. John Mason. Bartholomew Pearson. John Rayner. Lewis Roberts. Thomas Rowley. Sir Francis Tanfield. John Treworgie. Sir William Vaughan. Sir Richard Whitbourne. Thomas Willoughby. Edward Wynne.*

MARIE-EMMANUEL CHABOT (mère Marie-Emmanuel, O.S.U.). Professeur de rhétorique, monastère des Ursulines, Québec, Québec.
Hélène Boullé. Marie-Madeleine Chauvigny de La Peltrie. Marie Guyart, dite de l'Incarnation. Marie de Savonnières de La Troche, dite de Saint-Joseph. Marie-Catherine de Simon de Longpré, dite de Saint-Augustin.

SIMONE-L. CHARETTE (sœur Marie-Jean-d'Ars C.S.C.). Professeur d'histoire et bibliothécaire, collège Basile-Moreau, Saint-Laurent, Québec.
Claude Dablon. Marie-Françoise Giffard, dite Marie de Saint-Ignace.

THOMAS CHARLAND, O.P. Couvent des Dominicains, Montréal, Québec.
Jean Crevier de Saint-François.

J.-ROGER COMEAU. Archiviste, Archives publiques du Canada, Ottawa.
Jean Bourdon de Romainville. Dauphin de Montorgueuil. Nicolas Gargot de La Rochette. Ignace de Paris.

ALAN COOKE. Formerly Assistant Librarian, Stefansson Collection, Dartmouth College; Research Fellow, Centre d'études nordiques, université Laval, Québec, Québec.
George Best. Lorenzo Ferrer Maldonado. Sir Martin Frobisher. James Hall. Thomas James. John Scolvus.

CONTRIBUTORS

NORA T. CORLEY. Librarian, Arctic Institute of North America, Montreal, Quebec.
William Hawkeridge. Jens Eriksen Munk.

CLÉMENT CORMIER, C.S.C. Recteur de l'université de Moncton, Nouveau-Brunswick.
Alexandre Le Borgne de Belle-Isle. Charles Melanson. Philippe Mius d'Entremont.

EILEEN C. CUSHING. Genealogist; formerly Assistant Archivist, Department of History, New Brunswick Museum, Saint John, New Brunswick.
Messamouet.

JEAN DARBELNET. Directeur de la maîtrise ès arts en français à la faculté des lettres de l'université Laval, Québec, Québec ; reviseur des traductions françaises, *Dictionnaire biographique du Canada/ Dictionary of Canadian Biography.*

MARIE-CLAIRE DAVELUY. Ex-bibliothécaire adjointe, bibliothèque de la ville de Montréal, professeur de catalographie et de compilation bibliographique, École de bibliothéconomie, université de Montréal (1937–43) ; historien, auteur de romans et de contes historiques pour la jeunesse.
Louis d'Ailleboust de Coulonge et d'Argentenay. Paul de Chomedey de Maisonneuve. Raphaël-Lambert Closse. Jeanne Mance. Pierre de Puiseaux.

ARTHUR DAVIES. Dean of Social Studies, Professor and Head of the Department of Geography, University of Exeter, England.
João Fernandes.

K. G. DAVIES. Professor of History, University of Bristol, England. General Editor, Hudson's Bay Record Society, London, England.
John Nixon.

RAYNALD DESMEULES. *Dictionnaire biographique du Canada/Dictionary of Canadian Biography*, Les Presses de l'université Laval, Québec, Québec.

ERNEST S. DODGE. Director, Peabody Museum, Salem, Massachusetts, U.S.A.; Editor of *The American Neptune.*
William Baffin. William Gibbons.

RAYMOND DOUVILLE. Sous-secrétaire, secrétariat du Québec, Québec.
Achille Bréhaut Delisle. François de Champflour. François Derré de Gand. Charles Du Plessis-Bochart. Guillaume Guillemot. Jacques Hertel de La Fresnière. Thomas de Lanouguère. Michel Leneuf Du Hérisson. François Marguerie de La Haye.

ANTONIO DROLET. Bibliothécaire en chef, Archives du Québec, Québec.
Florent Bonnemere. Louis Chartier. Claude David. Adrien Du Chesne. Louis Maheut.

G.-M. DUMAS, O.F.M. CAP. Professeur d'histoire et de géographie, bibliothécaire, séminaire Saint-François, Cap-Rouge, Québec.
Germain Allart. Côme de Mantes. Pacifique Duplessis. Guillaume Galleran. Paul Huet. Georges Le Baillif. Chrestien Le Clercq. Léonard de Chartres. Gervais Mohier. Irénée Piat. Nicolas Viel.

THOMAS DUNBABIN. Author and researcher, Ottawa.
James Beare. Giovanni Antonio de Carbonariis. Juan de Fuca. David Ingram. George Johnson. Charles Leigh. Henry May. John Nutt. Jean Parmentier. George Waymouth. Thomas Young.

CÉLINE DUPRÉ. *Dictionnaire biographique du Canada/ Dictionary of Canadian Biography*, Les Presses de l'université Laval, Québec, Québec.
René-Robert Cavelier de La Salle.

ALED EAMES. Warden of Neuadd Reichel and Lecturer in Education, University College of North Wales, Bangor, Wales.
Sir Thomas Button.

W. J. ECCLES. Professor, Department of History, University of Toronto, Ontario.
Jacques Bizard. Claude de Boutroue d'Aubigny. Louis de Buade de Frontenac et de Palluau. Pierre Dubois Davaugour. Jean-Baptiste Patoulet. François-Marie Perrot. Daniel de Rémy de Courcelle. Denis-Joseph de Ruette d'Auteuil. Augustin de Saffray de Mézy.

C. BRUCE FERGUSSON. Archivist of Nova Scotia; Associate Professor of History, Dalhousie University; Chairman, Historic Sites and Monuments Board of Canada; Halifax, Nova Scotia.
Bergier. Charles Duret de Chevry de La Boulaye. Constance Ferrar. Charles La Tourasse, dit Chevalier. John Leverett. Sir James Stewart. Edward Tyng. Richard Walker.

JOHN F. FLINN. Associate Professor, Department of French, University College, University of Toronto, Ontario; Committee for the English translation of French biographies, *Dictionary of Canadian Biography/Dictionnaire biographique du Canada.*

ALLAN M. FRASER. Provincial Archivist and Curator of the Newfoundland Museum; General Advisory Editor for Canada, *Encyclopedia Americana*; St. John's, Newfoundland.
Sir George Calvert.

GEORGES-ÉMILE GIGUÈRE. Professeur d'histoire du Canada, collège Sainte-Marie, Montréal, Québec.
Charles Albanel. Pierre Chastellain. Isaac Jogues.

FRÉDÉRIC GINGRAS, O.F.M. CAP. Séminaire Saint-François, Québec, Québec.
Exupère Dethunes. Jean Dolbeau. Simon Girard de La Place. Denis Jamet. Charles Langoissieux. Joseph de La Roche Daillon. Joseph Le Caron. Eustache Maupassant. Zénobe Membré. Hyacinthe Perreault. Guillaume Poulain.

ALAN GOWANS. Professor and Chairman, Department of Art and Art History, University of Delaware, Newark, Delaware, U.S.A.
Claude Baillif. François Bailly, dit Lafleur. François Boivin. Jean Lemire. Didace Pelletier.

THOMAS GRASSMANN, O.F.M. CONV. Director, The Mohawk-Caughnawaga Museum, Fonda, New York, U.S.A.
Agariata. Eustache Ahatsistari. Annenraes. Capitanal. Flemish Bastard (Bâtard Flamand). Honatteniate (Le Berger). Kiotseaeton. Pierre Magnan. Makheabichtichiou. Joseph Manitougatche. Thérèse Oionhaton. Charles Ondaaiondiont. Otreouti. Oumasasikweie. Panounias. Pierre-Antoine Pastedechouan.

F. GRENIER. Professeur titulaire de géographie humaine et directeur de l'Institut de géographie, université Laval, Québec, Québec.
Pierre Allemand. Charles Bazire. Mathieu Damours

CONTRIBUTORS

de Chauffours. François Doublet. Antoine Pécaudy de Contrecœur.
FRANCESS G. HALPENNY. Managing Editor, University of Toronto Press, Toronto, Ontario.
JEAN HAMELIN. Professeur auxiliaire, Institut d'histoire, université Laval, Québec, Québec.
Charles Amiot. Jean Bourdon. Jacques Bourdon d'Autray. Jean-François Bourdon de Dombourg. Mathurin Gagnon. Charles Huault de Montmagny. Pierre Legardeur de Repentigny. Charles Legardeur de Tilly. Jean Nicollet de Belleborne. Étienne Pézard de La Tousche Champlain. François Viennay-Pachot.
MARCEL HAMELIN. Professeur, externat classique Saint-Jean-Eudes et faculté des arts, université Laval, Québec, Québec.
Thierry Desdames. Mathieu Gaillard. Claude de Godet Des Maretz. Raymond de La Ralde. Jean Paumart.
D. C. HARVEY. Archivist Emeritus of Nova Scotia, Halifax, Nova Scotia.
Sir William Alexander, Earl of Stirling. Sir William Alexander (the younger). Asticou. Segipt.
DAVID M. HAYNE. Second General Editor, *Dictionary of Canadian Biography/Dictionnaire biographique du Canada*, August 1965– ; Chairman, Committee for the English translation of French biographies, vol. I, *DCB/DBC*; Associate Professor, Department of French, University College; Fellow, New College, University of Toronto, Toronto, Ontario.
P. H. HULTON. Assistant Keeper, Department of Prints and Drawings, British Museum, London, England.
John White.
E. HUNT. Anglican clergyman (retired); broadcaster and writer on early Newfoundland history, St. John's, Newfoundland.
Thomas Dermer. Peter Easton. Sir Henry Mainwaring. Christopher Martin. Erasmus Stourton.
MAUD M. HUTCHESON. *Dictionary of Canadian Biography/Dictionnaire biographique du Canada*, University of Toronto Press, Toronto, Ontario.
Thomas Anderson. Walsall Cobbie. Thomas Draper. Leonard Edgcombe. John French. Thomas Garland. Daniel Lane. Richard Lucas. William Lydall. John Marsh. Samuel Missenden. Thomas Phipps. Richard Power. Pierre Romieux. Joseph Thompson. James Young.
WILLARD E. IRELAND. Provincial Librarian and Archivist, Provincial Archives of British Columbia, Victoria, British Columbia.
Bartholomew de Fonte.
ALICE M. JOHNSON. Archivist, Hudson's Bay Company; Assistant Editor, Hudson's Bay Record Society, London, England.
John Abraham. Charles Bayly. William Bond. John Fletcher. George Geyer. Thomas Gorst. Andrew Hamilton. Thomas Shepard. Hugh Verner. Nehemiah Walker.
OLGA JURGENS. *Dictionnaire biographique du Canada/ Dictionary of Canadian Biography*, Les Presses de l'université Laval, Québec, Québec.
Étienne Brûlé. Jacques Le Maistre. Guillaume Vignal.
ELSIE MCLEOD JURY. Researcher, in conjunction with Wilfred Jury, Fort Sainte-Marie, Midland, Ontario.
Anadabijou. Étienne Annaotaha. Atironta (Darontal) (fl.1615). *Jean-Baptiste Atironta* (d.1650). *Pierre Atironta* (d.1672). *Auoindaon. Batiscan. Begourat. Carigouan. Chomina. Iroquet. Miristou. Simon Pieskaret. Étienne Pigarouich. Savignon. Geneviève-Agnès Skanudharoua, dite de Tous-les-Saints. Taratouan. Tehorenhaegnon. Joseph Teouatiron. Tessouat* (fl.1603–13). *Tessouat (Le Borgne de l'Île)* (d.1636). *Paul Tessouat (Le Borgne de l'Île)* (d.1654). *Totiri.*
HELMUT KALLMANN. Supervisor of Music Library, Canadian Broadcasting Corporation, Toronto, Ontario.
François Dangé. André-Louis de Merlac.
W. KAYE LAMB. Dominion Archivist, Public Archives of Canada, and National Librarian, National Library, Ottawa.
Sir Francis Drake.
LÉOPOLD LAMONTAGNE. Doyen et professeur, faculté des lettres ; directeur des cours d'été de français, université Laval, Québec, Québec ; directeur, équipe des traducteurs français, *Dictionnaire biographique du Canada/Dictionary of Canadian Biography*, Les Presses de l'université Laval.
Thomas Crisafy. Simon-François Daumont de Saint-Lusson. Jacques Duchesneau de La Doussinière et d'Ambault. Dominique La Motte de Lucière. Gabriel de La Ribourde. Jacques Leneuf de La Poterie. Jacques de Mareuil. Jean Peré. Alexandre de Prouville de Tracy. Pierre de Troyes, dit Chevalier de Troyes.
GUSTAVE LANCTOT. Auparavant sous-ministre et archiviste du Dominion, Archives publiques du Canada, et professeur honoraire d'histoire et de méthodologie, université d'Ottawa.
Juan de Agramonte. Pierre Aigron, dit Lamothe. Thomas Aubert. Claude de Brigeac. Thomas Chefdostel. Jean Denys. Jean Fonteneau, dit Jean Alfonse. Troilus de La Roche de Mesgouez.
FLORIAN LARIVIÈRE, S.J. Recteur du collège Saint-Ignace, Montréal, Québec.
Charles Garnier.
MARGARET MONTGOMERY LARNDER. Geographer, Geographical Branch, Department of Mines and Technical Surveys, Ottawa.
John Davis.
ROBERT LA ROQUE DE ROQUEBRUNE. Écrivain et archiviste, Paris.
Jean-François de La Rocque de Roberval. Marguerite de La Roque. Joseph-Antoine Le Febvre de La Barre.
RENÉ LATOURELLE, S.J. Professeur de théologie et auparavant doyen de la faculté de théologie, université Grégorienne, Rome.
Jean de Brébeuf.
ÉMERY LEBLANC. Rédacteur en chef, *L'Évangéline*, Moncton, Nouveau-Brunswick.
Pasquine. Joseph Robinau de Villebon. Vincent Saccardy.
ESTHER LEFEBVRE, R.H.S.J. Bibliothécaire, bibliothèque médicale, Hôtel-Dieu de Montréal, Quebec.
Catherine Macé. Marie Maillet. Judith Moreau de Brésoles.

CONTRIBUTORS

JEAN-JACQUES LEFEBVRE. Archiviste en chef, cour supérieure, palais de justice, Montréal, Québec.
Bénigne Basset Des Lauriers. Pierre Gadoys. Éléonore de Grandmaison. Pierre Lamotte de Saint-Paul. Charles Le Moyne de Longueuil et de Châteauguay. Claude Maugue. Jean-Baptiste Migeon de Branssat. Louis Prud'homme.

MARINE LELAND. Professor Emeritus of French Literature and French-Canadian Civilization, Smith College, Northampton, Massachusetts, U.S.A.
Jacques Babie.

ELIZABETH W. LOOSLEY. Assistant to the General Editor, *Dictionary of Canadian Biography/Dictionnaire biographique du Canada*, 1960–65, University of Toronto Press, Toronto, Ontario.

A. J. E. LUNN. Chief of the Cataloguing Division and Editor of *Canadiana*, National Library of Canada, Ottawa.
Simon Denys de La Trinité.

GEORGE MACBEATH. Director, Centennial Centre of Science and Technology, Toronto, Ontario.
Introductory Essay: *The Atlantic Region. Mathieu Damours de Freneuse. Nicolas Denys. Pierre Du Gua de Monts. Andrew Forrester. Robert Gravé Du Pont. Marie Jacquelin. Pierre de Joybert de Soulanges et de Marson. Bernard Marot. Jeanne Motin. Jean Rallua u. Isaac de Razilly. Charles de Saint-Étienne de La Tour. Claude de Saint-Étienne de La Tour. Jean Thomas.*

CONSTANCE P. MCFARLAND. Textual Editor, *Dictionary of Canadian Biography/Dictionnaire biographique du Canada*, University of Toronto Press, Toronto, Ontario.

ARTHUR MAHEUX, P.D. Archiviste du séminaire de Québec, Québec, Québec.
Henri de Bernières. Nicolas Du Bos.

GÉRARD MALCHELOSSE. Auteur, généalogiste, bibliothécaire adjoint, Bibliothèque générale, université Laval, Québec, Québec.
François Pollet de La Combe-Pocatière.

MARIE-P. MARTIN (mère Sainte-Jeanne-de-Chantal, O.S.A.). Archiviste (section historique), Hôtel-Dieu de Québec, Québec.
Marie Guenet, dite de Saint-Ignace.

OLIVIER MAURAULT, P.S.S., P.A. Ex-recteur de l'université de Montréal, Québec.
Guillaume Bailly. René de Bréhant de Galinée. Gilles Pérot. François de Salignac de La Mothe-Fénelon. Gabriel Souart.

JOHN S. MOIR. Associate Professor, Department of History, Scarborough College, University of Toronto, Ontario.
Sir David Kirke. Sir Lewis Kirke. Thomas Kirke.

J. MONET, S.J. Chargé de cours en histoire, Loyola College, Montréal, Québec.
Charles-Joseph d'Ailleboust Des Muceaux. Mathieu Amiot, dit Villeneuve. Pierre Bailloquet. Charles Boquet. Antoine Dalmas. Ambroise Davost. François Du Peron. Jacques Frémin. Léonard Garreau. Philippe Gaultier de Comporté. Eustache Lambert. Jean de Lauson (père et fils). François Malherbe. Jacques Marquette. René Ménard. Noël Negabamat, dit Tekouerimat. Anne de Noüe. Philibert Noyrot. Jean Pierron. Claude Pijart. Pierre Pijart. Claude Quentin. Louis-Arthus de Sailly.

G. ANDREWS MORIARTY. Lawyer, genealogist, Ogunquit, Maine, U.S.A.
Zachariah Gillam. Esbon Sanford.

GÉRARD MORISSET. Conservateur honoraire du musée du Québec, Québec.
Claude François, dit frère Luc. Jean Guyon. Jean Levasseur, dit Lavigne. Pierre Levasseur, dit l'Espérance. Marc-Antoine Olivier, dit le Picard. Hugues Pommier. Jean-Baptiste Villain. Robert de Villeneuve.

WILLIAM F. E. MORLEY. Bibliographer, Douglas Library, Queen's University, Kingston, Ontario.
Pierre de Chauvin de Tonnetuit. Luke Fox. Hugues Randin. Giovanni da Verrazzano.

W. L. MORTON. Professor of Canadian History and Provost, University College, University of Manitoba, Winnipeg, Manitoba.
Introductory Essay: *The Northern Approaches to Canada* [in collaboration with T. J. Oleson].

GABRIEL NADEAU. Médecin, surintendant, Rutland Hospital, Rutland, Massachusetts, U.S.A.
Vincent Basset Du Tartre. Gervais Baudouin. Jean de Bonamour. Étienne Bouchard. François Gendron. Jean Madry. Louis Pinard. Timothée Roussel.

L. H. NEATBY. Professor and Head, Department of Classics, Acadia University, Wolfville, Nova Scotia.
Robert Bylot. Henry Hudson. John Hudson.

GRACE L. NUTE. Formerly Professor, Hamline University; Director of project for the preparation of the James J. Hill Papers, St. Paul, Minnesota, U.S.A.
Médard Chouart Des Groseilliers.

† T. J. OLESON. Formerly Professor, Department of History, University of Manitoba, Winnipeg, Manitoba.
Introductory Essay: *The Northern Approaches to Canada* [in collaboration with W. L. Morton]. *Bjarni Herjólfsson. Saint Brendan. John Cunningham. Eirikr (Eric) upsi Gnuppson. Eirikr Thorvaldsson (Eric the Red). Leifr heppni Eiriksson (Leif the Lucky). Nicholas of Lynne. Snorri Thorfinnsson. Thorfinnr karlsefni Thordarson. Nicolò and Antonio Zeno.*

JEAN-GUY PELLETIER. Archiviste, Archives du Québec, Québec, Québec.
Marie Forestier, dite de Saint-Bonaventure-de-Jésus. François-Marie Renaud d'Avène de Desmeloizes. René Robinau de Bécancour. Pierre de Saurel.

LÉON POULIOT, S.J. Ex-professeur d'histoire de l'Église et ex-provincial des Jésuites du Bas-Canada, actuellement engagé dans la recherche sur l'histoire religieuse du Canada français, collège Sainte-Marie, Montréal, Québec.
Claude Allouez. Noël Chabanel. Antoine Daniel. René Goupil. Jean de La Lande. Charles Lalemant. Gabriel Lalemant. Jérôme Lalemant. Paul Le Jeune. Simon Le Moyne. Jacques Quentin. Paul Ragueneau.

HONORIUS PROVOST, PTRE. Sous-archiviste, séminaire de Québec et université Laval, Québec, Québec.
Jean Amiot. Claude Auber. Jean Baudoin. Romain

CONTRIBUTORS

Becquet. Marie-Barbe de Boullongne. Pierre de Caumont. Zacharie Cloutier. Guillaume Couillard de Lespinay. Robert Drouin. Jean Dudouyt. Michel Fillion. Robert Giffard de Moncel. Jean Guyon Du Buisson (père et fils). Jacques-François Hamelin de Bourgchemin. Charles de Lauson de Charny. Jean Le Sueur, dit abbé de Saint-Sauveur. Nicolas Le Vieux de Hauteville. Pierre Miville, dit le Suisse. Thomas Morel. Louis Peronne de Mazé. Martin Prévost. Charles Sevestre. Barthélemy Vimont.

DAVID B. QUINN. Andrew Geddes and John Rankin Professor of Modern History, University of Liverpool; Vice-President, Royal Historical Society; Liverpool, England.
Étienne Bellenger. Thomas Bradley. Richard Clarke. Thomas Croft. Sir Bernard Drake. Hugh Eliot. Richard Fisher. Sir Humphrey Gilbert. Edward Hayes. Richard Hore. David Ingram. John Jay. George Johnson. La Court de Pré-Ravillon et de Granpré. Charles Leigh. Madoc. Anthony Parkhurst. Stephanus Parmenius. John Rastell. John Rut. Lancelot Thirkill. Robert Thorne. Sylvester Wyet.

W. STANFORD REID. Professor and Head of Department of History, University of Guelph, Guelph, Ontario.
Michel-Sidrac Dugué de Boisbriand.

JEAN DE LA CROIX RIOUX, O.F.M. CAP. Professeur d'histoire, séminaire Saint-François, Cap-Rouge, Québec.
Gabriel (Théodat) Sagard.

WILLIAM I. ROBERTS, 3rd. Assistant Professor of History, Pennsylvania State University, Abington, Pennsylvania, U.S.A.
Jurriaen Aernoutsz. John Rhoades. Robert Sedgwick.

RÉGIS DE ROQUEFEUIL. Conseiller technique au programme ARDA, Québec, Québec.
François Byssot de La Rivière.

JACQUES ROUSSEAU. Professeur d'ethnobiologie et chargé de recherches à l'université Laval, Québec, Québec.
Étude préliminaire: *Les Indiens du Nord-Est de l'Amérique* [en collaboration avec George W. Brown].

C. M. ROWE. John Carter Brown Library Graduate Fellow 1965-66, Providence, Rhode Island, U.S.A.
Sir John Berry. William Hinton.

HUIA G. RYDER. Formerly Acting Art Curator, The New Brunswick Museum, Saint John, New Brunswick.
Jean de Biencourt de Poutrincourt et de Saint-Just. Charles de Biencourt de Saint-Just. William Crowne. Sir Thomas Temple.

SISTER SAINT MIRIAM OF THE TEMPLE, C.N.D. Chairman, Department of English, Marianopolis College, Montreal, Quebec.
Marie Raisin.

SYLVIA SEELEY. Librarian, Royal Canadian Geographical Society, Ottawa.
João Gonsales.

R. A. SKELTON. Deputy Keeper and Superintendent, Map Room, British Museum; Honorary Secretary, The Hakluyt Society, London, England.
John Cabot. Sebastian Cabot.

W. AUSTIN SQUIRES. Curator, Natural Science Department, The New Brunswick Museum, Saint John, New Brunswick.
Sir Samuel Argall. Ouagimou. Secoudon. Tisquantum.

C. P. STACEY. Professor of History, University of Toronto, Ontario. Director, Historical Section, Canadian Forces Headquarters, Ottawa.
Sir William Phips.

ANDRÉ SURPRENANT, S.J. Professeur de latin et de français, collège de Saint-Boniface, Saint-Boniface, Manitoba.
Pierre-Joseph-Marie Chaumonot.

ALBERT TESSIER, P.D. Ex-visiteur en chef des instituts familiaux, séminaire de Trois-Rivières, Québec.
Eustache Boullé. François-Joseph Bressani. Jacques Buteux. René Gaultier de Varennes.

G. E. THORMAN. Vice-Principal and Head, Guidance Department; Teacher of English and History, St. Thomas Collegiate, St. Thomas, Ontario.
John Outlaw. Henry Sergeant. Nicholas Smithsend. Richard Smithsend.

VICTOR TREMBLAY, P.D. Auparavant professeur d'histoire, séminaire de Chicoutimi, Québec.
Jean de Quen.

BRUCE G. TRIGGER. Assistant Professor, Department of Sociology and Anthropology, McGill University, Montreal, Quebec.
Amantacha (Louis de Sainte-Foi). Cherououny. Joseph Chihwatenha. Erouachy. Daniel Garakontié.

MARCEL TRUDEL. Professeur et directeur, Institute of Canadian Studies, Carleton University, Ottawa. Directeur adjoint pour le volume premier du *Dictionnaire biographique du Canada/Dictionary of Canadian Biography*.
Étude préliminaire: *La Nouvelle-France, 1524–1713. Pierre Angibault, dit Champdoré. Marc-Antoine Bras-de-Fer de Chateaufort. Émery de Caën. Guillaume de Caën. Jacques Cartier. Samuel de Champlain. Charité, Espérance, Foi. Donnacona. Jean Duval. François Gravé Du Pont. Macé Jalobert. Olivier Le Jeune. Olivier Letardif. Jacques Noël. Claude Roquemont de Brison. André Thevet. Nicolas de Vignau.*

ANDRÉ VACHON. Directeur adjoint, Les Presses de l'université Laval, Québec, Québec. Secrétaire général pour le volume premier du *Dictionnaire biographique du Canada/Dictionary of Canadian Biography*, Québec, Québec.
Antoine d'Allet. Guillaume Audouart, dit Saint-Germain. Laurent Bermen. Jacques Boisdon. Josias Boisseau. Lambert Boucher de Grandpré. Claude Charron de La Barre. Louis-Théandre Chartier de Lotbinière. Michel Colin. Gilbert Courseron. Adam Dollard Des Ormeaux. Jean-Baptiste Dubois de Cocreaumont et de Saint-Maurice. Dubok. Pierre Duquet de La Chesnaye. Jessé Fléché. Louis Gaudais-Dupont. Jean Gloria. Jean-Paul Godefroy. Jean Godefroy de Lintot. Thomas Godefroy de Normanville. Jacques Godefroy de Vieuxpont. Rolland Godet. Noël Jérémie, dit Lamontagne. Louis Jolliet. Jean Juchereau de Maur. Noël Juchereau Des Chatelets. Gilles Lauson. Laviolette. Jean Liégeois. Nicolas Marsolet de Saint-Aignan. Martine Messier. Le sieur de Monts. Nicolas de Mouchy. Jean-Baptiste Peuvret Demesnu.

CONTRIBUTORS

Gilles Rageot. Jean de Saint-Père. Jean Talon. Louis Taondechoren. Gabriel Thubières de Levy de Queylus. Daniel Vuil.

L.-A. VIGNERAS. Professor of Romance Languages, George Washington University, Washington, D.C., U.S.A.
Gaspar Corte-Real. Miguel Corte-Real. Matias de Echevete. João Alvares Fagundes. Estavão Gomes.

MASON WADE. Professor of History and Head, Department of History, Middlesex College, University of Western Ontario, London, Ontario.
Emmanuel Le Borgne. André Malapart.

PAUL A. W. WALLACE. Fellow in the Humanities, Lebanon Valley College, Annville, Pennsylvania, and Consultant, Pennsylvania Historical and Museum Commission; New Cumberland, Pennsylvania, U.S.A.
Dekanahwideh.

BERNARD WEILBRENNER. Directeur des Archives du Québec, Québec, Québec,
Nicolas Juchereau de Saint-Denis. Louis Rouer de Villeray. Gabriel Testard de La Forest.

CLIFFORD P. WILSON. Assistant Director, National Museum of Canada, Ottawa.
John Bridgar.

J. S. WOOD. Professor, Department of French, Victoria College, University of Toronto, Ontario; Committee for the English translation of French biographies, *Dictionary of Canadian Biography/ Dictionnaire biographique du Canada.*

Index

Included in the Index are the names of persons mentioned in Volume I, except of those—artists, for example—who had no connection with Canada. The pages for biographies included in the volume are indicated by bold type.

AAOUANDIO, 458
Abancourt, Marie d' (Jolliet; Guillot; Prévost), 392, 554
Abbadie* de Saint-Castin, Jean-Vincent d', 63, 185, 510, 577, 649
Abbot, George, 678
Abraham, John, **39**, 107, 329, 493, 529
Abraham, Mary, 39
Achelacy, chef d', 169, 275
Achiendassé, 374, 413, 414
Acqueville. *See* Bernières
Actodin (Son of Memberton), 501
Adam (Indian), 559
Adams, Clement, 158
Adhasatah. *See* Togouiroui
Adriansdatter, Katherine (Munk), 514
Aenon, 133
Aëoptahon. *See* Atironta, Jean-Baptiste
Aernoutsz, Jurriaen, 25, **39–40**, 185, 399, 573
Agariata, **40–41**, 308, 556
Agathe (Indian, possibly a sister of Thérèse Oionhaton), 523
Agnello, 317
Agona, 168, 169, 276
Agramonte, Juan de, **41**
Ahatsistari, Eustache, **41–42**, 344, 388, 523
Ahinsistan. *See* Pastedechouan
Ahuntsic (Auhaitsique, Ahautsic), François, 661
Aiandacé, 637
Aigron, Marie. *See* Daquin
Aigron, Marie-Madeleine. *See* Doucet
Aigron, Pierre, 42
Aigron *dit* Lamothe, Pierre, **42**, 666
Aiguillon, Duchesse d'. *See* Vignerot
Ailleboust, Antoine d', 42
Ailleboust, Catherine d', 43
Ailleboust, Charles d', 42
Ailleboust, Dorothée d'. *See* Manthet d'Argentenay
Ailleboust, Jean d', 42
Ailleboust, Marie-Barbe d'. *See* Boullongne
Ailleboust, Suzanne d'. *See* Hotman
Ailleboust de Coulonge et d'Argentenay, Louis d', **42–47**, 60, 79, 110, 112, 128, 217, 218, 219, 230, 231, 339, 340, 344, 349, 353, 373, 412, 431, 447, 453, 473, 480, 494, 511, 538, 580, 606, 645, 662
Ailleboust de Coulonge-la-Madeleine, Nicolas d', 43, 45, 47
Ailleboust* de Manthet, Nicolas d', 466
Ailleboust Des Muceaux, Catherine. *See* Legardeur de Repentigny

Ailleboust Des Muceaux, Charles-Joseph d', 44, 45, **47**, 219, 447, 508, 592, 600
Aillon. *See* La Roche Daillon
Ainsworth, Henry, 391
Alard, Madeleine (Troyes), 653
Albanel, Charles, 35, **47–50**, 83, 108, 226, 227, 244, 282, 396, 402, 558, 625, 629
Albemarle, Duke of. *See* Monk
Albert, Guillaume, 256
Albert, Marie-Louise (Demosny), 256
Alden*, John, 576, 654
Alden, William, 576, 654
Aleman, Lazaro. *See* "Noremberguer"
Alençon, Duc d', 229
Alexander, Janet, Countess of Stirling. *See* Erskine
Alexander, Sir William, Earl of Stirling, 25, **50–54**, 55, 242, 311, 407, 497, 596, 597, 605, 613, 636
Alexander, Sir William, the younger, 25, 53, **54–55**, 311, 405, 499, 593, 597, 605, 613
Alexandre VII (Fabio Chigi), Pope, 111, 645
Alfonse, Jean. *See* Fonteneau
Alfonse, Valentine (Fonteneau), 309
Aliecte, Antoine, 167
Aliecte, Guillaume, 167
Aliomet, Isabelle (Prud'homme), 557
Alix, Marguerite (Boullé), 109, 110
Allart, Germain (baptized Théodore), **55**, 313, 420, 439
Allde, John, 670
Allemand, Claude, 56
Allemand, Louise. *See* Douaire
Allemand, Marie. *See* Mandet
Allemand, Pierre, **56**, 653
Allen, William, 641
Allet, Antoine d', **56–57**, 220, 612, 644
Allouez, Claude, 14, **57–58**, 121, 244, 249, 492, 626
Almodóvar, Duke d', 676
Aloigny* de La Groye, Charles-Henri d', 85
Alward, Robert, 369
Amantacha, Louis de Sainte-Foi, **58–59**, 247
Amaugère, Geneviève (Bourdon), 114
Ambault. *See* Duchesneau
Amboise, Michel d', 424
Ameau*, Séverin, 327, 550, 575, 579
Amelotte, Marguerite (Chartier), 202
Amiot, Anne. *See* Convent
Amiot, Charles, **59–60**, 60, 250, 387
Amiot*, Charles, 61
Amiot, Geneviève. *See* Chavigny
Amiot, Jean, **60**, 490
Amiot, Marie. *See* Miville

717

INDEX

Amiot, Philippe, 59, 60
Amiot* de Vincelotte, Charles-Joseph, 60
Amiot, *dit* Villeneuve, Mathieu, **60–61**, 61, 250
Amiscouecan. *See* Chomina
Amours. *See* Damours
Amyot. *See* Amiot
Anadabijou, **61**, 86, 508, 638
Andehoua, Jean-Armand, 637, 638
Anderson, Sir Edmund, 280
Anderson, Thomas, **61**
Andigné de Grandfontaine, Anne d', 62
Andigné de Grandfontaine, Gaston d', 62
Andigné de Grandfontaine, Hector d' (the elder), 62
Andigné de Grandfontaine, Hector d', **61–64**, 185, 398, 435, 436, 510, 637, 667
Andioura, 429
André*, Louis, 50
Andrewes, William, 334
Andros*, Sir Edmund, 537, 573, 654
Angé. *See* Dangé
Anghiera. *See* Martire
Angibault, *dit* Champdoré, Pierre, **64**, 69, 72, 189, 292, 293, 564
Anglesey, Earl of. *See* Villiers
Ango, Jean (the elder), 72, 532
Ango* Des Maizerets, Louis, 92, 291, 506
Annaotaha, Étienne, **64–65**, 267, 272
Anne de Saint-Bernard. *See* Le Cointre
Anne de Sainte-Agnès. *See* Bourdon
Anne of Austria, Queen of France, 129, 324, 328, 348, 389, 484
Annenraes, **65–66**, 524
Anonchiara, 295
Anotaha. *See* Annaotaha
An8ennen, 247
Antaïok. *See* Amiot, Jean
Anthoine, Dom, 167
Antonio, Don (of Portugal), 228
Aonetta, Marie (wife of Chihwatenha), 212
Aontarisati, 65
Aouandoie, 73
Apostolos Valerianos. *See* Fuca
Aprendestiguy, Jeanne. *See* Saint-Étienne de la Tour
Aprendestiguy, Joanis, 66
Aprendestiguy, Marianne (Bourgeois), 67
Aprendestiguy, Martin d', Sieur de Martignon, 25, 63, **66–67**, 595
Archambault, Anne (Chauvin), 557
Archambault, Françoise. *See* Toureault
Archambault, Jacques, 427, 463
Archambault, Marie (Lauson), 427
Arentson, *See* Aernoutsz
Argall, Mary. *See* Scott
Argall, Richard, 67
Argall, Sir Samuel, 24, 53, **67–69**, 69, 95, 98, 101, 299, 441, 470, 498, 560, 592, 596
Argenson. *See* Voyer
Argentenay. *See* Ailleboust de Coulonge; Manthet
Argyle, Earl of. *See* Campbell
Arioo, 203
Arnauld, Henri, Bishop of Angers, 512
Arnoult de Broisle de Loubias, 327

Arpentigny. *See* Aprendestiguy
Arran, Earl of. *See* Stewart
Arthus. *See* Sailly
Artigny. *See* Rouer
Arundel, Earls of, 121, 241
Arundell, Thomas, first Lord Arundell of Wardour, 667
Asenragéhaon, Jeanne (wife of Ondakion), 610
Asshehurst, Thomas, 302, 343, 386
Assour, Marie (Byssot), 145
Asticou, **69–70**, 101, 526
Aston, Sir Arthur, 672
Atarhea. *See* Tareha
Atetkouanon, *See* Pastedechouan
Athasata. *See* Togouiroui
Atholl, John, fourth Earl of. *See* Stewart
Atic. *See* Chomina
Atironta, fl. 1615, **70**
Atironta, Jean-Baptiste, **70–71**
Atironta, Jean-Baptiste, wife of. *See* Catherine
Atironta, Jean-Baptiste, son of. *See* Mathieu
Atironta, Pierre, **71–72**
Atontinon*, Marie-Barbe, 118
Atotarho, 253, 254
Auber, Anne (Baudoin), 80
Auber, Claude, **72**, 80
Auber, Félix, 72
Auber, Jacqueline. *See* Lucas
Auber, Jacques, **72**
Auber, Marguerite (Doublet), 277
Auber, Marguerite (Grouvel; Fillion), 305
Auber, Marie. *See* Le Boucher
Aubert, Thomas, 22, **72**, 658, 660
Aubert* de La Chesnaye, Charles, 21, 56, 84, 85, 104, 105, 178, 200, 224, 227, 289, 338, 387, 393, 396, 397, 400, 444, 445, 538, 602
Aubert de La Chesnaye, Marie-Louise. *See* Juchereau de La Ferté
Aubigné, Françoise de, Marquise de Maintenon, 631
Aubigny. *See* Boutroue
Aubry, Nicolas, 64, **72**, 192, 292
Aucher, Anne (Gilbert), 331
Au-Ciel. *See* Ogenheratarihiens
Audiepvre, Michel, 167
Audouart, *dit* Saint-Germain, Guillaume, **73**, 91, 224, 298, 430, 538
Auger, François d'. *See* Dangé
Auger, *dit* Le Baron, Jean, 109
Augier, *dit* Desjardins, Christophe, 267
Auhaitsique, François. *See* Ahuntsic
Aulnay. *See* Menou
Aulquoy, Ambroise d' (Thomelin), 213
Aumale, Duc d'. *See* Lorraine
Auoindaon, **73**
Aussillon de Sauveterre, Paul d', 423, 424
Auteuil. *See* Ruette
Autray, Jacques d'. *See* Bourdon
Auxillon. *See* Aussillon
Avamy, Jeanne (Viennay-Pachot), 661
Avaugour. *See* Dubois Davaugour
Avène. *See* Renaud
Ayala, Pedro d', 147, 148, 149, 150, 151
Ayolas, Juan d', 342, 343

INDEX

BABIE, Isabeau. *See* Robin
Babie, Jacques, **74**
Babie, Jeanne. *See* Dandonneau
Babie*, Raymond, 74
Baby*, François, 74
Baby*, Jacques Duperron, 74
Bacqueville. *See* Le Roy de La Poterie
Badon, Clémence de (La Motte), 415
Baffin, Mrs., 75
Baffin, William, 5, 20, **74–75**, 144, 145, 252, 360, 378
Baguleughe, Elizabeth (Pearson), 535
Bahamas, Baron des. *See* Caën, Guillaume de (the younger)
Bailey, Capt., 383
Baillargé*, Thomas, 76, 77
Baillargeon*, Charles-François, 356
Baillif, Catherine. *See* Sainctar
Baillif, Claude, **75–77**, 460, 536, 664
Bailloquet, Pierre, **78**, 282, 345
Bailly, Guillaume, 78
Bailly, Marie. *See* Fonteneau
Bailly, Robertus de, 659
Bailly, *dit* Lafleur, François, **78**
Baily (Baley). *See* Bayly
Baltimore. *See* Calvert
Baptiste, Pierre. *See* Maisonnat
Barbé, Jeanne (Villain), 663
Barbeau. *See* Lucault
Barbier*, Marie, *dite* de l'Assomption, 117
Barbier, Minime, 230
Barcelos, Pedro de, 234, 305
Bárdarson, Ivar. *See* Ivar; Herjólfr
Bardou*, Anselme (or Ignace), 55, 312, 420
Barker, Andrew, 74
Barker, John, 365
Barlow, Roger, 156
Barnard, Anne (Fox), 311
Barnoin, François de, 478
Barré, Charlotte, *dite* de Saint-Ignace, 43, 208, 217, 230
Barrow, Henry, 390
Barthélemy, **79**
Barthélemy*, Michel, 126, 127, 647
Basset, Bonaventure, 80
Basset, Catherine. *See* Gaudreau
Basset*, David, 530
Basset, Jean, 79
Basset Des Lauriers, Bénigne, **79**, 80, 201, 230, 266, 273, 465, 498, 557
Basset Des Lauriers, Jeanne. *See* Vauvilliers
Basset Du Tartre, Vincent, **79–80**
Bastille. *See* Le Breton
Bâtard Flamand. *See* Flemish Bastard
Batiscan, **80**, 222
Baubee. *See* Babie
Baudoin, Jean, **80**, 577
Baudouin, Anne. *See* Auber
Baudouin, Gervais (the elder), 80
Baudouin, Gervais (the younger), **80–81**
Baudouin, Gervais (son of Gervais Baudouin, the younger), 81
Baudouin, Jeanne. *See* Desrues
Baudouin*, Michel, 81

Baugé, Jeanne de (Le Royer de La Dauversière), 214
Baugy*, Henri de, 178, 444
Bavin, Thomas, 333
Bavis, Jean, 74
Bayley*, Henry, 308, 611
Bayly, Charles, 39, 47, 49, 50, **81–84**, 107, 129, 226, 328, 337, 343, 396, 477, 518, 519, 553, 657, 666
Bayly, Hannah, 83, 84
Bazire, Charles, **84–85**, 114, 238, 326
Bazire, Charles (the younger), 84
Bazire, Geneviève. *See* Macard
Bazire, Jean, 84
Bazire, Jeanne. *See* Le Borgne
Bazire, Marie (Gaultier de Comporté), 84, 326
Beare, James, **85–86**, 317
Beaubassin. *See* Leneuf
Beaudoin. *See* Baudoin
Beauharnais, Marie de. *See* Bonneau de Rubelles
Beaujeu. *See* Le Gallois
Beaujot, Jean, 311
Beaulieu. *See* Gourdeau
Beaupré, Vicomte de. *See* Guyon Des Granches
Beauregard. *See* Boudier
Beauregard*, Barthélemy de, 533
Beauvais. *See* Legardeur
Beauvoir Du Roure de Combalet. *See* Vignerot
Bécancour. *See* Robinau
Bécart* de Granville, Pierre, 387
Bechourat. *See* Begourat
Becquet, Anne. *See* Vasse
Becquet, Julien, 86
Becquet, Marie. *See* Pellerin
Becquet, Romain, 85, **86**, 106
Becquet, Romaine. *See* Boudet
Beddé, Gilles de, 474
Begourat, 61, **86**
Belestre. *See* Picoté
Belin, Madeleine (Le Febvre de La Barre), 442
Bellanger, Françoise (Gamelin), 321
Belleborne. *See* Nicollet
Bellecourt. *See* Pouteret
Bellefonds. *See* Genaple
Bellefontaine. *See* Fortin
Belle-Isle. *See* Le Borgne
Bellenger, Étienne, **87–89**, 421
Belleville, Catherine. *See* Gauchet
Bellevue, Mme de. *See* Dolebeau, Antoinette
Bellinger. *See* Bellenger
Bellois, Cornelis (Corneille) de, 291, 294
Bellot, *dit* Lafontaine, **89**
Belmont. *See* Vachon
Bémont. *See* Du Saussay
Benne, Le commandant de, 419
Bennet, Stephen, 450
Berchereau. *See* Chavigny
Bergeron, Pierre, 409
Berges. *See* Renaud d'Avène
Bergier (or possibly Clerbaud-Bergier), **89–90**, 258, 260, 298, 542
Bergier Deshormeaux (or Des Ormeaux), 90
Bérin, Marguerite (Daumont de Saint-Lusson?), 249, 250
Berlise. *See* Faure

719

INDEX

Bermen, Laurent, **90–91**
Bermen de La Martinière, Anne de. *See* Després
Bermen* de La Martinière, Claude de, 39, 56, 107, 329, 430, 529, 581, 611
Bernard, André, 383
Bernard*, *dit* Larivière, Hilaire, 76
Bernier, Jeanne. *See* Villain
Bernier, Mathurin, 663
Bernières, Henri de, **91–92**, 291, 355
Bernières, Jourdaine de, 91
Bernières d'Acqueville, Madeleine. *See* Le Breton
Bernières d'Acqueville, Pierre, 91
Bernières de Louvigny, Jean de, 91, 208, 291, 587
Bernou, Claude, 174, 175, 179
Berrin, Marguerite (Bouin), 250
Berry, Sir John, 24, **92–93**, 278, 370
Berthelot*, François, 661
Berthier*, Isaac-Alexandre, 494, 556, 565, 602
Bertrand* de Latour, Louis, 291, 551, 630
Bérulle, Pierre de, 115
Beschefer*, Thierry, 50, 108, 345, 445
Besouat. *See* Tessouat
Bessabes, 69, 529
Best, George, 5, 85, **93–94**, 153, 316, 317, 318, 670
Béthune, Maximilien de, Baron de Rosny, Duc de Sully, 293
Beuvy, Anne de. *See* Bury
Biard, Jean, 94
Biard, Jeanne. *See* Cluzel
Biard, Pierre, 67, 68, 69, **94–96**, 97, 98, 100, 101, 165, 299, 307, 347, 441, 442, 456, 470, 498, 500, 560, 604
Bica, Philippe (Massé), 497
Bidoux de Lartigue, 423
Biencourt, Charles de, 96
Biencourt, Florimond de, 96
Biencourt, Jacques de (brother of Jean de Biencourt), 96
Biencourt, Jacques de (son of Jean de Biencourt), 96, 99
Biencourt, Jeanne de. *See* Salazar
Biencourt, Jeanne de (sister of Jean de Biencourt), 96
Biencourt, Louis de. 96
Biencourt de Poutrincourt, Claude de. *See* Pajot
Biencourt de Poutrincourt et de Saint-Just, Jean de, 28, 64, 67, 94, 95, **96–99**, 99, 100, 101, 110, 189, 292, 293, 294, 299, 300, 307, 347, 367, 441, 469, 470, 476, 495, 500, 501, 507, 526, 527, 564, 592, 596, 604
Biencourt de Saint-Just, Charles de, 25, 51, 67, 69, 94, 95, 97, 98, **99–102**, 293, 299, 307, 347, 470, 471, 476, 501, 592
Bienville. S*ee* Le Moyne
Big Mouth. *See* Otreouti
Billy, Godefroy de, 469
Bisson, Julienne (Demosny), 256
Bissot, François. *See* Byssot
Bissot*, François-Marie, 146
Bissot*, Jean-Baptiste, 146
Bizard, David, 102
Bizard, Guillemette. *See* Robert
Bizard, Jacques, **102–3**, 231, 540, 600
Bizard, Jeanne-Cécile. *See* Closse

Bjarni Herjólfsson, **103–4**, 448
Black Cauldron. *See* Chaudière Noire
Blainville. *See* Céloron
Blair, Regent, 54
Blaise, Jeanne-Cécile. *See* Closse
Blaise* Des Bergères de Rigauville, Raymond, 103, 231
Blanchon, Anne. *See* Convent
Blarye, *dit* Titailt, 425
Blas, Hernando, 157
Bligh, William, 378
Blondeau, Isabelle or Isabeau (Villesavin), 484
Blundeville, Thomas, 678
Bocall, Stevan de, 306, 671, 672
Bochart. *See* Du Plessis
Bochart* Champigny, Jean, 56, 103, 114, 138, 141, 239, 299, 320, 338, 398, 488, 528, 577, 582, 664
Bochart de Champigny, Marie (Prouville), 554
Bodeau, Mme, 610
Boeve, Jacobus, 369
Boisbriand. *See* Dugué
Boisbuisson, Louis-Marin. *See* Boucher
Boisdon, Jacques, **104**
Bois-le-Duc. *See* Cnoyen
Boispineau. *See* Jard
Boisseau, Josias, **104–6**, 290, 396, 397, 541
Boisseau, Marie. *See* Colombier
Boisseau, *dit* Cognac, Jacques, 267, 273
Boissel, Marguerite (Bouchard), 109
Boisvert. *See* Rapine
Boivin, Anne (Lauson), 427
Boivin, Charles, 106
Boivin, François, **106**
Boivin, Guillaume, 106
Boivin, Pierre, 106
Boivin, Thiennette. *See* Fafard
Bonamour, Jean de, **106–7**
Bonaventure, Brother, 386
Bonaventure, Simon-Pierre. *See* Denys
Bonaventure Basset, 80
Bond, Susan, 107
Bond, William, **107**, 361, 493, 529, 657
Bondy. *See* Douaire
Bonneau de La Varenne, Roger de, 573
Bonneau de Rubelles, Marie (Beauharnais de Miramion), 117
Bonnemere, Florent, **107–8**
Bonnerme, 190, 300
Bonnet, Jeanne (Richard), 473
Bontemps, Capt., 348
Booth, Sir George, 369
Boquet, Charles, **108**, 315, 547, 635, 651
Borghese, Camillo. *See* Paul V
Borough, Stephen, 158
Borough, William, 333
Borromeo, Charles (St.), 91, 469
Bossuet, Jacques Bénigne, 488
Bouat, Abraham, 416
Bouchard, Étienne, **108–9**, 201
Bouchard, Marguerite. *See* Boissel
Boucher, 89
Boucher, Gaspard, 330
Boucher, Jeanne. *See* Crevier
Boucher, Marie (Gaultier de Varennes), 327

INDEX

Boucher, Marie-Madeleine. *See* Marie-Madeleine Chrestienne
Boucher, Marin, 330
Boucher*, Pierre, 32, 45, 109, 123, 172, 200, 238, 283, 349, 354, 404, 468, 511, 512, 543, 579, 619
Boucher de Grandpré, Lambert, **109**
Boucher de Grandpré, Marguerite. *See* Vauvril de Blason
Boucher, *dit* Boisbuisson, Louis-Marin, 619
Boudet, Romaine (Becquet), 86
Boudier de Beauregard, Antoine, 344
Boudier de Beauregard, Éléonore. *See* Grandmaison
Boudrot, Abraham, 427
Bouette, Jeanne (Roussel), 583
Bouge, *dite* la Corruble, Ange, 203
Bouillon, Duc de. *See* La Marck
Bouin, Julien, 250
Bouin, Marguerite. *See* Berrin
Boulay, Capt. *See* Boullet
Boullé, Eustache, **109–10**, 193, 195, 200, 311, 495, 509
Boullé, Hélène (Champlain), *dite* de Saint-Augustin, 109, **110**, 161, 190
Boullé, Marguerite. *See* Alix
Boullé, Nicolas, 109, 110
Boullet, Capt., 110
Boullongne, Eustache de. *See* Quéan
Boullongne, Florentin de, 43, 110
Boullongne, Marie-Barbe de (Ailleboust), 43, 44, 47, **110–11**, 113, 204, 206, 217, 230, 412, 612
Boullongne, Philippine-Gertrude de, *dite* de Saint-Dominique, 43, 44, 111, 217, 230
Bouquin*, Claude, 361
Bourbon, César de, Duc de Vendôme, 129, 434, 436, 514
Bourbon, Charles de, Cardinal, Archbishop of Rouen, 87, 88, 89, 421
Bourbon, Charles de, Comte de Soissons, 186, 191, 294
Bourbon, François de, Duc de Montpensier, 421
Bourbon, Henri II, Prince de Condé, 98, 186, 187, 191, 192, 193, 194, 294, 386
Bourbon, family, 510
Bourbonnière. *See* Gaudry
Bourcier, Françoise (Chartier), 202
Bourdon, Anne. *See* Gasnier
Bourdon*, Anne, *dite* de Sainte-Agnès, 112, 113, 430
Bourdon, Geneviève. *See* Amaugère
Bourdon, Geneviève, *dite* Marie de Saint-Joseph, 113
Bourdon, Jacqueline. *See* Potel
Bourdon, Jean (M. de Saint-Jean or Sieur de Saint-François), 45, 49, 106, **111–13**, 113, 114, 202, 204, 227, 339, 340, 344, 353, 359, 371, 372, 373, 389, 396, 397, 404, 430, 472, 480, 523, 538, 580, 584, 585, 587, 588, 589
Bourdon*, Marguerite, *dite* de Saint-Jean-Baptiste, 113
Bourdon, Marie (Gloria), 339
Bourdon, Marie, *dite* Marie-Thérèse-de-Jésus, 113
Bourdon, Nicolas, 114
Bourdon d'Autray, Jacques, 111, **113–14**, 178
Bourdon de Dombourg, Jean-François, 112, 113, 114
Bourdon de Dombourg, Jeanne. *See* Jannière
Bourdon de Romainville, Catherine, 114
Bourdon de Romainville, Jean, **114–15**, 257
Bourdon de Romainville, Madeleine. *See* Daguerre

Bourduceau, Anne-Françoise (Sailly), 592
Bourduceau, Médéric, 592
Bourgchemin. *See* Hamelin
Bourgeois, Guillaume, 67
Bourgeois*, Jacques, 67, 510
Bourgeois, Marianne. *See* Aprendestiguy
Bourgeoys, Abraham, 115
Bourgeoys, Anne, 115
Bourgeoys, Guillemette. *See* Garnier
Bourgeoys, Marguerite, *dite* du Saint-Sacrement, 31, **115–19**, 213, 220, 231, 344, 453, 486, 487, 564, 598
Boursier, Joseph, 461
Boussat*, Jean, 108
Boutet de Saint-Martin, Catherine. *See* Soulage
Boutet de Saint-Martin, Marie, 119
Boutet de Saint-Martin, Martin, **119**, 359
Boutilier, 503
Boutillac, Jean de, 424
Boutroue, Mlle de (daughter of Claude de Boutroue), 322
Boutroue d'Aubigny, Claude de, **119–20**, 322, 326, 534, 571, 624
Boutroue d'Aubigny, Marie. *See* Lescot
Bouvier (perhaps Boyer), 382
Bouvier*, Michel, 78
Bouvot de Chevilly, François, 213
Bouvot de Chevilly, Jacqueline. *See* Chomedey
Boves, Charles de, 386, 417
Boyer. *See* Bouvier
Boyer, Daniel, 193, 194, 291
Boyle, Robert, 385
Boyvinet, Gilles de, 468, 582
Bradford, William, 392
Bradley, Thomas, **120**, 150, 164, 641
Bragg, Sir James, 605
Branssat. *See* Migeon
Bras-de-fer de Chateaufort, Marc-Antoine, **120–21**, 127, 372, 454
Brassier, Jacques, 267
Bréanainn. *See* Brendan, Saint.
Brébeuf, Georges de, 121
Brébeuf, Jean de, 9, 31, 60, 64, 73, **121–26**, 130, 203, 205, 206, 219, 247, 253, 281, 369, 388, 390, 411, 413, 414, 420, 458, 459, 460, 461, 483, 521, 522, 527, 549, 561, 562, 609, 610, 639, 661
Brébeuf, Nicolas de, 121
Bréhant, Mathurin de, 126
Bréhant de Galinée, René de, 35, **126–27**, 173, 174, 248, 393, 572, 625, 647
Bréhaut Delisle, Achille (Antoine-Louis?) de, 121, **127–28**, 372, 446
Brekenmacher*, Jean-Melchior, *dit* Père François, 312
Brendan (Bréanainn), Saint, **675**
Brereton, John, 364
Brésoles. *See* Moreau
Bressani, François-Joseph (Francesco-Giuseppe), 59, 71, 124, **128–29**, 389, 549
Brétigny. *See* Poncet de La Rivière
Bretonvilliers. *See* Le Rageois
Brice, Mme de, **129**, 380, 434, 514
Brice de Sainte-Croix, 129, 434, 514
Bridgar, John, 39, 56, 83, **129–30**, 227, 337, 338, 518, 528, 601, 606

INDEX

Brigeac, Claude de, **130**, 274, 662
Briggs, Henry, 311, 312
Brijat. *See* Brigeac
Brinon, Marie de (Chauvin de Tonnetuit), 209
Brisac. *See* Brigeac
Brisay* de Denonville, Jacques-René de, 56, 103, 109, 112, 114, 119, 137, 138, 204, 239, 295, 308, 320, 327, 397, 446, 463, 465, 488, 523, 526, 528, 537, 572, 582, 650, 653, 664
Brison. *See* Roquemont
Broisle de Loubias. *See* Arnoult
Brooke, Sir John, 311
Brossard*, Urbain, 78
Brouet, Ambroise, 461
Brouillan*, Jacques-François de, *dit* de Saint-André, 246, 530
Browne, Maurice, 229, 334, 531, 532
Browne (Brownel), Oliver. *See* Brunel
Browne, Richard, 380
Browne, Robert, 390, 392, 450
Brucy, Antoine de. *See* La Frenaye
Brulart de Sillery, Madeleine (Faure), 484
Brulart de Sillery, Nicolas, 484
Brulart de Sillery, Noël, 263, 470, 484, 516, 565
Brûlé, Étienne, 16, 59, **130–33**, 190, 191, 192, 196, 381, 493, 494, 516, 590, 603, 639
Brunel (Brownel, Browne), Olivier (Oliver), 408
Bruyas*, Jacques, 321, 635, 651
Buache de La Neuville, Philippe, 676, 677
Buade, Anne de. *See* La Grange; Phélypeaux
Buade, Antoine de, 134
Buade, François-Louis de, 134, 142
Buade, Henri de, de Frontenac et de Palluau, 134
Buade de Frontenac et de Palluau, Louis de, 32, 35, 40, 47, 49, 83, 84, 102, 104, 105, 106, 109, **133–42**, 174, 175, 177, 178, 185, 201, 204, 226, 238, 239, 245, 250, 286, 287, 288, 289, 290, 291, 295, 297, 309, 320, 323, 326, 327, 340, 361, 398, 399, 400, 402, 410, 417, 420, 439, 440, 443, 444, 448, 464, 466, 488, 489, 498, 499, 502, 528, 534, 535, 539, 540, 541, 544, 545, 565, 572, 573, 575, 576, 578, 581, 582, 583, 584, 585, 599, 600, 602, 613, 620, 622, 627, 632, 634, 650
Buchanan, George, 50
Buchanan, Thomas, 50
Buckingham. *See* Villiers, George
Budai Parmenius István. *See* Parmenius
Bueil, Honorat de, 421
Bugaret, Catherine (La Tourasse), 427
Buil, Friar, 150
Buisset, Luc, 438, 501
Buisson, Paul, 352
Bullion, Claude de, 484
Bullion, Mme de. *See* Faure
Bunyan, John, 378
Burel, Gilbert, 121
Burghley. *See* Cecil
Bury, Anne de (Talon), 614
Buteux, Jacques, 106, **142–43**, 214, 287, 341, 432, 453, 481, 549, 551, 558, 566, 640
Buteux, Jean, 142
Button, Barbara. *See* Merrick
Button, Margaret. *See* Lewis

Button, Mary. *See* Rice
Button, Miles (father of Sir Thomas), 144
Button, Miles (son of Sir Thomas), 144
Button, Sir Thomas, 20, 74, **144–45,** 145, 312, 329, 362, 378, 515
Butts, Thomas, 371
Bylot, Robert, 20, 74, 75, 144, **145,** 329, 374, 376, 377, 378
Byssot*, Charles-François, 146
Byssot, Claire-Françoise (Jolliet), 146, 395, 396
Byssot, François-Marie. *See* Bissot
Byssot, Geneviève (Maheut), 480
Byssot, Jean-Baptiste. *See* Bissot
Byssot, Marie. *See* Assour
Byssot de La Rivière, François, **145–46**, 395, 447, 620, 622
Byssot de La Rivière, Marie. *See* Couillard
Byssot Du Hommée, Jean, 145

CABANAC. *See* Desjordy
Cabot, Catalina. *See* Medrano
Cabot, Elizabeth, 158
Cabot, John, 19, 21, 22, 41, 120, **146–52,** 152, 153, 154, 164, 166, 171, 234, 240, 304, 333, 386, 641, 643
Cabot, Juana (Joanna?), 158
Cabot, Lewis (Ludovico), 147
Cabot, Sancio, 147
Cabot, Sebastian, 19, 21, 146, 147, 148, 149, 151, **152–58,** 375, 565, 643
Caboto, Giulio, 146
Caboto, Mattea, 146
Caboto, Piero, 146
Cadieu, Charles, 584
Cadillac. *See* Laumet
Caën, Émery de, 30, 58, **159,** 159, 160, 161, 194, 195, 197, 211, 266, 296, 297, 405, 407, 411, 419, 441, 473, 479, 533, 546
Caën, Ézéchiel de, 159, 160
Caën, Guillaume de (the elder), 159, 419
Caën, Guillaume de, 30, 110, 159, **159–62,** 194, 247, 266, 346, 368, 411, 419, 433, 473, 521
Caën, Hélène de, 161
Caën, Marie de (daughter of Guillaume), 161
Caën, Marie de. *See* Langlois; Sores
Caën, Suzanne de. *See* Petit
Caesar, Dr. Julius, 89
Cailhault* de La Tesserie, Denis-Jacques de, 589
Cailhault de La Tesserie, Éléonore de. *See* Grandmaison
Cailhault de La Tesserie, Jacques de, 285, 344, 345, 537, 589
Cailleteau, Françoise (Denys de Fronsac), 260
Cair, John, 150
Callières*, Louis-Hector de, 103, 138, 139, 140, 204, 540, 541, 581, 583, 633, 634
Calmonotius. *See* Chaumonot
Calvert, Alice. *See* Crosland
Calvert, Anne. *See* Mynne
Calvert, Cecil, second Lord Baltimore, 163, 369, 406
Calvert, Sir George, Lord Baltimore, 23, **162–63**, 365, 369, 405, 406, 419, 522, 567, 614, 653, 655, 672
Calvert, Jane, 162
Calvert, Leonard (father of Sir George), 162

INDEX

Calvert, Leonard (natural son of Sir George), 163
Calvonotti. *See* Chaumonot
Camaret, Marie, 197
Cambridge. *See* Hamilton
Campan, Gabriel, 213
Campbell, Archibald, seventh Earl of Argyle, 50
Camus, Claude (Charron de La Barre), 200, 201
Canchy de Lerole, Louis de, 40, 308
Canger, M. de, 257
Cantino, Alberto, 235
Capelli, Fiametta (da Verrazzano), 657
Capitanal, **163–64**
Cap-Tourmente, Baron du. *See* Caën, Guillaume de (the younger)
Carbery. *See* Vaughan
Carbonariis, Giovanni Antonio de, 150, **164**
Carcy. *See* Pajet
Cardenat, M. de, 359
Cardin, Maurice, 553
Carheil*, Étienne de, 322, 331
Carigouan, 6, **164–65,** 533
Carion, M. de, 600
Carion, Jeanne. *See* Dufresnoy
Carleill, Christopher, 333, 336, 363, 364
Carli, Bernardo, 658, 659
Carlier, Anne (Du Saussay de Bémont), 583
Caro, Gregorio, 156
Caron, Antoinette (Du Bos), 286
Caron, François, 109
Caron, Marie. *See* Crevet
Caron, Robert, 417
Cartier, Catherine. *See* Des Granches
Cartier, Jacques, 7, 11, 19, 21, 22, 27, **165–72,** 188, 191, 275, 276, 301, 371, 372, 384, 409, 423, 424, 426, 432, 469, 500, 520, 553, 557, 612, 659, 680
Cartier, Jeanne (Noël), 520
Cartwright, Sir George, 226, 337
Cartwright, John, 667
Cary, Henry, later Lord Falkland, 365, 632, 655, 669
Casson. *See* Dollier
Castille, Pierre de, 470
Castro, Isabel de (Corte-Real), 236
Catherine (Indian). *See* Gandeacteua
Catherine (Indian, wife of Jean-Baptiste Atironta), 71
Catherine (Indian, daughter of Totiri), 652
Catherine de Medici, Queen of France, 367, 421, 679
Catherine de Saint-Augustin. *See* Simon de Longpré
Caulincourt, Marie de (Lespinay), 425
Caumont, Pierre de, 172
Cavagnial. *See* Rigaud de Vaudreuil
Cavelier, Catherine. *See* Geest
Cavelier*, Jean, 79, 180, 183
Cavelier, Jean, 172
Cavelier, Perrette (Godefroy), 340
Cavelier de La Salle, René-Robert, 35, 79, 113, 126, 136, **172–84,** 226, 248, 289, 290, 379, 415, 420, 438, 440, 444, 446, 464, 501, 502, 557, 572, 573, 600, 625, 653
Cavendish, Thomas, 252
Cecil, Robert, Earl of Salisbury, 162, 364, 365
Cecil, William, Lord Burghley, 306, 362, 363, 364, 391, 409, 450, 671

Cécile (Indian, possibly a sister of Thérèse Oionhaton), 523
Cécile de Sainte-Croix, 353
Cecilia (Indian, wife of Oumasasikweie). *See* Natoukwabekwe
Céleste. *See* Ogenheratarihiens
Cèllere, Giulio, Comte de, 187, 658
Celles Duclos, Mme, 464
Céloron de Blainville, Hélène. *See* Picoté de Belestre
Céloron* de Blainville, Jean-Baptiste, 410
Cendre Chaude. *See* Ogenheratarihiens
Certain, André, 504
Chabanel, Noël, **184–85,** 412, 414
Chabert, Jeanne de, 213
Chabot, Philippe de, Seigneur de Brion, Comte de Charny et Buzançais, 660
Chalain. *See* Fouquet
Chalifour, Paul, 460
Chaline, Jean-Daniel, 311, 593, 597
Challoner, Sir Thomas, 530
Chambalon, Geneviève. *See* Roussel
Chambalon*, Louis, 583
Chambellé, Perrine de (Dugué de La Boulardière), 295
Chambly, Jacques de, 40, 63, **185,** 399, 556
Chambly, Louise de. *See* Laulne
Chambly, Philippe de, 185
Champaigne. *See* Champion
Champdoré. *See* Angibault
Champernowne, Katherine (Gilbert), 331
Champflour, Bertrand de, 186
Champflour, François de, **186,** 370, 403, 489, 548, 640
Champigny. *See* Bochart
Champion (or Champaigne), Capt., 80
Champion, Pierre, 563
Champlain. *See* Pézard de La Tousche
Champlain, Anthoine de, 186
Champlain, Hélène de. *See* Boullé
Champlain, Marguerite de. *See* Le Roy
Champlain, Samuel de, 7, 10, 11, 12, 13, 16, 27, 28, 29, 34, 35, 36, 53, 59, 61, 64, 70, 72, 76, 80, 86, 87, 96, 99, 100, 101, 109, 110, 120, 121, 122, 123, 125, 127, 130, 131, 132, 143, 159, 160, 161, 163, 164, **186–99,** 200, 208, 209, 211, 222, 236, 237, 238, 253, 262, 263, 265, 283, 292, 293, 294, 297, 300, 302, 303, 307, 311, 339, 340, 341, 342, 345, 346, 347, 366, 367, 368, 372, 373, 381, 382, 386, 405, 406, 407, 411, 424, 428, 432, 433, 436, 437, 452, 454, 470, 471, 473, 479, 482, 487, 488, 493, 494, 495, 500, 501, 507, 508, 509, 511, 516, **517,** 526, 529, 557, 558, 564, 565, 567, 568, 569, **570,** 578, 579, 591, 593, 602, 603, 604, 613, 615, 638, 639, 659, 662, 663, 680
Champs, Guillaume de. *See* Des Champs
Champvallon. *See* Harlay
Chancellor, Richard, 158
Chaouerindamaguetch, 111
Chapelier, Marie (Drouin), 281
Chapouin. *See* Garnier
Chardon de Tressonville, Jacques de, 87
Charest, Étienne, 620
Charité (Indian), 196, **199–200,** 237, 366, 452, 494
Charles, Brother. *See* Langoissieux
Charles, Capt., 451

723

Charles I, King of Great Britain and Ireland, 50, 51, 52, 53, 54, 81, 163, 311, 369, 384, 405, 406, 407, 419, 605, 613, 655, 673
Charles II, King of Great Britain and Ireland, 62, 82, 226, 241, 242, 337, 369, 406, 407, 436, 481, 513, 604, 636, 637
Charles V, Holy Roman emperor (Charles I of Spain), 27, 155, 156, 157, 158, 168, 342, 423
Charles VI, King of France, 202
Charles VII, King of France, 107, 287
Charles IX, King of France, 96, 573
Charlevoix*, Pierre-François-Xavier de, 45, 76, 100, 112, 183, 239, 267, 355, 357, 424, 440, 455, 466, 471, 492, 522, 523, 545, 633, 635, 649, 650
Charlotte de Saint-Ignace. *See* Barré
Charly*, Marie-Catherine, *dite* du Saint-Sacrement, 117
Charnisay. *See* Menou
Charny. *See* Lauson
Charon, Geneviève (Pijart), 549
Charron de La Barre, Claude, **200-201**, 478, 588, 589
Charron de La Barre, Claude. *See* Camus
Charron de La Barre, Élisabeth. *See* Damours de Chauffours
Chartier, Alain, 202
Chartier, François. *See* Bourcier
Chartier, Joseph, 202
Chartier, Louis, 109, **201**
Chartier, Marguerite. *See* Amelotte
Chartier, Marie. *See* Lenoir
Chartier, Philippe, 202
Chartier, René, 452
Chartier, René (Prior), 202, 662
Chartier de La Broquerie, Louis, 201
Chartier de Lotbinière, Clément, 202
Chartier de Lotbinière, Élisabeth. *See* Damours
Chartier de Lotbinière, Louis-Théandre, 112, **201-3**, 245, 399, 588, 589, 617, 629
Chartier de Lotbinière, Marie-Françoise (Joybert de Soulanges et de Marson), 202, 399
Chartier* de Lotbinière, René-Louis, 202
Chartier de Lotbinière, René-Pierre, 202
Charton, François, 121
Charton, Nicolas, 48
Chartres, Léonard de. *See* Léonard
Chasle, Catherine. *See* Fol
Chasle, Claude, 255
Chaste, Aymar de, 27, 188, 209-10, 346
Chastelard* de Salières, Henri de, 286, 555, 570, 602
Chastellain, Pierre, 125, **203-4**, 324
Chatchmaid, William, 350
Chateaufort. *See* Bras-de-Fer
Châteauguay. *See* Le Moyne
Châteauneuf. *See* Meneux
Châtel, Edmée, 116
Chatillon, Jean. *See* Mignot
Chaton de La Jannaye, Étienne, 520
Chauchetière*, Claude, 651
Chaudière Noire (Black Cauldron), **204-5**
Chaudron. *See* Le Page
Chauffours. *See* Damours
Chaumonot, Pierre-Joseph-Marie, 111, 121, 123, 124, **205-7**, 244, 269, 271, 273, 345, 415, 461, 523, 563, 612, 633, 665

Chaumont*, Alexandre de, 554
Chaüosé, 458
Chaussegros* de Léry, Gaspard-Joseph, 76
Chauveau, François, 214
Chauveton, Urbain, 154
Chauvigny, Jeanne. *See* Du Bouchet
Chauvigny, Marie-Madeleine de (Gruel de La Peltrie), 43, 205, **207-8**, 215, 217, 230, 352, 354, 373, 457, 483, 485, 552, 604, 640, 665
Chauvigny et de Vaubougon, Guillaume de, 207, 208
Chauvin, Anne. *See* Archambault
Chauvin, François, 209
Chauvin, Michel, 557
Chauvin de La Pierre, Pierre, 80, 190, **208-9**, 209
Chauvin de Tonnetuit, Jeanne de. *See* Mallemouche
Chauvin de Tonnetuit, Madeleine de, 210
Chauvin de Tonnetuit, Marie. *See* Brinon
Chauvin de Tonnetuit, Pierre de, 27, 208, **209-10**, 291, 345, 422, 601
Chaverlange, Antoine de, 474
Chaverlange, Jeanne de (Levasseur), 474
Chaverlange, Marthe de. *See* Guérin
Chavigny, Geneviève de (Amiot), 59
Chavigny, Marguerite de (Fleury d'Eschambault), 309, 418
Chavigny de Berchereau, Éléonore de. *See* Grandmaison
Chavigny de Berchereau, François de, 56, 344, 345
Chavigny* de La Chevrotière François de, 345, 394
Chavilly. *See* Bouvot
Chavin. *See* Chauvin de La Pierre
Chazy, M. de, 40, 308
Chefdostel, Thomas, **210**, 421, 422
Cherououny, **210-11**, 302, 303, 479
Chesneau, Anne. *See* Lalande
Chesneau, Guillaume, 287
Chesnel, Judith (Du Gua de Monts), 291
Chettle, John, 567
Chevalier, 564
Chevalier. *See* La Tourasse
Chevalier, Catherine (Noyon), 250
Chevilly. *See* Bouvot
Chevrier, Baron de Fancamp, Pierre, 214, 215
Chevrières. *See* La Croix
Chevry, Marquis de. *See* Duret de Chevry, Charles-François
Chevry, Charles de. *See* Duret
Chicot, Jean, 463
Chihwatenha, Joseph, **211-12**, 344, 388, 523
Chiohoarehra. *See* Chihwatenha
Chkoudun. *See* Secoudon
Cholenec*, Pierre, 635
Chomedey, Hierosme de, 213
Chomedey, Jacqueline de (Bouvot de Chevilly), 213
Chomedey, Louis de, 212
Chomedey, Louise de, *dite* de Sainte-Marie, 115, 213, 220
Chomedey, Marie de. *See* Thomelin
Chomedey, Odard de, 213
Chomedey de Maisonneuve, Paul de, 32, 43, 44, 45, 46, 47, 109, 115, 130, 200, 208, **212-22**, 230, 231, 266, 273, 284, 297, 310, 319, 330, 344, 373, 412,

INDEX

427, 430, 447, 453, 457, 464, 485, 486, 487, 540, 543, 547, 548, 557, 558, 598, 640, 648
Chomina, 80, 211, **222–23**, 302, 509, 516, 578, 639
Chomonot. *See* Chaumonot
Chou, Juan, 263
Chouart, Jean-Baptiste, 39, 223, 227
Chouart, Marie. *See* Poirer
Chouart, Médard (father of Des Groseilliers), 223
Chouart, Médard (son of Des Groseilliers), 223
Chouart Des Groseilliers, Hélène. *See* Martin
Chouart Des Groseilliers, Marguerite, 223, 228
Chouart Des Groseilliers, Marguerite. *See* Hayet
Chouart Des Groseilliers, Marie-Anne, 223
Chouart Des Groseilliers, Marie-Antoinette, 223
Chouart Des Groseilliers, Médard, 16, 20, 39, 48, 49, 50, 56, 82, 83, 129, **223–28**, 250, 271, 282, 337, 338, 385, 397, 429, 464, 495, 518, 528, 578, 602, 607, 625
Choumin. *See* Chomina
Chrestien, Father. *See* Le Clercq
Chrestienne. *See* Marie-Madeleine
Christian I, King of Denmark, Norway, and Sweden, 679
Christian IV, King of Denmark and Norway, 243, 360, 514, 515
Christmas, Anne (Vaughan), 656
Christmas, John, 656
Chudleigh, Sir John, 669
Church*, Benjamin, 26, 427, 577
Churchill, John, first Duke of Marlborough, 493
Churchyard, Thomas, 335
Claret* de Fleurieu, Charles-Pierre, 280
Clarke, Elizabeth (Tyng), 654
Clarke, Elizabeth. *See* Mitton
Clarke (Clerke), John, 390, 391, 392
Clarke, Capt. Peter, 407
Clarke, (Clark), Richard, **228–30**, 334, 335, 363, 532
Clarke, Thaddeus, 654
Claudius Clavus. *See* Swart
Clément Du Vault (Vuault) de Monceaux, Anne de. *See* Gasnier
Clément Du Vault (Vuault) de Monceaux, Claire-Françoise (Ruette d'Auteuil), 585
Clément Du Vault (Vuault) de Monceaux, Jean de, 113, 585
Clerbaud-Bergier. *See* Bergier
Clerk, William, 386
Clermont, Comte de. *See* Orléans
Clignancour. *See* Damours
Clodoré (Closdoré), Jean de, 443
Closse, Cécile. *See* Delafosse
Closse, Élisabeth, 231, 266
Closse, Élisabeth. *See* Moyen Des Granges
Closse, Jean, 230
Closse, Jeanne-Cécile (Bizard; Blaise), 103, 231
Closse, Raphaël-Lambert, 103, 219, **230–32**, 266, 271, 274, 297, 463
Cloutier, Anne (Drouin), 232, 281, 330
Cloutier, Louise (Marguerite; Mignot; Matau), 490
Cloutier, Xainte. *See* Dupont
Cloutier, Zacharie, **232**, 330, 359, 473, 490
Cluzel, Jeanne de (Biard), 94
Cnoyen, James (Jacobus, of Herzogenbusch), 678

Cobbie, Diana (Hall), 233
Cobbie, Eliza, 233
Cobbie, Walsall, **232–33**
Cobreth, William, 667
Cocreaumont, Jean-Baptiste. *See* Dubois
Cognac, Jacques. *See* Boisseau
Colbert, Charles, Marquis de Croissy, 513
Colbert, Jean-Baptiste (the elder), 25, 33, 34, 49, 63, 74, 115, 116, 120, 127, 135, 136, 137, 185, 227, 283, 284, 285, 287, 315, 326, 327, 396, 410, 418, 442, 443, 499, 534, 541, 555, 556, 565, 571, 581, 587, 589, 600, 615, 616, 617, 618, 619, 620, 621, 622, 623, 624, 627, 628, 629, 630, 648
Colbert, Jean-Baptiste, Marquis de Seignelay, 56, 119, 138, 179, 181, 250, 289, 290, 443, 446, 448, 526, 537, 586
Colbert de Terron, Charles (intendant de Marine), 62, 418, 419, 443, 534, 621, 627
Coleridge, Samuel Taylor, 385
Coligny, Gaspard II de, *dit* l'amiral de Coligny, 27
Colin, Michel, **233**, 265
Collet, Anne (Raisin), 564
Colletet, Guillaume, 469
Colleton, Sir Peter, 519
Collier, 293
Coloma, Carlos, General and Spanish historian, 187
Colombier, Marie (Boisseau), 104
Colson, Nicolas, 109
Colston, Elizabeth. *See* Gittens
Colston, William (the elder), 233
Colston, William, **233–34**, 350
Columbier. *See* Pouteret
Columbus, Christopher, 12, 21, 147, 148, 150, 155, 157, 234, 303, 657, 658, 677, 678
Combalet, Mme de. *See* Vignerot
Côme de Mantes, **234**, 434
Comporté. *See* Gaultier
Condé. *See* Bourbon, Henri de
Condé, Louis II de, *dit* le Grand Condé, 42, 225, 283, 561, 563
Condé, Princesse de. *See* Montmorency, Charlotte-Marguerite de
Condren, Charles de, 115, 208
Coney, 93
Contarini, Gasparo, 148, 153, 155, 157
Contarini, Marcantonio, 153
Contrecœur. *See* Pécaudy
Convent, Anne (Amiot; Maheu; Blanchon), 59, 60
Cooke, Elizabeth (Lady Hoby, Lady Russell), 362
Cooper, Anthony Ashley, first Earl of Shaftesbury, 519
Cordé, Catherine de (Legardeur de Tilly), 446, 447
Corrivault, Marguerite (Maheut), 479
Corruble, La. *See* Bouge
Corte-Real, Gaspar, 19, 21, 151, 166, 171, **234–36**, 236, 304
Corte-Real, Isabel. *See* Castro
Corte-Real, João Vaz, 234, 236
Corte-Real, Miguel, 19, 21, 166, 171, 234, 235, **236**
Corte-Real, Vasco Añes, 236
Corwin, George, 242
Cosa, Juan de la, 148, 149, 150, 151, 304
Cosineau de Mareuil, Jacques-Théodore. *See* Mareuil

725

INDEX

Cosnier, Marie (Denys de La Thibaudière), 256, 261
Coste (Costa), Mathieu de, 452
Costé, Michel, 87
Costebelle. *See* Pastour
Côté, Anne. *See* Martin
Côté, Jean, 495
Coton, Pierre, 97, 100, 121, 498
Couillard, Élisabeth. *See* Vesins
Couillard, Guillaume (the elder), 236
Couillard, Guillaume (son of Guillaume, de Lespinay), 366
Couillard, Louise (Letardif), 473
Couillard, Marguerite (Nicollet de Belleborne; Macard), 84, 369, 517
Couillard, Marie (Byssot de La Rivière; Lalande), 145, 146, 395, 661
Couillard, Nicolas, 366, 367
Couillard de Lespinay, Élisabeth (Guyon Du Buisson), 359, 366
Couillard de Lespinay, Geneviève. *See* Després
Couillard de Lespinay, Guillaume, 109, 145, 200, **236–37**, 237, 287, 359, 366, 452, 473, 517
Couillard de Lespinay, Guillemette. *See* Hébert
Couillard de Lespinay, Jacques, 161
Couillard de Lespinay, Louis, 48, **237–38**, 420, 430
Couillaud. *See* La Roque
Coulogne. *See* Robin
Coulonge. *See* Ailleboust de Coulonge; Ailleboust de Coulonge-la-Madeleine
Courcelle. *See* Rémy
Co(u)rcelles, Motin de. *See* Motin
Courpont, M. de, 297
Courseron, Gilbert, **238**
Courval. *See* Poulin
Coussez, Capt., 422
Couture*, Guillaume, 42, 60, 124, 145, 227, 298, 344, 387, 388, 396, 403, 404, 523
Couture*, Jean, 79
Cox, William, 334, 335, 363
Cramolet, 64
Crapaut. *See* Chomina
Craston, William, 450, 451
Crespieul*, François de, 49, 396, 483
Crevel de Moranget, 182, 183
Crevet, Marie (Caron; Langlois), 417
Crevier, Christophe, 475
Crevier, Jeanne. *See* Énard
Crevier, Jeanne (Boucher), 109
Crevier*, Joseph, 239
Crevier, Louis, 239
Crevier, Marguerite (Gamelain de La Fontaine; Renou), 321
Crevier, *dit* La Meslée, Christophe, 238
Crevier de Saint-François, Jean, **238–39**, 321, 369
Crevier de Saint-François, Marguerite. *See* Hertel
Crignon, Pierre, 235, 532
Crisafy*, Antoine de, 239
Crisafy, Thomas, **239**
Crisasy. *See* Crisafy
Croft, Thomas, 19, 21, 147, **239–40**, 386
Croft, William, 239
Croissy. *See* Colbert
Cromberger. *See* Noremberguer

Cromwell, Oliver, 242, 406, 407, 474, 595, 604, 605, 636, 652
Cromwell, Thomas, 566
Crosland, Alice (Calvert), 162
Crosland, John, 162
Crout, Henry, 233, **240–41**, 670, 671
Crowne, Agnes. *See* Mackworth
Crowne, John, 241, 242
Crowne (Crown), William, 25, **241–42**, 434, 435, 595, 605, 636
Cruse, Thomas, **242–43**
Crusson, *dit* Pilote, François, 267
Cryn. *See* Togouiroui
Crynssen, Abraham, 443
Cuillerier*, René, 130, 598, 662
Cunningham, John, **243**, 360, 408
Curler, Arent van, 308

Dablon, Claude, 48, 49, 58, 205, 206, 207, **244**, 282, 393, 394, 395, 396, 445, 461, 491, 492, 523
Daguerre, Madeleine (Bourdon de Romainville), 114
Dailleboust. *See* Ailleboust
Daillon. *See* La Roche
Dalmas, Antoine, **244–45**
Damienne, 426
Damours, Élisabeth. *See* Tessier
Damours, Élisabeth (Chartier de Lotbinière), 202, 245
Damours, Jean, 245
Damours, Louis, 245
Damours de Chauffours, Élisabeth (Charron de La Barre), 201
Damours* de Chauffours, Louis, 245, 246
Damours de Chauffours, Marie. *See* Marsolet de Saint-Aignan
Damours de Chauffours, Mathieu, 137, 201, 202, **245**, 245, 289, 587, 588, 589
Damours* de Clignancour, René, 245
Damours de Freneuse, Louise. *See* Guyon
Damours de Freneuse, Mathieu, **245–46**, 245, 577
Damours* de Plaines, Bernard, 245
Dandonneau, Jeanne (Babie), 74
Dandonneau*, Pierre, *dit* Lajeunesse, Sieur Du Sablé, 74
Dangé, François, **246**
Daniel, 334
Daniel, André, 247
Daniel, Antoine (the elder), 247
Daniel, Antoine, 70, 122, 124, 125, 128, 206, **246**, 247, 252, 253, 388, 414, 461, 633, 637, 638, 639
Daniel, Charles, 25, 53, **247–48**, 252, 261, 305, 482, 521, 567, 613, 665
Daniel, François, 247
Daniel, Marguerite. *See* Martin
Daprandesteguy. *See* Aprendestiguy
Daquin, Marie (Aigron), 42
Dardaine, Françoise (Olivier), 524
Darontal. *See* Atironta (fl. 1615)
Dartmouth. *See* Legge
Daulac (Daulat). *See* Dollard
Daumont de Saint-Lusson, Jean-Baptiste, 250
Daumont de Saint-Lusson, Magdeleine, 249
Daumont de Saint-Lusson, Marguerite. *See* Bérin; La Verge

INDEX

Daumont de Saint-Lusson, Simon-François, 35, 57, 63, 127, 226, **248–50**, 345, 393, 394, 572, 625, 626
Dauphin* de La Forest, François, 178
Dauphin de Montorgueuil, **250**, 299
Davaugour. *See* Dubois
Davène de Fontaine, 424
David, Claude, 225, **250–51**
David, Suzanne. *See* Noyon
Davis, Faith. *See* Fulford
Davis, John, 20, 75, **251–52**, 336, 360, 375, 377, 378, 397, 676
Davost, Ambroise, 122, 125, **252–53**, 388
Davys. *See* Davis
Dawbeny, Oliver, 371
Day, John, 21, 148, 149, 150, 240, 302, 643
Debryeux, Marguerite. *See* Dizy
Dee, John, 148, 302, 316, 332, 333, 336, 643, 677, 678
Dekanahwideh (Deganawidah), 7, **253–55**
Delafosse, Cécile (Closse), 230
De La Warr. *See* West
Delestre, Alonié, 267
Delisle. *See* Bréhaut
Delisle, Joseph-Nicolas, 677
Demesnu. *See* Peuvret
Demeulle*, Jacques, 90, 178, 238, 265, 298, 327, 340, 443, 444, 445, 446, 508, 526, 578, 664
Demosny, Catherine. *See* Fol
Demosny, Jean (or Jean-Baptiste) (the elder), 249, **255–56**, 550, 583
Demosny, Jean (the younger), 256
Demosny, Julienne. *See* Bisson
Demosny, Marie. *See* Filleul
Demosny, Marie-Louise. *See* Albert
Demosny, Paul, 255
Denbigh. *See* Feilding
Denis, Father. *See* Jamet
Denis, Françoise (Outlaw), 529
Denis*, Joseph, 536
Denis. *See also* Denys
Denonville. *See* Brisay
Denys, Anne. *See* Parabego
Denys, Jean, 22, **256**, 256
Denys, Marguerite. *See* Lafite
Denys, Marguerite (Forsayth), 258
Denys, Marie (Leneuf de La Vallière), 258
Denys, Nicolas, 25, 32, 66, 89, 90, 114, **256–59**, 259, 260, 261, 277, 383, 433, 434, 476, 503, 505, 514, 568, 595, 597, 621
Denys de Bonaventure, Jeanne. *See* Jannière
Denys* de Bonaventure, Simon-Pierre, 114, 246, 576, 654
Denys de Fronsac, Françoise. *See* Cailleteau
Denys de Fronsac, Louis, 261
Denys de Fronsac, Marie-Anne (Merçan), 260
Denys de Fronsac, Nicolas, 260
Denys de Fronsac, Richard, 90, 258, **259–61**, 649
Denys de La Ronde, Catherine. *See* Leneuf de La Poterie
Denys de La Ronde, Marguerite-Renée (Lanouguère; Fleury d'Eschambault), 418
Denys* de La Ronde, Pierre, 85, 260, 418
Denys de La Thibaudière, Jacques, 256, 261
Denys de La Thibaudière, Marie. *See* Cosnier

Denys de La Trinité, Barbe (Pécaudy de Contrecœur), 535
Denys de La Trinité, Françoise. *See* Du Tartre
Denys de La Trinité, Jeanne. *See* Dubreuil
Denys de La Trinité, Simon, 257, 261, **261–62**, 514, 535, 589
Denys* de Saint-Simon, Paul, 35, 49, 226, 396, 625
Dermer, Thomas, **262**, 650
Derré de Gand, François, **262–63**, 297, 637
De Ruyter. *See* Ruyter
Des Bergères. *See* Blaise
Desbordes, Marie (Migeon), 508
Descelliers, Pierre, 170
Deschambault. *See* Fleury d'Eschambault
Des Champs, Guillaume, 293
Des Chatelets. *See* Juchereau
Desdames, Thierry, **263–64**, 266, 579
Des Forges. *See* Robin
Des Friches* de Meneval, Louis-Alexandre, 426, 436, 533, 542, 544, 576, 578
Des Goutins*, Mathieu, 577
Des Granches. *See* Guyon
Des Granches, Alizon (Jalobert), 384
Des Granches, Antoine, 167
Des Granches, Catherine (Cartier), 167, 170
Des Granches, Jacques, 170
Des Granges. *See* Moyen
Des Granges de Mauprée, Alixe. *See* La Feuillée
Des Granges de Mauprée, Louis, 415
Des Groseilliers. *See* Chouart
Deshaies-Gendron, Claude, 328, 550
Deshayes*, Jean, 56
Deshormeaux (or Des Ormeaux). *See* Bergier
Desjardins, Christophe. *See* Augier
Desjardins*, Philippe-Jean-Louis, 314
Desjardins Du Val, 383, 503, 504
Desjordy* de Cabanac, François, 361
Des Lauriers. *See* Basset
Desloges, Anne (Guenet), 347
Des Maizerets. *See* Ango
Desmarais. *See* Godet
Desmarais, Innocent, 264
Desmarets, 313
Desmarets. *See* Godet
Des Maretz. *See* Godet
Des Méloizes (Desmeloizes). *See* Renaud d'Avène
Des Muceaux. *See* Ailleboust
Des Ormeaux. *See* Bergier; Dollard
Desportes, Françoise. *See* Langlois
Desportes, Hélène (Hébert; Morin), **264**, 367, 495
Desportes, Pierre, 233, 264, 495
Desportes de Lignères, Pierre, 248, 264
Després, Anne (Lauson; Bermen de La Martinière), 428, 430
Després, Étiennette (Guillemot), 349
Després, Geneviève (Couillard de Lespinay), 237
Des Prinzèles. *See* Dubois d'Esgriseilles
Desrosiers, Anne. *See* Leneuf Du Hérisson
Desrosiers, Antoine, 468
Desrues, Jeanne (Baudoin), 80
Des Touches. *See* Peronne
Dethunes, Exupère, **264–65**, 438, 439
Devennes, Gilles, 109

727

Dézy. *See* Dizy
Díaz de Solís, Juan, 155
Didace, Brother. *See* Pelletier
Dièreville*, Sieur de, 577, 649
Diescaret. *See* Pieskaret
Digges, Sir Dudley, 374, 377
Dion. *See* Guyon
Dizy- (or Dézy)-Debryeux*, Marguerite, 361
Dizy de Montplaisir, Élisabeth (Hamelin de Bourgchemin), 360
Dizy de Montplaisir, Pierre, 360
Dobbs, Sir Arthur, 677
Dodier, Sébastien, 468
Dognon, Comte de. *See* Foucault
Dolbeau. *See also* Dolebeau
Dolbeau, Jean, 233, **265–66**, 266, 385, 437, 590
Dolebeau. *See also* Dolbeau
Dolebeau, Antoinette (Bellevue), 484
Dolebeau, Charles, 484
Dolebeau, Jean, **266**, 477, 483
Dolebeau, Nicolas, 483
Dolebeau, Simon, 483
Dollard Des Ormeaux, Adam (called Daulat in death certificate and Daulac by some historians), 11, 32, 40, 65, 201, 225, **266–75**, 463, 547, 612, 633
Dollier* de Casson, François, 35, 78, 126, 173, 174, 180, 213, 215, 217, 219, 220, 230, 231, 248, 266, 269, 270, 273, 274, 319, 393, 410, 416, 439, 483, 484, 485, 486, 540, 547, 556, 558, 572, 598, 599, 613, 625, 647
Dolphyn, William, 371
Dolu, 160, 194, 433
Domagaya, 11, 166, 167, 168, 275, 276
Dombourg, Jean-François de. *See* Bourdon
Donck, Adriaen van der, 525
Dongan, Thomas, 444, 445, 526
Donnacona, 11, 166, 167, 168, 169, **275–77**
Dorfeuille, Pierre, 361
Dornelos, Juan de, 41
Dorvelos. *See* Dornelos
Dorvilliers. *See* Guilloust d'Orvilliers
Douaire de Bondy, Louise (Allemand; Pinault), 56
Douay, Anastase, 180, 182, 183
Doublet, François (the elder), 277
Doublet, François, **277**
Doublet, Jean-François, 277
Doublet, Madeleine. *See* Fontaine
Doublet, Marguerite. *See* Auber
Doucet, Marie-Madeleine (Aigron), 42
Dourado, Fernan Vaz. *See* Vaz.
Doussin, René, 267, 273
Doussineau, Gillette (Gendron), 328
Dovan (Devon), Earl of. *See* Alexander, Sir William, Earl of Stirling
Downing, John (the elder), 278
Downing, John, 24, 93, **277–78**
Downing, William, **277–78**, 370
Dowse, Thomas, 417
Drage*, Thomas Swaine, 677
Drake, Sir Bernard, 23, **278–80**, 364, 668
Drake, Sir Francis, 278, **280**, 318, 336, 362, 364, 378
Drake, George, 306, 672
Drake, Gertrude. *See* Fortescue

Drake, Hugh, 278
Drake, John, 280
Draper, Thomas, **280–81**, 324
Dreuillettes. *See* Druillettes
Drew, John, 667
Drouillettes. *See* Druillettes
Drouin, Anne. *See* Cloutier
Drouin, Marie. *See* Chapelier; Dubois
Drouin, Robert (the elder), 281
Drouin, Robert, 232, **281**, 330
Drué*, Juconde, 312
Druillettes, Gabriel, 49, 59, 244, **281–82**, 340, 379, 396, 402, 491, 498, 516, 558
Drummond, William (of Hawthornden), 51
Dubocq, Laurent, 286
Dubocq, Marie-Félix (Indian), 286
Duboct. *See* Dubok
Du Bog, Jacques, 167
Dubois, Anne (Lemort; Pécaudy de Contrecœur), 535
Dubois, Jacques, 550
Dubois, Marie (Drouin), 281
Dubois Davaugour, Pierre, 32, 146, 200, 202, **282–85**, 305, 325, 387, 402, 494, 537, 538, 563, 587, 647
Dubois de Cocreaumont et de Saint-Maurice, Jean-Baptiste, **285–86**
Dubois d'Esgriseilles, Jean-Baptiste, 285
Dubok, **286**
Du Bos, Antoinette. *See* Caron
Du Bos, Nicolas (the elder), 286
Du Bos, Nicolas, **286**
Du Bouchet, Jeanne (Chauvigny), 207
Du Bourg. *See* Morillon; Rémy
Du Breuil. *See* Le Creux
Dubreuil, Jeanne (Denys de La Trinité), 261
Du Buisson. *See* Guyon
Ducharme, Pierre, 452
Du Chartran. *See* Gaudais
Duchesnay. *See* Juchereau
Duchesne. *See* Du Quesne
Du Chesne, Adrien, **287**, 463, 495
Duchesne, Anne. *See* Lefebvre
Du Chesne, Judith (Le Moyne), 287, 463
Duchesne, Léonard, 264
Duchesneau (the younger), 105, 137
Duchesneau de La Doussinière et d'Ambault, Jacques, 103, 104, 105, 136, 177, 179, 203, 238, 245, **287–90**, 340, 345, 396, 397, 399, 438, 445, 448, 464, 537, 553, 565, 575, 581, 582
Duclos, Mme. *See* Celles
Du Coudray. *See* Le Borgne
Du Creux, François, 523
Dudley, Ambrose, Earl of Warwick, 316
Dudley, Anne, Countess of Warwick. *See* Russell
Dudley, Joseph, 654
Dudouyt, Jean, 89, 92, 105, 249, **290–91**, 359, 506
Du Fay, Polycarpe, 590
Dufresne, 130, 662
Dufresnoy Carion, Jeanne (Le Moyne), 466
Dufrost* de La Jemmerais, Christophe, 204
Dugardin, L., 487
Dugas, Marie (Melanson), 500
Duglas, Mgr, 469
Du Gua, Claire. *See* Goumard

INDEX

Du Gua, Guy, 291
Du Gua de Monts, Judith. *See* Chesnel
Du Gua de Monts, Pierre, 23, 28, 69, 72, 95, 96, 98, 99, 186, 188, 189, 190, 191, 197, 209, **291–95**, 300, 346, 367, 422, 452, 469, 470, 495, 500, 526, 527, 529, 564, 565, 601, 603, 604
Dugué de Boisbriand, Marie. *See* Moyen Des Granges
Dugué de Boisbriand, Michel-Sidrac, **295**, 308
Dugué* de Boisbriand, Pierre, 308
Dugué de La Boulardière, Perrine. *See* Chambellé
Dugué de La Boulardière, Pierre, 295
Du Guesclin. *See* Lefebvre
Duhaut, Dominique, 182, 183
Duhaut, Pierre, 182, 183
Du Hérisson. *See* Leneuf
Du Hommée. *See* Byssot
Du Jardin (Huguenot merchant), 100
Du Jardin, Marie (Le Mercier), 458
Dulhut. *See* Greysolon
Du Marché, Charles, 214, 453
Dumesnil. *See* Peronne
Dumons, Sieur. *See* Monts, Sieur de
Du Mortier, Madeleine (Roussel), 583
Dumoulin, 302, 509
Du Parc. *See* Godet
Du Peron, François, 48, 205, 206, 217, **295–96**, 461, 602
Du Peron, Joseph-Imbert, 295, 296, 523
Du Perron, Thalour, 25, 89, **296**, 323
Duperron Bâby. *See* Bâby
Du Plessis. *See* Schomberg; Vignerot
Du Plessis, Armand-Jean, Cardinal de Richelieu, 29, 53, 115, 121, 124, 129, 159, 160, 161, 186, 195, 196, 203, 248, 261, 297, 372, 427, 428, 471, 482, 484, 504, 521, 567, 568, 579, 592, 615, 642
Du Plessis, Charles, Duc de Liancourt, Governor of Paris, 98
Duplessis, Nicolas. *See* Gastineau
Duplessis, Pacifique, 108, **296**, 368, 379, 385, 552, 590
Du Plessis-Bochart, Charles, 159, **296–97**, 349, 527, 633
Du Plessis de Liancourt, Antoinette. *See* Pons
Du Plessis-Kerbodot. *See* Guillemot
Dupont. *See* Gaudais
Dupont, Xainte (Cloutier), 232
Dupont de Neuville, Françoise-Thérèse (Renaud d'Avène de Desmeloizes), 572
Dupont* de Neuville, Nicolas, 114, 232, 325, 572
Du Pont-Gravé. *See* Gravé
Dupré*, François, 488
Du Prévert. *See* Sarcel
Dupuy, Jeanne. *See* Fauvenel; Groisard
Dupuy, Zacharie, 102, **297–98**, 416
Duquerny, Jeanne (Lomeron), 476
Du Quesne (Duchesne), 100
Duquesne, Abraham, 257
Duquesne, Jacob, 257
Du Quesnoy. *See* Talon, Jean
Duquet, Catherine. *See* Gauthier
Duquet, Denis, 298
Duquet, Françoise (Madry; Morel de La Durantaye), 479
Duquet de La Chesnaye, Anne. *See* Lamarre
Duquet de La Chesnaye, Pierre, 73, **298**, 305, 474, 479, 537

Durand, Jean, 91
Durand de Villegaignon, Nicolas, 469, 679
Durantal. *See* Atironta (fl. 1615)
Duret, Louise (Rageot), 560
Duret de Chevry, Charles-François, Marquis de Villeneuve, 89, 298, 436
Duret de Chevry de La Boulaye, Charles, 90, **298–99**
Durosoy, Geneviève, 117
Du Roure. *See* Vignerot
Du Sablé. *See* Dandonneau
Du Saussay de Bémont, Anne. *See* Carlier
Du Saussay de Bémont, Jacques, 583
Du Saussay de Bémont, Marie-Anne (Rouer de Villeray), 583
Du Tartre. *See* Basset
Du Tartre, Françoise (Denys de La Trinité), 261
Dutch Bastard. *See* Flemish Bastard
Du Thet, Gilbert, 68, 95, 98, 100, 101, **299**, 441, 470, 560
Du Tillet, Madeleine. *See* Hélie
Du Tremblay, François-Joseph, *dit* le Père Joseph, 428
Du Val. *See* Desjardins
Duval, Jean, 190, **299–300**, 346
Duval, Nicolas, 271
Du Vault (Du Vuault). *See* Clément
Dyer, Edward, 531

Easton, Peter, 24, 240, **300–301**, 350, 481, 668
Echevete, Matias de, **301**
Échon (Héchon), 121, 205
Eden, Richard, 153, 154, 155
Eder de La Fontanelle, Guy, 186
Edgcombe (Edgecombe), Leonard, **301–2**
Edward III, King of England, 678
Edward IV, King of England, 239
Edward VI, King of England and Ireland, 157, 158
Effingham. *See* Howard
Egede, Hans, 252
Eirikr Thorvaldsson (Eric the Red), 17, 103, 448, 612, 642, 643, **676**
Eirikr *upsi* Gnupsson, **675–76**
Eiriksson, Leifr *heppni*. *See* Leifr
Élie, Madeleine. *See* Hélie
Eliot, Hugh, 21, 148, **302**, 343, 386, 643
Eliot, Sir John, 522
Élisabeth (You de La Découverte) (Indian), 573
Elizabeth I, Queen of England and Ireland, 93, 229, 279, 331, 333, 365, 566, 667, 678
Elliott, Thomas, 242, 636, 637
Ellis*, Henry, 677
Ellis, Thomas, 318
Elyot, Hugh. *See* Eliot
Elyot, Richard, 371
Émery. *See* Particelli
Emonnot, Catherine (Mance), 483
Énard, Jeanne (Crevier), 238
Énault*, Philippe, 260
Endemare, George d', 388
Endicot, John, 241
Entremont. *See* Mius
Épernon, Duc d', 427
Eric, Bishop. *See* Eirikr *upsi* Gnupsson
Eric the Red. *See* Eirikr Thorvaldsson

Erondelle, 471
Erouachy, 211, 222, **302–3**, 479, 509
Erskine, Janet (Alexander), 50
Erskine, John, Earl of Mar, 50
Erskine, Sir William, 50
Eschaillons, Pierre de Saint-Ours d'. *See* Saint-Ours.
Eschambault. *See* Fleury
Eschaux, Bertrand d', 352
Esgriseilles, Jean-Baptiste d'. *See* Dubois
Esmanville, 180
Esmart, Barbe (Michel; Letardif), 473
Espérance (Indian), 196, **199–200**, 237, 366, 452, 494
Esrouachit. *See* Erouachy
Estrades, Godefroi-Louis, Comte d', (marshal of France), 185, 284, 554, 587
Estrées, Jean d', 443
Étienne, Claude, 223, 495
Étienne, Hélène. *See* Martin
Étouat, 516
Evelin, Robert, 673
Evertsen, Cornelis, 496
Exupère, Father. *See* Dethunes

FAFARD, Thiennette (Boivin), 106
Fagundes, João Alvares, 21, 166, 171, **303–4**, 422
Falkland. *See* Cary
Fancamp, Baron de. *See* Chevrier
Farr, Walter, 578
Farrar. *See* Ferrar
Faure, Madeleine. *See* Brulart
Faure de Berlise, Angélique (Bullion), 484, 485, 486
Faure de Berlise, Guichard, 484
Fauvenel, Jeanne (Dupuy), 297
Favery, Marie (Legardeur de Repentigny), 447, 637
Favre, René, 105
Feilding, Basil, second Earl of Denbigh, 241
Fénelon, Abbé de. *See* Salignac
Fenton, Edward, 317
Ferchaud, Laurent, 593
Fercourt. *See* Perrot
Ferdinand II, King of Aragon and Sicily (Ferdinand V of Castile), 41, 147, 154, 155, 241
Fernandes, Francisco, 228, 229, 302, 304, 343
Fernandes, João, 19, 21, 153, 234, **304–5**, 343
Fernandez, Simon, 332, 333
Ferrar, Constance, 248, **305**, 613
Ferrer Maldonado, Lorenzo, **676–77**
Feuillon, Michel, 305
Feuquières. *See* Pas
Fézeret*, René, 663
Fiennes, William, Viscount Saye and Seele, 435, 636
Filleul, Marie (Demosny), 255
Fillion, André 305
Fillion, Antoine, 305
Fillion, Antoinette, 305
Fillion, Gabrielle. *See* Senler
Fillion, Jean, 305
Fillion, Marguerite. *See* Auber
Fillion, Michel, **305–6**, 589
Fillon, François, 536
Fillon, Michel, 305
Fin, Louis, 221
Fisher, Anne (Leverett), 474

Fisher, Richard, **306–7**, 364, 409, 450, 671, 672
Fisher, Robert, 306
Fitzgerald, Gerald, eleventh Earl of Kildare, 168
Fitzgerald, James Fitzmaurice, 421
Fléché, Jessé, 95, 97, 99, **307**, 500, 501
Flemish Bastard, 7, 40, 41, **307–8**, 325, 555, 556, 602
Flesche. *See* Fléché
Fletcher, Benjamin, 634
Fletcher, John, **308–9**, 611
Fletcher, Mary, 308
Fleuche (Fleuchy). *See* Fléché
Fleurieu. *See* Claret
Fleury, Charles, 68, 299, 441
Fleury d'Eschambault, Charlotte (Rigaud de Vaudreuil de Cavagnial), 345
Fleury d'Eschambault, Jacques, **309**
Fleury* d'Eschambault, Jacques-Alexis, 309, 344, 418
Fleury d'Eschambault, Marguerite. *See* Chavigny
Fleury d'Eschambault, Marguerite-Renée. *See* Denys de La Ronde
Florin (Florentin), Jean, 658
Flowerday, Baron, 280
Foi (Indian), **199–200**
Fol, Catherine (Demosny; Chasle), 249, 255
Follin, Nicolas, 621
Fonblanche. *See* Martinet
Fontaine. *See* Davène
Fontaine, Jacques, 277
Fontaine, Madeleine (Doublet), 277
Fontarabie, Pierre, 143
Fonte, Bartholomew de, 676, **677**
Fonteneau, Jérémie, 78
Fonteneau, Marie (Bailly), 78
Fonteneau, Valentine. *See* Alfonse
Fonteneau, *dit* Jean Alfonse, Jean, **309**, 423, 680
Ford, John, 301
Forestier, Marie, *dite* de Saint-Bonaventure-de-Jésus, **310**, 347, 353, 609, 611
Forrester, Andrew, **310–11**, 568, 593
Forsayth, James, 258
Forsayth, Marguerite. *See* Denys
Fortel. *See* Robert
Fortelle. *See* Robinau
Fortescue, Gertrude (Drake), 278
Fortescue, Sir John, 546
Fortin, 116
Fortin, Louise. *See* Sommillard
Fortin, *dit* Bellefontaine, Julien, 432
Fossambault. *See* Nau de La Boissière
Foucault*, Nicolas, 361
Foucault de Saint-Germain-Beaupré, Louis, Comte de Dognon, 324
Foucher, **311**
Fougeray, 293
Fouilleuse, Louise de (Prouville de Tracy), 557
Fount, William de la, 239, 240
Fouquet (Foucquet), Nicolas (financial secretary), 296, 323
Fouquet de Chalain, Christophe, 257
Fourier, Pierre (Saint), 115, 118
Fournier, Catherine (Roussel), 583
Fournier, Françoise. *See* Hébert
Fournier, Guillaume, 264

INDEX

Fox, Anne. *See* Barnard
Fox, George, 81, 82, 84
Fox, Luke, 20, 144, **311–12**, 329, 362, 375, 384, 668
Fox, Richard, 311
Foxcroft, Samuel, 499
Francheville. *See* Poulin; Terrier
Francheville, Pierre, 393
Francis, Mr., 370
François (Indian, son of Oumasasikweie), 527
François, Père. *See* Brekenmacher
François I, King of France, 27, 126, 165, 166, 168, 309, 384, 423, 424, 658, 659, 660
François, Claude, *dit* Frère Luc, 55, **312–15**, 359, 420
François, Jeanne (Le Borgne), 435
François, Mathieu, 312
François, Perrette. *See* Prieur
Franklin, Benjamin, 255
Franklin*, Sir John, 20, 375, 378
Franquelin*, Jean-Baptiste-Louis, 119, 537, 664
Frémin, Jacques, 48, 108, **315**, 445, 461, 547, 635, 650
French, John, **315**, 605
French, Lawrence, 315
Freneuse. *See* Damours
Freydis (sister of Leifr *heppni* Eiriksson), 449, 643
Frin. *See* Fin
Frisius, Gemma, 154, 679
Frobisher, Bernard, 316
Frobisher, Dorothy (widow of Sir William Widmerpole; second wife of Sir Martin), 318
Frobisher, Isabel (first wife of Sir Martin), 318
Frobisher, Sir Martin, 19, 85, 86, 93, 94, 153, **316–19**, 332, 375, 385, 607, 669, 670, 677, 679, 680
Frobisher, Peter, 318
Fromont, *dit* La Bouille, Thomas, 167, 169
Fronsac. *See* Denys
Frontenac. *See* Buade
Frotté, 423
Froyer de La Baronnière, Jeanne (La Roche), 420
Fuca, Juan de, 676, **677**
Fulford, Andrew, 278
Fulford, Faith (Davis), 251
Fulford, Sir John, 251

GABOTO, Antonio, 304
Gabriel, Brother. *See* Sagard
Gabriel, Father. *See* La Ribourde
Gadois. *See* Gadoys
Gadoys, Françoise (Godé), 319
Gadoys*, Jean-Baptiste, 319
Gadoys, Louise. *See* Mauger
Gadoys, Pierre, 218, **319**, 464, 557
Gadoys*, Pierre, 319
Gadoys, Roberte (Prud'homme; Verier), 319, 557
Gagnon, Françoise. *See* Goudeau
Gagnon, Jean, 319
Gagnon, Madeleine-Renée. *See* Roger
Gagnon, Mathurin, **319–20**
Gagnon, Pierre (brother of Mathurin), 319
Gagnon, Pierre (the elder), 319
Gaignard, Philippe, 277
Gaignier, Marguerite (Pinard), 550
Gaignon. *See* Gagnon
Gaillard, Mathieu, **320**

Gaillard, Pierre Rey. *See* Rey Gaillard
Gailliard, Françoise (Moreau de Brésoles), 512
Gaingnon. *See* Gagnon
Galilée. *See* Galinée
Galinée. *See* Bréhant
Galinée, Seigneur de, 126
Galinier, Dominique, 220, 612, 644
Galleran, Guillaume, **320**, 417
Gallifet*, François de, 524
Galliot, Jacques, 313
Galvão, António, 154, 235
Gamard, 256
Gamelain, Françoise. *See* Bellanger
Gamelain, Françoise (Pinard), 321
Gamelain, Michel, 321
Gamelain de La Fontaine, Marguerite. *See* Crevier
Gamelain de La Fontaine, Michel, **320–21**, 418, 468, 550
Gand. *See* Derré
Gandeacteua, Catherine (wife of Tonsahoten), **321–22**, 651
Gangnon. *See* Gagnon
Ganneaktena. *See* Gandeacteua
Gannensagouas, Marie-Thérèse, 118
Garakontié, Daniel, **322–23**, 445, 462, 464, 525, 555
Garat, Pierre, 476
Garault, Anne de (Garnier), 324
García, Diego, 156
Gargas, M. de, 577
Gargot, Anne. *See* Lardeau
Gargot, Hilaire, 323
Gargot, Jean, 323
Gargot de La Rochette, Nicolas, 296, **323–24**, 594
Garhi. *See* Garhio
Garhio, Marie, 522
Garland, Katherine, 324
Garland, Thomas, **324**
Garneau*, François-Xavier, 112
Garnier, Anne. *See* Garault
Garnier, Charles, 41, 125, 203, **324–25**, 388, 461, 562, 652
Garnier, Françoise. *See* Grenier
Garnier, Guillemette (Bourgeoys), 115
Garnier, Jean, 324
Garnier*, Julien, 322
Garnier de Chapouin, Jacques, 590
Garohiaé (Garonhiagué). *See* Ogenheratarihiens
Garreau, Léonard, 282, 307, 308, **325**, 651
Gaschet, René, 81, 583
Gasnier, Anne (Clément Du Vault de Monceaux; Bourdon), 113, 585
Gastaldo, Giacomo, 659
Gastineau, *dit* Duplessis, Nicolas, 231
Gauchet de Belleville, Catherine (Migeon de Branssat), 508
Gaudais Du Chartran, Nicolas, 326
Gaudais-Dupont, Louis, 79, 248, 323, **325–26**, 428, 512, 538, 629
Gaudar, Marie (Lauson), 428, 429, 431
Gaudarville. *See* Peuvret
Gaudreau, Catherine (Basset), 79
Gaudry, *dit* Bourbonnière, Nicolas, 45
Gaultier de Comporté, Angélique (Riverin), 326

731

INDEX

Gaultier de Comporté, Marie. *See* Bazire
Gaultier de Comporté, Marie-Anne (Peuvret de Gaudarville), 326
Gaultier de Comporté, Philippe, 84, 105, 106, **326**
Gaultier de La Vérenderie, Adam-Pierre, 327
Gaultier de La Vérenderie, Bertran de. *See* Gourdeau
Gaultier* de La Vérendrye, Pierre, 11, 37
Gaultier de Rinault, Gillette. *See* Vernon
Gaultier de Rinault, Philippe, 326
Gaultier de Varennes, Marie. *See* Boucher
Gaultier de Varennes, René, **326–28**, 468
Gauthier, Catherine (Duquet), 298
Gauthier, Guillaume, 479
Gauthier de La Chenaye, Marie. *See* Pichon
Gauthier de La Chenaye, Philippe, 606
Gautier, Gabriel, 89, 90
Gayon, Jacques. *See* Lalande
Geest, Catherine (Cavelier), 172
Gellée, Pierre, 277
Genaple* de Bellefonds, François, 203, 561, 565, 664
Gendron. *See* Deshaies
Gendron, Éloi, 328
Gendron, François, **328**, 550
Gendron, Gillette. *See* Doussineau
Geneviève-Agnès, *dite* de Tous-les-Saints. *See* Skanudharoua
Gentilly. *See* Pelletier de La Prade
Georges, Father. *See* Le Baillif
Georges, Pierre, 476
Georges, Samuel, 98, 101, 293, 476, 565
Georges, Suzanne (Lomeron), 476
Germain, Father. *See* Allart
Gerrard, Sir Thomas, 333
Gervais, Brother. *See* Mohier
Gervais, Jean, 508
Geyer, George, 39, 301, **328–29**, 509, 606, 657
Gibbons, Edward, 223, 241, 594, 636
Gibbons, Margaret, 241
Gibbons, William, 20, 74, 144, 145, **329**
Gié, Maréchal de, 423
Gien, Comte de. *See* Séguier
Giffard, Jeanne. *See* Poignant
Giffard*, Joseph, 326, 331, 428
Giffard, Louise (Lauson de Charny), 331, 428, 431
Giffard, Marc, 330
Giffard, Marie. *See* Regnouard
Giffard, Marie (Juchereau de La Ferté), 331, 400
Giffard, Marie-Françoise, *dite* Marie de Saint-Ignace, **329–30**, 330, 348
Giffard*, Marie-Thérèse (Juchereau de Saint-Denis), 331, 402, 550
Giffard, Michèle-Thérèse. *See* Nau de La Boissière et de Fossambault
Giffard de Moncel, Robert, 30, 218, 232, 281, 297, 319, 326, 329, **330–31**, 344, 359, 401, 417, 428, 431, 447, 584
Gilbert, Adrian, 251, 336
Gilbert, Anne. *See* Aucher
Gilbert, Sir Humphrey, 19, 23, 154, 228, 229, 251, 278, **331–36**, 362, 363, 364, 380, 531, 532, 668, 677
Gilbert, Sir John, 279, 333, 335, 336
Gilbert, Katherine. *See* Champernowne
Gilbert, Otho, 331

Gillam (*alias*). *See* Kelly
Gillam, Benjamin (elder brother of Zachariah), 337
Gillam, Benjamin (father of Zachariah), 337
Gillam*, Benjamin (son of Zachariah), 39, 129, **130**, 227, 338, 528, 601
Gillam, Bridget (Sanford), 337
Gillam, Hannah (mother of Zachariah), 337
Gillam, Hannah (Sharpe), 338
Gillam, Martha, 338
Gillam, Phoebe. *See* Phillips
Gillam, Zachariah, 82, 83, 129, 226, 227, **336–38**, 385, 519, 601, 607
Gillam, Zachariah (son of Zachariah), 338
Giovio, Giulio, 660
Giovio, Paolo, 660
Girard* de La Place, Louis-Hyacinthe, 339
Girard de La Place, Simon, **338–39**
Giraud, Jeanne de (Saurel), 602
Girot, Jehan, 421
Gittens, Elizabeth (Colston), 233
Gittens, William, 233
Glandelet*, Charles de, 117, 506
Gloria, Jean, **339**
Gloria, Marie. *See* Bourdon
Gloria, Perrette. *See* Vaulthier
Gloria, Pierre, 339
Gnupsson. *See* Eirikr *upsi* Gnupsson
Godé, Françoise. *See* Gadoys
Godé, Mathurine (Saint-Père), 598
Godé, Nicolas, 319, 598
Godeau, Antoine, Bishop of Grasse, then of Vence, French poet, 644
Godefroy, Barbe, 340
Godefroy, Charlotte, 340
Godefroy, Jean-Paul, 45, 112, 145, **339–40**, 340, 341, 344, 447, 623
Godefroy, Marie. *See* Marteau
Godefroy, Marie-Madeleine. *See* Legardeur de Repentigny
Godefroy, Perrette. *See* Cavelier
Godefroy, Pierre, 340
Godefroy, Robert, 339
Godefroy de Lintot, Jean, 121, 223, **340–41**, 341, 369, 447
Godefroy de Lintot, Marie. *See* Leneuf
Godefroy de Normanville, Thomas, 340, **341**, 489, 490
Godefroy de Vieuxpont, Catherine. *See* Poulin de La Fontaine
Godefroy de Vieuxpont, Jacques, 274, **341**
Godefroy* de Vieuxpont, Joseph, 553
Godet, Rolland, 245, **341–42**
Godet Des Maretz, Christine de, 342
Godet Des Maretz, Claude de, 190, **342**, 346
Godet Des Maretz, Cléophas de, 342
Godet Des Maretz, François de, 342
Godet Des Maretz, Jeanne de. *See* Gravé Du Pont
Godet Des Maretz, Marie de. *See* La Marck
Godet Des Maretz, Paul de, 342
Godet Du Parc, Jean de, 190, 342
Goes, Damien de, 234–35
Gómara, López de, 154
Gomes, Estevão (Esteban Gómez), 21, **342–43**
Gonsales, João, 153, 302, 304, **343**

Gorges, Sir Ferdinando, 51, 262, 497
Gorribon, Pierre de, 400
Gorry, Jean, 216
Gorst, Thomas, 47, 49, 50, 83, 226, 337, **343**, 477
Gosnold, Bartholomew, 189, 364
Gouault, Gaspard, 108
Goudeau, François (Gagnon), 320
Goulaine de Laudonnière, René de (French sailor), 469
Goumard, Claire (Du Gua), 291
Goupil, René, 42, 124, **343–44**, 388, 389, 523
Gourdeau, Antoine, 345
Gourdeau, Bertrande (Gaultier de La Vérenderie), 327
Gourdeau*, Jacques, 345
Gourdeau de Beaulieu, Éléonore. *See* Grandmaison
Gourdeau de Beaulieu, Jacques, 344, 345
Gourdeau de Beaulieu, Jeanne-Renée (Macart), 345
Gourges, Dominique de, 381, 469
Gournay, Marie de (Rousseau), Parisian mystic, 484
Goutin. *See* Des Goutins
Gowding (Goudon), Elizabeth (Kirke), 404
Grand Agnier, Le. *See* Togouiroui
Grande Gueule (Big Mouth). *See* Otreouti
Grandfontaine. *See* Andigné
Grandison. *See* St. John
Grandmaison, Éléonore de (Boudier de Beauregard; Chavigny de Berchereau; Gourdeau de Beaulieu; Cailhault de La Tesserie), 56, **344–45**, 418, 537
Grandmesnil. *See* Véron
Grandmont, Sieur de, 507
Grandpré. *See* Boucher; La Court
Grandville (Granville). *See* Bécart
Grange, Geneviève (Levasseur), 473, 474
Grangula (Grangular). *See* Otreouti
Granpré. *See* La Court
Grape, The. *See* Chomina
Gravé Du Pont, Christine. *See* Martin
Gravé Du Pont, François, 28, 61, 64, 86, 98, 160, 188-91, 194, 208, 209-10, 265, 292-93, 300, 342, **345–46**, 347, 386, 422, 432-33, 470, 473, 601-2, 638
Gravé Du Pont, Jeanne (Godet Des Maretz), 342, 346
Gravé Du Pont, Robert, 95, 98, 346, **346–47**
Gravenor, Elizabeth (Stourton), 614
Great Khan. *See* Kubilay
Great Mohawk, The. *See* Togouiroui
Greene, Anne (Mason), 496
Greene, Edward, 496
Greene, Henry, 145, 374, 375, 376, 377, 378
Greenway, Richard, 476, 666
Grenet, Simon, 267
Grenier (Garnier), Françoise (Langlois), 417
Grenolle, 132
Grenville, Sir Richard, 278
Greysolon* de Dulhut, Daniel, 132, 227, 228, 289, 290, 400
Griffith, Sir John, 477
Griffyn, Owen, 316, 317
Grimington*, Michael, 308
Groisard, Jeanne (Dupuy), 297
Groseilliers. *See* Chouart
Grouvel, Marguerite. *See* Auber
Grouvel, Martin, 305
Gruel de La Peltrie, 207

Gruel de La Peltrie, Marie-Madeleine. *See* Chauvigny
Gudridr (wife of Thorfinnr *karlsefni* Thordarson; widow of Thorsteinn), 612, 642
Guémenée. *See* Rohan
Guenet, Anne. *See* Desloges
Guenet, Marie, *dite* de Saint-Ignace, 310, **347–49**, 353
Guenet, Roger, 347
Guenet, Toussaint, 575
Guénin*, Hilarion, 55, 420, 438
Guer. *See* Kirke
Guercheville, Marquise de. *See* Pons
Guérin, Jean, 282
Guérin, Marthe (Chaverlange), 474
Guignard, Gilles, 505
Guignecourt (or Guignicourt), 423, 425
Guillaume, Father. *See* Galleran
Guillemot, Anne, 349
Guillemot, Étiennette. *See* Després
Guillemot, François, 349
Guillemot, *dit* Du Plessis-Kerbodot, Guillaume, 297, **349**, 428, 430, 431, 574
Guillon, Jean, 296, 323
Guillot, Gefroy, 392, 554
Guillot, Marie. *See* Abancourt
Guillouet. *See* Guilloust
Guilloust* d'Orvilliers, Rémy de, 664
Guinet, Sieur de, 538
Guise, Duc de. *See* Lorraine
Guitton, Madeleine (Hamelin de Bourgchemin), 360
Gunnbjörn Ulfsson, 676
Gutiérrez, Diego, 157
Guy, Anne, 351
Guy, John, 23, 233, 240, 241, 243, 300, **349–51**, 351, 365, 496, 534, 584, 655, 656, 668, 670
Guy, Nicholas, **351**, 656
Guy, Philip, 233, 350
Guyar (Guyer). *See* Geyer
Guyart, Florent, 351
Guyart, Jeanne. *See* Michelet
Guyart, Marie, *dite* de l'Incarnation (Martin), 8, 30, 31, 32, 41, 55, 65, 108, 113, 198, 205, 208, 223, 225-26, 231, 268, 269, 274, 325, **351–59**, 414, 430, 446, 455, 457, 511, 512, 516, 523, 536, 551, 552, 555, 556, 603, 604, 610, 618, 624, 632, 647, 665
Guyon, Denis, 396
Guyon, Jean, **359**
Guyon, Louise. *See* Racine
Guyon, Louise (Thibault; Damours de Freneuse), 246
Guyon, Simon, 359
Guyon Des Granches de Beaupré, 169
Guyon Du Buisson, Élisabeth. *See* Couillard
Guyon Du Buisson, Jean (the elder), 232, 281, 330, **359**
Guyon Du Buisson, Jean (the younger), 238, **359–60**
Guyon Du Buisson, Mathurine. *See* Robin
Guyotte*, Étienne, 78
Gylberte. *See* Gilbert

HAIES. *See* Hayes
Hakluyt, Richard (the elder), 332, 333, 530, 531
Hakluyt, Richard (the younger), 88, 89, 151, 158, 170, 333, 336, 363, 364, 371, 380, 531, 532, 586, 659, 660, 672, 678
Hall*, Charles Francis, 94, 318

INDEX

Hall, Christopher, 316, 317, 318, 375
Hall, Diana. *See* Cobbie
Hall, James, 5, 20, 74, 243, **360**, 408
Hamel, Anne-Félicité. *See* Levasseur
Hamel, Jean, 473
Hamelin de Bourgchemin, Anne-Marie, 361
Hamelin de Bourgchemin, Élisabeth. *See* Dizy
Hamelin de Bourgchemin, François (the elder), 360
Hamelin de Bourgchemin, François (son of Jacques-François), 361
Hamelin de Bourgchemin, Madeleine. *See* Guitton
Hamelin de Bourgchemin, Marguerite, 361
Hamelin de Bourgchemin et de l'Hermitière, Jacques-François, **360–61**
Hamilton, Andrew, 107, **361**, 493, 657
Hamilton, James, Marquis of (later first Duke of), second Earl of Cambridge in the English peerage, 369, 405, 613
Hampshire, Sir Thomas, 229
Hampson, John, 611
Hangard, Catherine de. *See* La Roque
Hangard, Robert de, 425
Hannam, John, 584
Hannam, William, 584
Harakontie. *See* Garakontié
Harborne, William, 85
Harcourt, Comte d'. *See* Lorraine
Harcourt, Robert, 366
Harlay de Champvallon, François de, Archbishop of Rouen, 646, 647
Harman, John, 443
Harris, Elizabeth, 81
Harvey, Thomas, 574
Harwick, Abraham van, 450
Harwick, Stephen van, 391, 450
Hateouati. *See* Otreouti
Hathorne*, John, 26, 246
Hatton, Sir Christopher, 93, 94
Haubichon, Jean, 270
Hauteville. *See* Le Vieux
Hautmesnyl. *See* Philippe
Hawkeridge (Hawkridge), William, 144, **362**
Hawkins, Sir John, 316, 331, 380, 381, 530
Hawkins, William, 228
Hawthorne. *See* Hathorne
Hayes (Haies), Edward, 334, 335, 336, **362–65**, 531, 532
Hayes, Thomas, 365
Hayet, Madeleine. *See* Hénaut
Hayet, Marguerite (Véron de Grandmesnil; Chouart Des Groseilliers), 223, 228
Hayet, Sébastien, 223
Hayman, Amis. *See* Raleigh
Hayman, Nicholas, 365
Hayman, Robert, **365–66**, 584, 656, 669
Hayward, Nicholas, 226
Hearne*, Samuel, 378
Hébert, Anne, 264
Hébert, Anne (Jonquet), 368, 437, 578
Hébert, Françoise (Fournier), 264
Hébert, Guillaume, 264, 367, 368, 578
Hébert, Guillemette (Couillard de Lespinay), 109, 145, 236, 237, 264, **366–67**, 368, 386, 517, 578
Hébert, Hélène. *See* Desportes

Hébert, Jacques, 367
Hébert, Joseph, 264, **367**, 367
Hébert, Joseph (son of Joseph), 367
Hébert, Louis (apothecary), 367
Hébert, Louis, 29, 96, 101, 108, 189, 195, 236, 237, 238, 264, 347, 366, 367, **367–68**, 437, 578
Hébert*, Louis-Philippe, 221, 232
Hébert, Marie. *See* Rollet
Hébert, Marie-Charlotte. *See* Poytiers
Hébert, Nicolas, 367
Hébert, *dit* Larivière, Roland, 267
Héchon. *See* Échon
Hélène de Saint-Augustin. *See* Boullé
Hélie Du Tillet, Madeleine (Mius d'Entremont), 510
Hénaut, Madeleine (Hayet), 223
Hennepin*, Louis, 175, 176, 226, 379, 415, 438, 439, 440
Henri (servant of Mme Hébert), 302, 366, 509
Henri II, King of France, 372, 421, 424
Henri III, King of France, 261, 324, 421, 520
Henri IV, King of Navarre and France, 23, 42, 96, 97, 99, 100, 134, 187–88, 190, 209, 210, 214, 291, 299, 307, 323, 421, 422, 453, 471, 498, 501, 521, 601
Henrietta Maria (Queen consort of Charles I, King of Great Britain and Ireland), 81, 534, 596
Henry, Prince (eldest son of James I, King of Great Britain and Ireland), 144
Henry VII, King of England, 120, 148, 149, 153, 164, 239, 302, 304, 641
Henry VIII, King of England and Ireland, 155, 157, 565, 566, 585, 586, 643
Henry*, Alexander, 225
Herbert, Philip, Earl of Montgomery and fourth Earl of Pembroke, 369, 405
Herbert, Sir Thomas, 678
Herjólfr Bárdarson, 103
Herjólfsson. *See* Bjarni
Hermitière. *See* Hamelin
Héron, Antoine, 90
Herovin. *See* Irwin
Herrera y Tordesillas, Antonio de, 342
Hertel, Jeanne. *See* Miriot
Hertel, Nicolas, 368
Hertel de La Fresnière, Jacques, 238, **368–69**, 550
Hertel* de La Fresnière, Joseph-François, 185, 239, 368, 369
Hertel de La Fresnière, Marguerite. *See* Thavenet
Hertel de La Fresnière, Marguerite (Crevier de Saint-François), 238, 369
Hertel de La Fresnière, Marie. *See* Marguerie
Hertel de La Fresnière, Marie-Madeleine (Pinard), 369, 550
Herzogenbusch. *See* Cnoyen
Heylyn, Peter, 678
Hiawatha, 7, 253, 254
Hill, Master (of Rotherhithe), 306
Hill, Peter, 306, 450
Hill, Ralph, 450, 451
Hill, William, 163, **369**, 405
Hinton, Sir Thomas, 369
Hinton, William, 93, **369–70**
Hinton, William (the elder), 369, 370
Hiou, Anne, 116

INDEX

Hirouin. *See* Irwin
Hoby, Elizabeth, Lady. *See* Cooke
Holland. *See* Rich, Henry
Home, Sir George, 54, 311
Homem, Lopo, 304
Honarreennha, Louis, 185
Honatteniate, **370–71**, 404, 548
Hopton, Ralph, Lord Hopton, 653
Hore (Hoore), Richard, 5, 19, **371–72**, 565, 566
Horehouasse. *See* Ourehouare
Hot Ash (Hot Powder). *See* Ogenheratarihiens
Hoteouate (Hotrehouati, Houtreouati). *See* Otreouti
Hotman, François, 42, 43
Hotman, Suzanne (Manthet d'Argentenay; Ailleboust), 42, 43
Houel, Louis, 192, 386, 590
Howard, Charles, Lord Howard of Effingham, Earl of Nottingham, 668
Howard, Thomas, Earl of Surrey and Duke of Norfolk, 566
Howe, Elizabeth (Sedgwick), 604
Howting, John, 565
Huault, Jacques, 372
Huault de Montmagny, Charles, 43, 44, 45, 111, 121, 124, 127, 128, 186, 197, 203, 205, 215, 216, 217, 218, 237, 250, 324, 344, 348, 354, 370, **372–74**, 389, 401, 403, 404, 414, 446, 454, 472, 481, 482, 485, 523, 548, 567, 574, 595, 596, 602, 663, 665
Hubou (Huboust, Hubout), Guillaume, 554, 578
Hubou, Marie. *See* Rollet
Hudson, Hannah (Leverett), 475
Hudson, Henry, 20, 74, 83, 144, 145, 190, 252, 312, 318, 329, **374–79**, 384, 385, 668, 679
Hudson, John, 377, **379**
Huet, Paul, 296, **379**, 552
Hugo of Ireland, 678
Hull, Mary. *See* Spencer
Hume, Edward, 611
Humfrey, Laurence, 531
Hunt, Thomas, 262, 650
Huret, Grégoire, 551
Hutchinson, Anne, 601
Hutchinson, Bridget (Sanford; Phillips), 337, 601
Hyacinthe, Father. *See* Perreault

Iberville. *See* Le Moyne
Ignace de Paris, **379–80**
Imbert, Simon, 95, 98, 100, 299, 470
Ingram, David, 333, **380–81**
Irénée, Father. *See* Piat
Iroquet, 70, 131, 190, **381–82**, 603
Irwin, Marie, *dite* de la Conception, **382**
Isabel, Guillaume, 468
Itarey, 451
Ivar Bárdarson, 679

Jackman, Charles, 317
Jacquelin, Françoise-Marie (Saint-Étienne de La Tour), **383–84**, 505, 594, 595
Jacquinot, Barthélemy, 455, 539
Jager, Claude, 205
Jalleau. *See* Jallot
Jallot, Jeanne (Terrier; Poulin de La Fontaine), 553

Jalobert, Alizon. *See* Des Granches
Jalobert, Bertrand, 384
Jalobert, Jehanne. *See* Maingard
Jalobert, Macé, 167, 169, **384**, 520
Jamay, Denis. *See* Jamet
Jambe de Bois. *See* Gargot
James I (James VI of Scotland), King of Great Britain and Ireland, 23, 50, 51, 52, 67, 69, 144, 243, 369, 481, 496, 597, 667, 668
James II, King of Great Britain and Ireland (formerly Duke of York), 92, 227, 329, 544, 605, 631
James, Richard, 229
James, Thomas, 20, 83, 144, 311, 329, 349, 362, 376, 377, **384–85**, 408
James, Thomas (mayor of Bristol), 349, 384
James, William, 306
Jamet, Denis, 192, 265, 296, **385**, 437, 590
Jamin, Gilles, 265
Jamin, Pierre, 503, 504
Janes, John, 375
Jannière, Jeanne (Bourdon de Dombourg; Denys de Bonaventure), 114
Janson, Paul, 213
Jard-Boispineau, Charles, 108
Jard-Boispineau, Jean, 108
Jarret* de Verchères, Madeleine (Tarieu de La Pérade), 239, 418
Jay, John, 19, 21, 147, 239, 240, **386–87**
Jay, John (merchant of Bristol), 386
Jay, John (tucker of Bristol), 386
Jean, Father. *See* Dolbeau
Jean Alfonse. *See* Fonteneau
Jean-Armand (Indian). *See* Andehoua
Jeanne de Sainte-Marie, 348
Jeanne-Françoise de Saint-Ignace. *See* Juchereau de La Ferté
Jeannin, Pierre, *dit* le Président Jeannin (magistrate and French diplomat), 470
Jenkinson, Anthony, 331
Jérémie, Claude, 387
Jérémie, Hélène. *See* Macart
Jérémie, Jeanne. *See* Pelletier
Jérémie, *dit* Lamontagne, Noël, 60, **387**
Jilbert. *See* Gilbert
Jogues, Isaac, 11, 41, 42, 112, 124, 125, 203, 344, 370, 371, 373, **387–90**, 403, 404, 410, 411, 414, 454, 457, 459, 461, 462, 523, 524, 566
Johnson, Francis, 390, 391, 392, 450, 451
Johnson, George, **390–92**, 450, 451
Joibert. *See* Joybert
Joinville, Gabriel de, 434
Jolliet, Adrien, 173, 225, 227, 248, 393, 536, 626
Jolliet, Claire-Françoise. *See* Byssot
Jolliet, Louis, 11, 15, 35, 76, 84, 104, 105, 146, 173, 174, 175, 178, 225, 226, 227, 289, 345, **392–98**, 400, 452, 480, 491, 492, 565, 572, 625, 657, 665
Jolliet, Marie. *See* Abancourt
Jolliet, Zacharie, 394, 396, 606, 657
Jollyet, Jean, 392, 554
Jones, Rice, 671
Jonquet, Anne. *See* Hébert
Jonquet, Étienne, 437, 578
Joseph, Père. *See* Du Tremblay; Le Caron

735

INDEX

Joseph, Benjamin, 74
Josselin, Nicolas, 267
Joubert, Capt., 263
Jourdan. *See* Launé
Jourdan, Françoise (Simon de Longpré), 607
Jousserand, Nicole de (Menou), 502
Jousset, Louise (Mauguę; La Sague), 498
Joutel*, Henri, 79, 180, 182
Joybert, Jacques, 399
Joybert, Pierre-Jacques, 399
Joybert de Soulanges, Louise-Élisabeth (Rigaud de Vaudreuil), 399
Joybert de Soulanges et de Marson, Marie-Françoise. *See* Chartier de Lotbinière
Joybert de Soulanges et de Marson, Pierre de, 25, 40, 62, 63, 185, 203, **398–400**, 667
Joyeuse, Anne, Duc de, 87, 88, 89, 421
Joyeuse, François de, Cardinal, 386
Juan Chou (Indian), 263
Juana, the Mad, Queen of Castile, 41
Juchereau, *dit* de Saint-Denis, Paul-Augustin, 400
Juchereau de La Ferté, Charlotte, 400
Juchereau de La Ferté, Denis-Joseph, 400
Juchereau de La Ferté, Jean, 108, 202, **400**, 401, 402, 580, 584, 587, 588, 589
Juchereau* de La Ferté, Jeanne-Françoise, *dite* de Saint-Ignace, 111, 231, 310, 329, 359, 400, 487, 631
Juchereau de La Ferté, Marie. *See* Giffard
Juchereau de La Ferté, Marie, *dite* de Sainte-Thérèse, 400
Juchereau de La Ferté, Marie-Louise (Aubert de La Chesnaye), 400
Juchereau de La Ferté, Noël, 108, 400
Juchereau de Maur, Geneviève (Legardeur de Tilly), 448, 602
Juchereau de Maur, Jean, 60, 330, 400, **401**, 402, 448
Juchereau de Maur, Marie. *See* Langlois
Juchereau* de Saint-Denis, Charles, 508
Juchereau* de Saint-Denis, Charlotte-Françoise (Viennay-Pachot; La Forest), *dite* Comtesse de Saint-Laurent, 661
Juchereau de Saint-Denis, Joseph, 402
Juchereau de Saint-Denis, Marie-Anne (Pollet de La Combe-Pocatière; Ruette d'Auteuil), 550, 551
Juchereau de Saint-Denis, Marie-Thérèse. *See* Giffard
Juchereau de Saint-Denis, Nicolas, 48, 146, 331, 401, **401–2**, 448, 550, 661
Juchereau* de Saint-Ignace, Mother. *See* Juchereau* de La Ferté, Jeanne-Françoise
Juchereau Des Chatelets, Noël, 319, 401, **402–3**, 447, 448
Juchereau* Duchesnay, Ignace, 402, 543
Juchereau Duchesnay, Marie-Catherine. *See* Peuvret Demesnu
Juet, Robert, 374, 375, 376, 377, 378
Juillet, Blaise, 271
Julian, Étiennette (Saint-Père), 598
Jumeau*, Emmanuel, 438
Jurie, Robert, 267

KAHIKOHAN, 48
Kateri Tekakwitha. *See* Tekakwitha
Kaylus. *See* Thubières

Kelly, James (*alias* Gillam and Sampson Marshall) 301
Kelsey*, Henry, 227, 329, 529, 611
Kélus. *See* Thubières
Kepitanal (Kepitenat). *See* Capitanal
Kerbodot. *See* Guillemot
Kerdement, Capt., 421
Kerr, John, 544
Kertk. *See* Kirke
Ketelby, Thomas, 522
Khan, The Great. *See* Kubilay
Khipikiwam, Agatha, 481
Kildare. *See* Fitzgerald
King, John, 376, 377
Kiotseaeton, *dit* Le Crochet, 7, 65, 71, 112, 186, 371, 373, 389, **403–4**, 548, 665
Kiouet, 204
Kirke, Lady (wife of Sir David), 406
Kirke, Sir David, 24, 25, 76, 162, 163, 199, 200, 243, 278, 303, 366, 369, **404–7**, 494, 495, 498, 567, 593, 596, 613, 652
Kirke, David (son of Sir David), 406
Kirke, Elizabeth. *See* Gowding
Kirke, George (son of Sir David), 406, 567
Kirke, Gervase (Jarvis), 404
Kirke, James (also called Jarvis occasionally), 405, 406, 407, 652
Kirke, Sir John, 405, 406, 407
Kirke, Sir Lewis, 199, 242, 405, 406, **407**, 408, 473, 487, 495, 636,
Kirke, Philip (son of Sir David), 406
Kirke, Thomas, 405, **407–8**, 487
Kirke, Thomas (English consul at Genoa, 1689), 408
Kirke brothers, 29, 53, 54, 59, 110, 122, 133, 159, 160, 161, 196, 237, 287, 311, 313, 330, 340, 342, 368, 411, 428, 452, 453, 489, 494, 511, 521, 533, 561, 567, 579, 653, 665
Kirwin. *See* Irwin
Knight, Gabriel, 408
Knight*, James, 385
Knight, John, 5, 20, 243, 360, 375, 397, **408**
Knollys, Henry, 332
Knox, Andrew, Bishop, 496
Kolno. *See* Scolvus
Krainguille, 593
Kryn. *See* Togouiroui
Kubilay (The Great Khan), 21, 147, 149, 150

LA BARBOTIÈRE, Capt., 499
La Baronnière. *See* Froyer
La Barre. *See* Le Febvre
La Barre, Claude de. *See* Camus; Charron
L'Abbé, Capt., 100, 101
La Blanchetière. *See* Renardin
La Boissière. *See* Nau
La Borde. *See* Mullois
La Bouille. *See* Fromont
La Boulardière. *See* Dugué
La Boulaye, Charles. *See* Duret
Labrador, The. *See* Fernandes
La Broquerie. *See* Chartier
La Brosse, 423
La Cardonnière. *See* Rouer de Villeray

INDEX

La Chapelle, François de. *See* Renou
La Chenaye. *See* Gauthier
La Chesnaye. *See* Aubert; Duquet
La Chevrotière. *See* Chavigny
La Citière. *See* Lauson
La Colombière, Guillaume-Daniel. *See* Seré
La Colombière*, Joseph de, 78, 506
La Combe-Pocatière. *See* Pollet
La Corruble. *See* Bouge
La Cosa. *See* Cosa
La Court de Pré-Ravillon et de Granpré, 306, **408–9**, 450, 671
La Croix* de Chevrières de Saint-Vallier, Jean-Baptiste de, 56, 76, 77, 80, 92, 117, 141, 175, 286, 291, 338, 361, 439, 506, 507, 536, 540, 635, 649
La Dauversière. *See* Le Royer
La Découverte. *See* You
La Doussinière. *See* Duchesneau
La Durantaye. *See* Morel
La Ferre, Marie de, 478, 512
La Ferrière. *See* Erouachy
La Ferté. *See* Juchereau
La Ferté de La Madeleine, Abbé de, 494
La Feuillée, Alixe de (Des Granges de Mauprée; La Motte de Lucière), 415
Lafite, Marguerite (Denys), 258, 259
Laflèche (*coureur de bois*), 225
Lafleur. *See* Bailly; Richard
La Fleur, Guillaume Richard *dit*. *See* Richard
Lafontaine. *See* Bellot
La Fontaine. *See* Gamelain; Poulin
La Fontanelle. *See* Eder
La Forest. *See* Testard
La Forest, Sieur de. *See* Tavernier, Jean
La Forest, Charlotte-Françoise. *See* Juchereau de Saint-Denis
La Forest*, François de, 661
La Forest, François de. *See* Dauphin
La Forière (La Fourière, La Foyrière). *See* Erouachy
La Fount, William de. *See* Fount
Lafraynaye. *See* La Frenaye
La Frenaye, Geneviève de. *See* Lepage
La Frenaye, Martin de, 409
La Frenaye de Brucy, Antoine de, **409–10**, 547, 600
La Frenaye de Brucy, Hélène de. *See* Picoté de Belestre
Lafresnaye. *See* La Frenaye
La Fresnaye. *See* Rémy
La Fresnière. *See* Hertel
La Garenne, Marie (Peuvret), 542
La Giraudière, 257
La Grande Gueule (Big Mouth). *See* Otreouti
La Grange, Seigneur de Trianon et de Neufville, 134
La Grange, Anne de (Buade), 134, 135, 142
La Grenouille. *See* Oumasasikweie
La Groye. *See* Aloigny
Laguide Meynier, Madeleine (Perrot), 117, 540
La Haye. *See* Marguerie
La Haye, Père de, 356
La Héronnière, Sieur de, 582
Lahontan. *See* Lom d'Arce
La Jannaye, Étienne de. *See* Chaton
La Jemmerais. *See* Dufrost
Lajeunesse. *See* Dandonneau, Pierre

Lalande, Anne de (Chesneau), 287
La Lande, Jean de, 390, **410–11**, 414
Lalande, Marie. *See* Couillard
La Lande, Robert de, 288
Lalande de Gayon, Jacques de, 104, 105, 146, 289, 395, 396, 397
Lalemand, Pierre. *See* Allemand
Lalemant, Charles, 43, 111, 121, 125, 160, 197, 213, 214, 217, 246, 329, **411–12**, 413, 428, 447, 453, 456, 484, 493, 494, 498, 521, 561
Lalemant, Gabriel, 9, 31, 64, 124, 126, 219, **412–13**, 414, 459, 483, 561, 562
Lalemant, Jérôme, 91, 123, 246, 268, 284, 354, 355, 357, 374, 388, 389, 404, 410, 411, 412, **413–15**, 428, 430, 431, 456, 459, 461, 473, 477, 498, 561, 562, 640, 662, 665
Lallemant, Louis, 126, 387, 563
La Lochetière. *See* Tavernier, Jean
La Madeleine. *See* La Ferté
La Marche, Jacques de, 477
La Marck, Marie de (Godet Des Maretz), 342
La Marck, Robert IV de, Duc de Bouillon, Prince de Sedan, Maréchal de France, 424
La Marque, 246
La Marre, Sieur de, 473
Lamarre, Anne (Duquet), 298
La Martinière. *See* Bermen; Lomeron
Lambert, Eustache, 146, 396, **415**
Lambert, Marie. *See* Laurence
Lamberville*, Jacques de, 635
Lamberville*, Jean de, 322, 323, 443, 445, 465, 525, 526, 633
La Meilleraye, Sieur de, 434
Lamer, Marie de (Nicollet), 516
La Mer Monte. *See* Chomina
La Meslée. *See* Crevier
Lamoignon, Guillaume de, 220
Lamontagne. *See* Jérémie
Lamorille. *See* Lemaître
La Mothe, Nicolas. *See* Le Vieux de Hauteville
La Mothe, Nicolas de, 441
Lamothe, Pierre. *See* Aigron
Lamothe (La Mothe) de Cadillac. *See* Laumet
La Mothe-Fénelon. *See* Salignac
La Motte, Clémence. *See* Badon
La Motte, Jean de, 415
La Motte, Louis de. *See* La Rue
La Motte de Lucière, Alixe de. *See* La Feuillée
La Motte de Lucière, Dominique, 175, **415–16**, 416
Lamotte de Saint-Paul, Pierre, 415, **416**
La Motte-le-Vilin, 68
La Motte Saint-Lys. *See* Caën, Guillaume de (the younger)
La Nasse. *See* Manitougatche
Lanaudière. *See* Lanouguère
La Nauraye. *See* Niort de La Noraye
Lancaster, Sir James, 499
Landon*, Simple, 55, 420
Landron, Étienne, 56, 664
Lane, Daniel, **416–17**
La Neuville. *See* Buache
Langlois, Françoise. *See* Grenier
Langlois, Françoise (Desportes), 264, 495

737

INDEX

Langlois, Guillaume, 417
Langlois, Jeanne. *See* Millet
Langlois, Marguerite (Martin), 495
Langlois, Marie. *See* Crevet
Langlois, Marie (Caën), 159
Langlois, Marie (Juchereau de Maur), 400, 401
Langlois, Noël, 330, **417**
Langloiserie. *See* Piot
Langoissieux, Charles (baptized Pierre), 320, **417**
La Noraye. *See* Niort
Lanouguère, Jean de, 417
Lanouguère, Jeanne de. *See* Samalins
Lanouguère, Marguerite-Renée. *See* Denys de La Ronde
Lanouguère*, Pierre-Thomas de, 418
Lanouguère, Thomas de, 321, **417–18**, 600
La Palme (or de Palme), 89, 418
La Peltrie, Mme de. *See* Chauvigny, Marie-Madeleine
La Pérade. *See* Tarieu
La Pierre. *See* Chauvin
La Place. *See* Girard
La Place, Jacques de, 215, 485
La Pocatière. *See* Pollet
La Poippe, Sieur de, **418–19**, 530
La Pommeraye, Charles de, 167
La Potardière, Sieur de, 626
La Poterie. *See* Leneuf
La Potherie. *See* Le Roy
La Prade. *See* Pelletier
La Rade. *See* La Ralde
La Ralde, Raymond de, 162, 411, **419**, 521, 579
La Ramée, Sieur de. *See* Melanson, Charles
Lardeau, Anne (Gargot), 323
Lardeau, Jacques, 323
Largilier*, Jacques, 394
La Ribourde, Gabriel de, 55, 176, 177, 265, **420**, 438, 499, 501
La Rivière, François de. *See* Byssot
Larivière, Hilaire Bernard, *dit*. *See* Bernard
La Rivière, Joseph-Antoine de. *See* Poncet
Larivière, Roland. *See* Hébert
La Roche, Jeanne. *See* Froyer de La Baronnière
La Roche Daillon, Jacques de, 420
La Roche Daillon, Joseph de, 132, **420–21**, 533
La Roche de Mesgouez, Troilus de, 23, 27, 88, 209, 210, 345, **421–22**
La Roche-Guyon, Duchesse de. *See* Schomberg
La Rochette. *See* Gargot
La Rocque de Roberval, Jean-François de, 27, 159, 169, 301, 309, 384, **422–25**, 425, 469
La Ronde. *See* Denys
La Roque, Catherine de (Hangard), 425
La Roque, Charlotte de (Madaillan), 424
La Roque, Isabeau de (Isabeau de Poitiers), 422
La Roque, Jean de, 424
La Roque, Marguerite de, 423, 424, **425–26**
La Roque, Pierre de. *See* La Roque, Jean de
La Roque, *dit* Couillaud, Bernard de, 422
Lartigue. *See* Bidoux
Lartigue de La Salle, Jean. *See* La Salle
La Rue de La Motte, Louis de, 416
La Sague, Jean de, 498
La Sague, Louise de. *See* Jousset

La Salle. *See* Cavelier
La Salle, Jean de, 425
La Salle, Rose de (Marquette), 490
La Saussaye. *See* Le Coq
Lascaris* d'Urfé, François-Saturnin, 599, 600, 647
La Taupine. *See* Moreau
La Tesserie. *See* Cailhault
La Thibaudière. *See* Denys
Latour. *See* Bertrand
La Tour. *See* Saint-Étienne
La Tour d'Auvergne, Henri de, Vicomte de Turenne, Maréchal de France, 283, 615
La Tourasse, Catherine. *See* Bugaret
La Tourasse, Charles, *dit* Chevalier, **426–27**, 361, 544, 576
La Tousche. *See* Pézard
La Trinité. *See* Denys
La Troche. *See* Savonnières
Laud, William, Archbishop of Canterbury, 406
Laudonnière. *See* Goulaine
Laulne, Louise de (Chambly), 185
Laumet de Lamothe de Cadillac, Mme, 416
Laumet* de Lamothe de Cadillac, Antoine, 141, 201, 582
Launay-Rasilly, Claude de, 503, 504, 567, 569, 593, 594
Launé-Jourdan, M. de, 607
Laurence, Marie (Lambert), 396, 415
Lauson, Anne. *See* Boivin
Lauson, Anne de. *See* Després
Lauson, François de, 427, 428
Lauson, Gilles, **427**
Lauson, Jean de (the elder), 45, 112, 145, 146, 200, 202-3, 214, 232, 237, 245, 340, 349, 372, 401, 412, **427–29**, 429, 431, 473, 475, 542, 574, 579, 580, 606
Lauson, Jean de (the younger), 274, 428, **429–31**, 432, 574, 665
Lauson, Marie. *See* Archambault
Lauson, Marie de. *See* Gaudar
Lauson, Pierre, 427
Lauson de Charny, Charles de, 46, 91, 92, 146, 331, 400, 428, 429, **431–32**, 537, 579, 580, 589
Lauson de Charny, Louise de. *See* Giffard
Lauson de La Citière, Catherine de. *See* Nau de La Boissière et de Fossambault
Lauson de La Citière, Louis de, 428, 542
Lauson de Lirec, François de, 427
Lauson de Lirec, Isabelle de. *See* Lottin
Lauzières, Pons de, Marquis de Thémines, Maréchal de France, 193
Laval*, François de, 31, 32, 33, 42, 46, 55, 57, 72, 76, 77, 78, 80, 85, 86, 91, 92, 111, 112, 116, 117, 120, 137, 198, 202-3, 237, 245, 249, 264, 265, 283, 284, 286, 289, 290, 291, 310, 313, 315, 321, 322, 323, 325, 326, 331, 354, 355, 356, 359, 366, 393, 414, 431, 432, 438, 466, 472, 479, 507, 534, 536, 539, 542, 554, 555, 556, 563, 580, 587, 588, 589, 590, 599, 606, 609, 610, 629, 630, 644, 646, 647, 648, 649, 651, 665
Lavallée. *See* Pâquet
La Vallière. *See* Leneuf
La Varenne. *See* Bonneau
La Verdure. *See* Melanson
La Vérendrie (La Vérendrye). *See* Gaultier

INDEX

La Verge, Marguerite (Daumont de Saint-Lusson), 249
La Viazère. *See* Senau
La Vieuville, Charles, Marquis, later Duc de, 521
Lavigne. *See* Levasseur; Tessier
Laviolette, 121, 127, 143, **432**
La Violette, 666
Lawrence O'Toole, Saint, Archbishop of Dublin, 560
Le Baillif, Georges, 160, 194, 320, **433**, 437
Le Baillif, Olivier, 366, 452
Le Barbier, Marie (Marsolet de Saint-Aignan; Le Maistre), 494
Le Baron, Jean. *See* Auger
Le Barroys, Claude, 400, 617, 628, 629
Lebel, Guillaume, 66
Le Ber (Leber), Élisabeth. *See* Le Bret
Le Ber*, Jacques, 105, 178, 284, 289, 295, 410, 416, 444, 464, 508
Le Ber*, Jeanne, 117
Le Ber*, Pierre, 416
Le Berger. *See* Honatteniate
Lebon, Pierre, 114
Le Borgne, Emmanuel, 62, 90, 129, 234, 257, 258, 259, 379, 380, **433–35**, 435, 468, 469, 504, 505, 514, 595, 604
Le Borgne, Jeanne. *See* François
Le Borgne, Jeanne (Bazire), 84
Le Borgne de Belle-Isle, Alexandre, 62, 426, 433, 434, **435–36**, 513, 514, 636
Le Borgne de Belle-Isle, Marie. *See* Saint-Étienne de La Tour
Le Borgne de l'Île. *See* Tessouat (d. 1636); Tessouat (d. 1654)
Le Borgne* Du Coudray, André, 436
Le Borgne Du Coudray, Emmanuel, 434, 435
Le Boucher, Marie (Auber), 72
Le Bret, Élisabeth (Moyen Des Granges), 231, 295
Le Breton, Guillaume, 167
Le Breton, Madeleine (Bernières), 91
Le Breton-Bastille, Guillaume, 167
Le Cadet. *See* Chomina
Le Camus, Claude. *See* Camus
Le Caron, Joseph, 58, 193, 222, 223, 265, 385, 386, 433, **436–38**, 511, 546, 590, 591, 612, 661
Le Castor, Jacques, 491
Le Chasseur*, Jean, 286
Leclaire, R., 77
Leclerc, Alix, 115
Leclerc, Hilaire, 447
Le Clercq, Chrestien, 14, 211, 222, 223, 265, 411, 433, 437, **438–41**, 509, 552, 661
Le Clercq, Maxime, 438
Le Cocq. *See* Le Coq
Le Cointre, Anne, *dite* de Saint-Bernard, 310, 347, 353
Lecompte, Jean, 267
Le Coq, Robert, **441**
Le Coq de La Saussaye, René, 67, 68, 69, 95, 98, 101, 299, 367, **441–42**
L'Écossais. *See* Martin, Abraham
Lecoustre, Claude, 91
Le Creux Du Breuil, Anne. *See* Motin
Le Creux Du Breuil, Nicolas, **442**, 503, 514, 568, 642
Le Crochet. *See* Kiotseaeton
Ledesma, Jacques, 125

Lee, Dorothy (Temple), 636
Lee, Edmund, 636
Lee, Edward, 643
Le Faucher, 161
Le Febvre de La Barre, Antoine, 442
Le Febvre de La Barre, *dit* le chevalier de La Barre, 446
Le Febvre de La Barre, Joseph-Antoine, 103, 105, 114, 130, 137, 178, 179, 180, 227, 295, 338, **442–46**, 464, 465, 488, 523, 525, 526, 541, 554, 576, 650
Le Febvre de La Barre, Madeleine. *See* Belin
Le Febvre de La Barre, Marie. *See* Mandat
Lefebvre Du Guesclin, Dominique, 409
Le Gall, Jacques, 425
Le Gallois* de Beaujeu, Taneguy, 180, 181, 182
Legardeur* de Beauvais, René, 650
Legardeur de Repentigny, Catherine (Ailleboust Des Muceaux), 47, 447
Legardeur* de Repentigny, Jean-Baptiste, 517
Legardeur de Repentigny, Marguerite. *See* Nicollet de Belleborne
Legardeur de Repentigny, Marguerite (Leneuf de La Poterie), 446, 467, 468, 575
Le Gardeur de Repentigny, Marie. *See* Favery
Legardeur de Repentigny, Marie-Madeleine (Godefroy), 340, 447
Legardeur de Repentigny, Pierre, 216, 287, 330, 339, 353, 402, **446–47**, 467, 495
Legardeur de Tilly, Catherine. *See* Cordé
Legadeur de Tilly, Catherine (Saurel), 602
Legardeur de Tilly, Charles, 145, 288, 402, 446, **447–48**, 467, 468, 581, 582, 587, 588, 602
Legardeur de Tilly, Geneviève. *See* Juchereau de Maur
Legardeur* de Tilly, Pierre-Noël, 448
Legardeur de Tilly, René, 446, 447
Le Gaudier, Antoine, 411
Legendre, Lucas, 293
Léger, César, 557
Legge, George, Lord Dartmouth, 92
Le Grand Agnier. *See* Togouiroui
Le Héricy, Guillaume, 89
Leifr *heppni* Eiriksson (Leif the Lucky), 17, 104, **448–49**, 612, 642, 643, 676
Leigh, Charles, 391, 392, 409, **449–52**
Leigh, Joan. *See* Oliph
Leigh, John, 449
Leigh, Olyph, 452
Leisler, Jacob, 586
Le Jeune, Oliver, 366, **452**
Le Jeune, Paul, 70, 120, 122, 123, 124, 126, 143, 159, 164, 186, 197, 203, 205, 207, 214, 215, 287, 310, 341, 348, 404, 412, 432, 452, **453–58**, 473, 481, 482, 487, 494, 516, 517, 518, 527, 533, 549, 563, 633, 637, 661, 665, 673
Le Maistre, Denis, 495
Le Maistre, Jacques, **458**, 525, 612, 662
Le Maistre, Marie. *See* Le Barbier
Lemaître, Marguerite. *See* Poulin de La Fontaine
Lemaître*, *dit* Lamorille, François, 553
Le Marchant, Jeanne (Leneuf), 340, 467
Le Marié, Guillaume, 167
Le Mercier, François-Joseph, 125, 212, 244, 255, **458–60**, 461, 552, 562, 563
Le Mercier, Marie. *See* Du Jardin

739

INDEX

Le Mercier, Paul, 458
Lemire, Jean, **460**, 589
Lemire, Louise. *See* Marsolet
Lemort, Anne. *See* Dubois
Lemort, Jacques, 535
Le Moyne, Judith. *See* Du Chesne
Le Moyne, Pierre, 463
Le Moyne, Simon, 10, 66, 70, 130, 206, 244, 295, 307, 315, 322, 414, 429, 458, **460–62**, 502, 523, 525, 563
Le Moyne de Bienville, François, **463**
Le Moyne* de Bienville, Jean-Baptiste, **463**
Le Moyne de Châteauguay, Louis, **463**
Le Moyne d'Iberville, Marie-Thérèse. *See* Pollet de La Combe-Pocatière
Le Moyne* d'Iberville, Pierre, 26, 61, 80, 179, 227, 308, 339, 361, 400, 463, 465, 493, 529, 547, 551, 577, 582, 611, 641, 649, 653
Le Moyne* de Longueuil, Charles (the younger), 464
Le Moyne de Longueuil et de Châteauguay, Catherine. *See* Thierry
Le Moyne de Longueuil et de Châteauguay, Charles, 103, 105, 225, 231, 271, 287, 289, 295, 319, 322, 444, 445, **463–65**, 465, 507, 508, 555
Le Moyne* de Maricourt, Paul, 465, 653
Le Moyne de Sainte-Hélène, Jacques, 463, **465–67**, 545, 653
Le Moyne* de Sainte-Hélène, Jacques (the younger), 466
Le Moyne de Sainte-Hélène, Jeanne. *See* Dufresnoy Carion
Le Moyne* de Sérigny, Joseph, 463
Leneuf, Jeanne. *See* Le Marchant
Leneuf, Marie (Godefroy de Lintot), 340, 467
Leneuf, Mathieu, 340, 467
Leneuf* de Beaubassin, Alexandre, 90
Leneuf de La Poterie, Catherine (Denys de La Ronde), 418
Leneuf de La Poterie, Jacques, 60, 186, 446, **467**, 467, 468, 575, 589
Leneuf de La Poterie, Marguerite. *See* Legardeur de Repentigny
Leneuf de La Poterie, Marie-Anne (Robinau de Bécancour), 467, 575, 576
Leneuf de La Vallière, Marie. *See* Denys
Leneuf* de La Vallière, Michel, 90, 258, 260, 396, 399, 467
Leneuf Du Hérisson, Anne, *dite* Du Hérisson (Desrosiers), 468
Leneuf Du Hérisson, Michel, 340, 467, **467–68**, 550
Lenoir, Marie (Chartier), 202
Le Noir* Rolland, François, 47
Léonard d'Auxerre, 129
Léonard de Chartres, 434, **468–69**
Le Page, *dit* Chaudron, 425
Lepage, Geneviève (La Frenaye), 409
Lepage, Marie-Rogère (Peuvret Demesnu), 543
Le Piat. *See* Piat
Le Picard. *See* Olivier
Le Pont. *See* Gravé Du Pont
Le Prestre de Vauban, Sébastien, Maréchal de France, 664
Le Rageois de Bretonvilliers, Alexandre, 540, 600
Le Raisin. *See* Chomina

Lerole. *See* Canchy
Lerouge*, Jean, 619, 664
Leroux, Valentin, 439, 440
Leroy*, Henri, 265
Le Roy, Marguerite (Champlain), 186
Le Roy, Marie (Paumart), 534
Le Roy* de La Poterie, *dit* Bacqueville de La Potherie, Claude-Charles, 40, 77, 112, 249, 522, 611
Le Royer de La Dauversière, Jeanne. *See* Baugé
Le Royer de La Dauversière, Jérôme (the elder), 214
Le Royer de La Dauversière, Jérôme, 31, 109, 213–21, 412, 454, 457, 478, 480, 485, 487, 512, 648
Le Royer de La Dauversière, Joseph, 214
Le Royer de La Dauversière, Renée (or Marie). *See* Oudin
Léry. *See* Chaussegros
Léry, Jean de, 469
Lescarbot, Claude, 471
Lescarbot, Françoise. *See* Valpergue
Lescarbot, Marc, 12, 28, 64, 67, 69, 72, 95, 96, 97, 98, 99, 170, 188-89, 197-98, 292, 293, 294, 300, 307, 346, 367, **469–72**, 500, 501, 526, 527, 564, 568, 591, 604
Lescarbot, Marc (probably nephew of Marc), 471
Lescot (Lescault), Marie (Boutroue d'Aubigny), 120
L'Espérance. *See* Levasseur
Lespinay. *See* Couillard
Lespinay, Hutin de, 425
Lespinay, Marie de. *See* Caulincourt
Lespinay, Nicolas de, 423, 425
L'Estang. *See* Petit
Le Sueur, Jean, *dit* Abbé de Saint-Sauveur, 111, 112, 310, 339, **472**
Le Suisse, Pierre Miville *dit*. *See* Miville
Letardif, Barbe. *See* Esmart
Letardif, Louise. *See* Couillard
Letardif, Olivier, 72, 163, 344, 452, **473**, 517, 518, 554
Le Tellier, François-Michel, Seigneur de Chaville, Marquis de Louvois, 535
Le Vasseur (companion of La Rocque de Roberval), 423, 425
Levasseur, Anne-Félicité (Hamel), 474
Levasseur, G. (cartographer), 188
Levasseur, Geneviève. *See* Grange
Levasseur, Jeanne. *See* Chaverlange
Levasseur, Louis, 473
Levasseur, Marguerite. *See* Richard
Levasseur*, Noël, 473, 474
Levasseur, Noël (the elder), 473
Levasseur*, Pierre-Noël, 225, 474
Levasseur, *dit* Lavigne, Jean, **473–74**, 645
Levasseur, *dit* L'Espérance, Pierre, **474**
Le Veneur, Jean, 165
Leverett, Anne. *See* Fisher
Leverett, Hannah. *See* Hudson
Leverett, John, **474–75**, 573, 595, 605, 636
Leverett, Sarah. *See* Sedgwick
Leverett, Thomas, 474
Le Vieux de Hauteville, Marguerite. *See* Lyonne
Le Vieux de Hauteville, Marie. *See* Renardin de La Blanchetière
Le Vieux de Hauteville, Nicolas (the elder), 475
Le Vieux de Hauteville, Nicolas, 431, **475**

Lévis (Lévy), Henri de, Duc de Ventadour, 58, 186, 195, 521
Levy. *See* Thubières
Lewis, Edward, 144
Lewis, Margaret (Button), 144
Lexington, Lady, 82
L'Hermitière, Jacques-François. *See* Hamelin de Bourgchemin
Liancourt, Duc de. *See* Du Plessis
Liancourt, Marquise de. *See* Schomberg
Libert, Nicolas, 248
Liddall. *See* Lydall
Liégeois, Jean, **475–76**
Lignères. *See* Desportes, Pierre
Lily of the Mohawks. *See* Tekakwitha
Lindenow, Godske, 243
Lino. *See* Martin
Lintot. *See* Godefroy
Lionne. *See* Lyonne
Lirec. *See* Lauson
Livingstone, Mary (Stewart), 613
Lloyd (captain of the fireship *Owner's Love*). 308
Lloyd (commanded expedition in search of Isle of Brazil, 1480), 239
Lloyd, James, 545
Lloyd, John, 19, 386
Llwyd, Humphrey, 677
Locke, John, 519
Lok, Michael, 316, 317, 318, 332, 659, 676, 677
Lom* d'Arce, Louis-Armand de, Baron de Lahontan, 526
Lomeron, David, 101, 248, **476**, 592
Lomeron, Jeanne. *See* Duquerny
Lomeron, Suzanne. *See* Georges
Lomeron de La Martinière, Daniel, 476
Longpré. *See* Simon
Longueuil. *See* Le Moyne
Longueval, Robert de, 423, 425
Longueville, Henri, Duc de, 58
Lorimier*, Guillaume de, 109
Lorraine, Charles de, Duc d'Aumale, 96
Lorraine, Charles de, Duc de Guise, 214
Lorraine, Henri de, Comte d'Harcourt, 248
Lotbinière. *See* Chartier
Lottin, Isabelle (Lauson de Lirec), 427
Loubias. *See* Arnoult
Louis (French youth in service of Du Gua de Monts), 603
Louis (Montagnais, baptized by Mohier), 511
Louis (son of Membertou), 500, 501
Louis IX (or St. Louis), King of France, 121, 126
Louis XIII, King of France, 100, 102, 133, 134, 160, 191, 194, 196, 217, 405, 433, 437, 501, 502, 584, 592, 593, 594
Louis XIV, King of France, 32, 35, 40, 55, 60, 62, 74, 76, 92, 104, 108, 109, 117, 119, 134, 135, 136, 137, 138, 139, 141, 174, 180, 202, 216, 220, 227, 238, 249, 261, 284, 288, 290, 330, 429, 443, 446, 467, 487, 510, 511, 513, 528, 535, 541, 542, 556, 561, 570, 571, 572, 576, 585, 587, 615, 616, 624, 631, 636, 646, 647, 648, 664
Louis de Sainte-Foi. *See* Amantacha
Louise de Marillac, Sainte, 484

Louise de Sainte-Marie. *See* Chomedey
Louvigny, J. *See* Bernières
Louvois (minister). *See* Le Tellier
Luc, Frère. *See* François, Claude
Lucas, Jacqueline (Auber), 72
Lucas, Richard, 315, 417, **476–77**, 606, 666
Lucau, *dit* Barbeau, Léonard, 230
Lucière. *See* La Motte
Luna, Pedro de, 342
Lydall, Sir Richard, 477
Lydall, William, 83, 343, **477**
Lyonne, Marguerite (Le Vieux de Hauteville), 475
Lyonne, Martin de, **477–78**, 558
Lyschander, Claus C., 675

Macain, Jean, 98, 101, 293, 476, 565
Macard, Geneviève (Bazire), 84
Macard, Marguerite. *See* Couillard
Macard, Nicolas, 84
Macart*, Charles, 345
Macart, Hélène (Jérémie), 387
Macart, Jeanne-Renée. *See* Gourdeau
Macdowall, Margaret (Stewart), 613
Macdowall, Uchtred, 613
Macé, Catherine, 220, 458, **478**, 480, 487, 512
Macé, Guillé, 478
Macé, Philippe. *See* Martineau
Macé, René, 478
Mackenzie*, Sir Alexander, 378
Mackworth, Agnes (Watts; Crowne), 241, 242
Mackworth, Humphrey, 241
Macquin. *See* Macain
Madaillan, Charlotte de. *See* La Roque
Madaillan, Louis de, 424
Madeleine (Indian, wife of Totiri), 651, 652
Madoc, **677–78**
Madog ab Owain Gwynedd. *See* Madoc
Madry, Françoise. *See* Duquet
Madry, Jean, 47, 80, 109, 255, **478–79**
Magdelaine (Indian, wife of Paul Tessouat), 640
Magellan, Ferdinand, 155, 342, 658
Maggiolo (Maiollo), Vesconte de, 304, 659
Magnan, Pierre, 211, 303, **479**, 509
Magnus, Olaus, 680
Maheu, 645
Maheu, Anne. *See* Convent
Maheu, René, 494
Maheut, Geneviève. *See* Byssot
Maheut, Jean, 480
Maheut, Louis, **479–80**
Maheut, Louis (elder brother of Louis), 479, 480
Maheut, Marguerite. *See* Corrivault
Maheut, René, 479
Mahigan Aticq Ouche. *See* Miristou
Maillet, Jean, 480
Maillet, Marie. *See* Rivard
Maillet, Marie, 220, 458, 478, **480**, 487, 512
Maingard, Jehanne (Jalobert), 384
Maingart, Jacques, 167
Maintenon, Mme de. *See* Aubigné
Mainwaring, Sir George, 481
Mainwaring, Sir Henry, 24, **481**, 668
Maiollo. *See* Maggiolo

Maisonnat*, Pierre, *dit* Baptiste, 577
Maisonneuve. *See* Chomedey
Maître Abraham. *See* Martin
Maizerets. *See* Ango
Makheabichtichiou, **481–82**, 527
Malapart, André, **482**, 613
Malaspina, Alejandro, 676
Maldonado. *See* Ferrer
Malherbe, Father, 607
Malherbe, François, **483**
Malherbe, François de (French poet), 470
Mallemouche, Jeanne de (Chauvin de Tonnetuit), 209
Mance, Catherine. *See* Emonnot
Mance, Charles, 483
Mance, Jeanne, 31, 43, 78, 208, 215, 216, 217, 219, 220, 230, 231, 310, 344, 412, 453, 457, 478, 480, **483–87**, 512, 547, 640, 648
Mandat, Galiot, 446
Mandat, Marie (Le Febvre de La Barre), 446
Mandet, Marie (Allemand), 56
Manitouabeouich, Marie-Olivier-Sylvestre (Prévost), 554
Manitougatche, Joseph, **487–88**, 533
Manoel (Manuel) I, King of Portugal, 234, 236, 303, 304, 305
Mansel, Sir Robert, 144
Mantes, M. de, 89
Mantes, Côme de. *See* Côme de Mantes
Manthet. *See* Ailleboust
Manthet d'Argentenay, Dorothée de (Ailleboust), 45, 47
Manthet d'Argentenay, Jean de, 42
Manthet d'Argentenay, Suzanne de. *See* Hotman
Manuel. *See* Manoel
Manwaring. *See* Mainwaring
Mar. *See* Erskine
March. *See* Marsh
Marchand, Jean, 77
Marchin (Indian), 507
Marest*, Gabriel, 61
Mareuil, Jacques de, 139, **488–89**
Marguerie, François, 489
Marguerie, Louise. *See* Cloutier
Marguerie, Marie (Hertel de La Fresnière; Moral de Saint-Quentin), 238, 369, 550
Marguerie, Marthe. *See* Romain
Marguerie de La Haye, François, 60, 186, 341, 369, **489–90**, 639
Marguerite d'Angoulême, Queen of Navarre, 424, 425, 426
Marguerite de Saint-Jean-Baptiste. *See* Bourdon
Marguerite de Valois, *dite* la Reine Margot, Queen of Navarre, 549
Maricourt. *See* Le Moyne
Marie (wife of Membertou), 501
Marie (wife of Negabamat), 516
Marie, le Sieur, 505
Marie Aonetta. *See* Aonetta
Marie de la Conception. *See* Irwin
Marie de l'Assomption. *See* Barbier
Marie de l'Incarnation. *See* Guyart
Marie de' Medici, Queen of France, 98, 99, 100
Marie de Saint-Bernard. *See* Savonnières

Marie de Saint-Bonaventure-de-Jésus. *See* Forestier
Marie de Sainte-Thérèse. *See* Juchereau de La Ferté
Marie de Saint-Ignace. *See* Guenet; Giffard
Marie de Saint-Joseph. *See* Bourdon, Geneviève; Savonnières
Marie-Catherine de Saint-Augustin. *See* Simon
Marie-Catherine du Saint-Sacrement. *See* Charly
Marie-Félix (Dubocq), (Indian), 286
Marie-Madeleine Chrestienne (Boucher), (Indian), 200, 354
Marie Olivier. *See* Manitouabeouich
Marie-Thérèse. *See* Gannensagouas
Marie-Thérèse of Austria, Infanta of Spain, Queen of France, 499
Marie-Thérèse-de-Jésus. *See* Bourdon
Marillac. *See* Louise
Marin, Lancelot, 121
Marlborough. *See* Churchill
Marot, Bernard, 442, **490**, 505, 593, 642
Marot, Clément, 423, 424
Marquette, Jacques, 15, 35, 58, 174, 175, 178, 244, 248, 282, 394, 395, 453, 460, **490–93**
Marquette, Rose. *See* La Salle
Marquette de Tombelles, Nicolas, 490
Marre, Sieur de La. *See* La Marre
Marsh, Elizabeth, 493
Marsh (March), John, 39, 107, 361, **493**, 529, 657, 672
Marshall, Sampson. *See* Kelly
Marsolet, François. *See* Sasousmat
Marsolet, Louise (Lemire), 460
Marsolet de Saint-Aignan, Marie. *See* Le Barbier
Marsolet de Saint-Aignan, Marie (Damours de Chauffours), 201, 245
Marsolet de Saint-Aignan, Nicolas, 133, 196, 199–200, 245, 452, **493–95**, 516, 574
Marsollet, Nicolas, 473
Marson. *See* Joybert
Marsson. *See* Ari Marsson
Marteau, Marie (Godefroy), 339
Marteau, Renée (Robinau de Bécancour), 574
Martel, Isaac, 209
Martel*, Jean, 577
Martel, Marie-Anne. *See* Robinau
Martignon. *See* Aprendestiguy
Martin. *See* Mécabou
Martin, Abraham (*dit* l'Écossais or Maître Abraham), 223, 233, 263, 264, 287, 379, 417, **495–96**
Martin, Anne (Côté), 495
Martin*, Charles-Amador, 495
Martin, Christine (Gravé Du Pont), 346, 347
Martin, Christopher, **496**
Martin, Claude (the elder), 351
Martin, Claude (the younger), 351, 352, 355, 356, 357, 358, 552
Martin, Énarde (Pécody), 535
Martin, Eustache, 109, 264, 386, 495
Martin, Hélène (Étienne; Chouart Des Groseilliers), 223, 495
Martin, Louis, 267
Martin, Marguerite. *See* Langlois
Martin, Marguerite (Daniel), 247
Martin, Marguerite (Racine), 263, 379, 495

INDEX

Martin, Marie. *See* Guyart
Martin, Thomas, 496
Martin* de Lino, François-Mathieu, 56
Martineau, Philippe (Macé), 478
Martinet* de Fonblanche, Jean, 109
Martins, João, 234
Martire d'Anghiera, Pietro (Peter Martyr), 151, 152, 153, 154, 155
Maruffo, Raphael, 586
Mary I, Queen of England and Ireland, 157
Mary II, Queen of Great Britain and Ireland, 329, 426, 544, 545, 611
Mary (Stuart), Queen of Scots, 96, 382
Mason, Anne. *See* Greene
Mason, Isabella. *See* Steed
Mason, John (the elder), 496
Mason, John, 51, 243, 262, 350, **496–97**, 650, 655
Massé, Énemond, 67, 68, 94, 95, 97, 98, 100, 101, 121, 142, 214, 299, 307, 338, 387, 411, 441, 442, 453, 470, **497–98**, 501, 560
Massé, François, 497
Massé, Philippe. *See* Bica
Massillon, 488
Masso, Imbert de, 498
Masson, François, 439
Masson, Marie (Pézard de La Tousche), 543
Mataut, Jean-Pierre, 490
Mataut, Louise. *See* Cloutier
Mather, Cotton, 544, 545
Mather, Increase, 544, 545
Mathieu (Indian, son of Jean-Baptiste Atironta), 71
Matthews, John, 567
Maudoux*, Abel, 578
Mauger, Louise (Gadoys), 319, 557
Maugis, Charlotte (Miville), 511
Maugue, Antoine, 498
Maugue, Claude, **498**
Maugue, Françoise. *See* Rigaud
Maugue, Louise. *See* Jousset
Maupassant, Eustache, **498–99**
Mauprée. *See* Des Granges
Maur. *See* Juchereau
Maurice, Mrs., 605, 657
May, Henry, **499**
Mayer, André, 88
Maynwaringe. *See* Mainwaring
Mayrand, Sœur, 117
Mazarin, Jules, Cardinal, 44, 389, 442, 615
Mazé. *See* Peronne
Mécabou, *dit* Martin, 199
Medici. *See* Catherine de'; Marie de'
Medrano, Catalina de (Cabot), 158
Megapolensis, Jan, 462
Melanson, Anne (Saint-Étienne de La Tour), 514
Melanson, Charles, **499–500**
Melanson, Marie. *See* Dugas
Melanson, Marie-Marguerite. *See* Mius d'Entremont
Melanson, Pierre, *dit* La Verdure, 436, 499, 500, 510
Méloizes. *See* Renaud d'Avène
Membertou, Henri, 69, 97, 100, 307, 367, **500–501**, 526, 529, 604
Membertou, wife of. *See* Marie
Membertou, sons of. *See* Actodin; Louis

Membré, Zénobe, 176, 178, 179, 180, 420, 438, 440, **501–2**
Ménage*, Pierre, 572
Ménard, René, 65, 206, 225, 251, 461, **502**, 566
Méndez, Martín, 156
Mendoza, Pedro de, 342
Menendez, 310
Menescardi, Giustino, 152
Meneux, *dit* Châteauneuf, Jacques, 550
Meneval (Menneval). *See* Des Friches
Menou, Nicole de. *See* Jousserand
Menou d'Aulnay, Charles de, 25, 32, 62, 63, 66, 90, 129, 234, 256, 257, 258, 259, 261, 323, 379, 380, 383, 433, 435, 442, 468, 469, 490, **502–6**, 514, 569, 593, 595, 596, 604
Menou d'Aulnay, Jeanne de. *See* Motin
Menou d'Aulnay, Marie de, Canoness of Poussay, 436
Menou de Charnisay, René de, 433, 502, 505
Merçan*, Jean, 260
Merçan, Marie-Anne. *See* Denys de Fronsac
Mercator, Gerard, 678, 680
Mercier*, Louis, 108
Mercœur, Duc de. *See* Vandémont
Meredudd ap Rhys, 677
Merlac, André-Louis de, **506–7**
Merrick, Barbara (Button), 144
Merrick, Rhys, 144
Merveille, Capt., 347
Merville, M. de, 465
Mesgouez. *See* La Roche
Mesnu. *See* Peuvret
Messamouet, 96, **507**, 604
Messier, Martine (Primot), 465, **507–8**
Messou (Montagnais deity), 164
Mestigoït, 164, 533
Mésy. *See* Saffray de Mézy
Metiwemig (Metigonèque), 65
Meulles. *See* Demeulle
Meusnier, Anne (Richard), 573
Meynier, Madeleine. *See* Laguide
Mézy. *See* Saffray
Miçel, Gabriel (Gabriel Witzel?), 157
Michel, Barbe. *See* Esmart
Michel, Gilles, 473
Michel, Jacques, 405
Michelborne, Sir Edward, 252
Michelet, Jeanne (Guyart), 351
Middleton, Roger, 300
Migeon, Jean, 508
Migeon, Marie. *See* Desbordes
Migeon de Branssat, Catherine. *See* Gauchet de Belleville
Migeon de Branssat, Jean-Baptiste, 47, 79, 105, **508**, 541
Mignot, *dit* Chatillon, Jean, 490
Mignot, Louise. *See* Cloutier
Milan, Dukes of. *See* Sforza
Milet* (or Millet), Pierre, 322, 634
Miller, Thomas, 519
Millet, Jeanne (Langlois), 417
Mills, Edward, 672
Minet, 180
Miramion, Mme de. *See* Bonneau de Rubelles

INDEX

Miriot, Jeanne (Hertel), 368
Miristou, 61, 195, 479, **508–9**
Missenden, Samuel, **509–10**
Mitigoukwe (Jeanne) (wife of Joseph Oumasasikweie), 640
Mitton, Elizabeth (Clarke), 654
Mius d'Entremont, Madeleine. *See* Hélie
Mius d'Entremont, Madeleine, 510
Mius d'Entremont, Marie-Marguerite (Melanson), 500, 510
Mius d'Entremont, Philippe, **510**, 595
Mius* d'Entremont, Philippe (the younger), 510
Mius* de Plemazais, Abraham, 510, 514
Mius de Plemazais, Marguerite. *See* Saint-Étienne de La Tour
Mius de Pobomcoup, Anne. *See* Saint-Étienne de La Tour
Mius* de Pobomcoup, Jacques, 510, 514
Miville, Charlotte. *See* Maugis
Miville, François, 511
Miville, Jacques, 511
Miville, Marie (Amiot), 60
Miville, *dit* le Suisse, Pierre, **511**
Mohier, Gervais, **511**
Moireau*, Claude, 264
Molière (Jean-Baptiste Poquelin *dit*), 139, 141, 607
Molin, Laurent, 63
Molyneux, Émery, 252
Monceaux. *See* Clément Du Vault; Ruette d'Auteuil
Moncel. *See* Giffard
Monchy. *See* Mouchy
Monk (Monck), Christopher, second Duke of Albemarle, 544
Mons, Sieur de. *See* Monts
Montaigne, Michel de, 471
Montecalunya. *See* Cabot, John
Montgomery, Earl of. *See* Herbert
Montigny. *See* Rémy
Montmagny. *See* Huault
Montmorency, Charlotte-Marguerite de (Condé), 484
Montmorency, Henri II, Duc de, 159, 186–87, 194–95, 427, 433
Montorgueuil. *See* Dauphin
Montortier, 327
Montpensier, Duc de. *See* Bourbon
Montpensier, Duchesse de. *See* Orléans
Montplaisir. *See* Dizy
Montrénault, Seigneur de. *See* Puiseaux
Monts. *See* Du Gua
Monts, Sieur de, 325, **511–12**, 615
Montsaulnin, Adrienne de (Renaud d'Avène de Des Méloizes et de Berges), 572
Moral de Saint-Quentin, Marie. *See* Marguerie
Moral de Saint-Quentin, Quentin, 369
Moranget. *See* Crevel
More, Elizabeth (Rastell), 565
More, Sir Thomas, 565, 566
Moreau, *dit* La Taupine, Pierre, 394
Moreau de Brésoles, François, 512
Moreau de Brésoles, Françoise. *See* Gailliard
Moreau de Brésoles, Judith, 220, 458, 478, 480, 487, **512–13**
Morel, Capt., 292

Morel, Claude, 469
Morel, Fréderic, 469
Morel, Thomas, 108, **513**
Morel de La Durantaye, Françoise. *See* Duquet
Morel* de La Durantaye, Olivier, 444, 479
Morillon Du Bourg, 435, 436, **513–14**, 636
Morin, Hélène. *See* Desportes
Morin*, Germain, 264, 392
Morin, Jean-Baptiste, 264
Morin*, Marie, 78, 216, 221, 230, 231, 478, 480, 512
Morin, Marie-Madeleine (Rageot), 561
Morin, Noël, 264
Morley, Lord, 407
Morosini, Francesco, 135
Morris, Robert, 601
Mossion, Robert, 474
Motin, Anne (Le Creux Du Breuil), 442
Motin, Jeanne (Menou d'Aulnay; Saint-Étienne de La Tour), 114, 129, 257, 261, 433, 434, 436, 442, 469, 503, 505, 510, **514**, 595
Motin de Co(u)rcelles, Louis, 442, 503, 514
Mottin. *See* Motin
Mouchy, Nicolas de, **514**
Mouroy, Demoiselle de, 470
Mousseaux, Louise de (Pelerin de Saint-Amant), 256
Moyen Des Granges, Élisabeth. *See* Le Bret
Moyen Des Granges, Élisabeth (Closse), 231
Moyen Des Granges, Jean-Baptiste, 231, 295
Moyen Des Granges, Marie (Dugué de Boisbriand), 231, 295
Moyer. *See* Mohier
Moyne, Alayne, 371
Muis. *See* Mius
Mullois de La Borde, Madeleine (Pézard de La Tousche Champlain), 543
Munk, Erik Nielsen, 514
Munk (Munck), Jens Eriksen, 20, **514–15**
Munk, Katherine. *See* Adriansdatter
Münster, Bishop of, 142
Murderer, The. *See* Cherououny
Mychell, William, 158
Mynne, Anne (Calvert), 162

NAMEUR, Louis de, 313
Naneogauchit, 222, 578
Napagabiscou, 511
Naples, Queen of, 120
Natel, Antoine, 300
Natoukwabekwe, Cecilia (wife of Oumasasikweie), 527
Nau de La Boissière et de Fossambault, Catherine (Lauson de La Citière; Peuvret Demesnu), 428, 542, 543
Nau de La Boissière et de Fossambault, Jacques, 542
Nau de La Boissière et de Fossambault, Michèle-Thérèse (Giffard), 326
Navarre, Queen of. *See* Marguerite d'Angoulême
Negabamat, Noël, *dit* Tekouerimat, 222, 282, **516**, 640
Negaskoumat, 516
Nelson*, John, 576, 637, 654
Nelson, Robert, 144
Neogaouachit. *See* Naneogauchit
Nesmond, Duc de, 309
Neuville. *See* Dupont

Nevers, Duchesse de, 425
Newland, Robert, 82, 666
Nicholas of Lynne, **678-79**
Nicolas (clerk), 90, 238
Nicolas, Father. *See* Viel
Nicollet, Marie. *See* Lamer
Nicollet, Thomas, 516
Nicollet de Belleborne, Jean, 35, 186, 197, 367, 369, 410, 473, 489, **516-18**, 639
Nicollet de Belleborne, Marguerite. *See* Couillard
Nicollet de Belleborne, Marguerite (Legardeur de Repentigny), 517
Nicolls, Richard, 308
Nika, 183
Niort* de La Noraye, Louis de, 63
Nixon, Anne, 520
Nixon, Em, 520
Nixon, John, 39, 84, 232, 281, 324, 328, 416, 477, **518-20**, 543, 553, 605, 666
Noegabinat. *See* Ouagabemat
Noël, Étienne, 167, 169, 384, 520
Noël, Jacques, 23, 170, 384, 409, **520**
Noël, Jacques (servant of Nicolas Godé), 598
Noël, Jean (father of Étienne), 520
Noël, Jean (son of Jacques), 520
Noël, Jeanne. *See* Cartier
Noël, Michel, 520
Noirefontaine, 423, 425
Noremberguer, Lazaro (Lazaro Aleman or Cromberger), 157
Norfolk, Duke of. *See* Howard, Thomas
Normanville. *See* Godefroy
Nottingham, Earl of. *See* Howard, Charles
Nouë, Anne de, 121, 410, 453, **520**, 527
Nouel. *See* Noël
Nouvel*, Henri, 50, 59, 282
Noyon, Catherine de. *See* Chevalier
Noyon, Édouard de, 250
Noyon, Suzanne de (David), 250
Noyrot, Philibert, 160, 411, 412, **521-22**, 579, 596, 665
Nutt, John, **522**
Nutt, Robert, 522

OAGIMONT. *See* Ouagimou
Ochiltree. *See* Stewart
Ogenheratarihiens, Louis, **522-23**
Ogeratarihen. *See* Ogenheratarihiens
Ogilvie, Capt., 305
Oionhaton, Thérèse, 42, 212, 344, **523-24**
Ojeda, Alonso de, 151
Olaf I Tryggvason, King of Norway, 448
Oldmixon, John, 50
Olier, Jean-Jacques, Founder of the Compagnie des Prêtres de Saint-Sulpice, 45, 57, 111, 115, 213, 214, 215, 219, 220, 480, 486, 612, 644, 648
Oliph, Joan (Leigh), 450
Oliva, Paul (Giovanni Paolo), eleventh general of the Jesuits, 460
Olivier. *See* Le Jeune
Olivier, Françoise. *See* Dardaine
Olivier, Marie. *See* Manitouabeouich
Olivier, Simon, 524
Olivier, *dit* le Picard, Marc-Antoine, **524**

Olmechin. *See* Onemechin
Ondaaiondiont, Charles, 65, 66, 71, **524-25**
Ondakion, Pierre, 610
Ondakion, Pierre, wife of. *See* Asenragéhaon
Ondessonk, 388, 461, 462
Onemechin, 69, 507, 529
Onontio, 374, 414, 461
Onorotandi, 73
Oonchiarey, 590
Orehaoue. *See* Ourehouare
Orkney, Earl or Prince of. *See* Sinclair
Orléans, Duc d' (1607-1611), 436
Orléans, Duc d', Philippe II (regent of France), 328
Orléans, Anne-Marie-Louise d', Duchesse de Montpensier, 134, 135
Orléans, Charles, Duc d', Comte de Clermont, 425
Orléans, Jean-Baptiste-Gaston d', 134
Orpheus Junior. *See* Vaughan, Sir William
Ortelius, Abraham, 280, 680
Orville, Sieur d', 189, 293
Orvilliers. *See* Guilloust
Otsinnonannhont, Barnabé, 652
Ostryge, Henry, 157, 158
O'Toole. *See* Lawrence
Otreouti, 7, 322, 445, 458, **525-26**
Ouagabemat or Noegabinat, 222
Ouagimou (Oagimont), 69, **526-27**, 529
Ouane, 461
Ouary, Françoise (Renardin de La Blanchetière), 475
Oudin, Renée or Marie (Le Royer), 214
Oughtred, Henry, 228, 229
Oumasasikweie, 10, **527-28**
Oumasasikweie, wife of. *See* Natoukwabekwe
Oumasasikweie, son of. *See* François
Oumasasikweie, Joseph, 548, 640
Oumasasikweie, Joseph, wife of. *See* Mitigoukwe
Ouracha, 324
Ourehouare, **528**, 537
Oureouhat. *See* Otreouti
Outchetaguin, 381, 603
Outetoucos, 603
Outlan. *See* Outlaw
Outlaw, Françoise. *See* Denis
Outlaw, John (Outlan or Outlas, Jean), 39, 107, 130, **528-29**
Outlaw, Mary. *See* Saille
Outreouhati. *See* Otreouti
Outsitsony, 574
Owain Gwynedd Madog ab. *See* Madoc
Owain the Great, King of Gwynedd in North Wales, 677
Owen, John, 365
Oxford, Thomas, 24, 278, 370

PACHIRINI, 485
Pachot. *See* Viennay
Pacifique, Brother. *See* Duplessis
Pacifique de Provins, 129
Page, Mr., 93
Paizs (Paizsos), István. *See* Parmenius
Pajet, *dit* Carcy, Raymond, 473, 495
Pajot, Claude (Biencourt de Poutrincourt), 96, 98, 99
Pajot, Isaac, 96

INDEX

Palluau. *See* Buade
Palme. *See* La Palme
Palmer, Edward, 306
Panounias (Panoniac), 69, 293, 500, 526, **529–30**
Paquet*, Sister Joséphine, 487
Pâquet* *dit* Lavallée, André, 77
Paquine. *See* Pasquine
Parabego (Partarabego), Anne (Denys de Fronsac), 260
Parant*, Gilbert, 573
Parant, Suzanne. *See* Richard
Parat, Antoine, 26, 419, **530**
Paris, Ignace de. *See* Ignace
Parisel, Jean-François, 108
Parkhurst, Anthony, 332, 334, 363, **530–31**
Parkhurst, John, 530
Parmenius, Stephanus, 5, 333, 334, 335, 363, **531–32**
Parmentier, Jean, **532–33**
Parmentier, Raoul, 532
Parry*, Sir William Edward, 75, 312, 375, 378
Pars, Marie (Picoté de Belestre), 547
Partarabego. *See* Parabego
Particelli d'Émery, Michel, French financier, 198
Pas, Isaac de, Marquis de Feuquières, 296
Pascal d'Auxerre, 129
Pascal de Troyes, 468, 504
Pascaud*, Antoine, 400
Pasqualigo, Lorenzo, 148, 149, 150
Pasqualigo, Pietro, 235
Pasquine (Paquine), **533**, 586
Pastedechouan, Pierre-Antoine, 164, 265, 488, **533–34**
Pastour * de Costebelle, Philippe de, 530.
Patin, Guy, 80
Patiner, Henry, 156
Patoulet, Jean-Baptiste, 63, 120, **534**, 581, 621, 627
Patriarch, The. *See* Fléché
Patterson, George, 335
Paul (Indian; brother of Totiri), 652
Paul, Father. *See* Huet
Paul V (Camillo Borghese), Pope, 97
Paumart, Guillaume, 534
Paumart, Jean, **534**
Paumart, Marie. *See* Le Roy
Pearson, Bartholomew, 350, **534–35**
Pearson, Elizabeth. *See* Baguleughe
Pease, Capt, 567
Pécaudy, Charles, 535
Pécaudy de Contrecœur, Anne. *See* Dubois
Pécaudy de Contrecœur, Antoine, **535–36**
Pécaudy de Contrecœur, Barbe. *See* Denys de la Trinité
Pécaudy* de Contrecœur, Claude-Pierre, 536
Pécaudy* de Contrecœur, François-Antoine, 535
Pécaudy de Contrecœur, Jeanne. *See* Saint-Ours
Peckham, Sir George, 333, 334, 336, 363, 380, 531, 677
Pécody, Benoît de, 535
Pécody, Énarde. *See* Martin
Peiras, Sieur, 581
Peirese, Nicolas de 294
Pelerin, Ignace, 256
Pelerin, Philippe, 91
Pelerin de Saint-Amant, Louise. *See* Mousseaux
Pelerin de Saint-Amant, Pierre, 256
Pellerin, Marie (Becquet), 86

Pelletier, Catherine. *See* Vannier
Pelletier, Catherine, 439
Pelletier, Didace (baptized Claude), 439, **536**
Pelletier, François, 387
Pelletier, Georges, 536
Pelletier, Jeanne (Jérémie), 387
Pelletier de La Prade de Gentilly, Michel, 251, 494
Pelling, Mr., 578
Pembroke, Earl of. *See* Herbert
Peñalossa, Diego, Comte de, 179
Penn, William, 605
Pennasca, Sébastien, 396
Pépin, Marie-Ursule (Pinard), 550
Pepys, Samuel, 226
Peré, Arnaud, 226, 537
Peré, Jean, 226, 393, 528, **536–37**, 572, 626, 627
Père Joseph (Indian, son of Chomina), 222
Peronne de Mazé, Louis, 468, **537**, 589
Peronne Des Touches, Michel, 537, 538
Peronne Dumesnil, Jean, 112, 326, 401, **537–39**, 580, 606
Perosse, Valeron, 88
Pérot, Gilles, **539**
Perrault, Julien, **539**
Perreault, Hyacinthe, **539–40**
Perrier, Philippe, 43
Perrot, François-Marie, 66, 84, 102, 105, 117, 136, 175, 204, 287–88, 295, 409, 410, 418, 436, 464, 465, 508, **540–42**, 576, 581, 584, 600, 631
Perrot, John (Quaker), 81
Perrot, Sir John, 228
Perrot, Madeleine. *See* Laguide Meynier
Perrot*, Nicolas, 40, 132, 174, 248, 249, 308, 547, 548, 625, 640
Perrot de Fercourt, 541
Perthuis, Marie (Rouer de Villeray), 579
Pétau, Denis, 203
Petit*, Jean, 295
Petit*, Louis, 544, 649
Petit, Suzanne (Caën), 161
Petit de L'Estang, Marie (Troyes), 653
Petitchouan. *See* Chomina
Petitpas, Marguerite (Sevestre), 606
Petiver, James, 677
Pett, Phineas, 144, 362
Peuvret, Jacques, 542
Peuvret, Marie. *See* La Garenne
Peuvret Demesnu, Catherine. *See* Nau de La Boissière et de Fossambault
Peuvret Demesnu, François, 542
Peuvret Demesnu, Jean-Baptiste, **542–43**, 587
Peuvret Demesnu, Marie-Catherine (Juchereau Duchesnay), 543
Peuvret Demesnu, Marie-Rogère. *See* Lepage
Peuvret* Demesnu de Gaudarville, Alexandre, 326, 543
Peuvret Demesnu de Gaudarville, Marie-Anne. *See* Gaultier de Comporté
Pézard de La Tousche, Claude, 543
Pézard de La Tousche, Marie. *See* Masson
Pézard de La Tousche Champlain, Étienne, **543**
Pézard de La Tousche Champlain, Madeleine. *See* Mullois de La Borde

INDEX

Phélypeaux, Jean, Seigneur de Villesavin, 484
Phélypeaux, Louis, Comte de Pontchartrain (French statesman, successor to Seignelay in the Secrétariat d'État à la Marine), 138, 510, 534
Phélypeaux de Pontchartrain, Anne (Buade), 133
Philip II, King of Spain, 187, 316
Philip III, King of Spain, 676
Philipeaux, Charles, 201
Philipot, Michel, 167
Philippe de Hautmesnyl, Jean-Vincent, 508
Philippeau. *See* Philipeaux.
Phillips, Bridget, *See* Hutchinson
Phillips, Mary, 337
Phillips, Phoebe (Gillam), 337, 338, 601
Phillips, William, 337, 601
Phipps, Thomas (the elder), 543
Phipps, Thomas, 39, **543–44**
Phips, James, 544
Phips, Mary (mother of Sir William), 544
Phips, Mary (wife of Sir William). *See* Spencer
Phips, Sir William, 26, 76, 90, 139, 146, 250, 260, 397, 402, 426, 436, 466, 542, **544–46**, 576, 577, 586, 649
Phokus Valerian(at)os. *See* Fuca
Piat (or Le Piat), Irénée, **546–47**
Picard, Le. *See* Olivier
Pichery, Anne de, 265
Pichon, Marie (Gauthier de La Chenaye; Sevestre), 583, 606
Picoté de Belestre, François, 547
Picoté de Belestre, Hélène (La Frenaye de Brucy; Céloron de Blainville), 410, 547
Picoté* de Belestre, Jeanne-Geneviève, 547
Picoté de Belestre, Marie. *See* Pars
Picoté de Belestre, Marie-Anne (Tonty), 547
Picoté de Belestre, Perrinne, 547
Picoté de Belestre, Pierre, 266, 271, 273, 410, 508, **547**
Pierre. *See* Pastedechouan
Pierron, Jean, 108, 315, **547**, 635
Pierson, Philippe, 321
Pieskaret, Simon, 71, 370, 403, **547–48**
Pigarouich, Étienne, 6, **548–49**, 640
Pijart, Claude (the elder), 549
Pijart, Claude, 231, 459, **549**, 549, 566, 645
Pijart, Geneviève. *See* Charon
Pijart, Pierre, 125, 203, 328, 459, **549–50**
Piles, Roger de (painter, writer, and diplomat), 313
Pillet, Charles, 211
Pilote, François. *See* Crusson
Pinard, Claude, 321, 550
Pinard, Françoise. *See* Gamelain
Pinard, Jean, 550
Pinard, Louis, 321, 328, 369, **550**
Pinard, Marguerite. *See* Gaignier
Pinard, Marie. *See* Rivard
Pinard, Marie-Madeleine. *See* Hertel de La Fresnière
Pinard, Marie-Ursule. *See* Pépin
Pinault, Louise. *See* Douaire
Pinault*, Nicolas, 56
Pining, 679
Pinteado, Capt., 316
Piot* de Langloiserie, Charles-Gaspard, 295
Piraube, Martial, 372, 374, 554

Piron, Pierre, 109
Pithou, Pierre (jurist, advocate in the Parlement of Paris), 629
Pius IX, Pope, 354
Pius XI, Pope, 121, 184, 246, 324, 343, 410, 412
Pius XII, Pope, 121
Pivert, Nicolas, 233, 311
Plaines, Bernard de. *See* Damours
Plattier, Jean, 394
Plemarch. *See* Mius de Plemazais
Plemazais. *See* Mius
Plet, François, 177
Ploumelle, Jeanne (Poulin), 553
Pobomcoup. *See* Mius
Pocahontas, 67
Pocatière. *See* Pollet
Poignant, Jeanne (Giffard), 330
Poincet, Martin, 460
Poippe. *See* La Poippe
Poirier, Marie (Chouart), 223
Poisson, François, 635
Poitiers, Isabeau de, 422
Pollet de La Combe de La Pocatière, Catherine. *See* Rossin
Pollet de La Combe de La Pocatière, François (the elder), 550
Pollet de La Combe-Pocatière, François, **550–51**
Pollet de La Combe-Pocatière, Marie-Anne. *See* Juchereau de Saint-Denis
Pollet de La Combe-Pocatière, Marie-Louise (Rouer de Villeray et de La Cardonnière), 551
Pollet de La Combe-Pocatière, Marie-Thérèse (Le Moyne d'Iberville), 551
Polo, Marco, 147, 150
Pommier, Hugues, 314, 359, **551**
Poncet, Joseph-Antoine, 551
Poncet de La Rivière, Joseph-Antoine, 205, 208, 216, 217, 352, **551–52**, 563, 610, 645, 665
Poncet de La Rivière et de Brétigny, Jean, 551
Poncet de La Rivière et de Brétigny, Marguerite. *See* Thiersault
Pons, Antoinette de, Marquise de Guercheville (Du Plessis de Liancourt), 67, 68, 69, 94, 95, 98, 100, 101, 294, 299, 367, 441, 521, 560
Pontbriand, Claude de, 167
Pontchartrain. *See* Phélypeaux
Pont-Gravé. *See* Gravé Du Pont
Poole, Sir William, 93
Popham, Sir John, 69
Popincourt de Roberval, Alix de, 422
Porten, Robert, 107
Porteret, Pierre, 491
Portneuf, Baron de. *See* Robinau de Bécancour
Potel, Jacqueline (Bourdon), 113, 114, 430, 480
Pothier, Bishop of Beauvais, 534
Pothorst, Hans, 679
Potier* de Saint-Denys, Jacques, 25, 63
Poudre Chaude. *See* Ogenheratarihiens
Poulain, Guillaume, 379, **552**
Poulet, Capt., 626
Poulin, Jeanne. *See* Ploumelle
Poulin, Pierre, 552
Poulin de Courval, Jean-Baptiste, 553

747

Poulin* de Francheville, François, 553
Poulin de La Fontaine, Catherine (Godefroy de Vieuxpont), 553
Poulin de La Fontaine, Jeanne. *See* Jallot
Poulin de La Fontaine, Marguerite (Lemaître), 553
Poulin de La Fontaine, Maurice, **552–53**
Poulin de Saint-Maurice, Michel, 553
Poullet, Jehan, 167, 170
Pournin, Marie (Testard de La Forest), 641
Poussay, Canoness of. *See* Menou
Poussin, Nicolas, 313
Pouteret de Bellecourt *dit* Colombier, Jean-François, 225
Poutrincourt, Jean de. *See* Biencourt
Powel, David, 678
Powell, Daniel, 162, 672
Power (Powers), Richard, 324, 476, **553**
Powhatan, 67
Poytiers, Marie-Charlotte (Hébert), 367
Prato, Albertus de, 586
Pratt, James, 369
Pré-Ravillon. *See* La Court
Preston, Amias (Amyas), 278, 279
Prévert. *See* Sarcel
Prévost, Charlotte. *See* Vien
Prévost, Marie. *See* Abancourt
Prévost, Marie. *See* Manitouabeouich
Prévost, Martin, 392, **553–54**
Prévost, Pierre, 553
Pricket, Abacuk, 144, 145, 374, 375, 376, 377, 378
Prieur, Perrette (François), 312
Primot, Antoine, 465, 507
Primot, Martine. *See* Messier
Pring, Martin, 75
Prinzèles. *See* Dubois d'Esgriseilles
Prouvereau*, Sébastien, 60, 387
Prouville, Charles-Henri, 557
Prouville, Marie de. *See* Bochart de Champigny
Prouville, Pierre de, 554
Prouville de Tracy, Alexandre de, 11, 33, 40, 41, 47, 48, 62, 74, 108, 113, 185, 202, 221, 245, 277, 308, 322, 353, 355, 393, 398, 400, 401, 402, 409, 416, 418, 442, 464, 511, 516, 547, **554–57**, 570, 571, 580, 584, 589, 602, 616, 617, 624, 627, 630, 635, 650
Prouville de Tracy, Louise de. *See* Fouilleuse
Provencher, Sébastien, 49
Provost. *See also* Prévost
Provost*, François, 85, 664
Prud'homme, Claude, 557
Prud'homme, François, 557
Prud'homme, Isabelle. *See* Aliomet
Prud'homme, Louis, 177, 230, 319, **557**
Prud'homme*, Louis, 557
Prud'homme*, Pierre, 177, 557
Prud'homme, Roberte. *See* Gadoys; Verrier
Puebla, Gonsalez de, 148
Puiseaux, Pierre de, 215, 216, 217, 401, 485, **557–58**, 640
Purchas, Samuel, 74, 75, 101, 158, 329, 349, 360, 379, 471, 586, 677, 678
Pyle, William, 652
Pytheas of Massilia, 17

QUÉAN (Quen), Eustache (Boullongne), 43, 110
Quen, Jean de, 48, 341, 404, 459, 552, **558–59**, 645, 646
Quentin, Claude, 214, **560**, 560
Quentin, Jacques, 68, 95, 299, 560, **560**
Querbonyer, 210, 422
Quer(que). *See* Kirke
Queylus, Abbé de. *See* Thubières
Quignon, François, 314
Quintal*, Augustin, 312

RABELAIS, François, 170, 365, 424
Rabutin-Chantal, Marie de, Marquise de Sévigné, 117
Racine, Étienne, 495
Racine, Louise (Guyon), 359
Racine, Marguerite. *See* Martin
Radisson*, Pierre-Esprit, 16, 20, 35, 39, 42, 48, 49, 56, 82, 83, 129, 130, 223, 226, 227, 228, 270, 271, 273, 274, 282, 337, 338, 377, 397, 406, 464, 509, 518, 528, 529, 578, 602, 625, 653
Raffeix*, Pierre, 48, 108, 321, 651
Rageot*, Charles, 561
Rageot, François, 561
Rageot, Gilles, 394, 474, 550, **560–61**
Rageot*, Gilles (the younger), 561
Rageot, Isaac, 560
Rageot*, Jean-Baptiste, 561
Rageot, Louise. *See* Duret
Rageot, Marie-Madeleine. *See* Morin
Rageot*, Nicolas, 561
Rageot*, Philippe, 561
Ragueneau, François, 214, 453, 561
Ragueneau, Paul, 44, 64, 71, 123, 125, 128, 143, 184–85, 186, 205–6, 214, 225, 296, 328, 412, 414, 455, 459, 460, 461, 489, **561–64**, 607, 608, 609, 610, 637, 640
Rainborow. *See* Rainsborough
Rainer, Dr., 553
Rainsborough, William, 407
Raisin, Anne. *See* Collet
Raisin, Edmé, 564
Raisin, Marie, 116, **564**
Raisin, Nicolas, 564
Raleigh, Amis (Hayman), 365
Raleigh, Sir Carew, 279, 331
Raleigh, Sir Walter, 251, 278, 331, 332, 333, 335, 363, 364, 668, 669
Ralluau (Ralleau), Jean, 292, 293, **564–65**
Ramezay*, Claude de, 602
Ramusio, Giovanni Battista, 151, 153, 154, 170, 235, 658, 660
Randin, Hugues, **565**
Raoul, Jeanne (Savonnières de La Troche), 603
Rapine de Boisvert, Charles, 219, 484, 485
Rasilly. *See* Launay; Razilly
Rastell, Elizabeth. *See* More
Rastell, John (the elder), 565, 566
Rastell, John 371, **565–66**
Raudin. *See* Randin
Raudot*, Jacques, 452
Ravillon. *See* La Court
Raye, Pierre, 493
Raymbaut, Charles, 388, 549, **566–67**
Raymond, George, 279, 499

INDEX

Rayner (Reyner), John, **567**
Raynsforde, Thomas, 279
Razilly. *See also* Launay-Rasilly
Razilly, Catherine. *See* Valliers
Razilly, François de (the elder), 567
Razilly, François de (the younger), 209, 567
Razilly, Gabriel, de, 567
Razilly, Isaac de, 25, 32, 54, 63, 196, 234, 247, 256, 258, 311, 442, 471, 482, 490, 502, 503, **567–69**, 593, 594, 642
Ré. *See* Derré
Reconciled, The. *See* Cherououny
Redwood, Nicholas, 652
Regnault, Christophe, 124, 562
Regnouard, Marie (Giffard), 329, 330
Reinel, Pedro, 235, 303, 304
Rémus. *See* Romieux
Rémy de Courcelle, Daniel de, 33, 40, 48, 55, 62, 80, 108, 111, 120, 135, 174, 204, 308, 322, 327, 355, 393, 400, 402, 416, 452, 464, 539, 540, 543, 555, 556, **569–72**, 581, 599, 615, 616, 617, 624, 625, 627, 629, 630
Renardin de La Blanchetière, Françoise. *See* Ouary
Renardin de La Blanchetière, Marie (Le Vieux de Hauteville), 475
Renardin de La Blanchetière, Vincent, 475
Renaud d'Avène de Des Méloizes et de Berges, Adrienne. *See* Montsaulnin
Renaud d'Avène de Des Méloizes et de Berges, Edmé or Aimé, 572
Renaud d'Avène de Desmeloizes, François-Marie, **572–73**
Renaud d'Avène de Desmeloizes, Françoise-Thérèse. *See* Dupont de Neuville
Renaud* d'Avène de Desmeloizes, Nicolas-Marie, 572
Renaudot, Eusèbe, French scholar, 174, 175, 179
Renden (Rendin). *See* Randin
Renou, Marguerite. *See* Crevier
Renou *dit* La Chapelle, François, 321, 578
Rensselaer, Kiliaen van, 527
Renty, Gaston, Baron de, 214, 219
Repentigny. *See* Legardeur; Terrier de Francheville
Repentigny, Mlle. *See* Favery
Rey Gaillard, Pierre, 261
Reyner. *See also* Rayner
Reyner, William 567
Rhoades (Rhode), John, 39, 40, 185, **573**
Ribaut (or Ribault), Jean, French coloniser, 333, 469
Ribero, Pedro, 342
Riberpré, M. de, 88
Rice, Mary (Button), 144
Rice, Sir Walter, 144
Rich, Henry, Earl of Holland, 369, 405
Rich, Sir Robert, later Earl of Warwick, 67, 69
Richard III, King of England, 120, 239
Richard, André, 266, 477, 539
Richard, Anne. *See* Meusnier
Richard, Jean (father of Guillaume), 573
Richard*, Jean (grandson of Guillaume), 573
Richard, Jean-Baptiste, 573
Richard, Jeanne. *See* Bonnet
Richard, Marguerite (Levasseur), 473
Richard, Marie-Anne. *See* You de La Découverte
Richard, Suzanne (Parant), 573
Richard, *dit* Lafleur, Guillaume, **573–74**
Richards, John, 573
Richelieu, Cardinal de. *See* Du Plessis
Richelieu, Duc de. *See* Vignerot
Richer, Edmond, Gallican theologian, 629
Richer, Jean, 225
Richomme, Françoise (Sarcel de Prévert), 602
Rifos, Miguel, 156
Rigaud, Françoise (Maugue), 498
Rigaud de Vaudreuil, Louise-Élisabeth. *See* Joybert
Rigaud* de Vaudreuil, Philippe de, 138, 139, 140, 239, 399, 463, 634
Rigaud de Vaudreuil de Cavagnial, Charlotte de. *See* Fleury d'Eschambault
Rigaud* de Vaudreuil de Cavagnial, Pierre de, 345, 399
Rigauville. *See* Blaise
Rinault. *See* Gaultier
Rivard (or Pinard), Marie (Maillet), 480
Riverin, Angélique. *See* Gaultier
Riverin*, Denis, 326, 402
Robert, 32
Robert, David ap, 655
Robert, Elizabeth (Vaughan), 655
Robert, Guillemette (Bizard), 102
Robert de Fortel, Louis, 615
Roberts, Ann, 574
Roberts, Ann (wife of Lewis Roberts), 574
Roberts, Gabriel, 574
Roberts, Lewis, **574**
Roberval. *See* La Rocque; La Roque
Roberval, Dame de. *See* Popincourt
Robin, Isabeau (Babie), 74
Robin, Mathurine (Guyon Du Buisson), 359
Robin, *dit* Des Forges, Étienne, 267
Robin de Coulogne, Thomas, 97, 100
Robinau, Marie-Anne (Martel), 577
Robinau de Bécancour, Marie-Anne. *See* Leneuf de La Poterie
Robinau de Bécancour, Pierre (the elder), 349, 574
Robinau* de Bécancour, Pierre, Baron de Portneuf, 575
Robinau de Bécancour, René, Baron de Portneuf, **574–76**, 576, 582
Robinau de Bécancour, Renée. *See* Marteau
Robinau de Fortelle, François, 575
Robinau de Villebon, Joseph, 26, 80, 246, 250, 338, 426, 427, 436, 510, 529, 542, 575, **576–78**, 586, 649, 654
Robinson, Sir John, 82
Robinson*, Capt. Robert, 93, 370
Rodas, Miguel de, 156
Roe, Sir Thomas, 144, 312
Roger, Madeleine-Renée (Gagnon), 319
Rohan de Guémenée, Prince de, 533
Rojas, Francisco de, 156
Rolland. *See* Le Noir
Rollet, Marie (Hébert; Hubou), 110, 222, 302, 366, 367, 368, 509, **578**
Romain, Marthe (Marguerie), 489
Romainville. *See* Bourdon
Romieux (Romulus, Rémus), Pierre (Peter), **578–79**

Ronsard, Pierre, 425
Roquemont de Brison, Claude, 59, 263, 330, 402, 405, 411, 521, 561, **578**, 593, 596
Rosé, Sieur de, 538
Roselli, Francesco, 148
Rosier, James, 667
Rosny. *See* Béthune
Ross*, Sir John, 75
Rossignol, Jean, 292
Rossin, Catherine (Pollet de La Combe de La Pocatière), 550
Rouer d'Artigny, Louis, 583
Rouer de Villeray. Catherine. *See* Sevestre
Rouer de Villeray, Charles, 583
Rouer de Villeray, Jaques, 579
Rouer de Villeray, Louis, 91, 112, 202, 288, 448, 538, **579–83**, 584, 587, 588, 589, 606
Rouer de Villeray, Marie. *See* Perthuis
Rouer de Villeray, Marie-Anne. *See* Du Saussay
Rouer* de Villeray et de La Cardonnière, Augustin, 551, 583
Rouer de Villeray et de La Cardonnière, Marie-Louise. *See* Pollet de La Combe-Pocatière
Rouffray, Pierre, 479
Rougemont, Philippe, 168
Rousseau, Marie. *See* Gournay
Roussel, Catherine, 583
Roussel, Catherine. *See* Fournier
Roussel, Étienne, 583
Roussel, Geneviève (Chambalon), 583
Roussel, Jeanne. *See* Boutte
Roussel, Louise, 583
Roussel, Madeleine. *See* Du Mortier
Roussel, Timothée, **583**
Rouvray. *See* Rémy
Rouvroy, Louis de, Duc de Saint-Simon, 135
Rowley, Roger, 584
Rowley (Rowlie), Thomas, 241, 350, 497, **584**
Rubelles. *See* Bonneau
Ruette d'Auteuil, Claire-Françoise de. *See* Clément
Ruette d'Auteuil, Denis-Joseph de, 136, 202, 288, 289, 580, 581, 582, **584–85**, 587, 588, 589
Ruette d'Auteuil, Marie-Anne de. *See* Juchereau de Saint-Denis
Ruette* d'Auteuil de Monceaux, François-Madeleine-Fortuné de, 289, 551, 585
Rupert, Prince, 281, 406, 604, 642
Russell, Capt., 93
Russell, Lady. *See* Cooke
Russell, Mr., 567
Russell, Anne (Dudley), Countess of Warwick, 318
Rut, John, 19, 301, **585–86**
Ruysch, Johannes, 148, 678
Ruyter, Michiel Adriaanszoon de, 25, 443, 496

SABATIER, François, 514
Sablé, Sieur Du. *See* Dandonneau
Saccardy, Vincent, 533, 576, **586–87**
Saffray de Mézy, Augustin de, 32, 47, 113, 146, 202–3, 221, 245, 323, 325, 400, 448, 467, 537, 542, 543, 549, 556, 570, 580, 584, **587–90**, 592
Sagard, Gabriel (baptized Théodat), 70, 73, 121, 123, 125, 130, 132, 133, 160, 211, 222, 233, 263, 265, 346, 368, 382, 417, 419, 433, 437, 509, 511, 546, 578, **590–92**, 639, 663
Saille, Mary (Outlaw), 529
Sailly, Anne-Françoise de. *See* Bourduceau
Sailly, Louis-Arthus de, 47, **592**
Sainctar, Catherine (Baillif), 76
Saint-Aignan. *See* Marsolet
Saint-Amant. *See* Pelerin
Saint-Amours, 633
Saint-André. *See* Brouillan
Saint-Bernard, Raymond de, 352, 357
Saint-Castin. *See* Abbadie
Saint-Denis. *See* Juchereau; Potier
Saint-Dominique, Philippine-Gertrude Boullongne, *dite* de. *See* Boullongne
Sainte-Croix. *See* Brice
Sainte-Foy, Seigneur de. *See* Puiseaux
Sainte-Geneviève, seigneur de. *See* Perrot, François-Marie
Sainte-Hélène. *See* Le Moyne
Sainte-Marie, Louise de. *See* Chomedey
Saint-Étienne, Jacques de, 514
Saint-Étienne de La Tour, Anne de. *See* Melanson
Saint-Étienne de La Tour, Anne de (Mius de Pobomcoup), 510, 514
Saint-Étienne de La Tour, Charles de, 25, 32, 51, **53**, 54, 62, 66, 90, 97, 102, 223, 234, 241, 248, 257, 258, 311, 323, 383, 433, 434, 435, 436, 469, 471, 476, 490, 495, 503, 504, 510, 514, 567, 569, **592–96**, 597, 604, 605, 636
Saint-Étienne* de La Tour, Charles de, 436, 514
Saint-Étienne de La Tour, Claude de, 25, 53, 54, 77, 503, 579, 592, 593, 594, **596–98**, 605
Saint-Étienne de La Tour, Françoise-Marie de. *See* Jacquelin
Saint-Étienne de La Tour, Jeanne de. *See* Motin
Saint-Étienne de La Tour, Jeanne de (Aprendestiguy), 66, 595
Saint-Étienne de La Tour, Marguerite de (Mius de Plemazais), 510, 514
Saint-Étienne de La Tour, Marie de (Le Borgne de Belle-Isle), 436, 514
Saint-François, Jean. *See* Crevier
Saint-François, Sieur de. *See* Bourdon, Jean
Saint-Germain, Guillaume. *See* Audouart
Saint-Germaine-Beaupré. *See* Foucault
Saint-Jean, M. de. *See* Bourdon, Jean
Saint-Jérôme, Mère de, 353
St. John, Oliver, Viscount Grandison, 94
Saint-Jure, Jean-Baptiste de, 484, 485
Saint-Just. *See* Biencourt
Saint-Laurent, Comtesse de. *See* Juchereau de Saint-Denis, Charlotte-Françoise
St. Ledger, Sir Anthony, 82
Saint-Luc, Maréchal, de, 133
Saint-Luc, Marquis de, 133
Saint-Lusson. *See* Daumont
Saint-Martin. *See* Boutet
Saint-Mas, 433
Saint-Maurice. *See* Dubois; Poulin
Saint-Michel, Seigneur de. *See* Puiseaux
Saint-Ours, Jeanne de (Pécaudy de Contrecœur), 535
Saint-Ours* d'Eschaillons, Pierre de, 418

INDEX

Saint-Paul. *See* Lamotte
Saint-Paul, Claude de, 313
Saint-Père, Étienne de, 598
Saint-Père, Étiennette de. *See* Julian
Saint-Père, Jean de, 79, 218, 230, 231, **598–99**
Saint-Père, Mathurine de. *See* Godé
Saint-Quentin. *See* Moral
Saint-Sauveur, Abbé de. *See* Le Sueur
Saint-Simon. *See* Denys
Saint-Simon, Duc de. *See* Rouvroy
Saint-Vallier, Mgr de. *See* La Croix
Sakumow Sagma. *See* Segipt
Salazar, Jeanne de (Biencourt), 96
Sales, François de (St.), 91
Salières. *See* Chastelard
Salignac de La Mothe-Fénelon, François de, 127, 136, 175, 270, 287, 297, 410, 539, 584, **599–601**, 613, 647
Salignac de La Mothe-Fénelon, François de, Archbishop of Cambrai, 599
Salisbury. *See* Cecil
Salusbury, Sir Henry, 656
Samalins, Jeanne de (Lanouguère), 417
Sancé, Michel de, 229
Sanderson, William, 251, 252
Sandrier, Simon Imbert. *See* Imbert
Sandys, Sir Edwin, 69
Sanford, Bridget. *See* Gillam; Hutchinson
Sanford (Sandford), Esbon (Ezbon), 129, 337, 338, **601**
Sanford, John, 601
Sanford, Sarah, 601
Sanlerg, Gabrielle. *See* Senler
Santa Cruz, Alonso de, 156, 157, 304, 342
Saossarinon, 634
Sarcel de Prévert, Françoise. *See* Richomme
Sarcel de (Du) Prévert, Jean, 188–89, 292, 507, **601–2**
Sarrazin*, Michel, 107
Sasousmat (François Marsolet), 164, 533
Satouta, 637
Saulnier, Étienne, 264
Saunders, Mr., 370
Saurel, Catherine de. *See* Legardeur de Tilly
Saurel, Jeanne de. *See* Giraud
Saurel, Mathieu de, 602
Saurel, Pierre de, 308, 418, 555, **602–3**
Sauvaget, Jean, 553
Sauveterre. *See* Aussillon
Savage, Thomas, 545
Savignon, 131, 190, 381, **603**
Savile, Henry, 82
Savonnières de La Troche, Jeanne de. *See* Raoul
Savonnières de La Troche, Marie de, *dite* de Saint-Joseph (formerly *dite* de Saint-Bernard), 108, 352, **603–4**
Savonnières de La Troche, Simon de, 603
Savoy, Duke of, 300, 301
Savoy, Marquis of. *See* Easton
Saye and Seele. *See* Fiennes
Saymond, Daniel, 590
Schomberg, Jeanne de (Du Plessis, Marquise de Liancourt, later Duchesse de La Roche-Guyon), 484
Schuyler*, Peter, 239
Scolvus, John, **679**

Scot, Dominique, **495**
Scot, Sir John, 496
Scott, Mary (Argall), 67
Scott, Sir Reginald, 67
Scottee, Joshua, 242
Secoudon (Secondon), 96, 507, 526, 529, 564, **604**
Sedgwick, Elizabeth. *See* Howe
Sedgwick, Robert, 25, 39, 241, 259, 434, 435, 469, 474, 595, **604–5**
Sedgwick, Sarah (Leverett), 475
Sedgwick, William, 604
Segipt, 53, **605**
Séguier, Pierre, Comte de Gien, Duc de Villemor, Chancellor of France, 214, 484, 504
Seignelay. *See* Colbert
Seller, John, 337
Senau, *dit* La Viazère, Michel, 524
Senler, Gabrielle (Fillion), 305
Sergeant, Henry, 130, 315, 329, 519, **605–6**, 657, 666
Sergeant, Mrs. Henry, 657
Sergeant, Thomas, 606
Sérigny. *See* Le Moyne
Settle, Dionise, 670
Sevestre, Catherine (Rouer de Villeray), 580, 583
Sevestre, Charles (the elder), 606
Sevestre, Charles, 145, 429, 580, 583, **606**
Sevestre, Étienne, 606
Sevestre, Ignace, 606
Sevestre, Louis, 606
Sevestre, Marguerite. *See* Petitpas
Sevestre, Marie. *See* Pichon
Sevestre, Thomas, 606
Sévigné, Mme de. *See* Rabutin-Chantal
Sewel, William, 81
Sforza, Gian Galeazza, Duke of Milan, 164
Sforza, Lodovico The Moor [Lodovico il Moro], Duke of Milan, 22, 148, 150, 164
Shaftesbury, Earl, of. *See* Cooper
Shapleigh, Alexander, 652
Shapleigh, Catherine (Treworgie), 652
Sharpe, Hannah, 338
Shepard (Shepheard), Thomas, 343, **607**, 642
Shilling, Andrew, 75
Short, Richard, 546
Short*, Richard, 76
Sidney, Sir Henry, 331
Sikes, Walter, 652
Sillery. *See* Brulart
Silvy*, Antoine, 56, 244, 653
Simon, Father. *See* Girard de La Place
Simon de Longpré, Françoise de. *See* Jourdan
Simon de Longpré, Jacques de, 607
Simon de Longpré, Marie-Catherine de, *dite* de Saint-Augustin, 31, 204, 310, 314, 457, 472, 551, 563, **607–10**
Simpson, John, 107, 361, 493, 673
Sinclair, Andrew, 243
Sinclair, Sir Henry, Earl or Prince of Orkney, 680
Skanudharoua (Skannud-Haroï), Geneviève-Agnès, *dite* de Tous-les-Saints, **610–11**
Slany (Slaney), John, 233, 349, 350, 650
Sloane, Sir Hans, 669
Smith, John, 67, 101, 132, 262, 650

INDEX

Smith, Sir Thomas, 331, 335, 374
Smiths John. *See* Flemish Bastard
Smithsend, John, 612
Smithsend, Nicholas, 308, **611**, 611
Smithsend, Richard, **611–12**, 611
Smits Jan. *See* Flemish Bastard
Snorri Thorfinnsson, 5, **612**, 643
Soines, 66
Soissons. *See* Bourbon
Solís. *See* Díaz
Sommillard, Catherine, 116
Sommillard, Louise (Fortin,) 116
Sommillard, Marguerite, 116, 117
Soncino, Raimondo de, 22, 148, 149, 150, 164
Soranhes (Indian), 58, 59
Sorel. *See* Saurel
Sores (Sors or Soré), Marie (Caën), 159
Sorester. *See* Forrester
Soto, Hernando de, 171
Souart, Gabriel, 108, 206, 220, 273, 508, 539, 592, **612–13**, 644, 647, 648
Soulage, Catherine (Boutet de Saint-Martin), 119
Soulanges. *See* Joybert
Soulard, Mathurin, 271
Southack*, Cyprian, 90, 250, 299
Southampton, Earl of. *See* Wriothesley
Spencer, Miss (wife of John Treworgie), 652
Spencer, Mary (Hull; Phips), 544
Spencer, Robert, first Baron Spencer of Wormleighton, 632
Spencer, William, 239, 240
Spert, Sir Thomas, 155, 371, 565
Spicer, Richard, 565
Spinula, Agostino de, 150, 164
Squando, 650
Squanto (Squantum). *See* Tisquantum
Staffe, Philip, 375, 376, 378
Stannard, William, 343
Steed, Isabella (Mason), 496
Steenwijck, Cornelis van, 573
Stewart, Lady Elizabeth, 613
Stewart, James, Earl of Arran, 613
Stewart, Sir James, fourth Lord Ochiltree, 25, 53, 54, 248, 305, 482, **613–14**
Stewart, John, fourth Earl of Atholl, 613
Stewart, Margaret. *See* Macdowall
Stewart, Mary. *See* Livingstone
Stewart, William, 613
Stirling, Earl of. *See* Alexander, Sir William, the elder
Stokes, Jane, 81
Stourton, Edward, 614
Stourton, Elizabeth. *See* Gravenor
Stourton, Erasmus, 163, **614**
Stourton, Mary, 614
Stow, John, 151
Straunge, Robert, 239, 240
Street, Robert, 652
Strong, Richard, 306
Strozzi, Philippe, 87
Stuart. *See* Stewart
Stuart, Mary. *See* Mary, Queen of Scots
Studley, Daniel, 390, 392, 450
Sublet de Noyers, François (French administrator), 313

Suève, Edmond de, 321, 418
Suisse, Le. *See* Miville
Sully, Duc de. *See* Béthune
Surrey, Earl of. *See* Howard
Suzanne (Indian), 634
Swanley, Robert, 567
Swart, Claudius Clavus, 18, 680
Szkolny. *See* Scolvus

TAGASKOUÏTA. *See* Tekakwitha
Taiearonk, 354
Taignoagny, 11, 166, 167, 275, 276
Talon, Anne. *See* Bury
Talon, Artus, 614
Talon, Denis, 629
Talon, Jean (also called Talon Du Quesnoy), 29, 32, 34, 35, 36, 47, 48, 55, 60, 62, 63, 85, 86, 111, 116, 119, 120, 127, 135, 146, 174, 175, 185, 193, 198, 203, 226, 237, 238, 248, 260, 261, 287, 297, 313, 315, 326, 327, 340, 345, 355, 393, 394, 399, 400, 416, 418, 464, 494, 534, 535, 536, 539, 540, 550, 553, 555, 556, 560, 565, 570, 571, 580, 581, 582, 592, 600, 602, **614–32**, 648
Talon, Omer, 629
Talon, Philippe, 614
Tandihetsi, 71, 404
Tanfield, Anne, 632
Tanfield, Clement, 632
Tanfield, Elizabeth, 632
Tanfield, Sir Francis, **632**, 669
Tanfield, Sir Lawrence, 632
Taondechoren, Louis, 11, **632–33**
Taratouan (Taratwane), **633**, 637, 639
Tareha, **633–34**
Tarieu de Lanaudière. *See* Lanouguère
Tarieu de La Pérade. *See* Lanouguère
Tarieu de La Pérade, Madeleine. *See* Jarret
Tarihia, Christine (wife of Totiri), 652
Tarrigha (Tarsha). *See* Tareha
Tasquantum. *See* Tisquantum
Tassy, Félix de, 81
Tatnam, James, 553, 666
Tavernier, Jean, *dit* La Lochetière, Sieur de La Forest, 267, 269
Tayler, Henry, 228, 229
Téganissorens*, 445, 634
Tegakwitha (Tegaskouïta). *See* Tekakwitha
Tegonhatsiongo, Anastasie, 635
Teharonhiagannra, 460
Tehorenhaegnon, **634–35**
Tekakwitha, Kateri (Catherine), 522, **635–36**
Tekouerimat. *See* Negabamat
Temple, Dorothy. *See* Lee
Temple, Sir John, 636
Temple, Sir Thomas (the elder), 636
Temple, Sir Thomas, 25, 62, 63, 241, 399, 407, 434, 435, 436, 475, 500, 513, 595, 605, **636–37**, 654, 666, 667
Téondechoren, Joseph, 42, 212, 344, 523
Teouatiron, Joseph, 633, **637–38**
Terrier de Francheville et de Repentigny, Jeanne. *See* Jallot
Terrier de Francheville et de Repentigny, Marin, 553
Terron. *See* Colbert

INDEX

Tessier, Élisabeth (Damours), 245
Tessier, Laurent, 452
Tessier, *dit* Lavigne, Urbain, 427
Tessouat (Besouat, *c.* 1603-13), 6, 192, **638–39**, 662
Tessouat (Le Borgne de l'Île, d. 1636), 10, 222, 489, 516, 633, **639**
Tessouat (Tesswehas, Le Borgne de l'Île; d. 1654), Paul, 548, 558, **640–41**
Tessouat, Paul, wife of. *See* Magdelaine
Tesswehas. *See* Tessouat
Testard de La Forest, Gabriel, 180, **641**
Testard de La Forest, Jacques, 641
Testard de La Forest, Marie. *See* Pournin
Testu, capitaine, 300
Testu, Guillaume (pilot), 679
Teuleron, Pierre (La Rochelle notary), 401
Tewathiron. *See* Teouatiron
Tharca. *See* Tareha
Thavenet*, Marguerite de (Hertel de La Fresnière), 185
Thavenet, Marie-Françoise de, 185
Théberge. *See* Thiberge
Thémines, Maréchal de. *See* Lauzières
Théodat, Gabriel Sagard. *See* Sagard
Thérèse (Indian). *See* Oionhaton
Thevet, André, 88, 170, 276, 423, 424, 425, 426, **679–80**
Thewathiron. *See* Teouatiron
Thibault, Charles, 246
Thibault, Louise. *See* Guyon
Thiberge (Théberge), Jean, 394
Thierry, Catherine (Le Moyne de Longueuil et de Châteauguay), 463, 465, 507
Thiersault, Marguerite (Poncet de La Rivière et de Brétigny), 551
Thirkill, Lancelot, 120, 150, 164, **641**
Thomas, Jean, 442, 490, 569, **642**
Thomas, John, 343
Thomelin, Ambroise. *See* Aulquoy
Thomelin, Jean de, 213
Thomelin, Marie de (Chomedey), 213
Thompson, Joseph, 232, 281, 607, **642**, 666
Thorbjörn, 612
Thordarson. *See* Thorfinnr
Thorfinnr *karlsefni* Thordarson, 5, 448, 449, 612, **642–43**
Thorfinnsson. *See* Snorri
Thorgerdr, 103
Thorne, Robert (the elder), 302, **643–44**
Thorne, Robert, 21, 148, 302, **643–44**
Thorne, William, 302
Thorsteinn, 448, 449, 612, 642
Thorvaldr, 449, 612, 643
Thorvaldr Asvaldsson, 676
Thorvaldsson, Eirikr. *See* Eirikr
Thubières de Levy de Queylus, Gabriel, 46, 56, 57, 78, 126, 220, 310, 486, 552, 559, 599, 612, **644–49**, 662
Thury, Louis-Pierre, 309, 577, **649**
Tiblemont, Nicolas, 267
Tilliard, Henry, 369
Tilly. *See* Legardeur
Timothée, Capt., 292
Ting. *See* Tyng
Tipton, John, 85

Tisquantum (Squanto, Squantum), 262, **649–50**
Titailt. *See* Blarye
Toby, Maurice, 148, 149
Togoniron. *See* Togouiroui
Togouiroui, Joseph (Sosé), *dit* le Grand Agnier, 322, **650–51**
Tokhrahenehiaron, 370, 403
Tombelles. *See* Marquette
Tonnetuit. *See* Chauvin
Tonsahoten, François-Xavier (Pierre), 321, **651**
Tonsahoten, wife of. *See* Gandeacteua
Tonty*, Alphonse de, 416, 547
Tonty*, Henri de, 79, 114, 175, 176, 177, 178, 444
Tonty, Marie-Anne de. *See* Picoté
Torcapel, Jean, 91
Totiri (Totihri), Étienne, 42, 523, **651–52**
Totiri, brother of. *See* Paul
Totiri, daughter of. *See* Catherine
Totiri, mother of. *See* Tariha
Totiri, wife of. *See* Madeleine
Touaniscou, 69
Toupin, Toussaint, 404
Toureault, Françoise (Archambault), 427
Tous-les-Saints, Geneviève-Agnès, *dite* de. *See* Skanudharoua
Tracy. *See* Prouville
Traversy, Capt. de, 40, 308
Tregouaroti, 603
Tressonville. *See* Chardon
Trevor, Sir John, 144
Trewethy. *See* Treworgie
Treworgie, Catherine. *See* Shapleigh
Treworgie, James, 652
Treworgie (Treworgy, Trewerghey), John, 24, 406, **652–53**
Treworgie, John (the younger), 652
Tronquet, Guillaume, 557, 558
Tronson, Louis, 80, 117, 134, 180, 244
Trout, Nehemiah, 496
Trouvé*, Claude, 82, 544, 599, 647
Troyes, Madeleine de. *See* Alard
Troyes, Marie. *See* Petit de L'Estang
Troyes, Michel de, 653
Troyes, Pascal de. *See* Pascal
Troyes, Pierre de, *dit* Chevalier de Troyes, 39, 56, 107, 130, 315, 324, 329, 361, 417, 465, 509, 529, 537, 606, 611, **653–54**, 657, 672
Tryggvason. *See* Olaf I, King of Norway
Tsondatsaa, Charles, 42, 523
Tsondoutannen, Thomas, 143
Tuffet, Jean, 248, 490, 593
Tullibody, Lord Alexander of. *See* Alexander, Sir William, Earl of Stirling
Turenne, Vicomte de. *See* La Tour d'Auvergne
Turgis. *See* Saint-Étienne de La Tour
Turmenys, Philippe de, 221
Turner, Capt., 68
Turner, Ephraim, 337
Tuvache, capitaine, 208
Twide, Richard, 380
Tyng, Edward (the elder), 654
Tyng (Ting, Tynge), Edward, 426, 576, **654**
Tyng, Edward (son of Edward), 654

Tyng, Elizabeth. *See* Clarke
Tyrkir, 449

UBALDINI, Roberto, Cardinal, 97, 307
Ulpius, Euphrosynus, 659
Unton, Henry, 531
Urfé. *See* Lascaris

VACHON* de Belmont, François, 116, 273, 274, 445, 598
Valbelle, Chevalier de, 443
Valbringue, Robert. *See* La Rocque de Roberval
Valerianos, Apostolos (or Phokus Valerianatos). *See* Fuca
Valets, Jean, 201, 267, 269, 270, 273
Valliers, Catherine de (Razilly), 567
Valpergue, Françoise de (Lescarbot), 471
Van Curler. *See* Curler
Van der Donck. *See* Donck
Van Harwick. *See* Harwick
Van Rensselaer. *See* Rensselaer
Van Steenwijck. *See* Steenwijck
Vandémont, Philippe-Emmanuel de, Duc de Mercœur et de Penthièvre, 421
Vaner (Vannier), Hans, 383
Vannier, Catherine (Pelletier), 536
Varennes. *See* Gaultier
Vasse, Anne (Becquet), 86
Vauban. *See* Le Prestre
Vaubougon. *See* Chauvigny
Vaudreuil. *See* Rigaud
Vaughan, Anne. *See* Christmas
Vaughan, Elizabeth. *See* Robert
Vaughan, Francis, 655
Vaughan, John, Earl of Carbery, 655
Vaughan, Katherine, 654
Vaughan, Walter, 654
Vaughan, Sir William, 162, 365, 496, 632, **654–57**, 668, 672
Vault. *See* Vuault
Vaulthier, Perrette (Gloria), 339
Vaultier, 105
Vaulx, Jacques de, 88, 89
Vautrollier, Thomas, 531
Vauvilliers, Jeanne de (Basset Des Lauriers), 79
Vauvril de Blason, Marguerite (Boucher de Grandpré), 109
Vaz Dourado, Fernan, 304
Venables, Robert, 605
Vendôme, Duc de. *See* Bourbon
Ventadour, Duc de. *See* Lévis
Verchères. *See* Jarret
Verdun, Sieur de. *See* Dupuy, Zacharie
Vergil, Polydore, 151
Verier. *See* Verrier
Verner, Elinor, 657
Verner, Hugh, **657**
Vernon, Gillette de (Gaultier de Rinault), 326
Véron, Étienne, 223
Véron, Guillaume, 223
Véron de Grandmesnil, Jean, 223
Véron de Grandmesnil, Marguerite. *See* Hayet
Verrazzano, Bernardo da, 657
Verrazzano, Fiametta da. *See* Capelli

Verrazzano, Gerolamo da, 657, 659, 660
Verrazzano, Giovanni da, 19, 21, 27, 72, 165, 187–88, 332, 333, 342, 374, 469, 585, 586, **657–60**
Verrazzano, Nicolo da, 657
Verrazzano, Piero da, 657
Verrazzano, Piero Andrea da (the elder), 657
Verrier, Pierre, 557
Verrier, Roberte. *See* Gadoys
Vesins, Élisabeth (Couillard), 236
Vespucci, Amerigo, 151, 155, 658
Viel, Nicolas, 58, 263, 420, 437, 440, 590, 639, **661**
Viele, Aernout Cornelissen, 526
Vieille Robe de Castor. *See* Chomina
Vien, Charlotte (Prévost), 553
Viennay-Pachot, Charlotte-Françoise. *See* Juchereau de Saint-Denis
Viennay-Pachot, François, 56, 397, **661**
Viennay-Pachot, Jeanne. *See* Avamy
Vienne, Marguerite, 233
Vieux-pont. *See* Godefroy
Vieuxpont, Alexandre de, 453, 665
Vignal, Guillaume, 46, 130, 458, 612, **661–62**
Vignar (Vignard, Vignart). *See* Vignal
Vignau, Nicolas de, 191–92, 638, **662–63**
Vignerot, Marie-Madeleine de, Duchesse d'Aiguillon (Beauvoir Du Roure de Combalet), 203, 297, 347, 348, 373, 483, 484
Vignerot Du Plessis, Armand-Jean, Duc de Richelieu, 483
Villain, Jean (master jeweller of Paris), 663
Villain, Jean (father of Jeanne Villain), 663
Villain, Jean-Baptiste, **663**
Villain, Jeanne. *See* Barbier
Villain, Jeanne (Bernier), 663
Villaine, Louis de, 425
Villars, Mme de, 58
Villebon. *See* Robinau
Villegaignon. *See* Durand
Villemenon, Sieur, secretary of the Duc de Montmorency, 433
Villemor, Duc de. *See* Séguier
Villeneuve, Marquis de. *See* Duret
Villeneuve, Mathieu. *See* Amiot
Villeneuve, Robert de, **663–64**
Villeray. *See* Rouer
Villesavin, Mme de. *See* Blondeau, Isabelle
Villiers, Christopher, Earl of Anglesey, 614
Villiers, George, first Duke of Buckingham, 365, 419, 669
Villieu*, Sébastien de, 426, 427, 578
Vimont, Barthélemy, 124, 205, 215, 216, 248, 348, 382, 389, 404, 430, 453, 516, **665**
Vincelotte. *See* Amiot
Vincent de Paul (St.), also called M. Vincent, 91, 208
Visscher, N. J., 525
Vitry, Jean, 108
Vouet, Simon, French painter, 214, 313
Voyer* d'Argenson, Pierre de, 46, 48, 206, 224–25, 269, 270, 283, 288, 330, 431, 538, 563, 580, 588, 645, 646, 665
Vuault. *See* Clément
Vuil, Daniel, 284, **665–66**
Vyner, Sir Robert, 83

INDEX

Walker, Anne, 666
Walker*, Sir Hovenden, 36, 76
Walker, James, 666
Walker, John, 333
Walker, Nehemiah, 39, 84, 232, 324, 417, 476, 518, 519, 528, 543, 605, 606, 657, **666**
Walker, Obediah, 667
Walker, Richard, 62, 399, 637, **666–67**
Walker, Sarah, 667
Walker, William (the elder), 84, 666
Walker, William (the younger), 666
Walley*, John, 466, 545
Walsh*, Thomas, 329
Walsingham, Sir Francis, 251, 252, 332, 333, 363, 380
Warde, Richard, 343
Warwick, Ambrose, Earl of. *See* Dudley
Warwick, Robert, Earl of. *See* Rich
Watteau*, Mélithon, 420
Watts, Agnes. *See* Mackworth
Watts, John, 241
Watts, Richard, 241
Waymouth (or Weymouth), George, 20, 189, 318, 375, 397, 650, **667–68**
West, Thomas, Baron De La Warr, 67
Whalley. *See* Walley
Wheler, Sir Francis, 546
Whitbourne, Sir Richard, 229, 278, 279, 300, 362, 632, 655, 656, **668–69**
White, John, 5, **669–70**
Whittington, George, 350
Widmerpole, Dorothy. *See* Frobisher
Widmerpole, Sir William, 318
Willes, Richard, 154
William I, King of England (called The Conqueror), 121
William III, King of Great Britain and Ireland, 92, 329, 426, 544, 545
Williams, John, 376
Willoughby, Bridget, 670
Willoughby, Edward, 670
Willoughby, Sir Hugh, 158
Willoughby, Sir Percival, 240, 351, 534, 535, 584, 670

Willoughby, Thomas, 240, 584, **670–71**
Willoughby, William, 443
Wilson, Edward, 374, 375, 378
Wilson, William, 374, 376, 377
Winne. *See* Wynne
Winter, William, 229, 333, 532
Withipoll, John, 386
Witzel. *See* Miçel
Wolfall, Master, 85
Wolfe*, James, 76
Wolsey, Thomas, Cardinal, 155
Wolstenholme, Sir John, 362, 374
Woodhouse. *See* Wydowse
Worcester, William, 386
Worthington, William, 158
Wright, Edward, 144, 252
Wriothesley, Henry, third Earl of Southampton, 667
Württemberg, Frederick I, Duke of, 632
Wyatt, Sir Thomas, 157
Wydowse (Woodhouse), Thomas, 374, 377, 378
Wyet (Wyeth, Wyatt), Sylvester, 5, 306, 364, 451, **671–72**
Wyndham, Thomas, 316
Wynne, Edward, 162, 614, **672**

Yong (Yonge). *See* Young
York, Edward, Duke of. *See* Edward IV
York, James, Duke of. *See* James II
York, Sir John, 316
Yorke, Gilbert, 85, 317
You de La Découverte, Élisabeth. *See* Élisabeth
You de La Découverte, Marie-Anne (Richard), 573
You* de La Découverte, Pierre, 573
Young (Yonge), James, **672–73**
Young (Yong, Yonge), Thomas, **673**
Yroquet. *See* Iroquet

Zamet, Sébastien, French prelate, 483
Zeno, Antonio, 316, **680–81**
Zeno, Nicolò, 316, **680–81**
Zénobe, Father. *See* Membré
Zichmni, 680